P9-EED-153

formerly Editorial Research Reports

JANUARY — DECEMBER 1994

Published by Congressional Quarterly Inc.
1414 22nd Street, N.W., Washington, D.C. 20037

ISBN 1-156802-025-2
ISSN 1056-2036

Elements of The CQ Researcher

(formerly Editorial Research Reports)

Subscribers to *The CQ Researcher* receive 48 reports per year. Each report provides background on a current topic of widespread interest. Designed as a starting place for research, the reports define the issues and include a chronology and extensive bibliographies. A feature called "At Issue," which quotes opposing viewpoints from two experts, also is a part of each report.

The publication is available in various formats.

The Report

The report, about 12,000 words in length, is issued on Friday four times a month. Each report treats a subject that is in the news or likely to be in the news in the near future.

Bound Reports

The weekly reports are bound into quarterly paperback editions and an annual hardbound cumulation.

Index

A subject index to the reports is published each quarter and cumulated annually. The latest index may be found (in the blue pages) at the back of this volume.

For more information, call Congressional Quarterly, 800-432-2250 or 202-887-8500.

Citation

Recommended format for citing these reports in a bibliography, based on The Modern Language Association of America's *Handbook for Writers of Research Papers,* 3rd edition, follows.

Clark, Charles S. "The Obscenity Debate." *The CQ Researcher* 20 Dec. 1991: 969-992.

THE CQ Researcher
formerly Editorial Research Reports

CONTENTS

JANUARY - DECEMBER 1994

THE CQ Researcher

PUBLISHED BY CONGRESSIONAL QUARTERLY INC.

Racial Tensions in Schools

Is the dream of school integration starting to fade?

It has been 36 years since 15-year-old Elizabeth Eckford walked a gauntlet of jeering whites to attend Central High School in Little Rock, Ark., and 31 years since James Meredith became the first black student at the University of Mississippi. Today, the mobs and the protective soldiers are gone, but hopes that public school integration would lead to an inclusive atmosphere at colleges and universities have been battered by the reality of racial and ethnic tensions at campuses across the country. Indeed, the nationwide push for integration appears to have reached a turning point, an outgrowth of the nation's lingering legacy of segregated housing. Now some researchers are even questioning whether integration has a positive effect on black children's academic and social development.

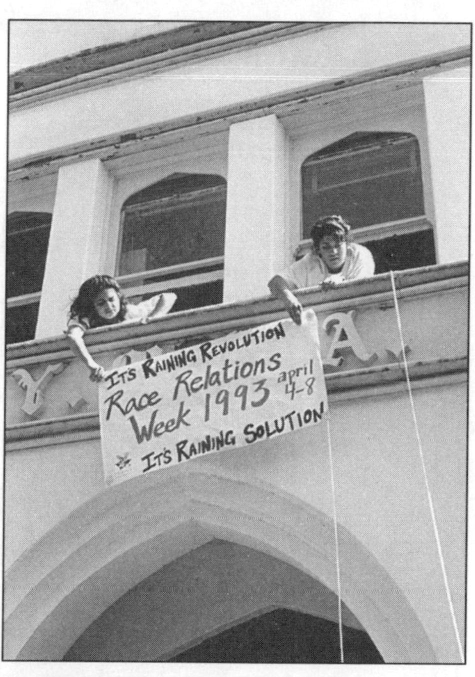

INSIDE THIS ISSUE

CQ January 7, 1994 • Volume 4, No. 1 • 1-24

Formerly Editorial Research Reports

Racial Tensions In Schools

COVER: STUDENTS HANG OUT A BANNER FOR RACE RELATIONS AT THE UNIVERSITY OF NORTH CAROLINA AT CHAPEL HILL (BRIAN PALMER).

January 7, 1994
Volume 4, No. 1

The CQ Researcher (ISSN 1056-2036). Formerly Editorial Research Reports. Published weekly (48 times per year, not printed the first Friday of any month with five Fridays) by Congressional Quarterly Inc., 1414 22nd St., N.W., Washington, D.C. 20037. Rates are furnished upon request. Second-class postage paid at Washington, D.C. POSTMASTER: Send address changes to The CQ Researcher, 1414 22nd St., N.W., Washington, D.C. 20037.

Racial Tensions in Schools

BY SUSAN PHILLIPS

THE ISSUES

Forty years after the Supreme Court ordered schools desegregated, racial disharmony continues to trouble high schools and colleges around the country. In the past two years, for example:

- Two white students were suspended for assaulting African American students at Millard South High School in Omaha, Neb. And a third white student was threatened by other whites for associating with the school's 25 blacks.
- Seven students at Norman Thomas High School in New York City were injured when a fight between two black girls in the cafeteria sparked a brawl involving dozens of Hispanic and African American students. The trouble began after a Puerto Rican girl tried to stop the original fight.
- Self-appointed censors at more than 25 colleges and universities, including the University of Maryland, have resorted to confiscating student newspapers containing articles deemed insufficiently sensitive to African Americans and other minorities.

While such tensions are not limited to blacks and whites, it is America's troubled effort to integrate black students into majority-white schools that defines the issue.

School integration has been plagued by the degree to which American society seems to treat blacks differently from other ethnic and racial groups. Blacks often live in residential areas so intensely segregated that some researchers call them "hyper-segregated." Indeed, African Americans are the only minority group for which increased income does not bring an end to racial isolation. [1]

With blacks and whites so estranged outside the classroom, it's not surprising that they often mix uneasily in integrated schools. Douglas A. Blackmon, a newspaper reporter who attended a newly desegregated high school in Leland, Miss., in the 1970s, wrote that "Fistfights on the playground between blacks and whites were routine, and being harassed by blacks as I walked home through their neighborhood after school was so common that I was later amazed to learn that anyone else had grown up differently. The school stopped sponsoring senior proms, student banquets, senior trips and other social gatherings long before I was old enough to know what they were." [2] The school is now 80 percent black, and most white children in Leland attend private schools.

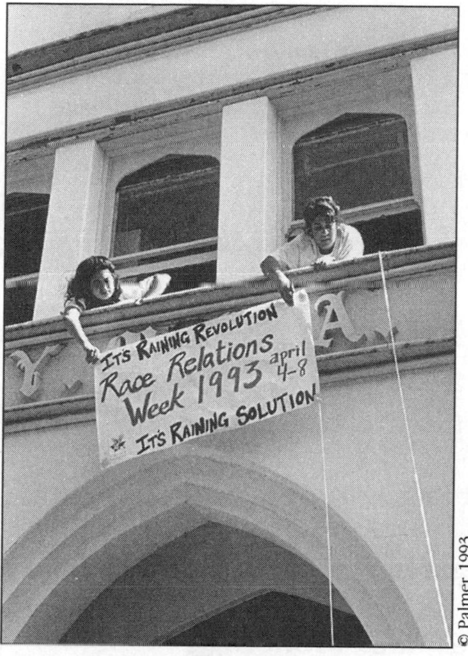

© Palmer 1993

The nationwide push to integrate schools appears to have reached a critical turning point. A Harvard University study released in December found that the percentage of black students attending classes where most of the students were minority had risen to 66 percent in 1991-92. It had fallen from 77 percent in 1968 to 63 percent in 1980. The decline in integration among Hispanics was even more pronounced, with 73 percent in predominantly minority classes, compared with 55 percent in 1968-69. [3]

The trend toward school re-segregation, according to some experts, can be linked to the nation's lingering legacy of segregated housing. "In the last two decades, the segregation of the cities has created a major-league nightmare," says Professor Robert L. Crain of Teachers College at Columbia University. "There is not much hope for school desegregation in Detroit, or in a number of other big cities. It's just a disaster, a disaster written into law because it is so difficult to break down the barriers between city and suburban school districts."

More than 90 percent of white Americans support school integration in principle, up from less than 40 percent in 1959, according to a 1991 survey by the National Opinion Research Corporation. But the same survey found no more than 5 percent of white parents will voluntarily transfer their children to a minority school unless it is a magnet school, which offers innovative and specialized courses. [4]

Researchers are divided over whether integrated schooling has a positive effect on black children's academic and social development. The achievement gap between black and white students has narrowed considerably in the last two years, but the role of integration is unclear.

Clifford Bennett, a professor of education at the University of Virginia (UVA), says that many blacks who grew up in segregated schools now question desegregation. (*See story, p. 15.*) "If you talk to blacks in their 40s and 50s, most of whom attended all-black institutions, they would say they received excellent educations and a good sense of who they are. Many feel that desegregation changed that, because of white teachers not really having high expectations and not really caring about black students."

Minority Enrollments on the Rise

Enrollment of African Americans in higher education increased steadily throughout the 1980s. By 1990, African American men and women accounted for 9.6 percent of all fulltime freshmen attending college for the first time. Blacks earned nearly 6 percent of all bachelor's degrees conferred, and 2.5 percent of all doctoral degrees.

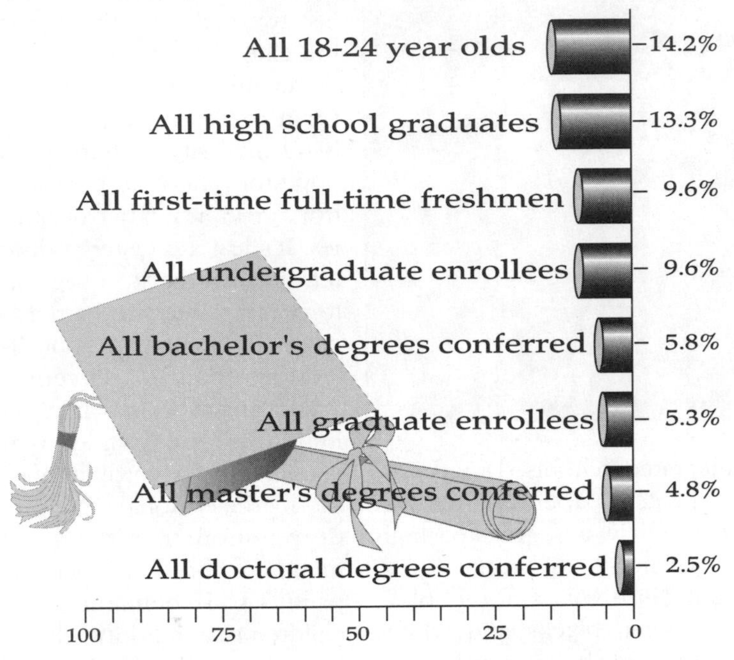

Source: "Minorities in Higher Education: Eleventh Annual Status Report," American Coucil on Education, 1992, based on Census Bureau, Department of Education and National Research Council data.

A Louis Harris survey of high school students released in November showed that 75 percent of the respondents had witnessed confrontations motivated by race or religion, up dramatically from 57 percent in 1990. And 57 percent of black students reported being the target in a racial incident, up from 46 percent in 1990. [5]

Many schools simply do not have a strategy for dealing with racial strife. A 1992 study of newspaper reports of racial and ethnic conflicts in schools over a two-month period found that the most common response was disciplinary or police action. Some schools also responded with a one-time educational event, such as a film or assembly. But fewer than 5 percent followed up with long-term programs to reduce tension. [6]

While most black students attend predominantly black schools in the primary and secondary grades, they are far more likely to attend majority-white colleges. In 1991, only 16 percent of black college students attended historically black colleges and universities.

Earlier experiences in segregated or hostile educational environments make the transition to majority-white colleges particularly difficult for some black students. John H. Bunzel, a senior research fellow at the Hoover Institution at Stanford University, found in 1990 that only 26 percent of white Stanford students had heavy exposure to blacks before arriving, while 41 percent reported little or no contact. Among African American students, 50 percent came from predominantly black neighborhoods, and 45 percent from majority-black schools. [7]

Behind these figures lie dramatically different world views. "Many white students, for example, believe that blacks now have equal access to a college education . . . and that dramatic progress has been made in providing racial equality in society at large," writes Bunzel. "Frequently questioning the validity of black students' concerns, they think blacks with lower grades and test scores today enjoy unfair advantages." For their part, black Stanford students "virtually all agree that white students have no understanding of the very different experience and culture they come from." [8]

When they look at college faculties, for example, black students still face a sea of white faces. In 1989, African Americans represented only 4.5 percent of the full-time professors on U.S. campuses — and almost half were teaching at historically black campuses.

While blacks remain very much in the minority at colleges — only 9.6 percent of all full-time freshmen in 1990 were black — there have been dramatic changes since W.E.B. DuBois attended Harvard in the late 19th century as one of the university's two black students. DuBois, who became the nation's pre-eminent black philosopher and scholar, was not allowed to live in the school's dormitories.

Although it's difficult to quantify the apparent rise in racial incidents on predominantly white campuses, it is evident that a disproportionate number of black students leave school before graduating and that increases in minority faculty and administrators have been slow in coming.

At the same time, serious strains appear to exist between black and white students, with the issue of self-segregation by blacks topping the white grievance list. Blacks, on the other hand, see pervasive subtle racism and a constant questioning of their academic credentials by white students.

As school officials, parents and students grapple with racial and ethnic tensions, they must answer the following questions:

Has school desegregation failed to help African Americans?

Boston University political science Professor Christine Rossell strongly supported the court-ordered 1974 plan to integrate Boston public schools. It is not a happy memory. "That is now a segregated system, and you can forget about it becoming desegregated," says Rossell. "It is a tragedy." Boston schools are now 81 percent minority, up from 43 percent in 1974.

© Brian Palmer 1993

Students rally in support of an African American cultural center at the University of North Carolina at Chapel Hill.

American public schools are certainly more integrated today than in the late 1960s, when intensive desegregation efforts began. According to federal statistics, in 1968 about 77 percent of black students attended schools that were over half minority, compared with 66 percent today. Nonetheless, there appears to be widespread acceptance of a status quo in which most black students wind up in primarily minority public schools.

"It has become increasingly difficult for whites to propose integration when they haven't really borne the burden of integration," says Willis Hawley, dean of the School of Education at the University of Maryland at College Park. "So many plans were achieved by placing the burden on blacks."

UVA's Bennett believes the essentially conservative nature of school bureaucracies makes them resistant to cutting-edge social policies. "People thought just putting black and white students together was going to solve all our racial ills," he says. "But major racial changes are not going to occur in the schools. Schools are always 20 years behind the times."

Crain at Columbia University says that support for desegregation has waned, in part because of "the symbolic insult it represents. If whites don't want it, then blacks will say, 'My kid doesn't have to sit next to a white kid in order to learn.' "

Indeed, there also appears to be a widespread feeling among black parents and educators that integrated schools fail black children to a large extent because overwhelmingly white teaching staffs don't bring out the best in black students. That runs counter to the theory that attending integrated schools boosts black students' self-esteem.

Based on that theory, psychologists Kenneth and Mamie Clark found persuasive support for desegregated schools in their famous experiments of the 1930s and '40s involving hundreds of black children in segregated schools. They discovered that 67 percent of the children, if given a choice between black and white dolls, chose white dolls. The result was considered proof of the extent to which black children had internalized the discrimination they faced in society. Desegregation, which would allow black children to compete and succeed in classrooms with white children, was supposed to reduce those feelings.

In 1985, however, the experiment was repeated by child psychologists Darlene Powell Hopson and Derek Hopson. They found that 65 percent of the black children from integrated schools still preferred white dolls, and 76 percent thought the black dolls "looked bad." [9]

The Hopsons point to the schoolroom as the place where black children first experience institutionalized racism. "Non-black school officials seldom appreciate or acknowledge how prevalent racial discrimination, even racial attack, is in their schools," they write in *Different and Wonderful*, their book of advice for black parents. "As a result, school personnel do not always explore the racial angle as a credible factor in children's behavior problems." [10]

There is a clear connection in the public mind between school desegregation and the image of public schools as increasingly dangerous, violent places. [11] The popular image of angry black children and adolescents settling schoolyard disputes at gunpoint, along with other stereotypes, feeds the wariness and even hostility black students often face when bused to majority-white schools.

But while desegregation undoubtedly contributed to increased racial tension in schools, the outcome was not inevitable, says Rossell. "When

Integration Progress Slows

The percentage of black students in schools where students were predominantly minority (top graph) rose from 63 percent in 1980 to 66 percent in 1990-91. The trend away from integration was even more pronounced among Hispanics, with 73 percent in predominantly minority classes, compared with 68 percent in 1980-81. Segregation also increased slightly in schools that are almost entirely minority (bottom).

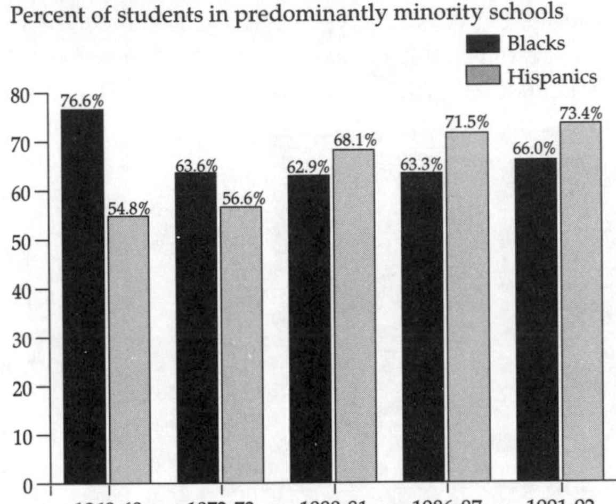

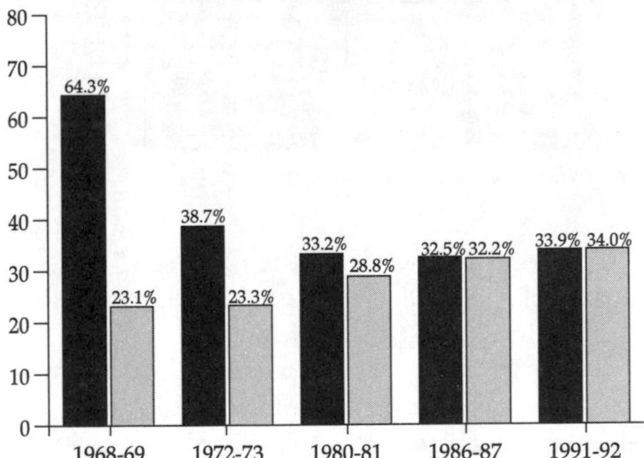

Source: "The Growth of Segregation in American Schools: Changing Patterns of Separation and Poverty Since 1968," based on U.S. Department of Education data.

you bring races together, you need to do something about it," she says. "Most schools don't. They have basically left it up to the kids, and that is ridiculous. The average teenager is a very confused person."

All of the problems with desegregation seem to be fueling a movement among black educators and parents to focus their energies on making black schools better, and more welcoming, to black children.

Spencer H. Holland is among many black educators prepared to exchange the ideal of integration for a more pragmatic goal: high-quality all-black schools. "White people are not going to move back to the inner city to go to school with these poor, black kids," says Holland, director of the Center for Educating African American Males at Morgan State University, in Baltimore.

Holland was an early proponent of all-black-male classrooms. (*See story, p. 18.*) He is also the driving force behind an effort to bring black male professionals into elementary schools as mentors to black boys.

"Functional illiteracy is the outstanding characteristic of African American males in jail, on parole and in the juvenile justice system," says Holland. "That is a real indictment of our schools."

Attempts to measure the benefits black students have received from integrated schools have not produced definitive answers. A 1991 statement filed in a Supreme Court desegregation case by 58 experts in the field summarizes research over the past 20 years. Written in support of continuing court-ordered desegregation in DeKalb County, Ga., the statement contends that:

- The desegregation of a school district can positively influence residential integration;
- Desegregation is associated with moderate academic gains for minority students and doesn't harm white students;
- Desegregation plans work best when they cover a large geographic area and as many grades as possible and stick to clearly defined long-term goals; and,
- Effective desegregation is linked to other types of educational reform. [12]

In hunting for signs of an impact outside the realm of test scores and grades, some researchers have found that blacks who attend integrated schools are more likely to plan professional careers in fields such as accounting, medicine and law. Another study found that black students who attended suburban schools through a voluntary busing plan in Hartford, Conn., had more realistic career plans than inner-city peers.

An integrated high school experience "affords black students the opportunity to develop confidence in their scholastic and coping skills in majority-white settings," says Jomills

Braddock, a professor of sociology at the University of Miami. [13]

Do teachers have lower expectations for black students?

There is strong evidence that teachers' expectations have a powerful effect on students' academic achievement. Teachers, of course, can form negative racial stereotypes like anybody else. And since only about 8 percent of all teachers are black, most black children are taught by white teachers, even if they attend majority-black schools. [14]

It is not surprising, then, that by the time black children complete elementary grades, they often are disenchanted with school, unsure of their own abilities and achieving less than they should. They are less likely than whites to take geometry and to complete two years of algebra in high school. But they are 2.3 times as likely as white students to be classified as "educable mentally retarded, trainable mentally retarded or seriously emotionally disturbed." [15]

The problems are particularly acute for black boys, who score lower than any other group of youngsters on standardized tests. They are twice as likely as whites to be placed in special-education classes but half as likely to enter classes for academically inclined students.

Behind these statistics are the everyday horror stories told by the parents of black children at both integrated and majority-black schools. There was the suspicious teacher who ordered a retest for a black student who received the top score on a math test. At the other extreme, there was the well-intentioned novice who gave black children good grades for poor work, explaining, "Things are so bad for them at home, I don't want to hurt anyone's feelings." And then there were the teachers who, after Black History Month ended, quickly took down the pictures of prominent blacks that had been put up on classroom walls — sending a not-so-subtle message to black *and* white children about the value of black heroes. [16]

Working with a national sample of 30,000 high school students, Will Jordan, co-director of the Center for the Social Organization of Schools at Johns Hopkins University in Baltimore, found a strong correlation between students' achievement in science and the racial composition of their schools. He then examined teacher attitudes in the schools, using a scale that measured workplace satisfaction and the teachers' perception of their students' abilities.

"I found that if you take teacher expectancies into account, much of the difference in science achievement is eliminated," says Jordan. "In plain English, teacher expectancies are one of the key reasons kids do poorly or well."

As educational psychologist Bruce R. Hare puts it, "This negative treatment of children becomes a self-fulfilling prophecy." [17]

Jawanza Kunjufu, an educational consultant in Chicago, calls the problem the "fourth-grade failure syndrome." In his multi-volume work *Countering the Conspiracy to Destroy Black Boys*, Kunjufu says that by fourth grade, teachers' expectations of their students largely determine whether or not a child will succeed. "If teachers see in black boys future engineers, computer programmers and doctors ... then they will produce those kinds of scholars." [18]

In addition to teachers' expectations, Kunjufu and others link learning styles to performance. Asa Hilliard, a professor of education at Georgia State University, has found that white children tell stories in a linear fashion, while black children employ a "spiral" style. Other researchers say black children are more sensitive to peer relationships and less interested in competing academically than white children.

The impact of learning styles leads some black educators to favor teaching black boys in classrooms without girls. "Most of the little girls in these schools are in single-parent households headed by their mothers," says Morgan State's Holland, "and most of their teachers are women, and I'll tell you what happens. These little girls become awfully bossy. And the little boys, they back away and let the girls do it. If everybody in the class is a boy, then one of the boys has to talk."

Like single-sex classes, grouping students by ability, or tracking, ranks among the most contentious issues in education — especially in relation to minorities. [19] Many educators contend that placing students in groups based on standardized-test results or on teacher assessments, which may also be racially biased, has a negative impact on student achievement.

In some school districts, students are assigned to tracks as early as two or three weeks into their kindergarten year. Children who attended preschool and learned the ABC song, their colors and their numbers may appear brighter and more promising than those who didn't go to preschool, or whose parents didn't read to them often.

Some school districts, however, rarely reassess tracking assignments unless a parent complains. Children tracked into lower-achieving classrooms are often taught by the least experienced teachers, using less challenging material.

Jeannie Oakes, in a definitive 1985 study, documented the deadening effect ability grouping can have on the intellectual development of low-income and minority children. "Those at the bottom of the social and economic ladder climb up through 12 years of ' the great equalizer,' as educator Horace Mann called public schools, and end up still on the bottom rung," Oakes wrote. [20]

Looking at tracking assignments in six integrated high schools, Oakes found that while 50 percent of the students were white, 62 percent of the students in high-track English classes were white, and only 29 percent of the students in low-track English were white. A similar pattern prevailed in math classes.

As a court case in Rockford, Ill., suggests, tracking may have served to segregate minority students within some supposedly integrated schools. Minority students in Rockford who scored high on standard achievement tests were nevertheless placed in the lower academic tracks in kindergarten, while low-scoring whites went into the high-achieving track. School administrators thus created schools that were numerically integrated but in which minority students ate lunch at different times than whites and used different classrooms, bathrooms and entrances.

Magistrate Judge P. Michael Mahoney concluded that Rockford's school district "has committed such open acts of discrimination as to be cruel . . . and committed others with such subtlety as to raise discrimination to an art form." [21]

Does self-segregation by black students at majority-white colleges contribute to racial tensions on campuses?

At the University of Massachusetts-Amherst (U-Mass), a black residential adviser is beaten up by a white visitor to his dormitory. At the University of Pennsylvania in Philadelphia, a white freshman shouts, "Shut up, you water buffalo!" at a group of noisy black women outside his room late at night. The young man faces charges of violating the campus speech code after "water buffalo" is ruled to be a racial slur. The charge eventually is dismissed. (*See story, p. 13.*)

The two 1992 incidents received wide publicity as indications of lamentable campus race relations. But each tells a different story. The attack on the adviser, coming after earlier racial conflicts on campus, was another signal to blacks that they could not be sure of their welcome even at a bastion of liberalism like U-Mass. The water buffalo incident reflected a growing tendency to blame campus tension on black and other minority students.

In a special report in April, *U.S. News & World Report* asserted that "the new segregation" on college campuses "is perpetuated by choice, not mandated by law." [22]

College administrators have actively supported the creation of a campus culture in which, according to the report, "all too many black and white students live apart, eat apart, play apart and eventually grow apart. Further complicating the situation: vocal organizations and suborganizations seeking separate-but-equal privileges for Hispanics, Asian Americans, Native Americans and other minorities."

Surveying 550 student editors about campus race relations, the magazine further found that 75 percent reported self-segregation by blacks was common on their campuses. The survey also uncovered "a statistically significant relationship between the degree of self-segregation by race and the number of racial incidents."

Similarly, a survey at Stanford University found that most black and white students agreed that minorities, chiefly blacks, do separate themselves from whites in the social sphere. The 1988-89 study by the Hoover Institution's Bunzel found the phenomenon far more troubling to white students than to blacks, though many blacks did report feeling pressured to avoid interracial dating or too much socializing with whites.

Bunzel, a former member of the U.S. Commission on Civil Rights, found that black and white students often arrive on campus having had little previous contact with other races. For example, more than 40 percent of the whites reported little or no contact with blacks in high school. Among blacks, 50 percent were from primarily black neighborhoods, and 45 percent were from majority-black

Doonesbury BY GARRY TRUDEAU

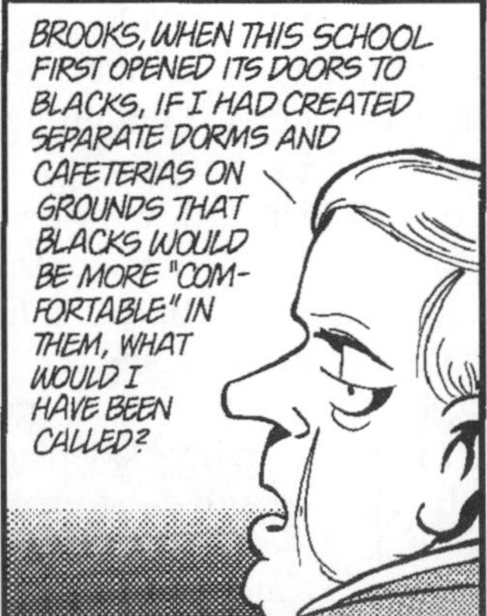

high schools.

One of Bunzel's central findings is that blacks and whites at Stanford define racism differently. White students generally see racism as a matter of personal attitudes and actions. Blacks, Bunzel discovered, are more likely to describe racism in institutional terms, as a matter of the racial group in power oppressing another racial group.

The black students' definition, Bunzel found, made them more likely to see some campus conditions as racist. More than 70 percent of blacks, but less than half of whites, described the large percentage of whites among tenured faculty as "definitely" or "probably" racist. Almost 84 percent of black students said the Western orientation of the curriculum is racist, because it is not sufficiently multicultural.

Bunzel also found that half the white students said they had experienced reverse racism at Stanford, such as having an application for a campus job refused because of a missed deadline, while applications were still being accepted from minority students, or being greeted coldly when sitting at a "black" table in the cafeteria.

Bunzel's discovery of widespread grievances among white students exposes one facet of the self-segregation debate. Another is that more than 40 percent of the black students interviewed by Bunzel felt teachers expected less from them than from white students.

With a 200-point gap between the average SAT scores of college-bound black and white students, and with black colleges and universities offering blacks a more welcoming alternative, elite schools have little choice but to alter their admissions criteria for blacks to increase minority enrollments. Yet high attrition rates for black students indicate that affirmative action in the admissions office has not been accompanied by effective strategies for helping black students succeed. Of the black students who entered the University of California-Berkeley in 1983, 37.5 percent graduated by 1988, compared with 71.5 percent of the whites.

Mary Berry, the newly appointed chair of the U.S. Commission on Civil Rights, argues that self-segregation is a form of self-preservation. Many blacks, said Berry at a recent press conference, "find the environment so hostile that it reinforces their desire for black [dormitories]. What most commentators on the subject of black self-segregation fail to recognize is that there is no great effort on the part of white students to integrate with black students. . . . The whole public debate makes it sound like black students have this duty to go out and integrate with whites." [23]

However, Sylvia Hurtado, a University of Michigan researcher, reports a different phenomenon. "One thing we found consistently across minority groups is the extent to which minority students are involved in cross-race interactions at a much higher rate than whites," she says. "That raises the question of whether this is self-segregation, or exclusion."

There is some reason to believe that the formation of a strong enclave can bolster black students in important ways. Psychologist G. Evelyn LeSure recently surveyed 540 students from five campuses of Claremont College in California. She found that while blacks were more likely to suffer from racist experiences than Hispanics or Asians, they also seemed to cope better. Hispanics and Asians said that racism made them less happy, and less successful, in their classes.

According to LeSure, black students make up a more homogeneous group than the other two minorities, and may be able to give each other more support. They may also expect more racism, and so be better prepared to deal with it. [24]

"For some reason," says Columbia's Crain, "people have a much harder time with what they see as black separatism than they do with the existence, say, of a Jewish fraternity. A lot of this is about fear, whites' fear of blacks and blacks' fear of whites. Fear is the underestimated great thing in life." ■

BACKGROUND

Desegregating Schools

Racial tension is one of the many legacies of a desegregation process that spent its energy simply on placing students of different races in the same schools — but had few resources left to help them get along.

"There was anger on both sides," says Vivian Paley, 64, a Chicago kindergarten teacher who is writing her eighth book about her teaching experiences. "There was ignorance and fear and a great gulf of suspicion. All that had to be lived through. I don't know why it should surprise any of us that it should take 25 years before we could begin to assess what needs to be done to make it work."

While desegregation took place at public schools and colleges at roughly the same time, it seems to have proved more painful in public schools. Beyond the obvious and profoundly threatening challenge to the status quo, desegregation represented an assault on two central tenets of American public education: community control of schools and attendance at neighborhood schools. [25] The net result, many observers say, was white flight to the suburbs.

The Supreme Court's historic but vague order to desegregate schools "with all due speed," as prescribed in the landmark 1954 *Brown v. Board of Education* decision, in practice permitted a lackadaisical pace because of its lack of specifics. In 1968, however, the court's *Green v. County School Board* ruling placed greater responsibility on local school officials to devise workable desegregation plans.

A brief period of intensive desegregation followed, until a 1974 Supreme Court case, *Milliken v. Bradley*, made it more difficult for lower courts to include suburbs in metropolitan desegregation plans. Detroit, the city directly affected by *Milliken*, saw black enrollments soar from 71 percent to nearly 90 percent in the next decade but remained unable to compel suburban districts to take part in any broad-based desegregation plan. Nationwide, desegregation continued at a slower pace until the early 1980s.

Curiously, court-ordered desegregation efforts in the late 1960s and early '70s did not address in-school issues. Says Columbia's Crain: "The courts began by saying, 'You have to desegregate. We won't make you do anything else, but you have to desegregate.' " Only later, as the need for support systems inside the schools became clear, did the courts begin to spell out solutions to problems. But by then, most of the desegregation cases already had been filed.

Mary Stuart Wells of the University of California-Los Angeles is working with Crain on a book studying the 1983 desegregation plan for St. Louis. It features the voluntary busing of 13,000 black students from the city to schools in predominantly white suburban districts.

"It's only now," says Wells, "that we're starting to see a change in the initial attitude, which was, 'We'll take these kids if we have to, but we're not going to change our schools to accommodate them.' "

Now, says Wells, the teaching force is changing, and more teachers are asking for in-service training and for lessons in black history and culture. On the political end, the suburban districts are receiving a considerable amount of state money for taking the black students. That creates a strong incentive to keep the plan in place.

Ironically, political support in St. Louis is waning. "The school board and the superintendent are now opposed" to the busing, says Wells. "They fear it is taking the cream of the crop of students out of the city schools. . . . [T]he tide is turning."

To some observers, the reaction in St. Louis reflects a new political equation: With blacks now wielding considerable political power in cities with large minority populations, the schools have inevitably become part of their power base. Thus desegregation plans that move students out of city schools — reducing the size of the school system — lose some of their appeal.

Changes at Colleges

The nation's colleges and universities have changed profoundly since the legal basis for desegregation was established in 1954. In 1962, when James Meredith enrolled at the University of Mississippi, just 6.5 percent of all undergraduates were black. In 1990, the number had risen by more than three percentage points, to 9.6 percent. Moreover, only 16 percent of black undergraduates were attending historically black institutions in 1990, compared with 36 percent in 1960.

The changes go far beyond numbers. "I remember being assigned no book by a black writer in all the years I attended Michigan," wrote Roger Wilkins in a memoir of his years at the University of Michigan, where he was a freshman in 1949. "I remember no blacks in any instructional capacity whatsoever. I do remember a white teaching fellow suggesting that elevator operator might be an occupation for which I was suited. . . . My girlfriend, Eve, was not permitted to try on clothes, as the white girls were, when she shopped on State Street. When I got to Michigan, no black had ever played on the basketball team." [26]

While the idea of public school for all children has long been accepted, college for any student who wants to go is a relatively new concept. As a result, some problems are only now beginning to emerge, as blacks begin to wield some clout at majority-white colleges.

In the case of elite private colleges and universities, administrators moved to admit more minorities, not under court order but in response to student pressure. Bunzel notes that it was black student protests following the assassination of the Rev. Dr. Martin Luther King Jr. in 1968 that led Stanford to recruit more minority students.

It was an era when many elite schools made such a commitment, and they still have a hard time fulfilling it. Because elite schools are more rigorous than other institutions, and because black students continue to lag behind whites in standard measures of achievement, top schools are competing for a scarce resource.

In the mid-1980s, only 4,200 black college-bound high school seniors had 3.75 grade point averages or better. Out of more than 71,000 black high school seniors who took the SAT, fewer than 1,000 had verbal SAT scores of 600 or better, and fewer than 1,700 had comparable math scores. [27] While some educators question the SAT as a measure of college potential, and consider it racially biased, it is nonetheless a key tool used by college admissions officers.

Affirmative Action

Poor performance by blacks has prompted the widespread adop-

Continued on p. 12

Chronology

1950s *The legal foundation for school desegregation is laid, but de facto segregation continues as social and political forces block integration.*

1954
The Supreme Court rules in *Brown v. Board of Education* that "separate but equal" schools for black and white students are inherently unequal.

September 1957
On Sept. 4, Arkansas Gov. Orval Faubus orders troops to prevent nine black teenagers from entering Central High School in Little Rock. A federal judge overrules Faubus, and the following day 15-year-old Elizabeth Eckford is spat upon and cursed by whites on her way to school, only to be turned away at the door by the National Guard. The nine students eventually attend classes under the protection of U.S. soldiers.

1958
Faubus closes all public schools rather than integrate them.

1959
Under court order, Arkansas schools are integrated.

1960s *Efforts to end segregation of schools proceed slowly until a new court ruling late in the decade.*

1962
James Meredith becomes the first black to attend the University of Mississippi, protected by federal troops ordered by President John F. Kennedy.

1968
The Supreme Court, in *Green v. County School Board*, places a greater responsibility for desegregation on local school officials. The decision spurs dramatic increases in integration efforts.

March 4, 1968
The Rev. Dr. Martin Luther King Jr. is shot and killed by James Earl Ray in Memphis, Tenn. Following the shooting, campus demonstrations spur promises of increased black enrollment and more attention to minority concerns.

1970s *Desegregation proceeds throughout the nation, but white resistance to busing grows, and new court decisions slow the process.*

1970
Parents in Charlotte, N.C., hang federal Judge James McMillan in effigy after he orders busing.

1974
Court-ordered busing in Boston spurs school boycotts and attacks on school buses. In *Milliken v. Bradley*, the Supreme Court rejects a desegregation plan for Detroit and its surrounding suburbs and limits local courts' authority to order interdistrict desegregation.

1980s *Residential segregation in urban areas continues to hamper school integration. While public support for integration and busing grows, economic and political factors place new stress on schools and families.*

1986
Federal statistics show that the 25 largest central city school districts serve 27 percent of the nation's black students and 30 percent of the Hispanic students, but only 3 percent of the white students.

1990s *Efforts to desegregate state university systems in the South are challenged by blacks; evidence mounts that segregation is increasing in public schools for the first time in 20 years.*

1992
Black educators, politicians and legal strategists say combining black and white schools in Mississippi and other states unfairly targets historically black institutions.

1993
In a survey of high-achieving high school students, 85 percent of blacks but only 30 percent of whites say minorities have fewer opportunities because of discrimination. And a Harvard University study indicates that the percentage of minority students attending predominantly white schools is declining.

Comparing High School Graduation Rates

High school completion rates for white, African American and Hispanic males dropped in 1991 (bottom graph). Women did better, with whites and African Americans maintaining steady completion rates and Hispanics improving over the previous year.

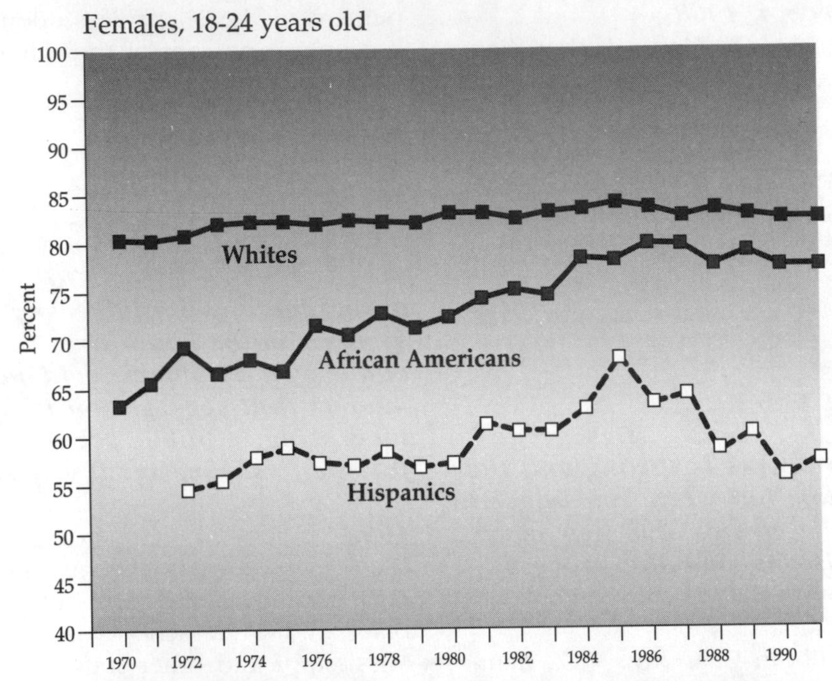

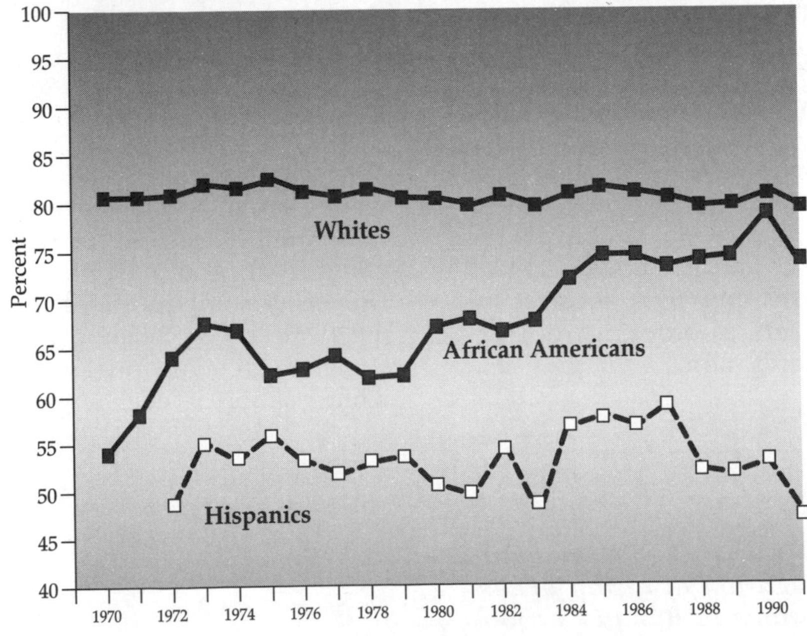

Source: "Minorities in Higher Education: Eleventh Annual Status Report," American Council on Education, 1992, based on Census Bureau data.

Continued from p. 10

tion of affirmative-action programs at colleges and universities — and a new source of student conflict. In 1991, for example, a white law student at Georgetown University in Washington, D.C., using confidential information on student applications, reported in the student newspaper that the average, white law student accepted at Georgetown scored 43 on the Law School Admission Test, compared with a 36 for the average black student. [28]

In response, the Georgetown Black Law Student Association demanded that the student and the paper's editorial board be expelled for using the confidential data; campus officials ordered the offending issue of the newspaper confiscated; and the law school dean claimed that race had not been a factor in the admissions process.

At selective state schools, such as California's Berkeley and Virginia's William and Mary, affirmative-action policies may be particularly unpopular with whites who do not gain admission but cannot afford to attend elite private institutions. Many contend that black and Hispanic students with lower grades were admitted, and they resent being asked to pay such a high personal price in the name of campus diversity.

Berkeley has moved aggressively to attract more minority students. Since a 1981 study found only 3.8 percent of Berkeley students were black and 4.4 percent were Hispanic, the university in 1988 set aside 31 percent of its openings for blacks and Hispanics.

To succeed, however, Berkeley must retain more minority students. In the class that started in 1983, 71.5 percent of the whites and 67.3 percent of the Asians graduated by 1988 — but only 43.5 percent of Hispanics and 37.5 percent of blacks. [29]

Even with affirmative action and financial assistance, many colleges

Are Campus Speech Codes Flunking Out?

There may be no animal more feared by University of Pennsylvania administrators than the water buffalo. This mild-mannered beast of burden, native to Asia, last year led the University of Pennsylvania into dangerous waters: attempting to define and punish hurtful speech.

Last February, a white student was charged with racial harassment for shouting "Shut up, you water buffalo," at five black women making noise outside his dormitory late one night. A university investigator determined that "water buffalo" qualified as a racial slur under the university's wide-ranging code barring harassing speech. Black scholars, however, stated that the term had no history of such use. And Eden Jacobowitz, the student who was charged, insisted that he had no racial intent.

The incident was seen in some quarters as a prime example of political correctness run amok. Commentators questioned whether Sheldon Hackney, president of Penn at the time, should be disqualified from heading the National Endowment for the Humanities for failing to come to Jacobowitz's defense. Eventually, the case was dropped, and early this year Penn administrators announced plans to eliminate the speech code.

Almost a year later, Hackney has his new job and Jacobowitz has seen his cause championed by *The Wall Street Journal*, and charges of wrongdoing eventually dropped. Jacobowitz had argued that he used "water buffalo" as a substitute for the Yiddish word "behameh," slang for a fool or stupid person.

But what was often glossed over in accounts of the incident was that Jacobowitz was just one of several students shouting at the women out the dorm windows that night, and that some of the other comments indeed were racial slurs. When the women complained, only Jacobowitz would admit to yelling. To some observers, it was hardly farfetched to think that Jacobowitz, who also told the women to go to the zoo if they wanted to party, had more in mind than a quaint Yiddish insult.

In the wake of the incident, one thing became clear: The university's speech code wasn't up to the job of improving race relations on campus. Rather, it seemed only to have fostered an adversarial proceeding. An increasing number of college administrations have reached similar conclusions about their speech codes, sometimes after they have failed to survive court challenges on free-speech grounds.

Hundreds of colleges and universities adopted policies intended to discipline students for displays of racial, ethnic or religious intolerance in the 1980s. They were responding to a wave of incidents, including racist graffiti scrawled on walls and blackboards, bomb threats against black dormitories and cultural centers and shouted racial slurs.

But in recent years, courts have struck down speech codes at the University of Michigan and the University of Wisconsin, among others. And in June 1992, a Supreme Court ruling overturning a St. Paul, Minn., hate-crime ordinance appeared to make it even more difficult to craft a speech code that would meet constitutional muster. †

The University of Pennsylvania plans to replace its code, which will remain in force for the rest of this academic year, with one that relies more on "informal conflict resolution," in the words of the university's interim president, Claire Faigin. Faigin has indicated that more speech, not less, is the direction to go.

"When you have guests in your home and they speak in ways that do not reflect the values you hold dear, you have a right to say, 'I don't really like the way you're talking,"' Faigin said recently. ‡

Faigin's views are in line with those of many who have studied prejudice, who say inhibitions on speech do nothing to help students overcome racial insensitivity or intolerance.

Alma Clayton-Pederson, a Vanderbilt University researcher, and Willis D. Hawley, director of the school of education at the University of Maryland at College Park, are developing an interactive video for use with a computer that will depict common scenarios of prejudice or harassment. Students will be able to choose various responses to the situation, and see what happens next. The program would be used to train small groups of college students to handle tense situations. Clayton-Pederson argues that this approach "communicates the value that higher-education institutions place on open and responsible discussion of all types of issues."

But not everyone at the University of Pennsylvania is ready to sit down for a frank talk about prejudice. "The situation here is so bad that if you tell students to talk it out after a racial slur," says Michael Chang, president of a predominantly black dormitory at the university, "you're going to have fistfights."

† For background, see "Hate Crimes," *The CQ Researcher*, Jan. 8, 1993, pp. 1-24.

‡ Quoted in *The Washington Post*, Nov. 17, 1993.

have failed to make much headway. In 1988, less than 4 percent of Smith College students were black, and the main University of Wisconsin campus at Madison was only approaching 2 percent.

The Roots of Bias

An infant's earliest interactions with parents and caregivers may affect its later relations with people of different races, according to some child-development experts. In this view, infants whose emotional needs are met evolve from happy, confident preschoolers who share toys into kindergarteners who aren't afraid of children who look or talk differently.

According to several studies published in the last decade, children notice differences in skin color as early as age 2. "By 3 years of age (and sometimes even earlier), children show signs of being influenced by societal norms and biases and may exhibit 'pre-prejudice' toward others," writes Louise Derman-Sparks in her anti-bias curriculum for preschool teachers. An example of pre-prejudice would be a child refusing to hold another child's hand because he saw that child's darker skin as "dirty." [30]

In addition to racial awareness, Derman-Sparks says that young children also pick up social clues about sex roles and attitudes toward disabilities. "By 4 or 5 years of age, children . . . use racial reasons for refusing to interact with children different from themselves," she writes. "The degree to which 4-year-olds have already internalized stereotypic gender roles, racial bias and fear of the [disabled] forcefully points out the need for anti-bias education with young children."

Derman-Sparks' curriculum includes guidelines for creating an inclusive environment through careful attention to the images, books and toys in the classroom; strategies for responding directly to children's observations about racial and ethnic differences; and suggestions for ways to use dramatic play to break down stereotypical views.

However, Derman-Sparks also notes that it is hard to know whether children who attend a preschool with an anti-bias curriculum can maintain more open attitudes in elementary school. "My guess is you'd need more than just the preschool years," she says. "It isn't enough to talk about diversity; you have to address the stereotypes and discomforts that kids are picking up. How much that is actually happening in schools, I can't judge."

Educational psychologist Robert Slavin, principal research scientist at the Center for the Social Organization of Schools at Johns Hopkins University, has found that by middle school, children have rather firm ideas about racial and ethnic identity. Slavin's studies of cooperative learning indicate that one of the most effective ways to promote tolerance is to give children the chance to work together toward a common goal.

Experts agree that one common strategy for responding to racial comments by children — telling them that differences in skin color don't matter — is ineffective and perhaps harmful. Developmental psychologists note that one of the primary tasks of early childhood is identity formation, which requires discerning and valuing one's own individual characteristics. Children who are told that people are all the same will simply not believe it, and may instead conclude that there is something shameful or negative about difference.

The "Black Table" Phenomenon

While youngsters are working out issues of individual identity, adolescents are often struggling to find their place in the group. They are also becoming sexually active. Since interracial dating and sex continue to be among the most troubling areas in race relations, high school students sometimes find it easier to separate into race-based cliques than deal with each other more openly.

The "black table" phenomenon that is so often noted on college campuses is commonplace in integrated high schools as well, and sometimes more acute. At some schools, students of different races use different entrances, bathrooms and cafeteria tables. The distinctions are enforced by the students, not by administrators. Black students at a Roslyn, N.Y., high school considered one corridor their own and would harass white males who used it; females were permitted to pass.

Norman Siegel, executive director of the New York Civil Liberties Union, and Galen Kirkland, a black attorney, team-teach a course in racial tolerance at New Utrecht High School in Bensonhurst, Brooklyn. It's near the spot where a young black man, Yusuf Hawkins, was shot and killed in 1989 by whites.

New Utrecht is an integrated school, 50 percent white, 25 percent black, 15 percent Hispanic and 10 percent Asian. Siegel says that students respond enthusiastically to the course and are enormously eager to talk about the racial issues that trouble them. The course has been adopted by 37 high schools and two junior high schools in New York City. But that doesn't mean New Utrecht students are ready to eat lunch together.

"I suppose one measure of success would be if we got to school one semester and the cafeteria was truly integrated," says Siegel. "That hasn't happened yet . . . Each group has their tables, and we say, 'What is this about?' and they tell us it's not about race, it's about liking different kinds of music. Or they'll say, 'Isn't it OK if you want to be voluntarily segregated?' " ■

CURRENT SITUATION

Learning to Get Along

There are three main approaches to helping students of different races get along in school: multicultural education; conflict resolution; and teaching tolerance directly.

Multiculturalism, something of an academic and political battleground in recent years, has become a necessity for many teachers, according to Chicago kindergarten teacher Paley.

Troubled Times for Black Colleges

William Sutton, president of historically black Mississippi Valley State University in Itta Bena, is a product of Howard University, one of the nation's top historically black institutions. He also attended Harvard University, the ultimate training ground for the white male power elite. Before coming to Mississippi Valley, Sutton was the first — and to date, the last — black vice president at Kansas State University.

"I know what the black schools are doing, and I know what the white schools are doing," says Sutton. "There is a mind-set in this country that what's black is bad, and what's white is good, but I can tell you there are some very weak white colleges, and some very strong black ones. I'd like to know why, when it comes to desegregation, it always means black people have to go to white people's places. . . . Why shouldn't white people come to our school?"

William Sutton

Mississippi Valley would be closed and its programs transferred to predominantly white Delta State University under a desegregation plan submitted to a federal court in October 1992 by the trustees of the Mississippi state college system. The plan would also merge predominantly black Alcorn State with predominantly white Mississippi State, leaving Jackson State as the only historically black campus in the system.

There is substantial opposition to the trustees' proposal, but supporters are worried that whatever plan the court adopts will not do enough to protect the state's historically black schools. Arguments in the case are scheduled for February.

Long a refuge from racism and a source of strength for the black community, historically black colleges and universities are entering an era in which their reasons for existence are increasingly called into question, both by their prospective clients and the wider academic and political world.

The state of Louisiana, like Mississippi, also is struggling to come up with desegregation plan for its state system, where historically black campuses also have been targeted for merger under some proposals. Other states as well are grappling over the public-policy implications of using taxpayer dollars to support what are essentially racially segregated institutions.

Meanwhile, private institutions such as Howard have seen enrollments stagnate after a burst of student interest in the mid-1980s. While black enrollments at majority-white colleges rose 7.8 percent from 1990 to 1991, the increase at historically black colleges was only 3.1 percent, mostly at less-expensive public institutions. †

One thing historically black institutions have going for them is considerable political clout. From Virginia Gov. L. Douglas Wilder (Howard law) to Congressional Black Caucus leader Kweisi Mfume, D-Md. (Maryland's Morgan State), their graduates are strategically placed within the political power structure.

Supporters argue that these institutions have proven themselves to be much better at nurturing black students who are academically or socially unprepared for the competition and racial tensions they would encounter at majority-white schools. They also argue that inequitable funding patterns have made it impossible for public black colleges to build themselves into first-rate institutions, and that the fairest solution is to give them the resources to do so.

Eddie N. Williams, president of the Joint Center for Political and Economic Studies, which researches issues of special interest to blacks, recently suggested a strategy that would include closing some black colleges in order to direct resources to the improvement of those that remain; raising academic standards; converting some black colleges into community education centers offering non-traditional, adult and continuing education programs; and accepting a greater white presence, both among students and faculty, at historically black schools. ‡

Sutton says Mississippi Valley has about a half-dozen white students this year out of 2,329, and he'd be happy to see more. "We're not anxious to stay as a black school. That's our history, but it doesn't need to be our future. We're willing to accept white people. I just want to know why desegregation always seems to go in one direction."

† *Minorities in Higher Education 1992: Eleventh Annual Status Report,* American Council on Education, 1993.

‡ "Reinventing Black Colleges," *Focus,* September 1993.

"For teachers, the students in their classrooms represent certain differences, and they recognize they need to deal with them," said Paley. "People are thinking very seriously, in a way they've never done before, about what it means to do that." [31]

Multicultural education takes many diverse forms. Paley invites parents of different backgrounds into her classes to tell stories from their cultures, to read children's books from those cultures and to talk about their experiences. In Milwaukee, Wis., La Escuela Fratney, a public elementary school, immerses students in an unusual bilingual program. Students speak English one day, Spanish the next, with proficiency in each language given equal weight. School systems across the country, meanwhile, are seeking textbooks and other materials with more nuanced views of the black and immigrant experience.

Paley believes that black parents have become much better advocates for their children in recent years. "African American families are being far more articulate and thoughtful and persuasive [about] racism in white-majority schools," says Paley. "No one thinks we've done a good job in the integrated classroom, but at least we are trying to start talking about it."

Conflict resolution programs often consist of training interested students as mediators in disputes. Mediators learn techniques for helping students talk and listen to each other without being pushed to violence. The effectiveness of these programs is difficult to gauge.

Numerous classroom materials have been developed for teachers who want to directly address such issues as racism, negative stereotypes and bias. For example, "Teaching Tolerance," a project started by the Southern Poverty Law Center in 1991, provides middle and high schools with a free videotape, textbook and other materials on the civil rights movement.

One of the most widely used anti-bias curricula is "Facing History and Ourselves," in which the events leading up to the Holocaust serve as a framework for examining racism, prejudice and anti-Semitism. The 17-year-old program is used by some 500,000 high school students annually.

Taking multiculturalism a giant step further, several all-black urban schools are turning to Afrocentric programs. Often controversial in the larger community because of concerns that lessons will be inaccurate and divisive, Afrocentric education is nonetheless popular in some school systems. In Atlanta, about 80 percent of public school teachers use "African-American Baseline Essays," a 533-page curriculum guide to teaching about the contributions of Africans and African Americans in every subject area. The essays originally were developed for Portland, Ore., schools.[32]

The Portland guide has been used in Atlanta for about four years now. Test scores have not improved over that time, but some principals and teachers report better attendance and students working harder.

Some scholars object to the essays' portrayal of Egypt as the cradle of civilization and Egyptians as black Africans. The ancient Egyptians "were African in the sense that they lived in Africa, but certainly they are not the same as the black Africans of this country," said University of Chicago historian William H. McNeill. "They are not the least bit the same, and anyone who thinks so is just talking nonsense." Moreover, he said, Afrocentrists "are not historians; they are agitators."[33]

However, the author of one of the essays, John Henrick Clarke, a professor emeritus of African history at New York's Hunter College, said, "Because the concession of Egypt's achievements would seriously undermine theories of white superiority in the modern period if Egyptians were black Africans, traditions of treatment of the Egyptian past have been created and preserved in Western thought that conceal and distort the true nature of the Egyptian experience."[34]

Black Studies

As black students continue to struggle at majority-white colleges, black and ethnic studies may reflect one way for minority students to find academic and intellectual areas where they see their own experiences reflected and valued. In that context, Afrocentrism has become a fierce battleground for scholars seeking to enhance the standing of black studies as an academic discipline.

Like the push for diversity at mostly white colleges, many black studies programs owe their existence to student protests more than two decades ago. Some programs are strong and rigorous. Others, lacking funding and student interest, were branded as academically second-rate. Spurred by increased enrollments and led by a new group of scholars, black studies is now moving to shed that stigma.

Two of the nation's most prominent black scholars, Henry Louis Gates Jr., and Cornel West, who head the African American studies departments at Harvard and Princeton, respectively, criticize Afrocentrism as a foundation for work in black studies. West finds Afrocentrism parochial. Gates argues that black Americans are so far removed from their African roots, and those roots are so varied, that it is misleading to interpret the black experience as primarily influenced by Africa.

"We need to explore the hyphen in African-American, on both sides of the Atlantic," Gates said. "We must chart the porous relations between an 'American' culture that officially pretends that an Anglo American *regional* culture is the true universal culture, and the black cultures it so long stigmatized. We must also document both the continuities and discontinuities between African and African American cultures, rather than to reduce the astonishing diversity of African cultures to a few simple-minded shibboleths."[35]

But other leading black academics take a different approach. Molefi Kete Asante, chairman of African American

Continued on p. 18

At Issue:

Does multicultural education contribute to racial tensions?

yes

Arthur M. Schlesinger Jr.

Albert Schweitzer professor of humanities, City University of New York

FROM "WRITING, AND REWRITING, HISTORY," *NEW LEADER*, DEC. 30, 1991

The current upsurge of multiculturalism in its militant forms has placed the idea of a common culture in jeopardy. Instead of a shared history, we see a congeries of separate ethnic and racial histories, each intended to promote group self-esteem, each subject to the veto of the group involved....

Let me be clear about this sensitive subject. When multicultural education means telling our children about other races, other cultures, other continents, it is a salutary development. We should surely teach black history, women's history, Hispanic history, African history, Asian history. We should teach American history, warts and all, with full accounting of the fact that America has been through most of its existence a racist nation. . . .

But when multiculturalism means, as the zealots insist, that our public schools should teach subjects like history and literature as emotional therapies, not intellectual disciplines, that is a different matter. When it means the assumption that ethnicity is the defining experience for every American, that the point of education is to make children feel good about their ancestors, that we must discard the idea of a common culture and celebrate, reinforce and perpetuate separate ethnic and racial communities, then multiculturalism not only betrays history but undermines the theory of America as one people.

Militant multiculturalism, portraying Europe as the root of all evil, goes on to denounce the alleged inequities of the "Eurocentric curriculum." Certainly Europe, like every other culture, has committed its share of crimes — not least against other Europeans. Yet, unlike other cultures, it has conceived and acted upon ideals that expose and combat its own crimes. No other culture has made self-criticism so organic a part of its being. Whatever the crimes of Europe, that continent is also the source . . . of those liberating ideals of individual liberty, political democracy, the impartial rule of law, human rights and cultural freedom to which most of the world aspires, ideals that empower people of every race, color and creed. To deny the European origins of American civilization is to falsify history.

Militant multiculturalism glorifies ethnic and racial communities at the expense of the common culture. It glorifies ethnic and racial myths at the expense of honest history. . . . [It] promotes fragmentation, segregation, ghettoization — all the more dangerous at a time when ethnic conflict is tearing apart one nation after another. James Baldwin once said, "To create one nation has proved to be a hideously difficult task; there is certainly no need now to create two, one black and one white."

no

Nathan Glazer

Professor of education, Harvard University Graduate School of Education

FROM "SCHOOL WARS: A BRIEF HISTORY OF MULTICULTURALISM IN AMERICA," THE BROOKINGS REVIEW, FALL 1993.

One might well ask why multiculturalism has become such an important issue today. It has been at least 20 years since public schools started adapting themselves to the presumed cultural distinctiveness and interests of blacks and Hispanics, by modifying textbooks, introducing new reading materials, changing examinations, instructing non-English-speaking students in Spanish for a few years. What has put the issue on the agenda today, not only in the public schools, but in colleges and universities, public and private?

I believe the basic explanation is a build-up of frustration in the black population in recent years over the failure of civil rights reforms to deliver what was expected from them. In the colleges, affirmative action — well-established as it is — has not increased markedly the number of black instructors or the number of black students who can qualify for the more selective institutions without special consideration. In the public schools, black achievement as measured by ... SAT scores and high school completion rates has improved, but the gaps between black and white achievement remain large. . . .

In short, I do not believe we would see the present uproar over multiculturalism were it not for the frustration among blacks over widespread educational failure, which leads them to cast about for alternatives, new departures, new approaches, anything that might help, including special schools for black boys featuring an Afrocentric education.

For the critics of multiculturalism, the issue that ultimately determines its acceptability is a judgment as to the underlying purpose of the curriculum reform. Is it to promote harmony and an acceptance of our society? Or to portray our society as so fatally flawed by racism, so irredeemably unfair and unequal that it must be rejected as evil? The critics fear that the second vision underlies the strong multicultural position. On one level, they are right. But if we look more deeply into the objectives of those who promote a strong multicultural thrust, and who in doing so present a somewhat lopsided view of our history, we will find that they promote multiculturalism not because they aim at divisiveness and separation as a good, not because they — to put it in the strongest terms possible — want to break up the union, but because they aim at a fuller inclusiveness of deprived groups.

In the short term, their vision may well mean more conflict and divisiveness, but they see this as a stage on the way to a greater inclusiveness. They are no Quebec separatists, Croatian nationalists, Sikh or Tamil separatists. They seek inclusion and equality in a common society.

Experimenting With All-Black, All-Boy Classes . . .

The boys stream into the cafeteria, jostling each other with elbows and backpacks, their 11-year-old energy bouncing off the cinder-block walls. But they settle quickly into chairs at the round tables facing the stage. Some sport brightly colored T-shirts and jeans, but most of the children wear dark pants and white shirts.

The fourth-graders at the Robert W. Coleman Elementary School in Baltimore, Md., have been together in all-boy classes since first grade, and on this day they are about to get a pep talk.

"I'm upset," says Spencer H. Holland, a black educator and champion of all-male classrooms for black boys from disadvantaged neighborhoods. "I'm upset because I've heard you are not doing the work you are capable of doing. I've heard you are giving your teachers a very hard time. . . . I'm upset, but I'm not worried, because changes can be made."

© Joslin Morgan

Spencer H. Holland

Pacing back and forth with a microphone, Holland wades into them, part coach, part preacher, part father. He talks about the departure of an admired teacher. "It was not your fault," Holland tells the boys. "He did not desert you, because he knew he had prepared you for fourth grade."

Holland tells them that the drug dealers they see on the streets have a problem. "You know what's wrong with them? They can't read," Holland says. "Why, some of them can't read as well as you can." A few of the boys laugh.

"What happens to drug dealers?" Holland asks.

"They go to jail," offers one boy.

"They get whacked," suggests another.

"That's right," says Holland. "Those are the only two things that happen to them."

When these boys started at Coleman, it was just another troubled elementary school in an all-black neighborhood in a poor city. About 85 percent of the students lived with a single parent or grandparent. Test scores were low.

In 1993, Coleman students scored in the top five among elementary schools in the city in some test categories. This is also the first year that all classes have been segregated by sex, the final step in a five-year experiment initiated by Principal Hattie Johnson.

Holland, director of the Center for Educating African-American Males at Morgan State University in Baltimore, has instituted a mentoring program at the school that brings in black male professionals and college students to work as classroom assistants. Holland's assistant, Kevin Mercer, runs an after-school program at the school and a summer camp for boys who keep their grades up and behave.

A few years ago, the concept of all-black-male classes, preferably taught by black male teachers, was one of the hottest ideas in education. The rationale was that the dismal academic performance of black boys often could be traced to the absence of positive male role models for boys in

Continued from p. 16

studies at Temple University in Philadelphia, says that black-studies departments that do not consider themselves Afrocentric should not call themselves black studies.

The controversial chairman of the black studies department at City College of New York, Leonard Jeffries, embraces Afrocentrism with what critics call an eccentric and racially inflammatory view of the differences between blacks and whites.

Jeffries was recently reinstated as chairman after being removed following a speech seen as anti-Semitic. But the widespread publicity given to his views of blacks as warm, giving "sun people" and whites as uncaring, deficient "ice people" during the uproar was seen by many scholars as casting a bad light on a field that has fought hard to gain credibility in the academic establishment.[36]

Some critics feel that the Afrocentric focus of many black studies departments discourages white students from taking courses offered by those departments, barring them from the kind of intellectual experience that might help them refine their own racial attitudes. But according to Asante, "This is not an idea to replace all things European, but to expand the dialogue to include African American information. . . . Afrocentricity is neither racist nor anti-Semitic; it is about placing African people within our own historical framework. In none of the major works of Afrocentricity has there ever been a hint of racism, ethnocentrism or anti-anybody."[37] ■

OUTLOOK

No Easy Answers

As the black middle class continues to grow and prosper, more blacks are moving to the suburbs. Some experts believe that with integration now a widely accepted social goal, suburban school systems may be

. . . Hopeful Signs in Baltimore

high-crime neighborhoods.

But many of the programs foundered when faced with legal challenges based on constitutional issues. The dearth of black male elementary school teachers also presented practical problems. In Holland's view, some proponents erred in combining the black-male classroom concept with an Afrocentric approach, thereby creating unnecessary political problems.

"I say, why go through that?" says Holland. "The problem is not the curriculum, the problem is these boys are not learning to read. I am a staunch supporter of multicultural education, but why set yourself up?"

In Baltimore, the idea of segregating students by sex has not generated much controversy, and three other elementary schools are experimenting with the idea. Coleman Principal Johnson is a strong believer in the benefits to girls as well as boys, so there is an effort to ensure that special programs for the boys are duplicated for the girls. "For the boys, we have to develop a bonding process," says Johnson. "I want them to remember, when they hit age 16 or 17 and go to pick up a gun, 'I was in first grade with this man, and we had fun.' So maybe they won't shoot." Now, she says, the boys are beginning to "talk it out when they have problems, to realize they can help each other."

Research has long shown benefits to girls from single-sex education, particularly in math and science, and that is Johnson's hope at Coleman as well. "We wanted to create young ladies very strong in math and science, and I believe we are doing that," says Johnson. "The girls are getting the idea this is not just a guy thing."

For a place built like a cinder-block bunker, Coleman is a cheery place. Teachers speak enthusiastically about their students and about special programs at the school. Students approach Assistant Principal Sandra Graves in the hallway to ask for hugs. Science teacher Robert DiSimone takes groups of students to nearby Coppin State College for advanced science classes.

Paradoxically, DiSimone feels that the single-sex classes benefit girls more than boys. "The girls adjust really well," he says. "They are great at working together on projects." The boys, however, still have trouble with teamwork and concentration. "I think we need to look more at the whole socialization issue, of how boys are taught to behave. It goes well beyond the six-hour school day," he says. He adds, however, that the boys will talk about some things in the all-male classes that they would probably never discuss in mixed classes. "I've had some kids admit they like to play with dolls. They'd never do that in front of girls."

But the unanswered question is how much of the improved test scores are due to single-sex classes, and how much to the presence of an energetic principal who has forged more than a dozen partnerships with local companies, private and public schools, colleges and government agencies to bring resources to her school; to the extra attention and tutoring the boys receive through Holland's mentoring program, after-school program and summer camp; and to Coleman's array of programs bringing parents into the schools.

Whatever the reason for Coleman's success, one thing seems clear: In a city where many schools are failing, here's one that works.

able to head off some of the problems encountered in areas where court-ordered desegregation occurred.

However, recent research indicates that housing patterns remain so segregated that newly integrated suburbs may quickly become majority-black neighborhoods. While whites profess support for integrated neighborhoods, research indicates that once the black population reaches around 8 or 10 percent, more whites will begin moving out than moving in. Blacks, by contrast, prefer neighborhoods with a higher concentration of black residents — 25 to 50 percent. [38]

That dynamic, along with parents' understandable preference for neighborhood schools, powerfully limits school desegregation. There is some reason to believe that integrated schools will continue to struggle with tense race relations as long as minority students are living different lives in different neighborhoods.

Similarly, racial problems are unlikely to disappear at colleges. For one reason, the policies developed by many colleges and universities to welcome students from different racial and ethnic backgrounds often backfire.

In many cases, affirmative-action policies designed to increase the percentage of black students have been obscured, inadequately explained or only half-heartedly defended by administrators. The result has been to increase grievances among some white students, who feel they have never been offered a compelling rationale for a policy that does have some costs for them.

A number of campuses turned in recent years to speech codes designed to protect minority students from harassment. However, the constitutional difficulties inherent in controlling speech, not to mention the impracticality of policing verbal exchanges between students, have slowed that trend.

Despite all the evidence of racial tension and insensitivity, some see a ray of hope. Surveys show that increasing numbers of black and white college students are learning to get along better. "We see a high degree of cross-race interaction in every dimension," says University of Michigan researcher Sylvia Hurtado, who is completing work on a survey of dining, studying and dating between students of different races.

In his book about race relations at Stanford, Bunzel offers an explanation for the apparent contradiction between racial tension and growing racial interaction: "Put very simply, the struggle against racism and the push for better race relations are two different things." [39]

But as long as housing patterns remain segregated, Harvard's Orfield notes, the trend toward school resegregation may be a painful reality for years to come. His report concludes that "the country and its schools are going through vast changes without any strategy. The civil rights impulse from the 1960s is dead in the water, and the ship is floating backward toward the shoals of racial segregation." [40] ■

Susan Phillips is a freelance writer in Washington, D.C.

Notes

[1] Douglas S. Massey, "The Residential Segregation of Blacks, Hispanics, and Asians: 1970 to 1990," to be published in 1994 in *Immigration and the Changing State of Race Relations*, Gerald D. Jaynes, ed.

[2] Douglas A. Blackmon, "The Resegregation of the Southern School," *Harpers*, September 1992.

[3] The December 1993 Harvard study, "The Growth of Segregation in American Schools: Changing Patterns of Separation and Poverty Since 1968," was authored by Gary Orfield, director of the Harvard Project on School Desegregation, for the National School Boards Association.

[4] For background, see "Magnet Schools," *Editorial Research Reports*, May 15, 1987, pp. 225-240.

[5] *USA Today*, Nov. 11, 1993. The survey was done for the Center for Study of Sport in Society at Northeastern University.

[6] Cynthia Coburn, "Racial and Ethnic Conflict in Schools: A Print Media Search," National Coalition of Advocates for Students, June 1992.

[7] John H. Bunzel, *Race Relations on Campus: Stanford Students Speak* (1992), p. 13.

[8] *Ibid.*, p. 4.

[9] Darlene Powell Hopson and Derek Hopson, *Different and Wonderful* (1990), p. xix.

[10] *Ibid.*, p. 152.

[11] For background, see "Violence in Schools," *The CQ Researcher*, Sept. 11, 1992, pp. 785-808.

[12] *The Chronicle of Higher Education*, Oct. 9, 1991, p. 1.

[13] Information in the above two paragraphs comes from Amy Stuart Wells and Robert L. Crain, "Perpetuation Theory and the Long-Term Effects of School Desegregation" (in draft).

[14] U.S. Department of Education, Schools and Staffing in the United States: A Statistical Profile, 1990-1991 (1993), p. 49.

[15] Unpublished data from the 1986 "Elementary and Secondary Schools Civil Rights Survey," U.S. Department of Education, Office for Civil Rights, cited in Percy Bates, *Can We Get There From Here?* September 1990.

[16] Hopson and Hopson, *op. cit.*, Chapter 1.

[17] Quoted in David J. Dent, "Readin', Ritin' & Rage," *Essence*, November 1989.

[18] Jawanza Kunjufu, *Countering the Conspiracy to Destroy Black Boys* (1990), Vol. III, p. 32.

[19] For background, see "Why Schools Still Have Tracking," *Editorial Research Reports*, December 28, 1990, pp. 745-760.

[20] Jeannie Oakes, *Keeping Track* (1985), p. 4.

[21] Quoted in the *Los Angeles Times*, Washington edition, Nov. 9, 1993.

[22] "Race on Campus," *U.S. News & World Report*, April 19, 1993 p. 52.

[23] Quoted in "Building Inclusive Universities," *FOCUS*, October 1993, p. 4.

[24] LeSure's findings are summarized in *USA Today*, Sept. 28, 1993.

[25] Christine H. Rossell, "The carrot or the stick for school desegregation policy?" *Urban Affairs Quarterly*, March 1990.

[26] Roger Wilkins, "A Modern Story," *Mother Jones*, September/October 1991.

[27] Bunzel, *op. cit.*, p. 17.

[28] Timothy Maguire, "My Bout with Affirmative Action," *Commentary*, April 1992.

[29] Andrew Hacker, *Two Nations: Black and White, Separate, Hostile, Unequal* (1992), p. 140.

[30] Louise Derman-Sparks, *Anti-Bias Curriculum: Tools for Empowering Young Children* (1989), p. 2.

[31] For background, see "Conflict Over Multicultural Education," *Editorial Research Reports*, Nov. 30, 1990, pp. 681-696.

[32] *Ibid.*, pp. 689-694.

[33] *Ibid.* p. 692.

[34] *Ibid.*

[35] *Newsweek*, Sept. 23, 1991, p. 47.

[36] James Traub, "The Hearts and Minds of City College," *The New Yorker*, June 7, 1993, p. 49.

[37] *Newsweek*, *op. cit.*, p. 46.

[38] Massey, *op. cit.*, p. 2.

[39] Bunzel, *op. cit.*, p. 61.

[40] Orfield, *op. cit.* p. 2.

Bibliography

Selected Sources Used

Books

Bunzel, John H., *Race Relations on Campus: Stanford Students Speak*, Stanford Alumni Association, 1992.
Surveys and interviews with Stanford University students form the heart of this close-up view of the complex racial dynamics at an elite liberal university.

Hacker, Andrew, *Two Nations: Black and White, Separate, Hostile, Unequal*, Scribners, 1992.
Hacker draws a bleak portrait of the many forces — social, political, economic — that contribute to the current climate of mistrust and misunderstanding between black and white Americans.

Kunjufu, Jawanza, *Countering the Conspiracy to Destroy Black Boys*, Vols. I, II and III, African American Images, 1982, 1986 and 1990.
This deeply felt but highly subjective analysis of the roots of black boys' poor academic performance and other problems suggests that schoolroom culture rewards white, feminine behavioral patterns that black boys cannot emulate.

Oakes, Jeannie, *Keeping Track: How Schools Structure Inequality*, Yale University Press, 1985.
This remains the definitive study on ability grouping of students and its effect on achievement. Oakes also demonstrates how race and class affect student assignments to learning tracks.

Hopson, Arlene Powell and Hopson, Derek, *Different and Wonderful: Raising Black Children in a Race Conscious Society*, Prentice Hall, 1990.
This practical handbook for black parents outlines difficulties black children may encounter in school and offers suggestions on dealing constructively with teachers and school administrators, countering negative messages received in school and building self-esteem.

Articles

Blackmon, Douglas A., "The Resegregation of a Southern School," *Harper's*, September 1992.
Blackmon describes his experiences as a white child attending newly desegregated schools in the Mississippi Delta town of Leland, and the process that has gradually resulted in a return to segregation.

Lefton, Terry, "Building Bridges in the Big Apple," *Teaching Tolerance*, spring, 1992.
This article describes the course in race relations taught by Norman Siegel, director of the New York Civil Liberties Union, and attorney Galen Kirkland at a high school in the Brooklyn community where a black teenager, Yusuf Hawkins, was shot and killed by young whites in 1989.

Maguire, Timothy, "My Bout With Affirmative Action," *Commentary*, April 1992.
The author tells of his experience at Georgetown University, where he was threatened with expulsion after writing an article about the difference in average Law School Admission Test scores between black and white students admitted to the law school.

"Race on Campus," *U.S. News and World Report*, April 19, 1993.
An overview of racial tensions at college campuses, with special attention to self-segregation by black and minority students.

Traub, James, "The Hearts and Minds of City College," *The New Yorker*, June 7, 1993.
Traub examines the uproar at the City College of New York surrounding the dismissal and eventual reinstatement of controversial Afrocentric Professor Leonard Jeffries as the chairman of the Black Studies Department.

White, Jack E., "Growing Up in Black and White," *Time*, May 17, 1993.
White offers a parents' perspective on the problems black children sometimes have with self-esteem and self-image, and presents evidence that the burdens of desegregation have fallen mostly on blacks.

Reports and Studies

Coburn, Cynthia, National Coalition of Advocates for Students, *Racial and Ethnic Conflict in Schools: A Print Media Search*, June 1992.
A summary of newspaper reports about racial incidents in public schools across the country during a two-month period in 1991 and 1992.

American Council on Education, *Minorities in Higher Education, 1992 Annual Status Report*.
This report includes high school completion rates, college attendance and completion information for various ethnic minorities.

Orfield, Gary, National School Boards Association, *The Growth of Segregation in American Schools: Changing Patters of Separation and Poverty Since 1968*, December 1993.
Orfield presents the first statistical evidence that integration in public schools is starting to decline after increasing or holding steady for more than two decades.

The Next Step

Additional information from UMI's Newspaper & Periodical Abstracts database

Opinions

"In sports, lessons on diversity are going untaught," ***Detroit News & Free Press*, Nov. 21, 1993, p. F2.**

An editorial says the effect of racial segregation, intentional or otherwise, in organized sports or any other school activity tends to make children more comfortable associating only with those people resembling them, and that is precisely the wrong lesson for them to learn in the classroom or on the playing field.

"New era of segregation demands new responses," ***USA Today*, Dec. 15, 1993, p. A10.**

An editorial discusses a Harvard study released in December 1993 that found racial segregation in schools worse than at any time since the 1960s. The study shows that black and Hispanic children are increasingly isolated in violent urban enclaves and bad schools.

Russakoff, Dale, "At Penn, can frank talk make racial tension walk?" ***The Washington Post*, Nov. 19, 1993, p. A2.**

Reporter Russakoff discusses the University of Pennsylvania's new leader's efforts to ease racial tensions.

Programs to Combat Tension

Dembner, Alice, "UMass will mentor minority youths, assure enrollment," ***Boston Globe*, Dec. 2, 1993, p. 1.**

A private foundation has awarded $600,000 to the University of Massachusetts at Amherst for an extensive partnership with Springfield middle schools designed to increase minority enrollment and improve race relations on campus.

Hall, Barbara, "School district gets grant for magnet plan," ***The New York Times*, Nov. 14, 1993, p. WC11.**

The New Rochelle, N.Y., school district has received a $1.39 million grant from the U.S. Department of Education. Local officials said the grant would be used to establish magnet schools at their Barnard and Columbus Elementary School sites. These conversions, part of the national trend to redress racial imbalance with magnet schools, are notable for their stress on change at early grade levels.

Heller, Carol E.; Hawkins, Joseph A., "Sowing the seeds of racial tolerance," ***Education Week*, Sept. 22, 1993, p. 29.**

The Southern Poverty Law Center's Teaching Tolerance project gives away its products and services free to teach students about the civil rights movement.

Holmstrom, David, "Boston-area teens target intolerance," ***Christian Science Monitor*, Dec. 6, 1993, p. 17.**

David Holmstrom describes activities at the 1993 National Conference for Christians and Jews, which taught 200 urban and suburban teenagers from the Boston area skills to combat racism and intolerance.

Konley, Patricia, "Glendora: Widening children's circle of tolerance and inclusion," ***Los Angeles Times*, Sept. 27, 1993, p. B4.**

The Glendora (California) School District's Green Circle program is featured. The program teaches second-graders the virtues of inclusion and appreciation of difference.

Love, Tru, "What I learned as a white girl in a black school," ***Ebony*, September 1993, pp. 44-50.**

The feelings of fear and prejudice toward blacks by whites can be overcome through a greater understanding of the black community. A white, female student discusses her experiences at Detroit's Finney High School, a black school.

Ryan, Bill, "New London's larger world in a school," ***The New York Times*, Nov. 7, 1993, p. CN1.**

The Regional Multicultural Magnet School in New London, Conn., is featured. The school is part of a plan to eliminate racial isolation in the state's public schools.

Research and Studies

Brady, Erik, "Survey: Racial, religious confrontations on rise," ***USA Today*, Nov. 11, 1993, p. C8.**

Three-quarters of high school students say they often witness confrontations that are motivated by race or religion, according to a Lou Harris poll. That is an increase from 57 percent in 1990. The study showed that a program using former athletes to counsel young people can help defuse tense conditions.

Jordan, Mary, "Segregation in schools increases: U.S. study says 70 percent of blacks, Hispanics are racially isolated," ***The Washington Post*, Dec. 14, 1993, p. A1.**

Racial isolation in America's schools is increasing, with 70 percent of black and Hispanic students studying in classrooms with a predominantly minority enrollment.

Segregation in Schools

Adams, Chris, "Our separate ways: Integration enrolled in name only," ***Times-Picayune*, Nov. 14, 1993, p. A1.**

In 1954 the U.S. Supreme Court declared the notion of

separate but equal schools inherently unequal. In New Orleans, almost half of the area's children attend schools that are nearly all-black or nearly all-white. (Part of a series).

Hornbeck, Mark; Basheda, Valarie, "School choice debate centers on the race issue," *Detroit News*, Dec. 1, 1993, p. A1.
Michigan lawmakers were expected to consider schools of choice again Dec. 1, 1993, after an impassioned six-hour debate that echoed the race-charged busing issue of the early 1970s ended Nov. 30 without a vote.

Schmidt, Peter, "U.S. judge rules educational practices led to student segregation in Illinois district," *Education Week*, Nov. 10, 1993, p. 9.
A federal judge found the Rockford, Ill., school district guilty of racial discrimination and school resegregation based, in part, on its use of some educational practices previously seen by the courts as racially neutral. The district was also faulted for its drawing of school boundaries, its use of open enrollment and its racially skewed distribution of teachers.

Tension in High Schools

Anderson, Eric, "School plans to apologize for alleged racial taunts," *Denver Post*, Sept. 23, 1993, p. B3.
On Sept. 22, 1993, a Golden (Colorado) High School official said that Golden's student council plans to apologize to Aurora (Colorado) Hinkley High School because black Hinkley cheerleaders allegedly were taunted with racial slurs during a football game between the schools on Sept. 14.

Hevesi, Dennis, "Cortines moves to devise new multicultural curriculum," *The New York Times*, Nov. 18, 1993, p. B3.
New York City Schools Chancellor Ramon C. Cortines has asked his staff and an advisory board to devise a new curriculum that bolsters multicultural education throughout the school system. The effort is designed to fight discrimination based on race, ethnic origin or sexual orientation.

Stein, Anne, "District 65's school test scores re-ignite racial imbalance battle," *Chicago Tribune*, Nov. 17, 1993, p. 2C6.
A wide disparity in test results on the 1993 state school report card in Evanston/Skokie District 65 re-ignited a heated debate over the question of racial balance within the district's schools, with some white parents warning that their children are being shortchanged by overcrowding and the racial imbalance of an enrollment that is more than 70 percent black.

"White girls jeered for acting black," *The New York Times*, Dec. 8, 1993, p. B7.
A nearly all-white rural school in Morocco, Ind., has been rife with tension over white girls wearing baggy clothes, braids and other fashions usually associated with young blacks. Since mid-November 1993, at least five girls have withdrawn from North Newton Junior-Senior High after being jeered and spit on by boys accusing them of "acting black."

Tension at Universities

"College hopes Maya Angelou can ease racial tension," *Jet*, Sept. 13, 1993, p. 22.
In an attempt to ease the campus racial tensions at Olivet College in Michigan, the school has gotten some help from poet Maya Angelou. Angelou offered a videotaped interview to the school that promotes multiculturalism.

Culver, Kate, "Campus fires: Dissenters, steal, destroy student papers," *Quill*, October 1993, pp. 12-15.
Dozens of college campuses have struggled to cope with the thefts of campus newspapers that began in May 1992. The thefts have become a way of protesting what many feel are racist remarks and have left school administrators unable to solve the problem.

Leff, Lisa, "Students detail racism complaints at U-Md. rally," *The Washington Post*, Nov. 4, 1993, p. C3.
More than 200 University of Maryland students and employees were on hand for a "speak out" that was organized to air grievances about the way ethnic minorities are treated by the campus newspaper and school administration.

McCabe, Coco, "Area colleges reach out to the world," *Boston Globe*, Nov. 14, 1993, p. N1.
The efforts of independent private colleges in the area north of Boston to attain a balanced cultural mix of students on their campuses are examined.

"Penn to alter harassment rules to balance free speech and privacy," *The New York Times*, Nov. 17, 1993, p. A25.
Officials of the University of Pennsylvania vowed on Nov. 17, 1993, to rework a racial harassment policy invoked against a white student, Eden Jacobowitz, who called five black women "water buffalo." Officals said that the policy used in disciplinary measures last spring against Jacobowitz will be replaced on June 30, 1994, with a "dramatically different approach" based on students' suggestions and comments.

Stains, Laurence R., "Speech impediment," *Rolling Stone*, Aug. 5, 1993, pp. 45-49.
University of Pennsylvania freshman Eden Jacobowitz was accused by the school of violating its racial-harassment policy when he shouted at fellow students making noise outside his dorm window. The investigation, race relations at the university, its racial-harassment policy and speech codes are discussed.

Back Issues

Great Research on Current Issues Starts Right Here...Recent topics covered by The CQ Researcher are listed below. Before May 1991, reports were published under the name of Editorial Research Reports.

JUNE 1992
Nuclear Proliferation
Food Irradiation
Lead Poisoning
Hard Times for Libraries

JULY 1992
Alternative Energy
Prescription Drug Prices
Alzheimer's Disease
Infant Mortality

AUGUST 1992
The Homeless
Work, Family and Stress
NATO's Changing Role
Marine Mammals vs. Fish

SEPTEMBER 1992
Domestic Partners
Violence in Schools
Public Broadcasting
Women in the Military

OCTOBER 1992
Depression
U.S. Auto Industry
Youth Apprenticeships
Hispanic Americans

Back issues are available for $4.00 (subscribers) or $7.00 (non-subscribers). Quantity discounts apply to orders over ten. To order, call Congressional Quarterly Customer Service at (202) 887-8621.

Binders are available for $15.00. To order call 1-800-638-1710.

NOVEMBER 1992
Physical Fitness
Privatization
Paying for College
U.S. Policy in Asia

DECEMBER 1992
Crackdown on Smoking
The New CIA
Eating Disorders
Women and AIDS

JANUARY 1993
Hate Crimes
Child Sexual Abuse
Nuclear Fusion
U.S. Trade Policy

FEBRUARY 1993
Community Policing
Europe's New Right
School Censorship
Violence Against Women

MARCH 1993
Gay Rights
Aid to Russia
War on Drugs
TV Violence

APRIL 1993
Head Start
High-Speed Rail
Children's Legal Rights
Muslims in America

MAY 1993
Cults in America
Preventing Teen Pregnancy
Software Piracy
National Parks

JUNE 1993
Food Safety
Prostitution
Childhood Immunizations
National Service

JULY 1993
Electric Cars
Population Growth
Downward Mobility
Intelligence Testing

AUGUST 1993
Mental Illness
Bilingual Education
Foreign Policy Burden
School Funding

SEPTEMBER 1993
Suburban Crime
Public Housing
Supreme Court Preview
Immigration Reform

OCTOBER 1993
Airline Safety
Disaster Response
Science in the Courtroom
The Glass Ceiling

NOVEMBER 1993
Paying for Retirement
Charitable Giving
Privacy in the Workplace
Adoption

DECEMBER 1993
U.S. Vietnam-Relations
Learning Disabilities
Child Care
Space Program's Future

Future Topics

- ***South Africa***
- ***Job Training***
- ***Pesticides***

THE CQ Researcher
PUBLISHED BY CONGRESSIONAL QUARTERLY INC.

South Africa's Future

Can South Africa make the transition to a non-racial democracy?

After four decades of domestic unrest and international condemnation, South Africa has jettisoned its policy of racial apartheid and started down the path to a non-racial democracy. Under a new, interim constitution — adopted after three years of difficult negotiations — the country's black majority will vote for the first time in national elections scheduled for April 27. Nelson Mandela, the once-imprisoned leader of the African National Congress, is all but certain to be chosen president of a five-year coalition government. But an alliance of white and black conservatives may boycott the election. Political violence also casts a shadow over the campaign. And observers question whether an ANC-led government will be able to meet the expectations of its newly enfranchised constituency.

INSIDE THIS ISSUE

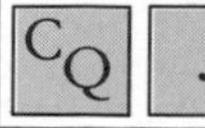
January 14, 1994 • Volume 4, No. 2 • 25-48

Formerly Editorial Research Reports

SOUTH AFRICA'S FUTURE

COVER: SOUTH AFRICAN PRESIDENT F.W. DE KLERK AND AFRICAN NATIONAL CONGRESS PRESIDENT NELSON MANDELA. (AP/WIDE WORLD PHOTOS)

THE *CQ Researcher*

January 14, 1994
Volume 4, No. 2

The CQ Researcher (ISSN 1056-2036). Formerly Editorial Research Reports. Published weekly (48 times per year, not printed the first Friday of any month with five Fridays) by Congressional Quarterly Inc., 1414 22nd St., N.W., Washington, D.C. 20037. Rates are furnished upon request. Second-class postage paid at Washington, D.C. POSTMASTER: Send address changes to The CQ Researcher, 1414 22nd St., N.W., Washington, D.C. 20037.

South Africa's Future

By Kenneth Jost

The Issues

The hour was late, the negotiators tired and the setting — a cavernous hall in the World Trade Center just outside Johannesburg — less than grand. But stop-and-start talks had finally produced a post-apartheid constitution for South Africa, and the mood in the early morning hours of Nov. 18 was euphoric.

"We are at the beginning of a new era," declared Nelson Mandela, the head of the African National Congress (ANC), who is all but certain to become the country's first black president after elections scheduled for April 27 — the first in which all races will participate.

F.W. de Klerk, the white president who has presided over the dismantling of South Africa's intricate legal apparatus of racial separation, said the new, interim constitution fulfilled his vision of a country "where freedom, peace and justice could walk hand in hand."

Ismail Mohamed, the Indian judge who presided over the constitutional negotiations, looked confidently to the future. "No force can now stop or even delay our emancipation from the pain and the shame of our racist past," said Mohamed, the only non-white judge in a country where whites constitute less than 15 percent of the population. [1] (*See table, p. 37.*)

Less than three weeks later, the nation marked another milestone: Black South Africans on Dec. 7 began exercising power at the national level for the first time as members of the newly created Transitional Executive Council. The council, made up of representatives from the 19 parties to the constitutional talks, will oversee government policy leading up to the election of a new, non-racial Parliament in April.

The agreement on the interim constitution, providing for a five-year "national unity" government and a bill of

AP/Wide World Photo

rights aimed at protecting minority rights, came after an often contentious, three-year process. Negotiators struggled to find accommodations that would satisfy the country's disenfranchised black population and simultaneously reassure the whites who have ruled South Africa since its creation as an independent nation in 1910.

Despite the undoubted accomplishments, the country still faces political dangers between now and April. Most worrisome is the threat of violence from a holdout alliance of conservative whites, the black Inkatha Freedom Party of Zulu Chief Mangosuthu Buthelezei and leaders of black "homelands" being abolished under the new constitution.

"There's an enormous amount of violence in South African society that will inhibit the easy run-up to elections and make dangerous the development of democracy," says Robert Rotberg, a Harvard University professor of African politics.

The new government will confront an agenda of pressing social, economic and political issues that would strain the most stable of democracies. "It's inevitably going to face severe difficulties," says Steven Friedman, director of the Center of Policy Studies in Johannesburg, the nation's largest city and financial center.

Friedman points to the risk of political instability in the new government, which must include representatives of any political party that gains at least 5 percent of the vote in the April balloting. "Unforced coalitions are sometimes not very easy," says Friedman. "Forced ones are even less so."

Other experts — in South Africa and in the United States — warn that the new government must work to revive a stagnant economy while trying to meet demands from blacks to create jobs, build housing, improve education and health care, provide land and redistribute wealth.

"South Africa is going to have to worry about fundamental transformation of its economy and at the same time worry about the distributive issues," says Jeffrey Herbst, a professor at Princeton University's Center of International Studies who recently spent a year in South Africa.

The economic statistics are daunting. Nearly half of South Africa's black labor force is unemployed or underemployed. Per capita income for whites is 10 times that of blacks. The government spends three or four times as much per pupil on white schools as it does on black schools. Health-care expenditures for whites are four times the spending level for blacks. More than 7 million people — nearly one-fifth of the population — live in "informal housing," the bureaucratic jargon for squatter camps, backyard shacks and other makeshift housing in urban or rural areas.

Overall, government spending for social welfare programs is less than half of what comparable industrialized countries spend. But the government has a massive deficit: about 9 percent of gross domestic product (GDP). By comparison, the U.S. budget deficit is only 5 percent of GDP.

South Africa Today . . . And Tomorrow

South Africa currently is divided into four provinces — Cape Province, Natal, Orange Free State and Transvaal — and 10 ostensibly self-governing black "homelands." The new constitution abolishes the homelands and divides the country into nine new provinces with broader powers but subject to laws passed by the national Parliament. Voters will cast a single ballot April 27 for Parliament and regional legislatures. The African National Congress is expected to win a majority of seats in Parliament. It is also favored to control legislatures in all the regions except the Western Cape, where mixed-race and white voters could give a majority to the National Party.

South Africa Today

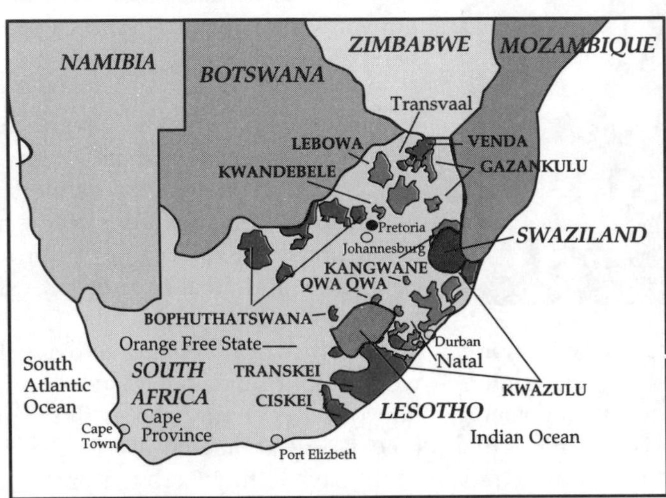

Homelands designated "Independent"

Other Homelands

Nine Provinces of the "New" South Africa

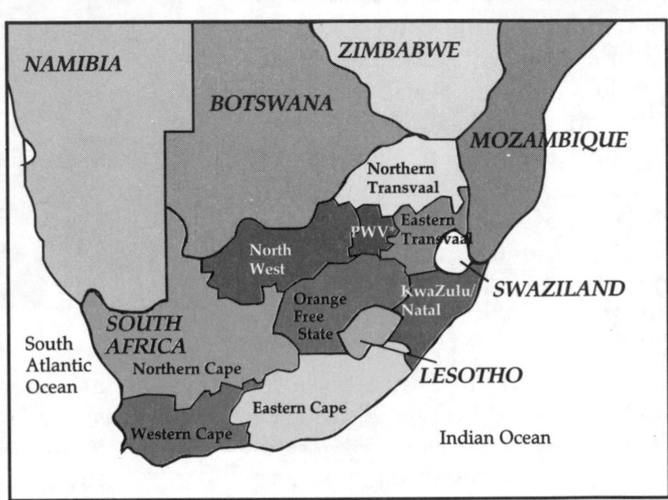

*(Pretoria-Witwatersrand-Vereeniging)

The country's economic landscape is not uniformly bleak, however. "It's got a good infrastructure, it's got good raw materials and it's got good revenue-earning capacity," says Pauline Baker, an expert on South Africa at the Aspen Institute in Washington. With moderate-sounding economic positions from Mandela and other ANC leaders, Baker adds, international investors are "poised to enter the market."

Mandela's presence represents another valuable asset in the national rebirth. Despite spending 27 years in prison for guerrilla activities against the apartheid government, Mandela has shown little bitterness over the past. He has also succeeded in steering the ANC along a moderate course without losing the support of more radical elements within an organization whose membership ranges from capitalists to communists, from professional elites to a vast downtrodden underclass.

Yet the pressures on Mandela will be immense as the ANC changes from a liberation movement to a governing party. The strains were evident last fall as he struck a statesmanlike pose for international audiences while sounding more strident notes in campaign appearances to mobilize black voters for the April election.

Meanwhile, a world community that has officially condemned apartheid for decades watches events in South Africa with a mixture of satisfaction and anxiety. Even with increased international trade, credit and aid, South Africa's economic rebuilding will be difficult. And white South Africans are already appealing to international audiences to measure the new, black-majority government by the same human rights standards that have been used to harshly judge the white-minority government.

As South Africa prepares for the dawn of a new era, these are some of the issues that are being discussed:

Does South Africa's new constitution establish the basis for a successful transition to a nonracial democracy?

South Africa's new constitution opens with befitting grandeur, proclaiming the need to "create a new order" that ensures "equality between men and women of all races." The interim charter then goes on for more than 220 typewritten pages to cover subjects ranging from the structure of the new government and individual rights to official languages and pensions for former officeholders and anti-apartheid fighters. (*See box, p. 32.*)

"It's not a terribly elegant constitution," says Friedman of the Center for

Policy Studies.

Cutting through the complexity, however, the constitution embodies two reciprocal compromises by the major negotiators: de Klerk's National Party government and the African National Congress. The ANC decided in the fall of 1992 to accept interim power-sharing with the white minority. For its part, the government yielded in the final days before the November agreement on its demands for some form of veto power within the new government.

"The National Party was very sensible in realizing that they couldn't have a white veto over policy," says Stephen Jay Stedman, a professor at Johns Hopkins University's School of Advanced International Studies in Washington who spent eight months in South Africa last year following the negotiations. "And the ANC was eminently sensible in putting forward the long interim period of five years when you would have a government of national unity and reconstruction."

The central government will be headed by a strong president, chosen by the new Parliament. The Parliament — which will propose a final constitution to take effect after five years — will be made up of a National Assembly directly elected on the basis of proportional representation and a Senate whose members will be elected by provincial legislatures. The judiciary is to include the existing court structure plus a newly created constitutional court.

To promote national unity, the constitution provides for a deputy president from the second-largest party or any party that receives 20 percent of the parliamentary vote. In addition, any party that receives at least 5 percent of the popular vote is entitled to Cabinet representation.

Some observers believe these features will cripple the new government. "The future government will be so constrained by the political compromises that have been arrived at that the government of national unity is going to be translated into a government of political paralysis," says Eugene Nyati, an independent political analyst in Johannesburg.

Other observers, however, see some advantages to the forced coalition arrangement. " They still have to rule in a coalition, which is a really good thing," says the Aspen Institute's Baker. "You don't get a winner-take-all mentality."

In a separate but related compromise, the constitution provides for power to be shared between the national government and nine newly created provincial governments.

AP/Wide World Photo

Mangosuthu Buthelezei
Inkatha Freedom Party

Whites favored regionalism to limit the power of a black-majority national government. While the national government has supreme power in most areas, some observers expect the regions to cause problems for the new government.

"The regional governments will have more powers than they've ever had in the past," says Nyati. "I expect some of the regional politicians will use their powers to undermine rather than complement the center."

A third area of uncertainty involves the constitution's lengthy listing of "fundamental rights" and the role of the constitutional court in protecting them. "The bill of rights is a very fuzzy document," says Richard Steyn, editor-in-chief of the *Star* newspaper in Johannesburg.

As one example, Steyn notes that individuals have a right to government information only where necessary to exercise other rights. Elsewhere, the constitution requires the state to provide a lawyer to a defendant only if needed to prevent "a substantial injustice." And, most broadly, the constitution provides that Parliament may pass laws limiting rights if they are "reasonable," "justifiable" and "necessary."

Even without the threat of parliamentary meddling, though, the judiciary has a difficult assignment to enforce constitutional rights. "South Africa has no tradition of judicial review," Rotberg notes.

The prospect of enhanced judicial power heartens many in South Africa's human rights community, but some observers are concerned about judicial overreaching. "It raises the question of how long does the court retain its legitimacy and credibility when it is continually intervening in political disputes," Friedman remarks.

Despite the questions and criticisms, the constitution gets a passing grade from political observers in and out of South Africa. "I give the interim settlement a six out of 10, which is a good enough pass for South Africa," says political analyst Nyati. The larger question is whether a country so badly divided for so many years can find the political will to make it work.

Will there be political stability both before the national elections and afterward?

Despite the success of the constitutional talks, South Africa must still overcome a host of unfavorable conditions to develop a politically stable democracy. The country's traditions

African National Congress leader Nelson Mandela and South African President F.W. de Klerk were awarded the 1993 Nobel Peace Prize. Excerpts are from their acceptance speeches at the award ceremony in Oslo, Norway on Dec. 10, 1993.

"We live with the hope that as she battles to remake herself, South Africa will be like a microcosm of the new world that is striving to be born.

This must be a world of democracy and respect for human rights, a world freed from the horrors of poverty, hunger, deprivation and ignorance, relieved of the threat and the scourge of civil wars and external aggression and unburdened of the great tragedy of millions forced to become refugees.

The processes in which South Africa and Southern Africa as a whole are engaged, beckon and urge us all that we take this tide at the flood and make of this region a living example of what all people of conscience would like the world to be."

— Nelson Mandela

Reuters

Mandela and de Klerk at the Nobel Peace Prize ceremony

"There is a growing awareness among all South Africans of our interdependence — of the fact that none of us can flour-ish if we do not work together — that all of us will fail if we try to pursue narrow sectional interests.

Five years ago people would have seriously questioned the sanity of anyone who would have predicted that Mr. Mandela and I would be joint recipients of the 1993 Nobel Peace Prize. And yet both of us are here today.

We are political opponents. We disagree strongly on key issues and we will soon fight a strenuous election campaign against one another. But we will do so, I believe, in the frame of mind and within the framework of peace which has already been established. We will do it — and many other leaders will do it with us — because there is no other road to peace and prosperity for the people of our country."

— F. W. de Klerk

of violence and intolerance, the limited education of many of the newly enfranchised black voters and the disaffection of white right-wingers and some black political leaders make a truly free election unlikely.

The most urgent concern is the threat of violence from groups that refused to sign on to the constitutional accord and threatened to boycott the election — the white Conservative Party, the Zulu-dominated Inkatha Freedom Party (IFP) and leaders of two black homelands: Bophuthatswana in the northern Transvaal and Ciskei in the eastern Cape.

After the constitutional talks ended, Inkatha leader Buthelezei promised "determined resistance" against the charter. On the right, Constand Viljoen, the former defense chief now leading the umbrella Afrikaner Volksfront (People's Front), said the country is "on the brink of war." [2]

"There is going to be considerable violence," says Robert Schirre, a political scientist at the University of Cape Town. Schirre notes that in many "no-go areas," political groups face the risk of violence when campaigning in hostile territory. ANC leaders are cautious about campaigning in rural KwaZulu, where Inkatha is strong, while ANC supporters are said to have broken up campaign rallies in black townships by the white liberal Democratic Party.

Despite the anticipated violence, Schirre and other observers believe the major holdout groups — Inkatha and the white right-wing — have little choice eventually but to join in campaigning for the April election.

Somewhat paradoxically, the threat from the right is viewed as the lesser danger. The Afrikaner Volksfront produced more ridicule than concern in late November when it said it plans to ignore the election and create a whites-only state. News accounts noted a recent poll showing that only 28 percent of whites support a white "homeland." [3]

"It's hard to take this war talk seriously," says Steven Friedman. The once-rural Afrikaners are now mostly urban mortgage-holders, he says. "These are not the people who throw it all up and head for the hills to fight wars," he concludes.

Inkatha seems to pose a greater danger to political stability. Buthelezei holds personal power as the tribal and governmental leader of the Zulus, South Africa's largest ethnic group. And ANC and Inkatha supporters have engaged in politically motivated violence throughout the constitutional negotiations. [4]

Even while Buthelezei hinted at boycotting the election, however, another high-ranking Inkatha official told a gathering in late November that 2 million rand (about $600,000) had been budgeted for campaign advertising. If it does compete in the April balloting, Inkatha is likely to surpass the 5 percent threshold needed to win one or more seats in the national unity Cabinet.

Buthelezei has suggested that he does not expect to join the Cabinet himself, pointing to the hostility between himself and Mandela.[5] But some observers believe Inkatha's representative could still play a spoiler's role. "I expect the IFP to use their position in the Cabinet to wreck the process from within," says political analyst Nyati.

In their campaigns, the two biggest political parties — the ANC and the National Party — have engaged at times in tough rhetoric toward each other. Mandela has promised to "bury" the National Party, while National Party ads have blamed the ANC for some of the recent political violence.

Meanwhile, there has been little substantive discussion of policy issues by any of the parties. "The campaign will go more on party personality than on anything else," says Harvard's Rotberg.

The ANC seems virtually assured of an absolute majority in the April balloting. Some observers predict it may gather 60 percent of the vote or more. The National Party fell in the polls during 1993, but it may gain strength as voters come to view it as the most viable counterweight to the ANC. If it polls the second-largest vote total, the party will be able to designate a deputy president — presumably de Klerk — in the national unity government.

Political Violence in South Africa

Political violence claimed nearly 12,000 lives in South Africa over the past three and a half years, according to an independent human rights monitoring group in Johannesburg.

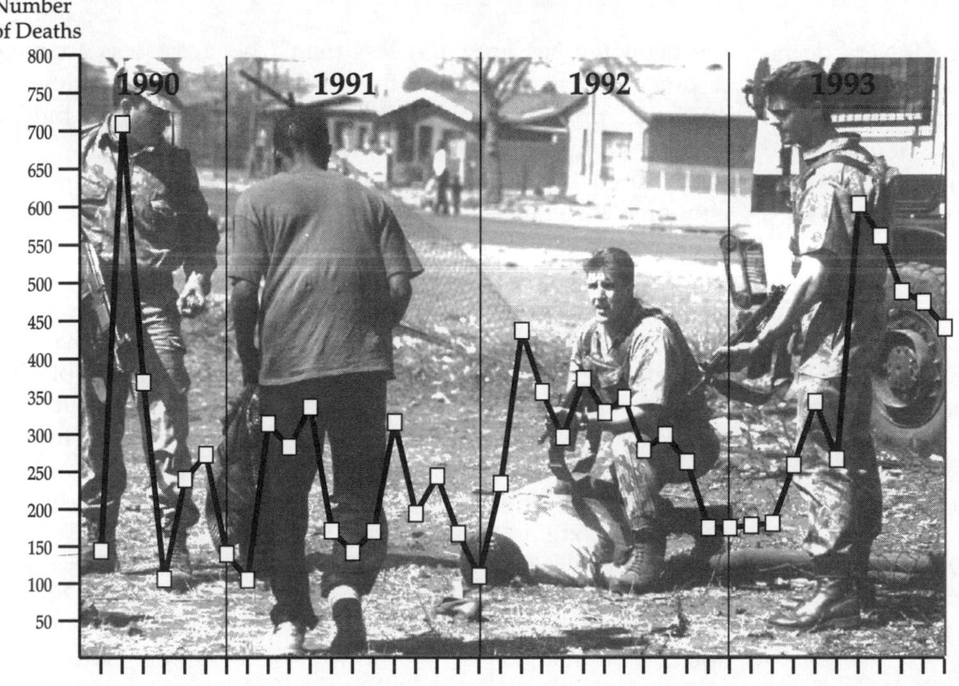

Source: Human Rights Commission, Johannesburg

South Africa Adopts New Constitution

On Dec. 22, 1993, the South African Parliament gave final approval to an interim constitution for a national unity government to be formed after national elections on April 27, 1994. Here are some of the major provisions of the new constitution:

Fundamental Rights: Broad provisions for individual rights, including freedom of speech and press; freedom of religion and conscience; political rights; right of privacy, including limits on search and seizure; right to travel; right to "fair labor practices," including right to strike; property rights; right to counsel in legal proceedings. Prohibits torture and cruel, inhuman or degrading punishment. Permits temporary state of emergency when declared by two-thirds vote of National Assembly; detention without trial permitted with restrictions.

Parliament: 400-member National Assembly, popularly elected from national and regional party lists on basis of proportional representation; 90-member Senate, elected by each of nine provincial legislatures. Bills to be passed by a simple majority of each house or a majority of the total number of members of both houses.

President/Deputy Presidents: Executive president to be elected by the National Assembly; executive deputy presidents to be designated by second largest party or any party that obtains 80 or more seats in National Assembly. President to have broad executive power: may refer bills back to Parliament in event of "procedural shortcoming in legislative process;" may refer constitutional disputes to Constitutional Court.

Cabinet: Multiparty Cabinet of about 27 members composed according to proportional representation of those parties that obtain 5 percent or more of the vote in the election; various portfolios to be designated by the president. Decisions to be made in a "consensus-seeking spirit."

Judiciary: Existing court structure to remain largely intact, with addition of an 11-member Constitutional Court to have final jurisdiction on interpretation, protection and enforcement of constitution at all levels of government; members of Constitutional Court to be appointed by president for non-renewable seven-year terms from list designated by new Judicial Service Commission.

Provinces: Nine provinces with legislatures, premiers and multiparty executive councils; provincial legislatures to have concurrent power with national government over many areas, including police, primary and secondary education, housing, health and welfare. Each province entitled to "equitable" share of national revenue.

Constitutional Assembly: National Assembly and Senate sitting together as Constitutional Assembly to draft final constitution within two years; two-thirds majority or approval by 60 percent of voters in referendum required. National unity government to function until next election, to be held April 27, 1999.

Schirre says that the ANC's dominant position eases some of the concerns about the coming campaign. "If the ANC gets 55 or 60 percent, and Inkatha gets 10 or 12 percent, it's very hard to say you were robbed," he says.

After the election, though, the ANC will confront a more difficult challenge. It must govern a country with a huge backlog of economic and social needs, a well-to-do population anxious for its economic and physical security, and a newly empowered black majority eager for a fairer share of the country's economic wealth.

What are South Africa's prospects for economic development and social change under a new government?

For nearly two decades, South Africa has had a sick economy. As Princeton's Jeffrey Herbst points out, the economy has grown at less than 2 percent per year since the mid-1970s and private-sector jobs failed to grow at all in the 1980s. The discontent caused by sluggish growth and economic inequalities will be destabilizing, Herbst warns, long after the first non-racial election is held. [6]

Apartheid contributed to the country's economic ills by swelling government expenditures, discouraging investment and failing to train a skilled black work force. Now, some people in South Africa hope that renewed growth and reduced government spending in some areas will produce a "liberation dividend" to meet the country's needs for jobs, education, housing, health care and social investments.

Many experts, however, caution that any liberation dividend may be smaller than hoped. "I think it will be a lot less than people believe," says Ann Bernstein, executive director of the Urban Foundation in Johannesburg.

Bernstein notes that the decision to preserve the jobs of white civil servants means that government employment "is not going to shrink overnight." In addition, she says, any savings from dismantling the governments in the 10 black homelands may be offset by creation of the nine new regional governments.

Economic growth may depend on outside help — foreign investment, loans and aid. "An ANC government cannot rebuild South Africa alone," says Solomon Terreblanche, an economics professor at the University of Stellenbosch. "We will get support," he adds. "My only worry is that it will not be enough."

The major international financial institutions — the International Monetary Fund and the World Bank — both are expected to provide substantial loans totaling several billion dollars once the new government takes office. But private investment and foreign aid are less certain.

Even though Congress repealed U.S. economic sanctions against South Africa in November, American companies may still be wary about investing in South Africa because of uncertain markets and unsettled political conditions. [7] (*See story, p. 39.*) And observers expect no increase in U.S. aid to South Africa, which currently totals $80 million a year — already more than to any other country in sub-Saharan Africa.

South Africa has several positive economic features, however. As political scientist Robert Price of the University of California at Berkeley notes, South Africa boasts established banking and legal systems, existing productive enterprises and substantial engineering and technical know-how. In addition, many needed improvements in the country's infrastructure — such as housing, roads and electrification — can generate jobs quickly if money can be found to pay for them.

The government will face an array of competing demands for money, however. Educational spending is likely to increase, but not by anything like the $18 billion per year that some advocacy groups say is needed to equalize spending on black and white schools.

The government also will be under pressure to increase spending on poverty programs. "The government will have to spend another 3 to 4 percent of GDP on poverty relief," Terreblanche says. "Will it be possible? That is one of the big questions."

In speeches before and after the constitutional talks had ended, Nelson Mandela has tried at times to lower the expectations of his emergent constituency. "A great number of our membership now understand the resource constraints that an ANC government will face," Mandela has said, "and that there will therefore be no quick fix to decades of apartheid destruction." [8]

Some analysts, however, say the pressures on the new government will be intense — and difficult to resist. "The masses are going to be very resentful," political analyst Nyati says. If the government does not deliver on expectations, he adds, radicals within the ANC "will be in a position to wrestle control away from the moderates."

Even before addressing economic issues, however, the new government will face urgent demands to restore law and order, especially in the major urban areas. Political violence, which has claimed more than 17,000 lives in the past nine years, is only a fraction of the problem. Violent crime — murders, robberies and assaults — has surged in recent years in central cities, white suburbs and black townships. The Johannesburg area, including Soweto and other adjoining black townships, registered 6,969 murders last year, according to police — about 1½ times the murder rate per capita in Washington, D.C. [9]

Experts agree, however, that the government must address the crime problem and economic issues at the same time. "So much of the violence is tied to high unemployment, crushing poverty, the lack of basic provisions in the townships," says Stephen Stedman. "Progress has to go hand-in-hand on these issues."

Like many other observers, however, Stedman ends by being optimistic about South Africa's future. "There are not going to be any simple answers," he says. "The only way out of the problems is for all sides to engage in a long protracted process, and that's been done over the last three years. That's the most impressive thing and gives you the most hope for that country." ■

BACKGROUND

Historical Legacy

The new South Africa inherits a legacy of violence, ethnic hatred and institutional oppression dating back more than three centuries to the arrival of the first European settlers. [10]

The Dutch East India Company brought Dutch settlers to the vicinity of modern Cape Town in 1652 to establish a refreshment station for ships traveling between Holland and the East Indies. At the time, native Africans lived in largely peaceful conditions as hunter-gatherers or herders in the western Cape or as farmers to the east.

The Dutch settlers, joined by Germans and French Protestant emigrés, established an autonomous, slave-holding agrarian society. European geopolitics led Britain to capture the Cape Colony from the Dutch in 1795 and, after relinquishing it in 1803, to retake the colony in 1806.

Tensions naturally arose between the commercially minded English and the Afrikaner farmers ("Boers"). In addition, the British government imposed more liberal racial policies, including the abolition of slavery in 1833. As a result, discontented Afrikaners migrated en masse into the interior in the Great Trek, a defining event in Afrikaner history.

For native Africans, the trek brought bloody wars with the Afrikaners, who triumphed because of superior firepower despite their inferior numbers. The British, meanwhile, fought a series of wars with Xhosa and other tribes that over time extended the Cape Colony as far east as present-day Ciskei. With their lands constricted, African tribes also clashed violently with each other.

For blacks living in white areas, the abolition of slavery brought no change in their servile status. Afrikaners "tolerated scarcely any social intervention with black people except as masters and servants," according to Yale historian Leonard Thompson, and British settlers "rapidly complied with the established mores." [11]

The Boer War

For imperial Britain, the Cape Colony and the Natal Colony, established along the Indian Ocean in 1843, ranked low in importance. But the discovery of diamonds in 1867 and gold in 1886 in the "Reef" — the plateau region centered around modern Johannesburg — raised the stakes. Britain moved to force the two independent Boer republics — the Transvaal and the Free Orange State — into the Empire.

The pressures culminated in the Anglo-Boer War of 1899-1902. Britain won, but its scorched-earth policies and use of concentration camps for Boer women and children further embittered Afrikaners against the English. The victory was pyrrhic, however. By 1906, Britain allowed the two former Boer republics to have their own, whites-only colonial governments. It then helped forge the four colonies — the Cape, Free Orange State, Natal and Transvaal — into the self-governing Union of South Africa, established in 1910.

Afrikaners dominated everywhere but Natal. Blacks were barred from voting except in the more liberal Cape region. The constitution preserved Dutch along with English as an official language. And it also permitted overrepresentation of rural areas, which in 1948 proved critical to the victory of the militantly Afrikaner National Party with its philosophy of racial separateness: apartheid.

Segregation to Apartheid

From its first days as a nation, South Africa established a web of laws to subjugate the black majority.

The Natives Land Act of 1913 prohibited blacks from buying or leasing land outside reserves that constituted less than 7 percent (later, 11 percent) of the country's area. Regulations under the Mines and Works Act gave whites a monopoly on all skilled jobs. A 1923 law empowered urban authorities to segregate blacks in "African locations." Other laws limited the travel rights of black Africans.

Blacks had no power to resist. Most were concerned only with immediate survival, not political or legal rights. The government provided no schools for blacks, so their only education came from a handful of missionary schools. Their only voice in national affairs was the Native Representation Council, a body created in 1936 that had no influence and was abolished after the advent of apartheid. And the only national black political group — the African National Congress, founded in 1912 — made no headway and by the 1930s was largely moribund. (*See story, p. 36.*)

White South Africans formed two major political parties: the pro-British Union Party and the National Party, which appealed to working-class and rural Afrikaners. The National Party came to power for the first time in 1924 after a Union Party government violently crushed a strike by white miners opposed to hiring blacks. Over the next decade, the National Party used its power to substitute Afrikaans for Dutch as an official language, open government jobs to Afrikaners and make more capital available to Afrikaner farmers.

The elections of 1938 returned the Union Party to power. The next year, Parliament narrowly voted to bring South Africa into the war alongside Britain against Germany. The vote split the Union Party, while the National Party, which had favored strict neutrality, gained ground as the war continued. Meanwhile, Afrikaner solidarity increased on the strength of economic discontent and a growing ideology that viewed Afrikaners as God's chosen people. [12] Campaigning in 1948 on a platform of Afrikaner nationalism and strict racial separateness, the National Party won a narrow victory — mainly in less populated rural areas — and began to construct an apartheid society.

Early apartheid laws — so-called "petty apartheid" — tightened racial segregation by prohibiting mixed marriages, classifying all South Africans by race and requiring racial separation in all public accommodations — from hotels and restaurants to trains and public beaches. The government also prevailed in a constitutional showdown with the country's highest court in eliminating mixed-race persons from the voting rolls in the Cape Province. And it moved to control the education of blacks by displacing the liberal missionary schools with government-run schools in 1953 and establishing segregated black universities in 1959.

The dream of "grand apartheid," however, was more ambitious. The government aimed to move all black South Africans into 10 "homelands" separated — indeed, isolated — from white areas. The policy, pursued for more than 35 years, was depicted as the equivalent of decolonization: Native Africans were to be restored to traditional lands that would eventually be made into self-governing nations.

In reality, most of the homelands — with the notable exception of KwaZulu — had only a loose tribal identity. Most consisted of scattered fragments of land in largely desolate areas. None had a realistic chance of being economically self-sustaining. And the chiefs installed in power were almost completely dependent on the white government, which provided money and the security forces that enabled them to remain in power.

Protests to Insurrection

Apartheid imposed unspeakable suffering on black South Africans

Continued on p. 37

Chronology

1900-1948 ***South Africa is forged into a single nation governed by a white minority with few rights for the majority-black population.***

1912
South African Native National Congress — later, the African National Congress — is formed.

1948
National Party gains control of government after campaigning on platform of Afrikaner nationalism and racial apartheid.

1949-1960 ***The National Party institutes apartheid, tightening racial segregation and moving blacks into 10 tribal-based "homelands." The ANC mobilizes against apartheid, but the government puts down dissent.***

1955
Anti-apartheid rally by ANC and other groups is broken up by government. More than 150 leaders are prosecuted for treason, but acquitted after four-year trial.

1960s-1970s ***ANC initiates "armed struggle" against apartheid, but neither domestic opposition nor international pressure dissuades the government from its racial policies.***

1960
Sixty-nine blacks are killed by police in protest at Sharpeville. Government bans ANC and Pan-Africanist Congress.

1963
ANC leader Nelson Mandela is captured, charged with sabotage and sentenced with others to life imprisonment.

1976
Riots erupt in the black township of Soweto outside Johannesburg over government plan to use Afrikaans language in black schools.

1980s ***The National Party government moves to reform — but not abolish — apartheid. ANC leads campaign to render the country ungovernable.***

1983
White voters approve new constitution creating separate parliamentary chambers for whites, mixed race "coloreds" and Indians. Blacks are still barred from voting.

1985
Chase Manhattan Bank leads other multinational banks in refusing to refinance South Africa's short-term debts.

1986
Government declares national state of emergency after three years of unrest in black townships. Some apartheid laws are repealed.

1989
F.W. de Klerk becomes National Party leader and president after hard-liner P.W. Botha is forced out.

1990s ***President de Klerk declares the end of apartheid and leads the government into negotiations with the ANC and other parties on a new constitution. Mandela, freed from prison, assumes leadership of the ANC. Constitutional talks proceed. Political violence increases.***

February 1990
De Klerk announces broad reforms in speech to Parliament on Feb. 2, including the lifting of the ban on the ANC. On Feb. 11, Mandela is released from prison to worldwide acclaim.

July 1991
The ANC holds its first national conference in 30 years. Moderates win major posts.

December 1991
Constitutional talks open, but break down.

March 17, 1992
White voters back de Klerk's reforms in a national referendum.

May 1992
A new round of constitutional talks also ends with no agreement.

April 1993
A third round of constitutional talks opens, with the ANC now prepared to share power with white minority. Chris Hani, black leader of South Africa Communist Party, is assassinated.

June 3, 1993
Constitutional talks agree on April 27, 1994, as date of nation's first all-races election.

Nov. 18, 1993
A draft constitution is completed, calling for a five-year government of national unity, a bill of rights but no veto by minority parties.

ANC's Journey From Liberation Movement to Governing Party

For nearly 40 years, the South African government denounced the African National Congress (ANC) as a terrorist, communist organization. For 30 years, the group was officially banned. Many ANC leaders were imprisoned, others were exiled and its headquarters was removed to the Zambian capital of Lusaka, 500 miles from South African soil.

Today, the ANC has a bustling political headquarters in a 20-story building in downtown Johannesburg. ANC President Nelson Mandela has been honored — along with South African President F.W. de Klerk — with the Nobel Peace Prize, while Cyril Ramaphosa, the ANC's general secretary, has gone on a private fishing trip with the government's minister for constitutional development.

In April, the ANC will complete the transformation from outlawed liberation movement to governing party following the country's first all-races election. Mandela, imprisoned for 27 years for directing a sabotage campaign against the white regime, will be installed as the head of a government expected to have a substantial black majority in Parliament and the Cabinet.

The ANC's accession to power has not been without problems, however. As Reuters correspondent Rich Mkhondo writes, the ANC has fallen short of its membership goal of 1 million, made few inroads among white voters and remained in the hands of older leaders who are out of touch with a younger, and often more militant, generation of blacks. [1]

Once it takes power as the dominant party in the five-year coalition government, the ANC can expect its internal divisions to become more evident. In addition, it will face — in exaggerated form — the problems that any political party meets when it replaces a prior government.

"You're dealing with people who've never been in power, who have to learn all this from scratch," says Steven Friedman, director of the Center for Policy Studies in Johannesburg. "It's inevitable that there will be some rough patches."

The ANC assumes its new role with two major strengths: its historic status as the oldest and largest black political organization in South Africa and Mandela's personal popularity and respect. But it has achieved a broad appeal in part by deferring specific policy choices.

"The ANC has never been a political party," Mandela himself said in an interview with *The Washington Post* in 1990. "Right from the start, up to now, the ANC is a coalition of people of various political affiliations." [2]

Mandela's campaign appearances so far have generally avoided specific stands, and the ANC has run newspaper advertisements soliciting views on policy priorities for the new government.

"The campaign will not proceed on the basis of particular policies as it would in this country," says Robert Rotberg, a professor of African studies at Harvard University. "It will go really on the basis of popular sympathy for the new ANC and everything it stands for and on the basis of those who are distrustful of the ANC."

Distrust of the ANC can be found among both blacks and whites. Chief Mangosuthu Buthelezei, leader of the Inkatha Freedom Party and the KwaZulu homeland, has criticized the ANC for its close ties to the South African Communist Party. He has also played on tribal sentiment among Zulus, South Africa's largest black tribe, by depicting the ANC as dominated by members of the rival Xhosa tribe.

Many young blacks in urban townships are discontented with the ANC because of the slow pace of constitutional negotiations and the decision to accept power sharing after the national election.

Meanwhile, many white South Africans harbor feelings that range from nervous skepticism to bitter hostility. Right-wing politicians continue to denounce the ANC as a terrorist or communist organization. But some liberals also view the ANC as less than committed to democracy. The mainly white Democratic Party, for example, says that ANC supporters have been breaking up its meetings in black townships.

The ANC's reputation was damaged by evidence of torture, executions and other abuses against dissident members in its exile camps in the 1970s and '80s. A three-member commission issued a report in August substantiating many of the accusations and reporting that some of the offenders still held positions within the congress. The ANC issued an apology, but said it would not discipline any of the offenders or pay compensation to victims. [3]

In three years of negotiations with the National Party government, the ANC shed some of its past image — for example, by accepting a property rights provision in the interim constitution. It has also sought to reassure Afrikaners. When the interim constitution was approved, Mandela — speaking in Afrikaans — vowed that Afrikaners would have "the fullest right to your own language, religion and culture."

As Steven Friedman points out, however, Mandela has been more critical of de Klerk and the National Party. Mandela has told gatherings that the ANC would "bury" the National Party. At one meeting, Mandela said he would keep de Klerk out of the new government. He backtracked the next day when he was reminded that de Klerk will be deputy president if the National Party finishes second in the balloting.

Notwithstanding occasional missteps, Mandela is getting good reviews as a political campaigner. And some observers view the ANC's lack of firm policy positions as a virtue. "It's a very flexible organization," says reporter Mkhondo. "They listen to the people. They listen to the mood of the world."

[1] Rich Mkhondo, *Reporting South Africa* (1993), p. 129.

[2] *The Washington Post*, June 27, 1990, p. A15.

[3] See *The New York Times*, Aug. 31, 1993, p. A9; *The Washington Post*, Oct. 26, 1992, p. A14.

Continued from p. 34

and, to a lesser extent, on the country's mixed-race and Indian populations. Over time, it also came to impose a huge cost on the country's white population in terms of economic growth, internal peace and international standing. Yet the policy persisted for four decades — maintained by a one-party government that cunningly cultivated popular support through political patronage and anti-communist propaganda and relentlessly crushed dissent through an intricate complex of internal security laws.

To establish the homelands, the government carried out one of the most massive displacements of population in history. By one estimate, more than 3.5 million blacks were uprooted from their homes and herded into homelands between 1960 and 1983. The newly established homelands constituted only 13 percent of the country's area, but by the 1980s held more than half of the nation's black population. As historian Leonard Thompson notes, overcrowding produced high levels of unemployment, poverty, undernutrition and disease.[13]

The government also sought to stop the influx of blacks into urban areas by intensifying enforcement of the pass laws that prevented blacks from being in white areas for more than 72 hours without a permit. Thompson cites figures showing that more than 100,000 blacks were arrested every year for pass law violations; the number peaked at 385,000 in 1975-76. In addition, the government razed black, colored and Indian squatter camps surrounding major cities and confiscated so-called "black spots" — lands owned or occupied by Africans in white areas.

Black opposition to the government's racial policies began to increase during World War II with the founding of the ANC Youth League by Nelson Mandela and others. In the 1950s, Mandela and his activist colleagues led the ANC in a campaign of demonstrations, picketing and other peaceful protest to try to soften apartheid policies.

Fiercely, the government cracked down. When the ANC joined with other anti-apartheid groups in sponsoring a huge freedom rally in 1955, the government broke up the meeting and put more than 150 leaders from the ANC and other groups, including Mandela, on trial for treason. In 1960, police shot into an anti-pass law demonstration by the radical Pan-Africanist Congress at Sharpeville, outside Johannesburg, killing 69 blacks and wounding 186 others.

The treason trial, which lasted more than four years, ended with a judge's acquittal of all of the defendants for lack of evidence. The failure to move the government through peaceful means, however, convinced the ANC of the need to shift tactics to violent confrontations. Under Mandela's leadership, it established a military arm — Umkhonto we Sizwe, the Spear of the Nation. Over the next several years, it carried out attacks on post offices and other government buildings and railroads and electrical facilities. But Mandela was captured in 1963, convicted of sabotage and sentenced along with other ANC leaders to life imprisonment.

The continuing crackdown brought an outcry at home and abroad that, seemingly, only stiffened the government's resolve. In 1961, South Africa pulled out of the British Commonwealth rather than take criticism for its policies. International sanctions were imposed: an arms embargo voted by the United Nations in 1977, broad trade sanctions adopted by the United States in 1986. The government insisted the international measures would have no effect. Domestically, it used the internal security laws to silence dissenters, jail opponents for extended periods without trial and ban opposition groups, including the ANC.

The crackdown did not bring stability, however. In the mid-1970s, riots broke out in black townships when the government moved to teach blacks in Afrikaans, a language they viewed as belonging to their oppressors. A decade later, the resistance moved from rebellion to insurrection — to use the characterization of U.S. political scientist Robert Price. The ANC combined school boycotts, po-

Population of South Africa, in millions, 1911-2035

Blacks comprise nearly 76 percent of South Africa's population. Whites make up about 13 percent of the population; about 60 percent of the whites are Afrikaners. South Africa's mixed-race persons — classified as "coloreds" — comprise about 8.5 percent of the population, and persons of Indian ancestry account for 2.6 percent. Demographers project that blacks will comprise 83 percent of the population by 2010, while the white proportion will fall below 10 percent.

	1911	1936	1960	1980	1987	1992	2010	2035
African	4.0	6.6	10.9	20.8	26.3	29.9	53.4	81.9
Colored	0.5	0.8	1.5	2.6	3.1	3.4	4.3	5.3
Indian	0.2	0.2	0.5	0.8	0.9	1.0	1.2	1.4
White	1.3	2.0	3.1	4.5	4.9	5.1	5.5	5.8

Sources: Leonard Thompson, A History of South Africa *(1990), p. 243 (historical figures; projections); 1992 figures from the Urban Foundation are cited in Institute of Race Relations,* Race Relations Survey 1992/93, *p. 254. Thompson notes that South African census figures likely underestimate the black population.*

litical strikes, consumer boycotts, rent strikes and huge community rallies with sharply increased sabotage in a deliberate effort to render the nation "ungovernable." [14]

The government declared a state of emergency in much of the country, but it failed to stem the protests. More importantly, by the 1980s white South Africans, including some within the National Party, began to recognize the costs of apartheid for themselves. The tangible costs included a bloated civil service, an expensive police force to maintain security at home and a large military establishment to carry out a policy of destabilizing the black countries bordering South Africa.

Apartheid was also dragging the economy down. Economic growth stalled in the late 1970s — in part because of a shortage of skilled labor. Economics dictated one retreat from racial apartheid: the government recognized black unions so that industry could have a means of achieving labor peace with its black work force. Apartheid was also contributing to white flight from South Africa. The country had depended on immigration for much of its growth in the 1960s and '70s, but it registered net emigration in 1977 and 1978 and again in 1986 and 1987.

Apartheid's Final Days

Through the 1980s, South Africans gradually came to recognize that apartheid could not survive. "The back was broken," says Michael Christie, director of the Washington office of the South Africa Foundation, a business-oriented group. "The question was how long the limbs would stay alive." Reforms were stalled, however, by a combination of stubbornness and craftiness by white leaders, including the country's president, P.W. Botha.

Botha took office as a hard-liner in the tradition of the earlier architects of apartheid, John Vorster and Hendrik Verwoerd. But he led the way in recognizing black labor unions in the late 1970s. In 1983, he turned to a plan that ostensibly reformed apartheid while preserving white minority rule. A new constitution created a new Parliament with three separate chambers representing the country's white, colored and Indian populations. Blacks still had no voting rights, however. And whites held majority power whenever the three chambers met together. Most mixed-race and Indian voters boycotted parliamentary elections.

The government also adopted other, more meaningful reforms. It eliminated some segregation laws, repealed some of the pass laws and tolerated blacks' presence in parts of Johannesburg and Cape Town supposedly reserved for whites. [15] The reforms brought some improvements for South African blacks and also helped supportive world leaders, such as U.S. President Ronald Reagan and British Prime Minister Margaret Thatcher, argue against economic sanctions.

The broad ANC-led campaign of insurrection in the mid-1980s, however, convinced the international financial system that South Africa was no longer a good investment. In August 1985, Chase Manhattan Bank led other multinational banks in refusing to refinance South Africa's short-term debts. As South African journalist Allister Sparks points out, the government was forced to devalue the rand and impose strict foreign exchange controls. [16]

Meanwhile, many U.S. businesses began to pull up stakes — partly because of pressure from domestic anti-apartheid groups and partly because of doubts about the country's economic viability. [17] In addition, domestic investment plummeted. "What the foreigners did was nothing compared to what the South Africans did to themselves in terms of stopping investment," Princeton's Jeffrey Herbst explains. And the country's economic situation also fell victim to sagging prices for gold and other minerals, which hurt South Africa's always tenuous balance of payments.

Despite the deteriorating economic and political situation, Botha turned after 1986 to a stubborn defense of white minority rule. In the face of intense criticism within his own party, he clung to power until February 1989, when he abruptly announced his resignation as National Party leader after suffering a stroke. As his successor, the party chose Frederik William de Klerk, a drab Cabinet member from the party's conservative wing, who beat out three opponents seen as more reform-minded. Botha initially refused to resign as president, but de Klerk and other party leaders finally forced him out in a tense confrontation in August. De Klerk was then elected president in September. [18]

Less than five months later, the lackluster de Klerk surprised his country and the world by using his opening speech to a new session of Parliament to announce a sweeping set of reforms. In his speech on Feb. 2, 1990, de Klerk said he would lift the ban on the ANC and the more radical Pan-Africanist Congress, release all political prisoners, lift the state of emergency in most of the country and repeal the 1953 law — the Separate Amenities Act — that established racial segregation in public accommodations. In a dramatic finale, he also said the government would release Mandela "unconditionally" and "without delay." [19]

Nine days later, Mandela walked to freedom arm-in-arm with his wife Winnie from a minimum security prison outside Cape Town, returning a clenched fist salute to thousands who lined the roads and thronged to hear his first speech as a free man later that day. The day's events were broadcast across the nation and around the world. Over the next year, Mandela assumed leadership of the ANC and was received in Washington and other world capitals as a hero and expected future leader of a black

Continued on p. 40

U.S. Policy on South Africa: From Sanctions to Investment

South Africa's recent moves to establish a non-racial democracy have ended a sharp debate within the United States over U.S. relations with Pretoria.

Since the 1950s, Republican administrations have maintained close ties with South Africa, while Democratic administrations have been more critical of its racial policies. The debate reached a climax in 1986 when the Democratic-controlled Congress enacted comprehensive economic sanctions against South Africa over a veto by President Ronald Reagan, who favored a policy of "constructive engagement" with the white regime.

President George Bush lifted many of the sanctions in 1991 as the reform process got under way in South Africa. Then on Nov. 23, 1993, President Clinton signed bipartisan legislation that repeals all remaining federal sanctions against South Africa and effectively requires state and local governments to follow suit by 1995. †

Clinton also dispatched Commerce Secretary Ronald H. Brown on a trade mission to South Africa and authorized the Overseas Private Investment Corporation (OPIC) to offer financial assistance to U.S. firms investing in South Africa. ‡ Brown is expected to name a high-level representative to work with U.S. businesses to expand trade and investment.

Herman W. Nickel

A wide range of experts now agree that the economic measures had some impact on South Africa. "They no doubt had an economic effect," says Herman W. Nickel, who opposed sanctions while serving as U.S. ambassador to South Africa during the Reagan administration. "The question is whether the political effect outweighed the lasting damage they did to the South African economy."

Nickel, who is now with an international consulting firm, Global Business Access Ltd., sponsored a meeting in Washington in October between Nelson Mandela, the head of the African National Congress who is all but certain to become the country's first black president, and U.S. investment firms interested in South Africa. The turnout — about 480 — was double the number expected, Nickel says. "Quite a bit of money is flowing into the South African stock exchange," he adds.

The now-repealed sanctions not only barred most U.S. trade and investment, but also required the United States to oppose loans to South Africa by the International Monetary Fund (IMF) and the World Bank. With the sanctions removed, the IMF in December quickly completed action on an $850 million loan to South Africa for drought relief — the first money to go to South Africa from the IMF in decades.

U.S. aid to South Africa currently totals about $80 million — the largest figure for any sub-Saharan nation — but all the funds go to non-governmental organizations. Direct aid may be resumed in the future, but observers do not expect the total amount to increase much, if at all.

For their part, anti-apartheid groups in the United States stress that some assistance should continue to go to private groups in South Africa. "If one asks the question, 'Who's going to guarantee democracy in South Africa,' it will be the people, the churches, the trade unions, the community organizations," says Imani Countess, director of the Washington Office on Africa. "U.S. support for those organizations is crucial."

Countess' group, which is sponsored by U.S. churches and trade unions, also wants U.S. firms investing in South Africa to abide by a business conduct code drawn up by the South African Council of Churches and the Congress of South African Trade Unions (COSATU). South African business leaders, however, fear such codes would hamper investment.

Generally, however, experts and interest groups agree that the United States now has relatively little leverage over events in South Africa. "The one thing we could do is to try to nudge the holdouts into participating in the [April 1994] election," says Pauline Baker, an expert on South Africa at the Aspen Institute in Washington who support-ed sanctions but now opposes investment codes.

Chad Evans Wyatt Photography

Pauline Baker

Nickel agrees. "What we need to do is be evenhanded in our approach in pushing all the players to act in a politically tolerant fashion," the former ambassador says. "We may not have all that much direct leverage, but over the years South Africans have been very sensitive to what the rest of the world thinks of them."

†States and localities that fail to repeal the sanctions by October 1995 risk the loss of federal transportation funds. See *CQ Weekly Report*, Nov. 27, 1993, p. 3281.

‡ OPIC, an agency of the federal government, provides assistance through risk insurance, direct loans and loan guarantees to qualified U.S. private investors to support their investments in less developed countries.

Continued from p. 38
majority government.

Mandela's release set the stage for negotiations between the government and the ANC. But the task of forging a new constitutional order took more than four years and had to survive a wave of brutal political violence, tense and exceedingly difficult negotiations and an often testy relationship between the two main negotiators, Mandela and de Klerk. ■

CURRENT SITUATION

Making a Constitution

South Africa's new constitution is very much a political document — a carefully calibrated calculus of broad provisions establishing political and civil rights and more ambiguous sections dispersing power between different parties, different levels of government and different branches of the new central government.

Many of the participants in the negotiations and outside observers found much to fault in the document. Richard Steyn, editor of the *Star*, called it "very much a second-best solution based on compromise." Billy Paddock, a columnist for a South African business newspaper, said the final constitution "will be changed and hopefully improved on in the next five years." [20]

In political terms, the ANC could count itself as the biggest winner in the negotiations. Provisions for universal citizenship and voting rights overturn the apartheid structure of separate homelands for blacks and fulfill the ANC's consistent position for non-racial voting. The ANC also successfully resisted proposals from de Klerk for a rotating presidency or minority vetoes of presidential or Cabinet decisions.

Reuters

Children celebrate a national day of peace in a black township east of Johannesburg on Sept. 2, 1993.

The National Party won some concessions, however. As columnist Paddock points out, it won greater power for regional governments than the ANC favored, a commitment to a five-year transition, a supermajority requirement for adoption of the permanent constitution and an effective 30 percent quota for non-black representation in town and city councils. The arrangement "gives solace to the right wing where it is fearful of straightforward majority rule," Paddock wrote.

The biggest losers in the deal-making included the Afrikaner groups that still dream of a separate white homeland and Zulu leader Buthelezei, who boycotted the talks and ended with less power over regional or national affairs for his Inkatha Freedom Party than he had hoped for. In addition, leaders of the black homelands of Bophuthatswana and Ciskei, fearful of losing their power base, vowed to oppose the new charter.

The 18-page chapter on fundamental rights reflects the country's unhappy experience with authoritarian rule. Under apartheid, the government sought to suppress dissent by censorship, detention without trial and physical and psychological torture of prisoners, including children. Judicial review of police actions was sometimes limited, and police were indemnified for any abuses committed under emergency powers.

The new rights sections protect freedom of expression for individuals and the media. They prohibit torture, cruel or inhuman treatment or neglect or abuse of children in custody. Detention without trial is permitted only under a state of emergency declared for a fixed period by a two-thirds vote of the National Assembly. Even then, a detainee is guaranteed legal representation, medical care and access to the courts.

Safoora Sadek, national director of the independent Human Rights Commission, calls the bill of rights "a fundamental break with the past" and praises a separate provision creating a permanent human rights commission within the government. But Sadek also questions the need for any use of pretrial detention. And she questions whether secret proceedings will be permitted under an amnesty provision, added at the National Party's insistence, that bars prosecution for political crimes committed between October 1990 and Dec. 6, 1993.

Continued on p. 42

At Issue:

Will there be political stability in South Africa after the April 1994 elections?

yes

Robert Schirre

Professor of political studies, University of Cape Town

The bad news in South Africa is that there will be considerable violence between now and the election. The violence will escalate. Passions are high, and there's no concept of tolerance. A completely free and fair election is not possible.

But the good news is that the overwhelming strength of the African National Congress (ANC) is so powerful that it will not make a difference. If the ANC gets 55 or 60 percent of the vote and Inkatha gets 10 or 12 percent, it will be very hard for them to say that they were robbed.

After the election, I do not think that South Africa will become ungovernable. Unlike most Third World countries, there is a sufficient layer of First World expertise not only among whites but among many blacks to carry the day. On that basis, there is a good chance that there will be a reasonably effective government for the next one to three years.

The big risk is the losers. I am not concerned about the white right. I do not think the white right after the election will be a problem. I am thinking of regional players, like the Inkatha Freedom Party (IFP) and the Transkei leadership. Right now, Transkei is on board, but this may not continue. The IFP remains a wild card, divided between the pragmatism of many of its lesser leaders and the irascibility of its principal leader, Chief Mongosuthu Buthelezei. It will be very hard to unify all these groups because they are not all committed to democratic government.

Redistribution will be the number one issue on the agenda for many people — a battle between the First World and the Third World of Africa. In the real world, though, the policy choices are very limited. We have all come to recognize the limits of redistribution. And one advantage of these long negotiations is that the top layers of the ANC have become socialized into the realities of the present world. It is coming to recognize that you cannot redistribute wealth, you have to create wealth.

The new government will have the responsibility of making significant progress over the next five years on a number of issues, such as housing, health and education. What is more important is a general perception that progress is being made. We all know that blacks are going to remain poor and whites are going to remain wealthy for a time and that unemployment is going to remain high. But psychologically there must be a perception that government is really concerned with these issues and that it has changed in the right direction.

no

Eugene Nyati

Independent political risk analyst, Johannesburg

Civil and labor unrest could resume in South Africa after the new government takes office and render the country ungovernable again. The government of national unity will not translate into effective government and will not be able to deliver on the expectations of the masses.

The masses will be very resentful. The unrest does not have to be a revolution. People refusing to pay rents, which they have done in the past, is enough to undermine political stability and economic growth. The government simply will not get the cooperation that it needs from the public to function effectively.

The future government will be so constrained by the political compromises that have been arrived at that the government of national unity will become a government of political paralysis. Any political party that can win 5 percent of the vote will be in the executive, not just the legislature.

You will have in the same government the African National Congress, the National Party, the Inkatha Freedom Party and quite possibly the Pan-Africanist Congress. These four parties have no history of working together. On any given issue, the cabinet will effectively become a debating society, where decisions are not taken and no one takes responsibility for anything.

The structure lends itself to spoiler tactics by the smaller parties. The smaller parties might begrudge any credit given to the larger parties for positive policies.

The hierarchy of the army, police and civil service will remain white for many years to come. White privilege will be preserved by these institutions more than by the constitution. White sectors will resist any attempt by the new government to dilute their influence. Five years is a long enough time to frustrate and paralyze the government.

If all the parties in the coalition government subordinated their interest to the national interest, the new government, with the assistance of the International Monetary Fund and World Bank, might be able to deliver on expectations for education, health and housing. If they could do that and deliver on market-friendly policies, come 1999 they might be able to go back to the electorate and say, "We've been able to deliver; please give us some more time."

The problem is that I do not believe that all the parties will necessarily subordinate their interest to the national interest. That presupposes a level of integrity that is rare and that I have not seen in South Africa.

South Africa's Major Political Parties

Name, Leader(s)	Description	Vote Forecast *
African National Congress Nelson Mandela, president Cyril Ramaphosa, secretary-general	Broad liberation movement transformed into political party; supported by most blacks; allied with parties representing colored and Indian constituencies; some white support; allied with South Africa Communist Party and parties in some black homelands.	55-65%
National Party President F.W. de Klerk Olaus van Zyl, executive secretary	Governing party since 1948; created apartheid and now has dismantled it. Supported by most whites; could win up to half of colored, Indian vote.	12-20%
Freedom Alliance Rowan Cronje, chairman Constand Viljoen [Afrikaner People's Front] Chief Mangosuthu Buthelezei [Inkatha]	Alliance between pro-apartheid Afrikaner groups, including Conservative Party, and Zulu-dominated Inkatha Freedom Party. Opposes new constitution; wants greater regional autonomy. Has not decided whether to participate in election.	10-18%
Pan-Africanist Congress Clarence Makwetu, president	Radical black organization; split from ANC in late 1950s. Opposes constitution, but decided to participate in election. Might win enough votes to gain Cabinet seat, but may decline and take role as opposition party.	3-5%
Democratic Party Colin Eglin, MP	Liberal parliamentary party that has opposed apartheid; scant voter support, but has influenced course of legislation and constitutional negotiations.	1-2%

** Speculative estimates based on published polls and interviews with political observers.*

Continued from p. 40

Most broadly, Sadek says the real test of the provisions will come after the new government takes office. "One can have a bill of rights on paper, but it's something that all South Africans need to make sure becomes a reality — creating a culture of human rights in this country," she concludes.

Preparing for Elections

Final action on the constitution required approval from South Africa's existing, racially based tricameral Parliament. The lawmakers ratified the charter Dec. 22, but only after a suspenseful series of ultimately unsuccessful talks between the ANC, the government and the Freedom Alliance — an alliance between pro-apartheid Afrikaner groups and Buthelezei's Inkatha Freedom Party. The ANC and the government hoped to win a promise from the holdout groups to take part in the coming election. [21]

The Freedom Alliance's demands focused on the powers of the regional governments. Afrikaner groups, the IFP and the two holdout homelands — Bophuthatswana and Ciskei — wanted a greater measure of autonomy for the regions. They also wanted two ballots instead of one to be used in the April 27 elections, so that voters could split their preferences for national and regional representatives.

The government and the ANC indicated some flexibility on the subject, but only if the Freedom Alliance first committed to participate in the election. When no commitment was forthcoming, however, the talks collapsed — and no amendments were offered in Parliament on the issue.

Meanwhile, the ANC and the Afrikaner groups engaged in parallel talks regarding the demand for a white homeland. At one point, the ANC and the Afrikaner People's Front, the least militant of the Afrikaner groups, announced an accord that proved to be only a vague promise to study the issue further. But at the last moment, Volksfront leader Costand Viljoen balked at signing the document, saying he felt "betrayed" by the collapse of the other talks on constitutional amendments.

New negotiations were expected this month, however, and observers speculated that Parliament could be called back into session to consider amendments if an accord could be reached. The parties have until February to decide whether to participate in the campaign.

In the meantime, the ANC and the National Party had already begun their campaigns for the April 27 elections — with Mandela getting better reviews than de Klerk. In December, *Africa Confidential*, a London-based newsletter, described Mandela as "a natural campaigner" who had gotten good receptions in more than 20 political forums in Natal and around Johannesburg.

De Klerk, on the other hand, was disappointing National Party supporters. "He is increasingly portrayed as a lame-duck president with nothing to offer fearful minorities after elections," the newsletter said. The newsletter even suggested that the Freedom Alliance could gain second place in the balloting over the National Party if the Afrikaner Volksfront and Inkatha take part in the election. [22]

Whatever the Freedom Alliance may decide, the threat of violence and disruptions in the months leading up to the election persists. Afrikaner and Zulu leaders continued to strike militant stands in December. Weapons are plentiful in the country. And some political groups question whether the central government or the black police forces in KwaZulu, Bophuthatswana and Ciskei will act to maintain order. "We still get reports of the security forces being part of the problem," said Sadek of the Human Rights Commission.

In their remarks after Parliament's approval of the new constitution, Mandela and de Klerk both acknowledged the threat of violence. De Klerk promised that the government will use force to prevent the holdout groups from disrupting the elections. For his part, Mandela issued a statement urging "all South Africans, regardless of race, creed or gender, [to] take hands and work together to bring an end to the terrible violence that is tearing our country apart." [23] ■

OUTLOOK

Rebuilding South Africa

South Africa is a nation of striking contradictions. It is a land of breathtakingly beautiful mountains and beaches and vast areas of arid desert and desolate highlands. It is a country where First World cities, like the busy financial center of Johannesburg or the relaxedly cosmopolitan Cape Town, stand amidst the Third World poverty of squatter camps and overcrowded townships.

South Africa's people — black and white — exude an easy warmth. Beneath the surface, however, lie the bitterness of a black population that has suffered grievously throughout South Africa's history as a nation and the resentment of a white population that has lived for decades under the burden of worldwide moral condemnation.

These contradictions cannot be resolved with a single election — or even in a single generation. The gaping inequities between the lives of white and black South Africans were built up over centuries. They will remain for years even if the new government takes on an ambitious program of social and economic transformation.

Political and economic realities, moreover, will work against bold initiatives by the government. The economy remains largely in white hands. The constitutional negotiations preserved whites' jobs in the military, the police and the civil service. And the government may hesitate to raise taxes for social programs in a country already highly taxed in comparison with other industrialized nations.

In addition, the ANC may temper its activism in order to hold the national unity government together and reassure domestic political constituencies as well as international audiences. "The ANC is probably the only liberation movement in history to speak of financial discipline before it assumes power," says Princeton's Jeffrey Herbst.

The climate for economic reconstruction appears to have been aided by recent events. The ANC's newfound moderation on business issues — including its support for a property rights provision in the interim constitution — has eased some concerns. "They used to have an essentially socialist manifesto," says Michael Christie of the South Africa Foundation. "Now, they're gung-ho market economists."

In addition, the adoption of the constitution has spurred U.S. businesses and investors to take a new look at South Africa. The same day that South Africa's Parliament approved the constitution, four U.S. companies — American Express, Merrill Lynch, Procter & Gamble and IBM — said they were re-establishing their business ties with South Africa. [24]

Political reconstruction may prove to be more difficult. Rural Afrikaners, Buthelezei's Inkatha supporters and the estranged black homeland leaders represent a continuing source of discontent and unrest. National Party supporters also may become disaffected once their party loses control of the government after 45 years in power. Meanwhile, moderate policies may aggravate internal divisions within the ANC — strengthening those on the left who have bristled at the accommodations Mandela and the rest of the ANC leadership agreed to during the constitutional talks.

Mandela's presence is seen as critical for keeping the confidence of blacks. "Mandela remains the only person who can carry their vote," says Reuters correspondent Rich Mkhondo.

Mandela's health — he is 75 — and his security cannot be taken for granted, however.

Moderates, such as Cyril Ramaphosa, the party's secretary general, hold many of the ANC's other major positions. But political analyst Eugene Nyati notes that other important posts are held by radicals, such as Peter Mokaba, the head of the ANC's Youth League, and Winnie Mandela, the just-elected president of the Women's League.* In addition, Nyati says, the ANC's rank-and-file constituency is "more radical than the leadership."

Despite the acknowledged risks, however, most observers in and out of South Africa end with an optimistic outlook about the future. Pauline Baker of the Aspen Institute notes that many of the difficult political issues of transition were resolved during the long constitutional talks — significantly, by South Africans themselves without the United Nations or other international mediation.

Reuters correspondent Mkhondo is optimistic, too, as he prepares — along with millions of blacks — for his first opportunity ever to vote for a democratic government. "My vote will bring an end to the humiliation and injustices of apartheid which we have suffered for decades," he writes. Despite the "enormous problems and challenges facing us," he concludes, "our hopes are high." [25] ■

*Winnie and Nelson Mandela were legally separated on April 13, 1992.

Notes

[1] Quotes drawn from *The New York Times*, Nov. 18, 1993, p. A1; *The Star* (Johannesburg), Nov. 18, 1993, p. 2.

[2] Quoted in the *Los Angeles Times*, Nov. 19, 1993, p. A10.

[3] See *The Washington Post*, Dec. 1, 1993, p. A20; *The Economist*, Dec. 4, 1993, pp. 44-47.

[4] See Eric Ransdell, "Freedom's Bloody Toll," *U.S. News & World Report*, Nov. 29, 1993, pp. 44-48.

[5] See *The Washington Post*, Nov. 21, 1993, p. A32.

[6] See Jeffrey Herbst, "Politics and the Post-Apartheid Economy," in Stephen Jay Stedman (ed.), *South Africa: The Political Economy of Transformation* (1994, forthcoming).

[7] See *The Wall Street Journal*, Oct. 7, 1993, p. A2; *The New York Times*, Oct. 21, 1993, p. D1.

[8] Quoted in Rich Mkhondo, *Reporting South Africa* (1993), p. 142.

[9] *The Washington Post*, Nov. 7, 1993, p. A42.

[10] Historical background is drawn largely from Leonard Thompson, *A History of South Africa* (1990).

[11] *Ibid.*, p. 108.

[12] See David Harrison, *The White Tribe of Africa: South Africa in Perspective* (1981), Chapter 8.

[13] Thompson, *op. cit.*, pp. 193-195.

[14] Robert M. Price, *The Apartheid State in Crisis: Political Transformation in South Africa, 1975-1990* (1991), pp. 192-202.

[15] Thompson, *op. cit.*, pp. 224-228.

[16] Allister Sparks, "A New South Africa: The Role of Sanctions," *The Washington Post*, Oct. 5, 1993, p. A19.

[17] See Mary Cooper, "The U.S. Role in South Africa," *Editorial Research Reports*, March 23, 1990, p. 164.

[18] Some of the recent history is drawn from David Ottaway, *Chained Together: Mandela, de Klerk and the Struggle to Remake South Africa* (1993). See also Mkhondo, *op. cit.*

[19] See Ottaway, *op. cit.*, pp. 75-76.

[20] Steyn spoke to the World Press Freedom Committee in Washington, D.C., on Dec. 7, 1993; Paddock wrote in *Business Day*, Nov. 19, 1993, p. 4.

[21] See *The New York Times*, Dec. 21, 1993, p. A3; *The Washington Post*, Dec. 22, 1993, A23.

[22] *Africa Confidential*, Vol. 34, No. 24, Dec. 3, 1993, pp. 1, 3.

[23] Quoted in *The New York Times*, Dec. 23, 1993, p. A3.

[24] See *The Wall Street Journal*, Dec. 23, 1993, p. C1; *The Washington Post*, Dec. 23, 1993, p. A16.

[25] Mkhondo, *op. cit.*, p. 177.

Bibliography

Selected Sources Used

Books

Friedman, Steven, ed., *The Long Journey: South Africa's Quest for a Negotiated Settlement*, Ravan Press, 1993.
This detailed account of South Africa's constitutional negotiations, prepared by the staff of the Center for Policy Studies in Johannesburg, goes from the preparations for the talks up to the beginning of the final, successful sessions in March 1993.

Harrison, David, *The White Tribe of Africa: South Africa in Perspective*, British Broadcasting Corporation, 1981.
Harrison, a documentary filmmaker, developed this history of the Afrikaners from an award-winning BBC television series. It recounts the Afrikaners' role from their defeat in the Anglo-Boer War in 1902 through the National Party's coming to power in 1948 and its increasingly embattled defense of apartheid through the 1970s.

Mallaby, Sebastian, *After Apartheid: The Future of South Africa*, Times Books, 1992.
Mallaby, formerly the Africa correspondent for *The Economist,* surveys some of the social, economic and political issues the new South African government will face.

Meer, Fatima, *Higher Than Hope: The Authorized Biography of Nelson Mandela*, Harper & Row, 1988.
Meer, a professor at the University of Natal and a co-defendant with Mandela in the 1956 treason trial, has written a favorable biography that relies heavily on Mandela's speeches and correspondence in prison. For a more journalistic biography, see Mary Benson, *Nelson Mandela: The Man and the Movement* (Norton, 1986).

Meli, Frances, *South Africa Belongs to Us: A History of the ANC*, Indiana University Press, 1988.
Meli, a member of the African National Congress' national executive committee, traces the ANC's history from its founding in 1912 through its defiance campaign in the 1950s, armed resistance in the 1960s and re-emergence in the 1970s and '80s.

Mkhondo, Rich, *Reporting South Africa*, Heineman, 1993.
This journalistic account of recent events by a black South African correspondent for Reuters is especially valuable for coverage of the ANC and conditions in black areas of South Africa. An 11-page chronology covers events from 1652 through summer 1993.

Ottaway, David, *Chained Together: Mandela, de Klerk and the Struggle to Remake South Africa*, Times Books, 1993.
Ottaway, who served as *The Washington Post*'s correspondent in South Africa from 1990 to 1992, recounts events from Nelson Mandela's release from prison through last summer's agreement on the date of the first all-races elections. The book includes a seven-page chronology.

Price, Robert, *The Apartheid State in Crisis: The Process of Political Transformation in South Africa, 1975-1990*, Oxford University Press, 1991.
Price, a political science professor at the University of California at Berkeley, analyzes the economic deterioration and political unrest that brought about the preconditions for broad political changes in South Africa.

Stedman, Stephen Jay, ed., *South Africa: The Political Economy of Transformation*, Westview, 1994 (forthcoming).
This book includes articles surveying political events by 10 experts: three South Africans and seven Americans. Stedman is a professor of African studies at Johns Hopkins University's School of Advanced International Studies in Washington, where some of the papers were originally presented at a conference in spring 1992.

Thompson, Leonard, *A History of South Africa*, Yale University Press, 1990.
This 288-page, carefully annotated history by the director of Yale's Southern Africa Research Program surveys events in South Africa from before the arrival of European settlers up to F.W. de Klerk's election as president. For a longer history, see T.R.H. Davenport, *South Africa: A Modern History* (3d ed.), University of Toronto Press, 1987.

Reports and Studies

Human Rights Commission, *Three Years of Destabilisation: A Record of Political Violence in South Africa from July 1990 to June 1993*, Johannesburg, 1993.
In this 24-page special report, the independent human rights monitoring group counted nearly 10,000 incidents of political violence, nearly 10,000 deaths and more than 16,000 injuries in a three-year period. The commission also publishes a monthly update on political violence.

***Race Relations Survey 1992/93*, South African Institute of Race Relations, Johannesburg, 1993.**
This annual volume is a comprehensive narrative and statistical report on social, economic and political conditions in South Africa. The institute also publishes valuable monographs on specific topics.

The Next Step

Additional information from UMI's Newspaper & Periodical Abstracts database

April Elections

Bartlett, Ellen, "South Africa transition council begins work," *Boston Globe*, Dec. 8, 1993, p. 2.

The multiracial council that will oversee the governing of South Africa until democratic elections in April 1994 met for the first time, as blacks and whites alike hailed the effective end of white minority rule.

Cherry, Michael, "South African agency faces new priorities," *Nature*, Nov. 25, 1993, p. 295.

With the way cleared for South Africa to hold its first open elections, science institutes in the country are concerned about how much government aid to expect in the future. South Africa's Council for Scientific and Industrial Research is discussed.

Shepherd, Anne, "Vetting the vote," *Africa Report*, November 1993, pp. 22-25.

The violence that has plagued South Africa in the past could jeopardize the country's April 1994 elections. The Transitional Executive Council is seeking to set up a National Peace-keeping Force to police the elections.

Taylor, Paul, "South Africa inaugurates nonracial rule," *The Washington Post*, Dec. 8, 1993, p. A25.

The era of exclusive white-minority rule in South Africa came to a formal close with the installation of the Transitional Executive Council, a multi-party, multi-racial body that will oversee preparations for the country's first universal suffrage election.

The Current Situation

Battersby, John, "At Blood River, a message of reconciliation," *Christian Science Monitor*, Dec. 17, 1993, p. 8.

On Dec. 16, 1993, rightwing Afrikaners commemorated a victory over the Zulus in 1838 at Blood River South Africa. Afrikaner Volksfront leader Constand Viljoen called for South Africans to behave as Christians, and called for people not to destroy each other, but to co-exist in the country.

Chabedi, Marks, "Wiseman Nkuhlu: Empowering communities," *Africa Report*, November 1993, pp. 20-21.

In an interview, South African Wiseman Nkuhlu, vice-chairman and CEO of the Independent Development Trust, discusses the Trust's approach to development, the role of international support, the problems the developing agencies now face and their role in a future government of national unity.

Collins, Carole, "Woman's death personalizes South African apartheid," *National Catholic Reporter*, Dec. 10, 1993, p. 32.

The killing in South Africa over apartheid continues every day, even though leaders in the country are trying to bring people together. The death of Claire Stewart and her life are discussed.

Darnton, John, "Note of unity pervades Peace Prize ceremony," *The New York Times*, Dec. 11, 1993, p. A7.

South African President F. W. de Klerk and African National Congress leader Nelson Mandela jointly received the Nobel Peace Prize in Oslo on Dec. 10, 1993, in recognition of their work to bring peace and non-racial democracy to their country. They joined together in a public expression of hope for South Africa's future.

Laurence, Patrick, "The diehards & dealmakers," *Africa Report*, November 1993, pp. 13-16.

An unlikely association of Chief Mangosuthu Buthelezei's Zulus and diehard Afrikaners is threatening the compact forged between South African President F. W. de Klerk and the African National Congress' Nelson Mandela. The Freedom Alliance is demanding a federal state and threatening new violence.

Smyth, Gareth, "Calling the shots," *New Statesman & Society*, Dec. 3, 1993, pp. 20-21.

Ronnie Kasrils, former intelligence head of the African National Congress' armed wing, Umkhonto we Siswe, believes that the struggle for change in South Africa is far from over. Kasrils is said to be responsible for the African National Congress's most violent campaigns.

"South Africa: Fighting bluster," *The Economist*, Dec. 4, 1993, pp. 44-47.

The South African Afrikaner Resistance Movement and the Afrikaner Volksfront are talking of forcibly resisting the upcoming new government. These groups' posturing may be little more than psychological warfare.

Education in South Africa

Mac Gregor, Karen, "Building a picture from snapshots," *Times Educational Supplement*, Sept. 24, 1993, p. 18.

South African schools will be largely responsible for creating a society in which blacks and whites can live comfortably together. Two South African secondary schools in Durban are profiled.

Penny, Alan, Stephen Appel, John Gultig, Ken Harley, and Robert Muir, "Just sort of fumbling in the dark: A case study of the advent of racial integration in

South African schools," ***Comparative Education Review*****, November 1993, pp. 412-433.**
By the end of 1990 in South Africa, legislation was enacted that made it possible for hitherto segregated white schools to admit children of other races. The ways that these schools are dealing with this open enrollment is examined.

Vergnani, Linda, "Universities after apartheid," ***Chronicle of Higher Education*****, Dec. 15, 1993, pp. A34-A35.**
South African universities are under pressure to make themselves more responsive to the country's black majority and more representative of it. Some of the changes taking place are discussed.

Investment in South Africa

"Colleges reverse divestment plans," ***The New York Times*****, Nov. 28, 1993, p. 33.**
Many of the American colleges that divested themselves in the 1980s of stock of companies with ties to South Africa have begun reversing their plans in the wake of Nelson Mandela's recent call for American reinvestment and the country's new constitution ending white rule.

Moose, George E., "U.S. support for new business opportunities in South Africa," ***U.S. Department of State Dispatch*****, Nov. 1, 1993, pp. 769-770.**
New business opportunities in South Africa as a result of the country's efforts to become a democracy are discussed. Outside investment and expertise will be valuable to South Africa during its economic transition.

Palmer, Elizabeth A., "Clinton signs bill to repeal anti-apartheid sanctions," ***Congressional Quarterly Weekly Report*****, Nov. 27, 1993, p. 3281.**
President Clinton signed legislation on Nov. 23, 1993, that repeals most of the sanctions in the 1986 Anti-Apartheid Act.

Shepherd, Anne, "Waiting for investment," ***Africa Report*****, November 1993, pp. 17-19.**
Foreign business reportedly considers South Africa a top investment prospect, but capital will come only after the April 1994 elections. Once an interim government is in place, it will make foreign investment a top priority.

Tannenbaum, Jeffrey A., "Focus on franchising: South Africa," ***The Wall Street Journal*****, Dec. 8, 1993, p. B2.**
With apartheid abolished and free elections scheduled for April 1994, some franchisers feel that South Africa may be one of the most lucrative markets for master licensees and franchisees.

"U.S. has high economic hopes for renewed ties with S. Africa," ***USA Today*****, Nov. 29, 1993, p. A4.**
Commerce Secretary Ron Brown, the highest-ranking U.S. trade official to visit South Africa in almost 20 years, said that the United States will have strong and growing economic ties with the post-apartheid state.

"World Wide: The U.N. General Assembly," ***The Wall Street Journal*****, Dec. 10, 1993, p. A1.**
The United Nations General Assembly lifted a non-binding oil embargo against South Africa that had been imposed because of Pretoria's racial policies. A mandatory arms embargo is expected to remain in force until a new South African government is formed after April 1994 elections.

The New Constitution

"Change comes to South Africa," ***Current Events*****, Dec. 6, 1993, pp. 1-2.**
A new constitution that grants equal rights to all races has been accepted in South Africa. The dramatic changes that brought this process to fruition are discussed, and 1993 Nobel Peace Prize winners F. W. de Klerk and Nelson Mandela are profiled.

Contreras, Joseph, "Apartheid on the ash heap," ***Newsweek*****, Nov. 29, 1993, p. 48.**
South African President F. W. de Klerk has endorsed a new Constitution that grants sweeping powers to the next president, who will almost certainly be Nelson Mandela. The deal empowers blacks, but includes protection for whites.

Sly, Liz, "Equality yes—But for women, too?" ***Chicago Tribune*****, Nov. 4, 1993, p. 1.**
Some of South Africa's traditional tribal leaders are beginning to realize that the high-sounding ideals of democracy being touted under the country's proposed new constitution could prove fatal to ancient privileges and powers they enjoy as hereditary chiefs. The chiefs are calling for the clause on gender equality to be struck from the constitution altogether.

"South Africa: A new dawn," ***The Economist*****, Nov. 20, 1993, p. 48.**
On Nov. 18, 1993, the African National Congress' Nelson Mandela and South African President F. W. de Klerk put their names to a final draft of the country's first non-racial constitution. The frantic finishing touches to the document are discussed.

Taylor, Paul, "Once hero, now holdout, Buthelezei wary of future," ***The Washington Post*****, Nov. 21, 1993, p. A29.**
Mangosuthu Buthelezei, head of the Zulu-dominated Inkatha Freedom Party, is losing power in South Africa after refusing to sign the new South African constitution, which he believes makes no allowance for the legitimate quest for self-determination of his "Zulu nation" and other ethnic groups.

Back Issues

Great Research on Current Issues Starts Right Here...Recent topics covered by The CQ Researcher are listed below. Before May 1991, reports were published under the name of Editorial Research Reports.

JULY 1992
Alternative Energy
Prescription Drug Prices
Alzheimer's Disease
Infant Mortality

AUGUST 1992
The Homeless
Work, Family and Stress
NATO's Changing Role
Marine Mammals vs. Fish

SEPTEMBER 1992
Domestic Partners
Violence in Schools
Public Broadcasting
Women in the Military

OCTOBER 1992
Depression
U.S. Auto Industry
Youth Apprenticeships
Hispanic Americans

NOVEMBER 1992
Physical Fitness
Privatization
Paying for College
U.S. Policy in Asia

Back issues are available for $4.00 (subscribers) or $7.00 (non-subscribers). Quantity discounts apply to orders over ten. To order, call Congressional Quarterly Customer Service at (202) 887-8621.

Binders are available for $15.00. To order call 1-800-638-1710. Please refer to stock number 648.

DECEMBER 1992
Crackdown on Smoking
The New CIA
Eating Disorders
Women and AIDS

JANUARY 1993
Hate Crimes
Child Sexual Abuse
Nuclear Fusion
U.S. Trade Policy

FEBRUARY 1993
Community Policing
Europe's New Right
School Censorship
Violence Against Women

MARCH 1993
Gay Rights
Aid to Russia
War on Drugs
TV Violence

APRIL 1993
Head Start
High-Speed Rail
Children's Legal Rights
Muslims in America

MAY 1993
Cults in America
Preventing Teen Pregnancy
Software Piracy
National Parks

JUNE 1993
Food Safety
Prostitution
Childhood Immunizations
National Service

JULY 1993
Electric Cars
Population Growth
Downward Mobility
Intelligence Testing

AUGUST 1993
Mental Illness
Bilingual Education
Foreign Policy Burden
School Funding

SEPTEMBER 1993
Suburban Crime
Public Housing
Supreme Court Preview
Immigration Reform

OCTOBER 1993
Airline Safety
Disaster Response
Science in the Courtroom
The Glass Ceiling

NOVEMBER 1993
Paying for Retirement
Charitable Giving
Privacy in the Workplace
Adoption

DECEMBER 1993
U.S. Vietnam-Relations
Learning Disabilities
Child Care
Space Program's Future

JANUARY 1994
Racial Tensions in Schools

Future Topics

- ***Job Training***
- ***Pesticides***
- ***Prison Overcrowding***

THE CQ Researcher

PUBLISHED BY CONGRESSIONAL QUARTERLY INC.

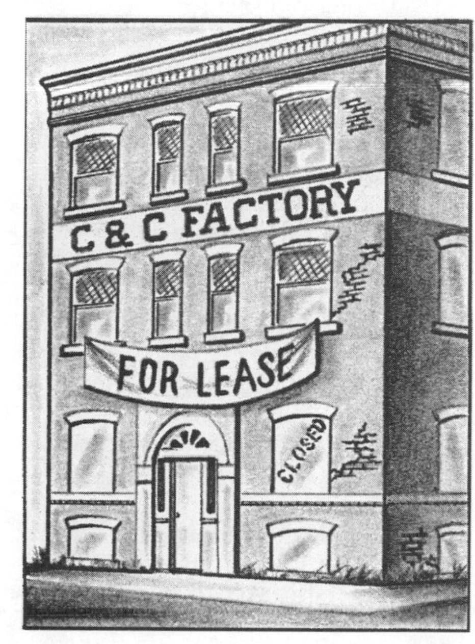

Worker Retraining

Do displaced workers get adequate training for new jobs?

About 20 million American workers were displaced in the 1980s, mostly from manufacturing jobs. Now, corporate restructuring and white-collar layoffs are adding highly trained workers and middle managers to the ranks of the displaced. Most laid-off workers will not get their old jobs back, and many are being forced to take new positions with less pay. The heated debate last year over the North American Free Trade Agreement (NAFTA) underscored concerns about the adequacy of U.S. programs for retraining displaced workers. In return for support on NAFTA, President Clinton promised additional assistance to laid-off workers. But now economists and other experts are questioning whether the country can afford a sweeping new plan — and what the consequences may be if the current system is not overhauled.

INSIDE THIS ISSUE

CQ January 21, 1994 • Volume 4, No. 3 • 49-72

Formerly Editorial Research Reports

COVER: ILLUSTRATION BY BARBARA SASSA-DANIELS

January 21, 1994
Volume 4, No. 3

Bibliographic records and abstracts included in The Next Step section of this publication are from UMI's Newspaper and Periodical Abstracts database, and are used with permission.

The CQ Researcher (ISSN 1056-2036). Formerly Editorial Research Reports. Published weekly (48 times per year, not printed the first Friday of any month with five Fridays) by Congressional Quarterly Inc., 1414 22nd St., N.W., Washington, D.C. 20037. Rates are furnished upon request. Second-class postage paid at Washington, D.C. POSTMASTER: Send address changes to The CQ Researcher, 1414 22nd St., N.W., Washington, D.C. 20037.

Worker Retraining

By Susan Kellam

The Issues

When he lost his job a year and a half ago, Brian Wessner drew comfort from knowing it had been a business decision. But the landing was still pretty rough. "It was like having a death in the family," Wessner says. "I had to grieve and move on."

Wessner had been earning about $100,000 a year at the Legent Corp., a software firm in Herndon, Va., when Legent acquired another software company. Although he had expected some downsizing, Wessner was still surprised when "my boss took me into a room and told *me* to go."

Harsh business realities affected Dwight "Doc" Iler, too, but the veteran steelworker didn't feel the pain initially. Iler had been an inspector at one of Bethlehem Steel Co.'s Baltimore mills for nearly 22 years when the plant closed a number of years ago.

At first Iler did nothing, explaining, "There used to be several weeks of layoff each year. So I'd gotten into a pattern where I didn't make a move." But soon a year had gone by, and he had no job and no prospects.

Although they represent different niches in the labor market, Wessner and Iler shared a common dilemma when the bottom fell out: At first, neither knew where to go for support services or job retraining.

Wessner eventually discovered that despite his bachelor's degree in aerospace engineering and master's in computer science, he didn't qualify for any federal programs for displaced workers. Iler was eligible for the Trade Adjustment Assistance (TAA) program, for workers whose jobs were affected by imports. But TAA's funding had been radically reduced in 1981. "By the time I got to it," says Iler, "[President Ronald] Reagan had cut it back. So I couldn't use it."

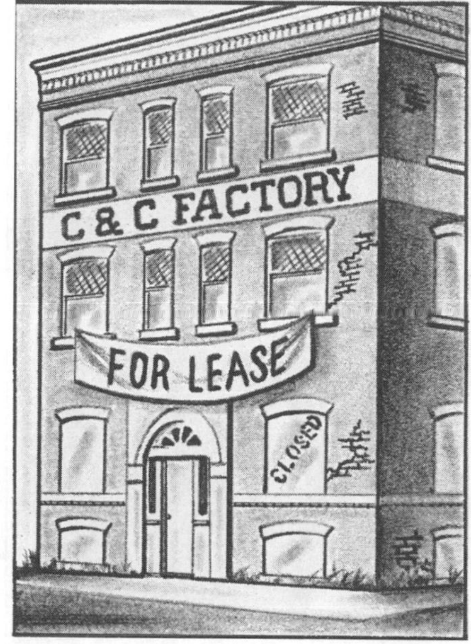

Thousands of jobless Americans face the same predicament today. Although there are several mostly small federal retraining programs for displaced workers (*see box, p. 53*), the majority of people who find themselves out of a job only receive the standard 26 weeks of unemployment insurance.

Under a sweeping plan to be unveiled in February, federal training programs for permanently laid-off workers will be expanded and consolidated into what Secretary of Labor Robert B. Reich calls a "seamless" new Workforce Security Program (*see p. 64*). In addition to providing more training and aid, the program will establish a nationwide network of one-stop offices where job-seekers can electronically tap into all available aid.

Roughly 20 million American workers were displaced throughout the 1980s, primarily from manufacturing jobs. However, a trend toward corporate restructuring and white-collar layoffs is altering the picture. As a result, the large share of blue-collar workers in the unemployment lines declined over the decade, falling from about 65 percent in 1982 to 55 percent in 1990. [1]

Cutbacks announced in recent years by such behemoths as General Motors, IBM, Sears and, early this month, K-Mart, reflect the massive changes likely to affect the current labor market. Among the casualties: highly trained workers who had ascended the corporate ladder, but not to job security. [2]

Thousands of defense workers face layoffs with the shutdowns ordered last year of 130 military installations, as well as those base closings anticipated in 1995. The Clinton administration also expects to cut 140,000 management jobs as it seeks to reduce the federal work force by 252,000 positions, or 12 percent, over the next five years. [3]

Middle managers from the private sector already are feeling the heat. Although they make up only 8 percent of the work force, middle managers shouldered 19 percent of the cuts at 8,000 companies in 1992-93, according to a survey by the American Management Association. [4]

"We now have a large number of [unemployed] workers who have never been out of work [before]," says Reich. "They don't know what hit them. They're 45 years old, and suddenly they're out on the street. They've got mortgages. They have cars to pay off. This isn't just a problem of the working poor; it's not just a problem of the manufacturing blue-collar; it's right across the board."

Reich already was on record as a critic of government's failure to retrain workers when he left Harvard University to join Clinton's Cabinet. In his 1992 book, *The Work of Nations*, for example, he wrote: "The official reason given for why America cannot invest more money in infrastructure, education and training is that we cannot afford it. . . . Even if the necessary funds cannot be reallocated from elsewhere in the federal budget — surely a heroic assump-

Displaced Workers on the Rise

An average of 2 million workers were displaced each year from 1984 to 1989, but in 1990 the number of workers who lost their jobs grew to 2.5 million.

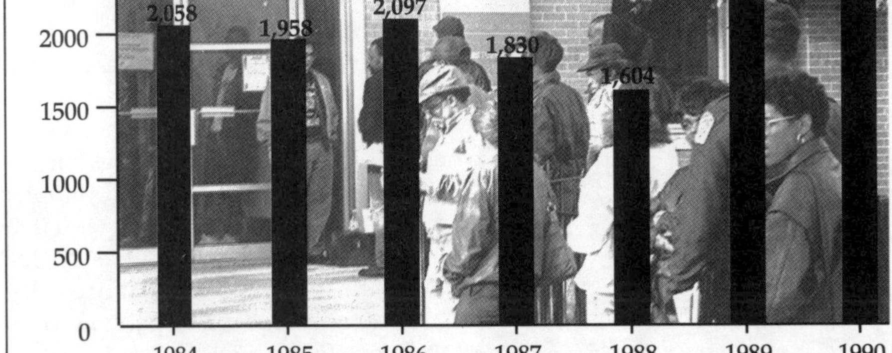

Source: Bureau of Labor, November 1993

tion, given the number of B-1 bombers and other military exotica being created to ward off communists, most of whom no longer exist (as such) — the claim that America cannot afford to spend more on the productivity of all its citizens remains a curious one."[5]

Many labor experts found it particularly odd that it took the opening of U.S. borders to Canada and Mexico to inspire a sharp re-evaluation of U.S. policy toward displaced workers. To win votes for the controversial North American Free Trade Agreement (NAFTA) during last year's rhetoric-filled debates, President Clinton pledged new attention to displaced workers' needs.*

Passage of NAFTA was a bitter loss for organized labor. According to AFL-CIO economist Sheldon Friedman, no aid program could fully offset the agreement's "damaging consequences for the vast majority of American workers."[6]

Now that NAFTA is a reality, Friedman acknowledges that the pact will have one benefit: It shines "a welcome spotlight on the glaring inadequacies of U.S. policies and programs to assist dislocated workers."

Labor experts generally agree that there will be winners along with the losers under NAFTA. Overall, U.S. employment is expected to increase, though many workers will lose jobs. Mexican industry, meanwhile, should continue to enjoy low labor costs for the next decade.

Given the likely trends, forecasters at DRI/McGraw Hill, a Boston consulting firm, say worker-assistance programs should stress training that exploits the competitive advantages of U.S. manufacturing, mainly areas where technological applications are fundamental.[7]

Sar A. Levitan, director of the Center for Social Policy Studies at George Washington University, argues that NAFTA is not the culprit in an eroding job environment. He blames weak government policies and the "culture of corporate downsizing" as the obstacles to greater worker security and a better job-training system.

House Majority Leader Richard A. Gephardt, D-Mo., said in September that he would not support NAFTA unless the White House pledged federal funds to retrain workers left unemployed in the treaty's wake. He said the trade pact did not protect U.S. workers because it didn't require Mexico to raise wages as its workers' productivity increases. Gephardt voted against NAFTA.

While job loss is a natural outgrowth of economic change, there is an especially "dark side" to today's dislocations, says Anthony P. Carnevale, president of the Institute for Workplace Learning at the American Society for Training and Development in Alexandria, Va. "Technology requires that companies build more flexible work systems," he says, "and flexible, in the end, is often just a fancy word for fired."

Carnevale, among others, feels that improving the economy will improve the lot of the displaced worker. And there are early indications that the picture may be brightening. Reich predicted Jan. 4 on ABC-TV's "Good Morning America" that about 2 million new jobs will be added to the U.S. economy in 1994 — the same number as in 1993. He also predicted that the unemployment rate, which stood at 6.4 percent in November 1993, would settle somewhere between that point and 6 percent during 1994.

Most of the new jobs, Reich says, will be higher-paid managerial and professional positions providing services to business; the others will be lower-paid restaurant and hotel positions.

"I want to stress that even though jobs are going to be in abundant supply, there still is going to be a greater and greater disparity between those who are prepared for them and those who aren't," Reich told TV viewers, emphasizing the importance of getting the nation in a "learning" mode.

Meanwhile, Brian Wessner and Doc Iler have experienced the despair and hope that accompany job seekers in the 1990s. Wessner is more optimistic since locating an outplacement assis-

---

*NAFTA went into effect Jan. 1, 1994.

Programs for Dislocated Workers

Trade Adjustment Assistance (TAA): Assists workers dislocated as a result of federal policies reducing barriers to foreign trade. A worker is certified for the program after the Department of Labor determines that increased imports contributed to decreased sales and, consequently, to worker layoffs. Established by the Trade Expansion Act of 1962, TAA provides training, employment services and job search and relocation allowances.

Economic Dislocation and Worker Adjustment Act (EDWAA): Provides retraining to dislocated workers who are unlikely to return to their previous industries or occupations. Offered through a network of local service-delivery offices, EDWAA provides basic education and literacy classes as well as on-the-job and skills training. EDWAA replaced Title III of the Job Training Partnership Act (JTPA) in 1988.

Clean Air Employment Transition Assistance: Provides retraining and readjustment aid to workers dislocated because of a firm's compliance with the 1990 Clean Air Act. The program is under the auspices of JTPA and offers services through the local service-delivery system.

Defense Conversion Adjustment: Provides retraining and readjustment aid to workers dislocated by defense cutbacks. The program was authorized in the 1991 Defense Authorization Act and comes under the JTPA.

Defense Diversification Program: Provides retraining and readjustment assistance to workers dislocated by defense cutbacks and base closures. Authorized by the 1993 Defense Authorization Act, the program comes under the JTPA and seeks to give workers slated to be displaced the skills needed to convent military facilities to civilian use. The program also provides limited funding to implement new production technologies to facilitate base conversions.

tance center for professionals. The federally funded center provides a reference library and a computer lab where he can scan job data bases. "It's given me a bridge to understanding the situation," he says. It also put him in touch with people who didn't treat him as if being a displaced worker is contagious.

Iler finally turned his termination into a rewarding new career. For the past eight years, he has counseled other displaced workers through a program sponsored by the United Steelworkers of America union and Bethlehem Steel. "When I first came down here 20 years ago," he says, "I didn't think I'd stay so long in the steel mills. I thought I'd go back to school. So this has been a blessing."

As the administration prepares to launch the Workforce Security Program, these are some of the issues that Congress will debate as it weighs the proposal against other domestic priorities:

Is the government doing enough to help laid-off workers?

Last year, about 360,000 displaced workers received federally sponsored classroom training, on-the-job training or job-search assistance.[8] That's a small fraction of the 2 million workers who lose their jobs annually.

The two principal federal job-training outreach efforts are the Trade Adjustment Assistance and Economic Dislocation and Worker Adjustment Assistance (EDWAA) programs. The Department of Labor, which administers TAA through state and local offices, spent $150 million on cash payments and services for 38,500 workers whose job losses were linked to imports in 1990.[9] Most of the affected workers were in the auto, apparel and electronics industries. For fiscal 1994, $190 million has been allocated.

Recent findings show that the TAA program has fallen short of its goals. Less than half the workers who used the program, for example, found employment that paid wages comparable to their previous earnings.[10] And only half of those accepted into the program sought job training; the others opted just to receive the program's trade adjustment allowances.[11]

In contrast to TAA, EDWAA programs help workers regardless of the reason for job loss. EDWAA aided more than 330,000 workers in 1991, mainly blue-collar workers and the chronically unemployed, while typically excluding professionals like Brian Wessner.

Figures released by the Congressional Budget Office (CBO) in February 1993 showed that roughly half of the displaced workers receiving unemployment benefits in the 1980s exhausted their benefits before finding another job.[12] CBO also noted that most displaced workers throughout the 1980s did eventually return to work, many with pay roughly comparable with that of their old jobs. Workers who incurred the largest pay cuts tended to be those who had been jobless the longest.[13]

"The truth is that most of the people that lose their jobs now are not going to get their old jobs back," says Reich. "The old concept of unemployment insurance as a bridge to tide you over until you got your old job back, until the recession ended, is simply obsolete."

Reich is equally convinced that "individualized, categorical job training programs for special groups of workers" are obsolete, too. Instead, Reich advocates a complete transformation from the current unemployment system to a re-employment system. (*See interview, p. 60.*)

Finding a Job Takes Longer

The percentage of displaced workers who were out of work for more than six months before finding new jobs has increased from 14.1 percent in the 1970s to 16.0 percent in the 1990s.

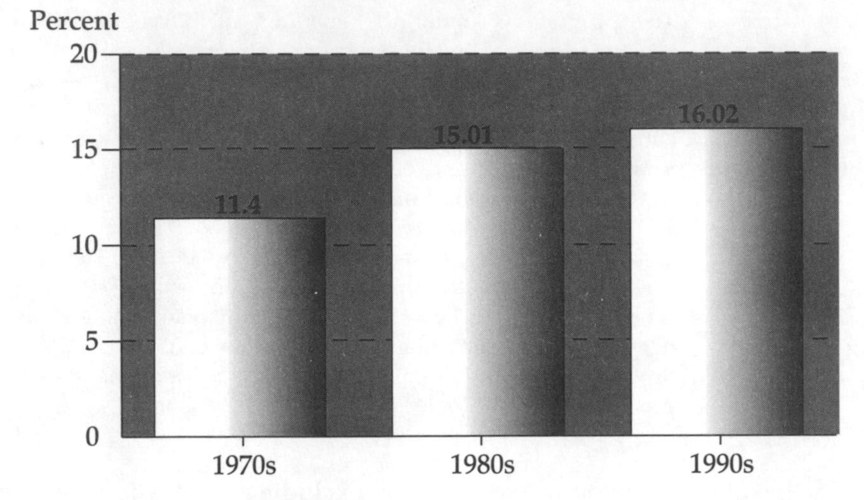

Source: Department of Labor, November 1993

Carnevale, an economist and job-training expert, counters that government programs aren't the problem. "We know how to treat dislocated workers," he says. "We can get them another job through job counseling and support groups. We just don't know how to guarantee them a job."

Although Carnevale agrees with Reich that U.S. labor market policy isn't particularly sensitive to workers, he blames the erosion of job security on the economy. Any proposal offered by the government for job retraining would only be "second best" to actually improving the economy, he says.

Similarly, many observers feel that job creation, either through jump-starting the economy with more funds or creating public-sector jobs, is the only way for government to soften the blow to displaced workers. In April, Clinton tried to pass a $16.3 billion stimulus package that would have funded construction and social service projects — and put thousands of people to work. But a bloc of Senate Republicans prevented a vote on the plan.

Joan Crigger, director of training at the U.S. Conference of Mayors, wonders whether Clinton has abandoned the stimulus concept, which was strongly advocated by many big-city mayors. "Is he just going to walk away from it?" she asks. "The mayors are still looking for more federal dollars for Community Development Block Grants, transportation and job training."

George Washington's Levitan advocates a jobs program akin to the Works Progress Administration (WPA), when President Franklin D. Roosevelt put tens of thousands of Americans to work building parks, bridges and roads. Later, the 1973 Comprehensive Employment and Training Act (CETA) had a public-jobs component, but it was viewed as scandal-ridden and too costly and abandoned when CETA was replaced with the Job Training Partnership Act (JTPA) in 1982. Nonetheless, Levitan says that what is missing from Clinton's vision of a new system for displaced workers is a job-creation component.

Many experts agree with Levitan that the current approach to job training and retraining should be enhanced but ask who will pay for a radical overhaul.

Carnevale thinks the answer is clear. "Community colleges are [going to be] the real winners," he says. Government can't afford to train all the workers who require more education, he explains, and four-year colleges haven't responded quickly enough to the need for more skills trainings.

David Pierce, executive director of the American Association of Community Colleges, says the government's short-term retraining programs have limited value in today's working environment and that many displaced workers will benefit from getting more training than existing programs offer, typically less than a year.

But government still can play an important role, indirectly, in job training, says Joseph F. Shopulski, director of industrial technology programs at Baltimore's Dundalk Community College. (*See story, p. 55.*) He defines that role as changing the rhetoric on job training, teaching workers how to learn and how to stay productive in a rapidly changing industrial world. "If the government doesn't do it, who does? People need leadership," he says.

Should industry assume more responsibility for training workers for new jobs?

There is a broad consensus that U.S. corporations, from the 1950s through the '70s, took advantage of a prosperous economy and legions of relatively unskilled workers with little consideration for the inevitable changes lurking on the industrial frontier. The downsizing and restructuring of businesses during the past decade are viewed as a natural, and necessary, response to industry's shortsightedness. What now alarms labor experts is how poorly equipped many of the displaced workers are to assume new jobs with higher skill requirements.

Continued on p. 56

Dundalk Community College: Putting People Back to Work

Dundalk Community College sits among the relics of Baltimore's industrial past and busily prepares for the future.

At the sprawling Bethlehem Steel Corp. just down the road from the modern campus, several mills have been shut down. Western Electric left the area a few years back. A General Motors plant nearby is still operating, but it's a pipsqueak compared with some of the facilities opening up overseas. This heavily industrialized section of the city has a new product now: large numbers of displaced workers.

That's why nearly 10,000 students a year flock to the college for some form of training or retraining.

"The only constant for the future is change," says President Martha A. Smith, adding quickly that today's student must "learn how to learn." At $50 a credit, or $1,200 annually (including books), it's "the cheapest education game in town," she says.

While two-year colleges may never achieve the prestige of four-year institutions, their training programs can efficiently position students for jobs. The country's more than 1,400 community colleges often work in tandem with local business and industry, preparing students or unemployed workers for immediate entry into the local work force.

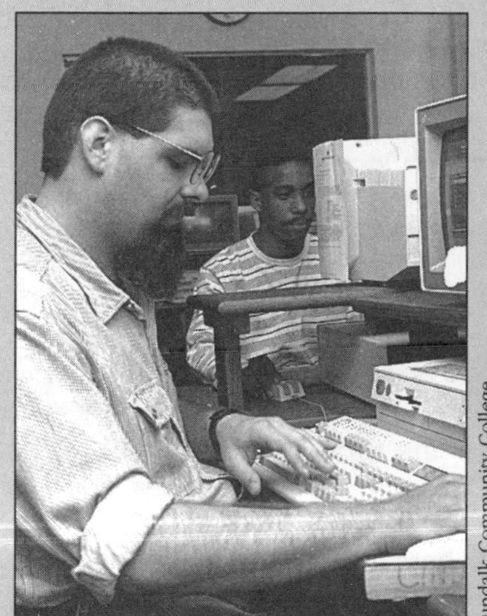

Dundalk Community College

Computer classes are among the most popular at Dundalk Community College in Baltimore.

Four-year colleges, on the other hand, have not responded quickly enough to the changing work environment, says Anthony P. Carnevale, an economist and the president of the Institute for Workplace Learning at the American Society for Training and Development. Consequently, he says, "Community colleges are going to be the real winners. The economy is headed their way."

Labor Secretary Robert B. Reich calls community colleges "one of the great untold success stories of America." Reich also emphasizes the important role he expects the community schools to play in his sweeping Workforce Security Program (*see p. 64*).

Despite all the new attention, community colleges really aren't doing anything very different, says David Pierce, president of the American Association of Community Colleges. "We've changed in an evolutionary, more than revolutionary way," he says. "It has been the mission of the community colleges to work closely with government and industry for the past 25 years. We serve communities, and business is part of those communities."

Joseph F. Shopulski, director of industrial technologies at Dundalk, knows the college is "overlooked and overshadowed by the broader school system," but he sees its role as vital, nonetheless: "We deal with the bulk of the workers."

Dundalk Community College

Dundalk Community College President Martha Smith, left, and students.

As industry attempts to retrain workers laid off from positions that no longer exist, Dundalk is pioneering a new program in customized training for particular industries, known as DACUM — or Developing a Curriculum. To do that, Smith and her staff maintain contacts in the career categories targeted for the training course. When they developed a leadership program for General Motors, for example, they gathered a panel of experts to help them ascertain what skills would be required by a contemporary manager in the automobile industry.

Dundalk's Cooperative Education (Co-Op) program combines classroom learning with paid employment in a related field. Yvonne Commadari, for example, earned college credits while assisting physical therapists at the Francis Scott Key Medical Center.

Dundalk also works closely with labor unions through its Center for Labor Education and Research, which offers courses customized to meet a particular union's training needs. "The ways in which our government, unions, higher education and businesses choose to address change will dictate the quality of life for our citizens in the 21st century," says Smith. "We must all be equal partners in the process of preparing workers for the future."

How Education Affects Earnings

The amount of education workers have is directly related to their earnings. Workers with college degrees made up the largest group with above-average earnings in 1992, while those with only high school educations constituted the largest group with below-average earnings. Similarly, a majority of workers with additional education beyond high school had above-average earnings.

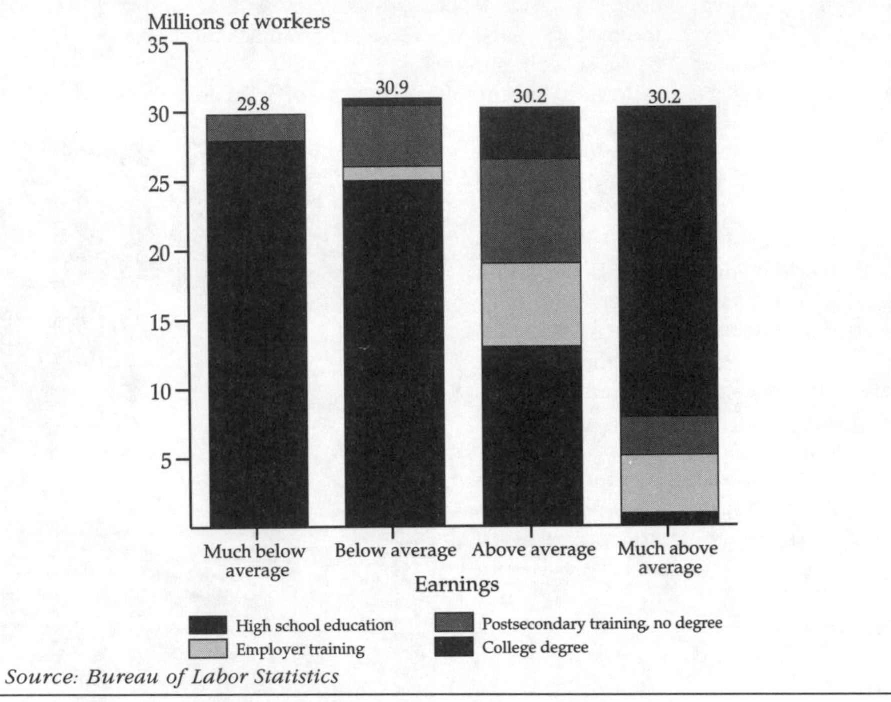

Source: Bureau of Labor Statistics

Continued from p. 54

An influential 1990 study, "America's Choice: High Skills or Low Wages!" demonstrated that most employers didn't expect work force skill requirements to be changing. "Despite the widespread presumption that advancing technology and the evolving service economy would create jobs demanding higher skills," the authors noted, "only 5 percent of employers are concerned about growing educational skill needs." [14]

Roughly $30 billion — about 1 percent of the payroll — is spent by U.S. business annually to train workers, according to the Institute for Workplace Learning. Most of the benefits, says institute President Carnevale, go to managers and upper-level workers. Foreign firms, by contrast, spend up to 6 percent of payroll on training and devote a significant portion of that to the front-line workers. [15]

Rae Nelson, executive director of the U.S. Chamber of Commerce's Center for Workforce Preparation, admits that "for a long time, corporations were not ahead of the curve." Now that NAFTA and the beleaguered defense industry have spotlighted displaced workers, Nelson says, business leaders are starting to take a "longer-term approach" to the problem.

In Pensacola, Fla., for example, the local Chamber is working closely with employees at the Naval Air Station and Naval Aviation Depot, both slated for closure. Bonny Johns, manager of the transition center established to help relocate the 3,000 civilian workers at the base and 3,500 workers in related activities, says she regularly gets a number of calls from local businesses that are attempting to match people losing jobs with opportunities for employment.

Bethlehem Steel is one of many corporations offering outplacement assistance. Doc Iler reports that counseling has helped some workers find good, new jobs nearby. "Others had to settle for temporary jobs," he says. "The vast majority of people generally had to be completely retrained out of manufacturing into such jobs as computer and electronics repair."

The United Steelworkers now has a new contract with Bethlehem, whose 1950s work force of 30,000 has dwindled to 5,000, that promises no more layoffs.

"I think that NAFTA has shaken up the business community a bit," says Reich. "It saw that deep anxieties and frustrations in the American work force are broader than just among organized labor."

Business may have a lot of catching up to do on the job-training front, according to some economists. The approach of private companies, says Carnevale, had been naive: "If we modernize, the work force will come." When the workers turned up at the new computerized factories, however, they were largely unskilled. In fact, the number of workers who received training to improve job skills surged 39 percent between 1983 and 1991, while total employment climbed 19 percent. [16]

More jobs now require reading, mathematics and communications skills. Even once-lowly service jobs like the checkout clerk have become "technologically empowered," as Reich puts it. A computer-equipped checkout clerk, for example, can control inventory and decide when to reorder items. "Instead of replacing her," Reich writes, "the computer empowers her to assume more responsibility and thus add greater value to the enterprise." [17]

To gear up for the increasingly

competitive global market, some companies are transforming the basic factory structure into what's known as the high-performance workplace. Corning Inc. reopened a ceramics plant in Blacksburg, Va., in the late 1980s with automated production lines tended by fewer but better-trained workers. Operating in teams, they are each capable of performing every task in the production process.

Corning sort of stumbled into the future. The company had shuttered the plant in 1983, but when it could not sell the building a decision was made to try again. This time around, Corning needed a very different work force. The average Corning production worker now has two years of college and solid math and writing skills. "Our people need basic algebra and pretty good math skills to deal with the statistical process control in the plant," said John C. Yearick, director of employee relations and services. [18]

Both Shopulski and Pierce say Corning's Blacksburg plant indicates that industry is doing what it can to change the structure of the workplace to stay competitive and to stem the flow of displaced workers. "It's not altruistic," says Shopulski. "They're doing it for survival."

Will training enable displaced workers to find new jobs matching their old salaries and responsibilities?

The Bureau of Labor Statistics (BLS) predicts that total U.S. employment will increase to 147.5 million workers in 2005, up 22 percent from 121.1 million in 1992. That's a slightly higher rate of growth than during the previous 13-year period, and the BLS says that jobs will continue to be generated for all levels of education and training. [19]

Few workers losing jobs today can expect their old jobs back, no matter how much the economy improves. Recent statistics indicate that only 14 percent of those laid off between July 1990 and June 1992 can expect to be recalled, compared with 44 percent of laid-off worker who returned to their former jobs over the prior four recession periods.

Traditional blue-collar factory workers will need the most training. About 1 million manufacturing jobs were lost annually between 1981 and 1990. [20] Yet fewer than 1 million manufacturing jobs are projected to open up in the next 10 years. Most of the more than 25 million new jobs expected will provide some type of service. [21]

And Reich insists that they should not be equated with low-echelon, minimum-wage positions. "The business service job is everything from technical sa[illegible] [illegible]pport, lab technicians and paralegals to systems analysts," he says. "These are good jobs, the new middle-class jobs, replacing the factory work of 20 or 30 years ago as the gateway to the middle class."

Even traditional low-wage service jobs in retailing, restaurants, hospitals and hotels are changing rapidly, Reich says. "Many of these people are technically trained, they understand what they're selling," he says. "They're paid well for their technical competence."

But Friedman, the AFL-CIO economist, counters that most of the jobs opening up now are low skill and low wage. "The fast growth is in jobs such as janitors and burger flippers," he says.

Indeed, earnings for service workers were about 40 percent below the average for all occupational groups in 1992. Part of the reason, according to the Department of Labor, is that almost a third of these employees had less than a high school education, and many worked only part time. [22]

Old Earnings Hard to Match

One to three years after losing their jobs in the 1980s, more than 60 percent of the affected workers either were not working or had new jobs that paid less than 95 percent of their old earnings. In contrast, more than a quarter of the workers had been re-employed and were earning at least 5 percent more than their previous earnings.

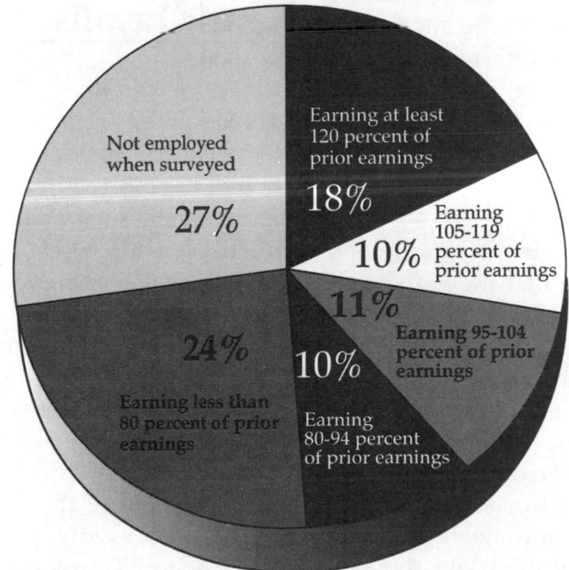

Source: Congressional Budget Office, Displaced Workers: Trends in the 1980s and Implications for the Future, *February 1993*

Friedman believes that it is important to offer training in new skills to displaced workers, even if they are being prepared for a letdown in wages. "I liken this to throwing a six-foot rope to someone drowning 12 feet offshore. Do you throw them a longer rope or take the rope away?"

He suggests that a greater investment in training, including longer programs, would offer a better shot at a different job with similar benefits, salary and security.

Reich intends to include longer training programs in his Workforce Security proposal. "A lot of research, experiments around the country show that for many people, a year of training is a wise investment and a good social investment," he says. "For the individual, the return is about 6 to 12 percent on future salaries."

In some cases, in fact, training in a new set of skills replaces once-valuable skills that have become obsolete. In its study of displaced workers in the 1980s, the Congressional Budget Office found that the level of wages earned in a previous job rewarded the worker for knowledge that might not be useful elsewhere. "This 'firm-specific human capital,' as economists call it, enables workers to be more productive and thus worth more to their employer than to other employers," according to the study. "The elimination of their job — for whatever reason — essentially destroys the value of such capital." [23]

Many workers re-entering the job market may find that they are over-educated and under-skilled for the jobs opening up in the 1990s. "There is still a very strong feeling that a B.A. degree is essential, an admission ticket to success," says Pierce, of the community colleges association. The unfortunate result, he observes, is a "mismatch between the level of education and the jobs that are available." The proof can be found, he says, on the campuses of community colleges around the country, where between 15 and 30 percent of the students graduated from four-year institutions, only to discover they had no marketable skills.

George T. Silvestri, a BLS economist, predicts faster-than-average growth for low-rung service jobs. Workers in these jobs will have the lowest earnings, and relatively few have college educations. In fact, a high proportion won't have high school diplomas.

However, employment also is expected to grow faster than average among workers in three occupational groups generally requiring advanced degrees: executives, administrators and managers; specialists in professional fields, such as certified public accountants; and technicians. In 1992, these areas boasted the highest-paying jobs and the largest proportion of workers with at least four years of college. [24]

"There is no question that people with more education are doing better," says Carnevale. ■

BACKGROUND

Early Layoffs

When Frederick Winslow Taylor went to work as a gang boss in 1878 at the Midvale Steel Co. in Philadelphia, the young engineer found the structure of the work force far more intriguing than the forging of metal. When he left Midvale a decade later, he brought with him the ground-breaking principles of production management he had formulated. He went on to organize manufacturing plants for such industry giants as Bethlehem Steel, and even to influence the development of Henry Ford's assembly line. [25]

In essence, Taylor applied "time and motion" studies to the most complicated manufacturing processes, breaking them down into simple, individual tasks that workers with little education and minimal training could master. By performing one task all day, each worker would develop machine-like efficiency.

"Taylor did not invent mass-production methods," write former Labor Secretary Ray Marshall and labor economist Marc Tucker, "but he perfected them, provided a rationale for them and served as their most effective champion." [26]

As inhuman as this system may seem now, it ignited the economy. The output of manufactures increased by 64 percent from 1919 to 1929, even as the labor force declined. [27]

While displaced workers typically are thought to reflect declining economies, they often characterize thriving ones, as well. Advancing technology and the increased globalization of the world economy have displaced American workers throughout the 20th century, forcing many to make several job transitions during their lives.

Some individuals can handle changes easily; others find them traumatic. Not surprisingly, work transitions are easier in times of prosperity, and it is quite possible that as many people must make work transitions during periods of growth as in periods of decline. [28]

According to Carnevale, there was as much churning in the workplace and concentration on job training during the 1950s as there is now. "The difference is that then we were facing an expanding economy. Now, the economy is restrained . . . making it more painful." As a result, he notes, a displaced autoworker at General Motors a few decades ago would most likely have stayed at GM, even at a higher-paying job, as the company evolved and expanded.

"The Most Profound of All Displacements"

The end of World War II was followed by the mass exodus of workers from farms to cities — "the most pro-

Continued on p. 60

Chronology

1940s-1960s

After World War II, the number of displaced workers skyrockets in the wake of technological changes and a loss of 3.64 million farm jobs. Concern about displaced workers eventually decreases as unemployment drops.

1947-54
The number of coal workers drops from 436,000 to 126,000 as oil and gas replace coal.

1962
President John F. Kennedy signs legislation creating two displaced-worker programs: the Manpower Development and Training Act (MDTA) and Trade Adjustment Assistance (TAA). In addition to emergency funding and job-search help, they retrain workers displaced because of technological changes or increased foreign trade.

August 1964
Congress creates the National Commission on Technology, Automation and Economic Progress in response to growing concerns that automation is causing unemployment.

1965
President Lyndon B. Johnson declares a War on Poverty that shifts attention and resources away from displaced workers.

1966
The Commission on Technology, Automation and Economic Progress reports to Congress after the unemployment rate has fallen to its lowest level in more than 10 years; concern over displacement and technology fades.

1970s

Economic boom times end, especially for the American worker, as the cost of living soars above wage levels.

1973
Congress folds a variety of employment and training services — including the War on Poverty's Jobs Corps — into the Comprehensive Employment and Training Act (CETA).

1974
As concerns about displaced workers rise once again, the Trade Act relaxes the requirements for Trade Adjustment Assistance to include any worker dislocated because of reduced barriers to foreign trade.

1975
Nearly 55,000 workers are certified for TAA, about one-half of those who request aid.

1980s

About 2 million workers lose their jobs annually. Congress creates a new program to aid displaced workers.

1980
About 585,000 displaced workers claim TAA benefits.

1982
During a recession year, Congress re-evaluates the CETA program before it is set to expire. The result is a new program built upon a partnership between government and industry, known as the Job Training Partnership Act (JTPA), which includes a Title III program to aid displaced workers.

1984
Displaced-worker issue enters the presidential-campaign debate. Democratic candidate Walter F. Mondale emphasizes the need to address unemployment problems stemming from the decline of basic industries and the displacement of workers whose job skills had become outmoded; Republican President Ronald Reagan counters that millions of jobs had been created during the previous two years of his administration.

1988
Title III is amended and renamed the Economic Dislocation and Worker Adjustment Act.

1990s

Growing concern about workers prompts Congress to take increasing responsibility for workers it displaces through the creation of new regulations, closings of military bases or the enactment of the North American Free Trade Agreement (NAFTA).

1990
The Clean Air Act provides relief to workers who lose their jobs because of the new regulations through a new program: the Clean Air Employment Transition Assistance Program.

1991
The JTPA is amended to provide retraining and readjustment assistance to workers dislocated by defense cutbacks.

Dec. 8, 1993
President Clinton signs the legislation implementing NAFTA.

Jan. 1, 1994
NAFTA goes into effect.

An Interview With Secretary of Labor Robert B. Reich. . .

Editor's note: Reporter Susan Kellam interviewed Secretary Reich at his office on Dec. 15, 1993.

Is it the role of government to help displaced workers?

The government position is that we all benefit as a society from a better-trained work force. We also all benefit if workers who have lost their jobs get new jobs quickly. A better-trained work force is a more productive work force, and a more productive work force means national income is higher. We all benefit from a better economy.

Getting unemployed workers back to work more quickly means we'll have productive individuals rather than individuals who are using up unemployment insurance and welfare. Individuals who are unproductive are not paying taxes.

How important is it that the displaced worker get help quickly?

Our research shows that the earlier someone who is not going to get their job back begins the training and the process of gearing up for the next job, the more likely it is that this person will relatively quickly get the next job. The longer the interval before someone begins gearing up, the longer it is until they get the next job. And people become quite demoralized quickly. . . .

Counseling in the psychodynamics is quite important. But what people need most of all is information: Where are the jobs? What are the jobs? What can they train for? How can they build on their present experience?

Do you expect individuals to work while they're getting trained in new skills?

Many can't get a part-time job while training. That's why some are going to need assistance beyond unemployment insurance, beyond the 26 weeks. You see, we have a system right now that, in a way, like health care, is an extremely expensive system that doesn't really go to where it's most useful. We have a federal-state unemployment system that costs about $22 billion a year. Recently, because of the recession, the federal government has been putting in another $12 billion to $14 billion a year on extended benefits across the board in every state. That totals more than $35 billion a year. And then we have a scatter shot of relatively small job-training programs, each for a special group of people deemed to be an exception.

Would the Workforce Security Program connect the unemployment insurance system with these scattered programs for displaced workers?

Yes, there are various pieces to it. One would be to consolidate the various job-training programs out there for dislocated workers and then fill in the blanks....We would fill in the patchwork so that we have a seamless program for people who need job retraining and can benefit from job retraining. But there's much more to it than that. In addition to providing reemployment services, we would identify people very early on who are not likely to get their old jobs back, and get them information as early as possible — where the jobs are and what the jobs are and what training is needed if they have to train. Also find out how they can build on their old skills, so that they can move as quickly as possible to the next job.

R. Michael Jenkins

Labor Secretary Robert Reich

There would be changes in unemployment insurance, such as a bonus if you leave unemployment before the scheduled 26 weeks. Also, unemployment insurance for people who want to work part time, can only work part time, but at the same time want training.

Would this proposal restructure the unemployment system?

A different part of this proposal would restructure the extended-benefits program so it was targeted during cyclical downturns to the states that were hardest hit, helping individuals hit by structural unemployment, those who will not get their jobs back regardless of what happens to the business cycle. Selective individuals who are hard hit by structural unemployment will get longer-term unemployment benefits, even when the business cycle turns up.

But it would gradually phase out this very, very expensive

Continued from p. 58

found of all displacements," noted the National Commission on Technology, Automation and Economic Progress. The postwar revolution in agricultural technology, marked by mechanical cotton pickers and harvesters, chemical pesticides and fertilizers and high-yielding crop varieties, forced many farmworkers off the land; others were lured by the promise of jobs in the cities. Employment in agriculture dropped by 3.4 million workers (43 percent) from 1947 to 1964. [29]

But for many, dreams of postwar prosperity were elusive. Countless displaced farmworkers, "suffering from

. . . on the Need to Retrain Displaced Workers

extended emergency unemployment system. We may not succeed in phasing it out entirely because if and when there is another recession it may be so deep that the federal government has to step in again.

Why does the United States have a history of handling job training inadequately?

Although Germany and Japan are going through deep recessions right now, I don't think many people disagree with the proposition that their work forces are highly competitive and that businesses in Germany and Japan are both actively engaged in training workers. Partly, our problems stem from the development of a business culture and an education culture that are quite separate. We have educational institutions and business institutions that never had very much to do with one another, although community colleges and technical institutes are just beginning to bridge that gap.

Also, American business has not until recent years had to face the problems of an inadequately trained work force. Not just with regard to the three Rs but also with regard to skilled training. Our primary business strategy was high volume, standardized, stable mass production. You didn't need well-trained workers, it was a matter of volume. The more volume the lower the unit costs. The lower the unit costs the larger the market. And we have caught on rather late to the idea that a well-trained work force is a key business asset.

Did the NAFTA debate raise the issue of displaced workers to a new level?

Absolutely, absolutely it did. It exposed something that was just not that visible. And that is the number of people who fear for their jobs and have experienced downward mobility.

We can't continue to globalize and do nothing for our work force. We need a work force investment strategy that's hand-in-glove with a strategy for open markets and a more global economy. The two are inseparable.

Are we training people for jobs that don't exist?

Let me say two things. One, it's not just training. For many people, the job-search assistance, early intervention and good-quality information about jobs are as important as training. For some people, it's more important than training.

There's nothing crueler than training someone for a job that doesn't exist. There are many jobs out there. What we're seeing in this recovery, interestingly, is a majority of the 1.7 million new jobs have required some postsecondary skill or training. This is relatively unusual because the jobs in the 1980s did not.

What's happened to the economy as we become a more global and technological society is that even relatively menial jobs, such a garage mechanic, demand more and more skills. Under the hood of a car today are electronics. You don't find mechanical equipment. To be trained in electronics, to be a garage mechanic requires some real, honest-to-goodness training. Those jobs pay $30,000 to $50,000 a year, and they're not bad jobs, they're good jobs. . . .

In the factories we have today, the robots and computers work machines. But you need people to work the robots and computers to service them, to program them. In factories around the country today, you see people sitting behind computer consoles. They are checking and servicing the robots.

But there is a little bit of confusion in the public's mind. People equate service jobs with poor jobs, but actually there are two big categories of service jobs. The business service jobs, that is everything from technical sales support, lab technicians, paralegals to people who are systems analysts. These jobs are good jobs. These are the new middle-class jobs, replacing the factory work of 20 or 30 years ago as the gateway to the middle class. But they require some post-high school credit.

The other category of service job is the low-wage retail, restaurant, hospital orderly, hotel job. These jobs are still out there, and they're coming back. But even here, interestingly, compare a place like K-Mart to Home Depot. At Home Depot, the floor sales people are technically trained. They understand what they're selling. They're paid well for their technical competence. Consumers come to rely upon their advice. They have responsibility for reordering and deciding what to order.

What role do you see unions playing in all this?

Some unions have been spearheading these changes. Of course, unions have for years been offering young people opportunities to learn trades. The unions have also been striking new contracts with employers in which employers agree to provide continuous retraining and upgrading of skills. Many workers are coming to understand that they have to stay competitive, and the only way they can stay competitive is if they are continuously trained. Lifelong learning is becoming a cliché, but it does reflect the necessity of everyone being continuously trained, including on the job. And many unions have put that into their contracts.

deficient rural educations, lacking skills demanded in urban areas, unaccustomed to urban ways, and often burdened by racial discrimination, exchanged rural poverty for an urban ghetto," the commission found.

Congress had created the commission in August 1964 in response to national concern about growing postwar unemployment and widespread fears that automation was the cause. The coal miners of Appalachia felt the tremors of that period when oil and gas took over most of the coal market, and technological advances in mining eliminated still more jobs. The number of coal miners fell from 507,333 in 1948 to 134,467 in 1968.

Blacks and Hispanics Hit Hardest by Displacement

Greater percentages of black and Hispanic workers lost their jobs than white workers during the three time periods shown below. Between the first and last periods, Hispanics replaced blacks as the group most affected by displacement.

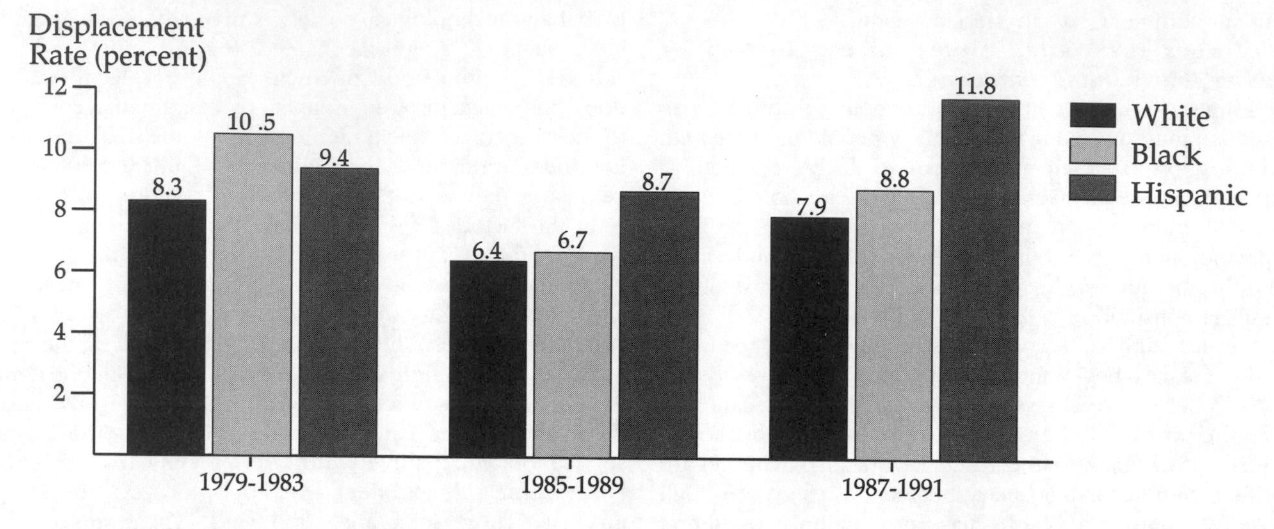

Source: Bureau of Labor Statistics, November 1993

Between 1947 and 1954 alone, coal-mining employment fell 42 percent. [30]

Despite numerous efforts to bring new jobs to Appalachia, the region has never recovered. Elsewhere, however, workers displaced by technology in the mid-1960s found new jobs. By the time the commission reported to Congress in 1966, the unemployment rate had fallen, and concern over displacement and technology had faded. [31]

Aid for Displaced Workers

Since public concern for displaced workers tends to be sporadic, it follows that support for worker-aid programs has been fragmentary. too. A job-matching agency _ the Public Employment Service _ was created by the Wagner-Peyser Act in 1933, with many amendments since. Marshall and Tucker sharply criticize the agency in its current form and compare it unfavorably with its European counterpart.

"Starved of resources," they write, "the Employment Service is not computerized in many of its offices, does not have adequate personnel to do a serious job of [finding] employment openings and [providing] funds for relocations and wage subsidies, that enable European employment offices to succeed in their mission." [32]

Similarly, two national displaced-worker programs signed into law by President John F. Kennedy in 1962 — the Manpower Development and Training Act (MDTA) and Trade Adjustment Assistance — also never received the resources or the attention to target workers requiring new jobs.

The primary objective of MDTA was to retrain workers whose skills were inadequate or obsolete and who had been displaced from jobs because of technological change. The program was designed to simultaneously rehabilitate a portion of the nation's unemployed and alleviate the scarcity of certain trained workers, among them nurse's aides, electronic assemblers, TV repairers, elementary school teachers and psychiatric social workers. Congress appropriated $70 million for the program in fiscal 1963, with Kennedy estimating that 400,000 workers would be trained. [33]

At about the same time, however, the economy received substantial boosts, first from a cut in personal income taxes and then as spending escalated for the Vietnam War and the Great Society programs of President Lyndon B. Johnson. By mid-decade, the unemployment rate for adult white males had fallen to 1.9 percent, and the focus of MDTA shifted from displaced to disadvantaged workers. [34]

Training for jobless workers faded as a public policy issue by the time that Johnson declared war on poverty. Nonetheless, many workers in troubled industries still needed help. A large automobile company — Studebaker — went out of business, and meatpacking plants were shut down as technology advanced and markets shifted.[35]

Workers who already had lost their jobs in import-troubled businesses also fell between the cracks of federal aid. For example, several restrictions in the Trade Expansion Act of 1962 were designed to weed out ineligible TAA recipients. A series of tests was to determine whether workers had really been laid off because of import competition, but some experts contended such determinations were difficult, if not impossible. In the end, no workers were certified to get TAA assistance between 1962 and 1969.[36]

The economic boom ended in the early 1970s, especially for the American worker. Wage increases could not catch up with the soaring cost of living, according to a 1974 year-end BLS report. And by the end of that year, the work force was facing mass layoffs that threatened to be the worst since the Great Depression of the 1930s.[37]

As concern about displaced workers grew, the Trade Act of 1974 relaxed the requirements for TAA assistance to include any workers dislocated because of reduced barriers to foreign trade. In 1975, nearly 55,000 workers were certified for the program, about one-half of those who requested aid. In 1980, 585,000 workers claimed benefits from TAA, which was the only major federal program in the 1980s that specifically benefited displaced workers.[38]

Under the Job Training Partnership Act, co-authored by Sen. Edward M. Kennedy and then-Sen. Dan Quayle, industry was given a subsidy to hold out a friendly hand to people facing barriers to employment.

1982 Training Act

The major focus for aid, however, remained on disadvantaged workers, primarily minorities and youths.[39] In 1973, Congress had folded a variety of employment and training services — including the War on Poverty's Jobs Corps — into the Comprehensive Employment and Training Act (CETA). It empowered local governments to operate training programs for unemployed adults and youths and to offer them public service jobs. Riddled with problems, CETA was amended and reauthorized several times in its nine-year history.[40]

Congress re-evaluated CETA before it was set to expire in 1982, another recession year, and came up with a new program built upon an industry-government partnership, the Job Training Partnership Act (JTPA). Co-authored by Sen. Edward M. Kennedy, D-Mass., and then-Sen. Dan Quayle, R-Ind., JTPA replaced CETA's scandal-plagued and costly subsidized public-employment concept with a business arrangement. Industry was given a subsidy to hold out a friendly hand to people facing barriers to employment. Congress also included a new JTPA program to aid displaced workers whose jobs had disappeared, known as Title III. It was amended in 1988 and renamed the Economic Dislocation and Worker Adjustment Act (EDWAA).

Any dislocated workers whose employment loss meant they were unlikely to return to their previous industries or occupations were eligible for assistance under EDWAA. This included workers who lost their jobs because of plant closings or mass layoffs; long-term unemployed persons with limited local opportunities for jobs in their fields; and farmers, ranchers and other self-employed people who became jobless due to general economic circumstances or natural disasters. In some circumstances, displaced homemakers (divorced women) could also receive aid.

In the mid-1980s, after three years of economic recovery, displacement again appeared to fade as a public policy issue. The administration proposed to reduce the funding for EDWAA, citing a slow rate of spending and lack of demand for its more expensive services, such as retraining. At the same time, concern was mounting over foreign competition and its effect on jobs.

Retraining became an issue in the 1984 presidential campaign when President Ronald Reagan's Democratic opponent, former Vice President Walter F. Mondale, D-Minn., called for attention to unemployment stemming from the decline of basic industries and the displacement of workers whose job skills had become outmoded. EDWAA funding amounted to $223 million a year, but Mondale called for a "much more ambitious" program for retraining and relocating workers. Reagan countered that millions of jobs had been created during the previous two years of his administration.[41]

New Solutions

The magnitude of worker dis placement was a matter of dispute, leading some economists to view broad-based tax incentives with skepticism. Marc Bendick, an economist at The Urban Institute, offered one of the most conservative estimates at the time, saying that about 100,000 workers a year lost their jobs and had trouble finding new work because of changes in technology, trade and consumer demands.[42]

But members of Congress from the Northeast and Midwest saw a broader phenomenon, estimating the number of workers displaced by industrial change at from 450,000 to 3 million.

Toward the end of the 1980s, several developments began to put the problems facing displaced workers back into the national spotlight. They included the increasingly common announcements of large-scale cutbacks by firms and the realization that cuts in the defense budget could cause massive job losses. In fact, the Bureau of Labor Statistics recently found that from 1981 to 1989, an average of 2 million workers lost full-time jobs each year. (*See graph, p. 52.*)

The 1990s are shaping up to be the decade when Congress attempts to take some responsibility for workers it displaces either through regulation or trade pacts. A precedent had been set in 1978, when Congress agreed to pay full salaries for up to six years to 2,900 timber industry workers displaced by the expansion of Redwood National Park. The deregulation era of the 1980s meant that Congress enacted few regulatory bills that directly cut jobs. But when lawmakers imposed new regulations on industry through the 1990 Clean Air Act, they provided relief through a new program — the Clean Air Employment Transition Assistance Program.[43]

The $250 million program was established in the belief that the Clean Air package's acid rain controls would shift jobs from the high-sulfur coal industry in the East to low-sulfur coal workers in Western states. The funding would stretch over five years to provide retraining and readjustment aid to affected workers. Jobs lost in the oil, chemical and auto industries would also be covered.

The job-training program was amended again in 1991, this time to provide $150 million in retraining and readjustment assistance to workers dislocated by defense cutbacks. The Defense Conversion Adjustment (DCA) Program targeted not only employees of the military but also individuals in corporations who were laid off as a consequence of reductions in U.S. expenditures for defense.[44]

With trade issues continuing to worry lawmakers and citizens alike, Bill Clinton took office keenly focused on concerns about making workers more competitive in the work force of the future. ■

CURRENT SITUATION

Clinton Initiatives

With a new administration in place, so is a new set of special programs and proposals to help displaced workers.

Clinton signed the Defense Diversification Program (DDP) into law last year. This new program, an addition to the JTPA, is similar to one signed by former President George Bush, except that it emphasizes conversion assistance to workers from facilities closed down by the Defense Department.

Clinton had signaled his concern for the defense industry within his first 100 days in office by visiting the Electronic Systems Group, a Westinghouse Corp. subsidiary near Baltimore. The firm had recently begun manufacturing such non-defense products as airline radar and home-security equipment. "You have given us a stunning example of just how brilliantly [defense conversion] can be done here in this fine facility," the president told workers.

But the company's viewpoint was somewhat different. Al Spencer, special assistant to the firm's president, told the *Los Angeles Times* that Westinghouse's diversification effort had been accomplished "pretty much on our cuff" without help from the federal government.

And Westinghouse officials conceded that despite success in finding new commercial markets, the corporation still had to lay off about 4,400 workers in Maryland between 1991 and 1993. The firm employed 17,000 workers in Maryland at its peak in the 1970s.[45]

Clinton also dived headfirst into the murky debate over protecting the northern spotted owl. The White House contends that 6,000 timber industry jobs would disappear if Clinton's plan to restrict logging — released July 1 and currently mired in legal challenges — goes into effect. Industry groups say that up to 85,000 jobs are at risk. A U.S. District Court in Seattle is reviewing Clinton's forest plan to determine if the logging ban should be lifted.[46]

To provide retraining and other assistance for displaced timber workers, Clinton proposed spending $270 million in fiscal 1994 through a new Northwest Economic Adjustment Fund. White House officials also said

Continued on p. 66

At Issue:

Should training for displaced workers be significantly upgraded?

yes

Sheldon Friedman and Jane McDonald-Pines

Friedman is an economist with the AFL-CIO. McDonald-Pines is assistant to the director of the Human Resources Development Institute, the employment and training arm of the AFL-CIO.

FROM *NORTH AMERICAN OUTLOOK*, SEPTEMBER 1993.

The training provided to dislocated workers is often of short duration and poor quality. Western Europe and Canada expend, on average, a far higher proportion of their gross domestic product (GDP) on worker training and provide training for a longer period than the United States. Federal programs intended to assist dislocated workers serve only 5 to 10 percent of the vast dislocated worker population, estimated to be 3.2 million in 1992.

There is little doubt that the U.S. training system needs reform. The number of workers (employed and unemployed) who need training and reemployment assistance continues to grow. A national strategy must be pursued that will restructure workplaces so that front-line employees can effectively utilize newly acquired skills. The system must provide workers with benefits and training services that will lead to high-wage, high-skill jobs and that will establish governance structures ensuring equal input from unions, employers and the community.

Even with its current limitations, Trade Adjustment Assistance (TAA) offers the best opportunity for education, training and income-support for trade-impacted workers. TAA should not be replaced with any program that provides less benefits or income support to workers affected by imports.

A redesigned employment and training system would provide workers with a wide range of benefits and services customized to meet their individual needs. It is important that workers have access to all information and referral services in a convenient and accessible location through a revitalized employment service.

Occupational skills training would provide tuition payments and income support to technical, vocational, undergraduate, graduate, professional, and post-graduate programs for a period of three years. Workers could choose to participate in class-size programs funded through direct contracts with training providers or could choose to utilize individual training grants for a specified period.

Basic literacy and math training, as well as English-as-a-second language training, would be guaranteed to any worker who could benefit from such training.

Employers would be encouraged to use on-the-job training for entry-level as well as incumbent workers who require skill-enhancement training.

no

Walter Corson

Vice President, Mathematica Policy Research, a for-profit public policy research organization based in Princeton, N.J.

Our findings do not indicate that making training mandatory had a significant impact on the estimated employment and earnings differences of Trade Adjustment Assistance (TAA) trainees and other Trade Readjustment Allowance (TRA) recipients. However, we also did not find strong evidence that training had a substantial positive effect on employment and earnings, at least in the first three years after the initial unemployment insurance claim. Given this uncertainty about the returns to training, we believe that training participation should be voluntary rather than mandatory for TRA recipients.

The TAA program offers TRA and reemployment adjustment services to workers who lose their jobs in the face of increased import competition. Established in 1962, the program initially emphasized compensating workers for their lost income, and relatively few workers received training, job-search assistance, or relocation allowances to support their adjustment to new jobs. Beginning in 1981, the emphasis of the program was shifted toward providing adjustment services, particularly training: TRA benefits were targeted more strictly at the long-term unemployed, and more funds were made available for training. Furthermore, as one of several major changes that were made to the program in 1988, training was made an entitlement for eligible workers, and TRA recipients were required to participate in an approved training program unless they received a waiver exempting them under certain circumstances.

The Mathematica study was designed to evaluate the pre-layoff characteristics and post-layoff labor-market experience of TRA recipients, based on data on nationally representative samples of TRA recipients who participated in the program either just before or just after the 1988 program changes.

[We found that] even if training were made voluntary, a relatively large proportion of TRA recipients would still probably participate in training; for example, more than a third of the members of our pre-1988 sample of TRA recipients, for whom training was voluntary, participated in training. At the same time, the training requirement could be replaced with a requirement to participate in a job-search program. This strategy was attempted in the TAA program between 1986 and 1988, but the job-search services were never fully implemented due to the absence of adequate funding. Recent research suggests that the combination of a job-search requirement and job-search assistance can reduce the receipt of unemployment benefits among recipients.

Sharing U.S. Know-How With Mexico

Thanks to the North American Free Trade Agreement (NAFTA), experts from the San Diego Community College District are sending their know-how south of the border. And along with a new source of revenue, they're getting a lesson of their own about America's new trading partner.

Officials from the district, which includes three community colleges and a large adult-education center, signed an agreement with the Mexican government in November 1993 that enables the colleges to share the latest manufacturing technology with Mexico's network of 200 vocational institutes, or Centros de Capacitacion Technologica Industrial (CECATI).

The arrangement is vital, said District Chancellor Augustin Gallego, because the vocational centers have not kept pace with the more advanced technologies that Mexican manufacturers must have to compete globally. Without up-to-date information, he said, "Mexican students will be prepared only for low-skill, entry-level jobs, such as assembly work." †

Mexican workers may have to play catch-up to take advantage of the opportunities NAFTA offers, but they are willing students. During a recent visit to Mexico, the San Diego contingent "was extremely impressed with the Mexicans' ability to instill pride in training," says Barry Garron, director of public information for the district.

You would never see graffiti on the walls of a learning institution in Mexico, he says. Indeed, the only slogan Garron saw on a building proclaimed (in Spanish): "When you stop learning, you begin to die."

American Association of Community Colleges

At a technical institute in Irapuato, Mexico, a student demonstrates his skill for, from left, State of Guanajuato CECATI Coordinator José Muñoz Garcia, San Diego Community College District Chancellor Augustin Gallego and San Diego City College Professor Jack Bollinger.

Mexican businesses are also supporting the country's vocational education efforts, Garron says. For example, a sophisticated satellite-communications system recently was installed linking the 200 CECATIs. The project was spearheaded by the regional Chamber of Commerce, headquartered in the city of Irapuato, which enlisted the support of thousands of businesses from six major cities. Their buying power reduced the cost of materials and equipment for the system.

Meanwhile, the Mexicans are seeking to improve wherever they can — even when it comes to some of their traditional products. As part of the San Diego pact, U.S. ceramics instructors will travel to the town of Dolores Hidalgo, where 80 percent of the people earn their living making pottery. There they'll teach artisans how to improve, among other things, the glaze on products that have been made there for centuries.

† Quoted in "After NAFTA: Are There Opportunities for Community Colleges in the Wake of Approval of the North American Free Trade Agreement?" *Community College Times*, Nov. 30, 1993, p. 1.

Continued from p. 64

that more than 15,000 new jobs repairing streams and roads damaged by logging would be created over five years. [47]

But it was NAFTA, not the spotted owl, that plunged President Clinton into the heart of the displaced-worker issue. In October, the White House unveiled a plan that would provide income-assistance payments and retraining, as well as help finding new jobs, to workers whose employers move to Mexico or whose industry is disrupted by more imports coming across the border.

In addition, the NAFTA implementing legislation signed by Clinton Dec. 8 included the Self-Employment Assistance Program, which allowed displaced workers to receive unemployment benefits while starting a new business.

Reich's Plan

Few would argue that Clinton hasn't tried to fulfill his promise to help displaced workers, least of all Labor Secretary Reich. His soon-to-be-announced Workforce Security Program will try to tie together all the divergent programs affecting displaced workers. The only criterion for acceptance would be a permanent loss of job.

"Anybody should have these services regardless of why they lost their jobs," Reich says. "With these categorical programs, we're spending more and more just trying to figure out who fits into the category. And by the time the decision is made, it's often too late for many of these workers."

The current system is so inequitable, he says, that in some factories that close, employees who worked on certain products would receive federal benefits, while those making non-qualifying merchandise would not.

All of the existing programs, including EDWAA and TAA, would be supplanted by the new comprehensive system. Funding for the new program, although still in the discussion stage, is projected to start at $1.1 billion next year and increase to $3.2 billion by fiscal 1998. Income support beyond the 26 weeks of regular unemployment insurance would be far more generous than the current system. Workers could receive up to additional 72 weeks of support if they meet certain tests, such as enrollment in training by the 16th week of unemployment and a fairly low probability of re-employment in the same or similar occupation.

Reich has even embraced a concept, conceived during the Bush administration, to eliminate the need for jobless workers seeking assistance to run around from center to center. Recognizing that displaced workers are often distressed and disheartened, one-stop centers would enable them to go to one centralized location for all unemployment assistance, even tapping into a nationwide network of possible job opportunities.

Meanwhile, the optimistic economic indicators released Dec. 23 tended to undercut the administration's arguments for its costly job-training overhaul. The average work week for manufacturing employees set a post-World War II record, and factory overtime reached the highest level since the government began keeping those statistics in 1956.

But, Reich counters, "even though we're in a jobs recovery and the economy has generated over 1.7 million new jobs since last January, the number of long-term unemployed has risen." The work-to-work transition, he says, is becoming extremely difficult. ■

OUTLOOK

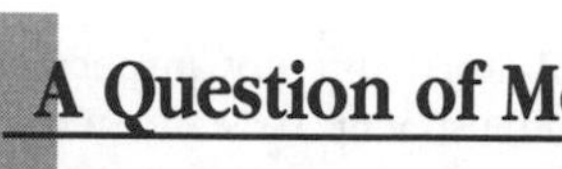

A Question of Money?

President Clinton fought an uphill battle to pass NAFTA, straight up a path littered with deals, promises and pledges. The most resounding of those public pronouncements was uttered Oct. 12: "We must create a continuous re-employment system so that people are always learning — even into their 50s and 60s and 70s, as long as they are willing to be productive citizens and keep going and growing."

The initial game plan was to offer Reich's Workforce Security proposal as a legislative package in September, just as the NAFTA debate started heating up. But the word back from the House and Senate committees with jurisdiction over the issues was to wait.

"While we were ready to move more quickly, that message from the committees opened up the opportunity for more extensive consultation with all parts of this community," says Douglas Ross, assistant secretary of Labor for employment and training. "That includes states, localities, delivery systems, the Congressional Budget Office, labor and business. In that sense, it was advantageous."

Ross is hoping the president will unveil the Workforce Security Program in his Jan. 25 State of the Union address, with actual introduction into the legislative process soon thereafter.

Although the various groups likely to be affected by the proposal all have expressed some reservations, Ross contends that there is "a surprisingly broad consensus."

"The concept is exceptionally good," says Jerry Abramson, the Democratic mayor of Louisville, Ky., and president of the U.S. Conference on Mayors. He already has met with Reich to express his concern over the proposal's funding formula, which he says may be inequitable. "There are significant-size cities that wouldn't get funds," he says. But such issues can be worked out easily before the program gets off the ground, Abramson says.

Economist Sheldon Friedman at the AFL-CIO says labor isn't commenting until the final package is released. But he is concerned about plans to terminate TAA. "Ideally, TAA should be improved and extended to other victims of government, such as defense downsizing and environmental compliance," he says.

Friedman is anxious about the final rules for eligibility. In the draft plan, he says, they were "so restrictive that Harry Houdini would have trouble qualifying for income support." He is also curious to see how the plan defines "permanent layoff" and "re-employment in the same or similar occupation."

Ellen Nissenbaum, legislative director of the Center for Budget and Policy Priorities, is watching to see how the long-term unemployed will fare under the plan, which reportedly revamps the extended-benefits provision.

Such details aside, the most overwhelming concern expressed by labor and government experts, as well as lawmakers, is simply whether there will be enough money for the ambitious overhaul. Nissenbaum acknowledges that Reich has discussed a very generous plan, but she notes that "prospects of the entire package are contingent on available financing."

And Treasury Secretary Lloyd Bentsen apparently doesn't think too highly of the prospects. When he was asked Dec. 19 on NBC's "Meet the Press" whether Reich's "idea of a payroll tax to finance worker retraining" was a good idea, he replied, "I don't see that happening next year."

Reich knows that in the current climate of austerity a proposal for new spending will face opposition, but he is undeterred by the challenge ahead. NAFTA, he says, "exposed something that was just not that visible. And that is the number of people who fear for their jobs and have experienced downward mobility."

As a nation, he maintains, "We can't continue to globalize and do nothing for our work force." ■

Susan Kellam is an assistant managing editor of the Congressional Monitor. *She covered social policy issues for* Congressional Quarterly Weekly Report.

Notes

[1] Congressional Budget Office, *Displaced Workers: Trends in the 1980s and Implications for the Future*, February 1993, p. 9.

[2] For background, see "Downward Mobility," *The CQ Researcher*, July 23, 1993, pp. 625-649.

[3] Stephen Barr, "Clinton Plan May Cut 140,000 Manager Jobs," *The Washington Post*, Dec. 23, 1993.

[4] See Tom Shoop, "Targeting Middle Managers," *Government Executive*, January 1994, p. 10.

[5] Robert B. Reich, *The Work of Nations* (1992), p. 259.

[6] Sheldon Friedman and Jane McDonald-Pines, "In Search of a 'New Convenant' for America's Dislocated Workers," *North American Outlook*, September 1993, pp. 67-99.

[7] National Commission for Employment Policy, *The Employment Effects of the North American Free Trade Agreement: Recommendations and Background Studies*, October 1992, Appendix b, p. 57.

[8] Congressional Budget Office, *op. cit.*, p. xiv.

[9] Department of Labor, Office of Inspector General, "Trade Adjustment Assistance Program: Audit of Program Outcomes in Nine Selected States," Sept. 30, 1993.

[10] General Accounting Office, *Dislocated Workers: Comparison of Assistance Programs*, September 1992, p. 1.

[11] U.S. Department of Labor, *op. cit.*, p. 2.

[12] Congressional Budget Office, *op. cit.*, p. 35.

[13] *Ibid.*, p. 12.

[14] "America's Choice: High Skills or Low Wages!" National Center for Education and the Economy, 1990, p. 25.

[15] *Ibid.*, p. 62.

[16] *The Wall Street Journal*, "Labor Letter," Nov. 9, 1993.

[17] Reich, *op. cit.*, p. 248.

[18] Quoted in *The Washington Post*, Aug. 2, 1992.

[19] U.S. Department of Labor, Bureau of Labor Statistics, "Monthly Labor Review," November 1993, p. 58.

[20] *Ibid.*

[21] Congressional Budget Office, *op. cit.*, p. 8.

[22] Bureau of Labor Statistics, *op. cit.*, p. 85.

[23] Congressional Budget Office, *op. cit.*, p. 2.

[24] Bureau of Labor Statistics, *op. cit.*, p. 84.

[25] *Who Was Who in America*, Vol. I, 1897-1942, p. 1219.

[26] Ray Marshall and Marc Tucker, *Thinking for a Living: Work, Skills and the Future of the American Economy* (1992), p. 5.

[27] Henry Pelling, *American Labor* (1960), p. 130.

[28] U.S Congress, Office of Technology Assessment, *Technology and Structural Unemployment: Reemploying Displaced Adults*, February 1986, p. 135.

[29] *Ibid.*, p. 138.

[30] National Commission on Technology, Automation, and Economic Progress, *Technology and the American Economy*, 1966, p. xii.

[31] Office of Technology Assessment, *op. cit.*, p. 139.

[32] Marshall and Tucker, *op. cit.*, p. 223.

[33] *1962 CQ Almanac*, p. 513.

[34] Office of Technology Assessment, *op. cit.*, p. 136.

[35] *Ibid.*

[36] *Ibid.*

[37] *1974 CQ Almanac*, p. 235.

[38] Committee on Ways and Means, U.S. House of Representatives, *Overview of Entitlement Programs* (1991), p. 453. (This publication is often referred to as "The Green Book.")

[39] For background, see "Youth Apprenticeships," *The CQ Researcher*, Oct. 23, 1992, pp. 905-929.

[40] Susan Kellam, "Parties Hope Job Training Bill Will Spin Political Gold," *CQ Weekly Report*, May 16, 1992, pp. 1341-1345.

[41] Janet Hook, "Private vs. Public Sector: Reagan and Mondale at Odds Over Jobs, Unions, Pay Issues," *CQ Weekly Report*, Oct. 13, 1984, p. 2652.

[42] *Ibid.*

[43] *1990 CQ Almanac*, p. 277.

[44] Department of Labor fact sheet.

[45] Art Pine, "Clinton Offers $19.5-Billion Package to Help Defense Industry After Cuts," *Los Angeles Times*, March 12, 1993.

[46] For background, see "Jobs vs. Environment," *The CQ Researcher*, May 15, 1992, pp. 409-433.

[47] Catalina Camia, "Clinton's Forest Compromise Is Assailed From All Sides," *CQ Weekly Report*, July 3, 1993, p. 1726.

Bibliography

Selected Sources Used

Books

Marshall, Ray and Tucker, Marc, *Thinking for a Living: Work, Skills, and the Future of the American Economy*, Basic Books, 1992.

A sharp-eyed and sharp-tongued critique of how American families, schools, policy-makers and employers all share responsibility for the failure to develop the skills of U.S. workers by a former secretary of Labor and a labor economist. The book also offers a comprehensive plan for reconciling the mismatch between the nation's needs and the skills provided by an outmoded education and training system.

Reich, Robert B., *The Work of Nations*, First Vintage Books, 1991.

The current secretary of Labor, while still a member of the faculty at Harvard's John F. Kennedy School of Government, wrote this lively critique of the challenge to the United States in the emerging global economy. He sees the country's traditional economic borders collapsing and questions the ability of the nation to come to the aid of those who are disadvantaged — and often lose their jobs — as a result.

Articles

Friedman, Sheldon and Jane McDonald-Pines, "In Search of a 'New Convenant' for America's Dislocated Workers," *North American Outlook*, Sept. 1993, pp. 67-99.

This article outlines the AFL-CIO's proposal for improving the nation's dislocated-worker programs.

Carnevale, Anthony P. and Eric R. Schultz, "Technical Training in America: How Much and Who," *Training and Development Journal*, November 1988, pp. 18-32.

A comprehensive examination of technical training and the general organization and structure of training in the United States.

Hansen, Janet S., "Making Sense of Worker Training," *Issues in Science and Technology*, winter 1993-94, pp. 21-25.

Hansen offers a strong rationale for why the country should improve the quality and coherence of training in the workplace, even as many U.S. firms appear to be moving toward a high-performance form of workplace organization that puts a premium on worker skills.

Reports and Studies

U.S. Department of Labor, Office of Inspector General, *Trade Adjustment Assistance Program: Audit of Program Outcomes in Nine Selected States*, Sept. 30, 1993.

This inspector general report scrutinizes the Trade Adjustment Assistance program, based on very comprehensive data, and draws the strong conclusion that the government job-training program for workers hurt by foreign trade is largely ineffective. It also points out that the emphasis of the program, despite its legislative mandate, is on financial assistance rather than on training.

Congressional Budget Office, *Displaced Workers: Trends in the 1980s and Implications for the Future*, February 1993

A detailed account of displacement throughout the 1980s, and what lessons may be learned from the experiences of roughly 20 million workers.

National Commission for Employment Policy, *The Employment Effects of the North American Free Trade Agreement: Recommendations and Background Studies*, October 1992.

This extensive special report offers a comprehensive look at NAFTA's implications for U.S. employment and the workplace.

National Center for Education and the Economy, *America's Choice: High Skills or Low Wages!*, 1990.

Ira C. Magaziner, the country's health-care czar, headed this ground-breaking account of what national resources it will take to improve the productivity of the country and of each worker.

U.S Congress, Office of Technology Assessment, *Technology and Structural Unemployment: Reemploying Displaced Adults*, February, 1986.

This report concentrates on the problems of displaced workers, especially those likely to face extended periods of unemployment, loss of health insurance and retirement benefits, and find reemployment only in a new job with lower pay.

The Next Step

Additional information from UMI's Newspaper & Periodical Abstracts database

Education

Kress, Gunther, "Paths to destruction," *Times Educational Supplement*, Nov. 19, 1993, p. 22.
A productive economy in a changing world requires a visionary shift in direction in the United Kingdom's education policy, according to Kress. Education must be securely anchored to economic and industrial policy to combine issues of employment, training and education with industrial and economic strategy, he writes.

McAuliffe, Sharon, "Reinventing education: The Chicago experiment," *Omni*, December 1993, pp. 62-64.
Nobel laureate Leon Lederman is heading a program dedicated to changing the way Chicago schoolchildren learn math and science. Lederman's goal is to retrain all of the more than 17,000 Chicago teachers responsible for math and science from kindergarten on up. To accomplish this, Lederman has established the Teacher's Academy.

Rudakewych, Lesia, "More bang for the buck in tech-ed," *Insight on the News*, Oct. 4, 1993, pp. 14-18.
As President Clinton calls for greater spending to train the "forgotten half" — youths who don't go to four-year colleges — some technical schools are going a long way with only a little federal money and a lot of ingenuity. The prospect of another federal program worries people in the technical-education field, who say job training and placement can be done through existing programs and local networks.

Sherwood, Jane, "Starting over," *Canada & the World*, November 1993, pp. 22-23.
The key to staying in and getting ahead in today's job market is education, Sherwood writes. Many older, experienced workers are finding it necessary to go back to school.

Federal Programs

"Clinton seeks plan to narrow United States wage gap," *The Christian Science Monitor*, Dec. 14, 1993, p. 10.
On Dec. 13, 1993, *The New York Times* reported that President Clinton is devising a multibillion-dollar strategy to narrow the gap between the wages earned by blue-collar workers and those who have college educations. The strategy will include job retraining and a loan program.

Dentzer, Susan, "Clinton's 1994 investment planning," *U.S. News & World Report*, Dec. 20, 1993, p. 54.
President Clinton doesn't seem to be truly serious about investing in job training, technology development and help for small manufacturers, Dentzer writes. He has failed to explain the difference between investments and garden-variety federal spending, she says.

Gerstenzang, James and Ronald Brownstein, "Job training for NAFTA victims is offered," *Los Angeles Times*, Oct. 2, 1993, p. A21.
On Oct. 1, 1993, senior Clinton administration officials said the White House would be willing to provide retraining assistance specifically for workers who might lose their jobs because of the NAFTA free-trade pact.

Lively, Kit, "Many states welcome Clinton's job-training plan, but some say it may not lead to significant change," *The Chronicle of Higher Education*, Sept. 8, 1993, p. A27.
The School-to-Work Opportunities Act is discussed.

Risen, James, "Clinton begins cutting federal spending plans," *Los Angeles Times*, Dec. 21, 1993, p. A1.
On Dec. 20, 1993, President Clinton began scaling back federal spending proposals as the White House admitted that its next budget will provide little or no growth in domestic "investments" such as public works, job training, education and children's programs.

Salwen, Kevin G. and David Wessel, "Reich weighs rise in payroll tax to fund training," *The Wall Street Journal*, Dec. 14, 1993, p. A2.
Labor Secretary Robert B. Reich is considering proposing an increase in the federal payroll tax to help expand federal worker-training programs; the department's dislocated-worker plan would require an additional $2 billion in training funds and $1 billion in benefits.

Stokes, Bruce, "American walls to rival Berlin's," *National Journal*, Sept. 11, 1993, pp. 2218.
The Clinton administration is pressing Congress to vote on NAFTA before a retraining program for U.S. workers is in place, but retraining is what is needed to ensure its approval, Stokes writes.

International Training

Ruess, Annette and Dietmar Student, "Fall of the German worker," *World Press Review*, January 1994, p. 37.
The declining technical knowledge of Germany's skilled workers and the factors that have influenced this decline are discussed. Germany has failed to capitalize on a broad-based plan to provide on-the-job training, company education and traditional trade-school education.

"UK graduates a bridge to Japan?," *Nature*, Sept. 23, 1993, p. 284.

Geoffrey Allen, chairman of a committee set up by the United Kingdom's Office of Science and Technology (OST) to make recommendations on strengthening scientific and technological links with Japan, has recommended that companies send graduate recruits to Japan for one year. The move could help the United Kingdom learn more about Japanese industry.

Wagster, Emily, "Many workers abroad hurt by culture shock," *USA Today*, Dec. 17, 1993, p. B1.

More workers than ever are taking overseas assignments, but many don't receive cross-cultural training first. A survey by the National Foreign Trade Council shows only 58 percent of companies provide pre-departure preparation.

Job Training Programs

Kleiman, Carol, "Training triumphs over traditional jobs," *Chicago Tribune*, Dec. 9, 1993, p. 3.

Carol Kleiman says many low-income women, most of them on welfare, benefit from special training programs resulting from the passage in 1991 of an amendment to the Job Training Partnership Act. The Employment for Women Act helps women get into well-paying, male-dominated jobs. (Part 2 of 2).

Lowther, William, "Work, not welfare," *Maclean's*, Dec. 6, 1993, pp. 28-31.

Starting in 1994, Wisconsin will introduce a series of rule revisions aiming to slash the welfare rolls. The program will provide physically able welfare recipients with two years of job training; after this time they will be denied benefits if they do not find employment.

McKenna, Joseph F., "NNS builds more than ships," *Industry Week*, Nov. 1, 1993, pp. 38-41.

Newport News Shipbuilding's Apprentice School carries on a tradition of craftsmanship through training. Company executives believe it makes good business sense to have a core of 2,500 apprentices among the company's 20,000-plus work force. (Part of a series)

Nickel, Lori, "Job training offers new chance to disabled man," *The New York Times*, Dec. 15, 1993, p. B7.

Nickel describes how a 36-year-old disabled man benefited from a job-training program operated by Adult Rehabilitation Services, a division of the Bureau of Community Service in Brooklyn, one of seven charities supported by *The New York Times* Neediest Cases Fund.

Panepinto, Joe, "Training expectations," *Computerworld*, Nov. 8, 1993, pp. 92-93.

Some companies are meeting significant information-systems training needs head on. The training programs at 3M Co., Carolina Power & Light Co. and Deere & Co. are described.

Sorohan, Erica Gordon, "Most likely to succeed," *Training & Development*, December 1993, p. 10.

Inc. magazine's "Best Small Companies to Work for in America," and their great training techniques, are discussed. Companies include Starbucks Coffee, which offers employees classes in everything from coffee knowledge to interpersonal relationships.

Waterman, Frederick, "Inside butler school," *Reader's Digest (U.S. Edition)*, November 1993, pp. 107-111.

There are 86 lessons in Ivor Spencer's training course for butlers, including how to bow, iron the morning newspaper and quietly remove a drunken party guest. The job of butler and the changing duties of the job are discussed.

Welty, Gus, "Training in tune with the future," *Railway Age*, November 1993, pp. 75-78.

Railroads and community colleges across the nation may soon be working together to train skilled workers, expanding on a program pioneered by Burlington Northern.

Retraining Programs

Griffin, Kate, "Program retrains homemakers to fill non-traditional jobs," *Chicago Tribune*, Nov. 28, 1993, p. 1.

Women re-entering the work force don't go in thinking "non-traditional," says Molly Howieson, who runs Target, a pre-employment program for displaced homemakers, through the YWCA in Du Page County, Illinois. Howieson's 12-week course offers counseling and hands-on experience to women trying to plan for life after divorce.

Kleiman, Carol, "Change in strategy for defense workers," Chicago Tribune, Nov. 28, 1993, p. 1.

Carol Kleiman comments on Rhode Island's full-time, 20-week intensive entrepreneurship training program sponsored by Bryant College, which retrains workers who have lost jobs because of reduced military spending.

Manspeaker, Jewell and John Krug, "Washington timber workers retrain for technical jobs," *Vocational Education Journal*, October 1993, p. 25.

Two work force training programs provided by technical and community colleges in Washington state that assisted displaced workers in the timber industry in obtaining jobs in other fields are discussed. The key lesson learned was that community colleges cannot retrain workers without help.

Mortwedt, Jim, "Starting over: In Wisconsin, Uniroyal workers face new reality," *Vocational Education Journal*, October 1993, p. 24.

The retraining of laid-off employees of the Uniroyal-Goodrich plant in Chippewa Valley, Wisconsin, by the Chippewa Valley Technical College (CVTC) is discussed. After retraining graduates, CVTC attempts to place them in jobs that utilize each worker's skills.

Back Issues

Great Research on Current Issues Starts Right Here...Recent topics covered by The CQ Researcher are listed below. Before May 1991, reports were published under the name of Editorial Research Reports.

JULY 1992
Alternative Energy
Prescription Drug Prices
Alzheimer's Disease
Infant Mortality

AUGUST 1992
The Homeless
Work, Family and Stress
NATO's Changing Role
Marine Mammals vs. Fish

SEPTEMBER 1992
Domestic Partners
Violence in Schools
Public Broadcasting
Women in the Military

OCTOBER 1992
Depression
U.S. Auto Industry
Youth Apprenticeships
Hispanic Americans

NOVEMBER 1992
Physical Fitness
Privatization
Paying for College
U.S. Policy in Asia

Back issues are available for $4.00 (subscribers) or $7.00 (non-subscribers). Quantity discounts apply to orders over ten. To order, call Congressional Quarterly Customer Service at (202) 887-8621.

Binders are available for $15.00. To order call 1-800-638-1710. Please refer to stock number 648.

DECEMBER 1992
Crackdown on Smoking
The New CIA
Eating Disorders
Women and AIDS

JANUARY 1993
Hate Crimes
Child Sexual Abuse
Nuclear Fusion
U.S. Trade Policy

FEBRUARY 1993
Community Policing
Europe's New Right
School Censorship
Violence Against Women

MARCH 1993
Gay Rights
Aid to Russia
War on Drugs
TV Violence

APRIL 1993
Head Start
High-Speed Rail
Children's Legal Rights
Muslims in America

MAY 1993
Cults in America
Preventing Teen Pregnancy
Software Piracy
National Parks

JUNE 1993
Food Safety
Prostitution
Childhood Immunizations
National Service

JULY 1993
Electric Cars
Population Growth
Downward Mobility
Intelligence Testing

AUGUST 1993
Mental Illness
Bilingual Education
Foreign Policy Burden
School Funding

SEPTEMBER 1993
Suburban Crime
Public Housing
Supreme Court Preview
Immigration Reform

OCTOBER 1993
Airline Safety
Disaster Response
Science in the Courtroom
The Glass Ceiling

NOVEMBER 1993
Paying for Retirement
Charitable Giving
Privacy in the Workplace
Adoption

DECEMBER 1993
U.S. Vietnam-Relations
Learning Disabilities
Child Care
Space Program's Future

JANUARY 1994
Racial Tensions in Schools
South Africa's Future

Future Topics

- ***Pesticides***
- ***Prison Overcrowding***
- ***Drinking Water Safety***

THE CQ Researcher

PUBLISHED BY CONGRESSIONAL QUARTERLY INC.

Regulating Pesticides

Do Americans need more protection from toxic chemicals?

Pesticides have long been suspected of causing cancer and other serious diseases. New studies lend support to these concerns, linking pesticides to diseases in children and breast cancer in women. The greatest worry is over pesticide residues in food and drinking water. But pesticides also pose a danger to agricultural workers and homeowners who use these chemicals. And runoff from fields pollutes groundwater, rivers and coastal areas, killing untold numbers of fish and animals. Farmers and chemical manufacturers agree with environmentalists and consumer advocates that current regulations governing pesticides are inconsistent, but they differ on a solution. Now the Clinton administration proposes to overhaul the laws regulating pesticide use, and Congress is expected to address the issue this year.

INSIDE THIS ISSUE

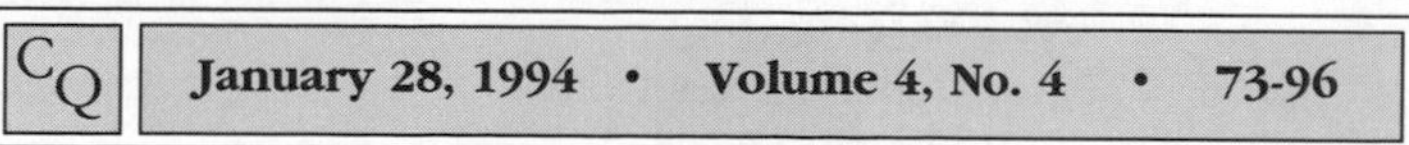

CQ January 28, 1994 • Volume 4, No. 4 • 73-96

Formerly Editorial Research Reports

Regulating Pesticides

Cover: A Crop-Duster In Action. (U.S. Department Of Agriculture)

January 28, 1994
Volume 4, No. 4

The CQ Researcher (ISSN 1056-2036). Formerly Editorial Research Reports. Published weekly (48 times per year, not printed the first Friday of any month with five Fridays) by Congressional Quarterly Inc., 1414 22nd St., N.W., Washington, D.C. 20037. Rates are furnished upon request. Second-class postage paid at Washington, D.C. POSTMASTER: Send address changes to The CQ Researcher, 1414 22nd St., N.W., Washington, D.C. 20037.

Regulating Pesticides

By Mary H. Cooper

The Issues

Health-conscious Americans will be able to learn more about the food they buy when new and improved labels begin appearing this year on most products at the grocery store. But missing from the lists of ingredients will be any mention of the chemical pesticides that almost certainly were used by growers to produce those ingredients.[1]

Farmers dust or spray pesticides — some 850 million pounds of them a year — on most of the food crops available to American consumers. Without pesticides, growers undoubtedly would suffer more than the $20 billion in estimated annual losses to insects, weeds, rodents and mold, and food would be more expensive and less blemish-free.

Ever since their widespread acceptance after World War II, however, chemical pesticides have been controversial. Opposition to the use of DDT and other chemical compounds known as chlorinated hydrocarbons crystallized in 1962 with the publication of *Silent Spring*, Rachel Carson's landmark work linking pesticides with serious damage to the environment and human health. Even after DDT was banned in the United States in 1972, deep concerns persisted about the toxic effect of other pesticides still in use.

To address consumers' concerns, Congress set up an elaborate system to regulate the sale and use of pesticides (*see p. 84*). The Environmental Protection Agency (EPA), established in 1970, was charged with overseeing the production, labeling and use of all pesticides. EPA requires extensive testing and safety studies on each pesticide to assure that it doesn't pose undue risks. The agency specifies acceptable application doses and the crops on which the chemical may be applied. (*See table, p. 76.*)

U.S. Department of Agriculture

EPA also establishes "tolerances," or maximum acceptable levels, for pesticide residues found in food, with enforcement by the Food and Drug Administration (FDA). In addition to the federal oversight system, individual states have their own pesticide regulations, some tougher than the federal rules.

Over the years, however, inconsistencies have crept into the federal pesticide regulatory system. One controversial rule, known as the Delaney clause, bans pesticide use on any crop that is used in processed foods if it has been found to cause cancer at any concentration. But another rule allows trace amounts of carcinogenic pesticides on raw foods as long as the economic benefits of their use outweigh the risk to human health. Over the years, regulators have allowed the use of these pesticides on processed foods as well if they deem the risk they pose to be "negligible."

Congress in 1992 failed to resolve the discrepancy in pesticide laws with new legislation, and in February 1993 the courts forced lawmakers to act. The Supreme Court let stand an appeals court ruling requiring the EPA to apply the stricter standard contained in the Delaney clause to raw foods as well as processed foods (*see p. 86*). EPA warned that more than 30 pesticides would have to be pulled from the market if Congress failed to rewrite the law.

"Under the current system of regulating pesticides, all of the agency's clients are underserved," said Lynn R. Goldman, assistant administrator of EPA's Office of Prevention, Pesticides and Toxic Substances. "The general public is concerned that its health and the environment may not be adequately protected. The pesticide industry feels that the regulatory system takes too much time and is unpredictable. And farmers are anxious because they feel they can't count on products being available for them when they need them."[2]

Last year also saw the release of new information implicating chemical pesticides in a number of diseases. A long-awaited study by the National Academy of Sciences concluded that children are especially susceptible to toxic effects of some pesticides because of their metabolic characteristics and because they consume greater amounts of fruits and vegetables relative to their body weight than do adults.[3] Another study presented new evidence linking DDT, which persists in the environment more than 20 years after it was banned, and breast cancer.[4]

Acting on the court decision and the scientific findings, the Clinton administration last September presented a sweeping proposal to overhaul the pesticide regulatory system. The plan would resolve the discrepancy involving the Delaney clause by applying a single safety standard to raw and processed foods that, unlike current law, would not take into consideration the

Estimated U.S. Usage of Common Pesticides

Pesticide	Type of Pesticide	Usage in Millions of Pounds (Active Ingredient)	Crops treated
Atrazine	herbicide	70-80	corn, sorghum
Alachlor	herbicide	55-70	corn, dry beans, peanuts, soybeans
Metolachlor	herbicide	50-65	corn, soybeans, sorghum, potatoes, cotton
1, 3-D (Telone)	nematicide, soil fumagant	45-65	soybeans, many vegetables, fruit
2, 4-D	herbicide	40-65	asparagus, corn, millet, rice, sugarcane, wheat, • soybeans
Methyl-bromide	gaseous fumigant	25-45	many row crops, including tomatoes, strawberries, asparagus, cauliflower, barley and fodder
Trifluralin	herbicide	25-45	alfalfa, apricots, asparagus, carrots, corn, cotton, cucumbers, sugarcane
Cyanazine	herbicide	20-30	field corn, cotton, sweet corn
EPTC	herbicide	20-30	beans, legumes, potatoes, corn, sweet potatoes
Metam sodium	soil fumigant, wide-spectrum pesticide	20-30	soil treatment before planting many crops
Glyphosate	herbicide	15-20	non-crop weed control, post-harvest use for small grains, alfalfa, beans, corn, also in orchards and vineyards
Chlorpyrifos Dursban, Lorsban	insecticide	10-20	citrus, corn, fruit, grain, nuts, vegetables
Chlorothalonil Bravo	fungicide	10-20	fruits, vegetables, peanuts
Carbary, Sevin	insecticide	10-15	citrus, fruits, nuts, fodder
Malathion	insecticide	10-15	many fruits and vegetables, nuts, grains, fodder
Terbufos	insecticide, nematicide	9-11	corn, sugar beets, grain, sorghum
Maneb/Mancozeb	fungicide	6-10	apples, onions, potàtoes, tomatoes, small grains
Butylate	herbicide	5-10	used to treat soil before planting corn

Source: Environmental Protection Agency and National Coalition Against the Misuse of Pesticides

economic benefits of pesticides. It would require that pesticides be evaluated according to their effects on children rather than adults. The administration also encouraged the use of "integrated pest management," a combination of agricultural techniques including crop rotation and modern tilling methods that can reduce the need for chemical pesticides.

Some environmental groups criticize the administration proposal because it scraps the zero-risk standard of the Delaney clause and replaces it with a less rigid measure. "The philosophy behind the Delaney clause — preventing unnecessary exposure to hazardous substances — should be preserved," writes Al Meyerhoff, a lawyer with the Natural Resources Defense Council (NRDC). "We still do not know whether humans are more or less sensitive than laboratory animals to carcinogens and whether one carcinogen may increase the cancer-causing effects of another." [5]

For their part, pesticide manufacturers, as well as many growers and food-processing companies, welcome the abandonment of Delaney but say the administration goes too far by eliminating economic considerations in deciding whether a pesticide may be used. Agricultural and food-processing businesses agree that current laws governing pesticides are flawed, but they question several administration proposals. "No one benefits from a failure of public confidence in EPA's ability to regulate pesticides," says John J. Aguirre, director of federal government affairs at the National Food Processors Association. "There's no argument about whether we want to move forward from current law on that issue. The question is, 'How far do you go?' "

Chemical manufacturers in particular take issue with the administration's proposals to reduce the use of pesticides. "There's been a lot of rhetoric coming out of this administration," says John McCarthy, a spokesman for the National Agricultural Chemicals Association. "The stark reality is that while it sounds good, just going in there with a meat ax to reduce use doesn't necessarily mean you're going to reduce that risk." The association advocates a system that would reduce the risks associated with pesticide use by providing the public with more information on the hazards pesticides pose and on ways to reduce exposure. (*See story, p. 85.*)

While the Clinton administration has yet to present legislation incorporating its proposed changes to pesticide law, some lawmakers have introduced measures reflecting both sides of the debate. A measure introduced by Sen. Edward M. Kennedy, D-Mass., and Rep. Henry A. Waxman, D-Calif., would permit pesticide residues in both processed and raw foods if they present a "negligible" cancer risk, defined as a one-in-a-million chance of causing cancer over a person's lifetime.

Chemical manufacturers, food-processing companies and agricultural businesses support another bill, sponsored by Reps. Richard H. Lehman, D-Calif., Thomas J. Bliley Jr., R-Va., and J. Roy Rowland, D-Ga., that would require the economic benefits of pesticides to be considered together with health risks in regulating pesticides.

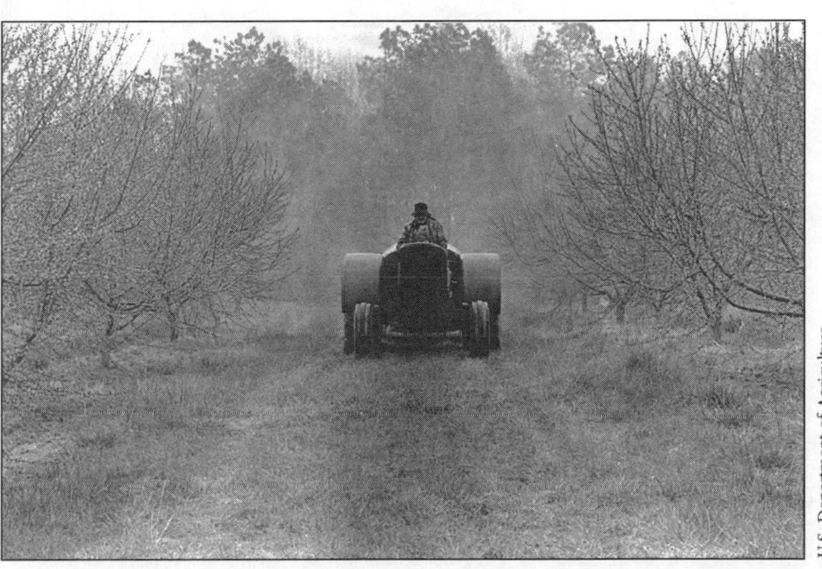
U.S. Department of Agriculture

Spraying fruit trees with insecticide.

As lawmakers prepare for the upcoming congressional debate over pesticide laws, these are key questions being asked:

Do chemical pesticides, as allowed under current law, pose a risk to human health?

There is a wide variety of pesticides, including many, such as insecticidal soaps, that pose no known risk to human health. "There are over 600 different active ingredients and over 20,000 different products," explains Jill Haukos, associate director of EPA's national Pesticides Telecommunications Network, a hotline set up to answer consumer queries about pesticides. * "That makes a generalized statement impossible to the question of whether pesticides pose a health problem."

Food industry spokesmen argue that fears over exposure to toxic levels of pesticide residues in food are overblown. "Categorically, pesticide residues in food today pose no significant risk to public health," says Aguirre.

Pesticide manufacturers agree. They also vehemently deny charges that pesticide manufacturers fail to adequately test their products for safety before selling them to the public. "We've been doing that for 30 years, and for sure we do it better today than ever," says McCarthy. New pesticides go through a testing period of seven to 10 years, on average, he says, at a cost to the industry of between $40 million and $50 million for each pesticide. "So it's a long-term, high-stakes game for the industry."

But public fears of contamination by pesticides persist. Concerns have long focused on DDT, which was banned following reports that it caused a dramatic decline in eagles and other wild birds. Because it deteriorates very slowly, DDT that leached into groundwater and rivers in agricultural runoff can still be found in the tissues of fish sampled in U.S. waters. It also is stored for a long time

*The EPA's toll-free hotline for consumer queries about pesticides is (800) 858-7378.

From Their Little Plot, a Healthful, Bountiful Harvest

Last year, Jess and Suzanne Unger set aside half an acre of their 160-acre farm in Lovettsville, Va., for organic farming. Using no chemical pesticides, they raised fresh produce for 60 customers. "We grew more than 40 varieties of vegetables," Jess Unger says, "from arugula to zucchini."

The variety of produce that sprouted from the modest plot is not all that distinguishes Brook Farm from many other producers that have adopted organic farming methods. Instead of selling their produce to a store or at a local farmers' market, the Ungers asked their customers to decide what they should raise. "Our customers sign up at the beginning of the year and fill out a questionnaire indicating what types of vegetables they want, and how much," Jess Unger explains. "They pay a lump sum at the beginning for weekly deliveries for 32 weeks from April to November."

Jess and Suzanne Unger

The Ungers are among a growing number of farmers who are adopting a marketing strategy called community-supported agriculture. In this reversal of the conventional food-marketing system, consumers contract directly with farmers to grow the commodities they want. The concept, which originated in Europe and quickly became popular in Japan, was introduced in the United States in 1985 with the first group in Massachusetts, Unger says. "From there it has spread throughout the country."

By eliminating the middleman — the grocery store — growers can offer fresher produce, including the more costly organic foods, at prices that often are below grocery-store prices.

"Our Washington customers tell us prices come in under what it costs them to buy at city outlets for organic foods, including the downtown food coops," Unger says. "Out here [in suburban Loudoun County], it costs more than Safeway produce, but we feel the cost shows consumers the cost of actually producing the food." Produce sold in grocery stores, Unger says, has hidden costs, such as poor quality and pesticide contamination, that are not readily apparent to consumers.

Although community-supported agriculture today poses little threat to Safeway and the other retail giants, demand for Brook Farm produce is growing. The Ungers are expanding their organic garden to two and a half acres this year. Apart from the lack of chemical residues, Jess Unger says, the main attraction his operation holds out to customers is freshness and the seasonal quality of his produce.

"Why buy something that was grown 2,000 miles away in December," he asks, "when you can get the same thing, grown locally, in May or June when it is in season?"

in the fatty tissues of humans and animals that ingest the pesticide. And DDT is still used in many developing countries, including Mexico. (*See table, p. 87.*)

Last April, researchers at Mount Sinai School of Medicine in New York City presented evidence linking DDT and breast cancer.[6] They found that DDT may have an action similar to the hormone estrogen in causing breast cancer. According to the study, women with the highest exposure to DDT had four times the breast cancer risk of women with the lowest exposure. Exposure to estrogen has been implicated in cancer and several other diseases, as well as reduced sperm counts in men.

"We know that more and more pollutants, industrial byproducts and pesticides are being discovered to have estrogenic properties, and that the total load of confirmed environmental estrogens is growing rapidly," said Richard Wiles, pollution prevention director of the Environmental Working Group, a nonprofit environmental research organization in Washington. "And we know that since the 1940s there has been a dramatic increase in toxic chemical pollution and pesticide use, and that breast cancer incidence in women has more than doubled from one in 20 to one in nine during that time."[7]

DDT is not the only pesticide implicated in breast cancer. In October, EPA announced it would examine other estrogenic pesticides currently in use for their possible link to breast cancer. These include endosulfan, an insecticide that is widely used on carrots, lettuce, spinach, tomatoes and about 40 other food crops. The Environmental Working Group reports that other commonly used pesticides, including the two most widely used herbicides — alachlor and atrazine — disrupt endocrine function in animals, causing cancer, reproductive failure, sexual dysfunction and birth defects.[8]

Another focus of public concern has been the potential risk to children's health from exposure to pesticides. In June 1993, the National Academy of Sciences released a long-awaited six-year study concluding that children's metabolisms and high intake of fruits and vegetables make them more vulnerable to pesticides than adults. [9] "Children are not just little adults; they are in many respects truly different," said Dr. Philip J. Landrigan, a professor of pediatrics at Mount Sinai School of Medicine and chairman of the study's research panel. "Unfortunately, current pesticide regulation does not adequately reflect that understanding." The study called for changes in the law to have pesticide tolerances measured separately for children.

As evidence continues to indicate potential health risks associated with pesticides, some scientists are seeking alternative ways to produce food. "There are a lot of things we don't know about pesticides," says Rhonda R. Janke, director of research into alternative farming at the Rodale Institute Research Center in Kutztown, Pa. "DDT was used for 20 years before they figured out what was going on, so I don't think human beings are clever enough to know what all the drawbacks are until it's too late. It's probably better to use few or no pesticides."

Do pesticides' benefits outweigh their dangers to the environment?

The environmental damage caused by chemical pesticides has been a focus of widespread concern since the 1962 publication of Rachel Carson's *Silent Spring*. Carson, a marine biologist with the U.S. Fish and Wildlife Service, linked DDT to an alarming decline in the number of eagles and other raptors, which ingested the pesticide in the flesh of fish and small mammals. DDT, Carson wrote, caused eggshell thinning, resulting in many eggs that never hatched.

Carson's work prompted further research that led to the 1972 ban on DDT in the United States. In place of DDT and similar pesticides, chemical manufacturers began producing pesticides that in many cases were more toxic but deteriorated more rapidly, making them less likely, when used properly, to persist in agricultural runoff and pollute rivers or harm wildlife.

Because it is still used in other countries and persists in the United States as well, DDT continues to take its toll on the environment. In addition, examples abound of environmental disasters caused by pesticides developed since DDT was banned. Numerous fish kills have been documented in Louisiana streams near sugar cane fields sprayed with azinphos-methyl (AZM), an insecticide used to kill the cane borer. [10]

Even though modern pesticides are designed to pose less danger to wildlife because they deteriorate quickly, they can wreak havoc after accidental spills. In July 1991, a freight train derailment near Dunsmuir, Calif., spilled tank-car loads of metam sodium, a chemical that kills a wide range of pests, into the Sacramento River, killing all fish and plants along a 40-mile stretch of the river. Afterwards, EPA revised the warning label for metam sodium and barred all products containing the pesticide for home use.

Alligators in Florida's Lake Apopka were also harmed by accidental spills, according to a recent report by Louis J. Guillette Jr., a professor of biotechnology at the University of Florida. Guillette linked the sudden decline of the lake's gators in the 1980s to a spill of the pesticide Kelthane from the nearby Tower Chemical Co. Kelthane, an insecticide used on apples, beans, citrus and cotton, contains the estrogenic chemical dicofol, which, like DDT, damages reproductive function and embryonic development. [11]

In addition to their fears about accidental spills, environmentalists worry that pervasive pesticide use is especially harmful because over time increasing amounts must be applied to obtain the same results. That's because insects or weeds that are resistant to a given pesticide will survive and reproduce, eventually replacing the weaker individuals that succumb and fail to reproduce. As more pesticide is required, runoff becomes increasingly contaminated, further jeopardizing the environment.

Industry representatives say this need not occur. "Now we know a lot more about managing that problem," says McCarthy of the agricultural chemicals association, "so you shouldn't use the same thing over and over because you're going to select out the hardiest and they'll take over." Rather than taking pesticides off the market, he says, growers should use an array of pesticides. "It's like having a big tool kit," he explains. "If you start taking the tools out of the tool kit and throwing them away, you can disrupt the whole system."

Can pesticide use be eliminated from agriculture?

Many environmentalists and consumer groups say that chemical pesticides are not needed to produce food. By using so-called organic farming methods, they say, growers can maintain current yields while avoiding synthetically produced chemicals altogether. Organic growers rely on crop rotation, which discourages the development of pests that thrive on a particular plant species. They also use natural biological pesticides to combat insects, weeds and other pests. Organic farmers release ladybugs and wasps, for example, which prey on certain insect pests.

Critics challenge the claim that organic agriculture is better for human health and the environment than farming with pesticides. "I haven't seen one shred of evidence to indicate that an organic commodity is safer than a commodity that has been grown using conventional farm practices," says Aguirre of the Food Processors Association. "No one has said

From Gerber to Gallo: How Growers Reduce Pesticide Use

While the debate over pesticide use continues to rage, many American farmers are battling bugs by combining elements of conventional and organic farming. Known as integrated pest management, or IPM, the approach combines the goal of reducing pesticide use with maintaining high crop yields.

Although definitions of IPM vary, it generally involves watching fields more closely to avoid applying chemicals before they are needed; rotating crops to discourage the development of pests that thrive on a given plant species; placing plants that repel certain pests between rows of vulnerable crops; and using so-called "biocontrols" instead of chemical pesticides when possible. Biocontrols include naturally occurring repellents and predators of insects as well as pheromone traps to interrupt insect breeding cycles.

Organic farming goes beyond IPM to eliminate the use of chemical pesticides and fertilizers altogether. Because they are considered labor-intensive and costly to use, organic methods have been limited largely to small-scale vegetable growers. Some have carved out niche markets, catering to health-conscious consumers. With the appearance of specialty stores, such as the Fresh Fields chain on the East Coast, larger-scale growers are beginning to find a market for organic commodities as well.

But most large-scale growers find it hard to abandon pesticides altogether. Chemicals enable them to grow a single crop year after year, using the least possible labor. To help farmers reduce their use of agricultural chemicals, the Rodale Institute in Kutztown, Pa., seeks alternative means of controlling pests. The institute, founded in 1947 to study organic farming, says that some crops now grown almost exclusively with pesticides can be cultivated with no chemicals.

"In our trials, we've been growing corn, soybeans and cover crops without pesticides successfully for over 13 years," says Research Director Rhonda Janke. "We've always been at or above county average for yields, so the economics are there." Convincing Corn Belt and other large-scale farmers to adopt their methods is the institute's ultimate goal.

Some food-processing companies are defying the conventional wisdom about the need for pesticides and are voluntarily reducing pesticide use for at least some of their products. Three years ago, Gerber Products Co. Inc., which accounts for 70 percent of the baby-food market, adopted a standard of no detectable pesticide residues in any jar of baby food it sells. Although the company allows growers to use pesticides, it monitors growing methods and tests for residues as a standard practice. [1]

Other large-scale food producers have adopted even stiffer standards, requiring their growers to use organic methods. Health Valley Foods Inc. of Irwindale, Calif., for example, uses certified organic commodities for 95 percent of the ingredients in its products, including cereal, bakery goods, crackers, canned soup and snacks. The remaining 5 percent comes from non-organically grown ingredients, such as rice, pineapple, papaya, mushroom, cinnamon and some other herbs and spices, according to Marketing Director Bernard M. Landes. For that reason, Health Valley's products do not meet strict California standards required of foods that bear the "organic" label.

"Health Valley does not represent our organic products to be free of pesticide residues, nor do we represent our organic products to be safer to eat or of higher nutritional value," Landes said. "We do, however, state our belief that organic foods taste better." [2]

The mammoth Gallo Wine Co. is also getting on the organic bandwagon. Of its approximately 9,000 acres of grapevines, the company says, 6,000 acres are grown organically. The entire 2,770-acre Ripperdan Ranch, a Gallo vineyard in California's San Joachin Valley, is cultivated organically, says ranch Manager Greg Coleman. "In lieu of chemicals, we plant cover crops down between the grapevine rows and release beneficial insects to create a balanced ecosystem where the beneficial insects can offset the pest populations," he says.

The cover crops, including peas, beans and oats, help enrich the soil and also provide a habitat for green lacewings, voracious insects Coleman releases into the vineyard to feed on the equally voracious grape leaf hopper and fruit-eating worms. Since introducing cover crops, Coleman has observed increasing numbers of naturally occurring insects, such as spiders, also thought to prey on grapevine pests.

The cover crops have enabled Coleman to completely eliminate both chemical fertilizers and pesticides at Ripperdan Ranch. But Gallo cannot advertise its wines as organically produced because 95 percent of the grapes used to make Gallo wines are grown by independent growers, many of whom use pesticides.

"More and more growers are taking a hard look at alternative methods, and some are trying organic," Coleman says. "But we're just in the infancy stage."

[1] See Carole Sugarman, "The New Baby Talk at Gerber," *The Washington Post*, July 28, 1993.

[2] Landes testified July 27, 1993, at hearings held by the House Government Operations Subcommittee on Human Resources and Intergovernmental Relations.

that people will live longer or that they will enjoy superior health" if they eschew pesticide-treated foods. Critics also contend that large-scale organic farming is more labor-intensive and costly because it involves more hands-on pest control, such as hand or mechanical weeding.

Jess Unger, an organic farmer near

Leesburg, Va., agrees — up to a point. (*See story, p. 78.*) "Spraying pesticides and monocropping [planting a single crop year after year] allows the farmer to do away with much of his labor costs, just as industrial mass production did away with craftwork," he says. "In much the same way, conventional farming results in reduced prices to the consumer, but with certain hidden costs in terms of quality. With organic farming, instead of just spraying with atrazine, I have to go out with a crew and shake the insects off the plants. It's labor intensive, and you have to expect some crop damage. But organic farming doesn't have the hidden costs of conventional farming in terms of potential health risks caused by pesticides."

Unger says his customers tell him his vegetables compete in price with those found in many food stores. But this may be due to the fact that he sells directly to the consumer. Organic foods sold in stores are generally expensive. This has limited its success in the market largely to gourmet shops and health-food groceries frequented by higher-income, health-conscious shoppers.

According to John Graham, a professor at the Harvard School of Public Health, organically grown produce costs up to 40 percent more than conventionally grown commodities. That comes to a $1,000-a-year premium for a family of four buying standard foods, he estimated. "For poor families and people on fixed incomes, higher food prices increase the risk of malnutrition and its associated illnesses," Graham said. "In short, banning numerous pesticides may have the same effect on poor people as cutting their food stamp payments." [12]

McCarthy of the agricultural chemicals group sees a place for organic farming, but only as a niche market. "People want organic produce and will buy it," he says. "But the stark reality is that you cannot produce food of the quantity, quality and price we now have by growing organic. There are things out there called bugs, diseases and weeds. They've always been with us, and they aren't going to go away. You've got to manage them. It doesn't mean you have to be a nozzlehead about it, just spraying the devil out of the land. But you need these tools in order to manage what we're up against in growing food."

There are no reliable estimates of what a total ban on chemical pesticides would cost farmers, and ultimately, consumers. However, Leonard Gianessi, director of the National Center for Food and Agriculture Policy, foresees severe losses for growers from a sweeping ban on pesticides. "Hops and apple growers in the Northwest would be severely affected by the loss of mitacides," he said. "Apple growers in North Carolina would be affected by the loss of fungicides. Rice growers in Texas would be severely affected by the loss of a key fungicide." [13] EPA has estimated that removal of three popular pesticides now used on tomatoes, peaches and apples would cost $900 million a year in crops lost to pests.

Even if farmers are able to continue growing crops profitably without pesticides, critics question whether there will be enough food for the growing world population if chemicals are eliminated. "We're not going to get the yields we're used to or be able to grow crops in areas where we can grow them now," says McCarthy. "We grow more food on less land with less people than we've ever done." Without pesticides, he says, farmers would have to use more land to produce the same amount of food. "You've got to go out and find the land, cut down the forest and plow up the grassland," he says. "You're going to wreak more environmental havoc by throwing away all this technology."

Modern technology holds out the promise of a potentially far-reaching solution to pest control in the form of bioengineered foods. Still in its infancy, biotechnology may enable scientists to transfer genes for disease or pest resistance from one plant or animal to a food crop, enabling growers to reduce pesticide use on that crop. Scientists at Cornell University working for the Human Genome Project broke new ground in November by isolating and cloning such a gene in wild tomatoes and transferring it into a cultivated tomato.

"Once we understand more about how it works," said Gregory B. Martin, an agronomist at Purdue University who participated in the research, "we'll be able to manipulate (disease-resistant genes) so we don't have to depend so much on chemical sprays." [14]

But in the view of some experts, biotechnology also presents health risks, perhaps even greater than those posed by pesticide residues. "Crops engineered to produce proteins toxic to insects and other pests clearly have the potential to be toxic to humans," said Rebecca J. Goldburg, a senior scientist at the Environmental Defense Fund. "Genetic engineering could also cause susceptible individuals to become allergic to foods they previously could safely consume." [15] A person who is allergic to eggs, for example, could have an allergic reaction after inadvertently eating a bioengineered tomato containing an egg gene.

Meanwhile, many growers who are concerned about the health and environmental risks associated with pesticides are adopting innovative methods of managing pests using fewer chemicals. Greg Coleman, manager of Gallo Wine Co.'s Ripperdan Ranch, a vineyard in California's San Joachin Valley, uses no chemical pesticides on his grapevines. But eliminating chemicals overnight is not the answer for all growers, according to Coleman. "It has to happen gradually," he says. "You can't just turn off the chemicals all of a sudden. Growers need tools, including pesticides, in case there is an outbreak of a pest, so we need to leave those options open." He advocates a move toward farming practices that enable growers to use the land without degrading it. "The bottom line is, we need to move in the direction of more sustainable practices and reduce our dependency on chemicals."

Janke of the Rodale Institute Research Center acknowledges that eliminating pesticides would mean a drastic change and some financial risk to farmers who use chemical pesticides and fertilizers. For example, she says, more than 95 percent of all the corn and soybeans grown in the United States are sprayed with herbicides, even though weeds can be effectively controlled using mechanical cultivation. "The reason farmers don't use mechanical methods is they are simply not set up for it," she says. "They already have herbicide sprayers, while modern cultivators cost anywhere from $3,000 to $10,000 for a fancy model with all the innovations of the past 10 years."

Once they buy the equipment, Janke says, it costs farmers no more to raise corn or soybeans using cultivators to kill weeds than it does to spray. But cultivating is more labor intensive than spraying, an important consideration for many farmers. "Labor is at a premium," Janke says. "Farmers all over the country report difficulty getting good farm labor, both in terms of affordability and quality of the work." ■

BACKGROUND

Postwar Regulations

Farmers have applied some form of pesticides for thousands of years. Their use goes back at least to the eighth century B.C., when the Greek poet Homer referred to the use of fungicides.[16] More sophisticated formulations containing sulfur compounds to kill molds and arsenic to control fruit- and vegetable-eating insects came into use in Europe and the United States during the 19th century. These earlier pesticides were highly toxic, however, and frequently poisoned livestock.

By accident, scientists searching for effective chemical weapons in the years leading up to World War II stumbled on a new substance that killed insects but appeared to have no effect on humans or other mammals. That chemical, DDT (dichlorodiphenyl-trichloro-ethane), had first been synthesized in the 19th century by German scientists. It was not until 1939, however, that Paul Mueller of Switzerland won a Nobel Prize for his discovery of DDT's usefulness as an agricultural insecticide.

DDT was assumed to be safe because it did not appear to harm the soldiers, refugees and prisoners who were dusted with DDT during the war to kill head lice. In the 1950s and '60s, it became the best known of a class of chlorinated organic pesticides that were widely adopted by farmers because they were long-lasting and lethal against noxious insects, yet apparently safe to use. Other chlorinated hydrocarbon insecticides used during those years included BHC (benzenehexachloride), aldrin, dieldrin and toxaphene.

Despite the general lack of concern about pesticides in the postwar years, lawmakers decided to set up a regulation system in the late 1940s. From the beginning, lawmakers confronted opposing interests in dealing with pesticides. Farmers want to use chemicals because they boost crop yields and reduce production costs. Consumers appreciate the high quality and low cost of foods produced with pesticides, but they also demand protection from the toxic effects of these poisons. The result of these conflicting interests led over the years to a hodgepodge of regulations involving several federal agencies.

Congress first addressed the problem of pesticide regulation with the 1947 Federal Insecticide, Fungicide and Rodenticide Act (FIFRA). By regulating the sale and use of pesticides, FIFRA attempts to satisfy both interests by stating that a pesticide must not cause "unreasonable adverse effects on the environment" when applied as the manufacturer intended. But FIFRA also requires regulators to take into account "the economic, social and environmental costs as well as the potential benefits of the use of any pesticide."

The regulatory system set up under FIFRA involves a registration process now administered by EPA. Each pesticide must be separately registered with EPA for every intended use. It is the manufacturer's responsibility to provide adequate data from safety tests it runs on each product, including potential effects on the environment and human health. EPA also must approve the label containing instructions for use and safety warnings before the pesticide can be sold.

The other principal law governing pesticide regulation is the 1954 Food, Drug and Cosmetic Act. It requires the appropriate federal agency (now the EPA) to establish tolerance levels — or the maximum quantity of pesticide residue that is allowable on raw foods and some processed foods.

In setting tolerances, which the National Research Council calls "the single most important tool by which the U.S. government regulates pesticide residues in food," EPA relies on manufacturers' data.[17] There are currently some 8,350 tolerances on the books for residues on raw fruits and vegetables and about 150 tolerances

Continued on p. 84

Chronology

1930s-1950s

The discovery of DDT's insecticidal properties helps fuel the "Green Revolution" after World War II.

1939
Paul Mueller, a Swiss scientist, wins the Nobel Prize for his discovery of DDT's effectiveness as an insecticide.

1947
Congress passes the Federal Insecticide, Fungicide and Rodenticide Act (FIFRA) regulating the sale and use of pesticides. The law specifies that pesticides must not cause "unreasonable adverse effects on the environment."

1954
The Food, Drug and Cosmetic Act is enacted. It requires regulators to set "tolerances," or maximum levels of pesticide residues allowable on raw foods, for each pesticide used on food crops.

1958
Rep. James J. Delaney, D-N.Y., adds an amendment to the Food, Drug and Cosmetic Act prohibiting the use of any cancer-causing pesticides on commodities that are to be used in processed foods. The Delaney clause establishes a stricter standard for processed foods than the one applied under FIFRA for fresh foods.

1960s

Consumers become increasingly concerned about pesticide use.

1962
Rachel Carson's bestseller, *Silent Spring*, links pesticides such as DDT to widespread damage to the environment and human health.

1970s

Congress strengthens the regulatory system governing pesticides.

1970
Congress creates the Environmental Protection Agency (EPA). The new agency's responsibilities include determining the safety of pesticides and registering each new product.

1972
DDT is banned on all food sources in the United States but continues to be used in many other countries.

1980s

Controversy breaks out over inconsistencies in the laws governing admissible levels of pesticide residues in food.

1989
Following a report by the Natural Resources Defense Council identifying Alar, a pesticide commonly used on apples, as a health threat to children, EPA withdraws the chemical from market. Later in the year, regulators discover traces of cyanide in a shipment of grapes from Chile.

1990s

Amid new reports linking pesticides with health risks, lawmakers prepare to reform pesticide laws.

July 1991
A train carrying 13,000 gallons of the pesticide metam sodium derails in California, dumping its lethal cargo into the Sacramento River and destroying all animal and plant life in the river for 40 miles. EPA subsequently restricts the pesticide's use.

July 1992
The 9th U.S. Circuit Court of Appeals in San Francisco rules in *Les v. Reilly* that EPA must strictly apply the terms of the Delaney clause to processed foods.

Feb. 22, 1993
The U.S. Supreme Court upholds the lower court ruling in *Les v. Reilly*. EPA announces soon after the decision that the agency will be required to take dozens of commonly used pesticides off the market unless Congress rewrites the law.

April 21, 1993
More than 20 years after DDT was banned in the United States, researchers release findings linking exposure to DDT to increased incidence of breast cancer.

June 28, 1993
The National Research Council, the administrative arm of the National Academy of Sciences, releases a study identifying pesticide residue as a potentially grave threat to children.

Sept. 21, 1993
The Clinton administration proposes overhauling the pesticide laws by replacing the Delaney clause with a single standard prohibiting residues in all foods that pose more than a one-in-a-million chance of causing cancer over a lifetime of exposure.

Continued from p. 82

for residues that are found in processed foods.

The decades following World War II also saw the development of more effective weed and mold killers, including phenoxy herbicides and dicarboximide fungicides. Pesticides using organic phosphorus, such as malathion and parathion, joined DDT in the farmers' arsenal against insects.

The new pesticides enabled farmers throughout the world to dramatically increase their yields. They were an important ingredient in the "Green Revolution," the postwar effort to alleviate hunger by improving agricultural methods in the Third World. The new pesticides also enabled tropical countries to effectively combat malaria by eradicating many of the mosquitoes that carry the disease.

Alarm Sounded Over DDT

The illusion that DDT was a harmless miracle chemical died in 1962, with the publication of Rachel Carson's *Silent Spring*. Carson, a marine biologist, blamed DDT and other chlorinated hydrocarbon pesticides for a dramatic decline in the number of birds and other wildlife that had been poisoned by ingesting contaminated plant material or animals. She also cited government findings of DDT in mothers' milk as evidence that the chemical is passed largely unaltered along the food chain: from contaminated animal fodder to cows, and then to their milk and ultimately to human infants.

"Along with the possibility of the extinction of mankind by nuclear war," Carson wrote, "the central problem of our age has therefore become the contamination of man's total environment with such substances of incredible potential for harm — substances that accumulate in the tissues of plants and animals and even penetrate the germ cells to shatter or alter the very material of heredity upon which the shape of the future depends." [18]

At about the same time that Carson's bestseller exploded on the scene, growers were observing another unintended effect of pesticides. The longer chlorinated pesticides were applied to crops, the more chemical was required to do the job, creating a feedback loop. As then-Sen. Al Gore, D-Tenn., wrote years later in his book, *Earth in the Balance*: "Pesticides often leave the most resistant pests behind as the more vulnerable ones disappear. Then, when the resistant pests multiply to fill the niche left by their dead cousins, larger quantities of pesticides are used in an effort to kill the more resistant pests, and the process is repeated. Soon, enormous quantities of pesticides are sprayed on the crops to kill just as many pests as were there when the process began. Only now the pests are stronger. And all the while, the quantity of pesticides to which we ourselves are exposed continues to increase." [19]

Regulations Criticized

By the late 1960s, evidence of this feedback loop, as well as the environmental damage caused by DDT and other chlorinated hydrocarbons, had led many growers to use alternative pesticides, such as organophosphates and carbamates, which break down more readily in the environment. Public concerns about DDT's toxicity were a factor in the creation in 1970 of the Environmental Protection Agency. Two years later, EPA banned DDT on all U.S. food sources.

In the years since the EPA's birth, critics have charged that the regulatory system is full of holes. One complaint involves the time it takes to remove a pesticide from use once it proves harmful. Under current procedures, after EPA has registered a pesticide, it may conduct a special review of the chemical if reports of adverse affects appear. But years may pass before a harmful pesticide is pulled from the market.

Granular carbofuran, for example, used to kill worms and insects on a variety of vegetables and grains, chiefly corn and sorghum, was found to kill birds as early as 1974. But EPA did not even begin its special review of the chemical until 1985. The reason for the delay, said John C. Martin, EPA's inspector general, was that the agency "did not have guidelines for evaluating the adverse effects carbofuran presented." [20]

In 1972, Congress amended FIFRA so that EPA would be required to keep track of all pesticides, including those already in use in the United States. To speed up the registration process, Congress in 1988 set a nine-year timetable to complete reregistration of previously approved pesticides. Because of inadequate funding and incomplete scientific data, however, the agency has made little progress. "Almost 20,000 pesticide products have been under review since 1972, and only 31 have been reregistered," said Rep. Mike Synar, D-Okla., chairman of the House Government Operations Subcommittee on Environment, Energy and Natural Resources, one of the panels that oversees pesticide legislation. "At that rate, it will take us to the year 15,520 A.D. to complete." [21]

Controversy Over Delaney Clause

A more basic complaint about the pesticide regulation system is the inconsistency of the standards it applies to raw and processed foods. Under current law, raw foods may have higher concentrations of pesticide residue than processed foods. That's because of a controversial provision of the Food, Drug and Cosmetic Act known as the Delaney clause. Named for Rep. James J. Delaney, D-N.Y., who attached it to the law in 1958, the clause prohibits the

Breaking the Circle of Poison

When the use of DDT was banned in the United States in 1972, many U.S. trading partners in the industrial world followed suit. Later, when modern pesticides were linked to new health and environmental risks, some European countries were even more cautious than the United States, banning several chemicals still used by American growers.

But many developing nations, heavily dependent on agricultural exports for revenue, have been slow to abandon pesticides. These countries, by combining low labor costs and the use of pesticides and other modern agricultural methods, can compete effectively on world markets with more industrialized nations.

Even though pesticide makers may not sell banned chemicals in the United States, they may continue producing them for export. Foods that are grown abroad with these pesticides may be exported to the United States, ending up on the plates of American consumers and completing what environmentalists call the "circle of poison."

There are even signs that the use of toxic pesticides in other countries causes environmental harm in the United States. Scientists in Florida have found evidence of contamination of the coral reefs off the Florida Keys by pesticides banned in the United States. They suspect agricultural runoff from Central and South America that made its way to the Keys along ocean currents. [1] Windborne particles of DDT applied to fields in Central America have been found as far away as the Great Lakes. [2]

Environmental and consumer groups, including Greenpeace and Consumers Union, have failed in the past to convince Congress to prohibit U.S. companies from exporting pesticides that are banned in the United States. Those efforts gained crucial support with the Clinton administration's pesticide reform proposal released Sept. 21. The plan would "prohibit export of any pesticide that has been canceled for all or virtually all uses in the U.S. based on health concerns or those pesticides that were voluntarily canceled in the U.S. by the manufacturer for health or safety reasons."

But pesticide producers call the circle of poison pure fantasy. "It sounds nice," says John McCarthy, a spokesman for the National Agricultural Chemicals Association, "but the fact is that it doesn't happen. If someone wants to make a law about it, that's OK, because we don't do it."

Environmentalists says pesticide exports are only one part of the circle of poison. Another crucial segment is the sale of tainted foods that have been imported from countries that permit the use of harmful pesticides. The Food and Drug Administration (FDA) is responsible for monitoring food residues on foods, including imports. But the agency's ability to perform that task is limited. "Right now, if there is a violative pesticide residue, we have to go first into federal court and file a formal seizure," said FDA Commissioner David A. Kessler. "By the time we do that, sometimes the product leaves and is not where we thought it was."

In fact, FDA has limited power to recall imports with pesticide residues. "People think we have the ability to recall products in the food area," Kessler said. "We don't. We only have voluntary recall authority." [3] He called on Congress to grant more monitoring and enforcement authority to FDA.

It is unclear how the new North American Free Trade Agreement (NAFTA) linking the economies of the United States, Canada and Mexico will affect the circle of poison. The treaty, which went into effect Jan. 1, calls for enforcement of existing U.S. health, safety and environmental standards. It also endorses the goal of "sustainable development," a relatively new concept that generally implies the use of agricultural methods that do not degrade the environment.

Whether or not pesticide use satisfies that standard is a matter of debate. Public Citizen, a consumer advocacy group, criticizes NAFTA for failing to provide sufficient protections of U.S. safety standards. The agreement was endorsed, however, by several environmental and consumer groups, including the Audubon Society, the Environmental Defense Fund and Consumers Union.

[1] See Dan Keating, "Pesticides in Reefs Scrutinized," *The Miami Herald*, May 13, 1991.

[2] See World Resources Institute, *The 1992 Information Please Environmental Almanac* (1993).

[3] Kessler testified Sept. 21, 1993, before a joint House and Senate hearing on reforms to pesticide legislation.

use of all cancer-causing pesticides on commodities that are to be used in processed foods.

At the time the Delaney clause went into effect, instruments could uncover only significant residues of harmful pesticide, so that any residue finding was cause for alarm. Three decades later, scientific advances have enabled regulators to detect increasingly minute traces of residue on foods. Because it is impossible to determine which fruits and vegetables will end up in a can and which in the fresh-produce section, regulators have permitted pesticide residues on both types of food as long as the residues pose no more than a "negligible risk" of causing cancer. [22]

Pesticide Use Rises

While the EPA has stopped the sale of some long-lived chlorinated hydrocarbons in the United States, it has done little to curtail the overall use of pesticides. American farmers today apply greater quantities of pesticide than ever before; an estimated 817 million pounds of active ingredients were used in 1991 alone. And they have more varieties than ever to choose from: about 600 ingredients contained in 23,000 pesticides registered with the EPA.[23]

Herbicides, or weedkillers, are the most commonly used pesticides today, accounting for about 495 million pounds, or two-thirds, of all agricultural pesticides used in 1991. By destroying plants that compete with crops for water, nutrients, air and light, herbicides boost yields. They also reduce labor costs by eliminating the need for labor-intensive hand weeding.

The vast majority of herbicides are used on corn, wheat, soybeans and cotton. Because many of the newly developed herbicides, such as atrazine and alachlor, are applied to fields before food crops are planted, they are less apt to be found as residues in food than insecticides or fungicides, which are applied directly to the fully developed food crops, or even after harvest.

Modern insecticides are used on a far broader segment of food crops than herbicides. They tend to be shorter-lived than DDT, but far more toxic. For this reason, insecticides are applied in smaller amounts to individual crops. Still, U.S. growers applied some 175 million pounds of insecticide in 1991. By eliminating bugs that can bore into plants, leaving holes and blemishes, these agents not only help boost crop yields but also improve the appearance of fresh produce. The new insecticide varieties include compounds known as organophosphates, such as parathion and malathion, as well as carbamates, including the highly toxic aldicarb, used on a wide variety of fruits and vegetables. Other insecticides are made of synthetic chemicals called pyrethrins, which are much less toxic to mammals.

Due to changes in farming techniques, farmers can use less fungicide today to kill molds on some crops, such as peanuts and wheat, but they continue to apply it heavily to fruits and vegetables. Because these crops cover much more acreage than they did 20 years ago, the amount of fungicide applied nationwide has remained steady at about 75 million pounds. By protecting plants from fungal infections that can produce aflatoxin, a poison to humans, fungicides are among the few pesticides that actually prevent consumers from geting sick.

Public Alarmed by Contamination Reports

Despite the substitution of DDT with shorter-lived pesticides, reports of contamination continue to surface. In 1989, for example, the Natural Resources Defense Council reported that Alar, a pesticide used on apples, may be harmful to humans, especially children, who consume more apples than adults. Although the report's conclusion was criticized as overly alarming, Alar was already under review by EPA, which subsequently blocked its use.

Later the same year, food inspectors reported unacceptably high concentrations of cyanide on grapes imported from Chile, further alarming consumers about the safety of the food supply.

Human exposure to pesticides is not limited to food residues, however. Consumers routinely come into contact with insecticides in a wide range of products, including lawn and garden chemicals, flea collars, sprays to kill termites, ants or roaches, and shampoo to kill head lice. In addition, handlers of these toxic chemicals, including farmworkers and lawn-care workers, are exposed to toxic levels of pesticide through faulty application or accidental spills. ■

CURRENT SITUATION

Pressure for Reform

After years of deadlock over the procedure for setting pesticide tolerances in raw and processed foods, Congress may finally be driven to draft new pesticide legislation. The Natural Resources Defense Council and other environmental and consumer groups sued EPA, charging that its policy of allowing residues that pose only a "negligible risk" of causing cancer violates the Delaney clause prohibiting any traces of cancer-causing pesticides in processed foods.

In July 1992, the 9th U.S. Circuit Court of Appeals in San Francisco ruled in favor of the plaintiffs in the case, *Les v. Reilly.* The court found that EPA did not have the right to dilute the Delaney clause's strict standard and must apply its terms literally. On Feb. 22, 1993, the U.S. Supreme Court upheld that decision. Unless Congress rewrites the law, EPA would likely be forced to ban dozens of commonly used pesticides in the United States.

"Efforts have been made for years to arrive at appropriate reforms to address the problems posed by the Delaney clause," said Sen. Nancy Landon Kassebaum, R-Kan., "but consensus has eluded us. Now we no longer have the luxury of time to resolve this issue."[24]

EPA identified 32 pesticides used on 29 different crops that may be banned as a result of the ruling. Because the cancer-causing potential of many other pesticides has yet to be determined, Kassebaum said that the decision could force EPA to revoke as many as 60 tolerances affecting up to 100 different crops, causing widespread economic hardship. "Increased costs of vegetables and fruit would deleteriously affect the health of low-income people," proclaimed an editorial in *Science* magazine. "Benefits to public health would be negligible." [25]

Not everyone agrees that EPA is required to act, however. Aguirre of the food processors association says the agency has failed to take advantage of another provision in the law that would permit it to declare a processed food safe if the pesticide residue in it does not exceed that allowed for the raw commodities it contains. "We think that EPA has not given appropriate attention to or made proper use of that provision," he says. "EPA has ample discretion to rethink its interpretation to minimize the scope of the Delaney clause, so that while we may still need new legislation, we would not see a major disruption in the food supply and hurt many agribusinesses and small farmers."

Reports Cite Danger

Calls for reform of pesticide law mounted in 1993 with the publication of several scientific studies implicating pesticides in various public health problems.

In April, a study linking DDT and breast cancer raised the issue of the potential hormonal effects of certain pesticides. [26] DDT was suspected of contributing to the development of breast cancer because it acts on human tissue in the same way as estrogen, a female hormone that is known to cause cancer under prolonged exposure.

Sen. Alfonse M. D'Amato, R-N.Y., greeted the findings with special interest because of an abnormally high rate of breast cancer among his female constituents in parts of Long Island. The rate is especially high among women living in housing developments in Nassau and Suffolk counties that were built on abandoned potato fields that had been treated with high concentrations of DDT to kill the golden nematode. D'Amato took EPA to task for failing to restrict 10 pesticides that cause mammary cancer in rats, even though the link to human breast cancer has yet to be proved definitively.

"I think the EPA's inaction on this matter is inexcusable, especially since the cost of screening to manufacturers is less than those of health and safety tests the EPA already requires," he said. "If we act now to determine

Restricting Hazardous Pesticides

*Many of the pesticides deemed particularly hazardous by the Pesticide Action Network are banned or restricted by nations throughout the world, including the United States, Canada and Mexico, new trading partners in the North American Free Trade Agreement (NAFTA) ***

■ Banned
⧅ Severely Restricted

	Canada	Mexico	United States	Total Banned or Severely Restricted*
Aldicarb (Temik)	⧅			13
Camphechlor (Toxaphene)		■		45
Chlordane		⧅	⧅	48
Heptachlor		■	⧅	43
Chlordimeform	■		■	51
DBCP	■	■	■	51
DDT		⧅	■	64
Aldrin	⧅	■	■	58
Dieldrin	⧅	■	■	66
Endrin		■	■	51
EDB	■		⧅	32
HCH/BHC		■	■	49
Lindane				28
Paraquat				10
Parathion				19
Methyl Parathion				11
Pentachlorophenol	⧅	⧅	⧅	33
2.4.5-T		■	■	46

** Pesticides without symbols are not banned or severely restricted.*
*** The totals represent the 78 countries from which data were available.*
Source: Pesticide Action Network International, May 1993

which pesticides are estrogenic, then we will be in a far better position to take the needed steps to protect the public should the science provide a conclusive link to cancer. I believe it will." [27]

The breast cancer study was especially alarming to some observers because many other pesticides that are in use today also have estrogenic effects in mammals. For example, atrazine, the most widely used herbicide, causes mammary cancer in laboratory animals. Other pesticides, including alachlor and dicofol, are known to interrupt normal endocrine activity, causing developmental and reproductive problems in animals. [28] Under current regulations, however, EPA does not routinely evaluate pesticides for dangerous hormonal effects.

Another study, released in May by EPA, announced that 132 different pesticides or their derivatives had been detected in groundwater in 45 states. [29] Although the agency said the levels of contamination fell short of posing an immediate threat to public health, the findings revealed that modern pesticides apparently are not as short-lived in the environment as was once believed. EPA announced that it would issue new rules in 1994 to protect groundwater from further contamination.

Lawmakers received yet another push to rewrite pesticide law in June, when the National Academy of Sciences released the results of its six-year study of the effects of pesticides on infants and children. The authors concluded that current regulations do not adequately protect children from pesticides in the food supply and recommended that pesticides be tested for toxicity in children and strictly limited if found to pose a threat to this vulnerable group. They specifically recommended that regulators place less emphasis on the economic benefits of pesticide use than they currently do when setting tolerances for residues in food.

"Children should be able to eat a healthful diet containing legal residues without encroaching on safety margins," the academy's study concluded. "This goal should be kept clear." [30]

Clinton Proposal

The Clinton administration, with strong support from Vice President Gore, an outspoken environmentalist, came to Washington with the enthusiastic endorsement of environmental and consumer advocacy organizations. It was thus not surprising when the administration responded to the events of 1993 with proposals to reform the pesticide laws. On Sept. 21, EPA, FDA and the Agriculture Department released a sweeping plan that featured a compromise in the debate over residue tolerances and emphasized health concerns over economic interests.

The plan calls for a new, single standard for pesticide residue tolerances that would replace the Delaney clause. Tolerances would be set for both raw and processed foods on the basis of a "reasonable certainty that no harm" would result, defined as no more than a one-in-a-million chance of causing cancer over a lifetime of exposure. Regulators would ignore most considerations of the economic benefits of pesticide use, which weigh heavily under current law, when setting tolerances for raw foods.

The administration's proposed change has long been sought by environmental and health interests. At the same time, the Clinton standard would not absolutely forbid all traces of cancer-causing residues in processed food, as the Delaney clause now mandates. This change is supported by growers and the food industry but strongly opposed by environmental and consumer advocacy groups.

The Clinton plan embodies many of the recommendations of the National Academy of Sciences in its June report on pesticides in children's diets. EPA Administrator Carol M. Browner recommended that tolerances be determined by their effects on children and infants rather than adults. "This administration is committed to making the 1990s a period of significant change in pesticide use and regulation," Browner said, adding that a central goal of the plan is to "provide additional assurance that our children are protected from pesticide risks." [31]

The plan also recommends that growers adopt pesticide-reduction methods, a primary goal of consumer groups and environmentalists involved in the issue. "We were very encouraged by the administration's statement that it intended to do whatever it could to promote use reduction," says Kristen Rand, a lawyer for Consumers Union, a consumer advocacy group that publishes *Consumer Reports* magazine. Even before Congress adopts a new pesticide law, she says, "We'd like to see the administration do as much as it can administratively toward that goal." Under prodding by the group, the Agriculture Department already has begun a pilot program to introduce food with no detectable pesticide residues into the school-lunch program it administers.

However, the companies that produce pesticides object to attempts to reduce pesticide use across-the-board. "We ought to talk in terms of risk reduction," says McCarthy of the agricultural chemicals association. "Use reduction may not be risk reduction because you may decrease the use of something and turn to an alternative that is riskier."

Finally, the Clinton proposal would speed up the registration process and the removal of pesticides found to be harmful, and require the testing and reregistration of all pesticides every 15 years. ■

Continued on p. 90

At Issue:

Do pesticides accumulate in the environment, posing a growing risk of cancer and other diseases?

yes

Dr. Theo Colburn

Senior Scientist, World Wildlife Fund

FROM *TESTIMONY BEFORE THE HOUSE ENERGY AND COMMERCE SUBCOMMITTEE ON HEALTH AND THE ENVIRONMENT,* OCT. 21, 1993.

An analysis of the information that has been generated over the past decade concerning the health effects of agricultural and industrial chemicals reveals that since the late 1930s, society has released large volumes of a great number of chemicals into the environment that act like or interfere with hormones, neurotransmitters, growth factors and inhibiting substances: compounds naturally produced by the body that control the development and function of vital physiological systems. . . .

Wildlife, laboratory animal, and human studies reveal that as a result of exposure in the womb of mammals including humans, or the eggs of birds, fish and reptiles, to chemicals of this nature, the endocrine, immune, and nervous systems of embryos do not develop normally. . . .

In the past it has been argued that these effects are insignificant compared with the benefits reaped from the use of agricultural chemicals. We can safely argue now that at the individual level the effects can be devastating. At the population level the effects could have significant social and economic impacts, far outweighing any benefits. . . .

It is important . . . to realize that our biosphere is saturated with chemicals that cause functional disorders. Humans are now carrying burdens of both industrial and agricultural chemicals at concentrations at which adverse endocrine, immune and reproductive effects have been reported in affected wildlife and laboratory animals. There is growing evidence that some of these humans also have been affected as a result of their parents' exposure. . . .

Unfortunately, most of the pesticides that were used in the past and are still in use today have not been tested for effects of this nature. Most of past testing focused on the individuals directly exposed and not on the functionality of their offspring. It is reassuring however, that protocols for studies of this nature are now being developed at the EPA Health Effects Research Laboratory. . . . The mothers whose babies have been, and are being, exposed to these chemicals in the womb had no choice. We now know enough to inspire grave concern about the fate of future generations.

Because so many chemicals of this nature already exist in the environment, it is cavalier to think that the global environment can assimilate more and not suffer dire consequences. Our goal should not be to replace old chemicals with new chemicals, but rather to seek non-chemical alternatives to meet the demands placed on agriculture and industry to meet society's needs.

no

Dennis T. Avery

Director, Global Food Issues Center, Hudson Institute, Indianapolis, Ind.

FROM *BIODIVERSITY: SAVING SPECIES WITH BIOTECHNOLOGY, HUDSON INSTITUTE,* 1993.

It is habitat loss, not chemicals, that we should be guarding against most diligently.

Why the misunderstanding? Rachel Carson's book *The Silent Spring* is responsible for some of it. . . . We know several things for certain, however, that Rachel Carson did not know.

First and foremost, we know that the natural chemicals within the foods we eat test out as toxic in our rat tests as frequently and about as dangerously as the synthetic chemicals she feared so deeply. Moreover, because we eat much larger amounts of them, these natural chemicals represent roughly a *thousand times greater* risk than do pesticide residues. The caffeic acid in lettuce, apples and carrots, the limonene in orange juice, and the hydrazines in mushrooms are all carcinogenic in rat tests. Many other foods contain natural carcinogens. We don't die from these carcinogens, because our bodies are able to handle such small carcinogenic insults from a wide variety of sources. It is only the large, repeated insults such as smoking. . . that have been directly linked to cancer.

In fact, health professionals throughout the U.S. are now aggressively telling their patients to eat twice as many fruits and vegetables as they do now, because this is the best known protection against cancer and heart disease — no matter what approved chemicals were used in their production. In cancer as in most other things, the dose makes the poison. Carson's theory of "cumulative pollution" is bunk. Her irrational fear of manmade chemicals has been revealed as hysteria. We have yet to find even *one* victim of pesticide residues. . . .

The opposition to pesticides is based on dubious factors such as the following:

- Discredited studies such as the one the Natural Resources Defense Council trotted out for its Alar scare.
- The almost mystical belief that manmade chemicals are more dangerous than "natural" chemicals.

These beliefs are untenable, however. In the Alar case, the EPA rejected the study presented by the NRDC because no cancer risk was found when the study was repeatedly run. And the belief in the extraordinary virulence of manmade chemicals is refuted by the fact that about half of both the manmade *and the natural* chemicals tested in our rat-tumor procedure have been ranked as carcinogens of about equal danger. . . .

The good news, then, is that the judicious use of modern pesticides can increase agricultural yields without creating any significant increase in the risk of developing cancer.

Tips on Cleaning Fruits and Vegetables

In spite of recent reports linking pesticides with cancer and other diseases, doctors warn consumers not to overreact by eating fewer fruits and vegetables.

"We are not saying that parents should rush out and radically change their children's diets to avoid certain foods," said Dr. Philip J. Landrigan, a professor of pediatrics at Mount Sinai School of Medicine in New York City and chairman of the National Academy of Sciences' recent study of pesticides in children's diets. "We do not say in our report that some particular food is terribly dangerous for children and needs immediately to be discarded. Parents should continue to emphasize fruits and vegetables in their children's diets." † Fresh produce is considered an important source of fiber and nutrients that help combat heart disease, high blood pressure and diabetes, as well as cancer.

Food scientists do suggest, however, that consumers follow a few simple safety tips for eliminating any pesticide residues from fresh produce:

- Wash fresh fruits and vegetables with water and scrub with a brush when appropriate.
- Remove the outer leaves of leafy vegetables, such as lettuce and cabbage.
- Peel and cook fruits and vegetables when appropriate, although some nutrients and fiber are lost when produce is peeled.

† National Research Council, *Pesticides in the Diets of Infants and Children* (1993). Landrigan made his comments June 28, 1993, on releasing the report.

OUTLOOK

Action This Session?

The Clinton administration has yet to introduce legislation incorporating its proposals for pesticide reform. Many lawmakers, sensitive to the conflicting interests that have stymied passage of pesticide reform for years, are reserving judgment until the White House formally submits its proposal to Congress.

"The administration's food safety plan announced in September is a credible start on the path toward reform," said Rep. Synar. "I believe many elements of the package as described up to now must be more precisely articulated so that we can better judge their likely effectiveness." [32]

Meanwhile, other lawmakers are going ahead with proposals of their own. "It is unconscionable that it has taken so long to solve the festering problems of food safety, and the federal government has clearly done an inadequate job of protecting the American people," said Sen. Kennedy. [33] While supporting the Clinton administration's proposals in concept, Kennedy is cosponsoring legislation with Rep. Waxman that would allow "negligible" pesticide residues in all foods, with more stringent standards for foods that figure heavily in children's diets, such as apples and bananas. The bill would go further than the Clinton proposal by eliminating all economic considerations of pesticide use when setting residue standards.

The food and chemicals industries have thrown their support behind legislation sponsored by Reps. Lehman, Bliley and Rowland. Under their bill, the Food Quality Protection Act, regulators would be required to continue considering the benefits of pesticide use, as well as potential health risks, in determining tolerances for all foods.

"Clearly, it would be ideal to live in a pesticide-free environment," Lehman testified Sept. 21. "But until we can achieve a pest management system that works entirely without chemicals, we need to act within current limitations. We must also consider the consumer who may take for granted the high quality and low cost of our domestic agricultural market but who understands the importance [that] eating a large variety of fruits and vegetables has in their diet."

Environmental and consumer advocacy groups are hedging their bets on pesticide reform. Most are disappointed that all major proposals now before Congress have abandoned the outright prohibition of all traces of cancer-causing pesticides currently mandated by the Delaney clause.

Even the Kennedy-Waxman bill falls short of expectations. "As introduced, it's going in the right direction, but it needs some improvements," says Rand of Consumers Union. "We will support it only if certain changes are made, the major one being that it include a phaseout of the most hazardous chemicals."

Participants in the longstanding debate over pesticide regulations generally expect Congress finally to enact reform legislation this year. But most are awaiting the Clinton administration's proposal, expected early this year, before they take a final stand on any bill.

Some agricultural experts, however, are looking far beyond regulatory reform. "It's great that the administration has set a goal of moving toward integrated pest management," says Janke of the Rodale Institute. "Now, however, they need to go further and give us a precise definition of what that means to farmers. Only then can we get people to adopt alternatives to pesticides." ■

Notes

[1] Food manufacturers must begin using the new labels, which will depict the ingredients in larger type and provide more information about nutrition and fats, by May 8, 1994. For background, see "Food Safety," *The CQ Researcher*, June 4, 1993, pp. 481-504.

[2] Goldman testified Oct. 29, 1993, before the House Government Operations Subcommittee on Environment, Energy and Natural Resources.

[3] National Research Council, *Pesticides in the Diets of Infants and Children* (1993).

[4] Mary S. Wolff, Paolo G. Toniolo, Eric W. Lee, Marilyn Rivera and Neil Dubin, "Blood Levels of Organocholorine Residues and Risk of Breast Cancer," *Journal of the National Cancer Institute*, April 21, 1993.

[5] Al Meyerhoff, "No More Pesticides for Dinner," *The New York Times*, March 9, 1993.

[6] Mary S. Wolff, et al, *op. cit.*

[7] Wiles testified Oct. 21, 1993, before the House Energy and Commerce Subcommittee on Health and the Environment.

[8] Environmental Working Group, *Pesticides in Children's Food*, June 1993.

[9] National Research Council, *op. cit.*, The council is the administrative arm of the National Academy of Sciences.

[10] AZM was responsible for 15 separate fish kills in Louisiana in 1991 alone. See Ted Williams, "Hard Views on Soft Pesticides," *Audubon*, March-April 1993, pp. 30-40.

[11] Guillette presented his findings at the Oct. 21 hearing of the House Health and the Environment Subcommittee.

[12] Graham testified Sept. 21, 1993, at joint hearings of the Senate Labor and Human Resources Committee and the House Energy and Commerce Subcommittee on Health and the Environment.

[13] Gianessi testified at the Sept. 21, 1993, joint hearings.

[14] Quoted by Anita Manning, "Clones May Wilt Use of Pesticides." *USA Today*, Nov. 26, 1993. For more on the Human Genome Project, see "Gene Therapy," *The CQ Researcher*, Oct. 18, 1991, pp. 777-800.

[15] Goldburg testified July 27, 1993, before the House Government Operations Subcommittee on Human Resources and Intergovernmental Relations.

[16] Unless otherwise noted, information in this section is derived from the National Research Council, *op. cit.*

[17] *Ibid*, p. 16.

[18] Rachel Carson, *Silent Spring* (1962), p. 8.

[19] Sen. Al Gore, *Earth in the Balance* (1992), p. 52.

[20] Martin testified Oct. 29, 1993, before the House Government Operations Subcommittee on the Environment, Energy and Natural Resources.

[21] Synar testified at the Sept. 21, 1993, joint hearing.

[22] For more information on this issue, see the National Academy of Sciences, *Regulating Pesticides in Food: The Delaney Paradox* (1987).

[23] See William M. Layden, "Food Safety: A Patchwork System," *The G.A.O. Journal*, spring/summer 1992, p. 50.

[24] Kassebaum testified at the joint hearing of Sept. 21, 1993.

[25] Philip H. Abelson, "Pesticides and Food," *Science*, Feb. 26, 1993, p. 1235.

[26] Wolff et al, *op. cit.*

[27] D'Amato spoke at the Sept. 21 joint hearing.

[28] See Joe Thornton, *Chlorine, Human Health and Environment: The Breast Cancer Warning*, October 1993.

[29] Environmental Protection Agency, *Pesticides in Ground Water Database — A Compilation of Monitoring Studies: 1971-1991*, May 14, 1993.

[30] National Research Council, *op. cit.*, pp. 8-9.

[31] Browner testified on the administration plan Sept. 21, 1993, before the House Agriculture Subcommittee on Department Operations and Nutrition.

[32] Synar spoke Oct. 29, 1993, while opening the hearings on EPA's pesticide reregistration program.

[33] Kennedy testified at the Sept. 21 hearings on the administration proposal.

Bibliography

Selected Sources Used

Books

Carson, Rachel, *Silent Spring*, Houghton Mifflin, 1962.
Carson, a marine biologist with the U.S. Fish and Wildlife Service, sparked a public outcry with her evidence that DDT and other chlorinated hydrocarbons used as pesticides were seriously hurting the environment. Her bestseller is credited with playing a key role in launching the environmental movement of the following decades.

Bormann, F. Herbert, and Stephen R. Kellert, eds., *Ecology, Economics, Ethics: The Broken Circle*, Yale University Press, 1991.
Environmental policies that fail to address the economic and moral burdens imposed on future generations by resource depletion today fall short of their purpose, the authors of this collection of essays write. A chapter on pesticides by David Pimentel, an entomologist at Cornell University, proposes cutting pesticide use in half.

Gore, Sen. Al, *Earth in the Balance: Ecology and the Human Spirit*, Houghton Mifflin, 1992.
Written before the author became vice president in the Clinton administration, this volume reflects Gore's longstanding interest in environmental affairs. In calling for a more rational use of pesticides, he cites an unintended effect of prolonged pesticide use: the development of increasingly resistant pests that require ever stronger applications of chemicals to control.

World Resources Institute, *The 1992 Information Please Environmental Almanac*, Houghton Mifflin, 1992.
The section on food contains valuable information on the most commonly used pesticides and the crops with which they are used. It also summarizes the terms of current pesticide laws and addresses the issue of pesticide exports, which may return to this country as residues in imported foods.

Articles

"Getting the Lead Out at the FDA," *Business Week*, Oct. 25, 1993.
Food and Drug Administration Commissioner David A. Kessler gets generally high marks for his efforts to speed enforcement action, crack down on fraudulent claims by manufacturers and streamline the agency's review process of new products it regulates.

Layden, William M., "Food Safety: A Patchwork System," *The G.A.O. Journal*, spring/summer 1992.
This extensive review of the federal regulatory system governing food safety concludes that it is rife with inconsistencies. "Its magnitude notwithstanding, this regulatory system did not develop under any rational plan," the author writes. "Programs emerged piecemeal, typically in response to particular health threats or economic crises."

Lee, Charles S., "Pass the Peaches, Hold the Poison," *Newsweek*, Nov. 15, 1993.
Scientists at Pennsylvania's Rodale Institute and other research centers reportedly are discovering many ways to reduce pesticide use while maintaining high crop yields. In the wake of recent reports linking pesticides with diseases, the search for alternative farming methods seems likely to accelerate, according to the author.

"Water: The Power, Promise, and Turmoil of North America's Fresh Water," *National Geographic*, special edition, 1993.
Among the many threats to the U.S. water supply is pollution from pesticides, the magazine says. Moreover, the contamination of whales that consume pesticide-tainted fish illustrates the fact that these chemicals also wreak havoc on wildlife as well.

Youth, Howard, "Flying into Trouble," *World Watch*, January/February 1994.
Although DDT was banned in 1972, pesticides have continued to kill wild bird populations in the United States. Granular carbofuran, for example, killed tens of thousands of birds in Virginia before EPA banned it in 1991. Meanwhile, DDT continues to take its toll on birds in Africa, where the pesticide still is commonly applied.

Reports and Studies

National Research Council, *Alternative Agriculture*, National Academy Press, 1989.
Because pesticides and chemical fertilizers are considered the main sources of water pollution, scientists are searching for farming methods that produce high yields without the use of chemicals. This study identifies numerous alternatives to conventional farming that require closer crop management and exploit naturally occurring pest-control methods.

National Research Council, *Pesticides in the Diets of Infants and Children*, National Academy Press, 1993.
This long-awaited report provides disturbing evidence that children are exposed to potentially harmful levels of pesticides in their daily diets. The report recommends that standards for pesticide residues in foods be set according to their potential damage to children, not adults.

The Next Step

Additional information from UMI's Newspaper & Periodical Abstracts database

Alternatives to Pesticides

Fanselow, Julie, "Organics: Hot debate," *Vegetarian Times*, August 1993, p. 16.
Rick Ihler's farm in Idaho was among the state's first to be certified chemical-free. Ihler was surprised when told he was in violation of Idaho's pesticide law for using a garlic and chili pepper mix to kill insects in his fields. The debate over the law and organic farming is discussed.

Gianessi, Leonard, "Viewpoint: Why chemical-free farming won't work," *Consumers' Research Magazine*, December 1993, pp. 15-18.
The goal of substituting non-chemical for chemical means of pest control is a politically popular one. However, some non-chemical alternatives may be as hazardous as the chemical pesticides they seek to replace, Gianessi says

Holden, Constance, "Organic farming with cocaine," *Science*, Oct. 29, 1993, p. 651.
Researchers at Massachusetts General Hospital suggest that the leaves of coca plants may be a natural pesticide. The pesticidal properties of cocaine are discussed.

Simons, Paul, "Could marigolds slay killer mosquitoes?" *New Scientist*, July 17, 1993, p. 18.
Chemists have discovered how marigolds ward off pests from neighboring plants—they give off volatile insecticides. The discovery has far-reaching implications because the marigold insecticide is especially toxic to the mosquitoes that carry malaria and yellow fever.

Spencer, Leslie, "Ban all plants — They pollute," *Forbes*, Oct. 25, 1993, pp. 104-108.
Organically grown tomatoes are about as likely to give one cancer as are the pesticides, Spencer writes. Moreover, she writes, naturally occurring pesticides in plants can cause cancer in rats as frequently as the synthetic ones.

Children and Pesticides

"Food pesticides may pose additional risk to children," *Medical World News*, July 15, 1993, p. 14.
Two new reports suggest that infants and children may be at increased risk of health problems due to pesticides on fruits and vegetables. A report issued by the National Academy of Sciences recommends that government agencies look at the diets of children and infants separately from adults, instead of calculating pesticide exposure for the population as a whole.

Marwick, Charles, "Pesticides pose concern about children's diet," *JAMA: The Journal of the American Medical Association*, Aug. 18, 1993, pp. 802-805.
The National Research Council is recommending that changes be made in regulating pesticides used on food products to reflect the "unique characteristics of the diets of infants and children." The concern over pesticides in children's diets is discussed.

"NRC report spurs changes in policies on pesticides in foods," *Nation's Health*, August 1993, p. 24.
The National Research Council has released a report calling on the government to change its method of measuring pesticides in foods. The current method ignores the differences between infants, children and adults.

Dealing with Pesticides

Hearn, Wayne, "Advising parents about pesticide peril, in wake of studies," *American Medical News*, Aug. 9, 1993, p. 12.
One of the best ways parents can minimize the danger from exposure to pesticides in fruits and vegetables is by eating a wide variety of fresh produce, Hearn writes. Doing so provides exposure to a wider variety of pesticides but less exposure to any one pesticide.

Kuczka, Susan, "Suburbs fight state on pesticide power," *Chicago Tribune*, Nov. 16, 1993, p. 2NW10.
Mayor Al Larson said that Schaumburg, Ill., and other northwest suburban communities will press ahead with a lawsuit challenging the state law that eliminates the authority of local governments to regulate the use of pesticides despite a move by the state attorney general's office to dismiss the suit.

Schindeler, Janice, "Pesticide claims cause consumer confusion," *Houston Post*, July 21, 1993, p. F1.
Janice Schindeler comments on grocery shopping in an era of pesticides, microorganisms, irradiation and the importance of nutritional information, saying that shoppers must now be math whizzes, and nutrition experts in addition to studying microbiology, toxicology, chemistry and environmental science.

Zupke, Mary, "Are pesticides in produce hurting your family?" *Ladies' Home Journal*, November 1993, p. 263.
There is concern that eating fresh fruits and vegetables can actually cause harm due to the pesticides used on them. Tips on preparing foods to reduce the dangers are presented.

The Federal Government

Hanson, David, "Pesticides and food safety: Administration proposes broad reforms," *Chemical & Engineering News*, Sept. 27, 1993, pp. 6-7.

The Clinton administration recently unveiled a broad reform policy for pesticides and food safety that will reduce the risks posed by pesticide use to Americans. Details of the reform policy are discussed.

Hermann, Mindy, "Pesticide alert," *American Health*, October 1993, p. 89.

Following a report indicating the government should be doing a better job controlling pesticide use on produce, the FDA, EPA and USDA are making a coordinated effort to reduce use of pesticides on the U.S.'s food supply.

Lauter, David, "Pesticide flap threatened crucial deal," *Los Angeles Times*, Nov. 18, 1993, p. A17.

In the final hours before the roll was called on the North American Free Trade Agreement, senior Clinton administration officials scrambled to defuse an uproar over a powerful pesticide before the controversy could unravel a key deal with members of Congress.

Meyerhoff, Al, "We must get rid of pesticides in the food supply," *USA Today: The Magazine of the American Scene*, November 1993, pp. 51-53.

Pesticides are deadly chemicals that can cause cancer, birth defects and neurological damage. The federal government's pesticide regulatory regime has failed repeatedly. The Clinton administration has called for national pesticide reform legislation.

"Reform would reduce pesticide use," *Farm Journal* (Central Edition), November 1993, p. D3.

President Clinton's proposed reform of pesticide and food-safety laws would scrap the Delaney clause and replace it with a consistent standard of "reasonable certainty of no harm" from pesticide-treated foods. The proposal is discussed.

"Washington wire: Food-safety delays," *The Wall Street Journal*, Nov. 26, 1993, p. A1.

Two months after proclaiming a new policy on pesticide regulation in early fall 1993, Clinton officials have not proposed a bill to carry it out. Few changes have been made in meat inspection despite Agriculture Secretary Mike Espy's pledge for an overhaul.

"White House seeks to break deadlock over pesticide policy," *Nation's Health*, October 1993, p. 4.

On Sept. 21, 1993, the Clinton administration delivered to Congress a blueprint for marrying two statutes that govern pesticide use and food safety and for grounding those laws in public health, not economic concerns. The deadlock over pesticide policy, the two statutes in question and proposed standards are discussed.

Pesticides Internationally

Bradley, David, "How to rob flies of their youth," *New Scientist*, Oct. 23, 1993, p. 15.

By working out the structure of a growth-and-reproduction hormone found in some flies, Australian chemists have come a step closer to making insecticides that block the hormone's action, killing the flies.

Lambrecht, Bill, "Chemical misuse makes land a Valley of Death," *St. Louis Post-Dispatch*, Nov. 28, 1993, p. A1.

The Dominican Republic's lush mountains and valleys with their bountiful plantations once stood as an agricultural showcase among developing countries, but now farmers call the land the "Valley of Death" because of the abuse of pesticides.

Lambrecht, Bill, "One worker's conclusion: Settling case was mistake," *St. Louis Post-Dispatch*, Nov. 14, 1993, p. A7.

Luis Chavez is among thousands of Central American banana workers who have accepted settlements for sterility and injuries suffered from working with the pesticide DBCP.

McConnell, Rob and Allan J. Hruska, "An epidemic of pesticide poisoning in Nicaragua: Implications for prevention in developing countries," *American Journal of Public Health*, November 1993, pp. 1559-1562.

A study was conducted to demonstrate the usefulness of the Northwestern Nicaraguan Ministry of Health surveillance system for detecting pesticide poisonings. During Jun-July 1987, an epidemic of 548 pesticide poisonings was detected in northwestern Nicaragua.

"Patently problematic," *Environment*, December 1993, p. 22.

Farmers in India are protesting a provision in the General Agreement on Tariff and Trade that Western patent laws be applied worldwide. Farmers believe they will no longer be able to obtain pesticides freely from native trees.

"Spare the pest and save the farmer," *New Scientist*, Oct. 30, 1993, p. 6.

A group of agricultural economists has suggested that pesticides used by rice farmers in the Philippines may cost the farmers more in medical bills than they earn from the extra rice they harvest. The Philippine government is encouraging farmers to give up pesticide use in favor of integrated pest management.

Research and Studies

Horowitz, John K. and Erik Lichtenberg, "Insurance, moral hazard, and chemical use in agriculture," *American Journal of Agricultural Economics*, November 1993, pp. 926-935.

A study examines how crop insurance affects corn farmers' fertilizer and pesticide use in the Midwest. The results suggest that insurance exerts considerable influence on corn farmers' chemical-use decisions.

Isensee, A. R. and A.M. Sadeghi, "Impact of tillage practice on runoff and pesticide transport," *Journal of Soil & Water Conservation*, November 1993, pp. 523-527.
A two-year study was conducted to evaluate the effect of no-till and conventional-till corn production practices on pesticide loss in runoff from natural rainfall. Runoff was measured, and runoff water samples were analyzed for atrazine, cyanazine and alachlor. The results are discussed.

"Pesticide report available," FDA Consumer, December 1993, p. 3.
According to the 1992 report of the FDA's pesticide monitoring program, almost 99 percent of food produced in the U.S. and over 96 percent of imports from 94 countries have either no pesticide residues or the levels detected are well within permitted limits set by the EPA.

"Pesticide residues are linked to breast cancer," *Better Nutrition for Today's Living*, November 1993, p. 22.
Women with high blood levels of dichlorodiphenyldichloroethylene (DDE), a chemical from the pesticide DDT, have an increased risk of breast cancer, according to a study of women in New York City. The link between pesticide residues and breast cancer is discussed.

Willis, Winnie O., Ann de Peyster, Craig A. Molgaard, Christine Walker and Tom MacKendrick, "Pregnancy outcome among women exposed to pesticides through work or residence in an agricultural area," *Journal of Occupational Medicine*, September 1993, pp. 943-949.
A study on pregnancy outcome among women exposed to pesticides through work or residence in an agricultural area found no difference between exposed and unexposed women regarding the risk of preterm birth or toxemia. Additional results are discussed.

Solutions to the Pesticide Debate

Gunset, George, "Wild tomato offers major clue to crop disease resistance," *Chicago Tribune*, Nov. 27, 1993, p. 1.
Purdue University agronomist Greg Martin's research, along with others', could shine light on the secret to crop plant resistance to diseases and reduce the need for chemical pesticides, Gunset writes. Martin was the lead researcher in a project at Cornell University that used a new method of gene isolation to clone a disease-resistant gene from a wild tomato plant.

Lichtenberg, Erik, Robert C. Spear and David Zilberman, "The economics of reentry regulation of pesticides," *American Journal of Agricultural Economics*, November 1993, pp. 946-958.
Government agencies frequently try to protect the public from industrial hazards by separating the two in time and/or space, according to the authors. A methodology for one such policy, re-entry regulation of pesticides, is developed.

Manning, Anita, "Clones may wilt use of pesticides," *USA Today*, Nov. 26, 1993, p. A1.
A disease-resistant gene from a crop plant has been successfully cloned for the first time using a technique that could lead to reduced use of pesticides.

Putnam, Clare, "Personal alarm flushes out aphids," *New Scientist*, Oct. 2, 1993, p. 14.
A group of Dutch scientists recently discovered that if aphids are exposed to the active chemical present in their "alarm" pheromone, they emerge from lettuce and can be killed by relatively small amounts of insecticide.

Stanley, Doris, "Scientists seek limits on pear pests," *Agricultural Research*, November 1993, pp. 4-9.
If scientists are successful in seeking limits on pear pests, it could mean expansion of the U.S. commercial production areas, Stanley writes. Efforts toward this goal, which include breeding new pear varieties, are discussed.

Whelan, Elizabeth, "Proposed food safety laws are starved for scientific merit," *Insight on the News*, Nov. 1, 1993, pp. 30-31.
The Clinton administration's proposal to revamp U.S. food safety and pesticide laws offers something to please and aggravate all parties in the pesticide debate, Whelan writes. There is no scientific consensus on the health risk of pesticides, and thus no scientific basis for increased regulation, she says.

Uses of Pesticides

Bonvie, Linda, Bill Bonvie and Michelle Kodis, "Flying in the mist," *Earth Journal*, November 1993, pp. 38-43.
The use of pesticides to disinfect airplanes on international flights is discussed. Most passengers are never warned that they are being exposed to these chemicals, which present definite health risks.

Richards, Rhonda, "Air quality on jets questioned again," *USA Today*, Dec. 21, 1993, p. B8.
The environmental magazine *Buzzworm's Earth Journal* is breathing new life into the controversy over air quality in airline cabins with its report that insecticides that are routinely sprayed toward overhead bins during some international flights are hazardous to passengers.

Back Issues

Great Research on Current Issues Starts Right Here...Recent topics covered by The CQ Researcher are listed below. Before May 1991, reports were published under the name of Editorial Research Reports.

JULY 1992
Alternative Energy
Prescription Drug Prices
Alzheimer's Disease
Infant Mortality

AUGUST 1992
The Homeless
Work, Family and Stress
NATO's Changing Role
Marine Mammals vs. Fish

SEPTEMBER 1992
Domestic Partners
Violence in Schools
Public Broadcasting
Women in the Military

OCTOBER 1992
Depression
U.S. Auto Industry
Youth Apprenticeships
Hispanic Americans

NOVEMBER 1992
Physical Fitness
Privatization
Paying for College
U.S. Policy in Asia

DECEMBER 1992
Crackdown on Smoking
The New CIA
Eating Disorders
Women and AIDS

JANUARY 1993
Hate Crimes
Child Sexual Abuse
Nuclear Fusion
U.S. Trade Policy

FEBRUARY 1993
Community Policing
Europe's New Right
School Censorship
Violence Against Women

MARCH 1993
Gay Rights
Aid to Russia
War on Drugs
TV Violence

APRIL 1993
Head Start
High-Speed Rail
Children's Legal Rights
Muslims in America

MAY 1993
Cults in America
Preventing Teen Pregnancy
Software Piracy
National Parks

JUNE 1993
Food Safety
Prostitution
Childhood Immunizations
National Service

JULY 1993
Electric Cars
Population Growth
Downward Mobility
Intelligence Testing

AUGUST 1993
Mental Illness
Bilingual Education
Foreign Policy Burden
School Funding

SEPTEMBER 1993
Suburban Crime
Public Housing
Supreme Court Preview
Immigration Reform

OCTOBER 1993
Airline Safety
Disaster Response
Science in the Courtroom
The Glass Ceiling

NOVEMBER 1993
Paying for Retirement
Charitable Giving
Privacy in the Workplace
Adoption

DECEMBER 1993
U.S. Vietnam-Relations
Learning Disabilities
Child Care
Space Program's Future

JANUARY 1994
Racial Tensions in Schools
South Africa's Future
Worker Retraining

Back issues are available for $4.00 (subscribers) or $7.00 (non-subscribers). Quantity discounts apply to orders over ten. To order, call Congressional Quarterly Customer Service at (202) 887-8621.

Binders are available for $15.00. To order call 1-800-638-1710. Please refer to stock number 648.

Future Topics

- ***Prison Overcrowding***
- ***Drinking Water Safety***
- ***Religion and Schools***

THE CQ Researcher

PUBLISHED BY CONGRESSIONAL QUARTERLY INC.

Prison Overcrowding

Will building more prisons cut the crime rate?

Public outrage over several recent murders has prompted politicians and crime-weary citizens to demand that dangerous criminals be locked away for life. But the get-tough campaign is colliding with the reality of a prison system bursting at the seams. The federal prison system is 37 percent over-capacity, while budget-strapped states are housing prisoners in tents, hallways and gymnasiums — or releasing them early. Conservatives cite government's duty to protect the public and argue that investing in new prison construction will pay off in long-range crime reduction. Liberals criticize the national trend toward mandatory sentences — enacted largely as part of the "war on drugs" — as a wasteful approach that is unaffordable and unlikely to cut crime.

INSIDE THIS ISSUE

CQ February 4, 1994 • Volume 4, No. 5 • 97-120

Formerly Editorial Research Reports

COVER: CELL DESIGNED FOR ONE INMATE HOLDS TWO AT THE FEDERAL PRISON IN JOLIET, ILL. (AMERICAN CORRECTIONAL ASSOCIATION)

February 4, 1994
Volume 4, No. 5

The CQ Researcher (ISSN 1056-2036). Formerly Editorial Research Reports. Published weekly (48 times per year, not printed the first Friday of any month with five Fridays) by Congressional Quarterly Inc., 1414 22nd St., N.W., Washington, D.C. 20037. Rates are furnished upon request. Second-class postage paid at Washington, D.C. POSTMASTER: Send address changes to The CQ Researcher, 1414 22nd St., N.W., Washington, D.C. 20037.

Prison Overcrowding

By Charles S. Clark

The Issues

In Georgia, some prison inmates are housed in trailers; in New Jersey many live in tents; and in North Carolina, hundreds of prisoners don't even remain in the state — they were sent to rented cells in Rhode Island.

Faced with such crowding, state corrections officials might be encouraged by recent action in Congress. "The toughest crime bill . . . in American history," as Sen. Phil Gramm, R-Texas, calls it, breezed through the Senate on Nov. 19, 1993. The bill was passed 95-4 in the wake of public outrage over the murder of 12-year-old Polly Klaas, abducted from her home in California, and the roadside shooting of basketball star Michael Jordan's father in North Carolina. In both cases, violent offenders free on parole were linked to the deaths. In the Carolina case, chillingly, defendant Daniel Andre Green had been released from prison early due to overcrowding.

Among other things, the Senate bill would provide $3 billion to build regional prisons to which states could send their inmate overflow. [1]

But there's a catch. To use the new federal cells, states would have to pass "truth-in-sentencing laws" requiring prisoners to serve at least 85 percent of their terms. In budget-crunched states, there is fear that such a federal "lock 'em up" policy might simply add to the corrections burden without reducing crime.

"Regional prisons would be devastating to states and would cost us millions if we took them up on it," says Chase Riveland, secretary of the Corrections Department in Washington state. "The crime bill is a lot of rhetoric that is not helpful in the long term. Justice is better meted out at the local level where it can be tailored to local needs."

American Correctional Association

In state capitals around the nation as well as in Washington, D.C., a gap is yawning ever wider between zeal for cracking down on crime and prison systems often described as bursting at the seams. There are more men and women in state and federal prisons than ever before, the Justice Department announced in October. In fact, the number of inmates grew by an average of 1,600 a week in the first half of 1993, with the federal prison population growing at twice the states' rate.

The number of inmates in state and federal prisons quadrupled from 1970 to 1990, according to the Sentencing Project, a Washington advocacy group. The country's incarceration rate of 455 for every 100,000 people has now surpassed that of South Africa to make it the highest in the developed world. (*See table, p. 115.*) Counting inmates in city and county jails, a total of 1.2 million adult men and women in the United States are behind bars.

Clearly, the amount of resources devoted to corrections has fallen behind the tough talk on crime. The federal prison system is 36 percent over capacity, according to the Bureau of Prisons. And 40 states and the District of Columbia are under court order or a consent decree to limit their prison populations due to overcrowding, according to the National Prison Project of the American Civil Liberties Union (ACLU). South Carolina, which except for the District of Columbia has the country's highest incarceration rate, spent $80 million to build two prisons but now doesn't have the funds to open them.

"In many parts of the country, you have to make a reservation to go to jail," says Rep. William J. Hughes, D-N.J., who specializes in prison issues on the House Judiciary Committee.

"Overcrowded? Underfunded?" asks an advertisement in a corrections journal. Try portable, modular correctional housing units. [2]

The reasons for the inmate explosion include new penalties against drunken driving and firearms violations, improvements in law enforcement and a rise in violent crime. The number of arrests nationally climbed 76.3 percent from 1973-89, noted a study by the Advisory Commission on Intergovernmental Relations. [3] But that alone wouldn't explain why the prison population swelled by 221 percent in the same period. The major force has clearly been the introduction of mandatory minimum sentences — enacted at the state and federal levels beginning in the mid-1980s — largely as part of the federal government's war on drugs. [4]

Currently on the books for more than 100 federal crimes, mandatory minimums have given new meaning to "doing time." In 1986, the average stay behind bars was 44.8 months for robbery, 23.1 months for drug offenses and 14.1 months for firearms offenses. By 1991, jail time had climbed to 90.8 months for robbery; 71.8 months for drug offenses and 35.3 months for firearms offenses, according to the U.S. Sentencing Commission. (*See table, p. 109.*)

Chief Justice of the United States

Most Prisons Are Above Capacity

At the end of 1992, an estimated 75 percent of all state prisons were operating over their maximum capacity. California topped the list, operating at 91 percent above capacity. Federal prisons were an average of 37 percent above capacity.

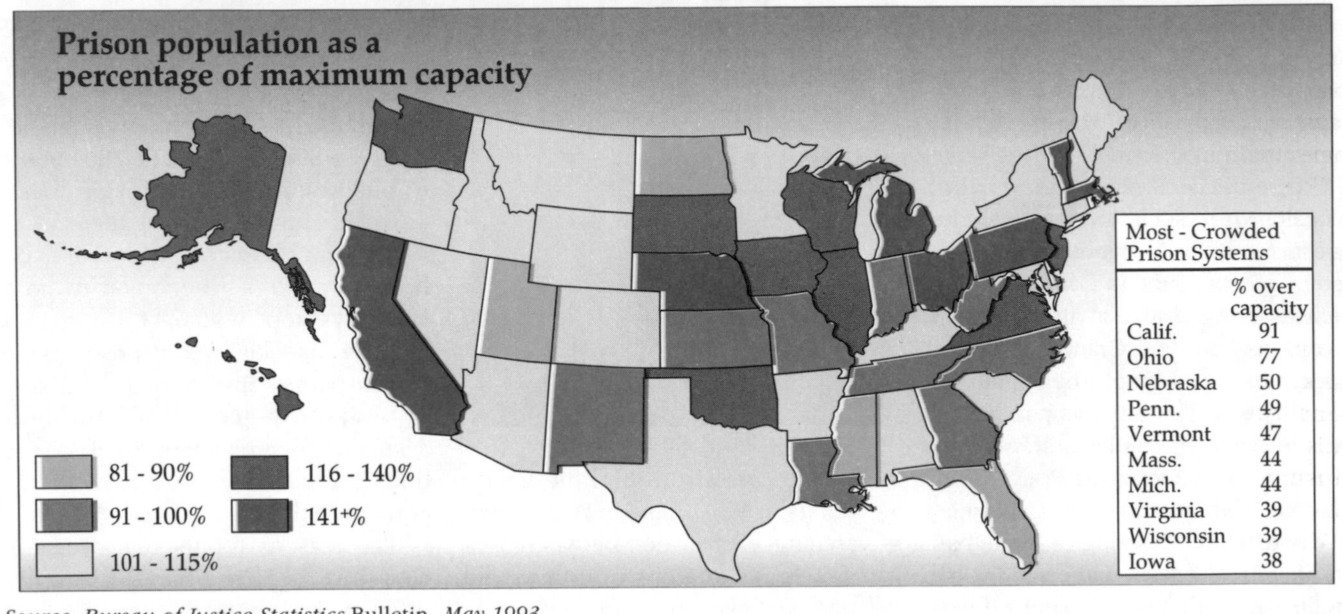

Source: Bureau of Justice Statistics Bulletin, *May 1993*

William H. Rehnquist, in a speech last June, called mandatory minimum sentences a "good example of the 'law of unintended consequences.' There is a respectable body of opinion which believes that these mandatory minimums impose unduly harsh punishment for first-time offenders — particularly for 'mules' [runners] who played only a minor role in drug distribution schemes. . . .[They] have also led to an inordinate increase in the federal prison population and will require huge expenditures to build new prison space." [5]

Mandatory sentences "represent a major shift in power from judges to prosecutors," says Beth Carter, spokeswoman for the Campaign for an Effective Crime Policy, which was mounted by corrections specialists rebelling against political "demagoguery" on crime. "Many state corrections officials say that prison overcrowding results when mandatory sentencing detracts from their ability to identify and put away the violent criminals."

Yet expanding the federal mandatory sentencing approach to the state level — with its accompanying demand for more prisons — is precisely the approach taken in the Senate crime bill and by proponents of a general crime crackdown. "The American criminal justice system must be reformed, particularly at the state level, to eliminate 'revolving door' justice," proclaims the founding statement of The First Freedom Coalition, an advocacy group headed by former Attorney General William P. Barr, who served during the administration of President George Bush. "Violent criminals must stay in prison for the entire length of their sentences. Releasing such offenders after a fraction of their sentences have been served results in more victimization."

To critics of the lock 'em up approach, the problem with building more prisons is that it's already been tried. The Bureau of Prisons has embarked on the most expensive expansion in its history, while corrections has been vying with Medicaid as the fastest-growing part of state budgets, according to the National Conference of State Legislatures.

"The public is confused into thinking that locking up more criminals is the same as reducing crime rates," writes Alvin J. Bronstein, executive director of the ACLU Prison Project. "It is not, and no jurisdiction has ever successfully built its way out of overcrowding or had an impact on crime rates by an expanded incarceration policy." [6]

Polls show the public see-sawing on the issue. When Yankelovich Partners, in an August 1993 poll for *Time* magazine and CNN, asked respondents whether they favored building more prisons even if that meant a significant hike in taxes, 60 percent said yes, while 35 percent said no. A January 1994 poll by NBC News and *The Wall Street Journal* showed that while crime is the top concern, only 39 percent think building more prisons would help.

"Because polls show crime to be the No. 1 concern and because there are governors' elections in many big states this year, the politicians want to out-demagogue each other," says Kenneth F. Schoen, director of justice programs at the Edna McConnell Clark Foundation, which supports alternatives to building prisons. "But back in the legislatures and state finance committees, they're looking for other ways out because all the tough talk comes without funds."

The problem of prison overcrowding is complicated by the fact that the American system of government is fragmented, notes Mary K. Shilton, an analyst with the National Association of Criminal Justice Planners. "The correctional crisis is an intergovernmental crisis that requires an intergovernmental response." [7]

What that response ultimately will be largely depends on answers to the following questions:

Will building more prisons reduce crime?

In 1992, the Bush administration's Justice Department released *The Case for More Incarceration*, a position paper arguing that prison was cheaper than the alternatives, that violent crime had been declining since the government began putting more people in prison and, most important, that much violent crime is committed by parolees and other individuals previously ensnared in the criminal justice system.

"The thing that almost everyone intuitively knows is so simple that it barely needs repeating," wrote commentator Ben Wattenberg, a conservative Democrat, in praising the paper. "A thug in prison cannot shoot your sister." [8]

The simplicity of such a solution impresses other conservatives as well. "If we have overcrowded schools, we build more schools; it's the same for prisons," says Paul Kamenar, executive legal director of the Washington Legal Foundation, a public interest law and policy center. "The public demands that criminals be put away rather than go through the 'revolving door' of the current justice system, and it is imperative that more prisons be built at the state level, where the crime is."

Florida Sheriffs' Association

Hundreds of New York City prisoners, most in pre-trial detention, live in plastic-covered 50-man "tents" on Rikers Island. The $72 million facility above was raised in three months.

A key proponent of the movement to build more prisons, *Reader's Digest* Senior Editor Eugene H. Methvin, has predicted that "if we again double the present federal and state prison population — to somewhere between 1 million and 1.5 million — and leave our city and county jail population at the present 400,000, we will break the back of America's 30-year crime wave." [9]

Essential to this conviction is the notion that most crime is committed by a core of hardened criminals who could be identified and "selectively incapacitated." That view was bolstered by a Bureau of Justice Statistics study released last March showing that 93 percent of federal and state prisoners are either violent offenders or recidivists. [10] Proponents also cite a study released in 1992 showing that the average violent offender serves only 37 percent of his sentence. [11]

Research suggesting that incarceration cuts crime comes from Texas A&M University economist Morgan Reynolds. He sees crime as a function of the potential criminal's perception of probable punishment. For example, in 1950, he reports, an offender risked spending an average of 24 days a year in prison, and serious crime was at 1.8 million incidents a year. By 1964, the imprisonment risk had dropped to 12 days, and crime had increased to 4.6 million incidents. During the turbulent 1960s, Morgan reports that the prison population dipped from 219,00 in 1961 to 195,000 in 1968, while the FBI's Uniform Crime Reports showed crimes rocketing from 3.4 million in 1961 to 8 million in 1970. Only in the late 1970s and '80s, when the movement toward mandatory sentences helped push prison risk back up, he says, did the rate of increase in crime level off. [12] *

* Discussions of crime rates are complicated by the differences in the two major national crime indicators. Under the FBI's Uniform Crime Reports, which measure crimes reported by police, the overall crime rate rose 7.9 percent from 1980 to 1990. But according to the Justice Department's National Crime Victims survey, the crime rate during that period dropped 14.5 percent. Analysts of all political persuasions agree that since the mid-1980s, the level of violent crime has been rising.

Overcrowding Is in the Eye of the Beholder

In North Carolina in recent years, prisoners in rural road camps have been triple-bunked in one-story dormitories with less than 28 square feet of living space per inmate. "They can't jump down from the top bunk without asking another prisoner's permission," says Susan H. Pollitt, an attorney with North Carolina Prisoner Legal Services in Raleigh. "And with the television on loudly, they can't read or write. Because the guards often can't see over the bunks, anything can happen — assaults, rapes, gambling, loan sharking."

Such conditions are the reason prisoners'-rights groups like Pollitt's and the American Civil Liberties Union (ACLU) file lawsuits charging that overcrowded prisons violate the Constitution's Eighth Amendment ban on cruel and unusual punishments.

Opponents say the suits would "have the Founding Fathers rolling over in their graves," in the phrase of Paul Kamenar, executive director of the Washington Legal Foundation, a public interest law and policy center. The Eighth Amendment is being "stretched every which way to cover frivolous lawsuits by prisoners who don't like the color of the paint on the walls or their brand of toothpaste," he says. "But living conditions aboard a submarine or in my college dorm were more cramped than many prison cells. These attempts to make prison a pleasant place simply reduce the deterrent factor."

The crowding debate is complicated by the absence of objective definitions of overcrowding that endure through changing times. All but the newest prisons were designed, for example, with one bunk per cell. Over the years, however, overcrowding forced most prisons to double-bunk, and by 1988, the practice was approved by the federal Bureau of Prisons and accepted under the standards of the Laurel, Md.-based American Correctional Association (ACA).

Accreditation by the ACA is voluntary, and only a little more than half the country's 1,200 federal and state prisons have sought such status, according to W. Hardy Rauch, the ACA's director of standards and accreditation. "It's up to the warden or the corrections commissioner," he says. "Just because a prison is not accredited, however, does not necessarily mean conditions are real bad, but it could mean it has inadequate structure, fire control or locking."

ACA standards, established in consultation with medical experts and the American Bar Association, vary among maximum- and minimum-security prisons. But typically they require cells in which prisoners are to spend more than 10 hours daily be 35 square feet, or 5 feet by 7, Rauch says. Individual spaces within dormitories need only be 25 square feet if there is a nearby communal area of 100 square feet.

"Square footage is important, but less important than having adequate exercise areas, education and medical programs," Rauch says. Double-bunking, for example, didn't increase violence or escapes if scheduling, staff supervision and training were adjusted accordingly. Overcrowding can also be eased with improved prison design — cells that open, for example, into a large day room with televisions, dining facilities and counselors' offices nearby.

The ACLU makes judgments on overcrowding using a multitude of considerations, according to Ed Koren, a staff attorney with the ACLU National Prison Project. The obvious first indicator is the prison's designed capacity.

But decades of Supreme Court decisions make the ACLU's case difficult. In *Bell v. Wolfish*, for example, the court ruled in 1979 that double bunking is not necessarily unconstitutional, nor is merely violating an ACA standard. "In order to have cruel and unusual punishment," says Koren, "we must show the impact on the prisoners, the increased risk." Violence alone in a prison is not deemed unconstitutional; the plaintiffs must show that violence is increasing with increases in the prison's population.

The general public, meanwhile, retains an image of some prisons — particularly in the federal system — as being "overly cushy," says Paul McNulty, executive director of the First Freedom Coalition in Washington. For example, Texas prisons are under a court order "that spells out every imaginable detail of human life," he says, including the size of prison bookshelves, a requirement that one of two TVs must have a "sports only" sign and that the temperature of food be taken three times before it is served.

Ultimately, says Chase Riveland, who heads the Department of Corrections in Washington state, prison staff and prisoners can put up with almost any level of crowding "if there's light at the end of the tunnel, if they know that other solutions are coming."

Prisoners themselves, of course, have their own perspectives. "Let us say you are in a cell 10 feet long and seven feet wide," writes convicted murderer Jack Henry Abbott in his acclaimed account of prison life. "That means 70 feet of *floor* space. But your bunk is just over three feet wide and six and a half feet long. Your iron toilet and sink combination covers a floor space of at least three feet by two feet. All tallied . . . [i]t works out to a pathway seven feet long and about three feet wide....If I were an animal housed in a zoo in quarters of these dimensions, the Humane Society would have the zookeeper arrested for cruelty."†

† Jack Henry Abbott, *In the Belly of the Beast: Letters from Prison* (1981), p. 45.

Applying such reasoning to individual states, Methvin cites the case of Michigan, where from 1981-1984 the prison population dropped from 15,157 to 14,606 (a 3.5 percent dip), and violent crime rose 25 percent. Then, he says, the state doubled the prison population from 1986 to 1991, and the crime rate dropped by 25-32 percent.

But drawing such direct links between prison building and crime reduction strikes critics as simplistic. The results may vary by time period, and correlations may well be coincidence. Perry Johnson, the former director of Michigan's Department of Corrections and now president of the American Correctional Association, says Michigan's violent crime rate actually rose all during the state's tops-in-the-country burst of prison construction. "It does not appear that Michigan got much value for the nearly $2 billion it has now spent for building and operating these new prisons. Certainly the back of the crime problem has not been broken, though that of the taxpayers may have been," Johnson says. [13]

Nationally, the prison population has grown by 102 percent since 1983, but violent crime still rose 40 percent, notes the Sentencing Project. A National Academy of Sciences panel last year concluded that increased incarceration had "apparently little effect" on crime. "While average prison time served per violent crime roughly tripled between 1975 and 1989," the panel said, "reported levels of serious violent crime [remained at] about 2.9 million per year." [14]

That level of violent crime shows the futility of putting more people away in prisons, says Scott Wallace, special counsel for the National Legal Aid and Defender Association. "If you build more prisons, you will fill them," he says, but jailing drug users and sellers and other non-violent criminals under mandatory-sentencing laws won't affect serious crime. That's why advocates of new prisons are "just skating across the surface of the criminal justice system," he says.

In fact, the percentage of state-imprisoned violent offenders actually declined, according to the Justice Department, from 54.6 percent in 1986 to 46.6 percent in 1991. Meanwhile, the percentage of drug offenders in state prisons rose from 8.6 percent to 21.3 percent over the same period. In federal prisons, the percentage of drug offenders is up to a startling 60 percent of the overall federal prison population. "The effect on crime is negligible," Wallace says.

Many observers note that crime related to illegal drugs has proven least responsive to the deterrent threat of prison. There are as many as 2 million hard-core American abusers of cocaine and heroin, and the current 300,000 individuals in prison on drug charges is barely one-eighth of the total, writes Elliott Currie, a professor at the Institute for the Study of Social Change at the University of California-Berkeley. "We have seen what this flood of offenders has done to the nation's courts and prisons," he notes, "but what is utterly sobering is that even this massive effort at repression has barely scratched the surface." [15]

"Selective incapacitation doesn't work," says Barry Krisberg, president of the San Francisco-based National Council on Crime and Delinquency (NCCD). "For every 100 victims of crime, only 30 report it. Of those, only about six result in a criminal being taken into custody. Only half of those get convicted, and only one in three go to prison. So you end up with 1 percent of criminals being incarcerated according to all data. And because the underclass is a large recruiting base, there's a replacement effect. You take one criminal out of circulation, and someone else comes off the bench."

Finally, there are those who argue that incarceration has the opposite of its intended effect. "The injudicious use of incarceration over the past 15 years has been partly responsible for *increasing* violent crime — particularly among youth," writes Virginia prisoner Evans D. Hopkins. "The imprisoned man all too often is further debilitated in a human warehouse where there is little real effort given to rehabilitation. After his release he is returned to the same environment from whence he came and, as often as not, because of his record denied entry into an ever-diminishing job market. And what has been happening while he has been in prison? Some woman has done without a man, some child without a father and a

Prison Population on the Rise

The number of individuals in state and federal prisons fluctuated during the Vietnam era but began a steady rise in 1973. By 1990, there were three times as many inmates as there were in 1961. The rise in the per capita rate of incarceration from 119 prisoners per 100,000 population to 293 prisoners indicates that the nation's rising population alone did not cause the increase.

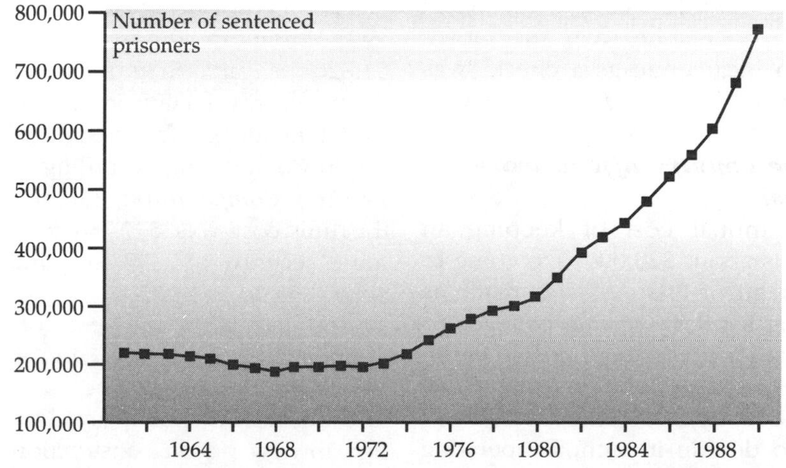

Source: "The Use of Incarceration in the United States," American Bar Association, April 1992

The Expanding Criminal Justice System

The number of adults in the criminal justice system, including those on probation and parole, rose from 1.8 million people in 1980 to 4.4 million in 1990.

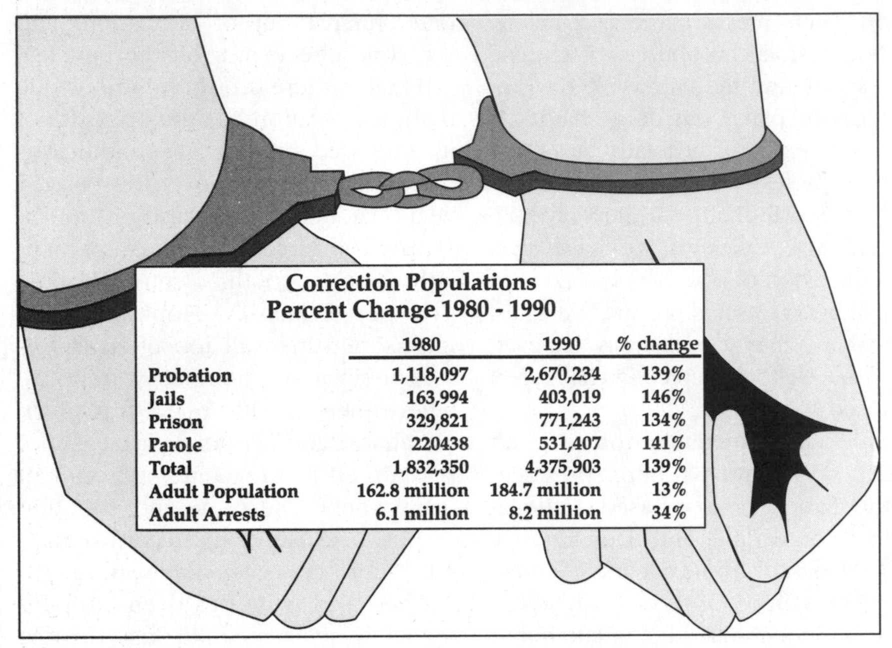

Correction Populations
Percent Change 1980 - 1990

	1980	1990	% change
Probation	1,118,097	2,670,234	139%
Jails	163,994	403,019	146%
Prison	329,821	771,243	134%
Parole	220438	531,407	141%
Total	1,832,350	4,375,903	139%
Adult Population	162.8 million	184.7 million	13%
Adult Arrests	6.1 million	8.2 million	34%

Source: National Council on Crime and Delinquency, February 1993

younger man has entered the street to supply a black market." [16]

Overall, counters McNulty of the First Freedom Coalition, the rise in prison population has cut crime. The effect would be more demonstrable, he says, were it not for the increased juvenile violence since 1987. "Until the mid-1980s," he says, the movement to incarcerate as a check "was on course."

Can the country afford more prisons?

The annual cost of keeping an inmate is about $20,000, according to the Bureau of Prisons — as much as a year at a pricey private college. To cope with a predicted increase in the federal prison population from 76,000 to 116,000 by 1999, the bureau expects to double its annual operating budget to $3.6 billion. [17]

California alone spends $7.6 million per day to incarcerate its 110,600 inmates, according to the Department of Corrections. Corrections spending by all state and local governments grew a whopping 232 percent from 1970-90, compared with increases of 79 percent for welfare and 71 percent for hospital and health care. [18]

Prison construction costs varied in 1993, from an almost infinitesimal $1,826 per unit in a minimum/medium security facility in Arkansas to $147,000 per bed for maximum security in Connecticut, according to *Corrections Compendium.* On average, the unit cost was $77,738 for maximum security, $55,173 for minimum, according to the ACLU.

And because of the need for bond financing, actual construction is only the short-term cost. "When a legislature decides to spend, say, $100 million in new prison construction, it is committing the taxpayers of that state to $1.6 billion in correctional expenditure over the ensuing three decades," the director of the National Institute of Corrections testified before Congress. "Construction is only 6 percent of the charge to taxpayers over 30 years. . . . The construction is only the down payment." [19]

Even granting, for the sake of argument, that incarceration reduces crime, many observers doubt that Americans will agree to pay for larger doses of it.

"Yes, these are difficult fiscal times," acknowledges Kamenar of the Washington Legal Foundation, "but this is an area that demands the highest priority. The primary function of government is to protect citizens. If it can't do that, we don't need millions of dollars on frills at the National Endowment for the Arts. People are willing to pay for it through higher taxes if they understand the purpose."

McNulty of the First Freedom Coalition adds that states can deal with the increased demand for funding because of the savings they will reap from reduced crime. Such a cost-benefit argument was advanced most notably by National Institute of Justice researcher Edwin Zedlewski in a controversial 1987 study. Zedlewski assumed that it cost $25,000 a year to incarcerate a prisoner, that the average offender commits 187 crimes per year and that the typical crime costs society $2,300 in property losses or physical suffering. He then calculated that the typical offender costs society $430,100 per year, compared with $25,000 for imprisonment, for a "benefit-cost ratio" of 17 to 1 in favor of imprisonment. [20]

"Unfortunately," Zedlewski wrote, "one side of the equation — confinement costs — is quite visible, while the other side — confinement benefits — is relatively invisible." Zedlewski added that "construction and financing costs can make building prisons seem overwhelmingly expensive when presented as a lump sum in a bond issue. [But] when these charges are amortized over the useful life of a facility, they become quite modest."

Many analysts scoffed at the notion that any government program could achieve such a high benefit-cost ratio. Zedlewski's "research has also been dismissed as basically irrelevant because it is premised on the notion that offenders not imprisoned will be left unsupervised in the community," according to the American Bar Association.[21]

John J. DiIulio Jr. and Anne Morrison Piehl of Princeton University found Zedlewski's numbers "incredible," but warned that his critics were too eager to pounce on a method that might one day prove useful. "The upshot of the debate," they wrote, "is that it is difficult to precisely identify [the hard-core offenders who commit most of the crime] with information generally available to the criminal justice system."[22]

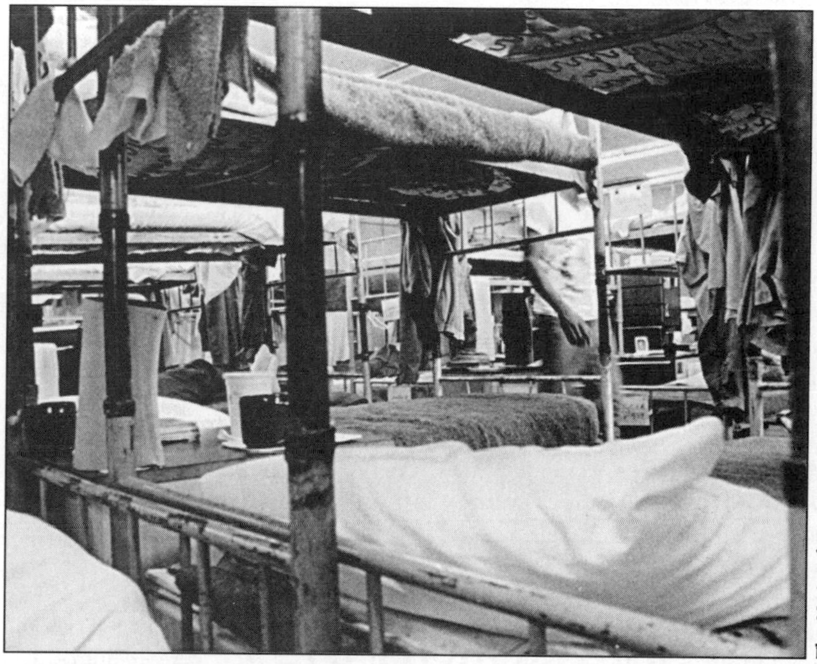

The National Council on Crime and Delinquency called Zedlewski's analysis "fatally flawed by political ideology." Moreover, says Krisberg, "It has never stood good scientific scrutiny. And like an economist's argument, it has never been implemented in a real place." He points to states such as Washington and Florida, where the opposite occurred: Incarceration and crime declined together.

His group warns that such thinking distracts decision-makers from opportunities to reduce crime while saving money by relying on alternatives to incarceration. An NCCD study for Illinois, for example, showed that when the legislature increased good-time credits for inmates, it saved about $100 million per year, with no impact on crime. Similarly, when Indiana turned more to community-based corrections, says the NCCD, it returned $40 million to the legislature.

"When there are limited resources, just like the rest of us do in ordinary life, you set priorities," observes Michael Tonry, a professor of law at the University of Minnesota who edits *Overcrowded Times*, a newsletter about prisons. "You can't send everyone to prison just because someone wants them there."

The National Prison Project

A crowded dormitory at the District of Columbia prison in Lorton, Va.

Are there feasible alternatives to incarceration?

Alfred Blumstein, dean of the School of Urban and Public Affairs at Carnegie-Mellon University, notes that there are three basic approaches to the prison-crowding problem: the "front-door approach," which involves non-incarcerative alternatives; the "backdoor approach," in which sentences are shortened; and building more prisons.[23]

The "backdoor approach," the use of parole and sentence reductions for good behavior ("good time"), is often applied unpredictably and inconsistently during overcrowding emergencies. It is as hotly debated as any aspect of the current prison debate. (*See below, p. 111.*)

The "front-door approach" offers a variety of planned alternatives to prison: probation, military-style "boot camps" for young offenders, halfway houses, electronically monitored home confinement, community service, financial restitution and drug/alcohol treatment.[24]

An NCCD survey showed that as many as 80 percent of inmates are non-violent and likely candidates for "front-door" programs, while the Bureau of Prisons estimates that some 1,612 federal inmates would be suitable for alternative sentences. Noting that the federal government had built 29 new federal prisons since 1979, Rep. Don Edwards, D-Calif., vice chairman of the House Judiciary Committee, says that if "we had sentenced these inmates to an alternative to prison such as probation or a halfway house, we could have saved $384 million in 1992 and, projections show, an astounding $438 million in 1993."[25]

The problem with prison, adds Rep. Hughes, is that "we haven't given more than lip service to how prisoners will come out of it if they go in with a drug habit, a lack of skills or psychological problems. If we concentrate better on their needs when they come into the system, we'd [help] them the *second* time, not the 14th time. Prisons harden people. That's why sentencing judges don't sentence people initially to prison but eventually are forced to, because we have not developed a myriad of alternatives."

Wallace of the National Legal Aid and Defender Association says that alternatives are particularly cost-effective for financial crimes. "People who write bad checks should be hit where it hurts, in the pocketbook," he says, though there also might be "a brief incarceration period to satisfy society's retributive component."

Several jurisdictions, the city of Los Angeles among them, are considering alternative programs modeled on Miami's Drug Court, which since the late 1980s has diverted first-time drug offenders to treatment instead of jail. [26]

Another increasingly popular alternative to prison, home confinement, has gone from a pilot program with 95 offenders in a few states in the mid-1980s to a nationwide program involving 12,000 people, according to Marc Mauer, assistant director of the Sentencing Project. It costs about $6.41 per day, compared with $31.37 for halfway houses, $46.54 for a federal inmate and $54.79 for a state inmate. [27]

Douglas Spencer, an Oregon circuit court judge, notes that "whenever the state floats a bond issue to build more prisons, there are immediately letters to the editor saying let's try some alternatives. But funds are scarce for probation as well. The Oregon Corrections Department claims that 80 percent of parolees successfully complete their transition. But that's not saying they're rehabilitated, only that they committed no new crime. To have the kind of group therapy and counseling it would take to intervene in lifetime patterns would be very expensive."

Opponents of alternatives, such as Methvin, cite a study of 350 high-repeat delinquents in Illinois by the American Institute for Research in Behavioral Sciences, a Washington think tank. Some of the youngsters were incarcerated, others placed in foster homes for community treatment programs. Subsequently, the incarcerated group registered fewer rearrests. [28]

"I'm not saying prisons are the only way," says Kamenar, adding that the Washington Legal Foundation would have favored an alternative sentence for a client who was sentenced to three years in federal prison (and actually served 27 months) for violating Environmental Protection Agency regulations in the course of landscaping his yard.

"I'll support meaningful alternatives," says McNulty, "but we don't have much to show that they're effective. After all, we've tried rehabilitation and we know it doesn't work. Thirty years of social spending hasn't worked, either."

Critics like Kamenar and McNulty fear that alternative sentences may backfire and fail to protect the public from crime by recidivists. "Every system of punishment will have its failures," counters Wallace. "A few highly published failures of an alternative option ends use of the option, while thousands of highly publicized failures of incarceration don't make a dent in its popularity."

Tonry of the University of Minnesota adds: "We can make some sensible choices, and bad things will still happen. After 30 years, a guy on house arrest will rape or rob or murder. But we can't keep everyone who ever committed an offense locked up. We can't lock up 60 million Americans. After all, we've decided it's worth it to tolerate 50,000 deaths a year in auto accidents."

Jerome Miller, a veteran corrections official who has consulted in the sentencing of hundreds of offenders for the National Center on Institutions and Alternatives, says the time isn't ripe for a move to alternatives. "The mood of the country is so bad," he says, "and things are so hyped and driven by irresponsible media and political figures, that even introducing alternatives now would be poison." ■

BACKGROUND

Early Prison Reforms

The earliest prisons in Colonial days — a time when hangings and public whippings were favored punishments — were scandalously cruel by today's standards. A prison in Simsbury, Conn., was converted in 1773 from a copper mine. During the day, convicts worked on the surface making such products as nails, barrels and shoes. "At night," a historian wrote, "prisoners were confined to the caverns below. Darkness, slanting floors, low ceilings and continually dripping water made this prison grossly uncomfortable and injurious to health." [29]

But during the Revolutionary War, a prison reform movement swept Britain and its colonies. Humane conditions were introduced and individual criminals isolated in the hope that they would become "penitent." When Quaker activist George Fox set up the earliest American prison, Philadelphia's Walnut Street Jail, in the late 1780s, he introduced fixed sentences and abolished the common practice of charging inmates for their upkeep. [30] Within a month, his 30 cells were full.

The prisoner-rights movement had taken root. When the Bill of Rights was adopted in 1791, the Eighth Amendment asserted: "Excessive bail shall not be required, nor excessive fines imposed, nor cruel and unusual punishments inflicted."

Prison space was always scarce in the United States, but never more so than after the Civil War devastated much of the South. Convicts worked on chain

Continued on p. 108

Chronology

Late 19th Century

Overcrowding leads to early prisoner-rights movement.

1876
Zebulon Brockway sets up Elmira Reformatory in upstate New York, offering the first prison programs in education, athletics and job training.

1891
Space shortages set the stage for the first experiments in probation, in Massachusetts.

1950s-1960s

Prison population stabilizes, then declines; first mandatory sentences enacted.

1951
Boggs Act introduces mandatory minimum sentences for federal drug offenses.

1968
Congress creates the Law Enforcement Administration Agency (LEAA), which over the next 12 years spends $8 billion to upgrade courts, state and local police and prisons.

1970s ***Prison philosophy shifts from rehabilitation to punishment, launching move to build more prisons.***

1970
Comprehensive Drug Abuse and Control Act repeals all mandatory sentences.

1971
At New York's Attica prison, 33 inmates and 10 prison staff die during a five-day inmate takeover quelled by police.

1974
Supreme Court rules in *Wolff v. McDonnell* that "there is no iron curtain drawn between prisons and the Constitution."

1975
In *Gates v. Collier*, Supreme Court holds that "a shortage of funds is not a justification for continuing to deny any citizens their constitutional rights."

1979
In *Bell v. Wolfish*, Supreme Court holds that 75 square feet of space for two inmates does not constitute cruel and unusual punishment unless other bad conditions are present.

1980s ***Many prisons are hit by rioting. Move to incarcerate more criminals leads to state action on overcrowding.***

1980
Riot at Santa Fe, N.M., prison. Minnesota becomes first state to enact sentencing guidelines that reflect available prison space. Michigan becomes first state to enact Emergency Powers Act allowing governor to order release of prisoners.

1981
Attorney General's Task Force on Violent Crime recommends $2 billion in federal aid for prison construction, but Reagan administration balks. Texas judge cites overcrowding in declaring the state's prison system unconstitutional.

1984
Omnibus crime bill seeks to eliminate sentencing disparities. Lawmakers abolish federal parole when new federal sentencing rules take effect Nov. 1, 1987.

1986
Prison riots occur at Arizona State Prison and other prisons. Congress enacts Anti-Drug Abuse Act, which ties minimum penalties to the quantity of drugs involved.

1988
Ads for Republican presidential candidate George Bush highlight Willie Horton, a convicted murderer who raped a Maryland woman while on furlough from a Massachusetts prison.

1990s ***Crime remains top political issue, with incarceration rates at record levels.***

1991
In *Wilson v. Seiter*, Supreme Court rules that prisoners complaining of cruel and unusual punishment must prove deliberate indifference by prison officials.

April 1993
Riot in Lucasville, Ohio, prison kills nine inmates and a guard.

Nov. 2, 1993
Ballot initiative in Washington state requires lifetime sentences for three-time violent offenders.

Nov. 19, 1993
Senate passes massive anti-crime bill, including a $3 billion proposal for regional prisons.

Crowding Seldom Deemed the Cause of Riots

Following a riot last April at the Southern Ohio Correctional Facility near Lucasville, in which nine inmates and a prison employee died, prisoners listed overcrowding among their complaints. But larger issues were to blame, according to Terry Collins, who recently took over as warden. Key among them were black inmates' resentment over sharing cells with whites, mandatory blood tests for tuberculosis and a perceived insensitivity among prison officials regarding Black Muslim religious beliefs.

"Lucasville was actually one of the least overcrowded prisons in the state," Collins says, holding 1,800 inmates in a facility designed for 1,620. Still, since the riot the population has been cut to 1,000, at least until more cell space can be created, he says.

Department of Correctional Services

New York State's Attica Correctional Facility.

Though frequently cited in news media accounts of prison riots, overcrowding by itself is seldom the major trigger for inmate violence, experts say. "Overcrowding has a role but it's overplayed," says Marc Mauer, assistant director of the Washington-based Sentencing Project. "Along with crowding come issues of management, programs, relations with administrators, the feeling of not being treated fairly. Most people I know in prison know they committed a crime and know why they're in prison. But once they're there, they expect rules and regulations to be reasonable, and they resent it if things are arbitrary."

Overcrowding played only a minor role in the country's worst prison riots, at New York's Attica prison in 1971 and in Santa Fe, N.M. in 1980, according to a study published in 1989. More often, prison riots occur in waves, as news coverage and prisoner activism from one riot influences inmates at other prisons the study said. "In 1967," the authors write, "there were five prison riots; 15 in 1968; 27 and 37 in 1970 and 1971, respectively; and in 1972 there were 48, more than in any other year in American history." [1]

Disturbances are often attributed by prison experts to violence-prone inmates who become ringleaders, rather than to overcrowding. An April 1986 riot at the double-capacity Kirkland Correctional Institution in South Carolina, in which two prison employees were wounded and fires caused $1.5 million in damage, was blamed by the state corrections commissioner on "hard-core, violent-time inmates . . . who don't want anything to improve their lives." [2]

Gerald G. Gaes, research director for the federal Bureau of Prisons, says the dangers of crowding can be averted if new resources are added accordingly. "There are instances in which prison populations have doubled or even tripled with no appreciable changes in the quality of inmate care or safety," he writes. The impact of overcrowding is often purposefully exaggerated, he adds. Complaints about overcrowding are a way for prison administrators, corrections officers, prisoners'-rights groups and prisoners themselves to request more resources and explain serious incidents. [3]

Edward Koren, a staff attorney with the American Civil Liberties Union National Prison Project, who handled legal work for Attica inmates after the 1971 riot, blames the rampage on a combination of "too many people, too little staff and no programs."

"If the population is growing," Koren says, "and you keep the same number of guards, that means less supervision. It's the same with the number of toilets, which will break down if not kept clean. There's a direct relationship."

---

[1] Bert Useem and Peter Kimball, *States of Siege: U.S. Prison Riots, 1971-1986* (1989), p. 18. A 1986 government study of 694 state prisons comprising 180,000 beds showed little evidence that crowding levels led to increased homicide rates, assault or major disorders. See study by statistician Christopher A. Innes for the Bureau of Justice Statistics, cited in John J. DiIulio Jr., *No Escape: The Future of American Corrections* (1991) p. 34.

[2] Ann E. Weiss, *Prisons: A System in Trouble* (1988) p. 11.

[3] Gerald G. Gaes, "Challenging Beliefs About Prison Overcrowding," *Federal Prisons Journal*, summer 1991, p. 19.

Continued from p. 106

gangs building canals and railroads in conditions tantamount to slavery. In the 1870s, the grim conditions were investigated and exposed by New Orleans newspaper reporter George Washington Cable. Often, he noted, "10 years, as the rolls show, is the utmost length of time that a convict can be expected to remain alive." [31]

In 1870 prison officials gathered in Cincinnati to form the National Prison

Association, the precursor of today's American Correctional Association. Its first chief, Ohio governor and future President Rutherford B. Hayes, sought to develop humane state prisons. By 1876, reform-minded Zebulon Brockway had set up the Elmira State Reformatory in upstate New York. Battling the Legislature for funds, he offered the first prison programs in education, athletics and job training and conducted the first experiments with parole.

Many states in the 19th century permitted the care of federal and state prisoners to be contracted out to farmers and businessmen, who exploited their labor. Congress outlawed the practice in 1887, prompting a feud with states that refused to house federal prisoners, whose number had risen from a few hundred in the 1840s to 15,000 at the end of '80s.[32]

In 1891, a space shortage set the stage for the first experiments in probation, in Massachusetts, and the creation by Congress of the first federal penitentiaries. (The first federal women's prison was added in 1925 in Alderson, W. Va.) In 1910, again prompted by overcrowding, Congress enacted federal parole and good-time laws.

The flagship facility at Leavenworth, Kan., meanwhile, saw its population climb to double designed capacity before it was fully completed in 1929, due largely to rising arrests of auto thieves and violators of Prohibition and drug laws. A 1925 FBI investigation found that many of the 3,262 prisoners were crammed into basements and hallways of a facility meant for 1,300, and that 2,000 inmates were without work. To cope with the overload, the warden was forced to dilute the milk supply with water and use inmate labor to file fingerprints.[33]

"From 1900-35, overcrowding at federal institutions left few resources for anything but custodial care," noted a history of the Bureau of Prisons, which was founded in 1930. "In this period, standards of administration and correctional theory were set by several progressive states rather than the federal government."[34]

Law and Order Era

The roots of the current debate over prison building can be traced to the 1960s, the era of the civil rights and anti-war movements. During this period, the rate of violent crimes rose from 190 per 100,000 persons in 1963 to 396 in 1971.[35] At the same time, a prisoners' rights movement took hold, average time served became shorter and rehabilitation through psychotherapy and education was emphasized.

By the early 1970s, however, faith in rehabilitation had been shattered. Its death knell was sounded in 1974 by City University of New York sociologist Robert Martinson, who studied 200 prison programs and found "little value" in rehabilitation.[36]

On the ascendancy was the thinking of management Professor James Q. Wilson of Harvard University, who wrote that the purpose of prison is not to rehabilitate but to isolate and punish. "It is a measure of our confusion that such a statement will strike many enlightened readers today as cruel, even barbaric. It is not. It is merely a recognition that society at a minimum must be able to protect itself from dangerous offenders and to impose some cost on . . . criminal acts; it is also a frank admission that society really does not know how to do much else."[37]

Beginning with the "law and order" emphasis of the Nixon administration and continuing into the 1980s under the Reagan administration, an ambitious and expensive prison-construction boom swept the country. The number of Americans in state and federal prison rocketed from under 200,000 in 1970 to more than

Jail Time Increases for Federal Inmates

After federal mandatory sentencing guidelines went into effect in 1987, the length of the average prison stay for drug and firearms offenses more than tripled. Prison terms also increased significantly for most other criminal offenses.

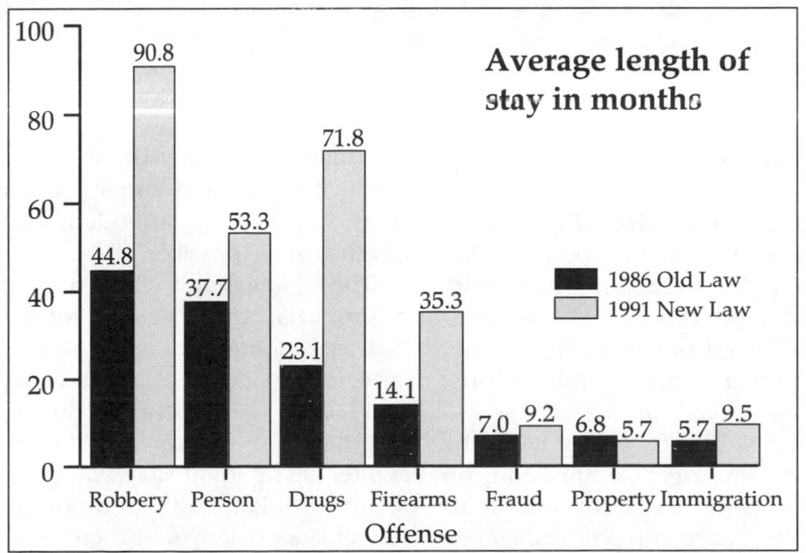

Source: American Correctional Association

Jails Often as Crowded as Prisons

Jails were simple affairs, in conception, designed for pretrial incarceration, or for terms of less than a year. Unlike prisons, jails were never designed to offer programs in work, education, behavior change or detoxification.

But many jails today are as crowded, and as busy, as prisons, partly because they are being asked to handle the prison system's overflow. "We're changing our jails into prisons, commingling pretrial and post-trial prisoners, and that's bad," says Charles "Bud" Meeks, executive director of the National Sheriffs' Association in Alexandria, Va.

Nearly half of jail occupants have already been convicted, according to the Bureau of Justice Statistics. Inmates awaiting trial also add to the crowding because officials are reluctant to release them while they wait to go to court.

"Prisoners prefer jails because they're close to their community and loved ones, and there's a local telephone and local paper," Meeks says. "They don't have to go to work, they don't have to get up in the morning, there's no rehabilitation or prison regulations, and girlfriends or mothers can visit three times a week."

Nationally, jails are at 101 percent of capacity, with larger jails (designed for more than 1,900 inmates) at 107 percent, according to Bobbie L. Huskey, president-elect of the American Correctional Association. [1]

The reasons for crowding are linked to the fact that sheriffs are elected, "and the last thing they want to do is appear soft on crime," says Paul Comiskey, an attorney and director of the California-based Prisoner Rights Union. [2] Other reasons cited by Comiskey include bail schedules set too high, a lack of alternative sentences and a tendency among police officers to use jails to dry out people who are intoxicated.

Exacerbating the crowding is the fact that jails house a disproportionate number of homeless, mentally ill and poor people — 35 percent of jail inmates in 1989 were unemployed, according to the Washington-based Sentencing Project, and 39 percent who had been free the previous year had annual incomes under $5,000.

Jail crowding also leads to serious health problems. The overcrowded Los Angeles city jails have been battling outbreaks of mumps and chicken pox, notes Rod Bottoms, a specialist in large jails at the National Institute of Corrections in Longmont, Colo. Faced last year with budget problems requiring the release of 5,000 criminals and lay-offs of 1,100 deputies, Los Angeles Sheriff Sherman Block called the situation a "crisis" that is forcing the dismantling "of the criminal justice system in this country." [3]

Short-term solutions to jail crowding have taxed the most innovative of sheriffs. In Hampden County, Mass., in 1990, a sheriff faced with an overcrowded jail invoked a 17th-century law dealing with the state militia and took over the local armory. [4] New York City since 1987 has been operating floating jails on the East River, using barges and a former Staten Island ferry. [5]

Long-term solutions such as new buildings and added deputies are expensive. But changes are occurring, Meeks notes, even in the most improbable jurisdictions. In some of the old, crowded jails of Mississippi, for example, he says that local authorities are making improvements under pressure from civil rights groups and the Justice Department, which have been suing and investigating a rash of alleged jail suicides.

---

[1] *County News*, Nov. 8, 1993.

[2] Writing in *California Prisoner*, fall 1993, p. 5.

[3] *USA Today*, May 19, 1993.

[4] *Sheriff*, January-February 1991, p. 17.

[5] *Sheriff*, December 1989-January 1990, p. 19.

823,000 in 1992.

Opposition to More Prisons

Critics of the prison boom quickly organized. In 1972, the ACLU successfully sued officials at the high-security federal prison at Marion, Ill., to force them to allow problem prisoners in a special unit to have access to attorneys. The following year, the National Advisory Commission on Criminal Justice Standards and Goals argued that "each correctional agency should adopt immediately a policy of not building new major institutions . . . unless an analysis of the total criminal justice and correctional systems produced a clear finding that no alternative is possible." [38]

The commission's report prompted a group of Unitarians to form the National Moratorium on Prison Construction. At the peak of its activism in 1980, the group tried to launch an international boycott of the 1980 Winter Olympics in Lake Placid, N.Y., to protest plans to build a dormitory for athletes that would then be converted to a prison. (The prison in Ray Brook, N.Y., opened in January 1981.)

In 1978, meanwhile, the American Bar Association, the National Association of Counties, the American Correctional Association, the National Sheriffs' Association and the National Council on Crime and Delinquency established the National Coalition for Jail Reform. Its goal was to tackle problems of the mentally ill, the poor and minorities housed in deteriorating, crowded jails. "It is not a new idea to say that jail conditions are inhumane and jails are crowded with the social misfits of a community," the group said. "But the jail crisis goes beyond the jail itself. Jails reflect the policies and procedures of all parts of the criminal justice and social service systems." [39]

Designers of new prisons were forced to respond to a series of court decisions requiring that prisoners be provided with minimal fresh air and natural light. That meant more cells had to face the outside wall rather than an interior corridor, a change that increased construction costs.

Overcrowding Crisis

Reacting to rising crime, states in the late 1970s began enacting mandatory-sentencing guidelines to reduce disparities in time actually served by individuals convicted of the same crime. Some 20 states enacted such laws while others considered them. But many states found that cracking down on crime collided with available prison space.

One of the worst situations confronted Texas, where the prison population doubled from 8,000 in 1972 to 16,000 in 1981. In response to an inmate lawsuit, Texas Judge William Justice in 1981 declared the state prison system unconstitutional, describing facilities as "strained beyond their limitations," creating a "malignant effect on all aspects of inmate life." [40]

The Texas Legislature and the Corrections Department worked through the 1980s to make amends, during which time the judge threatened to fine the state up to $800,000 a day. In the early 1990s, a state commission finally recommended coordinating sentences with available prison space; in 1991, Texas approved a $1.1 billion bond issue to create 25,300 more prison beds. Still, in March 1993, Senate Criminal Justice Committee Chairman John Whitmire described the state criminal justice system as "close to a meltdown, a mess." [41]

The mismatch between crime crackdowns and prison space was also evident in Florida. Following the abolition of parole and enactment of new penalties for drug trafficking in the early 1980s, crowding in prisons and jails brought a federal court ruling that threatened a forced mass release of prisoners. Republican Gov. Bob Martinez in 1987 called a special legislative session and won authority to grant prisoners "administrative gain time" when prisons were full. "When the program began, a state computer automatically granted most inmates five days off their sentences whenever state correctional officers learned the prisons were at 99 percent of capacity," a corrections official recalled. "Then we went to 10 days, but it wouldn't generate enough bodies out the door. "So, finally we went to 30 days." [42]

How Minnesota and Oregon Cope

Some states, however, took a different approach. In 1980, Minnesota "made corrections history," as a National Conference of State Legislatures analysis put it, with sentencing guidelines set out in a complex matrix. Taking into account such factors as the nature of the crime and the offender's previous record, sentences could be ratcheted up or down depending on the availability of prison beds. [43] The option of non-prison alternatives was also factored in.

The Minnesota method worked well from 1980-89, according to Professor Tonry, with the prison population stabilizing and crime rates leveling off, in defiance of national trends. "Most legislatures pass laws, and five to 10 years later they worry about the costs," Tonry says. "We showed that it is possible to establish a rational sentencing policy based on what we want and what we want to pay for." Similar approaches were later adopted by Oregon and Washington.

In 1989, following a number of shocking murders, the 1980 law was rescinded, and since then Minnesota has enacted some of the longest sentences in the country. In December, corrections officials asked the Legislature to expand prisons, buy a rent-a-cell facility or build a new prison for 800 felons at an estimated cost of $100 million. [44]

Oregon is now the only state to retain in pure form the built-in coordination between sentences and prison space. Oregon Judge Spencer says the "state legislature and Corrections Department did their best to sell the idea of sentencing guidelines as a progressive move, but their real motivation was to stop the widespread criticism of the parole board for releasing prisoners early. They were making a virtue of a necessity."

The upshot, in Spencer's view, is that in order to give adequate prison time to violent offenders, judges in Oregon have to release non-violent offenders. Moreover, because there's no room in the penitentiary, offenders don't take probation very seriously, he adds. "It's like threatening to send a student to the principal's office when there's no principal's office," he says. "Oregon still can't get adequate tax laws passed, and we're not building adequate penal facilities." ■

CURRENT SITUATION

Grab-Bag Crime Bill

The emerging federal crime bill contains prizes for all political camps, everything from bans on assault weapons to mandatory life sentences for three-time felony offenders.

And though financing is chancy — the $22 billion sought by the Senate bill would come from savings from reductions in federal jobs — the public's preoccupation with crime makes passage highly likely. President Clinton, in his "New Democrat" incarnation, has been supportive, though Attorney General Janet Reno says that scarce funds should be spent on preventive social programs as well as prisons. Senate Minority Leader Bob Dole, R-Kan., in his rebuttal to Clinton's tough talk on crime in the State of the Union address, charged that Democrats last year cut the federal prison construction budget by 20 percent.

Passage of the Senate bill in November with no hearings and serious alterations from the floor particularly upsets critics. "It's a lot of impetuous amendments in response to opinion polls drafted on the back of cocktail napkins that is merely a continuation of policies of the 1980s," says Wallace of the National Legal Aid and Defender Association. "And it will have the same effect — a tripled federal prison population and a doubled state population, a bottomless pit."

"If they'd had some hearings," Wallace adds, "they might have done a cost-benefit analysis and learned that drug addicts respond to shorter sentences combined with drug treatment. Instead, they're going to salt them away in warehouses."

The bill's proposal for 10 regional prisons, each with 2,500 beds, three-quarters of which would be reserved for states, came from Sen. Robert C. Byrd, D-W.Va., chairman of the powerful Appropriations Committee, and is backed by J. Michael Quinlan, former director of the Bureau of Prisons. "Regionalization is making sense in many different fields," he says; "by . . . using new technologies, we can now do things for large numbers of people and still do a good job."

Critics, among them the ACLU, warn that regionals will "result in increased prison overcrowding, increased costs to taxpayers and an exacerbation of the already disproportionate incarceration of African Americans and Hispanics." [45] Schoen of the Edna McConnell Clark Foundation predicted the federal government would build regional prisons but that the states would not enact the required "truth-in-sentencing" laws.

A panel from the National Conference of State Legislatures also has registered opposition to regional prisons. In a letter to President Clinton Nov. 19, 1993, Denton Darrington, chairman of the Law and Justice Committee, called the proposal a "poison pill." Citing the "conflicting public demands for longer sentences and lower taxes," he proposed that any crime bill "be accompanied by a prison impact statement."

Impact statements, which are intended to force lawmakers to put a price tag on new federal mandatory prison sentences, still survive in the House and Senate crime packages and are likely to make it through conference deliberations and into the final bill, according to Rep. Hughes. In the past, the New Jersey Democrat notes, "My colleagues more often than not haven't looked at the costs."

Sen. Jesse Helms, R-N.C., meanwhile, attached an amendment to the Senate bill ending the federal courts' power to cap the number of prisoners that states may incarcerate when systems are overcrowded. "Some prisoners may have to do with a few feet less of cell space," Helms told senators Nov. 16, "but that is far better than to continue to turn loose violent felons to kill or rape innocent citizens."

Sen. Joseph R. Biden Jr., D-Del., chairman of the Judiciary Committee, opposed the Helms plan, saying, "We would be stipulating that federal courts are no longer the final arbiters of the Constitution's Eighth Amendment," which prohibits cruel and unusual punishments. [46]

State Struggles

Few states have been grappling with prison overcrowding like North Carolina. As Helms has noted, crowding forced North Carolina to release 26,000 inmates early last year, among them 88 murderers and 37 rapists. "Too often criminals walk out of the courtroom laughing," Democratic Gov. James B. Hunt Jr. said in a Jan. 12 televised plea for a special legislative session to consider creating more prison space. "Even with a tough sentence, they can be back on the street in a matter of months, or even days." [47]

Following study by a special commission, the North Carolina legislature last year enacted new sentencing guidelines that take effect in January 1995. Among other things, they eliminate parole, give priority to locking up violent and career offenders, divert property offenders to alternative sentencing and match sentences with available prison space. "We're moving in the right direction," says Robin Lubitz, executive director of the Sentencing and Policy Advisory Commission, "but prison construction is not happening fast enough."

In the two most populous states, New York and California, Democratic Gov. Mario M. Cuomo and Republican Gov. Pete Wilson are running for re-election on anti-crime platforms that include new mandatory sentences. Wilson has proposed the building of six new prisons, and his support for mandatory prison for first-time drug offenders is being echoed by his Democratic opponents.

In Virginia, the new Republican governor, George F. Allen, continues to actively push his campaign pledge to abolish parole. The legislature plans a March special session on the issue. "If we can save one life by keeping a violent offender in prison for his entire sentence, then we have accomplished something," said Howard Gwynn, a prosecutor in Newport News. But, warned a corrections worker, "If you were to get rid of parole, we'd have to keep the prison on constant lockdown," which would eliminate prison labor

Continued on p. 115

At Issue:

Should states increase the length of time convicted criminals are incarcerated?

YES

JAMES WOOTTON

President, Safe Streets Alliance
FROM *"TRUTH IN SENTENCING," HERITAGE FOUNDATION STATE BACKGROUNDER,* DEC. 30, 1993.

Americans are increasingly alarmed at news stories of violent crimes committed by individuals who had received long sentences for other crimes and yet were released after serving only a small fraction of their time. This alarm is legitimate because a high proportion of such early-release prisoners commit serious crimes after being released. If crime is to be reduced in America, this trend needs to be reversed. Experience shows clearly that the first step in fighting crime is to keep violent criminals off the street. Keeping violent criminals incarcerated for at least 85 percent of their sentences would be the quickest, surest route to safer streets, schools and homes.

Government statistics on release practices in 36 states and the District of Columbia in 1988 show that although violent offenders received an average of seven years and 11 months imprisonment, they actually served an average of only two years and 11 months in prison — or only 37 percent of their imposed sentences. The statistics also show that, typically, 51 percent of violent criminals were discharged from prison in two years or less, and 76 percent were back on the streets in four years or less.

When these prisoners are released early, a high percentage commit more violent crimes. A three-year follow-up of 108,850 state prisoners released in 1983 from institutions in 11 states found that within three years 60 percent of violent offenders were rearrested for a felony or serious misdemeanor, 42 percent were reconvicted and 37 percent were reincarcerated. Of the violent offenders, 35 percent were rearrested for a new violent crime. Among non-violent prisoners released, 19 percent were rearrested within three years for a new violent crime. . . . Truth in sentencing will increase the length of time convicted violent criminals are incarcerated. . . . If required to serve at least 85 percent of their sentences, violent criminals would serve 2.3 times longer than they do now.

If the 55 percent of the estimated 800,000 current state and federal prisoners who are violent offenders were subject to serving 85 percent of their sentence, and assuming that those violent offenders would have committed 10 violent crimes a year while on the street, then the number of crimes prevented each year by truth in sentencing would be 4,400,000. That would be over two-thirds of the 6,000,000 violent crimes reported in the National Criminal Victims Survey for 1990. . . .

The time has come for states to enact truth-in-sentencing laws. There are few viable alternatives that protect citizens from the immediate threat of violent crime.

NO

CAMPAIGN FOR AN EFFECTIVE CRIME POLICY

FROM STATEMENT ISSUED IN NOVEMBER 1992.

Crime is a serious problem in the United States. While theories about cause and effect can be argued, there can be no debate about some of the facts.

- The U.S. has the highest rate of crime of any industrialized nation in the world.
- The U.S. has the highest rate of incarceration of any industrialized nation in the world.
- The cost of the criminal justice system, sustained mostly be state and local governments, has soared over the last decade and now threatens the ability to deliver many basic services.

Society will always need to incarcerate those who endanger the community, but for certain offenders, it is time to consider possibilities that already exist, cost less than prison and hold offenders accountable for their crimes. Too often sentencing practices, laws and prison-release policies needlessly hold offenders in prison, sometimes for long terms, when community-based alternatives would safely serve society's interest in punishment.

We recognize the extent to which crime degrades the lives of Americans. We believe that a wider network of intermediate sanctions is needed to create opportunities for offenders to repay their victims and their communities. And we believe that such sanctions could be used to control and rehabilitate offenders who would otherwise be incarcerated at great expense.

The unprecedented growth in the nation's prison population over the last decade has placed a heavy burden on taxpayers to build, maintain and operate prisons and jails. There have also been high costs associated with the disintegration of the families left behind. We are approaching — and, in some cases, have passed — the point at which it is no longer productive to invest in expanding our prison systems.

We urge those holding the public trust to refrain from politicizing crime and punishment policy. Policies founded on base human instincts and demagoguery will ultimately make the problem worse. We call on those in political office to engage in an informed debate about effective responses to the problem and to avoid the lure of simple and quick-fix solutions.

Court of Last Resort at an Overcrowded Prison

The basketball court has been sliced in half at the medium-security state prison in Jessup, Md., a gray, gritty town just south of Baltimore. A metal wall and scuffed wooden planks on the floor converted part of the facility to a dormitory for 82 inmates, who sleep in double-decker metal bunks jammed together in rows less than three feet apart.

Blaring radios compete with two prison-issued televisions throughout the day, while prisoners dressed mostly in sweat pants and athletic jerseys pass the hours reading, talking or just organizing the toiletries in their bedside lockers. Men lying in the top bunks stare at gaping holes cut in the ceiling panels to allow correction officers to check for contraband.

Designed to incarcerate 500 inmates when it opened in 1981, the prison now holds 1,140 of the state's convict population, which has multiplied from 8,000 in 1980 to more than 20,000. According to an inmate clerk at the facility, officials are regularly forced to accept new prisoners even if space is declared exhausted.

"We try and rotate new inmates through the dormitory so that no one is there permanently," explains a correctional officer. "Some don't like it because there are too many guys, and they feel more secure with just one roommate; but other guys are more social."

Maryland Department of Corrections

The state prison in Jessup, Md., turned its basketball court into a dormitory. Most prisoners live in the three-story "pods."

The advantage of the dormitory over standard units is the easy access to its larger shower room, its eight pay phones and its quieter, well-lighted side rooms where small groups can read or play cards.

But in the communal setting, "You can get in a fight over just about anything," says a correctional officer. "In here, whether or not to watch 'Oprah' is a big thing." Older, "more stable" prisoners enjoy a separate dorm. Prison rape, he adds, is not common in the dorm because "it's a private thing, a night thing, and nobody would want 36 witnesses."

Guards are outnumbered about 24-1 and don't carry weapons, but walkie-talkies assure that reinforcements are never far. They say it would be foolish to rely on force for discipline. "It's using your head, looking and listening," says a corrections officer. "You can see a situation building. And if you take a man away from his buddies, his anger level drops, but if you keep him with them, he has to save face."

Most inmates at Jessup live in pinwheel-shaped "pods," three-story units designed with a glass-floored central platform that affords guards a constant view of all cells, showers and even basement laundry and recreational facilities. The pod design also allows each cell to have an outside window, through whose mesh inmates can view the prison's gray brick buildings, lime-green sidewalks, athletic field, guard towers and 15-foot chain-link fences topped with curled barbed wire. The pods' double-bunked 11-by-7-foot cells contain their own sinks and toilets. Many are decorated with family photos and pinups.

Prisoners in the general population can walk unescorted through the prison hallways, bedecked with graffiti, AIDS warning posters and inmates' artworks, to the cafeteria, commissary, infirmary, library or chapel.

That freedom is denied to the 50 or so inmates confined to their cells in "segregation" or lockup, either because of rule infractions or as protection from other inmates. The men in lockup are less likely to enroll in courses or join other inmates in bidding for the limited number of 90-cents-a-day jobs in the laundry, print shop or maintenance and food service departments.

"The idle ones are unrefined," says Calvin Wilson, a case management specialist who handles inmate complaints at Jessup. "It's a matter of a guy wanting to do something for himself. And you don't hear complaints from the ones who're in school."

It costs $250,000 a week just to maintain security at the facility, says Warden Eugene M. Nuth. "It cost $19 million to build it," he says, "but that's now our annual budget, so we build it again every year."

Given tight state budgets, prospects for relieving the crowding at Jessup and other Maryland prisons are not bright, in Nuth's view, unless neighborhoods are stabilized against crime and non-prison alternatives are encouraged. "Crowding has been a permanent situation in this country since the 1770s," he says. "The system today was invented 500 years ago, yet we insist on repairing it. You don't repair old cars because you can't find parts. Incarceration in general is simply not a deterrent to crime. For those who've been incarcerated previously, however, it becomes a deterrent."

Continued from p. 112

and double costs.[48]

McNulty of the First Freedom Coalition, who is advising Allen, says the governor wants Virginia to become one of the first states to qualify for federal aid under the regional prison proposal. ■

OUTLOOK

Looking for Alternatives

In Alabama in 1990, legislators introduced a mandatory-sentencing bill that would have required a minimum one-year term for drug possession or trafficking, regardless of the drug. Analysts estimated that the bill would require 572 new prison beds at a cost of $14 million for construction and $7 million a year for operations. The bill was abandoned.

Some critics feel that the federal government may make the same turnabout. "Collectively, the Senate had a tantrum about crime, but cooler heads will prevail," says Krisberg of the National Council on Crime and Delinquency. As an alternative, the council has offered an array of social spending and prison and sentencing reforms estimated to save the government $9.6 billion. "The most valuable thing the federal government can do is provide seed money for programs of proven value in states," Krisberg says.

The American Bar Association and numerous state and local government organizations favor passage of so-called community corrections acts, already in effect in 19 states, which target state money and technical expertise at encouraging the use of nonprison alternatives.

"States do not have the money to finance complex sentencing systems or to build vastly larger prison systems," writes former Minnesota sentencing official Kay A. Knapp, who now runs the Institute for Rational Public Policy based in Takoma Park, Md. "State codes are in much better shape than the federal code and thus allow for easier drafting of guidelines. Moreover, state prosecutors typically do not have the essentially unrestrained charging discretion of federal prosecutors. Finally, there is a long history of state independence from federal influence in this area."[49]

Other alternatives also are being explored. South Carolina has begun making the parents of juvenile offenders pay $17-$24 in daily jail costs. Some jurisdictions are creating prison space by releasing elderly prisoners, who are generally deemed no longer a threat to society. Since 1989, the Project for Older Prisoners, run by George Washington University law Professor Jonathan R. Turley, has helped more than 50 inmates over age 55 obtain release.[50] And within a decade, futurists predict, "invisible prisons" will hold felons using electronic monitoring and behavior-altering drugs implanted in a prisoner's arm that can be activated remotely if the subject misbehaves.[51]

The movement to privatize prison construction and operation continues to be touted as a way to save money.[52] Charles W. Thomas, a professor of criminal justice at the University of Florida, points to savings of up to 14 percent —largely due to speeded up construction — at some of the 65 private prisons operating in 16 states (mostly in Texas).[53]

One possible quick fix — repatriating the more than 50,000 federal and state inmates who are not U.S. citizens — would require complicated international negotiations.

By the year 2000, predicts DiIulio of Princeton, the number of inmates, probationers or parolees in the corrections system could easily surpass 4 million, at a price tag of $40 billion a year — roughly 20 times the cost in 1975.[54]

U.S. Has the Highest Incarceration Rate

The United States has the highest per capita rate of incarceration of any industrialized nation in the world, followed by South Africa and Venezuela.

Nation	Rate of Incarceration per 100,000 population-1990/1991
United States	455
South Africa	311
Venezuela	177
Hungary	117
Canada	111
China	111
Australia	79
Portugal	77
Czechoslovakia	72
Denmark	71
Albania	55
Netherlands	46
Republic of Ireland	44
Sweden	44
Japan	42
India	34

Source: "Americans Behind Bars: One Year Later," The Sentencing Project, February 1992

The University of Minnesota's Tonry says a swing away from prison building is likely, but on financial rather than ethical grounds. "It won't be a conversion to a kinder, gentler nation," he says, "but the cold hard facts of costs."

According to McNulty, "the debate is over" because the public backs the movement to incarcerate. "Those in opposition will find themselves in opposition to what's happening across the country. We will spend the 1990s focusing on details."

Miller, the veteran corrections official, charges that the debate is being carried out through "soundbites, throwaway lines and the latest political speech" and is part of a hidden agenda to go after America's blacks. "When we say crime, we mean race," he says. "We will have a majority of black men in prison by the year 2000."

Beth Carter of the Campaign for an Effective Crime policy says that politicians have always raised fears and simplified the issues: "It's far less appealing to say, 'I'd like to talk with you about the facts on crime and punishment and discuss rational approaches to solutions.' People are naturally more attracted to simple solutions."

Whatever approach to crime reduction prevails, warns the Advisory Commission on Intergovernmental Relations, lawmakers must be realistic about the resources needed by the prison system or face jeopardizing the entire criminal justice system. "Ignoring the need for space," says the commission, "compromises the integrity of the actions of the police, prosecutor, defender, judge, probation and parole officers, as well as the penal system itself." [55] ■

Notes

[1] In addition to the sweeping anti-crime proposal passed by the Senate, several smaller crime bills have been approved by the House. For details, see "House Passes Anti-Criime Bills; More Debate in the Offing," *CQ Weekly Report*, Nov. 27, 1993, p. 3273.

[2] *Corrections Today*, August 1989, p. 122.

[3] Advisory Commission on Intergovernmental Relations, "The Role of General Government Elected Officials in Criminal Justice," May 1993, p. 14.

[4] For background, see "War on Drugs," *The CQ Researcher*, March 19, 1993, pp. 241-265.

[5] Speech to National Symposium on Drugs and Violence in America, June 18, 1993.

[6] Alvin J. Bronstein, untitled article, *GAO Journal*, fall 1989, p. 29.

[7] Mary K. Shilton, *Community Corrections Acts for State and Local Partnerships* (1992), p. 4.

[8] Column in *The Wall Street Journal*, Dec. 17, 1993.

[9] Eugene H. Methvin, "Doubling the Prison Population Will Break America's Crime Wave," *Corrections Today*, February 1992, p. 28.

[10] "Survey of State Prison Inmates 1991," Bureau of Justice Statistics, March 1993.

[11] Heritage Foundation State Backgrounder, "How States Can Fight Violent Crime: Two Dozen Steps to a Safer America," June 7, 1993.

[12] Methvin, *op. cit.*, p. 30.

[13] Perry Johnson, "Methvin's Incarceration Argument Doesn't Hold Up Under Scrutiny," *Corrections Today*, April 1992, p. 198.

[14] Albert J. Reiss Jr. and Jeffrey A. Roth (eds.) *Understanding and Preventing Violence* (1993), p. 292.

[15] Elliott Currie, *Reckoning: Drugs, the Cities and the American Future* (1993), p. 150.

[16] Op-ed column in *The Washington Post*, Dec. 19, 1993.

[17] Testimony from Bureau of Prisons Director Kathleen Hawk before the House Judiciary Committee, May 12, 1993.

[18] Advisory Commission on Intergovernmental Relations, *op. cit.*, p. 16.

[19] Edna McConnell Clark Foundation, "Time to Build? The Realities of Prison Construction," pamphlet, January 1994, p. 18.

[20] Edwin Zedlewski, "Making Confinement Decisions," National Institute of Justice, July 1987.

[21] Lynn S. Branham, "The Use of Incarceration in the United States," American Bar Association, April 1992, p. 24.

[22] John J. DiIulio Jr. and Anne Morrison Piehl, "Does Prison Pay? The Stormy National Debate over the Cost-Effectiveness of Imprisonment," *Brookings Review*, fall 1991, p. 28.

[23] Alfred Blumstein, "Prison Populations: A System Out of Control?" *Crime and Justice: A Review of Research* (1988), p. 231.

[24] Boot camps will be discussed in *The CQ Researcher* published Feb. 25, 1994.

[25] Column in *The Washington Post*, July 7, 1993.

[26] *Los Angeles Times*, May 17, 1993.

[27] Shilton, *op. cit.*, p. 3.

[28] Methvin, *op. cit.*, p. 40.

[29] Paul W. Keve, *Prisons and the American Conscience: A History of Federal Corrections* (1991), p. 3.

[30] Capsule history in *The Houston Post*, June 28, 1992.

[31] Keve, *op. cit.*, p. 20.

[32] John J. DiIulio Jr., *No Escape: The Future of American Corrections* (1991), p. 20.

[33] Keve, *op. cit.*, p. 53.

[34] Bureau of Prisons, "The Development of the Federal Prison System," 1979.

[35] Bert Useem and Peter Kimball, *States of Siege: U.S. Prison Riots, 1971-1986* (1989), p. 14.

[36] *The Public Interest*, spring 1974, reprinted in *The Public Interest on Crime and Punishment* (1984), pp. 1-34.

[37] James Q. Wilson, *Thinking About Crime* (1975), p. 172.

[38] Keve, *op. cit.*, p. 222.

[39] Pamphlet from the National Coalition for Jail Reform, 1985, p. 5.

[40] Susan Turner and Joan Petersilia, "Focusing on High-Risk Parolees," RAND Corp (1992).

[41] *The Houston Post*, March 7, 1993.

[42] Advisory Commission on Intergovernmental Relations, op. cit., p. 54, quoting from *The Washington Post.*

[43] Donna Hunzeker, "Can States Make Sentencing a Science?" *State Legislatures*, October 1991, p. 19.

[44] *Minneapolis Star-Tribune*, Dec. 22, 1993.

[45] ACLU press release on the Senate crime bill amendments, Nov. 19, 1993.

[46] For details, see Phil Kuntz, "Tough-Minded Senate Adopts Crime Crackdown Package," *Congressional Quarterly Weekly Report*, Nov. 20, 1993, pp. 3199-3201.

[47] Reuters dispatch, Jan. 12, 1994.

[48] Quoted in *The Washington Post*, Jan. 9, 1994.

[49] Kay A. Knapp and Dennis J. Hauptly, "State and Federal Sentencing Guidelines: Apples and Oranges," *U.C. Davis Law Review*, spring 1992, p. 679.

[50] *Business Week*, Aug. 16, 1993.

[51] Max Winkler, "Walking Prisons: The Developing Technology of Electronic Controls," *The Futurist*, July-August 1993, p. 34.

[52] For background, see "Privatization," *The CQ Researcher*, Nov. 13, 1992, pp. 985-1009.

[53] Charles W. Thomas, "Are 'Doing Well' and 'Doing Good' Contradictory Goals of Privatization?" *Large Jail Network Bulletin*, winter 1993.

[54] DiIulio, *op. cit.*, p. 4.

[55] Advisory Commission on Intergovernmental Relations, *op. cit.*, p. 138.

Bibliography

Selected Sources Used

Books

Currie, Elliott, *Reckoning: Drugs, the Cities, and the American Future*, Hill and Wang, 1993.

A veteran crime analyst from the Institute for the Study of Social Change at the University of California-Berkeley evaluates the effectiveness of the war on drugs, devoting a chapter to criticizing the movement to incarcerate.

John J. DiIulio Jr., *No Escape: The Future of American Corrections*, Basic Books, 1991.

A Princeton University professor of politics and public affairs gives opinions on controversial issues in the corrections field, from privatization to crowding to the debate over whether society gets its money's worth from incarceration.

Earley, Pete, *The Hot House: Life Inside Leavenworth Prison*, Bantam Books, 1992.

A former *Washington Post* reporter gives a highly personal account of months spent inside one of the nation's major federal prisons, offering profiles of inmates and examining daily tensions.

Keve, Paul W., *Prisons and the American Conscience: A History of Federal Corrections*, 1991.

A Virginia Commonwealth University historian traces the evolution of the federal penal system from Colonial days through the 1980s expansion of the Bureau of Prisons.

Shilton, Mary K., *Community Corrections Acts for State and Local Partnerships*, American Correctional Association, 1992.

An analyst with the National Association of Criminal Justice Planners reports on how states have implemented legislation to encourage community corrections, providing localities with funding and technical assistance for less-expensive alternatives to prison.

Useem, Bert, and Peter Kimball, *States of Siege: U.S. Prison Riots, 1971-198*, Oxford University Press, 1989.

Two sociologists examine the causes, context and reaction to major prison riots in recent U.S. history, concluding that overcrowding is not a major factor.

Weiss, Ann E., *Prisons: A System in Trouble*, Enslow Publishers, 1988.

A Maine-based author who popularizes discussions of legal issues evaluates the history, condition and future of the American penal system.

Reports

Edna McConnell Clark Foundation, *Americans Behind Bars*, March 1992.

This booklet from a New York City-based philanthropy with an interest in social issues offers analysis of the costs, causes, effects and prognosis for the movement to build more prisons, taking a skeptical approach.

Heritage Foundation, *How States Can Fight Violent Crime: Two Dozen Steps to a Safer America*, June 7, 1993.

A conservative Washington think tank presents an argument for enacting more mandatory sentences and building more prisons as a solution to rising crime.

Advisory Commission on Intergovernmental Relations, *The Role of General Government Elected Officials in Criminal Justice*, May 1993.

This special report to a congressionally mandated association of officials at the federal, state and local levels examines how crime is approached under the "fragmented" American systems of government and criminal justice.

Zedlewski, Edwin, *Making Confinement Decisions*, National Institute of Justice, July 1987.

A Justice Department analyst presents an early and influential argument as to why money spent on incarcerating the worst criminals ultimately will pay off.

The Next Step

Additional information from UMI's Newspaper & Periodical Abstracts database

Alternatives to Prison

"Alternatives to prison," *Futurist*, January 1994, pp. 53-54.

Overcrowded prisons and the ineffectiveness of probation have prompted judicial authorities to turn to alternative measures. Day fines, intensive supervision and electronic monitoring are among proposed alternatives.

Brenner, Elsa, "Alternatives to jail save $3 million," *The New York Times*, Aug. 15, 1993, p. WC7.

County Executive Andrew P. O'Rourke of Westchester County, N.Y., said that a program to move some non-violent criminals from the County Jail to rehabilitation services and shelters in 1992 saved the county $3 million. The merits of alternative punishments to jail terms are discussed.

Cottrell, James H. and John H. Shanahan, Jr., "A jail that floats," *Corrections Today*, April 1992, pp. 132-133.

The overcrowded conditions of prisons have led to innovative programs to incarcerate offenders. The use of water-borne facilities for inmates is discussed.

Smith, Linda G. and Ronald L. Akers, "A comparison of recidivism of Florida's community control and prison: A five-year survival analysis," *Journal of Research in Crime & Delinquency*, August 1993, pp. 267-292.

Florida's Community Control Program is the U.S.'s largest intermediate sanction (home confinement) program for felons. The effectiveness of this sanction compared with imprisonment is examined.

The Courts

Cole, Richard B. and Jack E. Call, "When Courts Find Jail and Prison Overcrowding Unconstitutional," *Federal Probation*, March 1992, pp. 29-39.

Since 1979, there have been 49 cases in which courts have ruled that prison overcrowding was unconstitutional. A look at how courts have sought to remedy overcrowding.

Greene, Andrea D., "U.S. Supreme Court backs ruling on felons in county jail," *Houston Chronicle*, June 22, 1993, p. A14.

The Supreme Court let stand an order requiring Texas prison officials to remove felony inmates from the Harris County Jail, a ruling that solidified local arguments that the state has a duty to provide housing for felons.

The Current Situation

Beck, Melinda, "Kicking the prison habit," *Newsweek*, June 14, 1993, pp. 32-37.

New incarcerations for drug offenses are growing much faster than those for any other crimes. The population in state prisons has more than doubled in 10 years. Possible solutions are discussed.

"Corrections chief makes argument for school prayer," *The Washington Times*, June 17, 1993, p. B6.

Peter G. Decker Jr., the outgoing chair of the Board of Corrections, placed some of the blame for Virginia's exploding prison population on the 30-year-old ban on school prayer.

Curtin, John J. Jr., "The Crisis in Corrections," *ABA Journal*, May 1991, p. 8.

Prison overcrowding threatens safety in and outside of the correctional facilities and diverts money from more beneficial domestic programs, Curtin writes.

Katel, Peter, "New Walls, No Inmates," *Newsweek*, May 18, 1992, p. 63.

Several prisons in Florida have been built but have been rendered unoperational due to budgetary constraints. Prison overcrowding in Florida is so widespread that many prisoners are being granted early releases to alleviate the problem.

McMillion, Rhonda, "Hard time," *ABA Journal*, March 1993, p. 100.

The impact of mandatory minimum sentencing is coming under congressional scrutiny as the nation continues its fight against crime. It is argued that mandatory minimum sentences are a primary cause of prison overcrowding.

Murphy, Sean P., and Gerard F. Russell, "Jail melee blamed on overcrowding," *Boston Globe*, Oct. 23, 1993, p. 13.

County corrections officials blamed overcrowding for a melee at the Worchester County (Massachusetts) House of Correction and warned that tension is increasing among inmates in other facilities across the state.

Turley, Jonathan, "A Solution to Prison Overcrowding," *USA Today: The Magazine of the American Scene*, November 1992, pp. 80-81.

The failure of the prison system to release geriatric low-risk prisoners to make room for younger, more dangerous ones is an emerging U.S. scandal, Turley writes.

Parole and Probation

Gondles, James A. Jr., "Let's take a look at the big picture when offering solutions to crowding," ***Corrections Today*****, October 1992, p. 6.**
The corrections profession as a whole needs to investigate alternatives to incarceration to solve the problem of prison overcrowding, according to an editorial. Probation and parole are going to be most affected by prison alternatives, it says.

Petersilia, Joan and Susan Turner, "An evaluation of intensive probation in California," ***Journal of Criminal Law & Criminology*****, fall 1991, pp. 610-658.**
Intensive supervision probation (ISP), a type of criminal sanction that is more stringent and punitive than traditional probation, but less expensive and coercive than incarceration, is discussed. ISP may be a viable solution to the problem presented by increasing numbers of felony offenders on probation because crowded prisons cannot accommodate them.

Prisons Overseas

Aduba, J. Nnamdi, "Overcrowding in Nigerian prisons: A critical appraisal," ***Journal of Criminal Justice*****, 1993, pp. 185-191.**
The special characteristics of the Nigerian prison population are examined, and "overcrowding" in Nigerian prisons is discussed.

Roth, Andrew, "Sideliners," ***New Statesman & Society*****, Oct. 22, 1993, p. 26.**
Home Secretary Michael Howard has risked the open contempt of his legal peers with his methods of dealing with prison overcrowding, according to Roth.

Travis, Alan, "Bail clampdown adds to jail pressures," ***Guardian*****, Nov. 10, 1993, p. 2.**
On Nov. 9, 1993, Home Secretary Michael Howard acknowledged that new powers to tighten the bail laws will add significantly to the rapidly rising population in Britain's prison. The powers are aimed at tackling "bail bandits" who commit offenses while awaiting trial.

Research and Studies

Joyce, Nola M., "A View of the Future: The Effect of Policy on Prison Population Growth," ***Crime & Delinquency*****, July 1992, pp. 357-368.**
The prison population in Illinois is projected to increase from over 28,000 to nearly 45,400 by the year 2000, costing $1.2 billion for construction to maintain prison crowding at 68 percent double and multicelling. The factors driving this growth and a variety of policy options to lower projections are examined.

Ruback, R. Barry, and Timothy S. Carr, "Prison crowding over time: The relationship of density and changes in density to infraction rates," ***Criminal Justice & Behavior*****, June 1993, pp. 130-148.**
The relationship between institutional density and institutional infractions was examined for 65 different institutions over a 10-year period. No consistent pattern of effects for density was found, the authors write.

Schurr, Carolyn, "Crime and Punishment," ***ABA Journal*****, May 1991, p. 23.**
A recent study indicated that the U.S. holds the world's record for the highest rate of incarceration, that taxpayers aren't spending their money wisely and that large-scale imprisonment provides no cure-all for crime.

Solutions

Cronin, Mary, "Gilded Cages," ***Time*****, May 25, 1992, pp. 52-54.**
New designs for jails and prisons are discussed. The new designs are the product of both urgent necessity and emerging philosophy: an exploding population of convicts on the one hand and, on the other, some new theories on how to treat convicts.

Eagleton, Thomas, "Prison cells and teen-age funerals," ***St. Louis Post-Dispatch*****, Nov. 21, 1993, p. B3.**
Thomas Eagleton discusses Congress' attempts to deal with prison overcrowding with new crime legislation.

Lemov, Penelope and Rob Gurwitt, "The Next Best Thing to Prison," ***Governing*****, December 1991, pp. 34-39.**
Alternative sentencing has not relieved the overcrowding in prisons as much as many believed it would, but the approach can still make a difference, the authors write. In these programs, prisoners are required to get a high school diploma and a job so they can be productive citizens after their term is over. The political clout of prison guards is also discussed.

McGinley, Laurie, "Program to free certain elderly inmates draws interest as way to help unclog crowded prisons," ***The Wall Street Journal*****, Aug. 18, 1993, p. A12.**
Jonathan Turley, a 32-year-old law professor in Washington, D.C., has worked with his nonprofit group, the Project for Older Prisoners, to help unclog the nation's crowded prisons by freeing elderly prisoners who no longer seem to pose a threat to society. So far, the group has helped free about two dozen inmates, not one of whom has been rearrested.

Mutch, David, "States take up prison reform," ***Christian Science Monitor*****, Dec. 30, 1993, p. 3.**
To lessen inmate crowding, Florida has become the first state to drop mandatory prison sentences for lesser drug offenses. Almost all state prisons in the U.S. are overcrowded, and some are facing the same dilemma Florida has faced: deciding which criminals to set free early.

Back Issues

Great Research on Current Issues Starts Right Here...Recent topics covered by The CQ Researcher are listed below. Before May 1991, reports were published under the name of Editorial Research Reports.

JULY 1992
Alternative Energy
Prescription Drug Prices
Alzheimer's Disease
Infant Mortality

AUGUST 1992
The Homeless
Work, Family and Stress
NATO's Changing Role
Marine Mammals vs. Fish

SEPTEMBER 1992
Domestic Partners
Violence in Schools
Public Broadcasting
Women in the Military

OCTOBER 1992
Depression
U.S. Auto Industry
Youth Apprenticeships
Hispanic Americans

NOVEMBER 1992
Physical Fitness
Privatization
Paying for College
U.S. Policy in Asia

DECEMBER 1992
Crackdown on Smoking
The New CIA
Eating Disorders
Women and AIDS

JANUARY 1993
Hate Crimes
Child Sexual Abuse
Nuclear Fusion
U.S. Trade Policy

FEBRUARY 1993
Community Policing
Europe's New Right
School Censorship
Violence Against Women

MARCH 1993
Gay Rights
Aid to Russia
War on Drugs
TV Violence

APRIL 1993
Head Start
High-Speed Rail
Children's Legal Rights
Muslims in America

MAY 1993
Cults in America
Preventing Teen Pregnancy
Software Piracy
National Parks

JUNE 1993
Food Safety
Prostitution
Childhood Immunizations
National Service

JULY 1993
Electric Cars
Population Growth
Downward Mobility
Intelligence Testing

AUGUST 1993
Mental Illness
Bilingual Education
Foreign Policy Burden
School Funding

SEPTEMBER 1993
Suburban Crime
Public Housing
Supreme Court Preview
Immigration Reform

OCTOBER 1993
Airline Safety
Disaster Response
Science in the Courtroom
The Glass Ceiling

NOVEMBER 1993
Paying for Retirement
Charitable Giving
Privacy in the Workplace
Adoption

DECEMBER 1993
U.S. Vietnam-Relations
Learning Disabilities
Child Care
Space Program's Future

JANUARY 1994
Racial Tensions in Schools
South Africa's Future
Worker Retraining
Pesticides

Back issues are available for $4.00 (subscribers) or $7.00 (non-subscribers). Quantity discounts apply to orders over ten. To order, call Congressional Quarterly Customer Service at (202) 887-8621.

Binders are available for $15.00. To order call 1-800-638-1710. Please refer to stock number 648.

Future Topics

- ***Drinking Water Safety***
- ***Religion and Schools***
- ***Juvenile Justice***

The CQ Researcher

PUBLISHED BY CONGRESSIONAL QUARTERLY INC.

Water Quality

Should safety standards for drinking water be tougher in the U.S.?

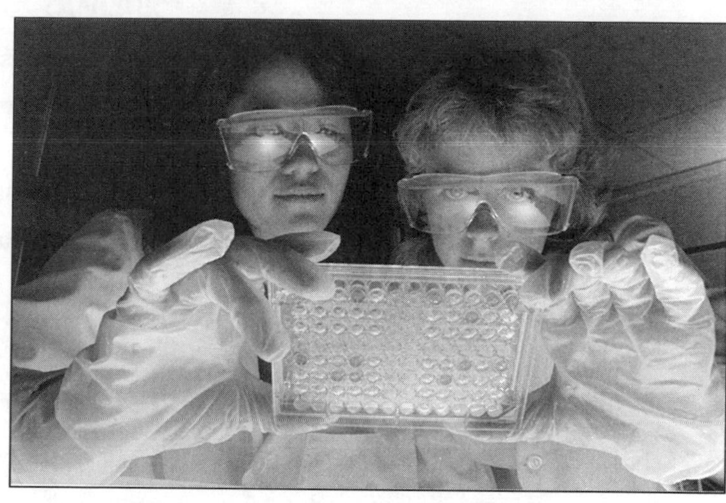

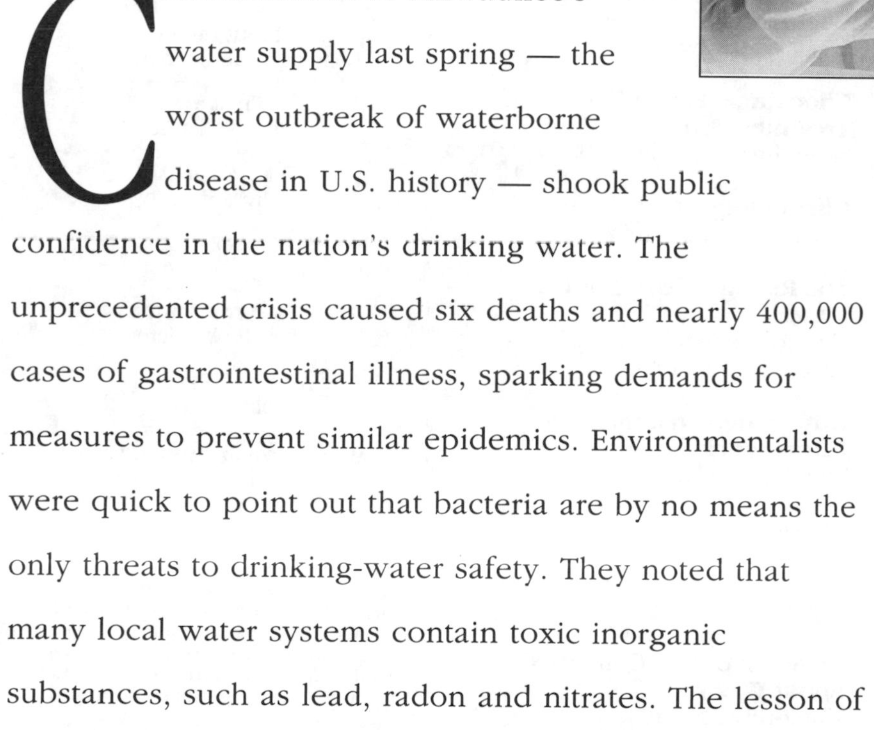

Contamination of Milwaukee's water supply last spring — the worst outbreak of waterborne disease in U.S. history — shook public confidence in the nation's drinking water. The unprecedented crisis caused six deaths and nearly 400,000 cases of gastrointestinal illness, sparking demands for measures to prevent similar epidemics. Environmentalists were quick to point out that bacteria are by no means the only threats to drinking-water safety. They noted that many local water systems contain toxic inorganic substances, such as lead, radon and nitrates. The lesson of Milwaukee, environmentalists say, is that federal rules regulating drinking-water safety need strengthening. But water industry officials, citing cost considerations, say the rules should be made more flexible.

Inside This Issue

CQ February 11, 1994 • Volume 4, No. 6 • 121-144

Formerly Editorial Research Reports

COVER: CHECKING WATER SAMPLES IN SOUTHERN CALIFORNIA FOR SIGNS OF BACTERIA. (METROPOLITAN WATER DISTRICT OF SOUTHERN CALIFORNIA)

February 11, 1994
Volume 4, No. 6

The CQ Researcher (ISSN 1056-2036). Formerly Editorial Research Reports. Published weekly (48 times per year, not printed the first Friday of any month with five Fridays) by Congressional Quarterly Inc., 1414 22nd St., N.W., Washington, D.C. 20037. Rates are furnished upon request. Second-class postage paid at Washington, D.C. POSTMASTER: Send address changes to The CQ Researcher, 1414 22nd St., N.W., Washington, D.C. 20037.

Water Quality

BY RICHARD L. WORSNOP

THE ISSUES

For most Americans, potable water is a birthright. "Americans expect to be able to turn on the faucet and be supplied with a clean, safe stream of water to brush their teeth, make their coffee, cook their spaghetti, wash the dishes and give the kids a bath," said Environmental Protection Agency (EPA) Administrator Carol M. Browner. Moreover, she added, they "are lucky enough to take safe drinking water for granted and hardly ever think about it." [1]

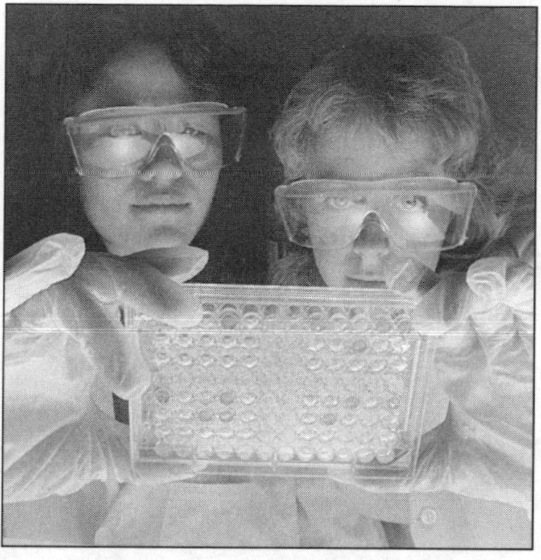

But millions of Americans did think about it last year, when cities and towns across the country faced unprecedented water emergencies — including the worst outbreak of waterborne disease in the nation's history. In March and April, nearly 400,000 people in the Milwaukee area alone became ill from an intestinal parasite that had invaded the municipal water supply. Similar but less serious problems occurred later in the year in New York City and Washington, D.C.

That wasn't all. Severe flooding of the Mississippi River and its major tributaries disabled the water-treatment systems in Des Moines, Iowa, and hundreds of other Midwestern communities.

To experts who say the nation's drinking water is not nearly as safe as it should be, the events of 1993 were only a grim warning of what could lie ahead. U.S. tap water is teeming with contaminants, these critics charge, adding that new harmful substances are joining the list virtually every day. The more worrisome contaminants include disease-causing microorganisms, lead, nitrates, arsenic and radon. (*See table, p. 125.*)

Even chlorine, the most widely used disinfectant in U.S. water-treatment systems, is now viewed as a potential health hazard. Scientists have found that chlorine reacts with decaying organic matter in water to form hundreds of chemical byproducts, some of which have caused cancer in laboratory animals (*see p. 126*).

Many current water-treatment problems are blamed on years of neglect by public authorities. "The main problem," says Professor Raymond Letterman, chairman of Syracuse University's department of civil engineering, is that water treatment "is the place where city fathers, or those in charge of water districts, like to skimp." The economizing even includes a tendency "not to hire the best people to operate these systems," Letterman adds.

The fragmented nature of U.S. drinking-water supplies also is seen as a problem. "It is an absurdity that there are 200,000 public water systems in the U.S. today . . . a substantial percentage of which are 'basket cases' that cannot even meet the most basic microbiological standards," wrote Erik D. Olson, a senior attorney for the Natural Resources Defense Council, an environmental group. "There is an urgent need for these non-viable and small systems to consolidate with larger systems." [2]

Smaller water-treatment systems are especially ill-equipped to deal with pollution of underground water, or groundwater, which is the main water source for more than half the country's rural population. Groundwater originates as precipitation and then seeps into the earth, forming subterranean rivers and pools. (The nation's most-populous areas depend on lakes, rivers and other surface-water sources.)

The difficulty with groundwater pollution is that toxic wastes follow the same underground route as the precipitation, eventually contaminating the groundwater reserves. While the pollution of surface water is often readily detected by telltale discoloration, groundwater pollution usually remains hidden until samples are brought to the surface. [3]

But the chief sources of groundwater pollution are present in staggering amounts, according to America's Clean Water Foundation. They include 390 million tons of municipal and industrial waste in 6,000 landfills; 23 million mostly residential septic systems; 1.7 million active and abandoned oil and gas wells; 72,000 active and inactive coal and mineral mines; 5 million active and inactive underground storage tanks at gas stations and other facilities; and vast quantities of pesticides, fertilizers, deicing salts and improperly disposed of motor oil. [4]

Protecting drinking water from contamination is considered all the more urgent in light of its relative scarcity and the world's spiraling population. Although 80 percent of the Earth's surface is covered by water, 97 percent of it is in oceans and seas and 2 percent is frozen in glaciers and polar ice, leaving only 1 percent for human use.

Freshwater's fragility as a natural resource doubtless will figure in the coming congressional debate on the

Many Sources of Pollution Remain

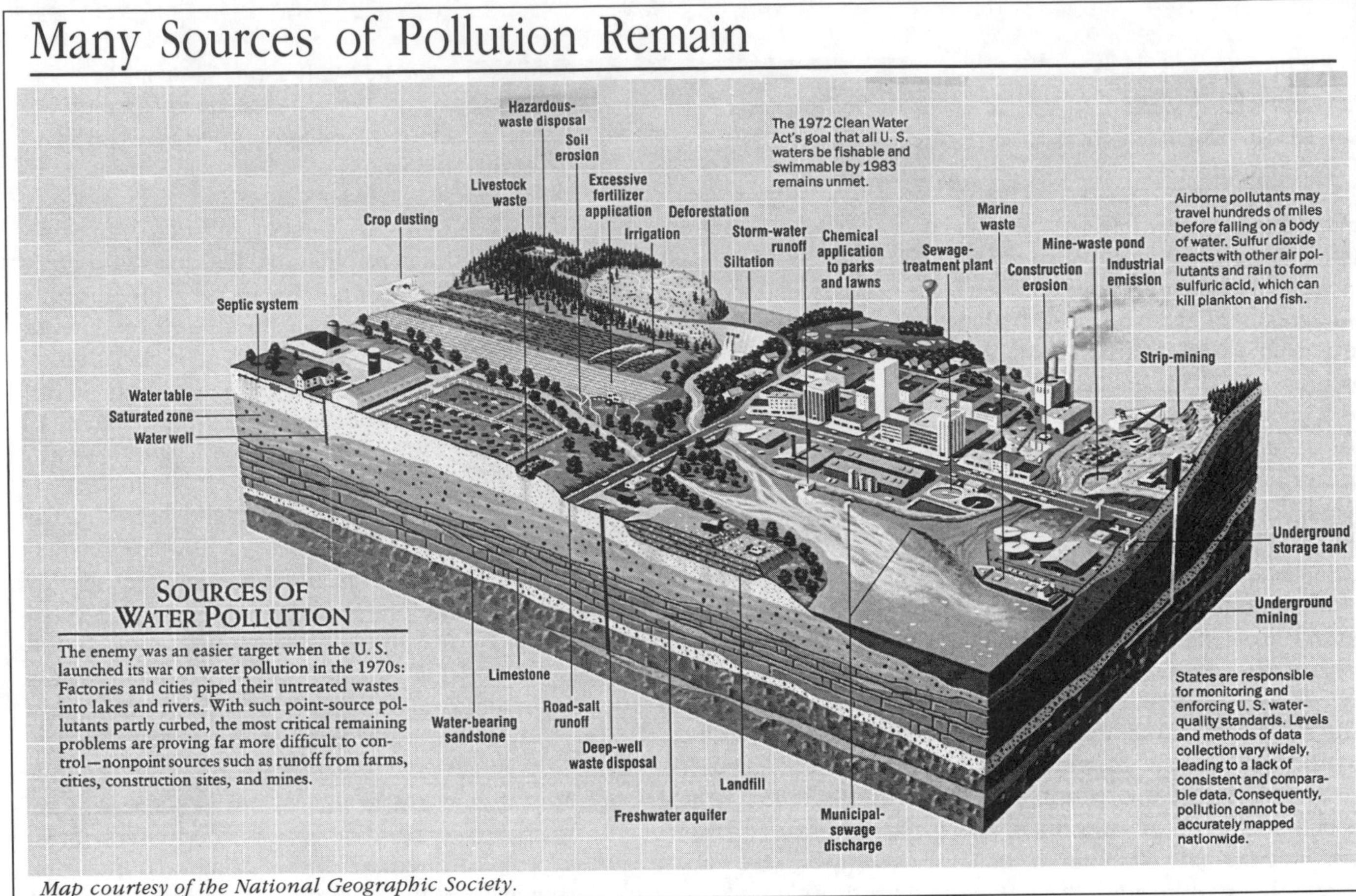
Hazardous-waste disposal
Soil erosion
Livestock waste
Excessive fertilizer application
Deforestation
Irrigation
Crop dusting
The 1972 Clean Water Act's goal that all U. S. waters be fishable and swimmable by 1983 remains unmet.
Storm-water runoff
Siltation
Chemical application to parks and lawns
Sewage-treatment plant
Marine waste
Mine-waste pond
Construction erosion
Industrial emission
Airborne pollutants may travel hundreds of miles before falling on a body of water. Sulfur dioxide reacts with other air pollutants and rain to form sulfuric acid, which can kill plankton and fish.
Septic system
Strip-mining
Water table
Saturated zone
Water well
Underground storage tank
Underground mining
SOURCES OF WATER POLLUTION
The enemy was an easier target when the U. S. launched its war on water pollution in the 1970s: Factories and cities piped their untreated wastes into lakes and rivers. With such point-source pollutants partly curbed, the most critical remaining problems are proving far more difficult to control—nonpoint sources such as runoff from farms, cities, construction sites, and mines.
Limestone
Water-bearing sandstone
Road-salt runoff
Deep-well waste disposal
Landfill
Freshwater aquifer
Municipal-sewage discharge
States are responsible for monitoring and enforcing U. S. water-quality standards. Levels and methods of data collection vary widely, leading to a lack of consistent and comparable data. Consequently, pollution cannot be accurately mapped nationwide.

Map courtesy of the National Geographic Society.

Safe Drinking Water Act (SDWA), which last underwent major change in 1986 (*see p. 128*). The battle lines for this year's contest already are clear. A Senate bill embodying the Clinton administration's thinking would relax some provisions of the existing law but retain what environmentalists regard as its heart: the procedure for setting drinking-water standards.

A rival House bill would go considerably further toward meeting the water industry's objections to the SDWA in its present form. For one thing, the measure would make it easier for small treatment systems strapped for funds to remain in compliance with the law. Environmentalists charge the bill caters too much to the water utilities and would gut the SDWA.

Affordability is sure to be a key debating point for proponents of both bills. Those favoring the House measure are likely to cite budget constraints in urging a more lenient regulatory approach. Supporters of the Senate bill may stress that drinking water, though traditionally priced low, is essential to life and well worth the cost of purifying.

As lawmakers prepare for the upcoming debate, these are some of the questions being asked by consumers, environmentalists and water-industry officials:

Is U.S. tap water safe to drink?

Blanket judgments about drinking-water safety in the United States are difficult to make, since water sources and treatment methods vary widely from community to community. In some isolated areas, water goes directly from the well to the home, where it may or may not undergo purification before use. More populous rural areas often have their own small water-treatment systems, but these often rely on antiquated equipment and methodology. The most advanced treatment systems, and consequently the safest drinking water, typically are found in and around large cities.*

Despite such differences in water quality, some experts give the nation's water supply a sparkling appraisal, among them Consumers Union. "Despite all the scary news reports," the product-testing organization declared

---

*The Safe Drinking Water Act regulates community and non-community public water systems. Community systems serve cities, towns, subdivisions and mobile-home parks with at least 15 service connections or 25 year-round residents. Non-community systems serve institutions, industries, camps, parks, hotels or businesses that are open to the public. Of the approximately 200,000 water systems in the country classified as public, 30 percent (60,000) are community systems and 70 percent (140,000) are non-community systems. The two types of systems serve 91 percent of the U.S. population; the remaining 9 percent of Americans get their water from non-public or individual sources, chiefly wells and springs.

in its 1993 buying guide to home water-treatment systems, "most people's drinking water in the U.S. is not seriously polluted. Public supplies are either comparatively clean to start with or are purified to bring them up to par." [5]

Syracuse's Letterman also feels that drinking-water quality "is good overall," though he's "not completely without concern."

Rep. Henry A. Waxman, D-Calif., chairman of the House Health and the Environment Subcommittee, takes a darker view. The December drinking-water alert in Washington suggested to him that "Here and across our nation . . . safe drinking water can no longer be taken for granted."

In Waxman's opinion, there were "startling" similarities between the crises in Washington and Milwaukee (*see p. 135*). "Both systems are vulnerable to source-water contamination," he wrote. "Both rely on an antiquated sand filter system. Both are operated by inadequately trained personnel. Both are subject to little meaningful oversight. And, incredibly, both cities routinely return contaminants caught by filters to the original-source water, where they can build up to overwhelm the filter and pose a threat of re-entering the drinking water." [6] Moreover, Waxman indicated, other cities suffer from similar deficiencies.

Experts agree that statistics are of little help in determining whether drinking water is safe. For instance, a recent report by the Centers for Disease Control and Prevention (CDC) on waterborne-disease outbreaks in 1991 and 1992 could easily be cited to support arguments that U.S. drinking-water quality is generally good. [7] During the two-year period, 17 states and territories reported a total of just 34 outbreaks associated with drinking water, causing 17,464 persons to fall ill. Significantly, 76 percent of the outbreaks were linked to well water, which often is untreated before use. (*See graph, p. 126.*)

The CDC report cautioned, however, that its data "should be interpreted with care" because the figures "probably do not reflect the true incidence" of waterborne-disease outbreaks. The report noted that "only a fraction" of such outbreaks "may be recognized, investigated, and/or reported to CDC or EPA, and the extent of underrecognition and underreporting is unknown." [8] By some estimates, only about one of every 25 cases of waterborne illness is reported to public health authorities.

Dr. Peter M. Schantz, deputy chief of the CDC Epidemiology Branch, cites a hypothetical situation to show why. Suppose, he says, that a wave of waterborne diarrheal illness strikes the New York metropolitan area, making 20,000 people sick. "It's theoretically possible that none of those patients would seek out the same physician for treatment," he says. "That's because there are 20,000 physicians in New York City alone. So, there would have to be an awful lot of cases before any given clinic got overwhelmed, realized something really strange was happening out there and made the phone calls to

Contaminants Found in Drinking Water

The Environmental Protection Agency (EPA) regulates safety levels for more than 80 contaminants sometimes found in drinking water. Some of the most common contaminants are listed below.

Contaminants	Health Effects	Sources
Organic Chemicals		
Benzene	cancer	fuel (leaking tanks); solvent commonly used in manufacture of industrial chemicals, pharmaceuticals, pesticides, paints and plastics
Toluene	kidney, nervous system, lung	chemical manufacturing; gasoline additive; industrial solvent
Vinyl chloride	cancer risk	polyvinyl chloride pipes and solvents used to join them; industrial waste from manufacture of plastics and synthetic rubber
Inorganic Chemicals		
Arsenic	dermal and nervous system toxicity effects	geological, pesticide residues, industrial waste and smelter operations
Asbestos	benign tumors	natural mineral deposits; also in asbestos/cement pipe
Copper	stomach and intestinal distress; Wilson's disease	corrosion of interior household and building pipes
Fluoride	skeletal damage	geological, additive to drinking water, toothpaste; foods processed with fluorinated water
Lead	central and peripheral nervous system damage; kidney; highly toxic to infants and pregnant women	corrosion of lead solder and brass faucets and fixtures; corrosion of lead service lines
Mercury	kidney, nervous system	industrial/chemical manufacturing; fungicide; natural mineral deposits
Nitrate	methemoglobinemia ("blue-baby syndrome")	fertilizers, feedlots, sewage; naturally in soil, mineral deposits
Radionuclides		
Radium 226/228	bone cancer	radioactive waste, geological/natural
Microbiological		
Giardia Lamblia	stomach cramps, intestinal distress (Giardiasis)	human and animal fecal matter
Legionella	Legionnaires disease (pneumonia), Pontiac Fever	water aerosols such as vegetable misters
Viruses	Gastroenteritis (intestinal distress)	human and animal fecal matter

Source: "Is Your Drinking Water Safe?" Environmental Protection Agency, September 1991

Causes of Waterborne Disease

Parasites in drinking water caused 21 percent of the 34 known outbreaks of waterborne disease in the United States in 1991-92; the cause of 68 percent of the outbreaks is unknown. A total of 17,464 individuals were reported ill in the outbreaks, though the actual number is considered much higher because contaminants are not always suspected.

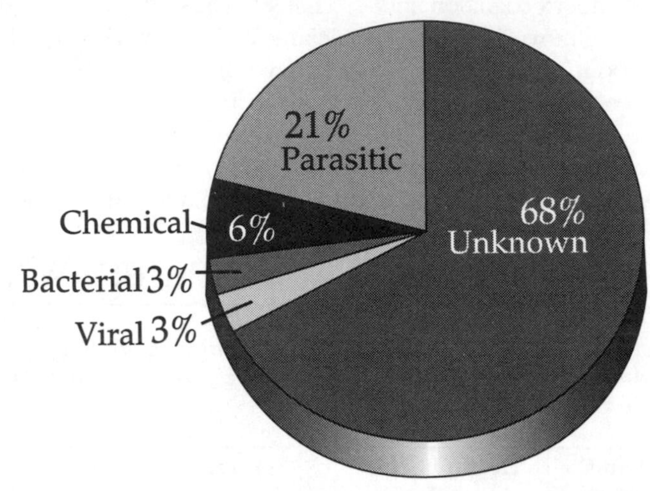

Source: Morbidity and Mortality Weekly Report, *Nov. 19, 1993; Centers for Disease Control. Figures don't add to 100 percent because of rounding.*

local health authorities that would trigger an investigation."

That's what happened in the Milwaukee area last spring, Schantz notes. "There were an estimated 400,000 cases of cryptosporidiosis. That overwhelmed the [local health-care] system and led to remedial action."

Since so many cases of waterborne illness apparently go unreported, experts in the field resort to informed guesswork to arrive at plausible data. One such study attracted considerable comment last summer. Based on estimates by CDC scientists, the study concluded that 940,000 Americans become ill each year from contaminated water and 900 die. [9]

Schantz reports that his CDC colleagues "did not feel the estimates in the study were particularly off base." Indeed, he says, "We do believe there probably are that many people out there becoming ill and dying" from waterborne disease.

But Dr. Dennis Juranek, chief of epidemiology at CDC, stresses that the study numbers "were strictly estimates; they weren't based on actual events or hard data. They could be overestimates or underestimates. We just don't have a good way of sorting that out."

Gathering hard data about waterborne illness is also difficult because "the total number of potentially pathogenic microorganisms in water is both unknown and continuing to increase," according to a recent report. The microbiologists who reached this conclusion noted that Cryptosporidium, for example, "was not generally recognized as a human pathogen until about 1976, and it was not incriminated in waterborne disease until 1985." [10] EPA has yet to issue a "maximum contaminant level" (MCL) for Cryptosporidium, the organism that caused the Milwaukee crisis.

In recent decades, scientists have found to their dismay that chemicals used to disinfect water can form toxic byproducts under certain conditions. A prime example is chlorine, which was first added to drinking water early this century to control the spread of typhoid, cholera and other once-common diseases. In the mid-1970s, researchers found that chlorine reacts with organic material in water to produce numerous chemical compounds, some of which have proved to be carcinogenic in laboratory tests on animals. One of the more dangerous substances is chloroform, which causes liver cancer in rats at high doses.

Some water-treatment experts want to replace chlorine with ozone for disinfection purposes. Others say chlorine is too effective to cast aside completely. They would concentrate instead on removing decaying leaves and other organic matter in stored water that combine with chlorine to form harmful disinfection byproducts (DBPs).

Is fluoridation of water harmful to health?

Concern over the presence of chlorine in water has revived interest in the decades-old debate over the merits of water fluoridation. The process involves adding a soluble compound of fluorine, a chemical element closely related to chlorine, to public water supplies to prevent tooth decay.

Despite the desirability of cavity-free teeth, fluoridation has stirred controversy from the start. In many a community in the 1940s and '50s, "forced" fluoridation was often portrayed as a communist plot. Opponents also claimed fluorides in water contributed to heart disease, cancer and mongolism, damaged bones and internal organs and constituted compulsory medication, thus infringing on individual and religious freedom. They also cited the risk of developing dental fluorisis — a mottling of the tooth surface that often appears initially as chalky white patches, which later darken.

Advocates of fluoridation, including the chief medical and dental societies, tended to dismiss anti-fluoridationists' charges as the rantings of a fringe group. To buttress their argument that fluoridation is benign, they cited numerous scientific studies. One of the earliest was a 10-year comparison, beginning in 1945, of children in Newburgh, N.Y., where the water was fluoridated, with kids in Kingston, N.Y., 35 miles away, where the water remained deficient in fluorides. At the end of the decade, Newburgh children had 58 percent fewer cavities than Kingston children. Similar studies elsewhere yielded similar results.

In recent years, however, cracks have begun to appear in the pro-fluoridation case. A key setback came in 1990 with a study by the National Toxicology Program (NTP), the federal government's chief evaluator of chemical risks. [11] In the study, five male rats among more than 100 that were fed large doses of sodium fluoride, the compound used in fluoridated water, developed bone cancer.*

Anti-fluoridationists hailed the NTP study as vindicating their cause. "It's like smoking," says Susan I. Pare, president of the Center for Health Action, an anti-fluoridation group in Springfield, Mass. "A single cigarette isn't going to kill you, but years of steady smoking can."

Pare's group does not object to fluoridated toothpaste and other topical applications of fluorides. "This is done at the user's discretion," she says. "And the user spits out the toothpaste afterward."

Pare argues that water fluoridation works a special hardship on poor people, who are least able to afford alternatives to fluoridated water. They also tend to be less healthy to begin with, making them more vulnerable to the adverse effects of fluorides, she says.

A recent report by the National Research Council (NRC) seemed to contradict the NTP study and affirm the safety of water fluoridation. The NRC asserted that more than 50 epidemiological studies did not "support the hypothesis of an association between fluoride exposure and increased cancer risk in humans." [12]

Indeed, drinking fluoridated water had only one harmful side effect, said the chairman of the study group, Barnard M. Wagner, a research professor of pathology at New York University Medical School. A minority of users developed "very mild to mild" cases of dental fluorosis," he said, indicating that the protection that fluoridation offers "far outweighs the small percentage of our population that shows fluorosis."

Biochemist John A. Yiamouyiannis, director of the Safe Water Foundation, in Delaware, Ohio, describes the National Research Council report as "just P.R. and damage control." He points to several passages in the document that seem to weaken its main conclusions. For instance, one passage states that "most dental researchers believe that the best approach to stabilizing the prevalence and severity of dental fluorosis is to control fluoride ingestion from foods, processed beverages and dental products rather than reduce the recommended concentrations of fluoride in drinking water." [13]

But Yiamouyiannis also cites this seemingly conflicting statement from the research council report: "applying such a policy would be formidable; reductions of fluoride in drinking water would be easier to administer, monitor and evaluate." [14]

Even the main benefit claimed for fluoridation — tooth decay prevention — has come under challenge. More recent surveys show the dental-health gap between fluoridated and non-fluoridated areas to be narrowing. In 1980, for instance, the National Institute for Dental Research (NIDR) found a difference of 33 percent between decay rates for children in fluoridated and non-fluoridated areas. A similar NIDR study in 1987 found a difference of only 25 percent. [15]

Dental-health experts disagree over

Test Your Freshwater IQ

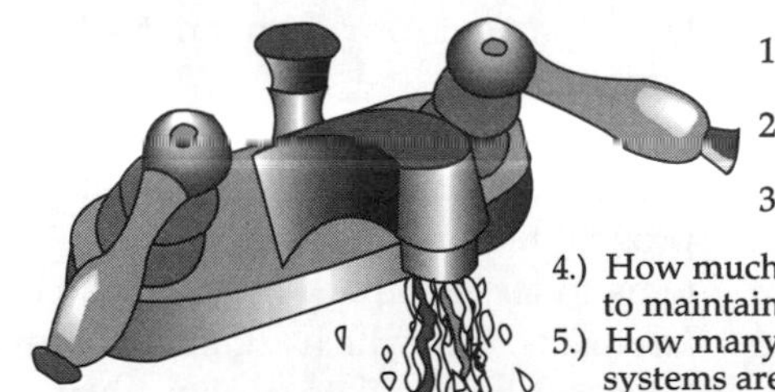

1.) How many households use private wells for their water supply?
2.) How long can a person live without food?
3.) How long can a person live without water?
4.) How much water must a person consume per day to maintain health?
5.) How many community public water supply systems are there in the United States?
6.) How much water do these utilities process daily?
7.) How much of the Earth's surface is water?
8.) Of all the Earth's water, how much is ocean or seas?
9.) How much of the world's water is frozen and therefore unusable?
10.) How much of the Earth's water is suitable for drinking water?

Answers: 1.) 17 million households; 2.) More than a month; 3.) Approximately one week, depending upon conditions; 4.) 2 1/2 quarts from all sources, i.e., water, food, etc.; 5.) 58,900; 6.) 34 billion gallons; 7.) 80%; 8.) 97%; 9.) 2%; 10.) 1%

Source: Environmental Protection Agency

*Of 50 male rats given fluoride in doses of 45 parts per million, one developed cancer; of 80 male rats given doses of 79 parts per million, four developed cancer. Sodium fluoride is added to public water supplies in concentrations of 1 part per million.

the cause of the trend. James Carlos, NIDR's chief epidemiologist, argued in 1990 that it is becoming increasingly hard to find a control group that is not benefiting from taking fluoride in some form, such as fluoridated toothpaste or bottled and canned beverages made from fluoridated water. Another explanation holds that dental health is improving in both fluoridated and nonfluoridated areas because of better nutrition and hygiene.

Should the Safe Drinking Water Act be relaxed?

The debate on drinking-water safety will become more focused when Congress takes up proposed legislation to reauthorize the Safe Drinking Water Act. Enacted 20 years ago, SDWA was extensively revised in 1986. Now there are calls for still more changes. But the two opposing sides — water-industry groups and environmentalists — have very different ideas on what to do.

The water industry favors a "more flexible" bill that would ease the regulatory burden on smaller treatment systems with limited financial resources. Environmental organizations, however, argue that recent outbreaks of waterborne illness point up the need to maintain strict quality standards.

Battle lines began to form last fall when Reps. Jim Slattery, D-Kan., and Thomas J. Bliley Jr., R-Va., introduced an SDWA reauthorization bill embodying many of the water industry's views. Most comments, pro and con, centered on the bill's proposed changes in the process for setting national drinking-water standards.

Under current law, EPA determines both a maximum contaminant level goal (MCLG) based on health data and an enforceable maximum contaminant level (MCL) that comes as close to the goal as is "feasible," taking costs and available water-treatment technology into account. In cases where an MCL is not feasible, the agency may specify a "treatment technique" to combat the contaminant in question. The law requires public water suppliers to test for contaminants on a regular basis and to notify the public when such sampling fails to occur or when an MCL has been exceeded.

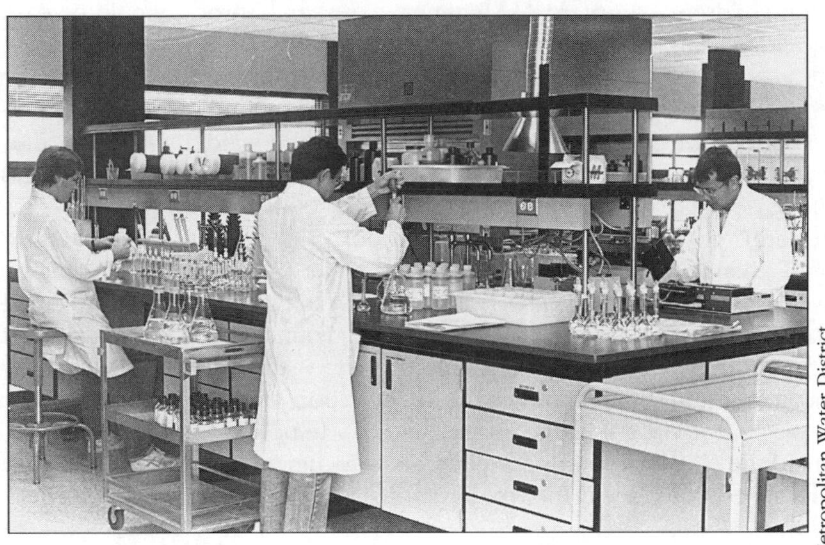
Metropolitan Water District

The water-quality lab at the Metropolitan Water District of Southern California.

Bliley and Slattery criticize these procedures as "a one-size-fits-all approach, requiring all public water systems to test for the same 80-plus contaminants for which standards have been established." In reality, they assert, "not all contaminants occur in every public water system."[16] Thus, their bill would give public water systems the authority — provided they obtain state approval — to focus on drinking-water contaminants that are most likely to cause trouble locally.

Slattery and Bliley also take issue with SDWA definitions of "goal" and "feasible" as they apply to contaminants. In many cases, they note, the goal becomes "zero risk," while feasible is generally interpreted as what a water system serving 1 million or more people can afford. Meeting such standards, they say, is too costly for many small water-supply systems.

Consequently, the Slattery-Bliley bill would require EPA to consider whether the "risk reduction benefits" of a "zero risk" standard are worth the cost of implementation. The measure would also direct the agency to identify what affordable "best technologies" are available to smaller water systems.

Industry groups embraced Slattery-Bliley. John H. Sullivan, deputy executive director of the American Water Works Association's (AWWA) Washington office, calls the bill's consideration of risk-reduction benefits and costs an "essential" provision. "We've got to do something that allows the utility industry to attack the biggest risks first," he says. "The industry just can't afford to do everything all at one time. People who say it can don't understand the magnitude of the problem."

Sullivan also likes the proposed changes in choosing which contaminants should be regulated. "The present method of dictating under the law without an in-depth scientific analysis is simply frivolous," he says. "And we like the additional options given to different-sized utilities. The law needs to be more flexible, more doable."

Vanessa M. Leiby, executive director of the Association of State Drinking Water Administrators, likes the bill's additional funding for state drinking-water programs. Moreover, "It provides flexibility for the states to

Choosing a Home Water-Treatment Unit

In rural areas, where wells serve many families, home water-treatment units are often used to make sure the water is pure and sweet.

Now even in urban areas with reliable water supplies, an increasing number of families also are installing home units. Some only want to improve the taste or clarity of the water flowing from the tap. Others want to reduce the water's "hardness" (dissolved mineral content). Still others are looking for extra protection against specific contaminants, such as radon, lead or nitrates.

Before a homeowner buys a home treatment unit for decontamination purposes, experts recommend that they find out precisely what's in their water first. Local water suppliers often will provide their latest laboratory test data.

A more expensive alternative is to have the water analyzed by a specialist recommended by the Water Quality Association, a trade group representing dealers and manufacturers of point-of-use water-treatment equipment. (Testing kits available from hardware stores are of limited help, since they can't detect most toxic pollutants.)

Assuming the test results show contaminants or other undesirable qualities are present, various types of devices can help alleviate the problem. Here are some of the most common ones:

Carbon filters: These vary in size from small, faucet-mounted devices to massive units capable of treating all the water in a home. Whole-house filters are especially useful for radon removal.

Reverse osmosis (RO) systems: An RO unit forces water under pressure through a semipermeable membrane, which blocks dissolved inorganic contaminants such as chloride, fluoride, nitrate, lead and salts. Most RO systems contain a carbon filter to remove organic chemicals.

Water softeners: Often bulky, water-softening units remove dissolved minerals that cause soap deposits, discolored laundry and damaged water heaters. Though the machines are highly effective against calcium, magnesium, iron and lead, they don't remove hazardous contaminants such as radon, nitrates or pesticides.

Distillers: Simple in principle, distillers boil water and cool the resulting steam until it condenses. Hazardous or unpalatable substances such as heavy metals and salts are generally left behind in the boiler.

Iron removers: These special-purpose devices use an oxidizing agent to rid water of dissolved iron, which, among other things, leaves rusty brown stains in bathtubs and sinks.

To give customers more options, manufacturers of home water-treatment equipment offer systems combining two or more technologies. R. Keith Reid, communications manager for the Water Quality Association, says no completely new technologies currently are available. Rather, researchers concentrate on making existing technology more efficient. For example, Reid cites efforts to improve the membranes in reverse-osmosis units by making them more resistant to breakdown from exposure to chlorine.

address monitoring requirements at the local level," she says. "And it looks at a different process for setting [water-quality] standards, so that EPA can place its priorities on the contaminants of greatest public health concern and set up a procedure to deal with contaminants that don't really fit into the normal mold."

One such contaminant is Cryptosporidium, the intestinal parasite behind the Milwaukee epidemic last spring. It is not among the substances that EPA requires public water systems to monitor, which, to Slattery and Bliley, highlights a serious flaw in SDWA. "[S]ince Milwaukee was using its limited resources to comply with the inflexible requirements of the Safe Water Drinking Act," they wrote, "it was not able to pay adequate attention to other contaminants that present obvious and serious threats to the public health." [17]

Environmental groups also have voiced concern about the Milwaukee outbreak. But they contend that the Slattery-Bliley bill would make things worse, not better. In 1993, EPA "was aware of the parasite's risks, but lacked sufficient funding to issue a standard to cover Cryptosporidium under the Safe Water Drinking Act," argued Marc Smolonsky, vice president for policy research at the Environmental Working Group. [18] Five other environmental and public-interest groups asserted in a joint statement that "it would likely take many years" if Slattery-Bliley became law "before EPA could even attempt to effectively control currently unregulated contaminants such as Cryptosporidium." [19]

The real moral of the Milwaukee epidemic, opponents of Slattery-Bliley say, is that current drinking-water standards should be strengthened. "Now is not the time to relax our guard against drinking-water contamination," declared NRDC attorney Erik D. Olson. Among other things, he noted, Slattery-Bliley would weaken existing safeguards against lead in drinking water and make it much easier for water utilities to obtain state variances from EPA health standards on grounds of unaffordability. [20]

Olson further argued that EPA has done a poor job of enforcing SDWA, noting that agency regulations "do not control some of the most widespread radioactive contaminants, such as radon." [21] Moreover, he said that water systems routinely fail to notify the public about outbreaks of contamination or failures to test for contaminants. "Even if this notice is purportedly provided," he said, "it is often done in a manner calculated to ensure that few if any customers ever actually are informed of or understand the problem.

"For example, many water systems typically place a notice in the 'Legal Notices' section of the newspaper to announce that they have violated the law. That's in full technical compliance with EPA rules, but in a way that virtually assures the public is never actually made aware of the problem." [22] ■

BACKGROUND

Early Water Woes

When people in early settlements did not live next to a river or a lake, they drew their drinking water from wells. The Chinese and the Egyptians are believed to have dug the first wells around 2000 B.C.

Aqueducts, used for transporting water long distances, probably were developed in ancient Mesopotamia. Their construction reached a peak, however, during the heyday of the Roman Empire. Romans preferred mountain water to well water, which often was tainted by sewage and other toxic wastes. Portions of some Roman aqueducts are still standing.

People in the ancient world had a sophisticated appreciation of water's many benefits, the historian Lewis Mumford observed. "The understanding of the importance of pure water not merely provided an incentive to municipal improvement," he wrote; "it led to the exploration of the curative properties of mineral springs; so that out of the original centers of medical treatment came their lineal descendants, the health resorts that specialized in natural hot and cold baths and copious water drinking." [23]

In the United States, efforts to provide a safe and reliable public water supply go back to Colonial times. A system built in Boston in 1652 consisted of wooden pipes and conduits to carry water from wells and springs to a wooden tank from which people could fill their water buckets. Almost a century later, in 1746, a Pennsylvania farmer named Schaeffer created what is considered the first water-supply system in the United States to serve an entire town, piping water from his farm to the community now called Schaefferstown.

Both in big cities in this country and throughout Europe, water availability and quality left much to be desired. Mumford noted that "In 1809, when London's population was about a million, water was available over the greater part of the city only in the basements of houses. In some quarters, water could be turned on for only three days a week."

The situation often was grimmer in the new industrial towns of the English Midlands. "Whole quarters were sometimes without water even from local wells," wrote Mumford. "On occasion, the poor would go from house to house in the middle-class sections, begging for water as they might beg for bread during a famine." [24]

Progress in 19th Century

New York became the first metropolis to assure itself of ample supplies of potable water when it opened a system of reservoirs and aqueducts north of the city in 1842. Nonetheless, contamination of water by sewage remained a problem there and elsewhere. It was only in the 1850s that scientists began to suspect disease could be transmitted by drinking water. The microscope and growing knowledge of bacteria helped confirm these suspicions. Around this time, moreover, following a typhoid epidemic in London, the first attempts were made to disinfect a city water supply with chlorine. [25]

In the United States, health and sanitary conditions did not show significant improvement until the turn of the century. Indeed, the increase in the number of water systems to more than 3,000 in 1900 actually contributed to major disease outbreaks; when contaminated, they provided a highly efficient vehicle for the spread of pathogenic bacteria. But the introduction in the mid-1870s of slow-sand filtration techniques and in the mid-1880s of rapid-sand filtration methods rapidly drove typhoid death rates down. The use of chlorination, at the turn of the century, virtually wiped out typhoid and cholera as public health threats.

Action in Congress

Epidemics in urban centers, coupled with growing knowledge of bacteriology, led to the formation of many state boards of health. In 1901, Congress authorized the construction of a Public Health Service Hygienic Laboratory "for the investigation of infectious and contagious diseases." The laboratory, completed in 1905, greatly improved the capacity of medical authorities to deal with water contamination.

In 1912, Congress enacted the first federal law aimed at water pollution by authorizing the Public Health Service (PHS) to investigate "the diseases of man and conditions influencing the propagation and spread thereof, including sanitation and sewage and pollution, either directly or indirectly, of the navigable streams and lakes of the United States."

World War I diverted attention from water quality, but after the war the PHS formulated a comprehensive program to meet pressing health needs. The program was based on close cooperation among federal, state and local gov-

Continued on p. 133

Chronology

Colonial Times

Efforts to construct water-distribution systems in the United States predate the American Revolution.

1652
Boston builds a water-distribution system consisting of wooden pipes and conduits.

1746
A Pennsylvania farmer pipes water from his farm to a nearby community in what is thought to be the first U.S. water system to serve an entire town.

—— • ——

1900s-1910s

Chlorination and other advances in combating waterborne disease bring dramatic improvement in overall U.S. water quality.

1901
Congress authorizes the construction of a Public Health Service Hygienic Laboratory "for the investigation of infectious and contagious diseases."

1912
President William Howard Taft signs the first federal law aimed specifically at water pollution.

—— • ——

1940s

The end of World War II reawakens interest in water-quality issues and many other domestic problems.

1948
President Harry S Truman signs the Water Pollution Control Act, the first such federal law.

—— • ——

1970s

During a decade that witnesses the birth of the U.S. environmental movement, Congress approves the two main federal laws governing water quality.

Oct. 18, 1972
Congress overrides President Richard M. Nixon's veto of the Federal Water Pollution Control Act Amendments of 1972, popularly known today as the clean water act. It sets a goal of eliminating all pollution discharges into U.S. waters by 1985.

Dec. 16, 1974
President Gerald R. Ford signs the Safe Drinking Water Act (SDWA), which allows the federal government for the first time to regulate drinking-water contaminants suspected of causing chemical poisoning or non-communicable diseases. The act authorizes the fledgling Environmental Protection Agency (EPA) to establish national standards for known or suspected drinking-water contaminants.

—— • ——

1980s

Dissatisfied with the slow pace of federal drinking-water regulation, Congress presses EPA to step up its efforts.

June 19, 1986
President Ronald Reagan signs legislation reauthorizing the Safe Drinking Water Act for five years. The measure lays out mandatory guidelines for regulating key contaminants, requires the monitoring of unregulated contaminants, establishes benchmarks for water-treatment technologies, strengthens enforcement and promotes protection of groundwater sources.

—— • ——

1990s

Growing awareness of groundwater contamination and mounting concern about waterborne disease spark demands for more effective ways of assuring drinking-water safety.

June 7, 1991
EPA issues a revised standard for lead in tap water that many critics condemn as inadequate.

April 1993
Milwaukee Mayor John C. Norquist tells residents on April 7 that the city's water supply is contaminated. By the time he lifts the advisory on April 14, some 400,000 persons have fallen ill from the organism; six people died.

July 1993
Unusually high levels of a common form of bacteria are found in the drinking water of two neighborhoods in New York. The bacteria, *E. coli*, thrive in human and animal waste and often signal the presence of other, less detectable organisms. The New York alert lasts only a few days and produces no reported cases of serious illness.

Dec. 8-11, 1993
Residents of Washington, D.C., and some adjacent suburban areas are warned by EPA to boil tap water before drinking it because of excessive cloudiness that could mean a harmful parasite had invaded the water supply. No parasites are found.

The Rising Tide of Bottled Water

In the world of bottled water, it's an iron law of nature: Wherever a drinking-water crisis strikes, sales of bottled water skyrocket. There's even a happy corollary to the law: Some of the sales gains are permanent.

About 10 to 15 percent of the people who switch to bottled water during an emergency "don't ever go back to water from the tap," says Lisa M. Prats, vice president of the International Bottled Water Association (IBWA).

Many regular users believe bottled water is inherently pure. However, the Association of State Drinking Water Administrators cautions that the bottled product "is not necessarily better than water provided by public water supplies."

The association notes, "Some bottled waters are disinfected spring water, while others may simply be water collected from a public water supply and treated with ozone to remove chlorine taste and odor. While bottled water may be necessary in some circumstances, it is important for the consumer to research the source and quality of the bottled water to determine if it is better than the water already being provided by the public water supply."

The bottled-water industry suffered a black eye in February 1990 when Perrier, a French bottler, discovered traces of benzene, a clear solvent suspected as a cause of cancer in animals, in 13 bottles of Perrier. In response, the company withdrew 72 million bottles from its 750,000 outlets in North America. The recall, which lasted three months, was largely responsible for a drop in U.S. bottled-water imports between 1990 and 1991. Imports (Perrier included) have since rebounded.

Though public water suppliers and bottled-water dealers distribute basically the same substance — H_2O — they answer to different regulatory bodies. Drinking water from a public system is regulated by the U.S. Environmental Protection Agency (EPA), working in tandem with its counterparts at the state level. Bottled water, on the other hand, is classified as a "food" and thus is governed by U.S. Food and Drug Administration (FDA) standards. The FDA requires that bottled water be clean and safe for human consumption as well as processed and distributed under sanitary conditions.

The agency is scheduled to release additional bottled-water rules in April. One will set the maximum contaminant level (MCL) for lead in bottled water at 5 parts per billion. That standard, the IBWA notes, is 10 times more stringent than the existing federal maximum, and also tougher than the EPA's limit of 15 parts per billion for lead levels at the tap.

In addition, the pending FDA rules will define terms commonly used on bottled-water labels, such as "mineral," "spring," "artesian," "well," "distilled" and "purified." A majority of IBWA members already meet or exceed the coming quality standards, the association reports. (Because seltzer, soda and tonic waters are classified as soft drinks, they are covered by different federal regulations.)

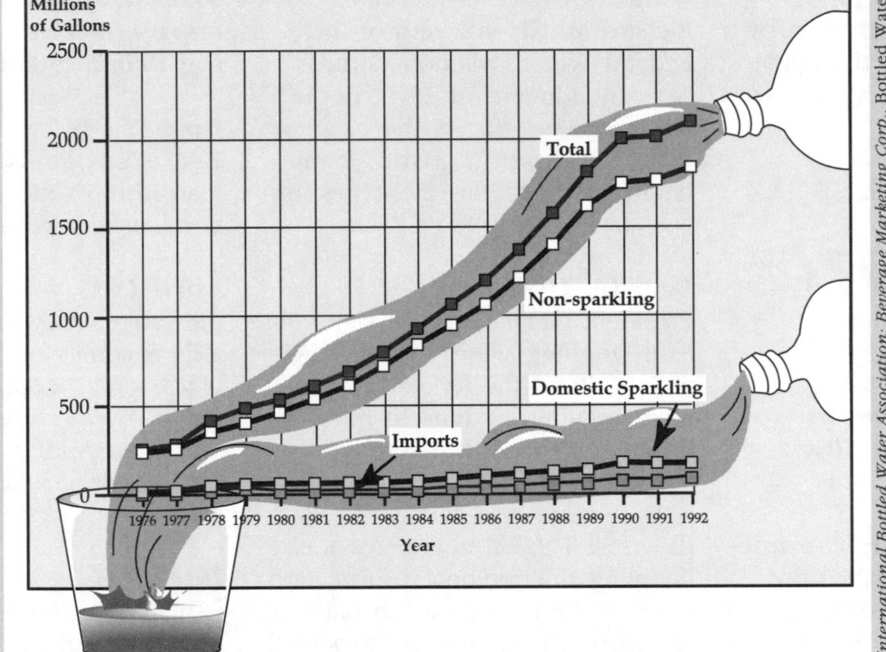

Bottled-water use in the United States has been rising steadily for nearly 20 years. In 1992, consumers quaffed more than 2 billion gallons, mostly of the non-sparkling variety.

International Bottled Water Association; Beverage Marketing Corp., Bottled Water in the U.S., 1993.

Beverage industry surveys show U.S. per capita consumption of bottled water is subject to striking regional variations. Thanks to Californians' nation-leading love of bottled water, the Pacific states are the top users of bottled water, with 19.4 gallons consumed per capita each year, followed by the Southwest states with 11.5 gallons. The West Central states bring up the rear at 3 gallons per person.

Such devotion made domestic and imported bottled water a $2.3 billion industry in the United States in 1992, and preliminary figures show 1993 was even better, says Prats. †

† Association of State Drinking Water Administrators, *The Regulation of Drinking Water Under the Safe Drinking Water Act* (1990), p. 9.

Continued from p. 130

ernments and volunteer groups to develop safe water supplies nationwide by encouraging water-purification treatment and sewage-system development. Actual control of water pollution, however, rested with the states until Congress passed the Water Pollution Control Act of 1948.

In 1920, the first Conference of State Sanitary Engineers was convened to discuss water pollution and water supply problems throughout the country.[26] Over the next three decades, the organization did much to educate citizens about water hygiene and improve purification practices throughout the country. It also pushed for federal research, investigation and assistance programs, and in 1935 won congressional approval of grants to help states expand their sanitary-engineering staffs. The infusion of federal funds greatly increased technical aid to cities and industries for water pollution and supply work, for training of water- and waste-treatment-plant operators and for the development of greater public awareness of water problems.

After another wartime interruption in water-quality progress — World War II — the efforts continued. The early postwar period saw the rise of popular concern over water pollution in general, marked by congressional approval of the Water Pollution Control Act of 1948. It was not until the mid-1950s, however, as the rising volume of chemicals in water became more apparent, that the public began to express uneasiness about drinking-water purity.

Federal standards for drinking water adopted before passage of the Safe Drinking Water Act of 1974 narrowly focused on the quality of water available to passengers in interstate travel. Added to the Interstate Quarantine Regulations in 1914, they established the furthest permissible deviation from purity rather than an ideal potable water. Physical properties, mineral content and chemical contamination were not dealt with, nor were the standards directed at municipal water supplies.

The 1914 standards were revised in 1925 and again in 1946 on orders of the U.S. surgeon general after many cities had begun to use them as guidelines. The American Water Works Association adopted a resolution voluntarily accepting the 1946 standards for all public water supplies. A revision of the federal standards in 1962 mentioned radioactivity and toxic chemicals for the first time.

The following decade brought passage of the Federal Water Pollution Control Act Amendments of 1972, popularly known today as the clean water act, the most far-reaching and costly environmental legislation in U.S. history to that point. President Richard M. Nixon vetoed the controversial bill shortly before Congress was due to adjourn, but the House and the Senate voted to override his action.

The clean water act (CWA) altered the basic approach to water-pollution control in the United States by limiting effluent discharges into U.S. waters as well as establishing water quality standards. It set a goal of eliminating all pollution discharges by 1985 and an interim goal of making all waters safe for fish, shellfish, wildlife and humans by July 1, 1983.

To help meet these objectives, the act contained authorizations totalling $24.7 billion, including more than $18 billion in federal grants to the states for construction of waste-treatment plants. Though the law did not deal expressly

Domestic Use of Groundwater

In most areas of the country, underground water, or groundwater, is used by at least 25 percent of the population. Serious groundwater pollution often occurs in areas of high population density.

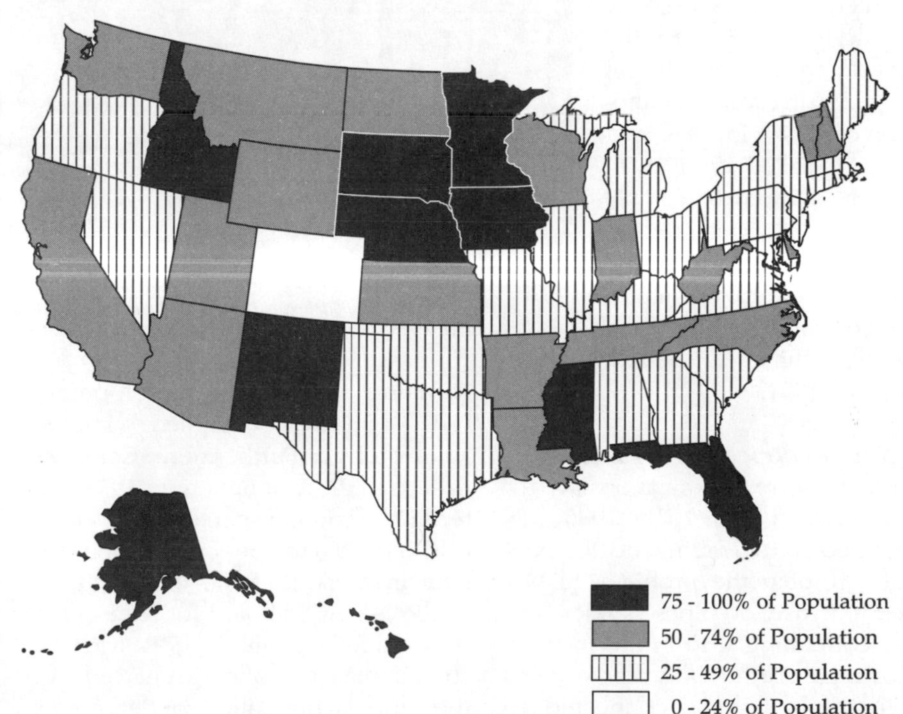

Source: U.S. Geological Survey, in Paul N. Cheremisinoff, Water Management Supply, *1993.*

with drinking-water safety, the improvements in water quality it sought were expected to help provide communities with potable water.

Safe Drinking Water Act

Two years later, on Dec. 16, 1974, President Gerald R. Ford signed the Safe Drinking Water Act into law. The measure allowed the federal government for the first time to regulate drinking-water contaminants suspected of causing chemical poisoning or non-communicable diseases. To this end, it authorized EPA to develop a uniform national drinking-water-protection program and to set "safe" levels for known or suspected contaminants. Over the next 12 years, however, the agency issued only about two dozen such standards.

Irritated by EPA's leisurely pace, Congress directed the agency to try harder when it approved a five-year reauthorization of SDWA in 1986. Specifically, it called on EPA to establish standards for 83 drinking-water contaminants by 1989. In addition, the agency was told to regulate 25 more contaminants in each subsequent three-year period, starting in 1991.

New Restrictions on Lead

Part of the reauthorization law focused on lead, which by 1986 was recognized as a leading health hazard. To combat the problem, SDWA barred the use of pipes, solder and fluxes containing lead in the installation or repair of public water systems or plumbing systems connected to them. It also required the states to carry out the ban through local plumbing codes or other means within two years of enactment.

Under the new restrictions, public water systems would have to provide customers with information on health hazards caused by lead and on ways to reduce them. New housing would not be eligible for guaranteed or insured mortgages from the Veterans Administration or the Department of Housing and Urban Development (HUD) unless it complied with the rules on lead. Furthermore, Congress ordered EPA to toughen its 1975 "interim" maximum contaminant level (MCL) of 50 parts per billion (ppb) for lead in drinking water at the tap.

American Water Works Association

In Cincinnati, a state-of-the-art granular activated charcoal filtration system similar to this is used for water treatment.

EPA's new standard for lead in tap water, adopted June 7, 1991, appears stricter than the one it replaced. All the same, many critics condemn it as inadequate. Instead of an MCL, the standard establishes an "action level" of 15 ppb. However, corrective measures come into play only when 10 percent or more of the homes tested are found to have lead levels in excess of 15 ppb in water drawn from the tap.

Even then, remedial action is far from immediate. EPA gives public water systems six to eight years, depending on their size, to take corrective action, such as adding corrosion inhibitors to the water supply. If this fails to lower the number of homes with action levels of lead below 10 percent of those tested, the water system gets up to 15 additional years to replace all lead pipes in its distribution network.

EPA officials defend the drawn-out enforcement timetable by citing the crushing cost burden many water systems would face if they had to meet a shorter deadline.

In a survey conducted between July and December 1992, EPA found alarmingly high lead levels in the drinking water of numerous small cities, which tend to have less advanced equipment than big cities. Communities with especially high lead concentrations included Grosse Pointe Park, Mich., 324 ppb; Goose Creek, S.C., 257 ppb; and Honesdale, Pa., 210 ppb.

Five cities in Massachusetts — Newton, Waltham, Brookline, Medford and Chicopee — ranked in the top 10 for lead levels in drinking water systems serving 50,000 or more people. The five communities have unusually "soft" water, which is more corrosive than "hard" water because it is low in dis-

How Water-Treatment Plants Work

In the United States, large cities usually draw their drinking water from rivers, lakes and streams or from a combination of surface and groundwater (underground) sources. Small cities, in contrast, often tap underground sources. Either way, the water supply is likely to be contaminated — by pollution, dissolved minerals or other contaminants.

Purification plants treating moderately polluted sources for a municipal water supply typically follow these steps:

1. Pretreatment: First, a process such as aeration or chlorination removes unpleasant tastes or odors, oxidizes some chemicals and breaks up emulsions.

2. Chemical coagulation and flocculation: This phase uses alum, iron salts, synthetic polyelectrolytes or other aids to coagulation; these substances combine with tiny particles of contaminants in the water to form clumps, or "flocs," large enough to settle out.

3. Sedimentation: Water is held in a settling basin, allowing the suspended matter and "flocs" to be removed. Water that is muddy or cloudy is clarified during sedimentation, and many bacteria, viruses, chemicals, metals and minerals are eliminated.

4. Filtration: Filters remove any turbidity still remaining, typically using sand or a combination of sand and crushed garnet or anthracite. The filters are back-flushed often to remove accumulated sediment.

5. Disinfection: In this final and most important step in the standard treatment system, chlorine is added in carefully controlled amounts to remove bacteria and other organisms without leaving an unpleasant taste. Enough chlorine remains in the water to provide a residual disinfection capacity as the water travels through the storage tanks and water mains to the consumer's tap.

6. Additional treatments: After purification, some municipalities also treat water with fluoridation, pH adjustment, softening, taste and odor removal, or chemical conditioning to prevent pipe corrosion.

solved minerals and thus, in effect, has more capacity to absorb lead. ■

CURRENT SITUATION

A Year of Crises

While lead-tainted drinking water clearly is a serious health hazard, mass outbreaks of illness from that source are nonetheless virtually unheard of. Popular concern centers instead on epidemics of waterborne disease that strike down many people more or less simultaneously. The United States experienced two episodes of this kind in 1993.

The first and worst outbreak occurred in Milwaukee, where Mayor John C. Norquist notified residents April 7 that the city's water supply had been contaminated by an intestinal parasite. He told people not to drink tap water unless they first boiled it to kill the parasite. Sales of bottled water soared. (*See story, p. 132.*)

Norquist's warning came too late for many. By the time he lifted the advisory on April 14, some 400,000 persons had fallen ill from the organism and six had died.

The parasite was identified as Cryptosporidium parvum, a protozoan that ordinarily lives in the digestive tracts of animals. Some public health officials speculated that it had infiltrated the local water supply after rains washed animal feces into Lake Michigan, which serves as the city reservoir. Once in the water mains, the organism was not affected by the normal purification technique of adding chemical disinfectants.

In humans, Cryptosporidium typically caused diarrhea, stomach cramps, nausea, fever and vomiting. The symptoms usually disappeared in a week to 10 days. But in people whose immune systems already had been weakened, such as AIDS patients, the microbe could be lethal. Of the six deaths in Milwaukee, only one, an elderly woman, could be linked directly to the microbe. The five other victims (including an AIDS patient) had terminal illnesses.

The contamination was traced to one of the city's two main water-purification plants, and the facility was promptly shut down. Inspectors believed the parasite had survived the normal sterilization process while employees were experimenting with a new purification chemical.

According to Raymond Letterman of Syracuse University, the Milwaukee experience suggests that it may be unwise to discard established disinfection techniques in favor of untested ones. He questions whether the water-treatment plant employees "really were aware of the chemistry and some of the possible outcomes when they made those changes."

The year's other water crises were relatively minor compared with Milwaukee's. In late July and early August, unusually high levels of a common form of bacteria were found in the drinking water of two neighborhoods in New York's Lower Manhattan with a combined population of about 25,000. The bacteria, E. coli, thrive in human and animal waste

Metropolitan Water District of Southern California

Control room technician monitors the Oxidation Demonstration Project in La Verne, Calif. The project tests the performance of ozone and an ozone-hydrogen peroxide blend in eliminating microorganisms and reducing disinfection byproducts.

and often signal the presence of other, less detectable organisms. The New York water alert lasted only a few days and produced no reported cases of serious illness (*see p. 140*).

A similar alert in the Washington, D.C., area in December turned out to be a false alarm. When EPA inspectors found that water in a District of Columbia reservoir was unusually cloudy, they warned area residents Dec. 8 to boil tap water first, since cloudiness often indicates the presence of harmful parasites such as Cryptosporidium. The order was lifted three days later after further testing found no trace of such organisms.

Last summer's severe flooding along the upper Mississippi River and its major tributaries disabled numerous drinking-water systems in the region. Smaller treatment systems were especially hard hit, as were isolated households that relied on wells for water. Moreover, some 250,000 residents of Des Moines were without tap water for almost three weeks after a levee on the Raccoon River broke July 11, knocking the area's principal water-treatment plant out of action.

New Initiatives

Congress, meanwhile, began to consider legislation to improve drinking-water safety. Spurred by the Milwaukee epidemic, the House Energy and Commerce Committee and the House Public Works and Transportation Committee approved separate bills that would set up revolving loan funds to help cities rebuild drinking-water facilities. Neither measure reached the House floor in 1993, however, since the two committees could not agree on who had jurisdiction over the issue. A ruling by the Speaker of the House is expected to resolve the dispute this session.

The Clinton administration also weighed in with proposed policy shifts. On Sept. 8, it recommended changes in the Safe Drinking Water Act to give state and local governments more flexibility in meeting its mandates. In addition, the administration proposed dropping an existing SDWA provision requiring EPA to set standards for 25 contaminants every three years. Instead, the agency would be free to regulate only those contaminants that pose the greatest risk to drinking-water safety.

Echoing the two House bills introduced earlier in 1993, the administration also proposed establishing a $4.6 billion revolving loan fund over five years to help states pay for improvements to water systems. Congress approved the money in the fiscal 1994 appropriations bill for Veterans Affairs, Housing and Urban Development and independent agencies, as long as a separate authorization bill is approved. The appropriations measure included $599 million for drinking-water programs in fiscal 1994.

On Oct. 27, the Senate Environment and Public Works Committee held a hearing on a bill embodying most of the administration's drinking-water program.[27] Introduced by Committee Chairman Max Baucus, D-Mont., the measure would authorize $6.6 billion over seven years for a revolving fund to help states and local governments pay for drinking-water treatment plants. It also would direct EPA to regulate 15 contaminants and evaluate each one within three years. Smaller water systems would receive more leeway in complying with the law. The Baucus panel may begin marking up, or finalizing, the bill as early as March.

The only SDWA reauthorization bill under consideration in the House at this point is the one introduced last fall by Reps. Slattery and Bliley (*see p. 128*). There is speculation, however, that a rival measure reflecting the Clinton administration's ideas will surface in the House before long.

Though the Baucus and Slattery-Bliley bills have some points in common, they differ sharply in one key respect. Baucus would retain the present formula for determining maximum contaminant levels (MCLs), while Slattery-Bliley would have EPA apply a cost-benefit test before setting standards. Defenders of cost-benefit analysis say it acts as a needed brake on

Continued on p. 138

At Issue:

Should the Safe Drinking Water Act be made more flexible?

yes

American Water Works Association

From* Press Release, *Dec. 10, 1993.

The American Water Works Association, along with a coalition of water organizations and public officials, is supporting a House bill (HR 3392) introduced by Rep. Jim Slattery, D-Kan., and Rep. Thomas J. Bliley Jr., R-Va., that would refine the existing Safe Drinking Water Act (SDWA). The National Resources Defense Council (NRDC) has accused AWWA and others of wanting to "weaken the Safe Drinking Water Act" with this bill.

"That accusation is false," says AWWA President Robert Reinert. "The NRDC wants status quo regulations, business as usual. Our experience as professionals shows that public health can be better protected by a better law."

At issue is the way contaminants are chosen for regulatory action. The current SDWA sets a specific number of chemical contaminants to regulate. The U.S. Environmental Protection Agency then must come up with regulations to fill that quota. AWWA and a number of other water groups and public officials say that rather than "playing a numbers game," the priorities for regulating contaminants should be based on how harmful the substance is and how often it occurs in the environment.

"For example, bacterial and parasitic organisms occur quite frequently in and around raw water sources," says Reinert. "Instead of spending limited time and money looking for a one-in-a-trillion chemical that may or may not cause cancer after 70 years, we think the public would be better served if water providers were allowed to concentrate on imminent threats to public health like Cryptosporidium and viruses. . . ."

Although most water providers meet all current federal standards for water safety, many face several problems; for example, the time it takes between finding a level of a substance in the water and actually building or installing new treatment systems. Designing and constructing new plants can take five years. Also, many small systems find that testing for so many random and sometimes obscure substances takes precious time and resources away from testing and treating for more simple and dangerous microbial organisms.

"We agree with the NRDC that there needs to be work done in updating some water-supply systems in the U.S. and in strengthening the SDWA," Reinert says. "We just don't agree with the method of accomplishing it. We want to see a new law based on setting priorities based on health risks, occurrence data, and to the extent possible, cost of removal."

no

Erik D. Olson

Senior Attorney, Natural Resources Defense Council

From* A Letter to Members of Congress, *Oct. 28, 1993.

Now is not the time to relax our guard against drinking water contamination. Earlier this year, the largest waterborne disease outbreak in U.S. history occurred in Milwaukee, Wis., causing over 370,00 to get sick and reportedly killing over 40 people with weak immune systems. Nationally, according to an estimate by scientists at the Centers for Disease Control, over 900,000 people get sick each year from germ-contaminated water, and as many as 900 may die. . . .

Other major drinking water problems abound, including lead-tainted drinking water . . . arsenic-contaminated drinking water . . . and radioactive cancer-causing drinking water. . . . Moreover, there is massive non-compliance with the Safe Drinking Water Act today; according to EPA data, 28 million Americans drank water more contaminated than EPA health standards allow in 1991-92, and over 100 million Americans drank water served by systems that had not tested their water or reported testing as the law requires. . . .

In addition to failing to implement many of the key recommendations of President Clinton's recent drinking-water reform package (such as a state revolving loan fund for drinking water, stronger enforcement and a small fee on water to pay for state drinking-water programs in states that fail to adequately fund their programs), the Slattery-Bliley bill includes the water-utility industry wish list of weakening amendments to the law, including provisions which would, among other things:

- Gut the act's two-decade-old health-standard-setting provision . . . [and] replace it with a vague and manipulable cost-benefit approach . . . that would tie EPA up in gridlock and devalue human life and health by requiring water-utility industry economics to override health protections. . . .
- Allow any water utility in the nation to get a state variance if it claims it can't afford to comply even with the weakened health standards. . . . Weaken health protection from lead in drinking water. . . . Extend from 1989 until 1997 or later the requirement that all public water systems disinfect their water unless it is found unnecessary to protect the public from disease. . . .

Instead of trying to solve the nation's drinking-water crisis by gutting health protection as the Slattery-Bliley bill does, we urge [Congress] to support additional funding to help water systems comply through a state revolving fund . . . and to work with the Clinton administration . . . to develop fine-tuned mid-course corrections in the Safe Drinking Water Act.

Growing Global Concerns About Water Supplies

Much of the world worries more about water availability than about water quality. And the concern is growing more urgent by the day. "In the 21st century, water will be in dangerously short supply in such diverse locales as Saudi Arabia, Central Asia and the Southwestern United States," Robert D. Kaplan writes in *The Atlantic Monthly*. [1]

Chances for water-related armed conflict seem especially great in North Africa and the Middle East. John Kolars, a professor of geography and Near Eastern studies at the University of Michigan, told a House subcommittee in 1990 that more than half the people in these two regions "depend either upon water from rivers which cross an international boundary before reaching them, or upon desalinized water and water drawn from deep wells." [2]

There are other complications as well, Kolar pointed out, such as the fact that two-thirds of all Arabic-speaking people in the area depend on river water that flows to them from non-Arabic-speaking lands, while another 24 percent have no access at all to perennial surface streams. "That is," said Kolars, "the latter must rely upon either well water from rapidly depleting sources or upon seawater which is expensive to purify in sufficient quantities and expensive to pump to its places of use."

Appearing before the same panel as Kolars, Thomas Naff, a professor of Asian Studies at the University of Pennsylvania, pointed to the Jordan River basin as one of the Middle East's main trouble spots for water. He noted that the basin's two main water users — Israel and Jordan — have both been overconsuming available stocks, creating a cumulative water deficit that may become irreversible.

"Neither known natural sources nor water technologies, now or in the foreseeable future, have the capacity to generate new usable water in needed quantities at an affordable cost" in the Jordan River basin, Naff said. "Failing a solution of scarcity, both Israel and Jordan will have to curtail their social and economic development."

Another water crisis is building over Turkey's Southeast Anatolia Project, a vast attempt to harness the hydroelectric and irrigation potential of the Tigris and Euphrates rivers. The project carries grave political implications: Much of the water being impounded by the Turks would otherwise flow into neighboring Syria and Iraq.

"It is true," said Erduhan Bayindir, site manager of the Ataturk Dam, centerpiece of the Turkish project, "we can stop the flow of water into Syria and Iraq for up to eight months without the same water overflowing our dams, in order to regulate their political behavior." [3]

---

[1] Robert D. Kaplan, "The Coming Anarchy," *The Atlantic Monthly*, February 1994, p. 58.

[2] Testimony before Subcommittee on Europe and the Middle East, U.S. House Committee on Foreign Affairs, June 26, 1990.

[3] Kaplan, *op. cit.*, p. 68.

Continued from p. 136

government spending.

But critics like Erik Olson retort: "Based on past experience with other laws, these proposals . . . would essentially give EPA a blank check in setting standards, condemning the agency to eternal analysis of risks and benefits, and weakening or stopping EPA from protecting the public." [28]

Cincinnati Model

Assuming some form of federal aid is forthcoming to help build water-treatment plants, the Cincinnati Water Works (CWW) will likely provide the model for many communities. In October 1992, CWW opened a state-of-the-art plant using granular activated carbon (GAC) technology, generally regarded as the most advanced water-purification process available. The 150,000-square-foot facility is the world's largest GAC operation, serving an estimated 800,000 people. [29]

Widely used in Europe, where it originated, GAC technology employs deep beds of carbon granules to trap contaminants. When the granules become saturated, they can be reactivated by baking at high temperatures. The technology's effectiveness depends largely on how frequently the reactivation process takes place.

According to Jack DeMarco, superintendent of CWW's water quality and treatment division, the chief advantage of GAC is that it "can effectively remove specific organic substances and precursors of disinfection byproducts" like harmful chlorine compounds. GAC also does a superior job of ridding water of synthetic organic chemicals such as gasoline or pesticides. Synthetic organics resist conventional treatment because they do not "clump" in the presence of coagulants and they are not trapped by sand, the standard filtration medium.

An added benefit of GAC, notes DeMarco, is that it filters out substances that cause unpleasant tastes and odors, permitting treatment plant technicians to use less chlorine. This has greatly improved Cincinnati's water, long notorious for its distinctive chlorine aftertaste. He hastens to add that the technicians' primary job still is "to make sure the water is microbiologically safe. That's the pact we have to have with everybody who drinks our water." ■

The reverse osmosis demineralization system serving Haywood, W. Va.

OUTLOOK

Aging Infrastructure

As drinking-water suppliers survey the future, they say that cost considerations limit their options. Americans, accustomed to water of high quality and low cost, could balk at the expense of maintaining that standard of safety in coming years.

American attitudes were shaped many years ago. "The proper value has never been placed on water, in part because water rates have been constrained by the political and social forces that developed when water was truly inexpensive to produce," noted a consumer education guide from the Association of State Drinking Water Administrators. "One of the ways rates have been kept low has been to defer expenditures needed for maintenance and replacement of water treatment facilities and distribution networks." [30]

Now the piper is demanding to be paid in many parts of the country. Not long after Washington's short-lived December water alert, for instance, the area experienced a rash of bursting water mains. The capital's water-distribution system, like those of many other older cities, is saddled with many miles of underground pipe in urgent need of replacement.

Upgrading the infrastructure of drinking-water systems may entail financial hardship for local residents. LaJuana S. Wilcher, EPA's assistant administrator for water during the Bush administration, estimated in 1991 that full compliance with the 1986 amendments to SDWA would "push homeowners' annual water bills up significantly, in some cases with increases reaching $500 to $800 a year." [31]

The biggest increases probably would occur in smaller communities. In big cities, where more customers could share the cost of improvements, the impact on individual households would be lessened. In Cincinnati, for instance, DeMarco says that GAC technology only costs about 6 cents a day, or about $22 a year per family.

Recruiting qualified personnel to operate advanced water-treatment systems, and then paying them salaries commensurate with their skills, also could become major expenses for many communities. Again, small treatment systems have the greatest needs. In some small communities, says the Natural Resources Defense Council's Olson, "the qualifications for obtaining a beautician's license are more stringent than they are for getting a job with the local water-treatment plant."

One problem in finding qualified personnel, says Letterman, is that "there aren't many academic programs in environmental civil engineering that train people to operate treatment plants." He sees a need for "people trained not just to run the physical facilities but also to deal with the public-administration aspects."

Joan Dent, public information director for the AWWA, agrees that running a water-treatment system "has become more sophisticated" and "probably is a higher-level job than has traditionally been the case." On the other hand, she says, "There isn't necessarily a problem in finding the right people," though she concedes, "There may be problems sometimes in being willing to pay them what they deserve."

Many of the right people, says DeMarco, may already be on a system's payroll. Before Cincinnati opened its GAC treatment plant, he says, "We had a large-scale field demonstration to be sure we could operate it with our typical in-house employees. Otherwise, we felt we couldn't be competitive in the marketplace."

One point on which most water-treatment experts agree is that measures for preventing water contamination should receive more attention. Dent notes that AWWA's Blue Thumb program gives tips on how consumers can help keep water supplies pure. [32] The philosophy behind the campaign, says Dent, is "conserve, protect and get involved." Family members are urged to "read the labels on household toxic materials, recycle plastics and paper and take paint and other potential contaminants to hazardous-waste collection sites."

New York's Problem

For operators of water-treatment systems, the top prevention priority is safeguarding water sources. More than

30 years ago, Lewis Mumford warned of the mounting population pressures on New York City's Croton and Catskills watersheds: "[T]he spread of the metropolis itself not alone closes down local sources of supply, but, by filling in swamps and denuding hillsides of vegetation lowers the water table; while the industrial use of water, plus its widespread utilization . . . for air-conditioning systems, brings [drinking-water] famine still nearer even at existing population levels." [33]

Now, under prodding by EPA, New York City has agreed to fund a 10-year program of watershed protection. A plan announced last September by then-Mayor David N. Dinkins calls for $750 million in improvements to community sewage treatment plants in the city's 2,000-square-mile Croton-Catskills watershed area.

The city adopted the pollution-prevention plan to avoid an EPA order to build a water-filtration plant that would cost an estimated $5 billion. Most big cities filter their water, but New York argued that its water is of such high quality that the city could meet federal standards simply by helping local communities keep pollutants out of the reservoirs.

The quality of water in reservoirs closer to the city is more problematic. In August, for example, environmental officials announced that the contamination in Lower Manhattan probably had been caused by sea-gull droppings in a reservoir in Yonkers, just north of the Bronx.

One prevention option under study at that reservoir is a concrete cover topped by a reflecting pool. In view of its estimated $177 million cost, some officials favor a flexible plastic shield for one-tenth as much.

Still, there is little question that action of some sort will be forthcoming. New York has long taken pride in its water, which has won numerous prizes in blind tastings against other municipal systems and even bottled sources. Albert F. Appleton, the city's former environmental protection commissioner, spoke for many New Yorkers when he said, "One of the things that has worked for this water system is to go first class." [34]

Other communities, with different drinking-water histories, might take another approach. Water "is a very local issue," says the AWWA's Dent. Similarly, she says, evaluating water content is often a "matter of degree," a case of one part per billion of a given contaminant being acceptable, but not 50 parts per billion.

That's why answers to questions about drinking-water safety typically are cloudy, and why water officials frequently view too much federal regulation as unnecessary. "It's frustrating, because we like clear answers," Dent says. The point to keep in mind is that a lot of the answers "in a sense are value judgments." ■

Notes

[1] Speech at annual conference of National Association of Towns and Townships, Washington, D.C., Sept. 8, 1993.

[2] Erik D. Olson, *Think Before You Drink: The Failure of the Nation's Drinking Water System to Protect Public Health*, September 1993, p. 25.

[3] For background, see "Garbage Crisis," *The CQ Researcher*, March 20, 1992, pp. 241-265, and "Preventing Groundwater Contamination," *Editorial Research Reports*, July 12, 1985, p. 517-536.el3¤

[4] America's Clean Water Foundation, *Water: The Source of Life, 1992*, pp. 8-9. The foundation is a nonprofit organization dedicated to educating people about clean water's importance. It is affiliated with the Association of State and Interstate Pollution Control Administrators.

[5] Consumers Union, "Water Treatment," *Consumer Reports 1993 Buying Guide*, 1993, p. 194.

[6] Op-ed column in *The Washington Post*, Jan. 19, 1994.

[7] Anne C. Moore, et al., "Surveillance for Waterborne Disease Outbreaks — United States, 1991-1992," *Morbidity and Mortality Weekly Report*, Nov. 19, 1993.

[8] *Ibid.*, p. 14.

[9] Joan Rose, "Waterborne Pathogens: Assessing Health Risks," *Health & Environment Digest*, June 1993, pp. 1-6.

[10] Mark D. Sobsey, et al, "Using a Conceptual Framework for Assessing Risks to Health From Microbes in Drinking Water," *American Water Works Association Journal*, March 1993, p. 45.

[11] National Toxicology Program, "Toxicology and Carcinogenesis Studies of Sodium Chloride," December 1990. The program is sponsored by the National Institute of Environmental Health Sciences, Research Triangle Park, N.C.

[12] National Research Council, *Health Effects of Ingested Fluoride*, Aug. 17, 1993.

[13] *Ibid.*, p. 43.

[14] *Ibid.*, p. 48, as cited in John A. Yiamouyiannis, "Questions about Fluoride Along with Answers from the National Research Council and Their Subcommittee on Health Effects of Ingested Fluoride."

[15] See Elliot Marshall, "The Fluoride Debate: One More Time," *Science*, Jan. 19, 1990, p. 277.

[16] Reps. Jim Slattery and Thomas J. Bliley Jr., letter to House colleagues, Nov. 5, 1993.

[17] *Ibid.*

[18] Statement issued to House members, Oct. 28, 1993.

[19] Statement issued to House members Nov. 2, 1993, by Citizen Action, Greenpeace, National Audubon Society, Sierra Club and the U.S. Public Interest Research Group.

[20] Erik D. Olson, letter to members of Congress, Oct. 28, 1993. For background, see "Lead Poisoning," *The CQ Researcher*, June 19, 1992, pp.538-562.

[21] Olson, *Think Before You Drink*, p. v.

[22] *Ibid.*, p. iv.

[23] Lewis Mumford, *The City in History* (1961), p. 142.

[24] *Ibid.*, p. 463.

[25] America's Clean Water Foundation, *op. cit.*, p. 7.

[26] The organization is now called the Conference of State Health and Environmental Managers, based in Austin, Texas. For background, see "California: Enough Water for the Future?" *The CQ Researcher*, April 19, 1991, pp. 221-245.

[27] For details, see "Issue: Drinking Water," *CQ Weekly Report*, Dec. 11, 1993, p. 3382.

[28] Testimony before Senate Committee on the Environment and Public Works, Oct. 27, 1993.

[29] According to a survey of 1,097 large and medium-sized U.S. water-treatment systems conducted from 1989 to 1992 by the American Water Works Association, 9.4 percent of surface-water systems and 3.7 percent of groundwater systems used GAC technology.

[30] Association of State Drinking Water Administrators, *The Value of Safe Drinking Water*, 1990, p. 2. For additional information, see the association's companion pamphlet, *The Regulation of Drinking Water Under the Safe Drinking Water Act*, 1990.

[31] Testimony before Subcommittee on Superfund, Ocean, and Water Protection, U.S. Senate Committee on Environment and Public Works, May 17, 1991.

[32] For more information on the Blue Thumb program, consumers can contact the AWWA in Denver, Colo., at (303) 347-6137.

[33] Mumford, *op. cit.*, p. 549.

[34] Quoted in *The New York Times*, Aug. 10, 1993.

Bibliography

Selected Sources Used

Books

Canter, Larry W., Robert C. Knox and Deborah M. Fairchild, *Ground Water Quality Protection*, Lewis Publishers, 1987.

The authors, who all have taken part in studies of groundwater availability and quality, explain how underground reserves of water become contaminated, and what the leading contaminants are. They also furnish background on how existing groundwater-quality management programs operate.

Cheremisinoff, Paul N., *Water Supply and Management*, PTR Prentice Hall, 1993.

Cheremisinoff, a professor of civil and environmental engineering at New Jersey Institute of Technology, reviews water's basic properties — color, odor, taste, alkalinity, hardness, and so on — as well as the goals of water treatment.

Tebbutt, T.H.Y., *Principles of Water Quality Control*, Pergamon Press, 1992.

Tebbutt, a senior lecturer in civil engineering at the University of Birmingham in England, focuses on contamination of water supplies by disease-causing microorganisms — a matter of current concern in the United States because of last year's outbreaks of waterborne illness in Milwaukee and New York.

Yiamouyiannis, John A., *Fluoride: The Aging Facto*, Health Action Press, 1993.

Yiamouyiannis, a leader in the campaign against fluoridation of public water supplies, presents a detailed indictment of "fluoride poisoning." He charges that fluorides cause genetic damage, weaken the immune system and cause cancer. He also disputes the claim that fluoridation reduces the incidence of tooth decay.

Articles

Carpenter, Betsy, "Is Your Water Safe?" *U.S. News & World Report*, July 29, 1991.

Carpenter gives a generally negative appraisal of U.S. drinking-water quality. "While the public-health danger is not as immediate or severe as in cholera-infested developing countries," she writes, "inept regulation, reckless land use and irresponsible handling of chemicals are all compromising the quality of the nation's drinking water."

Parfit, Michael, "Troubled Waters Run Deep," *National Geographic*, 1993 special edition titled "Water: The Power, Promise and Turmoil of North America's Fresh Water."

Parfit surveys the manifold sources of groundwater pollution and explains why it is more difficult to control than contamination of surface water. "Polluted runoff is what happens when you spill oil on the driveway, then hose it down," he writes. "It happens when a soybean field is treated with herbicide, and then it rains. It happens when someone throws a dead battery into a gully. It happens when a farmer's cows stroll through a stream."

Reports and Studies

Environmental Protection Agency, *Is Your Drinking Water Safe?* September 1991.

This EPA brochure summarizes the agency's role in protecting drinking-water quality under the Safe Drinking Water Act (SDWA). It also contains lists of primary (mandated) and secondary (recommended) drinking-water standards for various contaminants.

Moore, Anne C., et al., "Surveillance for Waterborne Disease Outbreaks — United States, 1991-1992," *Morbidity and Mortality Weekly Report*, Nov. 19, 1993.

Moore and her co-authors summarize what appears to be a remarkably uneventful two-year period in the annals U.S. waterborne-disease outbreaks. But the scientists caution that their data are based only on reported cases, and that the actual number probably was much higher.

Olson, Erik D., *Think Before You Drink: The Failure of the Nation's Drinking Water System to Protect Public Health*, September 1993.

Olson examines what he regards as lax enforcement of the Safe Drinking Water Act by both federal and state authorities. He charges, among other things, that falsification of water-quality test results is a common practice. He ends by setting forth his proposals for strengthening SDWA.

Subcommittee on Europe and the Middle East, U.S. House Committee on Foreign Affairs, *The Middle East in the 1990s* (published proceedings of hearings held April 4, May 8, June 26 and July 17, 1990).

Academic and government witnesses present their views on likely sources of conflict in the Middle East during the 1990s. A major concern is growing water scarcity in the region and the possibility that disputes over access to water supplies will lead to armed conflict.

The Next Step

Additional information from UMI's Newspaper & Periodical Abstracts database

Bottled Water

Burg, Dale, "Gulp: What's in the water?," *New Woman*, September 1993, p. 154.

Bottled water may contain higher levels of contaminants than water from the tap, Burg writes. The Food and Drug Administration has proposed guidelines that would mean tougher standards and labeling requirements for bottled water.

"In search of purity: People in panic resort to bottled waters," *Nutrition Health Review*, 1993, p. 5.

Because of deteriorating municipal water supplies, the public is pushing to find safety in bottled waters. Various bottled water brands and their ingredients are discussed.

LaMoreaux, Philip E., "Hot springs and bottled water," *Geotimes*, December 1993, p. 7.

Bottled water is becoming increasingly popular in the marketplace, but use of spring water dates back to earliest civilization. The FDA is working on additional regulations for bottled water.

Sietsema, Tom, "Water works," *San Francisco Chronicle*, Oct. 6, 1993, p. FOOD1.

The popularity of bottled water in the U.S. is examined, and sales figures for various brands of bottle water are discussed. In the late 1970s, Americans began to think of bottled water in terms of its snob appeal, as an alternative to alcohol and as part of a health regimen.

Squires, Sally, "On the (water) bottle: Concerns about safety spur sales of H_2O," *The Washington Post*, Dec. 14, 1993, p. WH6.

The rising popularity of bottled water is discussed, and purity regulations set forth by the FDA are discussed.

International Waters

"Bottled water: Eauverdose?" *Economist*, Aug. 14, 1993, p. 55.

Bottled water sales in the United Kingdom have surged by over 1,000 percent since 1982. Marketing spring water has fewer regulations to contend with, while selling natural mineral water is a tortuous process.

Freeman, Aaron, "Texaco's toxic legacy," *Multinational Monitor*, November 1993, p. 4.

Indigenous groups in Ecuador have filed a landmark $1 billon lawsuit against Texaco Inc., alleging that Texaco knowingly and intentionally used defective technology that resulted in the contamination of their drinking water. The oil company pulled out of Ecuador in 1992, leaving the government and local communities to deal with a legacy of oil spills, wastewater discharges and hundreds of unlined toxic waste ponds, Freeman writes.

Moore, Molly, "Around globe, water quality is matter of life and death," *The Washington Post*, Dec. 12, 1993, p. A39.

Water-related diseases are the single biggest killers of infants and the principal cause of illness in adults in the developing world, Moore writes.

"Pesticide row," *New Scientist*, Oct. 2, 1993, p. 12.

A conflict has recently emerged over a plan supported by the United Kingdom and France to revise the EC's rules on drinking water. The controversial plan is discussed.

Opinions

"H_2O-gate?," *The Washington Post*, Dec. 14, 1993, p. A24.

An editorial suggests that the drinking-water crisis in Washington, D.C., in December 1993 illustrates the need for people to get information about public health risks more quickly.

Kindinger, Paul, "Yes, drink the water," *St. Louis Post-Dispatch*, Sept. 21, 1993, p. B7.

Paul Kindinger discusses the effect that U.S. Geological Survey monitoring of drinking water has had on public perceptions of water quality.

"Water crisis? Well, sort of," *USA Today*, Sept. 29, 1993, p. A10.

An editorial discusses a study by the Natural Resources Defense Council that found 43 percent of the water systems in the U.S. violated safe-drinking laws in 1991 or 1992 and blamed dirty water for 900,000 illnesses a year, including 900 deaths.

Precautions and Solutions

"Drinking water: How safe is yours?" *Mayo Clinic Health Letter*, September 1993, p. 3.

Under the Safe Drinking Water Act of 1974 and its amendments, the EPA regulates 83 contaminants in drinking water, enforces compliance by public suppliers and promotes protection of groundwater sources. A few of those contaminants, such as lead and chemicals, are discussed, and some precautions regarding drinking water are presented.

"Ensuring water quality," *Home Mechanix*, December 1993, pp. 78-83.

Is the water coming from your tap fit to drink? A

complete guide to water-quality questions, including information on primary contaminants and their treatment.

King, Jonathan; Erik Olson and Bob Adler, "Something in the water," ***Amicus Journal*****, fall 1993, pp. 20-28.**
Milwaukee's Cryptosporidium outbreak caused by polluted drinking water has made cities and citizens more aware of the importance of proper filtration and healthy aquatic ecosystems. Ways people can protect their drinking water are discussed.

Pearce, Fred, "Fogs yield drinking water in the desert," ***New Scientist*****, Oct. 16, 1993, p. 19.**
Seventy-five large sheets of plastic mesh are suspended along a remote hilltop in the Atacama desert of northern Chile to capture the moisture in fogs that roll in off the Pacific Ocean. After a seven-year research project, the sheets have been hailed as the first new method for providing drinking water since 1869.

Problems with Drinking Water

Clifford, Frank, "Faucets pose prolonged lead risk, study says," ***Los Angeles Times*****, Sept. 9, 1993, p. A3.**
On Sept. 8, 1993, the Oakland, Calif.-based Environmental Law Foundation, which is suing 14 manufacturers of household plumbing fixtures, released a report showing that faucets commonly leach hazardous levels of lead into tap water for years after being installed.

Masters, Brooke A., "For cities, a big battle against microorganisms," ***The Washington Post*****, Dec. 10, 1993, p. A39.**
Microorganisms like the one that sickened nearly 400,000 Milwaukee residents last year have become an increasing concern to water specialists because more of the parasites are being identified, and they cannot be killed by chlorine, the standard disinfectant.

Newman, Alan, "Safe drinking water," ***Environmental Science & Technology*****, November 1993, pp. 2295-2297.**
There are serious problems in making sure safe drinking water remains available, Newman writes. Problems with providing safe water and policy issues regarding them are discussed.

Terry, Sara, "Drinking water comes to a boil," ***The New York Times Magazine*****, Sept. 26, 1993, p. 42.**
Problems in the U.S. with drinking water contaminated by chemicals and harmful microbes are examined and efforts to prevent such problems are discussed.

Wapner, Kenneth, "Water, water everywhere . . ." ***E: The Environmental Magazine*****, September 1993, pp. 10-11.**
Water from the Catskill Mountains of upstate New York is laced with pathogens that can cause illness. Research on the pathogens, such as bacteria, viruses or fungus, is discussed.

Research and Studies

Dunnick, June K. and Ronald L. Melnick, "Assessment of the carcinogenic potential of chlorinated water: Experimental studies of chlorine, chloramine, and trihalomethanes," ***Journal of the National Cancer Institute*****, May 19, 1993, pp. 817-822.**
Water chlorination has been one of the major disease-prevention treatments of the 20th century. Results of a study suggest that organic byproducts of chlorination are the chemicals of greatest concern in assessment of the carcinogenic potential of chlorinated drinking water.

Hileman, Bette, "Panel says no health risks from fluoride," ***Chemical & Engineering News*****, Aug. 23, 1993, p. 6.**
National Research Council research concluded that currently allowed levels of fluoride in drinking water do not cause cancer, bone disease or kidney failure. Research into fluoride toxicity is discussed.

Holmes, Hannah, "Getting the lead out," ***Garbage*****, November 1993, pp. 26-31.**
Old paint may be the biggest contributor to lead poisoning, but new studies suggest another source. The dangers of lead in drinking water are discussed.

Raloff, Janet, "Chlorination products linked to cancer," ***Science News*****, May 29, 1993, p. 343.**
A study found that chlorine byproducts can be linked to an increased risk of human bladder and rectal cancers. The ramifications of this finding on drinking-water protection are discussed.

Safe Drinking Water Act

Anderson, James; Mary Ann Dooley and Maureen McAvoy, "Good to the last drop," ***American City & County*****, November 1993, pp. 48-52.**
The authors discuss lead content in drinking water and what municipalities can do to clean it up.

Kocheisen, Carol, "Reps. Slattery and Bliley propose drinking water reforms," ***Nation's Cities Weekly*****, Nov. 1, 1993, p. 3.**
Reps. Jim Slattery, D-Kan., and Tom Bliley, R-Va., have introduced amendments to the Safe Drinking Water Act revising the current process for setting standards for drinking-water contaminants.

Pattison, Scott, "Less expensive water?" ***Consumers' Research Magazine*****, December 1993, p. 38.**
The federal govenment has proposed increasing the flexibility of states and localities when seeking to comply with federal government drinking-water requirements. Many local governments could not afford the costs of complying with the Safe Drinking Water Act amendments in 1986.

Back Issues

Great Research on Current Issues Starts Right Here...Recent topics covered by The CQ Researcher are listed below. Before May 1991, reports were published under the name of Editorial Research Reports.

AUGUST 1992
The Homeless
Work, Family and Stress
NATO's Changing Role
Marine Mammals vs. Fish

SEPTEMBER 1992
Domestic Partners
Violence in Schools
Public Broadcasting
Women in the Military

OCTOBER 1992
Depression
U.S. Auto Industry
Youth Apprenticeships
Hispanic Americans

NOVEMBER 1992
Physical Fitness
Privatization
Paying for College
U.S. Policy in Asia

DECEMBER 1992
Crackdown on Smoking
The New CIA
Eating Disorders
Women and AIDS

JANUARY 1993
Hate Crimes
Child Sexual Abuse
Nuclear Fusion
U.S. Trade Policy

FEBRUARY 1993
Community Policing
Europe's New Right
School Censorship
Violence Against Women

MARCH 1993
Gay Rights
Aid to Russia
War on Drugs
TV Violence

APRIL 1993
Head Start
High-Speed Rail
Children's Legal Rights
Muslims in America

MAY 1993
Cults in America
Preventing Teen Pregnancy
Software Piracy
National Parks

JUNE 1993
Food Safety
Prostitution
Childhood Immunizations
National Service

JULY 1993
Electric Cars
Population Growth
Downward Mobility
Intelligence Testing

AUGUST 1993
Mental Illness
Bilingual Education
Foreign Policy Burden
School Funding

SEPTEMBER 1993
Suburban Crime
Public Housing
Supreme Court Preview
Immigration Reform

OCTOBER 1993
Airline Safety
Disaster Response
Science in the Courtroom
The Glass Ceiling

NOVEMBER 1993
Paying for Retirement
Charitable Giving
Privacy in the Workplace
Adoption

DECEMBER 1993
U.S. Vietnam-Relations
Learning Disabilities
Child Care
Space Program's Future

JANUARY 1994
Racial Tensions in Schools
South Africa's Future
Worker Retraining
Regulating Pesticides

FEBRUARY 1994
Prison Overcrowding

Future Topics

- ***Religion and Schools***
- ***Juvenile Justice***
- ***Underground Economy***

THE CQ Researcher

PUBLISHED BY CONGRESSIONAL QUARTERLY INC.

Religion in Schools

Should the wall between church and state be lowered?

The longstanding battle over the place of religion in public schools is heating up again. Thirty years after the Supreme Court prohibited prayer in the classroom, religious conservatives want more religious activities in public schools. They are testing the Supreme Court's new decision to bar prayers at public high school graduations and seeking seats on local school boards. Civil liberties groups have responded by fighting in court and at the ballot box to keep schools from taking sides on religious issues. But courts have somewhat lowered church-state barriers in recent years. Now, a new case before the Supreme Court gives the justices another chance to define the relationship between religion and the schools.

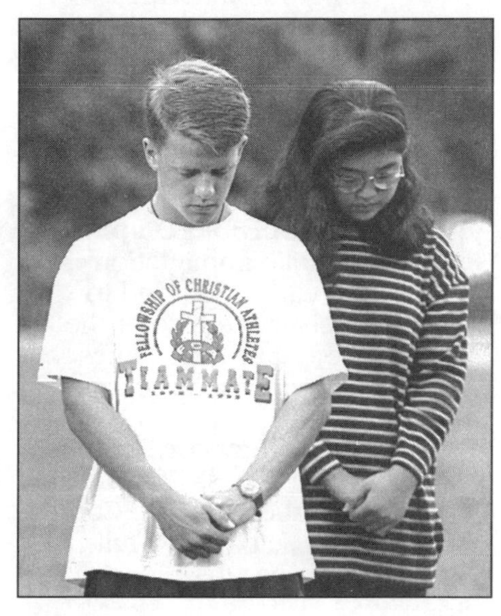

INSIDE THIS ISSUE

CQ February 18, 1994 • Volume 4, No. 7 • 145-168

Formerly Editorial Research Reports

Religion In Schools

THE ISSUES

BACKGROUND

CURRENT SITUATION

OUTLOOK

SIDEBARS AND GRAPHICS

FOR FURTHER INFORMATION

February 18, 1994
Volume 4, No. 7

The CQ Researcher (ISSN 1056-2036). Formerly Editorial Research Reports. Published weekly (48 times per year, not printed the first Friday of any month with five Fridays) by Congressional Quarterly Inc., 1414 22nd St., N.W., Washington, D.C. 20037. Rates are furnished upon request. Second-class postage paid at Washington, D.C. POSTMASTER: Send address changes to The CQ Researcher, 1414 22nd St., N.W., Washington, D.C. 20037.

Cover: Students at Langley High School, McLean, Va., last Sept. 15 during the nationwide Before-School Prayer Event launched four years ago for Christian students. (© 1993 Lisa Berg)

Religion in Schools

BY KENNETH JOST

THE ISSUES

When Brad Lucas rose to speak at his high school graduation last summer, the Northern Virginia teenager began — as uncounted commencement speakers had done in years past — with a prayer.

"Dear Heavenly Father, we thank you for the blessings you have bestowed upon us," Lucas said as the audience at Park View High School in Loudoun County, Va., reverently bowed their heads.

Lucas voiced thanks for families, teachers and friends. He prayed for strength, courage and wisdom for himself and his classmates. "Help us to spread your light wherever our paths may lead us," Lucas concluded, "and help us to always treat our fellow man with kindness and love. Amen."

Students delivered similar invocations at the county's three other high schools last June after the graduating classes had voted — with the support of school officials — to include prayer in the ceremonies. The class votes were aimed at circumventing a 1992 Supreme Court decision (*Lee v. Weisman*) that barred schools from inviting guests to deliver prayers at commencement exercises.

This year, however, Loudoun County will have no prayers at its official high school graduation ceremonies. Just before Christmas, a federal judge in Virginia ruled that the students' prayers violated the constitutional prohibition against governmental establishment of religion just as much as a school-sponsored prayer would.

"I think there's something that's going to be missing," county school board Chairwoman Connie Street says of the decision. But Street joined in the board's 7-3 vote last month to drop the court fight over the graduation prayers to avoid running up additional legal expenses.

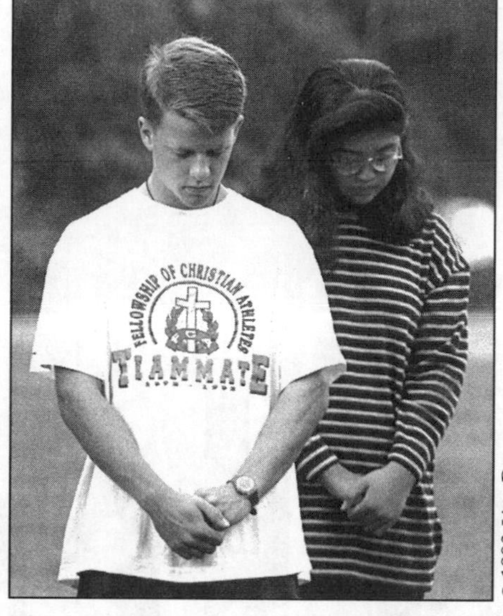

© 1993 Lisa Berg

In the rest of the country, however, the fight over graduation prayers — the newest battle in a 30-year-old war over religion in public schools — is far from over. As the annual graduation season nears, rival interest groups have been zeroing in on the legality of student-led graduation prayers.

"Students have the right to include an invocation and benediction in their graduation exercises," says the American Center for Law and Justice (ACLJ), a public interest law firm headed by televangelist Pat Robertson.

In a bulletin mailed to school administrators late last year, the center maintains that the Supreme Court only barred graduation prayers by officially invited speakers. The ACLJ cites a later ruling by a federal appeals court in Texas that upheld the right of "a majority of students . . . to incorporate prayer in public high school graduation ceremonies."

But the American Civil Liberties Union (ACLU) contends in its own legal advisory that the Supreme Court's 1992 ban does extend to student-initiated graduation prayers. "[W]hen public schools reserve time at a graduation ceremony for prayer," the ACLU says, "they violate the Constitution by putting the power, prestige and endorsement of the state behind whatever prayer is offered, no matter who offers it."

The Supreme Court has yet to settle the issue. [1] Last June, the justices declined to review the Texas case. Graduation-prayer supporters claimed the action showed the justices agreed with their view. "If the case posed a constitutional crisis," says Jay Alan Sekulow, the ACLJ's chief counsel, "you can bet the court would have heard it."

Since that time, however, the ACLU has won two rulings in lower federal courts. A federal appeals court in Philadelphia at the end of June issued an injunction barring a student from delivering a prayer at graduation ceremonies in Blackwood, N.J. And the ACLU represented the group of six students and teachers in the Loudoun County suit decided in December by U.S. District Judge Albert V. Bryan Jr., in Alexandria, Va.

Outside the courtrooms, however, prayer was very much a part of the nation's graduation exercises last year. In a survey by Phi Delta Kappa, a professional educators group, more than two-thirds of the school districts responding said prayer was included last year either in official commencement exercises or in separate baccalaureate services sponsored by outside groups. (*See story, p. 152.*)

The persistence of graduation prayers in the face of the Supreme Court's ruling parallels the reaction to the court's landmark decisions on school prayer three decades ago. Public opinion has remained strongly opposed to the court's rulings in 1962 and '63 that barred school-sponsored prayer or Bible reading in the classroom. But many principals and teachers continue to include prayer as part of the regular school schedule. Last fall, a high school principal in Jackson, Miss., won strong public support

Reactions to Supreme Court Ban on School Prayer

In the years since the Supreme Court banned organized Bible reading and prayer in public schools, a majority of Americans have disapproved of the decision. The rate of disapproval, however, has gradually dropped from a high of 70 percent in 1963 to 58 percent in early 1993.

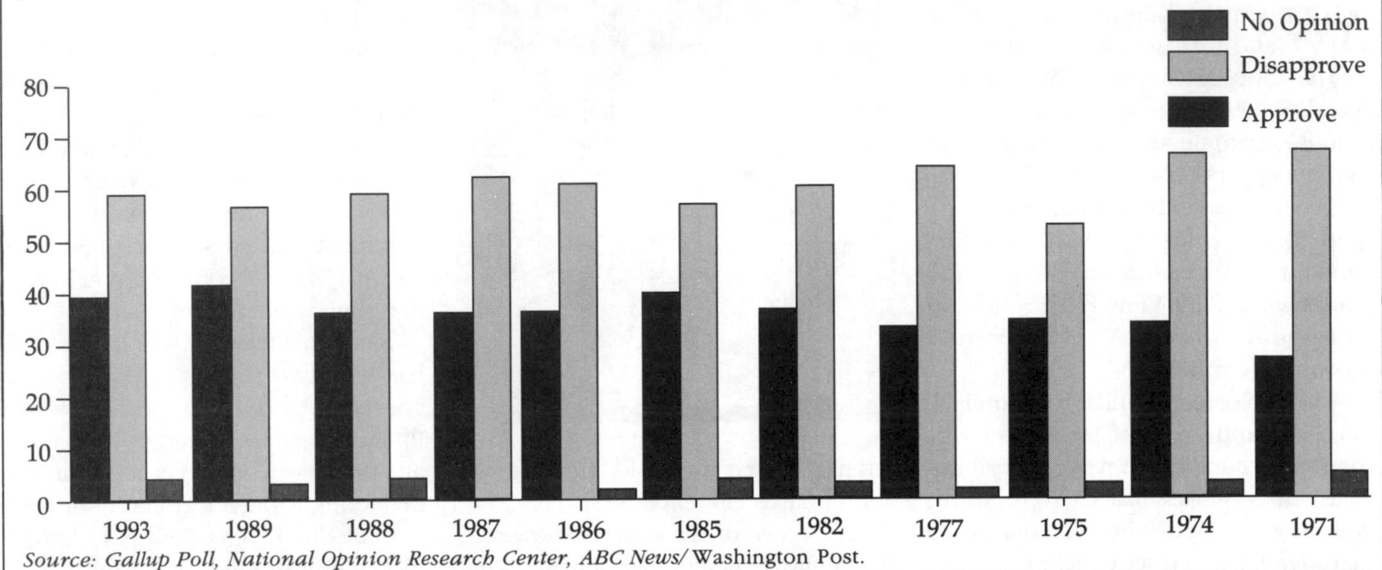

Source: Gallup Poll, National Opinion Research Center, ABC News/ Washington Post.

after he was suspended for permitting students to deliver prayers over the school's public address system. [2]

The battle over prayer is being fought in a politically charged atmosphere. Since the 1980s, religious conservatives have grown stronger and more assertive in political campaigns at the national, state and local levels. The "religious right" aligned itself closely with the Republican Party and buttressed the party's conservative stance on social issues such as abortion and homosexual rights under Presidents Ronald Reagan and George Bush.

In the past few years, religious conservatives have turned to local school board races and helped elect fundamentalist Christians to school board seats in a number of states. Members of the religious right reportedly gained majorities in five school districts around the country. In Vista, Calif. — just north of San Diego — the fundamentalist bloc has tried to have "creation science" taught along with the theory of evolution in high school biology classes.

Groups favoring the separation of church and state, such as the ACLU and People for the American Way, have tried to counter the religious right's resurgence. While the ACLU has pressed court fights, People for the American Way has conducted an energetic public relations campaign against the religious right's efforts to influence school policies. Since fall 1992, the group has warned that conservative religious organizations have been using "stealth" tactics to reshape school curricula and reintroduce what it calls "a degree of religious instruction and influence in the classroom." [3]

For their part, religious conservatives view public schools as increasingly hostile to religion. "Every day, Christian children all across America are quietly sitting in their public school chairs . . . being subjected to a subtle but systematic mind-altering and faith-destroying curriculum," says Robert Simonds, founder and president of Citizens for Excellence in Education. [4]

Simonds' group, founded in 1983 and based in Costa Mesa, Calif., has led the drive in recent years to elect religious conservatives to local school boards. Meanwhile, the ACLJ has been helping high school students use a 1984 federal law to form religious clubs or engage in other extracurricular religious activities on school property.

The often volatile disputes may obscure a subtle but unmistakable shift in attitudes toward religion and schools. Since the mid-1980s, a broad range of educators, religious advocates and civil libertarians have agreed that public schools have been giving short shrift to religion in courses such as history and literature where religion has played an important — and undeniable — role.

"Religion had been left out, and that was bad for students and bad for education," says Charles H. Haynes, executive director of the First Liberty Institute at George Mason University in Fairfax, Va. Haynes' organization has been working with textbook publishers and state and local school boards to develop ways to teach students about the history and beliefs of the world's major religions without advocating particular religious views.

More broadly, Yale law Professor Stephen Carter prompted a wave of rethinking last fall by arguing, in his book *The Culture of Disbelief*, that religious beliefs are generally frowned upon in schools and politics in the United States. Carter said he supports the Supreme Court's school prayer decisions, but still believes the educational system is "too often unresponsive to the needs or desires of parents concerned about their children's religious upbringing." [5]

Carter's argument struck a responsive chord among officials, policy experts and parents across the political and religious spectrums who say schools have given too little attention to teaching values to students. But the line between moral values and religious views can be difficult to draw.

Some religious conservatives, for example, have been promoting sex education course materials aimed at encouraging abstinence. But critics of the courses claim they promote sectarian views and have sued to block schools from using the materials in Shreveport, La., and Jacksonville, Fla.

The debate over the relationship between religion and schools in the United States is hardly new. Over the course of three centuries, schools have changed from sectarian institutions closely aligned with established Protestant churches into a secular system serving an increasingly diverse student body representing many religious faiths. Inevitably, the schools are faced with conflicting demands on what to teach and how to teach it.

The Constitution itself also seems to create conflicting requirements. The First Amendment bars any law "respecting the establishment of religion" or "prohibiting the free exercise thereof." Religious advocates argue that the free-exercise clause requires the government to accommodate religious observances in public life. Civil liberties groups, however, say that the establishment clause mandates a stricter separation of church and state.

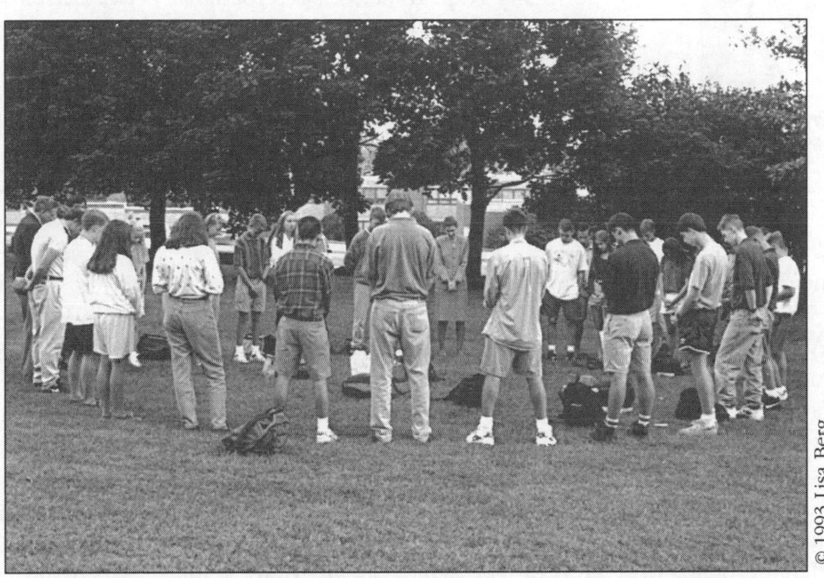

© 1993 Lisa Berg

For the past four years, Christian students at public schools around the country have gathered on Sept. 15 to pray before classes begin. Students at Langley High School in McLean, Va., are shown at last year's event.

As this perennial controversy is renewed in school boards and courtrooms around the country, here are some of the questions being debated:

Have efforts to keep religion out of public schools in order to protect separation of church and state gone too far?

For more than 30 years, religious advocates and political conservatives have been assailing the Supreme Court for "taking God out of the classroom." Church-state separationists, including civil liberties groups and some mainline Protestant denominations, have defended the court's rulings by saying the Constitution requires that schools be neutral in religious affairs.

Within some segments of the religious right, criticism of the school prayer rulings remains especially strong. Texas minister David Barton, for example, argues in a book-length tract — replete with graphs and charts — that the court's prayer and Bible-reading decisions led to a three-decade increase in violent crime, divorce and teenage pregnancies, and a sharp drop in college aptitude test scores among high school students. [6]

Some religious advocates, however, have become reconciled to the rulings that bar school-sponsored school prayer. "I don't anticipate any change in that doctrine, nor do I think we should change that doctrine," says the ACLJ's Sekulow. Instead, his group focuses on defending students' rights to engage in religious activities on campus but outside class (*see below*).

Civil liberties groups continue to defend the principle of government neutrality toward religion, but have also tried to take account of the apparent increase in religious sentiment. In a 35-minute video completed late last year, the ACLU uses a North Carolina minister to deliver the message that parents, not schools, should be responsible for youngsters' religious upbringing.

"Some people, however, want to take that right and responsibility away from parents," the Rev. W. W. Finlator, former pastor of a Baptist church in Raleigh, N.C., says on the video. "They want to bring religion to our children in another way. Not through parents at home, or in church, but through the

Charles H. Haynes
Executive Director
First Liberty Institute

public schools." [7]

The ACLU video also counters the charge that the Supreme Court's prayer rulings are to blame for social and educational decline. Author Jonathan Kozol, who has written extensively about education and poverty, says that college aptitude test scores have declined since the 1950s because more poor children are now taking the test. And Kozol similarly blames most other social problems in the United States on the gap between rich and poor, rather than the lack of religious observances in the public schools.

Even some religious advocates dismiss the notion that the Supreme Court bears the blame for taking religion out of public schools. Warren Nord, a religious historian at the University of North Carolina who favors teaching religion as a separate course in high schools, labels the charge against the Supreme Court "nonsense." Religion, he says, "had basically disappeared [from schools] by the end of the 19th century."

Still, other religious advocates insist that public education has become ever more secularized in recent decades. The result, they say, is that schools are not neutral but actively hostile to religion. They blame courts for taking the principle of separation of church and state too far — for example, by limiting school observances of Christmas. And they charge that school administrators and teachers have overreacted to the legal trend by virtually excising all mention of religion from the schools.

For the most part, separationists defend the rules against religious observances in schools. For example, they point with approval to court decisions and school board rules that generally require schools to focus on secular rather than religious aspects of Christmas. In many schools, that means "winter concerts" feature "Jingle Bells" rather than religious Christmas carols. In some areas, they may also include songs marking the Jewish holiday of Hannukah or the African American holiday Kwanza.

In some cases, however, separationists acknowledge their views are carried too far. When a Loudoun County high school principal urged the student newspaper last December to steer away from using the word "Christmas," Joseph Conn, a spokesman for Americans United for Separation of Church and State, told a reporter the principal was wrong. [8] And Ira Glasser, executive director of the national ACLU, says he strongly criticized a local ACLU chapter several years ago for trying to prevent a high school drama group from performing the rock-musical "Jesus Christ Superstar."

More broadly, many civil libertarians agree with religious advocates that schools have ignored religion in the curriculum. "Religion had been excluded from the teaching of American history," says Douglas Laycock, a constitutional law expert at the University of Texas who appears on the ACLU video. "That's bad history, and it was unfair to believers. I don't know how successful we've been in correcting it."

Haynes of the First Liberty Institute credits conservative Christians with raising the issue of whether education had been promoting an exclusively secular view of the world. But he also says the schools should not advance particular religious views.

"Public education cannot be a place where we impose religion on anybody," Haynes says. "But public education also can't be hostile to religion. That violates the ground rules, too."

Should public schools permit student-organized prayer, religious clubs and other religious activities outside class time?

For the past four years, tens of thousands of Christian students — perhaps as many as 2 million this past year — have gathered on Sept. 15 to pray around public school flagpoles before the beginning of the day's classes. This nationwide event epitomizes the new weapon that religious advocates have found to bring religion back to public school campuses: students' rights.

A one-page flyer distributed by the ACLJ lists 10 "student freedoms guaranteed under the First Amendment," including the right to form Bible clubs, wear religious T-shirts and buttons and hand out religious literature. Jay Sekulow often appears with Pat Robertson on the Christian Broadcasting Network (CBN) program "The 700 Club" urging students who are denied the right to engage in religious activities on school campuses to contact his organization for legal help.

Congress established the framework for students' religious rights on public school campuses in 1984. The Equal Access Act requires any public secondary school that receives federal funds to allow student religious organizations to meet and use school facilities on the same terms as other extracurricular student groups.

The Supreme Court upheld the act in 1990. But legal experts on both sides of the school prayer debate say authorities in many places continue to throw up roadblocks to religious activities on school grounds. "There are certainly some places where administrators don't fully understand the act and are not fully implementing it," says Elliot Mincberg, legal director of People for the American Way.

Sekulow criticizes authorities more strongly. "School administrators all over the country are hostile to Christian students' exercising their rights," he says. "The first year or so, you could say they're not clear about the ruling. Four years later, it's not misinformation. It's hostility."

Gary Marx, communications director for the American Association of School Administrators, insists that school authorities are trying to implement the act fairly. But he adds that public schools "are not meant to be religious centers."

"Proselytizing on school property is not part of our system," Marx says. "The school building is not the place to proselytize."

Marc Stern, a lawyer with the strongly separationist American Jewish Congress, agrees on the risks of what he calls "hard-core proselytizing" on campus, but says those dangers have yet to materialize. "As long as it stays that way, nothing is going to get litigated," Stern says.

Religious advocates have also used the banner of student rights to try to justify the practice of having students vote on permitting student-led prayer at graduation ceremonies. "Student-initiated prayer is constitutional," Sekulow says.

But civil liberties groups argue that school authorities are so closely involved in commencement planning that the prayer has to be viewed as school-sponsored. "They're selecting one particular topic, prayer, and saying they're willing to facilitate it," says Mincberg.

Federal courts have split on the legality of student-led graduation prayers. In its decision in the Texas case, the 5th U.S. Circuit Court of Appeals reasoned that student prayers "place less psychological pressure" on other students than invocations by an invited speaker because they "represent the will of their peers." But in the New Jersey case, the 3rd U.S. Circuit Court of Appeals said the fact that a fellow student gives a prayer "does not diminish the effect of a prayer on students who do not share the same or any religious perspective."

School authorities last year urged the Supreme Court to review the 5th Circuit's decision in order to settle the issue, but the justices voted not to take the case. Court observers are divided on whether the justices will take up the issue soon — or how they will decide it.

"I don't think the court wants to get involved in micromanaging the relationship between the principal's office and the president of the student council," says Douglas Kmiec, a constitutional law professor at the University of Notre Dame. "I think the court's going to say that if the record doesn't show that the principal and the school district are behind it, latitude will be given."

But Douglas Laycock says he expects the Supreme Court eventually will settle the issue — and will side against student-delivered graduation prayers. "Delegating control of [graduation] to a committee of students doesn't make a bit of difference," Laycock says. "If both sides continue to litigate about it, sooner or later the Supreme Court will have to take a case."

Should religion be included in public school curriculums — and, if so, how?

From its founding, the United States has been a strongly religious country. Many of the original colonists belonged to minority religions and came to America to escape religious oppression. Today, nine out of 10 Americans say they believe in God, seven out of 10 identify with a religious group and four out of 10 attend worship services in any given week. [9]

Despite this background, religion seemingly dropped out of the public school curriculum in the past few decades. Textbooks treated religion lightly, if at all. Pilgrims were defined in one text as "people who make long trips." The role of religion in the abolition or prohibition movements was barely discussed. The Rev. Dr. Martin Luther King Jr. was depicted as a civil rights activist with little attention to his calling as a minister or the central role of black churches in the civil rights revolution. [10]

Textbook publishers now say these acknowledged shortcomings resulted from an overreaction to the Supreme Court's school-prayer decisions and a fear of stepping on religious toes. "It was a very timid approach as a result of the issues of separation of church and state, which made avoidance the more comfortable route," says John Ridley, vice president and school publisher for Houghton-Mifflin Co., a leading textbook publisher.

Beginning in the late 1980s, several states took steps to fill the curricular gap on religion. California, the nation's largest textbook market, had the biggest impact when it adopted twin textbooks developed by Houghton-Mifflin that include chapters recounting the history and beliefs of Judaism, Christianity, Islam, Hinduism and Buddhism.

Some civil libertarians raised cau-

Jay Alan Sekulow
Chief Counsel
American Center for Law and Justice

Graduation Prayers, 1993

More than two-thirds of all public high school districts responding to a recent survey included prayer as part of their graduation activities last year.

More than 1,000 school districts out of 1,491 responding to the survey † said prayer was included either in the graduation ceremony or in a separate baccalaureate service not sponsored by the school. The survey was conducted by the Gallup organization for Phi Delta Kappa, a professional educators' society.

The U.S. Supreme Court in 1992 barred sponsored prayer at public high school graduation ceremonies. Religious and civil liberties groups disagree about whether schools can assist graduates in including a student-led prayer. The ruling said nothing about separate baccalaureate services.

Nearly one-fourth of the school districts reporting prayer at graduation said an adult had been invited to deliver the prayer. Where students delivered the prayer, 101 school districts said the prayers came as a "surprise" to the superintendent. But 92 districts said the wording of the student prayers had been approved in advance.

"It is clear from this survey," the authors of an article about the survey commented, "that court decisions seeking to limit prayer at formal public school commencements have not fully succeeded in doing so." ‡

† There are 15,173 school districts in the U.S.

‡ Martha W. McCarthy and Larry W. Barber, "Much Ado Over Graduation Prayer," *Phi Delta Kappan*, October 1993, p. 120.

Survey Results

Prayer included in graduation activities:	
At separate baccalaureate service	654 (43.8%)
At graduation ceremony	684 (45.8%)
At both baccalaureate and graduation	272 (18.2%)
Total at either baccalaureate or graduation service	1,066 (71.4%)
Prayer at graduation ceremony:	
Adult invited to give prayer	161
Student-offered prayer	526
Total (adult and/or student led; 3 schools had both)	684
Prayer at graduation ceremony (adult or student led) by region:	
South	76%
East	34%
Midwest	40%
West	36%

tion flags at the time. "This is fraught with practical, constitutional and intellectual perils," Barry Lynn, the ACLU's then-legislative counsel and now executive director of Americans United for Separation of Church and State, told *The Wall Street Journal* in 1991. "It isn't a violation to emphasize one political system over another, or capitalism over Marxism [in the classroom]. But promoting or emphasizing one religion over others or none can be a constitutional violation."

In California, religious groups raised specific concerns about Houghton-Mifflin's text and succeeded in making some changes before publication. Jackie Berman, an education specialist with the Jewish Community Relations Council of the San Francisco Bay Area, recalls, for example, that the text's chapter on Judaism originally had a time-line that stopped with the birth of Jesus, as if suggesting that Judaism had disappeared at that point.

Today, Berman is still dissatisfied with textbooks' treatment of Judaism. "I have not seen a model in curricular materials that does it in a way that, in our opinion, is satisfactory," she says.

The Houghton-Mifflin text describes Judaism as a religion founded on law and custom, Berman says, while Christianity comes across more favorably as emphasizing love and compassion. Moreover, she says, "Since Jews are in such a minority in this country, our beliefs are going to suffer in the classroom. It will be very hard for teachers to present them as equally valid."

Haynes concedes the pitfalls, but says teachers are working to minimize the problems. "Teachers have very little background in the teaching of religion," Haynes says. But he says teachers react enthusiastically to dealing with religion and work at treating the topic with sensitivity.

To help teachers, Haynes prepared a guide on classroom techniques to accompany the Houghton-Mifflin books. Haynes cautions against re-creating religious ceremonies or asking students about their religious beliefs. When asked about their own beliefs, Haynes says, some teachers may prefer not to answer. Those who do respond should describe their views "straightforwardly and succinctly . . . with little elaboration or discussion."

The re-entry of religion in some textbooks has not quieted criticism from religious conservatives. For the past two decades, groups on the religious right have attacked a number of public school curricula that they felt undermined religious beliefs. Most recently, they have criticized "Outcomes-Based Education," a curricular approach that in some versions teaches values through critical thinking rather than moral instruction. In at least one state — Virginia — the criticism forced school authorities to drop plans for adopting the curriculum. [11]

Given the importance of public school education, curriculum disputes such as these are certain to continue. Critics of the religious right accuse it of trying to control school curricula, censor reading lists and remove literary classics from library shelves. [12] In his book, Yale's Stephen Carter agrees that the curriculum disputes are "often nasty and usually depressing." But he also says that religious conservatives have a sincere fear that public schools are indoctrinating their children with anti-religious views and that liberals are "curiously intolerant" of their feelings.

Haynes says the best way to resolve these disputes is through negotiation and mutual accommodation — an approach that he says is dictated by the First Amendment. "The principles of the First Amendment ought to help us to include different perspectives within the schools rather than say that religion ought to be excluded or to suggest that we could somehow use the schools to promote our own particular religion," he says. ■

BACKGROUND

School Bible Disputes

Public education in America began, as writer Stephen Bates put it recently, as "an intrinsically religious undertaking." [13] Before the American Revolution, most schools and colleges were founded and operated by churches, not by Colonial governments. Religious instruction was a primary and ever-present mission.

For more than a century, countless numbers of American youngsters learned to read from a little book first published in 1690 entitled *The New England Primer.* This beginning reader taught the alphabet with rhyming couplets based on biblical events and two-line "lessons for youth" reflecting stern Puritan doctrine.

After the Revolution, Noah Webster's famous speller, *The American Spelling Book,* displaced the primer as the most widely used beginning reader. While Webster focused on establishing a common English language for the new nation, the book's instructional passages and stories had a strong religious orientation. "No man may put off the law of God," one passage declared. "My joy is in His law all the day."

By the 1830s, public education began to move away from overt religious instruction. Horace Mann, secretary of the country's first state board of education, in Massachusetts, from 1837 to 1848, provided the new philosophy toward religion in schools. He said schools in the state should teach America's "common religion," which closely resembled Mann's Unitarianism rather than more dogmatic Protestant denominations. He said students should read the Bible, but teachers should not comment on it. Massachusetts' school system "welcomes the Bible," he said, "but in receiving the Bible, allows it to do what it is allowed to do in no other system — speak for itself."

Mann's policy was aimed at reducing sectarian disputes over school curriculums between different Protestant denominations. But the wave of Catholic immigration from Europe led to a new, and more lasting, religious clash. The use of the Protestant King James Bible in public schools violated the religious beliefs of newly arrived Catholics. Catholic bishops in 1840 urged priests to oppose the practice, fueling anti-Catholic sentiment among the growing nativist groups.

The school Bible dispute erupted

into violence in New York City in 1841 after enactment of a Catholic-backed law that barred the teaching of any "religious, sectarian doctrine or tenet" in public schools. Protestants stoned the windows of the home of the city's Catholic bishop. Three years later, a more serious incident occurred in Philadelphia after the Catholic bishop's effort to exempt Catholic youngsters from Bible reading was taken as a step to prevent Bible reading altogether. Nativist groups started a riot that left 13 people dead and 50 others wounded.

Catholics responded to the rebuffs by starting their own schools. In New York, the state superintendent of education in 1853 approved Catholic youngsters' attendance at non-public schools. But in Maine, a Catholic father who withdrew his child from public schools lost a legal effort to have the state reimburse him for the cost of Catholic schooling. The Maine Supreme Court in 1854 said that the reading of the Protestant Bible in public schools was constitutional and "binding upon all the members of the schools, although composed of divers religious sects." [14]

The dispute was renewed after the Civil War when Catholics — aligned with the Democratic Party — won passage of a 1869 law in Cincinnati forbidding the reading of the Bible in public schools. Republicans, fearful of Catholic efforts to win public funding for parochial schools, proposed a constitutional amendment to bar any public moneys for sectarian schools. "Leave the matter of religion to the family altar, the church and the private school supported entirely by private contribution," President Ulysses S. Grant said in a speech to the Army of the Tennessee in 1875. The House passed the measure in 1876, but it fell short of a two-thirds majority in the Senate. Eleven similar measures proposed over the next decade also failed.

Enrollment in Catholic schools did increase through the 19th century — with some public assistance in places. Both then and now, however, most Catholic youngsters have attended public schools — and enrollment in Catholic schools has been declining since the mid-1960s. Jews, the country's second-largest religious minority, also have been educated for the most part in the public schools. Jewish immigration began increasing in the late 1800s, but most Jewish parents followed an assimilationist pattern.

Meanwhile, religion was being given a less and less visible role in public schools. The most popular textbook of the 19th century, *McGuffey's Reader*, taught moral behavior from a nondenominational point of view. Religious readings constituted about one-third of the book in 1837, but only 6 percent in the last edition in 1901. [15] At the turn of the century, only one state — Massachusetts — had a law requiring morning prayer or Bible reading in the schools.

Rise and Fall of Fundamentalism

In the early 20th century, the growth of a new brand of conservative Protestantism — called "fundamentalism" after the title of a popular series of conservative theological tracts — countered the secularizing trend in schools. After 1910, a dozen states, half of them in the South, passed laws requiring Bible reading or morning prayer in schools. In a more direct challenge, fundamentalists pushed for legislation — adopted in five states — to ban the teaching of evolution in public schools.

The fundamentalist movement suffered a setback in 1925 with the celebrated trial of John Scopes, a Dayton, Tenn., high school biology teacher, for violating the state's anti-evolution law. Scopes was convicted, but defense attorney Clarence Darrow won public opinion with a mocking cross-examination of William Jennings Bryan, the former Democratic presidential nominee who had volunteered to prosecute the case. Later, Scopes' conviction was overturned.

The 20th century brought a host of changes in the United States that combined to weaken the hold of traditional religion. Scientific advances challenged religious views of the nature of the universe. Urbanization, increased mobility and the communications revolution undermined the authority of family and church. Meanwhile, public education embraced the progressive philosophy of John Dewey, who based his social ethics on human experience rather than religious doctrine. [16]

Still, religion was a pervasive presence in American society, and in the schools, into the second half of the 20th century. Nearly two-thirds of Americans described themselves as church members in the 1960 census. In most places, business came to a halt on Sundays in deference to churchgoing. And Bible reading was standard practice in about two-fifths of the nation's school systems. The percentage was highest in the South and East, lowest in the Midwest and West. In those systems with Bible reading, less than half — about 40 percent — said that students who did not want to take part could be excused. [17]

School-Prayer Rulings

As part of a plan to strengthen moral education in the schools, the New York Board of Regents, the governing body for the state school system, wrote a 22-word prayer in 1951 that it urged local schools to use at the start of the day: "Almighty God, we acknowledge our dependence upon Thee, and we beg thy blessings upon us, our parents, our teachers, and our country."

This supplication seemed designed to give offense to none, but many people of minority religious view-

Continued on p. 156

Chronology

1600s-1800

Churches help establish primary and secondary schools and early colleges in America.

1690 [approx.]
A Boston publisher produces *The New England Primer* to teach Puritan children how to read using Bible verses and other religious lessons. The text, periodically revised, is used in much of New England into the early 1800s.

1800s-1960

Public schools and higher education in the United States gradually become secularized, but religion continues to play a part in many places.

1837-1848
Horace Mann, secretary of the Massachusetts board of education and a central figure in U.S. public education, urges schools to avoid "sectarian" doctrine.

1908
John Dewey, father of progressive education in America, writes an influential article contending that teaching religion in public schools is divisive.

1960s

Supreme Court bars government-sponsored religious observances in public schools, provoking controversy.

June 25, 1962
Supreme Court bars use of prayer written by New York state Board of Regents in public school classrooms (*Engel v. Vitale*).

June 17, 1963
Supreme Court extends school-prayer decision by barring government-sponsored recitation of Lord's Prayer or Bible reading. Court adds that religion can be included as a subject in public school curriculums (*Abington School District v. Schempp*).

Nov. 13, 1968
Arkansas law barring teaching of evolution in public schools overturned by Supreme Court.

1970s

Supreme Court skirts school-prayer issues but tries to clarify rules governing state aid for church-affiliated schools. Many experts find limits on assistance for parochial schools confusing and illogical.

June 28, 1971
Supreme Court bars state aid for teacher salaries at parochial schools. Decision establishes three-pronged test for judging whether state aid to religion violates Establishment clause (*Lemon v. Kurtzman*).

1980s

The religious right mobilizes to increase the role of religion in public schools but suffers setbacks.

1984
School-prayer amendment fails in Senate, but Congress passes Equal Access Act. The act requires schools to give religious clubs equal rights with other student organizations to use of school property and facilities.

June 4, 1985
Alabama "moment-of-silence" law struck down by Supreme Court (*Wallace v. Jaffree*).

June 19, 1987
Louisiana law requiring "balanced treatment" for creation science and theory of evolution struck down by Supreme Court (*Edwards v. Aguillard*).

June 25, 1988
Religious and civic leaders join in the Williamsburg Charter, which calls for teaching about religion in public schools.

1990s

Religionists make gains with moves by some states to include religion in public school curriculums. Religious right and civil liberties groups battle in school board elections.

June 4, 1990
Supreme Court broadly interprets Equal Access Act (*Board of Education of Westside Community Schools v. Mergens*).

June 24, 1992
Supreme Court bars school-sponsored prayers at public high school graduations (*Lee v. Weisman*).

November 1992
Religious right wins seats on many local school boards.

March 30, 1994
Supreme Court to hear arguments in case challenging creation of new school district for Hasidic Jewish village in New York (*Board of Education of Kiryas Joel v. Grumet*).

Major Groups in the Battle Over Religion in Schools

Conservative Religious Groups

American Center for Law and Justice
Virginia Beach, Va.
The Rev. Pat Robertson, president, Jay Alan Sekulow, chief counsel
Represents students seeking to engage in religious activities on public school campuses.

American Family Association
(formerly, National Federation for Decency)
Tupelo, Miss.
The Rev. Donald Wildmon, president
Has opposed some television programs, library books and elementary reading series, claiming they are anti-Christian.

Christian Coalition
Chesapeake, Va.
Ralph Reed, executive director
Has helped mobilize campaigns for election of Christian conservatives to local school boards.

Citizens for Excellence in Education/ National Association of Christian Educators
Costa Mesa, Calif.
Dr. Robert Simonds, president
Challenges variety of books, educational materials and curricula in public schools; helps elect members to local school boards.

Concerned Women for America
Washington, D.C.
Beverly LaHaye, president
Opposes sex education unless based on abstinence; materials widely used in challenging books and curricula in public schools.

Eagle Forum
Alton, Ill.
Phyllis Schlafly, president
Opposes sex education unless based on abstinence; opposes self-esteem programs; materials widely used in challenging local schoolbooks.

Civil Liberties Groups

American Civil Liberties Union
New York, N.Y.
Ira Glasser, executive director
Has been involved for decades in Supreme Court cases on school prayer, curriculum and church-school funding issues.

American Jewish Congress
New York, N.Y.
Marc Stern, co-director, Commission on Law and Social Action
Has advocated separation of church and state in several major cases before Supreme Court.

Americans United for Separation of Church and State
Silver Spring, Md.
Barry W. Lynn, executive director
Has lobbied and litigated on church-state issues since founding in 1947.

People for the American Way
Washington, D.C.
Arthur Kropp, president
Has opposed religious right on school and censorship issues since group's founding by TV producer Norman Lear in 1980.

Continued from p. 154

points did object. And the legal battle over the prayer transformed the relationship between schools and religion in the United States. [18]

The five parents who challenged use of the prayer by the New Hyde Park school district in suburban Long Island included two Jews, one Unitarian, a member of the secularist Ethical Culture Society and a self-described non-believer. They filed suit in a New York state court in 1958 contending that use of the prayer constituted an illegal establishment of religion. As the suit progressed, the families received abusive phone calls and letters and criticism in the Long Island press.

A lower court judge rejected their plea, as did the state's highest court. In a 5-2 decision, the New York Court of Appeals declared that the Constitution did not prohibit "mere professions of belief in God" in the public schools.

The U.S. Supreme Court had entered the controversy over religion and schools in the late 1940s. In 1947, the court issued a strong pronouncement about the importance of separation of church and state but nonetheless upheld, 5-4, public funding for transportation of parochial school students. In 1952, the court sidestepped a school prayer challenge, saying the parents of the child involved in the case no longer had standing because the child had graduated.

When the court agreed to take up the New York case in December 1961, battle lines were drawn. The parents' plea was supported by the ACLU, the American Jewish Congress and other Jewish groups and the American Ethical Union. On the other side were 19 states that joined in a brief urging the court to uphold the country's "religious heritage and tradition."

The court's decision — handed down on the last day of the 1961-62 term — read the country's religious traditions differently. [19] In a short opinion with few legal citations, Justice Hugo Black described use of the prayer as "wholly inconsistent with the Establishment Clause." After reciting the history of church-state conflicts in England and Colonial America, Black said the Constitution required government to "stay out of the business of writing or sanctioning official prayers and leave that purely religious function to the people themselves and to those the people choose to look to for religious guidance."

The reaction to the court's 6-1 decision was strong and overwhelmingly negative. Ten members of Congress filed statements the next day opposing the decision; none supported it. The ruling was also denounced by the country's most prominent religious leaders, including two Roman Catholic cardinals and the Protestant evangelist Billy Graham. "This is another step toward the secularization of the United States," Graham said.[20]

Despite the criticisms, the court extended its decision a year later in a pair of cases that challenged a Pennsylvania law requiring daily Bible reading in public schools and a Baltimore rule providing for the reading of a chapter from the Bible or the Lord's Prayer. In an 8-1 decision, the Supreme Court said both laws violated the Establishment clause.

Writing for the majority, Justice Tom Clark said that to pass muster under the Establishment clause, a law must have "a secular purpose and a primary effect that neither advances nor inhibits religion." Clark added a significant passage, however, that sanctioned the study of comparative religion or the history of religion in public schools: "Nothing we have said here indicates that such study of the Bible or of religion, when presented objectively as part of a secular program of education, may not be effected consistently with the First Amendment."[21]

The reaction to the court's new decision was less intense than a year earlier. Most Protestant denominations endorsed the ruling, and Catholic criticism was less vocal. Still, a poll taken in 1963 found 70 percent of the people opposed to the ruling.[22] In addition, members of Congress continued to push constitutional amendments to overturn the decisions. And schools in much of the country ignored or openly defied the court's pronouncements. In Texas, for example, 90 percent of the school districts in the state had rules requiring Bible reading four years after the ruling.[23]

More Setbacks

Over the next two decades, the court dealt more setbacks to religious groups that tried to use the schools to advance their views. In 1968, the court struck down an Arkansas law that barred the teaching of evolution in public schools. The unanimous court said that the law improperly singled out evolution "for the sole reason that it is deemed to conflict with a particular religious doctrine."

In the 1970s and '80s, the court wrestled with the question of public funds for church-affiliated schools. Financially strapped Catholic schools had urged state legislatures to find ways to subsidize their operations within Supreme Court guidelines. In a pivotal case in 1971 — *Lemon v. Kurtzman* — the court struck down two plans in Rhode Island and Pennsylvania that used public funds to supplement teacher salaries at parochial schools.

The decision, written by Chief Justice Warren Burger, added a new criterion to the secular-purpose and effect tests that the court crafted in the 1963 decision. To be upheld, Burger said, a law also must not result in "an excessive government entanglement with religion."

In applying this three-part test — called the *Lemon* test — the court made some exceedingly fine distinctions. Generally, it barred direct aid for parochial schools or students, but permitted plans — such as tuition tax credits — that benefited parents or students generally, whether in parochial or other private schools.

The Religious Right

In the 1980s, the debate over religion and schools became part of a broader political battle waged by a new force in American politics: the religious right. Conservative Christians, including many fundamentalist Protestants and some Catholics, entered politics with a vengeance, seeking to halt or reverse a host of trends that they found threatening to their religious beliefs.[24]

Religion, of course, has animated many of the important political movements in U.S. history — from the abolitionist and child-welfare campaigns of the 19th century through the temperance movement and civil rights revolution of the 20th century. The religious right, however, has focused on a broad agenda that has included outlawing abortion, combating promiscuity and opposing homosexual rights and the Equal Rights Amendment.

Two television evangelists — Jerry Falwell and Pat Robertson — personified the religious right and fostered its growth. In the late 1970s, Falwell, minister of a large Baptist church in Lynchburg, Va., joined with conservative activists in forming the Moral Majority, a political organization aligned with the Republican Party. Robertson, who founded the Christian Broadcasting Network, used the network to launch himself into politics, including unsuccessful runs for the Republican presidential nomination in 1988 and 1992.

Falwell and Robertson both assailed public education for turning away from what they regarded as traditional values. For them and like-minded Americans around the country, including President Ronald Reagan, the Supreme Court's rulings on prayer and Bible reading had started the schools down a path toward godless immorality.

In its most publicized initiatives, however, the religious right suffered one setback after another. In 1984, a school-prayer amendment was brought to a vote in Congress for the third time. But the measure fell 11 votes short in the Republican-controlled Senate of the two-thirds majority needed to send it to the states for ratification.

To circumvent the school-prayer ban, religious conservatives won passage of laws in 25 states to permit or require public schools to observe a "moment of silence" at the start of the day. But the Supreme Court in 1985 dealt that tactic a severe blow.

In a 6-3 ruling, the court held that an Alabama law that required a moment of silence for "meditation or voluntary prayer" improperly encouraged religion. The court left open the possibility of sustaining a moment-of-silence law with no mention of prayer. But in 1987, the court refused to reinstate a New Jersey moment-of-silence law that had been struck down by a lower court.

In the same year, the Supreme Court also turned back a new tactic by religious conservatives to put the biblical theory of creation back into public school curriculums as "creation science." In a 7-2 decision, the court struck down a Louisiana law that required balanced treatment for creation science and the theory of evolution. The court said that the purpose of the law was "to advance the religious viewpoint that a supernatural being created humankind."

Religious conservatives lost two other high-profile school legal battles in the 1980s. In Hawkins County, Tenn., a group of parents objected to a reading series that they said promoted secular humanism and offended their religious beliefs. In federal court, the parents asked only for their children to be exempted from reading the texts. A lower court judge in 1986 said the schools should accommodate the parents' request. But in 1987, a federal appeals court disagreed, saying that "mere exposure" to the books did not violate the students' or the parents' religious liberty.

In the same year, a federal judge in Mobile, Ala., ruling in another suit by conservative religious parents, ordered the removal of some 44 public school textbooks that he said established the "religion of secular humanism." But an appeals court quickly overruled him.

The Fourth 'R'

Despite the legal setbacks, religious forces made a significant gain by the end of the 1980s: They had moved educators and policymakers of all political stripes to a broad consensus that public schools had been shortchanging religion.

Haynes of the First Liberty Institute says the parents' defeats in the curriculum disputes actually helped the cause. "They lost in the courts, but they scored some important points," Haynes says. "They reminded us that we have excluded certain perspectives."

Indeed, two 1986 studies — one by a college religion professor and the other sponsored by People for the American Way — both found that public school textbooks sorely neglected religion.[25] Two years later, Haynes, who had also done research sponsored by a foundation affiliated with Americans United for Separation of Church and State, helped give voice to this new consensus. In 1988, he helped organize the drafting of the Williamsburg Charter criticizing "the exclusion of teaching about the role of religion in society."

The 23-page statement was signed by representatives of some of the country's largest religious groups, as well as Chief Justice of the United States William H. Rehnquist, former Chief Justice Warren E. Burger and former Presidents Jimmy Carter and Gerald Ford.[26]

Several states responded to the call to reintroduce religion into the curriculum, including California, the country's largest market for school textbooks. Working with California school officials, Houghton-Mifflin developed books for use by fifth- and sixth-graders that gave overviews of the history and beliefs of five major religions — Judaism, Christianity, Islam, Hinduism and Buddhism. The texts were adopted for the 1991-92 school year in California and at least nine other states.

Meanwhile, Congress had given students the right to participate in religious activities on school campuses not sponsored by the schools. Congress passed the Equal Access Act in 1984 as a bow to religious forces following the defeat of the school-prayer amendment. The act required high schools that received federal financing to give student religious organizations the same right to use school facilities enjoyed by other student groups.

In 1990, the Supreme Court upheld the act and gave it a broad construction. The justices said the equal access provision is triggered whenever a school allows use of its facilities by a club that does not "directly relate to the body of courses offered by the school."

The court's 8-1 ruling gave new encouragement to students seeking to form Bible reading or prayer clubs or to distribute religious literature on campus. School administrators often refused to recognize the clubs, however, and many disputes landed back in court.

The school-prayer controversy was also reignited in 1992, when the Supreme Court banned school-sponsored prayers at high school graduation ceremonies. Religious groups argued the ruling still allowed students themselves to decide to have prayers at graduation, but civil liberties groups questioned the tactic.

The controversies helped unsettle the developing consensus on religion and schools and give new impetus to the religious right. After a decade of activity in national and state politics,

The Curious Case of Kiryas Joel School District

Forty miles northwest of New York City lies the village of Kiryas Joel, an enclave of about 12,000 Hasidic Jews where religious rituals are scrupulously observed, television is shunned and almost all of the children are taught in private religious schools segregated — according to the Hasidim's religious views — by sex.

For the past four years, however, some 200 of the village's children — all of them handicapped or learning-disabled — have been going to a public school in a new school district created to try to accommodate the religious views of the Hasidim with the U.S. Supreme Court's mandate to keep church and state separate in public education.

The Kiryas Joel school district's lone public school has secular teachers and a secular curriculum. It has no religious trappings, not even a mezuzah on the door. But to church-state separationists, the school represents a clear violation of the Constitution's ban on establishment of religion.

The New York Legislature created the Kiryas Joel district in 1989 after the villagers reached an impasse with the Monroe-Woodbury School District on providing special-education services — as required by state and federal law — for youngsters with physical or mental disabilities.

Before 1985, the disabled youngsters had been getting special services in an annex operated by the school district adjacent to the religious schools. But in 1985, the Supreme Court ruled in a pair of cases that providing compensatory educational services at private religious schools violated the separation of church and state.

The school district told the Hasidim that if they wanted their children to receive special education, the youngsters would have to start attending a public school outside the village. Some did, but they reported feeling traumatized by attending school in what the village leaders called a "foreign setting."

So the Legislature responded in 1989 with a measure to make the village into its own school district so that it could establish a "public" school strictly for its special-needs students.

Even before the school district became operational, however, the New York State School Boards Association challenged the arrangement as unconstitutional. In July 1989, the New York Court of Appeals, the state's highest court, agreed. In a 4-2 ruling, the court said the act setting up the school district created a "symbolic union" between church and state.

When the U.S. Supreme Court agreed to review the case on Nov. 29, some observers speculated the case might prompt a fundamental rethinking of its doctrine in church-state cases. Religious accommodationists hoped the court would relax the relatively strict test it adopted for church-state issues in a 1971 case, *Lemon v. Kurtzman* (*see p. 157*). The ruling bars any laws benefiting religion unless they have a secular purpose and effect and do not entangle the government in religious issues.

In his brief for the village seeking to uphold the law, however, Washington attorney Nathan Lewin argues the school district passes muster even under the *Lemon* test. He says the law serves the secular purpose of providing special education to disabled youngsters, does not promote religious observances and does not foster any excessive government entanglement with religion.

But the American Jewish Congress has filed a brief opposing the law, arguing that it represents a more basic violation of church-state separation. "This case is about whether you can organize political units along religious lines," says Marc Stern, an attorney for the organization. "That goes very much to the core of the Establishment clause."

The justices are scheduled to hear arguments in the case — *Board of Education of Kiryas Joel v. Grumet* — on March 30. A decision is expected by late June or early July.

religious conservatives decided to move into local school board campaigns around the country. ■

CURRENT SITUATION

School Board Battles

When John Tyndall qualified as a school board candidate in 1992 in tiny Vista, Calif., near San Diego, he listed his place of employment as a "research institute." In fact, Tyndall is an accountant for the Institute for Creation Research, which publishes "creation science" textbooks.

Tyndall and a second candidate backed by religious-right groups — Cheryl Lee Jones, a substitute teacher in Vista — won in the November 1992 election. They joined Deidre Holliday, elected in 1991, to form a fundamentalist majority on the five-member board. And for the past year, they have pushed a number of initiatives critics say are aimed at increasing the influence of religion in schools.

The Vista school board election was one of many in recent years where candidates backed by the religious right have been victorious. The exact number is impossible to verify. Robert Simonds, a former minister and college professor who heads Citizens for Excellence in Education (CEE), claimed in 1992 that local CEE chapters had helped elect more than 3,500 school board members since 1989.[27]

People for the American Way more conservatively identified 283 school board candidates — and just under 100 winners — formally backed by religious-right groups in 1992 and 1993. In a 33-page report, the group counts five school boards where members of the religious right hold majorities: Duval and Lake counties in Florida; New Berlin, Wis.; Round Rock, Texas, and Vista. In addition, the report said, many of the unsuccessful campaigns "also had an influence on the community and the school board." [28]

Whatever the exact number may be, religious conservatives have been aggressive in using school board seats to challenge existing policies on a wide variety of curricular and other issues:

- In Greenville, S.C., three Christian conservatives on the 12-member school board unsuccessfully fought the "Framework for Learning" curriculum saying it undermines religious values.
- In Waterloo, Iowa, a conservative school board member elected in 1991 unsuccessfully opposed the district's AIDS education program and a school-based health clinic that she said promotes abortion.
- In Bozeman, Mont., three school board members on the religious right elected last April tried to give parents control of a curriculum committee composed only of educators. [29]

Fundamentalist board members in Vista tried three times last year to introduce creationism into high school science courses. Under threat of legal action from the local ACLU, the board backed off. Instead, the board adopted a resolution in August that says scientific theories should not be taught "dogmatically" and that "discussions of divine creation" should be included "at appropriate times" in history or literature courses. Jordan Budd, staff counsel for the ACLU of San Diego and Imperial counties, calls the resolution "meaningless" but says his group will go to court if teachers use the resolution to teach creationism.

Meanwhile, conservative-dominated school boards are already in court over another curriculum issue: sex education. In Shreveport, La., a state court judge last May blocked Caddo Parish schools from using "Sex Respect," a course published by a religious-oriented group in Illinois, Project Respect. The judge said the curriculum contained religious instruction in violation of state law.

In Jacksonville, Fla., the Duval County Board of Education, with a 4-3 fundamentalist majority, is also in court trying to protect another sex education curriculum: Teen-Aid. Planned Parenthood of Northern Florida contends the course materials promote sectarian views in violation of state law and the board's own rules.

LeAnna Benn, national director of Teen-Aid in Spokane, Wash., acknowledges the curriculum promotes sexual abstinence but says it isn't religiously based: "We do not discuss a deity or a theology; we discuss health measures."

But Carole Chervin, a senior staff attorney at Planned Parenthood, calls the Teen-Aid materials inaccurate and biased. On abortion, for example, she says the course "presents as fact that an abortion is the taking of an innocent human life." Moreover, Chervin adds, many students taking the course feel indoctrinated: "They say it was just like Sunday school."

Planned Parenthood's suit was filed in April 1992; a trial date has not yet been set.

Action in the Courts

Religious advocates also have turned to the courts in recent years, and the Supreme Court's most recent decisions have helped their cause.

The court's ruling on the Equal Access Act in 1990 was an important victory for religious advocates. Under the law, a school may bar religious clubs if it limits use of school facilities to student groups that are "curriculum-related." But the court defined that term so narrowly that few schools can qualify for the loophole.

"They refused to defer to the discretion of school boards in defining what's curriculum-related," says Laycock of the University of Texas. "They recognized that if they did that, compliance with the act would have become essentially voluntary."

Lower federal courts have generally backed religious groups' efforts to use the act. In East Brunswick, N.J., recently, the school district refused a student's request to form a Bible club. In ordering officials to recognize the club, the federal appeals court in Philadelphia said the school had "striven mightily" to avoid triggering the act. But the judges said that recognition of a student service club showed that the school recognized groups that were not "curriculum-related." [30]

The court's graduation-prayer ruling in 1992 seemed on the surface to be a clear defeat for religious advocates, but it contained the seeds of what could be a shift in legal doctrine. In his opinion for the court, Justice Anthony M. Kennedy avoided using the secular-purpose and secular-effect tests set out in the 1971 *Lemon* case for upholding laws affecting religion. Instead, he found the graduation prayer unconstitutional solely because it produced "coercion" on people who did not share the speaker's religious beliefs.

On that basis, Notre Dame's Douglas Kmiec calls the ruling "a moral victory" for religious accommodationists. "I assume coercion will continue to be the focus of the court in the prayer cases," Kmiec says. "Something which is spontaneous and led by students who are coming to this decision of their own free will, the court will find that to be more tolerable."

Last year, the court gave religious advocates two more victories in school cases. In one ruling, the court unanimously said schools must allow outside religious organizations to use school buildings after hours on the same basis extended to non-religious groups. And in a second deci-

Continued on p. 162

At Issue:

Should student-led prayers be permitted at public high school graduations?

yes

JAY ALAN SEKULOW

Chief counsel, American Center for Law and Justice

Not only should student-led and student-initiated prayer be permitted at public high school graduations, it is a legally protected right.

In 1969, the Supreme Court ruled that student expression against the Vietnam War could not be quashed in public schools. The court ruled that neither "students or teachers shed their constitutional rights to freedom of speech or expression at the schoolhouse gate."

It is now 1994, and once again there are those who seek to limit student speech. They claim that student-led prayers at graduation violate the Establishment Clause. That argument doesn't hold any water.

The First Amendment prohibits government from establishing religion. It leaves untouched private expression. In *Westside Community Schools v. Mergens* (1990), the Supreme Court said: "There is a crucial difference between government speech endorsing religion, which the Establishment Clause prohibits, and private speech, which the Free Speech and Free Exercise Clauses protect."

A student's right to free speech, including religious free speech, does not end when he or she stands up at the graduation podium to accept a diploma.

Our organization sent nearly 15,000 bulletins to public school administrators nationwide last year, urging them to permit students to exercise free speech rights. The bulletins helped educate school officials and students by providing an accurate analysis of the law.

Last year, the Supreme Court decided not to hear *Jones v. Clear Creek Independent School District*, a case in which a federal appeals court permitted a student-led prayer in a Houston-area school. If the case posed a constitutional crisis, you can bet the court would have heard it.

All of this sends a powerful message: Student-initiated and student-led prayer at graduation is protected free speech.

Don't be confused over the need for a separation of church and state. No one is suggesting that one religion be given preference over another. No one is suggesting that a school endorse any kind of religious belief. But religious speakers, even at school, must have equal access to the marketplace of ideas in America.

In 1969, when the Vietnam War controversy was raging, the Supreme Court ruled that students' expression against the war could not be squashed in public schools.

America survived those protests, some of which posed very real threats to life and property. Should not student prayers, which pose no threat to the Establishment Clause, also be permitted?

The answer has to be yes.

no

STEVEN R. SHAPIRO

Legal director, American Civil Liberties Union

Last June, the Supreme Court decided not to review a Texas decision that allowed a student to deliver a non-sectarian and non-proselytizing invocation at high school graduation if that were the choice of a majority of the graduating seniors.

In the days and months following the Supreme Court's action, the radical right claimed that the court's action was an endorsement of student-initiated prayer and a vindication of the decision by the United States Court of Appeals for the Fifth Circuit in *Jones v. Clear Creek Independent School District*. In fact, the Supreme Court's action neither indicated approval, nor did it transform the 5th Circuit's decision into a national precedent.

The Supreme Court agrees to review only a small percentage of the cases that are presented to it every year. As was true in the *Jones* case, the court rarely explains its decision to deny review. The court has consistently emphasized that a decision to deny review is not a decision on the merits.

Contrary to what some are claiming, therefore, the decision to deny review in *Jones* simply means that the law remains as it was when the Supreme Court last considered the issue of graduation prayer in *Lee v. Weisman* in 1992. And in *Weisman*, the court unambiguously held that even non-sectarian and non-proselytizing prayers at public school graduation ceremonies violate the Constitution's separation of church and state.

The fact that a majority of students may want the school district to permit graduation prayer, even though it is prohibited by the Establishment Clause, is as irrelevant in this context as it would be if a majority of students asked the school district to violate the First Amendment by engaging in censorship or to violate the Fourth Amendment by engaging in an unreasonable search of a student's belongings.

The American Civil Liberties Union strongly believes that *Jones* was wrongly decided and is flatly inconsistent with the Supreme Court's ruling in *Weisman*.

Since *Jones v. Clear Creek*, the ACLU has been engaged in several lawsuits over student-initiated prayers. In the most recent decision, federal Judge Albert V. Bryan in Virginia summed up the issue quite well when he wrote that "the notion that a person's constitutional rights may be subject to a majority vote is itself anathema."

"The graduating classes in Loudoun County certainly could not have voted to exclude from the ceremonies persons of a certain race," Judge Bryan said. "To be constructively excluded from graduation ceremonies because of one's religion or lack of religion is not a great deal different."

Are American Colleges Biased Against Religion . . .

Last year, after teaching introductory biology at San Francisco State University for 15 years, Professor Dean Kenyon was removed from the course in a controversy that tested the place of religious belief in American higher education. [1]

Kenyon, a tenured professor, spent part of the course discussing alternatives to the Darwinian theory of evolution. While he says he is not a biblical fundamentalist, Kenyon believes that an "intelligent design" played a part in the emergence of life — a theory that mainstream biologists reject as akin to the biblical story of creation.

In fall 1992, five students — out of a class of more than 100 — complained to the biology department chairman, John Hafernik, that Kenyon was including "unscientific views" in the course. Hafernik responded by telling Kenyon not to teach "biblical creationism" and then removed him from the course the next semester.

In June, the university's academic freedom committee concluded that the move violated Kenyon's rights as a teacher. In early December, the university's Academic Senate agreed. One week later, Hafernik told Kenyon that he could resume teaching the course this summer.

While Kenyon said he merely wanted to present all sides of a scientific dispute, the controversy can be seen as a prime example of what many professors of religion and theology regard as a pervasive hostility toward religion in American colleges and universities today. Last fall, one of the country's leading religious historians, George Marsden of Notre Dame University, charged that higher education has been biased against religion for more than a century — and that the prejudice is stronger today than ever.

"Traditional Christian perspectives, whether Protestant or Catholic, are discriminated against institutionally in American academia," Marsden said in an address to the American Academy of Religion. Without citing specific examples, he said he knew of cases in which applications for jobs or graduate admissions were "dismissed out of hand because applicants revealed Christian motivations for their work." [2]

Marsden's remarks were generally endorsed by a panel of professors the next day. "It's difficult for religious perspectives to be heard in universities outside specific religion courses or to be appreciated as legitimate," one of the panelists, Ellen Charry, a professor of theology at Southern Methodist University in Dallas, said later. At the meeting, Charry quoted a letter from her college undergraduate daughter who complained of what she termed an "anti-faith doctrine taught in the classroom" on her campus.

Marsden's critique brought to the surface views that have been gaining currency among religious experts in the past several years. But some experts on academic-freedom issues dispute the accusation.

"If anything, there is increasing receptivity in higher education to at least the study of religion," says Robert O'Neil, who teaches church-state issues at the University of Virginia Law School and heads the academic freedom committee of the American Association of University Professors (AAUP).

Matthew Finkin, a law professor at the University of Illinois in Urbana-Champaign and O'Neil's predecessor in the AAUP post, agrees there is little evidence of hostility toward religion in higher education. "I know of no respectable source to justify [Marsden's accusation],"

sion, the court ruled, 5-4, that school districts may pay for the cost of a sign-language interpreter for a disabled student attending a parochial school. The dissenting justices warned that the ruling opened the door to other forms of direct aid for parochial-school students. [31]

This year, the Supreme Court has another opportunity to relax the legal restrictions on church-state issues. The justices will hear arguments next month in a case challenging the creation of a special school district to serve a Hasidic Jewish village in a suburban area 40 miles northwest of New York City. (*See story, p. 159.*)

Legal experts and interest groups are divided, however, on the likely outcome of the case. Some separationists believe the court's conservative tilt on church-state issues may have reached its limit. "We are not likely to see major shifts by the court in this area," says Mincberg of People for the American Way, noting that Justice Ruth Bader Ginsburg appears to have a stricter stance on church-state issues than her predecessor, Byron R. White.

But others believe the case could open the door to more government aid for religious education. Kmiec says, for example, that the court could reaffirm the *Lemon* case but still expand on its 1993 ruling to permit other types of financial assistance for church-affiliated schools. ■

OUTLOOK

Disputes to Continue

Political, legal and social conditions suggest that the current wave of disputes over the role of religion in public schools is likely to continue.

Politically, the religious right has been encouraged by successes in local school board races. Because of their strongly committed followers and well-organized leadership, religious right groups have an advantage in school board races, which typically

. . . Or Are They Receptive to the Study of Religion?

he says.

Few experts on higher education would deny, however, that colleges and universities have become largely secularized since the mid-1800s. Most early colleges and universities were founded by churches. About 90 percent of college presidents before the Civil War were clergymen. Yale, the country's third-oldest college, founded in 1701, chose its first lay president nearly two centuries later — in 1899.[3]

Today, few of the older schools founded by Protestant denominations have any distinctive religious identity. Catholic universities have also undergone a partial secularizing process. In the late 1960s, the National Conference of Catholic Bishops called for Catholic colleges and universities to be part of mainstream higher education.

In recent years, however, the Catholic hierarchy has begun to re-emphasize the need for a distinctive Catholic approach to higher education. And fundamentalist Protestants have established at least one brand-new institution — Liberty University in Lynchburg, Va.

Finkin links the accusations of prejudice against religion to what he calls an intensified "combativeness" by some denominations. "Many organized religions have moved toward greater doctrinal purity and conformity," he says.

The complaints received by the AAUP's academic freedom committee tend to support Finkin's view. Jordan Kurland, the association's associate general secretary, says the committee receives "a steady stream" of complaints from professors at church-sponsored schools who say their rights have been violated because they were "deemed to be less than true to their particular faith."

By contrast, Kurland says the committee receives only about a half-dozen complaints a year from professors at secular institutions who say they have been mistreated because of their religious beliefs. "Often there's no evidence to support the allegation," he says.

Marsden counters that the number of formal complaints does not give a true indication of the extent of the problem. "What happens is that people feel under pressure to hide their religious views in most academic settings," he says. "People simply conform to whatever the prevailing expectations might be."

Marsden ended his speech by recommending that church-related colleges and universities should be encouraged to maintain their religious perspectives while other institutions "should be challenged to apply the principle of diversity toward religious perspectives in the curriculum." He also called for academics to rethink their attitudes toward the role of religious perspectives in scholarship.

"It's worth raising the question whether . . . hiding your religious commitments makes sense any more in the contemporary academic setting," Marsden says. "It seems to me you'd be doing a service in identifying your religious commitments and what relevance it might have to the work you're doing."

---

[1] See *Science*, Dec. 24, 1993, p. 1975; and Stephen C. Meyer, "A Scopes Trial for the '90s," *The Wall Street Journal*, Dec. 6, 1993, p. A1.

[2] George M. Marsden, "What Has Athens to Do With Jerusalem? Religious Commitment in the Academy," American Academy of Religion, Nov. 21, 1993. See *The New York Times*, Nov. 26, 1993, p. A21.

[3] Sydney E. Ahlstrom, *A Religious History of the American People* (1972), p. 641, n. 3; Bradley J. Longfield, "For God, for Country, and for Yale," in George M. Marsden and Bradley J. Longfield (eds.), *The Secularization of the Academy* (1992), p. 146.

draw little voter attention.

Legally, religious conservatives have been skillful in using the courts to gain greater leeway for religious activities in the schools. Barriers to school-sponsored religious activities appear likely to remain intact. Eventually, the Supreme Court may even decide to prohibit student prayers at graduation ceremonies. But students seeking to form religious clubs or engage in other religious activities outside class appear to be winning in court more often than not.

Social conditions also indicate that religious disputes will continue to swirl around public schools. With increasing public concern about crime, drugs and sex, many parents — actively religious or not — want schools to teach the "traditional values." And religious conservatives have a special stake in the public schools, according to Furman University political scientist James Guth.

Guth says fundamentalists are "younger, marry younger, and have more children." They have also come to realize that starting their own schools is too expensive. "So there was a natural strategic decision," he concludes, "to go back into the public school arena and try to 'take back the public schools.' "

Rival interest groups have only started to counter the religious right's forays into school board races. People for the American Way published a monograph last May describing how the religious right had been opposed in school board races in San Diego County. "The mainstream, once mobilized, is able to fight back successfully," the group says, but until then it "can be easily overwhelmed."[32]

Religious conservatives are also turning to legislative forums. At least one state — Tennessee — passed legislation last year to permit student-initiated prayer at graduations, sporting events and non-compulsory student assemblies. Even though the state's attorney general termed the law unconstitutional, similar measures have been considered in other states, including Mississippi, Oklahoma and Virginia. [33] And in Congress, the Senate on Feb. 3 easily approved an amendment to a federal education bill that would deny federal funds to any school district that prevented students from voluntarily engaging in "constitutionally protected" prayer.

For religious minorities and nonbelievers, the trend revives concerns that their children will feel isolated or alienated in public schools — or even suffer abuse or harassment if they speak out against religious observances. In the ACLU video, an Indiana family recounts receiving hate mail for several years after going to court to stop the Gideon Society from distributing Bibles in the public schools. And an Oklahoma family told how its home was firebombed after it sued to stop the local schools from sponsoring prayer sessions.

Civil liberties groups see the effort to keep religion and schools apart as very much in line with American traditions. "I don't think it's possible to find a more traditional value than the value that is reflected in the separation of church and state," says ACLU Executive Director Ira Glasser.

But religious conservatives remain convinced that they are the true protectors of traditional values and that religious influence in the schools is not harmful but absolutely necessary to youngsters' moral upbringing. "Christian teachers and Christian parents, in public schools, must . . . give each other support," says Simonds of Citizens for Excellence in Education, "working together to make the schools a spiritually safe environment for the children." [34]

Although feelings run strong on both sides of this debate, some experts advocate moderation. "We've got to find some common ground on this thing, and common ground is hard to find between extremists," laments Jimmy Allen, a minister and former president of the Southern Baptist Convention.

From his perspective, Charles Haynes of the First Liberty Institute believes the common ground can be found in the true meaning of the First Amendment.

"Religious indoctrination belongs in religious institutions and in the family," Haynes says. But schools should include a variety of religious and philosophical viewpoints in their curriculum. "The First Amendment not merely allows it, but requires it," he says. "For how can we say that a curriculum is fair if it does not include religion at all?" ■

Notes

[1] For a report on possible action by the court, see "Supreme Court Preview," *The CQ Researcher*, Sept. 17, 1993, pp. 817-840.

[2] See *The New York Times*, Nov. 19, 1993, p. A24; *The Washington Post*, Dec. 20, 1993, p. A1.

[3] "The Religious Right and School Boards, 1992 and 1993," People for the American Way, November 1993.

[4] Robert L. Simonds, *A Guide to the Public Schools: For Christian Parents and Teachers, and Especially for Pastors* (1993), p. 5.

[5] Stephen L. Carter, *The Culture of Disbelief: How American Law and Politics Trivialize Religious Devotion* (1993), p. 184.

[6] David Barton, *America: To Pray or Not to Pray?* (1993).

[7] American Civil Liberties Union, "America's Constitutional Heritage: Religion and Our Public Schools," November 1993.

[8] See *The Washington Post*, Dec. 11, 1993, p. B1.

[9] John Dart and Jimmy Allen, "Bridging the Gap: Religion and the News Media," Freedom Forum First Amendment Center at Vanderbilt University, November 1993, p. 3.

[10] Examples drawn from *The Christian Science Monitor*, Sept. 23, 1991. For other background, see *The Wall Street Journal*, May 1, 1991, p. B1; *Newsweek*, June 10, 1991, pp. 56-57; *Christianity Today*, September 1991, p. 47.

[11] *Time*, Nov. 1, 1993, p. 35; *Education Week*, Dec. 15, 1993, p. 25.

[12] For background, see "School Censorship," *The CQ Researcher*, Feb. 19, 1993, pp. 157-181.

[13] Stephen Bates, *Battleground: One Mother's Crusade, the Religious Right, and the Struggle for Control of Our Classrooms* (1993), p. 40.

[14] *Donahoe v. Richards*, cited in John H. Laubach, *School Prayers: Congress, the Courts and the Public* (1969), p. 28. See also Robert Michaelsen, *Piety in the Public Schools: Trends and Issues in the Relationship Between Religion and the Public School in America*, 1970

[15] Bates, *op. cit.*, p. 208. Bates' listing of references does not specify the source of this figure. See p. 355.

[16] Michaelsen, *op. cit.*, pp. 140-149.

[17] Richard B. Direnfeld, *Religion in American Public Schools* (1962), pp. 50-56, cited in Laubach, *op. cit.*, pp. 32-33.

[18] Paul Blanshard, *Religion and the Schools: The Great Controversy* (1963), chaps. 2 and 3. The Supreme Court's rulings in the New York case and the 1963 Bible reading cases are printed as an appendix.

[19] *Engel v. Vitale* (1962).

[20] Quoted in Laubach, *op. cit.*, p. 1.

[21] *Abington School District v. Schempp* (1963). Justice Potter Stewart, the lone dissenter, said he would permit classroom devotionals as long as teachers and students were not forced to participate.

[22] Cited in *Phi Delta Kappan*, September 1966, p. 30.

[23] Bates, *ibid.*, p. 50.

[24] See Bates, *ibid.*, pp. 51-55; Carter, *op. cit.*, pp. 264-268.

[25] Paul C. Vitz, *Censorship: Evidence of Bias in Our Children's Textbooks* (1986); O.L. Davis Jr., Gerald Ponder, Lynn M. Burlbaw, Maria Garza-Lubeck and Alfred Moss, *Looking at History: A Review of Major U.S. History Textbooks* (1986).

[26] *Christianity Today*, Aug. 12, 1988, p. 50.

[27] Sonia L. Nazario, "Crusader Vows to Put God Back Into Schools Using Local Elections," *The Wall Street Journal*, July 15, 1992, p. A1. See also David Hill, "Christian Soldier," *Teachers Magazine*, November/December 1992, p. 18.

[28] People for the American Way, "The Religious Right and School Boards, 1992 and 1993," November 1993.

[29] See *ibid.*; and *Time*, Nov. 1, 1993, pp. 34-35.

[30] *Pope v. East Brunswick Board of Education*, reported in *School Law News*, Vol. 22, No. 1., Jan. 22, 1994.

[31] *Lamb's Chapel v. Center Moriches Union Free School District* (1993); *Zobrest v. Catalina Foothills School District* (1993).

[32] People for the American Way, "A Community Battles the Religious Right," May 1993, p. 63.

[33] See *The Wall Street Journal*, Aug. 18, 1993, p. B5; *The Washington Post*, Feb. 5, 1994, p. B3.

[34] Simonds, *op. cit.*, p. 7.

Bibliography

Selected Sources Used

Books

Bates, Stephen, *Battleground: One Mother's Crusade, the Religious Right, and the Struggle for Control of Our Classrooms*, Poseidon Press, 1993.

Bates, a senior fellow at the Annenberg Washington Program of Northwestern University, relates the unsuccessful effort by a fundamentalist Tennessee family to exempt their daughter from school readings they found objectionable. The book also contains a historical overview of the relationship between schools and religion and useful source notes for each chapter.

Blanshard, Paul, *Religion and the Schools: The Great Controversy*, Beacon Press, 1963.

Lawyer-author Blanshard provides a good account of the background of the Supreme Court's 1962 and 1963 school-prayer decisions along with a historical overview of issues involving religion and schools. The court's decisions in the 1962 and 1963 cases are printed as an appendix. For another early book that takes the school-prayer controversy through the 1960s, see John H. Laubach, *School Prayers: Congress, the Courts, and the Public*, Public Affairs Press, 1969.

Carter, Stephen, *The Culture of Disbelief: How American Law and Politics Trivialize Religious Devotion*, Basic Books, 1993.

In this provocative work, Yale law Professor Carter argues that American law and politics in recent years have treated religious believers with disdain. Carter agrees with the Supreme Court's school-prayer rulings, but faults some other court rulings and school board policies aimed at keeping religion out of public schools.

Marsden, George, *Fundamentalism and American Culture*, Oxford University Press, 1980.

Marsden, a religious historian at Notre Dame University, sympathetically traces the history and beliefs of American fundamentalism from the early 20th century through the 1970s.

Marsden, George M. and Bradley J. Longfield, eds., *The Secularization of the Academy*, Oxford University Press, 1992.

Marsden and Longfield, a professor of religion at Duke University, edited this collection of 11 essays on the secularization of colleges and universities in the United States, Canada and Great Britain. Marsden's new book, *The Soul of the University*, is due to be published in April.

Michaelsen, Robert, *Piety in the Public School: Trends and Issues in the Relationship Between Religion and the Public School in the United States*, Macmillan, 1970.

Michaelsen, chairman emeritus of the department of religious studies at the University of California-Santa Barbara, recounts the changes in the relationship between religion and the public school from the Colonial era through the Supreme Court's school-prayer rulings of the 1960s.

Nelkin, Dorothy, *The Creation Controversy: Science or Scripture in the Schools*, Beacon Press, 1982.

Nelkin, a professor of science policy at New York University, provides a fairly balanced account of the creation controversy from the early attacks on Darwin's theory of evolution through the enactment of "equal time" laws for public school curriculums in the early 1980s.

Reports and Studies

People for the American Way, *The Religious Right and School Boards, 1992 and 1993*, November 1993.

The separationist civil liberties group published a 33-page report last fall describing what it called "a grassroots revolution that threatens to undermine an already challenged American public education system."

Simonds, Robert L., "A Guide to the Public Schools: For Christian Parents and Teachers, and Especially for Pastors," *Citizens for Excellence in Education*, 1993.

In this 112-page guide, Simonds appeals to Christian teachers and parents to work "together to make the schools a spiritually safe environment for the children."

Articles

Gibbs, Nancy, "America's Holy War," *Time*, Dec. 9, 1991, pp. 60-68.

Time provided a thorough overview of the legal and political battles over religion in public life on the eve of the U.S. Supreme Court arguments in *Lee v. Weisman*, the high school graduation prayer case from Rhode Island.

McCarthy, Martha A., and Larry W. Barber, "Much Ado Over Graduation Prayer," *Phi Delta Kappan*, October 1993, pp. 120-125.

McCarthy, a professor of education at Indiana University, and Barber, director of the Phi Delta Kappa Center for Education, Development and Research, explain that most school districts found ways to include prayer in high school graduation activities despite the Supreme Court's 1992 decision barring prayers by officially invited guest speakers.

The Next Step

Additional information from UMI's Newspaper & Periodical Abstracts database

Court Decisions

Berger, Joseph, "Public school leadership fight tearing a Hasidic sect," *The New York Times*, Jan. 3, 1994, p. A15.

The U.S. Supreme Court is expected to examine in March 1994 whether the New York Legislature's creation of a school district in 1989 for the benefit of handicapped children of the Satmar Hasidic sect in Kiryas Joel, N.Y., is constitutional. Dissidents within the sect criticize the religious community's management of the public school, however, and say that no matter what the Supreme Court says about the district's constitutionality, the religious community is too insular and hierarchical to run the system.

Boston, Rob, "Muddled message," *Church & State*, July 1993, pp. 9-11.

The Supreme Court recently declined to review a 5th Circuit Court of Appeals decision allowing "non-sectarian", student-led prayers at public school graduation ceremonies. Exaggerating the decision's significance, right-wing religionists immediately began to announce that prayer was now back in schools.

Gaffney, Edward McGlynn Jr., "Prayer at commencement," *Christian Century*, June 2, 1993, pp. 590-591.

The Supreme Court's decision in *Lee v. Weisman*, which bans the invitation of clergy to lead in prayer at graduation ceremonies, is discussed. The decision does not prevent prayer offered by private individuals under "free-speech" provisions.

Grady, William; Holt, Douglas, "Schools can't forbid leaflets, court rules," *Chicago Tribune*, Nov. 24, 1993, p. 2C4.

School officials cannot flatly prohibit students from distributing religious literature on school grounds, a three-judge panel of the Chicago-based U.S. Court of Appeals for the 7th Circuit ruled. But the panel also said school districts could adopt policies that effectively limit the distribution of such material.

Walsh, Mark, "Religious groups can use schools, high court rules," *Education Week*, June 16, 1993, p. 1.

The U.S. Supreme Court recently ruled that school districts must give religious groups the same access to school facilities after hours afforded to other community organizations. The court ruled unanimously that a New York State school district violated the free-speech rights of a Christian group when it refused permission to show a film series on Christian family values.

Current Situation

Doerr, Edd, "Church and state: Church-state separation still endangered," *Humanist*, July 1993, pp. 40-41.

President Clinton's election removed the threat to church-state separation from the White House, but the battle-grounds have shifted to the state and local levels. Three major areas are discussed: religion in public schools, abortion rights and tax aid to sectarian schools.

Farley, Christopher John, "Without a prayer," *Time*, Dec. 20, 1993, p. 41.

Bishop Knox, the former principal of Wingfield High School in Jackson Miss., was suspended because he allowed a 21-word, non-sectarian blessing to be read over the school's public address system. Many supporters of school prayer say the issue is values and not constitutionality.

Pae, Peter, "Christmas debate rages in Loudoun: Principal's alleged censorship blasted," *The Washington Post*, Dec. 17, 1993, p. D3.

Loudoun County, Va., supervisors have passed a resolution condemning high school principal Edward Starzenski for urging the school's newspaper staff to avoid using the word "Christmas" in its December 1993 issue.

Walsh, Mark, "Schools get free legal advice on religious-freedom issues," *Education Week*, Dec. 15, 1993, p. 9.

School superintendents are getting conflicting legal advice about such issues as the student-led prayers and Christmas observances in schools. The advice is coming in the form of legal bulletins from interest groups on opposite sides of religious-freedom issues.

Yardley, Jim, "Prayer improves the school climate," *Atlanta Constitution*, Dec. 14, 1993, p. A3.

Bishop Knox, the Mississippi high school principal who was suspended for allowing students to say a brief prayer over school intercoms in the morning, is interviewed about his decision to allow school prayer. Knox is appealing.

Graduation Prayers

"Federal appellate court allows graduation prayer in Virginia, despite AU/ACLU legal challenge," *Church & State*, July 1993, pp. 16-17.

On June 23, 1993, the U.S. Court of Appeals for the 4th Circuit removed a temporary restraining order blocking school-sanctioned prayer at public school graduation ceremonies in Loudoun County, Va. The ACLU and Americans United for the Separation of Church and State had sued to enjoin the worship ceremony.

Reske, Henry J., "Student-led prayers a tough subject," *ABA Journal*, November 1993, pp. 20-22.
Local school districts are caught between the Establishment and Free Exercise clauses of the First Amendment following the Supreme Court's June 7, 1993, refusal to review a decision by the 5th U.S. Circuit Court of Appeals permitting student-led prayers at graduation.

Walsh, Mark, "Court's action offers no peace in the war on graduation prayer," *Education Week*, June 16, 1993, p. 1.
The U.S. Supreme Court's decision to let stand an appeals-court ruling that approved student-initiated and student-led invocations and benedictions at public school graduation ceremonies is discussed. Supporters of strict church-state separation have vowed to continue their fight against prayers at public school graduation ceremonies.

Key Players

"Don't force us to pray," *American Legion Magazine*, July 1993, pp. 18-20.
Barry W. Lynn, executive director of Americans United for Separation of Church and State, is interviewed. He discusses the importance of the separation of church and state and reasons why prayer should not be allowed in public schools.

Lynn, Barry W., "New York, New York: If Pat can make it there . . ." *Church & State*, June 1993, p. 23.
New York City's recent school board elections, in which Pat Robertson's Christian Coalition exaggerated parts of a multicultural curriculum to persuade voters to elect conservative candidates, is recapped.

Moore, W. John, " 'Tis the season to be lobbied," *National Journal*, Dec. 4, 1993, p. 2896.
The ACLU and a conservative group in Texas are distributing competing videotapes on the issue of religion and the First Amendment. The videos' contents and the growing battle between the ACLU and Christian conservatives over the proper role of religion in school are discussed.

Smolowe, Jill, "Crusade for the classroom," *Time*, Nov. 1, 1993, pp. 34-35.
Since the religious right began targeting local school board races in 1990, school agendas have become increasingly politicized and controversial. Educators are beginning to complain that school board conservatives have a detrimental effect on the job of teaching.

Woodward, Kenneth L.; McGuire, Stryker, "Allies in a cultural war," *Newsweek*, Nov. 8, 1993, pp. 45-46.
A political alliance between two groups that have historically viewed each other as religious enemies — evangelicals and Roman Catholics — appears to be possible. Though they differ theologically, the two groups are quite concerned about the cultural antagonisms between secular liberals and serious believers of all faiths. Fundamentalist Christians on the Vista, Calif., school board are discussed.

Miscellaneous

"Catholic schools have little effect on religious attitudes," *Gallup Poll Monthly*, August 1993, pp. 26-46.
A poll found that attending Catholic school has little effect on a child's religious beliefs. Those attending Catholic schools showed no greater commitment to the church than other students.

Boston, Rob, "Prayer and Bible reading in schools: Dubious history," *Church & State*, June 1993, p. 11.
While the religious right's claims that Bible reading in public schools is a longstanding American tradition, a closer look at the practice's history shows that Bible reading was often sporadic and erupted in violence between Catholics and Protestants on several occasions.

Religion and Curriculum

Bushman, James, "Teaching about religions in world history courses," *Social Studies*, November 1993, pp. 249-255.
Using caution, objectivity and decorum, teachers can help students to comprehend their own religious heritage, Bushman writes. Students should also be taught about other religious traditions in order to understand other cultures, he adds. Incorporating these concepts into a high school world history class is discussed.

Lynn, Barry W., "Vista's school board: Model for disaster," *Church & State*, September 1993, p. 23.
Since the election of three activists running on a fundamentalist Christian slate to the Vista Unified School Board in California, there have been repeated efforts to introduce creationism into the district's schools, and arguments have erupted over other church-state issues. The actions of the board have brought strong responses from concerned faculty and parents.

Stafford, Jan, "How to teach about religions in the elementary social studies classroom," *Social Studies*, November 1993, pp. 245-248.
Most educators would like to teach about religions but hesitate because they are not exactly sure what they can legally teach, nor do they feel qualified, Stafford writes. The question of how teachers can teach about religions within their existing curricula is examined.

Back Issues

Great Research on Current Issues Starts Right Here...Recent topics covered by The CQ Researcher are listed below. Before May 1991, reports were published under the name of Editorial Research Reports.

AUGUST 1992
The Homeless
Work, Family and Stress
NATO's Changing Role
Marine Mammals vs. Fish

SEPTEMBER 1992
Domestic Partners
Violence in Schools
Public Broadcasting
Women in the Military

OCTOBER 1992
Depression
U.S. Auto Industry
Youth Apprenticeships
Hispanic Americans

NOVEMBER 1992
Physical Fitness
Privatization
Paying for College
U.S. Policy in Asia

DECEMBER 1992
Crackdown on Smoking
The New CIA
Eating Disorders
Women and AIDS

JANUARY 1993
Hate Crimes
Child Sexual Abuse
Nuclear Fusion
U.S. Trade Policy

FEBRUARY 1993
Community Policing
Europe's New Right
School Censorship
Violence Against Women

MARCH 1993
Gay Rights
Aid to Russia
War on Drugs
TV Violence

APRIL 1993
Head Start
High-Speed Rail
Children's Legal Rights
Muslims in America

MAY 1993
Cults in America
Preventing Teen Pregnancy
Software Piracy
National Parks

JUNE 1993
Food Safety
Prostitution
Childhood Immunizations
National Service

JULY 1993
Electric Cars
Population Growth
Downward Mobility
Intelligence Testing

AUGUST 1993
Mental Illness
Bilingual Education
Foreign Policy Burden
School Funding

SEPTEMBER 1993
Suburban Crime
Public Housing
Supreme Court Preview
Immigration Reform

OCTOBER 1993
Airline Safety
Disaster Response
Science in the Courtroom
The Glass Ceiling

NOVEMBER 1993
Paying for Retirement
Charitable Giving
Privacy in the Workplace
Adoption

DECEMBER 1993
U.S. Vietnam-Relations
Learning Disabilities
Child Care
Space Program's Future

JANUARY 1994
Racial Tensions in Schools
South Africa's Future
Worker Retraining
Regulating Pesticides

FEBRUARY 1994
Prison Overcrowding
Water Quality

Back issues are available for $4.00 (subscribers) or $7.00 (non-subscribers). Quantity discounts apply to orders over ten. To order, call Congressional Quarterly Customer Service at (202) 887-8621.

Binders are available for $15.00. To order call 1-800-638-1710. Please refer to stock number 648.

Future Topics

- ***Juvenile Justice***
- ***Underground Economy***
- ***Education Standards***

PUBLISHED BY CONGRESSIONAL QUARTERLY INC.

Juvenile Justice

Should violent youths get tougher punishments?

The number of juveniles under age 18 arrested for murder, rape, robbery and aggravated assault increased by 50 percent between 1987 and 1991, according to the FBI. Now lawmakers at the state and federal levels are scrambling to respond to Americans who see crime as their prime worry, and juvenile punishment as too short and too soft. Topping the agenda for many state legislatures are proposals to give adult sentences to violent youths, outlaw gun possession by minors and build more boot camps for juveniles. But while the public and many experts call for harsher penalties for violent youths, others say the current trend toward punitive treatment unfairly targets youths who are amenable to rehabilitation — and doesn't put a dent in the problem.

INSIDE THIS ISSUE

CQ February 25, 1994 • Volume 4, No. 8 • 169-192

Formerly Editorial Research Reports

COVER: BERNARD MILLER, 17, ENTERS THE HOWARD COUNTY COURTHOUSE IN ELLICOTT CITY, MD. HE WAS SENTENCED TO LIFE IN PRISON WITH THE POSSIBILITY OF PAROLE FOR DRAGGING PAMELA BASU TO DEATH WHILE STEALING HER CAR. (AP/WIDE WORLD PHOTOS)

THE CQ Researcher

February 25, 1994
Volume 4, No. 8

EDITOR
Sandra Stencel

MANAGING EDITOR
Thomas J. Colin

ASSOCIATE EDITOR
Richard L. Worsnop

STAFF WRITERS
Charles S. Clark
Mary H. Cooper
Kenneth Jost

PRODUCTION EDITOR
Sarah E. Merritt

EDITORIAL ASSISTANT
Michael M. Taylor

GRAPHICS
P. Eloise Fuller

PUBLISHED BY
Congressional Quarterly Inc.

CHAIRMAN
Andrew Barnes

VICE CHAIRMAN
Andrew P. Corty

EDITOR AND PUBLISHER
Neil Skene

EXECUTIVE EDITOR
Robert W. Merry

ASSOCIATE PUBLISHER
John J. Coyle

MARKETING AND SALES DIRECTOR
Edward S. Hauck

The CQ Researcher (ISSN 1056-2036). Formerly Editorial Research Reports. Published weekly (48 times per year, not printed the first Friday of any month with five Fridays) by Congressional Quarterly Inc., 1414 22nd St., N.W., Washington, D.C. 20037. Rates are furnished upon request. Second-class postage paid at Washington, D.C. POSTMASTER: Send address changes to The CQ Researcher, 1414 22nd St., N.W., Washington, D.C. 20037.

Juvenile Justice

By Sarah Glazer

The Issues

Marc insisted he was going straight. After serving two years for homicide, the maximum for juveniles in Washington, D.C., the 18-year-old said he was giving up the fast life.

He was already a veteran criminal. He had received his first gun at age 13 from a neighborhood drug dealer, who had recruited him to enforce drug deals. Even before his arrest for homicide three years later, he said that he had shot at dozens of people. But now that was behind him, he proudly told Claire Johnson, then-director of the District of Columbia Criminal Justice Research Center.

So Johnson was understandably startled when the young man mentioned casually over a meal later that he had enlisted another boy to shoot someone with whom he was having an argument. "For him, that was staying out of trouble," Johnson recalls incredulously. "That's how he saw it. He wasn't actually [shooting people] anymore: He was paying someone else" to do it. [1]

Youths like Marc — their value systems shaky at best — make the public scared about young offenders and dubious of the nation's juvenile justice system. Rather than rehabilitating juveniles who have gone astray, the system often seems to release hardened criminals only to enable them to claim new victims.

Across the country, lawmakers are scrambling to respond to Americans who see crime as their prime worry, and juvenile punishment as too short and too soft. Topping the agenda for many state legislatures are proposals to give youths adult sentences for violent crimes, outlaw gun possession by minors and build more boot camps for young offenders. Indeed, 73 percent of the respondents to a recent *USA Today*/CNN/Gallup survey said juveniles who commit violent crimes should be punished the same as adults. [2]

AP/Wide World Photos

In a special session on youth crime called last September by Gov. Roy Romer, D-Colo., the Colorado General Assembly lowered from 16 to 14 the age at which juveniles charged with violent crimes are tried as adults. Public concern in the state was galvanized by a string of shootings over the spring and summer in which several children were critically injured in crossfire from gang fights. In one instance, a 10-month-old at the Denver zoo was grazed in the forehead by a bullet apparently fired two blocks away. [3]

"These are kids committing very adult crimes," says Colorado Republican state Rep. Jeanne Adkins. One of the first juveniles held under the new law was charged with shooting a 4-year-old boy who has been paralyzed for life. "This [legislation] says there is a consequence for your actions, regardless of your age," Adkins says.*

* Under Colorado law, the maximum sentence for someone tried as a juvenile is generally two years. Murders by Colorado youths under 18 actually declined from 26 in 1991 to 22 in 1992, according to the Colorado Division of Criminal Justice.

Adkins, chair of the Colorado House Judiciary Committee, introduced a ban on juvenile gun possession after two youths, one white and one Hispanic, from a "relatively upscale" neighborhood in her suburban Denver district were convicted in the shooting death of a highway patrol officer. "In Colorado, this is an across-the-board problem from a racial and economic standpoint," she says. "We have continued to see in our 15-to-19-year-old male population an escalation from the kinds of petty offenses they were committing a decade ago to serious violent offenses that today's [outdated] children's code cannot address in any way."

Nationally, the statistics bear out the public perception that youth crime is becoming more violent. The number of youths arrested for murder and weapons violations has approximately doubled over the last decade, according to the Justice Department. (*See graph, p. 174.*)

Violent crime among youth started its most dramatic rise in 1988. Between 1987 and 1991, according to the FBI, there was a 50 percent increase in the number of juveniles under age 18 arrested for violent crimes — murder, rape, robbery and aggravated assault. [4]

Experts blame the rise on two main sources: guns and the drug trade. The unprecedented surge in violent youth crime coincided with a dramatic increase — over 700 percent — in the juvenile heroin and cocaine arrest rate during the 1980s, according to the Justice Department. The past decade also saw a 79 percent increase in the number of juveniles who committed murder with guns. Nearly three out of four murders by 10-to-17-year-olds are committed with guns. [5]

Actually, explains Delbert S. Elliott, a professor of sociology at the University of Colorado, there's been only a slight increase in the proportion of

Arrest Rate Rising for Violent Crime

From 1980 to 1990, the juvenile arrest rate for violent crime rose by 27 percent. Since 1965, the arrest rate has tripled. Murder, forcible rape, robbery and aggravated assault are classified as violent crimes.

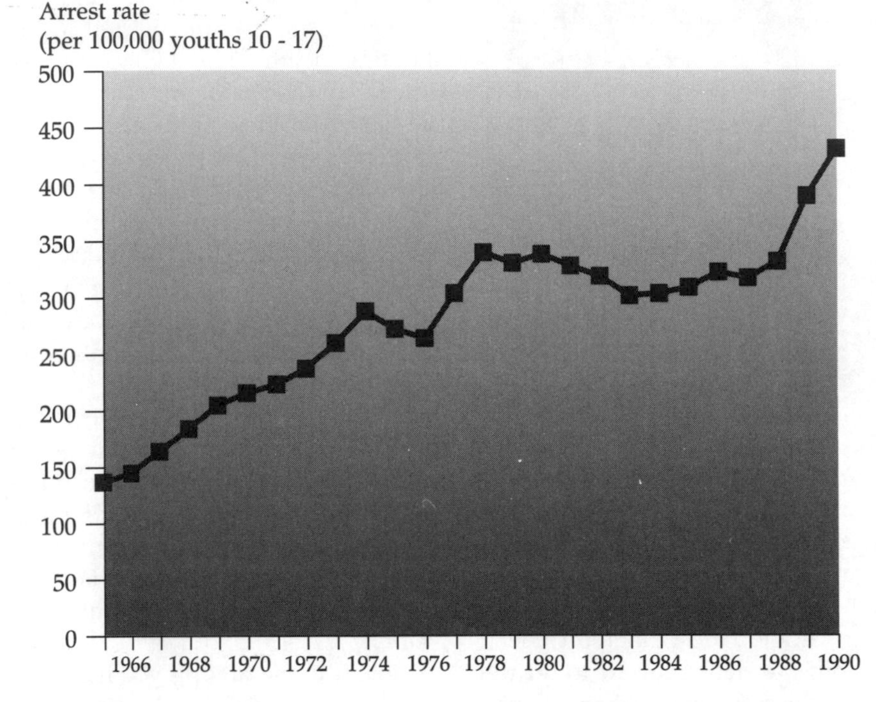

Source: FBI Uniform Crime Reports, Crime in the United States, 1991. *Statistics are based on data reported to the FBI by local law enforcement agencies.*

this age group involved in violent crime, according to surveys that ask high school seniors whether they have been involved in assaults or robberies. But while the percentage of teenagers committing violent crimes has not skyrocketed, the deadliness of their actions has reached a new level. In other words, an assault by a young thug that might have produced bruises 10 years ago is more likely to result in a gunshot wound or death — and consequently an arrest — today.

Some corrections officials admit this change caught them by surprise. "I think we were asleep on this," says Russ Van Vleet, who headed Utah's youth corrections system from 1978 to 1987. "The violent crime clearly has increased, and the accessibility of handguns has changed the way kids are reacting. I'm not sure any of the [juvenile corrections] systems were geared up for it."

Van Vleet oversaw a radical reform of Utah's juvenile corrections system in 1983, closing down the state's training school and moving most juveniles into small unlocked community-based programs. But that was before the Mormon-dominated state knew what it was like to have daily drive-by shootings among gang members in its largest city.

Now, he says, "What we have is a system in crisis." Utah is struggling with a shortage of the kinds of locked facilities needed for the growing number of violent juveniles. Last month, youths rioted at Salt Lake County's temporary detention facility, overcrowded with kids awaiting openings in Utah's secure facilities.

The Utah Legislature is considering legislation that would extend sentences for violent juveniles and transfer them to adult prisons when they become adults, rather than releasing them when they turn 18. In many states, such release policies have severely limited sentences for even the most serious violent juvenile offenders. "In most people's minds," says Van Vleet, "you can't take someone's life and walk away free in two to three years."

In fact, a growing number of experts say the juvenile system was not designed to deal with today's violent youths and must be harsher and more punitive. "I think it's fair to say that we do not know how to rehabilitate the serious repeat offenders," says James Q. Wilson, an authority on criminal justice at the University of California-Los Angeles. "So the goal has to be: to protect society and make it clear to [young offenders] that society is not going to tolerate this behavior by ignoring it or winking at it."

But criminologists point out that violent repeat offenders constitute a tiny fraction of the young people who end up in the juvenile system. [6] Even Wilson concedes that "most juveniles who are arrested once don't go on to become repeat offenders."

Thus, the current trend toward punitive treatment may unfairly target some youths who are amenable to reform, critics warn. "We are talking about a very small population" of chronic violent youths, says G. Larry Mays, a professor of criminal justice at New Mexico State University and a former police officer. "Whatever we do with these kids will not substantially impact the crime rate in this country. . . . Our tendency in this country is to kill the fly with an elephant gun sometimes. . . . It's clearly a movement towards retribution: 'Let's just punish them, whether we rehabilitate them or not.' "

Like adult murderers, most juveniles kill relatives or acquaintances. Sensational crimes against strangers are the exception, Mays notes. The most common violent juvenile crime, aggravated assault, usually victimizes other juveniles.

"A lot of the [youths] we see accused of violent crimes in New Mexico do things like kill their parents," says Mays. "I would call that kid dangerous, but I would not call that someone who is committed to a lifetime of crime."

Since their beginnings in the 19th century, the juvenile courts have been charged with acting, in effect, as surrogate parents. Juvenile court judges are expected to order treatment, not just punishment, depending on each youngster's individual potential for rehabilitation.

To youth advocates, laws that automatically slap adult sentences on juveniles undermine that philosophical foundation. James R. Bell, an attorney with the Youth Law Center, a youth advocacy firm in San Francisco, says an amendment to the omnibus crime bill passed by the Senate last year that would try youths charged with federal violent crimes as adults would be "the first step toward abolishing the juvenile justice system." [7]

"The juvenile system is based on the idea that there's hope," says Bell. "When you turn that around, you're saying, 'There's no hope. We want retribution.'"

As state and federal lawmakers respond to growing violence among youths, here are some of the questions being debated:

Should juveniles be tried as adults for violent crimes?

In the newspaper pictures, Cedric Green looks small. At age 13, he is the youngest of the four teenagers charged in the murder of British tourist Gary Colley at a highway rest stop near Monticello, Fla., last September. Green has pleaded not guilty. [8] But his brazen admission on TV that he enjoyed stealing cars, coupled with reports that he had more than 50 offenses on his record, jolted the public into the realization that children are committing frightening crimes at younger and younger ages. [9]

AP/Wide World Photo

Four youths age 13-16 leave the Jefferson County Courthouse in Monticello, Fla., Oct. 22, 1993, after bond was denied. They are charged with murder in the September slaying of a British tourist at a highway rest stop, and attempted murder in the wounding of his companion.

The Florida murder was one of the incidents that spurred a black, liberal, Democratic U.S. senator last November to push for an amendment to the Omnibus Anti-Crime Bill seeking adult trials for juveniles as young as 13 charged in violent crimes. * The successful move by Carol Moseley-Braun, D-Ill., signaled that the traditional division between punishment-minded conservatives and rehabilitation-minded liberals may be eroding.

Moseley-Braun reportedly had acted after learning that a teenager who shot an acquaintance had bragged in school that the courts couldn't do anything to him because he was a juvenile. Under her amendment, teenagers convicted of crimes like murder, armed robbery and drive-by shootings would build up a criminal record.

"[A]t the present time, we are grappling with a situation in which these juveniles leave no record, leave no fingerprints. They can shoot someone with impunity at 14 years of age . . . and do not have to account for their actions," Moseley-Braun declared on the Senate floor. Pointing to a dramatic increase in crime among the nation's youngest teenagers, she noted that 13-year-olds committed more than 14,000 aggravated assaults in 1992 alone. [10]

Opponents of the legislation maintain that, at least in theory, judges have the right to review an offender's juvenile record and weigh the sentence accordingly. State statutes keeping juvenile court and police records confidential are generally intended to protect the identity of a juvenile from the media and the public. Exceptions for court or law enforcement officials are common in state laws. [11]

"I think it's a phony issue," says Barry C. Feld, a professor of law at the University of Minnesota Law School. "Most states already count juvenile priors [prior offenses] when sentencing young adult offenders."

In practice, however, the existence of separate record-keeping systems for the juvenile and adult courts

---

* Among other things, the bipartisan, $22.3 billion Senate bill would boost spending for prison construction, expand the death penalty to dozens of new federal crimes, treat certain young criminals as adults and provide money for 100,000 additional police officers. The House has not considered its omnibus measure, but it has passed a number of smaller anti-crime bills.

Upsurge in Murder Arrest Rates

From 1980 to 1990, the murder arrest rate for black youths rose 145 percent. During the same period, the arrest rate among white juveniles rose 48 percent and declined 45 percent for youths of other races.

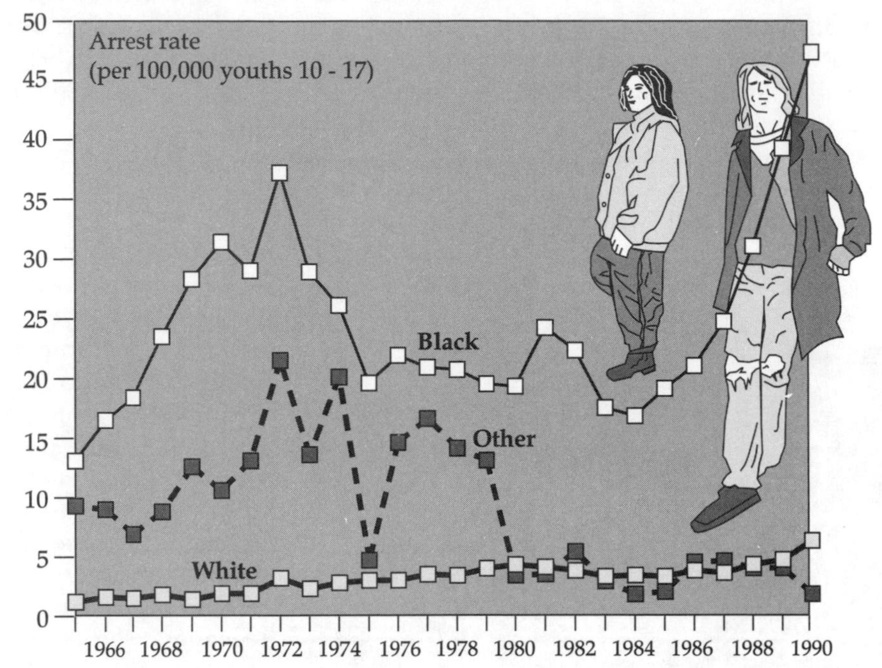

Source: FBI Uniform Crime Reports, Crime in the United States, 1991. *Statistics are based on data reported to the FBI by local law enforcement agencies.*

means that criminal judges may not be aware of an offender's prior juvenile record in the first place — or have easy access to it, experts around the country say.

In a national survey of prosecutors, half the respondents said they normally received little or no juvenile record information on even the most serious young adult offenders in their jurisdiction. When juvenile records were available, they were often incomplete or arrived too late to affect decisions on whether to file criminal charges, for example. Most prosecutors rely on local police files, the survey found, keeping many in the dark about a juvenile's police record in other cities or states. [12]

"One of the problems we have as police officers investigating juvenile crimes between jurisdictions is there is no [centralized] exchange of information about juvenile offenders," says Donald Cahill, a police officer in Prince William County, Va., and national legislative chairman for the Fraternal Order of Police. Cahill cannot run the fingerprints and photo of a juvenile suspect through a central national computer, as he can for adults, because the information is not compiled nationally. "We need to overcome this so we can exchange information with schools and with different police forces to combat juvenile crime," Cahill says.

Even within the same city, prosecutors and police officers may be unaware that a juvenile has committed a serious crime previously. In New York state, because of a traditional reluctance to stigmatize young offenders, the juvenile justice system does not permit the fingerprinting and photographing of juveniles, except for the most serious crimes, such as murder and rape.

Take the case of 15-year-old Shaul Linyear, who was arrested last year for the murder and attempted robbery of a delivery man on a Brooklyn street. Prosecutors initially were unaware that Linyear had been charged as a juvenile two months earlier for putting a loaded gun to the head of another man. That incident had been handled by New York's Family Court. But Linyear was charged as an adult in the murder, shifting the prosecution to the Brooklyn district attorney's office. Prosecutors there found out about Linyear's prior arrest after a Family Court prosecutor read of the murder in the newspaper and tipped them off. Linyear pleaded guilty and was sentenced to seven years to life in prison. [13]

Youth Law Center attorney James Bell, an outspoken opponent of the Moseley-Braun amendment, calls it "symbolic legislation" that would have virtually no impact on youth crime. Most crimes are prosecuted by states, he points out. Only 5 percent of the nation's crimes are federal, and juveniles are involved in a fraction of those.

Opposition to the amendment also comes from Sen. Joseph R. Biden Jr., D-Del., chairman of the Senate Judiciary Committee, which makes it unlikely the amendment will become law this year. Biden expressed the views of many progressive-minded juvenile justice experts when he reminded the Senate that "the philosophy that drives the juvenile justice system is that kids in trouble need something more than to be thrown in prison." [14]

But the direction taken by state legislatures over the last decade suggests that at least some Americans are growing impatient with rehabilitation. "Juvenile codes have been systematically revised to emphasize punishment," notes Ira M. Schwartz, dean of the University of Pennsylvania School of Social Work. And the citizens favoring such policies come from some surprising quarters.

A national survey conducted by Schwartz and two colleagues at the

Continued on p. 176

Do Juvenile Rehabilitation Programs Work?

In 1990, criminal justice researchers from both ends of the political spectrum got excited about a rehabilitation program that seemed remarkably successful.

Only six of the first 40 youths who finished the one-year residential program in rural Ohio had gone back to jail. In contrast, about half the youths held in traditional juvenile institutions get in trouble again.

Known as the Paint Creek Youth Center, the program featured a bucolic setting, small size and a dedicated and well-trained counseling staff. Unlike Ohio's training schools, it had no locked doors or fences. Nor did it have the broken-down furniture or surly staff that epitomized the Ohio training school where many of these juvenile offenders would normally have gone, one researcher recalls. [1]

But when Rand Corp. researchers analyzed the success rate for an expanded group of 75 Paint Creek graduates, the dramatic improvement in recidivism dwindled markedly. Compared with the 60 percent of Ohio training school graduates who were arrested again, about half of the Paint Creek graduates had been rearrested — a 10 percent decrease. [2]

"That surprised a lot of people, because this looked like a wonderful program," says Peter W. Greenwood, one of the researchers. "It's still a wonderful program. It just doesn't seem to make much difference."

Eugene E. Hebert/National Institute of Justice

A teenager in the Children at Risk (CAR) program in Austin, Texas, works in the public library. The program, sponsored by the Department of Justice and private foundations, aims at diverting inner-city youngsters from involvement in drugs, gangs and crime.

Greenwood's experience is typical. When the sample size is small — as it is in most such programs — statisticians say the results are not "statistically significant." That means the estimate is not stable: The next time the program is tested on another group of kids, the results could be a lot higher or a lot lower.

"The frustration for the researchers is that you can't easily do a study with thousands of kids trying out these more innovative programs," notes Mark W. Lipsey, director of the Center for Crime and Justice Policy Studies at Vanderbilt University, because it's too expensive.

Using a technique known as meta-analysis, Lipsey has analyzed over 400 studies, most of small rehabilitation programs, to elicit a statistically reliable pattern of successful approaches. On average, he finds that rehabilitation programs reduce recidivism only by about 10 percent. [3]

The most successful programs, Lipsey has found, are those that train juveniles directly to change specific skills or behavior. These include efforts to improve their scholastic performance, increase their job skills or change their anti-social responses to other people, by practicing more civilized approaches in role-playing, for example.

Lipsey finds weaker results for traditional "talk therapy," aimed at helping adolescents gain insight into the psychological roots of their criminal behavior.

At the bottom of the totem pole are scare-oriented programs. "They create more delinquency than they cure," Lipsey says. One variation that was popular in corrections systems in the 1970s was known as "Scared Straight." First-time offenders were given a one-day tour of a prison and then brought into a back room for a session of yelling and intimidation about the realities of prison life. The young-sters who experienced these day-in-the-life of a prisoner sessions were more likely to get arrested than comparison groups. Lipsey says he "suspects" that boot camps, which borrow similar scare tactics, will be equally unsuccessful.

"The idea of taking an acting-out adolescent and giving him a role-model for verbal abuse and macho behavior seems to me to be a poor strategy," Lipsey says.

Greenwood admits he was just as surprised as everyone else that Paint Creek had such little impact. But he has a few theories that might explain it. "These kids came from pretty disastrous homes, and apparently it overwhelms whatever good takes place," he says. Or, he adds, it may be that the traditional training schools, while no model of success, aren't as inferior to progressive approaches as reform-minded critics have contended.

"When I walk into the Training Institute of Central Ohio, I think it's a hellhole," he says. "But if you come from a housing project where nobody ever talks to you . . . maybe enough contact goes on in there — and those [staff] people who look bored and have been there 30 years still do a good-enough job."

[1] *Juvenile Rehabilitation*, videotape in "Crime File" series produced by National Institute of Justice, 1990.

[2] Peter W. Greenwood and Susan Turner, *Evaluation of the Paint Creek Youth Center*, 1993, p. 271.

[3] Mark W. Lipsey, "Juvenile Delinquent Treatment: A Meta-Analytic Inquiry into the Variability of Effects," in Thomas D. Cook, et al., eds., *Meta-Analysis for Explanation* (1992), pp. 83-126.

Continued from p. 174

University of Michigan found that African American parents have much tougher attitudes toward juvenile criminals than other racial or ethnic groups — including white parents. The majority favors adult trials and terms in adult prisons for juveniles who commit violent crimes. African American parents tend to be keenly aware that the violence is increasingly black-on-black and that juvenile violence most likely claims the lives of young, black males. "There's a lot of violence in these communities," Schwartz concludes, "and they're scared for their kids." [15]

Teens as young as 13 or 14 already can be tried as adults in a growing number of states. Twenty states automatically exclude youths from juvenile court if they commit certain crimes — usually violent ones — and if they meet the age threshold set out in state law, according to the National Center for Juvenile Justice, a private group in Pittsburgh, Pa., that collects statistics for the federal government. This year, several more states, including Minnesota and Utah, are expected to consider mandating adult trials for particularly violent juveniles.

More common are state laws that give judges or prosecutors discretion to try juveniles as adults. All but two states — Nebraska and New York — have such laws.

In most states, youths sentenced as adults go to adult prisons. And in most places that means sending them to schools for crime or handing them over to adult sexual predators, say reform-minded experts. In Florida, the nation's leader in sending juveniles to adult prisons, juveniles were even more likely to return to a life of crime after their release from adult prisons than the adults, according to Schwartz, a former head of the Justice Department's Office of Juvenile Justice and Delinquency. [16]

"The criminalizing effects of adult prison" may explain why youths commit more crime, says Schwartz. Sending juveniles to adult prisons "gives the community a false sense of public protection. It may be good politics, but it's not really very good public policy." In addition, he says, adult prisons usually deprive youths of the rehabilitation programs they likely would receive in a juvenile setting.

To avoid such drawbacks but at the same time give violent youths longer sentences, Colorado last year approved a unique hybrid: adult-length sentences in institutions specially designed for violent juveniles, including rehabilitation features. Not yet in operation, the Youth Offender System would apply to 14-to-18-year-olds charged with such crimes as assault with a deadly weapon, aggravated robbery and manslaughter.

Legislators say their prime concern is sending Colorado youths the message that violent crimes will result in longer, serious sentences. "If you're in the institutions talking to the kids, they see the juvenile system as a breeze, a joke," says Rep. Adkins. "You have adult gang members encouraging younger kids to commit crimes for them because, 'Hey, you'll get off easy' — and they do."

That in essence is what researcher Claire Johnson found after interviewing 19 young men serving sentences for homicide at Wash-ington's maximum-security facility for juveniles. "Some of them even said point blank that killing the person was worth it," she says, "because they were only going to be in here a couple of years." (*See story, p. 180.*)

If the public is looking for harsher punishment for juveniles, it is likely to be disappointed by treating them as adults, some researchers warn. "I think it's a myth that juveniles get treated leniently," says Peter W. Greenwood, a researcher at the Rand Corp., a Santa Monica, Calif., think tank. In 1988, for example, the California Youth Authority reported that juveniles typically spent 20 months in confinement for drug-related offenses, as opposed to 12 months for adult drug offenders. [17]

"[I]t does not appear that juveniles receive harsher penalties, on the average, when transferred to criminal courts for a broad range of offenses," conclude criminologists Dean J. Champion and G. Larry Mays in a wide-ranging review of the research on treatment of juveniles in adult courts. [18]

The penalties generally aren't stiffer because the majority of juveniles

Reuters

Sheriff Ken Fortune answers press questions about the shooting of British tourists Gary Colley and Margaret Jagger at a Florida highway rest stop.

transferred to adult courts are typically chronic, petty, property offenders sent there by judges often fed up with seeing them returning time and time again. They are not the violent criminals the public has in mind, explains Champion, who chairs the Criminal Justice Department at Minot State University in Minot, N.D. And roughly half the cases that get transferred to adult courts each year get dismissed for lack of evidence, says Champion. For those juveniles who remain, their age often becomes a mitigating factor, especially when eyed next to the hardened adult criminals surrounding them.

From the judge's perspective, says Champion, "The kids go from being big-time juvenile actors to small-time criminal actors. The likelihood is they will get probation."

Only about 10 to 12 percent of juveniles transferred to criminal court do any time in California, notes Champion, "which is an incredibly low rate of incarceration for juveniles who are supposed to be treated more harshly."

Champion supports tougher sentences for violent juveniles, but he says state laws should specify that only violent offenders should be transferred to adult courts. And he suggests that juvenile courts be given sentencing guidelines to counter judges' tendency toward leniency.

For the most violent of offenders who get transferred to adult court, however, the scenario is probably less rosy, says Mays. In New Mexico, for example, a juvenile who commits murder faces a maximum sentence of two years. If convicted as an adult, he faces life imprisonment or the death penalty.

Should the emphasis in the juvenile justice system continue to be on rehabilitation?

Taken as a whole, programs aimed at rehabilitating juvenile delinquents can't boast enormous success. On average, such programs reduce the number of youngsters who will be arrested again by about 10 percent, according to Professor Mark W. Lipsey, director of Vanderbilt University's Center for Crime and Justice Policy Studies.[19] Approximately 40 percent of those who go through a special-treatment program will get in trouble again, compared with about half of those in the juvenile justice system who don't get into such programs.

UCLA's Wilson believes the goal of rehabilitation is unrealistic, especially for juveniles who repeatedly commit violent crimes. "When you get to the small number of hard-core violent offenders, your underlying assumption must be . . . we do not know how to make these kids better at this stage in their life," Wilson says. "Maybe we know how to make them better when they're 3 years old and in preschool, but we don't know how when they're 15 or 17."

Other researchers counter that rehabilitation has never been tested specifically for chronic, violent delinquents. Most programs that have been studied include a broad range of delinquents, from petty thieves to the much smaller number of violent offenders. "There are violent offender programs out there," says Elliott, "but they're too new and haven't been evaluated. Under that circumstance, it is as unfair to say they don't work as to say they do."

Wilson is convinced, however, that juvenile courts need to crack down on delinquents, starting with the first offense and graduating to heavier penalties with each subsequent arrest. "There ought to be some penalty, something more serious than being told you are on probation, which in many states is relatively meaningless. You have to make a phone call once a week or once a month or [the probation officer] calls you and says, 'How are you doing?' "

But University of California criminologist Franklin E. Zimring sees probation as a useful screening device for teens who are only sowing their wild oats and not embarking on criminal careers. About 60 percent of all adolescents who get caught by police don't get into trouble with the law again, he notes.

"My guess is the average juvenile burglary has four actors in it, and I don't think they're all confirmed criminals," he says. "We don't have any way we can give a blood or urine test to find out who [the chronic criminals] are. What we can do is screen: Put them on probation. Some will be back real fast, and then you toughen policy on them."

Many juvenile justice experts agree that automatically sentencing juveniles to adult terms will unfairly penalize

Crimes by Young Children

In 1991, children 12 and under committed 35 murders and nearly 5,000 aggravated assaults; six of the murders and more than 1,000 of the assaults were by children under 10.

Type of Offense	Under age 10	Ages 10-12
Murder	6	29
Forcible rape	81	441
Robbery	238	1,924
Motor vehicle theft	253	2,423
Aggravated assault	1,068	3,859
Arson	1,068	1,571
Burglary	3,395	11,959
Larceny/theft	11,663	50,505

Source: FBI Uniform Crime Reports, Crime in the United States 1991, *Aug. 30, 1992.*

kids who would have grown out of their criminal tendencies or responded to counseling. "You get a couple of kids who kill and are remorseless and people say, 'Let's treat them all like adults,'" says Edward J. Loughran, director of the Robert F. Kennedy Memorial Juvenile Justice Project in Boston. "What happens is you widen the net and scoop in a lot of other offenders who could be handled adequately in the juvenile system."

Retorts Wilson: "'Don't Widen the Net' is the currently polite way of saying 'We don't like prison, we don't like jail, we don't like punishment. We are softies.' "

Juvenile courts need to act more like real-life parents raising children, Wilson insists. "Parents don't try to rehabilitate children. What they do is try to set rules and enforce them fairly, but consistently and relentlessly. So eventually your kid learns to pick up his room or start doing his homework . . . or whatever you're trying to enforce."

Ironically, some youth advocates on the left echo Wilson's criticism of rehabilitation philosophy. Approaching the issue from a concern for children's legal rights, they criticize the juvenile courts' broad sentencing discretion as too subjective and amorphous.

Minnesota law Professor Feld has long advocated abolishing the juvenile justice system, saying juveniles would be better served by the basic constitutional guarantees of adult jury trials. In many states, he estimates, less than half of all juveniles who enter the system receive a lawyer. [20]

"In the course of trying to do rehabilitation," says Feld, the juvenile justice system "perpetuates a variety of injustices by trying to individualize and make decisions in the best interests of the child. We treat black kids different than white kids. We institutionalize every form of racial, gender and class bias in the name of doing good. If the juvenile court is little more than a scaled-down criminal court for young people . . . that discrimination is indefensible."

The subjective nature of juvenile courts came under attack in the 1988 case of a 16-year-old Minnesota boy charged with the ax murders of his mother, father, brother and sister. The juvenile court judge refused to have the boy tried as an adult because he met the state's legal standard for staying in the juvenile system: The state could not prove he was not amenable to treatment. The boy, a B-plus high school student, had never been in trouble before and came from a white, middle-class family. The decision was eventually overturned by an appellate court, but not before it created a public uproar.

This year, a juvenile justice task force in Minnesota has recommended that the state move away from its therapeutic orientation in crimes of violence. The public's safety, rather than the best interests of the youth, would be the deciding factor in shifting a juvenile to adult court, says Feld, who helped draft the task force proposal. [21]

Rehabilitation advocates often point to the decline in youth crime that followed Massachusetts' decision in the early 1970s to close down its overcrowded, antiquated training schools. Hundreds of delinquent youths were transferred to small unlocked group homes that emphasized treatment. Only a minority, the most violent offenders, were placed in locked bunks.

But, Loughran says, "I don't think a claim really can be made to attribute [the decline in youth crime] to the closing of the institutions." A study of the system commissioned by Loughran noted that the declining number of juvenile arrests in the 1970s in Massachusetts mirrored the trend in many other states. Generally, the report noted, such declines were primarily influenced by demographic forces like the size of the at-risk youth population, unemployment, family instability and drug abuse. [22]

"The systems were changed not because anyone had any grandiose idea that going into community-based programs would change the crime rate," says Russ Van Vleet, who oversaw a similar transformation of the juvenile system in Utah. "No one's ever been able to show any relationship between the crime rate and corrections philosophy. What we did know is that we were going to stop abusing kids in the name of state protection."

The fact that Utah could tear down its crumbling training school and build small facilities for the same cost as building one large new reform school went a long way to making Utah's decision, according to Van Vleet.

Fundamentally, rehabilitation remains a somewhat mysterious concept. Most young people who are arrested in their teens stop committing crime. Either they're frightened by the experience or they simply grow out of it as they settle down, get jobs and start families. Other young arrestees return to a life of crime. Still others seem to respond to intensive programs aimed at putting them on the straight and narrow.

The problem, says Feld, is that "With respect to any given kid, we don't know into which group they would fit or what forms of intervention would be appropriate." ■

BACKGROUND

Rise of Juvenile Courts

In Colonial times, children were treated just as harshly as adults, if not more so. In 1648, the Colony of Massachusetts prescribed capital punishment for any child over 16 who "shall curse, or smite their natural father or mother." [23]

In 1825, the New York Society for the Reformation of Juvenile Delinquents opened the House of Refuge, the

Continued on p. 182

Chronology

1800s *Social reformers promote the idea of the child as a malleable creature who can be steered away from a life of crime.*

1825
The New York Society for the Reformation of Juvenile Delinquents opens the nation's first reformatory for juveniles.

1899
The nation's first juvenile court is established in Illinois, for children under age 16.

1960s *In response to studies showing that juvenile courts fail either to rehabilitate wayward youths or to protect their rights, juvenile courts increasingly reflect the policies and sentences of the adult criminal system.*

1967
The President's Commission on Law Enforcement and Administration of Justice issues report declaring that the juvenile system has failed to rehabilitate youthful offenders, stem delinquency or provide justice to child offenders.

1967
Supreme Court rules in *In re Gault* that a 15-year-old brought before a juvenile court is entitled to due process and to be represented by counsel. Gerald Gault had been sentenced to nearly six years in reform school for allegedly making an obscene telephone call to a female neighbor — a charge for which an adult might have been sentenced to 30 days in jail.

1969
Supreme Court rules in *In re Winship* that proof beyond a reasonable doubt is required to establish delinquency.

1970s *Reformers advocate sending juveniles to high-security institutions only as a last resort and only for the most serious offenders. Other states weaken traditional protections for minors under juvenile court laws.*

1972
Massachusetts shuts down all five of its youth training schools and moves most delinquents to unlocked group homes or other community-based programs.

1974
Congress enacts the Juvenile Justice and Delinquency Prevention Act, encouraging states to follow Massachusetts' example in moving toward deinstitutionalization.

1977
Washington state opens juvenile proceedings to the public and sets specific sentences for juvenile crimes.

1978
New York state mandates that all 13-year-olds charged with murder and all 14-and 15-year-olds accused of felonies be tried in criminal courts.

1980s *Juvenile crime surges as young people enter the illegal drug trade and the use of firearms increases dramatically, especially in inner cities.*

1983
Georgia and Oklahoma open boot camps for young offenders, starting nationwide trend.

1988
Violent crime arrest rate among youths begins climbing rapidly.

1989
Supreme Court permits states to pass death penalty laws for juveniles age 16 and older.

1990s *The public demands tougher penalties for minors as violent crimes by juveniles reach an all-time high.*

1993
The House and Senate pass crime bills expanding federal funding for boot camps, emphasizing that there should be "certainty of punishment" for young offenders. Federal penalties are also approved for the possession of guns by minors, and the Senate passes legislation to subject gang participants to stiff federal sentences.

1994
Crime becomes the public's No. 1 worry, according to opinion polls. In Minnesota, a juvenile justice task force recommends that the state move away from its therapeutic orientation when it comes to violent crimes. Public safety, rather than the best interests of the child, would be the deciding factor in shifting a juvenile to adult court.

Experts Question Effectiveness of Boot Camps . . .

Every time 17-year-old Roy smiles, he flashes his gold tooth embossed with a Jack of Spades — a menacing symbol of the drug-dealing life he once enjoyed. It supported him from age 14 until he was arrested three years later for attempted robbery.[1]

But Roy sounds like a religious convert when he describes his just-completed four-month stint at the Manatee County boot camp in Palmetto, Fla.

"It's changed me completely around," he says, citing the no-nonsense discipline as well as the talk-therapy sessions. Roy found the atmosphere a stark contrast from the state-run juvenile rehabilitation program he had previously attended, which offered "no self-discipline, no respect, no manners."

At boot camp, no profanity is allowed, and rule-breakers must do extra pushups or write essays on what they did wrong. The therapy convinced Roy that he can no longer blame his mistakes on his tragic childhood, although he still chokes up when he describes how his parents abandoned him at age 7.

A high school dropout at 14, Roy is realistic about attaining his dream career in engineering or computers. He also knows any job he could get right now can't match his drug-dealing income.

But he's determined to resist his old influences once he's released. His resolutions echo virtually word for word the reform strategy stressed at Manatee: "I used to think I had to be accepted by my friends. They'll bring you down just to bring you down to their standards." Now, says Roy, "They have to come up to my standards. If they can't do that, I just can't be with them."

Most boot camps sprouting up around the nation take adults arrested for a non-violent first offense. Manatee, one of about eight juvenile camps in the nation, targets violent offenders.

All the camps share the military-style drills, hard physical training and structured days. Youths at Manatee rise at 5 a.m. for several hours of running and other physical exercise, spend the afternoon in the classroom and have lights out at 9 p.m. There's no TV and no radio.

If adult boot camps are any guide, Roy may have trouble sticking to his resolution. The young men who go through adult boot camp are just as likely to be returned to custody for new offenses as prison inmates, says Doris Layton MacKenzie, a University of Maryland researcher who has studied several boot camps for the Department of Justice.[2]

That's despite the fact that boot campers are more upbeat than regular prisoners: They have better relations with the staff, like the program more, are proud to have become drug-free and generally think they've changed for the better.

Jeff Hooper

At Louisiana's Elayne Hunt Correctional Center, program focus is on treatment and education. . .

"There's something going on that may be positive," says MacKenzie, "but it's not carrying through on the outside. They get back with the same crowd, they still can't get jobs and whatever problems they had before are still there. Those who were drug-involved return to their old community, return to their drug-using friends and can't stay away from the problem."

These negative findings, however, have not dampened the popularity of boot camps. At least 30 states and 10 local jurisdictions, as well as the Federal Bureau of Prisons, have boot camp programs for adults, and more are considering or planning them.[3]

In Florida, "everyone wants one," says Neil Kaltenecker, who coordinates juvenile boot camp development for the state Department of Health and Rehabilitative Services. Communities have been so eager to donate funds, land or volunteer services, she says, that last May the governor approved $4.3 million to add two additional juvenile camps to Florida's four.

Since Manatee's camp opened last year, Kaltenecker says only one youth out of the 59 graduates has been rearrested — a remarkable record by most rehabilitation programs' standards. But she cautions that it will take several more years and more graduating classes before the state can say whether the approach is truly successful. Studies indicate that the recidivism rate rises significantly the longer camp graduates have been out on the street.

"Boot camps are so popular because it's perceived that we're finally doing something with these kids — not just putting them in a touchy-feely halfway house," says Kaltenecker. "It looks punitive, like the kids are really having to work for their crimes. And it has a fence around it, so kids don't escape."

Commander Lee Vallier, Manatee's tough-sounding

. . . But Politicians Think They're Terrific

director, designed the Manatee program and was instrumental in designing Florida's first adult camp. Despite his drill sergeant demeanor, he plays down the military aspects. "All the 'left faces' and 'right faces' — that's nothing but a ritual," he says. "The kid can't do anything with that when he leaves. So we added the educational component and therapeutic intervention that would change his criminal beliefs and values."

But prison boot camps lack a key aspect of military boot camps, says Dale Parent, a senior analyst at the Cambridge, Mass., consulting firm Abt Associates who studied boot camps in 1989. After military training, he says, recruits graduate to several years of guaranteed employment, education, housing and opportunity for advancement. Prospects are far dimmer for prison boot camp graduates.

In response to such criticism, some corrections officials have begun promoting boot camps as low-cost alternatives to prison overcrowding, rather than as rehabilitation tools.[4] But Parent says boot camps are actually more likely to increase prison overcrowding. That's because most boot camp inmates are drawn from populations that never would have gone to prison in the first place, Parent says. Typically, non-violent first offenders receive probation, not prison. In addition, about 30 to 40 percent of boot camp recruits drop out. Their penalty for failing to complete boot camp: a ticket to prison.

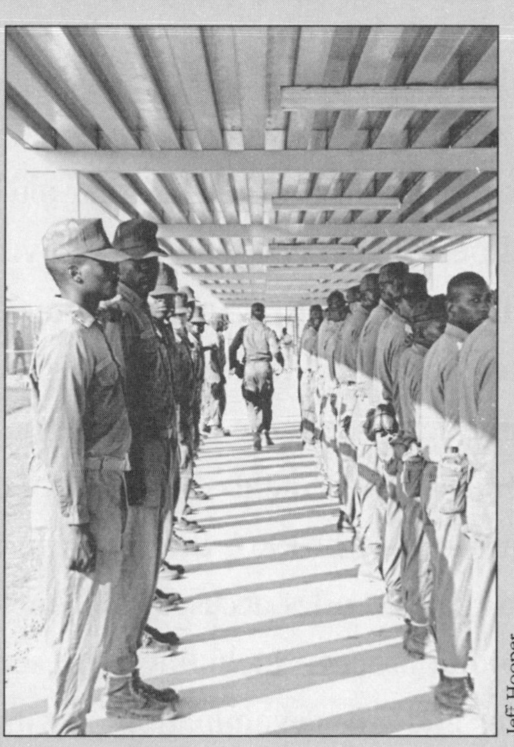
. . .but military discipline and physical training play important roles, too.

Jeff Hooper

"What you end up with is a very efficient feeder system for expanded prison populations," he says. "Now they're in prison only because they failed a very stringent, rigorous program."

MacKenzie says there's still potential to use boot camps to reduce prison populations and costs; it's just not targeted correctly in many states. She notes that South Carolina shifted its boot camp program from its focus on people bound for probation to offenders bound for prison.

"Even if boot camps don't reduce recidivism," she says, "they're getting the inmates out [of prison] earlier."

MacKenzie has estimated that Louisiana saved $7,828 for each boot camp inmate because of the shorter average stay — four months vs. 20 months in prison. That estimate took into account the state's high number of dropouts — 43 percent of entrants.[5]

Effectiveness is another matter. Six months after their stints, boot campers had as high a rate of new arrests or probation violations as prison parolees, MacKenzie reported.[6]

Two years after their release, MacKenzie found that compared with prison inmates, boot campers were more likely to get in trouble for violating their probation — for example missing appointments or using alcohol — but were less likely to commit new crimes.[7]

Despite the modest results, politicians are not likely to temper their enthusiasm for boot camps, to judge from Georgia's response.

After four years, slightly over half of Georgia's boot camp graduates were again in prison. By contrast, less than one-third of comparable offenders on probation and 56 percent of former prison inmates were in prison.[8]

Nonetheless, Democratic Gov. Zell Miller obtained $14.3 million from the legislature in 1992 to expand Georgia's program. "Nobody can tell me from some ivory tower that you take a kid, you kick him in the rear end and it doesn't do any good," Miller told *The New York Times*. "And I don't give a damn what they say, we're gong to continue to do it in Georgia."[9]

---

[1] Roy is not his real name.

[2] MacKenzie's latest study, of adult camps in Florida, Georgia, Illinois, Louisiana, New York, Oklahoma, South Carolina and Texas, is slated for release in March and reportedly will be the most extensive such study to date.

[3] Doris Layton MacKenzie, "Boot Camp Prisons in 1993," *National Institute of Justice Journal*, November 1993, pp. 21-28.

[4] For background, see "Prison Overcrowding," *The CQ Researcher*, Feb. 4, 1994, pp. 97-120.

[5] Doris Layton MacKenzie et al., "An Evaluation of Shock Incarceration in Louisiana," *National Institute of Justice Research in Brief*, June 1993, p. 6.

[6] *Ibid.*, p. 4.

[7] Doris Layton MacKenzie and James W. Shaw, "The Impact of Shock Incarceration on Technical Violations and New Criminal Activities," *Justice Quarterly*, September 1993, pp. 463-486.

[8] *Prison Boot Camps*, General Accounting Office, April 1993, p. 29.

[9] Adam Nossiter, "As Boot Camps for Criminals Multiply, Skepticism Grows," *The New York Times*, Dec. 18, 1993, pp. 1, 9.

Continued from p. 178

nation's first reformatory. Although it aimed to reform delinquents through prayer, work and study, the facility often resorted to whipping and leg irons.[24]

Americans generally continued to view children as little different than adults until the late 19th century, when reformers promoted a new view of children and adolescents as malleable creatures who could be shaped into God-fearing adults. Some argued that imprisonment with adults only increased a child's chance of falling into a life of crime. As industrialization and a massive wave of immigration brought dire poverty to the cities, other reformers blamed social and family conditions for delinquency.

In 1899, the nation's first separate juvenile court was established in Chicago, Ill., for youths under age 16. Before then, children were tried in the same courts and given the same sentences, often in the same facilities as adults. Like today's juvenile courts, the Illinois court became a substitute parent, its goal not to punish youthful offenders so much as to rehabilitate them with supervision and treatment. Judges looked at children's personal histories, not their crimes, to determine sentences. By 1925, juvenile courts existed in all but two states.

In the 1960s, the juvenile courts came under criticism for failing either to protect the rights of juveniles or to rehabilitate them. Responding to sentencing disparities stemming from juvenile judges' wide discretion, the U. S. Supreme Court granted more legal rights to juveniles. Gradually, the procedures of juvenile courts began to look more like those of adult criminal courts.

In a case known as *In re Gault*, 15-year-old Gerald Gault had been sentenced to nearly six years in the Arizona State Industrial School for making an obscene telephone call to a female neighbor. An adult committing the same offense would have been fined $50 and sentenced to 30 days in jail. Ruling on the case in 1967, the Supreme Court declared that juveniles accused of crimes are entitled to due process, including representation by a lawyer and cross-examination of witnesses.[25]

In a case known as *In re Gault*, 15-year-old Gerald Gault had been sentenced to nearly six years in the Arizona State Industrial School for making an obscene telephone call to a female neighbor. An adult committing the same offense would have been fined $50 and sentenced to 30 days in jail. Ruling on the case in 1967, the Supreme Court declared that juveniles accused of crimes are entitled to due process, including representation by a lawyer and cross-examination of witnesses.

In 1970, the Supreme Court ruled (*In re Winship*) that proof beyond a reasonable doubt is required to establish guilt for a juvenile charged with a criminal offense.

Rival Solutions

Starting in the 1970s and continuing into the '80s, two divergent philosophies battled for dominance in state and federal policy. One camp, inspired by Massachusetts' radical move to close its five training schools in 1972, urged a de-emphasis on punishment and the use of high-security institutions only as a last resort and for the most serious offenders.

Many state corrections officers were impressed that juvenile crime did not surge after most of Massachusetts' youthful offenders were moved to unlocked halfway houses or allowed to live at home while they participated in day programs. Like Massachusetts, many states had antiquated, overcrowded reform schools that were viewed as training grounds for crime.

Members of Congress were impressed, too, and in 1974 they passed the Juvenile Justice and Delinquency Prevention Act, which provided funding for other states to follow Massachusetts' lead. Several states, including Utah, Oklahoma, Oregon, Colorado, Pennsylvania and Louisiana, took steps to move away from locking most juveniles in institutions.

At the same time, however, a competing group of conservative thinkers began advancing a "just deserts" philosophy, saying the juvenile courts were too soft on crime. The state of Washington, breaking the tradition of individualized sentencing, passed legislation in 1977 linking specific juvenile sentences to particular crimes. A year later, New York state mandated that all 13-year-olds charged with murder and all 14- and 15-year-olds accused of felonies be tried in criminal courts.

In the late 1980s, violent juvenile crime began climbing dramatically, in-

Guns: Weapons of Choice

Guns were used in more than three-quarters of all homicides in the United States committed by juveniles in 1991.

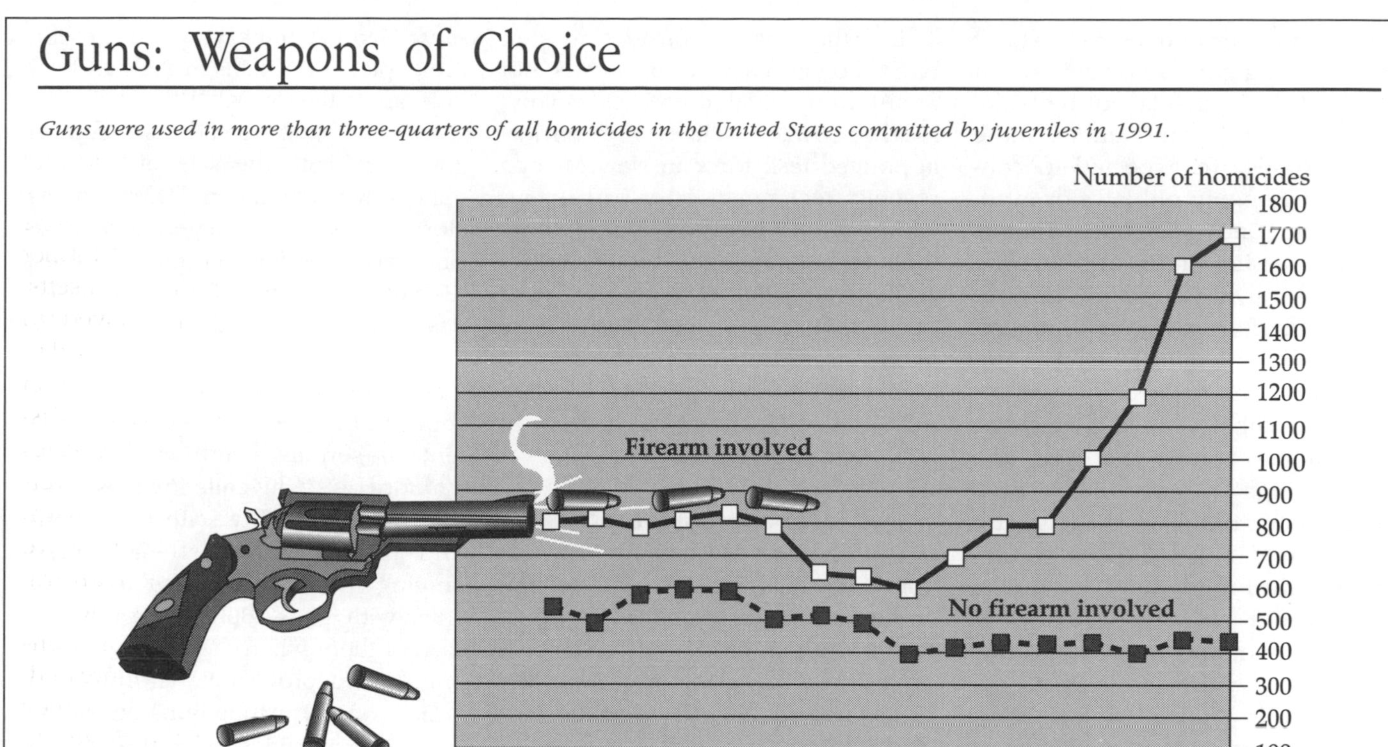

Source: Office of Juvenile Justice and Delinquency Prevention, Fact Sheet, *July 1993*

fluenced, experts said, by the growing availability of guns and the spreading drug trade. Juveniles entering reform-minded systems in Massachusetts and Utah included a growing proportion of youths who had committed violent crimes. Those states, among others, found themselves short of secure facilities, forcing overcrowding and early releases of dangerous youths.

As the public mood became increasingly punitive, Georgia and Oklahoma opened boot camps for first offenders in 1983, starting a nationwide trend. (*See story, p. 180.*)

In 1989, the Supreme Court upheld the death penalty for juveniles in *Stanford v. Kentucky.* Kevin Stanford was 17 when he and an accomplice raped, sodomized and eventually shot to death Baerbel Poore, 20, in Jefferson County, Ky. The 1981 murder took place during a robbery of a gas station where Poore worked as an attendant. Stanford later told police, "I had to shoot her [since] she lived next door to me and she would recognize me. . . . I guess we could have tied her up or something or beat [her up] . . . and [told] her if she tells, we would kill her." The jury found Stanford guilty of first-degree murder, and the judge sentenced him to death. The U.S. Supreme Court upheld the decision. [26]

Last year, crime bills passed by the House and Senate took a harsh line toward youthful offenders. Both houses approved expanded federal funding for boot camps, emphasizing that there should be "certainty of punishment" for the young. In addition, federal penalties were approved for the possession of guns by minors. And the Senate passed legislation to try juveniles as adults for violent federal crimes and to subject gang participants to stiff federal sentences. [27] By 1994, crime had climbed to the top of the nation's worries — even though crime rates were leveling out. [28] ■

CURRENT SITUATION

Targeting Guns

In the summer of 1992, gang members in Phoenix, Ariz., some as young as 13, came to a neighborhood crime-control meeting with guns strapped to their hips. But police were powerless to interfere. [29]

Like most states, Arizona prohibited the carrying of a concealed weapon. But like most states, it did not bar anyone — minor or adult — from displaying a firearm openly. The Arizona Legislature has since prohibited minors under 18 from possessing or carrying a firearm except under adult supervision. [30]

Legislatures around the nation have put controlling gun use by children at the top of their agendas in the battle against growing youth crime. More than 20 states are expected to consider strengthening old laws or introducing new ones prohibiting minors from possessing guns and barring adults from giving or selling guns to minors, according to Susan Whitmore, director of communications for Handgun Control Inc.*

Last November, Florida lawmakers, responding to tourist shootings and other killings by juveniles, voted unanimously to make it illegal for juveniles under 18 to possess firearms. Youths found guilty of carrying a gun would be sentenced to 100 hours of community service and one year's loss of a driver's license. [31]

The bill is similar to legislation passed in Colorado last September. In Colorado, however, the penalties are stiffer. A minor's second conviction for owning or carrying a handgun is a felony, carrying a sentence of up to three years. "It's hard to understate the difficulty of passing such a law in a state where the outdoors and guns are so much a way of life, and where the National Rifle Association (NRA) is so deeply entrenched in our politics," Colorado Gov. Romer wrote after the law's passage. [32]

Initially, the NRA mounted a $30,000 radio advertising campaign against the governor's handgun bill, according to news reports. [33] But eventually the association participated in negotiations and ended up supporting the new law. The statute makes exceptions for youths engaged in licensed hunting, target practice or shooting competition. The NRA supported Florida's gun ban after similar exceptions were included.

*According to Handgun Control, new firearms legislation will be considered by some 18 states, including states as diverse as Alabama and Vermont, while another six states are considering strengthening existing legislation. In all, 19 states now have juvenile gun-possession bans on the books.

In other states considering gun bans, however, NRA support is not assured. In rural areas, especially, local opposition is likely. A governor-appointed task force in New Mexico recently recommended a ban on juvenile gun possession with exceptions for hunting and shooting under adult supervision. "I doubt very seriously it will pass," says Mays of New Mexico State University. "This is such a frontier, open-range kind of state that a lot of kids hunt out here without adult supervision."

Action in Congress

Both houses of Congress last year approved bills making it a federal crime for a juvenile under 18 to possess a handgun or for an adult to give or sell one to a minor. Under the House-passed bill, the penalties include up to one year in prison for possession by a minor or transfer of a gun to a minor and up to 10 years in prison for someone who transfers a gun knowing it is intended to be used in a crime of violence.

The federal approach has been criticized by juvenile justice advocates as a symbolic vote-getting measure that will send more kids to overcrowded state and local facilities. The federal government does not maintain juvenile prisons or juvenile courts, they point out. (*See "At Issue," p. 185.*)

Some youth advocates argue that the federal proposal unfairly targets innocent kids. "The bill doesn't differentiate between an 8-year-old who takes his dad's gun to show to his friend and the kid who uses it for a drive-by shooting," objects Youth Law Center attorney Bell.

Bernard Horn, legislative counsel at Handgun Control, responds that the "No. 1 target for prosecution" under the federal legislation is interstate traffickers in guns. "People go and buy large quantities of guns in some state that has poor guns laws, they drive to New York City and sell them out of their trunk to kids," Horn says. "I don't think you can explain the explosion of guns in the hands of kids any other way." [34]

On the books already is a federal law prohibiting the sale of guns to minors by licensed gun dealers. But as Horn points out, it's largely ineffective since most kids don't buy guns in stores. "Someone can buy from a licensed dealer and turn around and sell it to the kid," he says. "It's perfectly legal."

A recent Justice Department study supports the view that guns are prevalent in serious youth crimes. The majority of 835 juvenile inmates at six mostly high-security state institutions said they committed their crimes, ranging from drug-dealing to homicide, with guns. But most said they carried them when they thought they might need protection. The problem is "less one of getting guns out of the hands of juveniles," the researchers concluded, than of "convincing them that they can survive in their neighborhoods without being armed." [35]

Shroud of Secrecy

Treatment of youthful offenders in juvenile courts remains murky, even to experts, since most proceedings are conducted in secret, and practices vary enormously from state to state.

"Nobody really knows how the juvenile court system works," asserts UCLA's Wilson. The reason, says Wilson, is the lack of reliable national and state data about a system that tries to protect children's transgressions from the public eye. "So you can have almost any opinion you like about the juvenile court system, and in some state you will be right and in another state you will be wrong."

Many experts agree with Wilson's description of juvenile court as "a low-status, underfunded, largely invisible operation," even if they disagree with his pessimistic view of

Continued on p. 186

At Issue:

Should juvenile possession of a handgun be a federal crime?

yes

SEN. HERB KOHL, D-WIS.

FROM *PRESS RELEASE*, SEPT. 13, 1993.

During the past few years, our country has had to cope with the effects of devastating natural disasters. . . . As a result of nature's wrath, lives were lost, communities were devastated. . . . But disasters are more than just destructive events. Each disaster represents an opportunity to define ourselves as individuals and as a nation. In each of these disasters, Americans . . . rose to the occasion to provide help wherever and whenever it was needed. . . . All levels of government marshalled their resources and developed responses to both the short and long-term effects of the devastation.

But those were natural disasters, acts of God, an accident of nature. We are also faced with a terrible man-made disaster: the deadly mix of kids and guns. . . . If anyone tells you that gun control alone will solve the problem, don't believe them. But if cynics tell you that government is not part of the solution, don't believe them either. . . .

We need a range of approaches: increased punishment for serious offenders; additional money for crime- and drug-prevention programs; more cops on the street, walking a beat; less violence on TV; more community-based programs to give kids something to belong to other than a gang; more economic opportunity; better education; the list goes on. And we have to go on, too. Because these are our kids. . . . And our kids are, in a very real sense, our future. . . .

We have tolerated a level of destruction in our streets that we would never have accepted if it had come from the skies. We measured the rise of the flood waters, but we ignore the rising tide of blood that runs through our cities. We watched the skies, but we close our eyes to the reign of terror in our communities. . . .

From our central cities to our rural communities — for kids who grow up in poverty and kids who grow up in middle-class areas — it is all the same. A world of threats and violence and death. This is not the kind of world that our children deserve. It is not the kind of world we ought to give them. But it is the world that they live in.

But we can change that world. Not easily. Not quickly. Not painlessly. Not with a single solution. But we can change it. . . . To that end, I recently introduced the Youth Handgun Safety Act. That bill would make it a federal crime to sell or give a handgun to a minor under age 18, and for a minor to possess a handgun under most circumstances. I also support the Brady bill, because it is the best way to keep guns out of the hands of adults who we know should not have them.

no

ROSE W. WASHINGTON

Commissioner, City of New York, Department of Juvenile Justice
FROM *A LETTER TO MEMBERS OF THE SENATE JUDICIARY COMMITTEE*, DEC. 2, 1993.

The New York City Department of Juvenile Justice opposes legislation that would create new federal crimes with regard to certain offenses committed by juveniles, such as . . . the Youth Handgun Safety Act of 1993, which would make possession of a handgun or ammunition by a juvenile a federal offense. While we agree that it is imperative to address problems such as the proliferation of gun- and gang-related violence among young people, we believe that federalizing such offenses would not be in the best interest of juveniles or the community and would have a detrimental impact on local detention facilities around the country.

Bills that would federalize state offenses do not adequately consider the administrative costs of such action. We anticipate that the federalization of state crimes committed by juveniles would significantly increase juvenile case processing time. Not only do federal courts lack the mechanisms developed by many state and local juvenile justice systems to expedite juvenile cases, but federal criminal calendars would be overwhelmed by the volume of cases involving juveniles charged with federal crimes. . . .

Local detention facilities such as ours would be adversely affected by prolonged federal cases. The increase in juvenile case processing time would result in a greater daily detention population, which could cause crowded and unconstitutional conditions of confinement and jeopardize the safety of staff and residents. In addition, longer periods of detention harm children by delaying their transfer or admittance to environments specifically designed to rehabilitate youth. Moreover, because of the high daily cost of detention per resident, the longer stays in detention for youth charged with committing federal crimes would be extremely expensive. . . .

Federalizing offenses committed by juveniles would also render children uniformly culpable for those offenses despite the discrepancies in their age and the circumstances behind each case. For example, under the Youth Handgun Safety Act, a 10-year-old child caught holding his parents' gun without permission could be treated the same as a 17-year-old who obtains a gun for the purpose of committing an armed robbery. State and local juvenile justice systems have implemented mechanisms to determine the appropriate course of action for each child depending on the child's level of responsibility; such mechanisms do not exist at the federal level.

We [support] the federal government's commitment to reduce crime . . . including efforts to prohibit the sale, delivery or transfer of handguns to juveniles. However . . . we believe that federalizing state offenses would be counterproductive to the goal of reducing juvenile violence.

A Researcher Talks to Youths Convicted of Homicide. . .

In 1988, faced with the highest murder rate in the nation, Washington, D.C., issued an in-depth report on the problem: *Homicide in the District of Columbia.* Three years later, the city issued a follow-up report as part of an ongoing effort to understand the factors that contribute to the proliferation of homicide.

The 1991 *Homicide Report* included a chapter based on interviews with youths incarcerated for homicide in the District. The interviews were conducted by Claire M. Johnson, then-director of the District of Columbia Criminal Justice Research Center, who wrote and edited the overall report.

The interviews were designed to gain insight into how the youths perceive themselves and their crimes. Johnson, now a senior associate at the Institute for Law and Justice in Alexandria, Va., has continued to follow the progress of the youths she interviewed at Oak Hill Youth Center, the city's secure detention facility for juveniles.

The following excerpts, in Johnson's words, are taken from the 1991 report:

"The typical sociodemographic profile of District youth involved in the juvenile justice system applies to the youth in this study. Their character profile reveals some insights that are not typically known. They have little understanding of alternatives to their actions and are not interested in changing their lifestyles or behavior or the probable course of their lives. They seem not to have a sense of remorse for the murders they have committed and accept the certainty of a very dismal and limited future. . . .

There were 19 youths serving commitments for homicide during the interview period. One declined to be interviewed, and one who agreed to be interviewed said he is not guilty of the homicide with which he is charged. The 17 that were interviewed fit the typical sociodemographic profile of juvenile offenders in the District. All are black males, and all had been involved in the juvenile justice system prior to their arrest for homicide. Eight were first arrested at age 12 or 13 and four at age 14 or 15. At the time of their homicides, seven were age 15 and five were age 14. Eight of the 17 said they were in school at the time, but did not attend regularly, and the others were not attending at all. Nine had completed seventh or eighth grade, six had completed ninth or 10th grade and one had completed 11th grade.

All of them have seen violence as a regular part of their environment, from witnessing robberies and brutal beatings to seeing people killed. Fourteen said they have been victims themselves of a range of violence including robberies, shootings, stabbings and beatings. . . .

Continued from p. 184

rehabilitation efforts.

"The Boston juvenile court is a circus; it's a disgrace," says Loughran, director until this year of Massachusetts' juvenile corrections system. "Kids walk into that chaos, and they don't know what's going on up there. . . . All they know is they have to report to a probation officer once a month and they say, 'I skated.' "

One solution would be more uniform sentences for juveniles from one jurisdiction to another. "As it is now, it's justice by geography," says Loughran. "A kid in one state could be subject to the death penalty and in another the kid could be out in a year or two."

To make the juvenile courts more accountable to society, some observers support opening the proceedings to the public — at least for serious offenses. Secrecy may have been appreciated in the past by young people who made a mistake and then went straight. But today notoriety is a "badge of courage" for some gun-toting youngsters, says Loughran. He points to one of the teenagers charged with opening fire at a Boston roller rink in January in a gang feud. When the boy left the courtroom after a hearing, according to *The Boston Globe*, his first question was whether his name had made it into the newspaper that day. [36] ■

OUTLOOK

Early Intervention

Liberals and conservatives alike agree that early and massive intervention in the lives of at-risk children is probably the only effective way to tackle violent juvenile crime.

"When a 13-year-old commits murder and has no remorse, what do you see there?" asks Frank Orlando, who presided over juvenile courts for 10 years during his 21-year career as a Florida circuit judge. "You see a kid that's never had any love, or any care. No one's ever bonded with him, his mother was probably 14 years old, so what do you expect? If you really want to stop the violent offense, you start dealing with that kid when he's born."

Attacking the problem at such an early stage calls for solutions that tend to be ambitious and expensive. UCLA's Wilson has proposed boarding schools for at-risk kids. Carnegie-Mellon University Professor Alfred Blumstein points to home-based programs that start at birth and continue into early childhood, teaching young, impoverished single mothers how to be parents. [37]

Finding solutions to the endemic social problems of poverty, family violence and poor schooling is considered equally important. Recently, some success has been reported by a Greenville, S.C., program for violent youthful offenders that tries to tackle

. . .To Understand Why They Resort to Violence

Their family situations also reveal concurrence with a typical profile. When asked, 'Who raised you?' nine said their mother, three said their grandmother, three said both parents, one said an aunt and two said they raised themselves. Five of these youths had children — and a few had more than one child. Thirteen said they had relatives in prison — most had several immediate relatives who were incarcerated.

With regard to violence at home, six of the youths were exposed to physical domestic violence among family members, and 12 say they received disciplinary beatings, but felt that these beatings were justified. . . .

The first common theme among these youths is their involvement in drugs. All of them said when asked that they did not use drugs; but, while not all of their homicide convictions were classified as drug-related, all but one of the youths stated they sold drugs. Research repeatedly has shown that involvement in the drug trade is likely to lead to being a victim or perpetrator of homicide. . . .

Interestingly, all of the youth mentioned their involvement in drugs as if it was a foregone conclusion for their lives. And there seemed to be little thought regarding whether or not there was something else in which to get involved. . . .

In questioning what brought these youths to decide to kill, an absence of the recognition of alternatives is another theme that emerged. . . . All but one . . . when asked why they killed, answered simply that they did what they had to do. . . . Virtually all summarized their alternatives with remarks tantamount to 'kill or be killed.'

All but one . . . carried guns for protection. . . . [They] were keenly aware of the significance of one's reputation and the ramifications of allowing a precedent to be set by letting a robbery or unpaid debt go unchallenged. . . . They considered killing as the ultimate message to others that they will not get away with being disrespected or robbed. . . . When asked if he wanted to kill or felt he had to, each invariably responded that he did not want to kill, but felt he had no choice. . . .

[These youths] seem to have no working understanding of the concept of the future. When asked, 'What are your thoughts about the future?' several youths asked for an explanation of the question. For too many of them, their thoughts about the future were the same as the past. . . . Most . . . said they would carry a gun again for protection. . . . This, combined with the resolution that they would kill again if faced with the same situations, makes the futures of these youths predictably a reenactment of their past."

all three problems at once. The approach, funded by the National Institute of Mental Health, treats youngsters' families and their communities as the root of the problem. Counselors teach parents of chronic delinquents to use words rather than beatings to discipline their children. Their goal: to break the cycle of physical abuse passed on from generation to generation. They help parents with jobs, housing and other basic needs often lacking at the bottom of the economic ladder.

Gary B. Melton director of the Center for Children, Families and the Law at the University of Nebraska, reports that the approach, known as "multisystemic family preservation therapy," has cut chronic delinquents' arrest rate in half and has sustained those results three years after the three-month program ends. [38]

Vanderbilt University's Marc Lipsey calls the early results "promising" but notes that the program will have to be tried with kids in a variety of settings before its effectiveness can be proven.

Yet is a public impatient with crime, and perhaps impatient with juvenile justice reformers like Loughran, willing to pay for such efforts?

Perhaps so, if combined with certain punishment, says Colorado state Rep. Adkins. Colorado's new intermediate program for juveniles who commit violent crimes is one such attempt to combine both treatment and punishment in one program.

"Even if you're going to give [juvenile offenders] a third chance and give them rehabilitation," she says, "you still have to say what kind of behavior is acceptable and what kind is not." The sentence "should encompass some element of punishment and justice from society's perspective as well as an element of rehabilitation." ■

Sarah Glazer is a freelance writer in Washington, D.C., who specializes in social-policy issues.

Notes

[1] See Claire Johnson, "Wounded Killers," *Focus*, February 1993, pp. 3-5. *Focus* is published by the Joint Center for Political and Economic Studies, which researches black-oriented issues. Marc is the fictitious name used by Johnson.

[2] Sam Vincent Meddis, "In a Dark Alley, Most Feared Face is a *Teen's*," *USA Today*, Oct. 29, 1993, p. 6A.

[3] Millicent Lawton, "Romer Calls Special Session to Focus on Youth Violence," *Education Week*, Sept. 15, 1993. For background, see "Youth Gangs," *The CQ Researcher*, Oct. 11, 1991, pp. 753-776.

[4] Barbara Allen-Hagen and Melissa Sickmund, "Juveniles and Violence: Juvenile Offenders and Victimization," *Fact Sheet*, Office of Juvenile Justice and Delinquency Prevention, July 1993.

[5] FBI Uniform Crime Reports, *Crime in the United States, 1991*, Aug. 30, 1992, p. 279. For background, see "Reassessing the Nation's Gun Laws," *Editorial Research Reports*, March 22, 1991, pp. 157-180, and "War on Drugs," *The CQ Researcher*, March 19,

1993, pp. 241-264.

[6] It's often said that a few delinquents commit most of the crime. In a pioneering 1972 study of 975 youths ages 10-18 in Philadelphia, chronic offenders — youths with at least five contacts with police — constituted only 18 percent of the delinquents but committed 71 percent of the homicides, 73 percent of the rapes, 82 percent of the robberies and 69 percent of the aggravated assaults. Later studies have produced similar results. See Wolfgang, M.E., et al, *Delinquency in a Birth Cohort* (1972).

[7] For background, see Kitty Cunningham, "Hitting Back at Youth Crime," *Congressional Quarterly Weekly Report*, Nov. 13, 1993, p. 3129.

[8] Jackie Hallifax, "Boy in Tourist Murder Case is Released," *St. Petersburg Times*, Nov. 13, 1993, p. 1B. Green is scheduled to be tried as an adult in April under a state law requiring adult treatment of juveniles indicted for first-degree felonies. All four teenagers were indicted by a grand jury in October for first-degree murder and attempted murder and could face the electric chair. Green was released from custody in November to await trial in the care of an unidentified adult.

[9] Between 1985 and 1991, arrest rates for homicide among 13-to-14-year-old males increased by 140 percent, according to Glenn L. Pierce and James Alan Fox, "Recent Trends in Violent Crime: A Closer Look," *National Crime Analysis Program*, Northwestern University, October 1992, Table 3.

[10] *Congressional Record*, Nov. 5, 1993, p. S 15175.

[11] Peter W. Greenwood, Joan Petersilia and Franklin E. Zimring, *Age, Crime, and Sanctions: The Transition from Juvenile to Adult Court*, RAND, October 1980, pp. 79-80.

[12] *Ibid.*, p. x.

[13] Bob Herbert, "15 and Armed," *The New York Times*, Jan. 23, 1994.

[14] *Congressional Record, op. cit.*

[15] Ira M. Schwartz, et al, "The Impact of Demographic Variables on Public Opinion Regarding Juvenile Justice: Implications for Public Policy," *Crime and Delinquency*, January 1993, pp. 5-28.

[16] Testimony of former Florida Judge Frank A. Orlando before the Senate Judiciary Subcommittee on Juvenile Justice, March 4, 1992, p. 8. According to Orlando, Florida transferred more than 6,000 juveniles into the adult system in 1991; approximately 1,000 were sentenced to adult prisons.

[17] The National Council on Crime and Delinquency, *Juvenile Justice Policy Statement*, April 1991, p. 14.

[18] Dean J. Champion and G. Larry Mays, *Transferring Juveniles to Criminal Courts* (1991), p. 80.

[19] See Mark W. Lipsey, *What Do We Learn from 400 Research Studies on the Effectiveness of Treatment with Juvenile Delinquents?* Unpublished conference paper, September 1992.

[20] Testimony of Barry C. Feld in Juvenile Courts: Access to Justice, hearing before Senate Judiciary Subcommittee on Juvenile Justice, March 4, 1992, p. 166. For background, see "Children's Legal Rights," *The CQ Researcher*, April 23, 1993, pp. 337-360.

[21] The task force presented a legislative proposal to the Minnesota Senate Judiciary Committee Jan. 19.

[22] National Council on Crime and Delinquency, *Unlocking Juvenile Corrections: Evaluating the Massachusetts Department of Youth Services*, 1991, p. 10.

[23] Leah Eskin, "Punishment or Reform? Juvenile Justice in U.S. History," *Scholastic Update*, April 5, 1991, p. 18.

[24] *Ibid.*

[25] Champion and Mays, *op. cit.*, p. 88.

[26] *Ibid.*, p. 102.

[27] For a summary of the bills, see "Issue: Crime," *Congressional Quarterly Weekly Report*, Dec. 11, 1993, pp. 3395-3396.

[28] Gwen Ifill, "Clinton to Stress Health and Crime," *The New York Times*, Jan. 24, 1994, pp. A1, B6.

[29] Center to Prevent Handgun Violence, *Kids Carrying Guns*, June 1993, p. 1.

[30] *Ibid.*, p. 2.

[31] William Booth, "Florida Bars Gun Possession by Juveniles," *The Washington Post*, Nov. 11, 1993, p. A18.

[32] Roy Romer, "Under 18? Hand over that Gun," *The New York Times*, Oct. 21, 1993, p. A27.

[33] John Sanko, "Romer Slams Down His 'Iron Fist' Plan," *Rocky Mountain News*, Sept. 8, 1993.

[34] Arrests in New York City of children ages 7 to 15 on gun charges increased 75 percent between 1987 and 1990. Statistics cited in editorial, "Mowing Down Our Children," *The New York Times*, Nov. 4, 1992.

[35] Joseph F. Sheley and James D. Wright, "Gun Acquisition and Possession in Selected Juvenile Samples," National Institute of Justice, Office of Juvenile Justice and Delinquency Prevention, Research in Brief, December 1993, p. 10. The survey took place at correctional facilities in California, New Jersey, Louisiana and Illinois.

[36] Mike Barnicle,"Dropping our eyes at true evil," *The Boston Globe*, Jan. 25, 1994, p. 17.

[37] For background, see Sarah Glazer, "Head Start," *The CQ Researcher*, April 9, 1993, pp. 297-320.

[38] Scott W. Henggeler, Gary B. Melton and Linda A. Smith, "Family Preservation Using Multisystemic Therapy: An Effective Alternative to Incarcerating Serious Juvenile Offenders," *Journal of Consulting and Clinical Psychology*, 1992, Vol. 60, No. 6, pp. 953-961.

Bibliography

Selected Sources Used

Books

Bernard, Thomas J., *The Cycle of Juvenile Justice*, Oxford University Press, 1992.

In this history of the juvenile justice system, the author asserts that punishment and rehabilitation tend to follow a cyclical pattern, in which periods of public concern about reforming delinquents are followed by periods in which harsher punishment is seen as necessary to insure public safety.

Champion, Dean J., and G. Larry Mays, *Transferring Juveniles to Criminal Courts: Trends and Implications for Criminal Justice*, Praeger, 1991.

The authors conclude that most juveniles transferred to adult court don't get harsher sentences. The basic differences between juvenile courts and criminal courts for adults are discussed.

Articles

Horowitz, Craig, "Law and Disorder: How the Juvenile Justice System is Letting Kids Get away with Murder," *New York*, Jan. 10, 1994, pp. 19-27.

Horowitz paints a dismaying portrait of the inability of New York City's juvenile courts to deal effectively with violent young criminals.

Kotlowitz, Alex, "Their Crimes Don't Make Them Adults," *The New York Times Magazine*, Feb. 13, 1994, pp. 40-41.

As he relates the stories of two Chicago teens drawn into serious crimes, journalist Kotlowitz argues that punishing children as adults is the wrong prescription for adolescent mistakes.

Loose, Cindy and Pierre Thomas, "Spread of Violence Poisons Well-being of Childhood," *The Washington Post*, Jan. 2, 1994, pp. A1, A19.

This portrait of growing youth violence in Washington, D.C., and throughout the nation looks at social causes, including rising child abuse and neglect.

Nossiter, Adam, "As Boot Camps for Criminals Multiply, Skepticism Grows," *The New York Times*, Dec. 18, 1993, pp. 1, 9.

This article reviews the numerous ways in which boot camps have not met expectations — in cutting recidivism, costs or prison overcrowding.

Reports and Studies

Allen-Hagen, Barbara and Melissa Sickmund, *Juveniles and Violence: Juvenile Offending and Victimization*, Office of Juvenile Justice and Delinquency Prevention, Fact Sheet, July 1993.

This statistical report based on the FBI's Uniform Crime Reports summarizes recent trends in youth crime.

American Psychological Association, *Violence & Youth: Psychology's Response. Volume I: Summary Report of the American Psychological Association Commission on Violence and Youth*, 1993.

This is a clear, concise summary of psychological research findings on the roots of childhood violence.

General Accounting Office, *Prison Boot Camps: Short-Term Prison Costs Reduced, but Long-Term Impact Uncertain*, April 1993.

Reviewing the results of studies on recidivism, the GAO concludes that "there is little difference between boot camp inmates and other inmates."

Office of Criminal Justice Plans and Analysis, District of Columbia Government, *Homicide Report*, April 1992.

This report, a follow-up to a 1988 report on homicide in Washington, D.C., contains compelling interviews with juvenile murderers as well as a discussion of homicide trends and causes in the nation's capital, the murder capital of the United States.

Senate Judiciary Subcommittee on Juvenile Justice, *Hearing on Juvenile Courts: Access to Justice*, March 4, 1992.

This hearing exploring the strengths and weaknesses of juvenile courts includes testimony from several prominent experts in the field, most of whom oppose increased use of adult courts for minors.

National Council on Crime and Delinquency, *Juvenile Justice Policy Statement*, April 1991.

This San Francisco-based reform group argues that expanding the use of punitive approaches to juvenile delinquents, such as more adult trials and adult prison sentences, is not effective.

National Council on Crime and Delinquency, *Unlocking Juvenile Corrections: Evaluating the Massachusetts Department of Youth Services*, 1991.

This widely cited report praises Massachusetts' pioneering decision to close down its juvenile reformatory. It concludes that the reform did not create excessive crime in the state and would be a good model for other states faced with overcrowded reform schools.

The Next Step

Additional information from UMI's Newspaper & Periodical Abstracts database

Alternative Actions

Dolan, James W., "Putting the cart before the horse in juvenile cases," *Boston Globe*, Oct. 27, 1993, p. 11.

James W. Dolan advocates trying juvenile offenders charged with serious crimes as adults in order to streamline the court system and save time and government money, commenting that judges could later decide whether a defendant should be sentenced as an adult or a juvenile.

Doyle, Jim, "State court holds parents to account," *San Francisco Chronicle*, July 2, 1993, p. A1.

The California Supreme Court ruled on July 1, 1993, that parents can be charged with criminal misdemeanor offenses if they fail to provide "reasonable care" in supervising a child who commits crimes or engages in delinquent acts.

Gottesman, Andrew, "2 cities can teach Chicago juvenile court lessons," *Chicago Tribune*, Dec. 22, 1993, p. 1.

While Cincinnati and Louisville, Ky., don't have the urban character or ills of Chicago, experts say that elements of their innovative juvenile court programs might be the key to reforming the clogged, inefficient Juvenile Court system in Cook County, Ill., that leaves abused children and their families adrift for years. (Part 2 of 2).

Jensen, Eric L. and Linda K. Metsger, "A test of the deterrent effect of legislative waiver on violent juvenile crime," *Crime & Delinquency*, January 1994, pp. 96-104.

The juvenile justice system has been moving away from its traditional rehabilitative orientation toward a model based on the adult criminal justice system, according to the authors. The deterrent effect of the 1981 Idaho legislative waiver statute is examined.

Lubin, Stuart Frederic, "Now is the time to revamp juvenile justice," *Chicago Tribune*, Dec. 2, 1993, p. 1.

Lubin says that juvenile justice is an expensive, lengthy process that has a dubious success rate. Lubin suggests a system of smaller, intensive center programs that give young offenders vocational, educational and therapeutic help.

Plummer, Don, "New program cuts case costs and juvenile detention stays," *Atlanta Constitution*, June 17, 1993, p. XG4.

A program to increase the number of lawyers assigned to help needy youngsters facing charges in Juvenile Court in Cobb County, Ga., has been cited as an example for other courts.

Schwartzkopff, Frances, "State asked to provide youth offenders' lawyers," *Atlanta Constitution*, July 29, 1993, p. F3.

Georgia should take the lead in the national debate over reforming juvenile justice systems by providing lawyers for offenders during hearings to decide whether they are sent to prison, according to Atlanta area child advocates. But the Department of Children and Youth Services is not supporting the idea.

Current Situation

Crawford, Jan, "Juvenile court judged a disaster," *Chicago Tribune*, Dec. 23, 1993, p. 1.

A 108-page report by the Illinois Supreme Court's Special Commission on the Administration of Justice paints a grim picture of an overburdened juvenile court system that all but ignores the children it should protect.

Davis, Patricia, "Top juvenile judge looking for help: Growing violence crowding the docket," *The Washington Post*, Oct. 14, 1993, p. VAF1.

A surge in juvenile and domestic violence has overwhelmed the Fairfax County, Va., Juvenile and Domestic Relations Court. The court's chief judge, Gaylord L. Finch Jr., says the youths who are being arraigned are younger, charged with more serious crimes and increasingly female.

Eisenman, Russell, "Society confronts the hard-core youthful offender," *USA Today: The Magazine of the American Scene*, January 1994, pp. 27-28.

There are two ways to handle juvenile offenders: juvenile courts and rehabilitation. Although no solutions are easy, the more that can be done to intervene to deal with the wide array of problems youthful offenders face, the better chance for turning youthful offenders into honest citizens.

Feld, Barry C., "Juvenile (in)justice and the criminal court alternative," *Crime & Delinquency*, October 1993, pp. 403-424.

The juvenile court has been transformed from an informal, welfare agency into a scaled-down, second-class criminal court as a result of a series of reforms that punish delinquent offenders and provide more formal procedures, Field writes. An alternative to the juvenile court is proposed.

Gibney, Jim, "Gun law upheld for first time," *Denver Post*, Dec. 8, 1993, p. B2.

Colorado District Judge Jane Looney ruled on Dec. 7, 1993, that the state's new juvenile gun law is constitutional, becoming the first judge to uphold the law. Looney ruled that the state has a compelling and legitimate interest in preventing juvenile violence.

Gottesman, Andrew, "Juvenile Court can rarely spare the time to care," *Chicago Tribune*, Dec. 21, 1993, p. 1.
Juvenile Court in Cook County, Ill., is too overloaded, underequipped and ill-conceived to fulfill its mission, experts say. The conclusions of a task force that investigated the death of 3-year-old Joseph Wallace have triggered a rare opportunity for massive overhaul, Gottesman says. (Part 1 of 2).

Makeig, John, "Judge letting juries hear teen gun cases," *Houston Chronicle*, Dec. 21, 1993, p. A21.
In Harris County, Texas, state District Judge Mary Bacon has decided to force all firearms cases involving first-offender teenagers to trial.

Root, Jay, "Deluge of pre-teens swamps courts," *Houston Post*, Nov. 26, 1993, p. A37.
Houston's teen court has reported that so many juvenile criminals ages 10, 11 and 12 are appearing before the court that the number of sessions has been doubled to handle the roughly 3,200 cases per month.

Saker, Anne, "Our society is failing to protect its children," *Detroit News*, Aug. 3, 1993, p. A2.
A sweeping report by the American Bar Association urges lawyers to play a more visionary role as children's advocates, saying children are mishandled, entrapped or often ignored in the nation's court system. A number of celebrated cases, including the adoption struggle over Jessica DeBoer in Michigan and Iowa, demonstrate the difficulties children often face in court.

Stanford, Duane D., "Juvenile court sheds light on problems outside," *Atlanta Constitution*, Nov. 4, 1993, p. XJA1.
Highlights of a day in DeKalb County, Ga., Juvenile Court are given as an example of the growing rate of juvenile deliquency in the county. Judge Madeline Griffin also sees parents brought before her court for neglecting and abusing their children. (Part of a series).

Torpy, Bill, "Exurban courts swamped," *Atlanta Constitution*, June 14, 1993, p. D1.
Part-time judges in once-rural counties surrounding Atlanta are getting overwhelmed by an explosion in the crime rate among children and teenagers.

A Question of Age

Greene, Andrea D., "Radack wants 14-year-olds tried as adults," *Houston Chronicle*, Dec. 11, 1993, p. A1.
Harris County, Texas, Commissioner Steve Radack urged that the governor call a special legislative session to allow the prosecution of 14-year-olds as adults.

Hirschi, Travis and Michael Gottfredson, "Rethinking the juvenile justice system," *Crime & Delinquency*, April 1993, pp. 262-271.
Special treatment of juveniles is based on an erroneous image of developmental sequences, and misrepresents differences between juvenile and adult crime, according to the authors. It is argued that one justice system would be better than two, and that of the models currently available, the juvenile system seems preferable to the adult.

Poulos, Tammy Meredith and Stan Orchowsky, "Juvenile offenders: Predicting the probability of transfer to criminal court," *Crime & Delinquency*, January 1994, pp. 3-17.
The legal and extralegal factors that play a significant role in the decision to transfer a serious juvenile offender to criminal court jurisdiction in Virginia are identified. Results are presented and discussed.

Research and Studies

Dao, James, "Cuomo names Stein to head a study panel," *The New York Times*, Nov. 24, 1993, p. B6.
Gov. Mario M. Cuomo, D-N.Y., on Nov. 23, 1993, announced the creation of a commission to study shortcomings in the state's juvenile justice system and appointed Andrew J. Stein, the departing New York City Council president, to head the panel. The new commission will be part of a broader study by his administration into crime and violence.

McGarrell, Edmund F., "Trends in racial disproportionality in juvenile court processing: 1985-1989," *Crime & Delinquency*, January 1993, pp. 29-48.
A study examined data on juvenile court processing to analyze a trend toward overrepresentation of non-white youths in correctional facilities. Findings indicate that non-whites were more likely to be detained and placed outside the home.

Pollock, Ellen Joan, "Legal beat: ABA unit finds children's courts in disarray, urges unified system," *The Wall Street Journal*, Aug. 4, 1993, p. B5.
A study by an American Bar Association commission found that the children's court system is in disarray, resulting in unnecessary delay, duplication and contradictory rulings and recommendations. The report endorses the creation of unified court systems to handle family-related issues.

Singer, Simon I., "The automatic waiver of juveniles and substantive justice," *Crime & Delinquency*, April 1993, pp. 253-261.
An analysis of juvenile court case processing decisions in a state with automatic transfer provisions revealed that offenders from single-parent households were more likely to face a grand jury indictment than juveniles from dual-parent households.

Back Issues

Great Research on Current Issues Starts Right Here...Recent topics covered by The CQ Researcher are listed below. Before May 1991, reports were published under the name of Editorial Research Reports.

AUGUST 1992
The Homeless
Work, Family and Stress
NATO's Changing Role
Marine Mammals vs. Fish

SEPTEMBER 1992
Domestic Partners
Violence in Schools
Public Broadcasting
Women in the Military

OCTOBER 1992
Depression
U.S. Auto Industry
Youth Apprenticeships
Hispanic Americans

NOVEMBER 1992
Physical Fitness
Privatization
Paying for College
U.S. Policy in Asia

DECEMBER 1992
Crackdown on Smoking
The New CIA
Eating Disorders
Women and AIDS

JANUARY 1993
Hate Crimes
Child Sexual Abuse
Nuclear Fusion
U.S. Trade Policy

FEBRUARY 1993
Community Policing
Europe's New Right
School Censorship
Violence Against Women

MARCH 1993
Gay Rights
Aid to Russia
War on Drugs
TV Violence

APRIL 1993
Head Start
High-Speed Rail
Children's Legal Rights
Muslims in America

MAY 1993
Cults in America
Preventing Teen Pregnancy
Software Piracy
National Parks

JUNE 1993
Food Safety
Prostitution
Childhood Immunizations
National Service

JULY 1993
Electric Cars
Population Growth
Downward Mobility
Intelligence Testing

AUGUST 1993
Mental Illness
Bilingual Education
Foreign Policy Burden
School Funding

SEPTEMBER 1993
Suburban Crime
Public Housing
Supreme Court Preview
Immigration Reform

OCTOBER 1993
Airline Safety
Disaster Response
Science in the Courtroom
The Glass Ceiling

NOVEMBER 1993
Paying for Retirement
Charitable Giving
Privacy in the Workplace
Adoption

DECEMBER 1993
U.S. Vietnam-Relations
Learning Disabilities
Child Care
Space Program's Future

JANUARY 1994
Racial Tensions in Schools
South Africa's Future
Worker Retraining
Regulating Pesticides

FEBRUARY 1994
Prison Overcrowding
Water Quality
Religion in Schools

Future Topics

- ***Underground Economy***
- ***Education Standards***
- ***Gambling***

THE CQ Researcher

PUBLISHED BY CONGRESSIONAL QUARTERLY INC.

Underground Economy

How much do "off-the-books" workers cheat on taxes?

This year at tax time, law-abiding Americans understandably may wonder if they have been bearing more than their fair share of the tax load lately. Recent news reports suggest that millions of employers and workers are skirting the Internal Revenue Service, among them: nominees to high government office who hired illegal aliens as housekeepers and didn't pay their Social Security taxes; immigrants paid in cash at urban sweatshops; welfare cheats who collect public benefits while earning untaxed income; and wealthy, self-employed professionals who significantly underreport their cash earnings. The underground economy by its very nature eludes measurement, but IRS estimates put the 1992 loss in potential taxes — the so-called tax gap — at some $114 billion.

INSIDE THIS ISSUE

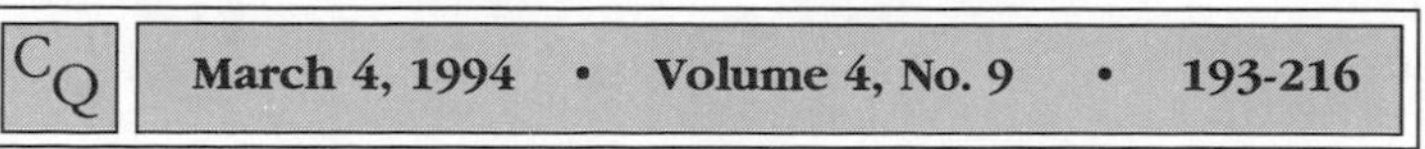
CQ March 4, 1994 • Volume 4, No. 9 • 193-216

Formerly Editorial Research Reports

COVER ART: BARBARA SASSA-DANIELS

March 4, 1994
Volume 4, No. 9

The CQ Researcher (ISSN 1056-2036). Formerly Editorial Research Reports. Published weekly (48 times per year, not printed the first Friday of any month with five Fridays) by Congressional Quarterly Inc., 1414 22nd St., N.W., Washington, D.C. 20037. Rates are furnished upon request. Second-class postage paid at Washington, D.C. POSTMASTER: Send address changes to The CQ Researcher, 1414 22nd St., N.W., Washington, D.C. 20037.

Underground Economy

By Mary H. Cooper

The Issues

"Taxes are what we pay for a civilized society."

Every year at tax time, the words of Oliver Wendell Holmes, inscribed above the entrance to the Internal Revenue Service (IRS) in Washington, assume a special significance. Behind the ritual gathering of wage and investment documents and the filing of Form 1040 by the April 15 deadline, lies a fundamentally American institution — voluntary compliance with various tax regulations.

But there are signs that this precarious institution is eroding. Last year saw President Clinton's first nominee for U.S. attorney general, Zoë Baird, go down in flames after it was reported that she and her husband hadn't paid Social Security taxes for their two household workers, both illegal aliens.

The public outcry over the so-called Nannygate incident was so strong that Clinton's second nominee, New York Judge Kimba M. Wood, voluntarily withdrew her nomination. Even though she had not broken the law then in effect by hiring an undocumented alien to work in her home, the appearance of impropriety was enough to ruin her prospects.

Nannygate has continued to touch nominees to high-profile posts. Adm. Bobby Ray Inman, who earlier this year withdrew as Clinton's choice to replace Les Aspin as Defense secretary, had acknowledged that he and his wife had not paid Social Security taxes for their housekeeper for six years. However, until Inman withdrew his name from nomination, he was nonetheless considered a shoo-in for the position.

The Nannygate housekeepers and their employers are part of what economists call the underground economy, a vast but largely unmeasured world of transactions that go undetected by the IRS. And they are far from alone. People who participate in the underground economy — also called the informal, invisible, subterranean and off-the-books economy — vary broadly. But they generally have two things in common: They use cash only, and they don't pay taxes on their transactions.

Media attention in recent months has pointed at yet another facet of the underground economy: the operation of sweatshops in New York, Los Angeles and other cities. These small factories are often manned by illegal aliens from China, who work at subminimum wages outside the taxed, or "formal" economy, to pay smugglers for bringing them to the United States. Compounding public outrage over this part of the underground economy are fears that recent immigrants, both legal and illegal, are profiting from the welfare system supported by taxpaying citizens.

Just how big is the underground economy? Because it eludes measurement by its very nature, nobody knows for sure. Most estimates date back to the early 1980s, when economists in the administration of President Ronald Reagan claimed it was equivalent to a fifth of the gross domestic product (GDP), the total value of the nation's economic output. What had happened, they said, was that overregulation and high taxes imposed by the previous Jimmy Carter administration had pushed many struggling Americans into taking off-the-books jobs.

The IRS estimated the 1992 loss in potential tax revenue — the so-called tax gap — at $114 billion. That's the tax revenue that would have been generated by an underground economy valued at $600 billion, experts estimated. [1]

And that doesn't even take into consideration the illegal economy, the businesses of drugs, prostitution and illicit gambling. The IRS has long since given up on that side of economic activity as a source of potential revenue. The last time the agency even tried to measure the illegal economy was in 1983, when it estimated its worth in lost tax revenues at some $10 billion.

"The drug economy today is a lot bigger than in 1983," says Bruce R. Wiegand, a professor of sociology at the University of Wisconsin-Whitewater and a former IRS analyst. "Since then, the IRS has decided to think of it as something to eliminate, not collect revenue from."

Excluding these illegal activities, the underground economy comprises myriad transactions that just about every American has engaged in at one time or another — the carpenter or plumber you pay in cash, the neighborhood teenager who babysits the kids, the rural entrepreneur selling firewood or the handyman shoveling snow off the driveway.

"These people who fail to report income are not a major deal," says David Levine, chief economist at

R. Michael Jenkins

© 1989 Faye Ellman

R. Michael Jenkins

The so-called Nannygate scandal scuttled the attorney general nominations of Zoë Baird (top left) and New York Judge Kimba M. Wood (top right). Adm. Bobby Ray Inman (left) withdrew his nomination as President Clinton's choice to replace Defense secretary Les Aspin. Inman, considered a shoo-in for the post, acknowledged that he and his wife had not paid Social Security taxes for their housekeeper of six years.

Sanford C. Bernstein & Co., a New York investment research and management firm. That's because many earn very little — often not enough to pay any taxes on in the first place.

More serious, in Levine's view, are people with enough income to pay taxes but who neither report the income nor pay the taxes. They account for 15 percent of the public, according to IRS estimates.[2] "The real problem," Levine says, "lies with self-employed people: the candy-store operator, the consultant, the gardener, the physician, the farmer — anyone who is a sole proprietor, who controls his own business, who has few or no employees and who does his own books. Is there a substantial tendency to underreport? Absolutely."

For some participants in the underground economy, tax cheating can be especially tempting. High-income professionals and business owners who report only part of their earnings to the IRS can save substantial sums on the unreported earnings.

Take the not-unusual recent case of a beer distributorship in Long Island City, Queens. "They were supplying about 90 percent of the Korean stores in the area," says Thomas Stanton, enforcement director of the New York City Finance Department. Acting on an informant's tip, Stanton's investigators discovered a second, parallel operation at work alongside the legitimate wholesale business.

"It was an all-cash business, and they kept two sets of books," he says. "They were written in Korean, but the numbers were good." Stanton found the owners were reporting about 60 percent of the business' $15 million annual income, taking home about $6 million a year tax-free.

But most underground workers have far less to gain by cheating the IRS, researchers in Detroit, Mich., discovered. "Three quarters of the people we talked to worked in the informal economy only because they couldn't find jobs in the formal economy," says Terry K. Adams, a senior research associate at the University of Michigan's Survey Research Center. "The pay was atrocious, and they were often out of work."[3]

Adams and his colleagues found that many workers went into the underground economy after they were laid off and failed to find new jobs. "The pay turned out on a hourly basis to provide them far less than the minimum wage," he says, "in part because their expenses ate up a very high proportion of what they made. They couldn't wait to get out of it."

If most participants in the underground economy are indeed there because they can't find regular work, there would appear to be little hope of eliminating it anytime soon. Even with the economy in a recovery, the unemployment rate in January was still a sobering 6.7 percent — meaning that 6.7 percent of the Americans who wanted work, or 2 million people, couldn't find jobs, according to the latest Labor Department figures, issued Feb 4.

Many of those job seekers are making ends meet by working "off the books," either on their own or for employers who choose to risk IRS penalties and possible labor law violations to skirt the tax laws. "The underground economy is as old as taxes, and it will stay with us as long as there are taxes," says Wiegand, author of *Off the Books: A Theory of the Underground Economy.*

As budget-minded policy-makers ponder ways to capture revenues lost to the underground economy, they must seek answers to the following questions:

Are more Americans participating in the underground economy even though economic conditions are improving?

After several years of stagnant growth, the economic recovery appears to be strengthening. The U.S. economy began picking up last year and is expected to grow by about 3 percent in 1994, according to Clinton administration economists. This is good news for unemployed workers looking for jobs in the formal economy because it means that many businesses will be hiring.

But several economic trends are driving some job seekers underground. One is corporate downsizing, a cost-cutting technique that has been in wide use since the 1980s, in which companies try to become more competitive by permanently shedding unnecessary employees. According to Challenger, Gray and Christmas Inc., a Chicago consulting firm, more than 600,000 jobs were lost last year through downsizing, twice as many as in 1990, which was a recession year. [4]

In addition, many production jobs are being transferred to countries with lower labor costs, while automation is eliminating still others. Workers who are displaced as a result of downsizing often find it hard to find new work without obtaining new skills. For many, the only alternative may be a low-skill job, but off the books and for much less pay.

Workers who find an opportunity to gain new skills may have to work during the training period. Even those who manage to keep working at their regular jobs during training may moonlight, working off the books at night or on weekends. "They report income from the regular jobs," says

What Households Spend in the Underground Economy

In a typical year, more than half of all American households bought food in the underground economy (column 1), with each household spending an average of $209 (column 2). By comparison, only 11.7 percent of U.S. households spent money in the underground economy on housekeeping, but each spent an average of $785 annually. Overall, more than twice as much money went into the underground economy for home repairs — $21.4 billion — as for food (column 3).

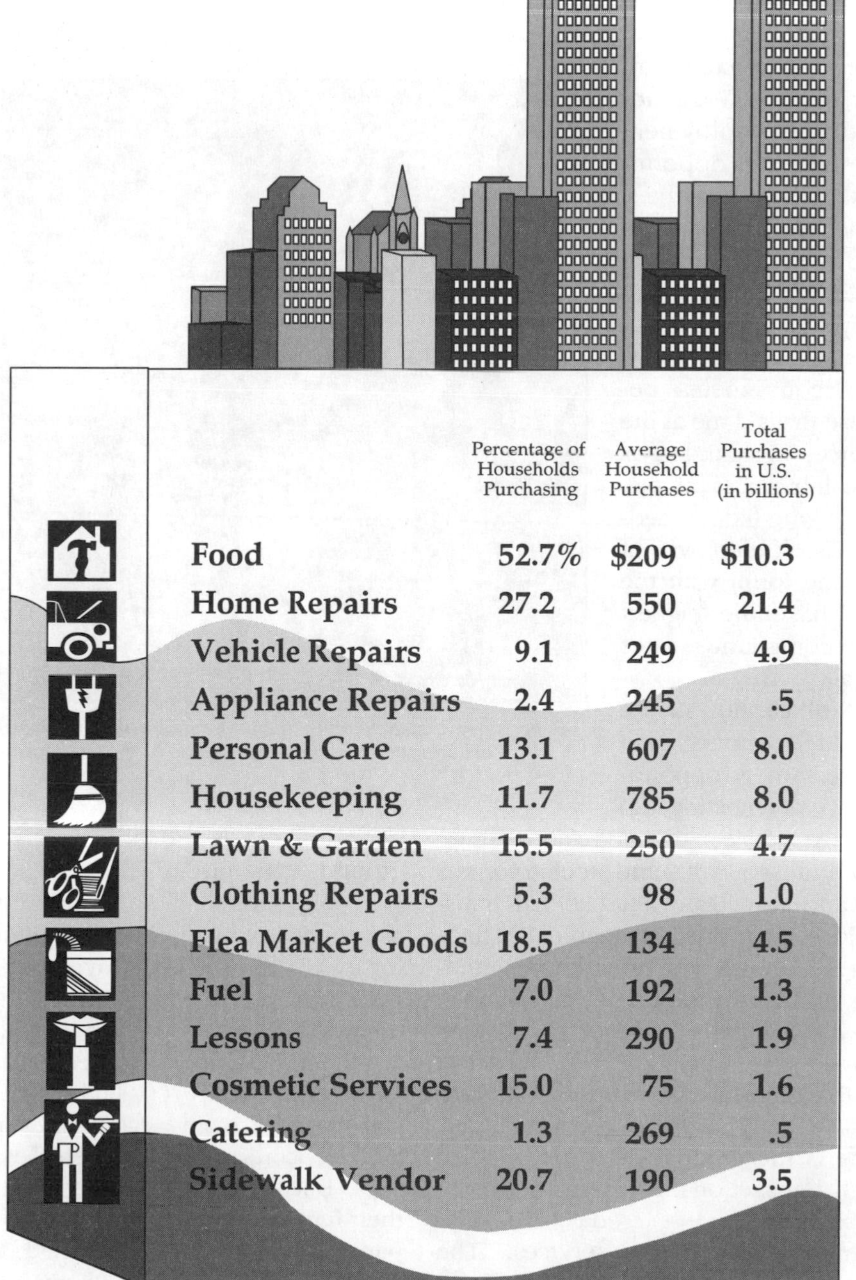

	Percentage of Households Purchasing	Average Household Purchases	Total Purchases in U.S. (in billions)
Food	**52.7%**	**$209**	**$10.3**
Home Repairs	**27.2**	**550**	**21.4**
Vehicle Repairs	**9.1**	**249**	**4.9**
Appliance Repairs	**2.4**	**245**	**.5**
Personal Care	**13.1**	**607**	**8.0**
Housekeeping	**11.7**	**785**	**8.0**
Lawn & Garden	**15.5**	**250**	**4.7**
Clothing Repairs	**5.3**	**98**	**1.0**
Flea Market Goods	**18.5**	**134**	**4.5**
Fuel	**7.0**	**192**	**1.3**
Lessons	**7.4**	**290**	**1.9**
Cosmetic Services	**15.0**	**75**	**1.6**
Catering	**1.3**	**269**	**.5**
Sidewalk Vendor	**20.7**	**190**	**3.5**

P. Eloise Fuller

Source: Institute for Social Research, University of Michigan, "Measurement of Selected Income Flows in Informal Markets 1981 and 1985-1986," April 1987.

Thomas A. Thompson, an economist in the IRS research division, "but not moonlighting income."

Like blue-collar victims of downsizing, laid-off managers find it hard to match the earnings they received in their old jobs with new ones available in the official economy. As a result, many executives with specialized skills go into business on their own, as consultants.

"The self-employed population is growing faster than [Form] 1040 wage earners," says Wiegand. And self-employment presents an opportunity to cheat on taxes. "The working stiff is tied to the withholding system through his employer and can't get out from under the reporting requirements because that's done at the source," Wiegand says. "Small-business people, those who file a Schedule C [self-employment income form] with the IRS, have the highest non-compliance rates of all."

Globalization of the world economy also presents new opportunities for cheating the IRS. As barriers to international trade continue to fall, and technological advances facilitate international transactions, even small companies are finding markets abroad. An unknown number of them evade taxes, for example, by declaring the value of goods sold abroad at less than the true sale price.

But there are other trends at work that make it harder to cheat on taxes. One is the gradual disappearance of cash transactions, as more and more businesses accept credit card payments for goods and services. "The 'credit cardization' of many businesses and restaurants leaves a paper trail that makes it harder to hide transactions," says Levine.

Another trend that hampers off-the-books activity, Levine says, is the automation of accounting services, which many firms contract out to firms such as ADP. "If you work for a corporation with 100 employees or more, the payroll is going to be done by a firm such as ADP, and nothing will be hidden," Levine says. "I would say that, not counting self-employed people, there is virtually no underground economy."

Clint W. Steib

Experts say that self-employed entrepreneurs like the ubiquitous street vendors in Washington, D.C., often participate in the underground economy. . .

A big slice of the underground economy, Levine reports, is accounted for by wealthy, self-employed people who don't report a significant part of their cash income. But even they have fewer opportunities to cheat, in his view. The nation's 700,000 physicians and dentists once accounted for a large proportion of tax evaders, Levine says, but they now receive most of their fees from private insurance companies, Medicare and Medicaid, not in cash from individual clients.

"Physicians account for about 10 percent of the self-employed but earn perhaps a quarter of all the self-employeds' income," Levine says. "But that group now accounts for a much smaller percentage of unreported income." Levine says the same goes for high-income lawyers, who now tend to work in partnerships that are run like corporations. "I guarantee you they report 100 cents on the dollar," he says.

Levine also downplays the significance of domestic workers in the underground economy. Nannygate, he says, is nothing more than "a bunch of 44-year-olds, who have nannies and don't pay taxes on them, talking to each other. Unfortunately, they are also the opinion-makers."

Despite the uproar over this sector of the underground economy, Levine says, "nannies don't earn anything. They're not even close to accounting for 1 percent of total employment, and they make about a quarter of the average wage."

Some studies show little change in the size of the underground economy under different economic conditions. Surveys conducted during the recession in 1981 and the mild recovery of 1985-86 showed little appreciable difference in the purchases by households of goods and services in the informal sector.

"One of our colleagues was trying to develop a theory that it was discretionary items, like babysitting or house-cleaning services, that people went to the informal economy to purchase in better times," says Adams at Michigan's Survey Research Center. According to this theory, however, "purchases of necessities in the informal economy, like food and plumbing repairs, increased in hard times." [5]

But the survey results did not support that theory. "The sums of all these things seem to have remained constant as a share of GDP between the two survey periods and after adjusting for inflation," Adams says. "It also seemed to us that the informal economy is quite a small chunk of the national economy — about the equivalent of 1 percent of GDP in both years."

Adams sees no evidence that the underground economy — at least the portion of it that he observed — has grown at all over the past decade. "Given the different economic situations between 1981 and 1985-86," he says, "there is no reason to expect that these kinds of household purchases in the informal economy have increased as a proportion of GDP."

Clint W. Steib

. . .because as self-employed entrepreneurs who take in cash, they are able to underreport their income to the Internal Revenue Service.

Is the informal economy placing a significant drag on tax revenues?

American taxpayers and businesses will hand over $1.25 trillion to the IRS this year. [6] That's the equivalent of almost a fifth of the total output of goods and services in the United States. That tax burden will be supported, of course, by workers who feel the pinch in withholdings from their paychecks and by businesses that comply with the tax laws. A sizable, but unknown, number of people pay no taxes or less than they should, while collecting the benefits of the federal programs supported by tax revenues.

In spite of the war on drugs and less visible attempts by law enforcement agencies to crack down on prostitution and illegal gambling, illegal transactions amount to tens of billions of dollars in value each year. From a fiscal standpoint, this vast illegal economy represents billions of dollars in lost revenues that could help reduce the federal budget deficit, which stood at $255 billion last year.

But the IRS excludes the illegal economy from most of its calculations on untapped sources of tax revenue. "These are activities that people are trying to keep secret, so they are hard to estimate," says Thompson of the IRS. "Where the illegal sector is concerned, the idea is not to collect tax revenue from this activity, but to stop it."

Thus, the IRS limits its enforcement efforts to the legal underground economy — the moonlighters, vendors and professional tax cheats involved in legitimate economic activities who break only the tax laws. "In the context of the legal sector, underreported income has implications for reducing the deficit and balancing the budget," Thompson says. "If you can start capturing this revenue, that helps the government financially.

From time to time, the IRS tries to calculate how much revenue it loses to the legal underground economy. This so-called tax gap includes taxes due on incomes earned in the legal sector of the economy that are not voluntarily paid or collected as a result of IRS enforcement activity. In 1992, the latest year for which estimates are available, the tax gap amounted to an estimated $114 billion. [7] And this was just for legal income. It also didn't count unpaid employment, estate, excise or gift taxes, or customs duties and other federal revenues that are lost in underground activities.

Individuals were responsible for about two-thirds of the tax gap, the IRS found. The vast majority of offenders underreported their incomes, while some overstated their tax credits, and a few made math errors on their returns. (*See graph, p. 200.*) Only 8 percent of the tax gap was the fault of individuals who failed to file an income tax form. About a quarter of the tax gap was traced to corporations — mostly large ones, those with assets of $10 million or more. [8]

To help the IRS better identify individuals responsible for the tax gap, Adams and his University of Michigan associates surveyed vendors in the informal economy selling goods and services in the Detroit area. "We found that people pretty much divided into two categories," he says. "One cat-

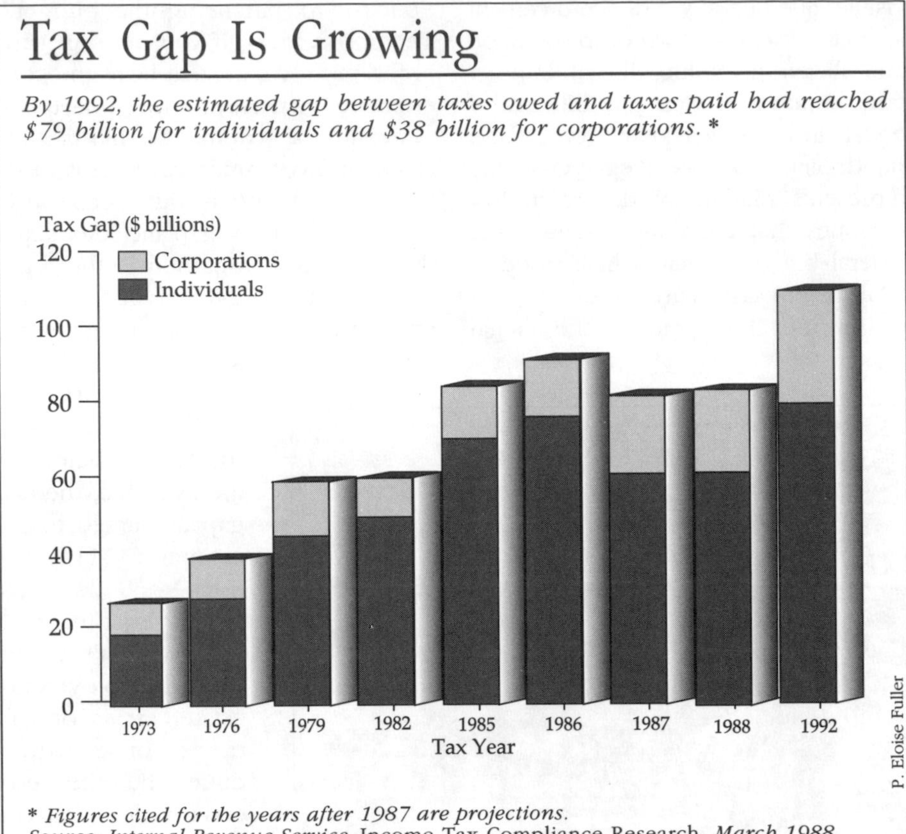

Tax Gap Is Growing

By 1992, the estimated gap between taxes owed and taxes paid had reached $79 billion for individuals and $38 billion for corporations. *

* *Figures cited for the years after 1987 are projections.*
Source: Internal Revenue Service, Income Tax Compliance Research, *March 1988.*

egory was people who were in skilled trades ranging from carpenters to accountants, who did this sort of work as their regular business, generally working for someone else, but also running their own much smaller business on the side."

Many of the building-trades workers they interviewed worked off the books while studying for their contractor's license. "Or, they may work for friends and neighbors for extra money on the weekends," Adams says, "and they tend to do that over the long term."

A much bigger category of tax cheats, Adams found, consisted of unemployed, low-skilled workers who turned to the informal economy out of desperation. "These were people who in large cities stood around in a bullpen area downtown where employers would drive by in the morning and say, 'You, you and you, come help me clear brush.' They thought it was better than nothing, especially because it wasn't being reported, and they weren't being taxed on it." These workers shouldn't shoulder much blame for the tax gap, Adams says, because they earn too little to tax.

But even including the higher-income vendors, Adams says the sector of the underground that supplies goods and services to households is "a trivial part of the total economy. From the IRS standpoint, it certainly looks like most of the money paid out by households ends up covering the workers' legitimate expenses in doing business, and as a result only a small portion of what they earn is taxable income."

Possibly more important than the actual revenue losses associated with the underground economy may be its unfairness to compliant taxpayers. "I suspect that there is a loss of government revenue that amounts to tens of billions of dollars," says Gary Burtless, an economist at the Brookings Institution. "But is that a large amount relative to total government revenues in the United States? It's just my guess, but I don't think that the government loses any more than 15 percent of potential total revenues as a result of the underground economy."

Federal coffers lose more potential tax revenue, Burtless says, through the perfectly legal exploitation by savvy taxpayers of loopholes in the tax code. "The bigger problem from the point of view of government revenue," he says, "is simply the loopholes in the law that you can drive a tank through. The big public policy issue is the evasion of taxation, because those people become freeloaders on the rest of us."

Public perception that others are getting away with not paying their taxes tends to erode the American tax system, based as it is on voluntary compliance in filing an annual return, says Burtless. "To the degree that the underground economy is large, and that many of us who are paying taxes resent the fact that there are freeloaders out there, we are going to look for more ways to escape taxes ourselves," he says. "That undermines voluntary compliance and thus raises the cost of collection. At that point, the underground economy becomes a very significant issue."

Are burdensome government regulations responsible for the underground economy?

Conservative economists argue that many American individuals and businesses now in the underground economy would shoulder their share of the tax burden if only the federal government would eliminate cumbersome regulations. Big businesses, they say, have the resources to hire accountants to handle complicated biweekly employee payrolls, including the withholding of income taxes and remittances of Social Security taxes, as well as reports of payroll and unemployment taxes. They also are better able to absorb the costs of complying with federal labor laws, including health and safety regulations, maximum working hours and the minimum wage.

Many small businesses and single proprietors, however, can't afford to spend valuable time and money on complying with the tax code and other federal regulations. Small businesses such as garment makers and laundries may produce goods and services with such low profit margins that compliance with tax and labor regulations may cut too deeply into profits. Operations that go underground rather than go out of business — or go underground to begin with — become the urban sweatshops that last year made headlines for hiring illegal aliens at subminimum wages.

Congress compounds the problem by periodically changing the laws, making it even harder for small companies to comply. Since 1977, Congress has passed eight major tax laws, each of which made significant changes in the rules businesses and individuals must follow. (*See "Chronology," p. 203.*)

In 1977 and 1983, lawmakers also changed the rates and effective dates for Social Security payroll taxes, further complicating the job of compliance for businesses. In 1986, Congress again added to the regulatory burden by shifting to employers the responsibility for determining whether a job applicant is an illegal alien and thus ineligible to work in the United States.

There is evidence that streamlining regulations and simplifying tax filing requirements would bring some violators into the official economy. If last year's Nannygate scandal is any indication, even knowledgeable professionals such as lawyers and accountants may find the regulations governing domestic workers burdensome enough that they risk penalties — and their careers — rather than comply with the rules.

The complications are not limited to federal regulations. Many local and state tax and labor rules are said to be even more convoluted. "The federal registration of domestic workers is very straightforward," says Kathleen Webb, president of Home/Work Solutions, a firm in Silver Spring, Md., that prepares tax returns and provides immigration forms for employers of domestic workers. (*See story, p. 204.*) "State registrations range from very straightforward to awesomely complicated."

Webb calls the District of Columbia one of the worst offenders. "They ask for your name and Social Security number no less than four times on the same registration form, which is six pages long," she says. "And that's just for registering. Then there are the quarterly and year-end tax returns to file to be in compliance with Social Security and unemployment laws that affect domestic workers."

Not everyone believes that simplifying the tax code and business regulations would draw many people back into the official economy. "Decades ago, the self-employed person had the same opportunity to evade taxes he has today, but that wasn't enough to make him cheat," says Bruce Wiegand. "What we have now is the opportunity plus the motivation to cheat, with a generational difference in attitudes toward paying your fair share between today's retiree population and the yuppie generation."

To Wiegand, whether people are willing to report their income or obey any other law comes down to a question of civic culture. "Our civic culture is the cornerstone of the voluntary compliance system," he says. "The tax system depends upon self-assessment and is based on trust.

"As support for Ross Perot shows, trust in government has been eroding for some time. We're developing a Third World notion of our government: that it is here to help itself first, and then to help the wealthy people." ■

What's Behind the Tax Gap

Individual taxpayers who filed returns but underreported their income accounted for more than half of the estimated $85 billion in lost tax dollars in 1987, the latest year for which actual figures are available. The rest of the tax gap was caused primarily by individuals who didn't file returns and corporations.

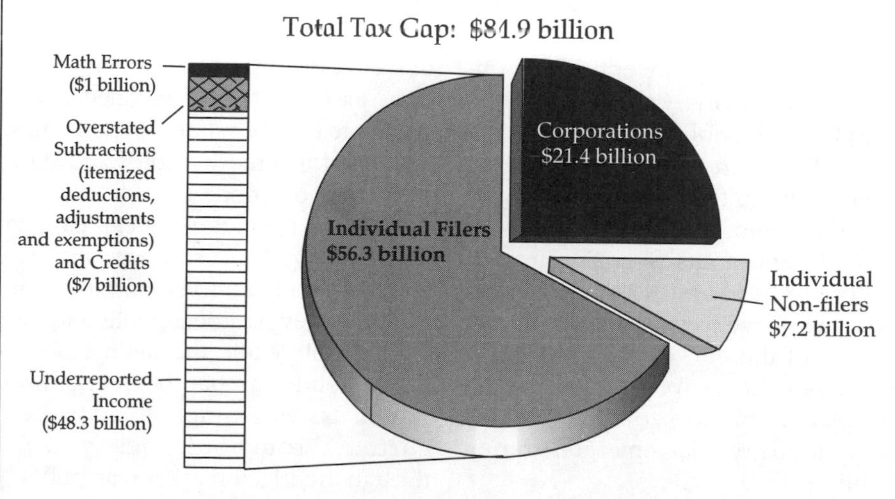

Source: Internal Revenue Service, Income Tax Compliance Research, *March 1988.*

BACKGROUND

Tax Evasion

Americans have always had ambivalent feelings about taxation. Resistance to taxes imposed by England found expression in the Boston Tea Party and eventually fueled the American Revolution. This tradition has continued to be a strong current in the American civic culture. Political candidates can always count on winning public support when they include tax cuts in their campaign platforms.

At the same time, Americans pride themselves on another component of the civic culture — voluntary compliance with the income tax laws. "Without the voluntary compliance of taxpayers," says Burtless, "it is hopeless to think that we could collect the amount of money that we do from the corporate or the personal income tax in this country."

The underground economy was not a significant issue in the United States until the income tax was introduced in the early years of this century. Since then, two periods stand out as boom years for underground transactions: Prohibition and World War II. [9]

Prohibition illustrates how declaring a booming sector of the economy illegal provides an incentive for underground activity. Congress banned the sale of alcoholic beverages in the United States in 1920 with the 18th Amendment to the Constitution. Tales of bathtub gin, speakeasies and underworld shootouts over liquor markets between gangster Al Capone and his rivals have become part of the folklore of the era. Beyond this anecdotal evidence, however, there is little information on the size of the bootleg liquor industry that emerged during Prohibition.

It has been estimated that sales of banned liquor totaled about $5 billion in 1929 and $4 billion in 1930. This was not only a huge market for the time, amounting to about 5 percent of total GDP, but it also was about the same size the industry would have been if Prohibition had never been imposed.

In 1933, Congress took heed of the failure of Prohibition and repealed the 18th Amendment. But the underground economy continued to thrive. The Depression, which began at the turn of the 1930s, led to widespread shortages of many goods, and the rise of black markets to meet the demand.

During World War II, price controls and rationing provided a different type of incentive to underground activity. The wartime Office of Price Administration (OPA) issued more than 600 price-cap regulations covering some 8 million goods and services. Through rationing, the agency also tried to control the distribution of essential goods and services to reserve adequate resources for the war effort and ensure that civilians had fair access to the products that were available.

The OPA had little more success against black marketeers than the liquor-control authorities had in enforcing Prohibition. Violations of wartime controls surfaced immediately, producing a vast black market in rationed goods that lasted throughout the war. From 1942 to 1947, the agency conducted more than a million investigations into the theft of rationed goods, counterfeiting of ration coupons, falsification of inventory records and short-weighting of goods.

Judging from the widespread nature of the violations, Americans were even less inclined to submit to rationing than they had been willing to give up alcohol. While the main violators of the liquor ban had been organized criminals, rationing violations occurred throughout society, even though the black market was publicly condemned as undermining the war effort. Some 20 percent of all meat eaten in the U.S. was sold on the black market, as was 5 percent of the gasoline. Tax evasion went hand in hand with rationing violations, and the tax gap amounted to several billion dollars by the end of the war.

One measure of the wartime underground economy was the vast amount of cash in circulation — $25.3 billion in 1945 compared with only $8.4 billion in 1941. A large portion of this extra cash was in $50 and $100 bills, the large denominations that serve as barometers of the underground economy because they are used for bulk purchases. At the same time, smaller-denomination bills, frequently used for individual cash purchases in the formal economy, diminished as a proportion of the money supply. By the end of the war, there was a $13 billion surplus in the cash in circulation above the amount that could be accounted for by legal cash purchases.

Rise of Labor Laws

In addition to tax evasion and black markets, another common characteristic of the underground economy long has been the exploitation of workers. Since the beginning of industrialization in the 1880s, sweatshops have employed workers at low pay and under poor conditions. Typically, sweatshops have operated in neighborhoods that are home to recent immigrants, whose lack of proficiency in English and knowledge of American customs make them easy prey to unscrupulous entrepreneurs.

Among the earliest sweatshops were garment factories, typically located in tenements of New York City and Chicago, where immigrants, including children, often worked 15- or 16-hour days for less than $10 a week. By 1901, at least 50,000 workers were employed in more than 20,000 apparel sweatshops in New York. The appalling conditions in these establishments were

Continued on p. 205

Chronology

1920s-1930s

Prohibition and the Depression spark the first major boom in the underground economy.

1920
The 18th Amendment to the Constitution bans the sale of alcoholic beverages in the United States, ushering in an era of widespread underground activity controlled largely by crime syndicates and based on the illegal sale of liquor.

1933
Faced with Prohibition's ineffectiveness in curtailing liquor consumption, Congress repeals the 18th Amendment. At the same time, black markets proliferate to make up for shortages of many goods caused by widespread business failures during the Depression.

1938
The Fair Labor Standards Act restricts employment of children, sets a minimum wage and requires employers to keep records of all employees' hours and earnings. The law is aimed in part at curtailing worker exploitation for underground activities.

1940s

Rationing during World War II sustains a sweeping black market in rationed goods.

1947
By the end of the war, about a fifth of all meat and 5 percent of all gasoline consumed in the United States come from underground suppliers. The annual revenue loss due to this untaxed black market activity amounts to several billion dollars.

1950s-1960s

Broader health insurance coverage and other changes in the ways consumers pay for goods and services restrict opportunities for underground transactions.

1965
Passage of Medicare and Medicaid, health insurance for the elderly and the poor, establishes a paper trail that makes it harder for dentists and physicians to evade taxation on much of their income.

1970s

Congress begins enacting a series of sweeping tax reforms, making it harder for individuals and small businesses to comply with the rules.

1970
The Occupational Safety and Health Act (OSHA) authorizes enforcement of workplace safety rules and requires employers to keep records of their employees' injuries and illnesses. The law strengthens the government's hand against the underground economy, as OSHA violators are frequently off-the-books businesses.

1977
Lawmakers enact changes in the rates and effective dates for Social Security payroll taxes.

1980s

Economists during the administration of President Ronald Reagan blame taxes and regulations imposed during the previous administration for a surge in underground transactions.

1983
The Internal Revenue Service (IRS) estimates that the Treasury loses about $10 billion a year in unrecovered tax revenue from illegal transactions in the underground economy, such as drug trafficking, prostitution and illegal gambling. Congress again alters the rules for reporting and paying Social Security payroll taxes.

1986
The Immigration Reform and Control Act shifts to employers the responsibility for determining whether a job applicant is an illegal alien and thus ineligible to work in the United States. The law is intended in part to curtail the exploitation of illegal immigrants, a mainstay of the underground labor force.

1990s

The underground economy is thought to total some $600 billion a year, about a tenth of the official economy.

1992
The IRS estimates that the tax gap — the amount of money the Treasury would have received if had taxes been paid on underground transactions — amounts to about $114 billion.

Hiring a Housekeeper Without the Hassle

Unfortunately for Zoë Baird, Judge Kimba M. Wood and a few other Clinton administration nominees, Home/Work Solutions came along too late to help them avoid problems with domestic workers.

But many other families who want to hire housekeepers have turned to the Silver Spring, Md., firm, which was founded in March 1993, as a direct result of Nannygate. The nationwide service even advertises by inviting prospective clients to "get legal" by letting it handle the paperwork associated with domestics employed in the above-ground economy.

"We take care of registering you with the state and federal governments for your employer identifications," says President Kathleen Webb, "and we work with you to decide which taxes are going to be withheld, particularly income taxes." Employers are not required to withhold income taxes for domestic employers, but Webb says many do so.

Domestic employment, though it generally involves few skills and low wages, accounts for a relatively large portion of the underground economy. (*See table, p. 197.*) Thus, the Internal Revenue Service and state financial agencies are eager to bring it into the official economy.

Kathleen Webb

Demographic trends suggest that the demand for domestic workers will continue to grow. As more and more women enter the labor force, families will need nannies and babysitters to care for children during the day. And the rapidly growing population of older Americans also enhances the demand for domestic workers.

"Although better than half of the workers employed by our clients are nannies, elder-care workers are becoming a growing portion of our business," Webb says. "Many elderly people are having companions live in, and even the adult children of the elderly will pay to have someone live in with their parent to delay the slide into a nursing home."

Bureaucratic red tape accounts for much of the firm's success, says Webb. Employers of domestic workers must deal with two types of confusing regulations. The first involves immigration laws, which apply because recent immigrants are frequently the main providers of babysitting, gardening and house-cleaning services.

Under the 1986 Immigration Reform and Control Act, it is the employer's responsibility to screen out illegal immigrants, who are not allowed to work in this country. Employers must verify a worker's status by examining a passport or other document, and they must keep records of hiring and termination dates, as well as wages paid. Hiring an undocumented alien is punishable by up to six months in prison and a $3,000 fine.

Employers face even more complicated regulations in complying with tax laws. The IRS requires employers to file forms every three months for the payment of Social Security withholding taxes on any employees making at least $50 a calendar quarter. These taxes, currently 15.3 percent of earnings, are paid by both workers and employers and entitle workers to receive disability and retirement benefits.

A household that pays a worker more than $1,000 during a calendar quarter must also pay a federal unemployment tax. At the end of the year, the employer is required to provide a completed W-2 wage statement for each domestic worker, who must then submit the form as part of the 1040 individual income tax declaration. Failure to file the forms or pay the required taxes carries fines plus the payment of any back taxes and interest. In addition to these federal requirements, each state taxes and regulates domestic employment.

For about $200 a year, plus an initial $60 registration fee, employers can hand the whole paperwork burden over to Webb. "Most of our clients are professionals who understand the value of time," she says. "Rather than spending an hour every quarter putting together the paperwork, they prefer to pay someone to do it for them."

Sobered by the lessons of Nannygate, many affluent Americans who long have skirted the law are pressing Congress to make it easier for them to legally engage nannies and other domestic workers. Lawmakers have responded to public protests that the regulations involving domestic employment are unnecessarily complex.

Sen. Daniel Patrick Moynihan, D-N.Y., has introduced a bill that would require tax payments only for domestic employees age 18 or older who earn about $610 a month. A less sweeping bill sponsored by Rep. Barbara B. Kennelly, D-Conn., would raise the earnings threshold to $800 a year and exclude payments for employees under 16.

The prospects for passage of either bill this year appear remote. Meanwhile, employers of domestic workers must continue to deal with the current regulatory headaches or find someone to help.

"Most average people who are hiring housekeepers or nannies don't even know where in the government to turn to get the forms and information," Webb says. "It's not like you can walk into the post office and pick them up. We know what needs to be filed, when it needs to be filed and how to go about doing it. We offer them peace of mind."

† For background, see "Child Care," *The CQ Researcher*, Dec. 17, 1993, pp. 1105-1128.

Continued from p. 202
brought to light by the Triangle Shirtwaist Factory Fire of 1911, in which nearly 150 women died. [10]

Congress tried as early as 1917 to ban perhaps the most egregious form of worker exploitation — child labor. But the Supreme Court declared that law unconstitutional, as well as a 1922 statute.

It was not until the 1930s that legislation prohibiting labor exploitation took effect. Once the new restrictions were in place, employers who violated them frequently became part of the underground economy. Employers who pay less than the minimum wage, for example, will often fail to report any wage payments to prevent the authorities from discovering their violations and subjecting them to financial penalties or prison sentences.

The 1938 Fair Labor Standards Act set minimal standards for child labor, restricting employment of children to certain jobs and setting maximum working hours according to age. The law also set a minimum wage and required employers to keep records of each employee's hours and earnings.

Although states and localities had long set building codes as well as health and safety regulations, it was not until 1970 that Congress established federal regulations with the Occupational Safety and Health Act (OSHA). The law authorizes enforcement of rules to assure "safe and healthful working conditions" by federal or state agencies and requires employers to keep records of their workers' injuries and illnesses. OSHA violations can cost employers up to $10,000 for each incident.

Finally, in 1986, Congress tried to stem the flow of illegal immigrants into the United States by cracking down on their employment — and, often, their exploitation — by American businesses. The Immigration Reform and Control Act imposes sanctions for hiring workers who lack valid documents that permit them to work in the United States.

The purpose of employer sanctions is twofold. In addition to diminishing the lure of the United States to aliens in search of employment, the law also is intended to discourage unscrupulous entrepreneurs from exploiting illegal immigrants by paying them less than the minimum wage and forcing them to work in substandard conditions.

U.S. Coast Guard

The underground economy includes the businesses of drugs, prostitution and illicit gambling. In 1983, the last time the IRS tried to measure the illegal economy, it estimated its worth in lost tax revenues at $10 billion. Here U.S. Coast Guardsmen confiscate smuggled marijuana off the Florida coast.

Economists Disagree

The slow growth and high inflation of the late 1970s and early '80s unleashed a tide of public indignation against government regulations and taxes. Conservative economists proclaimed that the cure for the nation's economic woes was to be found in the "magic of the marketplace," unfettered by unnecessary regulatory and fiscal burdens to free enterprise. Ronald Reagan, the Republican candidate in the 1980 presidential election, rode the anti-tax bandwagon to the White House, where he continued to promote tax cuts and deregulation as the centerpiece of his domestic policy.

Some economists at the time pointed to the underground economy as evidence of the distortions caused by taxation and regulation. [11] "There was a huge flurry of discussion about the underground economy at that time," says David Levine.

Peter M. Gutmann, an economics professor at Baruch College of the City University of New York, produced a typical analysis. Gutmann estimated that untaxed transactions amounted to $177 billion in 1976, the equivalent of 10 percent of the total output of goods and services in the official economy. [12] An even higher estimate was made by Edgar L. Feige, an economist at the University of Wisconsin-Madison, who placed the value of the underground economy as high as $704 billion, an astounding 27 percent of the GDP. [13]

These estimates were dismissed by critics such as Levine, who today says the studies amounted to little more than a "game of one-upmanship and very bad analysis. If you think about it carefully," he says, "even the figure of 10 percent of GDP is a joke."

At the same time that economists were describing an ever-growing un-

The Underground Economy Thrives Abroad

Experts peg the value of the U.S. underground economy at $600 billion — roughly 10 percent of the gross domestic product (GDP) — and all of it goes untaxed. By any measure, that's a lot of money — but it pales in comparison to the underground economies of many other countries.

Measuring the underground economy of other nations is at least as imprecise a science as assessing off-the-books activity in the United States. But accord-ing to Edgar L. Feige, an economics professor at the University of Wisconsin-Madison, "The world economy appears to subsume a hidden economy which employs U.S. currency as its medium of exchange and is roughly 90 percent as large as the U.S. economy." [1]

That would put the size of the global underground economy at a staggering $5.8 trillion.

According to Gary Burtless, an economist at the Brookings Institution, the underground economy "doesn't seem to be nearly as serious in the United States as it is in many Third World countries."

Bartering and cash purchases are typical of less-developed economies, making it hard for governments to collect taxes on many transactions. The United Nations International Labor Organization estimates that the informal economy employs 59 percent of the urban labor force throughout sub-Saharan Africa and accounts for as much as half the GDP of some countries in the region. [2]

AP/Wide World Photo

Cars enter the U.S. from Canada via the Peace Bridge in Buffalo, N.Y. Sales of contraband goods from the U.S. are a leading component of Canada's $25 billion underground economy.

Even among industrial nations, the United States does a better job of capturing tax revenues than many of its peers. "It's a much more severe problem in Italy than it is in the United States," Burtless says. "It's probably bigger even in countries that have very good statistical systems, such as Sweden, where enforcement is quite zealous and where they have terrific public servants."

One reason for the disparity among industrial nations, Burtless says, can be traced to tax rates. "If you look at tax burdens in the United States, they are not terribly heavy by world standards," he says. "I know Americans think they are, but that's because they don't compare them with those in other countries, and they don't realize how modest are the withholdings from our incomes in relation to those that citizens of other advanced industrialized countries have to pay."

In Sweden, he says, middle-class families pay as much as 80 percent of their incomes in taxes. "If you face a marginal tax rate like that in Sweden," he says, "there is a terrific incentive to be in the underground economy and to evade taxation by bartering services."

Closer to home, Canada long has tried to stem a burgeoning trade in contraband goods from the United States, where many items cost less. Contraband activity, a leading component of Canada's underground economy, has increased since 1991, when a 7 percent national sales tax was adopted.

In an effort to reduce one of the industrial world's largest budget deficits, Canada's newly elected Liberal Party government has pledged to crack down on Canada's estimated $25 billion underground economy. [3]

But when it comes to really big underground economies, Mexico is in a class by itself. South of the border, according to Mexico's National Chamber of Manufacturing Industries, the informal economy involves nearly a quarter of the entire labor force. [4]

[1] Edgar L. Feige, "The Underground Economy and the Currency Enigma," a paper presented at a conference of the International Institute of Public Finance, Aug. 23-26, 1993, in Berlin, Germany.

[2] See Michael A. Hiltzik, "Making Money Under Africa's Fierce Sun," *Los Angeles Times*, Washington Edition, April 30, 1991.

[3] See Anne Swardson, "Canadians Pay Cash and Skip the Tax," *The Washington Post*, Feb. 16, 1994.

[4] See "Mexico's Underground Economy," *The Wall Street Journal*, Oct. 9, 1991.

derground economy, Levine says, the percentage of workers who were self-employed had been dropping for several decades, largely as a result of the decline in the number of self-employed farmers. "Since the self-employed are the main cheaters and the ones with the main opportunity to cheat," he says, "it was certainly inconceivable that the underground economy had doubled or tripled as some were saying."

The reason for the flurry of studies had more to do with politics than economics, according to Wiegand. "All this talk about the underground economy helped relieve the decade-long angst middle-class Americans were feeling about their declining economic position," he wrote. "Two years of sensational publicity and dramatic news coverage articulated their sense of relative deprivation. . . . It legitimated their off-the-books income. Moreover, by coining a catchy new phrase ("the underground economy"), it was as if economists had finally discovered, and could now prescribe a (political) cure for, the root problems plaguing the American economy." [14]

Lending support to this argument was the fact that attention to the underground economy faded after the tax cut of 1981. Few studies, official or academic, have appeared since the early 1980s. ■

CURRENT SITUATION

Foiling Tax Cheaters

Some critics of the earlier estimates of a vast underground economy say it probably is even smaller today because of financial innovations and the stricter reporting requirements that appeared during the 1980s. "For years and years, people substantially underreported their interest income," says Levine. "That's no longer true because with the 1099 form, and computerization, the IRS has ways to find you."

Instituted in the late 1970s, the 1099 form reports dividends and interest from corporations, banks and mutual funds to the IRS, enabling the agency to compare information provided by tax filers with financial information supplied by the issuing bank or corporation. At the same time, the agency also began requiring restaurateurs to report estimates of the tips their waiters receive.

Another deterrent to tax cheating is the growing use of credit cards. Cash transactions, the main type of exchange as recently as 20 years ago, have been largely replaced by credit card transactions. Buying with plastic leaves a paper trail that includes receipts held by retailers and customers, as well as monthly statements. These statements and receipts are commonly used to document credits and deductions on income tax returns and are readily available to the IRS when it audits returns.

Another obstacle to hiding income, particularly among self-employed physicians and other health-care providers, is the spread of public and private health insurance over the past several decades. "Physicians were one of the main cheating groups in the 1950s because they were largely paid in cash by patients," Levine says. "Today, with Medicaid and Medicare as well as private insurance, physicians leave a visible paper trail."

New Immigration Laws

A potentially significant deterrent to underground activity is the requirement under the 1986 immigration law that employers screen potential employees to ensure that they are permitted to work in the United States. Congress passed the law in response to calls to strengthen the ban on the employment of illegal aliens following a dramatic increase in both legal and illegal immigration during the 1980s. [15] Employers are now responsible for determining the authenticity of immigrants' documents and must fill out a form — the I-9 — to prove they have complied with the law.

Because the law has been in effect only a short time, there is some disagreement about its effectiveness. Even less certain is its impact on the underground economy, which has been bolstered over the past decade by growing numbers of illegal aliens. To avoid detection by the authorities and certain deportation, they often are more willing than legal residents to work off the books and under substandard conditions.

The Immigration and Naturalization Service (INS) reports that about 10 percent of illegal aliens who became legal residents upon passage of the 1986 law were paid below the federal minimum wage of $3.35 an hour at the time they applied for legal status. Thirteen percent reported that they worked more than 40 hours a week but were not paid time-and-a-half for overtime, as federal law requires for most occupations. [16]

Violations of labor laws often go hand in hand with tax evasion. "Some of these jobs are in the informal economy as well as the formal economy," says Adams of the University of Michigan, who points out that some agricultural businesses are not required to pay the minimum wage. "Whether anybody should have access to this kind of cheap labor by ignoring the minimum wage laws ignores the argument that people could and should have a lot better job opportunities," he says.

But some economists say the underground economy, even with its often substandard working conditions, offers certain advantages to new immigrants. "No one is holding a gun to their heads and forcing them to work for $3 an hour," says Burtless. "Presumably, they're happier being in the United States working off the books for $3 an hour than they would have been in Nicaragua, Ireland or Southeast Asia, and the employer is certainly happier. The tax loss to the rest of us is a matter of some moment, but I'm not sure that the fact that they're working for less than the minimum wage is a significant issue."

Even among recent immigrants, enforcement records show that tax evasion occurs among the success stories as well as the downtrodden. "Here in New York, you have tax cheating anywhere you've got a cash business, be it retail or wholesale," says enforcement director Stanton.

Stanton says that immigrant neighborhoods are major centers of cash-based, off-the-books transactions. "It's found in ethnic marketplace areas, each of which may be a block with 17 to 20 retail stores that deal only with a certain ethnic group," he says. "In addition to restaurants, there are stores selling all sorts of things — electronics, beer, liquor, gold and jewelry — all for cash." he says. And the sums are often substantial. "One gold vendor took in $100,000 on a weekend."

In Stanton's view, cultural tradition plays a large part in tax evasion at all earnings levels in places that are home to many recently arrived immigrants, such as New York. When he asked an offender why many recent immigrants fail to collect or forward the local sales tax on their transactions, for example, Stanton says he was told, "That's the way it's done in other countries, and there's no reason to change when they get over here." (*See story, p. 206.*)

Evaders on the Rise?

If the underground economy is indeed expanding, poorly paid immigrants may be only a small part of the problem. "I suspect that most of the people in the informal sector are not paid less than the minimum wage," says the Brookings Institution's Burtless. "I suspect that the great majority of them are paid more than the minimum wage. It's just that they would prefer to receive the payments off the books."

These tax cheaters include doctors, lawyers and other high-earning professionals, he says. "I'm not sure that the typical underground economy transaction is between someone who is hopelessly exploited and gets a very, very low wage and a mean capitalistic employer," Burtless says. "I would think a lot of the people in the underground economy are actually themselves entrepreneurial capitalists seeking to avoid taxation, pure and simple."

Tax enforcement authorities confirm Burtless' suspicions. Despite the easy to follow paper trail being left today by public and private health insurance forms, physicians in private practice remain some of the biggest tax cheats, according to Stanton. "Most of them are in some kind of insurance plan," he says, "but if they should be fortunate to have cash-paying patients that aren't covered by insurance, many times those payments won't be shown."

In his 18 years in tax enforcement, Stanton says he's found it's harder to deter tax cheating by physicians than by other entrepreneurs, who tend to become compliant if they see one of their competitors caught and forced to pay heavy fines. "Doctors are not an industry that enforcement has a tremendous effect on," he says. "For them, it's every man for himself. They have their own individual pride and egos, so they'll continue to do it on their own anyway."

In Wiegand's view, off-the-books activities are on the rise, and not just because of physicians and immigrant entrepreneurs. "The trend toward downsizing and post-Fordism — getting out of the assembly-line mentality — has led to the breakdown of businesses into more flexible units through subcontracting," he says. "It used to be that when a company went out of business it went bankrupt. Now you get together for a project and work only for the duration of that project."

"All these new corporate [structures] popping up and disappearing offer a tempting lure to avoid taxation and a very fertile ground for doing creative accounting," Wiegand adds.

Another result of downsizing is the increase in numbers of self-employed consultants, many of them former corporate managers with specialized expertise they can sell to many different businesses. "You can be a company out of your own home now," Wiegand says, "and that makes it much more difficult to get a reading on tax compliance."

Today's work environment offers more opportunities for expansion of the underground economy on the labor side as well. The permanent layoffs that come with corporate downsizing leave large numbers of unemployed workers competing for jobs at the same time. For many of them, Wiegand says, off-the-books employment is an essential tool for survival. "The disappearance of whole sectors of the production process means that adaptations to unemployment have changed," he says, "and off-the-books employment has become part of the workers' strategy for dealing with the labor market."

Wiegand says the number of double jobholders has been growing as workers try to maintain the standard of living they enjoyed with the high-wage, full-time industrial jobs they lost to downsizing. "There is much more self-employment and double job-holding among workers today," he says. ■

OUTLOOK

Closing the Tax Gap

The IRS and state and local tax-collection agencies are expected to step up their efforts to capture more tax revenues from the underground economy, whatever its size. The rea-

Continued on p. 210

At Issue:

Are government regulations chiefly responsible for the emergence of the underground economy?

yes

JEFFREY TUCKER

***Associate Editor of the* Austrian Economics Newsletter and editor of the Free Market**
FROM *POLICY REVIEW,* THE HERITAGE FOUNDATION, SUMMER 1993.

Government policies usually have unintended consequences, but one effect is literally invisible to policymakers. When regulations get too complex or costly, or taxes too high, employers, workers and entrepreneurs sometimes move outside the official system and into . . . the "the informal sector. . . ."

The informal economy is as capitalistic as the formal economy, for it involves entrepreneurship, trade, saving, working, wages and capital, as in the formal economy. Moreover, the existence of the informal sector should be seen as a failing of government, not the market. Regulation drives people outside the official economy.

Today, nearly every industry and service, every profession and every dollar earned are subject to some dictate from Washington. The labor code mandates that only people of a certain age can work ("child" labor laws) and that people of low marginal product cannot ("minimum wage"). Laws mandate that businesses provide a myriad of benefits to employees that are often prohibitively expensive. State and local governments have their own regulations, from zoning ordinances to rental restrictions. These interventions create conditions that sometimes make going informal more attractive than staying official.

If, for example, you buy a cheesecake your neighbor baked in her kitchen, you are probably engaging in an illegal act, depending on local and state laws. There are health and equipment regulations, and specifications for the kitchen's size. The effect is to create a monopoly for restaurants, but it is also to criminalize what seems to be a perfectly natural economic arrangement. If a family rents a room to a student, even though the area is zoned to prohibit rental use, the family becomes informal. When parents employ their underage children in the family, they break the law and qualify as informal. The same is true for the informal handyman who has no office or license. . . .

If governments fail to change their legal structures to accommodate informals, and regulatory trends in this country continue . . . the informal sector will expand beyond its current scope. The growing informal economy is a testament to the resilience and ingenuity of people when confronted with governments that want to manage their economic life — and a reminder that total economic control will always be beyond government's reach.

no

SASKIA SASSEN

Professor of Urban Planning, Columbia University
FROM *"THE INFORMAL ECONOMY: BETWEEN NEW DEVELOPMENTS AND OLD REGULATIONS," THE YALE LAW JOURNAL,* JUNE 1994

The expansion of the informal economy in the U.S. is rooted partly in conditions that are an integral part of our economy. Immigrants have known how to seize the "opportunities" contained in this combination of conditions, but they cannot be said to cause the informal economy. . . .

The broader conditions in the U.S. that are contributing to the expansion of the informal economy can be briefly summarized as (a) the shift to a service economy and (b) the growing earnings inequality. . . .

Over the last 15 years, economic growth has assumed specific organizational and spatial forms. Large cities have lost manufacturing, warehousing, wholesaling and other such industries providing good jobs to low-income communities. Growth in these and other smaller cities has largely consisted of service growth, particularly business services and finance. Spatially, this type of growth tends to be concentrated in the downtowns of cities (or in suburban office complexes and edge cities). Thus low-income communities have lost blue-collar jobs and are not well-positioned to share in the new forms of growth. . . .

Different types of economic growth produce different types of earnings distributions. The forms of growth in the 1980s produced growing inequality in earnings, as has now been evident in large cities, which are now being seen as "dual cities." My research on New York City suggests that the growth of the informal economy in that city is related to this growth in inequality.

How should the government deal with this growing informal economy? The easiest way, perhaps, is to criminalize it . . . . New York City enacted such a policy. The result? Newsstands and small restaurants in low-income communities were closed; with them went not only some of the few economic activities around but also some of the few "public" space anchors in these communities. Such a policy may make sense from the perspective of a narrow reading of the regulations. But from an economic perspective it does not. Rather, we need to find ways to upgrade these activities, bring them under the regulatory framework without adding costs to the entrepreneurs involved. . . .

Why should we bother to upgrade the informal economy in low-income communities? Because it is one of the few forms of economic growth evident in these communities.

Continued from p. 208

son: Rising budget deficits are forcing governments to scramble for money. And closing the tax gap is always a more politically acceptable way to do that than the alternatives — raising tax rates or cutting services.

"We want to be certain that taxpayers believe that the tax laws are being applied fairly and uniformly," said Loretta Argrett, the newly appointed assistant attorney general for the Justice Department's tax division. "The mission of the division is to ensure that there is fair and uniform compliance and, furthermore, when there is not compliance, that those people who should be prosecuted are prosecuted. [17]

Agencies have several tools to collect revenues from the underground economy. Beginning in the mid-1980s, the IRS offered a carrot and stick to tax cheats with a program called Compliance 2000. The agency promised it would waive all penalties for past violations if cheaters started reporting their true income and paying taxes, coupled with the threat of severe penalties for future violations. "The IRS decided that fear doesn't increase voluntary compliance with the tax code," says Wiegand. "But more recently, the IRS has realized that it can't let down its enforcement guard. I think you're going to see more and more enforcement from the agency in coming years."

The IRS already recovers about 15 percent of unpaid taxes each year through enforcement. Computerization, which has been integrated into IRS activities over the past decade, is expected to continue to enhance the IRS's programs, such as computer matching of tax returns against third-party information documents, including W-2 employer withholding statements and 1099 interest statements filed by banks. Computers also greatly improve the agency's ability to verify math errors and collect overdue taxes. [18]

On the local level, attempts at strengthening enforcement efforts to catch tax cheaters are running into the same budget cuts the renewed enforcement efforts are designed to prevent. Like other government agencies, finance departments may be forced to reduce their staffs at the same time they are expected to capture additional revenues.

In New York City, for example, Stanton's tax enforcement unit has just 30 investigators for the entire city of 7.5 million people. "Let's put it this way," he says, "every agent we have earns his keep and then some."

Stanton says his department responds to all complaints of tax cheating. But with such a small staff, he has found that arresting the big offenders has the greatest effect because it sends a powerful message to other tax cheats. "Many times, we do a case in just one neighborhood or one industry, and the word gets out," he says. "There really is a ripple effect in all these cases because others see that they aren't impenetrable, that their own records could be found out, too."

Although he thinks tax violators are especially creative in New York City, Stanton faults tax accountants all over the country for encouraging people to cheat the government. "Maybe their industry has become so competitive that they feel they have to outdo the next guy to afford the taxpayer the biggest refund," he says. Although their clients are ultimately responsible for any unlawful behavior on their behalf, Stanton adds, "many accountants are part of the problem of the underground economy."

Like most experts on tax evasion, Stanton has little hope that his or any other government agency will ever be able to eliminate the problem entirely. "In the future, if all purchases go on plastic, replacing cash, it will have a tremendous effect on the small-time underground vendor," he says. "But the very bright — who can bring in large sums in cash and alter the books — will always find a way." ■

Notes

[1] See Internal Revenue Service, *Income Tax Compliance Research: Gross Tax Gap Estimates and Projections for 1973-1992*, March 1988. Another IRS study using different methodology estimated the tax loss at up to $127 billion for 1992. See also Karen Pennar and Christopher Farrell, "Notes from the Underground Economy," *Business Week*, Feb. 15, 1993, pp. 98-101.

[2] Internal Revenue Service, *ibid.*, p. 7.

[3] James D. Smith and Terry K. Adams, "The Measurement of Selected Income Flows in Informal Markets 1981 and 1985-1986," University of Michigan, April 1987.

[4] See Frank Swoboda, "U.S. Companies Speed Pace of Downsizing," *The Washington Post*, Feb. 9, 1994. For background, see "Downward Mobility," *The CQ Researcher*, July 23, 1993, pp. 625-648.

[5] Smith and Adams, *op. cit.*

[6] Congressional Budget Office, *The Economic and Budget Outlook: Fiscal Years 1995-1999*, January 1994.

[7] The 1992 figure is a projection. See Internal Revenue Service, *Income Tax Compliance Research: Net Tax Gap and Remittance Gap Estimates*, 1990.

[8] Internal Revenue Service, *op. cit.*, March 1988.

[9] Unless otherwise noted, information in this section is based on Barry Molefsky, "America's Underground Economy," in Vito Tanzi, ed., *The Underground Economy in the United States and Abroad* (1982).

[10] See U.S. General Accounting Office, " 'Sweatshops' in the U.S.: Opinions on Their Extent and Possible Enforcement Options," August 1988.

[11] For background on the theories presented at the time, see "The Underground Economy," *Editorial Research Reports*, April 6, 1984, pp. 249-268.

[12] Peter M. Gutmann, "The Subterranean Economy," *Financial Analysts Journal*, 1977.

[13] Edgar L. Feige, "How Big Is the Irregular Economy?" *Challenge*, November-December 1979.

[14] Bruce Wiegand, *Off the Books: A Theory and Critique of the Underground Economy* (1992), pp. 71-72.

[15] For background, see "Immigration Reform," *The CQ Researcher*, Sept. 24, 1993, pp. 841-864.

[16] Immigration and Naturalization Service, *Immigration Reform and Control Act: Report on the Legalized Alien Population*, March 1992. The minimum wage has since been raised to $4.25 an hour.

[17] Argrett spoke at a Justice Department press briefing Jan. 14, 1994.

[18] Internal Revenue Service, *op. cit.* (March 1988), p. 4.

Bibliography

Selected Sources Used

Books

Fix, Michael, ed. *The Paper Curtain: Employer Sanctions' Implementation, Impact, and Reform*, Urban Institute Press, 1991.

The authors present a collection of essays dealing with various aspects of the 1986 Immigration Reform and Control Act, which seeks to protect illegal workers from exploitation and control the underground economy by imposing sanctions on employers who hire illegal aliens.

Sassen, Saskia, *The Global City*, Princeton University Press Paperbacks, 1993.

A widening of the gap between rich and poor in big cities such as New York and London is fostering the expansion of underground activities, the author writes. High-income households demand the kinds of labor-intensive services and goods that low-wage, off-the-books workers can provide.

Tanzi, Vito, ed., *The Underground Economy in the United States and Abroad*, Lexington Books, 1982.

This collection of studies from several countries highlights the problem of measuring underground transactions as well as determining what policies promote or curtail them. Those who claim high taxes promote underground activities, for example, point to Sweden, where high taxes coexist with a burgeoning underground economy.

Wiegand, Bruce, *Off the Books: A Theory and Critique of the Underground Economy*, General Hall, 1992.

In contrast to conservative economists, who in the early 1980s claimed that tax cuts would greatly reduce the underground economy, Wiegand argues that off-the-books transactions are a permanent component of the country's economic activities.

Articles

Dalglish, Brenda, "Cheaters," *MacLean's*, Aug. 9, 1993.

Selling smuggled U.S.-made goods has long been a mainstay of underground activities in Canada. Following the introduction of a federal sales tax in 1991, however, the underground economy has expanded. Tax evasion has become so widespread that the tax gap, estimated at $30 billion, would pay off Canada's budget deficit, says the author.

McDonald, Richard J., "The 'Underground Economy' and BLS Statistical Data," *Monthly Labor Review*, January 1984.

The Bureau of Labor Statistics responds to critics of the early 1980s who claimed that the agency's data on unemployment and productivity were grossly inaccurate because they did not take underground transactions into account. The article presents an exhaustive review of the literature on the underground economy in refuting those claims.

Pennar, Karen, and Christopher Farrell, "Notes from the Underground Economy," *Business Week*, Feb. 15, 1993.

The authors contend that several factors are contributing to the spread of the underground economy, including the growing number of immigrants; a widening income gap between rich and poor; resistance to taxation; corporate downsizing and a sluggish job market.

Reports and Studies

Feige, Edgar L., *The Underground Economy and the Currency Enigma*, paper presented at a conference of the International Institute of Public Finance, Aug. 23-26, 1993, in Berlin, Germany.

Feige concludes that a vast global underground economy explains why about 80 percent of the U.S. currency in circulation outside the banking system cannot be found.

Internal Revenue Service, *Income Tax Compliance Research: Gross Tax Gap Estimates and Projections for 1973-1992*, Publication 7285, March 1988.

The IRS estimates that the income tax gap — the amount of taxes due but uncollected from underground transactions — amounted to $85 billion in 1987. The bulk of unpaid taxes was attributed to individuals who underreported their incomes.

Internal Revenue Service, *Income Tax Compliance Research: Net Tax Gap and Remittance Gap Estimates* (Supplement to Publication 7285), Publication 1415, April 1990.

This supplement to the 1988 tax gap report presents new estimates based on what the IRS was able to collect from delinquent taxpayers through enforcement efforts.

Smith, James D., and Terry K. Adams, *The Measurement of Selected Income Flows in Informal Markets: 1981 and 1985-1986*, University of Michigan, April 1987.

Households bought about $84 billion worth of goods and services from underground providers, according to this survey. The biggest outlays were for home repairs, catering services, car repairs and housekeeping services.

The Next Step

Additional information from UMI's Newspaper & Periodical Abstracts database

The Drug Economy

Applegate, Jane, "Cash: Fed Branch Is the Greenest Spot in L.A.," ***Los Angeles Times*****, Dec. 17, 1990, p. D1.**
The heavy use of cash in Southern California is discussed. The heavy use is attributed to a thriving underground economy based on the drug trade and under-the-table laborers.

Marshall, Jonathan, "Untaxable Billions," ***San Francisco Chronicle*****, July 28, 1991, p. WOR13.**
Behind the $73 billion in foreign capital that entered the U.S. in 1990 without leaving any trace as to its nature or origin may lurk the darker reality of the size and impact of the huge underground economy of drug money.

Wimberley, Michael, "Business Is Booming in Underground Economy of Drug Trafficking," ***Michigan Chronicle*****, Aug. 12, 1992, p. A3.**
Detroit's thriving underground drug market is discussed. With the dropout rate at some of the city's high schools exceeding 50 percent, drug trafficking proves to be a lucrative business for those blacks who cannot find gainful employment.

The International Underground

Alganaraz, Julio, "The Italian Miracle Begins Underground," ***World Press Review*****, June 1987, pp. 50-51.**
In 1977-78, foreign observers saw Italy as a country brought to its knees by the oil crisis, trade-union troubles, terrorist havoc and the Mafia's ability to operate with impunity. The underground economy — small and medium-sized businesses that were capable of making enormous efforts to adapt — is discussed.

Bronshtein, Boris, "Crime," ***Current Digest of the Post-Soviet Press*****, March 24, 1993, pp. 22-23.**
Many of the once-large youth gangs in Tatarstan Russia have turned their attentions to the lucrative black market. The organized underground economy in the region is discussed.

Bruner, Richard W., "Unreported business in Hungary spreads budget's red ink," ***Christian Science Monitor*****, Nov. 15, 1993, p. 10.**
Four million Hungarians—nearly half the country's population of 10.5 million people—take part in the underground economy. The money generated makes up 24 percent of the country's GNP. Since much of this income would normally be taxed at a 40 percent level, the loss to the government is enormous.

Demchenko, Irina, "The economy," ***Current Digest of the Post-Soviet Press*****, June 24, 1992, p. 25.**
The second congress of the Interregional Exchange Union asserted that the economic conditions in the territory of the former USSR are encouraging illegal business and corruption in the state. The shadow economy and black markets are discussed.

"Into the Black," ***The Economist*****, Nov. 5, 1988, pp. 76-77.**
Black South Africa's "informal sector," the unlicensed, unrecorded and untaxed underground economy, may account for as much as 40 percent of the officially recorded GNP. The informal sector is surveyed.

Landay, Jonathan S., "Black market becomes mainstay of teetering Serbian economy," ***Christian Science Monitor*****, Oct. 13, 1993, p. 9.**
Amid the ravages of war and economic upheaval in Serbia, fueled in part by United Nations sanctions, black-market gypsies and underground business dealings have become the norm.

Langan, Fred, "Canada's underground economy brings in the big bills," ***Christian Science Monitor*****, Nov. 24, 1993, p. 8.**
The growth of the underground economy in Canada is discussed. The Canadian Federation of Independent Business and other economists estimate that the underground economy is 15 percent of the entire economy and the amount of currency in circulation is high.

Lorinc, John, "The Outlaw Advantage," ***Canadian Business*****, April 1992, pp. 38-43.**
More than 25 percent of 11,000 respondents to the November 1991 Canadian Federation of Independent Business survey said they lost business to "competitors operating in the underground economy." Taxation of Canadian businesses is discussed.

Main, Jeremy, "Third World Economies: A New Proposal," ***Current*****, July 1989, pp. 38-40.**
The underground economies of Third World countries are flourishing, but they are restricted by government regulations. Hernando de Soto, a Peruvian economist, argues that the average citizen of these countries needs support to carry the energy to formal programs. The economist's ideas for developing economic policy in Third World countries are presented.

"Mexico's Underground Economy," ***The Wall Street***

***Journal*, Oct. 9, 1991, p. A12.**

Mexico's underground economy involved 23 percent of the labor force in 1990, up sharply from 13 percent in 1986. The value of enterprises working off the books and paying no taxes accounted for 10 percent of the gross domestic product.

Opinions

Akst, Daniel, "Our Economy Is Anchored Underground," *Los Angeles Times*, June 18, 1991, p. D1.

Daniel Akst discusses the massive underground economy in California, and suggests that the ability of sole proprietorships to cheat on their taxes provides jobs for those who would otherwise be unemployed.

"Asides: The L.A. Underground," *The Wall Street Journal*, Sept. 29, 1992, p. A16.

An editorial notes the apparent flourishing of an underground economy in Los Angeles because of the impossible tax and regulatory burdens placed upon inner-city businesses.

"Cuba Libre," *San Francisco Chronicle*, Dec. 26, 1992, p. A18.

An editorial notes the emerging signs of an underground economy in Cuba.

Research and Studies

McCrohan, Kevin F. and James D. Smith, "A Consumer Expenditure Approach to Estimating the Size of the Underground Economy," *Journal of Marketing*, April 1986, pp. 48-60.

A study attempts to determine the level of unmeasured economic activity in the U.S. economy, through the use of a probability sample of households. It is concluded that consumers' use of suppliers in the underground economy accounts for a minor portion of consumer expenditures.

Young, Jae-Bok, "Underground sector of economy rises, posing problems for IRS," *Christian Science Monitor*, April 1, 1993, p. 9.

A report is given on the money the IRS loses to the underground economy. Some economists estimate that the size of the underground economy is between $500 billion and $700 billion, with tax evasion totals as much as $127 billion a year. They say that a rise in tax rates contributes to dishonesty and tax evasion.

Stemming the Underground Economy

Cowell, Alan, "Bureaucratic monster, a new tax form, eats Italy," *The New York Times*, June 19, 1993, p. A5.

Italy's shock in June 1993 in dealing with a new and incredibly complex and bureaucratic tax form is described. Accustomed to an economy run on an underground business network that does not pay taxes, Italians are finding adherence to new tax laws difficult.

Glain, Steve, "South Korea acts to control black money," *The Wall Street Journal*, Aug. 13, 1993, p. A4.

South Korean President Kim Young Sam staged a surprise raid on the country's huge underground economy by introducing a real-names financial transaction system. The move is expected to rattle Korea's equity markets and could hinder efforts to get the country's economic engine chugging again.

Kutler, Jeffrey, "Attorney Revives the Case for Banning Use of Cash," *American Banker*, March 1, 1991, p. 2.

Attorney Harvey F. Wachsman is profiled for his proposals to mandate the use of electronic payments systems and end the use of cash in the U.S. as a way to tax the underground economy.

Murray, Allen E., "How to Catch Tax Cheaters," *Fortune*, March 17, 1986, pp. 124-125.

A consumption tax would be a method of bringing the underground economy within the grasp of the IRS. Details surrounding the tax and its Congressional proposal are provided.

"World Wire: Greece Targets Tax Evaders," *The Wall Street Journal*, July 30, 1992, p. A10.

Greece hopes to use computers to recover $5 billion a year and shrink an underground economy that could account for half the country's GDP. In an effort to plan for EC monetary integration, Greece must save as much as $7.5 billion over the next two years.

"World wire: Seoul boosts business lendings," *The Wall Street Journal*, Aug. 17, 1993, p. A10.

Trying to lessen the adverse effects of new financial reforms aimed at stamping out corruption and collusion among politicians and a huge underground economy, South Korea's Finance Ministry added $766.6 million to an announced package of $472.9 million of special loans for small business that have difficulty securing loans through normal channels.

Street Vendors

DePalma, Anthony, "Underground economy popping up at curbside," *The New York Times*, Oct. 11, 1993, p. A4.

The growing number of street vendors in Mexico City who attempt to sell merchandise to motorists while they are stuck in traffic is discussed.

Sontag, Deborah, "Unlicensed peddlers, unfettered dreams," *The New York Times*, June 14, 1993, p. A1.

About 10,000 street vendors work illegally in New York City, becoming the most visible and controversial representatives of the city's expanding underground economy.

Public debate about their livelihood heated up recently as then-Mayor David Dinkins announced a crackdown on peddlers. (Part 2 of 6).

Taxes and the Underground Economy

Lodge, Arthur, "Annals of Taxation — Sleeping on a Corncob Mattress," ***Journal of Accountancy*****, April 1988, p. 110.**

An examination of what a government can do with people who will not pay their taxes is presented. Estimates of the size of taxes lost to the underground economy, where transactions are either illegal or, if legal, are unreported, have ranged as high as $800 billion a year. The amount, if recovered, would go a long way toward ending the perennial budget deficit.

Newman, Peter C., "The secret boom: Our underground economy," ***Maclean's*****, Aug. 9, 1993, p. 38.**

A proposed wealth tax is causing a tax revolt in Canada, where citizens are still angry about the Goods and Services Tax (GST) that was introduced in 1991. An increasing number of Canadians are turning to the underground economy to avoid paying taxes.

Quint, Barbara Gilder, "How you may be cheating Uncle Sam," ***Glamour*****, July 1993, pp. 86-87.**

Without realizing it, many Americans are involved in the underground economy, through which between $500 billion and $750 billion changes hands in such areas as child care, street vending and restaurant work involving tips. The problem of unreported income is discussed.

Trager, Louis, "Underground economy costs billions in taxes," ***San Francisco Chronicle*****, Feb. 14, 1993, p. E1.**

Tens of millions of people and companies, engaged in lawful pursuits, neglect to pay income taxes. Examples are presented of common types of tax fraud.

White, Charles A., "Dodging the tax collector," ***Canada & the World*****, January 1994, pp. 6-7.**

Tax avoidance, which means taking advantage of every possible loophole in the tax laws to reduce the total tax payable, is legal while tax evasion is not. The emergence of a huge underground economy in Canada that cheats governments of revenue and penalizes honest taxpayers is discussed.

Underground Businesses

Langan, Fred, "Canada moving to check cigarette, alcohol smuggling," ***Boston Globe*****, Nov. 27, 1993, p. 5.**

Canadian politicians, worried by a growing tax revolt in the country, have announced steps to combat a sharp increase in smuggling to duck "sin taxes" on liquor and tobacco and a rise in the underground economy to avoid income and sales taxes.

Lyall, Sarah, "Trafficking in Parking for a Fast-Track Crowd," ***The New York Times*****, March 14, 1991, p. B3.**

An illegal underground economy has developed in Manhasset, N.Y., as thousands of out-of-town commuters pay $125 to $200 a month to park at gas stations, behind stores or even in driveways.

Michaeli, Ethan, "Cops put end to fake ID operation," ***Chicago Defender*****, Jan. 28, 1993, p. 3.**

Standing before stacks of fake auto titles, birth certificates and Social Security cards, Chicago police announced the arrests of two men, Alton Williams and Tyrome Williams, on charges they operated an illegal business that produced forged official documents.

Schneider, Howard and Graciela Sevilla, "America's homes hide an underground economy: Many workers want to pay taxes, but employers don't," ***The Washington Post*****, Feb. 14, 1993, p. A1.**

Maria de la Cruz Gonzalez is an example of immigrant workers who have suffered because their employers did not want to pay Social Security taxes and other taxes on their employees, even if the employees are willing to pay.

Tennison, Patricia, "Sale of old children's apparel has lots of cash appeal," ***Chicago Tribune*****, Oct. 20, 1993, p. 2D1.**

Fall is high season for children's used-clothing sales, and the amount of money changing hands belies their nickel-and-dime image. The system has spawned an underground economy.

Vobejda, Barbara, "America's homes hide an underground economy: U.S. is forced to confront pervasive hiring violations," ***The Washington Post*****, Feb. 14, 1993, p. A1.**

The overwhelming majority of Americans who employ household workers do so in an underground economy, and recent publicity about those migrant workers is forcing a discussion of public policy that government and society have long avoided.

Undocumented Workers

Dillin, John, "Economics Key to Halting Illegal Influx," ***Christian Science Monitor*****, July 24, 1990, p. 1.**

A recent congressional study of illegal immigration into the U.S. is discussed. The study recommends a long-term policy to strengthen the Latin American economies in order to reduce the incentive for residents of that region to work in the underground economy of the U.S.

Nieves, Evelyn, "Newcomers find success despite the barriers," ***The New York Times*****, June 18, 1993, p. A1.**

The underground economy of immigrants, which has exploited and virtually enslaved thousands of vulnerable undocumented aliens, has also served to sustain and nurture many thousands more who eventually surface to pay their taxes, gain legal status and achieve their goals. The story of the Vasquez family, immigrants from Panama whose journey through the underground economy ended in success, is related. (Part 6 of 6).

The U.S. Situation

Basheda, Valarie, "Chronicle Exploring City's Crime, Violence, Poverty," *Detroit News*, Aug. 12, 1992, p. B3.
In a special edition of the *Michigan Chronicle*, the newspaper will explore the "underground" economy of crime among blacks, segregation between the black middle class and underclass, and the influence of rap music on the community. The *Chronicle* is Michigan's largest black newspaper.

Harris, Scott, "Working the edge of fear," *Los Angeles Times*, March 31, 1993, p. B1.
The Westlake district of Los Angeles is featured. As densely populated as Manhattan, the downtown area is home to many immigrants and a largely underground economy.

Hendrick, Bill, "Underground economy costs Uncle Sam a bundle," *Atlanta Journal Constitution*, Jan. 23, 1993, p. A8.
When it comes to paying Social Security taxes for domestic help, the IRS says more employers break the law, as did Zoë Baird, than abide by it. Such activity is part of America's burgeoning underground economy, which cheats the government out of billions in tax money each year.

Kleinfield, N. R., "Pursuing tax cheats in land of opportunity," *The New York Times*, June 16, 1993, p. A1.
Trying to police New York City's swelling underground economy and the multiplying number of immigrants in it is grueling work nettled with frustration. The realm is too large, too amorphous and too difficult to deal with effectively. (Part 4 of 6).

Pennar, Karen and Christopher Farrell, "Notes from the underground economy," *Business Week* (Industrial/Technology Edition), Feb. 15, 1993, pp. 98-101.
The off-the-books economy produces annual income exceeding $500 billion. The IRS says the 1992 "tax gap" could be as high as $127 billion, enough to help make a nice dent in the national deficit.

Schiff, Lenore, and John Labate, "Labor Force Mysteries: The Working Poor and the Underground Economy," *Fortune*, Aug. 24, 1992, p. 22.
Approximately 5.7 million U.S. citizens hold jobs that pay the minimum wage or less, according to figures produced by the Bureau of Labor Statistics. The underground economy, those who work off the books, is worth some $600 billion or more.

Sontag, Deborah, "Emigres in New York: Work off the books," *The New York Times*, June 13, 1993, p. 1.
Legal immigrants in New York City are fueling a growing underground economy in the metropolitan region that is shaping the region's commercial life, changing the tempo of the city's streets and providing thousands of entry-level jobs for newcomers. However, it is also forcing some immigrants into a world of seven-day workweeks, meager pay and dangerous working conditions. Many believe this immigrant underground robs Americans of jobs. (Part 1 of 6).

Sprenkle, Case M., "The case of the missing currency," *Journal of Economic Perspectives*, fall 1993, pp. 175-184.
The household and business demands for currency added up to only about $28 billion, or under 16 percent of the total of $177 billion in the U.S. There are only three possibilities for holders of the remaining 84 percent of the currency—the domestic illegal (or "underground") economy, children under the age of 18 who are not included in the survey, or foreigners.

Young, David, "Underground Economy Doing Thriving Business," *Chicago Tribune*, July 10, 1992, p. 1.
University of Wisconsin sociologist Bruce Wiegand has made his career studying the black market, also known as the "underground economy." According to Wiegand, the shady, off-the-books economy may be one of the U.S.' largest and fastest-growing industries.

Back Issues

Great Research on Current Issues Starts Right Here...Recent topics covered by The CQ Researcher are listed below. Before May 1991, reports were published under the name of Editorial Research Reports.

AUGUST 1992
The Homeless
Work, Family and Stress
NATO's Changing Role
Marine Mammals vs. Fish

SEPTEMBER 1992
Domestic Partners
Violence in Schools
Public Broadcasting
Women in the Military

OCTOBER 1992
Depression
U.S. Auto Industry
Youth Apprenticeships
Hispanic Americans

NOVEMBER 1992
Physical Fitness
Privatization
Paying for College
U.S. Policy in Asia

DECEMBER 1992
Crackdown on Smoking
The New CIA
Eating Disorders
Women and AIDS

JANUARY 1993
Hate Crimes
Child Sexual Abuse
Nuclear Fusion
U.S. Trade Policy

FEBRUARY 1993
Community Policing
Europe's New Right
School Censorship
Violence Against Women

MARCH 1993
Gay Rights
Aid to Russia
War on Drugs
TV Violence

APRIL 1993
Head Start
High-Speed Rail
Children's Legal Rights
Muslims in America

MAY 1993
Cults in America
Preventing Teen Pregnancy
Software Piracy
National Parks

JUNE 1993
Food Safety
Prostitution
Childhood Immunizations
National Service

JULY 1993
Electric Cars
Population Growth
Downward Mobility
Intelligence Testing

AUGUST 1993
Mental Illness
Bilingual Education
Foreign Policy Burden
School Funding

SEPTEMBER 1993
Suburban Crime
Public Housing
Supreme Court Preview
Immigration Reform

OCTOBER 1993
Airline Safety
Disaster Response
Science in the Courtroom
The Glass Ceiling

NOVEMBER 1993
Paying for Retirement
Charitable Giving
Privacy in the Workplace
Adoption

DECEMBER 1993
U.S. Vietnam-Relations
Learning Disabilities
Child Care
Space Program's Future

JANUARY 1994
Racial Tensions in Schools
South Africa's Future
Worker Retraining
Regulating Pesticides

FEBRUARY 1994
Prison Overcrowding
Water Quality
Religion in Schools
Juvenile Justice

Back issues are available for $4.00 (subscribers) or $7.00 (non-subscribers). Quantity discounts apply to orders over ten. To order, call Congressional Quarterly Customer Service at (202) 887-8621.

Binders are available for $15.00. To order call 1-800-638-1710. Please refer to stock number 648.

Future Topics

- ***Education Standards***
- ***Gambling Boom***
- ***Private Management of Public Schools***

THE CQ Researcher

PUBLISHED BY CONGRESSIONAL QUARTERLY INC.

Education Standards

Will national standards improve U.S. schools?

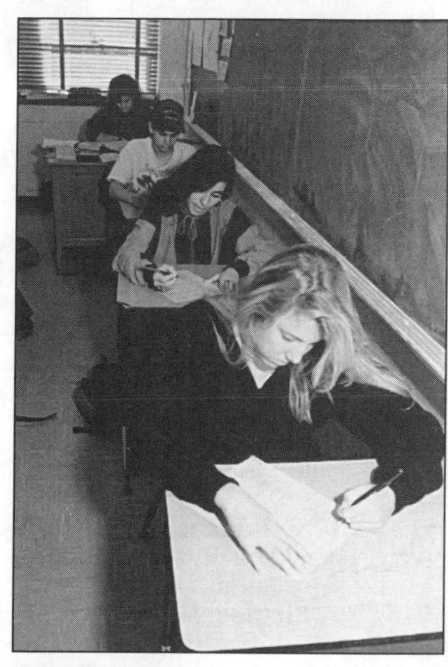

Nearly everyone agrees that U.S. education is in deep trouble. Many experts think the solution lies in establishing nationwide standards describing what every student should learn in core academic subjects. Spurred by 21st-century goals set by the Bush and Clinton administrations, teams of specialists are at work designing content standards in math, science, English and social studies. Many in the standards movement also advocate a nationwide system of state-administered tests to gauge whether content standards are met. Critics, however, warn of federal intrusion on local education prerogatives. Others worry that disadvantaged and minority children will suffer if standards are imposed without first equalizing education funding.

INSIDE THIS ISSUE

CQ March 11, 1994 • Volume 4, No. 10 • 217-240

Formerly Editorial Research Reports

THE ISSUES

BACKGROUND

CURRENT SITUATION

OUTLOOK

SIDEBARS AND GRAPHICS

FOR FURTHER INFORMATION

March 11, 1994
Volume 4, No. 10

The CQ Researcher (ISSN 1056-2036). Formerly Editorial Research Reports. Published weekly (48 times per year, not printed the first Friday of any month with five Fridays) by Congressional Quarterly Inc., 1414 22nd St., N.W., Washington, D.C. 20037. Rates are furnished upon request. Second-class postage paid at Washington, D.C. POSTMASTER: Send address changes to The CQ Researcher, 1414 22nd St., N.W., Washington, D.C. 20037.

COVER: STUDENTS AT ANNANDALE HIGH SCHOOL, ANNANDALE, VA. DAVID SNYDER/ DEPARTMENT OF EDUCATION

Education Standards

BY CHARLES S. CLARK

THE ISSUES

When Earlene Hemmer began teaching in the early 1970s, her grade-schoolers in Belgrade, Mont., tackled arithmetic largely by memorizing multiplication tables. "But they didn't understand why" the numbers worked, she recalls. "It was frustrating because by simply teaching according to the manual, I had stopped listening to myself, and I wasn't listening to the kids."

As she gained experience, Hemmer gradually moved toward more conceptual methods, showing students the reasons behind each process, bringing in her own visual aids. "There's still memorization," she says, "but things are done in a different order. The kids first think about how we learn and how we apply it."

By the late 1980s, Hemmer was gratified to realize that math teachers across the country had made similar discoveries. The National Council of Teachers of Mathematics [1] sent Hemmer and other math teachers the curriculum standards it had created through years of research and consensus-building in the profession — the first such standards in the nation.

"I felt reassured I was on the right track," Hemmer says. "I started to trust myself, and I got more out of reading the standards a second and third time."

Today, the council's math standards are used in schools in more than 40 states, and standards are being prepared in science, English, civics, history, geography and foreign languages.

In his State of the Union address last month, President Clinton promoted standards through legislation, called the Goals 2000: Educate America Act, which he said "links world-class standards to grass-roots reforms." Business groups, teachers unions, governors and many in the education field are rallying round the

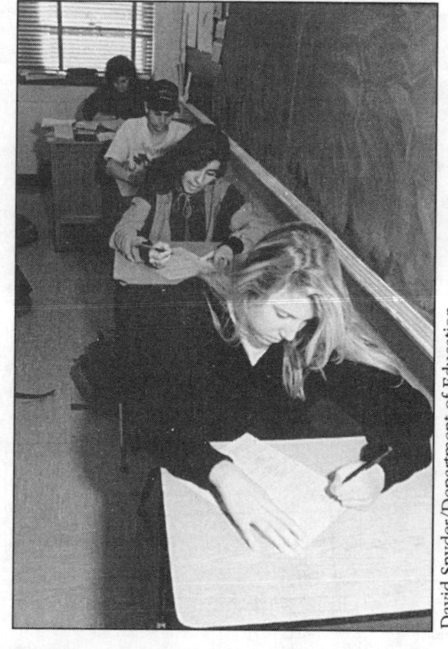

David Snyder/Department of Education

creation of standards through the bill, which would write the country's major education goals into law. [2] *(The six goals are listed on page 232.)*

Content standards — what students should know and be able to do — and performance standards — how good is good enough — will be spelled out. These standards are envisioned as a springboard for states, school districts and schools to work voluntarily toward systemic reforms that would revamp testing, teacher development, textbooks and methods for measuring each school's success.

Currently, "We have a system where everyone goes their own way," says Diane Ravitch, a Bush administration assistant Education secretary now at the Brookings Institution. "The textbook industry, the test makers, they design the standards based on what sells. But the theory is you can't improve schools unless you know where you want to go. Then everyone can work to make it happen, and the whole system is pushed in the same direction."

Diverse and locally controlled as U.S. education has always been, nearly everyone agrees that the modern system is in deep trouble. The average fourth-grader in Japan and Russia is said to be two years ahead of the average American fourth-grader. *(See story, p. 234.)*

"Colleges and universities complain bitterly that professors are now forced to add remedial courses to teach incoming freshmen how to write simple sentences and to compute basic mathematical formulas," notes the 1992 book *Failing Grades: A Teacher's Report Card on Education in America.* [3]

The "nation's report card," as the National Assessment of Educational Performance (NAEP) program is informally known, showed that 75 percent of students in 1992 scored below proficiency levels in math, while two-thirds scored below par in reading. As many as 47 percent of adult Americans cannot use a bus schedule or distinguish between two employee benefits, according to a 1993 Educational Testing Service study of literacy. [4]

Across the country, concerned parents and politicians point to "soft and fuzzy" curricula and the widespread practice of "social promotion" to the next grade. At Northridge Middle School outside Los Angeles, students in an "advisory class" on family and personal relations reportedly spent a class period practicing each other's names. [5] This fall, the District of Columbia schools announced, no first- or second-grader will be held back, regardless of achievement levels. [6]

The current panoply of local curricula means that students and teachers must grapple with frequent "repetitions, gaps and high mobility rates," observes University of Virginia English Professor E.D. Hirsch Jr., author of *Cultural Literacy: What Every American Needs to Know.* "If a second-grade teacher can't depend on students coming in knowing certain things, it means endless boring reviews and a third reading of *Charlotte's Web.*

Many States Considering Education Reforms

Sixteen states and the District of Columbia are considering comprehensive packages of education reforms in 1994, according to a survey conducted by the National Conference of State Legislatures. More than half the states in the nation will be dealing specifically with education standards this year.

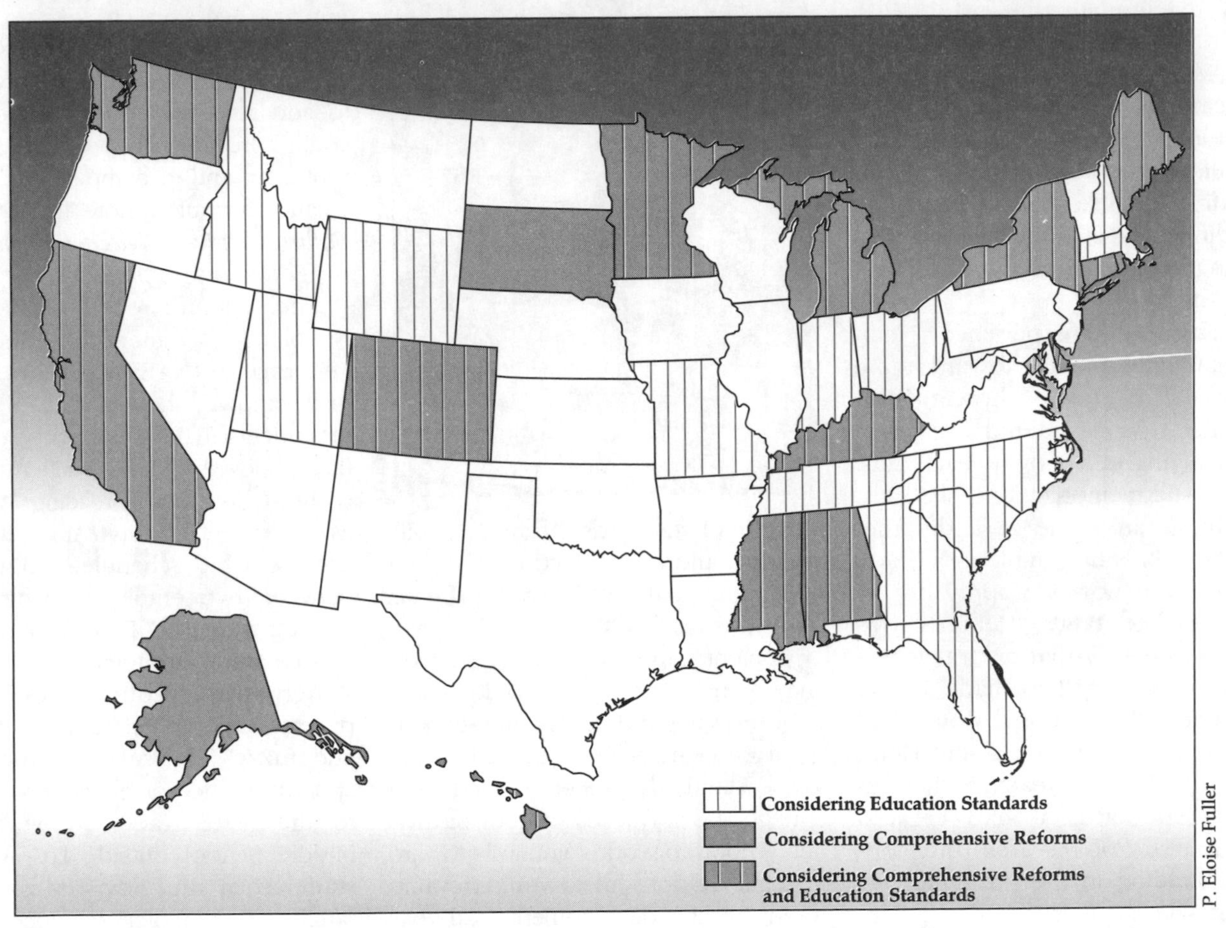

Source: National Conference of State Legislatures, Issues Outlook, *1994.*

"If disadvantaged or poor children are not made to understand the next step, they fall further behind. And mobility rates [the frequency with which families transfer to new schools in the middle of the year] in some districts are as high as 40-60 percent."

The movement to education standards — with their ambitious assumption that "all children can learn" if given clear goals, enough time and enough support — comes as employers express increasing dissatisfaction with the pool of job applicants.

"The attainment of basic skills in math and language is no longer sufficient for productive employment," says Gordon M. Ambach, executive director of the Council of Chief State School Officers. "Increasingly, American workers must have higher-order capacities. They must be able to communicate complex messages, organize their own teamwork, and ways to do it. They have to understand their work as part of a whole enterprise. Educators and policy-makers once thought that higher-order knowledge and skills were necessary for (and attainable by) only a small segment of the population, but we now recognize that these skills are vital for everyone."

The public appears disposed toward national standards. By a margin of 68 percent to 24 percent, respondents to a May 1991 Gallup Poll favored "requiring the public schools in this community to use a standardized national curriculum."

Critics, however, particularly political conservatives, are wary of a "federal power grab." They point out that the federal government is prohibited from dictating a national curriculum, and that 93 cents of every education dollar comes from state or local governments (*see below*).

Other resistance comes from educational innovators who worry that local experimentation will be quashed. "Who in America has the hubris or the right to set specific, measurable standards for all the people?" asks Brown University Professor Theodore R. Sizer, founder of the Coalition of Essential Schools. "Are the standards in things we value — taste, complex reasoning, historical meaning, economic fairness, imagination, the relative value of, say, life and property — widely agreed on? Or do reasonable people, including scholars in these areas, disagree?. . . Would the imposition of such standards be consonant with intellectual freedom?"[7]

And within the movement there are fears that a rush into standards will cause inordinate suffering among low-income and minority students. "Democratic standards-setting must keep equity central," writes Donald M. Stewart, president of the New York City-based College Board. "We cannot develop a list of new standards for all students and then ignore the savage inequalities in the opportunities students have to learn."[8]

In the education community, being in favor of standards is like being for "mom and apple pie," says Brian Curry, a policy analyst with the Association for Supervision and Curriculum Development (ASCD) in Alexandria, Va. "The question is, 'Are they in fact going to cure anything?' "

The answer is likely to hinge on the following issues:

Will national standards threaten local control of education?

During debate on Goals 2000 in recent months, several members of Congress responded to pressure from home states and softened the bill's language outlining what states must do to receive federal funds. Such tough-sounding phrases as "shall include" were changed to "might include," and the word "voluntary" appears no less than 59 times.

The House and Senate versions of Goals 2000 each offer slightly more than $400 million in grants to states if they do nothing more than adopt education reform plans "that address" issues of curricula, performance assessment and teacher training consistent with the nation's six education goals.

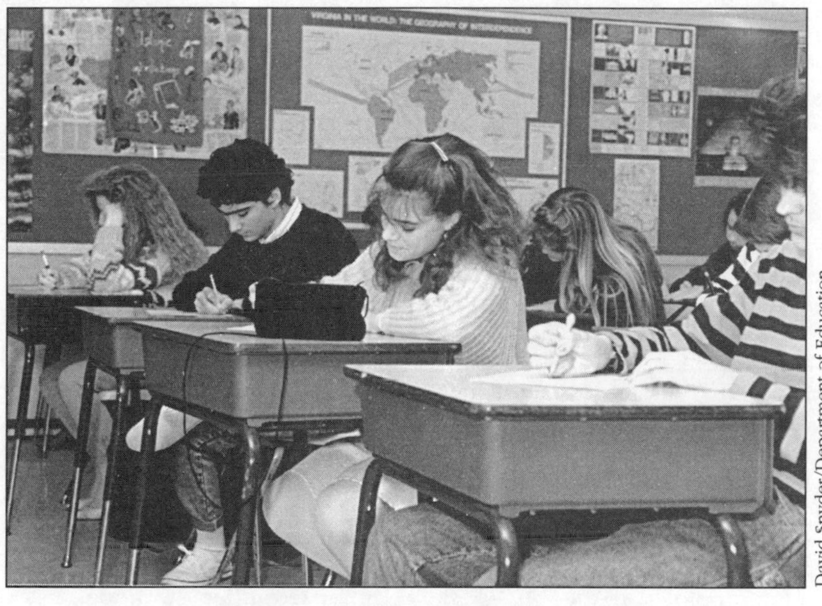
David Snyder/Department of Education

President Clinton's Goals 2000 legislation would write the country's major education goals into law.

To oversee the creation of standards by panels of educators in each subject area, the bill creates a National Education Standards and Improvement Council that would function, in the phrase of American Federation of Teachers (AFT) President Albert Shanker, "like the National Bureau of Weights and Measures."[9]

Conservatives complain that the bill creates "a national school board" that would be appointed by the Democratic-controlled White House and Congress. The Clinton Education Department "receives its marching orders from the education establishment, which has opposed every meaningful education reform proposal during the past 20 years," said a statement from Empower America, a Washington advocacy group led by former Education Secretary William J. Bennett. "Over the last 20 years, federal involvement has increased dramatically, and educational achievement has gone down."

Goals 2000 will create "a national outcome-based system, which would likely require attitude and belief changes of students, such as those we've seen at the state level," said a newsletter for Citizens for Excellence in Education, a Christian group based in Costa Mesa, Calif. "We do not believe the system will be voluntary, since students who don't attend certified schools will suffer limited employment and college opportunities."[10]

Sen. Judd Gregg, R-N.H., also scorned the bill's claim that state participation would be voluntary. "Anybody who has been in the government," he told the Senate Feb. 2, "knows the pressure which will be raised within the various states to obtain some of this funding."

Chief sponsor Sen. Edward M. Kennedy, D-Mass., responded that the plan represents "bottoms-up education reform with support from the top down. We do not federalize education. We do not establish a national curriculum or the equivalent of a national school board. We do not require that the states adopt national standards or submit state standards for federal government approval."

Composing a Standard: Too Specific? Too Vague? Too Long?

What does an education standard look like? Here's what students in grades five-eight should know about statistics, according to one of the few such standards in wide use:

"[T]he mathematics curriculum should include exploration of statistics in real-world situations so that students can systematically collect, organize, and describe data; construct, read, and interpret tables, charts and graphs; make inferences and convincing arguments that are based on data analysis; evaluate arguments that are based on data analysis; develop an appreciation for statistical methods as powerful means for decision making." [1]

The balancing act faced by creators of standards is how to make them useful and informative without barraging the reader with page after page of education jargon. That means a standard should pass "the barber shop and beauty parlor test," according to Shirley E. Malcolm, who chaired a technical panel on standards for the National Education Goals Panel.

"If you trot a standard in and show it to a randomly selected group of ordinary Americans, will they agree that it is both intelligible and important for kids?" asks Chester E. Finn Jr., another member of the panel and a former assistant Education secretary. "If it's gobbledygook or it offers things the citizens either don't value or find inappropriate, it won't be used. It's only if standards are accepted by voters, parents, taxpayers, mayors and council members that they will be effective."

Controversy has plagued past efforts at standards, notes Diane Massell, a research associate at Rutgers University's Consortium for the Study of Education Policy, because of a failure to generate more public involvement. "When the National Science Foundation tried to create a national framework for teaching anthropology in the 1970s," she says, "they emphasized expertise, and brought in Nobel laureates, and they felt that once the great leaders spoke, there was nothing more to do."

Today, Massell says, the various interests working to create standards "are more aware of the need to involve teachers, superintendents and principals, and to bring people along. The National Council of Teachers of Mathematics did it at the front end; they consulted people before preparing a document."

The Education Department has awarded grants to eight groups working on standards in the arts, citizenship and civics, English and language arts, foreign languages, geography, history, mathematics and science.

Drafts of standards (*see sample, p. 223*) have ranged from a single paragraph to hundreds of pages, a length that looms ominously to some teachers. Richard Aieta, chairman of a high school social studies department in Gloucester, Mass., read a draft of several hundred pages and declared, "If all these documents come out this way, somebody's going to have to take a sabbatical to read it all."

"Some of these 700-page documents are filled with illustrative lessons and learning activities," notes Charles N. Quigley, director of the standards project at the Center for Civic Education in Calabasas, Calif. His organization's civics standards, which run 150 pages in draft, are being designed in consultation with scholars and public officials, particularly in those states that are important textbook markets.

"The primary audience is curriculum developers, not teachers," Quigley says. "They're for people who design tests, texts and teaching materials. About 90 percent of teachers say, 'Don't give me standards, give me a textbook that embodies the standards.' It's like a carpenter doesn't want to know how to build an electric saw, he says just give me a saw."

Given the crazy quilt of approaches to creating standards, the question of whether the standards themselves must become standardized is now being raised throughout the movement.

And it will likely be addressed by the coming National Education Standards and Improvement Council, the body to be created by the new Goals 2000 legislation. The eight authorized groups working on standards are scheduled to complete their drafts on a schedule ranging from this summer to spring 1996. [2]

---

[1] National Council of Teachers of Mathematics, "Curriculum and Evaluation Standards for School Mathematics," Executive Summary, March 1989.

[2] Quoted in *Education Week*, Jan. 19, 1994.

"We do not create unfunded mandates," Kennedy continued. "We do not make the receipt of any other federal funds contingent upon the provision of Goals 2000. It does not dictate to the state how to spend, how to license teachers, or what textbooks to use. . . . It does not mandate or encourage value-based or outcomes-based education."

Even to some supporters of national standards, the bill raises problems. "It is an expansion of federal power," says Ravitch, "and there's a balancing act in creating national curriculum without creating a national curriculum."

"There is a tension in this bill that's not being addressed," says Arnold Fege, director of government relations for the National PTA. "They're saying the goals are voluntary and from the bottom up, on one hand, but there are all kinds of top-down structures that establish major new bureaucracies. Who develops the standards in the end? Clinton? [Sen.] Jesse Helms [R-N.C.]? Teachers? Parents? The feds say they like bottoms-up reform, but they kind of like being in control."

Those leading the standards movement emphasize that it would be the states and localities that ultimately decide whether national standards were applicable to them. When the National Governors' Association (NGA) met this winter to discuss education standards, governors pointed out that states all differ in their involvement in education reform.

"No one size fits all," as Susan L. Traiman, NGA director of education policy studies, put it, adding that some states have constitutions that prohibit statewide curricula. Gov. Thomas R. Carper, D-Del., told the gathering that the standards "are like a sandwich. The top piece of bread is the standard, the bottom piece of bread is the performance tests, but whatever is in the middle is up to the schools to decide."

The current framework of standards "doesn't say how to get there," argues Bella Rosenberg, assistant to AFT President Shanker. "If you believe there's a national interest in education — and I do — then there is a legitimate role for government in convening and stimulating the process. Every other advanced industrial nation operates that way. States are merely required to talk about the subject in a plan."

Others point out that standards will catch on only if they are attractive to states and localities. Though the standards are envisioned as "national in scope, they are not federal," write educators at the Center for Civic Education in Calabasas, Calif., which is helping create standards. "They are not mandatory, nor are they a national curriculum. . . .They must gain whatever influence they can muster from their character and quality alone."[11]

What's more, even if a standard is embraced by a state or locality, local curriculum planners would be free to tailor it to local needs, supporters say. When California adopted a uniform state history curriculum in the 1980s, recalls Diane Massell, a research associate at Rutgers University's Consortium for the Study of Education Policy, San Francisco's school superintendent objected to the short shrift given to Chinese-American history. When he offered supplementary material on the subject, the state approved and delivered his state funding.

"They can't just ship these standards off and expect them to be used," says Betty Ann Armstrong, assistant superintendent for instruction for the public schools in Arlington County, Va. "We would use them as a framework to develop our own. Arlington has never just accepted the state curriculum. We have always taken it and incorporated it and moved beyond to higher expectations."

Given today's competing education

What Students Should Know About Civics

This proposed draft of achievement standards in civics suggests what students in grades 9-12 should know about how governments are organized.

Content Standards

1. Students should be able to evaluate, take and defend positions regarding the relative merits of federal, confederate and unitary systems of government.

To achieve this standard, students should be able to:

- explain the difference among federal, confederate and unitary systems;
- identify historical and contemporary examples of federal, confederate and unitary systems;
- identify the relative advantages and disadvantages of federal, confederate and unitary systems of government.

2. Students should be able to evaluate, take and defend positions regarding the relative merits of systems of shared powers, presidential and parliamentary systems.

To achieve this standard, students should be able to:

- explain the differences among systems of shared powers, presidential and parliamentary systems;
- identify contemporary examples of systems of shared powers, presidential and parliamentary systems;
- identify the advantages and disadvantages of systems of shared powers, presidential and parliamentary systems.

Rationale

To understand and function effectively in one's own government, it is essential for citizens of a constitutional democracy to know how their government is organized and why it is organized in a particular way. But if citizens are to make informed political choices and judgments, it also is essential that they be knowledgeable about alternative means of organizing governments. That knowledge will enhance their understanding of their own government. It also helps them appreciate the meaning of events in the world, such as when parliamentary governments fall, federations threaten to break apart or confederations are found to be weak or unwieldy.

By comparing alternative means of organizing government, one becomes aware not only of their advantages and disadvantages, but of how one's own government might be improved. Thus, comparative study helps citizens of the United States evaluate criticisms of their government and enhances their ability to judge proposals for change.

Source: Momentum, *September/October 1993; Charles F. Bahmueller and Margaret Stimmann Branson, Center for Civic Education.* Momentum *is the official journal of the National Catholic Educational Association.*

Foreign Students Outperform Americans

American 13-year-olds were largely outperformed by students from several other countries in a 1991 assessment of science and math achievement. In math, for example, students in Korea, Switzerland and Taiwan bested U.S. students in all areas tested. None of the five foreign countries listed below scored lower than the U.S. in any math or science category.

Science Achievement

Academic Areas	Countries that scored lower than the U.S.	Countries where scores were similar to those of the U.S.	Countries that scored higher than the U.S.
Life Science		France, Switzerland	Taiwan, Korea, Hungary
Physical Science			France, Taiwan, Korea, Switzerland, Hungary
Earth Science		France	Taiwan, Korea, Switzerland, Hungary
Nature of Science		France, Taiwan, Korea, Switzerland, Hungary	

Mathematics Achievement

Academic Areas	Countries that scored lower than the U.S.	Countries where scores were similar to those of the U.S.	Countries that scored higher than the U.S.
Numbers and Operations		France	Taiwan, Korea, Switzerland, Hungary
Measurement			France, Taiwan, Korea, Switzerland, Hungary
Geometry			France, Taiwan, Korea, Switzerland, Hungary
Data Analysis, Probability and Statistics		Hungary	France, Taiwan, Korea, Switzerland
Algebra and Functions			France, Taiwan, Korea, Switzerland, Hungary

France   Taiwan   Korea   Switzerland   Hungary

P. Eloise Fuller

Source: The National Education Goals Report, *1993; Educational Testing Service, 1992.*

reform movements — among them multiculturalism, differing "learning styles" and magnet schools with special themes — many in alternative schools view the standards movement as a potential wet blanket.

Deborah Meier, the award-winning principal of Central Park East Secondary School in Harlem, whose teachers approach disadvantaged children by getting involved with their families, says: "The people in the school standards movement see themselves as the experts who know the answers, and are worried that their opinion might lose. The question is whether we all have to agree. I know of no evidence in pedagogy that says we have to agree. There is no other area of life where we have to agree. Piano teachers might all have high standards but disagree over what music to play."

William H. Kolberg, who as president of the National Alliance of Business has led a coalition of business groups pursuing standards for the past two years, says his group has no desire to let standards quash individuality and creativity.

"We're trying to raise the basic level of knowledge," he says. "We don't want to lose flexibility. If it becomes more rote-and-drill stuff, that's not what we're after. We're for graduating people who aren't afraid of new ideas and new teammates. It's a great thing if kids emerge with the basics and freedom to broaden their frontiers. How to do this for all kids is tough, but this is the first time we have a national strategy for change."

Will standards be unfair to minorities and disadvantaged students?

"The idea that all children can reach high and rigorous standards is a goal we must strive toward," says Glen Cutlip, a senior policy analyst with the National Education Association (NEA). "It is one of the major tenets of the NEA. But we seriously question the ability of the current educational system to make this a reality for all children, given the inadequate and unequal distribution of resources, the lack of technological innovation and the lack of flexibility for change."

In today's world, a curriculum "can't assume that all children have had the same experiences," notes Laurie Baker, principal at Tuckahoe Elementary School in Arlington, Va. "Thirty years ago, there was an assumption that we were homogeneous groups. Moms were at home for lunch, kids played in the yard, there were fewer divorces and the extended family was close by. Now we don't know our neighbors, kids are split between homes and you have a child from, say, El Salvador, who is used to buying fruit from on top of someone's head instead of going to the grocery."

Ramona Hoage Edelin, president of the National Urban Coalition, a Washington advocacy group that promotes education for minorities, argues that "until we can rectify the gross and savage inequalities that affect children of color [who are concentrated] in the inner city and some rural areas, the superimposition of goals on this inequality will not result in all children learning."

Under the current system, the best teachers are usually assigned to "cushy suburban schools," she adds, "while 80 percent of children of color are disqualified from technical courses in college for not having taken certain courses in high school because they weren't offered. For the same reason that we want national academic standards, we want national resource standards, and absent that, standards would be a fundamental and cruel hypocrisy."

To confront the issue of unequal resources, backers of standards have added "opportunity-to-learn" standards, a set of measurements intended to encourage states and localities to target disadvantaged schools with extra funding. The majority of states already have some form of opportunity-to-learn standards, according to a 1993 National Governors' Association survey, though their enforceability varies widely. [12] In Congress, the House version of the Goals 2000 legislation would require states receiving federal education grants to address the issue, while the Senate version would merely encourage them to do so.

"It's one thing to raise expectations, but another to be sure students have the wherewithal," says Richard Kruse, director of government relations for the National Association of Secondary School Principals in Reston, Va. "It's like trying to get a Volkswagen bug to 100 mph when it has a governor that stops it at 75. Yes, some states think this will force them to raise money, but the states do have veto power. And if it does mean spending more at all levels of government, it would be a [worthwhile] investment."

The problem, say critics, is that opportunity-to-learn standards would interfere with state budgeting prerogatives by imposing, as Sen. Gregg put it, a "federal methodology for teaching." The New Hampshire lawmaker also warns that the standards would become "the benchmark for the litigation community in this country." And, in fact, several observers predict a barrage of lawsuits from activists seeking a new vehicle for redressing longstanding issues of school funding. [13]

Rep. Jack Reed, D-R.I., says he doubts that there will be substantial lawsuits. "Opportunity-to-learn standards are not designed to be a backdoor way to leverage more resources," he says. But they are needed because "it is easy to talk about mastering subjects, but hard to create the right environment. Without that, we're just blaming the victims."

Others, however, are wary of allowing the standards movement to bog down in the broad and volatile issue of school funding. Those who fear standards will harm the poor, minorities, disabled and limited-English-proficiency students "would rather continue in the present state of mediocrity if the reforms result in some groups of youngsters surging ahead faster or farther than others," writes the AFT's Shanker. [14]

"Suppose we discovered a vaccine to cure some horrible disease . . . AIDS or cancer," he continues. "The vaccine cured half the victims, but for the other half it only prolonged life a bit. Would it be fair to distribute a vaccine that rescued some but not others? Would we withhold it and wait until we found one that could cure all?"

In the current climate, "I don't think we have enough money for equalization," says Shirley E. Malcolm, an official at the American Association for the Advancement of Science (AAAS), who chaired a key panel on standards. [15] "We must become smarter about how we spend the current money. Right now, we lack memory and coherence in our efforts, and we don't have information on what works, what doesn't and what is needed. There may be some differences between students, but schools shouldn't magnify those differences. In the end, it comes down to the interaction between student and teacher in a classroom. If one is not expected to perform, that is a denial of opportunity."

Others echo the view that classroom content is more vital than funding. Hirsch, whose Core Knowledge Foundation has assisted nearly 100 schools in implementing curricula using traditional standards he helped create, says, "the kids who can least afford it are the ones victimized by laissez-faire school content." His grade-by-grade guidelines to what every child should know were "originally conceived as the best way to help the downtrodden," he says. "It's not a matter of ideology."

"Money is not a panacea," says R.D. Harris, deputy state superintendent of education in Mississippi and a devotee of Hirsch's work. "If it were, why can some of the poorest districts turn out the brightest kids? If teachers stick to basic core knowledge, and they care, it doesn't matter where they are in the country."

Curriculum planner Armstrong ac-

"If this country is to have a great future, the first step. . .

Education Secretary Richard W. Riley, the former Democratic governor of South Carolina, has long been active in education reform. He spoke with *CQ Researcher* staff writer Charles S. Clark Feb. 18.

CQ: How you would rate national standards in importance to your over-all agenda?

Riley: I think that national standards, what a student should know and be able to do at a particular grade level, are extremely important in terms of bringing about education reform. Parents are interested in their child having a quality education. So you say to parents of a kid in the sixth grade, "What do you want for your child?" They say, "We want him to have a good education." And you say "Well, what's that?"

Reuters

Education Secretary Riley

Standards answer that question. It's not a black and white situation, but it is a consensus reached throughout this nation. It's not a federal thing because the great majority of it involves the people out in the local community: parents, teacher, leaders, etc., meeting and talking for hours and hours about these subjects. And this consensus process of arriving at academic standards is very good and healthy for this country. You don't want to set standards so high that they are out of focus with what a young person should know and be able to do. Goals are different. Goals should be out there, something we're reaching for. Standards are what we want to try to teach. I think it is extremely important, and if we are going to have fundamental change and real education reform, it has to be driven by high, world-class academic standards.

CQ: Is there a problem with local districts feeling that the federal government is intervening too much?

Riley: I don't see any reason for anyone thinking that, though there is some political rhetoric around that would raise those questions. That's the nature of our democracy. But the fact is, the "Goals 2000" legislation puts the challenge on the states. Then the states develop their process of involving people throughout the state and their responsibility to the school districts and then the school.

Our national consensus process is there for them to use for a model, as a lighthouse, as a North Star, but it is not mandated. Adopting the national standards has no relationship with receiving Goals 2000 money. But, it's part of the Clinton

knowledges that "standards will be tough on minorities, who are not doing well, and it may take some more time with some than others. There's no quick fix, and we'll have to keep plotting new programs. But you can see individuals in each group who are doing well. Middle-class blacks compare well with middle-class whites."

Kolberg of the National Alliance of Business says: "We'll start by concentrating on knowledge, and then you'll know which [students and schools] are meeting the standards and which are not. Then, once we have standards we believe in, it may well turn out that we will change our mind about opposing the court cases challenging school funding in 24 states. Business may have to say that it costs money, and we must pay a price to educate all children.

"My hope is that the standards movement will make it increasingly clear where we are, school by school, district by district, state by state. We can't keep saying, 'It'll always be this way.' We have to do something about it."

Should the effectiveness of standards be measured by nationwide testing?

It's one thing to be able to cook an omelet, says Chester E. Finn Jr., an assistant Education secretary in the Bush administration. It is another thing to cook an omelet that tastes good. [16]

Many who favor standards for content would like a concrete gauge of their effectiveness. Finn supports a more broad-based version of the biennial three-grade sampling that makes up the National Assessment of Educational Progress. The NAEP survey permits analysts, for example, to note that in 1992, 25 percent of eighth-graders met minimal levels of proficiency in math, compared with 20 percent in 1990, and that in Minnesota, proficiency rates were 37 percent, while in Georgia, they were only 16 percent.

In 1991, the Bush administration floated a proposal for a European-style standardized national test, an all-day affair for high-schoolers whose results would be made available to colleges and prospective employers. It was shot down, however, for fear that it would be expensive, unfair to disadvantaged school districts and would lead to the creation of a national curriculum. [17]

A single national test seems simple, says Lauren Resnick, chairman of the student-achievement group of the joint state-federal National Education Goals Panel, "but would penetrate into the social fabric of the country." [18]

"American students are already the

. . . is to define what students are expected to learn"

administration's new definition of the federal system and what the federal government's role should be in public education. It is not one of mandates, but of support, sharing and partnerships. It recognizes that the responsibility of education is, and always has been, with the states, and through the states, local school districts and schools.

CQ: Doesn't this make the American system different from the more centralized systems in European and Asian countries?

Riley: Yes. Some of them are [centralized] and some of them aren't. Of course, a country like France is totally centralized. The national government there [sets] a national education curriculum and [mandates] what would take place throughout the system. This has some advantages. It's certainly easier. The United Kingdom has been experimenting with a national curriculum, and they have had some negative results. Each country has its own style of governing, but I think our style works best. True education reform has to come at the point where learning touches the student, and that cannot be mandated from an office building in Washington, D.C. It has to come from the bottom up.

CQ: Do you think minority and disadvantaged students will respond better to higher expectations and higher standards than to watered-down ones?

Riley: Absolutely. I think that's really been a reason for lots of kids coming out of high school without a good education. I'm very sensitive to that because a lot of African American kids, a lot of Hispanic kids, poor white kids have really been denied adequate opportunity to get a strong education, or their parents or their grandparents were, and that's carried down from generation to generation. So we have that kind of tragic history of having low expectations for certain people, and that is a big explanation for a large segment of young people who have become disconnected from learning.

CQ: But is the fact that different areas of the country have higher percentages of disadvantaged children the reason why some people are uncomfortable comparing states in educational achievement?

Riley: Perhaps. I don't like to spend a lot of time ranking states and schools. I prefer to measure a state's educational success on improvement. Where they were last year, where they are this year, where they hope to get next year. The same with schools and students. You can't all of a sudden turn salt into sugar. In education, you have to do it in stages. You have to interest young people in connecting up with self-improvement.

CQ: Do you think the standards movement is a unique opportunity to have a long-term impact?

Riley: I really do, and I think that it is not only likely to be important in the future of this country, it is really necessary. If this country is to have a great future, we're going to have to connect the generation that's growing now in the public schools to learning in a much more significant way. The first step is to define what learning is and what students are expected to learn and be able to do.

most over-tested in the world as a result of . . . wrong-headed initiatives at the state and local level," writes Monty Neill, associate director of Fair Test, a Cambridge, Mass., advocacy group. "More than 100 million standardized achievement, aptitude, IQ, readiness and placement tests are administered in U.S. classrooms each year. The result: dumbed-down curricula and unfair barriers to equal opportunity." [19]

The current standards movement does envision a nationwide system of state-administered tests that are linked to content standards. "Performance standards are essential to gauging whether content standards are met," observed a report to the goals panel. "Certification of content standards should be provisional until associated performance standards are developed." [20]

But there is division over how soon such tests should count "for keeps" in such high-stakes decisions as promotion and graduation. The Senate version of the Goals 2000 bill would encourage tests to take real-world effect in three years; the House version would wait five years.

"It gets back to opportunity to learn, income and the basic fairness of assessment," says the NEA's Cutlip. "We don't think the field of assessment is firm enough to make high-stakes decisions, and they need to perfect it so as not to hurt children."

Rep. Reed says: "We want to move deliberately and not rush into standardized tests until we build up the whole education structure, reorganizing the way we operate, redirecting resources, bringing professional-development money directly to classrooms, bringing huge, monolithic high schools down to human scale. A premature assessment can be more damaging than none" among children who are educated at only $2,000 per pupil while competing with kids from affluent suburbs.

The value of national testing in comparing schools in different regions is challenged by Kruse of the Secondary School Principals Association: "Let's not compare Alabama with California; let's just look at Alabama, and say, 'You will achieve this level by eighth grade, this level by 12th etc.,' and then Alabama will have to reflect upon what it has adopted."

Kolberg of the National Alliance of Business thinks the go-slow thinkers are being "overly careful. What's the point of the tests if they can't be used?" he asks. "It's an old idea that we can't come up with a fair test, but tests should be linked to the new content standards, and teachers should be trained to use them."

"School is supposed to be a bridge," says the AFT's Rosenberg. "It's racist to assume automatically that poor and minority children can't meet standards. Yes, the costs are enormous, but we can't let schools off the hook like they did in the late 1960s, when they lowered standards to get over the equal-access hurdle instead of investing to bring them up."

Despite what some spokesmen say, Rosenberg adds, "poor and minority parents want the same thing as everyone else: for their kids to succeed."

Testing is not appropriate if it is done only to "find out where kids stand as opposed to seeing how to get where they ought to be," says Malcolm of the AAAS. "Assessment ought to inform us how to help teachers and students. Parents and kids trust schools to give them what's needed, yet the tests you see now have no connection to the curriculum. We want to make sure there's some relationship."

Rutgers' Massell agrees that national testing is politically problematic, and can have negative consequences for minority students. But there were similar concerns in the 1980s when new graduation requirements were introduced, she says. People thought many blacks would drop out, but they didn't. "There has to be some real consequences or stakes in testing in order for principals, teachers and students to take it seriously. It could be as mild as a public reporting of results."

Lawrence Feinberg, assistant director for reporting and analysis at the National Assessment Governing Board, which administers the NAEP, finds it puzzling that contents standards would be discussed without referring to testing. "Standards don't mean very much until they're used for something real, like promotions, grades or graduation," he says. "It's one thing to have a common curriculum, but you've got to have a test to know what level of attainment and complexity they've learned.

"There are pretty gentle ways of phasing them in, such as giving a bonus in college scholarship awards, or allowing tests to be considered along with other information. But a standard doesn't have much meaning unless it eventually can become a mark on some sort of exam."

The debate over testing also divides those who favor traditional multiple-choice standardized tests, and those who seek new approaches such as "portfolios" of students' best writing, videos, dance routines, speeches, or other work. "Multiple choice is an illusion of objectivity, valuing what you can measure as opposed to measuring what you value," says Malcolm. She envisions a combination of hard data on performance in such areas as math, and more subjective judgments by the teacher as to the students' powers of inquiry and ability to use reference material.

Others argue that standardized tests fail to motivate students who were raised on the entertainment of television and who demand more interactive learning. "Telling a kid that this is a test doesn't work anymore," says elementary principal Baker. "It's boring to spend two to three hours a day filling in bubbles."

Returning to Finn's adage about the omelet, alternative-education proponent Meier of Central Park East Secondary School says: "Most standardized tests can only tell whether someone can make an omelet. But there can be second opinions. You can go to different restaurants. You can't have a national standard on what tastes good."

IQ tests are often racially and culturally biased, she adds, and many other factors are predictors of success in later life. [21] "We want [evaluation] to be high-stakes, and all good schools should say, 'This is what you have to do to graduate.' But when there's too much weight put on assessment, students tend to mimic what's wanted on the tests. There are ways to make education more objective, but human work is not objective."

Finn calls such arguments "a slippery slope. Because we don't yet have a national consensus on some of the subjective results shouldn't mean we don't measure or try to compare anything," he says. "The question is, do kids know what the Declaration of Independence is? Can they write a coherent paragraph?

"There is no need to be embarrassed at the results unless the purpose of the measure is to humiliate. The result could be a discovery that they need to get up earlier in the morning, or that the teacher should teach geography instead of social garbage."

The more-subjective portfolio assessments, says Feinberg, "make it hard to know whether it's really the kid's work or the teacher or the parents', as often happens at school science fairs, where children from educated families have an advantage." Such alternative means are "all right as a teaching device in class, but not for public reporting or admissions decisions," he adds. "They aren't reliable, and they risk a scandal." ■

BACKGROUND

Unofficial Standards

When Gov. John R. McKernan Jr., R-Maine, was asked to draft academic standards for public schools, his response was, "Why didn't somebody do this 200 years ago?" [22]

Indeed, the tradition of local independence for the country's 16,000 school districts dates back to the founding of the Republic. The closest the country came to creating a national curriculum was in 1893, when

Continued on p. 231

Chronology

1980s

Reacting to a decade-long decline in standardized test scores, the administration of President Ronald Reagan launches a movement to improve education to compete with other countries.

1983
A Nation At Risk, a report published by the Education Department's National Commission on Excellence in Education, warns that American education has lost sight of its purpose.

1986
A report published by the National Governors' Association, *Time for Results*, proposes a "horse trade" in which states will give localities funding and flexibility on teaching methods in return for accountability on achievement results.

1987
E.D. Hirsch Jr. publishes *Cultural Literacy: What Every American Needs to Know*. It proposes a minimal framework of knowledge for all Americans.

September 1989
President George Bush convenes an education summit in Charlottesville, Va., with the National Governors' Association, headed by then-Gov. Bill Clinton, D-Ark.

1990s

Movement led by governors links up with federal efforts to set national goals and launch the creation of voluntary nationwide academic standards.

January-February 1990
Six national education goals are announced by Bush and accepted by the nation's governors. They include increasing high school graduation rates and giving students competency in English, mathematics, science, history and geography by the time they leave grades four, eight and 12.

July 1990
Bipartisan National Education Goals Panel, with eight governors, two administration officials and four members of Congress, is created to measure education progress.

April 18, 1991
Bush gives speech to the country on his "America 2000" initiative, outlining strategy to reinvent American education and set up 535 "break-the-mold" schools.

June 1991
Congress and the goals panel create the National Council on Education Standards and Testing to decide whether standards are feasible and desirable.

September 1991
The goals panel recommends setting up standards in the first annual *Goals Report: Building a Nation of Learners.*

Jan. 24, 1992
A National Council on Education Standards report urges national and state leaders to take on systemic change by setting ambitious state standards for curriculum, assessments and delivery of school services.

1992
The National Science Foundation releases part of its effort to create nationwide math and science standards. Twenty-three states began upgrading their math and science curricula. Education Department funds development of voluntary national curriculum standards.

Nov. 3, 1992
Clinton defeats Bush; Democrats prepare to take over White House.

April 1993
The Clinton administration offers education legislation, called the Goals 2000: Educate America Act, which would write national education goals into law.

Oct. 13, 1993
House passes its version of Goals 2000.

Feb. 8, 1994
Senate passes its version of Goals 2000.

March 1994
Congress expected to pass Goals 2000 legislation.

Results vs. Values: The Flap Over Outcomes-Based Education

Education reforms don't occur in a vacuum. The movement for national standards has been competing for attention with a related but more controversial reform known as outcomes-based education (OBE).

Since the late 1970s, OBE advocates have rallied round a simple notion: that measures of student progress should be based less on old-fashioned "inputs," such as how many course hours or how much "seat-time" a student has put in, and more on predetermined objectives or results in a given subject area.

University of South Dakota education Professors Floyd Boschee and Mark A. Baron, authors of a recent book promoting OBE, point to success stories across the country. In Frederick County, Md., they report, an outcomes-based system in use since 1986 has enabled 40-60 percent of the students to receive satisfactory or better marks on the state's performance exams, compared with 25-34 percent statewide. [1]

As the movement has grown — some two-thirds of the states have moved toward some form of outcomes-based education — specified outcomes have ranged from the purely academic to the hazy: "All students apply knowledge, demonstrate skills and examine attitudes in choosing behaviors that promote healthy lifestyles," reads one proposed outcome in Pennsylvania. [2]

In recent years, groups of conservative and religious parents have attacked outcomes-based education for promoting certain values and for delving into the realm of psychotherapy. OBE is "just another name for mastery learning, a method of manipulation based on B.F. Skinner's methods of repetitive reinforcement (training children the way he has trained animals)," said the Christian group Citizens for Excellence in Education. The Costa Mesa, Calif.-based group notes with concern that the movement's father, University of Chicago education Professor Benjamin L. Bloom, defines good teaching as "challenging the students' fixed beliefs." [3]

Phyllis Schlafly, president of the conservative Eagle Forum in Alton, Ill., attacks OBE on multiple grounds. "Computers play a big role in outcomes-based education," she says, "and parents are rightfully concerned about the accumulation of personal information on children that is not academic but deals with behavior, health and family. They're concerned about who will have access and whether it will be used to track children and be provided to prospective employers."

Schlafly adds that many business groups are promoting OBE because they want "a well-trained, compliant work force like that of Mexico" to compete in the global economy at a time when corporate downsizing is eliminating skilled blue-collar and mid-manager jobs.

"But OBE's biggest characteristic," Schlafly continues, "is that it's a dumbed-down, egalitarian system based on the notion that every child can learn to the same level. If you accept that, the level has got to be low. They recycle material until every child reaches a limited outcome. That is unfair to the faster learners because they can't go forward, and it's unfair to the slower ones because they quickly find out that if they sit around, someone will give them the answer."

The critics of OBE — now organized in 14 states, according to the liberal group People for the American Way — have had their impact. In Pennsylvania, in February 1993, the General Assembly backed off from its ground-breaking year-old OBE program following pressure from parents led by a 38-year-old former teacher named Peg Luksik, dubbed the "mother of the outcomes revolt." [4] In Virginia last fall, then-Gov. L. Douglas Wilder rejected the state's "Common Core of Learning" in its final stages because it was deemed too values-oriented.

According to a state summary, the Virginia plan was "not particularly concerned with what things are called or how they are accomplished or how one student is better than another. It is concerned with results: Can each student do those things necessary to learn, to prosper, and to benefit society?" [5]

Critics of OBE "want more competition and less cooperation, and they want more acquisition of facts," contends Laurie Baker, principal of Tuckahoe Elementary School in Arlington, Va. "But kids can no longer simply learn facts, because there are too many facts out there." Baker says what students need is *access* to information using a curriculum as a conceptually based body of knowledge.

"In the upper and middle classes," she says, "there is a level of discomfort at the [seemingly] low level of expectations of outcome-based education, but the goal is not what information is gleaned, it's what they can do with it. What facts do we need, for example, to solve the problem of homelessness? In our race to become career-minded professionals, we've lost some of the humanity in education."

The attacks on OBE have "muddied the waters" in the movement for national standards, says Susan L. Traiman, director of education policy studies at the National Governors' Association (NGA). The governors are being careful not to let others define their terms, she notes. "Yes, teachers teach values like honesty and hard work," she says, "but the governors want academic values that can be measured. You vary the time a student can take, but you don't vary the standards," which are designed to be "world class."

---

[1] Boschee and Baron's book is *Outcome-Based Education: Developing Programs Through Strategic Planning* (1993), cited in *Education Week*, Feb. 2, 1994, p. 31.

[2] *Education Week*, Sept. 22, 1993, p. 1.

[3] "Special Report on Outcomes-Based Education," by Citizens for Excellence in Education, 1992.

[4] *Education Week*, Sept. 22, 1993.

[5] Virginia Department of Education, "The Virginia Common Core of Learning," Draft, Oct. 20, 1992.

Continued from p. 228

a committee of college presidents and other luminaries headed by Harvard University President Charles Eliot issued the "Report of the Committee of Ten on Secondary School Studies."

This influential document recommended a traditional array of studies in Greek and Latin, math, chemistry, natural history, government and economy. It argued that studying Greek and Latin "trains the mind" and that geography "enhances the powers of observation and reasoning." [23]

The classics approach of the Committee of Ten was largely superseded by a 1918 report, "The Cardinal Principles of Secondary Education," prepared not by university chiefs but by education specialists, public officials and high school principals. Greatly influenced by the progressive, utilitarian philosophy of John Dewey, it emphasized "health, command of fundamental processes, worthy home membership, vocation, citizenship, worthy use of leisure and ethical character." [24]

The same emphasis on psychology and real-world applications was also apparent in *The Curriculum*, a groundbreaking book also published in 1918 by University of Chicago education Professor Franklin Bobbitt. It argued that human life "consists in the performance of specific activities. Education that prepares for life is one that prepares definitely and adequately for these specific activities." [25]

It was this philosophy, as interpreted variously by local school districts — many of them dealing with newly diverse populations brought about by immigration — that would hold sway in the United States for much of the 20th century.

Pressure for Standards

An antecedent of the current standards movement was launched in the 1950s, when the National Science Foundation (NSF) funded 53 local curricula projects in math, science and social sciences. "The perception that the federal government was getting involved in curricula meant they had to tiptoe around," says Rutgers' Massell.

The NSF's work, particularly in science, was adopted by an impressive number of schools, but in 1976 it ran into trouble in Congress. An NSF anthropology project called "Man: A Course of Study" (MACOS) brought protests from parents who objected to its emphasis on evolution and communal living. When Congress began investigating, the damage to the project's reputation hurt book sales, and the publishers abandoned the project. [26]

The nation's schools, in the late 1960s and '70s, were wracked with controversy. Alternative-education movements grew up favoring "open classrooms" and "schools without walls." Influential critic Charles Silberman charged that the current curriculum was filled with "banality and triviality." Another alternative advocate, Charles H. Rathbone, wrote that "there is no inherently indispensable body of knowledge that every single child should know." [27]

At the same time, curriculum decisions were further complicated by new social changes, such as busing controversies and demands both for black studies and bilingual education for recent immigrants. Moreover, plummeting SAT scores prompted new discussions of how to raise standards.

"A Nation At Risk"

"If an unfriendly foreign power had attempted to impose on America the mediocre educational performance that exists today, we might well have viewed it as an act of war."

So declared *A Nation At Risk*, the blunt and widely discussed report of an Education Department commission released in 1983. It spoke scornfully of a "cafeteria curriculum in which the appetizers and desserts can be easily mistaken for the main course" and worried that "in some metropolitan areas, basic literacy has become the goal rather than the starting point." [28] It called for a longer school day and school year, and for standards in content and expectations.

The impact of *A Nation At Risk* is still felt today. "It clearly affected all schools and brought pressure on them," Arthur Gosling, superintendent of schools for Arlington, Va., said recently. "On the negative side, it created a deep and abiding loss of confidence of people in the field." [29]

"It really was a report that seemed a little blind to changes in society," added Paul Masem, Gosling's counterpart in Alexandria, Va. "Part of it was it had a very strong conservative agenda. It was as much a political document as an education document." [30]

The report did prompt states to raise graduation requirements. But as Massell put it, many felt that was a pretty "blunt instrument," and most states did little to probe the reasons behind the schools' decline. One exception was California, which under education Superintendent Bill Honig instigated a statewide history curriculum with financial incentives for local jurisdictions to participate. The math teachers, meanwhile, embarked on their standards project, which would reach fruition in 1989.

By 1986, it was clear that the states needed more direction. A task force of governors led by Lamar Alexander, R-Tenn., who later became Education secretary in the Bush administration, released an influential report called *Time for Results*. It called for a "horse trade" between state governments and school districts, exchanging flexibility for local accountability.

"Presently," the report noted, "the school system controls both the production and consumption of education. The system tells the students what they will learn, at what speed and what quality. Students and their parents have little to say about it. A more responsive system would incorporate what students and their parents say they need with the education services necessary to meet it." [31]

1989 Education Summit

The current standards movement can be said to have been launched in earnest at the September 1989 education summit convened by then-President George Bush — the self-described "education president" — in Charlottesville, Va. There, Bush, who bucked his predecessors' reluctance to actively involve Washington in education, teamed with the president of the National Governors' Association, Bill Clinton, a future Democratic president who had been active in education reform in his home state of Arkansas. [32]

At the Charlottesville gathering, the governors laid the groundwork for developing six national education goals:

• By the year 2000, all children in America will start school ready to learn.

• The high school graduation rate will increase to at least 90 percent;

• American students will leave grades 4, 8 and 12 having demonstrated competency in challenging subject matter, including English, mathematics, science, history and geography, and every school in America will ensure that all students learn to use their minds well, so they may be prepared for responsible citizenship, further learning, and productive employment in our modern economy;

• U.S. students will be first in the world in science and mathematics achievement;

• Every adult American will be literate and will possess the knowledge and skills necessary to compete in a global economy and exercise the rights and responsibilities of citizenship;

• Every school in America will be free of drugs and violence and will offer a disciplined environment conducive to learning.

The governors also teamed with Congress and the Education Department to create the National Education Goals Panel, which was charged with compiling an annual report on how the country is progressing toward meeting the goals.

The new partnership spawned the Bush administration's "America 2000" program, which launched an effort to set up a "break the mold" schools program, a set of federal grants that would establish new schools — one in each congressional district — that would experiment with tutors, smaller classes, new curricula and a longer school year.

With the arrival of the Clinton administration, the America 2000 program was altered and renamed "Goals 2000." The big difference, says current Education Secretary Richard W. Riley, is scope. The Bush plan "focused on improving education in a small number of schools. Goals 2000 focuses on improving education for all children in all schools." [33] *(See Riley interview, p. 226.)* ■

CURRENT SITUATION

Flood of Initiatives

Goals 2000 is just part of the Clinton administration's education strategy. Congress is moving on Clinton's plan to help create education standards for non-college-bound youth through so-called school-to-work transition legislation. Lawmakers also are considering a major administration-sponsored overhaul of the key Title I section of the Elementary and Secondary Education Act Reauthorization, which would redirect federal education aid to concentrate on the poorest districts.

Clinton's fiscal 1995 budget request, released in February, would boost education spending by 7 percent, or $1.7 billion. "This request," Riley wrote, "coming as it does in a time of heightened budgetary consciousness, is a clear sign of the president's commitment and resolve to invest in children and youth — our future." [34]

The Goals 2000 legislation that Clinton sent to Congress last April was significantly altered by Democrats on the House Education and Labor Committee, who added the opportunity-to-learn standards that Republicans fear will cost school districts millions to comply with.

Critics charged that all the talk about "voluntary" participation for states in Goals 2000 is rendered moot by language in the Title I bill — whose $7 billion is where the real federal money lies — which conditions federal funding on states offering a Goals 2000 plan or something similar. "Congress out of one side of its mouth is saying Goals 2000 is voluntary," says Finn, "but on the other side is saying, 'Ha ha ha, fooled you.' "

Rep. Reed denies that the House is seeking to tie ongoing federal funds to participation in Goals 2000. The Title I program "has a requirement that some plan be adapted, and we would be accused of ludicrous redundancy if we didn't point out that states can use their Goals 2000 rather than come up with a separate plan for [Title I]."

Action in the States

The diversity of the standards movement is evident in the differences in how states are approaching it. Maine's "Common Core of Learning," for example, is organized by skills rather than subjects. California's social sciences framework closely mimics what the history, civics and social sciences standards groups are creating. And Alabama is planning to build its social science curriculum

Continued on p. 234

At Issue:

Will national standards improve education in the United States?

yes

ALBERT SHANKER

President, American Federation of Teachers
EXCERPTED FROM *"WHERE WE STAND,"* 1992.

There is a general recognition that students in other industrialized countries achieve at a much higher level than American students. They do better on the international examinations that allow us to make comparisons, and their school-leaving exams are more demanding than any our students face. What are these countries doing that we aren't?

. . . .There are many differences, but one of the most basic is that nearly all of these countries have national education standards. They have decided what their students need to learn, and they have developed a national curriculum and national system of tests to find out whether or not the students learn it. In some countries, the curriculum is so carefully prescribed that you could predict what math lesson a fourth-grader would be studying on a given day of the year. In other countries, there is more leeway. Still, national standards mean that a student graduating from high school has achieved a certain level of knowledge.

These systems have many advantages over ours. Each of our states and 16,000 school districts is more or less doing its own thing when it comes to curriculum. Some create their own or adapt curriculums from other districts; some take ideas from here and there. So our money and efforts are spread thin, and some districts have much better curriculums than others. With national curriculums, resources and talent can be concentrated, so children in every school district can benefit from excellent materials.

National curriculums mean that kids moving from one school district to another do not have to waste time by repeating material they already know or struggle to catch up on stuff they've missed. These curriculums also mean that you have an answer to the question of how to prepare teachers. Teach them to teach the national curriculum and test them on how well they do it. U.S. colleges and universities have no such guidance in preparing or assessing teachers. Their students will teach in different states and school districts with different curriculums. So what they get are abstract courses that most teachers say did not help them learn how to teach. . . .

There would be consequences for getting this system wrong, but there also are consequences for continuing to do things the way we are now. Our students don't know much, and no wonder. Except for the few students who hope to go to selective colleges, they don't work hard in school. And there's no reason for them to do so because they know it won't count. This is destructive for them and for our country.

no

DENNIS GRAY

Senior associate, Council for Basic Education
FROM "NATIONAL STANDARDS: A CONTRARY VIEW," *BASIC EDUCATION,* JANUARY 1994.

Count on this: The push for national standards, if successful, will mire schools more deeply in mediocrity. Why? Certainly not because high quality is a bad idea or that widespread excellence is unachievable. Rather, national standards will prove counter-productive because proposals in the name of standards for learning, with a couple of laudable of exceptions, trickle downward from the upper reaches of establishment subject-matter groups, academics whose job security depends on attracting renewed support for the turf they have always guarded and want to perpetuate.

It's hardly newsworthy to observe that schooling tends to operate less for the learning of young people than for the well-being of their guardians. What is new in the last decade is a growing recognition that conventional academic structures have little to do with the way that people encounter life. The tidy subdivision of schooling into subject matters ignores the messy reality of continuous coping, learning and adapting in adolescence and adulthood. The truth of this recognition threatens the barons of academe, so they're busily defining "What high school graduates should know and be able to do" as the core knowledge in their own subject-area enclaves. To know the standard-setters is to anticipate the standards.

If public schools try to perform up to the national standards now being enumerated by professional associations, academic subject by academic subject, the effect will be to intensify all the elements of the current system that do not work: segregated courses, syllabi, textbooks, tests, graduation requirements, all based on a misguided orthodoxy that bears little relation to how people live. . . .

If the standards-setters were thinking of real students, real needs and real life, what should they be doing? First, they should conduct broadly based conversations aimed toward restructuring curricula to breach discipline-drawn boundaries. They should focus instead on the qualities and habits that ought to characterize worthy graduates of public schools. The new focus should liberate the dialogue from control by subject-matter tories and should require the inclusion of broad-gauged generalists to argue for results that apply across traditional academic borders.

Doing so would necessitate a radical shift away from the current approach to national standards, which is producing prodigious lists of outcomes that one might expect from hard-working graduate students in conventionally organized universities. Such standards can only bury schooling more deeply in a past already gone bust.

Can U.S. Schools Learn From Other Countries?

In Paris, the French education minister for decades was said to be able to look at his watch at any hour and know which lessons were being taught in schools across France.

Such an ultra-uniform curriculum is no longer French practice, notes University of Virginia English Professor E.D. Hirsch Jr. But the modern French system of grade-by-grade standards administered by 20 regional bodies offers much that Americans can learn from.

In fact, he says, "Every major country in Europe and much of Asia offers curriculum standards except the Netherlands — and the Dutch students perform the least well." That suggests, Hirsch says, that rather than being unfair to some students, as some charge, standards actually improve performance.

American advocates of standards have long pointed with concern to international comparisons showing that American students do not stack up well in the intellectual Olympics. An international Educational Testing Service study of math and science scores among 13-year-olds in 1991 showed that American 13-year-olds were largely outperformed by students in five countries. (*See table, p. 224.*)[1]

American Federation of Teachers President Albert Shanker, in a speech last June, recalled having dinner with a couple who had just emigrated to New York City from economically devastated Russia. "They said that even though they had their eighth-grade daughter in a very good private school, she was learning what she had learned in the third grade back home."[2]

Critics of U.S. education also look approvingly on the way foreign countries maintain higher expectations by requiring their students to undergo tough national tests. France since the time of Napoleon has administered the baccalaureate to high-schoolers; Germany has its *abitur* after grade 13 for *gymnasien* students on the university track; and Japan has its Test of the National University Entrance Examination, which scares many students into attending commercial "cram schools" on weekends.

"The high expectations [other countries have] are manifest in the demanding questions they ask, not only about their own history and culture but also about those of other societies," said a National Endowment for the Humanities booklet on world testing. "Could American students answer the questions the French ask about the foreign policy of the United States? That the British ask about American progressivism? That the European schools ask about South Carolina's secession?"[3]

Others caution, however, that there are limits to how foreign techniques might apply in the United States, with its diverse population, tradition of individualism and local control of education.

"In many ways we're ahead of the Japanese and Russians," says Betty Ann Armstrong, assistant superintendent for instruction for the public schools in Arlington County, Va. "They do a lot of rote learning, while we've achieved a lot in creative thinking and initiative."

Hirsch agrees that "Americans are more independent-minded and challenge authority, but that's a cultural trait not owing to school arrangements," he says. "How flamboyant and critically thinking do you want someone to be in solving algebra problems? When you get down to cases, it's can they solve it?"

Tom Lavery, who directs the Board of Mathematical Sciences for the National Academy of Sciences, says the notion that foreigners are less creative is overstated. "I came to Taiwan with the standard Western attitude that we Americans may not learn all the facts, but that we sure are more creative," he says. "But in teaching a course in business math I found the Taiwanese to be two to three years more advanced than Americans, as well as highly creative. To be creative in the modern world, you have to have the basics down pat. You can't be creative in physics without knowing the parts of an atom."

Lavery also disputes the common notion that student populations in other countries are relatively homogeneous. "In Paris, there are North Africans; in Singapore, there are Chinese; in Germany, there are Turks and Spanish," he says. "There are school systems around the world that achieve high standards with heterogeneity far greater than ours."

Overall, American students are "just scraping to get by," he concludes. "Our best students are doing D work in Japan, and our middle-level students are not competing with the middle-level student in other countries. We've performed well by historical standards, but the rest of the world has gone beyond."

---

[1] National Education Goals Panel, "National Education Goals Report," Vol. 1: The National Report, 1993, p. 90.

[2] "Achieving High Standards," Albert Shanker's address to the 1991 AFT QuEST Conference, p. 6.

[3] National Endowment for the Humanities, "National Tests: What Other Countries Expect Their Students to Know," 1991, p. 2.

Continued from p. 232

around ecology.[35]

At least 45 states have created or are preparing new curriculum frameworks, according to a study released last April.[36] And at least 26 states and the District of Columbia will be dealing with education standards in 1994, according to a survey by the National Conference of State Legislatures. (*See map, p. 220.*)

The states that have made the most progress, says Julie Bell, the conference's

Denver-based director of education programs, include Vermont, Kentucky, South Carolina, Florida, Washington, Connecticut and California. Among those moving more slowly are South Dakota and Colorado, she says.

Educators' Proposals

Educators are not simply waiting for governments to act. The New Standards Project, a consortium of 19 states and six school districts operated by the National Center on Education and the Economy, is creating a set of assessments based on content standards that will combine written exams with students' portfolios to "reshape the way children learn." [37]

Meanwhile, Project 2061, named for the year Halley's comet returns, is under way by a group of teachers and administrators under the auspices of the AAAS. Dovetailing with the existing Council of Math Teachers standards, it has created "benchmarks" for grade-by-grade learning in math, science and technology by convening panels in six locales.

The project is seen as a boon to teachers because it "deliberately omits much of the traditional content of science, mathematics and technology found in today's curricula and textbooks yet contains material with which most teachers are not altogether familiar [such as] the history of science . . . themes that cut across disciplines [and] engineering concepts." [38]

Hirsch's Core Knowledge Foundation is circulating the curriculum guides from his book *Cultural Literacy* and setting up programs in individual schools, with 40 in Florida alone. The effort has met with particular success in minority-dominated schools such as the Mohegan School in the Bronx, where every student comes from a family poor enough to qualify for free school lunches. Test scores there have risen 4-18 percent, according to the foundation.

The Core Knowledge program also has been used successfully in four black schools in rural Mississippi. "The reason minorities don't do well in national standards tests is always geared to a lack of basic core knowledge," says Mississippi education official Harris. "In the Western world, certain facts never change, and 30 years ago we had a basic set of knowledge from which to springboard. Lots of kids are children of teenage mothers, and they never had the discussions about trips we had with our parents. This replaces what should have been expressed in the home."

Hirsch himself is well aware that his traditionalist approach is criticized as "educational fascism" that relies too much on the canon of "dead white males." "But it's voluntary fascism," he counters. "We have no power, only ideas. Only in a democracy can we make our way in the world. We don't even like to work at the superintendent level; it's better at the school level." ■

OUTLOOK

Hopes and Fears

"Children learn at different rates," observes Billy Sue Vogel, a teacher at Claude Pepper Elementary School in Miami, Fla. "They all learn to walk at different times. They all learn to talk at different times. Yet we plunk them in school when they turn 5 by Sept. 1, and we expect them all to do the same thing. Sometimes there is just a developmental lag there. It doesn't mean the child isn't bright." [39]

With national standards, teachers would vary the time and resources accorded each child, but the ultimate goals would be fixed. And unlike existing approaches, the standards would be set markedly high. Under preliminary 12th-grade math performance standards offered by the goals panel, for example, only 18 percent of boys and 14 percent of girls in 1992 would have measured up. [40]

The fear among many that such rigor will prompt low-performing students to drop out is contradicted by recent research. A study by researchers David Angus of the University of Michigan and Jeffrey Mirel of Northern Illinois University tracked the percentage of high school courses devoted to core academics over the past 70 years. It found that as more students (particularly blacks and Hispanics) moved to rigorous academics in the 1980s, the dropout rate fell 13-15 percent. [41]

The key, says Rutgers' Massell, will be developing teachers who can make the standards happen. "Some states pay only lip service to staff development and view it as a perk to teachers' unions," she says. But many states undergoing systemic reform of education — Vermont, Kentucky and California, for example — are devoting substantial attention and dollars to staff development, "getting teachers involved in *sustained* discussion of student learning, curriculum development and standards."

So far, the majority of teachers don't know about this "inside-the-Beltway argument," says the NEA's Cutlip. "It's been a national rather than a local debate."

Parents' groups, by contrast, have been deeply involved. The National PTA has been working to get a seventh education goal attached to Goals 2000, declaring that "by the year 2000, every elementary and secondary school will have a comprehensive school and home parental-involvement program."

Goals 2000 will "introduce a whole new paradigm of parental involvement," says the PTA's Fege. "Not that parents will decide what the basal readings will be, but they will be able to participate in developing and knowing the core curriculum and performance standards in order to make choices." He adds that standards may "democratize" the process by encouraging use of telecommunications technology to link up parents at town meetings.

"Yes, there will be parental involvement," says the AFT's Rosenberg, "but we shouldn't think that the patient can know more than the doctor. A lot of fads come whistling through, and the lines between professionals and lay people have become utterly blurred."

Like outcomes-based education, standards could founder on differences between the values and needs of inner-city and suburban schools. Brown University's Sizer this January warned that school reforms today are being driven by central-city schools, and that affluent suburban schools are not feeling pressure to change. [42]

As for students themselves, standards enthusiasts would do well to recall the survey of junior and senior high-schoolers taken in 1984 by educator John Goodlad. When asked what was the best thing about school, 50-60 percent of the youngsters cited "my friends," "sports" or "good student attitudes," while less than 10 percent mentioned teachers or classes. [43]

"If we get tightly crafted curriculum expectations, it won't work," says Michael A. Resnick, associate executive director of the Alexandria, Va.-based National School Boards Association. "But if we get broader ones that deal with what kind of broader skills students should have, then we'll be OK. It's one thing to be able to look at Shakespeare and with some facility understand the concepts, but it's another thing to say that students must know certain things about *Romeo and Juliet.*"

"There is more opposition to standards than is apparent," says Harlem principal Meier. "The debate could be a healthy and useful part of reform, but if they try for a single standard of what we must cover and a single assessment, then the reforms they claim they want in terms of teaching critical thinkers who analyze will go down the tubes."

Finn says he was once excited about standards, but now has misgivings. "Congress mangled the bill in areas where the federal government has no business, such as opportunity-to-learn standards," he says. He also regrets that the original plan for standards in five subject areas has grown to eight and more. "Pretty soon," he complains, "we could see national standards for driver's ed, home ec and bachelor living." ■

Notes

1 The council is based in Reston, Va.

2 Clinton requested $700 million for Goals 2000 in fiscal 1995. The Senate passed a $422 million bill for fiscal '95 on February 8, 1994; a similar House version for $427 million in fiscal '93 passed Oct. 13, 1993.

3 Philip Bigler and Karen Lockard, *Failing Grades: A Teacher's Report Card on Education in America* (1992), p. 14.

4 Reported in *Education Week*, Sept. 15, 1993. The National Assessment of Educational Performance (NAEP) is a series of tests that has been used to measure achievement in U.S. schools since 1969.

5 *Los Angeles Times*, Sept. 19, 1993.

6 *The Washington Post*, Nov. 8, 1993.

7 Theodore R. Sizer, *Horace's School: Redesigning the American High School* (1992), p. 110. The Coalition of Essential Schools helps public schools across the country locally define what they want their students to learn and then change to become more effective in meeting the students' needs.

8 Donald M. Stewart, "Setting Standards In a Democracy: Filling the Gap," *Education Week*, Feb. 2, 1994, p. 40. The College Board is a membership organization of colleges, universities, secondary school systems and educational associations that administers tests, conducts research and provides guidance, placement and other educational services.

9 "Achieving High Standards," American Federation of Teachers President Albert Shanker's address to the 1993 AFT QuEst Conference," July 1993, p. 25.

10 Citizens for Excellence in Education, *Education Newsline*, July-August 1993.

11 Charles F. Bahmueller and Margaret Stimmann Branson, "Renewing the civic purpose of the schools," *Momentum*, September-October, 1993. *Momentum* is the journal of the National Catholic Educational Association.

12 Susan L. Traiman, "The Debate on Opportunity-to-Learn Standards," National Governors' Association, 1993.

13 For background, see "School Funding," *The CQ Researcher*, Aug. 27, 1993, pp. 745-768.

14 Regular column as paid advertisement in *The New York Times*, June 13, 1993.

15 "Promises to Keep: Creating High Standards for American Students," National Education Goals Panel, Nov. 15, 1993.

16 Chester E. Finn Jr., column in *The Wall Street Journal*, Feb. 8, 1994.

17 *The Washington Post*, Jan. 31, 1991.

18 Quoted in Polly Wells, "Putting America to the Test," *Agenda*, spring 1991.

19 Writing in *The Washington Post*, April 5, 1992.

20 "Promises to Keep," *op. cit.*, p. iii.

21 For background, see "Intelligence Testing" *The CQ Researcher*, July 30, 1993, pp. 649-672.

22 Cited in Business Roundtable and National Alliance of Business Background Memo, "National Standards and Assessments."

23 E.D. Hirsch Jr., *Cultural Literacy: What Every American Needs to Know* (1985), pp. 117-118.

24 Diane Ravitch, *The Troubled Crusade* (1983), p. 48.

25 *Ibid.*, p. 49.

26 *Ibid.*, p. 264.

27 *Ibid.*, p. 249.

28 National Commission on Excellence in Education, A Nation at Risk: The Imperative for Educational Reform (1983).

29 Quoted in the *Arlington Journal*, Jan. 10, 1994.

30 *Ibid.*

31 Quoted in Gerald Leinwand, *Public Education: American Issues* (1992), p. 115.

32 For details on the Charlottesville meeting and Bush's education efforts, see "Scorned School Bill Dies in Senate," *1992 CQ Almanac*, pp. 455-460.

33 Richard W. Riley, letter to *USA Today*, Feb. 4, 1994.

34 *Ibid.*

35 *Education Week*, Jan. 19, 1994.

36 The study, "Status of New State Curriculum Frameworks, Standards, Assessments, and Monitoring Systems," was performed by Policy Studies Associates Inc., a Washington consulting firm.

37 Warren Simmons and Lauren Resnick, "Assessment as the Catalyst of School Reform," *Educational Leadership*, February 1993, p. 11.

38 American Association for the Advancement of Science, *Benchmarks for Scientific Literacy* (1993), p. 305.

39 Catherine Collins and Douglas Frantz, *Teachers Talking Out of School* (1993), p. 215.

40 The National Education Goals Report, 1993, Vol. 1, p. 60.

41 Cited in *USA Today*, Dec. 15, 1993.

42 Quoted in *Education Week*, Feb. 2, 1994, p. 1.

43 Leinwand, *op. cit.*, p. 97.

Bibliography

Selected Sources Used

Books

Bigler, Philip, and Karen Lockard, *Failing Grades: A Teacher's Report Card on Education in America*, Vandamere Press, 1992.

An author-lecturer and a high school teacher explore the current array of issues confronting public schools and suggest 19 reforms, among them school-based management and elimination of tracking.

Collins, Catherine, and Douglas Frantz, *Teachers Talking Out of School*, Little Brown, 1993.

Two *Los Angeles Times* reporters interviewed dozens of teachers at diverse schools around the country, gleaning frank and in-depth commentary on such issues as teacher motivation, grade inflation, racial tensions, poverty and discipline.

Finn, Chester E. Jr., *We Must Take Charge: Our Schools and Our Future*, The Free Press, 1991.

A former Bush administration assistant Education secretary now with Christopher Whittle's Edison Project on school privatization surveys education controversies in the late 1980s and early '90s, many of which helped lead the way toward the current standards movement.

Hirsch, E.D., Jr., *Cultural Literacy: What Every American Needs to Know*, Houghton Mifflin, 1987.

A University of Virginia English professor outlines his controversial argument for a minimal curriculum of basic Western knowledge for all citizens. Profits from the book have been funneled into the author's Core Knowledge Foundation, which has been setting up his curriculum in schools around the country.

Leinwand, Gerald, *Public Education*, Facts on File Books, 1992.

An editor at Facts on File and a former dean at Baruch College has written a survey of the history and current status of major issues facing public schools. He deals with such questions as what should be taught, who should teach and what education priorities should be for the 21st century.

Ravitch, Diane, *The Troubled Crusade: American Education, 1945-1980*, Basic Books, 1983.

A former Bush administration assistant Education secretary now at the Brookings Institution wrote this comprehensive history of postwar public education that tracks the increasing federal role in U.S. schools and the rise of powerful interest groups.

Articles

***Educational Leadership*, February 1991 and February 1993.**

The journal of the Alexandria, Va.-based Association for Supervision and Curriculum Development (ASCD) devoted two complete issues in the past three years to the emerging issue of national standards.

Reports

American Federation of Teachers, *National Education Standards and Assessments*, 1992.

The country's second-largest teachers' union published this convention resolution and background paper promoting the movement toward national standards.

National Education Goals Panel, *The National Education Goals Report*, Government Printing Office, 1993.

A panel made up of governors, four members of Congress and two members of the administration prepared this annual evaluation of the schools' progress toward fulfilling the national goals laid out after the Charlottesville, Va., education summit convened by President George Bush in September 1989.

The Next Step

Additional information from UMI's Newspaper & Periodical Abstracts database

Improving Education

Bash, Alan, "Kids' TV coming of age," *USA Today*, Dec. 21, 1993, p. D3.

Children's TV is finally embracing educational programming, and educational standards are improving, with the advent of shows like "Beakman's World" and the Disney-syndicated "Bill Nye the Science Guy," Bash writes

McCollister, Betty, "The terrible texts," *Humanist*, November 1993, pp. 40-41.

One necessary step forward improving public schools that can be taken immediately and at no cost to taxpayers is for schools to refuse to purchase textbooks until their publishers improve their generally wretched quality, McCollister writes. Today's schoolchildren are using books that contain leaden, clunky prose that is without resonance and that is guaranteed to turn children off reading, she says.

Musante, Fred, "Groups are divided on education plan," *The New York Times*, Jan. 9, 1994, p. CN5.

The dispute in Connecticut over a public education reform plan in which schools would be converted to an "outcomes-based" approach is examined. Supporters characterize the proposal as promoting higher standards for students, while opponents claim the plan is really motivated by a social agenda to indoctrinate children with values and attitudes their parents may not share.

Goals 2000

Farney, Dennis, "Beyond Washington: Middle America in Clinton's first year: Parents are skeptical of Washington's ability to upgrade the nation's educational system," *The Wall Street Journal*, Oct. 13, 1993, p. A24.

The House is tentatively scheduled to vote on a high-priority Clinton education measure called Goals 2000, the week of Oct. 18, 1993. The legislation has been seven years in the making, incubated by the bipartisan National Governors' Association, initially proposed by President Bush and now by President Clinton. For the first time in U.S. educational history, it would have Washington directly set voluntary academic standards.

Ohanian, Susan, "Clinton education recipe: Reheat old hash," *USA Today*, Feb. 2, 1994, p. A11.

Susan Ohanian criticizes President Clinton's Goals 2000: Educate America Act, arguing that by focusing solely on standards, the plan overlooks the real needs of children and the problems of education in the U.S.

Pitsch, Mark, "New Goals 2000 bill excises state standards requirement," *Education Week*, Nov. 17, 1993, p. 15.

The Clinton administration's new version of its education-reform plan eliminates requirements that states establish standards for curricular content and student performance. This change is discussed.

National Standards

Celis, William III, "Education panel states its mission," *The New York Times*, Nov. 26, 1993, p. B15.

In the strongest and clearest statement of intentions yet offered by the National Education Goals Panel, the 14-member board said that the educational standards being adopted in various subjects were not intended to become a national curriculum.

Cizek, Gregory J., "On the disappearance of standards," *Education Week*, Nov. 10, 1993, p. 32.

The absence of standards in education seems to have made experts grow more fond of them, Cizek writes. Applying any standard must result in some students meeting the standard and others falling short, he says.

Ordovensky, Pat, "Do we need national standards for schools? Let localities do it," *USA Today*, Dec. 13, 1993, p. A15.

Comments by Lauro Cavazos from a discussion and press conference with other former Education secretaries are presented. He says each state and school district should set its own standards and that developing a private school system is a mistake when the existing public one is already in trouble and meaningful changes won't come from Washington, D.C., but from the schools themselves.

Viadero, Debra, "Standards in collision," *Education Week*, Jan. 19, 1994, pp. 25-27.

As the national academic standards-setting movement continues to gain momentum, worries that the documents may turn out to be too numerous, too lengthy and too different from one another are being voiced with increasing frequency, Viadero writes. The movement to set national standards in precollegiate subjects is discussed.

The State of Education

Benning, Victoria, "U.S. educators renew debate on K-12, higher-ed roles," *Boston Globe*, Nov. 21, 1993, p. 40.

With a debate raging over whether Massachusetts' public colleges are lowering admission standards to accommodate poorly prepared students, educators across the nation are wrestling with similar issues, the author writes, including how to bring college and K-12 educators together for a restructuring.

Henry, Tamara, "Student standards in development," *USA Today*, Dec. 15, 1993, p. D6.

A special report on the quality of education in the U.S. looks at the work being done by U.S. educators, using other countries as models, to develop documents that could fundamentally alter how English, math, science and other subjects are taught in the classroom.

"Most students score poorly on new state test," *The New York Times*, Jan. 15, 1994, p. A24.

Only 1 in 5 public-school students meets or exceeds statewide academic standards, according to the results of the Connecticut Mastery Tests released on Jan. 14, 1994. Although lower scores had been expected in the first year of the new, more rigorous tests, education officials were disappointed.

Ravitch, Diane, "The war on standards," *Partisan Review*, fall 1993, pp. 685-692.

The war on standards in U.S. education is a generational phenomenon, Ravitch writes. The decline of standards can be traced to the 1930s, when many tenets of progressive education were institutionalized in public schools or to the campus rebellions of the 1960s, she says.

Tabor, Mary B. W., "Schools battle wide disparity in curriculums," *The New York Times*, Nov. 21, 1993, p. 39.

New York City's decentralized school system, which allows districts to choose their own books and curriculums as long as they follow city, state and federal guidelines, has produced wide variations in the quality and content of instruction in the city's 1,069 schools and 32 districts, Tabor writes. Schools Chancellor Ramon C. Cortines has announced plans to develop a core curriculum that would set citywide standards for different grade levels.

Subject-Specific Standards

Coleman, Trevor W., "Science educators push standards for kids," *Detroit News*, Oct. 25, 1993, p. A2.

The American Association for the Advancement of Science, a leading organization of science educators, has jumped into the national debate over student education standards by issuing a report with the first set of guidelines for what all kids should know and be able to do by the time they graduate.

Schloemer, Cathy G., "Aligning assessment with the NCTM's curriculum standards," *Mathematics Teacher*, December 1993, pp. 722-725.

Several mathematics teaching activities that help meet the National Council of Teachers of Mathematics' standards are described. Improved communication is the focus of assessment standards.

Schneider, Donald, "Teaching social studies: The standards movement," *Clearing House*, September 1993, pp. 5-7.

The movement to establish national educational standards has profound implications for students, teachers and schools, Schneider writes. It is to be hoped that the commonality of themes, concepts, perspectives and intellectual skills addressed in the various social studies standards development efforts may offer a basis for subsequent collaboration in the search for curriculum integration and coherence, he says.

Viadero, Debra, "Sampler of avenues to English standards offered," *Education Week*, Dec. 1, 1993, p. 8.

The National Council of Teachers of English, the International Reading Association and the Center for the Study of Reading at the University of Illinois are developing academic standards for the study of English. A sampler that the group has developed includes some examples of standards and vignettes describing how those standards might be reflected in real classrooms.

Teacher Standards

Bradley, Ann, "Teacher education and standards," *Education Week*, Nov. 24, 1993, pp. 22-23.

The parallel movements of developing standards for students and standards for teachers are coming together, and the concerns of teacher-educators are being addressed, Bradley writes. The standard-setting movement for teacher education is discussed.

Columba, Lynn and Kathleen Dolgos, "Professional development for teachers of mathematics," *Education*, Summer 1993, pp. 656-660.

The use of the "Curriculum and Evaluation Standards for School Mathematics" and the "Professional Standards for Teaching Mathematics" in preparing mathematics teachers is discussed.

Dillon, Sam, "Cortines calls for standards in teaching," *The New York Times*, Nov. 10, 1993, p. B1.

New York City Schools Chancellor Ramon Cortines said Nov. 9, 1993, that he has ordered the preparation of a core curriculum that would set citywide standards. The curriculum changes are similar in spirit to reforms he made in the San Francisco school system.

Wise, Arthur E., "A vision of the future: Of teachers, teaching, and teacher education," *National Forum: Phi Kappa Phi Journal*, Fall 1993, pp. 8-10.

The U.S. of the future will require more children to reach higher levels of cognitive functioning, Wise writes, but to reach this goal, every teacher must be fully prepared to carry out his or her responsibilities. Teaching and teacher education for the future, which he says have not been held to rigorous national standards, are discussed.

Back Issues

Great Research on Current Issues Starts Right Here...Recent topics covered by The CQ Researcher are listed below. Before May 1991, reports were published under the name of Editorial Research Reports.

SEPTEMBER 1992
Domestic Partners
Violence in Schools
Public Broadcasting
Women in the Military

OCTOBER 1992
Depression
U.S. Auto Industry
Youth Apprenticeships
Hispanic Americans

NOVEMBER 1992
Physical Fitness
Privatization
Paying for College
U.S. Policy in Asia

DECEMBER 1992
Crackdown on Smoking
The New CIA
Eating Disorders
Women and AIDS

JANUARY 1993
Hate Crimes
Child Sexual Abuse
Nuclear Fusion
U.S. Trade Policy

Back issues are available for $4.00 (subscribers) or $7.00 (non-subscribers). Quantity discounts apply to orders over ten. To order, call Congressional Quarterly Customer Service at (202) 887-8621.

Binders are available for $15.00. To order call 1-800-638-1710. Please refer to stock number 648.

FEBRUARY 1993
Community Policing
Europe's New Right
School Censorship
Violence Against Women

MARCH 1993
Gay Rights
Aid to Russia
War on Drugs
TV Violence

APRIL 1993
Head Start
High-Speed Rail
Children's Legal Rights
Muslims in America

MAY 1993
Cults in America
Preventing Teen Pregnancy
Software Piracy
National Parks

JUNE 1993
Food Safety
Prostitution
Childhood Immunizations
National Service

JULY 1993
Electric Cars
Population Growth
Downward Mobility
Intelligence Testing

AUGUST 1993
Mental Illness
Bilingual Education
Foreign Policy Burden
School Funding

SEPTEMBER 1993
Suburban Crime
Public Housing
Supreme Court Preview
Immigration Reform

OCTOBER 1993
Airline Safety
Disaster Response
Science in the Courtroom
The Glass Ceiling

NOVEMBER 1993
Paying for Retirement
Charitable Giving
Privacy in the Workplace
Adoption

DECEMBER 1993
U.S. Vietnam-Relations
Learning Disabilities
Child Care
Space Program's Future

JANUARY 1994
Racial Tensions in Schools
South Africa's Future
Worker Retraining
Regulating Pesticides

FEBRUARY 1994
Prison Overcrowding
Water Quality
Religion in Schools
Juvenile Justice

MARCH 1994
Underground Economy

Future Topics

- ***Gambling***
- ***Private Management of Public Schools***
- ***Reproductive Ethics***

THE CQ Researcher

PUBLISHED BY CONGRESSIONAL QUARTERLY INC.

Gambling Boom

Will the gaming industry's growth hurt society?

Only a decade ago, gambling was a simple mix of lotteries, parimutuel wagering and casinos aimed at adults. But in just a decade, gaming has evolved into a vast entertainment industry that is spreading across the American heartland and competing with Orlando for families' vacation dollars. Gross annual revenues from legalized gaming have reached $30 billion — six times the box-office revenues from motion pictures. Further growth is anticipated as casinos proliferate on Indian reservations and riverboats, and video-gambling devices and innovative "scratch" games spark additional revenues. Meanwhile, mental health professionals worry that greater access to wagering may lead to increases in compulsive gambling — a disorder that has been likened to alcohol and tobacco addiction.

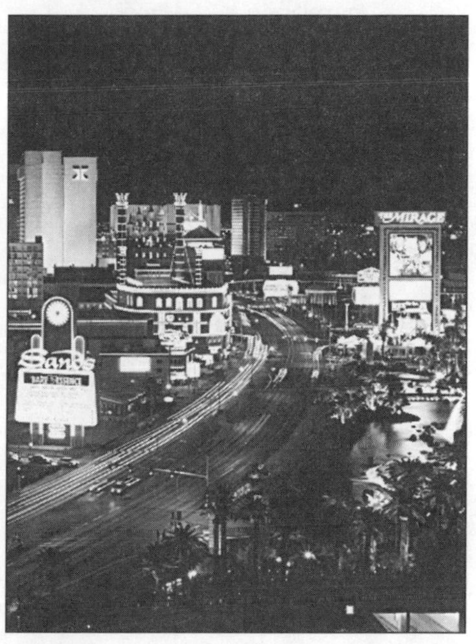

INSIDE THIS ISSUE

CQ March 18, 1994 • Volume 4, No. 11 • 241-264

Formerly Editorial Research Reports

Gambling Boom

The Issues

Background

Current Situation

Outlook

Sidebars and Graphics

For Further Information

Cover: In the last decade, Las Vegas has undergone ràdical change, luring families to mammoth new theme-oriented hotels. (Las Vegas News Bureau)

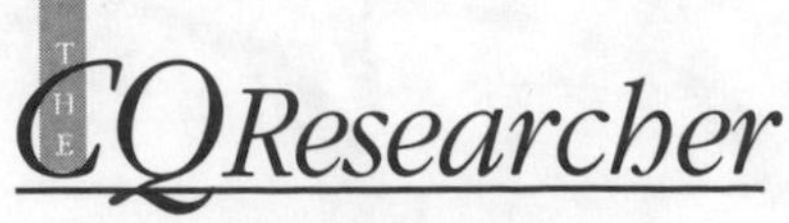

March 18, 1994
Volume 4, No. 11

The CQ Researcher (ISSN 1056-2036). Formerly Editorial Research Reports. Published weekly (48 times per year, not printed the first Friday of any month with five Fridays) by Congressional Quarterly Inc., 1414 22nd St., N.W., Washington, D.C. 20037. Rates are furnished upon request. Second-class postage paid at Washington, D.C. POSTMASTER: Send address changes to The CQ Researcher, 1414 22nd St., N.W., Washington, D.C. 20037.

Gambling Boom

By Richard L. Worsnop

The Issues

Many U.S. industries slumped during the recent recession, but gambling wasn't one of them. Capping a decade of robust growth, legal wagering rose to a record $329.9 billion in 1992—compared with a relatively anemic $126 billion in 1982.*

Gross gambling revenue — money lost by bettors — also surged in 1992, to $29.9 billion, or 12 percent above 1991. The rise is largely credited to the lure of new casinos and a new lottery in Texas. (The movie industry, by comparison, took in a modest $5.2 billion in box-office revenues in 1993.)

Today's U.S. gambling scene "is a world transformed," noted Eugene Martin Christiansen in his annual industry analysis for *Gaming & Wagering Business*, a leading trade journal. "A simple, lottery/parimutuel/Nevada-Atlantic City mix of traditional commercial games has evolved into an interactive device, casino/entertainment-driven behemoth that is at once spreading across the American heartland, revitalizing Indian economies and going head to head with Orlando for mainstream family leisure spending — the market with the biggest bucks of all." [1]

As Christiansen pointed out, gaming in facilities run by American Indian tribes has become an industry pace-setter. Despite resistance from the states, Indians have rushed to take advantage of a 1988 federal law allowing them to establish casino-style gaming (known as Class III gaming) on their reservations (*see p. 255*). In 1992, wagering at Indian casinos rose by nearly $10 billion over 1991 — a 240 percent increase.

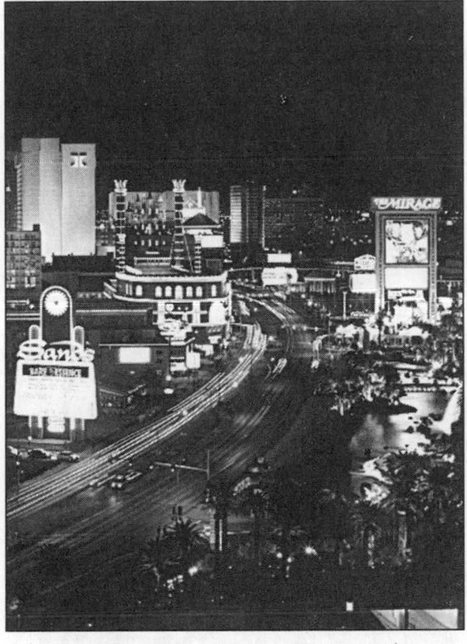

Las Vegas News Bureau

The take from riverboat gambling grew even faster. (Some of the "riverboats" are no more than huge barges moored fast to the shore.) Gross wagering in the floating casinos, licensed by six states along the Mississippi and Ohio rivers, increased by $6.2 billion in 1992 — a whopping 566 percent rise over 1991.

Video gambling also posted triple-digit growth in 1992, rising by $972 million, or 274 percent. Based on familiar card and number games like poker and keno, video machines attract heavy patronage because they offer virtually nonstop action and frequent jackpots. They are expected to remain a dependable state-lottery cash cow for many years to come.

Why all the growth? According to William Thompson, a professor of public administration at the University of Nevada-Las Vegas, the boom draws its energy from the gaming industry itself. "There's a public demand to gamble," Thompson says, "but there's no public demand for *legalizing* gambling." What the public wants above all, he says, is low taxes. The gaming industry senses this, "and it tells the politicians, 'Hey, here's a way to avoid taxes. Don't make the people mad, don't raise their taxes; give them gambling instead.' "

Public officials who embrace this view of gambling see it, in effect, as a voluntary tax. But they typically ignore the consequences of legalized gambling, Thompson says. "They don't look two, three, four years down the line and see that money will be drained out of other community resources — from retail sales, say — which otherwise would provide sales-tax revenue," he says.

Moreover, he notes, moral objections to gambling generally fall on deaf ears because "the public is worn out on the morality issue." And those who "are still into the morality issue are more concerned about abortion and school prayer than they are about gambling. Gambling's pretty low on the morality crusaders' list."

There's another reason for the muted moral criticism, according to a report on the gambling industry by Wertheim Schroder & Co. Inc., a New York investment-banking firm: Church and state, traditionally "two of society's moral arbiters and most outspoken critics of gaming," now hesitate to speak out "due to their dependence on revenues" from bingo and lotteries. [2]

Meanwhile, as Christiansen suggests, the gaming industry has disarmed critics by promoting itself as a source of wholesome entertainment. This marketing strategy can best be appreciated in Las Vegas, which boasts several new spectacle properties and theme parks that appeal to the U.S. family vacation trade. (*See story, p. 245.*)

As *The New York Times* recently noted about three of the new hotels, "There are no showgirls. There are no Runyonesque souls, even if there are people with glazed eyes playing five slot machines at a time with both hands. What one notices now is the children,

* The $329.9 billion represents what is known in the industry as the "handle," or the total amount wagered by players. The most recent statistics available are for 1992; figures for 1993 will be published in May.

Gambling in America: A $330 Billion Industry

Bettors in the U.S. legally wagered $329.9 billion in 1992, mostly at casinos in Nevada and New Jersey (column 1). They lost $29.9 billion, or 9 percent of the total amount they wagered (column 2). Bettors lost the highest percentage of their money (47 percent) on lotteries, while casino table games kept just 2.2 percent — the lowest percentage (column 3).

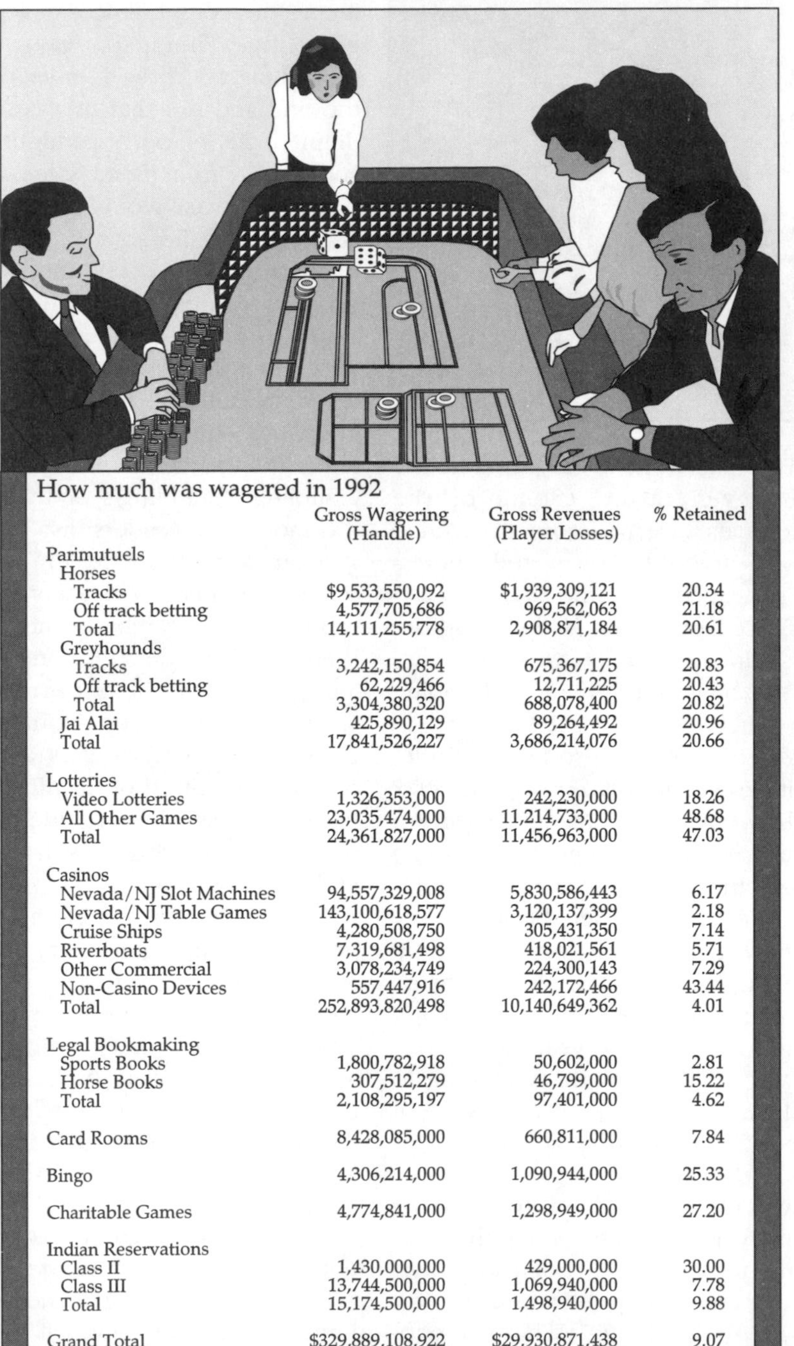

How much was wagered in 1992

	Gross Wagering (Handle)	Gross Revenues (Player Losses)	% Retained
Parimutuels			
Horses			
Tracks	$9,533,550,092	$1,939,309,121	20.34
Off track betting	4,577,705,686	969,562,063	21.18
Total	14,111,255,778	2,908,871,184	20.61
Greyhounds			
Tracks	3,242,150,854	675,367,175	20.83
Off track betting	62,229,466	12,711,225	20.43
Total	3,304,380,320	688,078,400	20.82
Jai Alai	425,890,129	89,264,492	20.96
Total	17,841,526,227	3,686,214,076	20.66
Lotteries			
Video Lotteries	1,326,353,000	242,230,000	18.26
All Other Games	23,035,474,000	11,214,733,000	48.68
Total	24,361,827,000	11,456,963,000	47.03
Casinos			
Nevada/NJ Slot Machines	94,557,329,008	5,830,586,443	6.17
Nevada/NJ Table Games	143,100,618,577	3,120,137,399	2.18
Cruise Ships	4,280,508,750	305,431,350	7.14
Riverboats	7,319,681,498	418,021,561	5.71
Other Commercial	3,078,234,749	224,300,143	7.29
Non-Casino Devices	557,447,916	242,172,466	43.44
Total	252,893,820,498	10,140,649,362	4.01
Legal Bookmaking			
Sports Books	1,800,782,918	50,602,000	2.81
Horse Books	307,512,279	46,799,000	15.22
Total	2,108,295,197	97,401,000	4.62
Card Rooms	8,428,085,000	660,811,000	7.84
Bingo	4,306,214,000	1,090,944,000	25.33
Charitable Games	4,774,841,000	1,298,949,000	27.20
Indian Reservations			
Class II	1,430,000,000	429,000,000	30.00
Class III	13,744,500,000	1,069,940,000	7.78
Total	15,174,500,000	1,498,940,000	9.88
Grand Total	$329,889,108,922	$29,930,871,438	9.07

Source: Gaming and Wagering Business *magazine, Aug. 15-Sept. 14, 1993; figures compiled by Eugene Martin Christiansen, Christiansen/Cummings Associates Inc.*

roaming the casinos and pumping quarters in video arcades as nimbly as their quite average-looking parents." [3]

Las Vegas appeals to foreign tourists as well. About 15 percent of the visitors now come from abroad, compared with 4 percent as recently as 1987.

But despite the gaming industry's prosperity, and also because of it, criticism of wagering persists. Much of the opposition comes from mental health professionals who treat compulsive gamblers — many of whom became addicted to betting at an early age.*

One such expert, psychiatrist Sirgay Sanger, wants the gaming industry to do more to help people who become pathological gamblers. (*See warning signs, p. 248.*)

"No casino or gambling operation really makes that much extra money on the problem gambler," says Sanger, past president of the National Council on Problem Gambling in New York City. To the contrary, it's in the operators' self-interest to identify and help patrons who "show signs of drinking too much, spending all their money and then using up their credit cards. Those are the people who get into fights, get involved in lawsuits, sometimes even commit suicide."

Sanger also thinks states that permit gambling should do more to combat the rise of pathological gambling. "If the state is going to advocate a risky business," he says, "then the state should dedicate some percentage of its gambling profits to the rehabilitation and study" of problem gamblers.

Advocates and opponents of legalized gaming agree that the nation's long gambling boom shows no sign of losing momentum in the foreseeable future. But they disagree over its

* The terms "pathological gambling" and "compulsive gambling" are used interchangeably by psychologists and other treatment professionals; "obsessive gambling" describes a less self-destructive behavioral pattern.

Continued on p. 246

The Lure of Las Vegas

Both Las Vegas and Atlantic City are gambling meccas, but gaming in the two cities couldn't be more dissimilar. Atlantic City players generally are elderly and blue-collar day-trippers from the New York-Washington corridor who stream in on buses and return home after a few hours. Aside from its famed boardwalk and long beachfront, the faded resort lacks the fine restaurants and other amenities that once made it one of the East Coast's most desirable summer vacation spots.

Las Vegas, by contrast, is a world apart. In recent years, it has transformed itself into a family-oriented tourist attraction by developing "spectacle properties" that combine the functions of hotel, casino and theme park. At the Polynesian-style Mirage, for example, a 54-foot artificial volcano erupts every 15 minutes after dark. The Excalibur, which opened a year later, in 1990, evokes the days of King Arthur with live reenactments of jousting matches and target shooting for prizes — with electronic crossbows.

Las Vegas News Bureau

The pyramid-shaped $395 million Luxor Hotel in Las Vegas is guarded by a giant replica of the sphinx.

Three more giant complexes opened last fall, adding 10,000 rooms to the mix and inspiring newspaper travel writers to appropriately monumental, and sometimes snide, coverage: "The dress code in Las Vegas is, of course, liberal," noted Stephen Drucker in *The New York Times.* "If you own anything angora, this is the place to wear it. A nylon warm-up suit? Most definitely. Armani, an undershirt, a wedding dress — everything is considered appropriate at a slot machine." †

Largest of the three new hotels is the MGM Grand. In fact, the Grand, with 5,005 rooms, bills itself as the largest hotel in the world. One of the attractions at its theme park is a recreation of the Yellow Brick Road from *The Wizard of Oz,* complete with talking statues of Dorothy, the Scarecrow and her other traveling companions.

The 2,526-room, $375 million Luxor Hotel, predictably, features an Egyptian motif, complete with sphinx and the "River Nile" flowing through the 30-story pyramid of black glass. On barge trips along the 3,000-foot river, guides give lectures on Egyptology. There's even a gift shop where well-heeled collectors can spend $14,000 for a seventh century B.C. bronze statue. At the 2,900-room Treasure Island, a 15-minute sea battle in the hotel's lagoon ends with a pirate ship in flames and the crewmen jumping overboard. The show is staged every 90 minutes starting in mid-afternoon.

Outdoing the other guy may seem to be the entrepreneurial philosophy in Las Vegas, but William Thompson, a professor of public administration at the University of Nevada-Las Vegas, says the city's casino operators have learned that cooperation spells prosperity for all.

"Steve Wynn [chairman of Mirage Resorts Inc., which owns the Mirage and other hotels] loves it when Caesars Palace expands next door," Thompson says. "He recognizes that will bring more people to Vegas from all over the country. So, even though Caesars might take some of his customers away from him, the net result will be increased patronage. Consequently, he'll advertise nationally, Caesars will advertise nationally and they'll both applaud Circus Circus when it builds a new property. They don't fear internal competition."

All that competition, of course, is designed to attract visitors who, after their brief fling, pile into their cars, or board planes, and go home. What concerns Thompson about legalized gambling in Las Vegas and other communities is gambling's daily lure to local residents, and the potential social problems that can arise. "I think urban areas that welcome in casinos will begin to feel some of those problems," Thompson says.

"It's bad to have casinos available to people on a day-to-day basis," he explains. "There are casinos off 'the Strip' in Vegas that cater to the local residents, and that does absolutely no good for our community. By making gamblers out of people who live here, we're going to wind up in pretty sad shape."

Moreover, he says, "Businesses stay away from here because they don't want their employees gambling. I don't think other communities will want that, either."

† Stephen Drucker, "Las Vegas, Theme City," *The New York Times,* Feb. 13, 1994.

Gambling Revenues Rise in 1992

In 1992, the amount of money that gamblers lost, known in the industry as gross revenues, rose by $3.2 billion, or 12 percent, compared with 1991. Especially strong revenue gains were posted by lotteries, riverboats and Indian reservations.

	Increase/Decrease in Gross Revenues (Player Losses)	
	Dollars	**Percent**
Parimutuels		
Horses		
Tracks	($51,632,475)	-2.59
Off Track Betting	110,184,412	12.82
Total	58,551,937	2.05
Greyhounds		
Tracks	(36,563,900)	-5.14
Off Track Betting	5,146,075	68.02
Total	(31,417,825)	-4.37
Jai Alai	(11,078,839)	-11.04
Total Parimutuels	16,055,273	0.44
Lotteries		
Video Lotteries	120,388,000	98.81
All Other Games	1,111,118,000	11.0
Total	1,231,506,000	12.04
Casinos		
Nevada/N.J. Slot Machines	588,287,443	11.22
Nevada/N.J. Tables Games	(80,830,601)	-2.53
Cruise Ships	14,544,350	5.00
Riverboats	338,335,781	424.59
Other Commercial	160,387,906	250.95
Non-Casino Devices	84,492,059	53.58
Total	1,105,216,938	12.23
Legal Bookmaking		
Sports Books	(1,698,000)	-3.25
Horse Books	(8,280,878)	-15.03
Total	(9,978,878)	-9.29
Card Rooms	1,697,000	0.26
Bingo	23,191,000	2.17
Charitable Games	55,606,000	4.47
Indian Reservations		
Class II	9,750,000	2.33
Class III	769,040,000	255.58
Total	778,790,000	108.14
Total	**3,202,083,333**	**11.98%**

Source: Gaming and Wagering Business *magazine, Aug. 15-Sept. 14, 1993; figures compiled by Eugene Martin Christiansen, Christiansen/Cummings Associates Inc.*

Continued from p. 244

likely impact on both society as a whole and individual gamblers.

As lawmakers, industry experts and other observers consider the gambling issue, these are among the questions they are trying to answer:

Does Indian-run gambling enjoy an unfair advantage over other gaming operations?

Debates on the pros and cons of legalized wagering often center on Indian-run gaming. Since a 1987 Supreme Court decision and a 1988 act of Congress affirmed the right of American Indians to establish casino gaming on their reservations, dozens of tribes jumped at the opportunity. (*See map, p. 254.*)

However, state governments and commercial gaming interests contend the Indian Gaming Regulatory Act of 1988 (IGRA) gives Indians an unfair — and possibly unconstitutional — competitive edge. They complain that IGRA exempts tribes from state taxes while allowing them to sue states that refuse to negotiate in good faith on gaming agreements, known as "compacts."

Critics say the gaming industry playing field would be made level if it were more difficult for tribes to obtain casino permits and if there were restrictions on the types of games permitted in tribe-operated facilities. Bills thus amending IGRA are now pending in Congress (*see p. 255*).

At the same time, several states have gone to federal court to overturn IGRA on constitutional grounds. They contend IGRA violates the 10th Amendment, which essentially says Congress can't force state governments to do anything — such as negotiate gaming compacts with Indian tribes — not spelled out in state law. They also say IGRA violates the 11th Amendment, which in effect bars states from suing each other. Their reasoning is that Indian tribes, which are sovereign entities under U.S. law, have the same legal standing as states.

Tribal officials indignantly deny getting any special advantages. Indeed, they say, the fundamental issue is tribal sovereignty. As far back as 1831, they note, the Supreme Court ruled in *Cherokee Nation v. Georgia* that tribal nations had the legal right to manage their own affairs, govern themselves internally and engage in legal and political relationships with the federal government and its subdivisions. Moreover, they say, in 1987 the court removed most remaining barriers to Indian gaming in *California v. Cabazon Band of Mission In-*

When Sports Betting Gets Out of Hand

When executives of sports teams discuss the perils of betting on games, the World Series of 1919 is usually Exhibit A.

The Chicago White Sox, one of the strongest teams of its era, was heavily favored to defeat the Cincinnati Reds. But the Reds won, 5 games to 3.

Rumors of a betting-related fix soon began circulating, and they eventually proved true. Eight Chicago players had conspired with gamblers to throw the series to Cincinnati.

To undo the "Black Sox" scandal's damage, club owners hired Judge Kenesaw Mountain Landis to be the sport's commissioner and gave him virtually autocratic powers. In his first official act, Landis placed all the players implicated in the fix on baseball's ineligible list. Later, even though they were acquitted in court on conspiracy-to-defraud charges, Landis banned them from the game for life. [1]

Other pro players have also been punished for involvement with gamblers. New York Giants football stars Frank Filchock and Merle Hapes were suspended for not reporting an attempted bribe to fix the 1946 National Football League championship game between the Giants and the Chicago Bears. Paul Hornung of the Green Bay Packers and Alex Karras of the Detroit Lions also were suspended in 1963 for betting on pro football games. And in 1989, then-Baseball Commissioner A. Bartlett Giamatti permanently banned former Reds player and manager Pete Rose from the sport because of his betting on baseball games.

In the late 1940s and early '50s, college basketball was shaken by several scandals involving point-shaving, or trying to beat the point spread by holding down the margin. One incident involved players at City College of New York (CCNY), which in 1950 became the only team ever the win the National Invitation Tournament and the National Collegiate Athletic Association championship in the same year.

The most recent point-shaving episode affecting a major college basketball program came to light at Tulane University in 1985. After eight persons, including three players and a bookie, were indicted in the case, Tulane's president abolished the university's basketball program.

More recently, reports of betting by players and others associated with big-time sports have centered on gambling's personal costs. Before retiring from the Chicago Bulls after the 1992-93 season, National Basketball Association star Michael Jordan was dogged by rumors that he had a serious gambling problem. Much was made of a casino-gaming trip he took to Atlantic City last spring on the eve of a playoff game with the New York Knicks. Shortly thereafter, San Diego businessman Richard Esquinas charged in his book about Jordan, *Michael & Me*, that Jordan had lost $1.2 million to him during 10 days of golf in 1991.

Jordan has acknowledged he gambles heavily but says it's not a problem and stems from his intensely competitive nature. "I am no Pete Rose," he said. [2] Jordan is now trying to start a second sports career as a baseball player for the Chicago White Sox.

Chet Forte, the former director of ABC television's "Monday Night Football," has said his career was wrecked by problems arising from compulsive gambling. Forte, who left ABC in 1987, says he lost at least $4 million as a casino and sports gambler, wagering on as many as 70 college and pro games a day.

In March 1992, Forte was sentenced to five years' probation for fraud and tax evasion in U.S. District Court in Camden, N.J. He also was ordered to perform 400 hours of community service and to make restitution of $850,000 to a savings and loan association and a former neighbor.

Forte insisted his betting never affected his television work — choosing which instant replays to show, for instance. "What we were doing — 'Monday Night Football' — was more important than my bet," he said. "I'd make my bets, then forget about them. I know it might be morally not right for me to direct a game and bet on the game. . . . But I wasn't going to live and die with one game." [3]

---

[1] The *Chicago Herald Examiner* printed this famous exchange between a small boy and "Shoeless Joe" Jackson, one of the implicated players, after Jackson left a grand-jury hearing: "Say it ain't so, Joe. Say it ain't so." "Yes, kid, I'm afraid it is." "Well, I never would have thought it."

[2] Quoted by Mark Starr, "The Gambling Man," *Newsweek*, June 14, 1993, p. 72.

[3] Quoted in *The Washington Post*, April 28, 1991, p. A24.

dians, once again treating the tribes as independent nations.

In view of these rulings, American Indians say IGRA violated tribal sovereignty by requiring tribes to negotiate compacts with state governments before setting up casino operations. IGRA's legislative history clearly shows, they say, that the compact requirement was added to the law at the states' insistence.

Now, according to the National Indian Gaming Association (NIGA),* "The states are reneging on the deal that they proposed and Congress accepted" when it approved IGRA in 1988. "When a tribe attempts to secure judicial enforcement of the state's obligation to negotiate a compact in good faith," NIGA charged in a 1993 study, "the state asserts immunity from suit under the 11th Amendment" and the states also claim that "the 10th Amendment renders unconstitutional any resulting obligation that the compact process may impose upon the state." This strategy "has successfully obstructed and delayed many tribal efforts to use Class III gaming as a

---

*NIGA, founded in 1985, is a nonprofit organization of tribes and associate members representing vendors and businesses involved in tribal gaming enterprises.

Signs of Pathological Gambling

A person who exhibits at least five of the following behaviors may be a pathological, or compulsive, gambler according to the American Psychiatric Association.

- Preoccupation with gambling (e.g., preoccupied with reliving past gambling experiences, handicapping or planning the next venture, or thinking of ways to get money with which to gamble).
- The need to gamble with increasing amounts of money in order to achieve the desired excitement.
- Repeated unsuccessful efforts to control, cut back or stop gambling. Restlessness or irritability when attempting to cut down or stop gambling.
- Gambles as a way of escaping from problems or of reliving dysphoric mood (e.g., feelings of helplessness, guilt, anxiety, depression).
- After losing money gambling, often returns another day in order to get even ("chasing" one's losses).
- Lies to family members, therapists or others to conceal the extent of involvement with gambling.
- Has committed illegal acts such as forgery, fraud, theft or embezzlement, in order to finance gambling.
- Has jeopardized or lost a significant relationship, job or educational or career opportunity because of gambling.
- Reliance on others to provide money to relieve a desperate financial situation caused by gambling.

Source: Diagnostic and Statistical Manual of Mental Disorders *(Fourth Edition), to be published spring 1994, American Psychiatric Association*

source of employment and government revenue." [4]

Indeed, Indian leaders cite jobs and income as the main benefits of tribal gaming. Gross revenue from wagering on Indian reservations in 1992 accounted for only 5 percent of the gaming industry total. But that minuscule share represented $1.5 billion, a huge windfall for the relatively small number of tribal members involved.

Minnesota's Mille Lacs tribe, for example, financed two new schools — the reservation's first — entirely from gaming proceeds. "That means kids on the reservation no longer have to be bused to school," says Gay Kingman, public relations director for NIGA.

In South Dakota, says Kingman, Indian tribes and the state government have joined forces to promote tourism. Visitors who come to see scenic attractions like Mount Rushmore are encouraged to stop at an Indian reservation and sample American Indian culture — "and also spend some time enjoying themselves in the reservation's casino."

Such cooperative efforts benefit both tribes and the states, Indian leaders say. "Indian casinos and bingo halls have created more than 30,000 taxpaying jobs in five states alone — Minnesota, Wisconsin, Michigan, California and Washington," wrote former NIGA Chairman Leonard Prescott. "The majority of those jobs are held by non-Indians." [5]

Meanwhile, Kingman says, many tribes are seeking to expand their gambling operations by "expanding their reservation landholdings." Some states and commercial gambling companies worry that the tactic will enable tribes to obtain more advantageous sites for casinos, draw business away from gaming establishments already in the area or discourage commercial operators from building rival casinos nearby. The IGRA provision permitting tribes to acquire more so-called "trust" lands, IGRA critics argue, is another example of the law's pro-Indian bias.

Neutral observers say fears about American Indians' expansion probably are overblown. They point out that prior approval must be obtained from the governor of the state where the trust land is located and from the U.S. secretary of the Interior. "Because of the rigor of this approval process," noted the report by Wertheim Schroder & Co., "it seems that Indians getting trust land for the purpose of gaming may happen occasionally, but will probably not become a widespread phenomenon." [6]

Would legalized betting undermine the honesty of college and pro team sports?

Next to casino table and slot games, sports betting is considered the most popular form of gambling in the United States. But since wagering on team sports is illegal in almost all jurisdictions, nationwide data are considered imprecise.

Former *Forbes* magazine Executive Editor James Cook wrote in 1992 that illegal betting in the U.S. may run "as high as $100 billion" a year. And that estimate doesn't include the "additional tens of billions" wagered on sports events in office pools and TV parties or bar-side bets among friends, he added. [7]

Most betting on college and pro games is against the law because politicians have accepted the argument that legalization would corrupt sports. They cite the fixed World Series of 1919 and the point-shaving scandals that surface periodically in college basketball. (*See story, p. 247.*)

Advocates of legalized sports betting retort that changes in gaming technology and higher player salaries have made it much more difficult to fix games. "This might be an instance where outrageous player salaries have made professional sports cleaner," Cook wrote. "What multimillionaire athlete would want to jeopardize his earnings by throwing a game?"

Testifying before a House Judiciary subcommittee in 1991, National Football League (NFL) Commissioner Paul Tagliabue cited four reasons for opposing legal wagering on team sports:

• "With legalized gambling, our games . . . would come to represent the fast buck, the quick fix, the desire to get something for nothing."

• "Sports gambling inevitably fosters a climate of suspicion about controversial plays and intensifies cynicism with respect to player performances, coaching decisions, officiating calls and game results."

• "Our players cannot be expected to serve as healthy role models for youth if they are made to function as participants in gambling enterprises."

• Legalized sports betting "would promote gambling among young people." [8]

Moreover, warned Boston Celtics President Arnold "Red" Auerbach, testifying before the same panel, legalized gambling would warp fans' outlook on sports. "Legalized sports betting creates a new type of fan," Auerbach said, "the 'point-spread' fan who is more concerned with whether the point spread is covered, not whether his team wins or how the players perform." To people with that mind-set, he said, "games are not entertainment events but only activities from which they hope to profit."

Some advocates of legalized sports betting insist it would reduce illegal bookmaking. But William L. Holmes, a forensic gaming consultant and former FBI agent, believes that people who use bookmakers will not shift to a legal sports lottery because bookies offer better odds, credit, tax-free payouts and greater convenience in placing bets and collecting winnings. Moreover, they generally set few if any restrictions on the amount an individual may wager. In fact, because of these advantages, Holmes feels illegal bookmakers would eventually lure many patrons away from legal sports betting.

Advocates of legalized sports betting continue to press their case all the same. One of their favorite arguments focuses on the social benefits gambling income would provide. "State-sponsored sports-pool lotteries could raise hundreds of millions in new non-tax revenue for the important state-run programs funded by lotteries, including education, economic development . . . senior citizen programs and state general funds," James E. Hosker, former president of the North American Association of State and Provincial Lotteries, told the House Judiciary subcommittee in 1991. [9]

Hosker also challenged the idea that legalized betting would undermine the integrity of college and professional sports and raise the risk of game-fixing. "Sports-pool lotteries are simply the 'office pool' on a slightly larger scale," he declared. Moreover, it would be no easy matter to rig a sports lottery drawing: A player would have to fix "14 or perhaps more professional sports events — practically speaking, an impossibility," he said.

But the main reason why sports lotteries are virtually tamper-proof, Hosker said, is that sophisticated computers "continually monitor the combinations that are being played, the amounts being wagered and where the wagers are being made, [and] any abnormal betting patterns would be quickly spotted." [10]

Bookmakers, for their part, contend that no one has a greater stake than they do in the absolute integrity of college and professional sports — chiefly football and basketball. "If there was widespread corruption in sports, there wouldn't be any bookmakers left," said Michael "Roxy" Roxborough, president of Las Vegas Sports Consultants Inc. and the man who sets the Las Vegas "line" — the nationally consulted point spreads on games. "They'd all be broke or looking to get out of business. If there's no integrity, nobody will come and watch. If there's no integrity, nobody's going to bet." [11]

Is compulsive gambling a mental disease?

Like NFL Commissioner Tagliabue, experts on compulsive gambling say legalized sports betting poses special hazards for teenagers. "With sports lotteries, the lottery industry is tapping a previously untapped resource, our young people" said Valerie C. Lorenz, executive director of the Compulsive Gambling Center in Baltimore, Md. "Compulsive gambling among our young people is already a serious problem, and we need to work together to prevent it from becoming a national tragedy." [12]

According to Lorenz, a psychologist, sports are "uniquely attractive" to youngsters. Furthermore, "The knowledge that children would acquire through sports lotteries would quickly lead them to illegal sports gambling, once they also discover the greater odds and thrill of risk such illegal gambling offers." [13]

Even now, says Lorenz, studies suggest that there is more compulsive gambling among teenage gamblers (7 to 11 percent are compulsive gamblers) than among adult gamblers (up to 5 percent). One reason for the disparity, she believes, is that, "We're telling our children it's OK to bet. Nowadays, a family will go to a restaurant where mom and dad can play a keno machine on the table. Or it'll take a pleasure cruise where mom and dad can gamble all the family's money away. That's what we're exposing our children to."

Compulsive (or pathological) gambling is defined by Beverly Hills, Calif., psychiatrist Richard J. Rosenthal as "a progressive disorder characterized by a continuous or periodic loss of control over gambling; a preoccupation with gambling and with obtaining money with which to gamble; irrational thinking; and a continuation of the behavior despite adverse consequences." [14]

According to Rosenthal and other experts in the field, winning is of secondary importance to compulsive gamblers. "While money is important," he writes, "most say they are seeking 'action,' an aroused, euphoric state comparable to the 'high' derived from cocaine and other drugs." [15]

Indeed, say compulsive-gambling counselors Arnie and Sheila Wexler of Bradley Beach, N.J., "most dual-addicted cocaine addict/compulsive gamblers will tell you gambling gives them the bigger high. Some drug addicts, who are also gambling addicts, will sell their drugs for gambling money." [16]

No consensus exists on the cause of compulsive gambling. One theory, advanced by Arnie Wexler, views the disorder as a product of family dysfunction. "There's a breakdown of the relationship between the gambler and the father, if the gambler is male," says Wexler, a recovering compulsive gambler. "Or there's a breakdown of the relationship between a female gambler and her mother. Also, about 50 percent of compulsive gamblers have a family member with some sort of addiction, be it gambling, drugs or alcohol."

Sanger of the National Council on Problem Gambling thinks compulsive gamblers suffer from one of a cluster of related disorders. Members of one subgroup "use the excitement of gambling the way some anorexics use starvation, or some runners use running: to give themselves a high," he says. For such people, these activities "slake an inner craving or inner absence."

The problem gamblers in a second subset "have neurotic qualities," Sanger says. That is, "they're compulsive in an opportunistic way; they have to keep repeating this behavior because it offers them some meaning in life."

Sanger describes a third group as "very angry people who are determined to continue gambling — behavior that's called 'chasing.' " These individuals typically have lost large sums of money, "and now they're going to force Lady Luck" to smile on them. They aren't angry at society per se, says Sanger. "They're just angry at the way they perceive their own lack of luck."

Not everyone considers compulsive gambling a mental, or organic, disorder. A rival school of thought holds that problem gambling is "learned behavior." Two leading proponents of this view are Richard E. Vatz, a professor of rhetoric and communication at Towson (Md.) State University, and Lee S. Weinberg, an associate professor at the University of Pittsburgh's graduate school of public and international affairs.

The American Psychiatric Association's (APA) *Diagnostic and Statistical Manual* "lists no medical criteria . . . for pathological gambling," Vatz and Weinberg wrote last fall, "only those referring to frequency of wagering and its social, financial and legal consequences. There is no credible evidence whatsoever of any neurochemical or neurophysiological status causally linked to heavy gambling, only changes such as increased adrenaline or palpitations caused by the excitement of the action." [17]

Vatz rejects the view that heavy gambling is beyond an individual's control. He likens it to cigarette addiction, observing that, "millions of people have quit smoking, and studies show that the majority of people who quit did so through willpower."

If willpower is all it takes, then why do some individuals keep on gambling until they lose their homes, jobs and families? "There always is a certain percentage of people who like that kind of exciting, high-risk action," Vatz explains. "And secondly, gamblers don't anticipate losing. They're wrong, of course. Since the odds are stacked against any gambler, all gamblers will lose over time."

Vatz doesn't scorn support groups like Gamblers Anonymous (GA). He cautions, however, that "the great majority of people who go to Gamblers Anonymous do so only because they're compelled to by courts as a result of lawbreaking. Also, most people don't return after the first meeting." Consequently, GA's claims of success are based on "an unrepresentative sample of people who stayed through the entire program — people who might have been sufficiently motivated to stop gambling on their own."

Vatz sees the current interest in problem gambling as "dovetailing with the societal focus now on compulsive behavior — on whether people can resist impulses. I'm thinking of the Lorena Bobbitt situation, the Menendez brothers situation, where people's behavior is attributed to compulsions and mental illnesses outside of their control." [18] ■

BACKGROUND

Ambivalent Attitudes

American attitudes toward gambling have always been deeply ambivalent — some would say hypocritical. In its first year in America, the Puritan-led Massachusetts Bay Colony outlawed not only the possession of cards, dice and gaming tables, even in private homes, but also dancing and singing. However, a century later, in 1737, Massachusetts legislators amended the anti-gambling law, stating: "All lawful games and exercises should not be otherwise used than as

Continued on p. 252

Chronology

19th Century

Gaming flourishes in frontier communities, but public opinion turns increasingly against it.

1832
Massachusetts and Pennsylvania become the first states to outlaw all lottery games.

July 6, 1835
Vigilantes lynch five gamblers in Natchez, Miss., one of the Mississippi River towns where gaming and other forms of vice had taken hold.

Aug. 2, 1876
Wild Bill Hickok, the legendary Indian scout and gambler, is shot dead while playing poker in the Number Ten Saloon in Deadwood, S.D.

1895
The Federal Lottery Act limits the distribution of lottery materials across state lines.

1930s

Nationwide economic distress spurs a revival of legalized gambling in several states.

1931
To build tourism during the Depression, Nevada legalizes most forms of gambling.

1931
Massachusetts decriminalizes bingo to help churches and charitable organizations raise money.

1933
Michigan, New Hampshire and Ohio legalize parimutuel betting.

1960s-1970s

Searching for new revenue sources, states turn to lotteries and other forms of gambling as forms of "voluntary" taxation.

1964
New Hampshire becomes the first state in the 20th century to sponsor a lottery, modeled initially on the Irish Sweepstakes.

1978
New Jersey becomes the second state to legalize casino gambling, though it is restricted to a single location — the rundown resort community of Atlantic City.

1980s

Indian tribes win the right to operate gaming facilities on their reservations.

Feb. 25, 1987
U.S. Supreme Court's ruling in *California v. Cabazon Band of Mission Indians* paves the way for Indian tribes to set up gaming operations if gambling is legal elsewhere in the state.

1988
President Ronald Reagan signs the Indian Gaming Regulatory Act (IGRA), which establishes regulations for three classes of gambling.

1989
South Dakota legalizes limited-stakes casino gambling in the historic mining town of Deadwood.

1990s

The gambling craze continues to gain momentum across the country, though limits are placed on betting on team sports.

1990
Following South Dakota's lead, Colorado voters approve casino-type gambling for three former mining towns.

1991
After a long absence, riverboat gambling returns to the stretch of the Mississippi adjoining Iowa.

Nov. 22, 1991
In a demonstration project, Massachusetts becomes the first state to allow residents to play the state's lottery by telephone.

Oct. 28, 1992
President George Bush signs legislation barring lotteries involving bets on team sports; four states that permit such wagering are exempted.

1992
Louisiana becomes the third state to legalize casino gambling, narrowly approving legislation to establish a riverfront facility in New Orleans.

1992
Legal wagering in the U.S. reaches a record $329.9 billion.

Nov. 22, 1993
Attorneys general from five New England states and New York issue a joint statement opposing the spread of legalized gambling. They warn, among other things, that, "Increased gambling will lead to increased crime."

Do Lotteries Really Make Cents for Education?

Supporters of legalized gaming often tout lotteries as a "voluntary tax" that funds education, economic development and programs for the elderly. Indeed, lottery proceeds in many states are specifically earmarked for such purposes. [1] But have lottery revenues lived up to expectations thus far?

When it comes to education, according to the Educational Research Service (ERS), the answer is no. "Scholarly examinations of lotteries for education have shown that as revenue sources, lotteries are: (1) a small part of education funding; (2) often substituted for regular funding; (3) an unstable revenue source; (4) an administratively inefficient way to gather revenue; and (5) similar to a regressive tax." [2]

Among other problems, said ERS, lottery proceeds tend to mingle with general funds, making it hard to evaluate the lottery's impact. "A second problem . . . is determining what the level of education funding would have been in the state without the lottery income."

Furthermore, said ERS, "Lottery schemes entail more administrative costs — printing tickets, paying prizes, marketing, personnel — to gather revenue than other methods, and the administrative costs of operating lotteries tend to grow over time."

The costs rise mainly because lottery officials must constantly search for new games to sustain the public's interest in playing. In 1991, ERS said, lottery administrative costs ranged from a low of 3 percent in New York and Pennsylvania to a high of 29 percent in Montana. "Nationwide, the average administrative cost was 6 percent of net income after vendor commissions."

The taxpayers, meanwhile, assume lotteries are meeting the state's education needs and thus are unreceptive to pleas for tax increases to finance school projects. Said ERS, "The net effect is that lottery funds may substitute for other sources of education revenue, rather than supplementing overall education funding."

But William Bergman, executive director of the North American Association of State and Provincial Lotteries, calls lottery revenues "found money. It wouldn't be there if you didn't have the lottery." [3]

---

[1] For background, see "State Lotteries," *Editorial Research Reports*, Feb. 27, 1987, pp. 89-100, and "Lucrative Lure of Lotteries and Gambling," *Editorial Research Reports*, Nov. 9, 1990, pp. 633-648.

[2] Educational Research Service (ERS), *State-Run Lotteries: Their Effects on School Funding*, 1993, pp. 4-5. Unless otherwise noted, information in this sidebar is from ERS, an association of individuals and agencies concerned with school management and policy.

[3] Quoted in *USA Today*, Aug. 17, 1993.

Continued from p. 250

innocent and moderate recreations, and not as trades or callings, to gain a living or make unlawful advantage thereby."

Games of chance found little favor among the Founding Fathers. Gambling, declared George Washington, is "the child of avarice, the brother of iniquity and the father of mischief." [19] Sounding a similar note, Thomas Jefferson warned, "Gaming corrupts our dispositions and teaches us a habit of hostility against all mankind." [20]

Nonetheless, Washington and Jefferson appreciated the money-making potential of gaming. At a time when the nation's banking and taxation systems were rudimentary, lotteries were seen as an alternative way of funding worthy projects. All 13 original Colonies established lotteries to raise revenue. The proceeds helped establish some of the nation's earliest and most prestigious universities — Harvard, Yale, Columbia, Dartmouth, Princeton and William and Mary.

Cardsharps on the Frontier

As the country expanded westward in the early 19th century, gambling acquired a less savory reputation. Cardsharps in the bustling river towns along the lower Mississippi, for example, were blamed for debasing local morals. Resentment exploded into violence July 6, 1835, when five accused hustlers were seized and hanged in Vicksburg, Miss. [21]

From that time until the Civil War, gambling operations in the area shifted to riverboats operating between New Orleans and St. Louis. This was the heyday of the flashy riverboat gambler, portrayed in such Hollywood films as "Mississippi," which starred comedian W.C. Fields as the flamboyant captain of the *River Queen*.

Today's moviegoers may assume that the nattily attired celluloid sharpers they see were figments of Hollywood's imagination. Not so. Riverboat gamblers "were acknowledged to be, as a class, the best-dressed men in the country," historian Robert K. DeArment wrote. The gambler's somber black outfit served merely as background for eye-catching accessories. These included a "snowy white shirt adorned with overlapping layers of ruffles" and a "garish flowered vest . . . studded with buttons of gold, pearl, or diamond." To complete the display, "Rings with precious stones sparkled on his fingers, and one very large stone, called the 'headlight,' gleamed in a stickpin on his chest." [22]

Gambling in the frontier communities west of the Mississippi was more rough-hewn. Colorful characters like Rowdy Joe Lowe, Poker Alice, Diamondfield Jack Davis and Madame Mustache abounded. But the frontier gambler best-remembered today is Wild Bill Hickok.

Once, DeArment noted, "when Hickok was in danger of being cleaned out by a pair of crooked poker sharks, he called the largest raise of the evening with his last greenbacks. At the showdown, one of his opponents displayed the winning hand and Bill tossed in his cards. 'Hold it!' he said, as the sharper reached for the pot. Drawing two revolvers, he leveled them at the swindlers. 'I have a pair of sixes, and they beat anything.' The slicks watched glumly as Hickok cleared the table." [23]

Hickok's fame was assured when he was fatally shot Aug. 2, 1876, while playing poker at the Number Ten Saloon in Deadwood, S.D. According to DeArment, he was holding two pairs, aces and eights, at the time — "a hand known ever since as the 'dead man's hand.' "

Rise of Oppositon

As the 19th century drew to a close, antigambling sentiment gathered force across the country, spurred by a series of scandals in 1890 involving the Louisiana State Lottery. (*See "Chronology," p. 251.*)

Much of the opposition to gambling at the turn of the century and later, however, came from organized religion, as in Colonial times. The Methodist Episcopal Church South declared in a 1930 policy statement: "To continue to gamble is to weaken the best qualities in the individual, no matter what the form of gambling may be, whether on the race track, in the popular sport of the day, at the card tables, or on the stock market." [24]

Historians Reuven and Gabrielle A. Brenner theorize that foes of gambling and speculation resist "the idea that chance, rather than divine will or talent, can have a significant effect on the allocation and reallocation of property." [25] Critics of gaming assume, they write, that "if gambling . . . was outlawed, and the laws were enforced, people would spend their time and money in more 'productive' ways." [26]

Legalized Gambling

Such thinking colored attitudes toward gambling until the Great Depression. As financial distress spread after the October 1929 stock market crash, legalized gaming came to be seen as a way to jump-start the economy. Nevada led the way in 1931, when it lifted bans on most forms of gambling. The same year, Massachusetts decriminalized bingo. And in 1933, Michigan, New Hampshire and Ohio legalized parimutuel betting. Chain letters and movie theater "bank nights," at which prizes were awarded, also flourished during the decade.

With the return of nationwide prosperity after World War II, Nevada's fledgling gaming industry boomed. But organized crime bankrolled many of the new facilities. The first big postwar Las Vegas casino, the Flamingo, was built in 1946 by mobster Benjamin "Bugsy" Siegel. At least four other major gaming properties in "Vegas" also had underworld ties: the Desert Inn (tied to the Cleveland crime syndicate headed by Moe Dalitz); the Stardust (opened by California mobster Tony Stralla); the Thunderbird (financed by New York gangsters Meyer and Jake Lansky); and the Tropicana (linked to New York mobster Frank Costello).

Las Vegas News Bureau

Slot machine players in Nevada and Atlantic City wagered nearly $96 billion and lost about $6 billion in 1992.

Televised hearings convened in 1951 by Sen. Estes Kefauver, D-Tenn., chairman of the Senate Special Committee to Investigate Organized Crime, did much to educate the public about the extent of mob influence in Nevada and elsewhere in the country.

The mob-gambling link has long been a prime argument against legalized gaming. To sculpt a more pleasing industry profile, gambling advocates now promote vacation trips to gaming resorts as a leisure activity the entire family can enjoy. Las Vegas' growth in recent years, which has drawn broad media coverage in this country and overseas, testifies to the effectiveness of this approach.

Lottery Fever

Mounting opposition to tax increases helped usher in the modern era of state-run lotteries in 1964. New Hampshire's pathbreaking game was based initially on just two horse races a year — a concept similar to

Indian Gaming Activity

Eighty-eight American Indian tribes in 19 states have agreements with their states, known as compacts, that permit them to operate sophisticated commercial gambling operations, including casinos, parimutuel wagering on horse and dog racing and electronic games. The number of compacts in each state is indicated below.

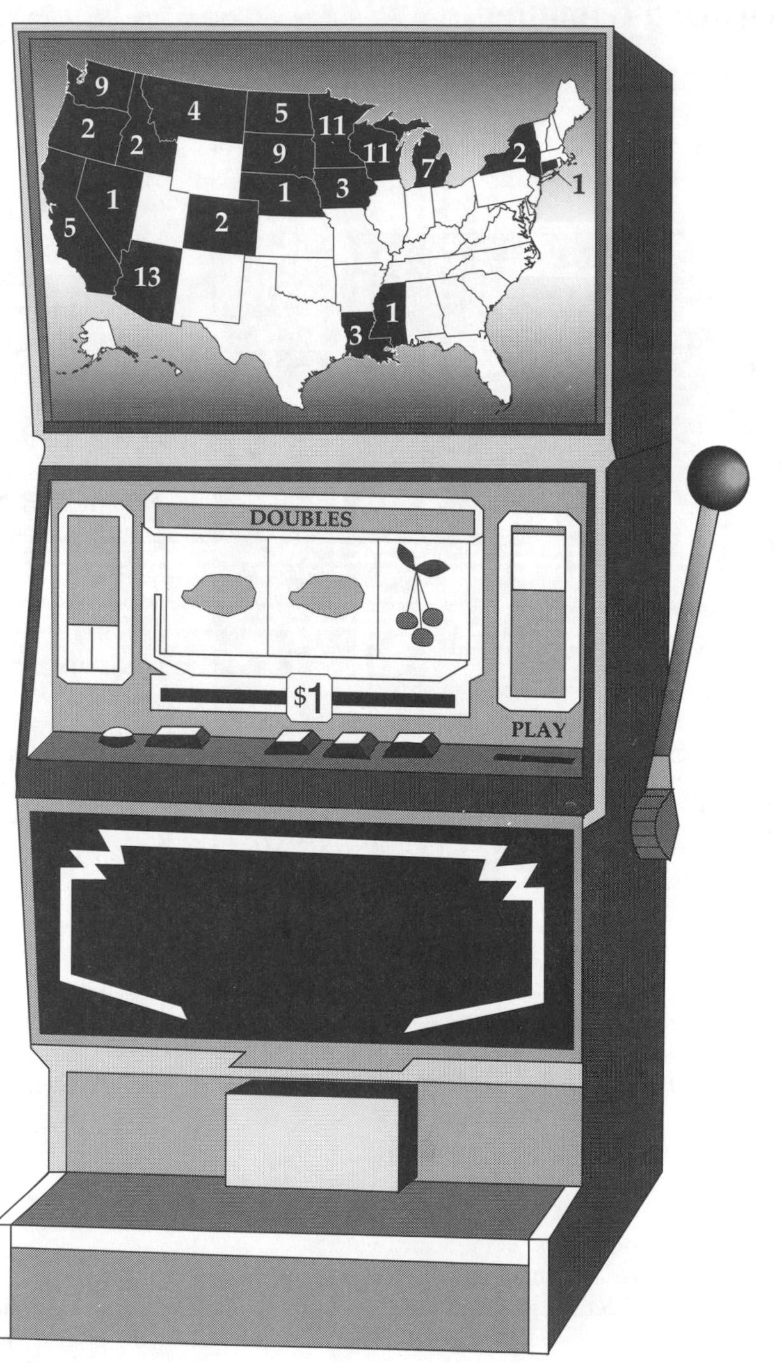

Source: National Indian Gaming Commission, Feb. 15, 1994; Bureau of Indian Affairs

the Irish Sweepstakes. But revenues fell well short of expectations both there and in New York, which in 1967 became the second state to institute a lottery.

It remained for New Jersey to launch the first financially successful modern lottery in 1971. The Garden State offered 50-cent tickets (half the price of those in neighboring New York) and weekly drawings (New York's were monthly), thus satisfying the habitual gambler's desire for frequent action at an affordable cost. New Jersey also put a higher percentage of lottery revenues into prizes than New Hampshire or New York.

New Jersey's innovations quickly became standard lottery practice, and three new twists soon were added. The first was the "instant game," in which players scratch a thin film off the ticket to uncover the numbers or symbols hidden beneath. Then came a legal daily "numbers" game, just like the illegal version long popular in big cities, but played on a computer network.

The third and most important lottery innovation was lotto, in which players typically choose six different numbers between 1 and 40 or 1 and 54. Though the odds of making a perfect lotto match are many millions to 1, the game has proved wildly popular. That's because the jackpot is rolled over each time it isn't won. Thus, when there are no winning tickets for several consecutive drawings, multimillion-dollar prizes and "lotto fever" invariably result.

Floridians got the fever as the jackpot headed toward $100 million in September 1990. During the week leading up to the Sept. 16 drawing, more than 100 million $1 tickets were sold. Computers showed that every possible combination of numbers had been purchased, guaranteeing there would be at least one winning ticket. In fact, there were six and they split a $106 million jackpot. But the nation's biggest jackpot ever — $118 million in California in April 1992 —

was split by 10 ticket holders.

Now that lotteries have spread to 37 states and the District of Columbia, including the 10 most-populous states, future revenue growth will hinge on aggressive marketing of existing products and development of new ones. In the meantime, the potential for gambling development on Indian reservations has barely been tapped.

Rulings Aid Indians

Until the late 1980s, gaming on tribal lands amounted to nothing more complex than bingo. In 1987, though, the Supreme Court's *California v. Cabazon Band of Mission Indians* decision elated Indian tribes and sent shock waves through the commercial gaming industry. In the case, the state challenged the right of two tribes to conduct bingo, poker and other card games on their lands.

The ruling held that state laws prohibiting a particular form of gambling cover tribes in the state. But if the state permits a form of gaming, tribes may operate such games, and operate them free of state control. In essence, said the National Indian Gaming Association (NIGA), the court "formally recognized the Indians' right to conduct gaming operations on their own land as long as [it] is not criminally prohibited by the state." [27]

Tribal self-sufficiency was at the heart of *Cabazon*. The court said federal agencies had sought to bolster tribal independence by promoting bingo and other games of chance. "Such policies and actions are of particular relevance in this case," declared the court, "since the tribal games provide the sole source of revenues for the operation of tribal governments and are the major sources of employment for tribal members."

Predictably, commercial gaming interests assailed *Cabazon*. State and federal law enforcement authorities also voiced misgivings, predicting that organized crime would infiltrate Indian gaming.

Congress tried to allay the concerns by passing the Indian Gaming Regulatory Act (IGRA) in 1988. The law defined three classes of gambling and applied differing regulatory standards to each:

Class I, consisting of traditional ceremonial gaming or social games for prizes of limited value, was placed under the tribes' exclusive control.

Class II, comprising bingo, lotto and certain card games, was made subject to oversight by a five-member National Indian Gaming Commission appointed by the president and confirmed by the Senate. Three seats on the commission were set aside for members of federally recognized Indian tribes.

Class III activities, including casino gambling, slot machines, horse and dog racing and jai alai, were prohibited unless they were legal in the state and the state and tribe entered into a "compact," as required under IGRA.

Indians denounced the compact requirement as a sop to the non-Indian gaming industry. "Regrettably, we had to make compromises and accept restrictions on our right of self-government and sovereignty in the enactment of the Indian Gaming Regulatory Act," said Leonard Prescott, then-chairman of NIGA, in 1992 congressional testimony. "Let the record be clear. IGRA did not confer any rights on Indian tribes to engage in, or regulate, gaming. We already had those rights." [28] ■

CURRENT SITUATION

Indians Cashing In

Today, six years after IGRA became law, Indian reservation gambling is on a roll. According to the U.S. Bureau of Indian Affairs, 88 American Indian tribes in 19 states have negotiated 92 gaming compacts, and 150-175 Class II and Class III gaming facilities (mainly bingo halls and casinos) are operating.*

But only Foxwoods High Stakes Bingo & Casino, in Ledyard, Conn., operated by the tiny Mashantucket Pequot tribe, is mentioned by industry experts in the same breath as casinos in Nevada and Atlantic City. Foxwoods, in fact, is believed to be "the single most profitable casino in the Western Hemisphere, raking in an estimated $600 million in profits in 1993." [29]

Foxwoods opened in February 1992 after a bitter legal struggle. State officials rebuffed the Pequots' initial proposal to operate a casino, prompting the tribe to sue. The Supreme Court eventually resolved the dispute in April 1991 by refusing to hear a final appeal by the state seeking to block the project.

Foxwoods only offered roulette, blackjack, craps and other table games in its first year, yet still posted revenues up to $300 million. The Pequots subsequently negotiated a pact with Gov. Lowell P. Weicker Jr., I-Conn., giving them the exclusive right to operate slot machines in Connecticut. In return, the tribe agreed to give the state 25 to 30 percent of annual slot revenues, depending on the total take.* In 1993, the state's share was

* According to the Bureau of Indian Affairs, there are 545 federally recognized Indian tribes in 35 states.

* Because of their sovereign status, Indian tribes are not required to pay local, state or federal taxes on their gaming revenues.

$113 million.

The tribe's staggering profits have built a community center, a child-development center and new housing. "The 280 [Pequots] now have no worries about college tuitions or health insurance," Thomas B. Allen recently wrote in *National Geographic.* "Foxwoods, with 8,200 people on its payroll, now rivals Electric Boat as a major employer in southeastern Connecticut." [30]

Deck Stacked?

For Indians, the Foxwoods story is an inspiring tale of bootstrap development. But for states and commercial gaming operators, the Pequots' success portends increasing competition — so much competition that the Indians say Congress and the courts have been asked to stack the deck against them.

That seems to be the aim of almost identical bills introduced in the House and Senate last May 26 by Rep. Robert G. Torricelli, D-N.J., and Sen. Harry Reid, D-Nev. Indian spokesmen, noting that Torricelli and Reid represent the only states with full-scale commercial casinos, promptly dubbed the bills "The Donald Trump Protection Acts" — a reference to the New York developer who owns three Atlantic City casinos.

The Torricelli and Reid bills would amend IGRA by providing that compact negotiations must be confined to games allowed under existing state law. No longer would states that offer one form of Class III gaming, such as a lottery, be compelled to negotiate with Indian tribes that want to set up full-scale casino gaming. The bills also would apply state gambling laws to Indian lands.

Torricelli and Reid said their bills were inspired partly by concern that organized crime was moving in on reservation gaming — a concern that Indian leaders called laughable. "There's no organized crime, reorganized crime or disorganized crime on Indian reservations," said NIGA Chairman Rick Hill. "What critics of Indian gaming are really afraid of is organized Indians." [31]

The Torricelli and Reid bills are currently languishing in committee. However, Senate Indian Affairs Committee Chairman Daniel K. Inouye, D-Hawaii, is trying to fashion a compromise acceptable to both supporters and critics of reservation gaming. Inouye, IGRA's principal author, has acknowledged the law needs clarification.

With Congress moving slowly on the Indian gaming issue, federal courts have become the main battleground. In a major decision on two long-pending cases, the 11th U.S. Circuit Court of Appeals in Jacksonville, Fla., ruled Jan. 18 that "the states retain their sovereign immunity" under the 11th Amendment, "and the federal courts do not have subject-matter jurisdiction over suits brought under IGRA." [32]

But in what the National Association of Attorneys General called "a surprise ending" [33] to the 11th Circuit decision, the court also held that Indian tribes blocked from negotiating a gaming compact by a state claim of sovereign immunity may appeal to the secretary of the Interior. "The secretary then may prescribe regulations governing Class III gaming on the tribe's lands." In other words, said the court, IGRA expressly provides for such redress.

The 11th Circuit decision was not the first on state claims of 11th Amendment immunity in gaming cases, and it will not be the last. In similar cases recently decided, several circuit and district courts have found for the states, while one circuit and two district courts have ruled for the tribes. The issue is also pending in the 4th, 9th and 10th circuits. And the U.S. Supreme Court may yet render a definitive judgment.

Gaming Action Spreads

Without making many waves in the national media, casino gambling has also spread in recent years to mining towns, riverboats and cruise ships. Low-stakes casino gaming returned in 1989 to Deadwood, S.D., the Black Hills town where Wild Bill Hickok was killed at a poker table. And in November 1990, Colorado voters approved a constitutional amendment allowing limited-stakes gambling in three old-time mining communities — Black Hawk, Central City and Cripple Creek.

Jack Hidahl, Central City's city manager, says his town's experience with casino gaming has been mixed. On the plus side, gaming revenue has spurred economic development, as was hoped. "No question about that," says Hidahl. "Our general-fund budget went from $350,000 in 1990 to $5.5 million this year."

But development and increased tourist volume have strained public services. "The police department went from two full-time guys and a part-timer in 1990 to 16 full-timers now," Hidahl reports. In all, the number of city employees has risen from 8 to 40 over the past four years.

The top challenge facing Central City, says Hidahl, is maintaining its squeaky-clean image despite the presence of 15 casinos. "We've always considered ourselves a family community," he says. "We have a lot more to offer than just gambling. We still have the summer opera, our annual jazz festival, museums and mine tours and arcades for kids.

"The gaming industry probably has not made Central City as attractive to families as it has been in the past. Initially, the casino operators were quite concerned about having kids in the casinos. And I think a number of families felt this was no longer an appropriate place to visit. So, we're making a concerted effort to change that impression, and attract even more family groups."

Riverboats Evoke Early Era

Riverboat gambling, evoking the pre-

Continued on p. 258

At Issue:

Is the Indian Gaming Regulatory Act (IGRA) unfair to the states?

yes

Rep. Robert G. Torricelli, D-N.J.

From *House Floor Speech,* May 26, 1993.

Some will argue that there is no problem with the Indian Gaming Regulatory Act (IGRA). I would respond that 49 governors, who have signed a petition calling for major reforms in Indian gaming laws, think there's a problem. The National Association of Attorneys General, which has called upon Congress to correct sections of the law that have resulted in repetitious litigation, thinks there is a problem. . . .

The problem is that we are facing the practical equivalency of de-regulated casino gaming across the country without the citizens of the United States or their elected representatives ever having made the decision to let that happen. Only two states in this country allow full-scale, for-profit casino gaming, yet there are now 124 commercial Indian gaming establishments of all sizes in 24 states. These operations gross roughly $7.5 billion a year — more than 10 percent of all gambling revenues in the country.

I come from one of two states that do allow high-stakes casinos. Gambling in New Jersey was a very difficult public-policy decision. It was made only after careful consideration by the people of New Jersey and their elected officials, and it was accompanied by an amendment to the state's Constitution.

The laws that were passed to implement that decision ensured that casino gaming would be highly taxed and closely regulated. Background checks for anyone even remotely connected with the games are thorough, and profits are earmarked for state programs to help the elderly and the disabled. The people of New Jersey carefully considered the pluses and minuses associated with casino gaming, and made a decision. But the people of other states that are now home to Native American gaming establishments had no say in the decision at all.

IGRA was supposed to be a compromise between Indian tribes seeking access to the revenues of gaming establishments, and state governments seeking to protect their citizens from the corrupting influences of unregulated gambling. But in practice, this law has greatly favored the tribes and has allowed the proliferating of gaming activities that the states had no intention of allowing. . . .

There is no doubt that many Native American tribes are in need of economic development to alleviate unemployment and other problems. But loosely regulated casino gaming in states that have not sanctioned such gaming is not the answer. We must give back to the states a reasonable opportunity to say no to gaming. It was not the intent of Congress in passing the Indian Gaming Regulatory Act to take away that opportunity.

no

Sen. Daniel K. Inouye, D-Hawaii

From *Senate Floor Speech,* May 27, 1993.

My colleagues have expressed what I believe to be a sincerely held concern that the state and tribal governments are not providing the kind of regulation of Class III Indian gaming that is provided by the states of Nevada and New Jersey.... [One] concern voiced by my colleagues . . . had to do with the interaction of state law and the federal Indian gaming law — a concern that somehow the federal law has somehow pre-empted what state law determines to be the scope of gaming that is authorized or allowed under state law. . . .

A number of the members of Congress yesterday expressed their understanding of the act at the time of its passage; namely, that state law would determine which Class III games could be conducted by tribal governments resident in the state. These members are correct in their understanding of the act's provisions. State law controls and determines which games are conducted in a state by all gaming operators — be they Indian or non-Indian. If states are opposed to the proliferation of any particular type of game, they retain their sovereign authority to amend state law to criminally prohibit the conduct of any specific game. . . .

The Indian Gaming Regulatory Act does not impose upon any state a requirement that the state must allow tribal governments to conduct a type of game that the state law criminally prohibits. The states are in full control in this area. . . . It is also true that the Indian Gaming Regulatory Act authorizes tribal governments to engage in the same kinds of gaming activities that are conducted by others in a state. State laws vary widely in this respect. Some states authorize the conduct of so-called casino nights for charitable purposes. . . .

Other state laws don't authorize certain types of games, but they knowingly look the other way when these games are being conducted in Moose Clubs and Elks Clubs and by police officers' associations. Other states authorize the conduct of some games only for social purposes, but in both instances anyone can see that these games are being actively engaged in year round — and yet, these same states would take the position that the tribal governments cannot engage in the same activity. . . .

These are the difficult areas that we are in the process of tackling in our dialog with state and tribal and federal officials. I have observed, on more than one occasion, that when Indian people see these games being played by everyone else in the state, we would be hard-pressed to tell them that there is or should be a different rule when it comes to tribal operation of the same games. So we must sort this out within the context of each state's laws.

Continued from p. 256

Civil War era of floating casinos, also staged a comeback. Gambling on riverboats is now legal in six states abutting the Mississippi and Ohio rivers — Illinois, Indiana, Iowa, Louisiana, Mississippi and Missouri. However, a bill that would have legalized riverboat gambling in Virginia's southeastern Tidewater region was defeated recently in the General Assembly. Advocates for the bill had said that gaming revenues would help offset defense spending cutbacks in the Norfolk-Hampton-Newport News area.

Riverboat gambling is not always what it would seem. "Some of the casinos in Mississippi are on riverboats (which are permanently moored to the dock), but others do not even resemble boats," noted industry analyst Wertheim Schroder. "The law does not require these 'riverboat' casinos to sail, but only that they be on the water." [34]

Waterborne gaming also is prospering on passenger ships offering "cruises to nowhere." That's industry shorthand for a brief round trip to international waters, where gambling is legal. Until recently, federal law barred American-flag vessels from offering gaming. To get around the ban, gaming operators ran cruises (usually from Florida) on foreign ships.

In 1992, President George Bush signed the U.S. Flag Cruise Ship Competitiveness Act, which repealed the prohibition against gaming aboard vessels with American registry. Cruise-ship gaming revenue that year totaled $305 million, a 5 percent increase over 1991.

Sports Betting

Other legislation signed by Bush in 1992 scored big with professional sports league officials. Sports gambling generates major revenues, but nearly all the action is illegal. That's because the leagues fiercely oppose all efforts to legalize wagering on their games. The legislation signed by Bush barred additional states from sponsoring sports-based lotteries based on college and professional basketball, football and baseball. The measure did not outlaw wagering on horse and dog racing, or on the state-run numbers games that are the most common form of lottery.

Tebo Photography/© Foxwoods Casino 1994

Foxwoods High Stakes Bingo & Casino in Ledyard, Conn., operated by the Mashantucket Pequot tribe, has been called the most profitable casino in the Western Hemisphere.

However, the legislation allowed Delaware, Montana, Nevada and Oregon, which permitted sports-based lotteries or casino gambling, to continue their policies. It also ordered New Jersey to decide whether to sanction wagering on team sports, and in November 1993 the New Jersey Casino Control Commission nixed legalized sports betting.

U.S. pro sports leagues scored another knockout against gaming in February, when the government of Ontario, Canada, agreed to remove pro basketball from the province's sports lottery. The move cleared the way for Toronto to become the National Basketball Association's (NBA) 28th team, effective next season. The NBA had threatened to rescind its award of a franchise to Toronto unless league games were stricken from the Ontario lottery menu.

Keno and "Scratch" Games

State-run lotteries, which provided much of the impetus for legalized gambling's growth in the 1970s and '80s, are fast becoming a "mature" segment of the industry. The lottery market is approaching saturation, with games operating in 37 states and the District of Columbia — jurisdictions containing about 90 percent of the country's population.

Nonetheless, lottery officials remain upbeat. William Bergman, executive director of the North American Association of State and Provincial Lotteries, is betting the future on Club Keno — a video version of the familiar casino game. Club Keno represents "a whole new market because it's played primarily in age-controlled venues — taverns and bars," says Bergman. "Those places traditionally have not been lottery agents."

Club Keno is popular because it delivers payouts every five minutes — a feature that "keeps people playing for a little longer." The average increase in playing time, Bergman says, is about 30 to 35 minutes.

So-called "scratch" games based on bingo and Monopoly are also seen as bettor-friendly. These games differ

Parimutuel Sports: Not a Great Bet

Though the gaming industry as a whole is booming, some of its components are lagging behind. Parimutuel sports — horse and greyhound races and jai alai games — lead the list of laggards. In 1992, industry analyst Eugene Martin Christiansen reported that the amount bet (the "handle") by players at thoroughbred, harness and quarter horse tracks fell by $330 million. On the other hand, the off-track betting (OTB) handle rose by $549.1 billion.[1]

But greyhound racing really went to the dogs, recording a loss of $221.3 million, or 6.4 percent, in the on-track handle. Though greyhound OTB increased by 60 percent, that segment of the market was too small to make up for sharply lower on-track action. "If this sport is going to withstand the coming shock of widespread casino gaming," wrote Christiansen, "it has got to get its product on television and out there in the off-track market and in the home and do all this real, real soon."[2]

Wagering on jai alai, the smallest parimutuel sport, continued its long-term downward spiral in 1992, dropping by 12.8 percent, or $62.2 million, over the previous year. Jai alai's prospects "remain cloudy," Christiansen wrote, describing the fast-paced sport as "regional and visibly contracting."[3]

Despite horse racing's slow pace, Christiansen doesn't see it turning into a "studio" sport — an activity that has few if any spectators and exists essentially for the TV cameras. "No other sports have become studio sports through the use of television," he says. "I don't see why horse racing should be different. What typically happens with televised sports is that parallel markets develop. There is a television audience and a live audience. If horse racing secures extensive television coverage, I would expect that process to repeat itself."

[1] Eugene Martin Christiansen, "Industry Rebounds With 8.4% Handle Gain," *Gaming & Wagering Business*, July 15-Aug. 14, 1993, p. 20.

[2] *Ibid.*, p. 22.

[3] *Ibid.*, p. 24.

from traditional ones in three ways, says Bergman: "The odds are generally higher, the payout is bigger and the cost is greater."

Moreover, says Bergman, resistance to paying more than $1 for a scratch ticket seems to have evaporated. "We've found that $5 tickets are in demand where they're available," he says. "A $2 bingo ticket that takes roughly 10 to 12 minutes to scratch everything off of also is doing extraordinarily well. Monopoly is popular because it's fun and everybody knows how to play it. And who knows what other [scratch] games are around the corner?" ■

OUTLOOK

An Interactive Future?

Looking ahead, industry analyst Christiansen says only one thing can hurt the gaming industry: a ban on gambling. Experience shows that the American consumer "likes to spend money on commercial games," he says. "And I think as long as these games are available, that spending pattern will continue." Christiansen is especially bullish on casinos, since "Casino games are one of the very few things . . . most consumers want that the U.S. economy does not supply in superabundance."[35]

Harold Vogel, a gaming and lodging securities analyst for Merrill Lynch Co. in New York, expects gaming stocks to perform "above average on the whole" over the next few years, though the situation is likely to be "very volatile." Investors "have to be selective" about gaming stocks, cautions Vogel, who adds: "For now, they're doing very well."

The University of Nevada's Thompson also foresees continued casino growth, provided casinos can attract gamblers from afar. Casinos generate significant new tax revenues "only if they can export their product," he says. "The local economy doesn't benefit if only local people are gambling."

Analyzing the situation in his state, Thompson says gambling on Indian reservations in Arizona and California is bound to affect Nevada gaming. "We get convenience gamblers from California and Arizona," he explains, "and the convenience gambler goes to the closest venue. So if a casino could be positioned in Palm Springs, a couple of hours closer to L.A. than Vegas, that could definitely draw off some of our business. But it's unlikely you're going to get the synergism from reservation gaming that you get from having 100 casinos."

Besides an abundance of casinos, Las Vegas "gives the best deals on hotels and meals because of the competitive atmosphere," Thompson says. "And then we have a multiplicity of entertainment — shows and theme parks and what have you. An Indian reservation wouldn't be able to compete with all that. It could attract the convenience gamers, but people who want a little more would drive the extra two hours" to Las Vegas.

The prognosis for casino gambling in Atlantic City is more guarded. Casinos there are expected to reap continued benefits from regulations approved in 1992 by the New Jersey Legislature and the state Casino Control Commission. The rules sanctioned 24-hour gaming; new games, including pai gow, an Asian card game; an increase in the amount of floor space that may be set aside for machines; TV simulcasts of horse races; and the temporary licensing of travel representatives, designed to attract tour groups from Asia.

At the same time, though, Atlantic City casinos face rising competition. For now, the Pequots' vast Foxwoods casino in Connecticut is the main threat. Near the Rhode Island border, Foxwoods is well-positioned to attract players from Providence and Boston as well as most of Connecticut.

The approval last year of gaming compacts with New York's Oneida Indian Nation and St. Regis Mohawk Tribe amounted to more bad luck for New Jersey. Each tribe won the right to offer 27 different casino games. Though the two reservations are in lightly populated areas, their casinos are expected to lure some business away from Atlantic City. Similarly, riverboat gambling in Virginia, though recently defeated by the General Assembly, could nibble at the southern edge of Atlantic City's territory if it passes in the future.

Still farther to the south, more casino activity is taking place. Harrah's, a subsidiary of Memphis-based Promus Cos., announced in mid-February that it is planning to open the world's largest casino in New Orleans in late 1995: a 200,000-square-foot, multistory riverfront operation with 6,000 slot machines and 200 table games.*

The future of gaming may lie, however, not with mammoth new casinos but with interactive communications within reach — literally — of every homeowner's favorite TV chair.

"Imagine the sports bettor who will be able to gamble, using the remote control of his or her set, not only on the outcome of a game, but on every play!" wrote psychiatrist and compulsive-gambling expert Rosenthal. "The clinician," he added with understatement, "can anticipate the need to know more about this disorder." [36]

But there is a catch. The sports lottery law enacted in 1992 bars most betting on team games. One traditional wagering sport wasn't affected by the ban, however. "By accident or design," wrote Christiansen, "the law would seem to have granted horse racing a legal monopoly on interactive sports betting. That can be a valuable franchise — perhaps a *very* valuable franchise." [37] ■

* Casino gambling in New Orleans was approved by the Louisiana Legislature in June 1992.

Notes

[1] Eugene Martin Christiansen, "Industry Rebounds With 8.4% Handle Gain," *Gaming & Wagering Business*, July 15-Aug. 14, 1993, p. 13.
[2] Wertheim Schroder & Co. Inc., *Gaming Industry Update: The Continuing Explosion in Gaming*, March 10, 1993, p. 8.
[3] Stephen Drucker, "Las Vegas, Theme City," *The New York Times*, Feb. 13, 1994.
[4] National Indian Gaming Association, *Speaking the Truth About Indian Gaming*, May 1993.
[5] Leonard Prescott, "Stop Picking on Indian Gambling," *USA Today*, Dec. 6, 1993, p. 11A.
[6] Wertheim Schroder & Co., *op. cit.*, p. 30.
[7] James Cook, "If Roxborough Says the Spread Is 7, It's 7," *Forbes*, Sept. 14, 1992, p. 353.
[8] Testimony before House Judiciary Subcommittee on Economic and Commercial Law, Sept. 12, 1991.
[9] *Ibid.*
[10] *Ibid.*
[11] Quoted by Cook, *op. cit.*, p. 362.
[12] Testimony before Senate Judiciary Subcommittee on Patents, Copyrights and Trademarks, June 26, 1991.
[13] Testimony before House Judiciary Subcommittee on Economic and Commercial Law, Sept. 12, 1991.
[14] Richard J. Rosenthal, "Pathological Gambling," *Psychiatric Annals*, February 1992, pp. 72-73. Rosenthal is an assistant professor of psychiatry at the University of California-Los Angeles and president of the California Council on Compulsive Gambling.
[15] *Ibid.*, p. 73.
[16] Arnie and Sheila Wexler, "Facts on Compulsive Gambling and Addiction," Center for Alcohol Studies, Rutgers University, 1992.
[17] Richard E. Vatz and Lee S. Weinberg, "Refuting the Myths of Compulsive Gambling," *USA Today* (magazine), November 1993, pp. 54-56. The fourth edition of the APA's diagnostic manual will be published this spring.
[18] Lorena Bobbitt, of Manassas, Va., was charged with sexual mutilation after she cut off her husband's penis in late 1993, claiming he had raped and abused her. She was found not guilty by reason of insanity and released in February 1994 after spending several weeks under observation in a state mental hospital. Lyle and Erik Menendez of Beverly Hills, Calif., were charged in 1993 with second-degree murder in the shotgun slayings of their parents. In February mistrials were declared after the juries couldn't reach a verdict. The boys contended they had been sexually abused by their father and feared for their lives.
[19] H.L. Mencken, *A New Dictionary of Quotations* (1962), p. 443.
[20] *Ibid.*
[21] Ann Fabian, *Card Sharps, Dream Books, & Bucket Shops* (1990), p. 29.
[22] Robert K. DeArment, *Knights of the Green Cloth* (1982), pp. 23-24.
[23] *Ibid.*, p. 335.
[24] Resolution of the General Conference of the Methodist Episcopal Church South, Dallas, Texas, May 1930.
[25] Reuven and Gabrielle A. Brenner, *Gambling and Speculation* (1990), p. vii.
[26] *Ibid.*, p. 49.
[27] National Indian Gaming Association, "History of Tribal Gaming" (undated fact sheet). For additional background, see "Native Americans," *The CQ Researcher*, May 8, 1992, pp. 385-408.
[28] Testimony before U.S. House Committee on Interior and Insular Affairs, Jan. 9, 1992.
[29] Francis X. Clines, "The Pequots," *The New York Times Magazine*, Feb. 27, 1994, p. 51.
[30] Thomas B. Allen, "Connecticut," *National Geographic*, February 1994, p. 91.
[31] Quoted by Matt Connor, "Nevada, N.J. Legislators Sponsor Indian Gaming Bills," *Gaming & Wagering Business*, July 15-Aug. 14, 1993, p. 45.
[32] The two cases are *Seminole Tribe of Florida v. Florida* and *Poarch Creek Indians v. Alabama.*
[33] National Association of Attorneys General, *Gaming Developments Bulletin*, January 1994, p. 1.
[34] Wertheim Schroder & Co Inc., *op. cit.*, p. 35.
[35] Christiansen, *op. cit.*, p. 17.
[36] Rosenthal, *op. cit.*, p. 77.
[37] Christiansen, *op. cit.*, p. 22.

Bibliography

Selected Sources Used

Books

Brenner, Reuven, with Gabrielle A. Brenner, *Gambling and Speculation*, Cambridge University Press, 1990.

The authors try to answer the questions, Why do people gamble? and, Why do people condemn gambling? They conclude that "behind the condemnation has lurked, at times, a resistance to the idea that chance, rather than divine will or talent, can have a significant effect on the allocation and reallocation of property."

DeArment, Robert K., *Knights of the Green Cloth: The Saga of the Frontier Gamblers*, University of Oklahoma Press, 1982.

DeArment, a historian of the American West, strings together numerous anecdotes about gambling in frontier towns. He trains his spotlight on raffish characters like Wild Bill Hickok, Poker Alice, Diamondfield Jack Davis and Madame Mustache.

Fabian, Ann, *Card Sharps, Dream Books & Bucket Shops*, Cornell University Press, 1990.

In explaining why gambling never seemed to want for supporters, Fabian, an assistant professor of American studies and history at Yale, writes that "Southern planters who bet with money made for them by their slaves could hardly condemn a gambler's search for easy gain, and Northern capitalists who celebrated the great profits that came of great risks could hardly condemn a gambler's small risks and tireless search for money."

Hornung, Rick, *One Nation Under the Gun*, Pantheon Books, 1991.

Hornung, a contributor to the *Village Voice*, recounts the violent dispute over reservation gaming that split the Mohawk tribe in 1989 and prompted intervention by U.S. and Canadian law enforcement authorities.

Articles

Christiansen, Eugene Martin, "Industry Rebounds With 8.4% Handle Gain," *Gaming & Wagering Business*, July 15-Aug. 14, 1993.

Christiansen, a noted analyst of the U.S. gaming industry, presents the latest of his annual surveys.

Cook, James, "If Roxborough Says the Spread Is 7, It's 7," *Forbes*, Sept. 14, 1992.

Cook explains how the Las Vegas "line" — the point spreads on major college and professional games — is calculated and how it works in practice. The key figure in his account is Michael "Roxy" Roxborough, the nation's leading oddsmaker.

Starr, Mark, "The Gambling Man," *Newsweek*, June 14, 1993.

Starr reviews the documented and alleged gambling activities of Michael Jordan, the basketball superstar who retired from the Chicago Bulls and is now pursuing a baseball career in the Chicago White Sox farm system.

Reports and Studies

Center for State Policy Research, *1993 State Gaming Issues*, 1993.

This survey covers gambling-related bills introduced in state legislatures last year.

Educational Research Service, *State-Run Lotteries: Their Effects on School Funding*, 1993.

ERS concludes that lotteries generally are an undependable source of funding for public education: "Despite the millions of dollars that lotteries collect, the net lottery proceeds available for state use are only a small part of both state revenue and education revenue."

National Indian Gaming Association, *Speaking the Truth About Indian Gaming*, May 1993.

NIGA, a nonprofit group composed of Indian tribes and businesses engaged in tribal gaming, sets forth the main "myths" about reservation gambling and contradicts them with "facts" of its own.

National Indian Policy Center, *Reservation-Based Gaming*, April 1993.

This study analyzes recent opinion polls on Indian gaming, the economic impact of such gaming, the provisions of compacts negotiated under the Indian Gaming Regulatory Act (IGRA) and case law interpreting IGRA.

Wertheim Schroder & Co. Inc., *Gaming Industry Update: The Continuing Explosion in Gaming*, March 10, 1993.

The investment firm covers most of the ground covered by Christiansen's 1993 survey and also reviews the financial performance of major gaming companies.

The Next Step

Additional information from UMI's Newspaper & Periodical Abstracts database

Advantages and Disadvantages

Gold, Steven D., "It's not a miracle, it's a mirage," *State Legislatures*, February 1994, pp. 28-31.
More and more states are legalizing gambling, but its benefits as a revenue source have become more and more dubious. Inflated expectations about the benefits of gambling and reasons why gambling has not been an economic boon for most states are discussed.

Parker, Laura, "Waiting for the payoff," *Detroit News & Free Press*, Feb. 6, 1994, p. A1.
For a year after the first casino opened in Tunica County, Miss., the poorest of poor counties, it seemed a miracle cure for generations of economic despair. Five gambling casinos operate within a dozen miles of the town of Tunica now, and the boom is forcing it to confront the deeper reasons for its poverty. Tunica's dilemma is a question any community, whether a metropolis like Detroit or a small town on the Mississippi River, must ask when dealing with gambling: Can gambling dollars resolve social problems or do they create new ones?

Zeller, Laurie Hirschfeld, "Distressed cities increasingly bank on casino gambling," *National Civic Review*, Summer 1993, pp. 302-304.
An increasing number of U.S. communities are turning to small-stakes casino gambling to raise cash. The advantages and disadvantages of using casino gambling to remedy economic ills are discussed.

Considerations

Holmstrom, David, "Casino gambling surges in U.S., tempting more teenagers," *Christian Science Monitor*, Feb. 17, 1994, p. 3.
A new gambling-industry survey indicates that casino gambling has grown explosively in the U.S. Spokesmen in the industry now define gambling as "entertainment" and refer to it as the "new American pastime," but critics say its rapid growth has a dark side, particularly among teenagers.

Weber, Jonathan, "Turning the tables," *Los Angeles Times*, Feb. 13, 1994, p. D1.
Just two years after the Mashantucket Pequot tribe of Connecticut replaced a modest bingo parlor with the Foxwoods High Stakes Bingo and Casino, the casino is now the largest in the U.S. outside Las Vegas, with revenue estimated at $600 million to $700 million a year. That fact troubles other residents.

Gambling a Problem?

"Gambling," *Mayo Clinic Health Letter*, November 1993, p. 6.
Compulsive gambling can start as an innocent pastime, but it can quickly turn into a habit that escalates into an addiction. Statistics on gambling in the U.S. and signs of an uncontrollable urge to gamble are discussed.

Schwartzkopff, Frances, "A payoff for DHR gambling program," *Atlanta Journal Constitution*, Feb. 6, 1994, p. D5.
Since officials with the Georgia Department of Human Resources scrambled to put an education-and-treatment program together for problem gambling, they've had to pay for it with money from other services. The lottery's $200,000 annual contribution to the program's budget comes out of unclaimed winnings, which are finally becoming available.

Gambling in the Sky

Lawrence, Jennifer, "Lady luck is my co-pilot for foreign travelers," *Advertising Age*, Nov. 22, 1993, p. 1.
If Transbrazil, Virgin Atlantic Airways and other foreign air carriers get electronic poker, blackjack and other gaming devices, U.S. citizens could be gambling on their way to foreign countries.

Magiera, Marcy, "Iacocca bets on future of in-flight gambling," *Advertising Age*, Feb. 7, 1994, p. 8.
Lee Iacocca has formed a new merchant banking company to create new revenue streams for the airline industry, including in-flight gambling.

Gambling on Reservations

Benjaminson, Wendy, "Indians weighing pros, cons of casino," *Houston Chronicle*, Jan. 23, 1994, p. D1.
Members of Texas' Alabama-Coushatta Indian tribe may decide to abandon their tranquil way of life and high unemployment rates in exchange for casino gambling, a trade-off they say could make them immensely wealthy, yet poor in less tangible ways.

Briancon, Pierre, "Betting with the Indians," *World Press Review*, December 1993, pp. 36-37.
Foxwoods Casino in Ledyard, Conn., owned by Mashantucket Pequot tribe, is profiled.

"California Indians: Buffalo stakes," *The Economist*, July 24, 1993, pp. 25-26.
Despairing Indian tribes in California have had their

hopes raised by a court ruling allowing them to operate slot machines on their reservations. Since California offers a lottery, the state forefeited its right to oppose the machines on Indian territory.

Horse Racing

Indrisano, Ron, "Expanded gambling a hot topic," *Boston Globe*, Feb. 6, 1994, p. 65.
Indrisano discusses several items of interest in horse racing, including expanded gaming at racetracks and casino boat gambling.

McKay, David, "Roundtable reflections," *Barron's*, Feb. 14, 1994, p. 34.
McKay notes that in Philadelphia this has been done for ten years. The races are on cable TV, he says, and calls are made from the telephone at home to the track.

Rubinstein, Julian, "Virginia to select 1st track by August," *The Washington Post*, Feb. 14, 1994, p. C11.
More than five years after Virginia made parimutuel horse racing legal, the Virginia Racing Commission is on schedule to announce the state's first track site in the summer of 1994. Six OTB locations also are allowed under Virginia law.

The Lottery

Grunwald, Michael, "R.I. town says buyback a safe bet," *Boston Globe*, Feb. 6, 1994, p. 29.
In Scituate R.I., firearms are traded for lottery tickets.

Krol, Eric, "Lottery officials blaming sinking revenues on riverboat gambling," *Chicago Tribune*, Feb. 8, 1994, p. 2C2.
Illinois lottery revenues fell $71 million short of projections during the last six months of 1993, prompting lottery officials to admit for the first time that riverboat gambling may be hurting sales.

White, Betsy, "Miller to nix school-grant allocations," *Atlanta Constitution*, Feb. 8, 1994, p. C1.
In a bid to keep lottery spending free from the taint of pork-barrel politics, Gov. Zell Miller, D.-Ga., said he will veto his plans to spend $9.8 million on a program that would have chiefly benefited schools in the home districts of the state's most powerful lawmakers.

Riverboat Gambling

Fefer, Mark D., "A grossly undersupplied consumer product," *Fortune*, Nov. 1, 1993, p. 14.
Since Iowa became the first state to initiate riverboat gambling in 1989, five other states have okayed the idea and a dozen more are mulling over it. Investors believe that casino gambling is a "grossly undersupplied consumer product in the U.S."

Kass, John and Douglas Holt, "Riverboat deal to set sail after the primary," *Chicago Tribune*, Feb. 16, 1994, p. 2C3.
The authors look at attempts by local politicians to bring riverboat gambling to Chicago and several suburbs.

Spending the Money

Hill, James, "Casino tie bolstered to schools," *Chicago Tribune*, Feb. 4, 1994, p. 2L1.
Officials in North Chicago and Waukegan are proposing an unprecedented revenue-sharing plan that would funnel money directly from proposed floating casinos into local school coffers.

Ratcliffe, R. G.; Rugeley, Cindy, "Lottery profits for schools urged," *Houston Chronicle*, Jan. 22, 1994, p. A25.
Republican George Bush has called for Texas lottery revenues to be dedicated to public education.

Walston, Charles and Ken Foskett, "School-grant dispute stalls budget," *Atlanta Journal Constitution*, Feb. 5, 1994, p. C1.
Georgia Senate Republicans criticized the process used to select schools for a pilot program, funded by the lottery, that would test computer equipment, raising concerns about how $8 million in lottery funds would be spent and stalling Gov. Zell Miller's proposed budget.

Sports Gambling

Frayne, Trent, "A vulnerable NBA hedges its bets," *Maclean's*, Dec. 6, 1993, p. 50.
Toronto is in danger of losing its newly granted NBA franchise because the province runs a lottery that encourages betting on sporting events. David Stern, the commissioner of the NBA, says the franchise will not be granted unless professional basketball is excluded from betting.

"Ontario action on lottery opens way for NBA team," *The Wall Street Journal*, Feb. 11, 1994, p. A4.
The province of Ontario cleared the way for an NBA franchise in Toronto by agreeing to drop basketball from its sports-betting lottery. The NBA and the new franchise agreed to help make up the province's lost gambling revenue by making various contributions to charitable causes.

Smith, Timothy K., "What is at stake in the XVII Olympiad?" *The Wall Street Journal*, Feb. 16, 1994, p. A14.
The wagering that is taking place in Las Vegas on events in the 1994 Olympic Games is discussed.

Taylor, Phil, "Don't bet on Toronto," *Sports Illustrated*, Jan. 17, 1994, p. 73.
There is a good chance that an NBA franchise will not be awarded to Toronto because of Ontario's refusal to remove NBA games from its sports lottery. The NBA might delay expansion plans altogether if Toronto loses its franchise.

Back Issues

Great Research on Current Issues Starts Right Here...Recent topics covered by The CQ Researcher are listed below. Before May 1991, reports were published under the name of Editorial Research Reports.

SEPTEMBER 1992
Domestic Partners
Violence in Schools
Public Broadcasting
Women in the Military

OCTOBER 1992
Depression
U.S. Auto Industry
Youth Apprenticeships
Hispanic Americans

NOVEMBER 1992
Physical Fitness
Privatization
Paying for College
U.S. Policy in Asia

DECEMBER 1992
Crackdown on Smoking
The New CIA
Eating Disorders
Women and AIDS

JANUARY 1993
Hate Crimes
Child Sexual Abuse
Nuclear Fusion
U.S. Trade Policy

Back issues are available for $4.00 (subscribers) or $7.00 (non-subscribers). Quantity discounts apply to orders over ten. To order, call Congressional Quarterly Customer Service at (202) 887-8621.

Binders are available for $15.00. To order call 1-800-638-1710. Please refer to stock number 648.

FEBRUARY 1993
Community Policing
Europe's New Right
School Censorship
Violence Against Women

MARCH 1993
Gay Rights
Aid to Russia
War on Drugs
TV Violence

APRIL 1993
Head Start
High-Speed Rail
Children's Legal Rights
Muslims in America

MAY 1993
Cults in America
Preventing Teen Pregnancy
Software Piracy
National Parks

JUNE 1993
Food Safety
Prostitution
Childhood Immunizations
National Service

JULY 1993
Electric Cars
Population Growth
Downward Mobility
Intelligence Testing

AUGUST 1993
Mental Illness
Bilingual Education
Foreign Policy Burden
School Funding

SEPTEMBER 1993
Suburban Crime
Public Housing
Supreme Court Preview
Immigration Reform

OCTOBER 1993
Airline Safety
Disaster Response
Science in the Courtroom
The Glass Ceiling

NOVEMBER 1993
Paying for Retirement
Charitable Giving
Privacy in the Workplace
Adoption

DECEMBER 1993
U.S. Vietnam-Relations
Learning Disabilities
Child Care
Space Program's Future

JANUARY 1994
Racial Tensions in Schools
South Africa's Future
Worker Retraining
Regulating Pesticides

FEBRUARY 1994
Prison Overcrowding
Water Quality
Religion in Schools
Juvenile Justice

MARCH 1994
Underground Economy
Education Standards

Future Topics

- ***Private Management of Public Schools***
- ***Reproductive Ethics***
- ***Democracy in China***

THE CQ Researcher

PUBLISHED BY CONGRESSIONAL QUARTERLY INC.

Private Management of Public Schools

Can for-profit companies reform public education?

Public schools have been under pressure for more than a decade to improve. Now, many school systems are considering a new idea: management by private companies. Education entrepreneurs say they can remake America's schools — and make a profit in the process. But critics say companies can profit only by shortchanging students or cutting the pay of teachers or other school employees. Despite the criticism, one company is now managing nine public schools in Baltimore, and a second venture will open three new schools in Massachusetts in 1995. Supporters and critics alike will be closely watching students' achievement scores and the bottom lines of the management companies as well.

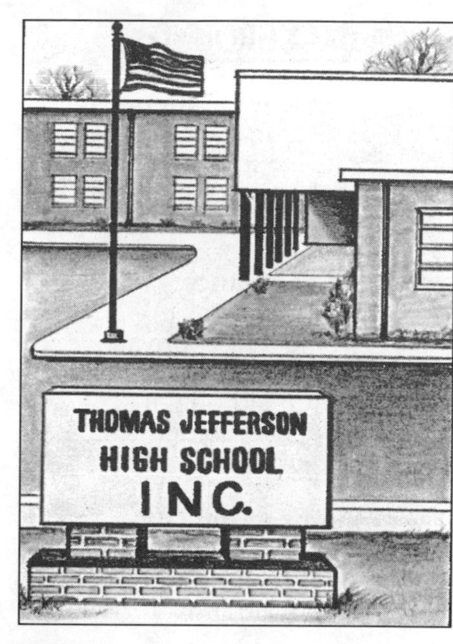

INSIDE THIS ISSUE

CQ March 25, 1994 • Volume 4, No. 12 • 265-288

Formerly Editorial Research Reports

Private Management Of Public Schools

The Issues

Background

Current Situation

Outlook

Sidebars and Graphics

For Further Information

Cover Art: Barbara Sassa-Daniels

March 25, 1994
Volume 4, No. 12

The CQ Researcher (ISSN 1056-2036). Formerly Editorial Research Reports. Published weekly (48 times per year, not printed the first Friday of any month with five Fridays) by Congressional Quarterly Inc., 1414 22nd St., N.W., Washington, D.C. 20037. Rates are furnished upon request. Second-class postage paid at Washington, D.C. POSTMASTER: Send address changes to The CQ Researcher, 1414 22nd St., N.W., Washington, D.C. 20037.

Private Management of Public Schools

By Kenneth Jost

The Issues

Linda Carter moves relentlessly around the gymnasium at Baltimore's Harlem Park Elementary School, exhorting the youngsters with the booming voice and compelling cadence of a tent-revival preacher.

"Do you know you're all heroes?" Carter asks the sea of eager black faces. Sitting on the gym floor, the children shout back yes. Then they join in singing a song with the repeated refrain, "when a hero comes along."

"You're all super kids," says Carter, the school's assistant principal, as the morning assembly draws to a close. "I want you to have a super day."

The daily meetings help the students "restart the day," an administrator tells a visitor. The kids do seem energized as they file out, winding their way through corridors lined with children's art and displays marking Black History Month. The hallways are clean, the grounds well-kept. Inside the classrooms, most youngsters appear alert and engaged as they take their places around group tables or at spanking-new computers.

Welcome to the showcase school of what admirers describe as a pioneering experiment in improving public education in America. (*See story, p. 269.*) Harlem Park is one of nine Baltimore schools that have been managed since September 1992 by Education Alternatives Inc. (EAI), which says it can remake America's schools — and make a profit in the process.

"If you match up rewards with risks, you can reward the risk of making the change in education," says EAI Chairman John T. Golle. His Minneapolis-based company is managing the Baltimore schools, with a combined $27 million annual budget, under a five-year contract based on a simple proposition: By using private-sector efficiencies and profit-motive

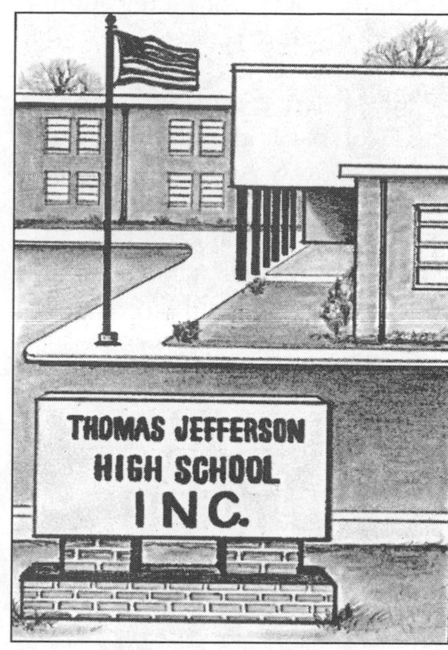

principles, EAI can make schools more accountable to their "customers" — students, parents, teachers and administrators.

Critics, however, see a host of overblown promises from a company with no track record in education. "It's hard not to get excited about the prospect that, for no money down and only pennies a week, we could raise kids' academic achievement to world-class levels, eliminate all the other social problems they bring to school every day and tame the bureaucracy," Albert Shanker, president of the American Federation of Teachers (AFT), told the Senate Education Appropriations Subcommittee in January. "The question is: Is this a solid idea or another chase after a quick fix that will end in disappointment?" [1]

Golle's company promises a lot. Working in partnership with KPMG Peat Markwick, a major accounting firm, and Johnson Controls World Services Inc., a national facilities-management company, EAI says it can save money, streamline school bureaucracies, clean up buildings and, above all, enliven classroom teaching and raise student achievement.

EAI's key contribution to the partnership, dubbed the Alliance for Schools That Work, is its trademarked curriculum, Tesseract, designed to turn bored youngsters into active learners. Tesseract takes its name from the trip through time in Madeleine L'Engle's popular children's science-fiction tale, *A Wrinkle in Time.* Tesseract teachers replace memorization and rote drill with flexible instruction tailored to the students' individual needs, with the progress of each student planned and tracked according to a "Personal Education Plan."

Golle claims EAI is accomplishing its goals in Baltimore, and Baltimore school officials say they are pleased with the results. But the company suffered two major setbacks this month when officials in Milwaukee and Washington, D.C., turned aside proposals from EAI to manage schools in their districts. "We have not met our sales objective," Golle acknowledged at a March 8 news conference in Baltimore, called to try to counter a newspaper report two days earlier that described the company's financial outlook as "bleak." [2]

EAI is not alone in trying to make a business out of private management of public schools. The Edison Project, a multimillion-dollar enterprise launched by Tennessee-based media entrepreneur Christopher Whittle, has been busy wooing school districts with a curriculum plan still on the drawing boards. Last week, the project scored an important breakthrough when Massachusetts officials awarded it charters to open three new schools in Boston, Lowell and Worcester in fall 1995.

Meanwhile, in Minneapolis, a private consulting firm, Public Strategies Group, has been hired to serve as superintendent of the 44,000-student school system under a three-year contract that ties the company's compensation to specified performance goals. At least two other companies have tried, but failed so far, to persuade local school boards to hire them to manage their schools.

The growing interest in private management reflects a prevalent feeling that something is deeply wrong with public education but that previous reform efforts have not produced results.

"Ten years after *A Nation at Risk*, things aren't that substantially different," says John M. McLaughlin, an associate professor of education at St. Cloud State University in Minnesota, referring to an influential critique of public education by a Reagan administration task force. "There's a feeling now that we're willing to look at things much differently."

McLaughlin, who follows for-profit school management in his newsletter, *The Education Investor*, says private companies bring more than new ideas to school reform. They also bring money. "Education is a capital-starved industry," McLaughlin says, noting declining public support for raising school spending. EAI offers up-front capital for schools — in Baltimore, it invested about $7.5 million — in hopes of future profits.

"Every other aspect of America operates on that market-driven notion," McLaughlin says, "so I don't have a problem with that. It doesn't make schools less public; it just makes them more efficient."

But critics of the new education entrepreneurs, including teachers' unions and liberal policy advocates, bristle at the notion of profiting from public schools. While they doubt that anyone will actually make money, they argue that any savings ought to be plowed back into education or returned to taxpayers.

"Why should the money recaptured go into private investors' pockets instead of back into the pockets of taxpayers?" asks Alex Molnar, a professor of education at the University of Wisconsin-Milwaukee.

Teachers' unions, school administrators and other public education traditionalists have been making similar arguments more and more forcefully. Their opposition lobbying has helped stunt the growth of the phenomenon, with unions playing the critical role in blocking private management plans in several cities.

Supporters of school privatization, already unsuccessful in introducing school choice and other forms of competition into the education marketplace (*see story, p. 277.*), say the aggressive lobbying proves their point. They contend that a well-entrenched "education lobby" will continue to block true reform until an outside catalyst — like a private company — forces the schools to change. "We've got to get rid of having education run as a monopoly," says Myron Lieberman, author of several books harshly critical of public schools.

The education management companies, however, carefully avoid harsh ideological attacks. Golle stresses that EAI is not promoting privatization but a "private-public partnership" that keeps public controls, public policies and most public employees in place while enabling teachers and principals to break the logjams that block school improvements.

© 1993 Rich Riggins

Education is a hands-on job for Assistant Principal Linda Carter of Baltimore's Harlem Park Elementary School.

As school systems around the country ponder the private-management idea, here are some of the questions being debated:

Should private companies be allowed to profit from educating children?

Supporters of private management say that many businesses already profit from education — from pencil makers and textbook publishers to food processors and construction companies. "I don't know anyone who works with schools who hasn't made a profit," says Katherine Henry, a former teacher and administrator hired by EAI to oversee teacher training in its Baltimore schools.

To save money and improve quality, schools also have "contracted out" a host of functions outside the classroom, including food services, transportation and janitorial work. EAI and its supporters say that hiring a for-profit company to manage the instructional program is a logical and equally legitimate way to improve the schools.

"We need people like [those who run] EAI who are willing to risk a lot of their money and a lot of their investors' money to create a different

Continued on p. 270

EAI Gets Mixed Report Card for Its Baltimore Schools

For more than a year, Education Alternatives Inc. (EAI) received high marks in Baltimore for its operation of nine inner-city public schools.

"In Baltimore, Capitalism Gets an 'A' in Education," trumpeted the headline to one especially favorable report. *Washington Post* business columnist James K. Glassman credited the firm with refurbishing the schools, cutting overhead, bringing new enthusiasm to students and teachers alike and making a profit to boot. [1]

But the favorable publicity for the closely watched experiment may stem more from astute public relations than from documented results. While the company draws nearly unanimous raves for the physical appearance of the schools, reports issued early this year question its school management and classroom instruction.

© 1993 Rich Riggins

Use of computers at Harlem Park elementary was criticized by an outside evaluator.

At Harlem Park elementary and middle schools, students sit at group tables instead of regimented rows of individual desks. Teachers appear to emphasize active learning techniques, such as reading aloud or manipulating objects, rather than tedious rote drill.

But a Pennsylvania educator commissioned by the Maryland Teachers' Association saw things differently. Olivia S. Reusing, visited Harlem Park and one other EAI-run school in December. In a 13-page report, Reusing said the classroom methods "fell short of the ideals described in Tesseract literature. . . . In no classroom during the two days of visits did I observe methodologies which encouraged students to act as self-directed learners and problem solvers." [2]

In an interview, Reusing was also critical of the use of computers, saying students worked mainly on elementary drill questions. In February, a reporter looking over the shoulders of sixth-graders using computers also saw seemingly basic, multiple-choice questions being worked on. One question asked what kind of book would be used to locate a country: (a) dictionary; (b) atlas; (c) encyclopedia.

Golle repudiates Reusing's report: "Paid for by the union, walked through the schools for two days, to my knowledge never done this kind of evaluation before." Nat Harrington, director of communications for Baltimore City Public Schools, is similarly dismissive. "It seemed like a rushing to judgment, of sorts," he says.

The school system's own evaluation of EAI's performance, however, is mixed. The 158-page January report found that the company had doubled the budgeted expenditures for facilities at the nine schools, conducted well-received teacher-training sessions and increased parental involvement. But the evaluation also found areas where it faulted EAI:

- An initial "Personal Education Plan" — a central component of the Tesseract method — was prepared for only 85 percent of the 4,800 students in the nine schools, not all students as promised. The preparation rate for scheduled second and third plans dropped to 56 percent and 23 percent.
- Repairs were found to have been completed faster than before, but the report also noted complaints that purchase orders "stayed on desks too long."

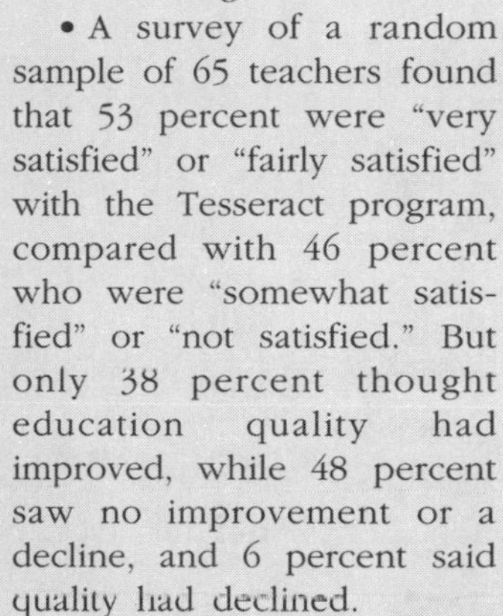

- A survey of a random sample of 65 teachers found that 53 percent were "very satisfied" or "fairly satisfied" with the Tesseract program, compared with 46 percent who were "somewhat satisfied" or "not satisfied." But only 38 percent thought education quality had improved, while 48 percent saw no improvement or a decline, and 6 percent said quality had declined.

On the all-important issue of student achievement, only fragmentary results are available so far. The Computer Curriculum Corp., which installed computers in the school last spring, found an average student gain of 88 percent (almost one grade level) three months later — considerably higher than the typical 30 percent grade-level gain. But results from standardized tests administered by the school system will not be available until the end of the current school year.

EAI failed to get hoped-for contracts to operate additional schools in February and March, but Baltimore school officials continued to voice confidence in the company. "They are doing everything they were pledged to do," Superintendent Walter Amprey told a news conference March 8.

On Wall Street, however, investors were less confident, and the stock price fell from a high of 48 in November to a low of 13¼ early this month.

In the March 8 session with reporters, however, Golle noted that the company made a 3.2 percent profit last year. "We believe that the prospect for our company has never been greater," Golle said.

[1] *The Washington Post*, Oct. 29, 1993, p. G1.

[2] Olivia S. Reusing, "A Report of Observations in Three Tesseract Schools," Jan. 2, 1994.

Learning the Tesseract Way

The Tesseract curriculum designed by Educational Alternatives Inc. replaces rote drill with flexible instruction tailored to students' individual needs.

- Each student experiences success in school every day.
- Parents are partners in their child's education.
- A Personal Education Plan™ is developed for each student.
- Real-life experience is the basis for learning.
- Students take responsibility for their own learning by planning, accomplishing and evaluating their own work, and making the best use of their time.
- Technology helps students learn and teachers teach.
- Hands-on projects provide experiences upon which students establish a solid foundation of understanding.
- Cross-disciplinary and thematic units produce learning that is relevant and challenging.
- All areas of curriculum are important.
- Students learn productive and positive behaviors.
- Creativity is fostered and celebrated.
- Learning styles vary. Teachers design and present learning experiences in a variety of learning modalities.
- Teachers use flexible grouping to meet the changing needs of individual students.
- Students develop communications skills through a literature-based program that includes phonics, reading, writing and spelling.
- Receiving instruction in a world language enriches students' understanding of other cultures and extends their language skills.
- Students develop a global perspective, learning to appreciate and accept all peoples of the world.
- Homework is a natural extension of classroom activities.
- Students, staff, parents and the community work, learn and share together.

Source: Educational Alternatives Inc.

Sarah Merritt

Continued from p. 268

system, build a better mousetrap," says McLaughlin.

Many public school educators, however, say that introducing the profit motive into the classroom will hurt rather than help education. "When the motive is reaping a profit, I don't believe the motive is going to be to provide the best educational system that there can be," says Keith Geiger, president of the National Education Association (NEA), the nation's largest teachers' union. He points as an example to EAI's moves to transfer all art, music, physical-education and special-education teachers out of its Baltimore schools.

Geiger and other critics argue as well that the companies are unlikely to make much profit, if any, out of the schools. Geiger says the company's first-ever profit last year came not from the Baltimore schools but from return on its investments. "They've made a profit because they've invested money," he says, "not off what they're doing in Baltimore."

In response, Golle insists that EAI's plan is not a "get-rich-quick idea." The company will make "a very, very small percentage in order to bring value to the children," Golle says. And he complains about what he depicts as contradictory criticisms from EAI's opponents.

"Sometimes I feel that I'm between the hydrant and the dog," Golle says. "If you make too much money, they say, 'How dare you make too much money off these children.' If you don't make any money, they say, 'You're a bad businessperson.' "

EAI's critics also worry about how to monitor its finances and check on its performance. "Who's going to certify that they're in fact doing all this?" asks the University of Wisconsin's Molnar.

Molnar says that school systems cannot rely on private companies to evaluate their performance. But any regulatory system, he says, will simply cost more money. "Far from saving money, you have a built-in mechanism for adding to the costs," he says.

AFT President Shanker says EAI's agreement in Baltimore illustrates the problem. He says the contract does not set specific student-achievement goals or provide for independent evaluation of EAI's performance.

Did Baltimore Get Better Education for Less?

The emphasis on cost-saving by John Golle's Educational Alternatives Inc. (EAI) reflects the widespread belief that public schools are wasting money on bloated bureaucracies and overpaid blue-collar workers. Golle cites statistics showing that education expenditures have been increasing faster than the rate of population growth, while the percentage going into the classroom has been declining.

"In 1950, as a country, we were spending about 50 cents of every dollar on teachers; today, that has declined to 38 cents," Golle says in his standard speech to legislators and school administrators. "More and more of those dollars are being siphoned off to the management of the enterprise as opposed to the direct, classroom education of our children."

Claiming that it could provide better education for less, EAI agreed to operate nine Baltimore, Md., schools with a budget based on the system's overall average per-pupil expenditure, or $5,918 this year.

But local union leaders, as well as American Federation of Teachers President Albert Shanker and National Education Association President Keith Geiger, insist that EAI is actually spending more money on the nine Baltimore schools than they would have received under previous budgeting. That contention was confirmed in a January report by Baltimore school officials.

The report concluded that EAI spent $1 million more than the school system would have spent on direct operation of the nine schools. EAI more than doubled the $1.9 million budgeted for facilities maintenance to $4 million. Meanwhile, the amount spent on regular instruction was cut by almost 10 percent — from $14.9 million to $13.5 million — and the budgeted amount for special education was nearly halved, from $2.3 million to $1.2 million, according to the report.

Golle acknowledges that the company has spent more on the nine Baltimore schools than the school system had budgeted. He says the company increased capital expenditures because "the facilities were in terrible condition" and hopes to recoup the investment "several years down the road."

But critic Alex Molnar, a professor of education at the University of Wisconsin-Milwaukee, says EAI's strategy creates an unfair standard to judge the public schools. "Given [enough] investment capital, public schools could do virtually every, single thing [the private companies] propose," he says. In addition, Molnar points out that any profit EAI makes ultimately will come out of the school system's budget.

"They have to recapture their capital investment over time," he says, "and the only way is to get it out of the operating funds of the school districts. It's almost a direct transfer of wealth."

Shanker calls the arrangement "an appearance of a conflict of interest."

EAI officials, however, insist that the company is fully accountable to public officials. They note, for example, that Baltimore can terminate the arrangement at any time. More broadly, they say the company can succeed — and make a profit — only by doing what it promises. "Accountability," Golle told the Senate Education Appropriations Subcommittee in January, "is the key to success."

Do private companies have a special contribution to make toward improving public education?

In its brochures, EAI promises "a new dimension" of learning. "The active learning process, not the teacher, is on center stage in an Education Alternatives classroom," the sales pitch continues. Students are "turned loose" in "dynamic learning areas" with "movable furniture" and "widely available" technology. With "two teachers" in every classroom, students get individual attention. And EAI "continually monitors performance" with standardized tests and "detailed reports to track progress."

"Virtually everywhere we've gone we have dramatically improved student achievement," Golle told the Senate subcommittee.

EAI's critics, however, contend that the company is offering nothing distinctive in the way of improving classroom instruction and has yet to prove its claims of raising student achievement.

These critics note that the progressive ideas that EAI touts — from group tables and computers to more fluid classrooms and individualized learning plans — are already being adopted in school districts all around the country. "There is absolutely nothing new there," Molnar says of EAI's instructional methods. "Given the investment capital, public schools could do virtually every single thing they propose."

Leaders of the Baltimore Teachers Union (BTU), an AFT affiliate, agree. "There isn't anything different in their style," says Irene Dandridge, the union's co-president.

The principal EAI selected to run both Harlem Park's elementary and middle schools agrees as well. "It's definitely not a new program," says Wayne Coger, who was transferred to Harlem Park from another Baltimore school a few months after EAI took over. He says the company's main contribution is financial. "It provides the additional resources that we would not ordinarily get," he says.

For their part, the Edison Project planners are dampening expectations that they will be unveiling a completely new curriculum.

Benno C. Schmidt Jr., the former Yale University president who heads the project, says the project's design group is "knitting together" features already found in "the world's most effective" schools. "Our distinctive

American Federation of Teachers

Albert Shanker
President, American Federation of Teachers

contribution," he told the Senate subcommittee, "lies, I believe, not in any one of those features but in their integration, both at the school level and at the system level."

Supporters of private management argue that critics are wrong to minimize that contribution. "To say that improved management technique is nothing is just incorrect," says John O'Leary, a senior fellow with the Los Angeles-based Reason Foundation and co-author of a report last fall on contracting-out options for schools. [3] "Management can make a tremendous difference in the final customer satisfaction. That's why very good managers prove to be very valuable in the market."

EAI's brochure promises that its partners — KPMG and Johnson Controls — will help schools get their finances in order and save up to 30 percent on facilities maintenance. But the company's appeal focuses on improving education, not just saving money. "I don't think the private sector is going to add much if they just do the same thing cheaper," comments McLaughlin.

As for its educational claims, EAI appears to be stretching the available evidence. The company's brochure says EAI offers "tested educational programs" and that EAI students "outperform the national norm, gaining, on average, 1.5 grade levels for each year in school."

Shanker says, however, that the Tesseract curriculum has never been discussed in a professional journal or presented at a professional conference. (*See box, p. 270.*) And the claims for improving student-achievement scores are based on EAI's record at the private schools the company operated in Minnesota and Arizona before it began working with public schools in Miami, Fla., and Baltimore. Comparison test scores from those schools are not yet available.

Will cost-cutting by private firms hurt teachers or other school employees?

School privatization has been fiercely resisted by unions representing teachers and other school employees, largely because they fear jobs or salaries would be cut. To allay those fears, EAI has promised to safeguard teachers' jobs and accept existing pay scales for teachers and principals.

In Baltimore, Golle and other EAI officials stress, no teachers have permanently lost their jobs. Teachers EAI didn't want were given the "opportunity" to transfer out of the EAI schools, but all of them have been "reabsorbed" elsewhere in the system.

Nonetheless, EAI's cost-cutting does rely heavily on reducing pay. Even though teacher pay is protected, EAI uses low-paid classroom assistants to "effectively lower the student-teacher ratio," in Golle's phrase. Meanwhile, Johnson Controls works to save money on secretaries, cafeteria workers, guards and other non-instructional personnel.

Union leaders in Baltimore acknowledge that no teachers have lost jobs under EAI, but say that 25-30 teachers still on the payroll have yet to find new placements. They also say that the company replaced all "paraprofessionals" — teachers' aides — at the nine schools with recent college graduates classified as "interns."

Salaries for paraprofessionals are in the $20,000 range, and the positions are permanent. The interns earn about $7 per hour (roughly $10,000 for the school year), with no health or other benefits. "What they wanted is a teacher and someone they could pay less," says Lorretta Johnson, president of BTU's paraprofessional chapter.

"Tesseract is supposed to manage schools cheaper, and salaries are one way to do that," says Rachel Gibson, a Harlem Park intern. "That's how it was explained to me."

EAI officials note that paraprofessionals did not need college degrees, while the interns are college graduates who are supposed to be considering teaching as a career. Still, the company has been inconsistent in describing the interns. EAI officials sometimes talk about having "two teachers" in the classroom. At other times, they say more precisely that the program calls for "two adults" per classroom.

BTU leaders also say that EAI initially told janitors and other non-instructional workers they could keep their jobs at lower pay or leave. Golle says the janitors were told they could stay at their present salaries.

In his congressional testimony, Golle said custodial workers' wages

National Education Association

Keith Geiger
President, National Education Association

Alternative Approaches to Managing Public Schools

Three school systems have hired Educational Alternatives Inc. to run or help run their public schools, and other systems are considering such moves. In addition, several states have passed or introduced "charter school" legislation allowing alternative approaches to managing public schools. Charters granted to private companies or to groups of teachers, parents or nonprofit organizations would set out terms for operating the schools, including possible performance goals.

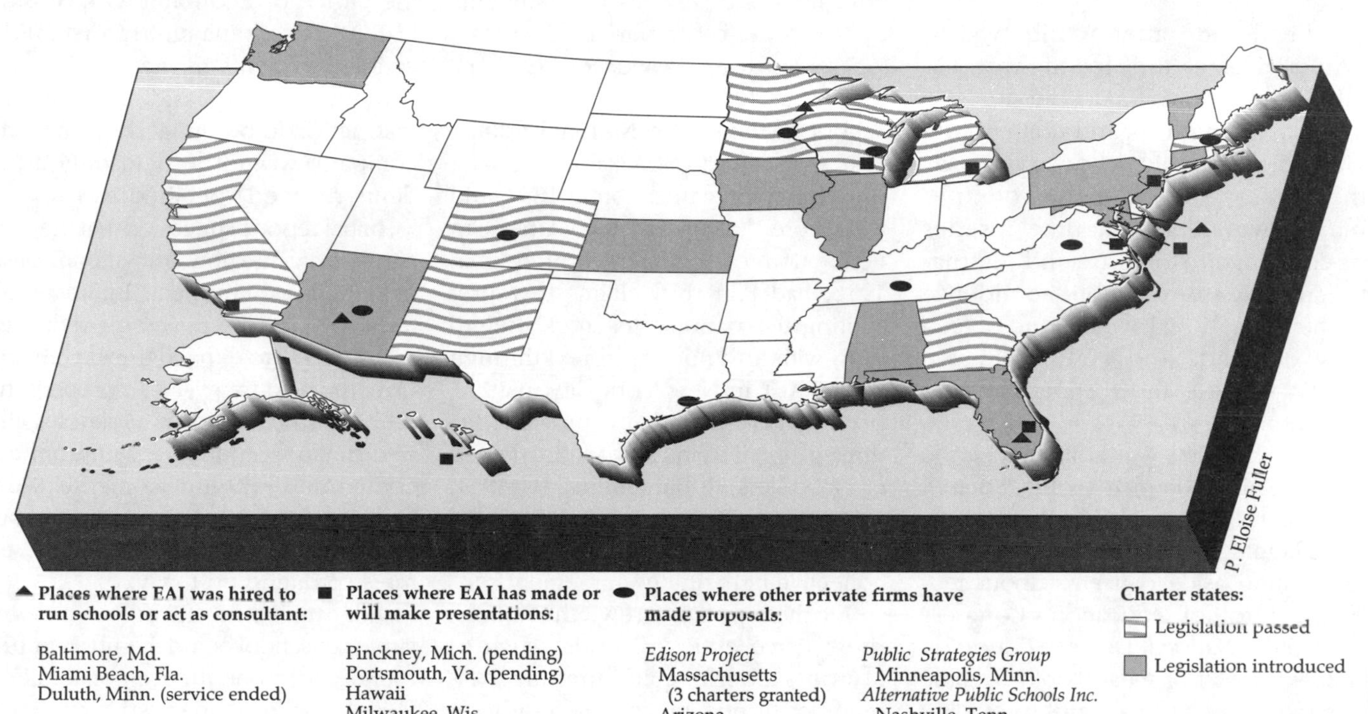

Source:

and benefits are "comparable" to previous levels. But he also told the senators that EAI's ability to increase spending on teacher training and technology depends on reducing labor costs for what he called "classified workers."

"We put more money into the classroom," Golle continued. "We buy more technology. We'll lower the [student-teacher] ratio in the classroom and we'll do significantly more staff development — without spending more dollars. And you do that by saving money from the classified work force."

For its part, Johnson Controls refuses to disclose pay scales for janitors or its other workers in Baltimore. "That's kept fairly proprietary to our company," says Marcia Jones, manager of business development for education for the Florida-based company. Jones says the company is spending about 20 percent less on non-instructional functions at the nine schools than the school system had spent, achieving savings from labor costs as well as energy efficiencies and bulk purchasing.

For some critics of public education, the potential cost-savings that private companies are promising is enough. "Even if they showed absolutely no improvement academically," says author Lieberman, "if they could do the job at half the cost, it would be great."

Labor is by far the biggest spending item for schools, however. Even if private companies can achieve some economies in energy, lighting or administrative costs, employee pay offers the biggest target for savings. And in Baltimore, union leaders say, those savings have come at the expense of low-echelon workers.

"Cutting through bureaucracy is positive," says NEA President Geiger, "but EAI and its business partners are taking part of their profits out of the pockets of the lowest-paid employees." ■

BACKGROUND

Postwar Challenges

In the decade after World War II, Americans felt they led the world in intellectual as well as economic and military strength — and contentedly viewed the public school system as the primary source of the country's brainpower. Since that time, a series of challenges, domestic and international, have shaken public confidence in the educational system and placed new demands and new strains on public schools and the people who run them.

With the Cold War at its height, the Soviet Union's launch of the Sputnik satellite in 1957 raised fears that schools were lagging in science and mathematics. Setting aside concerns about federal control of education, Congress passed the National Defense Education Act — the first of what would become a panoply of federal laws providing financial aid, with some strings attached, to local schools.

Three years earlier, the Supreme Court had more dramatically overridden the traditional autonomy of state and local school authorities by prohibiting legally mandated racial segregation in public schools. (*See "Chronology," p. 275.*) The landmark ruling began a still-unfinished process of court-ordered desegregation, initially in the South but later throughout the country. As desegregation battles continued, court orders to redraw school districts or bus pupils to schools outside their neighborhoods fueled discontent among many parents and, in places, contributed to "white flight" from central-city schools.

The population base for city school systems was eroding anyway as a result of the trend toward suburban living. Middle-class families disregarded city boundaries to move into tree-lined neighborhoods of single-family homes away from the ills of urban life. They left behind school systems with a narrowing tax base and a student population that was poorer and needed more remedial education and services than students in the better-off suburban districts.

The growing power of teachers' unions added to the pressures on school systems. The National Education Association (NEA), founded as a professional organization in 1857, and the more labor-oriented American Federation of Teachers, founded in 1916, had laid rival claims to representing the nation's teachers. Beginning with an important breakthrough by the AFT in New York City in 1961, both unions made rapid strides through the '60s in representing teachers in collective bargaining. By 1971, more than 70 percent of teachers across the country were covered by collective-bargaining agreements. [4]

As their power grew, the unions drew fierce criticism. Critics such as Myron Lieberman, a onetime AFT member turned management adviser on labor issues, blamed unions for driving up school system costs, protecting mediocre teachers and blocking any reforms, such as contracting out or school vouchers, that threatened teachers' interests. [5]

Public discontent with the schools collided with the teachers' unions in an important policy issue in the early 1970s. Since 1963, average scores on the Scholastic Aptitude Test (SAT), the most widely given college admissions examination, had been falling. Despite disagreement over the causes, the numbers were generally accepted as evidence of lagging student achievement. And an assortment of private companies emerged in the early 1970s claiming that they could succeed where teachers had failed. The result was a two-year experiment in using private companies to try to improve public education.

Performance Contracting

Texarkana, Ark., was the first school district to adopt what came to be called "performance contracting." [6] Using federal anti-poverty funds from the Office of Economic Opportunity (OEO), Texarkana hired Dorsett Educational Systems in the late 1960s to provide reading and mathematics instruction to potential dropouts. The company would be paid only if students reached specified levels.

Initial reports suggested that the company was achieving dramatic increases in student achievement. Impressed by those reports, the government decided in April 1970 to expand the experiment. Over the next two years, more than 100 school districts in some 23 states signed performance contracts with some 15 companies ranging from the Westinghouse Learning Corp. to tiny start-up firms akin to the entrepreneurial ventures sprouting up today.

Educators had mixed reactions. A survey of school board members in 1970 found about one-third emphatically in favor of the idea, one-third in favor with reservations and one-third opposed. [7] The teachers' unions, however, strongly opposed the idea. The NEA said it could support performance contracts with teachers, but not with private firms. The AFT opposed the idea in any form and began monitoring contracts to watch how they were implemented.

Performance contracting died within a few years — but not at the hands of the teachers' unions. First, a scandal was unearthed. Students in Texarkana, it turned out, had been given some of the questions used to measure their progress. Other results were untainted, but still unfavorable. A federal evaluation of 18 cities completed in 1972 concluded that there was "very little evidence that performance incentive contracting . . . had a beneficial effect on the reading and mathematics achievement of students participating

Continued on p. 276

Chronology

1800s-1950s

Free public education in government-operated schools advances throughout the 19th century. All states adopt compulsory attendance laws by early 20th century.

May 17, 1954
Supreme Court's *Brown v. Board of Education* ruling prohibits mandatory racial segregation in public schools.

Oct. 4, 1957
Soviet Union's launch of *Sputnik* satellite shakes Americans' confidence in education system.

1960s-1970s

Public education confronts a variety of new challenges, including white flight from inner-city schools, increased power of teachers' unions and growing discontent with school performance.

1962
Conservative economist Milton Friedman, in his book *Capitalism and Freedom*, proposes that the government issue vouchers to all families with children for use in the public or private school of their choice.

June 1972
Federal Office of Economic Opportunity (OEO) concludes after two-year experiment that private companies operating schools did not perform better than traditional public schools.

1974
East Harlem school district adopts school choice program.

1980s

A decade of political conservatism produces increased support for school privatization. School voucher proposals draw new interest, while many school districts contract out services.

1983
A Nation at Risk report warns of "a rising tide of mediocrity" in public education.

March 1988
Presidential Commission on Privatization recommends that private schools "be able to participate in federal programs providing educational choice to parents."

1989
Boston University takes over troubled school system in Chelsea, Mass.

1990s

For-profit companies seek to manage public schools. Voters in three states reject school voucher plans.

June 1990
Education Alternatives Inc. (EAI) forms partnership with Dade County school system to operate a Miami Beach elementary school beginning in fall 1991.

Nov. 3, 1990
Oregon voters reject school voucher initiative.

May 15, 1991
Media entrepreneur Christopher Whittle announces bold plan to establish a national chain of private, for-profit schools.

August 1991
Minnesota passes first state law permitting charter schools. Similar laws are passed by California in 1992 and six more states in 1993.

May 25, 1992
Yale University President Benno C. Schmidt Jr. says he will resign to head Whittle's Edison Project.

July 1992
Baltimore, Md., approves five-year, $133 million contract with EAI to operate nine inner-city schools beginning in September.

June 18, 1993
Massachusetts Gov. William Weld signs charter school law that includes option for private management of new schools.

August 1993
Edison Project fails to find financing for chain of private schools and shifts to plan to manage existing public schools.

Nov. 2, 1993
California voters overwhelmingly defeat school voucher initiative.

January 1994
EAI gets mixed reviews for its operation of schools in Baltimore.

March 1994
Milwaukee school system breaks off talks with EAI on March 2 but continues discussions with Edison Project. The next day, Washington, D.C., drops plans to ask EAI to manage 10-15 schools.

March 18, 1994
Edison Project is granted charters by Massachusetts to operate three new schools in Boston, Lowell and Worcester.

in the experiment." [8]

Supporters of performance contracting argued the idea had not gotten a fair test. They said OEO had rushed into the program without careful design and planning. The special instruction was too short, they said, covering only a couple of hours rather than the whole school day. Two years was too short a time to produce meaningful results. And, finally, they said, the built-in difficulties of motivating and teaching marginal students had been increased by resistance from administrators and teachers.

The conventional wisdom, however, quickly became that the experiment had simply failed. Today, critics of privatization cite the short-lived episode as proof that private contractors have little to offer in terms of educating students. "We put through a wave of it 22 years ago," says the University of Wisconsin's Molnar. "It disappeared without a blip on the radar screen."

Supporters of privatization barely acknowledge the history, if at all. Indeed, the widely cited 1993 report on school privatization by the libertarian Reason Foundation makes no mention of the 1970-71 experiment. [9]

Contracting Out

In the 1980s — after performance contracting had faded from memory — public education came under new pressure to turn to the private sector for help. With a conservative president, Ronald Reagan, in the White House, a free-market ideology gained ground in Washington and around the country. Advocates said that private companies could provide a wide range of government services — from garbage collection and building maintenance to running airports or even prisons — at lower cost with better results and greater accountability. [10]

Fiscal realities reinforced the push for privatization. At the federal level, Reagan pushed through a major tax cut and domestic-spending reductions in 1981 that presaged a decade of anti-tax sentiment and pressure on social programs. State and local governments also found increased resistance to higher taxes or bond issues to pay for public investments. For financially strapped governments, privatization offered an alluring promise of cost-savings and the hope of avoiding service cuts in lean budget times.

Education constitutes the biggest budget item for local governments, but much of that money is spent on non-instructional services seemingly well-suited for privatization. Private companies, it would seem, can transport children to school, run cafeterias or clean schools as well as government agencies. Advocates of privatization argue, indeed, that private companies would provide better service because, unlike government workers protected by civil service, they could be terminated at any time and would have a stronger incentive to keep their customers satisfied.

Schools did turn to private contractors more often in the 1980s. Many of the traditional yellow school buses bore the names of private companies rather than local school districts. Fast-food franchises such as Kentucky Fried Chicken and Taco Bell spiced up lunchroom fare. And an Illinois-based rug cleaning company turned into a national enterprise by contracting for janitorial services at hospitals and, later, public schools.

Schools even turned to private contractors for some instructional services, including special education for students with disabilities, driver's education and foreign language instruction. [11]

Despite the increase in contracting out, public employees continued to provide most non-instructional services for schools. In its November report, the Reason Foundation said that private contractors only provide about 30 percent of all school-bus services in the country and just 11 percent of school food services. [12]

The foundation found most school administrators satisfied with their private contractors. Among 30 school districts that had privatized bus service, for example, about 60 percent said they believed costs had been lowered, and 70 percent said service had been improved.

On the other hand, a study of public and private school bus service in California found that private contractors had a lower safety record than public school bus drivers. [13] For 1992, public school bus drivers of full-sized buses had 7.5 collisions per million miles driven compared with 10.3 collisions per million miles driven for private contractors.

As contracting out expanded, teachers' unions continued to voice skepticism. "Sometimes it works. Sometimes it doesn't," the NEA declared. "Cheapest doesn't always mean best — and the bottom line can't be a democratic society's only concern in deciding how to provide public services." [14]

School Choice

Advocates of privatization also pursued a more ambitious goal in the 1980s than simply contracting out selected school services. They wanted to break what they called the government monopoly on education by allowing families to choose the school their children would attend. Parents could pick from public schools or private schools, and the government would help parents participate in this free market by giving them cash vouchers equal to the cost of educating a child in public school to help pay for tuition at private schools. [15]

Conservative economist Milton Friedman had pioneered the school voucher proposal in a series of writings in the late 1950s and early '60s. In his 1962 book *Capitalism and Freedom*, Friedman argued that competition would force schools to im-

Continued on p. 278

Advocates of School Choice Undaunted by Setbacks

Critics of public education hoped to achieve a breakthrough last year in their campaign to break the "education monopoly." Voters in California, the nation's most-populous state, had the chance Nov. 2 to let parents use tax-funded vouchers to help pay their children's tuition at private schools.

When the votes were counted, however, it was the public-education establishment that was cheering, not the school choice movement. Proposition 174 had lost by more than 2 million votes out of 5 million cast.

"It is clear to me," Secretary of Education Richard W. Riley said the next day, "that the people of California will not abandon the historic American commitment to American public education."

The 2-to-1 defeat marked the third time in four years that Western voters had decisively rejected school voucher initiatives. (*See box, at right.*) And even though school choice advocates plan to continue their efforts, some observers now predict the movement will push limited voucher plans rather than try again for statewide measures.

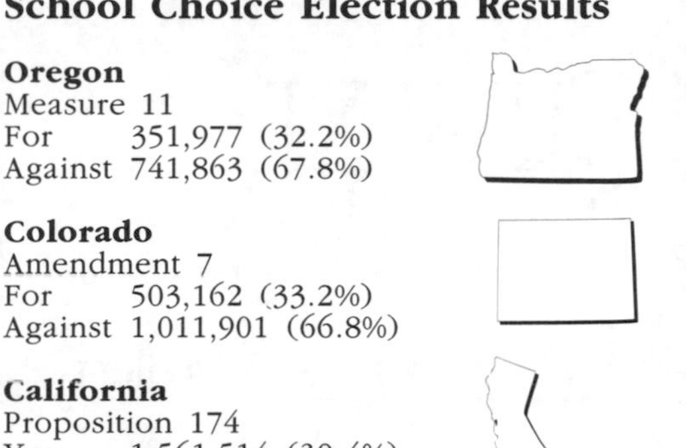

School Choice Election Results

Oregon
Measure 11

For	351,977	(32.2%)
Against	741,863	(67.8%)

Colorado
Amendment 7

For	503,162	(33.2%)
Against	1,011,901	(66.8%)

California
Proposition 174

Yes	1,561,514	(30.4%)
No	3,567,833	(69.6%)

"I think you'll probably see some more limited public-private choice programs," says John O'Leary, a policy analyst with the Los Angeles-based Reason Foundation and a strong supporter of school choice. "I don't think you'll see any statewide choice. I think you'll see choice plans limited to low-income people or to certain cities."

The defeat in California was a bitter blow to school choice supporters, who thought a multimillion-dollar campaign fund and 2-to-1 support in earlier polls would carry the measure to victory. [1] But the campaign failed to attract strong support from its natural constituencies, including business and the state Republican Party. The state's Republican governor, Pete Wilson, also opposed the measure.

In addition, the California Teachers' Association (CTA) mounted a strong, well-financed campaign against Proposition 174. CTA officials called the measure "evil" and levied a $57 assessment on the union's 200,000 teachers to defeat it. All told, opponents spent more than $17 million in the campaign.

Supporters spent only $4.1 million, much of it in 1991 and '92 to gather signatures needed to get the measure on the ballot. When a special off-year election brought the measure to a vote earlier than supporters expected, they were not well-organized or well-financed.

Proposition 174 would have amended the state constitution to give parents tax-funded vouchers to send children to the public, private or parochial school of their choice. The cost of the measure was a major issue in the campaign.

Proponents argued that spending on public schools would decline over time as families enrolled children in private schools. In the short term, however, the state's legislative analyst said that providing $2,600 vouchers to the 540,000 California students already in private schools would rob public schools of $1.3 billion. The opposition's media campaign blitzed the state in the last weeks before the election with TV commercials warning, "It's a risk we can't afford."

Opponents were also able to capitalize on other fears about the voucher measure. Affluent suburban school districts feared an influx of voucher-financed students from inner-city areas with lower-quality schools. Opponents also charged that the measure contained no safeguards for curriculum, teacher qualifications, teacher testing or disclosure. [2]

Despite the setback, supporters of the California measure said they may redraft the proposal for a future election. National school choice organizations — the Chicago-based Americans for School Choice and the Republican-affiliated Empower USA — are also eyeing moves to put voucher measures on the ballot in several other states, including Arizona, Colorado and Indiana.

Public-education groups vowed to fight hard against any use of vouchers for private schools. But support for public school choice has continued to grow. Nineteen states have laws that permit parents to choose between public schools within their home district or — under some of the laws — in other districts in the state. [3]

Educators who support public school choice plans evidently hope to deflect the push for broader voucher programs that include private or parochial schools. The movement to hire private companies to manage public schools may also slow the drive toward school vouchers.

John T. Golle, chairman of Education Alternatives Inc. (EAI), a private school-management firm, tells audiences that choice does not necessarily produce good schools. He also says that $2,500 vouchers — the amount given parents in a limited voucher program currently operated in Milwaukee — does not cover the $6,300 average per-student cost at private schools.

Choice, Golle warns, "is not much of a solution by itself."

[1] For background, see the *Los Angeles Times*, Nov. 3, 1993, p. A1.

[2] See Myron Lieberman, "The School Choice Fiasco," *The Public Interest*, winter 1994, pp. 19, 22.

[3] See Lynn Olson, "Choice for the Long Haul," *Education Week*, Nov. 17, 1993, p. 27.

Continued from p. 276

prove. New schools would "spring up" to meet parents' demands for high-quality education, while poor schools that could not attract students would close. The government's role would be limited to ensuring that schools met minimum standards.[16]

Friedman's voucher proposal made little headway over the next two decades. The federal government did conduct a limited experiment in the Alum Rock Unified School District near San Jose, Calif., from 1972 to 1976. Parents were given vouchers to use in any *public* school of their choice. Most parents, however, continued to send their children to their neighborhood schools, and the experiment produced little evidence of improved student achievement.

Still, conservatives began pushing the idea to the top of the education policy agenda in the 1980s. Public opinion was also shifting. In the early '70s, polls found the public narrowly rejecting the idea. By 1983, however, one poll registered majority support — 51 percent — for school vouchers, with 38 percent opposed and 11 percent with no opinion.[17]

Supporters of public education strongly opposed vouchers for private schools, arguing they would drain money from public schools and benefit well-to-do families. But some supporters favored choice plans limited to public schools. One such plan — instituted in East Harlem in 1974 — drew national interest and wide support from across the political spectrum. The 14,000-student school district won a large measure of autonomy to create a number of alternative schools with distinctive curricula and programs. Student test scores improved, parents were pleased and the district — which had ranked last in New York City — began attracting students from adjoining areas.[18]

Public school choice plans attracted greater interest in the '80s — partly as a liberal alternative to voucher plans that would include private schools. Minnesota carried the idea the farthest in 1989, allowing students to enroll in any districts within the state. Today, 11 states have some form of cross-district open enrollment, according to the NEA.

School voucher proposals, however, have failed to win approval — with one limited exception. In 1990, Milwaukee began giving vouchers to a limited number of poor students to use in either public or non-religious private schools. But voters in Oregon, Colorado and California decisively rejected initiatives to create broader voucher plans. (*See story, p. 277.*)

Despite the electoral defeats, school choice supporters remain hopeful, possibly for enactment of choice on a more limited scale. "It's an issue that's not going away," says O'Leary of the Reason Foundation. For the time being, however, reformers who wanted to create alternatives to public schools were forced to move in a different direction. ■

CURRENT SITUATION

Whittle's Edison Project

As the 1990s began, the American public was uneasy about the state of the nation's schools. Calls for broad educational reforms came from officials at all levels of government, from parents in all types of communities and from educators themselves.

Two entrepreneurs, Tennessee media entrepreneur Christopher Whittle and Minnesota businessman John Golle, met the discontent with sweeping — and controversial — plans to remake American schools.

Whittle was the first to capture the national spotlight in May 1991 when he announced an ambitious plan to open a multibillion-dollar chain of 150 to 200 for-profit private schools around the country by fall 1996. Whittle said the new schools would be better than existing public schools, but cost slightly less than the per-pupil spending in their communities. Educators voiced skepticism about the plan and dismay at the declared profit motive.[19]

A year later, Whittle made headlines again by hiring the nationally known president of Yale University, Benno C. Schmidt Jr., to head what was now being called the Edison Project.[20] Schmidt's hiring gave legitimacy to a project that had yet to complete a design plan or raise financing.

Last August, however, Whittle had to concede failure in efforts to raise money for his bold scheme. After pitching his plan to a host of giant corporations — including Apple Computer, Paramount Communications, Pepsico and Walt Disney Co. — Whittle fell well short of the $750 million to $1 billion he needed. Instead, the company announced scaled-back plans to seek management contracts with existing schools or to win public funds to charter some new schools.[21]

Schmidt insisted to reporters that the new strategy was not a retreat but a response to demands from educators for help in managing existing schools.[22] As the year ended, however, the Edison Project still had no published instructional plan and no commitments from school systems. Schmidt said vaguely that Edison officials had talked to officials in 20 states. But the strongest public expression of interest came in Massachusetts, where Republican Gov. William F. Weld and other officials appeared receptive to the idea of the Edison Project running some of the state's public schools. [23]

When he appeared before a congressional subcommittee in January, however, Schmidt reiterated that the first Edison schools would begin operating in fall 1995. Without specifying any of the likely locations, Schmidt also gave the Senate Education Appropriations Subcommittee more details about the philosophy of the planned schools.

Schmidt described a "national system" of schools that would integrate the best teaching methods, use more computers and operate on a seven-or eight-hour day with a shortened summer break of just six weeks. He said the schools would spend less on administration and more on instruction and would be accountable for meeting specified goals for students and teachers alike. "If we do not meet mutually established performance benchmarks," Schmidt said, "we're out of business."

Significantly, Schmidt also indicated the Edison Project would not necessarily work with existing teaching staffs. "Good teachers will be at the heart of the Edison school," Schmidt said. "We will search out the best from the areas where we establish schools as well as recruit promising young professionals from around the country."

Three months later, the Edison Project moved past the drawing-board stage. On March 18, Massachusetts officials awarded charters for the project, working with local partners, to operate new schools on a for-profit basis in three cities: Boston, Lowell and Worcester. The three elementary schools will initially enroll between 400 and 700 pupils but will eventually be expanded to include students from kindergarten through 12th grade.

At a Boston news conference, Schmidt described the schools as "in the first wave of Edison partnership schools." Edison officials said they were hoping to open other schools in Colorado, Arizona and possibly Virginia. [24]

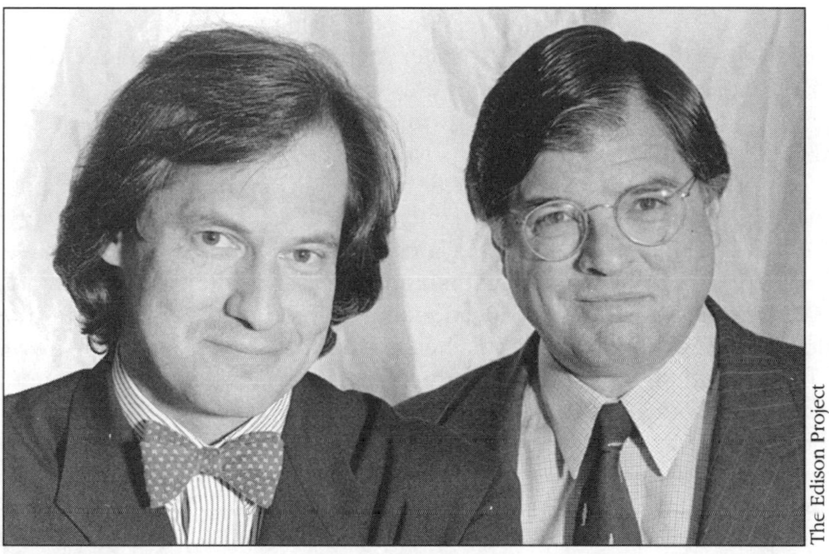

The Edison Project

Education entrepreneur Christopher Whittle, left, and former Yale University President Benno C. Schmidt, Jr., president of The Edison Project.

Golle Launches EAI

John Golle drew little notice in 1986 when he started Educational Alternatives Inc. by buying research from Control Data Corp. after the computer company abandoned its idea of operating private schools. Golle had been designing education and training programs for big corporations since 1970.

In addition, Golle had a personal reason for taking on the public schools. One of his sons had been classified as learning-disabled and consigned to a special-education class for severely disabled youngsters. As Golle recalls,"My son was stripped of his self-esteem and finally gave up on learning altogether." [25]

Golle thought he could find a market niche by offering low-cost elementary schools for families discontented with public schools. The company began small, opening its first school in 1987 in a converted warehouse in Minneapolis and later a second school in a Phoenix suburb. But the schools did not make money, and Golle was about to quit when he saw an ad from the Dade County, Fla., school system inviting proposals to operate a new public school. In June 1990, EAI signed a five-year contract to run a new elementary school in a Latino, Miami Beach neighborhood in partnership with the school system and the local teachers' union.

As its part of the "South Pointe partnership," EAI trained teachers in the Tesseract curriculum that Golle had developed earlier. The 600-student school, which opened in September 1991, was to get no extra public moneys. But EAI committed to raise $2.4 million to cover its management fee and supplement the school's budget. With the new money, EAI bought new computers and hired student teachers from the University of Miami to lower the staff-to-student classroom ratio.

School officials and visitors to the school describe a progressive, child-oriented learning environment backed up by an impressive array of computers. As of January, however, EAI's director of financial accounting acknowledged to *The Miami Herald* that the company had raised just half of the money it promised. [26] And, according to Principal Arlene Ortenzo, student achievement scores have been mixed. Students in some grades showed "substantial improvements," but in two grades students' scores declined. School officials have prepared an evaluation of student test scores, but in mid-March it had not yet been released.

Golle continued to look for more business in states considered receptive to outside vendors for educational services. In spring 1992, EAI was hired for a three-month period to run the Duluth, Minn., school district — the first time a private company had ever been given control of a U.S. public school system. But EAI and Duluth parted after the company completed its assigned tasks, including hiring a permanent superintendent.

Mixed Reviews in Baltimore

EAI finally made its first real breakthrough in June 1992 when it landed a five-year, $133 million contract with the Baltimore city school system to operate nine schools in inner-city neighborhoods. The company's task was daunting. Enrollment at the nine schools totaled about 4,800 — nearly eight times the size of South Pointe elementary.

In contrast to the limited role in Miami Beach, EAI and its partners — KPMG and Johnson Controls — had responsibility for teaching, financial management and building cleanup and maintenance. And EAI was to start operation in September, without the one-year lead time it had been given in Dade County.

The Baltimore experiment attracted national attention — and generally positive news coverage. [27] There were some rough spots in the first year. The Baltimore Teachers' Union (BTU) objected — in vain — when the company moved paraprofessionals out of the nine schools and replaced them with interns making substantially less. Some teachers said staff training was disappointing, parents' groups complained about lack of communication and promised computers were delayed. But the schools all looked cleaner and brighter. And when the computers arrived in spring 1993, critics and skeptics seemed to have little left to say.

Now midway through the second year, EAI and Baltimore school officials say they are pleased with the results of their experiment. "We think it's going splendidly," Golle told the Senate Education Appropriations Subcommittee in January. Appearing later, Baltimore Superintendent Walter Amprey cited a report crediting EAI with "significant, positive change in several areas," including parent involvement and facilities maintenance. [28]

The report, however, gave lower marks in other areas, including training for teachers and interns. In addition, an education expert hired by the Maryland Teachers Association issued a report in early January saying she observed teaching methods at two EAI schools that were "more representative of the old than the new perspective." [29] Meanwhile, the BTU also stepped up its pressure by filing a lawsuit in state court claiming that school officials exceeded their authority by turning over control of the schools to a private company.

In late February, EAI itself was charged in a shareholder lawsuit with misleading investors by overstating its revenues and making unfounded predictions about new business. The investors claimed that EAI exaggerated its revenues by counting the entire $27 million it received from the Baltimore school system since the company had to pay out the bulk of that money immediately as salaries. The suit also contended that Golle and two other company officials — President David Bennett and a director, Gale Mellum — had made six-or seven-figure profits from selling the company's stock.

Golle and other EAI officials call the lawsuit "frivolous." The firm's accountant, Arthur Andersen & Co., has defended the calculation of the company's revenue as proper. Golle has defended his stock sales and those by the other officials, noting that all three still have substantial holdings in EAI.

New Setbacks

EAI's market breakthroughs and the Edison Project's ambitious plans helped draw other entrepreneurs into what observers began to confidently describe as an emerging industry. More interest came from the movement to pass laws aimed at creating innovative new "charter" schools (*see below*) that could be run by groups of teachers, parents, nonprofit organizations or possibly private companies. So far, however, the new education entrepreneurs have produced more interest than action.

EAI itself has fallen short of its goals. It withdrew a proposal to operate 14 schools in Palm Beach County, Fla., last April just ahead of a likely rejection from the school board. The NEA took credit for persuading the school board in Piscataway, N.J., to reject a similar proposal last fall. And in Baltimore, two schools signed limited management contracts with EAI in November but didn't hire the company for curriculum and instruction. [30]

The bad news for EAI continued. On March 2, Milwaukee School Superintendent Howard Fuller picked the Edison Project rather than EAI to help in implementing a planned "school to work transition" initiative. The next day, Washington, D.C., school Superintendent Franklin Smith dropped plans to try to sell the school board on EAI management of 10-15 schools beginning this fall. Two local school-improvement groups had supported Smith, but he drew strong opposition from teachers' and principals' unions and a coalition of neigh-

Continued on p. 282

At Issue:

Should private firms be hired to manage public schools for a profit?

yes

John T. Golle
Chairman and CEO, Education Alternatives Inc.

Our claim is very simple: We can dramatically improve learner outcomes (or what individual students know) without spending more money, as long as we spend more of it on children in the classroom and *less* on the management of the enterprise. Then the very first question becomes, "What role can business play in all this?" That's our business. . . . We privately manage public schools. We enter into a contract with the school board such that all your public policy stays in place, and your elected officials make sure that the public gets the greatest value and service for the dollars expended. . . On a contractual basis, quite frankly, we are allowed to do those things that they would love to do themselves but because of the system they are not allowed to do.

There is a word that creeps into this new relationship. . . . "accountability." As a business, we are accountable for every single dollar that comes to us. . . . If we spend more than we receive (and we've done that in Baltimore schools, because the facilities were in such terrible condition), we take it out of our own pocket, hoping for a return. . . .

Private enterprise goes at risk, puts up their capital always asking themselves, "What is best for the children?". . . . So the word is "accountability," and the companion word is "flexibility" — the ability to do what's right from an investment point of view as well as from the children's point of view with that risk/reward ratio keeping you honest. . . .

People say, "That's a nice pitch, John, but my school is pretty good. Is it really necessary to be doing all this?" In a Harris poll, about 80 percent of the parents in the United States said they thought public schools in general need to be "fixed." Only around 20 percent believed *their* school needed to be fixed. It's always someone else's school.

. . . By inviting in private industry, you tap significant resources and provoke internal competition while maintaining local control by publicly elected or appointed school board members. It truly represents a "win-win" for all parties — especially the children.

Our contracts are performance-based and cancelable on 90 days' notice without cause by a simple majority of the school board. In a sentence, we either dramatically improve student performance *without* spending more money or our contract is canceled. That's what I call accountability! . . .

. . . [W]e are involved in a system that does not work. We do not need more evidence. We do not need more failures among our youth. It is not the people in the system: It is the system itself. It is something that Education Alternatives Inc. is trying to change.

no

Keith Geiger
President, National Education Association

Education Alternatives Inc. currently runs nine Baltimore City public schools. While teachers and princi pals remain school district employees, EAI has operational control of the schools and has put into place Tesseract — the company's education system.

Tesseract is based on sound educational theory. It calls for small classes, two adults in every classroom, cooperative and active student learning, professional development for teachers, flexibility in student grouping and education plans developed for each student with active parent involvement.

The problem comes in the gap between Tesseract theory . . . and EAI's practice in Baltimore. EAI has cut corners in Baltimore to save money and earn higher profits for itself and its business partners. . . .

EAI has drastically reduced the number of music, art, physical and special-education teachers in its Baltimore schools. The special-education program . . . has been absorbed into the regular classroom with little training or support offered to classroom teachers.

. . . No objective measure has shown improvement in student achievement. And attendance at EAI schools improved at about the same rate as at non-EAI schools in Baltimore last year. . . .

Cutting through bureaucracy is positive, but EAI and its business partners are taking part of their profits out of the pockets of the lowest-paid school employees — classroom aides and custodians. EAI replaced the aides and custodians, who were school district employees earning livable wages and benefits, with employees who work directly for EAI or Johnson Controls [World Services Inc.] Both earn considerably lower wages, and teacher aides receive no health insurance or health benefits.

The harsh truth is that there's no simple answer to the complex problems of troubled schools. Neither EAI nor any other company holds a magic key. . . .

. . .Superintendents need to fix their bureaucracies to make them responsive to students and the staff who work directly with students. It can and has been done within the public sector.

Radical solutions are needed for the serious problems of America's most troubled schools. And those solutions might include arrangements with private contractors on a straight fee-for-service basis. But allowing a for-profit company to take any savings out of the public schools and use them as profits for corporate executives and shareholders — as the EAI contract does in Baltimore — invites the company to cut corners and pocket the difference. Savings should be used to provide better education for students.

Continued from p. 280
borhood organizations. [31]

The reversals in Milwaukee and Washington appeared to leave EAI with only two immediate prospects for new business. In Pinckney, Mich., a predominantly white suburb outside Ann Arbor, the school board in January authorized the superintendent to negotiate a contract for EAI to operate the 4,000-student system beginning this fall. Meanwhile, the majority-black Portsmouth, Va., school system issued a "request for proposals" for management services after having initial discussions with EAI representatives.

Two start-up companies were also finding it slow-going in bids to manage public schools:

• In Nashville, the school board voted 5-4 last April to reject a proposal by Alternative Public Schools Inc. to create and operate an inner-city magnet school in which the company had complete freedom to hire and fire teachers.

• In Houston, the school board rejected a proposal last June from the Performing Schools Corporation, whose president, John Privett, wanted to bring a "highly regimented, highly structured" curriculum to inner-city elementary schools.

A 'Superintendent' for Minneapolis

Supporters of private management for public education did claim one step forward in November, when the Minneapolis school board hired a private consulting firm as "superintendent" of the 44,000-student system. But the decision stemmed from unique circumstances unrelated to the broader policy debate.

Businessman Peter Hutchinson, who heads the St. Paul-based Public Strategies Group, had straightened out the school system's finances last year after the superintendent resigned amid charges of financial mismanagement. The board subsequently voted 4-3 to hire Hutchinson's firm to provide "leadership services." Hutchinson will be designated superintendent for purposes of state law.

Hutchinson's three-year contract is a model of the performance-based accountability that advocates of private management envision. Over the next six months, the firm gets a base payment of $30,000, but it can earn up to $214,000 more by reaching specified goals in student achievement, financial management and community support. [32]

"Unless we improve student achievement," says partner Rick Heydinger, "we won't get paid. And that means raising all students' achievement and also decreasing the gap between majority and minority students."

Kenneth Jost

John Golle, founder of Education Alternatives Inc., and Baltimore school Superintendent Walter Amprey.

Charter Schools

Meanwhile, a growing number of states have adopted or are considering an idea that could offer new opportunities for private companies to improve public schools. Charter-school laws envision giving responsibility for individual schools to some designated group by a "charter" that sets out the terms for operating the school. Ted Kolderie, a Minnesota public-policy activist who is considered the nation's leading expert on charter schools, says a school's contract can be used to ensure accountability, including student performance goals.

The contract "expires unless affirmatively renewed and is renewed on the basis of meeting stated objectives," Kolderie explains. "It's a school that can be gotten rid of if it doesn't work, in contrast to most schools, which cannot be gotten rid of it they don't work." [33]

Eight states have enacted charter laws so far, and at least a dozen more are considering the idea. (*See map, p. 273.*) The laws vary significantly in their details, often because of pressure from teachers' unions. Minnesota's 1991 law, the first in the nation, limited the number of charter schools in the state to just eight; the number was raised last year to 20. California's law, passed in 1992, permits 100 schools.

Local school boards generally are given the power to decide whether to issue a charter. But charter school supporters prefer laws such as those in Colorado and Massachusetts, where state officials have a role in the decision. Significantly, Massachusetts' law is the only one that clearly permits applications from private companies.

Teachers' attitudes toward the idea vary — and have changed over time. In 1988, the AFT's Shanker called it "the best answer so far" to education reform.[34] But he has since changed his mind. "Charter schools are a very popular idea right now," Shanker wrote in November, "but does anybody really think we will be able to reform our education system one school at a time?"[35]

Locally, teachers have generally opposed charter school efforts. Minnesota's law was watered down because of opposition from the state teachers' union. More recently, the teachers' union in Sacramento, Calif., blocked a charter program because it would have permitted hiring of teachers on merit rather than seniority.[36]

On the other hand, once charter school laws are enacted, teachers may take advantage of the provisions. In Massachusetts, two of the 15 charter schools approved this month are to be run by teachers, and three others will be operated by boards that include parents and teachers.[37]

The charter school movement is too new to make predictions about where it is going, but critics of public education view it as one opportunity for change. "It may turn out," said a recent *Wall Street Journal* editorial, "that charters, either through success or failure, will make full competition in schooling possible later on."[38]

Both the NEA and AFT, however, have tried to raise doubts about the idea. The NEA describes charter schools as "a development with great promise — and quite a few pitfalls." It warns that charter plans can "allow unprepared people" to run a school, permit a school to select its own students and "undermine public school employee salaries and benefits." ■

OUTLOOK

Uncertain Future

Supporters and opponents of private management view the idea's future differently.

O'Leary of the Reason Foundation calls it "the tidal wave of the future." "We're going to see major differences in American education over the next five years," he says "and this is where it's going to come from. It's going to come from people who step outside the system. And once it starts happening, it's going to build on itself."

Liberal academic Molnar scoffs at that prediction. "It will not be a tidal wave, that's reasonably sure," he says. "There isn't money to be made in public education without taking it out of the public's pockets."

Less partisan observers make more tentative predictions. Harvard Professor Gary Orfield, a noted expert on education policy, says the future of private management depends on the companies' performance. "They're promising to do certain things," Orfield says. "If they do, there'll be more. If they don't, they'll be discredited."

EAI's inability to add new business since 1992 has dampened enthusiasm for the company in financial circles. EAI stock, which opened around $4 per share when the company went public in 1991, rose to $48 last fall but plummeted to $13¼ this month.

The Edison Project's entry into the market is still being awaited. The design team includes some major figures in education, and the project is working hard to line up business. But Denis Doyle, a senior fellow at the Hudson Institute and a supporter of school privatization, believes the project may come out with an overly elaborate plan. The project "has gotten sort of an Alfa-Romeo configuration," Doyle says, "when the market is really a Volkswagen or a Jeep."

More broadly, Doyle says any private company that develops ways to improve schools may be unable to protect its innovations from copycats. "Let's suppose somebody figures out something brilliant," Doyle says. "How's he going to protect it? It's just like IBM. They couldn't stop the clones."

Partly for that reason, Doyle thinks that a more important source of school management services could be nonprofit organizations, including existing private schools or service groups like the Boy Scouts, Girl Scouts or Urban League. He notes that with their tax-exempt status, nonprofit groups enjoy an important advantage over for-profit companies.

The new charter school laws invite nonprofit organizations, including existing schools or newly formed consortia of teachers or parents, to operate public schools. In Massachusetts, school charters were awarded this month to two service groups in predominantly black neighborhoods in Boston. In addition, Boston University received a charter to operate a school designed to serve children of homeless families, while Middlesex Community College will be allowed to open a school in the industrial city of Lowell for high school dropouts.

Boston University is already operating an entire school system in Massachusetts. The university was given a 10-year contract to run the financially strapped Chelsea schools in 1989. The university's management has been controversial, but a recent legislative report found evidence of "quiet and substantial" advances.[39]

Less controversially, the private Calvert School in Baltimore is in the third year of a four-year partnership with the public Barclay Elementary School. Since Calvert's curriculum has been adopted, students at the inner-city school reportedly have shown significant improvements. Superintendent Amprey says he would like to expand the experiment — currently being funded by the local Abell Foundation — to other public schools.[40]

Meanwhile, school choice supporters continue to push plans to provide vouchers for private school tuition despite rejection of the idea by California voters in November.

Even if proponents overcome the entrenched opposition to vouchers, however, the likely impact of choice plans is uncertain. So far, at least, public school choice plans appear not to have resulted in much movement of students out of their neighborhood schools. And none of the private school voucher plans have called for enough money to pay for full tuition at a typical private school.

In resisting school choice and privatization, supporters of public education have tried to avoid the appearance of being mere obstructionists. Opponents of the school voucher initiative in California vowed after its defeat to press ahead with other reform efforts.

But school choice supporters insist meaningful changes depend on pressure from outside the educational establishment. As proof, they say that legislation for public school choice and charter schools has advanced in part because public school educators view them as acceptable alternatives to the more sweeping changes that advocates of school privatization would like to see.

For now, the nation's 41 million public school students are getting their education from schools that vary widely in quality and funding. [41] Despite the widely voiced calls for broad reforms, opposing camps on school privatization appear sometimes to be more interested in attacking each other than attacking the problem.

"Caught in the middle are the opportunities for change and the opportunities for children," says Minnesota Professor McLaughlin. "I would hope we could have greater harmony and less bickering on the coming changes." ■

Notes

[1] Shanker was unable to deliver his prepared testimony for the subcommittee's Jan. 25 hearing on private management of public schools. In his absence, his assistant, Bella Rosenberg, delivered a condensed version of the statement.

[2] Ian Johnson, "EAI's promising future begins to look bleak," *The Baltimore Sun*, March 6, 1994, p. 1D.

[3] See Janet R. Beales and John O'Leary, "Making Schools Work: Contracting Options for Better Management," Reason Foundation, November 1993.

[4] Myron Lieberman, "The Future of Collective Negotiations," *Phi Delta Kappan*, December 1971, p. 214.

[5] See Myron Lieberman, Charlene K. Haar and Leo Troy, *The NEA and AFT: Teacher Unions in Power and Politics* (forthcoming, April 1994).

[6] See Myron Lieberman, *Privatization and Educational Choice* (1989), pp. 85-100; Edward M. Gramlich and Patricia P. Koshel, *Educational Performance Contracting* (1975).

[7] H.V. Webb, "Performance Contracting: Is It the New Tool for the the New Boardmanship?" *American School Board Journal,* November 1970.

[8] Battelle Columbus Laboratories, *Final Report on the Office of Economic Opportunity Experiment in Educational Performance Contracting*, 1972, cited in Lieberman, *op. cit*., pp. 88-89.

[9] Performance contracting has also received little recent attention. In Baltimore, however, a newspaper column warned recently of the potential for corruption or abuse in hiring private firms to deliver educational services. See M. William Salganik, "Education's Scandal to Come," *The Baltimore Sun*, Dec. 11, 1993, p. 10A.

[10] For background, see "Privatization" *The CQ Researcher*, Nov. 13, 1992, pp. 977-1000.

[11] For background, see "Learning Disabilities," *The CQ Researcher*, Dec. 10, 1993, pp. 1081-1104.

[12] Beales and O'Leary, *op. cit*., pp. 6, 11.

[13] *Ibid.*

[14] Undated NEA fact sheet.

[15] For background, see "School Choice," *The CQ Researcher*, May 10, 1991, pp. 253-276.

[16] Milton Friedman, *Capitalism and Freedom* (1962), p. 91. For an updated summary of Friedman's thesis, see Lieberman, *Privatization and Educational Choice*, *op. cit*., pp. 119-125

[17] Gallup Poll data cited in Lieberman, *ibid*., p. 135.

[18] See John E. Chubb and Terry M. Moe, Politics, *Markets & America's Schools* (1990), pp. 212-215; Seymour Fliegel with James McGuire, *Miracle in East Harlem: The Fight for Choice in Public Education* (1993).

[19] For background, see "Business' Role in Education," *The CQ Researcher*, Nov. 22, 1991, pp. 873-896.

[20] See *The New York Times*, May 26, 1992, p. A1.

[21] See *The Wall Street Journal*, May 5, 1993, p. B1; Aug. 3, 1993, p. B6; *The New York Times*, Aug. 9, 1993, p. A14.

[22] See Jolie Solomon, "Mr. Vision, Meet Mr. Reality," *Newsweek*, Aug. 16, 1993, p. 63.

[23] *The Washington Post*, Oct. 15, 1993, p. A4; *Education Week*, Oct. 20, 1993, p. 1.

[24] *The Wall Street Journal*, March 18, 1994, p. B3; *The New York Times*, March 19, 1994, p. A1.

[25] Quoted in Elizabeth Conlin, "Educating the Market," *Inc*., July 1991, p. 63. Some of the account of EAI's early history is drawn from Conlin's story.

[26] *The Miami Herald*, Jan. 16, 1994, p. 1B. For other accounts, see *The Miami Herald*, May 17, 1992, p. 1B; *The Christian Science Monitor*, April 20, 1992, p. 20; *The New York Times*, Nov. 6, 1991, p. B9.

[27] See William Celis 3d, "Hopeful Start for Profit-Making Schools," *The New York Times*, Oct. 6, 1993, p. A1. For an earlier, more critical account, see William Trombley, "For-Profit Public School Is Off to a Mixed Start," *The Los Angeles Times*, Dec. 22, 1992, p. A1.

[28] See Stephen J. Ruffini, Lawrence F. Howe and Denise G. Borders, "The Early Implementation of Tesseract, 1992-93 Evaluation Report," January 1994.

[29] Olivia S. Reusing, "A Report of Observations in Three Tesseract Schools," Jan. 2, 1994.

[30] See *The Miami Herald*, April 8, 1993, Palm Beach edition, p. 1B; *NEA Today*, February 1994, pp. 10-11; *The Wall Street Journal*, Nov. 24, 1993, p. A10.

[31] See *The Washington Post*, March 4, 1994, p. A1.

[32] See *Education Week*, Jan. 12, 1994, p.10, and Feb. 9, 1994, p. 31.

[33] For background, see Ted Kolderie, "Charter Schools," in Will Marshall and Martin Schram [eds.], *Mandate for Change*, Progressive Policy Institute, 1992, pp. 131-137; Ted Kolderie, "Charter Schools: The States Begin to Withdraw the 'Exclusive,' " Public Services Redesign Project, 1993.

[34] Albert Shanker, "A Charter for Change," *The New York Times*, July 10, 1988, p. E7.

[35] "'Charter' School Boards," *The New York Times*, Nov. 21, 1993, p. E7.

[36] *The Sacramento Bee*, Dec. 7, 1993, p. B6.

[37] *The New York Times*, March 19, 1994, p. 1.

[38] *The Wall Street Journal*, Feb. 16, 1994, p. A20.

[39] See *The* (Minneapolis) *Star-Tribune*, Nov. 29, 1993, p. 1A.

[40] See *The Baltimore Sun*, Dec. 12, 1993, p. 1F; Dec. 3, 1993, p. 1B.

[41] For background, see "School Funding," *The CQ Researcher*, Aug. 27, 1993, pp. 745-768.

Bibliography

Selected Sources Used

Books

Chubb, John E., and Terry M. Moe, *Politics, Markets, and America's Schools*, The Brookings Institution, 1990.

Chubb, a senior fellow at Brookings, and Moe, a professor of political science at Stanford University, propose a system of public and private school choice, with vouchers, as the key to educational reform. The book includes provocative data on school performance and extensive source notes.

Fliegel, Seymour, with James MacGuire, *Miracle in East Harlem: The Fight for Choice in Public Education*, Times Books, 1993.

Fliegel, a former educator and senior fellow at the Manhattan Institute's Center for Educational Innovation, and MacGuire, a fellow at the Center for Social Thought, tell the story of East Harlem's 20-year experience with public school choice.

Kraushaar, Otto F., *American Nonpublic Schools — Patterns of Diversity*, Johns Hopkins University Press, 1972.

Kraushaar, an author and former college professor, provides a useful overview of private education in America from the Colonial era to modern times. A new edition was published in 1988. Kraushaar also wrote a useful, pocket sized overview of the subject, "Private Schools: From the Puritans to the Present," for the Phi Delta Kappa Educational Foundation in 1976.

Lieberman, Myron, *Privatization and Educational Choice*, St. Martin's Press, 1989.

Lieberman, an education policy analyst and author, strongly argues that privatization and educational choice are essential to effective educational reform. He updates his arguments in a broader critique, *Public Education: An Autopsy* (Harvard University Press, 1993).

Articles

Conlin, Elizabeth, "Educating the Market," *Inc.*, July 1991, pp. 62-67.

The article describes the start-up of Education Alternatives Inc. (EAI) and analyzes its financial prospects as the company prepared to manage its first public school, South Pointe Elementary School in Miami Beach, Fla.

Morley, Jefferson, "Taking Public Schools Private: How It Would Work — And Why D.C. Didn't Do It," *The Washington Post*, March 13, 1994, p. C1.

The article analyzes the reasons why Washington's school superintendent dropped plans to invite Education Alternatives Inc. (EAI) to operate 10-15 schools beginning this fall.

Richardson, Joanna, "Superintendent for Hire," *Education Week*, Feb. 9, 1994, pp. 31-33.

An in-depth story recounts the Minneapolis school board's decision to hire a consulting firm to run the system under a contract that provides for payments based on the achievement of specific goals, including improvements in student test scores.

Solomon, Jolie, "Mr. Vision, Meet Mr. Reality," *Newsweek*, Aug. 16, 1993, pp. 62-65.

Solomon critically examines the prospects for Christopher Whittle's Edison Project after the company announced it was dropping plans to construct a chain of new private schools and instead would seek to manage existing public schools.

Reports and Studies

Beales, Janet R., and John O'Leary, "Making Schools Work: Contracting Options for Better Management," *Reason Foundation*, November 1993.

Policy analysts Beales and O'Leary say that private management of public schools is one of several contracting-out options that allow schools to gain "an infusion of expertise, accountability and cost-effectiveness" from the private sector.

Brown, Frank, and A. Reynaldo Contreras, "Deregulation and Privatization of Education: A Flawed Concept," *Education and Urban Society*, February 1991, pp. 144-158.

University professors Brown and Contreras argue that school choice and for-profit schools will not solve the nation's most-pressing educational problem — improving inner-city schools.

Gramlich, Edward M., and Patricia P. Koshel, "Educational Performance Contracting," *Brookings Institution*, 1975.

Gramlich and Koshel, then fellows at Brookings, evaluate the short-lived, federally funded experiment with "performance contracting" — the use of private companies to try to raise student achievement scores.

National Center for Education Statistics, *Digest of Education Statistics*, 1993, October 1993.

The most recent edition of this annual volume shows enrollment in public elementary and secondary schools at record levels and projected to continue to rise for the rest of the decade. It also reports some evidence of improvement in student achievement but notes "there is still reason for concern."

The Next Step

Additional information from UMI's Newspaper & Periodical Abstracts database

Both Sides of the Issue

Lytle, Robert J., "Reform: Let public schools go private," ***Detroit News*****, Oct. 15, 1993, p. A9.**

Lytle suggests various positive aspects that the implementation of educational vouchers, and school choice, would have for the U.S. educational system.

Merina, Anita, "Can the private sector save public schools?" ***NEA Today*****, February 1994, pp. 10-11.**

Merina says that educators on the front lines say the press isn't telling the whole story about Education Alternatives Inc., the first private firm to run public schools. Educators claim that morale is very low at some of the nine Baltimore public schools due to student discipline problems, curriculum cuts and poorly orchestrated mainstreaming.

Pipho, Chris, "Choice — Vouchers and Privatization," ***Phi Delta Kappan*****, September 1992, pp. 6-7.**

Support for the idea that a private, for-profit group should compete with the public schools in educating children and that it should do so at a profit has come from some surprising people, including the board of education in Baltimore, Pipho says. The issues of school choice, vouchers and privatization are discussed.

Rowe, Jonathan, "Whittle's Schools—3 R's and Lots of TV," ***Christian Science Monitor*****, July 6, 1992, p. 18.**

Rowe examines Christopher Whittle's since-aborted plan to create a national chain of for-profit private schools. He argues that for-profit private schools, such as the ones proposed by Whittle, negate the local community's input and expose students to nothing more than rampant consumerism.

Sutton, Judy, "Private investigation," ***American School & University*****, September 1992, pp. 33-35.**

The merits and pitfalls of privatizing school services are discussed. Privatization is being done primarily to save money and increase cash flow, Sutton says.

Tweedie, Jack, Dennis Riley, John E. Chubb and Terry M. Moe, "Should Market Forces Control Educational Decision Making?" ***American Political Science Review*****, June 1990, pp. 549-567.**

Opposing views on the question of whether market forces should exert more decision-making power in public schools are presented.

Contracting Services

Koprowicz, Connie L., "The private side of public education," ***State Legislatures*****, February 1994, pp. 17-19.**

In the quest for improvement, schools are looking at contracting for a number of services, including instruction and administration—much to the dismay of unions and certified education personnel. A look at the private side of public education is offered.

Mednick, Amy and Lucas Mearian, "Fast-Food Market Hits Cafeterias," ***Boston Globe*****, Nov. 15, 1992, p. SW1.**

Food service directors are vigorously debating the pros and cons of using fast-food chains in Boston-area schools, the author says. Some directors argue that using the chains helps subsidize the rest of the program, but others contend that fast-food restaurants could take over the lunch programs and put profits over nutrition.

Employee Reactions

Schmidt, Peter, "Employees Protest Firm's Tactics at Baltimore Schools," ***Education Week*****, Sept. 16, 1992, p. 1.**

Complaints by paraprofessionals and educators about the private management of eight elementary schools and one middle school in Baltimore by Education Alternatives Inc. are discussed.

Stevens, Mark, "DPS janitors fear move to privatize," ***Denver Post*****, Nov. 6, 1993, p. B1.**

The idea of letting a private company maintain Denver schools has touched a raw nerve with district custodians, who fear losing their jobs and claim replacements will be indifferent about the human side of the task, Stevens says.

Federal Government Involvement

Jordan, Mary, "Private operation of public schools gains," ***The Washington Post*****, Jan. 26, 1994, p. A4.**

As a rising number of cities, including Washington, D.C., consider turning to private firms to operate failing schools, the U.S. Education Department, state legislators and members of Congress are showing more support for private management of public schools, according to Jordan.

Lewis, Anne C., "Public Education and Privatization," ***Phi Delta Kappan*****, April 1992, pp. 580-581.**

The issue of public aid to private schools, which will undoubtedly reach the U.S. Supreme Court someday, is discussed. The Bush administration clearly believes that the public school system needs changing by privatization, Lewis writes.

Investment Possibilities?

Celis, William 3d, "Hopeful start for profit-making

schools," ***The New York Times*****, Oct. 6, 1993, p. A1.**

Harlem Park Elementary School in Baltimore, which is run by a private company for profit, has undergone a transformation since it was taken over by Education Alternatives Inc. The building is clean, attendance has improved and there are early indications that students are learning faster than expected, Celis says. And the company, which invested $1.3 million up front and is alloted $5,918 per student, is making a profit. The concept of privatization of public schools is examined.

Norris, Bill, "High Hopes for Hard Sell," ***Times Educational Supplement*****, Nov. 6, 1992, p. 20.**

Investors on Wall Street are gambling heavily on the privatization of U.S. public schools. Shares for Education Alternatives Inc., which runs nine schools in Baltimore and one in Miami Beach, Fla., were trading at more than $11 in October 1992—providing a 300 percent profit for those who invested early. Education Alternatives hopes to save on operating costs.

Model Plans

Berger, Debra R., "Model schools to start in the fall," ***Boston Globe*****, April 11, 1993, pp. 33.**

The work of the New American Schools Development Corp., which has raised some $55 million so far toward its goal of $150-$200 million to develop model schools, is examined.

Cohen, Muriel, "Edison Project forging into the public schools," ***Boston Globe*****, Jan. 9, 1994, p. 77.**

Media entrepreneur Christopher Whittle's plans to have 10-12 public schools participating in his Edison Project by September 1995 are discussed.

Hemp, Paul, "Desperate City Tries Schools-for-Profit," ***Boston Globe*****, Aug. 30, 1992, p. 1.**

In a move being watched by educators across the nation, a for-profit company, Minneapolis-based Education Alternatives Inc, has taken over for five years the management of nine inner-city Baltimore, Md., public schools, including classroom instruction.

Higgins, James V., "Pinckney school board considers privatization," ***Detroit News*****, Jan. 13, 1994, p. B1.**

The Pinckney, Mich., Board of Education has given notice that it would consider handing over responsibility for day-to-day operations of its seven schools to a private firm, Education Alternatives Inc. of Minneapolis.

Horwitz, Sari, "Shaking up the schools: D.C. superintendent pushes major changes," ***The Washington Post*****, Jan. 26, 1994, p. A1.**

Washington, D.C., School Superintendent Franklin L. Smith is lobbying hard to sell the city on a plan that would fundamentally alter the public school system, starting in the fall of 1994. He wants to turn over some public schools to private managers and make others independent.

Pattison, Scott, "Privatized schools," ***Consumers' Research Magazine*****, December 1993, p. 38.**

The Minneapolis school board has voted unanimously to privatize the management of the city's schools. No other large city has hired a private company to manage every school in the area's system. Baltimore hired a private firm to run some of its most troubled schools and is reporting a more positive attitude and cleaner schools.

Schmidt, Peter, "Dade County school is marketing tool for E. A. I.," ***Education Week*****, April 14, 1993, p. 1.**

South Pointe Elementary School in Miami Beach, Fla., is a showcase for Education Alternatives Inc., a for-profit company that aims to take over public schools and manage them profitably. Its contract with Dade County, Fla., to manage South Pointe is the firm's first move into the public school market.

The Privatization Concept

Branch, Eleanor, "Can Business Save Our Schools?" ***Black Enterprise*****, March 1991, pp. 38-50.**

U.S. corporations have launched programs to upgrade education in the public schools, Branch writes. Programs of several companies are described and highlighted. The issue of whether private industry can deliver results or not is examined.

Harris, Hamil R., "School privatization is tough sell," ***The Washington Post*****, Feb. 3, 1994, p. DC1.**

In scenes reminiscent of the 1993 debate over closing neighborhood schools, Superintendent Franklin L. Smith of Washington, D.C., has gone from one volatile community meeting to another to pitch his idea to privatize some of the city's schools.

Lewis, Anne C., "For-profit schools," ***Education Digest*****, April 1993, pp. 59-60.**

Interest in the privatization of U.S. schools has peaked among its supporters in Washington, D.C., Lewis writes. Projects are having trouble raising money, and grants are being awarded sparingly.

"Random walk," ***National Review*****, Feb. 21, 1994, p. 24.**

Private firms such as Educational Alternatives Inc. are starting to contract with school districts to operate their public schools. Washington, D.C., school officials have begun investigating the private-management concept.

White, George and Nicholas Morgan, "A Coordinated Development Program for K-12 Schools," ***Phi Delta Kappan*****, November 1992, pp. 260-262.**

The future of public education may come to rely more on private support, the authors write. The importance of having coordinated efforts for seeking financial support in the school system is discussed.

Back Issues

Great Research on Current Issues Starts Right Here...Recent topics covered by The CQ Researcher are listed below. Before May 1991, reports were published under the name of Editorial Research Reports.

SEPTEMBER 1992
Domestic Partners
Violence in Schools
Public Broadcasting
Women in the Military

OCTOBER 1992
Depression
U.S. Auto Industry
Youth Apprenticeships
Hispanic Americans

NOVEMBER 1992
Physical Fitness
Privatization
Paying for College
U.S. Policy in Asia

DECEMBER 1992
Crackdown on Smoking
The New CIA
Eating Disorders
Women and AIDS

JANUARY 1993
Hate Crimes
Child Sexual Abuse
Nuclear Fusion
U.S. Trade Policy

Back issues are available for $4.00 (subscribers) or $7.00 (non-subscribers). Quantity discounts apply to orders over ten. To order, call Congressional Quarterly Customer Service at (202) 887-8621.

Binders are available for $15.00. To order call 1-800-638-1710. Please refer to stock number 648.

FEBRUARY 1993
Community Policing
Europe's New Right
School Censorship
Violence Against Women

MARCH 1993
Gay Rights
Aid to Russia
War on Drugs
TV Violence

APRIL 1993
Head Start
High-Speed Rail
Children's Legal Rights
Muslims in America

MAY 1993
Cults in America
Preventing Teen Pregnancy
Software Piracy
National Parks

JUNE 1993
Food Safety
Prostitution
Childhood Immunizations
National Service

JULY 1993
Electric Cars
Population Growth
Downward Mobility
Intelligence Testing

AUGUST 1993
Mental Illness
Bilingual Education
Foreign Policy Burden
School Funding

SEPTEMBER 1993
Suburban Crime
Public Housing
Supreme Court Preview
Immigration Reform

OCTOBER 1993
Airline Safety
Disaster Response
Science in the Courtroom
The Glass Ceiling

NOVEMBER 1993
Paying for Retirement
Charitable Giving
Privacy in the Workplace
Adoption

DECEMBER 1993
U.S. Vietnam-Relations
Learning Disabilities
Child Care
Space Program's Future

JANUARY 1994
Racial Tensions in Schools
South Africa's Future
Worker Retraining
Regulating Pesticides

FEBRUARY 1994
Prison Overcrowding
Water Quality
Religion in Schools
Juvenile Justice

MARCH 1994
Underground Economy
Education Standards
Gambling Boom

Future Topics

- ***Reproductive Ethics***
- ***Democracy in China***
- ***Traffic Congestion***

THE CQ Researcher®

PUBLISHED BY CONGRESSIONAL QUARTERLY INC.

Reproductive Ethics

Is it ethical to tamper with the reproductive process?

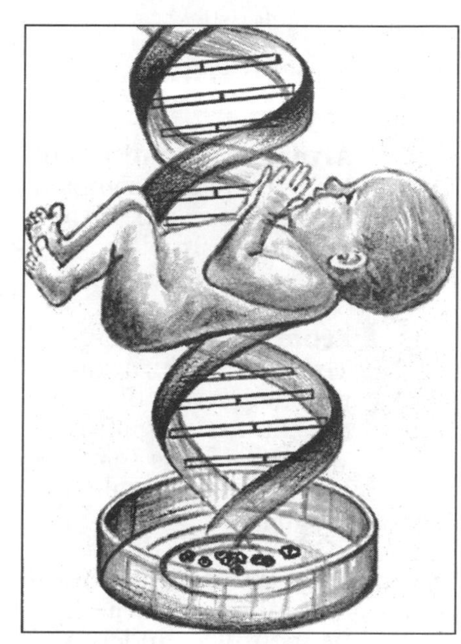

A 59-year-old woman gives birth to twins. A couple who lost two children to cystic fibrosis takes advantage of a new procedure that guarantees their next child will be free of the disease. A schoolteacher undergoes a new fertility treatment and gives birth to quadruplets. Are these people defying nature, or simply obeying one of its basic laws, when they enlist medical technology to aid the reproductive process? Is it fair to aid in the birth of children whose mothers may be ready for a nursing home by the time the children leave nursery school? Should medical insurance cover infertility treatments when millions of Americans have no health-care coverage at all? Should the government fund genetic research that might enable parents to choose the sex and the physical and mental characteristics of their unborn child?

INSIDE THIS ISSUE

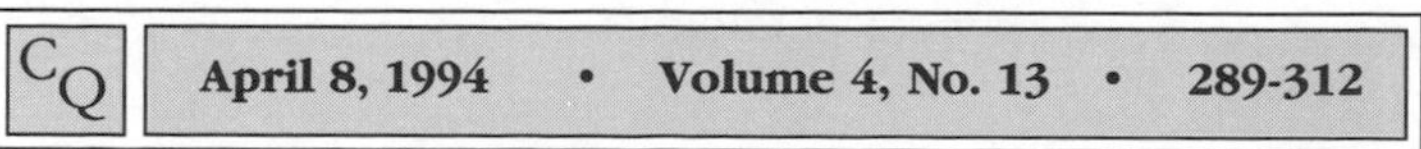

CQ April 8, 1994 • Volume 4, No. 13 • 289-312

Formerly Editorial Research Reports

THE ISSUES

BACKGROUND

CURRENT SITUATION

OUTLOOK

SIDEBARS AND GRAPHICS

FOR FURTHER INFORMATION

COVER ART: BARBARA SASSA-DANIELS

April 8, 1994
Volume 4, No. 13

The CQ Researcher (ISSN 1056-2036). Formerly Editorial Research Reports. Published weekly (48 times per year, not printed the first Friday of any month with five Fridays) by Congressional Quarterly Inc., 1414 22nd St., N.W., Washington, D.C. 20037. Rates are furnished upon request. Second-class postage paid at Washington, D.C. POSTMASTER: Send address changes to The CQ Researcher, 1414 22nd St., N.W., Washington, D.C. 20037.

Reproductive Ethics

BY SUSAN C. PHILLIPS

THE ISSUES

For Karen Reinhard, the darkest moment was not the stillbirth, at seven-and-a-half months, of the baby she had conceived through in vitro fertilization (IVF). It was not the failure, two months later, of a second attempt at assisted reproduction. It came instead last November, when the 40-year-old Reinhard tried a promising new technology: After her husband's sperm was mixed in the lab with eggs donated by another woman, some of the resulting embryos were inserted into Reinhard's uterus. But once again, she didn't get pregnant.

"Everyone was so upbeat, we really felt this would work," says Reinhard. "Then when this happened, it was the worst thing that ever happened to me. . . . I ask myself sometimes, why did God do this? Why can't I just adopt? Why am I pursuing this with such vigor?"

The condition that prevents Reinhard and her husband John from conceiving a child unassisted has never been diagnosed. Reinhard, a Baptist who lives in the Maryland suburbs of Washington, D.C., is active in her church. She has given considerable thought to the ethical issues surrounding her five-year odyssey in search of a way to bear a child.

For the growing number of infertile women and couples who turn to in vitro fertilization, those issues include deciding the fate of the extra embryos created during the IVF process. The development of cryopreservation, or embryo freezing, allows the tiny embryos to be preserved for years. But an estimated 20 percent will not survive the freezing or thawing process. Other options include disposal or donation, either to others suffering through infertility or to research.

In Reinhard's case, the decision to use eggs donated by another woman

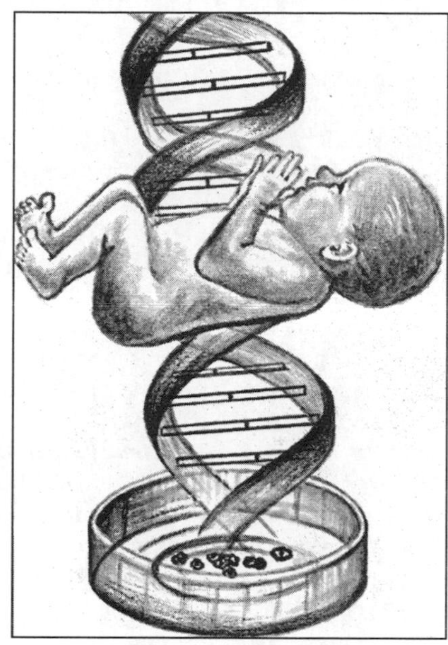

raises a host of new questions, including the ethics of bearing a child who will probably never know his or her genetic mother. But Reinhard believes she is destined to be a mother, and that her actions in pursuit of a baby are part of God's plan for her.

Sister Mary Brady, a professor of ethics at Catholic University in Washington, is sympathetic to the plight of infertile couples like the Reinhards, but she opposes IVF. "IVF might be motivated by love, but it is often motivated by something else — a presumed right to have a child," Brady says. "The Church has great compassion for those who are infertile. You can have compassion without thinking these things are all right." The Roman Catholic Church opposes virtually all assisted reproductive technologies because they remove the conception of children from the context of marital intercourse.

Biologist Ruth Hubbard, a professor emerita at Harvard University, opposes IVF for entirely different reasons. She sees in Reinhard's odyssey a tale of women's victimization by scientific arrogance. "I see these things, IVF and donor eggs, as exploitation of women by researchers who would have absolutely no way of studying human reproductive biology at this level if they did not feed the notion that this answers a health need of women," Hubbard says.

The Reinhards estimate that they have spent about $18,000 of their own money on infertility treatments. The rest of the close to $60,000 in expenses has been paid for by their insurance. *

Norman Fost, a pediatrician and medical ethicist at the University of Wisconsin in Madison, questions whether this is a fair use of medical resources in a country where 40 million people have no health-care coverage at all. "There needs to be a so-called decent minimum for everyone before you can begin supporting any elective, non-acute services being . . . subsidized," says Fost.

Lisa, a 38-year-old woman living in Rockville, Md., has little patience with the judgments of the fertile world. "Fertile people never examine what this means. . . . I have lost my genetic connection to the future," says Lisa, who is preparing to adopt after years of unsuccessful fertility treatments. "It's not like depression, it is like grief that never ends. Every time I menstruate, I grieve again; it is my body reminding me that I am not pregnant again."

The intersection between human procreation and medical science has always been an ethical battleground. In the 1960s, a British panel studying artificial insemination declared the practice "undesirable," saying sperm donation "is an activity which might be expected to attract more than the usual proportion of psychopaths." [1]

Early embryological research was carried out on embryos removed from women undergoing surgical sterilization, without their knowledge or

---

* Peggy Rubin, author of *How to Be a Successful Fertility Patient* (1993), says a single IVF cycle costs $5,000 to $12,000.

Reproductive Technology, From A to Z

Using the tools of science to help people make healthy babies is called ART — for assisted reproductive technology. Here are some of the terms of ART, and the related field of prenatal diagnosis.

AID: Artificial insemination by donor.

AIH: Artificial insemination by husband.

Alpha-fetoprotein screening (AFP): A blood test commonly administered between 16 and 18 weeks of pregnancy. Elevated levels of alpha-fetoprotein in the mother's blood can indicate a neural tube defect such as spina bifida (a spinal column deformity) or anencephaly, the absence of all or part of the brain. AFP screening is controversial because it produces a high rate of false positives: only one or two out of every 50 women with high AFP readings will eventually be shown to have an affected fetus. For this reason, a positive test requires follow-up in the form of amniocentesis or ultrasound.

Amniocentesis: A prenatal genetic test commonly recommended for pregnant women at higher-than-normal risk of having babies with birth defects, including those 35 or older and those with a family history of genetic disorders. Fluid in the amniotic sac surrounding the fetus is extracted and analyzed. The fluid is removed during the 15th or 16th week of pregnancy, and results are usually available within two to four weeks.

Blastomere analysis before implantation (BABI): A test for genetic diseases that involves removing one cell from an embryo and examining it for defective genes. Now used only with in vitro fertilization, BABI may soon be available more generally.

Chorionic villus sampling (CVS): A test for the same genetic defects revealed by amniocentesis that can be performed earlier in pregnancy — between 9 and 12 weeks. CVS involves removing and analyzing cells from the chorionic villi, tiny hairlike strands of tissue in the placenta that carry the same genes as the fetus.

Fetoscopy: Insertion of a miniaturized photographic instrument into the uterus, usually after the 16th week of pregnancy. Still used only rarely, fetoscopy carries a 3 to 5 percent chance of miscarriage.

Gamete intrafallopian transfer (GIFT): Multiple eggs produced during a hormone-stimulated cycle are removed from the ovaries, mixed with sperm and surgically reinserted in the woman's fallopian tubes. This is the only assisted reproductive technology that has not been specifically condemned by the Roman Catholic Church. It also is one of the most promising of the new technologies, with some clinics reporting a "take-home baby" success rate of over 30 percent, approximately the same as that which occurs in the general population.

Genetic Testing: Determining whether and to what degree a person is at risk of developing or passing on a disease.

Gene Therapy: Repairing or replacing an abnormal gene.

Host uterus (also known as surrogate gestational mother): A woman has her eggs fertilized in a laboratory dish with her husband's sperm, and the resulting embryo is transferred to another woman who will carry the pregnancy to term and then give the baby to its genetic parents.

Intracytoplasmic sperm injection (ICSI): A form of in vitro fertilization that involves propelling a single sperm to the center of an egg.

In vitro fertilization (IVF): Eggs are removed from the ovaries and mixed with sperm in vitro (within glass) in the laboratory. Resulting embryos are transferred to the uterus. It is often but not always accompanied by hormone treatments to produce multiple eggs for fertilization.

Peritoneal ovum sperm transfer (POST): Process similar to GIFT (see above), except that the eggs and sperm are placed just outside the opening of the fallopian tube rather than inside.

Pronuclear-stage transfer (PROST): Process that resembles ZIFT (see below), except that the transfer takes place sooner, right after the first signs of fertilization have occurred. It's thought that the sooner the embryo is returned to the woman's body, the better the chances for implantation.

Subzonal insertion (SUZI): A form of IVF in which a needle is used to puncture the outer shell of the egg and inject sperm.

Ultrasound or sonography: Through the use of sound waves, ultrasound provides a moving image of the fetus on a small black-and-white screen. It allows doctors to measure the fetus to determine fetal age, examine the position and condition of the placenta and determine the number of fetuses present. It is also used to insure the needle used to remove amniotic fluid for amniocentesis does not touch the fetus.

Zygote intrafallopian transfer (ZIFT): Eggs are removed from the ovaries and fertilized with sperm in a laboratory dish. Resulting embryos are surgically transferred to a woman's fallopian tubes. It differs from GIFT (see above) in that fertilization occurs in the lab, not in the fallopian tube, and from IVF (see above) in that embryos are transferred to the fallopian tubes rather than the uterus.

consent. Lesley Brown, the British woman who gave birth to the first IVF baby in 1978, had to agree that she would abort the fetus if it showed any signs of abnormality as a condition of receiving treatment.

Since then, the relatively new field of bioethics has developed some useful tools for doctors, scientists and society to evaluate reproductive technologies. But the science always seems to be one step ahead of any consensus on its ethical implications. In the United States, the lag is even greater, since a 15-year ban on federal funding of IVF research has limited public discussion and government oversight of the research that does continue. (*See story, p. 300.*)

Ethicists and researchers representing a broad spectrum of beliefs agree that the U.S. is overdue for a public airing of the many issues raised by the new technologies in order to avoid both an uncritical acceptance of potentially dangerous new treatments and unnecessary alarm over the implications of genetic knowledge. Here are some of the key questions in the debate:

Should there be limits on access to in vitro fertilization?

Last year, a 59-year-old British woman gave birth to healthy twins. A 62-year-old Italian woman is expecting a child in June. In the U.S., dozens of post-menopausal women in their 40s and 50s have become pregnant through in vitro fertilization. In each case, eggs obtained from younger women were fertilized in the lab, then transferred into the older women, who also underwent hormone treatments to prepare their bodies for pregnancy.

To hear French Health Minister Philippe Douste-Blazy tell it, these post-menopausal mothers represent a major threat to civilization. He has spearheaded a government effort to ban artificial impregnation of older women in France, and to lobby for a similar ban throughout the European Union. "I think it is absolutely shocking that a child can be 18 when his mother is 80," Douste-Blazy said in a radio interview. [2]

Only about 100 babies have been born to post-menopausal women around the world since the technology that makes such pregnancies possible was developed a little over three years ago as a way to help women with early menopause. Most observers believe that the vast majority of women have no interest in extending their childbearing years into their retirement years, and only a few of those who do will be able to afford the procedure. Supporters suspect that the uproar has more to do with preconceived notions about the role of older women than concern for the children produced.

Noting the general acceptance of fatherhood by older men — Charlie Chaplin became a father at 73, Sen. Strom Thurmond at 74, actor Anthony Quinn at 78 — *Washington Post* health columnist Abigail Trafford blames the scorn and censure being heaped on older mothers on "the familiar and unscientific Double Standard." [3]

Arthur Caplan, director of the Center for Biomedical Ethics at the University of Minnesota, notes that older men don't need expensive medical intervention to become fathers, so society is not in a position to regulate their decisions. But, he adds, society does have a stake in preventing births to elderly parents. "The primary goal of using reproductive technology, from the point of view of government and society, is to make sure children are born with a good start in life," Caplan says. "The major threat to that is to have two parents who are too old to parent."

Florence P. Haseltine, director of the Center for Population Research at the National Institutes of Health (NIH), has no patience with that sort of thinking. "If you're going to make it illegal for women to have babies when they are older, it should be illegal for men. . . . Men have children late in life because they want to be rejuvenated and feel there is no death. I don't see why women can't be just as bullheaded."

The focus on maternal age has obscured other ethical questions arising from this technique, which depends on the availability of donor eggs. IVF with donor eggs is a new but increasingly popular procedure, not only for post-menopausal women but also for those who have failed to conceive through IVF using their own eggs.

Egg retrieval for IVF carries with it a small risk of infection that can lead to infertility. And drugs used to stimulate a woman's ovaries to produce multiple eggs for retrieval sometimes trigger a dangerous reaction in which the ovaries become enlarged and may rupture. Potential donors are counseled about those risks, but some ethicists wonder whether a young, childless woman — the most common profile for an anonymous egg donor — should even be asked to undergo the procedure. The practice of paying donors adds to the ethical thicket. A serious short-term need for cash may seem more pressing to a young woman than the slight risk of future childlessness, until the day she wants a child herself.

"Are we trading one set of infertile couples today, for another set further down the road?" asks psychologist Linda Applegarth, who counsels egg donors and recipients for the IVF program at New York Hospital-Cornell Medical Center. "I don't know. There is no clear answer."

A 1993 study by epidemiologists from around the country suggested that the hormones used to stimulate women's ovaries to produce extra eggs for IVF might raise the women's risk for ovarian cancer. The methodology of the study has been sharply criticized. [4] But even critics acknowledge that there is a near-total lack of reliable information on whether there are long-term risks to women from using fertility drugs. Millions of American women have already taken these drugs, most commonly Clomid and Pergonal, either as part of less-aggressive fertility treatment plans, or in conjunction with IVF.

"I try not to think about it," says Reinhard of the possible dangers. "Probably if I ever have a baby, later, I'll look back and worry."

For those who have made peace with these questions, there are other,

The In Vitro Fertilization Process

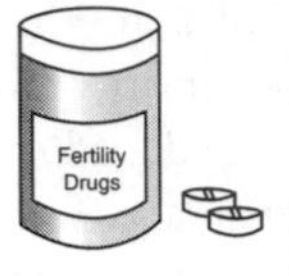

Ovulation induction: Fertility drugs prescribed and egg growth monitored. In 15% of cases, eggs do not develop properly and are lost to ovulation.

Semen analysis: A semen sample collected through masturbation is analyzed for viability of the sperm.

Sperm wash: The sperm are concentrated and impurities in the semen are removed.

Egg retrieval: Just before ovulation the eggs are retrieved using a needle guided by ultrasound. Depending on the drug regime used, the number can range from 5 to 10 or more eggs. Immature eggs are transferred to a culture medium to mature.

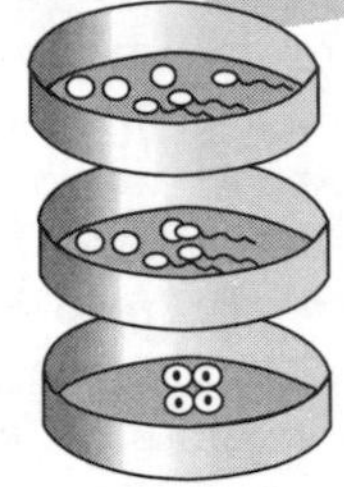

Egg fertilization: Four to 12 hours after the egg retrieval, sperm are added, and eggs are returned to an incubator. Within 20 hours of insemination, each egg is examined to determine if fertilization has occurred. In 13% of cases, a viable zygote does not result.

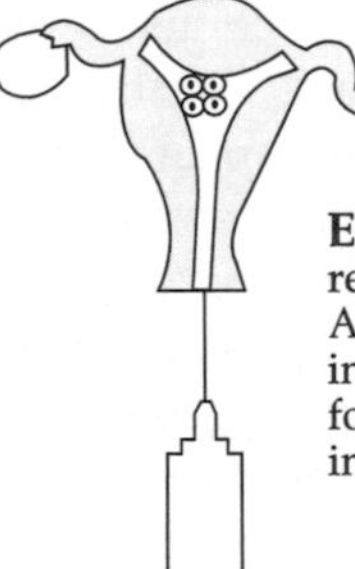

Embryo transfer: In about three days, when the zygotes have reached the two- to eight-cell stage, they are evaluated for viability. A number of them are transferred to the uterus using a fine catheter inserted through the cervix or to the fallopian tubes using laparoscopy for GIFT. (See glossary, p. 292.) About 80% of transfers do not result in implantation.

Implantation: If the zygote implants successfully in the wall of the uterus, a gestational sac can be detected by ultrasound and elevated hormone levels will be present in the woman's blood, indicating pregnancy.

Pregnancy: Pregnancy proceeds normally. More than one embryo may implant successfully and multiple pregnancy is common. About 30% of IVF deliveries are multiple. About 20% of clinical prgnancies are lost to miscarriage, and 5% are ectopic and must be terminated.

Live birth: For every 100 cycles initiated in 1991, 13 resulted in a live birth.

Source: Proceed With Care: Final Report of the Royal Commission on New Reproductive Technologies, *1993*.

broader issues to wrestle with. There has been little work done on whether IVF is appropriate for many of the women who undergo it. IVF success rates remain relatively low — about 13 live births per 100 attempts. Yet it is fast becoming a common treatment for women and couples with unexplained infertility.

Lisa now believes IVF would never have worked for her. After doing considerable research on her own, she believes her problem is related to implantation of the embryo in the uterine lining, a process biologists know little about.

"Given that, why would I be doing IVF? It's an absurdity," Lisa says. "I think it was the best decision we could make at the time, because we never had a diagnosis. But I wish they would pay more attention to figuring out what's wrong and tailoring the treatment to that diagnosis. . . . I remember my doctor saying to me, 'Forget diagnosis, let's just treat you.' I don't think that makes sense."

Last year, the Canadian Royal Commission on Reproductive Technologies concluded a three-year study of every aspect of infertility treatment. The commission concluded that IVF can be considered a proven treatment for only one type of infertility — blocked fallopian tubes. And the group recommended that no other form of the procedure receive health-care coverage. [5]

"It seems to us that everything except IVF for blocked tubes should be offered in the context of research trials, in which women are told these aren't proven treatments," said Patricia Baird of the University of British Columbia in Vancouver, the pediatrician and geneticist who headed the inquiry. [6]

Such restrictions seem unlikely in the U.S., where infertility treatment is a $2-billion-a-year business. But insurance coverage for the procedure, already only sporadically available, would be eliminated under President Clinton's proposal for health-care reform.

Should there be limits on prenatal testing?

Emily Pearl Kingsley of Chappaqua, N.Y., is the mother of a 19-year-old with Down's syndrome. Pregnant for the first time at 34, Kingsley considered and then rejected amniocentesis, a test that would have diagnosed her son's condition early enough in Kingsley's pregnancy for her to have an abortion.

"I talked to my doctor, and we decided I wasn't exactly high risk, so we decided to pass on the test. I'm ever so glad I did," says Kingsley. "I probably would have terminated the pregnancy, and missed the most enriching experience of my life."

Kingsley, who describes herself as strongly pro-choice, often speaks with couples and women who have learned they are expecting a baby with Down's syndrome. "The idea I try to get across is they need to do some homework, do some research, find some families and look at the kids," says Kingsley. "People should make this decision based on the most complete, up-to-date information possible, not on the fears and misconceptions of the past. . . . Some of the people I talk to are just so frightened."

Tests such as amniocentesis have become such a routine part of prenatal care for women in their mid-30s and older that the ethical uproar created by the development of the test a generation ago is largely forgotten. But advances in the understanding of human genetics raise the prospect of prenatal prediction, not only of susceptibility to thousands of diseases but also of countless other characteristics. One 1990 survey indicated that 12 percent of women would have an abortion if testing showed the fetus would suffer from uncontrollable obesity (no such gene has yet been identified). [7]

Advances in the understanding and treatment of conditions such as Down's syndrome complicate the decisions expectant parents face after a positive diagnosis. Kingsley was told her son would never speak, and would spend his life in an institution. He recently graduated from high school and may eventually attend a college specially geared to students with disabilities. With a friend, and helped by his mother, he has written a book about living with Down's syndrome. [8] Clearly, not all Down's children will do so well. But prenatal diagnosis tells parents nothing about the severity with which any condition will manifest itself, and probably never will.

"There's this excessive notion of predictability" with prenatal testing, says Harvard biologist Ruth Hubbard. "In most situations, knowing about a genetic predisposition doesn't tell you what is going to happen. . . . To look at human variability as something that needs to be controlled is extremely dangerous. We don't always know what we are in fact eliminating."

People with disabilities and advocates for the disabled are wary of prenatal testing. They fear that an expanded ability to diagnose various disabilities prenatally will increase discrimination against the disabled, reduce government support for the treatment of genetic diseases and disabilities and put increased pressure on parents to abort affected fetuses.

But Caplan at the University of Minnesota believes limits on prenatal testing are unworkable. "It is almost impossible to argue that people shouldn't be able to choose the traits of their babies if they can," he says.

There is already at least one fundamental human characteristic for which uncounted fetuses are aborted, even though few would characterize it as a disease or disability, and that is sex. Amniocentesis to determine the sex of an unborn child has been banned in India, in an attempt to curb abortion rates for women carrying female fetuses. Geneticists in the U.S. face frequent requests for prenatal testing to determine sex.

But sex selection is difficult, if not impossible, to control. "It's wrong to inhibit the technology for sex selection, since there are diseases [like hemophilia] that are linked to sex," says Dr. Paul Billings, chief of genetic medicine at Pacific Presbyterian Hospital in San Francisco. "There will always be some families where there are good reasons to have that information. . . . If the problem is a culture that values boys over girls, it is not a problem of the technology."

Expanded prenatal testing also raises the question of what pressures parents may face from outside, first to undergo tests, and later to act on them by terminating pregnancies.

"Certainly insurance companies and HMOs have reasons to want to limit the births of disabled children, and they can be expected to exert whatever direct or indirect pressure they can," says Billings. "That's an interest that may run counter to a general social interest in having a diversified populace, and it's not clear how that general social interest gets defended in the marketplace."

To date, insurers have been more interested in limiting coverage for prenatal testing than encouraging more tests. Many plans will not cover amniocentesis or a newer test, chorionic villus sampling (*see glossary, p. 292*), for anyone below the age of 35, unless there are some other identifiable risk factors for one of the diseases that the test can detect.

But a growing number of doctors and patients feel there is no reason to deny the test to younger women, if they want it. The current standard of 35 is used because that is the point at which the risk of miscarriage from the procedure, about one in 200, is somewhat less than the risk that the fetus will be affected by Down's syndrome. But women and doctors alike argue that the trauma of a miscarriage, while real, does not compare with the stress of bearing an affected child. And couples who would not have an abortion in any case can still benefit from having time to prepare themselves for the birth of a disabled child.

Should there be limits on technologies that make it possible to select a child's physical and mental characteristics?

Dr. Mark R. Hughes, a geneticist at the Baylor College of Medicine in Houston, is part of a team of researchers perfecting a technique, called preimplantation diagnosis, that permits examination of embryos for genetic defects before they are transferred to the uterus. One couple he has worked with, both carriers of the cystic fibrosis gene, recently gave birth to a healthy, unaffected baby following a modified IVF cycle in which fertilized embryos were screened for the cystic fibrosis gene before uterine implantation.

Some of the couples Hughes has worked with have already lost children to cystic fibrosis, a disorder of the lungs and digestive system, and undergone one or more abortions to avoid giving birth to another affected child. Preimplantation diagnosis allows the woman "to begin her pregnancy from day one, committed to completing it," Hughes says.

While preimplantation diagnosis can be seen as the logical extension of efforts to allow prenatal diagnosis earlier and earlier in a pregnancy, some doctors and ethicists see an important, and disturbing, distinction. French IVF pioneer Jacques Testart, for example, says preimplantation diagnosis is essentially eugenics in new-technology clothing. "Where prenatal diagnosis permits us to avoid the worst, by elimination, preimplantation diagnosis will elect the best, by selection," he says.[9]

Ethicist Andrea Bonnickson of Northern Illinois University says the technique is "the steppingstone to preimplantation genetic therapy. . . . It's not in the immediate future, but it is foreseeable that attempts will be made to correct the disorder at the preimplantation stage. Some would say we have a moral obligation to treat the embryos and correct genetic disorders, but that is at odds with the fears expressed over the last 20 or 30 years that this is genetic engineering."

The prospect of gene therapy carried out before transfer of the embryo to a woman's uterus is controversial because of the special characteristics of very early embryos. IVF embryos are usually transferred when they have only 32 cells, well before organ formation begins. Genetic alterations introduced at this stage would be present in all or most of the cells produced subsequently and, as a result, would be passed on to future generations. This is referred to as altering the germ line.

Harvard's Ruth Hubbard, who favors a complete ban on germ-line research, says she is leaning toward supporting a ban on preimplantation diagnosis as well. "I think that would be entirely warranted. It plays into all the wrong social impulses."

"Right now, you are talking about a technique used by not very many people," says Caplan. "But down the road, if you can use this technology to pick the traits of children, avoid disease and disability, it becomes attractive. . . . It will happen."

"I'm in favor of learning whether germ-line therapy is possible," says bioethicist John C. Fletcher of the University of Virginia. "If embryos or gametes [the scientific term for unfertilized reproductive cells — i.e., eggs and sperm] could be cured or treated, and then you said you wouldn't do it, I think that's pretty mean. On the other hand, if you make mistakes, they will be visited on the next generation." ■

BACKGROUND

Artificial Insemination

It was male infertility that prompted medical scientists to develop the first known example of an assisted reproductive technology, artificial insemination.

Some scholars have noted that this is one of the few instances in medicine where one person's condition — a man's infertility — is treated by subjecting another person — a healthy fertile woman — to an invasive and potentially risky procedure.[10] Those risks were considerably greater in the early days, when some doctors believed semen had to be deposited directly in the uterus, a procedure with a high risk of infection.

The first recorded instance of artificial insemination using sperm from a donor was performed in Philadelphia in the 1880s. "At the time, the procedure was so novel, so peculiar in its human ethics, that the six young men of the senior class who witnessed the operation were pledged to secrecy," wrote one participant, A.D. Hard, more than 20 years later.

The case involved a wealthy merchant, aged 41, who was puzzled by his inability to conceive a child with his wife, who was 10 years younger. An examination revealed the man was not producing any sperm.

"A joking remark by one of the class, 'the only solution of this problem is to call in the hired man,' was probably the incentive to the plan of action which followed," Hard's account continues. "The woman was chloroformed, and with a hard rubber syringe some fresh semen from the best-looking member of the class was deposited in the uterus, and the cervix slightly plugged with gauze."

Neither the man nor his wife was initially informed of the procedure, but according to Hard, the professor who performed the insemination later "repented of his action, and explained the whole matter to the husband. Strange as it may seem, the man was delighted with the idea, and conspired with the professor in keeping from the lady the actual way in which her impregnation was brought about."[11] The woman delivered a healthy son.

Continued on p. 298

Chronology

1880s ***Early experimentation with assisted reproduction.***

1884
The first recorded instance of artificial insemination with donated sperm takes place in Philadelphia, at the Jefferson Medical College, according to a disputed 1909 account.

1960s ***Amniocentesis, a procedure that allows for the diagnosis of Down's syndrome and other genetic disorders, is introduced.***

1970s ***In vitro fertilization in humans becomes a reality.***

July 25, 1978
Louise Joy Brown, the first child conceived through in vitro fertilization, is born in Great Britain. Media dubs her the world's first "test tube baby."

1979
The Ethics Advisory Board of the National Institutes of Health (NIH) concludes that federal support of research into human in vitro fertilization and embryo transfer could be ethically acceptable under certain conditions.

February 1979
First in vitro fertilization clinic in the United States opens at Eastern Virginia Medical School in Norfolk, Va.

1980s ***IVF techniques pioneered in Great Britain fuel the growth of an infertility industry in the U.S.***

1980
NIH Ethics Advisory Board is disbanded by the Carter administration before it approves any funding for IVF research. The action marks the start of a 15-year ban on federal funding for such research. The Northern California Sperm Bank in Oakland begins providing semen to unmarried as well as married women. Six years later, the bank reports that 70 percent of its clients are single.

Dec. 28, 1981
First American IVF baby, Elizabeth Jordan Carr, is born in Norfolk, Va.

January 1983
The first "donor baby" is born in Australia. The pregnancy occurred when an egg retrieved from one woman was fertilized with the sperm of another woman's husband, then implanted in the second woman.

1990s ***Advances in micromanipulation techniques allow both for new refinements of IVF technology and for the development of preimplantation diagnosis, which permits examination of embryos for genetic defects before they are transferred to the uterus. The U.S. moves toward resuming research funding.***

March 1992
A healthy baby girl is born to a British couple following the first successful application of preimplantation diagnosis. Both parents carry the cystic fibrosis gene, and normally any of their children would have a one-in-four chance of being born with the disease.

1993
Reauthorization bill for NIH eliminates requirement for Ethics Advisory Board approval of in vitro and human embryo research funding. The Canadian Royal Commission on Reproductive Technologies issues its 1,200-page report, after three years of study, and recommends strict limits on the use of IVF except within a research setting.

October 1993
Researchers at George Washington University in Washington, D.C., announce that they have successfully "cloned" some defective human embryos by splitting apart eight-cell human embryos into single cells, some of which had continued to grow and divide into new, genetically identical embryos in the lab.

December 1993
A British woman gives birth to twins at age 59, touching off a worldwide debate over the ability of new reproductive technologies to allow post-menopausal women to carry a pregnancy to term.

1994
NIH's Human Embryo Research Panel meets to establish new funding guidelines for research in the U.S. British researchers announce they have perfected a procedure allowing them to harvest immature oocytes from aborted mouse fetuses and grow them to maturity in the laboratory. They predict they'll be able to do the same with humans one day.

Continued from p. 296

Some doubt the veracity of Hard's account, but it is clear that doctors have long used their own idiosyncratic moral and ethical standards in matters regarding donor insemination. While states have various standards, many physicians employ a host of criteria entirely of their own choosing. These might include a woman's IQ, financial and marital status, sexual orientation and religious affiliation, as well as the doctor's assessment of her honesty, good character and motives for seeking the procedure. [12]

There were certain social benefits to giving doctors considerable control over reproductive technologies. Most important, a procedure that was regarded with loathing and suspicion by many religious and secular authorities gained a certain legitimacy. Donor insemination was initially perceived as an assault on the dignity of marriage and the sanctity of the family. And it raised troublesome issues of legitimacy and inheritance rights. Over time, the involvement of doctors has done much to remove that stigma. [13]

Medical control of artificial insemination eased considerably with the widespread realization in the 1970s that doctors are not necessary participants. A grass-roots self-insemination movement forced fertility doctors and clinics to become less restrictive in order to retain their clients. The fear of AIDS and other communicable diseases has reduced the use of fresh sperm for self-insemination, once a favored practice among single women and lesbian couples seeking to become parents. But some sperm banks will now sell frozen sperm to individuals without a doctor's request, even though self-insemination is considered a crime — practicing medicine without a license — in many jurisdictions.

Most people still choose to use a doctor's services for insemination, but the atmosphere surrounding the procedure has changed. What used to be a closely guarded family secret is now the topic of magazine articles with sidebars on "Sperm Banks and Clinics: Where to Go and What to Know." [14]

Resolve Inc.

Members of Resolve, an infertility support group with chapters nationwide, meet in Massachusetts.

There is also some movement toward lifting the veil of donor anonymity. The Sperm Bank of California in Oakland reports that about a third of its donors are willing to be identified to the children conceived from their sperm once the children turn 18. [15]

Nonetheless, there are still barriers to a woman's access to safe sperm. As recently as 1988, a survey found some sperm banks refusing women applicants for reasons including psychological immaturity, lack of a high school degree, a criminal record or a past history of drug or alcohol abuse. At the same time, 61 percent of physicians were refusing to inseminate women without male partners, and an even larger percentage were refusing to inseminate lesbians. [16] Canada's Royal Commission on New Reproductive Technologies concluded last year that artificial insemination services should not be refused on the grounds of marital status or sexual orientation. [17]

In the U.S., sperm donors are usually paid, though the payment is referred to as compensation for time and inconvenience to overcome strictures against paying people for body parts or tissues. There is little regulation or oversight of sperm banks, but most claim to screen donors and their sperm for disease. Some European nations have barred any payment to sperm donors, and many ethicists support that position.

Lack of regulation raises the possibility that a single donor may, over a period of years, provide the sperm for so many pregnancies that an unacceptable risk develops of his offspring meeting, marrying and producing children. Voluntary guidelines developed by the American Fertility Society call for the "retirement" of individual donors after 10 inseminations. But the case of Dr. Cecil B. Jacobson disclosed the shortcomings of a voluntary system. Jacobson, a fertility doctor from Vienna, Va., was convicted of fraud in 1992 for using his own sperm to impregnate dozens of patients who believed the sperm came from a sperm bank.

From Sperm to Eggs

Artificial insemination by a donor raises many of the ethical issues surrounding reproductive technologies today. Those issues are magnified and multiplied once the focus of treatment moves from male infertility to female infertility.

The reasons are both cultural and biological. On the cultural side, society seems more willing to accept the concept of anonymous fathers than that of anonymous mothers. Men produce multitudes of sperm, with great frequency. Women produce a single mature egg each month. The animal kingdom is filled with examples of fathers whose only responsibility is to impregnate as many females as possible.

Techniques to address female infertility, including in vitro fertilization, in vitro with donor eggs and surrogate motherhood (*see below*), do not lend themselves to the strong tradition of secrecy that initially surrounded artificial insemination. IVF and its variants are too complicated, expensive and time-consuming to take place unobserved. Women also seem less reluctant to acknowledge their own fertility problems, and more inclined to discuss their treatment with others. [18]

Egg retrieval for in vitro fertilization requires a woman to take fertility drugs for a month or more, to undergo repeated ultrasound screenings and blood tests as the expected date of ovulation approaches and to undergo the surgical removal of the eggs. Beyond its physical risks, the process is emotionally difficult, made more so by the effect of hormone treatments on women's emotional state.

"I see the whole IVF business as a way of luring women down not very rewarding paths," says Harvard's Ruth Hubbard. "They are lured down those paths by the story of the exceptional woman [who becomes pregnant], but that is not the story of most women."

Lisa, the 38-year-old Rockville, Md., woman, recently had to deal with another of the difficult choices IVF presents — what to do with the excess embryos produced by the procedure.

The use of hormones to stimulate women's ovaries can produce two dozen eggs or more per cycle. Almost all of them may become fertilized and progress to the early embryonic stage at which uterine implantation is attempted. Doctors usually insert no more than four embryos per attempt. Others may be frozen, destroyed or donated to another infertile couple or to research — sometimes for a reduction in the price of the IVF procedure.

"We talked about destroying them . . . but my husband felt strongly against it," says Lisa, who had two frozen embryos after her IVF. "I couldn't donate them to another couple. The idea of someone else having my biological child is unbearable." Lisa and her husband decided that she should return to the fertility clinic and have the frozen embryos implanted even though she has abandoned any hope of becoming pregnant this way.

Karen and Andrew Daniels of Upper Marlboro, Md., are the parents of IVF twins. They have 11 frozen embryos in storage. "We don't have a problem with it right now," says Karen. The Daniels are paying $1,000 to keep their embryos frozen for five years. But deciding to freeze excess embryos is not simple, since an estimated 20 percent will not survive the thawing process.

The Daniels faced a particularly wrenching decision early in Karen's pregnancy, when she found she was carrying triplets. After consulting with their doctors, the couple decided that Karen should undergo a procedure known as "selective reduction," an abortion of one of the fetuses, in order to give the remaining two a better chance at healthy, full-term delivery. "It was horrible," Karen says. "But we made the decision that the whole reason we did IVF was to have healthy babies, and we felt this was the best way to do that."

Women who become pregnant through IVF are more likely than others to find they are carrying more than one fetus. About 30 percent of IVF deliveries are multiple, compared with 1 percent in the general population. [19] Selective reduction is often recommended with three or more fetuses, because of the serious health risks of multiple gestations to both mothers and babies.

Questions Raised By Egg Donation

When in vitro fertilization is done with another woman's eggs, the person assuming most of the risks is the donor — either a friend or relative of the infertile woman, an anonymous donor motivated by altruism and/or a need for the $1,000 to $3,000 fee, or another fertility patient who may receive a reduction in the cost of her own IVF procedure if she donates some of the eggs she produces.

Each of these scenarios raises its own ethical questions. Can a sister or close friend truly be said to consent freely to something that may seem of such critical import to the future happiness of a much-loved individual? Is a woman with compromised fertility a logical egg donor for another infertile woman? Does any woman who has not already had a child truly understand what she may be giving up if she risks her own future fertility for another? Is it right to pay women for their eggs?

Cornell's Applegarth says that in an ideal world, the only women who would be allowed to participate in anonymous-donor programs would be in their mid-20s, with a child or children of their own. But there are simply not enough such women.

Applegarth says she has made peace with the concept of donations by IVF patients. "I think that by virtue of the screening process, the time I spend with them, I am able to pick apart their motivations," says Applegarth. "But many are comfortable with the idea of donating. The feeling is that they've been there, they understand what the recipient has

History of U.S. Ban on IVF Research

For the first time in 15 years, research involving in vitro fertilization (IVF) and human embryos will be eligible for federal funding later this year, ending a de facto ban supported by three consecutive presidents: Jimmy Carter, Ronald Reagan and George Bush.

In June, the Human Embryo Research Panel of the National Institutes of Health (NIH) is expected to issue its report on what types of research should be considered acceptable for federal funding, and to propose specific guidelines for review and conduct of this research. The panel itself will then be disbanded, and NIH will subject research proposals in these areas to its usual peer review process.

This rather low-profile process has been criticized by those who feel the ethical issues are so profound, and the science progressing so rapidly, that a permanent panel should be established. But the funding ban itself was always a rather backdoor affair.

It had its roots in the establishment, in 1975, of a permanent Ethics Advisory Board within NIH to review human IVF proposals. Regulations adopted that year required that "No application or proposal involving human in vitro fertilization may be funded . . . until the application or proposal has been reviewed by the Ethics Advisory Board (EAB) and the board has rendered advice as to its acceptability from an ethical standpoint."

In 1979, the EAB issued a report concluding that research into IVF and embryo transfer was ethically acceptable as long as certain conditions were met. The key conditions were: compliance with federal rules governing research with human subjects; that the human gametes (eggs and sperm) used in the research be obtained from persons who have given informed consent; and that no embryos are sustained in vitro beyond the stage normally associated with the completion of implantation in the uterine lining, 14 days after fertilization.

But before the EAB could approve a single research proposal, it was disbanded by the Carter administration. Some blame a decision by the administration and Congress to fold funding for the EAB into that for the National Commission for the Protection of Human Subjects of Biomedical and Behavioral Research. But pro-life activists claim that a massive letter-writing campaign to protest the board's expected approval of an IVF research proposal pushed Carter to act.

Whatever the reason for the initial disbanding of the EAB, abortion politics ensured its continued non-existence through the Reagan and Bush years. Without an ethics board in place, NIH could not by law fund any IVF research, so clinicians working at university hospitals and for-profit fertility clinics have had the field pretty much to themselves.

Some critics believe the result has been a lot of second-rate science, in part because researchers have not had the resources to rigorously design studies, and in part because the competitive atmosphere leads to the rapid spread of new techniques before they have been fully evaluated.

By 1990, the government's decision not to re-establish the Ethics Advisory Board was being presented by the Department of Health and Human Services as "a long-standing policy prohibiting support for in vitro fertilization or other harmful experimentation on live embryos." [1]

That same year, Congress began efforts to overturn the Reagan administration's 1989 moratorium on federal funding of fetal tissue transplantation research. [2] The American Fertility Society urged Congress to broaden its goal to include lifting the ban on federal funding for IVF research.

The House passed a 1990 NIH reauthorization bill that would have re-established the EAB for IVF research, but the Senate did not act before the 101st Congress adjourned. A bill was passed in both the House and Senate early in the 102nd Congress, but it was vetoed by President Bush.

With the election of a pro-choice Democrat to the presidency, supporters of resuming federal support for the research were able to simultaneously overturn the ban, and eliminate the requirement for a permanent ethics board to consider IVF research. They did this by inserting a single sentence in the 1993 NIH Reauthorization Act nullifying the federal regulation requiring such a board. The legislation was signed into law by President Clinton last June.

Though the new regulations do not require any special ethical review of IVF research, NIH established the new temporary panel to help develop guidelines for research. The 19-member panel includes experts in basic and clinical research, ethics, law, social science, public health and public policy.

Scientists say it will take years before researchers in the U.S. can catch up to their counterparts in other nations, where work in the field is strictly regulated, but funded. Most recent breakthroughs in assisted reproductive technologies and human embryology have come from Great Britain, France, Italy, and Australia.

[1] Letter dated Sept. 25, 1990, from HHS Secretary Louis W. Sullivan to Rep. John D. Dingell, D-Mich., chairman of the House Energy and Commerce Committee, quoted in Lynne D. Lawrence, "Overturning the Ban on IVF Research: A Case Study in Politics," *Assisted Reproduction Reviews,* Vol. 3, No. 3, 1993, p. 165.

[2] For background, see "Fetal Tissue Research," *The CQ Researcher*, Aug. 16, 1991, pp. 561-584.

been through. And there may be a fantasy that if they help somebody else, this will work for them."

Some programs use eggs donated by IVF patients to allow other patients who could not otherwise afford the procedure to undergo it at a reduced rate. Ruth Macklin, a professor of bioethics at the Albert Einstein College of Medicine in the Bronx, N.Y., argues that this benefit to others may outweigh the ethical questions. "A positive ethical feature is reciprocity," says Macklin. "In this situation, it seems everyone gains and no one loses."

Surrogate Motherhood

Surrogate motherhood has existed throughout history. Nevertheless, it has always been one of the most ethically questionable responses to infertility.

Society is uneasy about women who deliberately undergo pregnancy and childbirth, then walk away. There is ambivalence about the motives of couples who would seek access to a child this way, putting another individual at such risk of physical and psychological harm. There are questions about whether the children of surrogacy arrangements will have a harder time understanding the motives of their biological mothers than the children of adoption, because added to the issue of abandonment is that of having been created for the purpose of being abandoned.

Surrogacy doesn't fit neatly on a list of new reproductive technologies, since it does not necessarily involve any technology at all. In fact, unease with surrogacy is one of the forces driving the new technologies, as infertile individuals look for ways to achieve genetically related offspring without the emotional and legal risks attached to surrogate arrangements.

Between 1975 and 1990, an estimated 4,500 children were born in the United States through surrogacy arrangements. [20] There have been only a handful of cases in which surrogate mothers have tried to gain custody of the resulting children, but those few instances have received enormous publicity. Much of the debate over surrogacy centers on money: Many compare the practice to baby-selling. Eighteen states have passed laws sharply limiting surrogacy arrangements. [21]

New technologies have created a twist on the traditional surrogate arrangement — host uterus. In host uterus, a woman who produces viable eggs but is unable to carry a pregnancy to term undergoes egg retrieval; the eggs are fertilized with her partner's sperm; the resulting embryos are implanted in another woman, who carries the pregnancy to term.

One well-known and generally well-received instance of host uterus involved Arlette Schweitzer, the South Dakota woman who in October 1991 bore twin sons for her daughter and son-in-law. Her daughter, Christa Uchytil, had been born without a uterus. [22]

But the same arrangement between strangers, involving payment, raises ethical red flags. Who is the mother? "Gestational motherhood [the host uterus] is the one that should count the most, particularly where there are disputes," says Macklin at the Albert Einstein College of Medicine.

"Courts have looked to genetic parentage, as opposed to carrying the baby," counters Caplan. "I don't think pregnancy adds much from the point of view of law."

Prenatal Testing

Advances in the understanding of human genetics combined with more sophisticated technologies are providing parents with unprecedented amounts of information about their unborn children. While the medical community has generally regarded these tests as a boon, the rapidly expanding amount of prenatal genetic knowledge is causing concern in some quarters. (*See poll results, p. 306.*)

"I'm very interested in embryo diagnosis to avoid disease, but we have to be very cautious about where we are going with this stuff," says Fletcher at the University of Virginia. "As a society, we believe strongly in reproductive choice. But we may bend over backwards to make this information available, then wake up one day and find we've had a history of people making class- and race-based choices, and created sort of a back door to eugenics."

A study of older pregnant women in Georgia found that while 60 percent of white urban mothers over 35 received prenatal diagnosis, less than 1 percent of rural African American mothers did so. "If these inequalities continue, in the future, genetic disability could become a mark of low social class, because your parents had neither the education nor the money to prevent your birth," writes Dorothy C. Wertz, the author of the study and a senior scientist at the Shriver Center for Mental Retardation. [23]

Fletcher and others note that prenatal testing has been used so widely for sex selection in India that there is now a measurable sex imbalance in the population — with potentially serious social consequences. India has banned the use of amniocentesis for the purpose of determining the sex of an unborn child, but couples are now using ultrasound instead.

For 25 years, amniocentesis has allowed doctors to test a developing fetus for certain disorders. Most commonly, the procedure is used to detect Down's syndrome, a form of mental retardation. A woman's chances of bearing a child with Down's syndrome rise dramatically as she ages, from about a one in 1,250 chance in her 20s, to one in 365 at age 35 and one in 30 at age 45. [24]

The test is also used to screen for Tay-Sachs disease, which results in severe mental retardation and early death, sickle-cell anemia and the blood disorder Thalassemia. Testing is done when one or both of the parents are members of ethnic groups considered at high risk of carrying the genes for those disorders — Tay-Sachs testing for Jews of Eastern European origin; sickle-cell testing for African Americans; and Thalassaemia testing for those of Mediterranean descent.

Underlying Causes of Infertility

- Sexually transmitted diseases
- Smoking
- Delaying childbearing
- Exposure to harmful agents in the workplace or in the environment
- Personal and medical factors, such as alcohol and substance abuse, weight, eating disorders, exercise and stress
- Unintended consequences of medical intervention; sterilization; contraception
- Endometriosis, an inflammation of the lining of the uterus

Source: Proceed With Care: Final Report of the Royal Commission on New Reproductive Technologies, *1993.*

And parents who have already had a child affected by a genetic disorder such as cystic fibrosis often will have the test in subsequent pregnancies.

Amniocentesis has become a common part of prenatal care for a certain population of pregnant women — primarily white, well-educated and older. Yet the widespread acceptance of the test does not necessarily mean an equally widespread understanding of the reasons women agree to have it, or an understanding of its impact on their pregnancy.

Doctors, for instance, often assume a woman wants the test because she plans to abort a fetus with a serious abnormality. But there are few studies of the attitudes and experiences of women who undergo prenatal testing, and there is some evidence that many take the test on the advice of their doctors without having reached a decision on what they will do in the event of a positive diagnosis.

Amniocentesis takes place in the second trimester of pregnancy. An ultrasound exam, during which the pregnant woman can clearly see a moving image of the fetus, accompanies the procedure. Results are not available for two to four weeks, during which time many women will begin to feel fetal movement.

Both the experience of seeing the fetus on ultrasound, and of sensing fetal movement, are powerful milestones in a pregnancy. Many women speak of those moments as the time when their pregnancy becomes "real" to them. That they often occur before the results of the test are known can create enormous anxiety.

"One of the things that really irritates me is that most women who go through prenatal diagnosis talk about the extreme stress that they feel," says Hubbard. "They talk about those weeks of uncertainty between the test and the results. Meanwhile, these women are told not to drink a single glass of wine, or a single cup of coffee, to lead utterly healthful and impossible lives, but no one is paying any attention to these weeks of stress."

To avoid some of the stress associated with amniocentesis, some women have turned to a newer prenatal testing technique: chorionic villus sampling. CVS is performed earlier in pregnancy, at about the 12th week. Abortions at that stage are safer, easier and generally considered less emotionally traumatic than second-trimester abortions.

However, CVS is associated with a slightly higher risk of miscarriage than amniocentesis. And a recent study by the Centers for Disease Control and Prevention in Atlanta found an elevated risk of a rare deformation of the hands and feet in infants born to women who had undergone CVS. The CDC study is hotly disputed among supporters and critics of the test. [25]

Work is now under way on a technique that would allow the extraction of fetal blood cells from the mother's bloodstream. This would eliminate the need for invasive techniques such as amniocentesis and CVS, and further move up the time of testing.

Preimplantation Diagnosis

The logical endpoint of efforts to provide earlier and earlier diagnosis is preimplantation diagnosis — examination of embryos for genetic defects before they are transferred to the uterus. The procedure has already been used in a handful of cases involving couples at risk of having children with cystic fibrosis, Tay-Sachs disease and Lesch-Nyhan disease, a rare disorder characterized by retardation, seizures, self-mutilation and aggression.

For now, the technique can only be used in conjunction with in vitro fertilization. It involves removing a single cell from a fertilized embryo that has grown to contain about eight cells. At this stage, the embryo is large enough to work with, but at an early enough stage of development that cell division will continue normally despite the removal of a cell.

The cell that is removed is tested for the disease. Only embryos that do not carry the disease are selected for insertion in the uterus.

Hughes at Baylor College of Medicine, a pioneer in developing the technique, says he had expected that most of the people interested in the procedure would be those with a strong moral opposition to abortion, but who could accept discarding an eight-cell embryo created in a lab. In fact, 70 percent of the couples who contacted him did not fit that profile, and many had already undergone abortions to avoid bearing affected children. "They're coming because [the uncertainty of starting a pregnancy] becomes an emotional and family nightmare," says Hughes.

One Catholic family's first child was born with, and eventually died from, Lesch-Nyhan, which only manifests itself in boys. Pregnant for the second time, again with a son, the couple underwent a late abortion. A third pregnancy was also terminated, the next two ended in miscarriage and a sixth resulted in yet another abortion. Hughes reports that following preimplantation diagnosis, the couple is expecting an unaffected child this month.

But preimplantation diagnosis is viewed with alarm by ethicists across a wide spectrum of thought. Those with strong views on the human potential of laboratory-created embryos see this as another step down the road of devaluing human life. "The mentality is that whatever is defective is unwanted," says Catholic University's Brady. "It is a mentality that comes along with the technology."

Hubbard, who describes herself as resolutely pro-choice, nevertheless says she is leaning toward supporting a ban on preimplantation diagnosis. "It plays into all the wrong social impulses," says Hubbard. "From a health point of view, it is much harder than amniocentesis, and it fosters this dangerous illusion of predictability."

Work is already being done to refine an existing technique, uterine lavage, to allow preimplantation diagnosis on embryos conceived without in vitro fertilization. Uterine lavage involves washing an early-stage embryo out of a woman's uterus before it implants in the uterine lining. If this could be done reliably, preimplantation diagnosis would be available without the expense of IVF, bringing it within reach of a much larger population.

Fost at the University of Wisconsin says concern over preimplantation diagnosis is misplaced. "Unless one has a fundamental moral objection to prenatal diagnosis and selective abortion, I don't see that this expansion raises any new issues," he says. "There is one legal, ethical, very distressing and almost unsolvable issue that arises from all the advances in prenatal diagnosis, and that is the absolute inability of health providers to inform people of their options in a way that allows them to decide properly."

Fost notes that if 500 tests become routinely available for 500 different genetic disorders, it will be impossible for a pregnant woman to review all those tests, understand what they mean and make an informed decision. "Uninformed choices will be unduly influenced by doctors and others," Fost argues, noting that fear of malpractice suits provides doctors with a powerful incentive for offering every available test, while the costs of caring for individuals affected with various genetically determined conditions could provide incentives for insurers and others to encourage selective abortion even in cases of treatable conditions. Meanwhile, even healthy children born after extensive prenatal diagnosis may be affected in unexpected ways by the amount of genetic information contained in their medical records.

Controversy Surrounding Sickle-Cell Testing

Fost was an early critic of one early effort at widespread genetic screening, for sickle-cell anemia. The test involved was not a prenatal one, but many analysts see instructive parallels.

About one in 500 African Americans is likely to develop symptoms of sickle-cell anemia — symptoms that can range from mild to debilitating. About one in 10 African Americans is a carrier of the disease, meaning they can pass it on to their offspring but will not develop symptoms.

In the early 1970s, President Richard M. Nixon chose to fund a high-profile initiative against sickle-cell anemia, some say as a way of showing sensitivity to minority concerns. Several states instituted screening programs to detect carriers of sickle-cell trait. The screening was not accompanied by counseling, the test did not distinguish between carriers and those actually afflicted and the difference between carrier status and the disease often was not made clear. Some states made sickle-cell tests compulsory on entering school or before couples could obtain a marriage license.

In the early and mid-1970s, a number of major airlines grounded or fired employees with sickle-cell trait. The U.S. Air Force Academy made it a policy to exclude sickle-cell carriers until 1979, when one trainee filed a lawsuit. Some African Americans reported being denied employment or insurance, or having their insurance premiums raised, on the basis of their carrier status. Large-scale screening for sickle-cell stopped in the mid-1970s, but some experts believe the experience has made many African Americans suspicious of prenatal testing generally. [26] ■

CURRENT SITUATION

Scientific Frontiers

In Scotland, researchers have reported success at a disquieting experiment: Using ovarian tissue from aborted mouse fetuses, the scientists were able to mature the ovaries in the lab, harvest and fertilize eggs, implant them in a mature female mouse and produce baby mice whose genetic mothers had never been born. The researchers suggest that a similar feat will be possible with human ovarian tissue some day. [27]

Recent studies in South Korea demonstrate that human oocytes [eggs that are not fully mature] can already be harvested from a woman's ovaries and grown to maturity in the lab, for later fertilization and implantation. [28]

As a practical matter, such advances could eliminate the acute shortage of donor eggs for IVF. One researcher suggests that female fetuses miscarried late in pregnancy or anencephalic newborns with no chance of survival could become an important source of ovarian tissue. [29]

In an analogy to organ transplantation, doctors could harvest ovarian tissue or immature oocytes from a young woman declared brain dead after an accident. The ability to harvest immature oocytes from a woman's ovaries for maturation in the lab would allow the retrieval of many eggs at once, without the need for hormone treatments. And the technique could be used to remove and preserve healthy ovaries from young women about to undergo radiation treatment for cancer, in order to maintain their fertility.

These lab-grown oocytes would also be "ideal for screening potentially ovotoxic substances and could substitute for some toxicological studies that are still performed in whole animals," according to Roger Gosden, the leader of the University of Edinburgh research team working on ovary transplants. [30]

But that doesn't address what at least one scientist has dubbed an "unquantifiable yuck factor" — the sense that society is not yet ready to deal with children whose genetic mothers never drew breath. [31]

Last year in Washington, D.C., two doctors at George Washington University, Jerry L. Hall and Robert J. Stillman, cultured defective human embryos to the eight-cell stage then separated the cells, each of which then began to grow and divide as a separate embryo.

"Human Clones!" screamed the headlines. [32] Editorialists turned to their dog-eared copies of *Brave New World* to borrow bits and pieces of Aldous Huxley's bleak vision of the future of human reproduction.

Some researchers pronounced themselves amazed at the uproar. "This has been done for years and years in the animal industry," says Lucinda L. Veeck, a geneticist at the Jones Institute of Reproductive Medicine in Norfolk, Va. "It's an embryo-splitting technique, the same thing that happens when twins are formed."

For Stillman and Hall, the biggest problem may have been journalists' rather imprecise use of the word clone to describe the embryos that resulted from their experiment. The term clone is more commonly used to describe the hypothetical ability to take the genetic information contained in an ordinary cell, such as a skin or muscle cell, and use it to create a new individual with the exact same genetic makeup.

What Stillman and Hall did was actually quite different, since the embryos they worked with contained genetic material from two individuals. Such an experiment carried out with normal rather than defective embryos would result in numerous identical siblings, genetically no different from the identical twins that occur in nature. The researchers' rather modest goal had been to improve the odds for IVF patients by increasing the numbers of fertilized embryos available for implantation.

Nevertheless, their work raises real questions. Combined with embryo freezing techniques, it could allow couples to produce identical twins many years apart. Extra embryos could be preserved as a potential source for donated organs or bone marrow for their sibling, should the need arise. There is even the prospect that frozen embryos could be made available to infertile couples, perhaps on a commercial basis, with the existence of a living child as a powerful advertisement for the product in question.

Political and Legal Issues

As reproductive technologies succeed in simultaneously separating and tangling the threads of genetic, gestational and social parenthood, the political and legal implications are only beginning to emerge.

Last year, the U.S. Supreme Court declined to review a Tennessee court ruling that a man's right not to become a father against his wishes outweighed his ex-wife's claim to seven fertilized embryos created during an IVF cycle before the couple's marriage broke up. Mary Sue Davis had sought the right to have the frozen embryos thawed and implanted in an effort to become pregnant, but the court ordered the embryos destroyed. [33]

Feminists and pro-life activists found themselves united in opposition to the decision, just one of many odd alliances being created in response to the new reproductive technologies. "One of the most fascinating political aspects in the public response [to assisted reproductive technologies] concerns the configuration of groups skeptical of, or hostile to, these new capacities," Robert H. Blank wrote in his 1990 book, *Regulating Reproduction.* [34]

Blank notes that right-to-life groups and religious leaders have made common cause with advocates for the disabled, leaders of minority groups, women's health groups and civil libertarians in opposition to some of these technologies.

Richard Doerflinger, associate director of the Secretariat for Pro-Life Activities of the National Conference of Catholic Bishops, says that if and when researchers locate a gene for homosexuality, gays and lesbians will find "that the nasty right-wingers of the pro-life movement are going to be the best friends they ever had. We would fight any effort to abort based on disability or sexual orientation or

Continued on p. 306

At Issue:

Should the federal government fund research involving the human embryo?

yes

MARIA BUSTILLO, M.D.
Reproductive endocrinologist at Mt. Sinai Medical Center in New York and president of the Society for Assisted Reproductive Technology

FROM *TESTIMONY BEFORE NIH HUMAN EMBRYO RESEARCH PANEL,* FEB. 2, 1994

I am here today as a member of the Board of Directors of the Society for the Advancement of Women's Health Research. . . .

The society is pleased with the lifting of the de facto ban on [in vitro fertilization] research and commends the National Institutes of Health in the formation of this panel to develop ethical guidelines for the review and conduct of human embryo research. As we all know, advancement in the field of human assisted reproductive technology in the past 15 years has for the most part occurred because of research done outside of the United States, primarily in Australia and in Europe. As there had been no federal funding for such work, any research done in this country has been primarily self-funded by the clinics performing the assisted reproductive technologies. This lack of traditional academic participation has prevented the United States from being a leader in the international scientific community at a time of increasing interest in the issues of human reproduction.

Human reproduction is a very inefficient process. It is estimated that for every 100 in vivo exposures of egg to sperm, only about 30-35 ongoing pregnancies result. The study of gamete production and interaction as well as the metabolic, cytogenetic and molecular genetics aspects of embryo development would no doubt make it possible to increase our understanding of human reproduction. Ultimately, this would result not only in an increase in the efficiency and cost-effectiveness of treatments currently available but also in the development of new diagnostic tests and treatments for those couples affected with infertility. Research is also needed to help scientists understand maternal embryonic interaction; this work would not only help to explain implantation failure, but would delineate the frustrating problem of recurrent pregnancy loss. Additionally, enhanced understanding of human reproductive processes would no doubt lead to novel improved methods of contraception. . . .

It is the belief of the Society for the Advancement of Women's Health Research that with reasonable ethical guidelines, peer review and adequate funding, ethical scientists would have a responsible and leading role in advancing the progress already made by their colleagues elsewhere in the world. This progress would not only be in the best interest of American women's health but in the best interest of all people.

no

RICHARD M. DOERFLINGER
Associate Director for Policy Development, Secretariat for Pro-Life Activities, National Conference of Catholic Bishops

FROM *TESTIMONY BEFORE NIH HUMAN EMBRYO RESEARCH PANEL,* FEB. 2, 1994

The federal Ethics Advisory Board which last addressed the question of in vitro fertilization and embryo research, in 1979, came to no firm conclusion on whether human embryo experiments are justified. It concluded that some experiments are justified. It concluded that some experiments in this area should not be pursued; and after concluding that some other experiments would be "ethically defensible but still legitimately controverted," it declined to recommend whether the government should fund them. The board did conclude that "the human embryo is entitled to profound respect," but reached no consensus on whether such respect encompasses "the full legal and moral rights attributed to persons." Since that time, the federal government has declined to fund experiments in this area due to their controversial nature.

More recent attempts to draw a morally significant dividing line between the early embryo and other stages of human development have been unconvincing. . . . We have seen no proof that the early human embryo is somehow radically and qualitatively different from all later stages of fetal development. In the absence of such proof, this member of the human species should be treated with the same respect accorded any human subject who cannot give consent for himself or herself: Experiments should be permitted only if they will serve the health needs of that particular subject, or pose no significant risk of harm or death to him or her. . . .

Human in vitro fertilization (IVF) itself, especially as currently practiced, fails the test of concern for human life. Death rates for embryos produced through this process range as high as 96 percent. Success rates in achieving a live birth are so often misrepresented, and so low in reality, that Congress has acted to require more honest reporting on such matters from the IVF industry. . . .

Besides being concerned for the dignity of nascent human life, we are also deeply concerned about the integrity of marriage and family. When a child produced in the laboratory may have no parent in the ordinary sense (as in cloning), or as many as five (genetic parents, gestational mother and "social" parents); when prenatal girls may be harvested for their ovaries so they can be "mother" though never allowed to be born themselves; when researchers can seriously consider gestating human embryos in "alternative" sites . . . in such cases human parenthood and human dignity have been degraded. Such abuses should be rejected in federally funded research.

Public Concerns About Genetic Engineering

Because of advances in the understanding of human genetics, parents may soon be able to choose the characteristics of their unborn offspring. But not many people may elect to do so. The vast majority of women responding to a recent poll conducted for Redbook magazine opposed using techniques that would allow them to select the sex of their child or improve their child's intelligence or athletic ability. They did support genetic testing that enables parents to determine whether their child will have a disease or disability.

Should genetic testing and gene manipulation be used to:

Discover whether a child will have a disease or disability?	
Approve	76%
Disapprove	18%
Don't know	6%
Select the sex of the child?	
Strongly Approve	2%
Approve	10%
Disapprove	45%
Strongly Disapprove	41%
Don't Know	3%
Increase the child's IQ?	
Strongly Approve	1%
Approve	6%
Disapprove	49%
Strongly Disagree	42%
Don't Know	3%
Improve the child's athletic ability?	
Strongly Approve	1%
Approve	3%
Disapprove	45%
Strongly Disapprove	49%
Don't Know	2%

P.Eloise Fuller

Note: Some totals may not equal 100 because of rounding.

Source: Survey conducted by EDK Associates, New York City, for Redbook. The results are based on telephone interviews with 500 adult women conducted nationwide from Nov. 29-Dec. 3, 1993.

Continued from p. 304

anything else."

To date, there have been no reported cases of an egg donor seeking parental rights, but most observers believe such a case is inevitable. In 1991, an Oregon court granted visitation rights to a man who had donated sperm for artificial insemination.

While egg donors are far more carefully screened than sperm donors, in part to winnow out those who might cause problems in the future, psychological evaluation is far from an exact science. The relationship between known donors and recipients, including sisters or friends, may sour over the years of a child's life.

Genetic privacy is another looming issue, particularly as IVF providers develop new and better tests for preimplantation diagnosis. There has already been one reported case of an insurance company attempting to deny coverage for a child born to a couple who knew, through prenatal testing, that the infant would be affected by a genetic disease.[35] ■

OUTLOOK

Research Guidelines

Since 1980, the federal government has refrained from funding any research relating to human in vitro fertilization or human embryos. (*See story, p. 300.*) Though the Clinton administration has lifted the formal ban on such funding, there still are no guidelines in place for the National Institutes of Health to use in reviewing research proposals. A temporary NIH panel is now in the midst of an attempt to develop such standards.

The panel, headed by Steven Muller, former president of Johns Hopkins University, is due to issue its research and funding guidelines in June. The key policy questions being weighed by the panel include consideration of the moral status of the embryo; ethically acceptable sources of embryos and human oocytes for research; ethical methods of disposing of embryos after research; and whether additional mechanisms are needed to evaluate and monitor embryo research.

The NIH panel is expected to do no more than map out a general terrain for research that will be considered suitable for NIH funding. Even that will not be easy.

At their March meeting, panelists wrestled with a number of fundamental issues, including the troublesome question of whether or not to set a limit on how long or how fully embryos may be allowed to develop in the laboratory.

Right now, scientists here and abroad generally use 14 days as the outer limit for in vitro development for research. It's a limit that was initially chosen because it is somewhere around the 14th day that a developing human embryo first shows signs of what is called "the primitive streak," an organizing line running through what is until that point a mass of undifferentiated cells.

"It's totally arbitrary," argued one panelist, Kenneth J. Ryan, chairman of the ethics committee at Brigham and Women's Hospital in Boston. "It was not done with an eye to the scientific question."

But Ronald M. Green, an ethicist from Dartmouth College, insisted there are benefits to using an event like the appearance of the primitive streak as a signpost. "We always, in matters of life and death, are looking for marker events," Green told the panel. The primitive streak is the first sign that organogenesis, the formation of distinct organ systems, is beginning, Green said. "This is when genetic uniqueness comes into play."

The question has critical implications for researchers. For example, animal studies show there might be major benefits to allowing the unlimited maintenance in vitro, not of embryos, but of embryonic cells that could serve as factories producing supplies of blood, skin or other organ cells for transplant or study. But the embryonic cells needed for such work, known as stem cells, are not present until after the appearance of the primitive streak.

"Within a few years, it might be possible to . . . take a stem cell, and in an orderly way add chemicals, and begin producing blood cells or muscle cells or skin cells, then transplant them into someone who needs them," said Brigid L. M. Hogan, a professor of cell biology at Vanderbilt University School of Medicine. "You could have a cell bank, making these materials available to many people."

While most panelists seemed generally supportive of the idea of embryo research, and reluctant to impose hard-and-fast limits, several spoke of the need to be sensitive to public opinion. "Science is not going to impose a limit for us," said Thomas H. Murray, director of the Center for Biomedical Ethics at Case Western Reserve University. "We need to anticipate what the moral and social concerns might be that would cause us to put a brake on this research." ■

Susan C. Phillips is a freelance writer in Washington, D.C.

Notes

[1] See Ken R. Daniels and Karyn Taylor, "Secrecy and Openness in Donor Insemination," *Politics and Life Sciences,* August 1993, p. 156.

[2] Interview quoted in "France to Seek Legislation Curbing In Vitro Pregnancies," *The Washington Post,* Jan. 4, 1994.

[3] *Washington Post Health*, Jan. 4, 1994, p. 6.

[4] The study and the criticisms were summarized in Nancy Wartik, "Making Babies," *Los Angeles Times Magazine*, March 6, 1994, p. 18.

[5] *Proceed With Care: Final Report of the Royal Commission on New Reproductive Technologies,* Vol. 1, 1993, p. 564.

[6] Quoted in Wartik, *op. cit.,* p. 21.

[7] D.C. Wertz, J.M. Rosenfeld, S.R. Janes and R.W. Erbe, "Attitudes Toward Abortion Among Parents of Children with Cystic Fibrosis," *American Journal of Public Health,* Vol. 81, 1991, pp. 993-996.

[8] Jason Kingsley and Mitchell Levitz, *Count Us In* (1994).

[9] Quoted in Michael Balter, "Researchers Nervous About Bioethics Bill," *Science,* Jan. 28, 1994, p. 464.

[10] Daniel and Norma J. Wikler, "Turkey Baster Babies: The Demedicalization of Artificial Insemination," *The Milbank Quarterly,* Vol. 69, No. 1, 1991, p. 5.

[11] A.D. Hard, "Artificial Impregnation," *Medical World,* April 1909, p. 163.

[12] Wikler, *op. cit.,* pp. 13-15.

[13] Daniels and Taylor, *op. cit.,* pp. 5-35.

[14] See Tamar Abrams, "My Test-Tube Daddy," *The Washingtonian,* March 1994, p. 114.

[15] *Ibid.*, p. 116.

[16] *Artificial Insemination in the United States: Medical and Social Issues,* U.S. Congress, Office of Technology Assessment, 1988.

[17] *Proceed with Care, op. cit.*, p. 485.

[18] See Mary Briody Mahowald, *Women and Children in Health Care* (1993), p. 99.

[19] *Proceed With Care, op. cit.*, p. 527.

[20] *Ibid, op. cit.*, p. 663.

[21] "Surrogacy Under Siege," *People,* Sept. 28, 1992.

[22] *People*, Oct. 26, 1992, p. 165.

[23] Dorothy C. Wertz, "Ethical and Legal Implications of the New Genetics: Issues for Discussion," *Social Science and Medicine,* Vol. 35, No. 4, 1992, p. 496.

[24] March of Dimes, *Genetic Counseling,* 1992, p. 5.

[25] Study and criticisms summarized in Sandra Evans, "Study Finds Risk from Prenatal Genetic Test," *Washington Post Health,* March 22, 1994, p. 9.

[26] For background, see Ruth Hubbard and Elijah Wald, *Exploding the Gene Myth* (1993), pp. 33-35.

[27] R.G. Gosden, "The Biology and Technology of Follicular Oocyte Development In Vitro," *Reproductive Medicine Review,* Vol. 2, 1993, pp. 129-152.

[28] Paper presented by John Eppig to NIH Human Embryo Research Panel, March 14, 1994, p. 3.

[29] *Ibid.* Babies born with anencephaly are missing all or part of their brains.

[30] Gosden, *op. cit.*

[31] Eugene Robinson, "Furor over Fertility Options," *Washington Post Health,* Jan. 11, 1994, p. 6.

[32] See "Cloning Humans," *Associated Press,* Oct. 26, 1993; "Cloning Human Embryos," *The New York Times,* Oct. 26, 1993; "Researchers 'Clone' Human Embryos," *Science News,* Oct. 30, 1993

[33] See *Time*, March 8, 1993, and *The New York Times,* June 14, 1993.

[34] Robert H. Blank, *Regulating Reproduction* (1990), p. 220.

[35] Wertz, *op. cit.*, pp. 496-497.

Bibliography

Selected Sources Used

Books

Birke, Lynda, Susan Himmelwiet and Gail Vines, *Tomorrow's Child: Reproductive Technologies in the '90s*, Virago Press, 1990.

A comprehensive and readable review of the moral, ethical and political aspects of assisted reproductive technologies and prenatal tests. The book gives considerable attention to the impact of the technologies on women's experience of infertility and pregnancy.

Dyson, Anthony and John Harris, eds., *Experiments on Embryos*, Richard Clay Ltd., 1990.

Chapters by experts on the various social and ethical aspects of reproductive technology and research on human embryos cover a wide field. The second chapter provides a particularly interesting overview of the history of human embryo research.

Hubbard, Ruth and Elijah Wald, *Exploding the Gene Myth,* Beacon Press, 1993.

Hubbard and Wald argue against what they see as a dangerous overreliance on genetic explanations for everything from diseases and disorders to sexual and social behaviors. They review the hold that mistaken eugenic theories had in the United States in the early part of this century, and see a similar threat in the current emphasis on prenatal diagnosis and genetic screening.

Robin, Peggy, *How to Be a Successful Fertility Patient,* William Morrow and Co., Inc., 1993.

Written by a woman whose three years of fertility treatments resulted in two successful pregnancies, and intended as a survival guide for infertile couples and individuals, this book also provides a clear, often angry, look at how the new "miracle" technologies appear from the perspective of those who undergo them.

Articles

Abrams, Tamar, "My Test-Tube Daddy," *The Washingtonian,* March 1994.

Abrams tells the story of her decision, as a single woman past the age of 35, to become a mother through artificial insemination by donor. This is a personal account and a practical guide, but it illuminates some of the social forces behind the development and acceptance of assisted reproductive technologies.

Daniels, Ken R. and Karyn Taylor, "Secrecy and Openness in Donor Insemination," *Politics and the Life Sciences,* August 1993.

The authors review the history of artificial insemination by donor, and argue that a new understanding of the problems created for adopted children by the past practice of keeping adoption secret indicate that the children created through donor insemination may also be harmed by secrecy.

Fletcher, John C. and Mark I. Evans, "Ethics in Reproductive Genetics," *Clinical Obstetrics and Gynecology,* December 1992.

This article offers a clear analysis of ethical problems created by the availability of prenatal diagnosis, by the abortion choice that faces those who receive a positive diagnosis, by both the acceptance and the refusal of experimental fetal therapy, and by the absence of federal support for research in fetal diagnosis and therapy.

Gibbs, W. Wayt and Tim Beardsley, "Fertile Ground: IVF Researchers Pioneer the Bioethical Frontier," *Scientific American,* February 1994.

The recent controversial work by researchers at George Washington University, who "cloned" 17 dysfunctional human embryos in the lab, as well as new techniques to diagnose genetic disorders in lab-created embryos, are briefly explained and the ethical implications are reviewed.

Wartik, Nancy, "Making Babies," *Los Angeles Times Magazine,* March 6, 1994.

This article describes the infertility business from inside the lab. It also reviews the risks, high costs and uncertain returns of the new procedures.

Reports and Studies

March of Dimes Birth Defects Foundation, *Genetic Testing and Gene Therapy Survey,* September 1992.

A Louis Harris and Associates survey of 1,000 adults found broad support for gene therapy to treat genetic diseases. The survey also found few of those surveyed had even a basic knowledge of genetic testing or gene therapy.

Royal Commission on New Reproductive Technologies, *Proceed with Care: Final Report of the Royal Commission on New Reproductive Technologies,* Vols. I and II, 1993.

This massive 1,200-page work takes a deliberative look at virtually every imaginable aspect of every known human reproductive technology, with an eye toward recommending legislation and policy to the Canadian federal government.

The Next Step

Additional information from UMI's Newspaper & Periodical Abstracts database

Cloning

Adler, Jerry, "Clone hype," ***Newsweek,*** **Nov. 8, 1993, pp. 60-62.**
A technical advance in embryology by Jerry Hall and colleagues looking for a more efficient means for in vitro fertilization set off a storm of protest when media reports indicated that human embryos were being cloned. Hall's work and ethical questions surrounding its results are discussed.

"By large margin, Americans oppose cloning of humans," ***The New York Times,*** **Nov. 1, 1993, p. B9.**
A *Time*/CNN poll has found that three out of four Americans oppose human cloning, and 46 percent favor making it illegal. The cloning of human embryos at George Washington University Medical Center sparked debate among scientists and ethicists over a proper balance between research and the morality of human engineering.

Callahan, Daniel, "A threat to individual uniqueness," ***Los Angeles Times,*** **Nov. 12, 1993, p. B7.**
Daniel Callahan discusses the potential dangers of human cloning, and calls for public outcry against using the procedure even in the apparently benign practice of aiding infertile couples to conceive.

Fackelmann, Kathy A., "Cloning human embryos," ***Science News,*** **Feb. 5, 1994, pp. 92-95.**
The storm of controversy that has surrounded the Oct. 13, 1993, announcement that two researchers had "cloned" a human embryo is discussed.

Fackelmann, Kathy A., "Researchers clone human embryos," ***Science News,*** **Oct. 30, 1993, p. 276.**
For the first time, scientists have "cloned" human embryos. This accomplishment has raised a host of ethical and scientific issues regarding reproductive research.

Kolata, Gina, "The hot debate about cloning human embryo," ***The New York Times,*** **Oct. 26, 1993, p. A1.**
The debate that follows the announcement that scientists at George Washington University Medical Center had cloned human embryos is discussed.

Kolata, Gina, "Scientist clones human embryos, and creates an ethical challenge," ***The New York Times,*** **Oct. 24, 1993, p. 1.**
A researcher at the George Washington University Medical Center in Washington has cloned human embryos, the first time such a feat has been reported. The huge ethical questions that such an experiment generates are discussed.

McCormick, Richard A., "Should we clone humans?" ***Christian Century,*** **Nov. 17, 1993, pp. 1148-1149.**
The successful cloning of human embryos has sparked an interesting ethical debate, one that has focused primarily on the right to privacy. Cloning raises many ethical issues beyond personal privacy, including the integrity and individuality of life.

Ethical and Moral Questions

Babych, Art, "Reproductive technology report urges ethics," ***National Catholic Reporter,*** **Dec. 17, 1993, p. 9.**
Catholic church officials are concerned about ethical issues related to a report on new reproductive technologies in Canada. The Canadian Conference of Catholic Bishops will address the ethical implications of the technologies.

Baurac, Deborah Rissing, "Infertility: Technology of Conception Produces Ethics Dilemma," ***Chicago Tribune,*** **March 1, 1992, p. 1.**
Medical technologies that improve infertile couples' chances of having babies present a plethora of ethical decisions.

Dean, Malcolm, "New controversies over assisted conception," ***Lancet,*** **Jan. 15, 1994, p. 165.**
Several new controversies have emerged over controlled human fertilization research and treatment sponsored by the Human Fertilization and Embryology Authority (HFEA).

Elias, Marilyn, "Who controls reproductive technology?" ***USA Today,*** **Jan. 5, 1994, p. A1.**
The prospect of scientists creating babies from the eggs of aborted fetuses is igniting a furious debate over the ethical and emotional fallout spawned by such high-tech wizardry.

Gangelhoff, Bonnie, "The Heartbreak of Technology," ***Houston Post,*** **April 10, 1991, p. D1.**
Bonnie Gangelhoff says advances in reproductive technology are piling up so fast that doctors, lawyers and judges don't have time to sort out moral and ethical questions raised by artificial insemination, surrogates and in vitro fertilization.

Gershon, Diane, "New Panel for Ethical Issues," ***Na-***

***ture*, Jan. 17, 1991, p. 184.**
The American College of Obstetricians and Gynegologists and the American Fertility Society have announced that they will establish a national advisory board to set ethical guidelines in reproductive and fetal tissue research.

"Infertility Aid Has Ethics Snag," *Guardian*, May 7, 1991, p. 3.
Doctors have discovered a transplant technique that could help infertile women, but say ethical implications may overshadow the treatment. The procedure involves transplanting ovarian tissue from a fetus to an infertile woman.

Kolata, Gina, "Reproductive revolution is jolting old views," *The New York Times*, Jan. 11, 1994, p. A1.
Ethicists and many members of the public say they are shaken and often shocked by advances in reproductive technology. Although its aims are laudable — helping infertile couples to have children — the new reproductive science is raising piercing challenges to longstanding concepts of parenthood, family and personal identity.

Lauritzen, Paul, "What Price Parenthood?" *Hastings Center Report*, March 1990, pp. 38-46.
The author says current reproductive technologies challenge society to think seriously about social values surrounding childbearing.

Lieber, James, "A Piece of Yourself in the World," *Atlantic*, June 1989, pp. 76-80.
The moral and legal considerations surrounding cryopreservation, a technique for freezing human embryos for later implantation, are examined. Claiming that the process shows insufficient respect for human life, the Vatican has labeled the procedure unacceptable.

Macklin, Ruth; Delaney, Samuel R., "Artificial Means of Reproduction and Our Understanding of the Family," *Hastings Center Report*, January 1991, pp. 5-11.
New reproductive technologies force society to rethink the concepts "mother," "father," "family," the authors say.

"Women's Voices '94 — A declaration on population policies," *Population & Development Review*, September 1993, pp. 637-640.
The text of "Women's Voices '94 — Women's Declaration on Population Policies," a draft created by women's health advocates all over the world that focuses on ethical issues of women's reproductive health and reproductive rights.

Genetic Engineering

Annas, George J., "Crazy Making: Embryos and Gestational Mothers," *Hastings Center Report*, January 1991, pp. 35-38.
The ethical issues of whether individuals should be forced to agree on the disposition of embryos created from their own gametes, and whether genes, contracts, or biology alone determine the status of "mother" and child, are explored.

Busch, Lisa, "Designer families, ethical knots," *U.S. News & World Report*, May 31, 1993, p. 73.
The ethics involved with a controversial sex selection method for unborn babies are discussed. The Ericcson method is used in fertility clinics to choose a child's sex before conception.

Fennell, Tom, "Nearing the Final Frontier," *Maclean's*, July 15, 1991, p. 37.
With genetic engineering, scientists are able to change the genetic makeup of human embroyos. Some scientists have expressed reservations about the idea of re-engineering the unborn.

Pilkington, Edward, "We now have the means to select the baby of our choice but we are losing sight of the moral ground in the debate over reproduction-by-numbers as fears grow that medical technology is out of control," *Guardian*, Jan. 1, 1994, p. 2.
Edward Pilkington reports on how medical technology is allowing parents to basically create children in a paint-by-numbers process. Pilkington highlights the growing number of ethical dilemmas surrounding the issues of fertility.

Roan, Shari, "A Brave New World?" *Los Angeles Times*, Sept. 10, 1992, p. E1.
A controversial micromanipulation technique that can be used both for artificial insemination and to screen a human embryo for genetic diseases before it is implanted is discussed. Ethical questions abound, because the technique can be used to test for certain traits, including sex and eye color.

Smith, Lynn, "For Many, Picking a Child's Gender Is a Fertile Field," *Los Angeles Times*, Sept. 5, 1990, p. E1.
The controversial procedure of using artificial insemination of sperm treated to weed out chromosomes of an undesired sex is discussed.

In Vitro Fertilization

Burstyn, Varda, "Making Babies," *Canadian Forum*, March 1992, pp. 12-17.
The test-tube baby and the technologies that produce it — in vitro fertilization (IVF) and embryo transfer (ET) — are discussed. The powerful anti-woman dimension of medicalized reproductive technologies is examined. (Part 1 of a series.)

Kolata, Gina, "Fertility Advances Leave Trail of Ethical Questions," *The New York Times*, June 5, 1992, p. A10.
As the number of frozen human embryos lying in storage tanks continues to grow, so, too, do the ethical questions surrounding use of the high-tech in vitro fertilization

technique. The ethical problems are exacerbated by the lack of federal guidelines on the issue, something the American Fertility Society has urged.

Morgan, Derek; Nielsen, Linda, "Prisoners of progress or hostages to fortune?" *Journal of Law, Medicine & Ethics,* spring 1993, pp. 30-42.
New reproductive techniques, including in vitro fertilization, have raised questions regarding medical ethics and the law.

Montague, Anne, "Avoiding Misconceptions," *Guardian,* July 19, 1991, p. 30.
The 90 percent chance of infertile couples remaining childless following expensive in vitro fertilization procedures, and moves to force clinics specializing in the procedures to disclose their success rates, are discussed.

Rensberger, Boyce, "NIH panel looks at ethics, standards for human embryo research," *The Washington Post,* Feb. 7, 1994, p. A3.
The newly created NIH Human Embryo Research Panel assembled in Bethesda, Md., to begin reviewing the status of privately funded research in the field of in vitro fertilization and to ponder the thorny ethical and moral issues concerning human embryo research.

Spring, Beth, "Christian Doctors Approve in Vitro Fertilization," *Christianity Today,* June 18, 1990, pp. 56-57.
In an ethics statement passed recently, the Christian Medical and Dental Society (CMDS) approved in vitro fertilization and a number of other new reproductive technologies as long as the sperm and egg are provided by husband and wife.

Menopausal Maternity

Callahan, Daniel, "Babies in Late Life?" *The Washington Post,* Nov. 27, 1990, p. WH6.
Daniel Callahan discusses the ethical questions raised by the new medical technologies that enable infertile women to give birth to babies.

Carlson, Margaret, "Old enough to be your mother," *Time,* Jan. 10, 1994, p. 41.
The controversy surrounding women who bear children late in life is discussed.

Cowley, Geoffrey and Melinda Beck, "How far should we push mother nature?" *Newsweek,* Jan. 17, 1994, pp. 54-57.
Fertility technology is evolving faster than the ability to weigh the cost and ethics of some of the procedures. The latest controversy is women who are past menopause bearing children through in vitro fertilization.

Trafford, Abigail, "Menopausal maternity," *The Washington Post,* Jan. 4, 1994, p. WH6.
Abigail Trafford examines how a brave new technology that is breaking the menopause barrier to childbearing is challenging deeply rooted concepts of the body, as well as stereotypes about women and aging.

White, Michael and Madeleine Bunting, "Ethical hurdles which would thwart British case," *Guardian,* Dec. 28, 1993, p. 2.
The article discusses the ethical implications of a 1993 case involving fertility treatment of a 59-year-old British woman that resulted in the woman giving birth to twins. The treatments, which occurred in Italy, would not be passed under British National Health Service ethical guidelines.

Wolfe, Linda, "And baby makes 3, even if you're gray," *The New York Times,* Jan. 4, 1994, p. A15.
Wolfe blasts those who criticize older women who are having babies now that medical technology enables them to do so, noting that no such criticism has been aimed at men in their 50s and 60s who father children.

Back Issues

Great Research on Current Issues Starts Right Here...Recent topics covered by The CQ Researcher are listed below. Before May 1991, reports were published under the name of Editorial Research Reports.

SEPTEMBER 1992
Domestic Partners
Violence in Schools
Public Broadcasting
Women in the Military

OCTOBER 1992
Depression
U.S. Auto Industry
Youth Apprenticeships
Hispanic Americans

NOVEMBER 1992
Physical Fitness
Privatization
Paying for College
U.S. Policy in Asia

DECEMBER 1992
Crackdown on Smoking
The New CIA
Eating Disorders
Women and AIDS

JANUARY 1993
Hate Crimes
Child Sexual Abuse
Nuclear Fusion
U.S. Trade Policy

Back issues are available for $4.00 (subscribers) or $7.00 (non-subscribers). Quantity discounts apply to orders over ten. To order, call Congressional Quarterly Customer Service at (202) 887-8621.

Binders are available for $15.00. To order call 1-800-638-1710. Please refer to stock number 648.

FEBRUARY 1993
Community Policing
Europe's New Right
School Censorship
Violence Against Women

MARCH 1993
Gay Rights
Aid to Russia
War on Drugs
TV Violence

APRIL 1993
Head Start
High-Speed Rail
Children's Legal Rights
Muslims in America

MAY 1993
Cults in America
Preventing Teen Pregnancy
Software Piracy
National Parks

JUNE 1993
Food Safety
Prostitution
Childhood Immunizations
National Service

JULY 1993
Electric Cars
Population Growth
Downward Mobility
Intelligence Testing

AUGUST 1993
Mental Illness
Bilingual Education
Foreign Policy Burden
School Funding

SEPTEMBER 1993
Suburban Crime
Public Housing
Supreme Court Preview
Immigration Reform

OCTOBER 1993
Airline Safety
Disaster Response
Science in the Courtroom
The Glass Ceiling

NOVEMBER 1993
Paying for Retirement
Charitable Giving
Privacy in the Workplace
Adoption

DECEMBER 1993
U.S. Vietnam-Relations
Learning Disabilities
Child Care
Space Program's Future

JANUARY 1994
Racial Tensions in Schools
South Africa's Future
Worker Retraining
Regulating Pesticides

FEBRUARY 1994
Prison Overcrowding
Water Quality
Religion in Schools
Juvenile Justice

MARCH 1994
Underground Economy
Education Standards
Gambling Boom
Private Management of Public Schools

Future Topics

- ***Democracy in China***
- ***Soccer in America***
- ***Talk Show Democracy***

THE CQ Researcher®

PUBLISHED BY CONGRESSIONAL QUARTERLY INC.

U.S.-China Trade

Can U.S. trade policy improve human rights in China?

After the June 1989 massacre of pro-democracy demonstrators in Beijing's Tiananmen Square, the Communist Party tightened its grip over China, surviving though a combination of rigid political control and sweeping economic reforms. Now the United States faces a crisis in its relations with the 1.3-billion-population nation, which is rejecting U.S. demands for human rights improvements. Having threatened to raise tariffs on imports from China if these conditions are not met by June 3, President Clinton confronts the prospect of undermining America's share of the world's fastest-growing economy. If he yields to the lure of the vast Chinese market, however, he may undermine the United States' credibility as a defender of human rights throughout the world.

INSIDE THIS ISSUE

CQ April 15, 1994 • Volume 4, No. 14 • 313-336

Formerly Editorial Research Reports

U.S.-CHINA TRADE

April 15, 1994
Volume 4, No. 14

The CQ Researcher (ISSN 1056-2036). Formerly Editorial Research Reports. Published weekly (48 times per year, not printed the first Friday of any month with five Fridays) by Congressional Quarterly Inc., 1414 22nd St., N.W., Washington, D.C. 20037. Rates are furnished upon request. Second-class postage paid at Washington, D.C. POSTMASTER: Send address changes to The CQ Researcher, 1414 22nd St., N.W., Washington, D.C. 20037.

COVER: CHINA'S MOST-FAMOUS DISSIDENT, WEI JINGSHENG, IS SHOWN DURING HIS RELEASE IN MARCH AFTER 14 YEARS IN PRISON. HE WAS REARRESTED APRIL 1 ON UNSPECIFIED CHARGES. (REUTERS)

U.S.-China Trade

By Mary H. Cooper

The Issues

Within the next several weeks, President Clinton will face a critical test of his administration's foreign policy. By June 3, he must tell Congress whether China has improved its human rights record enough to continue enjoying favorable trade terms with the United States.

If Clinton adjudges China sufficiently changed, he risks alienating human rights advocates, who consider China one of the world's most repressive regimes. If he says acceptable progress hasn't been made, Congress by law must suspend China's favorable access to the U.S. market. China can be expected to retaliate, threatening sizable American business interests in what is potentially the world's biggest consumer market.

U.S. policy toward China has been shaped in part by the brutal repression five years ago of China's burgeoning democracy movement. On the night of June 4, 1989, the government sent troops into Beijing's Tiananmen Square to quash a student-led demonstration demanding democratic reforms. Hundreds of people died in the ensuing melee, and many others were subsequently executed for "counterrevolutionary" activities in connection with the uprising. [1]

Since the Tiananmen Square crackdown, the Chinese government, under aging Communist Party leader Deng Xiaoping, has maintained its iron grip over the country. Criticism of the political system is not tolerated, and reports abound of torture, the incarceration of political prisoners without trial and other abuses. According to the State Department's annual report on human rights around the world, "fundamental human rights provided for in the [Chinese] Constitution are frequently ignored in practice, and challenges to the Communist Party's political authority are often dealt with harshly and arbitrarily." [2]

Reuters

While the Chinese Communist Party has maintained its traditional disdain for civil liberties, such as freedom of speech and religion, it has strongly supported loosening of state control over the economy. Since they were introduced in 1978, economic reforms have sanctioned private enterprise, foreign investment in Chinese businesses and opening the vast country to international trade. In response, the gross domestic product grew by an astounding 13 percent last year for the second year in a row, making China the world's fastest-growing economy.

Lured by the tremendous potential for profits, American and other foreign businesses also are investing more and more money in China. They initially were drawn to China as a source of cheap labor to assemble products for export. But now that the man on the street in China has more money to spend, American and other foreign businesses also are vying to establish footholds in the country to sell their products locally.

Since China began opening its economy to the outside world in 1979, foreign investors have poured $141 billion into business ventures in the country, including $9 billion from the United States. The total value of U.S.-China trade already has skyrocketed from $14 billion in 1988 to $40 billion last year. (*See table, p. 316.*) Over the same period, U.S. sales in China have grown from $5 billion to $8.8 billion — a 76 percent increase.

Many experts feel that the best way to foster human rights in China is to facilitate the country's integration into the world economy. "There are demands that foreign trade and investment and an increasingly pluralistic economy place on the political system in China to decentralize control," says Richard Brecher, director of business advisory services at the U.S.-China Business Council. "That has been occurring for 15 years. The transformation of Chinese society is real and is one of the great stories of the second half of this century."

To a large extent, Clinton's foreign policy dilemma stems from Democratic Party criticism of then-President George Bush's reaction to Tiananmen Square. Although Bush firmly condemned the Chinese leadership for its brutal treatment of dissidents, he rejected congressional attempts to curtail U.S. commercial activity in China. And during the presidential campaign of 1992, Clinton himself accused Bush of coddling Beijing's leaders and abdicating the United States' traditional leadership role in the struggle for international human rights.

But Clinton also campaigned as a "new Democrat" ready to place U.S. economic interests at the top of his foreign policy agenda. With companies of other industrial countries clamoring to exploit the expanding Chinese market, any move to curtail U.S. corporate involvement in China would undermine that goal.

Last May, Clinton succeeded in convincing a skeptical Congress to extend

Comparing U.S.-China Trade

In the past six years, the value of U.S. exports to China has grown slowly compared with imports, creating an increasing trade imbalance.

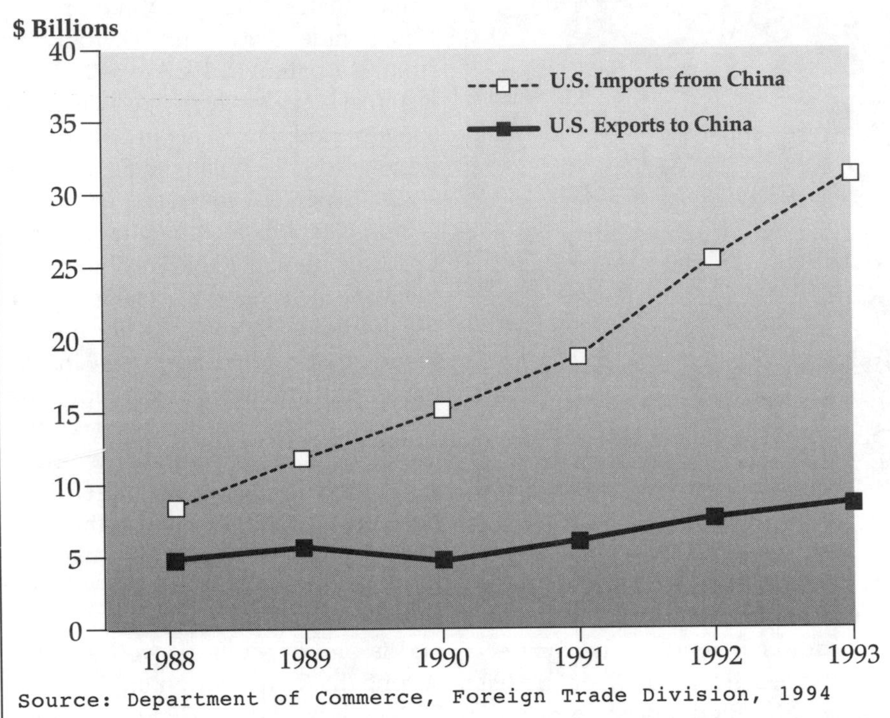

Source: Department of Commerce, Foreign Trade Division, 1994

for another year China's most-favored-nation (MFN) trade status, which allows Chinese imports to enter the United States at the same tariffs imposed on other U.S. trading partners. However, Clinton also issued an executive order listing seven improvements in China's human rights performance (*see p. 327*) that would have to be met if MFN were to be extended this year.

Over the past year, many observers say, China has somewhat improved its treatment of prisoners, releasing leaders of the democracy movement and even allowing a few of them to leave the country. But as the June deadline approaches, many observers say, China appears increasingly unlikely to meet Clinton's seven demands for improvements.

"[T]he government's overall human rights record in 1993 fell far short of internationally accepted norms as it continued to repress domestic critics and failed to control abuses by its own security forces," said the State Department. "In 1993, hundreds, perhaps thousands, of political prisoners remained under detention or in prison." [3] Torture, repression of minority populations, such as Tibetans, lack of due process and harassment of people for religious reasons were among the abuses reported.

The president has appeared determined to stand by his conditions. "As we build a more constructive relationship with China," he said in his Jan. 25 State of the Union address, "we must continue to insist on clear signs of improvement in that nation's human rights record." In recent months, administration officials and lawmakers have travelled to Beijing to underscore that message.

But a showdown with China appeared all the more likely following the firm and public rebuff received by Secretary of State Warren Christopher during his first official trip to Beijing. "China will never accept the U.S. human rights concept," Prime Minister Li Peng told Christopher March 12. "History has already proven that it is futile to apply pressure on China." [4]

Human rights advocates are calling on Clinton to stand firm. "Over the past year, there have been no substantial improvements in China's human rights performance," said Mike Jendrzejczyk, Washington director of Asia Watch, which recently published a report citing the cases of more than 1,700 people jailed in China for political, racial and religious reasons. "As the deadline for MFN renewal approaches, the Clinton administration should not squander the opportunity to obtain meaningful human rights concessions." [5]

Business leaders strongly oppose conditioning China's MFN status on its human rights performance. For one thing, they say, if the United States puts higher tariffs on China's exports, China will retaliate by imposing higher tariffs on U.S. exports and also by curtailing investment by American firms in the Chinese economy. The chief executive officers of AT&T and Ford Motor Co. are among the executives who have come out against suspending China's trade privileges. "Only America's competitors benefit if U.S. trade options with China are diminished," said Robert Allen of AT&T. [6]

More fundamentally, business representatives say, suspending China's favorable trade status won't improve human rights in China. In their view, the most effective way to accomplish that is to do everything possible to facilitate the country's passage toward a free market.

"The best lessons that China will learn about the dignity and treatment of workers, education and training, fair practice free of corruption, environmental consciousness and ethical conduct are being learned from American enterprises," said Lyn W. Edinger, chairman of the board of the American Chamber of Commerce in Hong Kong, which represents most American companies that do business in China.[7]

As an example, Edinger cited the firm he works for, Toronto, Canada-based Northern Telecom, which is building telecommunications networks in China. "Telecommunications do more than any other factor in a society to create the basis of enlightened politics and government," he said. "When information flows . . . abuse [is] more difficult. Any witness to history can see the impact on closed societies of access to information and telecommunications."

So far, the administration has refused to give in to critics of its human rights policy. "[W]e must not assume that a free market in goods can produce or protect a free market in ideas," Secretary Christopher said on his return from China. "Nor can we abandon our responsibility to support human rights around the world. The character of our relationship with China depends significantly on how the Chinese government treats its people. The American people would have it no other way."[8]

As President Clinton and lawmakers consider allowing China to continue enjoying normal trade relations with the United States, these are some of the issues that must be considered:

Has China made significant strides in its human rights performance?

Compared with conditions during Mao Tse-tung's rule, human rights in China today have improved dramatically. In the 1960s, at the height of the Cultural Revolution, millions of Chinese people were arrested, banished to "re-education" camps or summarily executed for criticizing Mao's regime.* Under Deng Xiaoping, who became head of the Chinese Communist Party after Mao's death in September 1976, the political climate is much less repressive.

Deng himself was a victim of the Cultural Revolution — he was stripped of his post as the party's secretary general for six years before returning to office as vice premier in 1973. Once back in power, he quickly embraced economic reforms that have increased the incomes of millions of urban workers, improved public health conditions and prolonged compulsory schooling.

Rising living standards were soon followed by looser political controls over the everyday lives of Chinese citizens. It was under Deng that the pro-democracy movement came into being, with students and workers joining in publicly demanding greater political freedom.

As long as the demonstrators did not threaten the government's one-party regime, freedom of speech and association were tolerated. But when demonstrators filled Beijing's Tiananmen Square, traditional site of Communist Party rallies and parades, calling for an end to the party's control, the leadership drew the line. On the night of June 4, 1989, the move toward greater political freedom came to an abrupt halt when government troops harshly suppressed the demonstrators.

During the five years since the Tiananmen debacle, thousands of Chinese citizens are believed to have been imprisoned for non-violent expression of political dissent. Thousands likewise are thought to have been detained for defying government rules limiting religious practices, including Chinese Christians and Tibetan Buddhists.* Internationally recognized norms of due process, such as the right to a fair trial, are routinely ignored in China, and reports of prison inmates being tortured are commonplace. Capital punishment is applied for a broad range of crimes, including such non-violent offenses as fraud and corruption.

Prison conditions have long been a focus of human rights concerns. In addition to the frequent reports of

* The Cultural Revolution was a nationwide campaign to instill the values of collectivism and class struggle that were the foundation of Maoist communism.

* China invaded and annexed Tibet in 1949.

Foreign Investments in China

More than $40 billion was invested in China by Hong Kong and Macao in 1992. The U.S. invested $3.1 billion, which represents 5 percent of all the foreign investments made in China that year.

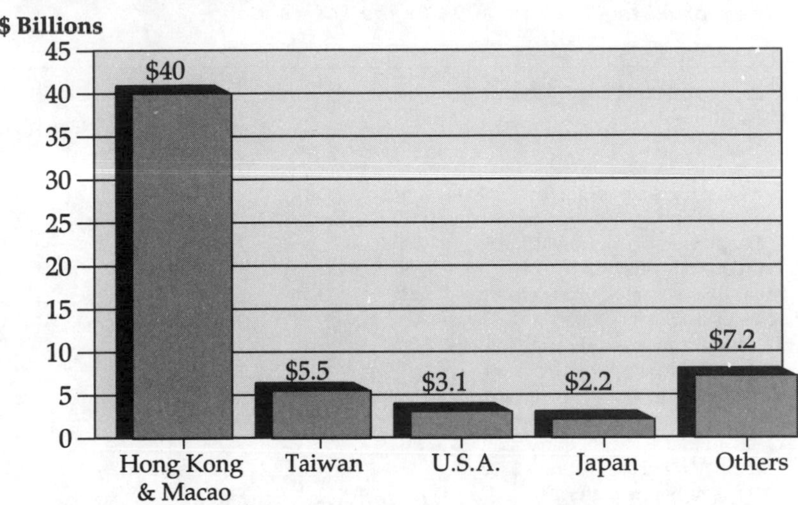

Source: Ministry of Foreign Trade & Economic Cooperation; U.S.-China Business Council.

The Top 20 Imports and Exports

Footwear, clothing and other consumer products requiring low-skilled labor comprised the bulk of the products imports from China by the U.S. in 1993 (top). Aircraft, motor vehicles and other high-technology products led the list of goods exported to China in 1993 by the U.S. (bottom).

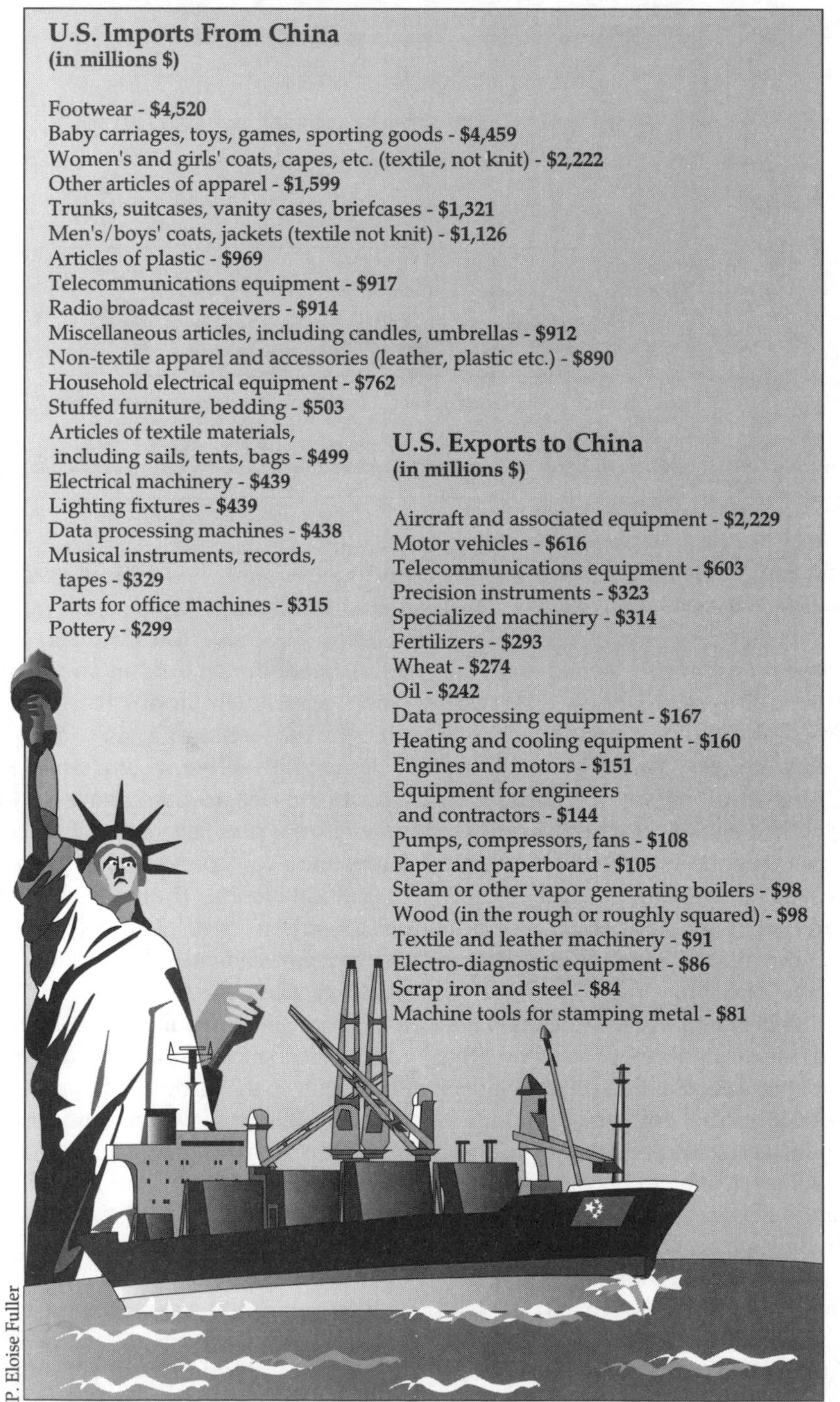

U.S. Imports From China
(in millions $)
Footwear - $4,520
Baby carriages, toys, games, sporting goods - $4,459
Women's and girls' coats, capes, etc. (textile, not knit) - $2,222
Other articles of apparel - $1,599
Trunks, suitcases, vanity cases, briefcases - $1,321
Men's/boys' coats, jackets (textile not knit) - $1,126
Articles of plastic - $969
Telecommunications equipment - $917
Radio broadcast receivers - $914
Miscellaneous articles, including candles, umbrellas - $912
Non-textile apparel and accessories (leather, plastic etc.) - $890
Household electrical equipment - $762
Stuffed furniture, bedding - $503
Articles of textile materials, including sails, tents, bags - $499
Electrical machinery - $439
Lighting fixtures - $439
Data processing machines - $438
Musical instruments, records, tapes - $329
Parts for office machines - $315
Pottery - $299
U.S. Exports to China
(in millions $)
Aircraft and associated equipment - $2,229
Motor vehicles - $616
Telecommunications equipment - $603
Precision instruments - $323
Specialized machinery - $314
Fertilizers - $293
Wheat - $274
Oil - $242
Data processing equipment - $167
Heating and cooling equipment - $160
Engines and motors - $151
Equipment for engineers and contractors - $144
Pumps, compressors, fans - $108
Paper and paperboard - $105
Steam or other vapor generating boilers - $98
Wood (in the rough or roughly squared) - $98
Textile and leather machinery - $91
Electro-diagnostic equipment - $86
Scrap iron and steel - $84
Machine tools for stamping metal - $81
P. Eloise Fuller

Source: Department of Commerce, Foreign Trade Division, 1994

mistreatment and torture, former inmates also charge that the estimated 10 million prisoners of China's vast labor-camp system, or *laogai*, are commonly forced to produce consumer goods for export without pay.

"These ordinary people, among them workers and religious believers, are still locked away as political prisoners, along with common criminals," wrote Harry Wu, a resident scholar at the Hoover Institution who spent 19 years in prison, without a trial, as a political detainee. "They are forced to work or starve, a practice that violates international law and basic decency." [9]

Diesel engines, hand tools and tea are among the products produced in labor camps that may be exported to the United States and other countries, according to Brecher of the U.S.-China Business Council. The Chinese government says it bars the export of goods made in prison and in 1992 signed a memorandum of understanding with the United States prohibiting trade in these products. The U.S. Customs Service, however, is investigating allegations that 31 Chinese prisons still produce goods for export, possibly to the United States.

Earlier this year, the Chinese government backed down on a previous agreement to allow U.S. customs officials to inspect Chinese prisons suspected of making goods for export to the United States. Although the government has agreed to talk with the International Red Cross about interviewing political prisoners, it has yet to allow such contacts.

Some observers cite China's strict population-control policy as a violation of human rights. In an effort to slow the growth of China's huge populace, the government in the late 1970s began rewarding couples for having only one child and fining those who had more. In some provinces, women who defied the policy were forced to undergo abortions or sterilization. The central government says it condemns such coercive measures and contends that local authorities have carried them out in defiance of government policy.

Since last May, when President Clinton defined the conditions of continued MFN status for China, the government has made a few conciliatory steps to soften international criticism of its human rights performance. Last fall, several well-known dissidents were released from prison in an apparent effort to help Beijing's unsuccessful bid to host the 2000 Summer Olympics. But on the eve of Christopher's trip to Beijing, a number of prominent dissidents were rounded up and detained.

This mixed record does not appear to meet Clinton's conditions for extending MFN this year. "In China, fundamental human rights provided for in the Chinese Constitution frequently are ignored in practice," said John Shattuck, assistant secretary of State for human rights and humanitarian affairs, "and challenges to the Communist Party's political authority are often dealt with harshly and arbitrarily." [10]

Human rights groups such as Amnesty International and Asia Watch are even more critical of China's record. Citing more than 250 known political arrests in 1993, Asia Watch concluded that "political repression is increasing, not decreasing," in China. [11]

Is MFN a suitable policy tool to pressure repressive governments into respecting human rights?

China is one of only 10 countries whose trade status with the United States comes up for reconsideration every year.* Under the terms of the 1974 Jackson-Vanik Amendment (*see p. 325*), Congress cannot permanently extend favorable tariff treatment to imports from countries that do not allow freedom of emigration. Aimed initially at pressuring the Soviet Union to ease its restrictions on the emigration of Soviet Jews, Jackson-Vanik has since been extended to cover a broader range of human rights. The law directs the president to certify each year that the country in question has satisfied human rights conditions before Congress can grant it MFN status for another 12 months.

Reuters

Chinese Communist Party leader Deng Xiaoping, appearing on state television in February.

The term most-favored-nation is something of a misnomer, inasmuch as all but 10 U.S. trading partners have MFN status and thus receive the same tariff treatment. In other words, an MFN country does not receive special advantages in the U.S. market but rather is spared being penalized with unusually high tariffs. Failure to receive MFN status may well force U.S. importers who are hit with higher duties to push up the price on Chinese goods to a point where Americans won't buy them.

For a developing country such as China, MFN status can be a crucial element of economic growth. Since Beijing initiated economic reforms in the late 1970s, China has achieved much of its phenomenal economic growth from exports to the United States of inexpensive consumer items. (*See table, p. 318.*)

China's exports to the U.S. amounted to $31.5 billion last year, up from $8.5 billion in 1988, according to the Commerce Department. In fact, Americans are buying so many Chinese imports that the United States ran a $22.7 billion trade deficit with China in 1993.

The American Chamber of Commerce in Hong Kong predicts that suspending China's MFN status will cost as many as 150,000 American jobs, mostly in agriculture, aviation and technology. [12] But human rights advocates are betting that the financial cost in lost exports would be so high that China will be forced to improve political freedoms. "By linking Beijing's abuse of its citizens with its urgent economic objectives," write Robert L. Bernstein and Richard Dicker of Human Rights Watch, "a firm and strategic use of advantageous trade terms is the most effective way to bring about human rights improvements." [13]

But critics of this policy say that past dealings with China offer little evidence that MFN withdrawal would improve the human rights situation there. "Prickly insistence on sovereignty is a particular attribute of the Chinese government," wrote Henry A. Kissinger, who as secretary of State during the Nixon administration spearheaded the U.S. rapprochement with China in the early 1970s. "In China, Western intervention [has been] perceived as an uninterrupted humiliation since the Opium Wars,

---

* The other countries are Azerbaijan, Afghanistan, Cuba, Cambodia, Laos, North Korea, Vietnam, Serbia and Montenegro. Under the terms of a recent bilateral trade agreement with the United States, Azerbaijan will gain permanent MFN status as soon as its legislature ratifies the agreement.

Taiwan: Holding Out Against Beijing

In 1949, Mao Tse-tung and his communist followers drove China's Nationalist government onto Taiwan (then called Formosa), an island off the southeastern coast of China. Ever since, the Nationalists have rejected the legitimacy of Communist Party rule on the mainland, claiming that they are the true government in exile.

When Hong Kong becomes part of China, due to occur in 1997, the Republic of China will remain the only independent territory that was once ruled from Beijing. (In addition to the island of Taiwan, the Republic of China includes Quemoy and Matsu islands and the Pescadores Islands.)

Although they have not regained political control of China, Taiwan's leaders have led their 32,000-square-mile country (roughly the size of South Carolina) on an independent path toward prosperity as one of East Asia's so-called Four Tigers, newly industrialized nations that also include Hong Kong, South Korea and Singapore.

Taiwan zeroed in on success from the beginning, inviting foreign investors from the United States, Japan and other industrial nations to use the island's low-cost labor to produce low-technology finished goods for export, such as shoes, textiles and clothing. As technological development and worker training advanced, Taiwan began manufacturing radios and other light industrial goods, then durable consumer goods such as refrigerators, cars and computers. Today, Taiwan boasts a fully industrialized economy with a modern service sector as well.[1]

Taiwan offers some support for the notion, advanced by supporters of continued business involvement in China, that economic development eventually leads to political reform and democracy. Shortly after establishing a government on Taiwan, Nationalist leaders imposed martial law and banned political parties and labor unions. For 20 years, Taiwanese citizens only could vote in local elections. It was not until the mid-1980s, long after the country's economic boom had begun, that martial law was lifted and national elections were held.

Supporters of continued most-favored-nation treatment of China also point to Taiwan as evidence of the mutual benefits of maintaining good relations with authoritarian governments. Reacting to China's involvement in the Korean War, the United States in 1954 signed a treaty with Taiwan promising to defend the island from invasion. Successive U.S. administrations largely ignored the human-rights abuses that abounded on Taiwan while encouraging American businesses to invest in the island.

The U.S. policy of engagement in Taiwan has been a "striking success" in the view of James R. Lilley, director of Asian Studies at the American Enterprise Institute. "Had America chosen economic disengagement or pulled back its security guarantees during this time — in the name of 'human rights' — the outcome would have been violence and government repression, the opposite of that intended," he writes.[2]

Meanwhile, political differences between Taiwan and mainland China remain deep. The Beijing government adheres to a "one-China policy," requiring foreign governments that want diplomatic relations with Beijing to terminate their official ties with Taipei, Taiwan's capital.

But the two governments have made some progress toward reconciling their differences. Ongoing negotiations begun last April have resulted in agreements on fishing rights, illegal immigration and other marginal issues. At the same time, Taiwanese businesses have become an important source of foreign investment for China's economic expansion.

---

[1] See William H. Overholt, *The Rise of China* (1993), pp. 132-133.

[2] Writing in James R. Lilley and Wendell L. Willkie II, eds. *Beyond MFN: Trade with China and American Interests* (due for publication by the American Enterprise Institute in April 1994), p. 38.

though America is blamed less than other societies. To base Sino-American relations entirely on Chinese progress toward human rights will therefore mortgage both the underlying relationship and progress on human rights — especially as every other industrial nation will eagerly fill the vacuum left by America."[14]

China's other main trading partners, in fact, show little interest in supporting the administration's human rights agenda in China. Japan and other East Asian powers are silent on the issue. And the prime minister of Canada, which currently exports $2 billion in goods to China, flatly rejects the policy. "I'm not allowed to tell the premier of Saskatchewan or Quebec what to do," said Prime Minister Jean Chretien earlier this month. "Am I supposed to tell the premier of China what to do?"[15]

As the United States finds itself increasingly isolated in its policy linking trade relations with human rights concerns, many observers are proposing alternatives that would "decouple" the two interests. While maintaining normal trade and investment relations with China, they say, the United States should turn to multilateral bodies to press for human rights improvements.

"The zero-sum game of MFN should be replaced by a more modulated policy similar to the terms of the Helsinki Accords," suggests Anne F. Thurston, a fellow at the U.S. Institute of Peace and a China specialist. "Rather than blanket withdrawal of MFN, particularly egregious violations of international human rights norms could result in the cancellation or withdrawal of specific deals that are highly attractive to China. Conversely, progress in specific areas could be rewarded." [16]

Would denial of MFN advance the cause of human rights in China?

Apart from the economic consequences of linking human rights with economic relations, there is considerable debate over the impact of current U.S. policy on ordinary Chinese citizens. Some evidence suggests that pressing for improvements in human rights has paid off since Clinton came to office. Numerous high-profile political prisoners have been released since his administration began intensifying the calls for human rights, among them Wei Jingsheng, a well-known leader of the democracy movement, who was released last September after almost 15 years in prison.

But in recent months the government has indicated less willingness to go along with the American demands, arresting several prominent political and religious dissidents. In January, Premier Li Peng signed two decrees barring unauthorized religious ceremonies and the work of foreign missionaries in China. In early March, a week before Secretary of State Christopher arrived in Beijing, Wang Dan, a leader of the 1989 Democracy movement, Wei and six other political activists were temporarily detained. Then, on April 1, the police arrested Wei again on unspecified charges, leaving open the possibility that he may be tried and sentenced to yet another prison term.

As the June deadline for China's MFN renewal approaches, the Chinese leadership's resistance to human rights appeals appears to be building, culminating most recently in the public rebuff last month of Christopher's request for more human rights improvements.

China's hardening stance may well be due to domestic circumstances. Christopher's visit to Beijing coincided with the opening of China's national legislature, and the arrests of dissidents may have been as much an attempt to prevent political protests during the legislative session as a signal of rejection aimed at Washington.

But even if this is true, it's small consolation to U.S. policy-makers. Deng Xiaoping is 89 years old and in poor health, and the struggle for the helm of the Communist Party is already well under way. Human rights advocates say the dangers of a political backlash make U.S. humanitarian efforts all the more urgent.

"We believe the administration should speak clearly, and with one voice," Jendrzejczyk of Asia Watch testified Feb. 24 before the House Ways and Means Subcommittee on Trade. "Only by holding Beijing publicly accountable, in a consistent and comprehensive manner, can the administration both maintain its credibility and exert effective pressure on China to make significant human rights improvements."

There is a risk, however, that any hostile action by the United States against China may strengthen the hand of hard-liners at the expense of moderate reformers. "The period following Deng's death will be inherently unstable," writes Thurston. "American influence over Chinese domestic politics is limited at best, but the withdrawal of MFN would alienate even those political reformers most open to that influence. To risk alienating those forces in China most worthy of our support at the period of greatest potential political instability since the death of Mao in 1976 is not in the interest of China or the United States." [17]

In fact, some critics say withdrawal of MFN might actually lead to a worsening of human rights in China. "If the United States were to withdraw China's MFN status, China's income would fall sharply and the expansion of its market would slow dramatically," writes Bryce Harland, a former ambassador to China from New Zealand. "The people most directly affected would be those in China producing for the U.S. market and those in America exporting to China. . . . Far from advancing the cause of human rights, it could prejudice that cause severely." [18]

Adds Brecher of the U.S.-China Business Council, "The jobs of millions of Chinese who are now employed in export-processing industries, as well as those employees who are now working for American joint ventures in China, would obviously be put at risk" if MFN was linked with human rights in China.

Brecher also predicts that suspend-

How MFN Affects Tariff Rates

Tariff rates are substantially lower on products from countries that enjoy most-favored-nation (MFN) status with the United States. For example, at the 6 percent MFN rate for sweaters, a U.S. importer would pay just $1.80 to bring in a $30 sweater; but at the 60 percent non-MFN rate, the tariff jumps to $18.

	MFN Tariff Rate	**Non-MFN Tariff Rate**
Footwear (uppers over 90 percent rubber or plastic)	6%	35%
Sweaters, shirts, vests	6%	60%
Stuffed toys depicting animals or non-human creatures	6.8%	70%
Artificial flowers, foliage, fruit	9%	71.5%
Cordless handset telephones	6%	35%
Parts and accessories for data processing machines	free	35%
Christmas tree lights	8%	50%

Source: U.S.-China Business Council

ing MFN would cause longer-term damage by undermining the very forces in China that support further reforms. "Clearly," he says, "by taking this unilateral trade action we would be undercutting political forces in China that are pressing not just for reform but for greater Chinese integration into the global community of nations, through membership in the General Agreement on Tariffs and Trade (GATT) and the United Nations."[19] ■

BACKGROUND

Isolation and Repression

China's recent rebuff of U.S. human rights conditions assumes a less hostile character when considered in the context of the country's history, especially its disastrous past contacts with the West. For thousands of years, Chinese rulers dominated much of East Asia and presided over a culture based on Confucian principles of strict social order.

Economically self-reliant and militarily superior to almost all its neighbors, China had few contacts with the outside world, and foreigners were considered to be barbarians. In recognition of their inferiority, foreign emissaries were expected to bring precious gifts and kowtow before the emperor, touching their foreheads to the ground in deference.

The clash between insulated China and the rapidly expanding West became inevitable after European explorers in search of spices and precious metals found their way to the Far East. The showdown came when Britain tried to expand its empire into China in the late 18th century. Rebuffed by the Chinese Emperor Qianlong, who showed little interest in the modern industrial products they offered him, the British eventually invaded China.

The treatment of China by foreign powers during the 19th century left an enduring legacy of mistrust toward outsiders. After the first Opium War (1839-42), Britain introduced opium from Bengal to China, and annexed portions of several major Asian seaports. After China lost a second Opium War to Britain (1856-60), France, Russia and Germany also claimed territories in China's seaports.[20]

China received no kinder treatment from its neighbor, Japan. After wresting the island of Taiwan from China in 1895, Japan returned in the 1930s and invaded the mainland, brutally massacring thousands of Chinese and annexing Manchuria. In 1949, after Japan's defeat in World War II, Chiang Kai-shek's Nationalists were driven from mainland China to Taiwan (then called Formosa) by Mao Tse-tung's communist revolutionaries.

Led by Mao until his death in 1976, the Communist Party ruled China with an iron grip. Social order was maintained at a high price. Tens of millions of Chinese died during a famine that resulted from the Great Leap Forward, a sweeping land-reform program launched in 1958 that organized land in the overwhelmingly agricutlural economy into communes.

Beginning in 1966, the 10-year Cultural Revolution, which sought to eliminate all opposition to the Communist Party, claimed still more victims. Millions of Chinese were denounced by militants citing quotations from Mao's "Little Red Book" and consigned to labor camps or executed for their alleged political crimes.

Push for Reform

Even before Mao died, there were moves within the party leadership to end China's isolation. While other developing nations were modernizing, China remained mired in the past, its economy dominated by agriculture and lacking the basic amenities that could come only through industrialization and trade. Deng Xiaoping, a reformer who was rehabilitated in 1973, won the leadership struggle after Mao's death in 1976 and in 1978 ousted party radicals led by Jiang Qing, Mao's widow.*

In December 1978, Deng launched an ambitious, two-part program of economic "adjustment and reform." The first part involved decentralizing economic decision-making, shifting the responsibility for economic performance from the central government to local authorities and individual enterprises. Agricultural communes were broken up, and farmers were allowed to choose what crops to grow and to keep part of the proceeds from their sale. Industrial enterprises also were freed to some extent from government control and allowed to produce goods according to consumer demand.

The reforms produced widespread benefits in China. With improvements in agricultural and light industrial output, the living conditions of most city-dwellers greatly improved. In 1988, 10 years after the reform effort was launched, the number of television sets per 100 people had risen from 0.3 in 1978 to 10.7 and the number of bicycles from 7.7 to 27.1. And per capita pork consumption — a key indicator of dietary protein — had increased from 2.7 kilograms to 14.5 kilograms a year.[21]

Growing Trade With the West

The second component of Deng's reforms entailed opening China's economy to trade and investment with the West. The opening initially was limited to four "special economic zones" (Shenzhen, Shantou, Zhuhai

* Jiang and the other members of the so-called Gang of Four were arrested in October 1976 and tried. Jiang received a death sentence, which was later suspended.

Continued on p. 324

Chronology

1940s-1960s

Mao Tse-tung takes control of China after World War II.

1949
Mao's communist revolutionaries drive the Nationalists of Chiang Kai-shek from mainland China to Taiwan.

1958
The Great Leap Forward, a sweeping land-reform program, is launched, resulting in a famine that leads to the deaths of millions of Chinese.

1966
The 10-year Cultural Revolution is launched to eliminate opposition to the Communist Party.

1970s *After the death of Mao, China introduces economic reforms.*

Feb. 27, 1972
After a two year diplomatic exchange with the Nixon administration, China signs the Shanghai Communiqué with the United States, paving the way for normalizing relations between the two countries.

1974
As part of the 1974 Trade Act, Congress passes the Jackson-Vanik amendment denying favorable tariff treatment — known as most-favored-nation status (MFN) — to imports from countries that do not allow freedom of emigration.

September 1976
Mao Tse-tung, the founder of the People's Republic of China, dies after 27 years as head of the Communist Party, sparking a struggle for his succession between reformers and hardliners.

1977
In support of President Jimmy Carter's focus on human rights, Congress creates the State Department's Bureau of Human Rights and Humanitarian Affairs.

1978
After emerging as Mao's successor, reform advocate Deng Xiaoping announces the creation of four "special economic zones" where foreign investors will be invited to set up factories to make goods for export. These are the first of many reforms that help bring China into the international trading system.

1980s *The United States and China develop extensive commercial ties.*

June 4, 1989
The Chinese government sends troops into Beijing's Tiananmen Square to quash a student-led demonstration demanding democratic reforms. Scores of people die in the ensuing melee, and many other are subsequently executed for "counterrevolutionary" activities in connection with the uprising.

1990s *Tensions mount in Sino-American relations in the wake of the Tiananmen Square massacre.*

1992
In response to U.S. protests over forced labor, China signs a memorandum of understanding with the United States prohibiting trade in products made in prison. President George Bush twice vetoes legislation that would restrict MFN status for China on the basis of its human rights violations. Democratic presidential candidate Bill Clinton criticizes the president for accommodating Beijing's repressive leadership.

May 28, 1993
President Clinton issues an executive order conditioning the renewal of China's MFN status for 1994-95 on seven specific improvements in human rights.

1993
Economic output in China rises by 13 percent for the second year in a row, sparking high inflation. With improving farm productivity, unemployment in the countryside mushrooms, prompting many rural Chinese to seek jobs in the cities.

Jan. 31, 1994
The State Department releases its annual report on human rights, which finds that the Chinese government "fell far short of internationally accepted norms."

March 12, 1994
During Secretary of State Warren Christopher's first official visit to Beijing, Prime Minister Li Peng publicly rejects U.S. efforts to pressure China to meet American demands on human rights. The preceding week, China's best-known dissident, Wei Jingseng, is detained by police, along with six other political activists.

April 1, 1994
Police arrest Wei Jingseng again on unspecified charges.

China's Top Trading Partners

Hong Kong was China's leading trading partner in 1992, by a wide margin. Different methods of record-keeping and the colony's role as a transshipment point for exports and imports largely account for its lead over other nations. China counts exports to Hong Kong that are re-exported to the U.S. as exports to Hong Kong; the U.S. counts them as imports from China.

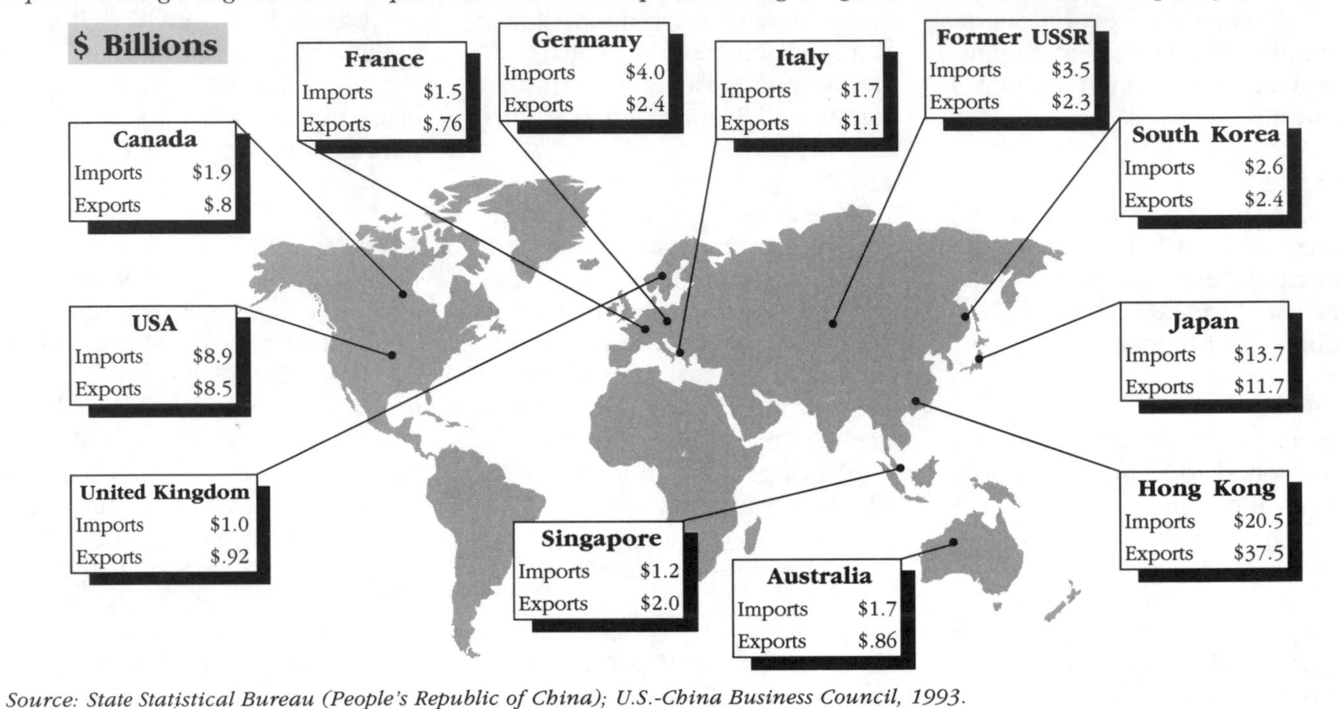

Source: State Statistical Bureau (People's Republic of China); U.S.-China Business Council, 1993.

Continued from p. 322

and Xiamen) in the southeastern coastal region, where industrial facilities were already in place. Foreign investors were invited to set up joint ventures in these areas, mostly to assemble parts into finished products that were then shipped to overseas markets. The foreign firms exploited China's cheap labor and enjoyed exemptions from taxes and bureaucratic interference, while the Chinese acquired technological know-how that enabled them to set up factories of their own. [22]

Because the state continued to control most large industrial facilities, the biggest impact of Western investment was felt in light industry, which produced consumer goods such as bicycles and refrigerators. The areas open to foreign investment were expanded along much of China's coast and eventually, in the late 1980s, encompassed the entire country, including Tibet. As incomes rose with the influx of new investment, local demand for consumer goods grew, and industries began producing for the burgeoning market in China as well as for overseas markets.

The growth in China's domestic market as well as its production of goods for export fueled a rapid increase in trade with the United States, with the total value of exports and imports rising from $4.4 billion in 1983 to $13.5 billion in 1988. [23]

By introducing reforms gradually, the Chinese government has avoided some of the pitfalls that can derail the transformation from state-controlled economy to market economy. In contrast to the former Soviet Union, where the sudden exposure of its economy to competition has caused widespread bankruptcy and scarcity of consumer goods, China has experienced phenomenal growth, reaching a blistering 13 percent in 1992 and 1993.

But the reform process is far from complete, and the threat of social upheaval still looms large in China. Decentralization of China's agricultural sector, for example, has made food production far more efficient but consequently has increased rural unemployment.

Unemployed peasants are flocking to urban industrial centers in search of work faster than jobs are being created. Rapid economic growth is fueling inflation, and government efforts to hold down inflation by keeping price controls on some essential items are far from effective. Today, inflation and unemployment are fanning widespread dissent that is reminiscent of the democracy movement that culminated in the Tiananmen Square tragedy.

U.S. Policy on China

During the postwar era, the United States had little contact with China until 1970, when President Richard M. Nixon began the process of restoring diplomatic relations with Beijing. Improving relations with China enabled Nixon to undermine the Soviet Union, the United States' chief Cold War adversary, whose relations with China had soured.

At the time, the United States avoided attempts to influence China's internal politics: "What is important is not a nation's internal political philosophy," Nixon told Mao during his historic visit to China in February 1972. "What is important is its policy toward the rest of the world and toward us." [24]

This principle was officially recognized in the Shanghai Communiqué of Feb. 27, 1972, which paved the way for normalizing diplomatic relations between the United States and China. "There are essential differences between China and the United States in their social systems and foreign policies," the document states. "However, the two sides agreed that countries, regardless of their social systems, should conduct their relations on the principles of respect for the sovereignty and territorial integrity of all states, non-aggression against other states, non-interference in the internal affairs of other states, equality and mutual benefit and peaceful coexistence."

But while U.S. policy toward the world's two biggest communist countries was following very different tracks, Congress laid the foundations for today's diplomatic conflict with China when it passed the 1974 Trade Act. Section 402 of the act bars most-favored-nation status for countries that do not respect freedom of emigration. Also known as the Jackson-Vanik amendment, this section was aimed at forcing the Soviet Union to allow Jews to emigrate.

Another section of the 1974 law holds that permanent MFN status may not be granted to any country that did not already have it as of Jan. 3, 1975. "That basically meant the Soviet Union and most of its Eastern European allies, as well as Vietnam and Laos," says David Moran, division chief of the State Department's Bureau of Economic and Business Affairs.

President Jimmy Carter, a Democrat, elevated human rights to a prominent place in American foreign policy. Reflecting the heightened concern, Congress in 1977 created the State Department's Bureau of Human Rights and Humanitarian Affairs. The Carter administration's human rights campaigns were aimed primarily at military regimes in Latin America, however. China was not a major focus of official U.S. attention.

The subsequent Republican administrations of Ronald Reagan and George Bush disavowed public condemnation of human rights abuses, preferring instead to press their cases through high-level "quiet diplomacy." Meanwhile, the scope of the Jackson-Vanik amendment was expanded beyond emigration to include a broader range of human rights concerns. "Technically, the law merely refers to freedom of emigration," Moran says. "But it's been interpreted in a very broad sense." [25]

Since the fall of the Soviet Union and the relaxation of bars to emigration in Russia and most of the other former Soviet republics, the United States has granted MFN status to these countries on a year-to-year basis. China also has received MFN treatment each year since its government opened the country to international trade and investment in the late 1970s.

Following the Tiananmen Square massacre, however, China's trade status has been a source of growing, largely partisan, disagreement. Democratic lawmakers, led by Senate Majority Leader George J. Mitchell, D-Maine, and Rep. Nancy Pelosi, D-Calif., criticized the Bush administration for failing to punish the Chinese government with limits on trade and investment. "The hope for freedom in China is as remote today as it was 10 months ago," Mitchell said May 18, 1990. "And, what is worse, the administration has signaled to the Chinese leadership and to the watching world that it views their actions with complacency. That is the wrong signal to send. It is unwise, it is profoundly inconsistent with American ideals, and it is a failure."

In 1992, Congress twice passed legislation requiring the president to certify that China had made "overall significant progress" in the areas of human rights, trade and weapons proliferation as a condition of China's MFN renewal. [26] Bush vetoed both laws, saying they would harm Sino-American relations and result in worse conditions for the Chinese people.

Clinton's Ultimatum

Bill Clinton held up the Bush administration's China policy for criticism during the 1992 election campaign. Only months after taking office as president, Clinton reached a compromise with human rights advocates and lawmakers supportive of business interests. On May 28, 1993, the president issued an executive order approving the renewal of China's most-favored-nation status for the following year. But in a break with previous policy, the order conditioned China's MFN renewal for 1995 on seven specific improvements in human rights.

Two of the conditions are seen as mandatory: They require the Chinese government to allow greater freedom of emigration and to comply with an earlier agreement banning the export of goods produced with prison labor.

The other five conditions — better observance of the 1948 Universal

Treasury Secretary Lloyd Bentsen meets with Vice Premier Zhu Rongji, China's economic czar, on Jan. 20 in Beijing.

Declaration of Human Rights, the release of political and religious prisoners, more humane treatment of prisoners, respect of Tibet's cultural heritage and an end to the jamming of Voice of America radio broadcasts in China — are more open to interpretation. The order requires the secretary of State to base his recommendation for a further extension of China's MFN status on whether the government had made "overall, significant progress" in these five areas.

Although MFN has dominated Sino-American relations in recent months, it was not the only area of foreign policy dialogue during the Clinton administration's first year. In January, trade negotiators reached an agreement on textile exports to the United States, long an area of concern for the American textile industry. China agreed to clamp down on the transshipment of Chinese textile exports through third nations, a violation of U.S. textile import quotas.

And Clinton himself met last November with Chinese President Jiang Zemin at the Asia Pacific Economic Cooperation (APEC) meeting in Seattle, the first meeting of the two countries' leaders since before the Tiananmen Square massacre. Other administration officials, including Treasury Secretary Lloyd Bentsen and Agriculture Secretary Mike Espy, led delegations to Beijing to broaden commercial relations with China.

U.S. negotiators have been less successful in halting arms proliferation, especially China's transfer of advanced missile technology to Pakistan. Charging that China had violated international non-proliferation rules, the United States last year blocked the sale to China of an American communications satellite, a loss to U.S. businesses of up to $1 billion. [27]

Meanwhile, the United States continues talks with Chinese officials as part of its effort to stymie the development of nuclear weapons by the communist regime in North Korea, which is allied with China in a mutual defense pact. In March, North Korea prevented a delegation of the International Atomic Energy Agency from inspecting nuclear facilities in the country. The agency subsequently announced that it could not certify that North Korea was in compliance with the United Nations' nuclear non-proliferation guidelines.

Thus far, China has cooperated with U.S. efforts to bring North Korea into compliance. "China is acting on Korea in its own self-interest," explained Winston Lord, assistant secretary of State for East Asian and Pacific affairs and the administration's leading China expert. "It doesn't want nuclear weapons on the Korean peninsula." [28] But strains between the United States and China are deepening on this issue as well, as China has threatened to veto any attempt by the U.N. to apply sanctions against North Korea if it continues to bar nuclear inspections. ■

CURRENT SITUATION

Phenomenal Progress

Fifteen years after Deng Xiaoping launched his first economic reforms, China has posted phenomenal gains in productivity, trade and living conditions. Economic output doubled during the 1980s and is expected to double again in the 1990s. If it does, China may boast the world's biggest economy by 2010. [29] The value of China's exports and imports with the rest of the world has roughly quadrupled over the past decade, from more than $50 billion in 1984 to almost $200 billion in 1993, according to the World Bank.

With such potential for growth, it is not surprising that American manufacturers and investors are eager to see the current crisis over human rights resolved. American businesses sold goods worth $8.8 billion to China last year, up 100 percent over 1990, while investors put some $3.5 billion into the country's development. [30]

The Americans are hardly alone. The Chinese government reports that

Two Deadlines Confront Hong Kong

On July 1, 1997, Hong Kong will revert to China's control, ending a remarkable chapter in Asia's economic history. [1]

While trade ties between Beijing and the diminutive economic dynamo have never been stronger, political tensions have been mounting as the colony's British governor tries to strengthen its democratic institutions before the Chinese Communist Party takes the reins of government. Negotiations over the terms of Hong Kong's return to mainland rule have run into snags over Beijing's refusal to accept Gov. Christopher Patten's last-minute election reforms. In response to a bill calling for full legislative elections in 1995, the Chinese government threatened to disband all elected bodies in the colony when it takes over in three years.

Despite the political tension, Hong Kong has been a key participant in China's export drive over the past 15 years. The colony has handled more than half the mainland's exports, re-exporting the bulk of goods it receives from China. In 1992, 45 percent of the $58 billion in foreign investments made in China came from investors in Hong Kong.

Most of the money from Hong Kong has funded joint ventures in Guangdong and other coastal provinces, which produce the bulk of China's exports. As a result, the economies of Hong Kong and neighboring Guangdong have become increasingly interdependent. Hong Kong has shifted much of its low-end manufacturing to Guangdong, where wages are lower, while developing its own higher-end manufacturing using the colony's more skilled work force. [2]

Although concern over the possible loss of China's most-favored-nation (MFN) status has focused on the mainland, President Clinton's upcoming June 3 MFN decision also is seen as crucial to Hong Kong. According to the American Chamber of Commerce in Hong Kong, withdrawal of China's MFN status would cost Hong Kong up to $21 billion in trade, $2.9 billion in income and 69,000 jobs. The approximately 900 American firms in Hong Kong, which employ 250,000 people (about 10 percent of the total work force), also would pay a heavy price. [3]

Because firms with foreign investors account for more than a third of China's total exports, Hong Kong and Taiwan — as the leading foreign investors in China — likely would suffer if MFN is suspended. "When we're talking about sanctioning Chinese exports," says Richard Brecher, director of business advisory services at the U.S.-China Business Council, "we're actually talking about sanctioning American, Taiwanese and Hong Kong investment China."

[1] Great Britain leased Hong Kong Island from China in 1898 for 99 years. In addition to the island, located off Guangdong Province, the colony includes several other small islands, Kowloon Peninsula and an area of adjacent mainland leased from China.

[2] The World Bank, *China: Foreign Trade Reform* (1994), p. 15.

[3] From testimony submitted by Lyn W. Edinger, chairman of the board of the American chamber, at the Feb. 24, 1994, hearings of the House Ways and Means Subcommittee on Trade.

in 1993 foreign businesses agreed to invest a record $111 billion in China, almost twice the amount promised the year before. More than 80,000 projects were initiated last year by foreign firms, which invested almost as much in China in 1993 alone as they had in the previous 14 years. [31]

The economic boom is now spreading from the southeastern coast, which was the first region to be opened to international trade and investment, into the rest of the country. Now the action has come to Shanghai, which in 1990 offered economic concessions to foreign investors. China's largest city, with 14.1 million inhabitants, Shanghai already has attracted investments from dozens of *Fortune* 500 companies and last year posted a 15 percent economic growth rate. [32]

China's economy is growing so fast that government leaders are beginning to worry that it may be getting out of control. In his opening address to the National People's Congress last month, Premier Li Peng announced government efforts to slow down the overheated economy, which has pushed the inflation rate to over 20 percent in big cities, posing a threat to political stability.

Citing "some major contradictions and problems in the midst of progress," Li said the government must "correctly handle the relations between reform, development and stability." He also called on the Chinese people to oppose "money-worship, ultra-individualism and decadent lifestyles," suggesting that economic progress has eroded the traditional communist principle of egalitarianism. [33]

Human Rights

With such vast economic interests at stake, the business community is understandably nervous about President Clinton's MFN decision, especially in light of the State Department's recent annual report on human rights in China.

The State Department concluded that China "fell far short of internationally accepted norms" in 1993. "The government detained, sentenced to prison, or sent to labor camps, and in a few cases expelled from country, persons who sought to exercise their rights of freedom of assembly and speech," the report said. Moreover, "Physical abuse, including torture by police and prison officials persisted [and] authorities continued to harass and occasionally detain Christians who practiced their religion outside the officially sponsored religious organizations." [34]

Some Western experts point out that there are real differences over the definition of human rights that may make the administration's demands appear unreasonable to many Chinese. Confucian values, which survive in China, place higher importance on conforming to society than on the needs of the individual.

Chinese human rights advocates "struggling with how to introduce new concepts of human rights . . . argue that the Chinese process of socialization ensures that few adults grow up with the sense of self-respect and individual autonomy that are basic underpinnings to a society where the rights of individuals are honored," writes Anne Thurston. She notes, in particular, the survival of the Chinese tradition of close-knit extended families. "Chinese children are not even taught that they can walk by themselves or stand on their own two feet, let alone that every individual has inalienable rights." [35]

Another fallacy in American human rights policy, according to some observers, may be its heavy focus on political prisoners. When he was released last fall after nearly 15 years in a forced-labor prison for his pro-democracy activism, Wei Jingsheng appeared before the television cameras in apparently good health. Ordinary prisoners, however, fare far worse, experts say. "Most of those incarcerated in Chinese jails would prefer the opportunity to work in prison-run factories, where the food is more plentiful, movement is permitted and prisoners can see the sun," Thurston writes. [36]

Indeed, some East Asian critics of U.S. human rights policy toward China say the United States misunderstands the nature of China's democracy movement. Bilahari Kausikan, director of the East Asian and Pacific bureau of Singapore's ministry of foreign affairs, suggests that Americans misinterpreted the democracy movement altogether and thus failed to grasp the motives for its suppression. "If dramatic scenes [of] students shouting defiance in Tiananmen stirred Western hearts," he wrote, "the emotion obscured the fact that the vast peasantry of China — among the first beneficiaries of Deng Xiaoping's reforms — were largely unmoved.

"Sympathy for the students came, if at all, after the massacre and probably had more to do with the disproportionate use of force against them than with their ideas," he continued. "What may have struck a chord with the peasants was not 'democracy' but complaints against inflation, corruption and nepotism." [37] ■

OUTLOOK

Clinton's Dilemma

Following the Chinese rebuff of Secretary of State Christopher over human rights, President Clinton faces a deepening crisis in Sino-American relations. Clinton must decide by June 3 whether China has shown enough human rights progress since his executive order last year. If his decision is negative, he cannot recommend that Congress extend most-favored-nation status to China for another year.

The loss of MFN status, the World Bank estimates, would effectively bar up to 96 percent of China's exports to the U.S. market. [38] China surely would retaliate by restricting U.S. exports to China. It also would likely favor foreign competitors of American firms in any bids for large purchases, such as aircraft, computers and telecommunications equipment.

In anticipation of just such an outcome, policy-makers are scrambling for a compromise solution. According to Lord, the administration may be considering a proposal by Sen. Mitchell and Rep. Pelosi to only partially suspend MFN. That would entail raising tariffs selectively on exports made by state-owned enterprises while continuing to allow products made by private firms to enter the United States under the normally low MFN tariffs.

"The point here was to try to preserve private enterprise in China, to try to lessen the impact on American business and joint ventures, and lessen the impact on innocent bystanders like Hong Kong and, perhaps, Taiwan," Lord told an audience at the U.S. Chamber of Commerce March 29. (*See stories, pp. 320 and 327.*) Noting the practical problems of such a policy, he added, "In principle, it's a good theory, and one should be looking at it."

MFN critics agree with Lord about the problems. They say it would be impossible, however, to apply sanctions selectively against state-owned enterprises, in part because the reform process is constantly transforming state-owned facilities into private ones. "What happens when a state enterprise starts to privatize and sell stock?" asks Brecher of the U.S.-China Business Council.

Another obstacle to selective sanctions is the multiplicity of sources of the components that go into a given export. "You don't know necessarily who produced a particular widget," Brecher says. "You're buying through a wholesaler who [buys parts] from state enterprises and collective enterprises, from township and village enterprises as well as foreign-invested enterprises. To be able to document the actual source factory is beyond the means of any of the documentation required in trading today."

Aside from the practical problems, Brecher says the policy "begs the question whether China would retaliate against U.S. exports, and I think they obviously would."

Wary of criticism that the adminis-

Continued on p. 330

At Issue:

Should the U.S. deny most-favored-nation trading status to China?

yes

U.S. Rep. Nancy Pelosi, D-Calif.

From *Statement to House Ways and Means Subcommittee on Trade*, Feb. 24, 1994.

On May 28th, 1993, President Clinton moved our U.S.-China policy forward by signing the executive order conditioning the renewal of China's most-favored nation (MFN) trade status on improvements in human rights. President Clinton's action, delineating a series of reasonable and achievable conditions, allowed Congress to speak with one voice regarding China for the first time since the Tiananmen Square massacre in 1989. . . .

The question before us today is whether China has made overall significant progress in meeting the human rights conditions contained in the executive order. Unfortunately, Mr. Chairman, to date China has not made the necessary progress.

The State Department's recently released *Country Reports on Human Rights Practices for 1993* states that the Chinese government's "overall human rights record in 1993 fell far short of internationally accepted norms as it continued to repress domestic critics and failed to control abuses by its own security forces. . . ."

In June, it will be five years since the world was shocked by the . . . massacre of pro-democracy activists in Tiananmen Square, and the repression continues. . . . The issue of forced labor, a must-meet condition in the executive order, illustrates clearly a gap between the Chinese government's words and actions. In 1992, under the threat of MFN revocation, the Chinese government signed a memorandum of understanding (MOU) regarding the export of prison labor goods to the United States. In my view, since the signing, the Chinese government's cooperation with the MOU's minimal standards has been less than satisfactory. . . .

There are three months remaining in which China must act to make overall significant progress in improving human rights. . . . I believe that without prompt and significant action by the Chinese government . . . Secretary [of State William] Christopher cannot recommend to the president that progress has been made.

In closing, I would like to remind my colleagues of why we turned to MFN as a tool to improve human rights in China. We tried moral suasion and conditioning World Bank loans. That accomplished nothing. Conditioning MFN provides real leverage. China's trade surplus with the United States was almost $23 billion in 1993. If it continues to grow at the same rate, it will reach $34 billion in 1994. Chinese government officials desperately want access to our markets, and I believe that they will meet our conditions if, and only if, they believe we are serious about using our leverage. . . .

no

Wendell L. Willkie II
Visiting Fellow, American Enterprise Institute, and former general counsel, U.S. Commerce Department, 1989-93.

Can the proclaimed "conditionality" of MFN really be expected to yield more than modest gestures — such as a few prearranged prison visits or the well-orchestrated release of a handful of political prisoners — from a government that relies on repression to survive. . . ?

Or is not systemic change in China far more likely to occur over time as a result of the inexorably increasing internal pressures — rising out of an exploding market economy and the growing exposure to Western values — for greater personal liberty and the establishment of a rule of law. . . ?

By June 3, 1994, the Clinton administration will be forced to choose between the retention and the withdrawal of MFN. Of course, the very existence of the issue can only be considered a historical accident. Virtually every country in the world today receives at least MFN status from the United States, irrespective of its human rights policies. . . .

[G]iven the disastrous implications for American interests of withdrawal of MFN, the Clinton administration now has a tremendous incentive to characterize any Chinese initiatives in human rights as meaningful progress. Furthermore, a determination by President Clinton in June 1994 that the Chinese had minimally satisfied his conditions would largely be spared the intense criticism from a Democratic Congress that George Bush had received for extending MFN.

But in diplomacy as elsewhere, it is generally unwise to engage in threats unless one is prepared to act on them. Brandishing a mutually destructive and therefore dubious weapon — in pursuit of worthy but very limited objectives — does little to enhance America's standing in the world. This has indeed been a policy that gives every appearance of having been dictated by yesterday's battles in Washington, not today's challenges in China. . . .

The United States has a vital interest in the further development of a stable, prosperous and more humane China, one that plays a constructive role in international affairs. The future of that country will primarily be decided by the Chinese themselves. The most sensible American policy will be one that takes full cognizance of the progress that has already occurred, moves beyond earlier political debates in Washington and effectively pursues the opportunities that China now presents for the advancement of American ideals and interests.

* Excerpted from James R. Lilley and Wendell L. Willkie II, eds., *Beyond MFN: Trade With China and American Interests,* AEI Press, due to be published in April 1994.

China's Growing Global Trade

China's trade with the rest of the world has been growing steadily since 1986. At the beginning of the period charted below, imports outpaced exports, but in 1990 exports took the lead.

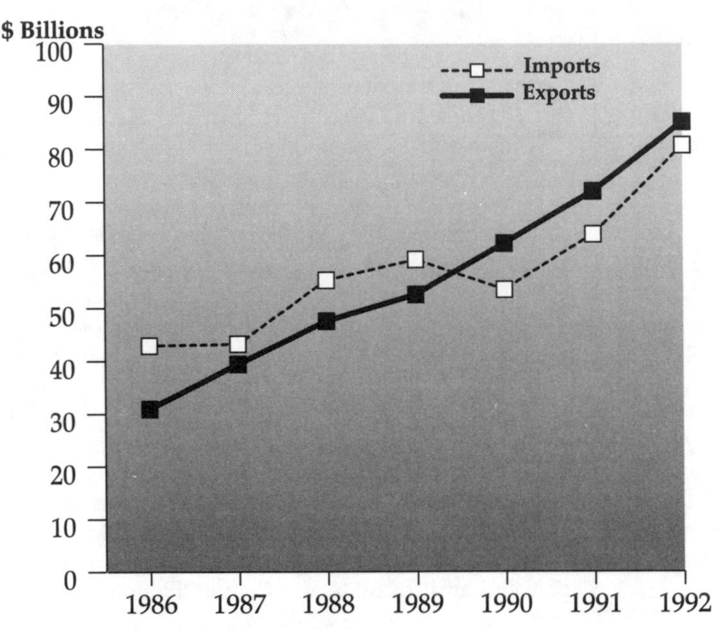

Source: State Statistical Bureau (People's Republic of China); U.S.-China Business Council, 1993.

Continued from p. 328

tration may be tempted to save the day by "moving the goal posts" closer to the Chinese and certifying progress where little has been made, some supporters of current policy point out that China already has taken significant steps toward meeting the June MFN deadline. "Despite all you've been reading and hearing," Lord said, "it is still possible to reach a credible outcome . . . between now and June 3. We made further progress on [Christopher's] trip. We're working very hard to continue that."

As marks of such progress, observers cite several actions by the Chinese government, among them agreeing to begin talks on access to Voice of America programming; providing information on the status of 235 political prisoners; allowing relatives of exiles to travel abroad; and promising to negotiate with the International Committee of the Red Cross on prison inspections.

"Before rushing to judgment about MFN for China," writes Rep. Lee H. Hamilton, D-Ind., chairman of the House Foreign Affairs Committee, "members of Congress and other analysts should judge Chinese actions against the agenda the Clinton administration laid out for it — and not by Beijing's rhetoric, which is mostly intended for a domestic audience. With firm and unified diplomacy, the administration has time to complete his agenda." [39]

Ultimately, many experts on both sides of the human rights debate would like to see commercial relations with China separated from human rights policy. For that to happen, however, Congress would have to pass new legislation specifically permitting China to receive multi-year MFN. That's necessary because of the Jackson-Vanik amendment's requirement that non-market (economists' shorthand for communist) economies be certified annually for MFN eligibility.

"The short-term objective," writes Kissinger, "should be to achieve sufficient progress on the existing human rights agenda to enable the administration to de-link human rights from MFN status once and for all. Afterward, the United States would pursue human rights objectives via normal diplomatic processes within the context of an overall political and strategic dialogue. Such a solution would preserve the dignity of both sides." [40]

While Democratic lawmakers are torn between their party's tradition as champion of human rights and their president's mandate to boost American businesses in the world economy, Republican lawmakers for the most part agree with Kissinger.

"Frankly, we need MFN," said Sen. Don Nickles, R-Okla., at a U.S. Chamber of Commerce meeting March 9. The Chinese people, he said, "are experiencing some economic freedom. I want them also to have some personal freedom and religious freedom. . . . I think through economic engagement we will help make that happen. . . . And if you don't have MFN, I'm afraid you'll lose a lot of that economic freedom, and you will have more punishment . . . and I'd hate to see that." ■

Notes

[1] For background on the democracy movement and the Tiananmen Square massacre, see Ross Terrill, *In Our Time* (1992).

[2] U.S. Department of State, *1993 Country Reports on Human Rights*, Jan. 31, 1994.

[3] *Ibid.*

[4] Cited in Elaine Sciolino, "China Rejects Call from Christopher for Rights Gains," *The New York Times*, March 13, 1994.

[5] Jendrzejczyk testified Feb. 24, 1994, before the House Ways and Means Subcommittee

on Trade. The Asia Watch report is *Detained in China and Tibet,* 1994.

[6] Allen spoke April 4 before a meeting of the Asia Society in New York City. See "AT&T, Ford Back China Trade Status," *USA Today,* April 5, 1994.

[7] Edinger testified at the Feb. 24 trade subcommittee hearing.

[8] Warren Christopher, "My Trip to Beijing Was Necessary," *The Washington Post,* March 22, 1994.

[9] Harry Wu, "China's Gulag," *The New York Times,* Feb. 4, 1994.

[10] Shattuck testified Feb. 1 before the House Foreign Affairs Subcommittee on International Security, International Organizations and Human Rights.

[11] From testimony by Mike Jendrzejczyk of Asia Watch at the trade subcommittee's Feb. 24 hearing.

[12] See "Renew China's Trade Status," *Heritage Foundation Backgrounder,* May 20, 1993.

[13] Robert L. Bernstein and Richard Dicker, "Human Rights First," *Foreign Policy,* spring 1994, p. 43. The authors are the group's chairman and associate counsel, respectively.

[14] Henry A. Kissinger, "China: The Deadlock Can Be Broken," *The Washington Post,* March 28, 1994.

[15] Quoted in Charles Trueheart, "Canada, Eyeing Vast Chinese Market, Deemphasizes Rights Issues," *The Washington Post,* March 29, 1994.

[16] Anne F. Thurston, "American Policy and the Sentiments of the Chinese People," in James R. Lilley and Wendell L. Willkie II, eds., *MFN: Trade with China and American Interests* (due for publication by American Enterprise Institute in April 1994), pp. 105-106.

[17] *Ibid.*, p. 104.

[18] Bryce Harland, "For a Strong China," *Foreign Policy,* spring 1994, pp. 51-52.

[19] For background, see "New Era in Asia," *The CQ Researcher,* Feb. 14, 1992, pp. 121-144, and "U.S. Policy in Asia," *The CQ Researcher,* Nov. 27, 1992, pp. 1025-1048.

[20] See "The Barbarians at the Gate," *The Economist,* Nov. 27, 1993.

[21] Chinese government statistics cited in Rensselaer W. Lee III, "Issues in Chinese Economic Reform," in *U.S. Foreign Policy and the USSR, China and India: Economic Reform in Three Giants,* Overseas Development Council (1990), pp. 79-80.

[22] For background, see "Trade With China," *Editorial Research Reports,* Dec. 5, 1980, pp. 885-904.

[23] See Harry Harding, *A Fragile Relationship* (1992), p. 146.

[24] Richard Nixon, *RN: The Memoirs of Richard Nixon* (1978), p. 562.

[25] For background, see *CQ Almanac,* 1992, pp. 157, 160, 161-62.

[26] HR 2212 would have restricted MFN status in 1992 for Chinese imports. HR 5318 would have conditioned the renewal of MFN status in 1993 for imports from Chinese state-owned enterprises.

[27] The satellite sanctions are under review and may soon be lifted. See Robert S. Greenberger, "U.S. Ban on Satellite Launches in China Is Reviewed Amid Human Rights Debate," *The Wall Street Journal,* March 8, 1994. For background, see "Foreign Policy Burden," *The CQ Researcher,* Aug. 20, 1993, pp. 721-744.

[28] Lord addressed a March 29 meeting of the U.S. Chamber of Commerce in Washington.

[29] See Jerome A. Cohen and Matthew D. Bersani, "Leveling the Playing Field for U.S. Firms in China," in Lilley and Willkie, *op. cit.,* pp. 107-113.

[30] See John. J. Curran, "China's Investment Boom," *Fortune,* March 7, 1994.

[31] See "Foreign Investment in China," *The Wall Street Journal,* Feb. 2, 1994.

[32] See Daniel Southerland, "Economic Boom Shakes Up Shanghai," *The Washington Post,* March 17, 1994.

[33] Quoted in Kathy Chen, "China's Premier Li Calls for Balance Between Economic Growth and Stability," *The Wall Street Journal,* March 11, 1994.

[34] U.S. Department of State, *op. cit.*

[35] Thurston, *op. cit.,* p. 97.

[36] *Ibid.*, p. 97.

[37] Bilahari Kausikan, "Asia's Different Standard," *Foreign Policy,* fall 1993, p. 37.

[38] The World Bank, *China: Foreign Trade Reform* (1994).

[39] Lee H. Hamilton, "Give Christopher Credit," *The Washington Post,* March 30, 1994.

[40] Kissinger, *op. cit.*

Bibliography

Selected Sources Used

Books

Harding, Harry, *A Fragile Relationship: The United States and China Since 1972,* The Brookings Institution, 1992.

One of the country's foremost China experts reviews China's development and its relations with the United States since the Nixon administration normalized diplomatic relations with Beijing more than two decades ago. Of particular interest is the collapse of political consensus on China policy after the 1989 Tiananmen Square massacre.

Lilley, James R., and Wendell L. Willkie II, eds., *Beyond MFN: Trade with China and American Interests,* The AEI Press, 1994 (due for release in April).

This collection of essays published by the American Enterprise Institute presents the views of some the country's most respected China experts on the implications of withdrawing most-favored-nation trade status from China.

Overholt, William H., *The Rise of China: How Economic Reform Is Creating a New Superpower,* W.W. Norton & Co., 1993.

The author, a Hong Kong banker, describes the potential political ramifications of China's phenomenal economic growth since the late 1970s. He warns that U.S. withdrawal of China's most-favored-nation status would jeopardize the progress in human rights that continues with economic development.

Terrill, Ross, *China in Our Time: The Epic Saga of the People's Republic from the Communist Victory to Tiananmen Square and Beyond,* Simon & Schuster, 1992.

A China scholar at Harvard University describes the events — often observed first-hand — leading from Mao Tse-tung's takeover of the country in 1949 to the current economic reform program and the changes they have brought to the lives of ordinary Chinese people.

Articles

"The Barbarians at the Gate," *The Economist,* Nov. 27, 1993, pp. 21-26.

China's rulers historically have treated foreigners as inferiors and resisted pressure from abroad as a challenge to their authority. The United States and other countries doing business with the current regime court failure in their dealings with Beijing if they ignore this lesson from the past, the authors conclude.

Curran, John J., "China's Investment Boom," *Fortune,* March 7, 1994, pp. 116-124.

The last few years have seen a flurry of foreign business investment in China. Attracted by the country's double-digit economic growth, investors also face high risks due to growing inflation and uncertainty over China's political future.

Greenwood, Gavin, "Hongkong: Running Out of Time," *Far Eastern Economic Review,* July 1993, pp. 16-17.

The lead article in a detailed study of Hong Kong reviews the economic and political problems that face the British colony as it prepares to revert to Chinese rule in 1997.

Oliver, April, "The Dragon's New Teeth," *The Nation,* Feb. 21, 1994, pp. 229-232.

While China's rapid economic development holds Americans' attention, some of its Asian neighbors are more concerned about recent moves to beef up China's military.

Segal, Gerald, "The Coming Confrontation between China and Japan?" *World Policy Journal,* summer 1993, pp. 27-32.

China's economic growth poses a direct challenge to Japan's postwar dominance of East Asia, the author writes. While China's integration into the world economy may diminish its threat as a hostile power, its military modernization program may signal new territorial ambitions.

Reports and Studies

U.S. Department of State, *1993 Country Reports on Human Rights,* Jan. 31, 1994.

The annual assessment of human rights around the world finds that China's progress in this area over the past year "fell far short of internationally accepted norms as it continued to repress domestic critics and failed to control abuses by its own security forces."

The World Bank, *China: Foreign Trade Reform,* 1994.

One of a series of reports the bank compiles on developing countries, this exhaustive study of China's economic reforms gained attention in the United States on its release last month because of its prediction that withdrawing China's MFN status would effectively end up to 96 percent of its exports to the United States.

The Next Step

Additional information from UMI's Newspaper & Periodical Abstracts database

China Today

Evans, Michael K., "The Great Wall (Street) of China," *GQ: Gentlemens Quarterly,* June 1993, pp. 64-66.
The Chinese quest for a stock market is discussed. Although the Chinese are far from any attempts at democracy, they are acutely interested in raising their standard of living.

Hutton, Will, "China goes for the big bite," *Guardian,* Dec. 21, 1993, p. 18.
Will Hutton discusses the growing Chinese economy, noting the decline in United Kingdom-Chinese relations due to the dispute over democratic reforms in Hong Kong.

Jian-Hua Zhu and Stanley Rosen, "From discontent to protest: Individual-level causes of the 1989 pro-democracy movement in China," *International Journal of Public Opinion Research*, Fall 1993, pp. 234-249.
Several individual-level causes of protest behavior are examined through a survey just months before the 1989 massive upheaval in China.

Owen, Wu, "Two Chinese rulers making the same history?" *History Today,* February 1993, pp. 6-7.
The Dowager Empress Ci Xi of the Qing Dynasty is compared with Deng Xiaoping. Both figures contributed to the same history by permitting significant advances toward Chinese modernization but suppressing movements of radical reform and democracy, Owen writes.

Solomon, Andrew, "Their irony, humor (and art) can save China," *The New York Times Magazine,* Dec. 19, 1993, p. 44.
The Chinese avant-garde is discussed. Contrary to popular Western conclusions, acts of defiance of the Chinese are not necessarily part of a fight for democracy, but function very legitimately within the system, Solomon writes. Several artists are featured.

Xunwu Chen, "The Chinese dream: Three ideologies in conflict," *America,* Feb. 19, 1994, pp. 4-7.
China's struggle toward modernization in the face of its two main ideological adversaries, conservative Marxism and a Western idea of democracy, is examined. The ideological conflict underlying this struggle is likely to continue, Xunwu writes.

Hong Kong

"A collision course in Hong Kong," *World Press Review*, December 1993, pp. 20-21.
Gov. Christopher Patten's role in the conflict between the United Kingdom and China over Hong Kong is discussed. Patten has gone public with proposals to broaden democracy in the territory before its return to China in 1997.

"China denounces Britain for pushing Hong Kong reforms," *Boston Globe,* Dec. 12, 1993, p. 25.
Chinese Prime Minister Li Peng denounced Britain for pushing ahead with democratic reforms in Hong Kong and urged a Chinese-appointed committee to come up with a plan for undoing them in 1997, when the United Kingdom will return the colony to China.

Frankenstein, John, "Britain, China, and Hong Kong: The pot keeps boiling," *USA Today: The Magazine of the American Scene,* July 1993, pp. 32-34.
The war of words between Hong Kong Gov. Chris Patten and Beijing, which stems from Patten's proposed election reforms, is discussed, and it is questioned whether democracy can exist in the United Kingdom colony after it transfers to Chinese rule in 1997.

Hines, Christopher, "For Hong Kong, prosperity comes before democracy," *San Francisco Chronicle,* Dec. 17, 1993, p. A14.
In light of the British government's December 1993 initiatives to bring democracy to Hong Kong over the objections of the Chinese government, a public opinion poll shows that few Hong Kong citizens support the British efforts if they will lead to political instability and jeopardize the economy. China vehemently objects to the British reforms and said it will dismantle them after taking control of the colony in 1997.

Long, Simon, "A quixotic tilt to Patten's lance in colonial joust," *Guardian*, Dec. 4, 1993, p. 15.
Simon Long discusses the battle between Hong Kong Gov. Christopher Patten and the Chinese government over electoral reforms for the colony, noting Patten's "quixotic idealism" in his efforts to bring democracy to Hong Kong before it reverts to Chinese rule in 1997.

Long, Simon, "Secret limit on HK democracy," *Guardian,* Feb. 14, 1994, p. 12.
New evidence emerged in February 1994 that Britain struck a secret deal with China in the 1980s to limit the development of democratic institutions in Hong Kong. The evidence is contained in the forthcoming memoirs of Sir Percy Cradock, a former British ambassador to Beijing.

Patten, Chris, "The letter and the spirit," *Spectator,*

Jan. 15, 1994, pp. 9-10.
The United Kingdom and China have signed a Joint Declaration spelling out Hong Kong's freedoms and values, but they continue to disagree about the process of democratization. Efforts to secure democracy in Hong Kong are discussed.

Polsky, Anthony, "Hong Kong: Will a free press be brought to heel?" *Columbia Journalism Review*, January 1994, pp. 34-35.
A look at what may happen to the free press when Hong Kong reverts to China is presented. China's communist government has never forgiven the Hong Kong media for their forthright reporting of the 1989 pro-democracy protests.

"World wire: Hong Kong pursues reforms," *The Wall Street Journal*, Feb. 28, 1994, p. A11.
The government of Hong Kong, ignoring China's wrath, has published plans to widen democracy in the British colony. The reform bill would allow Hong Kong to elect all 60 members of the Legislative Council in 1995.

Young, Hugo, "Patten and China battle out odium war over Hong Kong," *Guardian*, Jan. 18, 1994, p. 22.
Hugo Young discusses the status of democracy in Hong Kong in light of Hong Kong Gov. Chris Patten's upcoming January 1994 testimony before the United Kingdom Commons Foreign Affairs Committee, noting that there was no democracy as such until 1984 with the signing of the Joint Declaration.

Human Rights Issues

"China's most famous dissident is detained," *Boston Globe*, March 5, 1994, p. 6.
China's most famous dissident, Wei Jingsheng, was detained in a roundup of democracy activists a week before the arrival of U.S. Secretary of State Warren Christopher to push for human rights.

Courtney, Christine, "China releases 3 pro-democracy political prisoners," *Los Angeles Times*, Feb. 5, 1994, p. A5.
In an effort to deflect human rights pressure from the U.S., China has released three political prisoners jailed for their involvement in the 1989 pro-democracy movement, a U.S. human rights activist said on Feb. 4, 1994.

Dalai Lama, "APEC must challenge China, foster democracy," *Houston Chronicle*, Nov. 19, 1993, p. B15.
The Dalai Lama comments that with leaders meeting in Seattle at the Asia Pacific Economic Cooperation summit, Asia has a great opportunity and responsibility to develop a new sense of interdependence and common goals.

Goldstein, Carl, "Unrepentant dissident defies China's leaders," *Far Eastern Economic Review*, July 15, 1993, p. 86.
Chinese dissident Wang Xizhe is profiled. He spent 12 years in prison for his leadership role in the 1981 Democracy Wall movement.

Lawrence, Susan V., "Ancient games and modern politics," *U.S. News & World Report*, Sept. 20, 1993, p. 75.
Beijing wants to host the Summer Olympics in the year 2000, but international skepticism of China's human rights policies has weakened its bid. The issue of whether awarding the Olympics to China would push it toward democracy or simply encourage repression is discussed.

Quinn-Judge, Paul, "Rights issue is raised as China leader arrives in U.S.," *Boston Globe*, Nov. 19, 1993, p. 1.
President Jiang Zemin of China arrived in Seattle to hold the highest-level meeting between China and the U.S. since the 1989 suppression of pro-democracy demonstrators at Tiananmen Square. In a letter to President Clinton, 270 members of Congress called for the U.S. to take a tough line with China on human rights, trade and other issues.

Southerland, Daniel, "Beijing frees 3 political prisoners," *The Washington Post*, Feb. 5, 1994, p. A13.
Chinese authorities released Xiao Bin, Liao Yiwu and Ding Junze, three men jailed for alleged crimes connected with pro-democracy demonstrations in 1989.

Sun, Lena H., "As U.S., China trade barbs, Beijing gives dissident stern warning," *The Washington Post*, March 9, 1994, p. A13.
As China and the U.S. stepped up their criticism of each other over Beijing's human rights practices, Chinese police briefly detained democracy student leader Wang Dan for the second time in a week.

Moving Toward Democracy?

Evans, Mike, "Unstoppable China," *Industry Week*, Nov. 1, 1993, p. 68.
An economist believes that China will eventually emerge as the major world superpower. China is avoiding the pitfalls that tripped up the Russian Communists by moving toward democracy at a much more moderate pace.

Kelliher, Daniel, "Keeping democracy safe from the masses: Intellectuals and elitism in the Chinese protest movement," *Comparative Politics*, July 1993, pp. 379-396.
Popular protests can help push countries in a more democractic direction, and they can also lead to a tendency toward elite-mass conflict. China's protest movement and the transition from broad-based protest to democracy movement are examined.

Lerner, Marc, "Freedom's pioneers," *Reader's Digest*, May 1993, pp. 156-160.
Since China opened the door to private entrepreneurship in 1979, some 6 million privately owned enterprises now

exist. Lerner tells about four people whose success demonstrates to him the power of liberty at work.

Nathan, Andrew J. and Shi Tianjian, "Cultural requisites for democracy in China: Findings from a survey," ***Daedalus,*** **Spring 1993, pp. 95-123.**
The results of the first national-sample survey of Chinese political culture, which allow a more nuanced look at some related attributes and their distribution among the population, are offered. The overall pattern suggests that political culture may affect democratization in more complex ways than usually acknowledged, the authors write.

"Why China's people are getting out of control," ***The Economist,*** **June 12, 1993, pp. 41-42.**
China's economic changes are succeeding in 1993, where the 1989 pro-democracy movement failed, in breaking the power of the government over the people, according to *The Economist.*

Winchester, Simon, "A regrettable necessity," ***Spectator,*** **July 24, 1993, pp. 15-16.**
Li Sheng-yong, an appellate judge of the Shaanxi Province Higher People's Court in Xi'an China, is profiled. Li explains that he is opposed to democracy for China because he believes that democracy is good only for rich countries, and China is poor.

Taiwan

Chong-Pin, Lin and Man-Jung Mignon Chan, "Taiwan and mainland: A comparison on democratization," ***World Affairs,*** **winter 1993, pp. 117-119.**
The governments and rulers of China and Taiwan had various similarities throughout their histories that could manifest themselves in the years to come, the authors write. The democratization processes in China and Taiwan are examined and compared.

Radin, Charles A., "Taiwanese will vote in local polls that may send ripples overseas," ***Boston Globe,*** **Nov. 27, 1993, p. 8.**
Taiwan is poised for its next step toward democracy, a step certain to complicate foreign policy considerations for the U.S. and other nations with interests in East Asia, Radin writes. In island-wide elections, the Kuomintang, or KMT, which has ruled since losing the Chinese mainland to communists in 1949, is struggling to hold its own in the face of two growing opposition parties, the Democratic Progressive Party and the New China Party.

U.S. Policy

Awanohara, Susumu, "Caution to Peking," ***Far Eastern Economic Review,*** **Feb. 4, 1993, p. 15.**
Bill Clinton's nomination of Winston Lord as his key Asia specialist sends a strong signal to China that his administration will be tougher on China than the Bush administration was, according to the author. Lord will give priority to democracy and human rights, he says.

Awanhara, Susumu, "United States: Collision course," ***Far Eastern Economic Review,*** **Feb. 3, 1994, pp. 18-20.**
The predicted clash in the U.S. over high ideals and economic realities in dealing with China is becoming a reality, Awanhara writes. Democracy and human rights initiatives may be undercutting the U.S.'s ability to integrate into the fast-growing Asian economies, he says.

"China releases 3 prisoners in gesture to U.S.," ***The New York Times,*** **Feb. 5, 1994, p. A4.**
American businessman and human rights campaigner John Kamm said Feb. 4, 1994, that the Chinese government had released three political prisoners, including Xiao Bin, who was jailed for giving a foreign interviewer an exaggerated estimate of the number killed in the 1989 crackdown on the Tiananmen Square democracy movement.

"Education official on U.S. Chinese Student Act," ***Beijing Review*****, July 5, 1993, pp. 11-12.**
In May 1992, the U.S. passed the Chinese Student Protection Act of 1992, alleging that Chinese students participating in pro-democracy demonstrations would be persecuted if they returned to China. A spokesman for China's State Education Commission discusses the Act and Sino-U.S. relations.

Sun, Lena H., "Poetry-reciting apparatchik," ***The Washington Post,*** **Nov. 15, 1993, p. A13.**
Chinese President Jiang Zemin is scheduled to meet President Clinton Nov. 19, 1993, in Seattle for talks seen as a step toward easing relations between the U.S. and China, which have been strained since the Chinese army's bloody 1989 crackdown on pro-democracy demonstrators in Beijing's Tiananmen Square. Jiang, described as a gregarious, poetry-reciting apparatchik, is profiled.

Tyler, Patrick E., "Crossroads for China," ***The New York Times,*** **Jan. 29, 1994, p. A1.**
Tyler examines the new surge of democratic activity that seems to be occurring in China. The Clinton administration has pressured China for more openness, including a loosening of emigration restrictions and freedom for significant numbers of political prisoners. Clinton also is threatening to cancel China's low-tariff access to the U.S. market unless progress is made in human rights. Clinton has confronted China's leaders with a dilemma.

Zweig, David, "Clinton and China: Creating a policy agenda that works," ***Current History*****, September 1993, pp. 245-252.**
The Clinton administration faces a series of important questions as it develops a policy toward China. U.S. policy, with its two overall goals of promoting democracy and freedom worldwide while resuscitating the U.S. economy and the U.S. international economic strength, is discussed. China's territorial disputes with other countries are also highlighted.

Back Issues

Great Research on Current Issues Starts Right Here...Recent topics covered by The CQ Researcher are listed below. Before May 1991, reports were published under the name of Editorial Research Reports.

OCTOBER 1992
Depression
U.S. Auto Industry
Youth Apprenticeships
Hispanic Americans

NOVEMBER 1992
Physical Fitness
Privatization
Paying for College
U.S. Policy in Asia

DECEMBER 1992
Crackdown on Smoking
The New CIA
Eating Disorders
Women and AIDS

JANUARY 1993
Hate Crimes
Child Sexual Abuse
Nuclear Fusion
U.S. Trade Policy

FEBRUARY 1993
Community Policing
Europe's New Right
School Censorship
Violence Against Women

MARCH 1993
Gay Rights
Aid to Russia
War on Drugs
TV Violence

APRIL 1993
Head Start
High-Speed Rail
Children's Legal Rights
Muslims in America

MAY 1993
Cults in America
Preventing Teen Pregnancy
Software Piracy
National Parks

JUNE 1993
Food Safety
Prostitution
Childhood Immunizations
National Service

JULY 1993
Electric Cars
Population Growth
Downward Mobility
Intelligence Testing

AUGUST 1993
Mental Illness
Bilingual Education
Foreign Policy Burden
School Funding

SEPTEMBER 1993
Suburban Crime
Public Housing
Supreme Court Preview
Immigration Reform

OCTOBER 1993
Airline Safety
Disaster Response
Science in the Courtroom
The Glass Ceiling

NOVEMBER 1993
Paying for Retirement
Charitable Giving
Privacy in the Workplace
Adoption

DECEMBER 1993
U.S. Vietnam-Relations
Learning Disabilities
Child Care
Space Program's Future

JANUARY 1994
Racial Tensions in Schools
South Africa's Future
Worker Retraining
Regulating Pesticides

FEBRUARY 1994
Prison Overcrowding
Water Quality
Religion in Schools
Juvenile Justice

MARCH 1994
Underground Economy
Education Standards
Gambling Boom
Private Management of Public Schools

APRIL 1994
Reproductive Ethics

Future Topics

- ***Soccer in America***
- ***Talk Show Democracy***
- ***Traffic Congestion***

THE CQ Researcher

PUBLISHED BY CONGRESSIONAL QUARTERLY INC.

Soccer in America

Will the World Cup spread soccer fever to the U.S.?

The United States is a sports-loving nation, but there's a blind spot in its devotion. Although millions of Americans play soccer, they show little sustained interest in watching it in person or on television. That may change after the 52-game World Cup soccer finals are staged in the U.S. for the first time, starting in mid-June. An estimated 2 billion TV viewers worldwide will watch the July 17 championship game at the Rose Bowl, reaffirming its status as the world's premier sporting event. Meanwhile, organizers of a new professional U.S. soccer league are counting on World Cup enthusiasm to boost the venture's launch next spring. But the troubled history of pro soccer in the United States offers scant hope for instant success.

INSIDE THIS ISSUE

CQ | April 22, 1994 • Volume 4, No. 15 • 337-360

Formerly Editorial Research Reports

April 22, 1994
Volume 4, No. 15

The CQ Researcher (ISSN 1056-2036). Formerly Editorial Research Reports. Published weekly (48 times per year, not printed the first Friday of any month with five Fridays) by Congressional Quarterly Inc., 1414 22nd St., N.W., Washington, D.C. 20037. Rates are furnished upon request. Second-class postage paid at Washington, D.C. POSTMASTER: Send address changes to The CQ Researcher, 1414 22nd St., N.W., Washington, D.C. 20037.

COVER: COBI JONES, A MEMBER OF THE U.S. NATIONAL TEAM, GETS FIRED UP DURING A FEBRUARY ROBBIE CUP MATCH AGAINST BOLIVIA, IN MIAMI. (REUTERS)

Soccer in America

By Richard L. Worsnop

The Issues

The best teams in the world's top sport will showcase their skills in stadiums throughout the U.S. just weeks from now, yet most Americans don't seem to care. For the sport in question is soccer, a game that has never caught on in a big way in the United States at the professional level.

The World Cup championship tournament, the premier competition in international sports, comes to the United States for the first time starting June 17.* From then until July 17, when the two finalists meet at the Rose Bowl in Pasadena, Calif., teams representing 24 nations will play 52 games in nine cities across the country. (*See schedule and map, p. 340.*)

The coming tournament, the 15th in a series dating from 1930, could be the most successful yet. According to the Fédération Internationale de Football Association (FIFA), soccer's governing body, 3.6 million spectators will attend the games. Moreover, a cumulative television audience of 31 billion people in 170 countries is expected to watch some or all of the month-long competition. The World Cup championship game is expected to draw 2 billion TV viewers, or nearly three times the number who tuned in to this year's Super Bowl. (*See story, p. 354.*)

In almost any other country, the prospect of hosting the World Cup would be cause for jubilation. Soccer, after all, is by far the most popular sport on Earth. For many people, it is the *only* sport. Soccer enthusiasts consider the World Cup more prestigious than even the Olympics.

American sports fans feel differently. For nearly 30 years, U.S. soccer buffs have been saying the nation was ready to become a full-fledged member of the world soccer community. But the moment never arrived. Though Americans play and watch a wide variety of team sports, their interest centers on just four — baseball, basketball, football and hockey. One or more of these games is played year-round at the professional level, making it difficult for pro soccer to carve out a separate niche.

Consequently, many analysts doubt that American soccer ever will attain world-class status. "Television is weary of soccer in the United States," declared veteran sports journalist Frank Deford. "It's been led down the garden path too many times." While conceding the World Cup should be a "reasonably popular success," Deford predicted Americans would treat it merely as a novelty — "a little like the Bolshoi Ballet or the Chinese Acrobats coming to town." [1]

A recent Harris Poll indicated how far soccer has to go before achieving broad popularity in this country. Only 25 percent of the respondents to a survey in early February knew the World Cup involved soccer, and just 18 percent were aware it would be held this year. In addition, 53 percent said they weren't interested in watching a World Cup game on television.

Roy Wegerle, a likely member of the U.S. team, believes American attitudes are shaped by ignorance and unrealistic expectations. "The U.S. public is very uneducated as far as soccer goes," said Wegerle, a South African by birth. "They expect any team wearing the U.S. colors to win every time they play." [2]

At the 1992 Summer Olympics in Barcelona, Spain, Wegerle noted, Americans were confident the U.S. "Dream Team" would win every basketball game it played by a wide margin. The fans got their wish. Now "they expect their soccer team to do the same" in the World Cup.

U.S. sports fans "do not understand the power structure of world soccer," Wegerle added. "They don't appreciate the difference, for instance, between Italy and Greece, and they think a nation as small as Holland should prove no problem for the U.S." [3]

Even if most Americans haven't a clue about the professional game, many of them know a lot about amateur soccer. According to the Soccer Industry Council of America, 15.2 million people age 6 or older played soccer in 1992, the most recent year for which complete data are available. The council also found that 40 percent of the players were "frequent participants," playing 25 or more days a year. [4]

Three-fourths of the players in the council's survey — 11.6 million in all — were under 18. That makes soccer the nation's third-most-popular youth team sport, after basketball and volleyball — and well ahead of baseball, football and hockey. [5]

Moreover, anecdotal evidence suggests many U.S. youth soccer players were encouraged to take up the sport by

---

* Germany plays Bolivia at Soldier Field in Chicago in the opening game. Spain plays South Korea at the Cotton Bowl in Dallas later the same day.

Tracking the 1994 World Cup Tournament

The 24 teams competing in the first round of the World Cup tournament are divided into six groups. Each team plays three games with other teams in its group, each at a different site. The tournament begins June 17 with games between Germany and Bolivia, at Chicago's Soldier Field, and Spain and South Korea, at the Cotton Bowl in Dallas. After several more elimination rounds, the championship game will be held July 17, at the Rose Bowl in Pasadena, Calif.

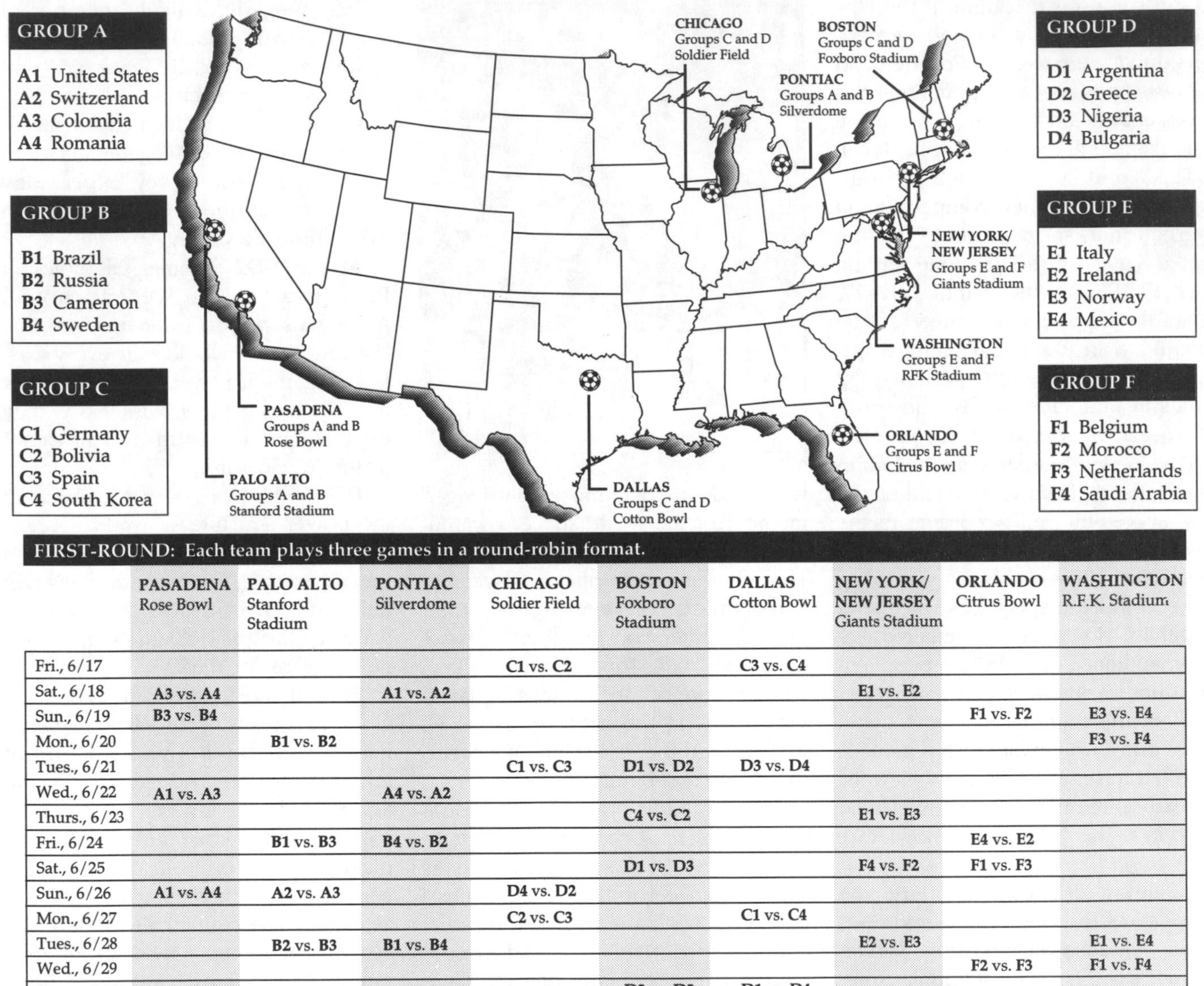

FIRST-ROUND: Each team plays three games in a round-robin format.

	PASADENA Rose Bowl	PALO ALTO Stanford Stadium	PONTIAC Silverdome	CHICAGO Soldier Field	BOSTON Foxboro Stadium	DALLAS Cotton Bowl	NEW YORK/ NEW JERSEY Giants Stadium	ORLANDO Citrus Bowl	WASHINGTON R.F.K. Stadium
Fri., 6/17				C1 vs. C2		C3 vs. C4			
Sat., 6/18	A3 vs. A4		A1 vs. A2				E1 vs. E2		
Sun., 6/19	B3 vs. B4							F1 vs. F2	E3 vs. E4
Mon., 6/20		B1 vs. B2							F3 vs. F4
Tues., 6/21				C1 vs. C3	D1 vs. D2	D3 vs. D4			
Wed., 6/22	A1 vs. A3		A4 vs. A2						
Thurs., 6/23					C4 vs. C2		E1 vs. E3		
Fri., 6/24		B1 vs. B3	B4 vs. B2					E4 vs. E2	
Sat., 6/25					D1 vs. D3		F4 vs. F2	F1 vs. F3	
Sun., 6/26	A1 vs. A4	A2 vs. A3		D4 vs. D2					
Mon., 6/27				C2 vs. C3		C1 vs. C4			
Tues., 6/28		B2 vs. B3	B1 vs. B4				E2 vs. E3		E1 vs. E4
Wed., 6/29								F2 vs. F3	F1 vs. F4
Thurs., 6/30					D2 vs. D3	D1 vs. D4			

Source: World Cup USA 1994, February 1994

a parent or sibling who also played it. As appreciation of the game passes from generation to generation, soccer promoters hope, an indigenous "soccer culture" may finally emerge in the United States.

This year's World Cup may be a crucial milestone for U.S. soccer. A more meaningful test will come next April, with the launch of Major League Soccer (MLS) in 12 cities (*see p. 352*). Establishment of such a league was one of the conditions laid down by FIFA in awarding the 1994 World Cup to the United States. Beverly Hills, Calif., lawyer Alan I. Rothenberg, president of the United States Soccer Federation, has said, "we will have failed" if a new league is not in place by 1995. [6]

However, a history studded with false starts makes some observers hesitant to predict a bright future for U.S. soccer. The sport's ultimate fate in this country, they believe, may hinge on the answer to this question:

Is the United States ready to embrace professional soccer?

Coaches and players agree that a first-rate professional league is needed to complete American soccer's transition to major-sport status. Otherwise, says George Washington University men's soccer coach George Lidster, "soccer will be in danger of becoming like softball" — a game that many Americans play but few take seriously. "Soccer won't grow without a professional league," says Lidster, "because the kids who play it will have no soccer aspirations beyond college."

The U.S. soccer community is divided on whether the country is ready to support pro soccer wholeheartedly. John Griffin, senior press officer for World Cup USA 94, credits the defunct North American Soccer League (NASL) with sparking the soccer-playing boom in schools and colleges.

"You could even say the NASL brought the World Cup to the United States," Griffin says, "because I doubt we could have been chosen without showing FIFA how many people play the sport in this country. We have the participants; now we have to develop soccer spectators." He believes the World Cup will help his group do just that, putting it "in perfect position to kick off Major League Soccer."

Others see pro soccer's prospects as more iffy. Clay Berling, publisher of *Soccer America*, a weekly tabloid, wrote that the soccer community "isn't big enough by itself, but more than that, it is suspicious of anyone 'making money in soccer.' To a large extent, people in soccer are content with their own involvement or with that of their children. This is soccer to them." [7]

Lidster feels television will determine the U.S. pro game's fate. "For a sport to succeed in this country, it's got to be accepted by the masses," he says. "And the only way that can happen in such a vast country is to be seen on TV. If soccer's not there, it has no credibility."

Reuters

Chris Henderson of the U.S. team and Pan Keun Kim of South Korea go for the ball during a March scrimmage in Los Angeles.

The situation overseas is quite different, notes Joe Morrone, men's soccer coach at the University of Connecticut. "In Europe, youngsters grow up with soccer on television, soccer on television and soccer on television," he says. "They're bombarded with one sport — and only one sport. In this country, we're exposed to a much greater variety."

Soccer has never become a TV sports staple in the United States for the most basic of reasons — few Americans watch it. As a result, ABC and ESPN paid only $11 million for the rights to televise this summer's World Cup tournament. (By comparison, Fox television recently paid $1.58 billion for the rights to the next four years of National Football League games.)

ESPN and ESPN2 also will televise 35 regular-season games when MLS soccer starts up next season, with ABC covering the championship.

Boosters of U.S. pro soccer fret that MLS won't be able to sign the best available players without a multi-million-dollar TV contract. But broadcasters and sponsors will remain wary of soccer until the sport develops a large group of home viewers.

Anson Dorrance, legendary women's soccer coach at the University of North Carolina, believes soccer in the United States is fundamentally more of a participatory than a spectator sport. "If there's a pro soccer game on TV at 2 o'clock on Sunday and a local pickup game is scheduled for the same time, I'll go play pickup soccer," he says. "Our sport actually competes with itself. All of us involved in the game would rather play it right now than watch it."

Some soccer enthusiasts have discussed the possibility of a women's professional league. But Dorrance, whose teams have dominated women's college soccer for more than a decade, doesn't think the time is ripe. "Even though our crowds are starting to get bigger, they'd have to become huge for a women's professional league to survive. And not just at North Carolina but all over the country." *

* Attendance at University of North Carolina women's soccer games averages between 1,000 and 2,000 during the regular season and between 3,000 and 6,000 during the playoffs.

Promotional Blizzard to Greet World Cup

Sports fans in the United States may not be fanatics about soccer, but they'll find it hard to ignore as the World Cup tournament draws closer. Between now and the opening games on June 17, nearly two dozen commercial sponsors will launch nationwide promotional campaigns aimed at whetting Americans' interest in the sport — and in their products.

World Cup tie-ins include Canon, Coca-Cola, Energizer, FujiFilm, General Motors, Gillette, McDonald's, Snickers, adidas, American Airlines, Budweiser, Electronic Data Systems (EDS), ITT Sheraton, Sprint and Sun Microsystems.

Much of the promotional activity will consist of television commercials on the two networks showing the World Cup, ESPN and ABC. (*See story, p. 354.*) But MasterCard has devised a more comprehensive approach, including a program through which shopping-mall patrons can receive World Cup premiums by presenting a MasterCard receipt from a designated mall. The company also has arranged World Cup promotions targeting fast-food outlets, movie theaters, supermarkets and restaurants.

Because soccer action is virtually nonstop, except in rare cases of player injury, World Cup games will not be interrupted by commercial breaks. Instead, the sponsors' logos will be prominently displayed on screen during periodic scoring updates. Most of the commercials that do appear are likely to run during pregame and halftime shows.

Alan Friedman, publisher of *Team Marketing Report,* a Chicago-based sports business publication, doesn't envision Americans "sitting down and planning big parties around the World Cup finals." He adds, however, that "if this doesn't sell soccer in the United States, nothing will." [1]

[1] Quoted in the *Los Angeles Times,* Feb. 2, 1993.

In Morrone's view, one reason why pro soccer has failed to find a permanent niche in the United States is that people from soccer-oriented countries don't understand American sports culture. "The people who were running the [NASL] came from abroad, they hired coaches who were from abroad and they went abroad for their players," he says. "They didn't see why it was necessary to promote the game, although most Americans don't understand it."

The foreign executives also failed to recognize that promoting soccer in America is a never-ending job. "We have parent coaches in this country," he says. "As a coach's children grow up, he drops out of soccer. Whenever that happens, the local soccer league needs to promote the game all over again." ■

BACKGROUND

Rugby vs. Soccer

In the winter of 1891, Dr. James Naismith attached two peach baskets to the balcony of a gym in Springfield, Mass. Thus was basketball born.

Tracing the genesis of soccer is far more difficult. That's because kicking games involving a ball and two or more bands of opponents have been played for centuries.

Despite soccer's murky beginnings, experts agree the modern game took shape in Britain's elite public schools during the mid-19th century. Two variations soon emerged. At schools with ample grounds, like Rugby, a rough-and-tumble version evolved that allowed some handling of the ball. Schools with more cramped playing fields stressed dribbling the ball with the feet.

In 1863, the founding of the English Football Association (FA) established the dribbling game as the standard form of soccer, and soccer's popularity soared, both in Britain and overseas.* A major boost came from the Football Association Challenge Cup (FA Cup) competition — the sport's first organized tournament and a distant forerunner of the World Cup. [8]

* The name soccer reportedly derives from the "soc" in association. The game, however, is still more popularly known as football throughout the world.

The first FA Cup was won in 1872 by Wanderers F.C. (football club), composed of public school graduates. Wanderers quickly established itself as the country's first soccer "dynasty," winning four additional trophies in the next six years.

Throughout the 1870s, in fact, British soccer was dominated by amateur teams of public school and university graduates. The 1880s witnessed the rise of professional clubs, many based in the industrial north of England. In the process, the sport acquired the working-class aura it still has in Britain and much of Europe and Latin America.

During this period, soccer began to attract a global following. On Nov. 30, 1872, England and Scotland played to a 0-0 draw in what is now regarded as the first international soccer match. At the same time, colonial administrators were taking the game to overseas outposts where it developed native roots and flourished. Little wonder that soccer was sometimes called, without irony, Britain's greatest cultural export.

Continued on p. 344

Chronology

19th Century

The basic rules of soccer are codified in Britain.

Oct. 26, 1863
The English Football Association is formed in London.

Nov. 6, 1869
Rutgers beats Princeton 6-4 in the first U.S. collegiate soccer match.

Nov. 30, 1872
England and Scotland tie in the first international soccer match.

1900s

Interest in soccer spreads beyond the British Isles.

1900
The 1900 Summer Olympics in Paris are the first to include soccer. Great Britain finishes first.

1904
Fédération Internationale de Football Association (FIFA) is founded to promote unity among national soccer associations.

1904
U.S. Intercollegiate Association Football League, forerunner of today's Intercollegiate Soccer Association of America, is started.

1930s

To demonstrate its authority over the sport, FIFA sponsors a global soccer tournament.

1930
The first World Cup competition, in Uruguay, attracts 13 nations.

1937
The first television broadcast of a soccer game shows part of the Football Association Cup final between two English teams.

1950s

England enters its first World Cup tournament as a favorite but is quickly humiliated.

June 29, 1950
The U.S. defeats England, 1-0, in a World Cup game at Belo Horizonte, Brazil. Some regard the win as the biggest upset in soccer history.

1960s

Inspired by live TV coverage of England's World Cup victory over West Germany, entrepreneurs launch pro soccer in the United States.

1968
The North American Soccer League (NASL) is established.

1970s

A few countries dominate World Cup competition.

1970
Brazil retires the original World Cup trophy by becoming the first nation to win three times.

1974
João Havelange of Brazil is elected president of FIFA and sets out to popularize soccer in countries — including the U.S. — where it is not widely played.

1980s

Though U.S. amateur soccer booms, efforts to establish a world-class professional league flounder.

1984
The NASL disbands after 17 years, devastated by inflated payroll costs and lack of a national television contract.

April 15, 1987
The U.S. Soccer Federation formally notifies FIFA that the United States wants to host the 1994 World Cup tournament.

July 4, 1988
The United States is selected to host the 1994 World Cup, beating out Morocco and Brazil.

1990s

Officials of World Cup USA vow that the 1994 tournament will be the most successful of all.

Dec. 19, 1993
The FIFA Final Draw in Las Vegas, Nev., is watched by an estimated 500 million viewers worldwide.

May 15, 1994
Application deadline for groups wishing to join Major League Soccer, the U.S. professional outdoor league scheduled to begin play in April 1995.

June 17, 1994
The World Cup finals begin as Germany plays Bolivia at Soldier Field in Chicago, and Spain plays South Korea at the Cotton Bowl in Dallas.

For World Cup Fans, the Grass Really Is Greener

For more than a quarter-century now, baseball and football have been played on plastic grass as well as the real thing. The shift to artificial turf began at the Houston Astrodome, the nation's first completely enclosed baseball-football facility, where not enough light filtered through the translucent roof to sustain plant life. Artificial turf also was installed in some undomed stadiums because it's cheaper to maintain.

However, the Fédération Internationale de Football Association (FIFA), soccer's governing body, insists that all World Cup games be played on natural grass. That posed a challenge for operators of Giants Stadium in East Rutherford, N.J., and the Silverdome in Pontiac, Mich., both selected to host World Cup games this year. Both are carpeted in plastic turf and required the temporary installation of real grass.

At Giants Stadium, the playing area was covered with protective layers of plywood and plastic sheeting, followed by a 10-inch layer of soil and rolls of Bermuda grass sod imported from Virginia. Charlie Stillitano, who supervised the installation, expects the grass to be firmly rooted by mid-May. "That gives us a full month to manicure and get the field right," he said. [1]

A radically different approach was taken to retrofit the Silverdome. That change from plastic to grass actually was made last summer for the England-Germany game during the U.S. Cup '93 tournament. Players and team officials were unanimous in praising the field's condition.

The Michigan State University researchers who worked on the Silverdome's field took a modular approach. After growing various mixtures of grass to determine which was the most durable in dim light, they chose a blend of 85 percent Kentucky bluegrass and 15 percent rye. Then they planted seeds in nearly 2,000 earth-filled, interlocking metal trays. After last summer's game, the grass-filled trays, each weighing 3,500 pounds, were stored in the stadium parking lot pending their reinstallation for the World Cup.

The switch to grass in the Silverdome had one unfortunate consequence, however. Real grass releases water vapor, and many spectators last year complained about the high humidity. The facility has massive air blowers but not air-conditioning, said World Cup USA 1994 President Alan I. Rothenberg, and "a lot depends on what the temperature is outside." [2]

---

[1] "Venue Meister," *Sidekicks*, February-March 1994, p. 19. *Sidekicks* is a recently launched bimonthly magazine devoted to soccer.

[2] Quoted in *The Washington Post*, April 12, 1994.

Continued from p. 342

Soccer Comes to the U.S.

Soccer was played informally at some Eastern U.S. colleges as early as the 1820s. But it didn't develop a substantial fan base until European immigrants came to America in large numbers later in the century. As various nationalities settled in urban neighborhoods in the Northeast and Midwest, they formed soccer clubs that served as emblems of group identity. Even today, many Americans look upon soccer primarily as an "ethnic game."

Around this time, American colleges faced the choice between "association football" (soccer) and the "handling game" (rugby) that had surfaced earlier in Britain. Initially, it appeared that soccer would prevail. For one thing, the Princeton-Rutgers game of Nov. 6, 1869, long regarded as the nation's first American-style college football contest, actually was played under soccer rules. Four years later, representatives of Columbia, Princeton, Rutgers and Yale met in New York to draw up rules modeled on the ones adopted by the FA in London in 1863.

Harvard, however, had a different concept of the sport. It favored a hybrid called the Boston Game, which allowed players to pick up the ball and run with it. The second of two 1874 games between Harvard and Canada's McGill University was played with an oval ball under Rugby Union rules. Though the game's significance was not apparent at the time, it marked "the beginning of American gridiron football" and, significantly, it "spelled doom for the future of soccer in the United States." [9]

Within two years of the Harvard-McGill games, the major Eastern soccer-playing colleges had switched to the rugby-style game. The dribbling game thus became even more closely associated with immigrant groups.

But even in ethnic enclaves, soccer's popularity tended to wane. "When immigrants first came here, they brought soccer with them, and it drew big crowds," says Connecticut's Morrone. "But the immigrants wanted to be considered Americans, not foreigners. So after a while, they didn't want anything more to do with soccer. And their children started to play typical American sports to win social acceptance."

Nonetheless, U.S. soccer staged a modest comeback around the turn of the century. In 1905, New York became the first city to make soccer part of its athletic curriculum. Several other cities followed suit, but most confined soccer to elementary schools.

"For many years, high schools . . . were reluctant to accept soccer as a varsity sport," wrote historians Sam Foulds and Paul Harris, "but in the elementary schools it was viewed as an acceptable physical activity." [10] Still, numerous prep schools and public high schools in the New England and mid-Atlantic states established soccer programs before World War I.

World Cup Evolves

The century's early years were notable also for the establishment of soccer federations in soccer-playing countries throughout the world and the selection of soccer in 1900 as the first Olympic team sport. Four years later, the Fédération Internationale de Football Association was formed in Paris to promote unity among national soccer associations. The U.S. Intercollegiate Association Football League, forerunner of today's Intercollegiate Soccer Association of America, also was established in 1904. And in 1913, the newly organized United States Football Association was recognized by FIFA as the country's governing body for soccer.*

The seven nations that brought FIFA into being sought to create a supervisory body independent of Britain's Football Association Board, then soccer's chief rule-making authority.** In one of its first acts, FIFA adopted the FA board's rules as its own. But though the board still exists, FIFA has long since supplanted it as soccer's supreme arbiter.

During FIFA's formative years, the Olympics emerged as a potential rival. The Olympic soccer champion, FIFA officials noted with chagrin, was widely recognized as the sport's world champion. In response, FIFA President Jules Rimet of France persuaded the federation in 1928 to "organize a competition open to representative teams of all affiliated national associations." The FIFA World Cup champion, it was hoped, would eclipse the Olympic soccer gold medalist in terms of prestige.*

The first World Cup tournament, held in Uruguay in 1930, was hardly the global playoff of champions envisioned by Rimet. Only four European national teams — Belgium, France, Romania and Yugoslavia — could be persuaded to make the three-week ocean voyage to Montevideo.

Pop artist Peter Max designed the official World Cup '94 poster.

Conspicuously absent were the four British Isles teams (England, Ireland, Scotland and Wales), which still regarded their annual championship series as the world's premier soccer competition.

The United States was one of the 13 nations that competed for the 1930 World Cup. Downing Belgium and Paraguay by identical 3-0 scores, the Americans won their group. But in the semifinals Argentina scored five goals in the second half to trounce the U.S. 6-1. Argentina, in turn, was beaten by Uruguay 4-2 for the championship.

The second World Cup, in 1934, was played in Italy by a full field of 16 teams, 12 of them from Europe. Only Argentina and Brazil represented the soccer stronghold of South America. Italy won the tournament and repeated as world titlist in 1938, establishing itself as Europe's dominant team of the decade.

World War II delayed the fourth World Cup until 1950. Brazil, the host country, was an early co-favorite with England, making its first appearance in the tournament. Though Uruguay downed Brazil 2-1 for the championship, the 1950 finals are remembered also for an early-round game regarded as the biggest upset in World Cup history. Against all expectations, the United States defeated England, 1-0.

According to the two-paragraph Associated Press account of the game: "The United States today defeated England 1-0 to add the latest and biggest upset in the world soccer championships. The favored British team and the spectators were stunned by the result. The lone tally of the match was scored by Joe Gaetjens at 39 minutes of the first half.

"Brazilian fans swarmed onto the field after the United States victory and took the Americans on their shoulders while the victors were given an ovation. The British forwards were uncertain in aiming for goal but their general play appeared superior to that of the winners except on the scoreboard."

Reactions to the game ranged from indifference to disbelief. In a 40th anniversary reminiscence, Clive Gammon of *Sports Illustrated* wrote: "Editors at *The New York Times* held off printing the score because they thought there had been a transmission error — the score must have been 10-1, England's favor. Most American newspapers that did print a paragraph or two attributed the goal to Eddy Souza. *The London Daily Herald* came out bordered in black." [11]

Through most of the 1970s, the

---

* In 1945, the name was changed to the United States Soccer Football Association. It was changed again in 1974 to its present name, the United States Soccer Federation (USSF), often called U.S. Soccer for short.

** The seven nations were Belgium, Denmark, France, the Netherlands, Spain, Sweden and Switzerland. Britain also was invited but declined to attend.

* The World Cup trophy was named the Jules Rimet Cup in 1946.

World Cup format remained basically the same. Sixteen teams qualified for the finals through a long process of elimination in regional tournaments. And with one exception, the finals alternated between Europe and South America, the two continents where interest in soccer was strongest. [12]

But the election of João Havelange of Brazil as president of FIFA in 1974 triggered changes that have begun to transform international soccer. At Havelange's urging, the World Cup field was expanded from 16 to 24 teams, starting in 1982. The number of teams could increase to 32 for the 1998 World Cup finals in France, according to a proposal introduced by Havelange in early April 1994. He has indicated that he would like to hold future championships in Asia, Africa and the Caribbean.

These changes conceivably will lead to more winners from other countries. Of the 14 World Cups held so far, 13 have been won by just five nations — Brazil, Germany and Italy (three times each) and Argentina and Uruguay (twice each). The only other cup champion was England, in 1966. Moreover, the World Cup seems to carry a "home continent" advantage. When Brazil claimed its first World Cup championship in Sweden in 1958, it became the first country — and still the only one — to win on a foreign continent.

Havelange also has encouraged the development of youth and women's soccer. FIFA staged its first World Youth Championship (for players under age 20) in 1977, its first Under-17 World Tournament in 1985 and its first Women's World Cup in 1991. The United States women's team won the inaugural cup competition and is expected to be one of the favorites in the 1995 tournament (*see p. 351*).

Pro Soccer Leagues

There have been several efforts to establish a world-class men's professional soccer league in the United States. One was prompted in part by the first television coverage of a World Cup final, the 1966 match between England and West Germany, which stirred considerable interest among American sports fans. Around the same time, several exhibition games featuring international teams drew big crowds to U.S. stadiums.

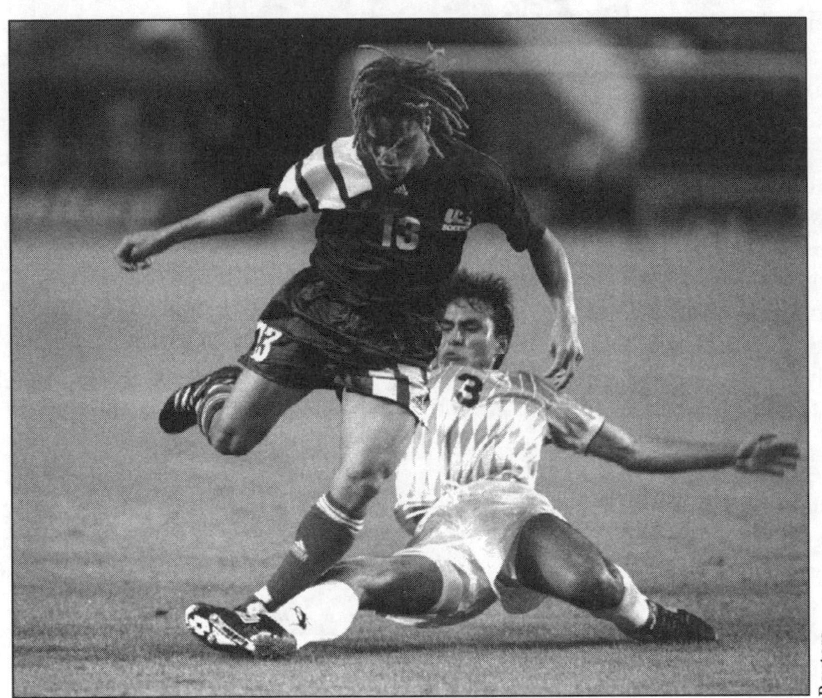

Reuters

Cobi Jones of the U.S. team, left, and Marco Sandy of Bolivia tangle during play in Miami in February.

Betting that America was at last ready to embrace the world's top game at the professional level, two groups of entrepreneurs announced plans to form soccer leagues, both to begin play in 1967. The leagues adopted radically different marketing strategies. The United Soccer Association (USA) imported entire professional clubs from overseas and gave them new local identities and nicknames. For instance, Bangu AC of Rio de Janeiro became the Houston Stars, while England's aptly named Wolverhampton Wanderers F.C. donned Los Angeles Wolves uniforms.

The second league, the National Professional Soccer League (NPSL), operated under a severe handicap from the start. Under FIFA regulations, each national soccer governing body may certify only one national (Division I) league. The USA was given that designation, forcing the NPSL to stock its franchises with American players of uncertain skill or with very young or aging veteran players from abroad. Some prospective recruits refused to sign up, not wanting to risk suspension by FIFA and their respective national associations by joining a renegade league. Consequently, the level of play in the NPSL was distinctly inferior to the USA's.

It hardly mattered, though, since the two leagues merged after the 1967 season to form the 17-team North American Soccer League (NASL). At first, it seemed the NASL also was destined to be a flash in the pan; by 1969 it was down to just five teams. But that year, stability arrived in the person of newly named Commissioner Phil Woosnam. A former Welsh player and NASL coach, Woosnam rebuilt the league, expanding it to eight teams in 1972, 15 teams in 1974 and 20 in 1975.

Even so, the NASL had a big problem. The dominance of foreign players meant that soccer was still a foreign game to most fans in the United States. And no foreign player had enough box-office appeal to fill stadiums. The New York Cosmos' signing of Pelé in the middle of the 1975 NASL season changed all that. The Brazilian superstar legitimized American soccer in the eyes of overseas stars, including Italy's Giorgio Chinaglia and West German World Cup hero Franz Beckenbauer, who joined Pelé on the Cosmos. The Cosmos and some other clubs moved out of small, aging arenas into modern football and baseball stadiums.

Still, pro soccer's popularity remained modest, with attendance averaging only 10,950 a game in 1976. But toward the end of the 1977 season, NASL soccer caught fire. On June 19, the Cosmos played the Tampa Bay Rowdies before 62,394 spectators at the Meadowlands in New Jersey, home of the pro football New York Giants. A playoff game against Tampa Bay on Aug. 10 drew 57,828. The pinnacle came on Aug. 14, 1977, when the Cosmos' home playoff game against Fort Lauderdale attracted a sellout crowd of 77,691, a league record.

However, the NASL wasn't able to sustain its growth momentum. The retirement of Pelé after the 1977 season removed the league's one sure gate attraction. Although the number of North Americans required to be in each team's playing lineup increased from two to three, foreigners continued to dominate. Attempting to imitate the Cosmos, several teams spent big dollars for foreign players, some of whom were past their prime. ABC's ratings for the NASL games were disastrous, and after two years the network dropped its regular-season coverage.

Average attendance peaked at about 15,000 per game in 1980, but after the season three teams went out of business. The NASL finally folded its tent in 1984. Since then, the United States has been without an officially recognized Division I pro soccer league.

Several factors sank the NASL, says *Soccer America* Publisher Berling. He contends that team owners in effect operated "a pyramid scheme, in which they kept trying to get new owners. Once they did, they'd split the franchise fees among themselves." But eventually they "ran out of people who were willing to pour money into pro soccer."

Nonetheless, Berling doesn't think it's accurate to say the NASL failed. As he sees it, the league "committed suicide." If it had "retrenched somewhat, taken a better look at what the situation was and developed a five-year plan, I think it would have done quite well."

Hindsight shows the expectations aroused by Pelé were illusory, says Berling. "Every time he came to town, it was an event. You can always draw people for an event, but you can't necessarily draw them for a league." Also, the owners of other teams "just didn't have the bucks" to sign comparable players.

Reuters

Bolivia's Sandy gets past Jones of the U.S. at the Robbie Cup in Miami.

Indoor Soccer Introduced

The 1970s vogue for pro soccer helped spawn an American innovation: indoor pro soccer. This variant of the game is played on hockey rinks covered with synthetic grass.

Although soccer skills and rules form the basis for the arena game, it is actually quite different from outdoor soccer. There are six players on each side, instead of 11. Hockey's sideboards are used, making the carom shot, which does not exist in outdoor soccer, a strategic weapon. The indoor playing area is much smaller. Players charged with major infractions are given timed penalties, forcing their teams to play shorthanded, as in hockey. There are elements of basketball as well, including zone defenses and certain set plays.

But the main difference is the high scoring. A 4-3 score would be considered high in outdoor soccer; scores in indoor soccer could easily be confused with those in football. On March 20, for instance, the Detroit Rockers of the National Professional Soccer League

(NPSL) beat the Baltimore Spirit, 16-13; the Cleveland Crunch downed the Dayton Dynamo, 27-18; and the St. Louis Ambush edged the Chicago Power, 26-24 in overtime.

A major reason for NPSL score inflation is that league rules assign a weighted value of 1, 2 or 3 points to each goal according to its degree of difficulty. This approach helps satisfy the U.S. sports fan's reputed craving for high point totals. According to Connecticut coach Morrone, indoor soccer appeals because it takes place in "a comfortable environment where fans can see the players' faces and there's a lot of action around the goals, which isn't usually the case with outdoor soccer."

Despite the NASL's demise and the rise of indoor pro soccer, world-class outdoor soccer retained a substantial fan base in the United States. This became evident at the 1984 Olympics in Los Angeles, the first in which professional players were allowed to compete. Total attendance for the 32 games was 1.4 million, or 44,400 per game. The championship final at the Rose Bowl in Pasadena, in which France defeated Brazil 2-0, drew 101,790 — the most people ever to attend a soccer match in the United States or Canada.

The big U.S. turnout was still fresh in mind as FIFA officials prepared in 1988 to choose among Brazil, Morocco and the United States as host country of the 1994 World Cup. The federation tipped its hand by setting July 4 — U.S. Independence Day — as the date for announcing its choice. During a tour of the United States in April, members of a FIFA technical inspection group had praised the stadiums they visited. The United States benefited also from possessing a sophisticated television and telecommunications network — no small consideration for an event that is televised worldwide, attracting billions of viewers. ■

CURRENT SITUATION

Spread of Youth Soccer

Soccer coaches in the United States often liken their sport to an unfinished pyramid. At the base of the structure is youth soccer, played by millions of boys and girls of school age. In the middle are high school and college programs for men and women, which also are thriving in most parts of the country. (*See graph, p. 350.*) Near the top are a handful of professional leagues, none ranking higher than Division II. *

All that's needed to complete the pyramid — the capstone, so to speak — is a Division I outdoor league that could compete with the top pro teams in other countries. Plans for such a league, due to begin play next spring, are now under way. Organizers hope that enthusiasm generated by the World Cup will turn soccer-playing Americans into pro soccer spectators as well.

If only 10 to 20 percent of U.S. soccer players attended pro games regularly, the future of the sport would seem assured. That's because the number of people in all age groups playing soccer has risen rapidly in recent decades.

Moreover, the potential for continued growth clearly exists, since the sport is especially popular in the youngest age groups. According to the Soccer Industry Council of America, 11.6 million youngsters under 18 played soccer last year, making it the third-most-popular team sport in that age bracket, after basketball (20.5 million participants) and volleyball (12.5 million). Soccer ranked second among kids under 12, with 6.8 million players, as against the 9 million under-12 who played basketball. [13]

Three organizations promote youth soccer participation nationwide — the American Youth Soccer Organization (AYSO), the Soccer Association for Youth (SAY) and the United States Youth Soccer Association (USYSA). Tournaments have proved to be an effective medium for selling the sport to youngsters and their parents. USYSA, for example, sponsors a wide range of contests for boys and girls of various age groups, culminating in national championships sponsored by Snickers candy bars.

Youth soccer groups also encourage children as young as age 5 to take up the sport. USYSA suggests that kids between ages 5 and 10 play shorter quarters on smaller fields, and with just five players on each team. To instill a spirit of sportsmanship, the association urges "participation awards for ALL — no trophies or awards just for the best team."

Soccer appeals to parents because both boys and girls can play, and unusual size isn't required but rather stamina, nimble footwork and an instinct for constant improvisation.

Parents also like soccer because the uniform is relatively uncomplicated and inexpensive, and there's less hazard of serious injury than in many other team sports. By some estimates, it costs as much to outfit a single well-padded, helmeted football player as it does to field an entire soccer team. In contrast, a soccer player needs only a pair of shorts, a jersey, knee-length socks (with padding) and cleats.

Despite the football player's protective armor, injuries to the knee, spine or head are a constant worry.

Continued on p. 350

* Under FIFA and U.S. Soccer guidelines, Division I leagues must have teams in all four quadrants of the United States and in at least four major media markets; Division II leagues must have teams in three of the four quadrants and in one or two major media markets; Division III teams generally are in minor media markets and play only teams from their own region.

On the Rampage With Soccer Hooligans

Some soccer fans say it's a shame that England, the birthplace of modern soccer, didn't qualify for this year's World Cup tournament. But to American journalist Bill Buford, it's just as well the English team — and its hooligan supporters — will be staying home.

In search of a story, Buford joined a renegade band of supporters of the Manchester United football club during an extended stay in England in the 1980s. From this vantage point, he came to know some of Britain's most notorious soccer hooligans and observed them in action at home and abroad. His insider's account will be an eye-opener for Americans who think rock-throwing and window-smashing after a Super Bowl or a World Series are the ultimate in fan misbehavior. [1]

Hooliganism has plagued British soccer for many years. As long ago as the 1955-56 season, Liverpool and Everton fans were involved in several train-trashing incidents while en route to games. At that time, members of the National Federation of Football Supporters' Clubs worried mainly that the vandalism would soil the reputation of law-abiding fans.

Over the years, however, violence during games became increasingly serious. To protect them from supporters of the local club, fans attending their teams' away games in Britain often are escorted to the playing grounds by mounted police. Inside the stadium, the opposing fans are kept apart, often by metal fences topped with concertina wire. Yet sometimes the precautions aren't sufficient.

This was made abundantly clear May 29, 1985, when England's Liverpool and Italy's Juventus of Turin met in a European championship final at Heysel Stadium in Brussels, Belgium. Liverpool supporters, some obviously drunk, began arguing and then fighting with Juventus fans. The fracas escalated into a full-scale riot as the English attempted to storm the Italian stands. During the attack, a cement wall separating the two groups collapsed, killing 39 people, mostly Juventus rooters.

Only the year before, Juventus supporters had felt the wrath of British soccer hooligans. In the spring of 1984, the Turin club hosted Manchester United in a semifinal game of a European championship tournament. Although Manchester management had banned its own fans from attending the game, many of them went to Turin, Buford among them.

Before and during the flight to Italy, Buford writes, his fellow passengers drank steadily, and as their convoy of buses headed into Turin from the airport, they screamed obscenities, threw bottles and cans and mooned through the windows. But this was only the beginning.

At the game, the British fans found themselves confined to an area where they were easy targets for debris hurled by Juventus fans. The British took their revenge after the game ended. Buford accompanied a pack of Manchester United fans as they roamed the city, smashing shop windows, vandalizing cars and viciously beating residents who happened to be in their path. When the group finally reached its destination, the railroad station, its leader declared, "'We did it. We took the city.' " [2]

Buford, like others who have written about British soccer violence, says he was surprised that many hooligans hold responsible, well-paying jobs. This prompts many observers to describe hooliganism as an expression of class antagonism. Author Lesley Hazleton likened destructive fan behavior to "a huge, obscene gesture directed at the ruling classes, at the rigid structure of English society. It is a working-class howl and, like most howls of the powerless, it ends up hurting themselves more than anyone else." [3]

Rampant hooliganism has altered the composition of British soccer crowds, says Hazleton. Few family groups, women, young children or blacks now attend games. They are repelled not only by the threat of verbal or physical abuse but also by the lack of spectator amenities. The bleacher-type seats often reek of urine, and many fans must stand jammed together on "terraces" behind the goals. British soccer fans who attend baseball or football games in the United States often marvel at the number of women in the stands as well as the prevalence of chair seating.

Soccer hooliganism is by no means an exclusively British phenomenon. In recent years, Dutch football fans also have gained a reputation for aimless violence. Many South American soccer fields are rimmed by moats and fences to prevent angry fans from assaulting players and officials. And in July 1969, Honduras and El Salvador actually went to war for five days — engaging troops and planes and inflicting casualties — after three hotly disputed World Cup qualifying games between the countries.

The "fútbol war" wouldn't have surprised George Orwell. Writing in 1945, the British author of *1984* said he was "always surprised" to hear others claim that "sport creates goodwill between the nations, and that if only the peoples of the world could meet one another at football or cricket, they would have no inclination to meet on the battlefield."

To the contrary, declared Orwell, "Serious sport has nothing to do with fair play. It is bound up with hatred, jealousy, boastfulness, disregard of all rules and sadistic pleasure in witnessing violence; in other words it is war minus the shooting." [4]

---

[1] Bill Buford, *Among the Thugs* (1992).

[2] *Ibid.*, p. 93.

[3] Lesley Hazleton, "British Soccer: The Deadly Game," *The New York Times Magazine,* May 7, 1989, p. 67.

[4] George Orwell, "The Sporting Spirit," *Tribune* (a weekly British newsletter), Dec. 14, 1945, quoted in Ian Hamilton, ed., *The Faber Book of Soccer,* 1992.

College Soccer on the Rise

Soccer programs for college men and women in the United States have increased steadily in the past decade, with programs for women showing dramatic growth. This academic year there are 445 programs for women — up from just 77 programs in 1981-82.

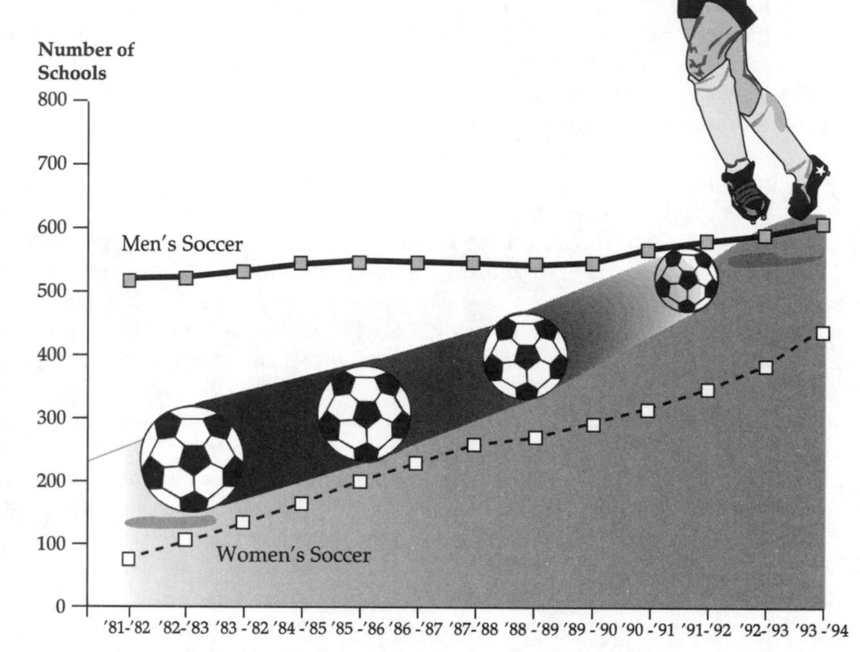

Source: National Collegiate Athletic Association; Sporting Goods Manufacturers Association

Continued from p. 348

The risk is lower for the soccer player. "We see a lot of the overuse kind of injuries, like shin splints, hip pointers and fractures in the growth plate," said Craig Hersh, a doctor of sports medicine in Westwood, N.J., who treats children with soccer-related injuries. "But we see more vertebrae problems with football." [14]

High Schools, Colleges

The spread of youth soccer has contributed to the sport's expansion in high schools and colleges. According to the National Federation of State High School Associations, the number of boys and girls in high school soccer programs rose from 127,345 in 1976-77 to 391,148 in 1992-93, embracing 7,137 high school programs for boys and 4,976 for girls. Soccer programs exist in all states except Arkansas, Indiana and South Dakota. [15]

Despite its explosive growth, high school soccer still should be viewed as a developing sport, says Morrone. "A quality player in one section of the country is not equal to a quality player in another section," he says. "It's not like basketball. If I were to get a kid from New York City and a kid from Chicago, chances are pretty good they'd be comparable. That's not true in soccer. A kid who makes the all-star team in one state may not even come close to doing that in another state."

Regional variations in the quality of soccer play are considered just as pronounced at the college level. St. Louis University once was the dominant team in men's college soccer, Morrone notes, winning 10 titles in the first 15 years of the National Collegiate Athletic Association (NCAA) championship tournament. Now the balance of power has shifted to the Atlantic Coast Conference (ACC). The last three NCAA men's soccer championships were won by the University of Virginia, which also tied Santa Clara University for the title in 1989.

In his 36 years as Connecticut's coach, Morrone has seen "tremendous changes in soccer, and all for the better." While putting together his first team in 1959, he recalls, "a young man tried out who had never played before. Today, to qualify for our team, you have played anywhere from 10 to 15 years, and you must have played on a regional team or higher."

High schools and prep schools are not the only sources of college soccer talent. George Washington University's Lidster regularly scouts local soccer clubs for player prospects. Most of his recruits from this burgeoning talent pool are Hispanic, he says, although "some good African players are now settling in the area."

Lidster, who came to the United States from England about 10 years ago, bemoans the fact that the best American athletes avoid soccer. "They veer toward basketball, baseball, football, because that's where the money is," he says. "Imagine Michael Jordan or Emmitt Smith playing soccer! This country could certainly take a vast leap with those superb athletes playing the game. But as youngsters, they don't see soccer on TV. So why should they bother playing it?"

In fact, some top U.S. athletes have played soccer but later dropped it. Jason Kidd of the University of California, who figures to be highly sought in the coming National Basketball Association college draft, credits soccer he played as a youngster for the stamina he displays on court as a point guard.

Grant Hill, who led Duke University to two NCAA basketball titles, also was introduced to sports through youth soccer. Not until he was 13 did he concentrate on basketball. "Soccer's my first love," Hill told sportswriter Barry Jacobs. "But it was as if I wasn't supposed to play soccer — you don't see tall, black kids playing soccer." [16]

U.S. Women's Teams

Perhaps the biggest story in U.S. high school and college soccer over the past 20 years has been the proliferation of women's teams. In 1976-77, only 11,534 girls nationwide were playing high school soccer. By 1992-93, the number had risen to 149,053. [17]

Women's college soccer can boast a similar growth curve. In 1981-82, NCAA figures show, only 77 of the association's 752 member institutions operated women's soccer programs. In 1992-93, institutions with such programs totaled 445, or slightly more than half of the NCAA's 895 members. (*See graph, p. 350.*)

Women's college coaches are quick to credit much of that growth to Title IX of the Education Amendments of 1972, which outlawed sex discrimination by all recipients of federal funds. NCAA efforts to exempt sports from Title IX got nowhere, leaving colleges with no choice but to practice "gender equity" in their athletic programs. [18]

Though new women's college soccer teams have been established at a much faster pace than new men's teams over the past decade or so, the momentum may be slowing. "I don't think we'll surpass men's soccer," says North Carolina's Dorrance, "but the gap will continue to close. What will eventually happen is that we'll come very close to the men's numbers."

Some soccer enthusiasts find women's soccer more adventurous and attack-oriented than the men's, featuring more running and a philosophy that stresses winning rather than averting a loss. Dorrance, whose North Carolina teams have won 11 of the 12 NCAA women's soccer championship games played to date, agrees with that assessment.

"There isn't the great pressure on all of us in the women's game to hold on to our jobs," he says, "so coaches can afford to be a bit more reckless. We encourage our players to attack. Since women aren't as quick and fast as men, they're playing, in effect, on a larger field. They're also protecting a larger goal, in a way, because a woman is shorter than a man, and doesn't jump as high, so the goal area she's protecting is bigger for her. The potential for scoring in our game is a lot greater." Dorrance's two most recent championship teams proved his point, winning by 9-1 and 6-0.

© 1992 David M. Minton

Players from the University of North Carolina-Chapel Hill and William and Mary go head-to-head during the NCAA quarter-finals in 1992.

U.S. women's soccer enjoyed its greatest triumph four years ago, when the American national team, coached by Dorrance, beat Norway 2-1 in Guangzhou, China, to win the first women's World Cup. The Americans were unbeaten in six games during the two-week tournament, outscoring their opponents by 25-5. Dorrance called the championship "proof to the world we are a developing soccer nation." [19]

Pro Leagues Growing

United States soccer is evolving at the professional level as well, though without the attendant hoopla of the NASL years. The top outdoor league is the American Professional Soccer League (APSL), formed by the merger in 1990 of the Western Soccer League and American Soccer League. The APSL now comprises eight teams, including three in Canada.* It plans to add four more teams next season, eventually reaching 16. This year's APSL season runs from July 1 to the weekend of Oct. 15. U.S. Soccer has classified APSL as a Division II league.

Like most other pro soccer leagues around the world, the APSL plays by FIFA rules. However, the APSL uses an unorthodox scoring system for team standings. A team is awarded six points for a win in regulation or overtime; four points for a win by shootout tie-breaker; and two points for a shootout loss. In addition, teams receive one point for each goal scored in regulation time (up to a maximum

* The eight APSL teams are the Colorado Foxes, Fort Lauderdale Strikers, Houston Force, Los Angeles Salsa, Montreal Impact, Seattle Sounders, Toronto Rockets and the Vancouver Eighty-Sixers.

of three) regardless of whether they win or lose.

APSL attendance, league spokesman Brian Bishop reports, averages 3,000 to 5,000 a game. "We're looking to improve on that, of course, with more marketing," he says. "But we also have to be careful we don't grow too fast."

Mindful of the NASL's overreliance on foreign players, the APSL makes a point of nurturing native talent. Of the 18 active players on U.S. teams, no more than two may be citizens of other countries. The Canadian teams are permitted to carry up to three non-Canadian players. "At least half or more" of APSL players have gone to college, says Bishop, though "some of them came right out of high school."

The U.S. Interregional Soccer League, composed of 71 teams in eight regional divisions, seems content with Division III status. This season it will conduct a number of rules-change experiments proposed by U.S. Soccer and the organizers of Major League Soccer, tentatively projected as the country's Division I league. The rules changes, concerning such things as goal size, penalties for major fouls and multiple fouls and corner kicks, are designed to develop crowd-pleasing rules for U.S. soccer that would meet with FIFA approval.

The National Professional Soccer League (NPSL), which just completed its 10th season, is currently the country's top indoor soccer league. Attendance has increased steadily, rising from an average of 1,706 per game in 1984-85 to 5,213 per game in 1992-93. Between 1991-92 and 1992-93, total attendance more than doubled, from 709,280 to 1,464,868. With this season's playoffs still in progress, 1993-94 attendance already exceeds 1.5 million, says Tom Morrison, NPSL director of team services.

Like the APSL, the NPSL is striving to Americanize soccer. League rules require that 14 of the 16 players on each team's active roster must be U.S. citizens. "The vast majority of those are drafted out of colleges," says Morrison. "The other two can be foreigners, but they must have a government-issued document that states that they are intending citizens and 'lawful permanent resident aliens.' "

The America-first personnel policy, says Morrison, is designed to counter the notion that soccer is "a foreigners' game that no one understands or cares about." NPSL soccer is "a heck of a lot more exciting" than the outdoor game, he says. "It's almost akin to hockey." Like hockey, NPSL soccer features power plays when a team is short-handed because of a penalty. Also, notes Morrison, the league's scoring system is similar to basketball's — allowing one, two or three points, depending on from where the goal was scored.

Meanwhile, as the World Cup draws closer, tournament organizers are accentuating the outdoor game's positives. They note that attendance averaged 47,793 per game at U.S. Cup '93 — a four-team, six-game tourney played last summer in five cities, including four 1994 World Cup sites.

A highlight of U.S. Cup '93 was the American team's 2-0 victory over England, which rekindled memories of the U.S. upset of England in 1950. Most observers, however, felt last year's American team played its best game against Germany, losing 4-3 at Soldier Field in Chicago. That contest, carried by ABC-TV without commercial interruption, marked the first appearance of the U.S. national team on network television in almost 10 years.

World Cup officials also were heartened by Americans' response to last June's sale of game tickets by telephone. Virtually all the seats allotted to the United States were snapped up within hours after the phones lines were activated. Many prospective buyers were stymied by busy signals.

The one sour note sounded thus far came at last December's World Cup Final Draw in Las Vegas, Nev. The ceremony, beamed to a worldwide television audience, divided the 24 participating teams into six groups and assigned the groups to the nine World Cup sites. (*See map, p. 340.*)

Many viewers wondered why Pelé did not participate. As it turned out, the retired Brazilian superstar was involved in a bitter legal dispute with his country's soccer federation, which is headed by the son-in-law of FIFA President Havelange. "Dropping him from the draw was a catastrophic error," wrote British soccer columnist Keir Radnedge. "The American media, much of which remains suspicious — to say the least — about the advance of soccer, leaped on the story as evidence of amateur incompetence." [20]

The Pelé flap overshadowed what World Cup USA executives hoped would be a highlight of the Final Draw weekend — the announcement that Major League Soccer would begin play in April 1995 in 12 U.S. cities. Nonetheless, soccer officials from abroad applauded the news. "We are optimistic about the future of soccer in the United States," said Joseph S. Blatter of Switzerland, FIFA's general secretary and chief executive officer. [21] ■

OUTLOOK

Uncertain Future

Major League Soccer expects to review applications from more than 30 cities before choosing the 12 that will be awarded teams. The deadline for submitting bids is May 15, with selections to be announced before World Cup competition gets under way.

Mindful of the woes that befell the NASL because of runaway spending by team owners, MLS organizers structured their league as a single entity. All teams and player contracts will be owned by MLS instead of by individual franchise holders. That is expected "to eliminate the financial disparities between large and small

Continued on p. 354

At Issue:

Will Americans catch soccer fever?

yes

THE EDITORS OF U.S. NEWS & WORLD REPORT
From *"Will America Catch Soccer Fever?" U.S. News & World Report,* Dec. 27, 1993.

Soccer is a game that has addled monarchs (four English kings banned it for causing too much noise), kindled riots (more than 300 people were killed in Lima, Peru, in 1964) and sparked wars (Honduras and El Salvador fought during a 1969 World Cup qualifying series; El Salvador won the series — the war was a draw).

Few American sports fans share such passion for "the other football," but the 1994 World Cup finals are about to change all that. In June and July, for the first time in the cup's 64-year history, America will host the quadrennial global phenomenon. The 24-team sports spectacle will be played in and around nine major American cities — Boston, Chicago, Washington, Los Angeles, Detroit, Dallas, New York, San Francisco, and Orlando — and culminate in a July 17 championship game at the Rose Bowl. Television viewership for the 52 games could reach 31 billion worldwide.

While America's soccer fever is low grade by world standards, it is rising steadily. More than 15 million Americans played soccer in 1992. Youth league participation has grown by 25 percent since 1980, and among Americans under 18, only basketball and volleyball attract more participants. The United States Soccer Federation recently announced plans to kick off a new professional league in 1995.

Soccer fever could become epidemic if the improving U.S. team can survive until late in the five-round tournament — a tall order against teams stocked with the world's best players. But America's women already have claimed a world soccer championship, and U.S. soccer officials are hoping against the odds that the men will be next.

---

no

WILLIAM F. REED
From *"It's Not My Cup of Tea," Sports Illustrated,* July 16, 1990.

I hate soccer, and I'm tired of being made to feel guilty about it. So there. I feel better now. Call me an ugly American, but please don't try to sell me the World Cup. I'm glad the blamed thing's over, so newspapers and magazines can start using the space they devoted to this endless yawner — was every final score really 1-0; wasn't there a 2-1 donnybrook in there somewhere? — to more exciting news. Such as softball scores. Or jai alai results.

For at least 20 years, maybe longer, I've been hearing that soccer is the coming sport in this country. Soccer advocates shrilly point out that more kids play soccer than play Little League baseball. Maybe so, but adolescent participation has definitely not carried over into adult interest. That's why there is no major U.S. pro soccer league worth talking about. And that's why TNT, the cable channel that carried the English-language telecasts of the World Cup, earned an average Nielsen rating of — what else? — 1.0, which is about as bad as it gets.

Whenever these points are raised, soccer buffs, who are about as tiresome as reformed smokers, act as if our lack of interest in the sport proves that Americans, instead of being the world's most sophisticated sports fans, are uncultured dunces. Or, as the argument always goes, how come soccer is the No. 1 sport nearly everywhere else in the world? Doesn't that prove there's something wrong with us? That we're too lazy or too arrogant to give soccer the respect it deserves, just as most of us are too lazy or too arrogant to learn a second language? Baloney, I say.

Soccer's global popularity has a lot to do with economics. To play soccer, all you need is a ball and a field, and I can appreciate the simple virtue of that: Nobody has to buy bats, helmets, gloves, pads or the other accoutrements of American sports. But that's why soccer is not only the most popular sport in most underdeveloped countries, but also the only sport.

As for the so-called soccer boom among this nation's youth, that also can be easily explained. Soccer has proved to be very useful in the important area of keeping the sons and daughters of yuppie America off the streets, out of the malls and away from MTV, at least for a few hours a day. You have noticed that soccer hasn't exactly taken hold in the inner cities, haven't you? And that the American kids who play the sport generally are white suburbanites who aren't tall enough, strong enough, fast enough or skilled enough to play football, baseball, basketball or tennis? Now, you moms who drive the station wagons to those dreary games, be honest. If Junior weren't out there bouncing that silly ball off his head, wouldn't you really rather be doing something — anything — else?

I'll concede that soccer requires conditioning and dedication, but so do jogging and mountain climbing. Those sports don't spin the turnstiles or light up the Neilsens much, either. When all is said and done, the reason so may American are turned off by soccer is that it's B-O-R-I-N-G. Americans love scoring, be it in the form of home runs or touchdowns or slam dunks, and soccer doesn't have nearly enough of it. Why, if it weren't for those ridiculous penalty-kick tiebreakers after two hours of play, most of the World Cup teams would still be playing.

We also like patterns to our games, with clearly discernible times of offense and defense, instead of all that milling around that we see in soccer. The sport most often compared to soccer is hockey, but that does hockey a great disservice. And what about strategy? We can think along with the manager or coach in baseball, football and basketball, but if there is a game plan in soccer — and experts insist there is — it remains a secret to me even after the game has blessedly ended.

And how about those European soccer fans? Wonderful, aren't they? The biggest upset in the World Cup was that nobody was trampled to death, although 246 English fans did have to be flown home at the expense of the Italian government after they battled police in Rimini. Given the choice between going to a soccer match in England or a professional wrestling match anywhere, I would take Randy (Macho Man) Savage and his crowd every time, even if the matches are fixed. At least the wrestlers will give you a few chuckles; they won't put you to sleep; and you have a good chance of getting home alive, even if you sit at ringside. Don't take my word for it. Ask the TV networks whether they would rather have the best soccer game in the world or a rerun of last week's wrestling card in Peoria.

So it's time to come out of the closet, fellow soccer haters. Don't be afraid to stand up and say that soccer doesn't provide the entertainment and excitement to which we have grown accustomed in exchange for our sports dollar. And don't let any of your yuppie friends try to make you feel bad because you didn't watch the World Cup on TV. Just say you had something more interesting to do. You wouldn't be lying, even if all you did was watch the grass grow.

Will U.S. Sports Fans Tune Out TV Soccer?

Television viewership surveys confirm what every sports fan already knows: Americans just don't watch very much soccer. What's surprising is that U.S. cable television broadcasts as much soccer as it does.

ESPN is "the biggest fish in the growing television soccer pond, having expanded its coverage of the game via ESPN2," wrote Steven H. Saltzman, managing editor of *Sidekicks,* a recently launched U.S. bimonthly magazine devoted to soccer.[1] On Sundays, ESPN2 shows a Dutch league game in the morning and a Brazilian league game late at night.

During the World Cup tournament, ESPN will broadcast 41 of the 52 games. ABC-TV will show the championship. But no one has a firm fix on how many Americans will tune in. During the 1990 World Cup in Italy, the Turner Broadcasting System's TNT cable channel broadcast 32 games in the United States. On average, the games were watched by viewers in 2 percent of U.S. cable homes, or about 1.2 million homes, World Cup officials say.

Prime Network and NewSport Television, two smaller cable distributors specializing in sports coverage, carry both European professional games and U.S. college soccer. Fans of the Italian league can follow it on local cable systems that show programming by RAI, Italy's television network. Univision and Telemundo, Spanish-language cable channels widely watched by members of the growing U.S. Hispanic community, also offer a generous menu of soccer, much of it originating from Latin America.

Worldwide TV Audiences for Major One-Day Events

Year	Event	Audience
1994	World Cup Championship Game (estimated)	2 billion
1993	NFL Super Bowl	750 million
1991	European Cup Final	526 million
1990	Wimbledon Men's Final	350 million
1981	Royal Wedding in England	420 million
1969	First man landing on the moon	490 million

Source: World Cup USA 1994 Inc.

Clay Berling, publisher of the weekly tabloid *Soccer America,* says he's "not sure that showing full games is necessarily the way to interest people" in soccer. In his view, highlight films would be more effective in introducing Americans to the game.

Weekly highlight films of National Football League games, Berling notes, helped make American pro football a cult sport in Britain, at least for a time. Beyond the games themselves, Berling feels Britons and other Europeans are drawn to American sports because of the marching bands, cheerleaders and other frills: "Americans transform sport into entertainment, and that's unusual in Europe."

[1] Steven H. Saltzman, "Grazing the Tube for Games," *Sidekicks,* February-March 1994, p. 26.

Continued from p. 352

markets, control player costs and offer commercial affiliates an integrated sponsorship and licensing program. Most important, MLS will be able to make decisions that are in the best interest of the entire league, rather than just one team."[22]

A "core problem" for pro soccer in this country, MLS officials feel, is the scarcity of suitable stadiums. Many U.S. baseball and football stadiums are too small to accommodate a regulation soccer field, and some are surfaced with artificial turf — unacceptable to FIFA. Moreover, the leading college and pro stadiums seat from 40,000 to 100,000 spectators, making them far too big for a typical U.S. soccer crowd. According to MLS, the ideal stadium for soccer in the U.S. would have 20,000 to 30,000 seats. To ease the stadium shortage, the league says it will provide money to remodel existing facilities and, possibly, help finance new ones.

By next year, the MLS may face another big headache from the APSL, which also covets Division I status. If MLS "does get off the ground, we welcome them as competitors," APSL Chairman William De La Peña said March 1. "The market will determine which survives. MLS has not received first-division sanctioning. All it has is a preliminary endorsement. USSF accepted its business plan. There are still a lot of things they have to do."[23]

Meanwhile, the APSL already has teams in four cities that MLS might want to occupy — Denver, Houston, Los Angeles and Seattle. And, APSL spokesman Bishop points out, "As of right now, MLS doesn't have any players. We have most of the players in the country under contract."

Both MLS and APSL are counting on the World Cup to give U.S. professional outdoor soccer a boost. However, Berling thinks their hopes may be misplaced. If the U.S. team doesn't advance beyond the first round, he says, "It'll be disappointing in the same way it's disappointing when we don't win medals at the Olympics. But the people who are interested in soccer will continue to support it. I don't think average American fans are going to be turned on by the World Cup, frankly. They don't understand what's going on because they don't have a vested interest in the sport."

In any case, FIFA has tinkered with the rules to liven World Cup action this year. A win during the 36-game first round will be worth three points in the group standings instead of the customary two, with a draw still worth one point to both teams. The change is designed to encourage teams to go for a win in each first-round game rather than settling for three draws and three points — usually enough to advance a team to the second round.

Regardless of what happens at the World Cup, the United States will be involved in two other major soccer tournaments in 1995 and 1996. The first will be next year's women's World Cup finals, in which the U.S. team will try to defend its title. Dorrance, expected to return as coach, says the 1995 team will include nine of the 11 starters from his 1991 championship squad.

Dorrance also is likely to coach the U.S. women's soccer team in the 1996 Summer Olympics in Atlanta. It will mark the first time the women's game has been an officially recognized Olympic sport. The Atlanta Olympics also will give the U.S. men's team additional experience against world-class competition.

Even if U.S. sports fans are still yawning after all this exposure to soccer, Berling feels the game is finally on firm footing in this country. "We're 25 years ahead of where we were back in North American Soccer League days," he says. "We have a fan base that indicates to me soccer can make it now."

Dorrance is less certain. "Soccer isn't part of the American cultural fabric yet," he says. "On Monday morning, when people come to work, they talk about football, basketball or baseball. I do, too. Soccer won't be part of American culture until we start to talk about it on Monday mornings." ■

Notes

[1] Remarks on National Public Radio's "Morning Edition," March 30, 1994. Deford is a contributing editor of *Vanity Fair.*

[2] Quoted by Mark Irwin, "U.S. Expects," *World Soccer,* February 1994, p. 4.

[3] *Ibid.*

[4] "1993 National Soccer Participation Survey," Soccer Industry Council of America. The council is a subsidiary of the Sporting Goods Manufacturers Association, and is affiliated with the United States Soccer Federation, the sport's national governing body.

[5] *Ibid.*

[6] Quoted in *The New York Times,* Dec. 9, 1991.

[7] Clay Berling, "Will Dem Bones Walk Again?" *Soccer America,* Dec. 20, 1993, p. 5.

[8] Michael L. LaBlanc and Richard Henshaw, *The World Encyclopedia of Soccer* (1994), p. 283.

[9] *Ibid.*

[10] Sam Foulds and Paul Harris, *America's Soccer Heritage: A History of the Game* (1979), p. 101.

[11] Clive Gammon, "A World Cup Day to Remember: The Day the U.S. Beat England," *Sports Illustrated,* May 21, 1990.

[12] Only once were two consecutive World Cup championships held on the same continent. The 1954 and 1958 World Cup finals were held in Switzerland and Sweden, respectively.

[13] "1993 National Soccer Participation Survey," *op. cit.*

[14] Quoted by Filip Bondy, "Now, Kids, That's the Way to Use Your Heads!" *The New York Times,* Dec. 24, 1992, p. B13.

[15] "1993 Sports Participation Survey," National Federation of State High School Associations.

[16] Barry Jacobs, *Three Paths to Glory: A Season on the Hardwood With Duke, N.C. State and North Carolina* (1993).

[17] National Federation of State High School Associations, *op. cit.*

[18] For background, see "Women and Sports," *The CQ Researcher,* March 6, 1992, pp. 193-216.

[19] Quoted in *The New York Times,* Dec. 1, 1991.

[20] Keir Radnedge, "Say It Ain't So, João!" *World Soccer,* February 1994, p. 8.

[21] Major League Soccer news release, Dec. 17, 1993.

[22] Major League Soccer, "Questions and Answers About Major League Soccer" (undated fact sheet).

[23] Quoted in *USA Today,* March 2, 1994.

Bibliography

Selected Sources Used

Books

Buford, Bill, *Among the Thugs,* W.W. Norton, 1992.
Buford, an American writer, describes his travels with "football hooligans" who were supporters (the British term for fans) of the Manchester United soccer club. Buford's account of the hooligans, who seem more interested in getting drunk and being violent than in watching their team play, is entertaining and appalling in equal measure.

Chyzowych, Walt, *The World Cup,* Icarus Press, 1982.
Chyzowych describes how Jules Rimet, former president of the Fédération Internationale de Football Association (FIFA), soccer's world governing body, hit upon the idea of a championship tournament open to all players. He also recaps each World Cup tournament from 1930 through 1982, providing first-round group standings and later-round scores for each.

Foulds, Sam, and Paul Harris, *America's Soccer Heritage,* Soccer for Americans, 1979.
This is a short book (150 pages), befitting the fact that soccer is not generally considered a major sport in the United States. Published 15 years ago, it is prescient in its appreciation of U.S. women's soccer.

Hamilton, Ian, ed., *The Faber Book of Soccer,* Faber and Faber, 1992.
This anthology consists mainly of contemporary accounts of notable soccer games and ruminations on the sport by such authors as Arnold Bennett, J.B. Priestley, Vladimir Nabokov, George Orwell, Albert Camus and Harold Pinter.

LaBlanc, Michael L., and Richard Henshaw, *The World Encyclopedia of Soccer*, Visible Ink Press, 1994.
Less exhaustive than a true encyclopedia, this book nonetheless covers the basics of soccer in satisfying detail. Included are a history of the game, an explanation of rules and tactics, brief biographies of soccer's greatest players and profiles of the world's soccer-playing nations, arranged alphabetically from Afghanistan to Zimbabwe.

Taylor, Rogan, *Football and Its Fans*, Leicester University Press, 1992.
Taylor is a founding member of the Football Supporters Association, organized after the 1985 clash between English and Italian soccer fans that led to 39 deaths at Heysel Stadium in Brussels, Belgium. He tracks the relationship between English fans and their soccer clubs from the 1880s to the present and speculates about the causes of hooliganism.

Articles

Gammon, Clive, "A World Cup to Remember: The Day the U.S. Beat England," *Sports Illustrated,* May 21, 1990.
Gammon reminisces about the U.S. team's stunning 1-0 victory over England in the 1950 World Cup.

Radnedge, Keir, "Say It Ain't So, Joáo!" *World Soccer,* February 1994.
British soccer columnist Radnedge takes FIFA President João Havelange to task for snubbing retired Brazilian superstar Pelé at last December's World Cup Final Draw in Las Vegas, Nev.

Reports and Studies

American Professional Soccer League, *APSL Media Guide,* Washington, D.C., 1993.
Highlights of the guide are the league history and all-time APSL player register.

Intercollegiate Soccer Association of America, *Intercollegiate Soccer Association of America Guide, 1993-1994,* St. Louis, Mo., Aug. 21, 1993.
The guide includes useful maps of the regions for Division I, II and III men's and women's college soccer, men's and women's intercollegiate records and explanations of how teams are selected for the national playoff tournaments.

National Professional Soccer League, *1993-94 Media Guide,* Canton, Ohio, 1993.
Histories and rosters for each team in the country's top indoor pro soccer league, plus statistics demonstrating the league's growing success as a gate attraction.

World Cup USA 1994 Inc., *World Cup USA 1994 Press Kit,* New York City, February 1994.
This magazine-size guide provides all the information the casual fan is likely to want about the coming tournament. Included are biographies of the leading officials of FIFA and World Cup USA 1994, description of the cities and stadiums where the games will be played, a history of U.S. soccer and a recap of the qualification rounds.

The Next Step

Additional information from UMI's Newspaper & Periodical Abstracts database

Coverage of the World Cup

Cooper, Jim, "No interruptions during World Cup," *Broadcasting & Cable,* June 7, 1993, p. 96.
The 1994 World Cup soccer matches, which will be the first to be held in the U.S., will be aired on network and cable telecasts without interruptions for commercials during the action. The plan of ABC and ESPN is discussed.

Starr, Mark, "Black, white and round all over," *Newsweek,* June 7, 1993, pp. 54-55.
The 1994 World Cup tournament that will be held in various sites across the U.S. is discussed, as is a U.S. Cup that will precede it. The World Cup could be the catalyst to increased appreciation of soccer in the U.S.

Verdi, Bob, "Open Arms or Cold Shoulders for World Cup?" *Sporting News*, July 30, 1990, p. 50.
The World Cup soccer tournament is scheduled for the U.S. in 1994, but the major networks say they will not bid for TV rights. The games will probably be seen on cable.

High School Soccer

Chin, Paula, Margie Sellinger and Brian Cazeneuve, "The Team from Hanoi High," *People Weekly,* Oct. 14, 1991, pp. 55-58.
A squad of high school soccer players from Hanoi, Vietnam, paid a visit to Alexandria, Va. There, they played a soccer game with the soccer team of Bishop Ireton High School and stayed in the homes of high school students. Students from both countries enjoyed the visit.

Gammon, Clive, "America's Teen," *Sports Illustrated,* June 12, 1989, pp. 68-73.
Todd Haskins, one of the stars of the U.S. under-16 national soccer team, is profiled. Haskins and his colleagues believe that they have what it takes to win the international competition.

Kerth, T.R., "Some Good Advice About Bad Refs," *Scholastic Coach,* August 1991, pp. 30-31.
The state of youth and high school soccer in the U.S. is promising, with young people exhibiting skill levels and knowledge that were rare 10 years ago. Referees' reactions to the skills at the younger level are discussed.

Nance, Roscoe, "Coach's dual role raises questions," *USA TODAY,* Nov. 23, 1993, p. C2.
North Carolina women's soccer coach Anson Dorrance agrees that as coach of the U.S. women's national team, he has an advantage on his collegiate colleagues. But he says it doesn't come from recruiting, as some feel, and that the edge isn't primarily responsible for the Tar Heels winning 11 of the past 12 national titles.

Profiles of the Players

Cart, Julie, "Vagabond," *Los Angeles Times,* Dec. 14, 1993, p. C1.
Soccer player Hugo Perez is profiled. A native of El Salvador, Perez is a member of the U.S. national team.

Ferro, John, "N.C. State teammates make mark in France," *USA TODAY,* Jan. 6, 1994, p. C11.
Henry Gutierrez and Dario Brose, former soccer teammates at North Carolina State, played on rival French teams before they were reunited on St. Brieuc in the new Super Second division. Brose plans to work out with the U.S. national team in January 1994.

Hersch, Hank, "Sports people: Alexi Lalas," *Sports Illustrated,* Jan. 31, 1994, p. 68.
U.S. national soccer team defender Alexi Lalas is profiled. Lalas has proved himself to be a versatile defender and a valuable scorer for the team.

Nance, Roscoe, "Balboa looks sharp; USA nips Norway," *USA TODAY*, Jan. 17, 1994, p. C6.
Sweeper Marcelo Balboa took another step on the comeback trail with a strong performance in the U.S. national team's 2-1 come-from-behind victory Jan. 15, 1994, against fellow World Cup qualifier Norway.

Nance, Roscoe, "Jones takes licking but keeps on ticking," *USA TODAY,* Feb. 3, 1994, p. C7.
U.S. National Soccer Team midfielder Cobi Jones has been getting roughed up and double-teamed and realizes that the physical play is being directed at him because he is regarded as an attacking force for a team not known for its offense.

Nance, Roscoe, "League dramas have hold on key U.S. stars," *USA TODAY,* March 10, 1994, p. C8.
Eric Wynalda of FC Saarbruecken (Germany) and Tab Ramos of Real Betis (Spain) might not be available to the U.S. national soccer team until Jun 1994 because their teams are in contention for promotion to the first division. The second-division season ends June 11, a week before the U.S.'s first World Cup match. The U.S. must submit its 22-man World Cup roster to FIFA by June 3.

Nance, Roscoe, "Raves abroad haven't put Keller on U.S. team," *USA TODAY*, Jan. 12, 1994, p. C4.

Goalkeeper Kasey Keller's play is a major reason Millwall is fourth in the first division and a serious contender for promotion to the Premier League in the 1994 season. However, Keller's status with the U.S. national team remains in limbo.

Nance, Roscoe, "Shaking off last year's rust, Burns displays polished game," ***USA TODAY,*** **Feb. 3, 1994, p. C7.**
Despite having hardly played soccer in 1993, U.S. National Soccer Team midfielder Mike Burns has impressed the team's coaching staff. Coach Bora Milutinovic said he wants Burns to remain with the team until the 22-man World Cup roster is picked in June 1994.

Nance, Roscoe, "Stewart fast becoming fixture in USA's one-forward attack," ***USA TODAY*****, Feb. 16, 1994, p. C2.**
Speed is the first thing many notice about U.S. national team forward Ernie Stewart.

Nance, Roscoe, "Wegerle hopes knee heals in time for Cup," ***USA TODAY*****, Feb. 1, 1994, p. C9.**
U.S. national soccer team forward Roy Wegerle is being positive about his chances of being able to participate in the 1994 World Cup. But it's difficult for him to conceal his disappointment after injuring his right knee.

Vincent, Charlie, "Lalas comes out of his soccer nutshell," ***Detroit News & Free Press*****, Dec. 4, 1993, p. B1.**
Charlie Vincent comments on U.S. soccer player Alexi Lalas, who is one of the three finalists for the 1993 Honda Player of the Year award.

Opinions and Concerns

Attner, Paul, "Crazy about a Cure for Insomnia?'" ***Sporting News,*** **July 23, 1990, p. 46.**
It is difficult for American sports fans to understand how an entire country can be so totally devoted to the details of something quite so boring as soccer, Attner writes.

Collins, Patrick, "No American Do," ***Punch,*** **Dec. 11, 1991, pp. 20-21.**
The 1992 World Cup will definitely be played in the U.S., which is a country that does not appreciate the game of soccer. The World Cup draw is criticized.

Diaz, Jaime, "Alive, but Barely Kicking," ***Sports Illustrated,*** **Oct. 27, 1986, pp. 62-63.**
Despite the predictions of coaches, promoters and players, soccer has failed to draw regular, large crowds across the U.S. The future of the game in America is described as in limbo.

Levine, Art, "Soccer: The Game America Doesn't Watch," ***U.S. News & World Report,*** **June 30, 1986, p. 56.**
Eight million people in the U.S. play soccer, but TV ratings for the sport in the U.S. are negligible. American indifference toward watching the sport on TV has been blamed on the game's low scores, lack of American superstars and the country's dismal international record.

"Person to person: Pelé on American soccer and the World Cup," ***Scholastic Coach,*** **December 1993, pp. A18-A22.**
In an interview, the retired Brazilian superstar discusses how he became interested in soccer and the teams he played on early in his career. Pelé believes that the World Cup is the most pressurized form of international sports competition, but he has enjoyed many of them and is looking forward to the one in 1994 in the U.S.

Starr, Mark, "Do you believe in miracles?" ***Newsweek*****, Dec. 20, 1993, pp. 104-105.**
A preview of 1993 World Cup soccer tournament is offered, as are plans by the FIFA (Fédération Internationale de Football Association) to use the World Cup to launch a major U.S. pro soccer league in 1995. There is talk that the FIFA may manipulate the draw to give the U.S. a favorable chance to compete.

Wilson, Jonathan, "Soccer apocalypse," ***New Yorker,*** **Jan. 10, 1994, p. 90.**
After the final draw Dec 19, 1993, it was determined that soccer's World Cup will be held in the U.S. Wilson calls soccer a dirty, stomach-churning, confusing, passionate and profane sport and says enthusiasts are afraid the U.S will curtail the traditional freedom associated with soccer.

Soccer and the Advertising Industry

Grimm, Matthew, "Adidas drives on soccer goal with $10M," ***Brandweek,*** **Sept. 28, 1992, p. 5.**
Adidas U.S.A. will spend at least $10 million in a 1993 media push to start a build-up to the World Cup '94, the global soccer tournament in the U.S.

Grimm, Matthew, "Soccer USA scores big with P&G," ***Brandweek,*** **Jan. 25, 1993, p. 1.**
Seven new sponsorship deals have been announced by Soccer USA Partners, the packager of pre-World Cup marketing and TV programs, and they include a sweeping multi-brand package with Procter & Gamble. A spate of sponsorships for Soccer USA is discussed.

Jensen, Jeff, "World Cup aims to score U.S. fans," ***Advertising Age,*** **May 24, 1993, p. 36.**
Even though people in the U.S. have traditionally shown little support for soccer, organizers are hoping to sell the 1994 World Cup with 11 major sponsorships. The campaign from Dentsu Corp. of America is detailed.

"On Wings of Gold," ***The Economist*****, July 25, 1992, pp. S8-S9.**
Sports are being invented for commercial gain, with TV

helping spread them across the globe. Soccer's expansion into the U.S., where the 1994 World's Cup will be held, and Africa, is discussed.

Smart, Tim, "This May Be the Kick American Soccer Needs," ***Business Week,*** **Sept. 16, 1991, pp. 98-99.**
Americans may finally begin to sit up and notice soccer when the U.S. hosts the World Cup championship in 1994. Many predict the World Cup will be a marketing bonanza as well as a boost for the U.S. soccer team.

"Soccer's last frontier," ***The Economist*****, Dec. 4, 1993, p. 100.**
The 1994 World Cup is giving soccer's promoters another chance to overcome U.S. resistance to the most popular sport on earth. U.S. TV executives remain skeptical about the commercial potential of a game that consists of 45-minute halves of unbroken action.

"The World Cup soccer games finally come to America," ***Business America*****, May 17, 1993, pp. 2-6.**
The U.S. will host soccer's premier event, the World Cup, for the first time in 1994, and more than a million international visitors are expected to attend. There will be special opportunities for the travel and tourism industry.

Soccer in the U.S.

Busby, Jim, "Soccer Kicks up in America," ***Current Health 2,*** **October 1992, pp. 16-17.**
The growing popularity of soccer in the U.S. is discussed, as are the similarities and differences between soccer and football.

McCormick, Mike, "The world cup of soccer," ***Europe: Magazine of the European Community,*** **December 1992, pp. 42-43.**
The importance of World Cup soccer to the sport's fans is discussed. The Féderation Internationale de Football Association (FIFA) is looking to expand soccer in the U.S.

Rose, David James, "Virginia: Not Just for Kicks," ***Hispanic,*** **September 1992, pp. 60-62.**
Many Hispanic Americans enjoy playing soccer. The Fairfax Soccer League in northern Virginia is discussed. It is one of only two Hispanic soccer leagues to be recognized by the U.S. Soccer Federation.

Saporito, Bill, "Soccer scores in the U.S.," ***Fortune,*** **July 26, 1993, pp. 13-14.**
There appears to be a tremendous pent-up demand for soccer in the U.S., as was evidenced by U.S. sales of World Cup tickets. The popularity of the game in the U.S. is discussed.

"What's the pitch," ***Scholastic Coach,*** **December 1992, pp. A14-A18.**
In an interview, Bob Gansler, U.S. Soccer Federation director of coaching and player development, discusses the soccer scene over the past several decades.

Yeomans, Matthew, "U.S. Cup '93: Boorish American scribes, half-decent U.S. players, and gracious English fans," ***Village Voice,*** **June 22, 1993, p. 145.**
Despite losing to the Brazilian team, the U.S. soccer team showed at the recent U.S. Cup that it can at last hold its own among international competition. Some xenophobic sportswriters still consider soccer a "foreign" sport.

Technology at the World Cup

Bannister, Nick, "Silicon Valley turns World Cup hi-tech," ***Guardian,*** **Jan. 24, 1994, p. 1.**
A group of computer companies in California's Silicon Valley is establishing an information network for the World Cup organization that will follow and detail all of the 1994 World Cup soccer matches in the U.S.

Bozman, Jean S., "World Cup soccer kicks into high tech," ***Computerworld,*** **Jan. 24, 1994, p. 51.**
The logistics of network management for soccer's World Cup, which will be staged in nine cities across the U.S. in the summer of 1994, are discussed. The World Cup promises to be the most technologically advanced major event in sports.

Crump, Andy, "Fair Play, Please," ***New Scientist*****, July 14, 1990, p. 63.**
The application of technology like instant replays would make soccer fairer all around. The U.S. will host the next World Cup match; perhaps the world can look forward to fairer and more professional control over play then.

Women's Soccer

Dillon, Susan R., "Global Goals," ***Women's Sports & Fitness,*** **March 1992, pp. 70-71.**
U.S. National Women's Soccer Team captain April Heinrichs talks about competition at the collegiate level, soccer training, the World Cup, being a team captain and the U.S. women's team.

Plummer, William and Tom Nugent, "Kicking up a Storm," ***People Weekly,*** **Nov. 25, 1991, pp. 99-100.**
U.S. soccer star Michelle Akers-Stahl is profiled. Akers-Stahl has twice been named soccer's Female Athlete of the Year.

Trotta, Gian, "Hail the Conquering Heroines," ***Village Voice,*** **Dec. 10, 1991, p. 162.**
Michelle Akers-Stahl led the U.S. women's scooer team to the first-ever FIFA Women's World Championship. The bravura performance of the U.S. in the 12-team tournament is described.

Back Issues

Great Research on Current Issues Starts Right Here...Recent topics covered by The CQ Researcher are listed below. Before May 1991, reports were published under the name of Editorial Research Reports.

OCTOBER 1992
Depression
U.S. Auto Industry
Youth Apprenticeships
Hispanic Americans

NOVEMBER 1992
Physical Fitness
Privatization
Paying for College
U.S. Policy in Asia

DECEMBER 1992
Crackdown on Smoking
The New CIA
Eating Disorders
Women and AIDS

JANUARY 1993
Hate Crimes
Child Sexual Abuse
Nuclear Fusion
U.S. Trade Policy

FEBRUARY 1993
Community Policing
Europe's New Right
School Censorship
Violence Against Women

MARCH 1993
Gay Rights
Aid to Russia
War on Drugs
TV Violence

APRIL 1993
Head Start
High-Speed Rail
Children's Legal Rights
Muslims in America

MAY 1993
Cults in America
Preventing Teen Pregnancy
Software Piracy
National Parks

JUNE 1993
Food Safety
Prostitution
Childhood Immunizations
National Service

JULY 1993
Electric Cars
Population Growth
Downward Mobility
Intelligence Testing

AUGUST 1993
Mental Illness
Bilingual Education
Foreign Policy Burden
School Funding

SEPTEMBER 1993
Suburban Crime
Public Housing
Supreme Court Preview
Immigration Reform

OCTOBER 1993
Airline Safety
Disaster Response
Science in the Courtroom
The Glass Ceiling

NOVEMBER 1993
Paying for Retirement
Charitable Giving
Privacy in the Workplace
Adoption

DECEMBER 1993
U.S. Vietnam-Relations
Learning Disabilities
Child Care
Space Program's Future

JANUARY 1994
Racial Tensions in Schools
South Africa's Future
Worker Retraining
Regulating Pesticides

FEBRUARY 1994
Prison Overcrowding
Water Quality
Religion in Schools
Juvenile Justice

MARCH 1994
Underground Economy
Education Standards
Gambling Boom
Private Management of Public Schools

APRIL 1994
Reproductive Ethics
U.S.-China Trade

Back issues are available for $4.00 (subscribers) or $7.00 (non-subscribers). Quantity discounts apply to orders over ten. To order, call Congressional Quarterly Customer Service at (202) 887-8621.

Binders are available for $16.00. To order call 1-800-638-1710. Please refer to stock number 648.

Future Topics

- ***Talk Show Democracy***
- ***Traffic Congestion***
- ***Women's Health Issues***

THE CQ Researcher

PUBLISHED BY CONGRESSIONAL QUARTERLY INC.

Talk Show Democracy

Are call-in programs good for the political system?

The proliferation of talk shows on radio and television has given politicians a new way to talk to their constituents. The public also gets a new way to make its views known and even sometimes to talk directly to its leaders — from President Clinton on down. But some critics view talk show democracy with concern, if not alarm. They fear that talk show hosts entertain more than they inform. They also complain that talk hosts like Rush Limbaugh and fellow conservatives are unfairly demonizing Clinton, Congress and all levels of government. But other political observers say talk shows are providing a valuable alternative to traditional news media and creating a new, interactive forum that will become more and more important in the years to come.

INSIDE

THIS ISSUE

CQ April 29, 1994 • Volume 4, No. 16 • 361-384

Formerly Editorial Research Reports

Talk Show Democracy

Cover art by P. Eloise Fuller. (Howard Stern photograph courtesy of E! Entertainment Television; Rush Limbaugh photograph by Kimberly Butler; Larry King photograph by Andrew Eccles © 1993 CNN Inc.)

The CQ Researcher

April 29, 1994
Volume 4, No. 16

The CQ Researcher (ISSN 1056-2036). Formerly Editorial Research Reports. Published weekly (48 times per year, not printed the first Friday of any month with five Fridays) by Congressional Quarterly Inc., 1414 22nd St., N.W., Washington, D.C. 20037. Rates are furnished upon request. Second-class postage paid at Washington, D.C. POSTMASTER: Send address changes to The CQ Researcher, 1414 22nd St., N.W., Washington, D.C. 20037.

Talk Show Democracy

BY KENNETH JOST

THE ISSUES

When legislation appeared in February that seemed to threaten parents' right to educate their children at home, the Home School Legal Defense Association sent out a nationwide alarm. Fax machines and computer bulletin boards first brought word of the offending provision in a federal education bill to thousands of home schooling families around the country. And then the group took to the airwaves.

Over the span of a few days, Executive Director Michael Farris and a half-dozen staff members appeared on more than 50 radio talk shows — all by telephone without ever leaving their offices in Purcellville, Va., just outside Washington. They asked listeners to call Congress and register their opposition to the provision. In no time at all, House switchboards were flooded with what Farris says were close to 1 million calls.

"We got a lot of calls on NAFTA, we got a lot of calls on gays in the military," says Brian Gunderson, administrative assistant to Rep. Dick Armey, R-Texas, "but I've never seen anything like this: going from no calls one day to the switchboards shut down the next."

Armey took on the fight in the House, and just 10 days later legislators removed the once-obscure provision from the bill by a vote of 422-1. Today, Farris gives credit to the talk shows for fueling the drive to kill the provision. "The talk shows were the jet fuel that helped the jet plane to really fly high," Farris says.

The episode demonstrates anew that America's growing corps of radio and television talk show hosts preside over a potentially powerful political weapon. Politicians in Washington and statehouses and city halls around the country have learned that lesson through bitter experience several times in recent years.

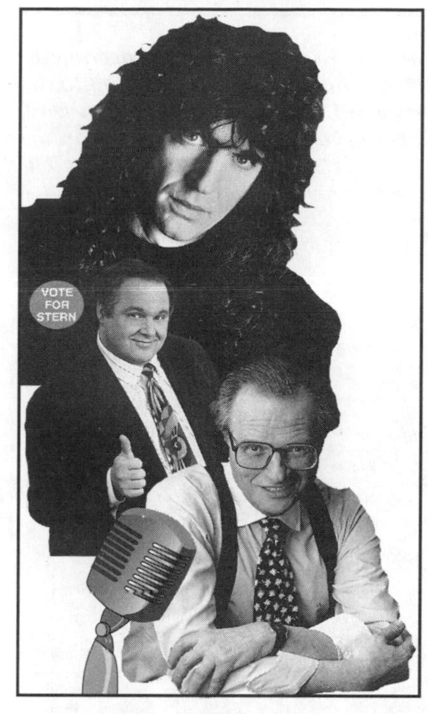

President Clinton fell victim to talk show democracy twice in his first month in office. He abandoned his first choice for attorney general, Zoë Baird, after talk show hosts and callers rose in near unison to protest her hiring of an undocumented alien for child care and failing to pay the employee's Social Security taxes. At the same time, the overwhelming opposition heard on call-in shows to lifting the ban on gays in the military helped force Clinton to back away from the proposal.

Congress, too, has felt the sting of America's talkmeisters. In 1989, they took the lead in mobilizing public opinion against a recommended pay raise for legislators. Under pressure, Congress blocked the increase. And for several years, talk show hosts have been among the loudest advocates for term limits for Congress — a proposition endorsed by voters in 15 states despite doubts about its constitutionality. [1]

For Farris, the home-school lobbying blitz was a vindication of direct democracy. "The grass roots works," he says. But direct democracy for one group may be viewed as mass hysteria by others.

"There have been occasions and likely will be again where members [of Congress] are overwhelmed with the kind of public reactions that comes from talk shows [and other news outlets] and which pushes them to a kind of rush to judgment," says Norman Ornstein, a resident scholar at the American Enterprise Institute and long-time Congresswatcher.

Talk shows have a predominantly conservative orientation, which has encouraged Republicans and other critics of the Clinton administration and congressional liberals. Rush Limbaugh, an unabashed conservative who has become the nation's most listened-to talk show host, was crowned "the leader of the opposition" in a recent cover story in the conservative *National Review* magazine. (*See story, p. 372.*)

David Keene, a political consultant and chairman of the American Conservative Union, credits talk shows with "revitalizing and refueling the conservatives and Republicans at the grass roots over the last year or so." But Keene also notes that Clinton has used talk shows both before and since his election "as a way of creating an alternative channel of communication to the public."

Clinton took questions from callers or a studio audience on more than 10 national TV programs between June and November 1992. [2] But he was not the only presidential candidate to make good use of talk shows that year. Billionaire Ross Perot launched his campaign on CNN's "Larry King Live" in February when he said he would run if supporters placed his name on the ballot in all 50 states. Even President George Bush took call-in questions on King's program late in the campaign — after having earlier dismissed "weird talk shows" as beneath the dignity of the White House.

The "talk show campaign" gener-

TV Talk Shows Outscore Traditional Media

*Television talk shows carried proportionally more "substantive" coverage of the 1992 presidential campaign than the traditional media, according to the Center for Media and Public Affairs. * Between Labor Day and Election Day, 74 percent of the 17 hours of campaign coverage by talk shows focused on the candidates' qualifications, policy issues or other substantive topics. By comparison, the eight traditional media outlets surveyed discussed substantive topics just 40 percent of the time, on average, though their overall amount of coverage was often much greater.*

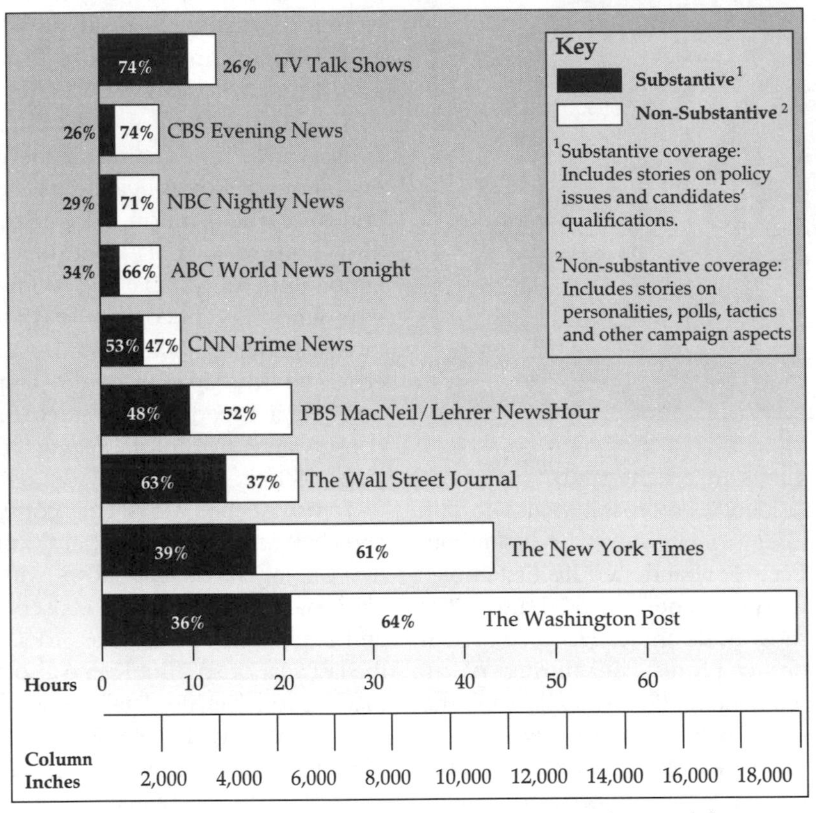

Talk shows were defined as shows that aired nationally on which a candidate appeared, including NBC's "Today," ABC's "Good Morning America," CNN's "Larry King Live" and the syndicated "Donahue."
Source: Center for Media and Public Affairs, February 1994

ated concern among many journalists, who complained that candidates were trying to avoid hard questions from print and broadcast reporters. But studies conducted after the election show that the talk shows focused more on substantive discussion of candidates' qualifications and policy positions than traditional news coverage did. (*See graph, above*).

"The talk shows were quite substantive," says Thomas Patterson, a political scientist at Syracuse University whose 1993 book, *Out of Order*, examines the role of the press in the campaign. "There was more issue content minute-by-minute on the talk shows than on the news."

The increased attention has encouraged some talk show hosts to make broad claims about their clout. Last fall, some 65 talk show hosts broadcast programs from the White House lawn the day after Clinton's health-care address to Congress. Afterward, Paul Lyle, a Long Island broadcaster and president of the five-year-old National Academy of Radio Talk Show Hosts, wrote in the organization's newsletter that the event marked the "elevation of our industry from gadfly to peer status with this country's policy-makers." [3]

Disinterested experts view the talkmeisters' impact a bit more modestly. "They can serve as a megaphone," says Randall Bloomquist, talk radio editor for the trade journal *Radio and Records,* "but they cannot set the agenda for what's going to be discussed on the megaphone."

Still, the consensus today is that talk shows — on radio and television — are here to stay. Indeed, call-in programming gives broadcasters and cable operators an economical way to fill more and more hours of air time and simultaneously build and hold audiences. And some hosts foresee a day when "interactive media" will be the nation's dominant means of communication.

"Talk radio is just the beginning of the new media of the 21st century," says Michael Harrison, who hosts a nationally syndicated radio program and edits *Talkers*, an industry news-magazine. "I foresee interactive media taking its place aside of and eventually replacing the traditional media as the main vehicle of communication in America in the next 20 years."

As Americans watch and listen to this new age of talk, talk, talk, here are some of the questions being debated:

Has the growth of talk shows been good for the political process?

When he campaigned for the presidency in 1992, Ross Perot said he would use "electronic town halls" to involve the public in policy-making if elected. While government by interactive telecommunications may not become reality for years — if ever — talk show hosts say they are already providing a new way for people to learn about and participate in the political process.

Larry King, in his book *On the Line* recounting the rise of talk shows in the 1992 presidential campaign, says call-in programs gave alienated and frustrated voters a feeling of empowerment. The public, he said, felt the country was being run "by a small group of people living comfortably under a bubble on the banks of the Potomac." Talk shows, he continued, "were like a glass cutter, a way for the public to reach the people under the bubble." [4]

After the election, talk show hosts continued to depict their programs as a powerful tool for bringing people closer to government. Gene Burns, a syndicated radio host on WOR in New York and incoming president of the talk hosts' association, calls such shows "the most efficient reconnect mechanism between the governed and those who govern."

One prominent media expert, however, discounts the notion that talk shows have changed the political system. Kathleen Hall Jamieson, dean of the Annenberg School for Communication at the University of Pennsylvania in Philadelphia, says call-in programs produce only "a voyeuristic sense of participation."

"Most of us aren't going to make that call, and most of us aren't going to get through," says Jamieson, who is working on a book for publication next year about politics and the media.

Jamieson's observation is borne out by a survey last summer. The Times Mirror Center for The People and The Press found that 61 percent of the public have listened to talk radio shows at some point, but only 17 percent say they listen "regularly." Eleven percent say they have tried to call in, but only 6 percent say they have ever talked on the air. [5]

King cites those figures himself but says people feel "empowered" anyway. "Just seeing that telephone number on their TV screens or hearing it on their radios, knowing they could call if they wanted to, hearing other people voice their own fears and frustrations was liberating enough," he writes.

Jamieson minimizes as well a second claim made by talk show hosts — that their programs promote an exchange of views between different segments of the public or between the public and the government. On radio in particular, she says, most talk programs "tend to have just one side ideologically" and merely "reinforce" the existing views of their audiences.

"Conservatives are listening to conservatives, liberals are listening to liberals, blacks are listening to blacks and young people are listening to Howard Stern," Jamieson says. Stern is the foul-mouthed "shock jock" who has drawn more than $1 million in fines from the Federal Communications Commission (FCC) for indecency.

Limbaugh's program — now heard on more than 600 radio stations with an estimated 20 million listeners each week — illustrates the point. In five years of syndication, the one-time disc jockey has built an avid following with what has been dubbed his "hard-edged humor and hard-right views." [6] Callers took up the habit of signaling their agreement with Limbaugh's views by simply saying "Ditto" — and now Limbaugh's followers proudly call themselves Dittoheads.

But the program manager at Limbaugh's home station insists that talk shows take pains to avoid airing just one side of an issue. "Anyone who wants to challenge the host always goes to the top of the line because we want debate," says John Mainelli, program director of New York's all-talk WABC. "The last thing we want is a series of yes-men. That would be boring."

Clearly, though, the need to produce entertainment places a higher premium on opinion than on information. And today, much of the opinion heard on talk programs has a sharply anti-government tone that troubles some media observers.

"The latest gaggle of talk show hosts tends to follow a very superficial, mechanistic, cheap, ill-considered view demonizing government and everything about it," says Andrew Jay Schwartzman, director of the liberal Media Access Project in Washington. "The impact of that has been unfortunate."

For their supporters, however, the populist denunciations of politicians and government officials heard on talk shows strengthen rather than threaten the democratic process. "Their combined impact is to put a lot of facts and a lot of information about what is going on in Washington before their publics," says conservative activist Keene. "They're reaching an attentive portion of the public, and that public responds."

Do talk shows present an accurate view of public opinion?

Talk shows may entertain and inform, but hosts and their audiences also believe the programs give a good picture of public opinion on the issues of the day. Evidence about the audiences for radio talk shows — which often are more ideological than television call-in programs — gives a mixed picture, however, about their usefulness in measuring popular sentiment.

When the Times Mirror Center surveyed radio talk show hosts, more than half — 56 percent — said they believe their callers are representative of the larger public in their listening area. And most listeners and callers — about 60 percent — said they believe the programs offer a diversity of viewpoints rather than being dominated by one perspective, liberal or conservative.

Under closer questioning, however, almost all of the hosts acknowledged some biases in the opinions of those who call — largely from conservatives. A solid majority of hosts said they think that conservatives are overrepresented and liberals underrepresented on their programs. Substantial numbers of hosts also felt that people who dislike the president or Congress or oppose abortion or homosexuality are overrepresented, while feminists and abortion rights supporters are underrepresented. [7]

The survey of talk show audiences confirmed some of those observations. Republicans and conservatives are more

Comparing Views of Radio Hosts and the Public

Talk radio hosts and listeners had more critical views of President Clinton and Congress than the public at large, according to a survey by the Times Mirror Center for The People and The Press. Hosts were also more critical than the public toward daily newspapers and network TV news.

	Favorable	Unfavorable
Bill Clinton		
Talk Hosts	46%	53%
Regular Listeners	48	48
General Public	60	34
Robert Dole		
Talk Hosts	56	42
Regular Listeners	60	27
General Public	48	28
Ross Perot		
Talk Hosts	39	58
Regular Listeners	65	30
General Public	64	31
Congress		
Talk Hosts	25	73
Regular Listeners	34	59
General Public	43	48
Daily Papers		
Talk Hosts	67	29
Regular Listeners	78	18
General Public	81	13
Network TV News		
Talk Hosts	54	42
Regular Listeners	76	22
General Public	81	15

Totals may not equal 100 because some respondents had no opinion.
Source: Times Mirror Center for The People and The Press, July 16, 1993

likely to listen to talk radio and to call in than Democrats or liberals, the survey found. And compared with the general public, talk show listeners were less likely to give favorable ratings to President Clinton, Congress and the Democratic Party and more likely to give favorable ratings to the Republican Party and to the one GOP leader asked about — Senate Minority Leader Bob Dole of Kansas.

On the other hand, talk show listeners roughly matched overall public sentiment on specific issues studied. The survey found that the general public and regular talk show listeners favored term limits for Congress and a school prayer constitutional amendment and opposed allowing gays and lesbians to serve in the military. The survey also found — in contradiction to talk hosts' perceptions — that most listeners, like most of the public, oppose laws making it more difficult for women to get an abortion.

Reporter Bloomquist says even the most listened to talk shows draw only a small fraction — perhaps 4 percent or so — of the total radio listenership. Even fewer people actually call a station. In addition, he says, callers are unlikely to be typical of the general public.

"They either have too much time on their hands or they have a wildly passionate feeling one way or another about an issue," says Bloomquist. "What you're hearing on the air is a very, very small sample of the public, and it's just not statistically valid."

Some hosts discount the criticisms that talk shows may be unrepresentative of overall public opinion. "They're probably as representative as the actual people who vote," says Harrison. "We're a nation of minorities. We're a nation of special interests."

But Bruce Williams, who hosts a nationally syndicated, determinedly apolitical radio program, agrees that political shows draw an unrepresentative audience. "If you take the politically oriented stuff, you don't get a representative sampling," Williams says. "That's not a criticism. It's an observation."

Interestingly, however, the Times Mirror Center study cast doubt on the common impression that talk shows are predominantly conservative. The 112 talk hosts included in the survey spanned the partisan and ideological spectrums. Politically, 38 percent described themselves as Republican or leaning Republican compared with 44 percent who described themselves as Democrats or leaning Democratic (18 percent gave no affiliation). Ideologically, 46 percent said they were conservative or leaning conservative while 43 percent were liberal or leaning liberal.

Still, conservative talkmeisters have been far more outspoken in recent days than liberal hosts, based on an in-depth sampling of recent broadcasts. Limbaugh's unabashed conservatism is matched by local talk hosts in a number of cities — such as Bob Grant at New York's WABC, Mike Rosen at Denver's KOA, David Gold at WLIF in Dallas and a growing number of black conservative hosts, among them Marie Kaigler at WJR in Detroit, C. Miles Smith of WGST in Atlanta and Armstrong Williams of WOL in Washington, D.C.

The most prominent liberal hosts, on the other hand, inject their views less forcefully, if at all. Larry King is a liberal Democrat, but his views are virtually undetectable on his television program and not especially

Cue the Talent: Profiles of Some of the Nation's Top Talkmeisters

Larry King, Mutual Broadcasting and CNN, Washington: Has conducted more than 30,000 interviews in four decades on air; 400 radio stations; TV program seen worldwide. "I am not a journalist," he writes. "I'm an interviewer, a TV and radio personality — an entertainer."

Gene Burns, WOR Network, New York: Talk host for 27 years; more than 100 stations; conservative/libertarian views; incoming president, National Association of Talk Radio Show Hosts. Talk radio, he says, "is raw, rough and tumble, occasionally hostile but basically honest and unfiltered."

Jerry Williams, WRKO, Boston: Forty years in broadcasting; at WRK0 since 1983; one-time liberal, now harshly criticizes taxes, government spending and politicians of all parties. He calls talk hosts "radio politicians without portfolio. . . . We can talk on anything."

Mary Beal and Doug Stephan, Independent Broadcasters Network, Wichita, Kan., and Framingham, Mass.: Paired on nationally syndicated program for three years; 135 stations, predominantly smaller cities and rural areas; Stephan takes conservative stands, Beal is more moderate. "We respect each other," Beal says, "but we don't always see eye to eye."

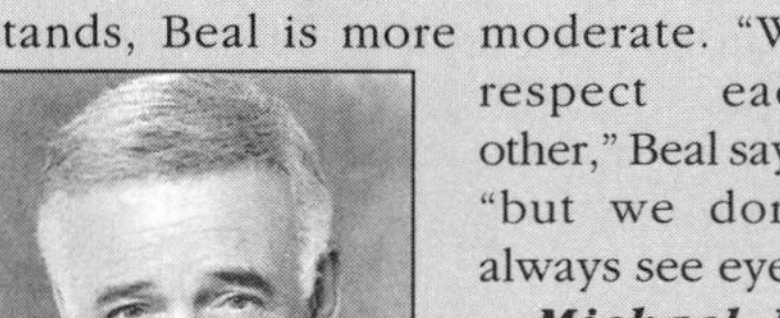

Michael Jackson, KABC, Los Angeles: Veteran of nation's first all-talk station; on air since 1965; British native, cerebral style; moderate to liberal views; critical of conservative hosts. "They don't generally welcome opinions different from their own," he says.

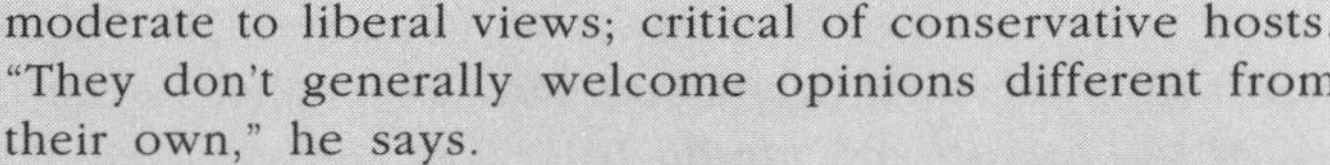

Howard Stern, Infinity Broadcasting (WXRK), New York: "Shock-jock" heard by 15 million listeners; on air since 1980; wrote best-selling autobiography, *Private Parts;* Infinity was fined more than $1 million by FCC for indecency. "I don't think that you can go too far on radio," he tells a reporter.

Don Imus, WFAN, New York: Irreverent morning host on all-sports station; on air for more than 20 years; topics range from scatology to politics. "I'm Howard Stern with a vocabulary," he tells an interviewer. "I'm the man he wishes he could be."

C. Miles Smith, WGST, Atlanta: Hosts "hippest trip on talk radio;" studied drama in college; on air since 1989; criticizes "so-called civil rights leaders;" endorses Nation of Islam leader Louis Farrakhan. "I think every black man ought to have a gun," he tells listeners.

Ray Suarez, National Public Radio, Washington: TV news reporter for 10 years; NPR host since April 1993; only Hispanic host of national talk program. "Listeners are driving the conversation," he says. "Calling 'Talk of the Nation' and saying 'Ditto, Ray,' is just not enough."

Bruce Williams, Talk Net, New Port Richey, Fla.: Top-rated nighttime syndicated program; about 325 stations; 19 years on air; listeners set the agenda, mostly personal or financial problems. "My program is vanilla," he says, "but vanilla is the most popular flavor."

prominent on radio. Similarly, the liberal-leaning Michael Jackson, who has been on KABC in Los Angeles since 1966, says he welcomes callers with opposing viewpoints. "If you have something to say, I don't care what your ideology is," Jackson says.

If there is a political or ideological imbalance on talk shows, the government has no legal tool for remedying the problem. Beginning in the 1940s, the FCC adopted a policy — called the "fairness doctrine" — that required broadcasters to present fair coverage of opposing viewpoints on major public issues. But the agency repealed the doctrine in 1987, and efforts in Congress to re-enact it have been unsuccessful. (*See story, p. 370.*)

Have talk programs displaced the role of the traditional media in covering politics and government?

For many political journalists and media observers, the 1992 campaign seemed to be ushering in a new — and unsettling — era of covering politics and government. As politicians learned new ways of using talk shows to deliver their messages to voters, some in the political press corps complained that the campaign was losing dignity and substance. And they grumbled that the candidates were ducking hard questions from trained journalists in favor of softball questions from poorly informed voters.

Some reporters even feared that talk shows were making them obsolete — unnecessary to the communication process between candidates and voters. "The candidates, tired of having their words sliced and diced into a few sentences in the paper, or challenged by the Sunday-morning pontificators, would simply cut out the middleman," Howard Kurtz, *The Washington Post's* media critic, wrote in a post-election assessment of what he and others called "the talk show campaign." [8]

As the Clinton administration took office, some staffers thought they could continue to use "the new media" to get their message to the voters rather than using traditional forums, like the presidential press conference. "You know why I can stiff you on the press conferences?" Clinton himself told a Radio and Television Correspondents Association dinner in March 1993. "Because Larry King has liberated me from you by giving me to the American people directly."

The voters who follow politics and government through talk shows appear to welcome this new media era. Thomas Rosenstiel, a *Los Angeles Times* reporter in Washington who covers the media and politics, says talk shows reached out to "new audiences that had tuned out the mainstream press." [9]

"The public was gravitating to shows like Larry King and Phil Donahue because they were rejecting the ways in which the traditional press operated — formats that cut up the news into little bits, the press' focus on attack tactics, horse race and politics and the press' boredom with policy," Rosenstiel says.

Today, more than a year after the election, political practitioners and people in and around the media are moving toward a more balanced view of both talk shows and the traditional press. This emerging consensus views talk shows as an important forum for candidates and officials to learn to use and a valuable source of information for the public. But voters should supplement that information with reporting and commentary from traditional print and broadcast journalism.

Talk Radio's Top 10 Topics, 1993

1. Crime and Violence
2. Health Care
3. The Economy
4. Civil Rights
5. Education
6. Natural Disasters
7. Foreign Affairs
8. Sex Scandals
9. Science and Technology
10. Sports and Entertainment

Source: Talkers *magazine, December 1993*

"The candidates have learned how to use a broad range of venues to reach a broad range of people," says Hal Bruno, political director at ABC News. "I don't see anything wrong with [talk shows] as long as they continue to be responsive and give access to the mainstream media, too."

Ellen Hume, media analyst with Northwestern University's Annenberg Washington program, says journalists are still necessary to straighten out the "uncorrected information" often broadcast on talk shows. "We still need journalists to provide carefully checked out facts," Hume says. "We still need thoughtful commentators. If you combine the wonderful free flow of talk with some more authoritative information and thoughtful commentary, then you have democratic discourse."

The Clinton administration, too, appears to recognize that it cannot dispense entirely with the "old media." While Clinton has used a variety of techniques — including town hall meetings and two appearances on Larry King's TV show taking call-in questions — he has also recognized the need to take questions from the White House press corps.

In March, for example, Clinton held a prime-time news conference to counter a growing clamor for answers about the Whitewater affair. David Lauter, White House correspondent for the *Los Angeles Times,* says aides considered but rejected other options, including an interview with CBS's Dan Rather on the network's magazine show "48 Minutes" or an interview with a weekly newsmagazine. Instead, Lauter says, "They decided that the public needed to see him answering questions from the press."

Larry King himself stresses the importance of traditional press coverage of politics. King subtitled his book on the role of talk shows in the '92 campaign "the new road to the White House." But he declares: "Talk shows should supplement the campaign press, not replace it. There's room enough for everyone." [10] ■

BACKGROUND

A Political Medium

From its inception, broadcasting in the United States has been a me-

Continued on p. 370

Chronology

1920-1949

Radio grows quickly from a handful of small stations to a national communications medium. National networks are established.

1921
The first commercial radio stations begin operating: KDKA in Pittsburgh and WBZ in Springfield, Mass. — now in Boston.

1924
National party conventions are broadcast on radio.

March 12, 1933
President Franklin D. Roosevelt makes the first of his 28 "fireside chats," reassuring Americans on the security of bank deposits.

Oct. 5, 1947
President Harry S Truman makes the first television broadcast from the White House — an appeal for public support of food conservation program.

1950s-1979

Television becomes dominant communications medium for entertainment and news. Talk radio becomes popular format.

Dec. 16, 1954
President Dwight D. Eisenhower permits radio and television to tape press conferences for later broadcast.

Aug. 1, 1960
KABC in Los Angeles becomes nation's first all-talk radio station, followed shortly by KMOX in St. Louis.

Sept. 26, 1960
Presidential candidates John F. Kennedy and Richard M. Nixon appear in the first of four televised debates. Kennedy's performance is widely viewed as a key factor in his narrow victory.

Nov. 5, 1968
Nixon is elected president after a campaign marked by deft use of television advertising.

May 17, 1973
Senate Watergate Committee opens televised hearings on the 1972 break-in into the Democratic National Committee and later coverup by the Nixon White House and campaign.

March 5, 1977
President Jimmy Carter answers questions on hour-long call-in program on CBS radio network.

March 19, 1979
C-SPAN — the Cable Satellite Public Affairs Network — begins operations, carrying floor proceedings of the House of Representatives and, later, the Senate along with additional news and information programming.

1980s

Cable television expands to reach most households in U.S. with dozens of channels of programming. Satellite technology facilitates growth of nationally syndicated radio talk shows.

1988
National Association of Radio Talk Show Hosts is founded. Group grows from 75 people at first convention in 1989 to about 3,000 members today.

February 1989
Congress rejects recommended pay raise after widespread public protest fueled in part by radio talk shows.

1990s

Presidential candidates make unprecedented use of talk shows on radio and television in 1992 campaign.

Feb. 20, 1992
Ross Perot, on CNN's "Larry King Live," says he will run as independent candidate for president if supporters place his name on ballot in 50 states.

Oct. 15, 1992
In their second campaign debate, President George Bush, Democratic nominee Bill Clinton and independent Ross Perot field questions from an audience of 200 undecided voters in Richmond, Va.

Jan. 22, 1993
Zoë Baird withdraws as President Clinton's nominee for attorney general after opposition from talk show hosts and callers.

Sept. 23, 1993
Sixty-five radio talk show hosts broadcast from White House lawn, interviewing officials on health-care proposal and other issues.

April 5-8, 1994
President Clinton appears in three televised town hall meetings to push the administration's health-care reform proposal and answer questions about other policies.

Will the "Fairness Doctrine" Be Reborn?

The Federal Communications Commission (FCC) did something back in 1987 that delighted broadcasters: It repealed the "fairness doctrine."

Now there's an effort in Congress to re-establish the doctrine. Opponents depict the move as an attack on talk radio. "The Beltway [crowd] is trying to pull the plug on its effective critics," a *Wall Street Journal* editorial said. [1]

To sharpen the point, the newspaper mocked the proposed legislation as "the Hush Rush Law" — with an accompanying picture of talk show host Rush Limbaugh, who has built an audience of 20 million listeners by bashing Congress, Democrats, feminists, environmentalists, civil rights groups and everything else on the liberal end of the political spectrum.

Proponents of the fairness doctrine say the legislative battle has nothing to do with the growth of talk radio or its predominantly conservative slant. "We've been trying to restore the fairness doctrine since Rush Limbaugh was spinning records in Sacramento," says Andrew Jay Schwartzman, director of the Media Access Project, a liberal Washington public interest lobbying group. [2]

The fairness doctrine required broadcasters to cover local issues and to provide a "reasonable opportunity" for discussion of contrasting viewpoints. Federal regulators had called for broadcasters to give fair coverage of opposing viewpoints as early as the 1920s, and the FCC formally adopted the policy in 1949.

In the 1960s, broadcast journalists mounted a legal attack on the doctrine, saying the policy abridged their First Amendment rights. But the U.S. Supreme Court unanimously upheld the policy in 1969. The court said the regulation was justified because of the scarcity of broadcast frequencies.

Today, with more than 11,000 radio stations and 1,500 television stations and the introduction of cable television, broadcasters say the spectrum-scarcity argument makes no sense. "You've got more diversity now than ever," says Steve Bookshester, associate general counsel for the National Association of Broadcasters (NAB). "If scarcity has to do with voices, then you certainly don't have scarcity."

A deregulation-era FCC voted to repeal the doctrine in 1987. Congress sought to write the policy into law the same year, but President Ronald Reagan vetoed the bill. The House of Representatives has passed similar bills three times since then, but the legislation died in the Senate.

The House Telecommunications Subcommittee took up the issue in hearings last July. But the effort stalled after religious broadcasters lobbied against it, saying the policy might force them to present opposing views on moral and religious questions.

Limbaugh himself has railed against the fairness doctrine, conjuring up an image of being forced to present liberal views on his show. " The fairness doctine is simply today's application of political correctness to the talk show business," he says. " Those with the real power are simply trying to stifle criticism, which, last time I looked, was protected speech." [3]

Schwartzman, however, says the policy would not affect Limbaugh or other "controversial, one-sided hosts."

"Nothing would require any talk show host to change anything they do in their program," says Schwartzman. "It might require the station in its programming to carry programs from an opposing point of view. I say 'might' because most stations are in compliance with the fairness doctrine in their overall programming anyway." [4]

---

[1] *The Wall Street Journal,* Sept. 1, 1993, p. A14.

[2] Limbaugh started his talk career with a Sacramento, Calif., radio station before going national in 1988.

[3] Quoted in Philip Seib, *Rush Hour: Talking Radio, Politics and the Rise of Rush Limbaugh* (1993), p. 264.

[4] See Gigi B. Sohn and Andrew Schwartzman, "Fairness — Not Silence," *The Washington Post,* Jan. 31, 1994, p. A21.

Continued from p. 368

dium for both entertainment and information. Radio brought Americans Jack Benny's comic patter and FDR's fireside chats. Television brought them "I Love Lucy" and the Kennedy-Nixon presidential debates. Today, cable television delivers a daily smorgasbord of movies, TV reruns and music videos along with proceedings in the House and Senate, courtroom trials and full-time news channels.

The new medium allowed politicians and public officials to reach millions of people instantly and, at the same time, create the illusion of intimate communication with each person in the audience. Politicians who were most successful with the new medium learned to make the most of this unique attribute.

As historian Edward W. Chester points out, President Calvin Coolidge was an effective speaker on radio but used it only to extend the reach of speeches prepared for other audiences. [11] In the next decade, President Franklin D. Roosevelt created what came to be called "fireside chats" — seemingly informal talks in plain language between the president in the White House and voters in their living rooms. Historian Arthur M. Schlesinger Jr. depicts FDR preparing for the first of the 28 chats — one week after his inauguration in March 1933 — by "look[ing] at a blank wall and trying to visualize the individuals he was seeking to help." [12]

Roosevelt also pioneered the use of broadcasting to bypass what today would be called "the old media." Facing strong opposition from newspapers controlled by Republican publishers, Roosevelt made radio the central element of his re-election campaign in 1936. His landslide victory showed for the first time that mastery of the broadcast medium could be an invaluable political asset.

When television arrived in the late 1940s and '50s, presidents were again slow to develop its potential. Harry S Truman conveyed determination and sincerity on TV, but he read from a manuscript as though he were still on radio. Dwight D. Eisenhower, the first president to permit radio and television to tape presidential news conferences, also draws middling reviews because of his tendency toward garbled sentences and tortured syntax. [13]

The Great Communicators: Kennedy and Reagan

Only in 1960 did the country see its first made-for-television politician. John F. Kennedy was youthful, energetic and handsome — even sexy. And he was comfortable on television — in a way that his opponent, Richard M. Nixon, was not.

Nixon had used television in his famous "Checkers" speech in 1952 to save his place as Eisenhower's running mate by appealing directly to voters over the heads of Republican Party chieftains who wanted to dump him because of ethics charges. In 1960, however, Kennedy defeated the better known, more experienced Nixon thanks in no small part to television.

Kennedy's superior performance in the first of four presidential debates is generally regarded as the turning point of the campaign. Kennedy is remembered as cool and poised, Nixon as sweaty, nervous and unshaven. But Theodore H. White, in the first of his presidential campaign chronicles, also stressed that Kennedy paid more attention to connecting with voters. "Nixon was addressing himself to Kennedy," White wrote, "but Kennedy was addressing himself to the audience." [14]

Eight years later, Nixon achieved a comeback by making better use of television. His 1968 campaign applied Madison Avenue advertising techniques to develop effective TV commercials on hot-button issues, especially law and order. In addition, Nixon presided over a series of televised panel discussion shows, fielding questions from voters who — unbeknown to the viewers — were handpicked Nixon supporters.

Both Nixon and his Democratic rival, Hubert H. Humphrey, held election eve telethons, but Humphrey took calls without screening them. "That's crazy," one of Nixon's media advisers commented. "He's got no control." [15]

Over the next two decades, politicians consciously worked to refine their skills in using radio and television. Ad executives and media advisers became essential members of campaign retinues and White House staffs. Jimmy Carter had his Gerald Rafshoon, Ronald Reagan his Michael Deaver and George Bush his Roger Ailes. For Carter and Bush, the techniques needed for radio and television were unnatural, and their awkwardness showed. But Reagan, who had been a radio announcer, actor and television pitchman before entering politics, was dubbed "The Great Communicator" on the strength of his media skills.

Reagan had kept his name in circulation as a radio commentator in the late 1970s and continued a weekly radio message as president. He demonstrated in these and other settings an ability to connect with average voters greater than any president since Roosevelt. Reagan was less nimble in news conferences, so his staff simply avoided such sessions. Instead, they contrived other opportunities for the president to deliver what the staff agreed was to be the "message of the day."

As early as the 1960s, political commentators came to view radio and television as a major factor in a shift of power to the president and away from Congress. Broadcasters were shut out of the House and Senate. Committee proceedings were typically long and disjointed — ill-suited for broadcast even if networks had been interested. And individual legislators could not command the attention of microphones or cameras as the president could.

Over the years, an occasional congressional hearing captured the public's attention. Sen. Estes Kefauver, D-Tenn., parlayed an investigation of organized crime in 1951 into a run for national office. Sen. J. William Fulbright, D-Ark., used a Foreign Relations Committee hearing to conduct a teach-in against the Vietnam War in 1965. And, most dramatically, the Senate Watergate Committee in 1973 laid out the Nixon administration's misuse of office in weeks of riveting testimony from one-time aides.

For the most part, though, Congress could not compete with the president's access to the airwaves. Even after the House in 1979 and the Senate in 1986 decided to allow televising of floor debates, Congress was simply no match for a media-conscious White House.

By the 1990s, however, politicians and public officials generally seemed to be losing control of an increasingly crowded media marketplace. The number of broadcast outlets had grown. Most viewers and listeners could now choose between at least a half-dozen television stations and 20 or more radio stations. In addition, cable TV was bringing subscribers anywhere from 30 to 60 channels of programming. And the medium that had allowed politicians to be seen or heard in people's living rooms was now being used to allow the people themselves to do some of the talking.

Radio Call-in Shows

Radio call-in shows date back to the 1940s, according to Bloomquist. For a time, however, federal regulations prohibited putting a telephone call on the air live. Instead, hosts listened to a caller's question and then paraphrased it on the air. This rudimentary technique was used

Rush Limbaugh Phenomenon . . .

Part showman, part ideologue, Rush Limbaugh has risen in the span of 10 years from a fledgling local talk show host to a national sensation unprecedented in the history of political broadcasting.

With 20 million listeners each week, the bombastic conservative has a radio audience unequaled since the days of Arthur Godfrey. His 300-page, 1992 political manifesto, *The Way Things Ought to Be,* netted him a six-figure advance, stayed on best-seller lists for more than a year and earned him millions of dollars in royalties. His second book, *See I Told You So* (1993), also was a best-seller. His new syndicated television show has the highest late-night ratings of any non-network program.

Kimberly Butler

Rush Limbaugh

A college dropout, Limbaugh these days ranks as a national commentator on the issues of the day. When ABC's "Nightline" had then-Sen. Al Gore, D-Tenn., on to push his environmentalist call to arms, *Earth in the Balance,* Limbaugh was picked to represent the other side. This month, Limbaugh debated media coverage of the Whitewater affair with, among others, *New York Times* Executive Editor Max Frankel.

Limbaugh's listeners light up the switchboards in the White House and on Capitol Hill. Former President Ronald Reagan and the conservative magazine *National Review* have called him the leader of the conservative opposition. Republican activists credit him with energizing the GOP grass roots.

Liberal commentators and observers acknowledge his skills. E.J. Dionne, a political columnist for *The Washington Post,* notes that Limbaugh uses rock and roll and other counterculture trappings to sell traditional conservatism to baby-boomers and younger generations. "His message is traditional, but his means are modern," Dionne says. [1]

Limbaugh himself is the show's only attraction. He has no guests and no sidekick. He begins a typical program by surveying the day's news and interspersing comments from an unabashed and undiluted conservative perspective. When Limbaugh turns to the phones, like-minded callers begin by registering their agreement with his views. "A Pacific Ocean full of dittos," a recent call from a West Coast "Dittohead" began.

Limbaugh takes callers of opposing viewpoints also and usually treats them with courtesy. But he keeps tight control of the conversation and never wavers in his own views. "The one thing I'm not is indecisive," Limbaugh says. [2]

Limbaugh, 43, grew up in Cape Girardeau, Mo., in a family

most commonly for interviewing celebrities either in the studio or at live performances.

Call-ins continued as an occasional supplement to music formats into the 1950s. The format's early practitioners included a twenty-something disc jockey named Larry King, who did celebrity interviews and took listeners' calls for a station in Miami. By the end of the decade, Bloomquist says, some DJs had moved into talking with callers about current events as well. Then, in 1960, a network-owned station in Los Angeles with lackluster ratings decided to try to sell listeners on a format of nothing but news and talk.

KABC combined 15-minute hourly newscasts with a variety of talk shows that would be regarded today as primitive. "There was very little two-way conversation," Ira Fistell, one of the station's later talk hosts, recalled in an article marking KABC's 25th anniversary as an all-talk station in 1985. [16] The station had only two time slots for call-in programs, and even on those programs hosts did not interact much with callers. "The on-air personalities just said hello," Fistell wrote, "and, after three minutes, said good-bye."

Later in 1960, a CBS-owned station, KMOX in St. Louis, Mo., became the country's second all-talk station, with a format consisting mainly of advice shows from lawyers, doctors and the like. But later the format began to open up. KABC introduced a legendary figure in talk radio who foreshadowed today's confrontational hosts: Joe Pyne, a political conservative who relished combat with his callers. "Go gargle with razor blades," Pyne once told a caller. Despite his bombast — or perhaps because of it — Pyne drew listeners. At KABC, his ratings were better than Dodgers baseball. Later, at another Los Angeles station — KLAC — he had the top-rated morning radio show.

Into the 1970s, however, the talk format was still primarily limited to large metropolitan markets. "Talk was very expensive to do," Bloomquist explains. Talk hosts needed to be better informed than disc jockeys. They worked shorter shifts. And a station needed a newsman for news updates. "It was very labor- and cost-intensive."

By the early 1980s, however, talk radio was expanding rapidly, encouraged by the development of satellite technology, which allowed easy, eco-

. . . How He Became 'The Leader of the Opposition'

of traditional Republican views. [3] His grandfather was a Missouri legislator and an ambassador in the Eisenhower administration. His father was a county GOP chairman.

From his youth, Limbaugh had a love affair with radio. He dropped out of his hometown state college in favor of the Elkins Institute of Radio and Technology in Dallas. After having been hired and fired from several radio jobs, he landed in 1984 at KFBK in Sacramento, Calif. — succeeding vitriolic Morton Downey Jr., who had been fired for racist comments.

Four years later, Limbaugh's program attracted the attention of a national radio consultant, Bruce Marr, who brokered the deal that took him to WABC in New York in 1988. By 1991 — with 400 stations — *Time* magazine was giving him feature-length attention ("A Man. A Legend. A What?"). The next year, he stayed overnight in the White House — despite his disparaging assessments of its then occupant, George Bush.

Now, with a Democrat at 1600 Pennsylvania Avenue, many Republicans pointedly recall that Ronald Reagan also started in broadcasting before starting his political career. But Limbaugh has repeatedly disclaimed any interest in politics.

"The countryside is strewn with the carcasses of many media types who thought they could get elected," he told Steven Roberts of *U.S. News & World Report* last summer. "Ten percent makes you No. 1 in the media, [but] 10 percent and you're a laughingstock in politics."

A poll accompanying the *U.S. News* cover story points up the perils Limbaugh would face in politics. He has what political consultants call "high negatives." Only a narrow majority of those surveyed said they had a favorable as opposed to an unfavorable opinion of Limbaugh (33 percent to 30 percent). And a mere 8 percent of those surveyed — and only 17 percent of his listeners — thought he should run for president.

Even as a broadcaster, Limbaugh's political impact may be smaller than it seems. The magazine's poll found that more of his audience said they listened to him for entertainment (28 percent) than for information (10 percent) or opinion (10 percent). Asked if they agreed with Limbaugh's views on most issues, 47 percent of his listeners said yes, 23 percent said no.

Some observers wonder whether Limbaugh can continue to draw audiences in the future. And some of his admirers concede that Limbaugh he may be preaching to the conservative choir more than making new converts for the cause.

But biographer Philip Seib thinks Limbaugh has staying power. Seib credits Limbaugh with working hard to master issues, performing skillfully on the air for 3-1/2 hours a day and nurturing the growth of a multimedia empire. "Rush Limbaugh is likely to be with us for a long time," he concludes. [4]

---

[1] Quoted in James Bowman, "The Leader of the Opposition," *National Review*, Sept. 6, 1993, p. 50.

[2] *Ibid.*

[3] Personal background is drawn from a variety of articles, including Peter Boyer, "Bull Rush," *Vanity Fair*, May 1992, pp. 156-160, 204-209, and Steven Roberts, "What a Rush," *U.S. News & World Report*, Aug. 16, 1993, pp. 26-35. See also Philip Seib, *Rush Hour: Talk Radio, Politics and the Rise of Rush Limbaugh* (1993), pp. 23-27.

[4] Seib, *op. cit.*, p. 276.

nomical distribution of nationally syndicated talk programs. "All of a sudden," says Bloomquist, "it became possible to have talk everywhere with a flip of a switch and a twist of the satellite dish." In addition, with improved voice quality on telephone calls, talk programs were easier to listen to. And with more stations on the air, many broadcasters were finding it easier to find and maintain audiences with talk than with music.

Talk on TV

Meanwhile, television also was doing more with talk. Early-morning and late-night talk programs had been a staple since NBC began "Today" in the early 1950s and "The Tonight Show" a little later. Many local stations had their own talk programs, combining interviews with local figures or visiting celebrities with a bit of news and tips on cooking, gardening and the like.

Then in the late 1960s, the variety of talk programs began to increase. In 1967, dynamic Phil Donahue introduced his nationally syndicated show — featuring questions from the audience. Over the next two decades, the format was copied by a host of personalities — Oprah Winfrey, Sally Jesse Raphael and Geraldo Rivera, to name just a few — and used to explore topics ranging from serious and substantive to titillating and sensationalistic.

The tube was also filling up with talking reporters. The early shows — such as the Public Broadcasting Service's (PBS) "Washington Week in Review" — were staid affairs, with a panel of journalists dispassionately analyzing the week's events. Then in the 1980s, sharp tongued John McLaughlin came on the air with a syndicated program that revolutionized the format. McLaughlin provoked his assembled panelists to fight with him and with each other. The format of hyperbole, invective and bad manners caused many journalists to sneer. But the program drew viewers and imitators.

The new kinds of talk shows were needed to satisfy a growing appetite for programming. During the 1970s, cable television began to reach a substantial percentage of households but offered subscribers little more than a larger selection of existing broadcast TV stations. Cable desper-

Not the 'Conversation' Hillary Clinton Had in Mind

Help us to start a "national conversation" on health-care reform, Hillary Rodham Clinton urged 200 radio talk show hosts and producers invited to the White House last September.

But the health-care conversation heard on a sampling of radio talk shows in early March was hardly what President Clinton and the first lady had in mind.

"I'd rather go to a witch doctor than to anything Bill and Hillary dreamed up," a Texas caller told conservative talk show host David Gold at KLIF in Dallas. A caller to Irv Homer, a conservative host on Philadelphia's WWDB, was also contemptuous. "I don't know if I want to buy health reform from the same people who pay $200 for a haircut," the caller said.

Talk show hosts, guests and listeners from 10 programs being studied by researchers at the University of Pennsylvania's Annenberg School for Communication served up big helpings of personal invective and dogmatic criticism for the Clinton health-care plan.

Conservative hosts bashed the Clinton proposal with gusto — and a smattering of information. "Nobody likes this health-care plan anyway," Bob Grant remarked during his afternoon show on WABC in New York. "It's dead."

Liberal hosts in the sampling were weaker and less informed in defending the plan. When a caller to WWDB's Susan Brey in Philadelphia complained that the Clinton plan would let major employers shift the cost of retirees' health-care to the public, Brey responded, "I don't know that that's true," and ended the call for a commercial.

Leading the attack on the Clinton plan was Rush Limbaugh, whose three-hour program can be heard on more than 600 stations around the country. Limbaugh began a program in early March by citing a new poll showing that the Clinton plan was opposed by a narrow majority of Americans. For the next several minutes, he questioned Hillary Clinton's qualifications on the issue, attacked the secrecy in drafting the plan and charged it would give the government too much control over health care.

When a caller sharply challenged him for attacking the Clinton plan without offering an alternative, Limbaugh shot back: "Have you not heard me say that what we have to do is get more private sector into this?. . . I've been specific about that."

The Annenberg School project was designed to analyze all references to health-care reform on programs in March in 10 major cities around the country. The sample included three programs — from Washington, Chicago and Los Angeles — with a pair of hosts representing opposing viewpoints. Of the remaining shows, four of the hosts were conservative while three were liberal or moderate.

Listening to several hours of excerpts from the shows, a reporter heard no one (host or guest) give a straightforward presentation of the president's proposals. Guests included several critics of the president's plan, but only one supporter — an author who spent more time plugging her book than talking about Clinton's proposals. However, Pat Korten and Mike Cuthbert of WRC's "Pat and Mike Show" in Washington told viewers they had interviewed administration officials during a previous week.

Callers also were predominantly critical of Clinton's plan, but a few supporters were heard. A caller told New York's Lynn Samuels at WABC that Clinton's proposal would "stop the doctors and the insurance people from having such control over people's lives."

A caller to Korten and Cuthbert mocked a plan offered by a guest from the libertarian Cato Institute that would allow anyone to establish a tax-free $3,000 savings account for medical expenses. "The solution is to tell unemployed people to sock away $3,000 in a savings account," the caller sneered. "It's not going to wash."

Some of the criticisms of Clinton's proposal reflected misunderstandings or oversimplifications. One caller said the proposal "would pay for health care for every bum in this country." In fact, Clinton's plan would require workers to pay 20 percent of the costs of their health insurance and would make significant cuts in the existing federal-state Medicaid program for health care for the needy.

Bob Chlopak, a Washington consultant whose firm is managing the Health Care Reform Project, an umbrella coalition supporting the Clinton plan, says the negative views heard on talk programs do not surprise him.

"By and large, the media coverage of the health-care debate has been critical," Chlopak says. "I would not be the least bit surprised that talk show coverage — which tends to be more conservative to begin with — would be more critical because I think the press as a whole has been unduly critical."

ately needed more "product" — and news and talk helped fill the need.

C-SPAN — Cable Satellite Public Affairs Network — came first, in 1979. The non-commercial network, funded by cable operators as both a public service and audience builder, debuted in 1979 with one programming mainstay: gavel-to-gavel coverage of the House of Representatives, newly opened to television cameras. A year later, to fill time, C-SPAN added call-in shows — mornings and evenings. In 1986, C-SPAN II was created to carry the U.S. Senate. Today, both channels operate round the clock, bringing a small but dedicated audience a full menu of congressional proceedings, academic and journalistic symposia, plus frequent call-in programs.

CNN — cable's full-time news network — was born in 1980, the brainchild of a brash Atlanta businessman, Ted Turner. Turner had recognized cable's potential years earlier while putting his Atlanta "superstation" on cable systems around the country. CNN seemed a dubious venture at first, but within a few years it had begun establishing itself along with ABC, CBS and NBC as a fourth national news network.

To help build audiences, CNN also turned to talk. In 1985, it brought in Larry King — who had a successful talk show on the Mutual radio network — to do a live, nighttime call-in show. Daytime call-in shows were added too — hosted by women and aimed at the predominantly female daytime audience.

The 'Blowhard' '90s

By the 1990s, viewers and listeners seemingly could not escape talk. The number of radio stations with all-talk or news-talk formats quadrupled in a decade — from 200 or so in the early '80s to more than 850 today. Nationally, news/talk is the second most listened to format — after adult-contemporary music — and many talk stations are No. 1 in their markets. Talk can also be heard on other stations. National Public Radio (NPR), for example, started a two-hour talk program, "Talk of the Nation," in 1991, now carried by 80 of NPR's 492 member stations.

With more talk on the air, the number of hosts was growing. About 75 people attended the radio talk show hosts association's first convention in 1989, according to Carol Nashe, the group's executive director. Today, the association counts more than 3,000 members, and its conventions are high-visibility events. Speakers in 1992 included Vice President Dan Quayle and presidential hopeful Bill Clinton.

Hosts have become more diverse in some respects — but not so diverse in others. Most hosts have worked their way up through radio, but an increasing number step into programs from other walks of life. Convicted Watergate co-conspirator G. Gordon Liddy has a program — called "Radio Free D.C." So does Jerry Brown, the former California governor and Democratic presidential hopeful.

But the roster of hosts still reflects little race or gender diversity. Bloomquist recently surveyed 73 mainstream, major-market talk stations — as opposed to black-oriented stations — and found only 14 black hosts. [17] Ray Suarez, the only Hispanic host on a national talk show ("Talk of the Nation"), says there are "damn few" Hispanic hosts on English-speaking stations locally. As for women, Bloomquist earlier this year counted 138 female hosts among 74 major-market talk stations, but only 57 of the women were doing issues-oriented programs. [18]

Many observers fret about the effect of all this talk on society. Dorothy Rabinowitz, a *Wall Street Journal* columnist, catalogued the array of titillating topics on TV talk shows that she said are "helping normalize pathology." [19] Edwin Diamond, a former *Newsweek* editor who now teaches journalism at New York University, complains of what he calls "a blowhard culture."

But other observers, as well as broadcasters themselves, insist that talk shows provide a valuable means of communication for a society in which face-to-face conversation seems to be dying out.

"Nobody talks to anyone in a neighborhood shopping center," says WABC Program Director Mainelli. "People just don't talk to strangers at all. And when people socialize, there's not as much political discussion going on as there used to be. People don't want to confront each other."

Talk shows also appeared to be having an effect on politics and government — and that, too, provoked disagreement. In 1989, hosts helped catalyze a broad public protest that forced Congress to roll back a recommended 50 percent pay raise. Some hosts urged listeners to send tea bags to congressmen with the slogan, "Read my lips: No pay raise." Tens of thousands did. [20] In New Jersey, talk hosts on a Trenton station fueled a tax revolt after an increase in the state's sales levy. In Denver, KOA's Rosen pushed an array of conservative causes, including an unsuccessful statewide tax-limitation initiative. [21]

Conservative activist Keene says listeners believe the talk shows are filling an information gap. "These people listen to these shows because they think they're getting information that's not available elsewhere," he says.

But media analyst Hume says some of the hosts are demagogues. "Fortunately, the demagogues haven't so swamped the air waves that they've taken over," she says. "But it's very important for people who are listening or watching to think carefully and use their judgment."

Talk Show Campaign

For the candidates in the 1992 presidential campaign, the variety of talk shows offered a forum for communicating directly with voters that had been little used in the past. Now, changes in the way television covered political campaigns increased the value of these new media.

Since the 1960s, the three major television networks had been giving presidential candidates less time to deliver their messages in news reports, according to researchers in 1990. They found that the average "sound bite" of candidates' remarks fell from a little over 40 seconds in 1968 to under 10 seconds in 1988. [22]

The new talk shows, however, offered candidates many, varied opportunities for so-called long-form interviews. In the past, candidates had disdained these programs, although Democratic presidential nominee Michael S. Dukakis appeared on a few talk programs at the end of his losing 1988 campaign. But in 1992, the candidates turned to interview programs more often. Russell Stevens, a researcher at the Joan Shorenstein Barone Center on Press, Politics and Public Policy at Harvard University, found that the major party candidates for president and vice president made twice as many appearances on long-form interview programs in 1992 as they did in 1988.

"You had a huge expansion of the number of formats in which you could see candidates interacting with other people," says Stevens. "That allows more chances to see a candidate as he really is."

The talk shows also provided some of the most memorable moments of the campaign. Clinton tried to humanize his image by playing the saxophone on the late-night "Arsenio Hall Show." Ross Perot used "Larry King Live" to launch his candidacy in February, but came under sharp questioning on a later program when Commerce Secretary Robert Mosbacher called in to challenge his criticisms of Bush administration policy toward Iraq. President Bush himself was bluntly challenged in his one appearance on King's program in October. After Bush said he had no prior knowledge of the Reagan administration's arms for hostage deal with Iran, Clinton campaign adviser George Stephanopoulos called in to dispute his account. [23]

For providing this forum, King earned the mocking title "master of ceremonies of the 1992 campaign" from columnist George Will. [24] Other media observers also sneered. "The talkshowification of America continues apace," Tom Shales, *The Washington Post's* television critic, wrote on the eve of the election. "[N]ow the political process is conquered too." [25] Some journalists worried that the candidates were escaping serious scrutiny by using "entertainment" and call-in shows so heavily in their campaigns.

King himself said he did not try to cross-examine his guests. "I am not a journalist," he wrote. [26] But studies of the 1992 campaign have concluded that the talk shows in fact gave greater emphasis to substantive campaign issues than traditional political coverage did.

In one study, the Center for Media and Public Affairs found that TV talk shows spent about three-fourths of the time on substantive coverage of campaign issues or candidates' qualifications as opposed to "non-substantive" discussion of campaign strategy and the like. By contrast, more than two-thirds of the coverage on the three commercial networks was deemed non-substantive, and even PBS's "MacNeil/Lehrer NewsHour" was judged to have had more non-substantive than substantive coverage. [27] (*See graph, p. 364.*)

As for call-in questions, Harvard's Stevens found that voters were more likely than journalists to ask about candidates' positions on the issues. But Stevens and Marion Just, a visiting professor at Harvard who is collaborating with Stevens on a book about politics and the "new media," agreed with the suggestions from journalists that voters were less likely to challenge candidates about their positions. "Journalists often have a great deal in their information base that they can draw on for a follow-up question," Just explains, "whereas members of the audience don't."

Nonetheless, it was a question from a voter rather than a journalist that stood out as perhaps the single most-defining moment of the campaign. For the second of their three debates, Bush, Clinton and Perot agreed to take questions from a studio audience of undecided voters. Toward the end of the Oct. 15 debate, a woman asked Bush how the national debt had affected him personally. Bush faltered badly in his answer, finally giving a limp response about mail he received from people who had been hurt by economic problems.

Clinton, who had already appeared in nine town hall settings during the campaign, used the debate format that night to maximum advantage. Throughout the evening, Clinton walked toward the audience to answer questions, while Bush sat stiffly on a stool. In replying to the question that had perplexed Bush, Clinton empathetically said he knew people — "by their names" — who were out of work or whose businesses had gone bankrupt in the economic downturn.

Four months earlier, Clinton had been behind both Bush and Perot. Now, after a campaign based in part on the use of talk shows to deliver his message, Clinton had become the front-runner. On Nov. 3, the talk show campaign ended — and the victor was the candidate who, the commentators agreed, had best mastered the new media politicking. ■

CURRENT SITUATION

Talk Show Government?

President Clinton returned to the talkathon format just three weeks after taking office. He traveled to Detroit Feb. 9 for a town hall-type broadcast linked by satellite to three other cities — Atlanta, Miami and Seattle — and covered nationally by CNN and C-SPAN. Press critic Kurtz gave Clinton good ratings for the performance, which he said marked the "birth of the talk show presidency." [28]

Talk shows, however, also took an early toll on the Clinton presidency. When his first nominee for attorney

Continued on p. 378

At Issue:

Should the fairness doctrine be reinstituted?

yes

GIGI B. SOHN
Deputy director, Media Access Project

FROM *QUILL MAGAZINE*, MARCH 1994.

The "fairness doctrine" has practical and symbolic importance for all Americans. It is a remarkably effective device for addressing one of the most difficult challenges facing a democracy: how to reconcile the public's right to receive information with the need to insure that journalists have the broadest possible editorial discretion. . . .

In operation, the "fairness doctrine" has fulfilled the objectives of the First Amendment by bringing more voices into the marketplace of ideas, thereby maximizing the discussion of issues in our democracy. . . .

The doctrine has had virtually no day-to-day impact on the operation of broadcasters. . . . By emphasizing citizen-broadcaster conciliation as a prerequisite to any FCC [Federal Communications Commission] involvement, the "fairness doctrine" . . . has actually restricted direct governmental interference in the operation of broadcast licensees. . . .

The hands-off approach used in "fairness doctrine" enforcement is a narrowly tailored, judicially approved scheme which does not constitute censorship. The doctrine is affirmative; it sometimes requires additional programming, but it never suppresses speech. . . .

It is said that nothing has changed since the FCC stopped enforcement in 1987, that broadcasters are now more willing to cover controversial issues of importance to their communities.

Things have changed, but not for the better. Since 1987, organizations and individuals which have tried to get controversial issues covered fairly have experienced ever-greater resistance from reticent broadcasters. In particular, there has been increasing imbalance in the coverage on ballot issues, where one-sided advertising blitzes now go unanswered....

Demand for scarce public airwaves has never been greater. It was this spectrum scarcity which the Supreme Court found to be the reason why broadcasters must serve as trustees for the public. Not only are broadcasters lined up for these frequencies and demanding even more for high-definition television, there is an ever-increasing crowd of other users . . . seeking spectrum space. . . .

[T]he growth of cable and the future arrival of the information superhighway do not lessen the need for the "fairness doctrine." The multi-channel, fiber optic future is at least a decade away for most Americans. Broadcasting remains — by far — the most important force for shaping public opinion. Forty percent of Americans do not even subscribe to cable. And, unlike broadcasting, most cable programming does not address local issues.

no

ROBERT CORN-REVERE
Communications lawyer, Washington, D.C.

FROM *QUILL MAGAZINE*, MARCH 1994

It is hard to imagine a government policy more deserving of historical obscurity than the "fairness doctrine."

The doctrine was predicated on the dubious proposition that, given a scarcity of broadcast frequencies, speech would remain free only if government intruded on the editorial decisions of radio and TV news editors. One would think that such reasoning would instantly be dismissed by an administration dedicated to "reinventing government" . . . to opening the electronic superhighway of unlimited video and information services.

Yet support for a new broadcast "fairness doctrine" keeps going and going. . . . To be fair, the drive for the doctrine's return comes from Congress and lobbyists, not from the Executive Branch. . . .

When the doctrine was first articulated in 1949, there were 51 TV stations and about 2,600 radio stations....Today, there are 1,520 TV stations and about 11,560 radio stations.

This does not count alternative technologies. . . . Now, cable television is available to more than 90 percent of homes in the U.S. and over 60 percent subscribe; three-fourths of American households have VCRs, 30 percent have personal computers and direct-broadcast satellites are beginning to offer hundreds of channels coast to coast.

Any continuing suggestion that scarcity still exists is transparently absurd. . . . The real issue is not scarcity; it is whether a society predicated on freedom of speech should allow the government to have this type of power over the press. . . .

It is well-documented that both the Kennedy and Johnson administrations carried on organized, covert campaigns to harass unsympathetic radio commentators with the filing of "fairness doctrine" complaints. And a 1969 memorandum from [White House aide] Jeb Magruder to [White House Chief of Staff] Bob Haldeman proposed "an official monitoring system through the FCC" and revealed that [President] Nixon directed his staff 21 times in a single month to take "specific action relating to what could be considered unfair news coverage. . . ."

More recently, support for a "fairness doctrine" bill has been linked to congressional displeasure with critical network news reports. Last August, the trade magazine *Broadcasting & Cable* reported that pressure for a new "fairness doctrine" grew after ABC's "Prime Time Live" ran a story featuring House Ways and Means Committee members being entertained by lobbyists in Barbados. . . .

There is no place in a free society for such legislative threats.

general, Zoë Baird, was disclosed to have hired an illegal alien for child care and to have failed to pay Social Security taxes for the employee, official Washington treated it as no big deal. But in a matter of days, people outside the Beltway voiced outrage — initially, on call-in talk shows. With public opinion solidly against her, Baird withdrew just two days after Clinton's inauguration.

Clinton's campaign promise to lift the ban on gays and lesbians in the military also fell victim to public opinion as voiced, in part, on call-in programs. In the week after his inauguration, the issue was — as *New York Times* reporter Elizabeth Kolbert put it — "the No. 1 topic" on talk radio stations. Within days, she wrote, "a near-record number of callers had phoned the Capitol to register their opinions." [29] Clinton backpedaled. By fall, he acceded to provisions in the 1994 defense authorization that barred questioning of recruits about their sexual orientation but allowed the military to continue to discharge servicemen or servicewomen for homosexual conduct.

As the year continued, however, talk shows faded into the background. Clinton used more conventional political and media techniques to win passage of his budget and to ride out criticism of foreign policy moves in Somalia, Haiti and Bosnia. But in November, Vice President Al Gore helped cinch congressional approval of the controversial North American Free Trade Agreement (NAFTA) by besting treaty opponent Ross Perot in a debate, with call-in questions, on King's program. And this month, Clinton hit the talkathon circuit again, with televised town hall meetings from three cities — Charlotte, N.C., Kansas City, Mo., and Minneapolis, Minn. — in a week to generate support for his health care reform plan.

"The president feels very strongly that the town hall meetings give him an opportunity to report to the people what he's been doing," Jeff Eller, a White House media adviser, told CNN White House correspondent Wolf Blitzer. But, as Blitzer and other reporters pointed out, members of the audience had some sharp questions for Clinton — not only on health care but also on the Whitewater affair and other issues. "He's finding that the questions can be just as tough, or even tougher, out here in the heartland," Blitzer reported. [30]

For many observers, Clinton's experiences during 15 months in office put the impact of talk shows in perspective. "You can't govern the country by town hall and talk show," the *Los Angeles Times'* Rosenstiel says.

The president and his people still have to use the traditional media techniques, Rosenstiel says. They have to try to sell administration policies to reporters for major news outlets. And the president has to face the White House press corps at critical times — as he did in March to try to quiet coverage of the Whitewater affair.

But Rosenstiel says an administration also has to master the new media and use them wisely to help deliver an intended message. As an example, he cites the invitation last September for talk show hosts to set up on the White House lawn the day after Clinton gave his health care address to Congress. "The message that day," Rosenstiel says, "was the extent to which [the administration was] reaching out for support."

The impact of talk shows was being seen and heard often in Congress. With talk radio covering the country, issues that once would have percolated for days or weeks before public opinion formed could now light up Capitol Hill switchboards in an instant. "When an issue catches fire," says conservative activist David Keene, "it tends to multiply the reaction that Congress gets back home."

But Congresswatcher Ornstein cautions against overreacting to the talk radio phenomenon. As an example, he points to last year's vote on the balanced-budget constitutional amendment. He notes that even though public pressure helped force the House leadership to permit a vote on the provision, it ultimately fell short of passage in both the Senate and the House.

Bloomquist agrees that talk radio may have less impact in the future than it seems to have today. "As time goes on," he says, "more and more lawmakers are going to realize that what they hear on talk shows is not always representative of how people feel." ■

OUTLOOK

Impact Questioned

When South Africans went to the polls this week to vote in the country's first all-race election, American talk radio was there. For five days, NPR's "Talk of the Nation" broadcast an hour a day from Johannesburg, with live callers from the U.S. as well as South Africa.

"As a neutral entity, NPR may be really able to get some air-clearing, ear-opening talk going in South Africa," host Ray Suarez said as he prepared to leave for the broadcasts. "We also want to give Americans a more intimate, ground-level view of what South Africans are feeling there."

Other hosts have felt the urge to take their programs global. Larry King, who is seen worldwide, went to Asia last year for a weeklong series of programs with call-in questions from Asia and the United States.

"This may be the real talk-show revolution," King wrote. While his show "is not going to solve the world's problems," King conceded, "we could promote understanding, involvement, interconnection." [31]

Critics of talk shows may scoff at the thought of this increasingly ca-

When Talk Radio Turns Into 'Hate Radio'

Listeners to radio station WOL in Washington, D.C., expect blunt talk from Cathy Hughes, the station's owner and host of a daily talk program. They got an earful Jan. 26 when Hughes complained that Hispanics had "taken over" parts of her city. [1]

"They're letting Hispanics bring 10 and 12 folks over, without green cards, stay in the buildings, open up businesses, get jobs, get on the welfare system, and there seems to be a tolerance. . . ," said Hughes, who is black, like most of her listeners. "It's almost as if everyone, starting off with the mayor and the city council, they just look the other way."

As the remarks circulated, leaders of Washington's Latino community denounced the comments as racist. But Hughes' son told *Washington Post* media reporter Howard Kurtz that he heard "nothing derogatory" in the remarks. Hughes herself met with a group of Hispanic journalists in Washington and agreed to host a segment on her program on Hispanic issues with Latino guests.

Talk shows always have had the potential for airing rank prejudice — racial, ethnic, religious, sexist or otherwise. In the 1930s, "Radio Priest" Charles Coughlin aired attacks on Jewish bankers in the United States and endorsed Adolf Hitler's efforts to get rid of Jewish Communists in Germany. Protests drove him from the air. [2]

A report by the American Jewish Committee in 1991 documented many instances of racist remarks about blacks by white talk hosts or listeners. A Rhode Island talk host was fired in 1987 for calling drug dealers "niggers." A caller to WABC in New York complained during the 1989 mayoral campaign that the city would be overrun by "black welfare parasites" if black candidate David Dinkins were elected. [3]

Today, Kenneth S. Stern, the author of the report, says talk shows still occasionally air some blatant prejudice, but hosts are doing a better job of countering bigotry. "Most of them see it as a matter of professionalism," Stern says.

Randall Bloomquist, talk radio editor for the trade journal *Radio & Records,* agrees, but says talk programs still give voice to feelings of racial prejudice. "No responsible talk radio station seeks or condones racism or race-baiting from either callers or hosts," says Bloomquist. "By the same token, talk radio is a mirror on society and reflects some of the racial hostility and bias that's out there."

Concern about less overt forms of prejudice has increased in recent years with the rising popularity of talk show hosts with conservative-populist views. In particular, Rush Limbaugh has reached the top of the talk show market with biting attacks on civil rights leaders, feminists, homosexuals and others. Some people view his humor as a medium for transmitting prejudice.

"I don't think he's funny," fellow host Larry King told a magazine interviewer in 1992. "Gay-bashing, bashing women, 'femi-Nazis,' bashing blacks, I don't think that's funny." [4]

Limbaugh himself denies charges of prejudice. He says he is only attacking black leaders in civil rights groups, not all blacks. He has apologized for old routines in which he mocked homosexual AIDS victims. As for his attacks on feminists, Limbaugh says, "I don't hate women. I don't hate anybody. I don't even dislike them." [5]

Black-oriented talk shows have also been viewed as sources of racial prejudice in recent years. Jewish groups and others complain that black stations have provided a forum for black groups, such as the Nation of Islam, that make harsh attacks on Jews and on whites generally.

"In some of these places, apologists for [Nation of Islam leader] Louis Farrakhan have kind of monopolized the air," says Stern. "You can hear people vilifying Jews, vilifying white people. . . . It's a little like a dirty, little secret because not that many people outside the black communities listen."

---

[1] For background, see *The Washington Post,* Feb. 22, 1994, p. D1.

[2] Edward W. Chester, *Radio, Television, and American Politics* (1969), pp. 193-198.

[3] Kenneth S. Stern, "Hate on Talk Radio," American Jewish Committee, 1991.

[4] Quoted in Peter J. Boyer, "Bull Rush," *Vanity Fair,* May 1992, p. 159.

[5] *Ibid.,* p. 208.

---

cophonous medium promoting peace and goodwill around the world. But the world has entered an era of global communications. The sounds and images of a famine in Somalia, a bombing raid in Baghdad or an attempted coup in Moscow can travel around the world in an instant — focusing worldwide attention on the events while they are still taking place.

Domestically, experts disagree about the long-term political impact of talk shows. Jamieson of the Annenberg School says the programs often have more "entertainment value" than political impact. "There's no evidence that [talk shows] change political views," she says. And even though talk shows may make it easier to mobilize public opinion, she notes that many popular uprisings — such as California's Proposition 13 tax revolt in 1978 — occurred without talk shows playing a significant role.

Reporter Rosenstiel also cautions against exaggerating the significance of talk shows. But he says they can be influential in specific situations. "When the Washington reaction is out of synch with public reaction, it can have an impact," says Rosenstiel, pointing to the public protest over the Zoë Baird nomination in early 1993. "And when Clinton wants to cajole a particular congressman, he now has the ability to target that congressman's media market — through talk shows and satellites — to narrowcast his message."

Talk show hosts themselves are now entering the political arena. At least seven radio hosts have filed papers to run in Republican primaries this year for seats in Congress. Two women are seeking Senate seats in Massachusetts and Michigan, while other hosts are running for House seats in Arkansas, Indiana and three Florida districts. In addition, "shock jock" Howard Stern is running for New York's governorship on the Libertarian Party ticket.

One Democratic campaign operative cast doubt on the hosts' viability as candidates. "There are still important questions to be answered," said Mike Casey, director of communications for the Democratic Congressional Campaign Committee. "To what extent do talk shows of a certain ideological bent preach to the converted? To what extent do their audiences act on what they hear on talk radio?" [32]

But political scientist Jeffrey Bell believes the talk hosts are reaching a broad range of potential voters. "This wouldn't be an important trend if the talk show hosts were just talking to the converted," Bell told *The New York Times*. "They are getting to middle America and middle-of-the-roaders. And maybe even liberals." [33]

Within the broadcast industry, talk shows continue to have a strong appeal. Talk shows have gained listeners in part on the strength of nationally syndicated programs. But industry observers say syndication has one downside: It reduces the number of local program slots for new hosts to use as a training ground. "There's a shrinking demand for local talkers," says Bloomquist. And that may be making it harder for women or minority hosts to break into the business.

Many political and media observers are likely to continue to sneer at the talk show phenomenon. The feeling persists that talk shows provide more entertainment than information, more confrontation than conciliation, more heat than light. These observers look to the "traditional media" — with their reporters and editors trained in "objective reporting" — to provide the nation with the most serious discourse about politics and government.

Even if the traditional media are not displaced, however, talk shows appear likely to take a lasting place alongside them as part of the public dialogue. The voices heard on these programs — whether from hosts, guests, listeners or viewers — may often be discordant. But for those who believe in talk shows, that discord is not a weakness, but a strength.

"I'm for talk radio as a medium — for all of its truths and all of its warts," says Harrison of *Talkers* magazine. "It's a valuable medium for a society that supposedly values free speech. Free speech can never be dangerous for a democracy." ■

Notes

[1] For background, see "Term Limits," *The CQ Researcher*, Jan. 10, 1992, pp. 1-24.

[2] See Larry King with Mark Stencel, *On the Line: The New Road to the White House*(1993) for a chronology of candidates' talk show appearances during the 1992 campaign, pp. xiii-xviii.

[3] *Open Line*, special edition 1993, p. 4.

[4] King, *op. cit.*, pp. 155-156.

[5] Times Mirror Center for The People and The Press, "The Vocal Minority In American Politics," July 1993, p. 6.

[6] See Steven Roberts, "What a Rush," *U.S. News and World Report*, Aug. 16, 1993, p. 27.

[7] Times Mirror Center, *op. cit.*, p. 16.

[8] Howard Kurtz, *Media Circus: The Trouble with America's Newspapers* (1993), p. 283.

[9] Rosenstiel is the author of *Strange Bedfellows: TV Anchors, Talk Show Hosts and Presidential Candidates in the Improbable Campaign of 1992* (1993).

[10] King, *op cit.*, p. 7.

[11] Edward W. Chester, *Radio, Television and American Politics* (1969), pp. 23-24.

[12] Arthur M. Schlesinger Jr., *The Age of Roosevelt: The Coming of the New Deal* (1965), p. 13.

[13] Congressional Quarterly, *Guide to the Presidency,* 1989, p. 738.

[14] See Theodore H. White, *The Making of the President 1960* (1961), p. 287.

[15] See Joe McGinniss, *The Selling of the President* (1969), Chapters 5, 13.

[16] Ira Fistell, "KABC Talkradio: The First 25 Years," *Let's Talk!,* September/October 1985, pp. 21-22.

[17] Randall Bloomquist, "'Waiting for Jackie Robinson,"' *Radio & Records,* Nov. 29, 1991, p. 40.

[18] Randall Bloomquist, "Female Talkers Making Slow Progress," *Radio & Records,* Feb. 18, 1994, p. 37.

[19] Dorothy Rabinowitz, "Talk and Consequences," *The Wall Street Journal,* July 12, 1993, p. A10.

[20] *1989 CQ Almanac*, p. 56.

[21] See Jeffrey Katz, "The Power of Talk," *Governing,* March 1991, pp. 38-42.

[22] Kiku Adatto, "Sound Bite Democracy: Network Evening News Presidential Campaign Coverage, 1968 and 1988," Joan Shorenstein Barone Center on Press, Politics and Public Policy, Harvard University, June 1990; Daniel Hallin, "Sound Bite News: Television Coverage of Elections, 1968-1988," Woodrow Wilson Media Studies Project, 1990. See also Thomas Patterson, *Out of Order* (1993), pp. 75-76, 160. Patterson, at Syracuse University, found that the networks in 1992 did not lengthen candidates' sound bites, as promised.

[23] King, *op. cit.*, pp. 21-22, 132-133.

[24] George Will, "Too Silly for Words," *The Washington Post,* Oct. 13, 1992, p. A21.

[25] *The Washington Post,* Nov. 2, 1992, p. D1.

[26] King, *op. cit.*, p. 132.

[27] Center for Media and Public Affairs, "The Media in Campaign '92," February 1994.

[28] *The Washington Post,* Feb. 12, 1993, p. A4.

[29] *The New York Times,* Jan. 29, 1993, p. A12.

[30] CNN, "Inside Politics," April 8, 1994. See also *The Washington Post,* April 6, 1994, p. A4; April 8, 1994, p. A9.

[31] King, *op. cit.*, pp. 187-88.

[32] Quoted in *Congressional Quarterly Weekly Report,* April 9, 1994, p. 853.

[33] Quoted in *The New York Times,* April 16, 1994, p. 7.

Bibliography

Selected Sources Used

Books

Chester, Edward W., *Radio, Television and American Politics,* Sheed & Ward, 1969.

This book by an American historian was described as the first complete history of the role of radio and television in American politics. The 19-page bibliography includes a host of books and articles about the early decades of radio and television.

King, Larry, with Mark Stencel, *On the Line: The New Road to the White House,* Harcourt Brace, 1993.

The noted radio and television talk show host chronicles candidates' increased use of call-in programs during the 1992 presidential campaign. He concludes call-in programs help "empower" the public but says the traditional press has a continuing role to play in covering politics.

Levin, Murray B., *Talk Radio and the American Dream,* Lexington Books, 1987.

Levin, a professor of political science at Boston University, studied hundreds of hours of talk radio tapes from two programs — one with a liberal host, the other a conservative — from 1977 and 1982. He says that "[n]o medium is more available to the disenchanted as talk radio" and "none is so prone to undermine the legitimacy" of government, business and other institutions.

Limbaugh, Rush, *The Way Things Ought to Be,* Pocket Books, 1992.

In his best-selling autobiography — written with a *Wall Street Journal* editorialist as collaborator — Limbaugh briefly recounts his path from local talk host to nationally syndicated master of the airwaves. He then lays out his views on topics ranging from abortion, AIDS and animal rights to crime, foreign policy and government gridlock.

Patterson, Thomas E., *Out of Order,* Knopf, 1993.

Patterson, a political science professor at Syracuse University, gives better marks to voters than to the news media in examining candidates' qualifications and policy positions in presidential campaigns.

Seib, Philip, *Rush Hour: Talk Radio, Politics and the Rise of Rush Limbaugh*, The Summit Group, 1993.

Seib, a journalism professor at Southern Methodist University in Dallas, traces Limbaugh's personal background and assesses his political impact. Two other journalists have also written Limbaugh biographies: Michael Arkush, *Rush,* Avon Books, 1993; and Paul D. Colford, *The Rush Limbaugh Story: Talent on Loan From God,* St. Martin's, 1993.

Articles

Hoyt, Mike, "Talk Radio: Turning Up the Volume," *Columbia Journalism Review,* November/December 1992, pp. 45-50.

Hoyt, *CJR's* associate editor, depicts talk radio as growing in terms of stations, listeners and political influence.

Katz, Jeffrey, "The Power of Talk," *Governing*, March 1991, pp. 38-42.

The story examines the impact of talk shows on state and local officials.

Lardner, James, "The Anti-Network," *The New Yorker,* March 14, 1994, pp. 48-55.

The article traces the birth and development of C-SPAN, cable television's full-time public affairs network.

Roberts, Steven, "What a Rush," *U.S. News & World Report,* Aug. 16, 1993, pp. 26-35.

This cover story includes a profile of Rush Limbaugh along with interesting data from a survey of Limbaugh's listeners.

Rosenstiel, Thomas B., "The Talk Is About New Media," *Los Angeles Times,* May 23, 1992, p. A1.

Rosenstiel, a reporter in the *Times'* Washington bureau who covers the media, recounts the expanded role that radio and television talk shows were playing in the 1992 presidential campaign. Rosenstiel also wrote a book, *Strange Bedfellows* (Hyperion, 1993), describing coverage of the campaign by one of the commercial television networks — ABC news.

Reports and Studies

Center for Media and Public Affairs, *The Media in Campaign '92,* February 1994.

The Washington think tank found that radio and television talk shows gave more attention to substantive issues in the 1992 presidential campaign than the "traditional media" did.

Stern, Kenneth S., *Hate on Talk Radio,* American Jewish Committee, 1991.

Stern, a program specialist on anti-Semitism for the American Jewish Committee, critically examines examples of bigotry from talk show callers and hosts. While he opposes government censorship, Stern lists steps for radio stations, community groups and others to take to combat intolerance.

Times Mirror Center for The People and The Press, *The Vocal Minority in American Politics,* July 1993.

The Washington-based center surveyed talk show callers and found them to be more hostile to President Clinton and Congress than the general public. The callers "caricature discontent . . . rather than genuinely reflect public disquiet," the report concludes.

The Next Step

Additional information from UMI's Newspaper & Periodical Abstracts database

The Impact of Talk Shows

"The danger of government by touchtone," ***Larry King Live—CNN,*** **Feb. 9, 1993.**
With voters now able to call talk shows and voice opinions as major events are occurring, there is a danger that politicians will tend to overreact to public opinion.

Jackson, Janine, "Talk radio: Who gets to talk?" ***St. Louis Journalism Review,*** **July 1993, pp. 8-9.**
The popularity of talk radio shows is discussed. The marketers of radio talk shows promote their programs based on entertainment value above all. Talk radio is heavily weighted toward the right. The influence of talk radio on politics and the democratic process is discussed.

Margolis, Jon, "Decency, fairness erode and Main St. loves every bit of it," ***Chicago Tribune,*** **Jan. 25, 1994, p. 17.**
Jon Margolis contends that Bobby Ray Inman was a casualty of something akin to McCarthyism, saying that mainstream America is where political decisions are made with respect to popular opinion found in TV and radio talk shows.

Opinions

Lupo, Alan, "When democracy gives way to talkmaster tyranny," ***Boston Globe,*** **Feb. 16, 1993, p. 15.**
Alan Lupo comments on the propensity for American citizens to air their political views on radio call-in shows every time President Clinton makes a decision, thus creating a "mobocracy."

Meadows, Donella H., "Rush and Larry, coast to coast: This is not democracy in action," ***Los Angeles Times,*** **Feb. 12, 1993, p. B7.**
Donella H. Meadows questions the common wisdom that call-in talk shows are democracy in action.

Ostrow, Joanne, "TV pundits brand call-in politics mere rabble-rousing," ***Denver Post,*** **Feb. 3, 1993, p. F1.**
Joanne Ostrow discusses the news media's unhappiness with call-in talk shows.

"Vox populi," ***Nation,*** **March 1, 1993, pp. 255-256.**
An editorial discusses the dangerous practice of subjecting civil rights, social policy issues and political decisions to public opinion expressed on call-in shows. The majority of those who call in to radio shows don't represent a cross-section of the U.S.

The Politicians

Carman, Tim, "Local talk radio gets new voice: Kathy Whitmire," ***Houston Post,*** **March 14, 1994, p. A9.**
Former Mayor Kathy Whitmire will host her own radio talk show on KPRC in Houston, beginning on March 14, 1994. Whitmire says the two-hour call-in program will focus on "current issues and politics."

Freemantle, Tony, "Race issue still never far from lips of radio host David Duke," ***Houston Chronicle,*** **May 9, 1993, p. A9.**
The racism and humorlessness of David Duke's radio talk show, "The David Duke Conservative Hotline," on Louisiana's WASO-AM is discussed. Duke, a former KKK klansman and attempted politician, is hosting the talk show on a trial basis.

Gillam, Jerry and Mark Gladstone, "Speaker Brown debuts as political talk show moderator," ***Los Angeles Times,*** **March 15, 1994, p. A3.**
California Assembly Speaker Willie Brown began his own morning talk show on March 14, 1994 on KCRA-TV in Sacramento, Calif., with a fast-paced debate on the "three strikes" criminal sentencing proposals.

Kurtz, Howard, "Look who's talking too: Ex-pols find a new home behind the mike," ***The Washington Post,*** **Feb. 1, 1994, p. C1.**
A striking number of umemployed politicians, among them former New York Mayor Ed Koch and perennial presidential candidate Jerry Brown, have been born again as rabble-rousing radio talk show hosts.

Paddock, Richard C., "Reincarnated on radio," ***Los Angeles Times,*** **Feb. 3, 1994, p. A3.**
Former California Governor Jerry Brown has been re-born as a political radio talk show host. Brown's show, "We the People," is seen by some as a liberal counterpoint to Rush Limbaugh.

Rush Limbaugh

"Limbaugh, Rush," ***Current Biography,*** **March 1993, pp. 34-38.**
Rush Limbaugh, political commentator, radio and TV broadcaster and writer, is profiled. Limbaugh, who is known for his conservative philosophy, has enjoyed much success by ridiculing liberal politics and has the most popular talk show on radio.

Montgomery, David, "Room with a view: Limbaugh has his niche in the land of Clinton," ***The Washington Post,*** **Sept. 23, 1993, p. MDP1.**
Peter Glass, a politically conservative barber and fan of radio talk show host Rush Limbaugh, has created the

"Rush Room" in his Clinton, Md., barber shop where customers can listen to Limbaugh's radio show from noon to 3 p.m. daily and engage in extended gripe sessions about President Clinton.

Stein, Harry, "You can make fun of Rush, but he's not going away," *TV Guide,* April 24, 1993, p. 35.
Even though Rush Limbaugh is an ideologue and prone to wild overstatement, he is still popular with millions of people. Limbaugh scores biggest by pushing buttons on issues that cut across ordinary political lines.

Stewart, Morgan, Ron Faucheux and Nicole King, "Pump up the volume," *Campaigns & Elections,* October 1993, pp. 22-26.
Radio talk show hosts, most notably Rush Limbaugh, are using radio as a populist soapbox to air their complaints about U.S. government. The question of whether this new form of populism will influence voters at the ballot box is addressed, and renowned conservative talk show host Rush Limbaugh is profiled.

Surveys and Polls

Berke, Richard L., "Poll says conservatives dominate talk radio," *The New York Times,* July 16, 1993, p. A12.
A survey by the Times Mirror Center for The People and The Press indicated that talk radio and call-in programs are dominated by Republicans who are more critical of President Clinton's programs than most people. The survey's results suggest that news organizations and politicians have put too much emphasis on the views of a very active and often very angry minority.

Bowman, Karlyn H., and Everett C. Ladd, "Public opinion and demographic report: Talk radio," *American Enterprise,* September/October 1993, pp. 96-97.
The results of two public opinion polls concerning talk radio revealed somewhat different political profiles for listeners. In another survey, 10 percent or respondents said they listen to talk show host Rush Limbaugh daily.

Talk Show Democracy

"Boom vox," *State Legislatures,* July 1993, pp. 62-63.
Political feedback, in the minds of the framers of the First Amendment to the Constitution, was a process for an elected official's constituents to let him or her know what they are thinking. The telecommunications explosion and age of instant opinions have created a new political noise machine for the voice of the U.S. public.

Carlson, Peter, "The heart of talkness: One man's fearless journey into the jungle of American talk shows," *The Washington Post,* April 25, 1993, p. WMAG19.
Peter Carlson comments that the art form of talk shows has changed American politics, American government and America itself.

Fineman, Howard, "The power of talk," *Newsweek,* Feb. 8, 1993, pp. 24-28.
The impact of call-in talk-show on the political process and other issues of current interest is explored. Government is responding to the public's voice as heard on talk-shows, but there is a threat to representative government.

Kolbert, Elizabeth, "The people are heard, at least those who call talk radio," *The New York Times,* Jan. 29, 1993, p. A12.
The belief among politicians that radio talk shows are becoming an increasingly potent force in American politics is explored. The Zoë Baird nomination and the questions of homosexuals being allowed in the military, both of which have generated heated public debate, are two issues that were given a great deal of air time on the call-in shows.

Matthews, Christopher, "Call-in democracy from the third house," *The Washington Times,* Feb. 7, 1993, p. B3.
Christopher Matthews describes his fantasy about a new Third House of Congress, commenting that the American people have created this deliberative body of their own: call-in radio and television.

Meadows, Donella H., "Talk shows don't make democracy," *Houston Chronicle,* Feb. 21, 1993, p. F1.
Donella H. Meadows points out the many ways in which radio and TV talk shows fail to represent a majority view on issues, despite the fact that many analysts are praising the medium as a way of restoring democracy in the U.S.

Peart, Karen N., "Congress tunes in," *Scholastic Update* (Teacher's Edition), Nov. 5, 1993, pp. 20-21.
Across the U.S., radio talk shows are filling the airwaves with politics, giving voice to angry voters and giving Congress an earful. The question of whether these shows have the power to reshape U.S. democracy is examined.

Spiegelman, Arthur, "Radio talk shows are popular channels for Americans' frustration," *Chicago Tribune,* Feb. 8, 1993, p. EV2.
Radio talk shows, once home to calls from kooks, cranks, insomniacs and the highly opinionated, have become the hottest lobbying tool going as ordinary Americans grab their home phones, their car phones or even phones on planes to vent their anger on politicians, especially President Clinton.

"Talk show politics, touch tone government," *Television Program: CNN & Company,* Feb. 4, 1993.
Betsy McCaughey, Tammy Haddad and Susan Page discuss the use of TV and radio talk shows by the candidates in the 1992 election campaign and the barrage of people calling Washington, D.C., on various issues.

Back Issues

Great Research on Current Issues Starts Right Here...Recent topics covered by The CQ Researcher are listed below. Before May 1991, reports were published under the name of Editorial Research Reports.

OCTOBER 1992
Depression
U.S. Auto Industry
Youth Apprenticeships
Hispanic Americans

NOVEMBER 1992
Physical Fitness
Privatization
Paying for College
U.S. Policy in Asia

DECEMBER 1992
Crackdown on Smoking
The New CIA
Eating Disorders
Women and AIDS

JANUARY 1993
Hate Crimes
Child Sexual Abuse
Nuclear Fusion
U.S. Trade Policy

FEBRUARY 1993
Community Policing
Europe's New Right
School Censorship
Violence Against Women

MARCH 1993
Gay Rights
Aid to Russia
War on Drugs
TV Violence

APRIL 1993
Head Start
High-Speed Rail
Children's Legal Rights
Muslims in America

MAY 1993
Cults in America
Preventing Teen Pregnancy
Software Piracy
National Parks

JUNE 1993
Food Safety
Prostitution
Childhood Immunizations
National Service

JULY 1993
Electric Cars
Population Growth
Downward Mobility
Intelligence Testing

AUGUST 1993
Mental Illness
Bilingual Education
Foreign Policy Burden
School Funding

SEPTEMBER 1993
Suburban Crime
Public Housing
Supreme Court Preview
Immigration Reform

OCTOBER 1993
Airline Safety
Disaster Response
Science in the Courtroom
The Glass Ceiling

NOVEMBER 1993
Paying for Retirement
Charitable Giving
Privacy in the Workplace
Adoption

DECEMBER 1993
U.S. Vietnam-Relations
Learning Disabilities
Child Care
Space Program's Future

JANUARY 1994
Racial Tensions in Schools
South Africa's Future
Worker Retraining
Regulating Pesticides

FEBRUARY 1994
Prison Overcrowding
Water Quality
Religion in Schools
Juvenile Justice

MARCH 1994
Underground Economy
Education Standards
Gambling Boom
Private Management of Public Schools

APRIL 1994
Reproductive Ethics
U.S.-China Trade
Soccer in America

Future Topics

- ***Traffic Congestion***
- ***Women's Health Issues***
- ***Mutual Funds***

THE CQ Researcher®

PUBLISHED BY CONGRESSIONAL QUARTERLY INC.

Traffic Congestion

Can America win the battle against gridlock?

When January's earthquake shook Los Angeles, it also jolted long-held assumptions about transportation in the nation's most car-dependent city. As commuters detoured around collapsed freeways, traffic experts, environmentalists and city planners framed the tragedy as a turning point in the ongoing war over the role of the car in U.S. life. Within months, however, it was clear that most commuters were returning to old habits, lured back by the freedom and convenience embodied in the private auto. Still, most policy-makers know the traffic crisis, and attendant pollution woes, will not ease without a concerted search for remedies. Most place their hopes in a combination of futuristic highway technology, regional land-use planning, alternative transportation modes and incentives to discourage solo driving.

INSIDE THIS ISSUE

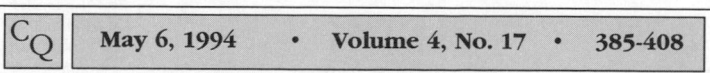

CQ May 6, 1994 • Volume 4, No. 17 • 385-408

Formerly Editorial Research Reports

TRAFFIC CONGESTION

THE ISSUES

BACKGROUND

CURRENT SITUATION

OUTLOOK

SIDEBARS AND GRAPHICS

FOR FURTHER INFORMATION

COVER: SOLO DRIVERS FIGHT TRAFFIC ON SEATTLE'S HIGHWAY 520 WHILE CARPOOLERS BREEZE ALONG IN THE RESTRICTED "DIAMOND LANE." (AMERICAN PASSENGER TRANSPORT ASSOCIATION)

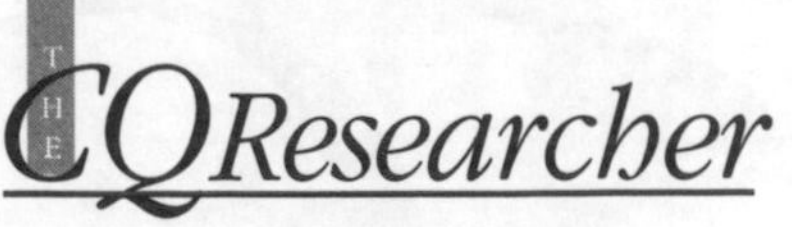

THE CQ Researcher

May 6, 1994
Volume 4, No. 17

The CQ Researcher (ISSN 1056-2036). Formerly Editorial Research Reports. Published weekly (48 times per year, not printed the first Friday of any month with five Fridays) by Congressional Quarterly Inc., 1414 22nd St., N.W., Washington, D.C. 20037. Rates are furnished upon request. Second-class postage paid at Washington, D.C. POSTMASTER: Send address changes to The CQ Researcher, 1414 22nd St., N.W., Washington, D.C. 20037.

Traffic Congestion

BY CHARLES S. CLARK

THE ISSUES

In the chaos following January's earthquake in Los Angeles, the one bright spot for panicked commuters turned out to be the city's fledgling commuter rail system.

The 14-month-old Metrolink, operating flawlessly while six collapsed freeways and 20 major streets were impassable, saw its ridership shoot up from a mere 900 daily to more than 22,000 a day the week after the quake. While many of L.A.'s 400,000 commuters sat stymied for hours in 15-mile backups, Metrolink used federal emergency funds and rushed in help from military construction teams to extend the system onto existing tracks and build seven new stations.

"The L.A. quake made people realize that freeways are fragile where rail is more robust," says John Holtzclaw, a transportation specialist at the San Francisco-based Sierra Club. "It's easier to get a rail back in place than a 50-foot concrete swath."

By April, Metrolink was holding onto an eightfold increase in riders, according to spokesman Peter Hidalgo. But talk in Los Angeles had turned to the Santa Monica Freeway, the nation's busiest thoroughfare, repaired 74 days ahead of schedule. "The most stirring symbol yet of California's endurance," Republican Gov. Pete Wilson called the reopened freeway, traveled daily by some 300,000 dedicated drivers.

"The earthquake produced changes in people's travel time, work schedules and mode of transportation," says Cheryl Collier, research director of Commuter Transportation Services, a Los Angeles research and consulting group that promotes ridesharing. "But the biggest changes were in work schedules," not in ridesharing or use of public transport. Bus use remained flat, she notes.

"Most drivers took side streets near the freeways, and the [temporary carpool] lane they set up around the devastation of the Santa Monica Freeway was surprisingly little used," Collier says. "People would rather wait in line on the exit ramp than carpool. It's a tough sell."

The reluctance of commuters to be weaned from their autos in the country's most car-dependent city goes deep in California — and American — culture. Traffic in the Golden State has grown five times faster than road capacity in the past two decades, and 79 percent of Los Angeles commuters drive alone, according to Collier.

The time people spend twiddling their thumbs in gridlock amounts to 510,000 hours per day, which costs the state an estimated $4.8 million daily in lost productivity, says California's Office of Traffic Safety.

"In L.A., driving is cheap," Collier says. "There are no tolls, and 93 percent of the people get free parking. We're building a subway, but lots of areas are not serviced due to the city's sprawl. And for buses to work, we'd need fewer transfers and more express buses." L.A.'s reputation as a car-loving city is also a product of culture, she adds. "Hispanics, for example, are more apt to rideshare, perhaps due to economics, but for the second generation of immigrants, the first thing they want to do is buy a car."

The traffic nightmare is so extreme in Los Angeles that the city's air pollution merits a special category from the Environmental Protection Agency (EPA). But such attachment to a car-based lifestyle is replicated in cities across the county. (*See table, p. 393.*)

In the past 15 years, notes Brookings Institution analyst Anthony Downs, the number of cars owned by Americans rose 41.9 percent and licensed drivers increased 29.3 percent, while the general population increased only 15.9 percent. [1] The average daily commuting time of America's estimated 108 million commuters lengthened by 7 percent from 1983-90, according to the Transportation Department's 1990 Nationwide Personal Transportation Survey. And the Federal Highway Administration (FHWA) predicts the extra time spent driving because of delays will rise from 2.7 billion "vehicle hours" in 1985 to 11.9 billion in 2005.

Though the 1970s and '80s witnessed modest traffic-flow improvements from HOV (high-occupancy vehicle) lanes and employer efforts to encourage ridesharing, the 1990 census showed that the percentage of workers driving alone actually *rose,* from 64 percent in 1980 to 73 percent in 1990. That's a gain of 22 million solo commuters.

One reason for the increase is the rise of suburb-to-suburb commuting, which is not conducive to public transportation. Fully 60 percent of office jobs are now in the suburbs, compared with only 25 percent in 1970, the census showed. [2]

Another contributor to traffic has been the rise of working women, who are more likely than other drivers to

California Commuters Consider the Alternatives

Last year marked a turning point in Southern California commuters' attitudes about driving alone, according to the state's fifth annual "State of the Commute" survey. More commuters said they were willing to try alternatives to solo driving, compared with 1992. The surveys help transportation officials develop travel-incentive programs, such as employer-sponsored ridesharing.

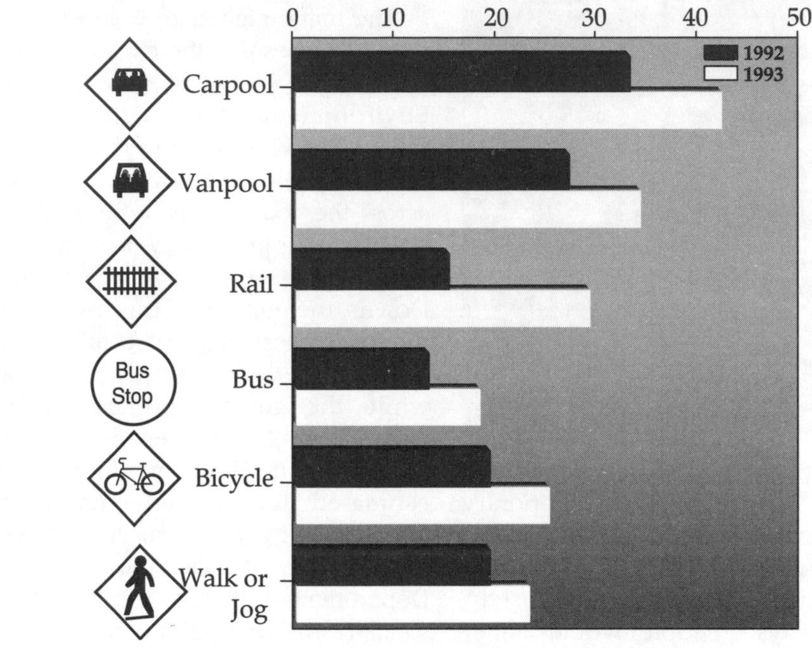

Source: "State of the Commute," Commuter Transportation Services Inc., 1993

take the children to school, shop and deal with emergencies at home. Women's daily rate of trip-making has increased 9 percent since 1983, while men's rose only 5 percent, according to the Personal Transportation Survey.

"Many women workers will continue to drive alone," noted a recent Labor Department study, "because driving still costs less than the additional child- or eldercare, or because they cannot obtain the needed care, or because they must use the time that would be required by an alternative mode to conduct their domestic responsibilities, or because they do not feel safe taking public transit." [3]

The task of easing the resulting gridlock has long been the province of highway engineers. But their prospects for success are rendered gloomy by what Downs calls the "triple convergence." Single solutions to traffic jams such as widening an expressway, for example, often backfire, causing drivers who formerly used alternative routes to switch back to the main one, drivers who traveled at alternative hours to return to peak hours and some who had been taking public transportation to try the newly widened roadway. "Any *initial* improvement in peak-hour travel conditions on high-capacity roadways will immediately elicit a triple convergence response, which will soon restore congestion during peak periods," he writes. [4]

Still, today's traffic problems are seen as solvable if engineers are joined by environmentalists, land-use planners and coalitions of businesses and local officials. "Half of traffic congestion comes from the lack of alternate routes, broken cars and accidents," says Hank Dittmar, director of the Surface Transportation Policy Project (STPP), a research and advocacy group representing more than 100 environmental and consumer organizations. "If there is no way to get cars off the road or to intercept cars after a toxic-waste spill, you get congestion. That's why our group has designed a system of choice, redundancy and flexibility that combines public transit with the wise use of arterial roads and information systems."

New computer technology — so-called smart cars and smart highways — is seen as a way to improve highway monitoring and alert drivers to backups. "Incident management is a good example of an activity that is easily implemented and would get immediate results," says Larry Darnes, chief of the FHWA's Traffic Management Branch. "Studies show that delay increases geometrically with the time it takes to clear up a traffic jam, meaning that a half-hour rather than a 15-minute delay translates to four times the delay to motorists."

The arrival of the Clinton administration has cheered some longtime advocates of buses, carpools, subways and commuter trains. The American Public Transit Association (APTA) points out that at rush hour every busful of passengers removes 40 cars from traffic, every full rail car eliminates 75-125 cars and every full van removes 13 cars. "Under Clinton, the public transit budget rose 20 percent, which is the biggest since the Carter years," says Chip Bishop, APTA's executive director for public relations. "We're very upbeat about the 1990s."

Observers agree, however, that the ultimate solution will not be some sort of transport revolution but a calculated mixture of modestly effective remedies. "When we talk about congestion mitigation, we're talking at the margin," says C. Kenneth Orski, a former Urban Mass Transit Administration official who is now president of the Urban Mobility Corp., a consulting firm. "We will never have radical restructuring of travel patterns because land uses have fixed the bulk of travel patterns for a long time to come. But from a transportation standpoint, the marginal 10 percent [we can affect] is extremely important. A single car added on a roadway is like one more grain of salt in a supersaturated salt solution. It can make traffic *congeal*."

Just what the remedies might be will depend on the following issues:

Are Americans permanently hooked on cars?

"If one agrees with the theory in vogue among some psychoanalysts that birth is a trauma we never forget or forgive, one can go even further and compare the car to the womb in which we were lying so snug, warm and cozy," writes German social scientist Wolfgang Zuckermann in his obituary for the automobile society, *End of the Road*. "Therefore the exit from that car to confront a cold, threatening, inhospitable world outside becomes a somewhat similar trauma." [5]

America's decades-old love affair with the car has long been remarked upon, the auto appearing as a symbol of control over one's fate, a natural part of the country's heritage of restless individualism. The car is "who we are; it's how we function," writes K.T. Berger; "it's more than a convenience, a mere possession, or a symbol of social status or identity. A car is a close friend, a family member, part of the family home. It even has its own room in the house — the garage." [6]

Orski point outs that while the car continues to be valued as a vehicle for freedom, privacy and status, "increasingly it is a necessity, particularly for women with small children, who may be insecure about using public transit at night because of crime. Most transit doesn't go where they want to go, is a problem in inclement weather and is not a comfortable way to travel. Most people don't want to wait," Orski adds, "they want to go on their own time."

Americans cherish their mobility, many say, even if it is punctuated by stints in bumper-to-bumper immobility. "We encourage voluntary, practical methods of reducing congestion such as van- and carpools, but we recognize the reality that most people use the auto," says Ken Vest, a spokesman for the Highway Users Federation for Safety and Mobility. "We want to preserve the freedom of choice that most people have come to enjoy."

But advocates for relying less on cars and concrete argue that in the long run, alternatives can be encouraged. "Traditionalists say mobility is cherished, but we say it's secondary to access to jobs and recreation," says Dittmar. "Today, Americans have a love-hate relationship with the car. When we were growing up as teens, it was the ticket out of the house, but we don't have a good time in cars anymore. Surveys show that pleasure driving has gone down since the 1960s. When you're moving at only 10 mph on the freeway, you're not inclined to spend weekends trying to have fun in cars." (*See story, p. 394.*)

The car is outpacing public transit currently because "the price of gas is cheaper today in real terms than at any time since before World War II," says APTA's Bishop. "There's free parking for commuters everywhere, for 90 percent of drivers" — a fringe benefit worth $12 billion-$50 billion a year, according to Marcia D. Lowe, a senior researcher at the Worldwatch Institute. [7]

Driving is also encouraged, Bishop continues, by an imbalance in federal spending. Federal aid for mass transit fell by 50 percent from 1981-91, while highway spending was doubled. "The message has been that the feds are behind highways and that they're getting out of the transit game."

The Campaign for New Transportation Priorities, a coalition of transit, rail and environmental advocates, argues that present policies favor the automobile with up to $300 billion in anti-pollution remedies and roadway services as well as lost tax revenues on land taken for roads.

Moreover, according to the coalition, the Transportation Department "says roadway user charges, taxes and fees account for only 60 percent of government expenditures for roads. The rest is out of general revenues. If such costs were internalized and reflected in highway user charges through increases in federal and state gasoline taxes, vehicle registration fees and weight-distance taxes on heavy trucks, motorists would be motivated to drive less, select more energy-efficient vehicles and make greater use of energy-efficient mass transit and other auto alternatives such as ridesharing." [8]

Public transit, however, with all its advertising touting the freedom of commuters to read their newspapers or

Commuting Preferences Vary From City to City

Among the nation's 40 largest cities, Baltimore was the carpooling capital in 1990, while Oklahoma City had the most solo drivers. New Yorkers used public transportation the most, and faced the longest commutes.

Most carpooling	Baltimore, Md.	16.8%
Least carpooling	New York City	8.5%
Most solo drivers	Oklahoma City, Okla.	80.8%
Least solo drivers	New York City	24%
Most use of public transit	New York City	53.4%
Least use of public transit	Virginia Beach, Va.	0.8%
Longest travel time to work	New York City	36.5 minutes
Shortest travel time to work	Albuquerque, N.M.	18.5 minutes

Source: Population Division, Census Bureau, May 29, 1992

California Quake Sent Message to Some Commuters . . .

Could the escape route from gridlock run through the electronic information highway?

For two decades, futurists eying the spread of computers, modems and fax machines have touted telecommuting as a way to reduce traffic by allowing workers to "punch in" from the comfort of their homes.

Some 7.6 million Americans telecommute at least part time during normal business hours, according to a 1993 survey by Link Resources, a New York City consulting firm, and the number has been growing 15 percent annually.

Not surprisingly, Los Angeles boasts the most telecommuters, some 600,000, with more expected since January's earthquake decimated local freeways.

In its wake, Southern California's major telephone companies, Pacific Bell and GTE Corp., set up new customer hotlines, and reported some 10,000 requests for enhanced telephone service. The Antelope Valley Telebusiness Center, a satellite installation that leases space to companies for telecommuting from a Los Angeles suburb, received so many new inquiries it made plans to multiply its building space tenfold. [1]

Potential Benefits From Telecommuting

If telecommuting continues to increase, up to 1.7 billion gallons of gas could be saved by the year 2002, and engine pollutants reduced by up to 3.4 percent.

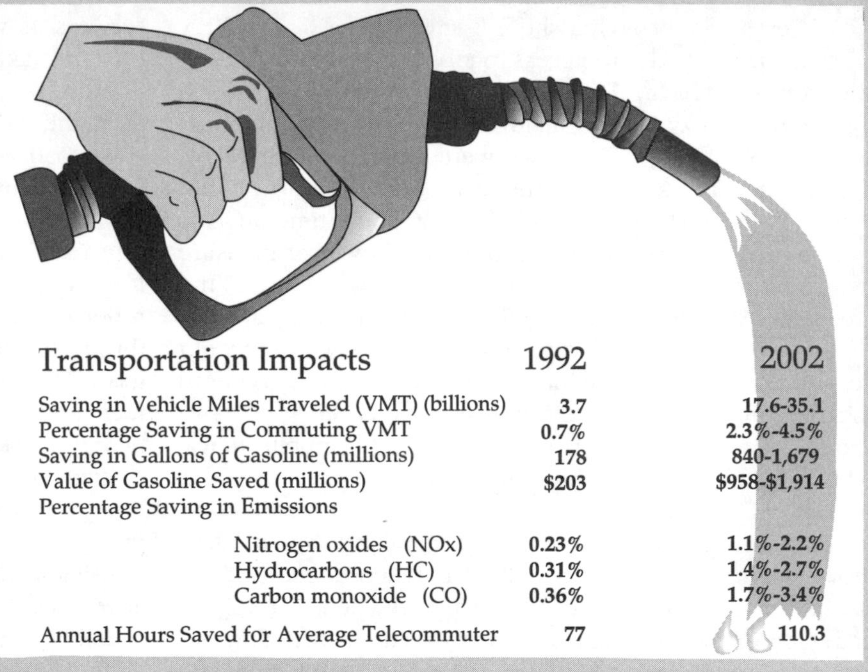

Transportation Impacts	1992	2002
Saving in Vehicle Miles Traveled (VMT) (billions)	3.7	17.6-35.1
Percentage Saving in Commuting VMT	0.7%	2.3%-4.5%
Saving in Gallons of Gasoline (millions)	178	840-1,679
Value of Gasoline Saved (millions)	$203	$958-$1,914
Percentage Saving in Emissions		
Nitrogen oxides (NOx)	0.23%	1.1%-2.2%
Hydrocarbons (HC)	0.31%	1.4%-2.7%
Carbon monoxide (CO)	0.36%	1.7%-3.4%
Annual Hours Saved for Average Telecommuter	77	110.3

Source: "Transportation Implications of Telecommuting," U.S. Department of Transportation, April 1993

The term "telecommuting" was coined in 1973 by Jack Nilles, a Los Angeles rocket scientist turned consultant. "I was looking for ways to apply space technologies to the real world," he recalls, "when I spoke to some urban planners who asked, 'If you can put a man on moon, why can't you do something about traffic?' "

Nilles' concept was picked up by futurist Alvin Toffler in his 1980 book, *The Third Wave,* as a staple of the future workplace. The movement also got a boost, says Nilles, during the1984 Olympic Games in Los Angeles, when there were predictions that the city would "congeal" with too many cars. Instead, experiments with telecommuting and alternative work schedules reduced traffic by 3-5 percent.

During the 1980s, numerous companies around the country began pilot programs in telecommuting, with the majority reporting gains in employee productivity of 10-20 percent. [2] By the start of the 1990s, there were bills in Congress to encourage telecommuting, and a federal pilot program had been started

catch up on work, has not kept up with the increasingly attractive comforts and privacy of the auto. Indeed, American drivers have purchased more than 5 million car phones, while the sales of books on audiocassettes have risen fivefold in the past five years. [9]

Polls show the public sympathetic to efforts to encourage ridesharing, but lukewarm toward public transit. An April 1993 poll commissioned by The Road Information Program (TRIP) showed that 52 percent of respondents say they're more likely to see car and van pools as practical and effective, compared with only 40 percent for mass transit.

"Public transportation faces a greater challenge in the United States than in virtually any other developed country," argue transportation analysts John Pucher and Ira Hirschman. They point out that America has the "world's highest level of auto ownership per capita and the most extensive, lowest-density suburbanization." [10]

Stephen Moore, director of fiscal

. . . Telecommuting's Time May Have Arrived

involving 13 government agencies. The landmark 1991 Intermodal Surface Transportation Efficiency Act (ISTEA) allows funds to be spent on telecommuting programs to reduce congestion and air pollution. And last year, the Clinton administration began promoting telecommuting as part of its effort to create a national information superhighway.

Even with all the fanfare, however, telecommuting has not taken the country by storm. "Despite the clear, positive benefits, it's still not being done," notes Bernadette Grey, editor in chief of *Home Office Computing* magazine. She says telecommuting remains the smallest portion of the universe of home-based workers, most of whom run traditional part- or full-time businesses. "It's more difficult than people anticipated to break down mid-managers' attitudes and fears of losing control of people who work for them," Grey says. "And employees express fear that, 'If I say I want to telecommute, it appears that my career is not important to me, and I will be overlooked for promotions.' It shouldn't be that way."

Labor unions worry about the opportunities for exploitation of hourly workers who are at home. Denise Mitchell, a spokesperson for the Service Employees International Union, says: "The hoopla over telecommuting is bigger than the reality. It has not grown in areas that affect large numbers of people. It's mostly for writers, editors and researchers, basically white-collar jobs such as consultants."

Many who've tried telecommuting say their colleagues can become resentful of their freedom, or that they miss the interaction with co-workers. "There is no doubt that the inability to see co-workers is an impediment causing resistance to telecommuting," says Milton Grodsky, director of the Center for the Study of Management and Organizations at the University of Maryland-College Park. He has hopes that the development of a video phone, such as the model recently developed by AT&T, may give telecommuters a visual element once the country is networked with fiber-optic cable. [3]

Some land-use planners fear that satellite telecommuting will bring unsightly "urban sprawl" to scenic isolated areas. "Already," a federal study noted, "there is an explosion in farm and village home prices in upstate New York, rural Maine [and] the Sierra Nevada that were once too distant from urban areas to be practical locations for home-based work." [4]

Commuter Transportation Services Inc. found that some 4 percent of the Angelenos it surveyed after the quake had begun to telecommute, but that 3 percent who were already telecommuting had to stop because of quake-related disruptions.

Still, the quake has added an urgency that may supersede many of the objections to telecommuting. *Los Angeles Times* columnist Michael Schrage suggests boosting telecommuting by requiring the phone company to cut local daytime phone service costs and to levy a special surtax on car phones to discourage driving. [5]

"The final say on telecommuting rests with corporate managers, who must decide whether it contributes to productivity and efficiency," says C. Kenneth Orski, president of Urban Mobility Corp., a Washington consulting firm. Top managers are divided, he says, with the most enthusiasm coming from those in computer and telecommunications companies, which regard telecommuting as a profit opportunity.

Nilles, the author of a forthcoming book, *Making Telecommuting Happen*, says: "Ultimately, half of our population will be eligible to telecommute. It's not for farmers or ditch-diggers, or, for a while, brain surgeons. But three out of five of our workers are in information-industry jobs."

As for the fear of loneliness, Nilles estimates that such complaints come from only 5 percent of the telecommuters. Much more common, he says, is the feeling, "What a relief not to have to talk to those turkeys at work."

---

[1] *USA Today*, Feb. 2, 1994.

[2] U.S. Department of Transportation, "Transportation Implications of Telecommuting," April 1993, p. 33.

[3] Julian M. Weiss, "Adding Vision to Telecommuting," *The Futurist*, May-June 1992, p. 16.

[4] Department of Transportation, *op. cit.*, p. 87.

[5] Column printed in *The Washington Post*, Jan. 28, 1994.

---

policy at the libertarian Cato Institute, points to studies showing that the $50 billion the government has spent on urban mass transit over the past 30 years had not benefited commuters. Ridership in most major cities is down, he notes. "The whole theory behind public transit was that if you build it they will come, if cities only have transit, then business will invest," he says. "And they keep building them in inner cities as if this were the 1950s commute, without anyone following the way people live and work in the 1990s."

In contrast to those who argue that government policy favors the auto, Moore says: "Washington is at war against the automobile, with its regulations, parking policies and gasoline taxes. As a libertarian, what bothers me is that a case could be made that over the past 100 years, the auto has been man's most liberating invention. The car lets you go where you want, and that troubles some people. What will defeat these plans to drive people out of their cars is that Americans

How Americans Travel to Work

The number of Americans driving to work alone increased from 1980-1990, while carpooling decreased. Bus and train commuting also declined during the period.

	1980 Census		1990 Census	
Means of Transportation	Number	Percent	Number	Percent
Total workers	96,617,296	(100%)	115,070,274	(100%)
Private vehicle	81,258,496	84.1%	99,592,932	86.5%
Drove alone	62,193,449	64.4	84,215,298	73.2
Carpooled	19,065,047	19.7	15,377,634	13.4
Public transportation	6,175,061	6.4	6,069,589	5.3
Bus or trolley bus	3,924,787	4.1	3,445,000	3.0
Streetcar or trolley car			78,130	0.1
Subway or elevated	1,528,852	1.6	1,755,476	1.5
Railroad	554,089	0.6	574,052	0.5
Ferryboat			37,497	0.0
Taxicab	167,133	0.2	179,434	0.2
Motorcycle	419,007	0.4	237,404	0.2
Bicycle	468,348	0.5	466,856	0.4
Walked only	5,413,248	5.6	4,488,886	3.9
Worked at home	2,179,863	2.3	3,406,025	3.0
All other means	703,273	0.7	808,582	0.7
Average travel time (minutes)	21.7		22.4	

Source: Population Division, Census Bureau, May 29, 1992

truly have a love affair with cars, and it is difficult to get them to change a whole lifestyle."

But Americans who move away from traffic-bound, polluting auto travel will not need to do so "out of altruism," says Andrew Clarke, project manager at the Bicycle Federation of America. "People will do what's easiest and quick and convenient. They're not wedded to the car if circumstances change. We need to have a plan ready for the time when gas goes up to $4 per gallon or air pollution reaches a crisis. Now we have all our eggs in one basket and are held hostage by the automobile. It's a monocultural transport policy that exists in no other country." (*See story, p. 398.*)

Should the country invest heavily in high-technology traffic management?

While debaters in the "car wars" argue human behavior and traffic policy, the nation is quietly entering an era when the solution to traffic congestion may be sought in high technology. "Smart cars" and "smart highways," as the new concepts are called, would be outfitted with computers and sensors to permit, for example, information on tie-ups or bad weather to be relayed to dashboard video maps that would point drivers toward a detour. Warnings would sound when cars got too close to one another, tolls could be collected electronically and special beacons would guide cars to vacant parking spaces.

Ultimately, high-tech cruise controls "would make it possible for vehicles to travel safely only inches apart, like railroad cars," writes Massachusetts Institute of Technology Professor Daniel Roos, who chaired a National Research Council panel on intelligent vehicles. "Each lane could thus carry far more vehicles, reducing the need for new roads. Drivers might even be free to read a book or enjoy the scenery during the trip." [11]

Programs to create such futuristic transport have been under way for years in Japan and in Europe, where 150 organizations from 11 countries are cooperating on development. In the United States, 1991 legislation authorized six years of pilot projects under the Intelligent Vehicle Highway System (IVHS) program, a diverse public and private research effort that has stirred excitement on Capitol Hill and drawn interest from American defense companies seeking to convert to civilian industries. About $1 billion in private and government money has been spent so far on dozens of research and operational test projects around the country. [12]

Transportation Secretary Federico F. Peña "has made it clear that IVHS is part of an effort to deal not only with congestion but with all transportation problems," says Darnes of FHWA. To fulfill his goal of "tying America together in a national transportation system," Peña has been accelerating IVHS in order "to create a new alliance linking transportation programs in the personal and economic universe with the technology industry. IVHS creates an environment to improve the way we go to work and the store, plus it's also good for the economy."

Like all newfangled technologies, however, smart cars and roads raise fears about unintended consequences. Cars with electronic maps, on-board tags for electronic tolls and highway video cameras that can read license plates present threats to civil liberties, warns *The Economist* magazine. "Besides collecting the money and enforcing the rules of the electronic road, it can have another, more sinister use: prying. A smart road would know where a motorist is at anytime." [13]

To Ross Capon, executive director of the National Association of Railway Passengers, the potential for IVHS "to reduce congestion is being dramatically oversold. IVHS is a vague term used for different things ranging from electric signage to sensors in the pavement, which are already on the New Jersey Turnpike. The fundamental problem is not that highway space is not used intelligently," he says, "but that there won't be anywhere near enough highway space to accommodate our present transportation modal split. This futuristic idea that you will be able to get on the highway and go to sleep implies little or no impact on people's lifestyles — that computers will battle congestion for us, and we won't ever have to get on the bus."

Others are even harsher. "IVHS is pure pork barrel, largely a sham," says Clifford Winston, a transportation analyst at the Brookings Institution. "Yes, it will solve the problem for an incredibly large amount of money, and then the highways will again fill up with others who'd been waiting in the wings using rail or whatever."

Indeed, the notion that the electronic advance warnings can help drivers avoid traffic congestion may well backfire, merely creating additional gridlock along the newly designated alternative route. "If we really want these systems to dramatically improve the flow of traffic, it may well be that traffic controllers will have to deliberately withhold accurate data or broadcast misleading information to commuters," says *Los Angeles Times* columnist Michael Schrage. [14]

IVHS is "the Star Wars of transit, and everyone is jumping on the bandwagon," notes Robert Dunphy, senior research director at the Urban Land Institute. "It has tremendous promise because there's lots we already know how to do, but are not doing." He is less impressed with the notion that travelers would "stumble off onto a smart highway without knowing how they're going to go. But if you could get more information to travelers before they depart, then maybe the report of a half-hour delay will cause someone" to postpone their trip.

Dittmar of the Surface Transportation Project says IVHS is worth developing for the technology but shouldn't be controlled by people who simply want to spend more to increase the capacity of highways. "We live in a complex society," he notes, "and people have multiple objectives. We can't just get the most cars on the road and provide safety. We must consider pedestrian access, business access, buses and transit. We must design multiple options with sometimes competing social objectives."

Many advocates for non-car transport, among them APTA, are participating in the planning of IVHS. "It has potential for transit buses as well," notes Bishop. "It could be useful in monitoring the location of buses, in rerouting and in telling you at the bus stop when the next bus is coming."

Bishop still worries, however, that IVHS could "obscure the real problem, which is the need to get more people in fewer cars, not more cars on the highways. We must find a way to combine the promise of technology with policies that encourage ridesharing in all forms. It won't solve the problem alone."

"IVHS can bridge the gap if we don't let technology drive the whole thing," agrees Collier of Commuter Transportation Services. "We can't just build it and assume people will come. We have to focus on people's needs. The map in the dashboard that shows an accident, for example. Will people use it?"

FHWA's Darnes reports that the 1994 list of IVHS projects includes research into the societal impacts of IVHS, including the likelihood of user acceptance and willingness to pay for it. "There's been some bad publicity emphasizing the image of smart highways and smart vehicles, but IVHS is more than that. It's a mixture of transport alternatives, the ability to flip on a TV before a trip and decide which mode is best for that trip. It's also about efficiency, comfort and safety. But if we can't provide good mobility that is also good for the environment, then it will fail."

The main purpose of IVHS is to produce "a more effective system, increased safety and improved infrastructure," notes Orski of Urban Mobility Corp. "One side effect might be that if it is successful, it will make highways more convenient and pleasurable and attract more drivers, but that is marginal."

Will new land-use planning reduce traffic congestion?

"Traffic congestion is caused by vehicles, not by people in themselves," writes urban planner Jane Jacobs in her classic work, *The Death and Life of Great American Cities*. "Wherever people are thinly settled, rather than densely concentrated, or wherever diverse uses occur infrequently, any specific attraction does cause traffic congestion. Clinics, shopping centers or movies bring with them a concentration of traffic — and what is more, bring traffic heavily along the routes to and from them. . . . This is tolerable where the population is thinly spread. It becomes an intolerable condition, destructive of all other values and all other aspects of convenience, where populations are heavy or continuous." [15]

Critics of the automobile society often argue that the roots of gridlock and air pollution can be traced to the city planner's drafting table. Each new

Coping With the Stress of Commuting

Todd Lewis rises at 3 a.m. every weekday and leaves his family in Sterling, Va., to brave his two-hour commute to the state capital in Richmond. The opportunity to broaden his experience as an air-traffic controller makes the daily 250-mile round trip worthwhile, even though he has put more than 100,000 miles on his Saturn in nearly two years of marathon commuting.

"It's like working a 13-hour day, and I resent not having the end of the day to relax," he says. "The fatigue accumulates during the week, and it becomes harder to decide whether I should spend my spare time sleeping or talking with my wife."

To head off the boredom, Lewis listens to books on tape, music or radio talk shows. "The trick," he says, "is to just view it as part of the day and don't make it into a bad, stressful thing."

In an age when telephones and fax machines are becoming commonplace in cars (indeed, Campbell Soup Co. predicts that by the year 2000 a quarter of all cars will contain microwave ovens), millions of Americans have made lengthy sessions behind the wheel a part of their workaday routines.

But psychically, there is a price to pay. "Long commutes are bad news," says Raymond W. Novaco, a professor of psychology and social behavior at the University of California-Irvine who studies traffic and stress. "Some people value that time in a car by themselves — away from home and work in their own private bubble — and can arrange comfort for themselves. But the longer the distance, the higher their blood pressure can become, and the more negative their mood."

In extreme cases, driver frustration leads to anti-social behavior. There were 3,600 episodes of freeway violence from July 1987 to September 1989, according to Novaco. In a survey of drivers, he found that 31 percent had chased another driver, 12 percent had thrown an object at another car, 5 percent had rammed another car and 3 percent had driven while carrying a gun. [1]

More commonly, however, people adapt. Their bodies absorb the effects of commuting stress, and the costs appear only over long periods. "It will show up in absences from work, illnesses such as colds or the flu, chest pain and in frustration, low-tolerance and negative moods at home," Novaco says.

Novaco found that women show the highest stress levels, the most need to wind down at day's end and the most negative effects on family life. This is most likely, he says, because their commutes are often complicated by the responsibility for transporting children to school or day care.

"Stress also depends on the context," Novaco adds. "In rural Indiana, 15 minutes sounds like a huge commute," but that is nothing in Los Angeles. Researchers have to study all the "vectors in a commuter's life," he says. Some, for example, have undergone the strain of having their company relocate and are suddenly faced with a long commute.

Evening commuting is the most stressful, Novaco says, when there is more traffic because people are also making non-work-related trips. "Add to that the strain and fatigue from the work day, and the stress is heightened."

To counteract commuter tension, Los Angeles health-management consultant Mark Strunin recommends breathing exercises, progressive-relaxation techniques (beginning with the legs and moving up to the shoulders and neck) and listening to quiet music. [2]

Will stress be eased by books on tape and car phones? No one knows, Novaco says. "Plausibly yes, because of the added security and the help in staying alert for long distances."

---

[1] Cited in K.T. Berger, *Where the Road and the Sky Collide: America Through the Eyes of Its Drivers* (1993), p. 60.

[2] Association for Commuter Transportation, Fact Sheet (undated).

auto requires nine parking spaces in a city or suburb, according to the Institute of Transportation Engineers. Office workers require 200-250 square feet of space while their cars require 400 square feet of land at both ends of their commute, according to the New York City-based Regional Plan Association. Individual houses use 15 times as much roadway and 40 times as much arable land as apartments, according to a study comparing detached housing in Davis, Calif., with apartments in San Francisco. [16]

Clearly, the amount of private automobile traffic in a community — and its receptivity to public transportation — depends greatly on the density of the population and the use of the land. Modern city planners sketching out the congestion-free town have already established "neotraditional" planned communities, such as Seaside, Fla., and Kentlands, in Gaithersburg, Md., which are designed "for people, not cars," as alternatives to suburban sprawl. They're characterized by cul de sacs and grids that allow travel between neighborhoods and shopping areas without the use of main roads, according to the Urban Land Institute.

Planners in Portland, Ore., surveyed the public on the type of streets they'd like to live on, notes the Bicycle Federation's Clarke. "People didn't pick the eight-lane divided highway but the traditional neighborhood with streets, people and shops. People want to live where people are, where it's safe. A blank wall with cars whizzing by is inhospitable."

Surveys show that people are willing to use public transit if their walk to the nearest station is a quarter-mile or less in the case of buses, and a half-mile or less for commuter rail, says the Sierra Club's Holtzclaw. According to a study by Holtzclaw that compared auto use in San Francisco neighborhoods of different population densities, doubling population density reduces the annual auto mileage per capita or per household by 20-30 percent in San Francisco. That's because apartment dwellers in the city often have better access to public transportation and use their cars less frequently.

But building such qualities into everyday communities is highly problematic. "The general perception," Holtzclaw says, "is that people don't like density and mixed use, and want to drive a lot." That, at least, is the view pushed by the highway lobby, he says — the American Automobile Association, the Association of State Highway Officials and the asphalt, concrete, tire and car companies.

In California, Holtzclaw continues, the 1978 cap on residential property taxes known as Proposition 13 means that cities feel the only way they can attract revenues is to encourage commercial development. Federal Housing Administration and veterans housing loan policy going back to the 1930s has required that housing be separate from commercial development, he says, and the requirements for front and side setbacks for single-family homes forbid high density. "A lot of the kind of development we would like is actually illegal."

Another obstacle, says Dunphy of the Urban Land Institute, "is resistance from neighbors to changing the residential character of their neighborhood, even though much vacant land and land currently in use have ideal characteristics for transportation for walkers, bicyclers or housing around a subway."

One of the key reasons that commuter rail travel hasn't caught on more rapidly, note rail advocates, is that the rail stations are not built near enough to workers' jobs. "Politicians often adopt the rhetoric of environmentalism, but their substance favors building roads," says Capon. "Changing land use smacks of communism — 'What? Tell developers what to do? This is America!' — so they keep increasing road capacity."

Coordination of traffic policy and land-use policy requires a forbidding degree of cooperation among governmental bodies. Local governments "will never voluntarily agree on how to make certain hard choices that affect congestion levels," writes Brookings' Downs. "Rather, each will seek to maximize its own residents' benefits and minimize their bearing of any social costs involved in cutting congestion.

"Hence the decisions necessary to reduce congestion effectively can only be made by one or more regional bodies with true authority and power not only over traffic flows but also over several other critical elements. These include highway and transit planning and construction, the location of key land uses and at what densities new urban development occurs." [17]

The ray of hope for advocates of better land-use planning is the 1991 Intermodal Surface Transportation Efficiency Act (ISTEA, pronounced "Iced Tea"). Hailed as a milestone that ended the country's decades-long embrace of highway building, ISTEA allowed states and localities to use federal money for non-road modes

Have Car, Willing to Travel

The distance Americans traveled for personal business increased by 137 percent from 1969-1990, with smaller increases for shopping trips and work travel. Trips to work still accounted for the most household travel in 1990.

Average Annual Vehicle Miles Traveled

Trip Purpose	1969	1977	1983	1990	Percent Change 1969-90
Home to work	4,183	3,815	3,538	4,853	16
Shopping	929	1,336	1,567	1,743	88
Other family or personal business	1,270	1,444	1,816	3,014	137
Social and Recreation	4,094	3,286	3,534	4,060	-1
All purposes*	**12,423**	**12,036**	**11,739**	**15,100**	**22**

*Includes trips for other purposes not shown, such as to school, church, doctor , dentist

Source: "Nationwide Personal Transportation Survey," U.S. Department of Transportation, March 1992

such as rail, bicycling and pedestrian projects. It also established an unprecedented level of community participation in transportation planning and shifted power from state transportation departments to regionwide groups called Metropolitan Planning Organizations.

"ISTEA has come along at a critical time," notes an analysis by the Bicycle Federation.[18] "Community-based planning efforts have been building steam for the past decade, as citizens and agencies across the nation have invented it over and over again in an attempt to find a better way to do planning. Now, with its mandates for public participation and a huge shift of power from the state to the local level, ISTEA has pushed the community-based planning movement to critical mass."

"Transportation is our largest investment of public capital," notes the STPP's Dittmar. "ISTEA says we have to look at the money available and make decisions as a region — in a way that integrates different transportation modes with the community and the environment. That kind of decision-making is new. Before, we proceeded incrementally.

"But solving problems by building is expensive. On San Francisco's I-880, they spent hundreds of millions of dollars to add four lanes and 10-foot walls and ended up changing the average rush-hour speed from 29 to 31 miles per hour. If we can coordinate information and land use, it could well prove cheaper than building."

So far, however, ISTEA has not delivered on its potential. Dittmar's group is one of several that have monitored state and local spending under ISTEA. They found that less than 1 percent of eligible funds were going to non-traditional, or non-highway projects, that bureaucrats had a limited understanding of how to involve the public in planning and that states were spending very little in urban areas, where the air is polluted, and a great deal in rural areas, even though the majority of the population is urban.

"It is a big change for these institutions to shift from a single-purpose engineering focus to the new multi-purpose paradigm of partnership, planning and public involvement," said an STPP report.[19]

"There is a learning curve," agrees Harriet Parcells, a transportation associate with the National Association of Railway Passengers. "States are still waiting for federal guidance on the regulations." A General Accounting Office survey of Metropolitan Planning Organizations noted that many officials said traffic-demand management activities of the type environmentalists and public transit advocates favor are "difficult to market politically" because they require changing commuter behavior, whereas traffic-supply projects focus mostly on engineering changes.[20]

Still, backers of regional planning remain hopeful. "ISTEA is an opportunity," says Dunphy. It shows that in order to solve traffic congestion, "we don't need just a bunch of aging hippies to move to a place with seven different garbage recycling bins, but that we must deliver land and housing at a price that average people can afford." ■

BACKGROUND

Triumph of the Auto

City streets have been congested at least since the days of Julius Caesar. One of the emperor's first acts on assuming power over ancient Rome was banning daytime wheeled traffic in the city center. The effect, notes historian Lewis Mumford, was to shift much of the traffic to night hours, an observation made by the poet Juvenal, who said the noise disrupted his sleep.[21]

In the United States, the arrival of the automobile at the dawn of the 20th century brought with it feuds between residents who valued their streets as communal gathering places, and the new visionaries who wanted to pave over the streets so that auto drivers could make their way to fledgling suburbs. In Brooklyn in 1896, a historian recently wrote, protesting residents petitioned to have cobblestones rather than asphalt on their roads, otherwise "the lives of our children would be in constant danger from reckless drivers and riders."[22]

Though subways, trolleys, trains and buses became as familiar as cars to many Americans, the flowering of suburbia that accompanied the economic boom after World War II set the country en route to its highway-centered lifestyle. Los Angeles became the car capital. "Back in the early '40s, when the first Southern California freeways were built, they were hailed as 'arteries' — lifelines of unrestricted travel enabling commuters to travel around the L.A. basin and escape from it swiftly and easily," writes David Rizzo. "In those early days, they worked. A driver could circle Los Angeles in an hour and a half or two hours."[23]

The 1956 Interstate Highway Act launched one of the world's greatest engineering feats. But as automobile historian James Flink put it, the system also "ensured the complete triumph of the automobile over mass-transit alternatives in the United States and killed off, except in a few large cities, the vestiges of balanced public transportation systems that remained in 1950s America."[24]

By the end of the 1950s, Los Angeles would already be experiencing its notorious traffic-induced smog, "partly owing to local eccentricities of circulation in the ocean of air, but also partly to the city's very scatter and amplitude

Continued on p. 398

Chronology

1940s-1950s

Interstate highway system planned as a result of wartime defense strategy.

1956
Congress passes Interstate Highway Act launching construction of $100 billion, 45,000-mile Interstate Highway System.

1960s

Traffic congestion affects suburbs; riots in inner-city Los Angeles underscore need for better public transportation.

1960
Time magazine cover story highlights problems associated with the nation's 43 million commuters.

1964
Urban Mass Transportation Act is passed, authorizing federal spending on transportation. Report after Watts riots shows that the lack of adequate public transport was a key reason for the isolation and frustration of inner-city residents.

1969
First HOV lanes established for buses only on Shirley Highway south of Washington, D.C.

1970s

The number of jobs rises in the suburbs twice as fast as elsewhere, leading to a surge in suburb-to-suburb commuting and increasing congestion and pollution.

1970
First Clean Air Act creates the Environmental Protection Agency (EPA) and the first national auto-emission standards.

1977
Clean Air Act Amendments require state and local governments to revise state air-quality plans if national quality standards have not been met.

1980s

Businesses concerned about productivity form public-private transportation management associations to plan curbs on traffic congestion. More Americans abandon public transport and embrace auto commuting.

1984
Tax reform bill continues employer-provided parking benefits as a non-taxable fringe benefit, limiting public transit subsidies to $15 a month per employee.

1988
California passes California Clean Air Act, with Regulation XV implementing Southern California's mandatory employer trip-reduction program.

1989
Earthquake hits San Francisco, prompting many to alter commuting habits; ridership on Bay Area Rapid Transit increases.

1990s

New Clean Air and highway legislation requiring regional planning alters the landscape for traffic-congestion mitigation.

1990
Census counts 108 million commuters. President George Bush signs Clean Air Act Amendments setting up inducements to large employers to reduce commuting trips in areas with extreme ozone and carbon monoxide problems.

Dec. 18, 1991
Bush signs Intermodal Surface Transportation Efficiency Act (ISTEA) diversifying government's role in transportation and giving increasing participation in decision-making to local citizens and authorities.

Oct. 24, 1992
Bush signs Comprehensive National Energy Policy Act including provisions to encourage alternatives to solo commuting by raising non-taxable employer subsidies for public transit.

Dec. 9, 1993
Clinton administration's transportation secretary, Federico F. Peña, announces detailed proposal for National Highway System.

Jan. 14, 1994
South Coast Air Quality Management District Board in Southern California votes to re-examine effectiveness of Regulation XV.

Jan. 17, 1994
Earthquake hits Los Angeles, collapsing six freeways and 20 streets, forcing many workers to alter commuting habits.

April 12, 1994
L.A.'s newly repaired Santa Monica Freeway, the nation's busiest highway, reopens 74 days ahead of schedule.

Bicycle Activists: From Militant to Mainstream

At a busy traffic circle in Washington, D.C., a beleaguered bicyclist curses at passing cars as he fights to maintain his place in a lane, and impatient drivers maneuver around him.

Such images of militance, often from long-haired, Spandex-clad bike couriers, represent the more radical wing of the movement against traffic congestion. In at least 12 U.S. cities, "auto-free" groups of cyclists have been organizing to pack roadways with enough riders to achieve "critical mass" and block cars, which they see as an unsustainable mode of transportation. The usual result: confrontations with angry motorists and arrests.[1]

Yet the campaign to promote the bicycle is also solidly mainstream. Of the 96 million Americans who own bikes, 27.5 percent ride them regularly. Bicyclists make up 1-3 percent of the commuter trips in most American cities, according to the Institute of Transportation Engineers. The institute says that trends over the past 20 years indicate that bicycling could soon make up 5-15 percent of all urban trips in America.[2]

Booster groups such as the Bicycle Federation of America highlight the potential: They say that half of all car trips in the United States are five miles or less, that in Tokyo 25 percent of all daily passenger trips are by bicycle and that in Denmark 33 percent of the people cycle to work.

Numerous American cities have factored bicycles into their transportation planning. Seattle, Wash., boasts 140 miles of trails and bike paths along main streets. San Diego last May hosted its second annual "Bike to Work Day" during its Clean Air Week, drawing 4,000 cyclists and participation from 55 local companies. Even freeway-dependent Los Angeles is set to build the West L.A. Veloway, an elevated 16-foot-wide bikeway stretching two miles from Westwood to West Los Angeles.

A 1990 Louis Harris poll for *Bicycling* magazine found that 20 percent of Americans would sometimes commute by bike if there were safe bike lanes and roads; 18 percent said they would bike in occasionally if their employers offered financial incentives.

The Federal Highway Administration last month released a study recommending that Americans double the number of trips made by bicycling or walking. It noted that traffic congestion and pollution would be reduced, injuries and deaths avoided and a healthy lifestyle promoted. "Government agencies, private organizations and citizen groups must work together to support one another's efforts to promote safe bicycling and walking," the report said.[3]

But the limits to bike commuting seem obvious. Bike-riding is physically demanding, often takes longer than driving (depending on traffic) and is tough during bad weather. Many would-be cyclists also fear riding alone, and face a lack of bike storage space at work, the risk of flat tires and the expense of bicycling equipment. The Transportation Department reports 1,000 fatalities a year among bicyclists, mostly due to cyclists who ride against traffic when visibility is limited.

"Obviously, cycling in good weather is more pleasant," says Andrew Clarke, project manager for the bicycle federation, "but you name a weather and I'll name you a city where people cycle through it. Madison, Wis., has 10 percent of [commuters] bicycling year-round; Tucson, Ariz. . . . has about 3 percent. In England, if you don't ride in the rain, you don't ride."

The advent of modern cycling clothing and mud guards, he points out, makes the ride more comfortable, though "some of it has become so trendy and faddish that people assume you need Spandex shorts and $100 helmets to ride.

"Even if you ride only one day a week," Clarke adds, "that would reduce the number of cars by a fifth, which would make any city manager happy."

Many potential barriers to cycling are being addressed by employers, particularly in California, where companies with more than 100 workers are required to reduce employee trips by car. Fleetwood Enterprises Inc., a maker of recreational vehicles and housing in Riverside, promotes a "Mud, Sweat and Gears" program that offers on-site bicycle repair facilities, backup rides for employees who cycle, forgiveness for cyclists' occasional tardiness and company-provided bicycle equipment. Six percent of the firm's workers participate.

Voluntary commuting by bicycle will do much to help reduce air pollution before the country is forced to resort to more mandatory employer sanctions and bans on such pollution sources as dry cleaning and barbecuing, Clarke notes.

"But to bring it closer to home, let's talk about health and fitness," he says. "As a way to exercise regularly, bicycling is better against all ailments for all ages, and much better than driving that quick mile to the health club so you can sit on some stationary bicycle. People can find a way of building cycling into their routine. I don't ride out of altruism. I ride because it's quicker, and I get crabby if I don't."

[1] See *The Washington Post,* March 14, 1994.

[2] Institute of Transportation Engineers, "The Traffic Safety Toolbox: A Primer on Traffic Safety," (1993), p. 204.

[3] Federal Highway Administration, "Final Report: The National Bicycling and Walking Study: Transportation Choices for a Changing America," April 1994, p. xvii.

Continued from p. 396

of open space itself," wrote Jacobs.[25]

Ironically, it was an event in Los Angeles in the 1960s that helped spawn the Great Society's massive program of federal spending on urban mass transit. The McCone Commission, convened to explore reasons behind the 1964 riots in the city's Watts area, wrote that "inadequate and costly public transportation currently existing throughout the Los Angeles area seriously restricts the residents of the disadvantaged areas such as south central Los Angeles. . . . handicaps them in seeking jobs, attending schools, shopping. . . . It has a major influence in creating a sense of isolation." [26]

This was also after a young scholar named Daniel Patrick Moynihan, now a Democratic senator from New York, authored an influential indictment of city-suburban traffic in a 1960 article in *The Reporter* magazine, "New Roads and Urban Chaos."

Fighting Air Pollution

By the 1970s, the environmental movement was added to the mix, with the creation of EPA and the first national auto emissions standards under the 1970 Clean Air Act. "There is a need to rethink the way this nation should go about developing a transportation system," a 1971 Transportation Department paper warned. "For the next three decades, all indicators point to more people, more affluence, more urbanization and a rapidly escalating intolerance for undesirable environmental side effects (of automobiles). In the face of this, the practices and policies of the past will almost certainly be inadequate for the future." [27]

In 1977, with passage of strong amendments to the Clean Air Act, emission standards were tightened effective with the 1980 model year, and new deadlines were imposed on cities for meeting national air-quality standards.

By the 1980s, traffic jams had become common in the suburbs, where so many jobs had migrated. Businesses worried about lost productivity among commuting employees who were arriving at work late and cranky. One result was the formation of transportation management associations, joint public-private efforts by employers, developers and local governments to reduce traffic congestion. Some 110 such associations have now been organized, 65 of them in California. They share information on how to manage transportation demand through alternative work schedules, new land-use planning, ridesharing and telecommuting.

"Draconian Methods"

Voluntary efforts by business, however, were not enough in the face of worsening air pollution. Governments in smoggy areas began cracking down on businesses with large numbers of solo drivers. The effort was sparked in 1988, when California passed a landmark Clean Air Act that required Southern California firms with more than 100 employees to reduce commuting through various recommended methods or face penalties. (*See "At Issue," p. 401.*) That approach was replicated in the nation's most-polluted metropolitan regions after Congress passed the 1990 Amendments to the Clean Air Act.

Under terms of the 1990 law, EPA identified 94 overly polluted "nonattainment" areas in California, Connecticut, Illinois, Indiana, Maryland, New Jersey, New York, Pennsylvania, Texas and Wisconsin. They must improve air quality by 15 percent by 1996 or lose federal funds and risk imposition of a federal plan.

Employer trip-reduction ordinances, which many states and localities have chosen as part of their pollution-reducing plans, remain controversial, and authorities in Illinois and Southern California are reconsidering them. Orski of Urban Mobility Corp. points out that they are costly and achieve only a 2-5 percent reduction in emissions, partly because of the relatively small number of people who work for companies with more than 100 employees at a work site, and because of the growing number of non-work-related driving trips. [28]

"Having to resort to draconian methods won't please everyone," says Darnes of FHWA. "But if we can't breathe the air, then drastic measures must take place. If transportation departments around the country would change their mindset to improve their infrastructures, we would be in a much better position to meet requirements of the Clean Air Act."

Ridesharing

Companies seeking to improve their employees' lives and comply with environmental regulations are actively promoting ridesharing, many of them appointing full-time staffers to tackle the selling job. At the Ritz-Carlton Huntington Hotel in Pasadena, Calif., the assignment went to Linda Brown, the human resources manager. "Before I can push someone to make a change, I need to walk in their shoes," she says. "So before I talked to employees about using the Metrolink [commuter train], I rode it. The same goes for taking the bus and biking to and from work." [29]

The most effective way of luring solo drivers out of their cars is cash incentives, rather than appealing to their public-spiritedness, according to a survey by California's South Coast Air Quality Management District.

But the first step for many companies is to simply launch a campaign and facilitate arrangements for van pools or carpools. At Minneapolis-based 3M Co., for example, maps are posted in employee common areas with numbered pins and sign-up sheets, colored to designate whether a person is willing to function as a driver, passenger or both. Employees make the contacts themselves, though computer matching is available by request.

One of the first companies to institute a vanpool program (back in 1972), 3M also offers to provide an employee unit with a 12-passenger van, operated by a 3M employee. Passengers pay a monthly fare that permits the operation to break even, and the van gets preferential parking. "Most riders are particularly taken by the social integrity of their pooling unit, which tends to stay together for many years and maintain its social bonds outside the workplace," a 3M official says. [30]

Many companies have gone to great lengths to overcome employee resistance to ridesharing, including offering emergency backup personal transportation. Among many employees, notes a Transportation Department study, there is "fear that they won't have a vehicle in an emergency or they can't leave at their usual time. Such fears have plagued transportation programs for years." Guaranteed Ride Home programs "counteract this often irrational fear with the reassurance of a reliable backup ride, at minimal or no cost, to get them to their destination quickly." [31]

In Northern Virginia, commuters to Washington often form ad hoc carpools on a day-to-day basis. Pedestrians arrive at shopping centers and other gathering points and call out their destinations to waiting drivers, who need extra passengers in order to qualify for carpool lanes. Despite dealing with total strangers, users report that they're comfortable with the arrangement because small talk is optional, and the groups are made up of professionals. "I guess it's an at-your-own-risk type thing," said John Wederman, a commuter from Burke. "But people are in dresses, suits and ties or military uniforms." [32]

The potential of ridesharing, however, is probably limited to those employees who can come and go at about the same time every day. In Southern California, the Commuter Transportation Services's 1993 "State of the Commute" survey showed that the ideal candidates for ridesharing are "drive-alone commuters who travel long distances, are dissatisfied with their commutes, have HOV lane access and view ridesharing as a means to save money." Most commuters, however, don't fit that description, it noted. Some 62 percent said they need a vehicle during the day for personal or business reasons.

Opening of HOV Lanes

Since the nation's first buses-only lanes opened on Northern Virginia's Shirley Highway in 1969, traffic planners have placed great hopes in HOV lanes (for high-occupancy vehicles) from which solo drivers are excluded. As of 1990, some 40 HOV lanes covered 332 miles in 20 North American cities, among them Houston, Minneapolis and Seattle, according to the Transportation Department. (In April, New York City announced its first carpool lanes ever, over the Queensboro Bridge.)

The California survey shows that 30 percent of commuters who travel near HOV lanes use them. Carpoolers with the requisite two, three or four passengers can often breeze down a stretch in five or 10 minutes while solo drivers in the regular lanes creep along for a half-hour or more. Violators (including occasional tricksters who post mannequins in the backseat) are given traffic tickets, and some jurisdictions have programs that encourage average drivers to phone in the license numbers of HOV-lane cheaters.

But HOV lanes do provoke resentment from ineligible drivers, and for policy-makers they can be political dynamite. In Los Angeles in the mid-'70s, Republican Gov. Ronald Reagan launched an effort to comply with the federal Clean Air Act that included introduction of carpool lanes (called "diamond lanes") on the busy Santa Monica Freeway. The problem was, the freeway wasn't widened; the engineers took over an all-purpose lane and gave it to carpoolers. Facing $271 fines for cheating, solo commuters who were at a standstill vented their anger on Adriana Gianturco, then director of California's Transportation Department. She received hate mail and eventually left her job. (She was interviewed following this year's earthquake, gleefully noting that new HOV lanes are now back on L.A.'s agenda.) [33]

Resisters to carpool lanes have had success elsewhere. In Northern Virginia, a carpool lane requiring a minimum of four passengers was relaxed to three passengers after political pressure. And in fall 1992, then-Gov. L. Douglas Wilder, D-Va., canceled new HOV lanes on the Dulles Toll Road paralleling the road to Dulles Airport after gridlocked commuters squawked upon seeing the lanes wastefully underutilized.

Rep. Frank R. Wolf, R-Va., led the effort to cancel the carpool lanes, arguing in a statement that while he was a strong proponent of ridesharing, "It is unfair to current toll road commuters — who have put up with more than two years of construction — to bar them from utilizing this additional capacity, which they are paying for with their user fees." [34]

The Washington Post blamed the debacle on a Virginia Transportation Department that had failed to make the public aware of carpool lanes. A 1990 federal Transportation Department report observed that HOV lanes often require an individual champion to be successful. [35]

Congestion Pricing

The traffic remedy regarded as most effective by many transportation analysts is the one method that is not being implemented. Congestion pricing, or charging drivers tolls for entering a crowded area during peak hours, is viewed by Brookings' Downs as the one method that would cut down on the number of cars without merely pushing those cars elsewhere to create new gridlock.

The method has been tested in Hong Kong, Singapore and several

Continued on p. 402

At Issue:

Should businesses be required to reduce solo commuting by their employees?

yes

CLEAN AIR COUNCIL

Environmental group in Philadelphia, Pa.
FROM *FACT SHEET* (UNDATED)

by now, many people have heard of the employer trip-reduction program required by the Clean Air Act Amendments of 1990 for geographical areas that have severe air-pollution problems for ground-level ozone (smog). Employers with more than 100 people at one worksite are responsible for implementing a worksite program that would increase the average passenger occupancy in cars driven by employees to and from work.

Employers have a wide range of options, which should involve the combined action of the county, state and the private sectors. These include ridesharing (carpools, vanpools and the provision of high-occupancy-vehicle lanes); transit (including park-and-ride lots); bicycling and walking facilities; alternative work schedules (i.e. every other Friday off, telecommuting); and reform of employer-paid parking benefits to encourage transit use.

A successful employer trip-reduction program might include incentives to rideshare or take transit, and/or disincentives to commuters who drive alone. Employers can provide preferential parking for vanpool and carpool vehicles, or direct financial incentives. For example, carpoolers could go through an express line in the company cafeteria.

A successful program will be difficult as long as there are so many strong incentives to drive alone. At least 90 percent of U.S. commuters who drive alone pay nothing for parking. Employer-paid parking actually encourages solo driving to work. Studies have shown that on average employer-paid parking shifts 27 percent of all commuters into solo driving from other modes.

Employer-paid parking obviously represents a cost to the employer. Analysts in Sacramento, Calif., estimated that an average company there spends $10,000-$15,000 for the construction and maintenance of a parking space for over 20 years, which is more than the cost of supplying employees with free transit passes.

One way to level the playing field would be to link the elimination of employee parking to a travel allowance for all workers. Employers could pay each worker a travel allowance of, for example, $75 per month and charge $75 per month for parking that formerly was free. According to a statistical model of 5,000 commuters and employers, offering the option of a cash travel allowance to employees who park in downtown Los Angeles could reduce single occupant driving by 20 percent and eliminate 9,000 vehicle commute trips a day. Other benefits of parking reform: It is cheap, simple to implement and will benefit employees by giving them a choice.

no

HIGHWAY USERS FEDERATION FOR SAFETY AND MOBILITY

***STATEMENT,* March 1994**

employee trip-reduction (ETR) regulations are costly, inflexible and they don't work. The regulations could cost businesses as much as $1,000 per employer per year. That doesn't count fines. ETR fines in California are $50,000 per day. Texas plans to impose fines up to $25,000 per day.

There are much cheaper and more effective ways to improve air quality. The General Accounting Office says ETR would produce a 0.7 percent to 1.0 percent gain in air quality. Removing old and poorly maintained polluting vehicles from the road would result in a 4.4 percent improvement. It's also cheaper. ETR in California got 54,000 vehicles off the road at $3,000 each. Clunker removal costs about $750 each.

There are other common-sense solutions. We could improve traffic system signals, widen roads *without* major construction, use remote sensing to get polluting vehicles off the road and respond to accidents faster.

The plain fact is that for most people today, the trip to work is not a simple ride from home to office. Daily life for working people in the '90s is complicated, and there never seems to be enough time. Working parents, especially working mothers, must juggle a host of family responsibilities on the way to and from work.

There are children to drop off and pick up from day care or school. Appointments with doctors or school officials have to be kept. Working people today are combining these trips along with other essential needs such as grocery shopping, stopping off at the dry cleaners and other destinations all just as important as getting to the office.

According to surveys conducted at suburban work sites, more than 70 percent of suburban workers make intermediate stops on a regular basis on their way to or from work, and nearly 80 percent run errands during the midday break. Transit and ridesharing cannot meet the needs of most people today. . . . Mass transit is useless in suburban and rural areas that will be forced to impose these regulations. These areas have either limited systems or no system at all. . . .

In the United States, we need both a good transportation system and a clean environment. Considering the progress we have made over the last 10 years with the development of cleaner cars, cleaner fuels and continued reduction of carbon monoxide emissions, and the experience we have gained, we do not need to sacrifice transportation for clean air. We can have both. This can be achieved by avoiding overly rigid interpretations of federal legislation and encouraging cooperation between transportation and the environment. A combination of flexible transportation and non-transportation solutions will insure that we have clean air for our children and our children's children.

Measuring Roadway Congestion

Los Angeles led the list of America's 11 most-congested cities in 1990, based on the relative amount of traffic on freeways and principal streets.

1. Los Angeles, Calif.
2. Washington, D.C.
3. San Francisco-Oakland, Calif.
4. Miami, Fla.
5. Chicago, Ill.
6. San Diego, Calif.
7. Seattle-Everett, Wash.
8. San Bernardino-Riverside, Calif.
9. New York, N.Y.
10. Houston, Texas
    New Orleans, La. (tied)

Commuter Transportation Services

Source: Texas Transportation Institute, Texas A&M University; U.S. Department of Transportation, March 1993

Continued from p. 400

cities in Norway, but no U.S. metropolitan area has implemented a complete system, even though some say the United States could use it to raise as much as $57 billion annually. Making it even more promising are the new technologies that would permit tolls to be collected electronically by equipment that remotely reads tags in each car and deducts the fare from a prepaid account.

But even proponents acknowledge the uphill battle. "By charging money for something that was formerly free — travel on highways during peak periods — the government is depriving citizens of income they could otherwise spend themselves," Downs writes. "This antagonizes people who believe that the government in our society is already too big and obtrusive." [36]

Orski recalls that in the 1970s, the Urban Mass Transit Administration offered a federal grant for a pilot project in congestion pricing, but there were no takers. (Under the current Intelligent Vehicle Highway Program, a pilot program is being developed in the San Francisco Bay area.)

Winston of Brookings says the limits of other traffic-mitigation approaches — such as smart highways, commuter rail and telecommuting — force the conclusion that the only way to cut traffic is to make drivers pay. "One reason we don't have it is the cultural love of the freedom to drive," he says. "The other is the notion that congestion pricing will hurt poor people. Economists have talked of this for decades, but the political types say people simply won't have it.

"In order to get re-elected, politicians must give people what they want. At the federal level, a pol can trade things off, and there's room for shirking on promises. But as you move down the totem poll, the closer the policy supplier is to the people, the less he can do. Congestion policy is really a local issue, and it's the one issue that can destroy someone politically." ■

CURRENT SITUATION

Focus on Incentives

The way to get more Americans to seek alternatives to driving is to go after incentives, such as subsidized parking, says Capon of the National Association of Railway Passengers. "That begins to get to the heart of the problem."

The Clinton administration is readying legislation to give workers the option of receiving in cash the free-market value of the employer-paid parking benefits given to so many solo commuters. The idea is that people who choose public transit or other alternatives should be on equal footing. The amount of parking subsidy employers can offer tax-free is currently capped at $155 a month under the 1992 Comprehensive National Energy Policy Act, which also raised the amount employers can offer to subsidize public transit from $21 to up to $60 a month.

The Clinton proposal would mimic a plan in use in California since 1992 that allows employers with more than 50 employees in areas with air-pollution problems to deduct the cost of transportation benefits from their corporate income tax regardless of whether employees opt for free parking or cash, which would be counted as part of the employee's taxable income. [37] A similar proposal is expected to be introduced by Sen. Arlen Specter, R-Pa. "The existence of free or subsidized parking is considered the single factor in determining the mode chosen by an individual commuter," Specter says. "The bill does not propose a mandate or require an employee to choose mass transit as transportation to work, but it attempts to level the playing field to allow an employee the choice to drive or use mass transit."

Studies have shown that subsidized parking definitely increases solo commuting. Lowe at Worldwatch notes that in 1975, when Canada began charging federal employees 70 percent of the local commercial parking rate, the number driving to work alone fell 21 percent, and use of public transit rose 16 percent. [38]

Marsha Williams, director of member services for the National Parking Association, says her group opposes the idea as "too burdensome on the employer, and tough to enforce. The employee who takes the cash might continue to drive and simply park elsewhere," she says, adding that in California, employees are asked to sign a statement saying that if they accept the money, they won't park near the office.

Furthermore, the effectiveness may be limited, she points out, because the policy would apply only to employers who contract space from third-party-owned parking facilities rather than using company-owned space, which means only 30-40 percent of cases.

New Highway System

Last December, in a ceremony at historic Union Station in Washington, D.C., Transportation Secretary Peña and FHWA Administrator Rodney Slater unveiled the Clinton administration's plan for the long-awaited National Highway System (NHS). The new system, which includes both existing and planned routes, is intended as a major boost to the nation's economy.

"The migration of population, business and manufacturing from Northeast urban areas to Southern and Western regions has placed new demands on the highway transportation system that the Interstate System alone was not designed to meet," says a TRIP paper on the potential benefits of the NHS. [39]

The new system would carry 40 percent of all U.S. traffic and 75 percent of the heavy truck traffic on 159,000 miles of roadway that includes much of the 45,000-mile Interstate Highway System. It would lead to major population centers, ports, airports, borders and public-transportation facilities while meeting the Defense Department's security needs. Backers also say the system will reduce traffic congestion costs by $40 billion a year.

The proposal, which under 1991 legislation must receive Congress' approval by September 1995 or lose its funding, has wide support as a concept, but the details have divided environmentalists and highway enthusiasts. "The National Highway System design happened outside the planning process" put in place under ISTEA, says Dittmar. "It's like the planners have said, 'Let's define the roads, then do engineering estimates on the costs, then we'll get a gas tax or take clean-air money so that engineers won't have to ask for a 30-year plan from elected officials.' "

Instead, he says, the NHS planning should be integrated with the work of the Metropolitan Planning Organizations that bring in community, alternative transport and environmental considerations.

"We're talking about 160,000 miles of important roadways that have to remain intact," says Vest of the Highway Users Federation. "Our concern is that some environmental groups want to ban all new highway construction, and they want local planners to delete some of the routes." He adds that money for non-highway transport programs such as railways and bicycle paths is available from other funding sources within ISTEA. "There is a disconnect in the environmental community about the gains we've made in recent years in clean fuel and lowered tailpipe emissions from cars and trucks," he adds. ■

OUTLOOK

Multiple Remedies

"We need to be more innovative," said Los Angeles Mayor Richard Riordan after the January earthquake, as local officials scrambled to set up new carpool lanes and help disoriented commuters with travel alternatives. "Are people willing to take the bitter medicine for a good, long-term goal? I think they are." [40]

"The dramatic need for an alternative to the automobile was clearly demonstrated by this disaster," Los Angeles County mass transit chief Franklin E. White told a U.S. Senate field hearing on April 4.

Following the 1989 earthquake in San Francisco, ridership on Bay Area Rapid Transit trains skyrocketed from 210,000 per day to 357,000, with the improvement now holding at 255,000 daily, says BART spokeswoman Vicki Mills. But after the Los Angeles quake, only 5 percent of the city's commuters had switched to ridesharing, mostly carpools, and only a fourth of those planned to stick with their new arrangements after highways were repaired.

The vast majority of Angelenos, it appears, are wedded to the car-based lifestyle, even when it means sitting dead still on a freeway and staring at a "Maintain your speed" sign. The California Transportation Department estimates that the state's average speed during rush hour (35 mph) will plummet to only 17 mph by the year 2000.

Attitudes toward the car seem to be affected by culture. In Los Angeles, 85 percent of whites and Asians drive alone to work, compared with 72 percent of African Americans and 68 percent of Hispanics, notes Commuter Transportation Services. The more money commuters earn, the more likely they are to drive alone to work.

Many Americans appear to view mass transit as beneath their status. Bus riding is "the ultimate test of democracy," writes humorist Garrison Keillor, describing the "surly drivers; exhaust odors; dingy, ripped seats with slimy stuff spilled on them and sickening obscenities scrawled in plain view; filthy windows and paper-littered aisles; standing shoulder-to-shoulder with silent, embittered persons and hostile teenagers lugging big, ear-busting radios and tape decks." [41]

Rail travel has a slightly "better cachet in people's minds," notes the Sierra Club's Holtzclaw, and not just in the United States. He recalls hearing of a doctor in Frankfurt, Germany, who hated the bus but enjoyed a new commuter train, claiming it was faster. In fact, the train and bus had identical schedules.

America's much-vaunted freedom to drive, says APTA's Bishop, "is being overcome by the congestion factor, and the illusion of freedom has dissipated."

But congestion, notes Orski, is also "an emblem of economic activity. We don't want deserted cities. It is the forces of land use that are driving employment outward. In the short-term, congestion will get marginally worse, but we won't be adding to highway capacity as rapidly as the population will grow."

Many agree that sudden, radical solutions are not in the cards. "We've subsidized auto use for so long," says Holtzclaw, "that to end it would be painful. We have to phase in solutions so people can make changes in their own lives."

"Congestion is a fact of life in the near term," says Dittmar. "The question is, 'Can we afford to live with congestion, and can we afford to solve it?' The mistake is making it 'either/or.' We need flexibility as we put things like ridesharing options and telecommunications into the mix and make people aware of them. Not everyone will go back to live downtown, nor should we design the world for the nuclear suburban family of the 1950s."

The people pursuing the multiplicity of remedies for the curse of traffic congestion are, in Downs' words, "like the woodsman who must cut down a huge tree with only a small axe. He cannot fell the tree or even make much of a cut in it with one swing. But he can eventually cut it down, with a hundred or more small cuts. A multifaceted approach offers the only hope of reducing traffic congestion significantly." [42] ■

Notes

[1] Anthony Downs, *Stuck in Traffic: Coping with Peak-Hour Traffic Congestion* (1992), p. 10.

[2] Cited in Neil Pierce, *Citistates: How Urban America Can Prosper in a Competitive World* (1993), p. 28.

[3] The study by Sandra Rosenbloom of the University of Arizona was summarized in *Innovation Briefs,* newsletter of Urban Mobility Corp., February 1994.

[4] Downs, *op. cit.,* p. 28.

[5] Wolfgang Zuckermann, *End of the Road: The World Car Crisis and How We Can Solve It* (1991), p. 57.

[6] K.T. Berger, *Where the Road and the Sky Collide: American Through the Eyes of Its Drivers* (1993), p. 13.

[7] Marcia D. Lowe, "Alternatives to the Automobile: Transport for Livable Cities," *Worldwatch Paper No. 98,* October 1990.

[8] *Transportation and Tax Policy,* newsletter of the Campaign for New Transportation Priorities, No. 2 (undated). For background, see "Electric Cars," *The CQ Researcher,* July 9, 1993, pp.577-600.

[9] *The Wall Street Journal,* March 15, 1994.

[10] John Pucher and Ira Hirschman, "Path to Balanced Transportation," International Association of Public Transport, October 1993, p. 1.

[11] Daniel Roos, "Getting Smart About 'Intelligent' Vehicles and Highways," *Headline News, Science Views II,* National Research Council, 1993.

[12] *The Washington Post,* March 14, 1994.

[13] *The Economist,* Aug. 7, 1993, p. 71.

[14] Printed in *The Washington Post,* June 7, 1991.

[15] Jane Jacobs, *The Death and Life of Great American Cities* (1961), p. 229.

[16] Zuckermann, *op. cit.,* p. 231. For background, see "Transportation: America's 'Quiet Crisis,' " *Editorial Research Reports,* Aug. 11, 1989, pp. 445-460, and "Gridlock in Suburbia," *Editorial Research Reports,* June 3, 1988, pp. 285-300.

[17] Downs, *op. cit.,* p. 4.

[18] "Community-Based Planning Under ISTEA: A Handbook for Citizens and Agencies," Bicycle Federation of America, March 1993, p. 4.

[19] "ISTEA: Year Three," Surface Transportation Policy Project, January 1994, p. 1.

[20] "Traffic Congestion: Activities to Reduce Travel Demand and Air Pollution Are Not Widely Implemented," General Accounting Office, November 1992, p. 8-9.

[21] Lewis Mumford, *The City in History* (1961), p. 218.

[22] Clay McShane, *Down the Asphalt Path: The Automobile and the American City* (1994), as reviewed in *The New York Times,* April 10, 1994.

[23] David Rizzo, *Freeway Alternates* (1990), p. ii.

[24] Berger, *op. cit.,* p. 89.

[25] Jacobs, *op. cit.,* p. 91.

[26] Christopher H. Lovelock, Gordon Lewin, George S. Day and John E.G. Bateson, *Marketing Mass Transit: A Strategic Approach* (1987), p. 6.

[27] Congressional Quarterly, *Congress and the Nation, 1969-1972,* p. 147.

[28] C. Kenneth Orski, "Employee Trip Reduction Programs: An Evaluation," *Transportation Quarterly,* July 1993, p. 327.

[29] *En Route,* newsletter of the South Coast Air Quality Management District, summer/fall 1993.

[30] J.Richard Kuzmyak, "Employers Manage Transportation," *Resource Guide Case Study,* Surface Transportation Policy Project, 1992.

[31] U.S. Transportation Department, "Guaranteed Ride Home: Taking the Worry Out of Ridesharing," November 1990.

[32] Quoted in the *Arlington Journal,* April 4, 1994.

[33] *Los Angeles Times,* Feb. 22, 1994.

[34] Statement released Aug. 3, 1992.

[35] "HOV Project Case Studies," Department of Transportation, December 1990, p. 151.

[36] Downs, *op. cit.,* p. 51.

[37] *Analysis in Transportation Demand Management,* Association for Commuter Transportation, January 1994.

[38] Lowe, *op. cit.,* p. 35.

[39] "The National Highway System and Its Benefits," *The Road Information Program* (undated).

[40] *Los Angeles Times* (Washington edition), March 11, 1994.

[41] Writing in *The New York Times* in 1985, quoted in Lovelock et al, *op. cit.,* p. 13.

[42] Downs, *op. cit.,* p. 34.

Bibliography

Selected Sources Used

Books

Berger, K.T., *Where the Road and the Sky Collide: America Through the Eyes of Its Drivers,* Henry Holt and Co., 1993.
Writing as K.T. Berger, two brothers traveled the country to gauge the role of the auto in American culture. They argue that "cars have reached a critical mass, their sheer numbers alone placing them in peril. Freedom of choice may be enhanced by being able to drive to 25 different restaurants, but we're seldom hungry after all that time fighting our way across town."

Cervero, Robert,*Suburban Gridlock*, Rutgers, the State University of New Jersey, 1986.
A scholar at the Institute of Transportation Studies at the University of California-Berkeley outlines the migration of jobs from cities to the American suburbs and the implication for traffic-mitigation policy. He discusses the role of transportation management associations and the need for new land-use planning.

Downs, Anthony, *Stuck in Traffic: Coping with Peak-Hour Traffic Congestion,* Brookings Institution, 1992.
Downs, an economist and urban-studies specialist, explores the causes and effects of traffic congestion, arguing that the best solution is the politically unpopular idea of making people pay extra to drive in congested areas during peak hours.

Lovelock, Christopher H., Gordon Lewin, George S. Day and John E.G. Bateson, *Marketing Mass Transit: A Strategic Approach,* Praeger Publishers, 1987.
A team of management and transportation experts explores why "mass transit in the United States is seen by many as desirable only for 'other' people." They include examples of the ways various cities have attempted to market public transit.

Zuckermann, Wolfgang,*End of the Road*, Lutterworth Press, 1991
A German social scientist has written an obituary for the automobile-dependent society, proposing an array of changes such as new land-use planning and increased use of public transit.

Reports and Studies

Institute of Transportation Engineers, *The Traffic Safety Toolbox: A Primer on Traffic Safety,* 1993.
This compendium by a Washington-based international professional society analyzes the major issues around traffic safety in different modes of transport from the perspective of a traffic engineer.

Pisarski, Alan E., *Travel Behavior Issues in the 90s,* Federal Highway Administration, July 1992.
A noted transportation expert analyzes data from the 1990 Nationwide Personal Transportation Survey, along with earlier findings, to paint a portrait of Americans' views and habits on commuting.

Transportation Department, *Estimates of Urban Roadway Congestion — 1990,* March 1993.
This report by the Texas Transportation Institute at Texas A&M University ranks U.S. cities according to traffic congestion, using various methods of measurement.

Federal Highway Administration, *Final Report: The National Bicycling and Walking Study: Transportation Choices for a Changing America,* April 1994.
A three-year study required under 1991 federal highway legislation makes recommendations for doubling the frequency of travel on foot and by bycicle through promotional efforts, new safety facilities and new land-use planning.

Transportation Department, *Guaranteed Ride Home: Taking the Worry Out of Ridesharing,* November 1990.
Citing examples of company and government ridesharing programs around the country, this handbook explains how to set up a workplace car- and vanpooling program that allays employee concerns about getting stuck without a ride in an emergency.

Transportation Department, *HOV Project Case Studies: History and Institutional Arrangements,* December 1990.
This report by the Texas Transportation Institute explores the history and current use of HOV (high-occupancy vehicle) lanes in Houston, Minneapolis-St. Paul, Orange County, Calif., Pittsburgh, Seattle and Northern Virginia.

Transportation Department, *Intelligent Vehicle Highway Systems Projects,* February 1993.
This is a compilation of high-technology "smart car" and "smart highway" projects currently being funded and researched under the federal government's Intelligence Vehicle Highway Systems (IVHS) program.

Transportation Department, *Transportation Implications of Telecommuting,* April 1993.
A discussion of the history, economic impact and outlook for the increasingly common practice of people using computers and telephone modems to avoid commuting by working at home or at satellite offices closer to home.

The Next Step

Additional information from UMI's Newspaper & Periodical Abstracts database

Congestion Pricing

McMullen, B. Starr, "Congestion pricing and demand management: A discussion of the issues," ***Policy Studies Journal,*** **summer 1993, pp. 285-295.**

The political, technological and economic issues involved in the formulation of congestion pricing policy are examined. Increased urban congestion combined with increasingly scarce resources is making policy-makers consider congestion pricing as an alternative to expanding highway capacity.

"The public's capital — Congestion pricing: Going somewhere slowly," ***Governing,*** **October 1993, pp. 49-52.**

Congestion pricing — policies that persuade people to drive less or to use alternative modes of transportation — would impose tolls that rise during peak commuting hours. Congestion pricing strategies are discussed.

Gate Communities

Mount, Charles, "Court backs Barrington Hills on road closure," ***Chicago Tribune,*** **Jan. 4, 1994, p. 2NW1.**

In a precedent-setting ruling that could allow suburbs to close more roads, the Illinois Appellate Court has upheld Barrington Hills' right to close Spring Creek Road at its border with Algonquin for safety, traffic congestion and maintenance expenses.

Grasmere, Robert, "Maplewood's wall of misunderstanding," ***The Wall Street Journal,*** **Dec. 22, 1993, p. A10.**

Robert Grasmere, the mayor of Maplewood, N.J., for 23 years, defends his city's decision to build five gates in an area to alleviate traffic congestion. The matter got national attention once the mayor of Newark accused Maplewood of building a wall to keep out predominantly black Newark.

The IVHS Plan

Ben-Akiva, Moshe and David Bernstein, et. al., "The Case for Smart Highways," ***Technology Review*****, July 1992, pp. 38-47.**

Intelligent vehicle/highway systems (IVHS) are a collection of technologies that would manage the flow of traffic in cities and on freeways to increase capacity, enhance safety and ease congestion. The IVHS concept is discussed.

Costantino, James, "The IVHS Strategic Plan for the United States," ***Transportation Quarterly,*** **October 1992, pp. 481-490.**

The problem of congestion on U.S. highways is discussed, and the intelligent vehicle/highway systems (IVHS), a potential solution to the problem, is detailed.

Keenan, Linda, "Technology aids traffic problems," ***Nation's Cities Weekly,*** **March 8, 1993, p. 3.**

The 1991 federal transportation legislation — the Intermodal Surface Transportation Efficiency Act — proposes to attack such problems as traffic congestion and air pollution partly through the implementation of intelligent vehicle/highway systems (IVHS). IVHS technologies are discussed.

International Traffic

"Idiocy in action," ***Bicycling,*** **March 1994, p. 18.**

The mayor of Guangzhou, China, in an effort to combat the daily traffic jams, has instituted a plan that bans bikes from the city's center while other vehicles are free to continue clogging the roads.

Sakamaki, Sachiko, "Road to nowhere," ***Far Eastern Economic Review,*** **Nov. 4, 1993, pp. 68-70.**

Tokyo's 225-km highway system is discussed. The highways, which offer a hard lesson in planning, turn into parking lots frequently each day.

Tsuruoka, Doug, "On the move," ***Far Eastern Economic Review,*** **Dec. 9, 1993, p. 72.**

Malaysia is considering relocating some of the capital's 250,000 government employees to a new city due to traffic congestion. The so-called twin city would be located 40-km south of Kuala Lumpur.

Tsuruoka, Doug, "Still on track," ***Far Eastern Economic Review,*** **Nov. 25, 1993, p. 54.**

Plans for an elevated light railway in Malaysia are discussed. Traffic in Kuala Lumpur, Malaysia, has become so congested that commuters are comparing the problem to the congestion in Bangkok.

Public Transportation

Baca, Stacey, "Santa Fe users due input on choices," ***Denver Post,*** **Nov. 17, 1993, p. B4.**

A Denver Regional Transportation District study indicates that motorists who are tired of driving along the much-used South Santa Fe corridor would prefer to hop on a light-rail train or take the bus as congestion on the road continues to grow. The district is considering options to deal with the traffic on the road.

Donegan, Lawrence, "Market forces drive rival buses into dead end," ***Guardian*****, July 10, 1993, p. 6.**

Lawrence Donegan describes how the United Kingdom Transport Department's deregulation of the public transport system in Darlington has led to fierce competition between the city's three bus companies and traffic jams on the once-quiet streets. An estimated 240 buses drive along the main street every hour.

George, Mary, "RTD pushed to ease jams in Boulder," *Denver Post,* Sept. 20, 1993, p. B1.

Convinced that buses are one antidote to their growing traffic problem, Boulder, Colo., officials are launching a $2.5 million push to increase supply and demand for Regional Transportation District (RTD) use. The initiative includes mall shuttles and issuing all-purpose passes to high school students and subdivision residents.

Research and Studies

Tipton, Virgil, "Congestion: Main cause of drivers' headaches," *St. Louis Post-Dispatch*, Nov. 15, 1993, p. A1.

A new study released by a national research group, The Road Information Program, found that Illinois' urban roads are the eighth most congested in the country, which puts Illinois ahead of New York state. Missouri's roads are the 11th most congested, ranking just behind New York.

Washburn, Gary, "Report: Driving fees could cut congestion," *Chicago Tribune,* Sept. 21, 1993, p. 2.

A new study on the "collision" between autos and American cities choked by congestion and pollution recommends drastic action that would force motorists who insist on driving to pay dearly for the privilege. The document calls for imposition of hefty fees to use expressways and enter central business districts during the busiest periods of the day and it proposes heavy increases in the federal gasoline tax.

Solutions

Atash, Farhad, "Mitigating traffic congestion in suburbs: An evaluation of land-use strategies," *Transportation Quarterly,* October 1993, pp. 507-524.

Traffic congestion is a major problem for many suburban communities and a source of frustration for all drivers. Strategies for mitigating suburban congestion are discussed.

Keebler, Jack, "Outsmarting traffic jams," *Automotive News,* April 12, 1993, p. 3.

The government has high hopes for the performance of the TravTek intelligent vehicle-highway system that was developed by GM. TravTek would be used as an alternative to highway construction because it is less expensive to design and implement than road expansions or rebuilds.

Krawczyk, Thomas, "Outsmarting traffic jams," *Technology Review,* February 1994, p. 14.

The Federal Highway Administration (FHWA) is one of the sponsors of a $13 million test that will equip some 3,000 cars with computers, CD-ROM drives, display screens and data-transmission equipment. This and a Chicago-area experiment called the Advanced Driver and Vehicle Advisory Navigation Concept are discussed with regard to finding solutions to the projected quadrupling of traffic problems by 2020.

Moore, Teresa, "First aid for commute congestion," *San Francisco Chronicle,* Feb. 1, 1994, p. A13.

On Jan. 31, 1994, the San Francisco Metropolitan Transportation Commission began its Freeway Service Patrol with shining white tow trucks and solar-powered cellular call boxes in the city's crusade against traffic congestion.

Pack, William, "Highway of the future — it's in Houston now," *Houston Post,* Feb. 21, 1994, p. A1.

Houston freeways in the upcoming years will utilize a variety of high tech devices — road sensors, closed-circuit TV cameras, remote-controlled road signs — to track commuters and divert traffic around congestion. Officials have instituted a $300 million plan for the Houston highway of the future.

Toll Roads

Fehr, Stephen C., "Panel opts not to raise fees on Dulles Toll Road," *The Washington Post,* Dec. 3, 1993, p. B3.

A panel formed to find ways to lessen traffic congestion on the Dulles Toll Road recommended building a carpool lane in each direction on the highway, but not raising tolls to pay for the lanes.

Pattison, Scott, "Toll tunnels," *Consumers' Research Magazine*, October 1993, p. 38.

Toll tunnels are being promoted as a solution to traffic problems in cities. The tunnels, which would provide relief from traffic congestion for those willing to pay the tolls, are discussed.

Riley, Kristyn, "Selling Automation to Toll Collectors," *New England Business,* April 1992, pp. 44-45.

AT/Comm Inc.'s solution to toll plaza traffic jams, Electronic Toll Collection, is discussed. A credit-card sized receiver mounted on the dashboard transmits a signal to a toll booth transmitter, allowing cars to pass through a toll booth on credit.

Transportation Problems

Daley, Beth, "Traffic runs afoul at bridge," *Boston Globe,* March 6, 1994, pp. SW1.

Despite an effort to restrict bridge openings, frustrated Route 3A commuters are looking to the Coast Guard to solve continuing traffic-congestion problems caused by rush-hour raisings of the Fore River drawbridge linking Weymouth and Quincy, Mass.

Zamichow, Nora, "Worst may come for motorists on Monday," *Los Angeles Times,* Jan. 22, 1994, p. B1.

Congestion on Los Angeles' earthquake-damaged freeways is expected to get worse on Jan. 24, 1994, as many people return to work. The city's plans to deal with the traffic are discussed.

Back Issues

Great Research on Current Issues Starts Right Here...Recent topics covered by The CQ Researcher are listed below. Before May 1991, reports were published under the name of Editorial Research Reports.

OCTOBER 1992
Depression
U.S. Auto Industry
Youth Apprenticeships
Hispanic Americans

NOVEMBER 1992
Physical Fitness
Privatization
Paying for College
U.S. Policy in Asia

DECEMBER 1992
Crackdown on Smoking
The New CIA
Eating Disorders
Women and AIDS

JANUARY 1993
Hate Crimes
Child Sexual Abuse
Nuclear Fusion
U.S. Trade Policy

FEBRUARY 1993
Community Policing
Europe's New Right
School Censorship
Violence Against Women

Back issues are available for $4.00 (subscribers) or $7.00 (non-subscribers). Quantity discounts apply to orders over ten. To order, call Congressional Quarterly Customer Service at (202) 887-8621.

Binders are available for $16.00. To order call 1-800-638-1710. Please refer to stock number 648.

MARCH 1993
Gay Rights
Aid to Russia
War on Drugs
TV Violence

APRIL 1993
Head Start
High-Speed Rail
Children's Legal Rights
Muslims in America

MAY 1993
Cults in America
Preventing Teen Pregnancy
Software Piracy
National Parks

JUNE 1993
Food Safety
Prostitution
Childhood Immunizations
National Service

JULY 1993
Electric Cars
Population Growth
Downward Mobility
Intelligence Testing

AUGUST 1993
Mental Illness
Bilingual Education
Foreign Policy Burden
School Funding

SEPTEMBER 1993
Suburban Crime
Public Housing
Supreme Court Preview
Immigration Reform

OCTOBER 1993
Airline Safety
Disaster Response
Science in the Courtroom
The Glass Ceiling

NOVEMBER 1993
Paying for Retirement
Charitable Giving
Privacy in the Workplace
Adoption

DECEMBER 1993
U.S. Vietnam-Relations
Learning Disabilities
Child Care
Space Program's Future

JANUARY 1994
Racial Tensions in Schools
South Africa's Future
Worker Retraining
Regulating Pesticides

FEBRUARY 1994
Prison Overcrowding
Water Quality
Religion in Schools
Juvenile Justice

MARCH 1994
Underground Economy
Education Standards
Gambling Boom
Private Management of Public Schools

APRIL 1994
Reproductive Ethics
U.S.-China Trade
Soccer in America
Talk Show Democracy

Future Topics

- ***Women's Health Issues***
- ***Mutual Funds***
- ***Political Scandals***

THE CQ Researcher

PUBLISHED BY CONGRESSIONAL QUARTERLY INC.

Women's Health Issues

Will women benefit from increased research funding?

Scientists are discovering that women respond differently from men to a surprisingly wide array of diseases and medications. Heart disease is the leading killer of women and men, but women are far less likely than men to survive heart attacks and heart surgery. Experts cannot explain why; the most influential studies of heart disease have studied only men. Women activists charge that medical research has focused on men long enough. Now, they say, it's their turn. Together, female consumers, lawmakers and doctors have won a string of impressive political victories boosting federal research attention to women's health. But some well-respected researchers in the scientific establishment attack this activism as special-interest politics that could ultimately undermine the validity of the scientific quest.

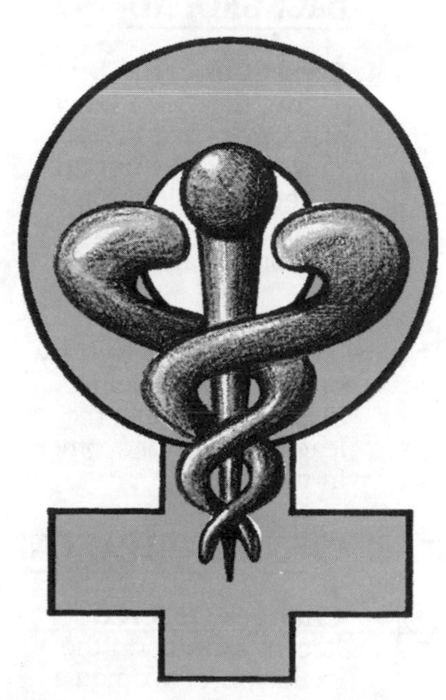

INSIDE THIS ISSUE

CQ May 13, 1994 • Volume 4, No. 18 • 409-432

Formerly Editorial Research Reports

WOMEN'S HEALTH ISSUES

COVER ART: BARBARA SASSA-DANIELS

May 13, 1994
Volume 4, No. 18

The CQ Researcher (ISSN 1056-2036). Formerly Editorial Research Reports. Published weekly (48 times per year, not printed the first Friday of any month with five Fridays) by Congressional Quarterly Inc., 1414 22nd St., N.W., Washington, D.C. 20037. Rates are furnished upon request. Second-class postage paid at Washington, D.C. POSTMASTER: Send address changes to The CQ Researcher, 1414 22nd St., N.W., Washington, D.C. 20037.

Women's Health Issues

BY SARAH GLAZER

THE ISSUES

It never occurred to 69-year-old Ethel Weichbrod that the crushing chest pain she felt one night in 1989 might signal trouble. But four days later, Weichbrod landed in the hospital with a heart attack. Plaque had been building up in her arteries for years, she learned, completely blocking one of them. But her doctor had never discussed heart disease with her or tested her blood cholesterol.

Seventy-year-old Helen Bryan didn't think anything was amiss either when, at her regular checkup, she mentioned the vague ache in her arm and her shortness of breath. When her doctor told her to leave for the hospital immediately, Bryan asked if she could walk. She did not realize she was having a heart attack.

More women in the United States die of heart disease than any other physical ailment. (*See graphs, pp. 412, 415.*) But until recently, many women were unaware of this fact, and the medical community paid scant attention to women in its most well-known studies of heart disease.

"When I was trained in the 1950s, everyone thought of heart disease as a man's disease," Suzanne Oparil, incoming president of the American Heart Association, told a symposium on women's health at the Smithsonian Institution. "If you saw a woman, it was an anecdote." [1]

Reviewing today's medical literature on women and cardiovascular disease is "a little bit depressing," Oparil continued, because "I can present just about everything we know in 45 minutes."

For years, many doctors waved away women patients' complaints of chest pains as psychological in origin, says Lila Wallis, clinical professor of medicine at Cornell University Medical College and past president of the American Medical Women's Association. (*See story, p. 414.*)

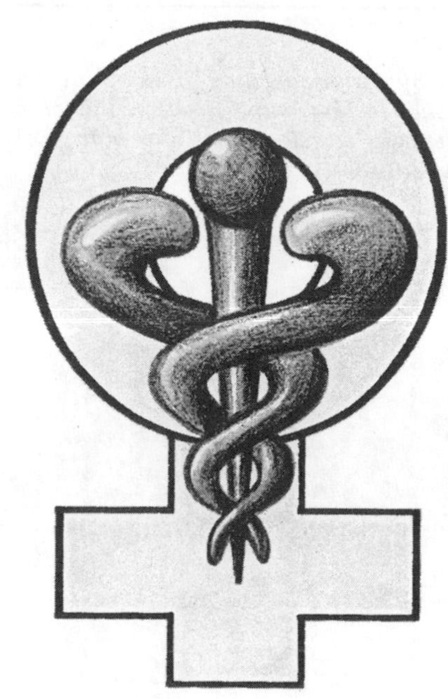

Recent studies have found that doctors tend to treat women with cardiac disease symptoms less aggressively than men with similar symptoms. Women may show up at the doctor's office with a range of complaints, including pain in the stomach or jaw, which don't fit the typical male profile. Yet women are almost twice as likely to die from a heart attack as men, notes Nanette K. Wenger, a professor of medicine at Emory University School of Medicine. [2]

Even when women do get high-tech treatment like coronary bypass surgery, they are more likely than men to die in the hospital. Researchers aren't sure why. There may be something biologically different about being a female with heart disease. Or it may be that women who show up with heart symptoms have neglected the disease for so long that it is less treatable. Age could also be a factor. On average, women who have heart attacks are at least 10 years older than men who are stricken.

So far, these are questions without answers, because the research has never been done, Wenger says. The "tacit assumption made in research" is that "the middle-aged white male is the prototype of disease, and that gets extrapolated to the universe," she says.

When Harvard University reported in 1989 that taking an aspirin every other day could prevent heart disease, some news reports implied that the results applied to all adults. [3] But the Physicians' Health Study involved 22,000 male doctors, and no women. Aspirin, which is supposed to help prevent blood clotting, "might not be useful in women" with heart disease, notes Oparil, because healthy women generally have faster rates of clotting than men.

Lately, heart disease has been garnering attention from the medical community because it affects men and women so differently. The fact that the rate of cardiovascular disease among women starts to rise after menopause suggests that reproductive hormones protect women from heart disease in their childbearing years.

But some prominent women in the medical community believe an entire universe of medical differences between the sexes has been neglected by researchers — not just heart disease. "Basically, what we need to do is rethink how we look at the disease process," says Florence Haseltine, director of the Center for Population Research at the National Institutes of Health (NIH) in Bethesda, Md. "There is a difference between men and women that in itself is interesting." [4]

"There's a very rich interaction between our ovarian hormones and every other organ of our body — whether it's the brain, the immune system, the liver, the heart or the bones," adds Eileen Hoffman, a New York City internist.

The women's health movement, started in the late 1960s by Boston feminists dissatisfied with their doctors' care, has picked up new clout in the

Leading Causes of Death for Men and Women

Most deaths in the United States are caused by cardiovascular disease, such as high blood pressure, heart disease and stroke. In fact, such diseases kill more women than men. Cancer was the second leading cause of death for both sexes in 1990, the latest year for which complete statistics are available.

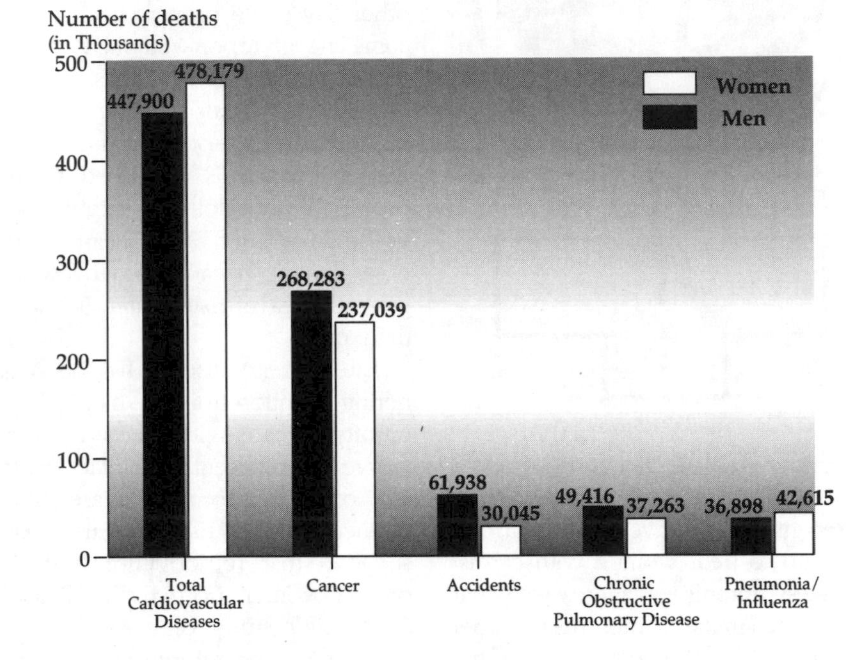

Source: National Center for Health Statistics; American Heart Association, 1993

1990s as women have invaded Congress and the medical profession and made the cause their own. In 1990, women lawmakers lobbied for and won a new infusion of federal dollars to study women's health (*see p. 424*).

Shortly after Bernadine P. Healy was appointed as the first female director of the NIH in 1991, she launched the Women's Health Initiative, a massive 14-year, $625 million study of some 160,0000 women. The initiative will examine three diseases of crucial importance to women: heart disease, breast cancer and osteoporosis. (*See story, p. 416.*)

Under pressure from the Congressional Caucus for Women's Issues, led by Reps. Patricia Schroeder, D-Colo., and Olympia J. Snowe, R-Maine, Congress last year required NIH, the nation's largest research funder, to include women in all applicable clinical trials of medical treatments. The Food and Drug Administration (FDA) also issued guidelines last year encouraging researchers to include women in tests of new drugs.

But these reforms face strong opposition from some researchers, who view them as an effort to politicize pure science. Curtis Meinert, a professor of epidemiology and biostatistics at Johns Hopkins University, describes the lawmakers' NIH mandate as "the forced busing of clinical trials." He doubts that the approach will uncover significant differences between men and women either in their responses to diseases or their treatment. "I believe men and women are more alike than they are different," he says.

The successful grass-roots effort to quadruple federal expenditures on breast-cancer research over the past two years has also come in for criticism from some scientists. Resentment in the research community has been aimed at a nationwide coalition of cancer patients, researchers and doctors who lobbied for the funding increases.

Some scientists have objected that earmarking so much money for one disease will starve basic laboratory research, where cures for diseases have often originated in the past. Even some physicians who specialize in breast cancer are doubtful.

"Most scientific discoveries are found serendipitously," says Helen E. Mrose, chief of breast imaging and assistant professor of radiology at George Washington University Medical Center. "The person who finds the key to breast cancer may not even be thinking about breast cancer. . . . Pouring millions of dollars into breast cancer is not the answer."

Susan Love, a surgeon from the University of California-Los Angeles who helped lead the coalition's lobbying campaign, stands firm. She has argued that as a scientist, " you will study what you fear. And if you're a white, middle-class male, it's more likely to [be] heart disease than breast cancer." [5]

"I get a little bit annoyed at people who say, 'You're trying to politicize research!' " Love continued. "That's baloney. It's always been political. It just was a matter of whose politics was calling the shots."

Michigan State University surgeon Janet Rose Osuch is also impatient with such arguments, noting that more women get breast cancer than any other form of cancer. "Very few citizens in our country understand that it's their tax dollars that fund the researchers' budgets in our country — that the entire budget of the National Institutes of Health is taxpayers' dollars. We're talking about taxation with representation. That's how our country works: The people that have their agenda and pay their money deserve a voice."

As the debate on women's health continues, these are some of the key questions being discussed:

Should there be a new medical specialty in women's health?

A century ago, physician Rudolf Virchow reflected medicine's view of women when he declared, "Woman is a pair of ovaries with a human being attached, whereas man is a human being furnished with a pair of testes." [6]

To hear some women doctors talk, medical education has not progressed much since then. Wallis notes that the typical medical school education is still based on the model of the 150-pound man as the norm. And medical students are not usually taught that women may metabolize medications differently from men because of their size, hormonal status and basic metabolic differences, she says.

"Any medical student can graduate and the only training they have in women's health is ob-gyn [obstetrics and gynecology]," protests San Francisco psychiatrist Karen Johnson. "Women's health is clearly not limited to the reproductive organs. The medical training we've had doesn't qualify us to take good care of women."

Unlike men, most women have to visit two doctors for their normal health care: the ob-gyn for pregnancy checkups and Pap smears and the internist for everything else. But sometimes this division becomes ludicrous, points out Michelle Harrison, clinical associate professor of family medicine at Robert Wood Johnson Medical School in New Brunswick, N.J. [7]

A woman who suffers abdominal pains may go to her internist, who will examine her abdomen — the liver, spleen, intestines and appendix. If the internist finds nothing wrong, the woman must continue on to the gynecologist, who examines her pelvis — the ovaries and the uterus. The woman must make two separate visits despite the fact that the two doctors are examining the same 8-by-10-inch cavity. "They're territorial and specialty divisions," Harrison says, "not anatomic ones."

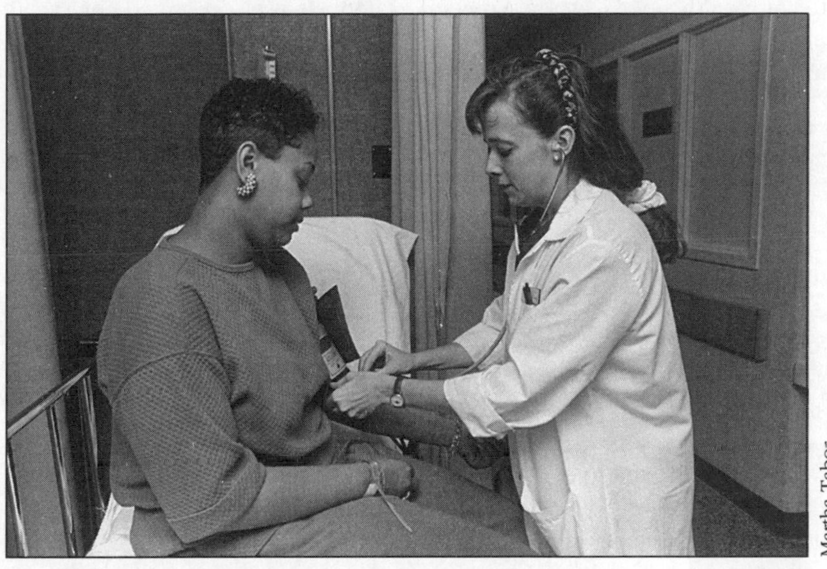

Martha Tabor

Nurse checks patient's blood pressure at George Washington University Hospital.

This artificial division dates from the mid-19th century, Harrison explains, when male doctors first defined childbirth as a surgical procedure. Up until then, female midwives had been responsible for childbirth as well as the larger universe of women's ailments. All that changed, however, once social mores permitted male doctors to examine women's genital areas.

"With the destruction of midwifery and the paucity of women's physicians," Harrison writes, "the woman's body . . . was now a foreign body to the overwhelmingly male medical profession." [8]

In an attempt to provide comprehensive medical care to women in one office, some doctors have begun to specialize in women's health, among them New York internist Hoffman. "There's no one practitioner looking at the woman as a whole human being," she says.

In 1992, Johnson, an assistant clinical professor of psychiatry at the University of California-San Francisco, proposed in a "debate" in the *Journal of Women's Health* that a new medical specialty be created and certified in women's health. She argued that "two or more physicians are required to provide complete care [for women], an inefficient and expensive process." Pointing to physicians' failures to diagnose such emerging problems as domestic violence and premenstrual symptoms, she noted that specialists "often fail to piece together the larger diagnostic picture." Johnson also argued that a women's specialty would stimulate more research on women, which in turn would improve medical school training. [9]

Harrison, who specializes in treating women with premenstrual syndrome, rebutted Johnson's proposal in the same issue. Creating a certified specialty in women's health, she wrote, "would allow the rest of those in medicine to feel absolved of responsibility for addressing the needs of women, and more inclined to leave the sensitive care of women to those few practitioners who are now the 'experts.' " She predicted that a field devoted solely to the non-surgical

Continued on p. 415

Grande Dame of Women's Health

Lila Wallis has always been a fighter. At age 18, she joined the Polish underground to fight the Nazis, working as a nurse in a field hospital for partisans.

Shortly after arriving in the United States in 1946, Wallis entered Columbia College of Physicians and Surgeons. It was a time when women comprised only about one-tenth of the class. She graduated in 1951 with honors.

Soon after starting her New York practice in internal medicine in 1955, Wallis began to see deficiencies in her education. "It was obvious to me that my training did not prepare me to respond to the health needs of my women patients," she says.

One of the problems was the pelvic examination. Wallis' patients recounted horror stories about the excruciating pain of exams at the hands of other doctors. At Columbia, as at many other medical schools, students in groups of four or five learned the exam by taking turns groping around in a clinic patient's vagina. Wallis had always thought that "this was a barbaric way to learn." The instructor could not tell whether the student was finding the correct organs with his fingers. The patient was usually too frightened to complain about the pain.

Lila Wallis, M.D.

"By instinct and guessing," Wallis developed a painless gynecological exam for her patients. In 1979, she created a radical program at Cornell University Medical College in which patients taught medical students from the examining table how to perform the pelvic exam painlessly and competently. She developed the idea together with two women from the feminist Boston Women's Health Book Collective.

Although Wallis' dean supported the idea, many faculty members did not. "There were poisonous letters to the dean about me — that I was a non-conformist . . . playing dangerously with the psyches of the students and these poor women," Wallis recalls.

But medical students loved the program, at one point marching on the dean's office to demand that funding continue. Some medical students traveled from other schools, paying extra tuition to attend the course.

The program caught on. Today most medical schools in the United States and Canada teach the pelvic exam through lay women instructors.[1] Wallis, now a clinical professor of medicine at Cornell, calls the program her proudest accomplishment. In her eyes, it created a "quiet revolution," turning women patients into respected teachers of physicians.

For Wallis, however, it was only the first step toward improving women's health. After stepping down as the widely quoted president of the American Medical Women's Association (AMWA) in 1989, she decided it was time to retrain practicing physicians in the treatment of women.

She created an advanced curriculum in women's health for doctors who had never learned the material in medical school. It was presented for the first time last October in a three-day AMWA seminar.

Wallis hasn't stopped there. After the seminar, she recalls, "We were so high because of the wonderful presentations and audience response" that she and another colleague cooked up a new organization over lunch — this one to convince medical schools to integrate women's health into their curricula (*see p. 427*).

The need was there, she once explained, because as in her student days, medical schools still consider men the model of a normal human. "Then there is a deviant subspecies — woman," she added in her droll, unflinching style.

Wallis' agenda would exhaust most normal mortals. In the wee hours of the morning, she is writing a textbook on women's health and another book on the same topic for lay people. She is founding president of the New York-based National Council on Women's Health, which teaches patients about their own health. And she is lobbying for legislation aimed at improving medical school training.

What keeps her pressing on? "I am stubborn," she confesses. But she is also flexible. Frequently, she says, she will think over her opponents' objections and try out her reform efforts again in a "non-adversarial way."

With all her accomplishments, it's little wonder that Wallis has been called the "grandmother" of the women's health movement.

But there is something else that makes Wallis — the mother of two sons, both doctors — especially proud these days. She recently added the title of biological grandmother to her spiritual title in the movement.

[1] Sarah Glazer, "Pelvic Exams from a Woman's Point of View," *Washington Post Health Section*, Dec. 8, 1992, pp. 12-13.

Continued from p. 413
care of women would become a "relatively low-paid, low-status field." [10]

Experts on both sides of the debate complain that traditionally trained doctors are notoriously insensitive to women as people. "Women frequently want to be partners in their own decision-making," says Glenda D. Donoghue, associate dean for postgraduate medical education at the Medical College of Pennsylvania. * "And doctors have quite a lot of difficulty sharing decision-making. They're accustomed to being in charge."

Several studies have suggested that female doctors do a better job of communicating with women patients and ultimately provide more comprehensive care. One survey showed that women doctors spend an average of 17 minutes on each visit, and male doctors spend 13 minutes. Several studies found that women doctors are more empathetic listeners and are less likely to interrupt their patients than men. [11]

A recent study at a large Minnesota health plan found that women were more likely to get Pap smears and mammograms — tests for cervical and breast cancer — if the internist or family physician they see is a female rather than a male. Surprisingly, young male physicians recently out of medical school had particularly low rates of screening, even though the tests are highly recommended. The authors suggested that young men may be uncomfortable examining women's breasts or vaginas, and that women patients may be more comfortable discussing issues of concern with doctors of the same sex. [12]

Harrison sympathizes with calls for more sensitive doctors and for one-stop shopping for women patients. But she says a new women's specialty is not the answer. "The issue, as I see it, is that all of medicine has to become user-friendly to women, not that we should designate separate doctors that are going to be nice to women."

Internists, for example, should provide gynecological exams as part of a routine physical exam, she believes. "When we're short of primary care to begin with, when many women can't get access to decent doctors, I can't see the rationale of allowing internists to go on not doing abdominal examinations. They're feeling for livers, they're feeling for spleens. Why can't they feel for ovaries too?"

As for stimulating women's research, Harrison argues that it is not doctors, but Ph.D.s in epidemiology and other academic fields who design studies. To fill the knowledge gap in women's health, she supports the development of an academic discipline at the graduate level and currently directs a new master's program in women's health that gives medical school graduates additional training after their residency.

Some doctors advocating improvements in women's health say the movement to create a new specialty for women has lost its appeal for them as the debate over health-care reform has picked up momentum. Under President Clinton's plan, insurance would cover visits to a general doctor for preventive or "primary" care but would require referrals by the

Women's Health Threats: Perception vs. Reality

Breast cancer is the disease that women fear most, according to a Gallup Poll, but heart disease is actually the No. 1 killer of American women (and men), though it arouses little concern.

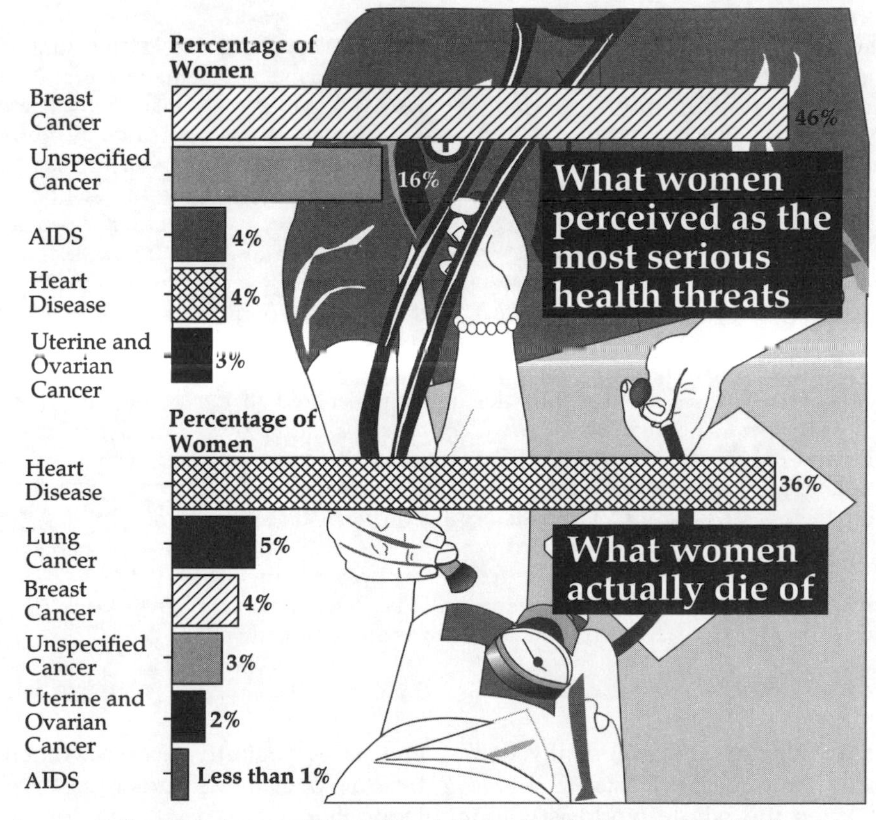

Source: Gallup Poll, August 1993; National Center for Health Statistics, 1990

* The college is the first medical school in the country to make women's health part of the required curriculum (*see p. 427*).

Women's Health Initiative: Is It Too Ambitious?

As director of the National Institutes of Health (NIH) in 1991, Bernadine P. Healy took a bold — some say ill-considered — step. Responding to the growing demand for more information about women's health, Healy launched the largest clinical trial in NIH history looking exclusively at women.

At first glance, the Women's Health Initiative — focusing on breast cancer, heart disease and osteoporosis — appears to attack many of the questions women have been concerned about. It has been welcomed by advocacy groups like the National Women's Health Network.

But critics say that in her eagerness to satisfy a spectrum of clamoring political constituencies, Healy created a patchwork study with somewhat sloppy results. "The worry is that there is too much stuffed into that box," says Curtis Meinert, a professor of epidemiology and biostatistics at Johns Hopkins University. "It's the Christmas tree approach to design."

The nine-year trial, involving 63,000 post-menopausal women, has three separate components to test what NIH dubs "promising but unproven" approaches to disease prevention.[1] One component will test the power of low-fat diets to prevent breast cancer, colon cancer and coronary heart disease. Another will examine hormonal replacement therapy to block coronary heart disease and osteoporosis. The last will evaluate the value of calcium and vitamin D supplements to forestall osteoporosis and colon cancer.

Last fall, an Institute of Medicine (IOM) committee expressed skepticism about the study, saying "much of the information could be obtained in better designed, smaller, more focused studies that could have a greater chance of success and probably be less costly."[2]

The panel saved its harshest criticism for the study's hypothesis that a change to a low-fat diet by women over age 50 could prevent breast cancer, calling the scientific link "quite weak." The theory is based largely on comparisons showing higher rates of breast cancer in nations that consume the most fat. But the committee noted that it's not clear whether fat in such countries is eaten by women, or by their husbands and children, or used as animal feed, or wasted. The committee recommended a shift in focus to the effects of dietary fat on heart disease, for which there is more evidence.

"There was a lot of pressure from breast cancer constituencies that want more research," says Susan Thaul, study director of the IOM report, "and it was all put together hastily."

The panel also was skeptical because eating habits in the United States already show a declining trend in fat consumption. By the end of the study, it said, there may be so little difference in the fat consumed by the treatment and control groups that it might be impossible to tell if fat had influenced cancer rates in either group.

According to Thaul, the initiative shows that "just including women won't be the answer" to improving women's health. "You have to design good studies."

Loretta Finnegan, director of the initiative, concedes "There is disagreement regarding diet and its use in preventing breast cancer. . . . However, because there is such disagreement in the scientific community, the only way you can demonstrate a link is to do a clinical trial."

Several members of the IOM panel also worry that other ongoing research may demonstrate the benefit of some therapies the Women's Health Initiative is studying, such as hormone replacement therapy, before the study is completed. If that happens, "it may become unethical to continue people on a placebo," said panel member Gary C. Cutter, president of Pythagoras Inc., a Birmingham, Ala., company that designs clinical trials. In response to such criticism, NIH will reassess the trial every three years and modify it if necessary, Harold Varmus, the NIH's new director, told the House Appropriations Committee in April.

At the National Osteoporosis Foundation, senior policy analyst Bente Cooney says the initiative will be only "marginally useful. It verifies a lot of the information that we already know."

Meanwhile, the high-profile study has made it harder for the foundation to raise funds for the research it believes is needed — basic data on how to grow bones again after osteoporosis has begun to weaken them, says Executive Director Sandra C. Raymond.

Florence Haseltine, director of NIH's Center for Population Research, acknowledges that in many ways the health initiative is "catch-up work." But there's another benefit to it, she says. It's establishing centers in women's health at the 45 medical schools and hospitals around the country involved in the study. "It's providing a framework."

[1] In addition to the clinical trial, the Women's Health Initiative includes an "observational study" of disease risk factors in about 100,000 women and a "community prevention" study of ways to promote healthy behavior.

[2] Susan Thaul and Dana Hotra, eds, *An Assessment of the NIH Women's Health Initiative* (1993). The institute report was requested by the House Appropriations Committee, spurred by concerns over NIH's escalating cost estimate for the study.

primary doctor and potentially extra charges to see specialists.

"When the whole world is talking about the need to create more generalists, to begin to create a women's health specialty is ludicrous," says Donoghue.

Obstetricians and gynecologists, who have been jockeying for position as women's primary doctors, won designation as "primary care" doctors in Clinton's legislative proposal, enabling women to see their ob-gyns without referrals.

Last year the American College of Obstetricians and Gynecologists publicized findings from a Gallup Poll showing that women were more likely to have a physical exam by an ob-gyn than any other doctor. However, ob-gyns were less likely than other doctors to perform cholesterol screenings or to discuss diet, exercise, medication or mental-health issues. [13]

Ob-gyns have traditionally taken care of a wide range of non-gynecological problems during a woman's pregnancy — everything from high blood pressure to diabetes, says Vicki Seltzer, vice president of the college and chairman of obstetrics and gynecology at Long Island Jewish Medical Center. "The realization has come during the last several years that it is important to women that care be expanded to a large spectrum of their life span because women are getting really fragmented care right now," Seltzer says.

With Seltzer as editor, the college launched a new journal this year aimed at updating gynecologists' knowledge of health-care issues outside their field, including diseases as diverse as cancer and cardiovascular disease. The college also has started offering postgraduate courses in primary health care for ob-gyns.

But some women's health activists doubt these steps will qualify ob-gyns beyond their traditional area of expertise. "You think if I had a thyroid disorder or clinical depression that I'm going to trust my ob-gyn — who's *read* about it [in the new journal]?" says Cynthia Pearson, program director of the National Women's Health Network, an advocacy group based in Washington. "I want to see a family practice doctor or internist or someone trained to do that."

Coming at the issue from the internists' perspective, several medical schools — including Harvard, Brown and Albert Einstein in New York — have developed one-to-two-year women's health fellowships for graduates who have completed an internal medicine residency.

While psychiatrist Johnson applauds such moves as "terrific steps in the right direction," she says they won't provide the kind of "woman-centered" care she envisions in a specialty. For example, she says, most of the new programs won't train physicians adequately to recognize "psychosocial" issues like depression — which is twice as common in women as men.

Johnson says she has been contacted by hundreds of medical students who want to become women's health specialists and have no place to train. She recently founded the San Francisco-based Women's Health Project with internist Hoffman to help medical schools develop programs in women's health.

But she concedes it's an uphill battle to create a new specialty. "Ob-gyns would lose the majority of their practice and become surgical specialists," she says. "I think this proposal is profoundly threatening to the medical establishment . . . economically and emotionally."

Will including more women in clinical trials improve women's health?

In 1984, NIH released a massive report entitled "Normal Human Aging," the results of its first two decades of studying aging. Although the study had involved more than 1,000 participants, no women were included in the findings. [14]

"It makes us wonder where we failed to qualify," Susan Calvert Finn, past president of the American Dietetic Association, quipped at a women's health symposium in Washington in March. "Were we not normal, human and aging?"

Finn's remark reflects long-standing frustration over the exclusion of women from several landmark medical studies. Women's health advocates have focused in particular on clinical studies, in which causes or treatments for a disease are tested in human subjects. In a clinical drug trial, one group of participants gets the experimental drug, another gets a placebo, but no one knows which treatment they are receiving. The studies can involve thousands of people, years of tracking and millions of dollars.

Generally, the federal government will not approve a new drug treatment for a given illness until it has passed the hurdle of a clinical trial. Almost overnight, the findings can change how doctors treat patients. So women activists raised an uproar in 1990 when the General Accounting Office (GAO) reported to Congress that women were "generally underrepresented" in drug trials funded by NIH. [15]

"Research studies were being reported as if they applied to everyone, when in fact most of them were done with only men," says Phyllis Greenberger, executive director of the Society for the Advancement of Women's Health Research. "So no one really knew if the results could be extrapolated to women." It was at the urging of the society that the Congressional Caucus for Women's Issues originally requested the GAO report.

Women's health advocates have leveled their harshest criticism at several well-known studies of cardiovascular disease that did not include any women participants. Three out of four major clinical trials on cholesterol-lowering drugs were conducted using only middle-aged men, yet half the prescriptions for those drugs subsequently were written for women over 60. [16] Extrapolating those findings to women is potentially faulty, critics say, because they ignore the importance of the hormone estrogen in women as a possible heart-attack preventive as well as the different course of the disease in women.

Traditionally, two major reasons have been given for excluding women from clinical trials. Some researchers fear li-

The Fight Against Breast Cancer

Although the number of women diagnosed with breast cancer has been rising since 1973, deaths from the disease have remained flat. The stable death rate indicates that more cases are being detected sooner and treated successfully.

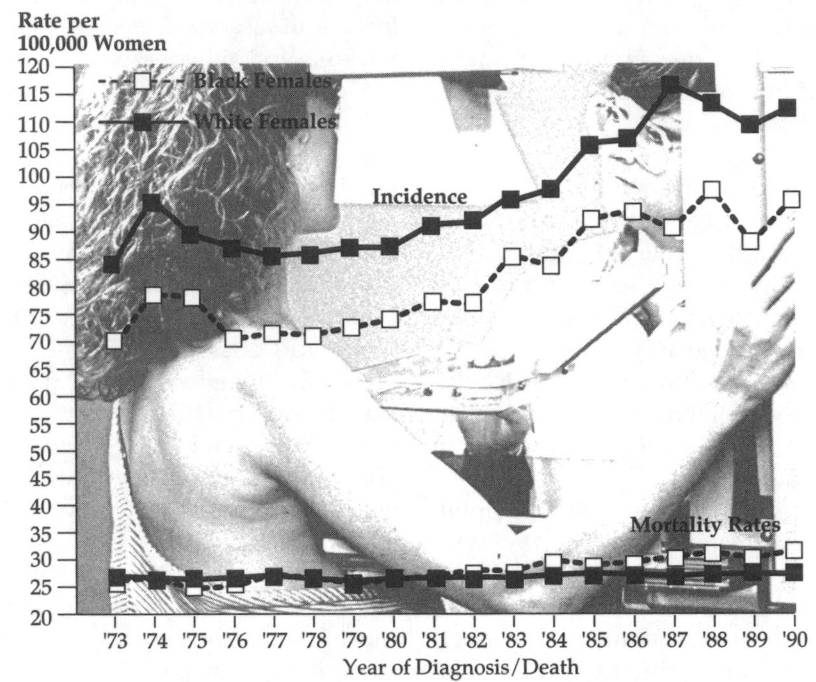

Source: National Cancer Institute, American Cancer Society. Photograph courtesy of the National Cancer Institute.

ability if drug treatments hurt pregnant women or their offspring. Other researchers, including drug companies, thought that women's varying hormonal levels during menstruation, ovulation, pregnancy and lactation would complicate the study. Indeed, when estrogen was first studied for its protective properties against heart disease a decade ago, it was tested only in men.

Harrison, who specializes in premenstrual syndrome, has long observed that her patients respond differently to medications depending on the point in their menstrual cycle. When she met with pharmaceutical industry representatives 15 years ago to urge them to study this phenomenon, however, she was told that they did not use women in their studies because they considered the menstrual cycle "a confounding factor."

Yet it is precisely this rise and fall in hormonal levels over the course of the monthly cycle that leads physicians like Harrison to suspect that women metabolize drugs differently at various points in that cycle. Very few studies have examined this impact. But it might make a crucial difference in how women should be treated.

One recent study suggested that the timing of breast cancer surgery in a woman's cycle could affect her chance of survival. Another recent report advised doctors to vary the doses of anti-depressant drugs over the menstrual cycle to reduce side effects and achieve optimal benefits. [17]

In the wake of the campaign launched in 1990 by female researchers and lawmakers, Congress last year required NIH to include women in all studies of diseases and conditions that affect them. [18] But some scientists are up in arms over the legislation, especially the requirement that researchers include enough women participants to perform a "valid analysis" of the differences between the sexes. [19]

New England Journal of Medicine Editor Marcia Angell reflected the medical establishment's viewpoint when she protested last year that the new requirements "assume that clinically important differences between men and women are the rule rather than the exception — a biologically implausible assumption." [20]

Meinert of Johns Hopkins, who designs clinical trials, says the new legislation will require so many additional participants that worthwhile studies will become prohibitively expensive. He cites the landmark MRFIT study (known as "Mr. Fit") in the late 1970s, which was influential in defining the risk factors for coronary disease as blood pressure, cholesterol levels and dietary fat. Women's health advocates have criticized the study for including 13,000 men and no women. But if enough women had been added to the study to analyze the differences between the sexes' risk factors in a statistically valid way, Meinert estimates that the cost of the trial would have skyrocketed from $115 million to $3 billion.

Already, he says, the mandate is discouraging researchers from pursuing projects. "When you sit and talk with people, they'll say, 'We can't come up with a sufficient number of women here. So let's forget it. It's not worth the battle.' "

"My biggest worry," Meinert adds, "is that the legislation will drive us to study those things more or less equal in the two sex groups and will drive us away from those things that are more prevalent in males than females because of the political risks involved."

Judith H. LaRosa, deputy director of NIH's Office of Research on Women's Health, agrees that in some cases the new requirement will increase costs. "But," she asks, "is it not better to spend the money now to find out the answers, rather than to pay in incomplete or inappropriate treatment later on?"

Meinert is skeptical, however, that clinical trials will find any differences of medical significance between the genders. "I don't think the search has produced much," he maintains, "and I don't think it's going to produce much." Meinert supports including women in trials but without the requirement for a separate analysis of sex differences. "We ought to be training people to go for sex neutrality as opposed to mandated mixes," he argues.

In Meinert's view, the legislative mandate is based on a faulty premise — that women have been unfairly excluded from most clinical trials. He says his own search of the medical literature in recent years found that most trials include both men and women. Out of some 2,000 projects conducted by researchers at Johns Hopkins, he says, studies focusing exclusively on women outnumber men-only studies by 4 to 1.

He also questions the assertion that women's health has been harmed by the orientation of past studies. Since 1960, he notes, women's death rates from cardiovascular disease have fallen at approximately the same rate as men's rates.

Because there is no central registry of clinical trials in the United States, it is not clear whether women have participated in clinical studies to the same extent as men, an Institute of Medicine panel recently concluded. It noted, however, that in two areas — heart disease and AIDS — important studies have either excluded women altogether or included them in numbers too small to yield meaningful information. [21]

Not everybody buys the argument that women were unfairly excluded from the early heart disease studies, which tended to study men in their 50s and 60s. For researchers to detect treatment effects in women at the same ages, when so few have heart disease, would have required a vast increase in the number of people studied, notes biostatistician Gary Cutter, president of Pythagoras Inc., a Birmingham, Ala., firm that designs clinical trials. "Part of this lack of female representation in studies has been a lack of budgetary funding to make these studies big enough," Cutter says.

To see a really big effect on women, researchers would have had to extend their studies another 10 or 20 years to the point when women start suffering heart attacks in large numbers, notes Valery T. Miller, who is leading two clinical studies of heart disease in women at George Washington University Medical Center. In the meantime, she says, the first studies of men have provided valuable information. Of the clinical studies of heart disease in women that are just now getting under way, she says, "I don't think it's been too long in coming."

Meanwhile, an Institute of Medicine panel on which Meinert served has recommended that the NIH move toward greater inclusion of women, including pregnant women, in clinical trials. But the panel also criticized the new gender-analysis requirement authored by Congress and NIH. In studies where no difference among men and women is anticipated, the panel said, requiring scientists to enroll sufficient numbers of women to ensure statistical reliability "would produce little additional information at a greatly increased cost." [22] ■

BACKGROUND

Breast Cancer

In spring 1992, 600,000 letters flooded Capitol Hill urging more federal spending to eradicate breast cancer. The letter campaign was organized by the National Breast Cancer Coalition, founded only the year before by cancer survivors, doctors and supporters. [23]

Today, two years later, the coalition can boast that it has more than quadrupled total appropriations for breast cancer research since its founding. * No other cancer research has received such increases.

Perhaps no other disease has inspired as much political militancy and passion among the physicians who work in the field day to day. Last May in *The Journal of the American Medical Association,* surgeon Love laid out the coalition's manifesto. Women, she wrote, want money to eradicate breast cancer before it is passed on to the next generation "and they want it now." She called the current approaches to breast cancer "crude and inadequate," equating medicine's arsenal of surgery, radiation and chemotherapy to "slash, burn and poison." [24]

One reason for the passion is that the cause remains unknown. Breast cancer last year killed 46,000 women. While more women die of lung cancer each year, the cause can at least be traced to the rising numbers of women smoking cigarettes.

It's that void of knowledge about breast cancer that makes Michigan surgeon Osuch despairing even as she exults in the coalition's recent political victories. "It's very frustrating to say 'I don't know' when patients ask, 'What caused this, and what can I do to prevent this from happening to my daughter?' "

Questions About Mammography

The frustration even embraces mammography, the highly touted, low-dose X-ray used to detect tumors

* Total appropriations for breast cancer research rose from $90 million in fiscal 1991 to $410 million in fiscal 1994. The coalition is seeking $697 million for 1995.

in women. In women over age 50, early detection with mammography decreases deaths from breast cancer by about 30 percent, notes Susan L. Troyan, a breast surgeon at Boston's Beth Israel Hospital and instructor in surgery at Harvard Medical School.

Since 1987, the National Cancer Institute (NCI) had urged women over 40 to get mammograms every one to two years. But an international workshop sponsored by the institute in February 1993 reviewed results of eight major studies and concluded that there was no statistically significant proof that routine mammography reduces death in women 40-49 without breast cancer symptoms. On Dec. 3, 1993, the NCI reversed its guidelines about screening for women in their 40s. It still recommends screening for women over 50. [25]

It's not clear why mammography should be so much less effective for the under-50 crowd. One theory is that younger women have denser tissue in their breasts, which shows up as a white area on the mammogram. Since tumors also show up as white masses, mammographers are studying pictures of "white on white" for younger women. As a result, almost 10 percent of tumors are missed for this age group, and many more lumps are suspected as cancerous than really are. [26] (After menopause, women's breasts become less dense and more fatty, so more of the normal breast area shows up as black.)

Until the institute revised its guidelines last year, the United States stood alone among major developed countries in urging women under 50 to get routine mammograms. The American Cancer Society and American College of Radiology both continue to support mammograms for women under 50, and both groups have questioned the validity of the studies cited by the NCI. "The problem is, we oversold [mammography], in the true American fashion," Love said. [27]

Rising Incidence Rate

Much is often made of the risk factors for breast cancer. Among them are a family history of the illness, a prior diagnosis of cancer, an early first period, late menopause and birth of a first child after age 30. One theory linking some of these factors stems from the fact that the female hormones estrogen and progesterone, which rise with menstruation and decline with menopause, stimulate the growth of breast tissue. It appears that the more time a woman lives with that hormonal stimulation — post menstruation and pre-menopause, for example — the more likely she is to get breast cancer.

Yet an estimated 60-80 percent of the women who develop breast cancer do not have any of these risk factors. "Just having breasts puts us at risk," Troyan says.

Scientists can't explain why the rates of breast cancer have been rising since 1930. One possibility is that as more women have gotten mammograms, more cancers are being detected than in the past.

Another explanation might be environmental influences. Last month, the New York State Health Department released what scientists called the first credible study outside a laboratory to suggest a link between breast cancer and industrial pollution. Women who once lived near a Long Island chemical plant ran a 62 percent higher risk of developing breast cancer after menopause than women who did not. But scientists cautioned that this one study was not enough to demonstrate cause and effect. [28]

At the same time that rates of breast cancer have been rising, deaths from the disease have remained almost static over the last two decades. (*See graph, p. 418.*) Apparently, modern advances in cancer detection and treatment have been offset by the rising incidence of the disease, most researchers believe. [29]

Some of these trends may be changing, however, according to preliminary data released by the cancer society. Since 1987, the incidence of the disease has dropped slightly, while deaths tapered off between 1990 and 1991.

Cancer society consultant Lawrence Garfinckel thinks the rise in the incidence of breast cancer over the 1970s and '80s stemmed from more women getting mammograms. Consequently, as the nation approaches the peak number of women who will get them, he expects to see a drop in the detection of new breast cancers. (According to a 1992 survey commissioned by the American Cancer Society, 41 percent of women 40 and older had had a mammogram in the past year or two.)

As for the drop in mortality, Garfinckel attributes that to successes in early detection and treatment. "You have to wait a few years before you can see if it's real or not," he says, "but it certainly is encouraging."

Research Controversy

On the horizon are a number of promising treatments, including bone-marrow transplantation and genetic analysis for an inherited form of the disease. Experts like Troyan and Osuch express the most hope for the synthetic estrogen known as tamoxifen. In an earlier trial of women with cancer in one breast, those who took tamoxifen were 50 percent less likely to develop cancer in their second breast. The theory for its effectiveness, explains Troyan, is that the chemical "looks enough like estrogen that it can fool breast cells into thinking it's estrogen" and play a protective role.

The NCI is testing the drug in healthy women at risk for breast cancer as a possible preventative. However, the trial has recently come under a cloud in the wake of reports that the trial's director, Bernard Fisher of the University of Pittsburgh, oversaw other breast cancer studies that included falsified data. In March, NCI temporarily suspended enrollment of

Continued on p. 422

Chronology

1950s-1970s

Birth defects caused by the drug thalidomide prompt action to reduce the risks of experimental drugs. Women start to agitate for more responsive health care.

1958
Thalidomide, a sedative and anti-nausea drug for early pregnancy, is approved for marketing in West Germany. Many children are subsequently born with deformities.

1962
Congress passes the Kefauver-Harris amendment, instituting a rigorous drug-approval process at the Food and Drug Administration (FDA).

1970
A primer on women's health written by Boston feminists becomes the popular book, *Our Bodies, Ourselves.*

1975
The congressionally created National Commission for the Protection of Human Subjects of Biomedical and Behavioral Research issues guidelines limiting research on pregnant women and fetuses.

1976
Feminists found the National Women's Health Network in Washington, D.C., to monitor and influence federal health policies.

1977
FDA issues guidelines recommending that women "of childbearing potential" be excluded from the early phases of drug trials.

1980s

Women of the baby-boom generation begin to reach mid-life and experience breast cancer and other illnesses. Growing numbers of female medical school graduates start questioning the amount of attention paid to women's health.

1985
The Public Health Service Task Force on Women's Health Issues concludes that the historical lack of attention to women's health concerns has "compromised the quality" of health care that women receive.

1986
A new National Institutes of Health (NIH) policy urges funding applicants to include women in clinical research.

1990s

The women's health movement gains momentum after it is revealed that women have been excluded from clinical research underlying standard medical procedures.

1990
The Society for the Advancement of Women's Health Research is founded to improve women's health by advocating expanded research, catalyzing congressional and media interest.

June 18, 1990
The General Accounting Office (GAO) reports that women have been excluded from major federally funded clinical studies and that NIH is not enforcing its policy of including women.

July 1990
Reps. Patricia Schroeder, D-Colo., and Olympia J. Snowe, R-Maine, introduce the Women's Health Equity Act, an omnibus bill authorizing additional funding for breast cancer and other women's diseases and requiring that women be included in clinical trials for other diseases.

September 1990
In response to GAO's report, the NIH establishes a new Office of Research on Women's Health.

1991
Bernadine P. Healy, the first female director of NIH, launches the Women's Health Initiative, a 14-year study of women's health.

October 1992
GAO reports that women are underrepresented in studies of drugs approved by the FDA.

1993
The FDA urges drug companies to include sufficient numbers of women in drug trials and lifts its 1977 ban on including women of childbearing age in early studies.

June 10, 1993
President Clinton signs the NIH Revitalization Act, requiring the inclusion of women in clinical research funded by NIH.

1994
A scientific panel appointed by the Institute of Medicine recommends that pregnant women be "presumed eligible" for participation in clinical studies.

Continued from p. 420

new patients in the tamoxifen trial. [30]

Under orders from NCI, the university removed Fisher in March as administrative head of the Pittsburgh project, which coordinates studies, including the tamoxifen study, at more than 400 medical centers across the U.S. and Canada. This month, federal health officials threatened to cut off all federal funding of the breast cancer project after the university proposed to keep Fisher involved as the project's scientific director. [31] In response, the university said it will bar Fisher from a leadership role. [32]

The tamoxifen trial has recently garnered controversy for another reason. In April, Fisher published a paper in the *Journal of the National Cancer Institute* revealing that the risk of uterine cancer from tamoxifen was greater than women in the trial had originally been informed and that some breast cancer patients on tamoxifen had died of uterine cancer. [33]

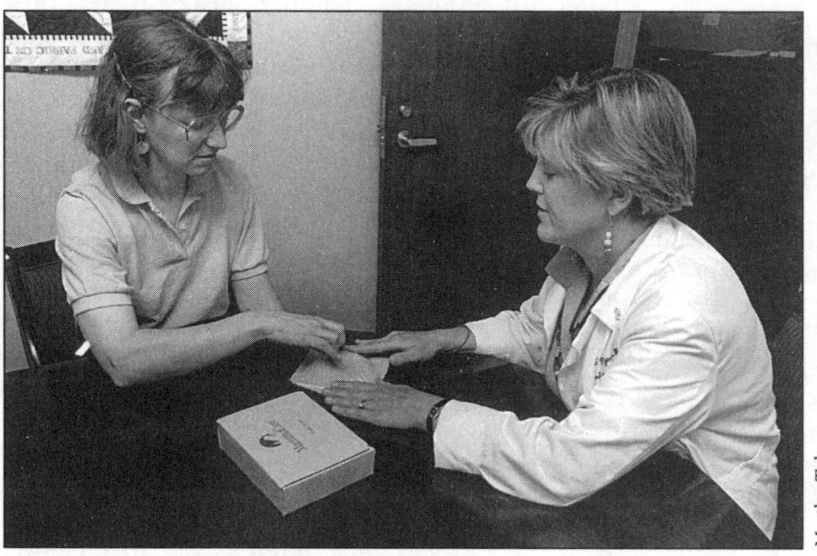

Martha Tabor

Nurse teaches breast self-examination technique at George Washington University Hospital.

Heart Disease

For some legislators and foundations, breast cancer has come to symbolize women's health issues. Many women's health activists say this makes it harder to draw their attention to other devastating diseases.

"We've come from women's health connoting reproductive health to women's health equaling breast cancer," says Greenberger of the Women's Health Research group. "So everyone thinks, 'If we've given money to breast cancer, we've taken care of women's health.' What we're trying to get the country to pay attention to is that women are different from men. We're not just talking about women's diseases."

The prime example is heart disease, the leading killer of women but only recently recognized as such. Each year approximately 2.5 million U.S. women are hospitalized for cardiovascular illness — including heart attacks, strokes and hypertension — and nearly 500,000 women die of it annually. Half of these deaths are due to heart disease. [34]

What is strikingly different about women is that they tend to get heart disease after menopause. Rates of disease increase gradually in postmenopausal women until they match the heart attack and death rates for men. Compared with men, women show the first signs of heart disease about 10 years later and suffer heart attacks about 20 years later.

"Suddenly there's an enormous amount of attention because this is a disease that is likely to grow as the population ages unless we can find out something about it," says Wenger of Emory University. The average American woman now spends 38 percent of her life in the post-menopausal phase. That proportion is likely to expand as women live longer.

Estrogen levels decline after menopause, and that's one reason researchers suspect that estrogen plays an important role in protecting women against heart disease. The primary hypothesis is that estrogen protects women by increasing their HDL (high-density lipoprotein), the "good" cholesterol in blood.

The recommendation that all adults lower their total blood cholesterol through low-fat diets and cholesterol-lowering drugs, which came out of the major studies of men, may be misplaced in women, some researchers suggest. "We know very little about whether specific interventions that have been shown to be useful in men are useful in preventing cardiovascular disease in women," says Oparil.

Yet several large studies that have had a widespread influence on the treatment and prevention of heart disease for both women and men included only men. Among those frequently cited are MRFIT, a study of almost 13,000 men at high risk for coronary heart disease, which recommended reducing blood pressure, cholesterol and dietary fat; the Physicians' Health Study, which recommended taking an aspirin every other day for prevention after studying 22,000 male doctors; and the Coronary Drug Project, which supported the value of cholesterol-lowering drugs in prolonging the lives of men with a history of heart attack.

The public perception that heart disease was "a man's disease" grew partly out of the so-called Framingham [Mass.] study, which was launched in 1948. It initially tracked men and

Weighing Risks in the Hormone-Therapy Debate

Since the mid-1960s, doctors have prescribed the female hormone estrogen to relieve some of the temporary unpleasantness of menopause — hot flashes, headaches, night sweats, sleeplessness and mood swings.

But in response to research suggesting that estrogen also prevents heart disease and osteoporosis, doctors have increasingly distributed the hormone for its health-promoting properties (*see p. 420*). In a recent survey of obstetricians and gynecologists, between 75 and 95 percent said they would prescribe hormones to most of their menopausal patients. [1]

The practice has precipitated a vigorous debate over the wisdom of giving the drug to healthy women. Starting in 1975, studies have shown that estrogen given alone increases the risk of endometrial cancer. The increased risk can be avoided by giving estrogen in combination with progestin — a synthetic form of the natural hormone progesterone. However, adding progestin may negate estrogen's protective power against heart disease.

What frightens many women is the possibility that the hormones will increase their risk of breast cancer. The evidence on this issue is conflicting, with some studies showing no effect or even decreased effect on breast cancer. However, the most recent data from the large-scale, 12-year Nurses' Health Study has found that women who take estrogen or estrogen-progestin combinations have an increased rate of breast cancer. [2]

The National Women's Health Network, an advocacy group in Washington, D.C., objects to the routine prescription of hormones, noting that there has never been a clinical trial to prove that hormones reduce heart disease or are safe. "In effect, women are being urged to take part in a risky, uncontrolled experiment without their fully informed consent," the group has charged. [3]

What's a woman to do? One approach is to look at the relative risks of the different diseases involved. From age 65-74, a woman has about a 6 percent risk of dying from heart disease, a 1 percent risk of dying from breast cancer, a 0.6 percent risk of dying from complications related to a hip fracture and a 0.4 percent risk of dying from endometrial cancer. One expert has calculated that the reduced risk of dying from heart disease as a result of taking estrogen would greatly outweigh the risk of death from other diseases, such as endometrial cancer. The risk of dying from endometrial cancer increases seven-fold with estrogen, for example, but it still is rarely fatal. [4]

In the last analysis, each woman has to decide for herself, based on her individual risk profile and how well she tolerates the drug. Many women discontinue it because of side effects like cramping, bleeding and water retention, or because of their fear of cancer.

"If you have a coronary heart-disease history, estrogen therapy is beneficial," says Suzanne Oparil, director of the vascular biology and hypertension program at the University of Alabama School of Medicine. "If you have a breast cancer history, it's virtually contra-indicated."

---

[1] Andrew Eccles, "The Raging Hormone Debate," *Health*, January/February 1994, p. 47.

[2] Cited in Paul E. Bechetz, "Drug Therapy: Hormonal Treatment of Postmenopausal Women," *The New England Journal of Medicine*, April 14, 1994, pp. 1062-1072.

[3] National Women's Health Network, *Taking Hormones and Women's Health: Choices, Risks and Benefits* (1993), p. 3

[4] Office of Technology Assessment, *The Menopause, Hormone Therapy and Women's Health*, May 1992, p. 105.

women between 30 and 59 and found that mortality rates for coronary heart disease were almost three times higher among men than women. As a result, researchers viewed heart disease as an epidemic among middle-aged men. Women were assumed to be relatively protected. [35]

Now it has been shown that women are not protected from heart disease. They just get it later. But the perception has persisted among some doctors and many women.

Miller, medical director of the Lipid Research Center at George Washington University, has seen many women with heart attacks. "Most of the women who come in here who've had heart attacks were badly taken care of," Miller says, citing high cholesterol levels, high blood pressures and poor living habits, including smoking. Part of it, she says, is that some doctors don't take the same aggressive steps they would with middle-aged men, insisting on serious exercise, diet regimens or even drug treatment.

Miller still encounters women whose heart disease was misdiagnosed. Rather than the classic crushing chest pain that characterizes most male heart attacks, she's more likely to see women whose attack masqueraded as indigestion or a pain in the pit of the stomach. Some went to the dentist because of jaw pain.

Yet conventional exercise tests and electrocardiograms (EKGs) — standard diagnostic techniques for men suspected of heart conditions — are about as accurate as "a flip of the coin" when it comes to women, notes internist Hoffman. "I have a large population of women who have chest-pain syndrome, abnormal EKGs but normal coronary arteries," she says.

Finally, it's a mystery as to why every kind of heart surgery is less successful for women than for men. One possibility is that the equipment designed for men's larger coronary arteries is too big for women, suggests Wallis. "My feeling is that everything in coronary surgery is targeted at men: the mind-set of the surgeon, the instruments, the technique."

Is Hormone Therapy the Solution?

Taking a cue from nature, leading researchers believe that the most promising approach to heart disease prevention is to replace the hormones a woman loses after menopause. For the first time, several full-scale clinical trials to test this theory are now under way. However, researchers have observed that healthy post-menopausal women who take estrogen pills have about half as many heart attacks as women who don't. [36]

It's hard to draw definitive conclusions about the hormone's benefits because women who decide to take estrogen tend to be healthier than women who don't. Generally, they go to doctors more often, can afford pills and return for checkups.

Researchers hope to settle the question in clinical trials, which assign women at random either to a group that gets estrogen therapy or one that gets a placebo. The first such trial, known as PEPI (the Post-Menopausal Estrogen Progestin Intervention Trial), and funded by NIH, is looking at the effect of estrogen and estrogen-progestin combinations on heart disease risk factors: cholesterol levels, blood pressure, insulin and blood clotting. The results are expected next fall.

Another trial, the Heart and Estrogen-Progestin Replacement Study, known as HERS, will investigate whether women who have had a heart attack get fewer subsequent attacks if they receive hormone therapy. The study started recruiting in December 1992 at 15 centers across the country, including Miller's Lipid Research Center. It will enlist approximately 2,500 post-menopausal women with heart disease. The five-year, $40 million clinical trial is funded by Wyeth-Ayerst Laboratories, a pharmaceutical company.

Hormone therapy remains a troublesome decision for women, however, because of side effects and increased risks of breast cancer and endometrial cancer. (*See story, p. 423.*) ■

Current Situation

Changes Ordered

The recent momentum in women's health can be traced to the 1990 GAO report requested by women in Congress. [37] The report attracted unprecedented media attention to the charge that women had been systematically excluded from research. GAO charged that NIH had failed to enforce a little-known policy requiring the inclusion of women and had consequently ignored women in studies of importance to their health.

In response to the ensuing outcry, NIH announced the creation of a new Office of Research on Women's Health in September 1990. The office's mandate was to strengthen research in diseases and medical conditions related to women and to ensure that women were represented in NIH-supported studies.

The office has been applauded by health activists for helping to create a whole new field of scientific inquiry. The office has made more than 150 research awards for the study of issues specific to women, including depression, endometriosis, eating disorders and incontinence in elderly women.

In October 1992, GAO issued a second blistering report. This time, it found women had been excluded on a large scale from trials conducted by drug manufacturers who subsequently had obtained FDA approval of their products. The GAO reported that for more than 60 percent of the drugs tested, the test population had a lower proportion of women with the corresponding disease. [38]

Even when enough women were included in drug trials, GAO found, drug companies did not analyze the results separately to determine if women had different responses to the drugs than men. GAO said this oversight was of concern because of "mounting health research" showing that women respond differently to drugs aimed at cardiovascular disease. For women of child-bearing age, GAO said such analyses were particularly important, since drug interactions with oral contraceptives can either decrease the effectiveness of contraceptives or increase the toxicity of the other drug. It noted that the potency of anti-depressants can increase "sometimes to toxic levels" when they interact with oral contraceptives.

After receiving the report, FDA urged drug companies on July 22, 1993, to include sufficient numbers of women and provide evidence of drug safety and effectiveness in both men and women. FDA also announced that it was lifting a restriction that barring women of childbearing age from participating in early clinical trials.

The restrictive policies of NIH and FDA grew out of public concern over protecting unborn children from drugs taken by pregnant women in the 1950s and '60s. In what came to be known as the "thalidomide disaster," doctors began giving thalidomide to pregnant women for use as a sedative and anti-nausea drug in the 1950s, although it had not been approved for marketing in the United States. Doctors began to notice a startling increase in the number of children born with severely deformed arms and legs. By 1962, approximately 8,000 American children had been affected by the drug.

Public aversion to including pregnant women and women of child-bearing age in studies was further bolstered by the tragedy over DES (diethylstilbestrol), a drug widely prescribed in the 1940s and '50s to pre-

Continued on p. 426

At Issue:

Should women's health be a separate medical specialty?

Karen Johnson, M.D.
Assistant clinical professor of psychiatry, University of California, San Francisco

FROM *"WOMEN'S HEALTH: DEVELOPING A NEW INTERDISCIPLINARY SPECIALTY," JOURNAL OF WOMEN'S HEALTH*, VOL. 1, NO. 2, 1992.

yes

No existing medical specialty is devoted exclusively to the comprehensive care of women. Many of us providing health care for women in a variety of existing specialties believe that the absence of such a comprehensively trained specialist is a significant problem in the health-care services offered to women. This problem could be solved through the development of an interdisciplinary specialty in women's health. . . .

The recent increased interest in women's health at all levels is gratifying; however, attention to the concerns of women has been inconsistent during this century. It would be a mistake to assume the current flurry of activity in women's health will continue without formalizing the specialty.

Having a medical specialty in women's health could be viewed much like having a room of one's own. Just as departments of women's studies have been instrumental in assuring that women's experiences are accurately represented in the academic community, a specialty in women's health would serve a similar purpose in medicine.

Those who believe it will be sufficient to simply add women's health to existing specialities would be wise to study the history of science, the sociology of knowledge and the role of values in science if the missed opportunities of other pioneers are to be avoided. Nineteenth-century scientists argued that the rigors of a university education would drain energy from women's reproductive organs. These and other socially expedient biases were used to justify the exclusion of women from positions of authority and decision making. Unless health issues are approached from a solid interdisciplinary, pro-woman perspective, I am not confident that current or future physicians will serve women significantly better than their earlier counterparts. We have already seen a great deal of the money targeted for new research in women's health funneled into the existing "old boys" research network. This is worrisome and disappointing to those of us who had hoped for more adventuresome funding and innovative projects.

Rest assured, the age-old debate of autonomy vs. integration will [rage] on as we struggle with how to include women's health in medical training. Common sense and experience suggest that we must do both. It is from the power base of a residency in women's health that efforts to mainstream are most likely to be successful. Furthermore, women's health is a separate body of knowledge and deserves to be treated as a legitimate area of inquiry.

Michelle Harrison, M.D.
Clinical associate professor of family medicine, Robert Wood Johnson Medical School, University of Medicine and Dentistry, New Brunswick, N.J.

FROM *"SHOULD WOMEN'S HEALTH BE A SEPARATE MEDICAL SPECIALTY?" GLAMOUR*, MARCH 1993.

no

Some prominent women physicians are exploring ways to make medicine more user-friendly to women. One proposal: a new medical speciality in women's health. Women's-health specialists would be trained not only in women's reproductive biology and in the different effects of certain diseases and therapies on women but also in the psychological and social issues that can come up in the treatment of female patients, such as domestic violence and sexual abuse. At first glance, this new speciality looks like a wonderful idea.

But it's not. For one thing, it would create the misleading impression that women's bodies are fundamentally different from men's. In fact, men's and women's bodies are much more similar than they are different. The vast majority of human organs and diseases behave the same way in men and women. . . .

Advocates for and against the new specialty agree that more and better medical research on women is needed. Although women utilize health-care services more often during their lifetime than men do (women need Pap smears, contraception and pregnancy care; they're usually the ones to take children to the pediatrician; and they live longer), there has been far less research on women's health than on men's. . . .

But what doctors do in their consulting offices has little or no impact on what goes on in the nation's research centers. Creating a specialty in women's medicine won't magically generate funding for research on women's health or for studies designed to take menstruation or pregnancy into account.

The campaign for a specialty in women's health takes the focus off the real problem: the need to make medicine user-friendly to women across the board. Research centers and funding institutions must include women in clinical trials. Internists should incorporate gynecology into their practices so that they can treat the whole woman, just as they treat the whole man and just as family physicians already do. Medical associations should educate their members about psychological and social factors that can influence women's physical well-being. Medical schools should teach all students to understand and respect women's bodies. Creating a corps of specialists in women's health will send a message to the rest of the profession that improving health care for women is someone else's job.

Experts Urge New Caution on Hysterectomies . . .

As appreciation grows for the disease-fighting power of women's hormones, experts are questioning the American habit of removing the organs that produce them.

At current rates, 38 percent of American women will have had their uterus surgically removed by age 60, according to the National Center for Health Statistics. The procedure, known as a hysterectomy, is the most common American surgery not related to pregnancy. European women are less than half as likely as American women to undergo hysterectomy yet can expect to live at least as long. [1]

Only about 10 percent of hysterectomies are performed for life-threatening conditions, such as cancer of the uterus. The remaining 90 percent are elective surgeries aimed at improving a woman's quality of life. [2]

The most common reason for removing a uterus is the appearance of uterine fibroids, usually benign growths that can be found in more than 25 percent of women over the age of 35. Fibroids may cause excessive bleeding, pain or no symptoms at all. Some women are convinced they must have a hysterectomy because their fibroids might become cancerous. Cancerous fibroids are rare, however, accounting for fewer than one in 1,000 cases. [3]

Half of the hysterectomies performed in the U.S. also involve the removal of both ovaries. Ovaries secrete the hormones estrogen, progesterone and testosterone. [4] These hormone levels drop dramatically when the ovaries are removed. Even when the ovaries are conserved, they may lose some of their functions once the uterus is gone, leading to menopauselike symptoms.

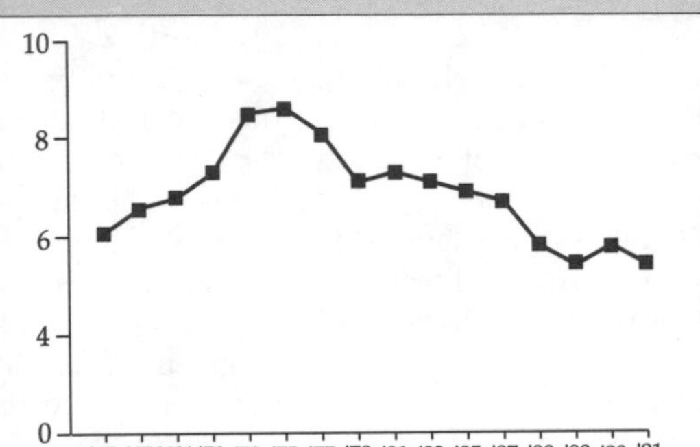

Rate at which women received hysterectomies peaked in 1975 then declined and leveled off.

** Data for 1969 are average estimates of 1968 and 1970.*

Source: National Center for Health Statistics

Scientists now believe that estrogen protects against heart disease and osteoporosis. Among pre-menopausal women, hysterectomy increases the risk of coronary heart disease up to three times. Women with hysterectomies suffer an increased rate of osteoporosis-related bone fractures. [5]

Although the role of testosterone in women's sex drive is hotly debated, some scientists believe it may be important. Doctors in England and Australia are more likely than American doctors to prescribe low-dose testosterone for women complaining of flagging libido and depression. [6] And diminished sexual response is one complaint of women who undergo hysterectomy.

Into the 1970s, doctors often told a woman who had completed her family that she had no more need for her uterus. One commonly reported but controversial reason for removing ovaries as part of a hysterectomy was to prevent ovarian cancer. It was widely believed that the only function of the uterus was to provide housing for the developing fetus and that ovarian hormones could easily be replaced. [7]

That view has come under challenge. "We're saying, 'Wait a minute. How can we intervene before it gets to the point of needing a hysterectomy?' " says Judith H. LaRosa, deputy director of the Office of Women's Health Research at the National Institutes of Health (NIH).

The medical community also has become more cautious. After peaking in 1975, rates of hysterectomy declined steadily

scribed in the 1940s and '50s to prevent miscarriage. By the late 1960s and early '70s, the daughters of women who had taken DES during pregnancy began suffering from a rare cancer and other health problems, including infertility.

In 1975, a national commission issued guidelines, still in effect, severely limiting the conditions under which pregnant women may participate in federally funded research. [39]

But in 1990, "policies once presented as protective were now labeled as paternalistic and discriminatory," observed an Institute of Medicine panel that recommended including pregnant women in studies earlier this year.* Politicians and scientists had begun to realize, the panel said, that "policies designed to protect certain populations from research risk may actually expose these populations to a greater risk of another kind: a lack of data about their health." [40] ■

* As of May 1994, NIH was reviewing its regulations regarding pregnant women but had made no changes.

OUTLOOK

New Initiatives

At the Medical College of Pennsylvania, students studying the case of a man suffering a heart attack now have to discuss how the symptoms might differ in a woman patient. In the hypothetical case of a woman patient rapidly losing weight, students

. . . as Importance of Hormones Is Recognized

until the late 1980s. Rates have remained level since 1988.

In the 1980s, doctors were less likely to recommend hysterectomy as a form of permanent birth control because of the growing use of tubal ligation, a form of female sterilization with fewer complications. Oral contraceptives also helped reduce some of the bleeding and pain symptoms that led to hysterectomies. [8] More recently, hormone therapy and new surgical procedures have been introduced as alternatives to hysterectomy for controlling pain and other symptoms.

Another major reason for the decline may be the rise of well-read consumers like Altadena, Calif., housewife Linda Wright. She was horrified when her doctor advised an immediate hysterectomy to deal with rapidly growing fibroid tumors six years ago. "I said I was not prepared for this castration and this instant menopause," recalls Wright, who was 48 at the time.

For several years, she searched for a doctor who was willing to remove the fibroids without taking out her uterus. Wright had read about menopausal symptoms like dryness in the vagina caused by hysterectomy. "I wanted to feel sexy and sexual," she says, "and I felt if I did not have my uterus, I would be kidding myself."

But as Wright found out, many doctors prefer to do a hysterectomy because it is an easier, faster surgery than removing fibroids one by one. Compared with the less-than-one-hour standard for a hysterectomy, it took seven hours of surgery to remove the 40 tumors that had grown in Wright's uterus.

Anthony Mora Communications

Vicki G. Hufnagel, M.D.

The doctor who performed the surgery, Vicki G. Hufnagel, specializes in preserving women's reproductive organs. Chairman of the department of female reconstructive surgery at Thompson Memorial Hospital in Burbank, Calif., Hufnagel says that there is growing use of the procedure known as myomectomy, in which fibroids are surgically removed but leave the uterus intact. "Surgeons are promoting it, and there's an awareness that didn't exist 10 years ago," she says.

But Hufnagel thinks hysterectomy rates are still too high. Medical schools, she says, have not yet overhauled their "why not?" attitude toward hysterectomy. And while growing numbers of women may push for alternatives to hysterectomy, she says, "There's not the volume of physicians [needed] to do high-tech, conservative surgery."

[1] Lynn Payer, "Hysterectomy," *Vogue*, June 1990, p. 152.

[2] Office of Technology Assessment, *The Menopause, Hormone Therapy and Women's Health*, May 1992, pp. 20-21.

[3] See Jane E. Brody, "Hysterectomies, the second-most frequent operation, need not be so common, some say," *The New York Times*, Jan. 3, 1991, p. B5.

[4] Lynne S. Wilcox et al., "Hysterectomy in the United States, 1988-1990," *Obstetrics and Gynecology*, April 1994, pp. 549-553.

[5] Office of Technology Assessment, *op. cit.*, p. 20.

[6] Natalie Angier, "Male Hormone Molds Women, Too, in Mind and Body," *The New York Times*, May 3, 1994, p. C1, and "Factor in Female Sexuality," p. C13.

[7] Office of Technology Assessment, *op. cit.*, p. 20.

[8] Wilcox et al., *op. cit.*, p. 554.

now add eating disorders to the list of possible causes.

The school is the first in the nation to integrate women's health throughout its curriculum as a required component. Faculty members hope to persuade other medical schools and accrediting bodies to incorporate women's health subjects into courses and exam requirements. This September, a new organization founded at the school, the National Academy on Women's Health Medical Education, will review a model curriculum to share with other medical schools.

To reach practicing doctors, the American Medical Women's Association in Alexandria, Va., held a three-day seminar last October on health problems of women 40-79 to teach physicians "what they didn't learn in medical school." [41] The organization, representing 13,000 female physicians and medical students, plans to hold a seminar on health issues for younger women this October in Philadelphia.

For medical research and education, incorporating women's health as a separate subject has been a revolutionary breakthrough in attitude in a few short years. "Now it's acceptable to look for gender differences and to study the gender differences as a field, not as 'a confusing variable,' " says Haseltine of the Center for Population Research.

Women's organizations are now turning their attention to health-care reform as "a unique opportunity to redress many of the inequities women have faced securing health care for themselves and their families," according to the Campaign for Women's Health, a coalition of 90 women's organizations lobbying to get women's health addressed by health-care reform legislation.

The campaign stresses the importance of including in any health-insurance package many of the preventive health needs that women have had to pay for out-of-pocket in the past, including mammograms, contraceptives and Pap smears.

The victories that women activists have won in only four years have given them new confidence about the future. "If we keep progressing at the rate we're going, eventually we'll be unstoppable," says Pearson of the National Women's Health Network. "Women professionals and women health activists will be so much a part of the process that we won't need a movement pushing or watchdogging." ■

Sarah Glazer is a freelance writer in Washington who specializes in health and social-policy issues.

Notes

[1] The symposium, "Women's Health: Critical Issues in the 1990s," was sponsored by the Smithsonian Institution and the American Dietetic Association, March 5, 1994. Oparil is a professor of medicine at the University of Alabama School of Medicine.

[2] Cited in Nanette K. Wenger et al., "Cardiovascular Health and Disease in Women," *The New England Journal of Medicine,* July 22, 1993, pp. 247-256. However, a recent study at Duke University found women were treated just as aggressively as men. See Daniel B. Mark, Linda K. Shaw, Elizabeth R. DeLong, Robert M. Califf and David B. Pryor, "Absence of Sex Bias in the Referral of Patients for Cardiac Catheterization," *The New England Journal of Medicine,* April 21, 1994, pp. 1101-1106, and "Study Suggests Equitable Female Heart Treatment," *The Washington Post,* April 21, 1994, p. A4.

[3] Steering Committee of the Physicians' Health Study Research Group, "Final Report on the Aspirin Component of the Ongoing Physicians' Health Study," *The New England Journal of Medicine,* July 20, 1989, pp. 129-135.

[4] Haseltine founded the Society for the Advancement of Women's Health Research in 1990 to push for increased study of disorders that afflict women alone or differently from men. See "Towards a Women's Health Research Agenda: Findings of the Scientific Advisory Meeting," the summary of an April 23, 1991, meeting convened by the society.

[5] Quoted in Janny Scott, "Susan Love: Setting the Agenda for the Politics of Breast Cancer," *Los Angeles Times,* Dec. 5, 1993, p. M3.

[6] Eileen Nechas and Denise Foley, *Unequal Treatment: What You Don't Know About How Women are Mistreated by the Medical Community* (1994), p. 15.

[7] The medical school is at the University of Medicine and Dentistry of New Jersey.

[8] Michelle Harrison, "Women's Health as a Specialty: A Deceptive Solution," *Journal of Women's Health,* Vol. 1, No. 2, 1992, p. 102.

[9] Karen Johnson, "Women's Health: Developing a New Interdisciplinary Specialty, *Journal of Women's Health,* Vol. 1, No. 2, 1992, pp. 95-99.

[10] Michelle Harrison, "Women's Health as a Specialty: A Deceptive Solution," *Journal of Women's Health,* Vol. 1, No. 2, 1992, pp. 103, 105.

[11] Cited in Linda Barthauer, "A Woman's Touch," *The New Physician,* September 1989, p. 16.

[12] Nicole Lurie et al., "Preventive Care for Women: Does the Sex of the Physician Matter?" *The New England Journal of Medicine,* Aug. 12, 1993, pp. 478-82.

[13] American College of Obstetricians and Gynecologists, Press Release, "Poll Shows Women Rely on Ob-gyns for Primary Care," Oct. 29, 1993.

[14] The study added a women's cohort 20 years after it started in 1958. Currently, 441 out of some 1,800 participants are women. See "Normal Human Aging: The Baltimore Longitudinal Study of Aging, National Institutes of Health" (1984), and Nechas and Foley, *op. cit.,* pp. 107-108.

[15] Anna C. Mastroianni et al., eds., *Women and Health Research,* Vol. 1, 1994, p. 48.

[16] *Ibid.,* p. 113.

[17] *Ibid.,* p. 91.

[18] The mandate is part of the NIH Revitalization Act, which was signed into law June 10, 1993.

[19] See Eliot Marshall, "New Law Brings Affirmative Action to Clinical Research," *Science,* February 1994, p. 602.

[20] Marcia Angell, "Caring for Women's Health — What is the Problem?" *The New England Journal of Medicine,* July 22, 1993, pp. 271-72.

[21] Mastroianni et al., *op. cit.* See also "Women and AIDS," *The CQ Researcher,* Dec. 25, 1992, pp. 1121-1144.

[22] *Ibid.,* p. 7.

[23] See Alissa J. Rubin, "New Breast Cancer Research Funding," *Congressional Quarterly Weekly Report,* May 29, 1993, pp. 1364-65.

[24] Susan M. Love, "Breast Cancer," *The Journal of the American Medical Association,* May 12, 1993, p. 2417.

[25] Charles Marwick, "NCI Changes Its Stance on Mammography," *The Journal of the American Medical Association,* Jan. 12, 1994, p. 96.

[26] Devra Lee Davis and Susan M. Love, "Mammographic Screening," *The Journal of the American Medical Association,* Jan. 12, 1994, pp. 152-153.

[27] Scott, *op. cit.,* p. M3.

[28] Diana Jean Schemo, "Long Island Breast Cancer is Possibly Linked to Chemical Sites," *The New York Times,* April 13, 1994.

[29] Institute of Medicine, *Strategies for Managing the Breast Cancer Research Program: A Report to the U.S. Army Medical Research and Development Command* (1993), p. 1.

[30] Lawrence K. Altman, "U.S. Halts Recruitment of Cancer Patients for Studies, Pointing to Flaws in Oversight," *The New York Times,* March 30, 1994, p. B8.

[31] Lawrence K. Altman, "Flawed Breast Cancer Study Faces Cutoff of Financing," *The New York Times,* May 4, 1993.

[32] Associated Press, "Cancer Study Bars Two From Leadership Roles," *The Washington Post,* May 8, 1994, p. A6.

[33] Robin Herman, "Research Fraud Breaks Chain of Trust," *The Washington Post Health Section,* April 19, 1994, pp. 6, 8, 9.

[34] Wenger et al., *op. cit.,* p. 247.

[35] Mastroianni, *op. cit.,* p. 64.

[36] Wenger et al., *op. cit.,* p. 249.

[37] The report was unveiled June 18, 1990, at a hearing of the House Energy and Commerce Subcommittee on Health and the Environment, chaired by Rep. Henry A. Waxman, D-Calif.

[38] General Accounting Office, *Women's Health: FDA Needs to Ensure More Study of Gender Differences in Prescription Drug Testing,* October 1992.

[39] The guidelines were issued by the National Commission for the Protection of Human Subjects of Biomedical and Behavioral Research.

[40] Mastroianni, *op. cit.,* p. 47.

[41] Elizabeth Rosenthal, "Is Women's Health Harmed by Medical Specialization?" *The New York Times,* Oct. 13, 1993, p. A1, C13.

Bibliography

Selected Sources Used

Books

Mastroianni, Anna C., et al., eds., *Women and Health Research: Ethical and Legal Issues of Including Women in Clinical Studies,* Vol. 1, National Academy Press, 1994.
This report gained press attention for its recommendation that pregnant women be eligible to participate in clinical studies of drugs and other new medical treatments. The report was prepared by an expert panel appointed by the Institute of Medicine, an arm of the National Academy of Sciences. It provides useful historical and medical background to the debate over women's participation in clinical research.

Nechas, Eileen and Denise Foley, *Unequal Treatment: What You Don't Know About How Women are Mistreated by the Medical Community,* Simon and Schuster, 1994.
Two journalists make an impassioned argument that there is pervasive prejudice against women in the medical community, using the exclusion of women from landmark medical studies as their starting point.

Articles

Angier, Natalie, "Male Hormone Molds Women, Too, in Mind and Body," *The New York Times,* May 3, 1994, pp. C1, C13.
As a byproduct of the growing interest in women's health, scientists are looking at how women's levels of testosterone affect their sex drive and whether the hormone is necessary to maintain bone density and muscle mass into old age.

"Breast Cancer: A Special Report," *Washington Post Health Section,* April 19, 1994, pp. 5-25.
This special section looks at new developments in breast cancer — bone marrow transplants as an unproven treatment and the search for the gene that causes familial breast cancer. The section also reviews ongoing debates over mammography, the experimental drug tamoxifen and lumpectomy vs. mastectomy.

Herman, Robert, "What Doctors Don't Know About Women," *Washington Post Health Section,* Dec. 8, 1992, pp. 10-14.
This is a good review of the burning questions in women's health and what research is needed to fill the gaps.

LaRosa, Judith H., and Vivian W. Pinn, "Gender Bias in Biomedical Research," *Journal of the American Medical Women's Association,* September/October 1993, pp. 145-151.
The director and deputy director of the Office of Research on Women's Health of the National Institutes of Health review the reasons why women have been excluded from several major medical studies.

Rosenthal, Elisabeth, "Is Women's Health Harmed by Medical Specialization?" *The New York Times,* Oct. 13, 1993, pp. A1, C14.
The author looks at the criticism that women's health is fragmented among too many medical specialties and discusses some emerging solutions.

Rubin, Rita, "Estrogen Anxiety," *U.S. News and World Report,* April 14, 1994, pp. 60-64.
The article discusses the scientific debate over the health benefits and risks of hormone therapy after menopause.

Turk, Michele, "The Neglected Sex," *American Health,* December 1993, pp. 54-57.
This article discusses the new National Institutes of Health study of women.

Reports and Studies

Institute of Medicine, *An Assessment of the NIH Women's Health Initiative,* National Academy Press, 1993.
This report, issued by an Institute of Medicine expert panel, raised questions about the link between dietary fat and breast cancer. The link is one of several women's health issues that the National Institutes of Health is studying in a large-scale study of women.

National Women's Health Network, *Taking Hormones and Women's Health,* 1993.
The advocacy organization takes a critical view of routine hormone therapy in this position paper.

Office of Technology Assessment, U.S. Congress, *The Menopause, Hormone Therapy and Women's Health,* May 1992.
This report provides a clearly written description of what is known and unknown about women's physiology after menopause.

Office of Research on Women's Health, *Report of the National Institutes of Health: Opportunities for Research on Women's Health,* National Institutes of Health, September 1992.
This report grew out of the institutes' first conference on women's health, held Sept. 4-6, 1991. It provides background on health issues of major concern to women and areas in which research is need.

The Next Step

Additional information from UMI's Newspaper & Periodical Abstracts database

Breast Cancer Issues

Kolata, Gina, "Breast implant companies dispute claim of settlement," *The New York Times,* March 19, 1994, p. A8.

Lawyers representing women who had silicone breast implants and the companies that made the devices earlier announced that they had reached a tentative agreement on a $4.75 billion fund to compensate the women for health problems. But several principals in the talks now say that while the deal is still progressing, it is not necessarily a foregone conclusion that it will be completed.

Points, Dana, "Breast cancer news flash," *Family Circle,* March 16, 1994, p. 66.

The age at which women should start having mammograms is at the center of one of the hottest women's health debates in decades. Recent developments in the study of breast cancer are discussed.

Tanouye, Elyse, "Mammograms: Should she or shouldn't she?" *The Wall Street Journal,* Feb. 22, 1994, p. B1.

Ever since the National Cancer Institute said it found no conclusive evidence that regular mammograms reduce the death rate from breast cancer for women under 50, health groups like the American Cancer Society and the American Medical Women's Association have been receiving inquiries from women confused about whether routine mammograms are necessary. The disagreement among medical professionals about the necessity of mammograms is examined.

Court Decisions

"Civil Rights Act — Section 1985(3)," *Harvard Law Review,* November 1993, pp. 332-341.

In the recent case of *Bray v. Alexandria Women's Health Clinic,* the Supreme Court rejected the claim that Operation Rescue blockades of abortion clinics constituted private conspiracies to violate civil rights and were remediable under Title 42 of the United States Code, Section 1985(3). The decision's implications are examined.

"Judge warns lawyers in implant suit," *Boston Globe,* March 13, 1994, p. 15.

Lawyers for women who claimed health problems from breast implants may keep no more than 25 percent of whatever their clients win, which could be in the billions, a federal judge has said.

"Obstacle to Pennsylvania abortion law is lifted," *The New York Times,* Jan. 30, 1994, p. 23.

Women's health clinics that provide abortions have decided against asking a federal appeals court in Philadelphia to reconsider its decision to allow a Pennsylvania abortion-control law to take effect. Barring an appeal to the Supreme Court, the appeals court will lift an injunction against the law Feb. 4, 1994. The law requires women seeking abortions to receive counseling, wait 24 hours, and, if they are under 18, get parental permission.

Federal Action

Hasson, Judi, "An impassioned plea for care for women," *USA Today,* March 9, 1994, p. A7.

Mourning the loss of two friends from ovarian cancer, Sen. Patty Murray, D-Wash., demanded that Congress make sure women's health issues are protected under reform. In a deeply personal speech on the Senate floor, Murray said women have gotten short shrift in coverage of preventive care.

Hasson, Judi, "Women say alternative health plan falls short," *USA Today,* Feb. 15, 1994, p. A4.

A group of 29 female lawmakers said they will not support Rep. Jim Cooper's, D-Tenn., health-reform proposal because it "short-changes women's health." The group, in a letter to the sponsor of a plan rivaling President Clinton's, criticized the plan because it does not specifically provide coverage for women's health needs, such as Pap smears and mammograms.

Kolbert, Kathryn, "The Clinton plan needs stronger safeguards against gender bias, especially in regard to women's reproductive services," *National Law Journal,* Feb. 7, 1994, p. 34.

In order to avert litigation, President Clinton's proposed health-care system must incorporate women's health needs fully. Health-care reform issues are discussed in the context of current sex-discrimination law.

Newman, Barbara, "Health care reform and women's needs," *San Francisco Chronicle,* Jan. 19, 1994, p. A21.

Newman comments that despite the well-publicized presence of three powerful women concerned with health, Donna Shalala, Joycelyn Elders and Hillary Clinton, the Clinton health-care plan, which they are promoting, comes nowhere near meeting American women's health needs.

"Optimism accompanies women's health legislation to Congress," *Nation's Health,* November 1993, p. 5.

The Congressional Caucus for Women's Health Issues introduced the Women's Health Equity Act of 1993 (WHEA) on Sept. 14, 1993. The WHEA addresses a broad range of women's health concerns, including osteoporosis.

Health-care Equity

Fugh-Berman, Adriane, "Training doctors to care for women," *Technology Review,* February 1994, pp. 34-40.

An ambitious proposal, already provoking criticism from the medical establishment, would create a specialty in women's health. Such a move not only might remedy deficiencies in the treatment of female patients but also provide a model for more effective care for everyone else.

Hirsh, Kim S., "Health gap," ***Chicago Tribune,*** **Jan. 23, 1994, p. 1.**

Leaders of the American Medical Women's Association say that American women must shuttle among too many doctors for their care because most doctors don't known enough about women's health to treat the "whole" patient.

Madison, Mary, "Women's health director talks of goals in new job," ***San Francisco Chronicle,*** **Jan. 18, 1994, p. C3.**

Getting American women a fair shake from science and medicine is the dream of Susan Blumenthal, whose new job is to make America's women healthier. Blumenthal heads the new Office of Women's Health in the Department of Health and Human Services.

Pinkney, Deborah Shelton, "AMWA program to reverse women's health inequities," ***American Medical News,*** **Nov. 22, 1993, pp. 4-5.**

The American Medical Women's Association has unveiled an advanced curriculum that is a model for redressing inequities in medicine's treatment of women. The three-day program is detailed.

Shepard, Robert, "2nd opinions," ***Chicago Tribune,*** **Jan. 30, 1994, p. 1.**

The $625 million Women's Health Initiative has wide support in the medical community and in Congress because of a consensus that diseases that primarily affect women have received too little study, but researchers disagree on priorities and whether the costs are justified. The controversy has landed in the lap of NIH Director Harold Varmus.

Tuller, David, "Second-class care motivates revolution in women's health," ***San Francisco Chronicle,*** **Nov. 22, 1993, p. A1.**

In a special report on women's health, "the second women's health movement" is featured. The movement is a broad-based effort to revolutionize the way American health care is researched, financed and delivered, and is vitally concerned with such issues as breast cancer, cardiovascular disease, lung cancer, AIDS research and the gender gap in health research.

Yamarick, Janelle R., "Women's health care," ***Atlanta Constitution,*** **April 8, 1994, p. A12.**

In a letter to the editor, Janelle R. Yamarick of the Georgia Abortion and Reproductive Rights Action League says that Rep. Jim Cooper's, D-Tenn., health-care reform bill shortchanges women's health.

Reproductive Concerns

Sedgwick, John, "The estrogen report," ***Self,*** **March 1994, pp. 132-135.**

Estrogen plays a central role in women's health beyond reproduction. The medical community's beliefs about estrogen and its connection with various medical problems are examined.

"Women's Voices '94 — A declaration on population policies," ***Population & Development Review,*** **September 1993, pp. 637-740.**

The text of "Women's Voices '94 — Women's Declaration on Population Policies," a draft created by women's health advocates all over the world that focuses on ethical issues of women's reproductive health and reproductive rights, is presented.

Research and Studies

Painter, Kim, "Goals aren't at issue; Cost and focus are," ***USA Today,*** **Nov. 2, 1993, p. A1.**

Experts assembled by the private Institute of Medicine say the 160,000-woman Women's Health Initiative study, the most hyped, most politically popular and most expensive health study ever launched by the federal government, won't answer long-neglected questions for which it is targeted and will cost more than the projected $625 million.

Sachs, Jessica Snyder, "Good news about women's health," ***New Woman,*** **January 1994, p. 122.**

Two important advances in women's medicine — one in heart disease and the other in breast cancer—are discussed. Cardiologists have begun to use more effective tests, such as the stress echocardiogram, with female patients.

Saltus, Richard, "Cranberry juice fights bacteria, study finds," ***Boston Globe,*** **March 9, 1994, p. 18.**

In a bit of good news for women's health and for the cranberry industry, a new study of an old remedy has shown that drinking cranberry juice squelches bacteria that cause urinary tract infections.

Tuller, David, "Advocacy groups quarreling over research funds, reforms," ***San Francisco Chronicle,*** **Nov. 22, 1993, p. A8.**

Several advocacy groups for women's health issues are in disagreement over which projects to fund, as well as which health-care problems are to be treated as priorities.

Younger, Lucille W., "Black women have 30 percent more fibroids than white women," ***Chicago Defender,*** **Dec. 28, 1993, p. 3.**

According to Nelson Stringer, a physician who specializes in women's health care, African American women have 30 percent more fibroids, non-cancerous tumors of the uterus that enlarge in women of reproductive age, than their white counterparts. The condition and its treatment are described.

Back Issues

Great Research on Current Issues Starts Right Here...Recent topics covered by The CQ Researcher are listed below. Before May 1991, reports were published under the name of Editorial Research Reports.

NOVEMBER 1992
Physical Fitness
Privatization
Paying for College
U.S. Policy in Asia

DECEMBER 1992
Crackdown on Smoking
The New CIA
Eating Disorders
Women and AIDS

JANUARY 1993
Hate Crimes
Child Sexual Abuse
Nuclear Fusion
U.S. Trade Policy

FEBRUARY 1993
Community Policing
Europe's New Right
School Censorship
Violence Against Women

MARCH 1993
Gay Rights
Aid to Russia
War on Drugs
TV Violence

Back issues are available for $4.00 (subscribers) or $7.00 (non-subscribers). Quantity discounts apply to orders over ten. To order, call Congressional Quarterly Customer Service at (202) 887-8621.

Binders are available for $16.00. To order call 1-800-638-1710. Please refer to stock number 648.

APRIL 1993
Head Start
High-Speed Rail
Children's Legal Rights
Muslims in America

MAY 1993
Cults in America
Preventing Teen Pregnancy
Software Piracy
National Parks

JUNE 1993
Food Safety
Prostitution
Childhood Immunizations
National Service

JULY 1993
Electric Cars
Population Growth
Downward Mobility
Intelligence Testing

AUGUST 1993
Mental Illness
Bilingual Education
Foreign Policy Burden
School Funding

SEPTEMBER 1993
Suburban Crime
Public Housing
Supreme Court Preview
Immigration Reform

OCTOBER 1993
Airline Safety
Disaster Response
Science in the Courtroom
The Glass Ceiling

NOVEMBER 1993
Paying for Retirement
Charitable Giving
Privacy in the Workplace
Adoption

DECEMBER 1993
U.S. Vietnam-Relations
Learning Disabilities
Child Care
Space Program's Future

JANUARY 1994
Racial Tensions in Schools
South Africa's Future
Worker Retraining
Regulating Pesticides

FEBRUARY 1994
Prison Overcrowding
Water Quality
Religion in Schools
Juvenile Justice

MARCH 1994
Underground Economy
Education Standards
Gambling Boom
Private Management of Public Schools

APRIL 1994
Reproductive Ethics
U.S.-China Trade
Soccer in America
Talk Show Democracy

MAY 1993
Traffic Congestion

Future Topics

- ***Mutual Funds***
- ***Political Scandals***
- ***Education and Gender***

THE CQ Researcher

PUBLISHED BY CONGRESSIONAL QUARTERLY INC.

ABS ABT ABW ABY ABZ

MUTUAL FUNDS

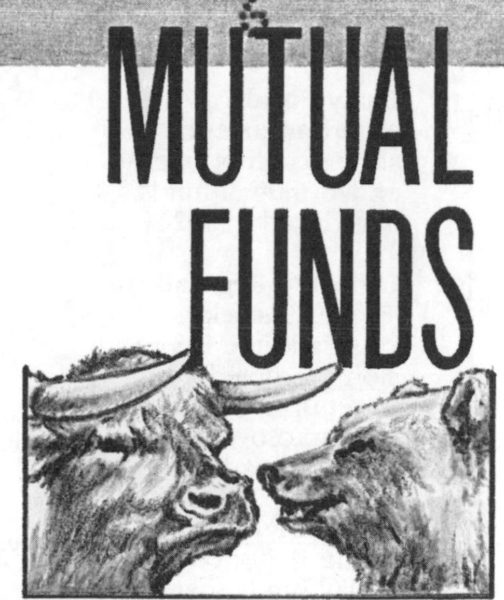

Are mutual funds safe investments?

Some 38 million Americans have invested more than $2 trillion in mutual funds. These investment pools have been around for years, offering small investors an opportunity to enter the stock and bond markets alongside wealthy individuals, pension funds and insurance companies. But never have mutual funds garnered the kind of attention — and money — that they have in the past few years. Lured by the promise of high returns at a time when interest rates on bank certificates of deposit were low, many consumers switched to mutual funds as an alternative means of saving for such big items as the down payment on a house, college tuition and retirement. Some economists worry, however, that newcomers to mutual funds may not fully understand the risks involved.

INSIDE THIS ISSUE

CQ May 20, 1994 • Volume 4, No. 19 • 433-456

Formerly Editorial Research Reports

Mutual Funds

COVER: BARBARA SASSA-DANIELS

May 20, 1994
Volume 4, No. 19

The CQ Researcher (ISSN 1056-2036). Formerly Editorial Research Reports. Published weekly (48 times per year, not printed the first Friday of any month with five Fridays) by Congressional Quarterly Inc., 1414 22nd St., N.W., Washington, D.C. 20037. Rates are furnished upon request. Second-class postage paid at Washington, D.C. POSTMASTER: Send address changes to The CQ Researcher, 1414 22nd St., N.W., Washington, D.C. 20037.

Mutual Funds

BY MARY H. COOPER

THE ISSUES

Last month's fall in the stock market jangled investors' nerves more than usual. It's not that the first major decline in three years came as a surprise. For months, market experts had warned that securities were overpriced and due for what they delicately call a "correction." In any case, volatility is a fact of life in the securities business.

What distinguished this downturn was mounting concern about its potential impact on a vast and growing component of the financial markets — the nation's 4,700 mutual funds. These investment pools have proliferated in recent years and today boast assets of $2.1 trillion. That's more than the combined gross domestic product of Britain and France.

In January alone, mutual funds of stocks and bonds attracted a record $32 billion in "net inflow" (new investments minus shares sold), according to the Investment Company Institute, the industry's trade group. The institute estimates that one American household in four now holds shares in mutual funds.

The recent market slide hit both stocks and bonds, the mainstays of the mutual fund industry.* Before the slide, stock prices had been pushed up as investors, sensing a long-awaited pickup in business activity, jumped into the market in search of higher returns than they could get with bank CDs (certificates of deposit). It was only a matter of time, economists predicted, before these inflated stock prices would fall.

Triggering the collapse was a move by the Federal Reserve Board to edge

up short-term interest rates in hope of slowing inflation in the expanding economy. The Fed's Feb. 4 action ended a decade-long decline in interest rates. It also ended the steady climb of the Dow Jones industrial average (*see glossary, p. 450*) from 2365 in October 1990 to nearly 4000 in January.* Higher interest rates can make savings accounts, which are risk-free, more attractive than stocks, pushing down share prices. Higher rates also put a damper on lending, potentially hindering future business expansion. Because bond prices fall as interest rates rise, the bond market slipped, too.

The market decline took a toll on mutual funds. According to Lipper Analytical Services, which tracks mutual funds, general, or non-specialized, stock funds lost 3.3 percent during the first quarter, which ended March 31. That was the worst performance for stock funds since the 1990 Persian Gulf crisis sent the market into a tailspin. Would shareholders sell off their shares at depressed prices for fear of losing even more of their savings? Or would they listen to the market experts and ride out the storm, anticipating higher returns in the future?

So far, mutual fund investors have remained relatively calm. Although the Dow dropped nearly 10 percent from its high in late January to the most recent low in the first week of April, only during that week did investors sell more shares in stock mutual funds than they bought. Since then, the market has picked up, as the Dow topped 3653 points May 12, though it still fell short of the January peak.

But many experts predict that last month's correction was the beginning of a slowdown in market performance that could last for years. If they are right, some fear that mutual fund investors may turn tail and pull out. Many investors are new to the stock market, drawn by recent annual returns of 40 percent or more for some funds.[1] "We just had the most remarkable period in history, when it was easy to make money in stocks and bonds," says Lipper President A. Michael Lipper. "New investors think this is normal, but it isn't."

Mutual funds have been around for 70 years, offering professional financial management to investors who want to tap into the superior long-term earnings record of the securities markets without having to manage their own holdings of shares of individual companies. Often accepting initial investments of less than $1,000, mutual funds make it easy for middle-income Americans to play the stock and bond markets, once seen as the exclusive realm of the rich. Because individual funds are diversified, containing a number of different holdings, the risks are distributed.

Despite such benefits, it was not until the 1980s that mutual funds became major players in the financial markets. Most Americans preferred to

* In addition to mutual funds containing stocks, bonds or mixtures of each, there are also funds specializing in money markets, international stocks, tax-free municipal bonds and many other investment vehicles.

* Between Feb. 4 and April 18, the Fed three times added a quarter-point to the federal funds rate, the interest that financial institutions charge each other for overnight loans. The rate rose from 3 percent to 3.75 percent over the period. In response to the Fed's action, banks raised the prime rate, the interest they charge for short-term loans to their best customers, from 6 percent to 6.75 percent.

Total Assets of Mutual Funds

The total assets of all mutual funds available in the United States have steadily increased over the past 15 years from $94.5 billion in 1979 to more than $2 trillion.

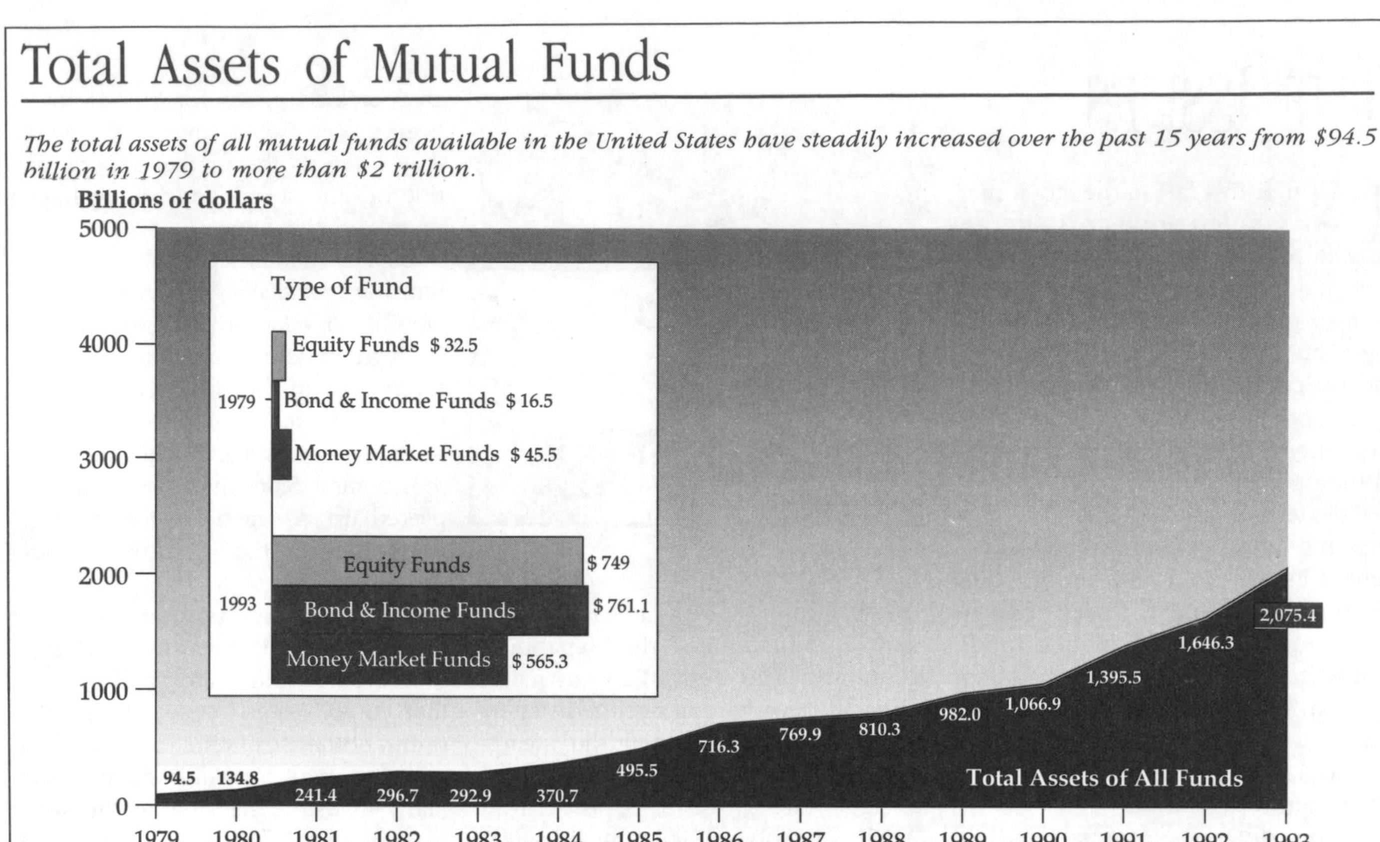

Source: Investment Company Institute, summer 1993

put their savings in banks and savings and loans, where deposits of up to $100,000 are protected by the Federal Deposit Insurance Corporation (FDIC). And while securities historically have appreciated much more over the long term than bank deposits and certificates of deposit, mutual funds offer no guarantees against losses.

Mutual funds have become more attractive in recent years as interest rates have fallen to their lowest levels in two decades. Eager to keep their customers, many banks have started selling mutual funds, enabling depositors to shift their savings from poorly performing CDs to funds without leaving the bank lobby. About a third of the more than 4,700 U.S. mutual funds are available in banks.

Another draw to the funds has been a proliferation of financial information in the news media. "All you have to do is open *Newsweek* or many of the newspapers, and you have this extremely readable, hard-nosed, commonsense but sophisticated approach to investment," says John Collins, a spokesman for the Investment Company Institute. "The information is better these days than it ever was, and it's everywhere."

One reason consumers are devouring financial news is the growing concern over job security and retirement income.[2] "People today are saving more, in part out of the uncertainty of the job market," Lipper says. "Another reason for the need to build capital is the threat posed by living too long."

Traditional, "defined-benefit" retirement plans, which guarantee retirees a fixed monthly income, are being replaced with less secure plans that shift the financial responsibility from the employer to the employee. These "defined-contribution" plans, which include 401(k) tax-deferred savings plans, leave it up to the employee to decide how much money to contribute to his retirement fund. More and more plans also let employees allocate their contributions among a number of investment options, including stock funds, bond funds and other vehicles.

Financial-planning columns warn workers that unless they tap into the stock market's superior long-term performance for their defined-contribution plans, they may face an unexpected decline in living standards upon retirement. Judging from the increasing volume of stock mutual fund purchases, consumers are following that advice. "There has been a big increase in cash flow to mutual funds," says Lipper. "A good bit of it is coming from 401(k)s and similar retirement plans."

While few dispute the allure of mutual funds, consumer advocates

Sorting Out Mutual Funds

A staggering array of mutual funds compete for investors' money. While making a choice can be daunting, the wide variety offers investors plenty of opportunity to find funds suited to their needs and to spread their investment dollars among different types of funds, thus reducing their risk of losses in any one. * In essence, there are four broad fund categories:

Common stock funds account for more than 1,400 of the 4,700 publicly traded mutual funds on the market today. They generally can be identified according to five different investment goals:

Growth funds primarily seek appreciation of investors' capital. Dividend income is a secondary concern.

Value funds try to achieve both growth and income.

Equity income funds strive for high dividend income.

Broad-based specialty funds make purchases in broad sectors of the market, such as international (non-U.S.) and global (including U.S.) stocks or the stocks of mid-sized companies.

Concentrated specialty funds buy only the stocks of one industry, such as high technology, health care or utilities.

Bond funds are more numerous and more diversified than stock funds. There are almost 1,700 bond funds in eight basic categories:

U.S. government funds invest in Treasury bills.

Mortgage-backed bond funds invest in securities issued by the Government National Mortgage Association (GNMA), known as Ginny Mae.

Investment-grade corporate bond funds invest in bonds issued by the soundest U.S. companies.

Medium-grade corporate bond funds pose higher risks, and offer greater potential returns, by focusing on loans to smaller or less creditworthy businesses.

High-yield corporate bond funds invest in so-called junk bonds, the riskiest corporate issues.

Investment-grade municipal bond funds focus on creditworthy local governments.

High-yield municipal bond funds invest in riskier local government bonds.

Global bond funds, the broadest of the lot, invest in bonds in the United States and abroad.

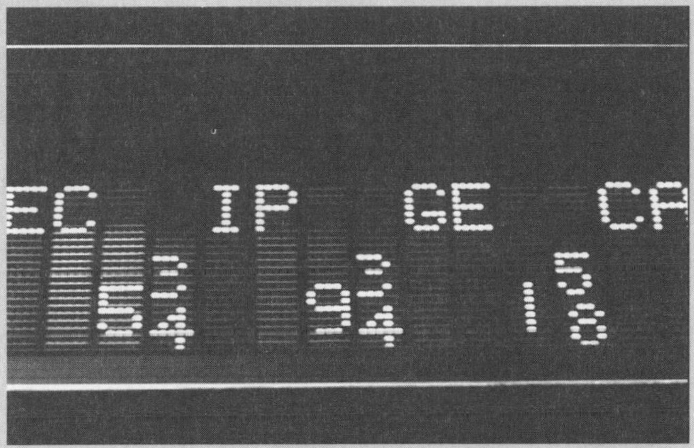

Stock market quotations on an electronic ticker.

Money-market funds come in taxable and tax-exempt varieties; there are about 1,000 on the market. Tax-exempts invest in municipal bonds, the others in short-term instruments such as bank CDs, Treasury bills and short-term corporate loans. They offer check-writing privileges and interest rates that are higher than bank rates. Money-market funds are generally considered to be quite safe, but they are not insured.

Balanced funds create broad diversification by investing in stocks, bonds and money-market instruments. There are about 600 balanced funds, generally falling into one of three categories:

Equity-oriented balanced funds invest slightly over half their assets in stocks, the rest mostly in investment-grade bonds.

Income-oriented balanced funds limit stock investments to no more than about a third of their assets to stocks with high dividend yields to satisfy their main goal of high current income.

Asset allocation funds give broader discretion to managers to shift their assets among stocks and bonds according to market conditions and consequently can be either conservative or risky.

* Mutual fund definitions are based on John C. Bogle, *Bogle on Mutual Funds* (1994).

worry that many buyers are lured into funds by dealers who don't disclose the risks involved. "There are problems in the quality of information and the assimilation or understanding of that [information] by the public generally, whether they are purchasing from a brokerage house or a bank," says Christopher Lewis, director of banking policy for the Consumer Federation of America. "This is particularly true among traditional bank customers who are not sophisticated investors and in many instances have never dabbled at all in what can be the cold world of investment banking."

The federation and other critics say the regulations governing mutual funds, especially bank involvement in their sales, need to be tightened. For while mutual funds can be viable options for many, they are not for everyone.

"Equity market investment is appropriate for long-term investment,"

Performance by Fund Category

*Most types of mutual funds declined in value in the most recent quarter. Over the past 15 years, however, all categories of funds showed substantial growth, with equity funds (stocks) generally outperforming mixed funds (equities and bonds) and fixed-income funds (bonds). **

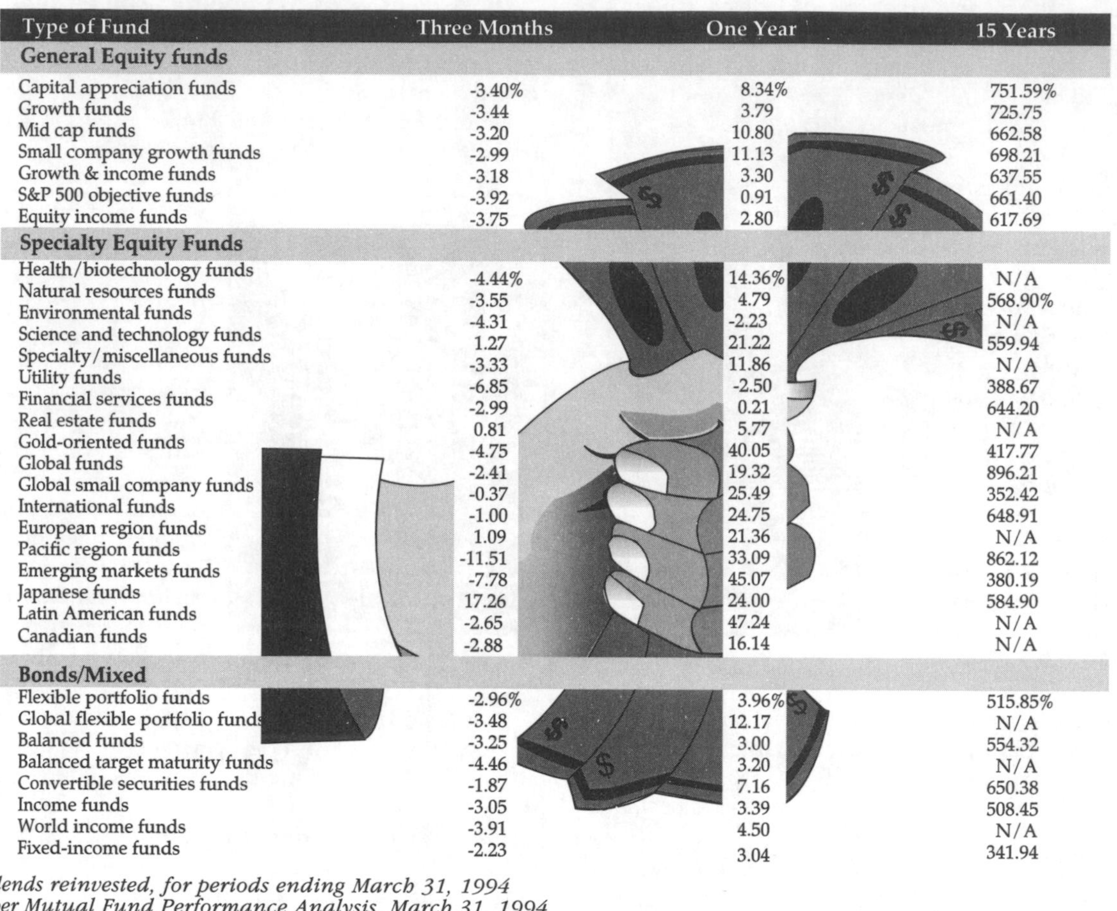

Type of Fund	Three Months	One Year	15 Years
General Equity funds			
Capital appreciation funds	-3.40%	8.34%	751.59%
Growth funds	-3.44	3.79	725.75
Mid cap funds	-3.20	10.80	662.58
Small company growth funds	-2.99	11.13	698.21
Growth & income funds	-3.18	3.30	637.55
S&P 500 objective funds	-3.92	0.91	661.40
Equity income funds	-3.75	2.80	617.69
Specialty Equity Funds			
Health/biotechnology funds	-4.44%	14.36%	N/A
Natural resources funds	-3.55	4.79	568.90%
Environmental funds	-4.31	-2.23	N/A
Science and technology funds	1.27	21.22	559.94
Specialty/miscellaneous funds	-3.33	11.86	N/A
Utility funds	-6.85	-2.50	388.67
Financial services funds	-2.99	0.21	644.20
Real estate funds	0.81	5.77	N/A
Gold-oriented funds	-4.75	40.05	417.77
Global funds	-2.41	19.32	896.21
Global small company funds	-0.37	25.49	352.42
International funds	-1.00	24.75	648.91
European region funds	1.09	21.36	N/A
Pacific region funds	-11.51	33.09	862.12
Emerging markets funds	-7.78	45.07	380.19
Japanese funds	17.26	24.00	584.90
Latin American funds	-2.65	47.24	N/A
Canadian funds	-2.88	16.14	N/A
Bonds/Mixed			
Flexible portfolio funds	-2.96%	3.96%	515.85%
Global flexible portfolio funds	-3.48	12.17	N/A
Balanced funds	-3.25	3.00	554.32
Balanced target maturity funds	-4.46	3.20	N/A
Convertible securities funds	-1.87	7.16	650.38
Income funds	-3.05	3.39	508.45
World income funds	-3.91	4.50	N/A
Fixed-income funds	-2.23	3.04	341.94

** With dividends reinvested, for periods ending March 31, 1994*
Source: Lipper Mutual Fund Performance Analysis, March 31, 1994

Lewis says, "but it is particularly inappropriate for an elderly investor who needs to protect principal at that point in life. So investor suitability is a big concern for us."

Even some champions of mutual funds warn consumers to beware. One of the industry's most vocal critics is John Bogle, founder and chairman of the Vanguard Group of Investment Companies, the country's second-largest mutual fund company. "Shareholders aren't active enough, don't consider costs enough and don't vote carefully enough on fee increases," says Bogle, who urges consumers to pick funds with low costs and proven track records. "The directors, who are supposed to be representing them, often don't represent them well, and as a result the shareholders are in the back seat. They deserve to be in the driver's seat."

Lawmakers and regulators will consider the following questions in coming months as they consider proposals to increase oversight of the mutual fund industry:

Are mutual funds safe investments for American savers?

Clearly, banks and savings and loan institutions are safe places to stash savings. If a bank or S&L goes belly-up — as many did during the 1980s real estate market crash — the federal government will reimburse customers for lost deposits up to $100,000 for each account.

Like other investments in stocks and bonds, mutual funds offer no such protection. The only federally backed insurance available to the mutual fund industry is the Securities Investor Protection Corporation (SIPC), a nonprofit membership group funded by securities brokers and dealers. But that only covers securities held by brokerage firms against losses due to theft, fire or bankruptcy. Investors have no protection whatever against the loss of market value of the securities themselves.

Except for periodic changes in the interest rates they pay customers for their deposits, banks and S&Ls also offer predictability. Securities, by contrast — whether they are purchased directly or through mutual funds — can fluctuate dramatically in value at a moment's notice. This market volatility can pose a problem for investors who need ready access to their investments. If they sell their shares when the market is low, as in March and April, they may have to swallow substantial losses.

But there is also a less obvious risk to the financial well-being of many Americans — their reluctance to save or invest money at all. The problem is especially severe among baby-boomers, many of whom are not putting aside enough money for retirement. According to a recent study, Americans are now saving less than one-fourth of the portion of their income that they saved during the 1950s and '60s. [3] And this at a time when employers are shifting more responsibility for setting up and managing pension funds to employees.

Over the long haul, stocks historically have outperformed both bonds and bank instruments. Thus, with many Americans ill-prepared financially for their retirement years, well-managed stock mutual funds, and bond funds as well, may offer a more desirable long-term investment decision than federally insured bank deposits.

Because money can be "lost" in an instant with equity investments, however, many long-term savers shy away from playing the stock market for fear of putting their money into a company whose stock does poorly and taking a big loss.* With professional managers overseeing portfolios of investments covering a wide array of businesses, equity mutual funds may offer them a way to cash in on the stock market's superior performance at far less risk, and with lower transaction costs.

Perhaps the biggest threat to safe investing in mutual funds is lack of understanding of the risks involved. The substantial shift of funds from maturing bank CDs into bond mutual funds over the past few years is a case in point. As interest rates fell over the period, the value of bonds held in mutual funds appreciated.

"Investors couldn't help but notice it because the information was in all the newspapers," says Collins of the Investment Company Institute, noting that $11.1 billion in new investments went into bond funds in January. "We became concerned that too much money was going into the bond funds without buyers noting that they can go down in value when interest rates go the other way."

But if care is taken to measure the risks, mutual funds can pay off, especially over the longer term. Although stock and bond values fall from time to time, they also occasionally register spectacular gains. "It makes sense to favor securities over CDs for long periods," says Lipper. "On average, the stock market grows faster than the population and the economy." But he warns that the averages may conceal the risk of loss. Do equity mutual funds perform better than CDs? "On average, yes," Lipper says. "Every year? No."

Do mutual funds threaten the overall stability of the financial markets?

Total assets held by the more than 4,700 funds sold in the U.S. now amount to an astounding $2.1 trillion. What if many shareholders, frightened by the markets' recent tremors, decided to cash in their shares and return to the safety of their bank CDs? With so much money in play, it is easy to imagine that a large-scale rush by fund shareholders to sell securities could send the entire market into a tailspin.

That scenario is not likely in the case of equities, since only a small percentage of all stocks are held in mutual funds (*see below*). But it may be more worrisome for the bond market. Many recent purchasers of bond mutual funds are traditional savers, not investors, who were lured away from their CDs by the promise of somewhat higher yields.

"People who bought bond funds were by definition more conservative investors, and for most of them the word 'bond' implied something that could be held to maturity, when it would pay off at par, with no danger to principal," writes Martin Mayer, a guest scholar at the Brookings Institution. "Holders of shares in bond funds have been shocked to see the value of these shares deteriorate, often by as much as 10 percent." [4] When bond prices fell as a result of rising interest rates, he writes, some shareholders of bond funds began selling off their holdings and taking losses.

Perhaps the most pessimistic views of mutual funds' potential to destabilize the financial markets come from Henry Kaufman, formerly chief economist at Salomon Brothers and now president of Henry Kaufman & Co. Inc., another New York brokerage. Kaufman, known as "Dr. Doom" for his often gloomy forecasts, says the rapid growth of mutual funds has undermined the financial markets' traditional strengths. He notes the growth in assets of stock mutual funds from about $180 billion to about $700 billion since the October 1987 market crash.

"What this means is that the average investor in equity mutual funds has never experienced a prolonged bear market," he said recently. [5] Since the bond market began its climb in 1982, Kaufman noted, assets of bond funds also have grown, from just $20 billion to more than $700 billion. "Up until last fall," he said, "only a minority of individuals had much personal memory as

* When a stock declines in value, money is only lost when the stock actually is sold. Generally speaking, stocks held over the long term will regain their "paper" losses.

investors of what happens to bond prices — and consequently mutual fund net asset values — when interest rates start a protracted cyclical rise."

"The fact is that we do not know how the ordinary investor in mutual funds will react when equity prices and bond prices continue to display spasms of [negative] volatility," Kaufman continued, "instead of the highly agreeable upside volatility to which most had become accustomed." Because of the tremendous growth of mutual fund assets and other destabilizing changes he says have occurred in the financial markets, Kaufman warned of a coming "plunge in financial asset values that will dwarf what we have experienced so far this year."

While Kaufman is not alone in predicting a worsening of the bear market, few experts share his view of the destabilizing impact of mutual funds. More than half the stock market is accounted for by individual investors, and pension funds own another quarter of the equities. Mutual funds account for only about 10 percent of the stocks in the stock market.[6]

"Very rarely has there been any hint of any wrongdoing in the mutual fund field. It's one of the reasons why it has grown so rapidly, because the public has more confidence in it than in savings and loans or banks or insurance companies."

Sir John Templeton

The only sector of the financial markets that may conceivably be vulnerable to a sudden decision by mutual fund shareholders to pull out, says Vanguard's Bogle, is the market in municipal bonds. According to the Federal Reserve, mutual funds account for about a quarter of the municipal bond market. "It's patently ridiculous to say that the taxable corporate bond fund or Treasury bond funds could have had any measurable impact on the marketplace," Bogle says. "We're just too small on those markets."

Because the latest industry data on purchases and sales of mutual funds cover only the period ending March 31, it's too early to know precisely how fund shareholders reacted to the latest market decline. But the picture that is emerging gives little cause for alarm. According to a survey by Quick & Reilly, a discount brokerage firm, most small investors did nothing after the 9.7 percent market drop in early April. "Overall, we found that most people sat out the recent market decline," says spokesman Leslie Zuke. "Fully 55 percent [of all Quick & Reilly clients] reported that they did nothing as a result."

The growing use of mutual funds as investments for retirement may also be a stabilizing element against massive redemptions in response to short-term market fluctuations. Although no one knows exactly how much money is invested in mutual funds for retirement purposes, Collins estimates that pensions and retirement plans account for as much as 30 percent of total fund assets.

Many 401(k) plans allow participating employees to change their investments no more than once a calendar quarter. The retirement objective of these investments also argues against a sudden pullout if the market were declining. "You're still going to be 65 in a certain number of years," Collins says, "and by pulling out early, you'd lock in your losses. My bet is you'd ride it out."

Do current regulations adequately protect consumers?

The Securities and Exchange Commission (SEC), established in 1934 to oversee the securities industry, has jurisdiction over mutual funds. The agency requires funds to provide essential information, such as past returns on their investments, in language that ordinary investors can understand. It also requires the National Association of Securities Dealers (NASD) to train and license brokers.

For the most part, there are few complaints about the agency's oversight of this growing sector of the securities industry. "I can't think of any other profession or industry that's been as successfully regulated," says Sir John Templeton, founder of the Templeton Group of mutual funds. "Very rarely has there been any hint of any wrongdoing in the mutual fund field. It's one of the reasons why it's grown so rapidly, because the public has more confidence in it than in savings and loans or banks or insurance companies."

Templeton gives much of the credit to the SEC. "Regulation has been necessary in order to provide the safety and confidence of the public," he says. "Very few of the public would be able to select the right mutual funds if there weren't somebody supervising the industry."

Lipper agrees that the regulatory system has worked well to protect shareholders of mainstream mutual funds from the kinds of abuses that have plagued other sectors of the financial services industry. "I'm not particularly concerned about large U.S. stock funds," Lipper says. "We have 50 years of experience doing that, and most of the problems involved in these investments we already know how to deal with."

The fly in the ointment, in his view, is the proliferation of new kinds of funds — such as adjustable-rate mortgage funds, short-term global funds and prime rate funds — managed by newcomers to the field. [7] "There are well over 100 different fund types," Lipper says, "and the SEC doesn't know how to regulate them all. Unfortunately, you need a market crash to measure the success of regulations, and today the safety nets aren't there for many of these new instruments."

Another area that has attracted scrutiny is the growing sale and management of mutual funds by banks, which are largely outside the existing regulatory framework. Nearly a fourth of the country's 14,000 banks are now involved in brokerage activities, and they account for about 15 percent of the $30 billion that U.S. consumers invest each month in mutual funds. [8] Regulators worry that many bank customers don't realize that the fund shares they purchase in the bank lobby do not have the same FDIC protection that their deposit accounts have.

Their concerns were borne out by a recent survey showing that only one in five bank customers knew that mutual funds are not federally insured. [9] This was especially true of low-income bank customers. "What concerns state securities regulators is that more and more we will see the financially unsophisticated consumers — those least able to recognize sometimes subtle distinctions between bank products — targeted by bank promotional campaigns," Denise Voigt Crawford, commissioner of securities for the state of Texas, told a congressional subcommittee. [10]

There is a point, experts say, beyond which regulators are powerless to protect consumers. "I think regulation has gone about as far as it can go," says Bogle. For example, the SEC four years ago began requiring each fund prospectus to show how much operating expenses reduce the fund's return to investors. "So the information about how much of a hit the return takes is probably as good as it can get," says Bogle, whose Vanguard Group funds are mostly no-loads (sold without sales commissions). "Now, if the investor doesn't want to read that or thinks it's too hard to understand, I'm not sure what to do about that." ■

Massachusetts Financial Services

A 1951 board meeting of the Massachusetts Investors Trust, the first U.S. mutual fund.

BACKGROUND

Early Funds

Until the 1920s, the only way Americans could invest in stocks was to purchase shares in a given company through a securities broker. Middle-income individuals, with only small sums available at any given time, tended to put their money in bank accounts, while investing in the financial markets was limited mainly to the more affluent.

The notion of pooling funds and investing them through a trustee who manages a portfolio of investments on the investors' behalf actually dates back to 19th-century Europe. [11] King William of the Netherlands authorized the first investment trust in 1822. Another appeared in Belgium in 1833. But it was in Great Britain that the concept was applied most broadly, and by the turn of the century large investment trusts existed in England and Scotland.

The first investment trust in the United States, the Boston Personal Property Trust, was set up in 1893, mainly for the professors and staff of Harvard University. But these early investment vehicles were "closed-end" funds, which are less flexible than most mutual funds today. Closed-end funds raise their capital only at the time they are set up, sell a fixed number of shares varying in price according to supply and demand and invest the proceeds.

"They were fixed pools and lacked the principle of constantly redeemable shares," says John Reilly, a spokesman for Massachusetts Financial Services, a Boston investment firm. "You couldn't just get out at any time. You had to find someone to buy your shares, and even then you weren't guaranteed to get the full value."

Reilly's firm started the first "open-ended" fund, introducing the notion of the redeemable share. The share can be sold at any time for the current value of the fund's assets — described in financial-page fund tables as net asset value, or NAV. Most mutual funds today are open-ended. The firm founded the first U.S. mutual fund, Massachusetts Investors Trust, in 1924. It started up with a portfolio of 45 stocks and $50,000 in assets. This fund, which is still operating, was joined later that year by two other trusts.

American investors were slow to accept the open-ended investment trusts, later known popularly as mutual funds. Even in the speculative fervor of the "Roaring Twenties," investors strongly preferred the closed-end trusts. By the end of the decade, there were hundreds of closed-end funds in the United States, with assets of some $7 billion, but only 19 open-ended funds, with less than $200 million in assets.

Industry Regulations

The stock market crash of 1929 and the ensuing Depression prompted Congress to set up a regulatory system to oversee the financial markets and prevent the kinds of speculative abuses that sparked the financial debacle. "Frequently, investment company assets were used by unscrupulous sponsors to further their own business interests," according to an SEC review of the period. "Failures to observe principles of fiduciary duty were widespread, and, as a consequence, holders of investment company securities, including the small, unsophisticated investors for whom the investment company product was so attractive, lost large sums of money." [12]

In addition to state laws, four federal laws enacted during the Depression or afterwards established the regulatory framework that oversees the mutual fund industry today. The 1933 Securities Act requires that all shares in mutual funds be registered, and that investment companies provide potential investors with a prospectus containing extensive disclosure information about each mutual fund. The disclosure statement must include the fund's investment objectives, the degree of risk involved and all fees and other costs.

The following year Congress passed the Securities Exchange Act, treating mutual fund firms as broker-dealers subject to regulation by the SEC. The 1934 statute also placed mutual funds under the jurisdiction of the NASD, which establishes advertising and distribution rules for mutual funds.

Two laws passed in 1940 complete the regulatory system governing mutual funds. The Investment Advisers Act requires all investment advisers to mutual funds to register with the SEC. The Investment Company Act — the most important law related to mutual fund operations — requires all mutual funds to register with the SEC. Signed into law Aug. 23, 1940, by President Franklin D. Roosevelt, the statute was written by SEC staff after five years of study and with strong support from the industry. It goes beyond the scope of other securities legislation by setting specific rules for the organization and operation of mutual funds.

The Investment Company Act requires funds to provide accurate and timely information to prospective clients as well as fair and accurate share prices and redemption amounts. It prohibits transactions between a fund and individuals affiliated with the fund, requires that fund officers and employees be bonded against embezzlement and sets strict rules for the management of fund assets. To further protect investors from mismanagement, the law requires that at least 40 percent of a fund's board of directors be independent of the fund's adviser. Unlike other financial instruments, mutual funds are required under the Investment Company Act to determine daily the current net asset value of their shares and to sell and redeem the shares at that value.

After World War II, mutual funds began to grow in popularity among American investors. From fewer than 80 funds with total assets of about $500 million in 1940, mutual funds grew to number almost 200 funds worth almost $19 billion by 1960. Over the next decade, the number of funds tripled and their total assets reached $50 billion. [13]

Along with new funds came new types of instruments, as managers sought to diversify their investments. The first international stock fund, for example, Towne, Templeton and Dobbrow, started up in a one-man office in New York City in 1940 with a $5,000 capitalization.

"We did what we thought was common sense, searching for the best opportunity and bargains everywhere," explains founder Templeton, who went on to create several other funds. [14] "If you limit yourself to one nation, you won't find as many as if you look everywhere. Also, if you're looking everywhere, you're more likely to find better opportunities. Thirdly, you reduce your risk because bear markets occur in every nation, but not at the same time."

Phenomenal Growth

Like Massachusetts Investors Trust and other early investment trusts, most mutual funds that came into being before the 1970s were stock funds. A few, known as balanced funds, also included bonds in their portfolios to reduce the impact of the stock market's periodic gyrations.

By the end of 1992, there were 1,432 stock funds, up from 463 in 1972. Bond funds grew even faster, from just eight in 1972 to 1,622 by the

Continued on p. 445

Chronology

1920s-1970s

The mutual fund industry begins slowly but later expands as confidence in securities grows following the establishment of an effective regulatory system and the end of the Depression.

March 21, 1924
Massachusetts Financial Services, a Boston firm, sets up the first open-ended stock mutual fund in the United States, Massachusetts Investors Trust.

1933
Congress passes several laws aimed at preventing a recurrence of the 1929 stock market crash, including the Securities Act. The first of four major statutes regulating mutual funds, the act calls for the registration of fund shares and the distribution to prospective buyers of detailed prospectuses describing each fund.

1934
The Securities Exchange Act sets up the Securities and Exchange Commission (SEC) to regulate the stock market, including mutual fund companies. The law also extends the authority of the National Association of Securities Dealers (NASD) to include mutual funds among the investment brokers and dealers it represents and certifies.

1940
The Investment Company Act, the principal law governing mutual funds, sets specific rules for fund operations, information disclosure, transactions by managers for their personal accounts and other matters affecting shareholder rights. Congress also passes the Investment Advisers Act, requiring that all mutual fund advisers be registered with the SEC. The first international stock mutual fund is started by Towne, Templeton and Dobbrow of New York City.

1970s ***Led by bond funds, mutual funds enter a phase of rapid expansion.***

1971
The first money market funds are set up, offering check-writing privileges and higher interest rates than bank savings accounts.

1976
Tax-exempt municipal bond funds first appear, offering tax shelters for higher-income individuals.

1979
Another tax-exempt vehicle, the tax-free money market fund, is created, combining the convenience of money market funds with the tax advantages of municipal bond funds.

1980s ***Spurred by the introduction of Individual Retirement Accounts (IRAs), mutual funds become major investment and retirement vehicles for many Americans.***

1982
Fueled by a long economic recovery, the stock and bond markets enter a period of relatively steady growth. Bond fund assets will grow from $20 billion to more than $700 billion by early 1994.

Oct. 19, 1987
On "Black Monday," the Dow Jones industrial average, the best-known measure of market activity, falls a record 23 percent (508 points). Stocks recover quickly, however, and stock mutual fund assets grow from $180 billion to about $700 billion by early 1994.

1990s ***Financial experts warn that fund performance will likely return to more normal, if less spectacular, levels.***

July 12, 1990
Iraq's invasion of Kuwait and the subsequent commitment of U.S. forces to the conflict triggers a bear market. Despite the decline in stock prices, mutual funds gain new shareholders.

Oct. 11, 1990
The stock market changes direction and begins rising again. The Dow will climb from 2,365 points to a peak of nearly 4,000 by January 1994.

Dec. 30, 1993
In the most visible of a flurry of bank acquisitions of mutual funds, Mellon Bank, N.A. announces its intention to buy Dreyfus Corp., the sixth-largest mutual fund company in the United States.

Feb. 4, 1994
The Federal Reserve Board announces the first of three quarter-point increases in short-term interest rates to combat inflation. The move triggers declines in the stock and bond markets.

Winners and Losers: How Funds Performed

The performance of individual mutual funds varies widely, depending on the period of time monitored and the type of fund. Over the past 15 years, finds have appreciated by up to 2,859 percent and lost as much as 44 percent. During the recent one-year period ending March 31, funds increased in value by up to 74 percent and declined by as much as 26 percent. In the first quarter of this year, funds gained up to 28 percent and fell by as much as 24 percent.

Top 15 Performers

Fifteen Years

Name of Fund	Type of Fund	Growth
Fidelity Magellan Fund	G	2859%
CGM Cap. Development	G	2466%
AIM Constellation, Retail	CA	1541%
IDS New Dimensions	G	1345%
Fidelity Destiny	G	1327%
Janus Fund	CA	1291%
New York Venture	G	1268%
AIM Weingarten, Retail	G	1251%
Fortis Growth Fund	CA	1234%
The New England Growth	G	1229%
Steinroe Special Fund	G	1212%
Merrill Pacific: A	PC	1176%
Twentieth Century: Growth	G	1139%
IDS Growth Fund	G	1126%
Phoenix Growth Fund	G	1116%

One Year

Name of Fund	Type of Fund	Growth
Lexington Strat. Invest.	AU	74%
Un. Svcs. World Gold	AU	62%
M. Stanley Instl: Emrg. Mkts	EM	62%
Excel Midas Gold Shares	AU	62%
Lexington Strat Silver	S	58%
Scudder Latin America	LT	57%
Merrill Latin Amer: A	LT	56%
Merrill Latin Amer: B	LT	55%
Blanchard Prec. Metals	AU	54%
Keystone Prec. Metals	AU	53%
Thomson: Prec. Metals: A	AU	51%
Thomson: Prec. Metals: B	AU	50%
Templeton Dev. Markets	EM	49%
Govett: Emerging Markets	EM	49%
Fidelity Select Prec. Metals	AU	49%

First Quarter 1994

Name of Fund	Type of Fund	Growth
DFA Group: Japan Small Co.	JA	28%
Capstone Nikko Japan	JA	22%
Wright Equity: Italian	EU	19%
T Rowe Price Intl: Japan	JA	17%
The Japan Fund	JA	17%
Fidelity Invest. Trust Japan	JA	15%
Merrill Technology: A	TK	15%
Merrill Technology: B	TK	15%
DFA Group: Contl. Sm. Co.	EU	13%
M Stanley Instl: Intl. Sm. Co.	IF	12%
GT Japan Growth: A	JA	11%
GT Japan Growth: B	JA	11%
Fidelity Select Electronic	TK	11%
Fidelity Select Computer	TK	10%
Fidelity Yen Perform.	WI	9%

Bottom 15 Performers

Fifteen Years

Name of Fund	Type of Fund	Growth
Steadman Tech & Growth	G	-44%
Steadman Amer Industry	CA	-38%
Steadman Investment	G	24%
American Heritage Fund	CA	49%
Steadman Associated Fund	EI	79%
Lexington Strat Investment	AU	84%
Centurion Growth Fund	G	106%
US: Gold Shares	AU	168%
Retire Plan Amer.: Bond	FI	179%
Capstone Govt. Income Fund	FI	196%
Rainbow Fund	CA	207%
First Inv. Fund for Income	FI	240%
Lexington GNMA Income	FI	244%
Merrill Spec Value: A	G	255%
ABT Utility Income Fund	UT	259%

One Year

Name of Fund	Type of Fund	Growth
Steadman Tech & Growth	G	-26%
Pilgrim Corp Utilities	UT	-22%
Excel Value Fund	G	-18%
Steadman Investment	G	-16%
Frontier: Equity Fund	G	-14%
Steadman Amer Industry	CA	-12%
Gintel Erisa	GI	-12%
Equity Strategies	S	-12%
Gintel Fund	G	-11%
Century Shares Trust	FS	-11%
Fidelity Select Insurance	FS	-11%
UST Master Environ.	EN	-10%
Dreyfus Edison Electric Indx	UT	-10%
Princor Utilities Fund	UT	-10%
Stratton Monthly Div	UT	-9%

First Quarter

Name of Fund	Type of Fund	Growth
Fidelity Southeast Asia	PC	-24%
BJB Intl. Equity: A	IF	-22%
BJB: Intl. Equity: B	IF	-22%
EV Trad. China Growth	PC	-22%
EV Mrthn Greater China	PC	-22%
M. Stanley Instl: Asian Eq.	PC	-22%
GT Global High Income: B	WI	-21%
GT Global High Income: A	WI	-21%
Fidelity New Mkts. Income	WI	-21%
T Rowe Price Intl: Asia	PC	-20%
Wright Equity: Hong Kong	PC	-20%
Merrill Dragon Fund: B	PC	-20%
Merrill Dragon Fund: A	PC	-20%
Govett: Dev. Markets Bond	WI	-19%
Scudder Pacific Oppty.	PC	-19%

AU= Gold Oriented Funds, CA= Capital Appreciation Funds; EM= Emerging Market Funds; EN= Environmental Funds; EU= European Region Funds; FI= Fixed Income Funds; FS= Financial Services Funds; G= Growth Funds; GI= Growth and Income Funds; GS= Global Small Company Funds; GX= Global Flexible Portfolio Funds; IF= International Funds; JA= Japanese Funds; LT= Latin American Funds; PC= Pacific Region Funds; S= Specialty/Miscellaneous Funds; TK= Science and Technology Funds; UT= Utility Funds and WI= World Income Funds

Source: Lipper Mutual Fund Performance Analysis, March 31, 1994

Continued from p. 442
end of 1992.

"The growth of bond mutual funds is one of the most remarkable aspects of the soaring popularity of mutual funds," Bogle writes. "Bond fund assets have grown from just $4 billion in 1970, representing 9 percent of total mutual fund assets, to $510 billion at the end of 1992, representing 32 percent of total fund assets." [15]

First appearing in the early 1970s, money-market funds quickly enjoyed tremendous success. Offering interest rates of a point or more above the average bank money-market account, these open-ended funds invest in relatively safe (but not federally insured) vehicles earning taxable interest, such as U.S. Treasury securities and short-term loans to financially sound corporations. "That was the first time that individuals could gain access to the prevailing rates that previously they could get only if they went through a broker," says Collins. Money-market funds have continued to lure bank customers by offering check-writing and other traditional banking services.

Another successful addition to fund offerings, tax-exempt municipal bond funds, first appeared in 1976 and have spread rapidly, as they offer a convenient tax shelter that is especially attractive to higher-bracket taxpayers. Three years later, tax-free money-market funds were introduced, combining the convenience of money-market funds with the tax advantages of municipal-bond funds.

As demand for different kinds of funds grew, the mutual fund companies themselves began offering an increasing number and variety of specialized funds. Stock funds mostly fall into one or more of five major investment sectors: broad-based specialty, concentrated specialty, equity income, growth and value. Bond funds are more varied, belonging to one of eight broad categories: U.S. government, mortgage-backed, investment-grade corporate, medium-grade corporate, high-yield (junk) corporate, investment-grade municipal, high-yield municipal and global. [16] They range from short-term to long-term.

Hundreds of millions of shares are bought and sold daily in the main trading room (above) of the New York Stock Exchange, founded in 1792. The nation's 4,700 mutual funds contain stocks and bonds from exchanges throughout the world, as well as money markets and other investment vehicles.

New Factors in Growth

Some mutual fund companies have grown into vast investment complexes offering dozens of funds and around-the-clock phone service, such as Fidelity Investments and Vanguard. These companies typically attract investors by allowing them to easily shift their investments among the company's funds.

Today the big companies account for about 85 percent of total mutual fund assets. [17] The biggest, Fidelity, has 210 funds with $164 billion in assets, accounting for just over 10 percent of the mutual fund market. The company owes much of its success to its Fidelity Magellan stock fund. Its phenomenal gains made its manager, Peter Lynch, one of the best-known figures in the industry before he left the fund in 1990.

Since the mid-1970s, when stock funds and balanced funds accounted for 86 percent of mutual funds' assets, the industry has become far more diversified. By the end of 1992, money-market funds made up the largest segment of the industry (35 percent), followed by bond funds (32 percent), stock funds (29 percent) and balanced funds (4 percent). [18]

Once the regulatory system was in place, mutual funds grew steadily in number and type. But in the early 1980s, several events sparked a continuing boom in the industry. "In 1980 alone, mutual fund assets popped 43 percent," Collins says. "There was a kick from the beginning of the decade caused by a long economic expansion that continued under both Reagan administrations."

Mutual fund sales were also boosted, he says, by Congress' introduction of the Individual Retirement Account. IRAs enabled workers to set aside up to $2,000 each year tax deferred in special accounts whose earnings would accrue free of taxation until the money is withdrawn at age 59 ½ or later. As part of the 1986 Tax Reform Act, Congress withdrew the tax deferral for annual contributions to IRAs for most participants, but maintained the deferral for accrued

Tips From the Experts on Buying Mutual Funds

Before buying mutual funds, understand that they are inherently riskier than bank deposits. By the same token, don't expect to make a killing with funds, which invest in a broad array of securities. That diversity reduces the risk of big losses, but it also dilutes big gains. "There's nothing worse than a shareholder who doesn't understand what he's getting into," says John Bogle, chairman of the Vanguard Group of Investment Companies, the second-largest U.S. mutual fund company. Experts also advise investors to:

Customer opens a new mutual fund account at Franklin Resources in San Mateo, Calif.

• Buy funds that meet your investment objectives. If you're young and saving for retirement, concentrate on stock funds, which typically have higher long-term growth potential than other investments. If you will need your money in a year or two, to pay for schooling or buy a car for example, consider parking your money in a money market fund or other safe investment so you won't risk having to cash in your fund during a down market.

• Look for steady performance, not the hottest return. Seek funds with consistent, above-average performance over several quarters and find out if the same manager is still at the helm. Find out how the fund weathers both up and down markets. Judge the fund's performance against others with the same investment objectives.

• Diversify your investments. Buy several funds with different objectives, including those with both stocks and bonds in the portfolio. That way, if one sector goes bad, all is not lost. Consider international stocks and bonds to spread the risk even further. "With the exception of Canada, bull and bear markets overseas almost never go together with the United States," says Sir John Templeton, who set up the first U.S. international mutual fund.

• Sell poorly performing funds at the right time. Don't dump a fund only because it makes a poor showing in a given quarter. All funds will have up and down periods. But a fund that has performed worse than others of its type for more than two years, has recently switched managers and has a high expense ratio may be ready for replacement.

• Don't neglect your funds. Changes in investment objectives, family composition or employment may all warrant changes in your investments. "People need to look at their funds on a regular basis over time and at least annually," says Michael Lipper, president of Lipper Analytical Services. "Around your birthday is a good time because that way not everyone is buying and selling at the same time."

• Don't panic when the market takes a dive or splurge when investments look too good to resist. "Invest against the headlines," Lipper advises. "They tend to greatly exaggerate trends in either direction. Americans are incredibly bright. Use your common sense."

earnings so long as they are not withdrawn before the age limit.

"So for all those years," Collins says, "you had strong market performance and tax incentives that would at least make people look at mutual funds as one place to plunk their money." Another incentive for people to put their money into the funds, he notes, was the widespread adoption by fund companies during the 1980s of toll-free telephone service. "It's a very lowly fact of life," Collins says, "and no one mentions it, but it was a very, very valuable thing for the mutual fund industry to be in touch with potential customers at no toll charge."

Investors' Profile

Just who are these fund shareholders? According to a survey by the Investment Company Institute, the typical mutual fund shareholder is middle-aged and married. Just over half the respondents who identified themselves as the main decision-maker in fund investments are male, indicating that women are involved in the financial affairs of almost half the households. Only a third of the households include children under 18. More than two-thirds of married shareholders have a spouse who is employed. Almost three-quarters said they have an IRA, indicating some awareness of the need to save for retirement beyond company pension plans. Finally, mutual fund shareholders have a median income of $50,000, almost $20,000 above the national median, and have completed more years of college than most Americans; half had a four-year college degree compared with about a fifth of the general population.[19]

Perhaps because they are a well-educated and knowledgeable group, mutual fund shareholders defied predictions that they would panic when the market turned sour on two recent occasions. During the October 1987 stock crash, Collins reports, only 2 percent of the money invested in stock funds was pulled out. Shareholders reacted similarly to a less drastic, but well-publicized slide in stock prices following the Iraqi invasion of Kuwait in August 1990.

"The market got a bad case of the jitters and was down by 15 percent by the end of September," Collins recalls. "But at just about that time, the mutual fund industry began to experience a new phenomenon: The decline in prices was seen by shareholders as a buying opportunity, and they purchased new shares."

Collins also credits the fund industry and improved media coverage of financial news for the stable investment habits of fund shareholders. The companies distribute vast amounts of literature to shareholders describing not only their funds' performance but also more general notions about the need for retirement saving, market trends and public-policy issues such as the impact of interest rate movements on fund performance.

Not all observers agree with Collins' upbeat assessment, however. "There has been a lot of ink flowing on the subject of mutual funds," says Lipper, "but I'm not sure it's good because much of it is performance-driven and not of long-term value." He worries that headlines announcing the most spectacular rise in value of a given fund or fund sector, such as funds specializing in stocks listed on industrializing nations' stock exchanges, can be interpreted by consumers as advice to buy.

These emerging-market funds, focusing on Asia and Latin America, were among the hottest funds in 1993, posting a 72 percent total return for the year. That compares with an average value increase of 15 percent for all funds in 1993. During the first quarter of 1994, however, emerging funds lost 7.8 percent of their value, and Pacific region funds fell 11.5 percent.[20]

Buying funds on the basis of recent performance rarely pays off, experts say. "Exceptional performance in a product, such as emerging markets, is usually followed by an exceptionally poor performance," Lipper says. People who choose top performers generally end up buying when shares are most expensive and losing money as the fund sinks toward average levels. "Thus you have a risk that some people, when the decline comes, will feel that they've been cheated or misled and become very anti-fund and anti-investing." ■

CURRENT SITUATION

Call for Reforms

Despite fears that mutual fund holders, by their sheer numbers, would destabilize financial markets, there is little indication that happened after the latest slump in the stock and bond markets. "The data suggest that the rush to invest new funds has been curbed somewhat," says Lewis of the Consumer Federation. "But people for the most part did not pull out."

That doesn't surprise Lipper, who says the recent market reversal was far less serious than it has been portrayed. "It's extremely mild," he says. "It's not even a downturn. We had been saying for more than year it had to happen because the market had been going up for so long."

Some mutual fund sectors have fared worse than others, of course. Although some funds managed to grow in value during the first quarter, virtually all major categories of stock funds and bond funds lost ground. Conservative investors holding shares in balanced funds, which include both stocks and bonds as a hedge against market declines, were surprised to be among the biggest losers.

Among the hardest hit have been municipal-bond funds, which have enjoyed a growing infusion of new capital with the introduction this year of higher tax rates for high-income Americans. During the first quarter, after the bond market fell following the Fed's boost in interest rates, municipal bond funds lost 6.2 percent of their value, more than any other kind of bond fund. Even so, "muni" bond funds experienced only a small net outflow of money during the first quarter.[21]

Concern About Banks' Involvement

While mutual fund investors are taking the recent market setback in stride, recent changes in the industry are prompting calls to reform the regulatory structure to better protect consumers and their savings. Supporters of reform point out that the 1940 Investment Company Act has been amended only once, in 1970, while the industry has continued to undergo rapid expansion.

Reformers' main concern is the growing role of banks in the sale and management of mutual funds. When the basic laws governing banks and investment companies were drawn up in the 1930s and '40s, the two industries were prevented from engaging in each other's activities. Banks accepted deposits and made loans, while investment companies dealt in securities. Consequently, the Investment Company Act and other laws creating the regulatory framework for the mutual fund industry made no mention of bank involvement.

Since then, however, the law has been reinterpreted in ways that permit a greater commingling of banking and investment activities. Today, banks account for a large portion of mutual fund sales, including a third of all money-market fund sales.[22] At the same time, however, shareholders of bank-sponsored funds do not enjoy the same protection as those who purchase fund shares outside banks. Unlike all other financial advisers who recommend investments to individuals, bank employees who advise customers about mutual fund investments are not required to be registered and tested for competence by the SEC. (*See "At Issue," p. 449.*) Moreover, many consumers believe — erroneously — that mutual fund shares sold in banks are protected by federal deposit insurance.

Concern over bank involvement in mutual funds has mounted since Pittsburgh-based Mellon Bank, N.A. announced its intention to acquire the $72 billion Dreyfus Corp., the nation's sixth-largest mutual fund company. The Dec. 30, 1993, transaction, which would create the largest bank mutual fund operation in the country, is only the most visible example of a recent flurry of acquisitions by banks.

According to Frank V. Cahouet, a Mellon officer, 79 banks now own mutual funds. "The growth in mutual funds has taken place to a large degree at the expense of bank deposits," he explained. "While mutual fund assets have been growing at a dramatic 23 percent annual rate, bank deposits have been expanding at a much slower rate. Since 1980, bank deposits have grown at one-quarter the rate of mutual funds."[23]

Bank regulators have issued voluntary guidelines aimed at ensuring consumer protection from unscrupulous practices involving bank sales of mutual funds. But SEC Chairman Arthur Levitt Jr. and many consumer advocates want the banks to be subject to the same SEC regulations as the rest of the financial industry.

The Securities Regulatory Equality Act of 1993, sponsored by Rep. John D. Dingell, D-Mich., chairman of the Energy and Commerce Committee and its subcommittee on Oversight and Investigations, would satisfy this goal by extending SEC regulations to bank mutual fund operations. The Investment Company Institute has endorsed this measure but rejects as duplicative an alternative approach proposed by House Banking Committee Chairman Henry B. Gonzalez, D-Texas. His bill would establish disclosure requirements and other safeguards to be administered under banking regulations.

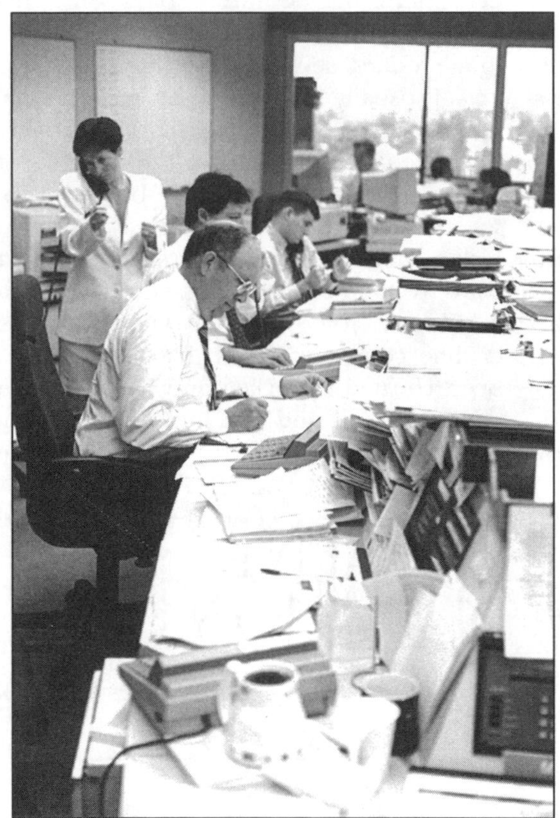

Trading desk at Franklin Resources in San Mateo, Calif.

Regulators also are looking at the role of mutual funds in certain high-risk securities, so-called "derivatives," which recently have suffered heavy losses. Derivatives are securities whose performance is based on such highly complex and risky vehicles as mortgage-backed securities, futures and options contracts. They can earn huge profits or crash in value.

Unlike privately held hedge funds such as George Soros' Quantum Fund, which recently lost $600 million on a bad currency deal, mutual funds offered to the public do not invest large portions of their assets in derivatives.[24] The problem for mutual fund shareholders, according to regulators, is that funds sometimes invest in derivatives without making it clear in their quarterly reports to shareholders.

Another concern has to do with personal trading by fund managers. This issue was largely ignored until January, when John Kaweske, a fund manager for Denver-based Invesco Fund Group, was fired for allegedly violating the company's rules on reporting trades he made on his own account. The Investment Company Act prohibits personal trading by fund managers if it is at their shareholders' expense, but the fund companies are left to set their own rules to carry out the law.

Some lawmakers, including Edward J. Markey, D-Mass., chairman of the House Energy and Commerce Subcommittee on Telecommunications and Finance, are considering proposals to bolster consumer protection in this area. ■

OUTLOOK

More Growth Seen

Unflinching though they may be, mutual fund shareholders will

Continued on p. 450

At Issue:

Do current regulations adequately protect consumers who purchase mutual fund shares through banks?

YES

Eugene A. Ludwig

Comptroller of the Currency
FROM *TESTIMONY BEFORE THE HOUSE ENERGY AND COMMERCE SUBCOMMITTEE ON OVERSIGHT AND INVESTIGATIONS,* MARCH 3, 1994.

Last year in a major policy address, I made it clear that any decision I make regarding the activities of banks will turn on whether I have the authority to approve an activity and, where I have that authority, on whether the activity can be conducted in a safe and sound manner by banks and on whether the activity benefits consumers of financial services. I developed those criteria because I recognized that in our dynamic financial services market supervisors must regularly decide what products and services banks may offer.

I believe that bank involvement in mutual funds meets those criteria and consequently represents sound public policy. . . . It offers customers greater convenience and greater choice in shopping for mutual fund services, and it permits banks to compete on an equal footing with other providers of financial services, enhancing competition in the market for mutual funds.

Supervisory diligence will be needed if consumers are to take the full measure of these benefits, and the [Office of the Comptroller of the Currency] has begun that effort. It has been clear to us for a long time that the safety of deposit insurance is inscribed on the minds of bank customers. Bank involvement in mutual funds sales puts that well-deserved sense of security to a new test, for there is a tendency among customers to believe that mutual fund products are as safe as insured deposits. They are not. Banks must take — and we will make sure they take — every step necessary to educate their customers about the true risks of mutual funds. This exercise in disclosure and public education will help to ensure that customers are not misled, and that they make intelligent and well-educated decisions when deciding to buy or not to buy bank mutual fund products. . . .

Our nation needs a strong banking system — not for the sake of having a strong banking system, but for the sake of the public. We need a banking system that can foster economic growth, and enable disadvantaged people to participate in that growth. For our banking system to remain strong, banks must be able to respond to changes in the market for financial services. To prohibit banks from responding to change would reduce both competitiveness and safety and soundness. To reduce the range of products and services from which consumers may choose would impoverish our marketplace and our economy.

NO

Arthur Levitt Jr.

Chairman, U.S. Securities and Exchange Commission
FROM *TESTIMONY BEFORE THE HOUSE ENERGY AND COMMERCE SUBCOMMITTEE ON OVERSIGHT AND INVESTIGATIONS,* MARCH 2, 1994.

Currently 113 banks or bank subsidiaries advise 943 mutual funds, and bank mutual funds have $204 billion in assets, an increase of 29 percent since Dec. 31, 1992. Banks also are increasingly active in selling mutual fund shares to the public. . . . The existing regulatory scheme for bank securities activities simply makes no sense. While bank affiliates and subsidiaries that engage in securities activities must register with the [Securities and Exchange] Commission like any other broker or dealer, banks that engage directly in securities activities continue to be exempt from broker-dealer regulation. . . . [T]he continued existence of a separate regulatory scheme for banks makes little sense in an era of regulatory consolidation. At a time when government resources are strained, it hardly seems appropriate for the federal bank regulators to hire and train a "mini-SEC" staff, to perform potentially duplicative and overlapping examinations, when a government agency already exists to do the job.

Regulatory gaps need to be eliminated. Under the existing fragmented regulatory scheme, the commission is unable to supervise bank securities activities, which are an increasingly important segment of the securities industry. As the regulator charged with oversight of the securities markets, the commission needs to have a comprehensive view of those markets and the participants in them. . . .

Investors deserve a single, consistent standard of protection, whether they purchase securities from a bank or a registered broker-dealer. Currently, investors who purchase securities directly from banks are not protected by the securities regulatory scheme that exists for broker-dealers. While banks that sell securities and advise investment companies are excluded from federal securities regulation, federal banking law does not provide a comparable regulatory scheme for bank securities activities. For example, bank securities sales personnel are not tested for competence, not are they subject to an examination and disciplinary program, such as the program administered by the National Association of Securities Dealers Inc. (NASD), that focuses on the potential for abuse that exists in connection with securities activities. Investor protection must be a priority. Bank regulation and examination generally seeks to ensure bank safety and soundness and depositor protection. Thus, bank regulators typically focus on maintaining the institution, rather than on investor protection. . . . In contrast, investor protection is paramount under the federal securities laws, and the commission's enforcement program is driven by investor-protection principles.

A Glossary of Mutual Fund Terms

Bonds: Interest-bearing certificates issued by governments and businesses, usually to raise capital. Bonds promise to pay a fixed rate of interest over a set period of time and return the investor's principal at the end of that time.

Bull and bear markets: When prices of most securities are rising, it's said to be a bull market; when prices fall, it's a bear market.

Distributions: Money paid by funds to shareholders, usually once a year. An income distribution, also known as a dividend, includes both interest and dividends earned from the securities owned by the fund. A capital-gains distribution is the net profit obtained by selling securities that have increased in price. Both are subject to taxation in taxable funds, but at different rates.

Dollar-cost averaging: An investment strategy intended to discourage panic selling in bear markets and wasteful purchases in bull markets. By investing a set dollar amount at regular intervals over a long period regardless of market conditions, an investor ends up buying more shares when prices are low and fewer when they are high. The technique also imposes the discipline of investing regularly, which builds up holdings over time.

Dow Jones industrial average: The oldest and most widely quoted barometer of stock market activity, based on the average price of 30 industrial stocks. It is computed daily by Dow Jones & Co., publisher of *The Wall Street Journal*.

Expense ratio: This is the main indicator of a fund's operating costs and is expressed as a percentage of the fund's total assets. The average ratio is around 1.2 percent. Some funds, such as international funds, are inherently more costly to manage than others.

Load: A fee or commission. A front-end load is the commission paid to the person who sells the fund and is subtracted from the shareholder's initial investment. Front-end loads can be as high as 8.5 percent. Some funds charge a back-end load, or redemption fee, when the investor sells shares. No-load funds don't charge sales commissions.

Management fee: All funds, including no-loads, charge a fee to pick and manage their investments.

Market timing: The opposite of dollar-cost averaging; market timers buy fund shares when they think the market or individual fund they want has hit bottom and sell when they think it has peaked.

Net asset value: Listed as NAV in newspaper mutual fund tables, this is the price per share an investor receives when selling a fund. The per-share price of buying a fund, or the asked price, is higher than the NAV if the fund charges a sales commission.

Portfolio turnover rate: The percentage of a fund's total asset value that the manager bought or sold in a year. High turnover in a fund that performs well may indicate astute management. It often means high costs.

Stocks: Also known as equities, common stocks represent an ownership stake in a company and offer possible capital gains or losses as well as dividend yields, which are periodic payments to shareholders based on the company's profits.

12b-1 fee: A sales commission that some funds charge shareholders' accounts each year, even when they claim to be no-load funds.

Continued from p. 448

be keeping a nervous eye on the financial markets in coming months. While the economic recovery appears to be firmly under way, suggesting higher profits and stock values, few analysts expect the recent market slide to be an isolated event.

Market analyst Kaufman recently predicted deeper turmoil in the markets. "The latest swings in bond and stock prices are likely to be merely a prologue to much greater volatility in the years ahead," he said. "At some point, after repeated bouts of volatility in the stock and bond markets, interest rates on CDs or other money-market instruments, which will have moved higher, will no longer be looked at contemptuously by many investors, new inflows into mutual funds will dry up and many individuals may become sellers. . . . The technology is in place for a cascade of selling by investors in mutual funds." [25]

While they reject the gloomy prediction of a general crisis in the financial markets, fund-industry executives say the joy ride of rapidly growing returns may be over for awhile. "The 1990s so far look a lot more like the 1970s than the 1980s," says Vanguard Chairman Bogle. "We've been warning people for at least the past four years that their returns in the 1990s won't be like they were in the 1980s."

The reason, he says, is that stock fund yields are low today, averaging 2.7 percent. Bogle cites two reasons: "People are buying the more speculative funds, which inevitably have lower yields. The other reason is that mutual fund expenses are so high that a nice 3 percent yield becomes 1.5 percent" after fees and other costs are factored in.

The solution to both problems, Bogle says, is a better-informed public. Educated investors will resist the lure of funds with high recent performance. "The long-term problem of grossly excessive costs in the fund business is only going to be solved by an enlightened shareholder group," he says. "If people stop buying high-cost funds, believe me, there will be no more high-cost funds left."

Nonetheless, most observers expect investor interest to continue to mount. They also foresee a continuation of the current proliferation of new funds coming on the market. Consumer demand for mutual funds is not only at an all-time high but it is also relatively easy for a would-be fund manager to start up a new fund. "The fact of the matter is that there are low barriers, so if you don't have a record of nefarious deeds, you can put up some money and start a mutual fund," says Collins. "It's expensive, but lots of people have money."

Another trend the industry experts predict will continue is consolidation of mutual funds into large complexes. "The advisers of most mutual funds are losing money," says Templeton. "The managers who are losing money are trying to make their funds bigger so they can cover their costs. If they don't do that, they will liquidate them. So there is a very active trend already toward the unprofitable funds being either liquidated or merged."

In addition, there are the tremendously profitable fund complexes already in existence, such as Fidelity, Vanguard and Franklin Resources, which bought out Templeton. "Those groups attract people who decide to team up," he says. "They have become enormous already and will be even bigger in years to come." ■

Notes

[1] See Shelly Branch, "Today's New Investors," *Money,* May 1994, p. 80.

[2] For background, see "Downward Mobility," *The CQ Researcher,* July 23, 1993, pp. 625-648, and "Paying for Retirement," *The CQ Researcher,* Nov. 5, 1993, pp. 961-984.

[3] Alan J. Auerbach and Laurence J. Kotlikoff, *Saving the American Dream,* Merrill Lynch & Co., April 1994.

[4] Martin Mayer, "Why Rates Are Rising," *The Washington Post,* May 6, 1994.

[5] Kaufman spoke April 25, 1994, at a global banking conference sponsored by the CS First Boston Corp. in New York City.

[6] See *USA Today,* April 28, 1994, p. 1.

[7] For more information on risks associated with new fund types, see John C. Bogle, *Bogle on Mutual Funds* (1994), pp. 292-293.

[8] See "Only Perform," (Survey of Investment Management), *The Economist,* Nov. 6, 1993.

[9] The "Bank Investment Products Survey" was released in January 1994 by the North American Securities Administrators Association and the American Association of Retired Persons (AARP).

[10] Crawford testified March 2 before the House Energy and Commerce Subcommittee on Oversight and Investigations, which was considering proposals to tighten regulation of bank involvement in securities.

[11] Unless otherwise noted, material for this section is based on H. Lee Silberman's untitled history of the Massachusetts Investors Trust, commissioned by the fund in November 1974.

[12] United States Securities and Exchange Commission, *Protecting Investors: A Half Century of Investment Company Regulation,* May 1992, p. xvii.

[13] *Ibid.*

[14] Templeton sold his funds, the Templeton Group, in 1992 to San Francisco-based Franklin Resources.

[15] Bogle, *op. cit.*, p. 97.

[16] *Ibid.*

[17] *Ibid.*

[18] *Ibid.*, p. 48.

[19] Investment Company Institute, *Profiles of Mutual Fund Shareholders,* fall 1992.

[20] Lipper Mutual Fund Performance Analysis, March 31, 1994, p. ii.

[21] See Carole Gould, "Tax Free Doesn't Mean Risk Free," *The New York Times,* April 10, 1994.

[22] See "Banks Turning to Mutual Funds as Shares in Household Assets, Credit Decline," *BNA Banking Daily,* Dec. 21, 1993.

[23] Cahouet testified March 3, 1994, before the House Energy and Commerce Subcommittee on Oversight and Investigations.

[24] See Susan Antilla, "A Concealed Danger for Funds," *The New York Times,* April 17, 1994.

[25] Speaking at the April 25 CS First Boston Corp. conference.

Bibliography

Selected Sources Used

Books

Bogle, John C., *Bogle on Mutual Funds: New Perspectives for the Intelligent Investor,* Richard D. Irwin, 1994.

The founder and chairman of the Vanguard Group Inc., the second-largest mutual fund company in the United States, offers specific advice on investing in various fund categories and how to allocate money according to investment goals.

Quinn, Jane Bryant, *Making the Most of Your Money: Smart Ways to Create Wealth and Plan Your Finances in the '90s,* Simon & Schuster, 1991.

This best-seller by the widely read personal-finance columnist covers the gamut of personal money management, from banking to buying a house. Mutual funds play a prominent role in her investment strategies.

Articles

"The Best Mutual Funds," *U.S. News & World Report,* Feb. 7, 1994.

In addition to a listing of 250 funds rated according to their performance over time, this cover story includes profiles of small equity and bond funds.

Edgerton, Jerry, "How Investors Can Get a Grip in Today's Wobbly Market," *Money,* May 1994.

Virtually every issue of *Money* magazine has advice about mutual fund investing. This issue suggests that funds with large cash holdings and growth funds may fare well in today's vacillating markets.

Laderman, Jeffrey M., and Geoffrey Smith, "The Power of Mutual Funds," *Business Week,* Jan. 18, 1993.

This overview of the mutual fund industry tracks the funds' rise in assets over the past two decades and discusses the implications of money flowing from bank deposits to equity funds.

"The New Bear Scare," *Newsweek,* April 11, 1994.

Compared with previous market downturns, the fall in stock and bond prices in early April was no more than a predictable market "correction," according to the magazine. Despite improving economic performance, however, markets are described as wary of future interest-rate increases.

"Only Perform: A Survey of Investment Management," *The Economist,* Nov. 11, 1993.

Professional investment managers are controlling a growing share of the world's wealth as mutual funds continue to attract investors. Mutual funds' main value to investors is reducing transaction costs as well as the risk associated with the securities markets by diversifying holdings.

"Should You Buy Mutual Funds from Your Bank?" *Consumer Reports,* March 1994.

Consumers Union found that banks rarely provide their customers with appropriate investment advice when selling them mutual funds. Many don't tell their customers that, unlike their deposit accounts, the funds are not federally insured.

Wyatt, John, "The Best Mutual Funds," *Fortune,* March 21, 1994.

Unlike many performance reviews, this one lists the best funds by their annual return after loads and fees are subtracted from the total, giving what the author says is a more than accurate reflection of each fund's performance.

Zweig, Jason, and Mary Beth Grover, "How to Decide When to Get Out," *Forbes,* Feb. 14, 1994.

Once investors buy into mutual funds, they often don't know when to sell them for something better. High costs and a below-average performance for the fund category for two years or more are among the signals investors should watch for.

Reports and Studies

Investment Company Institute, *The Organization and Operation of a Mutual Fund,* June 1986.

The organization representing the mutual fund industry describes the structure and operation of a typical mutual fund as well as the basic laws establishing regulatory oversight of the industry.

Investment Company Institute, *Profiles of Mutual Fund Shareholders,* fall 1992.

ICI found that the percentage of U.S. households investing in mutual funds has remained steady at around 25 percent since 1987, even as the amount of money invested in the funds has increased.

United States Securities and Exchange Commission, *Protecting Investors: A Half Century of Investment Company Regulation,* May 1992.

This detailed study of the regulatory treatment of mutual funds and other investment vehicles offers a number of reform proposals designed to reflect changes in the marketplace since the laws were passed more than 50 years ago.

The Next Step

Additional information from UMI's Newspaper & Periodical Abstracts database

Advice and Predictions

Calian, Sara and Robert McGough, "Mutual funds: Peter Lynch's advice: Ignore cash flows," *The Wall Street Journal,* April 28, 1994, p. C1.
Peter Lynch, the legendary former Magellan Fund manager, believes the rapt attention paid to mutual-fund cash flows is a waste of time. Lynch's advice to those who believe that the $794 billion in stock market funds has the power to yank markets up and down is discussed.

Edgerton, Jerry, "How investors can get a grip in today's wobbly market," *Money,* May 1994, pp. 52-53.
Advice is offered to help equity fund investors deal with the first unstable period since the summer of 1990. Investors should favor funds with tons of cash, lean toward growth funds and choose diversified international funds.

Kahn, Virginia Munger, "Should you invest through your bank?" *Working Woman,* May 1994, pp. 33-35.
Bank mutual funds promise higher returns than certificates of deposit, but they're just as risky as other investments. The question of whether one should invest through his or her bank is examined.

Ozanian, Michael K., "Does anyone remember earnings?" *Financial World,* April 26, 1994, pp. 56-62.
Many market analysts believe that per-share earnings for S&P 500 companies should climb a healthy 16.3 percent in 1994. A list of mutual funds that could see high rates of return is presented.

Sheets, Ken, "How to keep pace with rising yields," *Kiplinger's Personal Finance Magazine*, May 1994, pp. 62-67.
Returns from fixed-income investments have stopped sliding and are beginning to inch up again. Some tips on investing in income-producing mutual funds, including Treasury funds, municipal-bond funds, corporate-bond funds, corporate junk-bond funds, closed-end funds, REITs and preferred equity redemption cumulative stock are given.

Yip, Pamela, "Right path," *Chicago Tribune,* April 5, 1994, p. 1.
Tips for choosing a bond mutual fund are given, as well as the differences between bond mutual funds and stock mutual funds.

Broker Services

Englander, Debra Wishik, "Beware of mutual fund phone salesmen," *Black Enterprise,* April 1994, p. 49.
Some brokers allegedly are making wildly optimistic predictions on mutual funds while selling the funds by telephone.

Laderman, Jeffrey M., "Schwab gets mutually exclusive," *Business Week* (Industrial/Technology Edition), May 2, 1994, p. 6.
Giant discount broker Charles Schwab will expand OneSource, his successful broker-fee mutual-fund service, on May 9, 1994, to institutional customers such as 401(k) plans.

Talley, Karen, "Robert Thomas offers a discount brokerage plan," *American Banker,* April 19, 1994, p. 12.
Robert Thomas Securities' new Passport Investors Account would allow active bank brokerage customers to pay $33 to $50 per trade, no matter how many shares of stock or mutual funds they buy. An annual fee will also be levied.

The Future of Mutual Funds

Ellis, Junius, "Templeton's heir names the world's five best stocks," *Money,* May 1994, pp. 163-166.
When Sir John Templeton decided to retire from full-time portfolio management in 1987, he tapped Mark Holowesko to manage Templeton's Growth, Foreign and World stock funds. Holowesko says Georgia-Pacific, Stet Group, Telefonos de Mexico, Arbed Group and DSM Group could double their value within five years.

Kosnett, Jeff, "Mutual funds meet bank machines," *Kiplinger's Personal Finance Magazine*, April 1994, p. 20.
Wells Fargo Bank ATMs are being utilized to give the prices and account balances of Stagecoach funds that the bank runs. ATMs may one day serve as an interactive prospectus.

Gift Giving

"Brokers' trade group proposing more restrictive limits on gifts," *American Banker,* April 6, 1994, p. 17.
The NASD has proposed new limits on the amounts and types of gifts that securities firms, such as mutual fund companies, may give to brokers. The standards would help banks to police the perks doled out to their investment products sales representatives by mutual fund companies.

Holliday, Kalen, "Fund firm freebies sparking debate at banks," *American Banker,* April 6, 1994, p. 1.
Mutual fund companies are coming under fire for their

free flow of giveaways to bank-based sales representatives of their investment products. The melding of the banking and mutual fund industries has produced some violent cultural clashes. Among the banks responding with drastic measures are Chemical Bank of New York and First National Bank of Chicago.

Hedge Funds

Egan, Jack, "Giving hedge funds the third degree," *U.S. News & World Report,* April 18, 1994, pp. 72-73.
Hedge funds are highly leveraged and largely unregulated investment partnerships for the very rich, and these funds are being blamed for the turmoil that has gripped global financial markets for the past two months. The funds' use of derivatives and the role they may have played in producing the recent market confusion are examined.

Hansell, Saul, "A primer on hedge funds: Hush-hush and for the rich," *The New York Times,* April 13, 1994, p. A1.
Hedge funds have been blamed for many recent swings in financial markets, and their managers, like George Soros, have come under fire. But the funds continue to attract wealthy investors.

"Mind over matter," *The Economist,* April 23, 1994, pp. 73-75.
Influential investor George Soros says that human psychology is to blame for the financial markets' turbulence. Soros believes hedge funds stabilize markets because they bet against irrational trend-following.

"The return of the hedge," *The Economist,* April 16, 1994, p. 83.
The average hedge fund declined only 2.2 percent in the first quarter of 1994, compared with a 3.3 percent decline for the average equity mutual fund. Hedge funds have not been the disaster critics predicted they would become.

Taylor, Andrew, "New controls on hedge funds unnecessary, regulators say," *Congressional Quarterly Weekly Report,* April 16, 1994, p. 877.
Banking and securities regulators testified April 13, 1994, before a House Banking Committee that ongoing regulatory initiatives should be enough to protect the financial markets from hedge fund volatility and that new legislation is not needed.

Weiss, Gary, "Fall guys?: Mysterious and vilified, hedge funds are also the Street's trailblazers," *Business Week* (Industrial/Technology Edition), April 25, 1994, pp. 116-121.
Hedge funds are being blamed for the bond market collapse. Critics believe that hedge funds, run by operators such as George Soros and Julian Robertson, are overleveraged, undersupervised and disruptive to the markets.

International Markets

Gilpin, Kenneth N., "New Third World fear: Investors could walk away," *The New York Times,* April 24, 1994, p. 4.
Gilpin discusses a new trend in the credit and equity markets of Latin America and much of the rest of the developing world in which the primary source of foreign capital has become private investors, such as pension funds, mutual funds and investment firms, rather than banks.

Glasgall, William, "Is this any way to invest in South Africa?" *Business Week* (Industrial/Technology Edition), Feb. 28, 1994, pp. 90-92.
Stephen R. Goodwin wants to be the first independent black Wall Streeter to put together an open-ended mutual fund investing in South Africa. Goodwin is profiled, and his fund, the First South African Fund, is discussed.

Levinson, Marc and Daniel McGinn, "You can run but you can't hide," *Newsweek,* April 11, 1994, pp. 50-51.
The volatility of foreign stocks has hurt U.S. investors, who have recently seen overseas markets slide. The prospects for the performance of foreign stocks in the near future and turmoil in mutual funds markets are examined.

Spellman, James D., "Eurofunds," *Europe: Magazine of the European Community,* March 1994, pp. 18-20.
U.S.-based investors put more than $1.3 billion into mutual funds that invest solely in European stocks and bonds in 1993. The performance of these "Eurofunds" is examined.

Taub, Stephen, "Emerging markets mania: 1994 style," *Financial World,* March 29, 1994, p. 16.
The first emerging market fund directed at South Africa to be created is Morgan Stanley's Africa Investment Fund. South Africa should be the newest emerging-market-mania-fund country since trade sanctions have been lifted.

Investment Varieties

Black, Pam, "Index funds: A safer seat for the long-distance rider," *Business Week* (Industrial/Technology Edition), April 25, 1994, pp. 138-139.
The growing popularity of stock-index mutual funds is discussed. In the long run, these index funds are seen by many investors as a case of slow and steady wins the race. Several stock indexes are described.

Fink, Ronald, "Pale imitations," *Financial World,* April 12, 1994, pp. 70-72.
Unit investment trusts are among the hottest products on Wall Street. These trusts appear to be nothing more than an unmanaged version of mutual funds. Problems in investing in these trusts are discussed.

Laderman, Jeffrey M., "Sometimes diversity is no defense," *Business Week* (Industrial/Technology Edition), May 2, 1994, pp. 118-119.
Multi-market mutual funds are surprising investors with losses. These souped-up versions of balanced funds are called asset allocation funds and build on the old idea of diversification in the stock market.

Talley, Karen, "Mass. Financial offers do-it-yourself variable," *American Banker,* April 22, 1994, p. 12.
Massachusetts Financial Services is making available mutual funds that banks can use to create their own variable annuities, which are insurance contracts whose returns are linked to an underlying portfolio of investments, typically mutual funds. The Variable Insurance Trust contains 12 portfolios to supplement annuities that bank can seed with their own mutual funds.

Trumbull, Mark, "Hybrid funds promise stabler returns," *Christian Science Monitor,* April 28, 1994, p. 8.
Investing in hybrid mutual funds is discussed. Some financial counselors advocate investing in hybrid mutual funds that blend stocks, bonds, and cash in one investment package.

Regulating Mutual Funds

Bronstien, Barbara F., "FDIC chief opposes heavy-handed tactics," *American Banker,* April 20, 1994, p. 6.
FDIC Chairman Andrew C. Hove Jr. said on April 18, 1994 at the annual conference of the Conference of State Bank Supervisors that bankers who meet the needs of their communities and properly explain non-bank products such as mutual funds shouldn't be punished with regulatory overkill.

Cope, Debra, "Dalbar branching out into mystery shopping," *American Banker,* April 19, 1994, p. 12.
Louis S. Harvey, president of Dalbar Financial Services, says that while banks are more rigorous than brokers in terms of compliance when it comes to selling mutual funds, brokers are better at knowing the customer and matching needs. He plans to offer a "mystery-shopper" service to banks and brokerage houses to help firms selling funds comply with regulations about disclosure.

"Markey: Exemptions from SEC oversight archaic," *American Banker,* April 22, 1994, p. 13.
Excerpts from Rep. Edward J. Markey's, D-Mass., outline of his reasons for developing legislation that would remove banking regulators from oversight of mutual fund activity at banks, placing the risk squarely in the hands of the SEC, are offered.

Misra, Prashanta, "In the news," *Money,* May 1994, p. 53.
Misra discusses reports that the SEC is investigating whether Milwaukee's Strong/Corneliuson Capital Management fund family violated regulations governing so-called cross-trades. The investigation reportedly centers on whether Chairman Richard Strong shifted poor-performing junk bonds from favored institutional accounts to the Strong Total Return Fund between 1989 and 1990.

Prakash, Snigdha, "Levitt pushes for SEC oversight of fund sales," *American Banker,* April 15, 1994, p. 14.
SEC chairman Arthur Levitt Jr. on April 14, 1994 urged a key congressional panel to give his agency full authority to regulate the sale of mutual funds and other securities by banks.

Return on Investment

Berman, Phyllis, "Reaching . . . reaching," *Forbes,* April 25, 1994, pp. 50-52.
Pension fund managers are seeking to bolster their returns via private investments and direct deals. The pros and cons of using private investments to achieve bull market returns are examined.

"Investing for college," *Consumer Reports,* May 1994, p. 314.
A number of investments that offer special inducements for college savers are discussed. Advice on choosing stock and mutual funds for a college fund is offered as well.

Where to Invest?

Brown, Carolyn M., "A cause for investing," *Black Enterprise,* May 1994, p. 40.
The list of socially responsible mutual funds is growing. In general, these funds shun companies related to tobacco, liquor, gambling and weapons, and other funds that are even more focused are also available.

Del Valle, Christina, "The politically correct pension fund," *Business Week* (Industrial/Technology Edition), March 21, 1994, p. 108.
Economically targeted investing (ETI) is a concept whereby fund managers invest money in concerns owned by minorities or women. Critics fear that politics will decide which ailing businesses to prop up.

Grover, Mary Beth, "The garbage smells sweeter," *Forbes,* March 28, 1994, pp. 138-140.
Environmental stocks are one sector fund where investors stand to make money. Bargains abound in environmental funds because their prices have been depressed for three years.

Back Issues

Great Research on Current Issues Starts Right Here...Recent topics covered by The CQ Researcher are listed below. Before May 1991, reports were published under the name of Editorial Research Reports.

NOVEMBER 1992
Physical Fitness
Privatization
Paying for College
U.S. Policy in Asia

DECEMBER 1992
Crackdown on Smoking
The New CIA
Eating Disorders
Women and AIDS

JANUARY 1993
Hate Crimes
Child Sexual Abuse
Nuclear Fusion
U.S. Trade Policy

FEBRUARY 1993
Community Policing
Europe's New Right
School Censorship
Violence Against Women

MARCH 1993
Gay Rights
Aid to Russia
War on Drugs
TV Violence

Back issues are available for $4.00 (subscribers) or $7.00 (non-subscribers). Quantity discounts apply to orders over ten. To order, call Congressional Quarterly Customer Service at (202) 887-8621.

Binders are available for $16.00. To order call 1-800-638-1710. Please refer to stock number 648.

APRIL 1993
Head Start
High-Speed Rail
Children's Legal Rights
Muslims in America

MAY 1993
Cults in America
Preventing Teen Pregnancy
Software Piracy
National Parks

JUNE 1993
Food Safety
Prostitution
Childhood Immunizations
National Service

JULY 1993
Electric Cars
Population Growth
Downward Mobility
Intelligence Testing

AUGUST 1993
Mental Illness
Bilingual Education
Foreign Policy Burden
School Funding

SEPTEMBER 1993
Suburban Crime
Public Housing
Supreme Court Preview
Immigration Reform

OCTOBER 1993
Airline Safety
Disaster Response
Science in the Courtroom
The Glass Ceiling

NOVEMBER 1993
Paying for Retirement
Charitable Giving
Privacy in the Workplace
Adoption

DECEMBER 1993
U.S. Vietnam-Relations
Learning Disabilities
Child Care
Space Program's Future

JANUARY 1994
Racial Tensions in Schools
South Africa's Future
Worker Retraining
Regulating Pesticides

FEBRUARY 1994
Prison Overcrowding
Water Quality
Religion in Schools
Juvenile Justice

MARCH 1994
Underground Economy
Education Standards
Gambling Boom
Private Management of Public Schools

APRIL 1994
Reproductive Ethics
U.S.-China Trade
Soccer in America
Talk Show Democracy

MAY 1993
Traffic Congestion
Women's Health Issues

Future Topics

- ***Political Scandals***
- ***Education and Gender***
- ***Gun Control***

THE CQ Researcher

PUBLISHED BY CONGRESSIONAL QUARTERLY INC.

Political Scandals

Is the obsession with scandal hurting the nation?

President Clinton is being dogged by accusations of wrongdoing involving events long before he entered the White House — a failed real estate venture called Whitewater, Hillary Rodham Clinton's profits in commodities trading and an alleged sexual advance toward a state worker while Clinton was governor of Arkansas. The accusations dramatize the increased attention to political scandals in recent years. Yet polls show most Americans think that Whitewater has gotten too much news coverage and that the media are paying too much attention to Clinton's private life. Many experts believe an obsession with uncovering corruption and wrongdoing is hurting the political system. But they also say the media, political groups and the public show no sign of losing their appetite for scandal.

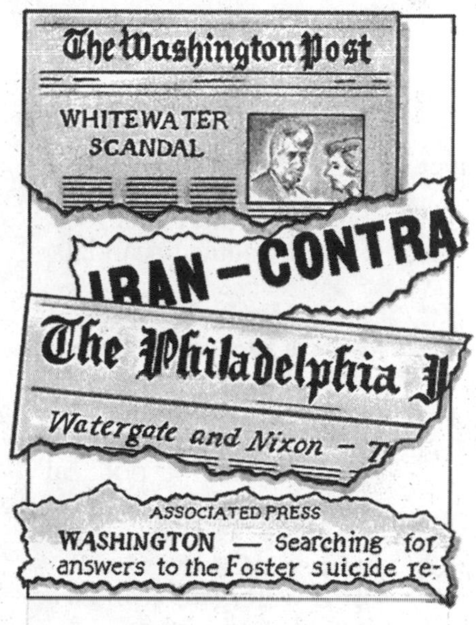

INSIDE THIS ISSUE

CQ May 27, 1994 • Volume 4, No. 20 • 457-480

Formerly Editorial Research Reports

POLITICAL SCANDALS

THE *CQ Researcher*

May 27, 1994
Volume 4, No. 20

The CQ Researcher (ISSN 1056-2036). Formerly Editorial Research Reports. Published weekly (48 times per year, not printed the first Friday of any month with five Fridays) by Congressional Quarterly Inc., 1414 22nd St., N.W., Washington, D.C. 20037. Rates are furnished upon request. Second-class postage paid at Washington, D.C. POSTMASTER: Send address changes to The CQ Researcher, 1414 22nd St., N.W., Washington, D.C. 20037.

COVER: BARBARA SASSA-DANIELS

Political Scandals

By Kenneth Jost

The Issues

As President Clinton began his second year in office, he faced a full plate of vexing issues from health care and crime at home to upheaval in Bosnia and Haiti, to name a few. But he was bedeviled as well by two of the oldest domestic issues in politics — money and sex.

Reporters and political opponents dissecting a failed real estate venture known as Whitewater were raising murky questions about possible financial conflicts while Clinton was governor of Arkansas. With the Whitewater affair churning, a new ethical issue was born when *The New York Times* disclosed that Hillary Rodham Clinton made $100,000 in the commodities market in 1978 and 1979 under the tutelage of a powerful Arkansas lawyer just before and during her husband's first term as governor. [1]

Then, just as White House damage-control efforts were moving Whitewater and commodity trading off the front pages, a new accusation made its way into an official forum. Paula Corbin Jones, a former Arkansas state employee, charged in a federal civil rights suit that Clinton, while governor, made an unwanted sexual advance toward her in a Little Rock hotel room in May 1991.

Clinton, through his privately retained lawyer, vehemently denied the sexual harassment charge. "Tabloid trash with a legal caption," attorney Robert S. Bennett, one of Washington's top white-collar defense lawyers, called the suit. The alleged incident, Bennett added, "never occurred."

In earlier times, accusations of this sort might never have reached the public. But in a more intense era of scandal politics, a public official's distant past remains fair game, and the line between public career and private life is blurred, if not erased. [2]

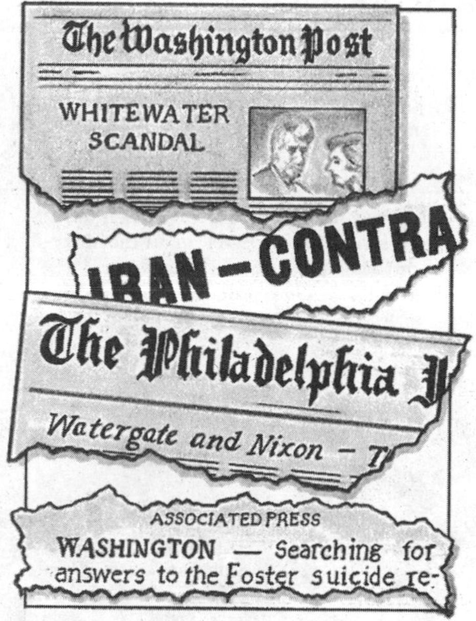

And allegations, once made, prove difficult, if not impossible, to dispel.

"The instant assumption in this town — not just about the president but about any official — is that if they can't prove they're innocent, they're guilty," Jack Nelson, Washington bureau chief of the *Los Angeles Times,* remarked recently. [3]

Within the past few years, scandal politics has become the weapon of choice for many political combatants. "It's become the standard operating procedure for the press, the public, public officials and opposition parties," says Larry J. Sabato, a professor of government at the University of Virginia and author of an influential book, *Feeding Frenzy,* criticizing the news media's handling of accusations against politicians and public officials.

Scandal toppled House Speaker Jim Wright, D-Texas, and now threatens the careers of such powerful lawmakers as House Ways and Means Committee Chairman Dan Rostenkowski, D-Ill., and veteran Republican Sen. Bob Packwood of Oregon. A new sensitivity to charges of personal misconduct derailed two candidates for attorney general at the start of Clinton's presidency and blocked President George Bush's first choice for secretary of Defense. And Anita Hill's allegations of sexual harassment continue to cast a shadow over Supreme Court Justice Clarence Thomas.

Despite the heightened emphasis on accusations of official wrongdoing or character flaws, many observers believe corruption or immorality among people in public life has declined, not risen, in recent times.

"There is no evidence that we are more corrupt than we were 25 years ago, but we certainly feel more corrupt," says Suzanne Garment, a scholar at the American Enterprise Institute. "And I would guess that we would find less 'unauthorized' sex than we would have found 25 years ago. But our standards have changed about what the public has a right to know."

In her book *Scandal,* Garment argued that the obsession with scandal has created a "culture of mistrust" that hurts the political system. She and other experts cite a variety of reasons for the new intensity of scandal politics.

The Watergate scandal increased public suspicion of government and invigorated a generation of investigative journalists. A wave of post-Watergate reform legislation established new standards for political life and brought some disclosure of checkered practices involving campaign financing and lobbying. And many Republicans complained during the Reagan and Bush administrations that the Democratic-controlled Congress preferred to cast political battles as scandals instead of mere policy disputes.

Brooks Jackson, an investigative reporter for CNN and formerly for *The Wall Street Journal,* links the stress on scandal to the decline of political parties and increased public cynicism about political candidates. "Politics has become largely a question of character," Jackson says. "If you can't

Public's View of Scandal Coverage

As Whitewater coverage peaked in late March, most Americans thought the media were giving the affair too much attention, according to a Gallup Poll. Many people also thought Watergate and Iran-contra received too much coverage as those scandals were breaking in 1973 and 1986.

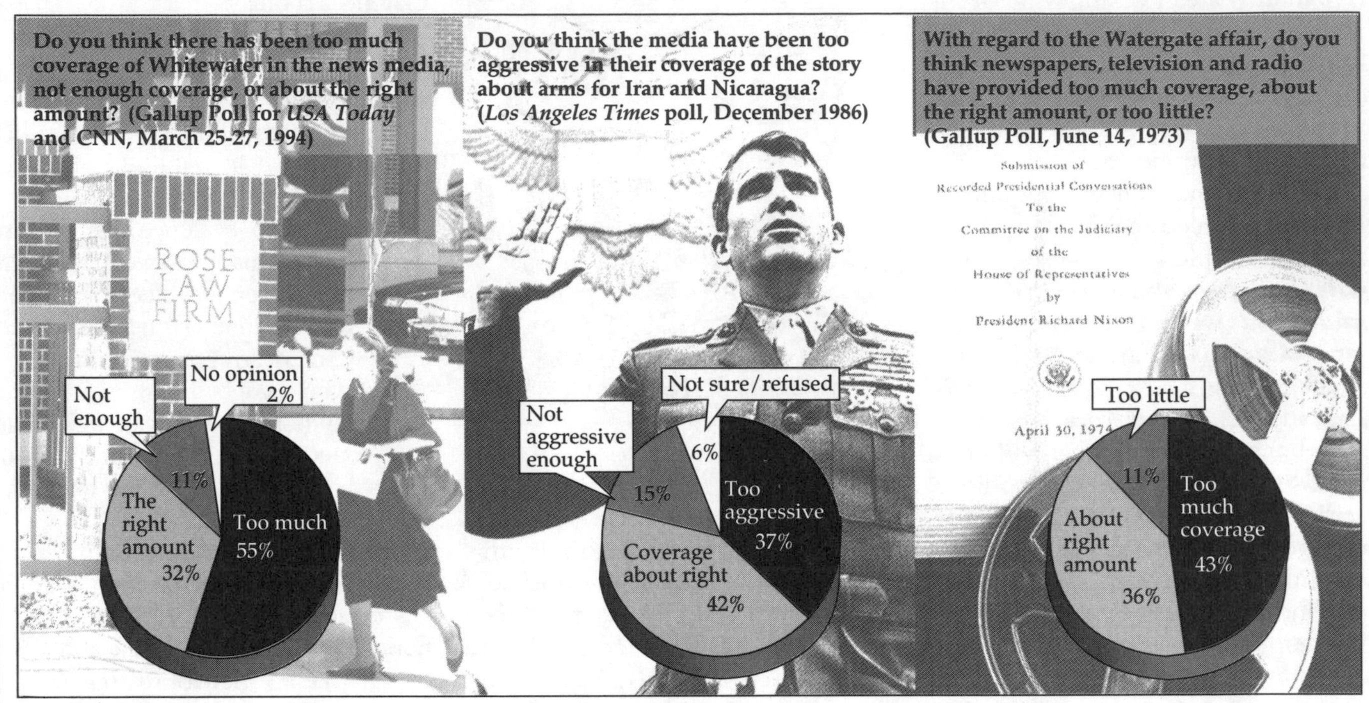
Do you think there has been too much coverage of Whitewater in the news media, not enough coverage, or about the right amount? (Gallup Poll for USA Today and CNN, March 25-27, 1994)
ROSE
LAW
FIRM
No opinion 2%
Not enough
11%
The right amount 32%
Too much 55%
Do you think the media have been too aggressive in their coverage of the story about arms for Iran and Nicaragua? (Los Angeles Times poll, December 1986)
Not sure/refused
Not aggressive enough
6%
15%
Too aggressive 37%
Coverage about right 42%
With regard to the Watergate affair, do you think newspapers, television and radio have provided too much coverage, about the right amount, or too little? (Gallup Poll, June 14, 1973)
Submission of
Recorded Presidential Conversations
To the
Committee on the Judiciary
of the
House of Representatives
by
President Richard Nixon
April 30, 1974
Too little
11%
About right amount 36%
Too much coverage 43%

Source: The American Enterprise, *May/June 1994*

depend on a candidate's party to see how they're going to behave in office, and you can't depend on a candidate to say how they're going to behave in office, you wind up relying on your gut feeling about what kind of person this candidate is."

Whatever the cause, many experts believe the emphasis on scandal has hurt the political system. "The overall impact is quite destructive to governance," says Thomas Mann, a fellow at the Brookings Institution. "It fuels a belief that everyone in public life is crooked. It turns our attention away from important issues. And it trivializes much of public life."

"The people are fed up to the gills with this kind of stuff," Morton Kondracke, executive editor of the Capitol Hill newspaper *Roll Call,* remarked on "The McLaughlin Group" May 6, the day Jones' suit was filed.

Polls support this view. A survey in late March by the Times Mirror Center for The People and The Press found that 55 percent of those responding thought the press was giving "too much attention" to Whitewater. And in early May, a *Newsweek* poll found that 59 percent of those surveyed said the media were paying too much attention to Clinton's private life.

The Times Mirror Center also found, however, that 52 percent of those responding thought the administration was "covering up" damaging information. And its poll showed a six-point drop in Clinton's approval rating from two months earlier. "The drip, drip, drip does take a toll," Eleanor Clift, *Newsweek's* White House correspondent, told a May 6 symposium sponsored by the Freedom Forum, a press study group.

Clinton has tried to disentangle himself from the web of accusations. In January, he ordered the appointment of an independent counsel to investigate Whitewater. (*See story, p. 474.*) A group of prominent Democrats formed an organization called "Back to Business" to counter Whitewater charges and focus public attention back on Clinton's health-care proposals and other policy initiatives. And this month, as Jones prepared to file her suit, Clinton told aides to adopt a strict no-comment policy and leave his defense to Bennett.

The accusations seemed unlikely

to go away anytime soon, however. Independent counsel Robert Fiske Jr. was giving indications his probe will last longer than the administration hoped. Congressional hearings on Whitewater are still expected — probably this summer. And Jones' lawsuit provides a potentially dangerous forum for renewing questions about Clinton's sexual behavior that he deflected but did not shake off during the 1992 campaign.

As those official inquiries proceed, these are some of the questions about political scandals that will be debated:

Do the news media devote too much attention to political scandals?

The press has played an essential role in raising charges of political scandal throughout American history. A partisan journalist was responsible for airing adultery charges against the country's first secretary of the Treasury, Alexander Hamilton. A century later, Lincoln Steffens and Upton Sinclair excoriated rapacious industrialists and crooked politicians — prompting Theodore Roosevelt to coin the term "muckraker" for crusading journalists. And in the 1970s, two young reporters for *The Washington Post,* Bob Woodward and Carl Bernstein, helped uncover the Watergate scandals and force the first-ever resignation of a sitting U.S. president.

The targets of scandal journalism routinely complain the press spends too much time on exposés. Richard M. Nixon charged the news media with "wallowing in Watergate." Bert Lance complained of "a pervasive and destructive cynicism" in the press corps after investigations of his banking practices forced his resignation as President Jimmy Carter's budget director. [4] House Speaker Wright commented he felt like "a hunted animal driven to his lair" as reporters hounded him for responses to ethics charges that ultimately forced him from office. [5]

As the Whitewater affair topped the news in March and April, critics of the coverage included not only Clinton supporters but also a number of leading journalists, among them National Public Radio's Daniel Schorr, PBS' Paul Duke, *New York Times* columnist Anthony Lewis and former *Washington Post* ombudsman Richard Harwood. In sum, these and other critics found too much innuendo made out of too little evidence and published too late — after Clinton was in office instead of during the 1992 campaign. [6]

Sabato echoed the critique, calling the Whitewater coverage a "classic feeding frenzy." "Headlines have outrun the facts," he told a National Press Club forum April 19. The coverage has reflected "a tremendous amount of hype," "a lack of balance" and "an insufficient attempt on the part of many in the press to explain this conglomeration of scandals."

Reporters and editors responsible for the coverage, however, find less to fault. Speaking on ABC-TV's "Nightline" on April 19, Max Frankel, executive editor of *The New York Times,* defended the newspaper's recent coverage, including its groundbreaking March 18 story disclosing Hillary Clinton's profitable commodities trading.

Frankel said the stories amounted to "unfinished business" from the newspaper's unsuccessful efforts during the campaign to document the Clintons' role in the Whitewater venture and their other business dealings in Arkansas. "We were confronted by a massive blockade," Frankel told host Ted Koppel. "We got very little help on this particular strand of the Clintons' background, and the chickens are coming home to roost."

Alan Murray, Washington bureau chief of *The Wall Street Journal,* also defends much of the Whitewater coverage. "The basic facts are very disturbing," Murray said at the press club forum, pointing to the Clintons' half interest in the Whitewater development while investing very little money. "It seems to me that it was a gift. It doesn't take a terribly highly refined sense of ethics to feel that it's not right."

To some media observers, the dogged pursuit of Whitewater stemmed less from the specific facts, however, than from a mind set born of previous scandals missed. "It is as though the media made a pact among themselves that, 'We will never again allow anyone to scoop us,'" says Stanley Kutler, a history professor at the University of Wisconsin and author of a history of Watergate. "Everybody is afraid to back off of Whitewater for fear of being called soft on the president."

In fact, many observers fault the news media for missing a number of genuine scandals while overemphasizing stories of relatively petty personal flaws and foibles. In his book *Media Circus,* Washington Post media critic Howard Kurtz lists the savings and loan industry and Department of Housing and Urban Development (HUD) scandals of the 1980s as two of the stories that major news organizations overlooked for years. [7]

While the media were slow to pick up on those stories, they had a field day in the late 1980s and early '90s with sex scandals. Media investigations of extramarital relationships forced Gary Hart to withdraw as a Democratic presidential candidate in 1987 and damaged the career of Sen. Charles S. Robb, D-Va., in 1991. Allegations of womanizing figured in the Senate's rejection of former Sen. John Tower, R-Texas, in 1993 to be secretary of Defense. And Rep. Barney Frank, D-Mass., one of Congress' two declared homosexuals, came under ethics scrutiny after *The Washington Times* disclosed that a male prostitute ran a gay escort service from Frank's apartment.

By the 1992 campaign, however, the press was in a period of self-examination. Major news organizations generally played down stories about Clinton's alleged womanizing

Continued on p. 463

When Paula Jones Spoke, the Press Wasn't Listening

Ever since *Miami Herald* reporters caught Florida model Donna Rice leaving the Washington townhouse of former Colorado Sen. Gary Hart before dawn one spring day in 1987, politicians' sex lives have seemed to be fair game — not only for grocery store tabloids but also for the establishment press and TV networks.

So when a former Arkansas state employee held a news conference in Washington on Feb. 11 to charge President Clinton with an especially crude sexual advance three years earlier, scandal watchers might have expected to see the story on the front page or the evening news.

Reuters

Paula Corbin Jones

In fact, however, the news media generally shied away from the story. Only when Paula Corbin Jones decided to file a federal civil rights suit 12 weeks later did her accusation of sexual harassment reach front pages, magazine covers and network newscasts.

The initial media silence has drawn varying interpretations. Journalists offered standard editorial reasons for holding the story — such as Jones' lack of solid corroboration or her use of a conservative forum to make the charges. Some media observers said news organizations had become more sensitive to investigations of sexual conduct by politicians since the Hart episode revealed just how powerful a sexposé could be.

But some conservative activists and media critics charged that "liberal" news media were simply letting Democrat Clinton off the hook. As proof, they pointed to the limited coverage given to Gennifer Flowers' claims in the 1992 campaign of a 12-year affair with Clinton and to the more recent allegations from former Arkansas state troopers of helping arrange Clinton's sexual liaisons while he was governor.

Others, including some non-mainstream feminists, saw evidence of a class bias. These critics charged that reporters and editors had less sympathy for a one-time clerical worker with teased hair than they had for law school Professor Anita Hill in her accusations against Supreme Court nominee Clarence Thomas three years earlier.

Once Jones went to court, however, the media could hardly ignore the story. Reporting the details of the suit posed some tricky editorial issues, however. The stories paraphrased Jones's central allegation by saying she accused Clinton of having lowered his pants and asked her to engage in oral sex. Within a few days, however, some columnists sympathetic to Clinton put into print the graphic quote ("Kiss it") that Jones attributed to Clinton — in order to show the anecdote was unbelievable.

Legal experts had conflicting views of the plausibility of Jones' allegation. Alan Dershowitz, a Harvard law professor, defense attorney and syndicated columnist, called Jones' charges stronger than Hill's. "By any standard of judgment, Miss Jones' charges against Mr. Clinton are far more serious, have more prima facie corroboration and are far more consistent with other allegations against the alleged perpetrator than were Miss Hill's charges against Mr. Thomas," Dershowitz wrote. But he acknowledged it was "too early to make an informed judgment." [1]

When the newspaper *Legal Times* asked eight well-known litigators to read and evaluate the complaint, however, most of them expressed strong skepticism. Fred Bartlit Jr., a corporate lawyer in Chicago, called Jones' central allegation "inherently not credible." Washington attorney Stephen Tallent said the suit was "drafted not with legal skill, but with talents more appropriate to a John Belushi/*National Lampoon* movie." [2]

Clinton's own lawyer, Robert S. Bennett, denied Jones' allegation within an hour after the suit was filed May 6. "The president adamantly denies that this incident occurred," Bennett said. He also raised the possibility of seeking to have the suit dismissed on grounds of presidential immunity.

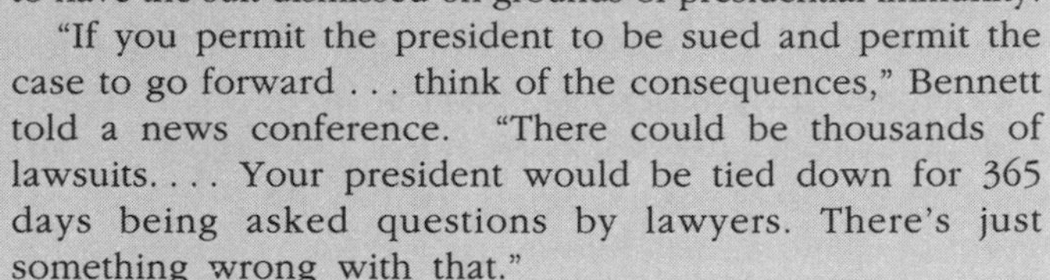

"If you permit the president to be sued and permit the case to go forward . . . think of the consequences," Bennett told a news conference. "There could be thousands of lawsuits. . . . Your president would be tied down for 365 days being asked questions by lawyers. There's just something wrong with that."

In 1982 the Supreme Court ruled in *Nixon v. Fitzgerald* that the president is immune from civil suit for any official actions. "Because of the singular importance of the president's duties," Justice Lewis F. Powell Jr. wrote in the 5-4 ruling, "diversion of his energies by concern with private lawsuits would raise unique risks to the effective functioning of government." The decision barred a wrongful termination suit against Nixon by a fired Air Force whistle-blower, Ernest Fitzgerald.

Legal experts say there apparently are no published court decisions involving suits against a president for conduct occurring before his presidency. The Justice Department is considered likely to support a presidential immunity plea by arguing that the suit against Clinton should either be dismissed or delayed until after he leaves office.

---

[1] *The Washington Times,* May 8, 1994, p. B1.

[2] *Legal Times,* May 16, 1994, pp. 30-32. The newspaper also published the text of the complaint.

Continued from p. 461

after he went on the CBS program "60 Minutes" to acknowledge "wrongdoing" in his marriage. And when conservative groups this year began pushing charges that Clinton had used Arkansas state troopers while governor to help line up sexual liaisons, the *Los Angeles Times* was the only major newspaper to give the story full coverage. [8]

Jones' charges — first made in February at a Washington news conference — were similarly shunned by major news outlets. (*See story, p. 462.*) Accuracy in Media, a conservative watchdog group, resorted to ads in *The Washington Post* and *The New York Times* to get the accusations into those papers. Once Jones said she would file suit, however, the story could not be ignored.

Rosemary Armao, executive director of the media organization Investigative Reporters and Editors, agrees with critics that the media have "overdone" some stories, but says the press must be "biased in favor of publication."

"That's our job," says Armao, formerly executive editor of the *Norfolk Virginian-Pilot*. "That's not an excuse to oversensationalize. But to cover or not to cover, that's pretty clearcut: You cover."

Has Congress misused its power to investigate allegations of government corruption or wrongdoing?

Congress also has played its part in airing political scandals throughout U.S. history. Early this century, a Senate investigation of government oil field leasing policies in 1923 uncovered the Teapot Dome Scandal. And the Senate Watergate Committee in May and June 1973 was the first official body to expose the full range of campaign misconduct and official abuses in the Nixon administration.

But congressional investigations also have engendered opposition. Many presidents have resisted congressional requests for information as intrusions on executive prerogatives. And in the 1950s, the anti-communist witch hunts by Sen. Joseph R. McCarthy, R-Wis., demonstrated the risks that unrestrained congressional investigations posed to individuals' reputations.

Both lines of criticism have gained strength since Watergate. In her book, Garment argues that partisan differences, institutional rivalries and the growth of congressional staff have led to "a perpetual scandal hunt" on Capitol Hill. A prosecutorial attitude pervades committee hearings, she suggests. Individuals are treated as "presumptive liars" and policy dilemmas "as the acts of swindlers and prevaricators." [9]

A former top lawyer for the House of Representatives agrees. "Proportionality and perspective in the investigation process have left us," says Stanley Brand, who served as House counsel from 1976-84. "It's left us for quite some time."

Norman J. Ornstein, a resident scholar at the American Enterprise Institute, also faults Congress for excessive zeal in some of its recent investigations. But he notes that some hearings have also deflated bogus scandals. In 1992, for example, he says a House committee discredited suggestions that George Bush, as a vice presidential candidate in 1980, was involved in secret contacts with Iran to delay the release of U.S. hostages until after the presidential election.

In recent years, however, Congress itself has been the target of many political scandals. "It's as much victim as perpetrator," says Brookings' Mann. He points to the ethics charges against Speaker Wright, the influence-peddling accusations against the "Keating Five" and the public furor in 1992 over overdrafts at the House bank.

Suzanne Garment thinks the wave of charges against lawmakers themselves has reduced the appetite on Capitol Hill for scandal politics. "I don't notice a lot of rhetoric these days about other people's sleaze," she says.

Still, when the Whitewater affair began churning last fall, congressional Republicans swung into action. In November, Republicans on the House Banking Committee called for broad hearings into the failure of Madison Guaranty Savings and Loan, the thrift headed by the Clintons' partner in the Whitewater venture, James McDougal. The committee's Democratic chairman, Henry B. Gonzalez of Texas, accused the Republicans of engaging in "a partisan fishing expedition or witch-hunt."

In January, Democrats also began warning that any congressional hearings might interfere with the Whitewater probe by special counsel Fiske. Fiske himself urged lawmakers to postpone hearings. But Republicans insisted they could be structured to avoid damaging Fiske's investigation and that the public's right to know took precedence anyway.

By March, Democrats began to give way. "There's no doubt there's going to be hearings," Senate Majority Leader George J. Mitchell of Maine acknowledged March 11. Still, Mitchell and House Speaker Thomas S. Foley, D-Wash., continued to talk of delaying hearings until after Fiske completed an initial phase of his investigation. And later that month, Gonzalez angrily put off a scheduled oversight hearing on the Resolution Trust Corporation to deny the committee's ranking Republican, Jim Leach of Iowa, a forum for probing charges that Clinton used his power as governor to slow regulatory actions against Madison Guaranty. [10]

Some observers, however, think the pressure for congressional hearings has diminished since March. "An awful lot of Republicans went back home, and the feedback they got was, 'Hey, you're overdoing it,' " says Ornstein. Barring new disclosures, he now predicts the eventual hearings will prove to be narrowly focused on technical issues about financial regulation.

Sabato agrees that hearings are "perfectly proper" but hopes they are not blown out of proportion. "I don't think it [should become] another Watergate or Iran-contra where the country is transfixed, and everything else is put on a back burner," Sabato says.

Has "scandal politics" hurt the political system?

A wide range of people in and around government believe that the obsessive search for wrongdoing in recent years has hurt the political system. They contend that scandal politics has made public service less attractive and distracted government and the public from more pressing issues.

Some observers, however, find the changed atmosphere in Washington less disturbing or, in some respects, healthy. Feminist groups view the Clarence Thomas hearings not as an inquisition but a watershed event forcing official Washington to take sexual harassment more seriously. Public interest groups regard the Keating Five scandal not as a persecution but a step toward reining in the influence of money on politics.

Still, even some of those who have helped uncover scandals confess to a sense of disquiet. "I think we have been obsessed by scandal," says CNN's Jackson. "It's always been a legitimate matter of inquiry whether someone is dipping into the public till. But when you start talking about other areas of personal behavior, there are no clear lines. People are confused."

Clearly, one effect of the country's greatest scandal — Watergate — was to set new constraints on presidential power. Watergate allowed Congress to enact the War Powers Resolution and a budget procedure act aimed at limiting executive prerogatives over war-making and spending. It also left a lasting legacy of mistrust of the president among journalists and, to a lesser degree, the public.

Today, that distrust is regarded as unfortunate even by liberals. "There's a difference between scrutinizing and crippling a presidency, so as to make it virtually impossible for them to govern," says historian Kutler.

On Capitol Hill, many lawmakers and people sympathetic to Congress fault the emphasis on campaign finance. "The biggest tempest in a teapot is election reform, and the second biggest is lobby reform," says Brand.

"I don't think campaign contributions really steer people," Brand adds. "I don't think PACs [political action committees] steer people. And there's a disproportionate amount of time spent worrying about whether a lobbyist who takes a member to lunch has corrupted the system."

But Fred Wertheimer, president of the public interest lobbying group Common Cause, argues that enforcing existing campaign finance and ethics laws and passing stronger restrictions will help rebuild public confidence in Congress. "There are practices and activities that are directly involved in building public cynicism," Wertheimer says, "and part of that is the way lobbies, lobbyists and interest groups use money in the political process."

As the threshold for scandal has been lowered, many Washington insiders believe that service in government has become less and less attractive. "You don't see the best people in any profession running for Congress — academia, law, business," Republican political consultant Eddie Mahe remarked recently. [11] And Reagan and Bush administration personnel officials often complained that tightened financial-disclosure rules made it difficult to recruit people for executive branch positions.

Some Washington observers are dubious, however. "I hear that said all the time," says Jackson, "but I don't see any vacancies." And Mann says he has seen no decline in the quality of people serving in Congress. But he adds, "I'm worried over the longer haul; if Congress continues to diminish in the eyes of the public, it will have an impact on the people who build the institution."

Scandal-watchers Garment and Sabato, however, say they see no signs that the political atmosphere is changing. "I feel very discouraged," says Garment. "I've been saying for five years that it's going to end any minute."

Sabato agrees that there's been no let-up in scandal politics. But he sees an encouraging sign in the public's ability to put scandals in better perspective. "We are the scandal generation," says Sabato. "Over time, we're becoming very good at interpreting scandal and determining what's important and what isn't about the myriad of scandals with which we're presented on a weekly basis." ■

BACKGROUND

Follow the Money

Money has been the most frequent source of political scandal in American history — from simple bribery and embezzlement to more elaborate methods of funneling money to politicians and officials in return for government favors. [12]

President George Washington set a high ethical standard for the new federal government that continued until the Jacksonian era. But Washington's secretary of State, Edmund Randolph, resigned in 1795 after an intercepted French dispatch indicated he had sought money in return for favorable treatment of French interests. Randolph denied the charge, and historians consider the accusation unresolved.

The election of President Andrew Jackson in 1828 opened an era of partisan strife marked by recurrent episodes

Continued on p. 466

Chronology

1950s-1960s

The age of television magnifies impact of political scandals in Washington, but news media generally skirt questions of drinking and sex.

Sept. 23, 1952
Richard M. Nixon counters "slush fund" charges with a nationally televised speech that helps save his place as the Republican vice presidential nominee.

Sept. 22, 1958
White House Chief of Staff Sherman Adams resigns after disclosures he accepted expensive gifts from financier Bernard Goldfine.

Oct. 7, 1963
Robert G. "Bobby" Baker Jr., protégé of Lyndon B. Johnson, resigns as secretary to Senate majority to avoid answering questions about conflict of interest and influence-peddling.

July 24, 1964
Senate votes to establish a permanent, bipartisan ethics committee to hear complaints against senators. The House establishes a similar committee in April 1967.

1970s

Watergate establishes a new benchmark for political scandal. News media give more attention to drinking by politicians.

Aug. 9, 1974
President Nixon resigns — climaxing two years of investigation into Watergate scandal.

Oct. 7, 1974
House Ways and Means Committee Chairman Wilbur D. Mills, D-Ark., is found drunk with a Washington stripper. His alcoholism exposed, Mills retires two years later.

Oct. 24, 1976
The Washington Post, in the first report of the "Koreagate" scandal, discloses a Justice Department investigation of payments by South Korean agents to members of Congress.

Oct. 26, 1978
President Jimmy Carter signs Ethics in Government Act, establishing procedures for appointment of special prosecutor to investigate charges of wrongdoing by high-ranking federal officials.

1980s

Partisan battles between Republican White House and Democratic-controlled Congress give sharper edge to scandals.

Nov. 25, 1986
Iran-contra scandal is disclosed when Attorney General Edwin Meese III announces that proceeds from sale of arms to Iran were diverted to aid Nicaraguan rebels.

May 3, 1987
Miami Herald stakeout discloses evidence of a relationship between presidential contender Gary Hart and a Florida model.

May 31, 1989
House Speaker Jim Wright, D-Texas, resigns while facing ethics charges.

1990s

Some political and media observers decry excesses of scandal politics, but news media and others continue to give prominent attention to wide range of charges of misconduct.

Feb. 27, 1991
Senate Ethics Committee concludes "Keating Five" inquiry by recommending discipline of Sen. Alan Cranston, D-Calif., and criticizing judgment of four other senators.

Sept. 18, 1991
A General Accounting Office report discloses that House members wrote more than 8,000 overdrafts on the House bank during 12-month period.

Jan. 26, 1992
Democratic presidential hopeful Bill Clinton, appearing with his wife on CBS' "60 Minutes," acknowledges "wrongdoing" in his marriage.

Jan. 12, 1994
President Clinton tries to lay Whitewater affair to rest by ordering appointment of special counsel to investigate matter.

May 5, 1994
House Ways and Means Committee Chairman Dan Rostenkowski, D-Ill., is notified that federal prosecutors have prepared a criminal indictment against him in House Post Office scandal.

May 6, 1994
Former Arkansas state employee Paula Corbin Jones files civil rights suit alleging President Clinton, while governor, made unwanted sexual advance.

Continued from p. 464

of politically motivated financial wrongdoing. The James Buchanan administration — viewed as the most corrupt of pre-Civil War governments — directed naval construction contracts and government printing work to favored concerns in return for campaign contributions. Investigations of the corruption by the Republican-controlled House undermined the Democratic Party and helped pave the way for the election of "Honest Abe" Lincoln in 1860.

After the Civil War, industrialization and national expansion brought an era of financial prosperity and a level of corruption in government unseen before or since. Congress was rocked in the early 1870s by evidence that stockholders in the Credit Mobilier construction company bribed members of Congress to ignore huge profits they were making on building the Union Pacific Railroad. Two House members were expelled, and others — including a future president, James A. Garfield — were widely thought to have received bribes too.

President Ulysses S. Grant was personally honest, but his administration was touched by a series of scandals. In the biggest episode — the so-called Whiskey Ring — more than 350 low-ranking officials and liquor distillers were charged with defrauding the government by falsifying production records and bribing inspectors.

The excesses of the Gilded Age brought calls for reform. Grant helped win enactment of the first federal civil service legislation in 1872. Over the next 40 years, other reforms aimed at breaking corrupt ties between government and business, including the establishment of independent federal regulatory agencies and use of the initiative, recall and referendum in state and local governments.

The boom era after World War I brought on the notorious Teapot Dome affair, which took its name from one of two oil fields that President Warren Harding's Interior secretary, Albert Fall, leased on favorable terms to oil millionaires Edward Doheny and Harry Sinclair. After Harding's death, a Senate investigation showed that Fall had taken $400,000 in gifts or loans from the two men. Fall was convicted of bribery, and the leases canceled, but Sinclair and Doheny were both acquitted.

From *Judge*, Sept. 27, 1884/Library of Congress

Scandals Arise Frequently After World War II

After World War II, most administrations have been beset by allegations of financial wrongdoing. Harry S Truman's was tarnished by bribe-taking Internal Revenue Service (IRS) officials and conflicts of interest in loans by the Reconstruction Finance Corporation. President Dwight D. Eisenhower had to accept the resignation of his chief of staff, Sherman Adams, for taking valuable gifts — including a vicuna coat — from financier Bernard Goldfine and intervening on Goldfine's behalf with a federal agency.

In the 1960s, President Lyndon B. Johnson was embarrassed by personal ties to two financial manipulators: Billie Sol Estes, who was convicted of fraud in connection with federal farm-subsidy programs; and Robert G. "Bobby" Baker Jr., the one-time secretary of the Senate majority who was convicted of stealing savings and loan funds for campaign donations.

It was also in the 1960s that a little-known governor of Maryland — Spiro T. Agnew — began taking kickbacks from state government contractors. Agnew's corruption was not proven until 1973, when he plea-bargained his way out of prison by resigning the nation's second-highest office just as President Nixon was trying to extricate himself from the Watergate scandals. [13]

Since Watergate, the smell of financial wrongdoing has hung heavier over Congress than the executive branch. In 1980, the "Abscam" sting operation snared a half-dozen members of Congress on bribery charges for taking cash from FBI agents posing as Arab businessmen seeking government favors. A decade later, Speaker Wright resigned after the House ethics committee found he had improperly taken favors from a Texas developer and used a book deal to circumvent limits on outside income.

Meanwhile, the Senate Ethics Committee began a two-year investigation of charges of influence-peddling by five senators on behalf of savings and loan executive Charles Keating. The probe ended in 1991 with a formal Senate action denouncing one of the senators — Alan Cranston, D-Calif. — and committee letters criticizing the other four.

Sex, Alcohol, Drugs

Sex has been a fitful source of political scandal in U.S. history. Ironically, accusations of sexual misconduct have proved to be more damaging in recent years than they were in supposedly more conservative times.

In the first years of the Republic, Alexander Hamilton had an affair with a woman who, with her husband, blackmailed him for two years. When he stopped making payments, the couple exposed him to opponents in Congress. But Hamilton dissuaded them from exposing him in 1792 by assuring them he had not abused his public office. And when the affair did become public later, Hamilton defended himself again. As Suzanne Garment concludes the story, "his career stayed afloat." [14]

Garment relates other episodes that failed to derail political careers. Thomas Jefferson was publicly charged with seducing married women. Andrew Jackson was accused of having married his wife Rachel before she had been divorced from her first husband. Grover Cleveland fathered a child out of wedlock but was elected president despite his opponents' mocking campaign chant — "Ma, ma, where's my pa? Gone to the White House. Ha, ha, ha!"

Two 20th-century presidents had extramarital affairs that came to light only well after their deaths. Franklin D. Roosevelt had an extended affair with Lucy Mercer, his wife Eleanor's social secretary, before entering national politics and renewed the friendship, perhaps on platonic terms, in the White House. [15] John F. Kennedy had sexual liaisons with numerous women both before and during his presidency, including the mistress of an organized crime boss. As Sabato points out, even though some reporters suspected or knew of FDR's relationship, and many had evidence of JFK's womanizing, nothing appeared in print during their presidencies. [16]

In the past two decades, however, evidence of extramarital sexual activities has helped cut short a number of political careers. Rep. Wilbur D. Mills, D-Ark., powerful chairman of the House Ways and Means Committee, was laughed into political oblivion after a chance encounter with police in 1974 exposed his alcoholism and his extramarital relationship with a burlesque dancer known as "the Argentine firecracker." Rep. Wayne L. Hays, D-Ohio, resigned in 1976 after *The Washington Post* disclosed that he had put his mistress on the congressional payroll.

"Nixon in Web," 1974/Library of Congress

More dramatically, a sex scandal in 1987 sank the presidential bid of Gary Hart, the former Colorado senator. A stakeout by *Miami Herald* reporters disclosed evidence of a relationship between Hart and Florida model Donna Rice — contradicting Hart's denials of womanizing.

Hart's withdrawal from the race helped prompt rethinking within the news media about coverage of politicians' private lives. In the 1992 presidential campaign five years later, established news organizations did display a restrained attitude toward Bill Clinton's sexual activities. Clinton's carefully worded acknowledgment of sexual indiscretion helped deflect attention too, but his incomplete admission also left him vulnerable to a renewal of the issue if more detailed accusations were to surface.

Recent decades have also seen more open coverage of alcohol or drug use by politicians or public officials. Years ago, as Sabato relates, the well-known drinking problems of prominent Washington figures — such as Sens. McCarthy and Russell B. Long, D-La. — were never put into print. [17] The Mills episode helped ease the taboo on the subject. Fifteen years later, allegations of excessive drinking figured heavily in the Senate's narrow rejection of Tower as President Bush's first nominee for secretary of Defense.

Two years earlier, Supreme Court nominee Douglas Ginsburg was forced to withdraw after news stories disclosed that the federal judge had used marijuana while he was a law school professor. The episode led to a rash of questions and stories probing drug use by other public officials. But a new strategy emerged of pre-emptive admissions. During the 1988 presidential race, for example, two Democratic contenders — Sen. Al Gore of Ten-

When Scandals Entangle Washington Officials . . .

Scandals have been part of the Washington scene since the earliest days of the Republic. Some officials have been permanently disgraced or banished from government, while others weathered the storm. Here are some of the people who have been embroiled in scandal or near-scandal in the past 40 years:

Richard M. Nixon

Sen. Richard M. Nixon, R-Calif.
GOP vice presidential candidate
"Slush fund" charges, 1952;
retained on ticket

Sherman Adams
White House chief of staff
Resigned, 1958;
accepted gifts from financier

Robert G. "Bobby" Baker Jr.
Secretary of Senate majority
Resigned, 1963; convicted, 1967;
influence-peddling; tax evasion

Justice Abe Fortas
Resigned, 1969;
accepted gifts from financier

Justice William O. Douglas
Charged with improper extra-judicial behavior; impeachment move failed, 1970

Spiro T. Agnew

Vice President Spiro T. Agnew
Resigned, 1973;
tax evasion (bribery probe)

Bert Lance

President Richard M. Nixon
Resigned, 1974;
cited in Watergate affair for obstruction of justice, abuse of power, contempt of Congress

Rep. Wilbur D. Mills, D-Ark.
Retired, 1976;
alcoholism

Hamilton Jordan

Bert Lance
Budget director
Resigned, 1977;
banking practices questioned

Rep. Edward Roybal, D-Calif.
Koreagate (unreported cash contribution); reprimanded, 1978; served until retirement, 1992

Hamilton Jordan
White House chief of staff
Drug-use charges, 1979;
cleared of charges

Sen. Harrison Williams, D-N.J
Resigned, 1982;
charged in Abscam bribery case

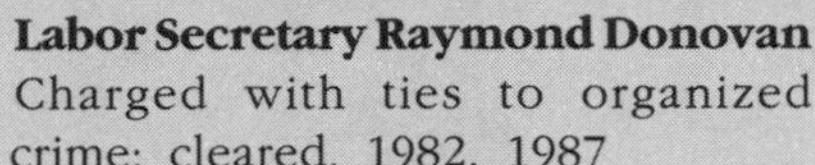

Labor Secretary Raymond Donovan
Charged with ties to organized crime; cleared, 1982, 1987

Edwin Meese III

John M. Poindexter

Anne M. Burford
EPA administrator
Resigned, 1983;
charged with political manipulation, contempt of Congress

nessee and Arizona Gov. Bruce Babbitt — both disclosed they had previously smoked marijuana. The disclosures had no noticeable effects on their campaigns.

By the end of the 1988 campaign, the public appeared largely willing to disregard past use of marijuana as long as a candidate was truthful in discussing the issue. But in 1992, Bill Clinton ran afoul of that rule. When questioned about using marijuana, Clinton first said that he had never broken a state law. Later, he acknowledged having tried pot in England, but claimed he "didn't inhale."

Abuse of Power

Watergate wrought a lasting change in the politics of scandal in the United States. While scandals involving money, sex, drinking or drugs continued, the array of campaign "dirty tricks" and official abuses that comprised the Watergate scandals established a new reference point for political misconduct.

The exact motive for the wiretapping of the Democratic National Committee headquarters in the Watergate Hotel complex remains a mystery more than 20 years after the fact. A break-in

. . . Some Lose Their Jobs, But Others Are Spared

Gary Hart

Edwin Meese III
White House counselor, attorney general
Financial disclosure questioned, 1984; no prosecution; confirmed as attorney general

President Ronald Reagan
Iran-contra role criticized; Completed second term, 1985-1989

John M. Poindexter
National security adviser
Resigned, 1986;
Iran-contra scandal

Lt. Col. Oliver L. North
National Security Council aide
Fired, 1986;
Iran-contra scandal

Jim Wright

Gary Hart
Democratic presidential candidate
Withdrew, 1987;
evidence of extramarital relationship

Theodore Olson
Assistant attorney general
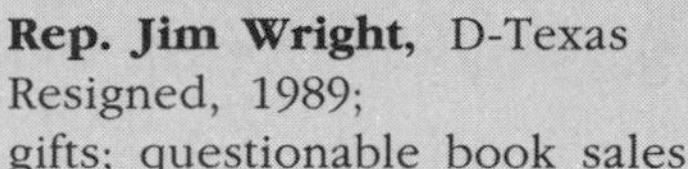
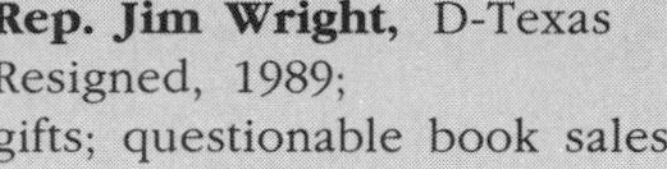
Charged with lying to Congress; cleared, 1988.

Rep. Jim Wright, D-Texas
Resigned, 1989;
gifts; questionable book sales

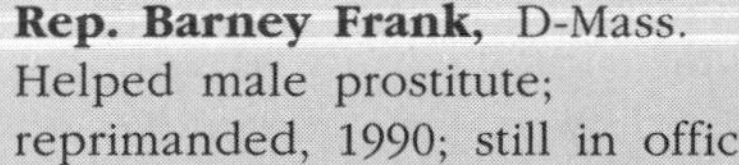

Barney Frank

Rep. Barney Frank, D-Mass.
Helped male prostitute;
reprimanded, 1990; still in office

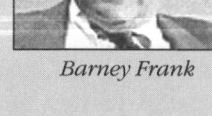

Alan Cranston

President George Bush
Iran-contra role studied;
"October surprise" charge probed; completed term, 1989-93.

Clarence Thomas
Accused of sexual harassment; confirmed as Supreme Court justice, 1991.

Sens. Donald W. Riegle Jr., D-Mich.
Dennis DeConcini, D-Ariz.,
John Glenn, D-Ohio,
John McCain, R-Ariz.
Investigated in "Keating Five" case; not disciplined; still in office.

Sen. Alan Cranston, D-Calif. Reprimanded, 1991; retired, 1992; aid to S&L executive (Keating Five case)

House bank
Closed, 1992;
105 members with overdrafts retired or were defeated for re-election

Clarence Thomas

Zoë Baird

Zoë Baird
Attorney general-designate
Withdrew, 1993;
did not pay "nanny" tax

Judge Kimba Wood
Attorney general candidate;
Withdrew from consideration, 1993; employed illegal alien for child care

to fix the wiretap in the early morning hours of June 17, 1972, went awry and led to the arrests of five men employed by Nixon's re-election campaign.

The arrests threatened to disclose other campaign misconduct as well as the existence of the White House's extralegal "Plumbers Unit" that had engaged in domestic covert activities against political opponents. To try to contain the scandal, Nixon personally approved a massive coverup that included cash payments to the burglars for their silence.

But their leader, James W. McCord Jr., broke his silence after receiving a stiff prison sentence. A select Senate committee was appointed to look into his accusations. In nationally televised hearings, the Watergate committee heard the president's former counsel, John W. Dean III, tie the coverup to Nixon. And the panel discovered the existence of the secret taping system that had recorded evidence of Nixon's wrongdoing.

When the Supreme Court upheld the Watergate prosecutor's subpoena for those tapes in July 1974, the scandal came to a rapid conclusion. Within a few days, the House Judiciary Committee approved three articles of impeachment against Nixon. And on Aug. 9,

Auth © 1992 *The Philadelphia Inquirer*, Universal Press Syndicate

1974, Nixon resigned the presidency.

The Watergate committee hearings, impeachment investigation and criminal trials of Nixon aides established a detailed record of the scandal. Still, to this day, Nixon's defenders insist he did little more than previous presidents or officials had done.

The Iran-contra Affair

A decade later, the Reagan administration tried to minimize any appearance of coverup when confronted with a scandal involving alleged abuse of power by White House officials. The Iran-contra affair — first disclosed by a Lebanese newspaper in early November 1986 — involved secret efforts to trade U.S. arms for American hostages held in Iran and a separate plot to use proceeds from the arms deal to support the right-wing rebels in Nicaragua. Both schemes arguably violated congressional restrictions on presidential prerogatives in foreign policy.

Three weeks after the story broke, the White House fired the mastermind of the schemes, Lt. Col. L. Oliver North, a National Security Council aide; accepted the resignation of national security adviser John M. Poindexter; and asked for appointment of an independent counsel to investigate the affairs. As Garment points out, the moves succeeded in distancing President Reagan himself from the scandals. [18]

The official investigations by independent counsel Lawrence E. Walsh and a select House-Senate committee laid out most of the events in the scandal but failed to bring about a public consensus about its significance. North's defiant denunciation of congressional meddling in foreign policy before the Iran-contra committee won wide public support. Walsh won a few convictions, but an appeals court threw out the biggest cases — against North and Poindexter.

As Walsh's investigation dragged on, critics denounced it as an expensive and unaccountable prosecution for what was ultimately a political dispute. On Christmas Eve 1992, President Bush effectively ended the prosecutions with pardons for a half-dozen Iran-contra figures, including former Defense Secretary Caspar W. Weinberger, whom Walsh had charged with lying to cover up the scandal.

'Post-Watergate Morality'

Watergate created a new nomenclature for political scandals in the United States. The news media blithely used a sinister suffix to focus public attention on allegations ranging from serious to nearly trivial.

First came Koreagate: accusations in 1977-78 of widespread bribery of members of Congress by Korean agents. There followed Billygate, the probe of lobbying by President Jimmy Carter's brother for the Libyan government, and Debategate, allegations that the Reagan campaign purloined a copy of Carter's briefing book for their 1980 debate. By 1993, the usage had reached a seeming low point when attorney general-designate Zoë Baird's failure to pay Social Security taxes for her child-care provider sent reporters looking for more "nannygate" culprits.

More substantively, Watergate fostered a wave of reforms aimed at preventing corruption or abuse in political campaigns, the executive branch and Congress, including:

- Campaign finance amendments in 1974 that set a $1,000 limit on the amount an individual could contribute to a campaign for national office.
- The Inspector General Act of 1978, protecting government whistleblowers and establishing independent inspectors general in a dozen Cabinet departments and agencies.
- The Ethics in Government Act of 1978, establishing procedures for court appointment of a special prosecutor to investigate allegations of wrongdoing against high-ranking executive branch officials.

Watergate also instilled a new zeal in a generation of journalists. Many viewed exposing political scandals as a mission and, not incidentally, a path to career advancement.

At first, the so-called post-Watergate morality was widely regarded as positive. Reformers said the heightened attention to abuses would help cleanse the political system. But a disquiet was born as early as the late 1970s and continued to grow through the '80s.

President Carter's chief of staff,

Hamilton Jordan, endured a special prosecutor's investigation before being cleared of charges of using cocaine. Carter's first budget director, Bert Lance, was forced to resign after a swirl of banking-misconduct charges. On Capitol Hill, Koreagate began with suggestions that up to 100 lawmakers had taken financial payoffs from Korean government lobbyists. But the scandal ended in 1978 with only one former House member convicted of a crime and three given mild reprimands.

The 1980s began with a more substantive episode of corruption on Capitol Hill: the FBI's Abscam sting investigation, which caught a half-dozen members of Congress taking cash payoffs from undercover agents. But the decade ended with a less clearcut scandal when Wright resigned following disclosures that he had accepted favors from a Texas developer and used book sales to skirt limits on outside income.

The House ethics committee concluded Wright broke House rules, but the investigation — pushed most strongly by Republicans — left partisan wounds. In resigning, Wright urged his colleagues to "bring this period of mindless cannibalism to an end."

The Reagan administration was also beset by charges of misconduct with partisan overtones. Many Republicans pointed to the Iran contra scandal as the prime example of a partisan dispute transformed into political scandal. Political fights also underlay two other investigations of Reagan administration officials by special prosecutors.

Theodore Olson, a former assistant attorney general, faced accusations of withholding documents from a congressional committee looking into the Environmental Protection Agency (EPA). And opponents of Attorney General Edwin Meese III raised ethics charges related to his financial affairs to block his confirmation as attorney general. Both men were cleared of wrongdoing.

The confirmation battle over Clarence Thomas in 1991 increased the concern in many quarters about scandal politics. He and his supporters insisted he had been unfairly hit, late in the process, with sexual harassment charges that he had no way to disprove. "This is a circus," he told the Senate Judiciary Committee in an impassioned defense that helped him win narrow approval from the full Senate.

But the accusations continued to hang over Thomas. One year after his confirmation, a *Wall Street Journal*-NBC News poll showed that more Americans — 44 percent to 34 percent — believed the accusations against him. [19] ■

CURRENT SITUATION

The Clintons' Woes

Ghosts from the past haunted Bill Clinton throughout the 1992 presidential campaign. He went on national television to make a veiled acknowledgment of extramarital sex. He struggled to get his story straight on how he avoided the draft. He admitted smoking marijuana — but said he never inhaled.

With those evident vulnerabilities, an obscure story about Bill and Hillary Clinton's role in a losing real estate venture with the head of a failed Arkansas savings and loan understandably stirred little interest among voters, political opponents, or the press. Just two days after *The New York Times* published the first major Whitewater-Madison Guaranty story on March 8, 1992, Clinton swept six Southern primaries. For Clinton, the road to the White House had many twists and turns, but Whitewater was not even a bump.

After Clinton took office, however, legal processes and a seemingly unrelated personal tragedy combined to revive the Whitewater issue.

In July, Vincent W. Foster Jr., the deputy White House counsel and a friend of Clinton's since childhood, committed suicide. Foster also had been a partner of Hillary Clinton's at the Rose Law Firm in Little Rock and had handled Whitewater matters for the Clintons. That connection prompted some Clinton detractors — in particular, *New York Times* columnist William Safire — to surmise that Foster's depression may have been caused in part by a fear that the Clintons faced damaging disclosures in the Whitewater affair.

Meanwhile, the Resolution Trust Corporation (RTC), the federal agency charged with disposing of assets of failed savings institutions, in October asked the Justice Department to open a criminal inquiry into Madison Guaranty. As part of its criminal referral, the RTC said that some funds from Madison may have benefited Clinton's gubernatorial campaigns.

The Justice Department finally assigned a team of prosecutors from Washington to the case, but critics called for an independent investigation. For weeks, those calls were resisted by Attorney General Janet Reno and key people inside the White House, including Hillary Clinton. In January, however, Clinton finally acceded to the pressure and directed Reno to pick an outside lawyer to lead the Whitewater investigation. Reno tapped Robert Fiske, a private attorney in New York and former Republican-appointed U.S. attorney.

Meanwhile, the issue of Clinton's sexual conduct while governor had also been revived. *The Los Angeles Times* and a conservative magazine, *The American Spectator,* published

Dan Rostenkowski

massive stories in December and January detailing accusations by four Arkansas state troopers that they helped arrange sexual liaisons for Clinton. [20]

Clinton's defenders responded by questioning some of the details, depicting the charges as old hat and attacking the motives of the man who was handling the troopers' press relations — Cliff Jackson, an Arkansas lawyer and longtime Clinton foe. The strategy worked. By February, when Jones aired her charge against Clinton at a Washington news conference, major news outlets were scandal-shy. The *Los Angeles Times* ran a medium-sized account of Jones' charges, but *The New York Times* carried only a four-inch story.

In March, however, *The New York Times* opened a new line of inquiry with its disclosure of Hillary Clinton's commodities trading. Despite the impenetrable complexities of commodities trading, the story's central points were easy to understand: Hillary Clinton, a novice in a risky field, made $100,000 profit in a year and a half with the help of a lawyer for Arkansas' biggest private employer, Tyson Foods, while Bill Clinton was beginning his first term as governor.

In the weeks of coverage that followed, the suspicion persisted that Mrs. Clinton's remarkable success might have depended on preferential treatment or left Clinton indebted to the lawyer for a company with a big stake in a variety of state regulatory issues. Mrs. Clinton tried to put the issue to rest with an extraordinary, hour-long news conference on April 22. She insisted there was "no evidence" of favoritism but acknowledged heavy reliance on Tyson's lawyer, James Blair, whom she described as a close friend.

In some respects, the charges swirling about the Clintons seemed thin. Whitewater could be viewed — in reporter Jackson's words — as "a penny-ante real estate deal that went bad." Journalists had uncovered no smoking gun of wrongdoing in the commodities trading. Troopergate could be dismissed as a partisan vendetta. And for many, aspects of Jones' account of her hotel-room encounter with Clinton strained credulity. According to a Times Mirror Co. poll in mid-May, most people — 54 percent to 23 percent — found Clinton far more believable than Jones.

Clinton's defenders stressed the meager evidence of wrongdoing as they urged his critics to let him get "back to business." As some observers point out, however, Clinton himself may be responsible for the cloud over the White House. During the campaign, he finessed some of the issues now being discussed — for example, by commissioning an incomplete auditor's report on Whitewater and withholding income tax returns that would have disclosed the commodities trading profits.

Now, the issues have returned. And questions persist, in part, because Clinton's performance in office itself has added to public doubts about his personal character. "There is still a significant doubt about Bill Clinton's trustworthiness," ABC White House correspondent Ann Compton told the Freedom Forum symposium last month.

Scandals on the Hill

When the U.S. attorney's office in Washington in 1991 began looking into suspected embezzlement and drug dealing by House Post Office employees, investigators did not expect the probe would lead to a possible indictment of one of the most powerful House members — Dan Rostenkowski, an Illinois Democrat and chairman of the tax-writing Ways and Means Committee. [21]

Nor did free-lance reporter Florence Graves imagine, when she began work on a story in 1992 about the treatment of female employees on Capitol Hill, that she would prompt an ethics inquiry into one of the Senate's strongest supporters of women's rights — Oregon Republican Bob Packwood. [22]

But today Rostenkowski and Packwood find themselves the latest congressional targets of serious, career-threatening charges of wrongdoing.

The new federal prosecutor in Washington has drawn up criminal charges against Rostenkowski that are now being reviewed by the Justice Department. The charges stem from allegations that Rostenkowski used the House Post Office to trade stamp vouchers for cash and misused official funds for personal expenses. Rostenkowski has denied wrongdoing. [23]

Meanwhile, the Senate Ethics Committee is moving toward formal hearings on charges that Packwood made improper sexual advances toward nearly two dozen women stretching back more

Continued on p. 474

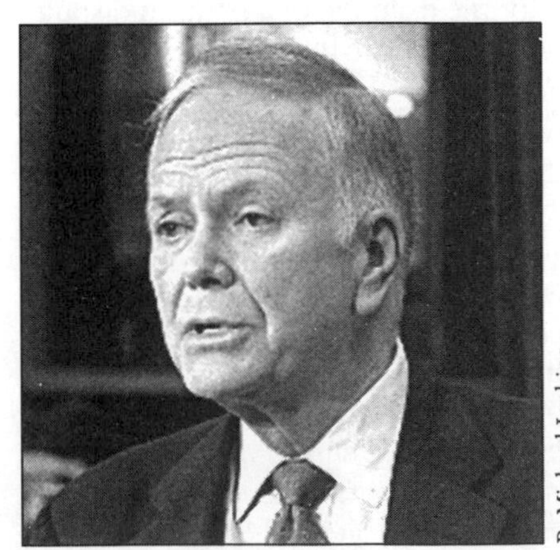

Bob Packwood

At Issue:

Have the news media gone overboard in covering Whitewater?

yes

JON KATZ

Media columnist, New York magazine

FROM *NEW YORK*, APRIL 11, 1994.

In modern American journalism, being arrogant and disliked has somehow mutated into a virtue. While politicians are supposed to reflect the people's will, journalists are trained to ignore it. The people's business can wait while campaigns, leaders and the business of governing itself become paralyzed by journalists' presumptions about their own self-important role. . . .

Of course, the media should do some investigating, especially when prosecutors and police fail to do their jobs. . . . But real investigative reporting has almost vanished from mainstream journalism, while variously disingenuous and Cotton Mather-ish obsessions with character and morality have become part of its central ideology. . . .

What's taken for investigative reporting today is actually closer to inquisition by mob, and journalism by leak and humiliation. . . . [R]eporters are free to pursue or explore any behavior their editors or producers deem immoral or improper or vaguely scummy. . . .

Although the details of Whitewater are profoundly confusing, the implications raised by the press are clear enough: WHITEWATER: ANGUISH INSIDE THE WHITE HOUSE ran a line at the top of March 28's *Newsweek*. And DEEP WATER said the cover line on *Time* last week: HOW THE PRESIDENT'S MEN TRIED TO HINDER THE WHITEWATER INVESTIGATION. That over an ominous black-and-white photo of a president looking as deep in crisis as anyone ever has. . . .

We all know the drill by now. Any other agenda gets shoved aside while journalists scrutinize every meeting, conversation, log and document. While the bloated Washington press corps is now in full pursuit, generating fire storms of heat but pinpoints of light, Whitewater is primarily a production of *The New York Times,* with crucial aid and comfort provided by the pit bulls of *The Wall Street Journal* editorial page. . . .

"You wouldn't believe the tenor of the Whitewater story-planning meetings," says a *Times* editor who has attended several. "I think I'm working for the Justice Department. Everybody's looking for the big break. There's a lot of deployment and memos and legal talk, but not much on the conceptual nature of the coverage, if you know what I mean."

. . . All of this makes one think that maybe Watergate wasn't such a journalistic high-water mark after all. Maybe the most salient lesson of our great modern presidential scandal isn't that the media should bring down a president but that journalists *could* — and get rich, famous and much more powerful in the process. . . .

no

THE NEW YORK TIMES EDITORIAL BOARD

FROM *NEW YORK TIMES EDITORIAL*, APRIL 10, 1994.

There is a kind of tidal rhythm to the attitude of the press — and the public's attitude toward journalists — when a political crisis is brewing. First come the revelations. Then follows a period of full media mobilization, with reporters scurrying everywhere. Then arrives the backlash. Officials complain that journalistic obsessions are derailing the nation's business. Politicians assert that the public is weary of incomprehensible details that, after all, give only an incomplete picture of events that would probably be innocuous if the full facts were available. . . .

We are now in this backlash phase. President Clinton and his allies are not alone in complaining that newspapers and television are making too much of Whitewater. Members of the media are also having second thoughts about whether they have lifted the incestuous behavior of Arkansas power brokers in the late 1970s and early '80s to the level of a national emergency, recklessly threatening the promise of Mr. Clinton's presidency. . . .

It is . . . true that any investigative exercise produces stories that are provocative but incomplete. But in the current situation, this is not the fault of writers, editors and broadcasters. They are, after all, operating in an information vacuum created by the people around Bill Clinton. . . . [T]hey have either stonewalled questions about Whitewater or answered them with irrelevancies. . . .

In this society, journalists have a constitutionally defined obligation to stick with a story as long as there are unanswered questions of political, legal, or moral consequence. . . .

Mr. Clinton's supporters have every right to believe that nothing improper was involved when Mrs. Clinton went into the commodities business under the tutelage of a lawyer for Arkansas' biggest agribusiness firm; or when the Clintons' campaign and real estate funds were passing through a sloppily run S&L owned by a key political supporter. They even have a right to condone the attempted politicization of law enforcement and regulatory agencies and the disinformation efforts of the Clinton press operation.

But for any journalist or news organization to be swayed by those arguments would be to abdicate responsibility. This page has argued from the beginning that the White House's most effective strategy would be fast, full disclosure. The White House has not adopted that advice. Until it does, there is a role to be played by Robert Fiske, the special prosecutor, by Congress — and by the press.

The Independent Counsel Rides Again

After several years of political and legal attacks, Republicans succeeded in 1992 in killing one of the most important legacies of the Watergate scandal: the law requiring court appointment of an "independent counsel" to investigate charges of wrongdoing by high-ranking officials.

Less than a year later, however, Republicans were clamoring for an independent lawyer to investigate President Clinton's role in the Whitewater affair. Clinton resisted the calls for months, but in January finally directed Attorney General Janet Reno to name a special counsel.

The role reversal highlights two of the issues surrounding use of the independent counsel — or special prosecutor, as the office was called until 1982. Administration officials who come under scrutiny may fear that an independent counsel will conduct a protracted investigation — as Iran-contra independent counsel Lawrence E. Walsh, among others, was accused of doing.

Critics, however, may doubt the ability of the Justice Department or a U.S. attorney's office to conduct an impartial investigation of a Cabinet member, top White House aide or the president himself. And if those doubts persist, the administration itself may decide an outside lawyer is needed to establish public confidence in the investigation.

Reagan administration officials recognized the benefit of independent counsels even while they criticized the law. Edwin Meese III called for an independent counsel in 1984 to investigate financial-disclosure questions that were holding up his nomination to be attorney general. The report clearing him of any criminal violations paved the way for his confirmation in President Ronald Reagan's second term.

Proponents of the independent counsel law, enacted as part of the Ethics in Government Act in 1978, said it was needed to prevent another Watergate-style coverup of wrongdoing by executive branch officials. But they also say that most investigations by independent counsels have ended with no charges brought — and with greater public confidence in the result. (*See box, p. 475.*) "There is no other way to ensure that there is credible investigation and where necessary prosecution of the highest officials in our executive branch system," says Fred Wertheimer, president of the public interest lobbying group Common Cause.

When several Reagan administration officials became targets of independent-counsel investigations, however, Republicans strongly attacked the law. They maintained that Congress had unconstitutionally intruded on presidential power. And they argued that independent counsels operated with no constraints and with every incentive to prolong an investigation even of the flimsiest of charges.

"The independent-counsel law has cost more in fairness to individuals and in the confidence of citizens in their government than it has gained us in stilled doubts about the system's integrity," Suzanne Garment wrote in her 1991 book, *Scandal.* Garment's husband, attorney Leonard Garment, represented Meese during his 1984 confirmation hearings.

As one example of the problems under the law, author Garment and other critics cited the probe of Theodore Olson, a former assistant attorney general, for allegedly lying to a congressional committee during its 1982-83 probe of the Environmental Protection Agency. Olson and his defenders insisted the probe was an attempt to criminalize a political fight between congressional Democrats and the Republican administration. After a 2 ½-year inquiry, independent counsel Alexia Morrison closed the case against Olson without bringing charges.

Olson himself prolonged the case by challenging the constitutionality of the independent counsel. The Justice Department sided with him in an appeal that reached the U.S. Supreme Court. But in June 1988, the justices upheld the law by a 7-1 vote (*Olson v. Morrison*). The previous year, Reagan had signed a five-year extension of the law while professing doubts about its constitutionality.

In late 1992, however, Senate Republicans stalled long enough to block a new reauthorization. President George Bush and GOP lawmakers had strongly criticized Walsh's investigation of the Iran-contra scandal, which ultimately lasted eight years and cost $35 million. But Republicans also argued that Democratic lawmakers limited their support for the law because of scandals swirling about Congress.

President Clinton came to office as a supporter of the law, but reauthorization measures moved slowly through Congress. So when calls for an outside investigation of Whitewater arose, Clinton had to direct Reno to use other powers to appoint a "special counsel" to handle the matter. In January, she chose Robert Fiske Jr., a New York lawyer and former Republican federal prosecutor.

Meanwhile, the Senate had passed an independent-counsel bill in November, and the House followed suit in February. A House-Senate conference reached agreement on a final version of the legislation May 17, and Clinton has promised to sign the measure. A last-minute provision clears the way for Fiske to be appointed as an independent counsel and continue investigating Whitewater.

Continued from p. 472

than 20 years. Packwood argues he is being judged for past actions by new, and uncertain, standards of conduct. [24]

The latest scandals contribute to a siege mentality on Capitol Hill that has been growing for the last several years. Lawmakers have come under attack for everything from tax increases and partisan gridlock to gifts from lobbyists and free parking spaces at Washington's National Airport. A record number of members have decided to call it quits this year. [25]

For many lawmakers and congressional sympathizers, the House bank scandal was a classic case of public overreaction to innocent practices on

Capitol Hill. The scandal erupted in fall 1991 after a General Accounting Office (GAO) inquiry disclosed that hundreds of current and former House members had routinely overdrawn their House bank accounts without penalty.

Some lawmakers likened the practice to overdraft protection available to customers in commercial banks. But public furor forced the House Democratic leadership to close the bank and ultimately agree to publish the names of all 269 members with overdrafts. Some 105 of the overdraft writers either retired or were defeated in the 1992 general election. [26]

Despite those electoral sanctions, some critics of Congress continue to believe the House was lax in handling the affair. "As an ethical matter, people who did this habitually were taking advantage of a perk of office that ultimately was at taxpayer expense," says David Mason, director of the Congress Project at the conservative Heritage Foundation. "And I think they should have been disciplined for that."

The bank scandal did force the Democratic leadership to accede to Republican demands for appointment of a professional manager to oversee House operations. And public discontent with Congress also has helped focus lawmakers' attention on a number of bills aimed at curbing the influence of money on the political process.

This month, the Senate passed a tough bill to prohibit members of Congress from accepting gifts, free lunches or recreational travel from lobbyists or anyone else except family members and close friends. The measure must be reconciled with a less restrictive House version passed in March. But proponents hailed the bill as a major step toward curbing the influence of special interests in Congress. "This will fundamentally change the way business is done on Capitol Hill," Wertheimer of Common Cause told a news conference.

Meanwhile, lawmakers were working behind the scenes to reach a

Investigations by Independent Counsels

There have been 13 investigations since the 1978 Ethics in Government Act authorized the use of court-appointed special prosecutors (known as independent counsels after 1982) to probe allegations of wrongdoing by high-ranking federal officials. [1]

Subject	Counsel	Issue	Outcome
Hamilton Jordan White House chief of staff (1979-80)	Arthur Hill Christy	Drug use	No indictment
Timothy Kraft White House aide (1980-81)	Gerald Gallinghouse	Drug use	No indictment
Raymond Donovan Secretary of Labor (1981-82; 1985-87)	Leon Silverman	Organized crime	No indictment [2]
Edwin Meese III White House counselor and attorney general designate (1984)	Jacob A. Stein	Financial	No indictment
Theodore Olson Assistant attorney general (1986-89)	Alexia Morrison	Lying to Congress	No indictment
Michael Deaver White House deputy chief of staff (1986-89)	Whitney North Seymour	Lobbying (perjury)	Conviction
Iran-contra (1986-94)	Lawrence E. Walsh	Official misconduct; lying to Congress	14 indictments: 7 guilty pleas; 4 convictions after trials; 2 overturned on appeal (Oliver North, John Poindexter); 1 dismissal; 2 withdrawn after pardons
Wedtech (1987-90)	James McKay	Lobbying activities	Two indictments: one conviction (Lynn Nofziger), overturned on appeal; one acquittal
Confidential (1987)	James R. Harper [3]		No indictment
Confidential (1989)			No indictment
Dept. of Housing and Urban Development (1990-present)	Arlin Adams	Official misconduct; misuse of funds	12 indictments: 7 guilty pleas; 3 convictions after trials; 1 acquittal; 1 trial pending
Confidential (1991-92)			No indictment
Clinton passport search (1992-present)	Joseph diGenova	Misuse of files	Pending

[1] *The Ethics in Government Act lapsed in December 1992 and is expected to be reauthorized by Congress this spring. In January 1994, President Clinton ordered the appointment of a special counsel to investigate the Whitewater affair, and Attorney General Janet Reno appointed Robert Fiske Jr.*

[2] *Donovan was indicted by a grand jury in New York and acquitted.*

[3] *Harper was identified in a report by the General Accounting Office.*

Source: Senate Governmental Affairs Committee, 1994

compromise on separate campaign-finance reform bills the two chambers approved last year. But the bills differ sharply on two critical issues — political action committees and public funding — and enactment of legislation is by no means certain, even with Democrats controlling Congress and the White House. ■

OUTLOOK

No End to Coverage?

When financial scandals rocked Italy and Japan recently, governments fell — a frequent occurrence in parliamentary systems. In the United States, however, there is no easy way out of a political scandal touching on the president. The trauma of Nixon's resignation remained painful enough 12 years later that even strong critics of Reagan's actions in the Iran-contra scandal steered the debate away from removing the president.

Today, no one is seriously suggesting impeachment for any of the charges being raised about Bill Clinton's conduct before becoming president or his responses to the charges while in office. For that reason, many observers are warning against allowing Whitewater, Troopergate or Jones' lawsuit to weaken Clinton's power. "He has 2½ years to serve in his term," says Sabato. "In our own self-interest, we have to keep it in perspective."

Nonetheless, the array of legal actions — including anticipated Whitewater hearings in Congress in late summer — are likely to be a continuing distraction for Clinton. Still, the administration can continue to function. As Washington waited for Jones' suit earlier this month, Clinton won a big victory when the House passed an assault weapons ban that he vigorously supported.

On Capitol Hill, the effects of scandal may also be blunted or delayed. In the House, Rostenkowski won renomination in March despite his leading opponent's concerted effort to capitalize on the charges against the lawmaker. In the Senate, Packwood deflected publication of the sexual harassment story in 1992 until after he had won re-election.

Scandal's effect on individual officeholders may be less important, however, than its overall impact on the political system. To many people in and around government, that impact is overwhelmingly negative: increased public distrust of government, disincentives to public service and distraction from policy issues. In the three years since Garment and Sabato published their critiques of scandal politics, few voices have been heard in Washington directly challenging the view that the hunt for wrongdoing has gone too far.

In individual cases, however, the public can sometimes make discrete judgments about officeholders charged with abusing their positions. In the House bank scandal, most of the lawmakers with the worst records of overdrafts lost or gave up their offices while voters spared most of those with lesser violations. And even when they seem to go overboard, the investigations of politicians' campaign financing, business affairs and sexual conduct do reflect — and reinforce — a heightened sensitivity among the public toward issues of ethics involving people in public life.

Whether harmful or beneficial, however, the machinery of scandal shows no sign of stopping. "It's a sad commentary that we've become so titillated by the downfall of celebrities, but that's very much a part of our popular culture now," says Brookings' Mann. "The foibles and failings of individuals are front and center these days." ■

Notes

[1] *The New York Times,* March 18, 1994, p. A1.

[2] For background, see "Politicians and Privacy," *The CQ Researcher,* April 17, 1992, pp. 337-360.

[3] "Washington Week in Review" (PBS), April 25, 1994.

[4] See William Safire, *Safire's Political Dictionary* (1978), p. 435.

[5] Quoted in Larry J. Sabato, *Feeding Frenzy: How Attack Journalism Has Transformed American Politics* (1991), p. 1.

[6] See *The New York Times,* April 10, 1994, p. E4 (quoting Schorr); April 4, 1994, p. A15 (Lewis column). Duke commented on WRC radio in Washington in early April; Harwood spoke at a National Press Club forum in April.

[7] Howard Kurtz, *Media Circus* (1993), chapters 2 and 3. Kurtz credits some regional and local newspapers for their reporting on the savings and loan industry but says the stories did not attract attention from major news outlets.

[8] *Los Angeles Times,* Dec. 21, 1993, p. A1.

[9] Suzanne Garment, *Scandal: The Crisis of Mistrust in American Politics* (1991), pp. 143, 168.

[10] See *CQ Weekly Report,* March 12, 1994, p. 585; March 26, 1994, p. 720.

[11] *CQ Weekly Report,* April 2, 1994, p. 788.

[12] See George C.S. Benson, with Steven A. Maaranen and Alan Heslop, *Political Corruption in America* (1978), chapters 5 and 19.

[13] Sabato, *op. cit.,* p. 188.

[14] Garment, *op. cit.,* pp. 17-18.

[15] Joseph P. Lash, *Eleanor and Franklin: The Story of Their Relationship Based on Eleanor Roosevelt's Private Papers* (1971), pp. 220-227, 714, 722.

[16] See Sabato, *op. cit.,* pp. 30, 33-41.

[17] *Ibid.,* pp. 32-33.

[18] Garment, *op. cit.,* p. 198. For a chronology of events, see Theodore Draper, *A Very Thin Line: The Iran-Contra Affairs* (1991), pp. 605-610.

[19] *The Wall Street Journal,* Oct. 5, 1992, p. A1.

[20] *Los Angeles Times,* Dec. 21, 1993, p. A1; *The American Spectator,* January 1994, pp. 18-30.

[21] See "Post Office Probe Hints at Larger Scandal," *1992 CQ Almanac,* pp. 47-51.

[22] *The Washington Post,* Nov. 21, 1992, p. A1.

[23] *The Wall Street Journal,* May 9, 1994, p. A4.

[24] Bob Packwood, "Bill and Me," *The Wall Street Journal,* May 13, 1994, p. A10.

[25] See *The New York Times,* April 28, 1994, p. A1, and *CQ Weekly Report,* April 2, 1994, pp. 785-789.

[26] *1992 CQ Almanac,* p. 39.

Bibliography

Selected Sources Used

Books

Benson, George C.S., with Steven A. Maaranen and Alan Heslop, *Political Corruption in America,* Lexington, 1978.

This work by three scholars at Claremont Men's College provides a historical overview of political corruption in America at all levels of government from the Revolutionary War into the 1970s. The book includes a 14-page bibliography.

DeLeon, Peter, *Thinking About Political Corruption,* M.E. Sharpe, 1993.

DeLeon, a professor at the University of Colorado's graduate school of public affairs in Denver, argues that reducing political corruption can best be accomplished not by increasing individual penalties but by making difficult systemic changes that reduce the opportunities for misusing government power.

Draper, Theodore, *A Very Thin Line: The Iran-Contra Affairs,* Hill & Wang, 1991.

Draper, a noted historian, writes the first comprehensive history of the Iran-contra scandal. The book contains a useful chronology and detailed source notes.

Eisenstadt, Abraham A., Ari Hoogenboom and Hans L. Trefousse (eds.), *Before Watergate: Problems of Corruption in American Society,* Brooklyn College Press, 1978.

Edited by three history professors at Brooklyn College, this book consists of essays by 14 contributors discussing political corruption in American history.

Garment, Suzanne, *Scandal: The Culture of Mistrust in American Politics,* Times Books, 1991.

Garment, a resident scholar at the American Enterprise Institute and former *Wall Street Journal* columnist, argues in this influential book that a preoccupation with scandal is harming politics and government. An updated edition in 1992 added discussion of sexual-harassment charges against Clarence Thomas and marital infidelity charges against then-candidate Bill Clinton.

Kurtz, Howard, *Media Circus: The Trouble with America's Newspapers,* Times Books, 1993.

Kurtz, media critic for *The Washington Post,* includes in this broad survey two chapters recounting how the news media largely missed two major scandals in the 1980s at the federal Department of Housing and Urban Development (HUD) and in the savings and loan industry.

Kutler, Stanley, *The Wars of Watergate: The Last Crisis of Richard Nixon,* Knopf, 1990.

Kutler, a historian at the University of Wisconsin, provides an exhaustive history of the Watergate scandals. Detailed source notes direct readers to the rest of the extensive literature on Watergate.

Sabato, Larry J., *Feeding Frenzy:How Attack Journalism Has Transformed American Politics,* Free Press, 1991.

Sabato, a professor of government at the University of Virginia, strongly argues that relentless media investigations of politicians' private lives are harming the democratic process. The book includes a useful listing of scandals, near scandals and mere rumors from the last several decades.

Articles

Lieberman, Trudy, "Churning Whitewater," *Columbia Journalism Review,* May/June 1994, pp. 26-30.

Lieberman examines the role of the conservative Republican organization, Citizens United, and its president, Floyd Brown, in disseminating information about President Clinton and the Whitewater affair.

Reports and Studies

Clark, Charles, "Politicians and Privacy," *The CQ Researcher,* April 17, 1992.

The report examines the issue of whether the news media should probe politicians' private lives.

Times Mirror Center for The People and The Press, "Whitewater Weighs Down Clinton in Public's Eyes," March 25, 1994.

A Times Mirror survey in late March found that coverage of the Whitewater affair was contributing to a drop in public confidence in President Clinton's performance in office.

Center for Media and Public Affairs, "Is the Attack Pack Back? TV News Coverage of the Whitewater Affair," *Media Monitor,* March/April 1994.

The media-study group found that television coverage of Whitewater emphasized the politics of the issue as much as the allegations themselves.

The Next Step

Additional information from UMI's Newspaper & Periodical Abstracts database

Capitol Hill

Groseclose, Timothy and Keith Krehbiel, "Golden parachutes, rubber checks, and strategic retirements from the 102d House," *American Journal of Political Science,* February 1994, pp. 75-99.

Political scientists have long been interested in the occupational decisions of politicians. Using preelection data on incumbents' decisions to retire or seek reelection, the effects of the House banking scandal and the discovery of a provision in the Federal Elections Campaign Act that allow certain members to keep campaign contributions are evaluated for the 1992 election.

Stone, Peter H., "Picking up the tab," *National Journal,* Feb. 26, 1994, p. 501.

At least 25 current and former aides to Rep. Dan Rostenkowski, D-Ill., have been called before a grand jury that is investigating Rostenkowski's role in the White House post office scandal, and more than $200,000 in legal bills for these witnesses have been paid by Rostenkowski's campaign fund. The ethics and legality of such payments are discussed.

Combating Scandal

Bartley, Robert L., "Agnew card bids to finesse Whitewater woes," *The Wall Street Journal,* April 21, 1994, p. A16.

Robert L. Bartley, editor of the *The Wall Street Journal,* says Spiro T. Agnew pioneered what is now a standard political card: In a corner, blame your troubles on the press. Bartley says President Clinton has championed the Agnew trump card to finesse his Whitewater woes but notes that although James Carville has done a masterful job in suppressing scrutiny of Clinton and his background, recent history suggests press-bashing is a sign of desperation.

Clift, Eleanor, "Where did David Gergen go wrong?" *Newsweek,* March 21, 1994, p. 36.

Spin doctor David Gergen's changing role in the White House is discussed. Gergen was hired to improve President Clinton's public image, but he mysteriously faded away when the Whitewater scandal came to the light.

Mollins, Carl, "See Ollie run," *Maclean's,* April 18, 1994, pp. 34-35.

Lt. Col. Oliver L. North, the man who admitted to lying to Congress during the Iran-Contra scandal, is running for a seat in the U.S. Senate. North is looking to upset Sen. Charles S. Robb, D-Va., in the race in Virginia in fall 1994.

Nichols, Bill, "A tough time staying the course," *USA Today,* March 16, 1994, p. A4.

As fallout from the Whitewater affair continues to swirl around the White House, President Clinton is apparently struggling to keep his temper in check and plow ahead with his message on issues such as health-care reform and national service. Clinton's appearance at a Nashua, N.H., town meeting is discussed.

Schneider, William, "What's next in Whitewater affair?" *National Journal,* April 2, 1994, p. 810.

President Clinton may survive Whitewater the way President Ronald Reagan survived Iran-contra — by making the case that the buck stopped elsewhere. Republicans don't want to destroy Clinton, just weaken him.

Thomas, Helen, "The presidency vs. integrity," *Chicago Defender,* March 28, 1994, p. 14.

Helen Thomas comments on the challenge facing President Clinton over how to defend himself against allegations of unethical conduct in the Whitewater case.

International Scandals

Epstein, Jack, "Probers link Rio rackets to Cali drug cartel," *San Francisco Chronicle,* April 14, 1994, p. A11.

Papers found in several safes belonging to Rio de Janeiro gambling boss Castor de Andrade in April 1994 are providing judicial officials in Brazil with the first documented link between Colombia's notorious Cali cocaine cartel and the politically powerful racketeers who run a popular illegal numbers operation in Brazil's cities. The papers also provide evidence of payoffs to top governmental officials in Brazil.

Kramer, Jane, "Dirty hands," *New Yorker,* March 28, 1994, pp. 70-81.

Raul Gardini, the billionaire who committed suicide after being caught in Italy's political scandal, is profiled. Gardini paid government officials a bribe of $140 million to buy his shares in Enimont, which had linked his chemical company, Montedison, and the government's oil company, Eni.

McAllister, J. F. O., "How scandal finally outran the reformer," *Time,* April 18, 1994, p. 45.

The resignation of Japan's Prime Minister Morihiro Hosokawa is discussed. Despite Hosokawa's vow to clean up big-money politics in Japan, his resignation was spurred by his own financial improprieties.

Sanger, David E., "Among blossoms in the dust, a pre-

mier departs,"*The New York Times*, April 21, 1994, p. A4.
One of the mysteries of the last two weeks of Japanese political upheaval is that Prime Minister Morihiro Hosokawa, who has resigned because of still-mysterious financial improprieties, still has high approval ratings. Public opinion regarding Hosokawa is discussed.

Waisbord, Silvio R., "Knocking on newsroom doors: The press and political scandals in Argentina," *Political Communication*, January 1994, pp. 19-33.
The causes for the rise of political scandals in Argentina in the early 1990s are examined. Available explanations fail to provide a satisfactory answer, mainly because they ignore the interplay of forces that produce media revelations of government wrongdoing.

Richard M. Nixon

Brownstein, Ronald, "Nixon's fall opened gate on scandal and scrutiny," *Los Angeles Times*, April 25, 1994, p. A1.
In light of former President Richard M. Nixon's April 1994 death, the impact the Watergate scandal has had on U.S. politics is discussed. Watergate changed the way the public and the press view politicians, influenced the way candidates raise money and institutionalized the use of scandal as a political weapon.

Laccetti, Susan, "He gained popularity after early defeats," *Atlanta Journal Constitution*, April 23, 1994, p. A11.
Georgia political experts and specialists in foreign policy hailed the late Richard M. Nixon as one of the greatest American presidents in making strides toward world peace but said his presidency always will be marred by the Watergate scandal.

Quindlen, Anna, "Living will," *The New York Times*, April 27, 1994, p. A17.
Quindlen says that in the days after his death, former President Richard M. Nixon was remembered in a wave of revisionist history as commentators, politicians and ordinary citizens were full of praise and hardly anyone mentioned his involvement in the Watergate scandal. Quindlen says that Nixon must be remembered accurately, misdeeds and all.

Opinions

Corn, David, "That was then . . .," *Nation*, May 2, 1994, pp. 581-582.
An editorial discusses the politics surrounding the Whitewater S&L scandal. Democrats are hoping the congressional hearings will be conducted by the Banking Committee, chaired by Rep. Donald W. Riegle Jr., D-Mich. They are also hoping the hearings will be tedious enought to bore the public.

"Get serious about limiting clout of money in politics," *USA Today*, April 27, 1994, p. A10.
An editorial contends that, as Richard M. Nixon is laid to rest, Congress must ponder the inadequacy of the reforms that followed the Watergate scandal and Nixon's resignation. The editorial states that Congress must limit the corrupting influence of special-interest money.

Kinsley, Michael, "TRB from Washington: Ox-goring festival," *The New Republic*, April 4, 1994, p. 6.
An editorial discusses the hypocrisy Republicans have shown over the Whitewater scandal. During the Iran-contra affair, Republicans were not so keen about Congressional hearings or a special prosecutor.

Matthews, Christopher, "It didn't start with Whitewater," *San Francisco Chronicle*, April 10, 1994, p. A19.
Matthews discusses the way voters see life on Capitol Hill, contending that a growing sense of distance between voter and lawmaker is the real scandal of 1994.

Whitewater

"The bottom line," *Progressive*, May 1994, pp. 11-12.
The Whitewater affair is discussed. The Republicans are doing their best to inflate the situation.

Church, George J., "Why it isn't Watergate," *Time*, March 21, 1994, p. 39.
Similarities between the Whitewater scandal and Watergate are discussed. Both concern allegations of impropriety directed at a president of the U.S., and both have triggered probes by a special counsel.

Donlan, Thomas G., "Riding the bull," *Barron's*, April 18, 1994, p. 50.
Donlan discusses several historical examples of political figures caught up in financial gain for favors and similarities with the case of Hillary Rodham Clinton's commodity trading speculation. Donlan declares that "hand-washing is the national political standard."

Lerner, Michael, "There's plenty of hypocrisy, but Whitewater is not the key," *Los Angeles Times*, April 18, 1994, p. B7.
Michael Lerner discusses the "politics of meaning" and how that theory applies to the Whitewater scandal in which President Clinton and Hillary Rodham Clinton find themselves in. Lerner says nothing the Clintons could have done would fully protect them from ruling elites terrified of substantial change.

Tisdall, Simon, "Clinton adviser may face criminal charge of cover-up," *Guardian*, March 28, 1994, p. 8.
George Stephanopoulos, one of President Clinton's closest advisers, faces possible criminal charges for his role in alleged White House efforts to obstruct official inquiries into the Whitewater ethics scandal.

Back Issues

Great Research on Current Issues Starts Right Here...Recent topics covered by The CQ Researcher are listed below. Before May 1991, reports were published under the name of Editorial Research Reports.

NOVEMBER 1992
Physical Fitness
Privatization
Paying for College
U.S. Policy in Asia

DECEMBER 1992
Crackdown on Smoking
The New CIA
Eating Disorders
Women and AIDS

JANUARY 1993
Hate Crimes
Child Sexual Abuse
Nuclear Fusion
U.S. Trade Policy

FEBRUARY 1993
Community Policing
Europe's New Right
School Censorship
Violence Against Women

MARCH 1993
Gay Rights
Aid to Russia
War on Drugs
TV Violence

APRIL 1993
Head Start
High-Speed Rail
Children's Legal Rights
Muslims in America

MAY 1993
Cults in America
Preventing Teen Pregnancy
Software Piracy
National Parks

JUNE 1993
Food Safety
Prostitution
Childhood Immunizations
National Service

JULY 1993
Electric Cars
Population Growth
Downward Mobility
Intelligence Testing

AUGUST 1993
Mental Illness
Bilingual Education
Foreign Policy Burden
School Funding

SEPTEMBER 1993
Suburban Crime
Public Housing
Supreme Court Preview
Immigration Reform

OCTOBER 1993
Airline Safety
Disaster Response
Science in the Courtroom
The Glass Ceiling

NOVEMBER 1993
Paying for Retirement
Charitable Giving
Privacy in the Workplace
Adoption

DECEMBER 1993
U.S. Vietnam-Relations
Learning Disabilities
Child Care
Space Program's Future

JANUARY 1994
Racial Tensions in Schools
South Africa's Future
Worker Retraining
Regulating Pesticides

FEBRUARY 1994
Prison Overcrowding
Water Quality
Religion in Schools
Juvenile Justice

MARCH 1994
Underground Economy
Education Standards
Gambling Boom
Private Management of Public Schools

APRIL 1994
Reproductive Ethics
U.S.-China Trade
Soccer in America
Talk Show Democracy

MAY 1993
Traffic Congestion
Women's Health Issues
Mutual Funds

Future Topics

- ***Education and Gender***
- ***Gun Control***
- ***Public Land Policy***

THE CQ Researcher

PUBLISHED BY CONGRESSIONAL QUARTERLY INC.

Education and Gender

Does the educational system shortchange females?

Two decades after winning battles for equal access, women's activists are seeking reform of what they see as an education system still weighted against females. They point to girls' declining self-esteem, a gender gap on SAT tests and new research showing that girls receive less attention from teachers than boys. Applications to women's colleges have shot up, and some schools are experimenting with girls-only science and math classes. Congress is moving to create a federal Office of Gender Equity and expand programs to train teachers in how to avoid giving girls short shrift. But critics of the gender-equity movement point to recent strides women have made in educational achievement. They warn that efforts to eliminate bias are a futile exercise in "political correctness."

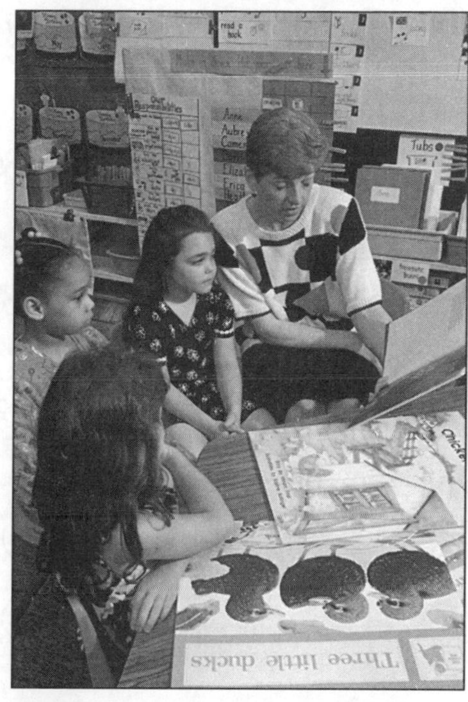

INSIDE THIS ISSUE

CQ June 3, 1994 • Volume 4, No. 21 • 481-504

Formerly Editorial Research Reports

COVER: KINDERGARTENERS WORK ON THEIR READING AT ST. CATHERINE'S SCHOOL, AN ALL-GIRLS PRIVATE SCHOOL IN RICHMOND, VA. (TONY SYLVESTRO)

THE CQ Researcher

June 3, 1994
Volume 4, No. 21

Bibliographic records and abstracts included in The Next Step section of this publication are from UMI's Newspaper and Periodical Abstracts database, and are used with permission.

The CQ Researcher (ISSN 1056-2036). Formerly Editorial Research Reports. Published weekly (48 times per year, not printed the first Friday of any month with five Fridays) by Congressional Quarterly Inc., 1414 22nd St., N.W., Washington, D.C. 20037. Rates are furnished upon request. Second-class postage paid at Washington, D.C. POSTMASTER: Send address changes to The CQ Researcher, 1414 22nd St., N.W., Washington, D.C. 20037.

Education and Gender

BY CHARLES S. CLARK

THE ISSUES

"When I was in fourth grade, I was a very assertive tomboy," says Cynthia Mahood, recalling her girlhood in South Dakota. "But sometime around the fifth grade I went from extrovert to painfully shy introvert. I was told by my teachers that my behavior before had been inappropriate, not like a young lady. It's amazing how influenced I was."

Mahood's shyness and reluctance to speak in class endured all the way through high school. It was only at all-female Mills College, in Oakland, Calif., that she broke out of her shell. "When I came home for Christmas after that first semester," says Mahood, a junior majoring in biochemistry, "my friends were telling each other, 'I finally had a full conversation with Cynthia.' They were amazed I even had an opinion. I hadn't seen the change until they mentioned it."

Surveys show that girls growing up in America often retreat inside themselves as Mahood did. "Going underground" is how Carol Gilligan, a co-founder of the Harvard Project on Women's Psychology and Girls' Development, describes the phenomenon. Many experts link it to declining academic performance as girls go through puberty.

"Girls and boys enter school roughly equal," says an influential 1992 report, *How Schools Shortchange Girls*. "On some measures of school readiness, such as fine-motor control, girls are ahead of boys. Twelve years later, girls have fallen behind their male classmates in key areas such as higher-level mathematics and measures of self-esteem." [1]

Girls' self-esteem is especially vulnerable. A 1990 poll of 2,400 girls and 600 boys commissioned by the American Association of University Women (AAUW) found that 60 percent of

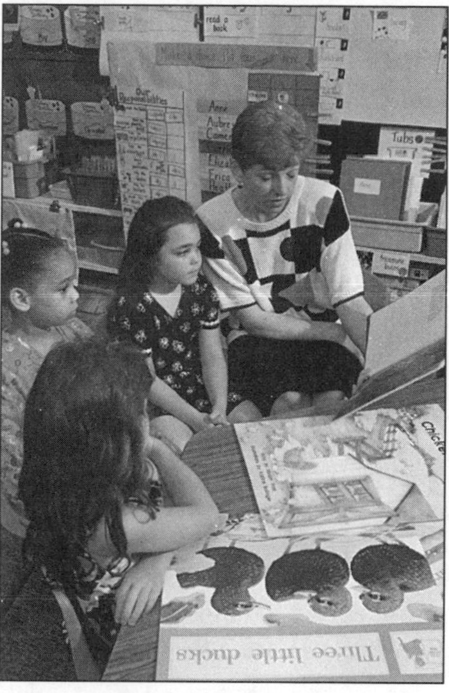

elementary school girls and 67 percent of boys agreed with the statement, "I'm happy the way I am." But when high school students were asked the same question, the percentage of girls who were happy with themselves dropped to 29 percent, compared with 46 percent for boys. [2]

As girls encounter adolescence, observers note, many begin prefacing their speech with disclaimers such as "I don't know," or, "I may be wrong, but. . . ." Adolescence "is hard and wonderful for most kids, but there are differences between the experiences of boys and girls," says Annie Rogers, an assistant professor at the Harvard Graduate School of Education. "Girls ages 12-13 no longer know what they knew. They doubt the grounds of their own perception. They question themselves as they hone their skills of abstraction of knowledge."

The reasons girls retreat inside themselves may be more than psychological. Advocates for gender equity were galvanized this spring by the publication of *Failing at Fairness: How America's Schools Cheat Girls* by American University education Professors Myra and David Sadker. Describing adolescence for girls as "the tightening of a corset," the Sadkers tied the shyness phenomenon to the education system's "gender-biased" tests and textbooks, the harms of sexual harassment and a culture in which expectations for achievement are lower for girls than for boys. (*See stories, pp. 488, 494.*) After evaluating teachers in action in 100 classrooms in four states, the Sadkers found "a syntax of sexism so elusive that most teachers and students were completely unaware of its existence." [3] (*See story, p. 486.*)

Bias against girls also has become the concern of groups working outside the school milieu. New York City-based Girls Inc., devoted to improving the health, academic performance and self-confidence of girls from low-income families around the country, recently published a handbook for its youth workers that asks, "Do staff assign tasks based on gender stereotypes — get girls to decorate, clean up, take minutes and do other secretarial tasks while boys get to carry or move things, climb ladders, make decisions and help fix things?" [4]

For increasing numbers of Americans, the solution to perceived gender inequity is to separate female and male students. Applications to the nation's 84 women's colleges are up 10 percent, on average, for the third year in a row, reports the Women's College Coalition. Despite a federal law against sex discrimination in public schools, all-girl science and math classes have been set up at high schools in Ventura, Calif., and at a school for gifted students in Aurora, Ill.

With encouragement from the Clinton administration, legislation is working its way through Congress to establish an Office of Gender Equity in the Education Department that

Girls Experience Greater Loss of Self-Esteem

Both boys and girls lose self-esteem as they get older, but girls show a far greater loss, according to a nationwide poll commissioned by the American Association of University Women. The sharpest drops in self-esteem occur between elementary and middle school.

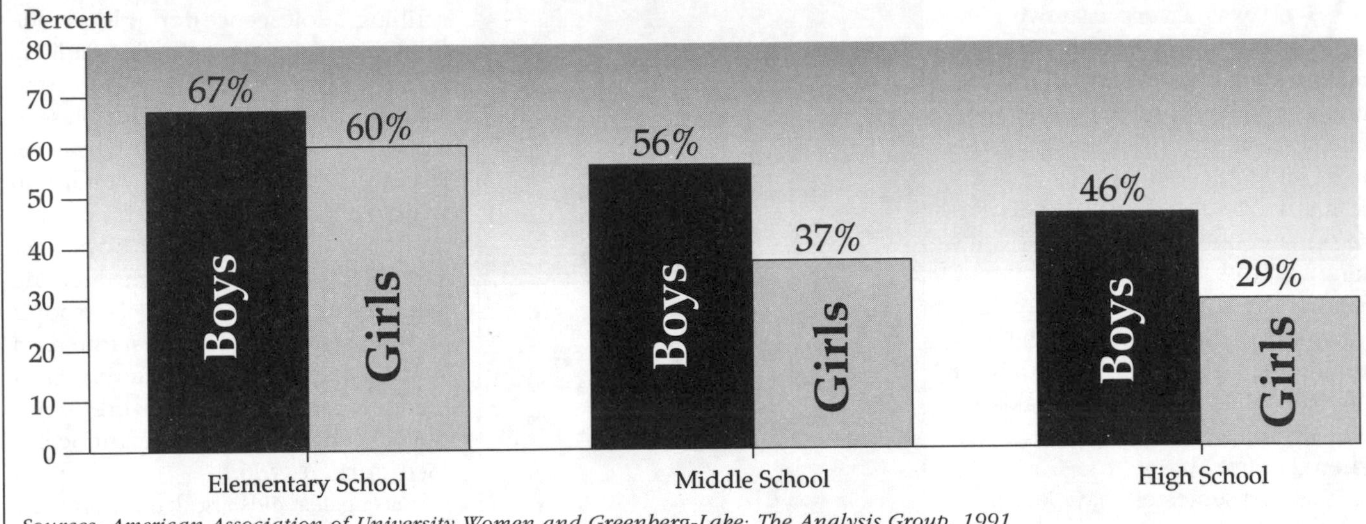

Sources: American Association of University Women and Greenberg-Lake: The Analysis Group, 1991

would distribute grants to train teachers in avoiding gender bias. "After 20 years, gender equity at long last is getting to the center of public debate," says Leslie Wolfe, president of the Center for Women Policy Studies, who ran women's educational-equity programs in the Carter administration. "It's very exciting that people are saying, 'Yes, damn it, that's true.' "

Detractors, however, speak disparagingly of the arrival of "feminist algebra." [5] Kristi Hamrick, spokeswoman for the conservative Family Research Council, says gender equity is a way for feminists to divide society and "judge people not by the content of their character but by their sex. Gender norming insinuates that boys are better, which is insulting to what it is to be a woman."

Diane Ravitch, a Bush administration education official who is now a senior research scholar at New York University, points out that women today outnumber men in college, making up 55 percent of undergraduates and 59 percent of master's candidates. "In every case of civil rights law, you end up relying on representation, so what more do they want?" she asks. "What will gender equity accomplish except provide money for people who advocate the legislation?"

Progress has been made, acknowledges Whitney Ransome, co-director of the National Coalition of Girls' Schools. But in the 1980s, she says, society and the women's movement underwent a "seismic shift." Previously, equality meant equal access. "But does access alone define equal treatment? Yes, there are equal numbers, but what is the quality of the experience? A level playing field doesn't always mean working side by side."

How the gender-equity debate plays out will hinge on the following issues:

Is the education system unfair to females?

The gender-equity debate pits data against anecdote and divides advocates over whether the metaphorical glass is half-full or half-empty.

The National Assessment of Education Progress — a set of achievement tests at three grade levels known popularly as "the nation's report card" — shows that girls score as well as boys in math at age 9, but then fall behind by age 17. [6] The reasons, the argument goes, are unequal expectations for girls, a lack of encouragement and too few female role models. A 1987 study of science classes, for example, showed that when teachers needed help carrying out a demonstration, 79 percent chose boys. [7]

The Sadkers cite research showing that boys call out in class eight times more than girls, which grabs the teacher's attention. Their evaluations of teachers in classrooms found that in their control group, more attention was consistently paid to boys than girls, worsening as the weeks went by and producing an overall attention gap as high as 14 percent. White males were most likely to receive attention, followed by minority males, white females and minority females. [8]

Teachers showed a sexist bias in about a third of the classes studied by University of Michigan psychology Professor Jacquelynne Eccles, though "the biggest gender difference is that boys get yelled at more than the girls," she says. [9]

Those who question the bias findings point to the sweeping progress made by females over the past 20 years. In 1973, only 43 percent of high school girls went to college, compared with 50 percent of boys, according to the National Center for Education Statistics. Nowadays, 67 percent of high school girls go to college, compared with only 58 percent of boys. Similarly, the number of girls enrolling in difficult math and science courses is up dramatically: The percentage of girls taking high school algebra rose from 35 percent in 1982 to 51 percent in 1990, those taking geometry rose from 46 percent to 65 percent and those in chemistry rose from 30.3 percent to 50 percent. [10]

"At a high school graduation, girls get the most prizes and honors," says feminism critic Phyllis Schlafly, president of the Eagle Forum, in Alton, Ill. "And most teachers are female. Are they saying there's a conspiracy against girls?"

If self-esteem can be measured in academic ambitions, it should be noted that freshman girls, for the first time in history, were more likely than men to plan on getting an advanced degree, according to the 28th annual survey of college freshmen conducted in 1993 by the Higher Education Research Institute at the University of California-Los Angeles (UCLA).

"Part of the drumbeat for gender equity is based on the idea that girls are burdened by low self-esteem, but it's demonstrably untrue," says Ravitch, citing the UCLA survey. "The Sadkers make their claim with no objective evidence. In the end, who wins the race? Maybe it's better if teachers don't call on girls. I've seen studies showing that Korean students had low self-esteem but the highest grades. This is a political-correctness kind of issue, but there are facts here."

The Sadkers deny that their research is as "soft" and anecdotal as critics say. "We spent one and a half years designing the evaluation form we used in 100 classrooms," says Myra Sadker. "The raters then circled items to show who was called on, and categorized the teacher's reaction as one of either praise, acceptance, remediation or criticism. We found that the gender gaps were greater when teacher feedback was more specific, both positive and negative. It certainly doesn't seem anecdotal."

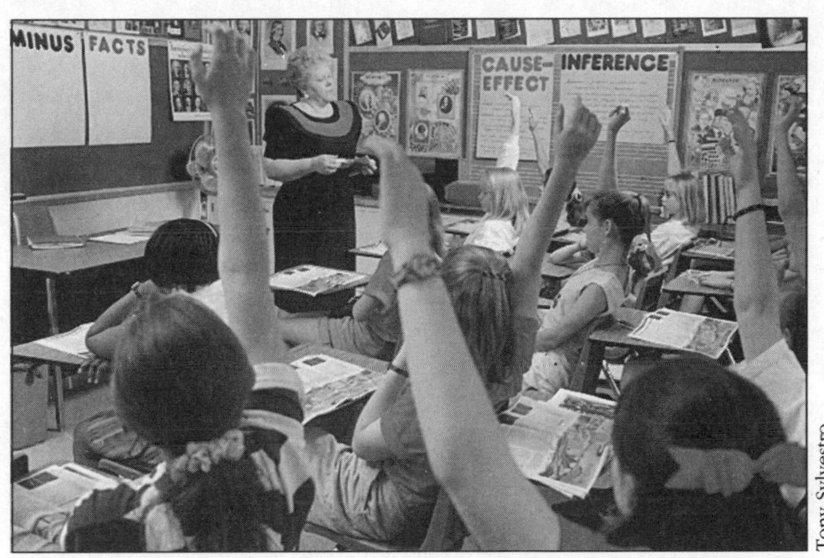

Tony Sylvestro

Middle-school girls participate enthusiastically in the "critical thinking" class at St. Catherine's School in Richmond, Va.

While there are encouraging signs at the national level, the argument that women have made great strides "is mixing apples and oranges," says Susan McGhee Bailey, executive director of the Wellesley Center for Research on Women. "We have made progress because women and men have worked hard at progress." The fact that females are a majority on campus "doesn't speak to those not making it. Feminists 100 years ago would have hoped we'd be further along by now. Look at the small percentages of professors who are female. It's 50 percent at Wellesley, but not at most places."

Continued discrimination in physical education programs "is obvious," says Nancy Huppertz, an equity specialist with the Northwest Regional Educational Laboratory in Portland, Ore. "There [also] are chronic patterns of disproportionate enrollment in science, computers and vocational ed. And look at what happens after college. There's only one female head of a medical school. There is still a glass ceiling and a sticky floor" of low-wage women's jobs. "It's subtle, but we need to look beyond the letter to the spirit of the law."

Do males and females learn differently?

When questions were raised about bias in the Scholastic Aptitude Tests (now called the Scholastic Assessment Tests), the College Board in 1989 issued a report on the politically delicate topic of differences between males and females. [11] Beginning soon after a child's birth, the paper noted, parents react more positively toward their toddlers when they engage in gender-appropriate behavior.

"Boys are more interested than girls in (among other things) guns, team sports and in making and fixing things," it said, citing research from the mid-1980s. "Girls prefer dolls, sewing, cooking and dancing." Current research shows no gross anatomical difference between male and female brains, the report also noted. There are "structural (and hormonal) differences related to the fact that women menstruate and men do not," but these differences "have not been

Researchers' Cameras Reveal Teachers' Bias

Myra and David Sadker were armed with camcorders when they researched their book on gender inequity. They needed the cameras to tape teachers in action — and to convince them that they sometimes showed biases against girls.

Some of the teachers "were stunned" at the results, say the education professors. "Only after several viewings of the videotape did [one teacher] notice how she let boys call out answers but reprimanded girls for similar behavior," they wrote. [1] Examples of teacher bias were also videotaped and broadcast by NBC's "Dateline" magazine show.

Still, the Sadkers and other advocates of gender equity decline to blame the teachers. "We're not teacher-bashers," says Myra Sadker, dean of education at American University. "They don't walk in there to do harm; they walk in saying, 'I don't want to get rich, I want to do good.' "

Gender bias is "so subtle and societally pervasive, it's unfair to make school the microcosm," says Claudia Edwards, a senior professional associate at the National Education Association. She replicated the Sadkers' experiments and also found that teachers were surprised at the bias. "Girls lose their voice in their families and in the media. In thousands of classroom interactions, gender simply doesn't get priority. It's a sin of omission."

To many observers, the tendency to call on boys more is understandable. "Boys are more apt to demand attention, and you're more apt to pay attention to them as a way of controlling the situation," says Susan McGhee Bailey, executive director of the Wellesley College Center for Research on Women. "Many teachers are aware of the issue, but receive little support from the administration or the community."

Others defend the tendency of girls to stay quiet. "If a girl doesn't respond with the same athleticism as a boy, it's not because she's lacking in academics," says Janet Parshall of the Concerned Women for America, "but that she might want to catch that boy's eye for a date Friday night. The wild flinging of arms is a turnoff."

Though some teachers deny they are biased or say the issue is blown out of proportion, most are receptive to new training in avoiding gender bias, according to Nancy Huppertz, an equity specialist with the Northwest Regional Educational Laboratory in Portland, Ore. She conducts workshops with teachers that seek to highlight disparities in treatment with an eye toward raising expectations for girls and minorities.

"We're supportive and non-judgmental," Huppertz says, noting that there are few differences between male and female teachers in their handling of students. "We look for who is being asked the who-what-when-where-type questions, and who is being asked the more analytical questions. Many teachers don't follow through with girls by using higher-order feedback. Is that a reflection of higher expectations for boys? What is the effect on those not called on? The females are getting good grades, but are they being graded merely on turning in their work and doing it neatly?"

Janice Damico, a sixth-grade math teacher in Arlington, Va., says the bias question is well-discussed in the training literature, though a survey showed that newer teachers are not as aware of the issue as experienced ones.

Meanwhile, she says, teachers should work hard to give girls a fair chance in the classroom. "I often make it a point to call on a girl, because boys are already getting enough."

[1] Myra and David Sadker, *Failing at Fairness: How America's Schools Cheat Girls* (1994), p. 48.

reliably associated with differences in cognitive functioning."

As they enter school, males are better at visualizing spatial relationships and performing tasks involving reasoning, with girls better at computation, the report continued. But such differences are narrowing. "With the exception of some limited domains of spatial ability and performance at the top levels of mathematics achievement, women are improving their position relative to men." [12]

Among gender-equity advocates, there is willingness to acknowledge gender differences. "Research shows differences for males and females on three of the major approaches to learning styles," according to two women's groups. "Schools are geared more to the learning styles of white males, which tend to be individualistic and competitive. In contrast, many girls prefer cooperation over competition, acknowledging and building on others' ideas to define common meanings over individual contributions, and understanding over assessment." [13]

Girls form leaderless groups, boys form hierarchies, Nancy Goldberger told a 1991 Educational Testing Service (ETS) conference. "Girls tend to see the role of peers as support. Girls acknowledge the uncertainty of knowledge and believe that peers, by listening to each other and sharing the floor, can create a relaxed and unpressured atmosphere in which disagreement can be addressed. Girls put less emphasis on reconciling disagreement than on understanding where others are coming from. Boys tend to see the role of peers as challengers and partners in argument. One speaks to show what one knows; one argues with others to sharpen one's position. Devil's advocacy is a strategy that is far more comfortable for and utilized by boys and men than girls and women." [14]

Many in the computer industry have

noted that men — the vast majority of computer users — buy new software, play games and experiment, while women more often simply use word processing. "Women consider computers the way they consider Cuisinarts. They're there for a purpose," says Katie Payne, president of Delahaye Group Inc., a Portsmouth, N.H., market-research firm. If the computer system crashes, women simply want to call in help and get back to work. "The guys want to solve the problem." [15]

Whether such differences are from nature or nurture remains a mystery. "My husband is an engineer," recalls Schlafly, "and he gave the same sales talk to our four sons and two daughters saying they should study engineering because there they won't teach you any untruths. All four boys did it, but neither of the girls. They couldn't get interested, and we couldn't make them, though they got good grades in different courses."

Still, gender-equity activists emphasize that many of the differences reflect problems that could be overcome. "As boys get older, those who do not like math are more likely to attribute this feeling to the subject itself; they don't like math, they say, because it is 'not useful,' " says the AAUW report. "Girls, instead, interpret their problems with math as personal failures." [16]

Anita Mattison, who teaches an all-girls math class in Ventura, Calif., noticed how in class discussions the "girls keep on with something that we'd pretty much exhausted, like each of them had to explain it their way," a tendency the teacher viewed as a sign that the girls "needed reinforcement." [17]

Ransome says there is too much emphasis in education on the vocabulary of sports and military metaphors — "going the distance, tackling a problem." With computers, there is talk of "commands, as if the wrong command will blow the thing up or kill someone," she says. By contrast, the word *menu* implies that you have a series of options and that if you make a mistake, you can choose another, which is a style more accessible to girls.

Many women are passive learners "because they see math as a prepackaged set of instructions to be followed exactly as their teacher presents it," writes math Professor Ann B. Oakes. "They do not consider that they might make sense of this material or ponder over it, nor do they see mathematics as consisting of ideas generated by human beings in response to human exploration." [18]

Janice Damico, who teaches sixth-grade math in Arlington, Va., says that girls do better when it is made clear that math is something that can be applied in the real world. "I think it's nuts to say that math is some kind of logic problem for girls. The key is coming up with strategies to attack a problem. Once they become more confident in that, math won't be the big bugagoo it has been."

Huppertz says studies show that girls who participate (raise their hands) in class perform better. "It helps if another girl starts off talking, setting a pattern that it is OK to discuss and that there is not a risk of getting it wrong and being chopped down," she says. "Boys have always had to have a thick skin, and there are greater expectations for them to become tough."

The notion of creating a non-competitive learning environment for girls, however, strikes some as a disservice. "The engine of our democracy runs on the fuel of competition," says Janet Parshall, assistant to the president of Concerned Women of America. "Competition is healthy in class. I married my high school sweetheart after we competed in class to see who got the best grade. It was the spark that lit the magic in our relationship."

Ravitch argues that "there is no evidence that boys and girls have differently wired brains. It's like saying there

Continued on p. 490

Doonesbury BY GARRY TRUDEAU

Do College-Bound Girls Face a Disadvantage . . .

When high school students sit down to confront that measure of adolescent success, the Scholastic Assessment Test (SAT), one outcome is virtually certain: Just as females earn only 71 cents on the dollar earned by males, girls' scores will be lower than the boys'. [1]

In 1993, the overall achievement gap was 53 points, with high school males registering an eight-point advantage on the verbal test and a 45-point edge in math. (The number of points possible on each test ranges from 200-800 points.)

Whether the problem lies with female performance or male-biased test questions is a debate that rages among gender-equity advocates and testing specialists. "SAT scores, which are designed to predict college success as defined by first-year grades, underpredict women's grades and overpredict men's," observes the American Association of University Women (AAUW). "Young women tend to receive higher college grades than young men with the same SAT scores." [2]

With gender gaps also showing up in graduate school exams and other national tests, the stakes in the debate are more than academic. "Those scores determine admissions to the best schools, scholarships and ultimately the best professions," notes Annie Rogers, assistant education professor at Harvard University.

In February, the National Center for Fair and Open Testing (FairTest) in Cambridge, Mass., filed a civil rights complaint with the U.S. Education Department charging that boys are favored over girls in the National Merit Scholarships. The scholarships are awarded in large part on the results of the Preliminary Scholastic Assessment Test (PSAT) taken by high school juniors.

FairTest estimated that boys receive $15 million of the $25 million in scholarship money awarded each year by the National Merit Scholarship Corp. A similar suit brought against New York State's Empire Scholarships in 1989 was successful. The judge noted "the probability that, absent discriminatory causes, that women would consistently score 60 points less on the SAT than men is nearly zero." [3]

The problem, say critics of such tests, is that they contain questions whose vocabulary and thought processes are most familiar to white males. Girls, they also point out, do better in written essays while boys thrive on multiple choice. "Girls look at problems more complexly, seeing shades of gray and intersections between answers," says Robert Schaeffer, public education director for FairTest. "Boys see things as 'either/or' and are more inclined to guess. Blind guessing gets results, and a fast-paced standardized test is a game which culturally favors the style of brash white boys."

The SAT contains far more questions that favor boys, writes Phyllis Rosser of the Center for Women Policy Studies, such as the following sports-related example from the November 1987 SAT:

(Fill in the blanks from the five pairs of choices below):

"Although the undefeated visitors . . . . . . triumphed over the underdog opponents, the game was hardly the . . . . . . sportswriters had predicted."

A) fortunately .... upset

B) unexpectedly .... classic

Comparing SAT Scores

Men invariably outperform women on the math section of the Scholastic Assessment Test (formerly the Scholastic Aptitude Test.) Since 1972, men also have scored higher on the verbal portion of the SAT.

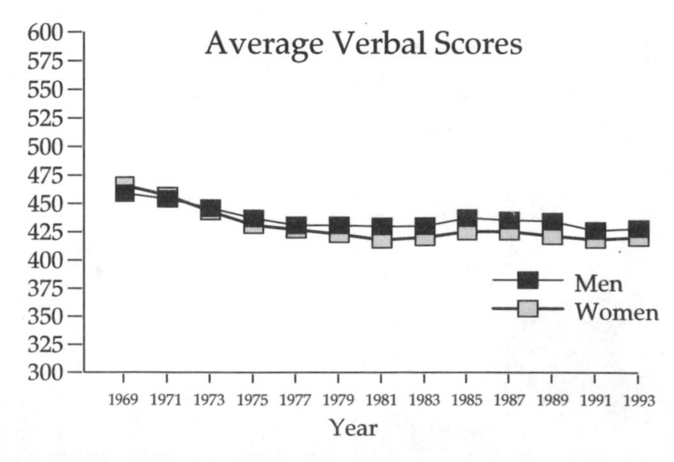

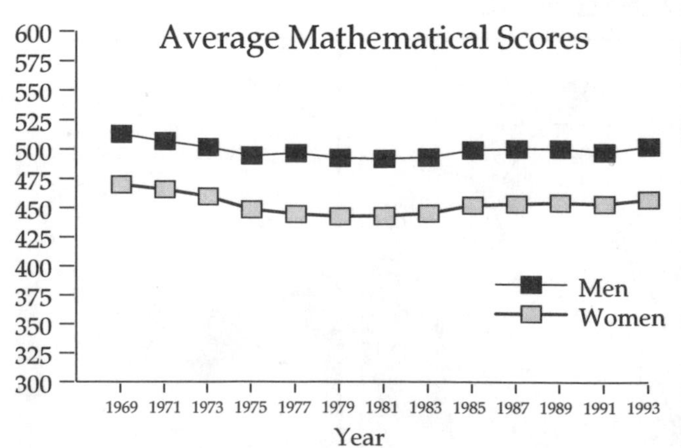

Source: The College Board, Aug. 19, 1993

. . . When They Sit Down to Take the SAT Test?

C) finally .... rout
D) easily .... stalemate
E) utterly .... mismatch

About 41 percent of boys chose the correct answer (C), but only 16 percent of girls. [4]

Finally, survey data show that females experience greater stress while taking the SAT, with 27.8 percent of girls reporting they were "extremely anxious," compared with only 10.8 percent of the boys. [5]

The College Board, which sponsors the SAT, and the Educational Testing Service (ETS), which creates the tests, have long acknowledged the gender differences, and try to adjust. Women "may do relatively better on quantitative problems that involve using a formula," says the ETS, "whereas men do relatively better when the route to solving the quantitative problems is unclear or when estimation provides shortcuts to solutions.

"Many men and women are included in the process of planning tests and writing test questions. There is a mandatory 'sensitivity review' process in which specially trained men and women examine every question to be sure there is no stereotyping or inappropriate content based on sex, race or ethnicity." [6]

But a senior College Board official argues that the gender gap results from factors other than flaws in the tests. She says that the same gap shows up on other national standardized tests. Moreover, more women than men take the SATs and more of those women come from low-income backgrounds. [7]

In recent years, however, research sponsored by ETS itself has pointed to bias, according to Rosser. She cites two ETS studies from 1991 and 1992. One surveyed a 1988 freshman class of 4,300 men and women at a state university and found a "statistically significant" underprediction of women's grade performance as compared with their SATs. A second study recommended that the tests be corrected "by adding some number of points to women's scores or by reworking the contents of the test." [8]

ETS reached a different conclusion. In 1992, it released a report on three ETS studies indicating that "when used in conjunction with other available information, the SAT accurately predicts the performance of women in college mathematics." According to one of the study teams, "A closer look at the current data shows that the large difference favoring men on the SAT [math] may be counterbalanced by the equally large difference favoring women on the high school grade-point average, resulting in little or no underprediction if both predictors are used." [9]

To FairTest's Schaeffer, the refusal to alter the SATs shows that The College Board and the ETS are run like businesses. "Do tobacco companies tell you their product causes disease?" he asks. "The heads of ETS and The College Board make a quarter of a million dollars a year in salary and benefits. They're selling a product and defending it." Schaeffer says the policy also reflects a reluctance to alter a test that has been in use since 1941 — when the vast majority of test-takers were white males — because analysts want comparable year-to-year-data.

ETS President Nancy Cole, who has written widely on test fairness, says that if ETS were run only like a business, her staff wouldn't be as cooperative as they are in offering test data for public scrutiny. "The only reliable evidence that critics have is from ETS," she says. "There is a continuing desire to have comparable year-to-year for short-term surveys, and there are uses for long-term data, but it's not something that drives us to the extreme."

Cole is concerned about the frequent charge — reflected in FairTest's complaint against the National Merit Scholarships — that important decisions on admissions and scholarships are too often made solely on the basis of SATs. "ETS guidelines strongly recommend the use of multiple types of information," she says. "But some colleges face thousands of applicants, so some may have cutting points. It's the same with the National Merit process. They get a great deal of information on the candidates, but the question is whether they can reduce it to a more manageable size."

ETS urges that SAT scores always be combined with grades, a position that in the future may help females beat the gender gap. "Test and grades put together are the most complete picture of the full range of skills relevant to college," Cole says. "Surveys and observations show that girls do better in showing a sense of social responsibility and fairness to the community, in persistence and willingness to work hard, and in use of language. The interpersonal skills of women are increasingly more valued in the business world, and grades are a way of getting at these other things."

---

[1] The Scholastic Assessment Test, or SAT, was originally known as the Scholastic Aptitude Test.

[2] American Association of University Women, *How Schools Shortchange Girls* (1992), p. 56.

[3] The New York suit was brought by the National Organization for Women, Girls Clubs of America, the American Civil Liberties Union and a group of high school students. The judge's quote is from FairTest documents.

[4] Phyllis Rosser, "The SAT Gender Gap: Identifying the Causes," Center for Women Policy Studies (1989), p. 52.

[5] *Ibid.*, p. 36.

[6] "Toward a Better Understanding of Gender and Testing," ETS Board of Trustees Public Accountability Project, 1989.

[7] Gretchen Wyckoff Rigol, "Why Do Women Score Lower Than Men on the SAT?" *College Prep*, 1989.

[8] Phyllis Rosser, "The SAT Gender GAP: ETS Responds, A Research Update," Center for Women Policy Studies, 1992.

[9] ETS researchers Brent Bridgeman and Cathy Wendler, quoted in *ETS Developments* newsletter, spring 1992.

Continued from p. 487

is a black or an Asian way of learning. Besides, some boys would learn more in a cooperative environment."

"Acculturation and socialization encourage traits and styles in girls and boys that are different," says Bailey. "But it is important that we think about the similarities rather than focus on the differences. By looking at the girls' situation and finding solutions, we may help boys, too."

Is female-only education a good idea?

Carol Denker, a vocational counselor at Madison Park High School in Boston, thinks many of the girls she sees would benefit from all-girl classes or schools. "The boys are loud and foul-mouthed, they dominate, and they need to be smarter than the girls," she says. "The girls are afraid to get good grades because that will threaten their boyfriends. I try to tell the girls to think of their future, but the culture is so strong, it's really difficult."

Women's colleges, private and parochial girls' academies and some experimental all-girl classes in public schools all recently have been the subject of fresh arguments for gender-segregated learning. "Young women from single-sex schools enter the coeducational community with a counterpoint to the messages of prime-time television and daily school immersion in the adolescent subculture," says Roberta Felker, principal of Seton Academy in South Holland, Ill. "They bring not only a sense of strength and possibility but also what [National Public Radio reporter] Linda Wertheimer calls 'the critical thing for women getting their education: a taste for power.' "[19]

In advertisements in *The New York Times,* the private Emma Willard School in Troy, N.Y., says it seeks to help girls "recognize that success need not be at odds with their femininity."

The National Coalition of Girls Schools advises prospective students that, "You will know it's OK to take intellectual risks because the classroom is an arena for cooperative discovery. . . . Self-confidence and self-esteem come from experiencing success . . . not just the brains and the beauties and the jocks, but every girl." Almost 100 percent of girls' school graduates go to college — all of them with four years of math under their belts — and they are four times as likely as their peers to plan careers in math, science and technology, the coalition says.[20]

In all-female schools, "girls are taken much more seriously because they're the only act in town," says Ransome. "That means they get the lead in plays and are the major sports players." And at many women's colleges, proponents point out, female students are offered more role models because more professors and guest speakers are female.

Peggy Skorpinski

In 1990, after protests by students at all-female Mills College, in Oakland, Calif., the school's Board of Trustees reversed its decision to admit men.

Critics of female schools often object less to the segregation of sexes than to their elitist or ideological orientation. "Feminists will support a liberal Smith or Wellesley, but would they support a conservative women's Bible college?" asks Parshall. Ravitch believes in single-sex education, but because they "focus more on academics and are less distracting, not because they're havens from oppression."

There is no question that women's colleges are for high-achieving, professionally oriented women, says Janet McKay, president of Mills College. "But 70 percent of our students marry and have careers, which is a higher rate than that of professional women across the board. Statistically, our graduates have a better chance of balancing work and home life."

The image of women's colleges as artificial environments that breed man-haters is contested by their students. "We get comments from people who think we're feminists running around with meat cleavers," says Mills student Mahood. "But I have a boyfriend, and Mills provides a van that goes to the nearby campus of Berkeley, where we can cross-register for courses. Some people say it's easier to meet men if they're in your classes and extracurriculars, but I haven't felt that way. My priority is to become a doctor, and everything else will come along by itself."

While many gender-equity specialists accept the option of female schools in the private sector, the recent experiments in all-girl classes within coed schools are more controversial. When St. Stephens & St. Agnes, a private middle and high school in Alexandria, Va., became coed in 1989, the faculty discussed ways to deal with gender inequity, according to David Carmen, a math teacher who directs the middle school. There was an agreement that in subjects such as English and history, where the general mode is discussion, the students "liked hearing what the other gender thinks because there are distinct girl and boy viewpoints." In math, however, "there is no *boys'* point of view, even though boys tend to appreciate the thrill of solving a quadratic equation while the girls appreciate the beauty of it."

It was decided to separate the genders in math from sixth to eighth grade, with all teachers teaching both types of classes. "We cover the same material, but boys are more individualistic, while the girls work in groups," Carmen says. Evaluations so far give the school reason for optimism.

General data on the success of single-sex experiments are scarce, but positive. Fifty-six percent of the students in an all-female math class at the University of Missouri-Kansas City went on to enroll in another math class, compared with only 17 percent of females in mixed classes, and the all-female class posted better grades and completion rates. [21]

As part of the UCLA survey of college freshmen, women who declared traditionally male majors — such as engineering — were asked whether their grades and levels of satisfaction were influenced by the number of women in their classes. "It turned out that women tended to be more satisfied with their field when they were in classes with many women," says Linda Sax, an associate director at the Higher Education Research Institute. "But that was because they were satisfied with their chosen field, not because of the composition of the classroom. The one exception was the area of persistence. If women have other women in their class, they're more likely to persist."

Wolfe of the Center for Women Policy Studies bemoans the fact that "people I love and respect have decided to get out of those 'awful' coed classes. But single-sex classes are wrongheaded. The message that gets out is that this is the only thing that works," she says. "Coed institutions need to learn from single-sex institutions about what works. We don't want to let teachers and administrators off the hook" in the schools that 90 percent of girls attend.

Huppertz quotes an educator who said, "'Single-sex classes are intervention, not prevention.' In the short term, it will help that group," she says, "but in the long run it is conceding defeat."

"We need more research on single-sex classes," says Bailey of Wellesley. "They can send a message that girls need special attention, which can be undermining rather than empowering. The real issue is what should go on in the classroom. If it works in single-sex, why not use it in mixed classes?" ■

BACKGROUND

Evolving Views

If differences between the sexes "consist only in women's bearing and begetting children, this does not amount to proof that a woman differs from a man in respect of the sort of education she should receive." [22] This egalitarian sentiment from the philosopher Plato did not carry the day in ancient Greece, which set Western civilization on a course that placed little value on educating females other than for domestic chores.

For centuries, the prevailing view was similar to that expressed by 17th-century French writer Jean de la Bruyere, who compared an educated woman with a gun that one shows as a collector's item, "but which has no use at all, any more than a carousel horse." [23]

There was a common fear that teaching a female to read would expose her to dangerously bawdy stories. Even the 14th-century French poet Christine de Pisan, one of the earliest advocates of female education, believed that it "should be narrower than men's because their tasks in life were different." [24]

During the 18th-century intellectual revolution known as the Enlightenment, French philosopher Jean Jacques Rousseau wrote that women should be educated for the sake of men, "to please them, be useful to them, get them to love and honor them, raise them when young, care for them when grown, counsel them, console them, render life sweet and agreeable to them." [25]

By the end of the 18th century, a movement for public education for women had been spurred by English writer Mary Wollstonecraft's treatise *A Vindication of the Rights of Women*. In 1787, statesman-physician Benjamin Rush created the Young Ladies Academy in Philadelphia with the goal of educating women to help promote political liberty, though it was not envisioned that the graduates would use their knowledge in the public arena. At about the same time, Quakers started the fledgling nation's first coed schools.

Wealthy families of the time often provided their daughters with tutors, but for the most part, girls seeking to learn were smuggled into schools after boys had gone home at night, to be given quick lessons from moonlighting schoolmasters who demanded extra fees. [26] Still, from 1819-35, 32 academies were incorporated in America with the word "female" in their names. [27]

In 1833, Oberlin became first college to make no distinction between the genders, and in 1837, Mount Holyoke, in Northampton, Mass., became the first of the elite Seven Sisters women's colleges. When there were concerns that educating women would turn them away from religious faith, Holyoke scientist Lydia White Shattuck assured worriers, "I have yet to learn that because of these studies, any of our students have become less reverent toward the Bible or less confident of the divine love and care." [28]

As more women's colleges were founded, often as part of the abolitionist movement, resistance to women applicants continued at male schools. In 1858, the University of Michigan rejected three female applicants after a nationally publicized debate. It held out until 1870, after passage of the federal Land Grant Act, when taxpayers began demanding college slots for their daughters. (Michigan professors, it is recorded, persisted in addressing women students as "Mr.") [29]

Coeducation Movement

A key proponent of coeducation was Elizabeth Cady Stanton, a 19th-century American suffragist who argued that "if the sexes were educated together, we should have the healthy, moral and intellectual stimulus of sex ever quickening and refining all the faculties, without the undue excitement of senses that results from novelty in the present system of isolation." [30]

Still influential, however, were the writings of Harvard Professor Edward Clarke, who warned in *Sex in Education* in 1873 that if newly menstruating women attended school during adolescence, blood would be diverted from [their] reproductive organs to the brain. The result would be "monstrous brains and puny bodies . . . flowing thought and constipated bowels." [31] In 1885, the AAUW undertook its first national study, designed to dispel the notion that higher education was harmful to women's health.

By 1900, 98 percent of public high schools were coed, and by 1910, 58 percent of colleges and universities. The coed movement, however, was driven less by philosophy than by economic demands of tax-weary citizenry. "In thinly populated districts," a historian wrote in 1896, "it was found that the number of pupils was too small to admit of separate schools being provided for boys and girls." [32]

Coeducation, of course, did not necessarily mean equal treatment. "There was no prejudice against women students" at the University of California-Berkeley, wrote industrial-engineering student Lillian Moller Gilbreth in 1900. "Consequently, it was a surprise, and a painful one, to aim for a Phi Beta Kappa key, only to learn there would be no girls on the list because, 'when it came to finding a job, men needed the help of this honor more than women did.' " [33]

Women's colleges were still disdained by many in academia as "institutions for glorified spinsterhood," as one critic called them, and when Radcliffe College was founded in 1893, its students could use the library at neighboring Harvard only at night. [34]

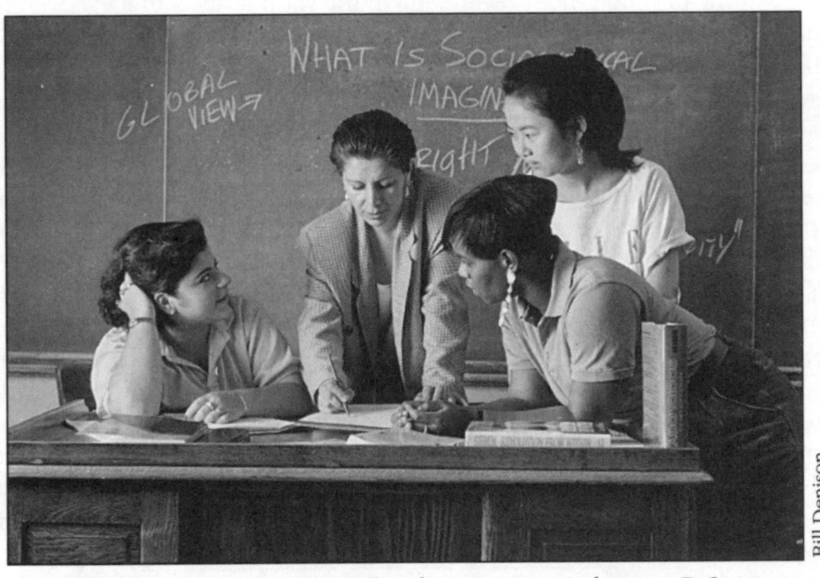

Bill Denison

Founded in 1897, Trinity College for women in Washington, D.C., is "dedicated to empowering women to make a difference in their careers, families and communities."

Gender Equity

The blossoming of the modern women's movement in the 1960s and '70s put women's colleges on the defensive, as the theme of the day became equal access. In one six-month period in 1968, almost a fourth of all women's colleges either closed or merged with men's institutions. [35]

The movement reached its pinnacle when Congress passed the Education Amendments of 1972. Its Title IX — permitting the government to withhold education funds from any school or college violating the act — became "the best stick we ever had," says Wolfe.

Under Title IX, "No person in the United States, shall, on the basis of sex, be excluded from participation in, be denied the benefits of, or be subjected to discrimination under any educational program or activity receiving federal financial assistance." To date, no Title IX funds have been withheld, though the threat to do so has influenced many institutions' policies. [36]

The states, during this period, began passing Equal Rights Amendments that affected schools, and in 1974, Congress passed the Women's Educational Equity Act (WEEA). Introduced by Rep. Patsy T. Mink, D-Hawaii (who introduced its reauthorization in 1993), the law channeled federal education dollars to enforcement of Title IX and research into reducing gender bias in education.

WEEA programs had high priority in the Carter administration, but in the Reagan-Bush era they were continually targeted for elimination. Funding for

Continued on p. 496

Chronology

1960s *During the Johnson administration's Great Society, federal role greatly increases in civil rights and education; birth of modern women's movement; women's colleges begin merging with men's.*

1964
Civil Rights Act includes ban on sex discrimination.

1965
Elementary and Secondary Education Act provides federal grants for schools.

1970s *Women's movement gathers steam; U.S. government enacts new protections against sex discrimination; women's studies point to bias in textbooks and instruction.*

1972
Congress passes Education Amendments including Title IX, prohibiting sex discrimination in any educational institution receiving federal money.

1974
Congress passes Women's Educational Equity Act (WEEA) providing grants for research into programs for gender equity.

July 21, 1975
Title IX takes effect.

1980s *Reflecting what some view as backlash against feminism, Reagan and Bush administrations cut funds for women's programs.*

Feb. 28, 1984
Supreme Court in *Grove City College v. Bell* narrows the scope of Title IX by ruling that the law applies only to programs that directly receive federal aid.

March 22, 1988
Congress passes Civil Rights Restoration Act, overriding President Ronald Reagan's veto and overturning *Grove City* ruling, reaffirming broad applicability of Title IX.

1989
Federal judge in New York City rules that New York State Empire Scholarships are unfair because SAT scores on which they're based are seen as gender-biased.

1990s *Applications to women's colleges and girls school rise; court cases favor harassment victims.*

Nov. 21, 1991
President George Bush signs civil rights bill that for the first time allows victims of sexual harassment to collect limited monetary damages.

Feb. 26, 1992
Supreme Court rules in *Franklin v. Gwinnett County Schools* that courts may award monetary damages for complaints brought under Title IX. The case involved a Georgia high school student who sued her school district after her teacher forced her to have intercourse.

1992
American Association of University Women publishes influential report, *How Schools Shortchange Girls*. Mattel Inc. introduces talking Barbie doll whose comment, "Math class is tough," draws ire from gender-equity activists and is eventually replaced.

February 1994
FairTest files civil rights complaint with Education Department saying National Merit Scholarships are unfair to girls because they're based in large part on "gender-biased" Preliminary SAT tests.

March 24, 1994
House passes reauthorization of the Elementary and Secondary School Education Act containing package of bills addressing gender inequity.

April 28, 1994
Ms. Foundation estimates 3 million girls ages 9-15 took the day off from school for the second annual Take Your Daughter to Work Day, intended to expose girls to career options. Critics complain of unfairness toward boys.

April 29, 1994
In an ongoing case challenging male-only admissions policy of Virginia Military Institute, federal district judge upholds legitimacy of creating a parallel military program for females at nearby Mary Baldwin College.

May 16, 1994
Trial begins in Charleston, S.C., on Shannon Faulkner's suit to become first woman to attend The Citadel, an all-male military academy.

Schoolyard Teasing Now Has a New Name . . .

When it's "Flip Skirt Day" on the playground, the little boys who grab at girls' clothing are acting out a ritual that for years was dismissed as just "boys being boys." But today, such antics among elementary school children bear the label of sexual harassment.

Nor is it considered innocent when a high school teacher requires hugs from girls who're late to class, or when students fill hallway chatter with details of one couple's "hot date."

Harassment can get so bad that "girls won't walk down certain halls or take certain courses," says Susan McGhee Bailey, executive director of Wellesley College's Center for Research on Women. "When it is allowed to continue in full view of everyone, the message is you have to get used to it, and this is appropriate behavior for boys."

As many as 85 percent of the nation's girls say they have experienced sexual harassment, along with 76 percent of the boys, according to a 1993 Louis Harris survey of 1,600 students in grades 8-11. Two-thirds of the boys and half of the girls surveyed admitted to being harassers. Some 13 percent of the girls said they had been "forced to do something sexual other than kissing."[1]

Responding to a survey questionnaire published in the March 1993 issue of *Seventeen* magazine, 39 percent of the girls ages 9-19 said they had been the target of sexual comments or looks, or had been touched, pinched or grabbed on a daily basis. In two-thirds of the incidents, other people were present, the survey noted.[2]

"I had four boys sexually harassing me," recalled one respondent. "I felt like they thought I was a slut. I even thought the whole bus thought I was a slut, because they would give me dirty looks and call me a slut. I hated it! I told the harassers to stop, but they wouldn't. So I wrote them a note saying it was sexual harassment, and if they didn't stop I would report them. They started saying, 'It isn't sexual harassment, we didn't lay a hand on you.' "

Investigators at the General Accounting Office recently released a study of the nation's military academies showing that 97 percent of the female students had experienced harassment. The episodes ranged from prank phone calls to name-calling to one incident in which a senior student commander reportedly dismissed a group of trainees but ordered one woman to stay behind so he could attempt to kiss her.[3]

Impact of Sexual Harassment

Sexual harassment in schools has a far greater impact on women than men, according to a survey by the American Association of University Women. For example, 33 percent of the girls who were harassed, and 12 percent of the boys, said they didn't want to attend school.

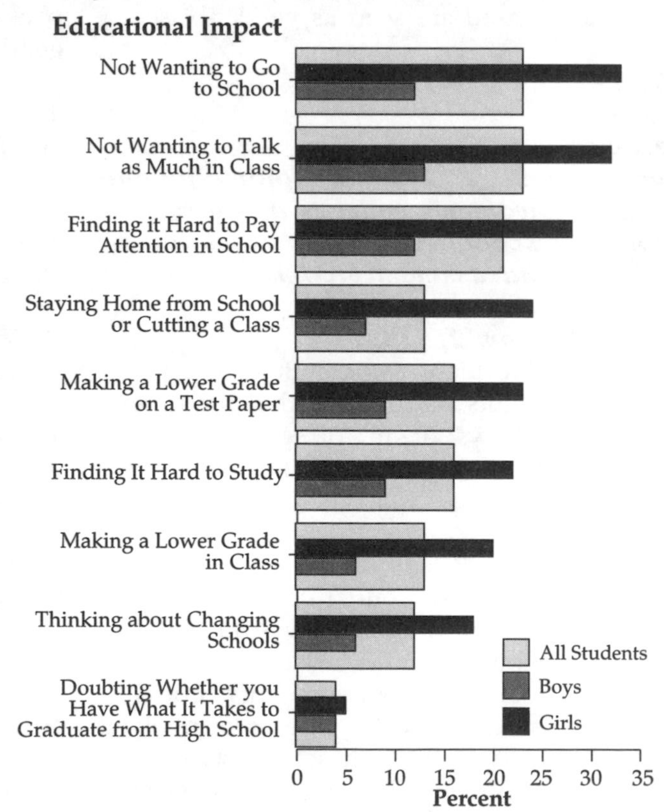

Sources: "Hostile Hallways: The AAUW Survey on Sexual Harassment in America's Schools," American Association of University Women, June 1993

Though harassment from teachers or staff made up only 4-18 percent of the incidents in the AAUW and *Seventeen* surveys, the ramifications from adult-to-student harassment tend to be more serious than those from peer harassment. In California, 145 teachers lost their licenses for sexual misconduct with students from 1985-90, according to Myra and David Sadker, authors of *Failing at Fairness.*[4]

And school districts have known they can be liable for monetary damages ever since the Supreme Court's 1992 ruling in *Franklin v. Gwinnett.* In that case, a Georgia high school student successfully sued her school district under the federal Title IX law after a teacher repeatedly questioned her about sex with her boyfriend and took her to his office and forced sexual intercourse.

"We're concerned about teachers getting due process," says Claudia Edwards, a senior professional associate at the National Association of Teachers. "Some lax school districts overreact and leak out the charges so that the teachers are hung out to dry and their careers are in jeopardy."

But Edwards acknowledges that problems do exist. "Girls are highly attuned to sexual harassment these days," she continues, even more than to sex discrimination. The number of sexual harassment complaints received by the Education

. . . Courts Often Call It Sexual Harassment

Department jumped from 27 in 1988 to 156 last year.

Katy Lyle, a student at Duluth Central High School in Minnesota, was mortified in 1987 to learn of obscene grafitti about her in the boys' restroom. Her complaints were first dismissed as a "building-maintenance problem," but Katy and her mother went to the Minnesota Human Rights Department. After an 18-month process, Katy was awarded $15,000. [5]

Cheltzie Hentz, a first-grader in Eden Prairie, Minn., told her parents of the older boys on the bus who constantly teased her because she didn't have a penis. In handling the complaint, the U.S. Education Department ruled that the school district violated Title IX because it "did not respond forcefully" in this and similar incidents. A settlement was eventually reached in which the district agreed to develop guidelines to help staff handle harassment complaints.

Tawnya Brawdy, a junior high schooler in Petaluma, Calif., was subjected to a daily chorus of cowlike mooing from boys making fun of her breasts. After a lawsuit and an Education Department investigation that produced a 211-page report, she received an out-of-court settlement of $20,000 in 1992. [6]

Another Petaluma student was less successful in her suit seeking $1 million from the school district after boys confronted her continually with a joke about masturbation. A U.S. District Court judge in San Francisco said she failed to "prove intentional discrimination on the basis of sex on the part of an employee of the educational institution." The case, however, was the first to affirm that "student-to-student sexual harassment is actionable under Title IX." [7]

Why do children sexually harasss? Observers point to an underdeveloped sense of empathy among young children. "I don't care, people do this stuff every day," a 14-year-old boy told the Harris survey. "No one feels insulted by it. That's stupid. We just play around. I think sexual harassment is normal." In the poll, 41 percent of boys who had harassed said it was just part of life, and 27 percent thought that the targeted person liked it.

Many common boys' comments, such as "Look at her shake her [backside]," or crude lyrics from rap songs, "would offend me, but I'm not sure about the girls," says Carol Denker, a vocational guidance counselor at Madison Park High School in Boston. "They kind of get off on it."

New York University scholar Diane Ravitch blames the media. "Society is saturated with this enticement to act out, to not repress any feelings," she says. "Freud said that civilization is not possible without a certain level of repression, but TV and the movies say don't repress."

"In negotiating for sex," says Annie Rogers, an assistant professor at the Harvard Graduate School of Education, "boys feel they can push as far as they can to get it, while girls feel that as soon as they say no or act demurely, that should mean stop. There's an incredible gray area." If the perpetrators were suspended from school, the behavior would stop, Rogers says. "We need policies."

California and Minnesota have enacted laws requiring public schools to create policies against sexual harassment. In a sample policy circulated in Minnesota, examples of harassment include: "Unwelcome verbal harassment or abuse; unwelcome, sexually motivated or inappropriate patting, pinching or physical contact [and] unwelcome behavior or words directed at an individual because of gender." [8]

Skeptics concerned about violations of free speech, however, raise eyebrows when the examples of harassment include such everyday banter as dirty jokes, "sexually descriptive letters or notes," spreading sexual rumors about other students, giving other students "the finger" and "making suggestive comments about cheerleading outfits." [9]

"Boys and girls are different, and you can't repeal human nature," says Phyllis Schlafly, president of the Eagle Forum and a longtime critic of feminism. "Boys like to hit, but they should be taught not to hit girls, except that the feminists are horrified because they want everyone treated the same."

Kristi Hamrick, spokeswoman for the conservative Family Research Council, adds that anger over sexual harassment in schools is "the feminists reaping their own whirlwind."

"Women are the permission-givers of society," she says. "Twenty or 30 years ago, if a girl was pinched she would slap the boy's face. Now she writes a letter to the editor. There's a difference between standing up for yourself and acting like an unempowered victim."

During the Reagan era, counters Leslie Wolfe, president of the Center for Women Policy Studies, it became common to portray harassment "victims as unequal and pitiful. But to acknowledge there is sexism doesn't diminish the person who is discriminated against." The fact remains, "you can't concentrate on doing well in school if you're afraid the boys will assault you on the playground."

---

[1] The survey, "Hostile Hallways: The AAUW Survey on Sexual Harassment in America's Schools," was commissioned by the American Association of University Women Educational Foundation.

[2] The survey, "Secrets in Public: Sexual Harassment in Our Schools," was commissioned by the Wellesley Center for Research on Women and the National Organization for Women (NOW) Legal Defense and Education Fund.

[3] The Associated Press, Feb. 4, 1994. The GAO study, "DOD [Department of Defense] Service Academies: More Actions Needed to Eliminate Sexual Harassment," was released Jan. 31.

[4] Myra and David Sadker, *Failing at Fairness* (1994), p. 114. The Sadkers teach at American University in Washington, D.C.

[5] *Los Angeles Times,* Oct. 3, 1993.

[6] *Newsweek,* Oct. 19, 1992, p. 77.

[7] *Education Week,* Sept. 15, 1993.

[8] Kathryn Wells Murdock and David Kysilko, "Sexual Harassment in Schools: What It Is, What do Do," National Association of State Boards of Education (1993), p. 21.

[9] From "Examples of Hostile Environmental Sexual Harassment," guidelines prepared by the Minnesota Department of Education, published in *Harper's Magazine,* June 1993, p. 14.

Continued from p. 492

the programs shrank from $10 million in 1980 to $500,000 in 1992.

As the 1990s dawned, an event on a West Coast campus highlighted the fact that the women's movement's call for equal access was no longer quite so simple. In 1990, the Board of Trustees of Mills College, citing a shortage of students and shaky funding, voted to admit men for the first time in the school's 138-year history. Students felt betrayed. "Mills is like a sanctuary from sexism and all the trash that goes with it," said freshman Elizabeth Bales. "They've taken that away from us." [37]

With alumni threatening to cease sending donations, students called a strike. Within two weeks, the board reversed its ruling, having developed a plan to boost the endowment and alumni giving. Applications began pouring in, and by fall 1993, Mills welcomed its largest entering class ever — still all-female.

"There was a feeling that we did something remarkable," said strike participant Giulietta Aquino. "In that period where we turned over the administration, that was worth the four-year education." [38]

Textbook Sexism

When feminist scholarship emerged in the 1970s, a key theme was gender bias in textbooks. "Dick and Jane as Victims," a 1975 study of 134 reading books used in elementary schools, found that "boy-centered" stories outnumbered "girl-centered" stories more than 2 to 1. [39]

In 1976, the Association of American Publishers issued a statement on bias-free materials, advising publishers to "avoid excluding women with the use of the pronoun 'he' by pluralizing . . . and employ generic terms such as doctor, lawyer, actor, teacher, secretary and poet for both male and females."

Today's equity activists still find flaws with textbooks. Prentice-Hall's 1992 *A History of the United States,* contains four illustrations of males for every female, and less than 3 percent of its text deals with women, according to the Sadkers. [40]

The AAUW and others note that textbooks nearly always portray settlers and scientists as men, and that Marie Curie is often the only female scientist mentioned. They cite the neglect of important women such as Catherine Littlefield Greene, who aided in Eli Whitney's invention of the cotton gin, and English author Aphra Behn, who wrote novels 30 years before Daniel Defoe, whose *Robinson Crusoe* is often called the first English novel. [41] Ironically, Defoe asserted that "one of the most barbarous customs in the world [is] that we deny the advantages of learning to women." [42]

"We do need women's heroes in history books, because we won't get them elsewhere," says Wolfe. "We're not changing facts, just how we look at them." The current curriculum is "still the macho star system, concentrating on oppression and conquest rather than social justice. If the curriculum is alienating to women, they won't learn. This is an attempt at supplying a corrective."

Roger Rogalin, vice president for the school division at the Association of American Publishers, says textbooks reflect the way society views the role of women. After complaints in the 1970s, an effort was made to show females in a variety of jobs. "But then there was a backlash, saying we never show women as homemakers."

Many of the critics are from special-interest groups and tend to generalize after flipping to a few pages of the book, he says. "The textbook publishers probably have more awareness of the issue than the state textbook-adoption boards." ■

CURRENT SITUATION

Legislative Solutions

Women's-equity advocates have rallied round the Clinton administration, which has called for a $3 million boost in funding for gender-equity programs in the Education Department. And the Congressional Caucus for Women's Issues, for the first time, has produced a broad legislative package addressing gender issues.

Originally comprised of nine bills, the package has been attached to the Elementary and Secondary Education Act reauthorization, which has passed the House. (*See "Chronology," p. 493.*) It would create a federal Office of Gender Equity; provide for more data collection on gender, race and socioeconomic status; boost math and science education; permit schools to use general funds to combat sexual harassment; and target funds toward girls who are pregnant or new parents.

"To increase the effectiveness of WEEA," said Rep. Patricia Schroeder, D-Colo., "we must shift the program's major focus to putting effective strategies in place in individual schools, while continuing the important research and development."

Critics, such as Parshall of Concerned Women, deride the bill as "a ridiculous Christmas list of feminism . . . mandatory political correctness." Schlafly calls the bill "a boondoggle for feminists to get government money." *U.S. News & World Report* columnist John Leo warns that it will

Continued on p. 498

At Issue:

Does the U.S. education system shortchange females?

REP. SUSAN MOLINARI, R-N.Y.

yes

In an age of ever-increasing global competitiveness, it is critically important we use all our resources to their fullest potential. As a nation worried about the future, we cannot afford to shortchange half our population. Studies show, however, we do just that by cheating our sisters and daughters in classrooms all across the United States.

Whether we look at pre-schools, elementary or high schools, research has proven that with both male and female teachers a child's gender helps decide what kind, and often how good, their education is.

Over the years, the findings have been consistent and disturbing. Boys tend to receive more attention, and in many cases more positive feedback, in schools than girls. Teachers are more likely to solicit responses from boys, and one study has shown they ask boys 80 percent more academically related questions than girls. Further, girls rarely, if ever, see their own lives and experiences, or the many accomplishments of women, reflected in our schools' curriculum. . . .

Traditionally in schools, encouragement and expectations for our daughters, especially in areas such as math and science, are so low the repercussions reverberate through our whole society. While girls and boys start schools with the same interests and abilities, today 64 percent of high school senior boys taking physics and calculus major in science and engineering. Only 19 percent of girls will do the same.

At a time when our economic competitiveness depends on the recruitment of qualified engineers, scientists and entrepreneurs, teachers, almost without realizing it, treat girls differently and unconsciously veer them away from these important career choices.

In short, current practices tend to give boys more attention, discourage girls from exploring certain important career choices and downgrade the importance of their contributions in class. All this leads to diminished self-confidence.

But perhaps the most disturbing barrier to learning today is that far too many girls in our schools are sexually harassed. A recent survey shows that 39 percent of girls ages nine to 19 said they were harassed once a day last year, and another 29 percent said it happened once a week. Sexual harassment and intimidation by boys and teachers strips girls and young women of their potential and distracts them from learning by leaving them feeling humiliated and angry. Worse, 45 percent of the reported cases are not acted upon by administrators, often with the excuse that "boys will be boys."

. . . . Schools should be a place where everyone, despite gender, has an equal opportunity to learn and therefore contribute their fullest later in life. Our sisters and daughters, as well as our nation, deserve no less.

DIANE RAVITCH

Senior Research Scholar, New York University

no

By now, you have seen or read the reports about how girls are being systematically maltreated in our nation's schools; how teachers consistently show favoritism to boys; how girls are suffering a crisis of self-esteem; how the hopes and dreams of girls are regularly shattered by the discriminatory treatment they receive in school. Every network, major newspaper and national magazine has repeated the same terrible story.

What they haven't told you, however, is that none of this is true. The real story — arguably the biggest, most underreported educational story of our time — has been the successful conquest of American education by girls and women. . . .

Those who claim gender bias in the schools purposefully ignore the remarkable changes that have occurred over the past generation. In 1970, women accounted for only 41 percent of college students in the United States, and fewer than 10 percent of degrees in law and medicine were awarded to women. Gender inequity, in education and society, was pervasive and triumphant.

Today, women are 55 percent of all undergraduates, and they are 59 percent of all master's degree candidates. Women are nearly 50 percent of the enrollment in American law schools and medical schools. In fact, women now constitute the majority of all graduate and professional students in American higher education.

The claim that girls and women are burdened by low self-esteem is demonstrably untrue. Surveys conducted by the U.S. Department of Education demonstrate that girls and young women have higher aspirations than their male counterparts. Eighth-grade girls are twice as likely as eighth-grade boys to aspire to a professional, business or managerial career. Twelfth-grade girls are more likely to aspire to get a college or graduate degree than 12th-grade boys. . . .

Another unfortunate consequence of the gender bias myth is that girls' schools and women's colleges have decided to capitalize on it and to advertise themselves as sanctuaries from male oppression. This is unworthy of them and leaves them open to the possibility that their reason for being will cease to exist when the claims of gender bias cease or prove unfounded.

There is a powerful case to be made for single-sex education, and it has nothing to do with cries of female victimization or male oppression. Research has convincingly demonstrated that students in single-sex schools, undistracted by the opposite sex, take their studies more seriously. . . .

It's difficult to slow a journalistic phenomenon when it is in full cry. . . . But sooner or later, the facts will prevail. One hopes.

Doonesbury BY GARRY TRUDEAU

Continued from p. 496
bring "indoctrination and federal monitoring. By identifying all girls as victims, it attempts to appropriate funding for one sex that ought to go generally to the schools." [43]

Single-Sex Schools

The women's movement has become divided in recent years on the controversial issue of male-only schools. Debate has swirled around court challenges to proposed all-male public schools in Detroit and to traditional, publicly funded, male military colleges, namely the Virginia Military Institute and The Citadel in South Carolina.

When the Detroit Board of Education in 1991 announced plans for special schools for African-American males, the American Civil Liberties Union (ACLU) joined with the National Organization for Women (NOW) in a challenge. "Parents are being asked to make a cruel and unusual choice," said Helen R. Neuborne, executive director of the NOW Legal Defense and Education Fund. "In the struggle for limited educational resources, they are being told that the way to save their boys is to give them a better education than is currently offered girls. This is unnecessary because having girls as classmates will in no way impinge boys' ability to benefit from quality education programs."

The ACLU is bringing the suit against The Citadel on behalf of Shannon Faulkner, a woman who won admission to the school but had not disclosed her gender when she applied. She has been permitted to attend classes but may not wear a uniform or live in the barracks pending the court's decision.

"It's an ancient idea: woman as tainted, polluted, corrupting, somehow diseased — Simone de Beauvoir's 'Other,'" wrote ACLU attorney Sara L. Mandelbaum. "The idea was echoed by a star graduate of The Citadel, who testified that the very word 'woman' (along with 'skirt' and other more vulgar terms) is one of the insults most frequently hurled at cadets by those superior to them in class or rank." [44]

The idea that the women's movement can attack male-only schools while promoting female-only education strikes critics as hypocritical. "Boys and girls are different," says Hamrick of the Family Research Council, "but if we split them up, who will complain? The feminists? The only time things can be separate is when feminists say they can be."

But advocates for women's colleges don't oppose male-only *private* colleges such as Morehouse, Hampden-Sidney and Wabash, notes Jadwiga Sebrechts, executive director of the Women's College Coalition. "VMI and The Citadel get public money," she says. "Also, women's colleges serve affirmative action purposes, so it's not exactly parallel. Women's colleges open a few more doors of extra opportunity, while VMI and The Citadel offer a glorious tradition and network of powerful alumni."

McKay of Mills adds that her all-woman's college doesn't offer a unique kind of education unavailable to men elsewhere. "VMI is a unique course of study in military leadership," she says. "There is a legitimate need for groups to affiliate with one another, even if they're all male, but there can be no federal grants for that."

The arguments about women vs. men and public vs. private are being confused, says Elizabeth Fox-Genovese, a professor of history at Emory College, who testified in defense of The Citadel at Faulkner's trial. "Research and common sense suggest that what single-sex schools offer especially benefits people from lower and middle-class backgrounds, precisely the people who need the public sector. If you're at Bryn Mawr or the Ivy League, you're in an elite world where a whole range of possibilities is available. If you're a minority whose parents didn't go to college, who went to a public high school where the whole issue of social life and dating was dominant, you may not know how to imagine ambition, and a single-sex school can help you."

Fox-Genovese argues that the choice of a single-sex school should be preserved for both sexes, even with public funding, if there is demand for it. "And to go on arguing that women need special treatment," she says, "is to fall back on paternalism, the potential dangers being dependency on other people to fight your battles and increasingly legitimate resentment on the part of men." ■

OUTLOOK

New Initiatives

Suzie Scibetta, a ninth-grader at Springfield High School in Northern Virginia, recalls how the "goof-off" boys were making fun of her perfect scores on geometry tests. "It's interesting to be with boys," she observes. "They make time to relax and laugh." At one point, her curiosity tempted her to deliberately botch a test to see if the teasing would stop, but she didn't.

Researchers have long noted that the so-called adolescent subculture — with its emphasis on physical attractiveness, cars and clothes — is of greater import to young people than academic achievement. But the impact is not the same for both genders. "Girls in grades six and seven rate being popular and well-liked [by their own sex] as more important than being perceived as competent or independent," says the AAUW. "Boys, on the other hand, are more likely to rank independence and competence as important." [45]

The documented shyness among girls — and the expectations held for them by adults — is a big reason that gender-equity activists propose remedial action. The movement is gathering steam. The Girls Scouts this month are releasing a "Gender Equity Module" training guide for volunteers and staff. The National Collegiate Athletic Association (NCAA) in January encouraged colleges to create more opportunities for female athletes by adding varsity teams in archery, badminton, water polo and other sports. [46]

And most dramatically, girls' shyness explains the current experiments in single-sex math and science classes. But segregated classes in the public schools are vulnerable to a legal challenge under Title IX.

"There are less segregatory means to reach the same end," Norma Cantu, assistant secretary for civil rights in the Education Department, said last November. "Have they really exhausted the possibilities of training teachers to handle the different learning styles of boys and girls?" [47]

Sen. John C. Danforth, R-Mo., is planning an amendment that would give demonstration projects for single-sex public schools, such as the Detroit academies for black males, a special exemption from legal challenge, provided that similar programs were offered for the opposite gender.

Women's colleges, with their hallowed traditions, "will be around for the foreseeable future, unless there are big societal changes," says Sebrechts. "In the long term, I would hope they would not be necessary, and that the advantages they provide will be available elsewhere. For now, the issue is not how many more woman's colleges can be constructed, but how much influence they can have."

In the 1970s, notes Ransome, "girls' schools had to justify their existence and were looked at as a dying breed. Now we're enjoying an incredible renaissance of interest because parents understand that we offer first-class education, not second-class citizenship."

The Sadkers report being surprised that their book, *Failing at Fairness,* has been so well-received among middle school and high school girls. Some critics say, "Oh, another victim book!" says Myra Sadker. "But it's an empowerment book. Girls [who read it] are then going to meet with their teacher. That's empowerment."

But special efforts for gender equity will prompt detractors. The Sadkers contribute to the "Balkanization of American society," writes education author Rita Kramer. "We should be worrying about why our youngsters of both sexes are near the bottom of the ladder in international tests of math and science and excel only in measures of self-esteem." [48]

"The feminist agenda's constant victimization of women is repugnant," says Parshall. "Self-esteem is caught, not taught. Good teachers know how to bring it out."

Wolfe says the much-discussed "backlash" against gender equity in the 1980s "is a rear-guard action. They're fighting the inevitable. My girls will have a real partnership with boys, and will try and revel in it."

"It's tricky when women speak out on behalf of women," says Wellesley's Bailey. "It's more acceptable socially to speak on behalf of others. So we must start speaking for ourselves and our daughters, which will speak for our sons, too." ■

Notes

[1] American Association of University Women, *How Schools Shortchange Girls* (1992), p. 2. The report, which summarized about a thousand research papers, was commissioned by the AAUW Educational Foundation and researched by the Wellesley College Center for Research on Women.

[2] The poll, "Shortchanging Girls, Shortchanging America," was conducted by Greenberg-Lake: The Analysis Group Inc.

[3] Myra and David Sadker, *Failing at Fairness: How America's Schools Cheat Girls* (1994), p. 2.

[4] Girls Inc., "What's Equal: Figure Out What Works for Girls in Co-ed Settings" (1993), p. 7.

[5] Cited in *The Wall Street Journal* book review of Paul R. Gross and Norman Levitt's *Higher Superstition: The Academic Left and Its Quarrels With Science,* April 19, 1994.

[6] AAUW, *op. cit.,* p. 25.
[7] *Ibid.,* p. 72.
[8] Myra and David Sadker, *op. cit.,* pp. 48-50, and interviews with the authors. The Sadkers evaluated teachers who received sensitivity training in gender equity as well as teachers in a control group who did not.
[9] Quoted in *Education Week,* March 30, 1994, p. 27.
[10] National Center for Education Statistics, *The 1990 High School Transcript Study Tabulations,* Education Department, 1993.
[11] Gita Z. Wilder and Kristin Powell, "Sex Differences in Test Performance: A Survey of the Literature," The College Board, 1989.
[12] *Ibid.,* p. 15.
[13] Mid-Atlantic Equity Consortium Inc. and The Network, "Beyond Title IX: Gender Equity Issues in Schools," September 1993, p. 16.
[14] Goldberger is an analyst at the Fielding Institute for Psychology and Human Development, in Santa Barbara, Calif. The ETS conference was held Oct. 26, 1991.
[15] Quoted in *The Wall Street Journal,* April 14, 1994.
[16] AAUW, *op. cit.,* p. 29.
[17] Quoted in *The New York Times,* Nov. 24, 1993.
[18] Ann B. Oakes, mathematics professor at Hobart and William Smith Colleges, writing in "Gender Equity in Math and Science" (Part 1), *Initiatives,* National Association for Women in Education, p. 32.
[19] "Single-Sex Schooling: Proponents Speak Out," Education Department (draft), Dec. 22, 1992.
[20] National Coalition of Girls Schools, "What Every Girl in School Needs to Know" (pamphlet).
[21] Cornelius Riordan, *Girls and Boys in School: Together or Separate?* (1990), p. 9.
[22] *Ibid.,* p. 15.
[23] Phyllis Stock, *Better Than Rubies: A History of Women's Education* (1978), p. 16.
[24] *Ibid.,* p. 41.
[25] *Ibid.,* p. 107.
[26] Myra and David Sadker, *op. cit.,* p. 16.
[27] Riordan, *op. cit.,* p. 30.
[28] Quoted in John Mack Faragher and Florence Howe, *Women and Higher Education in American History* (1988), p. x.
[29] *Ibid.,* p. 113.
[30] *Ibid.,* p. 108.
[31] Myra and David Sadker, *op. cit.,* p. 30.
[32] Riordan, *op. cit.,* pp. 34, 39.
[33] Faragher and Howe, *op. cit.,* p. 113.
[34] Myra and David Sadker, *op. cit.,* p. 24.
[35] Education Department, "Single-Sex Schooling: Perspectives from Practice and Research" (draft), December 1992.
[36] For background on Title IX, see "Women and Sports," *The CQ Researcher,* March 6, 1992, pp. 193-216.
[37] Quoted in *The San Francisco Chronicle,* May 4, 1990.
[38] Quoted in *The New York Times,* Sept. 1, 1993.
[39] Myra and David Sadker, *op. cit.,* p. 69.
[40] *Ibid.,* p. 130. The authors of the textbook are Daniel Boorstin and Brooks Mather Kelley. Editors at Prentice-Hall contend that the textbook, far from being biased, is a "paragon of diversity."
[41] Montana Katz and Veronica Vieland, *Get Smart!: What You Should Know (But Won't Learn in Class) About Sexual Harassment and Sex Discrimination* (1993), p. 15.
[42] Riordan, *op. cit.,* p. 20.
[43] *U.S. News & World Report,* Feb. 7, 1994, p. 23.
[44] Unpublished essay.
[45] AAUW, *op. cit.,* p. 11
[46] *The Chronicle of Higher Education,* Feb. 16, 1994.
[47] Quoted in *The New York Times,* Nov. 24, 1993.
[48] Book review in *The Wall Street Journal,* March 1, 1994.

Bibliography

Selected Sources Used

Books

Faragher, John Mack, and Florence Howe, *Women and Higher Education in American History,* W.W. Norton, 1988.
A Mount Holyoke historian and an editor at the Feminist Press collaborated on this anthology of writings highlighting the founding of women's colleges and the integration of previously male-only colleges.

Holland, Dorothy C., and Margaret A. Eisenhardt, *Educated in Romance: Women, Achievement, and College Culture,* University of Chicago Press, 1990.
Two anthropologists describe results of their longitudinal, in-depth study of women at two coed colleges, showing how greater dropout rates and lowered career expectations can be traced to the "adolescent subculture" on campuses that pre-empts academics and subjects women "to the sexual auction block."

Katz, Montana, and Veronica Vicland, *Get Smart! What You Should Know (But Won't Learn in Class) About Sexual Harassment and Sex Discrimination,* Feminist Press of the City University of New York, 1993.
Columbia and Barnard University scholars offer this handbook on how to counter unwanted sexual behavior and the "hidden curriculum" that shows up in classrooms in the form of lowered expectations for females.

Riordan, Cornelius, *Girls & Boys in School: Together or Separate?* Teachers College Press, Columbia University, 1991.
A Providence College sociologist gives a historical overview of how the two genders have been educated, citing current research to argue in favor of allowing the choice of single-sex learning.

Sadker, Myra, and David Sadker, *Failing at Fairness: How America's Schools Cheat Girls,* Charles Scribners' Sons, 1994.
Two American University education professors draw from 20-plus years of research in this non-technical survey of the issues that they say keep females from achieving as well as males. They include much history of education and describe their classroom observations of teachers' often-unconscious bias.

Skolnick, Joan, Carol Langbort and Lucille Day, *How to Encourage Girls in Math & Science,* Prentice-Hall, 1982.
Three doctors of philosophy in education have designed sample math and science lessons intended to boost female performance by emphasizing "success for each child, tasks with many approaches, tasks with many right answers, guessing and testing, estimating."

Stock, Phyllis, *Better Than Rubies: A History of Women's Education,* Capricorn Books, 1978.
A Seton Hall University historian discusses women's education in the Western world from ancient times through the "courtly love" period of the Middle Ages into the "limited victory" of the 20th century.

Reports and Studies

American Association of University Women, *Hostile Hallways: The AAUW Survey on Sexual Harassment in America's Schools,* June 1993.
Pollster Louis Harris conducted this survey of 1,632 eighth to 11th-graders in 79 American schools, documenting the extent of sexual harassment and examining the reasons, impact and possible solutions.

American Association of University Women, *How Schools Shortchange Girls: A Study of Major Findings on Girls and Education,* 1992.
Commissioned by the AAUW and researched by the Wellesley College Center for Research on Women, this overview summarizes major research on the self-esteem problems of adolescent girls, the gender gap in SAT tests, teacher treatment of girls and sexual harassment.

National Association of Women in Education, "Gender Equity in Math and Science," Parts 1 & 2, *Initiatives,* 1993.
This compendium of essays discusses ways to improve female performance in two of the most important fields in the arena of international economic competitiveness.

Connor, Katherine, and Ellen J. Vargyas, "The Legal Implications of Gender Bias in Standardized Testing," *Berkeley Women's Law Journal*, Vol. 7, 1992.
Two attorneys at the National Women's Law Center give the legal history and arguments in favor of correcting the alleged gender bias in SAT and college achievement tests.

Stein, Nan, Nancy L. Marshall and Linda R. Tropp, *Secrets in Public: Sexual Harassment in Our Schools,* NOW Legal Defense and Education Fund and the Wellesley College Center for Research on Women, March 1993.
Results of a survey among readers of *Seventeen* magazine giving detailed descriptions of the frequency and nature of schoolyard and campus sexual harassment.

The Next Step

Additional information from UMI's Newspaper & Periodical Abstracts database

Bias Against Girls

Downey, Maureen, "Sadkers write the book on gender inequity," ***Atlanta Constitution,*** **April 28, 1994, p. C3.**
Gender researchers Myra and David Sadker, authors of the controversial new book "Failing at Fairness: How America's Schools Shortchange Girls," are interviewed about the biases against girls they've found in the educational system.

Flynn, Valerie, and Roger David Chambers, "Promoting gender equity: What you can do," ***Learning,*** **January 1994, pp. 58-59.**
Gender inequality still exists in schools, with many girls starting their school careers auspiciously only to languish in later grades, the authors write. Four factors that contribute to this inequality—behavioral differences, gender segregation, teacher expectations and teacher/student interactions—are discussed, and steps to a bias-free classroom are offered.

Lawton, Millicent, "Girls will — and should — be girls," ***Education Week*****, March 30, 1994, pp. 24-27.**
Myra Sadker and David Sadker have written a book about how girls face gender bias in the classroom from kindergarten through graduate school. The question of whether this discrimination really exists is addressed.

Plucker, Jonathan A., "Educational benefits from equitable treatment," ***Science Teacher,*** **April 1994, pp. 49-51.**
Interventions, strategies and resources for eliminating gender bias in the science classroom and constructing an atmosphere of gender equity are discussed.

Winerip, Michael, "Merit scholarship program faces sex bias complaint," ***The New York Times,*** **Feb. 16, 1994, p. A18.**
The ACLU and the National Center for Fair and Open Testing have filed a federal civil rights complaint charging that the method of awarding National Merit Scholarships discriminates against girls. The selection method relies primarily on PSAT scores, which tend to be lower for girls than for boys.

In the Classroom

"Gender gap grants," ***Science Teacher,*** **February 1994, p. 60.**
The Teacher Education Equity Project, a national project designed to assist professors of teacher education in addressing gender equity in the fields of math, science and technology education, is discussed.

Sadker, Myra, and David Sadker, "Why schools must tell girls: You're smart, you can do it," ***USA Today,*** **Feb. 4, 1994, p. USW4.**
Teachers and students unwittingly shortchange girls up and down the educational ladder, from kindergarten through graduate school, the authors write. This problem is described, along with examples of what educators and students are doing to combat it.

Shea, Lois, "Teacher project aimed at gender parity," ***Boston Globe,*** **April 24, 1994, p. NH2.**
Lois Shea discusses teachers' efforts to achieve gender parity in the classroom with regard to differential treatment of boys and girls.

Thompson, Sheila, "May the force be walloped," ***Vocational Education Journal,*** **February 1994, pp. 21-23.**
Educators must overcome stereotypes to recruit students, Thompson writes. Tips for fighting years of sex-role stereotyping include reducing and eliminating gender bias in vocational labs.

Legislation

Stromquist, Nelly P., "Sex-equity legislation in education: The state as promoter of women's rights," ***Review of Educational Research,*** **winter 1993, pp. 379-407.**
A study examined federal legislation addressing gender inequities in education. Evidence indicates that women have made significant gains in access to education institutions as students rather than as educators or administrators.

Walters, Laurel Shaper, "Researchers assert girls get shortchanged in class," ***Christian Science Monitor,*** **March 31, 1994, p. 2.**
The House of Representatives in late March 1994 passed the Gender Equity in Education Act, calling for retraining of public school teachers to combat educational biases against girls. Bill supporters say it's needed because girls score lower on national achievement tests and are behind in math and science.

Math and Science

Irwin, Julie, "The new math: Experts divided on all-girls classes," ***Chicago Tribune,*** **Feb. 7, 1994, p. 1.**
The educational theory of putting girls in separate math and science classes is discussed. The idea is drawing mixed reviews.

Lee, Felicia R., "Cutting chains that still bind girls in school," ***The New York Times,*** **April 10, 1994, p. 27.**
Felicia R. Lee discusses the New York Project, a program started by Girls Inc. that offers girls-only classes for math and

science in East Harlem, Washington Heights and the South Bronx, where there is a high concentration of low-income girls.

Shepardson, Daniel P. Edward L. Pizzini, "Gender, achievement, and perception toward science activities," *School Science & Mathematics,* April 1994, pp. 188-193.
The science achievements of boys and girls in middle school life science are examined. The results indicate no significant differences in student achievement by gender or science activities and no significant differences in perception by gender.

Tousignant, Marylou, "An equation for equality: Same-sex classes target girls' math, science skills," *The Washington Post*, March 15, 1994, p. A1.
St. Stephen's & St. Agnes, a private Episcopal school in Alexandria, Va., separated by sex all its math and science classes, including honors courses, for grades, six, seven and eight. The intent is to focus on the different learning styles of girls and boys.

Turni, Karen, "Schools look to help girls in math, science," *Times-Picayune,* April 4, 1994, p. A1.
Math and science scores from students across the nation indicate that girls get short shrift in classrooms, leading some to determine that the glass ceiling truly does begin in kindergarten. Although it has taken 20 years, help to resolve this discrimination appears to be on the way, Turni writes.

Programs

Abramson, Rudy, "Women's school in Appalachia lights a beacon of hope," *Los Angeles Times,* April 14, 1994, p. A5.
The New Opportunity School for Women in Kentucky is featured. The school helps low-income women from southern Appalachia seize control of their lives.

Carroll, Nicole, "A good day's work puts girls on a professional path," *USA Today,* April 20, 1994, p. D3.
Girls around the world will be going to work April 28, 1994, as part of the Ms. Foundation's now-annual Take Our Daughters to Work Day. While the event is known largely for its efforts to bolster girls' self-esteem, teachers and parents are beginning to tap its educational value.

Franklin, Marie C., "Many schools trying not to short-change girls," *Boston Globe,* April 24, 1994, p. B25.
The efforts of Massachusetts schools to avoid short-changing girls, especially in science and technology studies, are examined.

Marks, Peter, "Encouraging schoolgirls to enter a mostly male world," *The New York Times,* Jan. 12, 1994, p. B4.
Eighth-, 9th- and 10th-grade girls were invited to the State University of New York at Stony Brook on Jan. 11, 1994, for a day of encouragement and exploration of academic disciplines that remain largely male bastions: the worlds of math and science.

Research and Studies

Banks, Michael H., and Debra Roker, "The political socialization of youth: Exploring the influence of school experience," *Journal of Adolescence,* February 1994, pp. 3-15.
A study is described that explored the possible role of educational experience in political socialization, comparing the political attitudes of girls from similar family backgrounds attending different types of school. A model of the role of the school in political socialization is proposed.

Thomas, Depelsha R., "Study: Schooling girls raises living standards," *Atlanta Constitution,* Jan. 31, 1994, p. A11.
Thomas discusses a report that said foreign assistance to close a gender gap that denies equal education to girls in less-developed countries would do more to improve living standards than the billions of dollars now going into military aid and technical assistance.

West, Peter, "N.S.T.A. handbook examines effective science instruction," *Education Week,* April 13, 1994, p. 11.
The "NSTA [National Science Teachers Association] Handbook on Research on Science Teaching and Learning: Implications for Classroom Instruction on Problem-Solving" is discussed. Researchers have found that classrooms that emphasize group learning may be less effective at encouraging girls to study mathematics and science.

Single-Sex Education

Couloumbis, Angela E., "A new-old experiment in separating girls, boys in schools," *Christian Science Monitor,* April 18, 1994, p. 1.
The educational experiment of introducing single-sex classes into coed public schools is discussed. Women's groups support all-girl science and math classes, but critics contend that gender segregation is demeaning and suggests that girls require special handling to keep up with boys.

Means, Marianne, "Separate and unequal," *Chicago Defender,* March 2, 1994, p. 12.
Marianne Means relates the Supreme Court's ruling in *Brown v. Board of Education* that "separate educational facilities are inherently unequal" to the state of Virginia's campaign to keep women out of its prestigious, taxpayer-supported Virginia Military Institute.

Watts, Claudius E. III, "Single-sex education benefits men too," *The Wall Street Journal,* May 3, 1994, p. A14.
Claudius E. Watts III, president of The Citadel in Charleston, S.C., discusses single-sex education. Watts says The Citadel is not trying to keep women out of the Corps of Cadets by protecting machismo; The Citadel is trying to preserve an environment that molds young men into grown men of good character, honor and integrity.

Back Issues

Great Research on Current Issues Starts Right Here...Recent topics covered by The CQ Researcher are listed below. Before May 1991, reports were published under the name of Editorial Research Reports.

NOVEMBER 1992
Physical Fitness
Privatization
Paying for College
U.S. Policy in Asia

DECEMBER 1992
Crackdown on Smoking
The New CIA
Eating Disorders
Women and AIDS

JANUARY 1993
Hate Crimes
Child Sexual Abuse
Nuclear Fusion
U.S. Trade Policy

FEBRUARY 1993
Community Policing
Europe's New Right
School Censorship
Violence Against Women

MARCH 1993
Gay Rights
Aid to Russia
War on Drugs
TV Violence

Back issues are available for $4.00 (subscribers) or $7.00 (non-subscribers). Quantity discounts apply to orders over ten. To order, call Congressional Quarterly Customer Service at (202) 887-8621.

Binders are available for $16.00. To order call 1-800-638-1710. Please refer to stock number 648.

APRIL 1993
Head Start
High-Speed Rail
Children's Legal Rights
Muslims in America

MAY 1993
Cults in America
Preventing Teen Pregnancy
Software Piracy
National Parks

JUNE 1993
Food Safety
Prostitution
Childhood Immunizations
National Service

JULY 1993
Electric Cars
Population Growth
Downward Mobility
Intelligence Testing

AUGUST 1993
Mental Illness
Bilingual Education
Foreign Policy Burden
School Funding

SEPTEMBER 1993
Suburban Crime
Public Housing
Supreme Court Preview
Immigration Reform

OCTOBER 1993
Airline Safety
Disaster Response
Science in the Courtroom
The Glass Ceiling

NOVEMBER 1993
Paying for Retirement
Charitable Giving
Privacy in the Workplace
Adoption

DECEMBER 1993
U.S. Vietnam-Relations
Learning Disabilities
Child Care
Space Program's Future

JANUARY 1994
Racial Tensions in Schools
South Africa's Future
Worker Retraining
Regulating Pesticides

FEBRUARY 1994
Prison Overcrowding
Water Quality
Religion in Schools
Juvenile Justice

MARCH 1994
Underground Economy
Education Standards
Gambling Boom
Private Management of Public Schools

APRIL 1994
Reproductive Ethics
U.S.-China Trade
Soccer in America
Talk Show Democracy

MAY 1993
Traffic Congestion
Women's Health Issues
Mutual Funds
Political Scandals

Future Topics

- ***Gun Control***
- ***Public Land Policy***
- ***Nuclear Arms Cleanup***

THE CQ Researcher

PUBLISHED BY CONGRESSIONAL QUARTERLY INC.

Gun Control

Will it help reduce violent crime in the U.S.?

The gun lobby suffered a pair of stunning setbacks in recent months. Congress passed the Brady bill, requiring a five-day waiting period for handgun purchases, and it moved closer to banning 19 models of assault weapons. Gun control opponents vowed to unseat lawmakers who voted for the bills and scoffed at the idea that restrictions will keep weapons away from criminals. They say such curbs infringe on Americans' constitutional right to bear arms. Further, they picture America under strict gun controls as a land where law-abiding citizens would be helpless against bands of well-armed hoodlums. Many gun control advocates, however, regard gun-related deaths and injuries as a public health problem that can be controlled only by rooting out firearms themselves.

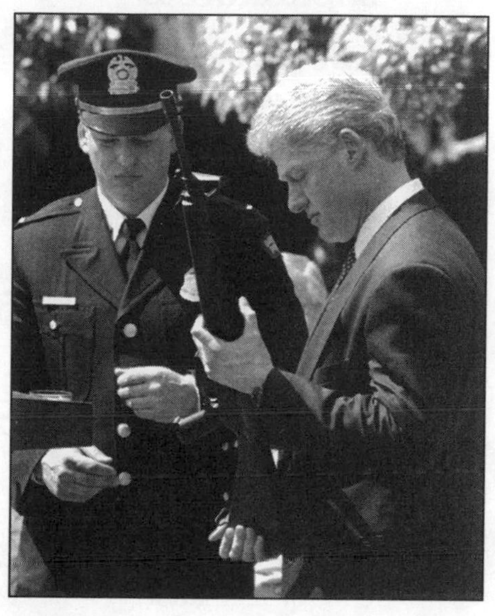

INSIDE THIS ISSUE

CQ June 10, 1994 • Volume 4, No. 22 • 505-528

Formerly Editorial Research Reports

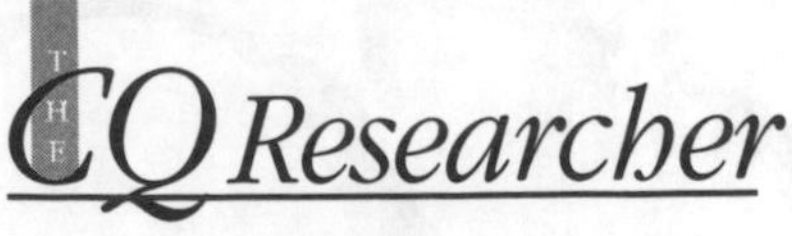

June 10, 1994
Volume 4, No. 22

EDITOR
Sandra Stencel

MANAGING EDITOR
Thomas J. Colin

ASSOCIATE EDITOR
Richard L. Worsnop

STAFF WRITERS
Charles S. Clark
Mary H. Cooper
Kenneth Jost

PRODUCTION EDITOR
Sarah E. Merritt

EDITORIAL ASSISTANT
Michael M. Taylor

GRAPHICS
P. Eloise Fuller

PUBLISHED BY
Congressional Quarterly Inc.

CHAIRMAN
Andrew Barnes

VICE CHAIRMAN
Andrew P. Corty

EDITOR AND PUBLISHER
Neil Skene

EXECUTIVE EDITOR
Robert W. Merry

ASSOCIATE PUBLISHER
John J. Coyle

MARKETING AND SALES DIRECTOR
Edward S. Hauck

The CQ Researcher (ISSN 1056-2036). Formerly Editorial Research Reports. Published weekly (48 times per year, not printed the first Friday of any month with five Fridays) by Congressional Quarterly Inc., 1414 22nd St., N.W., Washington, D.C. 20037. Rates are furnished upon request. Second-class postage paid at Washington, D.C. POSTMASTER: Send address changes to The CQ Researcher, 1414 22nd St., N.W., Washington, D.C. 20037.

COVER: AT AN APRIL ROSE GARDEN CEREMONY LAUNCHING EFFORTS TO PASS A BAN ON ASSAULT WEAPONS, PRESIDENT CLINTON EXAMINES A COLT AR-15 RIFLE USED TO KILL A DAYTON, OHIO, POLICEMAN DURING A ROUTINE TRAFFIC STOP. LT. RANDY BEAN, LEFT, WAS WOUNDED IN THE INCIDENT. (REUTERS)

Gun Control

By Richard L. Worsnop

The Issues

For gun control advocates, the past six months have seen one dream come true and another move close to realization. First came the passage last November of the Brady law, which requires a five-day waiting period for handgun purchases. Then, on May 5, the House joined the Senate in approving legislation banning 19 assault weapons linked to violent crime. The proposed ban is expected to become part of the omnibus crime bill that Congress will vote on this summer.

Gun control proponents feel confident the tide of opinion is rolling their way. (*See poll, p. 508.*) "The lesson of the Brady law and the assault weapons ban is that the American public wants more gun laws, not fewer," says Susan Whitmore, communications director for Handgun Control Inc., the largest group promoting firearms regulation.*

Groups opposing gun control reject Whitmore's appraisal. John M. Snyder, public affairs director of the Citizens Committee for the Right to Keep and Bear Arms, predicts gun owners will mobilize this fall to trigger a "major change in the makeup of Congress," unseating members "who heretofore have been foursquare on the pro-firearms side of the issue and then switched and voted the wrong way."

In fact, says Tanya K. Metaksa, chief lobbyist for the National Rifle Association (NRA), passage of the Brady law has prompted former NRA members to rejoin the organization at five times the normal rate. "Our biggest challenge is going to be harnessing the energy of our members," she says.

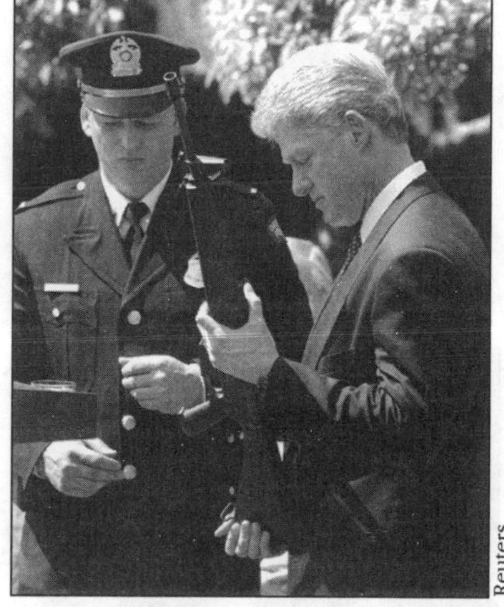
Reuters

Gun control experts credit law enforcement groups with their recent successes. "Not every law enforcement official agrees" that certain assault weapons should be outlawed, says Don Cahill, national legislative chairman for the Fraternal Order of Police (FOP), "but the majority of them do." Cahill says he "can understand someone from Utah or Wyoming complaining that this is not a problem, because it's not a problem in their states. But it's a problem in 75 percent of the rest of the country." Without a federal assault-weapons law, he says, "we'll have the same problem we had prior to Brady. That is, if a person can't buy a gun in one state, he'll go to another state." *

In some communities, the Brady law and the proposed assault-weapons ban don't figure to have much impact at all. For instance, Officer Denney Kelley of the Portland (Ore.) Police Bureau's Intelligence Division says Brady will have "virtually no effect on us." That's because Oregon already requires handgun purchasers to wait 15 days. Moreover, Portland and surrounding Multnomah County also have ordinances that "basically say people can't carry a lot of types of assault rifles," notes Sgt. Kathy Ferrell of the Sheriff's Office.

Though experts differ on how to combat gun violence, there's no disputing the problem's existence. In 1992, handguns were used in nearly 931,000 violent crimes — a 21 percent increase over the 1991 total of 772,000.[1] (*See graph, p. 510.*)

Such figures could fuel demands for tougher state and federal gun control laws. At the same time, they're likely to stimulate firearms purchases. Experience shows the two trends often move on parallel tracks.

The assassinations of the Rev. Dr. Martin Luther King Jr. and Sen. Robert F. Kennedy, D-N.Y., inspired Congress to pass the Gun Control Act of 1968 (*see p. 512*). But shortly before the law took effect, nationwide handgun sales doubled. Similarly, soon after the House banned assault weapons, gun dealers reported panic buying of those very weapons.

Nowhere is the demand for guns of all kinds stronger than in California. Attorney General Dan Lungren reported in January that Californians bought a record 665,229 firearms in 1993, about two-thirds of them handguns. The previous California gun sales record of 559,608, set the previous year, was attributed at the time to fears generated by the Los Angeles riots. But no single event seems to have sparked the '93 sales surge.

Advocates of stronger firearms laws and their opponents are not necessarily at loggerheads. Rather, they reflect intertwined concerns about gun-related crime on the one hand and

---

* The group is chaired by Sarah Brady, wife of James S. Brady, President Ronald Reagan's first press secretary, who was seriously wounded by a handgun during the attempted assassination of Reagan in March 1981 by John Hinckley. Brady himself is a board member of a sister group, the education-oriented Center to Prevent Handgun Violence.

* The Bureau of Alcohol, Tobacco and Firearms (ATF) generally describes assault weapons as copies of military-style firearms or machine guns. They usually have a large ammunition capacity. Many military firearms are automatics, which fire several bullets each time the trigger is pulled. The versions used on the street are semiautomatics: The trigger must be pulled each time to fire a bullet.

How Americans Feel About Gun Control

A majority of gun owners and the public at large favor stricter gun controls, including required safety classes, the Brady law and bans on assault weapons and cheap handguns, according to a national poll. But only 39 percent of the public backs a total ban on handguns.

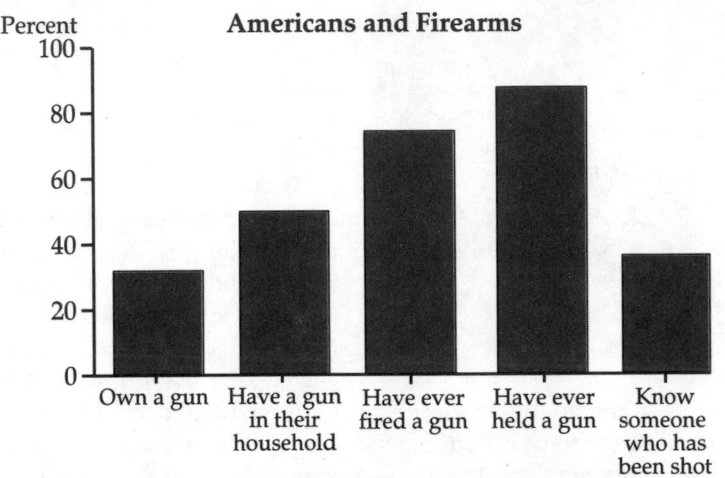

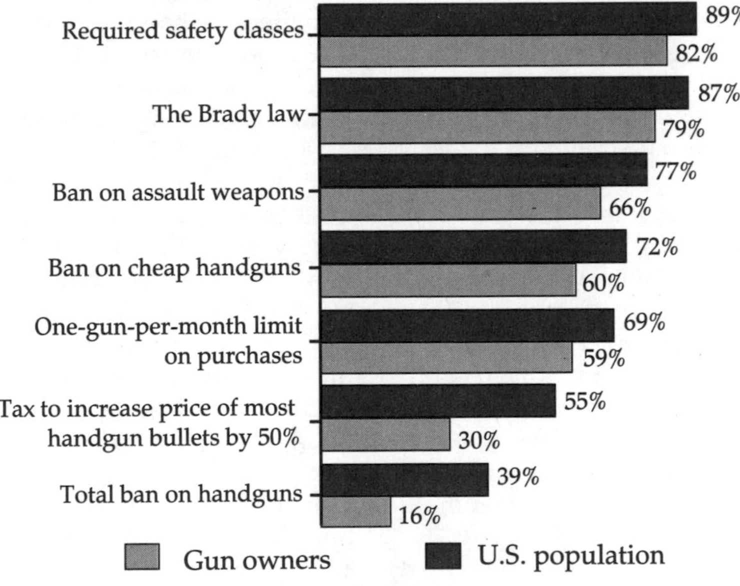

Source: USA Today/*CNN/Gallup Poll, Dec. 17-21, 1993*

appreciation of the Second Amendment "right of the people to keep and bear Arms" on the other.

Significantly reducing firearms violence while respecting the individual right to gun ownership has always been the central challenge facing gun control advocates. As the various parties to the firearms dispute vie for popular and legislative support, here are some of the key questions being asked:

Do gun control laws curb violent crime?

Gun control advocates argue that limiting access to firearms will reduce gun-related crimes and accidental shootings. They feel, in short, that firearms themselves are the key worry.

Gun control opponents, on the other hand, believe the problem with gun-related violence rests with the person holding the gun. As the National Rifle Association puts it, "Guns Don't Kill People — People Do."

Gun fanciers say that if firearms were made hard to obtain, or even outlawed altogether, criminals still would be able to get them by theft or through the black market. But law-abiding citizens would be deprived of an effective means of self-protection against armed criminals.

According to Franklin E. Zimring, a law professor at the University of California-Berkeley, available evidence tends to be ambiguous. "Ample data confirm that as guns become more available, people are more likely to die during violent crimes — a connection that opponents of gun control have tried to deny," he wrote. "Research also shows that many laws do not significantly diminish the number of guns used in violence, although many advocates of gun control have assumed they would." [2]

Gun control supporters have the harder case to prove, since it's impossible to count the firearms-related crimes that did not occur because a firearm wasn't available. Still, experience with the Brady law and similar state laws is cited to back the claim that guns can be kept out of criminals' hands. The Brady law's five-day waiting period allows local police to check the prospective buyer's background. During March, the first month Brady was in effect, 375,853 inquiries about gun purchasers were made to the FBI's computerized criminal information network. Of those, 23,610 — a little over 6 percent — were identified as possible felons.

Some prospective purchasers who flunked the background check doubtless turned to illegal channels, noted Northwestern University Law Professor Daniel D. Polsby, "but just as surely not all of them did." [3] To the extent that individuals with a criminal record or a history of mental illness or drug abuse are blocked from getting firearms, gun control supporters reason, crime is marginally reduced.

The Brady law "is breathing hope into this battle against crime involving firearms," declared John W. Magaw, director of the Bureau of Alcohol, Tobacco and Firearms (ATF). [4]

Gun control supporters say the proposed federal ban on assault weapons will further energize the fight against gun-related crime — and help save the lives of policemen. Two and a half years ago, Cahill recalls, several police officers were sent to arrest a Dale City, Va., man suspected of killing a policeman. One officer positioned himself behind a portable shield in front of the house. But he was killed when the suspect fired a round from an AK-47 rifle that pierced the shield and hit him in the head.

The AK-47 is one of the assault weapons that would be banned under the legislation pending in Congress. (*See table, p. 517.*) If the ban had been in effect then, says Cahill, "It wouldn't have been an AK-47 that killed that officer. The suspect might have pulled a different kind of gun, and it might not have penetrated" the shield.

Gary D. Kleck, a professor of criminology at Florida State University, dismisses the assault weapons ban. "There's no conceivable way that a federal ban could save a single life or prevent a single injury," he says, "unless you're willing to believe that there are criminals committed solely to using one of these particular 19 models, and not mechanically identical models among the 600 [other] unregulated assault weapons."

Polsby concurs. A partial assault weapons ban "will not affect the crime rate," he says. "Neither will the Brady bill. The crime rate's going to be worse four or five years from now, not better. Nobody will ever credit this kind of regulation with reducing any lawless or socially destructive behavior. It's pure gesture, pure theater."

To NRA Executive Vice President Wayne R. LaPierre Jr., the proposed assault weapons ban is merely "pretend crime control by people that don't want to spend the money to give us real crime control." [5]

Does gun ownership afford protection against violent crime?

Gun enthusiasts argue that weapons kept at home deter crime. In fact, some 8 million gun owners say they have used a gun to defend themselves or their family, according to a recent poll. [6] But gun control advocates contend that household guns often are fired in anger during family fights, causing injury or death. They also note that such guns are involved in numerous suicides and accidental shootings. (*See story, p. 514.*)

To resolve the issue, Arthur L. Kellerman, a physician at the University of Tennessee, and nine associates conducted a study on "Gun Ownership as a Risk Factor for Homicide in the Home." Published last fall in the respected *New England Journal of Medicine,* it concluded that "A gun kept in the home is far more likely to be involved in the death of a member of the household than it is to be used to kill in self-defense." [7]

The study evaluated 388 home homicides (half involving firearms) that occurred in the Cleveland, Memphis and Seattle areas between 1987 and 1992. A second set of 388 households in which no homicide had taken place served as a control group.

Among other things, the researchers found that 51 percent of the homicides "occurred in the context of a quarrel or a romantic triangle"; 77 percent of the victims "were killed by a relative or someone known to them"; and half of the victims died from gunshot wounds. According to the study, "the link between guns and homicide in the home was present among women as well as men, blacks as well as whites and younger as well as older people." [8]

Many gun control supporters hailed the study, saying it confirmed their warnings about the inherent hazards of firearms possession. Before long, though, other firearms experts pointed to what they termed serious flaws in the findings.

Kleck at Florida State University notes that given the study's premise, it will be assumed that "a lot of these people were killed with a gun kept in the victim's household. "But the study doesn't say a word about where the guns involved in the shooting homi-

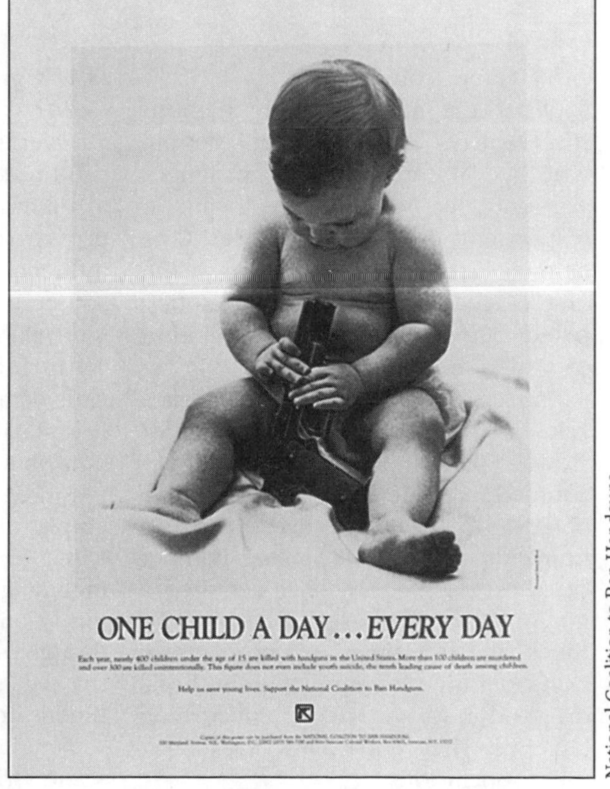
ONE CHILD A DAY... EVERY DAY

National Coalition to Ban Handguns

Handgun Violence on the Rise

Violent crimes involving handguns increased more than 21 percent from 1991 to 1992, according to the latest figures from the Justice Department's Bureau of Justice Statistics. Handguns were used in nearly 931,000 murders, rapes, robberies and assaults in 1992, up from 772,000 in 1991.

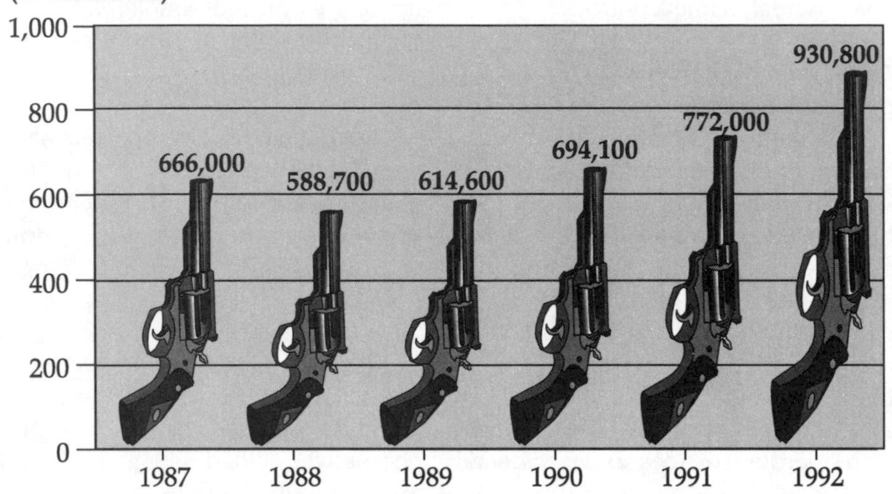

Source: Department of Justice, Bureau of Justice Statistics, May 15, 1994

cides came from."

What the study actually demonstrated, says Kleck, is that "people who live in dangerous circumstances are more likely to acquire a gun in response to those circumstances. One of the reasons they got a gun in the first place was because they anticipated being a victim of some kind of violence." [9]

Indeed, Kellerman and his colleagues acknowledge this possibility, noting that "reverse causation" could have "accounted for some of the association we observed between gun ownership and homicide — i.e., in a limited number of cases, people may have acquired a gun in response to a specific threat." To Kleck, the disclaimer is "one of those non-operative caveats [the authors] dropped in for the sake of anticipating criticism. They don't allow it to affect their conclusions."

Is the gun lobby losing its clout?

Over the years, the NRA and other pro-firearms organizations have built a reputation as one of the strongest pressure groups on Capitol Hill. Their influence stems largely from two sources: their ability to get members to bombard congressional offices with letters, faxes and phone calls demanding the defeat of hostile legislation, and their campaign contributions.

Since the 1992 election, for example, the NRA has given more than $535,000 directly to House members, including $150,000 in March. Handgun Control gave $12,000. [10] Now, though, some gun control advocates say they sense a shift of popular sentiment on firearms issues.

Noting that the NRA has "suffered some serious hits" over the past year, Handgun Control's Whitmore questions whether the nation's largest organization of gun owners "will ever be as strong as it once was." Even some NRA members "are finding fault with their leaders' policy of no compromise," she says.

Josh Sugarmann, executive director of the Violence Policy Center, cautions that "it would be hasty to declare that the witch is dead. Historically, every time it loses, there's a tendency for people to say, 'It's the end of the NRA.' That reaction is actually a testament to the organization's power." At the same time, he says, "the NRA has isolated itself to a great extent outside the mainstream [of public opinion]."

What's different now, says Sugarmann, is that "these losses are starting to accumulate. Every time a Brady bill or assault weapons ban wins approval, and the sky doesn't fall, gun violence becomes easier to talk about on Capitol Hill."

According to Polsby, "there's no doubt" that the NRA is losing influence, and that the House ban on assault weapons "is a great political victory for the gun control movement." But the NRA is only part of the story, he feels. "Democracy is working itself out, in the way that it will, bringing together a motley collection of potential allies who didn't previously know of one another's existence." Through this process, Polsby says, the gun control movement has emerged as "an effective counterweight to the NRA."

Since Kleck considers the proposed assault weapons ban "a nothing piece of legislation," he doesn't think its approval by the House says anything about the NRA's influence with Congress. "The only really quantifiable indicator of NRA strength is its membership," says Kleck. "And membership has been growing, not declining. The NRA now has 3.3 million members, each paying $25 or more a year." (Handgun Control claims about 1 million members.)

Moreover, Kleck notes, most legislation concerning guns is passed at the state level, not the federal level. "That's where the NRA gets its quiet victories," he says. "The big trend of the past 20 years, virtually unreported by the national media, and only lightly reported within the respective states, has been pre-emption statutes," which bar localities from regulating firearms more strictly than state laws (*see p. 517*).

"That's really significant," says Kleck. "It's like getting 100 defeats of gun control bills in each of those states, because each type of local regulation that might have been proposed in effect has been voted down already." ■

BACKGROUND

Love of Firearms

American attachment to firearms has its roots deep in English history. When the Anglo-Saxons ruled England 1,000 years ago, all able-bodied men were required to own weapons so they could respond to the "hue and cry" sounded when a criminal was being pursued. By the time English settlers arrived in the New World, they had decided that a militia composed of the entire male population was preferable to a standing army.

Indeed, the English jurist Sir William Blackstone listed the right to own arms as one of the five "auxiliary rights" needed by English subjects to maintain their "primary rights" — to personal security, personal liberty and private property. [11] Possession of arms, declared Blackstone, was a "natural right of resistance and self-preservation, when the sanctions of society and laws are found insufficient to restrain the violence of oppression." [12]

The harshness of life in North America reinforced the settlers' dependence on firearms. Guns killed game for food, warded off predators, protected travelers from bandits and imposed primitive justice where established agencies of law and order were either weak or non-existent. Firearms also were used against Native Americans.

It has been said that the Kentucky long rifle opened the frontier, the Winchester repeater won the West and the Colt revolver made men equal. In sum, wrote historian Philip B. Sharpe, the United States "was born with the rifle in its hand." [13]

Second Amendment

As the colonies moved toward independence, state militias assumed new importance. It was members of the Massachusetts militia, calling themselves Minutemen, who confronted British soldiers at Lexington and Concord in the opening battles of the American Revolution.

Several of the original 13 states required all adult men to serve in the state militia and guaranteed the right of citizens to keep and bear arms. When the Bill of Rights to the Constitution was being considered in 1789, those guarantees were a priority of legislators who feared that a strong central government with a standing army could usurp the power of the states.

The result was the Second Amendment to the Constitution: "A well-regulated militia being necessary to the security of a free state, the right of the people to keep and bear Arms shall not be infringed." Had the amendment simply guaranteed the right to keep and bear arms, it likely would stir little rancor today. However, the link between the right to own arms and the need for a trained militia has sown confusion among constitutional scholars for two centuries and remains at the core of the debate over gun control.

To those favoring private ownership of firearms, the Second Amendment implies an individual right to keep and bear arms. This belief is based in part on the theory, widely held in the early days of the republic, that a militia was to be composed of citizens.

Reuters

President Clinton and James S. Brady, former press secretary to President Ronald Reagan, meet to discuss strategy on the Brady bill. Congress passed the bill in November.

Many gun control advocates, on the other hand, stress the amendment's militia clause. They view the right to keep and bear arms as a collective right, applying to the people only as members of a militia and not as individuals. Some say even this collective right is an anachronism, since a standing army is now accepted as a necessity of national security, and state National Guards, funded and armed by the federal government since 1903, have become the militias referred to by the Constitution.

Supreme Court Rulings

The Supreme Court has addressed the Second Amendment question only rarely. Although it has never ruled directly on which interpretation is correct, the court has always decided against gun control opponents on the constitutional question.

In its first opinion on the issue, in *United States v. Cruikshank,* the court held in 1876 that the right to bear arms "is not a right granted by the Constitution" and that if such a right exists, it does so independently of the Second Amendment. The court also ruled that the amendment itself restricted the power of Congress, but not the state governments, to regulate firearms. In 1886, the court further endorsed the states' right to regulate firearms in *Presser v. Illinois,* upholding a statute banning the formation and parading of armed groups of men.

In 1939, the court held in *United States v. Miller* that Congress could regulate firearms as long as the regulations did not hinder state militias. That case involved the arrest of a man who had carried a sawed-off shotgun across state lines in violation of the National Firearms Act of 1934 — the so-called "machine gun act." It imposed a $200 excise tax on the sale of fully automatic weapons as well as short-barreled rifles and shotguns. [14] Because purchasers were identified upon payment of the tax, the law also indirectly entailed a requirement to register such weapons.

Since the parties in *Miller* had not produced "any evidence tending to show that possession and use of a [sawed-off shotgun] has some reasonable relationship to the preservation and efficiency of a well-regulated militia," declared the court, it could not say that the Second Amendment "guarantees the right to keep and bear such an instrument." In effect, Cornell University Law Professor David C. Williams noted, Miller "limits the scope of the [Second] Amendment to arms suitable for use by militia." [15]

Four years after the firearms act, the Federal Firearms Act of 1938 required gun dealers to obtain federal licenses and keep records identifying all gun buyers from across state lines. The law also prohibited dealers from selling firearms to individuals with convictions for violent felonies or to fugitives from justice. Moreover, it barred the shipment of stolen arms or arms with the manufacturer's serial number removed.

Reaction to Violence

The firearms question receded from public discourse during World War II but surfaced after peace returned. "By 1945, there was considerable pent-up demand [for guns] in a civilian market that had been neglected for nearly half a decade," noted the authors of *The Gun in America.* "The demand was further spurred by returning veterans," many of whom showed "continuing interest in weaponry." [16]

The postwar gun craze soon found expression in popular culture. Fess Parker, for instance, became an early TV star through his portrayals of gun-toting Davy Crockett and Daniel Boone. Westerns and crime series became staples on the home screen during the 1950s. All the while, sales of toy guns and antique firearms surged.

The NRA also drew strength from the gun revival. Before World War II, the NRA had about 50,000 members; by 1963, membership exceeded 500,000.

During the 1960s, however, popular opinion about firearms began to shift. To many people, the assassinations of President John F. Kennedy, his brother Robert and Dr. King signaled that gun violence in the United States was spinning out of control and that corrective action was needed.

Federal Gun Laws

Congress responded to these concerns with the Gun Control Act of 1968, which extended licensing requirements to all firearms dealers and prohibited handgun sales to out-of-state residents. It also banned the mail-order sale of guns and added most convicted felons, people with certain mental illnesses and illegal-drug users to the list of people to whom dealers were prohibited from selling firearms. Finally, the Gun Control Act banned the importation of guns that are not "particularly suitable for or readily adaptable to sporting purposes."

Enforcement of the 1968 law fell to the Treasury Department's Bureau of Alcohol, Tobacco and Firearms (ATF), which now devotes most of its energies to enforcing firearms laws.

Congress revised federal gun laws several more times after 1968. A measure passed in 1969 weakened the Gun Control Act by removing the record-keeping requirements for some types of rifle and shotgun ammunition. But a year later, lawmakers tightened the statute by making it a crime to carry a gun while committing a federal crime. The amendment, part of the Omnibus Crime Control Act of 1970, also established minimum mandatory sentences for these offenders. The mandatory-sentencing provision later was strengthened under the Crime Control Act of 1984, which set

Continued on p. 515

Chronology

19th Century

The Supreme Court attempts to define the scope of the Second Amendment after some states pass laws banning concealed weapons.

1876
The Supreme Court rules in *United States v. Cruikshank* that the right to bear arms "is not a right granted by the Constitution" and that if such a right exists, it does so independently of the Second Amendment.

1886
In *Presser v. Illinois,* the Supreme Court upholds a statute banning the formation and parading of armed groups of men.

1910s-1920s

After World War I, Congress takes tentative steps toward nationwide firearms regulation.

May 29, 1911
New York Gov. John A. Dix signs the Sullivan law banning the carrying, sale and possession of deadly weapons. Moreover, it makes carrying firearms without a license a penal offense.

1919
The War Revenue Act, the first federal firearms law, imposes a manufacturers' tax on firearms and ammunition.

1927
The Firearms in the U.S. Mails Act bars the interstate mailing of concealable firearms to private individuals. However, the law contains a loophole permitting the shipment of weapons by common carrier.

1930s ***Ruthless gunplay by gangsters heightens public concern about violence.***

1934
President Franklin D. Roosevelt signs the National Firearms Act (the "machine gun act"), which imposes a $200 excise tax on the sale of automatic weapons as well as short-barreled rifles and shotguns.

1939
In a challenge to the Firearms Act, the Supreme Court holds in *United States v. Miller* that Congress may regulate firearms if the regulations do not impede the efficiency of state militias.

1960s ***A decade of assassinations, antiwar protests and rising racial tensions brings enactment of a landmark federal gun control law.***

1968
The federal Gun Control Act, passed following the murders of President John F. Kennedy, the Rev. Dr. Martin Luther King Jr. and Robert F. Kennedy, strengthens restrictions on handguns and extends the restrictions to long guns and ammunition.

1970s ***Two of the country's liberal strongholds go in opposite directions on gun control.***

1976
Washington, D.C., bans possession of all handguns not already registered unless they belong to police officers or security guards. However, Massachusetts voters later in the year decisively reject an even stricter measure.

1980s ***States and localities assume a more visible role in gun regulation.***

1981
Morton Grove, Ill., becomes the first U.S. community to ban the possession and sale of handguns.

1988
Gov. William Donald Schaefer, D-Md., signs the nation's first statewide ban on the sale of cheap handguns. However, the law does not outlaw the possession of such weapons.

1989
After the 1989 killing of five children in a Stockton, Calif., schoolyard by a man with an AK-47, some states — notably California and New Jersey — limit access to assault weapons.

1990s ***Proponents of gun control demonstrate newfound clout at the federal level.***

Nov. 30, 1993
President Clinton signs the Brady bill, which imposes a five-day waiting period for handgun purchases.

May 5, 1994
By a tight 216-214 vote, the House approves legislation barring the manufacture and sale of 19 types of assault weapons.

Unanswered Questions About Suicide

Maybe it's because suicide is just too depressing. But whatever the reason, the media cover gun-related violence with almost morbid fascination but studiously avoid suicide — even though firearms kill far more suicide victims than homicide victims.

And scholars of violence don't seem terribly concerned about suicide either, according to University of California-Berkeley Law Professor Franklin E. Zimring. "Very few scholars have studied how firearms are related to two important forms of non-criminal violence: suicide and accidents," he writes.[1]

Suicide has "remained strangely outside" the mainstream of the gun control debate, according to a recent book on firearms violence published by the Violence Policy Center, a Washington research organization. The reason, the authors of *Cease Fire* suggest, is that suicide "does not fit into either side's schematics. Hence, it has been treated as something of an embarrassment and for the most part ignored."[2]

Among the questions yet to be answered about suicide, Zimring wrote, is what a person inclined toward suicide does when a gun is not readily available. How many suicide attempts "might be directed to less lethal means and how many lives would be saved?" he asked. "This question deserves far more attention than it has received."[3]

According to Josh Sugarmann and Kristen Rand, the authors of *Cease Fire,* persons "with pro-gun sympathies tend to brush the subject aside with the observation that suicide victims would find a way to kill themselves 'no matter what.'" At the same time, they say, gun control proponents are loath to take up the issue because it would mean acknowledging that "the problem lies not only with guns in criminal hands — but also in the [hands of the] law-abiding."[4]

Numerous studies show that the risk of firearms-related suicide is greatest among adolescents and young adults, who are more prone to impulsive acts than older people. Moreover, the victims of many fatal shooting accidents are small children who were playing with a gun kept at home for the family's protection.[5]

Broader recognition of the hazards guns pose to young people may give a lift to the campaign to transform gun regulation into a public-health crusade, an idea favored by Sugarmann and Rand. They note that the Children's Defense Fund and other organizations "outside the usual gun control suspects" are becoming involved in the debate.

"When you have new voices that don't carry the baggage of the traditional gun control advocates, you drive home the point that gun violence is not a special interest," they say. "It affects a broad range of constituencies who have a stake in reducing it."

Firearms and Suicide

Far more suicides than homicides were committed with firearms in the past three decades. The number of such deaths increased steadily during the period; there were more than 18,000 firearms-related suicides in 1989, the latest year for which statistics are available.

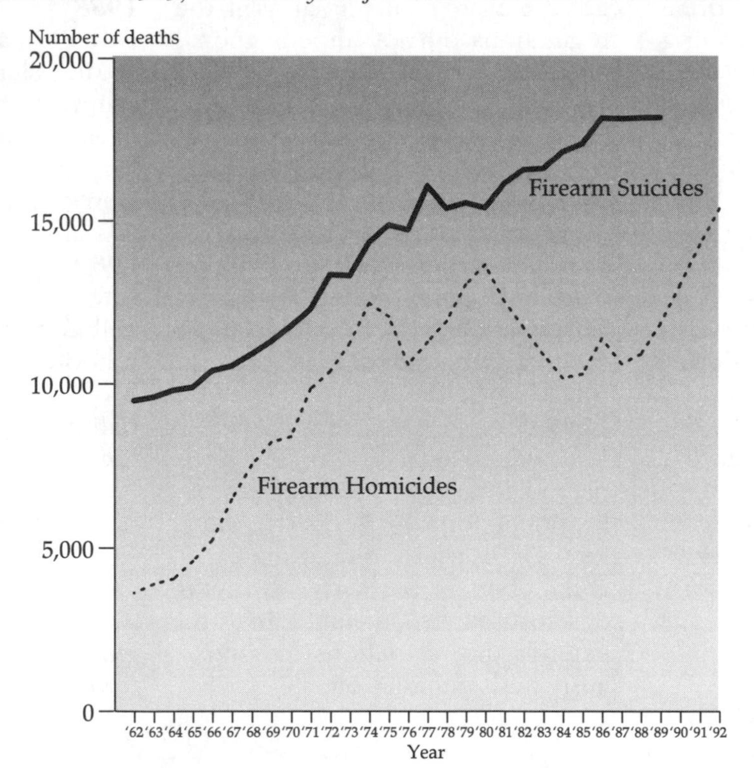

Sources: Cease Fire: A Comprehensive Strategy to Reduce Firearms Violence, *1994, Violence Policy Center; FBI,* Vital Statistics of the United States

[1] Franklin E. Zimring, "Firearms, Violence and Public Policy," *Scientific American,* November 1991, p. 52.

[2] Josh Sugarmann and Kristen Rand, *Cease Fire: A Comprehensive Strategy to Reduce Firearms Violence,* 1994, p. 5.

[3] Zimring, *op. cit.,* p. 52.

[4] Sugarmann and Rand, *op. cit.,* p. 5.

[5] For background, see "Teenage Suicide," *The CQ Researcher,* June 14, 1991, pp. 369-392.

Continued from p. 512

a mandatory, minimum five-year prison sentence for carrying or using a handgun with armor-piercing bullets while committing a violent crime.

In 1986, Congress passed two gun-related measures that prompted most police organizations to support gun control for the first time. One law curbed the sale of armor-piercing bullets, called "cop-killers" because they penetrate police officers' bulletproof vests. Congress also passed an NRA-sponsored measure, the Firearms Owners Protection Act, which eliminated some of the record-keeping requirements for gun dealers imposed by earlier legislation and allowed people once again to buy rifles out of state.

The bill also included an amendment banning the manufacture, sale or ownership of fully automatic machine guns after May 19, 1986. Machine guns made "under the authority of the United States" or any state agency were exempted from the ban.

ATF interpreted this provision to mean that only military and police forces were authorized to possess machine guns, an interpretation the NRA challenged as too restrictive. When a Georgia gun manufacturer was denied a license by ATF to make a machine gun in 1987, he sued the bureau. The case, *Farmer v. Higgins,* went all the way to the Supreme Court, which on Jan. 14, 1991, let the machine-gun ban stand.

In 1988, Congress banned the sale of plastic handguns that couldn't be readily spotted by metal detectors. Another law enacted that year, the Federal Energy Management Improvement Act, prohibited the manufacture and sale of toy or imitation firearms unless they had distinctive color markings that distinguished them from the real thing. The law was prompted by the rising number of assaults and robberies committed by criminals bearing imitation guns as well as shootings by police of people who appeared to be armed with lethal weapons.

In 1989, President George Bush — who like most Republican lawmakers generally opposed gun control — banned the importation of 43 types of semiautomatic assault weapons. He acted under authority granted to him by the 1968 Gun Control Act. But since almost three-fourths of such weapons were made in the United States, gun control advocates called on Congress to ban the domestic manufacture of these firearms, which include the AK-47 and Uzi rifles as well as the more easily concealed TEC-9 and MAC-11 pistols. However, support for such a far-reaching ban was slow to build.

The Brady bill, meanwhile, also was encountering difficulty. Despite support from President Reagan, the measure failed to win congressional support when it was first introduced in 1987. Though the bill was finally cleared by a wide margin in the House Judiciary Committee in July 1990, House Speaker Thomas S. Foley, D-Wash., an NRA member and longstanding opponent of gun con-

The Assault-Weapons Ban

The MAC 11 semiautomatic pistol is one of 19 military-style, rapid-fire weapons banned by the House May 5; the Senate approved a similar ban last fall. The proposed ban is expected to become part of the omnibus crime bill that Congress will vote on this summer.

	Approximate number in circulation in United States
Colt AR-15	*400,000*
Intratec TEC-DC9, TEC-9, TEC-22	*200,000*
AK-47	*100,000*
MAC-10, MAC-11, MAC-11/9, MAC-12	*100,000*
Fabrique Nationale FN/FAL, FN/LAR, FNC	*30,000*
Street Sweeper, Striker 12	*18,000*
Action Arms UZI, Galil	*10,000*
Steyr Army Universal Rifle	*10,000*
Beretta AR-70, SC-70	*1,000*
Total	***869,000***

Foreigners Baffled by U.S. Gun Freedom — and Violence

Foreigners often voice bafflement about the level of U.S. gun violence, and no wonder. In no other country does the Constitution set forth a "right of the people to keep and bear Arms." To the contrary, most nations impose strict curbs on individual ownership and use of firearms. With few guns in private hands, crime-related shootings abroad generally are much less common than in the United States.

Gun possession in Switzerland probably comes closest to the American model. Except for criminals, the mentally impaired and certain other classes of people, any Swiss citizen age 18 or older can buy and own a gun. Indeed, every Swiss citizen in the military keeps his weapon (including ammunition) at home until retiring from military service at age 50. Belonging to the militia is a duty of every male citizen of Switzerland. But despite the wide distribution of firearms, gun-related crime is rare.

British attitudes toward firearms once were nearly indistinguishable from American ones. Over the past 75 years, though, Britain has made it increasingly hard for individuals to obtain guns. "In the 1920s, gun controls were tightened because people were terrified of a Bolshevik revolt," *The Economist* noted recently. "In the 1930s, worries about American-style gangsters using sub-machine guns brought new restrictions. In 1988, ministers outlawed most semiautomatic weapons soon after Michael Ryan used one to kill 15 people in a Berkshire village." [1]

Notwithstanding these restrictions, British gun violence has risen to levels that law-abiding citizens find alarming. As in the United States, a disproportionate number of shootings are linked to drug dealers.

In a Gallup Poll published May 17, 67 percent of the Britons interviewed said they believed all of the country's traditionally unarmed police should carry guns. The poll results were issued as Scotland Yard disclosed that several dozen specially trained officers wearing sidearms would begin patrolling London streets this summer.

Germany also reports mounting gun violence despite a national system for registering and licensing handgun owners. The problem is that Germany is awash in handguns and other arms from the former Warsaw Pact nations of Eastern Europe. "Police report that in Frankfurt hand grenades are offered at about $17 apiece, and in Berlin and Munich a Russian automatic weapon can be had for less than $570," according to *Europe* magazine. [2]

Canada developed a case of gun jitters earlier this year after two random shooting deaths in Toronto and Ottawa. The incidents prompted the Canadian government to consider a nationwide handgun ban. Canada "must and will do everything it can to achieve . . . a safe society," Justice Minister Allan Rock told reporters in April. "Above all, I do not want to find Canada falling into a cycle where people believe they have to acquire a weapon for protection of themselves." [3]

---

[1] " Firing Up," *The Economist*, March 26, 1994, p. 69.

[2] Wanda Menke Glückert, "Gun Violence Rises," *Europe*, April 1994, p. 40.

[3] Quoted in *The Washington Post*, April 13, 1994.

trol, prevented the seven-day waiting period for handgun purchases from making it to the floor for a vote as part of the Omnibus Crime Bill. The ban on assault weapons also was dropped from the bill.

Action by States

According to some firearms experts, the news media devote excessive attention to gun control at the federal level. They point out that the vast majority of the nation's estimated 20,000 firearms laws originated with state and municipal governments, which are more responsive to regional and local differences of opinion on gun regulation.

This has been true since the nation's earliest days. Indeed, the first American gun-control law was approved by the Massachusetts colony in 1692; it forbade carrying "offensive" weapons in public places. In the 19th century, several states — Kentucky in 1813, Indiana in 1819 and Arkansas and Georgia in 1837 — prohibited the carrying of concealed weapons. Like most of the state and local laws still in effect today, the bans targeted small, concealable handguns, not rifles or shotguns.

The proliferation of guns in private hands after the Civil War initially prompted only sporadic concern, as when Presidents James A. Garfield and William McKinley were assassinated. For the most part, guns were casually accepted. Indeed, there were "more than a few instances in 1910 and 1911 in which [New York City] residents summoned police and firemen to their neighborhood by the simple expedient of firing pistols out of their windows. This was apparently quicker than going to an alarm box or telephone." [17]

Around that time, a gun-fueled crime wave erupted that shocked New Yorkers out of their complacency about firearms. Two incidents in particular stirred deep unease. The first occurred in August 1910, when Mayor William J. Gaynor was shot and wounded by a vengeful former city employee. Five months later, in January 1911, the popular novelist David Graham Phillips was fatally gunned down on a New York sidewalk.

Reacting to public pleas for an end

to the carnage, New York state Sen. Timothy D. Sullivan took the lead in drafting gun control legislation. The resulting Sullivan law, signed by Gov. John A. Dix May 29, 1911, was the most far-reaching statute of its kind in the nation up to that time. It broke new ground by banning not only the carrying of deadly weapons but also their sale and possession. Moreover, it required a license for the purchase of a handgun or other concealable weapon and made carrying firearms without a license a penal offense. To obtain a license, the applicant was required to show "proper cause" for wanting or needing the weapon. The Sullivan law is still on the books.

In more recent years, state and local gun control efforts have met with mixed results. A 1976 Washington, D.C., law regarded as one of the nation's strongest banned all handguns not already registered unless they belonged to police officers or security guards. It also required all firearms to be kept unloaded and dismantled or to be equipped with a locking device, except in business establishments.

An even stricter measure was placed before Massachusetts voters the same year. Under the proposed law, all firearms with barrels less than 16 inches long would have to be turned in, except for police and a few other groups. Conviction would have carried a minimum mandatory jail sentence of one year.

Two opinion surveys taken shortly before the election indicated the Massachusetts vote could go either way. But both polls were wide of the mark: The measure was defeated 69 percent to 31 percent. The decisiveness of the outcome, supporters and opponents agreed, would hamper future efforts toward gun control at the state level.

Maryland became a pivotal player in the gun control debate in 1988, when Gov. William Donald Schaefer signed into law the nation's first statewide ban on cheap handguns. The law made it illegal in Maryland after Jan. 1, 1990, to sell or manufacture pistols deemed easily concealed, inaccurate, unsafe and poorly made. However, the law did not outlaw the possession of such weapons.

Stung by its failure to block the law's passage by the Maryland General Assembly, the NRA mounted a $4 million campaign to place a repeal proposal on the November 1988 ballot. Voters rejected the initiative by a 2-1 margin. Vincent DeMarco, a spokesman for Marylanders Against Handgun Abuse, had predicted before the balloting that "If we win and the law stays, we expect other states and Congress to begin to follow our lead." [18]

In the aftermath of the burst of gunfire from an AK-47 that killed five children in a Stockton, Calif., schoolyard in January 1989, some states limited access to military-style assault weapons. The toughest, in New Jersey, banned the sale and restricted the ownership of many semiautomatics. Guns purchased before May 31, 1990 could be kept if their firing pins were removed.

A similar law in California banned the sale of some 60 types of semiautomatics and required the registration of semiautomatic assault-type weapons by Dec. 31, 1990. Most of the state's gun owners defied the law, however, and one group called a news conference to announce that its members would not register their semiautomatics. Of the estimated 200,000-plus assault-type weapons in the state, only about 18,000 were registered by the deadline.

Action at the Local Level

Though many firearms experts regard local gun control as unworkable, due to its limited geographic scope, numerous communities have enacted such ordinances. Morton Grove, Ill., a Chicago suburb, made nationwide headlines in 1981 by banning handguns for all but gun clubs, collectors and police and security personnel. Challenges to the ordinance were carried to the Supreme Court, which in 1983 declined to hear an appeal of a ruling by the Seventh Circuit Court of Appeals in Chicago that upheld the ban.

"The Second Amendment does not apply to Morton Grove and . . . possession of handguns by individuals is not part of the right to keep and bear arms," the appellate court declared.

While the Morton Grove controversy was raging, Kennesaw, Ga., just north of Atlanta, took a diametrically opposed approach to the firearms issue. In 1982, in an effort to reduce crime, the City Council required every household to have a firearm.*

Still, neither Morton Grove nor Kennesaw is a reliable guide to the effectiveness of firearms laws, according to University of San Francisco Professor David E. Newton. "First, crime was never a serious problem in either community," he wrote. "Second, in neither community was any serious effort made to enforce the gun laws. Thus, it has been almost impossible to say what the effect of these local gun laws has been." [19]

The Morton Grove ordinance did leave one legacy, however. It prompted the NRA to launch a nationwide campaign for state preemption laws. A few states, including California and Massachusetts, already had such laws on their books in the early 1980s. According to the NRA, the number now stands at 42 states.

The NRA argues that pre-emption "prevent[s] a hodgepodge of varying gun laws within a state, and thereby protect[s] the law-abiding citizen not only from unwitting violation of the law but also from arbitrary infringement of his or her rights." [20] ■

---

* Franklintown, Pa., approved a similar ordinance later the same year. On May 4, the Franklintown Borough Council voted 5-2 to repeal the measure.

Gun Buybacks: Gun Control for Fun and Profit

Gun control isn't just for governments, as New York City businessman Fernando Mateo showed last December. Prodded by a suggestion from his 14-year-old son, Mateo offered a $100 Toys R Us gift certificate to anyone who turned in a firearm. In five weeks, the toys-for-guns swap removed an estimated 3,000 weapons from the streets.

Similar variations on the same idea soon sprang up in other cities. In Denver, tickets to sports events were the bait; California cities offered concert tickets; participants in St. Louis received gasoline. And in Washington, D.C., former heavyweight boxing champion Riddick Bowe donated $100 in cash for every gun.

Reviews for gun buybacks, as the programs are called, have been decidedly mixed. St. Louis Police Chief Clarence Harmon hails the concept, noting that "the guns . . . we're taking out of circulation are the very same kinds of guns that are used by people in the heat of passion." Moreover, "they're the kinds of guns that young men . . . commit murders and robberies with."[1]

Franklin E. Zimring, a law professor at the University of California-Berkeley, was more guarded. Taking hundreds of firearms out of "an urban environment like New York's is not nothing," he acknowledged. At the same time, he cautioned that "People who are . . . keeping an eye on their watches waiting for the homicide rate to go down . . . are going to be disappointed."[2]

Gary D. Kleck, a professor of criminology at Florida State University, feels it's "impossible to know for sure" whether buybacks curb crime, "but it's highly unlikely." He notes that defenders of the approach argue that buybacks reduce the overall stock of guns. But Kleck suggests buybacks may actually increase the number of guns in circulation. That's because people may buy cheap handguns with the intention of swapping them for a premium that is worth more. But until they're swapped, they remain in circulation — and subject to misuse.

However, if a gun buyback was designed "as a surprise event, staged one time only, it wouldn't have that effect," says Kleck. "But if there are dozens of these programs all over the place, many of them held repeatedly, people will begin to anticipate them."

If a buyback plan offers $100 per gun, regardless of age or condition, "then every gun whose resale value is under $100 is fair game and quite possibly will be turned in. But that won't reduce the number of guns in private hands if those weapons are being replaced, or if they were obtained expressly to be sold to the buyback program."

Gun buybacks are hardly a novel idea, says Kleck, noting that U.S. officials in Cuba operated a similar program at the time of the Spanish-American War. "They bought back guns with gold. That's how old an idea it is."

[1] Remarks on National Public Radio's "Weekend Edition," Jan. 8, 1994.

[2] *Ibid.*

CURRENT SITUATION

Outbreak of Violence

Gun violence is so common today that most shootings draw only fleeting media coverage. In the past two years, though, several dramatic, gun-related incidents captured national attention because they seemed emblematic of underlying American attitudes toward firearms.

On Feb. 28, 1993, ATF agents tried to serve an arrest warrant on David Koresh, the head of the Branch Davidian religious cult, at its compound near Waco, Texas. Koresh and his followers were believed to have amassed an arsenal of machine guns, grenades and other explosives.[21]

The ATF raid quickly turned into a bloodbath in which four agents and six cult members died. The FBI was called in to handle the ensuing standoff, which ended April 19 after the agency pumped tear gas into the compound. Federal officials said cult members set the compound on fire, killing some 80 followers, including many children.

During congressional hearings after the Waco tragedy, Rep. Charles E. Schumer, D-N.Y., chairman of the House Crime Subcommittee, said he would seek legislation banning the sale of parts used to convert semiautomatic guns into automatics. He also urged a ban on the sale of high-caliber ammunition to all but police and military agencies.

Gun violence again came to the fore Dec. 7, when a gunman opened fire on a crowded Long Island Rail Road commuter train in New York, killing four persons and wounding 19. Two of the 19 later died of their injuries, raising the death toll to six.

Police and witnesses said that as the rush-hour train neared Garden City, Colin Ferguson, 35, began a three-minute shooting spree. The gunman, armed with a 9-mm handgun, was subdued by three passengers as he paused to reload for the third time, police reported.

The next day, President Clinton said he had asked Attorney General Janet Reno to review a proposal for a national system of gun licensing and registration. The idea originated with New York City's Republican mayor-elect, Rudolph W. Giuliani, who had met with Clinton at the White House. Reno said Dec. 9 she supported handgun licensing but felt states should handle the matter.

In recent years, U.S. gun violence has claimed several foreign visitors to the United States, stirring concern overseas. Nine foreigners were fatally shot in Florida during an 11-month period spanning 1992 and '93. Most of the slayings occurred in South Florida, prompting state officials and private businesses to worry about canceled bookings by tour groups. In fact, the state's tourist industry apparently suffered little damage.

Nonetheless, steps were taken to reassure foreign travelers. Shortly after British visitor Gary Colley was slain last September at a highway rest stop near Jacksonville, the Florida Division of Tourism faxed a statement, available in six languages, to 28,000 travel agents in North America and Europe to inform them of new safety measures, such as tightened security at major airports. On Nov. 24, Gov. Lawton Chiles, D-Fla., signed into law a bill prohibiting the possession of firearms by persons under 18 unless they were using the weapons for hunting or target shooting. Penalties were prescribed not only for youths but also their parents and gun dealers.

The Florida tourist slayings called to mind the fatal shooting on Oct. 17, 1992, of Yoshihiro Hattori, a 16-year-old Japanese exchange student living with a Louisiana family. The slaying occurred after Hattori, who was looking for a Halloween costume party, knocked at a home in suburban Baton Rouge. Homeowner Rodney Peairs, mistaking the costumed youth for an intruder, shouted "Freeze!" But Hattori understood little English and began to move toward Peairs, who shot him once in the chest with a .44-caliber magnum pistol.

News of Hattori's death met with anger and bewilderment in Japan, where access to firearms is tightly controlled and shooting deaths are rare. The Japanese media portrayed the slaying as typical of the violence prevalent in America. These feelings were reinforced when a state district court jury in Baton Rouge acquitted Peairs of manslaughter on May 23, 1993. His attorney argued that Hattori had behaved in what Peairs considered a threatening manner and thus his death was justifiable homicide under Louisiana's 1976 "shoot the burglar" law.

Guns and Politics

Though a cause-and-effect link is hard to prove, highly publicized cases of gun violence may have strengthened gun control sentiment in Congress and at least some states. Anecdotal evidence from the past year strongly suggests that groups representing gun owners and gun control proponents are nearing a balance of power.

In last year's gubernatorial elections, New Jersey Gov. James J. Florio and Virginia gubernatorial nominee Mary Sue Terry, both Democrats and outspoken gun control advocates, lost to Republican challengers. Anti-gun-control forces were quick to claim a major share of credit for the outcome of both races. However, many political analysts said New Jerseyites turned their backs on Florio mainly because he had raised state taxes. For her part, Terry was widely faulted for a lackluster campaign that caused her substantial early lead in opinion polls to evaporate by Election Day.

In California, meanwhile, the NRA put its prestige on the line this spring in an effort to unseat Democratic state Sen. David A. Roberti through a recall election that was widely viewed as a referendum on gun control. The NRA sought Roberti's defeat because he had been instrumental in persuading the Legislature to ban about 60 different semiautomatic assault weapons in 1989. However, the senator won the April 13 election handily, 30,743 votes to 21,276. The NRA, he said afterward, "vowed to drive me out of public office. Let's drive them out of California."

Two unforeseen developments contributed to Roberti's win. Burglars stole 15 guns from the home of one of his

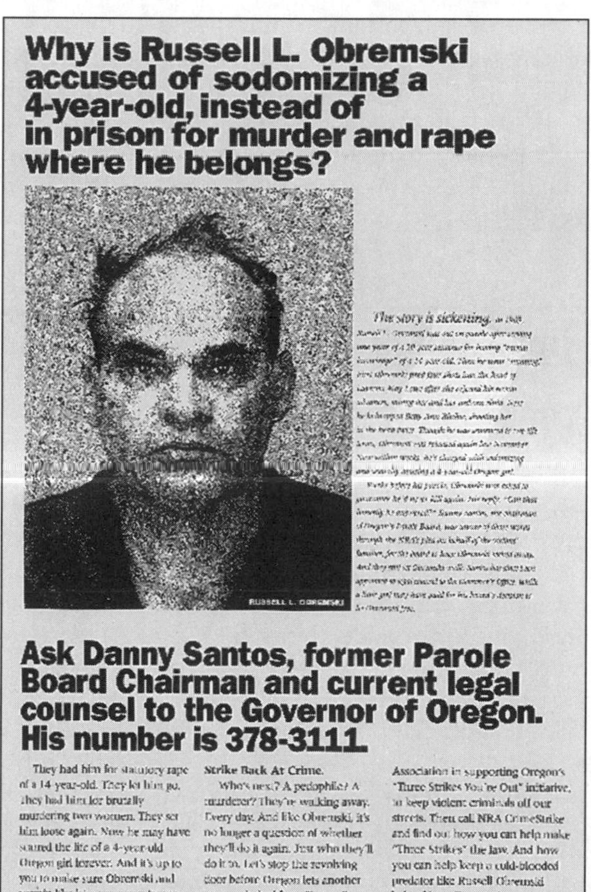

NRA Institute for Legislative Action

opponents during the campaign, presenting him with a public relations windfall. In addition, the Roberti camp revealed a confidential strategy memo that organizers of the recall drive had sent to the NRA in 1993.

"We may not win a particular election," the memo said, "but our methods have an extremely efficient 'political cost exchange ratio' making it exceedingly expensive, difficult and unpleasant for the target to remain in office. Victory springs from imparting excruciating political pain in unrelenting political attacks on a single politician as an example to others." [22]

In the past year, two other states have joined California and New Jersey in banning assault weapons. In Connecticut, Gov. Lowell P. Weicker Jr., (I), last June signed into law a measure prohibiting the retail sale of more than 60 types of semiautomatic rifles. And Maryland enacted a law in March barring the sale of 18 models of assault pistols as well as gun magazines that can hold more than 20 rounds of ammunition. The legislation took effect June 1.

Impact of Brady Law

Opinion is divided on whether passage of the Brady bill by Congress represented a major setback for the gun lobby, which had successfully kept it from becoming law for seven years. Gun control advocates hailed the bill as the most important federal legislation of its kind since the 1968 Gun Control Act. Their view was echoed by most organizations representing law enforcement officials, who also worked for the bill's passage.

But after Brady cleared Congress, opponents tried to downplay its significance. "This isn't a watershed issue for us," said the NRA's LaPierre. He pointed out that the NRA's chief aim at the end was ensuring an early shift from the five-day waiting period required by the bill to instantaneous background checks by computer. Indeed, the Brady bill in its final form provided that the waiting-period requirement would expire in five years, by which time a computerized identity-checking system presumably would be in place nationwide.

Kleck finds merit in the evaluations of both sides. The Brady bill, he says, "was serious gun control. Trying to impose a background check on all handgun purchasers is certainly a serious step in the right direction."

At the same time, Kleck feels the bill "ended up looking practically identical to what the NRA had proposed originally." Consequently, "it was hard for a lot of NRA people to say they seriously opposed" the measure when the final yeas and nays were taken. "All they really lost was five years' worth of a waiting period."

The NRA and other gun-owner groups generally support state programs to build more prisons and crack down on repeat felony offenders, including juveniles. Numerous laws of this kind have recently been passed or are awaiting consideration in legislatures across the country. [23] The most popular legislative formula is "three strikes and you're out," which mandates life in prison without parole for criminals convicted of a third serious felony.

Kleck questions the effectiveness of such laws. A new Florida program to expand the state prison system by almost one-third will have only "a little crime control impact," he feels. That's because Florida prisons already are packed with low-level drug dealers serving mandatory sentences, leaving scant room "for murderers, rapists, robbers and so on." Consequently, the Legislature has to provide more prison cells "to deal with genuine public outrage about violent offenders either being released early or not being put into prison in the first place because of a problem the Legislature created" by passing mandatory-sentencing laws.

Instead of expanding the prison system, Kleck favors "tinkering with the criminal justice system in other ways, like fooling with the gun control laws, hoping that some minuscule change in those laws will have an impact."

Some experts believe gun control should be treated as a public health or product-liability problem rather than a criminological one. A leading proponent of this approach is Sugarmann of the Violence Policy Center. "There definitely is a growing willingness to treat guns as inherently dangerous consumer products," he says.

Many public health experts share Sugarmann's opinion. "Communities should have the right, and governments should take the responsibility, to control the availability and safety standards of guns just as they do other public health hazards," noted an article by Daniel W. Webster, director of violence research at the Washington (D.C.) Hospital Center, and several colleagues. "Transferring the costs of gun injuries back to the gun industry through product-liability litigation is not only just, but should also act to reduce the number of gun casualties." [24]

The federal Centers for Disease Control and Prevention (CDC) in Atlanta also views firearms deaths and injuries as primarily a health issue. In the 1980s, CDC classified gun-related violence as a health hazard, "to be studied with the same kinds of epidemiological tools applied to suspected pathogens and toxins." [25]

At present, though, no regulatory framework exists for monitoring firearms safety and availability. The Violence Policy Center earlier this year proposed that the ATF be reconfigured as an agency with power to set firearms safety standards, oversee compliance with those standards and order recalls of defective weapons.

Continued on p. 522

At Issue:

Will gun control laws help reduce crime in America?

yes

SYLVESTER DAUGHTRY JR.
Chief of Police, Greensboro, N.C., and President of the International Association of Chiefs of Police

FROM TESTIMONY BEFORE HOUSE SUBCOMMITTEE ON CRIME AND CRIMINAL JUSTICE, APRIL 25, 1994.

The International Association of Chiefs of Police (IACP) does not object to the private possession of firearms by citizens in this country, understanding that this is a legitimate, constitutionally protected right. It does not, however, view that right as extending to any type of firearm whatsoever. Certain firearms, such as assault weapons, do not belong in civilian hands. . . .

Individuals are not born law abiding citizens or criminals. A law abiding citizen becomes a criminal when he or she commits a crime. The point here . . . is that ensuring public safety does not involve simply monitoring a specific segment of the population. It means looking after everybody. To suggest that every law abiding citizen with an assault weapon will never become a criminal is a pillow of fiction we cannot lay our head on.

We continue to see events which legitimate the concern of ours that individuals whom we in law enforcement have not identified as felons can still become so at any minute. On Jan. 25 of last year, just outside the District of Columbia on Langley, Va., an individual with no criminal record went on a shooting spree outside CIA headquarters, killing two and wounding three. On the other side of the country, on July 1 of last year, another individual with no criminal record entered a San Francisco law firm with over 450 rounds of ammunition, eventually killing eight and seriously wounding six. With these examples, the argument by gun control opponents that we will be restricting the rights of law abiding citizens rings very hollow. As we have said, we in law enforcement cannot make such a simplistic and dreamy distinction. . . .

[T]he reason there is no decrease in gun related mayhem as a result of stringent state and local gun control laws is that guns are easily purchased in less stringent locations and brought into these stricter areas. As you can imagine, chiefs do not have a laborer patrol, which allows us to prevent firearms purchased elsewhere from entering and being used in our jurisdictions. This is one of the logical reasons why the IACP supports federal legislation in the area of gun control. Gun control will work only if all the states are required to observe it.

Opponents of legitimate gun control legislation are losing popular support around the country as more and more citizens become resolved that we must do something about this gun madness.... The people of this country want gun control and it is time for Congress to show the same courage that members of state legislatures have shown.

no

JOHN M. SNYDER
Editor, Point Blank

FROM POINT BLANK (NEWSLETTER OF THE CITIZENS COMMITTEE FOR THE RIGHT TO KEEP AND BEAR ARMS), February 1994.

The American firearms industry represents a $24 billion segment of the nation's economy. . . . Our customers represent half of all the households in America. . . . [T]hey are ordinary everyday citizens who happen to own firearms. They commit no crimes and make no headlines. They represent mainstream America.

Society's criminal fringe create terrible destruction, cause real social unrest and threaten the very civil rights of the majority of Americans. Lawmakers, in their quest for real solutions to crime, are wasting their time and taxpayers' resources debating the irrelevant issue of gun control.

Remember, a minority of society are criminals and a minority of violent crimes — one in four reported violent crimes or one in eight if you use victimization studies — involve the criminal use of firearms. Yet a majority of time, energy and attention is spent in debating gun control issues that have no affect on criminal behavior. These red herrings do nothing more than pit honest, well-meaning and well-intentioned citizens against one another simply because one owns a gun and one fears a gun. . . .

President Clinton, during his State of the Union speech, called upon the firearms community to work with him in solving the seemingly unrelenting problem of violent crime. Mr. President, we answer your challenge with a resounding "Here we are!"

We made the guns that Americans used to make this country free. We made the guns that Americans used to fight tyranny and genocide all over the globe. We make the guns that protect law enforcement and honest citizens against criminal violation. We make the guns that Americans will use to keep America free and secure today, tomorrow and forever.

We are here in Washington, D.C., united as never before, to tell you, Mr. President, as well as the media and the public, that if we are to put an end to criminal violence we must concentrate on the cause of that violence — criminal behavior. Take away America's guns and you have criminals with guns and a nation of potential crime victims. Take away America's guns and you have criminals and crime. Take away the criminals and we ask you: who will be left to commit the crimes?

. . . .Mr. President, we challenge you, and the Congress, to join us in the search for a realistic solution to the crime problem in America.

Reuters

Vice President Al Gore talks about crime with students at Dunbar High School on Jan. 27, following a gang shooting at the school in northwest Washington, D.C.

Continued from p. 520

In addition, the center urged that ATF's jurisdiction embrace such related products as laser sights and rocket and grenade launchers. [26]

In Polsby's opinion, the center's approach is "silly." Firearms, he says, "are supposed to be dangerous. Their highest and best use is as weapons rather than as collectibles or hobby instruments. As far as I know, their danger stems not from defects in their manufacture but rather from the way they're used." ■

OUTLOOK

Still a Hot Issue

While still savoring their Brady law victory, gun control backers are now pushing a follow-up measure, known as "Brady 2." This bill would outlaw some firearms and require the licensing and registration of others. At a March 23 Senate Judiciary subcommittee hearing on Brady 2, Sen. Howard M. Metzenbaum, D-Ohio, said tighter controls are needed to reduce the supply of handguns and end the firearms "epidemic." To this end, the bill would:

- Require handgun purchasers to have a state handgun license that would be issued to persons who pass a background check and a firearms safety course.
- Strengthen the regulation and screening of gun dealers and require sellers of used guns to register sales with state police.
- Limit retail handgun purchases to one per person per month.
- Ban numerous semiautomatic assault weapons and other firearms that have no apparent sporting purpose.
- Require manufacturers to install safety devices on handguns to prevent small children from discharging them accidentally.

Over the past five years, safety devices have been required in a dozen states, notes Whitmore of Handgun Control. [27] Child-accident prevention laws, as they are called, generally make it a crime to store or leave a loaded firearm within the reach or easy access of a minor. Some states also require gun dealers to give purchasers a written warning about the law. Several additional child-accident prevention bills are now pending in legislatures that have not previously approved them, Whitmore reports.

The NRA's Metaksa calls Brady 2 "an abomination. It's everything that has been suggested before, but worse. The concept behind Brady 2 is to make law-abiding citizens who own guns criminals, and even take away our Second Amendment rights, one little step at a time."

Meanwhile, the NRA and other anti-gun-control groups are pursuing their own agendas. The NRA, for example, is trying to blunt the impact of the Brady law at the state level. In a suit supported by the NRA, U.S. District Judge Charles Lovell of Helena, Mont., ruled May 17 that local law enforcement officers cannot be required to perform the background checks on prospective gun buyers called for under the statute. "The Congress does not have the power to force local law enforcement, particularly the local sheriff, to carry out the federal government's mandates," Lovell declared. He cited the 10th Amendment, which circumscribes federal authority over state interests. [28]

The Montana decision may not apply to other states, and it does not affect the five-day waiting period prescribed by the Brady law. Similar court challenges are pending in Arizona, Louisiana and New Mexico, according to Montana NRA representative Bill Bigelow. He said that if courts in those states hand down conflicting opinions, the issue may end up in the Supreme Court. "The process is far from over, obviously," he said. [29]

As it happens, the Supreme Court already has a gun control case on its docket. The justices agreed in April to consider reinstating the federal Gun Free School Zones Act of 1990, which prohibited possession of a firearm within 1,000 feet of any school. [30] The Clinton administration is appealing a ruling by the U.S. Court of Appeals for the Fifth Circuit, in New Orleans, which invalidated the act on grounds that Congress had failed to specify it possessed power to enact the law.

Looking further down the road, Kleck predicts "current gun control trends will continue," though with "more and more focus on highly specialized sub-types of firearms." All that ever changes, he says, is "which particular gun is the flavor of the month." At one time "it was Saturday night specials, then it was plastic guns and now it's assault weapons. That'll evolve into something else, because new gun types are always coming along."

Kleck doesn't see the campaign to transform gun control into a public health or product-liability issue getting very far. In his opinion, "It's just old wine in new bottles. The public health people seem to have no sense of history on this at all. They don't realize they're going over the same ground that's been explored dozens of times by criminologists, sociologists and other social scientists."

Polsby's views parallel Kleck's. He foresees "no relaxation" of the campaign to regulate firearms, "because public opinion research tells us that this is people's No. 1 concern. We also know that gun control laws are popular. If you ask, 'Should we regulate assault weapons?' Or, 'Should we have gun control?' the ayes outnumber the nays by a 2-to-1 margin."

There's another reason why gun control will remain a hot issue, Polsby says: "It's very safe for a politician to support, notwithstanding all the chest-thumping you hear to the contrary. Voting for gun control doesn't have any budgetary impact, and as of now it's firmly linked in the public mind with a crime-busting agenda."

Sugarmann feels he and other gun control advocates are operating in "a two-year window of opportunity" to achieve their objectives. These include persuading the public to view gun violence as a public health issue, drawing the firearms industry into the debate on regulation and forging "a working coalition of organizations representing effective constituencies" that will press for gun control.

"To bring in new organizations — that's the key," says Sugarmann. "If we accomplish all that during this two-year period, we'll be way ahead of the game. But if we fail, which is a real possibility, we'll always have another chance. Because things will only get worse." ■

Notes

[1] Department of Justice, U.S. Bureau of Justice Statistics, "Guns and Crime," April 1994. For background, see "Reassessing the Nation's Gun Laws," *Editorial Research Reports,* March 22, 1991, pp. 157-172.

[2] Franklin E. Zimring, "Firearms, Violence and Public Policy," *Scientific American,* November 1991, p. 48.

[3] Daniel D. Polsby, "The False Promise of Gun Control," *The Atlantic Monthly,* March 1994, p. 62.

[4] Quoted in *The Washington Post,* March 31, 1994.

[5] Remarks on NBC-TV's "Meet the Press," May 1, 1994.

[6] *USA Today*/CNN/Gallup Poll, published in *USA Today,* Dec. 30, 1993.

[7] Arthur L. Kellerman, et al., "Gun Ownership as a Risk Factor for Homicide in the Home," *The New England Journal of Medicine,* Oct. 7, 1993, pp. 1084-1091.

[8] *Ibid.*, p. 1087.

[9] For background, see "Suburban Crime," *The CQ Researcher,* Sept. 3, 1993, pp. 769-792.

[10] "In Surprising Turnaround, House OKs Weapons Ban," *CQ Weekly Report,* May 7, 1994, p. 1122.

[11] The four other auxiliary rights cited by Blackstone were (1) the constitution, powers and privileges of Parliament; (2) limitation of the sovereign's prerogative; (3) the right to apply to courts of justice for redress of injuries; and (4) the right to petition the sovereign or either house of Parliament, and to seek the redress of grievances.

[12] Sir William Blackstone, *Commentaries* (1765-1769).

[13] Philip B. Sharpe, *The Rifle in America* (1938), p. 4.

[14] Congress had previously approved two other laws affecting firearms. The War Revenue Act of 1919 imposed a manufacturer's tax on firearms and ammunition to help cover World War I expenditures. The Firearms in the U.S. Mails Act of 1927 barred the interstate mailing of concealable firearms to private individuals. However, the 1927 law contained a loophole permitting the shipment of weapons by common carrier.

[15] David C. Williams, "Civic Republicanism and the Citizen Militia: The Terrifying Second Amendment," *Yale Law Journal,* December 1991, p. 557.

[16] Lee Kennett and James La Verne Anderson, *The Gun in America: The Origins of a National Dilemma* (1975), pp. 217-218.

[17] *Ibid.*, pp. 179-180.

[18] Quoted in *The New York Times,* June 5, 1988.

[19] David E. Newton, *Gun Control: An Issue for the Nineties* (1992), p. 56.

[20] National Rifle Association, "Why Does Your State Need a Firearms Preemption Law?" (1987 news release).

[21] For background, see "Cults in America," *The CQ Researcher,* May 7, 1993, pp. 385-408.

[22] Quoted by columnist George Skelton in the *Los Angeles Times,* April 11, 1994.

[23] For background, see "Prison Overcrowding," *The CQ Researcher,* Feb. 4, 1994, pp. 97-120.

[24] Daniel W. Webster, et al, "Reducing Firearms Injuries," *Issues in Science and Technology,* spring 1991, pp. 73-74.

[25] Gary Taubes, "Violence Epidemiologists Test the Hazards of Gun Ownership," *Science,* Oct. 9, 1992, p. 213.

[26] Josh Sugarmann and Kristen Rand, *Cease Fire: A Comprehensive Strategy to Reduce Firearms Violence* (1994), pp. 28-29.

[27] In 1989, Florida became the first state to pass a child-accident law. Similar ordinances have been approved in Baltimore, Houston and Elgin, Ill.

[28] Quoted in Reuter news dispatch, May 17, 1994.

[29] *Ibid.*

[30] For background, see "Violence in the Schools," *The CQ Researcher,* Sept. 11, 1992, pp. 785-808.

Bibliography

Selected Sources Used

Books

Furnish, Brendan F.J., and Dwight H. Small, *The Mounting Threat of Home Intruders: Weighing the Moral Option of Armed Self-Defense,* Charles C. Thomas, 1993.

Furnish and Small examine the religious and ethical issues involved in using a gun for self-defense against criminal intruders — especially those intent on burglary or rape.

Kennett, Lee, and James La Verne Anderson, *The Gun in America: The Origins of a National Dilemma,* Greenwood Press, 1975.

Kennett and Anderson provide detailed historical background on evolving American attitudes toward firearms. They conclude that "time works against the gun" because "social consciousness finds its excesses intolerable, whereas they were once accepted without thought."

Newton, David E., *Gun Control: An Issue for the Nineties,* Enslow Publishers, 1992.

Newton examines the role of firearms in American culture, presents the arguments for and against gun control, and speculates on what the future may hold.

Articles

Kellerman, Arthur L., et al., "Gun Ownership as a Risk Factor for Homicide in the Home," *The New England Journal of Medicine*, Oct. 7, 1993.

The authors' study of 388 homes in the Cleveland, Memphis and Seattle areas where homicides occurred indicates, they write, "that risks of keeping a firearm in the home may outweigh the potential benefits."

Levinson, Sanford, "The Embarrassing Second Amendment," *Yale Law Journal,* December 1989.

"For too long," argues Levinson, a law professor at the University of Texas, legal scholars "have treated the Second Amendment as the equivalent of an embarrassing relative." Now, he says: "It is time for the Second Amendment to enter full scale into the consciousness of the legal academy."

Polsby, Daniel D., "The False Promise of Gun Control," *The Atlantic Monthly,* March 1994.

"[T]he conventional wisdom about guns and violence is mistaken," writes Polsby, a Northwestern University law professor. "Guns don't increase national rates of crime and violence. . . ."

Webster, Daniel W., et al., "Reducing Firearms Injuries," *Issues in Science and Technology,* spring 1991.

Challenging the claim that guns afford self-protection against crime, Webster and his co-authors propose that gun manufacturers be held responsible for the costs of gun injuries. Such a policy, they argue, "is not only just, but should also act to reduce the number of gun casualties."

Wintemute, Garen J., "Homicide, Handguns, and the Crime Gun Hypothesis: Firearms Used in Fatal Shootings of Law Enforcement Officers, 1980 to 1989," *American Journal of Public Health,* April 1994.

The "crime gun hypothesis" holds that "all firearms are not at equal risk for use in a violent crime." Wintemute notes that handguns constitute about 40 percent of all firearms produced in the U.S. over the past 20 years but account for about 80 percent of gun-related crimes.

Zimring, Franklin E., "Firearms, Violence and Public Policy," *Scientific American,* November 1991.

Zimring, a law professor at the University of California-Berkeley, examines the various forms of gun control practiced in the United States and concludes that none of them is entirely satisfactory. One difficulty, he feels, is that "Neither supporters nor opponents of gun control laws have felt any great need to cite facts."

Reports and Studies

Bureau of Justice Statistics, U.S. Department of Justice, *Survey of State Prison Inmates, 1991,* March 1993.

This study constitutes a statistical profile of the nation's prison population. Included are tables showing how many inmates used guns while committing their offense.

Nay, Robert L., *Firearms Regulations in Various Foreign Countries,* May 1990.

Nay, a librarian at the Library of Congress, has collected brief surveys of firearms laws in 25 nations, each written by different contributors. "It is safe to assert," he writes, "that all countries have some form of firearms regulation, ranging from the very strictly regulated countries like Germany, Great Britain, Japan and Malaysia to the less stringently controlled uses in . . . Mexico and Switzerland, where the right to bear arms continues as a part of the national heritage."

Sugarmann, Josh, and Kristen Rand, Violence Policy Center, *Cease Fire: A Comprehensive Strategy to Reduce Firearms Violence,* 1994.

Sugarmann and Rand outline their arguments for treating firearms regulation as a product liability or public health issue. A highlight of the study is the set of proposals for transforming the Treasury Department's Bureau of Alcohol, Tobacco and Firearms into a regulatory agency like the Environmental Protection Agency.

The Next Step

Additional information from UMI's Newspaper & Periodical Abstracts database

Assault Weapons

Ayres, B. Drummond Jr., "This part's the barrel, I think," *The New York Times,* May 8, 1994, p. 4.
The oratory that preceded the House's vote to ban the production or importation of 19 assault weapons was nothing if not portentous, writes Ayers. Perhaps most tellingly, there was evidence of the lure of firearms. At Capitol Hill press conferences, the proponents of the ban could not resist fondling, however tentatively, examples of the hardware they had brought to underscore their pitch.

Dillin, John, "Vote on guns gives Clinton needed boost," *Christian Science Monitor,* May 9, 1994, p. 1.
President Clinton's high-profile victory on a bill to ban 19 assault-style weapons is discussed. The House of Representatives' 216-to-214 vote for the ban came with breathtaking drama and bolsters White House prospects when similar showdowns come on health-care reform, welfare, and crime, Dillin writes.

Eaton, William J., "Ford, Carter, Reagan push for gun ban," *Los Angeles Times,* May 5, 1994, p. A1.
Three former presidents, Gerald R. Ford, Jimmy Carter and Ronald Reagan, endorsed legislation on May 4, 1994 to ban the future manufacture, sale and possession of combat-style assault weapons as a closely divided House neared a May 5 showdown on the controversial issue.

Gun lobby criticizes president on assault-weapons proposal, *The New York Times,* May 2, 1994, p. A14.
NRA chief Wayne R. LaPierre Jr., speaking on the NBC News program "Meet the Press," said on May 1, 1994, that President Clinton did not understand guns and derided Clinton's open letter to hunters. LaPierre was criticizing proposed legislation, supported by Clinton, that would ban assault weapons.

Keen, Judy, and Leslie Phillips, "Gun debate on rapid-fire," *USA Today,* May 3, 1994, p. A4.
The White House upped the pressure on House members but estimated it was still 18-22 votes short of winning an assault-weapons ban. President Clinton, Vice President Al Gore and the Cabinet worked the phone, targeting about 70 House Republicans and Democrats from the South, West and suburbs who are usually loath to vote for anything that hints of gun control.

Scully, Michelle, A gun widow's request: Courage in Congress, *Los Angeles Times,* May 5, 1994, p. B7.
Michelle Scully, whose husband was killed on July 1, 1993, in the shooting at a San Francisco law firm, argues for the passage of a law to ban the manufacture and sale of assault weapons after describing how she watched her husband die.

Von Drehle, David, "In defeating the NRA, gun-controllers gain firepower," *The Washington Post,* May 7, 1994, p. A1.
As the May 5, 1994, vote on an assault weapons ban came down to the wire, undecided lawmakers were buffeted with calls and letters from lobbyists on both sides of the debate. The result was a reed-thin, 216-214 victory for the gun control crowd in the House.

Concealed Weapons

Ewegen, Bob, "NRA-ACLU Freedom is Indivisible Award goes to Kathy Bowers," *Denver Post,* April 25, 1994, p. B7.
Bob Ewegen comments on Article II, Section 13 of the Colorado constitution, which gives residents the right to keep and bear arms in defense of one's home, person and property, noting how Denver County Judge Kathy Bowers invoked the right to throw out the case against "Toolate Smart," a pseudonym, for transporting an unloaded, concealed handgun in his car.

Lindecke, Fred W., "Missouri bill goes forward," *St. Louis Post-Dispatch,* April 22, 1994, p. A1.
The Missouri House passed a bill containing anti-crime proposals including a provision that would allow Missourians to carry concealed weapons.

Pendleton, Scott, "Texans battle over the carrying of concealed weapons," *Christian Science Monitor,* May 9, 1994, p. 4.
In early May 1994 the U.S. House of Representatives voted to ban 19 assault weapons and look-alikes, but the fight over guns has just begun in Texas, where there is a strong move afoot to allow citizens to carry concealed weapons.

"Rap singer arrested in a weapons inquiry," *The New York Times,* May 2, 1994, p. A18.
Rap singer Tupac Shakur was arrested April 29, 1994, in Los Angeles on a concealed-weapon charge, the latest of several arrests for the performer. Shakur was released on $1,000 bail the next day.

Federal Action

Locin, Mitchell, "Bentsen talks of good guns, bad guns," *Chicago Tribune,* May 3, 1994, p. 4.

As the top pitchman for the Clinton administration's proposed ban on assault weapons, Treasury Secretary Lloyd Bentsen is trying to portray himself as a lover of guns in order to credibly pitch gun control.

Peterson, Doug, "Administration plans assault on licensed firearms dealers," *Nation's Cities Weekly*, Jan. 17, 1994, p. 11.
The federal government is prepared to furnish cities with lists of federally licensed firearms dealers and will help determine if those dealers are conforming to state and local laws. Regulation of federally licensed dealers is discussed.

Terry, Gayle Pollard, "Charles Schumer," *Los Angeles Times*, May 8, 1994, p. M3.
In an interview, Rep. Charles E. Schumer, D-N.Y., who led the surprisingly successful fight in the House of Representatives to ban 19 military-style assault weapons, discusses his work on gun control and crime legislation.

Guns and Schools

Greenhouse, Linda, "Justices to consider a ban on guns near schools," *The New York Times*, April 19, 1994, p. A15.
The Supreme Court on April 18, 1994, agreed to decide whether Congress has the constitutional authority to ban the possession of guns near school buildings. The case is an appeal by the Clinton administration from a federal appellate court ruling that invalidated the Gun Free School Zones Act of 1990, which makes it a federal crime to possess firearms within 1,000 feet of a school.

Merton, Andrew, "Don't take your gun to school," *Boston Globe*, May 1, 1994, p. NH2.
Andrew Merton comments on guns in schools and on New Hampshire legislation addressing the issue.

Walsh, Mark, "High court to weigh law outlawing guns near schools," *Education Week*, April 27, 1994, p. 13.
The Supreme Court has agreed to decide the constitutionality of a 1990 federal law that bans the possession of guns within 1,000 feet of a school.

International Gun Control

Clayton, Mark, "Canada considers plan for strict gun control," *San Francisco Chronicle*, April 25, 1994, p. A10.
Reacting to recent acts of random violence that have shocked millions of Canadians, Justice Minister Allan Rock unveiled a plan in April 1994 that would make owning a pistol illegal for all but soldiers and police.

Clines, Francis X., "Mandela tells backers to holster guns and vows gun control," *The New York Times*, April 24, 1994, p. 11.
Predicting victory in South Africa's upcoming presidential elections but furious at some celebratory gunfire, Nelson Mandela denounced some of his own supporters as criminals at a political rally on April 23, 1994, and vowed that gun control would be firmly enforced by the new government that he expects to lead.

Dickerson, Marla, "Random killings jolt Canadians," *Detroit News*, April 28, 1994, p. A17.
The aimless, "American-style" slaying of Georgina Leimonis in Toronto and a drive-by shooting death in Ottawa have some Canadians pushing for a total ban on handguns and a get-tough attitude on crime, though overall crime rates haven't increased much.

Miscellaneous

Corbin, Robert K., "The president's column," *American Rifleman*, April 1994, p. 49.
A number of federal lawsuits have been filed in response to the passage of the Brady Act. The new law may be unconstitutional, Corbin writes.

"Firearm violence and public health: Limiting the availability of guns," *JAMA: The Journal of the American Medical Association*, April 27, 1994, pp. 1281-1283.
Firearm violence has reached epidemic proportions in the U.S. and is now a public health emergency. Tougher gun control laws at the state and federal levels are called for and discussed.

McEvoy, Sharlene A., "Third-party liability unfair to gun dealers," *Human Rights*, spring 1994, pp. 22-23.
McEvoy argues that third-party liability is unfair to gun dealers. Many reputable gun dealers have gone out of business rather than risk facing charges if a gun they sell is used for unlawful acts.

Robinson, Bill, "Gunman arrested outside rally," *Atlanta Constitution*, May 4, 1994, p. B1.
A man carrying a pistol and three knives was arrested at an entrance to the CNN Center while President Clinton was at a rally inside, according to Atlanta police. Trevor Lawson, 23, was detained after he abruptly turned away from a metal detector. He was charged with carrying a weapon to a public gathering and carrying a pistol without a license.

Simpson, Kevin, "Lunch-time food court murder shortens chain of violence," *Denver Post*, April 28, 1994, p. B1.
Kevin Simpson comments on gun-related violence in light of the April 27, 1994, murder of restaurateur Wen-Cheng "Roc" Hsieh during the lunchtime rush at Denver's Republic Plaza Food Court.

Opinions

"Closer to the target," ***Boston Globe,*** **May 7, 1994, p. 10.**
An editorial praises members of the U.S. House who voted to ban 19 different types of assault weapons, but asserts that much more remains to be done.

"Easy access to death," ***USA Today,*** **May 9, 1994, p. A12.**
An editorial says the U.S.'s casual approach to firearms has resulted in minors' essentially unrestricted access to guns and calls for controls that emphasize responsible ownership, including registration and licensing requirements.

"Georgia Four stare down the NRA," ***Atlanta Journal Constitution,*** **May 8, 1994, p. H4.**
An editorial applauds the four Congressional representatives from Georgia who voted for the ban on assault weapons, saying two of them, Don Johnson and Sanford Bishop, may have political repercussions for their stance because they represent rural areas.

Mathewson, Joseph D., "Courts must lead fight against guns," ***Chicago Tribune,*** **May 3, 1994, p. 18.**
In a letter to the editor, Joseph D. Mathewson, a former Cook County, Ill., commissioner, says that handguns and assault weapons are so lethal and destructive that they should be legally classified as "abnormally dangerous" or "ultrahazardous" and the court system should take up the cause of banning such weapons.

"No purpose but to kill people," ***Chicago Tribune,*** **May 3, 1994, p. 18.**
An editorial comments on Rep. Henry Hyde (R-Ill.), who joined the majority in the House Judiciary Committee in supporting a ban on the manufacture and sale of 19 types of semi-automatic assault weapons. Seven representatives from Illinois are expected to vote against the ban on these deadly weapons.

Reese, Charley, "Gun owners, YOU are the target," ***American Hunter,*** **May 1994, p. 39.**
An editorial states that the Brady bill is not aimed at criminals but at honest citizens and is part of a scheme to deprive Americans of the right to firearms.

Research and Statistics

LaPierre, Wayne, "Standing guard," ***American Rifleman,*** **April 1994, p. 7.**
Fanatical legislators are attempting to ban shotguns, and no statistics on crime can be offered to support the bans, LePierre writes.

Lochhead, Carolyn, "Data support ban on assault weapons," ***San Francisco Chronicle,*** **April 26, 1994, p. A2.**
As Congress in April 1994 decides whether to include a ban on assault weapons in its new crime bill, early results from California's five-year ban seem promising, reflecting how many assault weapons were confiscated and showing that federal traces in California stabilized after the state ban.

"Will reduction of gun supply reduce crime rate?" ***National Public Radio, "Morning Edition,"*** **April 11, 1994.**
Law Professor Daniel D. Polsby suggests that no evidence exists that the Brady bill will have much effect on crime. Polsby says that criminals will go elsewhere other than retail outlets to purchase a more lethal weapon.

State and Local Action

Mason, Julie, "Foes of gun control fire verbal salvos at council resolution," ***Houston Chronicle,*** **April 27, 1994, p. A18.**
An angry crowd of more than 150 gun-control opponents jammed Houston City Council chambers in opposition to a proposed resolution supporting a federal ban on assault weapons.

Penn, Mary Sue, "Week may be just a start to end violence," ***Chicago Tribune,*** **May 3, 1994, p. 2S6.**
Organizers of the "Stop the Violence" campaign in Hammond, Ind., discuss violent crime and the weeklong activities to bring the problem to the public.

Quist, Janet, "Cities prepare to implement handgun purchase waiting period," ***Nation's Cities Weekly,*** **Jan. 17, 1994, p. 10.**
The Brady law, which will require a five-day waiting period and background check for handgun sales, goes into effect Feb. 28, 1994. Issues that cities need to clarify the implementation of this law are addressed.

Warrantless Searches

Leo, John, "Sweeping up the projects," ***U.S. News & World Report*****, May 2, 1994, p. 20.**
Politicians and pundits have been talking about police sweeps as a solution to the chaos at Chicago's most-troubled housing projects. The question of whether police should be able to search all apartments without notice or warrants is addressed.

Sutin, Phil, and Kathryn Rogers, "Tenants blast no-warrant plan," ***St. Louis Post-Dispatch,*** **April 18, 1994, p. B4.**
The no-warrant search policy for public housing announced by President Clinton has met with less-than-favorable response from the tenants of publing housing and the American Civil Liberties Union.

Back Issues

Great Research on Current Issues Starts Right Here...Recent topics covered by The CQ Researcher are listed below. Before May 1991, reports were published under the name of Editorial Research Reports.

DECEMBER 1992
Crackdown on Smoking
The New CIA
Eating Disorders
Women and AIDS

JANUARY 1993
Hate Crimes
Child Sexual Abuse
Nuclear Fusion
U.S. Trade Policy

FEBRUARY 1993
Community Policing
Europe's New Right
School Censorship
Violence Against Women

MARCH 1993
Gay Rights
Aid to Russia
War on Drugs
TV Violence

APRIL 1993
Head Start
High-Speed Rail
Children's Legal Rights
Muslims in America

Back issues are available for $4.00 (subscribers) or $7.00 (non-subscribers). Quantity discounts apply to orders over ten. To order, call Congressional Quarterly Customer Service at (202) 887-8621.

Binders are available for $16.00. To order call 1-800-638-1710. Please refer to stock number 648.

MAY 1993
Cults in America
Preventing Teen Pregnancy
Software Piracy
National Parks

JUNE 1993
Food Safety
Prostitution
Childhood Immunizations
National Service

JULY 1993
Electric Cars
Population Growth
Downward Mobility
Intelligence Testing

AUGUST 1993
Mental Illness
Bilingual Education
Foreign Policy Burden
School Funding

SEPTEMBER 1993
Suburban Crime
Public Housing
Supreme Court Preview
Immigration Reform

OCTOBER 1993
Airline Safety
Disaster Response
Science in the Courtroom
The Glass Ceiling

NOVEMBER 1993
Paying for Retirement
Charitable Giving
Privacy in the Workplace
Adoption

DECEMBER 1993
U.S. Vietnam-Relations
Learning Disabilities
Child Care
Space Program's Future

JANUARY 1994
Racial Tensions in Schools
South Africa's Future
Worker Retraining
Regulating Pesticides

FEBRUARY 1994
Prison Overcrowding
Water Quality
Religion in Schools
Juvenile Justice

MARCH 1994
Underground Economy
Education Standards
Gambling Boom
Private Management of Public Schools

APRIL 1994
Reproductive Ethics
U.S.-China Trade
Soccer in America
Talk Show Democracy

MAY 1993
Traffic Congestion
Women's Health Issues
Mutual Funds
Political Scandals

JUNE 1993
Education and Gender

Future Topics

- ***Public Land Policy***
- ***Nuclear Arms Cleanup***
- ***Vitamins***

THE CQ Researcher

PUBLISHED BY CONGRESSIONAL QUARTERLY INC.

Public Land Policy

Are sweeping management changes necessary?

The federal government owns a vast portion of the land in Western states, including national forests and rangelands that yield gold, timber and livestock forage. Westerners have always used those millions of acres of public lands, and their increasingly valuable resources, with little regulation by the government — and for very low fees. Now many in the West are rebelling against the Clinton administration's plans to raise more revenue from public lands by hiking user fees while tightening environmental controls over mining, logging and grazing. The intensifying battle over public land resources is raising fundamental questions about the federal government's control over those vast holdings. Some economists think the nation's public lands would be better managed by private owners.

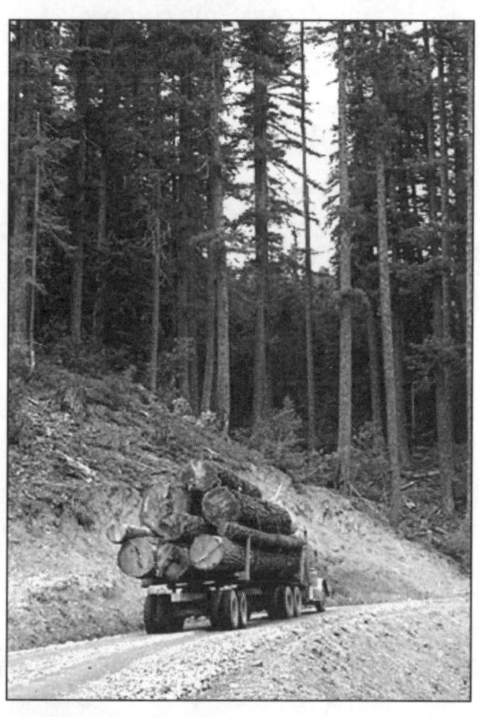

INSIDE THIS ISSUE

CQ June 17, 1994 • Volume 4, No. 23 • 529-552

Formerly Editorial Research Reports

THE ISSUES

BACKGROUND

CURRENT SITUATION

OUTLOOK

SIDEBARS AND GRAPHICS

FOR FURTHER INFORMATION

COVER: HAULING LOGS FROM A BLM TIMBER SALE IN WESTERN OREGON. (BUREAU OF LAND MANAGEMENT)

June 17, 1994
Volume 4, No. 23

The CQ Researcher (ISSN 1056-2036). Formerly Editorial Research Reports. Published weekly (48 times per year, not printed the first Friday of any month with five Fridays) by Congressional Quarterly Inc., 1414 22nd St., N.W., Washington, D.C. 20037. Rates are furnished upon request. Second-class postage paid at Washington, D.C. POSTMASTER: Send address changes to The CQ Researcher, 1414 22nd St., N.W., Washington, D.C. 20037.

Public Land Policy

BY TOM ARRANDALE

THE ISSUES

Few Americans will ever see the barren sweep of Sand Wash in northwestern Colorado or the Alvord Desert in eastern Oregon. Some may drive through Wyoming's Red Desert on the way to Yellowstone National Park, and others may speed across the gold-rich Great Basin rangelands along Interstate 80 between Elko and Battle Mountain, Nev. A few travelers may be drawn to the Alaskan tundra or the gloomy solitude of the towering Douglas fir groves in the Pacific Northwest. But usually, only ranchers, loggers, miners and the most adventurous hunters and backpackers ever venture into those back-country forests and wide open plains and deserts.

Many don't know it, but all Americans have a stake in these empty landscapes. They are public lands, part of an immense domain of 650 million acres owned by the federal government. Today, an intense political struggle is being fought for control of that common heritage.

Ever since white settlers first pushed west, ranchers, loggers and miners have been using federally owned forests and rangelands almost as if they owned them. In recent decades, however, environmental groups and recreation users have begun pushing their own agendas for how the U.S. Interior Department and Forest Service should manage those holdings. Over the last year and a half, the Clinton administration's efforts to revamp federal grazing, timber and mining policies and laws have provoked what could turn into a climactic showdown.

The battle for natural resources is being fought all over the West, where federally owned lands are concentrated. (*See chart, p. 535.*) The struggle over public land policy intensified on May 16, when a federal law passed 122 years ago forced Secretary of the Interior Bruce Babbitt to reluctantly sell 1,949 acres of federal lands in Nevada to a Canadian-based mining company (*see p. 534*). The lands hold an estimated $10 billion worth of gold, but the General Mining Law of 1872 required the government to sell them for $5 an acre, earning less than $10,000 for the federal Treasury. The sale was "the biggest gold heist since the days of Butch Cassidy," Babbitt declared. [1]

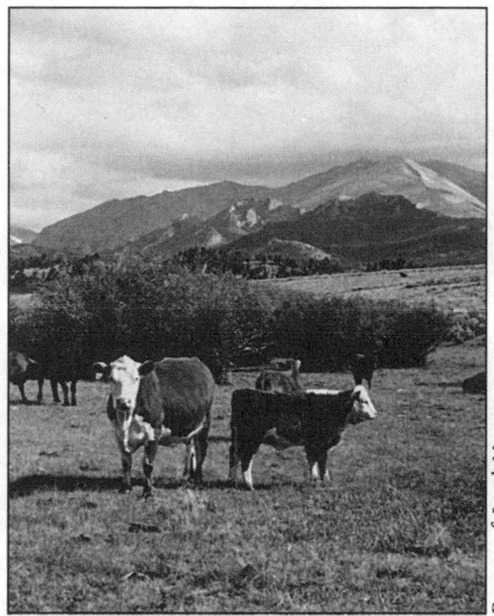

Bureau of Land Management

Federally owned rangeland in eastern Oregon.

When the 1872 mining law was passed, the West was still being settled. To encourage the region's development, Congress offered public lands for the taking by enterprising homesteaders, stockmen, miners and loggers. The frontier closed a century ago, and since then Congress has taken a number of steps to keep the remaining public lands under federal ownership. But public land agencies continued to make federally owned lands available for logging, mining and grazing livestock.

Environmentalists have been complaining for years about public land policies that they say subsidize extractive industries like mining and logging while ruining the ecological health of federal forests and rangelands. Critics contend that strategies for developing the West's federally owned resources are being determined by outdated policies — what University of Colorado law Professor Charles F. Wilkinson has described as "the lords of yesterday, a battery of 19th-century laws, policies and ideas that arose under wholly different social and economic circumstances but that remain in effect due to inertia, powerful lobbying forces and lack of public awareness." [2]

Wilkinson and other environmentalists argue that sustainable resource management has been frustrated by policies that include:

- Below-market livestock grazing fees and loose federal regulation of how ranchers manage sheep and cattle on public lands.
- Timber harvests on national forests that keep local sawmills going but threaten environmentally sensitive regions and endangered species like the northern spotted owl.
- The 1872 mining law, which still gives extracting gold, silver, copper and other "hardrock" minerals preference over any other use of federally owned lands.

President Clinton was elected in 1992 with environmentalists' support, and his administration came into office seeking fundamental changes in longstanding public land policies. Backed by environmentalists and some economists, the Interior Department and Forest Service have moved to reap higher financial returns from government-owned natural resources. They also are pressing for tighter environmental controls that they maintain are needed to end abusive development that is ruining federal lands.

Western-state governors and congressional delegations, however, see the administration's public land pro-

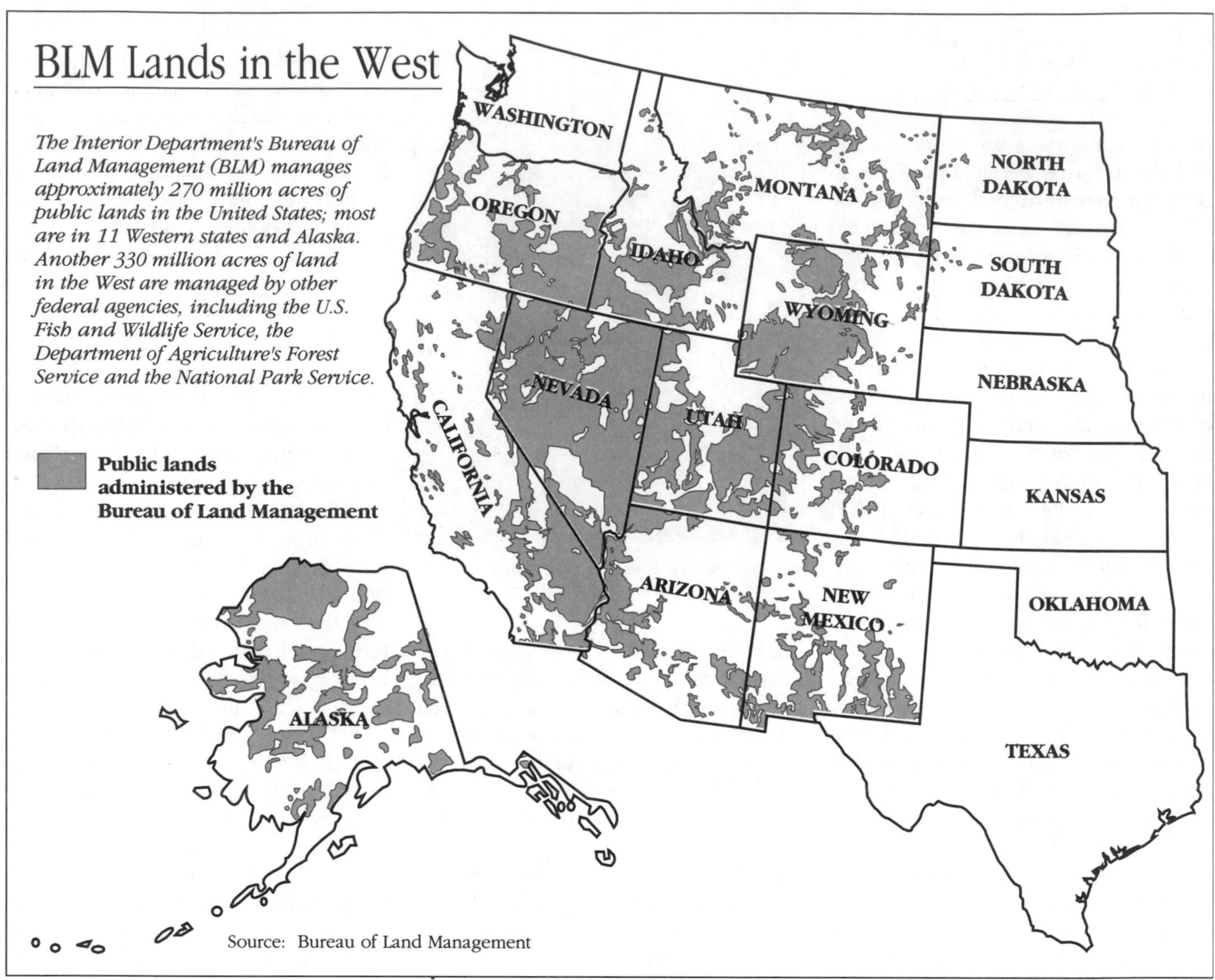
BLM Lands in the West
The Interior Department's Bureau of Land Management (BLM) manages approximately 270 million acres of public lands in the United States; most are in 11 Western states and Alaska. Another 330 million acres of land in the West are managed by other federal agencies, including the U.S. Fish and Wildlife Service, the Department of Agriculture's Forest Service and the National Park Service.
Public lands administered by the Bureau of Land Management
WASHINGTON
OREGON
IDAHO
MONTANA
NORTH DAKOTA
SOUTH DAKOTA
WYOMING
NEVADA
CALIFORNIA
UTAH
COLORADO
NEBRASKA
KANSAS
ARIZONA
NEW MEXICO
OKLAHOMA
TEXAS
ALASKA
Source: Bureau of Land Management

posals as part of a "war on the West" that is threatening the region's economic health, especially in rural towns that depend on resources from the federal lands that surround them.

Administration officials are "just shoving it to the West," Sen. Orrin G. Hatch, R-Utah, declared last fall. "We're just not going to turn over the West to total federal control; it's just that simple." [3]

Mining companies are trying to head off the administration's demand that Congress give the government authority to control a new gold rush on federal lands — and for the first time collect royalties when mining companies hit pay dirt on lands that belong to the entire nation. Loggers and wildlife protection groups are fighting over how national forests in the Pacific Northwest should be managed to protect the endangered spotted owl. Ranchers and small-town businessmen are rebelling against Babbitt's plans for raising fees and tightening government regulations for livestock grazing on public rangelands.

Western leaders say existing policies helped settle the West and remain essential to the region's economy. Based on the government's current land management goals, Western leaders say, mining and logging companies have invested billions of dollars to extract minerals and cut timber, and provided thousands of jobs in Western communities. At their own expense, ranchers have built fences, installed windmills and developed stock-watering tanks that have improved public rangelands for wildlife as well as livestock.

As a result of ranchers' efforts, range conditions have dramatically improved over the last 60 years, says Reeves Brown, executive vice president of the Colorado Cattlemen's Association. "From the ranchers' point of view, there's no reason to change things."

But environmentalists contend that most public lands suffer from too many livestock and too little protection for critical wildlife habitats. Many federal biologists and resource experts agree, and they have been pushing the Clinton administration toward a tougher stance on public land issues.

In all these public land disputes, the underlying issue comes down to whether authority to manage federal lands should be centralized in Washington or dispersed to the communities most directly affected. "It's all about power," says Sen. Larry E. Craig, R-Idaho, who comes from a ranching family. If the Clinton administration follows through on strengthening federal control over public land management, Craig adds, "you take away the power that the hinterlands once had to help determine how public policy could best manage the lands."

Congress is now reviewing the administration's most controversial public lands initiatives. As debates move forward, some basic questions remain to be answered about what the federal government should do with its public lands and the natural resources that they offer:

Should hardrock mining companies pay the same royalties that coal, oil and gas companies pay for minerals they extract from federally owned lands?

There has been long and bitter debate about whether ranchers, miners and loggers pay the federal land agencies enough for the use of the public's resources. Like any private landowner, the government can earn profits by selling products outright or by leasing the right to extract them to third parties. The Forest Service sells timber growing on national forests to logging companies that then cut it. The Interior Department leases the right to mine coal or pump oil and gas found beneath federal lands. The 1872 mining law opens most public lands for mining if prospectors find gold, silver, copper or other valuable hardrock mineral deposits.

"In recent years, the antagonisms between ranchers and environmental advocates have escalated sharply, increasingly dividing the West against itself. And this trend bodes ill for all of us, for in the absence of Western consensus, the making of federal

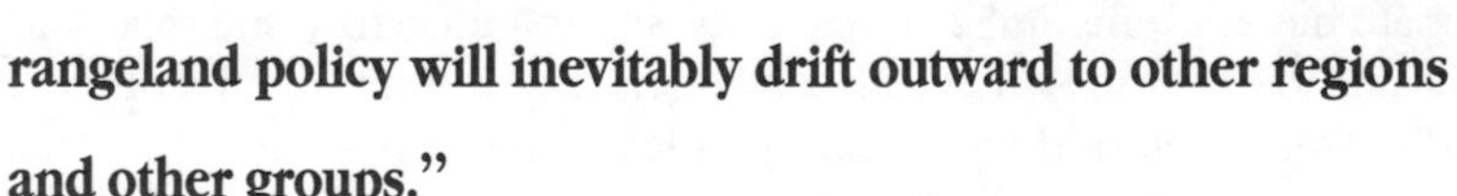

rangeland policy will inevitably drift outward to other regions and other groups."

— Secretary of the Interior Bruce Babbitt

For decades, environmentalists and some economists have contended that government agencies lose taxpayers' money because they charge less than private landowners command for developing valuable resources. By making public resources available at bargain rates, environmentalists say, the government also subsidizes overuse by politically influential ranchers and miners, who for years have headed off congressional efforts to charge them more for public resources.

For the last two years, Congress has been hotly debating how the government can earn taxpayers a better return for public resources without driving Western ranchers, miners and loggers out of business. This spring, public debate centered on the 1872 mining law, which Babbitt has called "the one area of federal resource law where the unrestrained, giveaway, environment-be-damned attitudes of the 19th century have persisted." [4]

Under the Mineral Leasing Act of 1920, the government collects royalties of 12.5 percent for coal, oil and gas produced from public lands. But hardrock minerals like gold, silver, copper and uranium on public lands are not covered by the leasing system, and they have remained available virtually free of charge to anybody who claims them.

Following procedures that developed during California's gold rush days, the 1872 mining law allows any prospector — or, more likely these days, a mining corporation — to explore federal lands to find and stake claims to valuable hardrock deposits. For $100 a year, the holder can maintain a claim indefinitely. If minerals are found, the law gives the claimholder the right to "patent" the claim by buying title to public lands and the wealth they hold for $5 or less an acre.

Not only must the government sell some of its most valuable lands, it loses the revenues it could collect by charging royalties for the minerals that are extracted. Every year, mining companies extract at least $1.2 billion in minerals from public lands, according to the General Accounting Office. [5] Some estimates go as high as $4 billion a year in mineral production, with no royalties going to the public.

Mining executives deny that they are ripping off the taxpayers. "Contrary to popular belief, our industry pays for the right to mine on federal lands" through federal taxes on mining company profits and the incomes of mine workers, says John A. Knebel, president of the industry's trade group, the American Mining Congress. "We also pay production taxes [and other taxes to the states] which are used to help finance highways, hospitals and schools."

Industry leaders and their congressional allies warn that tighter mining controls could force companies to abandon operations in Western states and look overseas for new mineral resources. Proposed changes in the mining law "would be devastating to mining on the public lands . . . without compensating gain to anybody else," Public Resource Associates, a group of geologists and mining attorneys, argued in a 1993 assessment of the legislation. Proposed regulations "would make mining the lowest use of the public lands and would create a whole new, complex, expensive and burdensome regulatory regime." [6]

The stakes in the mining debate have climbed higher over the last decade, especially in the gold-rich Carlin Trend formation beneath public lands in northern Nevada. Gold prices have risen to almost $400 an ounce, and new "heap leaching" technology uses cyanide solutions to extract minuscule amounts of gold from ores that earlier mining booms bypassed. In May, the 1872 law forced Babbitt to sell nearly 2,000 acres of Nevada lands to Toronto-based American Barrick Resources. The firm is now removing 325,000 tons of ore a day from its Goldstrike Mine, an operation that it plans to develop into the richest gold mine in North America. [7]

"The Barrick claims are only a fraction of the public wealth at risk," contends Phil Hocker, president of the Mineral Policy Center, a Washington, D.C.-based group that advocates revamping the federal mining law. [8]

Hocker and other industry critics contend that mining firms have been rushing to patent public land claims before Congress revises the mining law. The center has found 25 major mines that companies are moving to patent on public lands containing an estimated $86 billion worth of minerals. If the government kept those minerals and charged a 12.5 percent royalty for them, the center figures it would take in more than $10 billion for the U.S. Treasury. [9]

Environmentalists also have criticized the government for not requiring miners to restore mined sites once the minerals are gone, preventing wastes from polluting surrounding lands and nearby streams. "The hardrock mining industry has traditionally been able to 'externalize' costs, as economists say, simply by abandoning its played-out mines rather than reclaiming them," says former Interior Secretary Stewart L. Udall, now the chairman of the Mineral Policy Center. [10]

The center estimates that more than 500,000 abandoned mines, most in the West, are creating pollution problems in 32 states. Fifty-six abandoned mines have been declared federal superfund cleanup sites. The Environmental Protection Agency (EPA) is spending $40,000 a day to control cyanide leaking from a Summitville, Colo., gold mine that a mining company abandoned after declaring bankruptcy. The Mineral Policy Center says the cost of cleaning up every abandoned mine could range between $32 billion and $71 billion.[11]

The Clinton administration has proposed charging a 12.5 percent royalty on the gross value of hardrock minerals, the same levy that coal and petroleum producers now pay. Last Nov. 18, the House passed a comprehensive mining measure that would charge an 8 percent royalty on the gross value of the finished metal extracted from ore. The measure would channel the proceeds into a new fund for cleaning up abandoned mine sites scattered across Western states. Six months earlier, the Senate passed an industry-backed bill proposed by Sen. Craig that would levy a 2 percent royalty on net mining income after processing costs are subtracted. [12]

Mining executives warn that the royalty provisions in the House bill are so onerous that the industry will be forced to shut down mines and seek new mineral resources overseas. An industry study by Coopers & Lybrand, a national accounting firm, calculated that the House measure would cut mineral production by $5.7 billion and cost 44,000 miners their jobs. The study also concluded that an 8 percent royalty on gross production would cost the Treasury $420 million a year as personal and corporate income taxes plummeted. [13]

Industry officials generally recognize that they will wind up paying some kind of royalty. "Properly structured, a royalty can be beneficial to the country and not [have] a dramatic negative impact on mining," said Robert W. Schafer, the regional manager for Western U.S. exploration for BHP Minerals International Inc. "I believe most participants in the industry are willing to accept a net royalty in the neighborhood of 5 percent," Schafer continued. "Much more than that and the royalty becomes onerous." [14]

Should Western ranchers be charged more for grazing livestock on public lands?

Environmentalists and stockmen have been battling for more than two decades over whether the way the government figures grazing fees amounts to an unjustified subsidy for Western ranchers. Under a formula set by Congress in 1978, the agencies now charge Western ranchers $1.98 per "animal unit month" (AUM) — enough forage to feed one cow and a calf, five sheep or a horse for a month. In 1991, privately owned ranges in the West leased for nearly five times that amount, an average of $9.25 per AUM, according to U.S.

Department of Agriculture figures.

In 1993, the Clinton administration proposed raising federal grazing fees over three years to $4.28 per AUM. Last October, a Senate filibuster killed a compromise grazing package proposed by Harry Reid, D-Nev., that would have scaled the increase back to $3.45 per AUM. On March 17, 1994, Babbitt announced a new plan that would raise the monthly grazing fee to $2.75 per AUM in 1995, $3.50 in 1996 and $3.96 in 1997.

Western congressional delegations, which traditionally have dominated House and Senate natural resource committees, have steadfastly resisted raising the fees to market levels. A 1978 law linking the fees to livestock prices and ranchers' costs has worked to keep them lower than private leasing rates. Conservation groups, now joined by free-market economists who are critical of public land agencies, charge that below-market fees benefit "welfare ranchers" and give them an incentive to turn too many sheep and cattle out to graze on deteriorating public lands.

Because grazing fees are so low, "taxpayers spend millions of dollars subsidizing the damage of public lands," contends John Baden, chairman of the Foundation for Research on Economics and the Environment, a free-market group based in Seattle and Bozeman, Mont. That subsidy, Baden adds, "encourages commercially unviable ranching and ecologically destructive overgrazing." [15]

A 1992 survey by the Forest Service and the Interior Department's Bureau of Land Management (BLM) found that the value of public land grazing ranged from $4.68 per AUM in drier Southwestern states to $10.26 a month on Northern rangelands. [16] In 1990, critics point out, the Forest Service and BLM collected $52 million less in grazing fees than what the agencies spent to administer grazing on public lands.

If BLM alone had charged private land lease rates in 1991, a National Wildlife Federation study concluded, the agency would have collected $87 million in grazing fees, $68.5 million more than the congressional formula generated. The federation found that below-market fees were benefiting a few wealthy individuals and big corporations like Metropolitan Life Insurance Co., who collectively held permits to graze on 20.7 million acres, roughly 14 percent of BLM-managed rangelands. [17]

Ranchers say it's misleading to compare public and private leasing fees because private lands are more productive. Public lands, they point out, are often leftover tracts that early settlers passed over because they lie in rougher terrain and support only sparse grasses and other vegetation.

"Comparing the two is like comparing the price a renter pays for an unfurnished apartment in a less desirable section of town to a furnished one in a nicer area," Sen. Pete V. Domenici, R-N.M., said at a recent congressional hearing. [18] Domenici cited a 1994 study by New Mexico State University that concluded it takes 12.7 acres of Forest Service land and 11.1 acres of BLM land to match the productivity of 4.7 acres of private land.

Private land ranchers not only get better land, they get services not included in public land leases, says Brown of the Colorado Cattlemen's Association. "On a private lease, you drop your cattle off, then pick them up 90 days later," he says. "On public lands, you have to provide your own management, the fences, the water. . . . On top of that, you have to share the land [with hunters, hikers and others who are entitled to use it] and put up with cut fences, gates that get left open and other problems."

Western cattlemen deeply resent the "welfare rancher" label. The grazing debate is "not the story of big, rich cattle ranchers" ripping off the taxpayers, Sen. Craig said last fall. "It's the story of 27,000 ranch families with net incomes of less than $20,000 a year who make their sole livelihoods grazing cattle on public lands." [19]

Many of those ranchers are barely surviving as it is, Brown says. The way the livestock business has been

Federal Lands in the West

The federal government owns more than half the land in five of the 12 Western states: Alaska, Idaho, Nevada, Oregon and Utah. More than 90 percent of all public land is in the West

State	Federally Owned Land (millions of acres)	Percent Federally Owned	State	Federally Owned Land (millions of acres)	Percent Federally Owned
Alaska	248.0	67.9	Nevada	58.1	82.7
Arizona	34.2	47.1	New Mexico	25.7	33.1
California	44.5	44.4	Oregon	32.3	52.4
Colorado	24.1	36.2	Utah	33.6	63.8
Idaho	32.7	61.7	Washington	12.4	29.0
Montana	26.1	28.0	Wyoming	30.4	48.8

Total Federally Owned Land (in millions of acres):

U.S.	**649.8**
Western States	**602.1**

Source: Bureau of Land Management, Public Land Statistics 1992, *September 1993*

going, "some people really should have gone out of business two or three years ago." Any grazing fee increase at all will put more operations in financial jeopardy, he says.

"If ever implemented, Babbitt's proposals will drive nearly all small producers off the federal range," says Myron Ebell, a Washington lobbyist for the American Land Rights Association. "While some permittees might eventually obtain justice in court, it will be too late for the rural West. Hundreds of small communities will decline and disappear. Babbitt and his extremist allies will have achieved their long-pursued goal, to depopulate the rural West and turn an area three times the size of California into a nature museum."

Is protecting ecosystems compatible with economic growth?

Another debate is now shaping up over how strictly the federal government should regulate environmental impacts on national forests and rangelands. The most celebrated battle is still being fought over how much Pacific Northwest old-growth forests can be logged without dooming the threatened northern spotted owl. (*See story, p. 542.*)

Conservation groups contend that government management of its public lands has consistently served mining, logging and grazing interests at the expense of ecological quality. Now equally serious disputes are brewing over whether federal land managers should sharply curtail mining and grazing and halt timber sales in ecologically sensitive areas, even if that forces ranchers to sell off livestock and costs some miners and loggers their jobs.

The 1872 mining law, for instance, denies the Interior Department direct control over where mines are located and how environmental damage is contained. Once a mining company stakes a claim, the government has no authority to keep it from mining even though that would threaten critical habitat or pollute water supplies. Noranda Minerals, a Canadian mining firm, is now planning to open a major gold mine in the Montana high country 1.5 miles from Yellowstone National Park.

Environmentalists and Clinton administration officials contend that Congress should give the Interior Department power to declare critical areas unsuitable for mining as part of its revision of the 1872 law. In a letter to Sen. Max Baucus, D-Mont., National Park Service Director Roger G. Kennedy supported suitability review, contending that "the integrity of special places like Yellowstone may depend on it." [20]

Bob Armstrong, the assistant secretary of the Interior for land and minerals, says suitability reviews would save the mining industry the cost of exploring areas where mining will never be permitted. "You shouldn't be able to mine near the Washington Monument just because it's public land and you know gold is there," Armstrong said Feb. 15 at a mining conference in Albuquerque, N.M. [21]

The House-passed mining measure includes provisions favored by the administration that would require miners to obtain permits from Interior before exploring or mining on public lands. But the House dropped detailed suitability criteria from its version of the legislation. Sen. J. Bennett Johnston, D-La., chairman of the Senate Energy and Natural Resources Committee, has suggested a compromise measure that would confer more limited authority to deny exploration permits near national parks, wilderness areas and other protected lands.

While logging and grazing can be accommodated in many different areas, mining by its very nature can only be undertaken in a relatively few places where mineral deposits are located. Mining executives note that Congress and the Interior Department have taken various actions that, in effect, have put 263 million acres of public land off-limits for mining ventures. [22]

Federal and state officials already assess the suitability of lands for mining, they add, when they grant or deny permits required under various environmental laws. The House bill "adds a new layer of regulation and bureaucracy on top of what's already out there," says Debra H. Struhsacker, a mining consultant in Reno, Nev. "It's a way to give people yet another chance to say 'no' to mining."

For years, environmentalists have also been pressing the government to cut back livestock on public lands they say are close to ruin from overgrazing by too many sheep and cattle. Conservation groups contend that the government's own studies show that roughly 90 million acres, 60 percent of the lands BLM leases for grazing, are in unsatisfactory condition after a century of heavy use by livestock. [23] Grazing contributes to heavy erosion from dry, fragile soils and takes a heavy toll on "riparian" vegetation along the West's few streams that offer crucial habitat for several declining fish and bird species.

Unless grazing management improves, ranchers "are going to fall under a lot of heat from the Endangered Species Act," says Jim Baca, the controversial former director of the Bureau of Land Management who was forced to resign in February after angering Western governors with his aggressive approach to changing BLM policies (*see p. 544*).

So far, livestock interests have steadfastly resisted BLM attempts to regulate how many livestock they keep on public lands and where they let them graze. Environmentalists say congressional committees dominated by Western senators and representatives have kept the agency without the money and manpower to adequately manage the grazing program.

Grazing leases are granted for 10-year terms, and they go to ranch operators who control water supplies or

Continued on p. 538

An interview with Sen. Larry E. Craig, R-Idaho

"Nobody in the West is asking for a favor...."

Q. You grew up on your family's Idaho ranch. Do you feel that the U.S. government has a responsibility to preserve that way of life in managing public lands?

A. "The federal government doesn't have a responsibility for preserving our Western way of life. It's a way of life that has preserved itself pretty well over the years. But the federal government has no right to damage communities in the West, either, by enacting unreasonable fee hikes and regulations. Nobody in the West is asking for a favor; they are merely asking not to be strangled by an extreme federal presence."

Q. Because they live closer to public lands and earn their living from them, should ranchers or loggers or miners have more of a claim to public lands than other Americans?

A. "Not really. But their lives and livelihoods are more closely intertwined. While there has always been limited disagreement, Americans have developed a policy of shared land use over time. People use the land for different purposes, and, considering the number of competing uses, we've done a pretty good job of maintaining accessibility. Let's hope the current adjustment phase can maintain that balance."

Sen. Larry E. Craig

Q. The Interior Department has proposed giving ranchers a 30 percent break on grazing fees if they implement range-conservation practices. But how can Interior decide whether changes are needed on particular rangelands?

A. "That's a good question. The National Academy of Sciences has asked the same question. Certainly, the challenge will be for Interior to determine what *is* good and bad."

Q. Would the Interior Department's proposed local grazing advisory boards be better able (than existing range-management systems) to balance the local interest in grazing livestock with the national interest in environmental protection?

A. "I believe that those closest to an issue tend to find the best and most workable solutions to local problems. Entrusting local communities through the Multiple Resource Advisory Council is supposed to empower local communities. However, permitting Washington lobbyists to be members runs contrary to the administration's promise of local control. Further, it does not recognize that local environmental leaders are qualified and competent."

Q. With the federal deficit so high, shouldn't the federal government earn as much revenue as possible from royalties for hardrock mining on public lands?

A. "The time has come for a royalty. That's why my bill contains one, as well as calling for fair market value and other fees. But you can only go so far before reaching a point of diminishing returns. Remember the surtax Congress placed on luxury items like boats? It drove the domestic industry under, cost many jobs and cost the Treasury. If you tax something too much, you can create unintended effects. That simple economic principle must not be forgotten.

"The federal government should earn the optimum net royalty, which is based on a company's *profit*. A net royalty raises the largest net return to the U.S. Treasury of any of the proposals made to date. However, it is naive to believe that the revenue from royalties will significantly reduce the federal deficit, particularly if a gross royalty is established. It is estimated that a gross royalty could result in the loss of many more thousands of jobs. In addition, losses to the federal Treasury and to state and local governments would be large."

Q. How can federal agencies head off future conflicts like the spotted owl battle in the Pacific Northwest national forests?

A. "The Endangered Species Act must be amended to, at some point, consider the social and economic consequences of a decision. Further, any consideration, whether to list a species as threatened or endangered must be based on sound science. Our communities must be assured that decisions to list species are made fairly and intelligently. It is simply shameful to allow a species to be listed, disrupting the socio-economic stability of a community, and then have an agency change its mind and delist that species. The listing and delisting of the Bruneau Hot Springs snail is a fine example of this situation."

Q. Western cities are developing more diverse economies, but small communities still depend on ranching, mining and logging on federal lands. Should the federal government manage its lands to keep existing small-town economies going indefinitely?

A. "Cities and rural areas depend very much on each other. Cities could not exist without agriculture, grazing and other pursuits in rural areas. Where else does food come from?

"The same question could be posed for large cities. Should the government continue to pay for urban-renewal projects and the like in big cities and, if so, how long and how much? The big difference is that rural areas aren't asking for handouts. We are only asking not to be put out of business by huge federal fee hikes and stifling regulations."

Q. Could the federal government prevent conflicts by helping communities diversify by developing tourism and other environmentally sustainable industries?

A. "Certainly, it would be beneficial for any community, large or small, to have a diversified economic base. However, I believe that the decision of what businesses to diversify into should be made by the community and the marketplace, not the federal government. Central planning is a notion most Americans resist. Diversification is already occurring."

Counties to Uncle Sam: Pay Your Fair Share

It's not just ranchers, miners and loggers who are concerned about how federally owned lands are managed. And the concern is not limited to the rural West. Wherever the U.S. government is the largest landowner around, county governments say they often are left holding the bag for Uncle Sam's expenses.

Local governments rely heavily on property taxes to finance their operations. But the federal government's lands are exempt from local taxes. As a result, county officials say they must absorb the additional costs of providing services on public lands, such as law enforcement, trash disposal and search-and-rescue missions.

To raise the additional money needed to provide those services, county leaders say they are forced to turn to their limited base of private landowners, and raise the property-tax rate.

The cost of providing services on federal lands can mount up, particularly near national parks that draw millions of visitors yearly. But even remote counties that attract only the most adventurous tourists have to maintain roads, enforce the law and rescue stranded hunters on public lands. Several years ago, Clear Creek County, Colo., spent $300,000 in county funds for a two-week search for a hiker missing on federal lands.

Harney County in eastern Oregon covers more than 6 million acres, and 74 percent of the land is owned by the federal government. The county already spends $20,000 a year to operate eight solid-waste disposal sites in remote regions that are mostly public lands. That figure could jump to $800,000 a year when the county complies with new federal landfill standards. Public lands may belong to the entire country, "but when it comes time to pay the bill, all of a sudden they're our lands," complains Dale White, the Harney County administrator.

To compensate for those costs, Congress over the years has granted county governments a cut of federal agency revenues from resource development. The U.S. Forest Service gives 25 percent of its timber-sale receipts to county schools and road programs, and some states pass along part of their shares of federal oil and gas leasing revenues. Environmentalists complain that practice just augments pressure from local communities for all-out development of federally owned resources.

In May, for instance, three western Oregon counties joined labor unions and timber-company groups in filing lawsuits challenging the Clinton administration's plan to limit logging to preserve spotted-owl habitat in the region's federal forests. The lawsuit estimated that 13 national forests in Oregon and Washington affected by the plan generate more than $100 million a year for county governments in the two states. Clinton's plan could cut Forest Service payments to the counties to $55.2 million a year, the plaintiffs contended.

Some 1,789 counties in 49 states have some federal lands within their boundaries. Since 1976, the U.S. government has been paying such counties $104 million a year under a payments-in-lieu-of-taxes (PILT) program to compensate for the presence of tax-exempt federal lands.

The 1,789 counties embrace some significant federal holdings. In New Mexico and California, counties now get a total of $10.5 million a year in PILT funds. PILT funds cover more than half of the general operating budgets of six New Mexico counties, including 80 percent of the budget in Otero County, which includes BLM lands, the Lincoln National Forest and part of the White Sands National Monument.

Congress hasn't increased PILT appropriations in 17 years, so the National Association of Counties (NACO) has been pushing for legislation to raise the existing payment formula over the next five years from 75 cents to $1.65 for each acre of federally owned land. The Senate passed the measure by a 78-20 vote on April 13, but the House has not acted on the bill.

NACO officials say Congress needs to recognize the role local governments play in providing services for thousands of federal land-agency employees and their families, as well as the tourists drawn to federal lands. "If counties did not exist, the federal government would have to invent something like them" to provide those services, says Randall Franke, a Marion County, Ore., commissioner and a NACO vice president. [1]

[1] Testifying before the Senate Energy and Natural Resources Subcommittee on Public Lands, National Parks and Forests, Nov. 3, 1993.

Continued from p. 536

adjacent private holdings. Nobody else can bid for grazing rights, and critics say the agency never revokes a rancher's permit. BLM rangeland managers lack credible enforcement power to correct abuses, and environmentalists say that the agency has been reluctant to challenge politically powerful stockmen who set local policy on district grazing advisory boards.

Tom Dougherty, the National Wildlife Federation's Western division staff director, says Western congressional delegations have pressured BLM to transfer employees who try to enforce grazing cutbacks. If a BLM area manager in Wyoming had the temerity to take on livestock interests, Dougherty says, "that guy is dog meat for [Malcolm] Wallop and [Alan K.] Simpson," the state's two Republican senators.

For their part, stockmen insist that the range is in far better shape than it was 60 years ago when Congress first regulated public land grazing. Many ranchers privately acknowledge that a few stockmen have abused public lands, but they insist it's to their advantage to keep rangelands in optimal condition. "If you look at it Westwide, we've made tremendous leaps and bounds in range conditions," says Brown.

Ranchers whose fathers and grandfathers grazed livestock on the same public lands say they know the range better than BLM employees who spend just a few years in a district before transferring to new positions. "I was born and raised in a ranching family, having had conservation and proper [land] management put on my breakfast, dinner and supper plate from the day I can remember," says Sen. Craig. "I have always been very frustrated, and that frustration has grown into anger, at the environmental movement [which] really does not recognize the phenomenal love of the land and the stewardship that comes from the ranching families of the West."

Ranchers' resistance to higher grazing fees and livestock cutbacks is more than a matter of pride. Because federal leases cost less than private rangelands, ranchers can take financial advantage of a "permit value" that reflects the benefit they gain by grazing livestock on public lands. Purchasers pay for permit value when they buy an existing ranch, and bankers figure it into collateral when they make loans for yearly ranch operations. If BLM cuts the number of AUMS that a permit carries, that would reduce a ranch's total value as well as cut potential income.

For economically marginal ranch operations, the combination of higher fees and fewer AUMS could be enough to force them out of business. "A dramatic increase in government regulation and grazing fees will work to drive small and medium-sized ranches out of business," Sen. Domenici said at an April 20 hearing of the Senate Energy and Natural Resources Committee. "The family investment in ranches will be devalued, and this will have repercussions on the banks that secure these ranches."

Testifying at the same hearing, Babbitt said nothing in federal land law requires Interior to keep grazing fees artificially low "to preserve the market sale prices of an asset."

BLM has to consider multiple goals in managing public lands, adds former BLM Director Baca, "but keeping ranches in business is not one of them." What ranchers fear most "is losing control of the public lands," Baca suggests. "They really think it's theirs."

Would public lands be better managed by private owners?

Seventeen years ago, ranchers, miners and timber interests mounted a well-publicized "Sagebrush Rebellion," demanding that the federal government turn public lands over to Western states to be sold to private owners. [24]

Congress still is unlikely to comply with that request, and, in fact, is moving toward tighter federal regulation of public lands. But current controversies are raising new doubts about whether federal agencies can ever manage lands and resources so far from the nation's capital in a consistently efficient and equitable way.

Mainline environmental groups are fiercely opposed to any suggestions for privatizing public lands. But some economists and other free-market proponents are now arguing that federal lands will never be restored to health simply by charging higher fees or imposing new regulations.

"If we want improvement, we need to change existing institutional arrangements, not simply fiddle with prices," says Baden of the Foundation for Research on Economics and the Environment. "Ecological and social problems are caused by regulations that encourage poor management practices." [25]

Baden and other advocates of what they call "new resource economics" argue that free-market incentives to reap financial benefits from private property would conserve resources and protect natural values more effectively than the political institutions that now control federal lands. Bureaucratic management by the Forest Service and BLM helps perpetuate special economic interests that depend on federal largess, they say, while providing few incentives for protecting wildlife, encouraging recreation and preserving biologically diverse ecosystems.

Baden and his associates say that when lands are in private hands, owners have financial incentives to keep them in good shape, manage resources on a sustainable basis and profit by responding to growing public demand for recreation in open spaces. If they can profit from natural values, says Karl Hess Jr., a range ecologist affiliated with Baden's group, "people will be more responsible for the land because they will bear the financial risks of bad management and assume the potential benefits of superior management." [26]

In a 1992 book, Hess proposed that the federal government divest itself of all Forest Service and BLM lands over a 20-year period by distributing 100 shares free of charge to every U.S. citizen holding a Social Security card. Each recipient could either use his shares to buy public lands or sell them to others with stronger interests in them. Ranchers could maintain control over public rangelands, but they would have to outbid competitors. Environmental groups could collect members' shares and acquire wilderness and wildlife habitat. Western communities could organize associations to take control of public lands that surround them. [27]

But according to University of Maryland Professor Robert H. Nelson, a former Interior Department policy analyst, Hess' proposal would require "a pretty abrupt transfer" of public lands that would take no account of the rights that ranchers, miners and others already possess to develop federal resources. "It's not likely to happen, either," Nelson adds, because Congress would be reluctant to give up its power over federal land policy.

Environmentalists say there's little reason to conclude that private control of public lands would produce better environmental protection. "We have plenty of evidence that the private rangelands and forestlands have not been properly managed, no matter what the economic incentives have been," argues Johanna Wald, an attorney with the Natural Resources Defense Council (NRDC). "That clearly suggests that the market system we have now doesn't give the kind of economic incentives that could produce prudent management of natural resources."

Theories about private incentives for improving land management may be "an attractive idea," but they don't "work out on the ground," adds National Audubon Society Vice President Brock Evans. Federal land laws require federal agencies to conduct extensive public hearings and consider various interest groups' opinions before they make decisions, Evans notes, but private land owners have no obligation to consult with the public. "If I try to tell Weyerhaeuser or Plum Creek Timber Co. what they should be doing with their own forests, well, [they will just say] 'tough.' "

Baden and other proponents of new resource economics say those public participation requirements have further politicized public land management, making it harder for federal land managers to make final decisions. "When we allocate via politics, special interests and financial waste will prevail," Baden contends. "Property rights and voluntary arrangements are far more responsive — and often more responsible." [28] ■

BACKGROUND

Century-Old Struggle

The struggle for power over the public domain has been building since the Western frontier closed near the end of the 19th century. Before then, the central government encouraged settlers to move west by opening the public domain and its resources virtually free of charge to economic development. The Homestead Act of 1862, the 1872 mining law and other public land measures were drafted to encourage immigrants to develop the region's resources by plowing the prairies, grazing livestock on the plains, cutting timber and finding and extracting minerals.

Early settlers homesteaded the best lands along railroads and river valleys, and ranchers took de facto control over vast expanses of public rangelands by staking claims around critical water supplies. Congress also turned some lands over to state governments as they entered the Union. But for the most part, the region's high mountain forests, windswept rangelands and rugged deserts remained part of the public domain, still owned by a U.S. government headquartered 2,000 miles away.

To this day, the federal government owns more than half the land in five of the 12 Western states: Alaska, Idaho, Nevada, Oregon and Utah.

Nearly 70 million acres of federal lands in the region have been set aside in national parks to be preserved for their scenic and natural splendor. Another 82 million acres are managed as national wildlife refuges. But most of the remaining public lands, including 162 million acres in national forests and another 248 million acres in Interior Department holdings, generally are managed under "multiple use" policies that allow economic development for logging, grazing and mining along with hunting, hiking, whitewater rafting and other popular forms of recreation.

Congress established the Forest Service in 1905 as part of the U.S. Department of Agriculture. Its mission was to manage national forests through scientifically trained resources professionals for what Gifford Pinchot, its first chief, called "the greatest good for the greatest number in the long run."

In the Taylor Grazing Act of 1934, Congress gave Interior authority to regulate grazing on public rangelands by charging stockmen fees and issuing permits to limit livestock numbers. Critics say BLM, created in 1947 to manage Interior's multiple-use lands, has always been dominated by the livestock and mining interests it regulates.

After World War II, the Forest Service began accelerating timber harvests from national forests to supply lumber for booming housing markets. The rapid growth of cities in Rocky Mountain states also created new demands for recreation on public lands. More people began spending time in the forests and BLM lands, and environmental groups began questioning the way they were being managed.

A 1974 court decision in a lawsuit filed by the Natural Resources Defense Council (NRDC) ordered BLM to prepare a series of environmental impact statements reviewing its grazing program. In 1976, Congress passed the National Forest Management Act to strengthen the authority of the Forest Service over the national forests.

The same year Congress enacted the Federal Land Policy and Management Act (FLPMA), a law that for the first time gave BLM a formal mandate to administer multiple-use lands for a variety of goals. Both laws endorsed comprehensive land-use planning procedures in the hope that the agencies could blend their own scientific expertise with extensive participation by the public to forge agreement on how to manage the

Continued on p. 542

Chronology

1800s ***The federal government encourages settlers to move west by opening public lands for development. At the end of the century, however, the government begins setting lands aside for continued federal ownership.***

1872
The General Mining Law gives prospectors the right to stake claims to gold, silver and other hardrock minerals on public lands and acquire ownership from the government. Congress sets a precedent for preserving scenic parts of the public domain by creating Yellowstone National Park.

1897
Congress had given the president authority to create federal forest reserves in 1891. The Organic Act of 1897 requires that the forests be managed to protect watersheds and supply timber.

—— • ——

1900s-1930s

A growing conservation movement is led by President Theodore Roosevelt and Gifford Pinchot, founder of the U.S. Forest Service. New laws retain valuable public lands and regulate how resources are used.

1905
Congress creates the U.S. Forest Service and gives it control over national forests. Pinchot regulates logging and livestock grazing on the forests with the goal of producing resources "for the greatest good for the greatest number of people."

1920
The Mining Leasing Act gives the U.S. Interior Department authority to lease federal coal, oil, gas and potash for development, charging a 12.5 percent royalty.

1934
Alarmed by Dust Bowl conditions on public rangelands, Congress approves the Taylor Grazing Act to restrict grazing on federal lands to ranchers holding Interior Department permits.

—— • ——

1960s-1980s

The environmental movement pushes U.S. agencies to protect wildlife and watersheds as well as develop federal resources.

1964
The federal Wilderness Act orders the U.S. government to list endangered species and protect their habitat on public lands.

1976
The National Forest Management Act and the Federal Land Policy and Management Act strengthen federal authority to manage national forests and public lands for multiple users.

1977-80
A "Sagebrush Rebellion" by ranchers, miners and loggers forces the Carter administration to back away from stronger public land regulation.

1981-83
Secretary of the Interior James G. Watt angers environmentalists with policies favoring commodity production from public lands.

1990s ***Controversy over protecting the northern spotted owl sets off debate over national forest logging. Led by Interior Secretary Bruce Babbitt, the Clinton administration pushes for reform of public land policies.***

May 1991
U.S. District Judge William Dwyer prohibits the Forest Service from selling more timber in spotted owl habitat until protection plans are in place.

November 1993
The House of Representatives approves the first comprehensive reform of the 1872 Mining Law, including an 8 percent royalty on federal minerals.

March 17, 1994
Babbitt announces new proposals to raise federal grazing fees and create grazing advisory boards including environmentalists as well as ranchers.

April 14, 1994
The administration reveals its plan for solving the spotted owl issue by protecting 7.4 million acres of old-growth timber in the Pacific Northwest.

June 6, 1994
Judge Dwyer lifts his injunction blocking timber sales in the spotted owl's habitat in 13 Oregon and Washington national forests.

Spotted Owls vs. Northwest Loggers . . .

In the annals of political survival, the northern spotted owl is a breed apart. For years, the federal government and logging interests have battled over harvesting policies in the Pacific Northwest's old-growth forests, the shy critters' only habitat. Now, despite a new round of legal and legislative action, the battle shows no sign of letup.

U.S. Fish and Wildlife Service

On June 6, U.S. District Judge William Dwyer lifted his three-year-old injunction blocking timber sales in the owl's habitat in 13 Oregon and Washington national forests. Dwyer ruled that the Clinton administration's plan for resuming limited logging in the region, announced in April, addressed his concerns that federal forest plans consider the effects of logging on endangered species, including the spotted owl. But Dwyer withheld final approval of the Clinton plan, and both environmentalists and the timber industry are continuing legal challenges to it.

The spotted owl debate began back in the mid-1970s, when biologists began warning that owl populations were declining rapidly as the old-growth fir forests in the Pacific Northwest were logged. The spotted owl lives in the towering trees, and biologists consider it an indicator species whose decline reflects the rapid loss of the region's old-growth forest ecosystems. [1]

After several years of debate, the U.S. Fish and Wildlife Service in 1990 listed the spotted owl as a threatened species protected by the federal Endangered Species Act. [2] At the same time, a federal panel led by biologist Jack Ward Thomas, now chief of the Forest Service, concluded that the government should protect at least 3,000 pairs of spotted owls to assure its survival.

The next year, Dwyer barred timber sales until the agency prepared an environmental impact statement and plan for preventing the owl's extinction. Similarly, two 1992 court decisions blocked the U.S. Bureau of Land Management (BLM) from selling timber in owl habitat on 2.7 million BLM-regulated acres in western Oregon.

Timber interests blamed Dwyer's order for the loss of 12,000 logging and sawmill jobs as timber harvests fell off in the Northwest, and two dozen of the region's 150 sawmills closed. Also, notes Chris West, vice president of the Northwest Forestry Association in Portland, timber harvests have declined to between 200 million-400 million board feet a year [3] — "10 percent of what it's been over the last couple of decades."

The judge's order "held up all but very limited thinning sales for the last three years," West adds. Environmental groups contend, however, that timber-industry employment in the Northwest would have declined in any event because of economic factors.

Trying to resolve the conflict, President Clinton on April 2, 1993, conducted a one-day forest summit in Portland with environmentalists and industry workers and executives. On April 13, 1994, the administration laid out its proposed solution: the Pacific Northwest Forest Plan. Under the plan, comprehensive ecosystem management of publicly owned lands for the future.

Sagebrush Rebellion

The process hasn't worked the way Congress envisioned. In the late 1970s, ranchers, miners and other traditional interests rose in a "Sagebrush Rebellion" when the Carter administration began implementing the new public land laws. The rebels renewed the region's longstanding demand that Congress turn public lands over to state governments or, better yet, sell them to private owners. Their fury ebbed in the 1980s when Secretary of the Interior James G. Watt and his Republican successors reversed Carter's campaign for tighter BLM regulations.

As a result of Watt's policies, environmental groups grew more frustrated than ever with BLM's inability to crack down on rangeland abuses. Even the Forest Service, long regarded as a model for a highly professional government resource agency, came under increasing fire from conservation groups, and even within its own ranks, for neglecting recreation and wildlife habitat.

Professional foresters have dominated the service, critics say, and the supervisors of most national forests have been under pressure to meet nationwide timber sale goals set by Congress and agency headquarters. Logging may make sense in the Pacific Northwest, they add, but studies by the Wilderness Society, NRDC, congressional committees and forestry groups have found that the service sells timber from less productive Rocky Mountain forests for less than the agency spends to administer sales and build roads for logging operations.

. . . the Long-Running Battle Continues

old-growth forest habitat would protect spotted owls, enhance salmon runs and preserve biological diversity in the region.

In addition to the nearly 9 million acres of forests already protected in the region, the plan calls for setting aside 7.4 million acres of reserves to sustain the owl and other species that live in the old-growth forests, such as the Del Norte salamander and the marbled murrelet. The plan also proposes reopening about 5.5 million acres for logging, including 1.2 million acres in prime owl habitat.

The administration estimates that under the plan about 9,500 timber jobs will be lost. But timber executives say about 85,000 jobs will disappear.

In response to the plan, industry groups joined with loggers' unions, county governments and local citizens to file suits against the BLM and Forest Service, charging that the two agencies "made no attempt to determine what combination of resources will best meet the needs of the American people . . . and maintain a high-level output of the various renewable resources of the national forests." [4]

In lifting his injunction, Judge Dwyer withheld final approval of the administration's plan. Environmental groups say they will ask Dwyer to overturn the plan because it fails to protect the entire old-growth ecosystem adequately. "Their own data show they're not protecting the forest and all the species that depend on old-growth timber," says National Audubon Society Vice President Brock Evans.

Forest industry researchers, meanwhile, say they are finding that there are more spotted owls than previously thought, with 6,000 to 8,000 pairs in northern California. That raises the possibility that "Clinton's plan to shut down most Washington and Oregon logging may not only be unnecessary; it may be resting on an illusion," *Newsweek* environment writer Gregg Easterbrook has suggested. [5]

Still, Easterbrook and conservation groups contend, the government needs to start protecting entire ecosystems to keep species from declining to the point they need special protection. But with the Endangered Species Act up for renewal this year, the spotted owl controversy is stirring demands that Congress change the law to require the government to take economic impact into account when protecting critical habitat.

Secretary of the Interior Bruce Babbitt, meanwhile, is moving to create a National Biological Survey (NBS) within the Interior Department to study lands throughout the country and identify ways to preserve enough habitat on both public and private lands to assure that ecosystems will survive. The survey "will provide a map to help us avoid environmental and economic conflicts," Babbitt said in announcing the plan April 26, 1993. "Both economically and environmentally, the NBS will be a useful tool for sound resource management decisions."

Many Western commodity producers say the survey will interfere with development both on private and public lands. "Quite simply, we are talking about land-use zoning on a national level," says Al Schneberger, executive director of the New Mexico Cattle Growers Association. "Something doesn't smell right here," Schneberger adds, "Look what they've done just with the Endangered Species Act."

[1] For background, see "Jobs vs. Environment," *The CQ Researcher,* May 15, 1992, p. 409-432.

[2] For background, see "Endangered Species," *The CQ Researcher,* June 21, 1991, pp. 393-416.

[3] A board foot is 1 inch thick, 12 inches long and 12 inches wide.

[4] The two lawsuits, filed May 11 in U.S. District Court in Washington, D.C., were: *Northwest Forest Resource Council, et. al. v. Jack Ward Thomas, Chief, U. S. Forest Service, and Mike Espy, Secretary of Agriculture; and Northwest Forest Resource Council, et. al. v. Michael Dombeck, acting director, U.S. Bureau of Land Management, and Bruce Babbitt, Secretary of the Interior.*

[5] Gregg Easterbrook, "The Birds," *The New Republic,* March 28, 1994, p. 22.

As controversies have mounted, both BLM and Forest Service planning efforts have bogged down in testy public hearings and legal challenges. Nelson, the former Interior analyst, says the agencies' struggles have shaken public faith in the federal government's ability to manage public lands and resources based on the scientific findings and judgments developed by professional resource managers. In the last 25 years, "there has been an explosion of procedure. . . ," Nelson notes. "Yet, the managers of public lands do not seem to be able to get much decided." [29] ■

CURRENT SITUATION

Clinton Backs Down

The Clinton administration took office last year with high hopes that it could finally resolve long-smoldering public land issues.

Clinton encouraged environmentalists when he named Babbitt, a former Arizona governor who was chairman of the League of Conservation Voters, as secretary of the Interior. The White House also picked former New Mexico Commissioner of Public Lands Jim Baca as BLM director. Later in 1993, Jack Ward Thomas, who had led the Forest Service's scientific review of the spotted owl's decline, was named the first biologist to head that agency.

Clinton's first budget plan proposed that the government raise an additional $1 billion over five years by adopting mining reforms that would impose a 12.5 percent royalty on hardrock mining, implementing new grazing regulations that would raise BLM fees and phasing out money-losing timber sales on national forests. But the president backed away from the plan after Democratic senators from Western states complained that it would cost their party political support in the region.

In October 1993, Western senators mounted a successful filibuster to kill legislation in the annual Interior Department appropriations bill that would have implemented a modified administration plan for raising livestock grazing fees and imposed tighter BLM rangeland regulations. [30]

BLM Director Baca advocated plunging ahead with new rangeland policies despite ranchers' opposition. But Baca angered Idaho Gov. Cecil D. Andrus, a Democrat and former Interior secretary, and other influential Western politicians with his aggressive approach to changing the agency's policies. Over environmentalists' protests, Babbitt forced Baca to resign on Feb. 3, citing "different approaches to management style and consensus building."

Doughtery of the National Wildlife Federation says "scientifically, Baca was right on, but politically, he was 10 or 20 years ahead of anybody else" in his views on public land management.

Since then, Babbitt and congressional leaders have been searching for compromises on mining, grazing and timber issues.

Mining Reform Targeted

Congress, meanwhile, is working on a compromise mining measure to replace the General Mining Law of 1872.

The measure the House passed last November would (1) impose an 8 percent royalty to fund a reclamation program, (2) keep mining lands in federal ownership by abolishing the patent system, (3) review public lands for mining suitability and (4) set federal standards for controlling mine impacts and reclaiming abandoned sites. The Senate earlier passed an industry-backed measure that would charge a 2 percent royalty, maintain the patent system and rely on state enforcement of environmental and reclamation standards.

The House bill includes a provision applying the hardrock royalty on the gross value of minerals, but the Senate version applies its 2 percent levy to net value after processing costs are deducted. The government figures fossil fuel royalties at 12.5 percent of gross value, but mining officials say it would be unfair to levy hardrock royalties on the value of processed minerals.

"What we mine is not a marketable product, it's rock with minuscule amounts of valuable material," says mining regulation consultant Struhsacker. "We have to process the rock to get to a marketable product," she adds, and the Senate bill's net royalty "would allow us to do like other businesses do, deduct some of our costs before it is imposed."

To persuade House leaders to go to conference on mining bills, Sen. Johnston, the chairman of the Senate Energy and Natural Resources Committee, drafted a "chairman's mark" that suggested possible compromises between the House and Senate versions. Johnston's tentative proposal included a minimum 2 percent gross royalty, indexed to climb in stages to 7 percent, 12.5 percent and as high as 35 percent on gold and copper, depending on prices for those commodities. Gold royalties would stay at 2 percent of a price up to $300 an ounce and reach 35 percent on amounts over $475 an ounce if prices passed that level.

Since Johnston outlined the alternative proposals, the chairman has been negotiating with Craig and other key senators in an effort to agree on new legislation to take to conference with the House. Senate aides say the senators could reach agreement in June, and that would set the stage for conference negotiations to begin this summer.

Babbitt and the Ranchers

Secretary Babbitt is now trying to forge consensus among Western ranchers and environmentalists over scaled-back rangeland policy revisions. Last fall, senators from Western states successfully filibustered to force congressional leaders to drop provisions from Interior Department appropriations bill language that would have approved tighter range regulations and lifted federal grazing fees over three years to $3.45 per AUM.

Babbitt has now proposed new Interior grazing regulations including a new formula that would raise the fees to $2.75 in 1995, $3.50 in 1996 and $3.96 by 1997. The department also is considering granting a 30 percent break on the grazing fee starting in 1997 to stockmen who take part in stepped up efforts to improve and monitor range conditions on public lands.

For now, at least, much of the focus has shifted away from grazing fees onto how the government should go about tightening livestock regulations. Environmental groups have been demanding nationwide standards for protecting native wildlife and vegetation against overgrazing and keeping cattle out of critical streambank areas.

But in light of the Senate setback last year, Babbitt and his aides now have concluded that one-size-fits-all regulations will never be effective. "The command-and-control approach from the past, where Washington tells people what to do in the states and

Continued on p. 546

At Issue:

Is the Clinton administration's grazing plan fair to ranchers?

yes

Bruce Babbitt
Secretary of the Interior

FROM *TESTIMONY BEFORE THE SENATE ENERGY AND NATURAL RESOURCES SUBCOMMITTEE ON PUBLIC LANDS, NATIONAL PARKS AND FORESTS,* APRIL 20, 1994.

In recent years, the antagonisms between ranchers and environmental advocates have escalated sharply, increasingly dividing the West against itself. And this trend bodes ill for all of us, for in the absence of Western consensus, the making of federal rangeland policy will inevitably drift outward to other regions and other groups.

Therefore, I believe that one of the core issues of rangeland reform is the process by which we make decisions. The model for change already exists in the consensus groups. These new groups bring together ranchers, environmentalists and interested citizens to meet over coffee at the kitchen table and out on the range to listen to each other, to develop mutual confidence and search for consensus in solving public land issues. . . .

I believe that the time is now at hand for the Bureau of Land Management (BLM) to listen carefully to the changes taking place out on the land in this new West and to make fundamental changes, casting off the closed-shop practices of the past and moving to embrace a more open, diverse and public style of rangeland policy formulation. . . . Therefore, the first objective of the new governance provision in the draft regulations will be to assure balanced representation of all the diverse groups and interests that have a legitimate stake in the administration of public lands. . . .

In a second major area, we heard much criticism last fall. Producers said the proposed grazing fee was too high. Many conservationists and fiscal conservatives said it was too low. Having listened to the debate, our new proposal represents significant change.

In establishing the proposed fee, we determined that it should approximate fair market value and [be] comparable to fees paid for leasing on private lands. It should provide the public with a fair return for the use of its resources, but should not cause significant harm to the Western livestock industry and to ranching-dependent communities.

After full phase-in, the new fees would not have a significant impact on the vast majority of public lands ranchers: More than 73 percent of BLM permittees would have fee increases totaling less than $1,000 per year. . . .

[And] despite the fact that economic analysis continues to show the fee increases will not force ranchers out of business, our proposed rule contains language calling on the department to analyze the impact of increased fees after one year of the phase-in. If the fee does have a significant negative impact, it may be re-evaluated.

no

Myron Ebell
Washington Representative, American Land Rights Association

FROM *ARTICLE WRITTEN FOR THE CQ RESEARCHER,* MAY 1994.

Despite a propaganda campaign to the contrary, Interior Secretary Bruce Babbitt's latest grazing reforms differ little from last August's proposals that were exploded by a successful Senate filibuster. Babbitt's Rangeland Reform '94 is unfair to grazing permittees because it assumes a federal subsidy of ranchers when in fact most ranchers subsidize the government and because it imposes vast new costs to comply with regulations even though compliance costs are already too high.

No city dweller would pay the same rent for a vacant lot as for an adjacent lot with a house on it, but that is exactly what Babbitt wants grazing permittees to do. Rented private pasture includes fences, water, roads, corrals and dates certain when livestock can be put out.

Federal land ranchers must pay, or have paid through generations of hard sweat labor, to build and maintain fences, waterworks, roads and corrals. When livestock can be put out on the range is not written into contract, but is at the whim of federal bureaucrats.

Ranchers usually won water rights on federal range. Developing these water sources has greatly increased wildlife in the semi-arid West. Much of this wildlife winters on ranchers' private ground and eats their hay. These important environmental benefits are provided at no cost to the public.

Permittees do get something that renters of private pasture don't — federal bureaucrats and red tape. For the huge majority of permittees who are small mom-and-pop operations, the hundreds of hours required annually to deal with paperwork and meet with bureaucrats is a major cost of doing business.

Secretary Babbitt proposes a lot more regulation. As respected agricultural economist Frederick Obermiller of Oregon State University recently told the Oregon Cattlemen's Association. "It is the doubling of your regulatory costs that is going to put you out of business."

If ever implemented, Babbitt's proposals will drive nearly all small producers off the federal range. As their water rights and private base property become worthless, permittees will flood the U.S. Court of Claims with "taking" lawsuits.

While some permittees might eventually obtain justice in court, it will be too late for the rural West. Hundreds of small communities will decline and disappear. Babbitt and his extremist allies will have achieved their long-pursued goal, to depopulate the rural West and turn an area three times the size of California into a nature museum.

Out West, the 'County Movement' Picks Up Steam

It was a startling sight: rugged-looking ranchers in cowboy hats and boots parading back and forth on an Albuquerque, N.M., sidewalk, chanting slogans and holding picket signs. President Clinton was coming to town for a fundraising event that evening, and the cattle and sheep ranchers were protesting his "war on the West" and demanding that he fire Secretary of the Interior Bruce Babbitt.

Two decades ago during the Vietnam War, "most of us would have wanted all those protesters shot," one of the ranchers acknowledged. Picketing Clinton "is very traumatic for a lot of these guys," added Charles Cushman, executive director of the American Land Rights Association, who organized the protest.

But these days, the West's conservative ranching families, along with miners and loggers, are feeling desperate enough to steal some pages from environmentalists' protest book. They've always resented the power that the U.S. Forest Service and Interior Department wield over the lands they use, and now they are mounting grass-roots resistance to Babbitt's efforts to tighten regulation of public lands. And they're doing more than just carrying placards.

With financing from big mining and timber firms, Westerners from small communities have set up grass-roots organizations like People for the West to fight logging reductions, grazing restrictions and other policies that they feel threaten the economic life of the rural West. And they are finding allies among elected county government officials who have large federal landholdings within their jurisdictions.

Catron County, N.M., took the lead by adopting its own land-use plan for public lands within its boundaries and demanding that the federal government comply with the plan to preserve the area's traditional "customs and culture." Federal attorneys say there's no legal basis for such measures, but other local governments in the West have adopted similar tactics as part of what they call the "county movement."

Cushman and other activists say county governments should share authority to decide what happens on federal lands within their boundaries because they are the unit of government closest to the people. "I've been using county governments for years to yank the federal government's chain" during public land hearings, Cushman says. "Federal agencies are now finding they have to be more responsive to local concerns and local governments."

Following Catron County's initiative, county governments in five Arizona counties and eight New Mexico counties have joined together to form the Coalition of Arizona/New Mexico Counties for Stable Economic Growth. Counties in Wyoming, Idaho and other Western-range states have taken similar steps.

In southern Utah's canyonlands, county governments are trying to frustrate Interior Department wilderness-protection proposals by designating jeep trails as county road rights of way that must be kept open for future development.

In Idaho, the Owyhee County Commission contributed $5,000 to help farmers and ranchers win a lawsuit forcing the U.S. Fish and Wildlife Service to remove the Bruneau Hot Springs snail from the federal endangered species list. It didn't affect the county per se, says Chester Selmon, a rancher who is on the County Commission, but the commission was concerned about water supplies for local ranchers and farmers. "We felt some of our citizens were being treated unfairly. They couldn't afford to follow through on their own, so we had to chip in and help them out."

But Susan Shock, a Silver City, N.M., environmentalist, points out that county commissioners often have a vested interest in such fights. "You're looking at commissioners who have grazing allotments themselves" on federal lands, says Shock. In the case of Catron County, she contends that overgrazing is ruining mountain streams in the Gila National Forest and that Gila rangers have been intimidated by the county's demand to control forest policy. "They've turned the forest over to the county," she says.

Most observers think the county movement has no realistic chance of controlling public lands. But in Oregon, Marion County Commissioner Randall Franke argues that Forest Service and Interior officials need to consult local governments more closely as they seek to balance national environmental concerns and local economic consequences. "I don't think the counties by themselves are capable of striking the balance," says Franke, a National Association of Counties vice president, "but the counties need to be at the table and involved in exploring where the balance lies."

Continued from p. 544

the districts, either hasn't worked or could be improved on," Assistant Secretary Armstrong says.

Babbitt came up with his revised plan after extensive meetings with the Colorado Rangeland Reform Working Group, ranchers, environmentalists and state and local officials who had begun working together on range issues. Upon their advice, Babbitt scrapped his original proposal to limit grazing permits to five instead of 10 years; he also agreed to let BLM state offices set statewide standards and guidelines for range conditions.

Citing the Colorado group and other informal negotiations among public land interests around the West, the secretary also wants to set up expanded BLM advisory boards to assess local rangeland policies that would bring the growing number of environmentalists living in the West into the process of setting public land policy.

Babbitt suggests setting up boards that would include representatives from commodity producers, environmental groups and state game managers, land officials or other public representatives. "Today, the West is a different place," Babbitt says, where more and more people concerned about protecting public lands have been drawn to growing cities. "You no longer have to go to Washington or New York to find skillful environmental advocates; you can find them right next door. My wager . . . is that in the New West the stakeholders, in all their diversity, can come together and forge a new consensus for public land management." [31]

Many observers of the West don't share Babbitt's optimism. Ranchers and their congressional supporters want Interior to spell out what requirements permittees will need to meet to qualify for the 30 percent grazing fee break. "I'm intrigued by it, and so is a lot of the ranching community," says Brown of the Colorado Cattlemen's Association. But industry leaders say it would be unfair for Interior to start raising fees in 1995 without first putting the incentive program in place.

"Until ranchers are told what they must do to receive the 'incentive-based grazing fee,' [Secretary Babbitt] should not expect support for the proposal," Sen. Domenici said recently. "No standards exist, no rules have been written, no definitions apply. . . . If the Treasury secretary told the American people their taxes would go up for the next three years unless they change their behavior to meet a regulation that does not exist, the public would be enraged. The Interior secretary's 'trust-me-later' fee system should be seen through the same light." [32]

Many ranchers also are reluctant to accept expanded multiple-use advisory boards. In particular, they object to giving seats to the professional staffs of national environmental groups who live far from the rangelands in question. "Allowing Washington lobbyists on regional councils flies in the face of local control," Domencici said. [33]

Brown, as executive vice president of the Colorado Cattlemen's Association, took part in the Colorado Roundtable discussions that paved the way for Babbitt's advisory board proposal. He sees no need to require members to be local residents, although he suggests that "if somebody from New Jersey wants to be on there and somebody from Vail [Colo.] wants to be there, the person from Vail ought to get the nod."

Environmentalists say Babbitt has backed away from giving BLM real power to cut livestock numbers and eliminate grazing altogether on lands they consider too fragile. Many fear the advisory boards will turn into forums that ranchers can use to second-guess agency officials. The consensus-building process could "become an excuse for delaying decisions that need to be made, that you know need to be made if you just go out and look at the land," says NRDC attorney Wald. "It is a dumb way to manage an agency."

Environmental groups are planning to mount a nationwide campaign against Babbitt's program. We're going "to go to the people of Connecticut, Ohio and Florida and let them know what's happening to their lands," says National Audubon Society Vice President Evans, a veteran of many environmental lobbying battles. "Local control is what we've had for the last 60 years under the Taylor Grazing Act," Evans says, "and look at the trouble we're in."

Some environmentalists in the West agree, noting that it's hard to find residents in some small ranching towns willing to speak up against livestock interests. Dougherty, on the other hand, took part in the Colorado Roundtable process and thinks Babbitt's plan has a chance of working in some, but not all, Western ranching areas.

"If this thing is going to ever be resolved," he says, "it's going to be resolved by people who live in the area, care about the dirt, care about the wildlife and care about the local community." ■

OUTLOOK

Calls for Local Control

Eventually, current public land policy debates could lead to a basic reappraisal of how the government balances local and national interests. Since public lands belong to the nation, conservation lobbyists contend, the federal government ought to decide how they will be managed. But environmentalists have never had much faith in BLM, and they say Baca's dismissal frustrated his efforts to bring new blood into the agency.

Meanwhile, timber disputes have been eroding the Forest Service's once sterling reputation. Nelson at the University of Maryland says he detects a growing sense "in the environmental community that the Forest Service may be a hopeless institution after all."

Congress seems unlikely to sell public lands or turn them over to state or local governments. Even so, libertarian economists and the "deep ecology" wing of the environmental movement — who reject any human manipulation of the land — are now asking whether a decentralized system would produce better land and resource management.

Big corporations are now decentralizing their operations, Nelson points out, and public doubts have been growing about whether the national government can solve economic and social problems. As the country rethinks the federal government's role, Nelson suggests, "the public lands in the Western sections of the United States, the areas farthest removed from the federal headquarters in Washington, D.C., could be among the first places where these new directions become evident." [34]

Randal O'Toole, a prominent critic of the Forest Service, has suggested that the agency give each national forest the operating autonomy to set its own goals and collection fees from the public to finance its administrative costs. [35] Nelson has proposed a demonstration project that would turn management of both BLM and national forest lands within the same watershed or other ecological unit over to some type of local governing body representing the people who use them. Nelson thinks Babbitt's proposed advisory boards represent "a half-baked and highly compromised version of moving in that direction."

Some county governments in the West have drafted land-use plans and approved local ordinances demanding that federal land agencies manage forests and rangelands to preserve local residents' time-honored "customs and culture." Ranchers and other land-owning interests have joined together in what they call a "county movement," contending that units of government closest to the land are best qualified to make management decisions. Some ranchers say the county movement could empower communities to control their own destinies, but environmentalists see it as an effort by entrenched local interests to resist any changes in how public lands are managed. (*See story, p. 546.*)

County governments accurately reflect prevailing local opinions about how public lands should be used, Nelson notes, but they are not set up to consider the equally valid interests of outsiders who come to the region to hunt, backpack or birdwatch. "What you're really talking about is an alternative local government structure," Nelson adds, perhaps modeled on private associations that run condominiums, "that allows you to develop voting rights in different ways."

For now, it's up to the Interior Department and the Forest Service — and ultimately, Congress — to decide how public lands should be managed. Ranchers acknowledge they can never afford to buy public lands outright, and according to Brown, many now recognize that "the public wants to be included, wants to have more influence" in federal land policy.

Many environmentalists, on the other hand, have grown frustrated by what they see as the Clinton administration's backsliding on public land issues. NRDC attorney Johanna Wald acknowledges that many environmental activists have grown frustrated after trying to work with BLM and the Forest Service "then seeing very little change occur."

"On balance, I believe that both agencies are salvageable," she adds. "But in a real sense, time is running out." ■

Tom Arrandale is a free-lance writer in Albuquerque, N.M.

Notes

[1] Quoted by John H. Cushman Jr., "Forced, U.S. Sells Gold Land for a Trifle," *The New York Times,* May 17, 1994.

[2] Charles F. Wilkinson, *Crossing the Next Meridian: Land, Water and the Future of the American West* (1992), p. 17.

[3] Speaking Oct. 21, 1993, at a press conference held by Western senators who were filibustering the fiscal 1994 Interior Department appropriations bill to protest the administration's grazing-fee plan. For background, see *CQ Weekly Report,* Oct. 23, 1993, pp. 2875-2979.

[4] Remarks to the National Press Club, Washington, D.C., April 27, 1993.

[5] See Sharon Begley, "The Last Great Giveaway," *Newsweek,* May 30, 1994, p. 66.

[6] Public Resource Associates, "Critique of Title II of HR 322 and S 257," April 23, 1993, p. 1.

[7] See Begley, *op. cit.*

[8] Phil Hocker, "Mining Reform is an Urgent National Priority," *The Environmental Forum,* Environmental Law Institute, July/August 1993, p. 31.

[9] *Ibid.*

[10] Introduction to James S. Lyon, Thomas J. Hilliard and Thomas N. Bethell, *The Burden of Gilt,* Mineral Policy Center, 1993, p. 1. Udall was Interior secretary from 1961-1969.

[11] *Ibid.*

[12] The Senate bill passed on May 25, 1993.

[13] Stephen D. Alfers and Richard P. Graff, *A Comparative Analysis of Mining Fees and Royalties,* Coopers & Lybrand, 1993.

[14] Letter to Sen. Hatch dated Nov. 5, 1993, published in a media kit provided by the Society for Mining Metallurgy and Exploration Inc., a professional group of mining engineers, at their Feb. 14-15, 1994, annual meeting in Albuquerque, N.M.

[15] John Baden, "A Clash of Cultures in the Emerging West," *Northern Lights,* winter 1994.

[16] Bureau of Land Management and U.S. Forest Service "Grazing Fee Review and Evaluation Update of the 1986 Final Report," April 30, 1992.

[17] National Wildlife Federation, *Big Profits at a Big Price: Public Land Ranchers Profit at the Expense of the Range,* September 1992.

[18] Remarks at a hearing of the Senate Energy and Natural Resources Committee, April 20, 1994.

[19] Speaking at the Oct. 21, 1993, press conference held by Western senators.

[20] Quoted by Philip M. Hocker, "Bang or Whimper?" *Clementine,* Mineral Policy Center, winter 1994, p. 2.

[21] Armstrong spoke at the annual meeting of the Society for Mining Metallurgy and Exploration Inc.

[22] Debra H. Struhsacker, "Mining Law Reform and the Unsuitability Debate," *The Professional Geologist,* March 1994, p. 25.

[23] National Wildlife Federation, *op. cit.,* p. 1.

[24] For background, see "The Battle for Natural Resources," *Editorial Research Reports,* Oct. 28, 1988, pp. 537-548.

[25] John Baden, "A modest idea to create balance in range reform," *The Seattle Times,* Nov. 17, 1993. Also see John A. Baden, "Free-market forces favor public good, not privilege," *The Seattle Times,* March 9, 1994.

[26] Karl Hess Jr., *Visions Upon the Land: Man and Nature on the Western Range* (1992), p. 224.

[27] *Ibid.*

[28] Baden, *op. cit.*

[29] Robert H. Nelson, "Government as Theater: Toward a New Paradigm for the Public Lands," *University of Colorado Law Review,* 1994, p. 336.

[30] See *CQ Weekly Report, op. cit.*

[31] Prepared remarks to the Society for Range Management meeting in Colorado Springs, Colo., Feb. 14, 1994.

[32] Remarks at April 20 hearing of Senate Energy and Natural Resources Committee.

[33] *Ibid.*

[34] Nelson, *op. cit.,* p. 355.

[35] See Randal O'Toole, *Reforming the Forest Service* (1988).

Bibliography

Selected Sources Used

Books

Hess, Karl Jr., *Visions Upon the Land: Man and Nature on the Western Range,* Island Press, 1992.

Hess, a range-resource specialist affiliated with the Foundation for Research on Economics and the Environment, critiques what he considers politicized management by federal officials that he contends has caused overgrazing on federal rangelands. As an alternative, Hess proposes that public lands be transferred to private management.

Leshy, John D., *The Mining Law: A Study in Perpetual Motion, Resources for the Future,* 1987.

Leshy, a former Arizona State University law professor who is now the Interior Department's solicitor, contends in this analysis of the General Mining Law of 1872 that it both prevents environmental protection on public lands and interferes with orderly development of their minerals.

O'Toole, Randal, *Reforming the Forest Service,* Island Press, 1988.

O'Toole, a forest economist who has worked with several conservation groups, faults U.S. Forest Service budget policies for giving too much emphasis to cutting timber instead of providing recreation and protecting natural values. He proposes giving each national forest autonomy to develop its own budget priorities and charge fees to finance forest management.

Wilkinson, Charles F., *Crossing the Next Meridian: Land, Water, and the Future of the West,* Island Press, 1992

Wilkinson, a University of Colorado law professor, reviews the 19th-century laws and policies that still control public lands and resources. He suggests revising federal policies to encourage the West to develop a sustainable economy that would be more stable and less destructive than its current resource-extraction industries.

Articles

"Reforming the Hardrock Mining Law," *The Environmental Forum,* Environmental Law Institute, July/August 1993.

Congressional legislation to revise the Mining Law of 1872 is discussed by Sen. Larry E. Craig, R-Idaho, author of an industry-backed bill; Rep. Nick J. Rahall II, D-W.Va., author of House-passed legislation supported by environmentalists; American Mining Congress President John A. Knebel; and Mineral Policy Center President Phil Hocker.

Nelson, Robert H., "Government as Theater: Toward a New Paradigm for the Public Lands," *University of Colorado Law Review,* Vol. 65, Issue 2, 1994.

Nelson is a professor at the University of Maryland and a former Interior Department policy analyst. He describes what he sees as the failure of Interior and the Forest Service to provide professional, scientifically based management of federal lands and resources.

O'Callaghan, Kate, "Whose Agenda for America?" *Audubon,* September/October 1992, p. 80.

Writing for an environmental group's magazine, O'Callaghan traces the emergence of the "wise use" movement to a backlash against tighter federal control over economic development on public lands in Western states.

Struhsacker, Debra W., "Mining Law Reform and the Unsuitability Debate," *The Professional Geologist,* March 1994.

Struhsacker, an environmental-permitting consultant for the mining industry, argues that federal and state environmental laws provide adequate safeguards against damage from mining operations on public lands. She contends that new "unsuitability" criteria that would rule out mining on sensitive public lands would give environmental groups a powerful new tool.

Reports and Studies

Lyon, James S., Thomas J. Hilliard and Thomas N. Bethell, *The Burden of Gilt,* Mineral Policy Center, June 1993.

Published by a group advocating major changes in the Mining Law of 1872, the report estimates there are more than 500,000 abandoned hardrock mine sites in 32 states where untreated arsenic, asbestos and other mining wastes threaten to contaminate rivers, lakes and aquifers.

Mineral Resources Alliance, *Mining Law Reform: Industry View,* Washington, D.C., undated.

An industry-backed group analyzes pending congressional proposals for revising the Mining Law of 1872 and rebutts environmentalists' arguments on royalties, unsuitability rules and other potential changes in the law.

Carlson, Cathy, and John Horning, *Big Profits at a Big Price: Public Land Ranchers Profit at the Expense of the Range,* National Wildlife Federation, September 1992.

The authors review Bureau of Land Management (BLM) data on 18,000 ranches that graze livestock on public lands. They conclude that the 20 biggest operations owned by major corporations and wealthy individuals control BLM allotments covering 20.7 million acres, about 14 percent of the rangelands that BLM manages.

The Next Step

Additional information from UMI's Newspaper & Periodical Abstracts database

Compensation for Land Use

Kempner, Matt, "There goes the neighborhood," *Atlanta Journal Constitution,* April 10, 1994, p. D5.

The dilemma in Atlanta's suburbs of more people creating a demand for wider roads, more grocery stores and shopping centers, which in turn bring more people, is explored in terms of the residents seemingly having no recourse to protect themselves from zoning and land-use planning changes that could devalue their property.

Mathews, Jessica, "Takings exception," *The Washington Post,* Feb. 14, 1994, p. A15.

Jessica Mathews takes exception to the "takings agenda," whose supporters want to reinterpret the Fifth Amendment so that government would have to compensate property owners not just when it physically took possession of a piece of property for a road or school but whenever a regulation lowered a property's value.

Williams, Florence, "The compensation game," *Wilderness,* fall 1993, pp. 28-33.

Corporations and private landowners across the U.S. are besieging claims courts with demands for money, charging that government regulations have caused them a loss of profit for which they should be compensated. This conflict between land development and environmental protection is discussed.

Court Decisions

Bailey, Sandra, "Land use regulations and the takings clause: Are courts applying a tougher standard to regulators after Nollan?" *Natural Resources Journal,* fall 1992, pp. 959-975.

The U.S. Supreme Court's decision in *Nollan v. California Coastal Commission* has been interpreted as heightening the standard of review for government land-use regulations challenged under the takings clause of the Fifth Amendment. Whether the decision actually has made it more difficult for land-use regulations to survive constitutional challenges under the takings clause is discussed. Results indicate that it has not.

Coyle, Marcia, "High court again faces takings contention," *National Law Journal,* March 28, 1994, p. A10.

Dolan v. City of Tigard has set the stage for the next major clash in the Supreme Court between property rights advocates and government land-use regulators. The court will decide when regulation equals condemnation.

Lazarus, Richard J., "Symposium: Putting the correct "spin" on Lucas," *Stanford Law Review,* May 1993, pp. 1411-1432.

The U.S. Supreme Court ruling in *Lucas v. South Carolina Coastal Council* threatened to impose huge financial liabilities on governments that propagate environmental regulations violating the Fifth Amendment ban on takings of private property without "just compensation," Lazarus writes. The reasons why this case will result in fewer takings challenges are discussed.

"Takings clause — Regulatory takings: Lucas vs. South Carolina Coastal Council," *Harvard Law Review,* November 1992, pp. 269-279.

In the case of *Lucas v. South Carolina Coastal Council,* the Supreme Court held that when a regulation strips a parcel of land of all economic value then a state must compensate the landowner unless the prohibited use of the land constitutes a nuisance under the state's common law. The decision is discussed.

Environmental Issues

Armstrong, Scott, "Preserving California dunescape," *Christian Science Monitor,* April 15, 1994, p. 1.

Efforts to protect the California desert are discussed. U.S. Senate passage in April 1994 of a bill that would set aside a desert area the size of Vermont gives significant momentum to a decades-old drive by environmentalists to expand preservation of arid lands, Armstrong writes.

Dushoff, Jonathan, "Gold-plated giveaways: The Mining Act of 1872," *Multinational Monitor,* January 1993, pp. 16-20.

The Mining Act of 1872 gives companies the right to mine certain minerals from federal lands without paying royalties. The law and mining in the U.S., much of which has been environmentally disastrous, are discussed.

Rapp, David, "The President's sputtering green machine," *Governing,* April 1994, p. 92.

Pollution legislation in Congress continues to be bogged down. Environmental problems in 1994 are closer to people's homes and backyards, including local land use. Farmers, ranchers and ordinary property owners will be future targets of anti-pollution regulation.

Rangeland and Grazing Policies

"Babbitt offers new plan in grazing fee dispute," *Congressional Quarterly Weekly Report,* March 19, 1994, p. 670.

On March 17, 1994, Interior Secretary Bruce Babbitt presented a new plan to raise grazing fees and improve range conditions on federal lands. The proposal is discussed.

Camia, Catalina, "Democrats lash out at Babbitt over revised grazing plan," ***Congressional Quarterly Weekly Report,*** **March 12, 1994, p. 598.**

On March 7, 1994, four key Democratic allies, led by Sen. George Mitchell, D-Maine, dealt a serious blow to the Clinton administration's plan to charge higher grazing fees and improve federal rangeland conditions. Criticisms of the plan expressed in a scathing letter sent to Interior Secretary Babbitt by the four lawmakers are discussed.

Lustgarden, Steve, "Earth: Rangeland reform?" ***Vegetarian Times,*** **August 1993, p. 19.**

The controversial grazing of cattle on the fragile, arid Western rangeland is discussed. Western cattle ranchers have what some call a cushy deal where $1.86 is all it costs to graze a cow and her calf on federal land for a month.

Williamson, Lonnie, "All's not quiet on the Western front," ***Outdoor Life,*** **December 1993, pp. 38-39.**

The Clinton administration's proposal for managing public rangelands, the effects of which can be heard loud and clear across the West, is discussed. Range conditions as reported by the GAO and the reform package for improving them are described.

Research and Analysis

Feitelson, Eran, "The spatial effects of land use regulations," ***Journal of the American Planning Association,*** **autumn 1993, pp. 461-472.**

An approach for analyzing the likely spatial effects of land-use regulations and growth controls is presented. Planners must identify such effects to evaluate the success of different measures and their implications for economic growth and citizen welfare.

Gurwitt, Rob, "To see the impact on land use, press F1," ***Governing,*** **July 1993, pp. 21-22.**

Researchers at UCLA-Berkeley have come up with a computer model that mimics the land-use development process and its responses to different policy choices. The value of the computer to planning agencies is discussed.

O'Looney, John, "Framing a social market for community responsibility: Governing in an age of NIMBYs and LULUs," ***National Civic Review,*** **winter 1993, pp. 44-62.**

Two dominant but failing policy approaches to handling needed but locally unwanted land uses — a political regulatory approach and a deregulatory or market-mechanism approach — are examined. It is suggested that between these two policy poles, two more effective alternatives — an "organized market" approach and a "market framework" approach—may exist.

State and Local Policies

Gale, Dennis E., "Eight state-sponsored growth management programs: A comparative analysis," ***Journal of the American Planning Association,*** **autumn 1992, pp. 425-439.**

One of the most significant developments in the advancement of comprehensive land-use planning in the U.S. has been the enactment of programs designed to foster growth management by some state legislatures, Gale writes. Eight state-sponsored growth management systems, which reveal wide diversity in program features and provisions, are compared.

Hamilton, Joan, "A bolder BLM," ***Sierra,*** **July 1993, pp. 51-53.**

Jim Baca is the new director of the BLM, which is entrusted with protecting some 270 million acres of public land in Alaska and the West. Baca, whom Hamilton calls a master at figuring out ways for government to protect and profit from land it owns, is profiled.

"LESA bill passed in California," ***Journal of Soil & Water Conservation,*** **January 1994, p. 46.**

A bill requiring the development of a state land evaluation/site assessment (LESA) model has been passed in California. The California agencies will revise the model used by the federal government to suit their needs.

Maines, David R., and Jeffrey C. Bridger, "Narratives, community and land use decisions," ***Social Science Journal,*** **1992, pp. 363-380.**

The narrative character of community is explored, and it is argued that communities are intrinsically storied. State tourism and land-use decisions are ideographic situations in which entrenchment in institutions and in the political economy of communities is found.

Sherblom, Becky, "State land development standards project — A flawed concept," ***Public Management,*** **June 1993, p. 18.**

The National Association of Home Builders (NAHB) Research Center has been working on land development standards that could be adopted at the state level. The purpose of such standards is discussed.

"Tough decisions in the island state," ***State Legislatures,*** **July 1993, p. 8.**

Hawaii's Legislature has appropriated $137 million for the Office of Hawaiian Affairs for compensation of past wrongful uses of the state's lands since its statehood in 1959. Several bills and resolutions related to Hawaiian sovereignty are discussed.

Back Issues

Great Research on Current Issues Starts Right Here...Recent topics covered by The CQ Researcher are listed below. Before May 1991, reports were published under the name of Editorial Research Reports.

DECEMBER 1992
Crackdown on Smoking
The New CIA
Eating Disorders
Women and AIDS

JANUARY 1993
Hate Crimes
Child Sexual Abuse
Nuclear Fusion
U.S. Trade Policy

FEBRUARY 1993
Community Policing
Europe's New Right
School Censorship
Violence Against Women

MARCH 1993
Gay Rights
Aid to Russia
War on Drugs
TV Violence

APRIL 1993
Head Start
High-Speed Rail
Children's Legal Rights
Muslims in America

MAY 1993
Cults in America
Preventing Teen Pregnancy
Software Piracy
National Parks

JUNE 1993
Food Safety
Prostitution
Childhood Immunizations
National Service

JULY 1993
Electric Cars
Population Growth
Downward Mobility
Intelligence Testing

AUGUST 1993
Mental Illness
Bilingual Education
Foreign Policy Burden
School Funding

SEPTEMBER 1993
Suburban Crime
Public Housing
Supreme Court Preview
Immigration Reform

OCTOBER 1993
Airline Safety
Disaster Response
Science in the Courtroom
The Glass Ceiling

NOVEMBER 1993
Paying for Retirement
Charitable Giving
Privacy in the Workplace
Adoption

DECEMBER 1993
U.S. Vietnam-Relations
Learning Disabilities
Child Care
Space Program's Future

JANUARY 1994
Racial Tensions in Schools
South Africa's Future
Worker Retraining
Regulating Pesticides

FEBRUARY 1994
Prison Overcrowding
Water Quality
Religion in Schools
Juvenile Justice

MARCH 1994
Underground Economy
Education Standards
Gambling Boom
Private Management of Public Schools

APRIL 1994
Reproductive Ethics
U.S.-China Trade
Soccer in America
Talk Show Democracy

MAY 1993
Traffic Congestion
Women's Health Issues
Mutual Funds
Political Scandals

JUNE 1993
Education and Gender
Gun Control

Back issues are available for $4.00 (subscribers) or $7.00 (non-subscribers). Quantity discounts apply to orders over ten. To order, call Congressional Quarterly Customer Service at (202) 887-8621.

Binders are available for $16.00. To order call 1-800-638-1710. Please refer to stock number 648.

Future Topics

- ***Nuclear Arms Cleanup***
- ***Vitamins***
- ***Public Opinion and Foreign Policy***

THE CQ Researcher

PUBLISHED BY CONGRESSIONAL QUARTERLY INC.

Nuclear Arms Cleanup

What should be done with stockpiled plutonium and uranium?

The Soviet Union's demise five years ago brought an end to the Cold War, the 45-year arms race between the Soviet superpower and the United States. The euphoria that greeted the end of this bloodless conflict has dampened somewhat, however, as U.S. officials and their counterparts in the former Soviet republics come to grips with its legacy: thousands of highly toxic and politically destabilizing nuclear weapons. With no more perceived need for much of their vast arsenals, the governments have agreed to dismantle large numbers of nuclear warheads. But the agencies involved in this task face a daunting technical and political problem: what to do with the thousands of tons of plutonium and uranium that are the main ingredients of nuclear weapons.

INSIDE THIS ISSUE

CQ June 24, 1994 • Volume 4, No. 24 • 553-576

Formerly Editorial Research Reports

June 24, 1994
Volume 4, No. 24

EDITOR
Sandra Stencel

MANAGING EDITOR
Thomas J. Colin

ASSOCIATE EDITOR
Richard L. Worsnop

STAFF WRITERS
Charles S. Clark
Mary H. Cooper
Kenneth Jost

PRODUCTION EDITOR
Sarah E. Merritt

EDITORIAL ASSISTANT
Michael M. Taylor

GRAPHICS
P. Eloise Fuller

PUBLISHED BY
Congressional Quarterly Inc.

CHAIRMAN
Andrew Barnes

VICE CHAIRMAN
Andrew P. Corty

EDITOR AND PUBLISHER
Neil Skene

EXECUTIVE EDITOR
Robert W. Merry

ASSOCIATE PUBLISHER
John J. Coyle

MARKETING AND SALES DIRECTOR
Edward S. Hauck

The CQ Researcher (ISSN 1056-2036). Formerly Editorial Research Reports. Published weekly (48 times per year, not printed the first Friday of any month with five Fridays) by Congressional Quarterly Inc., 1414 22nd St., N.W., Washington, D.C. 20037. Rates are furnished upon request. Second-class postage paid at Washington, D.C. POSTMASTER: Send address changes to The CQ Researcher, 1414 22nd St., N.W., Washington, D.C. 20037.

COVER: WORKERS IN A PLUTONIUM-STORAGE FACILITY AT THE ROCKY FLATS PLANT, IN GOLDEN, COLO. (DEPARTMENT OF ENERGY)

Nuclear Arms Cleanup

BY MARY H. COOPER

THE ISSUES

High in the Texas Panhandle, rows of earth-covered concrete "igloos"add a bizarre look to the Southwestern landscape outside Amarillo. The thick-walled storage bunkers hold deadly plutonium, used in the weapons of mass destruction that have terrified the world for the past half-century.

On the other side of the globe, more nuclear storage facilities dot the landscape near the Russian cities of Chelyabinsk, Tomsk and Krasnoyarsk. Here in central Asia, most of the former Soviet Union's nuclear warheads were produced.

Since the Cold War ended with the Soviet Union's demise five years ago, the production of nuclear weapons has virtually ground to a halt. Today, the nuclear weapons complexes in Russia and the United States have a new mission — dismantling the arms they once produced and disposing of the lethal ingredients before they fall into the wrong hands and are fashioned into new warheads.

Empowering the new mission are the two key Strategic Arms Reduction Treaties (START). President George Bush signed START I in July 1991 with the Soviet Union, and START II with Russia and three other former Soviet republics in January 1993, after the U.S.S.R.'s breakup. Under the treaties, the U.S. strategic, or long-range, nuclear stockpile would be reduced from more than 12,500 operational weapons in 1991 to 3,500 in 2003. Russia's strategic arsenal would decline from more than 10,500 to 3,500 weapons over the same period.* Under subsequent agreements, sea- and land-based tactical, or shorter-range, warheads would be reduced, further shrinking the nuclear arsenals. [1]

Department of Energy

Negotiators for these landmark agreements stopped short, however, of deciding what was to become of these weapons once they were no longer deployed. But Presidents Bush and Clinton negotiated later accords with Russian President Boris N. Yeltsin to dismantle them. Now, the two superpowers are expected to dismantle a total of some 30,000 strategic and tactical nuclear weapons over the next decade. [2]

But dismantling weapons is only one step toward nuclear disarmament. If the terms of START I are followed, there will be 100 tons of plutonium to contend with. A man-made substance created in 1941, plutonium is produced by irradiating uranium in nuclear reactors and then chemically separating it from the other uranium byproducts. Both plutonium and highly enriched uranium (HEU), the other main component of nuclear weapons, are highly radioactive and persist in the environment for tens of thousands of years.* Exposure to tiny amounts of plutonium dust can cause cancer, and HEU is only slightly less toxic.

Dismantling nuclear weapons also poses a significant weapons-proliferation risk: It takes as little as 7 pounds of plutonium, or several times that amount of HEU, to make a nuclear weapon. HEU can be made unusable for weapons by converting it into fuel for power plants. But plutonium must be altered and ultimately removed from human access to eliminate the risk of its reuse for weapons.

"What we need to do is to find a solution to the radioactive-waste problem," says Martin Gelfand, research director for the Safe Energy Communication Council, a coalition of advocacy groups that are concerned about nuclear safety. "But we have to be sure that this doesn't come at the expense of the environment and public health."

For this reason, some experts say, the U.S. and Russian nuclear storage facilities only offer an interim solution to the disposal of nuclear weapons. Meanwhile, as weapons-grade plutonium piles up, policy-makers are still debating how to get rid of it.

Political instability in Russia lends special urgency to the problem. Beset by economic problems, the Russian government is viewed as unable to adequately protect its arsenals from theft or sabotage. There are fears that the country's powerful criminal cartels may gain access to Russian nuclear components and sell them to terrorist groups or other governments, such as North Korea or Iraq, that are thought to be developing nuclear arms. Although there have been no confirmed thefts from Russia's nuclear arsenal, numerous reports are circulating

* Belarus, Kazakhstan and Ukraine have agreed to transfer some 3,000 strategic nuclear warheads in their territories to Russia. The United States ratified START I Oct. 1, 1992, but the treaty has not entered into force, pending resolution of changes proposed by Ukraine. START II awaits ratification by all parties.

* Less than 1 percent of the uranium found, known as Uranium-235, can sustain a nuclear reaction. To create more concentrated amounts of U-235, uranium must be processed to produce either low enriched uranium (LEU), which contains 3-5 percent U-235 and is suitable for reactor fuel, or highly enriched uranium (HEU), containing more than 90 percent U-235, for use in nuclear weapons.

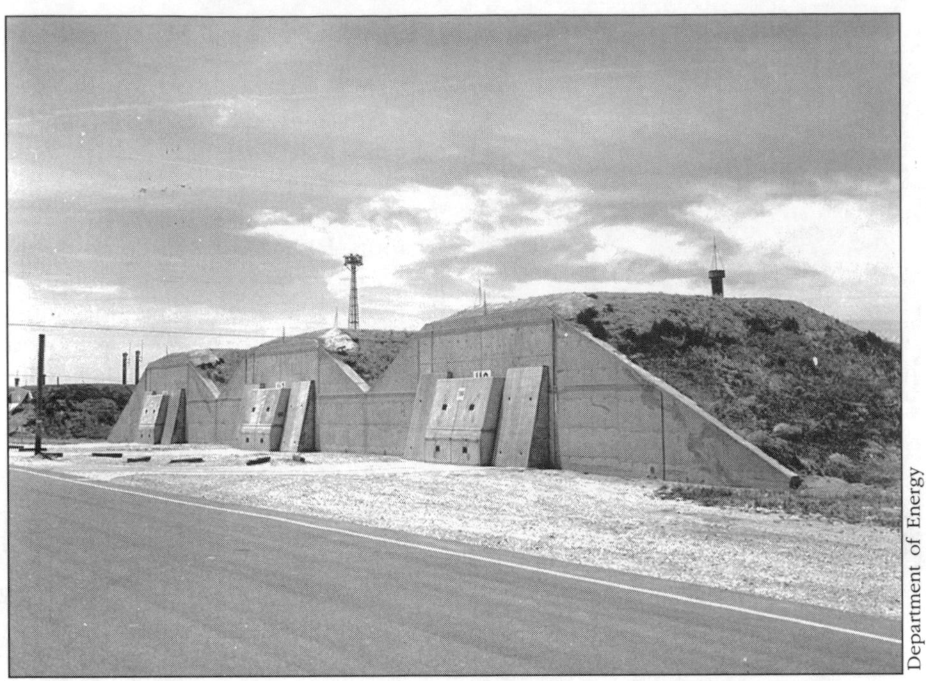
Department of Energy

Bunkers at the Pantex Plant in Amarillo, Texas, store nuclear weapons to be dismantled and plutonium from disassembled weapons. Double-steel doors to the concrete and steel "igloos" are shielded by 25-ton concrete slabs, which are moved by giant forklifts.

about attempted deals to sell weapons-grade nuclear material on the black market. [3]

The Clinton administration last year outlined a strategy for disposing of nuclear weapons. Announced Sept. 27, 1993, the new policy calls for:

- Safeguarding existing stockpiles of plutonium and HEU;
- Buying HEU from dismantled Russian weapons for conversion to fuel for civilian reactors;
- Seeking a multilateral ban on the creation of new plutonium and HEU for weapons;
- Reviewing the long-term options for plutonium disposition.

Because plutonium is also a byproduct of uranium-fueled nuclear reactors used to generate power, the problem of disposing of excess nuclear materials is not limited to the military. "In addition to military material, there are over 900 metric tons of plutonium in various forms within the civilian nuclear fuel cycle," said Richard J.K. Stratford, director of the State Department's Office of Nuclear Energy Affairs. "Almost 90 metric tons of this civilian material is directly weapons-usable, separated, reactor-grade plutonium. Clearly, therefore, policies on excess nuclear materials from weapons must be an integral part of our efforts to address these broader concerns." [4]

In the past six months, several American research groups have examined ways to dispose of weapons-grade plutonium and uranium. Most dismiss such exotic solutions as exploding the material underground or in space. Two alternatives have emerged as the most feasible, given currently available technology: using plutonium and HEU as fuel in nuclear reactors or processing the material into glasslike "logs," from which it could not easily be extracted and used for making bombs. The logs would be buried in deep underground repositories.

Using weapons-grade nuclear material as fuel in reactors would not only yield electricity but also a byproduct that is too "hot" to handle easily and would require sophisticated technology to turn into reliable weapons. "Instead of looking at military plutonium as a curse to be gotten rid of," said Edward D. Fuller, president of the American Nuclear Society, an industry group, "it should be brought fully into the civilian economy, to be looked upon as one more resource that can be recycled for civilian use to make electricity; analogous, for instance, to surplus tanks that can be cut up for steel scrap to be reused to make cars." [5]

But using plutonium for fuel would fly in the face of the Clinton administration's strategy for preventing proliferation announced last September. Clinton declared that the United States would no longer produce plutonium, either for defense or civilian purposes. And earlier this year, Energy Secretary Hazel R. O'Leary strengthened that policy by announcing that ongoing research into advanced reactors fueled by plutonium would be terminated. (*See "At Issue," p. 569.*)

The other main alternative for nuclear-waste disposal, vitrification, mixes plutonium from weapons with waste from civilian nuclear reactors to create glasslike logs, which would be buried in underground repositories. In 1982, Congress designated Yucca Mountain in Nevada as the country's sole deep geological repository for high-level nuclear wastes.

Although vitrification seems to be emerging as the most likely solution to nuclear weapons disposal, it too presents risks. Plutonium-239, the main ingredient of nuclear weapons, has a half-life of 24,390 years. That means it takes more than 240 centuries to lose half its radioactivity, a period many times longer than recorded human history. "We can't solve the problem by throwing the waste into a hole in the desert," says Gelfand. "Future generations will have to deal with this after we're dead and gone. You can't just cover this stuff up with some desert sand and make it go away."

For the same reasons that plutonium remains lethal for so long, the facilities where nuclear weapons were made and tested sustain enduring contamination from radioactive byproducts. The Department of Energy (DOE) estimates it will cost $300 billion over the next 35 years to clean up the weapons sites. And some of them appear to be virtually beyond salvation. The first land-use study of nuclear weapons sites, for the Hanford Reservation in Washington state, recommended that 9.4 square miles of the 560-square mile site be barred to human habitation "for the foreseeable future." [6]

As policy-makers debate the proposals for disposing of nuclear weapons and cleaning up the environmental damage they have caused, these are some of the issues they will consider:

Can the environmental damage resulting from bomb production in the U.S. be reversed?

For a half century, the government and the private contractors that made up the nuclear weapons industry made and tested warheads with national security as their overriding concern. Since the end of the Cold War, the Department of Energy, the federal agency that is responsible for all facets of nuclear energy, has shifted its focus from producing weapons to dismantling them and finding ways to dispose of the fissile, or radioactive, materials. Today, only one facility produces material for nuclear weapons. The Savannah River Plant in Aiken, S.C., continues to produce tritium, a short-lived gas that is an essential ingredient in nuclear weapons and must be renewed periodically.

Another key focus of the agency's activities is cleaning up the 14 major sites around the country involved in the research, production and testing of nuclear weapons. (*See map, p. 560.*) Only recently, the Energy Department has undertaken extensive land-use and environmental-impact studies to determine the extent of environmental damage those activities caused. The agency is undertaking the cleanup along with the private contractors that have worked since 1941 to develop the nation's nuclear arsenal, the Environmental Protection Agency (EPA) and state environmental agencies.

Hanford Reservation, formerly a plutonium-making facility (known as a reprocessing plant), is among the country's oldest nuclear facilities and one of the most contaminated weapons sites in the United States. It also is the object of the first long-term study of weapons facilities to be released. With cleanup efforts well under way, Hanford contains some areas that are expected to be decontaminated before the end of the year, according to Theresa Bergman, principal engineer at Westinghouse Hanford Co., DOE's contractor at the site. The rest of the site "is expected to be completed sometime between 2020 and 2030," says Bergman, who was involved in the land-use study.

There is one area of the reservation, however, that the study group predicts will remain off-limits for human residence "for the foreseeable future." That may mean forever, Bergman says. "They didn't want to use the term 'forever' because there is the expectation that we wouldn't stop working on the cleanup as long as there is a waste legacy left."

The area in question, the Central Plateau, today contains 149 tanks holding radioactive and other toxic waste. "Because wastes were also discharged directly onto the ground or buried in the soil, the Central Plateau is a unique waste situation," Bergman says.

Surprisingly, the worst long-term contaminants at Hanford are not plutonium or uranium wastes but nitrates and carbon tetrachloride, which are chemical byproducts of plutonium reprocessing. "In general, radioactive waste decays and eventually goes

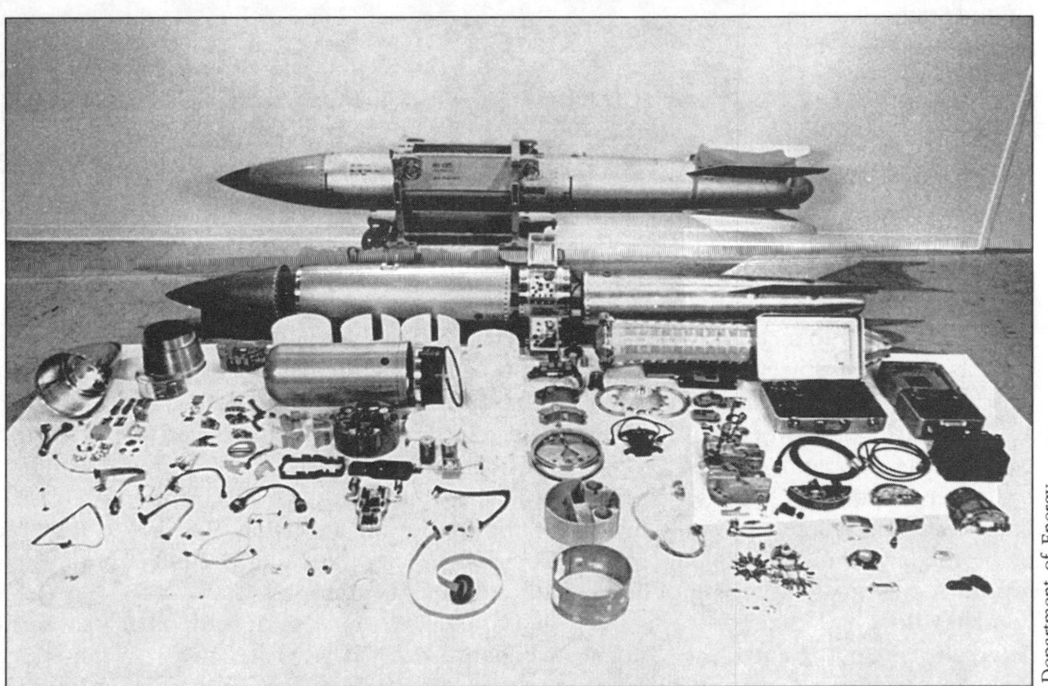

Department of Energy

Designed to be dropped by an airplane, the B-61 nuclear bomb (shown intact at rear) contains more than 6,000 parts, many shown here, including the cylinder-shaped nuclear core, in left foreground.

away, though it may be a very, very long time," Bergman says. "But unless they degrade naturally — and the ones in question here don't — chemicals won't go away at all."

Some participants in the land-use study, chiefly Yakima Indians who someday want to return to their ancestral lands on the Hanford reservation, recommended cleaning up the Central Plateau. "Cleaning up the plateau would be an extremely difficult and expensive proposition," Bergman says. "Lots more new technology would have to be developed to rid the area of contaminants."

Should the United States help clean up the former Soviet Union's nuclear weapons complex?

While cleaning up nuclear weapons production sites is a daunting task in the United States, it promises to be Herculean in the former Soviet Union. Not only did the state exercise complete control over the weapons complex, it subordinated environmental and health concerns to national security to a startling degree, experts say. The Soviet government's suppression of the nuclear explosion at the Chernobyl power plant in 1986 typified the problem.

Earlier incidents at Soviet weapons-producing plants are only now being made public, such as the recent report of systematic dumping of high-level radioactive waste from the Chelyabinsk plant into the Techa River, a short distance from population centers. [7] Recent Russian publications also document the exposure of nearby populations to high levels of radioactivity from hundreds of above-ground nuclear explosions, especially in Kazakhstan and the Altai area of Siberian Russia. [8]

Thus far, U.S. efforts to help Russia dispose of the weapons it inherited from the Soviet Union have focused almost exclusively on non-proliferation goals rather than environmental restoration. The 1991 Soviet Nuclear Threat Reduction Act helps pay for measures to speed the dismantlement process and safeguard the stockpiles of nuclear materials in Russia. Nunn-Lugar, as the bill is commonly known, after its chief sponsors, Sens. Sam Nunn, D-Ga., and Richard G. Lugar, R-Ind., authorized the president to establish and conduct programs to assist the demilitarization of the former Soviet Union. To date, Congress has appropriated $1.2 billion for programs to transport, store, safeguard and destroy nuclear and other weapons.

Many Republican lawmakers are reluctant to spend more money for aid to Russia. Citing political instability in Russia and budget concerns in the United States, Senate Minority Leader Bob Dole, R-Kan., has called for an aid freeze. [9] But some nuclear experts in the United States say that helping Russia clean up its nuclear contamination may be appropriate out of national security as well as environmental concerns. "I think we should embark on an environmental-restoration program in Russia as part of a broader effort to solve the brain-drain problem there," says Thomas B. Cochran, senior scientist at the Natural Resources Defense Council (NRDC) and a leading expert on Soviet nuclear issues.

Department of Energy

Storage buildings at the Idaho National Engineering Laboratory, in Idaho Falls, hold drums containing plutonium-contaminated waste awaiting shipment to the Waste Isolation Pilot Plant in Carlsbad, N.M.

Cochran's fear, which is shared by many, is that Russian nuclear scientists, deprived of their livelihoods by the shutdown of their country's weapons plants, may be tempted to either sell their technical knowledge or emigrate to countries that want to build nuclear weapons. Such defections would greatly undermine the international non-proliferation regime supported by the United States. "There are lots of joint programs," Cochran says, "that we could initiate to provide alternative employment for people involved in the Russian weapons programs."

Candidates for joint U.S.-Russian ventures to clean up nuclear sites in Russia abound, Cochran says, including Chelyabinsk. "After they quit dumping radioactive material into the Techa River, they put it into reservoirs along the river," he says. "We could help clean up those sites and also stabilize the groundwater contamination under nearby Lake Karachay, where there is a radioactive 'halo' caused by . . . radioactive cesium and other materials dumped there."

Should the United States try to reach an international agreement banning production of weapons-grade nuclear material?

As part of his counterproliferation strategy announced last Sept. 27, President Clinton proposed a multilateral convention banning the production of highly enriched uranium or plutonium unless it is monitored by the International Atomic Energy Agency (IAEA). That U.N. agency monitors adherence to the 1970 Nuclear Non-Proliferation Treaty banning the acquisition of nuclear weapons by any countries that did not already possess them. The following month, the U.N. General Assembly adopted a resolution in support of a "cutoff treaty" that would prohibit the production of fissile material for nuclear weapons.

The administration subsequently obtained agreement from the Russian government to halt plutonium production for weapons at the three remaining Russian production reactors near Tomsk and Krasnoyarsk. Because those cities depend on the reactors for heat and electrical power, however, the Russians conditioned their shutdown on U.S. help in setting up coal- and gas-fired plants to replace them. U.S. technical experts were expected to travel to the sites in early June to begin work on this project.

Clinton also announced that the United States would not reprocess plutonium for either nuclear weapons or as a fuel for civilian nuclear power plants and that the administration does not encourage the civil uses of plutonium anywhere. Accordingly, the administration has decided to phase out two experimental reactors — the integral fast reactor and the advanced liquid-metal reactor — built in the pursuit of a safer and more efficient energy source and run by the Argonne National Laboratory at the University of Chicago. That proposal awaits congressional action.

Advocates of these research programs criticize the administration for shutting them down because they offer a means of rendering plutonium less readily convertible to weapons. Critics also say the president sent a mixed message by declaring that the United States would maintain its existing commitments regarding the use of plutonium in civil nuclear programs in Western Europe and Japan. Under those commitments, entered into by President Ronald Reagan in 1981, the United States allows countries with advanced nuclear-power programs to use plutonium recovered from U.S.-supplied uranium for their reactors so long as they pose no proliferation threat. Because of their close relationship with the United States, that essentially means Japan and Western Europe.

In addition to Russia, in fact, Japan, France, Belgium, Germany and Switzerland already use or are considering plans to use mixed uranium-plutonium oxide (MOX) fuel to power their civilian nuclear reactors. Britain is about to bring a plutonium-burning reactor online. "The Reagan-Bush policy was highly discriminatory," said Paul Leventhal, president of the Nuclear Control Institute, a nonprofit research center in Washington. "It allowed Western European countries and Japan to have access to U.S.-origin plutonium while denying it to others." [10]

But many nuclear experts support the administration's efforts to curtail plutonium production for any purpose. "The chance to change the nuclear course is now better than ever," said Brian G. Chow, a senior physical scientist at the Rand Corp. in Santa Monica, Calif., and co-author of a recent study on plutonium disposition. [11] "Many countries, including some of the most ardent plutonium supporters such as France, Germany and the U.K., have scaled back their plutonium activities as a result of political and economic pressure. Even Japan's plutonium program faces delays. Considering that a continuation of the past course would lead to many countries being situated dangerously and ambiguously near the nuclear threshold, we have no alternative but to make a serious attempt to stem the plutonium tide." ■

BACKGROUND

Nuclear Age Begins

The atom bomb dropped by the United States on Hiroshima, Japan, Aug. 6, 1945, was the product of an intensive race by U.S. scientists to beat Nazi Germany to the atomic bomb. That effort, known as the Manhattan Project, built on the discoveries of Albert Einstein, Enrico Fermi, Glenn T. Seaborg and other pioneers in the field of nuclear physics to create the most powerful weapon in history.

The A-bomb that killed 142,000 people in Hiroshima and the one dropped over Nagasaki three days later that took 79,000 lives are the only nuclear devices ever used in combat. Those early weapons utilized the energy released in nuclear fission, which occurs when an atom of a rare isotope of uranium or its man-made derivative, plutonium, disintegrates when struck by a neutron. The result of this collision is the fission, or splitting, of the enriched uranium atom, producing two new atoms and heat. It also produces more neutrons, which then cause more atoms to fission in a chain reaction.

When nuclear fission is harnessed to produce electrical power, the fis-

Continued on p. 562

Efforts Launched at U.S. Nuclear Weapons Plants . . .

Cleanup efforts are under way to remove radioactive and chemical pollution at 14 major U.S. facilities that were involved in the production of nuclear weapons for the Department of Energy and its predecessor agencies. Four of these sites (indicated by asterisks) are also involved in dismantling warheads and storing excess plutonium and highly enriched uranium. A 15th site, near Carlsbad, N.M., is being set up to store nuclear wastes.

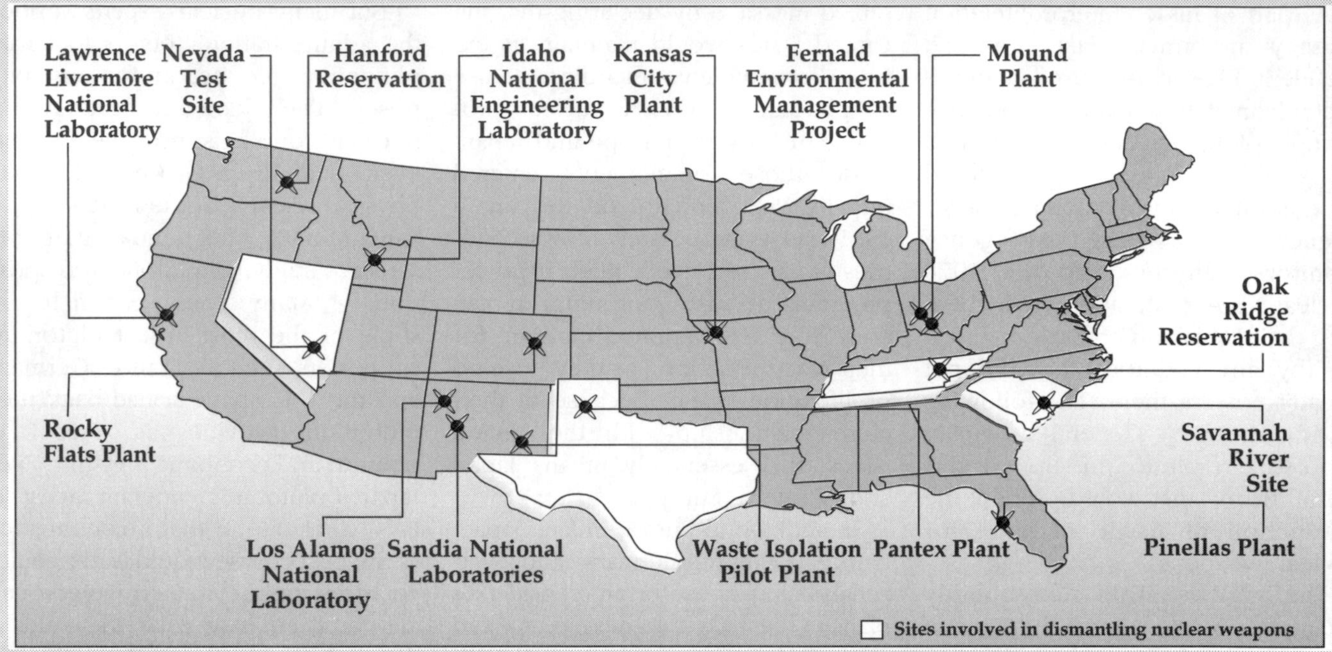

Weapons Research Sites

Lawrence Livermore National Laboratory, Livermore, Calif. (established 1952)

Built for weapons research and development. Now a superfund site. Problems include contamination of soil and groundwater on-site and beyond by tritium, lead, chromium and gasoline. May be consolidated with Los Alamos National Laboratory.

Cleanup cost: $362 million appropriated for FY 1990-94
$80 million requested FY 1995
Size: 7,680 acres

Los Alamos National Laboratory, Los Alamos, N.M. (1942)

Built for weapons research and development, nuclear fission and fusion, nuclear safeguards and environmental research. Now contains one of the world's biggest radioactive waste dumps. Some underground waste-storage tanks have been removed.

Cleanup cost: $608 million appropriated FY 1990-94
$180 million requested FY 1995
Size: 48,000 acres.

Sandia National Laboratories, Albuquerque, N.M. (1945)

Conducts research and development of all non-nuclear components of nuclear weapons, develops transportation and storage systems for nuclear weapons. Studies under way to assess extent of contamination from hazardous waste.

Cost: $259 million appropriated FY 1990-94
$52 million requested FY 1995
Size: 2,842 acres

Nuclear Materials Production Sites

Fernald Environmental Management Project (formerly the Feed Materials Production Center), Fernald, Ohio (1953; renamed 1991)

Produced nuclear reactor fuel until 1989, when all production operations stopped. Closed permanently in 1991 when cleanup began of on-site and surrounding areas contaminated with uranium dust. Now a superfund site, with groundwater cleanup under way; Great Miami Aquifer considered at risk.

Cost: $1.2 billion appropriated FY 1990-94
$294 million requested FY 1995
Size: 1,050 acres

Hanford Reservation, Richland, Wash. (1943)

Extracted plutonium from uranium for weapons and built and tested advanced reactor designs. All plutonium production shut down in 1989. Now a superfund site. Billions of gallons of radioactive and chemical wastes reportedly were released into the air, soil and groundwater, some reaching the Columbia River. Risk seen from explosion of hydrogen gas building up in waste-storage tanks. Highly radioactive reactor fuel rods were buried in shallow trenches on the site.

Cost: $5.3 billion appropriated FY 1990-94
$1.6 billion requested FY 1995
Size: 360,000 acres

Idaho National Engineering Laboratory, Idaho Falls (1949)

Develops reactors and manages nuclear waste and highly

. . . to Clean Up Contamination and Dismantle Warheads

enriched uranium (HEU) from spent naval reactor fuel. Now a superfund site. Has more than half the country's transuranic wastes (synthetic radioisotopes generated in reactors) stored in drums. Plutonium contamination from unlined burial trenches and chemicals in groundwater may be contaminating Snake River aquifer.

Cost: $1.9 billion appropriated FY 1990-94
$502 million requested FY 1995
Size: 570,000 acres

***Oak Ridge Reservation, Oak Ridge, Tenn. (1942)**

Consists of Oak Ridge National Laboratory, the K-25 site (uranium enrichment) and the Y-12 plant, original site of the Manhattan Project. Once produced enriched uranium and other weapons components; still fabricates materials for nuclear-powered submarines. Currently stores highly enriched uranium (HEU) from weapons dismantled at Pantex. Now a superfund site, it has caused extensive pollution from mercury, arsenic and other toxic materials. K-25 was shut down in 1987 due to environmental problems.

Cost: $2.8 billion appropriated FY 1990-94
$722 million requested FY 1995
Size: 5,400 acres

***Savannah River Site, Aiken, S.C. (1952)**

Produces tritium and once produced plutonium. Currently reprocesses tritium received from dismantled nuclear weapons. Vitrification facility may be used in future to dispose of excess weapons plutonium. Now a superfund site. Aging reactors shut down in 1988. Tuscaloosa Aquifer under the site is contaminated by solvents and tritium.

Cost: $3.2 billion appropriated FY 1990-94
$744 million requested FY 1995
Size: 192,000 acres

Warhead Production Sites

Kansas City Plant, Kansas City, Mo. (1949)

Produces electronic, plastic and metal components for nuclear weapons. Now a superfund site. Soil contamination from PCBs and other toxic chemicals poses threat.

Cost: $88 million appropriated FY 1990-94
$13 million requested FY 1995
Size: 320 acres

Mound Plant, Miamisburg, Ohio (1947)

Produced tritium and later detonators, cables and other non-nuclear components for nuclear warheads. Production discontinued in 1993, when mission shifted to cleanup. Now a superfund site. Plutonium contaminating soil may threaten groundwater.

Cost: $184 million appropriated FY 1990-94
$45 million requested FY 1995
Size: 306 acres

***Pantex Plant, Amarillo, Texas (1952)**

Assembled weapons; now responsible for maintaining nuclear weapons stockpile, dismantling excess weapons and temporarily storing plutonium cores and other materials from dismantled warheads. Radioactive and chemical contamination of storage areas, buildings and soil is now being assessed; cleanup of some areas is under way.

Cost: $128 million appropriated FY 1990-94
$46 million requested FY 1995
Size: 8,960 acres

Pinellas Plant, near St. Petersburg, Fla. (1956)

Manufactures neutron generators, thermal batteries and other components for nuclear weapons, as well as radioisotope thermoelectric generators using plutonium. Has 14 contaminated areas, including groundwater contamination from tritium, lead and other toxic metals.

Cost: $33 million appropriated FY 1990-94
$9 million requested FY 1995
Size: 128 acres

Rocky Flats Plant, Golden, Colo. (1952)

Produced plutonium "pits," or cores, and other radioactive components. Production has stopped, with cleanup now the main mission. Now a superfund site; drinking water in Denver suburbs may be at risk from plutonium and other contaminants.

Cost: $1.3 billion appropriated FY 1990-94
$640 million requested FY 1995
Size: 6,550 acres

Weapons Testing Site

***Nevada Test Site, 65 miles northwest of Las Vegas, Nev. (1951)**

Used to test nuclear weapons. Last used for underground testing Sept. 23, 1992. Currently used as dump for material from weapons dismantled at Pantex plant. Yucca Mountain, for deep underground storage of waste, is located here. Problems include contamination from radioactive plutonium, cesium and strontium, largely the result of more than 1,100 above-ground tests, which were banned in 1963.

Cost: $227 million appropriated FY 1990-94
$65 million requested FY 1995
Size: 864,000 acres

Future Waste Site

Waste Isolation Pilot Plant, Carlsbad, N.M. (1981)

Being built to demonstrate feasibility of storing plutonium waste underground. Ten miles of tunnels 2,150 feet below the surface are to receive radioactive waste from nuclear weapons now temporarily stored in 10 states.

Cost: $746 million appropriated FY 1990-94
$185 million requested FY 1995
Size: 10,240 acres

* Sites currently involved in dismantling and temporary storage of nuclear weapons and materials.

Sources: Department of Energy, World Resources Institute, Military Production Network (Belmont, Mass.)

Continued from p. 559

sion is carefully controlled to stop the chain reaction. In weapons, the chain reaction is enhanced to obtain the biggest possible explosion. The first successful nuclear weapon test surprised even its makers: The bomb exploded above the Mariana Islands on July 16, 1945, was equivalent to 20,000 tons of TNT.

Even before the bombs were dropped over Japan, work was proceeding to create an even more powerful device using the principle of thermonuclear fusion, which is similar to the reaction that creates solar energy and heat. Work on the "Super" project, centered at laboratories in Los Alamos, N.M., and Oak Ridge, Tenn., was suspended during the war. After the Soviet Union exploded its first fission bomb in 1949, however, President Harry S Truman gave the order to resume research to develop the far more destructive thermonuclear weapon.

A new site, on the Savannah River in South Carolina, was built to produce tritium, a key ingredient in this device, also known as the hydrogen bomb because the explosive energy it produces derives from burning an isotope of hydrogen. The project was declared a success when the United States exploded the first hydrogen bomb Nov. 1, 1952. The 10.4 megaton explosion targeted Eniwetok atoll in the Marshall Islands.

At the same time, scientists at the Argonne National Laboratory were developing the world's first breeder reactor, to produce plutonium out of uranium. Operating successfully by 1951, this project also showed how nuclear energy could be harnessed to produce electrical power.

Spread of Nuclear Technology

Despite the top-secret nature of early nuclear development, the technology spread rapidly to other countries. In the United States, the use of breeder reactors to stockpile plutonium for non-defense purposes was controversial from the start. Britain, however, embraced plutonium production in the early 1950s and took an early lead in the development of nuclear energy.

France quickly followed Britain's example. Spurred by a growing shortage of fossil fuels, the Common Market countries in 1957 established the European Atomic Energy Community (Euratom) to promote nuclear power in Europe. Japan, even more dependent on foreign energy sources than Europe, began buying nuclear technology and equipment from Britain and the United States in the 1960s.

Meanwhile, the arms race, launched by the Soviet Union's testing of its first nuclear device Aug. 29, 1949, continued between the two nuclear superpowers. For the next four decades, the Soviet Union and the United States engaged in a relentless competition to develop increasingly powerful nuclear weapons.

Although the Cold War created only two nuclear superpowers, other countries acquired much smaller nuclear arsenals. Britain had collaborated with the United States during its wartime programs and tested its first thermonuclear device in 1957.

France tested its first device in 1960 and China followed suit four years later. In addition to the five declared nuclear powers, India and Israel are believed to have developed nuclear devices by the 1970s. They reportedly were joined in the 1980s by Pakistan.

South Africa recently admitted to having developed nuclear weapons but stated that it would dismantle its arsenal. Iraq was well on its way toward developing a nuclear weapon when its reactor was destroyed by Israel in 1981.

North Korea has become the object of growing apprehension as it defies IAEA attempts to ensure that it also has not diverted plutonium to defense use.

First Test Bans

Attempts to control nuclear testing began in 1958, yielding U.S. and Soviet moratoria on atmospheric explosions. Britain later joined the Limited Nuclear Test Ban Treaty prohibiting atmospheric tests as well as tests in outer space and under water, which went into effect Oct. 10, 1963. Eager to prevent the further spread of nuclear arms, the three test-ban signatories also launched negotiations that in 1968 produced the Treaty on the Non-Proliferation of Nuclear Weapons; it went into effect in 1970 and today counts 163 signatories.

Compliance with the Non-Proliferation Treaty is monitored by the IAEA under the auspices of the United Nations. A third type of initiative to control defense uses of nuclear energy was a series of arms control talks between the United States and the Soviet Union. The Strategic Arms Limitation Talks (SALT) opened in 1969 and produced two treaties limiting the number of intercontinental nuclear warheads allowed to each superpower.

For the first three decades of the nuclear age, little attention was paid to the problem of nuclear waste. Operators of civilian nuclear power plants were free to recycle plutonium so long as the process adhered to technical guidelines. Concerned about the risk that growing stockpiles of plutonium might fall into the hands of unfriendly nations or terrorist groups, President Jimmy Carter finally banned plutonium recycling in the United States and tried to convince Britain, France and Japan to follow suit. But it was a time of severe energy shortages, and they rebuffed Carter's appeal, citing their need to develop reliable energy sources.

Reflecting the growing concern about proliferation, Congress in 1978 passed the Nuclear Non-Proliferation

Continued on p. 564

Chronology

1940s-1950s

The United States wins the race with Nazi Germany to develop the atomic bomb and then enters a race with the Soviet Union to build the most powerful nuclear arsenal.

1941
Researchers led by Glenn T. Seaborg produce plutonium, the key ingredient in later nuclear bombs.

Aug. 6, 1945
The United States drops an atom bomb over Hiroshima, Japan, killing 142,000 people. A second bomb dropped three days later over Nagasaki kills 79,000. These are the only times nuclear weapons have been used in combat.

Aug. 29, 1949
The Soviet Union tests its first nuclear device, marking the beginning of a 40-year arms race with the United States.

1960s-1970s

As the Cold War escalates, efforts are made to limit the spread of nuclear weapons.

Oct. 10, 1963
The Limited Test Ban Treaty goes into effect, prohibiting all above-ground nuclear explosions.

1969
The Strategic Arms Limitation Talks (SALT) begin and later produce two treaties limiting the number of intercontinental nuclear warheads allowed each superpower.

1970
After 19 years of negotiations, 98 countries ratify the Nuclear Non-Proliferation Treaty banning the acquisition of nuclear weapons by any countries that do not already possess them. In addition to the United States and the Soviet Union, the declared nuclear states are Britain, France and China.

1978
The Nuclear Non-Proliferation Act requires the United States to control the reprocessing of any nuclear fuel it provides other countries for their commercial reactors.

1979
An accident at a nuclear power plant at Three Mile Island, near Harrisburg, Pa., launches a national environmental movement aimed at curtailing the use of nuclear energy.

1980s

In the fourth decade of the nuclear era, the disposal of radioactive waste and toxic chemicals becomes an explosive political issue.

1982
After years of debate, Congress passes the Nuclear Waste Policy Act identifying Yucca Mountain in Nevada as the site for the country's first deep geological repository for high-level nuclear waste.

1986
A nuclear reactor in Chernobyl, Ukraine, explodes, spewing radioactive debris and dust across much of Europe. Nearly 100 people at the plant are killed in the blast, while thousands of deaths in the surrounding area are later attributed to the accident.

1990s

The Cold War's end prompts efforts to dismantle nuclear weapons and poses the problem of how to dispose of the fissile materials they contain.

1991
The Soviet Nuclear Threat Reduction Act, know as Nunn-Lugar after its chief sponsors, Sens. Sam Nunn, D-Ga., and Richard G. Lugar, R-Ind., authorizes programs to help Russia, Ukraine, Kazakhstan and Belarus dismantle weapons from the former Soviet Union and find ways to dispose of the excess plutonium and highly enriched uranium (HEU).

July 1991
The United States and the Soviet Union sign the Strategic Arms Reduction Treaty (START I), the first agreement to reduce the superpowers' nuclear arsenals.

1992
Congress bans further testing of nuclear weapons.

January 1993
The United States and Russia, the Soviet Union's most powerful successor state, sign START II calling for even deeper cuts in nuclear weapons.

Sept. 27, 1993
President Clinton announces a strategy for disposing of dismantled nuclear weapons.

1995
The 163 current parties to the 1970 Nuclear Non-Proliferation Treaty are scheduled to meet in New York City to decide whether to extend the accord indefinitely.

Weapons-Research Labs Seeking New Roles . . .

Since the end of the Cold War blasted the bottom out of the nuclear-weapons industrial complex, some parts of the vast industry have shifted easily to peacetime mode, but others been having a hard time making the transition.

Several production facilities that once churned out nuclear warheads — the Pantex Plant in Texas, Oak Ridge Reservation in Tennessee, the Savannah River Site in South Carolina and the Nevada Test Site — already have shifted and now are dismantling weapons and storing the excess plutonium and highly enriched uranium.

But the three main research laboratories engaged in designing nuclear weapons have not fared so well. Los Alamos and Sandia National Laboratories, both in New Mexico, and Lawrence Livermore National Laboratory in California served for the past half century as the brains behind the United States' vast nuclear arsenal. The three labs have some of the country's most advanced technology at their disposal, a combined annual budget of several billion dollars and a work force of almost 17,000 scientists and engineers. But they are struggling to find a new mission.

Energy Secretary Hazel R. O'Leary has assigned a task force to define a future role for the weapons labs and seven other research facilities the department operates, but the group is not expected to make its final recommendations until next year.

Eager to find ways to reduce the federal budget deficit, lawmakers are already getting involved. The Department of Energy National Competitive Technology Partnership Act of 1993 would shift research at the labs from weapons to "technologies critical to the economic, scientific and technological competitiveness of the United States." The measure also would promote joint ventures with the private sector to promote U.S. industrial competitiveness and create jobs for American workers.

After defeating proposals to mandate cuts in funding for the labs, the House Energy and Commerce Committee voted June 9 for a less restrictive measure that calls on the Energy Department to trim $1 billion from costs at all 10 labs it manages, including the three weapons facilities, over the next four years. [1]

The shift in focus called for in the bill is already under way. Scientists at Los Alamos, which helped build the first atom bomb, have adapted wartime laser technology to measure air pollution. The laser technique was originally developed to detect poison gas during the Gulf War. And at Los Alamos, scientists have turned another weapons technology, fiber optics, into a patented device to detect cancer without the need for biopsies. [2]

At Lawrence Livermore, where scientists worked on the Reagan administration's plan to establish a defense system in space (Star Wars), weapons still are the main focus of research. Since 1992, however, the lab also has signed more than 100 agreements worth about $375 million with private companies to research and develop civilian technology. One recently publicized result of that shift is a sensor to track bullets in

Continued from p. 562

Act, which required the United States to control the reprocessing of any nuclear fuel it provides other countries to develop nuclear energy. President Ronald Reagan adopted a less stringent approach to nuclear-fuel reprocessing than his predecessors, approving reprocessing of spent fuel from reactors in other countries that received their fuel from the United States.

Under a cooperation agreement with Japan, the Reagan administration granted long-term prior consent for reprocessing nuclear fuel provided by the United States for that country's civilian nuclear power program. Euratom also is allowed to reprocess the uranium it purchases from the United States into plutonium for its civilian reactors.

Despite efforts to curb the spread of nuclear technology for defense purposes, 22 countries today possess or have access to plutonium, the key ingredient of atomic weapons, either for defense or civilian purposes. [12]

Environment at Risk

Until last year, most information about threats to human health and the environment from nuclear facilities involved civilian reactors. The 1986 reactor explosion at Chernobyl, Ukraine, and the far less catastrophic accident in 1979 at Three Mile Island, in Pennsylvania, captured headlines for months. But little was known about the risks to plant workers and the environment at the 14 weapons facilities in the United States, much less in the Soviet Union.

But last December, Secretary O'Leary broke the traditional veil of silence surrounding the country's nuclear establishment and declassified documents revealing that from the 1940s through the '70s, thousands of Americans had been exposed, either intentionally through involuntary experiments on humans or as a result of accidental contamination, to dangerous levels of radioactivity. [13]

The full extent of environmental contamination at nuclear weapons sites that must now be cleaned up remains to be discovered by land-use studies. But incidents at several sites indicate the enormity of the problem. The Feed Materials Production Center

. . . in the New Post-Cold War World

flight and identify their origin in less than a second. The rifle-mounted tracking device, called Lifeguard, would enable police or military personnel to quickly return fire from a hidden source such as a sniper.

Despite such efforts to change course, Livermore faces the most uncertain future of the three labs. Its director, John Nuckolls, was forced to resign in early April by the University of California, which operates the Livermore and Los Alamos facilities for the Energy Department. Reportedly more concerned with weapons-related research than civilian applications, Nuckolls was replaced by Bruce Tarter, the lab's deputy director and a supporter of non-defense roles for the facility.[3]

Because the Livermore lab is near the heavily populated San Francisco Bay area, its future may be less certain than Los Alamos, which has a similar mission but poses fewer environmental and health risks because of its remote desert location. In addition, Los Alamos designed most of the submarine-launched weapons that are expected to comprise the bulk of the future nuclear stockpile, making it the more likely candidate to maintain the U.S. arsenal when the Energy Department completes its review next year.

There is less overlap with the Sandia lab, where Martin Marietta manages research into non-nuclear components of nuclear weapons, as well as their transportation and storage systems. Such work reportedly makes the lab less vulnerable to budget cuts than Livermore.

Growing concern over the development of nuclear weapons by North Korea and other aspiring nuclear powers is also throwing support to Los Alamos and Sandia. For the past two years, the labs have been developing remote-sensing satellites that can detect evidence of ongoing nuclear-weapons production, such as chemical residue released onto the ground during plutonium reprocessing.[4]

While the end of the Cold War spelled trouble for the weapons labs, its environmental legacy, ironically, may yet shore up support for them. While cleanup efforts are well under way in the United States, they have barely begun in Russia, where the environmental damage associated with nuclear arms production is thought to be far more extensive. Because Russia lacks the resources to undertake the massive cleanup alone, U.S. weapons labs could play a key role in developing a suitable technology.

"Cleaning up Russian nuclear-arms sites would be a good lab-to-lab project involving research facilities in both countries," says Thomas Cochran, a senior scientist at the Natural Resources Defense Council and a leading expert on Soviet nuclear issues. "It would have the added benefit of giving the U.S. labs an alternative mission."

[1] The House bill was sponsored by Sen. J. Bennett Johnston, D-La.

[2] See Shana Judge, "Sparing the Labs," *Government Executive,* November 1993.

[3] See Christopher Anderson, "Livermore Faces Forces of Change," *Science,* April 15, 1994.

[4] See Christopher Anderson, "Nonproliferation Boom Gives a Lift to the National Labs," *Science,* Feb. 4, 1994.

in Fernald, Ohio, processed uranium into fuel that was turned into plutonium at other plants. Several thousand former workers at the Fernald plant (renamed the Fernald Environmental Management Project in 1991) are suing the operators for exposing them to highly radioactive uranium dust, a million pounds of which also were found to contaminate the surrounding land.

The fuel processed in Ohio went to the plutonium reprocessing plant at Hanford, Wash. That facility, which operated throughout the Cold War, released massive doses of radiation into the atmosphere, some of it in a 1948 experiment involving radioactive iodine, known to be highly toxic to children. With vast chemical and radioactive contamination, Hanford is now the focus of the country's biggest nuclear cleanup project.

The next stop for much of the plutonium was Rocky Flats, a plant outside Denver that created the plutonium "pits" that constitute the core of nuclear weapons. Repeated incidents of radiation pollution and worker exposure at Rocky Flats prompted the government to close the facility in 1989. Most recently, the Energy Department revealed that hundreds of workers there had been exposed in the 1950s and '60s to higher levels of neutron radiation than they had been told.[14] The plant's contractor, Rockwell International Corp., already has paid $18.5 million in fines for violations of nuclear-waste standards.

After the weapons were assembled at the Pantex plant in Texas and elsewhere, some were tested. Before above-ground nuclear tests were banned in 1963, about 100 nuclear bombs were exploded at the Nevada Test Site, 65 miles from Los Vegas. Intensive study is being undertaken here, as elsewhere, to determine the extent of contamination and the potential for eventual environmental restoration.

START Treaties

During the 1980s, the United States and the Soviet Union agreed to stop their escalating race to build ever more nuclear weapons. With more than 50,000 warheads between them — enough, it was said, to destroy the human race many times over — the

Robert Del Tredici

The gaseous diffusion plant (K-25) at Oak Ridge Reservation, in Tennessee, produced enriched uranium for the atomic bomb dropped on Hiroshima. The plant, shown here in 1982, was closed in 1987 due to environmental problems.

superpowers shifted the emphasis of arms control from merely limiting to actually reducing the number of nuclear weapons in their arsenals.

Under the Strategic Arms Reduction Treaties (START I and II), signed in July 1991 and January 1993, the number of weapons in the U.S. strategic nuclear stockpile would fall from more than 12,500 in early 1991 to 3,500 in 2003. Russia's strategic arsenal would decline from more than 10,500 weapons to 3,500 over the same period. [15]

Tactical, or short-range, nuclear weapons also are being retired by the United States and Russia. President Bush announced in September 1991 that all U.S. ground- and sea-launched tactical nuclear weapons, then deployed in Western Europe and aboard submarines around the world, would be withdrawn to the United States. He further promised that all the ground-launched and about half the sea-launched tactical weapons would be destroyed.

Soviet President Mikhail S. Gorbachev followed suit that October, promising to destroy all ground-launched tactical warheads as well as nuclear mines and artillery. Russia's government has expanded on that commitment, promising to dismantle all tactical weapons by the year 2000. These unilateral moves would reduce the U.S. tactical nuclear arsenal from about 8,000 to 1,600. Russia would destroy as many as 12,000, though the size of the country's tactical nuclear arsenal is not known. [16]

As a result of all these arms reduction initiatives, the United States will likely retire up to 15,000 nuclear weapons by the early 21st century. That amounts to about 60 tons of surplus plutonium to be disposed of, though the exact amount will be determined by each weapon's design, which remains classified. The Russian government says it expects to have 50 tons of plutonium and 500 tons of highly enriched uranium left over after it reaches its arms-reduction goals. [17]

Like previous arms-control agreements, the START treaties simply call for the weapons in question to be retired. There are no provisions requiring the signatories to dismantle the warheads, destroy the missile systems designed to deliver them to their targets or dispose of the nuclear explosive material they contain.

Since the abortive coup against President Boris Yeltsin's government in August 1991, the United States has entered into a series of agreements with Russia to speed the dismantling and safe storage of retired warheads. During his June 1992 summit with Yeltsin, President Bush agreed to provide Nunn-Lugar assistance in dismantling Russian arms, including special rail cars and armored blankets for transporting warheads and other equipment to prevent accidents during transportation to dismantling sites.

Because the United States and Russia currently are dismantling a total of up to 4,000 nuclear weapons each year, the amount of fissile material to be stored is growing. In the United States, the dismantling operations are centered at the Pantex Plant outside Amarillo, where many of the weapons were made. More than 5,000 plutonium pits from these dismantled weapons are being stored in above-ground "igloos" at the plant. ■

CURRENT SITUATION

Plutonium Stockpiles

Today, the total worldwide stockpile of weapons-grade plutonium is estimated at 257 tons. There are also at least 1,300 tons — and possibly up to 1,800 tons — of HEU either contained in weapons or held in storage facilities. [18] The vast majority of this material is in or under the control of the United States or the former Soviet republics of Russia, Ukraine, Kazakhstan and Belarus.

The main concern today is the risk that some of Russia's material might be stolen or illicitly sold and end up in the hands of terrorists or rogue

Pushing for a Universal Test Ban Treaty

With nuclear test ban treaties, you get two deterrents for the price of one: Limiting nuclear test explosions can prevent the proliferation of nuclear weapons to states that want to get them, since they can't very well build weapons without testing them. And banning nuclear tests outright can also slow the arms race by convincing nations that no other country is competing to develop weapons of mass destruction.

Efforts to limit or ban nuclear testing have been under way almost since the beginning of the nuclear age. After years of negotiations, the United States and the Soviet Union in 1963 signed the Limited Test Ban Treaty prohibiting nuclear explosions underwater or in the atmosphere or outer space. The two superpowers later signed the Threshold Test Ban Treaty barring underground explosions of more than 150 kilotons and the Peaceful Nuclear Explosions Treaty extending its terms to all tests the two countries may conduct outside their territories. Both agreements went into force Dec. 11, 1990.

Now that the Cold War is over, President Clinton has proposed that all countries agree to a comprehensive ban on nuclear testing. Last summer, as an incentive for other countries to agree to such a ban, Clinton imposed a unilateral moratorium on nuclear explosions in the United States. "Today, in the face of disturbing signs, I renew my call on the nuclear states to abide by that moratorium as we negotiate to stop nuclear testing for all time," Clinton said in a Sept. 27 address before the United Nations General Assembly. In March, the administration extended the U.S. moratorium through September 1995.

The administration is trying to ready the text of a comprehensive test ban before April 1995, when negotiations begin among 163 nations to extend indefinitely the Non-Proliferation Treaty. But it is facing an uphill battle. The first round of negotiations among 38 nations produced little agreement in three months of talks in Geneva, Switzerland, that ended in April.

Although all participants said they support a comprehensive test ban in principle, some insisted that an exception be made for "peaceful explosions." Other countries, such as France, also say occasional weapons tests are necessary to ensure the safety of their existing nuclear arsenals.

regimes. "There are tens of thousands of nuclear warheads, hundreds of tons of weapon-usable, highly enriched uranium and tens of tons of separated plutonium stored in Russia," said Cochran of the NRDC. "Most, if not all, of these inventories are stored under inadequate physical security and material control and accounting." In his view, political unrest in Russia has made safeguarding nuclear materials "among the very highest U.S. national security concerns." [19]

To prevent proliferation of Russian weapons materials, Cochran says the United States should seek further reductions in nuclear weapons in all countries that now possess them; a global cutoff in the production of fissile materials for weapons; and a moratorium on use of plutonium and HEU for civilian reactors and a reduction in the global stockpile of these materials.

In announcing his non-proliferation policy last September, President Clinton endorsed many of these goals. Under the new policy, the United States will seek to eliminate the accumulation of HEU and plutonium, help safeguard existing stockpiles and propose a multilateral convention banning the production of HEU or plutonium to make weapons.

The Clinton administration has since entered into a series of agreements with the Russian government to safeguard the plutonium and HEU extracted from dismantled Russian weapons. The U.S. has agreed, for example, to buy from Russia HEU from dismantled weapons that has been blended down into low-enriched uranium (LEU) suitable for power plants.

In January, Ukrainian President Leonid M. Kravchuk signed a treaty with Russia and the United States providing for the shipment of nuclear warheads still deployed in Ukraine to Russia for dismantling. Two months later, the United States and Russia agreed to let each other inspect the storage facilities for plutonium pits from dismantled weapons as a means of verifying the pace of weapons dismantling and the quantity of plutonium in storage.

Despite the flurry of new agreements — at least 25 in the past year — critics say the Clinton administration is not moving fast enough to secure the growing stockpile of weapons materials in Russia. "As far as dismantling warheads is concerned, the Nunn-Lugar program has been a dismal failure," says Cochran. "The initiatives the United States has taken are better than nothing, but they're too little, too late and too slow."

Disposal Options

One of the components of Clinton's nuclear policy is to study options for the long-range disposition of excess plutonium and HEU, most of which is currently stored in vast underground tanks at Hanford and Savannah River. Since September, scientists from the National Academy of Sciences, the Rand Corporation, the Congressional Office of Technology Assessment (OTA) and other organizations have examined various options and released their recommendations. The ultimate goal, according to the National Academy of Sciences' long-awaited January report, is to make weapons plutonium as hard to acquire and use as the plutonium contained in spent fuel from commercial power reactors.

Unfortunately, this "spent fuel" standard for plutonium cannot be met fully with the available technology. The National Academy scientists ruled out as unfeasible or risky such previously suggested options as launching the material into space or exploding it underground (a proposal the Rand study did not dismiss, however). The National Academy study also recommended against developing new reactors specifically for burning weapons-grade plutonium as too costly.

"Development of advanced reactors and fuel types is of interest for the future of nuclear electricity generation, including the minimization of safety and security risks," the authors concluded, "but the timing and scope of such development need not and should not be governed by the current weapons plutonium problem." [20]

Both the National Academy group and OTA narrowed the best available options to two, based on currently available technology. [21] Vitrification turns plutonium and high-level radioactive wastes into a glasslike matter, making it hard to extract fissile material for weapons. The second option is to burn plutonium as fuel in nuclear power plants. A third option, which has received relatively little study, would be to bury the plutonium in bore holes several kilometers beneath the Earth's surface.

Cochran agrees that vitrification and burning plutonium in existing reactors are the two logical choices, given technological limitations. But vitrification doesn't necessarily meet the needs of Russia or other nuclear powers. "It depends on which country you're in," he says. "I prefer the vitrification option, but it doesn't have much support in Russia, where they want to use the fissile material for breeder reactors."

Gelfand of the Safe Energy Communication Council agrees that vitrification is an attractive way to help ensure that weapons plutonium does not find its way back into a nuclear device. But he has reservations about the safety of burying the waste. He says the problem needs to be discussed more broadly and combined with the overall issue of civilian nuclear waste, which has stalled the construction of nuclear power plants in this country since the 1970s.

Congress tried to break a deadlock over what to do with the mounting stockpile of spent nuclear fuel with the 1982 Nuclear Waste Policy Act, which identified a single high-level waste repository, to be built under Yucca Mountain on the Nevada Test Site. [22] Critics of the nuclear power industry such as Gelfand, however, say Congress caved in to the industry when it approved the site. "The nuclear industry wants to throw the waste in a hole," he says. "Then they can say, 'See, we've solved the problem. Now can we build more nuclear plants?' "

Up to now, the nuclear power industry has stayed out of the debate over what to do with defense-related fissile materials. Although it still has no official position on the matter, some industry representatives like the option of burning excess plutonium and HEU for later burial with civilian wastes.

"It makes a lot of sense to use existing reactors that are able to burn this material to produce power and therefore render them no longer powerful enough for weapons," says Cathy Roach, director of media relations for the Nuclear Energy Institute, the industry's trade group. "It would represent the notion of turning swords into plowshares at its very best."

Huge Cleanup Job

As the Energy Department turns its attention from developing nuclear weapons to cleaning up after them, it faces a monumental task. The department estimates that it will cost $300 billion over the next several decades to rid the environment of radioactive and chemical contamination at the agency's 14 major weapons sites around the country. And even that astronomical sum assumes that no more contamination will occur.

"Most of our money is spent on waste management and stability, hanging on to the waste we already have and preventing it from spreading," says James D. Werner, director of the department's Office of Strategic Planning and Analysis.

Because the extent of environmental damage at the sites has yet to be fully assessed, the cleanup is still at the beginning stages. For the most part, the private contractors that operated the 14 facilities for the government are primarily responsible for the cleanup effort as well.

At Hanford Reservation, for example, Westinghouse Corp., the facility's operator since 1987, now shoulders the main responsibility for restoring the environment. "There are more Westinghouse people out there than Energy Department people," explains Jenny Craig, a spokeswoman for the department's strategic planning and analysis office. "You could make the argument that they know what pollutants are there."

Hanford is the first nuclear weapons facility to complete a land-use study, which is an essential first step in assessing the environmental damage and planning cleanup operations. "Although Hanford is probably the

Continued on p. 570

At Issue:

Should the U.S. abandon efforts to develop a plutonium-fueled reactor?

yes

HAZEL R. O'LEARY
Secretary of Energy

FROM *A SPEECH BEFORE THE LAWYERS ALLIANCE FOR WORLD SECURITY, WASHINGTON, D.C.*, MARCH 15, 1994.

Controlling military fissile materials addresses just part of the proliferation problem. It leaves unchecked the continued production and separation of these materials, particularly plutonium, for *civilian* purposes. Because all plutonium can be used in nuclear weapons, its accumulation creates serious proliferation and security dangers, and it may thwart our goal of stopping new nations from developing nuclear weapons. We must create effective incentives to discourage international commerce in fissile materials. The department is working hard to identify alternatives to civil plutonium separation and will work with other government agencies to implement these strategies.

Our administration is providing leadership on this issue by proposing the termination of the Integral Fast Reactor (IFR) program. The Integral Fast Reactor program is inconsistent with the president's non-proliferation priorities for three basic reasons. First, employing the reprocessing technology associated with the IFR would require that the U.S. separate plutonium from spent nuclear fuel, an activity we are not now engaged in and which we seek to discourage worldwide. Second, if the IFR were employed as a weapons-grade plutonium burner, it is economically essential to produce power at the same time. This civil use of plutonium is an action the administration is seeking to reduce around the globe. Finally, the IFR was designed as a breeder reactor and can be used in this mode to produce more plutonium than it consumes. Continued pursuit of a breeder technology would send the wrong signal to the world and undercut our administration's desire to limit the stockpiling of plutonium for civil nuclear programs.

We cannot credibly urge that others not use technologies for separating and using plutonium if we are pursuing those same technologies ourselves. Such actions could provide an excuse for rogue nations to oppose international efforts to end their plutonium-separation efforts. It could also encourage the Russians to continue with similar breeder technologies at a time when we are actively seeking to have them end all plutonium separation for military purposes.

In short, continued support of the IFR would make it difficult, if not impossible, for the United States to help lead the world toward reducing the threat of plutonium proliferation.

no

RICHARD WILSON
Professor of physics, Harvard University, and member of the advisory committee for the Integral Fast Reactor.

FROM *TESTIMONY BEFORE THE SENATE ENERGY AND NATURAL RESOURCES COMMITTEE ON PLUTONIUM DISPOSAL*, MAY 26, 1994.

I believe that the decision of the administration to cut funding for the IFR out of the 1994-95 budget . . . was incorrect. . . . I believe that one of the most important things that we can do for our grandchildren is to develop technical options among which they may choose. This means an active research-and-development program and a recognition that many, if not most, of the options that have been developed to the point of feasibility will never be chosen. It is in this sense that I suggest that you continue to support the IFR. . . .

If fast reactors are never built, and the present U.S. policy of implementing a once-through fuel cycle [is implemented] by storing whole fuel rods in a repository, the quantities of plutonium will build up as nuclear energy continues to be used. Already, there are 1,000 tons of plutonium in spent reactor fuel compared to somewhat over 100 tons of weapons plutonium. Allowing it to increase is distasteful to many people, including myself. After several thousand years, when much of the radioactive material that makes the plutonium hard to use has decayed, there will be a plutonium mine. Moreover, it seems foolish to bury a useful fuel and at the same time talk about energy shortages and energy conservation! . . .

Japan, France and Russia have expressed their intention to proceed slowly but deliberately toward a breeder-reactor economy. Whether or not they are right to do so . . . we will have a hard time changing that view. If they do proceed with breeder reactors, I hope that they will use the proliferation-resistant IFR fuel cycle, where pure plutonium cannot be produced. . . .

I believe that we should exercise leadership in the world both in energy matters and matters such as ultimate management of plutonium. Thirty years ago, we did. About that time the fast-neutron reactor, EBRII, was built — one of the more successful reactors in the world. Of course, the pace of the program has (properly) slowed. We have more cheap uranium than we thought, and more oil and gas. The IFR is the only part remaining of our research program in advanced, safe, nuclear energy. To close this now seems to me utter folly.

The Hanford Reservation, near Richland, Wash., poses the nation's biggest nuclear cleanup challenge. Billions of gallons of radioactive and chemical wastes reportedly contaminated the site, possibly reaching the adjacent Columbia River.

Continued from p. 568

most contaminated of the federal nuclear sites, at least in terms of the sheer volume and total area of contamination, some other sites are close to the same [assessment and cleanup] stage we are," says engineer Bergman.

Under the terms of a 30-year plan agreed to by the Energy Department, EPA and the state of Washington, work is currently under way to restore parts of the 560-square mile facility. Although more than nine square miles of the site have been declared off-limits for human habitation indefinitely, the main focus of restoration efforts is protecting the Columbia River, which runs through the reservation.

"There is a significant amount of groundwater contamination on the site and some float [seepage] to the river," Bergman says. Just how dangerous that is is the subject of some debate. "The levels are fairly small and massively diluted once they get into the river," she says. "But there is disagreement whether it poses a health risk. Some say any amount of radioactive materials poses a risk."

Beyond the massive problem of assessing the damage and removing the most toxic pollutants, a major obstacle to restoring these sites is the lack of comprehensive standards governing radioactively contaminated sites. There are five different sets of standards and guidelines, including EPA's standards for drinking water and radium contamination near uranium mills, EPA guidelines limiting radioactive soil contamination and Nuclear Regulatory Commission standards for surface contamination and for decommissioning uranium-processing sites.

Congress may soon act to impose tighter control over the nuclear cleanup effort. Despite Secretary O'Leary's new policy of openness, some lawmakers want to take away the department's autonomy in defense-related nuclear programs. A bill sponsored by Rep. George Miller, D-Calif., would require the licensing of all new federal nuclear facilities by the Nuclear Regulatory Commission, the agency that controls the civilian nuclear industry. The bill, supported by environmental groups, also would launch a study of proposals for subjecting the Energy Department's existing nuclear sites to independent regulation.

Critics also charge that O'Leary undermined safety standards at the weapons sites when she merged the department's independent Office of Nuclear Safety into the Office of Environment, Safety and Health as part of her reorganization of the department last year. The General Accounting Office (GAO) reiterated that criticism in a report issued June 21. Sen. William S. Cohen, R-Maine, who requested the report, said he would introduce amendments to the defense authorization bill to force the Energy Department to maintain an adequate and independent staff to monitor the safety of nuclear weapons sites.

"Safety should be the highest priority of the Department of Energy," Cohen said. "The conclusions reached by the GAO are very disturbing in light of the potentially devasting consequences of a nuclear accident." ■

OUTLOOK

International Efforts

To date, most plans for disposing of excess weapons plutonium and HEU outside the United States seek to prevent these materials from falling into the hands of groups or countries that want to make nuclear weapons. This includes the Nunn-Lugar programs to safeguard weapons being dismantled in Russia as well as IAEA oversight of the Non-Proliferation Treaty.

But North Korea's recent refusal to allow IAEA inspectors to examine a nuclear reactor for evidence of plutonium reprocessing in violation of the treaty underscores the limits of the U.N. agency's ability to prevent nuclear proliferation. Although it is charged with monitoring the peaceful use of nuclear materials in all 163 nations that signed the treaty, the IAEA has no enforcement powers. All the inspectors could do when they were turned away from the Korean reactor last month was return to their headquarters in Geneva, Switzerland, and issue a statement of protest.

President Clinton, who called for strengthening the IAEA in his non-proliferation strategy announcement last September, has threatened North Korea with sanctions if it continues to evade oversight of its nuclear inventories. But unilateral sanctions may be ineffective or dangerous — the North Korean government has declared it would consider such a U.S. move to be an act of war. * China, a longstanding ally of North Korea, may veto any move to impose multilateral sanctions within the U.N. Security Council.

Proposals to strengthen the IAEA have been before Congress for several years. A bill introduced in 1991 by Rep. Edward J. Markey, D-Mass., for example, would require the president to enter into negotiations with other nations to improve the effectiveness of IAEA safeguards. Some conservatives, however, long suspicious of the United Nations as an agency of Third World and often anti-U.S. interests, are cautious about giving the IAEA enforcement power and advise the administration to reserve the right to intervene militarily to quash any threats stemming from nuclear proliferation.

"Rather than relying exclusively on the strengthened IAEA to curtail the spread of nuclear weapons," declared the conservative Heritage Foundation, "the U.S. needs a policy backing up a strengthened IAEA with stronger U.S. action." [23]

* After his recent visit to North Korea, former President Jimmy Carter told the White House June 19 that North Korea appeared ready to resolve the dispute.

With the international stockpile of plutonium and HEU growing steadily, however, momentum is building to broaden the IAEA's current mandate. Proposals to direct the IAEA to manage the storage and reduction of existing plutonium and HEU are likely to be considered when the 163 signatories to the Non-Proliferation Treaty meet in 1995 to consider extending the pact indefinitely. The Clinton administration strongly supports the extension as well as strengthening the IAEA.

"By making the treaty a permanent part of the international security structure," said Thomas Graham Jr., acting deputy director of the U.S. Arms Control and Disarmament Agency, "we would ensure that it continues to serve as a stable foundation upon which other vitally needed measures of nuclear disarmament can be built." [24] ■

Notes

[1] National Academy of Sciences, *Management and Disposition of Excess Weapons Plutonium* (1994), pp. 39-40.

[2] *Ibid.*, pp. 40-41.

[3] See R. Jeffrey Smith, "Freeh Warns of a New Russian Threat," *The Washington Post*, May 26, 1994. For background, see "Nuclear Proliferation," *The CQ Researcher*, June 5, 1992, pp. 481-504.

[4] Stratford testified May 26, 1994, before the Senate Energy and Natural Resources Committee at a hearing on plutonium disposal. For background, see "Will Nuclear Power Get Another Chance?" *Editorial Research Reports*, Feb. 22, 1991, pp. 113-128.

[5] Fuller testified at the May 26 hearing on plutonium disposal.

[6] Hanford Future Site Uses Working Group, *The Future for Hanford: Uses and Cleanup*, December 1992.

[7] See Office of Technology Assessment, *Dismantling the Bomb and Managing the Nuclear Materials*, October 1993, p. 134.

[8] See Jean-Marie Cadiou, "The Environmental Legacy of the Cold War," *NATO Review*, October 1993, pp. 33-35.

[9] See Carroll J. Doherty, "Anger Gives Way to Caution in Debate over Russia Aid," *CQ Weekly Report*, March 5, 1994, p. 556.

[10] Leventhal testified March 23, 1994, before the House Foreign Affairs Subcommittee on International Security, International Organizations and Human Rights.

[11] Brian G. Chow and Kenneth A. Solomon, *Limiting the Spread of Weapon-Usable Fissile Materials*, Rand, November 1993. Chow testified at the March 23 hearing.

[12] See George Perkovich, "The Plutonium Genie," *Foreign Affairs*, summer 1993, p. 154.

[13] For information on human exposure to radioactive materials, see "Scars and Secrets: The Atomic Trail," *Los Angeles Times Magazine*, March 20, 1994.

[14] See William Claiborne, "Workers' Radiation Exposure Is Upgraded," *The Washington Post*, May 25, 1994.

[15] National Academy of Sciences, *op. cit.*

[16] *Ibid.*, p. 40.

[17] *Ibid.*, pp. 40-41.

[18] See David Albright, Frans Berkhout and William Walker, *World Inventory of Plutonium and Highly Enriched Uranium* 1992 (1993).

[19] Cochran testified April 19, 1994, before the House Armed Services Panel on Military Applications of Nuclear Energy.

[20] National Academy of Sciences, *op. cit.*, p. 15.

[21] Office of Technology Assessment, *op. cit.*, p. 15.

[22] See Kai Erikson, "Out of Sight, Out of Our Minds," *The New York Times Magazine*, March 6, 1994.

[23] "Controlling the Bomb: International Constraints on Nuclear Weapons Are Not Enough," *Heritage Foundation Backgrounder*, May 19, 1993.

[24] Addressing the Committee on Disarmament's annual symposium in New York City, April 21, 1994.

Bibliography

Selected Sources Used

Books

Albright, David, Frans Berkhout and William Walker, *World Inventory of Plutonium and Highly Enriched Uranium 1992,* Stockholm International Peace Research Institute (SIPRI), 1993.

This is the most thorough worldwide inventory ever made of plutonium and highly enriched uranium, the essential ingredients of nuclear weapons. The authors estimate that there are 911 tons of plutonium and 1,330 tons of highly enriched uranium (HEU) worldwide and call for an international register to keep tabs on these lethal materials.

Hershberg, James, *James B. Conant: Harvard to Hiroshima and the Making of the Nuclear Age,* Alfred A. Knopf, 1993.

This exhaustive biography of a Harvard president and leader of the United States' nuclear program during World War II offers insights into the political environment surrounding the Manhattan Project and the race to produce the world's first atomic bomb.

World Resources Institute, *The 1993 Information Please Environmental Almanac,* Houghton Mifflin, 1993.

A chapter on the environmental damage wrought by the production of nuclear weapons in the United States describes the major research, production and testing sites, as well as programs for cleaning them up.

Articles

Carter, Luther J., "Ending the Gridlock on Nuclear Waste Storage," *Issues in Science and Technology,* fall 1993.

The author supports plans to use Yucca Mountain and the rest of the Nevada Test Site for storing excess nuclear materials. Controversy over the decision to build a vast underground repository under the mountain has slowed its construction.

D'Antonio, Michael, "The Atomic Trail of Tears," *Los Angeles Times Magazine,* March 20, 1994.

The legacy of exposure to radioactive materials during the early years of the Nuclear Age is only now coming into full view. Through accidents and deliberate testing in humans, thousands of Americans were exposed to potentially deadly amounts of radiation.

Erikson, Kai, "Out of Sight, Out of Our Minds," *The New York Times Magazine,* March 6, 1994.

Burying nuclear waste is not an ideal solution to the problem of long-term disposal, the author writes, in large part because there is no way of controlling access to the lethal material over the thousands of years it would take for it to become harmless.

Morrison, Philip, Kosta Tsipis and Jerome Wiesner, "The Future of American Defense," *Scientific American,* February 1993.

Three advocates of arms control call for more drastic reductions in U.S. military spending and the creation of a smaller, more flexible force that would be better suited to counter regional conflicts, what they call the greatest potential threat to peace in the post-Cold War era.

Rhodes, Richard, "Atomic Logic," *Rolling Stone*, Feb. 24, 1994.

The problem of nuclear proliferation has been overblown, according to the author, because nuclear weapons are of no military significance for offensive purposes. The superpowers' decision to dismantle many of their nuclear warheads demonstrates that these weapons serve only as deterrents to aggression.

Reports and Studies

Chow, Brian G., and Kenneth A. Solomon, *Limiting the Spread of Weapon-Usable Fissile Materials*, Rand, November 1993.

One of several studies of ways to dispose of plutonium and highly enriched uranium from dismantled nuclear weapons, this study by the California think tank argues against using plutonium for commercial nuclear power fuel but does not dismiss the possibility of exploding excess warheads underground and using the heat to generate electrical power.

National Academy of Sciences, *Management and Disposition of Excess Weapons Plutonium,* National Academy Press, 1994.

A panel of experts emphasizes the urgent need to ensure the safety of stored nuclear weapons material. The two most promising long-term solutions to plutonium disposal, they suggest, are processing it with other waste into glass logs (vitrification) and burning it in existing reactors.

Office of Technology Assessment, *Dismantling the Bomb and Managing the Nuclear Materials,* September 1993.

The technical research branch of Congress presents the alternatives currently under study for disposing of excess plutonium and uranium from dismantled U.S. nuclear warheads. The authors call on both the United States and Russia to quickly develop policies in this area to reduce the danger of proliferation.

The Next Step

Additional information from UMI's Newspaper & Periodical Abstracts database

Dismantling the Weapons

Deni, John; Lockwood, Dunbar, "DOD plan calls for more transparency in managing U.S.-Russian plutonium ," *Arms Control Today,* April 1994, p. 23.
The Pentagon has devised a plan for mutually monitoring U.S. and Russian warhead storage, transportation and dismantlement. Experts have advocated more transparency in warhead dismantlement.

Gordon, Michael R., "Pentagon offers new way to verify disarmament," *The New York Times,* March 10, 1994, p. A6.
The U.S. has devised a novel means to verify the dismantling of U.S. and Russian warheads, and the Pentagon wants to propose it to Moscow. Each side would continue to dismantle their nuclear warheads privately, then measure the amount of plutonium removed to determine the number of warheads demolished.

Jerome, Richard, "Bombs away," *The New York Times Magazine,* April 3, 1994, p. 46.
The U.S.'s drastic reduction of its nuclear weapons arsenal from 21,000 to 3,500 presents some weighty practical problems with dismantlement and the exacting business of disposing of the parts. The procedure of taking apart a nuclear weapon is described.

Komarow, Steve, and Juan J. Walte, "Ukraine has 7 years to dismantle warheads," *USA Today,* Jan. 11, 1994, p. A4.
Under the agreement announced by President Clinton, Ukraine would have seven years to dismantle 1,800 nuclear warheads left there after the demise of the USSR. Control of the weapons always remained with the Russian military, although Ukrainian scientists reportedly were working on overriding Russian firing codes and keys. A table indicates the number of nuclear warheads held by eight countries.

Renner, Michael, "Finishing the job", *World Watch,* March 1994, pp. 10-11.
The end of the Cold War brought about conditions that now permit a reversal of the nuclear weapons production process, though that process will not be without its hazards. The task of dismantling large numbers of weapons over a relatively short period of time is discussed.

Uhlenbrock, Tom, "Feds seeking Atomic Waste dump here," *St. Louis Post-Dispatch,* Jan. 14, 1994, p. A1.
After spending a decade and $50 million studying what to do with radioactive waste left in St Louis by the birth of the atomic bomb, the Department of Energy is about to recommend that it be buried in the area.

Wald, Matthew L., "Study faults U.S. program to dismantle atomic arms," *The New York Times,* Dec. 1, 1993, p. B8.
According to a report by the GAO, mishaps at a weapons plant in Texas have prevented workers at the plant from dismantling no more than two-thirds of the bombs that they had planned to disassemble in fiscal 1992. The report concludes that the disassembly schedule of 2,000 weapons a year is too ambitious.

Financing Cleanup

Obmascik, Mark, ''DOE knew cleanup pacts doomed,'' *Denver Post,* March 1, 1994, p. A1.
In an exit interview given to federal historians on his last day of work on Jan. 17, 1992, John Tuck, undersecretary of Energy during the administration of George Bush, said his department knew there wouldn't be enough money to pay for its cleanup contracts at nuclear weapons plants, including Colorado's Rocky Flats Nuclear Facility.

Inspections

Lippman, Thomas W., "Accord set on nuclear inspections," *The Washington Post,* March 16, 1994, p. A1.
The United States and Russia have agreed to permit each other to inspect the storage facilities where they keep the plutonium triggers from dismantled nuclear warheads, according to Clinton administration officials.

"U.S. and Russia agree on nuclear inspections," *The New York Times,* March 17, 1994, p. A16.
The U.S. and Russia on March 16, 1994, signed an agreement to allow inspectors from each country access to sites where nuclear weapons are being dismantled.

"U.S., Russia agree to permit visits to nuclear sites," *Boston Globe,* March 16, 1994, p. 19.
The U.S. and Russia have agreed tentatively to have representatives visit each other's storage sites for dismantled nuclear warheads, Energy Secretary Hazel O'Leary said.

International Issues

Berke, Richard L., "Prodded by Gore, Kazakhstan signs arms accord," *The New York Times,* Dec. 14, 1993, p. A15.
During a visit by Vice President Al Gore, Kazakhstan

endorsed an international treaty on Dec. 13, 1993 to halt the spread of arms and signed an agreement with the U.S. to dismantle the Central Asian republic's nuclear arsenal. They will receive $84 million in U.S. aid as a result.

Nichols, Bill, "Ukraine deal will aid Clinton in Yeltsin talks," *USA Today,* Jan. 12, 1994, p. A2.

Completion of a deal to dismantle nuclear warheads in Ukraine adds significant substance to President Clinton's second summit with Russian President Boris Yeltsin.

Patel, Tara, "France urged to come clean on military waste," *New Scientist,* April 2, 1994, p. 6.

France is being pressured to be more open about how it has handled waste from its nuclear weapons program. A team of French and U.S. researchers that traced the treatment and disposal of radioactive nuclear waste on 14 military sites discovered several accidental spills and called for a public inventory of military waste stored around the country.

Pine, Art, "Clinton shows confidence in Ukraine's arms efforts," *Los Angeles Times,* March 5, 1994, p. A12.

President Clinton said on March 4, 1994, that he is well satisfied with Ukraine's progress toward dismantling former Soviet nuclear weapons still on its territory, despite mixed assessments by government and private analysts on how much has been done.

"60 warheads leave Ukraine to be dismantled in Russia," *The New York Times*, March 6, 1994, p. 18.

Quoting Russian Defense Ministry officials, the Interfax news agency said on March 5, 1994, that the first 60 nuclear warheads taken from strategic missiles in Ukraine are on the way to neighboring Russia to be dismantled. The departure followed a visit by Ukrainian President Leonid M. Kravchuk to Washington, where Clinton announced on March 4 that the U.S. would double aid for dismantling weapons, to $350 million.

Nuclear Cleanup

Bettelheim, Adriel, "DOE details ways it's cleaning mess at nuclear sites," *Denver Post,* Nov. 30, 1993, p. A8.

On Nov. 29, 1993, the U.S. Department of Energy kicked off a two-day exhibit at its Washington, D.C. headquarters to demonstrate new technologies it will use in the nationwide effort to clean up nuclear bomb factories, including the contaminated Rocky Flats plant near Denver, Colo.

Bettelheim, Adriel, "Flats cleanup deadline missed; Fines at $285,000," *Denver Post,* Oct. 2, 1993, p. A9.

The Department of Energy has missed another deadline for cleaning up the Rocky Flats nuclear weapons plant in Colorado as of Oct. 1, 1993, bringing its total fines for delays this year to nearly $285,000.

Walker, Mary L., "Nuclear arms sites: Cleanup or setup?" *Christian Science Monitor,* Dec. 13, 1993, p. 23.

Mary L. Walker argues that the DOE's plan to clean up U.S. nuclear weapons facilities is insufficient, and argues for the transferrence of cleanup technologies from the national labs to the private sector. Walker urges the DOE to focus on results, not control.

Nuclear Disposal

Broad, William J., "U.S. begins effort to recast the law on atomic secrets," *The New York Times,* Jan. 9, 1994, p. 1.

The DOE is seeking to revamp or dismantle the Atomic Energy Act, calling it "obsolete." Energy Secretary Hazel O'Leary said in Dec 1993 that the act, which was adopted in 1946 and revised in 1954, needs to be revised because it has damaged American life and institutions by undermining trust in government. One proposed change would scrap the practice of automatically labeling all data on certain subjects as classified, a system known as "born secret."

Carter, Luther J., "Let's use it," *Bulletin of the Atomic Scientists,* May 1994, pp. 42-44.

The U.S. policy that has kept reprocessed plutonium out of civilian nuclear fuel should be changed to allow for the disposal of weapons plutonium. Obstacles to this goal are outlined.

Hazard, Anne, "Argonne reactor unnecessary for plutonium disposal, report says," *Chicago Tribune,* Jan. 29, 1994, p. 1D5.

A controversial advanced nuclear reactor being developed by Argonne National Laboratory will not be needed for the disposal of plutonium from dismantled nuclear warheads, a new report by the National Academy of Sciences said.

McGraw, Dan, "Weapons make some see red," *Boston Globe,* Jan. 23, 1994, p. 2.

Protests by Texas farmers and environmental groups have clouded the issue of nuclear dismantlement, and some residents of Amarillo, Texas, are questioning storage of plutonium bombs there without long-term plans to dispose of the plutonium.

Moss, Norman, "Hey presto — Atomic alchemy," *Guardian,* Nov. 11, 1993, p. 15.

Scientists believe they may be able to dispose of the unwanted plutonium piling up as the U.S. and Russia dismantle nuclear weapons by using particle accelerators to transform it into something else, in a form of "atomic age alchemy."

"Nuclear weapons: Defusing an explosive threat," *Current Science,* April 8, 1994, pp. 8-11.

Nuclear weapons are being dismantled in the U.S., Russia

and other countries of the former USSR. The question of how the leftover nuclear fuels will be disposed of is addressed, and the dangers of radiation experiments are examined.

Plaut, Josh, "Dangerous disposal," *Science World,* Dec. 3, 1993, pp. 16-18.
The U.S. is dismantling some of its nuclear weapons, but the question is how to safely dispose of the deadly leftovers, such as plutonium. The disposal of this highly radioactive element is discussed.

"Radioactive waste perilously stored at weapons plants, U.S. says," *Boston Globe*, Dec. 9, 1993, p. 10.
Tons of highly radioactive reactor fuel are being precariously stored, sometimes in rusting containers, at government weapons plants, the Energy Department says.

Opinions

Abelson, Philip H., "Need for enhanced nuclear safeguards," *Science,* March 18, 1994, p. 1543.
Although the Cold War is over, the hazards of nuclear terrorism are on the rise. As described in an editorial, the dismantling of weapons by both Russia and the U.S. could lead to warhead theft, and in turn to increased terrorism.

"A suitable site for nuclear waste," *Atlanta Journal Constitution,* Nov. 26, 1993, p. A12.
An editorial contends that the U.S. must accept foreign-produced, high-level nuclear waste for temporary storage at the Savannah River Site because the radioactive material could be used to build crude nuclear weapons and must not fall into the wrong hands.

"Ban the bomb," *Progressive,* January 1993, p. 10.
Scientific and managerial bungling, criminality and coverups have characterized the nuclear weapons program in the U.S., according to the magazine. Rocky Flats, Colo., is one of the sites considered.

"Base-closure process should be used for N-site cleanups," *Denver Post,* March 3, 1994, p. B6.
An editorial calls for the appointment of an independent commission to assess which former nuclear weapons facilities should receive federal assistance in cleaning up their plants and the environment surrounding them.

"China the key to unlock N. Korea," *Atlanta Constitution,* Nov. 5, 1993, p. A14.
An editorial notes North Korea's blatant disregard for the Nuclear Non-Proliferation Treaty and says the U.S. should cater to China by offering to help clean up its nuclear wastes in hopes that China would have a positive effect on North Korea's nuclear habits.

Heylin, Michael, "U.S. lacks plan to dismantle nuclear warheads," *Chemical & Engineering News,* Sept. 27, 1993, pp. 8-9.
The U.S. lacks a coordinated, comprehensive national policy for dismantling nuclear warheads, and the prospects of developing such a plan are uncertain, Heylin writes. Dismantling the warheads will be neither painless nor inexpensive.

"The plutonium glut," *The New York Times,* Dec. 1, 1993, p. A22.
An editorial warns that the dismantling of nuclear warheads since the end of the Cold War is creating a glut in supplies of plutonium that may result in the spread of atomic weapons. The editorial urges the Clinton administration to propose banning production of plutonium even under safeguards.

"Ukrainian arms," *San Francisco Chronicle,* Jan. 11, 1994, p. A16.
An editorial comments on Ukraine's voluntary dismantling of its nuclear arsenal.

Plutonium Threat

"Clear danger of plutonium theft," *USA Today,* Jan. 25, 1994, p. A6.
More than 100 tons of plutonium from dismantled U.S. and Russian nuclear missiles pose "a clear danger" because there is no sure way to keep stockpiles from terrorists, says the National Academy of Sciences.

Holdren, John P., "Dangerous surplus," *Bulletin of the Atomic Scientists,* May 1994, pp. 39-41.
The dismantling of many of the world's nuclear weapons has brought calls for increased safeguards on plutonium and highly enriched uranium (HEU). The National Academy of Sciences Committee on International Security and Arms Control's recommendations to control weapons-grade plutonium are described.

Hughes, David, "Arms experts fear nuclear blackmail," *Aviation Week & Space Technology,* Jan. 4, 1993, pp. 61-62.
As the dismantling of former Soviet weapons proceeds, enriched uranium and plutonium will be produced, creating concerns about who may obtain it. The threat of nuclear terrorism and blackmail is discussed.

Panofsky, Wolfgang K. H., "Safeguarding the ingredients for making nuclear weapons," *Issues in Science & Technology,* spring 1994, pp. 67-73.
With the end of the Cold War, countries are dismantling their nuclear weapons and storing the fissionable materials. Safeguards must be in place to prevent the theft of such materials, Panofsky writes.

Back Issues

Great Research on Current Issues Starts Right Here...Recent topics covered by The CQ Researcher are listed below. Before May 1991, reports were published under the name of Editorial Research Reports.

DECEMBER 1992
Crackdown on Smoking
The New CIA
Eating Disorders
Women and AIDS

JANUARY 1993
Hate Crimes
Child Sexual Abuse
Nuclear Fusion
U.S. Trade Policy

FEBRUARY 1993
Community Policing
Europe's New Right
School Censorship
Violence Against Women

MARCH 1993
Gay Rights
Aid to Russia
War on Drugs
TV Violence

APRIL 1993
Head Start
High-Speed Rail
Children's Legal Rights
Muslims in America

Back issues are available for $4.00 (subscribers) or $7.00 (non-subscribers). Quantity discounts apply to orders over ten. To order, call Congressional Quarterly Customer Service at (202) 887-8621.

Binders are available for $16.00. To order call 1-800-638-1710. Please refer to stock number 648.

MAY 1993
Cults in America
Preventing Teen Pregnancy
Software Piracy
National Parks

JUNE 1993
Food Safety
Prostitution
Childhood Immunizations
National Service

JULY 1993
Electric Cars
Population Growth
Downward Mobility
Intelligence Testing

AUGUST 1993
Mental Illness
Bilingual Education
Foreign Policy Burden
School Funding

SEPTEMBER 1993
Suburban Crime
Public Housing
Supreme Court Preview
Immigration Reform

OCTOBER 1993
Airline Safety
Disaster Response
Science in the Courtroom
The Glass Ceiling

NOVEMBER 1993
Paying for Retirement
Charitable Giving
Privacy in the Workplace
Adoption

DECEMBER 1993
U.S. Vietnam-Relations
Learning Disabilities
Child Care
Space Program's Future

JANUARY 1994
Racial Tensions in Schools
South Africa's Future
Worker Retraining
Regulating Pesticides

FEBRUARY 1994
Prison Overcrowding
Water Quality
Religion in Schools
Juvenile Justice

MARCH 1994
Underground Economy
Education Standards
Gambling Boom
Private Management of Public Schools

APRIL 1994
Reproductive Ethics
U.S.-China Trade
Soccer in America
Talk Show Democracy

MAY 1994
Traffic Congestion
Women's Health Issues
Mutual Funds
Political Scandals

JUNE 1994
Education and Gender
Gun Control
Public Land Policy

Future Topics

- ***Vitamins***
- ***Public Opinion and Foreign Policy***
- ***Crime Victims' Rights***

THE CQ Researcher®

PUBLISHED BY CONGRESSIONAL QUARTERLY INC.

Dietary Supplements

Should health products be less tightly regulated?

It turns out mother was right when she said, "Eat your vegetables." Nutritionists, citing dozens of scientific studies in recent years, say the vitamins and minerals in fruits and vegetables keep the body fit and strengthen its defenses against cancer, heart disease and other ailments. Now, some also endorse taking dietary supplements for added protection. Health-conscious Americans responded by buying more than $4 billion worth of nutrition supplements last year, including herbal products. Supplement producers want Congress to pass proposed legislation limiting the authority of the federal Food and Drug Administration (FDA) to regulate their products. Consumer-protection groups oppose such a law, saying it would stop the agency from cracking down on unsafe supplements and those that make questionable or misleading claims.

INSIDE THIS ISSUE

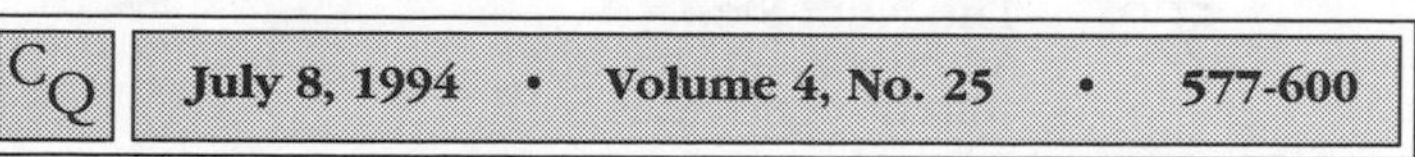
CQ July 8, 1994 • Volume 4, No. 25 • 577-600

Formerly Editorial Research Reports

DIETARY SUPPLEMENTS

COVER ART: BARBARA SASSA-DANIELS

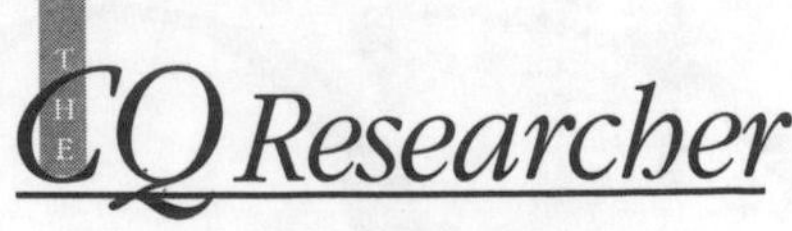

July 8, 1994
Volume 4, No. 25

EDITOR Sandra Stencel

MANAGING EDITOR Thomas J. Colin

ASSOCIATE EDITOR Richard L. Worsnop

STAFF WRITERS Charles S. Clark, Mary H. Cooper, Kenneth Jost

PRODUCTION EDITOR Sarah E. Merritt

EDITORIAL ASSISTANT Michael M. Taylor

GRAPHICS P. Eloise Fuller

PUBLISHED BY Congressional Quarterly Inc.

CHAIRMAN Andrew Barnes

VICE CHAIRMAN Andrew P. Corty

EDITOR AND PUBLISHER Neil Skene

EXECUTIVE EDITOR Robert W. Merry

ASSOCIATE PUBLISHER John J. Coyle

MARKETING AND SALES DIRECTOR Edward S. Hauck

The CQ Researcher (ISSN 1056-2036). Formerly Editorial Research Reports. Published weekly (48 times per year, not printed the first Friday of any month with five Fridays) by Congressional Quarterly Inc., 1414 22nd St., N.W., Washington, D.C. 20037. Rates are furnished upon request. Second-class postage paid at Washington, D.C. POSTMASTER: Send address changes to The CQ Researcher, 1414 22nd St., N.W., Washington, D.C. 20037.

Dietary Supplements

BY RICHARD L. WORSNOP

THE ISSUES

There's nothing in the Constitution, of course, about the right of Americans to take vitamins. But don't tell that to the health-conscious millions who religiously swallow nutrition supplements every morning with their orange juice. And don't even think about taking that "right" away.

In dark warnings last year, however, Americans were told they could lose their "nutritional rights." Widely distributed ads and flyers from the Nutritional Health Alliance (NHA), which represents health food stores and alternative medicine professionals, warned Americans to "kiss your vitamins goodbye" if Congress didn't pass legislation benefiting the dietary supplement industry. General Nutrition Centers, the largest U.S. chain of health food stores, installed cardboard letter-writing podiums during the campaign, with model letters for customers to sign and send to Congress.

The message hit home, triggering an avalanche of letters and faxes to members of Congress demanding unfettered access to dietary products. Veteran Capitol Hill observers termed the outpouring one of the largest grass-roots campaigns they had seen in years.

The protest also demonstrated that nutrition supplements are big business. According to industry figures, more than $4 billion worth of dietary products were sold in 1993, more than Americans spend every year at movie theaters. [1] Some 100 million Americans now use supplements, says John Cordaro, president of the Council for Responsible Nutrition (CRN), an industry trade group, and "millions more should be taking" them. [2] Supplement users include many prominent nutritionists and scientists,

including Nobel Prize-winning chemist Linus Pauling. (*See story, p. 594.*)

Most people take vitamins and minerals to safeguard their health and protect themselves against ailments ranging from the common cold to lung cancer.

Over the past 20 years or so, numerous studies have shown that people who consume large amounts of fruits and vegetables have markedly lower rates of most types of cancer and heart disease. Accordingly, the National Cancer Institute (NCI) recommends eating five portions of fruits and vegetables daily to assure an adequate intake of essential nutrients.

Ironically, says Jeffrey Blumberg, an industry consultant and professor of nutrition at Tufts University in Boston, people whose diet is based on the NCI model are "consuming two to four times the Recommended Dietary Allowance [RDA] of many vitamins and minerals."

Consequently, he believes the National Academy of Sciences' Food and Nutrition Board, which issues and periodically revises the RDAs, should promote the use of supplements to prevent chronic diseases. As it happens, the board is now considering whether to publish a new edition of the RDAs incorporating the results of recent nutrition research on chronic disease prevention (*see p. 595*).

As the board ponders its decision, dietary-supplement regulations drafted under the Nutrition Labeling and Education Act of 1990 have begun to take effect. Starting July 1, supplement makers are only allowed to make health claims that the U.S. Food and Drug Administration (FDA) believes are supported by "significant scientific evidence." And next July 1, supplement labels will have to carry nutrition information.

However, bills now pending in Congress would make it harder for the FDA to move against supplements it suspects of being unsafe. The legislation, sponsored in the Senate by Orrin G. Hatch, R-Utah, and in the House by Bill Richardson, D-N.M., would create a separate regulatory category for dietary supplements. This would bar the FDA from holding the products to the higher safety standards required of drugs or food additives. In addition, manufacturers could label products with "truthful and non-misleading" information that would not require prior FDA clearance.

"The effect of this legislation would be to eliminate any meaningful scientific standards for the validity of claims and any meaningful FDA role in evaluating the safety of those products," said Michael R. Taylor, deputy FDA commissioner for policy. [3]

"The 1993 Snake Oil Protection Act," a *New York Times* editorial called the proposed legislation. "Under the new food labeling rules," said the *Times*, "products that claim to contain essential ingredients to, say, cure baldness or male impotence might have to change their labels. But contrary to the industry's disinformation campaign, the products themselves wouldn't be banned." [4]

Sales of Nutritional Products on the Rise

Retail sales of nutritional products topped $4 billion for the first time in 1993, according to the Council for Responsible Nutrition, an industry group. The increase reflected higher sales of vitamins and other nutrition supplements, such as herbal products.

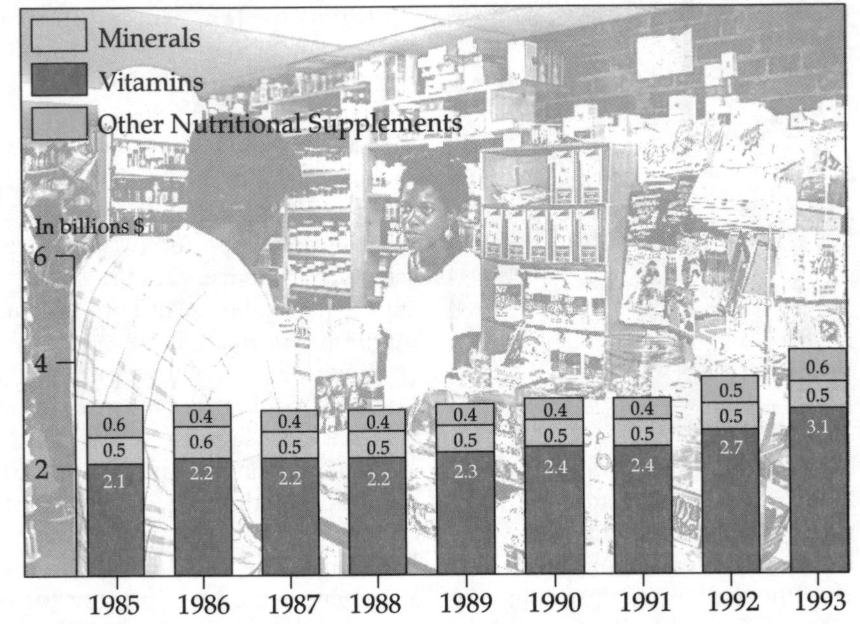

Source: Council for Responsible Nutrition. The council represents manufacturers, distributors and suppliers of nutritional supplements and products. Photograph by Clint W. Steib.

The legislation's fate is still uncertain. Hatch's bill, which has 65 cosponsors, was approved May 11 by the Senate Labor and Human Resources Committee, but no vote by the full Senate has yet been scheduled. Meanwhile, the House Energy and Commerce Committee has taken no action on the Richardson bill, which has 249 cosponsors.

All parties to the nutrition supplement debate agree that few products raise urgent safety concerns. "The overwhelming majority of dietary supplements currently on the market are safe," said Bruce Silverglade, legal affairs director of the Center for Science in the Public Interest (CSPI), in congressional testimony last summer. "Yet, serious questions have been raised about certain amino acids, some herbs and even large doses of particular vitamins. When consumers walk into a health food store, they have a right to expect that every product for sale there has been shown by the manufacturer to be safe." [5]

Supplements that make misleading health claims are a particular worry, says Silverglade. He notes that a product's name often implies a claim, citing Memory Booster, Sugar Control, Mental Wisdom, Viril Actin and Happy Camper as examples. "According to informal surveys [CSPI] took in the Washington metropolitan area, about 20 percent of the products on health food store shelves bear those types of claims," says Silverglade. "They are claims that would not be permissible under the Nutrition Labeling and Education Act."

Some consumers may choose a particular health supplement because it contains "natural" ingredients, which presumably are safer than synthetic ones. But that's a "misconception," says John Gleason, senior attorney for CSPI. "We should all keep in mind that alcohol, nicotine and coca are all naturally occurring substances," he adds. "It's important to recognize that the distinction is simply one of origin. It has nothing to do, necessarily, with safety or potency. Roughly 50-60 percent of pharmaceuticals are derived from plants, but that doesn't mean they're entirely safe."

As nutrition supplement makers and consumer watchdog groups debate the issues, here are some of the questions being asked:

Is the proposed Hatch-Richardson legislation in consumers' best interests?

Relations between the FDA and the nutrition supplement industry have long been marked by "an unusually intense antagonism," says Silverglade. CRN's Cordaro goes further, accusing the FDA of a "long-term bias" against supplements. He contends the agency needs to acknowledge that "Americans do not get all nutrients they need from food" and thus should "supplement their diets with nutritional products."

Beth Yetley, director of the FDA Office of Special Nutritionals, denies Cordaro's bias charge. "Dietary supplements can be regulated under either the food or the drug provisions of the Food, Drug and Cosmetic Act," she says. "Most of them are regulated as food. We use the same regulations for dietary supplements that we use for foods, if they are foods, or for drugs, if they qualify as drugs. The proportion of FDA resources committed to dietary supplements is smaller than the proportion devoted to conventional foods."

FDA regulation of dietary supplements as drugs or food additives is a

R. Michael Jenkins

Sen. Orrin G. Hatch, R-Utah

particular sore point among industry executives. Under FDA regulations, foods can be regulated as drugs if they contain directions for use or health warnings. As a result, Rep. Richardson wrote recently, "Often the FDA has sent warning letters to supplement companies demanding they make changes in their labeling — because they contained directions for use or warnings — or face seizure of their products as unapproved drugs."

But consumer groups also complain that the labels lack crucial information. "This situation places supplement companies in the Catch-22 position of being damned by the regulatory agency for providing accurate use information on their labels and damned by consumer protection organizations for not providing [enough] such information," declared Richardson.[6] Under the Hatch and Richardson bills, dietary supplements may not be classified as drugs simply because their labels include warnings or dosage instructions.

The supplement industry also seeks the following changes, which also are embodied in the Hatch-Richardson legislation:

- The right to make a health claim for supplements containing nutrients for which the FDA has approved a claim for conventional foods;
- Tightening of the standard used by the FDA to reject supplement health claims from "significant scientific agreement" to "the totality of scientific evidence";
- Permission to distribute printed matter about a product's potential benefits "without the need for a lengthy and cumbersome FDA approval process."[7]

Testifying on the legislation last July, FDA Commissioner David A. Kessler said, "The traditional vitamin and mineral products comprise more than 80 percent of the multibillion-dollar dietary supplement market and raise no serious concerns as long as they are sold without disease prevention or treatment claims, have reasonable potencies and are manufactured using appropriate quality-control standards."

Alluding to the NHA campaign, Kessler added: "Contrary to what members of Congress may be hearing, FDA has no intention of forcing consumers to get a doctor's prescription to obtain vitamins or minerals. Nor is the agency intent on forcing health food stores out of business."[8]

Nonetheless, Kessler insisted the FDA had a duty to move forcefully against dietary supplements with ingredients "that have been associated with serious and, in some cases, fatal adverse reactions." In this connection, he cited chapparal, comfrey and germander herbal products that can cause acute liver damage.

Even beneficial vitamins and minerals can be toxic if taken in sufficiently high doses, Kessler pointed out, especially niacin, vitamin A, and vitamin B6. (*See story, p. 584.*) Cordaro, insisting the industry is capable of regulating itself, notes that CRN's member companies have agreed to voluntary dosage limits for those three substances.

Kessler denied that FDA's proposed labeling rules for supplements would bar companies from distributing "reputable scientific publications" to buttress health claims. He also said the agency had no intention of trying to restrict publication of such material or preventing the flow of information to consumers, provided the information did not amount to improper labeling. He explained that FDA interprets the Food, Drug and Cosmetic Act of 1938 to mean that "printed material placed in close proximity to a product and used to promote the sale of the product constitutes labeling."

Furthermore, Kessler cautioned against easing the standards for proving health claims. While the Richardson bill "provides for notification of the fact that a particular claim is being made, it makes optional the submission of scientific [data] supporting the claim," he said. "FDA would have no basis for evaluating the scientific validity of that claim unless the scientific evidence is voluntarily submitted." Another flaw of the Richardson bill, he said, is that it "does not include a clear standard requiring that the validity of the link between the nutrient and the disease be established by scientific evidence."

Consumer watchdog groups tend to have mixed feelings about both dietary supplements and the Hatch-Richardson legislation. CSPI, for in-

R. Michael Jenkins

Rep. Bill Richardson, D-N.M.

Technician checks vitamins being processed in a high-speed tablet coater.

stance, supports the right of consumers to buy safe and properly labeled supplements. "Our position is based on the fact that a new era in nutrition has begun," said Silverglade. "In our view, the balance of evidence has tipped in favor of taking certain nutrients in supplement form, in doses significantly larger than what can be found in a normal diet." At the same time, he said, "as more and more consumers begin to rely on dietary supplements to protect and promote their health, it is all the more important that health claims on supplement labels be reliable." [9]

Silverglade thinks it's "a wise step" to create a separate regulatory category for dietary supplements, as proposed under Hatch-Richardson, "because under current law, the FDA has to pound a square peg into a round hole." As matters now stand, the agency must classify a supplement as either a food additive or a drug to require pre-market approval of the product's safety. Silverglade favors giving the FDA "more straightforward authority to require pre-market approval of the safety of products that are not generally recognized as safe."

This is precisely where CSPI parts company with the supplement industry and Hatch and Richardson. "The industry and Sen. Hatch say 'yes,' there should be a separate regulatory category for supplements. But they want that category modeled after the basic foodstuffs safety law. Foodstuffs like lettuce or potatoes are presumed safe because they've been in use for thousands of years, so there's no reason to require pre-market approval of their safety. The FDA can only take them off the market if they're proven to be poisonous.

"That's not the framework legislation should establish for dietary supplements. While supplements should have a niche in the law all their own, it should be based on the laws that have ensured the safety of food additives since 1958, when the first modern food additive safety law was enacted."

Gleason of CSPI suggests another reason for opposing the Hatch bill. "Under Sen. Hatch's definition of dietary supplements," he says, "it would be possible for a foreign drug manufacturer to label a foreign drug as a dietary supplement and import it into the United States."

Moreover, Gleason doesn't think much of proposals for distributing scientific studies to consumers to help them decide whether nutrition supplements are beneficial. "Preliminary scientific studies are meant to guide further research, not to be used for marketing purposes," he said. "It's inherently misleading to selectively distribute studies in order to hype products."

Numerous public health and consumer advocacy groups have come out against the Hatch-Richardson proposals, including the American Cancer Society, the American Association of Retired Persons, the Consumer Federation of America and the American Dietetic Association. All are concerned, said Silverglade, that the legislation "would make it more difficult for the FDA to take prompt enforcement actions against manufacturers of unsafe or improperly labeled products." [10]

Supporters of the two bills include the Society of Certified Nutritionists, in Aurora, Colo., the American Herbalists Guild, in Soquel, Calif., and the American Holistic Medical Association (AHMA), in Raleigh, N.C. "The Food and Drug Administration has consistently taken a biased stance against nutritional supplements, herbal remedies and other natural substances that have value in prevention and treatment of illness," said Sally Nicholson, executive director of the AHMA. "These FDA policies harm the public health and interfere with the freedom of Americans to choose the type of health care most appropriate for them." [11]

Do vitamins and minerals ward off disease?

Vitamins and other nutrients in food have long been prized for their health-enhancing qualities. For many years, however, the nutrition and public health establishments looked down on dietary supplements. Conventional wisdom held that all the nutrients needed for good health could be obtained by eating a balanced diet.

Now many scientists have changed their minds. "They point to mounting evidence that certain vitamins and other nutrients may offer protection against cancer, cataracts, Parkinson's disease and other disorders," noted *Consumer Reports* magazine. "They speculate that extra doses of those nutrients may slow the aging process. And, while few go so far as to make public recommendations, they freely admit that popping pills has become part of their own daily routine." [12]

Blumberg of Tufts, who is associate director of the Department of Agriculture's Human Nutrition Research Center on Aging, is one of the scientists who regularly take supplements — in his case, vitamin C, vitamin E and a form of vitamin A called beta carotene. These are the three antioxidant vitamins, so-called because they neutralize toxic compounds in the blood known as "free radicals." Free radicals are molecules missing an electron. They snatch electrons from other molecules to fill the void, thereby subjecting tissue to oxidation damage. Blumberg likens the process to "the way oxygen makes iron rust, or the way fish goes rancid after exposure to air." [13] Since antioxidants carry an extra electron, they can inactivate free radicals by giving up their spare.

Though scores of studies have strongly suggested antioxidants shield the body from cancer, clogged arteries and other diseases of aging, many scientists hesitate to accept the findings as conclusive. The FDA, for instance, has yet to approve any health claim for antioxidant supplements. And *The New England Journal of Medicine* stated in an editorial that "The chief limitation of even the best of these observational studies . . . is that the [health] benefits have not been very large and might therefore be due to other, unmeasured differences in lifestyle, including the composition of the diet, between those with high and low intakes of [antioxidant] vitamins." [14]

The editorial was written in response to a study of more than 29,000 male smokers from Finland that appeared in the same issue of the journal (*see p. 592*). Over a period of from five to eight years, the smokers were given vitamin E and beta carotene, singly or in combination, or a placebo. Contrary to expectations, those only receiving beta carotene showed an 18 percent higher rate of lung cancer than the other subjects. The finding sent shock waves through the nutrition community, which is still debating its significance.

Cordaro of CRN urges caution in evaluating the beta carotene finding, arguing that "We can't rely on one trial to set public policy" on nutrition supplements. The Finnish study, he believes, should be assessed in the context of earlier research that came to different conclusions.

For instance, a study in China suggested that vitamin A, beta carotene and selenium may help protect against stomach cancer. "That's the kind of information consumers ought to have access to," Cordaro said. "Let consumers decide what to do until a public policy can be formulated."

Gleason feels the supplement industry has been "largely irresponsible" in its criticism of the Finnish trial. In his view, the trial "raised some important warning signs." He further contends that "the industry's dismissal of it as a single study on smokers overlooks the fact that many previous studies indicating beta carotene is beneficial were also studies of smokers."

The Finnish and Chinese studies are not strictly comparable, Gleason argues, since "the Chinese trial centered on individuals who, unlike most Americans, suffer from acute vitamin deficiencies. As a result, they have a much higher rate of stomach cancer." The Finnish study, on the other hand, involved Europeans whose diet is "more like [that of] most Americans."

Blumberg asserts that the Finnish study "has some very significant flaws — or, at least, some significant limitations as to how it can be interpreted." One problem, he says, is that the researchers conducting it "didn't get the participants to stop smoking.

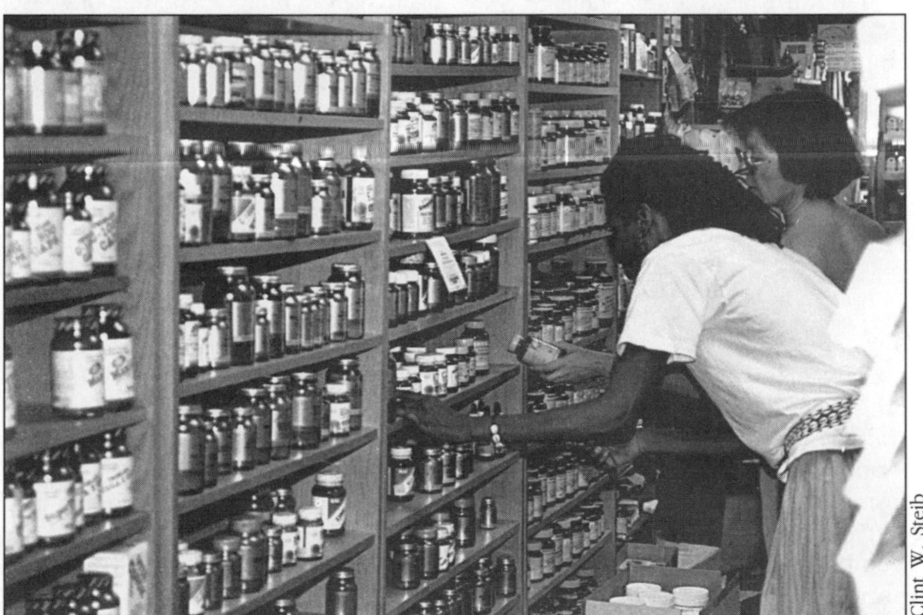
Clint W. Steib

Health-food store in Washington, D.C., offers a wide selection of supplements.

A Guide to Essential Vitamins and Minerals . . .

The 13 known vitamins, plus three minerals and four so-called trace elements, are usually deemed essential to human nutrition. With the exception of two of the vitamins (see below), the amount of each substance needed for good health, known as the "Recommended Dietary Allowance" (RDA) has been set by the National Academy of Sciences' Food and Nutrition Board (FNB). The RDA depends to some extent on the kinds and amounts of food eaten and on variations in metabolism. RDAs have not been issued for other minerals that may also be important to nutrition.

Vitamins

Vitamins are organic substances that are usually categorized as soluble in water (the B vitamins and vitamin C) or soluble in fat (vitamins A, D, E and K). Water-soluable vitamins pass out of the body faster than fat-soluable ones. The 13 vitamins are:

Vitamin A is especially important to children. Deficiencies, which are rare in the U.S., may result in retarded growth and poor development of teeth and bones, as well as night blindness and eye disease. In both children and adults, insufficient vitamin A may lead to dry skin and eczema. Good dietary sources are orange fruits and vegetables and milk. Excessive vitamin A can lead to vomiting, fatigue and headaches.

Vitamin B comprises a family (or complex) of several compounds: thiamin (vitamin B1), riboflavin (vitamin B2), niacin (vitamin B3), pantothenic acid (vitamin B5), pyridoxine (vitamin B6) and cobalamin (vitamin B12).

Thiamin plays an essential role as a catalyst in burning carbohydrates. Prime sources of thiamin include legumes and whole and enriched grains. The classic thiamin-deficiency disease is beriberi, typically found among heavy drinkers who don't eat enough to supply their minimum nutritional requirements.

Riboflavin is necessary for growth and tissue repair. Acute deficiency, which is very rare in the U.S., produces a condition similar to pellagra. In recent years, animal studies have suggested a correlation between cataracts and riboflavin deficiency. Good sources are milk, cheese, chicken, lean beef and pork.

Niacin, found in meats, enriched grains and poultry, is a term usually applied to both nicotinic acid and nicotinamide. Severe niacin deficiency is a leading cause of pellagra, whose telltale symptoms are diarrhea, dermatitis and dementia. Overdosage of nicotinic acid (though not of nicotinamide) almost always results in severe flushing of the face and hands, often accompanied by a stinging or burning sensation.

Pantothenic acid (vitamin B5) is found in all living things, and severe deficiencies in humans have never been known to occur naturally. The substance is converted in the body to a catalyst used in a variety of processes, including the metabolism of carbohydrates and the breakdown of fatty acids. Corn, lentils, eggs, nuts and lobster are leading sources. Pantothenic acid is non-toxic. The FNB has not yet issued an RDA for vitamin B5.

Pyridoxine is needed for proper functioning of the brain and central nervous system. It also aids in the manufacture of hemoglobin and the conversion of carbohydrates into energy. Meats, grains, fish, eggs and carrots are good sources. Researchers are trying to determine whether the substance can alleviate the symptoms of carpal-tunnel syndrome, a painful disorder that afflicts numerous users of computers and word processors. Also under study is whether pyridoxine can strengthen the immune systems of elderly people, who often consume only minuscule amounts of it. Megadoses of pyridoxine can result in severe nerve disorders.

Cobalamin, which contains the trace mineral cobalt, is the pure form of vitamin B12. Vitamin B12 acts in tandem with folate (see below) to facilitate normal cell division. Seafood, beef, poultry and dairy products provide abundant amounts of B12, whose classic deficiency disease is pernicious anemia. The vitamin is generally considered

They didn't provide any behavioral incentives, nicotine patches, or anything else. It's very odd to conduct a health-promoting trial without getting people to engage in other health-promoting behaviors."

It's also important to note, says Blumberg, that the Finnish smokers formed an "extraordinarily unhealthy" group. "They were all overweight, they all had high blood-lipid levels, very low intakes of other vitamins and minerals and a very high-fat diet. Thirty-nine percent of their calories came from fat. These are people at high risk for lots of diseases, including lung cancer. Also, 18 percent of the men in the study had occupational exposures to established carcinogens like asbestos."

In sum, says Blumberg, the Finnish smokers had "engaged in bad health practices" all their lives. "And then we say, 'Gee, can we reverse all this with a simple vitamin pill?' That's asking too much of any vitamin."

FDA's longstanding skepticism about health claims for dietary supplements is by no means confined to antioxidants. Far from affording protection against disease, wrote FDA nutritionist John N. Hathcock, overconsumption of certain vitamins and minerals can damage

. . . for Health-Conscious Americans

non-toxic even at megadose levels.

Vitamin C deficiency lowers resistance to infection and other ills. A plentiful supply of this vitamin, found chiefly in citrus fruits and vegetables, thus is highly desirable for both children and adults. Many regular users claim that moderate doses of vitamin C lessen cold symptoms. And researchers are trying to ascertain whether large doses can slow the onset of heart disease and cancer and lower the risk of cataracts. Serious deficiencies of vitamin C cause scurvy, now almost unknown in the developed world.

Vitamin D can be synthesized within the human body, provided the skin is exposed to sunlight or some other source of ultraviolet rays. The chief value of vitamin D lies in its ability to help the body absorb calcium, making it important for pregnant women and nursing mothers. Moreover, some nutritionists are confident that studies will show increased doses of vitamin D can halt or even reverse osteoporosis, a bone-loss condition afflicting many elderly people. However, excessive doses are toxic.

Vitamin E requirements can be easily met by including moderate amounts of green leafy vegetables in the diet. In recent years, sweeping claims have been made for vitamin E. Studies now seek to determine whether large doses can protect against heart disease and cancer; minimize heart damage when injected after a heart attack; improve immune system response in the elderly; and protect against cataracts.

Vitamin K (from the Danish word "koagulation") appears to play a key role in blood-clotting. In addition, low levels of vitamin K may be related to the development of osteoporosis.

Biotin (vitamin H) acts as a catalyst in the metabolism of carbohydrates and fats. Soybeans and brewer's yeast are especially good sources. However, deficiencies of biotin are extremely rare in humans because it's produced by microorganisms ordinarily present in the gastrointestinal tract. The substance is generally non-toxic in humans and has no known therapeutic uses.

Folate (often called folic acid) combines with vitamin B12 to promote normal cell division and synthesis of RNA (ribonucleic acid) and DNA (dioxyribonucleic acid). Green leafy vegetables are frequently recommended sources. Persons with folate deficiency display symptoms usually associated with anemia — irritability, weakness, lack of energy, sleeplessness and loss of facial color. Folate is considered non-toxic to humans.

Minerals

Minerals are inorganic elements or compounds. The FNB issues RDAs for three minerals: calcium, phosphorus and magnesium. All are crucial to building strong bones and teeth. In addition, calcium helps to transmit nerve impulses and regulate muscle activity; phosphorus is involved in nearly every key chemical reaction within the body; and magnesium plays a key role in controlling the flow of elements and nerve impulses across cell membranes. Calcium is found in milk, cheese and yogurt; phosphorus in dairy products, meat and fish, and magnesium in nuts, fish and whole grains.

FNB has prepared RDAs for four additional minerals that it classifies as "trace elements" because they are needed in smaller quantities. **Iron,** as most people know, is essential to healthy blood. **Zinc** is needed for cell division, repair and growth and for DNA and RNA synthesis. **Iodine** is vital to proper functioning of the thyroid gland, which regulates body metabolism. **Selenium** is the least familiar trace element, in part because direct evidence of its importance to human nutrition did not emerge until 1979. Some researchers are studying the possibility that selenium, as well as vitamin E, may afford protection against many types of cancer. [1]

[1] The most recent edition of *Recommended Dietary Allowances* (1989) discusses five additional trace elements: copper, manganese, fluoride, chromium and molybdenum. However, the Food and Nutrition Board did not establish RDAs for any of them.

health. "Megadoses of niacin have been known to result in liver toxicity," he noted. "High doses of vitamins A and D can cause liver damage. Too much vitamin B6 can produce nerve problems. People with kidney or liver complications are especially vulnerable to the potential side-effects of megadoses, because their ability to break down or excrete excess is reduced."

Furthermore, high doses of some nutrients can impair the body's ability to absorb others. "That's especially true with minerals," according to Hathcock. "High levels of calcium may precipitate iron deficiency, for example, and excess zinc can interfere with the body's absorption of copper." [15]

Are synthetic vitamins and minerals as effective as natural ones?

No one disputes that the vitamins and minerals in dietary supplements are chemically identical to the ones in foods. Moreover, numerous health professionals regularly take supplements to get nutrients that may be missing from their diets or for added protection against disease.

Even so, nutritionists generally recommend that people get the bulk of their essential nutrients from fruits,

Vitamin Use Heavier Among Certain Groups

*Vitamin use is heaviest among females, college graduates, adults between ages 45 and 54 and people living in the West. Easterners, non-high school graduates and young adults 18-24 are the least frequent users. **

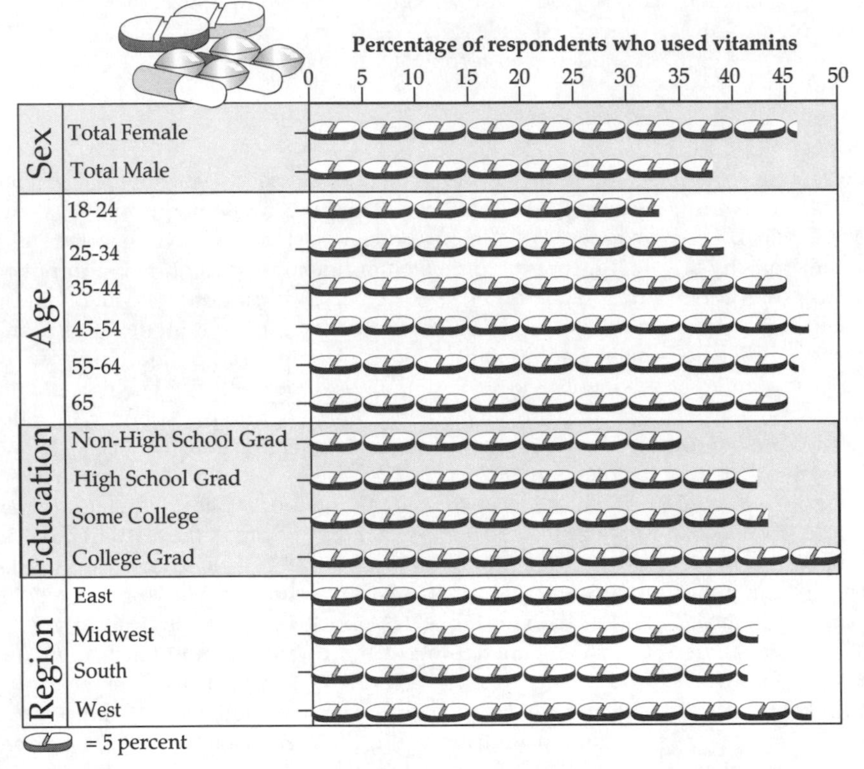

* *Respondents who were polled last year were asked whether they had used vitamins in the last 30 days.*
Source: Council for Responsible Nutrition. The council represents manufacturers, distributors and suppliers of nutritional supplements and products.

vegetables and grains. The reason is that studies suggest these foods contain a host of chemical compounds that seem to work in tandem with vitamins and minerals to keep bodies fit.

Many of these micronutrients already have been isolated, but many more remain to be identified. Called phytochemicals, they may not be nutrients in the usual sense of the word. Still, "in some sense, they could be regarded as just as essential as vitamins in maintaining us in a healthy, cancer-free state," said John Potter, director of the University of Minnesota's Cancer Prevention Research Unit. [16]

Potter believes phytochemicals will be marketed in pill form sometime in the next 10 years. "And while I think that they may have some value, what they'll mostly do is produce expensive urine," he said. "That's because we're still discovering more of these compounds, and a pill may lull people into thinking that a single compound — or even a small number of compounds — will do the job of hundreds." [17]

Cordaro also foresees the day when supplement makers will include phytochemicals in their products. "A whole new world of dietary supplements is being born," he says. "And those products are emerging for very precise health-nutrition reasons. They're designed to improve the wellness of the individual and lower the risk of disease. They may even be designed to treat or cure illness."

According to Cordaro, production of more sophisticated dietary supplements eventually will necessitate "more creative and innovative regulatory approaches." He views that as "a challenge that must be faced as the last decade of the 20th century ends."

At present, though, says CSPI Nutrition Director Bonnie Liebman, scientists know only that "there are so many chemicals — maybe thousands of them — in every food that it's hard to know whether any one is really making a difference in the human body." For that reason, nutritionists still recommend eating plenty of fruits and vegetables. Cruciferous vegetables, which include broccoli, Brussels sprouts, cabbage and cauliflower, are especially rich in phytochemicals.

The problem with that advice, says Liebman, is that consumers and the media tend to tune it out. "Telling people to eat their fruits and vegetables just isn't very sexy," she says. "And to some people, not very tasty, perhaps." ■

BACKGROUND

Capt. Cook's Discovery

Centuries before scientists identified vitamins and realized their importance to good health, the four main diseases caused by vitamin deficiency were known throughout the world. Beriberi, characterized by inflammation of the nerves, digestive system and heart, stems from lack of vitamin

B1 (thiamin). Pellagra, marked by skin and mouth lesions as well as gastrointestinal and nervous disorders, signifies a diet with insufficient niacin. Rickets, whose chief symptom is soft and deformed bones, is normally due to inadequate sunlight or vitamin D. And scurvy, whose victims suffer from sore gums, painful joints and hemorrhaging, results from vitamin C deficiency.

Scurvy was the first vitamin-related disease to yield to deliberate changes in diet. The ailment was long prevalent among seamen, who subsisted for months at a time on dried and salted foods. For similar reasons, it also was common among soldiers and prison inmates and in communities without access during winter to fresh foods rich in vitamin C.

It remained for Captain James Cook, the 18th-century English explorer, to demonstrate conclusively that eating fresh produce could keep scurvy in check. During his expeditions to the Pacific between 1768 and 1780, Cook ordered his men to gather fruits and vegetables whenever they went ashore. He began one voyage with nearly four tons of sauerkraut, a good source of vitamin C.

As a result, said chemist Pauling, "not a single member of his crew died of scurvy during his three Pacific voyages, carried out at a time when scurvy was still ravaging the crews of most vessels on such protracted voyages." [18]

However, Cook's dietary insights were more intuitive than scientifically grounded. For the most part, understanding of nutrition remained sketchy for the next 100 years.

"Until after the Civil War, it was widely believed that all foods had the same nutritive values," historian Daniel J. Boorstin wrote. "There was supposed to be one 'universal aliment' which helped the body grow, which kept it warm and working and repaired the tissues.

"This popular notion justified the monotony of the popular diet. . . . Seafarers knew that to prevent scurvy they should eat fresh fruits, but these were considered more medicinal than nutritive." [19]

Toward the end of the 19th century, researchers discovered that minerals such as calcium and phosphorus also were essential to good health. Many surmised that other nutrients, still unknown to them, might well be equally or even more important.

Casimir Funk, a Polish biochemist, confirmed this hunch when he published his "vitamine" theory of nutrition in 1911. Vitamines, as Funk described them, were a group of compounds vital to life; each was thought to have a nitrogen-containing component known as an amine. The "e" in vitamine was dropped when it was found that not all vitamins contain nitrogen and, therefore, not all are amines. In any event, Funk's hypothesis led to the identification of most individual vitamins over the next 20 years. (*See story, p. 584.*)

Concern About Nutrition

As knowledge about vitamins and minerals grew, nutrition became a public-policy concern. Between 1925 and 1937, for example, the Health Organization of the League of Nations published a series of documents examining aspects of food and nutrition. These culminated in a report on estimated requirements for vitamin and mineral intake. [20]

There also was growing recognition that a sound diet was important to national as well as individual well-being. After witnessing the poverty of British coal miners in the mid-1930s, novelist George Orwell wrote: "I think it could be plausibly argued that changes of diet are more important than changes of dynasty or even of religion." [21] In Germany, meanwhile, the Nazi government reportedly was stockpiling synthetic vitamins as a war-preparedness measure. [22]

Nutrition-consciousness was rising in the United States as well, as evidenced by passage of the Food, Drug and Cosmetic Act of 1938 (FDCA). The law broadened the definitions of adulteration, misbranding and lack of informative labeling first spelled out in the Federal Food and Drug Act of 1906. The 1938 law also provided for factory inspections and increased the penalties for violations.

On May 25, 1941, the National Research Council (NRC) announced a new dietary "yardstick" for individuals. It consisted of a chart setting forth the basic amounts of 10 essential food requirements — calories, proteins, calcium, iron, vitamin A, thiamin, riboflavin, niacin and vitamins C and D. This "nutritional gold standard" was the forerunner of Recommended Dietary Allowances, first published by the NRC's Food and Nutrition Board in 1943.

A National Nutrition Conference for Defense that had been called by President Franklin D. Roosevelt in May 1941 adopted the NRC yardstick as part of a program to spread nutrition knowledge among the lay public, spur greater production of foods needed in the average diet and "enrich" foods such as flour and bread with nutrients removed by the milling and refining process.

Experts viewed the program as a solid investment in the nation's future. Addressing the American Dietetic Association in St. Louis, Mo., in October 1941, Col. R.A. Osmun of the U.S. Army Quartermaster Corps said a revolution in American food habits and farm production could be expected from the training of more than 1.6 million soldiers in scientific nutrition. After eating balanced meals including milk, fresh vegetables and fruits, Osmun declared, the soldiers would demand a similar diet when they returned to civilian life.

Tougher Regulations

As the postwar era dawned, a fundamental weakness in FDCA became glaringly apparent: The law lacked a procedure for determining the safety of chemicals in foods and cosmetics before the products were marketed. To provide such a mechanism, Congress amended FDCA three times between 1954 and 1960. Under the Food Additives Amendments of 1958, for example, chemical additives were barred from any processed food unless the manufacturer had sought prior permission from the FDA, and the agency had then granted a tolerance indicating the amount safe for use. Where no approval or tolerance was granted, the additive could not be used at all. [23]

Relations between the FDA and the dietary supplement industry reached their nadir in 1966, when the agency proposed rules affecting supplements. Among other things, FDA recommended that labels on multivitamin and mineral preparations carry this announcement: "Vitamins and minerals are supplied in abundant amounts in the foods we eat. The Food and Nutrition Board of the National Research Council recommends that dietary needs be satisfied by foods. Except for persons with special medical needs, there is no scientific basis for recommending routine use of dietary supplements."

Not surprisingly, the label sparked protests from the health food and dietary supplement industries and from many nutritionists. As a result, the FDA stayed implementation of the 1966 rules and scheduled public hearings on nutrition supplements that were held from 1968 to 1970.

Then, in 1973, the agency unveiled a new labeling program affecting both foods and nutrition supplements. "Nutrition labeling for most foods is voluntary," the FDA stated. "However, if a product is fortified by the addition of a nutrient, or a nutritional claim is made in the labeling or advertising, that product label must then have full nutrition labeling."

The most controversial 1973 rule targeted vitamin and mineral supplements. It provided that supplements containing more than 150 percent of the Recommended Dietary Allowance (RDA) must be labeled and marketed as drugs, making them subject to stringent testing for effectiveness and safety. The FDA argued that Americans were overusing vitamins and minerals and that such overuse was potentially dangerous.

Manufacturers' Counterattack

As in 1966, the manufacturers of health foods and nutrition supplements mounted a fierce counterattack. It took the form of a protest campaign by consumers that "buried Congress under 2 million pieces of mail — said to be more than it had received on any other issue since Watergate," wrote Patricia Long in *Health* magazine. [24]

Congress responded by approving the Proxmire Amendment to 1976 legislation authorizing funds for a variety of health programs. The amendment, which is still in force, barred the FDA from ordering any dietary supplements off the market solely because it considered them worthless or overly potent. [25]

The 1976 legislation did, however, authorize seizure (or other enforcement action) by the FDA of vitamin or mineral products that had been falsely advertised. Except in cases of an imminent hazard to health, the FDA was directed to wait 90 days before seizing any product, thus giving the Federal Trade Commission time to investigate the alleged advertising violation.

The FDA's limited options on nutrition supplements became apparent during a public health scare linked to the amino acid L-tryptophan. On Nov. 17, 1989, the FDA announced it was seeking a voluntary nationwide recall of products containing L-tryptophan, which was suspected of causing a rare blood disorder known as eosinophilia-myalgia syndrome (EMS). More than 1,500 EMS cases, including 38 deaths, were reported to public health agencies, although the actual incidence was thought to be higher. A bad batch of L-tryptophan was blamed for the outbreak, and L-tryptophan was taken off the market.

The L-tryptophan recall prompted the FDA in 1990 to contract with the Federation of American Societies of Experimental Biology (FASEB) to review available safety data on amino acids. FASEB studied scientific literature on each amino acid, focusing on metabolism, genetic influences on metabolism and population groups potentially at higher risk for adverse health effects from nutrition supplements containing amino acids. The federation concluded there was insufficient information on which to base a safe maximum consumption level for any such supplement.

New Labeling Law Passed in 1990

Congress, meanwhile, approved legislation in 1990 that for the first time ordered manufacturers to display detailed nutritional information on most packaged foods and some seafood. The Nutritional Labeling and Education Act (NLEA) barred manufacturers from making certain nutritional claims about their products on the label — "low cholesterol," for example — when other equally important information, such as high fat level, was not mentioned. [26]

Manufacturers also were prohibited from making health claims for food if they were not verified by the FDA. In addition, the Department of Health and Human Services (HHS) was told to develop standards for such terms as "lite" and "low fat," which then could appear on labels only if the products met the standards.

Continued on p. 590

Chronology

18th Century

An antidote is found to a vitamin-deficiency disease that has plagued the world.

1768-1780
During three voyages to the Pacific, the English explorer Capt. James Cook demonstrates that fresh produce prevents scurvy.

1910s ***Important discoveries are made about individual nutrients.***

1911
Casimir Funk, a Polish biochemist, publishes his "vitamine" theory, which holds that four such substances are present in natural foods.

1920s-1930s

Governments around the world recognize nutrition as a key public-policy concern.

1928
Albert von Szent-Györgyi, a Hungarian biochemist, discovers vitamin C.

1938
President Franklin D. Roosevelt signs into law the Food, Drug and Cosmetic Act, which broadens the definitions of adulteration and misbranding.

1940s ***As World War II rages in Europe, the United States makes nutrition a defense-preparedness priority.***

May 25, 1941
The Food and Nutrition Board announces a dietary "yardstick" to serve as a "nutritional gold standard" for individuals.

May 28, 1941
A National Nutrition Conference for Defense called by President Roosevelt in May 1941 adopts the NRC dietary yardstick as part of a broader nutrition program.

1943
The FNB publishes the first edition of its *Recommended Dietary Allowances* (RDA).

1950s-1960s

As the dietary supplement industry expands, the FDA tightens its regulations.

1958
President Dwight D. Eisenhower signs into law the Food Additives Amendments barring chemical additives from processed foods without FDA permission.

1959
The FNB recognizes vitamin E as essential to human nutrition.

1966
The FDA proposes that labels on multivitamin and mineral preparations state that "there is no scientific basis for recommending routine use of dietary supplements." The agency later stays implementation of the rule.

1970s ***After another FDA attempt to rein in the dietary supplement industry, Congress steps in.***

1973
The FDA proposes that nutrition supplements containing more than 150 percent of the RDA be labeled and marketed as drugs.

1976
Congress approves the Proxmire Amendment, barring the FDA from ordering any supplements off the market solely because it considers them worthless or overly potent.

1980s-1990s

Tension between dietary supplement producers and the FDA persists.

Nov. 17, 1989
FDA announces it will seek a voluntary nationwide recall of the supplement L-tryptophan.

Nov. 8, 1990
President George Bush signs the Nutrition Labeling and Education Act, requiring detailed nutritional information on packaged foods.

1992
Bush signs the Dietary Supplement Act, which imposes a one-year moratorium — until December 1993 — on FDA action to implement health-claims rules for dietary supplements.

April 7, 1993
Sen. Orrin G. Hatch, R-Utah, and Rep. Bill Richardson, D-N.M., introduce legislation to relax FDA regulation of the supplement industry.

Dec. 29, 1993
The FDA issues final regulations requiring makers of vitamins and other nutritional supplements to provide scientific evidence supporting health claims, effective July 1, 1994.

Homeopathy Coming Back Into Fashion

If you're like most people, the definition of homeopathy probably has you stumped. But cheer up. *Webster's New World Dictionary* didn't quite get it right, either. Webster defines homeopathy as "a system of medical treatment, no longer practiced in the U.S." In fact, homeopathy is, once again, very much alive. But Webster can take heart too. Things are happening so fast in this field, it's hard to keep up.

Supermarkets and drug stores now stock homeopathic medicines, many of which contain herbs. Health-conscious consumers often gravitate toward remedies containing such "natural" ingredients, believing them safer — and often more effective — than prescription drugs.

As developed early in the 19th century by Samuel Hahnemann, a German physician, homeopathy is based on the premise that "like cures like." That is, the key to treating a disease is to use a drug or other agent that produces the disease's symptoms in a healthy person. Observers had noted, for example, that a healthy person who was given quinine, a chemical derived from cinchona bark, displayed malaria-like symptoms. Consequently, quinine became the treatment of choice for malaria.

Hahnemann also formulated the "minute dosage rule," which holds that physicians should prescribe no more than the smallest amount of any drug that produces the desired result. He believed that the more closely a drug's action mimics the disease's symptoms, the less is needed to prod the body into healing itself.

In practice, this means that many homeopathic preparations are so weak as to be indistinguishable from placebos. "Many of them are diluted to such a degree that, in theory, not even a molecule of the active ingredient remains" in the homeopathic product on the store shelf, *Consumer Reports* magazine declared in March.[1]

Why, then, hasn't the Food and Drug Administration moved against homeopathic medicines even more vigorously than it has against dietary supplements? The reason is that the Food, Drug and Cosmetic Act of 1938 exempted all substances in the *United States Homeopathic Pharmacopeia* from the safety and efficacy testing required of conventional drugs. Crafted by Sen. Royal S. Copeland, D-N.Y., a homeopathic physician, the exemption gave homeopathic preparations a marketing edge over herbal products and dietary supplements.

Though homeopathic remedies "are probably harmless," stated *Consumer Reports,* it urged Congress to lift the blanket protection for homeopathic preparations from federal drug laws. "In particular, remedies being marketed as treatments for specific illnesses should be removed from drugstore shelves unless and until they are tested and shown to be safe and effective."[2]

[1] "Homeopathy: Much Ado About Nothing?" *Consumer Reports,* March 1994, p. 201.

[2] *Ibid.*

Continued from p. 588

Under NLEA, most packaged food products were required to provide specific information on the amounts of fat, cholesterol, sodium, fiber, protein, carbohydrates and other nutrients per serving. For their part, retailers were directed to provide similar information for 20 types of raw agricultural products and raw fish. The measure preempted a variety of state nutrition-labeling laws but allowed states to require their own ingredient warnings.

With respect to dietary supplements, the 1990 law permitted FDA to stipulate the level of proof it required for health-benefit claims on labels. The agency chose the "scientific agreement" standard used for foods, which manufacturers complained was too strict. Most health claims would be disallowed, they said, in the absence of virtual consensus among scientific experts.

Sen. Hatch and Rep. John D. Dingell, D-Mich., thereupon agreed to passage of the Dietary Supplement Act of 1992, which Congress approved as part of a drug bill. The measure imposed a one-year moratorium — at least until December 1993 — on FDA action to implement health-claims regulations for dietary supplements. It further required the agency to take a fresh look at the issue and recommend how health claims for such products should be regulated.

Hatch acknowledged that he had a personal and political stake in helping the supplement industry. He testified at a 1993 congressional hearing that he takes supplements on a regular basis. Moreover, he said, "Utah has an important nutritional supplement industry that contributes over $700 million to the national economy. We must consider the adverse economic impact that burdensome regulations could have on Utah and other states."[27] ■

CURRENT SITUATION

FDA Initiatives

The FDA's final regulations for conventional foods, published in the *Federal Register* Jan. 6, 1993, suggested the agency wasn't planning to modify its policy on nutrition supplements. Despite the moratorium imposed by the Dietary Supplement Act, the FDA announced its "tentative conclusions" that dietary-supplement labels should be treated like other foods under NLEA, including requirements on nutrient content, mandatory nutrition labeling and health claims. Regarding health claims in particular, the agency indicated it would hold to its original position that standards and procedures for nutrition supplements should be substantially the same as those for conventional foods.

It came as no surprise, then, that the FDA proposed in June 1993 to regulate nutrition supplements on the same basis as ordinary food products. Specifically, the agency said it would require supplement makers to back up any health claims on labels with evidence supported by "significant scientific agreement" — the same standard of proof applied to breakfast cereal, fruit juice and other foods.

An accompanying advance notice of proposed rulemaking did raise eyebrows, however. It stated that FDA was "reviewing the manner in which it regulates dietary supplements, including products containing vitamins, minerals, amino acids, herbs and other similar nutritional substances." To facilitate its review, the agency asked for public comment on possible approaches to "assure the safety" of dietary supplements. To many in the nutrition-supplement industry, the tone and substance of the June 18 notice indicated that FDA planned to regulate supplements more stringently than in the past.

The FDA issued its regulations in final form on Dec. 29, just two days before the deadline set by Congress. The health-claim rule recently took effect, as noted, July 1. However, the agency delayed the effective date of the rule requiring nutrition information on supplement labels until July 1, 1995. The move pleased manufacturers, who had said that a mid-1994 deadline would have forced them to spend at least $100 million to relabel products already on the market.

On the same day it issued the final regulations, FDA announced its approval of a health claim that folate, a vitamin, can reduce the incidence of birth defects that affect the brain and spinal cord, such as spina bifida. Consequently, manufacturers may now state that products containing folate help prevent some common birth defects if taken before the onset of pregnancy.

The FDA had previously allowed supplement makers to claim that calcium helps prevent osteoporosis. However, the agency has yet to sanction any claims that supplements containing antioxidants (vitamins C and E and beta carotene) shield the body from cancer, heart disease and other serious illnesses.

Hatch-Richardson Bills

As FDA was putting the finishing touches on its dietary supplement

What Nutrition-Conscious Americans Are Buying

Among buyers of vitamins and minerals, multivitamins were the favorite product, capturing more than 44 percent of the 1993 retail market. The most popular individual vitamins were vitamins C and E.

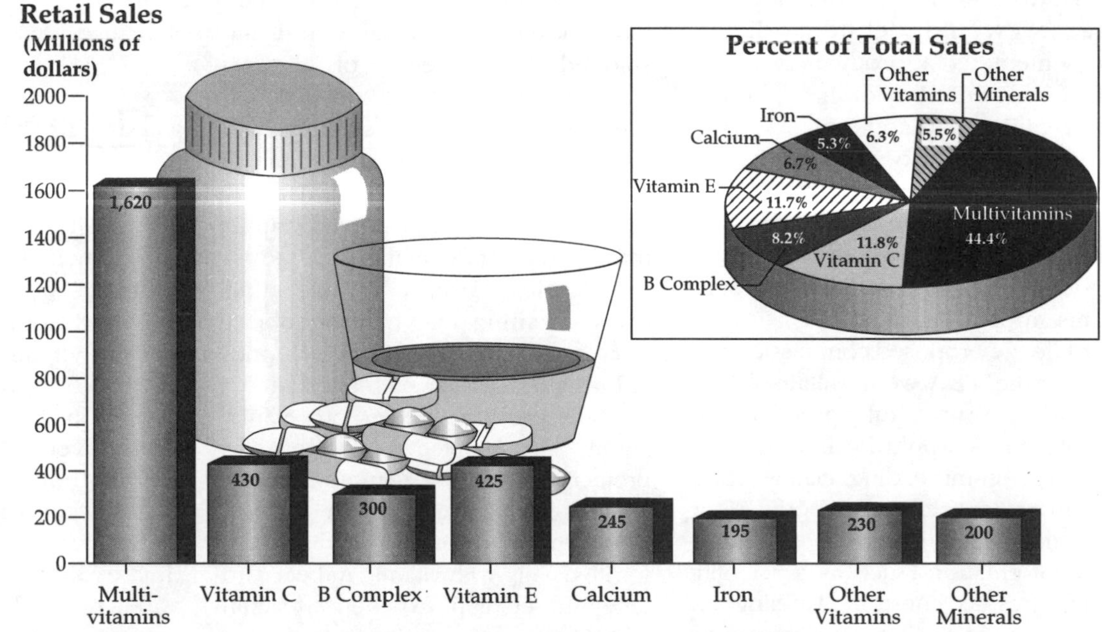

Source: Council for Responsible Nutrition. The council represents manufacturers, distributors and suppliers of nutritional supplements and products.

rules, moves were under way in Congress to curb the agency's power. On April 7, 1993, Hatch and Richardson introduced their similar bills. A key provision would undermine FDA's current standard of proof for health claims. Instead of requiring "significant scientific agreement," the legislation would allow a claim to appear on labels unless the FDA found through studies and the "totality of scientific evidence" that the claim was unsound.

FDA Commissioner Kessler, a former Hatch staff member, said this approach would tie his agency's hands. "In the absence of a clear standard, the only thing that FDA can do is go after the products on a case-by-case basis," he told a House subcommittee considering nutrition supplement legislation last summer. "Freedom of choice means little unless consumers have . . . accurate information." [28]

Though little has happened to the Richardson bill since it was introduced, the companion Hatch bill is now awaiting Senate floor action. As approved May 11 by the Senate Labor and Human Resources Committee, the measure would define a dietary supplement as a product that contains a vitamin, mineral, herb, botanical or amino acid and is meant to be taken orally. It also would direct the secretary of HHS to withdraw existing NLEA regulations and instead set up a temporary, independent commission to devise a more effective health claims approval process.

While the proposed commission was in existence, FDA would retain authority to move against faulty products, and manufacturers would be free to make truthful, non-misleading claims about how ingredients affect the body. Moreover, the Hatch bill states that third-party information (such as a scientific study) does not constitute labeling and may be made available to consumers so long as it is truthful and non-misleading; stipulates that a supplement is not a drug simply because it is accompanied by directions for use; and establishes an Office of Dietary Supplements within the National Institutes of Health.

Before the bill reaches the Senate floor, the committee is expected to approve a substitute version containing language allowing the "significant scientific agreement" standard to remain in force for the lifetime of the temporary commission. Hatch has said he will not oppose the provision.

Finnish Smokers Study

With the Hatch-Richardson legislation apparently enjoying broad support in Congress and among dietary-supplement users, nutrition regulation advocates had reason to feel glum. But then the Finnish smokers study seemed to vindicate those who had voiced doubts about health claims made for antioxidants.

The study, recently published in *The New England Journal of Medicine,* involved 29,000 middle-aged, male Finnish smokers who smoked a pack a day on average and had smoked for an average of 40 years. The participants were divided into four groups. Each received daily doses of either beta carotene, vitamin E, both substances or a placebo. To prevent the participants' expectations from unduly influencing the study, it was conducted on a "double blind" basis, meaning that neither subjects nor investigators knew which individual was taking which substance. [29]

Many previous studies of a similar nature had suggested antioxidants offer protection against certain types of cancer. For instance, a large trial in China found that persons whose diets were fortified daily with vitamin A, beta carotene and selenium experienced significantly fewer stomach cancer deaths than participants who didn't take the supplements. [30] More than 100 other surveys have suggested that smokers who ate fruits and vegetables rich in beta carotene had a lower risk of lung cancer. But it was not clear from those studies whether the lower risk was due to the beta carotene or some other factor.

The Finnish study's findings presented a different picture. No reduction in the incidence of lung cancer was noted among the men who received vitamin E. But "unexpectedly," the study's authors said, a markedly higher incidence of lung cancer was observed among the men who took beta carotene than among those who did not. They concluded that the trial "raises the possibility that these supplements may have harmful as well as beneficial effects."

The authors acknowledged, however, that the study data could be interpreted in other ways: "It is plausible that the intervention period was too short to inhibit the development of cancers resulting from a lifetime of exposure to cigarette smoke and other carcinogens . . . or the intake of beta carotene may be only a non-specific marker for lifestyles that protect against cancer."

Rising Sales

It's too soon to tell whether the Finnish study will affect nutrition supplement sales, which have been robust of late. According to the Council for Responsible Nutrition, retail sales of vitamins, minerals and other nutrition supplements totaled $4.2 billion in 1993, a 13.5 percent increase over 1992. Multivitamin preparations (both with and without minerals) accounted for 44.4 percent of vitamin and mineral sales. CRN estimates that 43 percent of American adults regularly take nutrition supplements and that consumption patterns are fairly uniform within groups de-

Continued on p. 594

At Issue:

Should the Food and Drug Administration have the authority to require manufacturers to demonstrate the safety of herbal dietary supplements?

yes

BRUCE SILVERGLADE
Director of Legal Affairs, Center for Science in the Public Interest

FROM *TESTIMONY AT A HEARING OF THE HOUSE ENERGY AND COMMERCE SUBCOMMITTEE ON HEALTH AND THE ENVIRONMENT,* JULY 29, 1993.

Questions have . . . been raised about the safety of particular herbs. Presently, FDA uses its authority over food additives to ensure the safety of supplements containing herbs. We believe this approach is cumbersome and inefficient. We recommend that Congress exempt herbs from the food additive provisions of the Food, Drug and Cosmetic Act and provide the FDA with express authority to ensure the safety of these products.

We believe, however, that such legislation should grant the FDA authority to require manufacturers to demonstrate the safety of herbs. Existing products should remain on the market until such evidence is forthcoming, unless the FDA believes that a particular substance is hazardous and needs to be removed from the marketplace. FDA should not be required to prove that such products may be injurious to health as the public might remain unprotected for years while FDA builds its case. Instead, the responsibility for demonstrating safety in such cases should rest with the manufacturer or retailer.

A brief review of supplements containing herbs indicates why it is essential that FDA be able to have such authority. Here is a product [that] contains chaparral as its primary ingredient. The ingestion of chaparral is associated with acute, toxic hepatitis. The FDA has issued a public warning concerning chaparral, and the industry has instituted a voluntary recall. If the FDA did not possess authority to demand evidence of safety, it is unlikely that these steps would be taken.

Regular consumption of large amounts of comfrey tea and comfrey pills . . . can lead to severe liver damage. Comfrey contains pyrrolizidine alkaloids that are metabolized by the liver into toxic substances. The herb is "prescribed" to treat abdominal pain, fatigue and allergies. Although comfrey is banned in Canada, FDA might not be able to ban comfrey promptly in the United States if it lacked appropriate legal authority. . . .

Black cohosh (cimicifuga racemosa) is used by Native Americans for a variety of ailments, but the safety of this substance has been questioned. Black cohosh may cause dizziness, headache, tremors, joint pains and a depressed heart rate. These adverse effects may occur at relatively small doses, and severe poisoning may occur at large doses. . . . It is imperative that FDA retain adequate authority to protect consumers from any harmful consequences of products containing this substance. . . .

no

KACHINAS KUTENAI
Apache medicine woman

FROM *TESTIMONY AT A HEARING OF THE HOUSE ENERGY AND COMMERCE SUBCOMMITTEE ON HEALTH AND THE ENVIRONMENT,* JULY 29, 1993.

I speak for the Hispanic, Oriental, Black and Indian Americans who exercise their rights to honor, respect and use those herbs which were planted by the Creator and blessed with secret healing powers to assist human beings to heal themselves.

The FDA's removal of chaparral and other healing herbs from stores, without sufficient evidence of clear and present danger to public health, is a violation of our cultural rights. Chaparral, in particular, is an herb known to my people for its ability to fight the growth of cancer cells in the brain, breast, bone and prostate. I suggest chaparral to people of all races, and I take it myself, daily.

The FDA is a biased organization, which has reacted to scanty information with regard to herbs such as chaparral and comfrey. The FDA operates on a double standard — they do not seem to feel it necessary to apply their supposedly scientific standards of acceptance and rejection to natural substances. Instead, the anecdotal evidence of a few cases has been enough to raid health-food stores in order to remove the herbs from public availability. No lengthy scientific studies were done. This invasive harassment has removed the freedom of choice, not just for ethnic minorities who depend on such substances as part of their cultural heritage, but for all free Americans. . . .

At the very least, this committee should recommend legislation which denies the FDA the power to ban such substances without substantial scientific evidence of genuine public health risks. Consumers who wish to use herbs which have been used traditionally for thousands of years deserve due process. Herbs, vitamins, minerals, amino acid and foods which are considered to have therapeutic value should be considered a separate category — neither food nor drug, but some intermediate category which can be considered independent of the FDA's current distinctions. Ideally, a new agency, which is completely separate and independent of the FDA, should be established by Congress. . . .

I know that government does not act morally or out of compassion, but rather reacts to economics. The bottom line that this committee and Congress should remember is that herbs, vitamins and minerals treat illness, and sustain wellness, more economically for all people, especially for the poor and ethnic minorities. The FDA destroys human rights when they take away the rights of ethnic minorities to use the herbs known to be effective for them.

Linus Pauling's Secret of Long Life

Linus C. Pauling won the Nobel Prize for chemistry in 1954 and the Nobel Prize for Peace in 1962. To many people, however, he is best known for his theories on vitamins — vitamin C in particular.

In his controversial best-seller, *Vitamin C and the Common Cold* (1970), Pauling asserted: "The evidence shows that ascorbic acid [vitamin C] decreases the average incidence of the common cold." He argued that extremely large doses of the vitamin could also cure schizophrenia and hasten the healing process.

Pauling's belief in the curative powers of vitamins is a central tenet of what he calls "orthomolecular medicine" — a strategy for fighting disease "by varying the concentrations in the human body of substances that are normally present in the body and are required for health." This approach is superior, he argued, to "treatment by the use of powerful synthetic substances or plant products, which may, and usually do, have undesirable side-effects." [1]

Now 93, Pauling discovered two years ago that he had prostate cancer. Typically, he insisted the disease had been "put off for 20, 25 years because of my high intake of vitamin C and other vitamins." [2] Similarly, he has written that by taking vitamins and "following a few other healthful practices from youth or middle age on, you can . . . extend your life and years of well-being by 25 or even 35 years." [3]

Pauling's ideas on vitamins initially met with skepticism or worse in the nutrition community. For instance, Philip L. White, secretary of the American Medical Association's Council on Food and Nutrition, wrote in the November 1970 *Today's Health:* "There is no reliable evidence that vitamin C has any preventive or therapeutic effects when given to a healthy person. . . .Unfortunately, it is still a widespread belief that extra ascorbic acid can not only prevent colds but also lessens the severity and duration of colds and other respiratory infections. Even when consumed at the first sign of a sniffle, large doses of the vitamin are useless."

More recent research indicates that high vitamin intake — especially of vitamin C — is indeed linked in some way to lower susceptibility to disease and longer life expectancy. However, skeptics note that the studies don't conclusively show a cause-effect relationship between vitamins and resistance to disease, nor do they prove the value of the doses advocated by Pauling. The chemist suggests vitamin consumption levels far higher than the Recommended Dietary Allowances (RDAs) published by the National Academy of Sciences' Food and Nutrition Board.

In any case, anecdotal evidence says it works. John Cordaro, president of the Council for Responsible Nutrition, which represents dietary supplement producers, reports coming down with "far fewer colds" since boosting his vitamin C intake. Moreover, "on those rare occasions when I've had a cold or flu, the severity and duration has been less."

Cordaro acknowledges that "If you look at the scientific literature, the results are non-conclusive. But the bottom line is, does vitamin C work for the individual? It works for me. Whether that's because the effect is real, or because it's a placebo, the outcome is the same."

---

[1] Linus C. Pauling, *How to Live Longer and Feel Better* (1986), p. 93.

[2] Quoted by John Horgan, "Stubbornly Ahead of His Time," *Scientific American*, March 1993, p. 36.

[3] Pauling, *op. cit.*, p. 3.

Continued from p. 592

fined by age, education and region. (*See tables, p. 586.*)

Analysts attribute much of last year's sales spurt to supplements containing antioxidants. American Cyanamid Co.'s Lederle Consumer Health Division introduced the industry's first antioxidant supplement, called Protegra, in March 1993. Bristol-Myers Products followed with Theragran AntiOxidant in October. And Bayer AG's Miles Inc. jumped on the antioxidant bandwagon early this year when it revamped its popular One-a-Day line.

Miles also included garlic in its One-a-Day makeover. According to Towne-Oller & Associates, herbal supplement sales rose by 70 percent to $22.7 million in supermarkets alone in 1993. Herbals were the second-fastest growing sales category for food and drugstores combined. Garlic, the No. 1 seller, posted a 67 percent increase in supermarket sales, while No. 2 ginseng recorded a 247 percent rise. [31]

Herbs are common ingredients of homeopathic medicines, which have gained wide acceptance in recent years. (*See story, p. 590.*) Once found mainly in health-food stores, homeopathic remedies are now stocked by supermarkets and drugstores. The preparations appeal to consumers who feel natural substances are safer and more effective than synthetic ones. ■

OUTLOOK

More Changes Ahead

Regardless of what happens to the Hatch-Richardson legislation, nutrition experts foresee continuing tension between the FDA and the dietary supplement industry. In Cordaro's opinion, "It's almost in the nature of the beast that there should be conflict between the regulator and the regulated industry. If it looked as if all was peace and harmony between them, people would suspect a 'cozy relationship.'"

Silverglade agrees. "There would be cause for concern if an industry totally felt comfortable with the regulators," he says. "That usually means a problem exists that watchdog groups like CSPI try to alert the public about."

The National Academy of Sciences' Food and Nutrition Board is likely to assume a more visible role in the nutrition debate in coming years. That's because a consensus is developing among nutritionists and within the board itself on re-evaluating the Recommended Dietary Allowances (RDAs). Although the current RDAs date only from 1989, many nutritionists contend they're badly outdated.

The main problem, says Liebman, is that the RDAs "are designed to make sure you don't develop a vitamin or mineral deficiency. What people really want to know is whether higher amounts — far in excess of what's needed to prevent a deficiency — can reduce the risk of some diseases. And the RDAs don't address that."

Liebman also feels the Food and Nutrition Board should determine what the upper safe levels of various nutrients are. "Right now," she says, "all most people have to go on is over-generalized advice from a health professional who says, 'Don't take more than the RDA.' And the fact is, two times the RDA can be harmful for some nutrients, while 100 times is safe for others."

Another drawback of the RDAs, says Rodney E. Leonard, executive director of the Community Nutrition Institute, a citizens' interest group, is that they're not intended for individuals. "They're recommendations for populations. And trying to prescribe nutrient intake based on general population recommendations is precarious. We have to find a way to enable each individual to develop a dietary pattern reflecting his or her genetic characteristics."

In a "concept paper" issued in May, the Food and Nutrition Board showed it was aware of the criticism being leveled at the RDAs and agreed that sweeping changes may be called for. A board meeting is scheduled for late July to consider what action to take. "A lot will depend on the comments we receive from professionals and other interested parties on the concept paper," says Bernadette M. Marriott, the board's acting director. "If people are favorably disposed toward revising the RDAs along the lines suggested in the paper, then the board will move forward more quickly than if it encounters a lot of criticism."

To make the RDAs more meaningful for individuals, the concept paper proposed establishing four "reference points" for key nutrients and food components:

• **Deficient** — The nutrient intake level below which almost all healthy people can be expected, over time, to experience deficiency symptoms.

• **Average Requirement** — The mean intake level that appears sufficient to maintain the desired biochemical-physiological function of a population.

• **Recommended Dietary Allowance** — The intake level deemed adequate to meet the nutritional needs of practically all healthy persons.

• **Upper Safe** — The intake level that seems safe for most healthy people, and beyond which there is concern that some individuals will eventually develop toxicity symptoms. [32]

Though most nutritionists expect the board to go ahead with its proposed RDA overhaul, it is under no deadline for making a final decision. And even if the project is approved, says Marriott, the first order of business will be raising money to pay for it.

The dietary supplement industry, meanwhile, is making preparations for

For More Information

Center for Science in the Public Interest, 1875 Connecticut Ave. N.W., Suite 300, Washington, D.C. 20009-5728; (202) 332-9110. The center conducts research on food and nutrition. Areas of particular interest include eating habits, food safety regulations, food additives, dietary supplements, organically produced foods, alcoholic beverages and links between diet and disease.

Council for Responsible Nutrition, 1300 19th St. N.W., Suite 310, Washington, D.C. 20036; (202) 872-1488. The council is a membership group consisting of manufacturers, distributors and suppliers of nutrition supplements. It provides information on the nutrition supplement industry and explains the industry's position on legislation. CRN also monitors regulations issued by the Food and Drug Administration, Federal Trade Commission and Consumer Product Safety Commission.

Food and Nutrition Board, 1055 Thomas Jefferson St. N.W., Washington, D.C. 20007; (202) 334-1737. The board, an arm of the National Academy of Sciences, publishes and periodically revises the *Recommended Dietary Allowances* (RDAs), widely used by nutritionists. It also publishes a chart listing the RDAs in a format easily grasped by consumers.

next year's battles in Congress, especially reauthorization of the farm bill. Among the many issues to be covered in the legislation will be nutrition research priorities and federal food assistance programs — both matters of obvious interest to supplement manufacturers. CRN would like the bill to allow food-stamp recipients to exchange their coupons for dietary supplements, now prohibited under current policy.

Nutritionists also are awaiting the results of several other clinical trials involving the health effects of beta carotene. They may shed new light on the unexpected beta carotene finding of the Finnish smokers study.[33]

Blumberg supports all three studies, but he doesn't expect them to provide clear answers to the questions raised by the Finnish trial. "They will give us more information, not definitive information," he says. "We need to consider other things besides clinical trials in making public health decisions." Since "science is an ongoing process," policy-makers "need to look more broadly at the totality of the scientific evidence."

To Liebman, however, clinical trials are crucial. "Without clinical trials," she says, "you can never get definitive information because you can't prove cause and effect. I can't argue with Blumberg when he says we should look at the totality of the evidence. Of course we should. But that's just the point. These new trials are part of that evidence." ■

Notes

[1] U.S. Department of Commerce, *Statistical Abstracts of the United States,* 1993, p. 775.

[2] Statement presented at field hearing on diet supplements conducted by Rep. Elton Gallegly, R-Calif., Ventura, Calif., Feb. 18, 1994.

[3] Quoted in *The Washington Post,* Sept. 14, 1993.

[4] Editorial, *The New York Times,* Oct. 5, 1993.

[5] Testimony before House Subcommittee on Health and the Environment, July 29, 1993. For background, see "Food Safety," *The CQ Researcher,* June 14, 1993, pp. 481-504.

[6] Bill Richardson, "Ease Up on Dietary Supplements," *Roll Call,* May 23, 1994, p. 13.

[7] Council for Responsible Nutrition, *Vitamin Issues: Rationale for Dietary Supplement Legislation,* May 1993, p. 25.

[8] Testimony before Subcommittee on Health and the Environment, House Committee on Energy and Commerce, July 29, 1993.

[9] *Ibid.*

[10] *Ibid.*

[11] Letter to Rep. Henry A. Waxman, chairman, Energy and Commerce Subcommittee on Health and the Environment, Aug. 12, 1993. For background, see "Alternative Medicine," *The CQ Researcher,* Jan. 31, 1992, pp. 73-96.

[12] "Can Vitamins Help?" *Consumer Reports,* January 1992, p. 12.

[13] Michelle Turk, "Do Antioxidants Reduce Disease?" (interview with Jeffrey Blumberg), *American Health,* May 1994, p. 38.

[14] Hennekens, Charles H., et al., "Antioxidant Vitamins — Benefits Not Yet Proved," *The New England Journal of Medicine,* April 14, 1994, pp. 1080-81.

[15] Quoted by Paul R. Thomas in "Which Supplements Should You Take?" *American Health,* March 1991, pp. 39-40.

[16] Quoted by David Schardt, "Phytochemicals: Plants Against Cancer," *Nutrition Action Healthletter,* April 1994, p. 11.

[17] *Ibid.*

[18] Linus Pauling, *How to Live Longer and Feel Better* (1986), p. 49.

[19] Daniel J. Boorstin, *The Americans: The Democratic Experience* (1973), p. 322.

[20] Food and Nutrition Board, National Academy of Sciences, *How Should the Recommended Dietary Allowances Be Revised?* May 1994, p. 7.

[21] George Orwell, *The Road to Wigan Pier* (1937), p. 91.

[22] "Nutrition and National Health," *Editorial Research Reports,* May 13, 1941, p. 332.

[23] Congress also gave FDA pre-market testing authority in the 1954 Pesticide Chemical Amendments and the 1960 Color Additive Amendments to the 1938 Food, Drug and Cosmetic Act. For background, see "Food Irradiation," *The CQ Researcher,* June 12, 1992, pp. 505-524.

[24] Patricia Long, "The Vitamin Wars," *Health,* May-June 1993, p. 47.

[25] The amendment was named for one of its two principal sponsors, Sen. William Proxmire, D-Wis. The other main sponsor was Rep. Paul G. Rogers, D-Fla.

[26] For additional background on nutrition labeling, see "Fast-Food Shake-Up," *The CQ Researcher, Nov. 8,* 1991, pp. 825-848.

[27] Testimony before House Subcommittee on Health and the Environment, July 29, 1993.

[28] Testimony before House Subcommittee on Health and the Environment, July 29, 1993.

[29] The Alpha-Tocopherol, Beta Carotene Cancer Prevention Study Group, "The Effect of Vitamin E and Beta Carotene on the Incidence of Lung Cancer and Other Cancers in Male Smokers," *The New England Journal of Medicine,* April 14, 1994, pp. 1029-35.The study was jointly sponsored by the U.S. National Cancer Institute and the Finnish National Public Health Institute.

[30] Blot, W.J.; Li, J-Y; Taylor, P.R., et al., "Nutrition Intervention Trialsin Linxian, China: Supplementation With Specific Vitamin/Mineral Combinations, Cancer Incidence, and Disease-Specific Mortality in the General Population," *Journal of the National Cancer Institute,* pp. 1483-92, Vol. 85, 1993.

[31] Emily DeNitto, "Herbal Remedies Peel Across U.S.," *Advertising Age,* April 4, 1994, p. 12.

[32] Food and Nutrition Board, *op. cit.,* pp. 18-19.

[33] The three trials are the Carotene and Retinoid Efficacy Trial (CARET), Harvard's Physicians' Health Study and the Women's Health Study.

Bibliography

Selected Sources Used

Books

Lieberman, Shari, and Nancy Bruning, *The Real Vitamin & Mineral Book: Going Beyond the RDA for Optimum Health*, Avery Publishing Group, 1990.
Lieberman and Bruning recommend Optimum Daily Allowances (ODAs) for leading nutrients that are generally much higher than the better-known Recommended Dietary Allowances (RDAs). They also offer advice on how to design a nutritional-supplement program tailored to individual needs.

Marks, John, *The Vitamins in Health and Disease: A Modern Reappraisal*, J. & A. Churchill, 1968.
Marks begins with a discussion of the nutritional significance of vitamins and the effects of vitamin deficiency. He then examines each vitamin separately, providing information on chemistry, sources, metabolism and physiology.

Pauling, Linus, *How to Live Longer and Feel Better*, W.H. Freeman, 1986.
The Nobel Prize-winning chemist, who has long advocated taking vitamin C to ward off the common cold, here offers a broader view of nutrition and disease. He writes, "By the proper intakes of vitamins and other nutrients and by following a few other healthful practices from youth or middle age on, you can, I believe, extend your life and years of well-being by 25 or even 35 years."

Articles

Alpha-Tocopherol, Beta Carotene Cancer Prevention Study Group, "The Effect of Vitamin E and Beta Carotene on the Incidence of Lung Cancer and Other Cancers in Male Smokers," *The New England Journal of Medicine*, April 14, 1994.
This study of 29,000 Finnish male smokers sent shock waves through the nutrition community because it appeared to contradict a large body of research.

Greenwald, Jeff, "Smart As You Wanna Be," *Los Angeles Times Magazine*, Dec. 22, 1991.
Greenwald reviews claims that certain vitamins, amino acids and prescription medicines are "smart drugs" that can improve concentration and memory as well as increase intelligence.

Reynolds, Robert D., "Vitamin Supplements: Current Controversies," *Journal of the American College of Nutrition*, April 1994.
Reynolds, a professor of nutrition and medical dietetics at the University of Illinois-Chicago, presents the chief arguments for and against dietary supplement use.

Sidak, Melinda Ledden, "Dietary Supplements and Commercial Speech," *Food and Drug Law Journal*, No. 3, 1993.
Sidak, an attorney, argues that health-claims provisions of the Nutrition Labeling and Education Act of 1990, as construed by the Food and Drug Administration, "prohibit truthful, protected speech." This prohibition, she contends, "cannot be justified as a narrowly tailored means of advancing the government's interests in protecting consumers from misleading statements in food labeling."

Thomas, Paul R., "Which Supplements Should You Take?" *American Health*, March 1991.
Thomas, a project director for the National Academy of Sciences' Food and Nutrition Board, asked prominent nutritionists to answer questions about dietary supplements. He presents their comments in Q&A format.

Reports and Studies

Council for Responsible Nutrition, *Rationale for Dietary Supplement Legislation*, May 1993.
The council, which represents nutrition supplement manufacturers, sets forth the case for giving the industry more latitude in making health claims for its products.

Food and Nutrition Board, National Academy of Sciences, *Recommended Dietary Allowances* (10th edition), 1989.
The most recent edition of this standard nutrition reference work gives recommended dosages for vitamins, minerals, trace elements and other substances commonly found in food. RDAs are defined here as "the levels of intake of essential nutrients considered, in the judgment of the ... board on the basis of available scientific knowledge, to be adequate to meet the known nutritional needs of practically all healthy persons."

Food and Nutrition Board, National Academy of Sciences, *How Should the Recommended Dietary Allowances Be Revised?* 1994.
The board outlines tentative proposals for revising its widely consulted RDAs to accommodate recent research on nutrition and chronic disease prevention.

Subcommittee on Health and the Environment, U.S. House Committee on Energy and Commerce, Regulation of Dietary Supplements (published proceedings of hearing held July 29, 1993).
Nutritionists, government officials and industry representatives present their views on pending legislation to loosen the Food and Drug Administration's regulatory grip on the dietary supplement industry.

The Next Step

Additional information from UMI's Newspaper & Periodical Abstracts database

Folic Acid

Brody, Jane E., "The incredible, edible miracle cure," *Family Circle,* June 7, 1994, p. 26.

The importance of folic acid in one's diet, which helps reduce heart disease and cancer risk and is vital for pregnant women, is discussed.

Schneider, Phyllis, "Folic-acid update," *Parents,* June 1994, p. 36.

Women of childbearing age are urged to consume 400 micrograms of folic B vitamin, daily. This can significantly decrease a woman's risk of giving birth to a child with a neural-tube defect.

Williams, Rebecca D., "To reduce birth defects: FDA proposes folic acid fortification," *FDA Consumer,* May 1994, pp. 11-14.

Recent studies have shown that women who eat diets rich in folic acid, a B vitamin, are less likely to give birth to babies with brain and spinal cord defects. The FDA has proposed adding folic acid to all bread and grain products.

General Information

Brody, Jane E., "Personal health," *The New York Times,* May 11, 1994, p. C11.

Researchers studying the effects of age on nutrition are finding that millions of older Americans are nutritionally deprived, either because they consume too little of various vitamins and minerals or because certain medical conditions or treatments prevent them from making full use of the nutrients in the foods they eat. The need for older people to take vitamins is discussed.

Kolata, Gina, "Challenging the faith of the vitamin culture," *The New York Times,* April 17, 1994, p. 6.

The publication of a study showing that vitamin E and beta carotene might not protect against cancer and heart disease and might even cause harm came as a shock to the public and to many scientists. However, there has never been conclusive evidence that vitamins help ward off disease, and people who take them hoping to stave off colds, alleviate stress or improve their sexual potency are acting largely on faith.

Legato, Marianne, "The latest word on vitamins," *Woman's Day,* Feb. 22, 1994, p. 24.

Doctors are studying the effects of vitamins and minerals on health more closely and have found that it may pay to take supplements.

"Marketscan: Shoppers look for healthier items," *The Wall Street Journal,* May 10, 1994, p. B10.

Consumers, reflecting growing concern about health in general, filled their supermarket cars in the first quarter of 1994 with products that enjoy a healthful image. Sales of minerals and herbal supplements rose 25.3 percent during the first 12 weeks of the year.

Trafford, Abigail, "A tale of two vegetables," *The Washington Post,* April 26, 1994, p. WH6.

Abigail Traffort discusses the results of studies showing that carrots are not as good as previously thought on the vitamin front and that broccoli helps prevent breast cancer.

Health Benefits

Bricklin, Mark, "Uncovering another nutritional good guy," *Prevention,* June 1994, pp. 17-18.

Several promising new medical studies in which glutathione seems to boost the body's immune system are discussed.

Hearn, Wayne, "Studies create confusion, but eating greens is good," *American Medical News,* May 9, 1994, p. 14.

Two recent studies exploring cancer-fighting properties in vegetables and vitamin supplements are discussed. One study suggests that vitamin E and beta carotene supplements may not inhibit cancer and that beta carotene may even be a contributing factor. Another study, however, found that the substance sulforaphane, found in vegetables rich in beta carotene, has powerful anticarcinogenic properties.

Turk, Michele, "Do antioxidants reduce disease?," *American Health,* May 1994, p. 38.

In an interview, Tufts University nutritionist Jeffrey Blumberg discusses the health benefits of antioxidants. Antioxidants are a broad class of compounds found in the diet and manufactured by the body, such as vitamins E and C and beta carotene.

Weininger, Jean, "Antioxidants lose some fans," *San Francisco Chronicle,* May 11, 1994, p. FOOD1.

Jean Weininger comments on the effects of antioxidants in light of a study completed in April 1994 in Finland that found no significant protective effect from two of the so-called antioxidant nutrients, beta carotene and vitamin E, in regard to cancer.

Willett, Walter C., "Micronutrients and cancer risk," *American Journal of Clinical Nutrition,* May 1994, pp. 1162S-1165S.

Substantial evidence indicates that a high intake of fruits and vegetables reduces the risk of cancers at many sites. There is accumulating evidence that vitamin A, folic acid and the carotenoids are important contributors to the reduced risk.

Legislation

Cordaro, J. B., "Let public get the facts," *USA Today,* April 18, 1994, p. A10.

J. B. Cordaro supports the Dietary Supplement Health and Education Act of 1993, saying that the legislation would permit manufacturers to provide sound, scientifically valid information on dietary supplement labels and in other materials, including pamphlets, brochures and package inserts. It would also ensure continued consumer access to safe dietary supplements, made to quality standards.

Michaelis, Laura, "Senate panel votes to restrict diet supplement regulations," *Congressional Quarterly Weekly Report,* May 14, 1994, p. 1228.

On May 11, 1994, the Senate Labor and Human Resources Committee approved S784, the dietary supplements legislation. The bill, which would curtail the FDA's plans to impose new regulations on dietary supplements, is discussed.

Ross, Michael, and Marlene Cimons, "Senate panel votes to delay vitamin rules," *Los Angeles Times,* May 12, 1994, p. A14.

The Senate Labor and Human Resources Committee approved legislation on May 11, 1994 that would delay the imposition of new FDA restrictions on the nutritional claims made by vitamin manufacturers, but approved a less restrictive proposal by Sen. Orrin Hatch on a 12-5 vote.

"Senate panel moves to ease vitamin rules," *The New York Times,* May 12, 1994, p. A23.

Congress took a first step on May 11, 1994, toward easing federal restrictions on dietary supplements and what they can claim to do for health. The Senate Labor and Human Resources Committee approved legislation that would water down the rules, which are due to take effect in July.

Opinions

"Are vitamins hazardous to your health?," *St. Louis Post-Dispatch,* April 18, 1994, p. B6.

An editorial discusses the conflicting reports that have been made concerning the link between the use of antioxidant vitamins and cancer occurrence.

"Regulate health claims for vitamins, supplements," *USA Today,* April 18, 1994, p. A10.

An editorial supports the FDA standards that go into effect July 1, 1994, that require the vitamin-supplement industry to label its products as food makers do now, listing all nutrients and the daily recommended requirements for them and making only health claims backed by "significant scientific agreement from qualified experts."

"Vitamin free-for-all," *The Washington Post,* May 11, 1994, p. A20.

An editorial discusses the problem of how to regulate the nutrition labels affixed to dietary supplements.

"Warning: This research . . . ," *Boston Globe,* April 16, 1994, p. 14.

An editorial comments on conflicting medical research reports on the benefits of beta carotene and vitamin E.

Supplements

Kolata, Gina, "Vitamin supplements are seen as no guard against diseases," *The New York Times,* April 14, 1994, p. A1.

A study designed to show if vitamins A and E reduce the incidence of heart disease and cancer has found no evidence of any such benefit and even hints at actual harm. Experts involved in the study say it is possible a benefit may emerge as the study continues, but they acknowledge that the case for vitamin supplements should be considered unproved for now.

Pugh, Clifford, "Are vitamin supplements a waste of money?" *Houston Post,* May 9, 1994, p. A11.

In a question-and-answer format, registered dietitian Lynne W. Scott discusses whether taking vitamin supplements will ward off major disease and lead to a healthier life.

Wade, Nicholas, "Method and madness," *The New York Times Magazine,* May 22, 1994, p. 20.

Nicholas Wade discusses the popular controversy over the use of massive doses of certain vitamins to promote health, and a recent study on vitamin supplements that found no evidence that they do any good at all and may even hurt.

Vegetarians

Herbert, Victor, "Staging vitamin B-12 (cobalamin) status in vegetarians," *American Journal of Clinical Nutrition,* May 1994, pp. 1213S-1222S.

There are six possible ways for vitamin B-12 deficiency to develop, and the deficiency is a problem for strict vegans because there is no vitamin B-12 synthesized by any plant. The four stages of negative vitamin B-12 (cobalamin) balance are described.

Specker, Bonny L., "Nutritional concerns of lactating women consuming vegetarian diets," *American Journal of Clinical Nutrition,* May 1994, pp. 1182S-1186S.

The nutritional inadequacies of lactating women on vegetarian diets may affect their well-being and that of their infant, Specker writes.

Back Issues

Great Research on Current Issues Starts Right Here...Recent topics covered by The CQ Researcher are listed below. Before May 1991, reports were published under the name of Editorial Research Reports.

DECEMBER 1992
Crackdown on Smoking
The New CIA
Eating Disorders
Women and AIDS

JANUARY 1993
Hate Crimes
Child Sexual Abuse
Nuclear Fusion
U.S. Trade Policy

FEBRUARY 1993
Community Policing
Europe's New Right
School Censorship
Violence Against Women

MARCH 1993
Gay Rights
Aid to Russia
War on Drugs
TV Violence

APRIL 1993
Head Start
High-Speed Rail
Children's Legal Rights
Muslims in America

Back issues are available for $4.00 (subscribers) or $7.00 (non-subscribers). Quantity discounts apply to orders over ten. To order, call Congressional Quarterly Customer Service at (202) 887-8621.

Binders are available for $16.00. To order call 1-800-638-1710. Please refer to stock number 648.

MAY 1993
Cults in America
Preventing Teen Pregnancy
Software Piracy
National Parks

JUNE 1993
Food Safety
Prostitution
Childhood Immunizations
National Service

JULY 1993
Electric Cars
Population Growth
Downward Mobility
Intelligence Testing

AUGUST 1993
Mental Illness
Bilingual Education
Foreign Policy Burden
School Funding

SEPTEMBER 1993
Suburban Crime
Public Housing
Supreme Court Preview
Immigration Reform

OCTOBER 1993
Airline Safety
Disaster Response
Science in the Courtroom
The Glass Ceiling

NOVEMBER 1993
Paying for Retirement
Charitable Giving
Privacy in the Workplace
Adoption

DECEMBER 1993
U.S. Vietnam-Relations
Learning Disabilities
Child Care
Space Program's Future

JANUARY 1994
Racial Tensions in Schools
South Africa's Future
Worker Retraining
Regulating Pesticides

FEBRUARY 1994
Prison Overcrowding
Water Quality
Religion in Schools
Juvenile Justice

MARCH 1994
Underground Economy
Education Standards
Gambling Boom
Private Management of Public Schools

APRIL 1994
Reproductive Ethics
U.S.-China Trade
Soccer in America
Talk Show Democracy

MAY 1994
Traffic Congestion
Women's Health Issues
Mutual Funds
Political Scandals

JUNE 1994
Education and Gender
Gun Control
Public Land Policy
Nuclear Arms Cleanup

Future Topics

- ***Public Opinion and Foreign Policy***
- ***Crime Victims' Rights***
- ***Contraceptives***

THE CQ Researcher

PUBLISHED BY CONGRESSIONAL QUARTERLY INC.

Foreign Policy and Public Opinion

Have Americans grown tired of world affairs?

With the Cold War over, Americans are divided and uncertain about the United States' role in the world. Polls find a strong desire to concentrate on domestic problems and a marked reluctance to send U.S. troops abroad. Yet the United States remains a world superpower. And most people still say they want the United States to be active in world affairs. The Clinton administration has grappled with these mixed views in responding to the war in Bosnia, the military junta in Haiti and North Korea's nuclear weapons program. Some critics say President Clinton should be doing more to develop public support for a stronger U.S. stance on these issues. But Clinton and his supporters say the administration has acted to protect U.S. interests without risking unnecessary military confrontations.

INSIDE THIS ISSUE

CQ July 15, 1994 • Volume 4, No. 26 • 601-624

Formerly Editorial Research Reports

FOREIGN POLICY AND PUBLIC OPINION

COVER ART: BARBARA SASSA-DANIELS. REUTERS PHOTOGRAPH SHOWS U.S. HELICOPTER PILOT, CHIEF WARRANT OFFICER MICHAEL DURANT, BEING HELD PRISONER IN SOMALIA.

July 15, 1994
Volume 4, No. 26

EDITOR
Sandra Stencel

MANAGING EDITOR
Thomas J. Colin

ASSOCIATE EDITOR
Richard L. Worsnop

STAFF WRITERS
Charles S. Clark
Mary H. Cooper
Kenneth Jost

PRODUCTION EDITOR
Sarah E. Merritt

EDITORIAL ASSISTANT
Michael M. Taylor

GRAPHICS
P. Eloise Fuller

PUBLISHED BY
Congressional Quarterly Inc.

CHAIRMAN
Andrew Barnes

VICE CHAIRMAN
Andrew P. Corty

EDITOR AND PUBLISHER
Neil Skene

EXECUTIVE EDITOR
Robert W. Merry

ASSOCIATE PUBLISHER
John J. Coyle

MARKETING AND SALES DIRECTOR
Edward S. Hauck

The CQ Researcher (ISSN 1056-2036). Formerly Editorial Research Reports. Published weekly (48 times per year, not printed the first Friday of any month with five Fridays) by Congressional Quarterly Inc., 1414 22nd St., N.W., Washington, D.C. 20037. Rates are furnished upon request. Second-class postage paid at Washington, D.C. POSTMASTER: Send address changes to The CQ Researcher, 1414 22nd St., N.W., Washington, D.C. 20037.

Foreign Policy and Public Opinion

BY KENNETH JOST

THE ISSUES

When President George Bush dispatched U.S. troops to the remote African nation of Somalia seven weeks before leaving office, most Americans supported his declared mission of delivering food to starving people. But last fall, the humanitarian mission turned deadly, and public opinion shifted in a TV instant.

Television newscasts on Oct. 4 brought Americans the grisly sight of a dead American soldier being dragged through the streets of Somalia's capital, Mogadishu. TV viewers also saw a bewildered, wounded U.S. helicopter pilot being questioned by his Somali captors.*

The disquieting images reached Americans just one day after a firefight between U.S. troops and Somali rebels left 18 Americans dead and nearly 80 wounded. On Capitol Hill, congressional offices were quickly flooded with calls demanding that the troops be withdrawn.

"What's happening is that 85 percent of the people back home are saying, 'Bring the boys home,' " Sen. Bob Kerrey, a Nebraska Democrat who supported the mission, told *The New York Times*. [1]

After three days of pressurized consultations, President Clinton bowed to public opinion. On Oct. 7, he announced plans to send reinforcements to Somalia but simultaneously set a firm deadline of March 31 for withdrawing all U.S. combat troops from the country. "Our mission from this day forward," Clinton said, "is to increase our strength, do our job, bring our soldiers out and bring them home."

* The pilot, Chief Warrant Officer Michael Durant, was captured Oct. 3 during a U.S.-led helicopter raid on the headquarters of Somali warlord Gen. Mohammed Farah Aidid. He was released 11 days later.

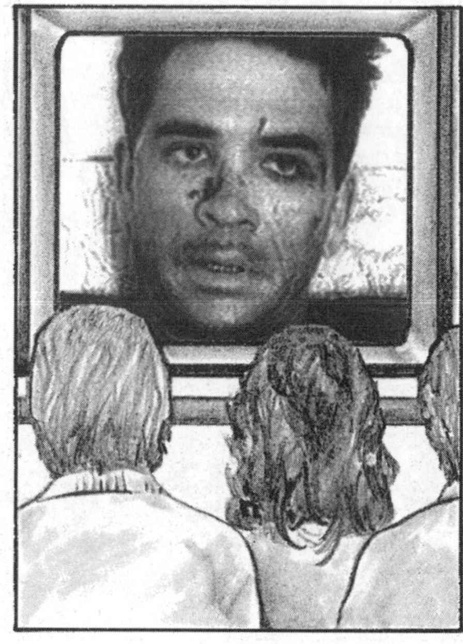

Clinton's pledge staved off an effort in the Senate a week later to force an immediate withdrawal. But the decision soon took on symbolic significance. To many commentators, the U.S. about-face in Somalia evidenced a lack of foreign policy leadership in Washington, a growing strain of isolationism among the public and an unnerving influence by television on the nation's foreign policy agenda.

"The image of a dead American soldier being dragged through the streets of Mogadishu turned ardent internationalists into instant isolationists," wrote Mortimer B. Zuckerman, editor-in-chief of *U.S. News & World Report*. [2]

Critics filled in this unflattering picture of U.S. foreign policy with other examples. Clinton was pictured as weak and ineffectual in the face of Serbian aggression in Bosnia and an oppressive military junta in Haiti. And the American public was depicted as preoccupied with domestic problems, weary of international leadership and unwilling to risk American lives to further foreign policy goals.

"I've got great sympathy for Clinton," says Yale historian Gaddis Smith. "I think he's reflecting the sentiments of the public on foreign policy, which is take no risks. There's really nothing worth the bones of an American service person at this point."

Some commentators see a drift toward isolationism in the public mood. They say Americans are turning inward even if the country is not trying to withdraw completely from world affairs as it did after World War I.

"The public is more self-centered," says Andrew Kohut, director of the Times Mirror Center for The People and The Press. "It wants a foreign policy directed to improving things here in the United States."

But other experts deny that the public is turning isolationist. "That's a bum rap," says Daniel Yankelovich, a veteran public opinion expert. "The public has not flagged for a moment in its commitments to the country's leadership responsibilities."

These experts also discount the accusation that Americans are unwilling to support the use of military force abroad. "They'll support the use of force if we go in to win, to solve the problem, to deliver the food, to get the Iraqis out of Kuwait," says William Schneider, a political analyst for Cable News Network (CNN) and resident scholar at the American Enterprise Institute (AEI). But Schneider says Americans "draw the line at getting involved in other people's politics, which is what we did in Vietnam and what we did not do in the Persian Gulf."

The uncertainty about U.S. policies in the post-Cold War era has also focused new attention on the role of public opinion in shaping foreign policy — and the role of television in shaping public opinion.

Since the Vietnam War, Americans have become less willing to trust the government or the so-called foreign policy establishment — the coterie of academics, think-tankers and Wash-

Clinton's Foreign Policy Ratings

Just 41 percent of those responding to a recent Washington Post-*ABC News poll approved of the way President Clinton was handling foreign policy. Half of those interviewed approved of the administration's handling of the North Korean situation, but more people disapproved than approved of the president's handling of the situations in Haiti, Bosnia and Rwanda.*

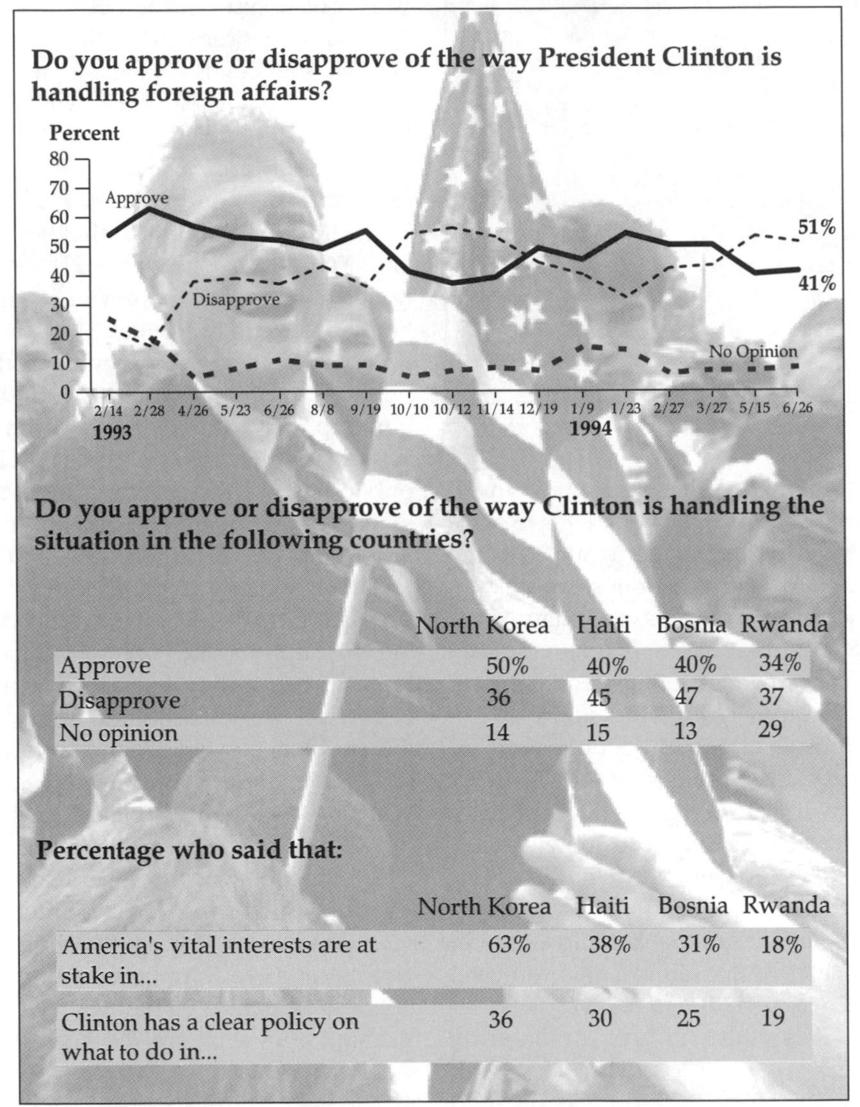

Do you approve or disapprove of the way Clinton is handling the situation in the following countries?

	North Korea	Haiti	Bosnia	Rwanda
Approve	50%	40%	40%	34%
Disapprove	36	45	47	37
No opinion	14	15	13	29

Percentage who said that:

	North Korea	Haiti	Bosnia	Rwanda
America's vital interests are at stake in...	63%	38%	31%	18%
Clinton has a clear policy on what to do in...	36	30	25	19

Source: Figures are from a Washington Post-*ABC News poll of 1,531 randomly selected adults conducted June 23-26, 1994. Margin of sampling error for the overall results is plus or minus 3 percentage points. Photograph courtesy of Reuters.*

ington in-and-outers with seemingly permanent ties to the formal foreign policy apparatus. At the same time, television gives Americans immediate access to events around the world, reducing the time for foreign policy-makers to weigh options and chart decisions.

With U.S. foreign policy in flux, public opinion seems likely to become even more important. "Leaders can expect a new aggressiveness and insistence on the part of the public that it be directly engaged in shaping the new post-Cold War foreign policy," Yankelovich and a colleague write in a new book examining public opinion and foreign policy. [3]

Yet presidential leadership clearly remains a vital element in shaping U.S. positions in international affairs. And on that score, Clinton gets low marks from a wide range of experts and commentators.

"He thought he could be a domestic affairs president, and that's an illusion," says Owen Harries, editor of *The National Interest,* a conservative journal on international affairs. "An American president must be as concerned with the one as with the other."

"There's no spine to American foreign policy," says Charles William Maynes, editor of *Foreign Policy,* a journal published by the Carnegie Endowment for International Peace. "The people who have been in power in the last days of the Bush administration and in the Clinton administration don't have a clear strategy for the country."

Clinton's supporters and sympathizers argue that critics are overlooking some real accomplishments. They say he persuaded European countries to join in a tougher stand on Bosnia, increased U.S. pressure for democratization in Haiti and won congressional support for aid to Russia and the controversial free trade treaty with Mexico.

Administration supporters also say that Clinton has acted wisely in resisting calls to use U.S. troops prematurely. "As a result, we've not been goaded into an untimely, unwise use of force, whether in North Korea or Haiti or Bosnia, that would have jeopardized American lives for an uncertain outcome," Senate Foreign Relations Committee Chairman Claiborne Pell, D-R.I., said in opening a foreign policy oversight hearing on June 30.

But even Clinton's allies concede that the administration has failed to give the public a clear idea of its foreign policy goals. "This administration has trouble articulating its foreign policy," House Foreign Affairs

Committee Chairman Lee H. Hamilton, D-Ind., told reporters in February.[4]

As the administration and the public sort out the priorities for U.S. foreign policy in the post-Cold War era, here are some of the questions being debated:

What role should public opinion play in making foreign policy?

Some people in the foreign policy community appear to view public opinion as an inconvenient necessity or, worse, a positive hindrance in shaping foreign policy. The public is seen as ill-informed about international affairs, preoccupied with bread-and-butter domestic issues and insensitive to the intricacies of diplomacy and statecraft.

This view of public opinion dates back at least to the beginning of the Cold War. In an influential book written in 1950, Yale political scientist Gabriel Almond argued that only a narrow segment of the population — the "attentive public" — follows foreign policy debates, while the general public participates in policy-making in "primarily indirect and passive ways."[5]

"Almond's view was that you can't trust a democratic public to make foreign policy," says Carl Everett Ladd, president of the Roper Center for Public Opinion Research at the University of Connecticut in Storrs.

Along with this restrictive view of public opinion sometimes comes an elevated sense of the president's role in undertaking foreign policy initiatives with little, if any, public discussion. "It is a fact of life that if a president is going to take an action that does not have full [public] support, he has to do it secretly, or else the issue goes into a public debate which probably frustrates what he intends to do," says David Newsom, a professor of international affairs at the University of Virginia and a longtime State Department official until his retirement in 1981.

Many foreign policy experts, however, fault this narrow conception of public opinion as historically inaccurate and politically unwise. They argue that the American public has generally supported U.S. foreign policy and that foreign policy-makers ignore public opinion at their peril.

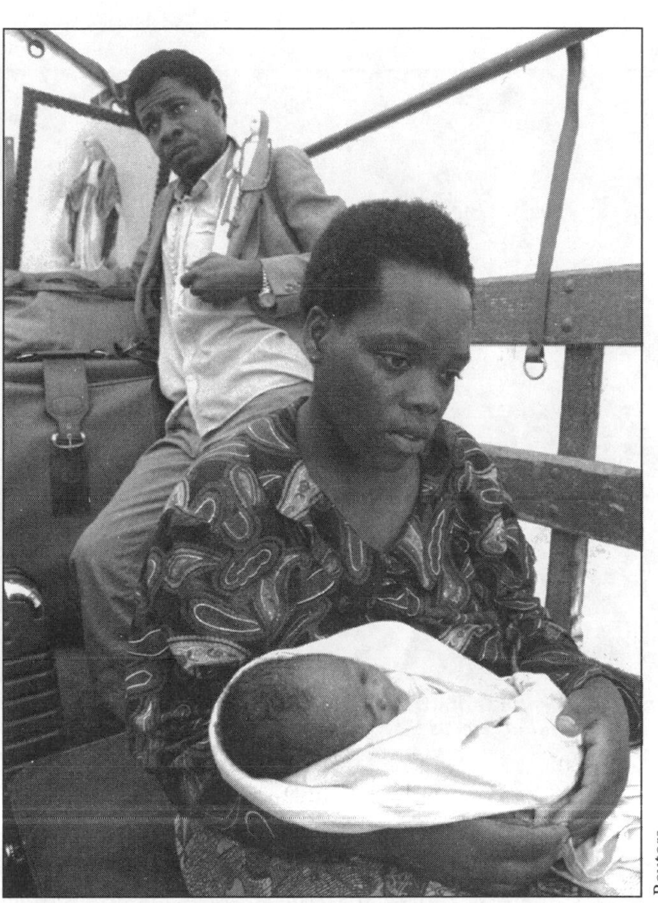

Reuters

U.N. evacuation of Rwandan refugees from the capital city of Kagali in May 1994.

"The public was broadly supportive of the outlines of defense and foreign policies throughout the Cold War years," Ladd says. "If the public had been resistant, I don't think you could have sustained the policies."

"If you don't consult the public or take its point of view into account, you won't get the kind of support needed for the kind of foreign policy commitment that entails real costs," says Yankelovich. "Every secretary of State has come to recognize that, including Henry Kissinger, who was not initially as concerned with public opinion. . . . If you don't take public opinion into account, you're going to be cut off at the knees."

Historian Stephen Ambrose, the author of celebrated biographies on Dwight D. Eisenhower and Richard M. Nixon, says that presidents are well served by "open and prolonged debate" about foreign policy moves. "The policies that have failed," Ambrose wrote in 1991, "have tended to be those adopted by presidents without meaningful debate." As examples, he cites the Bay of Pigs invasion under John F. Kennedy, Lyndon B. Johnson's intervention in Vietnam, Nixon's détente policies, Jimmy Carter's human rights policies and Ronald Reagan's Iran-contra policy.[6]

Advocates of a broader role for public opinion in foreign policy-making acknowledge that the public is not always well informed about the details of international affairs. Last fall, a Times Mirror survey recorded striking public confusion about the conflict in Bosnia. More than 40 percent of those surveyed thought that Bosnian Muslims had either invaded Serbia (7 percent) or attempted to drive Serbs out of Bosnia (36 percent). Only 32 percent correctly said that Serbians wanted large parts of Bosnia to be inhabited only by Serbs.[7]

With the collapse of the former Soviet Union, U.S. foreign policy now faces a bevy of ill-defined conflicts in places like Bosnia that the public knows little about. And polls document that the public wants the government to give top priority to domestic problems and pay less attention to foreign policy. (*See graphs, p. 615.*) In that setting, presidential leadership is all the more important in shaping public opinion — and President Clinton's widely perceived shortcomings all the more serious.

"I don't see any evidence of this administration using any kind of intelligent approach to bringing the public up to speed on the need for this or that policy or this or that commitment," says Yankelovich. "They're flying semi-blind, using some opinion poll data, but not really doing the kind of education and preparation job that's required."

Administration officials acknowledge the difficulty of fashioning a post-Cold War foreign policy. "The world is in a period of unusual turmoil," Vice President Al Gore said on the CBS program "Face the Nation" May 22. But Gore insisted the administration has a solid policy built around promoting market democracies, expanding trade and creating new security arrangements in Europe and Asia. "We're proceeding very carefully, very prudently, and very forcefully to assert American interests in the world," Gore said.

Turner Broadcasting System

During the Persian Gulf War, CNN correspondent Peter Arnett reported live from Baghdad even as U.S. bombs were falling on the Iraqi capital.

Are Americans becoming more isolationist?

The Clinton administration has struggled with foreign policy in part because Americans are thought to be weary of world responsibilities and especially wary of military involvement in international hot spots. Some foreign policy observers liken public attitudes to earlier periods of isolationism. But others say Americans are still willing to bear the burdens of international leadership.

Polls provide evidence for both interpretations of public opinion. Surveys show that Americans are more concerned with domestic issues than foreign policy. They find strong opposition to U.S. military involvement in such trouble spots as Bosnia or Haiti. On the other hand, polls also show Americans still support an active role in world affairs. And they show that Americans are willing to risk going to war in certain situations. (*See story, p. 610.*)

"There's no consistent evidence to support the view that the American public has turned isolationist," says Steven Kull, director of the University of Maryland's program on international policy attitudes. "There are some polling data [that indicate] they're not supportive on specific interventions."

Observers who see signs of isolationism are careful to qualify their assessments. "There is more isolationist sentiment compared to 10 years ago or certainly 30 years ago," says Kohut of the Times Mirror Center. "But it's not isolationist in the sense of wanting to withdraw from the world."

"It's not isolationism in the sense that this country wants to exclude itself from world affairs," says Newsom of the University of Virginia. "But it certainly amounts to non-involvement if we are going to be required to put our armed forces at risk."

In a wide-ranging survey released last fall, the Times Mirror Center found that the public favors a diminished role for the United States in world affairs. The poll found that nearly three-fifths of those surveyed want the United States either to take no leadership role in the world (7 percent) or to be no more or less active than other leading nations (51 percent). The survey also reported a 30-year high in the percentage of people who believe the United States should concentrate on national instead of international problems. [8]

The same survey also found, however, that most Americans (71 percent) believe the United States should "cooperate fully" with the United Nations. And the public strongly rejects stark isolationist attitudes. For example, nearly two-thirds of those surveyed disagreed that the United States "should go our own way in international matters." (*See graphs, p. 615.*)

Beyond these general propositions, however, the most critical tests of public opinion on foreign policy come on issues of war and peace. And on these questions, many observers believe Americans have simply lost the nerve to fight.

"Once we took casualties in Somalia, the prime concern in the country was to get our troops out and to minimize the risks while they were there," says Newsom. "It's very clear that the administration doesn't have any strong support in the Congress or in the public for deploying U.S. forces in Bosnia. And there doesn't seem to be a lot of support for military action against Haiti."

But Kull of the University of Maryland argues that Americans are more willing to endorse military intervention than most observers recognize. Kull cites polls by his program that show public support for U.S. participation in multilateral military actions in Bosnia. More than three-fourths of those surveyed favored the use of NATO airstrikes to try to stop Serb attacks on Bosnian cities. And substantial majorities favored committing U.S. troops to United Nations peacekeeping operations to enforce a peace accord or even to try to reduce conflict in the absence of a peace agreement.

"Support for peacekeeping as a principle is very strong," says Kull. "But there's a very strong feeling that we shouldn't do it unilaterally, that it should always be multilateral."

Other observers also believe that Americans will support military actions to protect vital U.S. interests. "A democratic public will always say, 'Do everything you can to avoid committing our sons to war,'" says Ladd of the Roper Center. "But that isn't the issue. The question is whether the public thinks the reasons for taking the action are overwhelming."

"Obviously, a democratic country is skittish about going to war," says Maynes of the Carnegie Endowment for International Peace. "On the other hand, the polls still show that [Americans] would like to see the government live up to its alliance commitments. Where they have trouble — and where they should have trouble — is in situations where the United States functions as a kind of colonial force. The American people are understandably quite reluctant to do that."

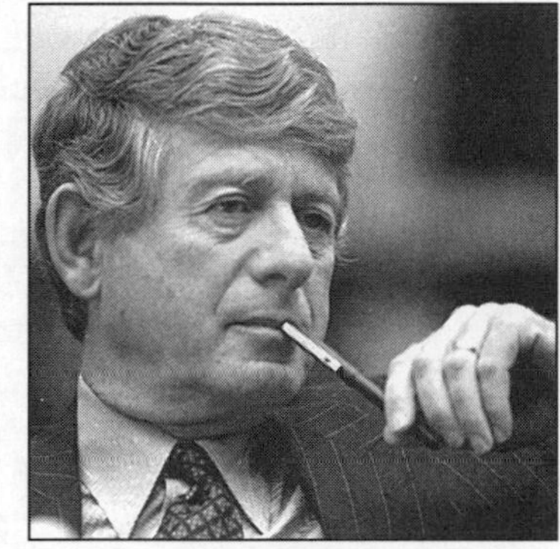

" The absence of a clearly formulated and enunciated [foreign] policy is like a vacuum. It will be filled by whatever is available: Congressmen having themselves publicly arrested . . . voices from the loyal opposition, or for that matter, television reports, which often contradict reality as presented by administration spokespeople."

— Ted Koppel, ABC News

Does television have too much impact on public opinion about foreign policy?

The news media have had strong influence on U.S. foreign policy many times in the past. William Randolph Hearst's newspapers spurred the United States to war with Spain in 1898. *Life* magazine's dramatic photographs of Japan's invasion of China hardened American feelings toward Tokyo in the 1930s. Edward R. Murrow's broadcasts from London prepared the public for U.S. entry into World War II.

The advent of television greatly magnified the impact that news coverage can have in shaping U.S. foreign policy. In the 1960s, television brought the Vietnam War into Americans' living rooms — and, according to some, weakened public support for the conflict. In the Iranian hostage crisis of 1979-1980, television kept the nation's attention riveted on the plight of the American captives, possibly dooming Jimmy Carter's presidency in the process.

Today, many people in and around government view television as perhaps the single most important influence in shaping U.S. foreign policy. "Ever since the breakup of the Soviet Union," Maynes wrote last year, "it has become clear to anyone who cares to notice that in Washington the real agenda-setters for foreign policy sit not in the White House but in editorial rooms and press cubicles." [9]

Maynes and other experts say television's influence has grown in part because of a lack of leadership in the White House. "TV has gotten more important in the last few years simply because Americans aren't clear what presidents have wanted to do," says former *New York Times* columnist Leslie H. Gelb, now president of the Council on Foreign Relations. "If there's a void, the television cameras will fill that void with pictures. If you have a policy, the pictures may cause problems, but they won't dictate what the White House should do or will do."

Television journalists and news executives insist that TV's impact is exaggerated. "If an administration has thought its own foreign policy through and is prepared and able to argue the merits and defend the consequences of that policy, television and all its new technologies can be dealt with," Ted Koppel, host of ABC's "Nightline" told the House Foreign Affairs Committee on April 26. "If, on the other hand, the foreign policy is ill-conceived and poorly explained, then it doesn't much matter whether the news arrives by satellite or clipper ship. Eventually, the policy will fail."

Technological changes have heightened the concern about television's impact. With the launching of communications satellites and the establishment of CNN as a 24-hour-a-day news service, television now often brings world events to Americans as they are happening. "Real-time television is quite an eye-opener for people," says Kohut of the Times Mirror Center.

The impact of "real-time" television was seen in the Persian Gulf War. CNN correspondent Peter Arnett reported live from Baghdad even as U.S. bombs were falling on the Iraqi capital. Bush administration officials have said that CNN's coverage of the bombing raids may have caused military planners to try harder to minimize civilian casualties.

"You'd probably have a hard time proving that it had an effect on decisions, but I think it probably did lead us to be more careful," Paul Wolfowitz, under secretary of Defense in the Bush administration, said in 1991. And Wolfowitz said that concern about televising further casualties may also have influenced Bush's decision to end the war once Kuwait was freed instead of allowing U.S. troops to move on to Baghdad. [10]

The Bush administration was again influenced by television in its final days in office. Gripping pictures of Somali children dying of starvation created a rush of public sympathy that Bush moved to satisfy. "If there had been no CNN, there probably would not have been the intervention in Somalia by President Bush," Elliott Abrams, an assistant secretary of State in the Reagan administration and now a senior fellow at the Hudson Institute, remarked recently. [11]

Ten months later, television again was credited with shaping public opinion on Somalia — this time pressuring President Clinton to withdraw U.S. troops. "It's probably not too much to say that the president's policy on Somalia changed in one day of press coverage," Abrams said.

Some experts, however, challenge this view of television's importance. John Mueller, a political scientist at the University of Rochester, says the U.S. casualties in Somalia changed public attitudes simply because Americans never regarded the mission as important. "It's the fact of what happened, not the fact that they saw a picture of it," says Mueller, who has written two books about public opinion toward military conflicts.

But according to historian and TV commentator Michael Beschloss, U.S. war planners have a different view of the effects of television coverage of military conflicts. They see television as "a key culprit" in reducing Americans' patience during the Vietnam War. The White House and the Pentagon have striven since then — in Grenada, Panama and the gulf war — to hold U.S. casualties to a minimum and to limit television's ability to transmit battlefield coverage back to the United States. [12]

The Clinton administration has similarly been convinced that Americans are unwilling to risk U.S. lives in such trouble spots as Bosnia or Haiti. As a result, its policies appear to many observers to be indecisive and at times inconsistent. Maynes says that even if television heightens the public's awareness of the risks of military conflict, the administration itself bears the blame for failing to develop clear policies and explain them to the public.

"It's not necessarily TV," says Maynes. "It's public opinion. Public opinion plays a larger role when we're not clear about our objectives." ■

BACKGROUND

Splendid Isolation

Foreign policy often appears to be more removed from the day-to-day lives of Americans than domestic issues. Foreign relations are the province of diplomats and career foreign service officers, serving in far-flung places with languages and cultures unfamiliar to most Americans. And in crises, foreign policy rests in the hands of the president and his national security team, huddling secretly in the White House with the public on the outside anxiously awaiting decisions that are, largely, out of their hands.

Yet, as the late historian Thomas Bailey pointed out, public opinion has always been a critical force in shaping U.S. foreign policy. "If the ordinary American wants to know who shapes fundamental foreign policy, all he has to do is look into a mirror," Bailey wrote in his authoritative book *A Diplomatic History of the American People.* [13]

The impact of public opinion — and public pressure — can be seen at critical junctures from the early days of the Republic on to the present, post-Cold War era.

Until the beginning of the 20th century, the United States stayed out of world affairs for the most part. As one historian wrote — specifically referring to the late 19th century — "foreign relations were composed of incidents, not policies." [14] But the effects of public opinion can be seen in the "incidents" that arose as the

Continued on p. 611

Chronology

1789-1900 ***The United States largely stays out of world affairs.***

1900-1950 ***The United States steps onto the world scene, returns to isolationism after World War I and then emerges as the dominant power after World War II.***

Nov. 19, 1919
The Senate rejects U.S. entry into the League of Nations, marking a return to isolationism.

September 1940
Congress narrowly passes the country's first peacetime draft as President Franklin D. Roosevelt prepares for possible U.S. entry into wars in Europe and Asia.

April 4, 1949
The U.S. signs pact creating the North Atlantic Treaty Organization (NATO), pledging to come to the defense of any member country under attack.

1950s ***The U.S. fights to a stalemate in the Korean War and settles into a Cold War with the Soviet Union.***

1960s ***John F. Kennedy's election as president brings rhetorical vigor to U.S. foreign policy, but after his death Lyndon B. Johnson leads the country into a quagmire in Vietnam.***

August 1964
Congress approves the Gulf of Tonkin Resolution, giving President Johnson wider authority to commit U.S. troops in Vietnam.

Nov. 6, 1968
Richard M. Nixon is elected president after promising to end the war in Vietnam.

1970s ***In a decade of malaise, the United States watches South Vietnam fall to the Communists and endures a 445-day hostage crisis with an anti-American regime in Iran.***

Jan. 23, 1973
U.S. involvement in the Vietnam War ends.

Nov. 4, 1979
Iranian students storm the U.S. Embassy in Tehran and seize more than 90 hostages. The hostages are released as Ronald Reagan becomes president.

1980s ***President Reagan directs U.S. military build-up, but also negotiates arms control accord with the Soviet Union. The collapse of the Berlin Wall marks the beginning of the end of the Cold War.***

October 1983
President Reagan sends U.S. troops into Grenada to oust pro-Communist military regime.

Nov. 9, 1989
The Berlin Wall is dismantled. By end of year, Communist regimes fall throughout Eastern Europe.

Dec. 19, 1989
President George Bush sends U.S. troops to Panama.

1990s ***The United States tries to construct a post-Cold War foreign policy.***

Jan. 12, 1991
Congress authorizes President Bush to use force against Iraq. "Operation Desert Storm" forces Iraq out of Kuwait by the end of February, with few U.S. casualties.

Dec. 31, 1991
The Soviet Union is dissolved after Mikhail Gorbachev resigns as leader.

Nov. 3, 1992
Bill Clinton is elected president after a campaign stressing domestic issues.

Dec. 9, 1992
U.S. forces land in Somalia — greeted by television cameras that broadcast their arrival around the world.

Oct. 3-7, 1993
Americans call for U.S. troops to withdraw from Somalia after deaths of Marines in firefight and photographs of soldier's body being dragged through streets of Mogadishu.

Feb. 5, 1994
A deadly mortar attack on a Sarajevo market in Bosnia galvanizes U.S. public opinion. Clinton backs NATO in threatening air strikes on Bosnian Serbs.

Public Sends Mixed Messages About the Use of Force

For months after Iraq invaded Kuwait in August 1990, Americans were ambivalent about what the U.S. response should be. *Washington Post*-ABC News polls taken from August to December found solid support — ranging between 65 and 74 percent — for taking "all action necessary, including the use of military force," to make Iraq withdraw. But Gallup polls during the same period found only a narrow plurality agreed that the "situation in the Mideast" was "worth going to war over."

Despite the uncertain state of public opinion, President George Bush became convinced that forcing Iraq out of Kuwait was of paramount importance. "The Bush administration decided to use force in the Gulf despite the fact that at times public opinion was not that much in favor," says Richard Haas, a Mideast specialist who served on Bush's National Security Council staff.

Americans typically have mixed views about the use of military force. Judging from public opinion polls, Americans are most willing to support military intervention when the United States is under direct attack, or when they are asked about vague, general situations. They are more likely to oppose the use of force when asked about specific situations.

Ninety-four percent of those responding to an October 1993 *Wall Street Journal*/NBC News poll said U.S. military intervention was acceptable if the nation was under direct military threat. Most people supported the use of military force to prevent mass starvation (67 percent), guarantee peace and security in key regions (63 percent), protect key economic needs such as oil (60 percent) or respond to aggression against innocent people (57 percent). And a narrow plurality (47 percent to 41 percent) said the use of force was acceptable to protect a democratic government from internal rebellion. [1]

But a Times Mirror poll taken around the same time found that most people opposed the use of American troops to respond to invasions of Israel or South Korea — two strategically important U.S. allies. [2] And most people said they opposed sending U.S. troops to African, Asian, Caribbean or Latin American nations to help restore law and order. [3]

"Americans don't want to be the world's policeman," says William Kohut, director of the Times Mirror Center for The People and The Press, "but they don't want to withdraw from the world either." [4]

John Mueller, a political scientist at the University of Rochester who has studied public opinion toward the Korean, Vietnam and Persian Gulf wars, says Americans are simply applying a "cost-benefit" test to issues of military involvement. "American foreign policy is not helpless," says Mueller. "It's just a question of what kind of price it's willing to pay for it."

Mueller says public support for the Korean and Vietnam conflicts fell sharply as casualties increased. And he says Americans would have an "extremely low tolerance for casualties" if U.S. troops were sent into action today in Bosnia, Haiti or Korea.

Haas, who is now a senior associate at the Carnegie Endowment for International Peace in Washington, points out that the president and Congress have "quite a lot of leeway" in deciding whether to commit troops abroad. "We don't conduct plebiscites before using force abroad," Haas says.

In fact, polls show that most Americans believe the president should be prepared to override public opinion on the use of military force. In three successive polls in the early 1990s, around two-thirds of those surveyed said that the president should send U.S. troops abroad if he was convinced it was "in the best interest of the country" even if the public was opposed. [5]

President Clinton has avoided sending U.S. ground troops into international hot spots. He authorized U.S. participation in airstrikes against Bosnian Serb positions last year, but said ground troops would be sent in only as part of a multilateral peacekeeping force after an accord was reached. He steered clear of sending U.S. troops to quell the fighting in Rwanda's bloody civil war. And he focused on economic sanctions rather than military action against North Korea in the dispute over Pyongyang's nuclear weapons program.

In the past two months, however, Clinton has hinted strongly at possible military action to force Haiti's military junta to step down. "It's in our back yard," Clinton told reporters in May. [6] And on July 5, Clinton's special envoy for Haiti, William H. Gray III, pointedly said that military action is "on the table."

Military action would come in the face of opposition in Congress. Republican and moderate Democratic lawmakers say U.S. interests in Haiti are insubstantial and U.S. forces would get bogged down in Haiti's bloody domestic conflicts. But Haas, who favors a U.S.-led multilateral action in Haiti, says Clinton can reshape public opinion on the issue if he tries.

"President Clinton has allowed himself to be heavily influenced by public opinion," Haas says. "If he thought it was in the national interest to use force against Haiti, or North Korea, or to have stayed in Somalia or gone into Rwanda, he could have brought the TV cameras into the Oval Office and made his pitch."

[1] Poll results reprinted in Peter J. Ferrara, "Foreign and Defense Policy," in *Issues '94*, The Heritage Foundation, 1994, p. 291.

[2] Times Mirror Center for The People and The Press, *America's Place in the World,* November 1993, p. 95.

[3] Times Mirror Center for The People and The Press, News Release, Nov. 2, 1993, p. 9.

[4] *Los Angeles Times,* Nov. 2, 1993, p. H5.

[5] See Alvin Richman, "American Support for International Involvement," *Public Opinion Quarterly,* summer 1993, p. 271.

[6] *The New York Times,* May 20, 1994, p. A1.

Continued from p. 608

United States sought to establish its rights in world commerce and to become a continental power.

The United States first established its presence in world affairs by besting Barbary Coast pirates who were marauding American merchant ships. With the public shouting "millions for defense, but not one cent for tribute," President Thomas Jefferson forswore his personal pacifism in 1801 to launch a naval war that ultimately forced the North African pirate states to respect U.S. freedom of the seas.

Britain and the United States also clashed over the same issue when the London government insisted on the right to board U.S. ships to impress deserting British seamen. The dispute helped fuel war fever in the United States. At the same time, Britain — which still ruled Canada — was helping Native American tribes resist U.S. expansion in what was then called the Northwest Territory. The two issues spurred Congress to declare war in June 1812. Two years later, the War of 1812 ended with a treaty that gained no new territory for the United States and left the impressment issue unsettled.

Three decades later, territorial expansion brought the United States into simultaneous conflict with Britain and Mexico. The public rallied to support American settlers in Texas, then part of Mexico, and in "Oregon Country," an expansive territory disputed by the U.S. and Britain. In 1844, the dark horse James K. Polk won the presidency by defeating the better known Henry Clay on a platform pledged to "the re-occupation of Oregon and the re-annexation of Texas at the earliest practicable period." [15]

Polk settled the dispute with Britain with a treaty establishing the existing boundary between the U.S. and Canada. The pact freed Polk to take a tougher stance against Mexico. The public approved. "Nine tenths of our people would rather have a little fighting than not," a New York newspaper declared in 1846. [16] The war with Mexico ended two years later with Mexico formally recognizing U.S. title over Texas and ceding New Mexico and California as well.

Americans' thirst for expansion was not yet sated, however. In the age of imperialism, the United States felt imperialistic urges that gained strength from traditional American policies of opposing foreign powers in the Western Hemisphere and protecting maritime and commercial rights. To safeguard Pacific Ocean sea travel, the U.S. tangled with Germany and Britain in Samoa — eventually acquiring half of the archipelago as an American territory. To protect American plantation owners, the U.S. moved to annex Hawaii — provoking a decade-long fight between Republicans who backed the move and Democrats who opposed it.

Public opinion exerted its greatest pressure, however, nearer to home, forcing a reluctant government to go to war with Spain in 1898 to free Cuba from colonial rule and acquire colonies for the United States in the process. Americans were enraged by sensationalistic news accounts of horrible conditions in Cuba published in the rabidly competitive newspapers of William Randolph Hearst and Joseph Pulitzer.

On Feb. 15, the battleship USS Maine was blown up in Havana harbor. No one knows who was responsible, but the public rallied to the slogan "Remember the Maine." For two months, President William McKinley resisted pressure for war, but acceded after his likely Democratic opponent in 1900, William Jennings Bryan, began orating in favor of an independent Cuba. The war ended just eight months later, with Cuba independent and other Spanish colonies — the Philippines, Guam and Puerto Rico — in U.S. hands.

While the spirit of isolation remained strong, the U.S. victory over Spain confirmed its status as a world power. And Theodore Roosevelt, who became president after McKinley's assassination in 1901, used that power with vigor. TR's slogan — "speak softly and carry a big stick" — encapsulates the transition from isolationism to what became, in *Time* publisher Henry Luce's phrase, "the American century."

Roosevelt reinforced the Monroe Doctrine, which called on European countries to stay out of Western Hemisphere affairs, by opposing the British and German blockade of Venezuela in 1902. He worked to protect an open door for U.S. business in China and took on a new role of peacemaker in settling the 1904-5 Russo-Japanese War. Some isolationists grumbled, but Roosevelt's foreign ventures had popular support.

World Wars, World Power

The principle of non-intervention remained strong, however. As Europe moved toward war, the United States hoped to stay out of the conflict. President Woodrow Wilson urged Americans to maintain strict neutrality and won re-election in 1916 on the slogan, "He kept us out of war." Popular sympathy tilted toward the Allies, however. Then, in 1917, Germany forced public opinion by launching unrestricted submarine warfare against neutral shipping. Support for freedom of the seas combined with hostility to German militarism to propel the United States into World War I.

After the Allied victory, Wilson dominated the Versailles Conference to draw up a treaty of peace. His goals were distinctively American: national self-determination and peaceful settlement of international disputes through a new League of Nations. He returned to the United States in 1919 with a treaty that started with public support. More than 30 state legislatures endorsed U.S. participation in the League.

Wilson blundered, however, by refusing to compromise when Republican opponents — led by the isolationist Sen. Henry Cabot Lodge of Massachusetts — tried to attach reservations to the treaty. After loyal Democrats blocked approval of the treaty with reservations, Republicans were able to kill it altogether. Emboldened Republicans campaigned for the White House in 1920 promising "a return to normalcy." America appeared to have turned its back on the world.

Franklin D. Roosevelt entered the White House in 1933 with a determined focus on economic recovery and a calculated disregard of foreign policy. But neither FDR nor the American public could ignore the developing wars in Asia and Europe.

In 1937, the re-elected Roosevelt went to Chicago, the seat of isolationism, to urge "quarantining" any nation that stirred up "international anarchy." Over the next four years, Roosevelt delicately led the country into becoming the world's arsenal for democracy and then rallied the nation when war finally came.

Roosevelt's policies are often depicted as clever manipulation to skirt public opposition to intervention. But public opinion polls belie that view. In 1940, a Gallup Poll found the public supported, 62 percent to 38 percent, Roosevelt's deal to trade Britain much-needed destroyers for base rights in the Western Hemisphere.

A year later, Roosevelt's lend-lease bill to help arm Britain had majority backing — 56 percent to 27 percent — as it moved toward congressional approval. And, in April 1941, 67 percent of those responding said they favored aiding the British even if it meant risking war. [17]

Cold War Consensus

The United States emerged from World War II as the world's dominant power. Germany and Japan were vanquished, and Western Europe and the Soviet Union lay in wreckage. Even before the war ended, the United States had begun laying the foundations for the postwar world order by spearheading the creation of the United Nations. A few isolationists grumbled, but Congress reflected popular sentiment in giving it overwhelming approval.

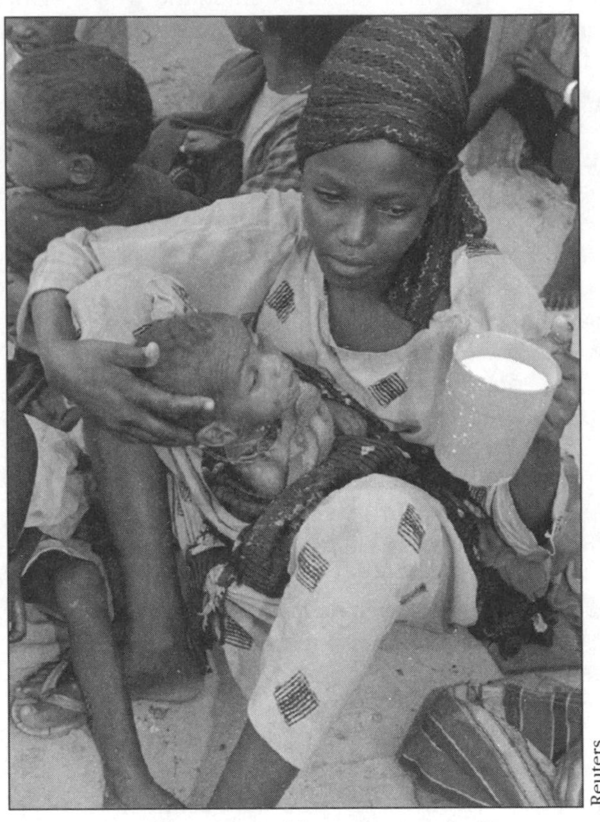

Reuters

A Somali mother and her infant at a feeding station in Mogadishu in December 1992.

Even if Americans had wanted to turn their backs on world leadership, however, events made that course impossible. The Soviet Union built what Winston Churchill in 1946 called an "Iron Curtain" over Eastern Europe. In China, a civil war ended with a Communist government on the mainland and the pro-American Nationalists forced onto the island of Formosa. With no respite, the United States found itself in a Cold War that was to last 40 years.

To counter the communist threat, President Harry S Truman and an extraordinary array of diplomats including George C. Marshall, Dean Acheson and George F. Kennan forged a bold and imaginative program. Truman went before Congress in March 1947 to plead for aid to Greece and Turkey and call for the United States to support "free peoples who are resisting attempted subjugation by armed minorities or by outside pressures." Secretary of State Marshall used a Harvard commencement speech that year to outline a plan for aiding the reconstruction of Western Europe. Kennan authored the "containment doctrine" that provided the basis for forming the North Atlantic Treaty Organization (NATO) to guarantee the security of European democracies.

Thanks to their leadership, those policies also won the support of the American public. Polls in 1947 showed the public supported aid for Greece (56 percent) and Turkey (49 percent). A poll of those who had heard of the Marshall Plan found 57 percent had a favorable opinion of it. Two years later, the NATO pact had the support of 67 percent of those surveyed. [18] In Congress, popular approval helped moderate Republicans lend bipartisan support to Truman's policies. In 1949, the Senate approved the NATO treaty by a vote of 84-12.

Bipartisanship did not end foreign policy disputes. Republicans blamed the Democratic administration for "losing" China and for fighting to a stalemate in Korea. Democrats countered in Eisenhower's second term by blaming him for setbacks in Hungary, Southeast Asia and Cuba. Kennedy won the White House in 1960 after blaming Eisenhower and his staunchly anti-communist vice president, Richard Nixon, for a "missile gap" with the Soviet Union.

Underlying those disputes, however, was a broad public consensus about the goals of U.S. foreign policy — a strong and resolute defense in aid of peace and democracy around the world. Those goals can be seen in Kennedy's most lasting foreign policy accomplishments as president: the creation of the Peace Corps, approval of the limited nuclear test ban treaty and the peaceful resolution of the Cuban missile crisis.

But Kennedy's bold rhetoric — pledging in his inaugural address to "bear any burden" in defense of freedom — also led to a humiliating defeat at the Bay of Pigs in 1961. It promised more than the United States could deliver in Africa, Asia and Latin America. And it started the U.S. toward a decade-long engagement in Southeast Asia that was to leave Americans deeply divided about foreign policy.

Vietnam Quagmire

The Vietnam War destroyed the Cold War consensus on foreign policy. The effects are still felt 20 years after the war's end: cynicism, divisiveness and doubts about America's strength and resolve.

Lyndon Johnson, who succeeded the slain Kennedy as president, won election in 1964 while promising to stay out of war in Southeast Asia. Within a year, he began the escalation that was to bring more than 500,000 U.S. troops to South Vietnam and claim more than 50,000 American lives. At home, the anti-war movement grew, but polarized what Nixon labeled "the silent majority."

By mid-1967, polls showed more Americans opposed the war than supported it. [19] Nixon won the White House in 1968 saying he had a secret plan to end the war. Opposition to the war continued to grow. But Nixon kept the war going for four more years before negotiating an agreement in 1973 that did not prevent a North Vietnamese victory two years later.

Vietnam had different lessons for different groups. Conservatives bitterly concluded that Americans were no longer willing to make the kind of sacrifices they had made during World War II in defense of freedom around the world. Liberals said Vietnam showed the danger of unrestrained presidential warmaking and pushed through the 1973 War Power Resolution requiring congressional approval before U.S. troops could be sent into combat abroad.

Politically, Vietnam produced what an article co-authored by Anthony Lake termed "a systemic breakdown" in seeking to fashion a coherent U.S. approach to the world. "The making of American foreign policy had entered a new and far more ideological and political phase," wrote Lake, who is now President Clinton's national security adviser, and his co-authors. [20]

The polarization complicated the making of foreign policy. President Gerald R. Ford sidetracked arms talks with the Soviet Union to deflect an intraparty challenge in 1976 by conservative Ronald Reagan. President Carter only barely won Senate approval of the Panama Canal treaty in 1978 and had to drop the SALT II accord in 1979 after conservative opposition was strengthened by the Soviet invasion of Afghanistan. In the 1980s, President Reagan waged an anti-communist campaign in Central America that liberals opposed and the public did not support. [21]

Militarily, the Reagan and Bush administrations put into practice the lesson that Americans would not support high-visibility, high-casualty conflicts abroad. Reagan invaded Grenada in 1982 and Bush invaded Panama in 1989 with similar strategies: keep casualties low and minimize television coverage of the fighting. Reagan sent in U.S. Marines to try to stabilize Lebanon in 1983, but withdrew them after 241 were killed in a suicide truck-bomb attack. Bush led the country into the Persian Gulf War in 1990-1991 only after assuring the public that the conflict would not be "another Vietnam." [22]

'New World Order'

Emboldened by the U.S. victory in the gulf war and the end of the Cold War, President Bush boldly proclaimed the United States would take the lead in establishing "a new world order" based on opposition to aggression anywhere in the world. But many Americans wanted the government to pay more attention to solving economic problems at home than serving as the world's policeman.

Polls showed fewer Americans were listing foreign policy issues among the country's biggest problems. In 1987, the Times Mirror Center found that 22 percent of persons surveyed listed an international issue as the most important problem facing the country. The figure dropped to 4 percent by 1992. [23]

As the 1992 election approached, polls showed that most Americans — 60 percent or more — thought President Bush had neglected domestic and economic problems. [24] To oppose him, Democrats nominated Bill Clinton, a five-term governor of Arkansas with no experience and little interest in foreign policy. In his acceptance speech July 16, Clinton devoted only one paragraph to foreign policy. He promised to maintain "the world's strongest defense, ready and willing to use force, when necessary," to work to protect the environment, and to champion "the cause of freedom and democracy."

By election time, Bush had become vulnerable on foreign policy. He had dropped the bold talk of a new world order. Saddam Hussein remained in power in Iraq. The former Yugoslavia had erupted in ethnic warfare. A military junta had overthrown Haiti's elected president. Bush was being criticized for siding too long with former Soviet leader Mikhail Gorbachev and for refusing to pressure China on human rights issues.

Clinton made some use of those weaknesses in his campaign. He accused Bush of coddling China and promised to link trade to human rights. He vowed to take the lead in standing up to Serbian aggression in Bosnia. He said he would reverse the Bush policy of returning Haitian refugees detained at sea to their country without giving them a chance to seek asylum.

The campaign turned on domestic issues, however. As AEI's Schneider noted recently, voters who said foreign policy was an important issue split 11 to 1 for Bush — "all 8 percent of them." [25] With economic growth stalled, Americans troubled about keeping a job and making ends meet gave Clinton a 43 percent plurality over Bush and independent candidate Ross Perot. Clinton took the vote to be a mandate for domestic change, but the election gave few helpful clues about voters' views on foreign policy. ■

CURRENT SITUATION

Clinton Under Attack

After a year-and-a-half in office, foreign policy has caught up with President Clinton. He has a nagging list of unresolved foreign crises: Bosnia, Haiti and North Korea. Republicans — and some Democrats — accuse him of weakness, indecision and inconsistency. Polls show that more Americans disapprove than approve of his handling of foreign policy — 51 percent to 41 percent, according to a *Washington Post*-ABC News poll in late June. [26]

President Clinton addresses the G7 economic summit in Naples, Italy, on July 9, 1994.

Clinton and his supporters are trying to counter the criticisms. In an op-ed column in *The Washington Post* in May, Nancy Soderberg, staff director of the National Security Council, offered a checklist of accomplishments, including aid to Russia, the North American Free Trade Agreement (NAFTA) and the Israeli-Palestinian accord — which actually was put together by a Norwegian mediator. She insisted the administration has stiffened U.S. policy in Bosnia and Haiti and was "working aggressively" to stifle North Korea's nuclear weapons program. [27]

For his part, Clinton asked for breathing room. As he prepared to fly to Europe to mark the 50th anniversary of D-Day, Clinton asked for "patience" on foreign policy and cautioned against "simplistic solutions that sound good on bumper stickers but that would have tragic consequences." [28]

"We cannot solve every outburst of civil strife or militant nationalism simply by sending in our forces," Clinton told graduates at the U.S. Naval Academy on May 25. U.S. interests were often "not sufficiently at stake" to justify military intervention. But he said the United States still has "an obligation to lead, or at times, when our interests and our values are sufficiently at stake, to act."

Rhetoric and Reality

When he announced the members of his foreign policy team in December 1992, President-elect Clinton had sounded an activist note. "Mine will be a foreign policy of engagement," Clinton told reporters, "one that strengthens democracy, promotes economic reform, opens markets and stands up to aggression and intolerance." [29]

In short order, however, Clinton had to temper that message. A week before taking office in January 1993,

Clinton said he would continue the Bush administration's policy of sending fleeing Haitians back to their country. Later, Clinton conceded he may have been "too harsh" in his criticism of Bush on the issue. [30]

In Bosnia, too, Clinton's rhetoric collided with reality. In May, Clinton dispatched Secretary of State Warren Christopher to consult with NATO allies on a plan to lift the arms embargo against the Bosnian government and authorize bombing strikes on Serb positions. European leaders turned the plan down. "I cannot unilaterally lift the arms embargo," Clinton told a news conference June 15.

Somalia provided Clinton an even harsher dose of reality. Bush sent U.S. troops to take part in a U.N.-led humanitarian effort to deliver food to victims of Somalia's civil war. After Clinton took office, however, the purpose of the mission broadened into establishing order and quelling the power of Somali warlords.

The scores of U.S. casualties in the unsuccessful Oct. 3 helicopter raid in Mogadishu brought home the dangers of taking sides in a civil war — dangers on graphic display in news coverage over the next several days. To quell congressional and popular outrage, Clinton set a March 31 deadline for getting all U.S. combat troops out. Clinton insisted the United States had accomplished its original mission, but the sequence of events left the undeniable impression that the United States was retreating under fire.

The United States suffered another humiliation in October, this time in Haiti. Armed Haitians prevented U.S. and Canadian engineers aboard a U.S. Navy ship from coming ashore to aid in public works projects that had been part of an agreement negotiated by the United States in the summer between the country's military junta and President Jean-Bertrand Aristide.

The accord called for the junta to step aside by Oct. 30, but the mob

How Public Views America's Global Role

Americans are more isolationist than they were 30 years ago and they want the government to concentrate more on domestic problems than international affairs, according to polling data compiled by the Times Mirror Center for The People and The Press. But most people reject suggestions that the United States "mind its own business" and "let other countries get along the best they can." And a large majority think the U.S. should cooperate fully with the United Nations.

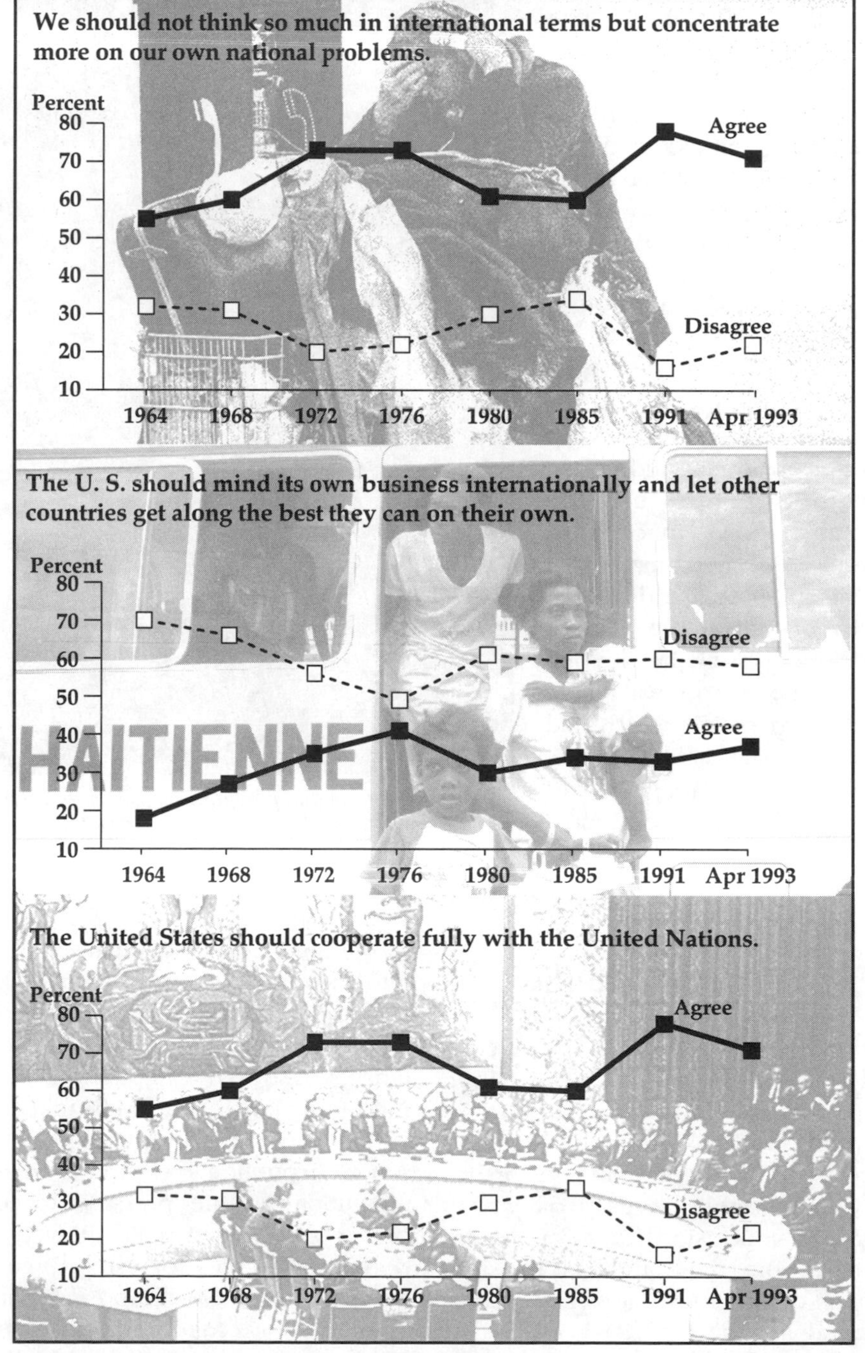

We should not think so much in international terms but concentrate more on our own national problems.
Percent
80
70
60
50
40
30
20
10
Agree
Disagree
1964
1968
1972
1976
1980
1985
1991
Apr 1993
The U. S. should mind its own business internationally and let other countries get along the best they can on their own.
Percent
Disagree
Agree
HAITIENNE
The United States should cooperate fully with the United Nations.
Percent
Agree
Disagree

Source: Times Mirror Center for The People and The Press, America's Place in the World, *November 1993. Photographs courtesy of Reuters.*

scene Oct. 11 at the docks in Port-au-Prince signaled the junta's decision to renege. Three weeks later, the deadline for Aristide's return passed with the junta still in power and Aristide still in exile in Wash ington.

In all three countries, the United States had invested enough prestige to have a stake in the outcome even though U.S. interests were hard to define. But in all three, the administration was finding that the United States lacked the power to determine the outcome unless it was prepared to commit more resources, including military force.

By fall 1993, the setbacks were damaging Clinton's standing in the polls. Several State Department aides had resigned to protest the administration's inaction in Bosnia. The combination of events in Somalia and Haiti in October made the United States look like a helpless giant. Clinton's approval rating on foreign policy, which had been gradually sliding all year, dipped sharply to its lowest point — below 40 percent.

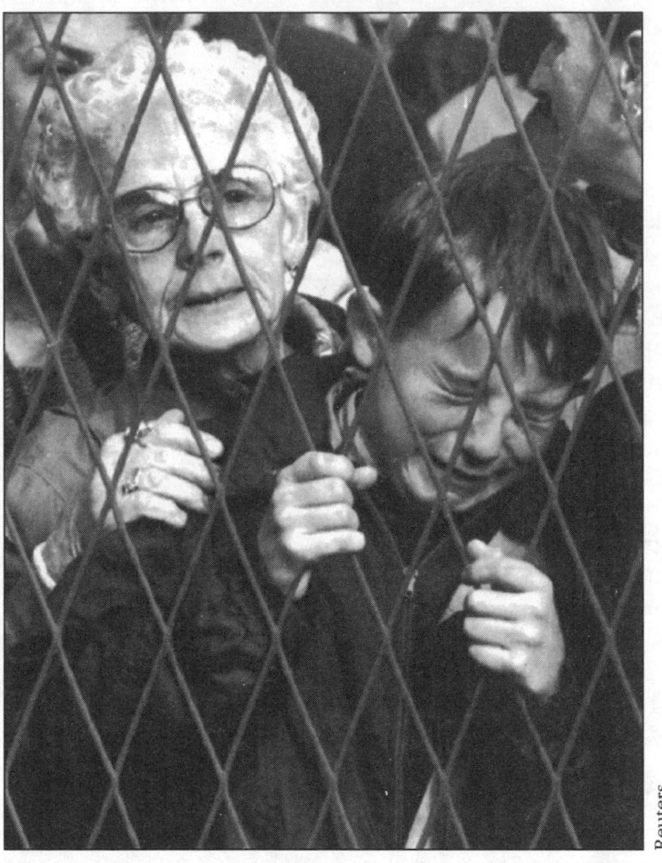

Reuters

A Muslim woman and her grandson cry as they watch the boy's Serbian father board a bus as part of an evacuation of 300 Serbs from the Muslim stronghold of Travnik in November 1993.

An Uncertain Public

Clinton's second year in office continues to be difficult. His public approval ratings hovered around 50 percent until March and then slid sharply to the 40 percent level again.

Clinton stands accused of vacillation and indecision from commentators on the right and on the left. Liberal columnist Anthony Lewis complained in *The New York Times* that Clinton's foreign policy seemed "driven by the vagaries of public opinion" instead of "firm beliefs" and "long-term vision." [31] Conservative Linda Chavez struck a similar note. "He just can't decide what to do," Chavez wrote in *USA Today*. "And even when he does, he's liable to change his mind." [32]

Former President Bush stepped into the debate as well. "Our leadership around the world is being eroded by a stop-and-start policy of hesitancy," Bush told a Republican Party fund-raiser May 17 in Milwaukee. [33]

Yet neither Congress nor the American public showed much greater resolution on the pressing foreign policy issues. Most polls showed no popular majorities for using force in Bosnia, Haiti or North Korea. In May, a center-right coalition in the House pushed through a non-binding amendment opposing U.S. military intervention in Haiti. The 223-201 House vote came just five days after Clinton had listed a number of reasons for taking military action if economic sanctions failed to dislodge the Haitian junta.

On Bosnia, the president faces pressure from the left to unilaterally lift the embargo on arming the embattled Bosnian government. But Clinton continues to maintain that the action would only anger European allies with peacekeeping troops on the ground. As Congress adjourned for the Independence Day recess, the outcome was uncertain. The House had voted 244-178 to lift the embargo, but the Senate defeated a similar provision on a tie vote — 50-50.

With Congress and the public divided, public opinion expert Yankelovich says he is "sympathetic" to Clinton's difficulties. "On the one hand, there's a consensus in this country that we are not to be the world's policeman," Yankelovich says. "On the other hand, the world needs a policeman, and our efforts with the U.N. have not succeeded. There's a question of how to carry out the leadership role in this strange new world we're in."

Clinton has brought some of the difficulties on himself. In his campaign, he promised to support U.N. peacekeeping and faulted Bush for weakness on Bosnia, Haiti and China. As president, however, he laid out tough conditions for U.S. participation in U.N. peacekeeping. He extended normal trading status with China — officially repudiating his position linking trade with human rights. And, even if he has marginally toughened the U.S. stance toward

Continued on p. 618

At Issue:

Does television distort public opinion on foreign policy?

yes

Rep. Lee H. Hamilton, D-Ind.
Chairman, House Foreign Affairs Committee

FROM *OPENING STATEMENT AT A HEARING ON THE IMPACT OF TELEVISION ON U.S. FOREIGN POLICY*, APRIL 26. 1994.

There can be little doubt that television has had an impact, perhaps a profound impact, on the conduct of U.S. foreign policy. Spurred by technological advances ranging from satellites to cellular phones, vivid images of conflict and deprivation are sent instantly to American homes from the world's trouble spots, whether in Haiti or Somalia or Bosnia or the Persian Gulf.

These televised images quickly become a central part of the foreign policy debate. They affect which crises we decide to pay attention to or which we ignore. They affect how we think about these crises, and I have little doubt these televised pictures ultimately affect what we do about these problems.

Television can educate the public and focus attention on far off trouble spots that may otherwise be ignored. It can provide world leaders the means to communicate with each other directly in a crisis.

But television also encourages policy-makers to react quickly, perhaps too quickly, to a crisis. It allows the media to set the agenda. It generates pressure for action selectively: why Somalia and not Sudan, why Bosnia and not Nagorno Karabakh?

Television, critics say, leads not to sound foreign policy, but [to] sound bites masquerading as policy. Secretary of State [Warren] Christopher has warned that television cannot be the North Star of our foreign policy, but it may be too late.

Pictures of the starving children, not policy objectives, got us into Somalia in 1992. Pictures of U.S. casualties, not the completion of our objectives, led us to exit Somalia last month.

Pictures of the market bombing in Sarajevo helped get us more deeply involved in Bosnia. Pictures of U.S. casualties, if they occur, could lead us to pull back.

What can be done, if anything, to counter the impact of television on our policy? What should policy-makers do, if anything, to prevent television from setting their agenda? What, if anything, should the media do to avoid inadvertently skewing American foreign policy one way or the other? These are some of the issues we hope to address in today's hearing.

no

Ted Koppel
Anchor, ABC News "Nightline"

FROM *TESTIMONY BEFORE THE HOUSE FOREIGN AFFAIRS COMMITTEE*, APRIL 26, 1994.

Television's influence increases in regions where an administration has (a) failed to enunciate a clear policy and/or (b) has done little or nothing to inform the American public on the dangers of intervention or failing to intervene. . . .

Prior to the appearance of the first television pictures from Somalia . . . the Bush administration had done little or nothing to marshal public support for any kind of massive aid operation . . . Neither the Bush nor the Clinton administration . . . clearly addressed the issue of what Washington would do in the event of U.S. casualties. Nor had it laid the groundwork for explaining to the American public why such a price might be necessary. . . .

In the absence of a clearly enunciated foreign policy toward the Serbs in Bosnia, we are left floundering in a sea of options. . . . We are still dealing with the possibility of up to 25,000 U.S. troops being sent to Bosnia to maintain peace if and when it has been agreed to by all sides. The suggestion is that if the peace breaks down, the troops would be withdrawn. In other words, we would send them if they are not needed, and withdraw them if they are. . . .

My point . . . is this: The absence of a clearly formulated and enunciated policy is like a vacuum. It will be filled by whatever is available: Congressmen having themselves publicly arrested in response to the leadership of a committed activist, voices from the loyal opposition or, for that matter, television reports, which often contradict reality as presented by administration spokespeople. . . .

No doubt, the speed of satellite communication, and the acquired sophistication of both friends and adversaries in using that technology to their own best advantage, require a great deal of further attention. Ultimately, though, it boils down to the same thing: If an administration has thought its own foreign policy through, and is prepared and able to argue the merits and defend the consequences of that policy, television and all its technologies can be dealt with. If, on the other hand, the foreign policy is ill-conceived and poorly explained, it does not much matter whether the news arrives by satellite or clipper ship. Eventually the policy will fail.

Continued from p. 616

Bosnia and Haiti, nothing has changed on the ground.

"You have to be very careful what you say in these campaigns," says Gelb, who served as assistant secretary of State in the Carter administration. "It's not just campaign rhetoric. It's your promise to the American people of what you're going to do if elected."

Some experts, however, say that there is latent public support for the tougher stands that candidate Clinton took if President Clinton would show more leadership. Kull of the University of Maryland says polls by his program on international policy attitudes show that Americans support U.N. peacekeeping in cases of civil wars (69 percent), large-scale atrocities (83 percent) or gross human rights violations (81 percent). And 49 percent of those surveyed said the United States should contribute troops to U.N. peacekeeping operations in "most cases." [34]

Kull says polls by his program also show that at least three-fourths of those surveyed backed the U.S.-NATO decision to threaten airstrikes against Bosnian Serbs after the dramatic shelling of a Sarajevo market on Feb. 5 that killed more than 60 civilians. He says a narrow majority — 53 percent — also backed lifting the arms embargo in Bosnia. [35] And he argues that Americans turned against the U.S. mission in Somalia only after events showed the Somalis "didn't want us there."

Kull says the administration is "accommodating" public opinion rather than "challenging" it. But he adds, "When the president does lead, there's a tendency for the public to follow."

A poll taken last month supports the view that Clinton's focus on Haiti and North Korea may have shifted public opinion. In late June, a *Washington Post*-ABC News poll found a sharp increase in support for military action if necessary to restore democratic government in Haiti — to 45 percent from 36 percent one month earlier. More than three-fourths of those surveyed said the U.S. and its allies should take all action necessary, including use of military force, to make sure North Korea does not obtain nuclear weapons. Two weeks earlier, a *Wall Street Journal*-NBC News poll found only 44 percent in favor of a military strike over the issue. [36] ■

OUTLOOK

Pressures on Clinton

As he prepared to take office, President Clinton wanted to be a domestic affairs president. In his first year, he concentrated on winning congressional approval of a budget package with politically unpalatable tax increases and a free-trade treaty with the politically treacherous risk of short-term job losses. He began laying the groundwork for a tough political fight over health care reform. And he took political hits on a range of other domestic issues — from gays in the military to the Whitewater affair.

Reuters

Secretary of State Warren Christopher

Foreign policy added to those headaches with few opportunities for political gain. As a result, Clinton appeared to give foreign affairs less attention than domestic policy. When he spoke to the U.N. General Assembly in September, *New York Times* correspondent Thomas Friedman called the speech "flat" and described Clinton's delivery as "subdued." [37] Six months later, in March, the administration answered criticism that Clinton was neglecting world affairs by saying that he had *recently* begun holding weekly meetings with his foreign policy team. [38]

By late spring, however, polls indicated that Clinton's low rating on foreign policy was contributing to an overall drop in popularity. "Clinton's losing points with the public, and it's hurting him politically," Schneider explains. "Other nations have gotten the message that they can defy him with impunity, and Americans are not very happy with that."

Clinton began looking at possible changes in foreign policy personnel. But when the *Los Angeles Times* readied a story on a possible shakeup that could even replace Secretary of State Christopher, Clinton personally called the *Times'* Washington bureau chief, Jack Nelson, to deny it. [39]

Two changes were made, however. Stephen Oxman, a "friend of Bill" who presided over the Bosnia policy as assistant secretary of State for European affairs, was replaced by a respected careerist, Richard Holbrooke, who had been ambassador to Germany. And David Gergen, a skillful spin-master, was moved from the White House to the State Department as "special adviser" to help "articulate" the administration's foreign policy goals.

Some insiders speculated that broader changes could take place later in the year. But the personnel moves struck some observers as inadequate. They said Clinton himself was the problem. "He talks like an internationalist and acts like an isolationist," Fred Barnes, conservative White

House watcher, said on the McLaughlin Group July 1.

No doubt, Clinton faced a difficult task in plotting a strategy to deal with the array of small to midsized foreign policy challenges around the world and then selling the strategy — and its costs — to a post-Cold War America. The current crises could be viewed as intractable. The war in Bosnia stems from centuries-old ethnic hostilities. Haiti has no history of democratic rule. And North Korea has set itself against world opinion for most of its 50 years as a nation.

Still, the United States stands as a world superpower, with the economic, diplomatic and military strength to influence, if not control, events around the globe. Polls show that Americans have not turned their backs on the international responsibilities that go with their power. The public may have a natural impulse to stay out of messy situations abroad, but they can be persuaded to bear the costs of an internationalist foreign policy with proper leadership. And that responsibility, many observers say, rests with the president.

"Clinton's got to put together a series of foreign policy positions that set a direction for U.S. foreign policy, which explain how he's going to proceed, and explain why it's important for Americans to back that course," says Gelb. "The public understands these problems are hard. The public doesn't expect easy solutions. But you still have to explain which way you're going and why we're going to pay a price to get there." ■

Notes

[1] *The New York Times,* Oct. 7, 1994, p. A7.

[2] *U.S. News & World Report,* Jan. 24, 1994, p. 75.

[3] Daniel Yankelovich and John Immerwahr, "The Rules of Public Engagement," in Yankelovich and I.M. Destler (eds.), *Beyond the Beltway: Engaging the Public in U.S. Foreign Policy* (1994), p. 45.

[4] Quoted in *The Christian Science Monitor,* Feb. 4, 1994, p. 3.

[5] Gabriel A. Almond, *The American People and Foreign Policy* (1960 ed.), pp. 136-139.

[6] Stephen E. Ambrose, "The Presidency and Foreign Policy," *Foreign Affairs,* winter 1991, p. 136.

[7] Times Mirror Center for The People and The Press, *America's Place in the World,* November 1993, p. 94.

[8] *Ibid.,* pp. 7-8, 28-31.

[9] Charles Williams Maynes, "A Workable Clinton Doctrine," *Foreign Policy,* winter 1993, p. 2.

[10] Quoted in Michael R. Beschloss, "Presidents, Television and Foreign Crises," Annenberg Washington Program, 1993, pp. 26-27.

[11] Abrams spoke June 8 at a Harvard College class reunion symposium, "Shaping the Public Agenda."

[12] Beschloss, *op. cit.,* pp. 20-21.

[13] Thomas A. Bailey, *A Diplomatic History of the American People* (10th ed., 1980), p. 3.

[14] Robert H. Wiebe, *The Search for Order: 1877-1920* (1967), p. 225.

[15] Bailey, *op. cit.,* p. 225.

[16] *Ibid.,* p. 258.

[17] *Ibid.,* pp. 719 n. 7, 722 n. 10, 723 n. 11.

[18] *Ibid.,* pp. 797 n. 3, 799 n. 5, 808 n. 10.

[19] John Mueller, *War, Presidents and Public Opinion* (1973), p. 56.

[20] I.M. Destler, Leslie H. Gelb and Anthony Lake, "Breakdown: The Impact of Domestic Politics on American Foreign Policy," in Charles W. Kegley Jr. and Eugene R. Wittkopf (eds.), *The Domestic Sources of American Foreign Policy: Insights and Evidence* (1988), pp. 17-29. The article was written in 1984.

[21] See Richard Sobel (ed.), *Public Opinion in U.S. Foreign Policy: The Controversy over Contra Aid* (1993), pp. 49-58.

[22] Quoted in John E. Mueller, *Policy & Opinion in the Gulf War* (1994), p. 45.

[23] Times Mirror Center, *op. cit.,* p. 83.

[24] *The New York Times,* Oct. 11, 1991, p. A8.

[25] William Schneider, "Clinton's Wobbly Foreign Policy Way," *National Journal,* May 28, 1994, p. 1274.

[26] *The Washington Post,* June 29, 1994, p. A10.

[27] *The Washington Post,* May 25, 1994, p. A23.

[28] *The Washington Post,* May 26, 1994, p. A31.

[29] Quoted in *National Journal,* Jan. 9, 1993, p. 64.

[30] Quoted in *National Journal,* March 13, 1993, p. 621.

[31] *The New York Times,* June 3, 1994, p. A27.

[32] *USA Today,* May 25, 1994, p. 15A.

[33] Quoted in the *Los Angeles Times,* May 26, 1994, p. A5.

[34] Steven Kull and Clay Ramsay, "U.S. Public Attitudes on U.N. Peacekeeping: Part I, Funding," Program on International Policy Attitudes, March 7, 1994, pp. 25-26.

[35] Steven Kull and Clay Ramsay, "U.S. Public Attitudes on U.S. Involvement in Bosnia," Program on International Policy Attitudes, May 4, 1994, pp. 5-6, 8-9.

[36] *The Washington Post,* June 29, 1994, p. A11; *The Wall Street Journal,* June 17, 1994, p. A1.

[37] *The New York Times,* Sept. 28, 1993, p. A16.

[38] *Congressional Quarterly Weekly Report,* March 26, 1994, p. 751.

[39] See the *Los Angeles Times,* May 28, 1994, p. A1.

Bibliography

Selected Sources Used

Books

Almond, Gabriel A., *The American People and Foreign Policy,* Praeger, 1960.
This famous work — written in 1950 and reprinted with a new introduction in 1960 — depicts public opinion as a secondary factor in the formation of foreign policy. Almond, then a political scientist at Yale and now at Stanford, argues that the general public is largely uninformed about and uninterested in foreign affairs. He says the government makes foreign policy by interacting with "policy and opinion elites" and the so-called "attentive public" that does follow international events.

Ambrose, Stephen E., *Rise to Globalism: American Foreign Policy Since 1938* (7th rev. ed.), Penguin, 1993.
Ambrose, a historian at the University of New Orleans, has periodically updated this survey of U.S. foreign policy since its first publication in 1971. The book includes a well organized, 10-page bibliographical essay.

Bailey, Thomas A., *A Diplomatic History of the American People* (10th ed.), Prentice-Hall, 1980.
This authoritative history contains well-indexed treatment of public opinion and foreign policy from colonial times to the present. Each chapter has detailed source notes.

Kegley, Charles W., Jr., and Eugene R. Wittkopf (eds.), *The Domestic Sources of American Foreign Policy: Insights and Evidence,* St. Martin, 1988.
The 20 essays in this collection include several that examine the role of public opinion, politics and elections on the formation of U.S. foreign policy. Most chapters include notes that point to other references.

Mueller, John E., *Policy and Opinion in the Gulf War,* University of Chicago Press, 1994.
Mueller, a political scientist at the University of Rochester, concludes that President George Bush won support for the Persian Gulf War by convincing the public that it was inevitable, rather than right or wise. In his earlier book, *War, Presidents and Public Opinion* (Wiley, 1973), Mueller examined public opinion during the Korean and Vietnam wars.

Sobel, Richard (ed.), *Public Opinion in U.S. Foreign Policy: The Controversy over Contra Aid,* Rowman & Littlefield, 1993.
Sobel introduces this collection of articles by saying that Americans opposed assisting the Nicaraguan contras, but the Reagan administration and, to a lesser extent, Congress continued the aid anyway. Sobel is an associate at Princeton's Center of International Studies.

Spanier, John, *American Foreign Policy Since World War II* (12th ed.), CQ Press, 1991.
Spanier, a professor at the University of Florida in Gainesville, opens this survey history with an insightful chapter on the American approach to foreign policy. The book includes a 12-page chronology and an 11-page bibliography.

Yankelovich, Daniel and I.M. Destler (eds.), *Beyond the Beltway: Engaging the Public in U.S. Foreign Policy,* The American Assembly/Norton, 1994.
The contributors to this collection of 11 essays conclude by agreeing that public participation in foreign policy making is "both a growing reality and an increasing necessity." Yankelovich is an expert on public opinion and president of the business research firm DYG, Inc. Destler is director of the Center for International and Security Studies at the University of Maryland.

Articles

Sharkey, Jacqueline, "When Pictures Drive Foreign Policy," *American Journalism Review,* December 1993, pp. 14-19.
The article examines the impact television coverage had on U.S. policy in Somalia and the media's influence on foreign policy generally.

Reports and Studies

Beschloss, Michael R., "Presidents, Television and Foreign Crises," Annenberg Washington Program, 1993.
Historian Beschloss analyzes the effects of television coverage on presidential decisionmaking in the Cuban missile crisis, the attack on the Mayaguez and the gulf war.

Cooper, Mary, "Foreign Policy Burden," *The CQ Researcher,* Aug. 20, 1993.
The report examines the debate over whether the United States should help police the world in the post-Cold War era.

Times Mirror Center for The People and The Press, *America's Place in the World,* November 1993.
The center surveyed nine groups of U.S. opinion leaders and found pessimistic and isolationist attitudes that pointed toward a more cautious and minimalist U.S. foreign policy.

The Next Step

Additional information from UMI's Newspaper & Periodical Abstracts database

Clinton and Foreign Policy

Barnes, James A., "Missing the boat?" *National Journal,* July 10, 1993, p. 1783.
The Clinton administration's lack of focus and emphasis on foreign policy and foreign affairs is discussed. The lift that a president can get from foreign policy accomplishments has been diminished by the collapse of Communism in the former USSR.

Cooper, Matthew, "Stress test," *U.S. News & World Report,* May 10, 1993, pp. 26-32.
President Clinton's first 100 days have been criticized by the public and the press, but even more challenges loom in the future of his second 100 days. Problems with the sagging economy, Bosnia and health care policy are discussed.

Church, George J., "Dropping the ball?" *Time,* May 2, 1994, pp. 52-57.
While President Clinton focuses on domestic affairs, U.S. world leadership suffers from a lack of attention and too frequent back-and-forth policy switches. Clinton's treatment of domestic and foreign matters and the results of a telephone poll are discussed.

Downs, George W., and David M. Rocke, "Conflict, agency, and gambling for resurrection: The principal agent problem goes to war," *American Journal of Political Science,* May 1994, pp. 362-280.
The problem of ensuring that chief executives act in accordance with the wishes of their constituency is particularly acute in the area of foreign intervention where the head of state can be expected to possess substantial information advantages. A formal analysis of strategies that can be used to deter overly passive and overly aggressive executives and a discussion of their side effects are presented.

"Ginsburg, economy, budget encourage upbeat Clinton," *Congressional Quarterly Weekly Report,* June 19, 1993, pp. 1601-1603.
During a news conference, President Clinton discussed the loss of confidence in his presidency, the policies toward Bosnia and Somalia and his Supreme Court nomination of Ruth Bader Ginsburg.

Kirschten, Dick, "Off shore, Bill Clinton's at sea," *National Journal,* April 30, 1994, p. 1040.
If President Clinton expects the voters to renew his contract in 1996, he is going to have to become a foreign policy president. Clinton's low marks for his handling of international affairs are discussed.

Neikirk, William; Atlas, Terry, "Clinton turns to global CNN forum to clarify foreign policy," *Chicago Tribune,* May 3, 1994, p. 7.
With perceptions that President Clinton's foreign policy is unfocused, unimaginative and reactive, eroding Clinton's support, the president will make a major attempt to demonstrate he is on top of foreign policy when he submits to 90 minutes of questioning on CNN. It will be his most lengthy public discussion of these issues since he took office and it will be watched not only by the American public but by foreign leaders taking stock.

Schneider, William, "Clinton tries new approach on trade," *National Journal,* Feb. 26, 1994, p. 506.
In talking tough with the Japanese and sweetly with the Saudis, President Clinton has scored points with the public for his aggressive trade policy. Clinton's mix of foreign policy and trade policy is discussed.

Seib, Gerald F., and Jeffrey H. Birnbaum, " Poll shows while Clinton's job approval is high, doubts about character, foreign policy persist," *The Wall Street Journal,* May 5, 1994, p. A16.
According to a recent *Wall Street Journal*/NBC News poll, despite a slight increase in President Clinton's overall job approval rating in April 1994, Americans are expressing significant doubts about his character and his base of support as a world leader is eroding.

Defining U.S. Policy

Sloan, Stanley R., "From U.S. deterrence to self-deterrence," *Christian Science Monitor,* May 3, 1994, p. 19.
Stanley R. Sloan contends that the mood of the American public is resulting in the U.S. becoming a self-deterred power, a country preventing itself from using force, which leaves the international system without the political credibility and military force needed to discourage aggressors.

Trubowitz, Peter, "Sectionalism and American Foreign Policy: The Political Geography of Consensus and Conflict," *International Studies Quarterly*, June 1992, pp. 173-190.
It is argued that U.S. foreign policy debates are regional in nature and part of a larger struggle over national priorities between the oldest and newest industrializing regions. The positions of the "manufacturing belt" and the "sunbelt" are contrasted.

Haiti

"Ask the Haitians," ***Progressive,*** **June 1994, pp. 8-9.**
President Clinton has begun sending signals that military intervention in Haiti is a possibility. According to a poll by National Public Radio, the vast majority of Haitians don't want to be "liberated" by the U.S.

Hines, Cragg, "New approach to Haiti," ***Houston Chronicle,*** **May 9, 1994, p. A1.**
President Clinton moved to stem the protest against his Haiti policy without significantly increasing the number of refugees from the beleaguered Caribbean nation who are granted political asylum in the U.S.

Mashberg, Tom, "Immigrants in Boston hail policy, talk of force," ***Boston Globe,*** **May 9, 1994, p. 1.**
Haitian-Americans across Boston expressed hope that President Clinton has shifted policy on Haitian refugees and chastised the island's dictators with his announcement that the Coast Guard would no longer forcibly return all of the refugees.

Preston, Julia, "U.S. shifts on Haiti, gets tougher on army," ***The Washington Post,*** **April 29, 1994, p. A41.**
The Clinton administration, smarting from public criticism of its stance on Haiti, unveiled a new policy that demands the resignation of Haiti's military rulers as a first step toward reinstalling President Jean-Bertrand Aristide.

Historical Trends

Bennett, W. Lance, and Jarol B. Manheim, "Taking the public by storm: Information, cuing, and the democratic process in the Gulf conflict," ***Political Communication,*** **October 1993, pp. 331-351.**
The framework of cues in which the Persian Gulf conflict was presented to the American people by the news media is examined, and the degree to which this portrayal facilitated or impeded timely and meaningful public debate of policy responses to the Iraqi invasion of Kuwait is discussed.

Bowman, Karlyn, and Everett C. Ladd, "Public opinion and demographic report: Sensible internationalism," ***American Enterprise,*** **March 1993, pp. 95-103.**
The results of public opinion surveys on U.S. foreign policy during various wars throughout history are presented. Americans support U.S. humanitarian efforts in Somalia, though they worry about an open-ended commitment.

Evensen, Bruce J., "A Story of 'Ineptness': The Truman Administration's Struggle to Shape Conventional Wisdom on Palestine at the Beginning of the Cold War," ***Diplomatic History,*** **summer 1991, pp. 339-359.**
Historical debate on the development of the Truman administration's policy toward Palestine frequently reflects personal attitudes toward Zionism and the Jewish state of Israel. The role of public opinion in the formulation of U.S. policy toward Palestine in the period before the creation of Israel is examined.

Holsti, Ole R., "Public opinion and foreign policy: Challenges to the Almond-Lippmann consensus Mershon series: Research programs and debates," ***International Studies Quarterly,*** **December 1992, pp. 439-466.**
World Wars I and II and the Vietnam War have had significant impacts on theories and research on public opinion and foreign policy. Three propositions about public opinion are drawn: It is volatile and thus provides inadequate foundations for stable and effective foreign policies; it lacks coherence or structure; and it has little if any impact on foreign policy.

Russett, Bruce, "Doves, Hawks, and U.S. Public Opinion," ***Political Science Quarterly,*** **winter 1990, pp. 515-538.**
The long-standing debate between so-called "realists" and "idealists" in international relations is usually perceived as contention between "hawks" and "doves" or conservatives and liberals. This is an overly simplistic comparison but serves as a suitable foundation from which to examine the effect of these characterizations on U.S. public opinion, and vice versa.

Russett, Bruce, Thomas Hartley, and Shoon Murray, "The end of the Cold War, attitude change, and the politics of defense spending," ***PS,*** **March 1994, pp. 17-21.**
The end of the Cold War has presented political scientists an opportunity to study the structure of U.S. foreign policy beliefs and the dynamics of public attitude change. The historic event also provides a chance to speculate about how changed and stable attitudes affect national security policy and defense spending.

Schneider, William, "No more rallying around the flag?" ***National Journal,*** **Oct. 30, 1993, p. 2624.**
In a part from historical precedent, Americans are no longer rallying around their president during foreign policy crises. The policy crises of the Clinton administration, in which no specific principles are involved, and public and political opposition to them are discussed.

Nixon and Foreign Policy

McGrory, Brian, "Voters take softer tone on Nixon," ***Boston Globe,*** **April 24, 1994, p. 23.**
In death, Richard M. Nixon appeared largely forgiven, as average voters talked not so much of Watergate, but of his deft hand in world affairs, not of stunning failure, but of human frailty.

Wowk, Mike, "In Detroit, Watergate will overshadow his achievements," ***Detroit News & Free Press,*** **April**

24, 1994, p. B5.

Whether they are old enough to have voted for him, or twentysomething, metro Detroiters seem to be surprisingly unanimous in their feelings toward former President Richard Nixon: Nixon was great in foreign policy, but he will forever be known for the Watergate scandal.

Opinions

Grier, Peter, "Clinton urged to use ultimatums sparingly," *Christian Science Monitor,* May 18, 1994, p. 1.

Peter Grier discusses U.S. foreign policy in Haiti, Bosnia and other areas, saying that a nation's basic values, its leader's personality, its past practices and public opinion are all part of the credibility equation in foreign policy.

McWhirter, Nickie, "Rethinking America's foreign policies," *Detroit News & Free Press,* May 21, 1994, p. C6.

Nickie McWhirter comments on the criticism President Clinton has faced because of his foreign policy, saying that Americans should stop worrying about Clinton's foreign policy and focus on more serious domestic issues.

Sperling, Godfrey, "Cautious involvement makes good foreign policy," *Christian Science Monitor,* May 31, 1994, p. 19.

In an open letter to President Clinton, Godfrey Sperling outlines the principles of "cautious involvement" as the foreign policy for the U.S., claiming that most Americans are more concerned with domestic issues than with sending U.S. troops to various global hot spots.

Public Opinion

Balz, Dan; Morin, Richard, "Public losing confidence in Clinton foreign policy," *The Washington Post,* May 17, 1994, p. A1.

Public confidence in President Clinton's handling of foreign policy has declined sharply in the wake of setbacks to his Haiti policy and criticism of other initiatives, and a majority of Americans now question whether Clinton understands difficult foreign policy problems.

Jordan, Donald L., and Benjamin I. Page, "Shaping Foreign Policy Opinions: The Role of TV News," *Journal of Conflict Resolution*, June 1992, pp. 227-241.

A study measured the connections between public opinion and U.S. foreign policy-making and assessed the impact of TV news broadcasts on public opinion. The results showed that the process of shaping opinion on foreign policy doesn't differ substantially from that affecting domestic policy preferences.

Greenfield, Meg, "Intervention fatigue," *Newsweek,* Oct. 25, 1993, p. 80.

Americans are having an attack of intervention fatigue. President Clinton's foreign policy will be overwhelmed by hostile public opinion unless he makes an honest, compelling case for those interventions he deems necessary and lets the rest go.

Moore, David W., and Lydia Saad, "Informed Americans support Yeltsin," *Gallup Poll Monthly,* March 1993, pp. 23-24.

A Gallup poll showed that Americans prefer that the US remain neutral in the current struggle between Boris Yeltsin and the Russian parliament, but among those who pay close attention to foreign policy, a majority would prefer that the U.S. support Yeltsin.

Newport, Frank, "Foreign affairs erodes public's confidence in Clinton," *Gallup Poll Monthly,* October 1993, pp. 29-32.

U.S. involvement in Haiti and Somalia has caused the U.S. public's confidence in President Clinton to decline. According to a Gallup Poll, Clinton's foreign affairs and overall approval ratings have begun to slip.

Schneider, William, "Test-marketing the Clinton doctrine," *National Journal*, Jan. 22, 1994, p. 214.

If President Clinton is serious about his new doctrine of U.S. engagement in Europe, he will have to sell it to the public. Internationalism does not come naturally to Americans.

Will, George F., "Since McKinley's cigar," *Newsweek,* June 13, 1994, p. 64.

The win by a Republican for Kentucky's House seat, which had been held by a Democrat for 129 years, is another example of President Clinton's failing popularity. The problems faced by Clinton, including his foreign policy fiascos, are discussed.

Yankelovich, Daniel, "Foreign Policy After the Election," *Foreign Affairs,* fall 1992, pp. 1-12.

The characteristics of the public mood regarding the U.S. recession are analyzed for foreign policy impacts in the 1992 presidential election. A strong industrial policy will likely be the heart of U.S. foreign policy after the election.

Somalia

Wheeler, C. Gray, and David W. Moore, "Clinton's foreign policy ratings plunge," *Gallup Poll Monthly,* October 1993, pp. 25-28.

In the wake of the deaths of U.S. soldiers in Somalia, President Clinton's foreign policy rating has dropped 15 points. According to a Gallup Poll, 40 percent approve of his foreign policy.

Back Issues

Great Research on Current Issues Starts Right Here...Recent topics covered by The CQ Researcher are listed below. Before May 1991, reports were published under the name of Editorial Research Reports.

JANUARY 1993
Hate Crimes
Child Sexual Abuse
Nuclear Fusion
U.S. Trade Policy

FEBRUARY 1993
Community Policing
Europe's New Right
School Censorship
Violence Against Women

MARCH 1993
Gay Rights
Aid to Russia
War on Drugs
TV Violence

APRIL 1993
Head Start
High-Speed Rail
Children's Legal Rights
Muslims in America

MAY 1993
Cults in America
Preventing Teen Pregnancy
Software Piracy
National Parks

Back issues are available for $4.00 (subscribers) or $7.00 (non-subscribers). Quantity discounts apply to orders over ten. To order, call Congressional Quarterly Customer Service at (202) 887-8621.

Binders are available for $16.00. To order call 1-800-638-1710. Please refer to stock number 648.

JUNE 1993
Food Safety
Prostitution
Childhood Immunizations
National Service

JULY 1993
Electric Cars
Population Growth
Downward Mobility
Intelligence Testing

AUGUST 1993
Mental Illness
Bilingual Education
Foreign Policy Burden
School Funding

SEPTEMBER 1993
Suburban Crime
Public Housing
Supreme Court Preview
Immigration Reform

OCTOBER 1993
Airline Safety
Disaster Response
Science in the Courtroom
The Glass Ceiling

NOVEMBER 1993
Paying for Retirement
Charitable Giving
Privacy in the Workplace
Adoption

DECEMBER 1993
U.S. Vietnam-Relations
Learning Disabilities
Child Care
Space Program's Future

JANUARY 1994
Racial Tensions in Schools
South Africa's Future
Worker Retraining
Regulating Pesticides

FEBRUARY 1994
Prison Overcrowding
Water Quality
Religion in Schools
Juvenile Justice

MARCH 1994
Underground Economy
Education Standards
Gambling Boom
Private Management of Public Schools

APRIL 1994
Reproductive Ethics
U.S.-China Trade
Soccer in America
Talk Show Democracy

MAY 1994
Traffic Congestion
Women's Health Issues
Mutual Funds
Political Scandals

JUNE 1994
Education and Gender
Gun Control
Public Land Policy
Nuclear Arms Cleanup

AUGUST 1994
Dietary Supplements

Future Topics

- ***Crime Victims' Rights***
- ***Contraceptives***
- ***Genetically Engineered Foods***

THE CQ Researcher

PUBLISHED BY CONGRESSIONAL QUARTERLY INC.

Crime Victims' Rights

Do victims need new laws and protections?

Long ignored as the "forgotten people" of the criminal justice system, victims of crime are now organized and vocal. The families of crime victims, as well as the survivors themselves, are seeking new laws and state constitutional amendments guaranteeing victims the right to participate in legal proceedings — to attend trials, to make statements in court on a crime's personal impact and to comment at plea bargainings and parole hearings. Opponents warn of threats to defendants' traditional presumption of innocence. Judges are wary of allowing emotionalism in their courtrooms, while prosecutors and police raise concerns about costs added to their heavy caseloads. Still, victims say that giving them an active role provides a needed catharsis and a chance to help in reducing crime.

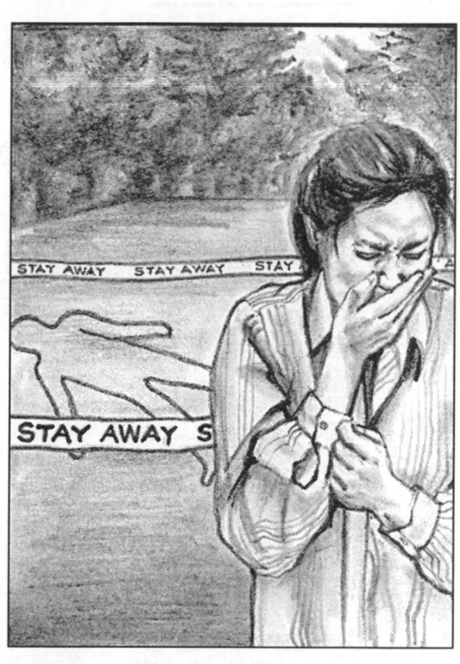

INSIDE THIS ISSUE

CQ July 22, 1994 • Volume 4, No. 27 • 625-648

Formerly Editorial Research Reports

CRIME VICTIMS' RIGHTS

COVER: BARBARA SASSA-DANIELS

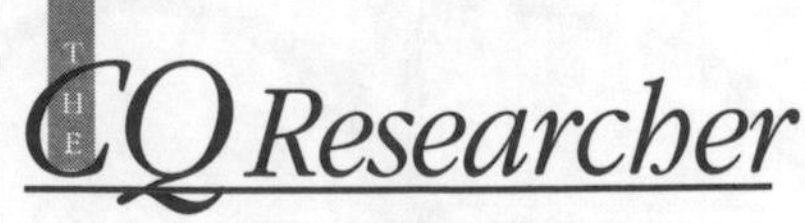

July 22, 1994
Volume 4, No. 27

EDITOR
Sandra Stencel

MANAGING EDITOR
Thomas J. Colin

ASSOCIATE EDITOR
Richard L. Worsnop

STAFF WRITERS
Charles S. Clark
Mary H. Cooper
Kenneth Jost

PRODUCTION EDITOR
Sarah E. Merritt

EDITORIAL ASSISTANT
Michael M. Taylor

GRAPHICS
P. Eloise Fuller

PUBLISHED BY
Congressional Quarterly Inc.

CHAIRMAN
Andrew Barnes

VICE CHAIRMAN
Andrew P. Corty

EDITOR AND PUBLISHER
Neil Skene

EXECUTIVE EDITOR
Robert W. Merry

ASSOCIATE PUBLISHER
John J. Coyle

MARKETING AND SALES DIRECTOR
Edward S. Hauck

The CQ Researcher (ISSN 1056-2036). Formerly Editorial Research Reports. Published weekly (48 times per year, not printed the first Friday of any month with five Fridays) by Congressional Quarterly Inc., 1414 22nd St., N.W., Washington, D.C. 20037. Rates are furnished upon request. Second-class postage paid at Washington, D.C. POSTMASTER: Send address changes to The CQ Researcher, 1414 22nd St., N.W., Washington, D.C. 20037.

Crime Victims' Rights

By Charles S. Clark

The Issues

In late January 1988, 21-year-old Kelly Rudiger received the news that changed her life: Her 16-year-old brother Jeffrey had been found beaten and stabbed to death not far from the San Diego, Calif., pizza restaurant where he worked. Within hours, a co-worker was arrested and charged with the murder.

Three months later, however, the 23-year-old suspect was released on bond. For the next two years, Kelly and her family felt like victims of the judicial system as a series of appeals considered the legality of the man's arrest and whether the evidence against him should be suppressed. As the matter wound its way to the U.S. Supreme Court, Rudiger's family, schoolmates and neighbors organized community meetings and a letter-writing campaign to protest the man's release and to keep her brother's case alive.

In July 1990, the case finally went to trial, and within three weeks defendant Mark Radke was convicted of first-degree murder in what police described as a sexual attack. He was sentenced to the maximum — 25 years to life.

Her brother's death turned Rudiger, now 27, into a victims' rights activist. Emotionally, she says, "I've been able to talk about the case only since I took this job" as director of the Doris Tate Crime Victims' Bureau in Sacramento.* "I don't put a sign on my forehead saying I'm a crime victim, but when I go into the state Legislature and mention the case, everyone remembers."

Rudiger is one of thousands of Americans who have turned a grim experience with crime into a springboard for action in one of the fastest-growing civil rights movements. Crime victims, because they lacked legal standing under state law and the U.S. Constitution, have long been known as the justice system's "forgotten people."

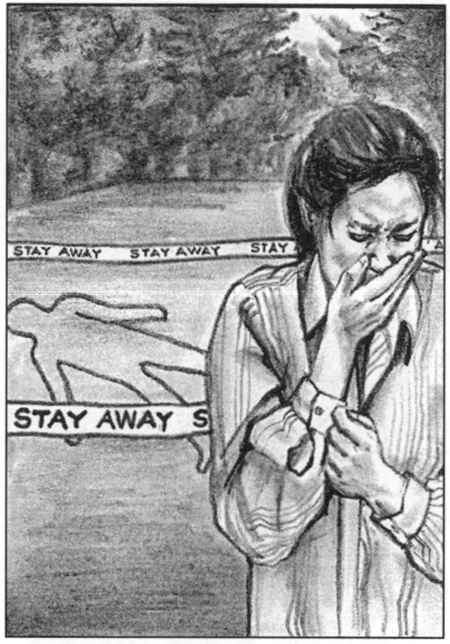

For years, "victims were treated as if they were no different from a bloody shirt or a sperm sample in a vial," says Deborah P. Kelly, a Washington attorney who chairs the Victims Committee of the American Bar Association. "Because of the myth that only the state has a case against the defendant, [crime victims] were kept outside the court so they couldn't find out what was happening. The result was they felt twice victimized."

Beckie Brown, the president of Dallas-based Mothers Against Drunk Driving (MADD), recalls that after a drunken driver killed her son in 1979, she had to depend on newspapers to follow the proceedings, suffering the further "indignity of having to pay $1 a page for a transcript of the trial."

Today, the legal landscape is vastly different. The number of local victims' rights organizations has exploded from 200 in 1980 to more than 8,000, according to the National Organization for Victim Assistance, a Washington nonprofit. All 50 states have crime victims' statutes, and 14 have enacted constitutional amendments to guarantee those rights. All 50 states now have victim compensation programs covering counseling, funerals and medical expenses, compared with only 27 states in 1980. And more than a third of the country's major police departments have their own victim assistance programs, according to the International Association of Chiefs of Police. (*See story, p. 636.*)

Most dramatically, at criminal sentencings it is now common for family members of victims to stand and deliver "victim impact statements," as the nation saw in May when an emotional widower told a New York City court how his life was shattered when his pregnant wife died in the 1993 World Trade Center bombing. [1]

"The movement has finally come to the forefront because of the incredible increase in crime — 18,000 homicides, 40 million victims a year," says activist John Walsh, host of the Fox Network TV show "America's Most Wanted." His 6-year-old son Adam was abducted and murdered in a case that became nationally famous in the early 1980s. "People from Beverly Hills to Watts are realizing that anyone can be a crime victim," he says.

What motivates many victims' advocates is a sense that the many recently passed laws affecting victims and criminals too often go unenforced. They want *assurances* that busy police, prosecutors, judges and parole officials will keep victims and families informed of progress through each stage of the criminal justice process. They want speedy trials for defendants. (In Arizona, an appeal by a rapist 15 years after his conviction required his victims to repeat their age-old testimony and, in some cases, discuss the rape with their spouses

---

*The bureau was named for the mother of actress Sharon Tate, who was murdered by followers of Charles Manson in 1969.

How Americans Feel About Victims' Rights

A majority of Americans consider victims' rights "very important," such as notification about trials and permission to attend them, according to a National Victim Center survey. Respondents also supported victims' right to be alerted about the release of criminals, to receive compensation and to present impact statements in court.

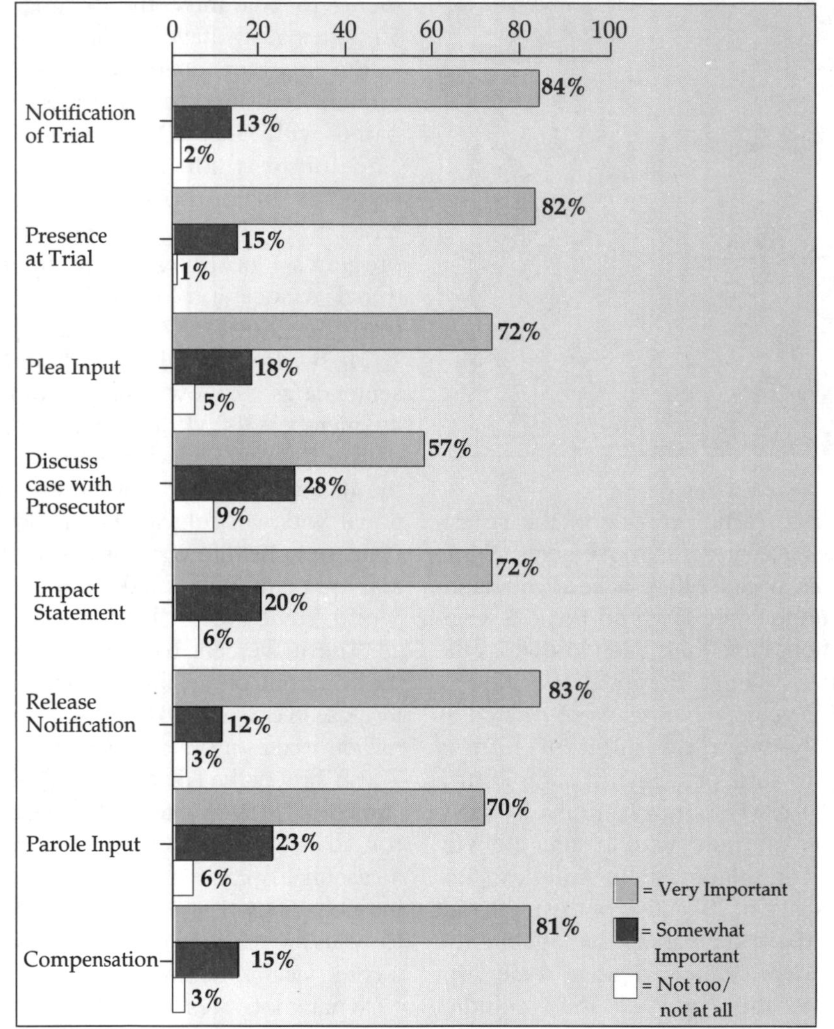

Source: Survey commissioned by the National Victim Center, "America Speaks Out: Citizens' Attitudes About Victims' Rights and Violence," April 18, 1991. The national telephone survey was conducted by Schulman, Ronca and Bucuvalas Inc.

and children for the first time.)[2]

Rape victims, in particular, are seeking to keep the news media from publishing their names and to require mandatory HIV testing for people accused of sex offenses.[3] And the survivors of homicide victims are seeking to prevent criminals from profiting from movie or book contracts, as many families feared might happen in the 1991 case of Milwaukee, Wis., serial killer Jeffrey L. Dahmer. (*See story, p. 632.*)

Politically, the movement is a hodgepodge of feminists and law-and-order purists, "a coalition of bleeding-heart conservatives and hard-nosed liberals," as one observer put it. Some groups, such as the Doris Tate Crime Victims' Bureau, actively lobby for tougher criminal sentencing. Others, such as the 300-chapter, 40,000-member group Parents of Murdered Children, based in Cincinnati, Ohio, counsel grieving families and help them navigate the legal system, monitor parole hearings and protest products that are offensive to crime victims, such as kids' trading cards featuring serial killers.

Crime victims are a vulnerable constituency. Psychologists have long noted how the violent death of a loved once can wreak emotional havoc for years and even destroy the survivors' marriage. The tendency to dwell on a crime gives victims a fear that friends will find them boring and self-pitying. "As a society, we do little to help victims to make them whole," notes George Kendall, assistant counsel at the NAACP Legal Defense Fund. "When we see a recent victim, we cross the street because we don't want to deal with them."

The public, however, appears solidly behind the victims' rights movement. A 1991 poll commissioned by the Arlington, Va.-based National Victim Center showed that 84 percent of the respondents supported a victim's right to be notified about dates and places of trials while 82 percent backed the victim's right to attend a trial and 72 percent backed the opportunity for a victim to discuss a case with the prosecutor during plea bargaining.

Critics, however, worry that the presence — and emotionalism — of victims and their families in court may jeopardize defendants' rights to a fair trial, particularly in death penalty cases where racial prejudice can affect sentencing. They argue that judges and juries alone are competent to dispense justice and charge, moreover, that guarantees and programs for victims are expensive.

"Victims have been victimized, and we don't want to sound like we don't care," says Nancy Hollander, an Albuquerque, N.M., attorney and former president of the National Association of Criminal Defense Lawyers. "But if you start a case and say, 'This is the defendant and this is the victim,' there's a presumption of guilt, and you decrease the public understanding of the presumption of innocence."

What's more, Hollander adds, "getting a victim involved with a trial won't solve crime in America. It's eye-for-an-eye retribution that risks institutionalizing vigilante justice. If we're concerned about preventing crime, let's use our resources for that."

Victims' rights advocates are fond of quoting Supreme Court Justice Benjamin N. Cardozo's phrase: "Justice, though due the accused, is due the accuser also."

Whether victims' advocates can transform the criminal justice system will hinge on the following questions:

After the murders of 16-year-old Jeffrey Rudiger of California and Stephanie Roper, 18, of Maryland, members of their families became crime-victim activists.

Do victims' rights infringe on the rights of defendants?

Roberta Roper is a Maryland victims' rights advocate who was stirred to action after the rape and murder of her daughter, Stephanie, in 1982. She recalls the vitriol that critics heaped on her and her allies when they first got involved with the case.

"We were barred from the guilt-innocence phase of the trial," she says. And, as the family of the deceased, they were blocked from offering testimony about Stephanie's life even as the defense attorneys raised questions about how many drinks she'd had on the night she died and why she had been driving alone at 3 a.m.

"The testimony I was offering was called emotional, irrelevant and probably cause for a mistrial," says Roper. "We were labeled a vigilante mob with blood dripping from our hands simply because we wrote letters saying we would be there."

Washington Post columnist Richard Cohen questioned whether the Stephanie Roper Committee, founded by Roper, her husband and some friends, was seeking justice or revenge. "From the legislation they propose," Cohen wrote, "it's hard to tell." [4]

Judges have traditionally sought to keep their courtrooms focused on facts rather than ruled by passion, and even the passage of victims' rights laws has not prevented defense attorneys from trying to exclude murder victims' family members from trials. (Indeed, a Maryland defense lawyer in 1991 tried to call as a witness the widow of the state highway patrolman his client was charged with killing, despite the fact that she had been at home asleep when the killing occurred. The reason? So the widow, under court rules, could be barred from the courtroom along with the other witnesses, who are not supposed to hear each other's testimony for fear they might coordinate their stories.) [5]

The victims' rights movement has sought to get around this roadblock through laws specifically permitting relatives of crime victims to sit in on trials after they've given testimony, to meet with prosecutors and to deliver, either orally or in writing, a victim impact statement before a sentencing or plea bargain (the so-called right of allocution). "The courts require that we treat defendants decently, but should not this be extended to victims?" asks Roper. "We trust juries to sift and weigh all information, and without the victims' input, they can't."

Ann Reed, the associate director of Parents of Murdered Children, complains that courtroom efforts to eliminate displays of emotion show that "the criminal justice system is all geared to justice for the criminal. The parent of the murderer can flop all over the court and scream, but if you're the parent of the murder victim, you can't even blow your nose without the judge calling you into his chamber," she says. (Reed's 18-year-old daughter Becky was raped and beaten to death in 1980.)

"Prisoners are guaranteed rights all at the expense of taxpayers," argues Walsh. "And not one victim I've met has said that criminals should be denied legal counsel and medical treatment or a parole hearing. All we're asking is to be treated the same."

The ABA's Kelly says that victims who don't know their rights under new victims' laws often leave the courtroom when the order is routinely given for all witnesses to leave.

"Defense attorneys don't want the human presence," she says, "not because there's a risk of tainting testimony but because a real person who's present makes the jury realize the human consequences of crimes. Removing the victim makes it easier for the defense to turn the case into a clash between a real person and the impersonal bureaucratic machinery of the state."

John Stein, deputy director of the National Organization for Victim Assistance, says "There is always the potential for prejudicing a jury when a relative of one party is present. That's true if it's the mother of the defendant or of the victim. But the message is only that this person has family and friends who love him," and the defense should be concerned with more important lines of argument.

David Price, president for litigation affairs at the Washington Legal Foundation, which sues on behalf of violent-crime victims, says the presence of victims "helps the triers of fact. They are part of the facts, you can't isolate them, just as the defendant's background prior to the crime is part of the facts." Price, however, believes the decision to include victims in a courtroom should be left to the prosecutor's discretion, based on whether it helps make the case.

Controversial for a different set of reasons are victim impact statements, which are allowed only after guilty verdicts have been rendered. Introduced in Fresno, Calif., in 1974, they were originally prepared by probation officers as part of pre-sentence investigations. Nowadays, they are often prepared by victims themselves and can be cited at sentencings, plea bargainings and in limited ways at bail hearings, often at the discretion of the judge.

"They're an important rite, a forum for an expression of passion," says Stein. "The victims frequently express rage against the offender, but just because it's discomforting for us doesn't mean they shouldn't be allowed to speak."

The victim's statement "gives the court complete information for use in parole, plea bargaining and the need for restitution," says Roper. "It isn't inflammatory, it's not prejudicial to any sentence and it doesn't take away from defendants' rights. It is limited to the crime's consequences emotionally, physically and financially. But it does help to sensitize the criminal justice system to the reality that the state is not the only victim, that it's human lives that are devastated."

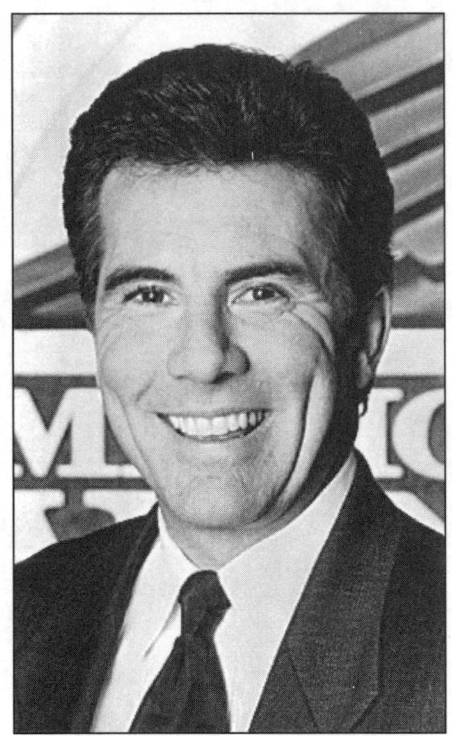

TV host and victims' activist John Walsh, whose 6-year-old son Adam was abducted and murdered.

To underscore their point, backers of victim impact statements cite the case of two youths convicted of the savage 1980s murder of a 79-year-old woman. Before their arrest for repeatedly stabbing the woman at the small store she operated, the boys were seen giving each other "high fives" and bragging about the crime.

Initially, prosecutors and defense attorneys agreed on a plea bargain to second-degree murder, carrying sentences of at least 38 years in prison. But the judge refused to accept the plea, noting the savagery of the crime and reading into the record a statement about the crime's impact from the victim's daughter and son-in-law. The defendants later switched to guilty pleas to first-degree murder and received sentences of 50 years to life. [6]

Impact statements are opposed, however, by many judges and prosecutors. A survey of their use in California commissioned by the National Institute of Justice in the mid-1980s showed that 69 percent of judges, 48 percent of prosecutors and 81 percent of probation officers said victim impact statements were not effective. [7]

Judge Vincent Femia of Maryland's 7th Judicial Circuit says that both victims and defendants have the right to allocution, but "neither side can get emotional in my court." He points to a recent case in which a victims' rights advocate asked to address the court. "I asked the lawyer, 'to what end?"' the judge recalls. "He said, 'Your honor should know how the family feels about the loss of a loved one.' I asked him what will that do for my judgment, make me more severe?

"There are only two reasons for victim statements: to increase the sentence and provide catharsis. I'm not competent in catharsis, that's for doctors and clergymen. But I'm competent in sentencing, and I don't need a victim to tell me how to do that. Being a judge isn't doing what's emotionally satisfying to the loudest of the multitude."

Douglas Spencer, a retired circuit judge in Eugene, Ore., disagrees. "Technically, a criminal trial is between a sovereign state and the defendants, and the victim is not a party," he acknowledges. "But having said that, I can understand why the victims' rights people are saying, 'We've got all these people wringing their hands over the defendant, saying what a good boy he was, how he loves his mother, how we don't know why he cut that guy's throat except that he fell in with evil companions.'

"You can't necessarily trust the district attorney to present the victims' information, because he's busy. So we passed legislation saying that the D.A. must notify the family of the time and place for sentencing. I like to have the family there to balance things out. I can't think of one case in which I had one sentence in mind and made it harsher after hearing the victim's family. But it feels good, even if I don't change the sentence, that the victims had their chance to be heard."

A major objection to victim impact statements, one that has been the focus of three recent Supreme Court cases, is the fear that their use in capital trials increases the risk of racially biased applications of the death penalty *(see p. 634)*

"Yes, victim impact statements are often the only opportunity a victim has to make a point," says the NAACP's Kendall. "But because race has always influenced the imposition of the death penalty, the statements become one more temptation for prosecutors in deciding in which cases to ask for capital punishment. Consciously or unconsciously, juries that are overwhelmingly white will identify with white victims, so we will have more death sentences applied to blacks."

On the contrary, counters Price, "The victim impact statement is a potentially valuable way to overcome racial bias in the criminal justice system. We all have preconceptions about race, and if the victim is a young black male, a juror may feel he had it coming. That's why a statement from people we don't rub shoulders with every day can bring a [victim] to life in the jury's mind and bridge the emotional distance."

In general, says Walsh, "When a person is convicted and sentencing recommendations are made, the defense can bring in 50 character witnesses including his clergyman. Why shouldn't the victim make a statement? Why can't a father hold a picture of his dead child to show that this child existed and now will never graduate from high school and will never get married? Since when is the law unemotional? Isn't somebody's life worth 10 minutes? If the judge is so smart, he will afford the victim this dignity and then go in his chambers and make a wise decision."

The names of murder victims are enshrined on the "memorial wall" at Parents of Murdered Children's Cincinnati headquarters.

Morton Bard, a longtime victims' rights activist and professor of psychology emeritus at the City University of New York, says: "The rights of defendants can be protected to the nth degree without sacrificing the victim. What's really involved is a turf battle among the players — the judges, prosecutors and the cops — who like to run the system. They don't want another system making problems. But we have a moral obligation to victims."

Are victims' rights a drain on the justice system?

In their psychological study *The Crime Victim's Book,* Bard and his co-author recount a woman's experience after her husband was murdered. A year after his death, when the killer had been sentenced and the woman was emerging from the grieving process, an envelope was delivered to her door. Inside, with no letter of explanation, was her husband's wallet, which the police had been keeping as evidence. It was still stained with blood. [8]

Doubtless, the harried evidence clerk who returned the wallet never meant to traumatize a widow but was acting out of habit dictated by the realities of short-handed staffs and tight budgets.

Victims' rights advocates say it doesn't have to be that way. "I don't see that being sensitive to the needs of people in extreme situations requires lots of money," says Bard. "But police are often like doctors who deal only with physical illnesses — it seems that people themselves count the least."

Victims' services, however, do cost money. State victim compensation funds, which are financed largely through fines levied against convicted criminals, "are facing financial pressure and some are delaying payments," says

Continued on p. 633

Laws That Make Sure Crime Doesn't Pay

The rock group Guns N' Roses tucked a macabre surprise inside its latest compact disc release, "The Spaghetti Incident." Listeners are treated, with nary a mention on the album cover, to a song called "Look at Your Game, Girl," written in the 1960s by California mass murderer Charles M. Manson.

Crime victims' advocates were appalled, and the Sacramento-based Doris Tate Crime Victims Bureau launched a boycott against the group's Hollywood label, Geffen Records Inc.

The controversy comes at a time when the imprisoned Manson is already accumulating royalties from a contract with a Newport Beach, Calif., T-shirt manufacturer, which sells shirts bearing Manson's eerie portrait to young surfers. Equally galling to many crime victims was the report that Chicago serial killer John Wayne Gacy, before his execution this spring, had found a market for sales of his clown paintings.

"It's a travesty," says victims' rights activist John Walsh, host of the Fox Network TV show "America's Most Wanted." Walsh, whose 6-year-old son Adam was murdered in the 1980s, deplores the way tabloid news shows pay criminals for interviews. "Any money made through victimization should go for compensation, therapy and rebuilding the lives of victims. No other society allows criminals to profit from crimes," he says.

The idea that criminals can become media stars and profit from their crimes is "a symbolic, gut issue that instantly outrages anyone," says David Beatty, director of public affairs for the Arlington, Va.-based National Victim Center. "It's the ultimate insult from the victim's perspective, and it calls into question the basic notion that crime doesn't pay."

Laws against profiteering from notoriety are known informally as "Son of Sam" laws. They are named for serial killer David Berkowitz, the postal worker who terrorized New York City with random shootings in 1977, and who left notes at the crime scenes signed "Son of Sam."

The crimes of Berkowitz, who eventually sold his story for $250,000, prompted an outraged New York assemblyman to introduce legislation to put such profits in an escrow account to be tapped by victims' survivors. Some 40 states imitated the New York law, and in 1984 the Federal Victims of Crime Act empowered federal judges to order the "literary profits" of criminals diverted to the Crime Victims Fund.[1]

The New York law, however, was challenged by publisher Simon & Schuster, among others, which called it a violation of the right to a free press. "The First Amendment has a broader social purpose, which is to serve as a counterbalance for the public to understand such issues as crime," says R. Bruce Rich, First Amendment counsel to the Association of American Publishers, which filed a friend-of-the-court brief in the case. Under the original New York law, Rich says, profits from a book could be seized even if "one page in a 500-page book recounted a youthful offense that was never prosecuted, like stealing a pen from a store.

"So who is to play God and decide how much of a chilling effect the law should have on publishing? It's an unpopular position. But our society incarcerates more people than any in the world, and therefore writings about the criminal mind and the criminal experience are deeply relevant."

In December 1992, the U.S. Supreme Court struck down the law, sending state and federal legislators back for creative ways to redraft it. "The court didn't strike down the whole idea, just the way it was drafted," says Washington attorney Deborah Kelly, who chairs the Victims Committee for the American Bar Association. The goal is to say that "It's OK to write the book, just that criminals can't then get rich and retire to Beverly Hills."

Revised in 1993, the New York law is "an improvement, but still doesn't get around our constitutional problems," says Rich. He says a number of the revised state laws appear to avoid singling out the criminals' media contracts and take the more evenhanded approach of confiscating all his assets.

Sentencing judges, meanwhile, are using disincentives to discourage defendants from writing books. When former student radical Katherine Ann Powers was sentenced last year for her role in the 1970 slaying of a Boston policeman, Suffolk Superior Court Judge Robert W. Banks forbade her from profiting from the killing by selling her story while in prison and while on probation for 20 years after her release.

In California, the Legislature is considering a bill to expand the state Son of Sam law to prohibit even indirect profits from notoriety, which would halt Manson's profits from T-shirts. And the Doris Tate bureau continues to canvass music stores to discourage purchases of Guns N' Roses albums or any Geffen products.

At one point, the record company offered a donation to settle the matter but backed out when it learned the money wouldn't be tax deductible, according to Kelly Rudiger, executive director of the Tate center.

"We've told them that we're not legally able to remove the track because Guns N' Roses has creative freedom in their contract," says Bryn Bridenthal, Geffen's vice president for media and artist relations. She points out that under California's law, all of Manson's royalties go to the surviving son of one of his murder ring's victims, the only one to file a claim.

"Guns N' Roses didn't know it was a Manson song when they chose it," she says, "but they later decided it was preferable to leave it in so that the victim's son gets some money. Everyone was comfortable that Manson wouldn't get a dime."

---

[1] James Stark and Howard W. Goldstein, *The Rights of Crime Victims* (1985), p. 267.

Continued from p. 631

Dan Eddy, executive director of the National Association of Crime Victim Compensation Boards.

In many states, claims have doubled or quadrupled in recent years, partly because the victims' rights movement has lent the programs new visibility. "I don't know of one that's not either facing a problem or nervous about the future," Eddy says. "Some states like New Jersey and Texas have tried boosting the fines, but there's a point of diminishing returns."

What's more, police departments and agencies that provide services for victims would be even more strapped if everyone who is eligible for the services were actually served. A January poll by the *Los Angeles Times* showed that 84 percent of U.S. crime victims in the previous 12 months had not received assistance from a victims' group or social service agency.

Prosecutors argue that victims' rights laws come with a price tag because they reduce prosecutors' discretion. "The victims' rights movement doesn't often consider the practicality of requiring us to give services that decency requires, but that when made mandatory become onerous," says Andrew L. Sonner, the Maryland state's attorney in Montgomery County. For example, "most people think victims are people like us. But many times they're not the people a prosecutor would want to talk and consult with, because, say, in a shootout in a drug war, the person who died may have been worse than the shooter."

Sonner also sees an unworkable costliness in cases with multiple victims, such as nationwide mail order fraud cases committed with television advertisements. If all the victims had the right to be kept informed throughout the trial, he says, the costs would be substantial.

Sonner recalls the 1981 case of Washington, D.C.-area burglar Bernard Welch, who had broken into at least 40 homes when he was arrested after shooting and killing a prominent doctor outside his house. In conducting the burglary prosecution, "we chose four cases, because it would have been ridiculous to go to trial 40 times. But several other victims still complained, even though it didn't affect their getting restitution."*

Victims' rights advocates counter that it's a matter of priorities. "If our government can spend billions for the Hubble telescope," says activist Walsh, "we can come up with money for a letter or a phone call from a D.A. saying that a parole hearing is next week."

Cost is a fair issue to debate, concedes Roper, but "look at the money we spend on incarcerating offenders vs. what we spend on their victims. Even if we could prove that victims' services were a financial drain, which they're not, it would be money well spent because it would preserve the system of justice by instilling faith and cooperation."

People who are concerned about costs too often see the problem "as a zero sum game, with the victims' rights coming at the expense of the offender," says David Beatty, director of public affairs for the National Victim Center. "But the relative amounts spent come to millions for defendants and pennies for victims. Nobody ever discussed costs during the civil rights movement or when the *Miranda* decision was made."**

Price of the Washington Legal Foundation says that whatever small costs occur are "outweighed by the value of having the victim's family as watchdogs, involved every step of the way to help the system avoid errors. Police are well-intentioned, but they are overwhelmed by the magnitude of their caseload, so there should be outside encouragement or pressure to maintain the human element."

---

*Bernard Welch was convicted of first-degree murder in the death of physician Michael Halberstam and sentenced to 143 years in federal prison. He was later sentenced to an additional 30 years for robbery.

**The Supreme Court's 1966 ruling in *Miranda v. Arizona* requires police to inform people being arrested of their rights to remain silent and to be represented by an attorney.

The National Victim Center poll indicated that 70 percent of Americans would pay higher taxes to improve services to crime victims. ■

BACKGROUND

Movement's Birth

The notion that individuals wronged by crime should take it upon themselves to seek redress goes back at least 3,500 years, to ancient Babylon, where the famous Code of Hammurabi required thieves to make restitution.

In England since Norman times, and later in Colonial America, it was common for victimized private citizens to take action themselves. In 18th-century Boston, for example, a victim could arrest a suspected wrongdoer assisted by a night watchman or constable, then pay for any warrants, conduct the investigation himself and hire an attorney to write the indictment and prosecute. Punishment was often servitude, since a jail sentence would require the victim to repay the government for incarceration costs. [9]

All this changed with adoption of the Constitution's Bill of Rights, which laid out the rights of defendants — but not victims — in its Fourth, Fifth, Sixth, Seventh and Eighth Amendments. By the 1830s, the nation's system of homemade criminal justice had been replaced by salaried police and prosecutors.

Victims' rights advocates, however, cite the earlier system of private justice as a key precedent. "In light of this history," said the Washington Legal Foundation in a 1991 Supreme Court brief, "it would be hard to say that the Framers thought that victim participation in criminal prosecution raised a constitutional doubt. Nor can it be said that the move to public prosecution reflected a desire to eliminate any role for the victim." [10]

Feminists and Rape Victims Spur Initiatives

The U.S. victims' rights movement had its first stirrings in the early 1960s, after Great Britain, New Zealand and other nations enacted the first victim compensation programs. (In the U.S., in 1964, Sen. Ralph W. Yarborough, D-Texas, introduced the first bill to create a federal victim compensation program, but it did not pass.) It was also in 1964, in New York City, that the murder of a woman named Kitty Genovese, whose screams for help were largely ignored by dozens of neighbors, dramatized for many the discomfort people feel when confronted with victimizations.

By the early 1970s, feminists and rape victims became the first victims' rights organizers when they staged urban rallies against rapists, often under the theme "Take back the night."

Law review articles began appearing at the same time proposing court reforms showing more respect for the needs of victims and witnesses. An academic publication, the journal of *Victimology* was launched while rape crisis centers, clearinghouses for information on missing children and telephone hotlines for battered women were set up. The first victim assistance programs were created in St. Louis, Mo., San Francisco, Calif., and Washington, D.C., and by 1974 the Law Enforcement Assistance Administration (LEAA) had spent $3 million to set up 19 victim assistance centers.

California, which had enacted the first state crime victimization fund in 1965, again led the way in 1978 with the nation's first law permitting crime victims to deliver impact statements at sentencings.

Reagan Takes Lead

It was the Reagan administration, in the early 1980s, that took the lead in bringing victims' rights reforms at the federal level, thanks largely to lobbying by Frank Carrington, a civic-minded Virginia Beach lawyer. In a 1982 White House Rose Garden ceremony announcing a new President's Task Force on Victims of Crime, President Ronald Reagan said: "The innocent victims of crime have frequently been overlooked by our criminal justice system. Too often their pleas have gone unheeded and the wounds — personal, emotional and financial — have gone unattended. They are entitled to better treatment, and it is time to do something about it." [11]

The task force's final report contained strong language. "Victims have discovered that they are treated as appendages of a system appallingly out of balance," it said. "They have learned that somewhere along the way, the system has lost track of the simple truth that it is supposed to be fair and protect those who obey the law while punishing those who break it. Somewhere along the way, the system began to serve lawyers and judges and defendants, treating the victim with institutionalized disinterest." [12]

Most important, the task force made 68 recommendations, among them a proposal that the Constitution's Sixth Amendment, which enumerates a defendant's rights to counsel and a speedy trial by jury, be amended as follows: "Likewise, the victim, in every criminal prosecution, shall have the right to be present and to be heard at all critical stages of judicial proceedings." [13]

Federal Fund for Crime Victims

The result was not a constitutional amendment, however, but a bipartisan movement in Congress led by Sens. Strom Thurmond, R-S.C., and Joseph R. Biden Jr., D-Del., to pass the 1984 Victims of Crime Act. The act set up a federal crime victims fund. Financed through fines paid by federal criminals, the fund sends grants ($137 million in 1992) to states to replenish their victim compensation funds and support some 2,500 victim assistance programs nationwide. [14] (*See map, p. 637.*)

Victims' funds cover a wide range of expenses incurred as a direct result of a crime, including medical bills, mental health counseling, funeral and burial costs, wage loss, loss of alimony or child support and job retraining. Such expenses are covered only if insurance and other sources aren't available. Property loss, including loss of cash, is not covered.

A state might finance its fund by assessing $25 from each felon, or $3 from each traffic violator, notes Eddy of the compensation board association. States differ in their generosity toward victims, with maximum benefits generally ranging from $10,000 to $25,000.

In recent years, there has been a shift in the types of services in demand, Eddy says. "The funds used to be just for physical injuries, and they'd patch you up and you'd get back on the job. But over the past 5-10 years, there has been more attention to mental health counseling for victims of child abuse, sexual assault and domestic violence. It's a big victory for the victims' rights movement." [15]

Supreme Court Reversal

Twice during the late 1980s, the Supreme Court heard cases on the delicate issue of whether victim impact statements should be permitted in racially tinged cases involving the death penalty. In 1987 in *Booth v. Maryland,* and in 1989 in *South Carolina v. Gathers,* the court sided with those who said the victim impact statements in such cases lead to an arbitrary imposition of capital punishment.

But in 1991, a reconstituted Supreme Court revisited the question in the case of *Payne v. Tennessee.** At issue was whether the grandmother of a young boy who had witnessed the murder of his mother and sister could testify about

Continued on p. 637

Chronology

1960s *First stirrings of victims' rights in U.S.*

1964
The murder of Kitty Genovese in New York City shows society's unresponsiveness to victims.

1965
California sets up first state victim compensation program.

1970s *Led by feminists and rape victims, victims' rights groups organize.*

1974
Brooklyn and Milwaukee prosecutors win grants to form first model victim/witness programs. Singer Connie Francis is raped, later becoming victims' activist.

1975
Formation of National Organization for Victim Assistance. First Victims' Rights Week is organized in Philadelphia.

1976
First issue of *Victimology*.

1978
California becomes first state to permit victim impact statements.

1978
Parents of Murdered Children founded in Cincinnati.

1980s *Federal government embraces victims' rights.*

1980
Mothers Against Drunk Driving (MADD) founded. Wisconsin becomes first state to pass a crime victims' bill of rights. American Bar Association releases study inspiring new state laws to prevent intimidation of victims and witnesses.

1981
President Ronald Reagan proclaims first National Victims' Rights Week.

1982
Reagan Task Force on Crime Victims offers 68 recommendations. Congress passes Victim Witness Protection Act, which makes victim impact statements a formal part of pre-sentencing reports.

1983
Reforms recommended by National Conference of the Judiciary on the Rights of Crime Victims. Federal Office for Victims of Crime created.

1984
Passage of Victims of Crime Act establishing Crime Victims Fund from criminal fines. American Psychological Association forms task force on victims.

1985
Bernard Goetz shoots four threatening teenagers on a New York subway. U.N. adopts Declaration of Basic Principles of Justice for Victims of Crime and Abuse of Power. National Victim Center founded.

1986
Fashion model Marla Hanson, slashed by thugs hired by her landlord, becomes victims' activist. Student Jennifer Levin is murdered in New York City's "Preppie Murder Case," spurring her mother Ellen to activism.

1987
MADD and other groups form coalition called Victims Constitutional Amendment Network.

1988
American Correctional Association releases report with 15 recommendations on improving victims services. Federal Anti-Drug Abuse Act says states getting federal money for victim compensation can't exclude victims of drunk drivers.

1989
TV actress Rebecca Schaeffer's murder by a fan prompts anti-stalking laws and gun control activism by her parents.

1990s *States consider new laws and constitutional amendments.*

1990
Des Moines Register story about rape victim who is named ignites debate on right to anonymity. Victims' Rights and Restitution Act instructs Justice Department to safeguard victims' rights.

1991
Congress declares National Parents of Murdered Children Week. In *Payne v. Tennessee,* Supreme Court allows victim impact statements in capital punishment cases. Rep. Ilena Ros-Lehtinen, R-Fla., introduces first joint resolution to place victims' rights in the Constitution.

Dec. 10, 1992
Supreme Court says New York's "Son of Sam" law violates First Amendment.

1994
Seven states have victims' rights constitutional amendments on November ballot.

Sensitizing Police to Victims' Needs

A sure sign of success for the victims' rights movement is the new way police officers handle victims. Almost unheard of 15 years ago, many of today's cops receive sensitivity training in responding to victims of such crimes as sexual assault, domestic violence and stalking.

Betsy Cummings, a rape victim who appears in a police training video produced by New York City's Victim Services agency, spoke of her fear at seeing that the police who first responded to her call were male. "Not that I dislike men, but I was embarrassed and humiliated. I wondered, what they would think of me?"

Cummings was surprised and reassured when the officers said, "I'm so sorry this happened, we want to help you." They prefaced their questions with comments such as, "I know this may be difficult," and explained why each intimate and detailed question about the rape was necessary, she noted. Finally, none of the officers implicitly blamed the victim by asking why she hadn't been more careful, and none made such statements as, "I understand how you feel," because it's not likely they could understand fully.

"Having all these people show concern rather than viewing me as just a statistic made a big difference in my decision to go through with the prosecution," Cummings said.

The new approach grew out of the feminist movement, new laws making arrests mandatory in cases of stalking or wife-battering and successful lawsuits against police departments that failed to respond when confronted with victims who were obviously bruised and blackened.

"There's been an explosion of laws against stalking in the past couple of years," says Deborah P. Kelly, a Washington attorney who chairs the Victims Committee of the American Bar Association. "Before, there were no statutes police could wrap their arms around, so there was nothing they could do other than get a temporary restraining order, which was costly and intimidating for the victim. Police would simply say, 'It's a free country,' which meant some guy could put a dead animal on a woman's windshield and say he's expressing his right to free speech."

In Iowa, some parents hired experts to prepare a manual on how police should notify next-of-kin in cases of sudden death. It was prompted after a couple returned home and learned that their daughter was dead when a policeman simply told them "the body" was inside their house. The guide advises officers to give the family a moment to prepare for the news and stay long enough to let it sink in.

"Don't make the notification at the screen door," explains a counselor who helped prepare the booklet. "Get the dogs under control. Turn off the TV. Tell the person that you have very bad news. Can we sit down? Should we call other people together?" [1]

The responsiveness of police is "improving, but we still have a ways to go," says Lucy Friedman, executive director of Victim Services. "At the top levels in the police department, we're seeing a verbal and attitudinal commitment" to victims' needs. Yet when there's an alleged sexual assault in which the victim knows the offender, she adds, "police are sensitive enough not to say 'We're too busy,' but they might exhibit subtle body language showing that they don't take the charge seriously, that perhaps [they think] the woman changed her mind when she felt guilty the morning after, or perhaps her parents found out she was sexually active. It becomes hard to disentangle."

Joyce St. George, a rape crisis counselor who co-directs a conflict-resolution consulting group in Kingston, N.Y., says victims' rights fare much better in New York City because of new laws such as those that prevent attorneys defending rape suspects from delving into a victim's sexual past.

"But in upstate New York, it's not taken seriously by police," she says. "The system is outmoded and lacks the tools for present-day issues. Rape, particularly acquaintance rape, definitely takes a back seat." And if survivors of a victim of a drug murder seek information on the trial, "the D.A. is liable to say there's nothing he can do, there are just too many cases."

Police are often heard to complain that they are overworked and, besides, they are cops, not social workers. "The reality is that training hasn't been booming, and police chiefs and sheriffs are angry at the lack of training funds," says Dennis Martin, executive director of the National Association of Chiefs of Police, in Miami, Fla. "Only the big cities like New York and Los Angeles have victim assistance programs. Most police departments are only one- or three-man operations, and police chiefs are interested mostly in how many arrests they make."

Kelly argues, however, that it is in the interests of police to aid victims. "They can't catch the criminal unless they have a victim who can give a valid, accurate description of a suspect, and you have to establish a base of rapport," she says. "The true hand-holding is done by rape crisis centers and witness-victim units. Police have to do a requisite amount, but they don't need to [literally] hold someone's hand and say, 'I feel your pain.' "

Crime victims whom police handle well, notes St. George, often go on to give something back to the criminal justice system in the form of volunteering. "If they receive the help they need at that most vulnerable time," she says, "the people who were so helpful become role models" who attract other volunteers.

---

[1] The Associated Press, *The New York Times,* June 12, 1994.

Continued from p. 634

how the boy continued to cry out for his dead family members. Bush administration Attorney General Dick Thornburgh appeared before the court to argue that the jury should be given "the full picture of the nature and extent of the harm that's been caused to the family."

ACLU attorney Diann Rust-Tierney expressed worry that the court would "sanction different punishment based on the worth of the victim and aggravate an already pronounced discrimination in the way the death penalty is applied." [16] Tennessee Attorney General Charles Burson countered by saying, "There can be no doubt that the taking of the life of the president creates much more societal harm than the taking of the life of the homeless person."

In the end, the court reversed its previous rulings and allowed the grandmother's statement, with Chief Justice William H. Rehnquist arguing that "victim impact evidence is simply another form or method of informing the sentencing authority about the specific harm caused by the crime." Justice Thurgood Marshall dissented, warning that the overturning of precedents was the first wave of a far-reaching assault on the rights of "minorities, women or the indigent."

That same year, the National Victim Center's poll showed that 69 percent of respondents favored allowing victim impact statements in capital cases.

Unlikely Allies

The victims' rights movement that emerged in the past two decades is "an interesting marriage" of liberals and conservatives, notes Beatty of the National Victim Center, uniting such groups as the National Organization for Women (NOW) and the Heritage Foundation.

The conservatives got involved after activist Carrington convinced the Reagan administration of its importance, notes Stein of the National Organization for Victim Assistance, "but [the fact that Reagan was then president] was just an accident." In the Clinton administration, he says, Attorney General "Janet Reno is equally persuasive with today's White House."

"Most people forget that the movement has [liberal] elements," says the ABA's Kelly. "They assume we must be to the right of Attila the Hun. But I'm a feminist who wrote a Ph.D. on rape victims. What's more, the left should be involved because crime victims are disproportionately minorities and the poor."

The right wing, says Bard, emphasizes "how we can make sure the victim feels better by punishing criminals more and depriving defendants of rights. The left emphasizes what services we can perform to help victims manage trauma, and sensitize the system to see the victim as a legitimate player."

The National Rifle Association (NRA), which conducts a victims' rights advocacy program called CrimeStrike, is involved "because of its long-standing commitment to crimi-

Continued on p. 639

Maximum Benefits Paid to Crime Victims

Victims of crime in nine states are eligible to receive more than $25,000 in compensation. Twenty-three states offer $25,000 maximums and 20 states provide up to $10,000. In all cases, awards are only for losses not reimbursed by insurance or other sources.

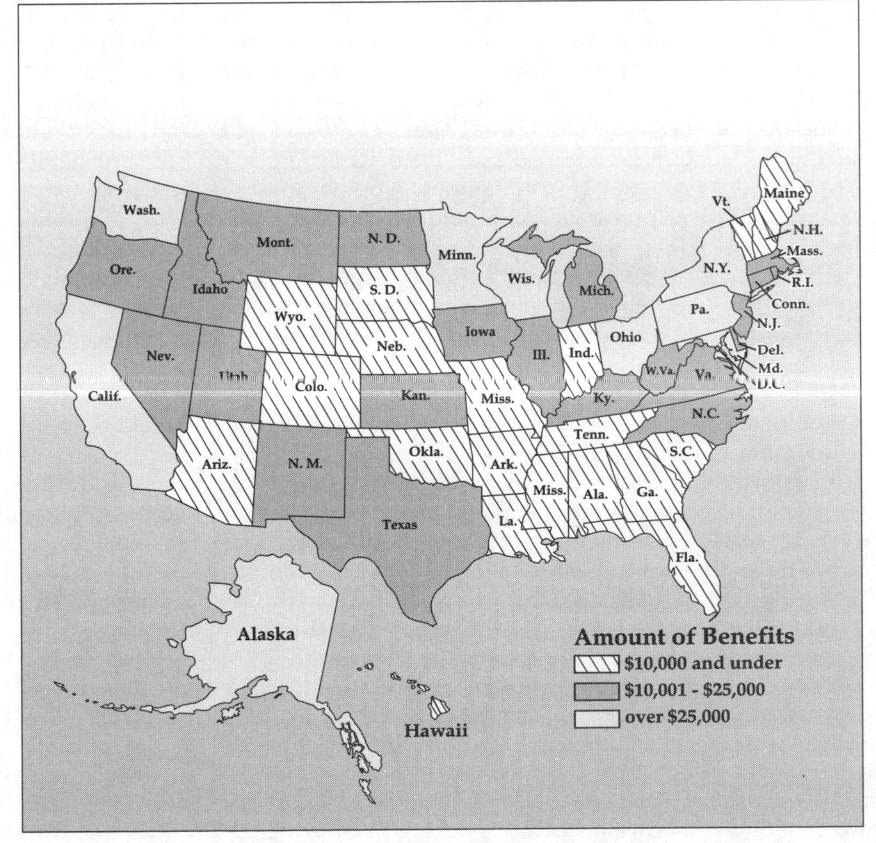

Source: National Association of Crime Victim Compensation Boards, July 1994.

---

*On Oct. 9, 1990, Justice David H. Souter replaced retiring Justice William J. Brennan Jr.

News Media Can Be Tough on Crime Victims

John Walsh can't forget the spectacle: hundreds of reporters packing his lawn on that morning in August 1981 that was the worst day of his life. The Florida hotel consultant and his wife were returning from a television appearance discussing the case of their missing son. They had just received word that 6-year-old Adam had been found, murdered.

"My wife was near heart-failure, and I was throwing up," says Walsh, now the host of the popular anti-crime show, "America's Most Wanted," recalling how he struggled to persuade the reporters to leave. That night at 3 a.m. he was awakened by a knock on the door. It was a young woman reporter. "My editor says I'll get fired if I don't get a quote from you," she said. Walsh admonished her, "You tell that cowardly S.O.B. to come over here himself, and I'll give him a quote he'll never forget."

Today, it remains common for victims who are reeling from the news of a tragedy to run a gauntlet of news cameras, shouted questions and microphones shoved in their faces. In Cincinnati recently, a mother whose son had been beaten to death by teenagers had announced that she would submit to no interviews at the trial. But when a guilty verdict was rendered, "The cameras hunted her down like a dog and broadcast shots of her running away," notes Ann Reed, associate director of the 40,000-member group Parents of Murdered Children, based in Cincinnati.

Though pressured by ratings competition to get the dramatic story, news professionals are instructed to behave "in a civilized way that doesn't trample on people's privacy," says David Bartlett, president of the Radio-Television News Directors Association, which includes such instructions in its ethics code. Reporters cannot force someone to be interviewed, and more people decline comment than accept, Bartlett says. "We grapple with whether an interview is relevant, but the judgment has to be on journalistic relevance, not sociological or law enforcement issues."

Some observers feel the news media have become more sensitive, but that the public continues to blame them even if subjects agree to be shown in moments of grief. "They want to tell us how wonderful their child was or maybe they just want to get something off their chests," says Brian Bracco, news director at KMBC-TV in Kansas City. "But the effect . . . is often anger at what [viewers] perceive as an invasion of privacy, and they'll call and scream, 'How dare you?' or 'How could you?' " [1]

Clearly, there is a gap between journalists and victims' rights advocates on how to handle the issue. In 1990, researchers at Texas Christian University and the National Victim Center polled 283 television news directors and 247 victims' advocates. Respondents were presented with case studies, such as: A woman's home is destroyed by a fire that kills her two children. Firefighters restrain the hysterical mother outside the house when she learns of the deaths. A news photographer has exclusive photos. Should they be used?

Fully 81 percent of news directors said yes, while only 14 percent of victim advocates agreed.

"Some journalists will do anything for the story and then cite the First Amendment," says Maryland victims' rights activist Roberta Roper, whose daughter Stephanie was raped and murdered. She notes that newspapers often publish the names and addresses of victims, and then people call to sell them security systems or intimidate them.

At other times, however, the media can be a big help, Roper adds, recalling how it was a reporter who helped her learn that her daughter's killer was applying for a transfer to a special prison that emphasizes therapy. In cooperating with the media, "you can sometimes win a friend and ally and sensitize another member of society," Roper says.

The National Victim Center offers a guidebook for victims with suggestions for how "the public's right to know about increasing crime and victimization can be balanced with a victim's right to privacy." It notes that reporters sometimes use hearsay information, lie to gain access to a home, hospital or funeral home, or broadcast crash-site footage — sometimes showing license plates — before families have been notified of a traffic death. "You have the right to say 'no' to an interview" and to select the time, place and spokesman, it advises. Victims can exclude children from being interviewed and can refuse individual questions.

A media code of ethics prepared by the National Organization for Victim Assistance recommends that news professionals advise victims of such rights, because the victims may be inexperienced.

Michigan State University recently won a grant to set up a program called "Victims and the Media" to help journalists develop better techniques for interviewing crime victims. Veterans of the experience say timing and restraint in the early stages may be crucial to winning a victim over.

Detroit News Picture Editor Stephen Haines, who co-authored a handbook on dealing with crime victims for the National Press Photographers Association, says, "In many cases, I've had people say, 'You're the one who didn't push me around,' " and then give him access that wasn't granted to other journalists. [2]

"Some news directors and editors have a conscience, others are jerks," says Walsh, who notes that he never uses names or photos of victims on his show without their consent.

---

[1] Quoted in Lou Prato, "It Was Like a Shark Attack," *American Journalism Review,* May 1994, p. 48.

[2] Quoted in *The Wall Street Journal,* Aug. 26, 1993.

Continued from p. 637

nal justice reform and mandatory sentences for armed offenders," says program director Steve Twist. "Our 3.4 million members are affected by crime, and frankly, if policies controlling crime are more effective, there will be less calls for attacks on the right to bear arms."

Crime doesn't discriminate between Republicans and Democrats, not by gender or economic status, says Roper, who before being pulled into activism by the murder of her daughter was a "full-time wife, mother and art teacher who had never even been in traffic court. We organized quickly, naively," she says. "I don't know if I would have preserved my sanity if we hadn't." ■

CURRENT SITUATION

Anti-Crime Bill

Every federal anti-crime bill for the past decade has included victims' rights provisions, and the current proposals are not exceptions. Backed by President Clinton, who also has endorsed National Victims' Rights Week, the Senate and House proposals contain tough initiatives to deny firearms to people convicted of domestic violence and to strengthen penalties for stalking and sexual assault. They would also train police and judges in handling child sexual abuse, expand the right to give victim impact statements at sentencings, toughen victim restitution laws and make housekeeping adjustments in the Crime Victims Fund to permit federally funded local experimental programs and to allow states to use federal money for administrative purposes.*

"Money from fines doesn't come in regularly, but with peaks and valleys," says Stein of the National Organization for Victim Assistance. "This [legislation] would allow the Federal Office for Victims of Crimes to put some aside for a rainy day."

One of the most controversial crime bill provisions is the so-called Racial Justice Act, a provision in the House-passed bill that permits defendants to use statistics to show that their states apply capital punishment in a racially discriminatory way. "Prosecutors are not going to own up to [bias], so you have to do it by circumstantial evidence," argued Rep. William J. Hughes, D-N.J. Opponents, such as Sen. Orrin G. Hatch, R-Utah, said such a provision "would put quotas on the death penalty." [17]

Action in States

The most dramatic action on victims' rights continues at the state level. This November, seven states — Alaska, Idaho, Maryland, Nebraska, Alabama, Ohio and Utah — will have ballot initiatives asking voter approval for constitutional amendments on victims' rights, according to the National Victim Center, which keeps a state legislative database. Intergovernmental groups such as the National Association of Attorneys General and the American Legislative Exchange Council (ALEC) are preparing model legislation or have endorsed state constitutional amendments providing victims' rights.

The Chicago-based National Conference of Commissioners on Uniform State Laws has drafted a prototype "Uniform Victims of Crime Act" to make state definitions of victims more consistent, to consolidate all related legislation in one place and to promote other improvements in running compensation and reparation programs.

Differences among states can be stark: Victim restitution, for example, is required in only 21 states for non-property crimes; 43 states notify victims when an offender is up for parole, but only 29 states do so if the offender escapes from prison; and 25 states require that victims be notified that a suspect made bail or was released before trial. Forty-eight states permit victims to make impact statements before or at sentencing. (In Alabama and Nevada, the practice is left to the judge's discretion.)

The steady stream of new legislation and proposed amendments to state constitutions reflects the lack of enforcement of laws already on the books, say victims' rights advocates. Indeed, in South Carolina, a study showed that only 15 percent of eligible victims gave victim impact statements, and three-quarters of the victims whose cases had cleared a grand jury were never given the opportunity to make a statement. In Texas, a study showed that only 1.8 percent of prepared impact statements were forwarded to parole boards, and only six victims out of more than 5,000 were notified of pending parole hearings. [18]

"Lots of states have statutes, but they haven't done enough to change the system's culture," says the NRA's Twist. "The need for constitutional amendments is profound." The National Victim Center poll in 1991 showed 89 percent of respondents saying they probably or definitely support amendments to state constitutions to increase victims' rights protection.

Maryland Among the Most Active

Few states have been as active as Maryland, where this May Democratic Gov. William Donald Schaefer signed

*A final version of the omnibus anti-crime bill is now being negotiated by House-Senate conferees. The $22.3 billion Senate version of the bill and the similar, $28 billion House version were passed in the spring.

victims' rights bills to provide better protection of witnesses, improve the collection of restitution and make parole hearings public if a victim requests it. Following active lobbying by the Stephanie Roper Committee, among others, the Maryland General Assembly also approved a November vote on a constitutional amendment guaranteeing the right of victims "to be informed of, to be present at and to be heard at appropriate criminal justice proceedings."

Prosecutor Sonner, who helped finalize some of the legislation, says that what the victims' rights advocates originally said they wanted would "have required prosecutors to keep every victim informed throughout a trial and would have marshalled all our resources. But they finally confessed that what they really wanted was something symbolic. So the final bill requires victims to make a request before we give them the services, which is the way we were already doing it."

Constitutional Amendments

Unlike proposals for new laws, campaigns for constitutional amendments often provoke resistance from lawmakers and legal scholars who believe that constitutions should be reserved for broad philosophical strokes and not be modified frequently with amendments to micromanage contemporary problems.

And judges often object to the way a constitutional amendment would make mandatory certain procedures that currently are at a judge's discretion. "What other person besides the accused is mentioned in the Constitution?" asks Judge Femia. The proposed amendments are "an effort to make victims feel that they're [entitled to] more than the Constitution allows, and this is utopian."

Furthermore, Sonner says, those who seek to give victims parity with defendants are unfairly misstating the Constitution. "Defendants' rights don't just attach to the criminal, they attach to everyone," he says. "The government can't do an illegal search and seizure in *anyone's* home, and the right not to incriminate yourself applies whether you're guilty or innocent."

Constitutional amendments, counters the ABA's Kelly, "don't risk a radical atrophy of defendants' rights. They give salience to the rights and make sure the laws already there are invoked and used."

California Politics

In most states, victims' rights advocates strive to be non-political. But in California, activists frequently have been charged with allowing partisan politicians to exploit them. In 1992, victims advocates converged on the state capital to show support for Republican Gov. Pete Wilson's budget proposal, attacking Democratic legislators for seeking to eliminate rape crisis centers and similar programs.

The move backfired, however, when it was pointed out that Wilson himself had earlier sought to cut them. "This is pathetic pandering," said Democratic Assemblyman John Vasconcellos. "It's sad that the governor has reduced himself to manipulating crime victims to make himself look good." [19]

One California group, Memories of Victims Everywhere (MOVE), is campaigning to repeal the state's "Inmate Bill of Rights" and to oust legislators who are "soft on crime." It is led by Collene Campbell, the staunchly Republican mayor of San Juan Capistrano, who suffered the murders of three close family members in two separate incidents. When Democrats accused her of exploiting crime for partisan reasons, she said, "If anybody thinks it's fun to talk about their murdered loved ones, they haven't been there yet." [20]

The Doris Tate Crime Victims Bureau also meets criticism, says Rudiger, for trying to reduce prisoners' rights and "because we have the audacity to think that capital punishment should be enforced. Ours is a small group that is not national, so it's easier for us to take clear positions." Though the group's efforts at tougher sentencing laws regularly meet resistance from the ACLU and the Prisoners Rights Union, Rudiger says, "We work both sides of the aisle. A criminal doesn't inquire as to your party affiliation before he hits you." ■

OUTLOOK

Death Penalty Debate

"Crime victims need three things," writes author and mugging victim Michael Castleman: "*support* from friends willing to listen throughout the grieving process; *permission* to recover in their own way; and the *power* to decide for themselves how to deal with the situation." [21]

But unquestionably, the ordeal of victimization can lead to a desire for revenge. In Virginia, this March, the state Senate narrowly rejected a House-passed measure to permit survivors of homicide victims to witness the killer's execution. "Naturally, there's a little bit of vengeance in the back of your mind, but that wasn't really it," said Earl Clark, a retired convenience store supervisor who sought to watch the execution of the man who had stabbed and beaten his daughter to death. "It was for closure. . . . I just wanted to put it behind me." [22]

The victims' rights movement, however, is divided over the death penalty, and many advocates consider witnessing executions, now permitted in six states, as distasteful and ineffective. "I believe in the principle of being informed at every stage," says Stein, "but the motives behind this legislation make me uneasy. There's not much evidence that it would bring a great catharsis of

Continued on p. 642

At Issue:

Are new laws needed to protect crime victims' rights?

DEBORAH P. KELLY
Chair of the American Bar Association's Victims Committee

YES

FROM *"HAVE VICTIM REFORMS GONE TOO FAR — OR NOT FAR ENOUGH?" CRIMINAL JUSTICE,* FALL 1991.

Victims' reforms reflect the consensus of most states that the interests of the 35 million people who are victims of crime annually should factor into the criminal justice system. Victims' reforms also reflect an effort to interject compassion into a system that often equates defending the accused with destroying the victim.

Victims who perceive themselves to be included or consulted in decision-making are more satisfied with the criminal justice system and more willing to cooperate with prosecutors in the future than those not informed. . . .

There is virtually no evidence that victims' participation in the system is at the defendant's expense. A national study of 36 states found that to the extent that victim-impact statutes had an effect on defendants it was to enforce restitution orders; the effect on sentence type and length was negligible. Further, judges interviewed in states with victims' rights legislation indicated that the legislation did not tip the balance in favor of victims.

A national study of victim participation in plea negotiations concluded that, contrary to what prosecutors originally envisioned, victims did not slow down the process or demand stiff sentences but instead, usually agreed to prosecutors' recommendations.

Despite the impressive count of statutes, it is clear that the integrity of victims' reforms is threatened because at present most "victims' statutes" are little more than paper promises. In many instances those charged with notifying victims of their rights do not. Ironically, the greatest resistance to correcting this and putting teeth in victims' reforms may come from prosecutors, who are concerned that their turf will be invaded and their ability to dispose of cases will be slowed considerably. Proposals to provide victims with a cause of action if they are not notified of their rights run the risk of causing this fragile alliance between prosecutors and victims' groups to disintegrate entirely.

Some victims' rights statutes, however, cry out for implementation if not reform. Compelling evidence exists that victims' reforms are at best honored in the breach, which is why many states have passed or are considering constitutional amendments that would make the rights more salient.

In spite of the quantity of statutes described above, if there is any truth to the adage that there is no right without a remedy, in the final analysis victims have no rights at all — merely privileges to be granted or withheld at the whim of criminal justice insiders.

ANDREW L. SONNER
State's Attorney for Montgomery County, Md.

NO

***WRITTEN FOR THE CQ RESEARCHER,* JULY 1994.**

In some jurisdictions, prosecutors, police and judges — not to mention defense attorneys — treat victims callously. A civilized justice system should not do that. It should ease the burdens of victims.

But legislative efforts designed to improve the treatment of victims should be subjected to rigorous scrutiny to assure that the collateral consequences of well-intentioned reforms do not damage public prosecution or fundamental fairness. Several states are finding that they have built in expensive delays and additional work without improving victim satisfaction. The solution should be no broader than the problem.

Victims' rights legislation first poses a fundamental philosophical question: How much should the personal feelings of victims influence the outcome of criminal cases? One of the goals of justice is the impartial administration of sanctions so that equally culpable defendants do not receive disparate punishment. American criminal justice is currently under attack by some informed observers for what is perceived as unfairly prosecuting and sentencing minorities. Will some vengeful victims, by injecting their wishes formally into the process, tip the scales so that the influence and standing of the victims drives the severity of the sentences?

There are also practical questions for legislators to consider in victims' rights legislation. To whom should the legislation apply? Making the rights apply to all victims of crime not only entails enormous costs, but often involuntarily injects victims more deeply into prosecution than is warranted or than many of them want. . . .

Some proposed legislation requires that law enforcement and the court "consult" with victims at every "significant stage." Does that include the charging stage, preliminary hearing, grand jury, plea negotiations, sentencing and appeal? And what will be the remedy for violations of victims' rights? How will those remedies be enforced? May victims address the court to express disagreement with prosecutors' charges, plea agreements or sentencing recommendations?

At the state level, the victims' rights movement's strategy has been to marshal crime victims with brutal experiences to recount their insensitive treatment by an impersonal system. Their stories can lead officials to legislate by anecdote. . . .

Some proposed reforms are tempting opportunities for a symbolic "going on the record for victims," but are poorly tailored to address defects in treatment. Ill-considered reforms themselves may quickly need reforming. Every citizen deserves understanding and courteous treatment from government officials, but a proper regard for justice calls for caution when trying to achieve it by legislation.

Continued from p. 640

healing. What is needed is a good crisis counselor or victim's advocate to assist the family in dealing with the emotionally charged event."

Members of Parents of Murdered Children "are often called avenging angels because we serve petitions at parole boards and get upset if a criminal gets off early or beats the death penalty," says Reed, adding that men tend to see vengeance as more important than do women. "But most people are so overcome with grief, they don't have room for those feelings."

The ABA's Kelly says: "Those Charles Bronson movies make it seem that it's normal to desire a slow death for criminals, but real-life crime victims have the opposite reaction. Rape victims are more concerned about how they are treated by the system than about the criminal's punishment."

According to the National Victim Center poll, nearly three-quarters of all Americans would join a crime-prevention or victims' rights group if they were victimized.

After 18-year-old Dominic Norman of Dallas, Texas, was killed by a drunken driver, his aunt, Debra Jones, and father, Archie Woulard (above), were spurred to activism. Dominic died a week before leaving for college on a full scholarship.

Other Approaches

Increasingly, in recent years, victims have shown an interest in mediated encounters with their victimizers. The practice began in the Canadian city of Kitchener, Ontario, in the mid-1970s and spread to the United States through prisoner, community, foundation and church groups.

"Through face-to-face communication, in the presence of a trained mediator, the conflict can be humanized, tension reduced and stereotypes of each other reduced," writes University of Minnesota social work Professor Mark S. Umbreit. "The mediation process is believed to result in a more satisfactory experience of justice for both the victim and offender." [23]

Though mediation is used most often for non-violent crimes such as vandalism and property theft, corrections departments in New York and Oklahoma now are experimenting with violent offenders. The Home Box Office cable channel in 1991 broadcast a dramatic encounter between New York City junior high school teacher Gary Smith and the young student who had beaten him nearly to death with a baseball bat. "I was at a boiling point, and you were the one I took it out on," the imprisoned boy told his victim as they shook hands in front of TV cameras. "It forms a closure of the whole thing for me," said Smith. [24]

Mediated negotiations for restitution following property crimes also have shown success in unclogging the court system and reducing repeat offenses. There are some 125 programs nationwide, according to Umbreit, whose study of results in four cities showed that the average amount of restitution was $200. [25]

Also gaining currency among victims is the use of civil suits to go after criminals' assets, including their wages, benefits, dividends and tax refunds, noted a 1992 bulletin from the federal Office for Victims of Crime. MADD advocates preventing offenders from using bankruptcy laws to escape their debts to victims, while the ACLU foresees new legal mechanisms such as "tripartite criminal proceedings," in which victims are active parties, and perhaps even legal aid and public defenderlike representatives for victims, as is now common practice in Europe. [26]

The 1991 victim center poll showed 76 percent of respondents in favor of allowing crime victims to sue public officials who don't provide them with their rights.

"What's new on the horizon is assisting with services and providing resources to help victims with recovery," says the center's Beatty. "We may have to create remedies, not just laws in books collecting dust."

"The American public as a society has to learn to take the view of the victim rather than be preoccupied with criminals," says Bard. People are reluctant to deal with victims partly because of pity and discomfort, he says. But it's also because they're more interested in criminals as society's "doers," while victims are merely passive. "We're intrigued by the entrepreneur, no matter if it's a criminal who's engaged in it. It goes to the soul of this society," he says.

The greatest failing of the victims' movement, says Stein, "is its lack of minority and poor people. It's a mostly white and female group. All of us share a more democratic vision of what we should be doing. If I could concentrate our resources, I would put more victims' advocates in urban public housing."

Albuquerque attorney Hollander says the movement is "going to grow because crime will continue to grow, and government will take advantage of it and make it a promising industry. We're at a juncture in history when there are larger numbers of people in the crime-creating age group. And we're not doing anything about that."

Many in the victims' movement speak of eventual plans to seek a victims' rights amendment to the Constitution. At that point, predicts Sonner, "We will see scholars taking a hard look at these people attempting to fool around with the Constitution, and the balance of the debate will change. Right now, on the state level, it's hard to turn down people who've been victims. As a politician, I recognize the strength of the movement, and I'm not anxious to take it on in battle."

Brown of MADD says she can clearly see the impact of the work done by victims' advocates in the many laws that have been enacted in the past decade or more. "But the constitutional amendments are needed because the most significant laws weren't adhered to, and in that respect we haven't come that far," she says.

Lucy Friedman, executive director of the Victim Services agency, a New York City nonprofit, points out that victim assistance services are now "part of the fabric of the criminal justice system. It would be politically impossible to say we won't provide services to victims anymore."

Still, grumbles Walsh, it's a "travesty that we have only 14 states with constitutional amendments," asking with frustration, "Will we see amendments in every state in my lifetime?"

"We need to tear down the barriers between political left and right and help victims so that the whole community is helped," says the ABA's Kelly. "We need to make victims more aware. If a right is not delivered to the victim, what good is it?" ■

Notes

[1] *The New York Times,* May 25, 1994.

[2] National Rifle Association, "CrimeStrike Special Report: Elements for an Effective Criminal Justice System" (undated), p. 10.

[3] For a discussion of whether the news media should use rape victims' names, see *Time,* April 29, 1991, p. 28.

[4] *The Washington Post,* Jan. 25, 1983.

[5] *The (Baltimore) Sun,* June 23, 1991.

[6] Robert C. Wells, "Victim Impact: How Much Consideration Is It Really Given?" *The Police Chief,* February 1991, p. 44. Wells is victim/witness coordinator at the Federal Law Enforcement Training Center, Glynco, Ga. For background, see "Juvenile Justice," *The CQ Researcher,* Feb. 25, 1994, pp. 169-192.

[7] Edwin Villmoare and Virginia V. Neto, "Victim Appearances at Sentencing Under California's Victims' Bill of Rights," National Institute of Justice, August 1987.

[8] Morton Bard and Dawn Sangrey, *The Crime Victim's Book* (1986), p. 153.

[9] James Stark and Howard W. Goldstein, *The Rights of Crime Victims* (1985), p. 20.

[10] Washington Legal Foundation, *amicus curiae* brief in *Payne v. Tennessee,* 1991.

[11] Office of Victims of Crime, *Report to Congress,* April 1990, p. 2.

[12] Bard and Sangrey, *op. cit.,* p. 212.

[13] Stark and Goldstein, *op. cit.,* p. 21.

[14] Justice Department, "Office of Justice Programs Annual Report for Fiscal Year 1992," p. 72.

[15] For background, see "Child Sexual Abuse," *The CQ Researcher,* Jan. 15, 1993, pp.25-48, and "Violence Against Women," *The CQ Researcher,* Feb. 28, 1993, pp. 169-192.

[16] Quoted in *Time,* May 27, 1991, p. 61.

[17] Quoted in *The Washington Post,* June 16, 1994. For background, see "Racial Sentencing Provision Snarls Crime Legislation," *CQ Weekly Report,* June 25, 1994, p. 1713.

[18] Deborah Kelly, "Have Victim Reforms Gone Too Far — Or Not Far Enough?" *Criminal Justice,* fall 1991, p. 26.

[19] *Los Angeles Times,* Aug. 18, 1992.

[20] *Los Angeles Times,* April 5, 1994.

[21] Michael Castleman, *Crime Free* (1984), p. 163.

[22] *The Washington Post,* March 1, 1994.

[23] Emilio Viano (ed.), *The Victimology Handbook* (1990), p. 339.

[24] Quoted in *The New York Times,* Sept. 14, 1991.

[25] *The Wall Street Journal,* Oct. 28, 1993.

[26] Stark and Goldstein, *op. cit.,* p. 8.

For More Information

DORIS TATE CRIME VICTIMS' BUREAU, 755 Riverpoint Dr., Suite 101, West Sacramento, Calif. 95605; (916) 372-6651. Named for the mother of slain movie actress Sharon Tate, this lobbying and educational group seeks changes in California laws and regulations to further the rights of crime victims.

NATIONAL ORGANIZATION FOR VICTIM ASSISTANCE, 1757 Park Rd. N.W., Washington, D.C. 20010; (202) 232-6682. This group of victims' activists, researchers and criminal justice professionals monitors legislation, offers support programs and provides information on victims' rights.

NATIONAL VICTIM CENTER, 2111 Wilson Blvd., Suite 300, Arlington, Va. 22201; (703) 276-2880. The center works to protect victims' rights through its public policy division; maintains a resource library; and provides training and technical assistance for victim services professionals.

PARENTS OF MURDERED CHILDREN, 100 East 8th St., B-41, Cincinnati, Ohio 45202; (513) 721-5683. This organization provides comfort and advice to relatives of murder victims primarily through 300 local chapters. It campaigns against early release of prisoners and against toys and popular literature that trivialize violence.

Bibliography

Selected Sources Used

Books

Bard, Morton, and Dawn Sangrey, *The Crime Victim's Book,* 2nd edition, Brunner/Mazel, 1986.

A professor of psychology and a writer on women and family issues produced this in-depth guide for crime victims on how to navigate the court system, fight for rights and cope with the anguish that accompanies victimization.

Castleman, Michael, *Crime Free,* Simon and Schuster, 1984.

An author who survived a mugging incident offers advice for crime prevention along with personal testimony: "After I was robbed at gunpoint, my life took some strange turns. On one level I felt lucky. I'd escaped a life-threatening situation without physical injury. But on a deeper level I felt profoundly violated. I haven't been quite the same since."

Gordon, Margaret T., and Stephanie Riger, *The Female Fear,* The Free Press, 1989.

Two academics discuss the impact of rape and the fear of rape on the lives of women, outlining the role of rape activists in the history of the victims' rights movement.

Mann, Stephanie, with M.C. Blakeman, *Safe Homes, Safe Neighborhoods: Stopping Crime Where You Live,* Nolo Press, 1993

A crime prevention consultant who helped found the Neighborhood Watch movement compiled this practical guide to organizing neighborhoods that includes a chapter on how to work with victims and witnesses.

Stark, James, and Howard W. Goldstein, *The Rights of Crime Victims,* Bantam Books, 1985.

This guidebook by two attorneys from the American Civil Liberties Union answers legal questions about how victims can participate in the criminal justice system and seek financial compensation and restitution.

Viano, Emilio (ed.), *The Victimology Handbook: Research Findings, Treatment, and Public Policy,* Garland Publishing, 1990.

Edited by an American University public affairs professor, this compendium of articles — many from *Victimology: An International Journal* — traces the development of the victims' rights movement and discusses related legal, medical and psychological issues. With an international scope, it also analyses crime issues such as family violence, rape and violence in the workplace.

Articles

Duggan, Paul, "A Giant Hold in Your Life," *The Washington Post Magazine,* Aug. 29, 1993.

A profile of Maryland victims' rights activist Roberta Roper recounting the gruesome rape and murder of her college-age daughter in 1982, with an update on the imprisoned perpetrators.

Quintanilla, Michael, "Promises to Keep: Patti Tate Leads a Justice Crusade in the Name of Her Sister Sharon," *Los Angeles Times,* Jan. 10, 1994.

The family of slain actress Sharon Tate, killed in the notorious Manson family murders in 1969, helps run a Sacramento-based victims' rights lobbying group, while monitoring the parole hearings of the criminals who victimized them.

Webb, Gary L., and James E. Hendricks, "Confronting Citizen Fear of Crime: Police Victim Assistance Training, *The Police Chief,* November 1992.

Two criminologists discuss how police are trained and sensitized to assure that victims are free from intimidation and told of their rights to financial assistance and social services.

Reports and Studies

Department of Justice, Office for Victims of Crime, *OVC Bulletin,* "Civil Legal Remedies for Crime Victims," December 1992.

This government bulletin explains how the crime victims' rights movement only recently has been encouraging the use of civil courts to win financial restitution.

National Institute of Justice, *Compensating Crime Victims: A Summary of Policies and Practices,* January 1992.

This government report surveys state crime-victim compensation programs, comparing which states pay the most to victims and which have the heaviest caseloads.

National Rifle Association, *CrimeStrike Special Report: Elements for an Effective Criminal Justice System,* undated.

This compendium of reform recommendations includes calls for tougher sentencing of criminals and outlines the basic victims' rights agenda for participation in the criminal justice system.

The Next Step

Additional information from UMI's Newspaper & Periodical Abstracts database

Advocates for Victims' Rights

Adler, Constance, "Besides that, really, he's a pretty nice guy," *Shape,* September 1993, pp. 100-105.
In the U.S. about 1 million women report intimate violence each year, with another estimated 2 million cases of battering that are never reported. Abusive relationships and the people who stay in them are discussed, and agencies that can help define victims' rights are listed.

Clinton, President William J., "Remarks honoring the 1994 Victim Service Award recipients and an exchange with reporters," *Weekly Compilation of Presidential Documents,* May 2, 1994, pp. 905-908.
The contributions of 11 people who have done great work in the cause of victims' rights are discussed, as is a tough crime bill designed to stem violent crime.

Faulkner, Mary Sue, "Crime Strike Fights for Victims' Rights," *American Hunter,* November 1992, pp. 32-33.
The NRA's CrimeStrike program is fighting to protect the rights of victims of crime. CrimeStrike recently supported two women, Susan Bromberg and Lori Bible, who spoke out on the justice system's failure to protect citizens from convicted criminals.

Golightly, Glen, "Victims' rights groups reach out for support," *Houston Chronicle,* Dec. 20, 1993, p. A19.
About 150 members of victims' rights organizations such as Parents of Murdered Children and Justice for All sought support by participating in a "life chain" in Houston.

Hensel, Deborah Quinn, "Victims' rights groups demonstrate against freeing killers," *Houston Post,* Dec. 20, 1993, p. A27.
Four victims' rights groups demonstrated in Houston on Dec. 19, 1993, to protest the leniency of the criminal justice system on violent offenders.

Roberts, Penny, "Victims find a safe place to speak out," *Chicago Tribune,* April 8, 1994, p. 2C4.
The Children's Advocacy Center, founded in 1988 in Waukegan, Ill., to champion the rights of young victims of sexual and physical abuse, is dedicated to helping prosecutors press cases that once might have been downplayed, if not avoided, by law enforcement.

Court Decisions

Bendor, Catherine, "Defendant's Wrongs and Victims' Rights: *Payne v. Tennessee,*" *Harvard Civil Rights-Civil Liberties Law Review,* Winter 1992, pp. 219-243.
In *Payne v. Tennessee,* the Supreme Court held that the Eighth Amendment does not bar capital sentencing juries from considering victim impact evidence. Details of the murder case are presented.

Sargeant, Georgia, "Victim Impact Testimony Allowed by Supreme Court in Death Penalty Hearings," *Trial,* October 1991, pp. 11-14.
The effect of victim impact testimony on death penalty hearings and the Supreme Court's recent ruling on the matter are discussed. Many believe that decisions on admittance of victim impact testimony should be weighted towards protecting the accused, but victims' rights activists are placing increased burdens on the defendents.

Sherman, Rorie, "Victims' advocate files novel suit in murder," *National Law Journal,* Mar 7, 1994, p. 9.
In an unusual victims' rights civil lawsuit, attorney Richard D. Pompello, whose son was murdered by five other boys, has sued the murderers' parents and their insurers, basing liability on the fact that the murder plot was hatched in the parents' homes.

Tiglao, Rigoberto, "Billion-dollar judgment," *Far Eastern Economic Review,* Mar 10, 1994, p. 21.
On Feb. 23, 1994, a jury in Hawaii ordered the estate of the late Ferdinand Marcos to pay $1.2 billion in so-called exemplary damages to some 10,000 victims of human rights abuses during his rule. The court decision and the complex legal tangles that must be resolved before payment can be made are discussed.

Federal Action

Clinton, President William J., "Proclamation 6678 — National Crime Victims' Rights Week, 1994," *Weekly Compilation of Presidential Documents,* May 2, 1994, pp. 908-909.
The proclamation of the National Crime Victims' Rights Week from April 24-30, 1994, is discussed. Americans are urged to remember innocent victims of crime and honor those who labor selflessly on behalf of these victims and their families.

Phillips, Leslie, "Bill makes sex crimes violation of civil rights," *USA Today,* May 28, 1993, p. A3.
The Senate Judiciary Committee approved legislation to extend civil rights protection to victims of gender-based crimes. The legislation is meant to persuade the public, law enforcement agencies and the courts that victims of gender-based crimes should receive equal protection under the law.

Seper, Jerry, "Reno vows to do what's right, scorns the politically popular," *The Washington Times,* April

7, 1993, p. A3.
Attorney General Janet Reno outlined her opinions on several topics in her first formal address to the Department of Justice, pledging to do what is right even if it is politically unpopular. Reno promised crime prevention programs and a focus on victims' rights.

Opinions

Hauser, Thomas, "Your Rights as a Crime Victim," *McCall's,* Nove,ber 1988, pp. 124-126.
An attorney answers questions regarding a crime victim's rights.

"Keeping track of child molesters," *Atlanta Constitution,* Jan. 6, 1994, p. A10.
An editorial comments on the national move to crack down on sexual predators of children by doing a better job of keeping track of them, saying Georgia lawmakers, unfortunately, rarely worry as much about child victims' rights as they do about criminals' rights.

"The Rights of Victims — And Others," *St. Louis Post-Dispatch,* Nov. 16, 1992, p. B2.
An editorial discusses the consequences of the overwhelming votes of approval in Missouri and Illinois on victims' rights amendments, noting that prosecutors and lawmakers must make sure that the rights of the accused are not violated or diminished.

"Victims' rights lost in the shuffle," *Atlanta Constitution,* March 2, 1994, p. A10.
An editorial supports Georgia's proposed Crime Victims' Rights Act, which would refocus the criminal justice system on the needs of victims, and criticizes those in the Georgia Legislature who would cite a lack of funds as an excuse for not enacting it.

Williams, Armstrong, "Victims deserve justice, too," *USA Today,* April 13, 1993, p. A10.
Armstrong Williams comments on the Ellie Nesler case, saying that victims should have the same rights as defendants and that when authorities can't or won't provide justice, it must be insisted on.

Privacy Issues

Case, Tony, "Naming Rape Victims," *Editor & Publisher,* Nov. 28, 1992, pp. 12-13.
The effects of Marshall University's student newspaper's adoption of a policy to print the names of rape victims, which has once again raised the debate of First Amendment rights vs. the right to privacy, are discussed. This editorial decision has opened a veritable Pandora's box of criticism and very public protest.

Kaplan, Joel, "State lawmakers are trying to seal key information in sex crimes," *ASNE Bulletin,* July 1993, pp. 14-17.
The broad legal and ethical debate over freedom of the press vs. a crime victim's right to privacy is considered. In order to shield victims of sex crimes, new state laws are requiring police and courts to keep "public" records secret. Laws that solidify victims' rights to privacy are discussed.

"State Lawmakers Eye Ban on Naming of Rape Victims," *Editor & Publisher,* May 25, 1991, p. 32.
State lawmakers are pushing for legislation that would make news organizations that name victims of sex crimes accountable to the law for doing so. The principal argument against the legislation is that it denies First Amendment rights.

State and Local Actions

Babington, Charles, "Md. Assembly endorses amending constitution for victims' rights," *The Washington Post,* Feb. 19, 1994, p. B3.
In an election year when crime is uppermost in voters' minds, the Maryland General Assembly approved a measure that had been rejected three times before: a proposed state constitutional amendment guaranteeing victims' rights.

Battle, Ursula V., "Coalition pushes for victim's rights," *Afro-American,* Feb. 5, 1994, p. A6.
In order to correct what many feel is an imbalance between the rights of victims and those accused of crimes, the Maryland Coalition for a Constitutional Amendment is working to change the state laws to ensure that victims have the right to be present and heard in court.

DeBenedictis, Don J., "Tackling Victims' Rights," *ABA Journal,* July 1991, p. 16.
The Arizona Legislature was presented with a bill relating specifically to victims' rights. Defining what those rights are and the details and controversy behind it are discussed. Victims' rights leader Karen Duffy argues that victims' rights issues should be decided by the legislatures, not by the courts.

Denniston, Lyle, "Victims law stuns Alaskan press," *WJR: Washington Journalism Review,* November 1991, p. 46.
The police and the press feel tension over the press' right to access to files and crime reports, Denniston writes. The Alaska Legislature passed the Victims' Rights Act, which guarantees confidentiality to crime victims and witnesses.

Johnson, Malcolm, "Crime bills aim to strengthen '85 victim's right law," *Detroit News & Free Press,* May 2, 1993, p. C4N.
Crime victims would have stronger rights to compensation, protection and consultation under legislation that cleared the Michigan Senate.

Jok, Debbie, "Peachtree City unveils victim/witness

assistance program," *Atlanta Constitution,* July 1, 1993, p. XM5.

Peachtree City, Ga., Police Chief Jim Murray said the "time has come to stop thinking so much about suspects' rights and to start thinking more about the victims" of crime as he unveiled department plans for a Victim/ Witness Assistance Program.

McGuire, Stephen, "Victims' Rights Laws in Illinois: Two Decades of Progress," *Crime & Delinquency,* October 1987, pp. 532-540.

The adjustments made by the criminal justice system in Illinois over the past 20 years in order to safeguard the rights of crime victims and to enhance their participation in the process of criminal adjudication are listed.

Reske, Henry J., "Helping Crime's Casualties," *ABA Journal,* November 1992, p. 34.

The Uniform Victims of Crime Act attempts to lend uniformity to the way victims are treated, and it is divided into three sections — victims' rights, victims' compensation and victims' restitution. The new act, which was drafted by the National Conference of Commissioners on Uniform State Laws, says that victims must be notified of their rights in order to receive their compensation.

Sargeant, Georgia, "Model victims' rights act prepared by Conference on Uniform State Laws," *Trial,* November 1992, pp. 100-102.

The National Conference of Commissioners on Uniform State Laws has prepared a multi-part bill standardizing the rights of crime victims. The proposals included in the bill are outlined.

Victims' Rights Movement

Chambers, Marcia, "Sua sponte: Victims of their success," *National Law Journal,* Nov. 22, 1993, pp. 15-16.

The birth of the victims' rights movement in the mid-1970s grew out of crime victims' lack of confidence in the justice system, Chamber writes. Today, however, TV shows like "Oprah" and "Geraldo" have turned the movement into a freak show, she writes.

Paege, Byron, "The Silent Sufferers Get Vocal," *Canada & the World,* September 1991, pp. 14-15.

The growing victims' rights movement, a movement in Canada which strives to assure the rights of victims in judicial proceedings, is discussed. The opinions of victim groups, defense attorneys and prosecutors are detailed. Politicians in Manitoba reacted to the movement by passing Bill C-89, a declaration of victim's rights.

Swasey, Elizabeth J., "NRA Woman's Voice," *American Hunter*, October 1992, p. 32.

Victims play so small a role in the criminal justice system that the very name of the system ignores victims. The victims' rights movement and proposed legislation to ensure victim's rights are discussed.

Victims' Testimony

Erez, Edna, and Ewa Bienkowska, "Victim participation in proceedings and satisfaction with justice in the continental systems: The case of Poland," *Journal of Criminal Justice,* 1993, PG- 47-60,

Typically, in adversary criminal justice systems, the role of the victim is a passive one; however, victims in the European criminal justice system have rights of participation in proceedings. The forms and extent of victim participation in legal proceedings are examined, and the effect of participation on victim satisfaction with justice in the Polish criminal justice system is assessed.

Greene, Donna, "Giving victims a voice in criminal trials," *The New York Times,* July 18, 1993, p. WC3.

Judge Anthony A. Scarpino of Westchester County Court in New York is interviewed concerning the rights of crime victims.

Hall, Donald J., "Victims' Voices in Criminal Court: The Need for Restraint," *American Criminal Law Review,* 1991, pp. 233-266.

The phenomenon of victims' rights is a full-fledged component of the U.S. criminal justice system. This has culminated in a significant number of state and federal statutes, many addressing the concern of compensation to victims of crime. "Victim participation" statutes ensure that a victim has the opportunity to be an active participant in some phases of the criminal case. These are discussed.

Harper, Jane, "Activists applaud judge's decision to let girl's father confront Cantu," *Houston Post,* Feb. 11, 1994, p. A25.

About 70 to 80 phone calls poured into District Judge Bill Harmon's court on Feb. 10, 1994, praising him for allowing the father of a murdered girl to tell her killer what he thinks of him. The callers were responding to emotional statements Randy Ertman made to Peter Cantu on Feb. 9 moments after Cantu was sentenced to die for the murder of Jennifer Ertman and Elizabeth Pena. Several victims' rights advocates said they hope the judge's move becomes the norm around the Harris County, Texas, courthouse.

Back Issues

Great Research on Current Issues Starts Right Here...Recent topics covered by The CQ Researcher are listed below. Before May 1991, reports were published under the name of Editorial Research Reports.

JANUARY 1993
Hate Crimes
Child Sexual Abuse
Nuclear Fusion
U.S. Trade Policy

FEBRUARY 1993
Community Policing
Europe's New Right
School Censorship
Violence Against Women

MARCH 1993
Gay Rights
Aid to Russia
War on Drugs
TV Violence

APRIL 1993
Head Start
High-Speed Rail
Children's Legal Rights
Muslims in America

MAY 1993
Cults in America
Preventing Teen Pregnancy
Software Piracy
National Parks

JUNE 1993
Food Safety
Prostitution
Childhood Immunizations
National Service

JULY 1993
Electric Cars
Population Growth
Downward Mobility
Intelligence Testing

AUGUST 1993
Mental Illness
Bilingual Education
Foreign Policy Burden
School Funding

SEPTEMBER 1993
Suburban Crime
Public Housing
Supreme Court Preview
Immigration Reform

OCTOBER 1993
Airline Safety
Disaster Response
Science in the Courtroom
The Glass Ceiling

NOVEMBER 1993
Paying for Retirement
Charitable Giving
Privacy in the Workplace
Adoption

DECEMBER 1993
U.S. Vietnam-Relations
Learning Disabilities
Child Care
Space Program's Future

JANUARY 1994
Racial Tensions in Schools
South Africa's Future
Worker Retraining
Regulating Pesticides

FEBRUARY 1994
Prison Overcrowding
Water Quality
Religion in Schools
Juvenile Justice

MARCH 1994
Underground Economy
Education Standards
Gambling Boom
Private Management of Public Schools

APRIL 1994
Reproductive Ethics
U.S.-China Trade
Soccer in America
Talk Show Democracy

MAY 1994
Traffic Congestion
Women's Health Issues
Mutual Funds
Political Scandals

JUNE 1994
Education and Gender
Gun Control
Public Land Policy
Nuclear Arms Cleanup

JULY 1994
Dietary Supplements
Foreign Policy and Public Opinion

Back issues are available for $4.00 (subscribers) or $7.00 (non-subscribers). Quantity discounts apply to orders over ten. To order, call Congressional Quarterly Customer Service at (202) 887-8621.

Binders are available for $16.00. To order call 1-800-638-1710. Please refer to stock number 648.

Future Topics

- ***Birth Control***
- ***Genetically Engineered Foods***
- ***Electing Minorities***

THE CQ Researcher

PUBLISHED BY CONGRESSIONAL QUARTERLY INC.

Birth Control Choices

Do American women need better birth control products?

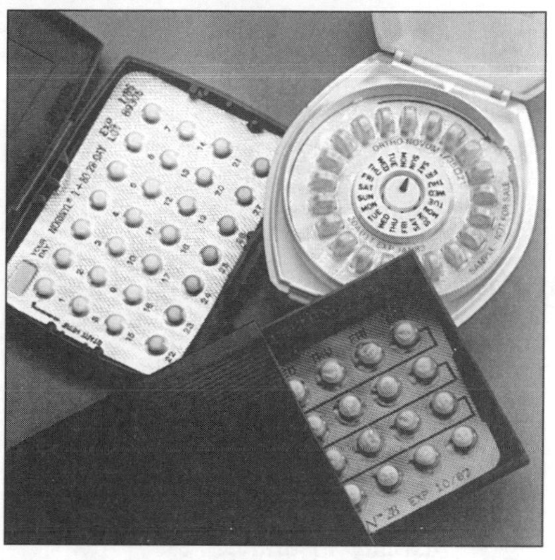

In the fourth decade of the sexual revolution spawned by "the Pill," women consumers and the medical community remain sharply divided over old and new birth control products. Some scientists had hoped by now to be offering more modern methods. But scientific, financial and political hurdles have kept those visions in the distance. Family planning organizations and contraceptive researchers continue to complain about the threat of lawsuits, cumbersome regulatory procedures and limited funding. Even when new contraceptives emerge from the laboratory, they often have serious drawbacks, consumer activists say. They blame researchers for paying too much attention to hormone-influencing products like the Pill. And they charge that safer products that would also protect against AIDS have been neglected.

INSIDE THIS ISSUE

CQ July 29, 1994 • Volume 4, No. 28 • 649-672

Formerly Editorial Research Reports

Birth Control Choices

Cover: Birth control pills, available today in a wide variety of formulations, are the most common form of contraception in the U.S. (Planned Parenthood Federation of America)

July 29, 1994
Volume 4, No. 28

The CQ Researcher (ISSN 1056-2036). Formerly Editorial Research Reports. Published weekly (48 times per year, not printed the first Friday of any month with five Fridays) by Congressional Quarterly Inc., 1414 22nd St., N.W., Washington, D.C. 20037. Rates are furnished upon request. Second-class postage paid at Washington, D.C. POSTMASTER: Send address changes to The CQ Researcher, 1414 22nd St., N.W., Washington, D.C. 20037.

Birth Control Choices

By Sarah Glazer

The Issues

American women face a dilemma when deciding on a contraceptive. They still have to choose between birth control methods that are highly effective but have side effects — like the birth control pill — and those methods with virtually no side effects but much higher failure rates, such as the diaphragm or condom.

Some scientists had hoped by now to be close to offering more modern methods: vaccines without hormonal side effects or even a male contraceptive beyond the condom. But scientific, financial and political hurdles have kept those visions in the distance. Family planning organizations and contraceptive researchers continue to complain about the threat of lawsuits, cumbersome regulatory procedures and lack of funding — all blamed for slowing contraceptive development in the mid-1980s. [1]

In the wake of multiple lawsuits against the Dalkon Shield intrauterine device (IUD) in the 1980s, all but one large American pharmaceutical manufacturer pulled out of contraceptive research and development. Several cited the difficulty of obtaining liability insurance and the threat of expensive lawsuits. In the ensuing years, some small drug firms — but few large ones — became involved in research.

All but alone in the field, along with the handful of American firms and several European companies, were three nonprofit organizations that depend on government and private grants: the Population Council in New York, Family Health International in Research Triangle Park, N.C., and the Contraceptive Research and Development Program (CONRAD) in Arlington, Va.

"I think that the liability situation is even worse than it was five or six

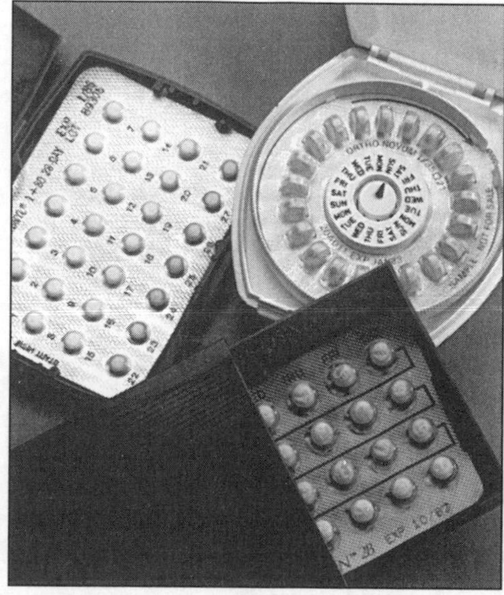

years ago, in spite of some reports to the contrary," says CONRAD Director Henry Gabelnick. [2]

A spate of recent lawsuits by women with silicone breast implants against Dow-Corning Corp., formerly the leading manufacturer of silicone implants, has led Dow to stop supplying silicone for new contraceptives. * Gabelnick says the move is likely to add costs and delays to CONRAD's work on a new one-size-fits-all diaphragm and a new cervical cap of silicone rubber.

Gabelnick says the breast implant suits also have discouraged other companies from entering the birth control field. Union Carbide recently dropped out of a joint effort with CONRAD to develop a new anti-AIDS spermicide, he reports. "It's just an overall corporate leeriness of getting involved in small-volume, high-risk operations," he says.

Some industry observers had predicted there would be renewed interest in contraceptive development in 1991, when Wyeth-Ayerst Laboratories started marketing Norplant, the first new contraceptive technology introduced in the American market in 30 years. (*See story, p. 662.*) But most of the expensive work of testing Norplant was carried out by the nonprofit Population Council. For the most part, substantial new investment by private companies didn't occur.

"We are losing our lead" in world contraceptive development, says Nancy J. Alexander, chief of contraceptive research at the National Institutes of Health (NIH).

One reason is money. A pharmaceutical company can expect to spend up to $250 million to bring a new contraceptive from concept to market. Yet altogether, the major nonprofit agencies and foundations spend only about $34 million annually on contraceptive research and development, according to a report prepared last year by a Seattle research firm. [3] NIH spends only about $16 million annually on contraceptive development, a sum Alexander considers "paltry."

In recent years, the AIDS epidemic has shifted scientists' attention to barrier methods like condoms and diaphragms, once ignored as the dinosaurs of contraceptives. The sense of urgency has increased now that women are the fastest-growing group of people becoming infected with HIV, the virus that causes AIDS. [4] The first condom for women, the Reality condom developed and marketed by Wisconsin Pharmacal Co. in Chicago, is due in stores in August. Since September 1993, the device has been bought by public health and family planning clinics in more than 170 U.S. cities.

"I think the newly emerging consciousness around sexually transmitted diseases and AIDS should develop a new public mandate and move the contraceptive discourse toward barrier methods," says Judy Norsigian, co-director of the Boston

* Major manufacturers of silicone breast implants, under the terms of a settlement agreement negotiated in federal court, have created a $4.3 billion fund to compensate claims, and numerous suits are being pursued outside the settlement. However, three large studies in the U..S. have found no harm from implants. (See *The New York Times,* June 16, 1994.)

Women's Health Book Collective, a feminist group that publishes the popular manual *Our Bodies, Ourselves*. "That's moving slowly. We've not done what we could there."

As women look at the array of products available, they often have questions on their minds very different from those of the scientists and population planners who develop them. Experts often point out that the health risks of hormonal contraceptives like the pill are far outweighed by the statistical risk of death from childbirth.

But Norsigian counters that many American women will deal with an unintended pregnancy not by giving birth but by having a first-trimester abortion, which is much safer than childbirth. Statistically, the use of barrier methods like the diaphragm, backed up by early surgical abortion, is safer than either the pill or childbirth.

"Risks that affect a woman's everyday life may be far more pressing than the risk of death," write Adrienne Germain, vice president of the New York-based International Women's Health Coalition, and sociologist Ruth Dixon-Mueller. Anxiety about going to a clinic and undergoing a gynecological examination or fear of the wrath of a husband, lover or parents may be far more influential in women's birth control decisions, they note. [5]

For a woman concerned about HIV infection, getting her sexual partner to wear a condom can turn into a no-win exercise in power relations. "In some cases, a woman will ask a man to use a condom, and he'll throw her across the room," says Holly Birnbaum Sherman, a spokeswoman for Wisconsin Pharmacal. "Until now, there has been no woman-controlled device to protect her against the disease."

The new Reality condom would provide some help. But because it is visible outside the vagina, it does not offer the clandestine protection that women in abusive relationships may need, says Marie Bass, director of the Reproductive Health Technologies Project, which advocates improved reproductive choices for women.

And diaphragms, which cover the cervix, are probably not sufficient to block HIV. In lab experiments, monkeys whose wombs and cervixes have been removed still contract HIV when the virus is inserted into their vaginas. That suggests that the virus can find its way into the body through the vaginal wall even when the cervix is blocked by a diaphragm, notes Alexander at NIH.

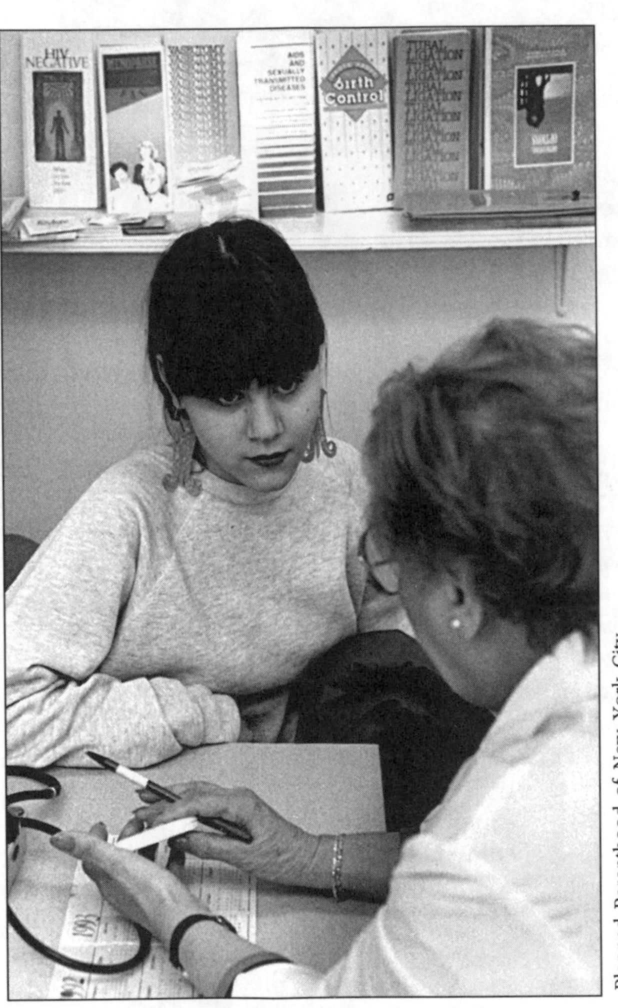

Planned Parenthood of New York City

A woman receives birth control counseling at a Planned Parenthood clinic.

Some scientists and consumers are now pushing for more powerful new microbicidal jellies or suppositories that would kill HIV and sexually transmitted diseases, as well as sperm, because women could use them secretively. But such new products are at best seven years away from the market, according to Christopher J. Elias of the Population Council. [6]

For now, it's not clear whether today's main over-the-counter spermicide — a compound known as nonoxynol-9 used in diaphragm jelly, sponges, suppositories and foams — actually prevents sexually transmitted diseases. In fact, because the spermicide is a biodetergent that can irritate the vagina, it may increase women's susceptibility to infection. Clinical data is inconclusive, Elias notes.

"Telling women, 'Just insist on a condom or don't have sex,' doesn't work for many women," Elias says, "because they are in violent or potentially violent relationships and can't raise the issue for fear of abandonment and abuse." He wants public health messages to take a clear stand on whether current spermicides do or don't protect against infection.

Meanwhile, close to half of all U.S. pregnancies that are unintended occur among women who were using contraception, according to the Alan Guttmacher Institute in New York, which tracks abortion data. Although abortion rates have declined somewhat recently, the United States continues to have one of the highest rates of abortion among comparable Western countries. [7]

While many experts say these statistics indicate the need for better contraceptives, some argue that most unintended pregnancies stem from flawed relationships. "It's important to develop new contraceptives, but the primary problem is not that our technology is so bad," says Norsigian. More important, in her view, are communication problems between sexual partners, people's discomfort with sex and the imbalance of power in sexual relationships.

Given the high U.S. contraceptive failure rate, some experts view the French abortion pill RU-486 as an easy, guilt-free way for women to end an early pregnancy. The inventor of the pill, chemist Etienne-Emile Baulieu, described RU-486 as somewhere between contraception and abortion, acting in a new realm he dubbed "contragestion." [8] But so far the pill's impending introduction to the U.S. market seems to have intensified the abortion controversy, not quieted it.

As lawmakers and activists continue the debate over contraceptives, here are some of the questions being asked:

Should RU-486 be made widely available in the U.S.?

By 1996, RU-486 * could be available in doctors' offices throughout the United States for women no more than seven weeks pregnant. [9]

The question of how widely the drug should be distributed already divides the pill's U.S. supporters. The opponents, a coalition of anti-abortion groups, have threatened to boycott whatever company markets the pill, suggesting that controversy will continue to dog the new medication.

Women's groups pushed hard for RU-486 during the Bush administration, arguing that it offered an easier, safer form of abortion to American women than surgical abortion. It avoids invasive surgery, reduces the risk of infection, eliminates the risk of perforation of the uterus and permits a woman to abort as soon as she misses a period.

In addition, some women activists hope RU-486 will defuse the abortion controversy. Broad distribution of the drug through family practitioners and gynecologists may make it harder for anti-abortion groups to mount the emotionally disturbing protests that have plagued abortion clinics recently, says Eleanor Smeal, president of the Feminist Majority Foundation, based in Arlington, Va.

"I think it forever transforms the debate about what abortion is," says Smeal. "What the opposition has done is make people picture an abortion killing a baby. When a pill works at a very embryonic stage, it smashes that argument."

RU-486 is known as an anti-progestin, because it blocks progesterone, the natural hormone that prepares the lining of the uterus for a fertilized egg to implant within it. Without the effect of progesterone, the uterine lining softens and breaks down. Any fertilized egg attached to the lining is dislodged from the side of the uterus and then expelled during menstruation.

In essence, an abortion with RU-486 is akin to experiencing a miscarriage and can occur either at the doctor's office or at home. The expelled embryo — a fraction of an inch long — resembles a blood clot and is accompanied by heavy vaginal bleeding that continues for several days.

But anti-abortion activists have not been assuaged by the fact that the drug works in the early stages of pregnancy. "We oppose RU-486 because it's going to kill millions more babies," says Richard Glasow, education director of the National Right to Life Committee, "which is exactly what the abortion lobby wants."

On June 1, the committee and other anti-abortion groups announced they would boycott the French manufacturer of RU-486, Roussel Uclaf and its parent company Hoechst A.G., and "any company contemplating using RU-486 as well."

Under pressure from the Clinton administration, Roussel announced May 16 that it was giving its patent rights to the Population Council. The council has said it will find another company to market the drug after it completes the clinical trials necessary for federal approval. Roussel Uclaf has consistently cited anti-abortion hostility as its main reason for refusing to seek marketing approval in the United States.

As the availability of the drug nears, experts now say that both sides, aided by the media, greatly exaggerated the ease of an RU-486 abortion. Actually, they say, RU-486 abortions take longer, produce more discomfort and offer less privacy than many women originally expected. In fact, it will normally require several days to complete the abortion — longer than the one day typically required for a first-trimester surgical abortion in the U.S.

The procedure is not without pain. Earlier this year, a *New York Times* account of American women undergoing RU-486 abortions in England portrayed them as extremely painful procedures, with up to six hours of severe cramping from prostaglandin, a drug that is used with RU-486 to aid expulsion of the embryo. [10]

But Population Council spokeswoman Sandra Waldman says the English clinics administered prostaglandin in suppository form, which is more painful than the oral version the council will administer to volunteers in this country. Although the prostaglandin pill also can cause cramps, bleeding or abdominal pain, the side effects resemble those of a heavy period, and Tylenol is usually sufficient to relieve the pain, according to Waldman.

The use of RU-486 won't guarantee that the abortion takes place in the privacy of one's home. In most cases, it will actually occur in a doctor's office or clinic.

Three or four doctor's visits will be required under the protocol for clinical trials of RU-486 that the Population Council plans to start this fall. The first visit will provide counseling, a physical

* The chemical name for the drug is mifepristone.

The Best-Kept Secret in Contraception . . .

The condom had broken during intercourse, and the Petaluma, Calif., woman was in a panic. Then she remembered reading in *Glamour* that oral contraceptives could be prescribed as a morning-after pill. She called 25 local physicians, but none had heard of it.

Finally, in desperation, she called the Sacramento gynecologist who had been quoted in the article, Felicia Stewart. To obtain the pills in time for them to work as "emergency contraceptives" — within 72 hours of intercourse — the woman drove to Stewart's office, 90 miles away.

"The tragedy is that an awful lot of people don't know about it," says Robert A. Hatcher, a professor of gynecology and obstetrics at Grady Memorial Hospital in Atlanta, Ga. Hatcher and Stewart have developed an emergency kit that explains how six common birth control pills can substitute as morning-after contraceptives.

Grady's Family Planning Clinic hands the "Personal Emergency Contraceptive Kit" to patients as a back-up to their regular contraceptive method. Some doctors tuck the required number of pills into the blue envelope, which also contains two condoms. "Use a condom so you do not need to use emergency contraceptive pills," the kit advises.

The procedure is well-known and widely prescribed on college campuses, according to Hatcher. But when it comes to the rest of the medical profession it's a well-kept secret.

One reason is that the method hasn't been advertised by pharmaceutical companies, says Michael Policar, vice president for medical affairs at the Planned Parenthood Federation of America. That's because the manufacturers of oral contraceptives have never sought Food and Drug Administration (FDA) approval to market the pills as morning-after contraceptives.

"What sells most pharmaceuticals these days is advertising," Policar explains. "So doctors don't hear about it much." Most of the federation's 165 affiliates give the pills to patients for emergency use, he says.

Another reason for the secrecy is that until recently most of the 4,000 family planning clinics receiving federal money to care for poor women thought federal regulations prohibited morning-after pills.

In addition, "the concern that emergency contraception would be considered a violation of the Title X abortion ban just caused people to be very cautious," a Public Health Service official said. Ironically, even the anti-abortion National Right to Life Committee does not consider this use of the pill an abortion agent, nor do most medical experts.

With the Clinton administration's liberalized attitude toward abortion, however, the U.S. Public Health Service started putting out the word last year through speeches and newsletters that the government is not seeking to limit use of oral contraceptives as morning-after pills, the official said.

"Word is getting out that there are actions women can take to ward off an unintended pregnancy before it gets established," says Anita L. Nelson, medical director of the Women's Health Care Clinic, a Title X clinic at the Harbor-University of California-Los Angeles Medical Center in Torrance.

One concern raised in the past about freely handing out the pills has been that women will come to rely on morning-after pills to the exclusion of regular contraception.

"Anybody who says that has not taken two Ovral and

exam and a determination of the length of the pregnancy. If there are no contraindications, the woman can take three mifepristone tablets then or at a subsequent visit, remaining under observation for a half-hour.

The woman will return for a second visit 36 to 48 hours later to take two prostaglandin tablets, which cause contractions of the uterus, helping to expel the fertilized egg. * She will remain under observation at the clinic for four hours. About two-thirds of women abort during this four-hour period.

The third and usually last visit will be a follow-up 12 days later to ensure the abortion is complete. If not, a surgical abortion will be performed. Doctors participating in the trial must be able to arrange surgical abortions, though not necessarily on site.

Norsigian contends that RU-486 "is not a better procedure [than surgical abortion] in any sense of the word." She points out that the vacuum suction procedure used in first-trimester surgical abortions in this country is "very, very safe," with an extremely low infection and complication rate. She predicts that many women will find the multiple visits required for RU-486 daunting. Moreover, a woman can't know ahead of time whether the abortion will take place at the clinic a few hours after taking the drugs or later that night at home.

"For many, many women," she says, "it's going to be unacceptable to have so much unpredictability about when the actual passing of the contents of the uterus will take place." Abortion can be "an emotional experience," she points out, and arranging for a supportive friend or relative to be there will be harder than with a scheduled surgical procedure.

Some experts contend that so many visits are not medically necessary. Women could, for example, receive the prostaglandin pills at the same time as the initial RU-486 pills and be told to take them at home later. That would reduce the procedure to two visits: one to receive the pills and one to make sure the abortion was successful.

In a symposium at the Institute of

* Mifepristone alone causes an abortion 65-80 percent of the time, according to the Population Council, but the effectiveness rises to 96 percent when prostaglandin is used.

. . .Using Birth-Control Pills for 'Morning-After' Emergencies

had to face two more 12 hours later," says Nelson. About a third of the women who take it experience nausea or vomiting. Because of these side-effects, says Nelson, "I don't think we're going to subtract from the numbers of people contracepting." On the contrary, she says, the crisis of impending pregnancy that brings a woman to the clinic provides an opportunity to educate someone who isn't using contraception regularly or to help someone find a more reliable method.

Of the approximately 3.5 million unintended pregnancies that occur each year in the United States, half are said to result from failures in contraception. Stewart and Hatcher estimate that the annual number of unintended pregnancies could be halved — and the number of abortions also cut by half, or 800,000 abortions — if emergency contraceptive pills were distributed more widely. The pills are generally considered at least 75 percent effective.[1]

Another contraceptive now under study as a morning-after pill could offer even greater effectiveness with less nausea, according to David Grimes, a professor of obstetrics and gynecology at the University of California-San Francisco. Grimes is studying the French pill RU-486, known most widely for stimulating abortions in early pregnancy. Grimes says it could prevent pregnancy if taken up to five mornings after intercourse. He plans to study the pill in 150 women volunteers as part of a worldwide study involving a total of 2,100 women.

The National Right to Life Committee opposes this use of RU-486 — as well as its use during pregnancy — because it "causes an abortion," says Education Director Richard Glasow. "It only functions after fertilization."

However, according to Grimes, it's unclear exactly when the drug exerts its influence. "It might work by preventing ovulation, it might work by preventing fertilization, it might alter transport of ovum in the [fallopian] tube, it might prevent implantation. We just don't know," he says.

Grimes does not consider morning-after use of RU-486 an abortion because it works before implantation of the embryo in the uterine lining. Implantation, which occurs one to two weeks after an egg is fertilized, is the generally accepted definition of pregnancy among gynecologists. Anti-abortion activists like Glasow believe life begins as soon as the egg is fertilized, which can occur from within a few minutes of intercourse to three days afterwards.

By contrast, Glasow's group does not oppose using birth control pills as morning-after contraceptives because "you don't know whether it's blocking ovulation or blocking implantation."

Scientists aren't sure either. "The basic mechanism we're counting on is that there will be a sudden increase in hormones," says Nelson. Once the artificially raised hormone levels drop, some scientists think, the uterus will respond as if it is time to have a menstrual period, sloughing off the endometrial lining before implantation can take place. However, it is also possible that the pills work by affecting ovulation or by disrupting the transport of the fertilized eggs through the fallopian tubes.

[1] James Trussel et al., "Emergency Contraceptive Pills: A Simple Proposal to Reduce Unintended Pregnancies," *Family Planning Perspectives*, November/December 1992, pp.269-273.

Medicine last year, David Grimes, who has conducted clinical research on RU-486, argued there is "no scientific foundation" for the frequent assertion that an RU-486 abortion requires "strict medical supervision." The scientific basis for more than two visits is "debatable," said Grimes, a professor in the Department of Obstetrics, Gynecology and Reproductive Science at the University of California-San Francisco.[11]

Grimes supports just one follow-up visit to make sure that all the fetal tissue has been expelled. He strongly favors bringing the drug to the United States, saying its safety and effectiveness were established long ago. "It would be a cruel hoax if we were to bring the drug to America and make it so cumbersome that women couldn't get access to it," he says.

The Feminist Majority Foundation, by contrast, points out that women often make three visits for surgical abortions: one to schedule the procedure, a second for the abortion itself and a third for a checkup.

Considering that surgical abortion services are unavailable in more than 80 percent of the nation's counties, Smeal predicts that pill-induced abortions will make abortion available to women who never had it locally. "Most people have family practitioners or gynecologists closer to them than they would have a clinic in rural areas," she explains. "It would seem to me when gynecologists and family practitioners realize how simple it is to do this procedure — and how much harder it would be to target them with protests — they would be more willing to do it."

One RU-486 activist questions why women should be limited to taking the drug in a medical setting, instead of buying it through a pharmacy like any other prescription drug. "It should be a matter decided between doctor and patient — not imposed by the manufacturer," says Simon Heller, an attorney at the Center for Reproductive Law and Policy in New York.

Heller represented Leona Benten, a pregnant San Francisco-area woman who challenged the Bush administration's import ban on RU-486 in 1992. Benten, 29, attempted to bring a dose of the drug into the country for her own abortion after a trip to Britain.

A Guide to Birth Control

The effectiveness ratings for birth control methods in the following chart are based on several studies. Sometimes birth control fails because of the method itself, and sometimes due to human error, such as incorrect use or failure to use. Each method has possible risks and side effects, and some cannot be used by individuals with certain medical problems.

Type	Estimated Effectiveness	Risks/Side Effects	Sexually Transmitted Disease (STD) Protection	Convenience	Availability
Male Condom	About 85%	Rarely, irritation and allergic reactions	Helps protect against STD, including herpes and AIDS	Applied immediately before intercourse; used only once and discarded	Non-prescription
Female Condom	An estimated 74 - 79%	Rarely, irritation and allergic reactions	Same as male condom, only not as effective	Applied immediately before intercourse; used only once and discarded	Non-prescription
Spermicides Used Alone	70 - 82%	Rarely, irritation and allergic reactions	Unknown	Applied no more than one hour before intercourse	Non-prescription
Sponge	72 - 82%	Rarely, irritation and allergic reactions; difficulty in removal; very rarely, toxic shock syndrome	None	Can be inserted hours before intercourse and left in place 24 hours; used once and discarded	Non-prescription
Diaphragm	82 - 94%	Rarely, irritation and allergic reactions; difficulty in removal; very rarely, toxic shock syndrome	None	Inserted before intercourse; can remain 24 hours, but more spermicide needed if intercourse is repeated	Rx
Cervical Cap with Spermicide	At least 82%	Abnormal Pap test; vaginal or cervical infections; very rarely, toxic shock syndrome	None	Can remain in place for 48 hours; may be difficult to insert	Rx
Pills	97 - 99%	Blood clots, heart attacks, strokes, gallbladder disease, liver tumors, water retention, hypertension, mood changes, dizziness, nausea; not for smokers	None	Pill must be taken regularly, regardless of frequency of intercourse	Rx
Implant (Norplant)	99%	Menstrual cycle irregularity; headaches, nervousness, depression, nausea, change of appetite, breast tenderness, weight gain, enlarged ovaries and/ or fallopian tubes, excessive body and facial hair; may subside after first year	None	Effective 24 hours after implantation for approximately 5 years; can be removed by physician at any time	Rx; minor outpatient surgical procedure
Injection (Depo-Provera)	99%	Side effects similar to those with Norplant	None	One injection every three months	Rx
IUD	95 - 96%	Cramps, bleeding, pelvic inflammatory disease, infertility; rarely, perforation of the uterus	None	After insertion, stays in place until physician removes it	Rx
Periodic Abstinence	Very variable, perhaps 53 - 86%	None	None	Requires frequent monitoring of body functions and periods of abstinence	Instruction from physician or clinic
Surgical Sterilization	Over 99%	Pain, infection, and, for female tubal ligation, possible surgical complications	None	Vasectomy is usually performed in a doctor's office; tubal ligation is performed in an operating room	Surgery

Source: "Choosing a Contraceptive," FDA Consumer, *September 1993.*

The drug was seized by customs officials in New York, and Benten underwent a surgical abortion. She sued the Food and Drug Administration (FDA), which administers the ban.

In January 1993, Clinton directed federal agencies to review the justification for the ban, which prevented even small amounts of RU-486 from being brought into the country for personal use under a doctor's supervision. But in May, FDA officials said they will keep the ban in place while the drug is being tested. Heller says he is considering reactivating the suit challenging the import ban. Although he concedes the ban is largely symbolic at this point, Heller objects to it as a precedent that the government "can single out women's reproductive health and treat it in a discriminatory fashion."

Several experts in the field believe the Population Council has taken a cautious approach to the drug's distribution in order to speed FDA approval. Most of the clinical data on the drug's safety come from France, where four visits are required. The drug has been used in combination with prostaglandin by some 25,000 women there.

"At some point way in the future, there is no reason why a woman couldn't take it in the safety of her home," says Waldman. But she adds: "This is a new drug here. The prudent thing is to treat it conservatively even though it's not a dangerous drug."

Should birth control pills be available over the counter?

It's the weekend, and you're out of town. You've run out of birth control pills, and your gynecologist's office is closed. Too bad you can't just run down to the drugstore and buy some more.

That's the picture painted frequently over the past year by prominent members of the medical community who urge the sale of oral contraceptives without prescriptions. Women may have achieved reproductive freedom with the advent of the pill, the British medical journal *Lancet* opined last September, but "these ex-prisoners remain on permanent probation — they must report to their doctors regularly for a prescription." [12]

"You find out that not getting a refill or not getting around to making an appointment or lack of insurance coverage are the kinds of things that keep women from initiating birth control use," says gynecologist Felicia Stewart of Sacramento, Calif., "and they end up with pregnancies they didn't intend." Stewart and four co-authors argue in the *American Journal of Public Health* that prescriptions impose "heavy costs" on women — not just in doctors' bills but in unintended pregnancies. [13]

The FDA scheduled a hearing last year to consider switching the pill's status but abruptly canceled it when the controversy heated up, saying they had not included a broad enough cross-section of views. [14]

Opponents of over-the-counter sales include consumer groups, many family planning clinics and doctors working with adolescents. "[F]or our clients — homeless women, runaway teens, women without health insurance, education or resources — it would be disastrous," the directors of the Los Angeles Free Clinic wrote last year. For many, noted Executive Director Mary Rainwater and Medical Director Susan Mandel, getting the pill is their only reason to see a doctor. About 75 percent of the clinic's patients have serious medical problems, they reported. In addition, buying pills at the drugstore would bypass the life-saving counseling about AIDS protection offered at the clinic. [15]

Moreover, Rainwater and Mandel added, low-income women can get birth control pills free or at reduced prices at family planning clinics. Even if, as expected, drugstore pills become cheaper, they wrote, "they will not be free . . . and how many women will decide to skip a day, week or month of pills because they ran out of money?"

In a survey of health-care providers for adolescents conducted in Boston this year by Tufts University researchers, 90 percent of the respondents opposed making oral contraceptives available over the counter. Most worried that without counseling adolescents would use pills incorrectly and that the shift wouldn't reduce unintended pregnancies. [16]

"At least we're getting some kids to take some form of contraception successfully," says Ann Davis, a survey co-author and director of pediatric and adolescent gynecology at Tufts New England Medical Center. "They need constant support to do it correctly. Adolescents don't think they're at risk; they think they're invincible."

"If a 17-year-old has normal side effects like bleeding and swelling breasts, she may stop taking the pill" if she has not been forewarned by a doctor, adds Michael Policar, vice president for medical affairs at the Planned Parenthood Federation of America.

Prescription pills provide an important source of revenue to Planned Parenthood's 165 clinics, which buy pills from manufacturers at heavily discounted prices and then resell them at a profit, using a sliding scale according to patients' income. The revenues help support many other clinical services, says Policar, especially for patients unable to pay.

James Trussell, director of Princeton University's Office of Population Research, is a leading proponent of over-the-counter distribution. "If we believe as a country that poor people's health care ought to be subsidized, there is a way to do it directly" — through health-care reform, he says.

But as Norsigian of the Boston Women's Health Book Collective points out, "We don't have national health care. If it comes over the counter, it's going to be harder for low-income women to get the pill."

As for the argument that prescription pills lure women into the doctor's office for physical exams, Trussell retorts, "Why don't we make provision of condoms conditional on physical exams for men? There's no question exams are good. But oral contraceptives don't have anything to do with this."

Underlying the policy debate is a fundamental difference in perception over the pill's safety. Over-the-counter advocates argue that the pill is safe for most women but that the prescription status makes it seem riskier than it really is. "A lot more women die every year from aspirin than from birth control pills," notes Grimes, "and there are no restrictions on aspirin."

Yet according to a 1993 Gallup Poll, nearly two-thirds of women believe oral contraceptives are at least as risky as childbirth. In fact, childbearing is twice as likely to cause death as taking birth control pills, according to the American College of Obstetricians and Gynecologists, which commissioned the survey. Only 6 percent of those surveyed were aware that birth control pills reduce the risk of ovarian and endometrial cancers. Eighty-six percent of those interviewed and 91 percent of those using the pill said oral contraceptives are not safe enough to buy without a doctor's prescription. [17]

One reason for the differing perceptions of the pill may be that its makeup has changed dramatically since the 1960s and '70s, when the pill "was considered dangerous," says Grimes. Since then the female hormone estrogen in the pill has fallen fivefold, and the progesterone has been reduced about tenfold, he estimates.

The pill is considered so safe now that experts say healthy non-smokers may use it well into their 40s. In 1990, the FDA removed the upper age limit on the information inserts included in packages. Previously, the inserts stated that women over 40 were at potentially higher risk for complications. The change resulted from "the reanalysis of earlier studies, the use of lower-dose pills and the recognition that it is primarily smoking and not pills which increases the risk of older women for cardiovascular complications," according to *Contraceptive Technology,* the bible of family planners. [18]

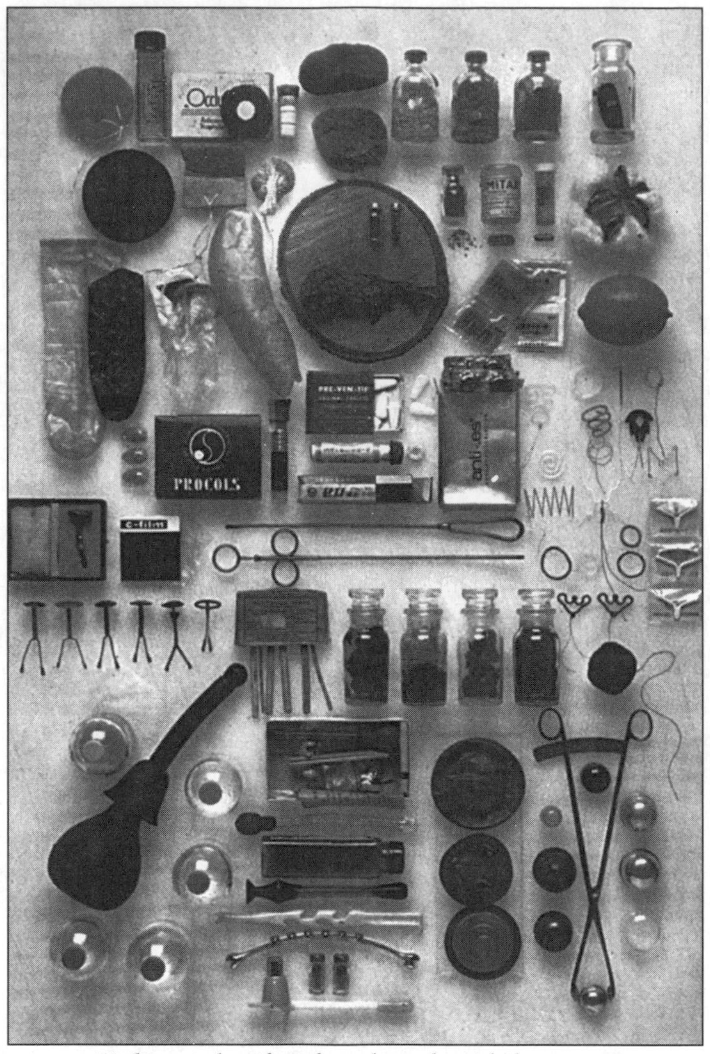

Poster courtesy Ortho McNeil Inc.

Birth control artifacts from down through the ages are displayed at the History of Contraception Museum in Don Mills, Ontario, Canada, maintained by Ortho Pharmaceutical Ltd.

However, most women apparently are unaware of the new outlook, according to a 1993 survey commissioned by Ortho Pharmaceutical Corp., the leading seller of oral contraceptives. Only 35 percent of the women surveyed thought healthy, non-smoking women could stay on the pill past age 35. But in the same survey, 96 percent of the physicians questioned thought it was safe.

Norsigian isn't convinced that pills should be sold over the counter, however. "What about the heavy smoker who happens not to read the pill package insert to learn that she should not take the pill?" Norsigian wrote last year. "Will we then blame her for any serious health consequences, such as stroke?" [19]

Norsigian notes there also are lingering questions as to whether young women under 35 who use pills for many years increase their risk of breast cancer (*see p. 660*). "That's the very group that's going to increase its use if it goes over the counter," she says. "That's why it's not smart policy at this point." ■

BACKGROUND

Sanger's Legacy

Since ancient times, people have used a wide variety of methods, some ridiculous and some effective,

Continued on p. 660

Chronology

19th Century

Many contraceptive methods exist, including condoms, diaphragms and cervical caps, but few Americans use them because of restrictive laws against birth-control information and distribution.

1873
Congress passes the anti-obscenity Comstock Act, forbidding interstate commerce in contraceptives and banning distribution of birth-control information.

1894
Charles Goodyear discovers the process for vulcanizing rubber, improving the potential distribution of condoms and diaphragms.

1900s to 1930s

Reformers fight to change birth-control restrictions.

1916
Margaret Sanger is arrested after opening the first American birth control clinic in Brooklyn, N.Y.

1918
A New York court says clinics can distribute contraceptives if prescribed by a physician.

1921
Sanger founds the American Birth Control League, forerunner of Planned Parenthood Federation of America.

1925
Margaret Sanger's husband establishes the first diaphragm manufacturing firm.

1936
In *United States v. One Package,* the Supreme Court allows the sale and importation of contraceptives by physicians to save lives or promote the well-being of their patients.

1960s

The birth control pill wins marketing approval in the United States and instant popularity, but reports of health risks rouse public concern. Manufacturers start reducing hormone doses in pills.

1960
Oral contraceptives first approved by Food and Drug Administration (FDA).

1963
By the end of the year, more than 2 million women are using "the Pill."

1969
Barbara Seaman's *The Doctor's Case Against the Pill* is published, alerting women to the dangers of the high-dose estrogen pill.

1970s to 1980s

The Dalkon Shield intrauterine device (IUD) causes serious infections in thousands of women users, spurring millions of dollars in lawsuits. Pharmaceutical giants drop out of contraceptive research, citing liability threats and regulatory burdens.

1985
A. H. Robins Co., maker of the Dalkon Shield, files under bankruptcy laws for protection against lawsuits. Upjohn Co. closes its contraceptive research lab.

1988
FDA approves the cervical cap for general use in the United States.

1990s

Several new contraceptives are introduced with support from nonprofit groups. Clinton administration liberalizes Republican anti-abortion policies and brokers agreement to bring RU-486 to the U.S.

1990
FDA removes any upper age limit on use of the pill. Drug makers stop warning women over 40 they are at higher risks for complications from the pill. Institute of Medicine panel says U.S. is lagging in world contraceptive development.

Dec. 10, 1990
Norplant is approved for use in the United States.

Oct. 29, 1992
Depo-Provera is approved for use as a birth-control injection in the United States.

Jan. 22, 1993
President Clinton orders federal agencies to review the import ban on the abortion pill RU-486.

April 27, 1993
FDA approves first female condom.

May 16, 1994
The maker of RU-486 says it will give its patent rights to the French drug to an American nonprofit group.

Continued from p. 658

to prevent conception. The Greek physician Soranus and the Roman naturalist Pliny the Elder described using honey as a spermicidal barrier and jumping backwards seven times after intercourse.

By 1900, virtually all the contraceptive methods now in use — except for hormonal methods such as pills, implants and injections — were available in Europe and North America. The earliest known description of the condom appeared in an account in 1564 by the Italian anatomist Gabriel Fallopius. Diaphragms and cervical caps were described in 1823 by the German physician F. A. Wilde. And vasectomy and sterilization were practiced in the 19th century.

Until the early 20th century, however, few Americans knew about, or could obtain, birth control. The legal suppression of contraception in the United States goes back to the anti-obscenity Comstock Act of 1873. The statute included contraceptives in its umbrella ban against the sale of pornography through the mail and interstate commerce. Under the act, explicit discussion of contraception was deemed obscene. The law continued to be influential for almost a century.

The movement to make contraceptives widely available in the United States is credited to Margaret Sanger, a public health nurse in New York. Sanger, who coined the term "birth control," began her crusade against restrictive laws in 1912 by publicizing the suffering and death among working-class women undergoing dangerous abortions.

Sanger was jailed soon after opening the first American birth control clinic in 1916 in Brooklyn; the clinic was shut down by police. In 1921, Sanger founded the American Birth Control League, the forerunner of Planned Parenthood.

Sanger challenged the Comstock Act but was only able to break the lock on contraceptives by making physicians the key to distribution. A New York state court, which upheld her arrest and conviction in 1918, found contraceptive advice to be within the law if physicians provided it. In 1936, the Supreme Court in *United States v. One Package,* a case involving a package of three diaphragms imported from Japan, ruled that contraceptives could be sold or mailed interstate if used by physicians to promote the well-being of their patients.

However, the legacy of the Comstock Act lingered into the 1960s and '70s. Although the first oral contraceptive was approved for marketing in 1960 by the FDA, it took two Supreme Court decisions — *Griswold v. Connecticut* in 1965 and *Eisenstadt v. Baird* in 1972 — to establish that the constitutional right to privacy includes the use of birth control devices. Not until 1970 did Congress remove contraceptives from the list of obscenities banned by the Comstock Act.

The Pill

The birth control pill helped usher in the so-called "sexual revolution." Starting in the 1960s, growing economic and social equality for women coincided with the freedom to defer childbirth offered by the pill with a new level of certainty. For many women, the pill also provided the psychological benefit of unhampered intercourse, answering the call issued by psychiatrist Sigmund Freud at the beginning of the 20th century: "The greatest invention some benefactor can give mankind is a form of contraception which does not induce neurosis." [20]

By the end of 1961, nearly a half-million American women were "on the pill." Within a year, the number of users had doubled; by 1973 there were 10 million. Since 1965, oral contraceptives have been the most common form of contraceptive in the country.

But early reports of the pill's negative effects soon clouded its image as a panacea. By the end of the 1960s, studies showed consistent associations between pill use and cardiovascular problems. [21] *The Doctor's Case Against the Pill,* a 1969 book by Barbara Seaman, alerted many women to the pill's potential dangers.

Protests by women and consumer activists, together with mounting research evidence, led to modifications of the pill starting in the late 1960s. Since most of the health problems were attributed to estrogen, manufacturers began to sharply reduce its dosage. Today's combined estrogen-progestin pill contains much lower doses of both hormones. And a so-called mini-pill, containing only progestin, also is available.

Cardiovascular problems are still linked to oral contraceptives, according to *Contraceptive Technology*. However, other factors predisposing women to cardiovascular disease, such as smoking and high blood pressure, are "far more important" than pill use in determining a woman's risk, the handbook notes. In addition, serious cardiovascular disease attributable to pills is rare in women who take today's low-dose pills, the book says. [22]

The Cancer Question

The most controversial question about pill use continues to be its effect on cancer. Because cancer takes so long to develop, there's no definitive word on what effect today's pills have on the disease. And it will be another 10 to 20 years before science can give the answer. (Most of the long-term studies were conducted with women who took pills with higher doses of hormones.)

The cancer question presents women with both positive and negative consequences. On the plus side, women who take pills are less likely to develop ovarian cancer and endometrial cancer than women who don't. And by age 55, women who take pills have no greater incidence of breast cancer than women who never take them.[23]

On the negative side, studies indicate that young women who took pills for many years face increased risks of breast cancer before age 35. The jury is still out on whether pill users are at increased risk for cervical and liver cancer.

The most recent study of pills and breast cancer, focusing on women under age 35 who used oral contraceptives for more than 10 years, reported a 70 percent increased risk for breast cancer compared with non-users of the pill. The authors also found a 30 percent increased risk for breast cancer among those who took the pill within five years after the start of menstruation. Most of the women used pills containing estrogen and progesterone.[24] The study focused on 1,500 women born after the mid-1940s — the first generation that had the pill available during their entire reproductive lives.

Biological differences may explain why younger pill takers are more susceptible to breast cancer than older women, the authors note. Under the influence of estrogen, breast tissue grows dramatically at puberty but slows after the first pregnancy. During this period between first menstruation and first pregnancy, cancer-causing damage could occur to the rapidly growing cells.

But the lead author of the study, epidemiologist Emily White of the University of Washington, does not recommend that young women avoid birth control pills. "It's my own personal feeling that the pills women are on today are not the same pills women were on during the course of the study, and it's possible the increased risk we saw would no longer apply to the current family of low-dose pills."

There's a lingering question about whether the increased risk experienced by this first generation of pill users will carry through into their 50s and 60s, when breast cancer becomes more common. Right now, breast cancer is so rare among women in their 20s and 30s that the increase in risk yields relatively small numbers of women with cancer. But at later ages, "If it's a small risk added on to a big risk, then it's more important," White says.

Most family planning experts conclude that, all in all, women who take pills have less risk of hospitalization or death than women who don't. "There's very unanimous opinion that the net effect on years of life is positive, not negative," says gynecologist Stewart.

Alexander of NIH calls the pill "amazingly safe. It's been unjustly maligned."

Yet many women remain leery. The National Women's Health Network argues that although today's pills with lower estrogen dosages do seem safer than pills from the 1960s, there is no data yet to support the claim that they have all the positive effects — such as reducing the risk of ovarian cancer — and none of the negative effects of higher-dose pills.

"Many of us are uneasy about taking a medication that affects almost every organ in our bodies each day for months and years, because its effects have not been conclusively tested," says the latest edition of *Our Bodies, Ourselves.*[25]

> "In the 1980s, the AIDS epidemic prompted new interest in the protective powers of barrier methods, which had attracted minimal interest from the scientific community since the advent of the Pill."

The Influence of AIDS

In the 1980s, the AIDS epidemic prompted new interest in the protective powers of barrier methods, which had attracted minimal interest from the scientific community since the advent of the pill. In 1988, the FDA approved the cervical cap, a thimble-shaped rubber cap that fits snugly over a woman's cervix. A woman can wear it and be protected for two days — twice as long as a diaphragm — and some people say it interferes less with sexual sensation.

Ironically, versions of the cap had been popular in the United States in the early 20th century. But the rise of the pill and the IUD eroded the cap's popularity, and by the mid-1960s U.S. companies had stopped producing it. It took nearly a decade for women's health groups and a coalition of doctors and nurses to shepherd it through the FDA's newly required trials for birth control devices.

Last April, the FDA approved the Reality Female Condom, which it called the first female product to offer "limited protection against sexually transmitted diseases." The device consists of a polyurethane sheath with a flexible ring on each end. One ring is inserted into the vagina much like a diaphragm. The other remains par-

Once Hailed as 'Dream' Contraceptive . . .

The woman calling Dr. Robert A. Hatcher at Grady Memorial Hospital in Atlanta last month was scared. She told Hatcher she was suffering severe headaches, temporary loss of vision, dizziness and nausea — all side effects associated with Norplant, a contraceptive that lasts up to five years. The problem, she explained, was that her own doctor wouldn't remove the small, hormone-filled capsules inserted just under the skin of her right arm. He feared a suit if the removal was difficult or painful.

That same week, newspapers were reporting that some 400 women were seeking to join a class action suit against the company that sells Norplant, Wyeth-Ayerst Laboratories. The women contend they suffered severe pain and scarring when their doctors removed the six matchstick-sized capsules. A Cook County, Ill., judge certified the suit as a class action in June, making any woman who has suffered injury from a Norplant removal eligible to join in the lawsuit. [1]

Creating further concern among Norplant patients and their doctors was a press report about a Birmingham, Ala., woman who died this spring after undergoing general anesthesia for Norplant removal. [2]

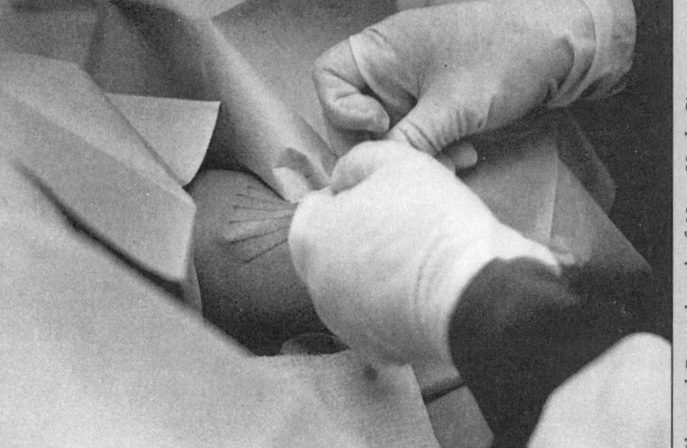

Planned Parenthood of New York City

A physician implants Norplant in a woman's arm.

Norplant was once hailed as a dream contraceptive by population planners because of its long-acting nature and its lack of interference with sexual intercourse. Yet practical problems with removal and ethical questions about its potential as a tool of social coercion have arisen as the nation gains real-life experience with the contraceptive.

Indeed, the demand for the implant has exceeded expectations. Over 900,000 women have had it inserted since its introduction in 1991, according to Wyeth-Ayerst. Some clinics have reported waiting lists for the implant.

Yet problems with side effects, which may also include heavy bleeding or disrupted menstrual patterns, lead some women to discontinue it. According to company surveys, about 10-12 percent of women request removal after the second year. That is lower than the company's initial prediction of 20 percent yearly based on clinical trials with women volunteers, according to Audrey Ashby, a Wyeth-Ayerst spokeswoman. By comparison, only about 50-75 percent of women taking birth control pills continue taking them after one year.

Wyeth-Ayerst contends that Norplant capsules can be removed in as little as 15-20 minutes, with minimal pain or scarring, if the doctor has had proper training in both insertion and removal. If the implant has been buried too deeply to begin with, the doctor will have a more difficult time removing it. The company says it has trained about 28,000 doctors in its technique. But there is no requirement that a doctor undergo training to obtain the device. In addition to damages, the lawsuit filed against Wyeth-Ayerst in Chicago seeks an injunction to prevent the company from selling the contraceptive to doctors who have not been trained to insert and remove it.

"We believe that class-action litigation is inappropriate because Norplant removal is an individual procedure that is affected by a number of variables," said the laboratory's medical director, Marc W. Deitch.

Hatcher, a professor of gynecology and obstetrics at Emory University School of Medicine and director of Grady Memorial Hospital's Family Planning Program, says he has seen patients for whom removal of the implants has taken much longer than 15 minutes. He described one patient who had suffered in agony for an hour as her doctor, using the small amount of local anesthesia recommended by Wyeth, unsuccessfully jabbed instruments into her arm.

Using his own removal technique, which calls for more local anesthesia and a deeper incision, Hatcher removed the implant in 18 minutes. The Emory technique is described in Hatcher's authoritative manual *Contraceptive Technology*.

In addition to removal problems, Norplant has faced a storm of controversy over its use to coerce poor, black women to stop having children.

Darlene Johnson, 27, unmarried and pregnant with her fifth child, was convicted in California of beating two of her children. At her January 1991 sentencing, Judge Howard

tially outside covering the labia. The female condom should start appearing on store shelves in August, according to Wisconsin Pharmacal, the distributor.

Development Hurdles

In the early 1970s, some 13 companies, eight of them American, were active in contraceptive research and development. By the mid-1980s, nine major companies had abandoned large-scale efforts, leaving only one big U.S. company, Ortho Pharmaceu-

. . . Norplant Faces Ethical and Practical Problems

Broadman of Tulare County Superior Court told Johnson that she could avoid prison by agreeing to use Norplant as a condition of her probation. Although Johnson originally agreed, she changed her mind a day or so later, and her attorneys appealed the order. In 1992, California's Fifth District Court of Appeal dismissed the case as moot because Johnson had violated her probation by using cocaine. [3]

"[W]e are witnessing the aggressive imposition of punitive birth control measures on poor women and women of color in the United States, just as sterilization and other so-called population control measures have been forced upon African-American women and new immigrants," said Julia Scott, director of public education and policy for the National Black Women's Health Project in Atlanta. [4]

"Your heart is torn when you see something like" Darlene Johnson's child-abuse history, concedes New York attorney Catherine Albisa. Her public interest law firm, the Center for Reproductive Law and Policy, represented Johnson. "These aren't sympathetic situations, but the fact is it's a violation of the constitutional right to privacy."

Albisa points to the famous 1942 Supreme Court case *Skinner v Oklahoma,* which declared it unconstitutional to sterilize a rapist. "If you had judges sterilizing women — even though in that particular case many people may not think it's a bad idea — it's going to end up being a bad policy decision that erodes all of our privacy rights and that is likely to be used arbitrarily, in a racially based way and only against women."

Johnson's case has continued to haunt the debate over contraceptives. As of June, legislation had been introduced in at least eight states that would make Norplant a condition of welfare benefits, according to the National Abortion and Reproductive Rights Action League. Scott says society should be dealing with root causes of poverty, like joblessness and health care, rather than "halting the fertility of certain women."

Norplant is "tempting" to policy-makers and judges as a tool for more general policy purposes because it "offers opportunities for surveillance and mandated compliance that other forms of contraception don't really lend themselves to," says Bruce Jennings, executive director of the Hastings Center in Briarcliff Manor, N.Y., which studies medical ethics.

Scott says her original fears about Norplant have been borne out in conversations with women on Medicaid who go to federally subsidized clinics. "We've heard from poor women that they've been moved toward Norplant as opposed to the full range of birth-control methods," Scott says. "The information has been slanted. They're not told the level of side effects — headaches, weight gain and depression that can put them more at risk of some diseases more prevalent in black populations [like] hypertension and diabetes."

A survey conducted last summer by Albisa's center found that some states will pay to insert Norplant in Medicaid recipients but will not pay to remove the capsules if the woman simply changes her mind. The three states — South Dakota, South Carolina and Oklahoma — required the woman to show a serious health problem before they would pay for removal, according to Albisa. A South Dakota woman who gained 50 pounds was told her implants could not be removed because her complaints were not on the official list of side effects, Albisa says.

"Basically, they didn't want these girls to be having kids," she says, "and they felt they could substitute their judgment for them."

But there's another side to the coin, notes Jennings. An unwanted pregnancy can be just as "coercive" to a teenager in the way it disrupts her life and hampers her future opportunities for education and work. Since it's probably impossible for contraceptive counselors to be totally objective, he still favors counseling, even if it is heavy-handed.

"It's puzzling that we have not greeted this development more positively as a society," Jennings says. "What might have been celebrated as an important new choice enhancing freedom of women at risk of unwanted pregnancy, we've greeted as a threat, a danger, a tool of repression."

In fact, some have complained that Norplant should be more widely available for poor women. At a congressional hearing in March, Surgeon General Jocelyn Elders said the high price of Norplant — $365 per kit — has deprived poor women of the most effective means of avoiding unplanned pregnancies. A spokesman for Wyeth-Ayers said the company planned to cut the price of Norplant substantially in December 1995. Until then, testified a witness for the company, the higher commercial price gives private doctors incentives to undergo training in removal and insertion. [5]

[1] Tamar Lewin, "'Dream' Contraceptive's Nightmare," *The New York Times,* July 8, 1994, p. 10.

[2] "Norplant removal death blamed on use of general anesthesia," *Contraceptive Technology Update,* July 1994, pp. 90, 97.

[3] The Associated Press, "Birth Curb Order Is declared Moot," *The New York Times,* April 15, 1992, p. 23.

[4] Quoted in Sarah E. Samuels and Mark D. Smith, *Norplant and Poor Women* (1992).

tical, and two European firms, Organon and Schering, still active.

Several of the companies, including Upjohn, cited the threat of multimillion-dollar lawsuits and difficulties in obtaining liability insurance. Others blamed FDA regulations that required years of study and deliberation to bring a product to market.

The liability difficulties stemmed to a great extent from the tragedy of the Dalkon Shield, an IUD manufactured by A. H. Robins Co. Before it was taken off the market in the late 1970s, the Dalkon Shield was found to have caused serious, at times fatal, pelvic inflammatory disease in thousands of users. In August 1985, Robins filed under bankruptcy laws for protection against the many suits against it. Other major manufacturers soon pulled their IUDs off the market.

In 1988, a small Somerville, N.J., company, GynoPharma Inc., started marketing a new IUD under the trade name ParaGard, after obtaining the license from the Population Council. While this IUD still commands barely 1 percent of the American market, it has not been plagued by either the health scandals or the litigation that doomed the Dalkon Shield. One reason, experts say, is that women must sign an informed-consent form that discusses the risks and limitations of the device in stark detail.

But some scientists blamed women for exaggerating the dangers of contraceptives and setting off a chain reaction of caution. In his 1992 autobiography, scientist Carl Djerassi, who developed the birth control pill, attributed declining industry interest in contraceptive development to "hysteria" whipped up by women activists over the pill's rare serious side effects. He blamed congressional hearings held in 1970 by Sen. Gaylord Nelson, D-Wis., which publicized emerging health questions about the pill, for setting off a new era of "hypercaution" within FDA that kept contraceptives off the market for years after they had been approved in Europe.

"[I]n the end, the combination of anti-pill women activists and this politically liberal Democrat [Nelson] . . . inadvertently caused the startling deterioration in contraceptive development which began around 1970," Djerassi contended.[26]

Role of Nonprofits

In response to dwindling industry interest in the 1980s, three nonprofit organizations — the Population Council, Family Health International and CONRAD — started to play a growing role in developing new contraceptives.

But these groups have been hampered by smaller budgets and less marketing experience than drug companies. In a 1990 report on contraceptive development, an Institute of Medicine panel described the United States as lagging years behind Europe and some other countries in getting new contraceptives to the public.[27]

The panel noted it had taken almost 20 years from the time the Population Council first proposed the Norplant concept to filing with the FDA for approval. "A large pharmaceutical company that routinely processes a number of new drug applications would probably have [acted] in a more timely manner," the panel said.[28]

Nevertheless, several new products have been introduced to the American market since 1990, and two of them — Norplant and the female condom — are due to nonprofit groups. In both cases, nonprofits paid for the expensive clinical trials to lure private industry onto the marketing stage. For the female condom, CONRAD conducted the trials for the manufacturer, Wisconsin Pharmacal, which promised discounted prices to family planning clinics and the U.S. Agency for International Development.

In the case of Norplant, which won FDA approval in December 1990, the Population Council paid for five years of studies on American women before handing the product over to Wyeth-Ayerst. In return, Wyeth provided its patented contraceptive steroid levonorgestrel for the product and agreed to keep the price of Norplant lower than birth control pills, says council President Wayne Bardin.

Other new products introduced in the 1990s include Upjohn's Depo-Provera, a synthetic hormone injection that provides contraceptive protection for three months, approved in October 1992, and the spermicidal Today sponge, approved in April 1993. ■

CURRENT SITUATION

Limited Profits?

The introduction of Norplant in February 1991 and its surprising popularity roused other American companies' interest in contraceptives. "For 30 years, there was nothing," says Audrey Ashby, director of public relations at Wyeth-Ayerst. "We feel that Norplant opened the door."

More than 900,000 women in the United States have had Norplant inserted since its introduction, according to Ashby, a sign the product is doing "very well."

But the interest in Norplant has not necessarily translated into big private-sector investments in contraceptive research. "There aren't great new things coming out of the labs of the pharmaceutical companies," says CONRAD's Gabelnick.

And Bardin detects a "dampening of interest" in the past year among pharmaceutical companies. He attributes it to uncertainty about how national health reform might affect drug companies' profits and the current FDA moratorium on silicone breast implants, which could stall development of future contraceptives.

"A few years ago, we were very optimistic that other companies would be coming back into the market," says Bardin. "I'm not so sure of that now."

One reason may be that big companies see no fundamentally new technologies with big enough profit potential to make investment worthwhile. That's the conclusion of a survey of the industry prepared last year by a Seattle

Continued on p. 667

At Issue:

Should oral contraceptives be available without a prescription?

yes

James Trussell, Felicia Stewart, Malcolm Potts, Felicia Guest and Charlotte Ellertson

FROM *AMERICAN JOURNAL OF PUBLIC HEALTH,* AUGUST 1993

In the United States, historical circumstances and health concerns once restricted all decisions regarding access to contraceptives to physicians. Eighty percent of American women now use oral contraceptives during their lives, yet these contraceptives have been provided only by prescription for the last 30 years. Because there is now considerable evidence for the safety of current low-dose oral contraceptives, we believe that it is time to rethink this practice. . . .

Whenever it is proposed that oral contraceptives be made available over the counter without prescription, two health concerns are commonly raised: safety and efficacy. First, women's health might be imperiled because some women who have conditions that preclude the use of oral contraceptives or who later develop medical contraindications would use these contraceptives, and because some women would cease to have regular gynecological exams. Second, efficacy during typical use might decline, and the risk of unintended pregnancy would consequently rise because women would be more likely to use oral contraceptives without clinical counseling. We argue that while both of these concerns are understandable, the health benefits of increasing the availability of this highly effective method of contraception by distributing it over the counter outweigh the possible health costs. . . .

Several over-the-counter options are possible. First, an over-the-counter system, managed by pharmacists, that uses a self-administered knowledge inventory could be organized to ensure that a woman understands contraindications and instructions for use before she is eligible to purchase oral contraceptives over the counter. Second, a toll-free telephone authorization process could be established, with a nurse available to administer a knowledge inventory and discuss the decision with a woman before authorizing a pharmacy to dispense oral contraceptives. Third, a fax or mail-in order form requiring answers to a self-administered questionnaire could be organized. Completion of this questionnaire would license a woman to purchase oral contraceptives over the counter or allow her to obtain them by mail order. Fourth, over-the-counter purchase of oral contraceptives could be allowed, but with the instruction that their purchase is not intended for first-time users (e.g., "If you have not previously used oral contraceptives, see your clinician before you start to use them"). Finally, over-the-counter purchase of oral contraceptives could be allowed with no restrictions.

no

Mary Rainwater and Susan Mandel

Rainwater is the executive director and Mandel is the medical director of the Los Angeles Free Clinic

FROM *LOS ANGELES TIMES,* SEPT. 17, 1993

There is one very good reason for making the Pill available over the counter: the prevention of unwanted pregnancies. But there are other consequences, unintended but certain to occur, that should make us reluctant to put the Pill on retail shelves next to the aspirin and cough drops.

At the Los Angeles Free Clinic, hundreds of women walk through our doors every day seeking birth control. Some of them are girls as young as 12; some are women who have already had four or five children. After taking their medical history, we give them a pelvic exam, as well as advice about the most appropriate form of contraception and life-saving education about protecting themselves from AIDS and other sexually transmitted diseases. They would get none of these things by walking into a drugstore and buying a month's worth of the Pill. . . .

For many of these women, getting a prescription for the Pill is their only impetus to see a doctor. Many of them are too embarrassed to ask for medical care, and too afraid of judgment or rejection for "shameful" conditions. However, their need for education and counseling about birth-control options is strong enough to get them through our doors.

Once they're here, we find that about 75 percent of them have medical problems that need immediate attention, ranging from dangerously high blood pressure to venereal disease to HIV infection. Some of these problems need to be addressed before they could safely take the Pill, or require monitoring after starting the Pill. When we talk with women during exams we hear about less evident underlying problems: domestic violence, homelessness, drug or alcohol abuse and depression. We can respond to these; the Pill cannot.

The Pill is an excellent form of birth control for many women; for others it is not the right choice. For instance, women with high blood pressure, diabetes, or a history of breast cancer, should not take the Pill. In addition to medical reasons, there are lifestyle reasons; women who have sex twice a year should not take the Pill.

Yet without counseling, women would not be able to make an educated choice about the method of birth control that is best suited for their lifestyles and their health. . . .

None of this is foolproof. The best doctor in the world can't show up every morning and make sure someone takes her Pill (or stick around every night to make sure she uses a condom). But at least we try to address the whole woman. She knows there's a human being she can turn to for help, not a printed information sheet that she may or may not be able to read.

Contraceptives for Tomorrow — and the 21st Century

Barrier Methods

Lea's Shield: A one-size-fits-all diaphragm-type device that has been approved in Canada and several European countries. A large-scale U.S. clinical study was completed last year. But an official of Yama Inc., the Millburn, N.J., developer and manufacturer, says it can't predict when the product will be available because additional studies may be required by the FDA.

Femcap: A cervical caplike device that comes in three sizes. Approval expected by end of the decade.

Disposable Diaphragm: A diaphragm that would release the traditional spermicide nonoxynol-9. Not clear whether it would be available before the end of the century.

Polyurethane male condom: A new polyurethane condom, produced by London International Group, was cleared for marketing by the Food and Drug Administration (FDA) last year. It reportedly has improved feel and durability. Other types are being tested in volunteers.

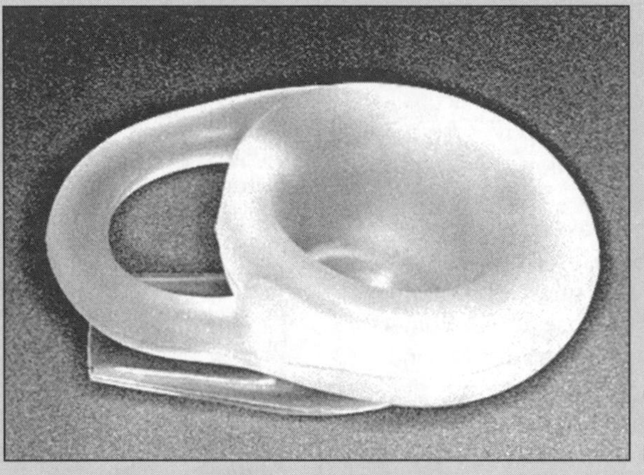
Yama Inc.

Lea's Shield

Chemical Barriers

Researchers are looking at alternatives to current spermicides in an effort to find something that would be less irritating to vaginal tissue and would also protect against sexually transmitted diseases. Some versions are in early testing. These products could be as long as 7-10 years away from marketing.

Hormonal Methods

Rings: The most likely candidate in the hunt for new contraceptives in the next few years is a doughnut-shaped rubber ring inserted into the woman's vagina that releases low doses of synthetic hormones. The advantage is that a woman could insert or remove it whenever she wished but it could be effective for six months or longer. Expected by the year 2000.

Implants: An improved version of Norplant containing two rods instead of six — easing removal — could go on the U.S. market as early as 1995. A one-capsule implant that would last two years is currently being tested. Biodegradable implants, which would eliminate the need for removal, are at least 3-5 years away.

Skin Patches: This device would deliver hormones through the skin and could be easily removed and replaced by the user. The Population Council has tested it in women volunteers and is seeking a manufacturer.

Injectables: Studies are ongoing on injectables that would contain estrogen as well as progestin in order to minimize the abnormal bleeding patterns that often occur with Depo-Provera and Norplant. One product being introduced by the World Health Organization, known as Cyclofem, could be registered in the U.S. within the next 2-3 years.

Intrauterine Devices (IUDs): A frameless IUD that would eliminate pressure against the uterus, minimizing cramping, is undergoing clinical trials in Europe. An IUD that releases the hormone levonorgestrel and reduces excessive bleeding has been approved in Finland and Sweden.

Vaccines for Women: The most advanced testing is on vaccines that interrupt the action of a hormone necessary to maintain pregnancy — human chorionic gonadotrophin (HCG). However, because the vaccine acts after the egg is fertilized, companies may be unwilling to pursue them in the face of political anti-abortion opposition. Vaccines that prevent fertilization are too early in development to be available this century.

Male Hormonal Methods: A drug known as testosterone enanthate has been tested in men for several years and may reduce sperm counts low enough to protect against pregnancy. Major drawbacks are a weekly injection schedule and a long lag time before it becomes effective.

Vaccines for Men: A vaccine currently being tested in men would suppress a brain hormone — luteinizing hormone-releasing hormone — which indirectly controls production of sperm. The vaccine shuts down the testes to eliminate not only sperm production but testosterone as well. To avoid impotence and loss of libido, the user would need to supplement the vaccine with testosterone. In contrast, a vaccine using another hormone important to reproduction — follicle stimulating hormone — has eliminated sperm but maintained normal testosterone levels in monkeys. Male vaccines are not expected to be available this century.

Sources: Robert A. Hatcher et al., *Contraceptive Technology (1994)* and the Population Council, March 1994.

Continued from p. 664
nonprofit organization with expertise in new contraceptive development, the Program for Appropriate Technology in Health (PATH).[29]

Representatives of several companies surveyed by PATH were doubtful of researchers' predictions that contraceptive vaccines would be available within the next two decades. Vaccines would be attractive because they could employ the body's immune system without causing hormonal side effects. However, researchers have not succeeded in developing a vaccine that is effective in at least 90 percent of women, the minimum standard for contraceptives, PATH experts said.

In clinical tests of women in India, 20 percent of the participants did not respond to the vaccine.[30] Many company representatives added that "vaccines would be extremely expensive to develop and, because they are long-acting, would not generate much profit."[31]

Authors of the Path report say that large pharmaceutical firms are more likely to tinker with marginal improvements in the big moneymakers — pills. "The profit margins on oral contraceptives are very large," says co-author Jacqueline Sherris, a PATH senior program officer. "Why should they bother to develop new methods?"

PATH suggested that nonprofits link up with smaller pharmaceutical companies — the "Ben and Jerry's" of the industry — because they tend to have less stringent requirements for profit margins on new products.

The PATH report also concludes that the bugaboo of the 1980s — consumer lawsuits over contraceptive products — has subsided as the main barrier to industry interest. "What we really found is that liability isn't a barrier in and of itself," says Steve Brooke, a PATH program officer. "It's always calculated into the risk of entering the market." What's more important to the pharmaceutical giants, says Brooke, is whether profits loom large enough to counterbalance future litigation costs.

One major problem has eased. Companies are now able to get once unobtainable liability insurance because many of them switched to self-insurance after the insurance crisis of the early 1980s, notes William Fay, executive director of the Product Liability Coordinating Committee.

Drug companies have shifted their concern from getting insurance to the cost of the lawsuits themselves, according to Fay, and the silicone breast controversy has only increased the concern. Fay represents a coalition of business organizations representing some 700,000 companies pushing for a new law that would shield a drug company from punitive damages if its product were approved by FDA and the company had complied with all FDA regulations.[32] Punitive damages are awarded in a small percentage of civil cases to punish and discourage flagrant conduct. By contrast, compensatory damages are awarded to the victim for harm sustained and tend to be much smaller in amount than punitive damages.

"The big thing that stifles development is punitive damages," Fay says. "Punitive damages are set at an amount to hurt a company financially."

A product-liability reform bill was under consideration in the Senate in June but appeared dead for this Congress following supporters' second failed attempt to block a filibuster June 29. The bill had strong opposition from consumer and women's groups, which said it removed important safety protections for consumers.

Getting FDA Approval

In recent years, the FDA has streamlined some of its processes for drug approval, according to nonprofit contraceptive development groups. But getting new devices approved, specifically those aimed at preventing AIDS, has become more difficult, they say.

Howard Miller, senior vice president for research and development at Family Health International, cites his organization's ongoing effort to get a new polyurethane condom approved. One advantage of the thinner plastic condom over existing latex condoms is that it permits greater sensation during intercourse and retains its strength if used with oil-based lubricants.

Because the condom uses a new material, FDA says the organization must prove not only that it doesn't break or slip but also that it prevents pregnancy among the volunteer couples who use it. That requirement has added another two to three years to what was once a six-to-eight-month study, says Miller, a requirement not made of the condoms now available for sale.

One reason conventional condoms have had to face less stringent requirements is that many of them went on sale before Congress passed a 1976 law requiring birth control devices to meet standards for safety and effectiveness similar to those for prescription drugs. If the FDA declares a new contraceptive device "substantially equivalent" to devices that were on the market in 1976, they can be exempted from the usual strict review. ■

OUTLOOK

Distant Visions

What if there were an IUD that didn't cause painful cramping and bleeding, or a birth control pill for men? What if women could protect themselves from AIDs without asking their partner to use a condom?

Contraceptives now under development would fulfill these and other visions — but the horizon for the most futuristic approaches, like vaccines and pills for men, continues to be at least 10 years away by some estimates. Male contraceptives under development that affect hormones tend to reduce men's libido, or sex drive, requiring them to take additional supplements of testosterone.

Michael J. K. Harper, a professor of obstetrics and gynecology at the Baylor College of Medicine, sees some hope for the new tools of biotechnology to manipulate genes to produce new, problem-free contraceptives. "Theoretically, if we make things more specific, they should have fewer side effects and should work only on the system you want it to," he says. He points to researchers' discovery of a mutant gene in mice that prevented a fertilized egg from implanting, and thus blocked pregnancy. No one knows if such mutant genes would work in humans, Harper notes, but "it's a lead. Maybe [researchers] can develop a specific anti-implantation drug or compound based around this."

In response to a Rockefeller Foundation request to reinvigorate contraceptive research, the IOM is launching a study in August examining promising new contraceptives that biotechnology research could bring to the fore. * Polly F. Harrison, senior study director at the IOM, says the study would also examine ways to engage industry's interest. "The sense is that pharmaceutical companies do not see brilliant lights at the end of any tunnels," she says. What they see instead is "no excitement, lots of risk, no profit."

Nevertheless, futuristic contraceptives will not be free of controversy. An Amsterdam-based international coalition of consumer and public interest groups, Health Action International, recently issued a call to suspend research on contraceptive vaccines. In a lengthy paper, it argued that several of the vaccines under study produce an autoimmune response, in which the body attacks itself.

In addition, with the versions developed so far, a vaccinated woman could unknowingly remain unprotected from pregnancy for several months while her antibodies gradually build up. Finally, the organization argued that vaccines could be used "coercively" by governments under pressure to implement population control as a precondition for foreign aid. [33]

"I suspect we're never going to get anything that's suitable for everybody," says Harper, noting that a 40-year-old woman who plans to have no more children may want something very different from a young woman or a woman living in a culture where AIDS is rampant. "Everyone in the field recognizes we're not going to have any silver bullet. We need an armamentarium of different things." ■

Sarah Glazer is a freelance writer in Washington who specializes in health and social-policy issues.

* The report is expected to be completed by spring 1996. It has funding from the National Institute of Child Health and Development, the Andrew J. Mellon Foundation and the U.S. Agency for International Development.

Notes

[1] For background, see "Birth Control: The Choices Are Limited," *Editorial Research Reports,* Nov. 11, 1988, pp. 565-580.

[2] The nonprofit group receives much of its funding from the U.S. Agency for International Development (AID).

[3] Program for Appropriate Technology in Health, *Enhancing the Private Sector's Role in Contraceptive Research and Development,* Feb. 25, 1993, p. 10.

[4] For background, see "Women and AIDS," *The CQ Researcher,* Dec. 25, 1992, pp. 1121-1144.

[5] Ruth Dixon-Mueller and Adrienne Germain, *Four Essays on Birth Control Needs and Risks* (1993), p. 8.

[6] Christopher J. Elias and Lori L. Heise, "Challenges for the development of female-controlled vaginal microbicides," *AIDS,* Vol. 8, No. 1, 1994, pp. 1-9.

[7] Susan Harlap et al., *Preventing Pregnancy, Protecting Health: A New Look at Birth Control Choices in the United States,* Alan Guttmacher Institute, 1991, p. 33.

[8] See Etienne-Emile Baulieu, *The "Abortion Pill"* (1991), p. 18.

[9] See "Accord Opens Way for Abortion Pill in U.S. in 2 Years," *The New York Times,* May 17, 1994, P. A1.

[10] Nina Darnton, "Surprising Journey for Abortion Drug," *The New York Times,* March 23, 1994.

[11] Molla S. Donaldson et al., *Clinical Applications of Mifepristone (RU-486) and Other Antiprogestins* (1993), pp. 183-4. The Institute of Medicine is an independent research organization chartered by the National Academy of Sciences.

[12] "OCs o-t-c?" (Editorial), *Lancet,* Sept. 4, 1993, p. 565.

[13] James Trussell et al., "Should Oral Contraceptives Be Available Without Prescription?" *American Journal of Public Health,* August 1993, pp. 1094-1099.

[14] Elyse Tanouye and Rose Gutfeld, "Talks Canceled on Making 'Pill' Nonprescription," *The Wall Street Journal,* Jan. 28, 1993, p. B1.

[15] Mary Rainwater and Susan Mandel, "Don't Sell the Pill Over the Counter," *Los Angeles Times,* Sept. 17, 1993, p. B7.

[16] L.J. Jacobsen et al., "Over-the-Counter Oral Contraceptives: The Adolescent Health Care Providers' Perspective," 1994, unpublished abstract.

[17] Sandra Evans, "Many Women Still Feel the Pill Is Hazardous," *Washington Post Health Section,* Feb. 15, 1994, p. 5. Neither the American College of Obstetricians and Gynecologists nor the American Medical Association (AMA) has taken a position on making birth control pills non-prescription.

[18] Robert A. Hatcher et al., *Contraceptive Technology* (1994), p. 249.

[19] Judy Norsigian, "Don't make the pill easier to acquire," *Chicago Tribune,* April 11, 1993, p. 9.

[20] *Encyclopaedia Britannica,* Fifteenth Edition (1993), p. 114.

[21] See Diana B. Petitti, "Safety of Birth Control Pills," pp. 77-116, in *The Pill: From Prescription to Over the Counter* (1994).

[22] Hatcher et al., *op. cit.,* p. 235.

[23] *Ibid.,* p. 277.

[24] Emily White et al., "Breast Cancer Among Young U.S. Women in Relation to Oral Contraceptive Use," *Journal of the National Cancer Institute,* April 6, 1994, pp. 505-514.

[25] Boston Women's Book Health Collective, *The New Our Bodies, Ourselves* (1992), pp. 279-80.

[26] Carl Djerassi, *The Pill, Pygmy Chimps and Degas' Horse* (1992), p. 132.

[27] Luigi Mastroianni et al., (eds.) *Developing New Contraceptives* (1990).

[28] *Ibid.,* pp. 63-64.

[29] Program for Appropriate Technology in Health, *op. cit.,* p. 29.

[30] Judith Richter, *Vaccination against Pregnancy: Miracle or Menace?* Health Action International, August 1993, p. 32.

[31] Program for Appropriate Technology in Health, *op. cit.,* p. 29.

[32] For details on the bill and debate, see Jon Healey, "Debate Over Limiting Lawsuits Nears Emotional Showdown," *CQ Weekly Report,* June 25, 1994, pp. 1687-1690.

[33] Richter, *op. cit.,* pp. 61-65.

Bibliography

Selected Sources Used

Books

Hatcher, Robert A., et al., *Contraceptive Technology*, Irvington Publishers, 1994.
This manual for clinicians contains clearly written chapters on each type of contraceptive, including descriptions of side effects and a summary of the existing research on safety.

The Boston Women's Health Book Collective, *The New Our Bodies, Ourselves*, Touchstone, 1992.
In this updated version of the groundbreaking self-help book first published in 1973 by the feminist Boston collective, the authors describe the pros and cons of birth-control methods in layman's language. Despite a wariness of hormone-containing contraceptives, the authors' description of each method's safety is generally balanced.

Articles

Barringer, Felicity, "Making Birth Control Easier Raises Touchy Political Issues," *The New York Times*, Nov. 18, 1992, Section 4, p. E6.
The approval of the contraceptive injection Depo-Provera raises questions about the potential for this drug to be used as a tool of social control.

"Clinicians, patients, Medicaid: Is anyone to blame for Norplant removal dilemma?" *Contraceptive Technology Update*, October 1993, p. 1.
Ethical and practical problems with Norplant removal are examined in this newsletter for health-care professionals.

Goldberg, Merle S., "Choosing a Contraceptive," *FDA Consumer*, September 1993, p. 18.
A concise, up-to-date discussion of the advantages and disadvantages of available birth-control methods.

Hoffman, Jan, "The Morning-After Pill: A Well-Kept Secret," *The New York Times Magazine*, Jan. 10, 1993, pp. 12-15, 30-32.
Many women and doctors still remain in the dark about using birth control pills as morning-after contraceptives, the author reports.

Trussell, James et al., "Should Oral Contraceptives Be Available Without Prescription?" *American Journal of Public Health*, August 1993, pp. 1094-1099.
This article by a group of prominent experts in the birth control field argues that oral contraceptives should be available without prescriptions.

Reports and Studies

Donaldson, Molla S., et al., *Clinical Applications of Mifepristone (RU-486) and Other Antiprogestins*, Institute of Medicine, National Academy Press, 1993.
This study conducted by a committee of the Institute of Medicine, a branch of the National Academy of Sciences, looks at the potential of RU-486 to treat a variety of diseases, such as breast cancer, as well as its application to medical abortion.

Harlap, Susan, et al., *Preventing Pregnancy, Protecting Health: A New Look at Birth Control Choices in the United States*, 1991, Alan Guttmacher Institute.
The New York-based institute, a leading contraception-research organization, provides valuable statistics and graphs on the health effects of contraceptives and contraceptive failure.

Institute of Medicine, *Oral Contraceptives and Breast Cancer*, National Academy Press, 1991.
This survey of the research discusses lingering questions about the link between birth control pills and breast cancer.

Samuels, Sarah E. and Mark D. Smith (eds.), *Norplant and Poor Women*, Henry J. Kaiser Family Foundation, 1992.
This collection of papers is a good cross-section of views on the potential for Norplant to help or hurt low-income women.

Samuels, Sarah E. and Mark D. Smith, (eds.), *The Pill: From Prescription to Over the Counter*, Henry J. Kaiser Family Foundation, 1994.
This collection of papers was presented at a June 1993 forum sponsored by the foundation to discuss the merits and disadvantages of turning birth control pills into a non-prescription drug. The report also contains a useful chapter summarizing the research on the safety of oral contraceptives.

The Next Step

Additional information from UMI's Newspaper & Periodical Abstracts database

Birth Control Worldwide

Baird, Jane, "Indian firms team up on contraceptives," ***Houston Chronicle,*** **Feb. 17, 1994, p. D4.**

Zonagen, a biotech company in Houston, said it has formed a collaboration with an Indian company, Reproductive Biotechnologies, to develop contraceptives.

"Cardinals back pope on population stand," ***Boston Globe,*** **June 15, 1994, p. 27.**

Roman Catholic cardinals from around the world gave their backing to Pope John Paul II's campaign to keep abortion and contraception off the agenda of a United Nations conference on ways of stabilizing population.

Kayal, Michele, "Czech abortions plummet," ***Atlanta Constitution,*** **May 26, 1994, p. A9.**

Contraception, long spurned as unhealthy, uncomfortable and just a great bother in the Czech Republic, is in vogue now as couples in the former Communist bloc abandon abortion as their primary means of birth control.

"World-wide: Clinton sought to find," ***The Wall Street Journal,*** **June 3, 1994, p. A1.**

President Clinton began his eight-day trip to Italy, England and France for D-day ceremonies with a visit to Pope John Paul II but conceded that disagreements over birth control and abortion may be unbridgeable.

Developments in Birth Control

Baurac, Deborah Rissing, "Sperm-sensing substance tested for contraceptives," ***Chicago Tribune,*** **March 20, 1994, p. 5.**

Researchers are working to develop an easy-to-use sperm-sensing vaginal contraceptive which would likely be used in diaphragms or cervical caps.

Beard, Jonathan, "Spermicide waits for the perfect moment," ***New Scientist,*** **Feb. 26, 1994, p. 22.**

A vaginal contraceptive that could be left in place for more than a day, ready to release spermicide at the needed moment, could be made possible in the near future by specially tailored polymers. This type of contraceptive would avoid the need for spermicide to be continually reapplied.

"Contraceptive may cut risk of breast cancer, study finds," ***Los Angeles Times,*** **March 16, 1994, p. A19.**

Efforts to find a hormonal contraceptive that also lowers a woman's risk of breast cancer look promising, according to a U.S.C. study published March 16, 1994, in the *Journal of the National Cancer Institute.*

Tanfer, Koray, "Knowledge, attitudes and intentions of American women regarding the hormonal implant," ***Family Planning Perspectives,*** **May 1994, pp. 60-65.**

Less than one-half of a national sample of 20-37-year-old women surveyed in 1991 report having been aware of Norplant, the hormonal contraceptive implant, within the year following its approval by the U.S. FDA. The considerable variation between groups of women in levels of awareness and in knowledge of the implant's attributes is examined.

Terrell, Gaynell, "Injections gain favor at clinics," ***Houston Post,*** **May 9, 1994, p. A1.**

Depo-Provera, a contraceptive shot that has been available in Houston's city clinics for less than a year, is rapidly becoming the preferred method of birth control among patients at Houston's seven public health clinics.

Vines, Gail, "Time to throw away your old contraceptives?" ***New Scientist,*** **April 30, 1994, pp. 36-40.**

There is a revolution going on in birth control for men and women. New birth control techniques are discussed, including those enabling men to produce their own gonadotrophin-blocking chemicals through gene therapy.

The Female Condom

Rodriguez, Patricia, "Female condom," ***Chicago Tribune,*** **May 19, 1994, p. E7.**

Years after first being announced, the long-awaited female condom should be in stores by August 1994. But early reports from the public health clinics already distributing the devices indicate that the condoms may not be the contraceptive breakthrough some had hoped for.

Trussell, James, Kim Sturgen, Jennifer Strickler, Rosalie Dominik, "Comparative contraceptive efficacy of the female condom and other barrier methods," ***Family Planning Perspectives,*** **May 1994, pp. 66-72.**

Comparisons using other female barrier methods as historical controls provide evidence that, among women in the U.S., the contraceptive efficacy of the female condom during typical use is not significantly different from that of the diaphragm, the sponge or the cervical cap.

Norplant

Holmes, Steven A., "Norplant is getting few takers at school," ***The New York Times,*** **May 3, 1994, p. A16.**

The Laurence T. Paquin School in Baltimore, established

for pregnant teenagers or those who have already given birth, is believed to be one of the first in the U.S. to provide students with the Norplant contraceptive. However, only 36 of the 700 students at Paquin have turned to Norplant in the 15 months that it has been available. The problems faced by schools and cities in trying to reduce the number of out-of-wedlock births are examined.

SoRelle, Ruth, "Psychiatrist: Norplant, depression may be linked," *Houston Chronicle,* June 8, 1994, p. A23.
Karen D. Wagner, a Galveston, Texas researcher, has identified two women who developed signs of clinical depression and panic disorder after the insertion of the contraceptive Norplant.

The Pill

Baurac, Deborah Rissing, "Pill a double protection," *Chicago Tribune,* Jan. 30, 1994, p. 1.
According to a report in the *Obstetrics and Gynecology* medical journal, women over 50 who have used birth control pills, even if only for a year, have half the risk of endometrial cancer compared with women who have never taken oral contraceptives.

Edwards, Sharon, "Reduced ovarian cancer risk quantified among women who use the pill," *Family Planning Perspectives,* May 1994, pp. 143-144.
A study found that women at risk of ovarian cancer who use oral contraceptives continuously for five years may have a 50 percent lower risk of developing epithelial ovarian cancer than do non-users of the pill. Additional findings of the research are discussed.

Winslow, Ron, "Study finds pill poses little risk of breast cancer," *The Wall Street Journal,* April 6, 1994, p. B7.
A new medical study shows hints of a slightly higher risk of breast cancer among baby-boom women who began using birth control pills two decades ago, when then were teenagers. Researchers are particularly interested in the impact of the pill on baby-boom women because they are the first generation to have had access to oral contraceptives throughout their reproductive lives.

RU-486

Adams, Jane Meredith, "150 women in U.S. to test RU-486 as contraceptive," *Boston Globe*, May 8, 1994, p. 2.
On the morning after, or even as late as five days after unprotected sex, 150 women will walk one by one into a room at San Francisco General Hospital, swallow up to three white pills and become the first Americans to test the French abortion drug RU-486 as an emergency contraceptive.

Caplan, Art, "What women don't know," *Los Angeles Times,* June 14, 1994, p. B7.
Caplan discusses the availability of the "morning after pill" in the U.S., and the need for women to know of their options.

Laird, Cheryl, "Morning-after pill remains secret to many," *Houston Chronicle,* Jan. 23, 1994, p. G1.
Some health experts say the "morning after pill," which disrupts conception by disturbing hormonal patterns if taken within 72 hours of intercourse, is America's best-kept contraceptive secret.

Perlman, David, "RU-486 volunteers jam S.F. clinic phone lines," *San Francisco Chronicle*, May 5, 1994, p. C3.
The Family Planning Clinic at San Francisco General Hospital was overwhelmed May 4, 1994, as scores of women telephoned the clinic volunteering for the nation's first clinical test of the French pill RU-486.

Use Among Young People

Greer, Germaine, "How careless talk costs sex lives," *Guardian,* May 2, 1994, p. 18.
Germaine Greer discusses why giving 12-year-old girls condoms isn't such a bad idea, saying that it doesn't mean they will suddenly become sexually active, rather that it gives them protection from pregnancy and disease and the freedom to proceed at their own pace.

Kreck, Carol, "Lincoln students to ask board for condom program," *Denver Post,* May 12, 1994, p. E3.
On May 12, 1994, at Montbello High School, students from Abraham Lincoln High School will ask the Denver School Board for a condom distribution program.

McMahon, Colin, and Carol Jouzaitis, "Taboos leave many teens unprotected," *Chicago Tribune,* May 24, 1994, p. 1.
Unlike their counterparts in Western Europe, American youngsters have unprotected sex at alarming rates, according to the authors. They consistently fail to use effective birth control because it's not readily available or because they are too naive, too embarrassed or too irresponsible. (Part 3 of a series).

Stacey, Julie, and Patti Stang, "USA snapshots: Sex without caution," *USA Today,* April 29, 1994, p. A1.
According to a survey commissioned by Upjohn, of the two-thirds of college students who say they are sexually active, 25 percent of men and 37 percent of women say they "often" discuss birth control with sex partners, and 47 percent of men and 32 percent of women say they have had sex without birth control within the past year.

Vobejda, Barbara, "Teens improve on prevention of pregnancy," *The Washington Post,* June 7, 1994, p. A1.
American teenagers have become more successful at preventing pregnancies, with at least 70 percent of those who are sexually active using contraceptives regularly, according to a two-year study by the Alan Guttmacher Institute that contradicts many common beliefs.

Back Issues

Great Research on Current Issues Starts Right Here...Recent topics covered by The CQ Researcher are listed below. Before May 1991, reports were published under the name of Editorial Research Reports.

JANUARY 1993
Hate Crimes
Child Sexual Abuse
Nuclear Fusion
U.S. Trade Policy

FEBRUARY 1993
Community Policing
Europe's New Right
School Censorship
Violence Against Women

MARCH 1993
Gay Rights
Aid to Russia
War on Drugs
TV Violence

APRIL 1993
Head Start
High-Speed Rail
Children's Legal Rights
Muslims in America

MAY 1993
Cults in America
Preventing Teen Pregnancy
Software Piracy
National Parks

Back issues are available for $4.00 (subscribers) or $7.00 (non-subscribers). Quantity discounts apply to orders over ten. To order, call Congressional Quarterly Customer Service at (202) 887-8621.

Binders are available for $16.00. To order call 1-800-638-1710. Please refer to stock number 648.

JUNE 1993
Food Safety
Prostitution
Childhood Immunizations
National Service

JULY 1993
Electric Cars
Population Growth
Downward Mobility
Intelligence Testing

AUGUST 1993
Mental Illness
Bilingual Education
Foreign Policy Burden
School Funding

SEPTEMBER 1993
Suburban Crime
Public Housing
Supreme Court Preview
Immigration Reform

OCTOBER 1993
Airline Safety
Disaster Response
Science in the Courtroom
The Glass Ceiling

NOVEMBER 1993
Paying for Retirement
Charitable Giving
Privacy in the Workplace
Adoption

DECEMBER 1993
U.S. Vietnam-Relations
Learning Disabilities
Child Care
Space Program's Future

JANUARY 1994
Racial Tensions in Schools
South Africa's Future
Worker Retraining
Regulating Pesticides

FEBRUARY 1994
Prison Overcrowding
Water Quality
Religion in Schools
Juvenile Justice

MARCH 1994
Underground Economy
Education Standards
Gambling Boom
Private Management of Public Schools

APRIL 1994
Reproductive Ethics
U.S.-China Trade
Soccer in America
Talk Show Democracy

MAY 1994
Traffic Congestion
Women's Health Issues
Mutual Funds
Political Scandals

JUNE 1994
Education and Gender
Gun Control
Public Land Policy
Nuclear Arms Cleanup

JULY 1994
Dietary Supplements
Public Opinion and Foreign Policy
Crime Victims' Rights

Future Topics

- ***Genetically Engineered Foods***
- ***Electing Minorities***
- ***Prozac***

THE CQ Researcher

PUBLISHED BY CONGRESSIONAL QUARTERLY INC.

Genetically Engineered Foods

Do they pose health and environmental hazards?

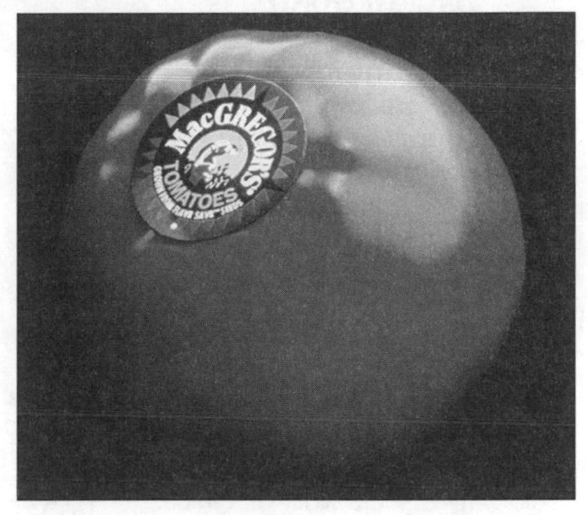

Genetic engineering, the science of moving pieces of DNA from one organism to another, is a high-profile component of the high-stakes world of biotechnology. It has produced new drugs, new ways of making old drugs, new insights into the genetic roots of disease, and aroused little public controversy along the way. But for years, genetic engineers have been using the same techniques to transform the plants and animals we use for food, and the fruits of their labors are beginning to reach the market. Supporters say genetic engineering will produce healthier, cheaper and better-tasting foods. But critics say scientists do not fully understand the impact genetic alterations will have on the nutritional quality or toxicity of foods. They also fear the technology has the power to produce unintended and dangerous environmental changes.

INSIDE THIS ISSUE

CQ August 5, 1994 • Volume 4, No. 29 • 673-696

Formerly Editorial Research Reports

Genetically Engineered Foods

The Issues

675 **Are genetically engineered foods safe? Will the public accept genetically engineered foods? Will genetic engineering hurt small farmers and milk producers?**

Background

681 **Technological Advances**
Sophisticated gene splicing techniques led to the creation of transgenic plants.

682 **Applications to Food**
Researchers say gene transfers will enable them to produce healthier foods, increase crop yields and reduce losses to insects and diseases.

685 **Risks and Benefits**
Critics say scientists do not fully understand the impact genetic alterations could have on the nutritional quality or toxicity of foods.

Current Situation

686 **Environmental Concerns**
Some critics fear that widespread cultivation of the new crops could lead to ecological disaster.

688 **Old Rules, New Foods**
Both the biotechnology industry and its critics worry about the adequacy of federal regulations governing genetically engineered foods.

690 **Consumer Confusion**
Supporters say consumer education will dispel the public's fears.

Outlook

690 **New Applications**
Common crop plants may one day be used to produce a variety of nonfood products.

Sidebars and Graphics

676 **Public Backs Labeling**
Public opinion is closely divided on the topic of genetically engineered foods, but most people want such products labeled.

677 **Will Public Buy It?**
More than half of those responding to a recent survey said they would switch brands or stop using a product if it was being genetically engineered.

683 **Chronology**
Key events since the 1960s.

684 **Regulatory Framework**
Three federal agencies share responsibility for regulating genetically engineered foods.

687 **The Labeling Dilemma**
Genetically engineered foods require labels only in unusual circumstances.

689 **At Issue**
Are genetically engineered foods safe?

For Further Information

692 **Bibliography**
Selected sources used.

693 **The Next Step**
Additional articles from current periodicals.

August 5, 1994
Volume 4, No. 29

Editor
Sandra Stencel

Managing Editor
Thomas J. Colin

Associate Editor
Richard L. Worsnop

Staff Writers
Charles S. Clark
Mary H. Cooper
Kenneth Jost

Production Editor
Sarah E. Merritt

Editorial Assistant
Michael M. Taylor

Graphics
P. Eloise Fuller

Published By
Congressional Quarterly Inc.

Chairman
Andrew Barnes

Vice Chairman
Andrew P. Corty

Editor and Publisher
Neil Skene

Executive Editor
Robert W. Merry

Associate Publisher
John J. Coyle

Marketing and Sales Director
Edward S. Hauck

The CQ Researcher (ISSN 1056-2036). Formerly Editorial Research Reports. Published weekly (48 times per year, not printed the first Friday of any month with five Fridays) by Congressional Quarterly Inc., 1414 22nd St., N.W., Washington, D.C. 20037. Rates are furnished upon request. Second-class postage paid at Washington, D.C. POSTMASTER: Send address changes to The CQ Researcher, 1414 22nd St., N.W., Washington, D.C. 20037.

Cover: A genetically engineered Flavr Savr tomato (Calgene Fresh)

Genetically Engineered Foods

BY SUSAN C. PHILLIPS

THE ISSUES

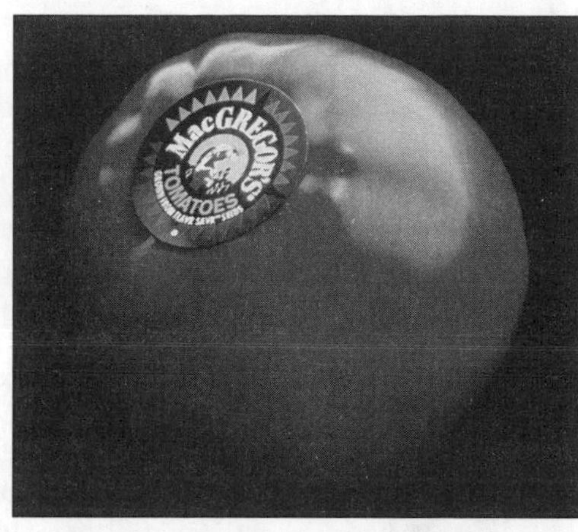

New Jersey milk distributor Mark Goldman has received almost 2,000 letters from customers thanking him for providing milk and dairy products from farmers who have pledged not to treat their cows with a new synthetic growth hormone. "People are talking about the impact [milk from treated cows] might have on themselves, on their small children," says Goldman, president of Farmlands Dairies in Wallington, N.J. "These feelings seem to go very deep."

James Corrigan, owner of the Carrot Top market in the Chicago suburb of Northbrook, Ill., has had a very different experience. He says people have been flocking to his store from all over the Midwest to buy genetically engineered Flavr Savr tomatoes. "It's been phenomenal," says Corrigan. "We started [selling the tomatoes] on a Saturday, very quietly, with our regular clientele coming through. We did samplings and the response was terrific. Then came a media blitz, and we've been shipping these tomatoes all over the country ever since."

Goldman and Corrigan are on the front lines of an emotional battle for the hearts, minds and taste buds of American consumers. Behind the uproar are recent advances in genetic engineering that are beginning to transform the foods we eat.

The synthetic growth hormone Goldman's customers worry about — known as recombinant bovine somatotropin, or rBST — was one of the first products of genetic engineering to be approved for use in food production. [1] Developed by Monsanto Co. and marketed under the name Posilac, it increases milk yields in lactating cows by an average of about 15 percent per cow.

The Flavr Savr tomato is the first genetically engineered food to reach the marketplace. (Monsanto's rBST is not a food, but a veterinary drug.) What distinguishes it from other tomatoes is an "antisense" gene, introduced through genetic engineering techniques, that slows the biological process by which a tomato ripens, softens and eventually rots. As a result, the tomato can remain on the vine longer before being harvested, yet remain firm enough to ship.

Most tomatoes sold in this country are picked while green and hard, shipped, then exposed to ethylene gas, which causes them to turn pink. The Flavr Savr, developed by Calgene Corp. in Davis, Calif., and marketed under the brand name MacGregor, is designed to offer a better flavor at a somewhat higher price during those months of the year when locally grown tomatoes, picked ripe, are not available.

Both the Flavr Savr and rBST seem somewhat modest products to bear the weight of the expectations and predictions being made on behalf of genetically engineered foods. Supporters say the powerful gene-splicing techniques of recombinant DNA will provide healthier, cheaper, better-tasting foods; reduce farmers' dependence on toxic chemicals to control weeds and pests; and increase the world's food supply to meet the needs of a growing population. [2]

Critics say scientists do not fully understand the impact these genetic alterations will have on the nutritional quality or toxicity of foods. They fear that as a result of genetic manipulations, allergy-producing proteins may spread more widely through the food supply. They also fear that the technology has the power to create unintended ecological disaster in the form of rampant weeds, voracious, oversized fish and rapidly evolving plant viruses.

Corrigan and Goldman have radically different attitudes toward these new gifts of science, and both claim to be answering the demands of their customers.

"I felt I'd rather be safe than sorry," Goldman says of his decision to spurn milk from cows injected with the new hormone, which was approved for use by the Food and Drug Administration (FDA) last November. "I was really concerned about consumer reaction, and I kept hearing different allegations made by some of the opponents about their health concerns. . . . Per capita consumption of milk has been on a steady decline for a long time, and I felt this was one more negative we didn't need."

Corrigan, on the other hand, believes properly educated consumers will embrace genetically engineered foods — as long as the price is right and the quality high. The much-hyped Flavr Savr tomato was approved for sale by the FDA in May, and Corrigan was one of the first to offer it to his customers. "I've eaten a lot of tomatoes, and I think the Flavr Savr compares favorably with most of what's out there," Corrigan says.

Among food retailers, Corrigan is a particularly enthusiastic champion of the union between food and technology. He does not sell milk that is identified as coming from cows *not* treated with rBST, noting that there is no reliable way to distinguish between milk from treated and untreated cows. He is one of a handful of retailers to sell irradiated produce and poultry. [3] And while he sells organic

Public Strongly Backs Labeling

Public opinion is closely divided on the topic of genetically engineered products, according to a recent survey by The Wirthlin Group, a consulting firm in McLean, Va. Forty-four percent of the respondents favored the technology while 47 percent opposed it. The vast majority of respondents said genetically engineered foods should be labeled as such.

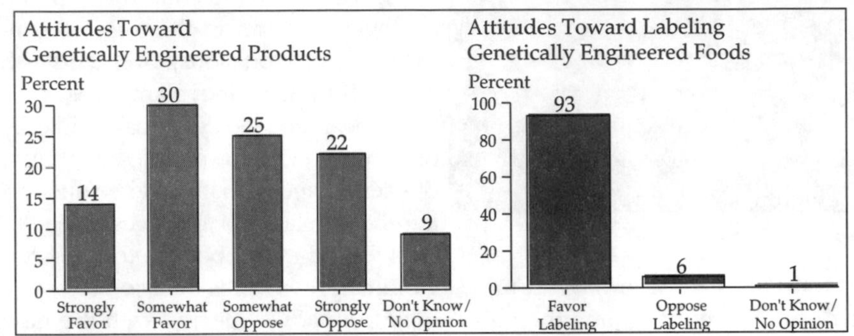

Source: Telephone survey of 1,036 adults conducted by The Wirthlin Group, March 14-16, 1994. Margin of error is ±3 percentage points.

produce, he does not label it as such, saying organic farmers do not follow reliable standards.

Anxiously watching the consumer response to both rBST and the Flavr Savr tomato are the creators of a new flock of genetically engineered products that are nearing commercialization. They include a recombinant growth hormone for pigs, which has been shown to reduce fat content in pork by up to 30 percent; potatoes that absorb less fat while frying, and others that resist bruising; tomatoes that resist freezing; and a virus-resistant squash.

As the controversy over genetically engineered foods heats up, here are some of the questions being asked:

Are genetically engineered foods safe?

Even some of the harshest critics of genetically engineered foods have conceded that the Flavr Savr tomato is probably safe. "Calgene, to its credit, has been extraordinarily willing to cooperate with the government in providing information on safety. . .," Margaret Mellon of the Union of Concerned Scientists noted in April, shortly before the FDA approved the commercial sale of the Flavr Savr. "To the extent the risk assessment on the tomato has been well done, it demonstrates that one biotechnology food product is safe." [4]

But the critics are not ready to accept the view of the FDA and many scientists that genetically engineered foods are as safe in principle as those produced through traditional breeding methods. (*See "At Issue," p. 689.*)

"Genetic engineering is, to my mind, in between conventional breeding and food processing in terms of safety risks," says Rebecca Goldburg, a senior scientist at the Environmental Defense Fund in New York. "In both genetic engineering and conventional breeding you are altering foods — but you now have access to a virtually unlimited number of traits that can be added, and that is certainly not true of conventional breeding."

"It's very clear that the only real answer to safety concerns is to have case-by-case studies done," says Michael Hansen, a research associate at the Consumer Policy Institute, a division of the Consumers Union, the group that publishes *Consumer Reports* magazine. "Right now there is no protocol for that."

Field tests on about 850 varieties of genetically engineered plants have already taken place or been approved by the U.S. Department of Agriculture (USDA), which shares regulatory responsibility with the FDA and the Environmental Protection Agency. (*See story, p. 684.*) The USDA also has approved a handful of tests allowing researchers to raise genetically engineered fish in carefully isolated outdoor ponds. Research on animals other than cows has been restricted to a small number of animals in carefully controlled laboratory settings.

A major seed company, Pioneer Hi-Bred International Inc. in Des Moines, Iowa, has added a Brazil-nut gene to a soybean plant, in hope of creating soybeans with a higher protein content for high-quality animal feed. But late last year, the company discovered that the new soybean causes a reaction in individuals who are allergic to Brazil nuts. * A company spokesman says Pioneer is continuing to test the soybean for research purposes but has no plans to commercialize it.

Scientists say the inadvertent transfer of genes that guide the production of allergens is likely to be a rare event, but Pioneer Hi-Bred's experience proves it can happen. Allergic reactions can range from mild discomfort to severe shock, and even death.

Under current regulations, genetically engineered foods containing genes from substances known to cause allergic reactions, such as nuts, have to be tested. If the new food is found to contain an identified allergen, it has to be labeled.

Critics point out that labeling would not guarantee that an allergic individual

---

* Even though the new soybean is intended for animal feed, the company is concerned about allergic reactions in humans; soybeans and their byproducts are used in so many aspects of food manufacture that it would be difficult to control the end uses of all plants grown from the altered seeds.

could avoid a certain food, particularly when eating in a restaurant or someone else's home. Children old enough to understand the need to avoid certain foods might not grasp the need to avoid a normally safe food containing the offending gene.

For people with unusual food allergies, genetic engineering will complicate an already difficult situation: Current regulations require premarket testing and possible labeling only in cases of gene transfer from food sources that are considered common allergens. The FDA has not issued a list of such allergens or guidelines to help companies determine what would qualify.

The possible introduction of substances known to cause food allergies isn't the only safety concern raised by agricultural biotechnology.

Some studies have shown an increased incidence of mastitis, an infection of the udder, in cows treated with the synthetic hormone rBST. Mastitis is treated with antibiotics, residues of which can turn up in milk. Exposure to low levels of antibiotics can make individuals resistant to those antibiotics.

State and federal regulations require dairy farmers to discard milk from cows that have been treated with antibiotics for a certain number of days, to make sure drug residues don't end up in the milk supply. Milk processors are required to test the milk they collect from farmers for antibiotic residues on a daily basis, and discard tainted milk. But critics say federal oversight of the testing is minimal and is only geared to detect residues of a dozen commonly used antibiotics.

The use of rBST also has been found to increase the levels of insulin-like growth-factor-1, or IGF-1, in milk. In humans, elevated levels of IGF-1 can cause abnormal enlargement of the hands, feet, nose and chin, and have been linked to the development of colon and breast cancers. Critics, led by Samuel S. Epstein, a professor of occupational and environmental medicine at the University of Illinois School of Public Health, argue that consumption of milk from treated cows could present a breast cancer risk to adult women. Critics also warn that fetuses and infants exposed to higher IGF-1 levels, either through maternal consumption, breast milk or milk-based formula, might be more susceptible to developing breast cancer as adults.

The FDA has concluded that the IGF-1 in milk is fully digested by humans, and therefore is not harmful. [5]

Many of the biotech foods now under development contain genetic material derived from non-food sources. For example, a gene from a wax moth is being used to develop a bruise-resistant potato. Since the safety of most foods has been established through a long history of safe consumption, these non-food genes may pose problems of allergenicity or toxicity that are not yet understood.

The bulk of genetic engineering experiments now under way on crop plants are intended to produce plants that are resistant to herbicides, viruses or insect pests. Could plants engineered to be toxic to certain bugs also harm soil bacteria, beneficial insects, birds or other organisms? Could pollen from herbicide-resistant crops transfer the resistance to related wild plants, creating super-invasive weeds? Could genetically engineered

Will Public Buy Genetically Engineered Foods?

More than half of those responding to a recent survey said they would switch brands or stop using a product if they discovered it was being genetically engineered. But the survey by The Wirthlin Group also found that lower prices might help combat some consumer resistance.

What would you do if you learned that a product you frequently use was being genetically engineered?

Look for another brand	41%	Don't know/Depends	6%
Keep using the product	38%	No Opinion	1%
Stop using that type of product altogether	14%		

Company A manufactures some food products that have genetically engineered ingredients and some products that have all natural ingredients. Company B manufactures food products that only have all natural ingredients. All other things being equal, would you buy products from Company A or from Company B?

Company A	5%
Company B	45%
Both	21%
No Difference	27%
Don't know	2%

If the products were consistently less expensive from Company A, would you buy products from Company A or from Company B?

Company A	26%
Company B	27%
Both	17%
No Difference	27%
Don't know	3%

Source: Telephone survey of 1,036 adults conducted by The Wirthlin Group, March 14-16, 1994. Margin of error is ±3 percentage points.

virus resistance spur the creation of new, more powerful plant viruses?

Charles Gasser, a former Monsanto researcher who is now an associate professor of molecular and cellular biology at the University of California-Davis, says most of the safety questions raised about genetic engineering are the same as those raised by traditional plant breeding techniques.

"In the 1930s or '40s, plant breeders introduced the trait for nematode resistance into tomatoes," Gasser says. (Nematodes are plant-eating worms.) "The trait doesn't come from an edible tomato; it comes from a different species, the fruits of which would make you sick. When breeders moved the resistance trait into the cultivated tomato, it brought with it 50 or 100 other genes. Now you can buy this product at organic farms. No one is worried about it."

Scientists using genetic engineering to accomplish a similar feat would be able to limit the amount of genetic information transferred into the cultivated host plant to the gene for nematode resistance. Gasser says this would be inherently safer.

Steven Taylor, a professor in the department of food science and technology at the University of Nebraska in Lincoln, was asked by Pioneer Hi-Bred to investigate the possibility that the company's new soybean might pose an allergy problem. It was Taylor who discovered that the Brazil-nut gene transferred into the soy was enough to transfer the Brazil-nut allergy to the new plant. Taylor says Pioneer's decision to call him in as a consultant shows that "industry will ask the right questions."

But Taylor also notes that genetic engineering makes testing more complicated. "If the genetic material doesn't come from a known food, there would be no history of it as an allergy producer, so there would be no way of testing for a reaction," Taylor says. To test the new Pioneer soybean for allergens, Taylor used blood serum gathered from individuals who are allergic to Brazil nuts. But he doesn't have any blood serum from people who are allergic to the wax moths that are being used to develop a bruise-resistant potato.

Calgene Fresh

Calgene's Flavr Savr tomato was the first genetically engineered food approved for sale in the U.S.

Ronald Cummins, director of the Pure Food Campaign, a Washington-based organization opposed to genetically engineered foods, argues that food technology has outstripped the regulatory framework that exists to ensure a safe food supply. "There are too many issues that need further study," he says.

Cummins' organization takes the position that genetically engineered foods should be regulated under the 1958 food additive amendments to the 1938 Food, Drug and Cosmetics Act, which call for strict regulation and exhaustive testing of new ingredients in food. "There's a need for long-term health tests," Cummins says. "The public supports us in that view. Survey after survey show significant consumer suspicion and opposition to unlabeled genetically engineered foods, and those concerns need to be addressed."

But federal regulators so far have agreed with researchers and the food industry that genetic manipulation is simply the next step in the long history of selective breeding to improve and change crop characteristics. "All plant breeding involves genetic manipulation," says James Maryanski, biotechnology coordinator for the FDA. "There are hundreds of new plant varieties introduced every year in the United States, and all have been genetically modified through traditional plant breeding techniques. The new biotechnology . . . is actually an extension of traditional plant breeding." [6]

Will the public accept genetically engineered foods?

Corrigan of Carrot Top market says he couldn't keep Calgene's Flavr Savr tomato on his shelves during its brief availability this spring. No one expects the superheated demand created by mountains of publicity and a limited supply to persist when the tomato becomes more widely available this fall. But supporters of genetically engineered foods were heartened by the public response.

"I haven't come across anyone who

[is] afraid of this tomato," Corrigan says. "The produce in this country is the safest, most beneficial produce on the market bar none."

"This tomato will cost more," says Robert M. Goodman, a professor at the Institute for Environmental Studies at the University of Wisconsin who worked as Calgene's head of research and development from 1982 to 1990. "But if it is better, and if people really do want good quality, good-tasting tomatoes year round, and if there is a regular supply adequate to meet the demand, it will be a hit."

Some observers predict that the Flavr Savr's acceptance will not translate to other products.

"This tomato is probably not that bad a thing," says Rick Moonen, executive chef of the Water Club restaurant in Manhattan. "It's the 50 to 100 things standing in line behind it that I worry about."

Moonen is the founder of a coalition of close to 2,000 chefs who have pledged to keep genetically engineered foods out of their restaurants. "I'm not closed-minded," he says. "But with so many greedy people out there, if the industry is allowed to be our curator for safety, we're going to have problems. We're going too fast."

It may be too early to tell what level of resistance genetically engineered foods will encounter. For one thing, many of the qualities now being engineered into foods are designed to help farmers and food processors. They don't offer a clear consumer benefit, so shoppers may be warier of them than they seem to have been with the Flavr Savr.

"This is why it has been so easy to make the argument against [the growth hormone] rBST," says Goodman. "It doesn't improve the taste, the quality or the nutritional value of milk. We already have a milk surplus in this country. . . . So there's nothing in it for the consumer."

Supporters of the new technology are calling for a comprehensive effort to educate consumers about genetically engineered foods. "Basically, the public is scientifically illiterate," says Donna Scott, an agricultural extension agent at Cornell University. "It's harsh to say, but it's true. People don't have the background to assess what's safe and what isn't, and that makes it easier for people to spread disinformation."

"There's been a big public education void in agricultural biotechnology," agrees Brian Shmaefsky of Kingwood College in Texas. "Right now, I'm in the process of trying to sell rBST back to the farmers — they've jumped on the anti-BST bandwagon and now they say it's bad." Schmaefsky, a professor in the college's biotechnology department, also directs a program that attempts to improve public understanding of biotechnology issues. "When you have Ph.D.s coming out with what seem like compelling arguments against it, and no one is really working the other side, then you worry," he says.

It's unlikely the food industry will be so thoroughly blindsided by consumer opposition in the future. Calgene's decision to seek FDA approval of the Flavr Savr tomato, an approval that is not required under existing regulations, was in part an acknowledgment of the risks of going forward without a thorough public airing of the issues. It was a decision that cost Calgene time, money and jobs, as delays in the FDA approval process forced the company to plow under its first crop and dramatically pare its work force. [7] But it may account for the fact that when the tomato finally made its debut, many news stories focussed on how it tasted rather than how it was made.

"This is an evolving process, and I think there is some new savvy within companies about what it is going to take to win consumer confidence," says Goodman. "One part of that is to come out with a product with clear nutritional and health benefits," such as lower fat content.

Will genetic engineering hurt small farmers and milk producers?

The National Family Farm Coalition, which opposed the approval of rBST, blames a recent drop in milk prices on the new hormone. "This product is continuing and worsening the problem of milk oversupply," says coalition spokeswoman Jane Kochersperger in Washington, D.C. "Why this product is on the market

"BOVINE GROWTH HORMONE MILK... GENETICALLY ALTERED BAKED POTATO WITH MARGARINE....
THE CRAZY FOOL WAS LIVING ON THE EDGE, CHIEF."

when we have a milk surplus and no supply management program to oversee it is mystifying."

Goldman of Farmlands Dairies also blames rBST for at least some of the recent price decline. "Milk has taken a lot of negative hits for a long time, and it has been outmarketed by a lot of beverages for a long time. People are already concerned that milk may be too fattening. They don't need more questions," Goldman says.

William Lesser, an agricultural economist at Cornell, says it is too early to say whether rBST has had any effect on milk sales or supplies. Lesser notes that milk prices usually drop in the spring because of a surge in supply. "We don't have any systematic surveys on the rate of adoption [of rBST], no information on how much rBST is out there. It will take six months to find out," Lesser says.

The National Family Farm Coalition is pushing for voluntary labeling standards that would allow dairy farmers who refuse to use the drug on their cows to advertise that fact. (*See story, p. 687.*)

The American Farm Bureau Federation, the nation's largest farm organization, takes the opposite position. "We don't think labeling should be allowed at all," says John Keeling, the federation's director of government relations. "As an organization, we tend to be market-oriented: If the scientific view is this is safe, then let the market forces determine if it will work."

Lesser believes rBST may push some small, struggling dairy farms over the edge, and that in general, the new technology will favor efficient, well-run farms of viable size.

If most farmers begin using rBST within the next few years, Lesser calculates, the number of cows and the number of dairy farms will drop by about 20 percent. "Right now, the unit profitability in dairying is so low, you need a certain size to meet an income expectation," he says. "Like a lot of sectors of the economy, the size you need for viability is increasing. . . . This technology may accelerate that process a little bit, but what you really have is the continuation of a long-term trend rather than a substantial shift."

U.S. Department of Agriculture

Consumer advocates say milk from cows treated with the synthetic growth hormone rBST should be labeled.

Lesser notes that recent improvements in breeding and feeding have increased milk output per cow by about 1 percent per year. Long term, the changes have been even more striking, with milk production per cow increasing from close to 6,000 pounds per year in 1955 to more than 15,000 pounds per year in 1992. The number of cows in the United States dropped from 21 million to 9.8 million over the same period. [8] The number of farms with dairy cows decreased from close to 1.8 million in 1960 to about 171,560 in 1992, according to the USDA.

Unlike some earlier improvements in dairy technology, such as milking machines and storage tanks, rBST does not require a heavy investment in equipment. What it does require, according to some farmers who have used it, is careful attention to feeding and overall conditioning of the cows being treated.

Posilac, the market name of the hormone, is now being sold in packages of 25 doses, priced at about $140 per package. Each dose is given by injection, and the cows are injected once every two weeks. Farmers who used the drug during pre-approval trials reported seeing an increase in milk yields two or three days after the first injection. Cows also eat more, and require a high-quality feed in order to sustain the higher levels of milk production.

Charles Slater Jr., a dairy farmer in Tyringham, Mass., says Posilac has had one particularly welcome effect: boosting the amount of milk he's getting from some marginally productive cows. Slater has been able to keep those cows in the milking herd longer, rather than have them slaughtered. "I can look out in the barn right now and see three or four cows I would have had to cull by now without the hormone," Slater says. "Now they're producing enough to pay their way. This time last year, I was so short of cows I had to go to the auctions and buy more. This year, I have more cows than I know what to do with."

Donald H. Beermann, a professor in the Department of Animal Science at Cornell who is researching the effects of recombinant porcine somatotropin, or rPST, says his work with pigs indicates that weekly or biweekly injections of the synthetic growth hormone make young pigs grow faster and leaner, while eating less. "It seems that the big uncertainty is the cost of the drug per pig," Beermann says. "My expectation is that it will be economically advantageous for producers of all sizes to use it, because the magnitude of the response is so great. . . . Even if there is no premium price for the leaner quality of the meat, the reduced feed intake is a big savings."

One potential disadvantage for small farmers, who have fewer hired hands, is the additional handling required to give young pigs the necessary injections. Cows are restrained in stanchions each day for milking, but pigs are not generally handled as much.

Monsanto, which is supporting Beermann's research, has not yet made a decision on whether or not to pursue commercialization of rPST. McDermott says the handling issue is one concern: If pork producers find the drug difficult to administer, then they are unlikely to use it. Pork also represents a smaller potential market than milk products, beef or poultry.

Lesser says that the genetic engineering now under way with major crop plants is unlikely to produce anything like the sharp milk supply increase expected from rBST use. The economic impacts are likely, therefore, to be muted. Smaller producers may benefit as much as larger ones, he adds, because higher crop yields or improved quality crops will be available in a simple, familiar, low-tech package: the seed.

"These kinds of changes should be quite neutral in terms of benefits, as far as farm size goes," says Lesser. "As with anything, if you're dealing with a technology that is more expensive or more complicated, the return is to better management. Enhanced productivity concentrates production on better-quality land, and leads farmers to abandon poorer quality land. The forces are pretty basic." ■

BACKGROUND

Technological Advances

The bovine growth hormone marketed by Monsanto is produced in vats by bacteria into which a snippet of cow DNA has been inserted. * The DNA contains the instructions for making the hormone, and the transformed bacteria work like tiny factories to produce it in large quantities.

The Flavr Savr tomato comes from a plant that contains an extra bit of tomato DNA that has been altered in the lab. The new DNA is a transformed version of a gene that would normally cause a ripening tomato to produce the enzyme that degrades pectin, leading the tomato to soften and rot. However, in this case, the gene has been "reversed" to block rather than promote production of that enzyme.

In each case, it is recombinant DNA technology that has allowed genetic material to be moved and manipulated in new ways. In the early 1970s, scientists first discovered how to replicate DNA in the laboratory, and how to introduce this genetic material into the cells of living organisms such as bacteria, clearing the way for the development of products like Monsanto's growth hormone. [9]

But while single-celled, rapidly reproducing organisms such as bacteria yielded relatively easily to the genetic engineer's manipulations, it took a decade for scientists to find a successful method for the genetic transformation of plants.

About 12 years ago, scientists at the Max Planck Institute for Plant Breeding in Cologne, Germany, pioneered what is still the most common method for creating transgenic plants. Not surprisingly, the technique relies on a bacterium for its success. The scientists modified the bacterium known as agrobacterium tumefaciens, which is responsible for a common plant disease. They removed its disease-causing DNA and replaced it with DNA producing resistance to kanamycin, an antibiotic.

The disarmed bacterium successfully invaded the cells of the target plants, in essence "infecting" the plant with antibiotic resistance. Since then, the disarmed bacterium has been successfully used to introduce dozens of other traits into plants, including the slow ripening characteristics of the Flavr Savr tomato.

The method has limits, however. It can only be used reliably with plants that are natural hosts for the bacterium. Some key crop plants are not, including rice, corn and wheat. New methods have been developed for genetically transforming plants, but none have proved as successful. They include introducing DNA into plant protoplasts, cells that have had their cell walls removed by enzymes; and shooting small metal particles coated with DNA through the cell walls of intact plant cells.

Gene-transfer techniques are far from foolproof. Sometimes the new genetic material is not successfully transferred to the target cells. Even when transfer occurs, scientists have limited control over where the new material ends up on the DNA chain of the target organism. This placement affects the way genes work, or whether they work at all. In one place on the chain, the new gene may inadvertently activate another

* Deoxyribonucleic acid, or DNA, is the material from which genes are made.

nearby gene that is normally inactive. In another spot, it may change or suppress the functioning of a different gene. In both cases, unexpected mutations may occur, making the resulting plant infertile or otherwise unsuitable.

One of the ways that scientists can determine if the gene transfer has been successful is by including a "marker gene" in the material to be transferred. The most common marker gene is that for kanamycin resistance, because of its history of successful incorporation into plant cells. After the transfer has taken place, the transformed cells are exposed to kanamycin. Those that survive can be assumed to have incorporated the new genetic material.

Unlike animal cells, plant cells are what is known as totipotent — each plant cell contains the necessary genetic information to generate an entire new plant. For genetic engineering purposes, that means individual transformed plant cells can be cultured to produce whole plants. Those plants must then be raised to maturity and fertilized to create seeds. If plants grown from the seeds also contain the new genetic information, then the transformation is said to be stable, a key to successful commercialization.

To date, there is no reliable way to remove the marker gene after the desired genetic trait has been transferred to the target organism. Some researchers have expressed concern that deliberately breeding antibiotic resistance into widely grown food crops may have unintended consequences, both for the environment and for humans and animals consuming the crop.

While scientists have the ability to perform similar genetic manipulation on livestock, to date the only transgenic animals that appear close to yielding commercial benefits are fish. This is largely because most fish eggs are fertilized outside the body. New genetic material can be injected into fish eggs without developing complicated and risky techniques for removing and then returning them into the bodies of female fish. In farm animals, the success rate in creating transgenic offspring is less than 1 percent. With fish, transgene DNA is successfully integrated in 10 percent to 70 percent of offspring. [10]

Applications to Food

In theory at least, genetic engineer ing techniques hold the potential to create limitless changes in the food supply.

"The beauty of it is, once you have the gene in one variety of melon or tomato or whatever, it's there in the seeds and people can move that gene into other varieties through traditional breeding techniques," says the University of California's Gasser. "It's incredibly low-tech."

Gasser says that if the slow-ripening characteristic Calgene introduced into its tomato could be replicated in other crops, there could be enormous benefits to farmers and consumers in the developing world, where refrigeration is unreliable and expensive, and transportation networks rudimentary. "In countries without the energy to preserve things such as frozen food, and without the technology for canned foods, the ability to have melons, squash or tomatoes that will last five times as long before rotting [would produce] an immediate additional supply of food with no additional cost or environmental effect," Gasser says.

Research by Beermann at Cornell has shown that pigs injected with rPST at critical stages of growth produce more meat while eating less, and that the meat itself is far leaner than that of pigs that do not receive the injections. "There is a dramatic growth in lean tissue," says Beermann. "We've seen no behavioral changes, no symptoms of pathologies or anything unusual at slaughter." He does warn that too much rPST results in meat so lean no one is likely to enjoy eating it.

Researchers at the University of Maryland Biotechnology Institute in Baltimore have created carp and catfish with the gene for rainbow trout growth hormone, and found that they grow larger faster than unaltered fish. Genetic engineers have armed Atlantic salmon with the gene for winter flounder antifreeze protein, in hope of giving the fish the ability to extend their range into colder waters. The same flounder antifreeze gene has been successfully introduced into tomatoes, in hope of creating a tomato that can be refrigerated without losing flavor.

One of the most active areas for research has been into the transfer of traits aimed at increasing crop yields and reducing losses to pests: insect-resistant apples, virus-resistant cantaloupes and cucumbers, and herbicide-tolerant corn, canola, potatoes, soybeans and tomatoes.

However, consumers may see a payoff in the next few years, as genetic engineers come up with solutions to all sorts of food quality problems — including a few that not everyone would recognize as such. Researchers at Cornell believe they may have found a way to eliminate the watery puddles that form in partially consumed containers of yogurt, through genetic engineering of a milk protein. And work is under way to develop potatoes resistant to the plant disease that causes the dark streaks in some potato chips.

Wide-ranging efforts are under way to reduce the levels of saturated and unsaturated fatty acids in some commonly used oils, such as canola oil and soybean oil, with potentially important health benefits. Fish, considered a particularly healthy source of dietary protein, could become cheaper if varieties genetically engineered to grow larger faster ever become commercially viable options for aquaculture.

Continued on p. 685

Chronology

1960s ***Development of a new type of potato proves that genetic alterations can have unexpected effects.***

1967
The U.S. Department of Agriculture (USDA) unveils the Lenape potato, a new variety bred for high solids content. Two years later, the potato is withdrawn from the market after being shown to contain high levels of a toxic glycoalkaloid, solanine. Critics of genetically engineered foods will later cite the Lenape example as proof that genetic alterations can have unintended and dangerous effects.

1970s ***Scientists develop the rudiments of recombinant DNA technology.***

1979
Cornell University initiates the first study on the effect of recombinant bovine somatotropin (rBST), a synthetic growth hormone, on the milk producing capacity of dairy cows.

1980s ***Development of more sophisticated recombinant DNA techniques allows for the genetic transformation of plants and animals.***

1983
Researchers at Monsanto Co. in St. Louis, Mo., and at centers in West Germany and Belgium succeed in disarming the bacterium responsible for a common plant disease so that it can be used to transfer new DNA into plants without causing the disease. This remains the most common method for genetically engineering crop plants.

1985
The Food and Drug Administration (FDA) rules that meat and milk from cows treated with rBST are safe for human consumption, but the agency holds off approving use of the hormone as a veterinary drug to allow for further research into its effects on animal health.

1986
The first field test of a genetically engineered crop plant takes place in Belgium. The test involves a canola plant altered to include a disarmed version of a disease-causing bacterium.

June 26, 1986
The Reagan administration issues a framework for regulating biotechnology through existing laws, to be implemented primarily by USDA, FDA and the Environmental Protection Agency.

1987
The USDA issues the first permits for field testing genetically engineered crop plants in the U.S.

1989
Calgene Inc. in Davis, Calif., holds initial conversations with the FDA about the possibility of seeking approval for its genetically engineered tomato.

1990s ***The first genetically engineered foods are made available to the public.***

1990
American Medical Association (AMA) and NIH Technology Assessment Conference conclude in separate reviews that meat and milk from rBST-treated cows are as safe as that from untreated cows.

1991
The American Academy of Pediatrics joins the AMA and NIH in issuing assurances that milk from rBST-treated cows is safe.

May 29, 1992
The FDA publishes its policy on food biotechnology, including decision not to require premarket notification or labeling for most genetically engineered foods from plants.

Nov. 5, 1993
The FDA approves the use of rBST in dairy cows, sparking controversy and protests.

January 1994
The White House, through the Office of Management and Budget, issues a report finding no evidence of a health threat to animals or humans from rBST use in dairy cattle. The report had been requested in 1993 by dairy-state senators critical of rBST.

April 1994
Maine passes a law directing farmers who use rBST to register that information with the dairies they supply, and establishing an official label for milk from untreated cows. Vermont passes a law requiring food companies to put a label on dairy products made with milk from rBST-treated cows.

May 18, 1994
The FDA issues final okay for Calgene's Flavr Savr tomato, which becomes the first genetically engineered whole food approved for the market.

The Regulatory Framework

There is no comprehensive law governing the activities associated with the development of genetically engineered foods. Instead, pieces of legislation such as the 1958 food additive amendments to the 1938 Food, Drug and Cosmetic Act, the 1957 Plant Pest Act and the 1947 Federal Insecticide, Fungicide and Rodenticide Act give various federal agencies authority over certain aspects of the process.

Three agencies play key roles: the Food and Drug Administration (FDA), the Department of Agriculture (USDA) and the Environmental Protection Agency (EPA).

Since 1987, the three agencies have had an informal agreement to work together on assessing the products of food biotechnology in order to avoid turf battles in areas where their authorities overlap. This arrangement has given USDA the key role in environmental assessment of the new crops, while the FDA takes the lead on food safety issues. The EPA is expected to play a more active role as crops engineered for herbicide and disease resistance come to market. (The National Institutes of Health, through its Recombinant DNA Advisory Committee, may play a key role in the future development of genetically engineered animals, including fish.)

What follows is a brief review of the responsibilities of the three federal agencies:

Food and Drug Administration: The FDA has broad authority over foods derived from genetically engineered plants. Under the 1958 food additive amendments, the FDA has the power to require premarket testing of any food containing an additive not generally regarded as safe.

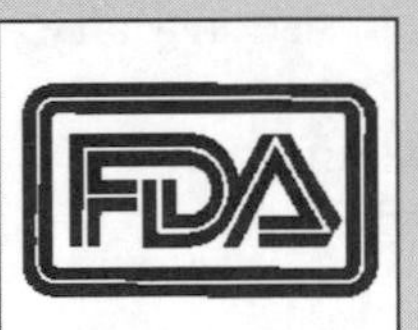

To date, the agency has taken the position that new genes do not in themselves qualify as a food additive. Instead, the focus is on the "expression product" of the new gene — the change that the presence of the new gene engenders in the plant.

In most cases, it is up to the manufacturer or developer of the new food to determine whether or not the expression product of the newly introduced gene is generally regarded as safe, or GRAS. In the case of non-GRAS expression products, the manufacturer is expected to submit a food additive petition to the FDA, and would be unable to market the new food until the petition was approved.

If the new gene comes from a food known to cause allergic reactions, such as peanuts, the manufacturer would need to develop scientific evidence that the allergy-inducing property has not been transferred to the new food. If the genetic alteration introduces a novel protein, carbohydrate, fat or oil into the food, it would probably require submission of a food additive petition and approval by the FDA.

The FDA is currently reviewing two controversial aspects of its policy: (1) that the producers of a new genetically engineered whole food do not, in most cases, need to notify the agency before putting the new food on the market (*see p. 688*); and (2) that genetically engineered whole foods do not, in most cases, require special labeling. (*See story, p. 687.*)

The FDA's lengthy review of the Flavr Savr tomato was not required by existing regulations, but was instead requested by the manufacturer.

Department of Agriculture: USDA scientists are deeply involved in research on developing transgenic plants and animals as part of the agency's mission to promote and improve agriculture. At the same time, it is the USDA, through the Animal and Plant Health Inspection Service (APHIS), that administers the major existing program for assessing the environmental risks of genetically engineered crops.

Under the authority of the 1957 Federal Plant Pest Act, APHIS issues permits for the field testing of genetically engineered plants and microorganisms, and prepares an environmental assessment for each release permit. After field testing, the producers of a new plant variety can apply to have the variety removed from the list of potential plant pests. If that application is granted, the plant may be freely transported and planted.

In some cases, this will be the only approval needed prior to commercial production of a new transgenic plant. In other cases, the manufacturer might need additional approvals from the FDA or the EPA.

Theoretically, the USDA has the authority to regulate the commercial sale and labeling of genetically engineered meat and poultry, through its Food Safety Inspection Service. To date, the agency has not issued any regulations in this area.

Environmental Protection Agency: A sizable percentage of the genetically engineered crops now approaching commercialization have been altered to express substances that are toxic to some common plant pests. That brings them under EPA review, through the 1947 Federal Insecticide, Fungicide and Rodenticide Act, also known as FIFRA. Since 1987, APHIS has routinely forwarded permit requests for field tests of such plants to the EPA for review.

EPA review is also required for plants developed to resist certain herbicides, such as the "Roundup ready" strain of soybeans being developed by Monsanto Co. (*see p. 688*). In these cases, EPA review is triggered by the need for a change in the label carried by the herbicide explaining its proper use.

Continued from p. 682

Risks and Benefits

A curious problem confronts those who are trying to determine whether genetically engineered foods are safe: While researchers generally have a pretty good understanding of the genetic material being transferred, they often know surprisingly little about the target food.

Until recently, researchers' understanding of which plants and animals humans can safely eat has been based almost entirely upon history and observation: We eat the things our ancestors ate without getting sick or dying. Regulatory systems that have been developed to ensure the safety and quality of food supplies have focused on additives and the dangers of contamination, unsanitary processing and poor storage and handling.

But even foods that are an important component of the human diet contain potentially toxic compounds. Among those that have been identified: protease inhibitors in legumes; goitrogens in canola species; cyanogens in cassava, sorghum and lima beans; glycoalkaloids in potatoes; pressor amines in plantain and bananas; myristicin in nutmeg and celery. The International Food Biotechnology Council has suggested that those plant foods not already known to contain natural toxicants have simply not been analyzed in sufficient detail. [11]

Ever since Austrian monk Gregor Mendel formulated the laws of heredity in 1865, humans have used selective breeding of plants and animals to increase yields, improve flavor or appearance, and confer resistance to drought, cold or pests. Sometimes, this breeds trouble.

In 1967, the USDA unveiled the Lenape potato, bred for high solids content — a valuable processing quality that is now the target of genetic engineering efforts. The Lenape was widely planted, and used by potato chip manufacturers. Two years after commercial release, a Canadian plant breeder became ill after consuming Lenape potatoes, which were later found to contain high levels of solanine, a toxic glycoalkaloid. The potato was on the market for two-and-a-half years before being withdrawn. Critics of genetically engineered foods often cite the Lenape example as proof that genetic alterations — even those introduced through traditional breeding — can have unexpected consequences.

In general, however, plant breeding has a good safety record, and has succeeded in reducing toxic elements in a number of common foods. The FDA has pointed to this record, and to the parallels between traditional breeding and the new genetic engineering techniques, in explaining why it does not generally require manufacturers to prove that foods created through genetic engineering are safe (*see p. 688*).

However, there are real differences between plant breeding and gene splicing. Usually, hybrid plants produced through breeding will have the same number of genes as the parent plants, arranged in an orderly sequence determined by processes of sexual reproduction. With gene splicing, there is an increase in the number of genes, and genetic engineers have little control over where the new DNA will wind up.

Random insertion can lead to secondary effects, by either inactivating or activating a nearby gene. These secondary effects, called pleiotropic effects, could result in the increased production or accumulation of toxins in edible plant material. Genetic alterations intended to make the inedible portions of a plant (the leaves, stems or roots of a tomato plant, for instance) toxic to pests could carry an increased risk of such unintended results.

There are similar concerns over the potential toxicity of genetically engineered fish. That is because some species of fish are known to contain toxins — most famously, the pufferfish, which is a sometimes fatal delicacy in Japan — and because close evolutionary neighbors of fish are known to produce toxins. That raises the prospect of an introduced gene accidentally "turning on" an inactive gene for toxin production in the cells of the target fish.

Some scientists argue this is unlikely, pointing to evidence that the toxins in most, if not all, toxic species of fish and shellfish are not actually produced by the animal itself, but rather by microorganisms such as bacteria. What the fish has that nontoxic varieties do not share is a genetically determined resistance to the toxin. Still, while that would eliminate the chances that genetic engineers might accidentally activate a toxin-producing pathway, it raises another possibility: that toxin resistance might be engineered into fish that do not currently enjoy that protection, and that those fish could become hosts for the poison-producing bacteria.

While a fair amount of attention has been paid to potential dangers of transgenic foods, such as toxicity and allergenicity, there is another category of concerns having to do with nutritional quality. Will a Flavr Savr tomato nearing the end of its extended shelf-life contain the same vitamins and nutrients it had when it was new? The tomato may be as attractive and flavorful as ever, yet still be nutritionally inferior. Calgene research showed the Flavr Savr to contain normal levels of vitamin C and other nutrients, but scientists are only now beginning to understand the dietary importance of some components of food that are present only in very small quantities.

It is in the area of nutritional and health benefits that some observers see the greatest payoff from genetic engineering. As Americans struggle to reduce fat in their diets, the prospect of low-fat pork chops from pigs treated with rPST is enticing. As the world struggles with the need to feed a growing population, the prospect of a more nutritious or more flavorful soybean is also appealing.

Recent cancer research reveals the importance of antioxidants — compounds that can slow or shut down oxidation, a biologically damaging chemical reaction that appears to promote the development of some cancers. [12] Using genetic engineering to increase levels of naturally occurring antioxidants could conceivably lead to a reduction in the rates at which certain cancers are found in the population. ■

CURRENT SITUATION

Environmental Concerns

As more transgenic plants approach commercialization, some scientists are raising a red flag about possible environmental risks posed by widespread cultivation of the new crops.

The Union of Concerned Scientists, in a 1993 report titled *Perils Amidst the Promise,* concluded that commercialization of transgenic crops poses serious environmental risks, including the following possibilities:

- that transgenic crops will become weeds, requiring expensive and environmentally dangerous chemical control programs;
- that new genes from transgenic crops will be transmitted, through pollen, to wild plant relatives that will then become weeds;
- that plants engineered to contain virus particles as part of a strategy to enhance resistance could facilitate the creation of new viruses;
- that plants engineered to express potentially toxic substances such as drugs and pesticides will present risks to other organisms that are not the intended targets;
- and that commercialization of transgenic crops will pose a new threat to crop genetic diversity, already endangered by current agricultural practices that favor the worldwide adoption of a few modern crop varieties. [13]

Peter Kareiva, an ecologist at the University of Washington in Seattle, believes that the risks are manageable, but real. "Ecologists see some of these problems in a fundamentally different way from industry and agriculture people," Kareiva says. "When it comes to insect and virus resistance in a crop with any weedy tendencies at all, for instance, the agriculture people will argue they don't know of any cases of plants whose spread is controlled by diseases or insects, and which would therefore become invasive if resistance were engineered in. But as ecologists, we know of lots of such plants. It's just that none of them are crops."

Crops are the 98-pound weaklings of the plant world, largely ill-suited to survive outside the shelter of a garden or farm field. Generations of selective breeding have made most crop plants more productive, but also more dependent: they are picky about soil, water and sun supplies, and susceptible to invasions by bugs, fungi and diseases. That's one reason many scientists believe there is little risk of transgenic crops becoming weeds.

However, many crop plants have some surprisingly hardy, even weedlike wild-plant relatives. Red rice, a close relative of the cultivated crop, is a major pest in rice fields. The cucumber/squash family contains many weedy and wild members. In cases where crop plants are grown in close proximity to sexually compatible wild or weedy relatives, there is a risk of gene transfer through pollen. According to the Union of Concerned Scientists, that's the situation for carrots, sunflowers, radishes and squash in some parts of the United States.

"I don't think anyone argues that the [Flavr Savr] tomato is going to become a weed," says Kareiva. "But Upjohn is very close to approval for its virus-resistant squash, and ecologists are concerned because it could become very weedy."

The USDA has already reached a preliminary finding that the squash (a yellow crookneck engineered to resist two common viruses) would have no significant environmental impact. The National Wildlife Federation, in 1993 comments opposing approval of the squash, argued that Upjohn had not produced sufficient experimental data to answer the question of whether the engineered plant had increased weediness potential, or whether cross pollination with the new squash variety might increase the invasiveness of Texas gourd, a weedy relative that grows in the wild. [14]

Environmentalists are also wary of industry claims that genetic engineering will lead to a dramatic reduction in chemical herbicide and pesticide use.

A prime example is the very active field of engineering insect-resistant crops. Most of these crops are engineered to contain genes for Bacillus thuringiensis (Bt) endotoxins, bug killing toxins produced by a soil bacterium. Crystalline spores of Bt are one of the most widely accepted "natural" pesticides, and are used by organic farmers to protect plants under attack from caterpillars. That's because they are not toxic to mammals.

When mammals consume the Bt crystals, they are not digested. The digestive systems of insects, however, are alkaline rather than acid, and break down the crystals into a toxic compound that dissolves the insects' guts.

Kareiva sees certain potential problems in placing the Bt gene directly into crop plants. First, while direct consumption of the spores poses no

The Labeling Dilemma

From a public-relations perspective, the labeling issue may present creators and regulators of genetically engineered foods with their biggest headaches.

The Food and Drug Administration (FDA) announced in May 1992 that genetically engineered foods would require labels only in unusual circumstances — if a transformed food were found to be newly allergenic, for example, or dramatically altered in its nutritional profile, such as an orange with greatly reduced amounts of Vitamin C.

The policy was controversial. After receiving more than 3,000 comments from consumers, FDA Commissioner David Kessler said in the spring of 1993 that the agency was reconsidering its no-label policy, and would issue a final decision in 1994. But since then the FDA has shown no inclination to embrace labeling. In May, the agency approved the commercial sale of Calgene's Flavr Savr tomato without requiring any special labeling. (Calgene decided to label the tomato anyway.)

Supporters of labeling say the FDA has put industry concerns over consumers' interests. "The thousands of individuals who commented on the FDA food policy are still awaiting a response," Margaret Mellon of the Union of Concerned Scientists said in April, shortly before the FDA issued its Flavr Savr ruling. "To respond to industry pressure and grant the Calgene tomato an approval before completing work on a new [labeling] policy would be an insult." [1]

But biotechnology boosters say the labeling confusion is no boon to industry, because fears of a change in policy are stifling investment. "I'm concerned that the FDA will not be able to proceed with their current policy, which is science-based, sensible and realistic," says Christine Bruhn, a researcher at the Center for Consumer Research at the University of California-Davis. "I fear that labeling would be taken as a warning, instead of information."

The struggle over recombinant bovine somatotropin (rBST) — a synthetic growth hormone manufactured by Monsanto Co. — demonstrates how difficult it would be for the FDA to develop a labeling policy that would begin to satisfy the competing claims of industry and consumer interest groups.

At the time it approved rBST for use on dairy cows in November 1993, the agency declared that milk from treated cows is indistinguishable from milk from untreated cows, and therefore it would not have to be labeled. The FDA went a half-step further this year, when it issued interim guidelines warning producers who label milk as coming from cows *not* treated with the synthetic hormone to take care that those labels are neither false nor misleading.

Because all milk contains natural bovine somatotropin, labels using the term "BST-free" would be false and potentially misleading, the agency said. The phrase "from cows not treated with rBST" is better, the guidelines stated, but it "has the potential to be misunderstood by consumers.... Such unqualified statements may imply that milk from untreated cows is safer or of higher quality than milk from treated cows. Such an implication would be false or misleading."

The FDA guidelines go on to suggest that labels indicating milk comes from untreated cows also include a disclaimer stating, for example, that "no significant difference has been shown between milk from rBST-treated and non-rBST-treated cows."

Dr. Samuel S. Epstein of the University of Illinois School of Public Health in Chicago blasted the FDA guidelines, saying they are "scientifically flawed and reckless and represent blatant disregard of consumers' right to know." [2]

Monsanto spokesman Tom McDermott says his company will vigorously oppose efforts to either mandate labeling of milk from treated cows or loosen the strictures on labels for milk from untreated cows. "It would turn the food label into a bumper sticker," McDermott says.

There are signs that the market will find a way to give consumers a choice — for a price. Two major dairy companies have already launched new product lines from untreated cows: Marigold Foods is offering Kemps Select, and Land O'Lakes is putting out Superior Brand Milk. The new products will be identified as coming from untreated cows through display signs on the dairy case. No such information will appear on the cartons themselves. Consumers can expect to pay about 10 cents more per gallon for the milk.

More than 90 percent of those responding to a recent poll said genetically engineered foods should be labeled. (*See poll, p. 676.*) "In a way, it comes down to trust," says Donna Scott, an agricultural extension agent at Cornell University. "People want to think they have a choice, and people have stopped trusting government."

---

[1] Comments to the Food and Drug Administration Advisory Committee on Genetically Engineered Food, April 8, 1994.

[2] Samuel S. Epstein, "A Needless New Risk of Breast Cancer," *Los Angeles Times*, March 20, 1994.

threat to mammals and insect-eating birds, there could be a risk in consuming insects that have already ingested the poison, and dissolved the Bt toxins. Similarly, the decomposition of Bt crops in alkaline soils could release the toxins into the soil, destroying soil bacteria and other fauna. Finally, the transformation of a large number of common crops to contain Bt might speed the process by which insects become resistant to the toxin.

Another active area of genetic engineering is the creation of "packages" of a particular herbicide paired with a transgenic plant resistant to that herbicide. Monsanto, for instance, is developing crops resistant to glyphosate, the active ingredient in Roundup, an herbicide that it manufactures. Monsanto spokeswoman Karen Marshall says "Roundup ready" soybean seeds may be commercially available by the 1996 growing season — the soybean has received USDA approval, and Monsanto is seeking EPA approval now. Corn and potatoes are in the works, but not as far along. The company is seeking Canadian approval for "Roundup ready" canola.

On one hand, this would seem to be a recipe for increased herbicide usage, since the threat of killing the crop plant is one of the brakes on usage of herbicides to kill weeds. On the other hand, glyphosate is considered one of the safest herbicides now on the market, so widespread availability of glyphosate-resistant crops could lead to a reduction in the use of more dangerous chemicals.

"My take is that it will encourage safer practices than the current ones, but that it may reduce the pressure to get rid of herbicides," says Kareiva. "Sometimes the industry makes it sound like there are no risks, and environmentalists make it sound like there is nothing but risks, while the truth is somewhere in between."

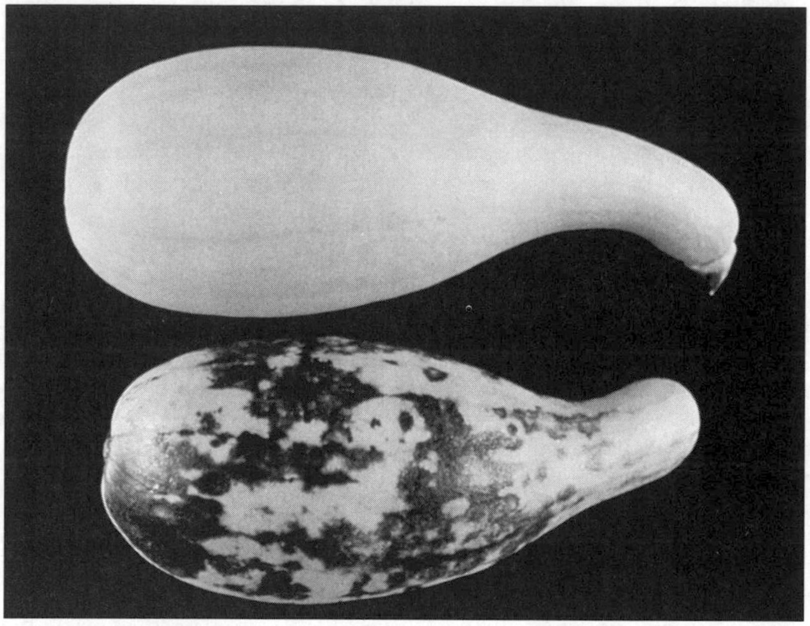

Asgrow Seed Company

The squash at the top of the photo has been genetically engineered to resist viruses that affect squash. The effects of one common virus can be seen in the squash at the bottom of the photo.

Old Rules, New Foods

So far, genetically engineered foods and foods produced with the help of genetic engineering have flowed from lab dish to dinner plate not in a stream, not in a trickle, but one drop at a time.

As groundbreaking products, both rBST and the Flavr Savr tomato were subjected to enormous amounts of scrutiny before they reached the market. However, there are signs that regulations governing the approval of such products, most of which predate the development of genetic engineering techniques for food, are not designed to withstand the expected onslaught of requests for new approvals.

It's an issue of concern to the food biotechnology industry and its critics alike. In such a fast-moving field, U.S. industry argues that a flexible regulatory system is necessary to maintain competitiveness with other nations, and that companies need clear guidance on what they must do to win marketing approval. Those concerned primarily with issues of health and environmental safety worry that an outmoded regulatory framework combined with pressure from industry for quick approvals will result in unsafe products reaching the marketplace.

The key federal agencies with actual or possible roles in regulating genetically engineered foods are the Food and Drug Administration, the Department of Agriculture and the Environmental Protection Agency. (*See story, p. 684.*)

The FDA's current policy on food biotechnology, announced in May 1992, takes the position that genetically engineered crops are not fundamentally different from plant hybrids created through traditional cross-breeding techniques. The 1992 policy does not require any special review or labeling of foods produced through genetic engineering of crops. In most cases, manufacturers are not required to notify the FDA before bringing such foods to market. The exceptions include instances when the introduced gene comes from a common allergen, or when the developing company itself determines that the new food is substantially different from its conventional counterpart.

FDA officials have indicated that they are reviewing certain aspects of their policy. The agency has requested public comment on what type of labeling might be appropriate for genetically engineered foods. It has consulted with experts in the field of food allergies. And it is considering establishing a program that would require companies to notify the FDA if they intend to market genetically engineered foods. Such notification would not include any additional safety review, but it would allow the FDA to maintain a database on the new foods, making them easier

Continued on p. 690

At Issue:

Are genetically engineered foods safe?

yes

David A. Kessler
Commissioner, U.S. Food and Drug Administration

FROM TESTIMONY BEFORE HOUSE APPROPRIATIONS SUBCOMMITTEE ON AGRICULTURE, RURAL DEVELOPMENT, FDA AND RELATED AGENCIES, APRIL 20, 1993.

The public is faced with what at times must seem like a bewildering assortment of new technologies. From pocket size computers to information superhighways to the latest medical improvement, consumers face a dizzying array of new scientific advances that are often accompanied by an equally confusing litany of new terms.

In this type of environment, it is very important for people to understand exactly how government is overseeing these developments and have confidence in that process. . . .

FDA is working diligently to be at the forefront of [food biotechnology]. We intend to ensure that these new products meet the same high safety standards as the foods we eat today. Unsafe food products are not going to make their way onto America's dining tables. . . .

I know that some are concerned and anxious about products developed through biotechnology, especially food products. But I believe there are many misconceptions about what bioengineered food products are and about how FDA intends to regulate them. . . .

Food products produced through biotechnology such as recombinant DNA techniques and cell fusion are emerging from research and development. It is these products that people normally refer to as "genetically engineered foods."

The new "gene splicing" techniques are being used to achieve many of the same goals and improvements that plant breeders have sought through conventional methods — the techniques that bring us hybrid peas, and disease resistant wheat. Today's techniques are different from their predecessors in two significant ways: First, they can be used with greater precision and allow for more complete characterization and, therefore, greater predictability about the qualities of the new variety. . . .

Second, today's techniques give breeders the power to cross boundaries that could not be crossed by traditional breeding. For example, they enable the transfer of traits from bacteria or animals into plants. It is this power, the ability to cross natural boundaries, that many in the public are concerned about when they hear about biotechnology. I understand this concern. That is why I disagree with those who say we need only concern ourselves with the final product and not the process that created it. While study of the final product ultimately holds the answer of whether or not a product is safe, knowing the process used to create the product helps in understanding what questions to ask. That is the way FDA currently regulates food products, and products derived through biotechnology will be treated no differently.

no

Jeremy Rifkin
Director, Foundation on Economic Trends

FROM A 1991 PRESS RELEASE

The full-scale use of biotechnology in agriculture and in food production raises profound environmental, economic and ethical concerns. The question of whether we should embark on a long journey in which we become the engineers of life is, perhaps, the most important ever to face the human family.

The biotechnology industry is preparing to release scores of genetically engineered viruses, bacteria, plant strains and transgenic animals into the environment in the next few years. In coming decades, hundreds, even thousands, of genetically engineered life forms may enter the world's ecosystems in massive commercial volumes. The release of novel genetically engineered organisms into the environment raises troublesome environmental questions and poses serious potential risks to human health.

Because they are alive, genetically engineered products are inherently more unpredictable than chemical products. Genetically engineered products can reproduce, mutate and migrate. Environmental scientists have compared the risk of releasing biotechnology products to those we have encountered in introducing exotic organisms to North America habitats. While most of these organisms have adapted to our ecosystems, several . . . have wreaked havoc on the environment.

The long-term cumulative environmental impact of releasing thousands of genetically engineered organisms could be equally destructive. Once released, it is virtually impossible to recall these living products back to the laboratory. . . .

Biotech products are also likely to have a deleterious impact on small family farms and could devastate farm communities. . . . Consider the case of bovine growth hormone (BGH). When injected into cattle on a daily basis, this hormone . . . can increase milk production by at least 20 percent per dairy cow.

Because of the already flooded milk market, BGH poses a serious threat to dairy farmers. It has been estimated that milk prices may fall 10 to 15 percent within the first three years of introduction of BGH.... [T]he number of dairy farmers may have to be reduced by 25 to 30 percent to restore market equilibrium. . . .

In an effort to find commercial applications for biotechnology, scientists are crossing species boundaries at an ever increasing rate, inserting human genes into animals, and animal genes into other animals and plants. Many recent achievements sound more like science fiction than science fact. . . .

The engineering of transgenic plants and animals goes far beyond traditional breeding techniques. Cross-species genetic transfers may be the ultimate offense to the dignity and integrity of the biotic community. Prolonged and expanded use of these cross-species organisms could mean the end of the natural world as we currently know it.

Continued from p. 688

to trace in the event of allergy problems or other concerns.

Right now, the major hurdle faced by foods from genetically engineered plants is that presented by the 1957 Plant Pest Act, under which the USDA regulates all genetically engineered crops. All engineered plants are considered potential plant pests under the act, so companies or researchers interested in field testing must apply to the USDA for permits. After field tests are completed, the applicants submit data to support deregulation of the plant as a plant pest. Once deregulated, the plant may go into commercial distribution.

The EPA will take a more active role as plants engineered to resist herbicides and viruses or to be toxic to pests near commercialization. Some observers feel the environmental agency is better placed to assess the environmental risks of such plants than is USDA, with its traditional mandate to boost agriculture rather than police it. USDA scientists are very active in genetic engineering research with both plants and animals.

Consumer Confusion

Surveys have shown considerable consumer resistance to genetically engineered foods. (*See poll, p. 677.*) But supporters say that resistance is linked to a lack of understanding of what genetic engineering entails.

Shmaefsky at Kingwood College says that in discussions with consumers, he finds most are fearful of two types of events: that microorganisms or "superplants" might be released during field trials, or that accidents in the laboratory might lead to the release of toxic agents or biological poisons.

"People are happy about the [Flavr Savr] tomato, about having french fries that taste better or chips without the brown spots," says Schmaefsky. "Once the technology is explained, it is not frightening to most people. . . . The questions I get are more along the lines of 'Why aren't we feeding the world with this stuff?' "

"Some would prefer not to have genetically engineered foods at all; for them, it's a philosophy of life," says Christine Bruhn, a researcher at the Center for Consumer Research at the University of California-Davis. "Then there are those people who are simply very risk-averse. Others, once they are familiar with the products and the technology, they have no concerns. And then there are some people whose employment in life is to be against change."

Corrigan at the Carrot Top market believes effective marketing could overcome much of the resistance to genetic engineering. "Listen, most of the vegetables in our store or any store are hydrocooled after picking. It gets rid of the heat from the field, it makes them ship better," Corrigan says. "I bet if I put up a sign saying 'All Our Vegetables Hydrocooled for Freshness,' I could get customers going into other stores and asking why their vegetables aren't hydrocooled. And the average person working in a supermarket produce section doesn't even know enough to tell this customer that those vegetables are hydrocooled, too."

Moonen, the chef at the Water Club restaurant, isn't looking for a marketing hard sell, or a seminar on probability and risk as it relates to gene transfer. He and many others in the food business are looking for something that may be harder to provide — the kind of assurances of safety and wholesomeness that until now have come from the simple experience of generations of safe consumption.

"Mother Nature's been doing a great job," Moonen says. "I don't see the need to improve foods. The focus should be on growing things locally, eating them in season and cleaning up pollution." ■

OUTLOOK

New Applications

While food producers, consumers and regulators wrestle with the implications of new foods produced through genetic engineering, researchers are busy on the next step — one that will raise its own array of health and safety issues.

That is the prospect of common crop plants, such as potatoes, cotton and tobacco, being transformed to manufacture a wide variety of materials, including human proteins such as albumin and interferon, and natural polymers, including a type of polyester.

Researchers in Switzerland have already shown that genetically engineered yellow turnips can produce large amounts of interferon, a substance that can slow or stop the growth of viruses. In Brussels, a variety of canola plant has been engineered to produce an opiate identical to one produced by the human brain. And in the Netherlands, potato and tobacco plants have been transformed to produce serum albumin in a form indistinguishable from that produced by humans. Serum albumin is widely used in medicine for fluid replacement. [15]

Many of these developments may never reach commercialization. Genetic engineers have had considerable success using bacteria to produce a wide array of medical and industrial products. Plants are harder to transform genetically. And even if a particular gene can be successfully introduced, the target plant often produces the desired product at such low levels that it would not be economically feasible to harvest it.

But in some cases, plant production may offer valuable advantages, producing larger amounts of the desired substance at less cost, or producing them in a form that is easier to store and transport, such as seeds.

Charles Hess, professor of environmental horticulture at the University of California-Davis, sees the potential for eliminating one of the most persistent problems facing American agriculture: overproduction. Fields now devoted to surplus crops such as corn, and socially questionable crops such as tobacco, could be turned over to the production of useful commodities, or substitutes for non-renewable resources like petroleum. [16]

Tobacco in particular has shown itself to be quite susceptible to genetic manipulation. Researchers in the Netherlands and the United States have shown that tobacco plants can be engineered to produce the enzyme alpha-amylase, which is used in the manufacture of foods such as bread and low-caloric beer, and to clarify wines and fruit juices.

Elsewhere, scientists have used tobacco to produce a mouse antibody. It's theorized that if plants could be engineered to produce human antibodies, their seeds would provide a stable, inexpensive source of genetic material for immunizing against common diseases. That would eliminate a major drawback of many existing vaccines, which have only a short shelf life and often require refrigeration or other expensive storage techniques. [17]

"The opportunity in [the non-food product] area . . . is as large as the production opportunity in agriculture was in the 1920s, 1930s, 1940s and 1950s," Ralph W. Hardy, a member of the Alternative Agriculture Research and Commercialization Board, told a congressional subcommittee last year. [18] The board was established by USDA in March 1992 to investigate non-food applications of agricultural biotechnology.

Among the potential benefits Hardy mentioned were increased biodegradability of plastics and other materials; a reduced reliance on polluting, non-renewable fossil fuels; a smaller tab for agricultural support programs; and new economic opportunities for rural areas. "It is critical to find new uses" for agricultural products, Hardy noted. ■

Susan C. Phillips is a free-lance writer in Washington, D.C.

Notes

[1] The product also is referred to as recombinant bovine growth hormone, or rBGH. Pfizer Corp.'s genetically engineered form of rennet, used in making cheese, was approved in 1990, but received little public notice.

[2] For background, see the following *CQ Researcher* reports: "Food Safety," June 4, 1993, pp. 481-504; "Regulating Pesticides," Jan. 28, 1994, pp. 73-96; "World Hunger," Oct. 25, 1991, pp. 801-824; and "Population Growth," July 16, 1993, pp. 601-624.

[3] For background, see "Food Irradiation," *The CQ Researcher,* June 12, 1992, pp. 505-528.

[4] Comments to the Food and Drug Administration Advisory Committee on Genetically Engineered Food, April 8, 1994, pp. 5-6. Mellon is director of the group's agriculture and biotechnology program.

[5] Food and Drug Administration, "Bovine Growth Hormone: Human Food Safety Evaluation," *Science,* August 1990, pp. 875-884. For an opposing view, see Samuel S. Epstein, "A Needless New Risk of Breast Cancer," *Los Angeles Times,* March 20, 1994.

[6] Quoted in Mary Alice Sudduth, "Genetically Engineered Foods: Fears & Facts," *FDA Consumer,* January-February 1993, p. 10.

[7] See "Flavr Savr-Related Losses Force Cuts," *The Packer,* March 12, 1994, p. 1.

[8] See Russ Hoyle, "Will the Market Let BST Strut Its Stuff?" *Biotechnology,* April 12, 1994, p. 353.

[9] For background on recombinant DNA technology, see these *Editorial Research Reports*: "Genetic Breakthroughs," Jan. 10, 1986, pp. 1-20; and "Genetic Business," Dec. 26, 1980, pp. 945-964.

[10] David B. Berkowitz and Ilona Kryspin-Sorsensen, "Transgenic Fish: Safe to Eat?" *Biotechnology,* March 1994, p. 247.

[11] Kent K. Stewart, "Food Composition and Analysis in the Assessment of the Safety of Food Produced by Biotechnology," *Food Technology,* March 1992, p. 103.

[12] For background, see "Dietary Supplements," *The CQ Researcher,* July 8, 1994, pp. 577-600.

[13] Jane Rissler and Margaret Mellon, *Perils Amidst the Promise: Ecological Risks of Transgenic Crops in a Global Market,* Union of Concerned Scientists, December 1993.

[14] National Wildlife Federation Comments to the USDA APHIS on a Proposed Interpretive Ruling Concerning Upjohn's Transgenic Squash, May 21, 1993. The squash is being developed by Asgrow Seed Company, a subsidiary of Upjohn.

[15] Anne Simon Moffat, "High-Tech Plants Promise a Bumper Crop of New Products," *Science,* May 8, 1992, p. 770.

[16] *Ibid.*

[17] Jaleh Daie and Faith Belanger, "Plant Factories: Production of Industrial Proteins and Non-Food Products in Transgenic Plants," *Agro Food Industry Hi-Tech,* January/February 1993, p. 7.

[18] Hardy testified before the House Appropriations Subcommittee on Agriculture, Rural Development, Food and Drug Administration, and Related Agencies.

Bibliography

Selected Sources Used

Books

Bills, Donald B., and Shain-Dow Kung, eds., *Biotechnology and Nutrition,* Butterworth-Heinemann, 1992.
This book is composed of papers presented at an international symposium sponsored by the U.S. Department of Agriculture, the University of Maryland and E.I. du Pont de Nemours & Co. It presents a broad, positive overview of developments in food biotechnology, with emphasis on the potential benefits to human nutrition.

Hallberg, Milton C., ed., *Bovine Somatotropin and Emerging Issues,* Westview Press, 1992.
This book provides a comprehensive overview of the scientific, social, ethical and economic issues surrounding use of the synthetic growth hormone recombinant bovine somatotropin, or rBST.

Articles

Comai, Luca, "Impact of Plant Genetic Engineering on Foods and Nutrition," *Annual Review of Nutrition,* 1993.
Comai offers a relatively clear explanation of genetic engineering technology as it relates to food, and reviews potential hazards and benefits of the results.

Council on Scientific Affairs, American Medical Association, "Biotechnology and the American Agricultural Industry," *JAMA,* March 20, 1991.
This article expresses strong support for genetically engineered foods, and argues that physicians are "uniquely positioned" to dispel patient fears about the safety of the new foods. It includes a brief review of recombinant DNA technology, examples of its use in plants and animals, and recommends that the American Medical Association and physicians generally speak out in support of agricultural biotechnology.

Kessler, David A., et al, "The Safety of Foods Developed by Biotechnology," *Science,* June 26, 1992.
Food and Drug Administration (FDA) Commissioner Kessler and other agency officials unveiled what is still the key framework for regulating genetically engineered foods in this article, outlining the reasoning behind the FDA's decision not to require labeling, premarket notification or safety testing for most genetically engineered foods.

Moffat, Anne Simon, "High-Tech Plants Promise a Bumper Crop of New Products," *Science,* May 8, 1992.
Moffat gives a brief review of developments in what has been described as the "third wave" in plant biotechnology: efforts to develop plants as factories for biological and chemical products, including medicines and substitutes for petrochemicals.

Seabrook, John, "Tremors in the Hothouse," *The New Yorker,* July 19, 1993.
Seabrook's article provides a concise history of the development of the Flavr Savr tomato, which recently became the first genetically engineered whole food to reach the marketplace. Seabrook's story ends before the FDA gave the tomato its final approval, but provides an interesting analysis of the market forces driving development of the tomato.

"Udder Insanity," *Consumer Reports,* May 1992.
This brief, unsigned article provides a sharply critical overview of the economic and health issues surrounding the use of rBST in dairy cattle, with a focus on the negatives for consumers.

Reports and Studies

Rissler, Jane and Margaret Mellon, *Perils Amidst the Promise: Ecological Risks of Transgenic Crops in a Global Market,* Union of Concerned Scientists, December 1993.
Mellon and Rissler offer their assessment of the potential ecological dangers inherent in widespread commercial planting of genetically altered crop plants, including the possible creation of invasive new weeds and the destruction of native species. They also propose a regulatory framework and methods for assessing these risks prior to commercialization.

Beermann, Donald H., "Use of Exogenous Agents to Regulate Growth Composition," paper presented to the Pork Industry Conference on Swine Growth, University of Illinois, Nov. 19-20, 1992.
Beermann reviews 10 years of research into the use of genetically engineered porcine growth hormone to spur rapid growth in young pigs, producing leaner meat while reducing feed consumption.

World Health Organization and Food and Agriculture Organization of the United Nations, *Strategies for Assessing the Safety of Foods Produced by Biotechnology,* Geneva, 1991.
This report attempts to outline an international framework for assessing the safety of foods derived from genetically engineered plants and animals, as well as microorganisms.

The Next Step

Additional information from UMI's Newspaper & Periodical Abstracts database

FDA Approval

"Genetically altered tomato approved," ***News for You,*** **June 8, 1994, p. 2.**
The Food and Drug Administration (FDA) has approved the first genetically altered food in the U.S. It's a tomato called Flavr Savr.

McGinley, Laurie, "U.S. clears Calgene tomato, the first genetically engineered food to be sold," ***The Wall Street Journal,*** **May 19, 1994, p. B8.**
The FDA has approved Calgene Inc.'s Flavr Savr tomato for sale in the U.S., making the fruit the first genetically altered food cleared by federal regulators. The tomato's genetic altering allows producers to leave it on the vine longer, becoming redder and riper.

Manning, Anita, "FDA: Time is ripe for longer-lasting tomato," ***USA Today,*** **May 19, 1994, p. D1.**
The first genetically engineered food to go on the market, a tomato with a long shelf-life, got the FDA's stamp of approval. It will be in stores in the West and Midwest by early June 1994. The Flavr Savr tomato will be sold under the brand name MacGregor's.

Naj, Amal Kumar, "Pre-emptive strike," ***The Wall Street Journal,*** **May 20, 1994, p. R6.**
By seeking unrequired FDA approval for its Flavr Savr tomato, which has an added gene engineered into it to delay rotting, Calgene Inc. hoped to allay public fears about genetically altered foods. Some companies, however, are concerned that Calgene's approach has put an undue burden on small companies, which may not be able to negotiate the bureaucratic maze as well as Calgene did.

O'Neill, Molly, "Move over, Elsie: Recasting the cow as a political animal," ***The New York Times,*** **May 18, 1994, p. C1.**
When the FDA in November 1993 approved the use of bovine somatotropin, a synthetic version of the hormone that stimulates milk production, the cow suddenly became a political animal. The debate over the safety of the hormone is examined.

Thayer, Ann, "FDA gives go-ahead to bioengineered tomato," ***Chemical & Engineering News,*** **May 23, 1994, pp. 7-8.**
The FDA has approved Calgene's genetically engineered Flavr Savr tomato. Calgene's tomato represents the first whole food produced by biotechnology to reach U.S. consumers.

Walters, Donna K. H., "1st genetically altered food approved by FDA," ***Los Angeles Times,*** **May 19, 1994, p. A1.**
On May 18, 1994, the FDA for the first time approved a genetically engineered food, clearing the way for Davis, California-based Calgene Inc. to sell its laboratory-designed tomato.

Flavr Savr

Lehrman, Sally, "Gene-altered tomatoes face new protests," ***Nature,*** **May 26, 1994, p. 268.**
As a result of the official approval of the genetically engineered Flavr Savr tomato, consumer groups are preparing a boycott and are demanding that biotech foods be labeled. Activists are going to ask every supermarket chain not to stock the tomato.

Shapiro, Laura, "A tomato with a body that just won't quit," ***Newsweek,*** **June 6, 1994, pp. 80-82.**
Most consumers seem to be impressed with the taste of the MacGregor Flavr Savr tomato and not overly concerned with the fact that it is genetically engineered. Some worry, however, about other biotech products waiting in the wings and the way the FDA regulates them.

Strauss, Larry A., "Calgene's crop not just tomatoes," ***USA Today,*** **June 3, 1994, p. B3.**
Like the product it has been engineering for over a decade, Calgene could ripen into a choice stock pick. The agricultural biotechnology company spent $25 million genetically re-engineering tomato seeds to design the Flavr Savr, which is billed as a better tomato with a shelf life of up to 14 days. The company is profiled.

Tyson, Ann Scott, "Chicagoans try genetic product: Designer tomato," ***Christian Science Monitor,*** **June 3, 1994, p. 5.**
Chicago consumers are tasting tomatoes that are the first genetically engineered whole food approved by the federal government for marketing in the U.S. Crates of the tomatoes, developed by Calgene Inc., arrived at a Chicago grocery chain on May 27, 1994, as part of a marketing trial.

General Information

"Foodless farming," ***Futurist,*** **May 1994, pp. 55-56.**
Biotechnology and engineering will greatly broaden the markets for farm crops and improve foods. Several new approaches to bioagriculture are discussed.

"Genetically engineered food," ***Mayo Clinic Health Letter,*** **March 1994, pp. 4-5.**
Through advances in genetic engineering, foods are becoming more plentiful, better-tasting and more nutri-

tious. The benefits of genetically engineered foods and regulatory issues are discussed.

Labeling Products

Barnum, Alex, "Berkeley studies bioengineered food," *San Francisco Chronicle,* Jan. 25, 1994, p. A20.
Stepping into a national controversy, the Berkeley (CA) City Council will consider a measure on Jan. 25, 1994, that would require labeling of genetically engineered foods and impose a one-year ban on milk from cows treated with a bioengineered hormone.

Burros, Marian, "More milk, more confusion: What should the label say?" *The New York Times,* May 18, 1994, p. C1.
The conflict over the use of the artificial bovine growth hormone, which increases milk production, is reflected in torturous confusion over labeling of milk products. The debate over the labeling of such products is examined.

Lustgarden, Steve, "Gene cuisine," *Vegetarian Times,* April 1994, pp. 62-67.
The FDA has ruled that there is no reason to require that genetically altered foods be labeled, unless the process introduces a known allergen or substantially alters a food's nutritional value. However, consumer groups are calling for mandatory labeling of all genetically engineered foods.

Steyer, Robert, "Maine allows no-BST label," *St. Louis Post-Dispatch,* April 15, 1994, p. E8.
Maine Governor John McKernan has signed a law letting dairy farmers put labels on their milk assuring that their herds have not been injected with the genetically engineered copy of a cow protein known as rBST (recombinant bovine somatotropin or bovine growth hormone (BGH)).

Steyer, Robert, "No need for BST labels, Missouri health chief says," *St. Louis Post-Dispatch,* March 26, 1994, p. A8.
Missouri Department of Health chief Coleen Kivlahan has branded as "unnecessary" labels that distinguish food containing milk from cows treated with a Monsanto Co. drug vs. those containing milk from untreated cows.

Livestock

Beck, Ernest, "Hungary's Hungapig Ltd. preparing a not-so-little-piggy for global market," *The Wall Street Journal,* April 4, 1994, p. B4B.
Hungapig Ltd. in Hungary is trying to reclaim the country's reputation as a producer of qualtity swine through a selective process of genetically engineered hogs.

Holden, Constance, "Raising a herd of therapeutic goats," *Science,* May 13, 1994, p. 902.
Genzyme Transgenics Corp. has announced that it has bought a 166-acre farm in Massachusetts to breed goats that have been genetically altered to produce human therapeutic and diagnostic proteins in their milk.

Howe, Peter J., "Genzyme Transgenics buys goat farm," *Boston Globe,* May 3, 1994, p. 37.
Marrying the ancient trade of goat-herding with cutting-edge biotechnology, Genzyme Transgenics Corp. said it had bought a farm southwest of Worcester, Mass., where it will raise genetically modified goats to produce drugs for humans.

Mazzola, Vince, "Toward retrovirus-resistant sheep," *Agricultural Research,* April 1994, p. 17.
The development of genetically engineered sheep may be the first step toward preventing difficult-to-control viral diseases of livestock that do not respond to vaccines.

Milk Hormone - BST

Abend, Paula, "Crying over split genes," *Animals,* May 1994, p. 40.
The controversy over genetically engineered bovine growth hormone is discussed. The process increases milk production between 10 percent and 25 percent in lactating cows.

Hertzel, Leo J., "Pus is an ugly word," *North American Review,* March 1994, pp. 4-7.
Protests over genetically engineered food, particularly the use of bovine somatotropin (BST), a growth hormone that stimulates cows to produce more milk, are discussed. Leaflets and the like proclaiming that BST-produced milk contains pus illustrate the lack of the public's science understanding.

"New cries over how the milk spills," *Tufts University Diet & Nutrition Letter,* April 1994, pp. 7-8.
Dairy farmers recently began injecting cows with a genetically-engineered growth hormone in order to produce more milk. Concerns over the hormone as a potential safety risk are discussed.

Ropp, Kevin L., "No human risks: New animal drug increases milk production," *FDA Consumer,* May 1994, pp. 24-27.
On Nov. 5, 1994, the FDA approved sometribove, a genetically engineered bovine somatotropin that increases milk production in dairy cows. Although the decision was based on solid research, it has generated controversy.

"Will they cry over this spilt milk?" *U.S. News & World Report*, Feb. 14, 1994, p. 6.
Consumer opposition to milk treated with BST, a bioengineered version of a natural cow hormone developed by Monsanto, is discussed. Many grocery stores and milk-production firms have announced that they will keep BST milk off their shelves.

Opinions

Dixon, Bernard, "We say tomato, they say Flavr Savr," *Guardian,* May 21, 1994, p. 24.
Bernard Dixon discusses a decision by the FDA to approve the sale of a genetically engineered type of tomato called the Flavr Savr, and argues why genetically engineered foods may prove better than the originals.

Hoppe, Arthur, "Go stuff a tomato," *San Francisco Chronicle,* May 29, 1994, p. PUN1.
Art Hoppe comments on the outrage over the new genetically engineered Flavr Savr tomatoes that are about to hit the market.

"Let's call the whole thing off," *Boston Globe,* May 21, 1994, p. 14.
An editorial comments on efforts to produce a better tomato through genetic engineering, asserting there is no need for consumer groups to boycott the product, as early reports indicate that people will not buy it anyway.

Miller, Henry I., "Doctoring the tomato," *San Francisco Chronicle,* May 31, 1994, p. A17.
Henry I. Miller argues in support of improving food products through biotechnology in light of Calgene's Flavr Savr tomato.

Moss, Chuck, "Genetically altered veggies a hot topic," *Detroit News & Free Press,* May 28, 1994, p. C12.
Chuck Moss comments on the uproar over genetically altered vegetables.

"Passing the tomato test," *Detroit News & Free Press,* June 4, 1994, p. C12.
An editorial says the FDA has approved the genetically engineered Flavr Savr tomato, the first genetically altered food to be approved by that agency. The tomato will hit Detroit grocery shelves in September 1994.

"Science and the tomato," *St. Louis Post-Dispatch,* May 21, 1994, p. B14.
An editorial asserts that the FDA is right to resist demands for labeling of all genetically engineered food products.

"Tomato catch up," *USA Today,* May 20, 1994, p. A10.
An editorial comments on the introduction of Calgene's Flavr Savr tomato, the first genetically manipulated new food to hit the market. The editorial states that biotechnology is new enough, and public concern is great enough, that all products should be inspected and labeled by the FDA.

Questions and Issues

Manning, Anita, "A brave new world of biotech food," *USA Today,* March 17, 1994, p. D1.
The prospect of markets full of genetically engineered food, some of it not labeled as such, raises a host of questions and triggers deeper concerns about the ethics of altering nature. So far, biotech food hasn't faced a warm welcome.

Miller, Susan Katz, "Genetic first upsets food lobby," *New Scientist,* May 28, 1994, p. 6.
The world's first genetically engineered food, a tomato called the Flavr Savr, made its debut in California and Chicago stores in May 1994. Activists agree with the FDA that the tomato is probably safe for consumption, but they worry about the safety of future genetically engineered foods.

Vegetables

Barnum, Alex, "More bio-engineered crops on the way," *San Francisco Chronicle,* May 25, 1994, p. B1.
The rush to bring bio-engineered food products to the supermarket shelf is examined. Calgene Inc.'s Flavr Savr tomato led the pack, but other companies are investing heavily to bring their own products to the market. Upjohn Company's bio-engineered squash is undergoing the U.S. Department of Agriculture's approval process in May 1994.

Barnum, Alex, "New soybean genetically engineered," *San Francisco Chronicle,* June 3, 1994, p. B3.
A soybean genetically engineered to tolerate Monsanto Co.'s popular weedkiller Roundup has been approved for widespread planting by the U.S. Agriculture Department in early June 1994.

Elmer-Dewitt, Philip, "Fried gene tomatoes," *Time,* May 30, 1994, pp. 54-55.
After years of promises and protests, the era of genetically engineered food has finally begun. The new genetically engineered tomatoes and other genetically altered vegetables that are in the works are discussed.

Mestel, Rosie, "Bean patent sweeps the field," *New Scientist,* April 30, 1994, p. 7.
Agracetus, a biotechnology company, has won patent rights in Europe to all transgenic soya beans. Scientists feel that the broad scope of the patent will discourage innovation.

Steyer, Robert, "Monsanto soybean nearer to market," *St. Louis Post-Dispatch,* June 3, 1994, p. B8.
Monsanto Co. moved a step closer to selling a genetically engineered soybean that resists the company's Roundup herbicide.

Back Issues

Great Research on Current Issues Starts Right Here...Recent topics covered by The CQ Researcher are listed below. Before May 1991, reports were published under the name of Editorial Research Reports.

JANUARY 1993
Hate Crimes
Child Sexual Abuse
Nuclear Fusion
U.S. Trade Policy

FEBRUARY 1993
Community Policing
Europe's New Right
School Censorship
Violence Against Women

MARCH 1993
Gay Rights
Aid to Russia
War on Drugs
TV Violence

APRIL 1993
Head Start
High-Speed Rail
Children's Legal Rights
Muslims in America

MAY 1993
Cults in America
Preventing Teen Pregnancy
Software Piracy
National Parks

Back issues are available for $4.00 (subscribers) or $7.00 (non-subscribers). Quantity discounts apply to orders over ten. To order, call Congressional Quarterly Customer Service at (202) 887-8621.

Binders are available for $16.00. To order call 1-800-638-1710. Please refer to stock number 648.

JUNE 1993
Food Safety
Prostitution
Childhood Immunizations
National Service

JULY 1993
Electric Cars
Population Growth
Downward Mobility
Intelligence Testing

AUGUST 1993
Mental Illness
Bilingual Education
Foreign Policy Burden
School Funding

SEPTEMBER 1993
Suburban Crime
Public Housing
Supreme Court Preview
Immigration Reform

OCTOBER 1993
Airline Safety
Disaster Response
Science in the Courtroom
The Glass Ceiling

NOVEMBER 1993
Paying for Retirement
Charitable Giving
Privacy in the Workplace
Adoption

DECEMBER 1993
U.S. Vietnam-Relations
Learning Disabilities
Child Care
Space Program's Future

JANUARY 1994
Racial Tensions in Schools
South Africa's Future
Worker Retraining
Regulating Pesticides

FEBRUARY 1994
Prison Overcrowding
Water Quality
Religion in Schools
Juvenile Justice

MARCH 1994
Underground Economy
Education Standards
Gambling Boom
Private Management of Public Schools

APRIL 1994
Reproductive Ethics
U.S.-China Trade
Soccer in America
Talk Show Democracy

MAY 1994
Traffic Congestion
Women's Health Issues
Mutual Funds
Political Scandals

JUNE 1994
Education and Gender
Gun Control
Public Land Policy
Nuclear Arms Cleanup

JULY 1994
Dietary Supplements
Public Opinion and Foreign Policy
Crime Victims' Rights
Birth Control Choices

Future Topics

- ***Electing Minorities***
- ***Prozac***
- ***College Sports***

THE CQ Researcher

PUBLISHED BY CONGRESSIONAL QUARTERLY INC.

Electing Minorities

Are new methods needed to help minorities get elected?

More minorities than ever before have won congressional office in recent years, thanks in large part to the creation of electoral districts with majorities of minority voters. Now a Supreme Court decision has imperiled such districts in five Southern states, spawning litigation that could diminish previous gains. Civil rights lawyers contend that requiring states to draw majority-minority districts in their legislative maps is an appropriate remedy for past voting discrimination. White plaintiffs who have challenged these maps say their rights are being denied. Some critics want to move away from the traditional single-member, winner-take-all voting schemes that breed such disputes and toward the proportional representation plans used in many countries overseas. Others dismiss such approaches as "social engineering."

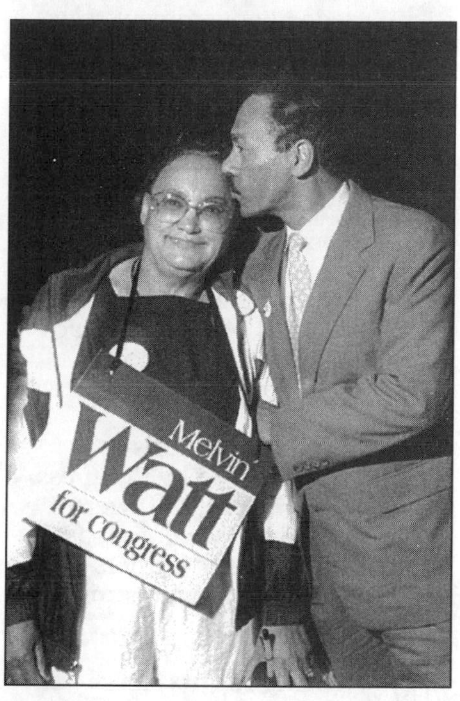

INSIDE THIS ISSUE

CQ August 12, 1994 • Volume 4, No. 30 • 697-720

Formerly Editorial Research Reports

ELECTING MINORITIES

August 12, 1994
Volume 4, No. 30

The CQ Researcher (ISSN 1056-2036). Formerly Editorial Research Reports. Published weekly (48 times per year, not printed the first Friday of any month with five Fridays) by Congressional Quarterly Inc., 1414 22nd St., N.W., Washington, D.C. 20037. Rates are furnished upon request. Second-class postage paid at Washington, D.C. POSTMASTER: Send address changes to The CQ Researcher, 1414 22nd St., N.W., Washington, D.C. 20037.

COVER: VICTORIOUS HOUSE CANDIDATE MELVIN WATT, A NORTH CAROLINA DEMOCRAT, KISSES HIS MOTHER ON ELECTION NIGHT IN 1992. (© 1994 *CHARLOTTE OBSERVER*/GARY O'BRIEN)

Electing Minorities

By Nadine Cohodas

The Issues

Victory has been sweet — but shaky — for Reps. Melvin Watt and Eva Clayton.

On June 28, 1993, barely six months after they celebrated becoming North Carolina's first black members of Congress in 90 years, the U.S. Supreme Court threatened to make them put the champagne corks back in the bottles. Ruling 5-4 in *Shaw v. Reno,* the court reinstated a lawsuit challenging the electoral map that created their two oddly shaped majority-black districts.

Justice Sandra Day O'Connor, writing for the majority, said that North Carolina appeared to have engaged in racial gerrymandering. Such map-drawing, she wrote, "even for remedial purposes may balkanize us into competing racial factions." In order for the districts to stand, O'Connor said, North Carolina would have to show that the map was not drawn for a racial purpose, or if it was, that the map was "narrowly tailored to further a compelling governmental interest."

This spring, the trial on the challenged map took place before a special three-judge federal panel in Raleigh, and on Aug. 1 Watt and Clayton, both Democrats, received some good news.

In a 2-1 decision, the judges ruled that while North Carolina may have indeed undertaken a racial gerrymander, "we nonetheless conclude that the plan passes constitutional muster because it is narrowly tailored to further the state's compelling interest" in complying with the 1965 Voting Rights Act.

Therefore, the panel added, the plan did not violate the constitutional rights of the white plaintiffs who had attacked the state's redistricting map. They had claimed that their right to equal protection, guaranteed in the 14th Amendment to the U.S. Constitution, had been violated in order to help ensure the election of black members of Congress.

"I'm very excited about the decision," says Watt, whose sinewy 12th District drew the most attention. He adds that he was not surprised by the outcome because he had been "confident of the rationale" the state had used to create the electoral map.

The decision is virtually certain to be appealed to the U.S. Supreme Court, and whether North Carolina's map ultimately will pass muster remains an open question. (*See "At Issue," p. 713.*)

After the 1990 Census, the state had drawn the new congressional district map under pressure from the U.S. Justice Department, which is charged with enforcing the Voting Rights Act.[1] Section 5 of the law requires states with a history of discrimination against minorities to get approval for election law changes — known as preclearance — from the Justice Department, and North Carolina fell under the act's coverage.

The subject of several contentious lawsuits over the last quarter-century, the Voting Rights Act has been interpreted to require states with sizable black populations to create electoral districts that give blacks a chance to elect a representative of their choosing — by inference a black. Watt's district is 56.6 percent black; Clayton's is 57.3 percent black.[2]

The law has been widely credited with helping minorities win elections. At the end of 1993, nearly 8,000 blacks and more than 5,100 Hispanics held public office in the United States.[3] (*See charts, pp. 708, 710.*)

The *Shaw* decision immediately imperiled the two majority-minority North Carolina districts and threatened similar districts in several other Southern states. Shortly after the decision, lawsuits were filed challenging majority-minority districts in Florida, Georgia, Louisiana and Texas. *

The high court decision also served to reignite a debate about race and electoral politics that was sparked by the failed nomination last year of civil rights lawyer Lani Guinier as assistant attorney general for civil rights. Key elements in this debate are the undisputed history of discrimination against blacks and other minorities in some states and localities, the fact of racial-bloc voting in racially mixed populations and the question of whether ethnic representation on governmental bodies is an appropriate goal, and if so, how it should be accomplished.

Guinier, a professor at the University of Pennsylvania Law School, has written extensively about race and politics, criticizing single-member districting and winner-take-all voting. She believes different electoral approaches are needed

---

* On July 25, a panel of three federal judges imposed a new congressional district map for Louisiana that has only one majority-black district. The judges ordered the court-drawn map after rejecting for the second time a district map containing two black-majority districts (*see p. 712*). The judges had ruled July 22 that the second map, like the first, also represented unconstitutional racial gerrymandering. Four Louisiana voters — two whites, one black and one of Asian descent — had challenged the new districts.

Black and Hispanic Officials by Category, 1993

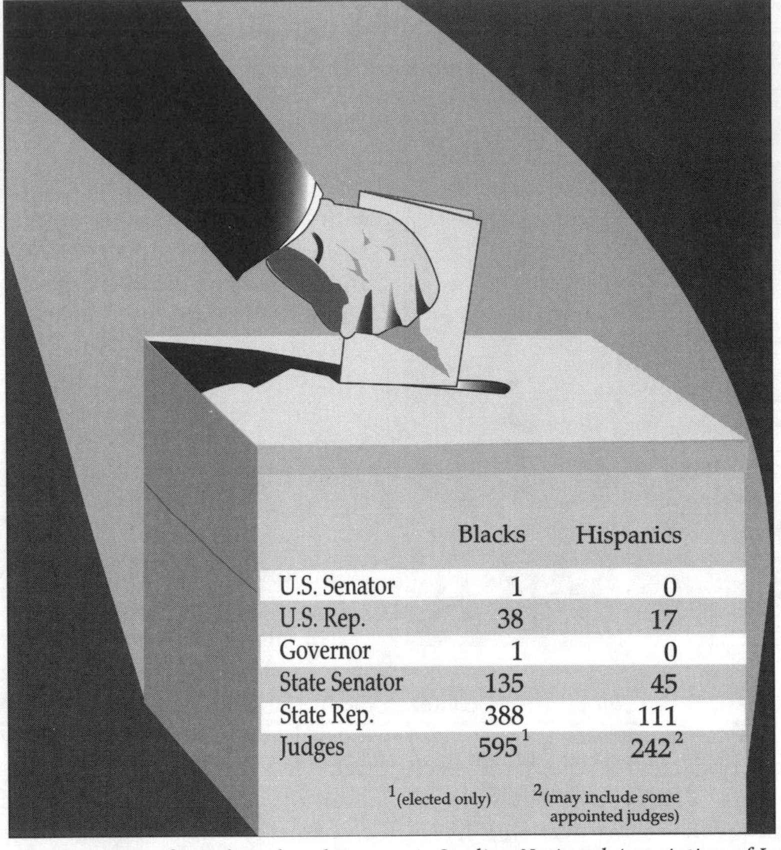

	Blacks	Hispanics
U.S. Senator	1	0
U.S. Rep.	38	17
Governor	1	0
State Senator	135	45
State Rep.	388	111
Judges	595[1]	242[2]

[1](elected only) [2](may include some appointed judges)

Sources: Joint Center for Political and Economic Studies; National Association of Latino Elected and Appointed Officials

to improve minorities' political representation and influence.

"Representing a geographically and socially isolated constituency in a radically polarized environment," she wrote in "The Triumph of Tokenism," an essay, "blacks elected from single-member districts have little control over policy choices made by their white counterparts. Thus, although it ensures more representatives, district-based black electoral success may not necessarily result in more responsive government." [4]

During Guinier's brief nomination, detractors blasted her as a "quota queen" whose ideas were well out of the mainstream of the current dialogue on race. One influential Republican, Sen. Orrin G. Hatch, R-Utah, called her views "frightening to many, even in the civil rights community." [5]

President Clinton subsequently withdrew her nomination June 3, 1993, saying he was troubled by some of the views expressed in her writings and that, "I cannot fight a battle that I know is divisive . . . if I do not believe in the ground of the battle." [6]

Guinier maintained that her ideas had been distorted and her writings taken out of context.

Shaw v. Reno brought new attention to her views and also gave new currency to voting proposals other academics and voting-rights specialists have been discussing. That interest only increased when, a year after the *Shaw* decision, the Supreme Court spoke again on voting rights. One case involved legislative districting in Florida, the other alleged dilution of minority votes on a county commission in Georgia.

On June 30, 1994, the last day of the term, the court upheld the Florida districting plan, which provided minorities with the chance to elect several state representatives. However, in the case, *Johnson v. De Grandy*, the justices declined to support a plan drawn by a lower court that would have provided even more minority representation.

In the other case, *Holder v. Hall*, the court ruled that the Voting Rights Act did not require Bleckley County in Georgia to expand its one-member county commission to give black residents a chance to win election to the government. Although blacks make up 22 percent of the county, they have never elected a commissioner.

As states with significant minority populations grapple with the thorny legal and political matters raised by the high court decisions, these are some of the central questions being raised in the debate:

Is proportional representation of minorities a legitimate goal?

The term "proportional representation" generally refers to representation in Congress or other elected bodies based on the proportion of a minority group in the general population. But that can mean different things to different people depending on the context.

If considered in the context of single-member districts, proportional representation looks to many like a quota because it so often can require what some consider extreme measures to guarantee that all segments of a community are represented. If the black population of a state is, say, 33 percent, under a strict notion of proportional representation one-third of the members of the state's congressional delegation would have to be black. Assuming that voters voted in racial blocs, an electoral map would have to be drawn with one-third of the districts majority-black to guarantee this result.

But in a different voting scheme, such as a large, multi-member district, proportional representation is seen by many voting-rights specialists as more egalitarian because voters have a wider choice of candidates. Instead of casting a ballot for only one candidate, as in a

Reuters

Justice Sandra Day O'Connor

single-member district, voters in a multi-member district would have a better chance to elect at least one of their chosen candidates.

The problem, says Clint Bolick, litigation director of the Institute for Justice, a conservative public interest law center, is that in the existing political terrain, all congressional elections and all but a handful of other contests are based on single-member districts and winner-take-all outcomes.

Therefore, proportional representation "operates as a ceiling, not a floor," Bolick adds, preventing minority candidates from flourishing outside particular boundaries. It also stifles healthy political competition, Bolick asserts, because whites and blacks, with their own essentially safe districts, don't have to compete for each other's votes.

Watt takes exception to the notion that majority-black districts are necessarily safe. In his district, he notes, the black voting-age population is around 53 percent. "You don't take a 53 percent district and guarantee a black person they are going to get elected," he says.

Robinson Everett, a plaintiff in the *Shaw* case and also one of the plaintiffs' lawyers, dislikes proportional representation. "While I think it is good to encourage diversity, I would not subscribe to that as a legitimate goal in and of itself," he says. "I think that the notion that only a black can represent the interests of blacks is erroneous and that whites can only represent whites is erroneous."

Watt agrees with Everett on this point, but he contends that political realities are altogether different. "OK, you want to be colorblind, and that's fine," he says. "But we've got 30 percent of white people who won't vote for anybody black. How is that colorblind?"

To Frank Parker, a professor at the District of Columbia School of Law, the proportional representation debate is a diversion, "a red herring. We don't say anywhere that if you don't have proportional representation it is a violation of the Voting Rights Act," says Parker, author of *Black Votes Count,* a 1990 book about Mississippi voting-rights litigation.

He notes that Section 2 of the act, which he helped revise in 1982, bars discriminatory voting schemes nationwide. The revisions note specifically that "nothing in this section establishes a right to have members of a protected class elected in numbers equal to their proportion in the population."

In other words, Parker argues, majority-minority districts are not based on proportional representation. They are simply "a remedy for exclusion" from the political process.

Vanderbilt University law Professor James Blumstein counters that such remedies go too far. "No one has a right to be in a particular district," he says, adding that voters are only guaranteed the right not to be "purposefully disadvantaged."

Justice David H. Souter, who had dissented in the *Shaw* case, did not specifically endorse proportional representation in his majority opinion in the Florida case, but he noted the dual importance of the proportion of minority representatives as well as the proportion of minorities in the relevant voting-age population when districting disputes arise.

In *Johnson,* the court found that Hispanics were adequately represented under the state Legislature's plan. "Treating equal political opportunity as the focus of the inquiry," wrote Souter, "we do not see how these district lines, apparently providing political effectiveness in proportion to voting-age numbers, deny equal political opportunity" to Hispanics.

It is the often-acrimonious debate over line-drawing and percentages that has prompted Guinier and others interested in voting rights to propose different electoral alternatives to achieve more diverse representation. Among the leaders in such efforts is the two-year-old Center for Voting and Democracy.

When these voting rights experts talk about proportional representation, says center Director Robert Richie, they do so outside the context of single-member districts. Indeed, the center presented a plan in the North Carolina case that would have divided the state into three large multi-member districts and provided a revised voting scheme. In the center of the state, the plan proposed a district with five representatives. Each voter in the district would have five votes. Under a system known as "cumulative voting," voters could cast all five votes for one candidate or they could divide their votes among the candidates. The five candidates

Clint Bolick

Challenging North Carolina's Districts

A North Carolina redistricting plan that created two oddly shaped black-majority congressional districts — the 1st, represented by Eva Clayton, and the 12th, represented by Melvin Watt — sparked a constitutional challenge last year. On Aug. 1, a special three-judge federal panel approved the plan. The decision is virtually certain to be appealed to the Supreme Court.

Source: Congressional Quarterly

with the most votes would win.

Members of minority groups could give their votes to one candidate and thereby increase the likelihood of that candidate's election.

"This has an enormous number of advantages," says Douglas J. Amy, a political science professor at Mount Holyoke College in South Hadley, Mass., and author of the 1993 book *Real Choices/New Voices: The Case for Proportional Representation in the United States*. "It doesn't require the drawing of these special districts that people have been complaining about."

Such a system, Amy adds, "doesn't assume anything about how people want to be represented. It doesn't assume that blacks want to be represented by blacks or whites represented by whites. It simply allows individuals to vote any way they feel depending on what criteria are important to them. Some may vote on the basis of race, some on the basis of gender, some on the basis of certain partisan considerations."

Bolick remains dubious of such schemes, even if they depart from the single-member district model. Dismissing the plans as "social engineering," Bolick rejects the premise that blacks, Hispanics or any other ethnic groups "have interests different from other voters based on their racial identity. The entire enterprise of trying to maximize racial strength in voting contexts is to me inherently divisive and counterproductive," he says, adding that cumulative voting schemes could favor radicals of any sort because they would stir the most passions and make it difficult for centrists to win election.

Some academics agree. "Proportional representation makes it more likely that deputies from the one-issue outskirts of political life will fill the legislatures," Daniel D. Polsby and Robert D. Popper wrote recently in the *Michigan Law Review*. Those elected, they said, would likely face "quite a challenge . . . to create and implement a common agenda of governance." They warned that a legislature could "disintegrate into a cafeteria-style of concessions to various factions that make up the governing coalition." [7]

Even if a proportional-representation scheme gained support, one large hurdle prevents it from working at the congressional level — a law passed by Congress in 1967 requiring states with more than one House member to use single-member districts. Ironically, lawmakers warned at the time that the use of at-large elections in Southern states could dilute the strength of the black vote.

Cumulative voting has been tried in local jurisdictions, however. Most recently, a federal judge ordered at-large elections with cumulative voting for county commission elections in Maryland's Worcester County. Black residents, who make up 21 percent of the population but who have never won countywide office, had challenged the existing district system. The case is on appeal. [8]

Should states still be allowed to draw congressional districts that virtually ensure the election of minorities?

Vanderbilt's Blumstein believes that the *Shaw* case will make majority-minority congressional districts a threatened species. The decision, he says, was not just about a district that looks strange but rather about a racial motive for creating a district. "The goal should not be to recognize racial polarization," he adds, "but to take appropriate steps that can build cross-racial coalitions."

Law Professor Parker contends that majority-minority districting is still appropriate under the Voting Rights Act. Where districts are drawn that dilute minorities' electoral strength, he says, "then lines should be redrawn to give minorities an opportunity to elect candidates of their choice."

Watt believes his situation illustrates the need for majority-minority districts. Citing the 30 percent of the white population that he says won't support a black candidate, Watt believes the only way to counter their bloc voting is by creating a district that gives a black a realistic chance to win.

Brenda Wright, director of the voting rights project of the Lawyers' Committee for Civil Rights, sees a double standard operating. Majority-minority districts, she says, "are denounced as 'segregated' while majority-white election districts that elect white representatives are considered 'colorblind.' "

Moreover, Wright says, majority-minority districts are said to foster "racial polarization, suggesting that the cause of racial unity is better served by the all-white governing bodies that we had for so long, when all election districts were majority white."

Once minorities are elected, Wright adds, they can more easily work to build the cross-racial coalitions described by Blumstein. She cites the case of Mike Espy, who was Mississippi's first black representative this century before becoming secretary of Agriculture in 1993. Espy, a Democrat, was initially elected from a majority-black district, receiving only 10 percent of the white vote. But after "proving that he could represent [all] the people of his district, his share of the white vote increased in subsequent elections," Wright says.

Voting-rights advocates say racial-bloc voting remains a difficult problem in electing minorities. "I found that under racially polarized conditions, white voters are reluctant to support a black candidate — even if he possesses identical credentials, background and experience to a white candidate," Keith Reeves recently wrote in a doctoral dissertation at the University of Michigan. In Southern congressional districts, Reeves adds in an interview, "We can assume race is always a factor."

Charles Cooper, a former Justice Department official in the Reagan administration, agrees that racial-bloc voting is "one of the arguments [for majority-minority districting] that has force and appeal. But it is just not enough. I have a problem with drawing lines in order to ensure a racial result," adds Cooper, who has represented several state and local governments in voting-rights challenges.

Richard Samp, general counsel of the Washington Legal Foundation, a public-interest law firm, shares Cooper's view. "As bad as the disease may be, the cure is worse," he says. "To the extent we are trying to get a colorblind society, we are going in the wrong direction."

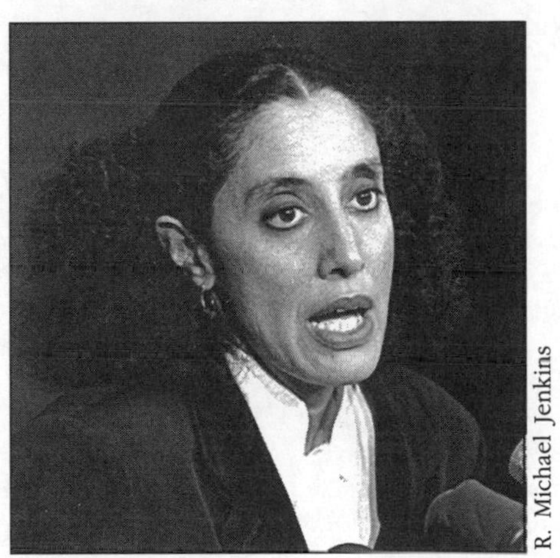
R. Michael Jenkins

Lani Guinier

Guinier believes that other options are preferable to majority-minority districting, but like Parker and Wright she agrees that it is a remedy, if an imperfect one. Any districting reflects the "social engineering" that Bolick complained of, Guinier says. "Districting is about a group of government individuals, incumbent politicians, drawing lines to determine who gets represented. It is completely arbitrary."

That view is shared by Penda Hair, an attorney with the NAACP Legal Defense and Educational Fund who helped try the Texas districting challenge. Referring to the several state congressional maps under attack, Hair says, "In none of these cases was the shape of the district determined by race. It was determined by political factors, mostly incumbent protection."

She contends that in each of the cases more compact majority-minority districts could have been created — but weren't — because they would have imperiled sitting members of Congress.

Like Guinier, Mount Holyoke's Amy favors a shift from single-member districts to the kind of multi-member electoral scheme suggested for North Carolina. "But if we stick with single-member districts," he says, "I do support majority-minority districts because they are the only way to get fair representation for minorities." Otherwise, he adds, blacks will be submerged in white-majority districts, and in states like North Carolina "there will be no minority representation in Congress."

Cooper finds this unduly pessimistic. "It is certainly true that individuals, white and black, have voted on the basis of race," he says. "But over time, that will abate. Fair and neutral" voting procedures will have an effect, though not as quickly as some minorities want. "But it seems the race-neutral route will enormously reduce the level of racial hostility that has been generated" over map drawing.

Should the federal government relax enforcement of the Voting Rights Act?

"The Voting Rights Act still exists and is being enforced and is still necessary," says Steven Rosenbaum, head of the Justice Department's voting-rights section.

Even those who part company on districting issues agree there is still the need for effective voting-rights enforcement. But they disagree over what constitutes effective and appropriate action. "The government should not relax its enforcement," says Vanderbilt's Blumstein, "but it should enforce the law according to court decisions."

In the North Carolina case, he says, the Justice Department in the Bush administration acted in "a lawless man-

Language Help Crucial to Hispanic Voters

In the nation's rapidly growing Hispanic community, as in other ethnic groups where language is often a barrier to voting, the 1965 Voting Rights Act is of paramount importance. The act has provisions requiring bilingual election materials and voting assistance for any language-minority group with over 10,000 voting-age citizens in a single county.

The growth of Hispanics, in particular, has been considerable. In 1900, according to the Census Bureau, only about 130,000 people living in the United States were Spanish-speaking. Now, almost one out of every 10 U.S. residents — roughly 24.1 million individuals — is of Spanish-speaking origin. By the year 2000, a Hispanic population of 30.6 million is projected, and by 2010 the total is expected to reach 39.3 million. [1]

The Hispanic population explosion was apparent in five congressional districting maps that were redrawn after the 1990 Census. Each created majority-Hispanic districts, boosting the Hispanic Caucus in the House of Representatives from 13 to 18 members. [2]

Hispanic leaders fear the Supreme Court's 1993 *Shaw v. Reno* decision may imperil some of their gains. Indeed, the congressional districting map for Texas, with two new Hispanic-majority districts, was challenged after *Shaw*. A federal trial on the issue ended July 1, and a decision is expected later this summer.

Richard Larson, legal director for the Mexican American Legal Defense and Educational Fund (MALDEF), worries that *Shaw* may go farther than just congressional districts. "It applies across the board," he says. "One of the problems for us about the Texas case is that the congressional districts are very similar to the state Senate districts. The fallout from a loss in the congressional case could be huge — and that's true elsewhere in the country."

Larson sees other ramifications from *Shaw*. "We are having to slow down our litigation," he says, "because we assume we are increasingly going to be in a defensive posture" on cases MALDEF thought were already completed. Still other cases are more difficult to settle because of the decision, he adds.

"We draw single-member districts [for local elections]," Larson says, "and now the defendants contend that those districts are bizarrely shaped and unconstitutional." In one case, involving City Council elections in Santa Maria, Calif., Larson said MALDEF had expected to reach agreement with city officials, who were defendants in the case. But because of the *Shaw* ruling, the officials were "heartened" about getting approval to draw a different council map, and they rejected MALDEF's proposal. The case went to trial July 6.

In addition to concerns about the impact of *Shaw*, Hispanic leaders also are concerned about the low rate of citizenship among Hispanics. "It almost doesn't make sense to do voter registration if 40 or 50 percent of the residents are not citizens," says Charles Kamasaki, a National Council of La Raza vice president. Trying to create legislative districts that will enable Hispanics to elect the candidate of their choice requires "a much more concentrated population."

This view is seconded by Larson, who says that such districts must be as much as 65 percent Hispanic, rather than just over a majority, in order to elect an Hispanic. The extra margin is needed, Larson says, because of unregistered voters and residents who are non-citizens or below the voting age.

Even heavily Hispanic districts do not always yield Hispanic victors, however, which leaders say tends to disprove the notion of racial-bloc voting. Kamasaki points to non-Hispanics like California Democrat Howard L. Berman, whose district is 52.7 percent Hispanic, and Texas Democrats Ronald D. Coleman and Gene Green, whose districts are 70.4 percent and 60.6 percent Hispanic, respectively.

But according to *The Washington Post*, at least one-fourth of the residents in Green's and Berman's districts are not citizens, and one-third of the eligible voters stayed home. [3]

Hispanic leaders believe citizenship and voting participation are related. "In the past, it did not matter how many people voted — Latinos could not get elected, so there was less appeal to citizenship," Rep. Lucille Roybal-Allard, D-Calif., told the *Post*. "Now that people see that voting can count for something, it is much easier to get them interested in becoming citizens and participating." [4]

[1] *Hispanic Americans Today*, U.S. Census Bureau, 1993. For background, see "Hispanic Americans," *The CQ Researcher*, Oct. 30, 1992, pp. 929-952.

[2] "Moving Ahead," *National Journal*, April 2, 1994, p. 781; "Black- and Hispanic-Majority Districts," *CQ Weekly Report*, July 10, 1993, p. 1829.

[3] *The Washington Post*, May 22, 1994, p. C-3.

[4] *Ibid*.

ner" because it pressured North Carolina to draw a congressional district map with two majority-black districts. He believes it is a misreading of the Voting Rights Act to require the drawing of majority-minority districts every time it is technically possible.

Samp shares that view, charging the Bush administration's Justice Department with "a misinterpretation of the Voting Rights Act." Some critics said the department was being "hypocritical, that they were doing this to help Republicans" by getting safe GOP districts, Samp adds. "Basically, they were being carried away" by the notion that, "If you can draw any kind of majority-minority district, then you must."

Samp and Blumstein argue that the relevant standard is whether or not a new districting map puts minorities in a worse position than they currently are in.

But the lawyers who represent

minority plaintiffs contend that this interpretation is erroneous and point to the department's own guidelines, put into effect in 1987, during the second administration of President Ronald Reagan. The regulations essentially require that if legislatures in states with racially polarized voting fail to create majority-black districts wherever they can be drawn, the Justice Department will object to that plan.

Rosenbaum put it this way: Even if a proposed election-law change "is not retrogressive but nevertheless is enacted with a discriminatory purpose, that is still a central component of Section 5 [the preclearance requirement]. We make an intense and fact-specific appraisal for each redistricting plan that we review."

Voting-rights specialist Wright says that hearings over the revisions of the law in 1982 provided "compelling" testimony that "merely striking down formal barriers to registration and voting would never permit minorities to achieve full participation in the political life of this country." Hence, more dramatic remedies, such as majority-minority districting, are required, she says.

Adds Parker, the "primary function of the Voting Rights Act is to protect minorities from methods of election that deny them the opportunity to elect their preferred candidate to office. There is no indication of any letup in that problem."

Cooper also agrees that enforcement of the voting act should not be relaxed. But he says the *Shaw* decision makes clear that "there should be fewer occasions to enforce it." The Supreme Court's recent Florida and Georgia decisions, while not about congressional districting, indicate that the court "is still unwilling to endorse some of the more exotic and extreme theories of voting rights" that, in his view, virtually guarantee electoral victories. ■

Districts with Black and Hispanic Majorities

The list below shows congressional districts with a majority population of blacks or Hispanics, and the percentage of minorities in each district. Districts in North Carolina, Louisiana, Texas, Florida and Georgia have been challenged.

Black-Majority Districts (32)

District	% of Blacks	Total % of Minorities	Representative
New York 11	74.0	84.2	Major R. Owens, D.
Maryland 7	71.0	73.1	Kweisi Mfume, D.
Michigan 15	70.0	75.1	Barbara-Rose Collins, D.
Illinois 1	69.7	74.1	Bobby L. Rush, D.
Michigan 14	69.1	71.2	John Conyers, Jr., D.
Illinois 2	68.5	75.4	Mel Reynolds, D.
Alabama 7	67.5	68.0	Earl F. Hilliard, D.
Louisiana 4	66.4	67.6	Cleo Fields, D.
Illinois 7	65.6	72.8	Cardiss Collins, D.
Virginia 3	64.1	66.6	Robert C. Scott, D.
Georgia 11	64.1	65.9	Cynthia McKinney, D.
Mississippi 2	63.0	63.6	Bennie Thompson, D.
Georgia 5	62.3	65.1	John Lewis, D.
South Carolina 6	62.2	62.9	James E. Clyburn, D.
Pennsylvania 2	62.2	65.9	Lucien E. Blackwell, D.
Louisiana 2	61.0	66.5	William J. Jefferson, D.
New York 10	60.7	79.0	Edolphus Towns, D.
New Jersey 10	60.2	73.6	Donald M. Payne, D.
Tennessee 9	59.2	60.7	Harold E. Ford, D.
Ohio 11	58.6	60.7	Louis Stokes, D.
Maryland 4	58.5	68.9	Albert R. Wynn, D.
Florida 17	58.4	80.2	Carrie Meek, D.
North Carolina 1	57.3	58.6	Eva Clayton, D.
North Carolina 12	56.6	58.6	Melvin Watt, D.
Georgia 2	56.6	58.7	Sanford D. Bishop Jr., D.
New York 6	56.2	77.2	Floyd H. Flake, D.
Florida 3	55.0	58.3	Corrine Brown, D.
Pennsylvania 1	52.4	64.0	Thomas M. Foglietta, D.
Missouri 1	52.3	54.2	William L. Clay, D.
Florida 23	51.6	60.7	Alcee L. Hastings, D.
Texas 18	50.9	68.7	Craig Washington, D.
Texas 30	50.0	68.6	Eddie Bernice Johnson, D.

Hispanic-Majority Districts (20)

District	% of Hispanics	Total % of Minorities	Representative
California 33	83.7	91.9	Lucille Roybal-Allard, D.
Texas 15	74.5	76.1	E. "Kika" de la Garza, D.
Texas 16	70.4	75.0	Ronald D. Coleman, D.
Florida 21	69.6	74.5	Lincoln Diaz-Balart, R.
Florida 18	66.7	70.8	Ileana Ros-Lehtinen, R.
Texas 27	66.2	69.3	Solomon P. Ortiz, D.
Illinois 4	65.0	73.2	Luis V. Gutierrez, D.
Texas 23	62.5	66.4	Henry Bonilla, R.
California 34	62.3	73.3	Esteban E. Torres, D.
California 30	61.5	84.8	Xavier Becerra, D.
Texas 20	60.7	67.8	Henry B. Gonzalez, D.
Texas 29	60.6	72.2	Gene Green, D.
Texas 28	60.4	69.6	Frank Tejeda, D.
New York 16	60.2	95.8	Jose E. Serrano, D.
California 31	58.5	82.5	Matthew G. Martinez, D.
New York 12	57.9	86.0	Nydia M. Velazquez, D.
California 20	55.4	67.4	Cal Dooley, D.
California 26	52.7	65.8	Howard L. Berman, D.
Arizona 2	50.5	61.8	Ed Pastor, D.
California 46	50.0	64.4	Robert K. Dornan, R.

Note: There are two districts, both in Hawaii, with majority-Asian populations. The total minority population percentages are based on 1990 Census data, subtracting the non-Hispanic white population from the total population in the district.

Sources: Polidata, Congressional Quarterly, Census Bureau

BACKGROUND

Early Barriers

The tensions in the nation's biracial electorate go back to the aftermath of the Civil War. Northern-enforced Reconstruction had thrust laws upon the Southern states that resulted in the election of hundreds of former slaves to public office. The existence of a large black voting population did not sit well with many Southern whites, and by 1880, with Northern interest in policing the South on the wane, white-supremacist groups such as the White League in Louisiana, the White Line in Mississippi and the White Man's Party in Alabama had formed to wrest political power from blacks by intimidation and outright violence.[9]

Southern blacks were deprived of political power by whites who prevented black voters from reaching the polls, stuffed ballot boxes or engaged in other electoral fraud. Between 1875 and 1901, for example, 107 of the 183 contested elections in the House of Representatives were from 12 Southern states.[10]

But such egregious misdeeds troubled many white leaders throughout the region. "It is true that we win these elections," editorialized a Louisiana paper, "but at a heavy cost, and by the use of methods repugnant to our idea of political honesty and which must, in time, demoralize the people of Louisiana." And a politician in Virginia complained that, "Cheating at elections is demoralizing our whole people."[11]

Inevitably, blacks were disfranchised and whites returned to unquestioned political power. Mississippi, the state with the second-largest black population, led the way. In 1890, the state constitution was rewritten to include literacy tests and property requirements that effectively denied the ballot to most black voters.

South Carolina followed suit in 1895, Louisiana in 1898, North Carolina in 1900, Alabama and Virginia in 1901 and Georgia in 1908. Florida, Arkansas and Texas, meanwhile, disfranchised many black voters by enacting poll taxes and other devices.[12]

These efforts were highly successful; the laws would endure for more than a half-century, and no Southern black would be elected to federal office for 70 years.

Challenging the White Primary

By forcing Reconstruction on the South, Northern Republicans made the GOP anathema to Southerners. Thus, anyone who aspired to a political career aligned himself with the Democratic Party. This made primaries the critical contest; November elections simply ratified the primary result. Shut out of the Democratic Party, Southern blacks were denied the opportunity to vote even though the 15th Amendment to the Constitution mandated that "the right of citizens of the United States shall not be denied or abridged by the United States or by any state on account race, color or previous condition of servitude."

In a challenge to the white primary system, a black Texan sued the Democratic Party. But the Supreme Court eventually ruled in *Grovey v. Texas* in 1934 that a political party was a private association and could set whatever membership rules it wanted.

A few years later, another black Texan, this time represented by NAACP lawyer Thurgood Marshall, again challenged white primaries. On April 3, 1944, the Supreme Court, in *Smith v. Allwright,* reversed the previous decision. Ruling 8-1, the court said that primary elections in Texas were conducted by the Democratic Party under state statutory authority. Hence, the court said, it became "an agency of the state" and was thus forbidden from discriminating against citizens in their right to vote.

In the wake of the decision, Georgia Gov. Ellis Arnall, perhaps the most moderate politician in the region, declared the white primary dead. But other Southern political leaders tried to get around the decision.

The reaction was perhaps most extreme in South Carolina, where the governor called the legislature back into session to repeal all primary laws in an effort to make the Democratic Party a completely private entity. Some 150 laws were stripped from the books in the short session, prompting *Newsweek* to label the state legislators "killbillies."[13]

Though it took two separate lawsuits in South Carolina, the effort by white political leaders to keep blacks from voting ultimately failed; blacks voted in the August 1948 primary in substantial numbers for the first time in more than 50 years.

Anti-Poll-Tax Drive

While black leaders were pursuing legal remedies, there was movement in Congress to repeal the poll tax — an effort that would ultimately prove unsuccessful despite House passage of the measure on five separate occasions over a period of years. The stumbling block was always the Senate, where Southerners, led by Georgia Democrat Richard B. Russell, held considerable power.[14]

What happened in 1948 was typical. On April 28, after the House passed an anti-poll-tax bill, a Senate committee sent its version of the legislation to the full Senate. But Senate debate did not begin until July 29. Six days later, senators voted to adjourn, killing the bill.

This effort to enfranchise Southern black voters had failed despite President Harry S Truman's support. On Feb. 2, 1948, he had sent a special message to Congress calling for a number of civil rights initiatives, including more protections for the right to vote. Indeed, later in the year he campaigned for election on a party platform containing the party's

Continued on p. 708

Chronology

1890 -1910 *Southern and border states revise laws to keep blacks from voting.*

1890
Mississippi becomes first of former Confederate states to rewrite constitution, imposing poll taxes, residency requirements and literacy tests to disfranchise blacks.

1908
Georgia is last of deep South states to revise constitution to disfranchise black voters.

1940s-50s *Congress attempts to enact anti-poll-tax legislation; Supreme Court decides an important voting-rights case.*

April 13, 1944
Supreme Court strikes down "white primary," ruling Texas Democratic Party was equivalent to a state agency and could not discriminate.

June 12, 1945
House passes bill outlawing poll tax.

July 31, 1946
Senate fails to stop filibuster on anti-poll-tax bill.

July 21, 1947
House again passes anti-poll-tax bill; no action in Senate.

Feb. 2, 1948
President Harry S Truman calls for greater protections for voting.

Aug. 4, 1948
Senate kills anti-poll-tax legislation.

July 24, 1949
House again passes anti-poll-tax bill; companion proposal dies in Senate.

Aug. 29, 1957
Following House approval, Senate passes major civil rights bill that includes new protections for voting. Critics call measure too weak.

1960s *Congress passes strong voting-rights legislation; black registration in Southern states increases dramatically, and blacks begin to win political office in sizable numbers.*

May 6, 1960
New civil rights bill signed with voting-rights protections; critics call bill "a fraud."

Aug. 4, 1965
Senate OKs Voting Rights Act one day after House action.

Aug. 7-10, 1965
Government sues to eliminate poll taxes in Mississippi, Alabama, Texas and Virginia and suspends literacy tests in Alabama, Alaska, Georgia, Louisiana, Mississippi, South Carolina, Virginia and North Carolina.

March 7, 1966
Supreme Court upholds Voting Rights Act.

1970s *Black electoral gains continue to increase in the South.*

June 17, 1970
Extension of Voting Rights Act enforcement section is approved.

November 1972
Rep. Andrew J. Young, D-Ga., becomes first black congressman from the South in 70 years.

June 18, 1973
Supreme Court allows challenge to election schemes alleged to dilute minority voting strength.

July 28, 1975
Voting Rights Act enforcement section extended; anti-bias provisions expanded to cover Spanish-speaking.

November 1978
Number of black elected officials in 11 states of old Confederacy rises to 2,256, up from 776 in 1970.

1980s *Congress renews enforcement sections of Voting Rights Act as Supreme Court rules on voting cases.*

April 22, 1980
Supreme Court rules that plaintiffs in voting cases must prove officials who created the election scheme acted with the *purpose* of racial discrimination.

June 1982
Congress extends Voting Rights Act, renewing critical enforcement section and adding language to overturn the 1980 Supreme Court decision.

June 30, 1986
In first application of 1982 Voting Rights Act changes, Supreme Court holds that six of North Carolina's multi-member legislative districts illegally diluted the strength of black votes.

1990s *Federal courts hear challenges to districts drawn with majorities of black voters.*

1991-92
States redraw electoral districts based on 1990 Census.

November 1992
Alabama, Florida, North Carolina, South Carolina and Virginia elect first blacks to House in this century. Illinois elects black woman to Senate.

June 28, 1993
Supreme Court reinstates lawsuit by white North Carolinians who challenged the state's congressional map.

Fall-Winter 1993
Majority-minority districts challenged in Florida, Georgia, Louisiana and Texas.

April 6, 1994
Federal judge orders "cumulative voting" in Maryland county to help blacks win countywide office.

Aug. 1, 1994
Federal panel says redistricting plan in North Carolina is not illegal.

Black and Hispanic Elected Officials, 1984-93

The number of black elected officials increased 40 percent from 1984-93, while the number of Hispanic elected officials increased 65 percent.

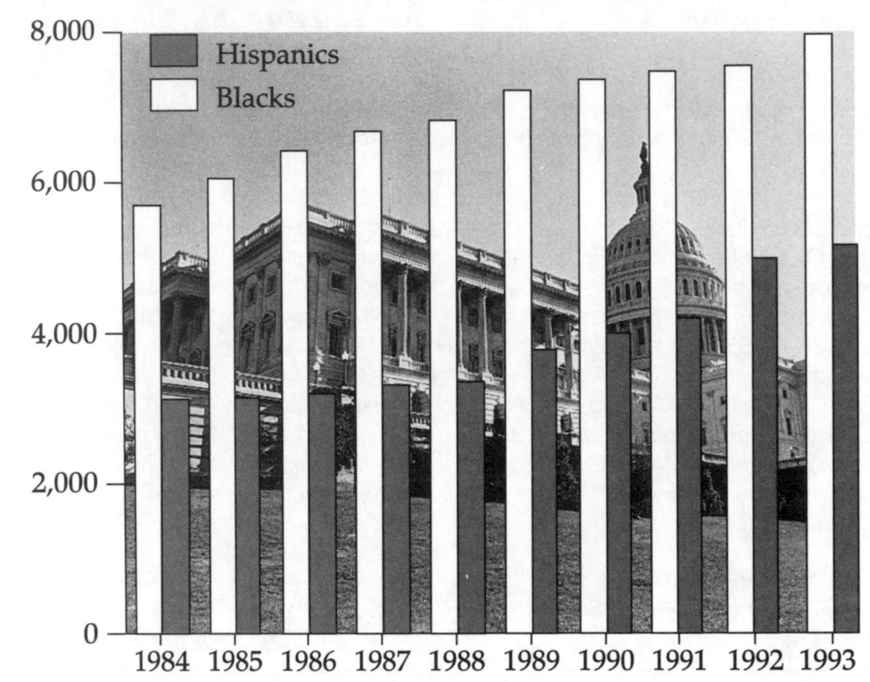

Sources: Joint Center for Political and Economic Studies; National Association of Latino Elected and Appointed Officials

Continued from p. 706

strongest civil rights language to date. It was so strong it prompted a walkout by some Southern delegates from the party's convention in Philadelphia and led to a third-party challenge from Southerners who called themselves States' Rights Democrats — the "Dixiecrats." [15]

When the Truman administration ended in 1953, black Southerners still faced numerous barriers to voting. The 1944 *Smith* decision had helped, but much more was needed.

Civil Rights Bills

Although President Dwight D. Eisenhower invariably invoked civil rights in his annual State of the Union addresses, he did not request legislation until 1956. Then he proposed new laws to protect voting rights, including a civil rights commission to investigate charges that "in some localities . . . Negro citizens are being deprived of their right to vote and are likewise being subjected to unwarranted economic pressure."

After a year of discussion, Congress agreed on legislation that was somewhat pared down from the bill Eisenhower and civil rights activists had wanted. In fact, the new law, approved Aug. 29, 1957, was considered something of a victory for Southern members. Although they had been unable to muster enough votes to kill the bill, Southerners nonetheless had cut some of the muscle out — mainly a section that would have given the attorney general broad authority to file lawsuits for deprivation of civil rights. [16]

The law's voting rights section only authorized the attorney general to seek an injunction when individuals were deprived or about to be deprived of their right to vote. And it gave federal district judges authority to hear such cases. But it soon became clear that the law was incapable of tearing down the voting barriers Southern blacks still faced.

Three years later, Congress took up another civil rights bill, one with a more ambitious voting-rights section.

The fledgling Civil Rights Commission had provided compelling evidence of the disparity between white and black voters. In Alabama, for example, 63.6 percent of the voting-age whites were registered to vote in 1960 compared with 13.7 percent of the blacks; in North Carolina, it was 92.8 percent of the voting-age whites vs. 38.2 percent of the blacks; and in Mississippi, only 6.7 percent of the eligible black voters were registered; (the percentage of registered whites was not available). [17]

Eisenhower had sent a civil rights bill to Congress early in 1959, but there was little action on it. Pressure to go forward increased early in 1960, and at the end of January the Justice Department announced that the administration would add a new voting-rights section to the measure that would allow court-appointed referees to help blacks register and vote.

After nearly two months of debate and procedural jousting, a bill was finally enacted. But once again, Southern lawmakers forced changes that made the new law, in the view of civil rights leaders, too cumbersome to be effective.

The law's complicated procedures for registering black voters required the attorney general to first win a civil suit for deprivation of civil rights. That enabled the attorney general to return to court to seek a separate finding of discrimination against potential black voters in the community. Only then could any black apply to the court for an order declaring that he was a qualified voter. State officials then would be required to permit that individual to vote.

Thurgood Marshall, then head of the NAACP Legal Defense and Educational Fund, called the new law "a fraud," and NAACP chief Roy Wilkins complained that "A Negro has to pass through more checkpoints and more officials than he would if he were trying to get the U.S. gold reserves in Fort Knox." [18]

Voting Rights Act

John F. Kennedy's narrow victory over Richard M. Nixon in the 1960 presidential election, with crucial help from Southern black voters, increased pressure on the new Democratic administration to move on civil rights. Black leaders were growing impatient with Kennedy's seeming recalcitrance. But the murder in 1963 of Mississippi civil rights leader Medgar Evers prompted him to action. The assassination of Kennedy himself then lent even more impetus to these efforts.

Blending his considerable political skills with poignant memories of his youthful predecessor, President Lyndon B. Johnson pushed through the landmark 1964 Civil Rights Act, which opened parks, restaurants, hotels and other "public accommodations" to all Americans. Then, in 1965, he turned to voting rights.

But civil rights activists had gotten there first. Led by the Rev. Dr. Martin Luther King Jr., they were seeking to register voters in Dallas County, Ala., where only 2.1 percent of the eligible blacks were on the rolls.

To dramatize the problem, the prospective voters wanted to march from Selma, the county seat, to Montgomery, the state capital. On March 7 they set off. Six blocks into the 50-mile trek, the demonstrators were confronted by local police, state troopers and unfriendly white citizens. As the marchers tried to retreat, they were clubbed and teargassed — the debacle captured by the national news media. [19]

Eight days later, in a televised speech to a joint session of Congress, Johnson vowed to present lawmakers with a tough, new voting rights bill. Adopting the slogan of the civil rights movement, he promised, "We shall overcome." [20]

The Senate began work on the new voting rights bill in April, passing it in August. The key provisions authorized federal supervision of voter registration in states, cities and counties that had used voter-qualification tests before the November 1964 elections and where fewer than 50 percent of the voting-age residents had participated in the presidential election.

The legislation also suspended the use of literacy tests in selected Southern states and in scattered counties elsewhere, and it required Justice Department approval before these states and counties could change election procedures or laws — the Section 5 preclearance requirement, which would be key to enforcement. Despite attacks by Southern opponents, these critical provisions survived.

The House passed its version of the legislation July 9, and three weeks later, after differences in the House and Senate measures were resolved, Congress approved the legislation and sent it to the president. On Aug. 6, Johnson signed the act. In a nationally televised ceremony broadcast from the imposing second-floor Rotunda of the Capitol, he noted that blacks had come to the United States "in darkness and they came in chains. And today we strike away the last major shackle of those fierce, ancient bonds."

Section 5 of the new law, the enforcement provisions, would have to be renewed by Congress after five years. Another part of the law, Section 2, barred the adoption of any elections or procedures that would deny or hamper the right to vote. Unlike Section 5, it was permanent and covered all states and political subdivisions.

The Justice Department swung into action following passage of the act. On Aug. 7, it sued to eliminate Mississippi's poll tax. Similar actions were taken three days later against Alabama, Texas and Virginia. Also on Aug. 10, the department suspended literacy tests and similar qualification devices in Alabama, Alaska, Georgia, Louisiana, Mississippi, South Carolina, Virginia, North Carolina and one county in Arizona.

Two days later, Attorney General Nicholas deB. Katzenbach named the first group of Southern counties and parishes where federal examiners would process voter-registration applications.

On Aug. 25, Johnson announced that in the first 19 days under the new law, examiners had registered 27,385 blacks in three Southern states. In Selma, on Aug. 14 alone, 381 blacks were put on the rolls — more than *all* the black registrants in the previous 60 years. By November, the number would rise to nearly 8,000. [21]

South Carolina officials had quickly challenged the Voting Rights Act, but on March 7, 1966, the Supreme Court upheld the new law. The justices ruled that Congress had properly exercised its authority to enforce the 15th Amendment to the Constitution, which empowered Congress to enforce the right to vote "by appropriate legislation."

For the next quarter-century, the voting law inspired dozens of lawsuits over voting rights, forever changing Southern politics. As black registration soared, and blacks were elected to local and state offices, white politicians learned to tailor their campaign pitches to an integrated electorate.

Supreme Court Tests

In 1968, in one of the first important cases testing the Voting Rights Act, the

Black and Hispanic Elected Officials, 1993

The list below shows the number of black and Hispanic elected officials from each state and Washington, D.C. The list includes federal, state and local officials.

State	Black	Hispanic
Alabama	699	0
Alaska	3	0
Arizona	15	350
Arkansas	380	1
California	273	797
Colorado	20	204
Connecticut	62	19
Delaware	23	1
D.C.	198	0
Florida	200	68
Georgia	545	0
Hawaii	0	0
Idaho	0	2
Illinois	465	797
Indiana	72	8
Iowa	11	0
Kansas	21	6
Kentucky	63	0
Louisiana	636	9
Maine	1	0
Maryland	140	2
Massachusetts	30	3
Michigan	333	10
Minnesota	16	3
Mississippi	751	0
Missouri	185	1
Montana	0	2
Nebraska	6	3
Nevada	10	5
New Hampshire	2	0
New Jersey	211	44
New Mexico	3	661
New York	299	93
North Carolina	468	0
North Dakota	0	0
Ohio	219	9
Oklahoma	123	1
Oregon	10	5
Pennsylvania	158	8
Rhode Island	12	1
South Carolina	450	1
South Dakota	3	0
Tennessee	168	0
Texas	472	2,030
Utah	0	4
Vermont	2	0
Virginia	155	0
Washington	19	15
West Virginia	21	0
Wisconsin	30	2
Wyoming	1	5
Total	**7,984**	**5,170**

Sources: Joint Center for Political and Economic Studies; National Association of Latino Elected and Appointed Officials

Supreme Court upheld Section 5's authority over two proposed changes in local election procedures: changing from districtwide elections to at-large elections, and from elected to appointed county superintendents of education. The court's ruling consolidated cases from Mississippi and Virginia, where state officials had contended that such electoral decisions were not covered by the Voting Rights Act. [22]

Five years later, the court again addressed at-large elections, ruling in a Texas case, *White v. Regester,* that so-called vote dilution violated the 14th Amendment's Equal Protection Clause. The court said that multi-member districts were not automatically unconstitutional but could violate the 14th Amendment if they were used "invidiously to cancel out or minimize the voting strength of racial groups."

To prove a claim of vote dilution, those challenging at-large voting must show that the political processes leading to nomination or election "are not equally open to participation" by those classes of citizens protected by the Voting Rights Act. The factors to be considered could include the extent of any history of official discrimination, the extent of racially polarized voting and the size of election districts.

Two years after *White,* in 1975, the Supreme Court further refined its views on enforcement in *Beer v. United States.* The issue was whether a New Orleans reapportionment plan providing for two majority-black districts, where there had been none, was acceptable even though a differently drawn map could have provided the chance for election of more black City Council members. The justices ruled that an electoral plan from a covered jurisdiction was acceptable under the law as long as there was "no retrogression in the position of racial minorities with respect to their effective exercise of the electoral franchise."

The decision was unpopular with voting-rights activists, who believed that jurisdictions should have been required to maximize opportunities for minority electoral success, not merely to make a bad situation somewhat better.

By the mid-1970s, the law's impact was clear. In Alabama, for example, black voter registration had risen from 23 percent of those eligible in 1964 to 58.1 percent in 1976; in Mississippi during those 12 years, it had gone from 6.7 percent to 67.4 percent. [23]

Figures for black elected officials tell a similar story. In 1970, according to the Joint Center for Political and Economic Studies, 1,469 blacks held office across the nation, including 86 in Alabama, 81 in Mississippi, 62 in North Carolina, 40 in Georgia and 38 in South Carolina. By 1975, there were 3,503 black officeholders, and the number had at least doubled in the Southern states. The total included two members of Congress, Democrats Andrew J. Young from Atlanta, Ga., and Harold E. Ford, from Memphis, Tenn. [24]

Congress Compromises

In 1980, the Supreme Court continued its key role in interpreting the Voting Rights Act and also set the stage for a difficult fight looming two years away. Ruling in *Mobile v. Bolden,* the court held that intent to discriminate had to be shown for there to have been a violation of Section 2 of the act — the permanent provision covering the entire nation.

Civil rights lawyers complained that the court had misinterpreted the voting law, setting a standard of proof that was virtually impossible to meet. They vowed to reverse the decision in 1982, when renewal of the act's Section 5 enforcement

Asian-American Community Fighting for Civil Rights

In the past decade, the nation's Asian-American population doubled to 7.5 million. Census Bureau projections and immigration patterns suggest there will be three times as many Asian-Americans by the year 2020.[1]

Ethnic diversity distinguishes the nation's Asian community, which encompasses large numbers of Chinese, Korean, Japanese, Filipino, Vietnamese, Cambodian and Laotian Americans.

Among the issues facing this diverse group are developing political cohesion and documenting discriminatory voting patterns. As a result, Margaret Fung, executive director of the New York-based Asian-American Legal Defense and Education Fund, told a congressional panel, the Voting Rights Act remains an important tool for Asian-Americans, particularly those provisions requiring bilingual materials and voting assistance.[2]

To work for the rights of Asian-Americans, a new organization, the National Asian Pacific American Legal Consortium, was started in Washington, D.C., last year. It embraces Fung's group, the Asian Law Caucus in San Francisco and the Asian Pacific American Legal Center of Southern California in Los Angeles.

The consortium asserts that "prejudice, misunderstanding, institutional barriers and violence continue to prevent Asian Pacific Americans from fully exercising their civil rights and civil liberties."[3]

Some of that experience, Fung told members of a House subcommittee, is reflected in voting-rights matters. In the past, Asian-Americans outside of Hawaii have been unsuccessful in persuading officials to create majority-Asian districts. She cited unsuccessful efforts in New York City to keep Manhattan's Chinatown in one state assembly district and to maximize Asian-American voting strength on the City Council. Although a "so-called Asian district" was created, Fung said, "Asian-Americans were totally submerged within a much larger white population." In the four primary and general elections for City Council held since 1991, she noted, Asian-American candidates "have been soundly defeated."

Fung said similar problems occurred in California, where in 1991, despite a broad-scale effort by Asian-Americans, their communities were split up in legislative districts drawn in the San Francisco area and central Los Angeles, where great numbers of Asian-Americans live.

Out of 120 state legislators in California, only one is an Asian-American, Fung said, and in San Francisco, where Asian-Americans account for 30 percent of the city's population, only one Asian-American has served on the Board of Supervisors. In New York City, where the Asian-American population exceeds a half-million, Asian-Americans have never been elected to legislative office this century, she said.

On a national level, there are four Asian-American representatives in the House. One, Democrat Patsy T. Mink, was elected from Hawaii, a state with a majority Asian-American population. The other three are from California: Democrats Robert T. Matsui and Norman Y. Mineta and Republican Jay C. Kim. Hawaii's two Democratic senators, Daniel K. Inouye and Daniel K. Akaka, also are Asian-American.

Among the reasons for what Asian-Americans believe is their political underrepresentation is their lower rate of citizenship in comparison with their actual population. Nationwide, according to Fung, 62 percent of all Asian-Americans are foreign-born, with the percentages even higher among certain Asian groups, particularly in urban areas.

As a result, large numbers do not speak English well. They can pass citizenship tests, she said, but are not able "to understand complicated electoral procedures or obscure ballot propositions and referenda." In New York City, for example, 44 percent of the Asians do not speak English well. In Los Angeles, with more than 950,000 Asian-Americans, roughly 40 percent do not speak English well; nearly two-thirds of them speak their native Asian language at home, according to Fung.

"Unequal educational opportunities as well as the difficulties of learning to read and write a language that utilizes an unfamiliar Romanized alphabet create special barriers for Asian-Americans," Fung said, "even though they may be well-informed about political issues through the Asian language media and other sources."

Coupled with these problems is a low voter-registration rate. New York City Asians, for example, represent 6 percent of the population but only 2 percent of the city's 3.4 million registered voters. And in San Francisco, Asians make up fully 30 percent of the population but less than 5 percent of its registered voters.

---

[1] For background, see "Asian Americans," *The CQ Researcher*, Dec. 13, 1991, pp. 945-968.

[2] Testimony at hearings of the House Judiciary Civil and Constitutional Rights Subcommittee, May 25, 1994.

[3] National Asian Pacific American Legal Consortium, *1993 Annual Report*, p. 1.

provisions would be decided.

The House-passed renewal bill, actually completed in 1981, overturned the *Mobile* decision by revising Section 2 to say that a violation of the law could be proved by showing that an election procedure "results in the denial or abridgment" of the right to vote.

In the Senate, a group led by Orrin Hatch strongly opposed the House approach and argued for retention of the "intent" standard spelled out by the Supreme Court. After days of hearings and weeks of backroom negotiations, Democratic and Republican members of the Senate Judiciary Committee reached a compromise. The "results" test inserted by the House would be kept, but language would be added based on the 1973 *White v. Regester* decision, which required a court to look at the "totality of the circumstances" before determining whether a violation existed.

The compromise, which was ultimately approved by Congress, also stipulated that minority groups did not have a "right" to proportional representation and that lack of proportional representation was only one circumstance a court could consider in a voting-rights case.[25]

Four years later, in 1986, the compromise got its first test at the Supreme Court. In *Thornburg v. Gingles* (pronounced "Jingles"), the court, upholding the new Section 2 language, set out the criteria to prove a violation under this provision. The key elements were whether a majority-minority district could be created, whether minority voters tended to vote for particular candidates and whether minority-preferred candidates are usually defeated by white-bloc voting. The court rejected the argument that once one or more black candidates have been elected from a challenged district, the district is immune from challenge under the Voting Rights Act.

Barely five months after the *Gingles* decision, Mike Espy became the first black elected to Congress from Mississippi in more than a century, bringing to four the number of black congressmen from Southern states. *

The 1990 Census required the redrawing of electoral districts, and black political leaders in the South, in particular, hoped for more electoral success. Despite some contentious battles in the states, majority-black districts were drawn across the South, and in Alabama, Florida, North Carolina, South Carolina and Virginia blacks were elected to the U.S. House of Representatives for the first time this century. In addition, a black woman, Democrat Carol Mosely-Braun, was elected to the U.S. Senate from Illinois. (*See table, p. 700.*)

In North Carolina and Florida, as well as in Louisiana, which had previously elected a black to Congress, the majority-minority districts had unusual shapes, not only to give black candidates a good chance at winning but also, some observers said, to protect white incumbents in their districts. The stage was set for the high court's *Shaw v. Reno* decision. ■

CURRENT SITUATION

Action in the States

Since *Shaw*, there have been trials on four state districting maps and three court decisions — two of them coming from Louisiana, the first state to provide a post-*Shaw* judicial opinion on such issues. On Dec. 28, 1993, a special three-judge federal panel had ruled that the districting plan in general and the 4th District in particular were "not narrowly tailored to further any compelling governmental interest," as *Shaw* had required. Therefore, the plaintiff's right to equal protection under the law had been violated, the court said, and the districting plan was declared null and void.

To several voting-rights specialists, the decision suggested that, at least in the eyes of the federal judges in Louisiana, *any* district drawn with a majority-minority population could be constitutionally suspect, not just those that looked funny.

Allan J. Lichtman, a history professor at American University, finds this view troubling because it ignores the 14th Amendment's role in safeguarding minority rights. "Thus is history inverted," he asserted, because individuals intended to be protected by the 14th Amendment now can be harmed by this interpretation of it.[26]

But those dubious about race-based districting applauded the opinion as an appropriate interpretation of *Shaw*, including Everett, the plaintiff's lawyer in *Shaw*, and Cooper, the former Justice department official. "I think the judges made it clear that there was overreaching by the Justice Department," Everett says, referring to the Louisiana decision.

This past spring, the Louisiana Legislature redrew the map, making the 4th District more compact. Blacks, who had been 63 percent of the old district, would be 55 percent of the new 4th. The Justice Department approved the new map in June.

Responding to an appeal, the Supreme Court on June 27 voided the three-judge panel's decision on the old 4th District and sent the case back to Louisiana for consideration in light of the new district map.

After a trial on the new map, the court on July 22 again rejected the districting plan as an unconstitutional racial gerrymander. Three days later, the court imposed a new congressional map with only one majority-black district. Louisiana's attorney general, Democrat Richard P. Ieyoub, has asked the U.S. Supreme Court to stay the imposition of the new map, pending an appeal.

The trial on the Texas districting map was heard from June 27 to July 1, and a decision is expected in late summer. The trial on the Georgia challenge was completed July 25. No date has been set for a trial on the Florida congressional district map, but a federal court has ruled that the upcoming 1994 elections will proceed under the current redistricting plan.

The North Carolina ruling Aug. 1 was the latest development, with a special three-judge federal panel deciding 2-1 that the state's districting plan was constitutional because it was "narrowly

Continued on p. 714

* The others, all Democrats, were John Lewis (Georgia), Harold E. Ford (Tennessee) and Mickey Leland (Texas), who died in 1989.

At Issue:

Did North Carolina go too far in drawing congressional districts that favor the election of minority candidates?

yes

JUSTICE SANDRA DAY O'CONNOR

Writing for the majority in* Shaw v. Reno, *June 28, 1993

It is unsettling how closely the North Carolina plan resembles the most egregious racial gerrymanders of the past. An understanding of the nature of the appellants' claim is critical to our resolution of the case. In their complaint the appellants did not claim that the General Assembly's reapportionment plan unconstitutionally "diluted" white voting strength. They did not even claim to be white. Rather appellants' complaint alleged that the deliberate segregation of voters into separate districts on the basis of race violated their constitutional right to participate in a "color-blind" electoral process. . . .

Classifications of citizens solely on the basis of race "are by their very nature odious to a free people whose institutions are founded upon the doctrine of equality." They threaten to stigmatize individuals by reason of their membership in a racial group and to incite racial hostility. . . . Accordingly we have held that the Fourteenth Amendment requires state legislation that expressly distinguishes among citizens because of their race to be narrowly tailored to further a compelling governmental interest. . . .

A reapportionment plan that includes in one district individuals who belong to the same race, but who are otherwise widely separated by geographical and political boundaries, and who may have little in common with one another but the color of their skin bears an uncomfortable resemblance to political apartheid.

For these reasons we conclude that a plaintiff challenging a reapportionment statute under the Equal Protection Clause may state a claim by alleging that the legislation, though race-neutral on its face, rationally cannot be understood as anything other than an effort to separate voters into different districts on the basis of race, and that the separation lacks sufficient justification. It is unnecessary for us to decide whether or how a reapportionment plan that, on its face, can be explained in non-racial terms successfully could be challenged. . . . We only hold that, on the facts of this case, plaintiffs have stated a claim sufficient to defeat the state appellees' motion to dismiss.

Racial classifications of any sort pose the risk of lasting harm to our society. They reinforce the belief, held by too many for too much of our history, that individuals should be judged by the color of their skin. Racial classifications with respect to voting carry particular dangers. Racial gerrymandering, even for remedial purposes, may balkanize us into competing racial factions; it threatens to carry us further from the goal of a political system in which race no longer matters. . . .

no

JUSTICE DAVID H. SOUTER

Dissenting opinion in* Shaw v. Reno, *June 28, 1993

Today, the court recognizes a new cause of action under which a state's electoral redistricting plan that includes a configuration "so bizarre" that it "rationally cannot be understood as anything other than an effort to separate voters into different districts on the basis of race (without) sufficient justification" will be subject to strict scrutiny. In my view there is no justification for the court's determination to depart from our prior decisions by carving out this narrow group of cases for strict scrutiny. . . .

Until today the court has analyzed equal-protection claims involving race in electoral districting differently from equal-protection claims involving other forms of governmental conduct. . . .

As long as members of racial groups have the commonality of interest implicit in our ability to talk about concepts like "minority voting strength" and "dilution of minority votes, and as long as racial bloc voting takes place, legislators will have to take race into account in order to avoid dilution of minority voting strength in districting plans they adopt. . . .

A second distinction between districting and most other governmental decisions in which race has figured is that those other decisions using racial criteria characteristically occur in circumstances in which the use of race to the advantage of one person is necessarily at the obvious expense of a member of a different race. . . .

In districting, by contrast, the mere placement of an individual in one district instead of another denies no one a right or benefit provided to others.

Under our cases there is in general a requirement that in order to obtain relief under the Fourteenth Amendment, the purpose and effect of the districting must be to devalue the effectiveness of a voter compared to what, as a group member, he would otherwise be able to enjoy. . . .

If a cognizable harm like dilution or the abridgment of the right to participate in the electoral process is shown, the districting plan violates the Fourteenth Amendment. If not, it does not. Under this approach, in the absence of an allegation of such cognizable harm, there is no need for further scrutiny because a gerrymandering claim cannot be proven without the element of harm.

The court offers no justification for treating the narrow category of bizarrely shaped district claims differently from other districting claims. . . . I [therefore] would not respond to the seeming egregiousness of the redistricting now before us by untethering the concept of racial gerrymander in such a case from the concept of harm exemplified by dilution. . . .

Louisiana's Troubled 4th District

Concern over the Z-shaped, majority-black 4th District (left), represented by Cleo Fields, prompted a panel of three federal judges to reject Louisiana's 1992 congressional district map last year. On July 25, the judges ordered the use of a new court-drawn map (right) that placed Democrat Fields, an African-American, and white Republican Rep. Richard H. Baker in the majority-white, Baton Rouge-based 6th District.

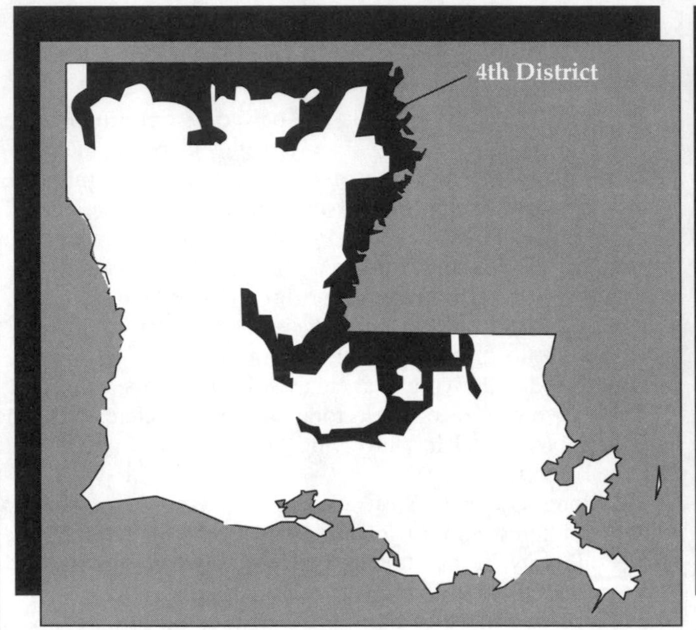

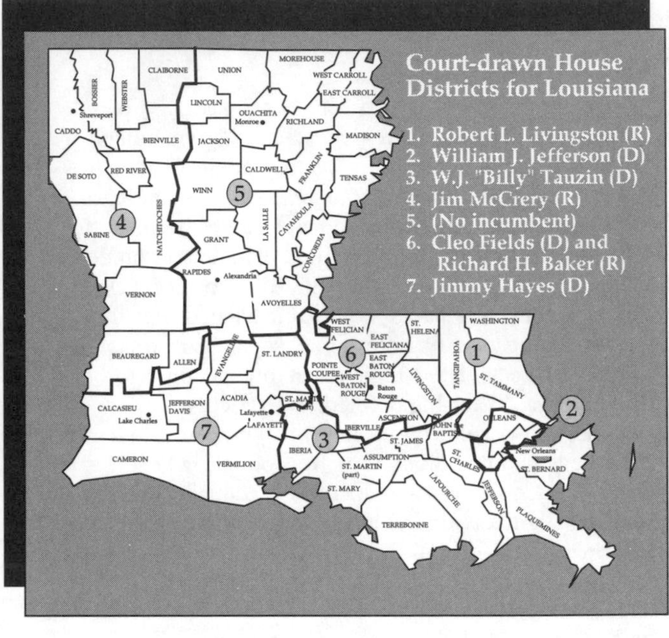

Source: Congressional Quarterly

Continued from p. 712

tailored to further the state's compelling interest in complying with the Voting Rights Act." Like the Louisiana decision, this ruling is expected to be appealed to the Supreme Court.

The Justice Department has been defending the redistricting plans in the challenged states. Deval Patrick, head of the Civil Rights Division, announced in the spring that he had created a Voting Rights Protection Task Force to handle any similar voting-rights claims.

And in June, the Rev. Jesse Jackson, perceiving threats to black electoral gains, went on a 10-day bus tour from Texas to Virginia to talk about the *Shaw* decision and its implications for the South. Funded by Jackson's Rainbow Coalition and supported by the Democratic National Committee, the tour was intended not only to educate voters about the case but also to build support for possible congressional action to reverse rulings that minority communities consider adverse.[27]

However, it is not clear just what Congress could do to overrule *Shaw,* if it were so inclined. As law Professor Parker noted, the case was a constitutional claim decided under the Equal Protection Clause of the 14th Amendment. It was not a matter of statutory interpretation that could be dealt with by rewriting the Voting Rights Act. ■

OUTLOOK

More Litigation?

Lawyers active in voting rights believe more litigation is in the offing, and that means that the future of majority-minority districting will rest in judicial hands. They also agreed that the high court's two most recent voting decisions — in Florida and Georgia — were relatively narrow (*see p. 700*), though attorneys who represent minorities said they feared the cases could be used as roadmaps for governmental bodies looking for ways to dilute minority voting strength but still avoid violating the Voting Rights Act.

Cooper, who has represented several governmental bodies in voting-rights challenges, considers *Shaw* "a clear and present danger to racial gerrymandering." Thus, he says, it could be used for challenging any electoral map that looks like it was drawn for racial reasons.

According to Parker, *Shaw* could affect not just congressional districting but other electoral maps as well, such as those for state legislatures, county commissions and city councils. "There's no limit to the number of the lawsuits that can be filed," he says. "What's bizarrely shaped was not defined in the Supreme Court decision."

But Vanderbilt's Blumstein contends that *Shaw* was not about "weird districts" but about the use of race to draw districts. The shape of the district, in his view, is just evidence that race was a motivating factor in the creation of the electoral map.

Rosenbaum, the Justice Department's voting-rights chief, believes that some post-*Shaw* decisions indicate that the ruling may be more limited than originally thought. He cites a recent decision in Mississippi, where a three-judge court declined to throw out a districting map for the Board of Supervisors election in Calhoun County. Blacks had sought a new districting plan, but the county had contended that would be seen as racial gerrymandering and violating *Shaw*. The court rejected that reasoning. The same result came in a similar case involving a districting map for the Bridgeport, Conn., City Council.

Whatever the court interpretations, voting-rights specialist Wright says governmental bodies "are becoming more recalcitrant about the types of districting plans they will draw." After *Shaw*, she notes, the attitude seems to be "how much they think they can get away with."

As evidence, she points to the greater willingness to challenge Justice Department objections about possible racial discrimination in districting plans. Where in the past these objections would have been accepted and dealt with, she says, jurisdictions are now more ready to go to court to fight the department's rulings.

And that means more lawsuits and more judicial decisions that will further define the 1965 law. ■

Nadine Cohodas is a Washington writer and the author of the 1993 book Strom Thurmond and the Politics of Southern Change.

Notes

[1] For background, see "Redistricting: Drawing Power With a Map," *Editorial Research Reports,* Feb. 15, 1991, pp. 97-112, and "1990 Census: Undercounting Minorities," *Editorial Research Reports,* March 10, 1989, pp. 117-132.

[2] "Black- and Hispanic-Majority Districts," *CQ Weekly Report,* July 10, 1993, p. 1829.

[3] *Black Elected Officials— A National Roster 1993,* 21st Edition, Joint Center for Political and Economic Studies; *Hispanic Elected Officials 1993, Statistical Summary* (September 1993), National Association of Latino Elected and Appointed Officials Educational Fund.

[4] Lani Guinier, *The Tyranny of the Majority* (1994), p. 43.

[5] Quoted in "Withdrawing Guinier Nomination a No-Win Situation for Clinton," *CQ Weekly Report,* June 5, 1993, p. 1427.

[6] *Ibid.*, p. 1425.

[7] Daniel D. Polsby and Robert D. Popper, "Ugly: An Inquiry into the Problem of Racial Gerrymandering Under the Voting Rights Act," *Michigan Law Review,* Vol. 92, No. 3, December 1993, pp. 665. The December issue includes two other articles on voting rights.

[8] See Dave Kaplan, "Alternative Election Methods: A Fix for a Besieged System?" *CQ Weekly Report,* April 2, 1994, pp. 812-813; and "Controversial Way To Vote Ordered," *CQ Weekly Report,* April 9, 1994, p. 857.

[9] Frances Butler Simkins, *A History of the New South* (1961).

[10] C. Vann Woodward, *Origins of the New South* (1961), p. 326.

[11] *Ibid.*

[12] *Ibid.*, p. 321.

[13] *Newsweek,* May 1, 1944, p. 33; James O. Farmer Jr., *The End of the White Primary in South Carolina: A State's Fight to Keep its Politics White* (1965, master's thesis).

[14] Congressional Quarterly, *Congress and the Nation,* Vol. I (1965), pp. 1615-17.

[15] *Ibid.*

[16] *Ibid.*, pp. 1619-21.

[17] *Ibid.*, p. 1626.

[18] *Ibid.*, pp. 1626-30; Steven F. Lawson, *Black Ballots: Voting Rights in the South* (1976), pp. 247-48.

[19] *The New York Times,* March 8, 1965, p. 1; see also Lawson, *op. cit.*, p. 310.

[20] *The New York Times,* March 16, 1965, pp. 1, 30; see also Merle Miller, *Lyndon* (1980), pp. 431-32.

[21] Congressional Quarterly, *Congress and the Nation,* Vol. II (1969), p. 362; Lawson, *op. cit.*, pp. 329-30.

[22] The case was *Allen v. State Board of Elections.*

[23] Voter Education Project of the Southern Regional Council (1964 statistics); U.S. Census Bureau/*1981 ALMANAC* (1976 statistics).

[24] Joint Center for Political and Economic Studies. The center, a nonprofit, non-partisan research organization, reports annually on black elected officials.

[25] *1982 CQ Almanac,* pp. 373-377.

[26] Testifying before House Judiciary Subcommittee on Civil and Constitutional Rights, "Roundtable on Voting Rights," May 11, 1994.

[27] *The New York Times,* June 5, 1994, p. 24.

Bibliography

Selected Sources Used

Books

Guinier, Lani, *The Tyranny of the Majority,* Free Press, 1994.

This collection of Guinier's law review articles about voting rights figured prominently in the dispute over her nomination to head the Justice Department's Civil Rights Division. Guinier has written a new introductory essay discussing the nomination dispute and providing new context for her articles, which had been written in previous years. The book also includes a spirited foreword by Yale University law Professor Stephen L. Carter.

Amy, Douglas J., *Real Choices/New Voices: The Case for Proportional Representation Elections in the United States,* Columbia University, 1993.

Amy takes issue with the existing winner-take-all plurality electoral system in the United States. He argues that the system favors men and the majority race, in effect limits choices to the two major political parties and ends up protecting them from competition. Proportional representation in large multi-member districts, as opposed to the single-member districts used in virtually all U.S. elections, gives all voters, even those in the minority, a chance to elect representatives, he says. Amy presents arguments against proportional representation, but he asserts that these are less significant than the positives that accrue from the model he describes.

Parker, Frank R., *Black Votes Count: Political Empowerment in Mississippi,* University of North Carolina, 1990.

Parker, who ran the Lawyers' Committee for Civil Rights office in Mississippi for eight years, provides a detailed case study of voting-rights litigation in Mississippi. Included with the narrative are charts, maps and descriptions of important Supreme Court cases interpreting the 1965 Voting Rights Act.

Lawson, Steven F., *Black Ballots: Voting Rights in the South 1944-69,* Columbia University, 1976.

Where Parker's book looks at voting rights in a particular state, Lawson provides a broader look at voting rights in the entire region. It includes several chapters on the state of the franchise for black Southerners before 1944 that are helpful in understanding the litigation and congressional fights that came later.

Woodward, C. Vann, *Origins of the New South,* Louisiana State University, 1961.

This classic on Southern history provides a thorough and readable explanation of how segregation developed across the South after the Civil War.

Articles

Sunstein, Cass R., "Voting Rites," *The New Republic,* April 25, 1994.

Based on a review of Guinier's book, this essay discusses the broad social issues that surround the voting-rights debate. Sunstein advocates "race-neutral and race-blind" voting reforms even if the problems they seek to address have racial dimensions.

Karlen, Pamela S., "End of the Second Reconstruction?" *The Nation,* May 23, 1994.

A professor of law at the University of Virginia, Karlen has written extensively about voting rights. Praising the Voting Rights Act for its effectiveness, she criticizes the Supreme Court and other federal courts for substituting their "narrow vision" of voting rights for the choices made by the political branches of government.

Reports and Studies

Joint Center for Political and Economic Studies, *Black Elected Officials — A National Roster 1993.*

The center, a nonpartisan, nonprofit research organization on black issues, publishes an annual roster of black elected officials. It includes state-by-state breakdowns of the elected officials by level of government and positions. These yearly reports are available going back to 1970.

National Association of Latino Elected and Appointed Officials Educational Fund, *Hispanic Elected Officials 1993 — Statistical Summary,* September 1993.

This report includes several charts and graphs showing the number of Hispanic governmental officials in the United States. There are breakdowns by level of government service, gender and party affiliation in states with large Hispanic populations.

National Asian Pacific American Legal Consortium, *1993 Annual Report.*

This is the first report of the group, which was formed in 1993 to monitor issues of concern to the Asian-American community. It provides an overview of these issues and the organization's activities. The consortium is made up of the Asian American Legal Defense and Education Fund in New York, the Asian Law Caucus in San Francisco and the Asian Pacific Legal Center of Southern California in Los Angeles.

The Next Step

Additional information from UMI's Newspaper & Periodical Abstracts database

African-Americans

Andrews, Brenda H., "In South Africa and America: After the vote," *Journal & Guide* (Norfolk, Va.), May 4, 1994, p. 2.

Brenda H. Andrews says that all blacks can celebrate the jubilation of black South Africans who are voting for the first time and that black Americans should use this occasion as a reminder of how far they have come and how far they must go to attain real political power of their own in America.

Burroughs, Todd, "Lessons of the reverse freedom rides," *Crisis (NAACP)*, January 1994, p. 26.

Lessons that the black community can learn from 1993 elections are discussed, as are the activities of the "Reverse Freedom Riders," blacks who sought to educate other black voters about political issues. Grass-roots activism and the elimination of voter apathy are crucial to achieving better black voter participation, Burroughs says.

Bustamante, Michael Tuan, "Black judicial candidates fare well in primary," *Call & Post* (Cleveland, Ohio), May 12, 1994, p. A2.

Despite a low turnout, especially in the black community, three of the six black judicial candidates who had opposition were victorious in the primary elections. With three other candidates running unopposed, a record six blacks will seek judgeships on the Ohio Supreme Court and the Cuyahoga County Court of Common Pleas.

Horowitz, Craig, "The Sharpton generation," *New York*, April 4, 1994, pp. 36-45.

The Rev. Al Sharpton and a group of young insurgents are making a power play in New York to purge and replace the established black leadership. Sharpton is running for the U.S. Senate against Daniel Patrick Moynihan (D-N.Y.) in the September 1994 Democratic primary. Sharpton and the new era of black leaders in New York are discussed.

Parker, Laura, "Incumbent blacks face opposition," *Detroit News*, June 8, 1994, p. A5.

It used to be that black politicians were immune to the anti-incumbent moods of voters. So few African-Americans held congressional office that their constituents were loath to turn them out. Times have changed, Parker writes. Rep. John Conyers' (D-Mich.) re-election peril is perhaps the clearest example in the U.S.

Sack, Kevin, "Coalition of minority officials to endorse Sharpton for Senate," *The New York Times*, May 7, 1994, p. A28.

A large coalition of black and Hispanic officials in New York, including half the black members of the Legislature, plans to endorse the Rev. Al Sharpton in his campaign to unseat Sen. Daniel Patrick Moynihan (D-N.Y.). Sharpton is given little chance of defeating Moynihan in the Sept. 13, 1994, Democratic primary, but he said the endorsements, to be announced May 7, will demonstrate his growing influence among black New Yorkers.

Worrill, Conrad W., "Electing a black mayor in Chicago," *Chicago Defender*, April 9, 1994, p. 22.

Worrill describes the efforts to mobilize Chicago's African-American community to help get five blacks appointed to the Chicago School Board and force the resignation of Thomas Ayers. Their success was the beginning of a movement that laid the foundation for the election of Harold Washington, Chicago's first African-American mayor. (Part 3 of 5).

Cumulative Voting

Ellison, Bob, "Cumulative voting," *Afro-American*, April 23, 1994, p. A13.

Senior U.S. District Judge Joseph H. Young on April 5, 1994, ordered Worcester Country, Maryland, to use cumulative voting in its election of county commissioners. Young's order stemmed from a suit filed earlier on behalf of seven black residents and two civil rights groups. In his order, Young said the at-large system of chosing commissioners perpetuated a system that made it virtually impossible for blacks to be elected to countywide office.

Kaplan, Dave, "Alternative election methods: A fix for a besieged system?" *Congressional Quarterly Weekly Report*, April 2, 1994, pp. 812-813.

Cumulative voting, preference voting and other alternative methods of ensuring representation for minorities are discussed. These alternatives are getting a second look from both judges and legislators.

Kaplan, Dave, "Controversial way to vote ordered," *Congressional Quarterly Weekly Report*, April 9, 1994, p. 857.

Senior U.S. District Judge Joseph H. Young ruled on April 4, 1994, that Worcester County, Md., needed to elect its commissioners using a controversial election method designed to give minorities a greater chance of winning a seat.

Van Biema, David, "One person, seven votes," *Time*, April 25, 1994, pp. 42-43.

A ballot-casting experiment called cumulative voting, one of a brace of methods hailed by some as the future of suffrage but labeled antidemocratic by no less an authority than President Bill Clinton, is discussed. Chilton County, Ala., is one district where the experiment is being tried.

General

Jacobs, Phil, "Bridges are being built," *Michigan Chronicle,* May 4, 1994, p. A6.
Phil Jacobs discusses relations between blacks and Jews in Detroit and efforts by members of both groups, particularly black congressional candidate Melvin "Butch" Hollowell Jr., to emphasize their similarities, not their differences.

Morrison, Patt, "Minorities, women gain in state races," *Los Angeles Times,* June 19, 1994, p. A3.
Although Californians who voted in the June 1994 primary were predominantly white males, they sent into the November general elections many candidates who are women, minorities and gays. The trend could be seen as a harbinger of the state's political future.

Latinos

Horvit, Mark, "Voting Rights Act may jeopardize Hispanic woman's bid for office," *Houston Post,* June 5, 1994, p. A31.
The election bid of Rosemary Garza, the Democratic candidate for the newly created Harris County, Texas, Criminal Court-at-Law, could be jeopardized by the federal Voting Rights Act — the very document designed to help minorities like Garza get elected. The Justice Department has refused the state's request to create the new county court because it believes that the countywide election process makes it difficult for minorities to win.

Lopez, Robert J., and Greg Krikorian, "Politicians battle over non-Latino candidate," *Los Angeles Times,* May 24, 1994, p. B1.
The Democratic primary race in northeast Los Angeles' 45th Assembly District has sparked a dispute among some politicians about whether a non-Latino should inherit the seat. The race has divided Latinos, who have strongly supported Assemblyman Richard Polanco (D-Los Angeles).

Lopez, Robert J., "Torres carries Latino hopes for state post," *Los Angeles Times,* June 13, 1994, p. A3.
California state Sen. Art Torres' campaign for state insurance commissioner in June 1994 is examined. If Torres is elected, he will become the first Latino to hold a statewide office since Romualdo Pacheco stepped down as governor in 1876. The Hispanic-American community's hopes for Torres are examined.

Ramos, George, "1 last obstacle on the long road toward the dream," *Los Angeles Times,* June 13, 1994, p. B3.
George Ramos discusses the attempts of California Senator Art Torres to get the Democratic nomination for the state insurance commissioner's post. Ramos examines the difficulties Latinos have gaining political ground and notes that the fall campaign will be difficult for Torres.

Thomas, Irene Middleman, "The Hispanic vote," *Hispanic,* January 1994, p. 10.
During his term as mayor of New York City, David Dinkins appointed a record number of Hispanics to senior-level positions. Dinkins lost the 1993 election, and he also received 10,000 fewer Hispanic votes than in the previous election. Insiders say Hispanics expected more from the administration.

Native Americans

Price, Richard, "Idaho candidate aims at history, being role model," *USA Today,* May 26, 1994, p. A10.
Idaho Attorney General Larry EchoHawk won the Democratic primary for governor in a landslide, and he leads his Republican opponent, former Lt. Gov. Phil Batt, by 12 points in a statewide poll conducted May 16-18, 1994. If he wins, he'll be the first Native American in U.S. history elected as a governor, one more milestone in a soaring political career that sets new precedents with every victory.

"Trailblazer," *People Weekly,* June 6, 1994, p. 128.
Larry EchoHawk may become the first Native American governor in the U.S. EchoHawk, an Idaho Democrat who is against abortion and who supports gay rights, is profiled.

Opinions

"Healthy signs," *Houston Chronicle,* April 13, 1994, p. C10.
An editorial states that the outcome in three local Democratic Party legislative runoff races in Harris County, Texas, showed the maturity of Houston's political climate, particularly in the Hispanic community.

"Shame in Cincinnati," *Call & Post* (Cleveland, Ohio), May 12, 1994, p. A4.
An editorial states that Cincinnati's black voters must bear, once again, the shame of a black congressional candidate going down in defeat by a slim margin, as State Sen. William Bowen lost a hard-fought primary battle to incumbent Rep. David Mann by less than 700 votes.

"Vote May 3," *Call & Post* (Cleveland, Ohio), April 28, 1994, p. A4.
An editorial urges black residents of Cleveland to vote in the May 3, 1994, primary elections, saying the historic events in South Africa should underscore the importance of exercising the right to vote.

"We must care," *Los Angeles Sentinel,* April 21, 1994, p. A6.

An editorial discusses the positive political implications for blacks in the U.S. of the historic all-race elections in South Africa April 26-28, 1994.

Political Parties and Organizations

Andrews, James H., "Bay State is home to small, influential black GOP group," ***Christian Science Monitor,*** **June 6, 1994, p. 10.**
Massachusetts is home to a small but dedicated band of black GOP activists. The group is the Massachusetts chapter of the National Black Republican Council (NBRC), headquartered in New York City, and is making gradual but discernible inroads in the African American community, Andrews says.

"Blacks back idea of separate political party," ***Jet,*** **May 2, 1994, p. 6.**
A poll of 1,200 blacks conducted by the University of Chicago found that 55 percent support the formation of a separate political party. Additional results of the poll are discussed.

Foskett, Ken, "Atlanta hosting Republican effort to woo black voters," ***Atlanta Constitution,*** **May 20, 1994, p. B3.**
The Republican National Committee is bringing its campaign to recruit black voters to the GOP to Atlanta, hosting a two-day conference called "Defining the Republican African-American Agenda." Organizers expect 300 black leaders to attend from Southeastern states.

Wickham, DeWayne, "Blacks should form political party," ***USA Today,*** **May 24, 1994, p. A13.**
DeWayne Wickham discusses the idea of America benefitting from the creation of a black political party. Not a black nationalist party like Louis Farrakhan's Nation of Islam, but a party similar to South Africa's ANC; an alliance across racial lines to create a government of national unity.

Redistricting

Anderson, Ed, "New La. remap may face court fight," ***Times-Picayune,*** **June 7, 1994, p. B4.**
Attorneys for four residents of Lincoln Parish, La., who oppose the creation of five majority-white congressional districts and two majority-black districts said they will probably mount another court challenge to the Legislature's latest redistricting plan. The Justice Department had approved the plan.

Wardlaw, Jack, and Ed Anderson, "House rejects remap plan with 2 black-majority districts," ***Times-Picayune,*** **April 20, 1994, p. B1.**
The congressional reapportionment train jumped the legislative tracks when the Louisiana House voted 54-50 to reject, in effect, a plan to retain two black voter-majority districts.

Single Transferable Vote

Fain, Howard, "P.R. elections in Cambridge, Mass.," ***National Civic Review,*** **winter 1994, pp. 84-85.**
Elections using the single-transferable-vote form of proportional representation have run smoothly in Cambridge, Mass., for 25 years and have insured fair African-American representation.

Sinha, Tito, "P.R. elections in N.Y.C.: Effects of preference voting on Asian-American participation," ***National Civic Review,*** **winter 1994, pp. 80-83.**
The single-transferable vote was used in the May 4, 1993, Community School Board elections in New York City. The effect that this type of proportional representation had on Asian-American participation is examined.

Voter Turnout

"Burris cites lack of black support as factor in losing bid for Illinois governor," ***Jet,*** **April 4, 1994, pp. 5-6.**
Illinois Attorney General Roland Burris recently expressed concern and disappointment over the lack of black voter turnout during his bid to become the first black governor of the state. However, Burris noted that he doesn't feel betrayed by black voters.

Colvin, Leonard E., "We need same enthusiasm as South Africans," ***Journal & Guide,*** **May 4, 1994, p. 9.**
Colvin comments on how black South Africans waited as much as 12 hours in line, some even being carried in, to vote in that country's first all-race election, saying it made him wonder why black Americans do not exercise their right to vote.

Strausberg, Chinta, "Burris seeks to awaken black giant," ***Chicago Defender,*** **April 13, 1994, p. 6.**
Former Democratic gubernatorial candidate Roland W. Burris is vowing to find out why more than 430,000 blacks opted out of Illinois' March 15, 1994, election and is bent on reawakening them in time for the November general election.

Back Issues

Great Research on Current Issues Starts Right Here...Recent topics covered by The CQ Researcher are listed below. Before May 1991, reports were published under the name of Editorial Research Reports.

FEBRUARY 1993
Community Policing
Europe's New Right
School Censorship
Violence Against Women

MARCH 1993
Gay Rights
Aid to Russia
War on Drugs
TV Violence

APRIL 1993
Head Start
High-Speed Rail
Children's Legal Rights
Muslims in America

MAY 1993
Cults in America
Preventing Teen Pregnancy
Software Piracy
National Parks

JUNE 1993
Food Safety
Prostitution
Childhood Immunizations
National Service

Back issues are available for $4.00 (subscribers) or $7.00 (non-subscribers). Quantity discounts apply to orders over ten. To order, call Congressional Quarterly Customer Service at (202) 887-8621.

Binders are available for $16.00. To order call 1-800-638-1710. Please refer to stock number 648.

JULY 1993
Electric Cars
Population Growth
Downward Mobility
Intelligence Testing

AUGUST 1993
Mental Illness
Bilingual Education
Foreign Policy Burden
School Funding

SEPTEMBER 1993
Suburban Crime
Public Housing
Supreme Court Preview
Immigration Reform

OCTOBER 1993
Airline Safety
Disaster Response
Science in the Courtroom
The Glass Ceiling

NOVEMBER 1993
Paying for Retirement
Charitable Giving
Privacy in the Workplace
Adoption

DECEMBER 1993
U.S. Vietnam-Relations
Learning Disabilities
Child Care
Space Program's Future

JANUARY 1994
Racial Tensions in Schools
South Africa's Future
Worker Retraining
Regulating Pesticides

FEBRUARY 1994
Prison Overcrowding
Water Quality
Religion in Schools
Juvenile Justice

MARCH 1994
Underground Economy
Education Standards
Gambling Boom
Private Management of Public Schools

APRIL 1994
Reproductive Ethics
U.S.-China Trade
Soccer in America
Talk Show Democracy

MAY 1994
Traffic Congestion
Women's Health Issues
Mutual Funds
Political Scandals

JUNE 1994
Education and Gender
Gun Control
Public Land Policy
Nuclear Arms Cleanup

JULY 1994
Dietary Supplements
Public Opinion and Foreign Policy
Crime Victims' Rights
Birth Control Choices

AUGUST 1994
Genetically Engineered Foods

Future Topics

▶ ***Prozac***

▶ ***College Sports***

▶ ***Home Schooling***

THE CQ Researcher

PUBLISHED BY CONGRESSIONAL QUARTERLY INC.

Prozac Controversy

Are drugs for treating mental illness being used too freely?

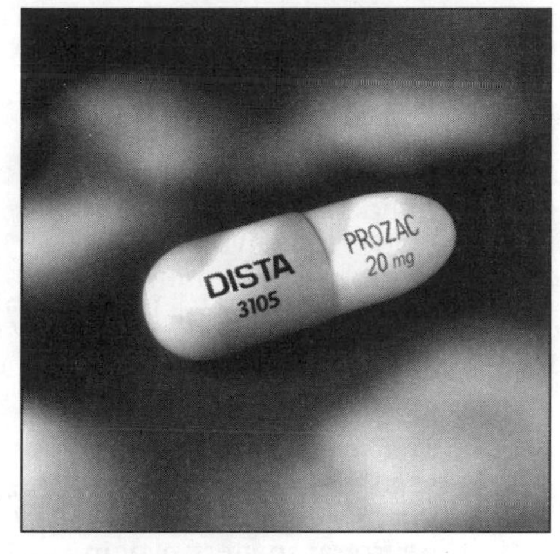

Officially, Prozac has been approved only for treating two serious mental diseases: clinical depression and obsessive-compulsive disorder. But millions of people in the U.S. are turning to the distinctive green-and-white capsules just to pull themselves out of the dumps. They've helped make Prozac one of the world's most widely prescribed medications. Prozac's extensive use has sparked an intense debate over the use of psychoactive drugs vs. talk therapy to treat mental illness, and raised questions about whether such drugs are tempting essentially healthy people to use "cosmetic psychopharmacology" to fine-tune their personalities. Even as the debate rages, there is agreement that the controversy has focused much-needed attention on depression — the most common, and most treatable, serious mental illness.

INSIDE THIS ISSUE

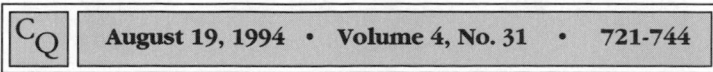

CQ August 19, 1994 • Volume 4, No. 31 • 721-744

Formerly Editorial Research Reports

Prozac Controversy

COVER: A 20 MG PROZAC CAPSULE. (PHOTO COURTESY OF ELI LILLY AND CO.)

The CQ Researcher

August 19, 1994
Volume 4, No. 31

The CQ Researcher (ISSN 1056-2036). Formerly Editorial Research Reports. Published weekly (48 times per year, not printed the first Friday of any month with five Fridays) by Congressional Quarterly Inc., 1414 22nd St., N.W., Washington, D.C. 20037. Rates are furnished upon request. Second-class postage paid at Washington, D.C. POSTMASTER: Send address changes to The CQ Researcher, 1414 22nd St., N.W., Washington, D.C. 20037.

Prozac Controversy

BY MARY H. COOPER

THE ISSUES

Three years ago, Rita M., a 60-year-old business owner in Northern Virginia, went to her family doctor because she was feeling depressed. She did not present the severe symptoms of clinical depression, such as profound sadness, hopelessness, insomnia or suicidal thoughts. "I'm not a typically depressed person," she says, "and I also have good coping skills." Rita (who asked that her real name not be used) was simply overwhelmed by "a lot of external blows," chiefly her schizophrenic son's unmanageable behavior and her husband's battle with multiple sclerosis.

Rita's doctor, an internist, handed her a prescription for Prozac. Every day since then, Rita has taken one 20 mg green-and-white capsule. After a couple of weeks on Prozac, Rita says she noticed a change in her mood. "I did feel much better, and I continue to feel very good," she says. "The interesting thing is, I've always been a positive person. But now I'm very positive, considering the circumstances that I'm living under. I don't at all feel depressed or sad."

Rita sees a connection between the Prozac and her smooth handling of a recent medical emergency, when her husband became temporarily paralyzed. "This had never happened before, but I didn't panic," she says. "I just knew that I was going to be able to take care of it." Rita called a neighbor, who helped carry her husband to his bed.

"It's very hard for me to distinguish what Prozac is truly doing for me because I always have been able to cope in a crisis," she says. "But now I feel pleasant, very pleasant, and things do not bother me too much."

Rita is not alone. Since it was introduced eight years ago, Prozac has been taken by some 11 million people worldwide. As the best-selling — and most visible — member of a new class of antidepressant drugs known as "selective serotonin reuptake inhibitors" (SSRIs), Prozac has become a catchword for the simmering controversy surrounding psychopharmacology.

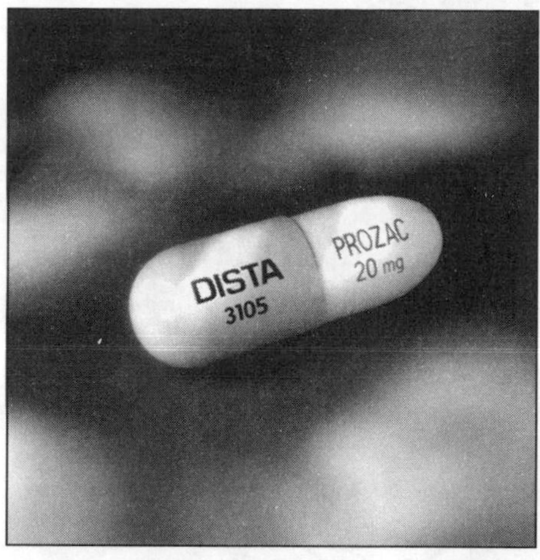

Made by Eli Lilly and Co. of Indianapolis, Ind., Prozac — the trade name for a synthetic compound known as fluoxetine — is one of three SSRIs now on the market in the United States. But because Prozac has attracted so much attention, the others — Paxil (made by SmithKline Beecham Pharmaceuticals of Great Britain) and Zoloft (made by New York-based Pfizer Inc.) — have a lot of catching up to do.

Drug companies are not complaining, however. "All the publicity about Prozac has helped stimulate a great increase in awareness of depression — that depression is prevalent, that it's serious and that it's treatable," says Richard Rudolph, senior director of clinical research at Wyeth-Ayerst Laboratories Co., which makes Effexor, another new antidepressant. "I think it's resulted in more people getting diagnosed and treated."

But the extensive publicity, including a cover story in *Newsweek* and Peter D. Kramer's 1993 bestseller, *Listening to Prozac,* also has made Prozac one of the most hotly debated drugs in recent memory.[1] The controversy stems in part from what the drug implies about ongoing changes in the field of psychiatry.

Sigmund Freud and his followers laid the foundation of contemporary psychiatry with their stress on the importance of understanding childhood experiences in treating mental illness. Today, however, psychiatry is moving increasingly toward biological explanations of mental illness.[2] Modern technological advances have enabled researchers to link physical disturbances in the brain to some mental disorders. Based on such findings, drug manufacturers are synthesizing new compounds that affect these disturbances. Prozac, for example, offsets imbalances of serotonin, a brain chemical that has been linked to depression.

Antidepressants have been in use since the late 1950s to treat mental illnesses. But two things make Prozac different from its cousins. It is relatively free of the unpleasant and occasionally serious side effects that discouraged many severely ill patients from taking earlier antidepressants. And Prozac improves the quality of life for people like Rita M., who do not have serious mental illnesses. As a result, Prozac is widely prescribed to combat a broad range of relatively minor symptoms, including coping with family problems.

Prozac has been formally approved by the U.S. Food and Drug Administration (FDA), however, for the treatment of two serious mental illnesses: clinical depression and obsessive-compulsive disorder. The agency's approval of Prozac for treating bulimia, an eating disorder, is expected soon.[3] *(See story, p. 726.)*

But once the FDA approves a drug, physicians may prescribe it as they see fit. With its reputation as a highly

How Antidepressants Work

Depression is thought to be caused by a chemical imbalance in the brain. Chemicals known as neurotransmitters, particularly serotonin and norepinephrine, act as "messengers" transmitting signals from one nerve cell (neuron) to the next at the gap, or synapse, between cells. When a nerve cell sends neurotransmitters to another cell, some bind to the receptors on the next nerve cell, but others are reabsorbed by the sending cell in a process called reuptake.

Scientists think that the excessive reabsorption of neurotransmitters from the synapse creates a chemical imbalance that may lead to a depressive disorder. Prozac and other "selective serotonin reuptake inhibitors" (SSRIs) block the reuptake of serotonin, allowing it to remain in the synapse for a longer time. Other antidepressants block the reuptake of both serotonin and norepinephrine, as well as other neurotransmitters.

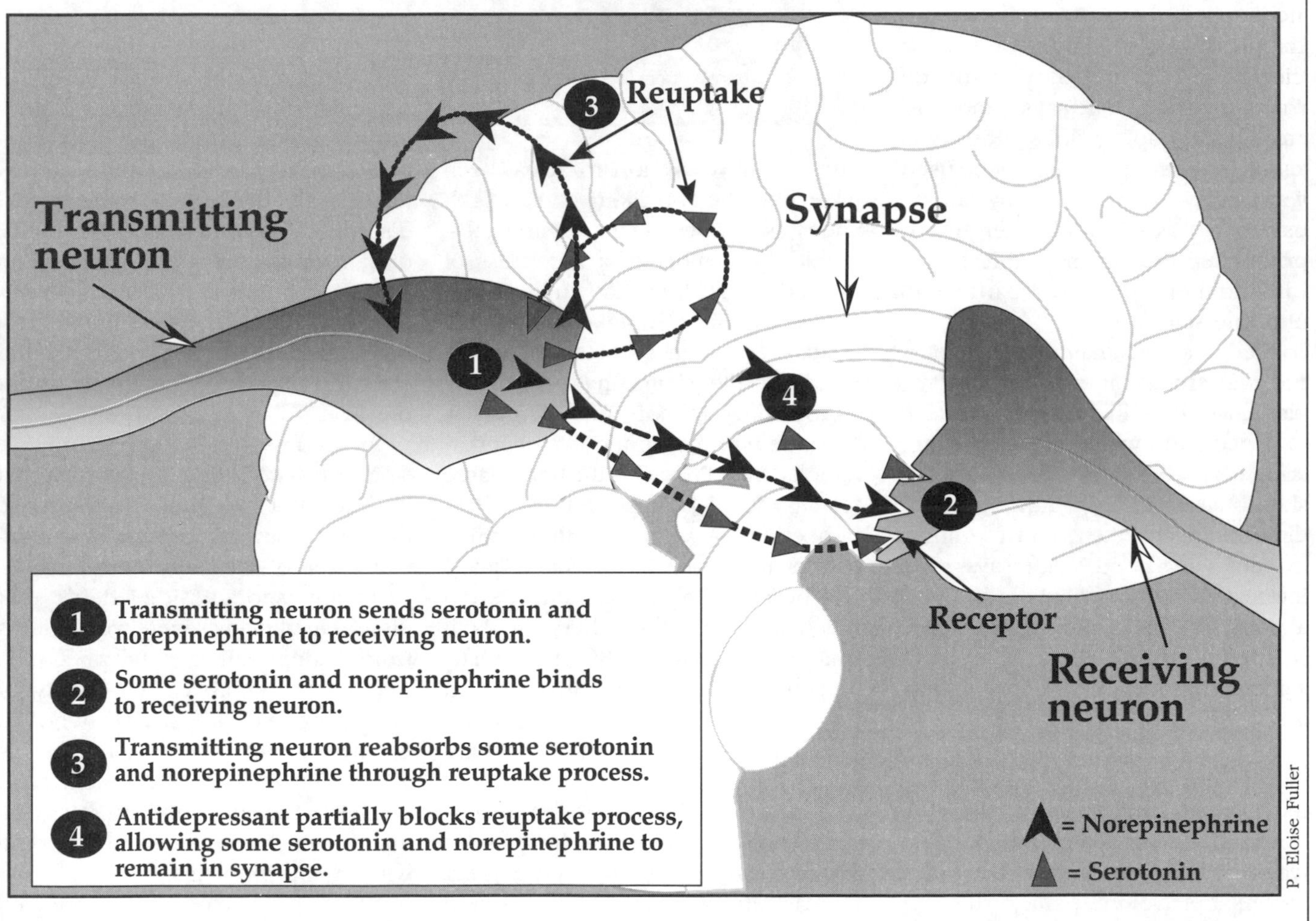
3 Reuptake
Transmitting neuron
Synapse
1
4
2
Receptor
Receiving neuron
1 Transmitting neuron sends serotonin and norepinephrine to receiving neuron.
2 Some serotonin and norepinephrine binds to receiving neuron.
3 Transmitting neuron reabsorbs some serotonin and norepinephrine through reuptake process.
4 Antidepressant partially blocks reuptake process, allowing some serotonin and norepinephrine to remain in synapse.
= Norepinephrine
= Serotonin
P. Eloise Fuller

effective drug with fewer side effects than other antidepressants, Prozac is being dispensed widely by physicians of all specialties. (*See list, p. 732.*)

Many Prozac users, like Rita, never consulted a mental health specialist about their problems, receiving the drug directly from their physician. Rita has had no "talk" therapy in conjunction with the drug, nor has her physician scheduled appointments, apart from routine annual physicals, to monitor Prozac's effect.

The fact that fewer than half the prescriptions for Prozac are written by psychiatrists worries many of the drug's supporters and critics alike. Author Kramer, a psychiatrist at Brown University, says that Prozac ideally should be one of several tools available to psychiatrists. "For me, the cutting edge of psychotherapy right now is the mixed use of medication within psychotherapy," he says. "The ideal therapy would be to work with the person first."

More troublesome, to some Prozac

watchers, have been allegations that the drug has precipitated violent or suicidal behavior in hundreds of Prozac users. (*See "At Issue," p. 737.*) Reports of severe reactions surfaced soon after the drug was introduced but were largely dismissed because many had been circulated by the controversial Church of Scientology, which has been critical of psychiatry and psychopharmacology.[4]

But many people who say they have no connection with the group report they have experienced violent or suicidal behavior while taking Prozac. The Prozac Survivors Support Group wants the FDA to study Prozac more thoroughly. "I'm not necessarily saying that Prozac should be removed or banned," says Guy McConnell, national director of the Clovis, Calif.-based organization. "But because research shows that Prozac poses a danger, it should be looked at. Instead, it's being prescribed for everything from hangnail to major depression."

James D. Goodwin, a clinical psychologist in Wenatchee, Wash., has been called the Pied Piper of Prozac for recommending the drug to hundreds of patients.[5] (Since Goodwin is not a medical doctor and thus cannot prescribe the drug himself, he works with a physician.) Goodwin himself began taking Prozac in 1989 for severe depression. He says the drug is an economically reasonable alternative to the traditional treatment of depression — years of costly counseling. But he rejects claims that drugs alone can cure psychological problems.

"Biological imbalances affect our central nervous system," Goodwin says, "but our central nervous system affects how we think, and our behavior. And those things also need to be dealt with in psychotherapy."

But because psychotherapy is time-consuming and expensive, efforts to cut health-care costs work against the use of extensive psychotherapy. Many prepaid health-care plans, for example, limit or exclude extensive talk therapy.

"A really good psychiatrist is probably going to charge $150 an hour," Kramer explains. "Prozac, which is one of the most expensive of these new drugs, costs just $15 or $16 a week. That means you could get 10 weeks' worth of medication for one hour's worth of psychotherapy. So using the drug alone is much cheaper."

Some professionals condemn the use of any drugs to treat psychological disturbances. Peter R. Breggin, a Bethesda, Md., psychiatrist and outspoken critic of psychopharmacology, says Prozac's success shows how far his profession has been won over by the pharmaceutical industry. "Modern psychiatry doesn't really have a psychological wing to it any more," says Breggin, the co-author of a recent book critical of Prozac.[6] "The leadership of psychiatry now is totally wedded to the drug companies." This union, says Breggin, has given rise to a "psychopharmaceutical complex" that decides what psychiatric therapies will be offered to Americans, much as the so-called military-industrial complex determines the state of U.S. defense.

Breggin says all the attention to Prozac reflects a quintessentially American response to life's difficulties. "People love to take pills when they're feeling hopeless," he says. "If a pill is declared to be magical by the medical profession and by *Time* and *Newsweek*, the placebo effect is enormous."

Rita M., for one, rejects Breggin's cynical view. "I would not consider myself a pill popper," she says. "I was not sick, and I was not depressed, but Prozac is helping my mental health."

Still, the fact remains that prescription drugs — from cancer treatments to cholesterol reducers to antidespressants — are big business in the United States, and getting bigger. Last year, sales hit an estimated $58 billion, almost double the figure in 1988.[7] In 1992, the latest year for which data are available, antidepressants accounted for about 3 percent of all prescription drug sales in the United States.[8]

As Americans debate the proper use of Prozac and similar psychoactive medications in maintaining mental health, these are some of the questions being asked:

Will Prozac's widespread use undermine the role of traditional psychotherapy?

In its guidelines for treating depression, the U.S. Public Health Service suggests that doctors consider medication, psychotherapy or a combination of the two. The agency says research shows that more than half of the depressed outpatients who are treated with antidepressants "experience marked improvement or complete remission of their depressive symptoms." The service recommends that doctors consider drug therapy especially for severely depressed patients — those with nearly all the symptoms of depression — as well as people with chronic or recurrent depression or a family history of the disease. Psychotherapy is recommended for mild or moderate depression.[9]

Too much enthusiasm for Prozac landed psychologist Goodwin in hot water with the Washington State Board of Psychology. In September he will answer complaints that he has recommended the drug too freely to his patients. But Goodwin says he doesn't favor medication over psychotherapy.

"I'm a clinical psychologist," he says. "I make my living teaching people cognitive and interpersonal therapies, which are the two recognized therapies for dysthymic disorder [a less severe form of depression], moderate depression and more severe depression. Those are the ways we deal with the disorder behaviorally. But from the biological approach, the SSRIs are the medicines of choice."

Goodwin insists that he views drugs merely as an effective adjunct to, and not a substitute for, psychotherapy. "All people are interested in is this silver bullet," he says. "They don't want to listen to the part that says you've got to do some work. But you have to do some psychotherapy, so you can learn

Prozac and the Treatment of Serious Mental Illness

Prozac has received final approval from the Food and Drug Administration (FDA) for the treatment of two serious illnesses and preliminary approval for a third:

Depression: The FDA first approved Prozac for treating clinical depression, a condition far more serious than the "blues" that everyone experiences from time to time or the temporary grief that follows a major loss. This severe form of depression strikes an estimated 15 million Americans each year and will affect more than 8 percent of the population during their lifetimes. A milder form of depression is called dysthymia. The American Psychiatric Association defines severe depression as the almost constant presence of five or more of the following symptoms for at least two weeks:

- depressed mood most of the day, nearly every day;
- loss of interest or pleasure in previously enjoyed activities;
- significant changes in weight or appetite;
- sleep disturbances (oversleeping, waking up early, trouble falling asleep);
- feelings of guilt, helplessness or lack of self-worth;
- decreased ability to concentrate;
- fatigue or loss of energy;
- anxiety, restlessness or slowed activity;
- hopelessness or thoughts about death or suicide.

Obsessive-Compulsive Disorder: This condition was recently approved by the FDA for treatment by Prozac. OCD, as it is known, is characterized by recurrent, unpleasant and unwanted thoughts (obsessions), or repetitive, ritualistic behaviors that a person feels driven to perform (compulsions). OCD affects about 4 million Americans, or 2 percent of the population. A person with OCD may experience obsessions or compulsions alone or in combination. Patients typically recognize the irrationality of their thoughts or behaviors but are unable to control them. Typical obsessions include:

- fear of dirt and contamination;
- fear of acting on violent or aggressive impulses;
- feeling overly responsible for others' safety;
- inordinate concern with order, arrangement or symmetry.

Typical compulsions include:

- washing, cleaning, counting, arranging, checking, saving and repeating.

Bulimia: In April, an FDA panel recommended approval of Prozac for treatment of bulimia nervosa, a chronic eating disorder. Uncommon in men, bulimia may affect as many as 2.8 percent of American women during their lifetimes, mainly between the ages of 18 and 35. Bulimia is accompanied by some or all of the following symptoms:

- recurrent episodes of binge eating;
- feelings of lack of control;
- self-induced vomiting;
- use of laxatives or diuretics;
- strict dieting or fasting or vigorous exercise to prevent weight gain;
- an average of at least two binge-eating episodes a week for at least three months;
- persistent concern with body shape and weight.

Sources: Eli Lilly and Co.; U.S. Public Health Service

how to think straight again."

Kramer also has been criticized for what has been viewed as his unqualified support of Prozac, but like Goodwin he says that few patients benefit from drug therapy alone. "You can't just give medication to most people with major depression and say, 'That's it,' " he warns. "Even for someone with dysthymia, it's very unlikely that person would just walk into your office and say, 'I don't want to know anything about myself, just give me the medicine,' walk out and then feel better."

Nonetheless, many physicians say they are being pushed to favor drugs over psychotherapy for a simple reason: cost. More and more Americans are being covered by managed-care schemes, such as health-maintenance organizations, which decide what services will be covered and at what cost before they are provided. Aimed at curbing costs, such policies encourage physicians to opt for less costly treatments — using drugs — since that is what HMOs are more inclined to approve. "I think there's a danger that the availability of these drugs will drive psychotherapy out," says Kramer, "because managed care won't approve psychotherapy."

Cost is not the only factor favoring medication over psychotherapy. "The majority of private mental health care in this country is given by non-psychiatric physicians," Kramer says. Although most doctors are not knowingly prescribing Prozac too casually, he says, many are ill-informed. "Some doctors don't really know whether they're giving it out for depression or dysthymia or some ordinary state of sadness."

Critics of modern psychiatry counter that neither drugs nor psychotherapy provide an adequate treatment for depression. "There are many approaches to overcoming human suffering besides going to a mental health professional," says Breggin. "Frankly, that often does more harm than good."

Breggin, who calls himself a "fairly traditional therapist," defines depression as despair and hopelessness, not a medical illness. "These are not issues of brain, they're issues of spirit, soul, psyche," he says. "America has become such an industrialized, materialistic society that we think that a product sold by a company is the answer to human suffering."

Does Prozac have dangerous side effects that outweigh its benefits?

When it was introduced in 1988, Prozac was greeted by mental health professionals as an attractive treatment alternative for depression. The new drug's main appeal was its absence of many of the adverse side effects associated with earlier antidepressants. Imipramine, the oldest successful antidepressant, can cause dry mouth, heart palpitations, urination difficulty and constipation. Antidepressants known as tricyclics, including such widely prescribed drugs as Elavil (amitriptyline) and Norpramin (desipramine), can cause similar, though less severe side effects.

Another class of antidepressants, monoamine-oxidase inhibitors (MAOIs), interacts with certain foods to cause severe reactions, even stroke and death. All MAOIs are potentially lethal if the patient overdoses, an important consideration in prescribing medication for depression, in which suicidal thoughts are among the distinguishing symptoms.

Prozac may be no more effective than imipramine and other antidepressants in curing depression. Studies show that like its predecessors Prozac helps about 60 to 70 percent of the people who take it. But because of its lack of side effects, patients are more willing to take the drug and stay on it. Physicians are more willing to prescribe it because it is harder for potentially suicidal patients to overdose on Prozac.

That does not mean that all Prozac users will be free of side effects. Eli Lilly's own clinical trials revealed a number of adverse reactions, including "anxiety, nervousness and insomnia; drowsiness and fatigue or asthenia [weakness]; tremor; sweating; gastrointestinal complaints, including anorexia, nausea and diarrhea; and dizziness or lightheadedness."[10] These were severe enough to prompt 15 percent of about 4,000 patients treated with Prozac during the clinical trials to discontinue treatment.

Shortly after Prozac was introduced, reports of violent and suicidal behavior began to surface among users. A 1990 study by Harvard University psychiatrist Martin Teicher and two colleagues at McLean Hospital, a renowned psychiatric institution in Belmont, Mass., reported that six of their depressed patients began having suicidal thoughts while on Prozac. The Citizens Commission on Human Rights, a Los Angeles-based group linked to the Church of Scientology, then launched a public relations campaign denouncing Prozac as a "killer drug" that caused hundreds of suicides among patients taking it.[11]

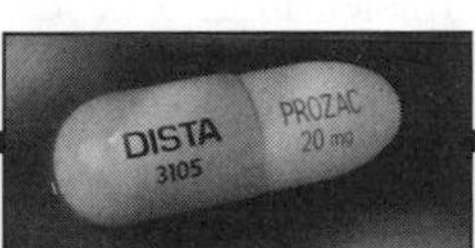

Shortly after Prozac was introduced, reports of violence and suicidal behavior began to surface among users . . . . In 1991, the FDA held hearings on these reports and concluded that the evidence was insufficient to change the agency's initial finding that Prozac is a "safe and effective drug."

In 1991, the FDA held hearings on these reports and concluded that the evidence was insufficient to change the agency's initial finding that Prozac is a "safe and effective drug." Prozac's sales, which had plummeted after the first reports of suicide and violence, recovered. Today Prozac is the world's best-selling antidepressant. *(See table, p. 730.)*

Prozac's market success, however, has not entirely quelled comments about harmful side effects. Breggin notes that little attention has been given to adverse reactions some Prozac patients have when they ill-advisedly take other antidepressants, especially imipramine and Elavil.[12]

Andrea N., a professional woman in Northern Virginia, has seen a variety of reactions to Prozac use in her family. Her husband, a 51-year-old podiatrist, has been taking Prozac for eight months to treat what she describes as "chronic, low-grade depression that runs in his family." Apart from becoming "real tired" when his psychiatrist raised the dosage above 20 mg a day, Andrea's husband has been free of adverse side effects and has benefited overall from the medication.

"One of his issues always has been trying to control obsessive thoughts, and now he feels much better," says Andrea, who asked that her real name not be used. "He feels much more relaxed. He doesn't seem to worry about things with the same intensity. He feels more at peace and is more balanced." Andrea says her sister-in-law also has done well on Prozac, which she began taking at about the same time.

But Andrea's father, a 79-year-old retired physician who has been taking antidepressants most of his adult life, had a negative experience after his psychiatrist switched him from imipramine to Prozac. "He lost his appetite and was sleeping all day," Andrea recalls. "When he started having trouble breathing, he was hospitalized with congestive heart failure."

After undergoing a coronary bypass and receiving a pacemaker, her father is "not doing that well." Doctors speculate that the withdrawal from imipramine and switch to Prozac may have aggravated a previously undetected heart condition. "The moral of this story," Andrea says, "is that Prozac is a drug that is not necessarily right for everyone."

Is "cosmetic psychopharmacology" a legitimate use of medication?

In *Listening to Prozac,* Kramer cites cases that suggest the drug's "transformative" powers, its ability to change an individual's basic personality. That ability distinguishes Prozac — and other SSRIs — from older antidepressants. "Prozac seemed to give social confidence to the habitually timid, to make the sensitive brash, to lend the introvert the social skills of a salesman," he wrote.[13]

Many of the people taking Prozac, Kramer noted, were not the clinically depressed for whom the FDA had approved its use, but often essentially healthy people with dysthymia or those who were especially sensitive to rejection. For these individuals, taking Prozac amounted to what Kramer called "cosmetic psychopharmacology," a treatment to make them "better than well."[14]

More than anything else, it was Kramer's description of Prozac's ability to effect a personality makeover that catapulted the drug to the headlines and contributed heavily to its phenomenal success. It may also explain in large part why Kramer has been criticized as an unabashed promoter of the drug.

According to Sherwin B. Nuland, a professor of surgery and the history of medicine at Yale University and himself the author of a bestseller, Prozac brings about wholesale personality transformations in no more than 10 percent of the cases. In a scathing review of Kramer's book, he charges the author with "unabashed self-congratulation" for misleading readers by suggesting that "cosmetic psychopharmacology" is one of Prozac's potential applications.[15]

Breggin says attributing to Prozac the power to improve one's personality is not only misleading, but dangerous. "One of the most twisted things about Kramer's book is that he's presenting one of the oldest ideas on the misuse of drugs to transform our personalities as if it were his new idea," says Breggin. "That's why people abuse drugs, from alcohol to cocaine. There's nothing unique in this notion of cosmetic psychopharmacology."

What's worse, in Breggin's view, is that the term makes Prozac seem far more benign than it really is. "This book is immoral because what happens isn't cosmetic, in the sense of it being on the surface," he says. "It's tampering with the basic neurotransmitters of the brain, and when you start tampering with a human brain chemical, it's anything but cosmetic."

In response to such critics, Kramer emphasizes that he is promoting neither Prozac nor its use as a tool of cosmetic psychopharmacology, but merely presenting issues for public debate. Cosmetic psychopharmacology, he says, involves "changing from one normal, but unrewarded, state to another normal, better rewarded, state."

"I don't think that one personality trait is necessarily better than the other," Kramer adds. "It's a matter of personal preference and of social rewards. The issue is that we as a society ideologically value a muscular form of self-esteem, and we reward it, so that people are actually deprived who don't have it." In that sense, Kramer says, introverts who take Prozac to change their personality are "not just participating in an arbitrary fad. We really don't value introversion that much. So people often really need to get out of that state."

Other mental health professionals say Prozac's effect on personality isn't as extreme as the term cosmetic pharmacology implies. As might be expected from a clinical psychologist, Goodwin thinks Prozac has only an indirect impact on personality. Since he began taking the drug to combat severe depression, he has noticed changes in the way he perceives reality, likening Prozac's effect to "putting glasses on your central nervous system."

"I think personality comes from our behaviors over long periods of time," he says. "If I perceive the world as a harmful place to be, and I'm frightened, I'm going to act a certain way, and I'll do that for a long period of time. But if my perception changes, I'm going to act differently. Now, is it my perception that is changing or my personality? I don't know." ■

BACKGROUND

Flawed Ancestors

Depression has afflicted humankind since earliest recorded history. It always has been attributed, at least in part, to physical causes of one sort or another.[16] But it was not until recent decades that modern pharmacologic research produced drugs designed specifically to combat the disease. At the time they appeared, Freudian psychoanalytic theory dominated psychiatry and treatment for depression.

Early antidepressants were actually designed initially to treat other illnesses.[17] Doctors stumbled upon their effectiveness in combating depression by accident. Iproniazid was introduced in the early 1950s to combat tuberculosis. But it also was found to "energize," or stimulate, patients. Intrigued,

Continued on p. 730

Chronology

1930s-1940s

Neurotransmitters are identified and found to play a key role in the central nervous system.

1936
Sir Henry Dale of England and Otto Loewi of Austria receive the Nobel Prize for their research into the role of neurotransmitters in brain activity.

1948
Scientists at the Cleveland Clinic isolate serotonin, a neurotransmitter with multiple effects on various organ systems.

1950s-1960s

Serotonin and other neurotransmitters are isolated in brain tissue and linked to mood states. The first modern antidepressants come on the market.

1957
Iproniazid, a tuberculosis medication, and imipramine, an antihistamine, are found to ease the symptoms of depression. Iproniazid causes jaundice and is quickly discontinued, but imipramine (Tofranil) becomes widely used. It is the first of the so-called tricyclic antidepressants, which are successful in more than half the patients using them but also have serious side effects.

1970s

Research continues on the role of neurotransmitters in depression, focusing on serotonin, norepinephrine and dopamine.

1972
Scientists at Eli Lilly and Co. synthesize fluoxetine, the first "selective serotonin reuptake inhibitor" (SSRI).

1976
Clinical trials with fluoxetine begin.

1980s

Trazodone (Desyrel) and other new antidepressants are introduced.

Sept. 6, 1983
Eli Lilly files application with the U.S. Food and Drug Administration (FDA) for use of fluoxetine to treat clinical depression.

1986
Prozac is introduced in Belgium for the treatment of depression.

Dec. 29, 1987
FDA approves Prozac for use in the United States. Lilly begins U.S. marketing of the drug the following year.

1989
After killing eight people and wounding 12 at the printing plant in Louisville, Ky., where he once worked, Joseph Wesbecker commits suicide. Wesbecker's son sues Eli Lilly, saying his father had been influenced by Prozac, which he had been taking for five weeks before the shootings.

1990s

Prozac sparks widespread media coverage, and controversy, for its use in treating a variety of less serious mental conditions as well as depression, and also for its possible connection to suicide.

1990
Several reports and studies allege that Prozac induces suicidal and violent behavior. In December, the FDA approves Paxil, another SSRI, for treating depression.

Sept. 20, 1991
The FDA examines claims linking Prozac to suicidal thoughts and behavior and issues a statement of support for Prozac's safety and effectiveness. In December, the agency approves Zoloft, another SSRI for treating depression.

1993
In his bestseller, *Listening to Prozac,* psychiatrist Peter D. Kramer raises ethical and medical issues posed by widespread Prozac use. Prozac's worldwide sales top $1.2 billion, up 20 percent from the year before.

March 1994
FDA approves Prozac for the treatment of obsessive-compulsive disorder.

April 1994
An FDA advisory committee approves Prozac for treating bulimia, an eating disorder.

Sept. 27, 1994
The lawsuit against Eli Lilly by Joseph Wesbecker's survivors is scheduled to begin. It would be the first product-liability suit involving Prozac to go to trial.

The Top Three Antidepressants

The three best-selling antidepressants in the world last year — Prozac (made by Eli Lilly and Co.), Zoloft (Pfizer Inc.) and Paxil (SmithKline Beecham) — had total sales exceeding $1.9 billion.

Brand	1993 Worldwide sales ($ millions)	1992 Worldwide sales ($ millions)	Percent change from 1992	Percent change from 1991	1993 U.S. sales ($ millions)	1992 U.S. sales ($ millions)	Percent change from 1992
Prozac	$1,210	$1,005	20.4%	10.4%	$875	$835	4.8%
Zoloft	$464	$195	137.9%	5,984.4%	$418	$135	209.6%
Paxil	$228	$45.5	401.1%	NA	$135	$0	NA

Sources: InfoScan Inc., 1994; Pharmaceutical Research and Manufacturers of America

Continued from p. 728

Nathan S. Kline, a New York City psychiatrist, tried iproniazid on depressed patients. After his finding that iproniazid was an effective antidepressant in 1957, hundreds of depressed patients were treated with the drug. Unfortunately, many of them developed jaundice, and the drug was withdrawn from the market.

A few months after iproniazid was hailed as an antidepressant, another drug was found to combat depression. Roland Kuhn, a researcher at J.R. Geigy, a Swiss drug firm, noticed that a new Geigy antihistamine, Tofranil (imipramine), also lifted the mood of depressed patients. Although imipramine, a sedative, and iproniazid, a stimulant, acted in different ways to combat depression, their introduction during 1957 launched the modern era of research into what Kramer calls "the biology of mood."

Imipramine alleviated many symptoms of clinical depression — insomnia, loss of appetite, listlessness and the "blues" — in 60 to 70 percent of patients. This relatively high success rate has made imipramine one of the leading antidepressants. But like other antihistamines, imipramine causes several unpleasant side effects, including heart palpitations, sweating, dry mouth, constipation and urination difficulty.

Although iproniazid had been quickly abandoned as an antidepressant, it led to the discovery of related compounds to combat depression called monoamine-oxidase inhibitors (MAOIs). By inhibiting the action of an enzyme that destroys certain amines, or chemicals, in the body, MAOIs are thought to maintain a normally elevated mood. During the 1960s, after a number of patients on MAOIs died from brain hemorrhages, the drugs were found to elevate blood pressure to lethal levels if taken in conjunction with foods containing the amino acid tyramine. Now patients on MAOIs observe strict diets, avoiding figs, aged cheese, red wine and other proscribed foods.

Because of these problems, MAOIs were temporarily withdrawn from use in the United States. Today, several MAOIs, including Nardil (phenelzine,) Marplan (isocarboxazid) and Parnate (tranylcypromine), are prescribed widely in England and other countries and have been reintroduced in the United States. But MAOIs have remained less popular among American psychiatrists than imipramine and similar "tricyclic" antidepressants, so called because their chemical structure has three carbon rings.

Other tricyclics have fewer side effects and act more quickly against depressive symptoms than imipramine. Some of them, such as Elavil and Norpramin have become leading antidepressants.

But despite these improvements, researchers couldn't eliminate some of the tricyclics' side effects, notably their potentially dangerous consequences for the heart. Another drug, Desyrel (trazodone), was introduced in the early 1980s. About as successful in combating depression as the tricyclics, Desyrel also caused adverse effects, chiefly dizziness and fatigue. As a result of the myriad side effects, many patients refused to take these older antidepressants.

Secrets of the Brain

For all the phenomenal advances in medical research in recent decades, the physiology of the brain remains largely a mystery. Modern imaging technologies have helped scientists link certain areas of the brain to specific functions, and new biological explanations for normal and abnormal behavior emerge almost daily. But much of our knowledge of brain function remains speculative.

The search for antidepressants has focused on the notion that mood is affected by naturally occurring chemicals in the brain called neurotransmitters. The vital role of these substances, which are found throughout the nervous system, was discovered by Sir Henry Dale of England and Otto Loewi of Austria, who in 1936 received the

Nobel Prize for their work.[18]

Neurotransmitters carry impulses from one neuron, or nerve cell, to the next, enabling the brain to receive, process and respond to information arriving from the body's sense organs. The neuron that receives an impulse, or message, releases neurotransmitters into the gap, or synapse, that separates it from the next cell, enabling the impulse to continue along the nerve pathway. Under normal conditions, some of the neurotransmitters are reabsorbed by the neuron that released them, and the process is ready to repeat itself.

Several types of neurotransmitters have been linked over the years with mental illness. One of them, serotonin, led to the development of Prozac. Serotonin (5-hydroxytryptamine) was first identified in 1948 by scientists at the Cleveland Clinic. Named for its property of constricting blood vessels ("sero" refers to blood serum, "tonin" to the chemical's ability to enhance vessel resilience, or tone), serotonin was found to have many effects on a variety of organs.

Serotonin was first detected in brain tissue in the early 1950s and was thought to mimic the effect of LSD and other hallucinogens, whose chemical structure it resembles. People who ingest these drugs say they experience increased sensory awareness and enhanced perception of their surroundings while losing inhibitions over their behavior. Other neurotransmitters, including dopamine, norepinephrine and acetylcholine, also are thought to affect mood and depression.

As evidence of neurotransmitters' role in brain function emerged in the 1960s and '70s, some researchers postulated that depression results from abnormally low concentrations of serotonin and other neurotransmitters at the synapse. One theory held that the low levels result when the transmitting neuron, after releasing neurotransmitters, takes them up again, removing them from the synapse where they are active. (*See diagram, p. 724.*) The relatively high success rate of tricyclic antidepressants such as imipramine was thought to be due to their ability to impede this "reuptake" of serotonin and the other neurotransmitters linked to mood and thus increase the level of these chemicals at the synapse. The host of side effects these drugs often cause is linked to their action on many brain chemicals.

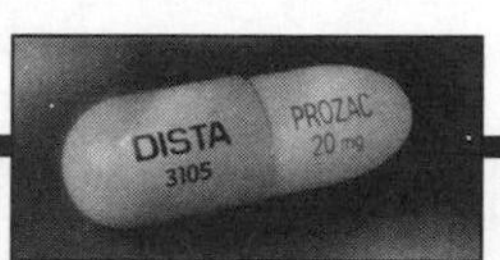

"Nobody told me, 'Go make an antidepressant,' " said Bryan B. Molloy, an organic chemist who was the project director. "It was simply Ray Fuller, Dave Wong and I pursuing our scientific inquisitiveness. When we started off on this journey, it's true that we didn't know exactly where we were going, but it got clearer as the experiment went along."

Creation of Prozac

In the early 1970s, researchers at Eli Lilly began searching for a substance that would prevent the reuptake of serotonin alone. In this way, they hoped to find an antidepressant as effective as the tricyclics but with fewer side effects, some of which were attributed to tricyclics' effect on norepinephrine.

From the outset, the quest for the new compound was controversial. In the past, many new drugs for mental disorders were discovered when doctors prescribed them for unrelated illnesses and then observed their effects on behavior or mood. In this case, Lilly's researchers started with a theory — that inadequate serotonin levels at the synapse were a cause of depression — and set about finding a drug to test the theory. Critics within the company derided the project as a quest for "a compound in search of a disease" and called for its termination.

"Nobody told me, 'Go make an antidepressant,' " said Bryan B. Molloy, an organic chemist who was the project director. "It was simply Ray Fuller, Dave Wong and I pursuing our scientific inquisitiveness. When we started off on this journey, it's true that we didn't know exactly where we were going, but it got clearer as the experiment went along."[19]

The three researchers looked for compounds that embodied the specific qualities they had identified: "If we can make a compound that retains the therapeutic activity of the tricyclic antidepressants, but gets rid of their [less desirable] activity and their effects on cardiac conduction, which kills people," Molloy explained, "such a compound would represent a major step forward."[20]

They examined randomly chosen substances from among some 200,000 synthesized compounds stored at Lilly and began making new ones by altering the chemical composition of exist-

Antidepressants Available in the U.S.

Type	Name	Effect	Side Effects
Tricyclics	Elavil (amitriptyline) Tofranil (imipramine) Norpramin (desipramine) and 29 other brand names (six other compounds)	Believed to increase levels of serotonin and/or norepinephrine, neurotransmitters associated with mood elevation.	Danger of overdose by suicidal patients. Serious side effects include irregular heartbeat, muscle tremors, nervousness, weight gain, sexual impairment.
MAO Inhibitors	Marplan (isocarboxazid) Nardil (phenelzine) Parnate (tranylcypromine)	Inhibits action of the enzyme monoamine oxidase (MAO), which breaks down serotonin, norepinephrine and dopamine.	Can be lethal if overdosed or taken with certain foods. Side effects include dizziness, difficult urination, blurred vision.
Bupropion	Wellbutrin	May inhibit reuptake of dopamine, a neurotransmitter.	Side effects include agitation, anxiety, irregular heartbeat, severe headache.
Selective Serotonin Reuptake Inhibitors (SSRI)	Prozac (fluoxetine) Paxil (paroxetine) Zoloft (setraline)	Enhances action of serotonin by increasing its concentration at the synapse between brain cells. Effective in about 60 percent of cases like earlier antidepressants.	Minimal overdose risk though some claim it prompts ideas of suicide. Fewer side effects than older drugs, including agitation, nausea, drowsiness.
Serotonin-Norepinephrine Reuptake Inhibitors (SNRI)	Effexor (venlafaxine)	Enhances action of both serotonin and norepinephrine.	Side effects similar to SSRIs. May help patients who don't respond to SSRIs.

Source: United States Pharmacopeial Convention Inc.

ing antihistamines and other drugs. In mid-1971, one of the compounds the researchers had synthesized, known as LY86032, met their requirements. This compound was later altered slightly to produce fluoxetine hydrochloride and named Prozac.

Battery of FDA Tests

Before the drug could be marketed, it had to undergo the FDA's extensive battery of tests and win FDA approval. Animal studies to test fluoxetine's effect on various organ systems, and how it was broken down and eliminated, were followed by human clinical trials. Healthy subjects (paid volunteers) were given small doses of the drug, followed by larger doses to determine safe dosage levels and whether the body builds up tolerance to the drug. These trials showed fluoxetine to be effective as a serotonin reuptake inhibitor that did not block the norepinephrine reuptake typical of tricyclics.

In the late 1970s, the next phase of clinical testing commenced, this time using depressed patients. Early results were inconclusive, but a second round of tests showed fluoxetine to effectively reduce common symptoms of depression. The trials also indicated that the drug might help combat other mental disorders, including obsessive-compulsive disorder, bulimia and addiction to alcohol and other substances. Unlike tricyclic antidepressants, which often cause weight gain, fluoxetine seemed to cause weight loss, suggesting its possible use in overcoming obesity.

In the final phase of testing required by the FDA, a much larger test population was used, and subjects who took the drug were compared with others who received a placebo. Neither the subjects not the doctors in these "blind" trials knew who received the actual drug.

On Sept. 6, 1983, more than 11 years after fluoxetine was discovered, Lilly submitted the required new-drug application for Prozac. Two years later, after the FDA's advisory committee examined the testing results, it recommended Prozac's approval for treating depression. Two years after that, on Dec. 29, 1987, the FDA formally approved Prozac.

By the time the FDA acted, Prozac had already been approved for use in Belgium and South Africa. By the end of the 1980s, the drug was allowed in most countries and had become the world's most widely prescribed antidepressant. Its sales skyrocketed as television talk shows and magazine cover stories hailed it as a "breakthrough drug."

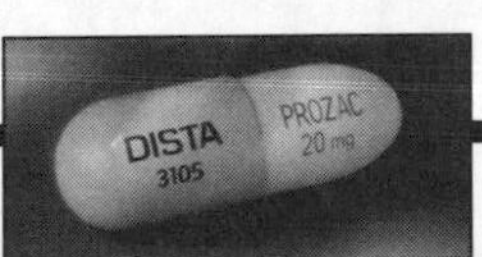

At the height of the anti-Prozac furor, Prozac's share of the U.S. antidepressant market fell from 25 percent in July 1990 to 21 percent a year later. The company defended its product aggressively, offering to pay the legal expenses of any doctors who were sued after prescribing Prozac. Company representatives and many doctors emphasized that antidepressants such as Prozac diminish suicidal thoughts and may also prevent violent behavior.

Critics Speak Out

Drug treatment for psychological disturbances has long been controversial. In the 1960s, Valium and other tranquilizers to combat anxiety were so widely prescribed to American housewives that they became known as "mother's little helpers." But even before they were found to be addictive, such drugs were criticized as instruments of oppression against women whose anxiety was nothing more than a healthy response to an unfulfilling role in life.

It wasn't long after Prozac's introduction that opposition to its growing use became apparent. Among the more vocal critics was the Citizens' Commission on Human Rights, which launched a campaign denouncing Prozac in 1989.

Later critics of Prozac found support for their views in the scientific findings reported in 1990 by Harvard psychiatrist Teicher and his two colleagues at McLean Hospital. They described six patients who, after several weeks on Prozac, developed "intense, violent suicidal preoccupation" for the first time,

Although they warned doctors to use caution when prescribing the drug, the three authors stopped short of attributing the suicidal impulses of the six to Prozac. "At the present time," they concluded, "we can only state that persistent, obsessive and violent suicidal thoughts emerged in a small minority of patients treated with fluoxetine."[21]

The article heightened public apprehension over Prozac. The Citizens' Commission bolstered its campaign against the drug with appearances on television talk shows and petitioned the FDA to withdraw its approval. Meanwhile, many patients who claimed Prozac had made them violent or suicidal, as well as survivors of suicide victims who had been taking Prozac, filed product-liability suits against Lilly and malpractice suits against doctors who had prescribed the drug.

Lawyers introduced the "Prozac defense" when representing Prozac users charged with committing violent crimes. The Health Research Group, a project of Public Citizen, a Washington-based consumer advocacy organization, petitioned the FDA to require Prozac to add a warning about the drug's suspected link to suicidal behavior.

At the height of the anti-Prozac furor, Prozac's share of the U.S. antidepressant market fell from 25 percent in July 1990 to 21 percent a year later. The company defended its product aggressively, offering to pay the legal expenses of any doctors who were sued after prescribing Prozac. Company representatives and many doctors emphasized that antidepressants such as Prozac diminish suicidal thoughts and may also prevent violent behavior.

They attributed the violent or suicidal ideas and actions of Prozac users to the underlying condition of depression. Prozac had not caused or aggravated the symptoms, the advocates said, but merely had failed to help those patients. ■

Yes, Prozac Is Going to the Dogs

It had to happen. Prozac has received so much attention for its effect on humans that, to no one's surprise, it is now being touted in the press as a tonic for what ails Fido.[1]

Veterinarians are now prescribing the drug for a variety of conditions ranging from severe depression in dogs to birds that obsessively pluck out their feathers. It does work, vets say, but in far fewer cases than the media coverage would suggest. And in most situations, experts say, other antidepressants are usually more effective and less expensive.

But serious dog depression, like human depression, does respond well to Prozac, says Bonnie Beaver, chief of medicine at Texas A&M University's department of small-animal medicine. "Prozac has been used primarily in true clinical depression in dogs," she says. Beaver has seen only three dogs with the rare condition, one of which she treated with Prozac. "In two of these cases, a human companion the dogs had been extremely close to had passed away," she says. "They didn't want to eat, they didn't want to drink, they didn't want to move. They just lay there."

On the dog Beaver treated with Prozac, "The drug worked very well," she says. "We saw very dramatic, though gradual changes." After a short course of treatment, Beaver says, the depression lifted.

Prozac has proved most useful in veterinary medicine to treat lick granuloma, a common skin lesion that typically appears on large dogs. "In many cases, lick granuloma will start as a local injury, then become infected as the animal licks the wound, removing the top layer of skin," says Bruce L. Hansen, a veterinary dermatologist in Springfield, Va. Hansen says Prozac has proved effective in about a third of the cases he has treated with the drug, presumably because the drug counters an obsessive component in the licking behavior.

Hansen also has used Prozac to treat extensive itching in dogs. "However, 99.99 percent of dogs can be treated for itching without using Prozac," he says. "Prozac is not the drug of choice except for lick granuloma, and even then only when conventional treatments fail." He usually treats the condition with antibiotics for at least a month.

Only for the 20 percent of cases in which antibiotics fail does he turn to antidepressants, and his first choice is Elavil or another tricyclic. "Elavil is much less expensive," he says, "and it does the same thing as Prozac."

Beaver also prefers tricyclic antidepressants over Prozac for veterinary use. "They have a faster onset of action, and they cost less," she says.

But there's another reason she avoids the drug. "Prozac has been blown so far out of proportion that it's become a fad," she says. Because of extensive press coverage, "clients are beginning to ask us for Prozac for their pets instead of bringing them in for diagnosis of the disease they want to treat."

[1] See "Listening to Prozac: 'Bow-Wow! I Really Love the Mailman!' " *The Wall Street Journal,* June 24, 1994, p. 1, and "Why Is This Dog Smiling?" *The Washington Post,* Aug. 16, 1994, p. D1.

CURRENT SITUATION

Success Amid Protests

After hearing testimony from patients, doctors and company researchers who had re-examined the earlier clinical trials of Prozac, the FDA's Psychopharmacological Drugs Advisory Committee gave Prozac a clean bill of health in October 1991. It found "no credible evidence of a causal link between the use of antidepressant drugs, including Prozac, and suicidality or violent behavior." The committee also recommended against changing the labels on antidepressants.[22]

Prozac soon resumed its upward climb in the sales charts and today is the world's most widely prescribed antidepressant. Its 1993 global sales topped $1.2 billion, up 20 percent from 1992. With U.S. sales at $875 million, Prozac ranks fifth among all prescription drugs sold in the United States and the world, and is Lilly's bestseller by far.[23]

Prozac's sales appeared likely to continue to grow after the FDA in March approved it for treating obsessive-compulsive disorder; a month later, the agency's advisory panel recommended its approval for treating bulimia.

Reports of adverse reactions to Prozac did not end with its FDA exoneration, however. A Canadian study found that Prozac appeared to speed the development of cancer in mice, suggesting the need for further research into the drug's long-term physical effects in humans.[24] The Prozac Survivors Support Group, started in 1990, quickly claimed members in 25 states and two Canadian provinces, offering help to people who say they have experienced adverse symptoms while on the drug or know someone who has.

A Story of Medication and Murder

McConnell, the group's national director, became involved in 1992 after his then-fiancée suffered a catastrophic experience during Prozac treatment for what he calls "minor depression." Gail Ransom, who was 39, became increasingly agitated and hostile after starting on 20 mg daily, a typical dosage. Her psychiatrist decided the problem was insufficient medication and increased the dose to 40 mg a day and then, when the symptoms worsened, to 60 mg. "After about two more weeks, she had lost touch with all reality," McConnell says. "This was a totally different person. I didn't know who this person was any more."

Three weeks after she began the high doses, McConnell says, Ransom strangled her mother with a drapery cord. She turned herself in to the police, confessed and was charged with first-degree murder. Ransom was convicted, but on a lesser charge — manslaughter — and received a three-year sentence instead of the six-to-12-year term typical of that charge, McConnell says. He attributes her favorable treatment by the court to the successful use of the Prozac defense by her attorney. "Although Prozac did not get her off," he says, "it was a mitigating factor in sentencing."

McConnell insists that his group is not out to get Prozac banned but just wants the FDA to exert closer scrutiny of it and all new drugs. "We're a completely independent organization," he says. "We're not funded by anybody, and we do this because we believe that Prozac is a dangerous drug when it's not closely monitored."

He points to earlier drugs that were initially approved only to be withdrawn from the market after causing widespread harm. In his view, the problem is especially serious with drugs used to treat mental disturbances, whose physical causes are still open to debate. "We have a real problem with psychiatric drugs because psychiatry is such a gray area," he says. "As far as I'm concerned, it's not an exact science, yet psychiatrists can prescribe these mind-altering drugs freely."

Professionals Voice Concern

Criticism continues to flow as well from many mental health professionals. Yale's Nuland says Prozac works well for its approved applications and is relatively safe. But he says the drug's use for less severe problems is inappropriate, the result of effective, but cynical, marketing. As for *Listening to Prozac,* "this is not called science, it's called hype, and it's well orchestrated by professional publicists," he wrote. "Many of [Kramer's] statements about Prozac are nothing more than a series of fanciful ruminations, mantled in the adornments of quasi-scientific logic and written in such a way that they cannot but mislead the unwary general reader." [25]

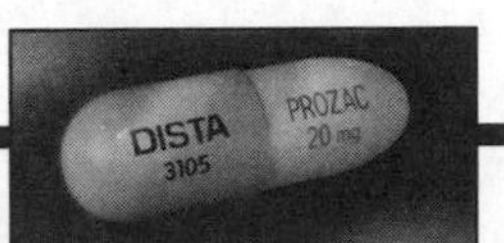

Yale's Nuland says Prozac works well for its approved applications and is relatively safe. But he says the drug's use for less severe problems is inappropriate, the result of effective, but cynical, marketing. As for *Listening to Prozac,* "this is not called science, it's called hype, and it's well orchestrated by professional publicists," he wrote.

Kramer rejects the portrayal of himself as a promoter of Prozac, pointing to his own natural bias, as a psychotherapist, toward traditional talk therapy rather than medication. "My vision of the future, given enough resources, is that it would be all psychotherapy, and the drug would be one element of psychotherapy," he says.

Other mental health professionals see Prozac as a symbol of what they disparagingly call the "medicalization" of psychological problems. A frequent target of these critics is the *Diagnostic and Statistical Manual of Mental Disorders,* the American Psychiatric Association's guide to diagnosing and treating mental illness. Writing in *The New York Times,* Stuart A. Kirk and Herb Kutchins note that the 1994 edition describes more than 300 mental disorders, up from 106 just 15 years ago. By linking more and more behavior patterns to mental illness, they contend, the profession is effectively saying that more and more people need treatment, possibly including medication.

A manual might be of use, they write, "only if it were much narrower in scope, included only clearly distinguishable mental disorders that entail severe consequences and didn't pander to insurers, drug companies and therapists by medicalizing so many social problems." [26]

Lilly has entered the fray with an unusual advertising campaign that criticizes the media for "trivializing a serious illness." The media have done this, says the ad, by emphasizing Prozac's reputed ability to alter personality and cure minor psychological disturbances, rather than its power to do what it was intended to do: control illnesses like severe depression. Appearing earlier this year in major medical journals, the ad cautions doctors against prescribing the drug too freely. "Prozac is intended — as are all Lilly medicines — for use only where a clear medical need exists and when the scientific data have determined safety and effectiveness," the ad warned.

Meanwhile, the first product-liability case involving Prozac is scheduled for trial this fall. Psychiatrist Breggin, who has testified in criminal cases involving defendants who blamed their violent acts on Prozac, is scheduled to testify.

The case involves Joseph Wesbecker, who in 1989 opened fire with a machinegun at his former workplace, a printing plant in Louisville, Ky. Wesbecker killed eight people and wounded 12 more before committing suicide. The gunman's son sued Lilly, saying his father had been under the influence of Prozac, which he had been taking for five weeks before the incident. Breggin says a key issue at the trial, scheduled to begin Sept. 27, is whether Wesbecker had a history of mental illness that could have induced his behavior.[27]

Growing Competition

Amid the publicity, both positive and negative, Prozac continues to claim a growing share of the market for antidepressants. But it is hardly alone. The older drugs, such as tricyclics and MAOIs, continue to be prescribed for depression. There also are two other SSRIs on the market that, like Prozac, act selectively on serotonin, increasing its concentration in the brain.

Zoloft (sertraline), which received FDA approval for treating depression in December 1991, is made by Pfizer, which had been marketing the drug in Britain as Lustral. In 1993, Zoloft's $464 million in worldwide sales ranked second to the $1.2 billion racked up by Prozac.

The third SSRI currently available to Americans is Paxil (paroxetine), produced by SmithKline Beecham. Already in use in several European countries, Paxil received FDA approval in December 1990 for depression. Paxil is the third-ranking SSRI, with worldwide 1993 sales of $228 million, but it nevertheless outsells all the older antidepressants on the market.

Paxil and Zoloft claim several advantages over Prozac, chiefly a shorter half-life, a measure of a drug's concentration in the body after a patient stops taking it. "Zoloft washes out of the body far more rapidly than Prozac," says Pfizer spokesman Andy McCormick. "If you have a bad experience with Prozac, it can be in your system as long as three or four weeks, whereas Zoloft will wash out in 10 days or so, and that can be a real benefit."

Not to be outdone, supporters of Prozac are suggesting new uses for it and similar drugs. Based on Lilly's premarketing clinical trials and anecdotal reports from people who have taken the drug, Prozac may help people lose weight.[28] Recent studies also provide evidence that the drug may help overcome social phobia, the clinical term describing extreme introversion.[29] Prozac is even being used to treat pets. (*See story, p. 734.*)

Despite such prospects, SSRIs may not dominate the antidepressant market much longer. Already a new class of pharmaceuticals called serotonin and norepinephrine reuptake inhibitors (SNRIs) is challenging Prozac. Like tricyclic antidepressants, these new agents target two neurotransmitters thought to influence mood, but like the SSRIs they do not cause the multiple side effects attributed to the older drugs. The first SNRI — Effexor (venlafaxine) — has been approved for use in depression and was introduced in April by Wyeth-Ayerst.[30]

The Pharmaceutical Research and Manufacturers of America reports that about 15 new drugs are in the process of seeking FDA approval for use in depression and other mood disorders, such as bipolar disorder. * Luvox (fluvoxamine) and Serzone (nefazodone) are two of the better-known new agents that the FDA may soon approve for use in the United States. ■

OUTLOOK

Health-Care Reform

One element of the ongoing debate sparked by Prozac — whether it is better to treat psychologically disturbed people with drugs or talk therapy — may be profoundly affected by health-care reform now under way in Washington. Although the final shape of legislation may not become apparent for months, if at all this year, most proposals contain some benefits for mental health care.[31]

Currently, more than 37 million people in the United States have no health insurance. Because most Americans would be covered under the proposals being discussed, many more people would gain access to psychological care than now receive it.

But broad insurance coverage is not the only goal of health-care reform. At least as important to many lawmakers is stemming the growth of health-care costs. Taking its cue from trends already under way in the health-care system, the Clinton administration is proposing, along with others, to rely on managed care, which rewards doctors for treating their patients using the least costly methods.

The emphasis on cost-cutting could be bad news for psychotherapy. "While they give lip service to psychotherapy," says Kramer, "the administration's direc-

Continued on p. 738

* Also known as manic-depressive disorder, this condition is characterized by alternating periods of mania and depression.

At Issue:

Has the link between Prozac and violence been exaggerated?

YES

PETER D. KRAMER

FROM* LISTENING TO PROZAC *(PENGUIN BOOKS, 1993)

The publicity attendant on stories of Prozac's violent dark side is intriguing. It represents, I think, our cultural conviction that there is no averting conservation of mood, that what goes up must come down. Because Prozac has done great good, we are ready to believe it can do great harm. . . .

Part of what makes people uneasy about Prozac is precisely that it works so well and has so few side effects. Prozac is enormously seductive. It is not addictive — patients do not crave Prozac, and there is no known withdrawal syndrome — but people who have experienced a good response to it are often leery about coming off medication, out of fear that they will return to their old way of feeling and behaving. Since we continue to believe in conservation of mood, we are suspicious of a drug that is so pleasant to take.

This seduction is legitimately worrisome because we know that some drugs, especially those that are taken chronically, will have unknown or even late-appearing (tardive) side effects. Psychotherapeutic drugs can sometimes cause tardive neurological disorders, which appear years after a drug is discontinued; and questions have already been raised whether Prozac can cause such syndromes. . . . Concern over unforeseen or tardive effects is realistic, because Prozac has been around too briefly for anyone to know its long-term effects.

But the panic about Prozac and violence seems to me to have gone beyond rational fear — to be what psychoanalysts call "overdetermined," that is, welcome because of the way it corresponds to our fantasies. The reports about Prozac and violence made good television because they meshed with science-fiction images of chemicals that turn Jekyll into Hyde. . . .

The television talk show title, "Medication That Makes You Kill," says something not only about medication but about "You." Within you is evil; not the evil of the conflicted unconscious but the evil of an animal — an injured, ostracized, low-status, impulsive cur who turns against his own kind and then himself. You have a personality that is readily subject to biological influence. Medication can reshape you in quite particular ways.

If these fantasies are credible, it is because medication has shaped our beliefs about how the self is constituted. In the final analysis, the uproar about Prozac and violence represents further testimony to our focus on biologically determined feelings and behaviors. The scare about violence contains a backhanded tribute to Prozac, an acknowledgment, albeit in nightmare form, that Prozac can transform the self.

NO

PETER R. BREGGIN

FROM* TALKING BACK TO PROZAC *(ST. MARTIN'S PRESS, 1994)

Prozac's horizon is full of storm warnings — including many tragedies that have already struck. In addition to the more dramatic cases of murder and suicide attributed to Prozac that have made the news, Eli Lilly declared in its 1992 annual report to the Securities and Exchange Commission that in "approximately 170 actions, plaintiffs seek to recover damages as a result of the ingestion of Prozac.". . .

A 1990 report by Natalie Angier in *The New York Times* confirms that most of the suits against Lilly are related to violent behavior and thoughts, suicidal obsessions and acts and self-mutilation. That most of the suits against Lilly are related to violent behavior or self-destructive behavior is further confirmed by my discussions and consultations with attorneys and clients who have brought suits or are initiating new ones against the drug company.

The suits against Lilly entail product liability in which the company is charged with failing to test the drug properly and failing to give warning of its adverse side effects, as well as negligence in regard to making, marketing or promoting Prozac. The allegations often hinge on the drug company's promotional materials, specifically whether or not they sufficiently warn doctors, patients and the public about drug-induced mental aberrations, including violence against self and others. As of now, to our knowledge none of these suits have come to trial.

The suits against Eli Lilly are only a portion of the legal actions being generated by Prozac. Dozens of malpractice suits — the total number is unknown, but attorneys estimate that it is very large — have been brought against physicians for alleged negligence in prescribing Prozac. According to lawyers involved in some of these cases, most of them also concern drug-induced violence and suicide. Many of these legal actions involve both malpractice and product liability resulting from the same patient's treatment.

In yet another court activity involving Prozac, people who were taking Prozac when they committed crimes are defending themselves in the criminal justice system on the grounds that Prozac caused or contributed to their actions. . . .

Meanwhile, I know firsthand that the number of those suits is growing and that the major ones have yet to be decided by a jury. No other psychiatric medication has ever generated such an outpouring of legal responses within its first few years on the market. There is nothing comparable. Not since amphetamines were used as antidepressants years ago has any antidepressant been so consistently and repeatedly associated with violence and suicide.

Continued from p. 736

tives essentially expect primary-care doctors to treat depression for at least the first 12 weeks. The combination of managed care and the emphasis on primary care would mean almost utter reliance on medication, which I believe is a failed strategy."

There is evidence supporting the argument that managed care gives short shrift to mental health care, especially psychotherapy. In its extensive "Medical Outcomes Study," the Rand Corp., a Santa Monica, Calif., think tank, found that depressed patients covered by prepaid health plans (a form of managed care), were 20 percent less likely to have their depression detected and treated than similarly affected patients covered by traditional fee-for-service insurance.[32]

Kramer, rejecting his label as a champion of Prozac, still insists that psychotherapy is essential for treating depression. But because it is so much more expensive than drug treatment alone, the only way patients will have access to psychotherapy under most reform scenarios may be to pay for it out of pocket, outside the official health-care system.

"There is infinite cynicism when it comes to money and mental health treatment," he says. "The drugs that are potentially wonderful may become a pretext for throwing psychotherapy off the train," he says. "I think we are going to leave vast segments of the population in the hands of not very good mental health care." ■

Notes

[1] "Prozac: A Breakthrough Drug for Depression," *Newsweek,* March 26, 1990. See also "Depression: The Growing Role of Drug Therapies," *Time,* July 6, 1992. (*Time's* coverage included a long sidebar on Prozac.)

[2] For background, see "Biology Invades Psychology," *Editorial Research Reports,* July 8, 1988, pp. 342-351.

[3] For background on bulimia, see "Eating Disorders," *The CQ Researcher,* Dec. 18, 1992, pp. 1097-1120.

[4] See Thomas M. Burton, "Anti-Depression Drug of Eli Lilly Loses Sales After Attack by Sect," *The Wall Street Journal,* April 19, 1991.

[5] See "A Washington Town Full of Prozac," *The New York Times,* Jan. 30, 1994.

[6] Peter R. Breggin and Ginger Ross Breggin, *Talking Back to Prozac* (1994).

[7] Congressional Budget Office, *How Health Care Reform Affects Pharmaceutical Research and Development,* June 1994, p. 3.

[8] Figures from the Pharmaceutical Research and Manufacturers of America. (The organization was known as the Pharmaceutical Manufacturers Association until its name change earlier this year.)

[9] U.S. Public Health Service, Agency for Health Care Policy and Research, *Depression in Primary Care: Detection, Diagnosis, and Treatment,* April 1993, p. 12.

[10] Warning information inserted in packages of Prozac after March 15, 1994, Dista Products Co., a division of Eli Lilly and Co.

[11] Burton, *op. cit.*

[12] Breggin, *op. cit.,* pp. 79-82.

[13] Peter D. Kramer, *Listening to Prozac* (1993), p. xv.

[14] *Ibid,* p. xvi.

[15] Sherwin B. Nuland, "The Pill of Pills," *The New York Review of Books,* June 9, 1994, p. 8. Nuland authored *How We Die* (1993), about the physiology of death.

[16] For background, see "Depression," *The CQ Researcher,* Oct. 9, 1992, pp. 857-880.

[17] Unless otherwise noted, information in this section comes from Kramer, *op. cit.,* pp. 47-60.

[18] Information in this section is based on Nuland, *op. cit.,* pp. 4-6.

[19] Pharmaceutical Manufacturers Association, *The Story of Prozac* (1993), p. 15. In 1993, Molloy, biochemist Ray W. Fuller and pharmacologist/biochemist David T. Wong received the association's annual Discoverers Award for outstanding work in drug research.

[20] *Ibid,* p. 16.

[21] Martin H. Teicher, Carol Glod and Jonathan O. Cole, "Emergence of Intense Suicidal Preoccupation during Fluoxetine Treatment," *American Journal of Psychiatry,* February 1990, p. 210.

[22] See "Antidepressants Update," FDA news release, Oct. 18, 1991.

[23] Infoscan Inc., 1994. The only drugs that exceeded Prozac in U.S. sales were Zantac, an anti-ulcer agent (Glaxo Inc.), Vasotec (Merck & Co. Inc.) and Capoten (Bristol-Myers Squibb Co.), both anti-hypertensives, which are used to lower blood pressure.

[24] See Mark Nichols, "Voice in the Wilderness," *Maclean's,* May 23, 1994.

[25] Letter to the editor, *The New York Review of Books,* July 14, 1994, p. 55.

[26] Stuart A. Kirk and Herb Kutchins, "Is Bad Writing a Mental Disorder?" *The New York Times,* June 20, 1994. The authors are professors of social work at, respectively, Columbia University and California State University-Sacramento.

[27] Burton, *op. cit.*

[28] See "Respect for Diet Pills Rises as Studies Shed New Light on Obesity," *The Wall Street Journal,* July 20, 1994.

[29] See Michael Van Ameringen et al., "Fluoxetine Efficacy in Social Phobia," *Journal of Clinical Psychiatry,* May 1993.

[30] Pharmaceutical Research and Manufacturers of America, *New Medicines in Development for Mental Illnesses* (1994).

[31] For background, see "Mental Illness," *The CQ Researcher,* Aug. 6, 1993, pp. 673-696.

[32] Kenneth B. Wells et al., "Detection of Depressive Disorder for Patients Receiving Prepaid or Fee-for-Service Care: Results from the Medical Outcomes Study," *Journal of the American Medical Association,* Dec. 15, 1989.

Bibliography

Selected Sources Used

Books

American Psychiatric Association, *Diagnostic and Statistical Manual of Mental Disorders,* Fourth edition, 1994.

The association's manual is widely used by mental health professionals and the insurance industry as a guide for diagnosing, treating and providing insurance coverage for more than 300 mental illnesses.

Breggin, Peter R., M.D., and Ginger Ross Breggin, *Talking Back to Prozac,* St. Martin's Press, 1994.

Peter Breggin, a psychiatrist, and his co-author and wife, who is director of research and public education at the Center for the Study of Psychiatry, criticize the use of Prozac and other drugs to treat psychological problems.

Kass, Frederic I., M.D., John M. Oldham, M.D. and Herbert Pardes, M.D., *The Columbia University College of Physicians and Surgeons Complete Home Guide to Mental Health,* Henry Holt, 1992.

This layman's guide includes a general discussion of psychiatry, definitions of recognized mental disorders and a discussion of diagnosis and treatment methods.

Kramer, Peter D., *Listening to Prozac: A Psychiatrist Explores Antidepressant Drugs and the Remaking of the Self,* Penguin Books, 1993.

This is the controversial bestseller that has sparked the recent debate over psychopharmacology. Kramer reviews Prozac's effects in a number of cases and speculates on what they mean for our understanding of mental illness. He calls the use of Prozac by essentially healthy people to change unwanted personality traits "cosmetic psychopharmacology."

Styron, William, *Darkness Visible: A Memoir of Madness,* Random House, 1990.

The novelist's account of his journey into the depths of depression vividly illustrates the difference between clinical depression and the blues or feelings of sadness that fall within normal human experience.

Articles

Debrovner, Diane, "Mind Menders," *American Druggist,* April 1994.

Prozac's success has prompted the development of new drugs with similar action, Debrovner writes. It is unclear whether the growing competition will drive prices for antidepressants down or whether growing demand for the drugs will make them more expensive, she says.

Nichols, Mark, "Questioning Prozac," *Maclean's,* May 23, 1994.

Nichols offers one of the more critical newsmagazine examinations of Prozac's growing use to treat conditions for which it has not been officially approved. The article describes recent findings that the drug speeds the development of cancerous tumors in laboratory animals.

Nuland, Sherwin B., "The Pill of Pills," *The New York Review of Books,* June 9, 1994.

This scathing review of *Listening to Prozac* describes the book as self-serving hype based on incompetent scientific research. Nuland, a professor of surgery and the history of medicine at Yale University, points out that neither the biological basis of depression nor the effectiveness of drugs in reducing its symptoms is universally accepted.

Rothman, David J., "Shiny Happy People," *The New Republic,* Feb. 14, 1994.

Rothman, a professor of social medicine and history at Columbia University, poses hard questions about the ultimate significance of "cosmetic psychopharmacology." At a time of escalating health-care costs, he asks where we are to draw the line in seeking to engineer physical or mental traits we don't like.

Thompson, Tracy, "Seeking the Wizards of Prozac," *The Saturday Evening Post,* March/April 1994.

The author writes that she suffered from major clinical depression for years before she tried Prozac. Its benefits were so great that she sought out the drug's developers to thank them and find out more about their research.

Reports and Studies

U.S. Public Health Service, Agency for Health Care Policy and Research, *Depression in Primary Care,* April 1993.

One in the federal government's series of clinical-practice guidelines, this two-volume booklet contains information on depression. The first volume is aimed at helping identify and diagnose this common illness. The second describes the various treatment alternatives.

Department of Health and Human Services, Alcohol, Drug Abuse and Mental Health Administration, National Institute of Mental Health, *Approaching the 21st Century: Opportunities for NIMH Neuroscience Research,* January 1988.

This report was published to spur Congress to increase funding for research in the field of neuroscience. It describes the department's view that "we are on the brink of discovering the biological basis for many of the major mental illnesses." The report reviews current knowledge and theories on the link between biology and mental illness.

The Next Step

Additional information from UMI's Newspaper & Periodical Abstracts database

General Information

James, Oliver, and Colette Camden, "Power of the psychodrug," *Guardian,* Nov. 23, 1993, p. 14.
James Oliver and Colette Camden discuss the effects of the antidepressant drug Prozac and examine public opposition to the use of drugs to treat psychological problems.

Rimer, Sara, "With millions taking Prozac, a legal drug culture arises," *The New York Times,* Dec. 13, 1993, p. A1.
In small towns and large cities and on college campuses across the U.S., Prozac, an antidepressant that has been prescribed for 6 million people since it was introduced in 1988, has become the focus of a legal drug culture. The enormous popularity of Prozac is examined.

Thompson, Tracy, "The wizard of prozac: Who is this man who made me sane? A pilgrimage to the center of a medical debate.," *The Washington Post,* Nov. 21, 1993, p. F1.
Tracy Thompson discusses the development of the drug Prozac, which helps alter the personality of those with depression.

Government Approval and Regulation

Jann, Michael W., Michael A. Jenike and Jeffrey A. Lieberman, "The new psychopharmaceuticals," *Patient Care,* Jan. 30, 1994, pp. 47-61.
The class of drugs known as selective serotonin reuptake inhibitors (SSRI) is discussed. Three SSRIs — fluoxetine (Prozac), sertraline (Zoloft) and paroxetine (Paxil) — have been approved by the FDA.

"Lilly's Prozac approved by FDA to treat OCD," *The Wall Street Journal,* March 2, 1994, p. B10.
Eli Lilly & Co. received approval from the FDA to market its Prozac drug to treat obsessive-compulsive disorder. The only drug that has thus far had FDA approval as a treatment for OCD is Ciba-Geigy's Anafranil.

McGinley, Laurie, "Lilly's Prozac is cleared by FDA to treat bulimia," *The Wall Street Journal,* April 27, 1994, p. B6.
An FDA advisory committee has voted unanimously to recommend approval of Eli Lilly & Co.'s hot-selling antidepressant Prozac for patients suffering from bulimia, a disorder characterized by binge eating and self-induced vomiting. The FDA usually follows advisory-panel recommendations.

Smith, Mark, "Group lobbies for Prozac warning labels," *Houston Chronicle,* Jan. 11, 1994, p. A16.
Texas' largest mental health consumer organization, Texas Mental Health Centers, has petitioned the Texas Department of Health to require a "suicide and aggressive behavior" warning on prescription bottles of Prozac, the nation's most widely prescribed antidepressant.

Impact of Prozac

Barondes, Samuel H., "Thinking about Prozac," *Science,* Feb. 25, 1994, pp. 1102-1103.
The effectiveness of Prozac and other drugs in treating problems once left to psychology has caused many to rethink fundamental assumptions about psychiatry. The impact of such drugs on the field of psychiatry is discussed.

Begley, Sharon, "One pill makes you larger, and one pill makes you small . . . ," *Newsweek,* Feb. 7, 1994, pp. 36-40.
The same scientific insights into the brain that led to the development of Prozac are increasing the prospect of made-to-order, off-the-shelf personalities, Begley writes. The revolution in psychopharmacology is discussed.

Brown, S. Avery, "Miracle worker," *People Weekly,* Nov. 15, 1993, pp. 153-155.
In an interview, psychiatrist Peter D. Kramer discusses the profound personality changes in depressed patients who use the drug Prozac. The changes have led Kramer to re-examine what constitutes the self.

Freudenheim, Milt, "The drug makers are listening to Prozac," *The New York Times,* Jan. 9, 1994, p. 7.
The antidepressant drug Prozac, manufactured by Eli Lilly and prescribed for more than 6 million people in the U.S. since its introduction in 1988, had record sales of $1.2 billion worldwide in 1993. Industry executives see a far larger market as more doctors prescribe such feel-better products even for problems other than clinical depression, and a host of similar antidepressants may soon be competing with Prozak for a share of the market.

Miller, Michael W., "A new antidepressant will challenge Prozac," *The Wall Street Journal,* Dec. 29, 1993, p. B1.
The FDA on Dec. 28, 1993, granted approval to American Home Products Corp.'s Wyeth-Ayerst unit for its breakthrough antidepressant drug, Effexor. The drug is expected to stir up the huge market for depression drugs due to the drug's claims that it offers Prozac's greatest advantage, reduced side effects, with added strength. Questions about the drug's lofty claims have been made throughout the industry, however.

Young, Jeffrey, "Lefties, righties and anxieties," *Forbes,* July 19, 1993, pp. 208-209.

Sepracor Inc., a firm that knows how to separate and purify drug mixtures, is using its technology to improve on already popular drugs. Sepracor is working on a "left-handed" version of the antidepressant Prozac that may eliminate the drug's original side effects.

Opinions

"Artificial paradise encapsulated," ***Lancet,*** **April 9, 1994, pp. 865-866.**

An editorial discusses the success of and the doubts surrounding the use of fluoxetine, known by its trade name Prozac, as an antidepressant. Prozac has been linked to violent behavior and suicide.

Endredi, Anita L., "Why insult Prozac," ***The Wall Street Journal,*** **Jan. 4, 1994, p. A11.**

Anita L. Endredi responds to the Dec. 23, 1993, editorial "Why Discourage Religion?" She says she and many others take offense at the derisive comments about those who take anti-depressive medications, i.e. Prozac.

Raymo, Chet, "In which Eeyore discovers Prozac," ***Boston Globe,*** **March 28, 1994, p. 26.**

Chet Raymo comments on Peter Kramer's book *Listening to Prozac: A Psychiatrist Explores Anti-depressant Drugs and the Remaking of the Self* by depicting a mood change in the perpetually gloomy character of Eeyore the donkey of Winnie-the-Pooh fame.

Rigby, Julie, "Prozac envy," ***Chicago Tribune,*** **March 27, 1994, p. 18.**

Julie Rigby comments on Prozac. Invented to treat depression, Prozac has become the "Have a Happy Day" drug of the 1990s, as ubiquitous, and perhaps as creepy, as a smiley face, she writes. The culture that has grown up around Prozac reeks of the desire to just target the positive-thinking molecules and get on with it, she says.

Robson-Scott, Markie, "Who is the real Ms Prozac?" ***Guardian,*** **Sept. 21, 1993, p. 16.**

Markie Robson-Scott discusses the popularity of the antidepressant drug Prozac in the U.S., and examines the claims that Prozac is the "feminist" drug because it makes the people who take it more assertive.

Ross, A. S., "Personal view of Prozac," ***Chicago Tribune,*** **Sept. 17, 1993, p. E7.**

Some psychiatrists like Peter Kramer are concerned that an entire society's psychological makeup is being transformed through Prozac, a 20 mg green-and-white antidepressant. The drug's popularity among patients and psychiatrists is examined.

Opposition to Prozac

Adler, Jerry, "A dose of virtual Prozac," ***Newsweek,*** **Feb. 7, 1994, p. 43.**

A writer's bout with mid-life crisis, which he solved by forgiving himself for worrying about the futility of existence, is discussed. People do not have to use Prozac to solve their problems, Adler writes.

Pregnancy and Prozac

Ezzell, Carol, "Prozac's Effects on Pregnancy and Diabetes," ***Science News,*** **May 9, 1992, p. 310.**

A study of the effects of the antidepressant drug fluoxetine, commonly known as Prozac, indicates that pregnant women taking the drug run no greater risk of having a baby with birth defects than women among the general population. The drug can also aid in weight loss and improve diabetes symptoms.

Healy, Michelle, "Prozac not found to increase birth defects," ***USA Today,*** **May 5, 1993, p. D4.**

A new study suggests that the use of the popular yet controversial antidepressant Prozac during the first trimester of pregnancy does not appear to increase birth-defect risks.

Pastuszak, Anne, Carol Zuber, Marcia Feldkamp, Maria Pinelli, et al, "Pregnancy outcome following first-trimester exposure to fluoxetine (Prozac)," ***The Journal of the American Medical Association,*** **May 5, 1993, pp. 2246-2248.**

Fluoxetine is an antidepressant used by many young women. A comparison of the pregnancy outcome following first-trimester fluoxetine (Prozac) exposure with pregnancy outcome in two matched control groups is discussed.

Spencer, Mary J., "Fluoxetine hydrochloride (Prozac) toxicity in a neonate," ***Pediatrics,*** **November 1993, pp. 721-722.**

A case of fluoxetine hydrochloride (Prozac) toxicity in a newborn of 38 weeks' gestation is presented. The newborn was asymptomatic at 96 hours of age, indicating that the parent compound may be the active part of the drug.

Questions and Controversies

Angier, Natalie, "Drug works, but questions remain," ***The New York Times,*** **Dec. 13, 1993, p. B8.**

Prozac and related compounds bear their own disturbing consequences and question marks, particularly in their long-term risks, and doctors fear that the problems associated with antidepressants are being ignored, Angier writes. Questions concerning the safety and legitimacy of widespread prescribing of the drugs are explored.

Bass, Frank, "Prozac: Wonder drug or '90s crutch?" ***Houston Post,*** **June 1, 1994, p. A17.**

Since its introduction in 1986, Prozac has taken the pharmaceutical market by storm—an estimated 11 million people have taken the pills for the blues, blahs or clinical depression and consider it the answer to their prayers. The question of whether

Prozac is just too good to be true is discussed.

Brink, Susan, "Singing the Prozac blues," *U.S. News & World Report,* Nov. 8, 1993, pp. 76-79.
Controversy over Prozac and about when and how all antidepressants should be prescribed is examined. Such drugs are considered by some to be virtual miracles, while others believe they are dangerous and over-prescribed.

Concar, David, "Design your own personality," *New Scientist,* March 12, 1994, pp. 22-26.
For a minority of psychiatrists, the era of the personality pill has already arrived. The controversy over the efficacy and social desirability of the antidepressant Prozac and the prospects for "cosmetic psychopharmacology" are discussed.

Egan, Timothy, "A Washington city full of Prozac," *The New York Times,* Jan. 30, 1994, p. 16.
James D. Goodwin, a clinical psychologist in Wenatchee Wash., has been called the "Pied Piper of Prozac," the antidepressant drug that has been used by more than 6 million Americans. Of the 600 people he has seen with depression in his practice, he has treated almost all of them with Prozac. Critics have brought charges against Goodwin, saying he is too quick to diagnose and overuses the drug. Goodwin and his supporters accuse other psychologists of preferring years of costly counseling to a treatment that works. The debate over Prozac is examined.

Wright, Robert, "The coverage of happiness," *New Republic,* March 14, 1994, pp. 24-29.
The growth of "cosmetic pharmacology," which will enable people to custom-build minds and personalties, raises a number of questions about mental health and mental illness. The debate over Prozac is discussed.

Research and Studies

Marchetti, Domenica, "Happy daze," *Detroit News,* Oct. 7, 1993, p. D1.
While researchers recognize the phenomenal success of Prozac as a treatment for major and minor clinical depression, as well as other mood disorders, they are wrestling with the ethical question of whether or not it is right to prescribe a drug that, in some cases, seems fundamentally to change the personality of those who use it.

Nichols, Mark, "Voice in the wilderness," *Maclean's,* May 23, 1994, p. 40.
Lorne Brandes, a doctor in Winnipeg, Canada, has conducted research that indicates that Prozac use accelerates tumor growth. Brandes, who is profiled, says he will not be upset if his research if proven wrong.

Side Effects

Burton, Thomas M., "Anti-Depressants May Speed Growth of Tumors in Mice," *The Wall Street Journal,* July 14, 1992, p. B6.
A study by University of Manitoba researchers found that two antidepressant drugs, Eli Lilly & Co.'s Prozac and the generic drug amitriptyline, appeared to speed the development of certain cancerous tumors in mice that had been injected with carcinogens.

Marx, Jean, "Do Antidepressants Promote Tumors?" *Science,* July 3, 1992, pp. 22-23.
A new animal study has raised the disturbing possibility that the antidepressants Elavil and Prozac might act as tumor promoters, accelerating the growth of existing tumors.

Nichols, Mark, and Patricia Chisholm, "Questioning Prozac," *Maclean's,* May 23, 1994, pp. 36-39.
The increased use of Prozac by Canadians is discussed. The ways in which Prozac affects the brain, and causes side effects, are examined.

Raskin, Valerie, "Cure-alls not always end-alls to problems," *Chicago Tribune,* Feb. 27, 1994, p. 11.
Valerie Raskin says that like penicillin, Prozac will not cure all that ails a person. While it's usually well-tolerated and a highly effective treatment component for diseases that commonly afflict women, Prozac is expensive, not uncommonly interferes with sexual pleasure and may cause jitteriness, nausea, headaches or insomnia.

Support for Prozac

Brooks, Alison, "Let's hear it for happiness," *New Scientist,* May 28, 1994, p. 44.
It is suggested that one of the most significant benefits that science could offer ordinary people is the ability to overcome unhappiness. Criticisms of the drug Prozac are refuted, and it is suggested that Prozac should be available without a prescription, as are other mind-altering chemicals like alcohol and nicotine.

Halprin, Sally, "Still life with Prozac," *San Francisco Chronicle,* Aug. 15, 1993, p. W16.
Sally Halprin discusses her experience taking Prozac for her depression. Halprin says it's not what she thought it would be like, but she's better than she was before.

Klyman, Cassandra, "Prozac's link to violence is refuted," *Detroit News,* Jan. 2, 1994, B2.
In a letter to the editor, Cassandra Klyman of the Michigan Psychiatric Society responds to a Dec. 19, 1993, *Detroit News* article on a murder in Chelsea, saying that there is no evidence that Prozac causes violent behavior.

McCallum, Jack, and Richard O'Brien, "Listening to Alberto," *Sports Illustrated,* June 20, 1994, p. 19.
Alberto Salazar, a world-class runner, is crediting his victory in the Comrades Marathon in South Africa to the drug Prozac. Salazar's support of the drug is discussed.

Metzner, Richard J., "Prozac is medicine, not a miracle," *Los Angeles Times,* March 14, 1994, p. B7.

Richard J. Metzner notes the media's love-hate relationship with the antidepressant drug Prozac, saying that he has prescribed that medication to hundreds of patients in six years without any of them having a personality change. Metzner disagrees with a quote calling the drug "cosmetic."

Miller, Michael W., "Listening to Eli Lilly: Prozac hysteria has gone too far," *The Wall Street Journal,* March 31, 1994, B1.

Drug maker Eli Lilly & Co. is launching an unusual ad campaign titled "Trivializing a Serious Illness" that deplores the media's role in exaggerating the power of its antidepressant, Prozac, and making light of clinical depression.

Wood, Chris, "Prozac's prophet," *Maclean's,* May 23, 1994, p. 41.

U.S. psychologist James Goodwin has an almost evangelical zeal for Prozac that has many people concerned. He maintains that using Prozac would make three-quarters of the population healthier.

Uses of Prozac

"All the feelings that fit?" *New Scientist,* March 12, 1994, p. 3.

The pharmaceuticals industry has the know-how to shower the public with drugs that interfere specifically with the brain's neurotransmitters and receptors. The use, safety and social desirability of drugs such as Prozac are discussed.

Clendinen, Dudley, "Prozac 101," *Lear's,* October 1993, pp. 70-73.

The question of whether Prozac should be given to adolescents, who are not yet biologically or emotionally stable, is discussed. Prozac is being doled out to college students by college health centers for mild worries, stress and depression.

Cowley, Geoffrey, "The culture of Prozac," *Newsweek,* Feb. 7, 1994, pp. 41-42.

The antidepressant Prozac has attained the familiarity of Kleenex and the social status of spring water. The trend of using Prozac when one has not been diagnosed as depressed is discussed.

Dolan, Carrie, "Listening to Prozac: 'Bow-Wow. I really love the mailman,' " *The Wall Street Journal,* June 24, 1994, p. A1.

Not only has Prozac become the designer drug of the '90s for humans, it could well become so for canines as well. The growing potential for the use of Prozac and other human psychiatric drugs to treat destructive and antisocial behavior will be one topic addressed at the July meeting of the American Veterinary Medical Association. The number of animals on Prozac is currently small, but evidence to its effectiveness seems to be encouraging, especially in cases of unruly behavior.

Mauro, James, and Peter Breggin, "And Prozac for all. . . ," *Psychology Today,* July 1994, pp. 44-49.

Prozac is becoming a common topic in the U.S. and is exiting the realm of clinical depression and entering the murkier world of subclinical, subsyndromal disorders. The effects of Prozac on people with dysthymia and the thoughts of several people concerning Prozac are discussed.

"Panel backs Lilly's Prozac to treat obsessive illness," *The Wall Street Journal,* July 21, 1993, p. B6.

An FDA advisory panel recommended that the agency allow Eli Lilly & Co's drug Prozac to be used for treating obsessive-compulsive disorder. The drug is already used to treat depression.

"Prozac and anti-epileptic effective for migraines," *Medical World News,* July 15, 1993, p. 13.

Results from a recent study conducted at the 35th annual scientific meeting of the American Association for the Study of Headaches suggest that an epilepsy drug, divalproex sodium, and an antidepressant, fluoxetine, may be effective for treating migraines in patients unresponsive to other treatments.

Rohrer, Trish Deitch, "LA confidential," *US,* June 1994, pp. 95-96.

Hollywood's obsession with antidepressants, most notably the drug Prozac, is discussed. Many actors erroneously believe that taking antidepressants is a panacea for the stress in their lives.

Sachs, Jessica Snyder, "Update on women and depression," *New Woman,* Feb. 1994, p. 146.

Clinical depression is a serious mental health problem in the U.S., affecting millions of Americans each year. Clinical depression in women and the use of Prozac to combat this illness are discussed.

Toufexis, Anastasia, "The personality pill," *Time,* Oct. 11, 1993, pp. 61-62.

The increasing use of Prozac for treatment of minor mental problems is discussed. Prozac is the hottest psychoactive drug in history, and more than 6 million Americans have used it since its U.S. introduction in 1988.

Back Issues

Great Research on Current Issues Starts Right Here...Recent topics covered by The CQ Researcher are listed below. Before May 1991, reports were published under the name of Editorial Research Reports.

FEBRUARY 1993
Community Policing
Europe's New Right
School Censorship
Violence Against Women

MARCH 1993
Gay Rights
Aid to Russia
War on Drugs
TV Violence

APRIL 1993
Head Start
High-Speed Rail
Children's Legal Rights
Muslims in America

MAY 1993
Cults in America
Preventing Teen Pregnancy
Software Piracy
National Parks

JUNE 1993
Food Safety
Prostitution
Childhood Immunizations
National Service

JULY 1993
Electric Cars
Population Growth
Downward Mobility
Intelligence Testing

AUGUST 1993
Mental Illness
Bilingual Education
Foreign Policy Burden
School Funding

SEPTEMBER 1993
Suburban Crime
Public Housing
Supreme Court Preview
Immigration Reform

OCTOBER 1993
Airline Safety
Disaster Response
Science in the Courtroom
The Glass Ceiling

NOVEMBER 1993
Paying for Retirement
Charitable Giving
Privacy in the Workplace
Adoption

DECEMBER 1993
U.S. Vietnam-Relations
Learning Disabilities
Child Care
Space Program's Future

JANUARY 1994
Racial Tensions in Schools
South Africa's Future
Worker Retraining
Regulating Pesticides

FEBRUARY 1994
Prison Overcrowding
Water Quality
Religion in Schools
Juvenile Justice

MARCH 1994
Underground Economy
Education Standards
Gambling Boom
Private Management of Public Schools

APRIL 1994
Reproductive Ethics
U.S.-China Trade
Soccer in America
Talk Show Democracy

MAY 1994
Traffic Congestion
Women's Health Issues
Mutual Funds
Political Scandals

JUNE 1994
Education and Gender
Gun Control
Public Land Policy
Nuclear Arms Cleanup

JULY 1994
Dietary Supplements
Public Opinion and Foreign Policy
Crime Victims' Rights
Birth Control Choices

AUGUST 1994
Electing Minorities

Future Topics

- ***College Sports***
- ***Home Schooling***
- ***Welfare Reform in the States***

THE CQ Researcher

PUBLISHED BY CONGRESSIONAL QUARTERLY INC.

College Sports

Will reform efforts help or hurt student athletes?

Over the past decade, a reform movement has reshaped the image of big-time college sports. At the insistence of college presidents, members of the National Collegiate Athletic Association (NCAA) have voted to raise academic standards for student athletes, reduce the number of sports scholarships, limit practice time and phase out separate dormitories for players. Despite all this, major college "revenue" sports — chiefly football and basketball — remain under constant threat of commercialism and corruption. Some say the best way of defusing the threat is to acknowledge that college football and basketball players are professionals and pay them accordingly. NCAA reform leaders reject this approach, arguing that constant vigilance is the best way to protect the integrity of both college education and college sports.

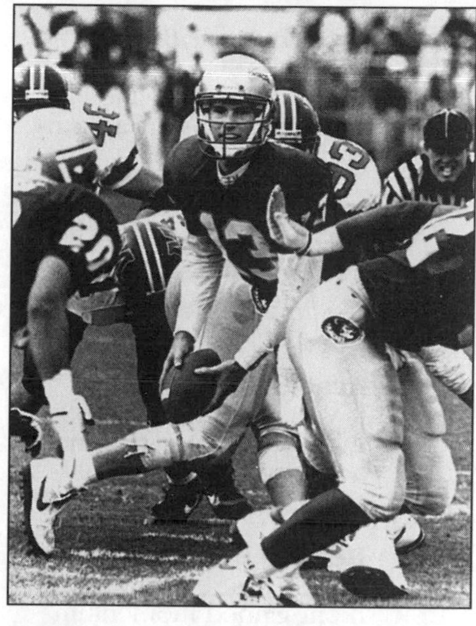

INSIDE THIS ISSUE

CQ August 26, 1994 • Volume 4, No. 32 • 745-768

Formerly Editorial Research Reports

College Sports

The Issues

Background

Current Situation

Outlook

Sidebars and Graphics

For Further Information

COVER: FLORIDA STATE UNIVERSITY QUARTERBACK DANNY KANELL. PAGE 747: UNIVERSITY OF NEVADA-LAS VEGAS GUARD REGGIE MANUEL.

August 26, 1994
Volume 4, No. 32

EDITOR
Sandra Stencel

MANAGING EDITOR
Thomas J. Colin

ASSOCIATE EDITOR
Richard L. Worsnop

STAFF WRITERS
Charles S. Clark
Mary H. Cooper
Kenneth Jost

PRODUCTION EDITOR
Sarah E. Merritt

EDITORIAL ASSISTANT
Michael M. Taylor

GRAPHICS
P. Eloise Fuller

PUBLISHED BY
Congressional Quarterly Inc.

CHAIRMAN
Andrew Barnes

VICE CHAIRMAN
Andrew P. Corty

EDITOR AND PUBLISHER
Neil Skene

EXECUTIVE EDITOR
Robert W. Merry

ASSOCIATE PUBLISHER
John J. Coyle

MARKETING AND SALES DIRECTOR
Edward S. Hauck

The CQ Researcher (ISSN 1056-2036). Formerly Editorial Research Reports. Published weekly (48 times per year, not printed the first Friday of any month with five Fridays) by Congressional Quarterly Inc., 1414 22nd St., N.W., Washington, D.C. 20037. Rates are furnished upon request. Second-class postage paid at Washington, D.C. POSTMASTER: Send address changes to The CQ Researcher, 1414 22nd St., N.W., Washington, D.C. 20037.

College Sports

BY RICHARD L. WORSNOP

THE ISSUES

To millions of armchair athletes, big-time college sports means entertainment, glamor, excitement. From late August to late March, television serves up a rich assortment of regular-season football and basketball games, followed by postseason football bowl games and the national basketball championship tournament. The TV networks pay dearly to broadcast all this, and spectators pay premium prices to attend games. Surely, one would assume, college sports programs must be turning a hefty profit.

In truth, most aren't. According to the Knight Foundation Commission on Intercollegiate Athletics, which has proposed a reform agenda for college sports (*see story, p. 756*), about 70 percent of major college programs "now lose money, many of them operating deeply in the red." [1] The commission also found that sports income "often represents fool's gold." It explained: "Expenses are driven by the search for revenues, and the revenue stream is consumed, at most institutions, in building up the program to maintain the revenue." [2]

Deficits are by no means the only problem plaguing college sports. More than 20 years after passage of Title IX of the Education Amendments of 1972, college athletic directors still are struggling to provide women with sports opportunities commensurate with men's. [3] And educators still are debating whether student athletes should be held to rigorous academic standards.

One of the most troubling questions about college sports concerns the exploitation of players by academic and athletic officials alike. Rules laid down by the National Collegiate Athletic Association (NCAA) [4] bar players from sharing the wealth they create for so-called "revenue sports," which typically include

just football and basketball. Student athletes are allowed to receive only an athletic scholarship, which can be lifted at any time for breaking NCAA rules.

Many student athletes, moreover, hold unrealistic expectations about their chances for a professional sports career. "The facts are that in football 4.5 million young men play high school football, 39,000 will play college ball, 1,500 will make the professional recruitment list, 500 will be drafted, but less than 100 will make it in professional football," LeRoy T. Walker, chancellor emeritus of North Carolina Central University, told a congressional panel. "The obvious answer is for coaches to insist that players obtain another option — a degree." [5]

College sports critics say the situation breeds cynicism among athletes. Rep. Cardiss Collins, D-Ill., touched on this point at a recent hearing on stipends for student athletes. "How can one explain to the athlete, who is attending ... practices, flying back and forth across the nation in tournaments, watching the coach cut lucrative deals with a shoe company, that this is amateur sports and that the acceptance of a pair of shoes is illegal?" she asked. "How can we set one set of rules for the coaches and administrators and a different set of rules for the student?" [6]

Improper gifts to Florida State University football players triggered a scandal uncovered this spring by *Sports Illustrated.* Last Nov. 7, the magazine reported, at least seven FSU players bought $6,000 worth of merchandise at a Foot Locker store in Tallahassee, Fla. Raul Bey, a visiting businessman from Las Vegas, Nev., used his credit card to pay for all the purchases.*

One of the athletes who took part in the shopping spree rationalized his behavior this way: "At Florida State you work so hard to give to that program and get nothing out of it. The most you can get out of it is a trip to the NFL [National Football League]. I felt I was entitled to money or clothing. Why couldn't I have it?" [7]

The FSU scandal drew heavy media coverage because the school's football team had won the unofficial 1993 national championship.** For similar reasons, the NCAA's decision last November to place the University of Nevada-Las Vegas on three years' probation made headlines across the country. UNLV had been one of the nation's top college basketball powers for a decade, winning the NCAA Division I tournament in 1990. Sanctions were imposed after the NCAA found that the school had committed 26 rules violations, including "substantial" inducements to recruits and payments to student athletes.

---

* Florida State on July 29 suspended four players involved in the Foot Locker incident. Linebacker Derrick Brooks and tailback Tiger McMillon were suspended for the first two games of the coming season, guard Patrick McNeil for the first three games, and tackle Forrest Conoly was suspended indefinitely. The NCAA has not announced whether it will impose penalties of its own on the FSU football program.

** According to NCAA public information director Kathryn M. Reith, commitment to the existing postseason bowl system is the main reason why there is no championship playoff for Division I-A football. She also cites widespread concern that a football playoff would interfere with the players' studies for midterm exams.

Student Athletes More Likely to Earn Degrees

Student athletes are now graduating at higher rates than the general student population. Black athletes are far more likely to graduate than black students in general. Graduation rates for athletes have been rising since 1986, when the National Collegiate Athletic Association toughened academic standards for student athletes. The new rule, known as Proposition 48, set minimum test scores and grade-point averages for freshman athletes.

SCORE BOARD

HOME 00 | 00:00 | VISITOR 00

College graduation rates

	All students	Athletes	Male students	Male athletes	Female students	Female athletes
1984	53%	52%	51%	47%	54%	62%
1985	54%	52%	52%	48%	55%	61%
1986	55%	57%	54%	52%	57%	68%
1987	56%	57%	54%	53%	58%	67%

	Black males	Black male athletes	Black females	Black female athletes
1984	28%	33%	34%	45%
1985	30%	34%	36%	44%
1986	30%	41%	36%	54%
1987	33%	43%	41%	53%

	White males	White male athletes	White females	White female athletes
1984	54%	55%	57%	66%
1985	55%	55%	58%	65%
1986	56%	57%	60%	70%
1987	57%	58%	61%	69%

Note: The figures show the percentage of full-time students who entered NCAA Division I colleges in 1984-87 who earned bachelor degrees within six years.

Source: National Collegiate Athletic Association

Indeed, numerous NCAA sports programs are on probation at any given time. The current total is 35. The prevalence of rule-breaking has prompted some college sports analysts to suggest the NCAA has too many regulations. They say the association might get better results by concentrating its enforcement weaponry on major abuses.

Another school of thought holds that rampant rule-breaking spotlights the hypocrisy of pretending that big-time college sports are played by amateur athletes. College football and basketball teams, it is argued, have long served as unofficial farm systems for the National Football League and National Basketball Association. A similar relationship seems to be evolving in college baseball and hockey. This being the case, why not allow college athletes in these sports to receive monthly stipends — or even salaries?

So far, the NCAA has turned its back on all suggestions that college sports be professionalized in any way. Over the past decade, though, the association has approved reforms aimed at boosting the academic performance of student athletes and ending their traditional isolation from the campus community. College presidents, intent on wresting control of intercollegiate sports from coaches and athletic directors, have been in the forefront of the reform movement from the beginning.

The presidents' reform agenda has stirred heated debate both within NCAA ranks and among media sports commentators. These two questions figure prominently in the debate:

Are NCAA academic standards fair to student athletes?

One of the most vexing issues facing the NCAA concerns academic standards for student athletes. Educators and sports officials have been at odds over the issue since 1983, when the NCAA approved Proposition 48, the association's first academic standards for incoming freshman student athletes. Prop. 48, as it is generally called, took effect in the fall of 1986.

To be eligible for sports competition in their first year of college, athletes at Division I schools (*see box, p. 750*) have to have at least a 2.0 high school grade-point average (out of 4.0) in a core curriculum of 11 academic courses, including English, history, math and science. They also are required to score a minimum of 700 points (of a possible 1,600) on the combined Scholastic Assessment Tests (SATs) or a minimum of 15 points (of a possible 35) on the American College Testing Program (ACT) exam.

Many black leaders argue that standardized tests like the SATs and ACT are culturally biased in favor of whites and that this explains why a disproportionate number of black students do poorly on them.[8] To ease the sting of the standardized test score requirement, black leaders have urged that prospective student athletes who fail to meet it be allowed to make up the deficit with a grade-point average (GPA) higher than the specified minimum.

The NCAA adopted even tougher academic standards at its 1992 convention. Under the new rules, scheduled to take effect in the 1995-96 academic year, freshmen will not be eligible for intercollegiate sports at Division I schools unless they have a high school GPA of 2.5 (up from 2.0) in 13 core courses (up from 11). In addition, they must score at least 700 on the SATs or a 17 on the ACT. However, the pending rules feature a sliding scale that will enable athletes whose grade-point average falls between 2.0 and 2.5 to offset the deficit with higher standardized test scores. For instance, a student with a 2.0 GPA could gain athletics eligibility by scoring 900 on the SATs or 21 on the ACT. Freshmen who fail to reach the standards may receive need-based financial aid, but they may not receive an athletic scholarship that year and they lose a year of eligibility.

Although the revised academic standards were approved by a nearly 3-to-1 margin, some campus officials said they would discriminate against minority-group athletes. "There are going to be kids who will be denied access to education," said Francis X. Rienzo, Georgetown University's athletic director. "I think the road to academic reform will be covered with the bodies of socioeconomically disadvantaged individuals. . . ." [9]

Unhappiness with the pending changes was one of the factors that impelled the Black Coaches Association (BCA), a nationwide group of college and high school coaches, to threaten a boycott of selected college basketball games last season. To help settle that dispute, the NCAA established a Special Committee to Review Initial Eligibility Standards.

The special committee's recommendation, announced June 9, called for a minimum GPA of 2.0 in 13 core courses. However, it prescribed no fixed cutoff point for standardized test scores. Instead, it proposed a sliding scale for both test scores and grade-point averages, ranging from a 2.0 GPA combined with an 810 on the SATs to a 3.0 GPA and a 410 SAT (test-takers are awarded 400 points for signing their names).

Delaware State College President William B. DeLauder, co-chairman of the special committee, said the panel's review had "provided dramatic evidence of the disparate impact of current rules on minority student athletes." Consequently, he said, "We chose a standard that would maximize access . . . [to college], allowing student athletes who have a reasonable chance of graduating to succeed. On the other hand, we made sure that the standard would still provide a graduation rate for student athletes comparable to that of all students." [10]

The NCAA Presidents Commission,

Current and Proposed NCAA Eligibility Standards

Tougher academic standards for student athletes are scheduled to take effect in the fall of 1995. Responding to criticism from the Black Coaches Association and others, two NCAA groups — the Presidents Commission and the NCAA Council — have proposed alternatives that would delay the effective date of new standards until the 1996-97 academic year. Both proposals feature a sliding scale that would allow students to offset lower grade-point averages with higher test scores. One proposal would allow athletes with lower test scores to practice with the team and receive financial aid, but not compete. They could qualify for a fourth year of eligibility if they meet academic progress requirements. NCAA Division I members will vote on the proposals at the NCAA's 1995 convention, to be held Jan. 7-11 in San Diego.

Current Standards

SAT Score	Core GPA for 11 courses
700 and above	2.0 and above

Standards Scheduled to Take Effect Fall 1995

SAT Score	Core GPA for 13 courses
700 and above	2.5 and above

Athletes with a GPA between 2.0 and 2.5 can offset deficits with higher test scores. Freshmen who fail to meet standards may receive need-based financial aid, but they cannot receive an athletic scholarship that year and they lose a year of eligibility.

NCAA Presidents Commission's and NCAA Council's Proposal

SAT Score	Core GPA for 13 courses
900	2.0
860	2.1
820	2.2
780	2.3
740	2.4
700	2.5 and above

Athletes with SAT scores of 600-690 and corresponding GPAs of 2.75-2.52 can get financial aid and practice as freshmen but not compete; they could earn a fourth year of eligibility.

NCAA Council's Proposal

SAT Score	Core GPA for 13 courses
810	2.0
770	2.1
730	2.2
690	2.3
650	2.4
610	2.5

Source: National Collegiate Athletic Association

NCAA Divisions at a Glance

At a special convention in August 1973, the National Collegiate Athletic Association (NCAA) placed its member institutions in three divisions with differing views on the role of competitive sports in an academic setting. The schools in each division tend to have similar policies on the number of intercollegiate sports and athletic scholarships they offer.

Division I includes the nation's top college football and basketball powers, most of which are grouped in powerful conferences like the Big Ten, Pacific-10, Southeastern, Atlantic Coast and Big East. Leading independents, such as Notre Dame, also are in Division I. [1]

In 1978, Division I was subdivided into Divisions I-A and I-AA for football only. I-A schools must have a home stadium with at least 30,000 permanent seats and must have averaged 17,000 in paid attendance per home game at least one year in the most recent four-year period. I-AA schools have no such requirements to meet, though they do operate football programs.

Division II schools, which include institutions like South Dakota State and the University of Puget Sound, often aspire to big-time sports status but lack the financial resources to reach that level. As a result, they generally offer fewer athletic scholarships than Division I colleges do.

Division III comprises small schools like Washington and Lee and Case Western Reserve, which maintain sports programs but do not field highly competitive teams. The NCAA prohibits Division III institutions from offering any athletic scholarships.

[1] Notre Dame joined the Big East basketball conference this year.

a 44-member board formed in 1984 (*see p. 755*), announced June 29 that it was rejecting the special committee's proposal. Commission Chairwoman Judith Albino of the University of Colorado said the group did not want to send a mixed signal to athletes. "We certainly want to send the message we're about student athletes, not professional athletes," she said at a news conference. "The first point needs to be academics." [11]

At the same time, however, the commission retreated from its longstanding insistence on a minimum 700 SAT score. Instead, it said it would propose "partial qualifier" status for prospective student athletes with at least a 600 SAT score (15 on the ACT). Under the commission's plan, such students would be able to practice with their team as freshmen and earn a fourth year of athletics eligibility if they made satisfactory progress toward a degree.

Gary R. Roberts, vice law dean at Tulane University and the faculty representative on Tulane's athletic council, finds this aspect of the Presidents Commission's recommendation troubling. In his opinion, it means nothing more than keeping student athletes out of competition their freshman year. "If they can practice with their team and get their fourth year of eligibility back toward the end of their college career, they're just being red-shirted," he says. "That, to me, is a backdoor way of throwing out the initial academic eligibility standards altogether."

Dana D. Brooks, dean of West Virginia University's school of physical education, says he's "not necessarily in total agreement" with the Presidents Commission's plan. He feels the plan submitted earlier by the Special Committee to Review Initial Eligibility Standards, "given time, would have had a positive impact on students entering college and even graduating."

The debate on academic standards became even more tangled when the NCAA Council, the association's policy-making board, offered still another formula for resolving the dispute. The council on Aug. 10 proposed a sliding scale ranging from a minimum SAT score of 610 plus a 2.5 GPA in 13 core courses to an 810 SAT combined with a 2.0 GPA. If approved, the council's measure would take effect in August 1996, the same implementation date suggested earlier by the special committee.

In addition to presenting its own recommendation, the council agreed to cosponsor the Presidents Commission's proposal. However, the council added language postponing the measure's effective date until August 1996. Both the council's and the commission's proposals will be voted on at the 1995 NCAA convention, to be held Jan. 7-11 in San Diego, Calif.

"This issue is a sensitive one," noted Joseph N. Crowley, the current NCAA president and the president of the University of Nevada-Reno. "We are balancing two important values for the association: academic standards to ensure student athletes are prepared for college-level work and educational opportunity for those student athletes who may not have had the best preparation but are capable of college-level work. Both of the council's proposals incorporate these important values. The council felt that the full Division I membership should debate and decide which proposal is better." [12]

Data on the college graduation rates of student athletes have done nothing to still the dispute over NCAA academic standards. The association's most recent set of graduation figures, issued June 30, showed that 57 percent of scholarship athletes who entered Division I colleges in 1987 — the second year Prop. 48 standards were in effect —

graduated within six years. That compared favorably with 56 percent of all full-time students who entered that year. (*See table, p. 748.*)

Though still lagging behind the general student population, black male athletes continued to post larger than average graduation gains. After rising 8 percentage points in the first year of Prop. 48, black male athletes recorded a further 2 percent improvement in the second year, to 43 percent. Only 33 percent of black males in the general student body graduated within six years.

To some analysts, the rising graduation rates for student athletes show that the NCAA standards are achieving their purpose. But opponents of Prop. 48 say the improvements were achieved at unacceptable cost. "This . . . may be just another indication that opportunities are being taken away from youngsters, and many more black youngsters in particular," noted John Chaney, men's basketball coach at Temple University. "If you want to have a great graduation rate, just keep raising the [eligibility] standards." [13]

Should major college football and basketball teams turn professional?

Some observers suggest turning teams at the major sports schools into bona fide professional enterprises, based in the academic community but operated independently of the school administration.

In his 1980 book *The Recruiting Game,* John Rooney proposed paying athletes on such teams for up to five years on an escalating salary scale. Players who wanted to take advantage of the college's educational facilities could do so. Non-revenue sports would return to the original philosophy of participation for its own sake.

Numerous variations on Rooney's idea have been floated over the years. For instance, *Washington Post* sports columnist John Feinstein wrote in January that money should be set aside for "football and basketball players who do not become millionaires" upon leaving college. "The money should be available only after a player graduates," said Feinstein. "That would give a lot of mid-level athletes an incentive to stick with their classes." He added that college coaches should be "fighting to get the players who make them rich a piece of the pie." [14]

"My position [is] that student athletes are compensated adequately by that scholarship, by that room and board. Let's remember that they're on campus to be students first and student athletes second."

— Dana D. Brooks, dean of West Virginia University's school of physical education

The case for paying college athletes often rests on the premise that a player who is later drafted to play pro ball generates as much as $1 million a year in TV and ticket revenue for his college while he's still in school. An athletic scholarship, by this measure, represents only a tiny fraction of the player's monetary worth to his alma mater.

Not only are college players unsalaried, wrote *Los Angeles Times* sports writer Bob Oates, but "universities deny them even a few cents" to spend on clothing, entertainment and incidentals. "Gifts of any kind are also out" under NCAA rules, Oates added. "So are personal or career-related loans. And so are in-season part-time jobs." [15]

Not surprisingly, play-for-pay plans appeal to many college athletes. Eric Ramsey, a former football player at Auburn University, told a House subcommittee in July that he "wholeheartedly" supports the concept. He favors a pay scale ranging from $3,000 to $5,000 per month, with the money being held in trust until the player's athletic eligibility ends. [16]

Testifying before the same panel, player advocate Dick DeVenzio* criticized the NCAA for "systematically depriving thousands of athletes (and their families) of the opportunity to receive just economic rewards" commensurate with their talents. "What negatives would occur if athletes were permitted to receive money from Nike or Chevrolet or any other commercial enterprise — the way coaches can now?" he asked. "What if trust funds, not actual cash, were permitted athletes? This would obviously benefit athletes and their families tremendously. . . . [And] trust funds linked to educational achievement would obviously encourage more athletes to get their diplomas."

College administrators and NCAA officials are generally cool to proposals for player stipends or salaries. Once you start paying student athletes, said former

* DeVenzio, a former basketball player for Duke University, is the co-founder of a group called Student Athlete Incentive Gifts.

NCAA Executive Director Richard D. Schultz, "you immediately establish an employee-employer relationship, and following that there are two things that happen that make it almost unaffordable for colleges: First, you now are liable for [workers'] compensation and all the other liabilities that go into an employer-employee relationship. Second . . . I'm sure the IRS would step in and say that . . . you are a professional, not an amateur, team." [17]

West Virginia's Brooks cites other reasons for opposing payments to college athletes. "My position has been, and will forever be, that student athletes *are* compensated adequately by that scholarship, by that room and board," he says. "Let's remember that they're on campus to be students first and student athletes second. They get quality coaching, trips to distant cities and access to a network of people with connections. Those athletes who don't go to the pros tend to get jobs in their own communities after college. If you cost all that out, it's worth quite a bit."

Tulane's Roberts disagrees. Although players receive athletic scholarships, he says, "the demands put on them by their coaches are such that they can't really take advantage" of their academic opportunities. "Or, they're shuttled into classes that don't really give them an education. And so their compensation is illusory rather than real."

To the extent that colleges "don't give their student athletes access to a full and meaningful education and make sure that have every chance to get a degree," says Roberts, "then you've professionalized the athletes, but you've paid them with bogus money, basically. You've paid them with an education that's not there. And that, I think, is just immoral." ■

Background

Prosperity and Scandals

The rise of college sports to big-business status didn't happen overnight. Ironically, some sports historians attribute the development to campus officials' aloofness toward extracurricular athletics. Educators allowed sports to evolve without adequate supervision, the argument goes, by failing to see that competitive games had a rightful place in the learning process.

Harvard established the first college gymnasium in one of its dining halls in 1826. College athletics grew slowly from that time until 1870, when they began to take their place in undergraduate life. Up to about 1880 there was neither specialized training nor coaching, and management was entirely in the hands of undergraduates. Then expansion began in earnest, with more types of athletics being introduced and professional coaches being hired. Equipment became more complex and more expensive. Funds were obtained from subscription fees, gate receipts and outsiders — especially alumni. The alumni, in turn, began to acquire the power and control over intercollegiate sport that they have retained to this day at many institutions.

Around the same time, some college administrators built up sports programs to attract talented scholars and students. A prime example was William Rainey Harper, the first president of the University of Chicago. To boost the fledgling institution's prestige, Harper hired the legendary Yale football coach Amos Alonzo Stagg, who proceeded to mold Chicago into a major Midwestern gridiron power. Between 1896 and 1909, enrollment at the university tripled.

Meanwhile, though, college football had acquired an unsavory reputation because of its brutality. Dangerous formations such as the "flying wedge" — in which blockers locked arms to guard the ball carrier and trampled anyone who got in the way — resulted in hundreds of crippling injuries and dozens of deaths. A threat by President Theodore Roosevelt to ban football if the situation was not remedied resulted in the formation of the NCAA in 1906 and the drafting of most of the rules familiar to football fans today.*

Because its early rules on amateurism were widely ignored, the NCAA called in 1916 for an investigation of college athletics by an independent body. The Carnegie Foundation, which accepted the challenge, spent the next 13 years evaluating sports programs at more than 100 colleges and universities. It found rampant corruption and commercialism. "Apparently the ethical bearing of intercollegiate football contests and their scholastic aspects are of secondary importance to the winning of victories and financial success," the foundation noted in its final report. [18]

Among the schools that took the Carnegie report to heart was the University of Chicago, then headed by Robert Maynard Hutchins. In 1932 Hutchins rescinded the university's "physical culture" requirement, which had been used to groom prospects for the football team. Stagg resigned as football coach the same year. After a string of losing seasons, Chicago dropped intercollegiate football in 1939. Dozens of other schools, most of them small private colleges, abandoned or de-emphasized varsity athletics, either because of the moral issues involved or because they could not afford to compete against the burgeoning state-funded public institutions.

Overall, though, college sports con-

*The organization was originally called the Intercollegiate Athletic Association. It became the NCAA in 1910.

Continued on p. 754

Chronology

19th Century

Early efforts to organize intercollegiate athletics involve mostly Eastern colleges.

Aug. 3, 1852
Oarsmen from Harvard and Yale stage the first U.S. intercollegiate sports contest, in rowing, on Lake Winnepesaukee, N.H.

—— • ——

1900s-1930s

As college sports grow in size and popularity, commercialization becomes a major worry.

March 31, 1906
The Intercollegiate Athletic Association is formed. In 1910, it changes its name to the National Collegiate Athletic Association (NCAA).

1929
In a landmark study, the Carnegie Foundation finds rampant corruption in college sports. "Apparently the ethical bearing of intercollegiate football contests and their scholastic aspects are of secondary importance to the winning of victories and financial success," the foundation states.

March 27, 1939
The NCAA sponsors its first national basketball championship tournament at Northwestern University in Evanston, Ill.

1939
After a string of losing seasons, the University of Chicago drops intercollegiate football.

—— • ——

1940s-1950s

Prosperity and scandal return to intercollegiate sports.

June 20-21, 1947
The NCAA holds its first baseball championship finals at Western Michigan University in Kalamazoo.

1951
Thirty-three basketball players at seven New York City schools, including 1950 national champion City College of New York, are indicted for point-shaving.

1952
Three University of Kentucky basketball players are convicted for gambling and point-shaving. The NCAA places Kentucky on probation — the first institution to receive such punishment — and cancels its basketball program for a year.

—— • ——

1980s

College presidents challenge the authority of athletic directors to determine college sports policy.

November 1981
The NCAA sponsors its first national championships in women's sports — cross country and field hockey.

1983
The NCAA approves Proposition 48, prescribing minimum academic standards for athletes.

1984
The NCAA forms a Presidents Commission consisting of 44 chief executive officers of institutions drawn from each of the association's three membership divisions.

January 1987
At their annual convention, NCAA members reject a set of cost-cutting measures proposed by the Presidents Commission.

1990s

Under the leadership of the NCAA Presidents Commission, the intercollegiate sports reform movement gathers momentum.

January 1990
NCAA Executive Director Richard D. Schultz calls for major cutbacks in recruiting, tougher academic standards, tenure for coaches and elimination of separate dormitories for athletes.

January 1991
The NCAA stiffens existing limits on recruiting contacts and player evaluations, mandates the phasing out of athletic dormitories and reduces the permissible number of athletic scholarships by 10 percent.

January 1992
The NCAA raises academic standards for entering freshman athletes, effective in 1995-96.

January 1993
The NCAA approves a certification or peer-review program for Division I sports departments.

January 1994
Black basketball coaches threaten to boycott selected games to protest NCAA policies on athletic scholarships and academic standards for student athletes.

March 23, 1994
The NCAA and the Black Coaches Association reach agreement on a number of issues, including athletic scholarships for entering freshmen who do not meet academic requirements.

More Women Are Playing College Sports

The number of women participating in college sports rose by about 8 percent over the past decade, while the number of men playing varsity sports fell by about 7 percent.

Year	Men	Women	Total
1984-85	201,063	91,669	292,732
1985-86	200,031	95,351	295,382
1986-87	190,017	91,101	281,118
1987-88	178,941	89,825	268,766
1988-89	180,144	91,406	271,550
1989-90	177,156	89,212	266,368
1990-91	184,593	92,778	277,371
1991-92	186,045	96,467	282,512
1992-93	187,041	99,859	286,900

Source: National Collegiate Athletic Association

Continued from p. 752

tinued to grow, especially after World War II. But once again, prosperity was accompanied by scandal. In 1945, for instance, five Brooklyn College basketball players were expelled after accepting bribes to throw a game. In 1951, 33 basketball players at seven New York City schools, including 1950 national champion City College of New York, were indicted for point-shaving; two spent time in prison.

However, the biggest shock came the following year when three University of Kentucky basketball players were convicted for gambling and point-shaving during the 1949 season. The NCAA thereupon put Kentucky on probation — the first institution to receive such punishment — and canceled its basketball program for a year.

The early 1950s also saw a number of former college football powers deemphasize or quit the sport. On Oct. 28, 1951, the presidents of Harvard, Yale and Princeton voted to de-emphasize athletics on the ground that rising costs and commercialization had made academic integrity and big-time college sports incompatible. The five other Ivy League schools — Brown, Columbia, Cornell, Dartmouth and Pennsylvania — soon followed suit. Scholarships based on athletic ability alone were banned, as were out-of-season practices.

Georgetown University announced the same year that it would no longer play intercollegiate football. The Very Rev. Hunter Guthrie, Georgetown's president, estimated that football brought in $1 million during the 1930s but cost his school $2 million. Football, he declared, "has as much reason to subsist on the campus as a nightclub or a macaroni factory." [19]

TV's Impact

It was during the early 1950s that television emerged as a key revenue source for college sports. Recognizing the medium's potential early on, the NCAA assumed a leadership role in TV programming of college games. At its 1952 convention, for instance, the NCAA ordered members to make no TV commitments for the coming college football season until its television committee had drawn up a schedule of its own. The resulting plan authorized TV coverage on 12 dates between late September and late November. It also called for a wide geographic distribution of games and, with a few exceptions, limited each team to one TV appearance.

The NCAA television control program was instituted over the protests of several powerful members, including Georgia Tech, the University of Kansas, Notre Dame, Ohio State and the University of Pennsylvania. Opponents argued that the program violated federal law. Nonetheless, the NCAA kept tight control over telecasts of major college football games for more than 30 years.

The end came in 1984, when the Supreme Court ruled in the case of *NCAA v. the University of Oklahoma* that the NCAA's exclusive rights to television contracts violated federal antitrust laws. But the decision turned out to be a Pyrrhic victory for college football powers. With many more games available for home viewing, TV networks no longer were willing to pay top dollar for broadcast rights. In 1983, the last year that the NCAA controlled television rights, ABC paid $32 million for one season's weekly broadcasts of college football. By contrast, ABC paid the College Football Association (CFA)* only $31.8 million for the rights to show roughly twice as many games during the 1985 and 1986 seasons.

According to a 1993 report by the National Association of College and University Business Officers, the dependence of college sports programs on TV money encourages disregard of student athletes' needs. "Allowing the networks to dictate the terms and conditions for televising college sports reduces institutional control over what are often educational as well as athletic decisions," the study said. "This is particularly the case where the terms

*Founded in 1976, the CFA represents the nation's top football powers, including most major conferences and independents.

of a television contract intrude into areas that are central to the university's educational mission. (For example, the effect on student athletes of playing in away games scheduled for 9 p.m. or later on weekday nights and attending classes early the next morning.)" [20]

The Knight Commission expressed similar concern. "Clearly, something must be done to mitigate the growing public perception that the quest for television dollars is turning college sports into an entertainment enterprise," the panel stated in its first report. It went on to assert that "Greater care must be given to the needs and obligations of the student athlete and the primacy of the academic calendar over the scheduling requirements of the networks." [21]

Academic Standards

Neglect of college athletes' classroom performance long antedates the television era, however. Before 1981, the only NCAA academic standard for athletic eligibility was that a student had to be making satisfactory progress toward a degree as defined by his or her institution. That year, a new rule required athletes to average a specified number of credit hours per semester or term. Not until 1983 was there a requirement that the credits be applicable to a specific degree.

Still, stories continued to surface about doctoring of grade transcripts to make athletes' academic records more presentable. And the media occasionally ran profiles of athletes who had completed their college athletic eligibility without receiving any education at all, let alone a degree.

The bad taste left by such reports prodded the NCAA into taking remedial action. At the group's 1983 convention, members approved Proposition 48, which for the first time established numerical academic standards for athletes entering Division I NCAA schools as freshmen (*see p. 748*). The standards took effect in 1986.

At the 1984 NCAA convention, members approved the creation of a 44-member Presidents Commission with largely advisory powers. Earlier, the convention had voted down a proposal by the American Council on Education to establish a "Presidents' Board" with authority to veto or modify NCAA rules and to impose new rules of its own design on association members, subject to review only by a mail vote of presidents of all member institutions.

In one of its first moves, the Presidents Commission called for a special NCAA convention in June 1985 to consider ways of punishing sports programs that flagrantly break NCAA rules. Two proposals passed by the delegates attracted particular attention. One authorized the suspension of a sports program found guilty of frequent and deliberate rules violations. The other provided that if a coach cheated at one college but left it before NCAA penalties were imposed, the infractions would remain on the coach's record at his or her next school.

At the 1987 NCAA convention, the Presidents Commission turned its attention to athletic scholarships and the length of sports seasons. The delegates approved a commission-backed proposal trimming men's basketball scholarships from 15 to 13. However, a measure to reduce the number of officially sanctioned baseball games from 80 to 60 was voted down. Despite that setback, the commission decided to seek scholarship cuts in football and minor sports at a special meeting that June in Dallas.

College athletic directors and heads of individual sports programs saw a chance to reassert their influence, and they did so with a vengeance. A commission proposal to cut Division I-A football scholarships from 95 to 90 was defeated, as was a measure providing for modest scholarship reductions in non-revenue sports like men's cross country and women's field hockey. To cap the panel's humiliation, the delegates voted to restore the two men's basketball scholarships that had been eliminated at the January convention.

For the moment, at least, the college sports reform movement was stalled. "After the Dallas debacle," Indiana University Professor Murray Sperber wrote, "the Presidents Commission became semi-moribund, retreating to what it termed a 'study phase' and hoping to hold 'national dialogues' about the main issues in college sports." [22]

Reform Revival

Though wounded, the reform movement was far from dead. It reinvigorated itself in 1990, thanks in large part to NCAA Executive Director Schultz. Addressing the association's convention that January, Schultz called for a "new model" of college sports, including major cutbacks in recruiting, tougher academic standards, tenure for coaches and elimination of separate dormitories for athletes. These objectives were to form the core of the Presidents Commission's agenda for the next four years.

A key aim of the 1990 convention was to ease the time demands on student athletes. To this end, the delegates voted to reduce spring football practice in Divisions I-A and I-AA (*see box, p. 750*) from 20 to 15 days and restrict contact drills to only 10 of those days. Spring football practice for Division II schools was trimmed from 20 to 12 days, with no contact allowed. In addition, the delegates cut the number of basketball games from 28 to 25, moved the start of basketball practice from Oct. 15 to Nov. 1 and pushed the basketball season's opening date from the fourth Friday in November to Dec. 1.

The 1990 convention also relaxed curbs on financial aid to athletes that

Knight Foundation Commission Sparks Reform

Reforms proposed by the NCAA Presidents Commission since 1990 owe much of their inspiration to the Knight Foundation Commission on Intercollegiate Athletics. Formed in October 1989, the commission was charged with finding solutions to the abuses then threatening to swamp college sports. [1] Many of the panel's recommendations were adopted by the Presidents Commission and approved by delegates to the NCAA's annual conventions.

The Knight Commission's core proposal, as outlined in the introduction to the first of its three reports, was that university presidents "must be in charge — and be *understood* to be in charge — on campuses, in conferences and in the decision-making councils of the NCAA." At the time, many major college sports programs were perceived as fiefdoms run by the director of athletics and the head coaches serving under him.

To help the presidents assert leadership, the Knight Commission urged that they implement a uniform model of athletics department oversight. Specifically, it urged presidents to ensure the academic and financial integrity of the department, and verify its status through annual independent audits. "With such a model in place, higher education can address all of the subordinate difficulties in college sports," the commission declared. "Without such a model, athletics reform will continue in fits and starts, its energy squandered on symptoms, the underlying problems ignored." [2]

In its final report, issued in March 1993, the commission noted that college presidents had pushed through NCAA reforms like sports-program cost reductions, tougher academic standards for student athletes and a certification program for athletics departments. The presidents' crowning achievement, said the report, was the approval in 1993 of a proposal to create an NCAA Joint Policy Board with authority to review the association's budget and legislative agenda and evaluate and supervise the executive director. "Presidential leadership is the hallmark of today's NCAA," the report concluded. [3]

Still, the Knight Commission acknowledged that much remained to be done. High on its list of unfinished business was curbing the independence of athletics foundations and booster clubs. Though some of these groups "have contributed generously to overall athletics revenues," the commission said, "too many seem to have been created either in response to state laws prohibiting the expenditure of state funds on athletics or to avoid institutional oversight of athletics expenditures." All funds raised for college sports, it declared, "should be channeled into the university's financial system and subjected to the same budgeting procedures applied to similarly structured departments and programs." [4]

At a Washington news conference after the final report was issued, panel members stressed the need for continued vigilance. Creed C. Black, president of the Knight Foundation and a member of the commission, said he was "optimistic that there's now a framework in place to handle many of the problems we set out to fix, but there's much more to do and there must be constant watch." [5]

---

[1] As originally constituted, the 22-member Knight Commission included college presidents, business executives, Rep. Tom McMillen, D-Md., and NCAA Executive Director Richard D. Schultz. The Knight Foundation is now known as the John S. and James L. Knight Foundation.

[2] Knight Foundation Commission on Intercollegiate Athletics, *Keeping Faith With the Student Athlete: A New Model for Intercollegiate Athletics*, March 1991, p. vii.

[3] Knight Foundation Commission on Intercollegiate Athletics, *A New Beginning for a New Century: Intercollegiate Athletics in the United States*, March 1993, p. 4.

[4] *Keeping Faith With the Student Athlete, op. cit.*, p. 20.

[5] Quoted in *The Chronicle of Higher Education*, March 24, 1993, p. A29.

it had adopted the previous year.* It did so by voting to allow incoming freshman athletes to receive need-based financial aid even if they failed to meet the academic requirements for an athletic scholarship. The revised rule still barred such freshmen from receiving athletic grants and from participating in intercollegiate sports for a year.

Responding to pressure from Congress, the 1990 convention voted to require Division I and Division II schools to furnish the NCAA with data on the graduation rates of athletes. [23] Rates for basketball and football players also were to be tabulated by race. The disclosure rule further required that the data be published on an annual basis and be made available to prospective student athletes, their parents and their high school or junior college coaches.

Once more showing a strong appetite for change, the 1991 NCAA convention adopted 37 of a package of 39 proposals known as the "reform agenda." The more noteworthy measures stiffened existing limits on recruiting contacts and player evaluations; required that academic tutoring and counseling services be made available to all recruited student athletes; mandated the phasing out of separate athletic dormitories; reduced the permissible number of athletic scholarships by 10 percent; and limited mandatory participation in a sport to

* An amendment to Prop. 48 adopted at the 1989 convention barred all institutional aid to freshman athletes who failed to meet minimum academic requirements. John Thompson, Georgetown University men's basketball coach, boycotted two 1989 games to protest the new rule, which he claimed worked a special hardship on black and other minority-group athletes.

20 hours a week.

In Sperber's view, the mandatory-participation rule contains a gaping loophole that renders it virtually meaningless. He notes that the rule sets no ceiling for non-mandatory participation, leaving coaches free to schedule "voluntary" practices, weight-room sessions and so on. Athletes quickly realize, says Sperber, that signing up for such drills is in their best interest.

At its 1992 convention, the NCAA turned yet again to the touchy issue of student athlete academic requirements. Existing test-score standards were retained, and GPA requirements were raised. At the same time, the delegates voted for a sliding scale to allow athletes failing to meet the minimum GPA benchmark to make up the difference with higher SAT or ACT scores (*see p. 748*). ■

CURRENT SITUATION

Reforms Continue

After the tumult of the three previous meetings, the 1993 NCAA convention was relatively staid. Its chief accomplishment may have been the creation of a certification or peer-review program for Division I sports departments (*see p. 760*). Under the program, each institution must conduct a self-study every five years that is to be evaluated by an outside team of sports officials. The review is to cover four main areas: governance and commitment to rules compliance, academic integrity, fiscal integrity and commitment to equity.

Convention delegates also voted to establish a national clearinghouse to certify the academic eligibility of all prospective Division I and Division II student athletes. Backers of the proposal, which took effect Aug. 1, said the clearinghouse would reduce paperwork by high schools and colleges and make eligibility decisions consistent nationwide. Previously, individual colleges had collected academic records from incoming freshman athletes and determined eligibility on a case-by-case basis.

In another significant vote, the delegates approved the establishment of a joint policy board comprising the members of the NCAA's administrative committee and the officers of the Presidents Commission. Among other duties, the board was empowered to review the association's budget and legislative agenda and to evaluate and supervise the executive director.

The 1993 convention also was memorable for a proposal that narrowly failed to carry. The measure would have awarded a fourth year of eligibility to athletes who had failed to meet the NCAA's eligibility standards as freshmen, but who were on track to graduate after four years in college. Supporters argued that the proposal would act as a powerful incentive to athletes who had lost their first year of eligibility under Proposition 48. But opponents said the change would undermine the chief aim of Prop. 48 — persuading college-bound athletes to upgrade their high-school classroom performance.

Prop. 48 returned to the spotlight on July 1, 1993, when the NCAA released a statistical report showing improved graduation rates for student athletes who entered college in 1986, the year that the academic standards took effect. The report was the first to cover an entire freshman-to-senior cycle of athletes in the Prop. 48 era. Graduation rates in the report reflected the percentages of student athletes receiving a degree within six years of enrollment.

According to the report, the largest increases in graduation rates occurred among black football players at Division I-A schools and black male basketball players in Division I. The rate for all black male athletes was 41 percent, as against 30 percent for all black male students. Among white male students, the graduation rate was 57 percent for athletes and 56 percent for non-athletes. In contrast, the average graduation rate for all athletes starting college in 1983-85, before Prop. 48 took effect, was 51 percent.

Supporters of Prop. 48 were encouraged by the numbers. "[T]his report is the most encouraging sign that we are getting to the heart of the issue by getting black students performing academically and involved in campus life the way we should be," said Richard E. Lapchick, director of Northeastern University's Center for the Study of Sport in Society. [24]

Coaches' Concerns

Grade and test requirements are only one of the complaints voiced by black coaches and college presidents. There is also concern about cutbacks in athletic scholarships and limited opportunities for blacks in college coaching ranks.* Moreover, black coaches chafe under NCAA rules that limit contacts with prospective athletes. The coaches say they feel a special obligation to help youngsters in black communities, where wholesome role models often are in short supply.

Over the past year, the Black Coaches Association has taken the lead in calling attention to these issues. Last October, for example, the BCA boycotted an issues forum sponsored by the National Association of Basketball Coaches, conferred in Washington with

*According to the NCAA's Minority Opportunity and Interests Committee, blacks accounted for only 10 percent of the athletic directors and 8 percent of the head coaches at Division I schools in the 1993-94 academic year. Of the 107 coaches in Division I-A, college football's top level, only three were black.

Participation in Varsity Sports at NCAA Colleges, 1992-93

	Division I No. of Teams	Division I No. of Athletes	Division II No. of Teams	Division II No. of Athletes	Division III No. of Teams	Division III No. of Athletes
Women's Sports						
Baseball	289	3,873	219	2,978	319	4,307
Cross Country	288	3,571	168	1,680	244	2,855
Fencing	25	210	0	0	17	167
Field hockey	71	1,626	20	496	120	2,496
Golf	123	1,070	18	151	36	263
Gymnastics	67	898	10	117	14	185
Lacrosse	35	945	11	266	80	1,792
Skiing	9	132	9	89	16	194
Soccer	103	2,338	69	1,394	215	4,494
Softball	186	3,236	172	2,804	260	4,316
Swimming	164	3,772	48	902	179	3,294
Tennis	283	2,632	160	1,440	289	3,035
Track, indoor	235	5,946	90	1,809	154	3,126
Track, outdoor	249	6,250	116	2,366	209	4,222
Volleyball	274	3,452	207	2,608	303	4,181
Crew	30	1,032	6	112	15	411
Squash	5	70	0	0	18	256
Total		**41,053**		**19,212**		**39,594**
Men's Sports						
Baseball	274	9,316	174	5,324	282	7,106
Basketball	298	4,410	220	3,300	313	5,321
Cross Country	290	4,263	174	1,984	259	3,419
Fencing	27	518	0	0	20	300
Football 1-A	106	12,529	129	10,849	229	17,885
1-AA	89	8,505				
Golf	269	3,282	138	1,366	212	2,290
Gymnastics	36	544	0	0	4	46
Ice hockey	51	1,591	12	361	58	1,711
Lacrosse	53	2,072	24	617	91	2,621
Rifle	31	310	6	33	13	86
Skiing	10	173	9	108	18	286
Soccer	191	4,985	116	2,738	284	7,072
Swimming	160	4,064	46	934	163	2,869
Tennis	271	2,981	152	1,474	282	3,074
Track, indoor	235	8,460	95	2,584	159	4,373
Track, outdoor	248	8,928	124	3,497	210	5,754
Volleyball	24	422	10	126	25	315
Water polo	30	690	6	105	11	183
Wrestling	108	3,251	44	1,135	113	2,192
Crew	30	1,311	7	153	14	514
Squash	5	90	0	0	17	238
Total		**82,695**		**36,688**		**67,655**

Source: National Collegiate Athletic Association

members of the Congressional Black Caucus and expressed dismay that only four of the top 46 NCAA executives were African-Americans.*

The group raised the ante at this January's NCAA convention. Frustrated by the delegates' rejection of a proposal to raise the number of Division I men's basketball scholarships from 13 to 14, the BCA threatened to stage a boycott of selected college basketball games. It claimed that black athletes, who constitute between 60 and 70 percent of Division I basketball squads, would be the main victims of the scholarship cutback.

As television networks scrambled to fill possible blank spots in their sports schedules, the BCA and the Congressional Black Caucus announced Jan. 15 that the threatened basketball boycott was being suspended. Around the same time, the Justice Department offered to mediate the black coaches' differences with the NCAA.

Nine weeks later, on March 23, the BCA and NCAA reached an agreement in principle on several issues. After talks assisted by federal mediators, the NCAA said it would set up a special committee to study proposals for athletic scholarships for incoming freshmen who do not meet academic requirements. It also acknowledged that racial equality is a goal of the same importance as other college sports-reform objectives, including cost containment and academic integrity.

After meeting May 31-June 1 in San Francisco, the special committee recommended a sliding scale of initial-eligibility standards. Under the committee's proposal, there would have been no minimum cutoff point for scores on standardized tests like the SAT. However, the NCAA Presidents Commission rejected the special committee's formula at its summer meeting (*see p. 749*).

At the same time, the commission said it would sponsor a compromise approach that would allow prospective student athletes to receive sports-related financial aid if they achieved a score of at least 600 on the SAT or 15 on the ACT. Such "partial qualifiers" could practice with their team but not compete as freshmen. On the other hand, they would have the opportunity to earn a fourth year of athletic eligibility if their academic progress was satisfactory.

The commission's proposal is one of two proposed changes to Division I eligibility standards that will be voted on at the 1995 NCAA convention. If either one is adopted, it will supersede the standards scheduled to take effect next year. (*See chart, p. 749.*)

Change in Leadership

Black coaches are not the only NCAA subgroup that feels its interests often are disregarded by other mem-

* The NCAA on July 22 announced the hiring of the first black to its top management staff. Daniel Boggan Jr., a University of California vice chancellor, will become the NCAA's group executive director for education services on Oct. 17.

Gender Equity: Seeking a Level Playing Field

When Congress passed Title IX of the Education Amendments of 1972, a new phrase entered the American sports lexicon. The law barred sex discrimination by all recipients of federal funds, including institutions of higher learning. As a result, college athletic directors shortly embarked on a quest for "gender equity." [1]

The chase is still on, with no end in sight. On many campuses, the Knight Foundation Commission on Intercollegiate Athletics noted last year, "fans would be outraged if revenue-generating teams were expected to make do with the resources available to women." [2] In this connection, a March 1992 study by the National Collegiate Athletic Association (NCAA) reported that women receive less than 33 percent of athletic scholarship money paid by universities, less than 23 percent of sports operating budgets and less than 18 percent of recruiting money. [3]

Funding disparities of this size expose colleges to the risk of potentially costly litigation. Ruling in the case of *Franklin v. Gwinnett County* in February 1992, the Supreme Court held that sex discrimination victims could sue colleges for monetary damages.

Lisa Helfert

Cecily Scarpelli of the University of Maryland's women's soccer team takes the ball downfield.

The ultimate goal of Title IX remains sports participation rates that precisely match the ratio of male and female students at a college. In practice, though, colleges are not being found in violation of the law if they can show they are making significant progress toward sexual equality or that they are satisfying fully the sports needs of their women students.

The NCAA, meanwhile, is hesitant to adopt a comprehensive set of gender equity rules binding on all its members. "It's a fact of life, given all the differences among NCAA institutions, that ultimately it will have to be up to each institution to address these issues," association President Joseph Crowley said last August after a meeting of the NCAA Council.

Delegates to the January 1994 NCAA convention voted on four gender equity guidelines. Only one of the four actually was adopted, and it provided little in the way of guidance. It merely established the principle of gender equity in intercollegiate sports to ensure that no one is discriminated against on the basis of sex.

[1] For background, see "Women and Sports," *The CQ Researcher*, March 6, 1992, pp. 193-216.

[2] Knight Foundation Commission on Intercollegiate Athletics, *A New Beginning for a New Century: Intercollegiate Athletics in the United States*, March 1993, p. 7.

[3] *NCAA Gender-Equity Study*, March 1992.

bers. Division I-A football coaches worry that the quality of their game will suffer if the number of scholarships they can award falls below the current ceiling of 85. They contend a football squad needs at least two players at every position on both offense and defense, plus kickers and special-teams players. Moreover, say the coaches, as many as 30 scholarships are held each year by athletes who are sidelined because of injury or red-shirting.

In January, the commissioners of eight of the 10 conferences that play Division I-A football* submitted a proposal for restructuring the NCAA to the organization's newly installed executive director, Cedric W. Dempsey. The overall thrust of the plan is to do away with the present one-college-one-vote system of governance. Instead, institutions with the largest sports programs would gain a proportionately larger rulemaking voice. The proposal has been forwarded to the NCAA Joint Policy Board for further consideration.

Meanwhile, many members of the NCAA's Division II and Division III are feeling restive, too. A major source of concern is the inequality among sports programs of colleges within each division. Some institutions field teams in the NCAA minimum of eight intercollegiate sports, while others compete in two dozen or more. Consequently, Division II and Division III reform proposals focus mainly on creating subdivisions of colleges grouped by enrollment size and sports competitiveness.

*Atlantic Coast, Big East, Big Eight, Big Ten, Pacific 10, Southeastern, Southwest and Western Athletic conferences. The commissioners of the Big West and Mid-American conferences did not participate.

Richard D. Schultz resigned as NCAA executive director in May 1993 after an NCAA-commissioned report concluded that he had known about rules violations at the University of Virginia while serving as that school's athletic director.

Agitation for NCAA structural change comes at a time when the organization is still adjusting to a change in leadership. Schultz resigned as executive director in May 1993 after an NCAA-commissioned report concluded that he had known about rules violations at the University of Virginia while serving as that school's athletic director.

During Schultz's tenure, the report stated, the Virginia Student Aid Foundation (VSAF) "made numerous loans to student athletes which constitute 'extra benefits' in violation of NCAA legislation." The document further charged that Schultz "had actual knowledge of at least some of the VSAF loans." [25]

The findings were especially embarrassing to Schultz because of his close identification with the college sports reform movement. In submitting his resignation, he maintained his innocence and said he was stepping down because doubts about his integrity would tarnish the NCAA's image and impede its efforts to clean up college sports.

As the NCAA began its search for a successor to Schultz, the sports and academic communities wondered if the association would break with precedent by picking a college president. The group instead picked Dempsey, athletics director at the University of Arizona. [26]

Some educators voiced disappointment with the choice. "Picking a president would have sent a very strong message that the NCAA is a presidential organization and its direction is largely in the hands of the presidents," said Robert H. Atwell, president of the American Council on Education. "The choice would have been more than symbolic." [27]

Sperber feels much the same way. "Picking a good old boy from the athletic establishment was intended to pacify the people who really run the NCAA — the athletic directors and the coaches," he says. "The schools don't run the NCAA, and the Presidents Commission doesn't run it."

Addressing his first NCAA convention this January, Dempsey dropped only a few clues to his thinking on college sports reform. He told the delegates he didn't want "to leave the impression that this association is in need of major repairs." At the same time, he said the NCAA must be willing to tinker with reforms that don't work: "Reform does not mean rigidity, and refinement does not mean retreat." [28]

Football Playoff?

NCAA Division I schools have been anything but rigid about realigning sports conferences to maximize their television revenue. In February, the Southeastern Conference (SEC) announced it would leave the 63-team College Football Association after the 1995 season and sign a separate TV contract with CBS.

The SEC's move prompted other major college athletic leagues to take similar action. For example, the Big East signed a football pact with CBS, while the Big Eight and Atlantic Coast conferences each arranged deals with ABC and a cable network. [29] The Big Eight, moreover, will gain four new members next season by adding Baylor, Texas A&M, Texas Tech and the University of Texas. All four schools belong to the Southwest Conference, which is disbanding after the 1995 season.

Some analysts view the current jockeying for TV money as the first step toward "super-conferences" — a handful of powerful leagues comprising the 50 or so football powers that regularly appear in the weekly newspaper rankings of top college teams. These polls, in turn, help determine the mythical Division I-A champion after the postseason bowl games.

The emergence of super-conferences could speed NCAA adoption of a Division I-A championship playoff system. At the association's 1993 convention, Schultz said such a playoff might be effective in raising new revenue at a time when many intercollegiate sports programs are losing money. The additional funds, he suggested, could help support new and existing women's teams.

Dempsey, in contrast, says he is neutral on the idea. Although a Division I-A playoff could be the "last major [sports] event opportunity for the American public," he said, it might not yield enough revenue to offset the damage it

Continued on p. 762

NCAA Executive Director Cedric W. Dempsey was director of athletics at the University of Arizona. Some leaders of the reform movement were disappointed that the NCAA did not select a college president for the post.

At Issue:

Is the National Collegiate Athletic Association unfair in investigating alleged violations of its rules?

yes

ORGANIZATION FOR UNDERSTANDING & REFORM
Nonprofit group in Champaign, Ill., interested in reforming the enforcement and infractions activities of the NCAA.

FROM *JUSTICE DENIED: THE NCAA'S STRANGLEHOLD ON COLLEGE ATHLETICS*, 1991.

In the college sports section of any American newspaper on any given day, there will be a story about allegations made by the National Collegiate Athletic Association (NCAA). The accused college will almost always proclaim [its] innocence. Rival colleges will almost always declare them guilty. And somewhere in between lies the truth.

But truth has little bearing in an NCAA investigation. What it's really about is money — the millions of dollars generated by collegiate athletics.

And the very source of all that money, the student athletes, are used as pawns in a struggle in which they are powerless to defend themselves.

While no one believes that abuses do not occur, the NCAA rule book is open to interpretation — their own. They prefer to operate on the assumption that a college, and thus its athletes, are "guilty until proven innocent."...

Athletes are especially vulnerable. They, not the schools they play for, ultimately pay the price. Colleges have huge financial resources to weather the blows inflicted by the NCAA. They also profit enormously from the talents of their athletes. Players, however, have no such resources.

Only approximately 2 percent of all colleges athletes go on to play professional sports. When an unfair ruling by the NCAA deprives players of the opportunity to participate on the college level, it may also deprive them of their only opportunity to play the game they love on a competitive basis.

Abuses within the system stem from the competition for players — teenagers — who are the hard currency in a big money game. And student-athletes are denied the right to a fair and impartial hearing of the facts....

Schools that have undergone the harrowing experience of an NCAA investigation are caught in a Catch-22. They are denied due process, and their claims of innocence are derided as "whining" by rival schools who stand to benefit from sanctions imposed....

But is everyone guilty? And is the harsh "justice" imposed by the NCAA applied consistently, without regard to personal friendships or a team's standing in the polls? A great many schools say no. But as many of them have discovered, any criticism of the NCAA is an open invitation to an NCAA investigation.

no

NATIONAL COLLEGIATE ATHLETIC ASSOCIATION

FROM *NCAA ENFORCEMENT PROCEDURES*

The Supreme Court [in the 1988 case *NCAA v. Tarkanian*] said a person did not have as a remedy a lawsuit against the NCAA for any alleged violation of the 14th Amendment. That is because the Supreme Court found that the NCAA is a private entity. The court found that the NCAA is not a state actor; it is not an arm of the government....

The fact that the NCAA has been held not to be a state actor does not mean that the NCAA membership has failed to adopt fair procedures in dealing with alleged violations of its rules. This brings up another false assumption; i.e., that the only model of due process is the one found in courtroom procedures or other governmental adjudicatory institutions that have the power to utilize court subpoenas, rules of evidence and punishment of reluctant witnesses for contempt of court. To the public that is used to seeing courtroom dramas on television, any procedure that does not involve the ability of an attorney to "break down a witness' story" is perceived to be unfair....

[T]he NCAA's procedures are much more elaborate and afford more procedural protections than do most private organizations. The NCAA has not ignored due process....

Any institution, coach, or student athlete involved in an infractions matter is given an opportunity to appear before the NCAA Committee on Infractions.... [They] are entitled to have legal representation present during an infractions hearing. In addition, an attorney can represent them at any stage of the process. An attorney may interrogate any witnesses the NCAA has talked with long before the hearing, and the attorney is given prior access to any materials or evidence the NCAA staff will be submitting to the Committee on Infractions....

The members of the [committee] are prominent educators. A number of them are law professors.... This "jury of peers" comprises people who are independent-minded educators of the highest caliber. They would not be part of any "kangaroo court" or "star chamber." They do not rubber-stamp the decisions of the NCAA enforcement staff. They do not automatically find violations of every charge....

Individuals and institutions have the right to appeal findings or penalties to the NCAA Council. This second "jury of peers" is a totally separate entity from the Committee on Infractions. It comprises college administrators representing institutions and conferences from around the country.

Playing by the NCAA's Rules

Jerry Tarkanian's nickname is "Tark the Shark," but lately he's the one claiming he was bitten. The former University of Nevada-Las Vegas (UNLV) basketball coach says he was hounded from his job in 1992 by a National Collegiate Athletic Association (NCAA) vendetta dating from the 1970s. The NCAA, for its part, insists it was only investigating a sports program it suspected of multiple rules infractions (*see p. 747*).

Testifying before a House subcommittee in 1991, Tarkanian said that NCAA enforcement procedures "pay lip service to fairness but are designed for prosecutorial efficiency." And after charges become public, he added, "a violation has been found in every case because the NCAA acts as the police officer, prosecutor, judge and jury." [1]

Tarkanian's bitter comments came three years after the U.S. Supreme Court held that the NCAA had not violated his rights when it sought to discipline him for recruiting and other violations at UNLV. Ruling in the case of *NCAA v. Tarkanian,* the court said the association's treatment of the coach had been "constitutionally inadequate." Nonetheless, it said, the NCAA was a private organization, not an arm of the government, and thus was not bound by the Constitution's due-process requirements. (Due process generally means fair procedure, including notice to the defendant and an open trial with the right to counsel.)

Tarkanian is not alone in believing the NCAA is high-handed toward the colleges, players and coaches it investigates. "The current NCAA enforcement system is rife with abuse, committed not by colleges, but by the very group [that] claims to be the watchdogs," states a publication of a Champaign, Ill.-based group called Organization for Understanding & Reform. [2] (*See "At Issue," p. 761.*) The group supports efforts to encourage states to enact legislation to ensure that schools and athletes are given due process.

Legislation requiring the NCAA to extend due-process rights to institutions and individuals has been enacted by four states — Florida, Illinois, Nebraska and Nevada. The immediate effect of the laws, observed the Knight Foundation Commission on Intercollegiate Athletics, was "to virtually forbid the NCAA from enforcing any of its rules without court action." [3]

In November 1991, the NCAA filed suit in U.S. District Court in Reno, Nev., challenging the constitutionality of the Nevada due-process statute. [4] The association said the law was impeding its investigation of the UNLV basketball program, which was suspected of 29 rules infractions. The court struck down the law, declaring that it violated the Constitution's commerce clause. The 9th U.S. Circuit Court of Appeals affirmed the district court's decision last November, and in April 1994 the U.S. Supreme Court declined to review the case further.

At present, the NCAA has no plans to contest the three remaining state due-process laws. "When we reach a point where it appears we can go no further in enforcing our rules without violating state law, then we'll have to decide what to do," says S. David Berst, the NCAA's assistant executive director for enforcement. "In Nevada, we determined that filing suit was appropriate. But obviously there are other options, such as not applying our rules in a given state."

Gary R. Roberts, vice law dean at Tulane University, says he's troubled by "the almost plenary authority" of the NCAA enforcement division. It has "discretion that's extraordinarily broad, and that is disturbing to a lawyer."

On the other hand, says Roberts, one must appreciate "the climate and the culture" in which the association is trying to enforce its rules. "If you assume the rules are good rules, and should be enforced, then it seems to me the enforcement mechanism has to be somewhat like the one the NCAA already has."

NCAA officials make a valid point, Roberts continues, in claiming they lack many of the powers available to police and prosecutors. For instance, "They don't have any legal authority to subpoena witnesses. They can't issue orders or grant witnesses immunity." Consequently, due process "is not something the NCAA can afford. If it was required to give legal due process to everybody, it simply couldn't operate."

Nonetheless, Professor John Weistart of Duke University Law School feels there are procedural reforms the association could adopt to enhance its credibility. One such change would entrust decision-making on enforcement issues to persons not employed by the NCAA. These individuals, Weistart says, would be "high-profile people with a long history of public service and a well-earned reputation for neutrality — [former Supreme Court Justice Byron R.] "Whizzer" White, for example."

Weistart notes that questions have been raised about whether the NCAA shows favoritism to some schools. "That problem would be solved by having more neutral decision-makers," he says.

[1] Testimony before Subcommittee on Commerce, Consumer Protection and Competitiveness, House Committee on Energy and Commerce, June 19, 1991.

[2] Organization for Understanding & Reform, *Justice Denied: The NCAA's Stranglehold on College Athletics,* 1991.

[3] Knight Foundation Commission on Intercollegiate Athletics, *A Solid Start: A Report on Reform of Intercollegiate Athletics,* March 1992, p. 8.

[4] The suit named as defendants Gov. Robert F. Miller, Tarkanian, two UNLV assistant coaches and a former UNLV academic adviser.

Continued from p. 760

would inflict on existing bowl games. [30]

Nonetheless, the NCAA appointed a special committee in March to examine the pros and cons of a Division I-A playoff. After meeting twice, the panel concluded that the proposal had merit but that some issues required further study. It cited the impact of playoffs on athletes, the championship format and the distribution of revenues.

Then, at its June 28-29 meeting in Kansas City, Mo., the Presidents Commission announced it was disbanding the special committee. "If there were any significant level of interest among the NCAA membership in a [Division I-A] championship, it would make sense to continue working," said NCAA President Crowley. "However, the level of interest simply isn't there. . . . [A]ll indications are that it is an idea whose time has not yet come." [31]

However, a recently announced postseason bowl alliance could be the first step toward an NCAA-sanctioned football playoff. During a telephone conference call Aug. 4, the commissioners of four Division I-A conferences and Notre Dame Athletic Director Dick Rosenthal agreed on a format to determine an unofficial national football champion, starting after the 1995 season.

Under the plan, six teams will be eligible for the postseason "title" game — the champions of the Atlantic Coast, Big East, Southeastern and Big 12* conferences, plus two at-large teams. The No. 1- and No. 2-ranked teams will meet in one of three bowls — the Fiesta, Orange or Sugar — while the four others will play at one of the two remaining sites. The opportunity to host the championship game will rotate among the bowls.

The three-bowl coalition will not necessarily boast the country's top six Division I-A teams every year. That's because the Big Ten and Pacific-10 still are contractually obligated to send their conference champions to the Rose Bowl. Big 10 and Pac-10 teams often are ranked high in the weekly newspaper polls. Consequently, pressure for a more inclusive playoff system seems likely. "I'd bet my mortgage on it," says Sperber.

According to Sperber, the football championship question has to be viewed "in the context of the financial squeeze in higher education right now. We're really rattling the tin cup," he says. [32] There's "no educational reason for a college football playoff," he adds, noting that it would greatly extend the season and put more pressure on players. But in the eyes of many campus administrators, a playoff represents "a pot of gold that will solve lots of their sports-related financial problems." ■

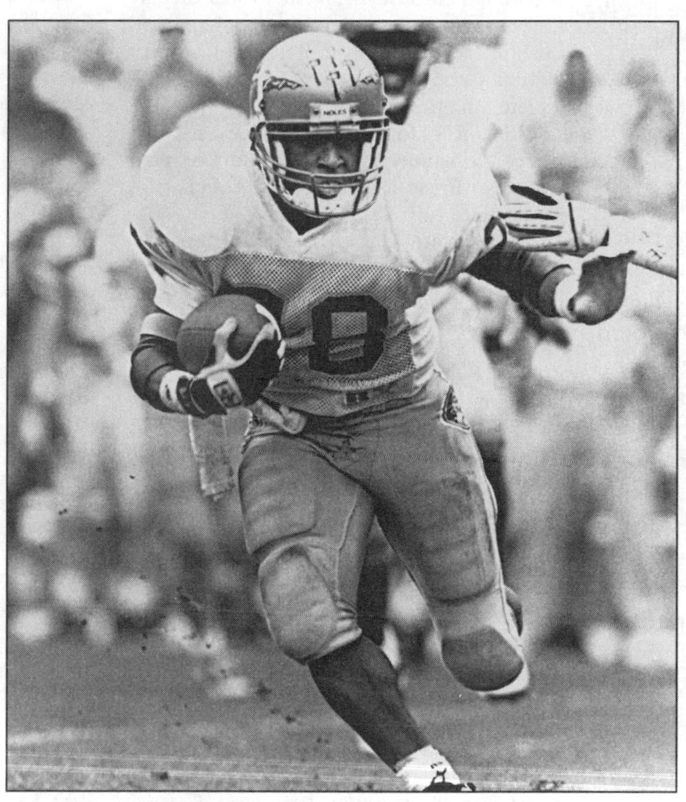

Florida State University tailback Warrick Dunn gains a few yards for the Seminoles.

* The Big 12 is the prospective name of the current Big Eight Conference, which will gain four members when the Southwest Conference disbands after the 1995 season.

OUTLOOK

Peer Review

Progress on NCAA reform issues may well depend on how the association's new certification program works (*see p. 757*). The first 62 Division I colleges are now taking part in the process, a yearlong self-examination designed to ensure that every institution's sports program is under control. The parent institution then prepares a report for a review team of officials from other colleges. That team, in turn, writes a separate report that is forwarded to the NCAA's Committee on Athletics Certification.

Proponents of peer review say it will keep the college sports reform movement alive by forcing Division I schools to engage in periodic soul-searching. It may take years, however, to pass judgment on the program. That's because the last group of Division I schools will not undergo review for the first time until the 1997-98 academic year, and a second complete cycle may be needed before pronouncing the program a success or failure.

In the meantime, skepticism about peer review abounds. The "clearly negative side," says Roberts at Tulane, is that "it's going to create an enormous amount of expense and paperwork, and take a lot of time that could be used to do more substantive things. It's adding an incredible amount of bureaucratic paperwork and rigamarole to a system where we're trying to cut costs."

On the other hand, he says, peer review could be healthy for some colleges. "If there are rogue institutions out there that are running amok without any real checks and balances, this sort of process will bring that to light and force them to clean up their act a little bit."

Sperber feels per review will work "only if the findings are made public." This may present no problem at publicly funded institutions, he says, but the booster clubs that help run sports programs at many major colleges are likely to resist outside scrutiny of their books. Such clubs are in good position to stonewall investigators, since many are organized as private foundations.

John Weistart, a law professor at Duke University and an authority on sports law, [33] says "the jury is still very much out" on peer review. In his opinion, it's a "classic problem of regulation. That is, are the reviewers going to get co-opted by the people they're reviewing?"

Other questions awaiting answers, says Weistart, are whether "colleges themselves really want to reform, and whether the American public wants college sports to reform." Over time, he has become "less and less convinced that there's a real undercurrent for change." That's because "people, by and large, like the entertainment value of the product as it is."

Weistart says he's "neither optimistic nor pessimistic" but rather "neutral and somewhat skeptical" about peer review. "It could end up turning into a really massive coverup," he believes. "If that happens, then it'll actually, in a very perverse way, set back considerably the process of college sports reform." ■

Notes

[1] Knight Foundation Commission on Intercollegiate Athletics, *A New Beginning for a New Century: Intercollegiate Athletics in the United States,* March 1993, p. 7.

[2] Knight Foundation Commission on Intercollegiate Athletics, *Keeping Faith With the Student Athlete: A New Model for Intercollegiate Athletics,* March 1991, p. 5.

[3] The law barred sex discrimination by all recipients of federal funds, including institutions of higher learning. For background, see "Women and Sports," *The CQ Researcher,* March 6, 1992, pp. 193-216.

[4] The NCAA, based in Overland Park, Kan., is a membership organization of colleges and universities that participate in intercollegiate athletics. It formulates rules of play for NCAA sports, conducts national championships, adopts and enforces standards of eligibility and studies all phases of intercollegiate athletics.

[5] Testimony before Subcommittee on Commerce, Consumer Protection and Competitiveness, House Committee on Energy and Commerce, July 25, 1991.

[6] Opening statement at hearing of the Subcommittee on Commerce, Consumer Protection and Competitiveness, House Committee on Energy and Commerce, July 28, 1994.

[7] Florida State cornerback Corey Sawyer, quoted by Sonja Steptoe and E.M. Swift, "Anatomy of a Scandal," *Sports Illustrated,* May 16, 1994, p. 21.

[8] For background, see "Racial Tensions in Schools," *The CQ Researcher,* Jan. 7, 1994, pp. 1-24.

[9] Quoted in *The New York Times,* Jan. 9, 1992.

[10] NCAA news release, June 9, 1994. The other co-chairman was University of New Mexico President Richard E. Peck.

[11] Quoted in *The Washington Post,* June 30, 1994.

[12] NCAA news release, Aug. 10, 1994.

[13] Quoted in *The Chronicle of Higher Education,* July 7, 1993, p. A42.

[14] John Feinstein, "Power Play Penalizes Both Sides," *The Washington Post,* Jan. 15, 1994, p. D7.

[15] Bob Oates, "The Big Steal," *Los Angeles Times,* Oct. 3, 1993.

[16] Testimony before Subcommittee on Commerce, Consumer Protection and Competitiveness, House Committee on Energy and Commerce, July 28, 1994.

[17] Interview in the *Christian Science Monitor,* Oct. 11, 1991, p. 14. Schultz resigned last year (*see p. 759*).

[18] Carnegie Foundation, *American College Athletics* (1929), p. 298.

[19] Quoted by Helen B. Shaffer, "Commercialism in College Athletics," *Editorial Research Reports,* Sept. 10, 1952, p. 613.

[20] National Association of College and University Business Officers, *The Financial Management of Intercollegiate Athletics Programs,* 1993, p. 16.

[21] *Keeping Faith With the Student Athlete, op. cit.,* p. 14.

[22] Murray Sperber, *College Sports: The Athletic Department vs. the University* (1990), p. 338. Sperber is an associate professor of English and American Studies. He also is the author of *Shake Down the Thunder: The Creation of Notre Dame Football* (1993).

[23] Later in 1990, Congress approved right-to-know legislation requiring colleges and universities to report yearly graduation figures.

[24] Quoted in *The Chronicle of Higher Education,* July 7, 1993, p. A44.

[25] Quoted in *The Chronicle of Higher Education,* May 19, 1993, p. A35. The report was prepared by James Park Jr., a lawyer hired by the NCAA to investigate the allegations against Schultz.

[26] The other finalists were William W. Cobey Jr., a former athletics director at the University of North Carolina-Chapel Hill, and Judith M. Sweet, director of athletics at the University California-San Diego. A fourth candidate, University of Mississippi Chancellor R. Gerald Turner, dropped out of the running shortly before the NCAA made its final choice.

[27] Quoted in *The Chronicle of Higher Education,* Nov. 10, 1993, p. A37.

[28] Quoted in *The Chronicle of Higher Education,* Jan. 19, 1994, p. A36.

[29] The Big Ten and Pacific-10 conferences, which do not belong to the CFA, have had separate long-term deals with ABC.

[30] Quoted in *The Chronicle of Higher Education,* Jan. 19, 1994, p. A36.

[31] NCAA news release, June 29, 1994.

[32] In *Campus Trends,* 1994, a study issued July 25, the American Council on Education reported that 71 percent of the public colleges and universities it surveyed said reduced state support had forced them to rely more heavily on tuition for revenue.

[33] Weistart is co-author (with Cym H. Lovell) of *The Law of Sports* (1979), a basic reference work on the subject.

Bibliography

Selected Sources Used

Books

Brooks, Dana D., and Ronald C. Althouse, eds., ***Racism in College Athletics: The African-American Athlete's Experience,*** **Fitness Information Technology Inc., 1993.**
Brooks, Althouse and the other contributors to this book examine the problems facing blacks in intercollegiate athletics, including racial differences in recruiting, retention and graduation rates and racial imbalance in coaching and managerial posts.

Chu, Donald, ***The Character of American Higher Education and Intercollegiate Sport,*** **State University of New York Press, 1989.**
Events since this book was published have overtaken Chu's rather gloomy assessment of the chances for meaningful college sports reform. He provides an excellent summary of the development of intercollegiate athletics.

Dealy, Francis X. Jr., ***Win at Any Cost: The Sellout of College Athletics,*** **Carol Publishing Group, 1990.**
Dealy is highly skeptical about college sports reform. "Big-time college football and basketball can never be abolished," he writes. "They mirror our national character traits, our aggressiveness, competitiveness and acquisitiveness too well. Only the University of Chicago could afford to drop football. Oklahoma or UNLV can't and shouldn't."

Lapchick, Richard E., and John Brooks Slaughter, eds., ***The Rules of the Game: Ethics in College Sport,*** **American Council on Education and Macmillan Publishing Co., 1989.**
The essays in this collection are grouped under three headings: historical background, ethical dilemmas of the 1980s and '90s, and "principals in the equation" — namely, coaches, athletic directors, college presidents, the NCAA and the mass media.

Sperber, Murray, ***College Sports Inc.: The Athletic Department vs. the University,*** **Henry Holt and Co., 1990.**
Sperber concludes his book by predicting that "massive change will come to college sports. The present situation is too unstable and the pressures upon it too great for college sports to continue in its current form to the end of this decade."

Sperber, Murray, ***Shake Down the Thunder: The Creation of Notre Dame Football,*** **Henry Holt and Co., 1993.**
Though he focuses on the rise of America's most famous college football power, Sperber chronicles the evolution of big-time intercollegiate sports in the process. He ends his story with the hiring of Frank Leahy as Notre Dame football coach in 1941.

Articles

Steptoe, Sonja, and E.M. Swift, "Anatomy of a Scandal," ***Sports Illustrated,*** **May 16, 1994.**
The authors describe a "midseason, two-handed, shelf-clearing, 90-minute shopping spree" by at least seven members of Florida State's 1993 national championship football team.

Wolff, Alexander, "Upstairs Downstairs," ***Sports Illustrated,*** **Oct. 14, 1991.**
Wolff shows why many college coaches like to house their players in athletic dorms, which the 1991 NCAA convention voted to phase out by 1996. "The athletic dorm is like a reactor core," writes Wolff. "Intensity, emotion and single-mindedness feed on themselves until they've grown into the hellish contagion that wins football games."

Reports and Studies

Knight Foundation Commission on Intercollegiate Athletics, ***Keeping Faith With the Student-Athlete: A New Model for Intercollegiate Athletics,*** **March 1991;** ***A Solid Start: A Report on Reform of Intercollegiate Athletics,*** **March 1992;** ***A New Beginning for a New Century: Intercollegiate Athletics in the United States,*** **March 1993.**
These three reports outline the college sports reform agenda that was adopted in large part by the NCAA Presidents Commission. The final report expresses satisfaction with progress to date and points to the major problems still awaiting solution.

National Association of College and University Business Officers, ***The Financial Management of Intercollegiate Athletics Programs,*** **1993**
NACUBO focuses on the tax problems that could plague colleges whose sports programs become too commercial. It also cites the danger of a "win at all costs" attitude: "Such a perspective is in and of itself antithetical to a fundamental premise of higher education institutions — that the processes of learning are as important as the end knowledge that is gained."

National Collegiate Athletic Association, ***1992-93 Annual Report,*** **January 1994.**
Highlights of this report are a statistical review of participation in NCAA-sanctioned sports, broken down by division, and 1993 financial reports for both the association and all championship competitions.

The Next Step

Additional information from UMI's Newspaper & Periodical Abstracts database

Academics in College Sports

Blum, Debra E., "The impact of tougher standards," *Chronicle of Higher Education,* June 1, 1994, p. A35.
Five studies funded by the NCAA are expected to give more ammunition to opponents of the association's plans to raise academic requirements for incoming freshmen.

Diegmueller, Karen, "New rules in play for college-sports eligibility," *Education Week,* April 13, 1994, p. 8.
A new academic-eligibility-assessment process has been implemented for high school seniors who want to play college sports as freshmen. The problems that the NCAA has had with the implementation of the clearinghouse are discussed.

Feezell, Travis, "Upgrading the at-risk student-athlete," *Scholastic Coach,* October 1993, pp. 4-6.
College athletes who are academically at risk need special attention. An overview of athletic department academic services is offered, including the why, who, how and what of the situation.

Lederman, Douglas, "Dubious path to the big time," *Chronicle of Higher Education,* June 29, 1994, pp. A31-A32.
The NCAA is concerned that many junior-college athletes may be taking courses of dubious academic merit in order to win the right to play at member colleges. The NCAA is looking into instances of possible fraud.

Budgeting College Sports

Blum, Debra E., "Top players produce up to $1-million in revenue for their universities," *Chronicle of Higher Education,* April 13, 1994, pp. A33-A34.
Robert W. Brown, an economist at the University of North Texas, has done studies to measure the revenue-generating abilities of top college players and their so-called income or athletics scholarships. According to the results of Brown's research, a top college player could produce as much as $1-million in annual revenue for his university.

Grimes, Paul W., and George A. Chressanthis, "Alumni contributions to academics: The role of intercollegiate sports and NCAA sanctions," *American Journal of Economics & Sociology,* January 1994, pp. 27-40.
An empirical analysis of the effect of intercollegiate athletics on alumni contributions to the academic endowment of an institution is presented. It is suggested that sanctions imposed by the NCAA for rules violation may slightly reduce contributions to academics.

McCallum, Jack, and Richard O'Brien, "Student save," *Sports Illustrated,* June 27, 1994, p. 14.
Students at the University of California-Davis voted to raise student fees to offset projected budget cuts for intercollegiate athletic teams. The measure was approved by a 52 percent majority and will protect nonrevenue sports from being eliminated.

Gender Equity Issues

Blum, Debra E., "Pay equity for coaches," *Chronicle of Higher Education,* April 6, 1994, pp. A53-A54.
A slowly growing number of coaches of women's college sports, expecially basketball, are receiving substantial salary increases in line with their counterparts in men's athletics. The salaries of several of the top women's coaches are discussed, including gymnastics coach Suzanne Yoculan and women's basketball coach Andy Landers, both of Georgia State University.

Lorenz, Matt, "A reality-based plan for achieving gender equity in college sports," *Chronicle of Higher Education,* March 2, 1994, pp. B1-B2.
Requiring colleges to have sports-participation ratios that match the proportion of men and women enrolled isn't the best way to achieve equality. A reality-based definition of equity and a compromise based on a national participation index are needed.

Schrof, Joannie M., "A sporting chance?" *U.S. News & World Report,* April 11, 1994, pp. 51-53.
The glitz and hype that surrounded the TV coverage of the women's Final Four NCAA basketball championship betray the truth of the sad state of women's college athletics. The lack of equity between men and women is examined.

"Sports lib," *The Economist,* April 9, 1994, p. 98.
Demands for gender equity in sports are increasing at college campuses. College sports equity in the U.S. is coming closer to fulfillment thanks to a dogged legal campaign by sportswomen angered by fewer choices and smaller budgets.

Ineligibility

Blum, Debra E., "Smarting from sports scandals, Ala. lawmakers weigh punishing athletes who take money," *Chronicle of Higher Education,* March 23, 1994, p. A48.
Alabama's Legislature is considering bills that would punish college athletes who accept money or extra benefits from college boosters. The proposed law includes a penalty of up to one year in jail.

Hodges, Jim, "Players caught in net profits," *Los Angeles Times,* April 9, 1994, p. C11.
The USC Trojans tennis team defaulted on April 8, 1994, to UCLA when four of their players were declared ineligible for accepting expense money beyond that allowed by the NCAA while competing in summer professional tournaments.

Opinions

Benjaminson, Wendy, "Few cheer for college sports," *Houston Chronicle,* April 9, 1994, p. A29.
Former U.S. Rep. Barbara Jordan, D-Texas, one of two dozen panelists at a University of Texas symposium on the value of college athletics, asserted that athletics served as the best teacher of self-esteem, ethics and "as an antidote to the balkanization of our society."

Blum, Debra E., "The undaunted kook," *Chronicle of Higher Education,* April 13, 1994, pp. A33-A34.
For years, Dick Devenzio has campaigned against the NCAA and its rules that govern college sports. At the top of his hit list are the association's regulations that prohibit athletes from receiving compensation for their participation in athletics beyond college tuition, room and board. Devenzio's ideas may be gaining acceptance.

Campbell, Bill, "Humility deserves more respect," *Times-Picayune,* May 15, 1994, p. C15.
Bill Campbell discusses the perceived lack of respect in college sports, citing the comments by Florida State football player Corey Sawyer, who considers the free university education he receives on scholarship as "nothing in return" for his services on the field.

Falls, Joe, "Duderstadt: If only the media would mind its own business," *Detroit News,* April 1, 1994, p. C3.
Joe Falls comments on a variety of sports topics, including University of Michigan President James J. Duderstadt's claim that the trouble with college athletics is the news media.

Kee, Lorraine, "Women's game shows signs of looming lunacy," *St. Louis Post-Dispatch,* April 1, 1994, p. D3.
Lorraine Kee comments on the status of women's college basketball and the lack of emphasis given to it.

Rhoden, William C., "Hen house guarded by foxes," *The New York Times,* April 16, 1994, p. A29.
William C. Rhoden says that Nigerian native Yinka Dare, who left George Washington University after only two years to pursue a career in the NBA, is yet another example of how college is becoming just a whistle-stop on the way to the pros.

Player Compensation

Blaudschun, Mark, "Player payment is debated by NCAA committees," *Boston Globe,* May 4, 1994, p. 45.
Although the idea of paying collegiate athletes is not yet an issue the NCAA is ready to address, it is an ongoing subject of debate among administrators and student athletes.

Dickey, Glenn, "Money for college players," *San Francisco Chronicle,* April 8, 1994, p. E7.
Glenn Dickey comments on sports news, including the debate over whether college athletes should be paid.

Dooley, Vince, "No: Schools offer a better benefit," *USA Today,* June 8, 1994, p. C2.
University of Georgia Athletic Director Vince Dooley says the concept of paying student-athletes cold, hard cash is, in fact, cold-blooded and hard-hearted, and he lists the benefits student-athletes are currently eligible to receive, including a free college education and Pell grants.

Gordon, Jeff, "Players deserve cut of the take in college sports," *St. Louis Post-Dispatch,* May 19, 1994, p. D1.
Jeff Gordon contends that college athletes should be paid, asserting that too much is given to the successful coaches and not enough to the kids themselves.

Roberts, Gary, "Yes: Trends make change inevitable," *USA Today,* June 8, 1994, p. C3.
Gary Roberts of Tulane Law School discusses the debate about paying college athletes, saying when courts and legislatures no longer see big-time college sports as mere extracurricular activities or their athletes as amateur students, revenue-sport players will be paid.

Reform

Blum, Debra E., "Accreditation for sports," *Chronicle of Higher Education,* March 23, 1994, pp. A47-A48.
The NCAA's new peer-review program is discussed. The program is designed to insure that college sports programs are kept in proper perspective and under control.

Blum, Debra E., "A watchdog growls," *Chronicle of Higher Education,* June 15, 1994, p. A33.
Some of those who served on the Knight Foundation Commission on Intercollegiate Athletics, a panel that pushed college sports on the road to reform, think that college sports may need their help again. Concerns over the NCAA's efforts to fine-tune eligibility standards and other rule changes are discussed.

Mangieri, John N., "The challenges of further reforming intercollegiate athletics," *Educational Record,* Spring 1994, pp. 63-64.
The problems of reforming college athletics are discussed. The plethora of events surrounding college athletics, including firings, player transfers and disciplinary actions, has added to the challenges.

Back Issues

Great Research on Current Issues Starts Right Here . . . Recent topics covered by The CQ Researcher are listed below. Before May 1991, reports were published under the name of Editorial Research Reports.

FEBRUARY 1993
Community Policing
Europe's New Right
School Censorship
Violence Against Women

MARCH 1993
Gay Rights
Aid to Russia
War on Drugs
TV Violence

APRIL 1993
Head Start
High-Speed Rail
Children's Legal Rights
Muslims in America

MAY 1993
Cults in America
Preventing Teen Pregnancy
Software Piracy
National Parks

JUNE 1993
Food Safety
Prostitution
Childhood Immunizations
National Service

Back issues are available for $4.00 (subscribers) or $7.00 (non-subscribers). Quantity discounts apply to orders over ten. To order, call Congressional Quarterly Customer Service at (202) 887-8621.

Binders are available for $16.00. To order call 1-800-638-1710. Please refer to stock number 648.

JULY 1993
Electric Cars
Population Growth
Downward Mobility
Intelligence Testing

AUGUST 1993
Mental Illness
Bilingual Education
Foreign Policy Burden
School Funding

SEPTEMBER 1993
Suburban Crime
Public Housing
Supreme Court Preview
Immigration Reform

OCTOBER 1993
Airline Safety
Disaster Response
Science in the Courtroom
The Glass Ceiling

NOVEMBER 1993
Paying for Retirement
Charitable Giving
Privacy in the Workplace
Adoption

DECEMBER 1993
U.S. Vietnam-Relations
Learning Disabilities
Child Care
Space Program's Future

JANUARY 1994
Racial Tensions in Schools
South Africa's Future
Worker Retraining
Regulating Pesticides

FEBRUARY 1994
Prison Overcrowding
Water Quality
Religion in Schools
Juvenile Justice

MARCH 1994
Underground Economy
Education Standards
Gambling Boom
Private Management of Public Schools

APRIL 1994
Reproductive Ethics
U.S.-China Trade
Soccer in America
Talk Show Democracy

MAY 1994
Traffic Congestion
Women's Health Issues
Mutual Funds
Political Scandals

JUNE 1994
Education and Gender
Gun Control
Public Land Policy
Nuclear Arms Cleanup

JULY 1994
Dietary Supplements
Public Opinion and Foreign Policy
Crime Victims' Rights
Birth Control Choices

AUGUST 1994
Genetically Engineered Foods
Electing Minorities
Prozac Controversy

Future Topics

- ***Home Schooling***
- ***Welfare Reform in the States***
- ***Courts and the Media***

THE CQ Researcher

PUBLISHED BY CONGRESSIONAL QUARTERLY INC.

Home Schooling

Is it a healthy alternative to public education?

Increasing numbers of American parents are keeping their children home for a custom-tailored education they feel only loved ones can provide. Home schooling has long been associated with hippie communes and fundamentalist Christians. But in recent years the practice also has attracted thousands of secular, career-minded families fleeing the public schools' violence, social stresses and low academic performance. Home-schoolers' numerous victories in loosening state compulsory-education laws have given them sizable political clout. Critics warn, however, that home schooling risks isolating children from other kids and society at large. Pointing to solid academic achievements by home-schoolers, practitioners reply that public schools have much to learn from home-schooling techniques.

INSIDE THIS ISSUE

CQ Sept. 9, 1994 • Volume 4, No. 33 • Pages 769-792

Formerly Editorial Research Reports

Home Schooling

September 9, 1994
Volume 4, No. 33

Editor
Sandra Stencel

Managing Editor
Thomas J. Colin

Associate Editor
Richard L. Worsnop

Staff Writers
Charles S. Clark
Mary H. Cooper
Kenneth Jost

Production Editor
Sarah E. Merritt

Editorial Assistant
Tonya Whitfield

Graphics
P. Eloise Fuller

Published By
Congressional Quarterly Inc.

The CQ Researcher (ISSN 1056-2036). Formerly Editorial Research Reports. Published weekly (48 times per year, not printed the first Friday of any month with five Fridays) by Congressional Quarterly Inc., 1414 22nd St., N.W., Washington, D.C. 20037. Rates are furnished upon request. Second-class postage paid at Washington, D.C. POSTMASTER: Send address changes to The CQ Researcher, 1414 22nd St., N.W., Washington, D.C. 20037.

Cover: Home-schoolers Yvonne and George Bunn of Murfreesboro, N.C., and their three children. (Home School Legal Defense Association); Page 771: Home-school graduate Tabitha Abbott of Gaithersburg, Md.

Home Schooling

BY CHARLES S. CLARK

THE ISSUES

Tabitha Abbott entered the University of Maryland last year having missed some of the defining experiences of adolescence. Unlike many of her new classmates, she had no memories of cheering for a high school football team, of lockers slamming in crowded hallways, or of crib sheets being furtively passed during tests.

"What I had," she says, "was an opportunity to home school, which gave me the personal attention and chance to move at my own pace that are not easy to get in public schools. I was never pushed faster or slower than I wanted, and I felt that what I learned was important to the instructor. I was given strong self-esteem and never made to feel dumb."

Ironically, Abbott plans to make a career in the very public schools that she and her parents decided to avoid. "The public schools are not past help," says Abbott, who lives in Gaithersburg, Md. "There's just lots of red tape that prevents teachers from doing what they want to do. I see an opportunity to give them a little taste of what I've had."

Like most home-schooled students today, Abbott used a religiously oriented curriculum. But her commitment to working in the public schools is a sign of how home-schoolers are rapidly moving into the mainstream of education reform.

"The vast majority of them are basic, biblical Christians," says Brian D. Ray, president of the National Home Education Research Institute at Western Baptist College in Salem, Ore. "But even though religion is at the top of their list, they quickly add in other reasons such as good academics, selective socialization and strong family interaction for relationships."

Susannah Sheffer, editor of *Growing Without Schooling*, a home-schooling magazine in Cambridge, Mass., says it is wrong to "stereotype home-schoolers as hippies or fundamentalists when people may have 10 reasons why they do it." She says there are newsletters for Jewish and Muslim home-schoolers and that home schooling can be found among single parents, African-Americans and in urban, rural and suburban areas.

"There's also a growing understanding and acceptance of home schooling," Sheffer says, "because it has become common to know someone who's doing it, not just some wacky people, but your neighbors."

What drives many home-schoolers are the well-documented social troubles and declining test scores in public schools. "The basic cause of all the problems is that we're pulling kids out of the home too early so that they're getting their values from other kids, especially boys in special education," says Raymond Moore, a founder of the modern home-schooling movement who heads an educational foundation in Washington state.

"It's called social contagion," Moore explains, "with the kids showing up at school tired and bringing pornography. Our problem is we've turned away from the warm response of mother every day to the relatively rare response of a certified teacher bound by the rules of schools."

Home schooling has long been popular among such itinerants as Foreign Service families, missionaries and touring musicians. But the desire for more family life and the advent of home computers has made it attractive to "what a few years ago were called yuppies, and people from urban schools who are concerned about crime, busing and violence," says Lawrence T. Williams, educational director of the Oak Meadow School, a home-schooling curriculum provider in Blacksburg, Va.

Estimates of the number of children being home-schooled vary. In 1991, the U.S. Department of Education put the total at between 248,500 and 353,500. [1] The Purcellville, Va.-based Home School Legal Defense Association says there are nearly a million. No one knows for sure because many home-schoolers may not notify education officials or respond to census questions.

What is clear is that the movement has exploded since the mid-1970s. (*See graph, p. 772.*) The legal defense association, with some 40,000 members, says it's growing 25 percent a year, and there is now an informal network of 3,000-4,000 local home-schooling support groups. Thirty-four states have enacted specific home-schooling statutes or regulations, says the association. The practice that was long illegal in much of the country is now permitted in all 50 states, though laws differ considerably on how closely it is regulated. (*See story and table, pp. 776, 777.*)

Politically, home schooling has achieved surprising visibility, as demonstrated in February when telephone lines on Capitol Hill were jammed by hundreds of thousands of calls and faxes from home-schoolers concerned that their families would be hurt by new teacher-certification requirements (*see p. 783*).

U.S. Home Schooling on the Rise

Estimates of the number of children being home-schooled have risen from 12,500 in 1978 to 500,000 this year, or about 1 percent of school-age children.

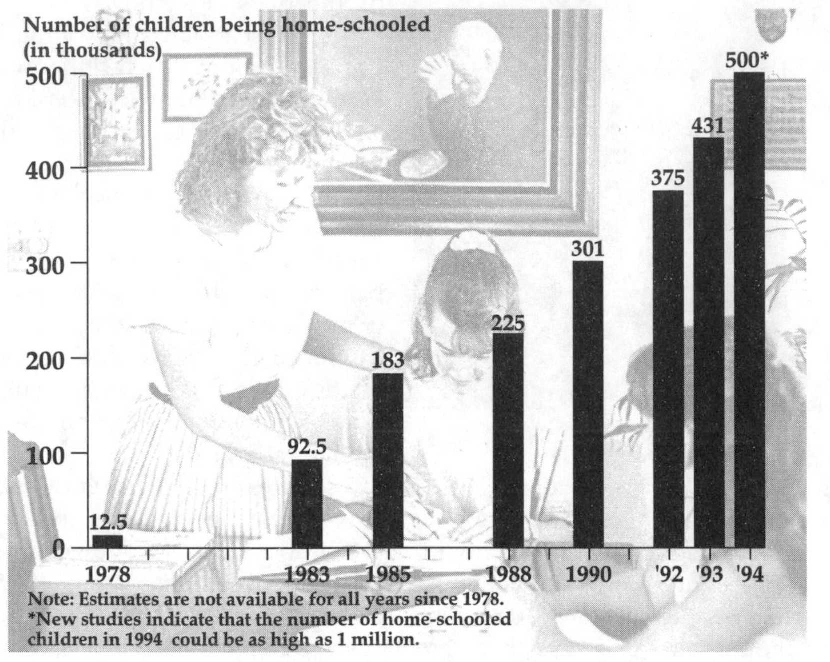

Source: Brian D. Ray, National Home Education Research Institute, 1994; Patricia M. Lines, "Estimating the Home-Schooled Population," U.S. Department of Education, October 1991; John Holt. Photograph courtesy of The Teaching Home.

"Home-schoolers are like gun owners and owners of radar detectors," says Elliot M. Mincberg, legal director of the liberal advocacy group People for the American Way. "They are passionate, and when called upon can be mobilized effectively."

Congress itself contains one product of home schooling and one current practitioner. Freshman Rep. Vernon J. Ehlers, R-Mich., is a nuclear physicist whose asthma kept him home from school as a child. Rep. Donald Manzullo, R-Ill., has three children who are taught by his wife, a microbiologist, to help the family cope with the hectic life of a politician.

When it comes to academic achievement, the data are consistently impressive. In one study in Washington state from 1986-90, 3,634 home-schooled students averaged in the top third of all students tested nationwide, and slightly better than students in public schools in the state. [2] And more than 200 colleges have accepted home-schooled children, according to the legal defense association, including up to 10 a year at Harvard.

Still, many professional educators share the concern of Thomas Shannon, executive director of the National School Boards Association, who has called home schooling "a giant step backward into the 17th century." [3]

Says Montana educator Robert Anderson: "I've gotten numerous calls from relatives, from grandparents who are upset that kids are being jerked out the public schools and are home watching TV," says Anderson, executive director of the Montana School Boards Association. "One home-schooling student was found to be working in his dad's construction business, and another drowned in a pond while driving the tractor on his family's farm."

Joe Nathan, director of the Center for School Change at the University of Minnesota, says he has met many people for whom "home schooling has been wonderful. But I've also talked to far-right ideologues in Idaho who want it to promote worldviews that are essentially Nazi. I've talked to home-schoolers in Minnesota who are racist, anti-Catholic and anti-Jewish, as well as members of a far-left lesbian commune near Grand Falls, Ore., who want their own schools" to promote anti-male views.

Bonnie Price Lofton, a journalist in Vienna, Va., who is currently a full-time mother, considered home schooling but rejected it "because I need time away from my children. Also, I didn't want to play the heavy in disciplining them to do algebra when I'm already doing that to get them to come home on time and clean up their rooms. Kids need to be exposed to other adults' styles," she adds.

Among the general public, only 28 percent favor home schooling over traditional schools, according to a June NBC News-*Wall Street Journal* poll. A September 1993 poll asked whether home-schooled children learn as well as children educated at public schools and found 44 percent agreed and 44 percent disagreed, according to the conservative Family Research Council.

"There is a learning curve for home-schooling families," says David Wagner, the council's director of legal policy. "They often start out disgusted with the public schools, and if there's no private school nearby or private [school] is too expensive, they choose home schooling in desperation, saying, 'Surely we'll send them back to public school next year.' But they soon discover the advantages, like you can get done in two hours what public schools take six to accomplish."

Early grades are the most popular

grade levels among home-schoolers. After fifth grade, according to a 1990 study by Ray, the number of home-schooled children tapers off as kids reach adolescence and gravitate back to the social amenities of middle and high school.

But many families move back and forth between home schooling and public schools, notes Patricia M. Lines, an Education Department analyst. "A fair number don't have a particular bone to pick with the public schools," she says.

The continued growth of the movement in the U.S. will depend on the following issues:

Can parents teach as well as professional teachers?

"Home-schooling parents can be of average intelligence, or even below it, but they have to be above average in willingness to work hard," says Michael P. Farris, a Baptist minister and attorney who is president of the Home School Legal Defense Association and who, with his wife, is home schooling their nine children.*

Parents "love their children to a depth I can't match," writes David Guterson, a public school teacher in Bainbridge Island, Wash., "and teaching is an act of love before it is anything else." Guterson's own children are educated at home. [4]

The home-schooler's belief in the superiority of parental teaching is often coupled with criticisms of professional teachers for spending more time managing than teaching. "Most educators don't like to answer questions," writes home-schooler Cheryl Gorder; "it messes up their schedule." [5]

Mothers provide about 88 percent of the home-schooling instruction. Only 1-2 percent of home-schooling parents are certified to be teachers, according to Farris' group. The lack of certification is one of the things that troubles many educators.

"Home schooling can benefit a small percentage of a nation of 45 million students," says Michael A. Resnick, senior associate executive director of the school boards association. "But most parents are not educationally able to provide a curriculum and don't have the instructional capability. Those who are doing it seem to be doing well, but there's no way of comparing it with how those kids would have done in public schools."

When uncertified parents teach, "Where's the accountability?" asks Janet Bass, a spokeswoman for the American Federation of Teachers. "And what about socialization? Kids do learn from other kids, especially since teachers nowadays are getting away from chalk and talk drills and moving to more cooperative class discussions."

William Martin, director of communications for the National Education Association (NEA), the nation's largest teachers' union, says children get a lot in a class setting that they can't get at home, such as help from other children, help from teachers trained in dealing with different learning styles and a chance to mix with kids of diverse backgrounds. "If, say, a fifth-grader goes through a book at an accelerated pace," he says, "it's good for him to see other kids who struggle with the same material, so when he goes into the work world he will know that not everyone learns at the same pace."

Teachers also are more aware of students with special needs, Martin says, and try hard to be flexible in managing the class so that individual needs come first. "From the beginning of teacher education," he says, "you learn that some kids learn better in a well-lit room, others next to the window, some with sound, others with quiet. Teachers go through hours of training on differences in attention spans."

Teachers, Martin adds, also are more likely to spot students' disabilities. "Parents will know their children quite well, but a vision problem is an example of something that might be pointed out by a teacher who notices a child squinting. Often it takes a teacher to spot it because the well-intentioned parent is so close he can't compare his child's progress with that of others."

But home-schooling advocates have long been skeptical of teacher-bestowed labels, such as "learning disabled" and "gifted and talented." Oregon home-schooling activist Grace Llewellyn recalled with irony the girl whose parents had once been denied permission to home school her because the public schools had identified her as learning-disabled. Her parents fought and won permission to proceed. Three years later, after she took the state's mandatory assessment test, the girl was told she couldn't be home-schooled anymore because she was gifted and wouldn't get the special attention she needed at home. [6]

Editor Sheffer says the resistance to home schooling comes from teachers "who after undergoing years of training do not welcome the thought of being confronted by someone" who says it can be done by parents. "But teaching in a classroom is different," she says. "It's all management. Teachers who are tired of disruptive students are very tempted when they hear from home-schoolers about kids who want to learn. That's part of their confusion about home schooling: They assume that kids will go to school only if they're made to."

Others say that teachers who criticize uncertified parents merely want to protect their jobs. "Because of recent demands for educational reform, teachers are left desperately trying to hang on to one credential that gives them standing," says Larry Kaseman, director of the Wisconsin Parents Association, a home-schoolers' group.

Kaseman says he doesn't blame teachers because they're simply reacting to the realities of the public education system. "The main attraction of home schooling," he says, "is that it is a more normal process for learning

---

* Farris was an unsuccessful Republican candidate for lieutenant governor in Virginia last year.

Couple's Decision to Home School Reflected Concern . . .

Sheldon Richman is senior editor at a libertarian think tank. His wife, Kathleen, runs a desktop publishing business from their comfortable townhouse. When the couple became disgruntled with their neighborhood public school in suburban Woodbridge, Va., home schooling their daughter Jennifer seemed a natural fit.

"The funniest thing about first grade," young Jennifer had told them, "is that it's easier than kindergarten." That was the first of several indicators that she was being held back by less capable classmates. The Richmans also had objected to the school's "political indoctrination," which they felt was turning pupils into "pliant, uncomplaining taxpayers" rather than independent thinkers.

"Of course, it wouldn't be fair to expect a teacher to spend a good portion of her time on work appropriate for Jennifer when the rest of the class is on a different level," they wrote in a local alternative newspaper about their decision to home school. "But we're not interested in fairness; we're interested in Jennifer." [1]

That was in 1991. Three years later, the Richmans are immersed in home schooling Jennifer, now 10, as well as 8-year-old Emily and 6-year-old Ben.

"There is no regular schedule and no real typical day," says Kathleen, who handles most of the weekday schooling. "But there is at least one formal hour after they wake up during which they must pick an activity: write a story, read a book, practice piano, or play a game that's on my list." Outside of that, the kids are free to go out and play, work on their grammar or read. There are field trips to museums or historical sites and extracurricular activities such as horseback riding and soccer. And there is vacation travel, which need not be scheduled around the conventional school year.

Thomas J. Colin

Sheldon and Kathleen Richman, with Emily, Ben and Jennifer.

The children "do some things most people wouldn't consider purely educational, such as cleaning house, which I consider a learning experience," she adds. What's more, the children earn money participating in Mom's business, helping to prepare text and artwork for laying out her clients' newsletters and brochures, each child managing his or her own computer file.

"The day doesn't end at any certain time, and the kids can stay up in their rooms and work all night," Kathleen says, noting that the process goes on year-round. "The informal style means there's no way to stop. You can't say, 'Don't learn anymore.' "

Under Virginia law, the Richmans are qualified to home school without teaching credentials because they have bachelor's degrees. If they didn't, they could still qualify but would have to submit a curriculum for state approval, or seek an exemption on religious grounds. (*See table, p. 776.*) The Richmans simply

from the real world from people who care deeply about you."

Moore says, "There is not a single reputable study in education research that supports a need for teacher certification." He recalls the New Jersey high school that tried to hire a New York Yankees coach for the school baseball team but was prevented from doing so by the teachers' union.

Lynn Maher, a spokeswoman for the New Jersey Education Association, says certification is essential. "You coach the Yankees to win," she says. "But the real goal in school is the education of children."

Teacher certification is based "on the premise that teachers are people who care whether children get a good education and that the person delivering the instruction [should be] well-qualified," says Gary Marx, senior associate executive director at the American Association of School Administrators. "It comes from something deep inside. It's a matter of conscience, not just politics."

To put home schooling in a better light, Ray recommends that proponents try to highlight the advantages to public educators by asking, "'How would you like to have just five pupils in your class, or just one, and be flexible so that when a red double-crested booby suddenly alights on the window sill, you can stop the lesson and show the children how to look it up in the bird field guide?' Home-schoolers need to better explain this, not necessarily to criticize the public schools, but to show what can be done."

Do home-schoolers miss out on social and community life?

"It takes a village to raise a child," goes the African proverb often cited by public educators. Home-schoolers,

. . . About Slow Learners and 'Political Indoctrination'

notify the state of their intentions every August.

Virginia requires educational assessments for home-schooled students and gives parents several options for complying: allow the school district to administer standardized tests for free; pay for private tests; show state officials portfolios of each child's work; or hire an approved evaluator, which is the option the Richmans selected. At the end of the school year, their free-lance evaluator interviews the children, gives them oral tests and reviews portfolios of their work. The Richmans also show the evaluator photographs from the kids' field trips.

The year's curriculum is roughed out in August, Kathleen says. "The first year, we spent a lot more time planning the curriculum than we needed." They ordered scads of catalogs of home-schooling materials for such subjects as math and grammar. "The catalogs give you a sense of what approach they take, whether the math is done with hands-on learning or visuals, and you decide what works," she says. "If your child is not getting it, then you throw the material away, which wouldn't happen in a public school."

Sheldon, who, like his wife, is a product of the public schools, harbored doubts that things would work out when they began home schooling. "But there's a large support network of home-schoolers, with newsletters, which is reassuring," he says. "I've even heard of home-schoolers' proms and graduations." The Richmans participate in a community children's theater run completely by home-schoolers.

"It is time-consuming," admits Kathleen, "and there are times when I'd like to ship the kids off." The Richmans realize that, as often happens when home-schooled kids grow older, they may have trouble getting access to such school staples as science labs or a chance to try out for the band.

But the thought of returning to public schools has little appeal. "Schools are an artificial and negative form of social training — you can't even get a drink of water or use the bathroom without raising your hand," says Sheldon. "It's a systemic problem, like the Post Office. It's not because of bad teachers. Managing 25 kids at a time calls for different skills than teaching."

Why not rejoin the schools and help to reform them? "If we'd thought that sticking with the system would improve schools, we would have," says Kathleen, "but we feel powerless to improve the education system because the flaws are so fundamental. Out of 25 students in a class, there will be some the teacher doesn't like, and you don't know if your kid is among them. With home schooling, at least you know the teacher likes the kid. That's more important than the teaching skills."

For the most part, both parents say, they've simply added some academics to the classic job of parenting. "People ask me, 'How do you know when your child is ready for multiplication?' " Kathleen says. "Well, how do you know when to instruct a toddler not to run into the street?"

Occasionally, such as when the family is at the grocery store during public school hours, they get odd glances from onlookers who suspect truancy. But society seems to be adjusting to the sight, the couple says, and other kids are even envious of the arrangement. "You're lucky," exclaimed a youngster their kids met at an amusement park. "You must be rich."

The Richmans envision staying with home schooling until the kids are ready for college, says Sheldon, who bemoans the "lack of motivation" among public high schoolers he sees.

"It would be so condescending to our children to send them back to the spoon-feeding of a high school after all this home schooling," says Kathleen, pointing to the children's strong motivation to learn. "The good thing about home schooling is that there's nothing to rebel against."

---

[1] *Washington City Paper*, July 19, 1991

however, are often accused of abandoning the proverbial village, denying their children needed social interaction and escaping from obligations to the community.

"The first thing people want to know about home schooling is, 'How do your kids make friends?' " notes Sheffer.

Among public educators, the supposed absence of social interaction is a major objection to home schooling. In a survey of 115 educators, more than 80 percent believed home-schoolers were at a disadvantage in the social development of the child, and 59 percent believed that a disadvantage of home schools was the lack of competition in the child's academic and social world. [7]

In fact, says Marx, "Much of the motivation for home schooling is to escape the diversity of society. While the parents may seem to be saving their children from confronting diversity in thinking, race, economic status and social skills, in the long run these young people will still have to go into the world. And these kids later will feel deprived."

It's true, acknowledges Wagner of the Family Research Council, that "if you never take your kids outside, and you throw up real or metaphorical walls, they can be isolated. But the 'village' concept is abused when used by the authorities to justify state power. A village can be one's parents and friends," he says. "There is socialization among home-schoolers; it's not just regimented by age group the way it is in [traditional] schools, which is unnatural. And it is not selfish to give kids the best education you can. What's good for kids is good for society."

Continued on p. 777

Home-Schooling Laws in the United States

Regulation of home schooling varies widely among the states. Overall, 34 states specifically regulate home schooling, and 29 require standardized testing or evaluations; 40 states, however, don't require parents to have specific qualifications for teaching.

	Have home-school laws or regulations	Don't require parents to have specific qualifications for teaching	Require parents to have high school diploma, GED or other qualifications	Generally require parents to be "competent" and instruction to be "thorough," but no specific requirements	Require standardized testing or evaluations of students	Permit groups of home-schoolers to qualify as private or church schools	Permit individual home schools to qualify as private or church schools
Alabama		X					X
Alaska		X			X		X
Arizona	X		X		X		
Arkansas	X	X			X		
California		X		X			X
Colorado	X	X			X	X	
Connecticut	X	X		X	X		
Delaware		X		X			X
District of Columbia		X					
Florida	X	X			X	X	
Georgia	X		X		X		
Hawaii	X	X			X		
Idaho		X		X			
Illinois		X					X
Indiana		X		X			X
Iowa	X	X		X	X		
Kansas		X		X			X
Kentucky		X					X
Louisiana	X	X			X		X
Maine	X	X		X	X	X	
Maryland	X	X		X			
Massachusetts		X			X		
Michigan		X		X			X
Minnesota	X	X			X		
Mississippi	X	X					
Missouri	X	X					
Montana	X	X					
Nebraska		X					X
Nevada	X	X		X	X		
New Hampshire	X	X			X		
New Jersey		X		X			
New Mexico	X		X		X		
New York	X	X		X	X		
North Carolina	X		X		X		
North Dakota	X		X[1]		X		
Ohio	X		X	4	X		
Oklahoma	2	X					
Oregon	X	X			X		
Pennsylvania	X		X		X		
Rhode Island	X	X		X			
South Carolina	X		X		X	X	
South Dakota		X			X		
Tennessee	X		X		X		
Texas		X					X
Utah	X	X				X	
Vermont	X	X			X		
Virginia	X	X			X		
Washington	X	X			X		
West Virginia	X		X[3]		X		
Wisconsin	X	X					
Wyoming	X	X					

1. Requires parents to pass teacher's test. 2. Constitutional amendment protects home schooling. 3. Parents must stay 4 years ahead of student. 4. Also requires parents to be "competent."

Source: Christopher J. Klicka, "Home Schooling in the United States: A Legal Analysis," Home School Legal Defense Association, 1994

A Patchwork of Home-Schooling Laws

During the 1980s, changes being made in home-schooling laws throughout the states left a patchwork of regulations affecting such areas as standardized-test requirements, home visits and teacher certification. Currently, 40 states and the District of Columbia do not require specific teaching qualifications for parents, according to the Home School Legal Defense Association. (*See table, p. 776.*)

Among the states with teacher requirements, eight states require a high school diploma or general equivalency diploma (GED); North Dakota requires parents to pass a standard test for teachers; and West Virginia allows parents to teach as long as their education level remains four years ahead of the student's.

In Wisconsin, parents who want to home school need only register by filling out a form. "It's not an application and not an approval," says Sally Sarnstrom, state director for school management services. "There's no assessment and no monitoring by either the state or the local district. By state statute, parents have the right to meet the state compulsory-attendance law in their own way."

In California, parents who want to home school have several options, says Barbara Beach-Courchesne, a consultant for Los Angeles County. They can teach their children themselves, if they are certified teachers; set up an independent study contract that follows the state curriculum and is monitored by a certified teacher; or establish their own home-based private school, which entails adhering to state regulations.

This third method is the most popular, Beach-Courchesne says, although it requires parents to have health and fire inspections, fingerprint the children and send the prints to the FBI and teach in English. "Parents might find these rules restrictive," she says, "but we receive complaints from neighbors and children's-services departments that there is too little monitoring of these private schools."

Often, state laws do not reflect what is actually happening among home-schoolers. "In Alabama, for example," says Christopher J. Klicka, senior counsel at the legal defense association, "if you call the state Education Department, they will say you have to have a certified tutor to home school. But there are 10,000-15,000 home-schoolers in Alabama who are operating under the state's church-school exemption statute."

In Michigan, home-schoolers were cheered last year by two state Supreme Court rulings involving home-school families that had been convicted of violating the state's compulsory education statute. [1] In reversing the lower court convictions, the Supreme Court permitted religious home schooling on First Amendment grounds and curbed the power of education officials to review home-schooling practices.

[1] The cases were *People v. DeJonge* and *People v. Bennett.*

Continued from p. 775

Other home-schooling proponents point to the proliferation of book clubs, Little League teams, charity projects and joint field trips that have been organized in recent years by home-schooling support groups.

"There are about 40 kids in our group," wrote one Michigan home-schooler, "and they all come from within about an hour's drive of Detroit. Of course, not everyone participates in every activity. . . . Sometimes we only get three or four people, and that can be fun, too. A lot of friendships have grown among kids in the group." [8]

What's more, many school authorities have begun cooperating with home-schooling families. Oregon, for example, permits home-schoolers to participate in interscholastic activities such as sports and debate, while Iowa and California schools open their music and art classes to home-schoolers.

"Kids' social needs can be met with good attention from adults, such as apprenticeships, or visits to museums, laboratories or courtrooms," says Sheffer. "People accuse us of being shut off from the real world, but we're the ones who're participating in the community." And, she says, "home-schoolers actually prefer their kind of social life, without all the cliques and snobbery you get in schools. They have a broader range of friends of all ages and types, and it doesn't matter if your friends disagree or don't wear the right clothes."

What home-schooling requires is an independent personality. "One key to a full social life when you are a home-schooler is being able to make your own fun," wrote Rebecca Marion, a 15-year-old from Danville, Ind. "If you wait around for the fun to come to you, you'll be waiting for a long time." [9]

Studies of home-schooled students appear to belie the notion that home-schoolers are isolated. A 1988 study by Seattle University researcher Linda Montgomery found that home-schoolers were just as involved as conventional students in music and dance lessons, scouting and 4-H clubs, and were even more likely to have jobs such as delivering papers, mowing lawns or baby-sitting. [10] Also in 1988, the Washington (state) Home School Research Project surveyed 219 home-schoolers and found that more than half spent 20-30 hours a month in community or volunteer activities. About 40 percent spent more than 30 hours a month with friends outside their families. [11]

Home School Legal Defense Association

The Teaching Home

Home School Legal Defense Association

Home Schooling Close-Ups

Home-school graduate Aaron Fessler gives computer help to Virginia home-schoolers Christy Farris, 18, and her sister, Jayme, 16, (*top left*).

San Antonio plays Houston in the championship game of last year's National Home School Basketball Tournament in Colorado Springs, Colo. (*bottom left*).

Richard Wheeler of San Antonio explains a Revolutionary War cannon to his son Joshua. Wheeler, a professional public speaker on "Christian roots in American history," and his wife Marilyn home school their three children, (*top right*).

In a 1991 study of adults who had been home-schooled, no respondents were unemployed or on welfare, 94 percent said home schooling prepared them to be independent persons and 79 percent said home schooling had helped them interact with individuals from different levels of society. [12]

Home-schooling proponents frequently cite a 1986 study based on self-esteem tests given to 224 home-schoolers by John Wesley Taylor V of Andrews University in Berrien Springs, Mich. On average, they ranked in the 91st percentile of the widely used Piers-Harris Children's Self-Concept Scale. [13]

As for the charge that home-schoolers are trying to escape diversity, Ray denies that home schooling amounts to a not-so-subtle form of bigotry. "Is home schooling a form of white flight?" he asks. "The black home-schoolers I've spoken to say it is not."

"And I know of no research showing problems with too much parental input in children's lives," Ray adds. "But there's a huge amount showing that there's not enough."

The notion that parents are a home-schooler's sole authority is exaggerated, says Farris, noting that home-schoolers frequently have contact with softball coaches, piano teachers and ballet instructors. "Kids generally commingle well," he says. "Some kids have problems no matter what, and some will get teased at school and withdraw while others who are home-schooled will turn inward. "But being a home-schooler gives them a healthy appreciation for the needs of minorities because of the stigma attached" to home schooling.

Farris also dismisses the fear that home-schoolers' isolation will lead to involvement with Nazis or other extremist groups. Such "horror stories" are concocted by critics as scare tactics, Farris says. "That's not to say there are not bad parents out there, but there will be whether or not there's home schooling. Home schooling is actually a more natural setting than any other I know. I don't know of any other form of education that's more like a village."

Does home schooling threaten the public schools?

After 17 years in public schools in Alaska and Idaho, one teacher was so frustrated with the system that she embraced home schooling. "I continuously grappled with the mammoth, unwieldy system that public education is," she said, "and became depressed at times with the stranglehold the system often administered to children's curiosity, creativity, thinking and sense of well-being.

"I taught alongside many excellent teachers who managed in their own corners of the school building to fashion as many miracles as they could — despite the system. However, I also taught alongside several of the dregs of the teaching vocation. They outstayed me, incidentally, and are still there. Their perpetual presence and the overpowering dominance of the colossus that the education system has become drove me away from the public schools." [14]

Conservative education critic Phyllis Schlafly, though not a crusader for home schooling, says parents' fear of crime in schools has made it a reasonable choice. [15] "If the public schools were doing their job," she says, "there wouldn't be a million home-schoolers."

Many home-schoolers express the fundamental complaint that public schools gear children to the needs of business at the expense of fostering individuality. Gorder recites a litany of objections that couldn't be remedied with just a few simple reforms. She chastises schools for putting too much emphasis on consumerism, conformity, excessive devotion to one's job, numerical performance measures and social-class distinctions. She also blasts schools for instilling "information vulnerability" in children, or encouraging them to believe everything they read in the newspaper. [16]

And plenty of home-schoolers see traditional schools as having a vastly different agenda. "Officially," says Ray, "school superintendents who oppose home schooling are concerned about academics and wonder how a mother with a high school education can teach algebra. But unofficially, they're concerned about maintaining what has been called the 'hidden curriculum,' about students becoming good democratic citizens, their socialization, their values and belief systems."

That is why, says Ray, when one home-schooler was asked what he would change about schools, he said, "'The question is wrong. The question is why go to public school at all?' "

Most visibly, home schooling has become a weapon in attacks on the school system from the politically active religious right. In 1992, for example, Washington state's Republican Party platform included a call for "deregulation of home and church schools" along with a ban on homosexuals in teaching jobs, a return to corporal punishment in schools and the teaching of creationism. [17]

Public educators, though respectful of the rights of home-schoolers, portray home schooling not as a threat to their institution but as a phenomenon that needs to be monitored to maintain high standards. "When I was principal of a school in Massachusetts," says Ronald Areglado, associate executive director of programs for the National Association of Elementary School Principals, "there was a family that wanted to home school [their son and daughter] based on some metaphysical concept of what school is all about, which I never understood. But I approved the program, then monitored it, as part of the agreement."

Areglado eventually concluded that the boy wasn't learning much and seemed dispirited. "I realized that basically the kids were home because the parents didn't want them in school," he says, "and the boy was baby-sitting for his younger sister." Areglado had to threaten to take the family to court if they didn't change the curriculum or return the children to school.

There are limits to home schooling because "it's hard to be a citizen in isolation," Areglado continues. "Schools become a forum in which you test basic tenets of democracy — cooperation, problem solving, exposure to different ethnic and racial groups. There are parents who home school well, and, to their credit, they often stretch to make it happen. But many are just taking away an important component of a child's overall growth."

Anderson of the Montana School Boards Association says that while there are plenty of good home-schoolers in his state, "we see a lot of the kids returning to public schools at the junior high and high school level whom I suspect are not satisfied. They want to be with other kids, and they're a discipline problem because they're not as easy to control.

"We also have the problem of where to place these kids because they have no transcripts or assessments. One parent wanted his kid to return as a freshman, but we knew he should be a sophomore because he was bored to tears. In another case, the parents wanted the kid to be a sophomore, but he was working only at the eighth-grade level. Parents don't have a fix on how their kids compare with other students."

Despite the concerns about public schools, Marx doubts that large numbers will abandon them. "We're not a nation of people who run from problems," he says. "The public school is an institution that has brought our society together. Historically, home-schoolers lived in isolated locations, but today's society has become more complex, and in this age of technology and information, it is difficult to have in your home the laboratories and expertise for such areas as math and science. And the future will require an understanding of people beyond our borders, so we need to stretch our view of where those borders are."

The frequent comment that educators resist home schooling because they fear a loss of teaching jobs is dismissed by Martin of the NEA. "We added more than 37,000 members last year and have reached an all-time high of 2.2 million," he says. "The number of public school pupils has also grown in the past 10 years."

Martin says the teachers' union gets a lot of calls from home-schoolers and critics "who have this feeling that the NEA is plotting against home schooling. But we devote little attention to it. It's not high on an agenda that includes taxes, teaching materials, quality of school buildings and employment practices."

"Home-schooling parents are sincere," Martin continues, "and they devote a lot of time to it. But we in the public schools are dealing with a different type of student — including the learning-disabled, those newly arrived in the country, those with language barriers, those in special education and those who get very little support at home. Most parents will choose public schools because they want that diversity. They want their kids to see that others are struggling financially, that not everyone can afford a car to drive to school, because that's what they will see in the real world."

From a political perspective, says Mincberg of People for the American Way, "there is an enormous tie-in between home-schoolers and the movement for prayer in schools and for government education vouchers [to help parents pay private school costs]. If they can assert the moral bankruptcy of public schools, they can foster the growth of the religious right" and argue that the state has no right to regulate education, he says. "Our main criticism of some home-school advocates is they are challenging the state's ability to see that education is happening effectively." [18]

Farris, whose candidacy for lieutenant governor in Virginia last year heightened the image of home-schoolers as religious rightists, acknowledges that there are "some shared values" between home-schoolers and those whose agenda includes restoring prayer in the schools and removing "value-laden" sex education. "But the legal defense association doesn't deal with any of those issues," he says. "Home schooling defies political characterization. In Pennsylvania, home-schooling legislation passed both houses unanimously, with liberal Democratic sponsors."

What home schooling shares with conservative politics, Farris says, is the desire to take schools back from "one-size-fits-all bureaucracies" governed by state and federal mandates. "If we get parental control and educational choice, who's to complain?"

Many home-schoolers object to being typecast politically and are nervous about the visibility of home-schoolers who are members of the religious right. "Home schooling is not a vote of no confidence in the schools," says Kaseman of Wisconsin. "It's done primarily for constructive and positive reasons." ■

BACKGROUND

Education System Evolves

George Washington, Abraham Lincoln, Frederick Douglass, Thomas Edison, Mark Twain, Andrew Carnegie, Theodore Roosevelt, John Philip Sousa, Winston Churchill, Margaret Mead, Charlie Chaplin, Albert Einstein, Douglas MacArthur, Grandma Moses and Agatha Christie — all are claimed as distinguished alumni by the home-school community.

Indeed, before the advent of American public schools in the mid-19th century, home schooling was the norm. Founding Father John Adams, whose diplomatic missions often took him away from his family, wrote at length to his wife Abigail about her role in educating their four children. She was inspired to compose a poem celebrating the "Parent who vast pleasure finds; in forming her children's minds; in Midst of whom with read delight; she passes many a winter's night." [19]

In the 1840s, instruction books for the home such as *Domestic Education and Fire-side Education* were popular in the United States and Britain. Even then, the difficulty of traveling to the fledgling system of community schools in the U.S. was provoking detractors.

Around the same period, author Lydia Sigourney wrote in *Letters to Mothers:* "Why expose [a child] to the influence of a promiscuous association, when it has a parent's house, where its innocence may be shielded, and its intellect aided to expand? Does not a mother's tutoring for two to three hours a day give a child more time than a teacher at school?" [20]

Public Schools Emerge

Most of the country, however, began moving toward public schools. As recounted by Roger D. Stephon, coordinator of the NEA's Preserving Public Education Program: "[O]ne of the first things [the pioneers] did . . . was to set aside a plot of land, hold a 'barn raising' to build a rudimentary schoolhouse and recruit the area's most educated resident [as the] schoolmarm. Later, they recruited graduates of Eastern Seaboard colleges to further the education of their children beyond that which they were capable of providing themselves." [21]

With the rise of the public school movement led by Horace Mann, states soon passed compulsory-education laws. They were designed primarily to prevent farmers, miners and other parents from keeping their kids home to work. (Ironically, another force behind public schools was the desire to use them to spread Christian morality, with its concern for the larger good over individualism.) [22]

Massachusetts enacted the first compulsory-education law in 1852. It required children ages 8-14 to attend school at least 12 weeks a year — unless they were too poor — and sometimes had to be enforced by militiamen. [23] The laws were effective; from 1870-1898, the number of children enrolling in schools outpaced population growth, a clear indication that many had been kept at home. [24]

By the early 20th century, public education in an increasingly urbanized society was firmly under the influence of community-oriented theorists such as John Dewey, who focused on the needs of each individual child in large group settings that cut across social classes. "The teacher is engaged," Dewey wrote, "not simply in the training of individuals but in the formation of the proper social life." [25]

As teachers and administrators became more professional, however, the parents' role was not neglected: From 1905-1910, no less than three international congresses on the role of the home in education were held in Brussels, Belgium, after which the U.S. Bureau of Education issued a report emphasizing the importance of home nursery schools and parental involvement in the Parent-Teacher Associations. [26]

Continued on p. 782

Chronology

1800s ***Before rise of public schools in the U.S., home schooling is the norm.***

1852
Massachusetts is first state to enact a compulsory-schooling law.

1910s ***Professional educators are influenced by the socially oriented education theories of John Dewey.***

1918
Mississippi becomes last state to enact compulsory schooling.

1920s ***Supreme Court rulings affect home schooling.***

1923
Supreme Court rules in *Meyer v. Nebraska* case that the state's right over education is not absolute.

1925
Supreme Court in *Pierce v. Society of Sisters* says Oregon parents can't be denied their own schools, noting, "The child is not the mere creature of the state."

1960s ***Rise of hippie counterculture spurs interest in child-centered, anti-establishment education.***

1964
Education reformer John Holt publishes his critique of public schools, *How Children Fail.*

1970s ***Fundamentalist Christians embrace home schooling. By mid-decade, home-schoolers are estimated at 10,000-20,000.***

1972
Supreme Court in *Wisconsin v. Yoder* allows an Amish child to be educated at home. Raymond Moore's articles in *Harper's* and *Reader's Digest* crystallize home-school movement.

1976
Libertarian gadfly and occasional congressional candidate Ed Nagel of Santa Fe, N.M., launches National Association for the Legal Support of Alternative Schools.

1977
Holt breaks with public school advocacy and founds *Growing Without School* magazine in Cambridge, Mass.

1978
In *Perchemlides v. Frizzle,* a Massachusetts judge rules that there is a constitutional right to home schooling.

1980s ***Number of home-schoolers rises from 60,000 in 1983 to 122,000-244,000 by 1988. Growth occurs among both religious and secular home-schoolers.***

1982
Holt publishes *Teach Your Own,* attacking both Dewey and public schools.

1983
Formation of Home School Legal Defense Association. Education Department releases study critical of U.S. education, *A Nation at Risk.*

1984
John Naisbett's best-selling book, *Megatrends,* cites home schooling as a wave of the future.

1987
Grant Colfax, son of California home-schoolers David and Micki Colfax, graduates magna cum laude from Harvard University. (Two brothers later follow.)

1988
Seven thousand delegates at National Education Association convention call for tighter restrictions on home-schoolers.

1990s ***Number of home-schoolers estimated at 350,000 to 1 million; home-schoolers mobilize politically.***

March 1993
National Association of Elementary School Principals adopts resolution criticizing home schooling.

May 1993
Michigan Supreme Court rules in favor of home-schooling parents convicted of truancy.

Nov. 2, 1993
Home School Legal Defense Association President Michael P. Farris fails in his bid to become Virginia lieutenant governor but raises visibility of the home-schooling movement during the campaign.

February 1994
Thousands of home-schoolers inundate House members with telephone calls and faxes over an amendment they fear will require parents to be certified teachers.

Rise of Home Schooling

Except among certain religious sects and users of correspondence schools, home schooling remained limited for much of America's 20th century. Schlafly recalls how in 1955 she became disturbed by the way reading was being taught in public schools and decided to teach her own children. "I didn't know a single living being who was doing the same thing," she recalls, "and I was treated with scorn, like I was doing something dreadful."

But in the 1960s, the hippie counterculture exploded on the scene. Its revolt against the education establishment prompted wide interest in the "child-centered" educational freedom espoused by John Holt (*How Children Fail*), Ivan Illich (*DeSchooling Society*) and A.S. Neill (*Summerhill*). Thousands of young Americans began "dropping out" of society and going "back to the land" to live on communes, generating the modern home-schooling movement.

In 1972, education theorist Moore, a former U.S. education official, published an influential article in *Harper's* and *Reader's Digest* criticizing U.S. schools for taking youngsters out of their homes too early. As Moore recalls it, the piece launched a correspondence between him and Holt — and energized the home-schooling movement.

Not long afterwards, Holt, after years of promoting public school reform, made his break with public education. In 1977, he founded the home-schooling magazine *Growing Without Schooling*, making it part of the mail-order book and music store he later started in Cambridge, Mass. In 1981, he published *Teach Your Own*. In 1983, he touted home schooling as an inexpensive "laboratory for the intensive and long-range study of children's learning and of ways in which friendly and concerned adults can help them learn." [27]

Public School Problems

The 1970s saw the resurgence of fundamentalist Christianity in the United States that would help elect Ronald Reagan president in 1980. By 1983, the year the Education Department issued its scathing critique of education, *A Nation at Risk*, the growing number of home-schoolers had prompted Farris and other conservative Virginia lawyers to form the Home School Legal Defense Association.

Problems in the public schools, meanwhile, had prompted many parents to complain about "unhealthy" and anti-religious values being taught in schools. The concerns led the Education Department to hold a series of public hearings around the country.

"This year we have taken our children out of public schools and are home-teaching them," Shannon Stearns, an Arizona parent, testified. "This has proven to be a great thing for our family. We have even discovered that we can read the books and answer the questions just like teachers do. I've discovered, too, that I have much to offer them. I believe my children can withstand the temptation of drugs, alcohol and smoking, and even bad language, but I fear that they cannot always recognize the lies that are found in the classroom at school." [28]

Susannah Sheffer, *Growing Without Schooling*

In an extra-curricular activity he chose himself, 7-year-old Eoin Gaj, a home-schooler in Cambridge, Mass., helps Pat Farren, editor of Peacework *magazine, attach mailing labels to envelopes.*

Studies began appearing that showcased the academic achievements of home-schoolers. In the early 1980s, the Alaska Education Department studied fourth-graders' reading and math scores and found that home-schoolers consistently outscored public school students. Similar results were found in Tennessee.

At the same time, many states cracked down on home-schoolers. "The two major ways they intimidate home-schoolers is by home visits and by the manipulation of teacher-qualification requirements," says Farris. His group fought court battles, organized the lobbying of state legislatures and helped promote home-schooling support groups that "know more about state law than the average truant officer."

By 1988, the Education Department estimated that 150,000-300,000 children were being home-schooled. The National School Boards Association weighed in with model legislation designed to help states and districts maintain the quality of home schooling.

Meanwhile, 7,000 delegates to the 1988 NEA convention passed a resolution stating that "home-schooling programs cannot provide the student with a comprehensive education experience." The resolution declared that instruction should be provided only by properly licensed teachers using a state-approved curriculum. And it said that home-schooling programs "should be limited to children of the immediate family, with all expenses being borne by the parents."

Into the Mainstream — and Harvard

In the late 1980s, the home-schooling movement got a boost from secular practitioners that propelled it into the mainstream. Prominent among them were David and Micki Colfax, anti-Vietnam War activists and community organizers who had dropped out of teaching to educate their three sons on a ranch north of San Francisco. "We weren't about to turn our kids over to an institution we felt was destructive of our kids and of the larger society," says David.

In 1987, Grant Colfax was accepted by Harvard University, a home-schooling feat that was accompanied by extensive media coverage. (His younger brothers Drew and Reed were to follow.) What everyone wanted to know was how they did it.

"Grant interviewed at nearly a dozen colleges and applied to two," the Colfaxes later wrote in *Homeschooling for Excellence,* one of their two books on home schooling. "We submitted a letter to each, describing his coursework and evaluating his strengths and weaknesses as objectively as possible. In lieu of teacher and counselor recommendations, Grant provided letters from a half-dozen people who could variously attest to his work in the community health center, his dairy goat business and, in general, his character and intellectual potential. He wrote a long essay that described his years on the ranch, his home-schooling experiences and his hopes for the future. He was admitted to Yale and Harvard and entered the latter that fall." [29]

State laws, meanwhile, were clearly loosening. In Ohio, for example, the Trumbull County education supervisor typically visited his district's 15-20 home-schooled children twice a year to review lesson plans and logs charting their progress.

"In 1989, new state guidelines came out, and it was like Parliament was dissolved," said Supervisor Joseph Casagrande. "You couldn't go to their houses anymore, you couldn't phone them unless they put their phone number down on the notification form. They didn't even have to put the grade level of the child." [30] ■

CURRENT SITUATION

Blitzing Congress

It was in February that the home-schooling movement showed its political muscle. The Home School Legal Defense Association coordinated the effort, firing up home-schoolers around the country through mailings, phone calls and radio talk show appearances. Hundreds of thousands of home-schoolers responded, calling or faxing members of Congress to protest legislation they feared would threaten home-schoolers. Phone lines in many offices were jammed for hours.

The clash began early in February, as the $12.7 billion Elementary and Secondary Education Act (ESEA) Reauthorization was being readied for floor debate in the House. Rep. George Miller, D-Calif., had proposed an amendment requiring all school districts seeking federal education grants under the bill to require all teachers to be certified by 1998.

Miller told colleagues he had been "confronted by many district teachers who tell me that they are forced to teach classes for which they have not studied, nor do they know the subject matter, for the convenience of their school and/or their school district."

As Farris tells it, his people told Miller that such a requirement would threaten home-schoolers and "small, rural schools where, if a history teacher happens to have been a college debate champ, he still couldn't teach debate. We gave him a chance to back off, and he refused," Farris says. "Miller wasn't thinking about home schools, he was just helping the teachers' unions."

Farris then put out the nationwide alert to home-schoolers and sent a letter to House members calling Miller's amendment "the equivalent of a nuclear attack upon the home-schooling community."

Democrats on the House Rules Committee offered to strike Miller's language in favor of a substitute amendment from Reps. William D. Ford and Dale E. Kildee, both Michigan Democrats, stating simply that the certification requirement didn't apply to home-schoolers. After debate on the House floor, it passed 424-1, with Miller dissenting. [31]

But Farris' group wasn't satisfied, pointing out that the substitute amendment could still threaten private schools and that "17 states have home-schoolers that operate under the name of private schools, including three of the biggest home-schooling states — California, Texas and Michigan."

As lobbyists from private, Catholic and Christian schools joined in, home-schoolers rallied behind another amendment prepared by Rep. Dick

Armey, R-Texas. Armey said his goal was to "write language that makes America's home-schoolers feel secure that they can continue to enjoy practicing their freedom in their home rather than defending their freedom in the courts." His amendment said the bill would not "permit, allow, encourage or authorize any federal control over any aspect of any private, religious or home school." It passed 374-53 on Feb. 24.

"There is nothing better than a positive, explicit prohibition to keep both federal and state education bureaucrats from using ESEA as a club to force home-schoolers into their 'school reform' agenda," Farris wrote to members of some 1,000 home-schooling organizations.

But to some home-schoolers, the Armey amendment was a step backward, simply because it called attention to home schools. Armey's proposal would introduce home schools "as a separate class of schools in a major federal statute," said the Wisconsin Parents Association. "Thus, the federal government would name 'home schools' and thereby gain dominion over them. Federal regulations would undoubtedly be written about 'home schools,' now or in the near future." [32]

Wagner of the Family Research Council disagrees. "In the context of legislation," he says, "it is a good thing to be marked as a class." Most of the home-school victories in the 1980s have been in the state legislatures, largely due to home-schoolers demonstrating an essential ingredient for succeeding in a democracy — group consciousness."

Farris' home-schoolers were ecstatic. "On Feb. 24, 1994, God protected the home-schoolers of America," wrote Douglas Phillips, director for government affairs at Farris' affiliate, the National Center for Home Education. [33]

Many in Congress, however, felt the Armey amendment was unnecessary, not least of all Miller. "I'm terribly sorry about the misinformation and the misconstruing of the language that I put into this bill," he said. "This amendment never did have any impact on home-schoolers. . . . Somebody could not pass up the political opportunity to gin those people up and arouse them and have them spend their time, their money and their resources beseeching the Congress on a problem that never existed."

Breyer Confirmation Opposed

In July, Farris was back on Capitol Hill, this time to speak against the nomination of federal Judge Stephen G. Breyer to the Supreme Court. Farris called Breyer "a clear and present danger to our freedoms" because of his ruling in a 1989 case involving a Massachusetts Christian school, which Farris had represented. [34] "We believe his opinion clearly indicates he would vote to uphold a state law which bans home schooling," Farris testified. [35]

The case arose over attempts by the local education committee of East Longmeadow, Mass., to review the credentials of teachers at the New Life Baptist Church Academy and periodically visit the school. School officials, however, considered it a "sin" to submit their educational enterprise to a secular authority, calling the supervision an "unnecessary burden" and proposing evaluation through standardized tests.

A three-judge federal panel led by Breyer, then the chief judge of the 1st U.S. Circuit Court of Appeals, backed the school committee. The panel argued that forbidding "*any* classroom observation or 'checkup' . . . could significantly inhibit the state's efforts to evaluate the secular education provided by religious schools (or home schools)" and that such a system of checkups "doesn't pose a likelihood of excessive entanglements and doesn't violate the First Amendment's Establishment Clause."

Breyer assured senators that he respected home schooling and went on to be confirmed.

Charter School Debate

In Berlin, Mich., an experimental "charter" school is provoking intense debate in and around the home-schooling movement. Last December, as part of the growing trend toward charter schools — publicly funded schools launched by parents or interested citizens — Michigan passed a charter school law. In April, the Noah Webster Academy, a network of home-schoolers connected to a small central office via computers, became the first school to win approval for state money. [36]

Opposition emerged, however, "because the original founders were all fundamentalists or evangelicals, and they originally said the curriculum would deal with religion and moral truths," says Pat Montgomery, founder and director of the non-religious Clonlara School in Ann Arbor.

Teachers' unions also objected because there were signs that the faculty would be non-union. "We have questions about the curriculum, real fears about public tax dollars going for a quasi-private interest," says Kim Root, spokeswoman for the Michigan Education Association. "We believe there's potential to shut kids out based on religious values and all kinds of criteria that are not a good use of $5,000 per pupil in tax money."

The founder of Noah Webster, lawyer David Kallman, a longtime defender of home-schoolers, says he recommends the curriculum from the non-religious Calvert School in Baltimore for grades K-8 and the curriculum from the University of Nebraska correspondence program for grades 9-12. "Our focus is to allow parents to choose a style that suits them. We're not saying 'Here's the Noah Webster

Continued on p. 787

At Issue:

Should parents be encouraged to try home schooling?

yes

M. Larry and Susan D. Kaseman

The Kasemans have been home schooling their four children since 1979, and working with a grass-roots home-schooling organization since 1984.

FROM *TAKING CHARGE THROUGH HOME SCHOOLING: PERSONAL AND POLITICAL EMPOWERMENT (KOSHKONONG PRESS, 1990)*

The decision to home school involves much more than where a child will learn to read and do long division. It is a big responsibility with serious consequences. It is also an adventure.

People decide to home school for many reasons and in different ways. Some decide intellectually that it will provide the best education for their child. Others are led through prayer or feel in their hearts that it is right for them. Still others reluctantly choose it as the best alternative, although they lack confidence in their own abilities or are reluctant for some other reason. Parents' feelings about home schools vary, too. Many embrace it joyfully and truly love it. Some begin out of a sense of duty and find they like it better than they had expected, while others persist only because they are convinced it is best for their children.

Among the strengths and advantages of home schooling are the following: A child can learn at his own pace, when he is ready, using the learning styles and approaches that work for him. Without the limitations of a conventional classroom, he can pursue special interests in depth; think creatively; and make the most of his strengths, abilities and talents.

Within the security of his own home and family, he can work one-on-one with a parent who cares deeply about him and gives him strong support. He does not have to contend with either the competition and peer pressure of a classroom or the stress of trying to learn something before he is ready. He has the opportunity to learn from direct experience with the real world, to interact with a wide range of people of different ages, to be of service to others, to participate in real activities that make sense and to discover how to learn in his own way.

A home-schooling parent has much more control over his child's environment and is able to provide important support. A parent also has many opportunities to learn with her child and through home schooling.

no

The National Association Of Elementary School Principals

FROM *A RESOLUTION ADOPTED AT NAESP'S ANNUAL CONVENTION IN ORLANDO, FLA.,* MARCH 1993.

The National Association of Elementary School Principals (NAESP) believes education is the cornerstone of American democracy. In order to guarantee an enlightened electorate capable of governing itself, the American people must ensure quality education for each citizen.

NAESP asserts that this is most effectively done through cohesive organization in formal settings in which resources can most beneficially be brought to bear.

NAESP is concerned with the increasing number of individuals and groups who are avoiding education in the traditional setting in favor of at-home schooling.

Home schooling may:

1. deprive the child of important social experiences;
2. isolate students from other social/racial/ethnic groups;
3. deny students the full range of curriculum experiences and materials;
4. be provided by non-certified and unqualified persons;
5. create an additional burden on administrators whose duties include the enforcement of compulsory school-attendance laws;
6. not permit effective assessment of academic standards of quality;
7. violate health and safety standards; and
8. not provide the accurate diagnosis of and planning for meeting the needs of children with special talents, learning difficulties and other conditions requiring atypical educational programs.

When alternative options such as home schooling have been authorized by state legislation, resources and authority should be provided to make certain that those who exercise these options are held strictly accountable for the academic achievement and social/emotional growth of children.

Quality of Home-School Curricula Varies Widely

For many parents, the notion of sitting kids down with a preplanned set of workbooks defeats the whole purpose of home schooling. "We emphasize that you don't *need* a packaged curriculum in order to home school successfully," advises Holt Associates, a clearinghouse for home-schooling information based in Cambridge, Mass. "Think of adults you know who can share a skill. . . . Think of real-life activities, writing letters, handling money, measuring, observing the stars, talking to older people. . . . These are some of the ways that home-schoolers learn." [1]

But a sizable number of home-schoolers — from 25 percent to 50 percent of the nationwide total, according to the U.S. Department of Education — rely on publishers and correspondence schools for materials, particularly when they're just starting. [2] "Those who're more likely to use them are the Christians," notes Education Department analyst Patricia M. Lines.

Indeed, fundamentalists and evangelicals account for the bulk of the dozens of home-curriculum providers that have sprung up in recent years, judging by the exhibitors' booths at home-schooling fairs. There are some 25 suppliers of year-round curricula with enrollments of at least 100 students, and some of the firms even grade the students' work.

The home-schooling market also attracts single-topic publishers who offer materials ranging from Bible lessons to phonics drills, as well as large religious marketers such as Bob Jones University Press in Greenville, S.C., and Alpha Omega Publications in Tempe, Ariz.

The oldest religiously oriented home curriculum comes from Home Study International, a Seventh-Day Adventist group in Silver Spring, Md. Founded in 1908, it is "the only entity in the world that offers state-approved and accredited school-at-home education from preschool through college," says Robert Burnette, the group's director of student services. The recent surge in home schooling boosted its enrollment by 60 percent last year and 34 percent in 1992.

Many of Home Study International's 5,000 enrollees are overseas military personnel, missionaries, foreign citizens who want an American education, critically ill patients and even students who have been expelled from public schools.

Some home-schoolers turn to Home Study International because its curriculum is less religiously oriented than others. "Many non-religious families feel discriminated against" by the heavy Christian emphasis of most home-schooling curricula, says Burnette. Others turn to Home Study "in distress" over deteriorating public schools.

Among non-religious curriculum providers, the oldest is the Baltimore-based Calvert School, which has been offering home-schooling materials since 1906. Long a favorite of Foreign Service families, Calvert currently enrolls 12,000 students from kindergarten to eighth grade. Calvert also runs a local day school, where more than 300 children use Calvert's home-instruction curricula "to test our courses in actual learning situations," the school says.

The boom in home schooling has been "fueled by the fundamentalists, and for that we are grateful," says Lawrence T. Williams, educational director of the non-religious Oak Meadow School in Blacksburg, Va. In addition to standard home-schooling materials, the school's telecommunications program enables high-tech families to receive coursework and return it for grading via computers and telephone modems. Oak Meadow's enrollment has been growing 15-20 percent in recent years and has now reached 3,000.

"There is a wide range of quality in the market, so it's caveat emptor," Williams says. "Religious materials that are centered on the Bible can be weak in academic areas, but there are also many Christian materials that are academically rigorous, so there's not necessarily a correlation."

Robert Anderson, executive director of the Montana School Boards Association, says many home-schooling parents have brought him their children's workbooks and marveled at how they whizzed through them. "But at what grade level?" he asks. Many of the parents had no idea of their child's level, based on the workbooks, he says, "and even when the book specifies a grade level, I'm not sure it's accurate."

Home curriculum materials are of varying levels of quality, says Ronald Areglado, associate executive director of programs for the National Association of Elementary School Principals. "The home-schooling people, to their credit, have taken the curriculum frameworks that are used by the major publishers and curriculum developers and aligned their home materials to them," he says. "The publishers want the kids to achieve, or they would be out of business. It's the small, mom and pop curricula developers that I'm worried about."

Parents seeking synopses and reviews of home-schooling materials often turn to Mary Pride, author of *The Big Book of Home Learning* series. Despite her popularity, she has been criticized within the home-schooling movement for her conservatism and her pro-Christian bias. For example, she criticizes Alpha Omega's science curriculum for distorting biblical passages and for liberal "green preaching" on the dangers of overpopulation." [3] And while generally praising Oak Meadow's curriculum for youngsters in lower grades, she faults its lessons for using fairy tales and fables, rather than biblical stories.

Pride has acknowledged that her views are biased, says Williams, "but most people accept her nonetheless."

---

[1] Holt Associates, "You Don't Have to Go to Grow!: Information About Home Schooling."

[2] Patricia M. Lines, "Estimating the Home Schooled Population," working paper, October 1991, p. 4.

[3] Mary Pride, *The Big Book of Home Learning,* Vol. 3, Teen and Adult (1991), p. 233.

Continued from p. 784

curriculum.' There are great programs out there, so we won't reinvent the wheel. But parents can choose the Accelerated Christian Education program if they want.

"And to people who ask, 'How can tax dollars pay for that?' I say, How can we have paid chaplains in the military? How can GI bill grants be used at religious colleges? It's permissible under the free-exercise clause" of the Constitution.

More than 1,000 families have signed up for Noah Webster's fall term, but Kallman says the school's grant money from the state won't arrive until December or January. Meanwhile, a legal challenge to the school is expected from the American Civil Liberties Union.

Not all home-schoolers support the concept of state-supported charter home schools. "We value our freedom," says Clonlara's Montgomery. "If we took that money, we'd have to take the Michigan Educational Assessment Program test and implement collective bargaining for our teachers."

Farris also opposes the Michigan school. "You can't have a religious curriculum and try to have public education at home. It's naive." ■

OUTLOOK

Growth Amid Controversy

Though home-schoolers are united in the effort to protect the freedom to home-school, they find plenty to feud about among themselves. On the various proposals that have been advanced for government school vouchers and tuition tax credits for private schools, for example, some welcome the prospect of financial help, but others are wary of government interference.

And the activism of the legal defense association and its religious followers has alienated many of the non-religious and less formally organized groups. "People with political ambition are causing distortion about what home schooling is," says Kaseman of the Wisconsin Parents Association, noting that some leaders of the "radical right" are not being clear about what they want. "We advocate a grass-roots, not a top-down, approach to maintain the freedom to home school built with the community and with state legislatures, but with distance from the federal government."

Kaseman criticizes the legal defense association for losing most of the court cases it has brought. "Its legacy for home-schoolers is court cases that can be used against us," he says. Home-schooling activist Moore complains that Farris' group "goes from state to state saying how bad the laws are just so they can make a lot of money. The only states we have trouble in are those he goes in and divides people over religion."

Farris responds that he solicits no money, only $100 annual contributions from his 40,000 members — potentially $4 million a year. "When we started in 1983," he says, "only three states had home-schooling statutes; now it's 34. But we never initiated legislation or lobbied until we were asked in after trouble started."

Some school districts have remained unsympathetic to home-schooling. In North Dakota in 1989, for example, a home-schooled student who was a spelling bee champion was barred from a subsequent contest because her parents were not certified teachers.[37]

But many districts have held out the hand of cooperation. In West Virginia, the movement has become so established that the Legislature sponsors an annual home-schoolers' day, when home-schooled children serve as pages and their parents get a chance to talk with lawmakers about home schooling. San Diego's Community Home Education Office has won praise for its six full-time teachers who work with 180 local home-schooled students.

In Cupertino, Calif., the school district receives $2,961 in state revenues for each of the 148 home-schooling students it supervises, $1,000 of which goes to each student for books, materials and field trips. "The success of Cupertino's home schooling is evidenced by the number of parents who remain in the program from year to year and continuously recruit others to join," wrote Superintendent Patricia Lamson. "While it is not actively promoted by the district, under the right circumstances and accompanied by a strong commitment to the concept, home schooling is a choice that is here to stay."[38]

Arnold Fege, director of federal relations for the National PTA, sees possibilities for more sharing between schools and home-schoolers. "Why isn't it possible for kids to come to school in the morning and take advantage of social studies-type things, and then have parents teach them in the afternoon?" he asks. "It would be a rich education, and it could help cement relations between the home and school as an equal partnership."

University of Michigan researcher J. Gary Knowles, who has studied home-schooling extensively, says he "would hope the school system is changing to be more responsive to individuals and that schools all over the nation begin to accept parents as a really important part of the system."

But, he adds, the tests showing high academic performance of home-schoolers are problematic. "We would expect these kids to achieve above the norms for public schools because they're in a special learning context. We need to see how they would do compared with kids in their own neighborhoods and similar socioeconomic and ethnic backgrounds."

Resnick of the school boards association says home schooling has "an overblown appeal." He worries that the advent of home computers may prompt parents to rely on long-distance education at the expense of "the interaction of a child in a class-room with a teacher. It has achieved a certain popularity, and the number of participants may grow, but it's not going to work on a broad scale."

Guterson writes that home schooling's success has given it a "public relations problem." It is perceived by many as an insult and by others as a severe admonition, he says: "'Take more interest in your children, like us!' " home-schoolers seem to say.[39]

Still, Farris predicts that ultimately the movement will grow to 5-7 percent of the nation's school-age population, aided by the sophisticated communications technology increasingly available in the home.

Ray of Western Baptist College says home schooling "is not the passing fad that some in the 1980s said it was. Indeed, he says, recent studies indicate that more and more parents plan to home school their children through high school. Ray predicts that the movement "will continue growing at 15-40 percent a year, limited by such factors as the number of parents who are willing to stay home and give up one income and do all that work."

The Christian practitioners, Ray adds, "believe what they're doing is part of Christianity and don't separate God from other aspects of life. They don't avoid talking religion and politics at parties. We don't take off our Christian coat when we enter a McDonald's, the state capital or the voting booth." ■

Notes

[1] Patricia M. Lines, "Estimating the Home Schooled Population," U.S. Education Department, working paper, October 1991, p. 4.

[2] "Fed Up With Schools, More Parents Turn To Teaching at Home," *The Wall Street Journal*, May 10, 1994. (The article was Part 1 of a series on education.) For a detailed examination of academic accomplishments, see Jane Van Galen and Mary Anne Pitman (eds.), *Home Schooling: Political, Historical, and Pedagogical Perspectives* (1991), pp. 43-62.

[3] Krista Ramsey, "Home Is Where the School Is," *The School Administrator*, January 1992, p. 22.

[4] David Guterson, *Family Matters: Why Home-schooling Makes Sense* (1992), p. 10.

[5] Cheryl Gorder, *Home Schools: An Alternative* (1990), p. 76.

[6] Grace Llewellyn, *Real Lives: Eleven Teenagers Who Don't Go to School* (1993), p. 295.

[7] Gorder, *op. cit.*, p. 34.

[8] "Teen Groups," *Growing Without Schooling* (No. 94, July-August 1993), p. 9.

[9] Llewellyn, *op. cit.*, p. 97.

[10] Guterson *op. cit.*, p. 55.

[11] *Harvard Education Letter*, May-June 1993.

[12] J. Gary Knowles and James A. Muchmore, "'We've Grown Up and We're OK': An Exploration of Adults Who Were Home-Educated as Children," paper presented at annual meeting of American Educational Research Association, April 1991. The authors are education professors at the University of Michigan.

[13] Borg Hendrickson, *Home School: Taking the First Step* (1989), p. 16.

[14] *Ibid.*, p. 2.

[15] For background, see "Violence in Schools," *The CQ Researcher*, Sept. 11, 1992, pp. 785-808.

[16] Gorder, *op. cit.*, p. 94.

[17] Fact sheet on the religious right from People for the American Way (undated).

[18] For background, see "School Choice," *The CQ Researcher*, May 10, 1991, pp. 253-276, and "Religion in Schools," *The CQ Researcher*, Feb. 18, 1994, pp. 145-168.

[19] Edward E. Gordon with Elaine H. Gordon, *Centuries of Tutoring: A History of Alternative Education in America and Western Europe* (1990), p. 263.

[20] *Ibid.*, p. 281.

[21] Testimony before the Interim Study Committee on Compulsory Attendance, Iowa State Education Association, Sept. 30, 1988.

[22] Van Galen and Pitman, *op. cit.*, p. 143.

[23] Guterson, *op. cit.*, p. 107

[24] Van Galen and Pitman, *op. cit.*, p. 149.

[25] Gorder, *op. cit.*, p. 90

[26] Gordon, *op. cit.*, p. 308.

[27] Van Galen and Pitman, *op. cit.*, p. 59.

[28] Gorder, *op. cit.*, p. 58.

[29] Quoted in Llewellyn, *op. cit.*, p. 308.

[30] Ramsey, *op. cit.*, p. 20.

[31] See "Home-School Movement Gives House a Lesson," *CQ Weekly Report*, Feb. 26, 1994, p. 479.

[32] *Prairie: A Bulletin on Parental Rights and Responsibilities in Education*, April 1994.

[33] "God Answers the Prayers of His People," *News Issues & Updates*, National Center for Home Education, February/March 1994.

[34] The case was *New Life Baptist Church Academy v. Town of East Longmeadow*.

[35] Testimony before the Senate Judiciary Committee, July 15, 1994.

[36] For more on charter schools, see "Parents and Teachers Battle Public Schools By Starting Their Own," *The Wall Street Journal*, May 19, 1994.

[37] Gorder, *op. cit.*, p. 108.

[38] Patricia Lamson, "Home Schooling," *The School Administrator*, January 1992, p. 27.

[39] Guterson, *op cit.*, p. 6.

Bibliography

Selected Sources Used

Books

Gorder, Cheryl, *Home Schools: An Alternative,* Blue Bird Publishing, 1990.

This author of books on business and social issues began home schooling her children because she and her husband traveled frequently, but she ended up embracing home education for philosophical as well as pragmatic reasons. She surveys the historical, legal, academic and practical considerations.

Gordon, Edward E., with Elaine H. Gordon, *Centuries of Tutoring: A History of Alternative Education in America and Western Europe,* University Press of America, 1990.

A historian and a librarian at DePaul University in Chicago have assembled a detailed history of tutoring and non-mainstream education, including a discussion of home schooling in early America.

Guterson, David, *Family Matters: Why Home-schooling Makes Sense,* Harcourt Brace Jovanovich, 1992.

A Bainbridge Island, Wash., high school English teacher surveys the state of modern education while agonizing over his ongoing dilemma of educating his own children at home while earning his living in public schools.

Hendrickson, Borg, *Home School: Taking the First Step,* Mountain Meadow Press, 1989.

A 17-year veteran of public school teaching describes the disillusionment that led her to embrace home schooling. This manual offers advice on curriculum selection, student assessments and state laws and procedures, including a state-by-state description of the climate for home-schoolers.

Kaseman, M. Larry, and Susan D. Kaseman, *Taking Charge Through Home Schooling: Personal and Political Empowerment,* Koshkonong Press, 1990.

Leaders of the Wisconsin Parents Association, a home-schoolers' group, offer advice on how to get started with home schooling, with particular emphasis on how average parents in informal home-schooling networks can mobilize to affect public policy.

Llewellyn, Grace, *Real Lives: Eleven Teenagers Who Don't Go to School,* Lowry House, 1993.

A former English teacher in Eugene, Ore., has compiled and edited these essays from adolescents who are being home-schooled. Writes one: "The world is full of interesting things. So much is happening everywhere and so much has happened through history, that I can't understand why kids are made to sit in classrooms and have everything interpreted to them through other people."

Pride, Mary, *The Big Book of Home Learning, Vol. 3, Teen and Adult,* Crossway Books, 1991.

This volume in a popular series by an Illinois-based writer includes reviews of available home-schooling curricular materials on a wide range of academic subjects, as well as "character education." She takes a conservative, Christian view.

Van Galen, Jane, and Mary Anne Pitman (eds.), *Home Schooling: Political, Historical and Pedagogical Perspectives,* Ablex Publishing, 1991.

Two professors of education prepared this anthology of major scholarship on the growing home-schooling movement, covering sociological, pedagogic, cultural, philosophical and legal aspects.

Wade, Theodore E. Jr., and others, *The Home School Manual: For Parents Who Teach Their Own Children,* Gazelle Publications, 1986.

A veteran home-schooler has assembled writings from home-schooling families who offer up their own experiences and advice, including what types of families should try home schooling and how to work with local authorities.

Articles

Knowles, J. Gary and James A. Muchmore, "From Pedagogy to Ideology: Origins and Phases of Home Education in the United States, 1970-1990," *American Journal of Education,* February 1992.

Two University of Michigan scholars review the sociological and pedagogic evolution of the modern home-schooling movement.

Reports and Studies

Home School Legal Defense Association, *The Home School Court Report,* March-April 1994.

A magazine-style report from a Virginia-based advocacy group recounts in detail the state-by-state participation of home-schoolers in the February 1994 lobbying effort that blitzed Capitol Hill with calls and faxes demanding passage of an amendment protecting home-schoolers.

Lines, Patricia M., "Estimating the Home Schooled Population," working paper, U.S. Education Department, October 1991.

A senior research analyst at the Education Department summarizes her pioneering work in estimating the growth and size of the home-schooling movement, using mostly surveys of home-schooling organizations and curriculum providers.

The Next Step

Additional information from UMI's Newspaper & Periodical Abstracts database

Certification Requirements

Kuntz, Phil, "Home-schooling movement gives House a lesson," *Congressional Quarterly Weekly Report,* Feb. 26, 1994, pp. 479-480.

Convinced that the House was about to require home-schooling parents to be government certified, thousands of concerned religious conservatives besieged members with phone calls, letters and faxes.

Mathis, Nancy, "U. S. House removes teacher provision," *Houston Chronicle,* Feb. 25, 1994, p. A14.

House members voted 424-1 to strip an education bill of a provision requiring schools to certify that their teachers are qualified to teach their assigned subjects, a clause interpreted by some home schools and private school backers as an attempt to license them as well.

Pitsch, Mark, and Lynn Schnaiberg, "Soldiering on," *Education Week,* March 2, 1994, p. 19.

The controversy in the House over the Elementary and Secondary Education Act and its effect on home schooling is discussed. HR6 requires school districts to certify by 1998 that teachers in selected disciplines are certified to teach in their subjects.

"The right runs amok," *NEA Today,* April 1994, p. 3.

A nine-line amendment to the Elementary and Secondary Education Act proposed by Rep. George Miller, D-Calif., is discussed. The legislation was immediately killed after several groups saw the amendment as an attempt to force those who teach their children at home to be certified teachers.

Curriculum and Instruction Materials

Colfax, David, and Micki Colfax, "The three R's," *Country Journal,* January 1994, pp. 45-47.

Advice and materials needed for starting one's child on home education in reading, writing and arithmetic are presented. Since home-educated children don't need to be sorted, a lot of individual attention can be paid, the authors write.

Lawton, Millicent, "Borrowing from the basics," *Education Week,* April 20, 1994, pp. 32-33.

For years, Baltimore's Calvert School has sold its kindergarten-through-eighth-grade home-instruction curriculum and instructional advice to parents and students all over the world. The Barclay School, a predominantly African-American neighborhood elementary school in Baltimore, has been using the curriculum and instructional program in a four-year, $400,000 experiment.

Marshall, Lisa, "Home schoolers not absent at education exposition," *Denver Post,* March 12, 1994, p. B2.

Catering to parents who want to teach their children at home, vendors at the News4 Education Expo at the Colorado Convention Center displayed books, videos, curriculum guides and other school supplies for the would-be parent-teacher.

"Valley Brook helps fill the gaps," *USA Today,* April 6, 1994, p. D5.

Valley Brook Academy in Silver Spring, Md., offers support for homeschooling with a menu of tough-to-teach-at-home electives. A $50 monthly fee gets home-school parents support with state regulations and curriculum planning.

Funding

Davis, Kristin, and Kim Quillen, "The economics of teaching your kids at home," *Kiplinger's Personal Finance Magazine,* July 1993, p. 30.

Many parents who have been disappointed by the public schools have turned to home schooling. Parents who educate their children at home must learn their state's legal requirements, choose a curriculum and plug into a local support group for home-schoolers, the authors write.

Dickerson, Ann, "Parent wants free testing for home-schooled kids," *Atlanta Constitution,* April 14, 1994, p. XJ.

Bill Webster of Peachtree City, Ga., who schools his two children at home, says the Fayette County system should allow his children to take state-mandated standardized tests free of charge. The system says it cannot afford to offer the testing to an estimated 200 home-schooled students.

Larson, Elizabeth, "Lesson time," *Reason,* June 1994, p. 16.

The Bennett Valley School District in Santa Rosa, Calif., has a new program that subsidizes home schooling. Most support the program, but there have been critics as well.

Lindsay, Drew, "Board backs charter for home-schooling academy in Mich.," *Education Week,* May 11, 1994, p. 3.

A Michigan school board has approved a publicly funded charter school for home-schooling students throughout the state. The board's decision will probably be challenged in court.

Government Regulation

Alpert, Bruce, "Schools bill hits a nerve," *Times-Picayune,* Feb. 24, 1994, p. AB1.

Legislation expected to sail through the House concerning a record $12.5 billion aid package for schools has hit a snag with Christian educational groups, religious broadcasters and organizations advocating home teaching. The bill and opposition to it are discussed.

Bell, Lydia, "Home schooling choices available," *Times-Picayune,* Nov. 4, 1993, p. OTG1.

Louisiana law permits home schooling as long as the lessons covered are the same as in the public schools. Guidelines and suggestions for parents considering home-schooling are presented.

Kennedy, John W., "House learns civics lesson," *Christianity Today,* April 4, 1994, p. 76.

The House of Representatives dropped a controversial proposal that would have put an end to home schooling. The Home School Legal Defense Association was instrumental in seeing that this amendment in the Improving America's School Act was defeated, Kennedy writes.

Mathis, Nancy, "Home school advocates jam Capitol phones," *Houston Chronicle,* Feb. 24, 1994, p. A10.

A nationwide protest was sparked by a provision in the Improving America's Schools Act that required school districts receiving federal funds to have all their full-time teachers certified in the subjects they were teaching. The protesters saw the provision as a potential threat to private and home schools.

Judicial Considerations

Benjaminson, Wendy, "Home schools win court fight," *Houston Chronicle,* June 16, 1994, p. A1.

The Texas Supreme Court has upheld parents' right to educate their own children, ending a decade-long legal battle over the state's authority to monitor home schools.

Goldberg, Stephanie B., "Education begins at home," *ABA Journal,* August 1993, p. 87.

Court decisions in *Michigan v. Bennett* and *Michigan v. DeJonge* simultaneously undercut and bolster the parental right to teach their children at home, Goldberg writes. Details on the two cases are offered.

Henderson, Alma C., "The home schooling movement: Parents take control of educating their children," *Annual Survey of American Law,* 1991, pp. 985-1009.

The constitutional foundations upon which parents assert the right to control their children's education by teaching them at home are examined. Home schooling is constitutionally supported, and severely restrictive home-education requirements unconstitutionally burden a parents' rights to control their children's education, Henderson writes.

Rothman, Robert, "Court Strikes S.C. Testing Requirement for Home Schoolers," *Education Week,* Jan. 8, 1992, p. 31.

The South Carolina Supreme Court threw out a state requirement that parents must pass a test in order to teach their children at home. Experts consider this a victory for "fair and appropriate testing."

Opinions

"Asides: Capitol flood," *The Wall Street Journal,* March 2, 1994, p. A10.

A brief editorial notes that hundreds of thousands of calls flooded Capitol Hill switchboards to protest a bill that would require all teachers, including those who instruct their kids at home, to be certified. The editorial concludes that home-schooling parents not only taught their kids, but Congress as well.

"Hands off," *Houston Chronicle,* Feb. 25, 1994, p. A22.

An editorial asserts that requiring teacher certification for private, parochial and home-school educators would represent an unwarranted federal intrusion in an area of education which appears to be functioning satisfactorily.

"Home school hitch," *Houston Post,* June 23, 1994, p. A30.

An editorial says that the Texas Supreme Court's decision affirming the right of parents to educate their children at home instead of sending them to public or private schools should also be complemented by a set of standards that will ensure that children are being legitimately educated.

Nelson, Tom, "Home is where the best education is," *The Wall Street Journal,* June 10, 1994, p. A11.

Nelson argues that children can be better socialized in a family setting in which there are many ages and points of view than they can by interacting in a peer group.

Pace, Nadine, "Parents' voices heard on home schooling," *St. Louis Post-Dispatch,* April 8, 1994, p. C11.

Nadine Pace comments on the rewards of home education and discusses Missouri and federal law governing the practice.

Saunders, Debra J., "House of wimps, home of schools," *San Francisco Chronicle,* March 2, 1994, p. A18.

Debra J. Saunders writes that an amendment to require teacher certification was used by Michael Farris, president of the Home School Legal Defense Association, to cry wolf and scare parents into thinking it might be used to require certification of home school and private school teachers.

Reasons for Home Schooling

Coyle, Pamela, "When school stays home," *Times-Picayune,* Dec. 20, 1993, p. A1.

At least five families in one Covington, La., neighborhood teach their children at home and are members of a support group with about 100 families that is starting a buddy system to pair veteran home schoolers with novices, Coyle writes. Concerns about values and violence are sparking the home-school movement, she writes.

Toch, Thomas, "The Exodus," *U.S. News & World Report,* Dec. 9, 1991, pp. 66-77.

Many parents view the public schools as ineffective and dangerous to their children and are exploring their options before it's too late, Toch says. Options to public schooling are discussed, including parochial schools, preparatory schools and home schooling.

Back Issues

Great Research on Current Issues Starts Right Here...Recent topics covered by The CQ Researcher are listed below. Before May 1991, reports were published under the name of Editorial Research Reports.

FEBRUARY 1993
Community Policing
Europe's New Right
School Censorship
Violence Against Women

MARCH 1993
Gay Rights
Aid to Russia
War on Drugs
TV Violence

APRIL 1993
Head Start
High-Speed Rail
Children's Legal Rights
Muslims in America

MAY 1993
Cults in America
Preventing Teen Pregnancy
Software Piracy
National Parks

JUNE 1993
Food Safety
Prostitution
Childhood Immunizations
National Service

JULY 1993
Electric Cars
Population Growth
Downward Mobility
Intelligence Testing

AUGUST 1993
Mental Illness
Bilingual Education
Foreign Policy Burden
School Funding

SEPTEMBER 1993
Suburban Crime
Public Housing
Supreme Court Preview
Immigration Reform

OCTOBER 1993
Airline Safety
Disaster Response
Science in the Courtroom
The Glass Ceiling

NOVEMBER 1993
Paying for Retirement
Charitable Giving
Privacy in the Workplace
Adoption

DECEMBER 1993
U.S. Vietnam-Relations
Learning Disabilities
Child Care
Space Program's Future

JANUARY 1994
Racial Tensions in Schools
South Africa's Future
Worker Retraining
Regulating Pesticides

FEBRUARY 1994
Prison Overcrowding
Water Quality
Religion in Schools
Juvenile Justice

MARCH 1994
Underground Economy
Education Standards
Gambling Boom
Private Management of Public Schools

APRIL 1994
Reproductive Ethics
U.S.-China Trade
Soccer in America
Talk Show Democracy

MAY 1994
Traffic Congestion
Women's Health Issues
Mutual Funds
Political Scandals

JUNE 1994
Education and Gender
Gun Control
Public Land Policy
Nuclear Arms Cleanup

JULY 1994
Dietary Supplements
Public Opinion and Foreign Policy
Crime Victims' Rights
Birth Control Choices

AUGUST 1994
Genetically Engineered Foods
Electing Minorities
Prozac Controversy
College Sports

Back issues are available for $4.00 (subscribers) or $7.00 (non-subscribers). Quantity discounts apply to orders over ten. To order, call Congressional Quarterly Customer Service at (202) 887-8621.

Binders are available for $16.00. To order call 1-800-638-1710. Please refer to stock number 648.

Future Topics

- ***Welfare Reform in the States***
- ***Courts and the Media***
- ***Tobacco Update***

THE CQ Researcher

PUBLISHED BY CONGRESSIONAL QUARTERLY INC.

Welfare Experiments

Are states leading the way toward national reform?

Reflecting widespread dissatisfaction with the national welfare system, Bill Clinton pledged an "end to welfare as we know it" during the 1992 presidential campaign. Now it appears unlikely that Congress will act this year on the welfare reforms proposed by Clinton. That means the states will continue to set the pace on reform. In recent years the states have been experimenting with a wide range of programs — from limiting benefits to two years to denying additional benefits to welfare parents who have more children. Some observers say these and other state experiments, typically being tested in one or two counties or communities, will show the country what works and what doesn't. But others question the use of states as testing grounds at the expense of people in need.

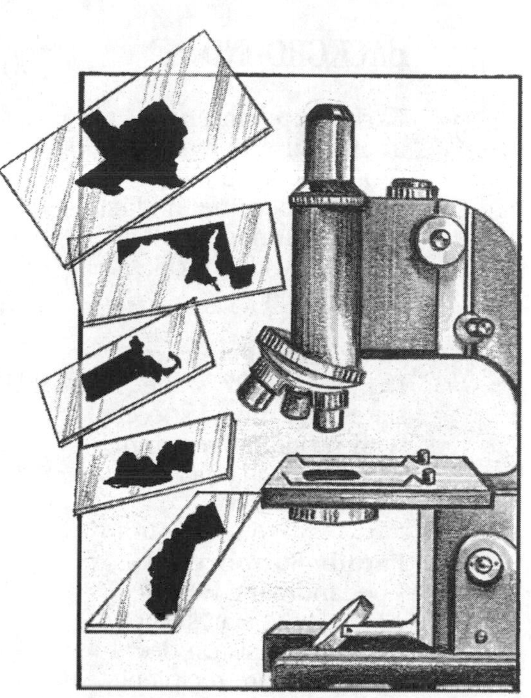

INSIDE THIS ISSUE

CQ Sept. 16, 1994 • Volume 4, No. 34 • Pages 793-816

Formerly Editorial Research Reports

WELFARE EXPERIMENTS

THE ISSUES

BACKGROUND

CURRENT SITUATION

OUTLOOK

SIDEBARS AND GRAPHICS

FOR FURTHER INFORMATION

COVER ART: BARBARA SASSA-DANIELS

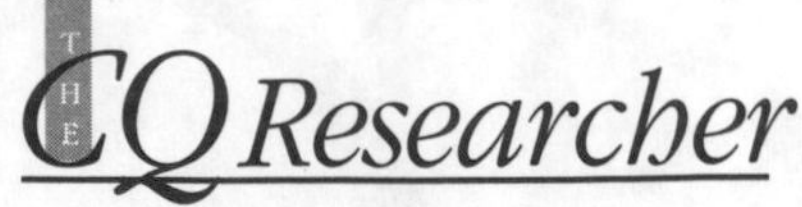

September 16, 1994
Volume 4, No. 34

The CQ Researcher (ISSN 1056-2036). Formerly Editorial Research Reports. Published weekly (48 times per year, not printed the first Friday of any month with five Fridays) by Congressional Quarterly Inc., 1414 22nd St., N.W., Washington, D.C. 20037. Rates are furnished upon request. Second-class postage paid at Washington, D.C. POSTMASTER: Send address changes to The CQ Researcher, 1414 22nd St., N.W., Washington, D.C. 20037.

Welfare Experiments

BY SUSAN KELLAM

THE ISSUES

For six decades, one program has stood as the cornerstone of U.S. welfare efforts: Aid to Families with Dependent Children (AFDC), the federal-state partnership that supports needy children. Now most observers think it's time to overhaul the $25 billion program. *

AFDC was born during the Depression, when the goal of welfare was to provide benefits to needy women and children without forcing mothers to work. Today, however, there is a growing feeling among most Americans that welfare recipients should be weaned from benefits and into jobs. As candidate Bill Clinton said during the 1992 presidential campaign, "Welfare should be a steppingstone, not a way of life."

This new attitude toward welfare has prompted most of the states to launch their own cutting-edge welfare experiments in recent years. The wide-ranging experiments, including some two dozen permitted under special "waivers" of AFDC rules, embrace a simple goal: to reduce dependence on welfare by putting people back on their feet. For example:

- Vermont cuts off benefits after 30 months and places recipients in public service or community jobs.
- Utah provides a one-time cash payment — in lieu of monthly checks — along with access to child care, health care and other services.
- Oregon plans to replace welfare checks and food stamps with commensurate salaries in private-sector jobs.

Through these and other experiments, typically being tested in one or two counties or communities, the states are trying to devise techniques for reducing their growing welfare caseloads. (*See graph, p. 796.*) Ten years ago, for example, fewer than 4 million families received welfare. Currently, 5 million families, about 14 million people, get an average monthly benefit of $374 per family. [1]

In the blunt assessment of A. Sidney Johnson III, executive director of the American Public Welfare Association, "The current system is broken."

This July, a nationwide survey by the National Governors' Association (NGA) underscored the states' commitment to welfare reform. Throughout the country, according to the NGA, 48 states and the commonwealth of Puerto Rico have set up welfare initiatives that go beyond those programs required by federal law. [2]

Among the initiatives are programs established under the trail-blazing Jobs Opportunities and Basic Skills Program (JOBS). Passed in 1988, JOBS offers states matching funds to create their own welfare-to-work programs, giving the states considerable flexibility to design programs offering such services as education, job training, job placement and child care. In Riverside County, Calif., a program known as Greater Avenues for Independence (GAIN) was credited with saving $2.84 in welfare expenses for every $1 invested in the job-training program (*see p. 802*). [3]

"We're learning that states are extremely eager to reform the welfare system," says Mary Jo Bane, assistant secretary for children and families at the Department of Health and Human Services (HHS), who oversees the granting of AFDC waivers. "They, too, want to orient their welfare systems toward work."

To David T. Ellwood, assistant HHS secretary for planning and evaluation, the experiments are fulfilling the vision of Justice Louis D. Brandeis, who saw the states as "laboratories of democracy."

"We really see the states as laboratories," says Ellwood, a former colleague of Bane's at Harvard University. "There's so much we've learned by watching the states. . . . Some things are better to observe on a small scale."

Bane, a former commissioner of social services in New York state, says the experiments can't be fully evaluated yet since "many have not been operating long enough to get clear results."

Some observers contend that the failures will be as important as the successes. "The waivers are designed to provide us with seriously evaluated projects," Johnson says. "If it makes sense, then take it nationwide. If not, I'd rather learn it in two counties in some state."

Douglas Besharov, a resident scholar at the conservative American Enterprise Institute (AEI), agrees. "I'm an old-fashioned Whig," he says. "I like to see something tested small first."

Others question the use of states as testing grounds at the expense of people in need. Mark Greenberg, a lawyer at the liberal Center for Law and Social Policy, argues that the states are "often testing only marginally different experiments. . . . It's very possible that at the end of five years of evaluation we will know nothing.

---

* Federal funds cover from 50 percent to 80 percent of the cost of cash grants to recipients, depending on a state's poverty rate.

Welfare Cases and Costs on the Rise

The number of families receiving benefits from the Aid to Families with Dependent Children program has risen steadily since 1970 (graph at left), along with the amount of federal and state contributions to the program (graph at right). The 5 million families enrolled in 1994 include nearly 10 million children, or 13 percent of all U.S. youngsters.

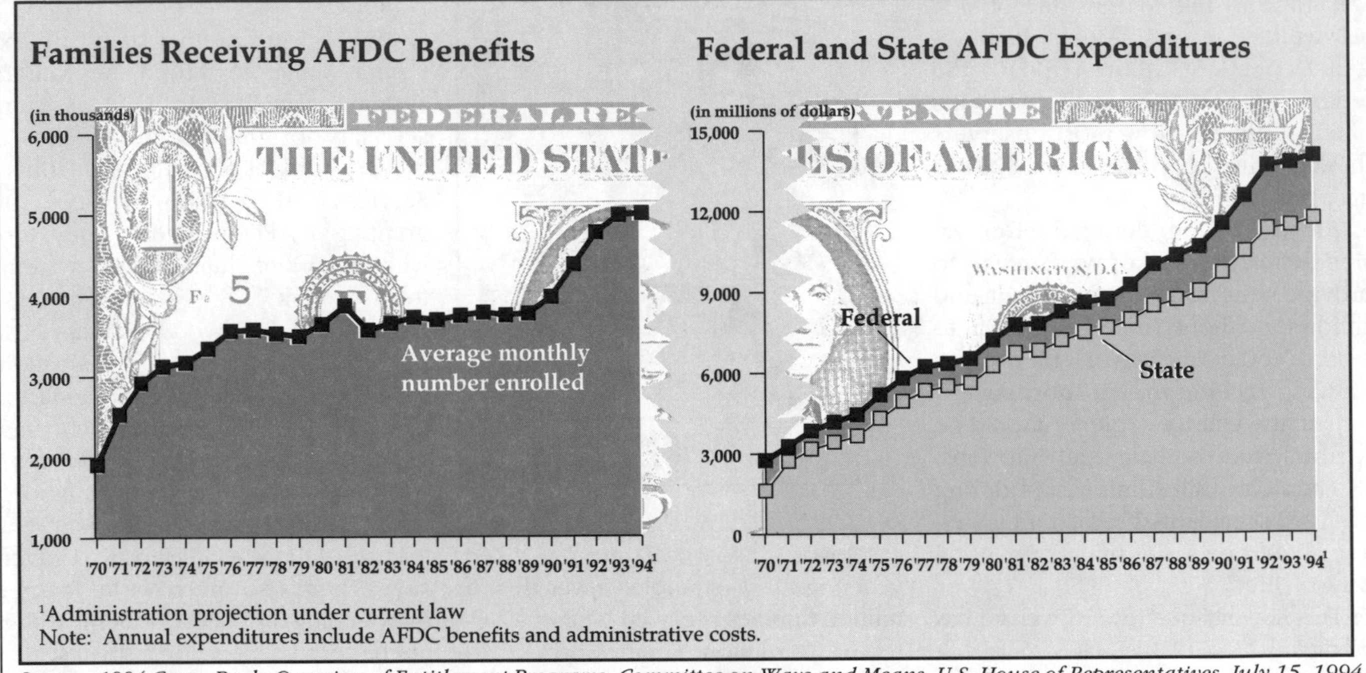

Source: 1994 Green Book: Overview of Entitlement Programs, Committee on Ways and Means, U.S. House of Representatives, July 15, 1994.

What we will have is chaos."

Ellwood counters that each experiment is different, even if the general policy outlines are similar. "It may be that some programs are tested in rural areas while another is in an urban setting," he says. "We've tried to encourage states to go in different directions."

Robert Rector, a senior analyst at the conservative Heritage Foundation, stands at the other end of the ideological spectrum from Greenberg. Rector describes many of the state efforts, including Riverside's acclaimed GAIN program, as "public relations farces."

Rector argues that the "bottom line on all of these reforms is that they don't have the right issue. The real issue is whether or not we find it significant that we're moving toward an even higher number of out-of-wedlock births. If that's all right, then we can continue to tinker around with these public relations exercises."

In fact, several state experiments touch on out-of-wedlock births as well as many aspects of family life. New Jersey, for example, pioneered the controversial "family cap," which seeks to limit the size of welfare families by restricting additional payments to mothers who give birth while on welfare. Forty-two states are experimenting with changes that allow families to earn more without reducing their AFDC grant; * 30 states are exploring ways to create jobs for AFDC recipients; and 25 states are considering two-year welfare cutoffs and work requirements similar to those proposed in President Clinton's welfare-reform proposal (*see below*). Several states are even testing electronic welfare cards similar to those used in automated teller machines.[4]

The welfare community has mixed feelings over the process for granting waivers for experimental projects. Bane says she bases her evaluations on what can be learned from the demonstration. "We want the project to be consistent with the objectives of the Social Security Act — support for children deprived of the support of their parents. We also want to help move families toward self-sufficiency," she says.

Actually, waiver requests are rarely turned down, and that occurs only when a state submits a plan that has been adjudged unconstitutional. In a case that drew wide attention, the Supreme Court in January rejected an attempt by California to limit the benefits paid to welfare recipients who had lived in the state only a short time. Based on that ruling, HHS nixed an Illinois experiment with similar limits.[5]

Johnson, whose bipartisan APWA represents local and state welfare

---

* Current AFDC rules reduce a family's AFDC grant by a dollar for every dollar the family earns.

agencies, would rather see a quicker, smoother route to state experimentation. The current waiver process is too "rigorous and cumbersome," he says.

Greenberg says he worries that the states now view waivers as "a matter of right." With states having such power, he argues that safeguards should be built into the process to protect needy children and families from losing vital benefits.

As a former governor who long argued for state flexibility, President Clinton has pledged to approve most experiments, even if he does not agree with them.

Under Clinton's proposed welfare overhaul — the Work and Responsibility Act of 1994 — many demonstration projects now being carried out by states under AFDC waivers would become state options. Those include the family cap as well as various incentives to keep young welfare recipients in school. The Clinton administration says the plan would cost about $9.3 billion more than the current program over five years. [6]

In the next few months, even as Clinton's proposal takes center stage, the ongoing work of the states will remain central to the debate over the nation's welfare system. As the discussion intensifies, these are some of the issues being considered:

Are some states going too far in cutting off benefits to the poor?

States scrambling to save tax money and reduce their welfare rolls have initiated a number of programs that some observers view as punitive and intrusive. Others say it's unfair to criticize a state initiative that may reduce benefits without first looking at the whole picture. That includes the supplementary services that are being offered to wean recipients from monthly checks to self-sufficiency.

Several states viewed by some observers as "hard-nosed" are triggering the debate:

Susan Kellam

Child-care services at Delaware's Northeast State Service Center make visits easy for Lonniea Peterson and her son Rakeem.

• In Wisconsin, the conservative Republican governor, Tommy G. Thompson, pioneered welfare experimentation in 1988 with his "Learnfare" program, which cuts government aid to families when their teenagers miss too many days of school. (*See story, p. 806.*) Now he wants to replace AFDC with a far less generous program.

• In Maryland, families can lose some AFDC benefits if they fail to immunize their children or to keep them in school and if they don't pay the rent on time.

• In Ohio, financial penalties are used to promote school attendance among pregnant and parenting teenagers on welfare.

• In California, Gov. Pete Wilson, a Republican, is attempting an across-the-board cut in AFDC benefits.

• In New Jersey, a two-year-old "child exclusion" rule, or family cap, denies additional cash aid to parents who have children while receiving benefits.

Such programs raise the hackles of welfare advocates, who accuse the states of experimenting on poor people, in effect punishing them for missing school or having babies. Meanwhile, they say, some states are spending millions of AFDC dollars on questionable programs, such as those that offer job training in areas where there are few available jobs.

Critics have sued to stop the experiments in California and New Jersey, and they are threatening suits in Wisconsin and several other states.

A San Francisco Superior Court judge issued a preliminary injunction in early August blocking a 2.3 percent reduction in AFDC payments that was to go into effect in California on Sept. 1. [7] A California Supreme Court decision on Aug. 30 backed the lower court. [8]

Greenberg applauds the court decision. Under the guise of calling it a research experiment, he says, California has "cut benefits indiscriminately." Welfare has been one of the main areas targeted for spending cuts by Wilson and the California Legislature in recent years as the state wrestles with its budget deficit.

New Jersey's child-exclusion rule has prompted a suit on behalf of eight

The "Waiver" and JOBS Programs at a Glance

Waivers: A 1962 amendment to the Social Security Act of 1935 allowed the states to design and run their own experimental welfare programs, but only if they received "waivers" of the rules regulating participation in the Aid to Families with Dependent Children (AFDC) program. The amendment authorized the secretary of Health and Human Services (HHS) to waive AFDC rules for "any experimental, pilot or demonstration project" that promoted AFDC program objectives, such as allowing AFDC recipients to earn more money and still receive benefits or encouraging teenagers in AFDC families to stay in school.

Only in recent years, however, have states begun to seek waivers. Since 1990, some two dozen states have received waivers permitting a wide range of programs. (*See story, p. 804.*)

Experimental or demonstration projects permitted under waivers must be "cost neutral" to the federal government, or cost no more than existing programs, and participating states must agree to rigorous evaluations of their experiments.

JOBS: The Family Support Act of 1988 included a provision creating the Job Opportunities and Basic Skills (JOBS) program, which helps states to provide education, job training and employment to welfare recipients. States are given flexibility regarding design and administration of their own JOBS programs.

States must match between 17 percent and 40 percent of federal JOBS funds with state and local dollars, depending on each state's poverty rate.

The 1988 legislation required each state to implement a JOBS program by Oct. 1, 1990. While all but a few states met the deadline, several with financial problems were unable to put up all the matching funds needed to get their full share of federal funding, according to Mary Jo Bane, assistant secretary for children and families at the U.S. Department of Health and Human Services.[1]

In fiscal 1993, the states claimed only about 70 percent of the eligible federal funds; only 16 states claimed their full allocations.[2]

In fiscal 1992 and '93, states were required to enroll at least 11 percent of AFDC families in their JOBS program — up from 7 percent in fiscal 1991. To meet these new requirements, 34 states expanded their JOBS programs.[3]

[1] Testimony before the House Education and Labor Subcommittee on Human Resources, April 19, 1994.

[2] Overview of Entitlement Programs: *1994 Green Book,* House Committee on Ways and Means, July 15, 1994.

[3] *Ibid.*

welfare recipients by the state chapter of the American Civil Liberties Union (ACLU), the state Legal Services Corporation and the National Organization for Women. State officials say the rule reduces the birth rate among welfare recipients; the advocacy groups counter that by withholding aid, the state is conducting "harmful research" on human subjects without their consent.[9]

Greenberg is particularly concerned about Maryland's Primary Prevention Initiative. Approved in 1992, it reduces a family's benefits by $25 per child each month if they do not adhere to federal immunization schedules.[10] He argues that AFDC "is a system that had never before asked whether the child was immunized." Now, he says, with no real understanding that the rules of the program have changed, a mother can unwittingly lose the money she needs to feed and clothe her children.

One shouldn't criticize a state's attempt to link welfare with behavior too quickly, admonishes Ellwood, who admits he learned from his own experience that "sometimes an experiment can surprise you."

Ellwood says that he had initially been skeptical of Ohio's Learning, Earning and Parenting (LEAP) program, which penalizes welfare recipients who don't go to school. Now he applauds it. LEAP is only the second statewide effort to enforce a school-attendance mandate for all teen parents on welfare. (Wisconsin was first.) "Sometimes carrots alone are not enough," Ellwood says. "Recipients need to be pushed."

LEAP has reached more than 20,000 eligible teens since its 1989 launch. A study released in April 1993 noted a significant increase — 10.3 percentage points — in the number of teens who stayed in school during the 12 months after entering LEAP.[11]

Ellwood has written that the program "appears to provide powerful evidence for an incentive-based strategy."[12] But Ellwood also notes that such penalty-based initiatives work only if accompanied by counseling and support programs. He believes a fundamental principle must be focused on when considering changes to welfare: "People playing by the rules should be able to make it."

AEI's Besharov believes that social-policy analysts "must put all the components together before saying whether a state is being punitive or not." He defends Wisconsin's attempts to reduce benefits by pointing out that the state has provided considerable assistance in the areas of job training and child care.

Johnson doesn't view states as treading ethical boundaries in their experiments. "If I looked across the board at all the waivers, I might see some I would question . . . but you have to look at the waivers compared to the status quo — that's what isn't working. Everyone wants [the welfare system] changed," he says.

At the Heritage Foundation, Rector

bristles at the idea that some states may be launching a backdoor war on the poor. "The word 'punitive' is wrong when talking about putting limits on free handouts," he says. "It's hard to call gifts punitive."

Should major changes to the welfare system be left to the states?

The federal-state AFDC partnership embraces a good deal of state-to-state variation in how the program operates. Most experts agree that a major overhaul of the welfare system shouldn't tamper with this basic equation.

As the system now exists, the federal government is the major benefactor to welfare offices throughout the country. Yet AFDC benefit levels are set by the states and vary quite dramatically. This year, maximums for a family of three range from $120 per month in Mississippi to $680 per month in Connecticut. To receive their AFDC funding, the states must heed an extensive array of federal regulations and rules, including submission of a plan to prevent payments to former recipients.

A few members of Congress feel that the states should be unshackled from their federal constraints. In fact, last March a group of Republican senators proposed a radical revamping of state and federal funding responsibilities. Under the new plan, states would take over control of welfare programs, and the federal government would pay a greater share of Medicaid costs. The lead sponsor of the legislation, Sen. Nancy Landon Kassebaum, R-Kan., said the proposal would free states to custom-design welfare programs that work for them.

The proposed swap in responsibilities calls for the states to assume full responsibility for funding AFDC, food stamps and the special supplemental food program for Women, Infants and Children (WIC). During the phase-in period for the changeover, state and federal governments would be required to maintain current levels of funding for welfare programs, and the federal government would kick in a little extra for state Medicaid costs.

Sen. Joseph I. Lieberman, D-Conn., has introduced legislation making states the central players in a national overhaul strategy, but without significant changes to the funding formula. His bill would ease conditions for granting waivers for state experiments. Most particularly, it would provide additional funding to the states to initiate these projects. Current rules require the state experiments not to cost the federal government any additional expense — to be "budget neutral."

Lieberman told his colleagues March 15 that his proposal "provides the flexibility, resources and guidance states need to implement innovative solutions not ready for application at the national level. It makes states full partners in our efforts to put people back to work, strengthen families, reduce teenage pregnancies and reinvent the welfare bureaucracy."

Among welfare activists, there's considerable debate over how to strike the right balance between state flexibility and federal standards.

A complete removal of all federal standards "would be a prescription for disaster," Greenberg says. He warns that poor states like Mississippi, which provides the lowest welfare benefits in the nation, might further reduce assistance to the poor. Nonetheless, he agrees with Lieberman that states should be free to launch welfare experiments that don't have to heed the federal budget-neutrality rule.

AEI's Besharov says that leaving welfare reform to the states "is an exceedingly good idea. The federal government doesn't really bring very much to the program except money." He disagrees with Greenberg that poor states might view a lack of federal mandates as an opportunity to deny aid. "The world has changed a lot since the 1960s," Besharov says, when discrimination toward the poor was more prevalent.

The United States is "a large, diverse country with very different welfare needs and different communities with differing values," he says. For example, he notes, there are large parts of West Virginia with virtually no jobs, rendering a welfare-to-work program nearly impossible to carry out. "You just can't have a government in Washington talking about kicking someone off the welfare rolls in Seattle," he says. "Different communities value different things."

"We believe states should be given substantial flexibility in shaping programs because needs and conditions vary," says the APWA's Johnson, speaking for welfare administrators across the country. "But there must be a basic national goal," and federal control. The National Governors' Association also asserts that state experiments "should not necessarily take the place of national reform." [13] ■

BACKGROUND

Early Experiments

Policy-makers have known for decades that when it came to infusing the nation's welfare system with an old-fashioned work ethic, the hard part would be up to the states. The challenge for the federal government was to provide the states with the right tools — financial and legislative — to do the job.

Ever since passage of the Social Security Act of 1935, the federal Treasury has been tapped to match a given percentage of state welfare payments. Title IV of the act established what was then called Aid to Dependent Children (ADC), a cash benefits program for children whose parents could not support them. [14]

It has been mutually beneficial to the states and the federal government

John F. Kennedy

to continuously explore options for reducing welfare expenditures.

Consequently, when President John F. Kennedy delivered a welfare message to the nation on Feb. 1, 1962, he set out two broad goals: to fight poverty with larger welfare payments and to encourage states to place a heavy emphasis on vocational training that would ultimately enable people to get off welfare. Congress passed major amendments to the Social Security Act that year incorporating the president's two aims.

Provisions designed to encourage self-support included more federal funds for welfare research, demonstration projects and training state welfare personnel.

Little noticed at the time, the 1962 amendments also allowed the federal government to waive, "for experimental, pilot or demonstration projects," state compliance with the ADC program, renamed that year as Aid to Families with Dependent Children. It was not until the 1980s that states would begin to take advantage of the waiver process. [15]

The first federally sponsored work requirement stemming from the 1962 legislation was the AFDC-funded Community Work and Training Program (CWT). States could require two-parent households deprived of financial support due to unemployment to "work off" the assistance they received at a community job. CWT remained a small program, except in West Virginia, which enrolled hundreds of unemployed men in public-sector jobs. [16]

However, the 1962 amendments generally failed to generate the kinds of social services, such as counseling and guidance, that would give welfare recipients an opportunity for independence. Bane and Ellwood have noted that a major problem was the lack of training among the staffs of local welfare offices.

"Though the Social Security amendments of 1962 had an important impact on the deployment of welfare workers," they wrote, "the goal of promoting self-sufficiency with a network of professional caseworkers remained elusive." [17]

Work Incentive (WIN) Program

The subject of AFDC work requirements came up again in 1967, when Rep. Wilbur D. Mills, D-Ark., chairman of the House Ways and Means Committee, blamed the states for the continued growth of the welfare rolls. Indeed, the number of recipients had grown 36 percent during the previous five years. [18]

Reacting to the increases, lawmakers in 1967 passed legislation creating the Work Incentive (WIN) program. Among other things, WIN required every state to participate in a program offering work training and work incentives to all AFDC recipients. It also mandated that states provide child-care services to program participants.

Defending WIN, Mills told his colleagues: "We want the states to see to it that those who are drawing [welfare checks] as unemployed fathers or drawing as mothers . . . take training and then work. Is there anything wrong with that?" [19]

To state and local officials, there was indeed something wrong. Many welfare workers found the WIN program cumbersome to administer. And the failure of social workers to enroll recipients was blamed in part on the program's skimpy funding. Nationwide, only about 173,000 people enrolled in any WIN activity between July 1968 and June 1970. [20]

The dismal statistics prompted Congress to put some teeth into the new program. In 1971 they amended the original WIN law to require all able-bodied AFDC recipients to register for the program. The amendment placed a new emphasis on employment-based training, which in turn required reallocation of funds: Under the new law, one-third of program funds were to be devoted to on-the-job training or public service employment. Compared with the first years of the program, WIN in the 1970s was considered a success in boosting enrollments and emphasizing employment-related activities.

'Workfare' Programs

During the 1970s, the states had mixed success with demonstration programs that required AFDC recipients to work in exchange for welfare

Continued on p. 802

Ronald Reagan

Chronology

1930s *The Depression throws millions of Americans into poverty, with no comprehensive policy in place for delivering aid and services to the needy.*

1935
Title IV of the landmark Social Security Act creates Aid to Dependent Children (ADC), a program to give the states matching federal funds "to assist, broaden and supervise existing mothers' aid programs."

1960s *The nation focuses anew on poverty with the goal of helping Americans to get off welfare and become self-sufficient.*

1962
President John F. Kennedy sets out two broad welfare goals: to fight poverty with larger welfare payments and to encourage more vocational training for Americans receiving welfare. An amendment to the Social Security Act allows states to request waivers of federal welfare rules "for experimental, pilot or demonstration projects." The same legislation renames the ADC program as Aid to Families with Dependent Children (AFDC), and permits states to require unemployed adults to participate in community work and training programs as a condition of AFDC aid to their families.

1967
Legislation creates the Work Incentive (WIN) program, which requires every state to offer worker training and work incentives to all AFDC recipients.

1970s *States have mixed success with demonstration programs that require AFDC recipients to work in exchange for welfare benefits. Programs in California and Massachusetts encounter administrative difficulties, legal challenges and staff opposition. Utah's Work Experience and Training (WEAT) demonstration project is small but successful in getting welfare recipients to work.*

1971
The WIN law is amended to require all able-bodied AFDC recipients to register for the program.

1980s *President Ronald Reagan advocates strict work requirements for AFDC recipients. A number of states start experimenting with welfare-to-work programs.*

1981
Congress rejects Reagan's proposal to require states to operate a Community Work Experience Program (CWEP) as a condition of receiving AFDC. But lawmakers give states greater latitude in administering WIN and in imposing work requirements

1987
The Manpower Demonstration Research Corporation evaluates a number of state programs and reports that most of them produce positive employment and earnings gains for welfare recipients. In some cases, there is also a reduction in state welfare outlays.

1988
The growing success of state welfare-to-work experiments translates into passage of the Family Support Act, which Reagan calls a "reform that will lead to lasting emancipation from welfare dependency." The legislation creates the Job Opportunities and Basic Skills (JOBS) program. One of the first federal waivers of AFDC rules goes to Wisconsin's "Learnfare" program, which reduces AFDC benefits if there is unreasonable truancy among the teenagers in an AFDC family.

1990s *A national recession hinders state efforts to implement the new JOBS program. States begin exploring new options for reforming welfare, including controversial "family caps" and looser earnings rules. President Clinton introduces his federal welfare reform plan.*

1992
President George Bush pledges in his State of the Union address to encourage and support state experimentation on welfare. The Department of Health and Human Services grants nine waivers.

Jan. 18, 1994
The U.S. Supreme Court strikes down a welfare experiment in California that seeks to limit the benefits paid to welfare recipients newly arrived from out of state.

June 1994
President Clinton introduces his $9.3 billion welfare program, known as the Work and Responsibility Act. It proposes a two-year time limit on welfare benefits followed by a transition into the workplace or community jobs.

JuJuanna Earl-Perkins' Prospects Were Slim . . .

Applying for welfare benefits five years ago wasn't a big deal to JuJuanna Earl-Perkins of Wilmington, Del. "I thought it was a reward," she recalls. "It was money. Those I grew up with were on it. My mother was on it."

The alternative to welfare, she adds, was back-breaking work at a printing plant where, for $5 an hour, she often had to carry heavy stacks of paper. "I just wasn't being treated like a human being," she says. "It was the lack of respect that finally pushed me to apply for AFDC."

Susan Kellam

JuJuanna Earl-Perkins (right) and Carmen R. Nazario, secretary of Delaware's department of Health and Social Services.

Earl-Perkins easily qualified: At age 18, she was unmarried and had a 2-year-old son, Antonio. After her eligibility for Aid to Families with Dependent Children was established, Earl-Perkins learned that welfare in Delaware didn't stop with a monthly check.

Enrollment in an educational program was required, and her caseworker sent her off to get her general equivalency diploma (GED) at the New Castle County Learning Center.

But that was only the beginning for Earl-Perkins, largely because Delaware has an active Jobs Opportunities and Basic Skills (JOBS) program (*see p. 803*). After completing her GED classes through JOBS, she was referred to Delaware Technical and Community College for eight weeks of training in "life skills." Earl-Perkins learned more than just how to write a résumé or present herself to a prospective employer. "I got to know a little bit about myself," she says.

Then she enrolled at the community college for another three years, this time for a degree in human services. Along the way she received regular monthly benefit payments, child care and Medicaid. But those days are over. She's now off AFDC and working for the state as a social worker/case manager.

In April 1986, three years before Earl-Perkins opted for the welfare route, Delaware's department of Health and Social Services (HSS) implemented its First Step Employment and Training Program. The fledgling initiative got its first federal dollars through the Work Incentive Demonstration (WIN) program (*see p. 800*).

After the Family Support Act was signed in 1988, First Step became a model JOBS program, giving new welfare recipients education and training along with financial resources.

By 1990, about $1.1 billion in federal dollars was available under the JOBS program to states capable of putting up matching funds. In Delaware, the federal government provided $1.8 million for Delaware's JOBS program last year, and the state put in $978,558. [1]

Continued from p. 800

benefits, dubbed "workfare."

Utah's Work Experience and Training (WEAT) demonstration was small but appeared to have reached its goal of getting welfare recipients to work. Of the state's 1,153 WIN registrants, 45 percent were assigned to WEAT. By contrast, the California and Massachusetts programs encountered administrative difficulties, legal challenges and staff opposition. In California, only 4,760 AFDC recipients actually worked out of nearly 183,000 eligible individuals. In Massachusetts, where the program was targeted to unemployed men, only 350 out of a potential group of 3,120 showed up to work. [21]

The poor showing on work programs throughout the country started to change when Ronald Reagan became president in 1981. Reagan immediately advocated a much stricter work requirement than had ever been incorporated in WIN. Congress rejected Reagan's proposal to require states to operate a Community Work Experience Program (CWEP) as a condition of receiving AFDC. But lawmakers did give states greater latitude in administering WIN and imposing work requirements.

In the early 1980s, a number of states started experimenting with welfare-to-work programs aimed at correcting WIN's shortcomings. In most cases, these programs were operated by the state welfare departments under federal waivers of the WIN rules.

The Massachusetts ET [Employment and Training] Choices Program was much-heralded. Although participation in ET was voluntary, state officials claimed considerable success in attracting clients to take part in education, training and employment activities. Proponents of ET claimed large employment gains and welfare savings. But Massachusetts' welfare caseload only went down 5 percent, a drop comparable to decreases in states without such

. . . Until Delaware's Welfare System Came to the Rescue

Delaware now operates 12 multi-service centers that serve as one-stop facilities for individuals and families seeking federal aid. At the Northeast Service Center in Wilmington, Delawareans can apply for welfare, receive food stamps and meet with a trained career counselor. There are also facilities at the center for child and elderly care.

"We're one of the few states who have really taken advantage of the JOBS money to help our clients find their niche in life," says Delaware HHS Secretary Carmen R. Nazario. "Smaller states like Delaware don't benefit from economies of scale. Here, we're just a few people carrying out the program from concept to fruition."

A few people, perhaps, but proud ones. The architects of the First Step program boast of offering such special features as counseling to help welfare recipients develop positive self images, and individualized instruction to help participants overcome daily challenges, such as balancing parenting and getting off to work in the morning.

Computers play a role, too. Qualified applicants for AFDC are automatically referred to First Step for education and job training. Then the system tracks the recipients' progress and ultimately provides listings of available jobs.

Former Gov. Michael N. Castle, now a Republican member of the House of Representatives, told his colleagues in a floor speech on Nov. 19, 1993, that more than 2,100 persons have used First Step — including 1,500 who were able to leave the welfare rolls entirely.

Gov. Thomas R. Carper, a Democrat who switched places with Castle in the 1992 elections (Carper had held Delaware's only House seat), is now pushing to take First Step a step further. A new program, A Better Chance, unveiled in March, would help the working poor by encouraging them to take better advantage of the federal Earned Income Tax Credit. To encourage families to stay together, the new program would also ease the rules limiting family earnings.

A Better Chance would, however, impose a two-year time limit on those enrolled in First Step employment and training programs, with the understanding that the training provided would result in a job or community service. Failure to participate in First Step would result in reduced AFDC benefits.

Carrying out Carper's blueprint for welfare reform would be much easier for Nazario with passage of a national welfare reform bill. That's because several of Carper's proposals would require waivers of AFDC rules, which can take several months to obtain. Part of the waiver-approval process involves showing that the experiments would not cost more than the current state program. That's a hoop that Nazario is not keen about jumping through, what with all the costly analysis involved.

"I'm very interested in seeing the [Clinton] Work and Responsibility Act happen," she says. "It would accommodate all of our waiver options." For example, without the national legislation, a federal waiver would be needed for Delaware to change the rules to allow families with incomes below the poverty level to keep more earnings and child support.

Nazario is a strong supporter of the need for federal welfare policy. "Fifty experiments wouldn't work," she says. But she is quick to add that Delaware already is ahead of the other states: "Our welfare ethic is already changed toward work."

[1] "Delaware's First Step Employment and Training Program: An Overview," Delaware department of Health and Social Services, June 1994.

"workfare" programs.

"Especially given the great strength of the Massachusetts economy during the period that ET was implemented," Bane and Ellwood noted, "the 5 percent drop in caseloads suggests that even an enthusiastically implemented and well-managed work-welfare program on this model is likely to have only a modest impact on who goes off welfare and how fast." [22]

In the early 1980s, another pioneering experiment in workfare, the Baltimore Options Program, claimed moderate success. Still serving AFDC clients, it offered job-search assistance, education and training programs, on-the-job training and 13 weeks of work experience.

The most impressive gains from a work-to-welfare program were racked up by California's Greater Avenues for Independence program. In Riverside County, the GAIN program was operated exceptionally well, according to Bane and Ellwood. The county commissioner was passionately committed to the program and set high expectations for both workers and clients.

This June, after three years of study, the effectiveness of the GAIN program in training welfare recipients for jobs was clearly established. In six counties throughout the state, 33,000 AFDC recipients were either assigned to GAIN or kept from participating. After three years, GAIN participants earned 25 percent more a month than non-participants, or an average of $636 a month. [23]

Family Support Act

By 1985, 47 states had adopted at least one of the options approved by Congress that were geared to putting welfare recipients to work. Virtually all the states relied heavily on job-search assistance programs. Some states, such as Massachusetts and California,

Welfare Pioneers Among the States

While many states are in the process of planning and developing welfare experiments, several pioneers already have embarked on a wide variety of efforts to restructure their welfare systems. The table below identifies states that have implemented significant changes in the Aid to Families with Dependent Children (AFDC) program and the date the changes were implanted.

Treatment of Earnings or Assets: To encourage recipients' self-sufficiency, several states increase the earnings family members can have without reducing their AFDC grants; extend the period of time a parent can receive a salary and still qualify for welfare; increase the amount of assets a family can save; and raise the limit on the value of the vehicle a welfare family can own.

Alabama	7/90	Alaska	5/93
California	12/92	Colorado	6/94
Florida	5/94	Illinois	11/93
Iowa	10/93	Michigan	10/92
Minnesota	4/94	New Jersey	8/93
North Carolina	7/93	Ohio	4/94
South Dakota	5/94	Utah	1/93
Vermont	7/94	Virginia	2/94
Wyoming	10/93		

Time Limits on Benefits: Several initiatives require AFDC recipients to work after a transition period of assistance. Programs include both strict and flexible timetables and placement in public-sector employment or community service.

Colorado	6/94	Florida	5/94
Iowa	1/94	Michigan	10/93
South Dakota	5/94	Vermont	7/94

Job Creation for AFDC Recipients: Strategies include diverting AFDC grants to subsidize wages; employing and training recipients to rehabilitate public housing; training AFDC recipients to create their own small businesses; and combining AFDC and food stamp benefits to create subsidized jobs.

California	6/86	Connecticut	1/94
Florida	5/94	Illinois	9/92
Iowa	1/88	Michigan	1/89
Minnesota	1/88	New Jersey	10/92
Pennsylvania	1/88	South Dakota	2/94
Utah	1/93	Vermont	7/94
Virginia	6/94	West Virginia	3/94

Support for Intact Families: Initiatives are designed to reduce the current penalties imposed on two-parent families, such as the "100-hour rule," which prohibits two-parent families from receiving AFDC if either of the parents works more than 99 hours per month, even if the family earns so little that it would still qualify for assistance.

Alabama	7/90	Alaska	5/94
California	12/92	Florida	5/94
Illinois	11/93	Iowa	10/93
Michigan	10/92	Minnesota	4/94
New Jersey	10/92	Utah	1/93
Virginia	4/94	Wisconsin	10/91

Family Cap on AFDC Benefits: Initiatives seek to deny families additional cash grants, or cut the grants they receive, if additional children are born after a family begins receiving AFDC.

Georgia	1/94	New Jersey	10/92
Wisconsin	7/94		

Source: "Final Report: Survey of State Welfare Reforms," National Governors' Association, July 1994. The report contains a complete listing of states that are planning or have implemented initiatives in a dozen areas.

also offered education, vocational training and support services. About half the states operated CWEP for at least some AFDC recipients. [24]

During the Reagan era, many states succeeded in increasing employment rates and producing some interesting results. The Manpower Demonstration Research Corporation (MDRC) evaluated a number of the state programs and reported that most of them produced positive employment and earnings gains for AFDC women. In some cases, there was also a reduction in state welfare outlays. MDRC concluded that the benefits of running the programs generally outweighed the costs. [25]

For policy-makers accustomed to negative results from social welfare experiments, this was good news. The information was also timely. Reagan and many congressional leaders were committed to welfare reform during the time the studies were released.

In the late 1980s, the momentum translated into the landmark Family Support Act, which Reagan signed on Oct. 13, 1988. The president called the massive welfare overhaul a "reform that will lead to lasting emancipation from welfare dependency." [26]

The new act ordered the states to put new emphasis on developing self-sufficiency, following in the footsteps of such innovative state programs as ET and GAIN. The tool provided for changing the culture of the welfare system was the Job Opportunities and Basic Skills (JOBS) program. In contrast to WIN, JOBS required participation, not just registration. JOBS programs had to include instruction in basic skills, job-skills training and job development and placement. States are expected to provide child care and other supportive services as needed.

Unfortunately, these requirements went into effect during a very difficult time for states. During the late 1980s, a national recession led to increasing welfare caseloads and decreasing state revenues. In 1992, $1 billion was appropriated for JOBS, but states were only able to use about one-third of that amount because they could not provide the matching funds, according to Rep. Matthew G. Martinez, D-Calif. [27]

Bush Boosts Waivers

Meanwhile, one of the states' most potent reform tools was being virtually ignored. Since 1962, states have had the right to request waivers from AFDC rules in setting up their own welfare experiments. But the waivers were seldom sought.

One of the earliest waivers went to Wisconsin's Learnfare program in 1988. Under Learnfare, the welfare benefits of parents on AFDC were reduced if there was unreasonable truancy among the teenagers in the family.

A year later, Ohio was granted a waiver for a program to improve school attendance among teenage parents. The Learning, Earning and Parenting (LEAP) program required all teen parents on AFDC to attend school or an educational program granting a diploma. Enrollment resulted in a monthly bonus of $62; failure to enroll brought a $62 reduction in benefits.

However, a new era began on Jan. 28, 1992, when President George Bush announced in his State of the Union address a commitment to encourage and support state use of the waiver process.

He told the nation: "States throughout the country are beginning to operate with new assumptions: that when able-bodied people receive government assistance, they have responsibilities to the taxpayer, a responsibility to seek work, education or job training; a responsibility to get their lives in order; a responsibility to hold their families together and refrain from having children out of wedlock — and a responsibility to obey the law. We are going to help this movement. Often, state reform requires waiving certain federal regulations. I will act to make that process easier and quicker for every state that asks our help." [28]

Above all, said Bush, waivers had to involve "rigorous evaluation" and be "cost neutral" to the federal government.

The states quickly responded to the call. In 1992 alone, HHS granted nine waivers. They went to California for two programs, one to cut recipients' benefits and another to block benefits to new residents (later struck down by the Supreme Court); Georgia and Maryland for preschool immunization projects; Michigan to make it easier for families to work and receive welfare; Missouri to expand the state's JOBS program to mandate school attendance; New Jersey for the controversial "family cap"; Oregon for expanding JOBS participation requirements; and Utah for a single-parent employment project. [29] ■

CURRENT SITUATION

Clinton's Proposal

After the difficult passage of the Family Support Act (FSA) in 1988, lawmakers understandably may have expected a respite from dealing with welfare-overhaul attempts. Getting that legislation through its final hurdles in 1988 had called for some strong lobbying from the governors, and one of the most aggressive efforts came from Bill Clinton of Arkansas. He was there in the Rose Garden when Reagan signed the bill into law.

"By 1993, however, welfare reform was once again on the agenda of the president and of most governors, as though the FSA had already become an irrelevance or a failure," wrote Bane and Ellwood. "By encouraging states to apply for waivers from federal mandates, the Bush administration had encouraged a wave of state experimentation with incentives and requirements aimed at shaping work and family formation." [30]

APWA's Johnson describes the Family Support Act as offering a "framework for reform." But as a major vehicle for changing the welfare system, he says the law has been "invisible."

Clinton, stumping the campaign trail to Washington, spoke loudly and clearly on the issue. He told voters he wanted to break the dependency that many observers linked to people who stayed on welfare too long. He talked about "empowering" Americans to leave welfare by giving them education, training and child care. There would also have to be some form of universal health protection. After a two-year transitional period, welfare benefits would be cut off.

Once in the White House, the new president tapped numerous experts, including Ellwood and Bane, to help him draft the type of sweeping plan that could deliver his campaign promises.

Working Paper Urged Caution

Ellwood had written a working paper on welfare reform in December 1992, not long before he joined the administration. In it, he suggests Clinton's bold plan should be introduced slowly in "a modest number of states," with more states gradually added "over time." He recommends more federal support for the participating states in exchange for radical reforms in their welfare systems.

In the paper, Ellwood laid out a six-point plan for the participating states:

- They would be required to de-

Wisconsin Continues to Try Welfare Experiments . . .

President Clinton may have vowed to "end welfare as we know it," but Wisconsin Gov. Tommy G. Thompson did him one better. The conservative Republican actually stamped an expiration date — Dec. 31, 1998 — on state participation in the Aid to Families with Dependent Children program.

"We think the best thing to do is to start afresh, rather than tinker around the edges," Thompson said last December, after signing the cutoff legislation. [1]

Wisconsin Gov. Tommy G. Thompson

The state has promised to set up a new program before its self-imposed 1998 deadline, using federal money. "It's not our intention to write off the federal dollars," says Gerald Whitburn, secretary of Wisconsin's Department of Health and Human Services. The conservative Hudson Institute in Indianapolis, Ind., is helping the department to devise its new approach to welfare.

Wisconsin, where 230,000 of the state's 5 million residents receive welfare benefits, has seen its caseload drop by about 60,000 recipients since 1986 — the year Thompson was elected governor. It is one of the few states where caseloads have actually declined in recent years.

Thompson is heavily favored to win a third term in November and continues to make welfare reform the centerpiece of his agenda.

"The constant Tommy Thompson drumbeat here has resonated across our state and is continuing to ripple, bringing dividends," says Whitburn. "There's a growing understanding among the AFDC population that it isn't business as usual any more."

The legislation to end the AFDC program in Wisconsin also created a new welfare-reform experiment — Work, Not Welfare, which begins Jan. 1, 1995, in Pierce and Fond du Lac counties with approximately 1,000 recipients. Under the experiment, families entering the welfare system will be required to find full-time work or enter a job-training program within 30 days of signing up for assistance. The program limits cash benefits to no more than 24 months over a four-year period; cash assistance would then be denied for the next three years. Child care is provided while parents work or receive training. [2]

Welfare advocates say there are fundamental differences between Work, Not Welfare and Clinton's welfare overhaul package.

"The president envisions that after . . . two years, assistance will be provided to a healthy individual only in return for work," writes attorney Mark Greenberg of the Center for Law and Social Policy. "For those who cannot find work in the private sector, community-service work will be provided. In contrast, [Work, Not Welfare] will terminate assistance to families when the parent is willing to work, actively looking for work and simply unable to find a job." [3]

Clinton stated in a February 1993 speech to the National Governors' Association that his administration would give states "more elbow room to experiment." But Greenberg argues that even recognizing Clinton's commitment to state flexibility, granting a waiver for Work, Not Welfare

---

velop policies that moved far larger numbers of people from welfare to work than past efforts.

- Welfare recipients' participation in work must be tracked.
- Some states would experiment with a CWEP-type work-for-welfare plan while others would be expected to implement time-limited welfare followed by a public/private jobs programs.
- All states must improve their child-support enforcement systems.
- Each program had to have a comprehensive evaluation plan.
- Federal matching funds for these program would be increased to 90 percent or more of state contributions.

This strategy, Ellwood wrote in "Major Issues in Time-Limited Welfare," would give the new administration the chance to pick the experimental states. "The reality is that we simply do not have all the answers about how to transform the welfare system," he wrote. "Serious time-limited welfare followed by jobs has never been tried."

Ellwood also pointed out the dangers: A state-by-state phase-in, rather than full-scale implementation, would make Clinton appear to be backing off on the sweeping promises of the campaign.

Even more of a problem, perhaps, was the likelihood that Clinton would be upstaged by members of Congress, including his own moderate Democrats. Clinton's attack on the welfare system invited other action plans: from Republicans, who wanted to show that they could take an even stronger stand on kicking people off welfare; from senators, who wanted the country to adopt the welfare plans initiated by their states; and from liberals, who didn't think it was fair to include a time-limit on welfare.

When Clinton finally delivered his Work and Responsibility Act to Con-

. . . as It Seeks New Ways to Reduce Caseloads

was "an exceedingly poor policy decision." He writes that it places state flexibility above the federal role in protecting poor families against extreme conduct and is unlikely to provide useful data to guide future federal policy decisions.[4]

Work, Not Welfare marks the seventh waiver that Wisconsin has received from the federal government since its pioneering "Learnfare" program was launched in 1988. That statewide project aims to ensure that more AFDC teenagers age 13-19 complete high school or its equivalent. If they do not attend school regularly, their family's welfare benefits are subject to reduction. The state recently found that during 1992 and '93, 97 percent of Learnfare teens complied with school attendance requirements.[5]

The state's other waiver experiments are just getting off the ground. In July, the state began the Parental and Family Responsibility Demonstration Project in six counties, limiting benefits for additional children born to welfare families. At the same time, the project liberalizes AFDC earning rules by allowing working parents to earn more without a reduction in benefits.

Wisconsin also received waivers this year to carry out statewide demonstrations to raise the federal AFDC asset limits so that welfare families can own more expensive cars and save more money. The goal is to provide the family with better transportation for work or training and the opportunity to save more money for educational advancement.

Wisconsin's benefits payments are the 12th highest in the country, providing a family of three, typically a parent and two children, $517 monthly. In neighboring Illinois, a similar family would receive $382; in Indiana, it would get $288.

To test whether its high benefits are attracting poor families from states with lower benefits, Wisconsin received permission to conduct a demonstration project. Beginning June 30 of this year, AFDC recipients from out of state received the same benefits as in their previous state during their first six months in Wisconsin.

"There has been a tremendous migration from Chicago to Wisconsin, and people resent picking up the tab," says Paul Soglin, mayor of Madison. "That is one of the reasons the governor has been given such a free hand in making changes to the welfare system."

Soglin, a Democrat and former anti-war protester, is often compared with the staunchly conservative Thompson in the local media. Nonetheless, he doesn't disagree with the governor on ending Wisconsin's role as a welfare magnet.

But Soglin disagrees with the governor on the meaning of the state's lower welfare rolls. "Are you going to judge success by a decrease in welfare rolls or by the elimination of poverty?" Soglin asks. "The disparity between the white and African-American populations is worse here than in any other state," he says. "And where the welfare rolls have been shrunk, there is not necessarily a reduction in poverty."

[1] Thompson signed the bill on Dec. 13, 1993. See "Wisconsin Pledges to Exit U.S. System of Public Welfare," *The New York Times,* Dec. 14, 1993, p. 1A.

[2] Wisconsin received a waiver for Work, Not Welfare from the U.S. Department of Health and Human Services on Nov. 1, 1993.

[3] Mark Greenberg, "On Wisconsin? What's Wrong With the 'Work Not Welfare' Waiver," Center for Law and Social Policy, February 1994.

[4] *Ibid.,* p. 19.

[5] "Wisconsin Welfare Reform: A Summary," Wisconsin department of Health and Social Services, June 1994, p. 4. For more on Learnfare, see "Learning From 'Learnfare' " in "Welfare Reform," *The CQ Researcher,* April 10, 1992, pp. 313-336.

gress in June, more than 300 legislative proposals were pending that touched on the welfare issue.

Clinton and Ellwood ultimately decided against starting with experimental states first. Instead, the legislation focused initially on younger women. The $9.3 billion plan would initiate a two-year time limit on welfare for women born after 1971.

The proposal does call for state demonstration projects, but those would occur in tandem with a major national welfare overhaul, rather than as isolated first steps. For example, the plan would allow up to five demonstrations with welfare cutoffs different from the two-year limit set out in the Clinton plan. There would be various demonstrations to encourage job placement through participation in the JOBS program, including placement bonuses to reward agencies or caseworkers who excelled at placing JOBS participants in private-sector jobs.

Now, sitting in his large office at HHS, Ellwood says that he was wearing a "different hat" when he drafted the working paper.

After traveling around the country as a member of the administration to see what the states are doing, he says too many states have "lost sight of the values of welfare." What's needed, he says now, is less tinkering at the state level and the "broad framework" of a strong national policy to get the system on keel.

States' Frustration

Some states would prefer the right to push welfare reform on their own, without federal officials peering over their shoulders. Oregon, for ex-

Key Clinton welfare advisers Mary Jo Bane, assistant HHS secretary for children and families, and David T. Ellwood, assistant HHS secretary for planning and evaluation.

ample, requested a federal waiver more than 10 months ago for Jobs Plus, a pilot workfare program the state wanted to launch in September.

Welfare recipients participating in the three-year program in six Oregon counties would be placed in private-sector jobs for nine-month stints. They would receive child-care assistance, health coverage and at least as much income as they got on welfare.

Their minimum-wage salaries would be paid through a combination of state funds and the money they now receive in the form of food stamps and welfare. Their employers would pay $1 an hour toward an education fund for each participant.

Delay over the program's approval irked Oregon Sen. Bob Packwood, a Republican. On July 13, at the Senate Finance Committee's opening hearing on the Clinton welfare-reform proposal, Packwood publicly scolded HHS Secretary Donna E. Shalala for the delay.

"We need this waiver, and it isn't fair for the administration to keep delaying [it]," Packwood said. "Our program is a shining example of what you want to achieve."

Shalala assured Packwood that the agency was still finishing up its recommendations and that there was "no problem."

"Just grant that waver," quipped Finance Chairman Daniel Patrick Moynihan, D-N.Y., and he would get Packwood to vote for the president's plan.

As of Sept. 12, Oregon was still waiting. Other states are equally frustrated. Massachusetts' Republican Gov. William F. Weld said that federal officials should "just get out of the way" and let the states experiment. [31]

Weld does not share the president's interest in job training or community work experiences. The Massachusetts plan he is pushing would kick welfare recipients off the rolls 60 days after signing up. Those who didn't find private-sector employment would have to accept public jobs through the state government. Weld predicts the state's caseload would drop by 50 percent within 18 months, saving taxpayers $360 million. [32]

But Massachusetts legislators don't buy Weld's plan. In June, both houses of the Democrat-controlled legislature rejected his reform package and passed an alternative that also promotes work and self-sufficiency. But that plan would increase spending by $22 million in the first year, so Weld vetoed it.

Paul Offner, an aide to Moynihan, wrote in *The New Republic* that "if Weld's own welfare proposal is any indication, a little federal oversight may not be such a bad idea." [33]

"By today's standards, though, Weld's proposal is hardly extreme," Offner continued. "All over the country, conservatives are concocting much harsher measures."

Wisconsin's Thompson would completely abandon the federal public welfare system. He signed a law last December that would withdraw the state from AFDC within five years and replace it with a yet-unspecified plan for public relief.

No state has sought to drop the federal welfare program since its inception during the Depression, and according to reporter Jason DeParle of *The New York Times,* Wisconsin's action "reflects the political turmoil engulfing the welfare system around the country." [34]

Meanwhile, welfare recipients in California will receive lower benefits this month despite court rulings against the reductions. The typical family of three on welfare will get $593, $14 less than before and $39 less than three years ago. Although California's Supreme Court blocked the action in August, the reduced checks to AFDC recipients were already in the mail; full welfare checks will be sent beginning in October, including the portions previously cut. [35] ■

OUTLOOK

Prospects for Change

If the unenthusiastic reaction to Clinton's health-care proposal is any barometer, Congress isn't likely to enact massive changes in welfare policy anytime soon. On Sept. 12,

Continued on p. 810

At Issue:

Is welfare a major cause of the increase in out-of-wedlock births?

yes

CHARLES MURRAY
Bradley Fellow, the American Enterprise Institute

FROM *TESTIMONY BEFORE THE HOUSE WAYS AND MEANS SUBCOMMITTEE ON HUMAN RESOURCES,* JULY 29, 1994.

Every once in a while, the sky really is falling, and this seems to be the case with the latest national figures on illegitimacy. The unadorned statistic is that, in 1991, 1.2 million children were born to unmarried mothers, within a hair of 30 percent of all live births. How high is 30 percent? About four percentage points higher than the black illegitimacy rate in the early 1960s that motivated [Sen.] Daniel Patrick Moynihan to write his famous memorandum on the breakdown of the black family. . . .

To restore the rewards and penalties of marriage does not require social engineering. Rather, it requires that the state stop interfering with the natural forces that have done the job quite effectively for millennia. Some of the changes I will describe can occur at the federal level; others would involve state laws. . . . I begin with the penalties, of which the most obvious are economic. . . .

Restoring economic penalties translates into the first and central policy prescription: to end all economic support for single mothers. The AFDC [Aid to Families with Dependent Children] payment goes to zero. Single mothers are not eligible for subsidized housing or for food stamps. An assortment of other subsidies and in-kind benefits disappear. Since universal medical coverage appears to be an idea whose time has come, I will stipulate that all children have medical coverage. But with that exception, the signal is loud and unmistakable: From society's perspective, to have a baby that you cannot care for yourself is profoundly irresponsible, and the government will no longer subsidize it.

How does a poor young mother survive without government support? The same way she has since time immemorial . . . she must enlist support from her parents, boyfriend, siblings, neighbors, church or philanthropies. . . .

We need to raise the probability that a young single woman who keeps her child is doing so volitionally and thoughtfully. Forcing her to find a way of supporting the child does this. It will lead many young women who shouldn't be mothers to place their babies for adoption. This is good. It will lead others, watching what happens to their sisters, to take steps not to get pregnant. This is also good. Many others will get abortions. Whether this is good depends on what one thinks of abortion. . . .

The reforms I have described will work for blacks as for whites, and have been needed for years. But the brutal truth is that American society as a whole could survive when illegitimacy became epidemic within a comparatively small ethnic minority. It cannot survive the same epidemic among whites.

no

ROBERT GREENSTEIN
Executive Director, Center on Budget and Policy Priorities

FROM *TESTIMONY BEFORE THE HOUSE WAYS AND MEANS SUBCOMMITTEE ON HUMAN RESOURCES,* JULY 29, 1994.

The welfare reform debate has broadened in recent months from a debate primarily about how best to move people from welfare to work to one that also includes discussion about the large numbers of children born outside of marriage. The enlargement of the debate reflects, in part, increasing awareness of the large and growing proportions of births occurring out of wedlock. . . .

Some argue that welfare is the primary cause of the rise in births outside marriage and propose eliminating all support for single-parent families with children . . . Anyone concerned about the well-being of children must be deeply troubled by the increasing numbers of children born outside of marriage. And in dealing with this difficult question we must weigh the research in the area very carefully. We must understand what it shows and be careful not rush to embrace conclusions and policy prescriptions that are not supported by the weight of the evidence. . . .

First, if welfare were the principal cause of the rising tide of out-of-wedlock births, one would expect out of wedlock births to be increasing primarily among low-income, less-educated women. However, the rise in childbearing by unmarried mothers has occurred among high school graduates, those with college educations and school dropouts alike. . . .

The question of whether welfare is a major cause of the increase in out-of-wedlock births is not a new one. It has been studied extensively. Most studies in the area find little relationship between welfare benefits and out-of-wedlock births. Several welfare reform bills now before Congress contain provisions that relate to these issues. Two bills include provisions that would make certain categories of single-parent families ineligible for basic cash assistance. The "House Republican welfare reform bill" [HR 3500, sponsored by Minority Leader Robert H. Michel, R-Ill.] requires states to deny AFDC benefits to minor single mothers and their children unless a state passes legislation opting out of this provision. . . . The Real Welfare Reform Act, HR 4473, introduced by Rep. Jim Talent, R-Mo., goes still further. Under this bill, children born to unmarried mothers under age 21 — or older at state option — would be ineligible for AFDC, food stamps and housing assistance. . . .

Given the research in this field, there is no basis for assuming that provisions such as these would have dramatic effects on out-of-wedlock childbearing rates. One virtually certain effect, however, is that poor children would become poorer.

Controversy Over New Jersey's "Family Cap"

Of all the state welfare experiments, none has been as controversial as New Jersey's so-called "family cap." Under the two-year-old initiative, also known as the "family-exclusion" program, women who give birth while on welfare can't receive additional benefits, which amounts to $64 a month.

New Jersey's family cap is being adopted by several other states and already has been incorporated into President Clinton's welfare proposal as a state option.

However, in a suit against the New Jersey and federal governments, the National Organization of Women (NOW), the American Civil Liberties Union (ACLU) and the Legal Services Corporation contend the family cap violates the constitutional right of a woman to decide about childbirth without government involvement. Two conservative proponents of state-based welfare reform, the American Legislative Exchange Council and the Empowerment Network Foundation, filed a friend of the court brief in March supporting New Jersey's right to reform welfare as it sees fit. [1]

Attitudes about family caps, however, don't always fall along expected ideological lines. New Jersey's program was initiated by state Assemblyman Wayne Bryant, a liberal Democrat who represents Camden, where 70 percent of the residents receive some form of public assistance.

Bryant told CBS-TV's "60 Minutes" in May: "You don't go to a job and tell the person you're going to have a child, and all of a sudden they say, 'Well, thank God. I'm going to give you a raise.'. . . We're saying that the same kind of norms, the same kind of values, ought to be in our poverty system." [2]

Charles D. Hobbs, chief welfare adviser to former President Ronald Reagan, views caps on family size and other "punitive" measures as "counterproductive" because they don't seem to reduce welfare dependency. For three decades, he says, there have been various attempts at cutting back benefits for those recipients who don't heed program rules, but with little improvement in the welfare system. "It seems we shouldn't be talking welfare reform," he says, "we should be talking welfare replacement."

[1] "New Jersey Effort to Cut Welfare Gets Support in Federal Lawsuit," *The Washington Post,* March 4, 1994.

[2] Quoted on "60 Minutes," May 15, 1994.

Continued from p. 808

House Speaker Thomas S. Foley, D-Wash., told reporters there wasn't enough time to pass welfare reform before the November elections. [36] That means the states will continue — at least for the next year or so — to set the pace on welfare-to-work experimentation.

Furthermore, the administration has stipulated that health-care legislation must precede any national efforts to revamp welfare.

Clinton's Work and Responsibility Act is built on the premise that former welfare recipients would be protected by universal health coverage, as envisioned by his ambitious health-care package. Current rules cut recipients off Medicaid (health insurance for the poor) a year after they start in the workplace, when they are often unable to pay for health insurance themselves.

Hundreds of proposals were introduced in the 103rd Congress seeking to change various aspects of the welfare system, from how to control welfare recipients' earnings to how the system handles teenage pregnancy and out-of-wedlock births. "This is a time of enormous frustration," says Ellwood. "No one is happy with the status quo."

A number of welfare advocates say it's too soon for national welfare reform, especially along the lines outlined in Clinton's $9.3 billion proposal.

"We would be committing a substantial number of dollars into the untried," says Greenberg. He argues that none of the states have really put in place firm time limits on welfare followed by public-service jobs. Vermont received a waiver in 1992 to use AFDC grant money to create jobs by subsidizing wages for recipients who reach their time limit on benefits. However, the state legislature didn't approve the plan until January 1994, and it was not implemented until July.

"There just isn't a good set of experiments out there yet," says Greenberg. "The failure of the current waiver process is that it has not guided us to shape the next round of welfare reform."

Besharov agrees with Greenberg that there should be some experimentation on the two-year time limit before it is mandated nationwide. He's also disappointed in what the states are doing but adds the caveat: "We don't need a lot of innovators.

"We talk about the states leading the way, but it's only a handful leading," Besharov says.

Thus in the minds of many welfare experts, the question of who should be providing leadership on welfare reform — the federal government or the states — remains unanswered.

Meanwhile, there's also the question of how much flexibility should be given to the states to implement programs within any national program.

Rep. Michael N. Castle, R-Del., was instrumental, along with Clinton, in pushing through the last round of welfare changes in 1988. Their passionate involvement was understandable. Both men were governors then, overseeing very active welfare-to-work programs on a state level.

"I feel much more removed from anything sitting here in Washington," says Castle. He admits it was easier to envision changes to a system that he worked with every day.

Castle is a lead sponsor on a comprehensive welfare proposal put forward last fall by 160 House Republicans that, like the Clinton bill, puts a limit on receiving welfare. He makes it clear that he's borrowed directly from his state experience. "While our bill is a logical extension of the Family Support Act," Castle told his colleagues on the House floor on Nov. 19, 1993, "it is, in fact, and perhaps more importantly, an attempt to do nationally what has worked on the state level in Delaware." (*See story, p. 802.*)

Indeed, many governors take fierce pride in their own efforts. Back in 1987, when the nation's governors approved an ambitious welfare reform plan calling for every able-bodied recipient to work or get training, there was one dissenter — Wisconsin's Tommy Thompson. Thompson said at the time that his state already had an advanced system for aiding the poor and feared that adoption of a new federal policy would interfere with Wisconsin's efforts. [37]

A delay in national welfare reform could give states more time to exert or demand certain rights. For example, a small but growing number of governors is trying to organize a "Conference of States" next year to correct what they see as an imbalance in the federal-state relationship. And support for a summit on "a new federalism" is coming from both the National Governors' Association and the National Conference of State Legislatures.

"In order to challenge [Congress] and compete for their rightful role, states require a rallying event, a means of consolidating their power," said Gov. Mike Leavitt, R-Utah. [38]

APWA's Johnson strongly supports the rights of states to carry out welfare programs that work in a particular locality, but within a national framework. He's also anxious for something to happen on welfare sooner rather than later. "This is the right time for reform," he says. "There is no one solution. But now is the time to act. Everyone is energized around this issue now." ■

Susan Kellam is an assistant managing editor for Congressional Quarterly's Congressional Monitor. *She covered social-policy issues for* Congressional Quarterly Weekly Report.

Notes

[1] Overview of Entitlement Programs, *1994 Green Book,* House Committee on Ways and Means, July 15, 1994, p. 395.

[2] Julie Strawn, Sheila Dacey and Linda McCart, *Final Report: Survey of State Welfare Reforms,* The National Governors' Association, July 1994. Idaho and New Mexico did not respond to the survey.

[3] Manpower Demonstration Research Corporation, "GAIN: Benefits, Costs and Three-Year Impacts of a Welfare-to-Work Program," June 1994. MDRC is evaluating the JOBS program under an eight-year contract awarded in 1989 by the Department of Health and Human Services.

[4] Strawn, et al., *op. cit.*

[5] Richard Carelli, "High Court Says States Can't Limit Welfare for Newcomers," The Associated Press, Jan. 18, 1994.

[6] See Jeffrey L. Katz, "Long-Awaited Welfare Proposal Would Make Gradual Changes," *CQ Weekly Report,* June 18, 1994, p. 1622.

[7] *The Washington Post,* Aug. 20, 1994, p. A2.

[8] *Los Angeles Times* (Washington edition), Aug. 31, 1994.

[9] *The Washington Postt,* March 4, 1994, p. A7.

[10] For background, see "Childhood Immunizations," *The CQ Researcher,* June 18, 1993, pp. 529-552.

[11] "Interim Findings on a Welfare Initiative to Improve School Attendance Among Teenage Parents," Manpower Demonstration Research Corporation, April 1993, p. 5.

[12] Mary Jo Bane and David T. Ellwood, *Welfare Realities: From Rhetoric to Reform* (1994), p. 108.

[13] Strawn, et al., *op. cit.*

[14] For background, see "Welfare Reform," *The CQ Researcher,* April 10, 1992, pp. 313-336.

[15] *1962 Congressional Quarterly Almanac,* p. 215.

[16] Bane and Ellwood, *op. cit.,* p. 11.

[17] *Ibid.,* p. 11.

[18] *1967 Congressional Quarterly Almanac,* p. 895.

[19] *Ibid.,* p. 893.

[20] Thomas Brock, David Butler and David Long, "Unpaid Work Experience for Welfare Recipients: Findings and Lessons from MDRC Research," Manpower Demonstration Research Corporation, September 1993, p. 6.

[21] *Ibid.,* p. 7.

[22] Bane and Ellwood, *op. cit.,* p. 22.

[23] Manpower Demonstration Research Corporation, *op. cit.*

[24] Brock et al., *op. cit.,* p. 9.

[25] *Ibid.,* p. 10.

[26] *1988 Congressional Quarterly Almanac,* p. 349.

[27] Testimony during oversight hearings on JOBS before the House Education and Labor Subcommittee on Human Resources, April 19, 1994.

[28] *1992 Congressional Quarterly Almanac,* p. 10-E.

[29] Mark Greenberg, "1992 Welfare Waivers," Center for Law and Social Policy, Jan. 5, 1993

[30] Bane and Ellwood, *op. cit.,* p. 1

[31] National Public Radio, "Morning Edition," Aug. 26, 1994.

[32] *Ibid.*

[33] Paul Offner, "Critical Mass," *The New Republic,* Sept. 5, 1994, pp. 17-18.

[34] Jason DeParle, "Wisconsin Pledges to Exit U.S. System of Public Welfare," *The New York Times,* Dec. 14, 1993, p. A1.

[35] National Public Radio, "Morning Edition," Aug. 26, 1994.

[36] "House Speaker Declares Welfare Reform Dead for the Year," The Associated Press, Sept. 12, 1994.

[37] "Governors Vote a Plan Linking Welfare to Work," *The New York Times,* Feb. 25, 1987.

[38] Quoted in *The Washington Post,* Aug. 29, 1994, p. A19.

Bibliography

Selected Sources Used

Books

Bane, Mary Jo, and David T. Ellwood, *Welfare Realities: From Rhetoric to Reform,* Harvard University Press, 1994.

The writings in this collection represent nearly a decade in the work of the two experts President Clinton selected to shape his welfare proposals. Bane and Ellwood, both assistant secretaries at the Department of Health and Human Services, include writings they each did while teaching at Harvard University's John F. Kennedy School of Government. The authors detail the nature of welfare offices, discuss the history and dynamics of welfare and set out various policy proposals.

Gueron, Judith M., and Edward Pauly, with Cameran M. Lougy, *From Welfare to Work,* Russell Sage Foundation, 1991.

This book summarizes and interprets the research findings of the Manpower Demonstration Research Corporation, which evaluates current efforts to overhaul the welfare system and tries to determine whether welfare-to-work programs are effective.

Murray, Charles, *Losing Ground: American Social Policy, 1950-1980,* Basic Books, 1984.

Murray broke ground a decade ago when he held a magnifying glass up to the social programs many Americans took for granted. Murray raises a question that continues to plague social-policy experts: Why do social programs so often seem futile?

Articles

DeParle, Jason, "States' Eagerness to Experiment with Welfare Jars Administration," *The New York Times,* April 14, 1994.

DeParle tries to answer the question of what happens when two-thirds of the states try to run their own welfare experiments. He says that some of the waiver experiments put the Clinton administration in the tough position of approving requests that didn't necessarily jibe with White House policy.

Ramos, Dante, "Rats: Welfare Reform and Human Experimentation," *The New Republic,* Aug. 8, 1994.

Ramos asserts that if the groups currently suing New Jersey and the federal government over the state's "child-exclusion" rule win their case, shock waves will be felt far beyond the Garden State.

Gueron, Judith M., "The Route to Welfare Reform: From Welfare to Work," *The Brookings Review,* summer 1994, Vol. 12, No. 3.

The president of the Manpower Demonstration Research Corporation makes her case for why welfare reform should be phased-in over five years and then carefully evaluated to answer such questions as whether the two-year limit on benefits is feasible and whether jobs can be created.

Wiseman, Michael, "Welfare Reform in the States: The Bush Legacy," *Focus,* Institute for Research on Poverty, Wisconsin, Volume 15, Number 1, spring 1993.

Wiseman analyzes the waiver process that has spawned so many welfare experiments, viewing it from a historical and policy perspective.

Katz, Jeffrey L., "The New Vision of Welfare: Offer More, Demand More," *Congressional Quarterly Weekly Report,* June 5, 1993.

Katz provides an early look at state welfare experiments that served as models for President Clinton's reform proposal, especially those programs that tie benefits to obligations.

Reports and Studies

Brock, Thomas, David Butler and David Long, *Unpaid Work Experience for Welfare Recipients: Findings and Lessons from MRDC Research,* Manpower Demonstration Research Corporation, September 1993.

A thorough study of welfare-to-work programs that assigned AFDC recipients to community-service jobs as a condition of public assistance. The research indicates that it was feasible to operate unpaid work-experience programs on a limited scale.

***GAIN: Benefits, Costs, and Three-Year Impacts of a Welfare-to-Work Program,* Executive Summary, Manpower Demonstration Research Corporation, June 1994.**

This well-publicized report illuminated the effectiveness of California's Greater Avenues for Independence (GAIN) program and helped set the stage for President Clinton's welfare proposal, which calls for more resources for such welfare-to-work programs.

Levin-Epstein, Jodie and Mark Greenberg, *The Rush to Reform: 1992 State AFDC Legislative and Waiver Actions,* Center for Law and Social Policy, November 1992.

The authors look at some early state initiatives to reform welfare, including many of the proposals that seek to use fiscal bonuses or penalties to reward or punish behavior.

The Next Step

Additional information from UMI's Newspaper & Periodical Abstracts database

Limits on Benefits

Reed, Thomas F., "No more welfare as we know it?" *Detroit News,* June 30, 1994, p. A15.
Thomas F. Reed criticizes President Clinton's proposal to reform welfare, focusing especially on imposing a two-year limit on benefits for younger mothers on welfare, and expanded job-training and day-care services for families receiving grants.

Shaw, E. Clay Jr., and Lynn Woolsey, Lynn, "Big issues: Should Congress set time limits on welfare benefits?" *American Legion Magazine,* July 1994, p. 8.
The issue of whether Congress should set time limits on welfare benefits as part of a welfare reform bill is debated. One congressional representative argues that the present system encourages illegitimacy and non-work, but another argues that time limits are not the solution to the problem.

Stotzer, Bea Olvera, "Mothering isn't a two-year job," *Los Angeles Times,* July 8, 1994, p. B7.
Bea Olvera Stotzer states that the Clinton administration's proposed two-year limit on benefits for welfare mothers is cruel. Stotzer claims that instead of unleashing anger on the most vulnerable mothers, society should give mothers the option of working either outside or inside the home.

Wright, James, "CBC wary of Clinton welfare plan," *Afro-American,* June 25, 1994, p. A1.
The Congressional Black Caucus is wary of the Clinton welfare reform plan that would impose time limits on how long a family can receive benefits and force low-paying, low-skill jobs on the poor of the black community.

The Clinton Plan

Cohen, Deborah L., "Clinton offers plan to break welfare cycle," *Education Week,* June 22, 1994, p. 1.
President Clinton's welfare reform plan includes both penalties against and resources for young single mothers. He also hopes to enlist schools in a national campaign to prevent teenage pregnancy.

Katz, Jeffrey L., "Long-awaited welfare proposal would make gradual changes," *Congressional Quarterly Weekly Report,* June 18, 1994, pp. 1622-1624.
President Clinton's welfare proposal is discussed. The plan, which would make gradual changes to welfare benefits, was unveiled on June 14, 1994.

"Welfare reform in America: You say you want a revolution," *The Economist,* June 18, 1994, pp. 21-24.
Devising a plan to end the U.S.'s current welfare program has been hard for the Clinton administration. Passing a welfare reform proposal and making it work will be harder still. President Clinton's plan is discussed.

The Controversy Over Welfare

Dart, Bob, "Clinton's welfare plan hit from right and left," *Atlanta Constitution,* June 14, 1994, p. A1.
Both Democrats and Republicans are attacking President Clinton's long-promised welfare reform plan, but House Minority Whip Newt Gingrich, R-Ga., called it a $9.3 billion "step in the right direction" and pledged bipartisanship.

Frame, Randy, "Is welfare redeemable?" *Christianity Today,* June 20, 1994, pp. 44-45.
The debate over how best to proceed with welfare reform is examined, focusing on the Center for Public Justice's draft vision of welfare reform. Many undesirable consequences of welfare reform could emerge if reforms are not carefully thought out.

Waldman, Steven, "Taking on the welfare dads," *Newsweek,* June 20, 1994, pp. 34-38.
President Clinton's controversial new welfare-reform program limits benefits and is supposed to deter teenage pregnancies. The current welfare program is compared to President Clinton's proposed welfare program, and welfare dads tell their stories.

Weaver, Kent, "Old traps, new twists," *The Brookings Review,* summer 1994, pp. 18-21.
An examination of the Clinton administration's welfare reform plans and rival plans is presented, focusing on the problems that will inhibit true reform. The key to making progress on welfare reform is sustained work — by welfare recipients and those who design and implement policy, Weaver writes.

Demand for Welfare

Burgo, Barbara, "Rent reform — A resident's view," *Journal of Housing,* May 1994, pp. 6-7.
A resident of a public housing project in Richmond, Va., who got a job as a social work assistant at a local nonprofit center found that her rent increased and she lost her Medicaid health insurance and food stamps. She found that her income after taxes, rent, food and health-care costs was almost less than when she received public assistance.

Claiborne, William, "Substance abuse among welfare's young mothers," *The Washington Post,* June 28, 1994, p. A3.
More than a third of young mothers on welfare, the group targeted for intensive education and job training by

the Clinton administration's welfare reform proposals, are addicted to or abuse drugs and alcohol, according to a new study released by the Center on Addiction and Substance Abuse at Columbia University.

Offner, Paul, "Kid stuff: How deadbeat dads can reform welfare," *The New Republic,* Aug. 1, 1994, pp. 10-11.
Many women who are supposed to receive child support end up on welfare because of delinquent fathers, Offner writes. President Clinton's welfare reform proposals must go farther and require more state enforcement to alleviate the problem, he says.

Usdansky, Margaret L., "Births-welfare link is disputed," *USA Today,* June 24, 1994, p. A6.
As the controversy over welfare reform and illegitimacy has been heating up, researchers say that welfare benefits aren't the main reason out-of-wedlock births are rising; more relaxed attitudes toward sex, poor job opportunities and increasing acceptance of single parenthood had more effect on the rise of illegitimacy, Usdansky writes.

Family Caps

Brownstein, Ronald, "Welfare reformers confront out-of-wedlock births," *Los Angeles Times,* July 14, 1994, p. A15.
On July 13, 1994, the first congressional hearing on the Clinton administration's welfare reform plan debated whether or not to cut off benefits entirely to young women who bear children out of wedlock. The proposal is favored by conservatives, but some Democrats raised red flags on the issue.

Hall, Mimi, "Abortion foes, backers unite against welfare plan's caps," *USA Today,* July 7, 1994, p. A5.
When congressional staffers gathered for a briefing on welfare reform "family caps," they were met by an unlikely coalition: Abortion rights supporters and opponents, working together for the first time to oppose a White House proposal to deny additional benefits to women who have more children while receiving welfare.

Popiel, Leslie Albrecht, "Critics see welfare reform increasing U.S. abortion rate," *The Christian Science Monitor,* July 22, 1994, p. 3.
In an unusual show of agreement, groups traditionally split over the issue of abortion are rallying to condemn a provision in President Clinton's welfare reform proposal that would allow states to cap payments made under the AFDC program to any welfare mother who has a child while on welfare.

Federal Action

Katz, Jeffrey L., "Welfare overhaul hearing set; Action pegged to other issues," *Congressional Quarterly Weekly Report,* June 25, 1994, p. 1723.
The House Ways and Means Human Resources Subcommittee is gearing up for hearings on President Clinton's proposal for welfare reform. The prospect has been raised that Congress could approve legislation that would overhaul the welfare system, Katz says.

Pianin, Eric, "Welfare overhaul prospects brighten," *The Washington Post,* July 14, 1994, p. A11.
Senate and House Democratic leaders raised prospects of congressional action before the end of 1994 during a hearing on the president's $9.3 billion welfare reform plan.

Tabin, Barrie, "Welfare reform could deal new mandates for local governments," *Nation's Cities Weekly,* May 2, 1994, p. 4.
Overall, the Clinton administration has been thoughtful about drafting a proposal that would move individuals from welfare to work in order to achieve long-term self-sufficiency, Tabin writes. However, some of the proposals of the welfare reform bill may create additional unfunded mandates for cities, he says.

Opinions

"For all the children left behind, eradicate poverty, not welfare," *National Catholic Reporter,* April 1, 1994, p. 28.
An editorial agrues that the need to eradicate poverty greatly overrides the need to get rid of welfare. A good welfare reform plan would offer new employment opportunities and better education.

"Lies, damned lies, and welfare reform," *The National Review,* July 11, 1994, pp. 14-16.
An editorial says that President Clinton's welfare reform plan has fallen way short of his promise to "end welfare." Under his proposal, there will be no two-year limit and work requirements are practically non-existent.

"New player in the welfare game," *The New York Times,* July 18, 1994, p. A14.
An editorial praises a welfare reform proposal from Rep. Robert T. Matsui, D-Calif., that would build on the 1988 Family Support Act, which required states to begin providing job-search assistance, training, education, child care and transportation to ease able-bodied welfare recipients into paying jobs. The editorial recommends combining the Matsui proposal with President Clinton's proposal for time-limited benefits.

"Punting on welfare," *The Wall Street Journal,* July 18, 1994, p. A12.
An editorial addresses Clinton administration proposals to reform the nation's welfare system. The editorial says the welfare "investment" has cost the equivalent of 20 Marshall Plans, and is far from ending poverty, adding that the administration's sounds-good but content-light proposal indicates that while Washington can elevate an issue to national attention, real reform is most likely to occur at the state level.

"States should be allowed to seek welfare solutions," *Atlanta Journal,* June 14, 1994, p. A24.
An editorial argues that the best approach to welfare reform

is for the federal government to give the states wide latitude to experiment with their own programs, and, if successful, Congress would have a better guide to national approaches.

"Why should welfare be anti-marriage?" *Los Angeles Times,* July 10, 1994, p. M6.

As part of a series, an editorial applauds California's new "Wedfare" approach to welfare reform that will allow single mothers who must leave welfare because they have married or returned to an estranged spouse to keep child care and medical benefits for 18 months.

Zuckerman, Mortimer B., "Starting work as we know it," *U.S. News & World Report,* July 4, 1994, p. 72.

An editorial discusses the need to shatter welfare dependency and instead emphasize the value of work and self-sufficiency. If the Clinton administration's welfare reform plan fails, states should be given the chance to craft their own welfare reform initiatives.

State Action

Bivins, Larry, "House plan urges more state input on welfare," *Detroit News & Free Press,* July 3, 1994, p. A5.

A growing alliance of moderate House members, including Reps. Sander M. Levin, D-Mich., and Dave Camp, R-Mich., is pushing for legislation that will offer states more authority to reform welfare programs than President Clinton has proposed.

Ellis, Virginia, "Court invalidates '92 welfare cuts," *Los Angeles Times,* July 14, 1994, p. A1.

A federal appeals court on July 13, 1994, invalidated millions of dollars in California welfare cuts, saying government officials had failed to consider the hardship they would impose on poor families. The 2-1 ruling said the Bush administration violated federal law in 1992 by approving the cuts.

Ellis, Virginia, "In tightening welfare, state encourages marriage," *Los Angeles Times,* July 6, 1994, p. A1.

California legislators have quietly inserted in the state's spending plan a major revision in welfare policy that will make the state one of the few to provide financial incentives for recipients to get married.

Howe, Peter J., "Democrats urge Weld to accept welfare plan," *The Boston Globe,* July 8, 1994, p. 25.

Two key Democratic legislators urged Republican Gov. William F. Weld to back off threats to veto the Massachusetts legislature's welfare reform plan, but the lawmakers seemed far from certain a Weld veto would be overridden, Howe writes.

Kreck, Carol, "State welfare changes to aid foster children," *The Denver Post,* July 7, 1994, p. B1.

Colorado children adrift in foster care edged closer to being rescued with an agreement filed in federal court on July 5, 1994, to overhaul the state's child welfare system. The settlement forces timely investigation of all child-abuse reports and timely resolution of cases of children removed from parents' homes.

"Wilson administration to appeal court's invalidation of welfare cuts," *Los Angeles Times,* July 16, 1994, p. A20.

California Department of Social Services Director Eloise Anderson announced on July 15, 1994, that the Wilson administration will seek reconsideration by the full 9th U.S. Circuit Court of Appeals in San Francisco of a decision striking down millions of dollars in welfare cuts.

Welfare Reform Ideas

Conniff, Ruth, "Big bad welfare," *The Progressive,* August 1994, pp. 18-21.

Democrats and Republicans alike have declared a war on welfare. Some of the ideas being tossed around Washington, D.C., include orphanages, penalties for single motherhood and what some describe as the total destruction of the safety net, Conniff writes.

Gueron, Judith M., "The route to welfare reform," *The Brookings Review,* summer 1994, pp. 14-17.

The historical basis of welfare and how the balance between opportunity and obligation has changed are discussed in relation to the Clinton administration's welfare reform plan. The best welfare reform plan is one that is gradually phased-in and evaluated for its efficacy after five years.

Teepen, Tom, "Education ends welfare," *Atlanta Journal Constitution,* June 19, 1994, p. D7.

Tom Teepen says a sharp and urgent upgrading in education, especially preschool for the unprepared, day care that would open access to employment and universal health coverage that would make minimum-wage jobs more remunerative, will solve the welfare problem.

Women and Welfare

Gibbs, Nancy, Ann Blackman, James Carney and Richard Lacayo, "The vicious cycle," *Time,* June 20, 1994, pp. 24-33.

When young, single women have children, it almost guarantees they will be poor, the authors write. The deep-pocketed welfare system has ended up subsidizing disaster, and welfare reform may or may not break the pattern, they say. In an interview, President Clinton discusses his plans for welfare reform.

Nyhan, David, "Mother, can you spare that dime?" *The Boston Globe,* June 26, 1994, p. 73.

David Nyhan attacks the scapegoating of welfare mothers with regard to the debate over welfare reform.

Pollitt, Katha, "Subject to debate," *The Nation,* July 11, 1994, p. 45.

The relative silence of feminists on the subject of welfare reform and its impact on single mothers is examined. Feminists need to point out that it is in the self-interest of most working women to preserve and even expand AFDC, Pollitt writes.

Back Issues

Great Research on Current Issues Starts Right Here...Recent topics covered by The CQ Researcher are listed below. Before May 1991, reports were published under the name of Editorial Research Reports.

MARCH 1993
Gay Rights
Aid to Russia
War on Drugs
TV Violence

APRIL 1993
Head Start
High-Speed Rail
Children's Legal Rights
Muslims in America

MAY 1993
Cults in America
Preventing Teen Pregnancy
Software Piracy
National Parks

JUNE 1993
Food Safety
Prostitution
Childhood Immunizations
National Service

JULY 1993
Electric Cars
Population Growth
Downward Mobility
Intelligence Testing

AUGUST 1993
Mental Illness
Bilingual Education
Foreign Policy Burden
School Funding

SEPTEMBER 1993
Suburban Crime
Public Housing
Supreme Court Preview
Immigration Reform

OCTOBER 1993
Airline Safety
Disaster Response
Science in the Courtroom
The Glass Ceiling

NOVEMBER 1993
Paying for Retirement
Charitable Giving
Privacy in the Workplace
Adoption

DECEMBER 1993
U.S. Vietnam-Relations
Learning Disabilities
Child Care
Space Program's Future

JANUARY 1994
Racial Tensions in Schools
South Africa's Future
Worker Retraining
Regulating Pesticides

FEBRUARY 1994
Prison Overcrowding
Water Quality
Religion in Schools
Juvenile Justice

MARCH 1994
Underground Economy
Education Standards
Gambling Boom
Private Management of Public Schools

APRIL 1994
Reproductive Ethics
U.S.-China Trade
Soccer in America
Talk Show Democracy

MAY 1994
Traffic Congestion
Women's Health Issues
Mutual Funds
Political Scandals

JUNE 1994
Education and Gender
Gun Control
Public Land Policy
Nuclear Arms Cleanup

JULY 1994
Dietary Supplements
Public Opinion and Foreign Policy
Crime Victims' Rights
Birth Control Choices

AUGUST 1994
Genetically Engineered Foods
Electing Minorities
Prozac Controversy
College Sports

SEPTEMBER 1994
Home Schooling

Future Topics

- ***Courts and the Media***
- ***Regulating Tobacco***
- ***Historic Preservation***

THE CQ Researcher

PUBLISHED BY CONGRESSIONAL QUARTERLY INC.

Courts and the Media

Can pretrial publicity jeopardize justice?

The massive publicity surrounding the O.J. Simpson murder trial has renewed an old debate: Can the constitutional rights to a free press and a fair trial be balanced? Nowadays, the clash between the First and Sixth amendments is occurring in televised courtrooms amid saturation media coverage. Some observers fear that the traditional legal tools for assuring impartial juries — the questioning of jurors for bias and the change of venue — are no longer effective in cases where the basic facts are widely known. Others say juries can put aside the impressions received from blanket news coverage. Meanwhile, all agree that the issue is far from resolved and that the media will remain a powerful player in the criminal justice system.

INSIDE THIS ISSUE

CQ Sept. 23, 1994 • Volume 4, No. 35 • Pages 817-840

Formerly Editorial Research Reports

COURTS AND THE MEDIA

COVER: CAMERAMEN AND JOURNALISTS BESIEGE O.J. SIMPSON'S LEAD ATTORNEY, ROBERT L. SHAPIRO. (REUTERS)

September 23, 1994
Volume 4, No. 35

EDITOR
Sandra Stencel

MANAGING EDITOR
Thomas J. Colin

ASSOCIATE EDITOR
Richard L. Worsnop

STAFF WRITERS
Charles S. Clark
Mary H. Cooper
Kenneth Jost

PRODUCTION EDITOR
Sarah E. Merritt

EDITORIAL ASSISTANT
Tonya Whitfield

GRAPHICS
P. Eloise Fuller

PUBLISHED BY
Congressional Quarterly Inc.

CHAIRMAN
Andrew Barnes

VICE CHAIRMAN
Andrew P. Corty

EDITOR AND PUBLISHER
Neil Skene

EXECUTIVE EDITOR
Robert W. Merry

ASSOCIATE PUBLISHER
John J. Coyle

MARKETING AND SALES DIRECTOR
Edward S. Hauck

The CQ Researcher (ISSN 1056-2036). Formerly Editorial Research Reports. Published weekly (48 times per year, not printed the first Friday of any month with five Fridays) by Congressional Quarterly Inc., 1414 22nd St., N.W., Washington, D.C. 20037. Rates are furnished upon request. Second-class postage paid at Washington, D.C. POSTMASTER: Send address changes to The CQ Researcher, 1414 22nd St., N.W., Washington, D.C. 20037.

Courts and the Media

By Charles S. Clark

The Issues

When historians look back on the trial of O.J. Simpson, their accounts will focus on much more than just the wealthy ex-football star and his team of celebrity attorneys. Equally significant in the shocking tale of double murder will be the controversial role of the news media.

Since the June 12 slaying of Simpson's ex-wife Nicole Brown Simpson and her friend Ronald L. Goldman, the broadcast, print and tabloid media have:

- broadcast the tapes of two 911 emergency calls from Nicole Simpson revealing Simpson's past as a wife-batterer; airing the tapes prompted a judge to dismiss a grand jury for fear that jurors had heard potentially prejudicial information;
- broadcast, and then retracted, a report saying that video tape showed Los Angeles prosecutor Marcia Clark on the grounds of Simpson's Brentwood estate before police had obtained a search warrant;
- paid potential witnesses for exclusive interviews, including a woman who said she saw Simpson driving away from the murder scene and who now may not be called as a witness because prosecutors fear her testimony would be tainted.

The press' willingness to use any information it could get its hands on has drawn multiple calls for restraint. Loud among them was the lament of Sylvester Daughtry, president of the International Association of Chiefs of Police, who deplores the "pitched contest for public opinion played out by certain parties pandering to the public's appalling appetite for sensationalism." [1]

Indeed, in what many call the most heavily scrutinized murder case in history, there is no question that both the prosecution and defense in the Simpson case have overtly played to the gallery. Taking advantage of California's loose regulations on pretrial publicity, Clark used what normally would have been a brief pretrial hearing to release a vast array of evidence, even as her boss, Los Angeles District Attorney Gil Garcetti, flew to New York to discuss prosecution strategy on talk shows.

And Simpson's chief lawyer, Robert L. Shapiro, who last year authored a primer on working the press to advantage, showed he follows his own advice about speaking in "sound bites" and picking and choosing among reporters' questions. "Immediately upon the arrest of a well-known person," he wrote, "initial headlines of the arrest often make the sacred presumption of innocence a myth. In reality, we have the assumption of guilt. This is why dealing with the media is so important. To make inroads into the mindset that 'if the press reported it, it must be true,' is the lawyer's most challenging task." [2]

Though unmatched in its drawing power, the Simpson case is only the most recent chapter in an age-old clash between the First Amendment guarantee of a free press and the Sixth Amendment right to a fair trial. * The ongoing collision of competing worthy goals is described in a prominent legal textbook: "Judges and lawyers are accustomed to seeking the truth in a courtroom where hearsay and illegally obtained evidence have no place; speed in arriving at the truth takes second place to faith that the process will lead eventually to the truth. For journalists, on the other hand, speed is of major importance, and even hearsay and illegally obtained evidence may be deemed newsworthy." [3]

Experts and the public alike are torn about how to resolve the tension. "Unfortunately, this kind of balance makes it difficult to make categorical rules," says Washington lawyer David E. Kendall, who served on a recent American Bar Association (ABA) panel on the fair trial-free press issue. "With a high-visibility case, there is a legitimate interest in having the public know what's going on so that they see that the rules of justice are not bent. But the public also has an interest in tribunals that conduct fair trials. In recent years, there's been an intensity of coverage of celebrities that probably was not there before. But that doesn't justify drastic solutions."

Others think that strong steps may be needed. "We're still looking at the question of pretrial publicity the same way we did 30 years ago, when there were only three TV networks," observes Richard T. Kaplar, vice president of the Media Institute, a First Amendment advocacy group. "Technological changes will change the way we look at the justice system because theoretically, every citizen or juror might be swayed by the coverage. We have to redefine what we mean by bias in an age of ubiquitous information."

But even before the age of 24-hour-a-day news, there was a wide and deep hunger for coverage of sensational court

---

* The Sixth Amendment guarantees: "In all criminal prosecutions, the accused shall enjoy the right to a speedy and public trial, by an impartial jury. . . ."

battles. "Popular trials become more important than other news and government events because they appeal to lots of different people, media and interest groups," says Robert Hariman, professor of communications at Drake University and author of *Popular Trials: Rhetoric, Mass Media and the Law.* "Since ancient Greece and Rome, they've been a very important way for people to make sense of an issue.

"Now, the development of mass media technologies has made the popular trial an important source of communication. But if there's been a change in degree, I don't know if it's been a change in kind. Before there was television, newspapers seemed like enough coverage. Once you fill up all the media and dominate public consciousness, the effect could be no greater than it was when a trial filled up newspapers in the 19th century."

Few dispute that media coverage can impact a legal proceeding. The lawyer who represented a 13-year-old California boy in a molestation suit against pop singer Michael Jackson last year said he relied on media coverage of his suit to turn the case. "I saw polls that showed 85 percent of the people believed that Michael Jackson was innocent," he told *Editor & Publisher.* "That potentially could influence a jury. Something had to be done to turn the tide so at least we could have a jury that was open-minded." [4]

Still, in the Simpson case, most observers say that the barrage of press coverage has not closed off chances for a trial decided on the merits. "O.J. Simpson can't get a perfect trial," says Richard Stack, a professor of communications at American University. "But under the Constitution, a defendant is entitled to an 'impartial jury.' That doesn't mean an unaware jury. To look around for a jury made up of people who've been living under a rock would be a waste of the court's time and resources."

The pretrial publicity has probably eliminated some people as jurors, but not everyone, says Louis Hodges, a professor of journalistic ethics at Washington and Lee University. "There's a difference between prejudgment and prejudice. A prejudgment can change with the introduction of new evidence, while prejudice can't. Prejudice is more a belief and an attitude."

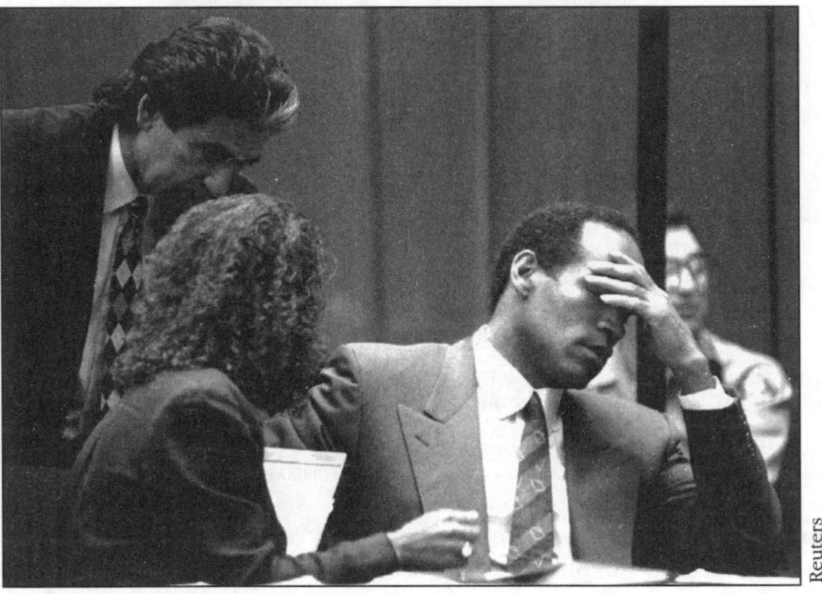

Reuters

Defense attorneys confer with O. J. Simpson during a pretrial hearing July 29.

The first trial of the four white officers charged in the 1991 beating of black Los Angeles motorist Rodney King proved that fair trials are possible, says John Burkoff, a professor of law at the University of Pittsburgh. Although the videotaped beating was seen by most Americans, the officers were acquitted by a jury in predominantly white Simi Valley of all but one relatively minor charge.

The acquittals showed that courts "have been able to find jurors who are not biased," says Burkoff. "Jurors today really don't know much [about specific cases] because they're so barraged with media stuff. It's a sad commentary, but they can easily go on to the next mass murder or sexy serial rape case." *

The coverage accorded the Simpson case has been extraordinary. From June 12-Aug. 23, according to a data base search, *USA Today* published 313 stories on Simpson, compared with only 235 on President Clinton's health-care initiative and 136 on the massacres in Rwanda. (A tally of television coverage on CNN showed roughly the same proportions.)

More than 75 percent of the public has been following the Simpson case, according to a July poll by the Times Mirror Center for The People & The Press. In California, the fear has been expressed that daily coverage of Simpson's trial, coming simultaneously with the trial of alleged Hollywood madam Heidi Fleiss, will overshadow news coverage of this fall's important races for governor and U.S. Senate.

"It's hard to imagine a case more freighted with public curiosity," says Miami attorney Richard Ovelmen, a former general counsel for *The Miami Herald.* "It's a black man accused, a powerful person who can afford the best defense. It makes you wonder what it says about our system working better for the rich than for the average person. But the amount of coverage is ridiculous. I can think of 50 cases as important that are not being reported on. The public has limited resources to devote

Continued on p. 822

* In a second trial, on federal civil rights charges, two of the officers were convicted and two were acquitted.

An Interview With Court TV Founder Steven Brill

Legal journalist and publisher Steven Brill was riding in a New York taxi in 1989 when a radio broadcast of a trial gave him the idea for a courtroom television channel. With backing from Time Warner, he founded Court TV. Launched in July 1991, the 24-hour channel now reaches 14 million viewers in 125 communities.

Q Has the O.J. Simpson trial been a boost for the proponents of courtroom TV coverage?

A In some respects, it's raised new problems because it has raised a question I thought had been almost settled. The problem is that lawyers and people writing articles confuse the issue of media coverage with the question of whether there should be a camera in the courtroom. Every stupid "A Current Affair" segment that has someone who has been paid to tell a story or a gory photograph or a leak from the prosecution or defense — a lot of which we as media critics criticize — somehow washes over into a question of whether there should be cameras in court. I think cameras in the courtroom is the best antidote to that other garbage.

Steven Brill

Q Do judges and lawyers become too theatrical when they're on camera?

A It doesn't happen, or at least doesn't happen any more than a judge or a lawyer will ham it up in any high-profile case. Does anyone think the prosecutor in the William Kennedy Smith case went Hollywood when the cameras went on?

Q How about the question of witnesses losing their privacy and being intimidated outside the courtroom?

A Any decent rule about cameras allows the judge to turn the camera off or not show a witness' face if there's any belief at all that the witness will be intimidated. But if a witness is simply going to be embarrassed or uncomfortable by being thrust in the public limelight, that's going to happen with or without the camera. Trials are public. We make a tradeoff in our society as a result of our being an open society.

Q Is the reason a lot of judges and lawyers resist cameras because they don't want their "legalese" to be demystified?

A I take exception to your question. In any polls and surveys we've done, a lot of judges and lawyers don't resist cameras. If you call a hundred lawyers at random, my guess if that you'd find 80 that either aren't against it or in favor of it.

Q But they used to be against it, and the Supreme Court is still against it.

A The Supreme Court is not against cameras, they're against cameras in the Supreme Court. In the Supreme Court, all the arguments good or bad against cameras don't even exist. What they're really concerned about, which is appropriate, is that they are the last important power for people in this country whom no one recognizes. I'm not saying that the Supreme Court wants to preserve hidden power, but a justice likes to be able to go to the supermarket and not be accosted by people seeking autographs or seeking to do him harm.

Q How about the argument that coverage of trials misrepresents the legal system since most legal proceedings are not trials?

A I think that's true if you don't take pains to emphasize the other aspects. But that's not an argument to have a law [against coverage]. Legislators are not supposed to be editors. I think that is one very legitimate criticism of Court TV. In fact, someone wrote a law review article about it. So I started a weekly show called "The System," which covers the whole pipeline from crime reports to arrests to plea bargaining to imprisonment to parole.

Q How about the argument that Court TV overemphasizes visual drama over something more dull like class-action suits.

A That's why we cover both class-action suits and murder trials. There is a fight even internally here among people who want to do instinctive television, which means a good picture, and I think anyone watching Court TV would agree that we don't succumb to that temptation very much.

Q Some have said the emotional testimony in the Menendez brothers' trials may have changed the public's view, making them appear more sympathetic. Was that a function of having it televised?

A Why does that matter? The only thing that matters is what the jury thinks. Whether our cameras were there or not, the jury was going to see that same testimony.

Q Has media coverage in general affected jurors' impartiality?

A It's there, but again you have to cut through the debate and use a little common sense. . . . Name the defendant in the most highly publicized trial you can think of, and they have one thing in common: Usually they got acquitted. William Kennedy Smith, Jimmy Hoffa, John Connally, [auto executive] John Delorean on national TV holding up the bag of cocaine and a glass of champagne in the other hand. I have a theory that some of that stuff has a backlash effect. Jurors get into a courtroom and realize that's it's more complicated than the little soundbites they saw that go the other way. If O.J. Simpson gets convicted in a slam dunk, and after you've seen it on Court TV you say "Boy, those jurors must have been prejudiced and that's why they've convicted him," then you'll have a good argument.

Court TV

Court TV

Court TV covered the trials of Lyle and Erik (top) Menendez, charged with killing their parents.

Continued from p. 820

to courts, and the media has limited resources, so it's unfortunate so much space is taken up."

Nancy Hollander, an Albuquerque attorney and former president of the National Association of Criminal Defense Lawyers, says she has accepted that the media are "here to stay. I've moved in my feelings on allowing the press in the courtroom because the Simpson case has become a constitutional law course for all of America."

Because many people watching TV believe Simpson, Hollander adds, they are open to the possibility that the police did something wrong while searching for evidence. "If the media can teach something like that, people will see why criminal defenders are so adamant, that everything is not just a technicality."

How the fair trial-free press conflict is ultimately reconciled will hinge on the following issues:

Are the news media covering the courts responsibly?

"I don't want to belabor knocking the press, but I can't believe what is being said," Simpson said in the dramatic farewell letter he wrote before his extraordinary flight — captured live on TV — along the L.A. freeways. "Most of it is totally made up. I know you have a job to do, but as a last wish, please, please, please, leave my children in peace."

Similar pleas were heard from Jesse Jackson, concerned over racial bias in the coverage, and from the Los Angeles Police Department. "Detectives are requesting that the media not attempt to contact potential witnesses in the case," Cmdr. David Gascon said June 13, "as those contacts may delay and negatively impact the course of this investigation." [5]

In the clash between free press and fair trial, the aggressiveness of the media has long sparked complaints from the legal community. "Too often the media appear to attach significance to the fact that their rights are defined in the First Amendment and all other amendments follow," wrote Michigan Judge Avern L. Cohn. "I see a great deal of self-righteousness and little of self-instruction. I do not find a text. I see constantly changing personnel. I see editors remote from the courtroom. I see a highly competitive environment. I find no mechanism for review or a window to receive complaints." [6]

Indeed, a study in the early 1980s found that 90 percent of trial reporters lacked any form of legal education. [7] And the public appears to share in the criticism. In a June 28 *Los Angeles Times* poll, 67 percent of the respondents said the media had been irresponsible in reporting on the Simpson case.

Efforts by the press to satisfy the public's hunger for details — and solutions — before trials start can be risky. The sensational 1989 case of Boston businessman Charles Stuart proved just how risky. Stuart breathlessly phoned 911 from his car phone to report that he and his pregnant wife had been shot by a black robber. From that moment on, the press played Stuart's story for all it was worth, which turned out to be not much. Several months after Stuart's dramatic call, Willie Bennett, a black ex-convict, was arrested in the shooting and his photo was prominently displayed in the news media. [8] Only later, after Stuart jumped off a bridge to his death, did the public learn that he had arranged his wife's death to collect insurance money. [9]

But as Hariman points out, there are many instances in which press coverage prevented a miscarriage of justice, among them the infamous Scottsboro case in Alabama in the 1930s. Nine black teenagers falsely charged with raping two white girls might have been hung if the press hadn't trumpeted their case.

Journalists invariably cite "the public's right to know" in defending their hot pursuit of criminal cases. "Our judgment is based on two questions: Will this advance the story, and does the public need to know it?" says Leo Wolinsky, metro editor of the *Los Angeles Times*. "Our reason for being is not to assure whether someone gets a fair trial but to get facts out to the public in a way that's accurate and fair. Not to report is a disservice, because the public needs to know whether the police are operating fairly. Imagine if O.J. Simpson had been arrested and you had no information on why or what evidence linked him to the crime. You'd have rumors out of control."

Nor is Wolinsky sympathetic to the criticism that pretrial press reports on evidence can bias potential jurors if the evidence is later ruled inadmissible. "We don't consider ourselves part of the court system," he says. "We don't think we should wait until a trial unfolds; that's not our job."

Cynthia McFadden, who has been covering the Simpson trial for ABC News, says the prospect of causing a mistrial does not concern her. The media are part of the process of a trial, says McFadden, who has a law degree. "It isn't a sanitized trial, like a

Star Chamber, which would be more efficient and antiseptic, if not more just. Such a trial would be less tainted by publicity, but would not result in something the public could count on with confidence."

Jane Kirtley, executive director of the Reporters Committee for Freedom of the Press, who is also an attorney, says she is troubled by arguments that the press is constitutionally duty-bound to avoid undermining the government's case in a criminal trial. "If a case is jeopardized by government leaks or because a competent defense counsel has filed a motion for a mistrial," Kirtley asks, "is the problem the government leaking or the press reporting it?"

Finally, journalists point out that cases in which the press is ahead of the police are rare. "Reporters have no subpoena power; they can't conduct ballistics tests or force people to talk," writes *Washington Post* media critic Howard Kurtz. "In 99 percent of crime stories, they get their information from police and prosecutors, who generally provide their own 'spin' on a not-for-attribution basis. This produces an inherent bias toward the law enforcement version of events." [10]

In covering crime, goes the complaint, the press risks biasing potential jurors in any number of ways: by covering a prosecutor's press conferences and displaying photos of seized evidence; by scheduling "recap" stories that repeat past details of a case just as the jury is being selected; and by publishing details of pretrial hearings, lawyers' sidebar conferences and interviews with jurors after the verdict.

But editors are also willing, notes Wolinsky, to "think of safety" and exercise restraint by withholding the names of rape victims, juveniles, undercover cops or government agents and witnesses to crimes if the criminal is still at large.

Gary Deckelnick, assistant managing editor for legal affairs at the *Asbury Park Press* in New Jersey, said his paper delayed the story of an indictment for four days at a judge's request. The delay was sought because the indictment was against a defendant who was already on trial, and the jury in the case was home for the weekend and so couldn't be reached with a warning not to read newspaper stories of the indictment. [11]

But as McFadden cautions, "It's too easy to talk about the media as one thing, when there are actually vastly different media and individuals within news organizations."

Nowhere does this diversity become more apparent than in the practice of "checkbook journalism," or paying for interviews. In "Cash for Trash," which focused on the Simpson trial, writer Jeffrey Toobin of *The New Yorker* described the rise of brokers who represent witnesses to crimes who are seeking payment for talking to reporters from tabloid TV shows and magazines. Critics fear that witnesses will embroider their stories to make them more salable. [12]

"It's disgusting to think that I could have a good case weakened by the greediness of witnesses," says Andrew Sonner, state's attorney in Montgomery County, Md. "I think [taking money] impeaches the witness, that the defense lawyers will argue that it does and jurors will buy it."

After it was revealed in court that *The National Enquirer* had paid employees of a Los Angeles sporting goods store for their exclusive story about selling O.J. Simpson a knife, prosecutor Clark quickly moved to defend the employees, who were prosecution witnesses. She told reporters that the witnesses had told the same story all along.

"There is a risk with everything" in journalism, says Iain Calder, editor-in-chief of the *Enquirer.* "We felt comfortable [with the knife stories]. We check out what can be checked out."

Kirtley says critics who worry about paid witnesses embroidering stories are acting as if witnesses have never been paid. "The *National Law Journal* classified ads are filled with experts offering their services," she says. "It doesn't mean they will lie, or that the evidence is no longer any good. If they change their story, of course, [their testimony] can be impeached."

"As the practice of buying interviews becomes more common, juries will disregard it," says Kendall. "And in high-profile cases, they will even anticipate it."

Toobin himself has been criticized by fellow journalists for not naming his sources. In late July, he published an anonymously sourced scoop revealing that the Simpson defense team was planning a strategy based on charges that LAPD detective Mark Fuhrman, who said he discovered a bloody glove outside O.J. Simpson's house, was a racist with a history of psychological problems. "In a series of conversations last week," Toobin wrote, "leading members of Simpson's defense team floated this new and

Continued on p. 825

Lorena and John Bobbitt testify during her trial on malicious wounding charges.

Cameras in the Courtroom: a Survey of State Rules

News media cameras and microphones are permitted in courtrooms in 47 states, with varying limitations. In 23 states, coverage occurs routinely, though with some minor restrictions. In 24 states, tougher rules severely limit coverage. The only jurisdictions that prohibit coverage are Indiana, Mississippi, South Dakota and the District of Columbia.

States That Allow the Most Coverage

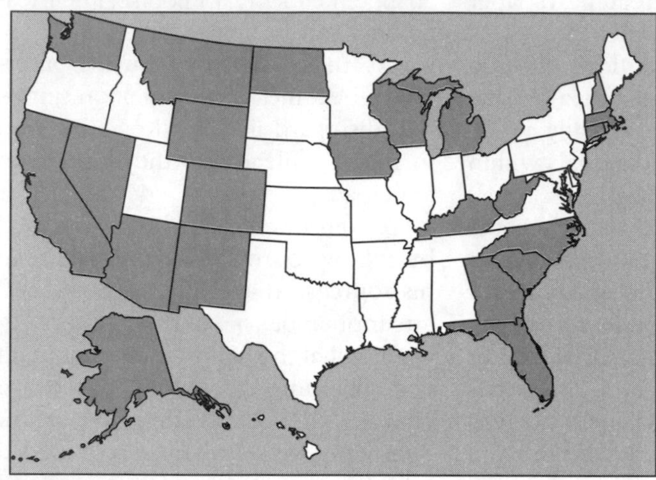

Alaska — sex offense victims cannot be covered without consent of court and victim
Arizona — prohibits coverage of proceedings involving juveniles and adoptions
California — judge has broad discretion
Colorado — judge has broad discretion
Connecticut — prohibits coverage of cases involving trade secrets and family matters such as adoptions
Florida — individuals seeking to block cameras must prove coverage will cause harm
Georgia — judge has broad discretion
Iowa — victims and witnesses in sexual-abuse cases must consent to coverage
Kentucky — judge has broad discretion
Massachusetts — judge may prohibit coverage if harm to an individual could result
Michigan — judge may prohibit coverage of certain witnesses
Montana — judge has broad discretion
Nevada — judge has broad discretion
New Hampshire — judge has broad discretion
New Mexico — judge may prohibit coverage of certain witnesses
North Carolina — prohibits coverage of certain types of cases and witnesses
North Dakota — witnesses can block coverage but news media may respond to objections
Rhode Island — judge has broad discretion
South Carolina — judge has broad discretion
Washington — judge has broad discretion
West Virginia — judge has broad discretion
Wisconsin — judge has broad discretion
Wyoming — judge has broad discretion

States That Allow the Least Coverage

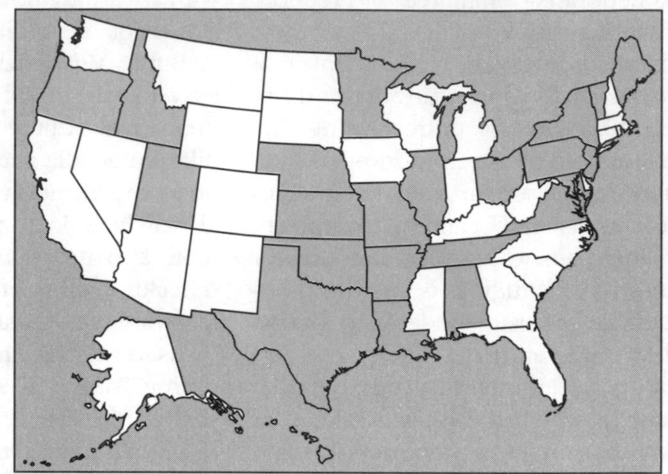

Alabama — requires consent of all parties and attorneys
Arkansas — coverage must cease after objection by attorney or principal party in case
Delaware — only permits appellate coverage
Hawaii — judge has broad discretion to limit coverage of many types of cases and witnesses
Idaho — only permits appellate coverage
Illinois — only permits appellate coverage
Kansas — wide range of witnesses may object to coverage
Louisiana — only permits appellate coverage
Maryland — only permits coverage of appellate and civil trials
Maine — cameras allowed in trial courts but prohibited during testimony in criminal trials and cases involving children, sex offenses and trade secrets (as amended July 1994)
Minnesota — permits appellate and trial coverage only with consent of all parties
Missouri — wide range of witnesses may object to coverage; judge decides
Nebraska — permits full appellate coverage and audio coverage of trials
New Jersey — prohibits coverage of sexual penetration, trade secret and family cases
New York — numerous restrictions on coverage of witnesses
Ohio — prohibits coverage of objecting witnesses and victims
Oklahoma — coverage requires consent of criminal defendant
Oregon — prohibits coverage of objecting witnesses
Pennsylvania — permits coverage of non-jury civil trials only
Tennessee — requires consent of accused parties in criminal proceedings; objection by any party terminates all coverage
Texas — allows appellate coverage, civil trial coverage if county rules OKd by Texas Supreme Court and criminal trial coverage on case-by-case basis determined by judge
Utah — permits full appellate coverage but only still photography of trials
Vermont — judges generally don't approve coverage
Virginia — prohibits coverage of cases involving sex offenses, trade secrets and domestic matters

Source: "News Media Coverage of Judicial Proceedings with Cameras and Microphones: A Survey of the States," Radio-Television News Directors Association, Jan. 1, 1994

Continued from p. 823

provocative theory as part of both the public relations war surrounding the case and their continuing effort to keep the prosecution off balance." [13]

To ABC's McFadden and others, the Toobin article was irresponsible. "You have to be careful when using unnamed sources," she said, "because chances are good that you're being used for another's agenda."

Publication of uncorroborated theories and evidence "worries me because it gets into the public's mind but may not be admissible in court," says Washington and Lee's Hodges. "There ought to be a rule that you don't publish if it is not likely to be admissible." He acknowledges, however, that "journalists aren't equipped to make that judgment, so it's an impossible standard."

Are legal professionals doing all they can to preserve fair trials?

"An attorney in a popular trial has to play to multiple audiences, within the court and without," observes Hariman. While the practice can create problems — such as "a riot or harm to a party's family" — it can be beneficial, he says. "Greater public attention means that greater resources go into a case, and you will get good litigators. And it becomes harder to get off on a technicality."

The age of the media-savvy attorney has gotten a mixed reception in the legal community. "The biggest problem when cases get tried in the media is that people take lawyers' words as gospel" and forget that they're all playing roles in the advocacy process, says Burkoff of the University of Pittsburgh. "This can harm people."

Burkoff notes that comedian Woody Allen suffered last year when a Connecticut prosecutor announced that he would not prosecute Allen for alleged child abuse but that in his opinion Allen was still guilty. "That prosecutor had no right," he says. "A regular person can say someone is a sleazebag, within the strictures of slander, but for a lawyer or a prosecutor to do so is unprofessional."

Indeed, in 1991, then-Attorney General Dick Thornburgh wrote, "it is time . . . to remind all concerned of the true role of the prosecutor. His duties do not encompass the exposure of suspected criminal activities for exposure's sake. . . . Much as the defendant has the right to remain silent before the court, the prosecutor has the obligation to remain silent outside the court." [14]

The 1991 Palm Beach rape trial of William Kennedy Smith illustrated how lawyers' pretrial maneuvering can significantly affect a trial. The prosecutor placed sworn statements in the public record from three women claiming to have been sexually assaulted by Smith in 1983-88. When opinion polls showed an abrupt shift in sympathies against Smith, the defense requested and was granted a postponement. The judge ultimately disallowed the statements as evidence because the episodes described were old and no charges had been filed. Smith was eventually acquitted. [15]

In the Simpson case, observers agree, the prosecution used the pretrial hearing to unveil much more evidence and strategy than is usual. "With everything being televised, I would never do that," says Maryland's Sonner. "DNA testing and videotape are whole new kinds of evidence that could be very prejudicial [to a defendant], and if they're ruled not admissible, the [prosecution's case] could be jeopardized."

The Simpson defense has worked the media in subtler ways. Johnnie Cochran referred in court to a police report about a burglar who said he was at Nicole Simpson's condo on the night of the murder and saw two white men fleeing the scene. Actually, according to the *Los Angeles Times,* the report was one of hundreds of "tips" police have received. Yet Cochran suggested that police were investigating the report as an alternative "theory" to the proposition that Simpson was the killer. Cochran's statement was duly reported in the press' routine coverage of the hearing, thus putting the "theory" in public view. [16]

The tactic of prosecutors and defense attorneys putting pretrial "spins" on the facts can turn into a judicial nuclear arms race, in which each side blames the other for accelerating the conflict. "Not only does the defense lawyer have the right to respond to prosecutorial leaks," said Pennsylvania attorney William Costopoulos, "it's my view that the defense attorney *owes* it to the client, and it can be done constitutionally and ethically." [17]

In theory, attorneys on both sides are restrained in what they say publicly before a trial by standards set by bar associations and chief state judges. Violators can prompt judges to crack down by issuing contempt citations. In the Simpson case, Judge Lance Ito has threatened both the prosecution and the defense because of news leaks.

"Judges can impose restrictions on comment" if prosecutors make prejudicial statements before a trial, notes attorney Kendall, and they can compensate the defense by giving them more chances to strike potential jurors. "They can also sequester the jury."

"But it's hard for judges to really crack down because of the First Amendment," says Burkoff.

"More free speech is generally better than less," says Ovelmen. "If a lawyer's statement is accurate, it should be allowed, the only caveat being with statements about evidence that is likely to be inadmissible. Here in Florida, there's lots of concern about making sure the public understands a prosecution so that there will be confidence, and there won't be a riot. Prosecutors have a duty to tell the public their probable cause [for an arrest]."

Though modern media coverage has complicated matters, lawyers and judges continue to place faith in time-tested methods for avoiding prejudiced juries: the voir dire, or questioning of prospective jurors, and the change in venue, or shifting of a trial to another jurisdiction.

As the celebrated jurist Learned Hand once said, "any examination in the voir dire is a clumsy and imperfect way of detecting suppressed emotional commitments to which all of us are to some extent subject, unconsciously or subconsciously." [18]

Potential jurors are not always candid in admitting their prejudices, notes the ABA's book of standards for fair trials. The ABA does "not encourage undue reliance upon the surgical precision of voir dire. It appears to be something much more of a blunt instrument. But both the scientific and anecdotal evidence do suggest that it can be used, in the hands of skilled practitioners, to eliminate some of the untoward effects of pretrial publicity." [19]

Lawyers who conduct the voir dire are often aggressive, says Burkoff, "saying, for example, 'If you knew my client had a past as a rapist, could you still acquit him based on the evidence presented?' It's a challenge to [the jurors] sense of civic duty. And it can work, though you occasionally get a screwy or duplicitous juror."

Others argue that the risk of news coverage prejudicing a juror is exaggerated and that only perhaps 2 percent of jurors are affected. [20] Experiments have shown that even when jurors read news accounts of crimes, they often forget key details in the weeks or months before the trial. One study showed that fewer than 1 ½ facts per crime were recalled by readers of common crime stories, while another study of high-profile cases found that 94 percent of prospective jurors could not remember key facts about the crime. [21]

"You have to look carefully at what the local people are reading," says Hariman. "We're too quick to assume everyone is reading national media. But neighbors talking over the back fence is equally powerful, and people might be reading their local Catholic paper, or black newspapers in Los Angeles."

Similarly, the dawn of mass media has not eliminated use of the change in venue if one party can show through opinion surveys or other court-approved evidence that there is prejudice in the original community.

"The change in venue is less an option in high-profile cases, but those are rare," says Kendall. "It often is a viable alternative in cases involving local publicity for a heinous crime in which people often know the victim and have strong feelings about the accused."

"It hasn't become irrelevant in the media age," says Kirtley, "because there is a diminishing amount of interest in a trial the farther away you get from it."

A cartoonist's view of O. J. Simpson press coverage.

Others disagree, noting that changing venue has more to do with demographics than jurors prejudiced by news coverage. American University's Stack cites the decision to move the first Rodney King trial from inner-city Los Angeles to the largely white suburb of Simi Valley. "Given the media deluge," he says, "moving from south-central L.A. did nothing except frustrate the community where the event took place."

Overall, legal professionals agree that none of these preventive steps can guarantee a fair trial. Mere claims of neutrality by prospective jurors are not adequate, according to Norbert Kerr, a professor of psychology at Michigan State University: "If you take only those potential jurors who saw or read something about a case but say they can put that information aside, and compare them with those who saw nothing, you continue to find differences in their ratio of voting to convict that are in line with what they had seen.

"The assertions of attorneys and trial consultants who say they can tell [if prospective jurors are prejudiced] during voir dire are not well-documented. They're asking people to pretend they don't know something they've been told or seen. Can we really expect a human being to do that?"

Should television cameras be permitted in courtrooms?

For most of the 20th century, trials have been largely off-limits to photographers, microphones and television cameras, necessitating the journalistic tradition of the courtroom sketch artist. The fear was that "as-it-happens" media coverage would distract court participants, detract from the dignity of the proceedings and violate the privacy of witnesses or subject them to outside intimidation.

Since the 1970s, however, states have been permitting live TV coverage, touting, among other things, its educational value. Today it is allowed by all states except Indiana, Mississippi and South Dakota and Washington D.C. (*See table, p. 824.*) In other developments, the federal courts are completing a pilot project permitting cameras in civil trials; interest has been renewed in televising oral arguments at the Supreme Court; and the meteoric rise of Court TV (*see story, p. 821*) has highlighted the strong public interest in live coverage.

Still, the divisiveness of the issue was dramatized by ABC's "Nightline" on Aug. 30. Press advocate Kirtley argued that William Kennedy Smith's acquittal "was tolerable for most people only because the proceedings were televised, and they saw how the trial was conducted." She was countered by Leslie Abramson, the defense attorney in the recent trials of Lyle and Erik Menendez, accused in Los Angeles of murdering their parents. Abramson said that the prospect of a televised trial with its "notion of total exposure . . . kept people that we discovered during our investigation from being willing to be witnesses."

Objections to cameras in court are multifold. During Smith's rape trial, then-President George Bush said he was "concerned about so much filth and indecent material coming in through the airwaves and through these trials into people's homes." [22] And Kathryn Ross, a criminal defense lawyer in Lynnwood, Wash., recently charged in an op-ed piece that trials suffer if lawyers for either side are affected by the pressure of having their performance "reviewed daily by network lawyer-commentators and scrutinized by a national audience." [23]

George Gerbner, dean emeritus of the Annenburg School of Communication, worries that TV coverage of criminal trials is undermining the court system: "While I can understand the fascination, and I think it has been a great educational experience, I think judgment, moderation and, eventually, a reconsideration of the policy of admitting cameras in the courtroom . . . is in order." [24]

"Many trials are long, tedious and complex," writes Hartwick College political scientist Paul Raymond. "They appear to be impersonal, with an overabundance of legal quibbling. Unlike fictionalized trials on television, poor people often do not emerge victorious in actual trials. Consequently, some televised trials may reinforce people's belief that trial outcomes are unfair and courts are biased against the disadvantaged." [25]

Raymond, however, goes on to report the results of a revealing experiment. He showed 30 residents of Madison County, Ky., a videotape of a 1989 trial involving a man who claimed he had been illegally fired. Afterwards, Raymond had them fill out a questionnaire about whether the trial was fair. Raymond then compared their answers with questionnaires filled out by people from the community who hadn't seen the videotape. He concluded that the TV coverage did not make the viewers less confident in courts, and that it even made most more supportive of live coverage.

"It is important to have the camera as a truthful record for the public to measure lawyers for both sides who come out on the courthouse steps and spin [the facts] and say, 'We had a great day in court,' " says McFadden.

"Cameras in court is a change for the better," says the ABA's Kendall. "When lawyers and judges know they're on camera, they are better prepared and better behaved. I hope the Supreme Court will allow coverage of oral arguments so that the public can see the issues the court is wrestling with." The fear that witnesses will lose their privacy and have their lives endangered outside of court can be addressed by judges, who can order the cameras turned off or a particular witness' face blotted out, he notes.

Since the debate over cameras began, one of the fears has been that judges and lawyers would alter their behavior and grandstand for the public.

"Yes, lawyers and judges behave differently when they're on TV, but that's not a bad thing," says Burkoff. "Lawyers emote more, and judges avoid falling asleep, and they smile where they used to be mean. It's not bad for the public to see things in a way they can't see in the print media." In the trials of the Menendez brothers, he surmises, people at first might have been 100-1 for a guilty verdict, but after the emotional TV coverage, the majority favoring a guilty verdict might have dropped to 80-20.

In Florida, says Ovelmen, cameras haven't adversely affected the performance of litigants, who were conscious of the cameras only at the beginning. What is disappointing, he says, is the way the news media have handled their courtroom access. "They don't show enough of each trial, only tiny snippets."

Hodges concurs, noting that cameras in court "don't give the public a real sense of the legal system. The ins and outs of a trial are complicated, so you lose the educational benefit unless it all is explained. But it won't have an effect on a trial. The idea that lawyers will dance a jig in front of the camera is silly."

Hariman dismisses the argument that cameras don't reflect the realities of the legal process, pointing out that trials take place in only a fraction of the cases. [26]

"There is no pure form of legal education," Hariman says. "You have 'Night Court' and 'Perry Mason' and all kinds of garbage. Besides, the legal professionals all have their own ideology, so we need to identify those biases when they come up in popular trials." ■

BACKGROUND

Fair Trial vs. Free Press

The unresolved tension between the Constitution's First and Sixth amendments was quite evident to the Founding Fathers. Indeed, in an early version of the First Amendment, James Madison combined both freedom of the press and the right to fair trial by jury, but it was rejected by the U.S. Senate. [27]

The question of whether jurors can be kept impartial also goes back to the early years of the Republic. In 1807, in the famous treason trial of Aaron Burr, Chief Justice John Marshall turned aside Burr's lawyers' charge that jurors had a bias toward Burr's nemesis, Thomas Jefferson.

"Light impressions which may fairly be supposed to yield to the testimony that may be offered, which may leave the mind open to a fair consideration of that testimony, constitute no sufficient objection to a juror," Marshall wrote." [28] His view would be affirmed in 1878, in *Reynolds v. United States,* when Chief Justice Morrison Waite added that the burden was on the defense to show that a juror's opinion was strong enough to raise a "presumption of partiality." [29]

Journalists, meanwhile, were already arguing that press coverage of trials is as American as apple pie and doesn't prevent a just verdict. None other than Mark Twain wrote in *Roughing It* in 1872 about the futility of trying to avoid well-informed jurors. "[I]n our day of telegraphs and newspapers" the jury system "compels us to swear in juries composed of fools and rascals, because the system rigidly excludes honest men and men of brains."

Courtroom Bedlam

The first major trial to receive electronic media coverage was Tennessee's famous "monkey trial" in 1925, during which radio listeners could hear teacher John Scopes being tried for teaching evolution in schools.

In 1935, the burgeoning armies of the American press showed their forces in the trial of Bruno Richard Hauptmann, who was convicted for the notorious kidnapping and slaying of the infant son of aviator Charles A. Lindbergh. The courtroom in Flemington, N.J., was packed with 141 reporters and photographers from all over the world, 125 telegraph operators and a public that openly cheered on the witnesses. [30] In reaction to the pandemonium, the American Bar Association in 1937 adopted Canon 35 of its Judicial Ethics, recommending that courts bar photographers from courtrooms.

In 1952, the ABA called for courts to broaden the ban to include cameras from the newfangled medium called television, but not all agreed. The following year, an Oklahoma station broadcast what is believed to be the first live TV broadcast of a trial.

In 1954, the murder trial of Dr. Samuel Sheppard transformed the fair trial-free press debate. Sheppard, from suburban Cleveland, was accused of bludgeoning his pregnant wife to death. He claimed he had fought off an intruder who had entered his house and committed the crime. (His story reputedly sparked the popular 1960s television drama "The Fugitive.")

But the press was aggressively suspicious. "Why Isn't Sam Sheppard in Jail?" demanded a front-page editorial in the *Cleveland Press,* then Ohio's largest paper, which ran banner headlines about the case for 23 days leading up to the trial. "This is not the time to permit anybody — no matter who it is — to outwit, stall, fake, or improvise devices to keep away from the police," it editorialized. Other papers uncovered and wrote of Sheppard's extramarital affairs.

When the trial got under way in a packed courtroom, reporters were seated right next to the defendant and relayed every whispered conversation with his counsel. Supreme Court Justice Tom Clark later described the trial as "bedlam" and recalled that when "Sheppard's chief counsel tried to place some documents in the record, he was forcibly ejected from the room by the coroner, who received cheers, hugs and kisses from the ladies in the audience." [31]

So skewed was the trial that convicted Sheppard that his appeal was championed by an up-and-coming legal star named F. Lee Bailey, now a member of the Simpson defense team. Bailey took Sheppard's case to the Supreme Court and won an acquittal for Sheppard in 1966. As the high court noted, "the pervasiveness of modern communications" and "unfair and prejudicial news comment on pending trials has become increasingly prevalent." [32] In response, judges all over the country began issuing gag orders.

In 1967, for example, the judge in the Chicago trial of Richard Speck, accused of killing eight student nurses, banned artists' sketches of participants, extrajudicial statements from participants and the release of news leads from police or lawyers. "[T]he news media are placed upon notice as to the impropriety of publishing material not introduced in the proceedings," he added. [33]

The press opposed gag orders as a violation of the First Amendment, and in practice they were not always foolproof. In 1969, as Charles Manson and his followers were coming to trial for multiple murders in Los Angeles, then-President Richard M. Nixon got into hot water for observing to reporters that Manson was "guilty, directly or indirectly, of eight murders without reason." Jurors in the trial had to be shielded from the banner headlines reporting the comment. [34]

Search for Guidelines

In the mid-1960s, when the Warren Commission issued its report on the

Continued on p. 830

Chronology

1930s-40s *First efforts at regulating mass media coverage of courts.*

1935
Massive publicity surrounding trial of Bruno Richard Hauptmann in Lindbergh kidnapping case prompts American Bar Association (ABA) ban on cameras.

1948
Supreme Court in *In re Oliver* affirms openness of courtrooms, arguing that a public trial is an important outlet for community concerns, hostility and emotions.

1950s *First televised trials.*

1954
Dr. Samuel Sheppard convicted of murdering his wife following a chaotic trial and massive pretrial sensationalizing by the press. He appeals.

1960s *Major court cases show how media can affect criminal justice.*

1961
In *Irwin v. Dowd,* Supreme Court establishes test for determining juror bias.

1963
In *Rideau v. Louisiana,* Supreme Court strikes down conviction of man who confessed to murder before a TV news crew.

1965
In *Estes v. Texas,* Supreme Court's reversal of Billy Sol Estes' swindling conviction is interpreted as a ban on courtroom cameras.

1966
In *Sheppard v. Maxwell,* Supreme Court cites "bedlam" of media coverage in overturning 1954 murder conviction of Sheppard.

1968
First report of ABA commission on fair trial and free press.

1970s *Press wins cases for open courts.*

1975
In *Murphy v. Florida,* Supreme Court says jurors' exposure to information about a defendant's prior convictions does not inevitably lead to prejudice.

1976
Supreme Court in *Nebraska Press Assn. v. Stuart* rejects a judge's gag order on a murder trial; establishes test for gag orders.

1979
In *Gannett v. DePasquale,* Supreme Court backs judge's right to close a pretrial hearing. ABA issues second report on fair trial-free press issues.

1980s *Rulings favor cameras; federal courts pressed to open up.*

1980
In *Richmond Newspapers Inc. v. Virginia,* Supreme Court OKs closing trials only under extreme circumstances.

1981
In *Chandler v. Florida,* Supreme Court permits states to experiment with courtroom cameras.

1982
In *Globe Newspaper Co. v. Superior Court,* Supreme Court rejects closing trials to protect minors.

1983
Twenty-eight news organizations ask federal courts to allow cameras.

1984
Supreme Court in *Press-Enterprise Co. v. California* opens voir dire to press during rape and murder trial.

1990s *Criminal attorneys become "media savvy"; rise of Court TV on cable.*

September 1990
Three-year test of cameras OKd in federal civil courts.

1991
Supreme Court in *Gentile v. State Bar of Nevada* says speech of lawyers may be regulated.

January 1994
Mistrials declared in trials of Menendez brothers.

June 12, 1994
Nicole Brown Simpson and her friend Ronald L. Goldman are found dead outside her L.A. condo.

June 17, 1994
O.J. Simpson arrested.

Sept. 26, 1994
Simpson's trial slated to begin.

Canadians Chafe at Their Media Bans . . .

In Canada, a sensational murder gets the same flood of news coverage it might in the United States, with one gigantic exception: News blackouts can be ordered by judges to prevent potential jurors from forming prejudices.

The propriety of such bans has been hotly debated recently throughout the country as Canadians have gradually learned the gruesome details of the murders of two teenage girls.

Paul Teale, a 29-year-old accountant from a suburb of Toronto, was charged in 1993 with first-degree murder, kidnapping and other charges following the discovery of the dismembered body of 14-year-old Leslie Mahaffy of Burlington, Ont., found encased in concrete at the bottom of a lake.

Teale's 23-year-old ex-wife, Karla Homolka, was also charged, but when her separate trial began last year in June, Ontario Court Judge Francis Kovacs worried that a full airing of the evidence against her would jeopardize Teale's trial, which may not begin until 1995. "The considerations for a fair trial outweigh the right to freedom of the press in these exceptional circumstances," Kovacs wrote, explaining the ban he was imposing. [1]

The Homolka ban, as it came to be called, allows Canadian reporters to attend the proceedings but forbids them to publish any details of the evidence. Foreign reporters and the public (except for immediate family members of the litigants) are barred from attending, though foreign reporters are free to gather details outside the courtroom. Canadian subscribers to American publications such as *Newsweek* and *USA Today* receive special editions with the Homolka story missing.

As a result, details of the evidence against Homolka are known to American readers of major magazines and big-city papers but not to average Canadians. This evidence includes prosecutors' statements that Homolka procured girls for sex with Teale, that she drugged her own sister so that she and Teale could have sex with her (covering up the fact of the drugs after the sister subsequently choked to death on her vomit), and helped him abduct 15-year-old Kristen French, whose nude body was found in April 1992 near a Burlington, Ont., cemetery. [2]

And when Karla Homolka and Crown prosecutors agreed to two concurrent 12-year prison sentence on July 6, 1993, the Canadian public got the news with no information about the evidence or whether there had been a plea bargain. "It's hard to tell whether she got a fair sentence, because we don't really know how much she was involved," said Richard Rice, a 28-year-old Canadian banker. [3]

The ban has been challenged by the Canadian Broadcasting Corporation and Toronto's three English-language dailies and is pending in the Ontario Court of Appeals.

It "should be lifted," editorialized Robert Lewis, editor of *Maclean's*, Canada's newsweekly. "No one can say with certainty that if the details of Homolka's crimes were released, an impartial jury could be assembled. But the dissemination of the details *has* happened on a global scale. They have appeared in Ontario border papers, like *The Buffalo News*, in certain copies of *The New York Times* and *USA Today*, in an issue of the French daily *Le Figaro* available for weeks in at least one public Toronto library until it was removed recently and on the proliferating networks via modem on home computers." [4]

Canadians frustrated by media bans in other cases have seen articles from foreign papers posted on telephone poles outside of courtrooms. Also in protest, a retired police officer has been distributing videotapes of a segment about the Teale-Homolka case that was broadcast on the American TV show "A Current Affair."

"I can't remember when we've had to spend so much time on the phone with lawyers," says Lewis, explaining how a publication's reporters, editors and lawyers are permitted to learn all the facts but are subject to contempt penalties of fines or imprisonment if they print any banned details. "It's an uncomfortable position for an editor," he says. "It's bizarre that we can't even talk about it, because the facts are all over our business and the legal community. Even the guy in our local sandwich shop knows the details. Plus there are rumors going around that are wildly untrue, and we aren't allowed to say which ones are true."

Scott Fairley is a Toronto attorney representing a major cable company that has joined the lawsuit to overturn the ban. "It didn't bother us until the ban took effect," he says, "but then it turned us into a censor. On newspapers, the effect was prior restraint, meaning you could have the story in your computer but you just couldn't uncork it."

But as a cable TV company that receives American broadcasts of such shows as "Hard Copy," says Fairley, "we had to set up a way to bleep things out. We didn't know

Continued from p. 828

assassination of President John F. Kennedy, it noted that suspected assassin Lee Harvey Oswald might never have received a fair trial because of massive publicity surrounding his arrest. (He was shot by Jack Ruby only days after Kennedy's death.)

Also in the 1960s, the Justice Department, American Society of Newspaper Editors, International Association of Chiefs of Police, Twentieth Century Fund and the ABA all began the search for guidelines striking a balance between free press and fair trial.

The ABA assigned Paul Reardon, an associate justice of the Massachusetts Supreme Court, to chair a panel that in 1968 published the legal community's first standards on pretrial publicity. The document provided sanctions against any lawyer who disseminated extrajudicial statements about a defendant that went beyond

. . . But Frown on American Press Excesses

exactly what was banned, so we had to guess. Millions of our customers were seeing a blank screen on their TVs, and many were reinstalling their rabbit ears to pick up coverage from the border stations. As a 24-hour operation, we realized the magnitude of the problem because it was costing us big bucks."

Canadian law, like the British common law from which it evolved, has long permitted restrictions on press coverage of crime. But specific media bans — which can be requested by the defense or the prosecution and are nearly always approved — have become more common in recent years. In 1982, Canada amended its constitution by adding a Charter of Rights and Freedoms. It covers a wide range of areas, including press freedom, and is still being tested in the courts.[5]

"The marked distinction between the situations in Canada and the U.S. is that in Canada the courts have mostly ruled that fair trial trumps free press," says Fairley.

Jon Festinger, a Canadian Bar Association specialist on media bans who is also general counsel to Vancouver-based Western International Communications, says: "A certain amount of the opposition to the Homolka ban is the press stirring up the pot for self-serving purposes. But among non-press people, a real anger and frustration at the government and the courts has showed through.

"We should have a more realistic and targeted approach [to bans]," Festinger says. "Not everyone sees the papers, or TV, and even if they have, it doesn't mean they've formed an opinion."

Among the defenders of the Homolka ban is Toronto lawyer Austin Cooper. "It's a delay, not a ban. Once Teale's trial is over, the press can write anything it wants," he says. As for the argument that the ban has been ineffective because of smuggled-in foreign coverage, Cooper says: "In my circles, most people really don't know what happened with Karla Homolka, other than speculation and rumor. The people I meet at cocktail parties have not had their partiality affected."

Cooper, like many Canadian attorneys, is uncomfortable with many aspects of the American legal system, including the heavy reporting of pretrial evidence, the questioning of jurors by American attorneys and the freedom reporters have to interview jurors after a verdict.

Compare the coverage of the Homolka case with the "publicity surrounding the O.J. Simpson trial," says Cooper, "and ours looks reasonable. With all these lawyers giving their opinions on the Larry King show and discussing evidence that may never be admitted, people at cocktail parties have clearly formed opinions on whether Simpson is guilty. Now the prosecution and defense will have to act as spin doctors to disabuse the jury of a partiality that's there. It shouldn't happen that way."

Festinger would like Canada to adopt some of the American-style openness while preserving Canada's traditional restraint and respect for individual privacy. "A uniquely Canadian solution would be to allow cameras in the courtroom to afford public scrutiny but to retain some of the contempt restrictions so that you don't have psychiatrists on the news speculating about the motives of someone like O.J. Simpson," he says. He would take away the judge's option of prior restraint on the press and let the media take their chances on acting in contempt of court. "The big difference is that the American system is more realistic about effects of new technology in the 2,000-channel universe," he says.

"It's generally a bad idea to have secrets," says editor Lewis. "And experience in the United States with cases involving massive publicity — the first Rodney King trial, the Menendez brothers, and the Bobbitts — shows that the system does work, that it is possible to find" jurors who aren't overly influenced by the coverage.

"But the circus aspect to some trials is disturbing," Lewis adds. "Putting potential evidence on TV before a trial raises the danger of slanting jurors and causing a wrong conviction. I favor openness, and much of it in the United States is admirable. But to see evidence related to a trial on Eyewitness News is, shall we say, inelegant."

---

[1] *Maclean's,* Jan. 31, 1994, p. 2.

[2] *The Washington Post,* Nov. 23, 1993.

[3] Quoted in *Maclean's,* July 19, 1993, p. 19.

[4] *Maclean's,* Jan. 31, 1994, p. 2. The Ontario Appeals Court is not expected to rule on the challenge to the Homolka ban until the Canadian Supreme Court rules on a challenge to a similar media ban in a child sexual-abuse case tried last year in Saskatchewan.

[5] For background on the charter, see Philip Aniseman and Allen Linden (eds.), *The Media, the Courts and the Charter* (1986).

the public record or who violated a judicial order. "The primary burden for ensuring a fair trial is on the legal branch and the agencies which serve and minister to it," it said.[35]

The Reardon report has been updated periodically and published as the ABA's model rules of professional conduct for prosecutors and defense attorneys. These principles have been adopted in full by the highest courts in 39 states, according to ABA ethics counsel George Kuhlman, while other states have used it as a basis for creating modified rules. Violators are subject both to contempt citations by trial judges as well as to disciplinary action by the state bar or special state agencies representing the bar.

Under the rules used in Maryland, for example, prosecutor Sonner reports that lawyers during a pretrial period may not make public statements "about a suspect's confession, prior criminal record, the possibility of a guilty plea, the results of a search or scientific tests, or a suspect's refusal to make a statement." Nor can any lawyer or other officer of the court offer "an opinion on guilt, the character or credibility of one party, the identities of witnesses or their expected testimony, or discuss evidence or whether it's inadmissible."

What can be commented on, Sonner adds, is "an investigation in progress, a request for a police agency's help, a warning of danger, the residence and family status of an accused and the time and place of a suspect's arrest."

The ABA modified its rules this August to permit a so-called right of reply. It allows an opposing attorney to answer, without being disciplined, the remarks of another attorney who was found by a judge to have violated the ABA's standards of conduct on pretrial publicity.

The police chiefs, meanwhile, wary of frequent tension between police and journalists, have created a similar set of guidelines. It includes advice on how police should prevent journalists from invading crime scenes and a prohibition on releasing information from police personnel records.

Judges, in addition, frequently take steps to discipline the press. Detroit Judge George Crockett III last year briefly jailed a cub reporter who had accidentally contacted a sitting juror by phone. And he slapped a contempt charge on a *Detroit Free Press* photographer for violating his ban and taking a picture of a witness outside the courtroom. [36]

As for the press, its energies in the past 20 years have been spent resisting the legal profession's efforts to assign it rules of conduct. [37] What the press calls the "public's right to know," though not mentioned in the Constitution, appears in the Society of Professional Journalists' (SPJ) code of ethics as "the overriding mission of the mass media." (The code, purely voluntary, also admonishes journalists to "guard against invading a person's right to privacy" and "not to pander to morbid curiosity about details of vice and crime.")

A survey of 304 media outlets showed that 42 percent of newspapers and 31 percent of television stations have written codes of ethics for such questions as naming rape victims, juveniles and suspects or accused persons in crime stories. Others rely on verbal policies, according to the SPJ. [38]

TV in the Courts

The early experiments with televised trials lasted until a 1965 Supreme Court ruling in the case of *Estes v. Texas*. Billy Sol Estes, an associate of President Lyndon Johnson, had been convicted of swindling in 1962. Estes' trial attracted massive press coverage. Press clippings about the trial filled some 11 notebooks, and a preliminary hearing drew 12 television cameramen with the attendant — and obtrusive — bundles of cables, wires and microphones for national commentators. [39]

Even though live telecasting was prohibited for much of the trial, Estes' attorneys appealed on the grounds that the cameras' presence had been disruptive. The appeal was supported by the ABA and the American Civil Liberties Union (ACLU). The Supreme Court agreed that the judge had been harassed by the presence of cameras, which effectively banned them from courtrooms.

But with the ABA's consent, experiments were resumed again in the 1970s, led by courts in Florida. In 1977, 2,750 participants in recent Florida trials that had been covered electronically — witnesses, lawyers, court personnel and jurors — were polled. The conclusion was that the cameras had had little effect. [40]

On March 9, 1983, 28 news organizations petitioned the Judicial Conference of the United States, asking that the judges' code of conduct be amended to permit broadcasting and camera coverage of federal court proceedings. The conference held hearings, took a survey and concluded that 78 percent of 600 active judges felt that "the alleged public benefits of the requested changes . . . are outweighed by the risks to the administration of justice." They cited distractions and diversion of judicial time, psychological effects on jurors, witnesses, judges and lawyers and preserving the solemnity of judicial proceedings. [41]

Also during the 1980s, a string of proposals from news organizations to broadcast the Supreme Court in action elicited little enthusiasm from Chief Justice William H. Rehnquist: "I don't think that's in the works right now. . . . A majority of the court was not in favor of it. . . . I hope we don't get to the time where the members of our court are trying to get on the 6 o'clock news every night, and I think if they did, it would lessen to a certain extent some of the mystique and moral authority" of the court. [42]

Associate Justice Stephen G. Breyer, during his confirmation hearings this July, seemed a bit more open to the idea. He testified that he had permitted cameras while he had been an appeals court judge and would be willing to discuss the possibility with his new colleagues on the Supreme Court.

The Judicial Conference, meanwhile, in 1991 began a pilot project permitting cameras to cover civil trials in eight federal district and appeals courts for three years. The Federal Judicial Center found that in the first two years of the experiment, the media filed for coverage in 257 cases, 82 percent of which were approved.

"Attitudes of judges toward coverage of civil proceedings were initially neutral and became more favorable . . . under the pilot program," the report said. "[M]ost participants believe electronic media presence has no or minimal detrimental effects on jurors or witnesses." [43]

Nonetheless, on Sept. 20 the Judicial Conference decided not to permit cameras in federal civil proceedings on a nationwide basis. The pilot program ends Dec. 31. ■

Continued on p. 834

At Issue:

Has media coverage of the O. J. Simpson case been excessive?

EVERETTE E. DENNIS
Executive Director, The Freedom Forum Media Studies Center

FROM *COMMUNIQUÉ,* JULY/AUGUST 1994.

yes

As this is written, coverage of O. J. Simpson continues with firehose ferocity in the news media. . . . The story . . . was for a time a who-done-it with wild speculations pieced together from many sources. That phase of the case ended with Mr. Simpson's flight from justice that culminated in a freeway chase watched live by 95 million Americans on several TV channels.

Real-time television was showcased at its best in following the breaking story with compelling bravado. But the coverage was replete with errors and rumors, which most observers forgave in light of the fact that news gathering in real time does not allow for editing and confirmation.

Subsequent coverage of this tragedy has been equally intense, with the monitoring of Mr. Simpson's movement through the judicial system. Though such a journey is always a slow and tortured process, in this case it has been made into a daily soap opera involving police, lawyers and grand jurors as they add new elements and bits of often uncorroborated "evidence. . . ."

The relentless presence of the media in this case has once again threatened the balance between First Amendment press freedom rights and Sixth Amendment fair trial rights. While few doubt the right of the press and the public to gather information and express opinions as they wish, the use of the press by police and law enforcement personnel, prosecutors and defense attorneys, grand jurors and others to leak information, has, in many instances, violated legal ethics with reckless abandon. This case recalls the appalling prejudicial press treatment of Dr. Sam Sheppard in his first trial for the murder of his wife. . . .

In the 1960s, the Reardon Commission Report adopted rules for the legal system and voluntary guidelines for the media to protect the fragile balance between the First and Sixth amendments. Those guidelines are all but forgotten today, and the chances for their return are not good. That, however, does not absolve law enforcement officials and press for their repeated trammeling of rights, so dramatically illustrated in the O. J. Simpson case.

One can hope that some media will establish a "zone of decency," offering the public a "Good Housekeeping Seal" on information that is at least fact-checked in this instance, but even that is a lot to hope for. . . .

Of course, the republic will not fall because of this case, but our commitment to the values of the Constitution may be a bit less firm when resolution finally comes.

JANE HEALY
***Managing Editor,* Orlando (Fla.) Sentinel**

FROM *ASNE BULLETIN,* AUGUST 1994.

no

Have the media gone nuts on O. J.? Absolutely. Is that justified? Absolutely. Why is it that every time a great story breaks these days we want to beat ourselves up over our coverage? It's as if we can't stand the fact that our readers might actually be enjoying a story. We write column after column about our "overreaction" and wring our hands over whether we should be paying attention to it at all. . . .

Yes, some of the coverage has been dead wrong. The media are usually wrong some of the time in a huge story like this, mostly because television is going with the story before broadcasters have had time to thoroughly check it out. They go with one source, rather than two, and too often a flimsy one at that. This is why newspapers have been more accurate than TV on this story. They have had the time and patience to double-check the sources.

And, yes much of the coverage has been repetitive. After all, there can only be so many interpretations of what is in "the envelope." But so what? Most people couldn't watch — or read — all of the coverage anyway. They tried to channel-surf their way through the broadcast news magazines to get the latest legal expert each night and then got another interpretation in their paper the next morning. It's all part of a fascinating legal debate.

That said, we still need to know when to shut up. It's one thing to have reams of coverage during the preliminary hearing; trying to keep that up the following week is a stretch. Face it, we ran out of things to say. We need to be willing to get a life until the next chapter begins. . . .

Actually, the biggest problem I've had with this story is that newspapers haven't been able to carve out enough of a niche for themselves. Readers hungry for more on the story turned to their newspapers the next day, but we gave them little that was different from television. With its myriad legal experts, TV was able to give instant analysis. And, obviously, cameras in the courtroom gave TV a huge advantage over us.

Perhaps during the trial we can learn how to better deal with this, maybe by focusing on stories previewing the upcoming day's events rather than rehashing the day before. Or we could help readers find the O. J. TV specials on that night rather than forcing them to switch channels. If we're smart, we'll use TV as a huge promotional device for our next day's paper and then complement its coverage in a big way.

CURRENT SITUATION

Preparing for Simpson

As Los Angeles prepared for the Simpson trial, few expenses were being spared. The courtroom in the Criminal Courts Building was being outfitted with the latest electronic gear, including computers for attorneys to search through texts and transcripts, large-screen TVs to display documents and a "light pen" to allow witnesses to augment their testimony with electronic sketches. [44]

Local TV stations spent a quarter of a million dollars preparing the press room, according to the *Los Angeles Times*. And the city was mobilizing to call up to 1,000 potential jurors, a major expense for taxpayers.

Prosecutors, it was revealed in late August, had repaired to Phoenix, Ariz., where they staged what in effect was a mock trial — and lost. Simpson's defense, meanwhile, hired a jury consultant to study potential jurors' backgrounds, body language and comments during questioning to detect bias.

Both sides had agreed earlier that gruesome photographs of the bloodied bodies of Nicole Simpson and Ronald Goldman would be withheld from the news media, a decision that drew protests from a coalition of news organizations that included Gannett, *Newsweek,* CBS, and Times Mirror. The Fox television network, meanwhile, acceded to pleas from Simpson's defense team and postponed a planned Sept. 13 made-for-TV movie about Simpson until after the trial.

Judge Ito in August floated the possibility of a gag order on the press. "The problem is that I think we're in a different dimension because of the improvements in the electronic media," he said. [45] The news organizations argued that such a ruling would violate the First Amendment and was overly broad, citing past high-profile cases where impartial juries had been found. The ACLU also objected, saying, "Not only would Judge Ito's proposed order harm the public's right to know how its court system is operating, it will do nothing to enhance Mr. Simpson's right to a fair trial." [46]

Also in August, California lawmakers introduced legislation to prevent prosecutors and defense attorneys from making prejudicial statements outside court. (California is the only state where the Legislature, rather than the judicial branch, plays such a role in regulating the legal profession, according to the ABA's Kuhlman.)

Kendall of the ABA task force says that while the Supreme Court has ruled that a lawyer's speech rights "can be circumscribed, that's a task for a judge, not the blunderbuss of legislation. I don't see how a statute would get around the First Amendment."

Law Professor Burkoff says that such legislation would make little difference, if the rules other states have on pretrial statements are any indication. They "typically don't have a restraining effect," he says. "Also, defendants could go around their lawyers and leak through friends."

Media Protests

In other cases, judges have cracked down on pretrial press reports with mixed success. In July, a Stockton, Calif., judge stunned attorneys and the media when he ordered 18 news agencies to save all published and unpublished materials they had assembled concerning the coverage of the high-profile kidnapping of a 12-year-old girl.

The prosecutor had joined with the defense in favoring the move to stave off additional pretrial publicity that could lead to a change of venue. "The court has no jurisdiction over the news media," protested Debra Bruns, in-house counsel for McClatchy Newspapers. News professionals vowed to fight and predicted the order would be overturned. [47]

The media were more successful in Philadelphia. A U.S. Appeals Court ruled in January that the press could attend the post-trial questioning of jurors necessitated by allegations of juror misbehavior. One juror in the racketeering and extortion trial of a criminal defense attorney had reported after the verdict that jurors had defied a judge's admonition not to watch TV news reports, read newspapers or discuss the case with outsiders. A lower court had ruled against the newspapers, saying the presence of the press would interfere with candor and that public interest was outweighed in the "interest of justice to conduct a hearing in the least coercive atmosphere." [48] ■

OUTLOOK

An Enduring Debate

Until the Supreme Court decides, in effect, whether the First or Sixth Amendment should take precedence, the two amendments are not likely to cease clashing. One reason is that the court "has not acknowledged the crucial link between the extent of media freedom [that should be allowed] and the ability of the accused to receive a fair trial," said Professor Alfredo Garcia of St. Thomas University Law School in Miami, Fla. Secondly, he noted, "the court has ignored the contradictory purposes served by a free press and a fair trial." [49]

It is difficult to set rules for all cases, notes prosecutor Sonner. "We inevitably judge what goes on day in and day out [in the legal system] by what happens in a case like O.J. Simpson's that comes along once in a century." But rules that apply to high-profile cases would be "oppressive to the First Amendment" in average cases,

How Journalists Cover the Simpson Case

Immediately after police responded to the discovery of the bodies of Nicole Brown Simpson and Ronald L. Goldman, reporters were hard on their heels.

The *Los Angeles Times* interviewed a jogger who said she'd passed Nicole Simpson's condo on the night of the murder and had seen a Ford Bronco similar to O.J. Simpson's parked nearby. *The Los Angeles Sentinel* contacted a man who had been on Simpson's flight to Chicago that night, saying Simpson had seemed normal. And the tabloid TV show "A Current Affair" emerged with an exclusive report from a man who had caddied for Simpson earlier on the fateful day: He described an angry and depressed Simpson turning to him and saying, "I'm a pathetic person." [1]

The upshot of all the journalistic activity was a number of early stories containing investigative details that observers took to be leaks from the Los Angeles Police Department. Journalists and police both deny it. "The Simpson defense team, the LAPD and the prosecuting attorneys all have reasons to want information out in public," says Leo Wolinsky, metro editor of the *Los Angeles Times*. "But at the beginning, we were really using our traditional [police and court] sources. The defense wasn't organized. The police didn't yet know what they had."

"I'm not sure where the reporters get their information," says Cmdr. David Gascon, an LAPD spokesman. "But my belly tells me that anyone who makes the assumption that it's from a single source is wrong. The majority of the information comes from outside the LAPD. The DA, the defense teams, the coroners, they all talk. We have an interest in not having things leak because of the overwhelming number of calls we then get. An investigator who thinks he has eight hours to do his work spends 12 hours fighting off the media." However, Gascon adds, "I'm in a position to know what's accurate, and we feel comfortable looking at what has come out."

The notion that the LAPD would use leaks to work with Los Angeles newspapers seems absurd to Jim Newton, a *Times* reporter covering the Simpson case. "I've never been in any journalistic environment where there was as deeply felt an antagonism as exists between the LAPD and the *Times*," he says. "During the Rodney King trial, the police said the *Times* was unfair, and [then-Police Chief Daryl] Gates said the only good thing about the [subsequent] riots was that people tried to set fire to the *L.A. Times*."

The notion of leaks from police also represents "a misunderstanding of the process," Newton adds. "I've been on the beat for a year and a half, and I've had to ferret things out in little bits and pieces. There's been no stream of revelations all dropping at once."

The tabloid press has had a field day with the Simpson story, and has broken several exclusives. But the tabloids have also published numerous stories that would appear to serve the interests of one side or another. In late August, for example, an anonymously sourced *Globe* story reported that Nicole Simpson had stalked O.J. in the months before her murder, surprising him at restaurants and screaming at him. *The National Enquirer* that week broke the story of the prosecution's secret mock trial in Phoenix, in which Simpson was found not guilty. And the *National Examiner* quoted friends and ex-girlfriends of the accused, saying, "O.J. Simpson loved his wife so much there's no way he could have murdered her." [2]

None of the parties in the case "have planted evidence in the *Enquirer*," says Iain Calder, the Florida tabloid's editor-in-chief. He finds the charge that tabloids take sides "totally ridiculous. We run stories on both sides. We're blind to which side it would help," he says. "We don't say, 'Bring me a story that's pro-O.J.' We say, 'Just get me a great story that will help sell 3.5 million copies.' It's just digging by dozens of people working seven days a week," he adds. "We work on 10-12 leads every week, and most die because they don't check out or we can't source them."

Louis Hodges, professor of journalistic ethics at Washington and Lee University, worries about the use of unnamed sources in stories that are likely to influence a trial. "If they really wanted to inform rather than attract attention and entertain, they would slow down." News leaks, he says, have been a fundamental problem in the Simpson case, "but it is unrealistic to expect a news organization not to publish information it has. The media's disposition that the public needs to have such information serves a public good. But if a reporter gets a leak from the LAPD or other source, he has a positive duty to check out its validity. There's no point in publishing rumors."

Cynthia McFadden, who is covering the Simpson case for ABC News, says that "all journalists who've been around for a while know they're occasionally used" by sources trying to leak information. "It's the power of your organization, and you have to second-guess as to why. ABC has been aggressively conservative in following the story, and we have still have moved the investigative ball forward. But being first is not as important as being right. Temptation can be resisted in our business if we care about the truth."

[1] Quoted in Jeffrey Toobin, "Cash for Trash," *The New Yorker*, July 11, 1994, p. 33.

[2] *The National Examiner*, Aug. 30, 1994, p. 24.

he says, adding that the ABA has considered a separate set of standards for "megacases."

"Rather than quash freedom, let's open up," says American University's Stack, who teaches public relations techniques to attorneys to help them "make a strong case in the court of public opinion. But attorneys need to keep an eye cocked on justice as well as the interests of their client," Stack adds. "Unfortunately, in our adversarial system no one is rewarded or encouraged or trained to engage the public's interest."

As for the effects of stepped-up media coverage, ABC's McFadden says, "We're turning a corner. We're instilling in people a revitalized interest in what happens in this branch of government. In covering 250 trials, I'm astonished at how well the system worked. Look at the New England town squares that are built around courthouses — people are expected to come out to trials."

Media lawyer Ovelmen says he "never bought the idea that the media tries cases. And there's not much of a workable alternative to allowing the press to report what it can get," he says. "But that doesn't mean they can't exercise some restraint, and we've lost that."

Justice Breyer, when asked during his confirmation hearings whether he favored a law to stop witnesses from selling their stories to the media, said: "The kind of restraint we may talk about may be discussed at prestigious panels of either press associations or bar associations, and the discussion will be forgotten the first time there's competition for a story." [50]

Many observers argue that after 200 years of practice, the public and the court system can handle the competing claims of free press and fair trial. "Sometimes in a democracy," says Burkoff, "you have to hear a cacophony of voices. But because we hear so many, we don't always believe every one, particularly when they contradict each other." ■

Notes

[1] Press release, June 30, 1994.

[2] Robert L. Shapiro, "Using the Media to Your Advantage," *The Champion*, January-February, 1993, p. 7. The magazine is published by the National Association of Criminal Defense Lawyers.

[3] T. Barton Carter, Marc A. Franklin and Jay B. Wright, *The First Amendment and the Fourth Estate: The Law of Mass Media* (1991), p. 438.

[4] *Editor & Publisher*, March 12, 1994. Jackson reportedly settled the suit for several million dollars before the case went to trial.

[5] Quoted in Jeffrey Toobin, "Cash for Trash," *The New Yorker*, July 11, 1994, p. 34.

[6] Avern L. Cohn, "Fair Trial v. Free Press: A Trial Judge's View," *Michigan Bar Journal*, February 1992, p. 190.

[7] Robert Hariman (ed.), *Popular Trials: Rhetoric, Mass Media and The Law*, (1990), p. 90.

[8] For background on police policies on releasing mug shots, see "Access to Police Mug Shots Varies Widely," *The News Media and The Law*, spring 1994, pp. 16-18. The magazine is published by the Reporters Committee for Freedom of the Press.

[9] See Howard Kurtz, *Media Circus* (1993) p. 84.

[10] *Ibid.*, p. 87.

[11] "That Delicate Balance: Fair Trial vs. Free Press," *New Jersey Law Journal*, June 7, 1990, p. 9.

[12] Toobin, *op. cit.*

[13] "An Incendiary Defense," *The New Yorker*, July 25, 1994, p. 56.

[14] Dick Thornburgh, "Prosecutors and the press in the search for the truth, the whole truth and nothing but the truth," *Judicature*, Vol. 75, No. 1, June-July 1991, p. 20. The magazine is published by the Chicago-based American Judicature Society.

[15] Peter E. Kane, *Murder, Courts and the Press* (1992), p. 93.

[16] Bill Boyarsky, "Comment on California," *Los Angeles Times*, Aug. 4, 1994.

[17] "Fair Trial v. Free Press," *Pennsylvania Law Review*, Nov. 15, 1993.

[18] Quoted in Alan Barth, *Rights in Conflict: Report of the Twentieth Century Fund Task Force on Justice, Publicity and the First Amendment* (1976), p. 11.

[19] American Bar Association, *ABA Standards for Criminal Justice, Fair Trial and Free Press, Third Edition* (1992), p. 44.

[20] Ralph Frasca, "Estimating the Occurrence of Trials Prejudiced by Press Coverage," *Judicature*, Vol. 72, No. 3, October-November 1988, p. 162.

[21] *Ibid.*

[22] Bruce Kauffman, "Living Room Law," *Washington Journalism Review*, March 1992, p. 17.

[23] *USA Today*, Aug. 10, 1994.

[24] Comments on National Public Radio's "Morning Edition," July 12, 1994.

[25] Paul Raymond, "The Impact of a Televised Trial on Individuals' Information and Attitudes," *Judicature*, Vol. 75, No. 4, December-January 1992, p. 204.

[26] Only 10 percent of all felony arrests resulted in jury trials, according to a 1979 Department of Justice Survey of major metropolitan areas. In the rest of the arrests, no criminal charges were filed, charges were dismissed, or cases were handled through plea bargaining.

[27] Thornburgh, *op. cit.*

[28] Frasca, *op. cit.*, p. 162.

[29] Alfredo Garcia, "Clash of the Titans: The Difficult Reconciliation of a Fair Trial and a Free Press in Modern American Society," *The Champion*, July 1994, p. 9.

[30] Alfred Friendly and Ronald L. Goldfarb, *Crime and Publicity* (1967), p. 12.

[31] Kane, *op. cit.*, p. 10.

[32] ABA, *op. cit.*, p. 3.

[33] Barth, *op. cit.*, p. 71.

[34] Kane, *op. cit.*, p. 30.

[35] Friendly and Goldfarb, *op. cit.*, p. 132.

[36] *Editor & Publisher*, July 24, 1993.

[37] Cohn, *op. cit.*

[38] *Quill*, November-December, 1992, pp. 31, 38. The magazine is published by the SPJ.

[39] Friendly and Goldfarb, *op. cit.*, p. 217.

[40] Philip Aniseman and Allen Linden (eds.), *The Media, the Courts and the Charter* (1986), p. 452. The Florida poll did not include judges.

[41] "Report of the Judicial Conference Ad Hoc Committee on Cameras in the Courtroom," Sept. 6, 1984.

[42] Quoted in Tony Mauro, "Justices Keep Out Cameras, Preserve Their Rite of Privacy," *Washington Journalism Review*, November 1988, p. 24.

[43] Molly Treadway Johnson, "Electronic Media Coverage of Federal Civil Proceedings: An Evaluation of the Pilot Program in Six District Courts and Two Courts of Appeals," Federal Judicial Center, Nov. 4, 1993.

[44] *USA Today*, Aug. 18, 1994.

[45] *The Washington Post*, Sept. 1, 1994. As of Sept. 20, Judge Ito had not issued the gag order.

[46] *Los Angeles Times*, Washington Edition, Aug. 31, 1994.

[47] *Editor & Publisher*, July 30, 1994, p. 9.

[48] *The News Media and The Law*, winter 1994, p. 28.

[49] Garcia, *op. cit.*

[50] Testimony before Senate Judiciary Committee, July 12, 1994.

Bibliography

Selected Sources Used

Books

Aniseman, Philip, and Allen Linden (eds.), *The Media, the Courts and the Charter,* Carswell, 1986.
This Canadian legal text anthologizes essays providing a thorough discussion of how fair trial-free press issues are handled in Canada and how the Canadian and U.S. systems compare.

Barth, Alan, *Rights in Conflict: Report of the Twentieth Century Fund Task Force on Justice, Publicity, and the First Amendment,* McGraw-Hill, 1976.
A New York foundation commissioned this background paper giving various specialists' views on the clash between free press and fair trial, including a history of how legal authorities have confronted the problem.

Carter, T. Barton, Marc A. Franklin and Jay B. Wright, *The First Amendment and the Fourth Estate: The Law of Mass Media*, The Foundation Press, 1991.
Professors in law, communications and journalism examine all aspects of media law, with a 100-page section devoted to the conflict over free press and fair trial.

Friendly, Alfred and Ronald L. Goldfarb, *Crime and Publicity: The Impact of News on the Administration of Justice,* Twentieth Century Fund, 1967.
In this classic on the subject, a former *Washington Post* editor and a Washington attorney explore the history and debate surrounding the clash between the courts and the news media, revealing how little has changed in the past 25 years.

Hariman, Robert (ed.),*Popular Trials: Rhetoric, Mass Media and the Law,* University of Alabama Press, 1990.
This collection edited by a Drake University communications professor explores the role of the trial in society, discussing historical, psychological, political, social and legal aspects of court cases that capture popular attention.

Kane, Peter E., *Murder, Courts, and the Press: Issues in Free Press/Fair Trial,* Southern Illinois University Press, 1992.
An academic reviews high-profile cases over the past three decades that have raised the conflict between the First and Sixth amendments. Also included is an appendix of key court rulings on the subject.

Kurtz, Howard, *Media Circus: The Trouble With America's Newspapers,* Times Books, 1993.
The media critic for the *The Washington Post* discusses how modern newspapers cope with declining circulations and ethical dilemmas. He includes some discussion of crime reportage.

Siebert, Fred, Walter Wilcox and George Hough III, *Free Press and Fair Trial: Some Dimensions of the Problem,* University of Georgia Press, 1970.
Three academics examine empirical research on the question of whether jurors are overly influenced by news media coverage of crimes. They also discuss early efforts to arrive at conduct codes for lawyers and reporters.

Articles

Kerr, Norbert, "Behavioral Research and the Effects of Pretrial Publicity," *In the Mind's Eye,* Vol. 1, No. 3, 1992.
A University of Michigan psychology professor surveys research on juror behavior, arguing that most jurors are not able to put aside information that they have been exposed to in the news media.

Reports

American Bar Association, *ABA Standards for Criminal Justice: Fair Trial and Free Press,* Third Edition, 1992.
The history and legal arguments behind the fair trial-free press debate are outlined in this set of guidelines designed to help attorneys avoid prejudicial publicity.

American Society of Newspaper Editors, *The Bulletin,* August 1994.
The magazine for a major journalists' organization devoted an entire issue to examining the news coverage of the murder trial of football hero O.J. Simpson.

The Next Step

Additional information from UMI's Newspaper & Periodical Abstracts database

Cameras in Court

Gerbner, George, "Challenging the mythology of the television courtroom," *Governing,* June 1993, p. 11.
The issue of whether TV cameras should be allowed into court hearings and proceedings is discussed. Before courtrooms are open to more TV coverage, whether such coverage enhances or diminishes the integrity of the criminal justice process should be determined, Gerbner writes.

"He-e-ere's justice," *New Yorker,* Oct. 11, 1993, pp. 6-8.
The U.S. Supreme Court is discussed. For better or worse, the magazine says, the rise of TV has been one of the most important changes in U.S. society since World War II; it is time for TV and the judiciary to learn to live with each other, which would probably raise the level of both.

Kolbert, Elizabeth, "A full docket, but no profits, for Court TV," *The New York Times,* Jan. 31, 1994, p. D6.
The chances for success of Court TV, founded by Steven Brill, are examined. Court TV has been hailed as the CNN of the legal system, and although it is not making a profit, it is clearly making a big splash. Court TV's schedule includes several hours of live trial coverage every day, making it unattractive to advertisers who routinely avoid current-affairs programming.

Mauro, Tony, "Cameras go to court," *Quill,* October 1993, p. 39.
The experiment involving cameras and microphones in the courtroom has been a success, Mauro writes. No problems have occurred during the experiment, and broadcasters have found a good news source, he says.

Quindlen, Anna, "Order in the court," *The New York Times,* July 13, 1994, p. A19.
Quindlen addresses the publicity surrounding the preliminary hearing in the case of accused murderer O. J. Simpson, saying that the notion that the publicity forecloses Simpson's ability to get a fair trial is a simplistic reaction to a complex process. Quindlen says that all people have the right to observe courtroom proceedings and that cameras in the courtroom are merely the manifestation of that right.

Sherer, Michael, "A case of now or never?" *News Photographer,* August 1993, p. 14.
Questions concerning the evaluation of broadcast coverage in federal appeals courts—including the extent and nature of news media coverage, the types of cases covered and how courtroom footage was used — are examined, and a three-year experimental program analyzing photographic coverage is discussed. (Part 2 of 2)

Civic Education

Bils, Jeffrey, "Simpson case gives rare, but warped, civics lesson," *Chicago Tribune,* July 10, 1994, p. 2C1.
For a national TV audience, the O. J. Simpson murder case coverage has been a rare view into the inner workings of the American judicial system. For a TV audience that grew up with Perry Mason and has come to expect at least one good thrill in any courtroom scene, the broadcast of Simpson's banal preliminary hearing was an eye-opener, Bils says.

Boyarsky, Bill, "TV conveys drama — And opens up courts," *Los Angeles Times,* July 2, 1994, p. A4.
Boyarsky comments on how televising the O. J. Simpson case in Los Angeles is exerting an influence on the opinions of millions of viewers, including potential jurors. Boyarsky says the event will educate people about the courts.

Brill, Steven, "The eye that educates," *The New York Times,* July 15, 1994, p. A27.
Court TV founder Brill argues that televising trials and court proceedings is not only educational for the public but also protects defendants' rights. Brill asserts that the publicity surrounding the O. J. Simpson case, and the media abuses that have occurred, will likely continue to occur in connection with the case, making it all the more necessary for the public to have access to the "real-reality TV of a camera in the court."

Mauro, Tony, "A public civics lesson," *USA Today,* Jan. 24, 1994, p. A3.
The face of justice has been on public view to an unprecedented degree, Mauro writes. From the Lorena Bobbitt trial to the Menendez murder trials, the public has been given a rare civics lesson about the usually invisible justice system. Courts are rapidly catching up with the visibility of the other two branches of government brought about by C-SPAN, CNN and local and national broadcast outlets.

Gag Orders

Fitzgerald, Mark, "Canadian gag," *Editor & Publisher,* Dec. 11, 1993, p. 18.
Newspapers in Canada are challenging a judge's gag order, while U.S. newspapers are abiding by the order. The gag order involves a murder trial and was invoked by Justice Francis Kovacs. The gag order is discussed.

Harman, Alan, "Canadian judge bans U.S. media from trial," *Editor & Publisher,* July 10, 1993, p. 11.
A Canadian judge's ban on U.S. reporters from the courtroom while allowing their Canadian counterparts to attend the manslaughter trial of the ex-wife of a man charged with

murder is discussed. Members of the public were banned from the courtroom, and Canadian reporters were warned against reporting anything other than the judge's verdict.

Jenish, D. Arcy, "Leaks in a gag order," ***Maclean's,*** **Dec. 13, 1993, pp. 16-18.**
Canadians can get the details of the trial of Karla Homolka by watching TV stations in Buffalo, N.Y. A judge had placed a publication ban on information about the trial in Canada. Homolka is accused of helping her husband kill two teenage girls.

"When a gag order is a first resort. . ." ***The News Media and The Law*****, summer 1993, p. 3.**
While gag orders can be justified to a degree, judges who gag the news media, prohibiting them from reporting on criminal proceedings, often have an overwhelming desire to censor, according to the magazine. Gag orders should be the last resort of a thoughtful judge, not the option of choice, it says.

Manipulating the Press

Hoffman, Jan, "May it please the public," ***The New York Times,*** **April 22, 1994, p. B1.**
Defense lawyers in high-profile cases are increasingly using a new strategy: speaking about the case to the news media. Though legal experts are dismayed by the increasing number of lawyers who consider a news conference part of the job, they question whether the remedy, court-ordered silence, can be fairly enforced or is even necessary. The controversial issue is examined.

Stein, M. L., "Lawyer says it's OK to lie to the media," ***Editor & Publisher,*** **Aug. 28, 1993, pp. 9-10.**
The attorney for Amy Fisher, the woman who shot the wife of her alleged lover, says that he has no qualms about misleading reporters to benefit his client. Attorney Eric Naiburg has stated that he routinely and successfully manipulates "sympathetic" reporters to write stories favorable to his clients.

Spotlight on Lawyers

Bart, Peter, "Agents of change," ***Variety,*** **June 14, 1993, p. 5.**
More and more showbiz attorneys and agents have dropped their protective cover and are issuing pronouncements and volunteering quotes to the press, Bart writes. Many are even hiring press agents to enhance their public presence. The issue of confidentiality among attorneys, talent agents and their clients is examined.

Drell, Adrienne, "In the spotlight," ***ABA Journal,*** **November 1993, pp. 60-65.**
Most lawyers find that their efforts on behalf of clients go unnoticed, but sometimes they are thrust to the center of media attention and public controversy. Four lawyers who took on cases that put them in the center of controversy discuss how to cope with the attention and scrutiny.

"High court denies prosecutors immunity," ***The News Media and The Law,*** **summer 1993, pp. 60-61.**
The U.S. Supreme Court ruled in June 1993 that prosecutors may be liable for making false and defamatory out-of-court statements about criminal defendants to the news media. The court's unanimous ruling in *Buckley v. Fitzsimmons* is discussed.

Samborn, Randall, "ABA floats trial publicity rule," ***National Law Journal,*** **Sept. 20, 1993, p. 3.**
A proposal to revise a model ethics rule governing trial publicity is drawing some opposition, Samborn writes. Since the U.S. Supreme Court's 1991 ruling in *Gentile v. State Bar of Nevada,* the American Bar Association has been working to amend the rule affecting an attorney's right to make out-of-court statements.

The Supreme Court and the Media

Denniston, Lyle, "The news media won't miss Byron White," ***American Journalism Review: AJR,*** **July 1993, p. 46.**
The news industry has had a love/hate relationship with retiring Supreme Court justice Byron White for years because of his stance on the First Amendment. White tended to be suspicious of rights protecting the press.

Hohler, Bob, "Backers, critics vie for spotlight; family seeks to survive it," ***Boston Globe,*** **July 13, 1994, p. 12.**
The impact of the intense media spotlight on friends and backers of Supreme Court nominee Stephen G. Breyer is discussed.

"No, it doesn't please the court," ***U.S. News & World Report,*** **Sept. 13, 1993, p. 14.**
Most states allow some judicial broadcast coverage, but the U.S. Supreme Court has refused. The court is also considering taking legal action against a political scientist who has published audiotapes from the National Archives of 23 landmark cases.

Sableman, Mark, "Ginzburg contribution: Making free speech work," ***St. Louis Journalism Review,*** **July 1993, p. 12.**
The replacement of Byron White by Ruth Bader Ginsburg will mean replacing a vote against free speech with a vote for free speech, Sableman writes.

"Summary of Ginsburg's media opinions," ***The News Media and The Law,*** **summer 1993, p. 59.**
During her tenure on the Washington, D.C., Circuit, Judge Ruth Bader Ginsburg participated in numerous cases concerning the news media. Several of Ginsburg's significant decisions are outlined.

"Supreme Court vs. the media circus," ***The New York Times,*** **April 22, 1994, p. B7.**
The Supreme Court's 1966 ruling overturning the murder conviction of Sam Sheppard is briefly remembered as one of the court's most important rulings on the news media and fair trials. The court overturned the conviction because, it said, virulent pretrial publicity had tainted a jury.

Back Issues

Great Research on Current Issues Starts Right Here...Recent topics covered by The CQ Researcher are listed below. Before May 1991, reports were published under the name of Editorial Research Reports.

MARCH 1993
Gay Rights
Aid to Russia
War on Drugs
TV Violence

APRIL 1993
Head Start
High-Speed Rail
Children's Legal Rights
Muslims in America

MAY 1993
Cults in America
Preventing Teen Pregnancy
Software Piracy
National Parks

JUNE 1993
Food Safety
Prostitution
Childhood Immunizations
National Service

JULY 1993
Electric Cars
Population Growth
Downward Mobility
Intelligence Testing

AUGUST 1993
Mental Illness
Bilingual Education
Foreign Policy Burden
School Funding

SEPTEMBER 1993
Suburban Crime
Public Housing
Supreme Court Preview
Immigration Reform

OCTOBER 1993
Airline Safety
Disaster Response
Science in the Courtroom
The Glass Ceiling

NOVEMBER 1993
Paying for Retirement
Charitable Giving
Privacy in the Workplace
Adoption

DECEMBER 1993
U.S. Vietnam-Relations
Learning Disabilities
Child Care
Space Program's Future

JANUARY 1994
Racial Tensions in Schools
South Africa's Future
Worker Retraining
Regulating Pesticides

FEBRUARY 1994
Prison Overcrowding
Water Quality
Religion in Schools
Juvenile Justice

MARCH 1994
Underground Economy
Education Standards
Gambling Boom
Private Management of Public Schools

APRIL 1994
Reproductive Ethics
U.S.-China Trade
Soccer in America
Talk Show Democracy

MAY 1994
Traffic Congestion
Women's Health Issues
Mutual Funds
Political Scandals

JUNE 1994
Education and Gender
Gun Control
Public Land Policy
Nuclear Arms Cleanup

JULY 1994
Dietary Supplements
Public Opinion and Foreign Policy
Crime Victims' Rights
Birth Control Choices

AUGUST 1994
Genetically Engineered Foods
Electing Minorities
Prozac Controversy
College Sports

SEPTEMBER 1994
Home Schooling
Welfare Experiments

Back issues are available for $4.00 (subscribers) or $7.00 (non-subscribers). Quantity discounts apply to orders over ten. To order, call Congressional Quarterly Customer Service at (202) 887-8621.

Binders are available for $16.00. To order call 1-800-638-1710. Please refer to stock number 648.

Future Topics

- ***Regulating Tobacco***
- ***Historic Preservation***
- ***Religion and Politics***

THE CQ Researcher

PUBLISHED BY CONGRESSIONAL QUARTERLY INC.

Regulating Tobacco

Can the FDA break America's smoking habit?

The Food and Drug Administration (FDA) has been accumulating evidence that may enable the agency to regulate tobacco as a drug. Testifying at dramatic congressional hearings in March, FDA Commissioner David A. Kessler presented lawmakers with documents he says prove that cigarette manufacturers have long known of tobacco's addictive qualities and manipulated nicotine levels to keep smokers hooked. This latest offensive in the 30-year campaign against tobacco comes amid growing public intolerance of smoking, a new wave of litigation against cigarette manufacturers and a nationwide flurry of new local and state restrictions on smoking in public buildings. Cigarette makers deny wrongdoing and reject the assertion that nicotine is addictive. And they promise a stout defense of their beleaguered $50-billion-a-year industry.

INSIDE THIS ISSUE

Sept. 30, 1994 • Volume 4, No. 36 • Pages 841-864

Formerly Editorial Research Reports

REGULATING TOBACCO

COVER ART: BARBARA SASSA-DANIELS

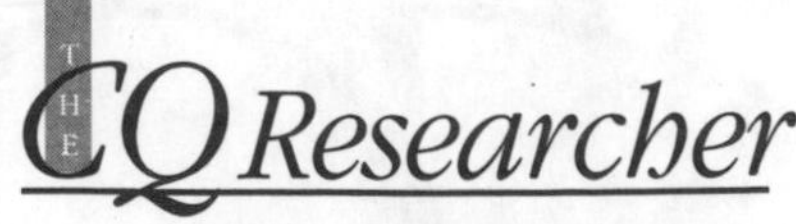

September 30, 1994
Volume 4, No. 36

The CQ Researcher (ISSN 1056-2036). Formerly Editorial Research Reports. Published weekly (48 times per year, not printed the first Friday of any month with five Fridays) by Congressional Quarterly Inc., 1414 22nd St., N.W., Washington, D.C. 20037. Rates are furnished upon request. Second-class postage paid at Washington, D.C. POSTMASTER: Send address changes to The CQ Researcher, 1414 22nd St., N.W., Washington, D.C. 20037.

Regulating Tobacco

BY MARY H. COOPER

THE ISSUES

Anti-smoking activists have come a long way since the surgeon general branded tobacco as a leading cause of disease and death 30 years ago. And the fight over the $50-billion-a-year industry goes on, with increasing intensity. [1]

There have been victories and defeats for both sides. Anti-smoking advocates have blocked smoking in airplanes and many offices and forced cigarette manufacturers to curtail advertising and place warning labels on tobacco products. The tobacco industry, meanwhile, has staved off more aggressive measures by Congress to tax and regulate tobacco, while winning numerous product-liability lawsuits brought by smokers and their families.

Now anti-tobacco forces have opened a major, new front in the war on tobacco. The call to arms came from David A. Kessler, commissioner of the Food and Drug Administration (FDA), who announced Feb. 25 that he was considering trying to regulate the entire tobacco industry.

To succeed, Kessler must make a compelling case that nicotine is an addictive substance and that tobacco companies intentionally maintain nicotine levels high enough to keep smokers addicted. That, Kessler said, would make nicotine a drug under his interpretation of the Food, Drug and Cosmetic Act and thus make tobacco subject to FDA regulation. [2]

Thus far, however, the tobacco industry's potent lobbyists and coalition of tobacco-state lawmakers have successfully fought off many past efforts at regulation. To lose the latest fight could be disastrous for the industry. If the FDA successfully claims jurisdiction over tobacco, the agency could not only determine how much nicotine would be allowed in cigarettes but also how they are labeled, marketed and distributed. In short, the FDA would gain virtual control over cigarette production and could even totally ban tobacco products.

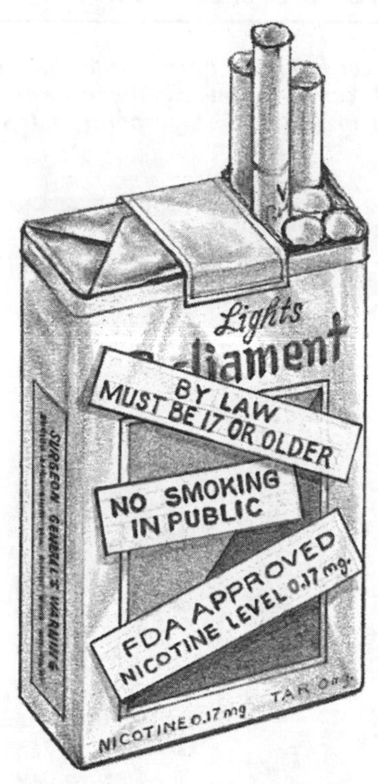

FDA regulation "could mean, ultimately, removal from the market of tobacco products containing nicotine at levels that cause or satisfy addiction," Kessler wrote in February. "Only those tobacco products from which the nicotine had been removed or, possibly, tobacco products approved by FDA for nicotine-replacement therapy would then remain on the market."

Not long after Kessler agreed to consider a new offensive against cigarettes, the FDA's key Drug Abuse Advisory Committee concluded Aug. 2 that, on the basis of mounting scientific evidence, cigarettes and other tobacco products are addicting and that nicotine is the drug in tobacco that causes addiction. The finding could be crucial in new regulatory efforts because it signals that there is a scientific basis for the FDA to assert jurisdiction over tobacco.

The push to regulate tobacco stems from the ever-growing body of evidence linking tobacco products with disease and death. According to the Coalition on Smoking OR Health, tobacco is responsible for 419,000 deaths a year, or one of every five American deaths.

Smoking also exacts a huge economic toll. Health-care expenditures caused directly by smoking came to $50 billion last year, according to the coalition, and lost economic productivity caused by smoking amounted to more than twice as much. The coalition estimates that every pack of cigarettes smoked is directly responsible for more than $3.90 in health-care costs and lost productivity. [3]

As the evidence of tobacco's harmfulness mounts, public opinion has turned increasingly against tobacco. State and local ordinances banning smoking in public buildings and raising excise taxes on cigarettes have spread across the country. [4] As a result of the growing public intolerance of tobacco smoke, and widespread health concerns, cigarette consumption in the United States has been falling since the early 1980s. It fell by 3 percent from 1992-93. (*See graph, p. 844.*)

Teenagers, not surprisingly, buck the trend. Cigarette consumption among teenagers has held almost steady since the mid 1980s. Today, Surgeon General Joycelyn Elders reported, 28 percent of high school seniors smoke. "Nearly all first use of tobacco occurs before high school graduation," she said. "So smoking is not just an adult habit, it is an adolescent addiction." [5]

Indeed, Kessler has targeted young people as the main focus of his regulatory efforts. "In many respects, this is a children's disease," says FDA spokesman Jim O'Hara. "Children will try cigarettes anywhere from age 11 to 14 and become regular smokers within two to three years. If you look at the

Smoking on the Decline in the U.S.

After nearly four decades of growth, cigarette consumption in the United States began declining in the early 1980s. In 1993, consumption was down to 485 billion cigarettes, compared with 640 billion in 1981, the high point of U.S. consumption.

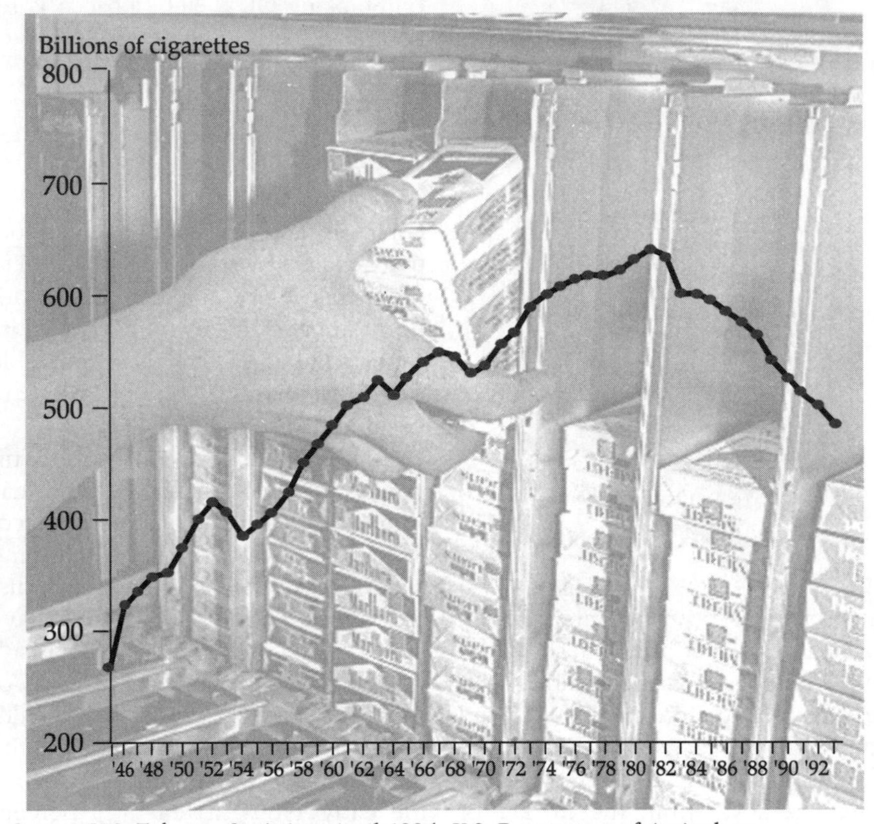

Source: U.S. Tobacco Statistics, *April 1994, U.S. Department of Agriculture*

data, it's pretty clear that if people have not begun smoking by 18 or 21, they will not become smokers."

The FDA's latest assault on tobacco is the most visible of several threats to the tobacco industry this year. Labor Secretary Robert B. Reich joined the fight in March, directing the Occupational Safety and Health Administration (OSHA) to draw up regulations restricting smoking in all workplaces. Reich based his action on a 1993 Environmental Protection Agency (EPA) report tracing disease and death among non-smokers to secondhand smoke in their home and work environments.

Anti-smoking initiatives also have emerged in the courtroom, where innovative lawsuits were brought against the industry, and in Congress, where lawmakers debated a health-care reform bill that included higher excise taxes on cigarettes.

The tobacco industry has held its ground on the tax front, at least for now. As part of its health-care reform proposal, the Clinton administration had called for the federal excise tax on cigarettes to be increased from 24 cents a pack to 99 cents. Intended to help pay for broader health coverage as well as deter smoking, the 75-cent hike was later whittled down to 45 cents by tobacco-state lawmakers before Congress abandoned the controversial proposal for this year. [6]

Over the years, cigarette manufacturers have fought off numerous courtroom attacks in the form of product-liability suits. Such suits, typically brought by a smoker or a smoker's family, blame manufacturers for disease or death caused by using the product as intended. Juries to date have rejected such suits, accepting the manufacturers' argument that smokers are free to choose whether or not to expose themselves to the hazards of smoking. But the traditional freedom-of-choice defense may not work in some innovative class-action suits initiated earlier this year in Louisiana and Minnesota. (*See story, p. 854.*)

Also this year, Florida enacted a law authorizing the state to recover from cigarette manufacturers the costs of treating Medicaid recipients with smoking-related diseases, such as lung cancer, heart disease and emphysema. On May 23, Mississippi also sued cigarette makers, seeking compensation for treating such diseases under Medicaid, the state-federal health insurance program for the poor and disabled.

To guard against the success of any of the anti-tobacco initiatives, the industry is hedging its bets, mainly by diversifying its product mix and focusing marketing efforts overseas. As to the likelihood of Kessler putting the industry under FDA jurisdiction, "I'd say he's got two chances — slim and none," says Walker Merryman, vice president and chief spokesman of The Tobacco Institute, the industry's lobbying organization. "The agency itself consistently over the years has maintained that, absent any claim by a manufacturer that the product is therapeutic in some way, the FDA has no regulatory jurisdiction."

Financial analysts aren't sounding the retreat either. They point to rising tobacco-company stocks as a sign that few investors expect regulation to succeed. "On Wall Street, we take the view that much of this stuff is a lot of noise," says Gary D. Black, a tobacco analyst at Sanford C. Bernstein & Co., an investment research and management firm in New York City.

Tobacco embraces a vast segment of American industry. In addition to the growers in 16 states, there are the cigarette manufacturers, which have become multinational behemoths selling everything from bagels to beer, and the legions of retail outlets from nationwide grocery chains to corner newsstands and vending machines.

With growing global prosperity, the smoking habit is taking hold in countries where cigarettes were once an unaffordable luxury. In addition to American cigarettes, many countries are buying unprocessed American leaf to make their own.

But when it comes to threats against the industry, tobacco growers are more vulnerable than the manufacturers. Acre for acre, no other crop is as big a money-maker as tobacco. It brings in an average of $3,862 an acre, according to Lisa Eddington, managing director of the Tobacco Growers Information Committee, based in Raleigh, N.C. Cotton, the next most lucrative crop that can survive on tobacco land, brings only $380 an acre.

"There's too much restriction already on tobacco," she says, "and these efforts by FDA and OSHA to create even further restrictions are totally unnecessary. As far as taxation goes, taxes have the power to put the growers out of business."

But most observers predict that if anyone breaks America of its smoking habit, it will be federal regulators. Proposals include improving warning labels, banning cigarette machines and gradually reducing nicotine levels in cigarettes to a non-addictive level.

"The thought of FDA regulation of nicotine has been so unthinkable for so many years that public health officials and researchers in this area need time to think and work on what is the best way to go about it," says Lynn Kozlowski, an addiction expert at Pennsylvania State University and a consultant to the FDA advisory committee.

In considering FDA regulation of tobacco, these are some of the issues Kessler and federal officials will be examining:

Reuters

Food and Drug Administration Commissioner David A. Kessler displays a cigarette ad during June 21 testimony before a House subcommittee hearing on tobacco.

Is nicotine addictive?

For the definitive answer to this key question, anti-smoking activists say, one need look no further than the 1988 surgeon general's report on smoking and health. "Careful examination of the data makes it clear that cigarettes and other forms of tobacco are addicting," Surgeon General C. Everett Koop, then the nation's top health official, declared unequivocally. "An extensive body of research has shown that nicotine is the drug in tobacco that causes addiction. Moreover, the processes that determine tobacco addiction are similar to those that determine addiction to drugs such as heroin and cocaine." [7]

Koop's view reflects that of most health professionals who have spoken out on nicotine and addiction. "The main definition of addiction is a loss of personal control over the use of the drug, where the drug is a chemical substance that has effects on the body and that, unlike food, is not a necessary part of one's life," says Neal Benowitz, chief of clinical pharmacology and professor of medicine at the University of California-San Francisco. "It's clear that nicotine is what sustains cigarette smoking. People don't smoke cigarettes without nicotine."

Benowitz, who served as a consultant at the FDA's Aug. 2 advisory committee meeting, points out that smokers who try to cut down on the number of cigarettes they smoke often switch brands or puff more intensely on each cigarette to obtain the desired nicotine level.

Perhaps most telling, Benowitz says, is the difficulty smokers face when they decide to quit. "The vast majority cannot quit," he says. "They try multiple times, and many spend a lot of money going to doctors and clinics for help. Some addicted smokers can't quit even when there's an immediate threat to their lives, such as those who've had a heart attack or lung cancer."

The tobacco industry has consistently rejected the assertion that nicotine is addictive, or that there is a

R. Michael Jenkins

Surgeon General Joycelyn Elders testifies during the House subcommittee hearings on tobacco.

direct link between cigarettes and health problems. "Dr. Koop said that cigarettes are more addictive than heroin, completely ignoring the fact that up until that point, 40 million people had quit smoking over the previous 25 years, virtually all of them without any external assistance," says Merryman of The Tobacco Institute. "I think what Koop began and what Kessler is attempting to expand upon is a radical change in the definition of the word addiction in order to cast the net wide enough to include smoking. If you do that, however, inevitably you have also to include caffeine. That would bring in not only coffee and tea but also a lot of soft drinks, chocolates and other things."

The industry's claim that scientists are arbitrarily changing the definition of addiction to help them ban cigarettes is "just nonsense," says addiction expert Kozlowski. He notes that the first surgeon general's report on smoking, issued in 1964, contained only 36 references to scientific studies on the tobacco "habit."

"In that first document," he says, "what they really say is that there's not much to go on. Now there is a lot to go on, such as the development of things like nicotine-containing gum and plasma assays, which have caused an explosion of research on the topic." Nicotine gum is used to help smokers quit, suggesting that it is the nicotine, not merely the act of smoking, that sustains the habit. Plasma assays are laboratory analyses that measure blood nicotine levels.

Cigarette manufacturers do not deny that they change nicotine levels in cigarettes, but they say they do so indirectly: By cutting levels of tar, they also cut nicotine levels. But the tobacco industry adamantly denies "spiking" cigarettes with nicotine and insists that what drives smokers to demand nicotine in their cigarettes is not an addictive craving but rather the taste it lends to smoke. [8] *(See "At Issue," p. 857.)*

"Nicotine certainly does measurably affect taste," Merryman says. "That's why it's there. In my way of thinking, it's approximately the same thing as the difference between caffeinated and decaffeinated coffee. I don't like the way decaffeinated coffee tastes."

Merryman's view of nicotine and addiction, needless to say, is at great odds with the view of addiction experts. "Nicotine is clearly addictive," Kozlowski says flatly. "It's not even a close call. If you think of all the classic drugs of abuse — heroin and so on — nicotine is really the champ at getting into the brain. There's nothing quite like it."

Would tobacco regulation lead to eventual prohibition?

Although the FDA has yet to say what form regulation would take if it claims jurisdiction over tobacco, regulatory measures would likely include measures to restrict access to cigarettes. One of the most widely discussed proposals would gradually lower the nicotine allowed in cigarettes until it falls below the threshold at which the chemical causes addiction in smokers. This would spare current smokers from having to stop "cold turkey" while ensuring that within a few years future generations would have no pharmacological incentive to start or continue smoking.

Tobacco industry representatives say that attempting to regulate tobacco would lead to an extensive black market similar to today's trade in illegal drugs. Regulation will fail, they add, just as Prohibition ultimately was unable to stop alcohol use. "If you force the manufacturers to produce a product that is rejected by most of the marketplace," says Merryman, "then obviously someone is going to rush to fill that vacuum with smuggled cigarettes."

In the industry's view, raising excise taxes on cigarettes would have the same effect. "That's why Canada rolled back their taxes by several dollars a pack," Merryman says. In February, the Canadian government cut the federal tax on cigarettes by $5 a carton in an effort to stamp out a thriving black market in smuggled U.S. cigarettes. [9]

Reuters

Former Philip Morris scientist Victor DeNoble tells a House subcommittee hearing April 28 that the company ordered him not to publish his findings on nicotine addiction a decade ago.

"Whether you skew the market by economic means with taxes or by forcing changes in the product that are unacceptable to the consumer through regulation," Merryman says, "you have the very real specter of giving organized crime an engraved invitation to get into the marketplace."

Addiction experts say the industry's argument contains a fatal flaw. "I don't doubt that there is going to be a black market in cigarettes," says Benowitz, who co-authored a proposal for reducing nicotine levels to non-addictive levels. [10] "But I think it's interesting to have them talk about a black market when they say that nicotine is just in there for the taste. A black market makes this product sound a lot like alcohol or heroin."

While acknowledging the risk of encouraging the creation of a black market, many scientists see regulation as the only way to stop young people from becoming addicted to a lethal product. The most recent surgeon general's report on tobacco and health, issued in February, called cigarette smoking an adolescent addiction. The report estimated that 3.1 million 12-to-18-year-olds — 13 percent of all children in that age group — smoke cigarettes. And another million use snuff or chewing tobacco. If adolescents can be kept free of tobacco addiction, the report concluded, most will never use tobacco when they get older. [11]

In its recent push to regulate tobacco, the FDA also has identified teenagers as the group most vulnerable to nicotine addiction. As a result, most regulatory proposals are aimed at reducing their exposure to tobacco. "The policy is really aimed at preventing youth from becoming addicted," Benowitz says. "Kids start smoking for social reasons that are unrelated to nicotine addiction, and within two or three years they become addicted and can't stop for pharmacologic reasons. So the idea behind the low-nicotine content cigarettes would be that it would prevent this transition from experimental smoking and social smoking to addictive smoking."

U.S. Cigarette Exports Dropped in 1993

Considered vital to the tobacco industry, U.S. cigarette exports rose from just 6.9 billion cigarettes in 1945 to 205.6 billion in 1992 (graph at right). Last year, however, cigarette exports declined for the first time in eight years, to 195.5 billion. Japan, the leading importer of U.S. cigarettes, purchased 55.6 billion in 1993 (graph at left).

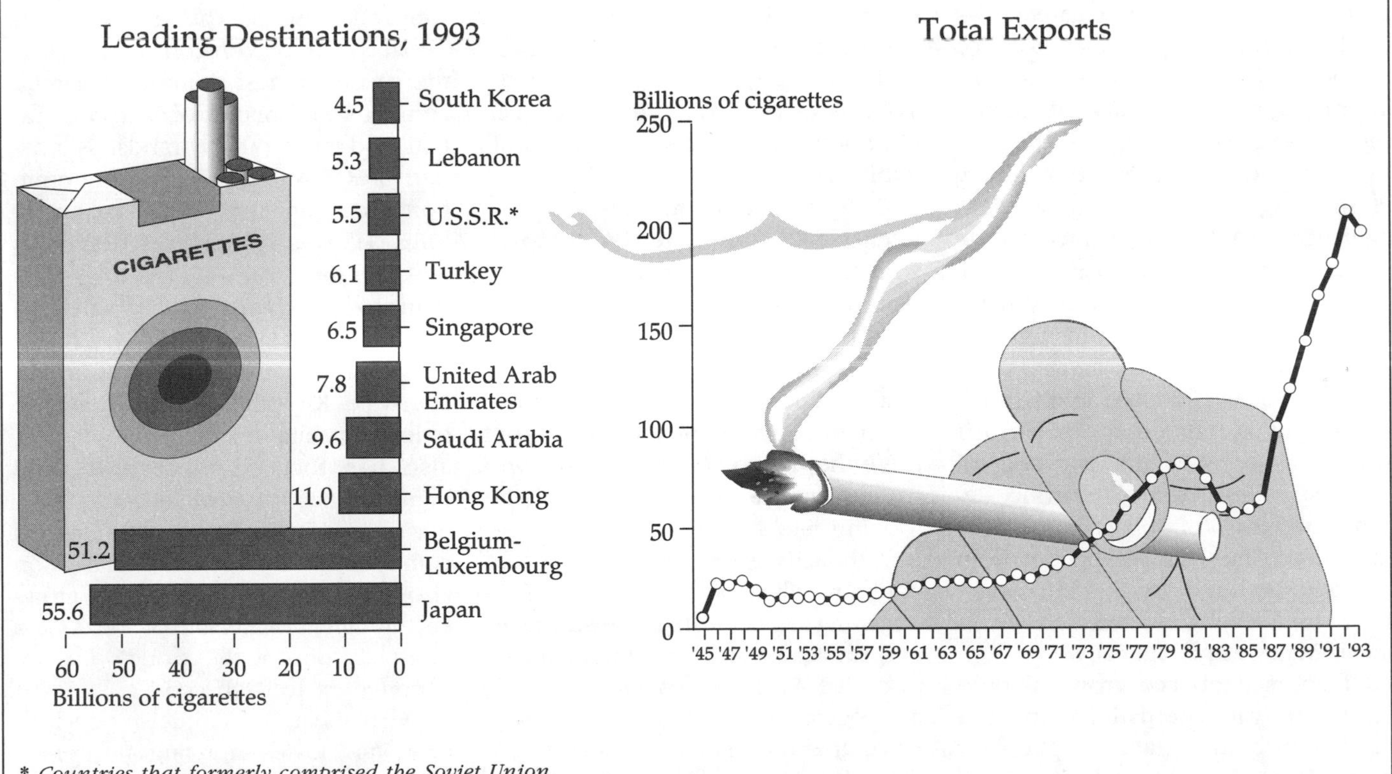

* *Countries that formerly comprised the Soviet Union*
Source: U.S. Tobacco Statistics, *April 1994, U.S. Department of Agriculture*

Major Tobacco-Growing States

The six leading tobacco-growing states generated $2.74 billion from tobacco sales in 1993. Tobacco accounted for nearly a third of Kentucky's agricultural revenues last year. In North Carolina, the nation's leading tobacco producer, tobacco generated 18.8 percent of the state's revenues from crops and other farm commodities.

State	Tobacco sales (in millions $)	Percentage of total revenues
North Carolina	$1,030	18.8%
Kentucky	$919	31.3%
Tennessee	$266	13.1%
South Carolina	$186	15.1%
Virginia	$182	8.8%
Georgia	$157	3.7%

Source: Tobacco: Situation and Outlook Report, *June 1994, Department of Agriculture*

Would tobacco regulation cause economic problems?

For the tobacco industry, regulation could not come at a worse time. Per-capita consumption of cigarettes — which comprise 95 percent of tobacco products sold in the U.S. — has been declining for years. Meanwhile, there's rising concern over the health effects of smoking, and restrictions are mounting on smoking in public buildings. FDA regulation of tobacco products would only accelerate the anti-tobacco trend.

Growers would be especially hard-hit by a further decline in cigarette consumption. In addition to falling domestic demand for tobacco leaf, growers are finding it harder to export their crops because of a glut in world tobacco supplies. Despite growing demand overseas for tobacco products, U.S. growers face stiff competition from relatively new and lower-cost producers in the developing world, such as Brazil, Malawi and Zimbabwe.

Of course, tobacco growers could always cultivate alternative crops. But that is hardly an attractive option for most. "Tobacco is a weed, so it naturally grows better [in poor soil] than any other type of cultivated crop in many parts of the country," says Eddington of the Tobacco Growers Information Committee. "Especially in the rolling hills and mountainous areas of eastern Tennessee and Kentucky, you can't grow a lot of crops. Tobacco is best suited to the land in the Southeast, and it's the [most profitable] crop as well."

Indeed, Eddington says, tobacco fetches $3,862 an acre. By comparison, the next most lucrative crop is peanuts, worth $691 an acre, followed by cotton at $380 an acre. "Tobacco growers have to put up with so much attack," Eddington says, "it seems to me if there were something else out there they could earn a living on, you can believe they would they would be looking into it."

Although cigarette manufacturers are naturally allied with the growers in opposing regulation, higher excise taxes and smoking restrictions, the manufacturers are in a better position to weather any regulatory assaults on the industry. Since the anti-smoking assault began three decades ago, the major companies have moved to protect their profits by expanding exports and diversifying into non-tobacco businesses.

The leader in diversification is the Philip Morris Companies Inc., maker of Marlboro cigarettes and eight other brands as well as discount, or generic, cigarettes. Already the biggest domestic tobacco manufacturer, Philip Morris has turned itself into the world's largest and most profitable international cigarette maker as well. Marlboro alone generated more than $15 billion last year in operating revenues and is the world's best-selling consumer-packaged product. Its sales, plus those of Kraft foods and Miller beer, which the company also owns, make Philip Morris the world's biggest maker of packaged goods. Only a sixth of that came from domestic tobacco sales. Even if FDA regulation eventually ended domestic tobacco sales, it's unlikely that Philip Morris would be dealt a serious blow.

While no other cigarette manufacturer has diversified as broadly as Philip Morris, the others have adopted similar strategies. The R.J. Reynolds Tobacco Co. of Winston Salem, N.C., the second-largest domestic cigarette company and maker of Winston, Salem and nine other brands, is now part of RJR Nabisco, Inc., an international consumer products manufacturer. Like its competitors, Reynolds makes more from cigarette exports than it does from domestic sales.

The third-largest U.S. producer, Brown & Williamson Tobacco Corp. of Louisville, Ky., maker of Kool and five other premium brands and generics, also has focused on exports and branched out into insurance and other businesses. In an ironic twist to this complex industry, Brown & Williamson also competes with U.S. tobacco growers through its ownership of Souza Cruz of Brazil, one of the world's leading exporters of leaf tobacco.

What the tobacco industry sees as economic losses resulting from new regulations, health professionals view as even greater economic gains. According to the Coalition on Smoking OR Health, tobacco use costs the U.S. economy more than $100 billion a year. And these costs appear likely to grow.

According to the federal Centers for Disease Control and Prevention (CDC), the medical costs of smoking have more than doubled since 1987, to $50 billion.[12] Any measure to reduce this sum, which includes health-care costs and lost productivity due to tobacco-related illness and death, would provide a valuable stimulus to the U.S. economy, the CDC says. ■

BACKGROUND

Birth of an Industry

Ever since Europeans set foot on American soil, tobacco has played a fundamental role in the New World's economy. Native Americans introduced European explorers to tobacco, which was indigenous to the Western Hemisphere. Tobacco smoking was an instant hit in Europe as well as in the Colonies, where Southern growers quickly developed an economy centered on exports of pipe tobacco.

The tobacco industry continued to grow after independence and, together with cotton formed the basis of the South's predominantly agricultural economy. Overcultivation of cotton depleted the soil, and after the Civil War cotton production declined, leaving tobacco, with its weedlike ability to thrive in weak soil, as a mainstay of the Southern economy.

The invention of the cigarette rolling machine in 1881 marked a turning point in tobacco production. Until then, cigarettes had to be hand-rolled, and most tobacco leaf was produced for pipes or cigars. James Albert Bonsack's cigarette machine turned out 120,000 cigarettes a day and enabled James Buchanan Duke, the son of a North Carolina tobacco farmer, to build a vast cigarette empire. Until the Supreme Court broke up Duke's so-called tobacco trust in 1911 because it violated the Sherman Antitrust Act, the trust wielded ruthless power over the tobacco growers, forcing them to sell their crops at low prices. Today's tobacco giants are the offspring of the old monopoly.

Cigarette consumption took off in the United States in the early years of this century. The government distributed free cigarettes to soldiers at the front in both world wars, promoting cigarette smoking to entire generations. Astute advertising and Hollywood movies further associated smoking with glamour and sophistication. Cigarette smoking grew steadily: By 1963, Americans 18 and over were smoking an average of 12 cigarettes a day.

Changing Attitudes

Publication in 1964 of the first surgeon general's report linking tobacco and cancer initiated a radical change in Americans' smoking habits. Then-Surgeon General Luther L. Terry stated as public policy what many scientists had been claiming since the early 1950s — that cigarette smoking causes lung cancer and other diseases. By 1992, per capita consumption had declined from 12 to seven cigarettes a day, and overall national consumption had dropped to 500 billion cigarettes. The percentage of adult smokers also has fallen, from 40 percent in the mid-1960s to 29 percent in 1987.[13]

Per-capita consumption of most other tobacco products — cigars, pipe tobacco and chewing tobacco — also has declined dramatically since the mid-1960s. The sole exception is snuff, which since the early 1980s has grown in popularity, mostly among teenage males.[14] This smokeless tobacco, which is "dipped," or wadded, between the cheek or lip and gum, is said by users to deliver a slight "buzz," or high. Snuff users avoid the risk of lung cancer and emphysema associated with smoking, but snuff is associated with oral cancer, which kills about 8,000 Americans a year, and other diseases.[15]

The shift toward snuff among some smokers and the overall decline in tobacco use reflect not only smokers' fear of disease but also growing restrictions on smoking and rising prices for cigarettes. In addition to the 24-cent federal excise tax on a pack of cigarettes, 43 states impose additional sales taxes on cigarettes. Last year, 14 states and the District of Columbia raised cigarette taxes by an average of 11 cents a pack, and this year at least six states have raised the sales tax by an average of 12 cents. In May, Michigan hiked the cigarette excise tax by 50 cents to 75 cents a pack, the highest in the country.[16]

About half of all living Americans who ever smoked have quit, a fact that the tobacco industry presents as evidence that nicotine is not addictive. Despite the decline in tobacco use, however, some 51 million Americans continue to smoke regularly.[17]

Regulatory Initiatives

Anti-tobacco sentiment is not a recent phenomenon. The spread of cigarette smoking early in the century met with strong opposition, and 14 states briefly outlawed tobacco as part of the Temperance movement in the early 1920s.[18] But it was not until the 1960s that the modern war on smoking began.

As the evidence mounted linking cigarette smoking with disease, federal, state and local governments launched efforts to reduce access to tobacco products through taxation and regulation. Bolstered on the one hand by an array of anti-smoking groups, they were fought every step of the way by the powerful tobacco lobby. The resulting 30-year war on smoking left a patchwork of restrictions and taxes.

The first major regulatory move against tobacco came just two years after the landmark 1964 surgeon general's report on smoking and health. The Cigarette Labeling and Advertising Act, which went into effect in 1966, required all cigarette packs and advertisements to warn: "Caution: Cigarette smoking may be hazardous to your health."

Four years later, after the 1967 surgeon general's report called smoking the main cause of lung cancer, Congress strengthened the warning labels to read, "Warning: The Surgeon General has determined that cigarette smoking is dangerous to your health." In the 1980s, warning labels were also required on snuff and chewing tobacco packages as well.

In 1970, lawmakers took a different approach to curbing cigarette consumption with the Public Health Cigarette Smoking Act, which banned all television and radio advertising for cigarettes beginning in 1971. Denied access to their principal advertising outlets, the tobacco industry stepped up magazine advertising and turned increasingly to sales promotions, coupons and price wars to market their products. [19]

Workplace Bans

The first federal restrictions on smoking in public places came in 1973, when the Civil Aeronautics Board (CAB) required commercial airlines to offer non-smoking sections. By 1990, smoking was banned on all domestic flight of six hours or less, as well as on all intercity buses. [20]

State and local anti-smoking initiatives have been more extensive in scope than federal measures. Since 1973, when Arizona became the first state to enact smoking bans in public places, nearly all states have imposed some restrictions on smoking in government offices, schools and other public buildings.

Workplace smoking bans were extended to federal offices in 1987, starting at the Department of Health and Human Services. As one of his first acts in office, President Clinton banned smoking in the White House. Since then, more federal agencies have restricted or banned smoking in offices. This year the Pentagon banned smoking in all military workplaces, and the Labor Department in March proposed regulations that would ban smoking in all private workplaces.

Until this year's campaign to seek jurisdiction over tobacco products, the FDA has played a minor role in regulating cigarettes. The only time the agency has moved to restrict tobacco products was in the mid-1950s, when low-tar brands were briefly promoted as healthful alternatives to regular cigarettes. Citing the Food, Drug and Cosmetic Act, which gives FDA jurisdiction over any products intended for therapeutic use, the FDA ordered the "healthful" cigarettes withdrawn from the market.

Tobacco's Clout

Although they stand united philosophically against anti-tobacco efforts, the tobacco growers and cigarette manufacturers represent different interests within the industry. "Whatever legitimacy smoking has, whatever sanction of tradition claimed by the industry, comes from the growing of tobacco in the South," writes Larry C. White in his history of the industry. "The cigarette companies like to hearken back to this heritage, but the mass marketing of cigarettes is in fact a relatively recent phenomenon." [21]

In addition to the legitimacy the growers receive from their ties to the nation's founding farmers, they also have had the more tangible legitimacy of strong support in Congress. Although tobacco is grown in only 51 of 435 congressional districts, White points out, in 27 of those it is a mainstay of the local economy. As the recent deadlock over health-care reform demonstrated, tobacco-state lawmakers often hold the key to passage of laws. [22]

Although tobacco interests appear to carry more clout in Congress than their numbers seem to warrant, tobacco still holds a key place in the U.S. agricultural economy. An acre of tobacco is worth far more than a comparable crop of any other agricultural commodity, and tobacco is the sixth-largest cash crop grown in the United States. (Corn is the biggest.) From an international perspective, the United States is the world's leading exporter and importer of tobacco and is second only to China in tobacco production.

Although tobacco is cultivated in 16 states, the bulk of the crop comes from the six "tobacco states" — North Carolina, Kentucky, Tennessee, Virginia, South Carolina and Georgia. North Carolina and Kentucky account for about two-thirds of the crop. They also are the leading producers of the prized tobaccos used in American-blend cigarettes — North Carolina's flue-cured and Kentucky's burley, which account for more than 94 percent of U.S. tobacco output. [23] Oriental tobacco, a third type used in this blend, is imported, mostly from Turkey. Twenty-one other types of tobacco, used for cigarettes, cigars, chewing tobacco, snuff, pipes and roll-your-own cigarettes are produced as far from the Tobacco Belt as Massachusetts and Wisconsin.

Price Supports to the Rescue

The economics of the tobacco industry are nothing if not complex. Wages are starkly divided between the growing and manufacturing sectors. According to the accounting firm Price Waterhouse, the average compensation for agricultural workers was $5,627 in 1990, compared with $51,517 for tobacco-manufacturing employees. [24]

Many smaller tobacco growers have

Continued on p. 852

Chronology

1950s-60s ***Early studies linking tobacco use and disease prompt federal efforts to warn consumers of the health risks of smoking.***

1952
Richard Doll, a British researcher, publishes findings linking smoking and cancer.

1963
Cigarette smoking peaks in the United States at an average of 12 cigarettes a day among people age 18 and older.

1964
The first surgeon general's report on smoking and health links smoking and cancer.

1966
The Cigarette Labeling and Advertising Act takes effect, requiring cigarette packaging and advertisements to include a label warning consumers that cigarette smoking "may be hazardous to your health."

1970s ***Congress passes increasingly stringent measures against cigarette smoking.***

1970
The required cigarette package and advertising warning is strengthened to read: "Warning: The Surgeon General has determined that cigarette smoking is dangerous to your health."

Jan. 2, 1971
The 1969 Public Health Cigarette Smoking Act goes into effect, banning cigarette advertising on television and radio. Challenged by the tobacco industry, the ban is upheld a year later by the U.S. Supreme Court.

1973
The Civil Aeronautics Board requires commercial airlines to offer non-smoking sections. Arizona becomes the first state to enact smoking bans in public places.

1975
The military stops providing cigarettes free to U.S. soldiers.

1980s ***Despite opposition by conservatives, anti-smoking activists continue to win restrictions on tobacco.***

1982
The No Net Cost Tobacco Program Act requires that the federal price-support system for tobacco be financed entirely by the tobacco industry. Congress doubles the federal excise tax on cigarettes to 16 cents a pack.

1984
Congress passes the Comprehensive Smoking Education Act requiring rotating health warnings on cigarette packages and advertisements.

1987
A workplace smoking ban goes into effect at the Department of Health and Human Services, the first smoke-free federal agency.

May 16, 1988
Surgeon General C. Everett Koop declares that nicotine is addictive in much the same way as cocaine and heroin. Smoking is banned on domestic flights of two hours or less.

1990s ***New studies linking nicotine with addiction and passive smoking with disease prompt efforts to regulate tobacco.***

1990
Smoking is banned on all domestic airline flights of six hours or less and on intercity buses.

1992
Per-capita consumption of cigarettes stands at seven per day among adult Americans, down from 12 a day in 1963.

1993
The Environmental Protection Agency releases its report linking environmental, or secondhand, tobacco smoke with cancer and other diseases among non-smokers.

February 1994
Food and Drug Administration Commissioner David A. Kessler announces plans to consider regulating tobacco as a drug. Surgeon General Joycelyn Elders reports that most smokers become addicted to nicotine by age 18, emphasizing the importance of preventing smoking among teenagers.

May 23, 1994
Mississippi sues the tobacco industry, becoming the first state to seek reimbursement for the costs of treating smoking-related illnesses incurred by Medicaid and other public health-care programs in the state.

Cigarette Advertising Skyrockets

From 1987-91, advertising and promotional expenditures for cigarettes nearly doubled, to about $4.7 billion. The amount spent on ads in magazines and newspapers declined during the period, while more was spent on outdoor, transit and direct-mail advertising.

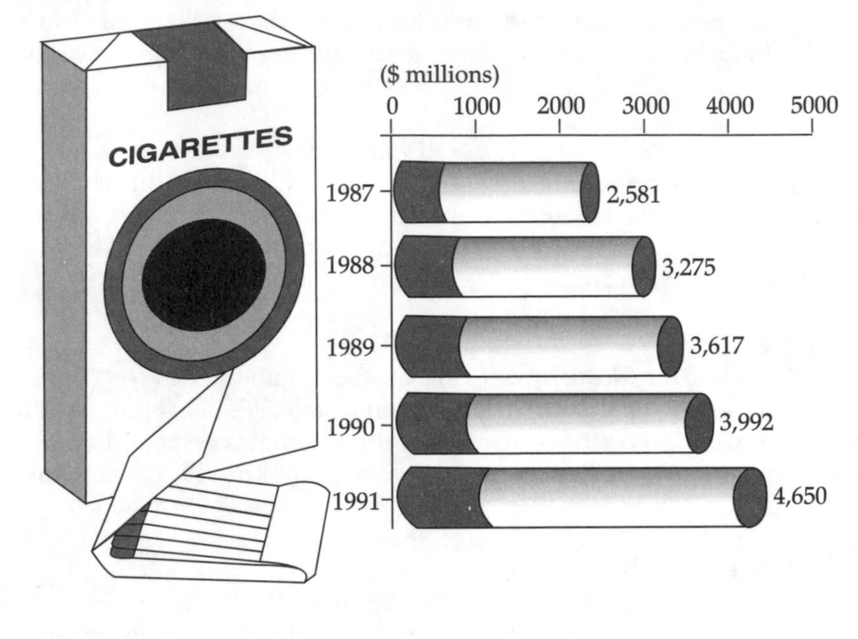

Source: Tobacco: Situation and Outlook Report, *June 1994*

Continued from p. 850

failed to weather the hardships posed by growing foreign competition and falling domestic demand. As a result, the total acreage used for growing tobacco has shrunk in recent decades. From 1954 to 1987, the number of acres planted in tobacco fell by more than half, from 1.5 million acres to 633,000. During the same period, the number of tobacco farms plummeted from 512,000 to 137,000, as small farmers sold out to bigger concerns. [25]

Tobacco growing is a labor-intensive enterprise with many hands-on steps — planting, harvesting, bundling, hanging leaves in drying sheds, baling and shipping. To keep tobacco prices high enough to support the many workers involved, the federal government has supported prices for tobacco (and other commodities) since the 1930s. Under the 1938 Agriculture Adjustment Act, production quotas are set low enough to sustain government prices for the commodity. Farmers must agree to grow no more than their allotted quota each year, with the expectation that they will earn in return a predictable income from their crop.

Of course, prices at the annual tobacco auctions do not always come in at the government-set levels. They may fall short when especially favorable weather conditions produce an abundant harvest or when foreign suppliers such as China or Brazil flood the world market with their own tobacco exports. American cigarette manufacturers do not limit their purchases to domestic growers; in fact, they have been importing more and more of the tobacco they put in U.S. cigarettes. This year Congress required that at least 75 percent of the tobacco in U.S. cigarettes be U.S.-grown.

When auction bids fall below the set price, the second part of the federal tobacco program kicks in. Each year the Agriculture Department sets a guaranteed average price for tobacco. This year, for example, the support price is $1.58 a pound for flue-cured and $1.71 for burley. When buyers' bids come in below those amounts, the government buys the tobacco at the guaranteed price and stores the tobacco until it can be sold at full price. [26]

In recent years, anti-smoking activists have stepped up their condemnation of the tobacco support program, charging that the government is supporting an industry through the Agriculture Department that it is combating through the surgeon general's office. As a result, Congress passed the 1982 No Net Cost Tobacco Program Act, requiring the government's Commodity Credit Corporation, which pays for the government tobacco purchases, to recover all the money it spends on the program. The law means that taxpayers no longer pay for losses incurred by the program, though they still get the bill for about $16 million a year in administrative costs to run the price-support program. [27]

Survival Strategies

Apart from price supports, growers have little to help them stay afloat in the dwindling domestic tobacco economy. But overseas demand for American tobacco offers long-term hope. The value of tobacco leaf exports has nearly quadrupled since 1967, totaling nearly $1.7 billion in 1992. [28]

"The future for U.S. growers lies in the export market," says Eddington of the Tobacco Growers Information Committee. "That market is a very important thing for us to develop and protect."

The same forces that have cut into

the growers' earnings — higher excise taxes, smoking restrictions and declining domestic consumption — threaten the cigarette manufacturers as well. But the "Big Six" U.S. cigarette makers have developed a far more flexible response to adversity. *

In response to the first published reports linking smoking and disease, in the early 1950s, the industry began selling filter-tip cigarettes, allegedly lower in tar and nicotine than regular brands. By 1992, filtered cigarettes accounted for 97 percent of the domestic cigarette market. [29] After the 1964 surgeon general's report, the industry also began marketing cigarettes containing 15 milligrams or less of tar, the substance in cigarette smoke that has been most closely associated with lung cancer. Their success led to brands containing as little as 1 milligram of tar. [30]

But with Americans gradually shaking the tobacco habit, the industry searched for other markets — and Third World countries beckoned. Since 1960, cigarette consumption has grown sevenfold in China, sixfold in Nigeria and fourfold in Indonesia, to name only a few. While some large consumers, such as China, produce tobacco leaf and manufacture their own cigarettes, Third World markets for prized American-blend exports have provided an expanding outlet for U.S. manufacturers. Japan, which imported 56 billion American cigarettes in 1993, tops the U.S. export market, but Belgium and Luxembourg, Hong Kong and the countries comprising the former Soviet Union also serve as important regional export markets. (*See chart, p. 847.*)

The cigarette manufacturers are still fighting, however, to retain their share of the domestic market. Over the past few years, discount cigarettes known as "generic" brands selling at much lower prices than premium brands have captured a growing share of the market. In an effort to stop the trend, Philip Morris last year cut the prices of Marlboro and other premium brands. The other companies followed suit, causing a drop in earnings until early this year, when R.J. Reynolds broke ranks and raised prices. The others soon followed its lead, ending the price war. *

Diversification has provided another essential survival tool for cigarette manufacturers. Industry leader Philip Morris, for example, last year made more than twice as much — $21 billion — from its North American food division, including General Foods and Kraft (Jell-O, Kraft cheeses, Post cereals) as it did from U.S. tobacco sales ($10 billion). The company, which last year earned $60 billion in operating revenues, also relies increasingly on its beer sales (including Miller and Molson), international foods, financial services and real estate. [31] R.J. Reynolds, the second-largest cigarette maker, also has benefited from its purchase of Nabisco, maker of Life Savers, Oreo cookies and other familiar foods. ■

* The six leading U.S. cigarette manufacturers are Philip Morris, RJR Nabisco, Brown & Williamson, Lorillard, American Brands and Liggett Group.

* The average price of a pack of cigarettes in the U.S., including premium and generic brands, is $1.85. Average prices range from $1.65 a pack in Virginia to $2.35 in Michigan.

CURRENT SITUATION

The FDA's Threat

Despite Surgeon General Koop's 1988 admonition that "it is reprehensible for this wealthy nation to export disability, disease and death to the Third World," the Reagan and Bush administrations supported the efforts of U.S. cigarette manufacturers to penetrate Third World markets. [32] The Office of the U.S. Trade Representative, for example, repeatedly charged Japan, Thailand, South Korea and Taiwan with unfair cigarette trade practices, forcing them to open their markets to American manufacturers.

Last November, a new interagency task force of trade and Health and Human Services officials was set up to re-examine U.S. trade policy on tobacco. Expected to issue a new policy this fall, it has been instructed to reconcile the federal government's conflicting aims of protecting human health and boosting U.S. business overseas. Meanwhile, the trade representative's office has taken no further action on behalf of the tobacco companies.

The biggest challenge to the tobacco industry came in February, when FDA Commissioner Kessler announced he would consider bringing tobacco products under FDA jurisdiction. Under the Food, Drug and Cosmetic Act, the FDA can regulate products as drugs if the vendor intends that they be used as drugs. Cigarettes have never come under FDA regulation in the past, Kessler wrote, because the agency has given the industry "the benefit of the doubt as to whether they intend cigarettes to be used for this purpose, because some people smoke for reasons other than the drug effect."

This spring, however, Kessler confronted the tobacco industry head-on. He presented evidence to lawmakers aimed at proving that the tobacco industry for decades has been aware that nicotine is addictive, hid that fact from the public and manipulated nicotine levels in cigarettes to maintain smokers' addiction. During the hearings, the top executives of the Big Six tobacco companies made an unprecedented joint appearance, insisting that

Continued on p. 855

New Weapon in Suits Against Tobacco Firms

"The tobacco industry spends $4 billion a year on advertising a product that maims, disables and kills," says J.D. Lee, a Knoxville, Tenn., lawyer involved in tobacco litigation. "And they know that it maims, disables and kills."

Since 1954, when the first lawsuit against a tobacco company was brought, some 350 suits have been filed. The industry has never paid a penny in compensation. Tobacco companies have consistently persuaded juries that the plaintiff's lung cancer, emphysema or heart disease could not be traced to a single cause — smoking.

"The companies use [the doctrine of] causation in a very tactical fashion, to [block] cases that otherwise would have been successful," says W. McKinley Smiley Jr., a law professor at Stetson University College of Law in St. Petersburg, Fla. "They have the financial resources to go back into the medical histories of the plaintiff and his family. Then they claim that tobacco didn't kill them all, hence there's no proof it killed the plaintiff."

The companies also have argued successfully that smokers exercise free will in choosing to smoke and thus assume the responsibility of any risks that may be associated with smoking.

In the most visible case in recent years, *Cipollone v. Liggett Group Inc.*, Rose Cipollone claimed in 1983 that cigarettes had caused her lung cancer and that the manufacturer had misled her into believing that cigarettes were safe. Although Liggett eventually won the suit, the industry suffered a blow when the Supreme Court ruled in 1992 that the federal law requiring warning labels on cigarette packs does not protect cigarette manufacturers from state damage suits alleging fraud.

Now lawyers have a new weapon in their suits against cigarette manufacturers. It's nicotine addiction — the same weapon that Food and Drug Administration Commissioner David A. Kessler is using in his campaign to regulate tobacco as a drug. During congressional hearings in March, Kessler said that internal tobacco company documents suggested that tobacco companies have known for decades that nicotine is addictive. [1] Kessler now has given lawyers the legal ammunition they needed to open a new generation of suits against the tobacco companies.

The new element in cases filed this year is what Lee calls "conspiracy to conceal and failure to reveal." In past product-liability cases, he says, "the industry has focused on the concept that the person assumes responsibility for his own health. If they got evidence that the plaintiff lied, they would win." Now the documents reviewed in congressional hearings this year may bolster the evidence that the cigarette makers lied.

Signs that tobacco litigation had entered a new phase began to emerge May 9, when Louisiana lawyer Wendell Gauthier and some 50 law firms around the country filed a class-action suit in New Orleans on behalf of all nicotine-addicted smokers — potentially including all 50 million smokers in the U.S. The suit, *Castano v. American Tobacco Co.*, is the first to cite nicotine addiction as the cause of action and to seek damages from companies for manipulating nicotine levels. The lawyers allege that the companies knowingly produced an addictive product and that once the plaintiffs realized the product was dangerous they were too addicted to quit and thus unable to freely assume the risks associated with smoking. [2]

Another new line of attack in tobacco litigation this year has been taken by states seeking to recover Medicaid expenses related to treating diseases caused by smoking. On May 23, Mississippi became the first state to sue the tobacco companies on behalf of taxpayers to recover the costs of treating tobacco-related diseases paid by the state-financed insurance fund for the poor and disabled. At least eight states have followed Mississippi's lead.

Florida has given such suits extra strength by passing a law that specifically authorizes the state to sue tobacco companies on behalf of all smokers who are Medicaid recipients. The Florida Third Party Liability Act also allows statistics to be used to prove causation. [3]

That undercuts one of the industry's strongest traditional defenses: that since all smokers don't fall ill, there is no proof that cigarettes cause disease. The law, which Philip Morris challenged in court June 30 as unconstitutional, further prohibits the companies from arguing that plaintiffs are free to choose whether to smoke and thus to assume any risks associated with smoking. Philip Morris and The Tobacco Institute decline to comment on pending anti-tobacco litigation, although the institute does acknowledge the added clout Florida's Legislature handed to the industry's opponents. "Florida differs to the extent that it [passed] legislation," says institute spokesman Walker Merryman, "whereas the other lawsuits spring from the same idea but are not specifically authorized by law."

More recently, Minnesota Attorney General Hubert H. Humphrey III sued on behalf of the state and its largest private health insurer, Blue Cross and Blue Shield. The Aug. 3 suit charges the tobacco companies with conspiracy, fraudulent concealment in violation of consumer-protection laws and antitrust violations. Like the other state suits, the Minnesota action seeks to recover the taxpayers' share of smoking-related health-care expenses. But Minnesota's is the first state action to charge the tobacco companies with conspiracy and fraud, the same allegations that were made in the congressional hearings.

---

[1] Kessler testified before the House Energy and Commerce Subcommittee on Health and the Environment.

[2] See "Class Actions Claim Tobacco Industry Deceived Smokers About Nicotine," *Trial*, July 1994. The magazine is published by the American Trial Lawyers Association.

[3] Gov. Lawton Chiles, D-Fla., signed the legislation into law May 26.

Continued from p. 853

nicotine levels are adjusted solely to enhance cigarette flavor and that they didn't think nicotine was addictive.[33]

The FDA proceeded with its investigation into nicotine's addictiveness as the main issue involved in any decision to regulate tobacco. An important step in that direction came Aug. 2, when the FDA Drug Abuse Advisory Committee studying the issue concluded that nicotine is indeed addictive.

If the FDA decides to claim jurisdiction over tobacco, it will be faced with an immediate dilemma that Kessler recognized from the outset. If nicotine is addictive, its sudden removal from tobacco products would mean millions of current smokers would be required to quit cold turkey, possibly experiencing adverse health effects associated with withdrawal. Any steps to restrict access to tobacco also would invite the creation of a black market. Faced with this dilemma, Kessler has asked Congress to provide guidance with new legislation defining a framework for tobacco regulation.

Focus on Addiction

Meanwhile, addiction experts have proposed several ways to regulate tobacco. The most widely publicized approach would gradually lower the nicotine content of cigarettes below the threshold amount that causes addiction.

One study of blood nicotine levels in "chippers," apparently non-addicted smokers who smoke no more than five cigarettes a day, puts the threshold at 5 milligrams a day. Assuming that a smoker consumes up to 30 cigarettes a day, and takes in no more than 40 percent of the nicotine contained in a cigarette (the rest goes up in smoke), the study concludes that lowering the nicotine level to 0.5 milligrams per cigarette would result in an intake of 6 milligrams of nicotine, possibly low enough to prevent addiction. That would mean a dramatic change for smokers, since nicotine levels of American cigarettes average 8-9 milligrams.[34]

AP/Wide World Photo

Top executives of U.S. cigarette makers, here being sworn in, told a House subcommittee hearing April 14 that they did not think nicotine is addictive.

The beauty of this proposal, says researcher Benowitz, is that young, first-time smokers might stop after a short period. "The idea behind low-nicotine cigarettes would be to prevent the transition from experimental and social smoking to addictive smoking," he says. "If this idea were to hold true, it would prevent the whole next generation from becoming addicted."

Heavier smokers probably would not fare so well under this approach, even if regulators phased it in over 10 to 15 years as Benowitz proposes. Smokers likely would compensate for declining nicotine levels by smoking more cigarettes, puffing more often and inhaling more deeply in an effort to maintain blood nicotine at the habitual level. Because the most lethal ingredients of cigarettes are in the smoke, addicted smokers would face greater risks of cancer and other diseases, at least in the short term.

"There is no painless way to do this," Benowitz concedes. "There would be a period of time when people are exposed to higher levels of tobacco toxins. There wouldn't be any way to get around that. In the long run, though, even if smokers were exposed for a brief period of time to higher levels of toxins, if you could prevent the whole next generation from becoming addicted, the health trade-off would certainly be worthwhile."

Benowitz says that many smokers who want to quit, but can't, support his proposal. "They welcome this possibility because it may actually help them wean themselves from cigarettes," he says. Over the longer term, even the most tenacious smoker may stop if nicotine levels are low enough. "When nicotine is low enough, no matter how much people smoke they're not going to be satisfied by it," he says. "So I think that eventually they would just give it up."

Critics of the low-nicotine approach to regulating tobacco say there are more humane ways to reduce smoking. Penn State's Kozlowski, who like Benowitz presented his ideas at the Aug. 2 advisory committee meeting, agrees with tobacco industry spokesmen who predict that drastically low-

For More Information

The Tobacco Institute, 1875 I St. N.W., Suite 800, Washington, D.C. 20006; (202) 457-4800. The tobacco industry's main lobbying group, representing manufacturers of tobacco products, provides the public with information on the economics and history of the industry.

Food and Drug Administration, 5600 Fishers Lane, Rockville, Md. 20857; (301) 443-1130. The federal agency that develops safety standards for foods and drugs now is considering regulating tobacco products as well.

Coalition on Smoking OR Health, 1150 Connecticut Ave. N.W., Suite 820, Washington, D.C. 20036; (202) 822-9380. The leading anti-smoking coalition, comprised of the American Cancer Society, the American Lung Association and the American Heart Association, alerts lawmakers and federal agencies to the hazards of smoking.

U.S. Department of Agriculture, Tobacco Analysis Section, 14th St. and Independence Ave. S.W., Washington, D.C. 20250; (202) 219-0890. The leading source of historical data on the tobacco industry provides information on smoking trends and the economic status of tobacco growers and cigarette manufacturers.

ering nicotine levels would result in a vast black market for full-strength cigarettes. "I think there are complicated issues with respect to running a free society that is also a regulated society," he says. "To me, banning nicotine in cigarettes is the same as banning smoking."

A more reasonable approach, Kozlowski says, would entail stricter labeling requirements. "Smokers need to know that the tar and nicotine yields of a cigarette aren't [as precise as] the contents on the side of a pill box," he says. "It depends on how you smoke." The tar levels reported on a cigarette pack, for example, are determined by smoking machines taking in standard, measured puffs. "But if you adjust the machine to simulate a very hungry smoker, taking as many puffs as they can, a cigarette that delivers 15 milligrams of tar in a standard assay delivers 70 milligrams of tar," he says. "You could easily take a Marlboro Light and take two or three extra puffs on it and it becomes a Marlboro. You don't sit there counting puffs when you smoke." Cigarette labels, Kozlowski asserts, should reflect that reality.

Kozlowski also recommends banning vending machines to make cigarette purchases harder for teenagers. "We don't have vending machines for beer or whiskey, but machines for cigarettes are everywhere," he says. "They should be viewed as inappropriate under any circumstances, and I think FDA regulation could probably contribute to their elimination." ■

OUTLOOK

Showdown Coming?

The FDA's Drug Abuse Advisory Committee concluded Aug. 2 that nicotine is addictive. It is now up to the agency to decide whether to use that finding to begin regulating tobacco.

"The advisory committee's determination is an important step for the agency toward answering the question of whether or not nicotine-containing cigarettes affect the structure or function of the body," says FDA spokesman O'Hara. "The hearings put a lot of information on the public record that speaks toward the question of intent. Now we're in the process of deciding whether or not we have a basis to assert jurisdiction under the statute."

Meanwhile, Kessler is getting additional help from anti-smoking forces in Congress. The leader of this group is Rep. Henry A. Waxman, D-Calif., chairman of the House Energy and Commerce Subcommittee on Health and the Environment, who has presided over this year's tobacco hearings. Tobacco-state lawmakers such as Rep. L. F. Payne Jr., D-Va., did succeed in reducing the proposed increase in the federal cigarette excise tax to pay for health-care reform. But anti-smoking forces are advancing their cause in other ways.

Legislation that would specifically grant the FDA jurisdiction over tobacco products awaits congressional action. The Tobacco Health and Safety Act, introduced by Sen. Jeff Bingaman, D-N.M., on March 30, 1993, would amend the Food, Drug and Cosmetic Act to regulate the sale and distribution of tobacco products containing nicotine, tar or other harmful ingredients. Rep. Mike Synar, D-Okla., introduced companion legislation, the Fairness in Tobacco and Nicotine Regulation Act, on May 18, 1993. It remains to be seen whether Synar's Sept. 20 defeat in a runoff primary election will affect Kessler's efforts.

The tobacco industry is fighting regulation with an unprecedented public relations initiative. During the summer, R.J. Reynolds and Philip Morris placed full-page advertisements in the country's leading newspapers debunking the EPA's 1993 report on secondhand smoke and warning consumers that if cigarettes are regulated, caffeine, high-fat foods and other items posing health risks will be next.

But the 30-year war on smoking may have reached a decisive turning point. Kessler is expected to announce his decision on whether or not to regulate tobacco at any time. Even if the FDA decides not to try, anti-smoking forces are regrouping along an-

Continued on p. 858

At Issue:

Is there evidence that cigarette makers manipulate nicotine levels in cigarettes?

yes

David A. Kessler
Commissioner, Food and Drug Administration

FROM *A STATEMENT BEFORE THE HOUSE ENERGY AND COMMERCE SUBCOMMITTEE ON HEALTH AND THE ENVIRONMENT,* MARCH 25, 1994.

The cigarette industry has attempted to frame the debate on smoking as the right of each American to choose.

The question we must ask is whether smokers really have that choice. Consider these facts: Two-thirds of adults who smoke say they wish they could quit. Seventeen million try to quit each year, but fewer than one out of 10 succeed. For every smoker who quits, nine try and fail. Three out of four adult smokers say that they are addicted. By some estimates, as many as 74 to 90 percent are addicted. . . .

Accumulating evidence suggests that cigarette manufacturers may intend this result — that they may be controlling smokers' choice by controlling the levels of nicotine in their products in a manner that creates and sustains an addiction in the vast majority of smokers. . . .

The public thinks of cigarettes as simply blended tobacco rolled in paper. But they are much more than that. Some of today's cigarettes may, in fact, qualify as high technology nicotine delivery systems that deliver nicotine in precisely calculated quantities — quantities that are more than sufficient to create and to sustain addiction. . . .

The history of the tobacco industry is a story of how a product that may at one time have been a simple agricultural commodity appears to have become a nicotine delivery system. Prior to the 1940s, the waste products from cigarettes . . . were discarded. The tobacco industry had identified no use for these materials in the cigarette manufacturing process.

Then, in the 1940s and '50s, the industry created reconstituted tobacco from the previously unusable tobacco stems, scraps and dust. This gave cigarette makers the ability to reduce the cost of producing cigarettes by using fewer tobacco leaves and making up the difference by using reconstituted tobacco. While the motive appeared to be purely economic, the reconstitution process was nevertheless a critical development that started the industry down the path toward controlling and manipulating nicotine levels.

The ability to control and manipulate nicotine levels becomes important in light of another key realization. Industry patents show that the industry recognized that nicotine is the active ingredient in tobacco smoke. It is what produces the psychoactive effects that lead smokers to crave cigarettes. . . .

It is prudent to keep in mind that patents do not necessarily tell us what processes are currently being used in manufacturing cigarettes. Nevertheless, the number and pattern of these patents leaves little doubt that the cigarette industry has developed enormously sophisticated methods for manipulating nicotine levels in cigarettes.

no

Charles O. Whitley
Senior consultant, The Tobacco Institute

FROM *A STATEMENT BEFORE THE HOUSE ENERGY AND COMMERCE SUBCOMMITTEE ON HEALTH AND THE ENVIRONMENT,* MARCH 25, 1994.

Commissioner Kessler [has] suggested that the cigarette manufacturers "commonly add nicotine to cigarettes to deliver specific amounts of nicotine" and deliberately manipulate the amount of nicotine in cigarettes in order to "produce and sustain addiction." Similar allegations have been aired in the media . . . I am here today to tell you — unequivocally — that these suggestions are false.

The cigarette manufacturers do not "spike" their cigarettes with nicotine. In fact nicotine is *lost* in the manufacturing process. There is not a single cigarette on the market in this country today that does not contain *less* nicotine than is found in the raw tobacco used in its manufacture.

Generally, nicotine levels are a function of "tar" levels. When "tar" levels are set, nicotine levels follow. As manufacturers have reduced "tar" levels and yields over the years to satisfy changing consumer tastes, nicotine levels and yields have fallen correspondingly.

The nicotine in the average cigarette today is lower than it has ever been. Between 1954 and 1993, the average nicotine level in cigarettes fell from 2.6 milligrams to 0.89 milligrams — a two-thirds decline. The suggestion that nicotine is being "added" to cigarettes or "manipulated" to keep smokers "hooked" is absurd. . . . More ironic still, Dr. Kessler's letter accusing cigarette manufacturers of this practice came in response to petitions filed by anti-smoking groups alleging that the manufacturers have been *reducing* "tar" and nicotine levels in cigarettes in order to mollify the health concerns of smokers! The manufacturers clearly are damned if they do and damned if they don't. . . .

Despite the attention that Dr. Kessler and others are now calling to the issue of nicotine in cigarettes, the fact is that the cigarette manufacturers have been publicly reporting "tar" and nicotine yields for their advertised brands for over 20 years. The reconstituted tobacco process has been in use for at least 30 years, denatured alcohol has been used for over 40 years and tobacco extracts also have a long and well-documented history of use in the manufacture of tobacco products.

These processes are not new. They have not been hidden from the government. And they do not add measurable amounts of nicotine to the final product. During all this time, FDA has never suggested that cigarettes should be subject to ongoing regulation as a drug. Yet Dr. Kessler suggests that "the evidence now available" to FDA could support "a different approach." We disagree. Nothing has occurred during this time to warrant a change in FDA's long-standing policy toward tobacco.

Continued from p. 856

other front. Efforts to impose high excise taxes on cigarettes, which weakened during the summer's abortive debate over health-care reform, will not be abandoned permanently, according to anti-smoking advocates. Next year, or whenever Congress takes up health reform again, observers predict that a less ambitious health package will gain bipartisan support. Although it may cover fewer Americans than Clinton's original plan for universal coverage, any new reform bill is likely to retain higher excise taxes on tobacco products.

The proposal to raise the tobacco tax presents a bitter irony to tobacco growers. "Growers are among the very group of people who need meaningful health care," says grower representative Eddington. "But because a massive tax naturally would lower demand for tobacco products, there would be a domino effect all the way down the production chain. So the growers may end up with health care, but they'll be indigent, too."

Anti-smoking activists stand firm in their support for a tobacco tax increase. "Tobacco taxes are one of the few things that almost everyone agrees make good sense as a matter of health policy and economics," says John Bloom, the American Cancer Society's chief lobbyist on the tobacco tax issue.

And supporters include members of Congress from both parties, Bloom says. "Congressional support for tobacco-control measures like this has never been stronger." ■

Notes

[1] Jasper Womach, *Tobacco Price Supports: An Overview of the Program,* Congressional Research Service, March 16, 1994.

[2] Kessler outlined the prospects for regulating tobacco products in a letter to Scott D. Ballin, chairman of the Coalition on Smoking OR Health, which includes the American Cancer Society, American Lung Association and American Heart Association. Kessler's letter was in response to earlier coalition petitions requesting FDA regulation of tobacco.

[3] Coalition on Smoking OR Health, "What Tobacco Costs America" (undated).

[4] For background, see "Crackdown on Smoking," *The CQ Researcher,* Dec. 4, 1992, pp. 1049-1072, and "Tobacco Under Siege," *Editorial Research Reports,* Oct. 5, 1984, pp. 737-756.

[5] Elders spoke at a Feb. 24 news conference following release of "The Report of the Surgeon General: Preventing Tobacco Use among Young People," February 1994. For background, see "Who Smokes, Who Starts — and Why," *Editorial Research Reports,* March 24, 1989, pp. 149-164.

[6] See Alissa J. Rubin, "Prospects for Major Overhaul Fade as Senate goes Home," *Congressional Quarterly Weekly Report,* Aug. 27, 1994, pp. 2486-2487.

[7] U.S. Department of Health and Human Services, *The Health Consequences of Smoking: Nicotine Addiction,* May 16, 1988, p. iii. The department has issued annual reports on smoking and health since 1979.

[8] See Philip J. Hilts, "Cigarette Makers Debated the Risks They Denied," *The New York Times,* June 16, 1994. Other articles on cigarette spiking appeared June 17 and 18.

[9] See "Pack of Trouble," *Maclean's,* Feb. 21, 1994.

[10] See Neal L. Benowitz and Jack E. Henningfield, "Establishing a Nicotine Threshold for Addiction," *The New England Journal of Medicine,* July 14, 1994.

[11] Department of Health and Human Services, *op. cit.,* February 1994.

[12] Department of Health and Human Services, "Medical-Care Expenditures Attributable to Cigarette Smoking — United States, 1993," *Morbidity and Mortality Weekly Report,* July 8, 1994.

[13] Bruce K. Mulock, *Cigarette Advertising Bans and Other Tobacco-Related Proposals,* Congressional Research Service, Dec. 12, 1991.

[14] *Ibid.*

[15] For a comparison of the health effects of cigarettes and snuff, See Brad Rodu and Philip Cole, letter to the editor, *Nature,* July 1994. Rodu is an oral pathologist and Cole is an epidemiologist at the University of Alabama-Birmingham.

[16] U.S. Department of Agriculture, *Tobacco Situation and Outlook,* June 1994.

[17] Mulock, *op. cit.*

[18] See Steven B. Duke and Albert C. Gross, *America's Longest War* (1994), p. 24.

[19] For background, see "Advertising Under Attack," *The CQ Researcher,* Sept. 13, 1991, pp. 657-680.

[20] The 1978 Airline Deregulation Act eliminated the CAB as of Dec. 31, 1984, and parceled out its functions to other agencies.

[21] Larry C. White, *Merchants of Death* (1988), pp. 48-49.

[22] See David S. Broder, "Panel Rejects Big Tobacco Tax Increase," *The Washington Post,* June 30, 1994.

[23] Womach, *op. cit.,* p. 5.

[24] Price Waterhouse, *The Economic Impact of the Tobacco Industry on the United States in 1990,* October 1992, p. II-2. Average compensation for manufacturing employees is substantially higher than for agricultural workers because professional employees, including researchers and administrative personnel, are included in the total.

[25] Department of Agriculture, *op. cit.,* p. 67.

[26] Womach, *op. cit.,* p. 5.

[27] *Ibid.,* p. 6.

[28] U.S. Department of Agriculture, *op. cit.,* April 1994, pp. 244-248.

[29] *Ibid.,* p. 15.

[30] See Robert H. Miles, *Coffin Nails and Corporate Strategies* (1982), pp. 214-216.

[31] See Jay Mathews, "For Tobacco Giant, the Future Is Glowing," *The Washington Post,* July 5, 1994.

[32] Margaret Ebrahim and Charles Lewis, "Will Washington Kick Tobacco?" *The Nation,* April 25, 1994, p. 556.

[33] Kessler and the tobacco chiefs testified before the House Energy and Commerce Subcommittee on Health and the Environment. Kessler testified several times, but presented his most compelling case March 25. The tobacco executives testified together April 14.

[34] Benowitz and Henningfield, *op. cit.* pp. 123-125.

Bibliography

Selected Sources Used

Books

Duke, Steven B., and Albert C. Gross, *America's Longest War: Rethinking Our Tragic Crusade Against Drugs,* G.P. Putnam's Sons, 1993.

The authors propose to end the failed war on drugs by legalizing drugs that now are banned and placing them, as well as tobacco, under a new regulatory system aimed at minimizing their harm to society.

Miles, Robert H., *Coffin Nails and Corporate Strategies,* Prentice-Hall. Inc., 1982.

The author provides a detailed account of the "Big Six" U.S. cigarette manufacturers' reactions to health reports since the 1950s linking smoking and disease. The companies have turned to different methods of advertising, cigarette exports and diversification to defend their market share.

Reynolds, Patrick and Tom Shachtman, *The Gilded Leaf: Triumph, Tragedy, and Tobacco: Three Generations of the R.J. Reynolds Family and Fortune,* Little, Brown, 1989.

A grandson of the founder of RJR Nabisco traces his family's path to fortune — and sometimes disaster — in the tobacco industry. Mainly a personal account by an anti-tobacco activist, the book provides an insider's view of the development of the second-largest U.S. tobacco company.

White, Larry C., *Merchants of Death: The American Tobacco Industry,* Beech Tree Books, William Morrow, 1988.

Beginning with the scientific community's early reports linking tobacco use with disease, the tobacco industry has made strategic moves to remain profitable. By diversifying into food, beverages and other businesses, the cigarette companies have built a broad corporate structure able to defend their core business against attempts to reduce tobacco use.

Articles

Benowitz, Neal L., and Jack E. Henningfield, "Establishing a Nicotine Threshold for Addiction," *The New England Journal of Medicine,* July 14, 1994.

The authors describe one of the most widely discussed proposals for implementing tobacco regulation if the FDA decides to begin regulating tobacco products as drugs. They would gradually reduce nicotine levels in cigarettes to a point where there is too little to cause addiction.

Finkel, David, "Life Among the Leaves," *The Washington Post Magazine,* Oct. 25, 1992.

The tobacco price-support program guarantees growers a higher price for their crop than most could get for any other commodity. But life is hard for workers in this segment of the tobacco industry, Finkel writes: Just as it is to smokers, the tobacco leaf is toxic to those who handle it.

Rosenblatt, Roger, "How Do They Live With Themselves?" *The New York Times Magazine,* March 20, 1994.

The author interviewed executives of Philip Morris, the world's largest tobacco company, and concludes that they may be in denial as a psychological response to repeated evidence of their products' lethal effects.

"Should Cigarettes Be Outlawed?" *U.S. News & World Report,* April 18, 1994.

This cover story explores the likely economic impact that FDA regulation would have on the tobacco industry, including the possibility of a ban on cigarettes.

Reports and Studies

National Academy Press, *Growing Up Tobacco Free: Preventing Nicotine Addiction in Children and Youths,* September 1994.

Because most regular smokers started smoking before age 18, the National Academy of Sciences calls for regulations that make it harder for young people under 18 to have access to cigarettes.

U.S. Department of Health and Human Services, *The Health Consequences of Smoking: Nicotine Addiction. A Report of the Surgeon General,* May 1988.

In the surgeon general's 20th annual report on smoking, then-Surgeon General C. Everett Koop asserts that nicotine is addictive in much the same way as heroin and cocaine and calls for a policy that treats cigarettes as addictive substances.

U.S. Department of Health and Human Services, *The Health Consequences of Smoking: Preventing Tobacco Use Among Young People. A Report of the Surgeon General,* February 1994.

In this year's report, Surgeon General Joycelyn Elders concludes that if young people can be prevented from taking up their first cigarette, they will never become regular smokers as adults. Steps to deter teenage smoking, she writes, offer the greatest promise for reducing smoking-related sickness and death.

The Next Step

Additional information from UMI's Newspaper & Periodical Abstracts database

Advertising Regulation

Colford, Steven W., "Joe Camel on trial," Advertising Age, July 4, 1994, p. 1.
The California Supreme Court has ruled that an unfair-advertising suit against R. J. Reynolds Tobacco Co.'s Joe Camel campaign can go to trial. Advertising agencies McCann-Erickson Worldwide and Young & Rubicam are also named in the suit, which alleges that the campaign is aimed at children.

Crain, Rance, "Miles couldn't read the smoke signals," *Advertising Age,* July 4, 1994, p. 13.
The tobacco industry seems to be interested only in getting sales and profit from a dying business for as long as possible and not interested in market share, notes an editorial. This is what the argument over Joe Camel is really about.

de Silva, D. Richard, "Targeting alcohol, tobacco ads," *The Washington Post,* July 7, 1994, p. DC5.
An array of witnesses called on city officials to ban all alcohol and tobacco advertisements in Washington, D.C., to address a "public health crisis" that has disproportionately plagued young people and African-Americans.

Mahaney, Francis X, Jr., "Oldtime ads tout health benefits of smoking: Tobacco industry had doctors' help," *Journal of the National Cancer Institute,* July 20, 1994, p. 1048-1049.
Advertising during the tobacco industry's heyday often showed doctors, dentists and nurses (or people posing as such) lighting up cigarettes. The health claims for tobacco made by cigarette manufacturers are discussed.

Ban on Smoking

Lucas, Greg, "Measure would ban almost all smoking," *San Francisco Chronicle,* July 8, 1994, p. A19.
The California Legislature on July 7, 1994, sent Gov. Pete Wilson what supporters say would be the toughest statewide anti-smoking law in the nation.

Rickard, Leah, "Burger lovers show distaste for smokes," *Advertising Age,* July 4, 1994, p. 34.
According to one survey, a majority of fast-food consumers are in favor of a no-smoking policy in restaurants. Around 25 percent of those surveyed said they would visit fast-food restaurants more often if they banned smoking.

Florida Ruling and Its Impact

"Blowing smoke," *New Yorker,* June 13, 1994, pp. 6-8.
Florida plans on suing the tobacco industry to recoup the cost of treating smoking-related illnesses in the Florida's Medicaid system. The argument that smokers cost the state more money than non-smokers is somewhat flawed, says the magazine. A third of all smokers die before age 65, which means they never collect Social Security.

"Mississippi sues tobacco companies; Florida law empowers state to sue," *Health Letter,* July 1994, p. 6.
Mississippi has filed a lawsuit demanding that cigarette makers repay the cost to taxpayers of medical services rendered to victims of smoking-related illnesses. A similar law in Florida is discussed.

Spayd, Liz, "Md. may sue tobacco firms over health," *The Washington Post,* July 7, 1994, p. MDP1.
Maryland officials are considering filing a lawsuit against tobacco companies in hopes of recovering millions of Medicaid dollars the state has spent on smoking-related illnesses.

Sullum, Jacob, "The rule of Lawton," *Reason,* August 1994, pp. 6-7.
An editorial discusses Florida's recently approved Medicaid Third Party Recovery Act, which is aimed at forcing tobacco companies to reimburse the state for the cost of treating smoking-related illnesses under Medicaid. The legislation clearly violates the Due Process and Equal Protection clauses of the Constitution.

International Regulations

Kondro, Wayne, "Ontario's tough anti-tobacco package," *Lancet,* July 9, 1994, pp. 118-119.
Ontario, Canada has passed the toughest anti-smoking legislation in North America, which will take effect Dec. 31, 1994. The law, which prohibits the sale of cigarettes to anyone under 19 years old, is discussed.

Nandan, Guru, "Indian government," *British Medical Journal* (International), June 11, 1994, pp. 1528-1529.
The government of India has drafted anti-tobacco legislation aimed at curbing India's rising consumption of tobacco. It is estimated that about 142 million men and 72 million women in India use tobacco.

"Provincial differences in health practices," *Canadian Social Trends,* summer 1994, pp. 30-34.
Health practices in Canada differ by province. Smoking, drinking, drug use, exercise and women's care are some of the topics discussed.

Waxman, Sharon, "French take tobacco ban with a puff of smoke," *Chicago Tribune,* June 30, 1994, p. 6.

In the two years since France adopted ambitious no-smoking laws, banning cigarettes in public places, outlawing tobacco advertising and imposing smoke-free zones in restaurants and in the workplace, the response has been underwhelming.

Issues Surrounding Regulation

Cohen, Richard E., "Where they'd rather fight than switch," *National Journal,* July 2, 1994, p. 1583.
The stormy hearings into tobacco-industry practices and the reaction of the industry's backers are discussed. It may be impossible to find a balanced perspective given the heated emotions.

Jones, Laurie, "Balancing approval, prohibition," *American Medical News,* July 11, 1994, p. 3.
The debate over FDA regulation of tobacco and FDA head David Kessler's efforts to build a case for FDA regulation of tobacco are discussed. House bill HR2147 would authorize the FDA to regulate tobacco products without banning them.

McCarthy, Michael, "Attack and counterattack in U.S. tobacco war," *Lancet,* July 2, 1994, p. 49.
The Justice Department is reviewing evidence suggesting that tobacco companies may have illegally concealed information about the hazards of cigarette smoking. Attacks against the tobacco industry that have provoked the tobacco industry to counterattack are discussed.

Scott, Steve, "Year of decision: Plethora of smoking issues tests tobacco industry's clout," *California Journal,* June 1994, pp. 25-28.
The tobacco industry's status as the best all-purpose villain since the "Commies" of the 1950s was confirmed in 1994 with congressional hearings and news reports lending suspicions about evil intent. The plethora of smoking issues testing the industry's clout in California is examined.

Nicotine

Benowitz, Neal L., and Jack E. Henningfield, "Establishing a nicotine threshold for addiction," *New England Journal of Medicine,* July 14, 1994, pp. 123-125.
Studies have demonstrated that nicotine intake can be limited by restricting the amount of nicotine in the tobacco, according to the authors. The absolute level of nicotine in a cigarette could be regulated for the purpose of preventing and limiting the development of addiction in smokers while providing enough nicotine for taste.

Colford, Steven W., "Nicotine fit," *Advertising Age,* June 27, 1994, p. 1.
A preliminary inquiry is being made by the Department of Justice into possible criminal, civil and antitrust violations by tobacco advertisers. Such an inquiry would investigate whether marketers, perhaps aided by their advertising and public relations agencies, trade associations and lobbyists, knowingly misled the public and Congress about the health hazards of tobacco.

Gavaghan, Helen, "FDA claims nicotine levels were manipulated," *Nature,* June 30, 1994, p. 696.
FDA Commissioner David Kessler recently testified before a congressional subcommittee that tobacco companies add ammonia to tobacco to increase nicotine levels in cigarettes. The question of nicotine's addictiveness is crucial to whether the FDA may regulate the drug.

Kleiner, Kurt, "Cultivating a taste for addiction?" *New Scientist,* July 2, 1994, p. 8.
A congressional committee has found that tobacco companies have thoroughly researched the addictive properties of nicotine. Tobacco industry representatives have denied that nicotine levels are manipulated to keep smokers addicted.

Raloff, Janet, "Some cigarette makers manipulate nicotine," *Science News,* July 2, 1994, p. 7.
FDA Commissioner David A. Kessler has laid out evidence that tobacco manufacturers manipulate the amount of nicotine in U.S. cigarettes. Details of Kessler's findings are presented.

Schwartz, John, "Easing of nicotine levels in cigarettes is proposed," *The Washington Post,* July 14, 1994, p. A4.
Neal L. Benowitz and Jack E. Henning, two prominent tobacco researchers, have proposed a system for gradually reducing the amount of nicotine in cigarettes to render them non-addictive.

Opinions

"Smoke and piety," *National Law Journal,* July 4, 1994, p. A18.
An editorial discusses the moral and social implications of the current anti-smoking movement. The tobacco industry has had the temerity to suggest that alcohol and bad thoughts will be neo-Puritans' next targets.

Sullum, Jacob, "Smokenders," *Reason,* May 1994, pp. 6-8.
An editorial notes that anti-smoking groups' shift in focus from banning tobacco smoke to banning tobacco is a sign of the times. The arrogance of the anti-smokers is said to be resurgent paternalism.

"Tobacco criminals," *Advertising Age,* July 4, 1994, p. 13.
Legislators appear fixated on smoking and passing anti-tobacco legislation, notes an editorial. One group of Congressmen has urged Attorney General Janet Reno to consider using the RICO Act against tobacco companies, their lobbyists, ad agencies and public relations agencies.

"Tobacco loses a round in California," *Atlanta Constitution,* July 25, 1994, p. A12.

An editorial discusses the legislation in California eventually banning or restricting smoking in public places, noting that it will be interesting to see if California voters recognize another anti-smoking bill on the November 1994 ballot for what it is: a tobacco industry-sponsored initiative shot full of loopholes.

"U.S. shouldn't be exporting cancer," ***Denver Post,*** **July 5, 1994, p. B6.**
An editorial suggests that the tobacco industry not be allowed the same tax benefits that other businesses enjoy and should be taxed more heavily, including higher export fees.

"When will cigarettes be smoked out?" ***Nature,*** **June 30, 1994, pp. 691-692.**
An editorial discusses growing restrictions on smoking in the U.S. and increasing pressure on the tobacco industry. Eventually, tobacco and marijuana will be dealt with similarly.

"Wilson to smokers: Get lost," ***Los Angeles Times,*** **July 23, 1994, p. B7.**
An editorial praises California Gov. Pete Wilson for signing an anti-smoking bill on July 22, 1994, which outlaws smoking in nearly all enclosed places of employment, and maintains that the bill gives Californians the best protection from unwanted smoke of all Americans.

Proponents of Regulation

Duke, Stephen B. and Albert C. Gross, "Regulate tobacco. Regulate all drugs," ***The New York Times,*** **July 24, 1994, p. 15.**
Stephen B. Duke and Albert C. Gross argue that the U.S. needs to rethink its entire approach to drugs, saying that it needs not only a sensible new policy to address the problems posed by smoking but also a rational alternative to the "disastrous prohibition of drugs in general." Duke and Gross propose steps to regulate, rather than prohibit, all drugs, including tobacco.

"FDA's tobacco plan: Tight rules but no ban," ***U.S. News & World Report,*** **July 4, 1994, p. 10.**
FDA Commissioner David Kessler's fight to regulate tobacco, rather than banning it altogether, is discussed. Kessler wants to get public opinion on his side so that Congress will be forced to pass a bill giving the FDA special regulatory powers over the tobacco industry, the magazine says.

"New regulations on cigarettes? FDA now considering," ***Cancer News,*** **summer 1994, p. 20.**
For many years, the American Cancer Society has encouraged a stronger role by the FDA in the scrutiny of tobacco products. Now that more information about the contents of cigarettes is coming to light, the FDA is reconsidering regulating tobacco products.

"People in the news: David Kessler," ***News for You,*** **July 13, 1994, p. 2.**
David Kessler, head of the FDA, is profiled, and his efforts to get FDA approval to regulate the tobacco industry are discussed. Kessler does not support a ban on cigarettes, but he argues that regulations governing them should be tightened.

Research and Studies

Brimelow, Peter, "Thank you for smoking. . . " ***Forbes,*** **July 4, 1994, pp. 80-81.**
Lost in the frenzied attacks on the tobacco industry is the fact that smoking might be, in some small ways, good for people, Brimelow writes. Research findings show that cigarettes really do stimulate alertness, dexterity and cognitive capacity and that smoking offers subtler health rewards against some diseases, including Parkinson's and Alzheimer's.

"Cigarette smoking among adults — United States, 1992, and changes in definition of smoking," ***JAMA: The Journal of the American Medical Association,*** **July 6, 1994, pp. 14-16.**
The use of tobacco in the U.S. is monitored continually to evaluate efforts to control and prevent its use. To determine the prevalence of smoking among adults during 1992, the "National Health Interview Survey-Cancer Control and Epidemiology Supplements" collected self-reported information on cigarette smoking; the results are discussed.

Jenks, Richard J., "Attitudes and perceptions toward smoking: Smokers' views of themselves and other smokers," ***Journal of Social Psychology,*** **June 1994, p. 355-361.**
A sample of smokers in the U.S. completed a questionnaire regarding their motivations for and opinions about smoking, as well as their perceptions of how other smokers feel about the same issues. The results indicate that the subjects perceived psychological addiction as the primary reason for their own smoking.

Muirhead, Colin R., "Radon risks," ***Lancet,*** **July 16, 1994, pp. 143-144.**
Various studies that were conducted to determine the health risks associated with exposure to radon are described. The uncertainty about the joint effect of radon and smoking is also discussed.

"Poor circulation," ***Mayo Clinic Health Letter,*** **July 1994, pp. 4-5.**
The causes of intermittent claudication, otherwise known as poor leg circulation, are examined, and two lifestyle changes that often improve the pain — quitting smoking and exercising — are discussed. In nine out of 10 cases, leg pain is a sign that the leg muscles aren't getting enough oxygen and nutrients.

"Smokers quitting in concern for families' health," ***American Medical News,*** **July 4, 1994, p. 14.**
More and more smokers appear to be dropping the cigarette habit because of concern about how secondhand smoke will affect their families. The results of a recent study on the effects of secondhand smoke are discussed.

Swift, W. Bradford, "High-tech tobacco: Finding new uses for an old plant," ***Omni,*** **August 1994, p. 18.**
North Carolina State University crop scientist Raymond Long believes that tobacco is an ideal source of protein for food additives. Tobacco produces a large amount of biomass in a single season and has a high concentration of Fraction-1 protein.

Taxing Tobacco

Feingold, Eugene, "Tobacco tax hike would pay wide dividend," ***Nation's Health,*** **July 1994, p. 2.**
Increased tobacco taxes worked in Canada to help prevent and control tobacco use, especially among teenagers. The need to increase tobacco taxes in the U.S. is discussed.

"Hill support for tobacco dwindles as prospects for tax hike rise," ***Nation's Health,*** **May 1994, p. 4.**
Members of Congress are rethinking long-held positions on tobacco taxes and a range of other smoking legislation, which is partly driven by accumulating evidence of health dangers. The result is that the once formidable clout of the tobacco industry appears shaky amid the prospect of being legislated and regulated into full retreat.

Jordan, Jerie, "All this and high taxes too?" ***Cancer News,*** **summer 1994, p. 16.**
The bad news that 1994 has brought the tobacco industry in the way of bans, taxes and health reports is discussed. Congress is no longer considering whether to raise tobacco taxes, but rather how much to raise them.

Passell, Peter, "Economic scene," ***The New York Times,*** **July 14, 1994, p. D2.**
A discussion is presented of the reasons why economists generally are not supporting a proposal to tax cigarettes to pay for health care despite a study that showed that smoking-related diseases have "an enormous economic impact."

The Tobacco Lobby

Eaton, William J., "Tobacco industry strikes back to curb anti-smoking onslaught," ***Los Angeles Times,*** **July 18, 1994, p. A11.**
Reeling from an unprecedented assault on smoking, the tobacco industry in mid-1994 has revamped its lobbying and public relations strategy and is aggressively striking back with campaigns that include attempts to portray Big Government as the enemy of individual choice.

Garland, Susan B., "Clinton vs. the sin lobby: All bark," ***Business Week*** **(Industrial/Technology Edition), July 18, 1994, pp. 82-83.**
President Clinton has found out how difficult it is to implement social programs funded by tax increases. Clinton briefly considered a new gambling tax to help pay for welfare reform until the alcohol, tobacco and gambling industries mounted stiff opposition to the proposed tax increases.

Teinowitz, Ira and Julie Liesse, "Philip Morris mounting tobacco offensive," ***Advertising Age,*** **June 27, 1994, p. 8.**
Philip Morris Co. is mounting a vigorous response to attacks against the tobacco industry from a variety of critics. The response, which kicks off June 27, 1994, with full-page ads in eight markets, is discussed.

Women and Smoking

Marino, Gigi, "Parents' smoking damages their kids' lungs," ***Science News,*** **July 2, 1994, p. 5.**
The effects of a woman smoking during pregnancy appear to be irreversible. Strong evidence has been found that both maternal and paternal smoking create long-term, and even lifetime, health dangers for children.

Morain, Claudia, "Still a long way to go, baby . . . ," ***American Medical News,*** **July 4, 1994, p. 11-14.**
As smoking rates among girls vie with boys' and women's cessation rates trail men's, public health experts are looking anew at the reasons why women take up smoking and the forces that keep them from stopping. Several reasons why women can't stop are explored, and a protocol for helping female smokers kick the habit is outlined.

Tamkins, Theresa, "Smoking and your child's intelligence," ***American Health,*** **July 1994, p. 90.**
Smoking during pregnancy is discussed. A new study has found that, in addition to causing low birth weight and decreasing head circumference, prenatal smoking may also lower the child's intelligence.

Sachs, Jessica Snyder, "Women and smoking: Quitting time?" ***New Woman,*** **August 1994, p. 58.**
Although smoking rates have fallen dramatically among men, rates among women have not declined significantly over the last 35 years. The risks smoking poses for women and the difficulties women have in quitting are discussed.

Villarosa, Linda, "Body and soul," ***Women's Review of Books,*** **July 1994, p. 13-14.**
Although cigarette and liquor ads target black women, health messages for these same women are few and far between, the author writes. An excerpt from "Body and Soul: The Black Woman's Guide to Physical Health and Emotional Well-Being" focuses on this advertising and the effects that alcohol and cigarettes have on the body.

Back Issues

Great Research on Current Issues Starts Right Here...Recent topics covered by The CQ Researcher are listed below. Before May 1991, reports were published under the name of Editorial Research Reports.

MARCH 1993
Gay Rights
Aid to Russia
War on Drugs
TV Violence

APRIL 1993
Head Start
High-Speed Rail
Children's Legal Rights
Muslims in America

MAY 1993
Cults in America
Preventing Teen Pregnancy
Software Piracy
National Parks

JUNE 1993
Food Safety
Prostitution
Childhood Immunizations
National Service

JULY 1993
Electric Cars
Population Growth
Downward Mobility
Intelligence Testing

AUGUST 1993
Mental Illness
Bilingual Education
Foreign Policy Burden
School Funding

SEPTEMBER 1993
Suburban Crime
Public Housing
Supreme Court Preview
Immigration Reform

OCTOBER 1993
Airline Safety
Disaster Response
Science in the Courtroom
The Glass Ceiling

NOVEMBER 1993
Paying for Retirement
Charitable Giving
Privacy in the Workplace
Adoption

DECEMBER 1993
U.S. Vietnam-Relations
Learning Disabilities
Child Care
Space Program's Future

JANUARY 1994
Racial Tensions in Schools
South Africa's Future
Worker Retraining
Regulating Pesticides

FEBRUARY 1994
Prison Overcrowding
Water Quality
Religion in Schools
Juvenile Justice

MARCH 1994
Underground Economy
Education Standards
Gambling Boom
Private Management of Public Schools

APRIL 1994
Reproductive Ethics
U.S.-China Trade
Soccer in America
Talk Show Democracy

MAY 1994
Traffic Congestion
Women's Health Issues
Mutual Funds
Political Scandals

JUNE 1994
Education and Gender
Gun Control
Public Land Policy
Nuclear Arms Cleanup

JULY 1994
Dietary Supplements
Public Opinion and Foreign Policy
Crime Victims' Rights
Birth Control Choices

AUGUST 1994
Genetically Engineered Foods
Electing Minorities
Prozac Controversy
College Sports

SEPTEMBER 1994
Home Schooling
Welfare Experiments
Courts and the Media

Back issues are available for $4.00 (subscribers) or $7.00 (non-subscribers). Quantity discounts apply to orders over ten. To order, call Congressional Quarterly Customer Service at (202) 887-8621.

Binders are available for $16.00. To order call 1-800-638-1710. Please refer to stock number 648.

Future Topics

- ***Historic Preservation***
- ***Religion and Politics***
- ***Arts Funding***

THE CQ Researcher®

PUBLISHED BY CONGRESSIONAL QUARTERLY INC.

Historic Preservation

Will the fight over Disney's America spark more clashes?

In the face of strong opposition from preservationists, the Walt Disney Co. recently abandoned plans to build a $650 million history theme park in Virginia's heritage-rich Piedmont. The company's pullout pointed to the preservation movement's increasing clout, but it also raised two longstanding criticisms: that preservationists are anti-development and that they tend to embrace elitist values. Preservationists respond that most of the nation's designated historic sites actually reflect the accomplishments and views of a broad cross-section of American society, and that the anti-Disney campaign succeeded because it had grass-roots support all across the country. One thing seems likely: As preservationists increasingly challenge business interests over quality-of-life issues, additional battles are inevitable.

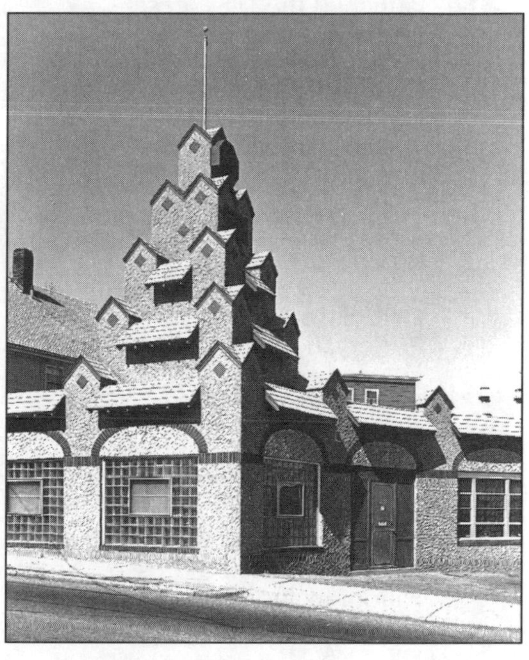

INSIDE THIS ISSUE

CQ Oct. 7, 1994 • Volume 4, No. 37 • Pages 865-888

Formerly Editorial Research Reports ®

Historic Preservation

The Issues

Background

Current Situation

Outlook

Sidebars and Graphics

For Further Information

Cover: Built as a gas station in about 1931, Gilbane's Service Center in Pawtucket, R.I., is now used for retail shops and offices. It's listed on the National Register of Historic Places. (Warren Jagger/National Park Service)

The CQ Researcher

October 7, 1994
Volume 4, No. 37

The CQ Researcher (ISSN 1056-2036). Formerly Editorial Research Reports. Published weekly (48 times per year, not printed the first Friday of any month with five Fridays) by Congressional Quarterly Inc., 1414 22nd St., N.W., Washington, D.C. 20037. Rates are furnished upon request. Second-class postage paid at Washington, D.C. POSTMASTER: Send address changes to The CQ Researcher, 1414 22nd St., N.W., Washington, D.C. 20037.

Historic Preservation

By Richard L. Worsnop

The Issues

No corner of America has a richer history than the rolling hills of Northern Virginia's Piedmont. The region extending westward from Manassas to the Blue Ridge Mountains and southward from Harpers Ferry to Charlottesville contains more than two dozen Civil War battlefields, the homes of four of the first five presidents and countless other historic sites, humble and great.

To many historians, the Piedmont is nothing less than sacred ground. "This is the ground of our Founding Fathers," says Pulitzer Prize-winning historian David McCullough. "These are the landscapes — small towns, churches, fields, mountains, creeks and rivers — that speak volumes." [1]

Given such sentiments, it was hardly surprising that historians launched a campaign this spring to stop the Walt Disney Co. from building a 3,000 acre development in the heart of the Piedmont, including a history theme park.

The opponents claimed Disney's America would ruin the bucolic area by attracting haphazard commercial development and increasing air pollution and traffic. Manassas National Battlefield Park, site of two key Civil War battles, * was seen as especially imperiled because it lies barely five miles east of Disney's property.

Disney's $1 billion project was not without its supporters, including government leaders in Virginia and neighboring Washington and Maryland, residents of Prince William County, where the park would have been built, and even a few historians. They viewed the theme park as an engine of job creation and tourism growth and a popularizer of the nation's history.

To a large extent, the project's supporters also viewed the opposition as just so many wealthy and intellectual elitists. "Freedom admittedly is difficult for a certain sort of mind to abide," a Virginia paper editorialized, "because most people aren't as smart as they are, and given freedom of choice, most people choose things intellectuals consider tawdry, appalling and vulgar. But those tawdry . . . things provide happiness to lots of jes' plain folks." [2]

But the support was not enough, and on Sept. 28, Disney blinked. "We recognize that there are those who have been concerned about the possible impact of our park on historic sites in this unique area," said Peter S. Rummell, president of Disney's theme park division, "and we have always tried to be sensitive to the issue." [3]

The next day, Disney sketched its next steps, which included seeking a more acceptable site in Virginia. "We are starting afresh and are reaching out to historians who have opposed us to make sure our portrayal of the American experience is responsible," said John F. Cooke, president of the Disney Channel, who was tapped as the new chairman of Disney's America. [4]

The company's abrupt turnabout brought a flood of relief from the project's opponents. "We see this not as a defeat for Disney, but as a victory for common sense," Robert Dennis, president of the Piedmont Environmental Council, told reporters.

"The outpouring of support [for blocking the project] was so great that it may in fact represent a turning point in the long and continuing struggle to protect our nation's most important historic assets," said Richard Moe, president of the National Trust for Historic Preservation. "It was the first time that historians, preservationists, environmentalists and ordinary citizens have come together in such numbers and with such determination to achieve a common goal. We hope the experience will encourage citizens everywhere to organize and fight for what's important to their own communities as well as to the nation." [5]

The controversy over Disney's America has focused new attention on the historic preservation movement — including its considerable clout. Once dismissed as a pastime of the idle rich, preservation of the nation's historic heritage has indeed taken on the trappings of a populist movement in recent decades.

"There may have been a time when preservation was about saving an old building here and there, but those days are gone," Moe said earlier this year. "Preservation is in the business of saving communities and the values they embody — and we find ourselves battling policies that seem bent on destroying both." [6]

To a great extent, those values are reflected in the National Trust's 1994 list of "America's 11 most endangered historic places." In addition to Virginia's Piedmont, the list includes Cape Cod, Mass., which the Trust said faces "the sort of "uncontrolled sprawl [that could endanger] the quality of

* The first Battle of Manassas (also known as Bull Run) was the first major conflict of the Civil War. It ended July 21, 1861, when Confederate troops forced unseasoned Union volunteers to retreat. Confederates also triumphed at the Second Battle of Manassas, Aug. 28-Sept. 2, 1862.

Historic Virginia Countryside Lured Disney

Disney's America was planned for a 3,000-acre site near Haymarket, Va., 35 miles west of Washington. The heritage-rich region embracing the site includes 20 historic towns and districts and 18 Civil War battlefields. In addition to a controversial 400-acre theme park, the $1 billion project would have included 1,340 hotel rooms, 2,200 homes and nearly 2 million square feet of commercial space.

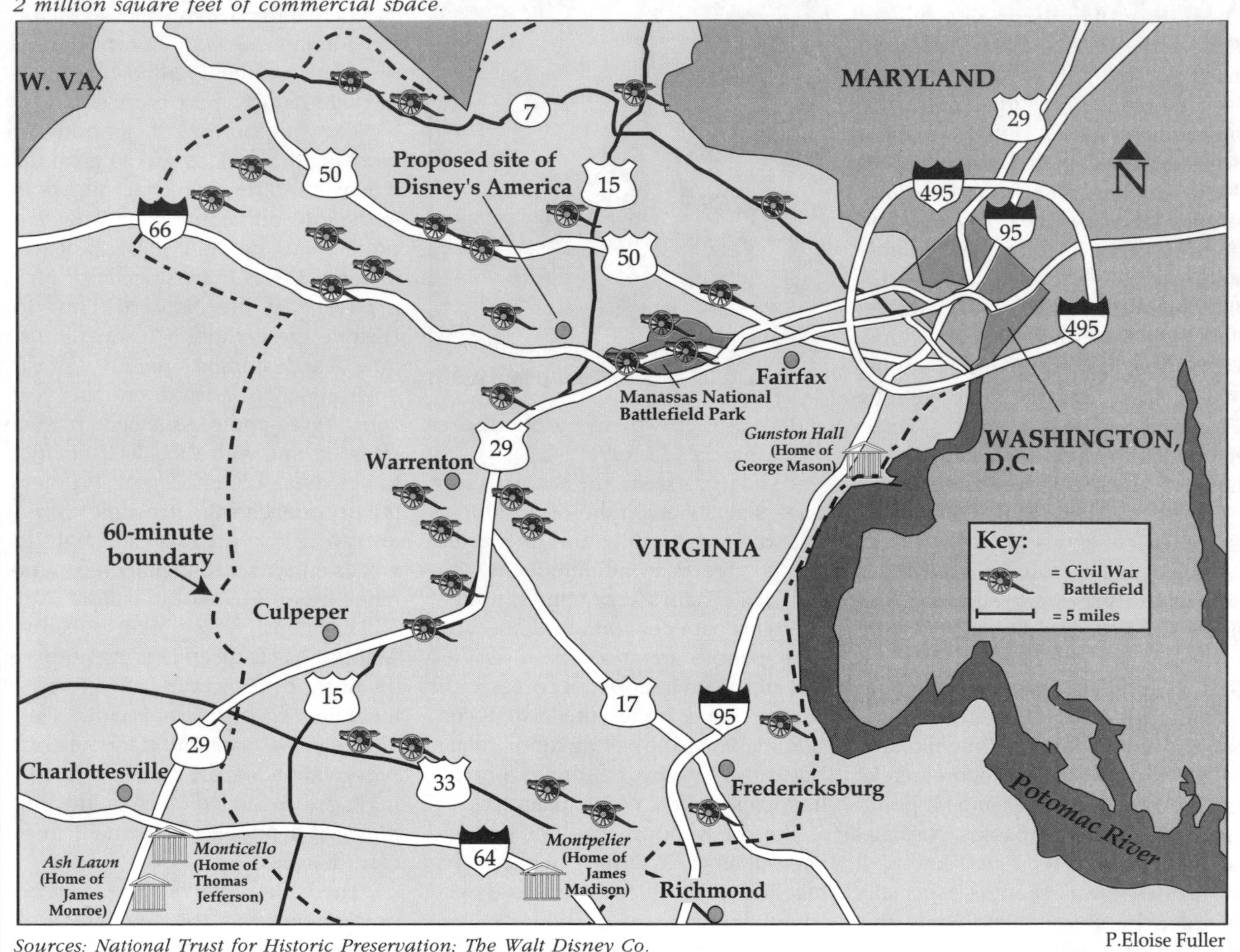

Sources: National Trust for Historic Preservation; The Walt Disney Co. P.Eloise Fuller

life in a very special part of America" *

Other sites on this year's list reflect how far preservationists have branched out in recent years. There's an archaeological complex in New Mexico, the deteriorating schooner USS *Constellation* and the buildings of Harlem, "one of the most distinctive architectural and cultural enclaves in America."

As the battle royal over Disney's America showed, the interests of historic preservationists, property owners and developers often conflict. But preservationists also have learned to join hands with commercial interests, proving that their interests are not irreconcilable. The federal government's investment tax credit program has encouraged thousands of investors to undertake historic rehabilitation projects since 1977. (*See graph, p. 877.*)

And the National Trust's Main Street program encourages downtown business owners in small communities to properly restore their storefronts as a way to use the charm of a community's historic ambience to revive struggling local economies. Scores of communities across the country have benefited from the downtown face-lifts under Trust guidance, finding new hope for battling the often overpowering competition from regional malls and discounters.

But even as the preservation move-

---

* Last year's endangered list included the entire state of Vermont, which the Trust said was threatened by a national problem known as "SprawlMart," or "uncontrolled, large-scale commercial development on the periphery of town that saps the vitality from traditional main streets and destroys open space."

ment continues to broaden its focus beyond the stately homes of the wealthy, championing the cause of what Moe calls "ordinary citizens," many observers still question its methods and goals.

One of the questioners is Jerry Baxter, district director of the California Department of Transporation in Los Angeles. As project director for a planned six-mile stretch of highway through historic neighborhoods in several communities, including Pasadena, he has encountered intense opposition from preservationists (*see p. 882*). "There are many single-purpose organizations that are only concerned about their own issue and want zero impact," he says. "From their standpoint, they'd prefer that we never touch any buildings. But that's not realistic. It's hard to imagine any project that doesn't have some construction associated with it. In the final analysis, there are statewide and regional needs that have to be balanced against the needs of individual communities.

"It's a tough problem, and sometimes you have to make sacrifices. We've done our best to minimize the impact on historic resources. We've reduced the number of lanes, reduced the freeway width and eliminated interchanges. But the bottom line is, the project is needed for the vitality of this region."

In Virginia, meanwhile, Disney's decision to seek a new site for its theme park demonstrated the preservation movement's muscle, but it also raised anew a question that long has dogged the movement:

Is historic preservation an elitist movement?

The dispute over Disney's America has given fresh currency to the argument that historic preservation is a movement run by and for elitists.

Indeed, historic preservationists themselves acknowledge there is a kernel of truth in the charge. "Until very recently, most national preservation programs have been preponderantly upper-class and urbane in their emphasis," wrote architectural historian James Marston Fitch in the early 1980s. "Because of this inherent bias, most of the artifacts studied and conserved have been monumental — palaces, castles, cathedrals, and parliaments: the seats of the powerful and famous." [7]

Much of the opposition to Disney's America, supporters of the theme park contended, came from members of the "horse country gentry" whose estates are located nearby. "The foes of Disney's America include folks whose family wealth involved trashing vast stretches of water or land: Firestone, du Pont, Mellon," declared Tony Snow, a former speechwriter for President George Bush. "Suddenly threatened by the potential invasion of what one heiress termed 'lesser types,' wealthy Virginians want the federal government to hold the riff-raff at bay." [8]

The *Richmond Times-Dispatch* sounded a similar theme in numerous editorials. The paper branded the park's opponents as "purists and elitists" [9] whose ranks include "numerous swells from academia and the Piedmont." [10] "The pink jackets and the tweeds can wave their riding crops and speak of pristine fields steeped in history," the paper stated, "but growth in Prince William and throughout Northern Virginia will occur." [11]

However, others challenge the notion that foes of Disney's America were all charter members of the fox-and-hound set. "It ain't the clenched teeth Ivy League types who are opposing this," said Washington public relations executive Frank Mankiewicz, who claimed to be neutral in the dispute. "These are people who have taken a night off from bowling." [12]

Historic preservationists insist their

National Park Service (all)

Among the 63,000 structures, sites and objects listed in the National Register are (clockwise from top left) the Frederick Douglass Home, Washington, D.C.; Francis Canyon Ruin, New Mexico; the Main Street/Market Square Historic District, Houston, Texas; and a Pratt through-truss bridge in Cherrytree Township, Pennsylvania.

Even the Lowly Diner Has Its Boosters

Who says historic preservation has to be stuffy — or even historic? Certainly not the Society for Commercial Archeology (SCA), which treasures structures and artifacts of the recent past. Commercial archaeologists are especially fond of relics of roadside architecture. They dig diners, for one thing, and those quaint, whitewashed tourist cabins from the early years of motoring, the ones that people stopped using after the Interstates came through.

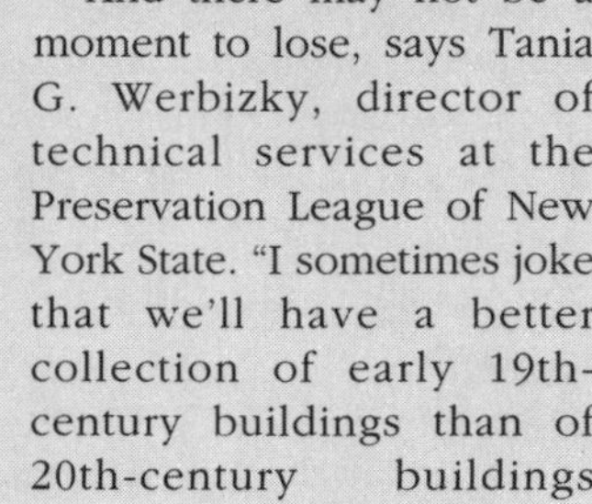
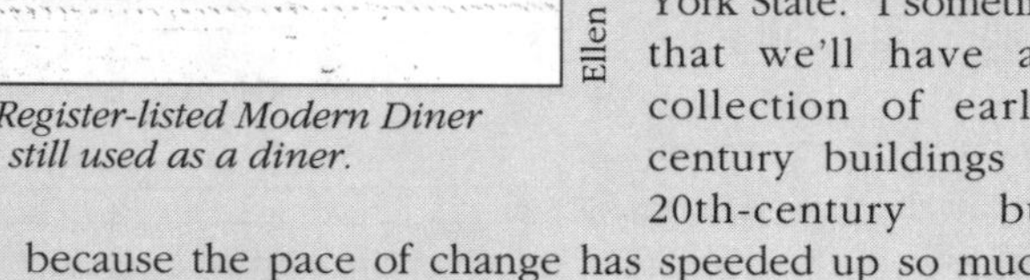

Ellen Weiss/National Park Service

Built in 1940, the National Register-listed Modern Diner in Pawtucket, R.I., is still used as a diner.

These icons of a past that is still a living memory for millions of Americans are disappearing at an alarming rate, commercial archaeologists say, which is why they are trying desperately to salvage the best examples of what little remains.

Getting official landmark status for a diner or a quirky filling station shaped like a coffee pot is especially difficult because buildings and artifacts less than 50 years old must possess "exceptional importance" to qualify for listing on the National Register of Historic Places. A National Register rule of thumb holds that "the more recently that a property has achieved significance, generally the more difficult it is to demonstrate exceptional importance." [1]

Still, some structures of that vintage have passed the test, including six diners, says Beth L. Savage, an architectural historian at the National Register and an SCA member.

But as diners, tourist courts, mammoth neon signs and other artifacts recede further into roadside history, commercial archaeologists must be prepared to preserve the relics of more recent times. Areas of future evaluation could include "post-World War II developments, the growth of suburbs, shopping malls and commercial strip development, the expansion of educational, recreational and transportation facilities, the civil rights movement, the Vietnam War and the impact of historic preservation." [2]

And there may not be a moment to lose, says Tania G. Werbizky, director of technical services at the Preservation League of New York State. "I sometimes joke that we'll have a better collection of early 19th-century buildings than of 20th-century buildings because the pace of change has speeded up so much in the 20th century," she says.

[1] U.S. Department of the Interior, *National Register Bulletin*, No. 22 (undated), p. 6.

[2] *Ibid.*

movement has a broadly based constituency. "The term 'elitist' is no longer relevant as far as historic preservation is concerned," says Frederick C. Williamson Sr., an African-American and the longtime state historic preservation officer for Rhode Island. "There's a great effort today to spread the message that historic preservation is in everybody's interest. Everyone in this nation — black, white, red — has contributed to its history and traditions. That heritage needs to be protected so that future generations can appreciate it. And as this realization grows, historic preservation becomes more and more meaningful to the average person."

Elizabeth Merritt, associate general counsel at the National Trust, shares Williamson's view. People from all walks of life have come to realize, she says, that historic preservation "isn't primarily about restoring rich people's houses. It's actually about much broader quality-of-life and community-preservation issues." She is heartened that residents of the Washington metropolitan area debated the pros and cons of Disney's America in these terms. "To have people thinking so much about what a development like this would do to traffic and their overall quality of life was a very positive thing," she says.

Like Merritt, Nellie Longsworth, president of Preservation Action, a national preservation group, feels the movement "is changing very dramatically" as it reaches out to groups not previously involved in it in a significant way — Native Americans and Native Hawaiians, for instance.

"There's also growing concern nationally with preservation at the local level of government," says Longsworth. "Trying to bring back Main Street is one part of it. The overall goal is to make the quality of life for everybody better. That's not elitist." The trend in historic preservation, she adds, is to "embrace and bring in" all kinds of people.

As part of this outreach effort, the National Trust invited a number of persons involved in community preservation to attend its annual meeting in St. Louis, Mo., last year. The invitation came with free tickets for students and reduced rates for individuals and groups with limited means, many from inner-city neighborhoods.

"All of them had the sense, as we got into conversations with them, that what they were doing was the same thing we were doing — but they would never, ever think of their work as historic preservation," recalls Longsworth. "Still, they could see we were all trying to improve the community. Historic heritage is one of the things that can really bring a community together."

As further evidence of their field's growing popularity, historic preservationists cite the recent emergence of commercial archaeology, a preservation specialty aimed at protecting relics of the roadside environment, such as tourist courts, filling stations, neon signs and diners. (*See story, p. 870.*)

Since many of these structures and artifacts are less than 50 years old, they rarely are regarded as "historic." And for that very reason, they often are more vulnerable to destruction or mutilation than older buildings. Commercial archaeologists report that saving recent-vintage landmarks has helped make historic preservation more relevant to younger people.

Tania G. Werbizky, a commercial archaeology buff and director of technical services at the Preservation League of New York State, points to a June 1993 conference on diners to illustrate the society's approach. "We had about 200 people, many of whom probably don't get that excited about history," she says. "But they really had a heartfelt interest in diners and what they represent on the American landscape. Many could look at a diner and tell you exactly when it was made and who the manufacturer was."

Werbizky belongs to the Society for Commercial Archeology, which tries hard to dispel the idea that historic preservation is elitist, but she concedes it's "one of those stereotypes that's based partly on truth." She adds, "Our members never lose sight of the fact that this stuff is fun. Sure, you get some serious talks on some strange topics at our meetings, but usually they're delivered with a sense of humor. You can be scholarly and enjoy yourself, too, which is what we're trying to do." ■

BACKGROUND

Birth of the Movement

The first U.S. preservation efforts focused mainly on saving buildings linked to historic events or persons. Fittingly, the first recorded preservation action was the 1816 purchase by the city of Philadelphia of Independence Hall — site of the signing of the Declaration of Independence — from the Commonwealth of Pennsylvania. Restoration of the building, which otherwise would have been razed, entailed reconstruction of its distinctive tower, which had been removed around 1790.

The nation gained its first historic house museum in 1850, when the New York Legislature bought Hasbrouck House in Newburgh, George Washington's headquarters during the last two years of the Revolutionary War. The legislative committee appointed to study the purchase said: "No traveler who touches upon the shores of Orange County will hesitate to make a pilgrimage to this beautiful spot . . . and if he have an American heart in his bosom, he will feel himself a better man; his patriotism will kindle with deeper emotion; his aspirations of his country's good will ascend from a more devout mind for having visited the 'Headquarters of Washington.' "[13]

The next major U.S. preservation project also involved Washington, but it wasn't as easy as the purchase of the Hasbrouck House. A South Carolina woman, Ann Pamela Cunningham, launched a campaign in 1853 to buy George Washington's Mount Vernon from John A. Washington, a descendant, who demanded an exorbitant $200,000 for the deteriorating house and 200 acres of land. Spurred by rumors that the plantation would be sold for use as a resort hotel, Cunningham organized the Mount Vernon Ladies' Association of the Union. With fund-raising chapters in every state, the association succeeded where the governments of the United States and Virginia had failed; in 1858 they acquired title to the property.

Cunningham announced the following year that Mount Vernon was almost clear of debt — famed orator Edward Everett had raised nearly $70,000 of the $200,000 purchase price on a cross-country speaking tour — and kicked off a new campaign to raise $150,000 to maintain the estate in the future.

By contrast, the campaign to save Thomas Jefferson's Charlottesville, Va., home, Monticello, limped along from 1862 to 1923, when a New York-based foundation finally succeeded in buying the house. However, the foundation did not make the last payments on the mortgage until 1940.

The Mount Vernon-Monticello formula has been applied to a number of other preservation projects, including the Hermitage, Andrew Jackson's home near Nashville, Tenn. James Marston Fitch observed: "It is significant that all three of these monuments have been preserved by private organizations of women, without any assistance from government agencies."[14] (*See story, p. 878.*)

Americans of a century ago also recognized that sites associated with recent history could well be worthy of preservation. For instance, the campaign to make a permanent memorial of the Gettysburg battlefield began just three weeks after the battle ended. David McConaughy, a Gettysburg lawyer,

Chronology

19th Century

Efforts to preserve America's historic heritage begin during the republic's early years.

1816
To preserve Independence Hall, the city of Philadelphia purchases the landmark from the state of Pennsylvania.

1853-59
The Mount Vernon Ladies' Association wages a successful campaign to save George Washington's Virginia estate on the Potomac River.

September 1863
The Gettysburg Battlefield Memorial Association is founded to "hold and preserve the battlegrounds of Gettysburg . . . with the natural and artificial [defenses] such as they were at the time of said battle."

1920s-1940s

The pace of historic preservation quickens as the federal government becomes a key participant.

1924
Charleston, S.C., establishes the nation's first historic district.

1935
President Franklin D. Roosevelt signs into law the Historic Sites Act, which creates the National Register of Historic Places.

1949
Congress charters the National Trust for Historic Preservation to provide a national focus for preservation activities.

1960s

Destruction of a beloved urban landmark imparts fresh vigor to the preservation movement.

1963
Razing of New York's Pennsylvania Station to make way for a new Madison Square Garden arena and an office building sparks a nationwide outcry.

1966
President Lyndon B. Johnson signs the Historic Preservation Act into law. The measure creates an Advisory Council on Historic Preservation and sets up other programs that expand the federal government's role in preservation.

1970s

Many historic structures across the country gain a new lease on life through conversion to different uses, or "adaptive re-use."

1976
Developer James Rouse converts Boston's Faneuil Hall, a famed Revolutionary-era meeting place, and the Quincy Markets into a huge shopping complex.

1978
Supreme Court blocks plan by the Penn Central Transportation Co. to build a 53-story office tower atop the landmark Grand Central Terminal. The decision is seen as affirming the right of cities to control development through landmarks commissions.

1980s

The federal government's commitment to historic preservation is reaffirmed during the Reagan administration.

1981
President Ronald Reagan signs into law the Economic Recovery Tax Act, which sets up a 25 percent tax credit for the rehabilitation of historic, income-producing properties.

1983
Congress decides to spend $49 million to restore the last original wall of the U.S. Capitol — the West Front — rather than destroy it to build a $70 million extension to the building.

1990s

The Disney company's plan to open a theme park in Northern Virginia ignites fierce opposition.

November 1993
The Walt Disney Co. discloses its plans for a historical theme park, Disney's America, near Manassas National Battlefield Park.

March 1994
Urged by Gov. George F. Allen, the Virginia General Assembly approves a $163.2 million aid package for Disney's America.

May 1994
Protect Historic America, composed of prominent historians and journalists, is formed to block Disney's development.

Sept. 29, 1994
Disney President Michael D. Eisner announces that Disney will seek another site for its theme park.

wrote to Gov. Andrew G. Curtin of Pennsylvania on July 25, 1863, about his plan to buy portions of the field to be retained in the "actual form and condition they were in, during the battles."

McConaughy's initiative led to the founding of the Gettysburg Battlefield Memorial Association in September 1863. The association's goal was to "hold and preserve the battlegrounds of Gettysburg . . . with the natural and artificial [defenses], such as they were at the time of said battle . . . to commemorate the heroic deeds, the struggles, and the triumphs of their brave defenders." [15]

Government Action

Historic preservation remained primarily a grass-roots movement in the United States throughout the 19th century. The federal government did not become involved on a continuing basis until 1906, when President Theodore Roosevelt signed the Antiquities Act into law. The measure authorized U.S. presidents to set aside national monuments in the public domain. In 1916, the National Park Service Act created a federal bureau in the Interior Department to administer national parks and monuments.

During the 1930s, the Depression-era government began to take an active role in preservation. In the Historic Sites Act of 1935, Congress declared it "a national policy to preserve for public use historic sites, buildings and objects of national significance for the inspiration and benefit of the people of the United States."

Beginning in 1934, the Park Service, in collaboration with the American Institute of Architects and the Library of Congress, started the Historic American Buildings Survey, which embarked on a continuing effort to make highly accurate surveys — including measured drawings, photographs and written descriptions — of important architectural landmarks. [16]

It was around this time that the preservation movement began to broaden its field of vision to embrace structures and sites not necessarily commemorative in nature. Citizens' groups and some city governments concluded that buildings of varied architectural styles also merited protection.

These early efforts were especially successful in cities where economic decline had kept historic areas, usually low-income neighborhoods, relatively free of development pressure. Charleston, S.C., created the nation's first historic district in 1924; New Orleans followed by protecting the Vieux Carré (the French Quarter) in 1936. Development and alterations of architectural details were strictly controlled in all such areas.

National Trust Founded

Largely dormant during World War II, the U.S. historic preservation movement gained fresh impetus after 1945. Establishment of the National Trust for Historic Preservation was perhaps the most significant development. Chartered by Congress in 1949 and modeled after England's National Trust, it is authorized to acquire and preserve historic sites and structures for the public and to encourage public participation in preserving the nation's heritage. The Trust relies primarily on dues and contributions from some 250,000 members to finance its activities. Since 1966, however, it has also received substantial federal aid. *

Along the way, the Trust has acquired its own diverse collection of historic properties. The first was Woodlawn Plantation, near Mount Vernon, built in 1802-05 for George Washington's foster daughter, Nelly Custis, and her husband Lawrence Lewis, Washington's nephew. It now shares its grounds with the Pope-Leighey House, a 1940 house designed by Frank Lloyd Wright that was whisked from the path of a Virginia highway in 1964. Other Trust properties include Casa Amesti, a 19th-century adobe house in Monterey, Calif., Lyndhurst, a Gothic Revival mansion overlooking the Hudson River in Tarrytown, N.Y., and the Trust's ornate beaux-arts headquarters building in Washington, originally one of the city's first luxury apartment buildings.

The National Trust's Main Street revitalization program, established in the late 1970s, strives to preserve America's urban past by reviving downtown commercial centers suffering from loss of business to suburban shopping malls. In a desperate attempt to modernize, downtown shop owners turned to aluminum siding and other false fronts, covering up the classic Main Street look and destroying the architectural unity of their areas.

"Clearly this handling of old buildings reflected the American attitude toward used artifacts in general," wrote Fitch. "Unless the artifact was a 'genuine antique' (in which case it was subject to an entirely different evaluation), it was 'used,' 'secondhand,' 'old-fashioned'; hence all traces of the aging process were to be concealed." [17]

The Main Street program, in contrast, seeks the restoration and rehabilitation of existing building stock and the reintroduction of appropriately designed street "furniture," such as benches and street lights. Moreover, merchants are encouraged to create an economically balanced retail mix and to convert unused upper floors into housing and offices. Main Street programs typically are run as independent, nonprofit organizations that provide ongoing guidance.

Criticism Surfaces

While the Main Street movement has been widely praised, preser-

Continued on p. 874

* Last year, the National Trust's annual grant from the Department of the Interior was $6.9 million.

Tracing the Roots of U.S. Preservation

Three schools of thought dominated preservation efforts in 19th-century Europe, all of which helped shape the U.S. movement. Destruction caused by the French Revolution of 1789 inspired the first known preservation activity. The government took a commanding role from the outset. King Louis Philippe appointed an inspecteur général des monuments historiques in 1830, followed by a monuments commission in 1837.

The commission's inventory of old buildings in France laid the groundwork for subsequent preservation efforts. The government reserved the right to prevent alterations of privately owned historic buildings and even hired its own architects to restore some castles and churches.

The most famous of these architects was Viollet-le-Duc, an ardent exponent of the Gothic Revival style whose penchant for design unity led him to remove newer parts of old buildings and substitute his own version of the "correct" Gothic features.

In Britain, meanwhile, the preservation movement was being pushed by private, rather than government, organizations. Led by essayist John Ruskin and poet William Morris, preservationists concentrated on preserving buildings in their current state, rather than trying to restore them to some other condition or appearance. Indeed, Ruskin contended in his classic work, *Seven Lamps of Architecture,* that restoration was impossible. Restoration "means the most total destruction which a building can suffer," he wrote, adding that "it is *impossible,* as impossible as to raise the dead, to restore anything that has ever been great or beautiful in architecture."

In 1877, Morris founded the Society for the Protection of Ancient Buildings, the first private organization formed expressly to save buildings. The society has been followed by other non-governmental organizations, including the pre-eminent National Trust, founded in 1894. At first chiefly concerned with preserving scenic areas, Britain's Trust since 1940 has focused on preserving domestic architecture, including the great country houses that many private owners no longer can afford to maintain.

Preservation took a different turn in Sweden, where Artur Hazelius in 1891 began to assemble the world's first outdoor museum in a Stockholm park. The museum, called Skansen, presented a living display of Swedish cultural history, complete with costumed guides who depicted various aspects of daily life. Colonial Williamsburg is one of many American offshoots of the Skansen living-history concept. It has been followed by many other outdoor museums — Henry Ford's Greenfield Village in Michigan, Old Sturbridge Village in Massachusetts, Mystic Seaport in Connecticut, Old Salem in North Carolina and Schoenbrunn Village in Ohio, to name only a few.

Sweden also has been a leader in maritime archaeology. In the 1960s, the Swedish government decided to conserve the wooden warship *Vasa,* which sank in Stockholm Harbor on its maiden voyage in 1628. Investigation showed that the hulk and its cargo had been surprisingly well-preserved in the cold salt water. But organic material that has been submerged for long periods will turn to dust if allowed to dry out. *Vasa* was saved by impregnating its wooden components with transparent epoxy resins, which filled cavities in the wood and held it together. The ship is now housed in a climate-controlled harborside museum.

The savage destruction of World War II inspired a major boom in historic rehabilitation and re-creation throughout much of Europe. Some of the most dramatic efforts occurred in Warsaw, Poland. Though little remained of the city's historic core, the Polish government resolved to rebuild as many important landmarks as it could.

At the top of the wish list was the Stare Miasto, a 1,000-year-old square in the city center. Detailed architectural plans that survived the war gave direction to the rebuilding program, as did the paintings of Bernardo Belotto (Canaletto), who worked in Warsaw in the mid-1700s. "His views of various sites have proved so accurate," architectural historian James Marston Fitch observed, "that they are used by conservationists as guides to vanished monuments." [1]

[1] James Marston Fitch, *Historic Preservation: Curatorial Management of the Built World* (1982), p. 389.

Continued from p. 872

vation efforts involving extensive re-creation of vanished structures have drawn mixed reviews. A notable example is Colonial Williamsburg, the first large-scale attempt in this country to recover the physical form and atmosphere of an entire community.

Williamsburg, the capital of Colonial Virginia from 1699 to 1780, was a sleepy backwater in 1926 when a local minister, the Rev. W.A.R. Goodwin, asked John D. Rockefeller Jr. to help restore it. About 80 major buildings that survived from the 18th century were restored, and 600 of later vintage were razed or removed. The old Capitol and the Governor's Palace, among other structures no longer standing, were reconstructed on their original foundations. In addition, the College of William and Mary was radically restored to its pre-1775 appearance. By the time of Rockefeller's death in 1960, he had given $68.5 million to Williamsburg restorations.

Although Williamsburg is one of the most popular tourist attractions in the nation, its value as a re-creation has been questioned. "The present-day streetscapes — even though they are composed of excellent antiques, excellently restored and excellently conserved, are in one sense fictitious," Fitch wrote a decade ago. "There are other anomalies: the relative absence of workaday activities and artifacts; the improbably high level of maintenance and housekeeping; the snobbish connoisseurship of much of the interpretive program." [18]

Now, to a large extent, Williamsburg is a different place. To reflect the real world of the times, Williamsburg leaves some of the once pristine buildings unpainted, and fields untrimmed. Indeed, costumed slaves are even seen about town. *(See story, p. 876.)*

Although Fitch took issue with Colonial Williamsburg, he thought that even a structure as preposterous as San Simeon, the huge California mansion built by newspaper publisher William Randolph Hearst, could acquire "historic and aesthetic merit" over time. That's because "history itself has its own paradoxical power of validating historical fakes." Though buildings like San Simeon "are anomalous artifacts which fail to meet the strict standards of art historians and museologists, they are an integral part of our cultural heritage," Fitch declared. [19]

Plimoth Plantation, a museum village in Massachusetts that makes no pretense of being an authentic relic of the past, also stretches the meaning of preservation. The entire community is a conjectural reconstruction of the original Pilgrim community near Plymouth Rock, some seven miles away. The houses and artifacts are all based on meticulous research and scholarship, but no attempt has been made to give them a false patina.

"In this sense," Fitch noted, "Plimoth's anti-antiquarian, anti-connoisseurship emphasis is the reverse of that found at . . . Williamsburg, where everything in the field of view is authentic in its [provenance] even if it is displaced in space." [20]

Key Initiatives

The historic preservation movement witnessed setbacks as well as advances in the 1960s and '70s. Many New Yorkers still mourn the razing of stately Pennsylvania Station in 1963, torn down to make way for the new Madison Square Garden sports arena and an office building. The loss of that urban landmark and others of comparable quality were blamed on federal tax laws that then allowed write-offs for the costs of demolition.

Concern over the disappearance of cherished old buildings led New York City to establish its Landmarks Preservation Commission in 1965. The commission has authority to designate individual landmarks and historic districts, subject to approval by the City Council. Once a structure has been designated as a landmark, its exterior may not be altered without commission approval. The commission also has authority to block the demolition of a designated landmark or delay demolition for up to one year while it seeks a new use for the building; in all cases, owners are assured a reasonable return on their property.

In 1966, Congress enacted three major statutes dealing with preservation. The National Historic Preservation Act authorized matching grants to the states and the National Trust for a variety of preservation projects; authorized an expanded National Register of Historic Places * to serve as a record and index of the "districts, sites, buildings, structures and objects significant in American history, architecture, archaeology and culture"; and created a national Advisory Council on Historic Preservation to advise the president and Congress and to coordinate preservation activities at all levels.

* The National Park Service had begun a limited register of nationally significant landmarks in 1935. Today the National Register has some 63,000 listings encompassing a total of more than 926,000 sites, buildings and objects.

Another of the 1966 statutes, the Demonstration Cities Act (later called the Model Cities Act) allowed cities to credit the costs of preservation against their required local share of urban-renewal costs. It also permitted the secretary of Housing and Urban Development to make grants to the National Trust and municipal governments to cover portions of the cost of identifying and restoring historic properties. Finally, the Department of Transportation Act of 1966 provided statutory protection for historic sites threatened by highway construction.

The Supreme Court's decision in a 1978 case, *Penn Central Transportation Co. v. City of New York,* gave historic preservation another big boost. Spurred by a protest movement led by Jacqueline Kennedy Onassis, New York's Landmarks Preservation Commission denied a request by Penn Central to build a 53-story office tower atop Grand Central Terminal, which it owned. Because the terminal site was zoned for taller buildings, Penn Central sued the city, charging that its "air rights" over the terminal had been confiscated in violation of the Fifth Amendment, which bars the "taking" of private property for public use "without just compensation." The Supreme Court ruled 6-3 against Penn Central.

Trust attorney Merritt calls the Penn Central ruling "one of the real turning points nationally for the historic preservation movement." That's because the decision "gave the green light to communities all over the country to enact preservation laws patterned after New York's. Local laws to protect historic resources spread very quickly after that."

Tax Incentives for Rehabilitation

Tax incentives dating from the mid-1970s likewise have fueled the preservation movement's growth. Building upon smaller incentives provided by the 1976 Tax Reform Act, the 1981 Economic Recovery Tax Act allowed for rehabilitating historic, income-pro-

Role of Blacks Finally Being Recognized

African-Americans, like women, have long been underrepresented or ignored at the nation's historic sites, even where they played a prominent role. "Until recently, docents at Monticello never uttered the word 'slave,' " history Professor James Oliver Horton of George Washington University noted. "Visitors to Gettysburg would never know from the exhibit there that slavery was an issue in the Civil War or until recently that black troops played a key role." [1]

Architectural historian James Marston Fitch made the same point about Colonial Williamsburg a dozen years ago, noting "its evasion of a crucial aspect of its history: the fact that its culture and economy alike were based upon the institution of human slavery." [2]

Today, Williamsburg is a much different place. "We have a whole department on African-American preservation that deals with specific slave issues of the time," says Lorraine Brooks, a Williamsburg spokeswoman. "Visitors get to hear what slave life was like on a day-to-day basis — from the domestic or house slave to the field slave."

And, says Brooks, the complete story of the slave experience is told. "One of the tours talks about how people were packed in ships for the trip to the Americas — loose-packed or tight-packed depending on how much cargo they had — and how they were auctioned off."

Colonial Williamsburg Foundation

Interpreters at Colonial Williamsburg re-enact a slave marriage, known as "jumping the broom."

The unvarnished new tours and exhibits, she says, are part of an ongoing program "to recognize that Colonial Williamsburg was 52 percent black during the 18th century and that the slaves were a major part — indeed, the backbone — of the growth of Williamsburg."

Similarly, the contributions of blacks are being openly acknowledged at Civil War battlefields and other historic sites. According to Edwin C. Bearss, the National Park Service director's special assistant for military sites, "It was well-known, up till about 1910, that large numbers of black soldiers had served in the Union Army. But then people seemed to forget about all that as Jim Crow took hold across the country." In fact, says Bearss, there were some 186,000 black Union soldiers and about 15,000 black sailors in the Union Navy. Now black participation on the Union side of the Civil War is getting its due again, partly because of the popular 1989 movie "Glory." Bearss notes, for instance, that African-American units have been formed to re-enact Civil War battles.

In addition, legislation is pending in Congress to establish a national historic site at Honey Springs, Okla., "where on the 17th day of July 1863," Bearss says, "a battle took place in which, I like to say, you had a Rainbow Coalition long before you had Jesse Jackson. On the Union side, you had the First Kansas Colored Infantry [the first black military unit to see action in the Civil War], which fought like tigers, you had white units and you had units composed of Native Americans from the Cherokee, Creek and Seminole nations. On the Confederate side, you had whites and Hispanics, plus Indian units from the Cherokee, Choctaw, Chickasaw and Seminole nations."

On Sept. 7, ground was broken in Washington for a memorial honoring the black soldiers who fought with Union forces during the Civil War. The African American Civil War Memorial Freedom Foundation believes the memorial will be the first to feature the inscribed names of black Americans who served in the Union military.

[1] James Oliver Horton, "A House Divided: Historians Confront Disney's America," *OAH Newsletter,* August 1994, p. 8. The newsletter is published by the Organization of American Historians. Horton is director of the Afro-American Communities Project at the National Museum of American History.

[2] James Marston Fitch, *Historic Preservation: Curatorial Management of the Built World* (1982), p. 96.

ducing properties. Only buildings listed on the National Register of Historic Places were eligible for the credit, and the owners of even those buildings had to undergo review by the National Park Service. Despite these restrictions, the tax incentives sparked a boom in the utilization of historic buildings for commercial, industrial or housing purposes.

Concerned about abuses of the tax credits by large investors and developers, Congress passed the Tax Reform Act of 1986 to scale back the incentives. The 1986 law reduced the main tax credit from 25 percent to 20 percent and generally prevented investors from using losses on their "passive" investments — such as real estate, cattle feeding and equipment leasing — to reduce their taxes on other income from wages and capital gains.

The aim of the passive-loss rule was to eliminate a tax shelter for the wealthy. But the 1986 law ended up undercutting rehabilitation efforts. According to the National Trust, the 1986 changes have resulted in an 80 percent drop in rehabilitation tax-credit use.

Battlefields at Risk

Around this time, meanwhile, some of the nation's most famous battlefields became the focus of preservation controversies. In a dispute foreshadowing the Disney's America flap, preservation groups in 1988 challenged plans by a Northern Virginia developer to build a 1.2 million-square-foot shopping mall next to Manassas National Battlefield Park. The proposed development site included Gen. Robert E. Lee's headquarters during the second Battle of Manassas in 1862.

The Prince William County Board of Supervisors had approved the proposal because it would have strengthened the tax base. But preservationists argued it would have ruined the national park site. In the end, Congress rescued the battlefield by approving legislation to buy the disputed 600-acre parcel for $118 million and add it to the park.

Changes at Antietam National Battlefield in Maryland also caused recent anxiety in some quarters. The Civil War battleground, which witnessed the single bloodiest day in American military history, * grew by 151 acres in 1991 when two conservation groups donated a plot of privately owned farmland in the battlefield park to the National Park Service (NPS).

The additional property solidified Antietam's reputation as the best-preserved Civil War battlefield. However, some private landowners in the area were wary that their use of their own nearby properties would somehow be restricted. At issue is a 20-year NPS restoration plan that calls for ripping out roads and replacing wire fences with more authentic-looking wooden ones, re-creating 345 acres of woods and 35 acres of orchards, and sharply restricting recreational activities like ballgames and horseback riding.

Park Superintendent Susan Moore reports the project is proceeding on schedule and that criticism "has calmed down quite significantly since the original plan was introduced. Everyone is very supportive of it now."

A controversy of a different sort has swirled for years around the site where Gen. George A. Custer and all 264 men under his immediate command were killed by Sioux and Cheyenne warriors led by Chief Crazy Horse. "Far from being a placid tourist attraction amid the rolling prairies of Montana," noted Edward Tabor Linenthal, a professor of religion at the Univer-

Tax Credit Program Spurs Development

Since the federal tax incentives program started in 1976, more than 25,000 historic buildings have been rehabilitated, representing total investment of about $16 billion. The number of projects shot up after the Economic Recovery Tax Act of 1981 boosted the tax credit for rehabilitating historic, income-producing properties to 25 percent. The subsequent decline in rehab activity reflects changes in the program under the Tax Reform Act of 1986 as well as the period's economic slowdown.

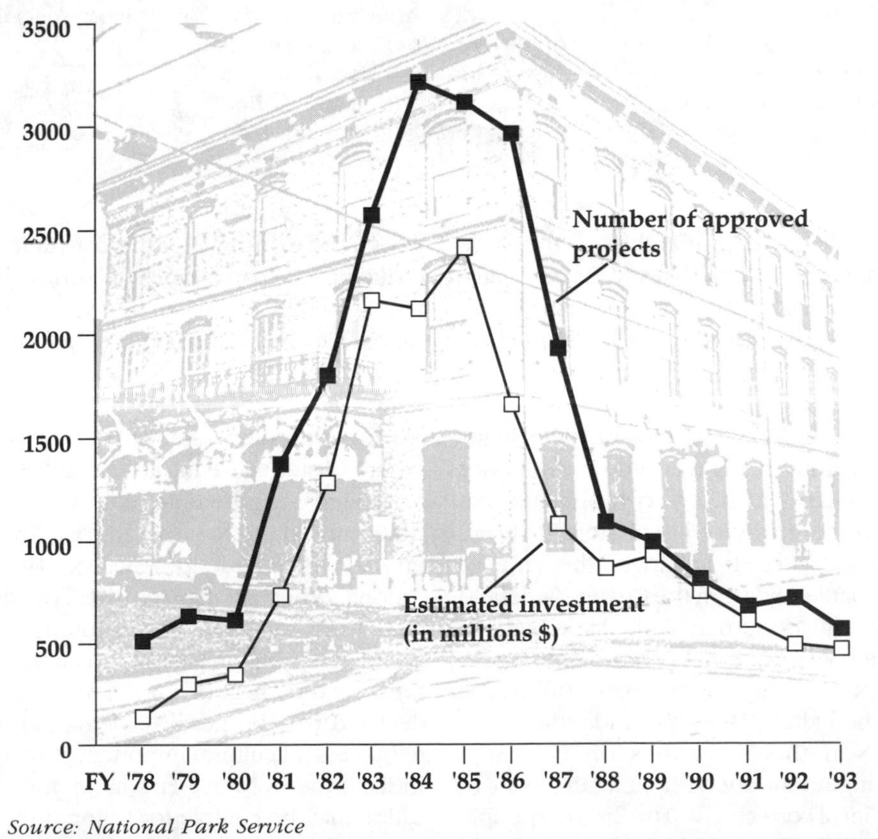

Source: National Park Service

* During the Battle of Antietam (also called Sharpsburg) on Sept. 17, 1862, more than 22,000 Confederate and Union soldiers were killed, wounded or missing.

It's a Women's (Preservation) World

For most of its history, the U.S. historic preservation movement has been largely a women's movement. The Mount Vernon Ladies' Association set the pattern in the 1850s by raising funds to buy George Washington's dilapidated Virginia estate, Mount Vernon, from his heirs and restore it (*see p. 871*).

Other women's organizations attempted to emulate the Mount Vernon model, not always successfully. The Ladies' Hermitage Association was unable to raise enough money to purchase former President Andrew Jackson's home near Nashville, Tenn. However, the association did prevent the Hermitage from being converted into a home for Confederate veterans, and in 1889 Tennessee Gov. Robert L. Taylor turned the building over to the group.

The Daughters of the American Revolution (DAR) have long been active in preservation. In 1892, for example, DAR chapters across the country rallied to save Philadelphia's Betsy Ross House, though there was little firm evidence that Ross had ever lived there, or indeed had actually made the first U.S. flag with the Stars and Stripes. The DAR also has helped maintain Independence Hall and various Revolutionary War battle sites.

Individual women figure prominently in the early preservation movement, too. During the 1920s, Elizabeth Thomas Werlein did much to draw attention to the architectural and historic importance of New Orleans' French Quarter. It was largely due to her efforts that the neighborhood gained protection as one of the nation's first historic districts. In the 1930s, du Pont heiress Louise du Pont Crowninshield was instrumental in persuading her father to buy Eleutherian Mills, the original home of industrialist E.I. du Pont de Nemours, which now forms part of the Winterthur Museum complex near Newark, Del. The National Trust named its highest preservation honor, the Crowninshield Award, for her.

Toni Lee, a historian at the National Park Service, says women are still prominent in the preservation movement, outnumbering men by roughly 2 to 1 in both professional work and as volunteers and community activists. One reason, she says, is that women tend to gravitate toward liberal arts subjects in college, including history. In addition, more women than men are likely to have sufficient leisure time to do volunteer work for preservation groups.

Despite this level of involvement over the years, relatively few historic sites pay tribute to the accomplishments of American women, historians say. "If Americans had to rely on existing historic sites for their understanding of women's history, a very limited and distorted picture would emerge," wrote Page Putnam Miller, director of the National Coordinating Committee for the Promotion of History. "About 50 historic sites, mostly house museums, have as their primary mission the preservation of structures and the development of interpretive programs about women, with most specializing in the life of a particular woman." [1]

[1] Page Putnam Miller, "Landmarks of Women's History," in *Reclaiming the Past: Landmarks of Women's History,* Page Putnam Miller, ed. (1992), p. 3.

sity of Wisconsin-Oshkosh, "the Little Bighorn remains the site of an ongoing clash of cultures that is less violent but just as spirited as the military clash that took place there in 1876." [21]

The confrontation reached a climax in 1991, when Congress approved legislation authorizing a monument to honor American Indians who fought to preserve their way of life at Little Bighorn. The measure also changed the name of the battlefield from the Custer Battlefield National Monument to the Little Bighorn Battlefield National Monument. Under Park Service policy, battlefields are named after places, not individuals.

Nonetheless, critics of the name change denounced it as a surrender to political correctness. The 250,000 people who visit Little Bighorn each year "do not go there because of the convenient location," said Lowell Smith, board chairman of Little Big Horn Associates of Albertville, Ala., in testimony before a Senate subcommittee in July 1991. Rather, he said, "They visit there for one reason and one reason only — to see where Custer made his last stand." [22]

Congress again deferred to Native Americans in the National Historic Preservation Act Amendments of 1992. Among other provisions, the law directed the secretary of the Interior to establish a program to help Indian tribes preserve their historic properties. It also declared that properties "of traditional religious and cultural importance" to an Indian tribe or Native Hawaiian organization may be eligible for listing on the National Register of Historic Places. ■

CURRENT SITUATION

Disney's America

Residents of the national capital area were startled last November when the Walt Disney Co. announced plans to open a $650 million history theme park, Disney's America, about 35 miles west of Washington near tiny Haymarket, Va. The facility, to be built on a 3,000-acre tract, would feature "painful, disturbing and agonizing" exhibits on slavery, American Indian life and the Vietnam War, said Disney Chairman Eisner. [23]

Initial reaction to the news was mainly favorable. Local and state government leaders in Virginia said the park's projected payroll of 1,000 workers and average daily visitorship of 30,000 would spread economic benefits over a wide area. An additional boost was expected from construction of some 1,200 hotel rooms, 2,200 homes, a campground, golf courses and nearly 2 million square feet of office and retail space. In all, some 19,000 new jobs were anticipated for the region.

"What attracts me is the idea of breaking out of the academic mode [of teaching history] with the opportunity to reach a broad public that we rarely address," said history Professor Eric Foner of Columbia University, a Disney consultant. [24]

Even the Smithsonian Institution, a Washington tourist attraction in its own right, was in Disney's corner. "It isn't very likely that visitors would come to Washington only to see Disney's America," wrote Robert McCormick Adams, secretary of the museum complex, "but it is quite likely that some family decisions to come would be tipped favorably in the end by the additional presence of a Disney attraction." [25]

Opposition was not long in surfacing, however. Critics included established environmental groups such as the Chesapeake Bay Foundation and the Piedmont Environmental Council as well as newly formed ones like Protect, a Prince William County citizens organization. Their objections centered on the project's impact on regional traffic and air and water quality.

"Make no mistake," wrote Pulitzer Prize-winning historian James M. McPherson, president of Protect Historic America (PHA), the national group that spearheaded the anti-Disney effort. "Disney's America will turn the unique historical landscape of Northern Virginia into another Orlando." [26] Columnist George F. Will wrote, "Disney has decided to build something that would radically transform, beyond recognition, an area that is, arguably, America's most defining landscape." [27]

Nonetheless, Disney's America kept

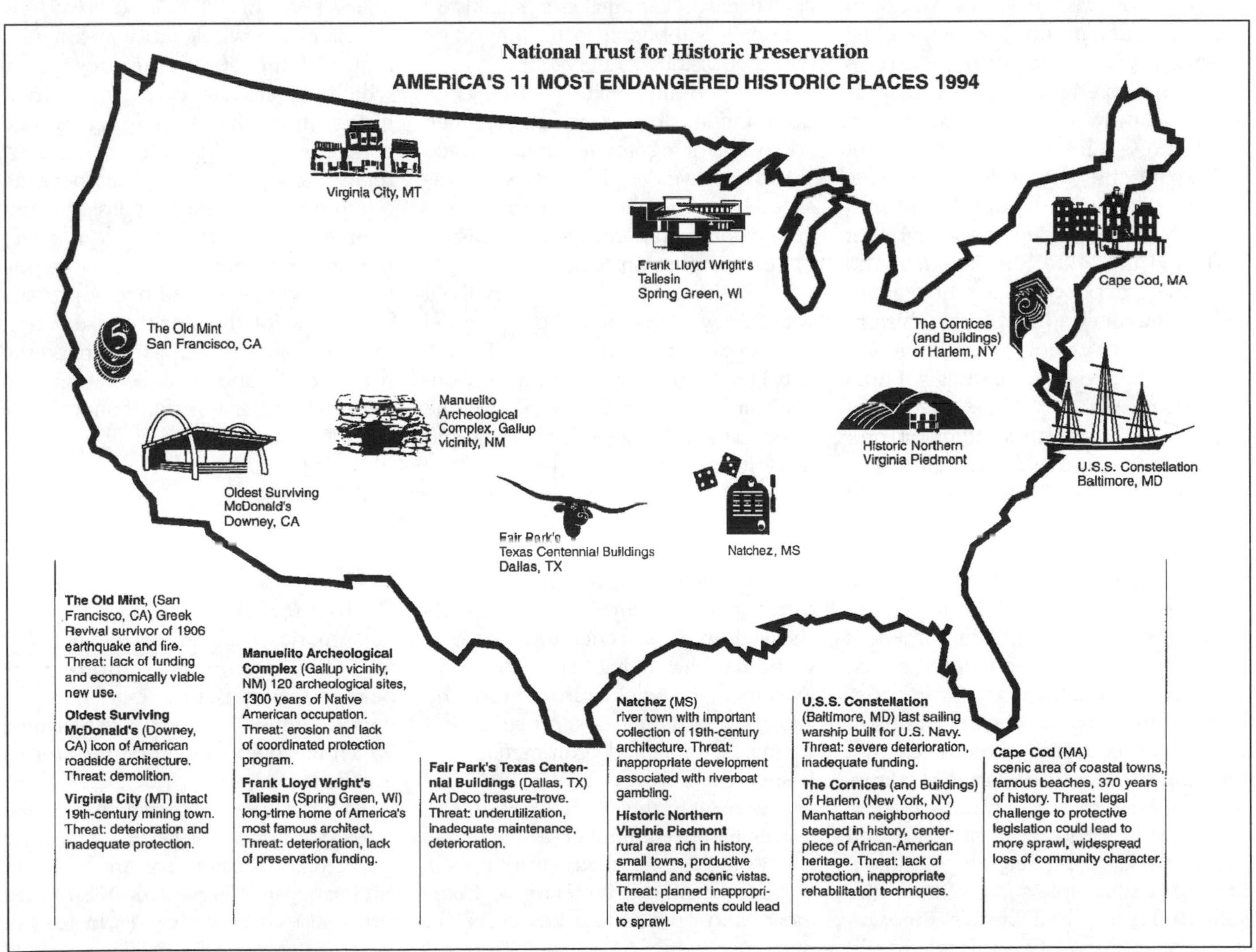

National Trust for Historic Preservation
AMERICA'S 11 MOST ENDANGERED HISTORIC PLACES 1994
Virginia City, MT
Frank Lloyd Wright's Tallesin Spring Green, WI
Cape Cod, MA
The Cornices (and Buildings) of Harlem, NY
The Old Mint San Francisco, CA
Manuelito Archeological Complex, Gallup vicinity, NM
Historic Northern Virginia Piedmont
U.S.S. Constellation Baltimore, MD
Oldest Surviving McDonald's Downey, CA
Fair Park's Texas Centennial Buildings Dallas, TX
Natchez, MS
The Old Mint, (San Francisco, CA) Greek Revival survivor of 1906 earthquake and fire. Threat: lack of funding and economically viable new use.
Oldest Surviving McDonald's (Downey, CA) icon of American roadside architecture. Threat: demolition.
Virginia City (MT) intact 19th-century mining town. Threat: deterioration and inadequate protection.
Manuelito Archeological Complex (Gallup vicinity, NM) 120 archeological sites, 1300 years of Native American occupation. Threat: erosion and lack of coordinated protection program.
Frank Lloyd Wright's Taliesin (Spring Green, WI) long-time home of America's most famous architect. Threat: deterioration, lack of preservation funding.
Fair Park's Texas Centennial Buildings (Dallas, TX) Art Deco treasure-trove. Threat: underutilization, inadequate maintenance, deterioration.
Natchez (MS) river town with important collection of 19th-century architecture. Threat: inappropriate development associated with riverboat gambling.
Historic Northern Virginia Piedmont rural area rich in history, small towns, productive farmland and scenic vistas. Threat: planned inappropriate developments could lead to sprawl.
U.S.S. Constellation (Baltimore, MD) last sailing warship built for U.S. Navy. Threat: severe deterioration, inadequate funding.
The Cornices (and Buildings) of Harlem (New York, NY) Manhattan neighborhood steeped in history, centerpiece of African-American heritage. Threat: lack of protection, inappropriate rehabilitation techniques.
Cape Cod (MA) scenic area of coastal towns, famous beaches, 370 years of history. Threat: legal challenge to protective legislation could lead to more sprawl, widespread loss of community character.

moving forward, propelled by the unwavering support of George F. Allen, Virginia's new Republican governor. Under Allen's prodding, the Virginia General Assembly on March 11 approved a compromise package of $163.2 million in state subsidies for the project, mainly for new roads.

Critics Step Up Pace

Criticism of Disney's America shifted direction this spring, as the park's possible effect on nearby Civil War battlefields and other historic sites moved to the forefront of the debate. The change in emphasis came about largely through the efforts of Protect Historic America.

PHA board member McCullough, president of the Society of American Historians and author of a best-selling biography of President Harry S Truman, blasted the Disney project at a May 11 news conference at the National Press Club. "The very idea of bulldozing the land of [Robert E.] Lee, Stonewall Jackson, Thomas Jefferson, James Monroe, the legions who fought and died there and the families who lived there exposes those who want to do it as having no heart for the history they want to exploit," he charged.

PHA stepped up its assault at a June 21 hearing before a U.S. Senate subcommittee. Historian McPherson predicted that commercial development spawned by the Disney park would "crawl back to surround the [Manassas] battlefield and squeeze it to death." National Trust President Moe declared that the "centuries-old heritage and rural character" of the Piedmont would "be swept away, plowed under, paved over, utterly destroyed."

The drumfire of hostile comment clearly nettled Disney executives. At a meeting with *Washington Post* editors in June, Eisner said he was "shocked" by the vehemence of those opposed to the park. "I expected to be taken around on people's shoulders," he said. If Eisner "had known this was going to happen," he said, he "would have delayed it for a year." [28]

Meanwhile, the opposition continued to fight. The Piedmont Environmental Council, based in Warrenton, Va., said the project would have a negative impact on regional air, water, transportation, crime, schools, safety services and, not least, taxes.

Disney indignantly denied its park would defile the Piedmont's landscape. Disney's America "not only will not replace historic sites but rather will add to their luster by enthusing our guests about events that occurred there and the people who took part in them," asserted Eisner. "We are confident our project will actually encourage more people to visit historic areas. And we believe our presentation of the American heritage can make a significant national contribution to the important cause of historic preservation." [29]

The opposition seemed to have been dealt a serious blow on Sept. 21, when county planning commissioners voted 7-1 to approve the plan. The issue was slated to go to the Board of County Supervisors for final review when Disney pulled the plug on Sept. 28.

At the root of the decision to pull out was Disney's basic desire to be a good corporate citizen, said Disney Design and Development chief Rummell. "Implicit in our vision for the park is the hope that it will be a source of pride and unity for all Americans," he said. "We certainly cannot let a particular site undermine that goal by becoming a source of divisiveness." [30]

Gov. Allen was reportedly at an office party when Disney officials showed up at his office in Richmond with the bad news. The governor, who had led the cheerleading for the project, later issued a short statement saying he remained "committed to a Disney theme park in Virginia" and "pleased that the Walt Disney Co. shares that commitment." [31]

"We're just shocked," said Robert T. Skunda, Allen's secretary of Commerce and Trade and a key player in wooing Disney. Skunda blamed Disney's decision on "misinformation and meddling" from "well-financed, out-of-state interest groups." [32]

Similar sentiments were sounded by Warren Dahlstrom, a vice president of the Carey Winston Co., a real estate brokerage firm, who saw at work the economic clout of "a very quiet but powerful landed gentry who wrested control from the average folks who wanted the project." [33]

News of Disney's decision brought statements of relief from a wide range of organizations, from the Sierra Club and Clean Water Action to Citizens Against Gridlock and the Fairfax County Federation of Citizens Associations.

Historian McCullough said Disney's decision represented a victory for the nation's history. "We feel that few events in our whole story as a nation better demonstrate the degree to which Americans care about their history than what has happened here concerning the Piedmont," he told reporters Sept. 29. "This has been an overflow of sentiment, passion, concern, money and voices from every part of the country. I think in the future it will be looked back upon the way some of the great conservation turning points of the past changed the whole ethic about conservation and the environment in this country."

New Battles Ahead

Given the media focus on Disney's America, it sometimes seemed that few other preservation efforts were being pursued. But there are many of import. Ironically, one involves Disney, which has been widely praised for its involvement.

Earlier this year, the company agreed to lease, restore and modernize the New Amsterdam Theater, an Art Nouveau landmark on Manhattan's West 42nd Street, just off Broadway. From 1913 to

Continued on p. 882

At Issue:

Would Disney's America have endangered the Virginia Piedmont region?

yes

RICHARD MOE, JAMES MCPHERSON, DAVID MCCULLOUGH
Moe is president of the National Trust for Historic Preservation; McPherson is president of Protect Historic America; McCullough is a trustee of the National Trust and a board member of Protect Historic America

FROM *JOINT STATEMENT ISSUED SEPT. 29, 1994.*

On behalf of the National Trust for Historic Preservation and Protect Historic America, we commend the Disney Co. for the decision it has announced today. It was undoubtedly a difficult decision but it was certainly the right decision. It is good for Disney, it is good for Virginia and it is good for the country. . . .

It's never easy for a company to reverse its position on such a highly visible issue. But it is to Disney's great credit that it has done so, recognizing in the process the important preservation, environmental and other issues involved. As a result, future generations of Americans will be able to enjoy and appreciate the unique historic and natural beauty of the Northern Piedmont of Virginia.

We have said from the outset that we want to be part of the solution to this controversy. It's not sufficient simply to oppose an inappropriate development. The issue all along has been location, and that is now settled. We believe that a Disney theme park, if done well, can be an effective means of bringing our nation's history to millions of Americans in an intelligent and responsible way. That has never been an issue with us. Therefore we wish Disney well in its efforts to find another location in Virginia for this purpose. If there are ways that we can contribute positively to that effort, we would be happy to do so. . . .

Finally, we want to thank the thousands of individuals and scores of organizations across the country who voiced their support for this effort. We would like in particular to recognize the critical role played by the Piedmont Environmental Council and others in the area who initiated and sustained the local effort. Because an important part of our nation's heritage was at risk, this quickly became a national issue. It struck a chord with people everywhere who care about preserving the best of our past, and for us that was the most gratifying part of the entire effort.

The outpouring of support was so great that it may in fact represent a turning point in the long and continuing struggle to protect our nation's most important assets. It was the first time that historians, preservationists, environmentalists and ordinary citizens have come together in such numbers and with such determination to achieve a common goal. We hope the experience will encourage citizens everywhere to organize and fight for what's important to their own communities as well as to the nation. If so, this effort will have been a landmark moment in the life of the historic preservation movement in America.

no

SCOTT E. GIBB
Past president, Prince William County Chamber of Commerce

FROM *STATEMENT WRITTEN FOR THE CQ RESEARCHER,* OCT. 3, 1994

The recent fight between historians, preservationists and environmentalists and the Disney Co. wasn't simply a fight over a theme park in historic Virginia. It was a critical battle over development. Disney's defeat sets a precedent that will have a detrimental impact on Prince William County, Va., and the nation as a whole.

The opposition declared Disney's America would have an adverse effect on the Historic Piedmont, an 8,000-square-mile area encompassing almost one-fifth of Virginia. They argued Disney would be a catalyst for unwanted growth, destroying forever this legacy of all Americans.

If this is true, and if it is also true this region is so historically valuable it must be protected at all cost, then it follows there must be other types of development not suitable for this region. And if this is true, then any and all future development in these supposedly historically sensitive areas will have to pass a litmus test designed by historians before any project is allowed.

What this precedent effectively, and unfortunately, does is deny the citizens and communities of this region, and similar areas in the country, the same property and economic-development rights enjoyed by everyone else. They have denied these citizens their rights simply because of where they happen to live.

These groups have usurped the power, wishes and desires of the local citizenry, planning boards and elected officials through the use of negative, media-attracting demonstrations, boycotts, misinformation, strong-arm tactics and costly legal battles and corporate defamation of character to achieve their ends. How will they replace the tax revenues, jobs and economic stimulation in these communities? Through quaint bed and breakfast inns, cozy restaurants and over-priced antique shops?

If given a fair chance, Disney's America would have passed all local, state and federal laws and regulations. But the real and perceived damage to the company's reputation and bottom line ultimately led to its withdrawal from Haymarket, Va. If an upstanding, all-American company like Disney can't build in this area, then who can? Who will want to? Who will be allowed to?

It's no wonder corporations in America are taking their factories, jobs and money out of the United States. The triad of historians, environmentalists and preservationists are making the business climate in this country intolerable. Their power and influence grows every day, and every day America loses more and more of its ability to successfully compete in the world marketplace.

The past has been preserved. The future may not be quite so lucky.

Continued from p. 880

1927, the theater hosted the "Ziegfeld Follies," the legendary series of musical revues featuring stars like Fannie Brice, Bert Williams, W.C. Fields, Ina Claire, Will Rogers, Ed Wynn, Marilyn Miller and Eddie Cantor.

Whereas Disney's America was assailed as a threat to historic landmarks, the New Amsterdam project is being counted on to spark New York's effort to revitalize the Times Square theater district. Tentatively scheduled to reopen in September 1996, the theater reportedly will boast as much of its opulent decorative detail as can be restored or re-created, plus updated heating, cooling, lighting and plumbing systems. An earlier Disney theater restoration, of the El Capitan Theatre on Hollywood Boulevard in Los Angeles, was chosen by the National Trust as one of its 15 national honor award winners for 1992.

Merritt and other attorneys at the National Trust have been involved in a wide range of projects suggesting the movement's new breadth. They recently helped to persuade Interior Department officials to deny approval for gold-mining exploration at a Native American sacred site in Montana; won a suit to protect and restore the Devils Island lighthouse in Wisconsin after the Coast Guard removed and damaged the original historic Fresnel lens; and won major lawsuits stopping freeway projects in Atlanta, Ga., Fort Worth, Texas, and Mobile, Ala., based on their impact on historic resources.

Now the Trust is fighting on a number of fronts:

- to protect historic buildings from demolition for a casino parking garage in Cripple Creek, Colo.;
- to protect historic South Pass, Wyo., where the Oregon Trail crosses the Continental Divide, from construction of a huge pipeline;
- to protect the Dr. Pepper [soft drink] headquarters building in Dallas from demolition by a developer who wants to build a strip mall;
- to stop the Route 710 freeway in Los Angeles, which would destroy more than 1,000 homes in Pasadena, South Pasadena and predominantly Hispanic El Sereno.

In addition to these battles, the Trust is concerned about the properties on its latest annual list of "America's 11 Most Endangered Historic Places." The Northern Virginia Piedmont made the list, naturally, as did Frank Lloyd Wright's Taliesin in Spring Green, Wis., and all of coastal Cape Cod, Mass. (*See map, p. 879.*)

Los Angeles Conservancy

Preservationists are trying to save the original McDonald's in Downey, Calif., closed after it was damaged in the Los Angeles-area earthquake Jan. 17.

Burger Joints to Battlefields

But the most attention-grabbing entry was the original McDonald's hamburger carryout in Downey, Calif. Built in the once ubiquitous "golden arches" and red-and-white tile mode, the facility is one of a rapidly vanishing group of McDonald's originals.

Chances of saving this "icon of roadside architecture," as the National Trust calls it, don't appear bright. McDonald's closed and boarded up the Downey property shortly after it was damaged in the Los Angeles-area earthquake last Jan. 17. But company officials had announced plans to shut down the establishment even before then, saying sales had slumped due to its lack of amenities.

Complicating matters further, McDonald's already has built a replica of an old-style McDonald's carryout in Des Plaines, Ill., the hometown of the late Ray Kroc, who took over the company in 1961. Moreover, Des Plaines was the home of the first Kroc-franchised McDonald's, which opened in 1955.

Michael Jackson, chief architect in the preservation services division of the Illinois Historic Preservation Agency, nonetheless feels it's a shame the Downey facility is being given short shrift. "The Downey building is the one that clearly qualifies as a memorial to the McDonald brothers," he says. "It's the one that Richard and Maurice McDonald actually worked in when they founded the company. After all, we call it McDonald's, not Kroc's."

The prognosis for many Civil War battlefields could be as gloomy as that for the Downey McDonald's. "I don't think the American public understands how threatened this part of our heritage is," said Walter Powell, chief preservation officer for the borough of Gettysburg, Pa. "This next decade will be the turning point. What we consider important is [very] close to being destroyed. Even Gettysburg is not safe." [34]

Indeed, the Gettysburg National Military Park recently suffered significant damage as the result of a 1990 land swap between the National Park Service (NPS) and Gettysburg College, which abuts the battlefield. Under the exchange, the NPS gave the college 7.5 acres of federal land so that it could relocate a private rail line to the edge of its campus. In return, the NPS received an easement on 47 acres of college playing fields to assure that the land would remain undeveloped.

In moving the rail line, however, the college built a spur that sliced off part of a ridge crossed by Union troops during their retreat into town at the end of the 1863 battle's first day. NPS Director Roger G. Kennedy called the incident "a tragedy," and the Gettysburg park superintendent, who had arranged the land swap, was transferred to Texas. [35]

According to Edwin C. Bearss, former chief historian at the NPS, Civil War battle sites are imperiled because they lie close to major transportation arteries. "At the time of the Civil War, unlike the Revolution, the basic infrastructure of the United States was in place," says Bearss, now the NPS director's special assistant for military sites. "The capital and other major cities were well-established, and the nation's transportation network was tied into rivers and railroads. It was these areas — these corridors — that drew the armies and determined where the battles would be fought."

Since World War II, Bearss adds, the areas near Civil War battlefields have experienced robust growth. "The corridor from New York to Richmond has become a strip city, and the strip expands outward from it. The same thing is happening between Chattanooga and Atlanta. So battlefields in those areas are endangered because the greatest threat to historic sites is the urban population explosion."

Surviving Revolutionary War battlefields tend to be less threatened, says Bearss. Many of the battles took place in remote areas that still are rural, he says, among them Kings Mountain and Cowpens on the Piedmont frontier of South Carolina. "They have survived because the course of the Revolution was not dictated by a transportation network that already existed." ■

OUTLOOK

"Hard Stuff" Ahead

Historic preservationists see no easing of their workload in coming years, for structures and artifacts worth saving are getting older, and the boundaries of what's important are constantly changing. Who could ever have guessed, a quarter-century ago, that an ordinary McDonald's hamburger stand would someday be regarded as a historic treasure? Or a Saturn rocket, a carousel horse or slave dwellings on a Mississippi plantation?

Major global and economic changes are having a profound effect on preservation's agenda. With military down-sizing, for example, has come a flood of base closings, many with historic properties that face potential threats.

The wave of gambling casinos being built in historic towns around the nation, like Cripple Creek, Colo., poses a serious threat to historic resources. And there is the ongoing effort of the Federal Deposit Insurance Corporation to quickly unload properties, many of them historic, that it has acquired through bankruptcies.

A priority aim of preservation groups is to revive the rehabilitation tax credit that the Tax Reform Act of 1986 modified. Subsequent efforts to persuade Congress to reinstate the credit in its original form failed, mainly because the projected loss of tax revenue was deemed too high.

Now, however, a new effort to provide tax incentives for homeowners who rehab historic properties is under way at the National Park Service. A proposal being developed by Harry K. Schwartz, a special projects adviser in the preservation services division, would extend the existing 20 percent tax credit to individuals who rehabilitate a building on the National Register — or buy a newly rehabilitated one — and live in it.

Under existing law, notes Schwartz, the rehabilitation tax credit is limited to "commercial properties — those held for the production of income or used in a trade or business." Giving the credit to homeowners, he argues, would encourage rehabilitation of rundown buildings without activating the passive-loss rule. He reasons that a homeowner's tax credit "would not be treated as a 'passive loss' because the taxpayer would be actively living in the building." [36]

Before approaching potential congressional sponsors, Schwartz wants to make sure that the projections for lost tax revenue are within lawmakers' acceptable range. The ultimate goal is to have the legislation incorporated into the next major overhaul of the federal tax code, which Schwartz expects Congress to tackle in 1995 or 1996.

In the meantime, preservationists are seeking to counter the burgeoning private property rights movement. Legisla-

For More Information

National Park Service, P.O. Box 37127, Washington, D.C. 20013-7127; (202) 343-9540. The Park Service administers the National Register of Historic Places and the Investment Tax Credit program, designed to encourage the rehabilitation of historic, income-producing buildings.

National Trust for Historic Preservation, 1785 Massachusetts Ave. N.W., Washington, D.C. 20036; (202) 673-4000. The 250,000-member private organization, patterned after a similar group in Britain, supports preservation activities at the local, state and national levels.

Piedmont Environmental Council, 45 Horner St., Warrenton, Va. 22186; (703) 347-2334. Founded in 1972 to preserve Northern Virginia's Piedmont region, the council helped lead the fight against Disney's America.

Society for Commercial Archeology, National Museum of American History, Room 5010, Washington, D.C. 20560; (202) 882-5424. The society strives to preserve the roadside environment of the 20th century, including gas stations, diners, tourist courts, drive-in restaurants, neon signs and the like.

tion introduced in March by Senate Minority Leader Bob Dole, R-Kan., was particularly alarming to preservationists. Called the Private Property Rights Act of 1994, the measure would require all federal agencies to analyze any regulation that could result in a "taking" of private property.

"Although the sponsors of the bill have portrayed it as a moderate approach to the protection of property rights," George Abney wrote in *Historic Preservation News,* "a close analysis reveals some provisions that could severely limit the government's ability to administer public-interest policies — among them, historic preservation laws." [37]

Over the years, the Supreme Court has held that establishing whether a taking has in fact occurred can be determined only on a case-by-case basis. The Dole bill takes a more sweeping approach, requiring agencies to conduct an impact analysis before issuing "any policy, regulation, proposal, recommendation or related agency action [that] could result in a taking or diminution of use or value of private property."

The National Trust contends this provision would generate red tape and allow property owners to use their property in ways harmful to the property values of millions of Americans. On May 19, Dole offered his bill as an amendment to the Safe Drinking Water Act reauthorization. However, Sen. Dale Bumpers, D-Ark., offered a compromise measure that still required impact analysis but narrowed the definition of a taking. Bumpers' version was acceptable to Dole and was passed by the Senate on a voice vote. Preservationists were still troubled by Bumpers' approach, but less so.

In the opinion of Preservation Action's Longsworth, the historic preservation movement needs "to figure out how we present ourselves" to the public as well as "bring more people into it to understand what we're about." And to do that, preservationists have to show that older historic areas "can really pull together, bring in tourism, become economically productive and also end up as good places to live."

Historic preservation "isn't antigrowth," she adds. "We're just against bringing that growth and development into existing historic areas. We're looking for tools to go into the really disinvested city neighborhoods, where we've got lots of buildings but few people living in them, plus high crime and high unemployment. We're trying to find ways to make those areas viable again.

"So, we're looking at some hard stuff. We'd like to roll up our sleeves and see what we can do, knowing that we're looking at the long term, not a short-term solution." ■

Notes

[1] Quoted in "The Cradle of Democracy: Virginia's Historic Piedmont," program from Sept. 12, 1994, celebration sponsored by Protect Historic America and the National Trust for Historic Preservation.

[2] "Disney vs. the Elites," editorial, *Richmond Times-Dispatch,* May 13, 1994.

[3] Quoted in *The Washington Post,* Sept. 29, 1994.

[4] Quoted in *The New York Times,* Sept. 30, 1994.

[5] Moe read his statement at a press conference at National Trust headquarters in Washington. It was co-signed by historians McCullough and James M. McPherson, a professor at Princeton University and president of Protect Historic America (PHA), the group that spearheaded opposition to the Disney project.

[6] Address before Town Hall Los Angeles, a nonpartisan issues forum, March 10, 1994.

[7] James Marston Fitch, *Historic Preservation: Curatorial Management of the Built World* (1982), pp. 23-24. For background, see "Historic Preservation," *Editorial Research Reports,* Feb. 10, 1984, pp. 105-124.

[8] Tony Snow, "Disney Foes: There Goes the Neighborhood," *USA Today,* June 27, 1994, p. 13A. Snow is a Washington columnist for *The Detroit News.*

[9] "Family's Value," *Richmond Time-Dispatch,* June 29, 1994, p. A10.

[10] "Scarlett Duvall," *Richmond Times-Dispatch,* June 10, 1994, p. A22.

[11] "Time for Disney," *Richmond Times-Dispatch,* March 5, 1994, p. A8.

[12] Quoted by Dennis Wharton, "Disney Park Battle Heats Up in Virginia," *Variety,* June 20-26, 1994, p. 16.

[13] Quoted by Charles B. Hosmer Jr., *Presence of the Past: A History of the Preservation Movement in the United States Before Williamsburg* (1965), p. 36.

[14] Fitch, *op. cit.,* p. 89.

[15] Edward Tabor Linenthal, *Sacred Ground: Americans and Their Battlefields* (1991), pp. 89-90.

[16] The survey lapsed during World War II but was reactivated in the 1960s. The surveys provide a precise record of buildings in case they are destroyed.

[17] Fitch, *op. cit.,* p. 165.

[18] *Ibid.,* p. 96.

[19] *Ibid.,* p. 218.

[20] *Ibid.,* p. 203.

[21] Linenthal, *op. cit.,* p. 130.

[22] Testimony before Senate Energy and Natural Resources Subcommittee on Public Lands, National Parks and Forests, July 25, 1991.

[23] Quoted by Michelle Singletary and Spencer S. Hsu, "Disney Says Va. Park Will Be Serious Fun," *The Washington Post,* Nov. 12, 1993, p. A1.

[24] News release, Feb. 14, 1994.

[25] Robert McCormick Adams, "Smithsonian Horizons," *Smithsonian,* February 1994, p. 8.

[26] James M. McPherson, "Battling to Preserve our History," *Chicago Tribune,* July 15, 1994. Approximately 200 historians serve on Protect Historic America's advisory board.

[27] George F. Will, "Where much of American history was made, Disney is threatening to unmake it," *The Philadelphia Inquirer,* July 18, 1994.

[28] "Eisner Says Disney Won't Back Down," *The Washington Post,* June 14, 1994.

[29] Michael D. Eisner, "Let's Celebrate America," *The Washington Post,* June 20, 1994, p. A15.

[30] Quoted in *The Washington Post,* Sept. 29, 1994.

[31] *Ibid.*

[32] *Ibid.*

[33] *Ibid.*

[34] Quoted by David Lamb, "The Battle to Save the Battlefields," *Los Angeles Times,* Sept. 9, 1994, p. A12.

[35] Testimony before House Government Operations Subcommittee on the Environment, Energy and Natural Resources, May 9, 1994.

[36] Harry K. Schwartz, "Outline of Proposal for 'Historic Homeownership Assistance Act of 1994,'" Aug. 25, 1994.

[37] George Abney, "Washington Watch," *Historic Preservation News,* June-July 1994, p. 5. Abney is a legislative assistant in the National Trust's center for preservation policy studies.

Bibliography

Selected Sources Used

Books

Boatner, Mark M. III, *Landmarks of the American Revolution,* Stackpole Books, 1973.
Readers of this state-by-state guide to Revolutionary War sites may be surprised to find how many such landmarks have survived. One reason is that many key events occurred in rural areas that still are off the beaten path more than 200 years later.

Cantor, George, *Historic Black Landmarks,* Visible Ink Press, 1991.
This is a guidebook to historic sites of special interest to African-Americans. Not surprisingly, many are in the South. A number of sites in Western states pay tribute to blacks who helped settle the region after the Civil War. For instance, Omaha's Great Plains Black Museum spotlights the contributions of black pioneers and settlers in the Dakotas, Montana, Nebraska and Wyoming.

Fitch, James Marston, *Historic Preservation: Curatorial Management of the Built World,* McGraw-Hill, 1982.
Fitch, an architectural historian, surveys the development of historic preservation worldwide, though the United States is his primary area of interest. In his opinion, citizen participation is crucial to the preservation movement's success. "[T]he battle to save the habitat must parallel the battle to save the inhabitants of that habitat," he argues. "These are, in fact, two complementary aspects of the battle to save the built world."

Jacobs, Jane, *The Death and Life of Great American Cities,* Vintage Books, 1961.
"Cities need old buildings so badly it is probably impossible for vigorous streets and districts to grow without them," writes Jacobs, a firm believer in diversity as a source of urban health.

Linenthal, Edward Tabor, *Sacred Ground: Americans and Their Battlefields,* University of Illinois Press, 1991.
Linenthal, a professor of religious studies at the University of Wisconsin-Oshkosh, examines five pivotal military engagements in U.S. history — Lexington and Concord, the Alamo, Gettysburg, Little Big Horn and Pearl Harbor. A central concern is maintaining the integrity of the sites in the face of unrelenting pressures to commercialize them.

Miller, Page Putnam, ed., *Reclaiming the Past: Landmarks of Women's History,* Indiana University Press, 1992.
This book is useful chiefly for the articles on "Landmarks of Women's History" and "Women and Architecture," which discuss American women's crucial contributions to the historic preservation movement, especially during the 19th century.

Murtagh, William J., *Keeping Time: The History and Theory of Preservation in America,* The Main Street Press, 1988
"In a country as large as the United States, the future of preservation lies at the local level," writes Murtagh. "The success of local preservation efforts stands in direct relationship to the ability of experts at national, state, and international levels to sense this eventuality and serve it well."

Articles

Bates, Angela, "New Promise for Nicodemus," *National Parks,* July-August 1992.
Bates, president of the Nicodemus Historical Society, tells the story of the Kansas town settled by freed slaves after the Civil War. Today it is the site of an annual Emancipation-Homecoming Celebration that draws black visitors from throughout the country.

Society for Commercial Archeology, *SCA Journal,* winter 1993-1994.
The contributors to this issue write on various aspects of the diner, the subject of a society-sponsored conference in June 1993.

Reports and Studies

Beaumont, Constance E., *How Superstore Sprawl Can Harm Communities,* National Trust for Historic Preservation, 1994.
Beaumont shows how communities can combat the adverse economic and social effects of giant discount stores, typically situated near highway interchanges on the edge of town.

National Trust for Historic Preservation, *Landmark Yellow Pages,* 1990.
This reference work contains an extensive listing of historic sites and preservation groups across the country, with addresses and phone numbers. Other useful features include background on the National Trust and capsule descriptions of federal legislation and important court decisions on historic preservation.

Senate Energy and Natural Resources Subcommittee on Public Lands, National Parks and Forests, *Miscellaneous National Park Legislation,* July 25, 1991.
In this report, witnesses testify in often emotional terms on proposed legislation to change the name of the Custer Battlefield National Monument to Little Bighorn Battlefield National Monument. The bill was approved by Congress and signed into law later that year.

The Next Step

Additional information from UMI's Newspaper & Periodical Abstracts database

Patrons of Preservation

Daly, Christopher B. "Removing the 'eyesore' near Thoreau's pond," *The Washington Post,* April 16, 1994, p. A3.

A dedicated band of preservationists has won a series of victories that could secure enough of the woods surrounding historic Walden Pond to help restore the pond's ecosystem and make it look much more like the "perfect forest mirror" that Henry David Thoreau wrote about. A landfill site near the pond will be removed.

Millburg, Steve, "The phantom of the Fox," *Southern Living,* January 1994, p. 64.

Atlanta's Fox Theatre, an exotic movie palace built in the 1920s, found a friend in Joe Patten. Patten worked to preserve the building when it was threatened with demolition, and now he helps to keep the machinery working.

Scott, Liz, "Richard Baumbach: A tribute," *New Orleans Magazine,* June 1994, pp. 123-124.

Richard Baumbach, who died in 1993, was responsible for the aggressive lobbying that prevented an expressway project from edging in on New Orleans' historic French Quarter. Baumbach is profiled.

Zollinger, John, "To preserve, protect and defend," *National Journal,* Jan. 29, 1994, p. 252.

Richard Moe, president of the National Trust for Historic Preservation, is profiled. Moe views his biggest task as changing people's perceptions of preservation.

Preserving Sites

"Action needed to preserve Weir Farm," *National Parks,* July 1994, p. 14.

The Weir Farm National Historic Site in Connecticut was established in 1990 to preserve the summer home and studio of artist J. Alden Weir. Legislation that has been introduced to extend the park's boundaries is discussed.

"Civil War sites face grave threats," *National Parks,* November 1993, pp. 10-11.

A study released in the summer of 1993 claims that the U.S.' Civil War heritage is in danger because of infringing development. The nation could lose two-thirds of the major battlefields before the early 21st century if action is not taken now.

Fish, Peter, "Pasadena old & new," *Sunset* (Central West Edition), January 1994, pp. 58-63.

The history of Pasadena, Calif., and various places to visit there are discussed. Efforts to preserve downtown Pasadena — called Old Pasadena — are discussed.

Gattuso, Greg, "Back to the future," *Direct Marketing,* December 1993, pp. 32-35.

After 65 years of restoration, Colonial Williamburg, Va., is a historic recreation of an era gone by. Retail and mail order sales are helping support The Colonial Williamsburg Foundation's "museum without walls."

Geist, Darrell, "Agreements: The best medicine," *E: The Environmental Magazine,* March 1994, p. 10.

On a wind-swept plateau atop Wyoming's Medicine Mountain lies an ancient "Medicine Wheel." The conflict between modern tourism and ancient religion that eventually led to an agreement among the Bighorn National Forest, Wyoming State Historic Preservation Office and the Advisory Council on Historic Preservation are discussed.

Malles, Ed, "Hallowed ground," *Southern Living,* June 1994, pp. 128-131.

People from all walks of life are uniting in a fight to preserve the memory of forefathers who fought in the Civil War. The battle to save Civil War memories and sites is examined.

Nash, Rebecca, ''Adopt-a-Cemetery program leaving its mark,'' *Atlanta Constitution,* March 10, 1994, p. XJG7.

Cobb County, Ga., Cemetery Preservation Commission members will unveil new signs at five cemeteries targeted by their Adopt-a-Cemetery program. The preservation commission was established in 1990 by the Cobb County Commission to provide a uniform procedure for identifying, preserving, protecting and maintaining cemeteries.

Preserving Buildings

''A McDonald's goes the way of the Edsel,'' *The New York Times,* April 2, 1994, p. A7.

The McDonald's Corp. has decided not to renew the lease on its 41-year-old restaurant in Downey Calif., near Los Angeles, citing earthquake damage. Preservationists and local residents are fighting to save it, because it is the nation's oldest McDonald's, and local officals have denied McDonald's a permit to tear down the restaurant, which has the only remaining Speedee mascot.

Battista, Carolyn, ''A house for the future finally lives up to its billing,'' *The New York Times,* April 10, 1994, p. CN2.

After a careful four-year restoration, the Winslow Ames house at Connecticut College in New London, Conn., is now headquarters for the college's Center for Arts and Technology, whose symposiums and other events focus on topics like virtual reality and computer-assisted sculpture. Just a few years earlier, the college had planned to demolish the Winslow Ames, but local preservationists recognized it as a valuable architectural experiment and rallied support for its restoration.

Gray, Christopher, "A stopped clock sired the preservation movement," *The New York Times,* April 3, 1994, p. 5.

The history of the Jefferson Market Courthouse at West 10th St. and Avenue of the Americas in Manhattan is discussed. The building was the object of New York's earliest major struggle for historic preservation, one in which a band of Greenwich Villagers saved one of the city's greatest structures before there was a landmarks law. Now the city's Department of General Services is beginning a restoration of the original slate roof.

Gray, Christopher, "The changing centerpiece of a 'city within a city'," *The New York Times,* May 15, 1994, p. 7.

Two small parks created by Fred French for the Tudor City apartment complex he built in the late 1920s in New York City are being made over by the Tudor City Greens, a nonprofit group that owns them. The history of the parks, which have been declared a landmark, and the plans for reconstruction are described.

Hallam, Linda, "A homeplace reborn," *Southern Living,* June 1994, pp. 154-156.

The historic restoration of a 182-year-old Georgia home is described. Old photos and remnants of a garden offered clues to how the house must have once looked.

Levinson, Nan, "Kipling's house — A treasure," *Boston Globe,* April 24, 1994, p. C13.

The restoration of Rudyard Kipling's home in Brattleboro, Vt., is discussed.

"Lighthouse moved to new home," *Civil Engineering,* December 1993, pp. 14-18.

The historic Southeast Lighthouse on Block Island, R.I., was moved inland about 250 feet because erosion was threatening the structure. The $2.3 million project to move the lighthouse is discussed.

Noel, Tom, "Fort Collins Taco Bell reuses the real thing instead of 'Santa Fake,' " *Denver Post,* April 30, 1994, p. B11.

Tom Noel comments on the efforts of Carol Tunner, a Fort Collins, Colo., preservation planner, in getting Taco Bell to use a Spanish Revival style home for a new Taco Bell restaurant instead of demolishing the home and building their usual plastic, stucco and cement building in the "Santa Fake" style.

"Patterns and styles in a country house," *Early American Life,* June 1994, pp. 18-29.

The Howard House in central Massachussetts provides a glimpse at history through its unique structural and stylistic design, which dates back to 1813. An interior design pictorial is presented showing the various historical aspects of the home.

Railroads

Barth, Linda, "Preservation and the real world," *Trains Magazine,* May 1994, p. 74.

Preserving steam locomotives is discussed. The contemporary real world of museums and railroads must be a part of preservation, the author writes.

Cupper, Dan, "No power line over EBT," *Trains Magazine,* April 1994, pp. 18-19.

East Broad Top (EBT), a narrow-gauge steam tourist railroad in south-central Pennsylvania, is a designated National Railroad Landmark and is often cited as an excellent example of preserved industrial history. A plan that would have resulted in a controversial 268-mile power line that would cross the EBT 10 times has been rejected.

Ibata, David, "New life possible for old station," *Chicago Tribune,* May 2, 1994, p. 7.

Preservationists and bank officials from Skokie, Ill., toured Lake Forest's stately downtown railroad station, hoping the sight of a successfully renovated depot would boost efforts to save an old station in their community.

Keefe, Kevin P., "Steamtown deserves a fresh appraisal," *Trains Magazine,* August 1994, p. 6.

A symposium entitled "Railroad Heritage Preservation: Toward a National Policy," which was sponsored by the Smithsonian and the National Park Service, is discussed in an editorial. The symposium was designed to get people to start thinking about the future of railroad preservation.

Technology and Preservation

"Archiving masterpieces," *Futurist,* November 1993, p. 7.

More than $5 million worth of irreplaceable music, literary and artistic masterpieces have been destroyed by major fires in Southern California within a two year period. The "Phoenix Project," a new project through the California Polytechnic State University at San Luis Obispo aimed at minimizing such damage in the future by scanning and transferring historic documents to CD-ROM, is described.

Williams, Barry, "Historic stoplights retain old fashioned charm and practicality," *Nation's Cities Weekly,* March 14, 1994, p. 9.

Classic traffic lights have nearly vanished from the U.S. streetscape over the last several years, replaced by uninspiring arrangements. While classic four-way signals may not be suitable for complex intersections, they are often ideal for historic districts and older urban neighborhoods, Williams writes.

Wyatt, Kyle K., "The very image of the past," *Journal of the West,* April 1994, pp. 42-51.

Good, clear photographs are an invaluable resource for restoring an old railroad car or locomotive from the 1800s, but these photographs do not show original color. The uses of photographs in restoration projects are discussed.

Back Issues

Great Research on Current Issues Starts Right Here...Recent topics covered by The CQ Researcher are listed below. Before May 1991, reports were published under the name of Editorial Research Reports.®

MARCH 1993
Gay Rights
Aid to Russia
War on Drugs
TV Violence

APRIL 1993
Head Start
High-Speed Rail
Children's Legal Rights
Muslims in America

MAY 1993
Cults in America
Preventing Teen Pregnancy
Software Piracy
National Parks

JUNE 1993
Food Safety
Prostitution
Childhood Immunizations
National Service

JULY 1993
Electric Cars
Population Growth
Downward Mobility
Intelligence Testing

AUGUST 1993
Mental Illness
Bilingual Education
Foreign Policy Burden
School Funding

SEPTEMBER 1993
Suburban Crime
Public Housing
Supreme Court Preview
Immigration Reform

OCTOBER 1993
Airline Safety
Disaster Response
Science in the Courtroom
The Glass Ceiling

NOVEMBER 1993
Paying for Retirement
Charitable Giving
Privacy in the Workplace
Adoption

DECEMBER 1993
U.S. Vietnam-Relations
Learning Disabilities
Child Care
Space Program's Future

JANUARY 1994
Racial Tensions in Schools
South Africa's Future
Worker Retraining
Regulating Pesticides

FEBRUARY 1994
Prison Overcrowding
Water Quality
Religion in Schools
Juvenile Justice

MARCH 1994
Underground Economy
Education Standards
Gambling Boom
Private Management of Public Schools

APRIL 1994
Reproductive Ethics
U.S.-China Trade
Soccer in America
Talk Show Democracy

MAY 1994
Traffic Congestion
Women's Health Issues
Mutual Funds
Political Scandals

JUNE 1994
Education and Gender
Gun Control
Public Land Policy
Nuclear Arms Cleanup

JULY 1994
Dietary Supplements
Public Opinion and Foreign Policy
Crime Victims' Rights
Birth Control Choices

AUGUST 1994
Genetically Engineered Foods
Electing Minorities
Prozac Controversy
College Sports

SEPTEMBER 1994
Home Schooling
Welfare Experiments
Courts and the Media
Regulating Tobacco

Back issues are available for $4.00 (subscribers) or $7.00 (non-subscribers). Quantity discounts apply to orders over ten. To order, call Congressional Quarterly Customer Service at (202) 887-8621.

Binders are available for $16.00. To order call 1-800-638-1710. Please refer to stock number 648.

Future Topics

- ***Religion and Politics***
- ***Arts Funding***
- ***Embargoes and Sanctions***

THE CQ Researcher

PUBLISHED BY CONGRESSIONAL QUARTERLY INC.

Religion and Politics

What impact will the religious right have on politics?

Religion is playing a greater political role this campaign season than at any other time in recent memory. Conservative religious organizations — sometimes called the religious right — are now a major force in the Republican Party despite predictions two years ago that they were on the decline. The largest of the groups, Pat Robertson's Christian Coalition, has helped lead the opposition to President Clinton and his policies. Administration supporters say the coalition is using religion to mask a purely partisan agenda. Other organizations, such as the liberal People for the American Way, say the religious right threatens the American tradition of separation of church and state. Religious conservatives say they will remain politically active, and some observers believe their political influence will continue to grow.

INSIDE THIS ISSUE

CQ Oct. 14, 1994 • Volume 4, No. 38 • Pages 889-912

Formerly Editorial Research Reports

Religion and Politics

The Issues

Background

Current Situation

Outlook

Sidebars and Graphics

For Further Information

Cover Art: Barbara Sassa-Daniels

October 14, 1994
Volume 4, No. 38

The CQ Researcher (ISSN 1056-2036). Formerly Editorial Research Reports. Published weekly (48 times per year, not printed the first Friday of any month with five Fridays) by Congressional Quarterly Inc., 1414 22nd St., N.W., Washington, D.C. 20037. Rates are furnished upon request. Second-class postage paid at Washington, D.C. POSTMASTER: Send address changes to The CQ Researcher, 1414 22nd St., N.W., Washington, D.C. 20037.

Religion and Politics

By Kenneth Jost

The Issues

Religion and politics made for an explosive combination last month as 3,000 members of the Christian Coalition gathered in Washington to praise God and denounce President Clinton. Amid a revival atmosphere and high-tech staging, speaker after speaker blamed "Clinton-style liberalism" for a decline in moral values in the United States. [1]

"This administration and those in its employ have displayed a disturbing insensitivity to religious values, religious people and religious institutions," Ralph E. Reed, the group's executive director, declared. "Faith in God is not what is wrong with America," Reed continued. "It's what's right with America."

Across town, Democratic Party chief David Wilhelm fired back, charging that the coalition and its founder — television evangelist and former Republican presidential candidate Pat Robertson — were trying to brand opponents as anti-religious.

"Pat Robertson's Christian Coalition does not speak for all, or even most, people of faith," Wilhelm told a news conference deliberately scheduled during the coalition's opening session. "There are millions and millions of people who go to church every week who are Democrats, independents and Republicans who do not share Pat Robertson's political goals."

The debate between the administration and the Christian Coalition, Wilhelm went on, "is not about who is more religious, who has greater faith. The debate is about policy."

For the Christian Coalition, the "Road to Victory" conference confirmed its status as an important political interest group and a major constituency within the Republican Party. Claiming more than 1 million supporters and dues-paying members, the coalition drew four GOP presidential contenders — former Vice President Dan Quayle, former secretary of Education and Tennessee Gov. Lamar Alexander, Sen. Phil Gramm of Texas and Dick Cheney, the former secretary of Defense and House member. A fifth hopeful, Senate Minority Leader Bob Dole of Kansas, sent his wife, Elizabeth H. Dole, a former secretary of Labor.

Since its formation in 1989, the coalition has grown into the biggest and most visible of the panoply of organizations on the religious right. (*See story, p. 898.*) But even as the coalition celebrated its growth in Washington, religious conservatives faced major hurdles in increasing their political clout.

Some within the Republican Party believe religious conservatives have been a divisive force. They note that religious conservatives have had bitter clashes recently with more traditional Republicans in such states as Minnesota, Texas and Virginia.

"They're tough for the Republican Party to handle," says Matthew Moen, chairman of the political science department at the University of Maine-Orono and author of two books on the Christian Right. "The party has been rent asunder in some places. But there's no question that they're a plus in certain venues, especially in converting lifelong Southern Democrats into Republicans."

After Clinton's election victory over President George Bush in 1992, many observers said the religious right was on the decline. Religious conservatives, who had claimed credit for three consecutive GOP victories, by Ronald Reagan in 1980 and '84 and Bush in '88, were blamed in some circles for Bush's defeat in 1992.

Less than two years later, however, the influence of religious conservatives within the GOP appears to be growing. A recent survey by the magazine *Campaigns & Elections* rated the Christian right as dominating Republican Party organizations in 18 states and wielding substantial influence in 13 others. [2]

But religious conservatives have often been unable to translate their influence within the Republican Party into election victories. In Minnesota, a religious right-backed gubernatorial candidate, Allen Quist, won the backing of the state Republican convention in June over the moderate incumbent, Arne Carlson. But Carlson beat Quist by a 2-1 margin in the party's Sept. 13 primary.

Stuart Rothenberg, editor of *The Rothenberg Report,* a political newsletter, says the religious right's emphasis on morality cuts both ways as a political issue. "There are people who overplay the religion card, overplay the abortion card, overplay the morality card without understanding that rhetoric turns off as many people as it turns on," Rothenberg says.

Americans are undoubtedly worried about moral values. A new survey by pollster Peter Hart for the liberal group People for the American Way found that most people blamed the country's "most serious problems" on declining moral values rather than economic or financial pressures. [3] The survey also

How the Public Views the Religious Right

Q **If a candidate for Congress had the endorsement of organizations associated with the religious right (which refers to conservative Christian groups active in politics) would you be more or less likely to vote for that candidate?**

A

More likely to vote for candidate	16%
Less likely to vote for candidate	27%
Would not affect vote either way	51%
Not sure	6%

Q **In your view, does the religious right have too little influence in the Republican Party, just enough influence or too much influence?**

A

Too little influence	17%
Just enough influence	25%
Too much influence	31%
Not sure	27%

Q **How would you rate your feelings toward the religious right?**

A

Very positive	11%
Somewhat positive	13%
Neutral	18%
Somewhat negative	13%
Very negative	16%
Have not heard of them	25%
Not sure	4%

Q **President Clinton and some other Democrats have recently criticized the political tactics of some members of the religious right, saying their tactics are unfair and extreme. Do you agree or disagree?**

A

Agree	25%
Disagree	11%
Haven't heard enough to say	60%
Don't know/No answer	4%

Q **Do you think members of the religious right are trying to impose their religious beliefs on others through their political activities, or do you think members of the religious right are just exercising their right to free speech through political activities?**

A

Imposing their beliefs	36%
Exercising free speech	45%
Both	2%
Don't know/No answer	17%

Q **In general, do you think the media are too harsh in their coverage of the religious right, too easy in their coverage or do the media treat the religious right fairly?**

A

Too harsh	20%
Too easy	8%
Fair	51%
Don't know/No answer	21%

*Sources: Questions 1-3 from NBC/*Wall Street Journal *poll conducted by Hart and Teeter Research Companies, July 1994; questions 4-6 from CBS News/*New York Times *poll, July 1994.*

found that most people are unconcerned about the rise of the religious right, although they also disagree with positions identified with religious conservatives on such issues as abortion, gay rights and school curriculums.

"Voters are drawn to the religious right's 'traditional values' rhetoric," Arthur J. Kropp, president of People for the American Way, commented, "but Americans will have to look elsewhere for solutions they can support." [4]

To many, the use of religion as a political weapon against President Clinton may seem surprising. Clinton was raised as a Southern Baptist, attends church regularly, often uses religious imagery in his speeches and meets periodically with members of the clergy in private breakfasts at the White House.

But Clinton also has lashed out at attacks from religious conservatives. In June, the president called a St. Louis, Mo., talk radio program and complained about personal attacks on him from religious conservatives. "That's fine, I deal with them," Clinton said. "But I don't believe that it's the work of God." [5]

Three days earlier, Rep. Vic Fazio, D-Calif., head of the Democratic Congressional Campaign Committee, accused the religious right of attempting to "impose their personal religious views and ethical beliefs on the party system." [6]

Leaders of the religious right have responded by accusing their critics of religious intolerance. "Bigotry and Christian-bashing have no place in American political discourse," says Reed.

But liberal groups, such as People for the American Way and the Anti-Defamation League of B'nai B'rith (ADL), a Jewish civil rights organization, contend that the religious right itself has been guilty of intolerance. In a 190-page report this summer, the ADL called the religious right an "exclusionist" movement that "traffics with bigots and conspiracists." The Christian Coalition countered that the ADL report was "filled with fabrications, half-truths, innuendo and guilt by association." [7]

At its conference last month, the Christian Coalition vowed to step up its political mobilization in the remaining weeks before the off-year congressional elections. "We are fed up with Clinton-style liberalism," Reed declared, "and in six weeks it's going to end."

But party chief Wilhelm insisted that Democrats would be competing for the votes of the religious faithful, too. "We're a party that in the 1980s lost the flag somehow," Wilhelm told reporters. "I do not want to let the party lose God or the Bible in this election."

As the clash between Democrats and the religious right continues, these are some of the questions being asked about the relationship between religion and politics:

Should religious views play a major role in politics and government?

In Virginia, Oliver L. North, the Republican nominee for the U.S. Senate, wears his Christianity on his shirtsleeves. "I stand before you as a Christian — unashamed to say so," North tells audiences.

In Texas, religious conservatives took control of the state's Republican convention. State Rep. Steve Ogden, who headed the platform committee, got a standing ovation when he said that the Republicans' platform, "unlike the Democrats'," endorses "traditional Judeo-Christian values." [8]

In Washington, Reed exhorts Christian Coalition members to go to the polls in November. "Our goal in the next two months," Reed tells a conference crowd, "is to see the largest turnout of evangelical and pro-family Roman Catholic voters in the history of this country."

Across the country, religion is being injected into politics more explicitly than at any time in recent memory. Religious activists say they are following a long tradition of bringing their faith into the political arena. "Martin Luther King organized the civil rights movement directly out of the churches," says Reed. "Many of the anti-war organizations organized out of the churches."

But critics say today's religious conservatives are misusing faith for political purposes. "Some of these religious right politicians use the Bible and their faith in a very manipulative way," Kropp remarked on ABC's "Good Morning America" in a joint appearance Aug. 10 with Reed. "It is a very mean-spirited movement. It seeks to divide people at a time when the country is looking to be brought together."

Kenneth Jost

"We are fed up with Clinton-style liberalism," says Christian Coalition Executive Director Ralph E. Reed (left), with founder Pat Robertson at the group's September conference.

Religion has always been an important factor in American political life, even though the Constitution limits official ties between church and state. For one thing, a person's religious tradition is a powerful influence on voting behavior. Roman Catholics have been solidly aligned with the Democratic Party from the first wave of Catholic immigration in the 1830s until the 1980s. Jews have voted predominantly Democratic since the 1920s. White Protestant voters, on the other hand, have been predominantly Republican, except in years of Democratic landslides.

Moreover, religious activists have been at the core of many of the most important social and political movements in U.S. history — from the anti-slavery movement in the 19th century to the civil rights and anti-war movements of the mid-20th century. Many of the ministers who led those struggles braved strong criticism from some religious adherents arguing that the pulpit was no place for politics.

Advocates of separation of church and state draw a distinction between these past movements and the religious right of today. They accuse the religious right of trying to use government to impose particular religious doctrines on society.

"The minute they start to use the political system to impose a narrow perspective on others, then it becomes a very serious issue in terms of religious freedom," says Herbert Valentine, executive director of the Baltimore presbytery of the Presbyterian Church (U.S.A.). Valentine chairs a group called the Interfaith Alliance, formed this summer to counter the religious right.

Similarly, People for the American Way accuses groups on the religious right of claiming divine authority for "extreme" positions on issues ranging from abortion and gay rights to public education and health care. "It is these positions — coupled with their willingness to claim or suggest God's endorsement for the positions — that define the movement," the liberal group said in a critique released in June. [9]

Some religious conservatives also fault the political tactics of some of the groups on the religious right. For example, George S. Weigel Jr., president of the Ethics and Public Policy Center, has criticized the use of "Christian scorecards" that list opposing candidates' votes or stands on policy issues. Speaking to a conference sponsored by the center last December, Weigel said the scorecards "demean the Gospel by identifying it with an ideological agenda." [10]

In his appearance on "Good Morning America," Reed defended the voter guides distributed by the coalition. He said they show candidates' stands on such issues as "a balanced-budget amendment, term limits, lower taxes and tougher laws against crime and drugs." He continued, "These are things that every survey shows 75 or 80 percent of the American people favor."

In an interview, Reed also insisted the coalition is not trying to enact a particular religious doctrine into law. "I don't think you should take a particular scripture verse and try to legislate that scripture verse," he says. "We are not attempting to legislate our theology. We are trying to legislate our public policy views."

But Reed also says religious views have a legitimate role in political debate. "To try to cut that out of American political discourse is a mistake," he says.

Are religious conservatives being unfairly criticized for their political activities?

As the religious right has come under attack, some of its leaders have responded by charging opponents with trying to exclude religious conservatives from politics altogether. They claim that religious conservatives are victims of a double standard since religious activists who back liberal political causes have been widely praised.

"As long as you're on the left, religious faith and vernacular can inform your dialogue," says Reed. "But if you're on the right, that becomes unacceptable. We have to stop dividing people on the basis of where they go to church or synagogue."

Critics of the religious right deny the accusation. They call it an effort to divert attention from a debate over the political stands being advocated by the Christian Coalition and other groups on the religious right.

Kenneth Jost

"I do not want to let the party lose God or the Bible in this election," says David Wilhelm, chairman of the Democratic National Committee.

"When you challenge their political views, the response will be that it's some sort of conspiracy to prevent Christians from taking part in the process," says Matthew Freeman, research director for People for the American Way. "That's not the case. My disagreements with Pat Robertson are not theological. They're political."

"We're not denying their right to participate in political issues, not at all," says Valentine. "We just want them to be honest about it."

The controversy has flared during the current political season, but it can be traced to an influential 1993 book, *The Culture of Disbelief,* by Yale University law Professor Stephen L. Carter. Carter, who describes himself as a liberal and a "committed Christian," argued that much of the criticism of the religious right appeared to assume that religious views have no place in politics. [11]

"I am offended," Carter wrote, "by suggestions that our politicians are wrong to discuss their views on the will of God, or that members of the clergy have no business backing what candidates they will, or that voters should never choose among candidates based on their religious beliefs."

Carter, who is black, said civil rights leaders like the Rev. Dr. Martin Luther King Jr. and anti-war activists like the Rev. William Sloan Coffin Jr. and the Roman Catholic priests Daniel and Philip Berrigan were not criticized for bringing religion into politics. "Probably the reason," Carter wrote, "was that the causes in which the word of God was enlisted were causes that were more popular, particularly among opinion-makers who have ever since been dumping on Republicans for daring to mix church and state."

Carter's book received favorable reviews, and a wide range of commentators generally accepted his thesis. Political analyst Rothenberg notes, however, that there is a difference between the civil rights and anti-war movements of the past and today's religious right.

"The religious liberals brought their religious values to issues that were not defined as religious issues," Rothenberg says. "The moral-issue types now want to address more explicitly religious issues, like teaching creationism, or books in the library, or gay rights or abortion, where the issue seems to be fought more along purely moral grounds."

Martin Bailey, director of communications for the liberal National Council of Churches, also sees a difference between the civil rights movement and the religious right. "One of the [distinguishing characteristics] that I see in the churches that take a more central position is that they see themselves as reconcilers and are looking for ways to bring people together rather than divide them," Bailey says.

Religious conservatives continue to insist that they are, in fact, subject to what Reed calls "a cruel and unfair double standard." Reed notes that Clinton praised passage of the administration-backed crime bill by saying that it was "the will of God" and that Hillary Rodham Clinton cited her Methodist beliefs in explaining her passion about health-care reform.

"I do think that these people should be allowed to use their religious beliefs to press their political positions," Reed says of the critics of the religious right. "What I don't think is fair, or the American way, is when they question our right to act on our religious views."

For their part, some of the religious right's critics acknowledge that some of their comments have gone too far. In a July 20 memo to "Progressive and Mainstream Leaders," Kropp of People for the American Way warned against using "epithets that belittle the religious faith of the [religious right's] leaders or followers."

"In all our discussions of this movement," Kropp continued, "we have to be careful never to suggest that they're not welcome to participate in the process. . . . We can't afford to suggest that this movement is not entitled to take part. They have every right."

Is the Republican Party helped or hurt by its support from the religious right?

Religious conservatives have been an important Republican voting bloc in the last four presidential elections. As their visibility and apparent influence increased, however, some political observers and some leaders and strategists within the Republican Party suggested the religious right was hurting the party by alienating moderate Republican and independent voters.

That speculation increased after President Bush's defeat by Bill Clinton in 1992. During the campaign, Bush agreed to give religious conservatives a high-profile role at the party's national convention, including Robertson and political commentator Patrick J. Buchanan, who had unsuccessfully challenged Bush in the party primaries. After the November election, many observers said that on balance Bush lost votes by being identified with unpopular social issues pushed by the religious right.

The argument has been refuted, however, by a team of political scientists who analyzed voter surveys from the Bush-Clinton campaign. In their paper, the scholars concluded the Christian right "appears to be a modestly helpful ally" for the Republican Party. [12]

Specifically, the researchers said Bush won more votes from "social-issue conservatives" by identifying himself with policy stands of the Christian right than Clinton won from "social-issue liberals." But Clinton won more than enough votes from people who ranked economic issues as most important to offset Bush's advantage on social issues. "Social-issue conservatism is simply not strong enough to be the sole basis for winning elections," the researchers concluded. But, they added, "Social issues helped keep the election close."

Nonetheless, as the 1994 elections neared, observers continued to warn Republicans against relying too much on the religious right. "The narrow, negative fervor of the religious right offends many Americans," Albert Hunt of *The Wall Street Journal* wrote in one widely noted column. [13]

Similar warnings were voiced two weeks later both from within and without the Republican Party. Democratic congressional campaign Chairman Fazio told reporters June 21 that

How Religious Groups Voted in 1992

President George Bush received a majority of the Protestant evangelical vote and a plurality of the mainline Protestant vote in the 1992 election. Bill Clinton got a near majority of the votes from Roman Catholics and secular (non-religious) Americans. Voters from "other" religious traditions — including black Protestants and Jews — backed Clinton overwhelmingly.

	Evangelical Protestant	Mainline Protestant	Catholic	Secular	Other *
Bush	56%	43%	33%	27%	13%
Clinton	29%	34%	45%	49%	79%
Perot	15%	23%	22%	23%	10%

** Includes black Protestants, smaller Christian denominations outside the major traditions, Jews and other non-Christians.*

Note: Totals don't necessarily equal 100% because of rounding.

Source: John C. Green, James L. Guth, Lyman A. Kellstedt and Corwin E. Smidt, "Murphy Brown Revisited: The Social Issues in the 1992 Election," in Michael Comartie (ed.), Disciples and Democracy: Religious Conservatives and the Future of American Politics *(1994).*

Republicans "accept the religious right and their tactics at their own peril" because their views were "out of touch" with moderate voters.

Four days later, Sen. Arlen Specter, a GOP moderate from Pennsylvania, took the same message to a state party convention in Iowa. Speaking to an audience with a large number of religious conservatives, Specter criticized the takeover of the Texas GOP by religious conservatives, called for scrapping the party's anti-abortion platform plank and warned against the divisive effects of the religious right. "In politics," Specter said, "the power to divide is the power to destroy." [14]

In the face of these criticisms, leaders of the Christian Coalition have shifted tactics a bit but remain largely unapologetic. In a newspaper interview on the eve of the group's annual meeting in September 1993, Reed said he wanted to put "a friendlier face on who we are." [15] He has staked out stands on a wide range of policies beyond the hot-button social issues. And he has proclaimed his intention of reaching out to blacks, Hispanics and other minorities.

But in an interview shortly before the Christian Coalition's conference last month, Reed was anything but conciliatory about the political importance of religious conservatives. He confidently declared that evangelical Christians comprise between one-fourth and one-third of the population, making them "the largest single voting bloc" in the country. "Anybody who underestimates the strength of that constituency does so at their hazard," Reed said.

For his part, Robertson issued a blunt warning at the conference that moderate Republicans should not expect religious conservatives to temper their stands on social issues. "There are some members of the Republican Party who say they don't need us," Robertson said. "They find the social and moral issues an embarrassment and wish that these issues, and people like us who care about them, would just go away."

Robertson said he and his followers have "no intention of advocating bizarre positions which will lose elections." But, he concluded, "We also have no intention of surrendering our deeply held moral stands just to please a handful of moderates who don't stand for anything."

The parade of GOP notables who spoke at the conference indicated that many Republicans considered the Christian Coalition an asset, if not a necessity, in trying to capture control of Congress this fall and regain the White House in 1996. "Welcome to the Republican Party," Senate Minority Whip Trent Lott, R-Miss., told the conference on its opening day. "We're glad to have you."

Still, many observers say the party has to walk a fine line between attracting and maintaining support from the religious right and also reaching out to other voters. "I agree it is absolutely critical to the Republican Party as long as it does not define the Republican Party," Rothenberg says. "The key is to find a candidate who is stylistically acceptable to the moderates but has enough of the basic conservatism to appeal to the evangelicals." ■

BACKGROUND

Church and State

Religion and politics have been an emotional mixture since the beginning of American history. Many of the original colonies were founded in the 1600s by people who fled England and its established Anglican Church to escape religious persecution. These religious dissenters all professed commitment to freedom of conscience, but they took different approaches in structuring the relationship between church and state.

New England's Puritan settlers — so named because they wanted to "purify" the Anglican Church — created "holy commonwealths" in four colonies: Massachusetts, Plymouth, Connecticut and New Haven. Religious practices were dictated by law. Town meetings made sure that religious worship was supported. Dissent was unwelcome. As Thomas J. Curry writes in his history of church-state relations in the Colonial and Revolutionary eras, "no one who refused to follow the canons of Scripture was to be tolerated." [16]

In other colonies, religious dissidents established something more akin to modern ideas of religious freedom. In Rhode Island, Roger Williams established a colony where religious liberty was recognized, and church and state were separate. In Pennsylvania, William Penn founded a Quaker colony based on radical notions of religious freedom and enlightened government. And in Maryland, Cecil Calvert, the second Lord Baltimore, allowed freedom of religion for all Christians after the colony was carved out of Virginia to provide a safe haven for Roman Catholics. [17]

Religion played a lesser role in the settlement of other colonies, and in many of them — notably Virginia — the Anglican Church became an established church much as it was in England. Indeed, as Curry points out, all the colonies imposed religious tests for office, and many of them levied religious taxes. [18] But by the late 17th century, religious freedom was making gains, owing to what historian Sydney E. Ahlstrom calls the "inescapable pluralism of the Colonial peoples." These "libertarian trends" continued in the 1700s and acceler-

Continued on p. 898

Chronology

Colonial Times

Religious dissenters settle many of the original 13 Colonies, but most Colonial governments adopt religious tests for office and religious taxes. Some colonies, however, establish models for religious freedom.

1789-1900

The Constitution prohibits government establishment of religion, but churches play an important part in politics on issues ranging from slavery and social reform to prohibition and public morality.

1900-1960

Strains increase between traditionalist and modernist religions.

1908
The Federal Council of Churches of Christ in America is formed and, as its first action, publishes a pro-labor report called "The Church and Modern Industry."

1910
The first of a series of conservative theological tracts published under the name "The Fundamentals" lays the groundwork for the formation of 20th-century fundamentalism.

July 1925
John Scopes, a high school biology teacher in Dayton, Tenn., is convicted of violating state law against teaching the theory of evolution. The conviction is overturned two years later by the state Supreme Court.

1941-1942
Rival fundamentalist organizations are formed: the combative American Council of Christian Churches in 1941, now defunct, and the more moderate National Association of Evangelicals in 1942.

1954
Congress adds the phrase "under God" to the Pledge of Allegiance.

1960s-1970s

Liberal religious groups are active in civil rights and peace movements, while religious conservatives are less active.

September 12, 1960
Democratic presidential nominee John F. Kennedy neutralizes the "Catholic issue" by telling a group of Southern Baptist ministers that his religious beliefs will not dictate his actions if elected.

June 25, 1962
U.S. Supreme Court bars state-written prayer in public school classrooms as an improper establishment of religion; the decision is extended a year later to cover Bible reading in class.

January 22, 1973
U.S. Supreme Court rules in *Roe v. Wade* that women have a right to an abortion during most of a pregnancy. The ruling is supported by most Americans but prompts strong opposition from Catholics and evangelical Protestants.

November 2, 1976
Jimmy Carter, a self-described born-again Christian, is elected president with support from most evangelical voters. Later, evangelicals spurn Carter's policies.

1979
The Rev. Jerry Falwell, a Baptist preacher and television evangelist, is recruited to head a new advocacy group, the Moral Majority, to lobby on abortion, pornography and other moral issues.

1980s

The religious right solidly backs Republicans Ronald Reagan and George Bush in presidential elections, but most of its agenda is not enacted.

1987-1988
Televangelist Pat Robertson campaigns unsuccessfully for Republican nomination for president.

1989
Robertson forms the Christian Coalition, hiring political activist Ralph E. Reed as executive director.

1990s

Conservative religious groups mobilize in many states.

November 3, 1992
Democrat Bill Clinton, a church-going Southern Baptist with liberal views on social issues, is elected president.

July 1993
Christian Coalition says it will broaden its agenda to economic issues.

June 21, 1994
Rep. Vic Fazio, chairman of Democratic Congressional Campaign Committee, criticizes religious right in speech to National Press Club.

Christian Coalition Views Mission as Divine Calling . . .

The minister delivering the invocation at the Christian Coalition's "Road to Victory" conference last month had a special prayer for the coalition's leaders — Pat Robertson, its founder and president, and Executive Director Ralph E. Reed. "Their calling is so heavy, Lord; their critics so harsh," Dr. Billy McCormack prayed. "Please place your angels in protection around them." [1]

To its supporters, the Christian Coalition's mission is nothing less than a divine calling. "We are seeing the Christian Coalition rise to where God intends it to be in this nation," Robertson told the conference last month, "as one of the most powerful political forces that have ever been in the history of America."

Its critics view the coalition quite differently. Some regard it as nothing more than a partisan political organization disguised in religious clothing. "Behind family-values rhetoric," says Democratic National Committee Chairman David Wilhelm, "the Christian Coalition fights the fight of the economic elite."

Other critics view the coalition more ominously — as a threat to the American tradition of religious liberty. In a critique published last month, the liberal group People for the American Way charged that the coalition favors "the formation of a Christianized government, which disavows the separation of church and state." [2]

In the five years since its founding, the Christian Coalition has grown from a little-noted spinoff of Robertson's failed 1988 campaign for the Republican presidential nomination into a sophisticated political operation with a $20 million budget this year and a claimed following of 1.4 million supporters and dues-paying members. [3] Its annual "conference and strategy briefing" — for the past two years held in Washington and open to press coverage — has become an important political event that attracts most of the major Republican presidential candidates.

The coalition holds a critical position among the panoply of religiously oriented conservative organizations that make up what is variously called the Christian right, the religious right or the radical right. (Reed himself rejects the term religious right as connoting "an intolerant and extremist political agenda" and prefers "religious conservative" or "pro-family conservative." [4]) Like the Christian Coalition, these other groups are also increasingly active and increasingly visible.

The Mississippi-based American Family Association, headed by the Rev. Donald Wildmon, has squared off against the National Endowment for the Arts over funding of what it calls pornographic art. In California, Citizens for Excellence in Education, headed by Robert Simonds, has mobilized campaigns to elect religious right candidates to school boards across the country. Concerned Women for America, headed by anti-feminist activist Beverly LaHaye, opposes abortion, homosexuality and sex education. The Washington, D.C.-based group claims 600,000 members, more than twice as many as the liberal National Organization for Women.

Unlike these other conservative groups, however, the Christian Coalition has a broad policy agenda and a focused political strategy to accomplish it. In the past two years, the coalition has expanded its focus from social issues such as abortion and gay rights to economic questions as well. In February, Reed said the group's highest priority this year was defeating President Clinton's health-care legislation. [5]

The coalition's political strategy has been crafted by the 33-year-old Reed, who has a doctorate in American history and experience in conservative Republican politics since his college days in the late 1970s. In place of the political televangelism of his mentor Robertson, Reed concentrates on local grass-roots organizing. Initially, he kept the coalition's profile low — prompting critics to accuse him of "stealth" tactics.

Now that the coalition has emerged as a significant player in GOP politics, it faces other criticisms, including its very

Continued from p. 896

ated during the Revolutionary era, Ahlstrom writes. [19]

After the Revolutionary War, many of the states wrote laws embodying religious toleration, at least for all Christian denominations. While many states maintained religious qualifications for office, the federal Constitution provided in Article VI that "no religious test" could be required for any federal office. According to Cornell University government Professor Isaac Kramnick, opponents warned during the debate over ratification that the provision could allow "Pagans, Deists and Mahometans" to hold office. [20] After ratification, however, advocates of religious liberty went further and wrote into the Bill of Rights a broad prohibition against any law "respecting an establishment of religion, or prohibiting the free exercise thereof."

Today, partisans in religio-political conflicts differ over the meaning of the First Amendment's so-called establishment clause. Strict separationsts argue that it created what Thomas Jefferson called "a wall of separation between church and state" prohibiting any government action benefiting religion. Others — so-called accommodationists — argue that the First Amendment prohibits the government from establishing a "national religion" or preferring one denomination over another, but does not preclude non-discriminatory aid to religion or religious institutions.

The accommodationists emphasize that the adoption of the First Amendment did not prevent the federal government from acknowledging religion as part of public

. . . But Critics See a Threat to Religious Liberty

name. Critics say the coalition's name implies that it regards its political adversaries as un-Christian.

"We need to be careful about appropriating the name 'Christian,' " says *Washington Post* political columnist E.J. Dionne Jr. "You are implying a lot if you claim to be speaking for Christianity and Christians."

Supporters disagree. Speaking to the coalition's conference last month, former Education Secretary William J. Bennett noted that many other organizations, such as the American Jewish Committee, have religious identification in their names. "They surely recognize that there are American Jews who don't belong to the committee," Bennett said.

The coalition also has been challenged on its right to claim tax-exempt status as a nonpartisan educational organization. One of the coalition's major activities is preparation of what it calls "voter guides" showing the positions of opposing candidates on selected issues in the weeks before an election. "We're like a League of Women Voters for people of faith," Reed often tells reporters.

Critics, however, view the guides as blatantly partisan. "If you read their voting guides," says Matthew Freeman, research director of People for the American Way, "you can't help but come to the conclusion that they are pressing the tax laws to the limits, if not beyond. It's hard to conclude that their interest is in providing good, solid, nonpartisan voting information."

The coalition has also been criticized by other organizations in the Christian right, according to Clyde Wilcox, a professor of political science at Georgetown University. "They take credit for everything, but don't send the soldiers out to do the work," Wilcox said.[6]

The coalition's political clout is by no means proven. Wilcox, for one, has predicted that religious conservatives will fall short of taking control of the Republican Party — a Robertson goal[7] — and become one of several factions within the GOP.[8] Stuart Rothenberg, editor of *The Rothenberg Report,* a political newsletter, says the coalition can help candidates capture GOP nominations, but they have to move to the center to win in general elections.

Other observers, however, believe that religious conservatives have wrought a lasting shift in the U.S. political landscape. "In one sense, 1992 may be remembered as the 'Year of the Evangelical,' " a team of academic experts on the religious right wrote in a paper last fall. "It is safe to predict that this mobilization will continue or even intensify in future local, state and national elections."[9]

Reed is similarly confident that the Christian Coalition will have a lasting impact on American politics. "This is a long-term cause for us," Reed says. "We expect to be a permanent part of American politics for the next half century or longer."

---

[1] Dr. McCormack is minister of University Baptist Church in Shreveport, La.

[2] People for the American Way, "The Two Faces of the Christian Coalition," Sept. 16, 1994.

[3] See David Von Drehle and Thomas B. Edsall, "Life of the Grand Old Party," *The Washington Post,* Aug. 14, 1994, p. A1; Sidney Blumenthal, "Christian Soldiers," *The New Yorker,* July 11, 1994, pp. 31-37.

[4] Ralph E. Reed, "What Religious Conservatives Really Want," in Michael Comartie (ed.), *Disciples and Democracy: Religious Conservatives and the Future of American Politics* (1994).

[5] See *The Washington Post,* Feb. 16, 1994, p. A6.

[6] Presentation to American Political Science Association, Sept. 2, 1994.

[7] See "Republicans' next battle is internal," *The Miami Herald,* Nov. 14, 1992.

[8] Clyde Wilcox, "Premillennialists at the Millennium: Some Reflections on the Christian Right in the Twenty-first Century," *Sociology of Religion,* Vol. 55, No. 3, fall 1994, pp. 259-260.

[9] Lyman A. Kellstedt, John C. Green, James L. Guth and Corwin E. Smidt, "Religious Voting Blocs in the 1992 Election: The Year of the Evangelical?" *Sociology of Religion,* Vol. 55, No. 3, fall 1998, p. 323.

life. They note that Jefferson and James Madison, the principal draftsman of the First Amendment, both issued presidential proclamations recognizing national days of thanksgiving.

Nevertheless, the amendment clearly foreshadowed a weakening of the ties between church and state in the new democracy. States began dismantling laws establishing religion or imposing religious taxes in the 1790s. Jefferson counted as one of his three greatest accomplishments the adoption of his Statute of Religious Freedom in his home state of Virginia in 1796. In 1833, Massachusetts became the last of the original states to repeal laws giving special privileges to designated denominations, and no new state except Vermont ever passed similar laws.[21]

Religion in Politics

Despite the substantial separation of church and state, religion has played a vital role in American politics since the founding of the new democracy. Religious institutions and individuals have continually brought their faith into the public square, seeking to elect candidates or shape government policy in line with their religious beliefs.

As the French statesman and author Alexis de Tocqueville wrote in his 19th-century account of American life, "Religion in America takes no direct part in the government of society, but nevertheless it must be regarded as

Religious Liberals Prefer Social Action to "Politics"

The religious right loudly criticized President Clinton last month when he announced plans to invade Haiti. But Clinton also came under attack from religious activists of a different political stripe. Religiously based peace groups that played a prominent part in opposing the Vietnam War in the 1960s also spoke out against the use of U.S. military force in Haiti.

"We opposed the invasion," says Leslie Withers, acting director of Clergy and Laity Concerned. "We believed there were ways to remove that illegal regime without sending in our military."

The Atlanta-based group and other religious segments of the peace movement had no visible impact on events during the critical days before the U.S. occupation. But their work represents one of many areas where people of faith are active on the side of liberal and progressive causes usually quite different from the issues being pushed by the religious right.

"The Christian Coalition does not have a monopoly on religion in politics," says Withers, whose group includes 35 chapters and about 10,000 members. "We encourage people to act out their own particular religious imperatives through work for social justice, through work in advocacy for people who are oppressed."

Sojourners *Editor Jim Wallis: "Evangelical Christians are not all right wing."*

Despite the work by liberal religious activists on issues ranging from civil rights and social justice to environmental protection and world peace, hardly anyone talks about a "religious left" today. For one thing, liberal religious groups themselves shun the label.

"Our churches would not want to be seen as the left," says the Rev. Martin Bailey, director of communications for the liberal National Council of Churches, which traces its origins to the founding of the pro-labor Federal Council of Churches in 1908. "We see ourselves as more central."

In addition, the news media have given far more attention to conservative religious groups in recent years. Jim Wallis, editor of the progressive evangelical magazine *Sojourners,* charges the news media with "a myopic focus on the Christian right" that has misled the public into equating evangelicalism with political conservatism.

"Evangelical Christians are not all right wing," Wallis wrote recently. "In fact, most are not." [1]

In his new book, *The Soul of Politics,* Wallis cites a number of examples of political activism by progressive religious groups. He says church-affiliated groups have helped form a campaign called Barrios Unidos to try to stop gang violence in inner-city neighborhoods across the country. Church groups were also at the forefront of raising the issue of "environmental racism" — the placement of toxic-waste sites near minority neighborhoods. And he recalls the role that church groups played in the 1980s in supporting a nuclear freeze, fighting apartheid in South Africa and opposing Reagan administration policies in Central America.

In contrast to the religious right, groups on the religious left have generally not gotten involved in electoral politics. "We would not claim that the Democratic Party is God's only way of working in the world, [nor is] the Republican Party," says Bailey.

Wallis agrees that religious progressives should emphasize social action instead of political campaigns. "The religious community is best served," he says, "when we're talking about the conscience of the nation rather than giving religious sanction to partisan politics."

[1] Jim Wallis, "Beyond the Christian Right," *Sojourners,* September/October 1994, p. 4.

the foremost of the political institutions of the country." [22]

The first half of the 19th century was a period of intense religious activity in the United States. Two distinctively American denominations — the Methodists and Baptists — grew with the country's westward expansion, on their way to becoming the two largest Protestant denominations in the country today. In New England and elsewhere, religious zeal fueled humanitarian reform movements on issues ranging from mental health and prison conditions to women's rights and urban poverty. Messianic visions led to the establishment of utopian communities in the East and the westward trek of Joseph Smith to found a Mormon community in what later became the state of Utah.

Clashes Over Schools, Slavery

Clashing religious beliefs fueled two important political disputes that continue to echo today. Public schools and colleges and universities were, as historian Ahlstrom writes, molded according to the specifications of an American Protestant "quasi-establishment." But the Catholic migration from Europe that began growing in the early 1800s produced controversy over the use of the Protestant King James Bible in public schools. Catholic leaders sought public funds for their own schools but met with strong — sometimes violent — opposition from the Protestant majority.

The schools issue was part of a bitter clash between Protestants and Catholics in the decades leading up to the Civil War. Anti-Catholic sentiment combined with social and economic concerns about the new immigrants to produce a strong nativist movement culminating in the sudden rise of the Know-Nothing Party in the 1850s. In the mid-1850s, the secretive, exclusively Protestant party held nearly 50 seats in Congress on the strength of an explicitly anti-Catholic platform. The party abruptly collapsed — superseded by the new Republican Party — but anti-Catholicism returned as a potent political factor after the Civil War.

The nativist movement faded when it was eclipsed by the second of the great religio-political issues of the 1800s: slavery. The abolitionist movement owed much of its fervor to the strong religious beliefs of such leaders as William Lloyd Garrison and Henry Ward Beecher, a Presbyterian minister who raised money from his pulpit to help arm anti-slavery groups in Kansas. More broadly, as Ahlstrom notes, churches were "a powerful factor" in the hardening of popular attitudes against slavery in the North. [23]

In the South, however, religion was used to help support the slave system. Elaborate scriptural arguments traced blacks to the disgraced descendants of one of Noah's sons. Hebrew prophets and St. Paul were cited as authorities for the moral validity of slavery. When the Methodist Church insisted in 1842 that a Southern bishop emancipate his slaves, the Southerners seceded and formed a pro-slavery church. A similar split occurred two years later when the Baptist church barred slave owners as missionaries. More than a century later, the Southern Baptist Convention continues as a separate entity with a powerful political influence in many Southern and border states. [24]

The Civil War ended slavery, but not sectional differences on issues of race, politics or religion. In the North, many churches supported Reconstructionists in Washington, and some provided help for freed blacks through ecclesiastical channels. In the South, the separate Methodist and Baptist churches continued in existence and grew in membership. They adopted moralistic stands on such issues as dancing, gambling, smoking and drinking while lending their support to the advent of racial segregation.

Religious Activists

In the ensuing decades, there was a ferment of activity among socially conscious religious activists. The 1870s saw the founding of the Salvation Army, the YMCA and the YWCA as missionary societies to the nation's rapidly growing urban centers. When the populist and progressive movements came to life near the turn of the century, a parallel theological movement called "the Social Gospel" invoked the teachings of Jesus in behalf of justice for farmers and workers. In 1908, the Federal Council of Churches, precursor of the National Council of Churches, was formed and immediately put out a pro-labor report entitled "The Church and Modern Industry."

As Ahlstrom points out, however, the ferment on the religious left did not represent the majority sentiment among American Protestants. "The hard fact," Ahlstrom wrote, was "that most American Protestants were conservative evangelicals who . . . strove chiefly to maintain the faith and practice of yore." [25]

The religious left and religious right of the early 20th century made common cause on one issue — prohibition — but saw other political questions from completely different perspectives. And despite continuing activity on the religious left, the story of politics and religion in 20th century America focuses mostly on the religious right.

Fundamentalism Emerges

A new branch of American Protestantism arose at the start of the 20th century. It took the name "fundamentalism" from a series of religious tracts called *The Fundamentals* that began appearing in 1910. The movement grew out of social and theological views much like those of conservative religious activists of today: discontent with liberal theology and the growth of religious indifference in society and discomfort with the impact of science and economic materialism on traditional faith.

Fundamentalism grew out of political unease, but many adherents shunned politics as irrelevant because of their belief in the imminent second coming of Christ. Yet fundamentalists did engage in political action on some issues of special religious significance. They supported prohibition, an issue that united Protestants. They also pushed, and became lastingly identified with, a more divisive cause: the anti-evolution movement.

For fundamentalists, the Darwinian theory of evolution was a direct challenge to the Bible's story of creation. Fundamentalist groups such as the World's Christian Fundamentals Association, formed in 1919, and Bible Crusaders of America won enactment of laws in five states in the 1920s to prohibit the teaching of evolution in public schools. In some other states, local school boards acted on their own to bar evolution from the classroom.

The issue made national headlines in 1925 when a high school biology teacher, John Scopes, was convicted of violating Tennessee's anti-evolution law. The trial, which pitted William Jennings Bryan as prosecutor against Clarence Darrow for the defense, was a public relations disaster for the cause; and the conviction itself was later thrown out. After the trial, support for the anti-evolution campaign became limited to extreme fundamentalists. [26]

In the 1930s, fundamentalism fell into a period of political retreat, according to Georgetown University Professor Clyde Wilcox, an expert on the Christian right. Public support for

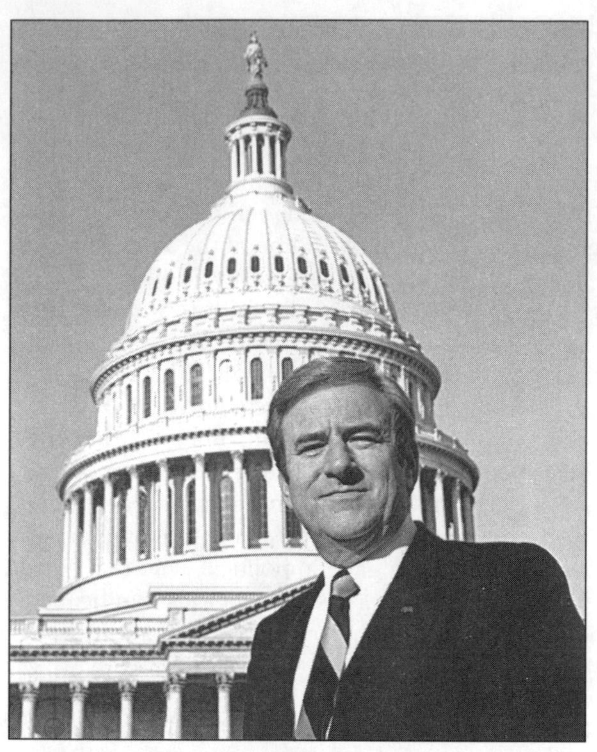

The Rev. Jerry Falwell was selected to head the Moral Majority in 1979.

fundamentalist organizations declined, he writes, and some of its leaders began taking racist, anti-Semitic and anti-Catholic stands.

The decade also witnessed the birth of a new political phenomenon: the radio preacher. Gerald L. K. Smith, a fundamentalist preacher from Louisiana, and Father Charles Coughlin, a right-wing Roman Catholic priest from Detroit, used their broadcast pulpits to attract national followings for platforms that amounted to a kind of populist fascism. But Coughlin's influence faded quickly after he backed a third-party challenge to President Franklin D. Roosevelt in 1936; and other radio preachers suffered the same fate.

Fundamentalism did make gains, however, on the religious front, as Wilcox notes. Bible colleges were built, and fundamentalist churches grew. At the beginning of the 1940s, fundamentalism spawned two rival organizations: the American Council of Christian Churches, founded in 1941 by a fiery anti-communist, Carl McIntire, and the more moderate National Association of Evangelicals, founded a year later.

With the advent of the Cold War, opposition to communism became the hallmark of political fundamentalism. New organizations, such as the Christian Crusade and the Christian Anti-Communism Crusade, depicted "godless communism" as a religious as well as political enemy. And, as Wilcox points out, they viewed domestic political issues through a religious lens. For example, sex education was opposed as part of a communist plot to undermine the United States' moral foundations.[27]

These Christian right groups never attracted large followings and sank into obscurity after the landslide defeat of conservative Republican presidential candidate Barry Goldwater in 1964. But the nation did experience an upsurge in public religiosity — or what one political scientist called "civil religion" — in the 1950s. In 1954, the phrase "under God" was added to the Pledge of Allegiance; two years later, "In God We Trust" was declared the nation's official motto. As Ahlstrom wrote, "Religion and Americanism were brought together to an unusual degree."[28]

This fusion of government and religion was challenged by a series of events in the 1960s. John F. Kennedy's election as the country's first Roman Catholic president was viewed by some as a vindication of separation of church and state. Kennedy made a crucial campaign appearance in September 1960 before a group of Baptist ministers, where he pledged not to allow his religious views to dictate his policy decisions if elected.

Two years later, the Supreme Court handed down the first of a pair of decisions that prohibited organized prayer and, the next year, Bible reading in public schools. The court said the decisions were necessary to protect religious freedoms, but they provoked strong opposition, especially among fundamentalists and other religious conservatives.[29]

Religious conservatives also faced challenges during the 1960s from religious activists on the left. Churches and church leaders were in the forefront of the civil rights revolution, the anti-war movement and the war on poverty. These religious liberals used their faith to challenge rather than support prevailing government policies and social practices. One effect, as Ahlstrom points out, was to depict most of churchgoing America "not as a moral leaven but as an obstacle to change."[30]

Rise of Religious Right

Religio-political activism on the right and on the left ebbed for most of the 1970s. On the left, the civil rights and anti-war movements receded; on the right, the school prayer issue waned after efforts to overturn the Supreme Court rulings by constitutional amendment failed. The high court touched off a new dispute involving religion and politics with its 1973 abortion rights ruling, *Roe v. Wade,* but the right-to-life movement took several years before it began moving toward its present strength and zeal.

In 1976, evangelical Christians were encouraged by the presidential candidacy of Democrat Jimmy Carter, a self-described born-again Christian. Post-election studies showed Carter drew strong support from evangelicals, but his liberal policies on social issues proved disappointing to religious conservatives. By the third year of Carter's one-term presidency, the groundwork was being laid for the rise of a new political force on the religious right.

In 1979, a group of archconservative political activists, including Howard Phillips, Richard A. Viguerie and Paul Weyrich, persuaded the Rev. Jerry Falwell, a Baptist preacher and television evangelist in Lynchburg, Va., to lead a new conservative Christian political organization. Falwell, who had previously shunned politics, agreed. The new organization was named the Moral Majority and quickly became the largest group in the Christian right. [31]

The Moral Majority set up state chapters, a Washington lobbying office and a political action committee. It backed Ronald Reagan in the 1980 presidential campaign, and Falwell took credit for Reagan's victory. Supporters and opponents saw it as a powerful political force.

Later, some of the Moral Majority's apparent clout was shown to have been exaggerated. Moen of the University of Maine says vote studies indicated that the religious right amounted to only about 6 percent of the vote in the 1980 presidential election. Journalists and scholars showed that the Moral Majority had not set up chapters in all 50 states as it said and could not document its claim to have registered 3 million new voters. Still, Falwell was a national figure, and the Moral Majority was an organization to be reckoned with.

Televangelist Pat Robertson

A second major leader of the Christian right was the Rev. Pat Robertson, who used his Christian Broadcasting Network (CBN) to become a national figure and Republican presidential contender. As liberal scholar Sara Diamond points out, Robertson began building his broadcasting empire by buying a run-down television station in Portsmouth, Va., in 1959. Four years later, he created a new format: a religious talk and variety show called "The 700 Club." The program's name came from Robertson's appeal for 700 viewers to donate $10 a month in order to keep the show in the black. Over time, the program became more lucrative: $100 million was raised from viewers in 1985. [32]

CBN also became more and more politically oriented. By the 1970s, the "700 Club" was featuring more political guests. A news department was added in 1978 to produce stories and reports from a conservative Christian perspective. A year earlier, Robertson had converted CBN into a 24-hour cable network, which went on to become the country's second most watched cable channel. In 1986, Robertson decided to enter politics himself by running for the Republican presidential nomination. He made some unexpectedly impressive showings in caucuses and straw polls in 1987 and early 1988. But, as Moen points out, the campaign effectively ended in March when Robertson won only one of 17 primaries and caucuses held on "Super Tuesday." [33]

Despite their increased visibility and influence in Washington in the 1980s, religious conservatives fell short of their goals. In assembling his new administration in 1981, President Reagan gave only one slot to a notable Christian right activist: a mid-level adviser's post in the Department of Education. [34] Religious conservatives complained the administration did not work hard enough to push their issues on Capitol Hill. Congress failed to enact the most important items on the Christian right's legislative agenda, including either a school prayer or anti-abortion constitutional amendment. The Supreme Court also reaffirmed its school prayer and abortion rulings even after six appointments to the court by Presidents Reagan and Bush in 11 years.

"The Christian right did a good job in terms of agenda-setting," Moen says, "but they did not do a particularly good job of enacting things into law."

The setbacks led religious conservatives to shift their focus to local and state political organizing as the 1980s ended. Falwell's Moral Majority had folded, but Robertson provided the mailing list from his presidential campaign to spawn a new organization in 1989 that called itself the Christian Coalition. As Sidney Blumenthal of *The New Yorker* points out, the new organization differed from religious right groups of the 1980s by focusing on grass-roots political organizing instead of using radio and television shows to spread its message. By September 1994, the coalition claimed to have 1.4 million supporters; Reed told Blumenthal about half of the supporters contributed $15 per year in dues. [35] ■

CURRENT SITUATION

Clinton's Agenda

Campaigning for the presidency in 1992, Democrat Bill Clinton blended religious imagery with liberal positions on most social issues. In his acceptance speech at the Democratic National Convention, he borrowed a biblical term to label his domestic program a "new covenant." As his running mate, Clinton picked then-Sen. Al Gore, D-Tenn., who is also a Southern Baptist and who studied theology for a year at Vanderbilt Divinity School before being elected to Congress.

Clinton's religious roots failed, however, to overcome the ties forged between the Christian right and the White House under 12 years of Republican rule. President Bush kept the support of the organized Christian right even though he never enjoyed the same popularity among religious conservatives as his predecessor, Ronald Reagan.

"The research suggests that evangelicals were the only group that consistently stayed with Bush," Moen says. "In many ways, that was his strongest voting constituency."

Clinton displeased religious conservatives with policy stands even before he took office. Shortly after his election, he repeated his campaign pledge to lift the ban on homosexuals in the military. Religious conservatives helped amplify the widespread outcry that eventually forced Clinton to retreat on the issue.

Clinton's stand on abortion rights further angered religious conservatives. On his first day in office, Clinton signed an executive order to overturn anti-abortion regulations promulgated in the Reagan and Bush administrations. Later, Clinton strongly lobbied for a bill to protect abortion clinics from violent demonstrations. Anti-abortion groups said the measure, enacted last year, violated their First Amendment rights.

The president's selection of Joycelyn Elders to be U.S. surgeon general became another lightning rod for criticism from the religious right. Elders won confirmation only after overcoming opposition from religious conservatives and others, who criticized her for, among other things, advocating distribution of condoms in high schools. In June, the criticism intensified after Elders, speaking to a gay audience, referred to "the unchristian religious right." Two days later, 87 Republican House members signed a letter calling for Elders to resign. [36]

Beyond administration policies, Clinton also became estranged from religious conservatives because of the lingering effect of his acknowledged marital infidelity. That issue — raised and then largely forgotten during the 1992 campaign — was revived in late 1993 and early '94. News stories detailed charges that Arkansas state troopers helped then-Gov. Clinton arrange sexual liaisons and disclosed an allegation of sexual harassment brought by a former state employee, Paula Jones. In addition, Clinton's assignment of a high-profile policy role to his wife, Hillary Rodham Clinton, was also a sore point with religious conservatives with traditional views of the role of women in family life.

The combination of political and personal issues produced among many religious conservatives an intense feeling of dislike and distrust for Clinton. "There's an unbelievable amount of hate against the man that goes on in Christian circles," Os Guinness, a conservative-leaning theologian, told *The New York Times* last month. [37]

Leaders of the religious right have stoked those feelings. Randall Terry, leader of the anti-abortion group Operation Rescue, has called Clinton "an enemy of righteousness." [38] The Christian Coalition called Clinton's inauguration a "repudiation of our forefathers' covenant with God." And Falwell, emerging from a period of political hibernation, has used his "Old Time Gospel Hour" to sell a videotape that contains an unsubstantiated charge that Clinton arranged for the murder of an investigator who allegedly had proof of Clinton's sexual liaisons. [39]

Despite the criticisms, Clinton has, in fact, been attentive to religious issues and religious leaders. He has had at least eight private breakfasts in the White House with religious leaders representing a range of theological and political viewpoints. After one of those breakfasts — on Aug. 30, 1993 — Clinton specifically agreed with the thesis in Carter's *The Culture of Disbelief*. "Sometimes I think the environment in which we operate is entirely too secular," Clinton said. [40]

Clinton also has used religious settings as a backdrop for some major policy addresses. In November 1993, he delivered an emotional anti-crime speech at the predominantly black Memphis church where Dr. King delivered his last sermon. [41] And last month, Clinton called for reducing the number of out-of-wedlock births in a speech to another largely black denomination meeting in New Orleans. [42]

Meanwhile, Democratic campaign strategists have been trying to devise steps to blunt the political impact of the religious right. Since Clinton's election, Democrats had suffered a series of setbacks at the polls. In May, a Republican candidate backed by religious right groups won a House seat in eastern Kentucky held by Democrats since the Civil War. A month later, Democratic congressional campaign chief Fazio took the offensive with his National Press Club speech warning against the influence of what he variously called the radical right or the religious right.

Clinton followed two days later with his call to the St. Louis talk radio show. Asked about the attacks from the religious conservatives, Clinton replied indignantly that he had "bent over backwards as a governor and as a president to respect the religious convictions of all Americans."

"But that is very different," Clinton continued, "from what is going on when people come into the political system and they say that anybody that doesn't agree with them is godless, anybody who doesn't agree with them is not a good Christian, anyone who doesn't agree them is fair game for any wild charge, no matter how false, for any kind of personal, demeaning attack." [43]

In the weeks after Fazio's speech, the administration appeared to soften its strategy of confronting the religious right. Some party leaders viewed the speech as too hostile. And the Christian Coalition sharply counterattacked. In a printed statement July 1, the group's communications director, Mike Russell, called Fazio's remarks "an assault on people of faith."

New Coalition Tactics

As Congress moved toward serious work on President Clinton's health-

Continued on p. 906

At Issue:

Are critics of the religious right guilty of bigotry?

yes

WILLIAM J. BENNETT
Co-director, Empower America

FROM THE WASHINGTON POST, JUNE 26, 1994.

Christians active in politics are now on the receiving end of an extraordinary campaign of bias and prejudice.

Consider a few recent examples. Democratic Congressional Campaign Committee Chairman Vic Fazio [D-Calif.] labeled conservative Christians the "fire-breathing Christian radical right." Texas Gov. Ann Richards calls them "hatemongers." The Anti-Defamation League [of B'nai B'rith] published a book accusing the "religious right" of bringing "a rhetoric of fear, suspicion and even hatred" to cultural disagreements. . . .

This is not political discourse. It is argument by invective. It is worth reflecting on how liberals and the mainstream media would respond if similar things were said by conservatives about, say, homosexuals. Or feminists. Or blacks. Or Jews. Or virtually any group actively engaged in politics *except* conservative evangelical Christians. Such criticisms would of course unleash, and rightfully so, a tidal wave of criticism and condemnation. But when it comes to Christians, apparently it is open season.

There are inherent dangers in politicizing religious faith — from the standpoint of politics *and* religion. And some of the Christian right are guilty of overheated, offensive and reckless statements. But every political movement has extremists who do not represent the movement as a whole. What is fundamentally unfair is the attempt to take the fringe element of this (or any) movement and argue that it is central and defining. The vast majority of conservative Christians are promoting a responsible (and mainstream) political agenda. What do they seek? Things like safe streets, good schools, strong families, non-intrusive government and communities where people care for one another. Good things all. And not, one would think, particularly controversial or divisive. . . .

[S]ome liberals would have us believe that the greatest threat to our Republic are people with strong religious convictions who are actively involved in politics. This is nonsense. . . .

Our political culture has sunk to the point where people who have time-honored religious beliefs that inform their politics now become the object of scorn and ridicule. On the issues, the "religious right" now stand where most Americans stood 30 years ago. The irony is that the critics of the "Christian right" are often guilty of the things they profess to be offended by: intolerance, mean-spiritedness, divisiveness and even bigotry.

no

MICHAEL KINSLEY
Co-host, CNN's "Crossfire"

FROM *THE NEW YORK TIMES*, JULY 5, 1994

It seems the self-proclaimed Christian right can dish it out, but they can't take it. They have called President Clinton every name in the book. The Rev. Jerry Falwell is selling videotapes that — without a shred of evidence — accuse the president of murdering political opponents back in Arkansas. The Christian Coalition has said Mr. Clinton's inauguration was "a repudiation of our forefathers' covenant with God." They have strayed far from traditional religious issues to proclaim the "Christian" position on matters like health-care reform and the gasoline tax.

Yet when Clinton supporters dare to hit back, these religious warriors retreat to their cloister and piteously accuse their critics of bigotry. . . .

Religious people have every right to be involved in politics. More than that: They have every right to argue that their political positions derive from their religious beliefs. If the Christian Coalition feels that Christ would want us to avoid universal health care, it should feel free to make that case in those terms.

But they cannot have it both ways. Having entered the political arena determined to play hardball, they cannot complain if their opponents decide to play hardball back. Labeling themselves Christians does not give them the right to complain of religious prejudice whenever anyone takes issue with them. And if they wish to declare the "Christian" position on every issue under the sun, they cannot logically scream "bigotry" when opponents call them "un-Christian" for those same positions.

The religious right is playing the same victimization game that conservatives often accuse interest groups on the left of playing. Its leaders are stoking the resentments of their followers, and attempting to intimidate political opponents by striking a pose of martyrdom. Yet what could be more absurd than the idea that genuine anti-Christian prejudice is a major force in America?. . .

As a non-Christian, I am not entitled to pass judgment on whether the political and social agenda of the religious right reflects the true spirit of Christianity. Nor can I judge whether Jerry Falwell and Pat Robertson, with their vicious and dishonest attacks on Mr. Clinton, are good Christians (though I have my suspicions). But I do know that neither Christianity nor political decency requires Mr. Clinton, when under attack from political enemies claiming to represent the Christian point of view, to turn the other cheek.

Continued from p. 904

care plan early this year, the Christian Coalition launched a $1.4 million lobbying drive against the legislation. The effort included regional forums, newspaper and radio ads and distribution of 30 million postcards in 60,000 evangelical and Roman Catholic churches for people to use in urging lawmakers to oppose the bill. [44]

The lobbying campaign grew out of the coalition's decision, announced in July 1993, to move into a broad spectrum of economic issues. In a news conference and an article in a conservative policy journal, Reed said that "the pro-family movement" had limited its effectiveness by giving disproportionate attention to issues such as abortion and homosexuality. In fact, Reed said, a survey of conservative Protestant and Catholic churchgoers showed they ranked those issues below such broad-based topics as the economy, welfare, the budget deficit and crime. [45]

The shift in tactics could be seen at the coalition's conference in Washington last month. Speakers drew fervent applause for a litany of conservative stances, including opposition to Clinton's health-care plan and support for lower taxes and congressional term limits. But the broadened agenda has also opened the coalition to criticism.

Liberals criticized the coalition for giving a religious cast to secular political issues. "What troubles many people," *Washington Post* columnist E. J. Dionne Jr. remarked at the Ethics and Public Policy Center conference in December, "is that certain planks of conservative ideology are made to seem synonymous with being Christian or being religious." [46]

From a different perspective, anti-abortion activists criticized the coalition for appearing to soften its stance on abortion. In an op-ed article published at the conclusion of the coalition's conference, anti-abortion activist Terry noted that Reed had credited evangelicals with helping to elect two Republican senators — Paul Coverdell in Georgia and Kay Bailey Hutchison in Texas — who are conservative but also favor abortion rights. "We cannot — in the name of the Christian Coalition — sell out the law of heaven for short-term political gain," Terry wrote. [47]

Events at the conference gave anti-abortion activists more cause for concern. The subject was given relatively short shrift by the major speakers, including GOP presidential hopefuls Quayle, Gramm, Alexander and Cheney.

Reed said that "the pro-family movement" had limited its effectiveness by giving disproportionate attention to issues such as abortion and homosexuality. In fact, Reed said, a survey of conservative Protestant and Catholic churchgoers showed they ranked those issues below such broad-based topics as the economy, welfare, the budget deficit and crime.

In addition, Phyllis Schlafly, the longtime opponent of the Equal Rights Amendment who now heads the Eagle Forum, a conservative advocacy group, outlined a plan to rewrite the Republican Party platform plank. Currently, the platform calls for a "human life" constitutional amendment to ban abortion. Schlafly called instead for a platform plank that would declare that an "unborn child" has a "fundamental, individual right to life" but would not endorse specific legislation.

Reed minimized the significance of the possible change. "There are lots of words you can use to say you are pro-life," he told a reporter at the conference. [48]

Mixed Election Results

The Christian Coalition met in Washington just three days after Minnesota voters dealt a setback to religious conservatives. Carlson, the state's moderate incumbent Republican governor, won a decisive 2-1 victory in the GOP primary over Quist, who had been strongly backed by the religious right.

Political analysts said the results of the Sept. 13 voting showed the dangers for candidates in being too closely associated with religious conservatives. "If you get effectively tagged as a candidate of the religious right, it's a loser," Charles Cook, editor of *The Cook Political Report,* remarked on National Public Radio's "Morning Edition" the next day.

But Reed was philosophical about the election. "There's no guarantee you're going to win every campaign, every contest, every time," he says. "You win some, you lose some. That's part of the give and take of politics."

Overall, religious conservatives can claim a handful of victories since the November 1992 elections. They helped Republicans capture Senate seats in a runoff election in Georgia in December 1992 (Coverdell) and in a special election in Texas (Hutchison) in June 1993. The religious right strongly backed Republican George Allen Jr. in his successful run for the Virginia governorship in November. And Republican Ron Lewis, a Baptist minister and Christian bookstore owner, won a special election to the House from Kentucky's 2nd Congressional District May 24 with support from religious conservatives.

But religious conservatives also suffered a number of defeats. Most significantly, Michael Farris, a religious right activist and head of the Home School Legal Defense Association, was defeated in the race for Virginia lieutenant governor in November 1993 even while other GOP candidates were winning handily. Republican voters in Georgia also defeated evangelical candidates for governor and one congressional seat in the state's Aug. 9 primary runoff.

Robertson also suffered an embarrassing defeat close to home in May when voters in Virginia Beach elected a school board slate backed by the local teachers' union over one backed by the Christian Coalition. [49]

Still, as religious conservatives looked toward the November elections, they saw two chances for high-profile victories for candidates strongly associated with the religious right. In Virginia, Oliver North, the former National Security Council aide and Iran-contra figure, was drawing enthusiastic backing from conservative religious groups in his senatorial campaign. North won the nomination earlier in the year in a GOP convention dominated by religious conservatives. He is opposing incumbent Democrat Charles S. Robb and former state Attorney General Marshall Coleman, running as an independent.

In South Carolina, David Beasley, a former legislator with close ties to the Christian Coalition, won the Republican gubernatorial nomination in the Aug. 23 primary. Beasley scored an upset victory over an opponent who had criticized his ties to religious activists. "The Christian-bashing that took place in the last several months, it didn't work," Beasley said afterward. [50] ■

OUTLOOK

Battle Lines Drawn

As he spoke at the Christian Coalition's conference last month, Robertson exulted in the group's increased political sophistication. Recalling his failed presidential campaign — staffed mainly by "political novices" — Robertson said he "never would have dreamed" that someday there would be "so many people who love God, love their country, love their families and who know how to win elections."

The forging of evangelical activists into a skillful political operation, with some support from conservative Roman Catholics and Jews, does distinguish the religious right of the 1990s from previous movements of religious conservatives. But the religious right has yet to prove that it can win enough elections to put its policies into effect.

Apart from local school board contests, the organized religious right can point to only a handful of victories in congressional or other elections. And the winning candidates typically have not come from the religious right itself and sometimes have had more moderate positions on some issues, such as abortion.

Still, religious conservatives have established themselves as a political presence that cannot be ignored. For the Republican Party, they are clearly an important — and some say essential — base of political support. "The Republican Party does not stand a chance of becoming a majority party in America or electing another president without the religious right," Fred Barnes, senior editor of *The New Republic,* remarked last year. [51]

For their part, Democrats appear to be concentrating on blunting the strength of religious conservatives instead of competing for their votes. "The Democrats have gone out of their way to tell these people that they're not welcome in the party," says analyst Rothenberg.

In countering the religious right, Democrats and other opponents appear to be adopting a toned-down strategy along the lines advocated by Democratic pollster Hart. In his survey for People for the American Way on voters' attitudes toward the religious right, Hart found the public shared the movement's concern about a decline in moral values and did not view the movement as a political threat. Hart's

For More Information

Anti-Defamation League of B'nai B'rith, 823 United Nations Plaza, New York, N.Y. 10017; (212) 490-2525. This Jewish civil rights organization seeks to combat anti-Semitism and other forms of discrimination and bigotry.

The Christian Coalition, Box 1990, Chesapeake, Va. 23327-1990; (804) 424-2630. The coalition works to promote what it calls "pro-family legislation and family-friendly public policy" at the local, state, and national level.

National Council of Churches, 475 Riverside Drive, New York, N.Y. 10115; (212) 870-2511. This ecumenical organization of Protestant and Orthodox churches has been active in issues involving church-state relations, racial equality, social welfare, economic justice and world peace.

People for the American Way, 2000 M St., N.W., Suite 400, Washington, D.C. 20036; (202) 467-4999. The organization works on a variety of First Amendment issues, including church-state questions. It was founded in 1980 by television producer Norman Lear.

advice was to debate the specific policy positions advocated by religious conservatives rather than the strength of the religious right or the role of religion in society.

Progressive religious groups have concerns about the strength of the religious right but have taken few steps to counter it. Instead of supporting specific candidates, these mainstream religious groups have limited their political activities to specific issues, such as civil rights or war and peace, or to social action at the local level. The Interfaith Alliance, formed this summer to try to counter the religious right, has had little visible impact.

The emergence of religious conservatives as an organized political force has undoubtedly created some strains. "Religious people always create problems," Irving Kristol, editor of the neoconservative journal *The Public Interest*, has observed, "since their ardor tends to outrun the limits of politics in a constitutional democracy." [52] ■

Notes

[1] The conference was held Sept. 16-17, 1994.

[2] John F. Persinos, "Has the Christian Right Taken Over the Republican Party?" *Campaigns & Elections,* September 1994.

[3] People for the American Way, "Nationwide Voter Survey on American Attitudes Toward Values, Religion and Politics and the Religious Right Political Movement," Sept. 14, 1994.

[4] *Ibid.*

[5] Quoted in *The New York Times,* June 25, 1994, p. A12.

[6] *The Washington Post,* June 22, 1994, p. A12.

[7] Anti-Defamation League of B'nai B'rith, *The Religious Right: The Assault on Tolerance and Pluralism in America,* July 1994, p. 145; The Christian Coalition, "A Campaign of Falsehoods: The Anti-Defamation League's Defamation of Religious Conservatives," July 28, 1994, p. 1.

[8] *The New York Times,* June 20, 1994, p. A20.

[9] Press release, June 6, 1994.

[10] George S. Weigel Jr., "Talking the Talk: Christian Conviction and Democratic Etiquette," in Michael Comartie (ed.), *Disciples and Democracy: Religious Conservatives and the Future of American Politics* (1994), p. 92.

[11] Stephen L. Carter, *The Culture of Disbelief: How American Law and Politics Trivialize Religious Devotion* (1993), pp. 48-49.

[12] John C. Green, James L. Guth, Lyman A. Kellstedt and Corwin E. Smidt, "Murphy Brown Revisited: The Social Issues in the 1992 Election," in Comartie, *op. cit.,* p. 63. A version of the paper was presented at the American Political Science Association meeting in Washington, D.C., in September 1993.

[13] *The Wall Street Journal,* June 9, 1994, p. A15.

[14] Quoted in *The Washington Post,* June 26, 1994, p. A6; *USA Today,* June 27, 1994, p. 8A.

[15] *The Wall Street Journal,* Sept. 7, 1993, p. A18.

[16] Thomas J. Curry, *The First Freedoms: Church and State in America to the Passage of the First Amendment* (1986), p. 4.

[17] See Sydney E. Ahlstrom, *A Religious History of the American People* (1972), pp. 182-183 (Rhode Island), pp. 207-209 (Pennsylvania), pp. 331-332 (Maryland).

[18] Curry, *op. cit.,* p. 133.

[19] Ahlstrom, *op. cit.,* p. 379.

[20] Isaac Kramnick, "Jefferson vs. the Religious Right," *The New York Times,* Aug. 29, 1994, p. A15.

[21] Ahlstrom, *op. cit.,* p. 380.

[22] Alexis de Tocqueville, *Democracy in America* (1835), quoted in Ahlstrom, *op. cit.,* p. 386.

[23] Ahlstrom, *op. cit.,* p. 668.

[24] See Samuel Eliot Morrison, *The Oxford History of the American People* (1965), pp. 512, 514; Carter, *op. cit.,* p. 72.

[25] Ahlstrom, *op cit.,* p. 304.

[26] See Ahlstrom, *op. cit.,* pp. 909-910; Clyde Wilcox, *God's Warriors: The Christian Right in Twentieth-Century America* (1992), pp. 4-8.

[27] Wilcox, *op. cit.* , pp. 9-10.

[28] Ahlstrom, *op. cit.,* p. 954.

[29] For background, see "Religion in Schools," *The CQ Researcher,* Feb. 18, 1994, pp. 145-168.

[30] *Ibid.,* p. 1093.

[31] See Sara Diamond, *Spiritual Warfare: The Politics of the Christian Right* (1989), pp. 60-61; Matthew Moen, *The Christian Right and Congress* (1989), pp. 72-77; Bill Keller, "Evangelical Conservatives Move From Pews to Polls, but Can They Sway Congress?" *Congressional Quarterly Weekly Report,* Sept. 6, 1980, pp. 2627-2634.

[32] Diamond, *op. cit.,* pp. 12-21.

[33] Moen, *op. cit.,* pp. 174-175.

[34] *Ibid.,* p. 72.

[35] Sidney Blumenthal, "Christian Soldiers," *The New Yorker,* July 11, 1994, p. 36. See also Robert Sullivan, "An Army of the Faithful," *The New York Times Magazine,* April 25, 1993, pp. 32-34, 40-44.

[36] See *The Washington Post,* June 26, 1994, p. A6.

[37] *The New York Times,* Sept. 13, 1994, p. A19.

[38] *The Washington Post,* Feb. 2, 1994, p. A3.

[39] *The New York Times,* June 26, 1994, p. A1.

[40] Quoted in *The Washington Post,* March 10, 1994, p. A30.

[41] *The New York Times,* Nov. 15, 1993, p. A1.

[42] *The New York Times,* Sept. 10, 1994, p. A1.

[43] Quoted in *The New York Times,* June 25, 1994, p. 12.

[44] See *The Washington Post,* Feb. 16, 1994, p. A6.

[45] See *The Washington Post,* July 18, 1993, p. A7; and Ralph Reed Jr., "Casting a Wider Net," *Policy Review,* Heritage Foundation, summer 1993, pp. 31-35.

[46] Comartie, *op. cit.,* p. 17.

[47] Randall Terry, "Selling Out the Law of Heaven," *The Washington Post,* Sept. 18, 1994, p. C9.

[48] Quoted in *The Washington Post,* Sept. 18, 1994, p. A6.

[49] *The New York Times,* May 5, 1994, p. B14.

[50] Quoted in *The Washington Post,* Aug. 25, 1994, p. A4.

[51] Fred Barnes, "Afterword: Why the Nation Needs the Religious Right," in Comartie, *op. cit.,* p. 114.

[52] Irving Kristol, "Foreword: Taking Religious Conservatives Seriously," *ibid.,* p. xi.

Bibliography

Selected Sources Used

Books

Ahlstrom, Sydney E., *A Religious History of the American People,* Yale University Press, 1972.
Ahlstrom's award-winning history traces the varied strands of religious beliefs in America from Colonial times through the 1960s. The book has a 30-page bibliography.

Carter, Stephen L., *The Culture of Disbelief: How American Law and Politics Trivialize Religious Devotion,* Basic Books, 1993.
Carter, a Yale law professor, touched off a vigorous debate by arguing that people of religious beliefs are often treated with disdain when they enter the political arena.

Comartie, Michael (ed.), *Disciples and Democracy: Religious Conservatives and the Future of American Politics,* William B. Eerdmans Publishing, 1994.
The book contains papers and responses from a variety of experts on religion and politics given during a conference in fall 1993 sponsored by the Ethics and Public Policy Center in Washington. Comartie is a senior fellow and director of the evangelical studies project at the center.

Curry, Thomas J., *The First Freedoms: Church and State in America to the Passage of the First Amendment,* Oxford University Press, 1986.
Curry, a Roman Catholic priest with the Archdiocese of Los Angeles, examines the relationship of church and state in Colonial America and the development of religious liberty through the writing of the First Amendment.

Diamond, Sara, *Spiritual Warfare: The Politics of the Christian Right,* South End Press, Boston, 1989.
Diamond, a journalist and university teacher in California, presents a detailed, critical account of the formation and activities of groups on the Christian right in the 1980s.

Kosmin, Barry A., and Seymour P. Lachman, *One Nation Under God: Religion in Contemporary American Society,* Harmony Books, 1993.
This book describes the relationship between religion and politics in the United States based on a telephone survey of more than 113,000 people. Kosmin is a professor of sociology and Lachman is university dean at the City University of New York.

Moen, Matthew S., *The Transformation of the Christian Right,* University of Alabama Press, 1992.
Moen, chairman of the political science department at the University of Maine, says the Christian right has shifted strategy since the mid-1980s by de-emphasizing Congress in favor of litigation and grass-roots organizing. In an earlier book, *The Christian Right and Congress* (University of Alabama Press, 1989), Moen says the Christian right largely failed to enact its agenda during the 1980s.

Wilcox, Clyde, *God's Warriors: The Christian Right in Twentieth-Century America,* Johns Hopkins University Press, 1992.
Wilcox, a professor of government at Georgetown University in Washington, provides a history and political science analysis of the Christian right since the beginning of the 20th century.

Articles

Bruce, Steve (ed.), "The Rapture of Politics: The Christian Right as the United States Approaches the Year 2000," *Sociology of Religion,* Vol. 55, No. 3, fall 1994.
This academic journal published a collection of eight articles by leading experts examining the political impact and prospects of the Christian right.

Persinos, John F., "Has the Christian Right Taken Over the Republican Party," *Campaigns & Elections,* September 1994.
A state-by-state survey finds that the Christian right is "dominant" in Republican Party organizations in 18 states and has "substantial" influence in 13 others. The issue also includes a demographic analysis of the Christian right and opposing evaluations of its strength by Republican and Democratic strategists.

Von Drehle, David, and Thomas B. Edsall, "Life of the Grand Old Party," *The Washington Post,* Aug. 14, 1994, p. A1.
Political reporters von Drehle and Edsall provide an in-depth look at the resurgence of the religious right since the 1992 election and the rise of the Christian Coalition as "the political heart of the movement."

Reports and Studies

Anti-Defamation League of B'nai B'rith, *The Religious Right: The Assault on Tolerance and Pluralism in America,* July 1994.
This 190-page report strongly criticizes the religious right as a threat to religious freedom and tolerance.

Christian Coalition, *A Campaign of Falsehoods: The Anti-Defamation League's Defamation of Religious Conservatives,* July 28, 1994.
In its response to the Anti-Defamation League's critique, the Christian Coalition charges the report is based on "innuendo, half-truths and outright falsehoods."

The Next Step

Additional information from UMI's Newspaper & Periodical Abstracts database

The Clinton Administration

Cummings, Jeanne, "Religious right backs president's accuser," *Atlanta Journal Constitution,* May 15, 1994, p. A1.
The Rev. Jerry Falwell is offering a $40 videotape about the Whitewater controversy that suggests complicity by President Clinton in a murder, and a videotape covering Paula Corbin Jones' sexual harassment charges against Clinton will soon be available, Cummings writes.

Eastland, Terry, "Religion, politics & the Clintons," *Commentary,* January 1994, pp. 40-43.
President Clinton has quietly been making friends with the Christian left, though no one has accused him of trying to give religion more of an "official" role, Eastland writes.

"Health care wars," *Christian Century,* March 9, 1994, p. 248.
Efforts by religious groups to forcefully articulate their views on health care reform in the U.S. are discussed.

"Religious Right and Clinton," *Christian Century,* July 13, 1994, p. 675.
Activists of the religious right are being accused by Clinton and other officials of using religion to divide the country, the magazine says.

Solomon, Burt, "His public embrace of religion ... gives Clinton a political boost," *National Journal,* April 16, 1994, pp. 912-913.
President Clinton's public embrace of religion has yielded him many political benefits, Solomon writes.

"Those troublesome Christians," *The Wall Street Journal,* June 30, 1994, p. A10.
An editorial argues that the attack on the "religious right" from President Clinton and other Democrats shows that Evangelicals and other Christians have committed the crime of getting into politics to make their views heard.

Conservatism and Religion

Best, Kathleen, "In God they trust," *St. Louis Post-Dispatch,* June 12, 1994, p. B1.
Ideological battles for control of the Republican Party are blowing up around the country with more Christian conservative activists taking power, Best writes.

Miller, Julie K., "Conservative Christians talk tactics," *Atlanta Journal Constitution,* June 26, 1993, p. E6.
The Christian Coalition is holding workshops around the U.S. to teach its foot soldiers how to polish a political image and be more sophisticated about hometown politics.

Page, Clarence, "Candidates share Christian backing, criminal background," *Chicago Tribune,* June 8, 1994, p. 25.
Page examines how Oliver North and former Washington Mayor Marion Barry are getting the support of Christian conservatives.

Stone, Judith, "The trivializing of religion in American life," *Glamour,* February 1994, p. 108.
In an interview, Yale law professor Stephen L. Carter discusses how religion is trivialized in the U.S. and the link between religion and conservative politics.

Opinions and Editorials

Bray, Thomas J., "Conspiracy of the religious right?" *Detroit News & Free Press,* June 26, 1994, p. B2.
Bray says most Democrats and more than a few Republicans feel outrage about the religious right's move into the Republican Party.

"Demagoguery in America," *New Republic,* Aug. 1, 1994, p. 7.
An editorial discusses the newly energized religious right's rhetorical violence, as illustrated by Jerry Falwell's videotape accusing President Clinton of arranging the murder of an Arkansas detective.

Dionne, E.J. Jr., "Our messy democratic bargain," *The Washington Post,* Dec. 21, 1993, p. A23.
Dionne argues that public life should be more hospitable to religious voices but that government policies should not be based solely on religious views.

McCarthy, Colman, "How Christian the Christian right?" *The Washington Post,* July 9, 1994, p. A21.
McCarthy criticizes the Christian right for interpreting selected teachings of the Bible to support political attacks against people of whom it disapproves.

"Politics and fair play," *The Christian Science Monitor,* June 27, 1994, p. 18.
An editorial criticizes attacks on and ridiculing of President Clinton's religious beliefs by talk-show host Rush Limbaugh and televangelist Jerry Falwell.

Religious Minorities

Abou El Fadl, Khaled, "Legal debates on Muslim minorities: Between rejection and accommodation," *Journal of Religious Ethics,* spring 1994, pp. 127-162.
The religious and political status of Muslim minorities is being questioned in Europe and North America, the author writes.

Kent, Stephen A. and James V. Spickard, "The other civil

religion and the tradition of radical Quaker politics," ***Journal of Church & State,*** **spring 1994, pp. 373-387.**

In 1981, Jim Corbett, an Arizona Quaker, defended his illegal aid to Central American refugees by asserting that the U.S. government acts against God's desire for peace.

Religious Right

Benedetto, Richard, "Faith, politics stir a debate within GOP," ***USA Today,*** **June 27, 1994, p. A8.**

Members of Iowa's Christian Coalition and thousands of conservative Christians like them are under fire as they become increasingly involved in grass-roots politics, Benedetto writes.

Broder, John M., "Frustrated Clinton assails Falwell and Limbaugh," ***Los Angeles Times,*** **June 25, 1994, p. A21.**

On June 24, 1994, Broder writes, President Clinton attacked Jerry Falwell and radio personality Rush Limbaugh by name, saying that their brand of politics and religion feeds a spreading intolerance and cynicism across America.

Fineman, Howard, "Some hard right turns for the GOP," ***Newsweek,*** **June 20, 1994, p. 38.**

Fineman examines the growing influence of religious conservatives.

Frum, David, "Myth of religious right," ***USA Today,*** **July 25, 1994, p. A11.**

Frum, a conservative commentator, argues that the power of the religious right is overstated.

Kamber, Victor, "Politics under the cloak of religion," ***Boston Globe,*** **July 15, 1994, p. 17.**

Kamber, a Democratic campaign consultant, calls the religious right fundamentally un-Christian and intolerant.

Lowry, Rich, "Crucifying the Christian Right," ***National Review,*** **Aug. 1, 1994, pp. 21-22.**

Lowry argues that the Democratic attack on the religious right failed because the Democrats were unable to support their charges of extremism.

The Role of Religion in Politics

Demerath, N. J. III, "The moth and the flame: Religion and power in comparative blur," ***Sociology of Religion,*** **summer 1994, pp. 105-117.**

A major shift that occurred in religion's perceived political prominence, especially following key events in 1979, and a current project to investigate religion, politics and the state in more than a dozen countries are described.

Hattersley, Roy, "Politicians with faith but no hope or charity," ***Guardian,*** **May 23, 1994, p. 23.**

Hattersley examines the problems that arise when politicians use their religious beliefs as a platform, and argues against the concept of politics that are governed by religion.

Solzhenitsyn, Aleksandr, and Douglas Coupland, "Bring God back into politics," ***New Perspectives Quarterly,*** **spring 1994, pp. 4-10.**

The role of morality in politics is examined. Humankind must learn to subordinate its interests to moral criteria or it will be torn apart as the worst aspects of human nature bare their teeth, the authors write.

Wall, James M., "Spiritual changes," ***Christian Century,*** **Jan. 5, 1994, pp. 3-4.**

President Clinton has been influenced by his religious views in using the "bully pulpit" to push high-priority items on his political agenda, Wall writes.

West, John G. Jr., "Politics from the Shadowlands," ***Policy Review,*** **Spring 1994, pp. 68-70.**

Lessons that can be learned from popular author C. S. Lewis about the proper relationship between religious faith, moral principle and political action are discussed.

Statement of Ownership
Management, Circulation

Act of Aug. 12, 1970: Section 3685, Title 39, United States Code

Title of publication: The CQ Researcher. Date of filing: October 12, 1994. Frequency of issue: Weekly (Except for 4/1, 7/1, 9/2 and 12/30/94). No. of issues published annually: 48. Annual subscription price: $299.00. Location of known office of publication: 1414 22nd Street, N.W., Washington, D.C. 20037-1097. Names and addresses of publisher, editor and managing editor: Publisher, Neil Skene, 1414 22nd Street, N.W., Washington, D.C. 20037-1097; Editor, Sandra Stencel, 1414 22nd Street, N.W., Washington, D.C. 20037-1097; Managing Editor, Thomas J. Colin, 1414 22nd Street, N.W., Washington, D.C. 20037-1097. Owner: Congressional Quarterly, 1414 22nd Street, N.W., Washington, D.C. 20037-1097. Known bondholders, mortgagees and other security holders owning or holding 1 percent or more of total amount of bonds, mortgages or other securities: none.

Extent and Nature of Circulation	Average Number of Copies Each Issue During Preceding 12 Months	Actual Number of Copies of Single Issue Published Nearest to Filing Date
A. Total number of copies printed *(Net Press Run)*	6,443	6,703
B. Paid Circulation		
1. Sales through dealers and carriers, street vendors and counter sales	—	—
2. Mail subscriptions	4,957	4,995
C. Total paid and/or requested circulation	4,957	4,995
D. Free distribution by mail carrier or other means. Samples, Complimentary and other free copies	358	550
E. Total distribution *(Sum of C and D)*	5,315	5,545
F. Copies not distributed		
1. Office use, left over, unaccounted, spoiled after printing	1,128	1,158
2. Returns from news agents	—	—
G. TOTAL (sum of E and F — should equal net press run shown in A)	6,443	6,703

Back Issues

Great Research on Current Issues Starts Right Here...Recent topics covered by The CQ Researcher are listed below. Before May 1991, reports were published under the name of Editorial Research Reports.

APRIL 1993
Head Start
High-Speed Rail
Children's Legal Rights
Muslims in America

MAY 1993
Cults in America
Preventing Teen Pregnancy
Software Piracy
National Parks

JUNE 1993
Food Safety
Prostitution
Childhood Immunizations
National Service

JULY 1993
Electric Cars
Population Growth
Downward Mobility
Intelligence Testing

AUGUST 1993
Mental Illness
Bilingual Education
Foreign Policy Burden
School Funding

Back issues are available for $4.00 (subscribers) or $7.00 (non-subscribers). Quantity discounts apply to orders over ten. To order, call Congressional Quarterly Customer Service at (202) 887-8621.

Binders are available for $16.00. To order call 1-800-638-1710. Please refer to stock number 648.

SEPTEMBER 1993
Suburban Crime
Public Housing
Supreme Court Preview
Immigration Reform

OCTOBER 1993
Airline Safety
Disaster Response
Science in the Courtroom
The Glass Ceiling

NOVEMBER 1993
Paying for Retirement
Charitable Giving
Privacy in the Workplace
Adoption

DECEMBER 1993
U.S. Vietnam-Relations
Learning Disabilities
Child Care
Space Program's Future

JANUARY 1994
Racial Tensions in Schools
South Africa's Future
Worker Retraining
Regulating Pesticides

FEBRUARY 1994
Prison Overcrowding
Water Quality
Religion in Schools
Juvenile Justice

MARCH 1994
Underground Economy
Education Standards
Gambling Boom
Private Management of Public Schools

APRIL 1994
Reproductive Ethics
U.S.-China Trade
Soccer in America
Talk Show Democracy

MAY 1994
Traffic Congestion
Women's Health Issues
Mutual Funds
Political Scandals

JUNE 1994
Education and Gender
Gun Control
Public Land Policy
Nuclear Arms Cleanup

JULY 1994
Dietary Supplements
Public Opinion and Foreign Policy
Crime Victims' Rights
Birth Control Choices

AUGUST 1994
Genetically Engineered Foods
Electing Minorities
Prozac Controversy
College Sports

SEPTEMBER 1994
Home Schooling
Welfare Experiments
Courts and the Media
Regulating Tobacco

OCTOBER 1994
Historic Preservation

Future Topics

- ***Arts Funding***
- ***Embargoes and Sanctions***
- ***Sex on Campus***

THE
CQ Researcher

PUBLISHED BY CONGRESSIONAL QUARTERLY INC.

Arts Funding

Is boosting the status of the arts a wise investment?

The arts world has been buoyed by Clinton administration initiatives to promote arts funding and to give the arts a new status in public school curricula. To encourage corporate and foundation giving as well as new state and local support, arts enthusiasts are emphasizing the value of dance, music, theater and fine art as universal communications tools. The arts are also being touted for their ability to stimulate local economies and to build a sense of community in areas beset by social problems. Critics, however, oppose government activism in the arts, especially at a time of federal budget deficits. They see the arts as an elitist luxury best left to the private sector. They also point to continuing scandals over publicly funded art deemed obscene.

INSIDE THIS ISSUE

CQ Oct. 21, 1994 • Volume 4, No. 39 • Pages 913-936

Formerly Editorial Research Reports

ARTS FUNDING

COVER ART: BARBARA SASSA-DANIELS

October 21, 1994
Volume 4, No. 39

The CQ Researcher (ISSN 1056-2036). Formerly Editorial Research Reports. Published weekly (48 times per year, not printed the first Friday of any month with five Fridays) by Congressional Quarterly Inc., 1414 22nd St., N.W., Washington, D.C. 20037. Rates are furnished upon request. Second-class postage paid at Washington, D.C. POSTMASTER: Send address changes to The CQ Researcher, 1414 22nd St., N.W., Washington, D.C. 20037.

Arts Funding

BY CHARLES S. CLARK

THE ISSUES

For the past five years, the arts have generated anything but the genteel and sophisticated discourse one might expect from discussions about dance, theater and music. Rather, the debates emanating from Washington were laced with heated rhetoric about obscenity and censorship, about sexually graphic photographs and defaced religious icons.

But today there is a new sound coming from Washington. And to the nation's arts community, it's as sweet as a symphony. The Clinton administration has launched a multipronged push for the arts ranging well beyond the traditional arts and humanities programs.

In September, the president made his feelings about the arts clear when he named several entertainers and corporate leaders to the reactivated President's Committee on the Arts and the Humanities. * "At a time when our society faces new and profound challenges, when we are losing so many of our children and when so many people feel insecure in the face of change, the arts and humanities are fundamental to our lives as individuals and as a nation," he said.

To help sell his vision, Clinton picked the celebrated actress Jane Alexander to chair the National Endowment for the Arts (NEA). Since her confirmation in late 1993, she has traveled to some 43 states and 80 cities, making the case for the arts as vital to education, the economy and family life. "The arts are not fiscally stable, but they are flourishing," she told the National Press Club in October. "The young man who picks up a clarinet or even a paintbrush or a pen

is not likely to pick up a needle or a gun."

Education Secretary Richard W. Riley included the arts in the administration's recently enacted Goals 2000 plan to set national education standards. "Any teacher knows how frustrating it is these days to get students enthusiastic about their subject — any subject," Riley said last year. "But recently we have seen some great successes in schools that either focus on the arts in the curriculum or use the arts in inventive ways in other courses." [1]

The Housing and Urban Development Department is talking up arts as a way to build stronger communities, and arts programs for troubled youth were included in both the recently enacted federal crime bill and the reauthorized Elementary and Secondary Education Act.

Initiatives are being launched beyond the Capital Beltway, too. The U.S. Conference of Mayors, meeting in Portland, Ore., in June, joined with the president, the NEA and a coalition of thousands of arts groups known as the National Cultural Alliance in calling for boosts in arts funding. Noting that 84 percent of local arts agencies in the 50 largest cities address social problems, the mayors also passed a resolution supporting this October's designation as National Arts and Humanities Month.

It is the indefatigable Alexander, however, who is carrying the message to every corner of the country — and winning rave reviews. "It's great that she's getting around the country to meet people and pay attention to what they say," says Sandra Hyslop, editor of the American Symphony Orchestra League's *Symphony* magazine. "In the last few years, the NEA has concentrated on controversies in Washington, but that's not what the arts are all about."

Luis R. Cancel, president of the New York City-based American Council for the Arts, is another fan. "Jane is a tremendous asset," he says. "She is healing the rift of recent years between the NEA chairman and the cultural community, recognizing the importance of creative integrity and public support for respecting the creative individual."

"I am hopeful because when she says the arts are important to the everyday life of this country, she believes it," says Serena Rattazzi, director of the American Federation of Arts, another New York group. "If I had to criticize the new NEA, it would be for taking the spotlight off the large institutions, such as orchestras and museums, and concentrating more on the grass-roots, local and small arts groups."

Among average Americans, interest in the arts is on the upswing. The proportion of adults who go to an art museum or gallery at least once a year rose from 22 percent in 1982 to 27 percent in 1992, according to the NEA. (*See table, p. 919.*) Participation is strongest among people with higher levels of education. [2] Opera audiences have grown 30 percent since 1980, to 4.3 million opera lovers in 1992, according to the Washington-based group Opera America.

* The committee's 45 members include composer Quincy Jones, actress Rita Moreno, American Express Chairman Harvey Golub and Atlanta Newspapers Chairman Anne Cox Chambers. President Clinton named Hillary Rodham Clinton as honorary chairman.

Where the Money Comes From

Funding for orchestras and dance and theater companies held steady during the past decade. Ticket sales, gift shops and other sources of earned income provided the most money, followed by private contributions (foundations, corporations and individuals). The smallest amount of support came from local, state and federal sources.

	1985	1989	1993
Symphony Orchestras			
Earned income	58%	59%	59%
Private contributions	33%	33%	34%
Public support	10%	9%	7%
Theaters			
Earned income	63%	61%	62%
Private contributions	29%	31%	32%
Public support	8%	8%	6%
Dance Companies			
Earned income	63%	58%	59%
Private contributions	29%	34%	32%
Public support	8%	8%	6%

Note: Totals don't necessarily add to 100% because of rounding

Sources: American Arts Alliance, American Symphony Orchestra League, Theatre Communications Group, Dance/USA

A February 1993 poll commissioned by the National Cultural Alliance showed 81 percent of Americans agreeing that the arts and humanities contribute to the economic well-being of society, with 80 percent saying that the arts make their local community a better place to live. Only 31 percent, however, said the arts and humanities play a major role in their lives. (*See poll, p. 920.*)

With the arts of major importance to fewer than a third of all Americans, some observers worry that the efforts of arts boosters could be easily thwarted in this era of budget deficits and shrinking roles for government. Corporations and foundations report that giving to the arts has not fully recovered from the recession of the late 1980s and early '90s. Federal arts spending — often the most visible catalyst for local government and private spending — was cut by 2 percent this summer (*see p. 928*). Several lawmakers clearly stated the reason: continued NEA funding of art that some consider offensive.

"The 2 percent cut is a signal," says the Rev. Donald Wildmon, founder of the Tupelo, Miss.-based American Family Association and a frequent critic of NEA funding. "There's been lots of signals, and the endowment has ignored every one of them. The same radicals are still there. If they're going to continue funding art that involves cutting bodies on stage with an AIDS-infected patient, and making a film about hard-core homosexual sex dedicated to [NEA critic Sen. Jesse Helms, R-N.C.] they will [upset] fair-minded people and taxpayers."

Others oppose government funding on fiscal and philosophical grounds. "Congress has created a nearly $5 trillion national debt," argued Rep. Philip M. Crane, R-Ill. "We need to get our fiscal house in order. How can we rationalize spending millions on the NEA when we do not even have enough money to effectively deal with the illegal immigration crisis or the crime in our streets?" [3]

Arts professionals respond to threats of federal cutbacks by noting that the NEA accounted for only 16 percent of government arts funding in 1993, compared with the 61 percent provided by local governments. Moreover, the National Assembly of Local Arts Agencies notes, private arts groups raise five times as much money as public ones. [4]

The NEA's contribution, however, is regarded as vital in attracting private money. Edward H. Able, president of the American Association of Museums (AAM), calls it "a key, symbolic commitment of the federal government in supporting the accessibility of the arts to the American people. It's the critical third leg of a stool that also includes science and the humanities."

Robert Lynch, president of the assembly of local arts agencies, views the 2 percent NEA cut as a victory because "it could have been more massive. But we want to move beyond defining success as a 2 percent cut." That, he says, means focusing on the social problems that the arts can help solve — youth at risk, crime and drugs.

"People don't realize the role that the arts play in the economy," he says. A study by his group showed that the arts accounted for 1.3 million jobs and $37 billion in spending last year, plus $3.5 billion in tax revenues that went back to Washington. [5] "The NEA budget is only $170 million, so we're not just freeloading," he adds.

Whether the new push for arts

funding succeeds will hinge on the following issues:

Should the federal government fund the arts?

"Art is the ultimate ambassador," said former New Jersey Republican Gov. Thomas H. Kean in one of many recent paeans to the arts. "Art is the passport that opened Soviet Russia to [pianist] Vladimir Horowitz — and to Billy Joel, for that matter. Art is the proof that genius has no race or nationality, no ideology or class." [6]

To such egalitarian ideals, the NEA adds hard economic facts: The creative arts represent 6 percent of the nation's gross domestic product (GDP), yet the NEA costs each American only 65 cents a year. In nearly 30 years of existence, the NEA can list many success stories among the more than 11,000 artists who have received grants, including choreographer Alvin Ailey, playwright Wendy Wasserstein, novelist John Irving and filmmaker Barbara Kopple. The NEA sponsored the contest that selected the design for the Vietnam Memorial in Washington and has helped produce 125 hours of public television programming.

Many nonprofit local theater productions received NEA support before going on to national fame, among them "Driving Miss Daisy," "Children of a Lesser God," "Annie" and "A Chorus Line." NEA-backed writers have won 42 Pulitzer Prizes, 28 National Book Awards and 47 MacArthur Foundation "genius awards." Over the past five years, the NEA and state arts agencies have given out more than $2 billion in grants, which has been matched by $4 billion in private funds. [7] (*See story, p. 918.*)

"We have seen the wonderful arts organizations the endowment has made possible . . . from the most rural to the most dense inner city," wrote Alexander in a letter to Rep. Crane, "organizations which built communities through the celebration of heritage, or that address the needs of at-risk youth in after-school programs or go into the classrooms to teach music, or painting. . . . The National Endowment for the Arts is an unqualified success as an agency." For every dollar the NEA awards, she added, from $11-$26 is leveraged from other public and private community sources. [8]

Many political conservatives, however, object to federal funding on principle. "Funding art, regardless of its content, is not a proper role for any form of government, especially one that's in debt," says Peter Sepp, director of media relations for the National Taxpayers Union. "Popular culture comes from society, not government."

Martha Swope

NEA Chairman Jane Alexander

Paul Hodge, a federal budget analyst at the Heritage Foundation, which has long called for abolishing the NEA, says "arts funding should be as local as possible so that it reflects each community and so people can influence it to reflect their values." In the absence of federal funds, Hodge adds, there would be more private giving for the arts. "People now are more likely to say, 'I gave at the office through the recent tax bill,'" he says.

Laurence Jarvik, Washington director of the Center for the Study of Popular Culture, says the notion of the NEA leading an arts renaissance "sounds good but is bad theory. Necessity is the mother of invention, and the arts can flourish without government putting its thumb on the scale. Subsidies have actually hurt the arts," he says. "We don't have better art than we had in 1965," when the NEA was founded.

Jarvik, who often shows up at NEA meetings to voice criticism, believes that artists should be forced to try to find their own audiences, without government help. "The average actor is never going to make it and should give up," he says. "People resent too many no-talents getting money. They should be discouraged from the professional area, but should be encouraged to do community theater for the joy of it and keep their day jobs. Whether they are recognized by the government is irrelevant."

Jarvik also is skeptical of the argument that spending on the arts exposes average or underprivileged Americans to quality art. Much of the funding "has gone to people who want a nice sound system and cushy auditorium seats," he says, "but what's on the stage isn't any good."

Hyslop of the orchestra league replies that she occasionally hears "fatuous statements about cushy concert halls, but American symphonies are widely recognized to be the best performing bodies in the world. You can go to a small town like Des Moines or Tucson and hear wonderful music, and the concert hall is part of their equipment and helps them play their best." All the government help combined, she adds, is only about 7 percent of orchestra budgets. "But it would be difficult to replace because it is an investment that brings in tremendous matching support from the community."

Lynch of the assembly of local arts

Continued on p. 919

Peer-Review Panels: Democracy or Cronyism?

Everybody's an expert. That's what makes giving away money for art so difficult. To decide which art gets taxpayers' money, the federal government relies on a network of peer-review panels set up by the National Endowment for the Arts (NEA).

The NEA sends the 16,000 or so grant applications it gets annually to these specialized committees, which cover about 100 arts categories. Some 1,100 people are on call to serve on the panels. Though made up mostly of arts specialists, the panels since 1990 have included at least one non-specialist.

After meeting in secret to discuss the candidates, panelists winnow down the applications to about 4,000 deemed worthy of funding. Those are sent on to the National Council on the Arts, whose 26 members are appointed by the president and confirmed by the Senate. After accepting or rejecting the peer panels' selections, the council sends its selections to the NEA chairman for final approval.

To many in the arts world, the peer process, with its mixture of experts and average citizens, is the fairest way to honor freedom of expression in the face of ever-present controversy. "Peer review provides insulation between the political and the creative process, you can't improve on it," says Luis R. Cancel, president of the American Council for the Arts in New York City. "As long as we want to support living artists, we must take the risk that their views may not match the norm."

But to critics, peer review is an "old-boy crony network of friends or funding people who think they're on the cutting edge," says Paul Hodge, a budget analyst at the Heritage Foundation. "It has nothing to do with what taxpayers want."

Carol Pratt

Derek Smith is Prince Hal in "Henry IV" at the Shakespeare Theatre, in Washington, D.C.

Louisiana State University political scientist Kevin V. Mulcahy has written that the NEA panels are a "cultural coterie" that serves the arts institutions better than it serves average Americans. "Policy-making by panel has distorted the mission of the NEA," he says. "Overall, the agency might be better served by a system of interdisciplinary panels [with] broadly representative panelists, who would ensure some approximation of a public perspective on public culture." [1]

Laurence Jarvik of the conservative Center for the Study of Popular Culture attacks the peer system for giving power to anonymous "bureaucrats who perpetuate a cult of infallibility." He notes that peer panels have been reversed only 40 times in NEA history. And he castigates as "hush money" the $252,000 that the NEA agreed to pay last year to settle a lawsuit brought by artists Karen Finley, John Fleck, Holly Hughes and Tim Miller. They were seeking damages because their peer-approved grant applications had been turned down by the NEA for what they said were political rather than artistic reasons.

The peer panels are "remarkably free of cronyism," says Robert Lynch, president of the National Assembly of Local Arts Agencies. "Some of the members know each other, but that's true in any industry." There are various checks and balances, he adds, and the panels look at an artist's or an organization's whole work or work history, not just the work that's submitted.

The reason some meetings are secret, he says, is "to protect the careers of rejected artists and their ability to work in the marketplace. If you have 100 applications and choose only 10 or 12, you must talk about the reasons why. Those comments can be taken out of context, which is dangerous to artists."

Helen Brunner, executive director of the National Association of Artists' Organizations and a peer-panel veteran, says: "Some of the best minds in the country often agonize and work from 9 a.m. to midnight for five straight days trying to create a tapestry of grants" reflecting the best work being done in that particular field.

Brunner was disappointed this summer when the national council overruled the peer-recommended grant application of Andres Serrano, the photographer who created the controversial 1980s photo of a crucifix in urine. Serrano was seeking a grant to prepare a photography exhibit showing bodies in a morgue wearing toe tags labeled with the cause of death. Brunner believes the rejection was a political sop to Congress and the political right as well as a reflection of a lack of communication between the national council and the peer panels. "Morgues have been artists' subjects since the early days of photography," she says, adding that Serrano "is a highly spiritual and religious artist."

After Serrano's application and two others were rejected, members of the photography peer panel told the council in a letter: "By appointing yourselves pre-emptive guardians of artistic decency, you have achieved precisely the effect that Sen. Jesse Helms and others have labored unsuccessfully to achieve: the evisceration of the endowment's 25-year commitment to artistic quality, independently addressed and assessed, without compromise or concession to non-aesthetic issues." [2]

---

[1] Kevin V. Mulcahy, "The Public Interest in Public Culture," *Journal of Arts Management and Law,* spring 1991, p. 19.

[2] Bulletin of the National Association of Artists' Organizations, September-October 1994.

Continued from p. 917
agencies points out that local government funding for the arts in 1993 was $650 million, compared with $250 million from the states and only $170 million from Washington (delivered through the NEA).

"The local money comes from leveraging by the state or federal government, or is inspired by their models," Lynch says. "Yet even that $1 billion in government money is still less than 10 percent of what supports the arts. Over 60 percent of arts revenues are earned, through ticket sales and spinoff products, such as mugs and T-shirts. People don't realize how much it's market-driven."

Cancel of the Council for the Arts says the cultural community has always viewed the NEA as comparable to a Wall Street venture capitalist. The amount of money involved is not great, he says, but "it plays an important role in pointing the way" for other investors. The NEA "has brought so much goodwill throughout the country with a small budget," he says. "No other agency comes close to matching it."

Moreover, says the museum association's Able, "Policy is led on a national level. There was no state and local funding for the arts until Congress established it on the federal level."

Hodge of Heritage says the idea of using government to leverage other funds might be a good argument for state and local arts funding. "But on the federal level it will inevitably break down into a [shouting] match over the quality and nature of the art."

Have the arts been harmed by controversies over art deemed obscene?

When Bill Clinton arrived in Washington early in 1993, many assumed that the debate over government-funded art that erupted during the Bush administration had faded. The shouting over the homoerotic photos of Robert Mapplethorpe and the nude performance art of Karen Finley may have quieted, but flare-ups over art have continued in many areas.

People for the American Way, a liberal advocacy group, this spring compiled a report on 204 recent challenges to publicly displayed paintings, sculpture, plays, performance art, storytelling and poetry. Fully 63 percent of the protesters' attacks resulted in the art being removed or restricted. "Attacks on art reflect the sharp divisions in our society around politics, race, religion, gender and sexuality," noted Arthur J. Kropp, the group's president. "And we're finding that the knee-jerk impulse to censor art that touches these raw nerves is now coming from both the left and right." [9]

In Congress, the decision this summer to trim NEA funding by 2 percent was directly linked to a June performance in Minneapolis by Ron Athey, a performance artist who is gay and HIV-positive. Athey dramatized his banishment from his church by drawing blood from a fellow performer with an acupuncture needle (*see below*).

As for arts funding in general, "We don't know the impact of the NEA controversy," says Nancy Meier, executive director of the New York-based Arts and Business Council. "There are definite cutbacks, but no one is saying that's the reason. Corporations are refocusing, thinking more strategically, and looking

Attendance at Arts Activities

Several arts activities posted attendance gains in the decade from 1982-1992, according to the most recent surveys. Art museums had the period's biggest increase in attendance. Historic sites, the second most popular arts destination following art and craft fairs, showed the greatest drop in popularity.

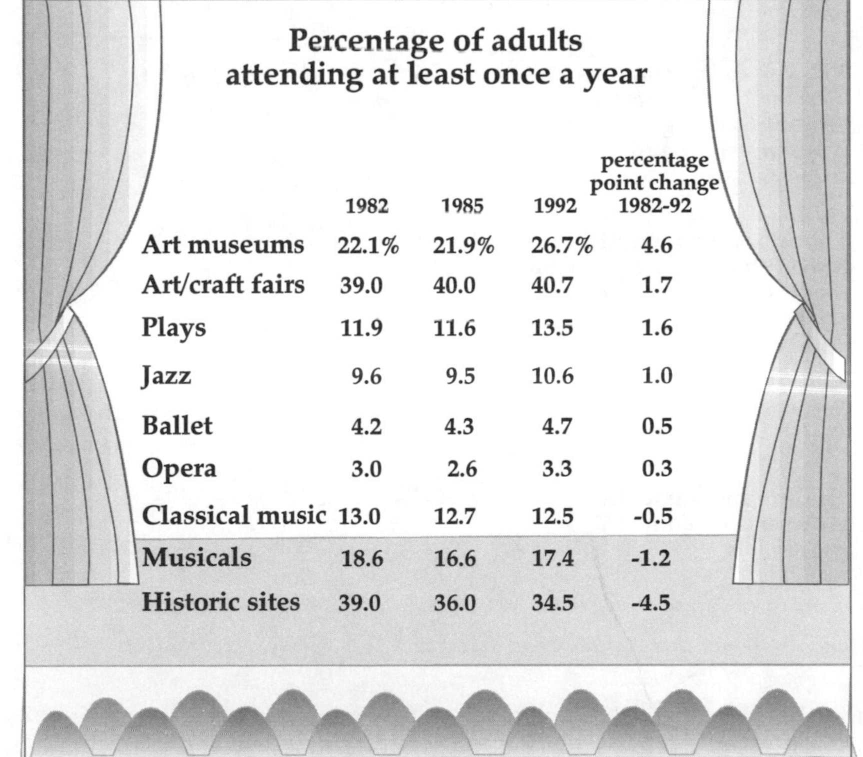

Percentage of adults attending at least once a year

	1982	1985	1992	percentage point change 1982-92
Art museums	22.1%	21.9%	26.7%	4.6
Art/craft fairs	39.0	40.0	40.7	1.7
Plays	11.9	11.6	13.5	1.6
Jazz	9.6	9.5	10.6	1.0
Ballet	4.2	4.3	4.7	0.5
Opera	3.0	2.6	3.3	0.3
Classical music	13.0	12.7	12.5	-0.5
Musicals	18.6	16.6	17.4	-1.2
Historic sites	39.0	36.0	34.5	-4.5

Source: National Endowment for the Arts

How Americans Feel About the Arts

	Strongly Agree	Somewhat Agree	Somewhat Disagree	Strongly Disagree
The arts and humanities are not essential to a healthy American society.	8%	10%	19%	55%
Without public financial support, the arts and humanities would be available only to the wealthy.	31%	28%	16%	16%
The arts and humanities contribute to the economic health and well-being of society.	38%	43%	9%	3%
People have an inborn need to experience the arts and humanities.	42%	36%	9%	4%
In spite of economic hardship, public and private support of the arts and humanities should not be curtailed.	41%	31%	11%	7%
The arts and humanities help me in understanding and appreciating different types of people and cultures.	58%	30%	4%	3%
The arts and humanities provide a form of expression that is essential in a democratic society.	51%	32%	7%	4%
The arts and humanities make my own local community a better place to live.	47%	33%	7%	4%
The arts and humanities represent freedom of expression.	68%	22%	2%	1%

Note: Totals don't necessarily add to 100% because some people expressed no opinion.

Sources: National Cultural Alliance; Research & Forecasts Inc., February 1993

at how something fulfills their corporate goals. Arts education does an excellent job of making the case. There is strong support for large groups and those that draw tourists, but what is falling between the cracks are the small groups, whose art is maybe less accessible, less well-known, maybe controversial."

The controversies "can't help but adversely affect attitudes," says Able, "but it is difficult to determine the degree when there are other factors." He cites the general malaise in the private economy, the drop in interest rates, which affects endowment giving, tax policy modifications and competition for fewer dollars due to government cutbacks, particularly during the past 12 Republican years. "Museums are very fragile," Able adds. "We're experiencing financial challenges we haven't seen before."

Other arts groups point to similar setbacks. A report by the New York-based Theatre Communications Group describes "a financially bleak environment" that has seen 21 local theaters throughout the country close in the past five years. For the first time in five years, city and county grants to theaters decreased, while the budget deficit of the top 67 theaters doubled from $2.5 million to $5 million. [10]

The orchestra league reports that while private support for the nation's 1,600 symphony orchestras grew by 18.5 percent from 1989-93, government support declined by 10 percent. The industry speaks of a "financial crisis" in noting that its annual deficit was $23.2 million in 1991 and is projected to exceed $60 million by the year 2000. [11]

Opera, by contrast, boasted record box office earnings in 1992-93, up 9 percent from the previous year, with total deficits dropping 10 percent and private support outpacing public aid by 5-1.

Private philanthropy, though contributing $9.5 billion to the arts in 1993, actually amounted to 1.22 percent less than the previous year, if inflation is factored in, says the compendium *Giving USA*. What's more, the book noted, "It is crucial to an accurate understanding of arts fund-raising to recognize that acquisitions of art or other property do not contribute to operating revenue. Thus, art institutions may post large gains in contributions without substantial improvement in their ability to meet operating costs." [12]

Because of concerns over obscene art, a fifth of the 140 corporate and foundation grant makers surveyed by the Foundation Center said they would probably award fewer grants to the arts and more to social service programs. Of the arts organizations surveyed, nearly one-fourth said they were engaging in more advocacy and coalition-building with other arts groups. [13]

"In the booming economy of the 1980s, the arts could do no wrong," says Cancel. "That atmosphere doesn't exist now. The controversies have cast a long shadow and form a pincer effect with the recession." With scarcer resources, he adds, funders are likely to "shy away from avant-garde and contemporary artists."

Stephen Butler, director of public affairs for the New York State Arts and Cultural Coalition, says the impact of the controversies is double-edged. "For as many corporations and foundations that would take away money, there are others that have redoubled their efforts to make sure funding is kept up."

"It's a chilling environment," says Ella King Torrey, president of Philadelphia-based Grantmakers for the Arts, a coalition of foundations. "Though private philanthropy is insulated and hasn't been financially affected, having had the previous two administrations so openly hostile to publicly funded art has made it difficult to form private-public partnerships. It becomes hard to work as colleagues."

Politically, says Jarvik of the Center for the Study of Popular Culture, the arts lobby has "alienated its supporters and made mistakes by assuming unanimity around the idea that you have to fund Ron Athey or you can't fund the New York Philharmonic."

But Judith Golub, executive director of the American Arts Alliance, says today's attacks on obscenity may be as virulent as always "but are not picked up by as many people." The anti-NEA amendments by Sen. Helms and others "were voted down consistently by 70 or so votes. The radical right opposition has changed from attacking the arts for obscenity to talking about the budget and the deficit."

Through all the controversy, individual artists haven't toned down their work, says Cancel. "If anything, some artists have recognized that they can gain notoriety by trading on hot-button art. As long as there are living artists, there will be controversy. The true measure of one's success isn't whether it avoids controversy, but whether it is helping to promote the arts."

Helen Brunner, executive director of the National Association of Artists' Organizations, says the controversies have made artists and gallery owners more cautious. "It's extremely exhausting to be attacked and be on the defensive," she says. "The only positive result is that artists and owners are making more of an effort to educate audiences about challenging artwork. There is an ignorance about what the art is. People either demonize artists or put them on a pedestal, when they're actually just struggling human beings like all others."

In the end, Brunner says, efforts to cut the NEA because of controversial art show the need to stand on principle. "There is a reason for the First Amendment," she says. "Once you give the playground bully your lunch money, he will demand your sneakers or coat."

Joan Marcus

Placido Domingo and Victoria Vergera starred in The Washington Opera's 1986 world premier of Gian Carlo Menotti's "Goya."

Rattazzi of the American Arts Federation says the controversies won't go away "because there will always be people who want to take advantage of it for political [gain]. There is no evidence that museum professionals are being more cautious, thank God," she adds. "Given the fact that they have always wanted to serve a larger audience, they pay attention while trying new approaches to education and museumology. But it's all within the normal evolution."

Is improving the education system a good rationale for arts funding?

The link between arts and education was forged during the 1980s, when the current school-reform movements began. In 1987, the NEA published *Toward Civilization,* a report focusing on the history and importance of the arts in education. "The

An Artist's Struggle to Follow Her Dream

There's a saying in the dance profession, observes modern dancer Randi Meares of Arlington, Va.: "If you miss one day of practice, you will notice. If you miss two days, your fellow dancers will notice. And if you miss three days, your audience will notice."

The need for a daily commitment — to avoid losing what Meares calls "muscle memory" — turns the life of a dancer, like that of most artists, into a constant struggle to make ends meet.

Meares, who's in her 30s, spends part of her time in New York City, where she rehearses for road trips with the Doris Humphrey Repertory Dance Co. and earns $225 a week. The remainder she spends in the Washington, D.C., area, where she teaches dance at local colleges and works as a library aide for a publisher.

"If you don't break in with a big company, it's hard to make it," she says. "For every three or four job openings, 500 people show up. And in dance, you get typecast by your height and what you look like in addition to your talent." Meares recently auditioned for a Broadway show produced by Tommy Tune but didn't get the nod. "I was tall enough for what he wanted, but I wasn't enough of the all-American type."

Meares is fortunate that her company's namesake, Doris Humphrey, is a giant of 20th-century dance in a league with the legendary Martha Graham. "Only a few big names really pack the crowds in," she says. "But even the Graham company recently ran out of funds to write checks to its performers."

When times get tough, Meares explains, companies like hers are forced to rehearse without pay, or to give up their professional managers. This means that the same people who dance or choreograph also have to create costumes and do the bookkeeping.

"It's depressing," she says. "There are always bad tempers, and you get exhausted, but if you're also having problems financially, it's that much harder to get out there."

Dancing, Meares notes, is a young discipline that is often recognized more as entertainment than as art. "People who try tap dancing, for example, think it's going to be entertaining, but it's actually much harder," she says. "Still, the more you do it, the easier it gets. The aesthetic look makes it what's called dance, the emotional and movement qualities that go beyond just a motor skill or an athletic exertion."

Like most artists, Meares has firm opinions about publicly funded art. "Should we only be funding math and science?" she asks. "Does that define our culture? In Europe, the funding is there. Most artists just want to get paid something, and they work all day but don't get half of what they need. It comes down to how important the arts are to the country."

Don Jacobsen

"Should we only be funding math and science?" asks Randi Meares. "Does that define our culture?"

Individual communities, she adds, will get back the money they spend on the arts, particularly when dance companies come to rural areas and local schools. "We shouldn't have to count on the economic times, on whether people have the money to go to a show," she says, pointing to cuts in arts programs in public schools and universities and to "decrepit" buildings in which many dancers work. "If we have to continue using makeshift studios, we will never keep a high level of teacher. Funding affects the level of dance," she says. "We're expected to be perfect when we perform, even though we're not well-paid."

Not everyone can be a superstar, but everyone wants to excel in their field, says Meares. With a master's degree in performing arts and some experience in journalism, choral arts and musical theater, she recalls the day in the late 1980s when "I dropped everything in order to dance all day because I didn't want to do anything else with my life." She has since received numerous thumbs-up reviews, developed a personal style and worked her way up in her company from corps member to soloist with a say in selecting repertoire.

In the long-term, Meares may seek a permanent job teaching at a university. "I made the choice to suffer now with the low pay in order to get the experience," she says. "I will have something to show for it."

same tools of thought that an artist needs to paint or sculpt or that a writer needs to write or a musician to compose are those which a scientist needs to discover or a technologist needs to invent," wrote biochemist Robert Root-Bernstein. "But these skills are not taught within any standard scientific or technological curriculum.

Virtually their only source is in the arts and humanities." [14]

The arts-education link was formalized last April, when arts educators became the first in the education community to publish proposed national curriculum standards in accordance with the new federal Goals 2000 legislation. "Arts cultivate a direct experience of the senses; they trust the unmediated flash of insight as a legitimate source of knowledge," the proposed standards say. "Their goal is to connect person and experience directly, to build the bridge between verbal and non-verbal, between the strictly logical and the emotional — the better to gain and understand the whole." [15]

The standards specify which tasks in dance, music, theater and visual arts students should master at each grade level to help them compete with students in other industrialized nations. In visual arts, for example, students in kindergarten through fourth grade should "understand there are different responses to specific artworks," while advanced students of theater in grades 9-12 should be able to "explain and compare the roles and interrelated responsibilities of the various personnel involved in theater, film, television and electronic media productions." [16]

"People unfamiliar with the arts," the standards observe, "often mistakenly believe that excellence and quality are merely matters of opinion ('I know what I like'), and that one opinion is as good as another. The standards give the arts 'academic' standing. They say there is such a thing as achievement, that knowledge and skills matter and that mere willing participation is not the same thing as education." [17]

A smattering of criticism was heard from people who oppose the notion of "world-class" voluntary standards as an intrusion of the federal government or just another education gimmick. *USA Today* columnist Joe Urschel ridiculed the arts standards for adding even more "non-academic distraction" at a time when it should be emphasizing the discipline of math and science. "I have never heard parents say the school system was failing because their kids couldn't dance well enough," he wrote. [18]

"It is wonderful for kids to learn the arts and have standards," says Chester Finn, an assistant Education secretary in the Bush administration, "but I don't know what will happen to the principle by which we will ever say no." Finn, now an executive with Christopher Whittle's Edison Project, points out that the original plan called for standards in only five subjects but was expanded to nine under Clinton. "If every subject gets a standard, eventually the school boards will have to choose," he says, "because we still have to make budget priorities."

John Mahlmann, executive director of the Music Educators National Conference, who headed the arts standards committee, denies that elevating arts education will detract from math and science. "I've met with representatives from Japan, Germany, Great Britain and Australia to discuss our [economic] competitors' programs, and if I were a businessman, I would say that you don't have to choose between one [approach] and the other."

Mahlmann points to the example set by Thomas Jefferson High School for Science and Technology in Alexandria, Va., a public magnet school that produced a record 94 National Merit Scholars last year and "also has the best orchestra and chorus. Education is a logical starting place for the arts," he says. "Education is where everyone goes, so if you're not there, you're missing a pretty big boat."

American Symphony Orchestra League

The Fort Worth Symphony Orchestra has received $48,600 from the NEA for educational concerts and tours to 17 Texas communities in 1994-95.

Analysts of the job market agree. Arnold Packer, an economist with the Institute for Policy Studies at Johns Hopkins University, recently cited several trends that favor arts in education: the disappearance of blue-collar work, the demands for improvements in routine mass production work and the continuing evolution from the industrial age to the information age. All indicate that non-verbal communication techniques are becoming all-important, he says. Multimedia technology and computers will "increase the demand for workers who are knowledgeable in the visual and the performing arts." [19]

Judith Jedlicka, president of the New York City-based Business Committee for the Arts, says, "the education system is broken, and business has decided that it must invest in it. Our last two surveys of giving to the arts show a threefold increase in giving to education." What's more, she adds, "local companies are giving 90 percent of their funding to their local communities."

Arts organizations, for the most part, are pleased. "The Education Department produced aggressive standards, where they could have done lip service," notes Lynch of the assembly of local arts agencies. And the arts community, "where everyone has suffered for so long and for so long has been in competition, is now collaborating," he says. "Arts organizations and education organizations are advising each other."

Others, however, are concerned that more money for arts education means less for the performing arts. "It's wonderful to have new talent and young people who may go on to big things, but there has to be somewhere for them to go," says Meier of the Arts and Business Council. "Hopefully, there will still be someone who's creating. Remember, for every actor who makes it on Broadway, it takes 15 years of nurturing."

Robert Murray, general director of the Shreveport Opera in Louisiana and a former president of the National Opera Association, is enthusiastic about the education push. "There's no future for any business unless you create an audience or customer base. Until opera gets enough years of exposure in schools, it won't be accessible to the man on the street. You don't dilute the quality of a performance for students," he adds. "They're one of the toughest audiences you run into, because they get restless, and they know when something's not working."

Butler of the New York arts coalition says: "No one is unhappy that art is mentioned in Goals 2000. The problem is that it's a small [funding] pie, and there are many hungry people." And that "is a symptom of a much bigger problem of the social agenda at a time when the United States is running a budget deficit."

Laura Loyacono, an arts policy analyst with the National Conference of State Legislatures, says today's "political realities dictate that it is safer for the NEA to play the arts education card. Some sacrifices must be made or we could lose the whole thing," she says, referring to the NEA. "As unreasonable as some of the complaints [about obscenity] are, they have an effect, and they won't go away." ■

BACKGROUND

A Frontier Without Art

In the nation's earliest days, "the American environment was not particularly conducive to art, even at the close of the 18th century, and not many Americans expressed great interest in it," wrote historian Russell Blaine Nye. "The United States possessed very few private collections or galleries, no art schools, no native artistic tradition and no court or aristocracy to provide encouragement or patronage." [20]

Indeed, as Rep. Crane likes to note, the notion that the arts were the province of government was dismissed at the 1787 Constitutional Convention. "Charles Pinckney from South Carolina wanted to fund literature, arts, scientists," Crane writes, "and it was overwhelmingly rejected by those people who crafted our Constitution as not a proper function of the national government." [21]

All the same, Congress in 1790 established the Marine Band, and in 1814 commissioned John Trumbull to paint four Revolutionary War scenes to hang in the Capitol. (Ten years later, Trumbull would lobby President John Quincy Adams, to no avail, to fund a national fine arts effort.)

The American artists who did emerge often lived lives of the desperation described by 19th-century painter Thomas Eakins: "The life of an artist is precarious. I have known very great artists to live their whole lives in poverty and distress, because the people had not the taste and good sense to buy their works." [22]

Help from the New Deal

During the throes of the Great Depression, representatives of President Franklin D. Roosevelt traveled to Mexico, where they were impressed by paintings and murals celebrating the Mexican Revolution being created by government-funded artists. Mexico's approach was embraced by New Deal planners as they sought solutions to record levels of unemployment in the United States among all social classes, including ways to provide "white-collar relief."

In late 1933, Roosevelt aide Edward Bruce developed an aid program designed to give artists "complete liberty to express themselves, with the single provision that their work, in the broadest sense, should be appropriate in design and quality for the adornment of public buildings." In addition to financial security, Bruce noted, the program also "brought to the artist the realization that he was not a solitary worker." [23]

Bruce's plan spawned the Works Progress Administration's arts program. At its peak in 1936, the multifaceted program employed some 40,000 artists. The Federal Art Project hired 5,300 artists to produce murals and oil paintings for schools, libraries and community centers; the Federal Theatre Project generated stage plays, among them Sinclair Lewis' controversial "It Can't Happen Here"; the Federal Writers' Project put hundreds of writers to work on a series of guides for each state; and the Federal Music Project employed 6,600 in bands and orchestras.

"[T]he people of this country know now," Roosevelt declared, "that art is not a treasure in the past or an importation from another land, but part of

Continued on p. 926

Chronology

1930s ***During the Depression, the federal government begins unprecedented direct funding of artists.***

1935
Congress launches Works Progress Administration (WPA) to fund arts.

1938
Newly created House Un-American Activities Committee attacks WPA art as radical.

1950s ***First private arts councils formed.***

1954
Rockefeller Foundation sponsors study of arts councils by American Symphony Orchestra League.

1955
President Dwight D. Eisenhower endorses report recommending a federal commission on the arts within the Health, Education and Welfare Department.

1960s ***Great Society legislation creates agency to dispense arts grants.***

1963
President John F. Kennedy signs executive order creating President's Advisory Council for the Arts.

Sept. 29, 1965
President Lyndon B. Johnson signs bill creating National Endowment for the Arts (NEA) and National Endowment for the Humanities.

1970s ***Some lawmakers angered over sexually explicit poems, books and stage shows with profanity.***

1972
Publication of sexually frank novel *Fear of Flying,* in which author Erica Jong thanks the NEA for a grant, angers newly elected Sen. Jesse Helms, R-N.C.

1975
Business Volunteers for the Arts founded in New York City.

1977
Sen. William Proxmire, D-Wis., gives his "Golden Fleece" award for government waste to artist who used an NEA grant to drop crepe paper from an airplane.

1980s ***Republicans call for cuts in arts funding.***

1981
President Ronald Reagan targets arts for 50 percent cut but a panel he appoints recommends keeping the current system and strengthening federal arts council.

1982
Reagan creates President's Committee on the Arts and Humanities to boost private support for arts.

April 1989
The Rev. Donald Wildmon launches campaign against NEA after museum displays Andres Serrano's photograph of Christ on the cross in a jar of urine.

June 1989
Corcoran Gallery in Washington cancels exhibit of Robert Mapplethorpe's homoerotic photographs.

July 1989
President George Bush appoints John E. Frohnmayer as NEA chairman.

October 1989
Congress passes Helms amendment barring NEA funding of sexually explicit art.

1990s ***NEA controversies continue; Clinton administration launches campaign for the arts***

1990
Artists known as the NEA Four file suit after they are denied NEA grants that had been approved by peer panels; independent commission report on NEA emphasizes importance of arts in education; Congress drops Helms amendment restricting NEA grants.

February 1992
Frohnmayer quits.

June 1992
A Los Angeles judge rules that blocking the NEA Four's grants violates the First Amendment.

October 1993
Clinton appointee Jane Alexander assumes chairmanship of NEA.

April 1994
Arts educators release national standards for arts education.

June 1994
HIV-positive performance artist Ron Athey does controversial show in Minneapolis.

July 25, 1994
Senate cuts NEA budget by 5 percent in response to Athey show; a House-Senate conference later reduces cut to 2 percent.

When It Comes to Public Art . . .

In museums and galleries, art is encountered voluntarily. At public plazas and airports, it reaches out to passersby and demands attention.

Many a public space has been spiffed up with the creative fruits of local artists — often reflecting the latest version of modernism. But to a taxpaying public more partial to conventional heroes on horseback, public art often stirs up outrage and debate.

Still, many public art projects are well-received. Denver's new airport, set to open in February, is proudly offering tours of its $7.5 million collection of new works by 32 artists, including sculptures, floor mosaics and light fixtures that double as direction finders for passengers.

The parking lot of one of the nation's largest shopping centers, Potomac Mills in Woodbridge, Va., outside Washington, boasts a new 20-foot high driftwood sculpture paid for by the Corcoran Gallery of Art and the German government's Goethe Institute.

And on the side of a building on Washington's Connecticut Avenue, a giant mural of actress Marilyn Monroe has become a landmark.

Many public art projects are funded through "percent for art" laws, in force in 31 states and hundreds of localities, which require all construction projects using public funds to earmark some money for art. At first, many public art projects were thrown in as afterthoughts, or "plop art," says Laura Loyacono, who monitors arts issues for the National Conference of State Legislatures. But in recent years, artists and architects have collaborated to integrate the art into building designs.

"The artists view it very favorably, as an important expenditure, but the architects have always resisted," notes Luis R. Cancel, president of the American Council for the Arts and a former commissioner for cultural affairs for New York City.

Even when the works are chosen by independent panels with citizen input, controversy can erupt. In Rhode Island this year, talk radio hosts had a field day ridiculing a plan — kept secret until the last moment — to spend $500,000 for an artist to create a work of art featuring cascading water and a "cloud machine" at the Providence airport. [1]

In Raleigh, N.C., Revenue Department headquarters features a new "non-visual sculpture" exposing visitors to a panoply of recorded sounds ranging from birds

Philipp S. Ritterman

NEA funds supported Alexis Smith's tiled "Snake Path" at the University of California's La Jolla campus.

Continued from p. 924

the present life of all the living and creating peoples." [24]

Birth of the NEA

The years that followed saw numerous attempts to create national arts companies by Sens. Claude Pepper, D-Fla., and Jacob K. Javits, R-N.Y., but they made little headway. Many of the WPA works had drawn criticism for being politically radical or too avant-garde. (President Harry S Truman, in an oft-told story, was shown a WPA painting that later sold for hundreds of thousands of dollars, and commented, "If that is art, I am a Hottentot.")

In the 1950s, art exhibits were frequently attacked and canceled because critics charged that the artists were communists. A commission's proposal to re-establish a federal role in the arts won the backing of President Dwight D. Eisenhower, but Congress declined to act.

It was the administration of President John F. Kennedy that gave birth to modern federal arts policies. The Rockefeller Foundation had commissioned a study recommending a federal grant-making body. Showing his willingness to get involved in the arts, Kennedy sent Labor Secretary Arthur Goldberg to arbitrate a labor dispute at New York's Metropolitan Opera, and he appointed August Heckscher, director of the prestigious 20th Century Fund, as his special adviser on the arts.

"Government," said Kennedy, "can never take over the role of patronage and support filled by private individuals and groups in our society. But government surely has a significant part to play in helping establish the conditions under which art can flourish — in encouraging the arts as it encourages science and learning." [25]

It fell to President Lyndon B. Johnson

. . . the Public Often Fails to See the Art

and thunderstorms to blacksmiths at work. Local columnist Dennis Rogers complained, "For $150,000, you could pay six teachers or police officers for a year instead of buying a tape that offers two minutes and 48 seconds of boiling lard." [2]

The public art movement traces its roots to the John F. Kennedy administration. In 1963, the General Services Administration (GSA) launched an Art in Architecture program to put art into federal buildings. In 1967, the National Endowment for the Arts (NEA) inaugurated its Art in Public Places program. The first two cities to benefit were Grand Rapids, Mich., and Seattle, Wash. By 1973, public arts programs also had been set up in Baltimore, Philadelphia and Honolulu.

By the early 1980s, two famous works of public art were sparking controversies. Architect Maya Lin's design for the Vietnam Memorial in Washington D.C., which lists the 58,000 Americans killed in Vietnam on panels of black granite, was denounced by critics as too bleak. (A statue of three American soldiers by Frederick Hart was added to the site following lobbying led by billionaire H. Ross Perot.)

Richard Serra's steel sculpture "Tilted Arc" also caused waves when it was erected at New York's Federal Plaza in 1981. It prompted thousands of citizens, among them 1,300 employees of the Federal Building, to circulate complaints that the work was a nihilistic and rusted "piece of junk." The government held hearings, and the art world debated it, in one writer's phrase, "as a test case of the 'coming struggle' between reaction and progress, the rabble-rousers and the intelligentsia." [3] In 1989, the work was removed.

Often, public art results from initiatives by the artists. In Brooklyn's Prospect Park, after a Haitian artist clandestinely carved faces in a tree stump, a park administrator spent a year leaving business cards to contact the artist and eventually commissioned another piece. [4] Less fortunate was the Detroit street artist whose two-block-long sculpture made literally of junk was removed by city workers as a health hazard.

"People's taste is all over the map, so you'll never please them all," says Nancy Meier, executive director of the New York-based Arts and Business Council. "And sometimes a work is simply what the CEO of a company says he wants. Many people tend to dislike a work of art when it's first unveiled, but they later get to like it." Maya Lin's memorial, for example, now enjoys widespread acclaim for its emotional impact.

The debate over public art, says Judith Golub, executive director of the Washington-based American Art Alliance, "reflects the power of art, and the fact that people are responding. In a democracy, we can disagree, but does that mean one or two people can stop something from happening?"

"There will always be arguments over whether public art is acceptable," says Stephen Butler, director of public affairs for the New York State Arts and Cultural Coalition. "And it's healthy for society to debate it." Efforts should be made to use peer panels to select artists with proven track records, he says. "But if you are defending something on artistic merit, and it turns out to be offensive to some on sociopolitical grounds, that's not the same argument. Both views might be valid."

[1] See *Governing* magazine, June 1994, p. 9.

[2] Raleigh *News & Observer,* Aug. 29, 1993.

[3] Arlene Raven, *Art in the Public Interest* (1989), p. 281.

[4] *Ibid.*, p. 6.

to sign the 1965 legislation that would create the National Endowment for the Arts. It was not without resistance. Republicans in Congress, and even some artists, warned of the "deadening hand of the federal bureaucracy [[on] the palate, the chisel and the pen" and predicted "attempts at political control of culture." [26]

Differing economic climates produced fundamental differences between the federal arts apparatus of the 1930s and the '60s. "In 1934," observes Michael Straight, the NEA's deputy chairman from 1969-78, "private patrons were impoverished, the private sector of our economy was foundering, artists were unemployed; radical measures were in order. Accordingly, the federal government became a direct and predominant patron of the arts. . . . In 1965, in contrast, private patrons of the arts were prosperous, the private sector of our economy was flourishing, an alliance of conservatives was in effective control of Congress and artists themselves were fearful of government control. The act of 1965, in consequence, is not a populist measure." [27]

Straight recalls how at the bill-signing ceremony the ambitious Johnson "announced to the startled crowd assembled in the Rose Garden of the White House that the endowment would establish a national theater, a national ballet company, a national opera company and an American film institute. It would commission new symphonies. It would create residencies for 'great artists' in our schools and colleges."

Of all these grand visions, only the American Film Institute became reality. Still, the NEA, with its modest first budget of $4.5 million, was up and running. Vice President Hubert H. Humphrey awarded the first grant ($100,000) to the private American Ballet Theater. By awarding most of its funds to states and institutions, and only 5 percent to individual artists, the NEA hoped to spawn replicas of itself at the state level.

Along the way, the agency's beneficiaries expanded from the classical arts to include folk art, literature, design arts, international programs, radio, television and special programs for rural and ethnic neighborhoods. For the most part, however, NEA remained a small, little-noticed agency until 1989, when politicians and other critics began decrying its role in funding controversial exhibitions, such as photographs showing a figure of Christ in a jar of urine and gay sex acts. ■

CURRENT SITUATION

Art and AIDS

Accounts of a controversial performance last June at the Walker Art Center in Minneapolis reverberated back to Washington and affected arts funding. The Walker, a recent recipient of $104,500 in NEA money, had given its stage over for one night to performance artist Ron Athey. After the audience had been warned of the show's controversial nature, Athey, who is HIV-positive, used needles to cut into the bare back of a fellow performer. He then wiped a line of blood on a paper towel and hoisted it over the audience on a clothesline. Several members of the 100-member audience apparently were upset at a perceived risk of exposure to AIDS and walked out. Angry letters followed in the Minneapolis newspapers.

In Congress, Sen. Robert C. Byrd, D-W.Va., chairman of the Appropriations Committee, wrote to NEA Chairman Alexander saying, "We expect you to ensure that NEA funding in the future does not put the public at health risk." He called for a 5 percent cut in the NEA's budget, targeted directly at grants to controversial art. Rep. Robert K. Dornan, R-Calif., who called the Minneapolis performance "nuts," said, "Most people here [in Congress] are terrified of the homosexual lobby, but some of us are not."

Walker officials argued that the performance had been conducted according to health guidelines from the Centers for Disease Control and Prevention and estimated that Athey's performance involved less than $150 of NEA money. Alexander defended Athey's show as "a disturbing but important contemporary subject." [28] Athey's fellow performer, in fact, had not been HIV-positive.

Helms, during floor debate on the Athey performance, said: "I asked [Alexander] if just one cockroach in a pot of soup would be too many. The dear lady sort of avoided the question. . . . But how about the human cockroaches who have repeatedly bullied their way into the pocketbooks of Americans who pay taxes to provide the money for the National Endowment for the Arts to hand out?"

Though a House-Senate conference reduced Byrd's proposal to a 2 percent cut ($3.4 million), [29] the punitive cutback was a blow to arts advocates such as Brunner of the National Association of Artists' Organizations. "This is [art] that's breaking new ground," she says. "Some people may not like the subject, but it is society that creates the context for the image. The artist just holds up a mirror."

Local Funding Outlook

In the states and localities, meanwhile, the arts are facing a mixed financial picture. Twenty-five of the 56 states and territories cut arts appropriations in fiscal 1994, according to the National Assembly of State Arts Agencies, with cuts of more than 15 percent enacted by legislatures in Louisiana, Alabama, Hawaii, Oregon and Washington. Increases of more than 15 percent were enacted in Florida, Kansas, Maryland, Michigan, Minnesota, North Carolina, Ohio, Tennessee and the Northern Mariana Islands. *

In Colorado, this November's ballot will give citizens a chance to reaffirm or withdraw support for a sales tax to support the arts enacted in 1988. Covering the six counties around Denver, it produces an estimated $17 million a year that is shared by 200 nonprofit arts groups. It was passed after a five-year effort by arts groups responding to a cutoff in state arts appropriations.

"In the 1980s, when state spending was rising, the trend was to rely on an appropriation for state arts councils because tax revenues were down," says Loyacono of the National Conference of State Legislatures. "Nowadays, the trend is [to rely on taxes] because state revenues are up, and there are fewer new appropriations." Other states are funding the arts through lotteries, hotel taxes, video rental taxes, or admissions taxes on cultural or sporting events.

In New York City, arts enthusiasts were pleased last February when the city's opera-loving new mayor, Republican Rudolph W. Giuliani, announced a plan to largely spare the arts from his wide-ranging budget cuts. The mayor said he would restore the nearly $4.2 million he cut from the city's share of local arts funding, and add even more money, if the city's cultural institutions raised matching contributions from private sources.

Though grateful, some in the arts were skeptical that matching funds would materialize. "It will encourage shifting within arts organizations from one program to another, and to a certain extent among funders from one organization to another," said Norma Munn, chairwoman of the New York City Arts Coalition. "No one will be able to verify what the level of increase is." [30]

Continued on p. 930

* The three states with the biggest appropriation increases were Florida, Tennessee and Minnesota; the three with the largest cuts were Washington, Oregon and Louisiana.

At Issue:

Is the National Endowment for the Arts making a good case for arts funding?

yes

AMY E. SCHWARTZ
Editorial writer, The Washington Post

FROM *THE WASHINGTON POST,* MARCH 11, 1994

Sometimes the best freshener for a worn-out debate is an abrupt change of context. Giving the National Endowment for the Arts a new context has been the main goal of Chairman Jane Alexander as she dashes from state to state and from conference to convention, describing the way support for the arts can benefit the economy, tourism and education, bring dying communities back to life and avert the spread of violence. There may still be people out there who want to talk about two photographers who got grants five years ago, but Alexander, for one is not going to oblige them by providing a conversational vacuum. . . .

On the trail, Alexander's story line is simple. She talks about the huge amount of money the arts can generate in jobs, community rebuilding and tourism — conveniently broken down when possible by congressional district — and the dramatic way the arts enrich, in particular, children's lives. Talking about drugs and violence at a recent panel, she reminded an audience that helping kids resist drugs requires giving them "something they can say yes to." Arts education, she argues . . . gives kids one fewer reason to "pick up a needle or a gun." It also feeds back into bigger future audiences and yet more economic benefits. . . .

To arts education audiences, she sprinkles her speeches with irresistible anecdotes picked up on the road, like the one about the children in Mississippi who held onto the legs of a visiting dance troupe and wouldn't let them leave. . . . To the travel people, she described the dramatic way European cities have increased the yield of tourism by factoring in cultural events.

It's talk, of course, and between trips such talk must yield to more chewy, and still sticky, parts of the agenda-like cutting the budget or dealing with some of the more substantive of the persistent partisan complaints from outside. . . . But then the arts themselves are perhaps best understood as a form of heightened and high-quality talk, an endless series of crystallized entries in the conversation about who we are and what's going on. Either your ear is inclined to that stream of talk, old and new, or it isn't; and if it isn't, there's always the danger that opportunistic rhetoric will tempt you to be the NEA's reflexive enemy. But when the stream of talk laps at your school or your district, you're a lot more likely to listen if the NEA chairman has been through town lately to bathe it in a demonstration of what's engrossing and worth funding about the arts.

no

LAURENCE JARVIK
Director, Center for the Study of Popular Culture, Washington Office

Jane Alexander's sales pitch, repeated no doubt with regional variations as she travels to towns in key congressional districts, is that support for the NEA will help the economy, aid tourism, improve education, resurrect dying neighborhoods and stop violence. Step right up and buy a case! Jane Alexander is selling the NEA as a good tonic for what ails America. . . .

Of course, one can always cite an occasional case of an individual whose life was turned around by the "magic" of the arts, just as some people swear by the effectiveness of snake oil. But these are the exceptions, not the rule. Art may in fact be indispensable for civilization, but it is dangerous to present the panacea of "the arts" as a substitute for family, religion, hard work, thrift, educational discipline, sound economic investments or swift and sure criminal justice.

Alexander says the arts create business, and so help create jobs. But does support for the arts really benefit the economy, as Alexander testifies? Obviously not. If it were so, why would the center of the American "arts community" be found in New York, a crumbling ruin of a city on the brink of financial collapse, whose industries and population shrink daily? Have the millions of dollars the NEA, New York City and New York State spent on the arts brought Harlem, the South Bronx and Bedford-Stuyvesant "back to life?" No. Have the NEA dollars poured into the District of Columbia stopped the exodus of some 200,000 residents over the last 30 years, improved the District's business climate, or helped balance the budget? Of course not.

Do the arts really help kids stay off drugs, as Alexander asserts? Has Alexander read ballet dancer Gelsey Kirkland's story, *Dancing on My Grave?* Have the drug addictions of actor River Phoenix and musician Charlie Parker, or Jean Michel Basquiat's $1,000-dollar-a-day heroin habit been forgotten so quickly? . . .

Does arts education really keep kids from violence? Have the arts helped "avert the spread of violence" in New York City, the NEA's largest beneficiary? How does the violent crime rate around New York's Times Square . . . compare [with] that on the cattle ranges of rural Montana, far from any major cultural institution?. . .

When Alexander recently visited schoolchildren in Richmond, Va., they greeted her singing the Munchkin chorus from "The Wizard of Oz." It must have been a charming photo op, and a punchy sound bite, although clearly the children did not intend to remind Alexander of the tragic fate of Judy Garland, yet another drug victim in the arts. Nor, evidently, did they succeed in doing so.

Eddie J. Shellman is a principal dancer with the Dance Theatre of Harlem, which received $325,000 from the NEA in fiscal 1994 for its professional school, dance company and community outreach program.

Continued from p. 928

New York's arts community was thrown into another funding quandary recently when the City Council considered a bill to outlaw smoking in public places. The Philip Morris Co. was among those scrambling to head off the ban, and it wanted help from arts organizations. For more than 35 years, the New York-based tobacco giant has supported the arts enough to earn a reputation as the nation's "corporate Medici."

Officials at such Philip Morris beneficiaries as the Metropolitan Museum of Art, the Brooklyn Academy of Music and the International Center of Photography were put in the uncomfortable position of receiving pointed phone calls from the company alerting them to the proposed ban. And virtually none of the groups could afford the luxury of turning down the tobacco money. As a New York dance company spokesman confessed, "I don't smoke and I hate people smoking, but Philip Morris is a great supporter. I say thank God for sinners; they're the only people to support the arts." [31]

Local funding for the arts continues to be buffeted by controversial art. Cobb County, Ga., made national news last year when the County Council passed a resolution condemning homosexuality and eliminating the county's $110,000 arts budget. (Marietta is the major city in Cobb County.) The move followed citizen complaints about references to gays in a play at the county's Theater in the Square. Council members were tired of the gay agenda being "crammed down our throats," said the resolution's sponsor, Gordon Wysong, and didn't want to confront the tricky issue of deciding which arts are offensive. "It's about redefining government's role," he said. "You can't make these kinds of decisions for the arts . . . so we got out." [32]

Arts groups staged protest rallies but so far have had no effect. "This is a true embarrassment, because I know most of my friends don't feel this way," said actress Suzi Bass, who moved to the county 15 years ago. "You will find that Cobb contains loving and giving . . . sensitive people." [33] ■

OUTLOOK

Rethinking the NEA

The next few years will bring proposals for new federal arts policies. Clinton has asked the President's Committee on the Arts and Humanities to issue a report next year on critical issues in the nation's cultural life. Meanwhile, the NEA is drafting a five-year plan for approaching the turn of the millennium.

The museum association's Able would like the government to "reexamine the whole issue of financing, to consider creating a true endowment, not just an annual appropriation, to stabilize the NEA's finances." It could be paid for perhaps through a small tax on publishing, recordings or movies, he says, "or a direct appropriation not subject to ebb and flow, whim and fancy."

Arts consultant Joseph Wesley Zeigler, author of the new book *Arts in Crisis: The National Endowment for the Arts versus America*, has examined several proposals to revamp the NEA, including some that recommend shifting all NEA money to the states. That, he points out, would reduce any scandals over controversial art to local affairs but would deny the NEA its role as national arts leader.

Other proposals would concentrate NEA money on supporting individual artists rather than institutions, but Zeigler points out that the NEA's current budget would fund less than 1 percent of the country's artists. He rejects as politically unrealistic a proposal to require the estates of wealthy artists such as Andy Warhol and Mapplethorpe to help start an endowment for other artists.

"The NEA has gotten into trouble by being too active," Zeigler writes. "The future may rest in finding ways to be creatively and dynamically passive, to fund the arts by doing as little as possible." [34] This might mean providing automatic NEA grants to institutions based on what money they raise from other sources. Alternatively, he would propose allowing individual taxpayers to take an extra 10 percent tax deduction on donations to arts institutions, which would replace the annual NEA funding bill.

Another idea being floated is to reform copyright laws so that visual artists could profit more from the resale of their work. "There's funding in the art world, but artists don't have access to it," says artist George Koch, president of the Washington-based National Artists Equity Fund. He argues that the United States is one of the few countries not to give its artists more long-term rights to proceeds from their works. "You give us our rights and let the marketplace decide, and the NEA wouldn't have to exist," he says.

The Political Right

Across the political spectrum, there is agreement that controversies over art, like funding shortages, will endure. "Michelangelo, one of the great, great, artists in the history of the world, was criticized by Pope Julius II about his work on the Sistine Chapel," Rep. Sidney R. Yates, D-Ill., said in June on the House floor. "And he had to change it. His heavenly and beautiful sculpture of David was criticized by the church because he had failed to place a fig leaf at an appropriate place. The fact is, artists have always rebelled against the academicians because the academicians required little deviation from their established norms."

Though protests against controversial art are a mainstay of the political right, this year's cut in NEA funds was clearly the work of Democratic Sen. Byrd. The party lines became especially murky during the tenure of John Frohnmayer as NEA chief from 1989-92. A longtime Republican, he was fired by President Bush, he says, to stave off attacks on Bush from the presidential campaign of conservative Patrick J. Buchanan. Frohnmayer's memoirs show his political evolution. "What I found . . . was that the Democrats typically played straight with me. It was some of the Republicans who were devious, self-serving and hostile." [35]

Alexander has declined to pressure artists to tone down work that some find offensive. In her October press club speech, she said that during her travels, "it is unusual to receive more than one question about [the controversies]. That's because Tucson, Ariz., or Jackson, Miss., are not terribly concerned with what happens in Minneapolis. Overall, our critics tend to be well-organized, to disseminate misinformation and distortion about a few of our grantees, and the media feeds on it."

Forging a national consensus in favor of the arts, says Lynch of the assembly of local arts agencies, can be done if "Alexander and the rest of the arts community can continue to focus on the positive and not get tricked into focusing on a few controversial grants, which we can't win on."

The political right, notes Able, "have found NEA-bashing a great bully pulpit for their own agenda. I question whether they have any substantive interest in the work of the NEA. Maybe they will find another horse to ride."

"Politically motivated attacks have little to do with real issues of arts in society," says Torrey of Grantmakers for the Arts. "If cutting the federal budget were the issue, they would go after far more lucrative agencies."

To the argument that controversial grants are a small fraction of the NEA's work, the Rev. Wildmon has a ready reply. "If it is a tiny part, then there should be no big problem getting rid of it," he says. As for the charge that groups such as his American Family Association use NEA scandals as a bully pulpit and fund-raiser, he says: "If that's true, then [his opponents] can kill two birds with one stone by cutting off the funding for bad art and put our group out of business."

Ongoing Advocacy

Arts advocates are fond of quoting President John Adams, who wrote

For More Information

American Arts Alliance, 1319 F St. N.W., Suite 500, Washington, D.C., 20004; (202) 737-1727. This coalition represents 2,600 nonprofit visual and performing arts organizations, including theaters, orchestras, art museums and dance and opera companies. It monitors legislation affecting federal arts funding.

American Council for the Arts, One East 53rd St., New York, N.Y., 10022; (212-223-ARTS). This group of corporate, civic and arts leaders organizes conferences, publishes books and engages in policy debates to support the contributions of art and artists to American life.

Center for the Study of Popular Culture, 1155 15th St. N.W., Suite 712, Washington, D.C., 20005; (202) 223-3081. This group of conservative art and media analysts publishes criticism and testifies against strong government involvement in cultural affairs.

National Endowment for the Arts, 1100 Pennsylvania Ave. N.W., 20506; (202) 682-5442. The NEA is a federal agency that awards grants to individual artists and to institutions for training museum professionals, conserving and preserving museum collections and developing arts-related educational programs.

to his wife that he must study politics and war so that his grandchildren may study and enjoy the arts. [36]

But two centuries later, the politics and the wars persist. The same people who were delighted to see the arts elevated to core curriculum status also bemoan the cuts in art and music programs that education districts have seen in places such as Baltimore, Md., and Alexandria, Va.

In New York City, the number of music educators and assistant principals concentrating on music are only one-fourth the number they were 20 years ago. "The opportunity to play a trumpet or sing a choral piece in harmony with other wonderful young people as they lift their voices in song has been withheld from most of this generation of students," the Music Educators Association of New York City told Education Chancellor Ramon Cortines in an October letter.

Uncertainties about funding, though a constant in the arts world, extract their toll. "Each year that funding shrinks, expectations shrink as well," Alberta Sebolt George, president of Old Sturbridge Village, a popular Massachusetts tourist attraction, told lawmakers in May. "Museums that have invested the time in applying and that have been turned down, not from any problems with the application but simply from lack of funds, decide it is not worthwhile to apply again." [37]

A bright spot on the horizon is the continued business interest in the arts. "Those companies that have been in it for long time, like Philip Morris, Mobil and AT&T, will continue," says Jedlicka. "I am also optimistic that small and medium companies, which by 2000 will employ most Americans, are now jumping in and making major contributions."

Steven D. Gold, a former director of fiscal studies at the National Conference of State Legislatures, has written that "the best way to foster adequate funding of the arts is to have a strong state and local tax system. An anorexic tax system tends to starve all spending purposes, including the arts." [38]

Indeed, a strategy paper prepared by the National Assembly of State Arts Agencies recommends that agencies seek a revenue source for which no other agency has a claim. "The need for ongoing advocacy to maintain a state's commitment to support the arts as a function of good government never diminishes," it said, "regardless of the state's revenue mix." [39]

"We know the arts will never be at that first tier of things government funds," says Loyacano. "Arts are not a social services entitlement or life and death. We will always have to be creative in order to fund them, because when times get tough, they're always the first thing to go." ■

Notes

[1] Riley spoke March 17, 1993, at a meeting of the American Council for the Arts, in Washington. For background, see "Education Standards," *The CQ Researcher,* March 11, 1994, pp. 217-240.

[2] *American Demographics,* February 1994, p. 9.

[3] Rep. Philip M. Crane, Op-Ed article, *Los Angeles Times,* Aug. 9, 1994.

[4] "Local Arts Agency Facts 1994," p. 7.

[5] "Jobs, the Arts and the Economy," National Assembly of Local Arts Agencies, January 1994.

[6] *Why We Need the Arts: 8 Quotable Speeches by Leaders in Education, Government, Business and the Arts* (1988), p. 2.

[7] See National Endowment for the Arts, *Arts in America: A Report to the President and to Congress,* 1992.

[8] Letter reprinted in the *Congressional Record,* June 22, 1994, p. H4846.

[9] People for the American Way, "Artistic Freedom Under Attack," Vol. 2, 1994.

[10] Barbara Janowitz, Theatre Communications Group, "Theatre Facts '93."

[11] Wolf Organization Inc., "The Financial Condition of Symphony Orchestras," June 1992.

[12] AAFRC Trust for Philanthropy, *Giving USA 1994,* p. 109.

[13] Nathan Weber and Loren Renz, "Arts Funding: A Report on Foundation and Corporate Grantmaking Trends," Foundation Center (1993), p. 114.

[14] Cited in *Why We Need the Arts, op. cit.,* p. 95.

[15] Consortium of National Arts Education Associations, "National Standards for Arts Education," 1994, p. 6.

[16] *Ibid.,* pp. 34 and 65.

[17] *Ibid.,* p. 15.

[18] "Fixing Education: Why Johnny Can't Dance," *USA Today,* March 15, 1994.

[19] Arnold Packer, "Meeting the Arts Standards and Preparing for Work in the 21st Century," paper prepared for a conference of the American Council for the Arts, September 1994.

[20] Russell Blaine Nye, *The Cultural Life of the New Nation, 1776-1830* (1960), p. 277.

[21] Crane, *op. cit.*

[22] Michael Straight, *Nancy Hanks: An Intimate Portrait* (1988), p. 92.

[23] William F. McDonald, *Federal Relief Administration and the Arts* (1969), p. 363.

[24] *Why We Need the Arts, op. cit.,* p. 48.

[25] See "Tying Down Federal Funds for the Arts," *Editorial Research Reports,* May 25, 1990, pp. 301-315.

[26] *1965 CQ Almanac,* p. 626.

[27] Straight, *op. cit.,* p. 96.

[28] Quoted in *Newsweek,* July 25, 1994. p. 52.

[29] *CQ Weekly Report,* Sept. 24, 1994, p. 2678.

[30] Quoted in *The New York Times,* Sept. 13, 1994.

[31] Quoted in *The New York Times,* Oct. 5, 1994.

[32] Quoted in *The New York Times,* Aug. 26, 1993.

[33] Quoted in *The New York Times,* Aug. 29, 1993.

[34] Joseph Wesley Zeigler, "Striving for Positive Passivity: Ideas for a Future NEA," *Journal of Arts Management, Law and Society,* spring 1994, p. 67.

[35] John Frohnmayer, *Leaving Town Alive: Confessions of an Arts Warrior* (1993), p. 55.

[36] Straight, *op. cit.,* p. 91.

[37] Testimony on behalf of the American Association of Museums before the House Appropriations Interior Subcommittee, May 9, 1994.

[38] Steven D. Gold, "Magic Formulas for Funding the Arts: Is There Any Hope?" Paper presented at NCSL annual meeting, Aug. 9, 1989.

[39] National Assembly of State Arts Agencies, "Supplemental Funding Strategies of State and Jurisdictional Arts Agencies," June 1993.

Bibliography

Selected Sources Used

Books

Frohnmayer, John, *Leaving Town Alive: Confessions of an Arts Warrior,* Houghton Miflin, 1993.

The Bush administration's chairman of the National Endowment for the Arts (NEA) has written a memoir of his stormy tenure, during which numerous controversies erupted over government-funded art. Attacks from the political right eventually forced him out of his job.

McDonald, William F., *Federal Relief Administration and the Arts: The Origins and Administrative History of the Arts Projects of the Works Progress Administration,* Ohio State University Press, 1969.

This 800-page compendium funded by the Rockefeller Foundation describes the inauguration and conduct of the Depression-era federal program that from 1933-39 "supported and subsidized an arts program that in material size and cultural character was unprecedented in this history of this or any other nation."

Raven, Arlene, *Art in the Public Interest,* UMI Research Press, 1989.

An art historian who writes for *The Village Voice* and a variety of art publications assembled this anthology of essays detailing the history and controversies surrounding the three-decade-old movement for art in public places.

Straight, Michael, *Nancy Hanks: An Intimate Portrait; The Creation of a National Commitment to the Arts,* Duke University Press, 1988.

The deputy chairman of the NEA from 1969-72 wrote this biography of his close colleague, the major force behind federal arts policy in its early years and the woman for whom the NEA building is named.

***Why We Need the Arts: 8 Quotable Speeches by Leaders in Education, Government, Business and the Arts,* American Council for the Arts, 1988.**

This compilation from a national arts convention sponsored by the New Jersey State Council on the Arts and the American Arts Council offers rhetorical support for the importance of the arts from such luminaries as playwright Edward Albee, education scholar Ernest Boyer and former congressman and New York University President John Brademas.

Reports and Studies

"Arts Funding: The Changing Environment," *Journal of Arts Management, Law and Society,* Vol. 24, No. 1, spring 1994.

The articles, commentary and book reviews in this issue of a quarterly devoted to the performing, visual and media arts provide an overview of the history of art funding as well as proposals for revamping the NEA.

Consortium of National Arts Education Associations, *Dance, Music, Theatre, Visual Arts: What Every Young American Should Know and Be Able to Do in the Arts,* 1994.

A nationwide group of arts educators last April became the first of nine academic advisory committees to release proposed voluntary education standards in accordance with the federal Goals 2000 legislation. The standards are organized by grade and by arts discipline.

National Assembly of State Arts Agencies, *Supplemental Funding Strategies of State and Jurisdictional Arts Agencies,* June 1993.

An advocacy group for the arts examines funding strategies used in the various states and territories, including endowment funds, bond issues, income tax checkoffs, special fees and state lotteries.

National Endowment for the Arts, *Annual Report,* 1992.

This lavishly illustrated 367-page compilation explains the NEA's mission and structure and lists recent grants by subject and recipient.

Weber, Nathan, and Loren Renz, *Arts Funding: A Report on Foundation and Corporate Grantmaking Trends,* Foundation Center, 1993.

This study by a group devoted to collecting data on foundation and corporate philanthropy evaluates trends in giving to the arts, mainly during the 1980s, and includes opinion surveys of donors and recipients.

The Next Step

Additional information from UMI's Newspaper & Periodical Abstracts database

Federal Policy and Funding Issues

Crane, Philip M., "It's curtains for federal arts funding," *Los Angeles Times,* Aug. 9, 1994, p. B7.

Crane explains his objection to the existence of the National Endowment for the Arts, saying it is not a constitutionally defensible responsibility of the federal government. Crane says the $171.1 million of taxpayer money for the agency could be replaced by the private sector.

Fitzpatrick, James F., "Decency clause still haunts the NEA," *American Theater,* November 1993, pp. 56-57.

Most attempts to impose content restrictions on federal funding in the arts have been beaten back in Congress, with the exception of the "decency clause" that provides that grant applications to the National Endowment for the Arts are to be judged "taking in consideration general standards of decency and respect for the diverse beliefs of the American public." This standard and legal challenges to it are discussed.

Kester, Grant H., "After the culture wars: Is there a future for public funding of the arts?" *Afterimage,* January 1994, pp. 2-4.

In November 1993, the Eastman School of Music in Rochester, N.Y., played host to leading figures from politics and the arts who came together to discuss the future of public arts funding. The conference included a symposium entitled "Federal Funding for the Arts: Is the NEA the best approach."

Plagens, Peter, "Act two, scene one," *Newsweek,* July 25, 1994, p. 52.

Actress Jane Alexander is facing cuts as chairman of the National Endowment for the Arts (NEA). A 5 percent cut in the NEA's $170 million budget that the Senate will consider in July 1994 is discussed.

Sabrin, Amy, "Thinking about content: Can it play an appropriate role in government funding of the arts?" *Yale Law Journal,* March 1993, pp. 1209-1233.

Both sides of the debate over government funding of the arts collide on the issue of First Amendment free speech rights, differing on whether the government can censor artistic content while paying for its production. It is argued that opponents and proponents of content-based criteria must first agree on what they mean by "content."

Urschel, Joe, "The gross art of federal spending," *USA Today,* June 24, 1994, p. A11.

Urschel comments sarcastically on the fact that Congress continues to fund the National Endowment for the Arts, which continues to provide grants for controversial art.

Zuckman, Jill, "National endowments renewed as opponents are thwarted," *Congressional Quarterly Weekly Report,* Oct. 16, 1993, p. 2818.

On Oct. 14, 1993, the National Endowment for the Arts (NEA) once again withstood conservative assaults aimed at slashing its budget or abolishing the agency outright. The bill to reauthorize the NEA is discussed.

Gays and Arts Funding

Bull, Chris, "Shot through the art," *Advocate: The National Gay & Lesbian Newsmagazine,* Oct. 5, 1993, pp. 42-45.

The controversy over funding of gay-themed art is heating up once again. The Cobb County, Ga., commission voted to cease all arts-related funding for fear of inadvertently subsidizing gay-themed works, Bull writes. Meanwhile, the NEA is reversing many of its more conservative policies.

Deitcher, David, "The Gay Agenda," *Art in America,* April 1994, pp. 27-35.

In an ongoing battle over public arts funding mounted by fundamentalist religious groups, the gay community of Cobb County, Ga., a conservative suburb of Atlanta, has become the focus of sophisticated right-wing hate propaganda. Cobb County's anti-gay "community standards" campaign is discussed.

"Georgia: The colour of money," *The Economist,* Sept. 25, 1993, p. 34.

Cobb County, Ga., has become the first county government in the U.S. to condemn the homosexual lifestyle. The county has become a rallying point for protesters on both sides of the homosexual issue, and arts funding in Cobb County has suffered.

Kaplan, Paul, "Theatre in the Square staying in Cobb," *Atlanta Journal Constitution,* April 17, 1994, p. H2.

The Theatre in the Square in Marietta, Ga., lost its annual $40,000 Cobb County grant in 1993 after a reference to homosexuality in its production of "Lips Together, Teeth Apart" ignited an arts controversy and the County Commission passed a resolution opposing the "gay lifestyle." Theatre officials have decided to stay in the town, however, because after Cobb pulled its funding, art patrons and corporations contributed $115,000 to the group.

National Endowment for the Arts

Cembalest, Robin, "NEA grants: 'Smaller or fewer'," *ARTnews,* March 1994, p. 40.

Congressional cutbacks have hit the National Endowment for the Arts (NEA) hard. The agency was forced to eliminate two categories and reduce funding for 17 others after a $4.2 million budget cut.

Dorf, Michael C, "Artifactions: The battle over the National Endowment for the Arts," ***Brookings Review,*** **winter 1993, pp. 32-35.**
Government funding for the arts can be controversial when legitimate questions are posed by reasonable people. However, compromise becomes impossible when viewpoints are transformed into moral opinion, Dorf writes. The National Endowment for the Arts is discussed.

Gannon, James P, "There's a solution for equitable arts funding: None for all, and all can pay," ***Detroit News & Free Press,*** **July 3, 1994, p. B1.**
James P. Gannon comments on the latest attack on "art" funded by the National Endowment for the Arts, a performance by HIV-positive artist Ron Athey and suggests that the NEA should be abolished.

Grimes, William, "U.S. arts endowment makes a new batch of grants," ***The New York Times,*** **July 25, 1994, p. C14.**
The National Endowment for the Arts has announced $31.5 million in grants for the third quarter of 1994. The 1,127 grants will go to arts organizations and a scattering of individual artists in all 50 states, the District of Columbia, Puerto Rico, the Virgin Islands and American Samoa.

Grundberg, Andy, "An insider's look at how NEA awards its grants," ***Los Angeles Times,*** **Aug. 17, 1994, p. F1.**
Grundberg, chair of the photography panel that recommended National Endowment for the Arts grants, discusses how the awards were granted and the current state of affairs at the endowment.

"NEA 1993 Media Arts Centers grants," ***Afterimage,*** **March 1993, p. 15.**
A list of the NEA's 1993 grant recommendations in the Media Arts Centers category is presented. A total of 83 grants were recommended totaling $1.8 million.

"The Talk of the Town: NEA Monkey Business," ***New Yorker,*** **Aug. 22, 1994, pp. 45-46.**
A flap over NEA funding of writer-director David O. Russell's debut feature film, "Spanking the Monkey," is detailed. The NEA gave Russell $20,000 but is demanding its money back.

Trescott, Jacqueline, "NEA awards $78 million: Arts grants go to both tried-and-true and controversial," ***The Washington Post,*** **May 16, 1994, p. B1.**
The first batch of National Endowment for the Arts grants approved by Chairman Jane Alexander May 16, 1994, shows that she is true to her word about the agency continuing to support established, albeit struggling, institutions, but not shying away from controversy either, Trescott writes.

Trescott, Jacqueline, "NEA balks at funding Serrano," ***The Washington Post,*** **Aug. 6, 1994, p. C1.**
The National Council on the Arts, the advisory arm of the National Endowment for the Arts, turned down photographer Andres C. Serrano's application for a fellowship. Ever since "Piss Christ" in 1986, a photograph of the crucifix in a jar of urine, Serrano's name, along with Robert Mapplethorpe, has been a rallying cry for opponents of the NEA.

Walker, Sam, "Jane Alexander works to recast NEA image," ***Christian Science Monitor,*** **Jan. 21, 1994, p. 16.**
Actress Jane Alexander is profiled about her new position as chairwoman of the National Endowment for the Arts, focusing on the difficult budget cuts she has had to make.

Opinions and Editorials

"Byrd as MacBeth," ***Houston Chronicle,*** **Aug. 2, 1994, p. A20.**
An editorial expresses disappointment that Sen. Robert Byrd, D-W.V., was successful in his efforts to have the National Endowment for the Arts cut its 1995 budget by 5 percent because Byrd took strong exception to a performance-art piece by an AIDS-infected artist.

Kilian, Michael, "Byrd's nest," ***Chicago Tribune,*** **Aug. 4, 1994, p. 6.**
The author comments on the controversy surrounding the National Endowment for the Arts and the efforts by some congressmen to do away with it, especially after it was discovered that $150 of the NEA's money was used to fund a "performance art" piece by HIV-positive artist Ron Athey.

"The Offensive Art of Grandstanding," ***Atlanta Constitution,*** **July 15, 1994, p. A14.**
An editorial says if Congress passes cuts in the National Endowment for the Arts grants that fund groups such as Atlanta's Woodruff Arts Center and Seven Stages, among others, then it should also cut the defense budget by 5 percent so it cannot provide soldiers with *Playboy.*

Rich, Frank, "Trail of lies," ***The New York Times,*** **July 17, 1994, p. 17.**
Rich comments on the peril the National Endowment for the Arts is in due to wildly exaggerated accounts of a performance by Ron Athey, who uses ritual tattooing as part of his autobiographical art.

School Programs

Rohner, James T., "Elusive excellence," ***Instrumentalist,*** **April 1994, p. 2.**
It seems that the more money is spent in pursuit of educational excellence, the more elusive it becomes, Rohner writes. Although government spending on education increased 70 percent from 1970 to 1992, several noticeable trends emerged, including a decline in the amount of money for school music programs.

Zimmer, Elizabeth, "Meditations in an emergency," ***Village Voice,*** **June 14, 1994, p. 16.**
Arts programs in the public schools offer kids encounters with every art form, and provide potential for budding artists to explore their talents. Zimmer says that New York City Mayor Giuliani's budget cuts will cripple the Department of Youth Services, which will lose up to $19 million, and the Board of Education.

Back Issues

Great Research on Current Issues Starts Right Here...Recent topics covered by The CQ Researcher are listed below. Before May 1991, reports were published under the name of Editorial Research Reports.

APRIL 1993
Head Start
High-Speed Rail
Children's Legal Rights
Muslims in America

MAY 1993
Cults in America
Preventing Teen Pregnancy
Software Piracy
National Parks

JUNE 1993
Food Safety
Prostitution
Childhood Immunizations
National Service

JULY 1993
Electric Cars
Population Growth
Downward Mobility
Intelligence Testing

AUGUST 1993
Mental Illness
Bilingual Education
Foreign Policy Burden
School Funding

SEPTEMBER 1993
Suburban Crime
Public Housing
Supreme Court Preview
Immigration Reform

OCTOBER 1993
Airline Safety
Disaster Response
Science in the Courtroom
The Glass Ceiling

NOVEMBER 1993
Paying for Retirement
Charitable Giving
Privacy in the Workplace
Adoption

DECEMBER 1993
U.S. Vietnam-Relations
Learning Disabilities
Child Care
Space Program's Future

JANUARY 1994
Racial Tensions in Schools
South Africa's Future
Worker Retraining
Regulating Pesticides

FEBRUARY 1994
Prison Overcrowding
Water Quality
Religion in Schools
Juvenile Justice

MARCH 1994
Underground Economy
Education Standards
Gambling Boom
Private Management of Publiç Schools

APRIL 1994
Reproductive Ethics
U.S.-China Trade
Soccer in America
Talk Show Democracy

MAY 1994
Traffic Congestion
Women's Health Issues
Mutual Funds
Political Scandals

JUNE 1994
Education and Gender
Gun Control
Public Land Policy
Nuclear Arms Cleanup

JULY 1994
Dietary Supplements
Public Opinion and Foreign Policy
Crime Victims' Rights
Birth Control Choices

AUGUST 1994
Genetically Engineered Foods
Electing Minorities
Prozac Controversy
College Sports

SEPTEMBER 1994
Home Schooling
Welfare Reform in the States
Courts and the Media
Regulating Tobacco

OCTOBER 1994
Historic Preservation
Religion and Politics

Back issues are available for $4.00 (subscribers) or $7.00 (non-subscribers). Quantity discounts apply to orders over ten. To order, call Congressional Quarterly Customer Service at (202) 887-8621.

Binders are available for $16.00. To order call 1-800-638-1710. Please refer to stock number 648.

Future Topics

- ***Embargoes and Sanctions***
- ***Sex on Campus***
- ***Blood Supply Safety***

THE CQ Researcher

PUBLISHED BY CONGRESSIONAL QUARTERLY INC.

Economic Sanctions

Can they replace combat in the post-Cold War era?

The United States has long been a leader in using sanctions to discourage unwanted behavior by other countries, including terrorism and human rights abuses. But the erosion of U.S. economic predominance has undermined Uncle Sam's ability to wield the sanctions weapon. With more countries producing essential items, the threat of a cutoff of U.S. goods and services is far less daunting than it once was. Nor is the American consumer market such a vital outlet for other nations' exports. As unilateral U.S. sanctions pose less of a threat, the United Nations is increasingly using sanctions to preserve international peace. Some experts say a new U.N. agency is needed to enforce multilateral sanctions in the post-Cold War era.

INSIDE THIS ISSUE

CQ Oct. 28, 1994 • Volume 4, No. 40 • Pages 937-960

Formerly Editorial Research Reports

ECONOMIC SANCTIONS

THE ISSUES

BACKGROUND

CURRENT SITUATION

OUTLOOK

SIDEBARS AND GRAPHICS

FOR FURTHER INFORMATION

COVER ART: BARBARA SASSA-DANIELS

October 28, 1994
Volume 4, No. 40

The CQ Researcher (ISSN 1056-2036). Formerly Editorial Research Reports. Published weekly (48 times per year, not printed the first Friday of any month with five Fridays) by Congressional Quarterly Inc., 1414 22nd St., N.W., Washington, D.C. 20037. Rates are furnished upon request. Second-class postage paid at Washington, D.C. POSTMASTER: Send address changes to The CQ Researcher, 1414 22nd St., N.W., Washington, D.C. 20037.

Economic Sanctions

By Mary H. Cooper

The Issues

Life has always been difficult in Haiti, the poorest nation in the Western Hemisphere. But for the past three years, Haiti has struggled with an additional burden: economic sanctions that sent the Caribbean nation's already fragile economy into a tailspin.

The United States and United Nations imposed the sanctions to protest the Sept. 30, 1991, military takeover that forced the democratically elected president, Jean-Bertrand Aristide, into exile. * During the tenure of Lt. Gen. Raoul Cédras, who led the coup, some 3,000 Haitians were reported killed by the military and tens of thousands more forced into hiding.

With Aristide now restored to power, the punishing economic sanctions have been lifted. But the effects of the country's near total isolation will be felt for some time to come.

The intense controversy sparked by the use of sanctions in Haiti reflected a broader debate over the effectiveness of the so-called "economic weapon" as an alternative to war. In contrast to arms embargoes, which simply block weapons shipments, economic sanctions include a broad range of actions, including boycotts of certain goods, general cutoffs of imports and exports and the freezing of financial assets.

Throughout this century, the United States has been the world's leading user of sanctions. Seven countries currently are targets of major U.S. economic sanctions — Cuba, Iraq, Iran, Libya, North Korea, Yugoslavia and Angola. (*See story, p. 944.*)

Supporters of sanctions value them as useful tools of diplomacy offering a variety of responses to objectionable behavior ranging between no action and declaring war. "In some cases, imposing sanctions is a way to appear to be doing things that are not as painful to us as war would be," says Robert B. Oakley, a former U.S. ambassador to Pakistan, Somalia and Zaire and now an international consultant.

Sanction supporters often point to the sweeping U.S. ban on trade and investments with South Africa from 1986 to 1991 that helped end apartheid. (*See story, p. 942.*)

"But sanctions are a mixed bag," Oakley notes. "Is it really serving our humanitarian objectives if, because we don't like human rights abuses in Haiti, we apply sanctions that make the lives of most of the people on the island much more difficult? I think there is a real question there."

While government leaders, who are the ultimate targets of sanctions, often have the means to insulate themselves from the impact of sanctions, average citizens, and especially the poor, must bear the hardship they cause. Under the recent U.S. and U.N. embargoes, for example, Haiti's military leaders and their wealthy civilian supporters continued to enjoy a high standard of living — with full access to smuggled goods — while most Haitians suffered immense privation as the fragile economy was set back even further.

On a more practical level, critics argue that sanctions rarely work. It was U.S. troops, not sanctions, they say, that finally forced the military in Haiti to cede power. * The critics invariably cite Cuba, which has been under a strict U.S. embargo since 1960, shortly after Fidel Castro took power. "The embargo is exacerbating trouble for Castro's regime, but it clearly has not gotten rid of it," Oakley says. "Sanctions haven't gotten rid of [Iraqi leader] Saddam Hussein, either, but in the case of Cuba they've certainly created a lot of misery for the people." (*See "At Issue," p. 953.*)

Sanctions have long been a successful and accepted element of wartime strategy, imposed to destabilize an adversary's economy and enforced with naval blockades. Even after the United States began to impose sanctions to achieve peacetime goals after World War I, they tended to work more often than not. Of 35 instances of U.S. sanctions against other countries imposed before 1973, 18 were successful, according to an authoritative 1990 study by the Institute for International Economics in Washington, D.C. [1]

The United States remains the world's leading user of economic sanctions. But as global trade ties spread, it is becoming harder for any nation, even the United States, to impose its will on another through unilateral sanctions. For sanctions to work in today's economy, the United States needs the cooperation of other countries. The United Nations has become increasingly willing to impose sanc-

---

* Unilateral sanctions imposed by the United States in November 1991 prohibited all trade between the U.S. and Haiti except humanitarian supplies such as food and also banned ships trading with Haiti from visiting U.S. ports. U.N. sanctions imposed in May 1994 included a general embargo, or cutoff of trade, and a specific ban on oil shipments.

* A delegation led by former President Jimmy Carter negotiated Cédras' departure in September, as U.S. troops were flying to Haiti to force him out.

tions to deter aggression around the world, such as in Yugoslavia and Iraq.

As a dominant force on the U.N. Security Council, the United States has often sought U.N. help in getting the multilateral support needed to make sanctions work. Following Iraq's 1990 invasion of Kuwait, for example, it was the Security Council that imposed an embargo against Iraq. The stated goal was forcing Saddam Hussein's regime to allow U.N. inspectors to ensure that it was not developing weapons of mass destruction.

When Iraqi forces again began making threatening moves near the Kuwait border recently, questions were raised about the embargo's effectiveness in curbing Iraq's territorial ambitions in the oil-rich region. (*See story, p. 951.*) Meanwhile, the multilateral consensus necessary to keep the sanctions in place has begun to weaken, as France and Russia, eager to resume commercial ties with Iraq, press the United States to agree to lift them.

The U.N. has proved even less successful in applying economic sanctions in the Balkans. The full trade embargo against the Yugoslav Federation of Serbia and Montenegro, imposed to discourage Serbia from supplying arms to Serbian forces in Bosnia's civil war, has been violated repeatedly. "These are not very well constructed sanctions," says Michael Malloy, director of graduate studies at Fordham University in New York and an expert on sanctions. "They have not been applied very vigorously, and in many respects they exacerbate the problem."

For all their perceived weaknesses, sanctions are likely to gain growing support in the years ahead, especially in U.N. efforts to maintain peace in the post-Cold War era. "Our expectation is that sanctions are increasingly going to be the resort of choice of the international community for dealing with middle- to lower-grade threats to, and breaches of, the peace," says Jeffrey Laurenti, director of multilateral studies at the United Nations Association of the USA, a research and educational organization. "Their costs to member states are relatively low. Also they don't take you to the difficult threshold of summoning troops to deal with 'a distant quarrel among faraway people of whom we know nothing,' in Neville Chamberlain's memorable phrase."

As government officials examine the usefulness of sanctions in pursuing foreign policy goals, these are some of the questions they must consider:

Do economic sanctions work?

In the past, when embargoes and other economic sanctions were used in conjunction with military action, they often were successful. "Blockades have always been part of war," says Laurenti. "A key element of the strategy against Germany in World War I was just to make life hard for the civilians back home and promote discontent. It was sanctions, rather than casualties at the front, that led to unrest in Germany in 1918 and to its ultimate defeat."

In the absence of combat, however, sanctions have a spottier track record. There are too many variables in a country's trade ties to identify hard-and-fast guidelines for applying peacetime sanctions. Still, experts point to several general principles for crafting sanctions that work.

Reuters

Residents of Port-au-Prince wait to buy kerosene in October 1993. Severe trade sanctions were imposed on Haiti by the U.S. immediately after the 1991 takeover by Lt. Gen. Raoul Cédras.

One rule is to clearly identify the goals of any sanction effort. "If you have narrow goals and are able to target a vulnerable sector of the target country, your chances are much better of achieving them," says Hurst Hannum, a U.N. expert at the Fletcher School of Law and Diplomacy in Medford, Mass.

Critics of China's human rights policy criticized the Clinton administration for renewing favorable trade status with the country earlier this year. [2] Hannum disagrees. "To say we're not going to trade with China until China becomes a democracy, for example, doesn't make any sense."

It also helps to have broad international support for sanctions. Hannum cites the 34-year-old U.S. embargo against Cuba as an example of a unilateral sanctions policy gone awry. [3] "Cuba shows the potential worthlessness of sanctions," he says. Until the Soviet Union collapsed in 1990, it subsidized Castro's regime with oil and other essential goods. But with few countries sharing the U.S. antagonism to Castro, the Soviet Union's demise has not forced democratic reform in Cuba. "Today, the U.S. embargo is still worthless because the rest of the world is propping Cuba up," Hannum says.

When other nations, especially U.S. trade competitors, don't go along with U.S. sanctions, American businesses often become the loudest critics of sanctions. Unilateral U.S. sanctions designed to force Vietnam to provide information on missing American servicemen were finally abandoned in February. The cutoff of sanctions followed years of complaints by U.S. businesses that the sanctions were denying them the chance to compete with foreign firms in Vietnam's rapidly developing economy. [4]

Critics of sanctions say the loss of international support for sanctions is a clear signal to drop them. But supporters respond that the United States should just try harder to make them work. "The embargo against Cuba is an effective strategy that the United States needs to pursue," says José Cardenas, director of the Washington office of the Cuban American National Foundation, the leading anti-Castro organization. "We would like to see more cooperation from the international community. The only way Castro is going to get the message is when other countries also start putting economic pressure on Cuba."

The absence of a carefully targeted approach often is a recipe for failure, experts say. "The real problem with the great, big trade measures such as general embargoes is that they're quite indiscriminate," says Holly Burkhalter, Washington director of Human Rights Watch. While the poor suffered dire economic privation on top of human rights abuses, she says, "the people responsible for Haiti's plight actually made out like bandits during the embargo." Although the sanctions were designed to squeeze the wealthy supporters of Haiti's military, they were able to monopolize sales of food and propane, which were exempted from the embargo. [5]

The success or failure of sanctions depends on the goal. Sanctions are widely thought to have succeeded in preventing the further development of Iraq's nuclear arsenal. "But they haven't done much for human rights," Burkhalter says. "In some of the worst regimes in the world, such as Burma [Myanmar] and Sudan as well as Iraq, I have yet to see evidence that sanctions are bringing human rights violators around."

Recent sanctions have worked best when imposed swiftly, multilaterally and comprehensively, according to the 1990 study by the Institute for International Economics. Broadly supported U.N. sanctions were slapped on Iraq less than a week after it invaded Kuwait. The U.N. quickly set up naval and air embargoes to enforce the sanctions, as well as secondary boycotts of countries violating them. "Nearly all these backup mechanisms — and the political will that made them possible — are missing in both the Serbian and Haitian cases," Gary Hufbauer, a study co-author, wrote recently. [6]

Joe Lopez\New York Times

Economic sanctions against Haiti were lifted after President Jean-Bertrand Aristide returned to power.

Do the costs suffered by countries imposing sanctions outweigh their benefits?

Sanctions don't come without cost to the country imposing them. When the target country is a major trading partner, sanctions can mean lost exports and jobs, as well as lost overseas investment opportunities. Unilateral sanctions impose the highest penalty to firms in the sanctioning country because they may never regain the market share lost to foreign competitors, even after the sanctions are lifted.

"When you don't have multilateral sanctions, they do not work," says Oakley. "You end up punishing U.S. business to the benefit of others. It lets companies from other countries come in and take the business that the United States can't have."

Such commercial punishment finally led the Clinton administration last February to lift the 30-year-old U.S. embargo against Vietnam. After Vietnam began inviting Western investment in the late 1980s, British, French and Dutch oil companies won offshore oil and gas exploration rights, but American oil companies were shut out of the potentially lucrative South China Sea reserves.

The potential loss of foreign business posed by sanctions is of special concern to American firms because of the large number of U.S.-imposed sanctions. Between 1973 and 1990, for example, the 12-nation European Community (now called the European Union) imposed sanctions only 12 times, and Japan on just four occasions. But the United States imposed sanctions 45 times over the 17-year period, placing a disproportionate competitive burden on American industry.

How much sanctions cost U.S. business is open to question, but the frequent corporate opposition suggests that the price tag may be considerable. "It would be a tough thing to calculate the costs because so much of the information is speculative," says Iain S. Baird, deputy assistant secretary of Commerce for export administration. "How you estimate how many people didn't enter into transactions that they might have if the sanctions hadn't been in place is

Continued on p. 943

Economic Sanctions and the Fall of Apartheid

Few issues have galvanized public support for economic sanctions as strongly as apartheid. South Africa's ruling National Party formally institutionalized the system of discrimination against the country's black majority in the 1940s. Since 1959, when the black-supported African National Congress (ANC) first called for an international boycott of South Africa "to precipitate the end of the hateful system of apartheid," the U.S. and other countries have grappled with the costs of using sanctions to influence behavior. [1]

"South Africa is a good example of a place where economic sanctions were hugely important," says Holly Burkhalter, Washington director of Human Rights Watch. "But they certainly didn't happen in the short term."

At the time of the ANC's appeal, South Africa was vulnerable to sanctions because the economy depended on foreign capital to develop its gold and diamond mining and manufacturing industries. When the country's black majority protested its exclusion from the benefits of rapid economic development after World War II, government repression intensified.

The U.N. General Assembly answered the ANC's appeal in 1962 by calling for a ban on trade with South Africa. But the Security Council, the only agency that can impose U.N. sanctions, repeatedly blocked the imposition of a general trade embargo. In 1977, the council did apply an arms embargo against South Africa but stopped short of imposing multilateral economic sanctions. Of the five permanent council members, each of which has veto power, two — the United States and Britain — had especially high stakes in South Africa's continued prosperity and voted against the full sanctions.

Reuters

Shortly before receiving the 1993 Nobel Peace Prize, African National Congress leader Nelson Mandela and South African President F.W. de Klerk met in Oslo, Norway. Mandela was elected South Africa's first black president in April.

A general trade embargo would have had the strongest impact on the United States, Britain and Japan, which absorbed half of South Africa's exports, mainly gold, diamonds and other minerals. South Africa depended on the same three countries and West Germany for more than half its imports, chiefly heavy machinery, high-technology goods and oil. By the early 1980s, South Africa imported more than $8 billion worth of goods and exported more than $12 billion, trading primarily with the same countries.

With the U.N. powerless to impose a multilateral embargo, support for sanctions against South Africa depended on grass-roots anti-apartheid movements in the country's main trading partners. In the United States, early protests were aimed at Chase Manhattan and nine other banks that lent money to South Africa. Workers at Polaroid Corp. and other U.S. companies forced their employers to stop selling goods there. After student uprisings in Soweto in 1976, a campus-led divestiture movement pushed U.S. companies, universities and local governments to sell their holdings in South Africa.

The anti-apartheid movement faced considerable economic obstacles. By 1982, total U.S. financial interests in South Africa amounted to some $14 billion. But the effort paid off, with many state and local governments as well as businesses refusing to do business in South Africa.

The grass-roots campaign claimed a key victory when Congress passed the 1986 Comprehensive Anti-Apartheid Act with enough support to override President Ronald Reagan's veto. The law banned new investments and bank loans to South Africa and prohibited bilateral trade in a number of goods. By the end of the decade, some 200 U.S. firms had pulled out of South Africa.

Shortly after his election in 1989, President F.W. de Klerk opened negotiations with leaders of the black majority and freed political prisoners, including ANC leader Nelson Mandela. In 1991, as political reforms were enacted, President Bush lifted the sanctions imposed under the Anti-Apartheid Act. All remaining U.S. sanctions were lifted last fall, and South Africa finally lost its status as a pariah state with Mandela's election in April as South Africa's first black president.

During the anti-apartheid struggle, South Africa suffered a severe recession. By 1993, economic growth had fallen and unemployment approached 50 percent. [2]

Just how great a role sanctions had in prompting constitutional reform is impossible to quantify, experts say. "At no time did sanctions supporters believe the sanctions by themselves could achieve the desired end — bringing human equality and political democracy to South Africa," writes Jennifer Davis, executive director of both the American Committee on Africa and the Africa Fund, based in New York City. "Rather, the imposition of sanctions was a strategy to provide direct support for an active and ongoing struggle for liberation." [3]

---

[1] See Jennifer Davis, "Squeezing Apartheid," *Bulletin of the Atomic Scientists,* November 1993, pp. 16-19. For background see "U.S. Role in South Africa's Future," *Editorial Research Reports,* March 23, 1990, pp. 157-172 and "South Africa's Future," *The CQ Researcher,* Jan. 14, 1994, pp. 25-48.

[2] International Monetary Fund, *Annual Report,* 1994, pp. 66-67.

[3] Davis, *op. cit.,* p. 19.

Continued from p. 941
very difficult."

Nonetheless, some loss appraisals have been made. In 1987, according to the most recent available data, U.S. firms lost an estimated $7 billion in potential exports because of U.S. sanctions. As a result, about 175,000 American workers lost their jobs. [7]

Similar economic repercussions arise from the unilateral U.S. embargo against Cuba, critics of the policy say. While European and Latin American firms are investing in Cuba's burgeoning tourism industry and generally expanding their trade ties with Cuba, American firms, banned from dealing with Cuba, find themselves at a disadvantage in their own back yard.

The United States, for example, is the second-largest rice exporter after Thailand. Cuba was once its best customer, buying more than half of all U.S. rice exports. "The U.S. rice industry views the Cuban market as one of great potential," David Graves, president of the Rice Millers' Association, testified this spring at congressional hearings on trade with Cuba. "Once the embargo is no longer in place, the U.S. industry will expect to re-enter the Cuban market." [8]

"As the largest country in the Caribbean, Cuba offers excellent prospects for U.S. trade and investment if it remains politically stable," said Carmen Diana Deere, director of the Latin American Studies Program at the University of Massachusetts-Amherst. "It represents a market of 11 million people only 90 miles from U.S. shores." Among the main beneficiaries of lifting the embargo now, Deere added, would be U.S. agriculture and the animal feed, fertilizer and farm equipment industries. [9]

Even when sanctions enjoy multilateral support, some of the sponsoring countries may suffer heavy losses. Since U.N. sanctions were imposed against Iraq, for example, an oil pipeline connecting Iraqi oil fields with tanker loading terminals in Turkey has been shut down. With the loss of this important source of income, Turkey is paying a high price for complying with the multilateral sanctions. "We're going to have to take far more seriously the need for some process for collectively offsetting the unusual economic hardships on some member states," says Laurenti of the U.N. association. "These are the states that, by complying with the Security Council sanctions, have suffered disproportionate economic losses themselves."

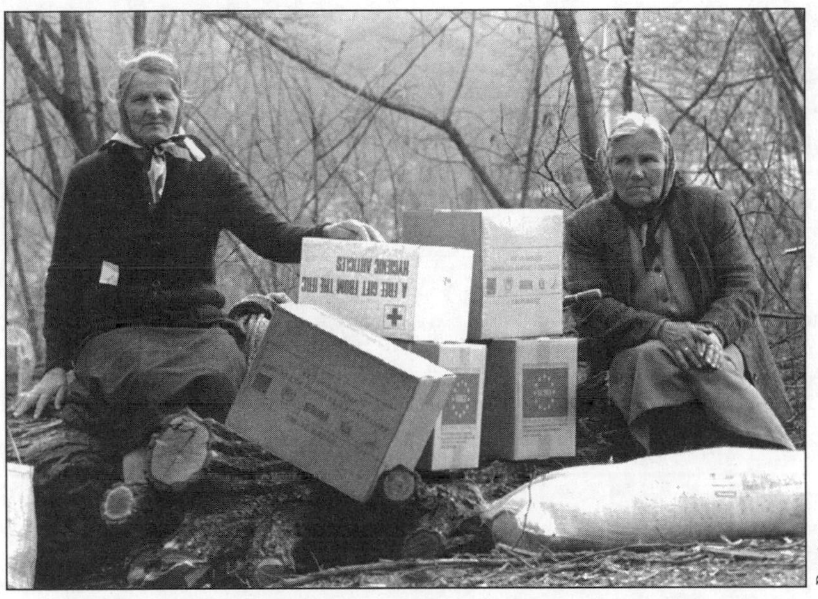

Reuters

Caught up in Yugoslavia's civil war, Bosnian Serb women wait for help last year in transporting humanitarian aid to their homes.

Although the greatest attention focuses on their costs, embargoes sometimes can help industries in sanctioning countries. Cuba, for example, is a major producer of grapefruit and already competes successfully in Europe with Florida growers, who are not anxious to see Cuban products enter the U.S. market.

"While our growers must meet certain socioeconomic standards for their employees, we understand that the Cuban government utilizes schoolchildren and others in almost a forced-labor situation to produce and harvest the citrus crop," said Carl B. Loop Jr., president of the Florida Farm Bureau Federation. "This translates into a massive subsidy and gives unfair advantage to Cuban citrus growers in the world market." [10]

When a sanctioning country has a perceived stake and involvement in fostering the target country's long-term stability, it can continue to pay a steep price for its policy. With U.S. troops in Haiti overseeing the transition to democratic rule, the United States is now faced with the task of helping to rebuild the country's shattered economy. Unemployment stands at 70 percent, about half the population is illiterate and the vast majority are without electrical power, safe drinking water or basic sanitation facilities. Barring a massive infusion of foreign aid, Haiti's prospects are dim. The United States already has pledged about $200 million in emergency aid over the next five years. [11]

Does the post-Cold War era offer better conditions for the successful outcome of sanctions?

The collapse of the Soviet Union in 1991 signaled the end of the Cold War between the world's two superpowers and their allies. Although the United States frequently imposed unilateral sanctions to achieve foreign policy goals during the 45-year nuclear standoff, it seldom achieved broad multilateral support. The Security Council, which must approve U.N. backing of

Seven Nations Currently Feel the Sting. . .

The United States regulates trade and financial exchanges with many countries to advance U.S. foreign policy goals. For example, all countries (except members of NATO, Japan, Australia and New Zealand) are subject to export controls limiting their access to certain U.S.-made weaponry. But the most sweeping restrictions, the ones most commonly associated with the term "economic sanctions," are the sanctions that are imposed under the Trading with the Enemies Act or the International Economic Emergency Powers Act. Implemented by the Treasury Department's Office of Foreign Assets Control, these embargoes currently affect the following seven countries:

Cuba: Since the U.S. banned economic and military aid to Cuba in May 1960, the government of Fidel Castro has been targeted by numerous U.S. sanctions. As Castro forged ties with the Soviet Union and seized American property on the island, the U.S. stance toward Cuba progressively hardened. In October 1960, President Dwight D. Eisenhower imposed a total embargo on exports to Cuba (except food and medicine) and broke diplomatic relations in 1961. In February 1962, 10 months after the unsuccessful U.S.-sponsored Bay of Pigs invasion, President John F. Kennedy imposed a further trade embargo and later barred any vessel engaged in trade with Cuba from entering U.S. ports.

After the October 1962 Cuban missile crisis brought the world to the brink of nuclear war, the embargo was tightened to bar virtually all financial transactions between Cuban and U.S. citizens (except for family remittances) and to freeze all Cuban assets under U.S. jurisdiction. The 1992 Cuban Democracy Act further tightened the embargo by prohibiting foreign-based subsidiaries of U.S. firms from trading with Cuba and by allowing the Treasury Department to fine U.S. citizens traveling to Cuba up to $50,000. The bill also let private U.S. groups deliver food and medicine to Cuba and permitted the president to establish telecommunications links with Cuba.

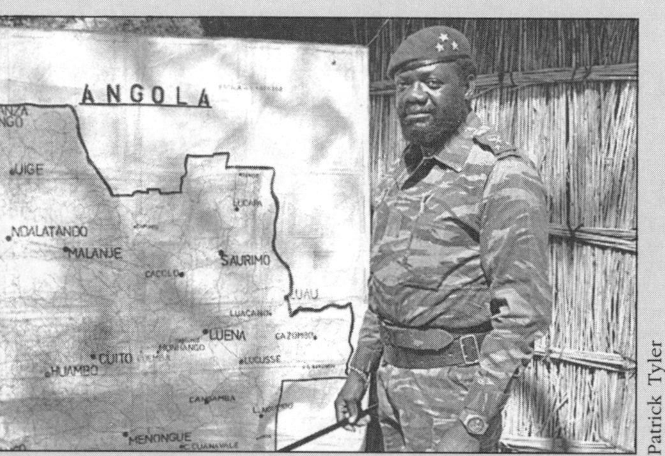

Patrick Tyler

The U.S. imposed sanctions last year in parts of Angola controlled by Jonas Savimbi, leader of the rebel UNITA Party, after he rejected elections that renewed the socialist government's mandate.

Iran: The revolution that ousted longtime U.S. ally Shah Mohammed Reza Pahlevi in February 1979 and brought the Ayatollah Ruhollah Khomeini to power culminated in November of that year with the seizure of more than 60 Americans at the U.S. embassy in Teheran. The Carter administration responded with a failed attempt to rescue the hostages and a freeze on Iran's considerable financial assets in the United States. The hostages were later released, but the Reagan administration in 1984 declared Iran a state sponsor of terrorism and suspended most trade, plus all U.S. aid and arms sales. In 1987, when Iran was not listed among countries that cooperate with U.S. anti-drug policies, a total trade embargo and ban on dual-use exports (civilian products that have military applications) were added to the sanctions.

Iraq: A Soviet ally and reputed supporter of anti-Israeli terrorist organizations during most of the Cold War, Iraq received limited U.S. support during its 1980-88 war with Iran, already the target of comprehensive U.S. sanctions.

sanctions, has five permanent members, each of which has veto power over any resolutions that come before it. * During the Cold War, sanctions resolutions — usually proposed by the United States — routinely were vetoed by the Soviet Union, often with the backing of China.

Today, U.S. relations with Russia, the Soviet Union's major successor state, are friendly. Despite tensions related to human rights abuses, China also is less likely than it was during the Cold War to veto U.S. sanctions proposals, to a large extent because of its extensive trade ties with the United States. "Multilateral sanctions are more possible now," says Hannum of the Fletcher school, "because of the end of the Cold War. They are a useful tool that we couldn't use as easily before."

The current U.N. sanctions against the Serbian-dominated Yugoslav Federation, for example, would have been much harder to achieve during the Cold War. Although Yugoslavia broke with the Soviet bloc in the late 1940s, it is unlikely that the Soviet Union would have agreed to sanctions against a fellow socialist government such as Serbia's. "Today, there is at least a possibility that if you have sanctions against Serbia, you're not going to have the Russians on the other side undermining them," says Burkhalter of Human Rights Watch.

---

* The five permanent members of the 15-member Security Council are the United States, Russia, France, Britain and China. The other 10 members are drawn from the U.N.'s general membership and sit on the council on a rotating basis.

. . . of Major Economic Sanctions Imposed by the U.S.

When Iraqi President Saddam Hussein invaded Kuwait in August 1990, however, U.S. policy reversed course. Together with other Western nations, the administration of President George Bush imposed a trade embargo, froze Iraqi assets and sent troops and warships to the Persian Gulf. Following the U.S.-led alliance's military victory against Iraq in February 1991, the U.N. Security Council kept a multilateral trade and arms embargo in place, allowing Iraq to sell only a specified amount of oil to fund purchases of food, medicine and other vital commodities until Iraq complies fully with the terms of the U.N.-brokered cease-fire. Despite pressure from European countries eager to expand trade ties with Iraq, the U.N. and U.S. embargoes and asset freezes remain unchanged.

Libya: Military strongman Muammar el-Qaddafi, in power since he ousted pro-Western King Idris in 1969, has been the target of U.S. sanctions since 1973 for his support of terrorism against Israel and other countries. After the administration of President Jimmy Carter declared Libya a state sponsor of terrorism in 1979, sanctions were strengthened to ban all trade, aid and arms sales. Following a spate of terrorist attacks linked to the Libyan government, President Ronald Reagan in January 1986 further tightened the embargo to include a freeze of Libyan assets, a ban on transportation between the two nations and a prohibition on the involvement of U.S. citizens in commercial interests between Libya and third countries. Because Libyan-supported terrorists are suspected of continuing their attacks, including the December 1988 downing of Pan Am Flight 103 over Lockerbie, Scotland, U.S. policy remains unchanged. It was reinforced in April 1992 by a U.N. arms and air-traffic embargo against Libya.

North Korea: The United States has imposed a total trade embargo and asset freeze against North Korea since the outbreak of the Korean War in 1950, when northern forces invaded South Korea. In an effort to support South Korea's attempt to improve relations with the North, the Bush administration eased the embargo in 1989 to allow the export to North Korea of commercial goods intended to meet basic human needs. The administration reversed course in 1992 on evidence that North Korea was selling missiles to Iran and Syria. As part of a nuclear accord reached Oct. 18, President Clinton is to ease the embargo's terms within the next three months in exchange for North Korea's commitment to freeze and eventually eliminate its capability to make nuclear arms.

Angola: An embargo against areas of Angola controlled by Jonas Savimbi's rebel organization UNITA was imposed in summer 1993 after Savimbi resumed hostilities against the government. The embargo marked a reversal of longstanding U.S. policy in the southern African nation. During Angola's 1975-1991 civil war, the United States supported Savimbi in his quest to overthrow the MPLA, the Soviet-backed socialist government. But when Savimbi resumed hostilities after U.N.-monitored elections in 1992 renewed the MPLA's mandate, the United States slapped an embargo on arms, petroleum and petroleum products destined for territory under the control of the former U.S. Cold War ally.

Yugoslavia (Serbia-Montenegro): Yugoslavia began breaking apart in 1989 with the fall of communist governments throughout Eastern Europe. By 1990, all that remained of Yugoslavia were Serbia and Montenegro. As Serbia tried to maintain control over parts of the former federation, civil war broke out in 1991. That year, the United Nations imposed an arms embargo against all the warring parties. In December 1991, the United States followed the European Community's lead by suspending trade to Serbia and Montenegro, identified as the main aggressors in the conflict, by then centered in Bosnia. In 1992, the United States strengthened sanctions to include a trade embargo, a freeze of Yugoslavian assets in the United States and a ban on flights to the U.S. by JAT, Yugoslavia's airline.

Similarly, she says, "If you're going to try to have an embargo against Angola, you can at least have the hope today that the Russians aren't going to feed things into the country as fast as you keep them out." Beginning in the mid-1970s, the superpowers waged a proxy war in the southern African nation's civil conflict pitting the Soviet-backed government against the U.S.-supported rebel leader Jonas Savimbi and his UNITA Party. Although the civil war continues, the United Nations last year imposed an embargo against both sides in an effort to end the hostilities.

For its part, the United States last year placed new sanctions against UNITA, its former ally, after Savimbi rejected the outcome of elections that renewed the socialist government's mandate. "The sanctions against UNITA have not had much impact," says Robert Deutsch, director of the State Department's Office of Economic Sanctions Policy. "We did so little business with Angola in the first place, and UNITA controls only part of the country."

Despite the improved prospects of multilateral sanctions through the United Nations, Hannum sees a danger that they will be overused now that the Soviet veto threat has disappeared. "Sanctions are a very important tool," he says, "but I think they are being used almost automatically and thoughtlessly."

Part of the problem, in Hannum's view, is the lack of adequate oversight. "One of the great scandals today," he says, "is that there are seven or eight entirely different U.N. sanctions in place, all of which are being monitored in secret by committees that report to the secretary general and the Security Council and are accountable to no one." Sanctions against Serbia, for example, are widely reported to have fallen short of their goal, as oil and other goods are smuggled into Belgrade. "So sanctions in some ways may be getting a bad name as being ineffective because the enforcement issue is not being adequately addressed," he says.

Because it has broken up the neat East-West divide in Third World conflicts, the Cold War's demise also has made it harder to discern the myriad interests involved in local disputes that are targets of sanctions today. While Russia and the United States are no longer waging a proxy war through their clients in Angola, for example, other countries with interests in the civil war's eventual outcome, including Zaire, are assuming roles as arms suppliers.

"It's not the superpowers any more that undermine international sanctions in the post-Cold War era," Burkhalter says, "but there are other actors out there to take their place." ■

BACKGROUND

Tools of Diplomacy

From the beginning of recorded history, economic sanctions have served as tools of diplomacy. More often, sanctions have been vital elements of a country's war arsenal. In one celebrated early use of sanctions, the Athenian leader Pericles punished the Greek city-state of Megara in 432 B.C. for kidnapping three women and trying to seize territory by banning Megara's exports to Athens. The Megara decree soon touched off the Peloponnesian War. [12]

Embargoes, blockades and other economic offensives have been used throughout the world ever since. Indeed, as all schoolchildren know, economic sanctions played a prominent role in the birth of the United States. Starting in the mid-1760s, American colonists began boycotting British goods to protest taxes imposed by the crown under the Stamp and Townsend acts. The nine-year boycott culminated in the 1774 Boston Tea Party, when frustrated colonists dumped a shipment of British tea into Boston Harbor, setting the stage for the American Revolution.

Later, an independent United States embargoed British goods in response to Britain's attempt to interrupt U.S. trade with France, leading to the War of 1812. A half-century later, the four-year U.S. blockade of the Confederate States during the Civil War contributed greatly to the industrial North's victory by preventing the largely agrarian South from obtaining weapons and other manufactured goods.

Naval blockades used to enforce sanctions played an equally crucial role in other 19th-century conflicts. The United States won independence for Cuba during the 1898 Spanish-American War by preventing reinforcements from aiding Spanish troops on the island who were battling native insurgents. France wrested the territory of Annam — later Vietnam — from China in 1883 after blocking rice shipments to China for two years. And Britain added South Africa to its empire after blocking shipments of goods to the country and defeating the Dutch inhabitants during the 1899-1902 Boer War.

Naval blockades have not always proved successful. After trying to cut off shipments of fuel, rice and cotton to Japan during the 1904-1905 Russo-Japanese War, a defeated Russia was forced to hand over parts of its territory to Japan and recognize Korea as within Japan's sphere of influence.

League of Nations Tries "Economic Weapon"

After the unprecedented devastation caused by modern weaponry during World War I, sanctions found limited use as alternatives to combat. President Woodrow Wilson led the push to substitute the "economic weapon" for warfare to settle disputes.

"A nation that is boycotted is a nation that is in sight of surrender," Wilson said in 1919. "Apply this economic, peaceful, silent, deadly remedy, and there will be no need for force. It is a terrible remedy. It does not cost a life outside the nation boycotted, but it brings pressure upon the nation which, in my judgment, no modern nation could resist." [13]

During the 1920s and '30s, the short-lived League of Nations had only limited success in using sanctions to forestall the renewed outbreak of hostilities in Europe. League sanctions forced Greece to withdraw from territory it had occupied in neighboring Bulgaria in 1925.

But in its last and most important use of the economic weapon, the league failed. After Italian forces under Fascist dictator Benito Mussolini invaded Abyssinia (now Ethiopia) in 1935, the league imposed a limited embargo blocking exports to Italy and a boycott of all Italian goods. But the embargo was not strong enough, excluding such essential products as oil, coal and steel. Italy refused to withdraw, and nine months later the sanctions were lifted. The league's failed initiative was viewed as a signal by Nazi Germany and imperialist Japan that the world lacked the resolve to forcibly intervene with their expansionist plans. The stage was set for the outbreak of World War II.

Dominated by isolationist sentiment, the United States never joined the League of Nations. Before the out-

Continued on p. 948

Chronology

1960s *Cold War politics drives sanctions policy in the United States, which takes the lead among Western powers in applying sanctions.*

October 1960
The United States imposes a trade embargo against Fidel Castro's Cuba, the Soviet Union's sole ally in the Western Hemisphere.

1965
In its first use of economic sanctions, the U.N. Security Council bans exports of oil and other commodities to southern Rhodesia to prevent white settlers from seizing control of the country. The sanctions remain in place until the election of a black-majority government in 1979 in the nation, which is renamed Zimbabwe.

1970s *Terrorism becomes a focus of U.S. sanctions policy.*

1973
Sanctions are imposed against Libya to protest Libyan dictator Muammar el-Qaddafi's support of terrorist groups in the Middle East and elsewhere. The sanctions are later strengthened to bar all trade and freeze Libyan assets.

1979
The Carter administration freezes Iranian assets in the United States after revolutionary forces take Americans hostage in Teheran. The sanctions are later expanded to include a broad trade embargo to curtail Iran's support of international terrorism.

1980s *Globalization of trade undermines U.S. unilateral sanctions.*

Jan. 20, 1981
The American hostages in Teheran are released on the day Ronald Reagan is inaugurated, in exchange for a partial lifting of the freeze on Iranian assets.

1986
The Comprehensive Anti-Apartheid Act bars new investments and bank loans to South Africa and prohibits bilateral trade in a number of goods. As a result of the law and a strong grass-roots campaign, some 200 U.S. firms eventually pull out of South Africa.

1990s *The United Nations steps up use of economic sanctions in the post-Cold War era.*

August 1990
The U.N. Security Council imposes an embargo against Iraq after Iraqi forces invade Kuwait.

July 10, 1991
Following the introduction of political reforms in South Africa, President George Bush lifts sanctions against the country.

November 1991
The United States imposes a trade embargo against Haiti after a military junta overthrows President Jean-Bertrand Aristide.

May 30, 1992
The United Nations hits Serbia and Montenegro with a full trade embargo, commercial flight ban and ban on Yugoslavian participation in sporting and cultural events for their role in arming Serbs in Bosnia's civil war.

October 1992
Congress passes the Cuban Democracy Act, tightening the embargo to include remittances to family members in Cuba.

Summer 1993
The United States blocks shipments of arms and oil to territory in Angola controlled by UNITA rebel leader Jonas Savimbi after he rejects the results of elections and renews the country's 19-year-old civil war.

Nov. 23, 1993
President Clinton signs legislation lifting all remaining sanctions against South Africa and requiring all state and local governments to follow suit by 1995.

February 1994
Bowing to U.S. companies eager to do business in Vietnam, President Clinton lifts a 30-year-old unilateral trade embargo against the Southeast Asian country.

Sept. 26, 1994
President Clinton lifts most U.S. economic sanctions against Haiti. U.N. sanctions that were imposed in May are lifted Oct. 15.

Oct. 18, 1994
An arms agreement with North Korea calls for the partial lifting of a U.S. trade embargo in place since 1950 in exchange for a Korean commitment to freeze and eventually eliminate its nuclear capability.

Continued from p. 946

break of hostilities, however, the Roosevelt administration applied sanctions against Japan, but only gradually. After Japan invaded China in 1937, the United States banned exports of aircraft and aviation fuel to Japan. When Japan joined Germany and Italy in the Tripartite Alliance in 1940, the U.S. embargo was strengthened to include iron and steel. After Japan occupied southern Indochina in July 1941, the U.S. embargo covered all goods, including oil. But these efforts were to no avail. Four months later, Japan bombed Pearl Harbor, and the United States was drawn into the conflict. [14]

During World War II, the Allies used sanctions somewhat more effectively than they had in peacetime. The naval blockade of Europe, in particular, helped deny Germany and Japan access to strategic materials needed to maintain their war effort. [15]

Cold War Sanctions

With the postwar development of nuclear weapons, the potential for hostilities to escalate into nuclear holocaust made economic sanctions increasingly attractive foreign policy tools. Sanctions were among the few non-belligerent means available to the United Nations, the successor to the League of Nations set up in 1944 to prevent another world war. But the division of the world into two camps dominated by the United States and the Soviet Union made it hard to achieve multilateral support for sanctions.

With the two superpowers holding veto power within the Security Council, the U.N. was able to agree on economic sanctions only once during the Cold War. In 1965, the council imposed sanctions to counter white settlers' efforts to seize control in Rhodesia. Although the sanctions were not lifted until 1979, they resulted in the transfer of power to the black majority and the establishment of Zimbabwe.

Unilateral sanctions continued to be used to counter military action, however, and they were often imposed by the United States. In the late 1940s, for example, U.S. sanctions forced the Netherlands to pull out of Indonesia and grant the island nation independence. It was again U.S. sanctions that forced Britain and France to abandon the Suez Canal in Egypt in 1956. And in the early 1960s, Egypt withdrew from the Congo and Yemen only after the United States canceled food and development assistance to Egypt.

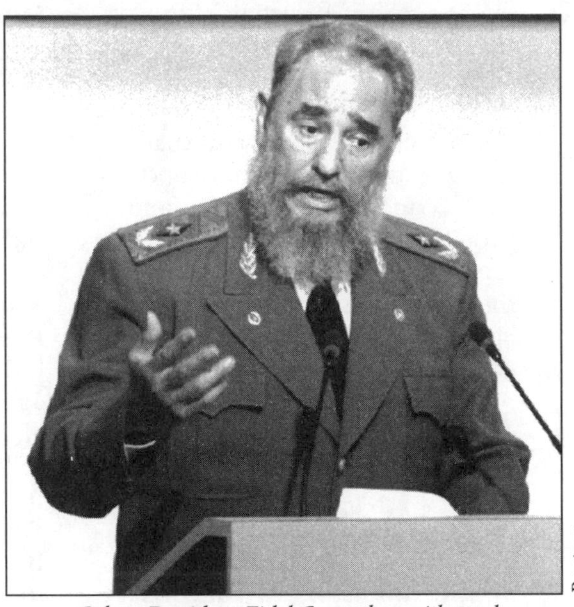

Reuters

Cuban President Fidel Castro has withstood a U.S. trade embargo for 34 years.

Perhaps the best-known unilateral Cold War sanction involves Cuba. In October 1960, nearly two years after Castro came to power and seized U.S. assets on the island, President Dwight D. Eisenhower embargoed all exports to Cuba (except food and medicine). President John F. Kennedy later froze all Cuban assets in the United States. The embargo was later broadened to include all imports from Cuba as well, notably sugar and cigars.

During the 34-year embargo, the United States has enjoyed little support for isolating Cuba. Following the 1962 missile crisis, the Organization of American States (OAS) joined the United States' "quarantine" of Cuba in 1964, but the OAS lifted its sanctions in 1975. Further undermining the unilateral U.S. effort was the Soviet Union's active support of Castro with regular shipments of oil, industrial equipment and consumer goods that were vital to the island nation's economic survival.

Although the United States, as the West's lone superpower, often imposed sanctions unilaterally, it also acted in concert with its allies to create a system of sanctions against the Soviet Union and other communist countries. In the late 1940s, as the nuclear arms race began, the United States gained the support of members of the North Atlantic Treaty Organization (NATO) and Japan to limit exports to the Soviet Union of so-called "dual-use" technology — products designed for civilian use that can be adapted for military use.

A special agency, the Coordinating Committee for Multilateral Export Controls (COCOM), was created to oversee the alliance's export controls. * Most of the COCOM nations also joined the United States in the China Committee (CHINCOM), set up in 1952 to keep strategic goods and technology out of China. After CHINCOM was disbanded in 1958, China came under COCOM rules. The ban on strategic technology transfers held throughout the Cold War.

The United States continued to include sanctions in its efforts to achieve foreign policy objectives. According to the 1990 study by the Institute for

* Iceland was the only NATO member that did not participate in COCOM.

International Economics, the United States has used sanctions repeatedly — and often successfully — to overthrow unfriendly governments in the Western Hemisphere.

U.S. sanctions helped overturn the oppressive regime of Rafael Trujillo of the Dominican Republic in 1961, as well as Chilean President Salvador Allende in 1973, who was assassinated in a coup. The regime of his successor, Gen. Augusto Pinochet, was later subjected to U.S. sanctions when it refused to extradite Chilean suspects in the 1976 assassination in Washington, D.C., of former Allende supporter Orlando Letelier.

Mixed Results

In contrast to their early postwar success in quelling military adventurism around the world, economic sanctions gradually became less effective in stopping aggression. The sanctions imposed by President Jimmy Carter in the mid-1970s still have not induced Turkey to withdraw from Cyprus. The Carter administration also failed to force the Soviet Union to withdraw after its 1979 invasion of Afghanistan, even with the one-two punch of a grain embargo and U.S. boycott of the 1980 Moscow Olympics.

Economic interests proved stronger than Cold War loyalties after the Soviet-backed Polish government declared martial law in November 1981. The following month, President Ronald Reagan announced sanctions against Poland as well as the Soviet Union. Among the U.S. sanctions was the withholding of export licenses to American firms that had contracted to provide equipment for a $15 billion pipeline to transport Soviet natural gas to Western Europe.

When the United States' NATO allies refused to join the sanctions effort, Reagan also banned the sale of equipment to U.S. subsidiaries involved in the project. As tensions built within the alliance, France and Britain ordered the subsidiaries operating in their countries to defy the ban, while West Germany declared the ban a violation of national sovereignty. After a year of acrimonious debate, Reagan lifted the sanctions, and pipeline construction went forward.

The economic weapon has not always been enough to topple hostile neighbors, however, or bring about reform. Despite harsh sanctions, Panamanian strongman Manuel Antonio Noriega held onto power until President George Bush sent the U.S. military to arrest him.

Sanctions had a more positive outcome in Poland, however. The sanctions were kept in place for six years and included limits on the financially strapped government to reschedule its debt of some $10 billion. Worn down by economic hardship, the military regime eventually released political prisoners and agreed to sweeping political and economic reforms in the late 1980s.

The economic weapon has not always been enough to topple hostile neighbors, however, or bring about reform. Despite harsh sanctions, Panamanian strongman Manuel Antonio Noriega held onto power until President George Bush sent the U.S. military to arrest him.

But the most glaring failure of U.S. sanctions to destabilize governments in this hemisphere remains Cuba. Until the Soviet Union's demise in 1991, Castro received massive aid from the U.S.S.R. enabling the Cuban leader to survive the U.S. trade cutoff. Since then, the shaky Cuban economy has faltered even more. Congress added to the pressure with the 1992 Cuban Democracy Act. The law, sponsored by Rep. Robert G. Torricelli, D-N.J., extends the embargo by prohibiting foreign-based subsidiaries of U.S. firms from trading with Cuba.

The United States also led the way in using sanctions to further less controversial foreign policy objectives during the Cold War, including building support for nuclear non-proliferation, combating terrorism and advocating human rights. After Iranian revolutionaries led by the Ayatollah Ruhollah Khomeini took more than 60 Americans hostage in 1979, President Carter imposed an embargo against Iran, froze Iranian assets in the United States, banned all financial exchanges with Iran and barred Americans from traveling to Iran.

Although the hostage crisis contributed to Carter's defeat at the polls in November 1980, the hostages were released Jan. 20, 1981, the day his successor, Ronald Reagan, was inaugurated, in exchange for a partial lifting of the freeze on Iranian assets. "Even though we were still in the Cold

War, indeed at a particularly delicate time of it," says Fordham's Malloy, "those sanctions were really quite effective on their own terms."

The United States and other countries rarely have imposed economic sanctions solely to improve human rights. A notable exception is South Africa, whose economic isolation by the United States and much of the rest of the world community during the 1980s helped dismantle the white-ruled country's racist policy of apartheid. Between 1986, when Congress passed the Comprehensive Anti-Apartheid Act banning new U.S. investments in South Africa, and 1991, when the Bush administration lifted the sanctions, more than 200 U.S. firms sold or otherwise abandoned subsidiaries there. [16] ■

CURRENT SITUATION

Clinton's Record

Until the recent dispatch of U.S. troops to Haiti and the Persian Gulf, the Clinton administration appeared less committed to sanctions than its predecessors, or at least unwilling to hurt the economy by imposing sanctions to further foreign policy goals. During the 1992 presidential campaign, Clinton had promised to focus on domestic issues, such as jobs and the economy. [17]

"You have to remember that this is the 'It's the economy, stupid' president," says Hannum.

"For this president, the arguments of grain producers in the Midwest are automatically going to be more persuasive than arguments about protecting human rights or other diplomatic or foreign affairs issues."

On Sept. 29, 1993, Clinton initiated the loosening of COCOM restrictions on exports of strategic technology to the former Soviet Union. With the move toward democracy in Russia and the other former Soviet republics, the president said, the rationale for limiting many exports of civilian technology had weakened. Economic reforms in these countries also were opening up new overseas markets for U.S. manufacturers of computers, software, telecommunications equipment and other goods.

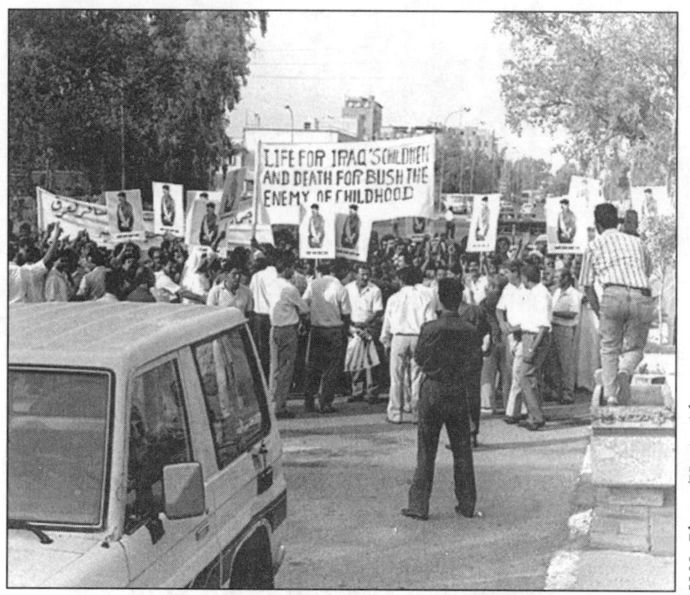

U.N. Photo/H. Arvidsson

Iraqi demonstrators protest U.N. arms inspectors in July 1992. After Iraq invaded Kuwait in 1990, the Security Council embargoed Iraq to force it to allow the inspections.

Meanwhile, in another move prompted, at least in part, by economic considerations, the administration in May renewed China's most-favored-nation status, despite continuing reports of human rights abuses in the country. [18]

It came as little surprise, therefore, when Clinton lifted the 30-year-old embargo against Vietnam in February. A broad array of U.S. businesses had argued that the sanctions were preventing them from cashing in on valuable investment opportunities in this rapidly developing country, costing not only corporate profits but also American jobs in companies that might export goods to Vietnam under normal trade conditions.

While business leaders welcomed the lifting of the sanctions, critics attribute the action less to anything the Clinton administration did than to earlier diplomatic efforts. Previous administrations had used the sanctions as leverage to gain information on U.S. servicemen still missing since the end of the Vietnam War in 1973. "There was a consistently strong policy of enforcement of the sanctions over a long period of time, together with a fair amount of experimentation [with different types of sanctions], even during the Reagan and Bush years," says Malloy. "The end result of the lifting at this particular moment is not something that can be tagged to this particular administration."

Haiti has posed far different challenges, and the administration's use of sanctions there has come under harsher criticism. For three years before U.S. forces helped return President Aristide to power Oct. 15, Haiti was under a series of heavy sanctions, including an oil embargo, enforced by the United States, the OAS and later the United Nations that caused widespread hardship among the poorest inhabitants. [19]

"We can pretty much [tie] the Haiti sanctions to the Clinton administration," Malloy says, "and they have done very poorly with these sanctions."

In July 1993, after Haiti's military leaders met with Aristide forces at Governors Island, N.Y., and agreed to step down by Oct. 30 of that year, the administration lifted the U.S. sanctions, as did the OAS and the United Nations. "Sanctions were lifted on the strength of a promise of future performance," Malloy says, "and of course

Iraq Reveals Complexity of Sanctions

If Iraq is any indication, lining up multilateral support for U.N. economic sanctions in the post-Cold War era will be a snap — but keeping them in place may take some fancy diplomatic footwork.

The United Nations imposed the sanctions just four days after Iraq's Aug. 2, 1990, invasion and occupation of Kuwait. The Security Council approved Resolution 661 imposing a full trade embargo barring all imports from and exports to Iraq, except medical supplies, food and other humanitarian items. The resolution also authorized the 15-member council to act as a sanctions committee to oversee the embargo.

The U.N.'s first application of economic sanctions in the post-Cold War era initially attracted widespread support, even as the U.S.-led military coalition succeeded in restoring the government of Kuwait to power.

"Sanctions have had a largely positive effect in Iraq because they were applied to prevent them from developing a non-conventional military capability," says former U.S. Ambassador Robert B. Oakley. "Sanctions have forced them to comply with Security Council resolutions that allow the International Atomic Energy Agency and others to put up a whole network of controls and constraints to make sure they're not developing weapons of mass destruction."

Reuters

Iraqi President Saddam Hussein greets a crowd in Qurna in November 1992. France and other countries are calling for lifting the sanctions against Iraq.

But other aims of international sanctions against Iraq have not been met. "Sanctions haven't done the populace any good from a human rights standpoint," Oakley says. "Nor have they led the government to recognize the boundaries of Kuwait. So they have been a mixed bag in Iraq, but on balance probably a plus given all the things that are at stake there."

Now, with Iraqi citizens suffering from the lack of food and other consumer goods that are normally imported, President Saddam Hussein is pressuring the Security Council to lift the embargo. [1]

Iraq, as a major oil supplier, has found allies in its quest to lift the sanctions, chiefly Russia and France, both Security Council members eager to secure lucrative trade arrangements with Iraq. Russian Foreign Minister Andrei V. Kozyrev specifically proposes lifting the oil embargo in exchange for Iraq's recognition of Kuwait's borders. France supports an easing of sanctions as a means of de-escalating the crisis that arose during the recent deployment of Iraqi troops near the Kuwait border.

As leader of the military coalition in the region, the United States is reluctant to ease sanctions now, lest Hussein view the move as a sign of weakness and take further hostile action against Kuwait. Moreover, the U.S. has fewer trade ties to Iraq than Russia and France. Britain sides with the United States on not lifting the sanctions now.

As support for easing the sanctions from Russia and France shows, the same economic incentives that make sanctions work can also undermine them. "In this day and age, with international trade so linked to a multinational market, you need the fairly active cooperation of a wide range of states to make sanctions effective," says Michael Malloy, a sanctions expert at Fordham University in New York. "On the other hand, the fact that we are now in a post-Cold War era does not necessarily mean that sanctions automatically will work better than they did before."

[1] See Edwin Chen, "Gulf War Leaves Legacy of Hard Times for Iraqi People," *Los Angeles Times* (Washington Edition), Oct. 17, 1994.

the Haitian colonels reneged." The administration reimposed the sanctions but could not dislodge the military without sending U.S. troops. "We lost a lot of ground," Malloy says. "Giving away that counter before the deal was done strikes me as very short-sighted and bad tactics."

Cuba and Iraq

With the Clinton administration's emphasis on domestic economic concerns and readiness to lift sanctions against other target nations, lawmakers once again are taking up the long-simmering debate over Cuba. The fact that sanctions have failed to unseat Castro after 34 years fuels arguments on both sides of the debate. Embargo supporters say it has not been enforced strongly enough to have the desired effect; opponents call it a vestige of the Cold War and that renewed trade with Cuba would actually hasten the island's entry into the world trading community.

Torricelli, whose 1992 Cuban Democracy Act tightened the embargo to block foreign remittances to Cuba, warns against dropping the embargo just as he says it is taking effect. He rejects the notion that Cuba poses no threat to U.S. interests now that the Cold War is over. "That attitude," he writes, "confirms the accusations of our worst critics, who argued during the Cold War that the United States was never really interested in securing human rights or democratic governments for the people of Latin America — that our actions were cynical attempts to gain an advantage against the Soviets. The Cuban Democracy Act defines the situation for Castro in unambiguous terms. When a free and fair election is scheduled, the embargo ends." [20]

Torricelli's position is supported by many Cuban-Americans. "Those who advocated dropping the embargo against Vietnam and sanctions against China at least had something to their argument because they could point to concrete, fundamental reforms that were going on in those countries, such as allowing individual citizens real economic freedoms," says Cardenas of the Cuban American foundation. "Those don't exist in Cuba. Lifting the embargo today would only strengthen the regime by providing it with more economic resources at a time when its lack of resources is forcing it to address and recognize the need for basic reform."

But Torricelli's fellow Democrats, Sen. Claiborne Pell, D-R.I., and Rep. Lee H. Hamilton, D-Ind., take issue with this argument. "U.S. policy has done little to advance the cause of human rights in Cuba," they write. "Instead, it creates an atmosphere of hostility, reinforcing a siege mentality and providing a justification for repressive policies." [21]

Some critics of the Cuban embargo say an unstated goal is not merely to encourage democratic reform on the island but to get rid of Castro altogether. That may have been justified during the Cold War, they say, when Cuba sent troops to defend the communist government of Angola against U.S.-backed rebels and to help leftist insurgents in other countries. "Frankly, I don't like the idea of getting rid of any government," says Oakley. "It clearly is not a legitimate goal, and nobody that I know of in the Western Hemisphere or anywhere else shares the view that it is. In any case, Castro isn't in the business of exporting revolution. He gave that up long ago."

Rep. Robert G. Torricelli, D-N.J.

Torricelli warns against dropping the Cuban embargo just as he says it is taking effect. "The Cuban Democracy Act defines the situation for Castro in unambiguous terms. When a free and fair election is scheduled, the embargo ends."

When it comes to Iraq, the Clinton administration has shown itself to be tougher on sanctions than other members of the Security Council. After Iraqi forces invaded Kuwait in 1990, the Security Council agreed to maintain a comprehensive embargo against Iraq until Saddam Hussein allowed U.N. arms inspectors to monitor the country's arsenal of chemical and nuclear weapons. The embargo bars exports to Iraq, which had imported three-quarters of its food and virtually all its military equipment. [22]

The sanctions appear to have achieved their stated goal, as Iraq has been deterred from developing weapons of mass destruction. But recent events suggest that Hussein is turning the sanctions to his advantage. Anti-American demonstrations in Baghdad indicate that the regime has convinced at least some Iraqis to blame the sanctioners for hardships incurred by the loss of international trade. Further, by holding out the prospects of lucrative business ventures, Hussein has driven a wedge between the sanctions' sponsors. France, Russia and other European countries, lured by Iraq's oil and other economic interests, have been pressing the Clinton administration for months to ease the sanctions, saying Iraq has complied with U.N. demands.

The United States, which has borne the main military burden in the Persian Gulf, is holding out for more concessions from Iraq, chiefly its formal recognition of the existing boundaries with Kuwait. "It would be a grave mistake," the president said, "for Saddam Hussein to believe that for any reason the United States would have weakened its resolve on the same issues that involved us in the conflict just a few years ago." [23] ■

OUTLOOK

U.N. Reform Proposals

If the past four years are a guide, sanctions will play an increasingly important role in post-Cold War di-

Continued on p. 954

At Issue:

Should the United States lift its embargo against Cuba?

yes

Rep. Charles B. Rangel, D-N.Y.
FROM *STATEMENT BEFORE HOUSE AGRICULTURE SUBCOMMITTEE ON FOREIGN AGRICULTURE AND HUNGER,*
MAY 19, 1994.

While I know that there are strongly held views on both sides of this issue, I believe that few Americans hold to the view that the denial of food should be used as a weapon to bring down a government, even one that we may not agree with. Unfortunately, that is the attitude attributed to some people . . . who have made the destruction of the Castro government their first priority. . . .

As an American, it is impossible to defend the morality of the reasoning behind the embargo — especially of those items that result in the greatest hardships to the common people, such as food.

Should we discard our most deeply held beliefs in the fundamental rights of all people — even our enemies — to the basic necessities of life? Should our desire to see a government changed blind us to the injustice of trying to foment a revolution by starving the mothers and their babies?

It has been said that allowing trade of any kind — whether in machinery, medicine or food — helps bolster the government of Fidel Castro. On the contrary, our misguided attempts to incite an uprising among the hungry poor provides the most persuasive defense to those who resist change.

And what if we were to succeed? What if the women and children and men who were too weak to endure any more took to the streets in revolt? Would we supply them with arms to overcome the most powerful military in Latin America? Would we dispatch Cuban-American freedom fighters to the Bay of Pigs? What would we do with the thousands who boarded rafts in flight to Florida? Would we welcome them?

. . . I believe it is my responsibility to speak out for what is best for America, not only for opportunities in trade, but as a moral nation and model of democracy and fairness around the world.

If we were to live up to that standard, as it relates to Cuba, we would lift the embargo and work to normalize relations. Rather than remaining stuck in a dead-end posture of confrontation and isolation, we should free ourselves of the political failures and grudges of the past — as we have in Vietnam.

There is no argument but that the collapse of the Cuban economy is due to the failure of the communist economic system. But for every day that the embargo prevents us from sharing the wealth of our fields and factories, and shackles the competitive spirit of our own entrepreneurs, we lose another opportunity to spread our most potent seeds of democracy.

no

The Cuban American National Foundation
FROM *STATEMENT ON U.S. POLICY TOWARD CUBA,*
JANUARY 1994.

The U.S. embargo remains the primary non-violent policy option for influencing change in Cuba. It serves as the major disincentive for the continuation of the Castro regime. It presents an alternative to the Cuban people. . . . [W]hat the Cuban people can have instead of Castro is normal diplomatic and economic relations with the U.S.

Removing the U.S. embargo of Cuba gives up the only leverage we have to bring about meaningful change there. Once the embargo is removed, it can never be reinstituted. What options will we be left with should no positive change in Cuba materialize? In short, lifting the embargo would provide in the short-term a critical boost to the regime with uncertain results of the long term. . . .

The Cuban people's suffering is caused by an inefficient system imposed on them by Fidel Castro, who refuses to allow any reforms with which Cuban citizens can improve their individual lives. For example, several years ago he abolished the Farmer's Free Markets because some Cubans became very effective in providing goods to the Cuban people independent of the state.

The Cuban people are suffering because Fidel Castro continues to deny Cuban citizens individual political and economic freedom because those freedoms mean autonomy from state control, and autonomy from state control means the state cannot exact reprisals if you refuse to conform. And without that climate of fear — fear of losing one's job when the state is the sole employer, fear of your children being expelled from the state's schools — Fidel Castro cannot retain power.

When you provide resources to Cuba, all of those resources go into the hands of Fidel Castro. Despite the tremendous assistance that Cuba received from the Soviet Union over three decades, the Cuban people since 1960 have been receiving food through a ration book. Castro has used such foreign assistance not to establish a viable economy to meet the needs of the Cuban people, but to buy the loyalty of the *nomenklatura,* the party officials, to sustain himself in power. . . .

The end of the Castro regime is only a question of when, not if. So at this critical juncture in U.S.-Cuban relations and no less Cuban history, there is no compelling reason why the course of events should be arrested by some woolly initiative from Washington, especially in light of the historical record. Such initiatives by the U.S. were only used by Castro to his advantage. And while international conditions have certainly changed in the last few years, no evidence exists that Fidel Castro has.

For More Information

Cuban American National Foundation, 1000 Thomas Jefferson St. N.W., Suite 505, Washington, D.C. 20007; (202) 265-2822. The leading organization representing anti-Castro Cuban Americans supports tougher sanctions against Cuba.

Institute for International Economics, 11 Dupont Circle N.W., Washington, D.C. 20036; (202) 328-9000. A research organization that has published an extensive analysis of economic sanctions.

U.S. Treasury Department, Office of Foreign Assets Control, Main Treasury Building, Washington, D.C. 20220; (202) 622-2510. The federal office that enforces the most sweeping economic sanctions imposed by the U.S..

United Nations Association of the USA, 485 Fifth Ave., New York, N.Y. 10017-6104; (212) 697-3232. A research and educational organization focusing on ways to enhance the United Nations' role in peacekeeping.

Continued from p. 952

plomacy. To strengthen their impact in today's global economy, however, sanctions must have the broadest possible support among the leading economic powers. As the multilateral body dedicated to keeping the peace, the United Nations is seen as the only feasible existing organization to apply and enforce multilateral sanctions.

But some U.N. experts say the Security Council is not up to the task. Lloyd J. Dumas, a professor of political economics at the University of Texas-Dallas, for example, proposes the creation of a new Council on Economic Sanctions and Peacekeeping within the United Nations. By including all U.N. nations, the agency would have to gain far broader international support for any sanctions it imposes, Dumas writes, lessening the risk sanctions could be subverted and making them achieve their goals faster.

The proposed council also would have authority to enforce sanctions. Perhaps most importantly, the council would set out specific actions that would automatically lead to the application of U.N. sanctions. "In principle, any nation that violated the sanctions would automatically and immediately be subject to the same sanctions," Dumas writes. "Since the sanctions would be automatic, potential violators would know about them in advance and know they would be imposed." [24]

Anticipating the U.N.'s growing recourse to sanctions as a non-violent peacekeeping tool, the United Nations association also recommended Security Council changes. In a 1992 study by Laurenti, it called for the Security Council to set up a standing committee on sanctions and to consider creating a special office to closely monitor the impact of sanctions on the target countries' economies as well as their effectiveness in achieving diplomatic goals. [25]

"We don't think that when a state has gone to the ultimate recourse of war to satisfy its ends that those ends will lightly be abandoned because of economic hardship," says Laurenti. "But there are lower thresholds of violations where sanctions can tip the balance."

Critics of such changes say new agencies will not make sanctions work better in the absence of political will. "I love the idea of multilateralism," says Burkhalter of Human Rights Watch, "but we've just been through the Rwanda genocide, when the international community didn't lift a finger. The U.N. secretary-general was haranguing people about it, and there were mechanisms in place, not to mention all the wealth in the world that could have made sanctions work, and they still let upwards of a million people get killed."

Oakley also rejects expanding the U.N. bureaucracy as "a wild idea." If sanctions are applied through the United Nations, he says, "the Security Council is the best place to deal with them." For sanctions to work, Oakley says, they have to exact a higher cost on the offending country. "One of the most important things that you can do is to really go after the money supply and shut off the financial flow" to the country under sanctions, he says. "But the international community has not shown the political will to go after the international banks to do that."

Balkans Test Case

The stalemate in the Balkans civil war reflects the reality that multilateral sanctions are only as strong as the political will of their supporters. Four years after they were imposed by the United Nations, economic sanctions against Serbia are weakening under the pressure of conflicting interests among the world powers. European countries propose a relaxation of sanctions against Serbia, which has supplied weapons and moral support to the Serbian faction in the civil war that has ravaged Bosnia since April 1992.

The United States has held out for a harder line against Serbia. At the same time, the Europeans oppose a Clinton administration proposal to lift an arms embargo aimed at keeping weapons out of the hands of all parties in the civil war. [26] To do so at this juncture, the Europeans say, would endanger their troops on the ground. The majority of U.N. peacekeeping forces in Bosnia are from Britain, France and other European countries.

In a pitch to convince the Security Council to lift the sanctions, Serbian President Slobodan Milosevic agreed in August to allow the European Union to post observers along the Yugoslav border to ensure that only humanitarian aid passes into Serb-controlled Bosnia. In return for this concession, the Security Council Sept. 23 passed a resolution allowing Yugoslavia to open its airport in Belgrade, run passenger ferries to Italy and participate in sports and cultural events.

But observers of the Bosnian war caution the United States against caving in further to European pressure to ease economic sanctions against Milosevic. "Milosevic has once again outwitted the West," writes Frederick Cuny, a consultant in disaster relief working in Sarajevo. "The U.S. administration should be wary of being suckered again by the Europeans, who are anxious to ease the economic sanctions against Serbia. . . . At a minimum, the United States should make it clear that the 'reward' for Milosevic's recent maneuvers to avoid tougher sanctions will be limited to *not tightening* them, at least for now. Instead, we're talking about *easing* sanctions. Who's snookering whom?" [27]

To many experts, the situation in the Balkans is a barometer of just how far the international community must go before it will have a clear model for applying sanctions as a peacekeeping tool.

"Even in this new era, the sanctions now in place in Yugoslavia — mandated by the U.N. Security Council — are almost totally ineffective, arguably disastrous," says Malloy. "They demonstrate that there is no magic linkage between the post-Cold War environment and the effectiveness of sanctions. If they're not timed correctly, if they're not constructed properly, if they don't have a fairly broad and aggressive consensus behind them, they're not going to work, regardless of the geopolitical situation we find ourselves in." ■

Notes

[1] Gary Clyde Hufbauer, Jeffrey J. Schott and Kimberly Ann Elliott, *Economic Sanctions Reconsidered* (1990).

[2] For background, see "U.S.-China Trade," *The CQ Researcher,* April 15, 1994, pp. 313-336.

[3] For background, see "Cuba in Crisis," *The CQ Researcher,* Nov. 29, 1991, pp. 897-920.

[4] For background, see "U.S.-Vietnam Relations," *The CQ Researcher,* Dec. 3, 1993, pp. 1057-1080.

[5] See Douglas Farah, "Haitian Elite Set to Profit from U.S. Presence," *The Washington Post,* Sept. 25, 1994.

[6] Gary Hufbauer, "The Futility of Sanctions," *The Wall Street Journal,* June 1, 1994.

[7] Gary Hufbauer, *The Impact of U.S. Economic Sanctions and Controls on U.S. Firms,* National Foreign Trade Council, April 1990.

[8] Graves testified May 19, 1994, before the House Agriculture Subcommittee on Foreign Agriculture and Hunger.

[9] Deere testified May 19, 1994, before the House Agriculture Subcommittee on Foreign Agriculture and Hunger.

[10] Loop testified May 19, 1994, before the House Agriculture Subcommittee on Foreign Agriculture and Hunger.

[11] See Douglas Farah, "Toughest Task in Haiti: Reviving the Economy," *The Washington Post,* Sept. 23, 1994.

[12] Unless otherwise noted, information for this section is from Hufbauer et al., *op. cit.,* pp. 4-33.

[13] *Ibid.,* p. 9.

[14] See David A. Baldwin, *Economic Statecraft* (1985), pp. 165-166.

[15] Hufbauer et al., *op. cit.,* p. 10.

[16] For background, see "South Africa's Future," *The CQ Researcher,* Jan. 14, 1994, pp. 25-48.

[17] For background, see "Foreign Policy and Public Opinion," *The CQ Researcher,* July 15, 1994, pp. 601-624.

[18] See Holly Burkhalter, "U.S. Should Punish China's Rights Abuses by Raising Tariffs," *Human Rights Watch,* winter/spring 1994, p. 2.

[19] See Howard W. French, "Study Says Haiti Sanctions Kill Up to 1,000 Children a Month," *The New York Times,* Nov. 9, 1993.

[20] Robert G. Torricelli, "Keep the Embargo," *The Washington Post,* Sept. 11, 1994.

[21] Claiborne Pell and Lee H. Hamilton, "The Embargo Must Go," *The Washington Post,* Sept. 8, 1994. Pell is chairman of the Senate Foreign Relations Committee, and Hamilton chairs the House Foreign Affairs Committee.

[22] See Keith Bradsher, "Trade Embargoes: Do They Work?" *The New York Times,* July 14, 1991.

[23] Clinton spoke Oct. 10 at a White House news conference where he announced the dispatch of additional U.S. troops to the Persian Gulf.

[24] Lloyd J. Dumas, "Organizing the Chaos," *Bulletin of the Atomic Scientists,* November 1993, p. 48.

[25] Jeffrey Laurenti, *Partners for Peace* (1992).

[26] See Roger Cohen, "At Odds Over Bosnia," *The New York Times,* Oct. 2, 1994.

[27] Frederick Cuny, "Milosevic Outwits the West, Again," *The Washington Post,* Oct. 5, 1994.

Bibliography

Selected Sources Used

Books

Baldwin, David A., *Economic Statecraft*, Princeton University Press, 1985.

The author presents the historical and theoretical background of economic sanctions and assesses their effectiveness in achieving foreign policy objectives.

Hufbauer, Gary Clyde, Jeffrey J. Schott and Kimberly Ann Elliott, *Economic Sanctions Reconsidered*, Institute for International Economics, 1990.

This updated two-volume edition of the 1985 original work remains the most widely cited study of economic sanctions imposed after World War I by the United States and other countries. The main volume, *History and Current Policy,* presents a general overview and 11 recent cases. A second volume, *Supplemental Case Histories,* reviews more than 70 other sanctions and their impacts.

Articles

Brittain, Victoria, "Savimbi, Bloody Savimbi," *The Nation,* July 11, 1994.

Brittain writes that U.S. support of Jonas Savimbi's UNITA forces against the Soviet-backed socialist government of Angola enabled the rebel leader to wreak havoc on the country's economy for almost 20 years. Savimbi, now the target of U.S. sanctions for his rejection of recent elections in Angola, continues the civil war.

Hendrickson, David C., "The Recovery of Internationalism," *Foreign Affairs,* September/October 1994.

One of the Clinton administration's many foreign policy challenges is the crafting of a more coherent sanctions policy, the author writes. As the situation in Haiti shows, he writes, sanctions can backfire, causing greater suffering among ordinary citizens than among oppressive governments that are the policy's target.

Kornbluh, Peter, and James G. Blight, "Dialogue with Castro: A Hidden History," *The New York Review of Books,* Oct. 6, 1994.

In the 1970s, Kornbluh recounts, the Nixon administration conducted secret negotiations with Fidel Castro in an unsuccessful effort to normalize relations between the two countries. Two decades later, the trade embargo is still in effect and was even tightened two years ago.

"Serbia: Another Country," *The Economist,* July 23, 1994.

Serbian President Slobodan Milosevic clings to power despite a U.N. economic embargo levied against his country for his arming of Serbian nationalists in Bosnia's civil war. He retains popular support by blaming the worsening economic situation on unwarranted foreign antagonism toward Serbia, the magazine says.

Reports and Studies

Day, Erin, *Economic Sanctions Imposed by the United States Against Specific Countries: 1979 Through 1992,* Congressional Research Service, Aug. 10, 1992.

Of the 79 countries that were the focus of U.S. sanctions of all types during the period examined — including arms embargoes and other non-economic measures — seven nations are still under broad trade embargoes. The report provides a history and status of all the U.S. sanctions that were applied over the 13-year period.

Gunn, Gillian, *Cuba in Transition,* Twentieth Century Fund Paper, September 1993.

If the United States wishes to ease Cuba's transformation into an economically viable democracy, it should distance itself from the conservative Cuban-American community and its determination to oust Castro by increasing economic hardships on the island, writes Gunn, director of Georgetown University's Cuba Project.

Hufbauer, Gary, *The Impact of U.S. Economic Sanctions and Controls on U.S. Firms,* National Foreign Trade Council, April 1990.

Whether or not they achieve their foreign policy objectives, sanctions can be highly costly to U.S. firms trying to do business overseas, Hufbauer writes. In 1987, which the author calls "a representative year," U.S. companies may have lost $7 billion worth of potential exports due to economic sanctions and related export controls against more than 25 countries.

United Nations Association of the USA, *Partners for Peace: Strengthening Collective Security for the 21st Century,* October 1992.

The post-Cold War era offers new opportunities for the United Nations to assume a broader role in international peacekeeping, according to this study. As the strongest non-combat measure available to the U.N. to enforce the peace, economic sanctions are likely to play an important role. The authors recommend creating a new U.N. agency to oversee multilateral economic sanctions.

The Next Step

Additional information from UMI's Newspaper & Periodical Abstracts database

The Bosnian Situation

"Bosnia's Serb leader threatened," ***The Wall Street Journal,*** **Sept. 2, 1994, p. A1.**
Bosnia's Serb leader threatened to cut gas, water, power and food supplies to Muslim and Croat communities unless the Serbia-led Yugoslav government ends an economic blockade against the Bosnian Serbs.

Carter, Hodding, "Punishing Serbia," ***Foreign Policy,*** **fall 1994, pp. 49-56.**
Marten van Heuven's theory on restoring stability in the Balkans is criticized. It is unrealistic to expect either the U.N. or the European Union to take steps toward punishing the wrongs that have been committed in Yugoslavia, Carter says.

Christopher, Warren, "Foreign ministers contact group meeting on Bosnia-Herzegovina," ***U.S. Department of State Dispatch,*** **Aug. 15, 1994, pp. 553-554.**
Issues discussed and decided upon by a group of foreign ministers concerning the Bosnian Serb rejection of a proposed peace settlement are reported. Since the Serbs have rejected this plan, economic sanctions and an extension of U.N.-protected safe zones will be more rigidly enforced, Secretary of State Christopher says.

Doder, Dusko, "Divided town feels psychological effects of Serb blockade," ***Boston Globe,*** **Aug. 14, 1994, p. 4.**
Zvornik, Bosnia-Herzegovina, is a town divided. The left bank, in Bosnia, has been "cleansed" of its Muslim majority. The right bank, in Serbia, still has a functioning mosque. This town will most likely feel the majority of the effects of the blockade of supplies to Bosnian Serbs.

Morrison, David C., "How Bosnia is becoming a priority," ***National Journal,*** **Aug. 20, 1994, pp. 1976-1977.**
The Senate has approved an amendment to the fiscal 1995 defense appropriations bill directing President Clinton to lift the embargo on arms to Bosnia-Herzegovina by Nov. 15, 1994.

O'Sullivan, John, "Deja views," ***National Review,*** **Sept. 12, 1994, p. 4.**
An editorial discusses Margaret Thatcher's position on lifting the arms embargo on Bosnia-Herzegovina and then compares it with President Clinton's. Another campaign promise to admit Haitian refugees into the U.S. is embarrassing Clinton because of his flip flops on the issue of refugees from Haiti and now Cuba.

Pomfret, John, "Bosnian Serbs still get supplies despite Belgrade's blockade," ***The Washington Post,*** **Aug. 14, 1994, p. A31.**
Commerce is continuing to flow across the Drina River between Serbia and Bosnia despite an order by Serbian President Slobodan Milosevic barring everything but humanitarian aid from being sent to the Bosnian Serbs.

Shchedrunova, Yelena, "Yugoslavia," ***Current Digest of the Post-Soviet Press,*** **Aug. 24, 1994, p. 23.**
Russian special envoy Vitaly Churkin believes that Russia may "have to start using negative incentives" in the effort to broker peace in Yugoslavia. Punitive measures could come in the form of sanctions.

Crisis in Haiti

"Chronology of events," ***Congressional Digest,*** **August 1994, p. 202.**
A chronology of events through July 1994 relating to the crisis in Haiti is presented.

Ellison, Mike, "Haitian divorce," ***Guardian,*** **July 26, 1994, p. 6.**
Mike Ellison comments on several July 1994 performances by the Haitian band Boukman Eksperyans in Britain. Ellison comments on how the band has been unable to return to Haiti due to the intensified embargo on the nation.

Hackworth, David H., "A soldier's-eye view," ***Newsweek,*** **Aug. 22, 1994, p. 33.**
The "elite" Haitian presidential guard lacks the skill and equipment to put up much of a fight. Since there is no threat to U.S. national security, the U.S. invasion fleet should be brought home and the costly embargo lifted.

Chavannes Jean-Baptiste, "Tying Aristide's hands," ***The Progressive,*** **Sept. 1994, p. 26.**
Instead of supporting effective sanctions against Haiti's elites, the U.S. has used a weak embargo that impoverished the Haitian majority while enriching those in power, Chavannes writes.

Katz, Nancie L., "Haitian parents charge U.S. backlog trapped children at home," ***The Washington Post,*** **Sept. 4, 1994, p. A44.**
More than 200 Haitian children of U.S. citizens or legal residents are trapped in strife-torn Haiti, even though they should have had visas to leave before U.N. sanctions ended commercial flights in August 1994.

Klarreich, Kathie, "Haitians struggle to school children," ***Christian Science Monitor,*** **Sept. 9, 1994, p. 6.**
The difficulties involved in educating Haiti's poor children are discussed. Parents have been known to sell the

roofing off their houses to pay for their children's education, but the 1994 embargo against the country has worsened the state of education.

Spencer, Peter, "Haitian flight song," ***Rolling Stone,*** **Sept. 22, 1994, p. 36.**
More than ever, world music artists are at the mercy of global politics. The circumstances that led to the death of Michel-Melthon "Olicha" Lynch, bassist for the Haitian roots-pop group Boukman Eksperyans, on June 4, 1994, are discussed. Antibiotics that had cured his bacterial meningitis once before had become unavailable in Haiti after the U.S. embargo.

Other International Points of Interest

Brandon, Karen, "Vietnamese-Americans divided on Hanoi trade," ***Chicago Tribune,*** **Aug. 29, 1994, p. 4.**
Westminster, Calif., with 72,000 ethnic Vietnamese in its Little Saigon neighborhood, is the cultural crossroads of Vietnam and the U.S. Area residents have intense and conflicting emotions concerning the Clinton administration's decision to lift its 30-year embargo on trade with Hanoi. Various viewpoints are discussed.

"Iraq, hit by U.N. sanctions, may recognize Kuwait," ***Boston Globe,*** **Aug. 16, 1994, p. 11.**
Iraq has promised to issue a statement about recognition of Kuwait's sovereignty and U.N.-demarcated borders before the Security Council's next review of sanctions against Baghdad, said the body's president, Yuli Vorontsov.

LaBudde, Sam, "U.S. orders sanctions on Taiwan," ***Earth Island Journal,*** **summer 1994, p. 8.**
The Clinton administration has announced that the U.S. will suspend trade in Taiwanese wildlife products. Violations of international conservation treaties prompted the trade sanctions.

Rodman, Kenneth A., "Public and private sanctions against South Africa," ***Political Science Quarterly,*** **summer 1994, pp. 313-334.**
The influence of multinational business corporations' use of economic sanctions in the anti-apartheid movement in South Africa is examined. In many ways, the behavior of these private corporations was more significant than were the sanctions legislated by Congress.

Shirley, Edward G., "The Iran policy trap," ***Foreign Policy,*** **fall 1994, pp. 75-93.**
The U.S. government's dual containment policy, initiated for countering the lingering menace of Iraq and the intimidating threat from Iran, is discussed. The policy calls for collective economic action against Iran.

"Trouble on oily waters," ***The Economist,*** **July 23, 1994, p. 33.**
The tone of China's and Vietnam's regular diplomatic row has turned more dangerous as a result of a series of actions over competing oil claims in the South China Sea. The turmoil has been sparked by Chinese warships blockading a Vietnam oil rig in an area claimed by China.

Wright, Robin, "Libya thrashing about to shake U.N. sanctions hook," ***Los Angeles Times,*** **Sept. 1, 1994, p. A1.**
As part of a bid to ease the tightening grip of U.N. sanctions, Muammar el-Quaddfi's troubled regime in Libya has held out the prospect of turning over an indicted CIA renegade to appease the U.S. Libya also may be willing to pay compensation to the families of the victims in the 1988 bombing of Pan American Flight 103 over Scotland.

Trade Sanctions and Japan

Chappell, Lindsay, "Japanese need strong finish to meet parts target," ***Automotive News,*** **July 11, 1994, p. 28.**
Japanese carmakers need to buy $19 billion worth of U.S. auto parts in 1994 as part of an agreement to help smooth over trade tensions. Japan's failure to meet the deadline would create problems, and President Clinton has set a Sept. 30, 1994, deadline for deciding whether the U.S. should impose Super 301 trade sanctions.

Shear, Jeff, "The Bradley solution," ***National Journal,*** **Aug. 20, 1994, p. 1997.**
Sen. Bill Bradley, D-N.J., has a plan that he hopes will move the U.S. and Japan off a collision course on trade. In September 1994, the Clinton administration will put sanctions on Japan under Title VII of the 1988 Omnibus Trade and Competitiveness Act.

"The struggle to slim Japan's surplus," ***The Economist,*** **July 30, 1994, pp. 29-30.**
Japan says it will not negotiate trade policy with the U.S. if sanctions are implemented. The source of the row is growing. In June 1994, Japan's monthly trade surplus with the U.S. hit $11.3 billion, up 14 percent over June 1993.

"Washington wire: Sanctions loom," ***The Wall Street Journal,*** **Sept. 2, 1994, p. A1.**
Japan has not responded to a trade proposal made in July 1994, and six weeks later the prospects of sanctions loom greater as the U.S.-Japanese trade fight worsens. U.S. negotiators see no progress on Japanese government purchases and autos.

Trade With Korea

Bowman, Karlyn H., and Everett Carll Ladd, "Public opinion and demographic report: North Korea," ***American Enterprise,*** **July 1994, p. 83.**
A supposedly inward-looking public believes that the U.S. has vital interests at stake in the North Korean situation and supports economic sanctions and increasing

U.S. military involvement in South Korea. In most polls, over four people in 10 support allied military action if the situation deteriorates.

"Jimmy Clinton?" ***Far Eastern Economic Review,*** **June 30, 1994, p. 5.**
An editorial notes that just as the Clinton administration was laying the groundwork for sanctions against North Korea, Democratic predecessor Jimmy Carter was back in Seoul, South Korea, thumping against them. Moreover, a U.S. president who came to office announcing a U.S. pullout from South Korea and who left his name synonymous with indecision seems an odd choice of envoy.

Scheer, Robert, "You thought the Cold War was dead?" ***Los Angeles Times,*** **Aug. 19, 1994, p. B7.**
Scheer criticizes the Clinton administration's continuance of the trade embargo against Cuba, despite the end of the Cold War and the opening of trade relations with communist countries such as North Korea and Vietnam.

Tuna Fishing Embargoes

French, Hilary F., "The Tuna Test," ***World Watch,*** **September 1994, p.9.**
A GATT ruling that the U.S. embargo against tuna from Mexico violated the GATT has prompted a heated international debate on the proper role of trade sanctions in environmental policymaking. GATT rules should be updated so that they encourage, rather than undermine, efforts to protect the Earth's deteriorating natural resource base, French writes.

Myers, Paul, "Ferry hit by blockade," ***Guardian,*** **July 28, 1994, p. 9.**
Vacationers attempting to travel to the Spanish port of Santander were frustrated on July 27, 1994, by a blockade of the harbor by local fishermen waging a "tuna war" with French trawlermen. The Spanish fisherman have accused the French of using nets contrary to European Union regulations.

Smithers, Rebecca, "Ferries return to normal as Spanish lift blockade," ***Guardian,*** **July 30, 1994, p. 9.**
On July 29, 1994, the blockade of northern Spanish ports, which disrupted services for thousands of ferry passengers, was lifted. The four-day blockade was the climax of a long-running dispute over tuna fishing rights.

United States Policy and Cuba

Borrus, Amy, "Castro just might reach for the olive branch," ***Business Week*** **(Industrial/Technology Edition), Sept. 12, 1994, p. 56.**
The U.S. is considering easing Cuba's economic isolation in response to positive steps by Fidel Castro. The refugee crisis building at Guantanamo Bay is prompting concern from both the U.S. and Cuba.

Carpenter, Ted Galen, "Lift the embargo, clinch democracy," ***Insight on the News,*** **April 25, 1994, p. 20-22.**
The embargo imposed on Cuba should be lifted, Carpenter writes. It has been in place since 1964 and has failed to dislodge communist dictator Fidel Castro. A strategy based on increasing trade and tourism will hasten Castro's fall.

Kirschten, Dick, "What next for Cuba? Stay tuned," ***National Journal,*** **Sept. 3, 1994, pp. 2032-2033.**
President Clinton's decision to reverse a three-decades-old policy of granting political asylum to Cuban refugees and instead detain them at Guantanamo Bay Naval Base is discussed. Critics claim that Clinton should rescind the economic embargo against Cuba if he wants to loosen Fidel Castro's grip on the country.

Post, Tom, "We want freedom," ***Newsweek,*** **Sept. 12, 1994, p. 31.**
Negotiations over halting the mass exodus of Cuban refugees are examined. The crowded conditions at Guantanamo also are discussed.

"Stemming the tide of Cuban refugees," ***Atlanta Constitution,*** **Aug. 19, 1994, p. A18.**
An editorial urges the Clinton administration to lift the embargo on Cuba, saying the U.S. can stop fleeing refugees from boating to its shores by helping with the inevitable transition to democracy.

"To ease the Cuban crisis, end the trade embargo," ***USA Today,*** **Aug. 22, 1994, p. A10.**
An editorial says it is shortsighted for the Clinton administration to use economic restrictions and threaten a naval blockade to try and force Cuba into democracy. Instead, Cuba's leaders should be encouraged to stay put; they should be given an economic base to support a peaceful transition to democracy.

Williams, Ian, "A rum policy," ***Nation,*** **Sept. 19, 1994, p. 260**
An editorial discusses how U.S. foreign policy toward Cuba is designed to bring about the downfall of the Castro government. President Clinton should drop the economic embargo against Cuba and hasten the introduction of democratic reforms there that will preserve the educational, health, social and cultural achievements of the country.

Back Issues

Great Research on Current Issues Starts Right Here...Recent topics covered by The CQ Researcher are listed below. Before May 1991, reports were published under the name of Editorial Research Reports.

APRIL 1993
Head Start
High-Speed Rail
Children's Legal Rights
Muslims in America

MAY 1993
Cults in America
Preventing Teen Pregnancy
Software Piracy
National Parks

JUNE 1993
Food Safety
Prostitution
Childhood Immunizations
National Service

JULY 1993
Electric Cars
Population Growth
Downward Mobility
Intelligence Testing

AUGUST 1993
Mental Illness
Bilingual Education
Foreign Policy Burden
School Funding

SEPTEMBER 1993
Suburban Crime
Public Housing
Supreme Court Preview
Immigration Reform

OCTOBER 1993
Airline Safety
Disaster Response
Science in the Courtroom
The Glass Ceiling

NOVEMBER 1993
Paying for Retirement
Charitable Giving
Privacy in the Workplace
Adoption

DECEMBER 1993
U.S. Vietnam-Relations
Learning Disabilities
Child Care
Space Program's Future

JANUARY 1994
Racial Tensions in Schools
South Africa's Future
Worker Retraining
Regulating Pesticides

FEBRUARY 1994
Prison Overcrowding
Water Quality
Religion in Schools
Juvenile Justice

MARCH 1994
Underground Economy
Education Standards
Gambling Boom
Private Management of Public Schools

APRIL 1994
Reproductive Ethics
U.S.-China Trade
Soccer in America
Talk Show Democracy

MAY 1994
Traffic Congestion
Women's Health Issues
Mutual Funds
Political Scandals

JUNE 1994
Education and Gender
Gun Control
Public Land Policy
Nuclear Arms Cleanup

JULY 1994
Dietary Supplements
Public Opinion and Foreign Policy
Crime Victims' Rights
Birth Control Choices

AUGUST 1994
Genetically Engineered Foods
Electing Minorities
Prozac Controversy
College Sports

SEPTEMBER 1994
Home Schooling
Welfare Experiments
Courts and the Media
Regulating Tobacco

OCTOBER 1994
Historic Preservation
Religion and Politics
Arts Funding

Back issues are available for $4.00 (subscribers) or $7.00 (non-subscribers). Quantity discounts apply to orders over ten. To order, call Congressional Quarterly Customer Service at (202) 887-8621.

Binders are available for $16.00. To order call 1-800-638-1710. Please refer to stock number 648.

Future Topics

- ***Sex on Campus***
- ***Blood Supply Safety***
- ***Term Limits Revisited***

THE CQ Researcher

PUBLISHED BY CONGRESSIONAL QUARTERLY INC.

Sex on Campus

Will new programs cut the sexual assault rate?

Dire warnings about date rape together with the specter of AIDS have cast a grim shadow over sexual relations on campuses in the 1990s. Colleges are getting tougher with male students who press unwanted sex on women. The date rape movement, started by victims protesting insensitive treatment by campus police and administrators, has become institutionalized. The federal government now requires virtually every college to offer programs aimed at stopping sexual assaults. Rape-prevention educators argue that the heightened awareness of rape will help place sexual relations between men and women on an equal footing, reducing sexual exploitation by men. Critics say the movement is creating needless hysteria on campus, encouraging women to cry rape over miscommunication and regretted sex.

INSIDE THIS ISSUE

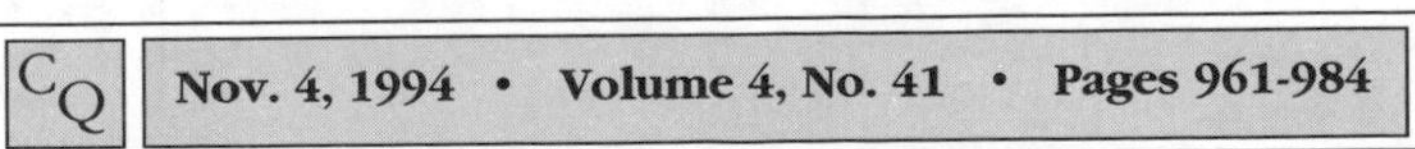
CQ Nov. 4, 1994 • Volume 4, No. 41 • Pages 961-984

Formerly Editorial Research Reports

COVER ART: BARBARA SASSA-DANIELS

November 4, 1994
Volume 4, No. 41

The CQ Researcher (ISSN 1056-2036). Formerly Editorial Research Reports. Published weekly (48 times per year, not printed the first Friday of any month with five Fridays) by Congressional Quarterly Inc., 1414 22nd St., N.W., Washington, D.C. 20037. Rates are furnished upon request. Second-class postage paid at Washington, D.C. POSTMASTER: Send address changes to The CQ Researcher, 1414 22nd St., N.W., Washington, D.C. 20037.

Sex on Campus

By Sarah Glazer

The Issues

At Brown University this fall, school officials sponsored an orientation skit that sent an ominous message to newcomers.

The skit began innocently enough, painting a scene that many in the audience found familiar, and even amusing. "Donna," a freshman, asks a friend to invite "Mike," a sophomore, to visit her dorm. After drinking some beer in her friend's dorm room, Donna says she feels dizzy and wants to go to her room to lie down. But Mike follows her back, and the couple begins making out on the bed. He mistakenly interprets her affectionate behavior as an invitation to sexual intercourse.

To most of the audience, it's clear that Donna doesn't want to have intercourse. "Mike, I like you," she says, "but I'm just not comfortable with the pace. I mean, can we just take it slow?"

"The next thing I knew," a stunned Donna tells the audience, "he was having sex with me." She explains that she tried to protest, but the "words wouldn't come out."

Mike, however, is unaware of her distress. "When we were done," he says, "I was feeling pretty good."

Similar performances — invariably followed by spirited discussions — are being staged at colleges around the nation this fall. They serve to warn young women to be on their guard against male students who seem perfectly well-behaved but may take advantage of them sexually. And they warn men that such behavior — having intercourse without first obtaining the woman's consent — may be grounds for expulsion.

Before new students arrived at Cornell University, their parents received a letter informing them that sexual assault is a serious issue at the Ithaca, N.Y., school. Once on campus, the newcomers hear a litany of warnings about sexual assault during a week of activities and speakers devoted to the topic. Indeed, a pamphlet widely circulated on U.S. campuses warns that 1 in 4 college women will be victims of rape or attempted rape. [1]

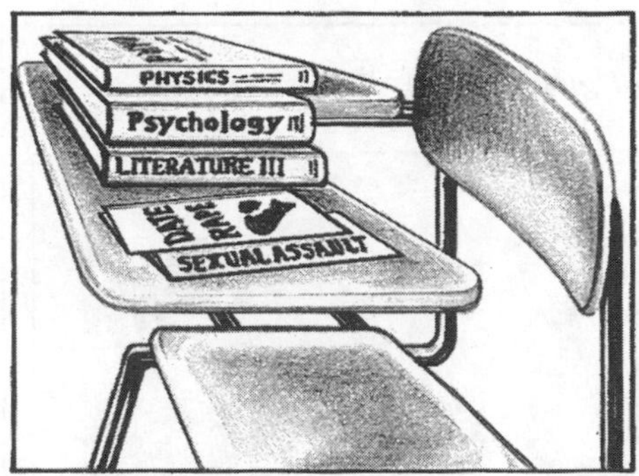

These fearful messages strike an odd note with some parents who attended college in the 1960s. Then, confined to separate-sex dorms, male and female students alike chafed against limited visiting hours and curfews. Those restrictions are relics of the past at most of today's campuses, where it's not unusual for boyfriends and girlfriends to spend the night in each other's dorm room.

In the 1960s and early '70s, Professor Mary L. Roark of the State University of New York-Plattsburgh recalls, "Sex was fun, joyful and liberating. . . . Right now, the focus on sex on campus is its downside. It's, 'Be careful or you will get AIDS and die; be careful or you will be taken advantage of in a way that might be [psychologically] difficult for you to overcome.'"

At progressive Antioch College, in Yellow Springs, Ohio, a mandatory orientation seminar recommends the use of a latex "dental dam" during oral sex and latex gloves so a lover's hangnail won't draw blood and transmit AIDS or other sexual infections. "We're talking about lives," says Andy Abrams, 25, a 1993 Antioch graduate who values these discussions. "Each sexual encounter is a risk at some level."

In the era of AIDS, some campus counselors report students are becoming more cautious about engaging in sex than those who came of age during the sexual revolution. At the University of California-Santa Cruz, one of the more liberal campuses in the California system, sexual activity "has taken a more conservative swing," notes Gillian Greensite, campus coordinator of rape prevention education. Compared with the sexually experimental atmosphere of the 1970s, when many students had multiple sexual partners, the current trend is toward monogamous relationships, she says.

A recent nationwide study led by researchers at the University of Chicago finds a similar trend toward monogamy for 18-to-24-year-olds. College-age Americans today engage in premarital sex at an earlier age than older generations did, and they marry later. But they tend to live with just one partner at a time, thus limiting the number of overall partners before marriage, according to Robert T. Michael, dean of the university's Harris Graduate School of Public Policy Studies and a study co-author. [2]

Those "living together" relationships tend to be short-lived, however, lasting no more than a year in about half the cases, Michael says. As a result, young adults soon move on to new partners. Looking at today's countervailing trends of earlier sex combined with monogamous cohabitation, Michael confesses, "I don't know whether there's a whole lot more or a little less" sexual activity than the 1960s' college generation.

The most widely publicized example of the new caution is the sexual code of conduct introduced at Antioch in 1992. It requires students to obtain "verbal consent . . . with each new level of physical and/or sexual contact/conduct in any given interaction." The policy warns, "Asking, 'Do you want to have sex with me?' is not enough."

Sex Among Teenagers

More than half of all teenage boys and girls remain virgins through age 16, though the likelihood of having intercourse increases steadily with age. *

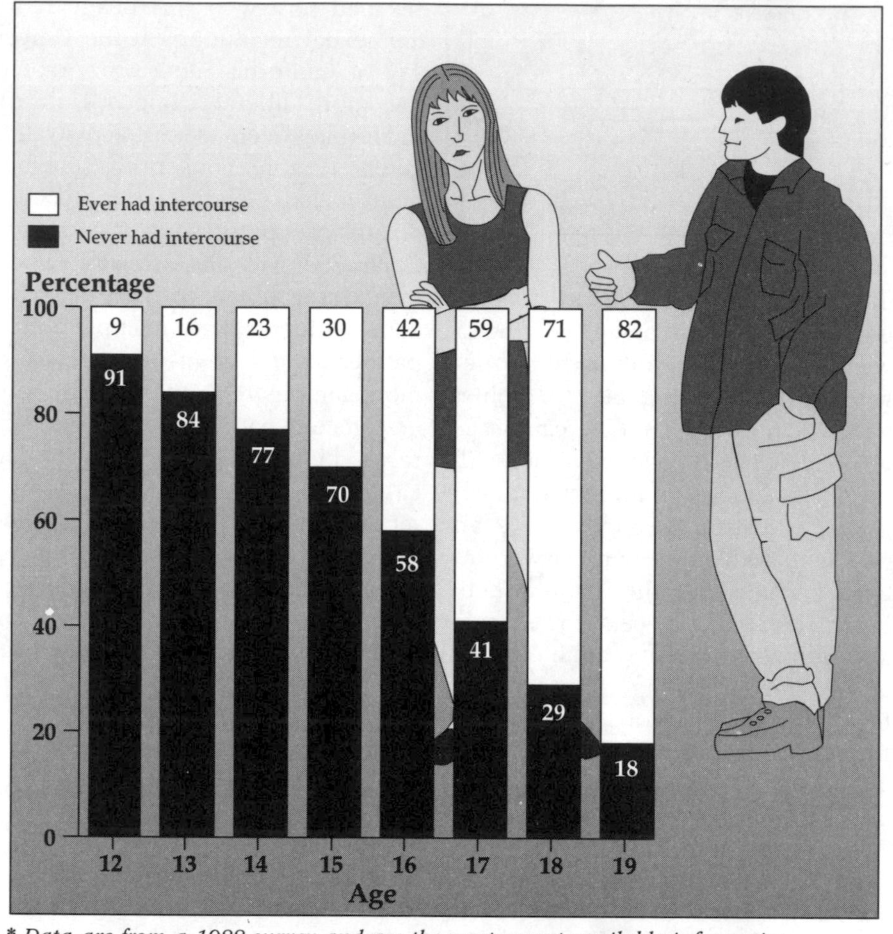

** Data are from a 1988 survey and are the most recent available information.*
Source: "Sex and America's Teenagers," The Alan Guttmacher Institute, 1994

The policy has been widely ridiculed on TV and in newspapers as an unrealistic restriction on romantic encounters. One sitcom portrayed a young girl becoming increasingly disgusted as a boyfriend assiduously questioned whether he could touch each part of her body. But Antioch Dean of Students Marian Jensen points out that students themselves demanded the policy.

"It gives them some boundaries, which is what students said they needed from the beginning," she says. "I've got male students who say, 'Suddenly I don't feel like I have to perform.' I've got female students saying, 'I have something behind me that allows me to say no.' "

In some ways, college orientation workshops that impart skills in setting limits resemble the old rules of courtship and sexual behavior that were tossed out in the 1960s. Pamphlets warning women to clearly communicate their limits to men — and not to drink too much or go to a man's room — "have actually begun to sound like Victorian guides to conduct," writes Katie Roiphe, a Princeton University doctoral candidate in English, in her controversial book deriding the date rape movement, *The Morning After.* [3]

The difference is that the new advice is for an environment complicated by heavy sexual activity and excessive drinking. The percentage of college women who drink primarily to get drunk has tripled since the mid-1970s and now nearly equals the percentage of college men who drink for the same reason — about 33 percent — according to a recent report. [4] The trend is significant because alcohol is involved in most campus crimes, including date rape.

Drinking is no longer viewed as a mere social lubricant at campus parties. "Now drinking has become the activity," says Jan Sherrill, assistant dean of students at George Washington University in Washington, D.C. Throwing up after drinking — or "hurling" — is part of the drinking ritual. To boost attendance at parties, some students videotape partygoers throwing up.

College administrators like Sherrill view date rape as a subset of the larger problem of alcohol abuse. "I don't know of one case of sexual assault where students haven't been drinking," he says. "One of the things we warn students is, 'Get drunk, and you run the risk of being raped.' " In a national survey of 10,000 undergraduates in 1989, the most frequent perpetrators of date rape were athletes or fraternity members who drank. [5]

The proportion of students who arrive on campus as virgins — and stay that way for very long — is also diminishing. Many students come to college sexually experienced already. The average age of first intercourse has been falling steadily over the past four decades, studies show.

Approximately 30 percent of teens have experienced sexual intercourse by age 15, according to The Alan Guttmacher Institute, a New York research organization. [6] Through the 1970s and '80s, only 15 percent of the men and 17 percent of the women were still virgins by age 19, according to the University of Chicago survey. By contrast, among those who came of age in the 1950s and '60s, 25 per-

Skit at Cornell dramatizes how a date . . .

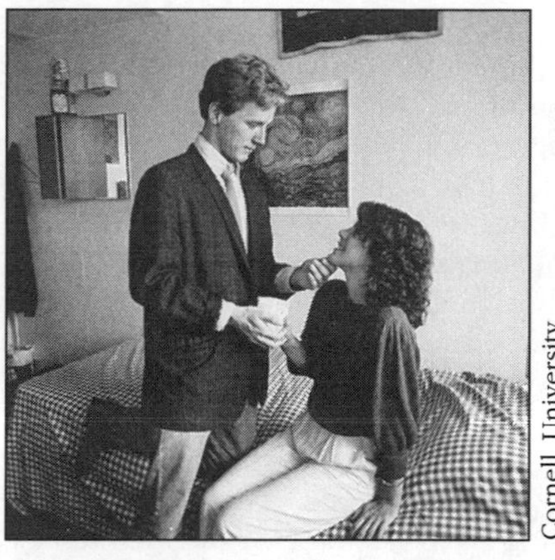

Cornell University

cent of the men and 45 percent of the women were still virgins by 19.[7]

"We know this generation is having a lot more sex than we did," Jensen says. Defending the college's new code, she adds, "I don't think we're stopping anybody from having sex. We're trying to prevent unwanted sex."

In that sense, Antioch is part of a trend among progressive colleges to expand the definition of rape and sexual assault. Traditionally, says Bernice Sandler, senior scholar in residence at the National Association for Women in Education, rape has been defined as occurring where a woman said "no" to intercourse but was forced into it against her will. Under the new definition, says Sandler, the burden of proof is shifting to the accused to show that his partner said "yes."

This expanded definition of rape has come under attack from a handful of women in academia. Christina Hoff Sommers, a professor of philosophy at Clark University in Worcester, Mass., and author of *Who Stole Feminism?,* says feminists who hold this view of rape are "criminalizing male lust." She charges that "Take Back the Night" demonstrations, where college women recount rape experiences before an open microphone, create a hysterical, "medieval" atmosphere, encouraging women to embroider their sexual experiences and describe themselves as victims.

To Princeton's Roiphe, the feminist movement's preoccupation with date rape "peddles an image of gender relations that denies female desire and infantilizes women."[8]

"Date rape has become a synonym for bad sex, for sex that is pressured, drunk or regretted the next day," she says. "If we call all of this rape, then I would guess that almost everybody has been 'raped' at one point or another."[9]

As college officials and students grapple with the changing definitions of sexual interactions, here are some of the questions being debated:

Has the extent of date rape been exaggerated?

The pamphlet that many college students received this fall from the American College Health Association has been widely cited in rape prevention literature. It warns: "1 in 4 college women have experienced rape or attempted rape since age 14." The pamphlet also notes that 84 percent of these victims were raped by someone they knew.

However, a few academics say the study that produced these numbers exaggerates the extent of date rape. Neil Gilbert, a professor at the University of California School of Social Welfare, in Berkeley, attacks the study as an example of "advocacy research" that "demonizes men and defines the common experience in heterosexual relations as inherently violent and menacing." The consequence, he charges, is an unnecessarily "frightening atmosphere" on college campuses.

The much-publicized study stems from a survey of 3,187 women students on 32 campuses conducted in 1984 and '85. Known as the *Ms.* Magazine Campus Project on Sexual Assault, it was funded by the National Institute of Mental Health and authored by Mary P. Koss, a clinical psychologist at the University of Arizona.[10]

Gilbert charges that Koss comes up

. . . can turn into a sexual assault

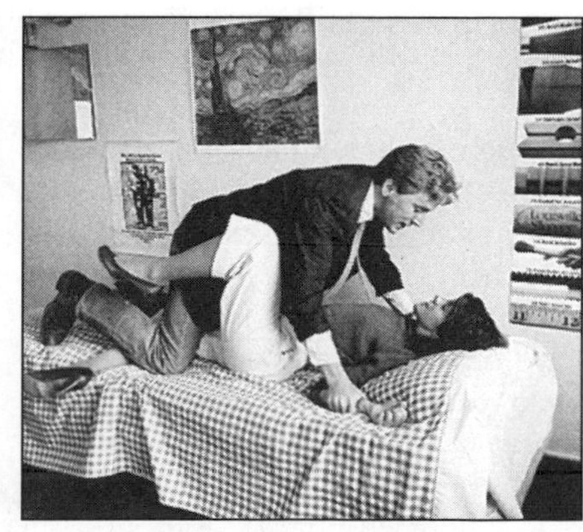

Statistics Leave Uncertainty About Campus Rape Rate

In 1986, Jeanne Clery, a sophomore at Lehigh University, in Bethlehem, Pa., was raped and murdered in her dormitory room. Her death prompted a vigorous campaign to make campuses safer, led by her parents.

The result was passage of a new federal law, the Campus Security Act of 1990, requiring colleges and universities to collect data on rape and other campus crimes. Schools also were required to publish the crime statistics annually to enable current students, as well as prospective students and their families, to make informed judgments about the safety of a campus.

Rather than clarifying the debate over the extent of rapes on campus, however, the statistics-gathering exercise has so far served only to cloud it.

According to data compiled by *The Chronicle of Higher Education,* approximately 1,000 rapes were reported in 1991 among 2,400 colleges participating in the first reporting period mandated by the new law.[1] That amounts to less than one-half rape per campus, a figure that casts doubt on the claim that a date rape epidemic is sweeping campuses.

But many sexual assault experts said the colleges underestimated the numbers of sex offenses against college women because the law originally required that colleges report only rapes — the most serious type of sexual assault.

The law was amended by the Higher Education Act of 1992 to expand the reporting of sex crimes. For 1992, colleges were instructed to replace the rape statistics with two broader categories: forcible and non-forcible sex offenses. Under the FBI definition, forcible sex offenses are "any sexual act directed against another person, forcibly or against that person's will." In addition to forcible rape, the category includes forcible sodomy, sexual assault with an object and forcible fondling. Non-forcible sex offenses cover incest and statutory rape.

As a result of these changes in definition, the statistics from 1991 and 1992 are not comparable, making it impossible to tell whether sexual assaults have gone up or down.[2] For 1992, many campuses continued to provide statistics only for rape, despite the new requirements. Further confusing things, some colleges reported all incidents occurring in the 1992 calendar year while others reported for the 1991-92 academic year.

In the latest campus crime reports, again compiled by *The Chronicle of Higher Education,* 774 academic institutions reported 466 rapes and 448 forcible sex offenses for 1992.[3]

That comes out to slightly more than one sex offense per college. But the figures remain fraught with problems. Some campuses purposely underreport crime on their campuses, presumably because they don't want prospective students or donors to shy away, some critics told the *Chronicle.*[4] Also, colleges are more likely to report sexual offenses if they have an active program for reaching out to victims of sexual assault. Colleges with highly professional police departments may pursue crime more aggressively than colleges that handle most incidents through a campus disciplinary system.

Finally, colleges had questions as to what counted as a reportable crime. Should they report only charges filed with campus security police, or should they count the confidences of a student to a dean or dormitory residence adviser? In its final regulations issued in April, the Department of Education said colleges should count any offenses reported to an official with "significant responsibility for student and campus activities."[5]

---

[1] Douglas Lederman, "Colleges Report 7,500 Violent Crimes on Their Campuses in First Annual Statements Required Under Federal Law," *The Chronicle of Higher Education,* Jan. 20, 1993, pp. A32-44. To date, the federal government has not added up nor compiled in a single report the rape statistics it collected from individual colleges. The figure of 1,000 rapes is based on the *Chronicle's* collection of college safety reports directly from the colleges.

[2] Campus sexual assaults are declining, according to the Campus Violence Prevention Center at Towson State University in Maryland, which has surveyed 2,700 college administrators on the issue since 1987. During the 1992-1993 year, 47 percent reported rapes or sexual assaults on campus, down from 64 percent in 1990.

[3] Douglas Lederman, "Crime on the Campuses," *The Chronicle of Higher Education,* Feb. 2, 1994, pp. A31-A41.

[4] *Ibid.,* p. A31.

[5] "Student Assistance General Provisions; Campus Safety; Final Rule," *Federal Register,* April 29, 1994, p. 22315.

with such high numbers because she includes gray areas that could be described as miscommunication between dates. Included in Koss' rape count are women who answered "yes" to the question, "Have you had sexual intercourse when you didn't want to because a man gave you alcohol or drugs?"

Gilbert says, "You can imagine cases where young people go out together, and the woman says, 'I don't want to go to bed with you.' They have drinks, her inhibitions are lower, she wakes up the next morning and says, 'What did I do that for?' "[11]

"I'm not of the utopian view that we can get all women to say no when they mean no," Gilbert adds, "because I think there's a legitimate area of ambiguity — not knowing what you want."

Koss responds that she tried to fashion the survey questions to reflect the legal definition of rape in Ohio, where she was working at the time of the survey. Ohio's 1980 rape statute includes situations where the offender "for the purpose of preventing resisting . . . impairs the other person's judgment or control by administering a drug or intoxicant to that person."[12] However, Gilbert says, it's not clear from the survey question whether the man intentionally got the woman drunk or whether her judgment was so impaired that she could not resist.

Once the drinking question is removed, Koss says, the numbers drop but are still high: 1 in 5 college women — rather than 1 in 4 — has been the victim of rape or attempted rape.[13]

Gilbert maintains the figures are still much too high when compared with other studies of rape. In essence, he sees Koss' method as faulty because the rape numbers aren't based on the women's characterizations of the incident as rape. Rather, Koss extrapolates the numbers after asking women whether they have been in situations that she considers rape.

Koss counts a woman who answered yes to the drinking question as a rape victim. But only 27 percent of the women counted by Koss as rape victims labeled their experience as rape. Some labeled it as miscommunication. Gilbert sees this as further evidence that few of them were really raped, but Koss puts it down to women's ignorance about the legal definition of rape. Rape counselors who support Koss' work say it is not unusual for women who describe an incident that is legally rape to resist that term.

Gilbert questions why 42 percent of the rape victims return to have sex with their rapist, as Koss reports. Rape counselors respond that this is a well-known phenomenon among victims of domestic abuse.

Though Gilbert concedes some women may fit into these categories, he doubts there are enough to account for Koss' high figures. For example, Koss calculates that about 16 percent of women on campuses are victims each year of rape or attempted rape. If this rate continued over four years, Gilbert estimates, over half of college women would be victims of rape or attempted rape during their college careers, a proportion he calls "implausible."

According to Gilbert, Koss' annual rape rate is 1,000 times higher than the rate reported to the FBI by about 500 major colleges and universities in 1992. Gilbert says that only 408 cases of rape or attempted rape were reported to campus police in 1992, less than one rape incident per campus.[14]

Yet rape counselors say that official college reports vastly undercount rape because of the stigma many women

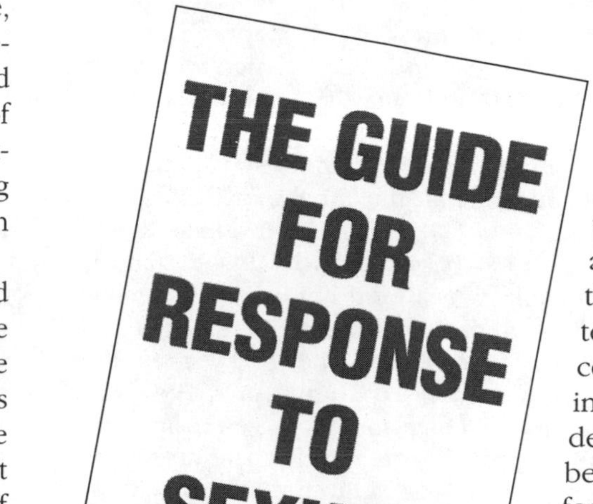

attach to rape. (*See story, p. 966.*) Experts in the date rape field estimate that about 90 percent of rape cases are never reported to police.

Jennifer Stromer-Galley, a student volunteer at the University of Minnesota who works with assault victims, says only about half the students who phone her following a sexual assault also call the campus police. A main concern is whether their anonymity will be protected. In the past, she says, police descriptions of rape victims published in the student newspaper enabled fellow students to identify the victim.

Who defines an incident as rape may explain why another national study, by the Campus Violence Prevention Center at Towson State University in Maryland, came up with a lower rate of campus rape. Only 1 percent of the women surveyed said they had been raped, and 10 percent said they were victims of acquaintance rape, since entering college.[15] Dorothy Siegel, the center's director, says the 1990 mail-in survey was returned by 12,000 students and produced lower numbers because it did not try to define rape for the women.

"I think you drive a lot of people away from really taking the problem seriously if it's trivialized by saying almost everyone is a victim," Siegel says of Koss' 1 in 4 figure.

Is all the attention prompting women students to cry rape in situations where it's not justified? Yes, argues Clark University's Sommers, pointing to this statement from a widely cited date rape prevention manual: "Any sexual intercourse without mutual desire is a form of rape." Charges Sommers: "By such a definition, privileged young women in our nation's colleges gain moral parity with the real victims in our community at large."[16]

But campus experts say few students report regretted sexual encounters as rapes. Toby Simon, associate dean of student life at Brown, says she has encountered only two such cases in her 13 years at Brown. More common is the woman who is afraid to report a sexual assault because she anticipates the disbelieving reactions, says Andrea Parrot, who developed Cornell University's date rape education program and co-authored the 1993 book *Sexual Assault*

She Would Have Said "No" If He Had Asked . . .

It started with a long night of drinking. Fresh from a girls' Catholic school, she was a newly arrived freshman at Pomona College, in Claremont, Calif. He was a sophomore honor student.

By the time she arrived at the campus Halloween party, she had had four beers. But she bought a wristband that entitled her to unlimited drinking from the party keg.

During the evening, they got to talking. When he bent over and kissed her, she was happy. Around midnight, they went out for a walk and ended up at his dorm room. "I was so drunk that I remember I did not hear nor understand what he had said," the young woman wrote in the rape complaint she filed with the college.

According to her complaint, she took her blazer off, he undressed her and she gave him oral sex, "which I did not feel comfortable refusing to do." They were lying on his bed, kissing, and he said, "I should get a condom." She shook her head and said "uh-uh." She meant she did not want to have sex with him, according to the complaint. He apparently assumed she meant she did not need contraceptive protection, she theorizes in her written account, and proceeded to have intercourse with her.

A week later, they discussed the encounter. She explained that had he asked her beforehand to have sex with him, she would have said "No." "It seemed like he understood the seriousness of this because he sat back very stunned, and all he could muster was an "Oh," she recalled in her complaint.

Last March, two-and-a-half years after the incident, she filed a rape charge with the college. The accused student, only a month away from graduation, sued to block the college from conducting a disciplinary hearing on the charge. Pomona's punishment for rape is expulsion.

The young man contended that the college violated his constitutional due process rights by not permitting an attorney to represent him at the hearing, by providing no statute of limitations on the filing of a rape charge and by failing to require an investigation before referring the case for a hearing.

The man's attorney also objected to the standard of proof applied by the university to prove rape — "clear and convincing evidence" — which is weaker than the "beyond a reasonable doubt" standard used in criminal courts.

"We're talking about people being charged with extremely serious felonies that if pursued and prosecuted in the criminal system would subject them to many years of incarceration," says Howard Z. Rosen, the man's attorney. "Imagine if you're in your fourth year of school, you're charged with date rape and your family has spent $25,000 per year to go to this school. Your whole career is down the toilet."

Rosen also objects to the way Pomona's sexual assault rules define consent. They require an explicit agreement to engage in sexual intercourse — something the Pomona woman says she never gave. "In life, we agree by our conduct," he says. "We don't always verbally agree to things."

But Nina Ellerman, a spokeswoman for Pomona, defends the college's procedures by noting that Pomona is a private

on Campus: "Why did you get drunk?" Or, "People who go to frat houses deserve what you got."

Indeed, these criticisms were echoed by provocative writer Camille Paglia in a contrarian essay on date rape that attracted wide attention in 1991. "A girl who goes upstairs alone with a brother at a fraternity party is an idiot," she wrote. "Feminists call this 'blaming the victim.' I call it common sense." [17]

As the storm over Paglia's essay showed, beneath the blizzard of statistics rages a fundamental disagreement over the nature of male-female relations. That theme emerged in a recent debate between Gilbert and Sandler, who advises colleges on how to deal with date rape. In her own date rape manual, Sandler cites individual university studies that find anywhere from 15 to 25 percent of students have had forced intercourse with someone they knew. [18]

If the startlingly high statistics published by scholars like Koss and Sandler are true, Gilbert said during a recent seminar on date rape at the American Enterprise Institute, a Washington think tank, "we are driven to conclude most men are pedophiles and rapists."

"We're not trying to demonize men but make relations between men and women better," Sandler retorted. But she agreed that the rise of the date rape concept has reshaped the way many women see normal sexual relations, as well as rape.

"Rape is no longer an aberrant sexual act but part of a larger pattern," Sandler said. The fundamental debate, she said, is over the "trend of these [sexual] relations to become more equal."

Should colleges adopt Antioch-style written policies on sexual conduct between students?

Under new federal requirements, all colleges must have a written policy on date rape and sexual assault, including a definition, a disciplinary policy and educational prevention programs (*see p. 975*). Some colleges also mete out discipline for lesser "sexual misconduct" offenses, such as unwanted touching.

Antioch goes further toward codifying sexual behavior than any other school in the nation. Its nine-page policy makes any unwanted advances without "verbal consent" a potential "sexual offense" subject to a range of penalties, including expulsion.

At a mandatory workshop at Antioch last fall, the leader explained the policy to freshmen this way: "If

. . . But He Assumed That She Meant "Yes"

institution. "Our rules are based on protecting members of the community, not necessarily on what is the legal definition of an offense," she says. "It's like a private club having its own rules that everyone who joins the club agrees to live by."

In the end, the judge postponed the hearing until after the young man's graduation, ruling May 24 that he should be represented by an attorney before the college's all-student disciplinary board. The decision "basically left us powerless," says Ellerman. "You can't expel someone who has graduated." In response, the university dropped the charge, and the young man dropped his suit.

Rosen believes the college buckled under student pressure despite weak evidence against his client. After the judge postponed the hearing last spring, students protested that the university was not doing enough to prosecute the rape case. "Dead Men Don't Rape," said an inscription on the school's graffiti wall.[1]

"One reason they didn't dismiss the case is it's very political," Rosen says. "Date rape is one of the issues of the '90s."

Since the judge's ruling, Pomona has revised its disciplinary process. It now allows an accused student to have an attorney in cases where criminal charges also have been filed. But Rosen says that means the alleged victim can control whether the accused is allowed a lawyer simply by waiting until after the disciplinary hearing to file criminal charges.

The Pomona case contains many of the ingredients that frequently accompany sexual assault charges on campus: a surfeit of alcohol, an inexperienced freshman woman interacting with an older male student and an outraged student community demanding action. It also illustrates the inexperience of colleges in dealing with the newly visible problem of date rape. This was Pomona's first date rape case, according to Ellerman.

"The majority of universities haven't dealt with more than one or two cases," says Boston attorney Philip Burling, who represents academic institutions. "No one has established a standard operating procedure for dealing with these cases."

Colleges that are most sensitive to the issue of date rape have leaned over backwards to make victims feel comfortable. In the 1980s, several studies found that rape victims were reluctant to report sexual assaults because of the insensitive treatment they received at the hands of university administrators as well as police. In response to these studies, the University of Rochester set up a hearing process in 1986 that allows the complainant to sit in a different room from the accused and listen to his testimony through audio equipment.

"The more we try to make educational institutions into courtrooms, the more unlikely people are to report" sexual assaults, says Gary Pavela, director of judicial programs (for student discipline) at the University of Maryland-College Park.

[1] Deborah Sullivan, "Date Rape Allegation Ignites a Furor at Pomona College," *Los Angeles Times*, May 21, 1994, p. B1.

you want to take her blouse off, you have to ask. If you want to move your hand down to her genitals, you have to ask. If you want to put your finger inside her, you have to ask."

One young man protested, "If I have to ask those questions, I won't get what I want."[19]

Advocates cite that remark as evidence that Antioch-style policies are desperately needed to reform the male idea that sex is something to be exploited, that the goal of dating is to "score." But critics say it shows the Antioch policy won't work in real life. (*See "At Issue," p. 977.*)

"What Antioch is asking students to do is completely reject 18 years of socialization and do something completely foreign without giving them the skills to do it," says Cornell's Parrot, who teaches campus athletes to change their sexual attitudes. Without years of training, she says, it's unfair to slap a new code of ethics on students with harsh new penalties.

Mention of the Antioch policy provokes laughter from administrators and faculty around the country. "When we talk to our students about it, we get comments like: 'Do we need a contract?' " reports Gary Pavela, who is in charge of student discipline at the University of Maryland-College Park. "It's not something in the real world that most young people are willing to do."

But Antioch graduate Abrams says the romantic vision of the unspoken magical moment is what's unrealistic. "Life is not like what you see on the big screen," he says. "People don't just throw themselves into each other's arms without knowing anything about each other."

Abrams concedes that asking a girl's consent each step of the way takes practice. But, "You can get the hang of it," he says. "Sex is better, more exciting, more fun when you can talk about it."

Stromer-Galley says that women need to be more assertive in their sexual relations, but she doesn't want an Antioch policy at Minnesota. "I don't believe in legislating common sense," she says.

Some campus experts see problems with enforcement. To Katie Roiphe, "The Antioch code of conduct represents a sort of Orwellian nightmare of cameras in our bedroom."[20] Elsa Kirchner Cole, general counsel at the University of Michigan, asks, "How do you monitor whether someone truly consented?"

But Antioch's Jensen says having a written policy makes it easier to discipline students for rape and other inappropriate sexual behavior. A group of students developed the policy because of dissatisfaction with how the university handled two earlier cases of acquaintance rape.

"Nobody can say, 'I had sex with this girl because she invited me into her room, and if that didn't mean yes, what did it mean?' We're saying if she didn't say 'yes,' it didn't mean yes," says Jensen.

In the two years since the policy was instituted, only one Antioch student has been disciplined, according to Jensen. He received a 10-day suspension for improperly touching a girl at a dance.

Other colleges don't codify rules as elaborately as Antioch, but some of them implicitly tell students to follow an Antiochlike code of behavior to protect themselves against charges of rape. The point was driven home at the close of the skit about Donna and Mike, when it was performed at Manhattanville College in Purchase, N.Y. "The boy and the girl both made mistakes," Mike told the audience, "but one of the mistakes the guy made was he raped a woman."

While Mike's behavior might not meet a court's definition of rape, associate dean Simon concedes, it fits Brown's definition of "sexual misconduct" and could warrant expulsion.

"What the Antioch code is essentially doing is protecting potential rapists, saying, 'Be Smart. Ask and get affirmative consent,' " says Sandler.

Should colleges ban sex between faculty and students?

According to Lisa Topol, the affair she began with her English professor at the University of Pennsylvania quickly became a 12 ½-week nightmare. The professor tied her sexual performance to her grade, assigned her increasingly abusive sexual "homework" and routinely spanked her with a riding crop or whip, she charges in lawsuits against the university, the professor and his former employer. A Phi Beta Kappa senior hoping to attend graduate school in the professor's field of Victorian literature, she said she felt trapped by her need for a good recommendation, and eventually fell into a severe depression that kept her from graduating with her class.[21]

Courtesy Antioch College

Students and faculty meet during development of Antioch College's Sexual Conduct Policy, requiring students to obtain "verbal consent" before each stage of sexual contact.

For Professor Malcolm Woodfield, the affair was nothing but a one-time fling by mutual consent. "I was hotly pursued by this woman," he claims.[22]

Recently there has been a flurry of activity on campuses to develop policies that discourage consensual sexual relations between professors and their students. The University of Virginia gained national attention last year when it debated a proposal that would have banned all sexual relations between professors and undergraduates.

Last August, the school issued a more limited admonition to faculty members warning that it is their "responsibility . . . to avoid" sexual relationships with students who are in their classes or whom they supervise in some other capacity. Violators are subject to dismissal. Universities with similar policies include the University of Iowa and William and Mary.

Ann J. Lane, director of women's studies at Virginia and a leading advocate of the broader ban that was initially proposed, says tough prohibitions would help avoid the kind of situation described by Topol. "Women of this age are very vulnerable and have enough trouble dealing with their peers," she says. "It's far more complicated dealing with someone in authority whom you have been taught to respect."

But critics of such policies, students as well as professors, say such bans ignore the rights of consenting adults to engage in private sexual activity. "We don't want to be in the business of telling people with whom they can fall in love," says Lesley Lee Francis, associate secretary at the American Association of University Professors. Because of growing pressure to respond to sexual-harassment charges, however, most universities are trying to develop policies governing sexual relations between students and faculty, Francis says.

Leslie Cole, a University of Southern California graduate student who had a relationship with a professor, strongly opposes such bans. She calls the picture of the professor as predatory lecher and the student as helpless victim an "archaic stereotype."

"The wide-eyed undergraduate is

still an adult," she says. "I don't think undergraduates want to be reduced to not having adult status."

Counters Lane, "I think the trouble is they are not adults. Part of the role of teachers is to help them [have] a few safe years" to get there.

Yet university personnel trying to formulate such policies are surrounded by happy marriages between faculty and former students. Several members of the University of Michigan Board of Regents, which instituted a policy discouraging faculty-student relations in 1991, married former students or secretaries, notes general counsel Cole. Indeed, the president of the University of Virginia is married to a former student.

"I think we hear about the happy marriages," says Sandler, "but we don't hear about the others, which are far more prevalent." She says more relationships start out as mutual affairs but end up with the student feeling exploited. "We don't hear about women who drop out or change majors or schools" after soured relationships. According to Sandler, 20 to 30 percent of undergraduate women and 30 to 40 percent of women in graduate programs report that professors have subjected them to sexual harassment, ranging from sexual jokes to direct threats or bribes for sexual activity. [23]

Barry Dank, a sociologist at California State University-Long Beach, recently formed a group of faculty, student and staff opposed to sex bans, known as CASE — Consenting Academics for Sexual Equality. Many of them are in long-term romantic relationships and object to "institutional intrusion," he says. He views the policies as the product of "authoritarian feminism" and suggests that middle-aged faculty women are jealous of the attention lavished on younger women. Advocates of such bans, he says, want to "put women back in the category of women and children."

In issuing Virginia's new policy last year, the university said its primary concern, however, was the conflict of interest created by a liaison that could affect a teacher's grading or evaluation of students. "The principal focus of this policy is on the question of fairness to other students, rather than on whether a particular relationship was 'consensual' or not," the university said in a press release.

Dank pooh-poohs questions of preferential treatment, noting teachers face similar conflicts in grading the children of colleagues. But Sandler says, "I think it's difficult to evaluate someone fairly when you're sleeping with them."

Some legal scholars say that at public universities, sweeping bans on sexual relations between faculty and all students — not just those in their classes — would violate the constitutional right of privacy. [24] The strongest college bans, such as one at the University of Iowa, only cover situations in which a professor directly teaches or supervises a student. Most campus administrators say they have no interest in prohibiting liaisons between, say, a nursing student and an engineering professor.

Experts on both sides say, however, that clearer prohibitions may be necessary to prevent lawsuits against universities. In past years, notes Francis, professors have protested that they have not been given due process in the investigation of such complaints.

But the university's enforcement can be as important as the written policy in determining the outcome. Pennsylvania's policy, for example, is considered one of the stronger statements in academia against faculty-student sexual relations. Although it has no outright ban, it declares sexual relations between students and faculty to be "unethical." As an added discouragement, the policy states, "we will presume that any complaint of sexual harassment by a student against an individual is valid if sexual relations have actually occurred between them while the individual was teaching the student."

The written policy appears to come down squarely on the side of students like Topol, who filed a harassment complaint after Woodfield admitted to administrators that he had had sexual relations with her, according to her suit. But the university demonstrated "an abject failure to enforce" the policy, says Topol's attorney, Alice W. Ballard. The university took a year before bringing the issue to a hearing and then agreed to a settlement that permitted Woodfield to "declare victory," Ballard says.

At the hearing, held last spring, the administration presented its case against Woodfield before a faculty committee but settled the case before completing hearings to determine if he should be fired for cause. Woodfield admitted to "unethical conduct" and to having sex with Topol once. But he said, "I've always denied there was harassment." He agreed to resign before starting the third year of his contract. [25]

Topol's lawsuit demonstrates the problems that almost inevitably result in such situations of unequal power, Lane and others say, even if the relationship begins amicably. [26] Woodfield first wooed Topol while she was in a required course he taught but then refused to let her drop her second course with him — one that she needed to graduate — while she was in an increasingly abusive sexual relationship, according to her attorney.

"Certainly the biggest argument we have to face in the case is that she consented," says Ballard. "However, sexual harassment is not about non-consensual sex; it's about unwelcome sex, and it's about sex extracted or manipulated out of a student in the context of a teacher-student relationship."

Some critics, including Princeton's Roiphe, say such university policies are already starting to have a chilling effect on the informal relations between students and faculty, traditionally the pride of academia. Some faculty members say they are now reluctant to close their doors during office hours with a woman student or take a female student out to lunch for fear they will be charged with harassment.

When Lane hears these complaints from her male colleagues, she advises, "Don't take them out to lunch. It's a small price to pay, and it will enhance friendly relationships. The students will know it's not an overture." ■

BACKGROUND

Changing Sexual Mores

The current controversy over sexual mores on campus takes place in a university setting where the freedom of the sexes to mingle has changed radically from a generation ago. The battles that college students fought and won in the 1960s to loosen parietal hours look almost quaint in retrospect.

In 1963, sex was the concern when Harvard College students protested over plans to cut back on dormitory visiting privileges at the then all-male school. At the time, women could visit students' rooms from 4-7 p.m. on Sundays and weekdays and from noon to midnight on Saturdays.

To Harvard Dean John U. Monro, the rules promised "to bring us closer and closer to outright scandal. . . . [W]hat was once considered a pleasant privilege has . . . come to be considered a license to use the college rooms for wild parties or sexual intercourse." [27]

In a similar vein, the president of Vassar College, then all-women, made it clear that students who wished to indulge in premarital sex should withdraw from the Poughkeepsie, N.Y., college.

But a student rebellion against the old sexual mores was already brewing. A sizable minority of Vassar students considered their president's position "Victorian," student polls showed. And Harvard students reacted to their dean's threat by calling for longer visiting hours. At Columbia University, where an "open-door" policy required doors to be kept open the width of a book during women's visits, students decided the rule could be met with a matchbook. [28]

By the early 1970s, parietal hours were mostly a thing of the past. Co-ed dormitories, an innovation of the 1960s, had become common, in some cases housing men and women on the same floor. And most schools no longer attempted to curtail sexual activities in dormitories. Today, at Vassar, men and women not only live on the same floor but share unisex bathrooms.

Historically, changes in college students' sexual habits have reflected broader societal trends. The 1953 Kinsey report on sexual habits of American women shocked the American public with its findings that premarital sex was becoming increasingly common among women. Alfred Charles Kinsey traced the trend to the liberalized sexual attitudes of the "roaring '20s." By 1963, researchers estimated that about half of all college males and about a quarter of college women had experienced intercourse by age 21. [29]

As more women have entered college and the labor force over the past few decades, delaying marriage, the period of premarital activity has lengthened. In 1960, most women were married before 21. Today women at that age are entering graduate school or looking for jobs, Gilbert points out. In 1960, women on average spent one year between the time they became sexually active and got married. Now the average is 7½ years. [30]

The sweeping away of old moral restrictions against premarital sex during the sexual revolution also created new tensions between men and women over appropriate sexual behavior. "In the 1960s, women still had a shield of morality," says Gilbert. "If a guy said 'Why not?' she could say 'It's wrong.' Now they have to look the guy in the eye and say, 'Because I don't like you enough.' "

Journalist Robin Warshaw, who popularized the 1985 *Ms.* date rape study in *I Never Called it Rape,* looks back almost wistfully on the protective college rules prior to the 1970s. Acting as "substitute parents," colleges punished students for bringing alcohol on campus and for violating the "three-feet-on-the-floor" rule during coed visits. "Although those regulations did not prevent acquaintance rape, they undoubtedly kept down the number of incidents by making women's dorms havens of no-men-allowed safety," Warshaw writes. [31]

New Views of Rape

Notions about rape have also shifted significantly over the past two decades. In September 1982, *Ms.* offered disturbing evidence of a hidden kind of rape between a man and a woman who know one another. The magazine introduced "date rape" into the American vernacular. [32]

Although press stories about date and acquaintance rape have proliferated since then, experts say they don't have good enough records to say if the phenomenon has actually increased. Before the term entered the language, notes Roark of the State University of New York-Plattsburgh, "If people were abusing and assaulting one another, it was not common knowledge among us. What we don't know is: Does that mean there was less of it or does it just mean we wouldn't talk about it?"

The date rape concept challenged the traditional idea of rape as a violent encounter with a stranger. It also jarred the view of American judges that when it comes to women and sex, "consent is presumed," writes legal scholar

Continued on p. 974

Chronology

1950s ***Surveys reveal changing sexual habits in America.***

1953
The Kinsey report, a national survey of sexual habits, reveals premarital sex is widespread among American women.

1957
Purdue University researcher Eugene J. Kanin finds 30 percent of women suffered forced or attempted forced sexual intercourse on a high school date.

1960s ***The sexual revolution takes hold on college campuses. Students agitate to remove parietal hours; coed dormitories are introduced.***

1963
Harvard College considers cutting back women's visiting hours in men's dorm rooms, prompting student demands for expanded hours.

1970s ***Visiting hours and curfews become a relic of the past on most college campuses. Under pressure from feminist reformers, state rape laws begin changing to allow for easier prosecution.***

1976
Susan Brownmiller publishes *Against Our Will,* a historical treatise on rape, focusing new attention on societal attitudes toward rape.

1978
Senate approves the Criminal Code Reform Act of 1978 restricting questioning of sexual assault victims about past sexual conduct and removing the requirement that a rape victim's testimony be corroborated in federal rape cases.

1980s ***The term "date rape" is introduced; sexual harassment becomes an issue of concern on some campuses.***

1982
The term "date rape" is used for the first time, in a *Ms.* magazine article describing research by psychologist Mary P. Koss.

1985
Nationwide survey of college campuses by Koss concludes that 1 in 4 college women have experienced rape or attempted rape.

1986
University of Iowa adopts the policy that faculty members shall not have amorous relationships with students enrolled in their courses or under the faculty members' supervision.

1987
Susan Estrich publishes *Real Rape,* criticizing the legal system's treatment of acquaintance rape.

1990s ***Highly publicized celebrity trials give new visibility to date rape; federal legislation spurs colleges to develop date rape programs; critics attack studies that conclude date rape is widespread on campus.***

Spring 1991
University of California Professor Neil Gilbert publishes article in *The Public Interest* charging that the extent of campus date rape is exaggerated.

July 1991
Boxer Mike Tyson is charged with raping a young beauty contestant on a date; he is later convicted and sentenced to prison.

December 1991
William Kennedy Smith, a member of the politically prominent Kennedy family, is tried in Palm Beach, Fla., on charges of raping a woman he met in a bar. He is later found innocent.

July 23, 1992
President George Bush signs amendments to the Higher Education Act, requiring colleges to develop date rape awareness programs and publish statistics on sex offenses.

July 30, 1992
New Jersey Supreme Court rules that a teenager in an acquaintance rape case is guilty of sexual assault because he did not get affirmative permission to have intercourse.

1993
Princeton University graduate student Katie Roiphe publishes *The Morning After,* criticizing the date rape movement on college campuses.

1994
In *Commonwealth v. Berkowitz,* an acquaintance rape case involving two college students, the Pennsylvania Supreme Court rules that saying "no" to a sexual assailant is not sufficient grounds to prove a woman was raped.

The Cautious Generation

Young men and women born between 1963-72 were more likely to have had no sexual partners by age 20 than previous generations of 20-year-olds. Researchers link the slowdown to the fear of AIDS and other sexually transmitted diseases.

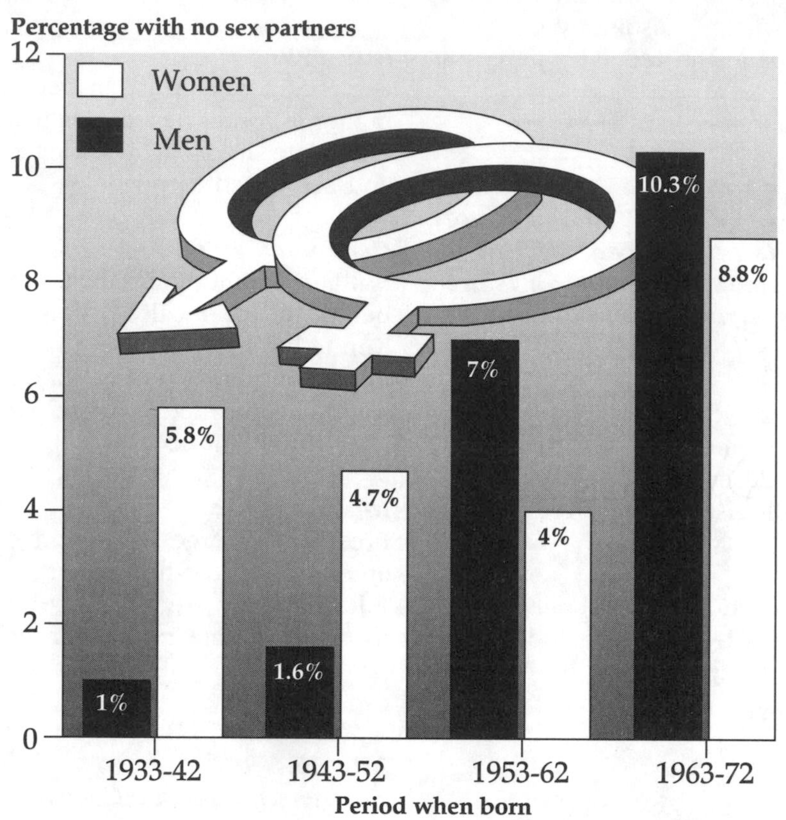

Source: The Social Organization of Sexuality: Sexual Practices in the United States, *1994*

Continued from p. 972

Susan Estrich. Since dates are consensual situations, most courts reasoned, a woman had to "do more than merely say no to sex" in order to forewarn a man who "viewed her words of protestation as nothing more than words." [33] She had to fight like a boy.

Under traditional rape law, in order to prove that a rape had occurred, the state had to show both that force had been used and that the penetration had been against the woman's will. What was "unique" about rape law, Estrich noted, was that a rape victim — unlike a robbery victim — had to prove her lack of consent by the vigor of her physical resistance. [34]

This resistance requirement stemmed from the traditional view of English courts that the testimony of rape victims could not be trusted, because they might be lying to cover up a consensual affair or to blackmail a man. Often quoted was the statement by 17th-century English Lord Chief Justice Matthew Hale that the woman had to be of good fame, suffer signs of injury and cry out for help. [35]

By the 20th century, it had become increasingly difficult in U.S. courts for the victim to prove she had been raped. She had to prove that she had not provoked the rape and that violence had been threatened. Many jurisdictions would not uphold a rape conviction without corroborating testimony from a witness.

During the 1970s, feminists and other rape-law reformers argued that distrust of women complainants had led to an exaggerated emphasis on evidence of resistance. They pointed to research indicating that women who resisted forcible intercourse often suffered far more serious injury as a result. Reformers also argued that the burden of showing non-consent should not fall on the victim of the crime.

Starting in the 1970s, some states began to remove provisions that defined force in terms of the victim's resistance. Another legal reform of that period — rape shield laws — placed sharp limits on testimony about a victim's sexual history. These laws aimed to remove the emphasis on what Hale would have called the "good fame" of the woman.

However, rape cases still remain difficult to prosecute. Almost half of all rape cases in the United States are dismissed before trial, according to a Senate Judiciary Committee report released last year. [36]

Rape cases involving acquaintances are even less likely to get a hearing in the legal system. "Prosecutors don't like those cases because it's very difficult to get a conviction," says Boston attorney Philip Burling, author of a handbook on acquaintance rape for the National Association of College and University Attorneys. "In the typical case, two people are in a room, and one says one thing happened, and the other says something else happened." ■

CURRENT SITUATION

College Programs

The prevalence of date rape may be hotly debated, but virtually every college in the nation is required to have a program to combat it. Any college that receives federal student aid must provide educational programs promoting students' "awareness of rape, acquaintance rape and other sex offenses," under the Higher Education Act amendments signed into law July 23, 1992. The act also requires schools to collect annual statistics on sex offenses, distribute them to current students and establish disciplinary procedures for dealing with sex offenses.[37]

According to Parrot of Cornell, rape education programs were becoming widespread even before the regulations took effect in July, although they vary in the extent of services offered. Cornell, which has one of the more extensive programs, pioneered the skit approach, in which students enact a sexual encounter and then answer questions from fellow students while they stay in character. Other colleges sponsor annual "speak-outs" for rape victims. Many have established rape crisis centers to counsel victims of sexual assault.

Judging from a recent national conference, rape prevention education is a burgeoning industry, complete with independent consultants offering videotapes, instructional handbooks and other educational materials to universities trying to develop programs. More than 400 participants from campus sexual-assault programs and related fields attended the Fourth Annual Conference on Sexual Assault and Harassment on Campus, in Cherry Hill, N.J., organized by the Safe Schools Coalition of Holmes Beach, Fla.

But some rape educators who attended said they felt besieged by skeptics like Katie Roiphe, whose book and articles have received national press attention. A University of Pennsylvania group, Students Together Against Acquaintance Rape (STAR), distributed a list of retorts to "Backlash Myths," including the charge that the 1-in-4 rape statistic is exaggerated. Some directors of campus rape programs said their colleges are reluctant to publicize or adequately fund prevention and counseling programs for fear that alumni and other donors will think the campus has an extraordinary rape problem.

The most treacherous area faced by universities is how to define sexual offenses and how far to go in disciplining them. Because date rape cases are notoriously difficult to prosecute, schools have generally created rules that are broader and easier to apply than criminal codes.

Sometimes this approach opens them up to lawsuits. Last spring, a Pomona College junior claimed that she had been raped by a fellow student 2 ½ years previously after an evening of drinking and after having oral sex with him. She concedes that she never objected at the time.

Like California's penal code, Pomona's policy defines sexual assault as intercourse against a person's consent. But Pomona's rules go one step further, stating "consent requires a clear, explicit agreement to engage in specific activity." The female student claims she never gave that consent. (*See story, p. 968.*)

To Estrich, who has long advocated that date rape be taken seriously in the courts, the Pomona accusation diminished the growing national consensus that date rape is real rape. "The greatest threat to that consensus is no longer those who argue that no means yes but those who claim that a woman or a man doesn't even need to say no. Punishing poor mind readers or even discourteous drunks is the surest route to a furious backlash."[38]

"When a Kiss is not just a Kiss"
SEX WITHOUT CONSENT
AN INTERACTIVE EDUCATION/AWARENESS PROGRAM

Mumbleypeg Productions

A wide range of videos and educational materials is available to rape-prevention educators, including Brown University's skit about "Donna" and "Mike."

Disciplinary Action

Universities are often squeezed between opposing interests as they struggle to formulate date rape policies. Haunting many a college administrator is a 1992 suit filed by four women students against Carleton College in Minnesota. The college knew of previous assaults by the male students who assaulted the four women, but it had failed to take proper disciplinary action that could have prevented the later attacks, the women charged.[39]

On the other hand, Valparaiso University in Indiana discovered that being too sympathetic to rape victims carries its own legal costs. The university developed a policy two years ago to combat sexual assault after President Alan Harre said he was "touched" by the stories several women told of their rapes on campus at a Take Back the Night demonstration.

Following the lead of schools that have attacked the issue aggressively, Valparaiso developed new disciplinary procedures, posted suggestions in every dormitory room on how students could avoid assault and set up a special counseling office for victims. Shortly thereafter, a woman accused a man she had known since high school of raping her at a fraternity drinking party. He responded that she had accused him of rape after having second thoughts about betraying her steady boyfriend.

Valparaiso's disciplinary panel ruled that the man would be suspended for violating Valparaiso's sexual assault guidelines. He sued the school, seeking $12 million in damages, saying his rights had been violated because the school had refused to allow testimony by students on his behalf. The woman who complained was also unhappy, saying that she had lost her anonymity on campus through the process. [40]

In February, Valparaiso brought in sexual-assault expert Simon from Brown University. She recommended a variety of new programs, including changes in the disciplinary process to help guard against lawsuits. "I think they were responding very much to student voices and student activism," says Simon, whose college overhauled its own disciplinary system after women scrawled the names of men they said were rapists in campus bathrooms. "Their heart was in the right place, but they didn't realize they have to pay attention to the rights of the accused."

Pavela, at the University of Maryland, observes that problems are almost inevitable when universities take on complicated cases the larger society won't deal with. But he says it's hard for an administrator to turn down a young woman after a prosecutor has refused to pursue her charge against a fellow student. "You feel you're not meeting your responsibilities in protecting your students when they have to sit next to each other in the classroom," he says.

At the same time, universities are coming under new pressure from the federal government to prosecute rape charges more energetically. The Department of Education's Office for Civil Rights (OCR) recently found two California universities in violation of anti-bias laws in their handling of sexual assault complaints. At the University of California-Santa Cruz, the OCR said, lenient punishments and delays in proceedings involving rape charges had created a "hostile environment" for women. [41]

Universities are coming under new pressure from the federal government to prosecute rape charges more energetically. The Department of Education's Office for Civil Rights (OCR) recently found two California universities in violation of anti-bias laws in their handling of sexual assault complaints.

"Colleges are very much caught in the middle," says Pavela. "On the one hand, you have OCR jabbing you with the stick saying you should be faster, tougher. On the other hand, there are lawsuits where judges say you can't proceed unless you allow a lawyer to be present for the accused."

Trends in State Laws

The debate on campuses over what constitutes rape mirrors to some extent the widely varying state rape statutes and court decisions in the nation at large. Like Pomona, at least one state court has decided that it is rape if a woman does not say "yes" to having sex.

In a 1992 case, the New Jersey Supreme Court ruled, "any act of sexual penetration engaged in by the defendant without the affirmative and freely given permission" of the other person constitutes sexual assault. The case involved two teenagers. A 15-year-old girl charged that a 17-year-old boy living in her home had crawled into her bed while she was asleep. She said she awoke to find him having intercourse with her. [42]

The New Jersey court found the boy guilty of sexual assault. Attorney Burling observes that the opinion can be seen as the logical extension of Antioch's sexual offense policy, which requires a verbal "yes" before engaging in intercourse.

However, Pennsylvania's Supreme Court recently interpreted a similar rape law in the opposite direction, making it harder for women to charge rape. Saying "no," the court declared, is not sufficient grounds for a woman to prove she was raped.

The case, *Commonwealth v. Berkowitz,* involved two East Stroudsburg University students who knew each other. The female student came into Berkowitz's dorm room looking for his roommate, who was not there. Berkowitz sat beside her, pulled up her blouse and bra and attempted without success to get her to give him oral sex, the opinion said. He then locked the door, pushed the girl on the

Continued on p. 978

At Issue:

Should colleges adopt written policies on sex between students?

yes

Alan E. Guskin
Chancellor, Antioch University

FROM *THE WASHINGTON POST,* NOV. 10, 1993.

An Antioch College policy . . . that makes verbal consent a requirement for campus sexual relationships has stimulated comment from national columnists, and conversations in classrooms, boardrooms and newsrooms. Apparently the policy raises eyebrows with its explicit language and its seemingly reasonable request that both parties involved in a sexual relationship get verbal consent at each level of sexual activity. Can it be that the public's reaction is a result of our breaking the taboo on speaking aloud about sexual behavior?

The growing avalanche of requests from other colleges and universities reinforces my sense that the Antioch policy is attracting attention because we may well be the first college that has found a path through the thicket of campus sexual abuses to a higher ground where we can educate people to deal with each other in healthy human relationships rather than attempt the hopeless task of policing student behavior.

Critics ask, how can Antioch, for so long the bastion of progressive thought, education innovation and student freedom from institutional regulation, create a policy that places restrictions on student sexual behavior? It seems as if the college, they say, has returned to an image of the helpless women of the 1950s. The policy, however, does not deal with the reimposition of constraints on freedom; it is not puritanical; it is not anti-romantic; it does not reimpose the perspectives of the 1950s. The Antioch College policy was developed by students' initiative and direct involvement to deal with the realities they face in the 1990s.

Antioch's sexual offense policy reflects the frustration and anger of students, particularly women, regarding the lack of responsiveness of colleges and universities to students who have experienced some form of sexual assault. The Antioch students did not push for this policy out of weakness but out of strength and their insistence that the college community acknowledge the depth of their concerns. They were not asking the institution to intervene on their behalf; rather, they were asserting their right to be treated fairly, with dignity and respect. . . .

The underlying philosophy asserts only one moral value: that each person has the right to have healthy human relationships and to define for himself or herself what that means. The goal is also rather simple but no less profound: that all students have a right to feel safe on the campus and to learn how to assert their interests in a sexual relationship.

no

Diana Trilling
Author

FROM *"MY TURN" COLUMN,* NEWSWEEK, JUNE 6, 1994.

A half-century ago, the gifted humorist James Thurber created a cartoon series — "The War Between Men and Women" — in which he satirized the often-bizarre marital struggle between the sexes. We have only to compare Thurber's bloodless war with the death-dealing spirit which animates the sexual manual which was recently drafted by the students of Antioch College to recognize the dangerous distance we have traveled in the relation of men and women.

According to the Antioch rules, verbal permission must be requested and received before one's sexual partner may proceed from one "level" (their word) to the next in sexual intimacy. Although the manual is at pains to address itself to men as well as women, it does a poor job of disguising its basic assumption that men are natural predators and that women are at one and the same time sacred vessels, shatterable at a touch, and the traffic managers of love.

This is scarcely a useful axiom to disseminate in our society, but for several years now it has been establishing itself in our sexual culture, and it accounts, of course, for the increase in charges now being brought by women against men, the most recent and unpleasant of them the charge of sexual harassment brought by Paula Jones against President Clinton. A woman who doesn't flinch at alleging that the president of the United States attempted to seduce her by letting down his pants demands legal and financial recompense for the damage which this is supposed to have done to her delicate sensibility!

We live in a world which runs with the blood of hostility between racial and religious groups, between ethnic and national groups. To these lamentable separations among people, we now add another division, a separatism of the sexes. Where it used to be that the act of love (as it was then called) was regarded as an aspect, and even a celebration, of our shared humanity, it now becomes a dehumanized exercise and a new arena for conflict. . . .

It is still possible for this trend to be reversed in our society if feminism will take warning from all the other separatisms which now divide our world. Surely nothing is gained for society, nothing is gained for either men or women, by fostering the idea that men are ruthless aggressors against women and that women need to keep themselves in cautionary command of any relation which they have with men. Ours is not a moment in history in which to widen the divisions among people.

For More Information

American Association of University Professors, 1012 14th St. N.W., Washington, D.C. 20005; (202) 737-5900. This organization can provide information on sexual harassment policies at colleges and universities.

American College Health Association, P.O. Box 28937, Baltimore, Md. 21240-8937; (410) 859-1500. This organization produces numerous publications on student health issues, including sexually transmitted diseases and acquaintance rape.

Campus Violence Prevention Center, Towson State University, Towson, Md. 21204-7097; (410) 830-2055. This research center conducts national surveys of such campus issues as date rape and alcohol consumption.

Center for Women Policy Studies, 2000 P St. N.W., Suite 508, Washington, D.C. 20036; (202) 872-1770. This feminist research and advocacy group produces publications addressing women's issues, including acquaintance rape and sexual harassment on campus.

Continued from p. 976

bed and had intercourse with her. [43]

Pennsylvania's law requires force or threat of force for a rape. But the judges concluded that the boy had not used enough force for the incident to qualify as rape. The court opinion acknowledged that the girl said "no" throughout the encounter. But it added, "the weight of his body on top of her was the only force applied." The court upheld a lower court's decision reversing the man's rape conviction but reinstated his conviction for indecent assault, a misdemeanor.

The ruling aroused a furious reaction among rape-crisis activists. "The message here is that a woman has to physically resist and risk serious bodily injury to prove she was raped," said Katherine Geller Myers, a spokeswoman for the Pennsylvania Coalition Against Rape. [44] The coalition is supporting a bill in the Pennsylvania legislature that would create a new category of offenses, sexual assault, to cover situations in which there is lack of consent. A second-degree felony, it would carry a maximum of 5-10 years in prison.

Myers said the new felony would cover "a heck of lot of date rapes" where lack of consent, not violence, is the issue. Noting that most sexual assault victims are attacked by someone they know, she said, "If you know someone and trust someone, the chance of him using a weapon against you is pretty rare." ■

OUTLOOK

Changing Attitudes

Whether the growing emphasis on the dangers of sexual assault will drive men and women further apart or closer together in understanding remains an intriguing question. Meanwhile, recent federal legislation indicates that lawmakers view campus sexual assault as a problem in need of action. In 1992, Congress authorized $10 million to the neediest colleges to fund rape education and prevention programs and services. [45]

For critics like Gilbert, such legislation is an example of how the "distortion of statistics" exaggerating campus rapes have "distorted social policy." He calculates that a $10 million rape prevention fund would spend $10,000 for every campus rape reported to the FBI. By contrast, he says, recent federal legislation ends up spending only $650 per reported rape case in the community at large, "where most rape occurs." [46]

But for those convinced that sexual relations between young men and women need to change, rape prevention programs do more than just prevent rape: They move relations in the direction of greater mutual consent between the sexes. Campus rape programs, such as the sexual encounter staged by Brown University students, are among "the few places" where college men and women can discuss their expectations of sexual situations, maintained Sandler in the recent American Enterprise Institute debate with Gilbert. "In those programs, young men and women have the chance to say what it is like be a man or woman . . . what's exploitative," she said.

During orientation week, rape prevention educator Greensite tries to show Santa Cruz students that sex can mean kissing and fooling around, not just "scoring" — with intercourse the goal at the end of the line. "As long as our sexuality remains male-centered," she says, "everything a female does is seen as contributing to that goal, so women don't have any sexual independence that's recognized." One of her missions, Greensite says, is to teach women to be more assertive as well as teaching men to be more sensitive to women.

Sandler points to a recent revision of Canada's sexual assault law as a reflection of the evolution in society's perception of male-female relations. In 1992, Canada added a provision to the law defining consent as "voluntary agreement of the complainant to engage in the sexual activity in question." *

Catherine Kane, an attorney at Canada's Department of Justice, said the change was made in response to acquaintance-rape decisions in which males accused of sexual assault were acquitted even though the woman, in most people's eyes, had not consented. In one "appalling" case that

* Canadian law does not use the term rape. Instead it covers three categories of sexual assault.

raised a public outcry, she said, a man was acquitted after having intercourse with a woman who was passed out drunk at a party. His defense was that he believed she had consented. Under the new law, defendants who use that defense — the belief that the woman has consented — "have to show they took reasonable steps to ascertain the complainant was in fact consenting," Kane said.

"Remember the Antioch policy everyone laughed at?" asked Sandler at the recent AEI debate. "That's what's law in Canada."

Not quite, says Kane. Antioch requires verbal consent before sexual intercourse. In Canada, however, "You don't have to say yes," Kane says. "But certainly your conduct and all the facts have to indicate a real genuine agreement to engage in the activity."

Gilbert is disturbed by this legal trend. "Between force and consent is a gray area of verbal persuasion," he says. "You begin treating a person who uses verbal persuasion the same way as violent criminals using force."

College students active in the rape prevention movement concede it's a big order to change behavior ingrained through the ages. Jacques Louis, a senior at Brown and a volunteer "peer educator" in its sexual assault program, says he often gets an incredulous reaction from males at other colleges and inner-city high schools at the thought that they have to ask, " 'Can I take off your shirt, can I touch your breast?' It's almost unrealistic," he concedes. But "If I ask, and she says 'yes,' it's more of a turn-on."

"We do work from an idealized model," says Alysia Turner, a Brown junior who also works in the program. "We say consent should be verbal, but we know that's not how it works. The best we can do is hope to change attitudes." ■

Sarah Glazer is a freelance writer in Washington, D.C., who specializes in health and social-policy issues.

Notes

[1] American College Health Association, "Acquaintance Rape," 1992.

[2] Edward O. Laumann et al., *The Social Organization of Sexuality: Sexual Practices in the United States* (1994).

[3] Katie Roiphe, *The Morning After: Sex, Fear and Feminism* (1993), p. 66.

[4] *Rethinking Rites of Passage: Substance Abuse on America's Campuses. A report by the Commission on Substance Abuse at Colleges and Universities,* Center on Addiction and Substance Abuse at Columbia University, June 1994.

[5] R. Barker Bausell et al., *The Links Among Alcohol, Drugs and Crime on American College Campuses: A National Follow-up Study* (1991). For background, see "Underage Drinking," *The CQ Researcher,* March 13, 1992, pp. 217-240.

[6] The Alan Guttmacher Institute, *Sex and America's Teenagers* (1994), p. 19.

[7] Laumann et al., *op cit.,* p. 326.

[8] Katie Roiphe, "Date Rape Hysteria," *The New York Times,* Nov. 20, 1991, p. A19.

[9] Anne Roiphe, "Fear and Feminism," *Mirabella,* August 1993, pp. 54-55. Anne Roiphe conducts an interview with her daughter, Katie Roiphe, in this article.

[10] See Robin Warshaw, *I Never Called It Rape: The Ms. Report on Recognizing, Fighting and Surviving Date and Acquaintance Rape* (1994), and Mary P. Koss et al., "The Scope of Rape," *Journal of Consulting and Clinical Psychology,* April 1987, pp. 162-170. (A 1982 article describing research by Koss in *Ms.* inspired the study.)

[11] Sarah Glazer, "Date Rape: A Campus Obsession?" *Glamour,* June 1993, p. 86.

[12] Warshaw, *op. cit.,* p. 207.

[13] *Ibid.,* p. xxiv.

[14] Neil Gilbert, "Was It Rape?" *The American Enterprise,* September/October 1994, pp. 68-77.

[15] Bausell et al., *op. cit.* Almost 8 percent said they were victims of "other sexual assault." It is not clear whether the 1 percent, 8 percent and 10 percent figures overlap, since participants in the questionnaire could check off several categories of crime simultaneously.

[16] Christina Hoff Sommers, *Who Stole Feminism?* (1994), p. 220.

[17] Reprinted in Camille Paglia, *Sex, Art, and American Culture* (1992), p. 51. Paglia is professor of humanities at the University of the Arts in Philadelphia.

[18] See Bernice Sandler, *"No Means No:" Sexual Harassment and Date Rape* (1993), Association of Governing Boards of Universities and Colleges, p. 36.

[19] The seminar leader and the young man were quoted in Jane Gross, "Combating Rape on Campus in a Class on Sexual Consent," *The New York Times,* Sept. 25, 1993, p. 1.

[20] Katie Roiphe, *The Morning After, op. cit.,* p. xiv.

[21] Sabrina Rubin, "12½ Weeks," *Philadelphia,* October 1994, pp. 83-87.

[22] *Ibid.,* p. 84.

[23] Sandler, *op. cit.,* pp. 6-7.

[24] Elizabeth A. Keller, "Consensual Amorous Relationships Between Faculty and Students: The Constitutional Right to Privacy," *Sexual Harassment on Campus: A Legal Compendium* (1990), pp. 81-102.

[25] "In Box," *The Chronicle of Higher Education,* May 4, 1994, p. A18. See also Courtney Leatherman, "Ex-student Sues Professor at U. of Pennsylvania for Sexual Harassment," *The Chronicle of Higher Education,* April 13, 1994, p. A16.

[26] For background, see "Sexual Harassment," *The CQ Researcher,* Aug. 9, 1991, pp. 537-560.

[27] Helen B. Schaffer, "Sex on Campus," *Editorial Research Reports,* Dec. 30, 1963, pp. 945-992.

[28] *Ibid.,* pp. 945-948.

[29] *Ibid.,* p. 952.

[30] Gilbert, *op. cit.,* p. 76.

[31] Warshaw, *op. cit.,* p. 24.

[32] *Ibid.,* p. 2. For background, see "Violence Against Women," *The CQ Researcher,* Feb. 26, 1993, pp. 169-192.

[33] Susan Estrich, *Real Rape* (1987), pp. 31, 40. Estrich discusses several key legal cases involving rape and also writes the personal story of her own assault.

[34] *Ibid.,* p. 29.

[35] Supreme Court of New Jersey, *State of New Jersey in the Interest of M.T.S.,* July 30, 1992.

[36] George Lardner Jr., "Justice System Lax in Cases of Rape, Senate Report Says," *The Washington Post,* May 28, 1993, pp. A1, A20.

[37] See *1992 CQ Almanac* (1993), p. 450, and *Federal Register,* April 29, 1994, pp. 22314-21.

[38] Susan Estrich, "This case demeans real date rape victims," *USA Today,* May 26, 1994, p. 15A.

[39] Sandler, *op. cit.,* p. 43. The suit was settled out of court.

[40] Edward Felsenthal, "The Risk of Lawsuits Disheartens Colleges Fighting Date Rape," *The Wall Street Journal,* April 12, 1994, pp. A1, A9. The suit is still pending.

[41] Scott Jaschik, "U.S. Says 2 Cal. Universities Mishandled Harassment Complaints," *The Chronicle of Higher Education,* May 11, 1994, p. A32. Pomona State University, the other institution cited, was found to have a "discriminatory environment."

[42] Supreme Court of New Jersey, *ibid.*

[43] See Dale Russakoff, "Where Women Can't Just Say 'No,' " *The Washington Post,* June 3, 1994, p. 1.

[44] *Ibid.*

[45] Originally introduced as part of Sen. Joseph R. Biden Jr.'s, D-Del., Violence Against Women Act during the 102nd Congress, the legislation was finally incorporated into the Higher Education Act Amendments of 1992 enacted in July 1992. To date, no appropriations have been approved to fund the $10 million authorization.

[46] See Gilbert, *op. cit.,* p. 77.

Bibliography

Selected Sources Used

Books

Bohmer, Carol and Andrea Parrot, *Sexual Assault on Campus: The Problem and the Solution,* Lexington Books, 1993.

Two experts present sexual assault as a widely prevalent but underreported crime on campus.

Laumann, Edward O., et al., *The Social Organization of Sexuality: Sexual Practices in the United States,* University of Chicago Press, 1994.

The most comprehensive survey of American sexual habits since the 1953 Kinsey report finds that college-age Americans are becoming more conservative in their sexual behavior than their sexual-revolution peers.

Roiphe, Katie, *The Morning After: Sex, Fear and Feminism,* Back Bay Books, 1994.

Roiphe, a doctoral candidate in English at Princeton University, portrays the campus date rape movement as a form of emotional indoctrination, restoring the myth of lost female innocence. The danger, she argues, is that rape-crisis feminists "are chasing the same stereotypes our mothers spent so much energy running away from."

Robin Warshaw, *I Never Called It Rape: The* Ms. *Report on Recognizing, Fighting and Surviving Date and Acquaintance Rape,* HarperPerennial, 1994.

First published in 1988, this classic of the date rape movement popularized the 1985 *Ms.* campus survey, which concluded that 1 in 4 college women has been the target of rape or rape attempts. This edition includes an afterword by Mary P. Koss, the study's author, describing how the survey was conducted.

Articles

Gilbert, Neil, "Was It Rape?: An Examination of Sexual Abuse Statistics," *The American Enterprise,* September/October 1994, pp. 68-77.

Social scientist Gilbert, a University of California-Berkeley professor, contends that the college surveys repeatedly cited in the media vastly exaggerate the extent of campus date rape.

Hellman, Peter, "Crying Rape: The Politics of Date Rape on Campus," *New York,* March 8, 1993, pp. 32-37.

The author questions "how real the campus rape threat is," as Columbia University students agitate for a 24-hour rape crisis center on campus. The previous year, Columbia received only two rape reports, both questionable according to Hellman.

"New Rules about Sex on Campus," *Harper's Magazine,* September 1993, pp. 33-42, and "Letters," November 1993, pp. 4, 85.

Harper's sponsors a forum among five academics to discuss Tufts University's new ban on student-professor romances. The participants' generally rosy view of student-faculty liaisons sparked outraged letters in subsequent issues of *Harper's.*

Rubin, Sabrina, "12 1/2 Weeks," *Philadelphia,* October 1994, pp. 82-87, 119-125.

A University of Pennsylvania student who has charged sexual harassment against a professor with whom she was sexually involved tells her story — and the professor tells his — in this fascinating in-depth account.

Span, Paula, "Date Rape 101," *The Washington Post,* Oct. 22, 1993, pp. C1, C4.

The author discusses the controversy over campus date rape generated by Katie Roiphe's book (see above).

Wagner, Betsy, "Struggling with Sex," *U.S. News and World Report,* Sept. 26, 1994, pp. 117-119.

A magazine reporter who spent a week at the University of Iowa describes an atmosphere in which casual, unprotected sex is surprisingly common.

Reports and Studies

Burling, Philip, *Acquaintance Rape on Campus: A Model for Institutional Response,* National Association of College and University Attorneys, 1993.

How universities should punish acquaintance rape in the face of new federal requirements and possible lawsuits is the focus of this clearly written monograph aimed at campus administrators.

Center on Addiction and Substance Abuse at Columbia University, *Rethinking Rites of Passage: Substance Abuse on America's Campuses,* June 1994.

A blue-ribbon panel finds an alarming rise in the number of college women who drink to get drunk and notes that 90 percent of all campus rapes reported occur when the assailant or victim is using alcohol.

Sandler, Bernice R., *"No Means No:" Sexual Harassment and Date Rape,* Association of Governing Boards of Universities and Colleges, 1993.

This report, aimed at helping universities prevent sexual assault, contains a useful summary of the landmark cases and campus surveys, some of them recently challenged by University of California Professor Neil Gilbert.

The Next Step

Additional information from UMI's Newspaper & Periodical Abstracts database

Coercive Sexual Conduct

Bachman, Ronet, Sally Ward and Raymond Paternoster "The Rationality of Sexual Offending: Testing a Deterrence/Rational Choice Conception of Sexual Assault," ***Law & Society Review,*** **1992, pp. 343-372.**
Male college students read and respond to five scenarios each describing a hypothetical sexual assault by a male.

Fields, Suzanne, "Could Rhett Beat the Rape Rap," ***The Washington Times,*** **April 16, 1991, p. G1.**
Fields discusses campus sexual politics and rape, especially at Dartmouth College in Hanover, N.H.

Span, Paula, "Date rape 101: It's this semester's hottest course. But author Katie Roiphe says it doesn't belong in the curriculum," ***The Washington Post,*** **Oct. 22, 1993, p. C1.**
As concern about sexual assault has become virtually part of the curriculum at U.S. colleges, Princeton University is undergoing an intense debate over Katie Roiphe's controversial book *The Morning After: Sex, Fear and Feminism on Campus.* Roiphe's thesis is that college activists have so exaggerated the dangers of date rape that the old stereotypes of bestial male predators and fragile female victims have been reawakened.

Struckman-Johnson, Cindy and David Struckman-Johnson, "Men pressured and forced into sexual experience," ***Archives of Sexual Behavior,*** **Feb. 1994, pp. 93-114.**
A predominantly heterosexual sample of 204 college men were asked to report incidents of pressured or forced sexual touch or intercourse since age 16. About 34 percent indicated they had received coercive sexual contact.

Faculty and Student Relations

Brown, DeNeen L., "U-Va. may limit faculty-student sex liaisons," ***The Washington Post,*** **March 25, 1993, p. B1.**
Officials at the University of Virginia are considering a proposal that would ban all sexual relationships, including consensual ones, between faculty members and undergraduates.

Chant, Cate, "Professor's sex views cause stir at U Mass," ***The Boston Globe,*** **Sept. 24, 1993, p. 22.**
The faculty senate at the University of Massachusetts at Amherst voted to dissociate itself from the views of William Kerrigan, who said in the September 1993 edition of *Harper's* magazine that sexual relations between students and faculty can have positive effects.

Jacobs, Sally, "Romance not in the books," ***The Boston Globe,*** **April 12, 1993, p. 1.**
The University of Virginia is considering a proposed ban on all sexual and romantic interaction between faculty and students, the first of its kind in the nation.

Leatherman, Courtney, "Trustees oust chief of Arkansas State, accusing him of sexual misconduct," ***The Chronicle of Higher Education,*** **April 20, 1994, p. A20.**
Arkansas State University President John N. Mangieri was fired by the school's board of trustees after being accused of sexual misconduct and harassment.

Meikle, James, "No Sex Please, We're Lecturers," ***Guardian,*** **May 15, 1992, p. 4.**
A ban on affairs between university lecturers and their students will be proposed at the conference of the Association of University Teachers in Avon on May 16, 1992. Some lecturers believe the ban is needed to prevent potential abuse of power.

Root, Jay, "Rice Faculty Waters Down Policy on Sex with Students," ***Houston Post,*** **Sept. 26, 1991, p. A17.**
After almost a year of debate, faculty members at Rice University have released a set of guidelines calling sexual relationships with students "usually unwise." The language in the document is much more lenient than in the originally proposed guidelines.

Schodolski, Vincent J., "Campus quandary: Teacher-student love," ***Chicago Tribune,*** **Sept. 5, 1993, p. 21.**
Deciding where affairs of the heart cross the line into manipulation and abuse of power is proving difficult on college campuses across the U.S. as schools try to set policies to protect the rights of students and faculty without taking away traditional freedoms.

Yardley, Jonathan, "When passion's academic," ***The Washington Post,*** **March 29, 1993, p. D2.**
Yardley discusses the proposal presented by the Committee on Women's Concerns to the University of Virginia that would ban all sexual relationships between faculty and undergraduates, between faculty and graduate students in the same department and between faculty members controlling fellowships and student applicants for such assistance.

HIV Issues

Chu, Henry, "Coming of age in the era of AIDS," ***Los Angeles Times,*** **Feb. 9, 1993, p. S4.**
In a special section on colleges, students attending college in 1993 say they are the first generation of students to have grown up in the shadow of the deadly disease AIDS. Statistics on students' sexual behavior are provided.

Hankins, Justine, "The Years of Living Dangerously,"

***Guardian,* July 7, 1992, p. 37.**

Hankins examines the bizarre and illogical responses given by many British college students when they were asked about AIDS and practicing safe sex. She examines the extent to which media coverage about AIDS and the HIV virus has been effective in informing young people about safe sex.

Lee, Felicia R., "College couples are now asking for AIDS tests," *The New York Times,* Oct. 4, 1993, p. A1.

More and more college students are rolling up their sleeves to take AIDS tests, often right on campus. Men and women, gay and straight, are demanding the test as a prerequisite for intimate relationships.

Safer Sex Practices

Caron, Sandra L., Clive M. Davis, William A. Halteman and Marla Stickle, "Predictors of condom-related behaviors among first-year college students," *Journal of Sex Research,* August 1993, pp. 252-259.

A study of condom use among 330 first-year college students is presented. Logistic analyses were also used to investigate the relationship between condom-related behaviors and attitudes toward condoms and sexuality.

Netting, Nancy S., "Sexuality in youth culture: Identity and change," *Adolescence,* winter 1992, pp. 961-976.

A study that explored the reasons behind sexual choices and that investigated whether the possibility of contracting AIDS will eventually lead adolescents to better balance their needs for sex, love, freedom and self-preservation is presented. Working against the choice of caution is the fact that, in our culture, sexual expression is an important element of becoming an adult.

Stacey, Julie and Patti Stang, "U.S.A. snapshots: Sex without caution, *USA Today,* April 29, 1994, p. A1.

According to information from David Michaelson & Associates for Upjohn, of the two-thirds of college students who say they are sexually active, 25 percent of men and 37 percent of women say they "often" discuss birth control with sex partners and 47 percent of men and 32 percent of women say they have had sex without birth control within the past year.

Young, Monica R., "Study says most at B.U. don't use condoms," *Boston Globe,* April 28, 1993, p. 83.

Despite a high awareness of AIDS and the risk of unprotected sex, 72 percent of sexually active Boston University students say they do not use condoms regularly, according to a new survey.

Sex Roles and Sexual Differences

Anderson, Peter B. and Ronelle Aymami, "Reports of female initiation of sexual contact: Male and female differences," *Archives of Sexual Behavior,* August 1993, pp. 335-343.

College women's reports of initiating sexual contact and college men's reports of experiencing female initiation were compared. Overall, males reported experiencing female initiation more frequently than females reported initiating. Traditional gender roles may influence male and female perceptions of female initiation of sexual contact in a way that contributes to significant differences in reporting.

Lottes, Ilsa L., "Nontraditional gender roles and the sexual experiences of heterosexual college students," *Sex Roles: A Journal of Research,* November 1993, pp. 645-669.

Heterosexual college students were studied to specify gender differences and similarities in sexual beliefs and experiences and to determine the prevalence of women enacting traditional male roles in dating and sexual interactions. The relationship between women's enactment of traditional male roles and their sexual experiences was also examined.

Lottes, Ilsa L. and Peter J. Kuriloff, "Sexual socialization differences by gender, Greek membership, ethnicity, and religious background," *Psychology of Women Quarterly,* June 1994, pp. 203-219.

A study was conducted to examine how parental and peer sexual socialization influences are related to gender, ethnicity, religious background and college membership in a fraternity or sorority. The results indicated that, compared with women, men continue to experience a more permissive sexual socialization from both parents and peers.

"Sexual Correctness" at Antioch

Abrams, Andy and Kristine Herman, "Antioch is not legislating sexual correctness," *The Chronicle of Higher Education,* Jan. 26, 1994, p. B3.

The news media in the U.S. and abroad have misrepresented college requirements that students obtain verbal consent for each state of intimacy, the authors write. It is argued that Antioch College, which adopted such a policy, is not legislating "sexual correctness."

"Ask first at Antioch," *The New York Times,* Oct. 11, 1993, p. A16.

An editorial says that Antioch College's insistence on a couple's clear, verbal consent before proceeding to increasingly intimate levels of a relationship will be almost impossible to implement.

Giles, Jeff, "There's a time for talk, and a time for action," *Newsweek,* March 7, 1994, pp. 54-55.

Antioch College's controversial sexual-conduct code is discussed. The policy hasn't seemed to put a damper on campus sexual activities, Giles writes.

Grenier, Richard, "Some advice on consent: This is going way too far," *Insight on the News,* Nov. 1, 1993, pp. 28-29.

Antioch College's new rules on sexual consent promote the old stereotype that women are weak and men are beasts, Grenier writes.

Page, Clarence, "On Today's campus, consent for a kiss is in Romance 101," *Chicago Tribune,* Sept. 15, 1993, p. 21.
Page comments on Antioch College in Yellow Springs, Ohio, which has come up with a code of sexual conduct that governs just about every aspect of private romantic moments between students.

Stanford, Duane D., "Will sexual codes be adopted on state's campuses?" *Atlanta Constitution,* Oct. 28, 1993, p. 2.
There is concern and sometimes fervor on DeKalb County, Ga., college campuses about the perils of date rape, but many local students say Antioch College has gone too far.

Wolff, Jennifer, "Sex by the rules," *Glamour,* May 1994, pp. 256-259.
For some students, making love using the rules established at Antioch College works well and keeps them out of trouble. The college's protective, strict policy is detailed, and students' opinions of the policy are presented.

Sexuality on Campus

Bryan, Janice Westlund and Florence Wallach Freed, "Abortion research: Attitudes, sexual behavior, and problems in a community college population," *Journal of Youth & Adolescence,* February 1993, p. 1-22.
Community college students were surveyed regarding their attitudes toward abortion, their sexual behavior and their problems. Of the 150 students asked, 82 percent supported abortion choice.

Elias, Marilyn, "Collegians drink to loosen up sexually," *USA Today,* Nov. 8, 1993, p. D7.
Many college students drink heavily so they can live up to a popular ideal of "recreational sex" that they are not really comfortable with, according to campus surveys.

Porter, James F. and Joseph W. Critelli, "Measurement of sexual aggression in college men: A methodological analysis," *Archives of Sexual Behavior,* December 1992, pp. 525-542.
Methods of measuring sexual aggression that rely on a self-reported history of the behavior are described and critically examined. It is suggested that the construct validity of these approaches can be enhanced through a systematic consideration of instrumentation and methodological issues.

Roche, John P. and Thomas W. Ramsbey, "Premarital sexuality: A five-year follow-up study of attitudes and behavior by dating stage," *Adolescence,* spring 1993, pp. 67-80.
The state of premarital sexual attitudes and behavior among college students during the 1980s is examined.

Shea, Mary E. Craig, "The effects of selective evaluation on the perception of female cues in sexually coercive and noncoercive males," *Archives of Sexual Behavior,* October 1993, pp. 415-433.
One-hundred eighty-two college students participated in brief heterosexual interactions and rated each other's behavior in terms of sexual expressiveness, flattery and interest in future interactions. Results support the hypothesis of selective evaluation in men, and in sexually coercive men in particular.

Simon, Toby, "Sexuality on campus — '90s style," *Change,* September 1993, pp. 50-56.
The chief concerns of college students regarding sexuality are virginity, pregnancy, disease, non-consensual sexual encounters, sexual orientation and sexual functioning. Sexuality on today's college campuses is discussed.

Wagner, Betsy, "Struggling with sex," *U.S. News & World Report,* Sept. 26, 1994, pp. 117-119.
Many people hoped that the sexual revolution would encourage responsible relationships between men and women on college campuses. Just the opposite seems to be the case, Wagner writes.

Women's Concerns

Corne, Shawn, John Briere and Lillian M. Esses, "Women's attitudes and fantasies about rape as a function of early exposure to pornography," *Journal of Interpersonal Violence,* December 1992, pp. 454-461.
In a study about how social forces such as pornography can shape women's attitudes and behavior about sexual violence, 187 female college students were questioned about childhood exposure to pornography, current sexual fantasies and endorsement of rape-supportive attitudes. Results showed early exposure to pornography was related to subsequent "rape fantasies" and attitudes supportive of sexual violence against women.

Gilbert, Neil, "Counterpoint: A Few Women Want to Speak for Both Sides," *San Francisco Chronicle,* June 26, 1991, p. A17.
Gilbert disputes statements regarding the extremely high incidence of date rape on college campuses.

Powers, Ann, "Let's talk about sex," *Village Voice,* Sept. 14, 1993, pp. 29-35.
Six college women comment on feminism's impact on their lives. None knows the solution to the current campus sex and power crises. Each has her own stories to tell about date rape, activism, sexuality and the reality of being a young woman in the 1990s.

Stein, Ruthe, "Date-Rape Debate Stirs up Young Women's Anxiety," *San Francisco Chronicle,* June 17, 1991, p. D4.
Ruthe Stein discusses the extreme concern college women have regarding date rape, comparing sexuality now and in the early 1960s, when she attended college.

Back Issues

Great Research on Current Issues Starts Right Here...Recent topics covered by The CQ Researcher are listed below. Before May 1991, reports were published under the name of Editorial Research Reports.

APRIL 1993
Head Start
High-Speed Rail
Children's Legal Rights
Muslims in America

MAY 1993
Cults in America
Preventing Teen Pregnancy
Software Piracy
National Parks

JUNE 1993
Food Safety
Prostitution
Childhood Immunizations
National Service

JULY 1993
Electric Cars
Population Growth
Downward Mobility
Intelligence Testing

AUGUST 1993
Mental Illness
Bilingual Education
Foreign Policy Burden
School Funding

SEPTEMBER 1993
Suburban Crime
Public Housing
Supreme Court Preview
Immigration Reform

OCTOBER 1993
Airline Safety
Disaster Response
Science in the Courtroom
The Glass Ceiling

NOVEMBER 1993
Paying for Retirement
Charitable Giving
Privacy in the Workplace
Adoption

DECEMBER 1993
U.S. Vietnam-Relations
Learning Disabilities
Child Care
Space Program's Future

JANUARY 1994
Racial Tensions in Schools
South Africa's Future
Worker Retraining
Regulating Pesticides

FEBRUARY 1994
Prison Overcrowding
Water Quality
Religion in Schools
Juvenile Justice

MARCH 1994
Underground Economy
Education Standards
Gambling Boom
Private Management of Public Schools

APRIL 1994
Reproductive Ethics
U.S.-China Trade
Soccer in America
Talk Show Democracy

MAY 1994
Traffic Congestion
Women's Health Issues
Mutual Funds
Political Scandals

JUNE 1994
Education and Gender
Gun Control
Public Land Policy
Nuclear Arms Cleanup

JULY 1994
Dietary Supplements
Public Opinion and Foreign Policy
Crime Victims' Rights
Birth Control Choices

AUGUST 1994
Genetically Engineered Foods
Electing Minorities
Prozac Controversy
College Sports

SEPTEMBER 1994
Home Schooling
Welfare Experiments
Courts and the Media
Regulating Tobacco

OCTOBER 1994
Historic Preservation
Religion and Politics
Arts Funding
Economic Sanctions

Back issues are available for $4.00 (subscribers) or $7.00 (non-subscribers). Quantity discounts apply to orders over ten. To order, call Congressional Quarterly Customer Service at (202) 887-8621.

Binders are available for $16.00. To order call 1-800-638-1710. Please refer to stock number 648.

Future Topics

- ***Blood Supply Safety***
- ***Term Limits Revisited***
- ***Religion in America***

THE CQ Researcher

PUBLISHED BY CONGRESSIONAL QUARTERLY INC.

Blood Supply Safety

Is the nation's blood supply safe enough?

The nation's blood supply is safer than ever, blood-banking officials say, and industry critics generally agree. But the critics also say it's not as safe as it could be. And many Americans, fearful of contracting the AIDS virus, remain wary of receiving transfusions. Increasing numbers of people facing elective surgery now give blood in advance that is earmarked for their exclusive use. At the same time, researchers report progress in developing taint-free artificial blood with a long shelf life. Still, there will always be a need for natural blood, especially in times of emergency. But Red Cross officials say that the nation's pool of donors has been steadily shrinking, and that this winter, once again, blood stocks will dip to perilously low levels.

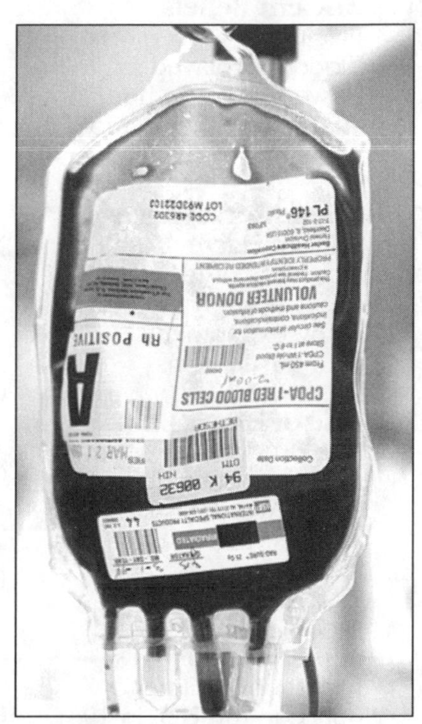

INSIDE THIS ISSUE

CQ Nov. 11, 1994 • Volume 4, No. 42 • Pages 985-1008

Formerly Editorial Research Reports

Blood Supply Safety

The Issues

Background

Current Situation

Outlook

Sidebars and Graphics

For More Information

Cover: Americans donate 14 million units of whole blood annually. (C. Ashley Jackson/*Consumers' Research*)

THE CQ Researcher

November 11, 1994
Volume 4, No. 42

The CQ Researcher (ISSN 1056-2036). Formerly Editorial Research Reports. Published weekly (48 times per year, not printed the first Friday of any month with five Fridays) by Congressional Quarterly Inc., 1414 22nd St., N.W., Washington, D.C. 20037. Rates are furnished upon request. Second-class postage paid at Washington, D.C. POSTMASTER: Send address changes to The CQ Researcher, 1414 22nd St., N.W., Washington, D.C. 20037.

Blood Supply Safety

BY RICHARD L. WORSNOP

THE ISSUES

The holiday season is a time for giving. Increasingly, though, it's not a time for giving blood. Last winter's shortage was the worst since World War II, and this year promises to be no better. "At this time of year, stocks of blood barely exceed patient demand," says Liz Hall, a spokeswoman for the American Red Cross. "A three-day supply is considered optimal in this country. But during holidays, we typically have only a one to one-and-a-half-day supply on hand. It's a dangerous time of year." *

To some extent, the holiday blood-donation slump is weather-related. Snowy and icy roads deter many prospective donors from rolling up their sleeves, as do colds and flu. Travel and other holiday-linked activities also claim time that might otherwise be devoted to blood donation.

But while the year-end shortfall stirs deep concern, blood-collection agencies have a greater worry: The country's pool of donors is steadily shrinking. Hall reports that blood donations have dropped by about 2 percent annually over the past five years. To slow the trend, blood banks eliminated the age limit on donors, which had been set at 65. **

Blood banks are also trying to make donating more convenient. They are opening up on weekends and holidays and staying open later on weekdays. And the Red Cross now conducts a donor-recruitment drive in one of its six regions during each major holiday period, with special events, press conferences and stepped-up mail and telephone appeals.

* According to the American Association of Blood Banks, about 8 million persons — fewer than 5 percent of the number eligible to give — donate 14 million units of blood each year. A unit is about one pint.

** The minimum age for donating blood remains 17.

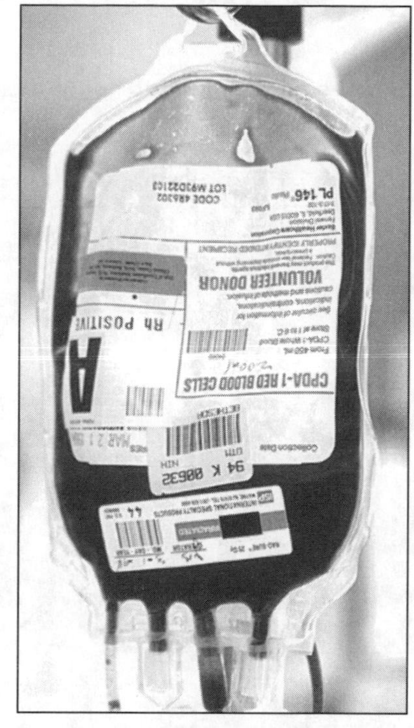

But many experts say the blood-supply crisis won't be solved until research pinpoints its underlying causes. "We need sociologists and anthropologists to do the studies to learn why we are not replacing with younger donors the aging generations that regularly gave gallons of blood over their lives in a community spirit that grew out of World War II and the Korean War," said Dr. Arthur J. Silvergleid, a past president of the American Association of Blood Banks (AABB). [1] The Red Cross estimates that 9 out of 10 blood donations come from repeat donors.

Fear of contracting acquired immune deficiency syndrome (AIDS) undoubtedly has dulled the blood-giving impulse. News reports have documented again and again over the past dozen years that the fatal illness can be spread by transfusions of infected blood products — but there's no risk to donors giving blood. Yet many people seem unconvinced, even though blood banks constantly issue reminders that needles used to draw blood are thrown away immediately afterward.

Aversion to giving blood is more pronounced in some groups than others. African-Americans, for instance, have long been underrepresented among U.S. blood and marrow donors. To justify their decision not to give, some blacks cite an old rumor about Charles R. Drew, a noted black surgeon and blood specialist. They mistakenly believe that he died shortly after a 1950 auto accident in North Carolina because a segregated hospital refused to give him a transfusion. [2]

Drew's daughter, Charlene Drew Jarvis, a City Council member in Washington, D.C., discovered during her term on the local Red Cross board that the rumor had gained wide credence. In fact, she says, her father received at least one transfusion at the hospital and died from his injuries. "[I]f the myth is going to be an impediment in people's decisions to save lives, then it's necessary to dispel it," she said. [3] For the past year, Jarvis has been touring the country on behalf of the National Marrow Donor Program to raise the donation rate of blacks. [4]

In the meantime, efforts are under way to stretch the nation's existing blood supply. In some cases, the need for transfused blood can be sharply reduced or even eliminated by treating surgical patients in advance with a synthetic copy of the human hormone erythropoietin (EPO), which stimulates the production of red blood cells in bone marrow. [5]

Surgeons also are finding that much of the blood lost during an operation can be retrieved and returned to the patient's body. Before being reinfused, the blood is filtered to screen out flesh and bone fragments and similar debris and then "washed" to remove other contaminants. Up to 90 percent of the blood lost during surgery can be salvaged, says Janis Smith, managing director of laboratories at the Red Cross regional blood center in Baltimore.

Some experts feel the best way to

Some Donors Give to Themselves

Donors who want to be 100 percent sure about the blood they receive in a transfusion use their own. And ever since the AIDS crisis arose in the 1980s, more and more people have been doing just that.

Autologous donations, as they are called, now account for about 5 percent of all donations nationwide. They are typically given in advance of elective surgery.

Most blood centers and large hospitals accept autologous donations, which usually occur weekly over a three-to-six-week period. In fact, because the body makes new blood so quickly, blood experts say blood may be given as often as every fourth day, with the final collection occurring no sooner than 72 hours before the operation.

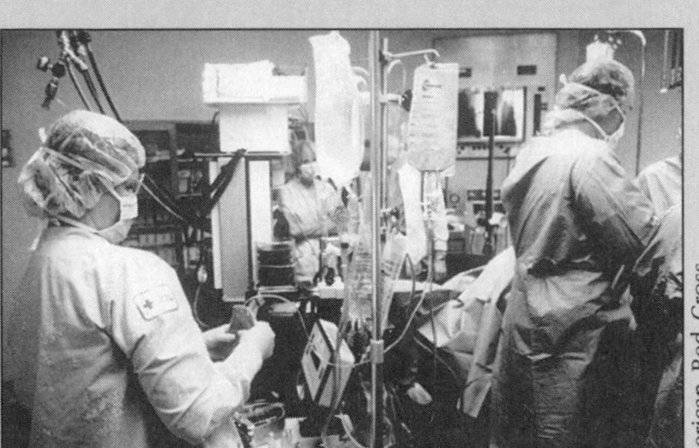

American Red Cross

Up to 90 percent of the blood lost during surgery can be recovered and reinfused in the patient during the operation, after it is filtered and cleaned.

To provide a margin of safety, many autologous donors give more blood than they're expected to need for their operation. The chief appeal of autologous blood, of course, is that it contains no contaminants that are not already present in the donor's body — and it's a perfect match. Moreover, there are no age or weight requirements for donors. Children and the elderly often are deemed suitable.

Often, however, patients who feel they have not donated sufficient blood of their own may ask family members or friends to give blood earmarked for their use. Surgeons discourage this practice, since experience has shown that relatives and friends are no more likely than volunteer donors to have taint-free blood.

The chief shortcoming of autologous donations and directed donations, which are designated for someone else, is that much of the blood is never used. In 1989, the non-utilization rate was reported at 44 percent for autologous blood and 55 percent for directed blood. [1]

And blood banks generally will not transfuse autologous or directed blood into persons for whom it was not intended, even in an emergency. That's because autologous and di-rected donors are subjected to less rigorous pre-donation screening than are volunteer donors.

[1] Wallace, E.L., et al., "Collection and Transfusion of Blood and Blood Components in the United States, 1989" *Transfusion,* Vol. 33, 1993, pp. 139-144.

ease the chronic blood shortage is to develop a safe and effective substitute (*see p. 989*). If artificial blood can be perfected, it will largely eliminate the problem of recruiting donors. But until that day arrives, the supply of blood must depend on the relative handful who, prodded by unavoidable circumstance, self-interest or community spirit, come forward to give.

As blood officials seek to increase the supply of blood, these are two of the key questions being debated:

Is the nation's blood supply safe?

Defenders and critics of the U.S. blood industry agree that the blood supply is far safer today than in the early 1980s. But they part company over whether blood stocks are as safe as they could or should be.

The Red Cross, the AABB and other blood-collection agencies — as well as federal health officials — say the screening tests introduced over the past decade (*see p. 991*) have greatly reduced the risk of infection from transfused blood. But critics contend that the infection rate is still unacceptably high for the AIDS-causing human immunodeficiency virus (HIV) and hepatitis.

To Harvey Klein, chief of the National Institutes of Health's Department of Transfusion Medicine, the situation warrants both confidence and caution. "With advanced screening methods, the nation's blood supply is safer today than ever before, but it can never be 100 percent safe," he said. "The risk of infection from hepatitis and HIV, as well as from future unknown viruses, remains a major concern among medical and scientific communities, not to mention the general public." [6]

According to the Red Cross, about 1 in 2,500 people had a chance of becoming infected with HIV from a blood transfusion in March 1985, just before a laboratory screening test was introduced nationwide. Today the Red Cross estimates the risk at 1 in 225,000. Improved donor screening and education programs also played a part in slashing the HIV infection rate.

Similar progress is claimed in curbing the incidence of hepatitis. Less than 30 years ago, nearly 1 of every 3 patients receiving a blood transfusion contracted hepatitis. The Red Cross credits improvements in the donor-selection process, plus more stringent testing methods, with lowering the infection rate from transfusions to about 1 in 100 patients. "The probability of a patient actually developing clinical hepatitis, rather than simply harboring the infection, is as low as 1 in 3,000," the Red Cross says. [7]

James P. Reilly, executive director of the American Blood Resources Association (ABRA), an industry group, calls the U.S. blood supply "probably as safe as it can be with the technology that we have to screen donors and test units of blood and plasma." He cautions, though, that "it's important to recognize there are differences between the blood supplies for transfusion and for plasma, which is used for further manufacturing. They're two very different products, with slightly different donor pools, and the technology to safeguard the products is somewhat different also."

Robert M. Winslow, a pioneer in blood-substitute research, believes the blood supply is "as safe as it *can* be," though not necessarily as safe as it should be. "'Should' is a hard word," explains Winslow, chief of the hematology/oncology section at the Veterans Administration Medical Center in San Diego. "You'd like donated blood to be totally safe, but I don't think we're ever going to get there. There are too many accidents that can happen. It's like asking, 'Is anybody in the United States absolutely free of the possibility of dying in an earthquake?' The answer is no, but the odds are very small. There's a similar situation with the blood supply. Safe as it is, could it become contaminated with something new? Yes."

Critics of the blood industry contend too much tainted blood enters the system despite all the safeguards adopted to detect it. HIV will remain a blood-transfusion hazard, the critics argue, as long as there is a "window." That's the period — lasting about six weeks in most persons — between initial exposure to the virus and the appearance of antibodies. During that time, an infectious donor may not be detected by the screening test, which is triggered by the antibodies.

Economics Professor Ross D. Eckert of Claremont McKenna College in Claremont, Calif., believes that hepatitis is a greater transfusion hazard than HIV. Testifying before a congressional subcommittee four years ago, Eckert estimated that from 1987 to the introduction of the first test for hepatitis C in 1990, 5 percent of the estimated 4 million Americans who received transfusions each year were infected with hepatitis viruses. He further estimated that every year 4,000 of the people with infections would develop fatal cirrhosis of the liver within five to 10 years. *

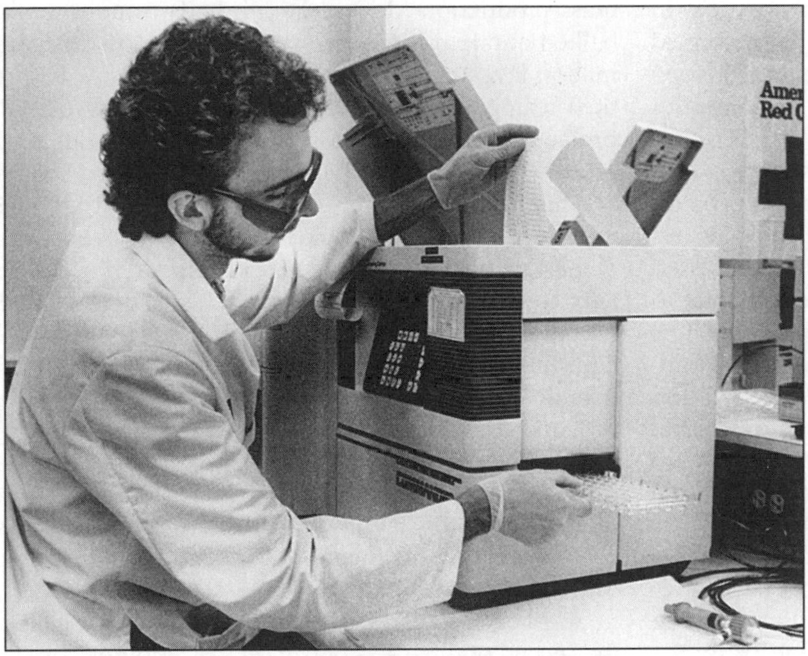

American Red Cross

Technician tests blood for HIV, the virus that causes AIDS, at the Red Cross regional blood center in Baltimore.

"Losing 4,000 people per year is about like losing a fully loaded DC-10 each month," Eckert said. "I doubt that Congress would tolerate in airline travel the rate of casualties we have had in blood banking." [8]

Eckert and some other blood-industry critics blame many safety problems on blood banks' reliance on a large pool of random donors. The problems would fade or vanish, they say, if collecting agencies accepted blood only from persons drawn from a registry of low-risk, repeat donors.

According to Eckert, "Registry donors would be limited to persons who are in good health; who have not been transfused since 1977; who agree to a detailed, confidential medical history, including questions about venereal diseases and sexual promiscuity; and who agree to more extensive testing than is now routine. Registry donors would give only as often as good health allowed and be replaced only with new, equally well-tested and well-screened donors from the same groups when absolutely necessary." [9]

Will artificial blood end problems of safety and supply?

If medical researchers succeed in developing artificial blood products, many of today's concerns about blood supply safety would be eased. Ideally, synthetic blood could be stored for years at room temperature, would not have to be typed and cross-matched and would be free of HIV, hepatitis and other potentially lethal viruses.

Winslow predicts that some such

* Of the several strains of hepatitis that have been identified, hepatitis B and hepatitis C pose the greatest danger in blood transfusions.

product will be available within five years. It's likely to have "rather limited use" at first, he says, "possibly in trauma or emergency situations where nothing else is available." Synthetic blood won't totally replace human blood for transfusion purposes, says Winslow, "but it will replace some blood, and as experience grows, it will replace more and more."

An effective blood substitute must perform one critical function: pick up life-supporting oxygen from the lungs, deliver it to tissues elsewhere in the body and then release the oxygen. In the bloodstream, this job is performed by the hemoglobin protein in red blood cells, which accounts for 97 percent of cell volume.

Researchers have long known that hemoglobin doesn't work as a blood surrogate. When hemoglobin is removed from the red cells, or isolated in its "free" state, it binds so tightly to oxygen that not enough oxygen is released to the body's tissues. Moreover, hemoglobin molecules soon break in two after being removed from red cells. These fragments, in turn, are rapidly filtered out of the bloodstream by the kidneys, which may suffer irreparable damage in the process.

To surmount these obstacles, researchers have focused on creating products based on genetically or chemically altered forms of human hemoglobin or hemoglobin extracted from pigs, cows or "outdated" human blood — donated blood too old for direct transfusion. In one such approach, hemoglobin is modified so that its protein chains are cross-linked, or polymerized. The resulting molecule is stable and capable of delivering and releasing oxygen as desired. Even so, some patients have experienced shortness of breath and chest tightness after receiving polymerized hemoglobin.

With a potential market estimated at $2 billion to $5 billion in annual sales, artificial blood has drawn the interest of numerous biotechnology and pharmaceutical companies, including Eli Lilly & Co., Upjohn Co., Baxter International Inc. and Northfield Laboratories Inc. However, their commitment has its limits.

In October 1993, for example, the DNX Corp. of Princeton, N.J., said it was shelving plans to develop a blood substitute derived from genetically altered pigs because it was unable to find sufficient financial backing. DNX President Paul J. Schmitt said the company had approached several drug manufacturers about a joint testing and mass-production deal, but all had balked at taking on a five-year, $150 million investment. Most pharmaceutical companies were "prioritizing projects and looking for near-term returns," said Schmitt. [10]

This June, on the other hand, Somatogen Inc. of Boulder, Colo., embarked on a joint venture with Eli Lilly to test and market Somatogen's blood substitute. The product contains human hemoglobin produced by genetically engineered E. coli bacteria. Since the supply of E. coli is virtually limitless, the Somatogen process presumably could supply greater quantities of artificial blood than techniques that rely on human or animal blood as raw material.

Somatogen's blood substitute is in the second of three sets of clinical trials that most new drugs must undergo before obtaining marketing approval from the Food and Drug Administration (FDA). Under the two firms' agreement, Lilly will take charge of production for the final test phase and for the product's commercial introduction.

Meanwhile, other approaches to making artificial blood remain in the research and development pipeline. Besides DNX's transgenic-pig process, now on hold, they include Baxter's technique for harvesting hemoglobin from outdated blood and a perfluorocarbon chemical developed by Alliance Pharmaceuticals Inc. that can transport oxygen through the bloodstream for short periods. ■

Background

Ancient Beliefs

Blood has always figured prominently in the medical arts, but it has always been much more than just a "medicine." Since ancient times, when humans learned that it was essential to life itself, blood has had a unique emotional dimension. Magic powers were ascribed to blood. Sacrifices to propitiate the gods, blood pacts to bind members of tribal brotherhoods and blood feuds to avenge blood brothers all testify to the powerful feelings associated with blood.

"The history of every people assigns to blood a unique importance," British sociologist Richard M. Titmuss observed. "Symbolically and functionally, blood is deeply embedded in religious doctrine; in the psychology of human relationships; and in theories and concepts of race, kinship, ancestor worship and the family. From time immemorial, it has symbolized qualities of fortitude, vigor, nobility, purity and fertility. Men have been terrified by the sight of blood; they have killed each other for it; believed it could work miracles; and have preferred death rather than receive it from a member of a different ethnic group." [11]

The ancients suspected the great curative powers of blood. The Egyptians used blood for baths to resuscitate the sick, and many believed that they could be cured of their ailments by drinking the blood of a healthy animal. Similarly, spectators at the fights between gladiators in Rome often rushed into the arena afterwards to drink the blood of the dying. And during the French Revolution, executioners sometimes offered the blood of beheaded aristocrats to a favored few of the poor.

Continued on p. 992

Chronology

17th Century

First attempts at blood transfusion fail, largely because little is known about blood's composition and the hazards of contamination.

1665
British physician Richard Lower performs the first authenticated blood transfusion, between dogs.

1667
Jean Baptiste Denis, a French doctor, performs the first recorded blood transfusion on a human. Blood taken from a lamb is administered to a 15-year-old boy, who dies afterward.

1678
Pope Innocent XI prohibits blood transfusions.

1900s-1910s

Giant steps are taken in understanding the makeup of blood and devising ways to preserve it.

1900
Austrian physiologist Karl Landsteiner discovers that there are different types of blood and that if the donor's and the recipient's types don't match, the red cells clump and disintegrate.

1914
Sodium citrate is introduced as an anti-coagulant. It permits the storage of refrigerated blood for up to seven days.

1930s-1940s

The U.S. blood-banking system begins to emerge.

1937
The first nonprofit U.S. blood bank is established at Cook County Hospital in Chicago.

1941
Irwin Memorial Blood Bank, the nation's first communitywide blood bank, opens in San Francisco.

1941
At the request of the military, the American Red Cross begins a nationwide blood-collection program to aid the war effort.

1947
The American Association of Blood Banks is founded in Dallas.

1947
U.S. blood banks begin testing donated blood for syphilis.

1960s

Hemophiliacs are the major beneficiaries of an advance in the manufacture of blood derivatives.

1962
The Council of Community Blood Centers is established.

1965
Concentrated preparations of factor VIII (blood-clotting factor) become commercially available for the first time and soon are widely used throughout the world to treat hemophilia.

1980s

The virus that causes AIDS contaminates blood supplies worldwide before scientists are able to identify the organism.

July 16, 1982
The first three cases of AIDS in hemophiliacs are reported by the federal Centers for Disease Control.

April 1984
Teams of French and U.S. researchers independently report the discovery of a virus thought to cause AIDS.

March 1985
The first direct blood-screening test for AIDS becomes generally available at U.S. blood banks.

1987
An enhanced test for hepatitis B is introduced.

September 1988
The Red Cross signs an agreement with the FDA under which it pledges to "standardize, revise and update standard operating procedures used by all regional blood services."

1990s

Health officials in the U.S. and other countries take tougher measures to assure the safety of donated blood.

1990
Testing of blood for hepatitis C begins in the U.S.

September 1991
An official report discloses that in 1985, French government ministers knowingly approved transfusions of blood contaminated with HIV.

May 1993
In a consent decree enforceable by court order, the Red Cross agrees to establish a comprehensive quality-assurance program and to improve its computer system and employee training.

Blood Types at a Glance

All people belong to one of four inherited blood groups: A, B, AB, and O. The letters A and B refer to the kind of antigen found in an individual's red blood cells. An antigen is a substance that triggers an immunological reaction, such as the formation of antibodies. Before a transfusion is given, it is important to know which blood group a person is in because the blood plasma contains strong antibodies, called anti-A and anti-B, that react against the red cells with A or B antigens. (Type O blood does not have antigens.)

If anti-A antibody came in contact with A antigen (or if anti-B antibody met B antigen), the result would be a dangerous, possibly fatal, clumping of red cells. To prevent such clumping, blood for transfusions is matched with that of the recipient for its ABO group. The four basic groups in the ABO system are:

Group A: blood has A antigen in red cells, anti-B in its plasma.

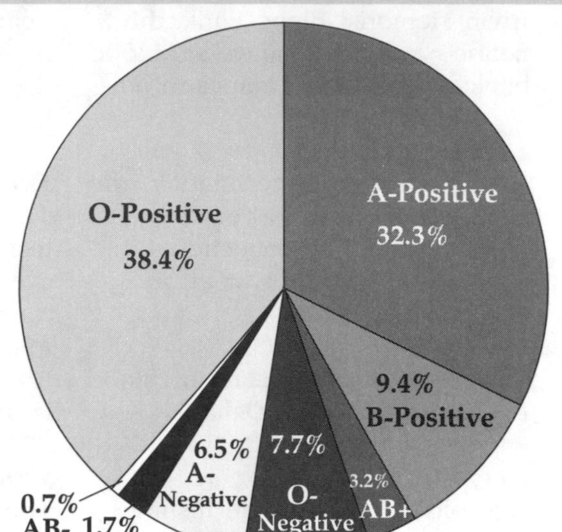

Two out of every three Americans have either A-Positive or O-Positive blood. Less than 1 percent of the population, or about 1 in 143 people, are AB Negative.

Source: American Red Cross

Group B: blood has B antigen in red cells, anti-A in its plasma.

Group AB: blood has both A and B antigens in red cells but neither anti-A nor anti-B in its plasma. AB blood cannot cause the clumping of red cells of any other groups, and therefore persons with AB blood are called universal recipients.

Group O: blood has neither A nor B antigens in red cells, and both anti-A and anti-B in the plasma. Group O blood cannot be clumped by any human blood, and therefore persons with Group O blood are called universal donors.

Most people also have an inherited condition of the red blood cells known as the Rh factor, or antigen D. When the D antigen is present, a person's blood type is designated as positive, or Rh positive. When antigen D is missing, the blood type is classified as negative, or Rh negative. A transfusion of Rh positive blood may cause kidney damage, even death, to an Rh negative person, because anti-D antibodies are produced in the plasma.

Continued from p. 990

Even in recent times, emotional attitudes about blood had the power to override scientific knowledge. During World War II, at the request of the military, the Red Cross provided blood to white and black servicemen that had been donated only by persons of their own race. The organization's central committee said in 1947 that "on the basis of recorded scientific and medical opinion, there is no difference in the blood of humans, based upon race or color." Nevertheless, said the Red Cross, "chapters will collect and hold blood in such manner as to give the physician and the patient the right of selection at the time of the administration." Three years later, however, a committee of the Red Cross Board of Governors said that "racial designation on donor cards should be withdrawn."

Scientific Advances

The idea of transfusing blood — transferring it from one person to another — took hold after 1628, when the British physician William Harvey published proof of his discovery that blood circulated throughout the body. A number of scientists in the 17th century experimented with animal and human transfusion. The first authenticated transfusion was performed by a British physician, Richard Lower, between dogs in 1665. That prompted Samuel Pepys to note in his celebrated *Diary,* "This technique may be of mighty use to man's health for the amending of bad blood by borrowing from a better body."

The next year, Jean Baptiste Denis, physician to King Louis XIV of France, attempted to transfuse the blood of a lamb into a 15-year-old boy. The youth died, and Denis was charged with murder. Although he was acquitted, France — followed by Italy and England — prohibited further transfusions. Pope Innocent XI forbade them in 1678.

Interest in blood transfusion revived in 1818, when James Blundell of London invented a direct transfusion device that he used successfully to control hemorrhaging in women after childbirth. The great breakthrough came in 1900 with the discovery by Karl Landsteiner, an Austrian physiologist, * that there are different types of blood and that if the donor's and the recipient's blood don't match, the red cells will clump and disintegrate. (*See story, p. 992.*) This solved the mystery of why some transfusions had been successful while others resulted in death.

Another great advance came in 1914 with the development of anti-coagulants to prevent clotting, and a few years later with the introduction of a syringe-valve device that made it possible to regulate the flow of blood during a transfusion.

As new knowledge in the biosciences accumulated, the complexity of the blood system became apparent. The great diversity of blood types and the variable combinations of blood components confounded old assumptions. A major milestone was the discovery in 1940 of antigens in red blood cells, known as the Rh factor. Equally important was the knowledge gained of the way the body's immunization mechanism functions through the production of antibodies in the bloodstream.

Improvements in Safety

All these advances had clinical applications. Among other things, they led to refinements of blood-handling techniques, improvements in separating blood components and the production of derivative products. (*See diagram, p. 996.*) While the new knowledge disclosed some previously unrealized hazards of blood transfusion, such as contaminated tubing, they also spurred the development of measures that increased transfusion safety.

As respect for the hazards grew, physicians became more cautious about recommending blood transfusions. "The hazards of the administration of blood are so great that only when there is an urgent need is blood prescribed," the College of American Pathologists said in 1964. [12]

Sounding a similar note, the American Medical Association six years later said a physician "must . . . recognize that the transfusion of blood carries with it a risk of hepatitis and other disease entities in addition to the danger of incompatibility that may result in disaster for a particular patient. As with any drug with known side effects, the physician must weigh the potential danger against the expected benefit before ordering a blood transfusion. A blood transfusion should never be ordered or given unless it is worth the risk." [13]

Rise of Blood Banking

In the early days of modern blood transfusions, the giving of blood was usually an impromptu affair. When a patient needed blood, friends or relatives were called. The transfusion was direct, with the blood flowing from the vein of one person into the vein of the other. The idea of a blood bank did not become feasible until a method of storing blood was developed following the introduction in 1914 of sodium citrate as an anti-coagulant. It permitted the storage of refrigerated blood for five to seven days. During World War II, an improved mixture of acid-citrate and dextrose extended storage time to three weeks.

The first blood "depots" were set up by the British army at casualty stations during World War I. During the 1920s in the United States, a number of "walk-in donor banks" were opened. The first nonprofit hospital blood bank was established in 1937 at Cook County Hospital in Chicago, and the first communitywide blood bank came along four years later — the still functioning Irwin Memorial Blood Bank of the San Francisco Medical Society.

The American Red Cross entered blood banking in the year before Pearl Harbor at the request of the U.S. Army and Navy, which wanted blood to be processed into dried plasma for military needs. * During the war, the Red Cross procured 13 million units of dried plasma and serum albumin (derived from plasma) for overseas use, and provided more than 300,000 pints of whole blood or plasma to military hospitals in the United States. The Red Cross program for the armed forces was terminated after World War II but reactivated after the outbreak of the Korean War.

Meeting Civilian Demand

Meanwhile, demand had swelled for a steady blood supply in civilian medicine. A number of hospitals established their own blood banks during World War II and in the early postwar years. Others cooperated with founders of community or regional blood banks to serve hospitals in their areas. The Red Cross, with the blessings of organized medicine, launched a program in 1947 to establish regional blood centers throughout the United States. **

Also in 1947, a group of hospital and community banks, fearing a Red Cross "invasion" of their territories, formed the American Association of Blood Banks (AABB) to serve as a trade association for its members. Since then, the two organizations have developed extensive programs of donor recruitment, professional education and research support. Today the Red Cross, the AABB and the Council of Community Blood Centers (CCBC),

* Landsteiner had become a U.S. citizen by 1930, when he won the Nobel Prize for physiology or medicine for his discovery.

* The Red Cross was called on because it had several thousand local chapters for recruitment of donors and because it had gained some experience in donor recruitment in a special program in Augusta, Ga., in 1937. And in the months before Pearl Harbor, the Red Cross had conducted "Blood for Britain" drives.

** The first Red Cross regional blood bank opened in Rochester, N.Y., in February 1948.

Screening Test Gives Hemophiliacs a Brighter Future

No population group has benefited more from advances in blood transfusions than hemophiliacs. But no other group has been more vulnerable to infection from donated blood.

Because they are born with impaired blood-clotting capability, hemophiliacs often require transfusions — some as many as 50 a year. U.S. public health officials estimate that half of the nation's estimated 20,000 hemophiliacs contracted HIV, the virus that causes AIDS, from transfusions of contaminated blood products before adequate testing was implemented in the mid-1980s. About 2,000 of the afflicted hemophiliacs have died as a result, according to the National Hemophilia Foundation (NHF).

Hemophilia once was thought to affect only royal families, which spread the disease among themselves through inbreeding. History's most famous hemophiliac doubtless was the son of imperial Russia's last czar, Nicholas II. Scientists now know, however, that hemophilia respects no boundaries of race, class or ethnicity. The disease is carried by females but almost always affects males — about 1 in every 4,000.

Hemophiliacs lack the proteins needed for blood to clot, and without proper treatment they can bleed profusely from cuts or bruises, which often cause internal bleeding. For most sufferers, the deficient blood-clotting agent is a substance called Factor VIII, although some lack Factor IX, which causes a milder form of the ailment.

Until the 1960s, hemophilia was invariably a tragic affliction. The only known therapy was transfusions of fresh blood plasma (the amber-colored, liquid part of blood, which contains anti-coagulants). But supplying enough anti-coagulant required such massive amounts of plasma that the body could not absorb the volume. Most hemophiliacs died before age 30, and few of those who did reach adulthood were able to hold steady jobs because of the danger of venturing into the world of bumps and bruises.

Then, in 1965, researchers discovered a plasma derivative that was rich in clotting factors. The body could accommodate the smaller volumes of the substance that were required to clot hemophiliacs' blood. By the 1970s, scientists had learned how to concentrate the derivative further and to freeze-dry it so that hemophiliacs could easily reconstitute the blood-clotting agents with water and inject them. No longer did persons with hemophilia have to seek hospital treatment for each bleeding episode.

Hemophiliacs had little time to savor their newly won independence, however. HIV was detected in blood-clotting agents in the early 1980s, and hemophilia sufferers became infected in large numbers.

Testifying before a congressional panel in 1990, NHF Executive Director Alan P. Brownstein explained why hemophiliacs were at such extraordinarily high risk of becoming HIV-positive:

The plasma from which blood clotting factors are derived, noted Brownstein, "is collected from many donors and pooled." As a result, a hemophiliac is "potentially exposed to anywhere from 4,000-48,000 donors at any one time." And since severe hemophilia patients "can treat bleeding episodes as many as 30-50 times annually, they can be exposed to hundreds of thousands of donors. The opportunity of infection is immense." [1]

Health and Human Services Secretary Donna E. Shalala last year asked the U.S. Institute of Medicine (IOM) [2] to study blood-supply safety and policies from 1982-86. "Such a review would give us better insight into how medical knowledge and practice contribute overall to public health decisions regarding disease transmission in the earliest stages of an epidemic," Shalala said in a letter to Sen. Bob Graham, D-Fla., who with Sen. Edward M. Kennedy, D-Mass., and Rep. Porter J. Goss, R-Fla., had urged a probe. [3]

The three lawmakers sought the review at the urging of a Florida couple whose three hemophiliac sons contracted HIV from contaminated blood products; one son died. Drug companies have been charged by hemophiliacs and their families with knowingly distributing contaminated products in the early 1980s, before the screening test was developed.

Though many HIV-positive hemophiliacs blame the blood-banking industry and clotting-factor producers for their plight, the IOM report, due at the end of 1995, apparently will point no fingers. In a September statement, the institute said the report "will not seek to determine liability or affix blame for any individual or collective decisions."

Meanwhile, thanks to HIV screening begun in 1985, there have been no cases of HIV infection since 1987 among hemophiliacs who use virally inactivated clotting factor to control their condition (and don't engage in at-risk behavior), says Anne King, an NHF spokeswoman. "The blood supply is safer than it has ever been," she says.

[1] Testimony before House Energy and Commerce Subcommittee on Oversight and Investigations, July 13, 1990.

[2] The IOM is an arm of the National Academy of Sciences.

[3] "Shalala Seeks Probe of Tainted Blood," *The Washington Post*, July 10, 1993.

founded in 1962, together account for approximately 98 percent of the whole blood collected from volunteer donors in the U.S. (In 1989, about 2 percent of the blood supply was imported from Europe.) [14]

The Red Cross now operates 45 regional blood centers. The AABB has about 2,400 institutional members, including the American Red Cross, hospitals and community blood-gathering facilities, plus more than 9,000 individual members working in the field. The CCBC comprises 62 regional and community blood centers. Institutional members of the AABB, like the Red Cross and CCBC blood banks, must be nonprofit enterprises.

The commercial growth of blood banking has been encouraged by the development of plasmapheresis, the process by which red cells are separated from the plasma and returned to the donor — all in less than an hour. This method permits donors to give plasma as often as twice a week, compared with only five times a year for donations of whole blood. Large pharmaceutical firms depend on a plasma supply for the production of blood derivative products, such as gamma globulin for immunization purposes. Plasma donors generally are paid $15 or $20 per donation.

Tensions between the Red Cross and the AABB in the early days of blood banking have eased considerably, and the two organization now cooperate amicably, for the most part. A reciprocity agreement, concluded in May 1961, facilitated the exchange of blood and blood-replacement credits between agencies in the two systems. Files for locating rare-blood donors have been coordinated with each other and with a similar file maintained by the International Society of Blood Transfusion, based in France. This permits rapid worldwide exchange of rare blood as need arises.

In 1971, the Red Cross Board of Governors voted to expand the organization's cooperation with other nonprofit blood-collecting agencies. In addition, chapters not involved in Red Cross regional blood programs were asked to assist other blood-collecting agencies in their areas by helping them recruit volunteer donors and giving other "appropriate volunteer service support."

It was also in the early 1970s that other nonprofit U.S. blood banking organizations followed the lead of the Red Cross — which has never paid donors — and stopped paying for blood. The shift to an all-volunteer blood supply was prompted by concern that individuals who regularly sold their blood were more likely than other donors to be carriers of hepatitis. In 1971, blood banks introduced a screening test for the so-called hepatitis B surface antigen.

The AIDS Plague

Blood collectors and processors were wholly unprepared for AIDS, which first came to notice in the United States in 1981.[15] Initially the condition was informally known as the "gay plague," since the earliest known victims were nearly all homosexual men. * Many were found to be suffering from one or another of two rare diseases: Kaposi's sarcoma, a form of skin cancer usually associated with elderly people, and pneumocystis carinii, a pneumonia caused by infectious protozoa. It was determined that the victims were vulnerable to these maladies because their natural immunological defenses had been drastically weakened.

At first, the search for the cause of AIDS centered on the victims' homosexual life style. They were, typically, sexually promiscuous and had histories of sexually transmitted disease and frequent drug use. A theory thus arose that these activities had progressively weakened the complex system by which the human body wards off disease.

However, circumstantial evidence surfaced in 1982 suggesting that AIDS might actually be spread by a specific substance or organism in the bloodstream, possibly a virus. This hypothesis was based on reported AIDS outbreaks among 32 Haitian immigrants and three hemophiliacs, none believed to be homosexual. Victims of hemophilia, a hereditary defect marked by delayed clotting of the blood, are dependent on clotting factors derived from the blood of numerous donors. (*See story, p. 994.*)

Despite the warning signs, the FDA and nonprofit blood banks initially did little to tighten screening of donors or donated blood. The FDA finally issued screening recommendations to all blood collectors in March 1983, though Hall says the Red Cross had started questioning donors about at-risk behavior, such as travel to Haiti, three months before the FDA issued its recommendations.

Those recommendations, wrote Herbert Burkholz in *The FDA Follies,* "were of the simplest sort [and] most blood bankers simply ignored them." Burkholz added that the agency's proposals "did not include a physical examination, they did not include direct questioning of donors and they did not include the signing of an affidavit."[16]

Meanwhile, public concern about the safety of blood transfusions was growing. Worry nearly reached the panic level after TV journalist Geraldo Rivera reported on the ABC-TV program "20/20" in May 1983 that AIDS had contaminated the nation's blood supply and that "the safest thing to do is store up your own blood."[17] Many people postponed elective surgery. Others asked friends and family to make donations for their use. In some cities, blood donations declined because people mistakenly believed they could get AIDS from donating.

In the same month that Rivera delivered his report, the U.S. Public Health Service recommended that homosexuals and intravenous drug users — the two groups most at risk of contracting AIDS — refrain from giving blood. Blood centers around the country took immediate steps to screen out high-risk donors while maintaining strict confidentiality.

Research Breakthrough

The AIDS breakthrough that medical researchers had been hoping for finally came in April 1984. In announcements made only two days apart, French and U.S. officials said researchers at the Pasteur Institute in

* AIDS was first named gay-related immunodeficiency disease (GRID) and then acquired severe immunodeficiency disease (ASID).

The Many Uses of Blood

The two major components of whole blood, plasma and cellular elements, can be broken down into derivative products that are used in treating a wide range of medical conditions.

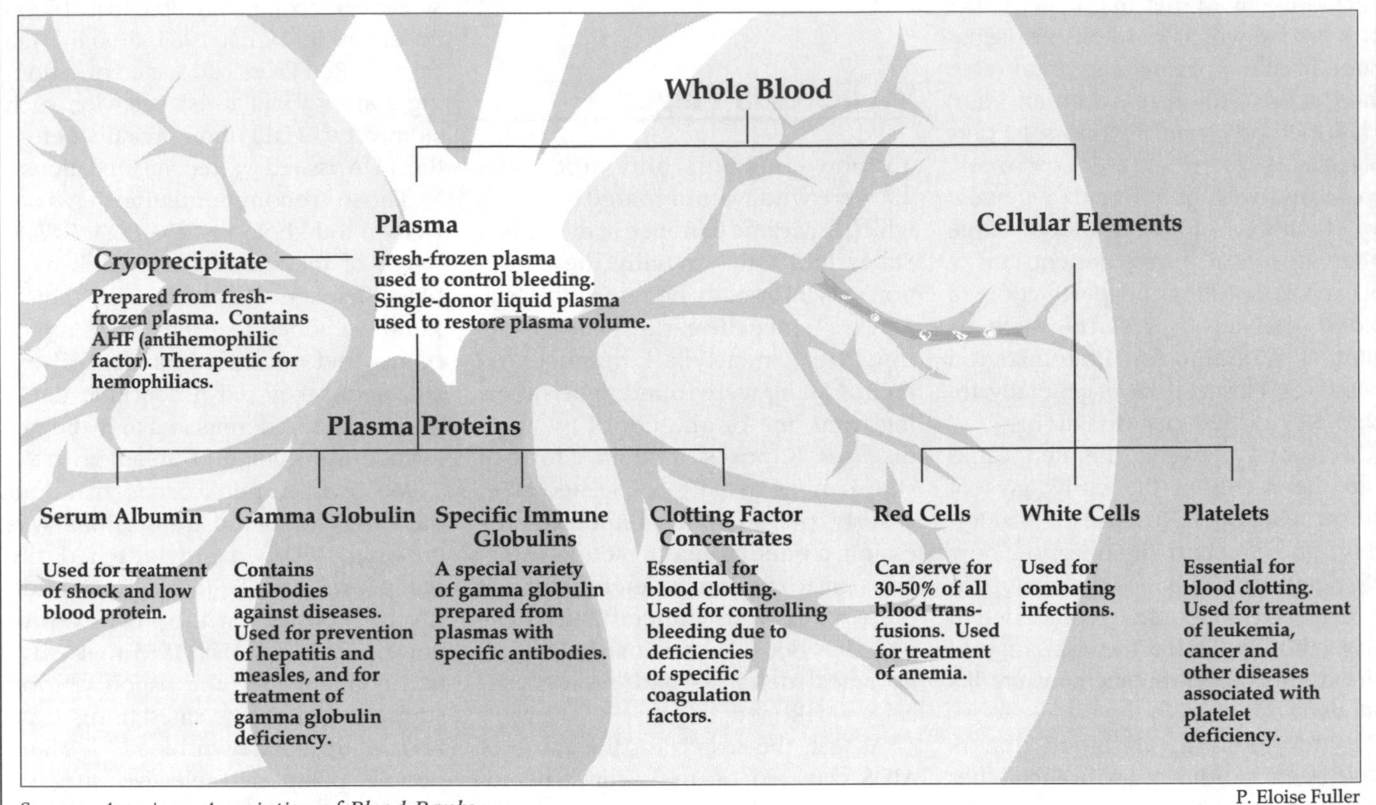
Whole Blood
Plasma
Fresh-frozen plasma used to control bleeding. Single-donor liquid plasma used to restore plasma volume.
Cryoprecipitate
Prepared from fresh-frozen plasma. Contains AHF (antihemophilic factor). Therapeutic for hemophiliacs.
Cellular Elements
Plasma Proteins
Serum Albumin
Used for treatment of shock and low blood protein.
Gamma Globulin
Contains antibodies against diseases. Used for prevention of hepatitis and measles, and for treatment of gamma globulin deficiency.
Specific Immune Globulins
A special variety of gamma globulin prepared from plasmas with specific antibodies.
Clotting Factor Concentrates
Essential for blood clotting. Used for controlling bleeding due to deficiencies of specific coagulation factors.
Red Cells
Can serve for 30-50% of all blood transfusions. Used for treatment of anemia.
White Cells
Used for combating infections.
Platelets
Essential for blood clotting. Used for treatment of leukemia, cancer and other diseases associated with platelet deficiency.

Source: American Association of Blood Banks

P. Eloise Fuller

Paris and the U.S. National Cancer Institute, working independently of each other, had isolated a virus believed to cause AIDS.

Identifying the HIV virus enabled scientists to devise a test for detecting its presence in donated blood. Health and Human Services Secretary Margaret M. Heckler said that the test, introduced in March 1985, "assures a higher level of safety for our nation's blood supply." [18]

The HIV test does not diagnose the disease nor does it indicate whether a person is carrying the virus. Rather, it registers the presence of an antibody produced by the immune system in response to the virus. The Red Cross and other blood-collection agencies quickly adopted the test and today routinely destroy any blood that registers positive.

In addition to the HIV test, researchers have since developed screening tests for hepatitis C, the form of hepatitis most frequently transmitted through blood; HTLV-1, a rare leukemia virus found mainly outside the United States; and HIV-2, a form of the AIDS virus that is rare in this country. A total of seven screening tests are now routinely used, including a test for syphilis.

Industry Criticized

Even critics of the blood industry acknowledge that the proliferation of tests has made the nation's blood supply significantly safer than it was only a decade ago. All the same, many critics still take the industry and the FDA to task for what they perceive as inaction and foot-dragging during the early years of the AIDS epidemic.

One such critic is Marcus A. Conant, a professor at the University of California Medical Center in San Francisco and co-chairman of the California AIDS Leadership Committee. Testifying in 1990 before a U.S. House subcommittee, Conant declared: "While blood bankers do much good, it is also irrefutable that if donors do not come to blood centers, there will be no product to sell to hospitals and patients. Blood bankers were terrified [in the early 1980s] that if they questioned donors about high-risk behaviors, donors would cease to present themselves voluntarily to blood centers" and thus "would threaten the financial viability of the blood banks." [19]

Blood banking officials clearly were irked by Conant and other unfriendly witnesses who testified at the same hearing. Gerald Sandler, then head of Red Cross Blood Services, complained that the witnesses "were all highly critical, and not one of them made any mention of the success of the [Red Cross] to reduce the risk of transfusion AIDS." [20]

Blood bankers got another public spanking last year, when the House panel held another hearing on blood-supply safety. FDA Commissioner David A. Kessler testified that his agency's "stepped-up inspection program over the last several years has revealed breaches" in the blood safety systems "at far too many blood banks." The "most significant" breaches, he said, occurred "in the areas of inadequate training of the staff conducting the screening tests, poor record-keeping so that suspect units of blood cannot be readily tracked down if a problem is discovered and problems in the required donor-deferral registry intended to keep high-risk donors out of the system."

The FDA "will continue to relate to this industry as colleagues and consultants," said Kessler, "but when enforcement is warranted, we will not walk away from our responsibilities to the public." [21]

Scandal in France

The U.S. problems, however, paled in comparison with those in France. Flagrant disregard for the public welfare helped set in motion a French blood-contamination scandal in the mid-1980s that has yet to run its course. According to a 1991 report by Michel Lucas, France's inspector general of health affairs, government health officials knowingly authorized transfusions of blood containing HIV during a five-month period in 1985.

At that time, procedures to rid blood supplies of the virus were available. The problem was that the technique had been developed by Baxter Travenol, an American company. Rather than embrace the Baxter model, French officials chose to continue using the country's tainted blood stock until a French-developed purification method was ready for introduction later in 1985.

The Lucas report further charged that French health officials delayed the use of a test for HIV that had been developed by Abbott Laboratories, another U.S. firm. But even without such assurances, wrote Jane Kramer, European correspondent for *The New Yorker,* the great majority of French people were supremely confident that their nation's blood supply was pure. In 1985, the French viewed AIDS as "the American disease," she observed, "and the name evoked everything that France supposedly was not — permissive, promiscuous, perverted, a country of meat-rack morals that had nothing to do with the way Frenchmen led their proper, womanizing lives." [22]

Four health officials implicated in the scandal were tried in 1992, and three were found guilty. Michel Garretta, former director of the National Blood Transfusion Center, received four years in prison and a 500,000 franc ($100,000) fine. He was convicted on fraud and negligence charges involving "deception over the basic quality of a product." Jean-Pierre Allain, the former chief of transfusion research at the center, received a four-year sentence, with two years suspended.

Moreover, Allain, Garretta and the center were ordered to pay a total of 9.2 million francs to persons who received the tainted blood. The victims were eligible for additional compensation under a government program. Jacques Roux, a public health director, was found guilty of negligence for failing to aid a person in danger, and received a suspended four-year sentence.

All three defendants insisted they were being made scapegoats for decisions made by higher-ranking officials, including then Premier Laurent Fabius, a Socialist, and members of his Cabinet who set health policy. But efforts to bring the former officials to trial were blocked at the time by the Socialist-controlled French National Assembly.

There is no official tally of the number of victims of the French scandal, but Kramer wrote last fall that "Four or five thousand transfusion patients are known to be contaminated now." [23] Most were hemophiliacs. ■

CURRENT SITUATION

Other Nations' Troubles

It now seems that Fabius and some of his former colleagues may stand trial after all. Popular indignation over the blood scandal contributed to the Socialists' crushing defeat in the March 1993 parliamentary elections, which left the party with only 70 seats in the 577-member assembly. Moreover, a Court of Justice of the Republic was created last year expressly to prosecute former government officials for crimes allegedly committed while in office.

In recent weeks, the court has formally accused Fabius and two members of his Cabinet with complicity in poisoning — a charge carrying a maximum 30-year prison sentence. The two others are former Social Affairs Minister Georgina Dufoix and former Health Minister Edmond Hervé. * Four advisers to the ex-min-

* Documents published in February by the Paris newspaper *Libération* indicate that Fabius, Dufoix and Hervé all attended meetings at which the delay in approving the Abbott HIV screening test was discussed.

isters also are under investigation by the court.

As the French blood scandal continues to unfold, other countries are grappling with similar problems. Germany, for example, was shaken last fall when Health Minister Horst Seehofer announced that nearly 400 hospital patients had received transfusions of HIV-tainted blood. Ute Braun, head of the German Hemophilia Society, said the actual number of infected patients was between 1,500 and 2,000, of whom almost 400 had died. [24]

Two weeks after Seehofer's disclosure, a small company in Koblenz called UB-Plasma was shut down for conducting inadequate HIV tests on plasma it had sold to hospitals and blood-product manufacturers. Soon afterward, several European countries halted the sale of blood products purchased from UB-Plasma. Public anxiety mounted when a second German firm, Haemoplas of Osterode, was closed in November because of flaws in its screening procedures. Around that time, the German Red Cross reported that blood donations had dropped 5-10 percent below normal levels.

Subsequent investigation showed that both UB-Plasma and Haemoplas collected plasma from paid donors and cut costs by failing to test individual donations for HIV. "UB-Plasma apparently tested pooled samples from several donations — and then judged results by eye, rather than using a photometer to detect the yellow coloration that indicates a positive result," wrote reporter Peter Aldhous. "Haemoplas is alleged to have tested only about every fifth donation from each individual, and so could not have known immediately if one of its donors became HIV-positive." [25]

Still, the public prosecutor's office in Koblenz suggested that fallout from the AIDS scare may be lighter than initially feared. According to a report from the prosecutor, only two of some 5,000 UB-Plasma donors were HIV-positive. The finding was based on new tests conducted on samples from more than 25,000 donations collected by the company over the previous two years. Although Haemoplas had not kept a complete set of samples of its plasma donations, German public health experts said its donors probably were about as infection-free as UB-Plasma's.

Technician uses a bar-code reader to log in blood samples to be tested.

American Red Cross

Last spring, Switzerland became the third European country to experience a blood-supply scandal. Alfred Hässig, the former director of the Swiss Red Cross' central laboratory, was charged in May with inflicting grievous bodily harm by allowing the use of possibly contaminated blood. [26] According to Swiss health officials, 68 hemophiliacs became HIV-positive from tainted blood products in the mid-1980s, and between 100 and 200 other persons were infected by hospital blood transfusions during the same period.

Complacency apparently helped set the stage for Switzerland's blood crisis. In the early 1980s, many Swiss assumed AIDS was a serious problem only in the United States, Haiti and Africa. Affluent, well-educated Switzerland, proud of its traditions of prudence and cleanliness, thought itself immune from an epidemic of such a "disreputable" disease. Consequently, Swiss public health officials — like their counterparts in France — were slow to respond to mounting evidence that AIDS can be spread by blood transfusion as well as by sexual contact and intravenous drug use.

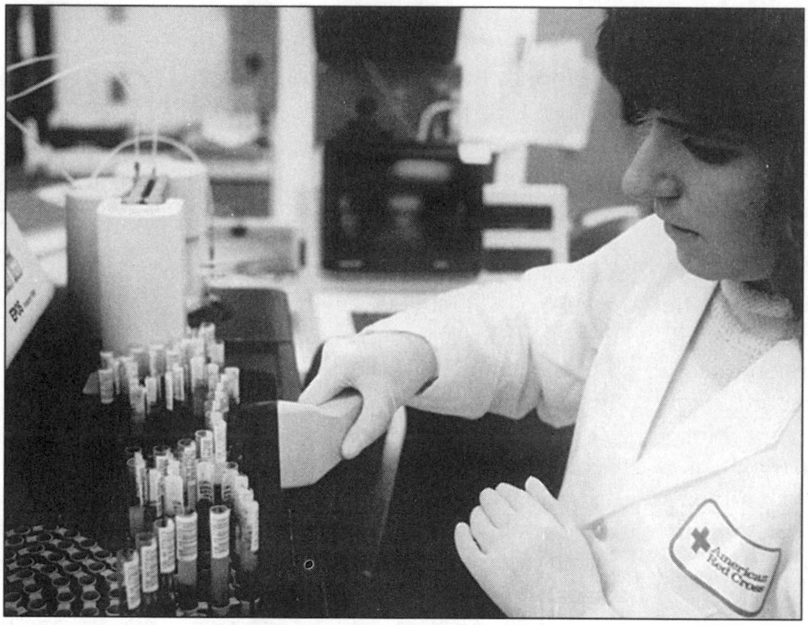

Double Trouble for Canada

Over the past year, Canada also has been rocked by disclosures that its blood supply was contaminated by HIV in the early 1980s. Before 1985, when the Canadian Red Cross Society began heat-treating blood to rid it of HIV, approximately 1,050 persons were infected with the virus through blood transfusions. An estimated three-fourths of the victims were hemophiliacs.

To get to the bottom of the tragedy, the federal government in October 1993 appointed Judge Horace Krever of the Ontario Court of Appeal to conduct an investigation, expected to last until the end of next year. Krever was told to find out how the contamination occurred, recommend ways of preventing a recurrence and consider whether the Canadian blood collection and distribution network should be restructured to accommodate new technologies.

Hearings to date have done nothing to restore faith in the Canadian system. According to D'Arcy Jenish of *MacLean's*, the Canadian newsweekly, witnesses have painted "a damning portrait of the Canadian Red Cross as a rigidly bureaucratic organization, and of government officials who misread warnings that the blood supply had been infected by the virus." [27]

Canadians' confidence in their blood system took yet another hit in early September, when the U.S. FDA ordered the Canadian Red Cross to stop sending some blood products to a plant in North Carolina that fractionates blood, or breaks it down into derivative products. (Canada does not yet have a fractionation plant.) The FDA said it issued the ban because a Toronto blood bank had violated American safety regulations.

The Canadian blood product targeted by the FDA was "source plasma," which is extracted directly from the donor's body rather than from donations of whole blood. An FDA inspector had found that the Toronto center's physical and oral examinations of prospective plasma donors were less rigorous than those required in U.S. facilities. * In addition, the inspector faulted the center's record keeping and product labeling.

Red Cross Faulted

The FDA has been no less demanding of U.S. blood-collection centers in recent years, especially those affiliated with the American Red Cross. In September 1988, the Red Cross signed an accord with the agency in which it agreed to institute standard operating procedures (SOPs) at its blood banks across the country. It also agreed to consolidate its computer systems and start an employee training program to enhance blood-supply safety.

Despite the agreement, FDA criticism of Red Cross operations continued. FDA field inspector Mary Carden told a congressional oversight panel in 1991 that inspections of Red Cross facilities "continue to reveal serious problems at the regional level." In some instances, she said, there is "a complete lack of SOPs in some very critical areas." In other cases, employees "are not trained properly, and they're not following these SOPs." As for the computer system, Carden said "most target dates . . . have come and gone with no corrections made." [28]

The month after Carden testified, the Red Cross announced it was launching a long-range, $148 million program to transform its blood collection, testing, processing and distribution systems into "a state-of-the-art operation." [29]

But the FDA still felt that the Red Cross wasn't living up to the 1988 agreement. Consequently, the agency filed a lawsuit that led to a May 7, 1993, consent decree in which the organization agreed to take further action to ensure that the nation's blood supply is safe from contamination by HIV and other blood-borne diseases.

In announcing the new accord, both parties sought to reassure the public. "For any patient requiring a blood transfusion, the risk of not receiving that transfusion outweighs the risk of receiving blood," said FDA Commissioner Kessler. "We are committed to maintaining the safety of the blood supply." Red Cross President Elizabeth H. Dole declared: "As a humanitarian organization, our only goal is to ensure an adequate supply of the safest possible blood to the American people. As long as we provide this service, we will not only fulfill the requirements of the FDA, we will surpass them." [30]

As part of the transformation program it launched in 1991, the Red Cross announced in February that it would open a Blood Services Training College in the Washington, D.C., area. The facility, to be located in Fairfax, Va., is to be named for U.S. blood-banking pioneer Charles Drew (*see p. 987*). It will "teach the latest in [blood-handling] techniques and instill . . . the most exacting standards of disci-

* According to the FDA, the Canadian blood clinics did not weigh donors nor take their temperature and blood pressure. The Toronto clinic, moreover, did not inspect plasma donors' arms for needle marks or other signs of intravenous drug use, nor did clinic staffers ask donors whether their life style put them at high risk of HIV infection.

For More Information

AMERICAN ASSOCIATION OF BLOOD BANKS, 8101 Glenbrook Rd., Bethesda, Md. 20814-2749; (301) 907-6977. The AABB is a nonprofit association representing approximately 2,400 independent hospital and community blood banks and transfusion services, and some 9,000 industry personnel.

FOOD AND DRUG ADMINISTRATION, 5600 Fishers Lane, Rockville, Md. 20857; (301) 443-1544. The FDA develops and administers programs to assure the safety and effectiveness of all drug products intended for human use, including blood.

AMERICAN RED CROSS, 17th and D Streets, N.W., Washington, D.C. 20006; (202) 737-8300. The ARC operates 45 regional blood centers that collect, process and distribute blood and blood components.

AMERICAN BLOOD RESOURCES ASSOCIATION, P.O. Box 669, Annapolis, Md. 21404-0669; (410) 263-8296. ABRA represents for-profit companies that collect, market or use blood and plasma to make therapeutic and diagnostic products.

pline," Dole promised.[31]

Other elements of the transformation also are on track, the Red Cross said in the progress report it issued earlier this year. For instance, five of nine proposed national testing laboratories are now open, each handling blood from more than one region. The other labs are due to be completed in December. A single nationwide computer system linking the organization's 45 blood regions also is being installed, and is slated to be fully operational by late 1996.

However, the Red Cross and other blood-banking organizations still face millions of dollars in lawsuits involving persons infected with HIV from transfused blood received before the donor screening test was in place. In one such case, involving a $10 million suit filed by a Montana rancher, the Red Cross in March 1993 settled the case during the trial.

Meanwhile, the FDA continues pressing to improve blood safety. In July 1993, the agency issued draft regulations aimed at helping blood centers throughout the country to identify blood-safety problems in advance. A key guideline calls for the use of uniform "look back" procedures if a repeat donor tests positive for HIV. When that happens, the center is to perform an additional test on the donor's blood. If the second result also is positive, any blood given previously by that donor must be destroyed. In addition, the blood bank must try to contact the physicians of patients who received blood from the donor in the past. The FDA look-back procedure also requires blood banks to keep donor records in such a way that donations can be easily identified and traced. ■

Outlook

Improving Safety

Experts may differ on the current safety of the nation's blood supply, but few would deny there's room for improvement. One new technique being explored involves the use of stem cells, which are found in minute quantities in bone marrow and the bloodstream.

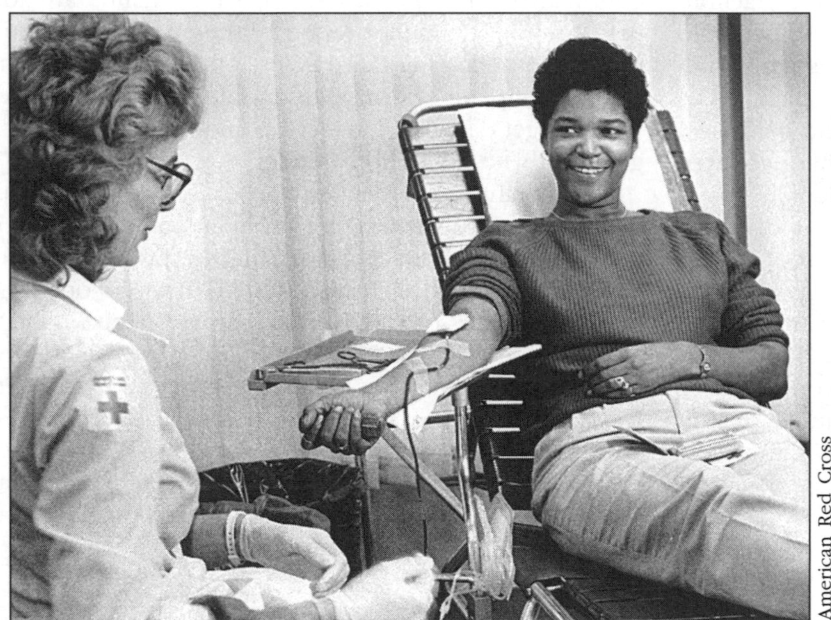

American Red Cross

Blood donors don't risk getting AIDS or other diseases, blood experts say.

Stem cells are blood cells at the earliest stage of development. They are important because as they mature they differentiate into the more numerous specialized cells of the blood and immune systems. These include the blood system's red cells and platelets and the immune system's T cells and B cells, which guard against disease. Stem cells also replicate themselves, so that a fresh supply is always present in the body.

Hematologists have known of the existence of stem cells for years. But because the body contains so few of them, only recently have ways been found to isolate and extract enough of them to be useful. In bone marrow, stem cells account for only one of every 10,000 to 100,000 cells. They are rarer still in the bloodstream, averaging about one of every million cells.

In the past, bone-marrow transplants represented the only way of obtaining enough stem cells to treat patients whose immune systems and blood-forming ability had been devastated by leukemia, cancer, chemotherapy or other causes. And extracting marrow from a donor's bones is an involved process that usually requires general anesthesia and can be hazardous to the donor.

Now, though, stem cells can be extracted from the bloodstream, though three donations on consecutive days generally are needed to obtain a sufficiently large number. The key to harvesting a usable supply is centrifugation. By setting a centrifuge at the proper speed, all the components of blood can be retrieved separately.

At the Red Cross regional blood center in Baltimore, all stem-cell donations currently are autologous. That is, they are intended for reinfusion into the donor at some future time, typically within a few weeks. (*See story, p. 988.*)

"The prospect of storing one's own stem cells for ready use at any moment opens up possibilities for dis-

Continued on p. 1002

At Issue:

Is the blood supply in the United States safe?

yes

AMERICAN RED CROSS

FROM *"THE SAFETY OF THE BLOOD SUPPLY,"* OCTOBER 1994

The blood supply is extremely safe today — safer, indeed, than it has ever been. And we are constantly working to improve that level of safety.

The estimated risk of HIV infection as a result of a blood transfusion immediately before testing was implemented in March 1985 was about 1 in 2,500. . . . The current risk is estimated to be 1 in 225,000, a 99 percent decline. . . .

New tests are being developed and implemented all the time. The introduction of hepatitis C testing in May 1990 reduced the rate of infection with hepatitis C by more than 90 percent . . . and it is estimated that the introduction of an improved test in March 1992 has reduced that risk by another 40 percent. . . .

Donors are carefully recruited and screened for risk factors related to HIV and other serious diseases. The Red Cross makes every effort to recruit a healthy donor population. Every Red Cross donor is given a minimum of four separate opportunities each time he or she gives blood to understand his behavioral risks and to self-defer. . . .

In addition to maintaining local records which identify all unsuitable donors, the Red Cross also maintains a national computerized database of over 250,000 donors (since the early 1970s) who are deferred from donating blood due to a history of risk-associated behavior, signs or symptoms which could be associated with various transmissible diseases or a positive result for any of the viruses tested.

Every donation received by the Red Cross is cross-checked against these Red Cross deferred donor lists to determine whether the blood should be destroyed based on past test results. A 1989 study concludes that donor recruitment practices plus careful education, donor screening and the use of donor referral registries are eliminating 49 of every 50 donors likely to be HIV positive prior to donation. . . .

The risk of contracting HIV from a blood transfusion today is extremely low. The latest [Centers for Disease Control and Prevention]-sponsored studies suggest that the overall risk of HIV infection from a blood transfusion due to the donor being in the infectious "window period" (the time between infection and the formation of detectable antibodies) is approximately 1 in 225,000 per unit. This means that a blood recipient is about 15 times less likely to receive a unit of HIV positive blood than an individual undergoing surgery is likely to have a fatal reaction to anesthesia.

no

MICHAEL CHAPMAN
Former associate editor, Consumers' Research

FROM *"HOW SAFE IS THE BLOOD SUPPLY?" CONSUMERS' RESEARCH*, APRIL 1994.

The Red Cross' Blood Service, which collects half of the nation's blood supply (about 6 million units) each year, has encountered many problems in the screening of donors and the collection, testing, labeling and distribution of its product. In [congressional] hearings in 1990 and 1991, it was found that . . . "various Red Cross collection centers [had] released infected blood, mixed up records, violated AIDS testing procedures, and failed to deter infected or undesirable donors." Also, the Red Cross violated a 1988 agreement with the Food and Drug Administration (FDA) to implement standard operating procedures for its blood centers. . . . In May 1993, the FDA took the Red Cross to court, where it was decided that the Red Cross had to improve its blood service operations by specific deadlines, or answer to a federal judge. . . .

Since 1988, the Red Cross' Blood Service has had over 3,000 blood safety violations, according to the FDA. At a center in Pennsylvania, blood contaminated with hepatitis B was released even after it was found to be contaminated, and blood components made from the blood of two HIV-positive donors were released from another center. . . .

But the Red Cross is not alone when it comes to violating FDA blood safety regulations. Both the Life Source blood bank in the Chicago area and the Irwin Memorial Blood Center in San Francisco were cited by the FDA for testing blood improperly. Other blood banks have had similar problems.

The quality of the blood supply is lower than possible primarily because blood banks rely on a large pool of random donors. . . . In 1973, the U.S. government adopted the National Blood Policy, which was based on the hypothesis that "blood bought by for-profit firms necessarily transmitted more disease than blood donated to nonprofit blood banks." This policy changed the incentive for people to donate blood, but it did not address the real problem: a large pool of random, walk-in donors. . . .

Although the blood supply has improved in quality, risks still exist — not only HIV and blood safety violations but also different strains of hepatitis and other pathogens. . . . Blood banks today will tell you that the blood supply is safer than ever, but except for improved testing and donor screening, the blood banks have not changed essentially. As long as public health policy is vulnerable to political pressure, consumers are at risk — which in these matters can prove fatal.

Continued from p. 1000

ease treatments that go well beyond reconstitution of the blood-producing system," David W. Golde wrote in *Scientific American*. "As researchers learn to grow certain stem cells in the laboratory, they should also be able to discover ways to remove a patient's stem cells, manipulate them for some therapeutic effect and then reintroduce them. For example, one might be able to alter stem cells so that when transplanted back, they differentiate into immune cells able to carry out specific new functions." [32]

For Red Cross lab director Smith, the key to blood safety is perfecting a way to inactivate viruses. Heat treatment kills off certain viruses, and various chemicals and detergents are effective against others. But she says the ultimate weapon remains out of reach — "something that'll wipe out all the viruses and bacteria, but not harm red cells, platelets or plasma. And that's asking a lot."

Such a process might have prevented Dana Kuhn, a hemophiliac, from getting HIV from a transfusion in 1983. Kuhn, a clinical counselor at Medical College of Virginia Hospitals in Richmond, says the nation's blood supply will never be totally safe until 100 percent viral inactivation is a reality. "It's something we have to have," he says. "No ifs, ands or buts about it."

Unfortunately, Smith says, viral inactivation "isn't at a stage where it would ever replace testing. Testing is still the best way to get the safest blood."

Reilly of the American Blood Resources Association says the blood supply is "going to continually become safer, because as technology advances, the tests we employ for known diseases will improve. There are other diseases out there that we either don't know anything about, or don't have a test for, that science may provide answers to eventually.

"Blood is a biological product, so it's not an absolute," adds Reilly. "You can't say it's 100 percent safe, guaranteed forever. But the blood industry is always looking for opportunities to improve its products. And safety is clearly an aspect of that." ■

Notes

1 Quoted in *The New York Times*, Feb. 1, 1994, p. C3.

2 In 1941, Drew became director of an American Red Cross program for the U.S. armed forces, developing techniques for using dried instead of liquid plasma. He resigned after only three months, following a military ruling that Caucasian and non-Caucasian blood would have to be stored separately.

3 Quoted in *The Washington Post*, April 10, 1994, p. B5.

4 Of the 1.2 million people on the program's donor registry, 67,555 (6 percent) are African-American. Blacks comprise about 11 percent of the U.S. population.

5 Because EPO increases the blood's oxygen-carrying capacity and thus improves performance, it has been abused by some athletes in endurance events, even though it poses a health risk because it thickens the blood. For background, see "Athletes and Drugs," *The CQ Researcher*, July 26, 1991, pp. 513-536.

6 "AIDS Scare Creates Interest in Blood Substitutes," Reuter dispatch, Dec. 8, 1993.

7 American Red Cross Biomedical Services, "Providing America's All-Volunteer Blood Supply" (undated fact sheet).

8 Testimony before House Energy and Commerce Subcommittee on Oversight and Investigations, July 13, 1990.

9 *Ibid.*

10 Quoted in *The Wall Street Journal*, Oct. 10, 1993, p. B4.

11 Richard M. Titmuss, *The Gift Relationship: From Human Blood to Social Policy* (1970), pp. 15, 16.

12 Statement submitted to Senate Judiciary Antitrust and Monopoly Subcommittee hearings on blood banking, Aug. 20, 1964.

13 American Medical Association, *General Principles of Blood Transfusion*, June 1970, p. 1. Italics were the AMA's.

14 Jeffrey McCullough, "The Nation's Changing Blood Supply System," *Journal of the American Medical Association*, May 5, 1993, p. 2239.

15 For background, see "Good News and Bad About AIDS," *Editorial Research Reports*, Oct. 6, 1989, pp. 553-568, and "Women and AIDS," *The CQ Researcher*, Dec. 25, 1992, pp. 1121-1144.

16 Herbert Burkholz, *The FDA Follies* (1994), p. 147.

17 Quoted by David Black in "The Plague Years," *Rolling Stone*, April 25, 1985, p. 57.

18 "Results of AIDS Tests," *The New York Times*, March 26, 1985, p. C2.

19 Testimony before House Energy and Commerce Subcommittee on Oversight and Investigations, July 13, 1990.

20 Quoted by Burkholz, *op. cit.*, p. 156.

21 Testimony before House Energy and Commerce Subcommittee on Oversight and Investigations, July 28, 1993.

22 Jane Kramer, "Bad Blood," *The New Yorker*, Oct. 11, 1993, p. 74.

23 *Ibid.*, p. 90.

24 Quoted in *The New York Times*, Oct. 10, 1993, p. 8.

25 Peter Aldhous, "German HIV-Blood Scandal Reveals Flaws in the System," *Science*, Nov. 19, 1993, p. 1205.

26 The Red Cross of Switzerland is a separate organization from the International Committee of the Red Cross, which is also based in the country. The Swiss Red Cross collects all the country's blood donations and manufactures about 80 percent of its blood products.

27 D'Arcy Jenish, "Bad Blood?" *MacLean's*, Sept. 19, 1994, p. 28.

28 Testimony before House Energy and Commerce Subcommittee on Oversight and Investigations, April 18, 1991.

29 American Red Cross, "Blood Services Transformation — Progress Report, 1994," p. 1.

30 "Red Cross Agrees to Tighten Its Blood Safety Measures," *Los Angeles Times* (Washington Edition), May 8, 1993.

31 Red Cross news release, Feb. 24, 1994.

32 David W. Golde, "The Stem Cell," *Scientific American*, December 1991, pp. 86-93.

Bibliography

Selected Sources Used

Books

Burkholz, Herbert, *The FDA Follies,* Basic Books, 1994.
Burkholz's chapter on the hesitant response of the Food and Drug Administration (FDA) to the AIDS crisis in the early 1980s forms just part of the author's wide-ranging critique of the agency's performance. Burkholz concludes on a hopeful note, however, citing the reforms instituted by current FDA Commissioner David A. Kessler.

Drake, Alvin W., Stan N. Finkelstein and Harvey M. Sapolsky, *The American Blood Supply,* The MIT Press, 1982.
The authors warn of a growing concentration of the U.S. blood industry among very few suppliers. "Once blood banking is totally cartelized," they write, "the public interest will require governmental monitoring of the performance of the industry, just as in every other case of a private monopoly of a vital public service."

Goldstein, Jack, ed., *Biotechnology of Blood,* Butterworth-Heinemann, 1991.
Goldstein groups the contributions (by 29 authors) to this reader-friendly book under four general headings: oxygen-delivery systems, plasma fractions, in vivo and in vitro regulation of blood cell production and blood-borne viral diseases.

Harmening, Denise, et al., eds., *Modern Blood Banking and Transfusion Practices,* F.A. Davis, 1989.
Written primarily for medical technologists and blood bank officials, this book nonetheless remains accessible to non-specialists. Among the topics covered are transfusion safety and federal regulatory requirements, transfusion-transmitted viruses, paternity testing and future trends in blood banking.

Madhok, R., et al., eds., *Blood, Blood Products and HIV,* Chapman & Hall Medical, 1994.
The contributors to this book, most of whom are associated with the federal Centers for Disease Control and Prevention in Atlanta or the University of Aberdeen, Scotland, examine the effects of HIV on the immune system, donor screening for HIV infection and procedures for preventing virus transmission through blood products, among other issues.

Titmuss, Richard M., *The Gift Relationship: From Human Blood to Social Policy,* Pantheon Books, 1971.
Though his perspective is now outdated, Titmuss offers observations on the philosophical differences in the American and British approaches to the giving of blood that remain provocative.

Articles

Jenish, D'Arcy, "Bad Blood?" *MacLean's,* Sept. 19, 1994.
Jenish reviews the blood-contamination scandal that has shaken Canadians' faith in the safety and credibility of their blood-supply system. An earlier report on the scandal by Jenish appeared in the magazine March 7.

Kramer, Jane, "Bad Blood," *The New Yorker,* Oct. 11, 1993.
Kramer, the magazine's European correspondent, tells the tangled story of how AIDS-contaminated blood was knowingly distributed to hundreds of French hemophiliacs in 1985. Similar scandals have since come to light in neighboring Germany.

Moffat, Anne Simon, "Three Li'l Pigs and the Hunt for Blood Substitutes," *Science,* July 5, 1991.
Moffat looks at the status of the search for hematology's Holy Grail — a safe, effective and abundant source of artificial human blood. As in all such quests, the prospects are mixed.

Newman, Richard J., and Doug Podolsky, with Penny Loeb, "Bad Blood," *U.S. News & World Report,* June 27, 1994.
Newman and Podolsky acknowledge that the U.S. blood supply is significantly safer today than it was a decade ago. Nonetheless, they conclude that blood transfusion remains a risky procedure.

Stone, Bradford Wind, "How the FDA Safeguards the Blood Supply," *FDA Consumer,* June 1991.
Stone, a press officer for the FDA, describes how the agency regulates the blood industry. He concludes that "the chances of contracting the AIDS virus from a blood transfusion are now estimated to be rarer than dying from an adverse reaction to penicillin."

Reports

Subcommittee on Oversight and Investigations, U.S. House Committee on Energy and Commerce, *Blood Supply Safety,* July 13, 1990; April 18 and May 15, 1991; and July 28, 1993 (published proceedings of three hearings with the same name).
Academic and government experts on blood safety issues assess the status of the U.S. blood supply in light of the AIDS and hepatitis contamination scares of the past two decades.

The Next Step

Additional information from UMI's Newspaper & Periodical Abstracts database

Blood Banks

Katz, Sidney, "How Safe Are Our Blood Banks?" *Chatelaine,* March 1992, p. 28.

With AIDS being widespread, blood transfusions, like most medical procedures, entail some risk for contracting the deadly disease. The testing of blood banks by the American Red Cross, which can minimize health risk, is discussed.

Rosenthal, Elisabeth, "Blood Banks Vigilant but Vouch for Safety," *The New York Times,* July 27, 1992, p. B2.

Officials at the nation's blood banks say they see no immediate need to change blood donation guidelines in the wake of recent revelations of a possible new strain of AIDS virus, but rather asserted that guidelines for screening out at-risk groups should protect the blood supply.

Segal, Marian, Ruth Weisheit and Rebecca Williams, "Plasma Center Closed," *FDA Consumer,* June 1991, pp. 37-38.

The Denton Plasma Center in Texas was closed by the FDA recently for not screening donors properly and falsifying records. The investigation is detailed.

Blood Supplies and HIV

Alter, Harvey J., Jay S. Epstein, Sally G. Swenson, John W. Ward, Richard A. Kaslow, et. al., "Prevalence of Human Immunodeficiency Virus Type 1 p24 Antigen in U.S. Blood Donors — An Assessment of the Efficacy of Testing in Donor Screening," *New England Journal of Medicine,* Nov. 8, 1990, pp. 1312-1317.

The finding that no donation studied was positive for p24 antigen and negative for HIV-1 antibody suggests that screening donors for p24 antigen with tests of the current level of sensitivity would not add substantially to the safety of the U.S. blood supply.

Bailey, Marvin E., "Developing a National HIV/AIDS Prevention Program Through State Health Departments," *Public Health Reports,* November 1991, pp. 695-701.

The basic direction and development of the HIV/AIDS Prevention Program has been shaped by the Centers for Disease Control and Prevention (CDC) through technical support and financial assistance for state and local health departments and other organizations. The CDC has responded to the course of the HIV-AIDS epidemic through such things as creating programs to preserve the safety of blood supply and by developing counseling and testing centers.

"Blood industry: Standard of Care — United Blood Service v. Quintana," *American Journal of Law & Medicine,* 1992, pp. 281-282.

The case of *United Blood Service v. Quintana* is discussed. The Supreme Court of Colorado held that a plaintiff should be allowed to submit expert testimony challenging the adequacy of the blood banking community's standard of care regarding HIV screening.

Brownworth, Victoria A., "Who Is Minding the Blood Supply?" *Advocate: The National Gay & Lesbian Newsmagazine,* May 19, 1992, pp. 46-47.

The safety of the U.S. blood supply is discussed in light of Arthur Ashe's admission that he contracted AIDS from a 1983 blood transfusion. The FDA estimates that current standards place the odds of contracting HIV from a blood transfusion at one in 50,000; some medical professionals claim that the guidelines for preventing HIV infection are incomplete and outdated.

Burkholz, Herbert, "Bad Blood?" *Town & Country Monthly,* March 1992, pp. 98-99.

The safety of the U.S. blood supply in the age of AIDS is discussed. On the one hand, Burkholz writes, the blood supply has never been safer as the result of the direct screening test for the HIV-1 antibody; on the other hand, the American Red Cross has had serious and persistent problems with its procedures for testing and keeping track of blood.

Dodd, Roger Y., "The Risk of Transfusion-Transmitted Infection," *New England Journal of Medicine,* Aug. 6, 1992, pp. 419-421.

An editorial discusses the risk of HIV transmission through a blood transfusion. The safety of the blood supply continues to increase as the result of major innovations and incremental improvements in test sensitivity.

Fennell, Tom, "Voices of the victims," *Maclean's,* Sept. 19, 1994, pp. 28-29.

In the early 1980s, nearly 1,000 people received blood tainted by AIDS in Canada. Some people in Canada continue to question whether the Red Cross and other organizations should even be involved in the distribution of blood.

Fettner, Ann Giudici, "Blood Simple? — New Doubts About Transfusion Safety," *Village Voice,* Jan. 19, 1988, p. 11.

Problems with HIV contamination of New York City's blood supply are surveyed.

Jackson, James O., "Very bad blood," *Time,* Nov. 15, 1993, p. 65.

Unexplained cases of HIV infection in Germany have been traced to UB Plasma, a small blood-supply company that has sold 7,000 units of blood since 1992. The discovery raises questions about the ability to ensure safe blood supplies worldwide.

McKeown, L. A., "Baffling AIDS-Like Illness Surfaces," ***Medical World News,*** **Aug. 1992, pp. 12-15.**
AIDS researchers are baffled by a new AIDS-like illness that is characterized by an absence of HIV and by CD4-cell depletion. Twenty-six cases of the new virus have been reported, and there is concern for the safety of the U.S. blood supply.

Neel, Joe R., "AIDS-Like Illness Stirs Concern on Blood Supply," ***Boston Globe,*** **Aug. 15, 1992, p. 3.**
Federal officials say that a new AIDS-like disease presents no threat to the nation's blood supply, but some scientists say that unless a cause is found soon, new and expensive measures may be needed to protect blood safety.

Weller, Robert, "AIDS Epidemic: Safe Blood Hard to Find in Zaire," ***Los Angeles Sentinel,*** **Nov. 21, 1991, p. A5.**
In Kinshasa, Zaire, a city with one of the world's highest known AIDS rates, the main blood bank has run out of testing agents for the AIDS virus, and some hospitals are dispensing untested blood.

FDA Regulations

Hilts, Philip J., "F.D.A. seeks tighter rules on safety of blood supply," ***The New York Times,*** **July 2, 1993, p. A11.**
The FDA issued new guidelines on July 1, 1993, to require blood blanks to meet safety standards similar to those for pharmaceutical manufacturers. For example, blood banks will be required to track each unit of blood until it is used and monitor the performance of workers and equipment.

Petit, Charles, "FDA threatens to close Irwin blood bank," ***San Francisco Chronicle,*** **July 21, 1993, p. A1.**
On July 20, 1993, FDA officials threatened to close the Irwin Memorial Blood Center in San Francisco if it does not come up with a better plan than the one it submitted the week before to meet government safety regulations.

Schwartz, John, "Red Cross, FDA agree on blood safety regulations," ***The Washington Post,*** **May 8, 1993, p. A5.**
The American Red Cross and the FDA agreed to a consent decree over how the Red Cross runs its blood-collection operations. The two organizations agreed to a number of measures intended to ensure the safety of the nation's blood supply.

Snider, Sharon, "Plasma Center Closed," ***FDA Consumer,*** **October, 1990, p. 33.**
The El Paseo Plasma Inc. blood plasma center in Las Cruces, N.M., was closed down by the FDA for flagrant violations of health and safety standards in 1989. The work of the FDA to regulate such operations is discussed.

Swardson, Anne, "FDA closes U.S. border to Canadian blood plasma," ***The Washington Post,*** **Sept. 8, 1994, p. A32.**
The FDA has ordered the Canadian Red Cross to stop sending some of its blood products to the U.S. for processing, saying a Toronto blood bank has violated American safety regulations. The organization has been criticized for failing to implement measures that would have stopped contamination by the AIDS-causing HIV virus.

General Blood Supply Safety

"Blood center licenses suspended," ***FDA Consumer,*** **July 1993, p. 6.**
The FDA suspended the establishment and product licenses of Inland Northwest Blood Center in Spokane, Wash., when it found the center had violated federal standards for ensuring the safety and quality of blood and blood components. Details of the FDA's investigation of the matter are presented.

Callery, Marjana F. and Bridget M. Culhane, et al, "Building a Safe Community Blood Supply," ***American Journal of Nursing,*** **June 1991, pp. 51-52.**
While the U.S.'s blood supply is at its safest point in history, the public is more skeptical than ever, the authors write. Donor education, laboratory screening, viral inactiviation of plasma products and other methods for insuring a safe blood supply are discussed.

Chapman, Michael, "How safe is the blood supply?" ***Consumers' Research Magazine,*** **April 1994, pp. 10-16.**
The national blood banking industry's initially slow response to the possibility of blood being contaminated by AIDS and other infectious diseases is examined. The trouble with the blood banks and what scientists knew in the 1970s and 1980s are discussed.

Chakravarty, Subrata N., "Seeing Red," ***Forbes,*** **June 1, 1987, p. 76-80.**
The safety of the country's blood supply — the chance of getting hepatitis from a transfusion is 4-8 percent — is no longer assured. The practice of using one's own blood for transfusions is becoming more popular.

Cowley, Geoffrey, "In Search of Safer Blood," ***Newsweek,*** **Aug. 10, 1992, pp. 44-45.**
Proven and experimental strategies for keeping anonymous blood out of one's veins are given. Although the blood supply is more reliable than ever, there are reasons to avoid transfusion, Cowley writes.

Day, Janet, "Safe Blood Concerns Put Electromedics in Pink," ***Denver Post,*** **May 29, 1992, p. C1.**
Electromedics Inc. rode a wave of concern over blood-supply safety to record revenues in 1991, and the company seems headed for an even better year in 1992. The Englewood, Colo.-based company makes products designed to cleanse a surgical patient's blood.

McCullough, Jeffrey, "The nation's changing blood supply system," ***JAMA: The Journal of the American Medical Association,*** **May 5, 1993, pp. 2239-2245.**
The U.S.' blood bank system is operating in a changed regulatory environment and is under public scrutiny. The safety, adequacy and cost of the blood supply are discussed.

Pekkanen, John, "How Safe Is Our Blood Supply?" ***Saturday Evening Post,*** **Sept. 1988, p. 50-55,**
Every year about 3.5 million Americans receive one or more units of blood in a transfusion. The risks and chances of contracting AIDS and hepatitis from blood transfusions are examined.

Stone, Bradford Wind, "How FDA Safeguards the Blood Supply," ***FDA Consumer,*** **June 1991, p. 12-15.**
New donor screening methods and testing, as well as FDA monitoring and inspection of blood banks, have made blood products in the U.S. safer to use than ever before.

Thomas, Duncan P., "Viral contamination of blood products," ***Lancet,*** **June 25, 1994, pp. 1583-1584.**
The viral contamination of blood donations and what can be done to improve the safety of blood storage are examined. Absolute safety of the blood supply is a mirage, Thomas says.

Wowk, Mike, "Contaminated blood killed Southfield safety director," ***Detroit News,*** **March 18, 1994, p. A1.**
The Oakland County, Mich., medical examiner has ruled that a contaminated blood transfusion, not natural causes, caused the death of Southfield Public Safety Director Rollin "Jerry" Tobin.

International Blood Safety

Dawood, Richard, "Bad blood overseas, and how to avoid it," ***Conde Nast Traveler,*** **January 1993, p. 28.**
Exposure to AIDS from blood transfusions or non-sterile needles while traveling overseas is uncommon since few travelers need such extensive medical treatment, but such risks do exist. Ways travelers can avoid the threat posed by tainted blood are suggested.

Hambley, Henry, "Revised guidelines on preoperative autologous blood donation," ***British Medical Journal*** **(International), Dec. 11, 1993, p. 1510.**
An editorial discusses the U.K.'s revised guidelines regarding preoperative autologous donation. The guidelines provide a framework that should ensure the quality and safety of autologous transfusion.

Harris, Derek, "Global Blood Safety Initiative," ***World Health,*** **Oct. 1989, pp. 28-29.**
The World Health Organization's Global Blood Safety Initiative is a cooperative effort among national and international agencies to prevent the transmission of AIDS via donated blood and ensure a health blood supply.

Kondro, Wayne, "Canada: Blood transfusion inquiry," ***Lancet,*** **June 5, 1993, pp. 1465-1466.**
Canada will conduct a public inquiry into the efficiency, safety and management of its blood-supply system. Possible HIV contamination of blood products and the transfusion-associated HIV infections that occurred in the mid-1980s are discussed.

Kondro, Wayne, "Tainted-blood commission," ***Lancet,*** **July 3, 1993, pp. 40-41.**
Canada is to appoint a commission to investigate the efficiency, management and safety of the country's blood-supply system. In the early 1980s, more than 1,000 Canadians were infected with HIV by contaminated blood.

Lewis, Sara, "EU health council meeting," ***Lancet,*** **Dec. 18, 1993, p. 1546.**
The European Commission is expected to audit national blood collection, treatment and control systems in the European Union (EU). The audit could lead to legislative proposals for EU rules laying down minimum safety criteria.

MacKenzie, Debora, "How safe is Europe's blood?" ***New Scientist,*** **Jan. 15, 1994, pp. 12-13.**
Cases of HIV in Germany have highlighted the risks of blood transfusion. However, better technology may not be enough to ensure clean blood supplies across Europe.

Marwick, Charles, "AIDS Commission Making Its Final Report," ***JAMA: The Journal of the American Medical Association,*** **June 24, 1988, p. 3529.**
The Presidential Commission on the Human Immunodeficiency Virus Epidemic is scheduled to send its final report to the White House this week. The report is to cover a myriad of topics concerning the blood supply.

Masters, William, Virginia Johnson and Robert C. Kolodny, " Is the Blood Supply Really Safe?" ***Newsweek,*** **March 14, 1988, p. 52.**
The authors disagree with the experts who believe that the nation's blood supply is now essentially safe from the threat of AIDS.

McClelland, D. B. and P. L. Phillips, "Errors in blood transfusion in Britain: Survey of hospital haematology departments," ***British Medical Journal*** **(International), May 7, 1994, pp. 1205-1206.**
The incidence of recognized transfusion errors in Britain in 1990-91 and the cause and clinical outcome of the errors are examined. Several ways of improving the quality and safety of Britain's blood transfusion process are proposed, including setting up pilot projects to find cost-effective ways to improve the process.

Turner, Craig, "Safety of Canadian blood supply questioned after mishandling revealed," ***Los Angeles Times,*** **Sept. 9, 1994, p. A1.**
Canadians were questioning the safety of their blood

supply on Sept. 8, 1994, after disclosures that U.S. and Canadian health officials had detected substandard practices at collection centers.

The Risk of Hepatitis

"Can you bank on the blood supply?" *University of California at Berkeley Wellness Letter,* May 1993, pp. 6-7.
While AIDS is typically on the minds of people who worry about the blood supply's safety, the risk of contracting hepatitis is much greater. Recent statistical research on both hepatitis and HIV in the blood supply is discussed.

Laurence, Leslie, "Beware the Quiet Killer," *Redbook,* October 1991, pp. 24-32.
Five forms of hepatitis are discussed: hepatitis A, hepatitis B, hepatitis C, hepatitis D and hepatitis E. Cases of hepatitis A and B are on the rise among the general population. The risk of vaccinating children and the safety of the blood supply are addressed.

Steinbrook, Robert, "New Blood Test Able to Identify Type of Hepatitis," *Los Angeles Times,* April 21, 1989, p. 3.
Researchers from Chiron Corp have developed an experimental blood test for the most common form of blood-borne hepatitis, which could improve the safety of the world's blood supply and speed vaccine development against "non-A, non-B hepatitis."

Role of the American Red Cross

Cimons, Marlene, "Red Cross agrees to tighten its blood safety measures," *Los Angeles Times,* May 8, 1993, p. A2.
Under orders from the FDA, the American Red Cross has agreed to take further steps to ensure that the nation's blood supply is safe from contamination by the AIDS virus and other blood-borne diseases, the FDA announced on May 7, 1993.

Cowley, Geoffrey, "How Safe Is the Blood Supply?," *Newsweek,* June 3, 1991, p. 58.
The Red Cross is going to spend more than two years and $120 million making its blood supply safer. The safety of stored blood supplies and techniques for improving the safety are discussed.

Gutfeld, Rose, "FDA's probe prompts Red Cross to agree to tighten its blood-safety procedures," *The Wall Street Journal,* May 10, 1993, p. B6.
In response to an FDA investigation that found violations in blood-safety laws, the Red Cross agreed to tighten its procedures to ensure the safety of its blood supply. The FDA's concerns involved a lack of safeguards and inadequate record-keeping, not an increase in tainted blood.

Toufexis, Anastasia, "AIDS Moves in Many Ways," *Time,* June 3, 1991, p. 56.
An announcement by the Red Cross that it is revamping its facilities and procedures for handling blood donations was perceived by the public as an admission that the current system is not as safe be. Public anxiety about medical professionals is running high, Toufexis writes.

Zachary, G. Pascal, "New managers of Red Cross blood banks will have hard time improving safety," *The Wall Street Journal,* Aug. 15, 1994, p. B6.
The thorny problems at the American Red Cross's troubled blood banks make rapid gains in the safety of much of the nation's blood supply unlikely. The Red Cross recently named Jim D. Ross as its new blood and biomedical chief and also filled its top two deputy slots.

Transfusions

Bohner, Kate, "Blood strategies," *Forbes,* Sept. 27, 1993, p. 152.
How to protect yourself against contracting AIDS from a blood transfusion is discussed. The best way to play it safe is to have your own blood stored and frozen for a transfusion.

Crenshaw, Theresa L., "A Surgical Patient's Transfusion Survival Guide," *Saturday Evening Post,* March 1989, pp. 60-63.
Tips for those who may need blood transfusions on how to avoid the risks of receiving blood at random are presented. Topics include: recycling your own blood with the Intraoperative Autologous Transfusion (IAT) process, plasmapheresis, pre-donation, and directed donations.

"Helpful or hazardous?" *Nursing,* February 1993, p. 49.
Although screening tests have made blood supplies safe, some risks still exist in blood transfusions. Some of those risks are discussed.

Perl, Rebecca, "Ashe Transfusion Was at Risky Time," *Atlanta Constitution,* April 9, 1992, p. A6.
Arthur Ashe, who revealed he has AIDS, had a blood transfusion during heart surgery in 1983, when the nation's blood supply harbored thousands of units of contaminated blood and was considered the least safe, Red Cross officials say.

Skolnick, Andrew A., "As the Blood Supply Gets Safer, Experts Still Call for Ways to Reduce the Need for Transfusions," *JAMA: The Journal of the American Medical Association,* Aug. 12, 1992, pp. 698-700.
Even though the FDA has taken measures to increase the safety of the blood supply, hazards still exist. Ways to reduce the need for homologous transfusions, such as preoperative autologous blood collection, are discussed.

Sutton, Darinda E., "One step closer to safe transfusions," *RN,* December 1993, pp. 38-39.
More than 2,600 transfusion errors occur each year in the U.S. The innovative Bloodloc system provides a safeguard against blood mismatches, Sutton writes.

Back Issues

Great Research on Current Issues Starts Right Here...Recent topics covered by The CQ Researcher are listed below. Before May 1991, reports were published under the name of Editorial Research Reports.

MAY 1993
Cults in America
Preventing Teen Pregnancy
Software Piracy
National Parks

JUNE 1993
Food Safety
Prostitution
Childhood Immunizations
National Service

JULY 1993
Electric Cars
Population Growth
Downward Mobility
Intelligence Testing

AUGUST 1993
Mental Illness
Bilingual Education
Foreign Policy Burden
School Funding

SEPTEMBER 1993
Suburban Crime
Public Housing
Supreme Court Preview
Immigration Reform

OCTOBER 1993
Airline Safety
Disaster Response
Science in the Courtroom
The Glass Ceiling

NOVEMBER 1993
Paying for Retirement
Charitable Giving
Privacy in the Workplace
Adoption

DECEMBER 1993
U.S. Vietnam-Relations
Learning Disabilities
Child Care
Space Program's Future

JANUARY 1994
Racial Tensions in Schools
South Africa's Future
Worker Retraining
Regulating Pesticides

FEBRUARY 1994
Prison Overcrowding
Water Quality
Religion in Schools
Juvenile Justice

MARCH 1994
Underground Economy
Education Standards
Gambling Boom
Private Management of Public Schools

APRIL 1994
Reproductive Ethics
U.S.-China Trade
Soccer in America
Talk Show Democracy

MAY 1994
Traffic Congestion
Women's Health Issues
Mutual Funds
Political Scandals

JUNE 1994
Education and Gender
Gun Control
Public Land Policy
Nuclear Arms Cleanup

JULY 1994
Dietary Supplements
Public Opinion and Foreign Policy
Crime Victims' Rights
Birth Control Choices

AUGUST 1994
Genetically Engineered Foods
Electing Minorities
Prozac Controversy
College Sports

SEPTEMBER 1994
Home Schooling
Welfare Experiments
Courts and the Media
Regulating Tobacco

OCTOBER 1994
Historic Preservation
Religion and Politics
Arts Funding
Economic Sanctions

NOVEMBER 1994
Sex on Campus

Back issues are available for $4.00 (subscribers) or $7.00 (non-subscribers). Quantity discounts apply to orders over ten. To order, call Congressional Quarterly Customer Service at (202) 887-8621.

Binders are available for $16.00. To order call 1-800-638-1710. Please refer to stock number 648.

Future Topics

- ***Term Limits Revisited***
- ***Religion in America***
- ***Arms Sales***

PUBLISHED BY CONGRESSIONAL QUARTERLY INC.

Testing Term Limits

Will the movement continue sweeping the country?

In just four years, 22 states have adopted laws to limit the tenure of members of Congress. Term limits also have been adopted for state legislators in 20 of those states and for local officials in some 240 cities and counties. Advocates say term limits will restore popular control over government. Opponents warn that they will hurt Congress and other legislative bodies, but their arguments haven't swayed voters. Term limits face a critical legal test Nov. 29, when the Supreme Court hears arguments in a case testing whether the Constitution allows states to limit congressional terms. If the justices say no, term-limit supporters will seek a constitutional amendment — and House Republicans promise an early vote on a term-limit measure in the new, GOP-controlled Congress.

INSIDE THIS ISSUE

CQ Nov. 18, 1994 • Volume 4, No. 43 • Pages 1009-1032

Formerly Editorial Research Reports

Testing Term Limits

The Issues

Background

Current Situation

Outlook

Sidebars and Graphics

For More Information

COVER ART: BARBARA SASSA-DANIELS

THE CQ Researcher

November 18, 1994
Volume 4, No. 43

The CQ Researcher (ISSN 1056-2036). Formerly Editorial Research Reports. Published weekly (48 times per year, not printed the first Friday of any month with five Fridays) by Congressional Quarterly Inc., 1414 22nd St., N.W., Washington, D.C. 20037. Rates are furnished upon request. Second-class postage paid at Washington, D.C. POSTMASTER: Send address changes to The CQ Researcher, 1414 22nd St., N.W., Washington, D.C. 20037.

Testing Term Limits

BY KENNETH JOST

THE ISSUES

Supporters of term limits for members of Congress did not wait long before celebrating on election night. Among the many towering lawmakers they had targeted was House Speaker Thomas S. Foley, a 30-year veteran and symbol of the opposition to term limits. And when he started to topple, champagne corks started popping.

"I want to toast Speaker Foley and the pension benefits he will get when he leaves Congress," a gleeful Paul Jacob, executive director of U.S. Term Limits, told an exuberant crowd as he raised a glass at a celebration in downtown Washington.

Even though the official results from Foley's Washington state district would not be known until the next day, voter exit polls signaled that the 15-term Democrat had been beaten by a Republican challenger. The winner, George Nethercutt, a Spokane lawyer, had attacked Foley's opposition to congressional term limits and promised himself to serve no more than three terms if elected.

Term-limit supporters had much more to celebrate in the midterm elections that gave Republicans control of both houses of Congress for the first time since 1954.

In addition to Foley, two other high-profile Democrats fell victim to the voter anger that term-limit activists had helped fuel. In Illinois, voters ousted Rep. Dan Rostenkowski, an 18-term lawmaker who had been satirized as the term limits "poster child" of 1994 after his indictment in the House Post Office scandal. In Texas, a GOP challenger defeated Rep. Jack Brooks, a 42-year House veteran who term-limit supporters said had "bottled up" term-limit measures as chairman of the House Judiciary Committee.

Meanwhile, voters in seven states approved ballot measures to limit the tenure of members of Congress. The voting brought to 22 the number of states that have adopted term limits for federal lawmakers since 1990.

Most significantly, the prospects for action on term limits by Congress had improved with the Republican victory. Republican House candidates had committed themselves to an early vote on term limits in a GOP-controlled Congress. And election results indicated that term-limit supporters could make their cause a potent political issue — or weapon — in individual House and Senate campaigns.

"We're going to get a vote on term limits in the first hundred days," Jacob promised the election night celebrants. "So this is real big."

For term-limit supporters, the 1994 election capped an astounding run of ballot-box successes. Since 1990, voters in 21 states, from Maine to California and Florida to Alaska, have overwhelmingly approved ballot measures to limit members of Congress to 12 years in office or less. In one other state — Utah — the Legislature approved a qualified term-limit measure for members of Congress. [1]

Term limits are also on the books for state legislators in all but two of those 22 states, Alaska and North Dakota. In addition, term limits have been adopted in about 240 cities or counties, including New York and Los Angeles. (*See map, p. 1012.*) On Nov. 8, voters in the nation's capital joined the movement by giving better than 2-to-1 approval to a measure to limit the mayor, members of the City Council and other officials to two four-year terms.

"It's virtually unstoppable," says Jacob, whose 70,000-member, libertarian-influenced organization has come to dominate the term-limits movement. "Our opposition, which thought it could just stonewall this issue, is waking up to the fact that the world has changed." (*See story, p. 1020.*)

Opponents of term limits have argued that term limits are unnecessary because voters already have the power to throw out incumbents at the ballot box. They also contend that term limits will hurt rather than improve legislative performance and will shift power from Congress and state legislatures to the president and state governors.

But the term-limit movement has simply rolled over its opponents. In the 1992 balloting, coalitions of Democrats, good-government groups, corporate interests and lobbyists mounted campaigns in some states to try to defeat term-limit initiatives. But term limits won approval in all 14 states where the issue was on the ballot by an overall 2-to-1 margin.

This year, opponents did little to try to block the third wave of state ballot measures. Though the victory margins were somewhat lower, term-limit supporters enthused over the results. And they took credit for replacing 19 anti-term-limit Democrats in Senate and House races with pro-term-limit Republicans. "This year marks the first time that term limits has been a cutting-edge issue in political campaigns," Jacob said.

Term Limits in the United States, 1994

Twenty-two states have passed term limits for members of Congress, and all but two of those states — North Dakota and Alaska — also have limits on state legislative seats. More than 240 cities and counties limit terms for local offices. The U.S. Supreme Court will decide on the legality of congressional term limits by next summer.

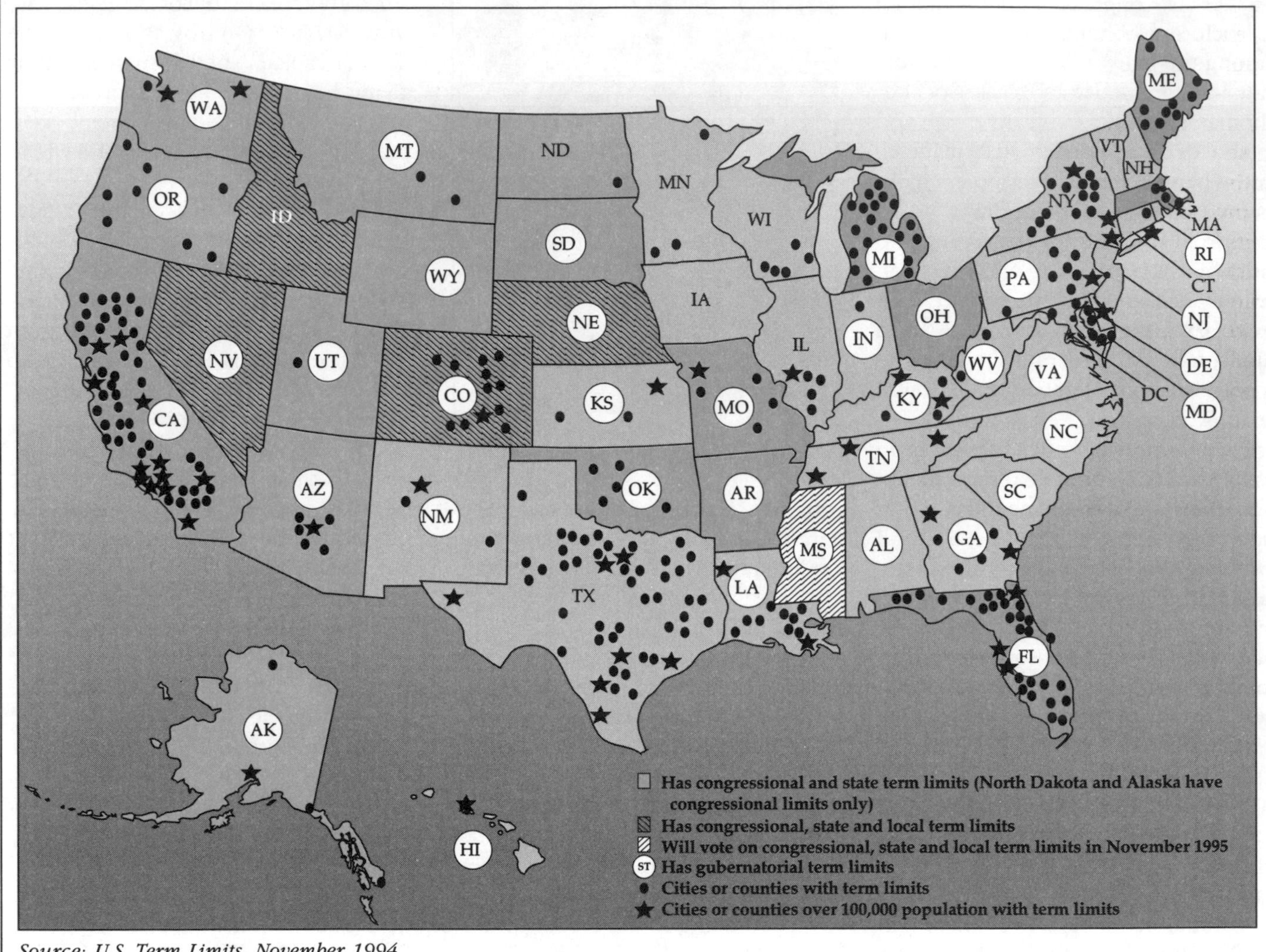

Source: U.S. Term Limits, November 1994

Term-limit supporters, such as the next Speaker of the House, Newt Gingrich, say the popular upswell stems from discontent with career lawmakers. "The system is frankly so out of touch with America and so pathetically sick that the country genuinely believes you've got to break up the current generation of professional politicians," the eight-term Georgia Republican said on NBC's "Meet the Press" a month before the election.

Critics, however, say the reflexive public support for term limits shows that the movement is more about political protest than about governmental reform.

"The American public is all prepared to limit the terms of any politician in any office anywhere in this country," Thomas Mann, director of governmental studies at the Brookings Institution, said on a radio talk show before the election. "It's reflective of the fact that this is not a well-reasoned, deliberative solution to a set of problems but rather a way of expressing frustration with the present system." [2]

Despite its stunning success at the ballot box, the term-limits movement could see its most important victories wiped out. The U.S. Supreme Court will hear arguments Nov. 29 in an Arkansas case testing whether states have authority under the Constitution to limit the tenure of their representatives in Washington. (*See "At Issue," p. 1025.*)

Courts so far have upheld state and local term-limit measures. But congressional limits pose a different issue because the Constitution lays out qualifications for serving in Congress: age, citizenship and residency in the state. Opponents of term limits say states cannot add to that list.

Supporters maintain that the list in the Constitution was never meant to be exclusive. But to try to skirt the issue, term-limit supporters revised their proposals. Early versions had imposed an absolute limit on service in a specified legislative post. Newer proposals prohibit long-term incumbents from being listed on the ballot but allow voters to cast write-in ballots for them.

So far, the courts that have ruled squarely on the term-limits issue have sided with opponents. A federal district court judge in Washington state and the Arkansas Supreme Court both ruled that term-limit measures approved by the states' voters in 1992 were unconstitutional.[3] They agreed with opponents that the U.S. Constitution specifies the only qualifications for serving in Congress. And they dismissed the write-in option for long-term incumbents as illusory.

In the legal showdown in the U.S. Supreme Court, the justices will review term-limits advocates' appeal of the Arkansas decision. Defending the measure, which voters approved by a 3-to-2 margin, are the state's Democratic attorney general, Winston Bryant, along with U.S. Term Limits and other term-limit groups. Opposing the measure are a former president of the Arkansas League of Women Voters and two Democratic House members from Arkansas — Ray Thornton and Blanche Lambert. In addition, the Clinton administration joined the case in August in opposition to the proposal (*see p. 1027*).

Most legal experts expect the justices to rule that states cannot set limits on congressional service. "They get very few cases on which the law is as one-sided as it is in this case," says Daniel Lowenstein, an election-law expert at the University of California-Los Angeles (UCLA) Law School, who filed a brief against term limits on behalf of the California Democratic Party.

Term-limit advocates say the issues are not so clear-cut. "Any expert who jumps to the automatic conclusion that we're going to lose hasn't studied the issue," says Cleta Deatherage Mitchell, executive director and general counsel of the Term Limits Legal Institute, which has helped defend term-limit measures in court. "You can't study this issue without realizing that this is a case of first impression. There really isn't a case in point" to compare it with.

Term-limit advocates satirized Rep. Dan Rostenkowski, D-Ill., as the term-limit "poster child" for his indictment in the House Post Office scandal. The 18-term Democrat was defeated Nov. 8.

Whatever the Supreme Court decides, the ruling will not end the term-limits fight. Supporters point to the targetting of anti-term-limit lawmakers like Foley and vow to use more hardball political tactics if necessary to force a reluctant Congress to submit a constitutional amendment to the states for ratification. Some opponents and political observers believe that strategy will succeed over time, thanks to the overwhelming public support for term limits — as high as 80 percent in a recent NBC News/*Wall Street Journal* poll.[4]

As the term-limits battle continues, here are some of the questions that will be debated:

Will term limits for lawmakers help or hurt the performance of legislative bodies?

In the campaign season just ended, "career lawmaker" was about the deadliest epithet a candidate could use against an opponent. Legislative seniority, once prized as a source of political clout and occasional wisdom, hung like an albatross around the neck of many lawmakers seeking re-election.

Term-limit supporters stoked the anti-incumbency fires. And they confidently predicted that setting limits to long legislative careers in Congress and elsewhere would improve, not hurt, lawmaking.

"You're going to get people in office who are more connected to the people they're representing," says Jacob. "When they decide questions of public policy, they won't decide it in an aloof fashion but will understand how it will affect them in their future life once they leave office."

Less partisan advocates voice similar criticisms of career lawmakers. Testifying before the House Judiciary

Subcommittee on Civil and Constitutional Rights in November 1993, Mark Petracca, an associate professor of political science at the University of California-Irvine, called term limits "an antidote to the professionalization of legislative politics in America."

Opponents counter that term-limit supporters ignore the importance of legislative experience. "It demeans the job of the legislator to say there is no learning curve, no knowledge, nothing peculiar to the job of legislator whereby you might actually learn something over a period of time," says Mann.

John Hibbing, author of *Congressional Careers,* a book about legislators' work in Congress, warns that the loss of legislative experience will hurt the quality of laws passed. "You'd have laws passed by people with less experience, who didn't have the knowledge," says Hibbing, a political scientist at the University of Nebraska. "I'm sure bills would still be passed, but there are bills, and there are bills."

Term-limit supporters mock the need for legislative experience. "Politics is not brain surgery," says Mitchell of the Term Limits Legal Institute, a former Democratic legislator in Oklahoma. And they also blame senior lawmakers for some of the major faults of Congress, including legislative gridlock and pork-barrel spending.

Opponents say the term-limit advocates paint with too broad a brush. "The assumption is that if you've been there for six years, for 12 years, you can't be for changing the system," says Becky Cain, president of the League of Women Voters, which opposes term limits. "If you look at the members of Congress who've been there for that long, that's not true. Some of them are, and some of them aren't."

For his part, Hibbing scoffs at the notion that term limits will eliminate pork-barrel spending. "There's still going to be plenty of pork ladled," he says.

Term-limit supporters respond that opponents are simply too tied to thinking about the present system to appreciate the changes that restricting lawmakers' tenure will bring.

"It will not be business as usual," says Roger Pilon, director of constitutional studies at the Cato Institute, a libertarian think tank. "We will have a much smaller government with a citizen legislature."

"If people come to Washington for one, two, or three terms, they're not going to come for the normal careerism reasons," says Jacob. "They will be people whose goal in life is not to climb the political ladder but to give something back to their community, their state and their country. Those people are going to function in a different way."

Opponents of term limits, however, predict that most lawmakers will continue to be political careerists even if tenure in particular posts is limited. They forecast a political version of musical chairs, with politicians working to move from office to office as they reach the end of their term. "We'll still get professional legislators who will adjust their careers one way or another," says Rebekah Herrick, a political scientist at Oklahoma State University, who has studied the careers of members of Congress after retirement.

Kathleen Beall

TV ads in Washington state attacked House Speaker Thomas S. Foley, a 15-term Democrat, for challenging the state's term-limit initiative in court. He was narrowly defeated Nov. 8.

But even if lawmakers simply scramble for other positions, term-limit supporters say the effects will be beneficial. "They will encourage people to be competitive for another office and open up competition for that seat," says Gerald Benjamin, a political scientist at the State University of New York-New Paltz. "That to me is a double plus."

The opposing sides disagree about other changes that term limits might or might not bring. Opponents warn that term limits will increase the power of lobbyists and unelected staff. Supporters disagree and say there is no evidence of that so far. Opponents warn that term-limited lawmakers will become beholden to special interests because of the need to find employment after their political careers end. Supporters again predict that citizen-legislators will return to their earlier careers after political life.

For the present, those arguments turn mostly on conjecture. In states where term limits have gone into effect, there has been too little time to make anything but the most tentative judgments about their effects. (*See story, p. 1016.*)

Do term limits imposed on members of Congress by state legislatures violate the Constitution?

Along with the political argument over term limits, the opposing sides have conducted a parallel debate over their legality. That debate, which reaches a critical stage later this month before the Supreme Court, turns on divergent interpretations of the text and history of the Constitution and of Supreme Court precedents from the past 25 years.

Ever since the first congressional term-limit measure reached a state ballot in 1990, opponents have confidently argued that states have no power to restrict the tenure of their representatives in Washington. They argue that the Constitution sets the only qualifications for serving in Congress: minimum age (25 years for the House, 30 years for the Senate); U.S. citizenship for specified periods; and residency in the state from which they are elected.

"[T]he text and structure of Article I leave no room for States to establish additional qualifications for membership in Congress," attorneys for the two Arkansas representatives opposing the state's term-limit measure argued last month in their brief to the U.S. Supreme Court.

Term-limit supporters, however, point to another constitutional provision that gives state legislatures authority to regulate the "Times, Places and Manner of holding elections for Senators and Representatives." The provision goes on to state that Congress "may at any time by Law make or alter such Regulations."

Lawyers for U.S. Term Limits argue in their brief that that provision "explicitly assigns the States broad power over congressional elections." They contend that the later term-limit measures, limiting long-term incumbents to running as write-in candidates, fall within the states' authority, subject to override by Congress if it wishes to do so.

In the four years since Colorado became the first state to approve a congressional term-limit measure, opposing sides have fleshed out their positions by poring over the 200-year-old records of the Constitutional Convention.

Term-limit opponents emphasize that the Framers considered, and rejected, term limits as well as any property requirement for serving in Congress. They also cite passages emphasizing the need for uniform qualifications from the debates at the convention and from the *Federalist Papers,* the pro-ratification tracts written by John Adams, Alexander Hamilton and James Madison.

Supporters of term limits counter with passages from the debates more favorable to states' rights positions. And they emphasize that after the Constitution was ratified, some states did enact laws setting qualifications for members of Congress, including property requirements and laws requiring representatives to live in the district, not only the state, from which they were elected.

Finally, the opposing sides both

House Members Tend to Keep Their Seats

*Term-limit supporters point to the steady decline in the turnover rate * in the House of Representatives since the 19th century as proof that limits are needed. From 1950 to 1990, the percentage of House members who were replaced by newcomers topped 20 percent only twice. Opponents of limits say the higher turnover rates in 1992 and this year show that term limits are unneccesary.*

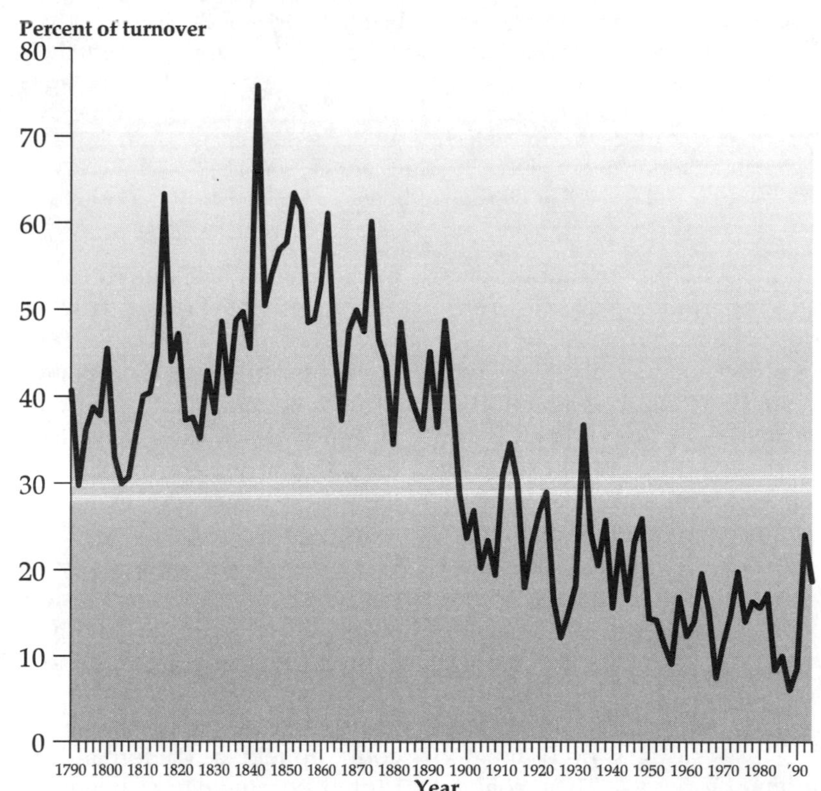

** The turnover rate includes members who retired or were defeated in primary or general elections.*

Source: Norman J. Ornstein, Thomas E. Mann and Michael J. Malbin, Vital Statistics on Congress, 1993-1994, *1994.*

Four Years After California Passed Term Limits . . .

Three decades ago, California's Legislature led the way in a national trend toward increased professionalization in state legislatures, switching to full-time lawmakers and higher staff salaries. In 1990, the state capital in Sacramento was hit by the early wave of another national trend: term limits for state lawmakers.

Four years later, term limits are beginning to have an impact in Sacramento. Even though only one lawmaker has actually been forced out of office, many others have moved out — or tried to move up — in anticipation of hitting the term limit set by the 1990 measure.

Supporters credit California's term limits with bringing about this increased turnover along with more competitive elections and improved legislative performance. "You get a better breed of legislator better able to do the public business," says John C. Armor, an election-law attorney who studied the changes in California as a resident scholar for U.S. Term Limits in Washington. [1]

But opponents either discount or deny any claimed benefits from term limits while insisting that the Legislature is already losing valuable expertise and giving up power to the governor and state bureaucrats. "It's almost impossible to believe that it's going to produce a better Legislature," says Ed Costantini, a professor of political science at the University of California-Davis.

On the surface, things have changed a lot in Sacramento in four years. In 1992, the first election under term limits, 27 freshman members were elected to the state's 80-member Assembly, and four lower house incumbents moved on to the 40-member Senate. This year, nearly one-fourth of the lawmakers — 29 out of 120 in all — decided to move on either to take jobs outside government or to run for other political positions. [2]

Some observers say the changes in 1992 were due to legislative redistricting, not to term limits. "The state is more diverse, and the districts have been redrawn to reflect that diversity," says Bernard Grofman, a professor of political science at the University of California-Irvine. "The impact of term limits is at the margin, if at all."

The effect on competitive elections is also subject to doubt. Mark Petracca, an associate professor of political science at UC-Irvine and a strong proponent of term limits, says there were somewhat more competitive races for the Legislature in 1992, but no real increase this year. In the long run, however, Petracca says he does expect increased competitiveness.

The relatively high exodus of lawmakers in 1994 does seem to be a clear result of term limits, but opposing camps view the change differently. Critics say the number of lawmakers seeking other offices has merely created what Costantini calls a game of "musical chairs" instead of bringing new blood into the Legislature, as term-limit supporters suggested. But Armor says the scramble for other political jobs is "an extreme positive."

"There isn't room for all these people to move up," says Armor. "Only the best of the lot is going to move up, which is fine. That's what the game is all about."

Critics also discount claims that term limits has changed

point to modern Supreme Court decisions to support their positions. Term-limit opponents rely primarily on the court's 1969 decision, *Powell v. McCormack,* arising from an effort by the House to deny Rep. Adam Clayton Powell his seat following his election because of corruption and misconduct charges. In a near unanimous decision, the court held that the House could not refuse to seat the New York Democrat because the qualifications for serving in Congress were "fixed in the Constitution."

Supporters of term limits respond that the *Powell* case has no bearing on the current proposals. They contend that requiring long-term incumbents to run as write-in candidates does not establish a "qualification" for Congress. And, even if it does, they argue that the *Powell* case dealt with Congress' power to determine qualifications for service. The states, they argue, have greater power because of the explicit constitutional provision giving states power to regulate elections and because of general principles of states' rights, including the 10th Amendment, which reserves to the states powers not granted to the federal government.

Term-limit supporters rely instead on other Supreme Court decisions that have upheld state election laws that control who can appear on the ballot. They point in particular to two decisions. In *Storer v. Brown* (1974), the court upheld a California law that prohibited candidates from running as independents if they had been registered with a political party within the previous 11 months. In the other case, *Clements v. Fashing,* the court in 1982 upheld a Texas law that prohibited incumbents in certain state offices from running for other state offices.

But opponents of term limits say these cases provide no legal basis for restricting the service of members of Congress or forcing them to run as write-in candidates. They argue that the court's election-law cases have been aimed at ensuring the integrity of the election process. By contrast, lawyers for the Arkansas representatives argued in their brief, the term-limit proposal "manipulates [election procedures] in order to disable an identifiable class of persons from service in the federal legislature."

Most legal experts agree with the opponents of term limits on the constitutional issues — as have the two courts to rule squarely on the issue so far. But some legal observers said they found the briefs filed with the Su-

. . . Critics and Supporters Debate Impact on Legislature

the political culture for the good in Sacramento. Sherry Bebitch Jeffe, a senior associate at the Center for Politics and Policy at the Claremont Graduate School in Pomona, says the election of so-called "term-limit babies" has not reduced lawmakers' ties to special-interest groups.

"They've all joined the system," says Jeffe. "They're not as independent as the proponents of term limits claimed they would be."

But Armor says freshman legislators are raising less money from special-interest groups than their more senior colleagues. And he says the new lawmakers are proving to be less partisan and more intent on accomplishing results in a short time.

"For the first time in seven years, they passed a budget on time," Armor says. "They were willing to work together, across the aisle."

California voters approved the term-limit measure in 1990 with 52 percent of the vote after a sharp partisan battle between the state's Republican Party and the leadership of the Democratic-controlled Legislature. Among the chief targets of the GOP campaign were two long-time Democratic lawmakers — Senate President Pro Tem David Roberti of Los Angeles and Assembly Speaker Willie Brown of San Francisco.

Roberti this year became the first California lawmaker to be forced from office by term limits when he became subject to the two-term limit (eight years) for senators by running in a new district in 1992. This year he ran for state treasurer but lost in the Democratic primary. Brown will be forced to give up his Assembly seat at the end of 1996; he has said he may run for a seat in the state Senate or become a television talk show host. Meanwhile, Brown's speakership was thrown in doubt when Democrats and Republicans ended with 40 seats apiece after the Nov. 8 elections.

In addition to setting six-year limits (three terms) for Assembly members and eight-year limits for senators, the 1990 measure also slashed the Legislature's budget by 40 percent. Lawmakers and others say the loss of experienced staff has combined with other changes from term limits to cede power to the governor, to bureaucrats and to special interests.

"I think that some people forgot that when you limit the power in the Legislature, you're limiting the power of people who represent them," said Democratic Assemblywoman Delanie Eastin, who gave up her seat to make a successful bid to become the state superintendent of education. [3]

But supporters say they see only positive changes from term limits so far in California. In a brief urging the U.S. Supreme Court to uphold state term limits for Congress, the conservative Pacific Legal Foundation pointed to the changes in California as proof that term limits would benefit Congress as well. "The infusion of new legislators," the group's lawyers wrote, "helped break the gridlock that has paralyzed the California Legislature, leading to a promising new trend that should be replicated in Congress."

[1] See John C. Armor, " 'Foreshadowing' Effects of Term Limits: California's Example for Congress," *U.S. Term Limits,* June 1994.

[2] *Los Angeles Times,* March 20, 1994, p. A3.

[3] National Public Radio, "Morning Edition," April 18, 1994.

preme Court by term-limit supporters more persuasive than they had expected. In any event, the Supreme Court often confounds predictions, and the justices will all be confronting the issue for the first time when arguments are held Nov. 29.

Will congressional term limits become law even if the Supreme Court strikes down restrictions imposed by the states?

The political fight over term limits will continue no matter what the Supreme Court decides on the constitutionality of the state measures.

If the state limits are upheld, supporters still face the task of getting similar restrictions passed in other states or uniform limits passed by Congress. If the court rules the state measures unconstitutional, term-limit supporters will have the more difficult challenge of getting a constitutional amendment approved by two-thirds majorities in Congress and then ratified by three-fourths of the states.

Despite the challenges, term-limit supporters are confident about the eventual outcome. "Term limits will happen," says Norman Leahy, research director for U.S. Term Limits. "It's just a matter of when."

Many political observers, on both sides of the issue, agree. "Term limitation will take time," term-limits advocate George F. Will wrote in fall 1992. "But it is coming." [5]

Fifteen months later, David Broder, the veteran *Washington Post* columnist and an opponent of term limits, came to the same conclusion. "Unless something unexpected happens," Broder wrote, "my guess is that before this decade is out, term limits will be in force in Congress and in most if not all the states." [6]

Term-limit supporters have used a multitrack strategy to reach their goal of restricting long-term service in Congress. In addition to working for state term-limit measures for Congress, they have also been pushing for term limits for state legislators and local lawmakers. Term-limits advocates call this the "trickle-up theory." They hope local and state lawmakers who no longer can stay in their posts indefinitely will add to the pressure to force members of Congress to relinquish their posts as well.

In addition, the term-limits movement this year stepped up the pressure on Congress itself. "We're really moving from the initiative sphere to a new arena: direct lobbying of Congress," Jacob of U.S. Term Limits remarked before the election. [7]

The strategy appeared to be paying off early in the election year. U.S. Term Limits spent $15,000 on a mailing to voters in a special House election in Kentucky that ended with the election of a pro-term-limit Republican, Ron Lewis. In September, the group financed another $15,000 mailing in an Oklahoma Democratic primary where eight-term Rep. Mike Synar, a term-limits opponent, was toppled by a political newcomer.

Despite the pressure on Congress, some political observers doubt that lawmakers on Capitol Hill will succumb. "Congress will never pass term limits," says David Magelby, a political science professor at Brigham Young University. "It's not in their interest."

Magelby, an expert on voter initiatives, also doubts that the term-limits movement can sustain its strength for a second round of political fights after a Supreme Court setback. "The history is these groups are not as strong the second time around," he says.

The leaders of U.S. Term Limits contend they have built a solid grassroots movement. "Over 5 million signatures have been collected by term-limit proponents to put this on local ballots and state ballots," says Jacob. "I don't think any other movement in this country has put as many measures on the ballot for people to vote on."

Within the term-limits movement, however, U.S. Term Limits has been criticized for building a "top-down" organization that pays little attention to developing local and state organizations. "They think they've built a great grassroots organization, but they haven't," says Mitchell of the Term Limits Legal Institute. "They've built a mailing list."

Jacob dismisses the criticism. "We have sometimes made people [at the local and state levels] unhappy because we don't spend money on overhead," he responds. And he reiterates complete confidence in the ultimate outcome of the term-limits fight whatever the Supreme Court says.

"One way or another, 80 percent of the American people are not going to be denied retaking control of their elected officials," he says. "If we have to get a constitutional amendment, I think that's what's going to happen. It means a more protracted battle, maybe a longer battle, but I think Americans are ready for that battle." ■

BACKGROUND

"Rotation in Office"

Supporters of term limits trace the idea to ancient times. In a paper on the history of "rotation in office," political scientist Petracca says that in the fourth and fifth centuries B.C., Athenians selected their governing council of 500 annually by lot and limited membership to two years. Both Aristotle, the Greek philosopher, and Cicero, the Roman leader, advocated rotation so that rulers would understand that they in turn would be ruled themselves. The idea was practiced in the Renaissance city-states of Florence and Venice and endorsed in the 17th and 18th centuries by such English figures as political philosopher John Locke and jurist Sir William Blackstone. [8]

Petracca says that rotation in office was practiced in the 1600s in at least three American colonies — Delaware, New York and Pennsylvania — and then widely discussed in the Revolutionary era. By 1777, he says, seven of the 10 new state constitutions limited the tenure of the chief executive. Pennsylvania, the most radical of the original states, also limited members of its assembly to four years' service over a seven-year period. But no other state limited tenure for the members of its larger legislative chamber, or "lower" house. [9]

Significantly for the current debate, the Articles of Confederation, adopted in March 1781, just before the end of the Revolutionary War in October, did limit the tenure of members of Congress. Under Article V, delegates to the Continental Congress were to be appointed by the respective states and limited to three years in office over a six-year period. When the provision was first applied in 1784, a sharp controversy erupted over the refusal of two Rhode Island delegates to relinquish their seats. Petracca says Congress left the controversy unresolved to avoid interfering with other business.

The Rhode Island episode is cited by lawyers for Rep. Henry J. Hyde, R-Ill., a term-limits opponent, in a friend of the court brief filed in the Supreme Court case. The dispute, Hyde's lawyers say, "may have led many of the Framers [of the Constitution] to doubt the wisdom of limiting legislative terms." Petracca acknowledges that support for rotation in office waned through the 1780s. He says opposition resulted from the disintegration of the Confederation and the forced retirement of six popular governors under state term-limit provisions. [10]

The Constitutional Convention

The opposing sides in today's term-limits debate agree that the Constitution, written in 1787 to replace the Articles of Confederation, contains no provision for rotation in office. But they disagree sharply about the reasons for, and the significance of, the deletion.

The initial draft of the Constitution — the so-called Virginia plan, presented at the opening of the convention on May 29, 1787 — included a rotation provision that would have barred members of "the first branch" of Congress (the House) for an unspecified number of years after the

Continued on p. 1020

Chronology

1700s

"Rotation in office" is adopted in some American colonies and states for executive officials and for lawmakers in one state — Pennsylvania — but not included in the Constitution.

1781
Articles of Confederation limit delegates to the Continental Congress to three-years' service in a six-year period.

1787
The Constitutional Convention rejects provision to require "rotation in office" for members of Congress.

1800s

Congressional service is widely viewed as unattractive, and turnover is high through most of the century.

1900-1950

The length of congressional careers increases with the institutionalization of party rules and committee structure and the growth of the federal government.

1913
Seventeenth Amendment providing for direct election of senators is ratified.

1947
Congress approves 22nd Amendment to limit president to two four-year terms after rejecting provision to limit congressional terms as well; states complete ratification in 1951.

1950-1989

Proposals to limit tenure of members of Congress gain attention and public support, but no action is taken.

1978
Senate Judiciary subcommittee holds hearing on congressional term limits, but takes no further action.

1988
Republican Party platform endorses congressional term limits, but issue receives little attention.

1990s

Twenty-two states put limits on congressional tenure despite constitutional challenges. Term-limit measures also are approved for state legislators in 20 states and for local lawmakers in some 240 cities and counties.

Nov. 6, 1990
Colorado voters approve 12-year limit for members of state's congressional delegation along with limits for state legislators. California voters also approve state legislative term limits; Oklahoma voters had adopted limits for state lawmakers in September balloting.

Oct. 10, 1991
California Supreme Court finds no state or federal constitutional bar to limiting terms of state legislators.

Nov. 5, 1991
Washington state voters narrowly reject retroactive congressional term-limit initiative.

Nov. 3, 1992
Voters in 14 states approve congressional term-limit ballot measures by an overall 2-to-1 margin.

Nov. 2, 1993
New York City voters approve term limits for mayor and City Council members by 3-to-2 margin. Los Angeles voters had approved term limits for local officials in April.

Feb. 10, 1994
Federal judge in Washington state rules congressional term-limit measure approved by state's voters is unconstitutional.

March 7, 1994
Arkansas Supreme Court rules 5-2 that 1992 ballot measure to limit congressional terms is unconstitutional.

Sept. 20, 1994
Oklahoma voters approve congressional term limits by 2-to-1 margin.

Sept. 27, 1994
Some 300 Republican candidates for the House endorse "Contract for America" calling for early vote on congressional term limits.

Nov. 8, 1994
Congressional term limits are approved in six additional states and tightened in Colorado. Republicans gain control of the House and Senate, and GOP leaders say they will act on term-limit proposals.

Nov. 29, 1994
U.S. Supreme Court hears arguments in constitutional challenge to Arkansas congressional term-limits initiative.

Well-Funded Group Backed by Libertarians . . .

The political and legal strategy behind the national term-limit movement has been plotted and financed by a multimillion-dollar organization based in Washington headed by one-time leaders of the national Libertarian Party. *

U.S. Term Limits and its president, Howard Rich, a New York City developer, reportedly provided the major financial backing for state term-limit measures in 1992 and again this year. The group, which claims 70,000 due-paying members, has aggressively pushed state ballot drives but has been criticized for doing too little to build up local organizations. The group has also been responsible for shifting the movement's goal to a six-year limit for members of the U.S. House of Representatives, instead of 12 or eight years as called for in earlier proposals.

U.S. Term Limits President Howard Rich

U.S. Term Limits, Rich and other leaders of the group contributed more than $2 million out of the $5.9 million spent on signature-gathering and campaigning for the 14 congressional term-limit measures on state ballots in 1992, according to *Common Cause* magazine. This year, the group donated more than $500,000 out of about $700,000 reported spent in six of the nine states that voted on term limits this fall, according to *The Washington Post*. [1]

Rich says he has personally contributed $600,000 to the term-limit movement since 1990. "I'm a lunatic for term limits," Rich said in an election-night interview. "My wife won't talk to me about it. She's bored with it."

U.S. Term Limits came to dominate the term-limit movement after taking over a defunct rival group, Citizens for Congressional Reform (CCR), in January. CCR had been controversial because it was bankrolled by two billionaire oilmen, brothers Charles G. and David H. Koch of Wichita, Kan., who had also funded libertarian causes.

The leaders of U.S. Term Limits also trace their political roots to the Libertarian Party. Rich was on the party's national committee in the early 1980s and was credited with directing the petition drives that got the party's presidential candidate listed on all 50 state ballots for the first time in 1980. [2]

Paul Jacob, the organization's executive director, was the Libertarian Party's national director in 1987 and '88. He became a celebrity in libertarian circles in the early 1980s when he served a five-month prison term for refusing to register with the Selective Service System.

But Rich and Jacob both say they are not active members

* The Libertarian Party calls for minimalist government, opposing even such universal programs as Social Security and public schools.

Continued from p. 1018

expiration of their terms. Two weeks later — on June 12 — the convention deleted the provision without dissent or recorded debate.

Term-limit supporters say the rotation provision was dropped because it went into too much detail. They also contend that convention delegates viewed it as unnecessary because frequent elections would ensure regular turnover. "For most of this country's history," U.S. Term Limits argues in its brief before the Supreme Court, "that faith of the Framers proved essentially correct. More recently it has not."

Opponents of term limits counter that convention delegates carefully considered a host of detailed provisions regarding Congress, including elections, salary, length of terms and qualifications. And they contend that the delegates must have been aware of the growing opposition to rotation. "Viewed in this historical context," Rep. Thornton argues in his brief, "the deletion of the rotation provision was a fully informed, deliberate rejection of the concept."

The convention went on to impose only three qualifications for members of Congress — age, residency and citizenship. Term-limit opponents say the Framers intended the requirements to be uniform in all states and wanted only the most minimal restrictions on voters' choices. "The qualifications of electors and elected were fundamental articles in a Republican" government, James Madison said during the convention, "and ought to be fixed by the Constitution." [11]

But term-limit supporters insist the convention's decision to leave states free to run elections — subject to override by Congress — shows that the Framers expected the states to be free to set additional qualifications for serving in Congress. They cite other convention delegates as proof. For one, Oliver Ellsworth, a states' rights advocate from Massachusetts, opposed a property requirement because it might "by implication tie up the hands of the Legislature" from writing other requirements. [12]

After ratification, some states did impose property qualifications or other requirements for serving in Congress. Term-limit supporters insist the early Congresses accepted those laws, prov-

. . . Directed the Campaign to Pass Term Limits

of the party today. And Jacob minimizes libertarian themes in explaining his support for term limits.

"It's very difficult to say that term limits are going to give us a smaller or bigger government or more active or less active government," Jacob says. "I don't favor term limits because I think it will give us smaller government, because I don't think you can make that extrapolation."

Some term-limit supporters accuse U.S. Term Limits of pushing local and state organizations aside. "They're a completely top-down organization," said Sherry Bockwinkel, a Washington state term-limits organizer. "If it were up to them, there would be no local people." [3]

The group has also drawn criticism, and legal scrutiny, from outside the term-limit movement. Earlier this year, the Democratic Congressional Campaign Committee accused U.S. Term Limits of violating federal campaign-disclosure laws with "voter education" drives in congressional districts where term-limit opponents are on the ballot. In its pending complaint with the Federal Election Commission (FEC), the Democratic group says contributions and expenditures should be disclosed because the drives are really aimed at influencing the elections.

U.S. Term Limits is also under investigation in four states — Oklahoma, Nebraska, North Dakota and Utah — for alleged irregularities in petition signature-gathering. [4] In North Dakota, a measure to tighten the 12-year limit for House members to six years was thrown off the ballot this year after it was discovered that more than half of the signatures were not collected by North Dakota residents, as required by state law.

Jacob says he regrets the problems with the petition drives and depicts the Democrats' complaint as an effort to curb the political rights of term-limit supporters.

A new round of "voter education" drives was financed in the weeks before the Nov. 8 election by a new group formed by two of U.S. Term Limits' board members. The new group, Americans for Limited Terms, paid for more than $1 million in broadcast and direct mail advertising in states or congressional districts where term-limit opponents were running against term-limit supporters. The group spent more than $300,000, for example, in eastern Washington, where House Speaker Thomas S. Foley was running against a pro-term-limits Republican, George Nethercutt.

Paul Farago, an Oregon investor who served as vice president of the new group, insisted the advertising was not aimed at defeating the anti-term limit candidates. On election night, however, Farago joined other U.S. Term Limits supporters in cheering the defeats of three Democratic lawmakers they had targeted with their ad campaigns: Foley, Dan Rostenkowski in Illinois and Jack Brooks in Texas.

"If Foley loses," Farago said as Foley's likely defeat became known, "I don't think any incumbent in Congress will dare oppose term limits."

[1] Amy E. Young, "The Money Behind the Movement," *Common Cause*, summer 1993, pp. 37-39; Dana Priest, "'Grass-Roots' Movement to Impose Term Limits Lacks Local Funding," *The Washington Post*, Nov. 5, 1994, p. A9.

[2] Jon Margolis, "Libertarians Buy a Piece of Term Limits Movement," *Chicago Tribune*, May 26, 1994, p. A1.

[3] Susan B. Glasser, "Fraud Charges Hit Term Limits Crusade," *Roll Call*, Sept. 22, 1994, p. 1.

[4] *Ibid.*

ing that the Framers expected the states to have that authority. As opponents point out, however, the House ignored one such state law in seating William McCreery as a congressman from Maryland in 1807 even though he may not have satisfied a state law requiring him to live within Baltimore County.

On the other hand, term-limit supporters insist that 19th-century Congresses continued to tolerate differences among the states on qualifications and elections of House members. They note, for example, that Congress passed a law in 1842 requiring that House members be elected from districts instead of at large, but that the next Congress nonetheless seated members from four states that continued statewide elections despite the law.

Congressional Careers

The historical record is less ambiguous on another central point of the term limits debate. Congressional careers have gradually become longer since the country's early days, especially in the last 40 years.

In the 19th century, turnover in Congress was high: above 40 percent for the House in most years. Few lawmakers made a career out of Congress. Voluntary retirement was common, due in part to the tradition of rotation in office. Columnist Will notes that of the three great lawmakers of the first half of the 19th century — John C. Calhoun, Henry Clay and Daniel Webster — only Webster would have been affected by a prohibition on more than 12 years' consecutive service. [13]

Political scientist Hibbing lists other factors besides the tradition of rotation in office to explain the prevalence of short congressional careers in the 1800s. Washington was viewed as a "swampy, mosquito-infested, rural outpost." Congress was a raucous place. Debate was laced with ridicule and sarcasm and occasionally punctuated with physical violence. Moreover, until the 1890s, lawmakers had limited power. "Congress was a part-time body with a part-time role in a limited federal government," Hibbing writes. [14]

Term-limit advocates have traced the beginning of congressional careerism to the enactment of tariffs in the late 19th century that they say gave lawmakers the power to grant or take away economic favors from specific business interests. Others have linked the rise in longevity to the growth of the federal administrative state that began in the early 20th century. Finally, Washington became a much more important place for Congress and the president alike after World War II as the U.S. became the world's leading superpower.

Whatever the reasons, long congressional careers have become common since the 1950s. There have been more than 100 House members with 12 or more years' consecutive service in each Congress since the end of World War II; the number reached 198 — close to half the House — in the 102nd Congress (1991-1993). [15] Seniority also increased in the Senate, although more gradually. The average length of service of current senators increased from seven years in the 83rd Congress (1953-1955) to 11 years in the 102nd Congress (1991-1993).

The record for congressional longevity was set by Arizona's Carl Hayden, who ended his 57 years' service in the House and Senate in 1969. The House record is held by Mississippi Democrat Jamie L. Whitten, who is retiring this year after 53 years in office. [16]

Hibbing sees benefits from congressional seniority in terms of legislative productivity. He calls senior members "the heart and soul of the legislative side of congressional service" and presents data showing that lawmakers become more effective in getting legislation passed the longer they are in office. [17]

"Junior members tend to have a very unfocused legislative agenda," Hibbing explains. "They're throwing bills in the hopper, and their chances of getting anywhere are slim."

But James K. Coyne and John Fund argue in their 1992 book, *Cleaning House,* that new members will improve the legislative process. "This new blood will be able to have greater impact, whether in Congress or in state legislatures, than before, and perhaps finally put an end to some of the log-rolling and mutual back-scratching that characterize the legislative process today," the authors wrote. [18]

Congress in Disrepute

Until the 1970s, most Americans seemingly took the more favorable view of congressional careerism. Veteran lawmakers such as House Speaker Sam Rayburn, D-Texas, longtime Senate Appropriations Committee Chairman Warren G. Magnuson, D-Wash., and Senate Republican leader Everett McKinley Dirksen of Illinois achieved national stature while enjoying immense popularity at home. Incumbent lawmakers routinely sought re-election by promising that their seniority would give them greater clout in Washington.

Rep. Jamie L. Whitten, D-Miss., is retiring after 53 years in office.

Voters apparently heeded the message. As Will notes, the re-election rate for incumbent House members who run for another term has traditionally been high — above 70 percent in all but seven elections since 1791. Since 1932, however, the re-election rate has been above 80 percent in all but two elections (1938 and 1948) and above 90 percent in 17 out of 21 elections from 1950 to 1990. The success rate for senators seeking re-election has been lower and more volatile, but it too has been relatively high in recent years — above 70 percent in all but three elections since 1960. (*See graph, p. 1023.*)

By the 1970s, however, popular approval of Congress was eroding. Congress was beset by a succession of political scandals, ranging from straightforward cases of bribery and corruption such as Koreagate in the 1970s and Abscam in 1980 to more intricate charges of misuse of office such as more recent House Bank and House Post Office scandals. [19] In addition, partisan differences between Republican presidents and the Democratic-controlled Congress led many people to view Congress as weak on foreign policy, extravagant on taxes and spending and generally indecisive or obstructionist or both.

Individual lawmakers found consolation in the high re-election rates that persisted even as Congress' institutional standing fell. By the mid-to late 1980s, however, a new, predominantly conservative cadre of critics was challenging that source of comfort for incumbent lawmakers. They argued that incumbents had, in effect, rigged the system for their own benefit. Congress, they said, had become an "automatic re-election machine," with lawmakers using all the powers and perquisites of office with the single-minded goal of staying in office.

Setting fixed limits on tenure, these critics said, offered the only way to increase electoral competition and restore public accountability.

Term-Limit Movement

Term limits for Congress have been advanced throughout U.S. history.

One House member during the First Congress proposed that representatives be limited to six years' service over an eight-year period and senators be limited to five one-year terms during any six-year period. The plan never came to a vote.

In fact, Congress has voted on a term-limit proposal only once, in 1948, when it was considering the 22nd Amendment, limiting presidents to two terms. Sen. W. Lee "Pappy" O'Daniel, D-Texas, introduced an alternative plan to limit the president and members of Congress to a single six-year term. It failed, 82-1.

Support for term limits was greater outside Congress. President Harry S Truman endorsed 12-year term limits for lawmakers in 1951. President Dwight D. Eisenhower backed the idea after he left the White House. A Gallup Poll in 1964 found a 49 percent plurality in favor of term limits; support increased to 59 percent in polls taken in 1977 and 1981.

Congress finally gave the idea official attention in the late 1970s. Lawmakers had introduced a flurry of proposed constitutional amendments aimed at increasing congressional effectiveness either by limiting tenure, increasing House terms to four years, or both. A Senate Judiciary subcommittee held hearings on the term-limit issue in 1978. Proponents included two senators sponsoring term-limit amendments who are, coincidentally, both retiring this year. Republican John C. Danforth of Missouri and Democrat Dennis DeConcini of Arizona. A panel of political scientists called to testify on the proposal unanimously opposed it. No further action was taken.

Ten years later, the Republican Party platform in 1988 called for limiting congressional terms, but the issue received almost no attention during the campaign. In early 1989, however, two Republican political consultants — Eddie Mahe Jr. and LaDonna Lee — created the first national term-limits group, Americans to Limit Congressional Terms. Two more national groups were formed in late 1990: Citizens for Congressional Reform, bankrolled by two Wichita, Kan., billionaire oilmen with libertarian views, Charles G. and David H. Koch; and Americans Back in Charge, the successor to a Colorado group founded by a Republican state senator, Terry Considine. [20]

Sweeping the Country

It was local politics, however, that put the term-limits issue before voters in its first three electoral outings in fall 1990. In Oklahoma, a disgruntled political activist and one-time legislator capitalized on public discontent with the state Legislature to win approval in September of an initiative to limit lawmakers to 12 years in office. In California, Republicans pushed state term limits to bring down a powerful Democratic lawmaker, Assembly Speaker Willie Brown. In Colorado, Considine, who had run unsuccessfully for the U.S. Senate four years earlier, used a term-limits initiative to keep his name before the voters for a future statewide race.

The disparate genealogies of the state initiatives produced the same result: victory for term limits in all three states. And Considine had added a distinctive touch to his measure: a provision to limit the tenure of the

The Power of Incumbency

The re-election rate of House members has been at or near 90 percent in every election since 1946. Senate races are more volatile, but the re-election rate for senators has been above 70 percent in all but three elections since 1960.

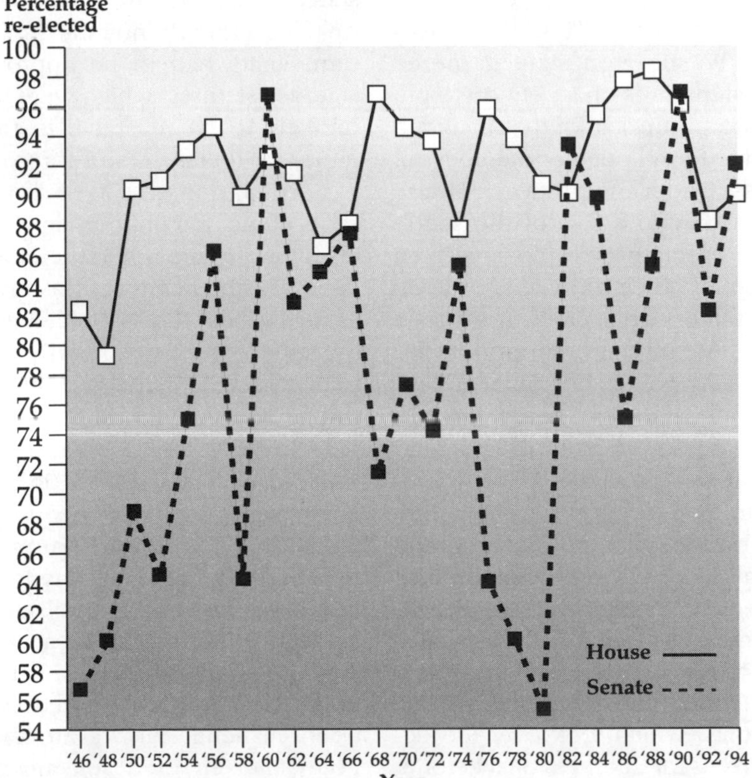

Source: Norman J. Ornstein, Thomas E. Mann and Michael J. Malbin, Vital Statistics on Congress, 1993-1994, *1994.*

Presidents Harry S Truman and Dwight D. Eisenhower both backed term limits.

members of Colorado's congressional delegation to 12 years as well. With no organized opposition in the state, the measure won 70 percent of the vote.

A year later, in 1991, the energized term-limits movement suffered a setback, largely because of overreaching and overconfidence. Term-limit advocates in Washington state garnered enough signatures on a petition to put a measure on the ballot that included retroactive term limits for members of Congress. Under the proposal, House Speaker Foley and five of the state's other representatives would have been forced out of office by the end of 1994. Foley campaigned actively against the measure. Meanwhile, supporters allowed themselves to be outspent 2-to-1 in the fall campaign. Voters rejected the measure, 54 percent to 46 percent.

The setback proved to be only temporary. In 1992, congressional term limits were on the ballot in 14 states — and won in all 14. The margins ranged from 52 percent in Washington, where a rewritten measure called for prospective instead of retroactive limits, to 77 percent in Florida and Wyoming. At U.S. Term Limits, which took over the defunct Citizens for Congressional Reform, the reaction was exultant. "It's a 14-state sweep, better than we ever hoped for," said spokesman Jeff Lanagan. [21]

Hitting Obstacles

After the ballot-box sweep, however, the term-limit movement faced three imposing obstacles. First, the initiative strategy was nearing the end of its course since only about half the states allowed voter-initiated measures on the ballot. [22] In non-initiative states, term limits had to be approved by state legislatures, which were thought unlikely to be receptive to the idea either for themselves or for Congress.

Second, Congress itself showed no signs of moving on term-limit proposals soon. In late 1993, the House Judiciary Subcommittee on Civil and Constitutional Rights yielded to growing support for term limits by agreeing to air the issue in the first hearings on the topic since 1978. The hearings, held in November 1993 and this past June, gave some junior Republican lawmakers the chance to endorse term limits. But committee Chairman Don Edwards, D-Calif., and Hyde of Illinois, the ranking Republican, both strongly criticized the idea.

Third — and most important — congressional term limits faced constitutional challenges. In Washington state, Foley himself filed suit against the voter-approved term-limit proposal. A similar suit was filed in Arkansas by the state's League of Women Voters.

Early this year, judges ruled against both measures. In Seattle, U.S. District Court Judge William Dwyer ruled Feb. 10 that the Washington ballot measure improperly attempted to add a new qualification for Congress to those set out in the Constitution. [23] Less than a month later, the Arkansas Supreme Court reached the same conclusion in a splintered 5-2 decision. [24]

U.S. Term Limits promptly asked the Supreme Court to review both rulings. At the same time, the group continued working to place term-limit measures on state ballots.

Both efforts bore fruit. In June, the Supreme Court agreed to hear the Arkansas case. The justices declined to review the Washington case, however, and left it pending before the 9th U.S. Circuit Court of Appeals.

By summer's end, term-limit supporters had also qualified ballot measures in nine states. Alaska, Idaho, Maine, Massachusetts, Nebraska, Nevada and Oklahoma all were to vote on congressional term limits for the first time, while Colorado and Utah had measures to change the 12-year term-limits measures for House members approved previously to six years and eight years, respectively. At the same time, term-limit groups moved into a new phase of their campaign by making term limits an issue in House and Senate campaigns from coast to coast. ■

CURRENT SITUATION

The 1994 Elections

Term-limit supporters turned congressional longevity, political clout and opposition to term limits into potent campaign weapons against veteran Democratic lawmakers in the

Continued on p. 1026

At Issue:

Is Arkansas' congressional term-limit initiative constitutional?

yes

FROM BRIEF OF U.S. TERM LIMITS

Amendment 73 does not set a qualification for office. Certainly it was advocated by supporters of turnover in elective offices, and is designed to lessen the overwhelming election advantages . . . that are enjoyed by multi-term incumbents. But it does so only by not continuing to print such incumbents' names on ballots. It does not disqualify them from running, being elected, or serving in office. . . .

The holding of the Arkansas court is that not printing a multi-term incumbent's name on the ballot amounts to a prohibition on holding office. But both history and the record in this case fail to support that assertion. Members of the House and Senate have been elected by write-in, including a Representative from Arkansas. . . .

States are not free, of course, to pass any ballot restrictions they want. State ballot-access laws can properly be, and regularly are, subjected to constitutional testing — but under the familiar standards of the Fourteenth Amendment. To . . . equate a state ballot regulation with a disqualification for office would open to Article I challenge the state primary laws and hundreds of other provisions by which fifty states regulate congressional elections.

Even if the Arkansas Supreme Court were correct in its assertion that Amendment 73 added qualifications for holding congressional office, still Article I would not be violated. Article I, in both [section] 2 and [section] 4, explicitly assigns the States broad power over congressional elections. It restricts such state regulations only by establishing Congress' power to annul them. . . . Its disqualification provisions, in Article I, [sections] 2 and 3, set minimums, but contain no restrictions on state laws. . . .

It is no accident that the Constitution's text is barren of the prohibition the Arkansas Supreme Court implied. A clause that would have made the disqualifications in Article I, [section] 2 exclusive was deleted from an early draft. . . .

What the Constitution allowed the States to do was demonstrated by the added qualifications for Congress that over half of them promptly enacted. Immediately upon ratifying the Constitution, States passed laws requiring that Representatives be district residents; establishing nominating and screening processes for candidates; and even requiring that Representatives be landed property owners. . . .

It would be late in the day, given the volume of contemporaneous state, and even federal, disqualification legislation and the ballot-restriction and disqualification laws in dozens of jurisdictions, now to hold that it all was and is unconstitutional. . . . The voters of Arkansas were not altering the structure of the federal government. They were simply trying . . . to remove one of the many election advantages that long-term incumbents enjoy. . . .

no

FROM BRIEF OF REP. RAY THORNTON, ET AL.

Article I of the Constitution creates the national legislature and comprehensively regulates its composition and selection. As part of this comprehensive scheme, the so-called "Qualifications Clauses" prescribe the uniform and exclusive attributes for membership in each House of Congress. . . .

Although Article I grants States authority to prescribe the qualifications of electors, it delegates no similar authority to the States (or to Congress) concerning the qualifications of who may be elected. . . .

[T]he text and structure of Article I leave no room for States to establish additional qualifications for membership in Congress. Given the uniquely national concerns at stake in the composition of a national legislature, the Tenth Amendment can reserve no authority to the States in this area. . . . Rather, Article I's comprehensive regulation completely pre-empts State authority to prescribe the characteristics of federal legislators.

The history surrounding the drafting, ratification and early interpretation of the Constitution shows overwhelmingly that the Framers intended what the text and structure plainly reveal — *viz.*, that the qualifications set forth in Article I are exclusive. Writing at a time when state constitutions prescribed numerous and varying qualifications, the Framers explicitly considered and rejected a number of requirements, including a rotation or term-limit proposal. . . .

This Court's precedents confirm that the constitutional qualifications are exclusive. Relying on the foregoing history, this Court has held that the *only* qualifications that may be imposed for membership in Congress are those specified in the Constitution. . . .

Petitioners' suggestion that Amendment 73 is permissible because it does not bar from Congress an incumbent who somehow manages to win as a write-in is fundamentally flawed. . . . Whether a law creates an additional qualification is to be determined not by resort to narrow dictionary definitions, but by reference to the essential democratic principles that the Framers sought to enshrine in Article I — namely, that the door to the national legislature should be open to all and that voters should be allowed to vote for whomever they please. Judged under this standard, a ballot-exclusion law that disqualifies persons based upon prior service is plainly an improper qualification.

Nor can Amendment 73 be justified as a mere ballot-access regulation. Unlike earlier laws that this Court has sustained, Amendment 73 is not an even-handed regulation designed to facilitate voter choice, nor does it regulate the conduct of state officeholders. Rather, the term-limit law manipulates election procedures in order to disable an identifiable class of persons from service in the federal legislature. Such manipulation is entirely outside the authority of States under the Times, Places and Manner Clause.

Continued from p. 1024

1994 midterm elections.

In Texas, a mailer sent to voters shortly before the election complained that 42-year House veteran Brooks had served in Congress "longer than the kings of England."

In Illinois, radio ads linked 18-termer Rostenkowski to a litany of political troubles from "midnight pay raises" to "lavish perks and privileges."

And in Washington state, television ads said Foley had "sued his own constituents" by challenging the state's term-limits initiative in court.

By election night's end, term-limit supporters were taking credit for the defeat of all three men. "What we saw last night was the power of an idea," Oregon businessman Paul Farago told a news conference the next day. Farago's group, Americans for Limited Terms, spent more than $1 million — including $300,000 in Illinois and Washington and $100,000 in Texas — on so-called voter-education drives aimed at publicizing the opposition of incumbent lawmakers such as Foley, Rostenkowski and Brooks to term limits.

Term limits were not the only factor in all three races. Rostenkowski carried the baggage of a 17-count federal indictment. Brooks angered gun owners by voting for an assault-weapons ban. And Foley was seen as having lost touch with his district.

Political analyst Stuart Rothenberg said the issue was not as critical in individual races as supporters claimed. "I don't think it was the cornerstone of campaigns," says Rothenberg. "I think it was part of a basket of congressional-reform issues that Republicans used — and used effectively — as part of their anti-Congress themes."

Term-limit supporters also fell short in many other races. Term-limit opponents were defeated in only six out of the 17 congressional districts where Americans for Limited Terms ran ads. Republican term-limit supporters won Senate races in two of the three states the group targeted: Michigan and Oklahoma. But in Massachusetts, Democratic Sen. Edward M. Kennedy, a 32-year veteran, beat a Republican challenger who campaigned with "Term Limits for Teddy" bumper stickers.

Overall, however, term-limit supporters claimed that 19 lawmakers opposed to restricting congressional tenure had been defeated by pro-limits candidates. And they vowed to target anti-term-limit lawmakers in the future. "Any member of the 104th Congress who wants to be re-elected should be a supporter of term limits," Farago warned.

But Rothenberg questions whether opposition to term limits will be a political liability in two years. "Pointing to this election as proof of that is poppycock," he says.

Success in State Balloting

The Republicans' capture of Congress overshadowed the term-limit movement's renewed success in state ballot initiatives. Voters approved congressional term-limit measures in all but one of the eight states — Utah — where the issue appeared on the ballot.

The margins of victory for the seven initiatives ranged from 51 percent in Colorado and Massachusetts to 70 percent in Nevada. Oklahoma voters also approved a congressional term-limits initiative in September by a 2-to-1 margin.

All but one of the newly approved measures called for limiting House members to six years in office and senators to 12. The Massachusetts initiative called for eight years for representatives. Colorado's measure tightened the 12-year limit for House members contained in its 1990 term-limit initiative.

Term-limit supporters dismissed the significance of the defeat of the Utah measure, noting that it included a controversial election runoff provision. In addition, the measure would have given the current members of the state's congressional delegation a lifetime exemption from term limits. Jacob called the initiative "phony term limits," even though his group had supported it during the campaign. The measure failed 35 percent to 65 percent.

Nevertheless, the Utah Legislature had already enacted a form of congressional term limits. State lawmakers this spring approved a measure that would set 12-year limits for representatives and senators if 24 other states vote to impose similar restrictions. A similar triggering feature was also included in two of the state initiatives approved Nov. 8 — Alaska and Nevada.

The Nov. 8 voting marked the virtual end of the ballot-measure strategy for term-limit supporters. Mississippi is scheduled to vote on a combined congressional, state and local term-limit measure in November 1995, but that is the last remaining state where a congressional initiative can be put on the ballot.

Term-limit groups in New Hampshire and Virginia already have begun mapping campaigns to lobby state legislatures for congressional limits. Jacob predicts that New Hampshire could become the first state to approve term limits by legislative action sometime next year.

But the same constitutional issues that threaten the state ballot measures could also doom any legislatively enacted term limits. So, for now, the term-limit battle shifts to nine unelected justices who are subject to no term limits at all.

Supreme Court Case

As a presidential candidate in January 1992, then-Gov. Bill Clinton said he was "personally opposed to term limits for Congress because I think it hurts small states, and it takes power away from the people." [25]

But the five-term Arkansas governor also said the issue was for the people to decide. "If people want to vote them in, it's their perfect right to do it."

Ten months later, Arkansas voters did just that: They approved, by a 3-2 margin, a 1992 ballot measure that bars from the ballot incumbent U.S. representatives after six years in office and bars incumbent senators after 12 years.

Now Clinton is asking the U.S. Supreme Court to rule the Arkansas measure unconstitutional. Solicitor General Drew S. Days III notified the court in August that the administration wanted to join the constitutional challenge to the Arkansas term-limits measure, calling it "a particular threat to the federal system."[26]

Term-limit supporters immediately assailed the administration's stance. "Taxpayers are being forced to pay tax dollars to the federal government to overturn their votes for term limits," said Jacob.

When the administration filed its legal brief in the case in October, Days echoed opponents' arguments that neither Congress nor the states had power to restrict lawmakers' tenure. "By fixing the qualifications for congressional service in the Constitution," Days argued, "the Framers prevented state legislatures from altering the popular character of the House by manipulating its membership."

Term-limit supporters acknowledge that most experts predict the court will vote to strike down the state-passed measures. "It's an uphill fight in that the Supreme Court has tended to side with the federal government," says Stephen Safranek, an assistant professor at the University of Detroit Mercy School of Law. "They've tended to say more power to the courts and more power to the Congress."

The most likely votes to uphold term limits, court-watchers speculate, will be from justices sympathetic to states' rights, including Chief Justice William H. Rehnquist and Justices Sandra Day O'Connor, Antonin Scalia and Clarence Thomas. Safranek, who filed a brief supporting term limits on behalf of Michigan's Republican governor, John Engler, says he thinks O'Connor and Justice Anthony M. Kennedy are critical to forging a majority for his side.

The more liberal-leaning justices — John Paul Stevens, David H. Souter and President Clinton's two appointees, Ruth Bader Ginsburg and Stephen G. Breyer — are viewed as less sympathetic to the states in cases involving federalism issues. But Neal Devins, who teaches constitutional law at the College of William and Mary's Marshall-Wythe School of Law in Williamsburg, Va., says he thinks all the justices' votes are "up for grabs."

"This is not an ideological battle," Devins says. "I don't think you can count to five in terms of sure votes against term limits." ■

OUTLOOK

Will Congress Act?

Term-limit supporters profess optimism about the Supreme Court case. "I think we're going to win," says Jacob. But legal experts who follow the court predict the justices will invalidate the state measures.

"I would be very surprised if they did anything different," says Dennis Hutchinson, a professor at the University of Chicago Law School.

"It's a hard question, but I'm inclined to think that the court will strike it down," says Susan Bloch, who teaches a Supreme Court seminar at Georgetown University law school.

Even before the court rules, however, Congress will come under intense pressure to act on the issue. "We're going to get real term limits out of Congress," says Howard Rich, president of U.S. Term Limits, "and it does not depend on what seven men and two women in black robes say."

Republicans captured Congress after some 300 GOP candidates for House and Senate seats signed a "Contract With America" that promised, among other things, a vote on term limits within the first 100 days of a Republican Congress. Jacob says term-limit supporters will press Republicans to honor that commitment. "You can bet we'll be there, holding their feet to the fire," Jacob says.

They could encounter difficulties, however, from the new Republican chairmen of both Judiciary committees. The House panel will likely be led by Hyde of Illinois, who filed a brief urging the Supreme Court to

For More Information

Brookings Institution, 1775 Massachusetts Ave., N.W., Washington, D.C. 20036; (202) 797-6000. The think tank's director of governmental studies, Thomas Mann, is one of the most outspoken national experts on Congress to oppose term limits. William Frenzel, a former Republican member of Congress and a supporter of term limits, is a guest scholar.

League of Women Voters, 1730 M St., N.W., Washington, D.C. 20036; (202) 429-1965. The 91,000-member voter-education and lobbying group has opposed term-limit initiatives in state elections and in court.

Term Limits Legal Institute, 900 2nd St., N.E., Suite 200A, Washington, D.C. 20002; (202) 371-0450. The institute, successor to an earlier pro-term-limits group, Americans Back in Charge, has worked on legal challenges to term-limit measures for Congress and state legislators.

U.S. Term Limits, 1511 K St., N.W., Suite 540, Washington, D.C. 20005; (202) 393-6440. The 70,000-member group has come to dominate the national term-limit movement since 1992.

strike down the state-passed measures. The new Senate Judiciary chairman, Orrin G. Hatch, opposed term limits in his home state of Utah.

In addition, many lawmakers may find the six-year limit favored by U.S. Term Limits too restrictive. The most popular of the term-limits amendments introduced in the 103rd Congress — sponsored by Rep. Bill McCollum, R-Fla. — set a 12-year limit for House members.

Whatever the figure, political experts continue to doubt that advocates can produce the two-thirds majority needed in Congress for passage of a term-limits constitutional amendment. "It's going to be a hell of a heavy lift to get it through Congress," political science Professor Benjamin said after the election. "I think there are sufficient numbers of well-placed persons in both houses who can prevent it from being passed."

Moreover, term-limit opponents are now using the high turnover in the House in the past two congressional elections to argue that mandatory tenure restrictions are unnecessary. (*See graph, p. 1015.*) "So who needs term limits?" columnist Broder wrote. "The voters on Tuesday cleaned house the old-fashioned way." [27]

But supporters say term limits are still needed to counteract the political advantages of incumbency. Jacob noted that even with the widespread criticism of career lawmakers this year, the re-election rate for congressional incumbents was still 90 percent. "The strength of incumbents' advantage is still there," he says. "The fact that powerful incumbents who try to block term limits get beat doesn't seem to be an argument against term limits."

Some critical observers, however, say the term-limits movement has diverted attention from more meaningful steps to increase electoral competition or to improve the performance of Congress generally. "I'd like to see all that energy channeled into a broader coalition to see what's really wrong with the system and how we can fix it," says Linda Fowler, a professor of political science at Syracuse University, who testified against term limits in the House subcommittee hearings in June.

In fact, the 103rd Congress considered but failed to adopt a number of proposals to reorganize its operations and revise laws on campaign finance and lobbying disclosure. A Republican-led filibuster blocked final action in September on a bill designed to limit campaign spending and provide partial public funding for campaigns. Another GOP filibuster prevented passage of a lobby-reform bill that would have prevented lawmakers from accepting meals, gifts and entertainment from lobbyists.

But term-limit supporters scoff at the notion that they have slowed the pace of reform. "No one has stood in Congress' way of passing reform," says Jacob. "Term limits, which is the reform that's needed, is also the reform that has created pressure for other reforms. The problem is that the leadership of Congress was simply not listening." ■

Notes

[1] Utah's term-limit measure will take effect when at least 24 other states approve similar restrictions. For background, see "Term Limits," *The CQ Researcher,* Jan. 10, 1992, pp. 1-24.

[2] "The Derek McGinty Show," WAMU-FM, Washington, D.C., Sept. 28, 1994.

[3] The cases were *Thorsted v. Gregoire* (Washington) and *U.S. Term Limits v. Hill* (Arkansas). In addition, in *Stumpf v. Lau,* the Nevada Supreme Court in 1992 blocked a state vote on a congressional term-limits measure on constitutional and state election-law grounds. A new term-limit measure was put on the Nevada ballot in 1994, without legal challenge, and approved by voters Nov. 8.

[4] *The Wall Street Journal,* April 17, 1992, p. A12. In a survey in October 1993, the same poll found 76 percent in favor, 20 percent opposed and 4 percent not sure.

[5] George F. Will, *Restoration: Term Limits and the Recovery of Deliberative Democracy* (1992), p. 227.

[6] *The Washington Post,* Jan. 9, 1994, p. C7.

[7] *Congressional Quarterly Weekly Report,* Oct. 15, 1994, p. 2970.

[8] Mark P. Petracca, "Rotation in Office: The History of an Idea," in Gerald Benjamin and Michael J. Malbin (eds.), *Limiting Legislative Terms* (1992), pp. 20-26.

[9] *Ibid.,* pp. 26-28. Petracca says three states — Delaware, New York and Virginia — required rotation for members of the state Senate. In a friend of the court brief filed in the U.S. Supreme Court by Rep. Henry J. Hyde, R-Ill., in opposition to term limits, only one state — Virginia — is listed as requiring rotation of state senators in the 1770s. The most detailed listing of Colonial and Revolutionary era provisions for rotation in office is found in Arkansas' brief in the case; it includes a term-limit provision for legislators in Pennsylvania and Virginia, but not in Delaware or New York. See *Brief for State Petitioner.*

[10] *Ibid.,* pp. 29-30.

[11] Quoted in *Brief for Congressman Ray Thornton,* p. 18.

[12] Quoted in *Brief for U.S. Term Limits,* p. 41.

[13] Will, *op. cit.,* p. 220.

[14] John R. Hibbing, *Congressional Careers: Contours of Life in the House of Representatives* (1991), p. 3.

[15] Will, *op. cit.,* pp. 76, 78-80.

[16] Hibbing, *op. cit.,* pp. 1-2. See also *Congress A to Z* (1993), p. 264.

[17] Hibbing, *op. cit.,* pp. 108-128.

[18] Coyne is a former Republican congressman from Pennsylvania; Fund is a *Wall Street Journal* editorial writer.

[19] For background, see "Political Scandals," *The CQ Researcher,* May 27, 1994, pp. 457-480.

[20] For the early history of the term-limits movement, see Stuart Rothenberg, "Transplanting Term Limits: Political Mobilization and Grass Roots Politics," in Benjamin and Malbin, *op. cit.,* pp. 97-113.

[21] *The Washington Post,* Nov. 4, 1992, p. A31; see also *The New York Times,* Nov. 5, 1992, p. B8.

[22] For background, see "Initiatives: True Democracy or Bad Lawmaking?" *Editorial Research Reports,* Aug. 17, 1990, pp. 461-476.

[23] See *The Washington Post,* Feb. 11, 1994, p. A1, and *The New York Times,* Feb. 11, 1994, p. A20.

[24] *Congressional Quarterly Weekly Report,* March 12, 1994, p. 622, and Oct. 1, 1994, pp. 2802-2804.

[25] NBC's "Meet the Press," Jan. 5, 1992.

[26] See *The Washington Times,* Sept. 8, 1994, p. A4; *The New York Times,* Sept. 9, 1994, p. A20.

[27] *The Washington Post,* Nov. 10, 1994, p. A25.

Bibliography

Selected Sources Used

Books

Benjamin, Gerald, and Michael J. Malbin (eds.), *Limiting Legislative Terms,* CQ Press, 1992.

The book features contributions from 11 academic experts on legislative term limits originally presented at a conference sponsored by the Rockefeller Institute of Government in October 1991.

Coyne, James K., and John H. Fund, *Cleaning House: America's Campaign for Term Limits,* Regnery Gateway, 1992.

Coyne, a former member of Congress and founder of the now-defunct Americans to Limit Congressional Terms, and Fund, an editorial writer for *The Wall Street Journal,* published this forceful, sometimes polemical tract in favor of term limits just before the November 1992 election.

Crane, Edward H., and Roger Pilon (eds.), *The Politics and Law of Term Limits,* Cato Institute, 1994.

The book includes contributions from 11 experts representing both sides of the term-limits debate presented at a conference sponsored by the pro-term-limits Cato Institute in December 1993.

Hibbing, John R., *Congressional Careers: Contours of Life in the House of Representatives,* University of North Carolina Press, 1991.

Hibbing, a political scientist at the University of Nebraska, examines the political behavior of members of the U.S. House of Representatives based on detailed statistical analyses covering four decades. The book includes an 11-page bibliography.

Ornstein, Norman J., Thomas E. Mann, and Michael J. Malbin, *Vital Statistics on Congress, 1993-1994,* Congressional Quarterly, 1994.

This biennial volume presents comprehensive statistics on members of Congress, congressional operations and elections, campaign finance and other topics. Ornstein is a senior fellow at the American Enterprise Institute; Mann is director of the governmental-studies program at the Brookings Institution; Malbin is professor of political science at the State University of New York-Albany.

Will, George F., *Restoration: Term Limits and the Recovery of Deliberative Democracy,* The Free Press, 1992.

Political columnist Will uses history and current events to present a strongly argued case for congressional term limits.

Articles

Armor, John C., "'Foreshadowing' Effects of Term Limits: California's Example for Congress," *U.S. Term Limits,* June 1994.

Armor, a resident scholar with U.S. Term Limits, argues that term limits have had a positive impact on the California Legislature since their enactment in 1990.

Hills, Roderick M., Jr., "A Defense of State Constitutional Limits on Federal Congressional Terms," *University of Pittsburgh Law Review,* Vol. 53, No. 1, fall 1991, pp. 97-151.

Hills, who now teaches at the University of Michigan Law School, wrote one of the most comprehensive law-review articles in support of the constitutionality of state-imposed term limits for members of Congress.

Lowenstein, Daniel Hays, "Are Congressional Term Limits Constitutional," *Harvard Journal of Law & Public Policy,* Vol. 18, No. 1, fall 1994, pp. 301-372.

Lowenstein, a law professor at the University of California-Los Angeles, argues that states cannot impose term limits on members of Congress.

Petracca, Mark P., and Karen Moore, "Testing Limits: The Experience With Municipal Term Limits in Orange County, Calif.," paper presented to Western Political Science Association, Pasadena, Calif., March 18-20, 1994.

Petracca, an associate professor of political science at the University of California-Irvine, found evidence that term limits improved government in California's Orange County.

Rausch, John David, "Testing Legislative Term Limitations: The San Mateo Board of County Supervisors as Laboratory," *National Civic Review,* spring 1993, pp. 149-156.

Rausch, an assistant professor of political science at Fairmount State University in West Virginia, says term limits have been in effect in California's San Mateo County for 14 years, but have had little impact on government.

Weisberger, Bernard A., "Term Limits? Not Again!" *American Heritage,* April 1993, pp. 24-25.

Weisberger, a contributing editor of *American Heritage,* briefly surveys the history of congressional term limit proposals from the Constitutional Convention up to the present.

Reports and Studies

Mann, Thomas E., and Norman J. Ornstein (dirs.), *Renewing Congress: A First Report,* American Enterprise Institute and Brookings Institution, 1992; *Renewing Congress: A Second Report,* 1993.

Mann, director of governmental studies at the Brookings Institution, and Ornstein, resident scholar at the American Enterprise Institute, serve as directors of a joint project aimed at improving congressional effectiveness. The reports do not discuss term-limit proposals, but critically examine congressional operations and recommend a number of changes ranging from consolidating committees and reducing staffs to providing for partial public funding of campaigns.

The Next Step

Additional information from UMI's Newspaper & Periodical Abstracts database

Anti-term-limit Sentiment

Ely, Jane, "A great argument against term limits," ***Houston Chronicle,*** **Sept. 25, 1994, p. C2.**
Jane Ely comments that the defeat of Oklahoma Rep. Mike Synar, an eight-term incumbent, illustrates why term-limits are not needed: The voters can always limit the terms of elected officials by voting them out of office.

Herschensohn, Bruce, "Voters, not laws, should set terms," ***Insight on the News,*** **April 11, 1994, pp. 23-25.**
Reasons why term limits would further erode voters' choices in electing their officials are discussed.

"No need for term limits," ***St. Louis Post-Dispatch,*** **May 1, 1994, p. B2.**
An editorial states that there is no need for congressional term limits since the number of retirements in Congress has increased dramatically in recent years.

Congressional Careers

Cohen, Richard E., "When seniority is a two-edged sword," ***National Journal,*** **Sept. 10, 1994, p. 2097.**
Rep. Jack Brooks, D-Texas, and Rep. Neal Smith, D-Iowa, have become symbols for the term-limit movement, and their positions in the House are in danger as the Nov. 8, 1994, elections loom closer. The manner in which their opponents are using their seniority in the House against them on the campaign trail is discussed.

Greene, Donna, "The 'ins' and 'outs' of 2 congressional races," ***The New York Times,*** **Oct. 9, 1994, p. WC1.**
The races between Republican Andrew C. Hartzell Jr. and incumbent Rep. Nita M. Lowey, D-N.Y., in the 18th District and between Democrat Gregory Julian and incumbent Rep. Benjamin Gilman, R-N.Y., in the 20th District are discussed. Hartzell and Julian both have endorsed term limits, which Lowey and Gilman oppose.

Hook, Janet, "Two careers confuse term limit debate," ***Congressional Quarterly Weekly Report,*** **March 19, 1994, p. 702.**
The congressional careers of Rep. William H. Natcher, D-Ken., and Sen. George J. Mitchell, D-Maine, are discussed. The careers of Natcher and Mitchell shatter the unflattering image of congressional stereotypes deployed on both sides of the term-limit debate.

The Constitution and Term Limits

"Administration asks to join suit against term limits," ***Congressional Quarterly Weekly Report,*** **Sept. 10, 1994, p. 2544.**
The Clinton administration has asked the Supreme Court for permission to join the suit against congressional term limitations. The administration claims such limits violate the Constitution.

Mitchell, Cleta Deatherage, "Arrogant senators snub taxpayers," ***Insight on the News,*** **Aug. 22, 1994, pp. 36-37.**
Senate leaders from both parties managed to pass a resolution that allows the Senate legal counsel to represent Dale Bumpers, D-Ark., in a term-limitation case that will be argued before the Supreme Court.

Previdi, Robert, "The people--Not term limits — Must decide who governs," ***Presidential Studies Quarterly,*** **summer 1994, pp. 667-668.**
An editorial asserts that term limits are a poor answer to the perceived problem of corruption or incompetence in office.

"What will be the effect of term limits?" ***USA Today: The Magazine of the American Scene,*** **April 1994, p. 3.**
Although several states have term-limit legislation, the constitutionality of state-imposed term limits has not yet been established.

Pro-term-limit Sentiment

Mitchell, Cleta Deatherage, "Limit terms and let others lead," ***Insight on the News,*** **April 11, 1994, pp. 20-23.**
Contrary to the Founders' intent, Congress has become an arrogant, power-hungry ruling class, Mitchell writes.

Moore, Stephen, "To achieve fiscal reform, we need term limits," ***Insight on the News,*** **July 18, 1994, pp. 38-39.**
Congress has frustrated every attempt to cut the federal budget, even though all such initiatives have had strong public support. The chances for real fiscal reform are remote unless term limits are imposed, Moore writes.

Runyon, Keith L., "Limiting terms will aid democracy," ***Chicago Tribune,*** **Oct. 3, 1994, p. 12.**
In a letter to the editor, Keith L. Runyon of Citizens Changing America comments on a letter written by Ira Glover published in the Sept. 3, 1994, *Tribune,* saying that Glover's support of unlimited terms for political office-holders is an alarming denial of the inherent weaknesses of democracy as it is implemented in the U.S.

Public Opinion

Nelson, Michael, "Why Americans hate politics and

politicians: Term limitations and a balanced budget," ***Vital Speeches of the Day,*** **Sept. 1, 1994, pp. 693-698.**

Public cynicism and indifference toward politics and politicians in the U.S. are examined, focusing on the utility of passing a balanced-budget amendment and term-limit legislation for members of Congress. Americans must try to start honoring politics and politicians if they want honorable people to consider running for office.

State and Local Initiatives

Ehrenhalt, Alan, "If term limits are the answer, what's the question?" ***Governing,*** **May 1994, pp. 7-8.**

South Pasadena, Fla., city Commissioner Fred Held was affected by the city's term-limitation laws and forced to resign after nine years on the commission. Problems within the commission ended with Held being elected the city's mayor two days after resigning.

Hook, Janet, "Arkansas case a crucible in term limit debate," ***Congressional Quarterly Weekly Report,*** **June 25, 1994, pp. 1679.**

On June 20, 1994, the Supreme Court agreed to decide whether states can constitutionally limit the number of terms a member can serve. The court's decision to review the Arkansas case is discussed.

Idelson, Holly and Sondra J. Nixon, "Review to be turning point for term limits issue, " ***Congressional Quarterly Weekly Report,*** **Oct. 1, 1994, pp. 2802-2806.**

New laws in 16 states and perhaps a constitutional amendment are riding on the decision about the length of service of individuals in Congress. During fall 1994, the U.S. Supreme Court will review a decision by the Arkansas Supreme Court that struck down that state's term limits as unconstitutional.

Leonard, Lee, "The end of an era in Ohio," ***State Legislatures,*** **July 1994, pp. 24-29.**

Ohio House Speaker Vern Riffe's retirement, along with the retirements of seven other veteran lawmakers, is discussed. Caucus dissension, a GOP-leaning reapportionment map and term-limit legislation were the main factors that led him to his decision to retire.

Moss, Bill, Nancy Rhyme and Brenda Erickson, " Rotation: One chance for the brass ring," ***State Legislatures,*** **July 1994, pp. 17-23.**

Florida's tradition of rotating leaders in the state House and Senate is examined, focusing on how tradition limits them to one two-year term. Although term limits won't change the tradition, the training time for leaders being groomed to assume speaker positions will be shortened considerably.

"State initiatives: Term limits, taxes," ***Nation's Business,*** **October 1994, p. 34.**

On Nov. 8, 1994, voters in eight states will act on ballot initiatives to limit the terms of their congressional and state lawmakers.

Thomas, Stephen, "Backers of term limits say some judges tainted," ***Chicago Defender,*** **Sept. 10, 1994, p. 5.**

Term-limit proponents are expected to petition the Illinois Supreme Court to rehear the case in which a referendum on the matter was ruled unconstitutional. Activists have argued that three of the seven judges should not be involved in the decision because they have been members of the Chicago Bar Association, which has been fighting the term limits.

Term Limits and Political Parties

Anderson, Jack and Michael Binstein, "Tom Foley on the line," ***The Washington Post,*** **Oct. 2, 1994, p. C7.**

Jack Anderson and Michael Binstein comment on House Speaker Tom Foley's decision to file suit against term limits in Congress, even though the move was certain to hurt him politically.

Barone, Michael, "The dawn of 'just say no' politics," ***U.S. News & World Report,*** **Sept. 19, 1994, p. 49.**

In 1994, candidates for public office are calling for strict limits on government and politicians, including term limits and caps on public spending. The implications of this trend for Democrats are ominous.

Baxter, Tom, "GOP hopefuls vow reform if they win power," ***Atlanta Constitution,*** **Sept. 28, 1994, p. A6.**

With Rep. Newt Gingrich,R-Ga., cheering them on, some 300 Republican congressional candidates pledged to support a legislative platform that includes term limits, tax breaks and a balanced-budget amendment.

Calmes, Jackie, "GOP 'contract' vows action on crime, tax cuts, welfare and term limits," ***The Wall Street Journal,*** **Sept. 28, 1994, p. A5.**

House Republicans, hoping to spur big gains in November, rallied at the Capitol steps to highlight a voter "contract" that vows action on tax cuts, crime, welfare and term limits.

Gilmour, John B. and Paul Rothstein, "Term limitation in a dynamic model of partisan balance," ***American Journal of Political Science,*** **August 1994, pp. 770-796.**

A model that captures the direct effect of term limits is presented. An analysis identifies the condition that determines which party is favored by term limits.

Trumbull, Mark, "More Democrat blues: House Speaker may lose," ***Christian Science Monitor,*** **Oct. 4, 1994, p1.**

In 1994, Democratic House Speaker Tom Foley faces the toughest race of his political career. Residents of Washington were upset by Foley's recent filing of a lawsuit to overturn a state ballot initiative limiting congressional terms to six consecutive years in the House and 12 in the Senate.

Back Issues

Great Research on Current Issues Starts Right Here...Recent topics covered by The CQ Researcher are listed below. Before May 1991, reports were published under the name of Editorial Research Reports.®

MAY 1993
Cults in America
Preventing Teen Pregnancy
Software Piracy
National Parks

JUNE 1993
Food Safety
Prostitution
Childhood Immunizations
National Service

JULY 1993
Electric Cars
Population Growth
Downward Mobility
Intelligence Testing

AUGUST 1993
Mental Illness
Bilingual Education
Foreign Policy Burden
School Funding

SEPTEMBER 1993
Suburban Crime
Public Housing
Supreme Court Preview
Immigration Reform

OCTOBER 1993
Airline Safety
Disaster Response
Science in the Courtroom
The Glass Ceiling

NOVEMBER 1993
Paying for Retirement
Charitable Giving
Privacy in the Workplace
Adoption

DECEMBER 1993
U.S. Vietnam-Relations
Learning Disabilities
Child Care
Space Program's Future

JANUARY 1994
Racial Tensions in Schools
South Africa's Future
Worker Retraining
Regulating Pesticides

FEBRUARY 1994
Prison Overcrowding
Water Quality
Religion in Schools
Juvenile Justice

MARCH 1994
Underground Economy
Education Standards
Gambling Boom
Private Management of Public Schools

APRIL 1994
Reproductive Ethics
U.S.-China Trade
Soccer in America
Talk Show Democracy

MAY 1994
Traffic Congestion
Women's Health Issues
Mutual Funds
Political Scandals

JUNE 1994
Education and Gender
Gun Control
Public Land Policy
Nuclear Arms Cleanup

JULY 1994
Dietary Supplements
Public Opinion and Foreign Policy
Crime Victims' Rights
Birth Control Choices

AUGUST 1994
Genetically Engineered Foods
Electing Minorities
Prozac Controversy
College Sports

SEPTEMBER 1994
Home Schooling
Welfare Experiments
Courts and the Media
Regulating Tobacco

OCTOBER 1994
Historic Preservation
Religion and Politics
Arts Funding
Economic Sanctions

NOVEMBER 1994
Sex on Campus
Blood Supply Safety

Back issues are available for $4.00 (subscribers) or $7.00 (non-subscribers). Quantity discounts apply to orders over ten. To order, call Congressional Quarterly Customer Service at (202) 887-8621.

Binders are available for $16.00. To order call 1-800-638-1710. Please refer to stock number 648.

Future Topics

- ***Religion in America***
- ***Farm Policy***
- ***Arms Sales***

PUBLISHED BY CONGRESSIONAL QUARTERLY INC.

Religion in America

Will younger generations return to organized religion?

For the last three decades, church and synagogue membership has been mostly declining or stagnant. Experts trace the decline to the baby-boomers — the 78 million Americans born from 1946-65. But now boomers are raising children themselves, and a surprising number who rejected religion have returned to organized worship. Churches and temples find themselves marketing faith to a population once known for its skepticism toward authority. But by emphasizing such attractions as child care and informal dress codes, religious bodies invite charges that they are watering down traditional faith. Parishioner-hungry congregations also seek to attract members of the "baby-bust" generation, now in their 20s. Unlike the boomers, they largely grew up with no religious grounding at all.

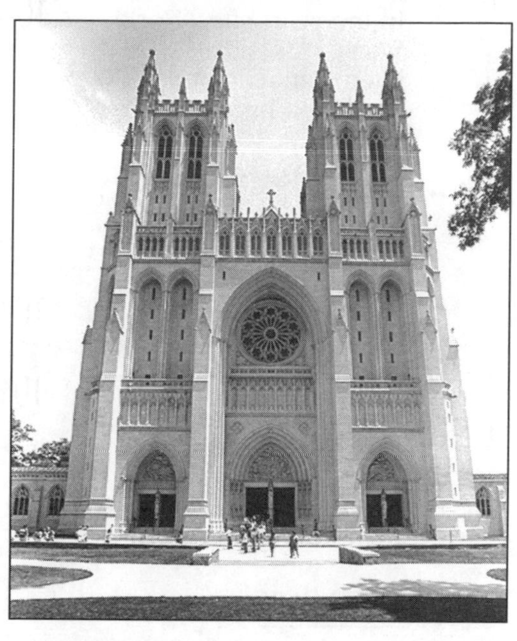

INSIDE THIS ISSUE

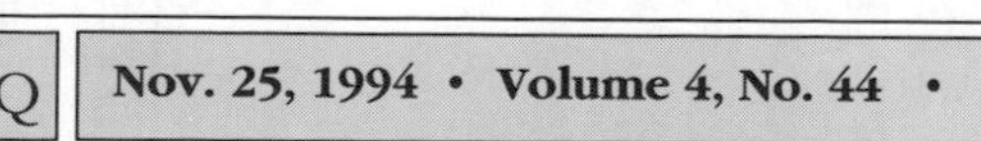

CQ Nov. 25, 1994 • Volume 4, No. 44 • Pages 1033-1056

Formerly Editorial Research Reports

Religion in America

COVER: WASHINGTON NATIONAL CATHEDRAL, WASHINGTON, D.C. (BOB BURGESS)

November 25, 1994
Volume 4, No. 44

The CQ Researcher (ISSN 1056-2036). Formerly Editorial Research Reports. Published weekly (48 times per year, not printed the first Friday of any month with five Fridays) by Congressional Quarterly Inc., 1414 22nd St., N.W., Washington, D.C. 20037. Rates are furnished upon request. Second-class postage paid at Washington, D.C. POSTMASTER: Send address changes to The CQ Researcher, 1414 22nd St., N.W., Washington, D.C. 20037.

Religion in America

By Charles S. Clark

The Issues

For Jeff and Nancy Wilson of Lake Oswego, Ore., churchgoing over the years has been on-again, off-again. Now in their late-30s, they attended Sunday school as youngsters, drifted away from religion during adolescence but renewed their devotion after taking on marriage and parenthood. It is a history they share with many in their generation.

"The kids are the main reason I want us to be in a church," says Jeff, who sells steel for machine parts. "I talk to my sons about the difference between what is real and what is the make-believe of television and music, which are so preoccupied with sex and show business. Some sort of religious input is important to their developing an understanding of real people, real friends, real life."

To Nancy, who does mail marketing from home, a key attraction of their Methodist church south of Portland is "the closeness of the small congregation" and the fact that "as our children have gotten into school and local athletics, so many in our community are also going to church."

What the Wilsons also share with many of their peers is the way they shopped around — turning away from one Lutheran church because of the long drive and burnout from too many church activities. They settled on a church with a "traditional service that uses the Methodist hymnal but is still accessible and informal," says Jeff. "The minister can get people to laugh, and he's good at giving pointed sermons that deal with the issues of the day but are still Bible-related."

Such exacting demands from the vast group known as baby-boomers — the 78 million Americans born from 1946-65 — have become pivotal to the outlook for organized religions, which over the past three decades have faced mostly declining or stagnant memberships.

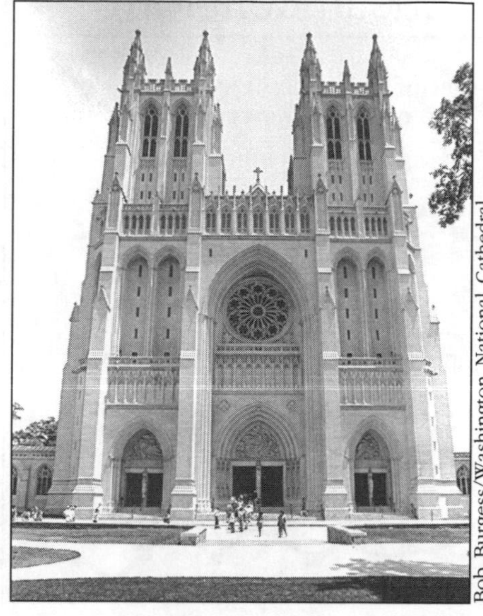

Bob Burgess/Washington National Cathedral

The 1990s, demographers note, have become the baby-boomers' long-delayed family years. In 1983, only 12.9 million of the boomers ages 20-34 had children under 18, according to the Census Bureau. By 1993, the number of parents from that same group (now ages 30-44) had risen to 21 million.

Eyeing the boomers' impending family-mindedness, church-watchers for a decade have been heralding a return to religion by the generation so famous for its youthful rebellion during the 1960s. David A. Roozen, a professor of religion and society at Connecticut's Hartford Seminary, reports that regular church attendance among the older baby-boomers (those born from 1945-54) climbed steadily from 32.8 percent in 1975 to 36.6 percent in 1980 to 41.1 percent in 1990. [1]

"Boomer families are busy and often have dual working spouses," Roozen notes, "and with kids being more complicated to raise these days, they are pulled in many directions. But they're so gung-ho to be the leaders of everything, they are taking charge and making time to serve on all the committees."

Baby-boomers are seen as special in other ways. Every generation has had members who drop out of religion during adolescence. But with the boomers, the dropouts for the first time encompassed record numbers of highly educated, middle- and upper-class youth. "This is a generation of seekers," writes Wade Clark Roof, professor of religion and society at the University of California-Santa Barbara. "Diverse as they are — from Christian fundamentalists to radical feminists, from New Age explorers to get-rich-quick MBAs — baby-boomers have found that they have to discover for themselves what gives their lives meaning, what values to live by.

"Not since the cataclysm of World War II have most of us been able simply to adopt the meanings and values handed down by our parents' religion, our ethnic heritage, our nationality. Rather, what really matters becomes a question of personal choice and experience." [2]

Nationally, the boom in boomers' devotion is visible on numerous fronts. "There is a sort of spiritual energy flowing through this country right now," Bill Clinton, the first baby-boomer president, told ABC News this spring. [3] One of the top-selling record albums this year is a collection of 1,300-year-old Gregorian chants sung by a group of limelight-shunning Spanish monks. And a previously unknown author's novel about ancient spirituality, *The Celestine Prophecy,* has sold nearly 2 million copies.

U.S. News & World Report, in an April cover story describing the baby-boomers' nostalgia for their childhood religion, reported poll results showing a religious mood around the country: 76 percent of Americans believe "God is a heavenly father who can be reached by prayers," and 62 percent say religion is increasing in influence on their lives. [4]

The return to religion is also being

How Americans Feel About Religion

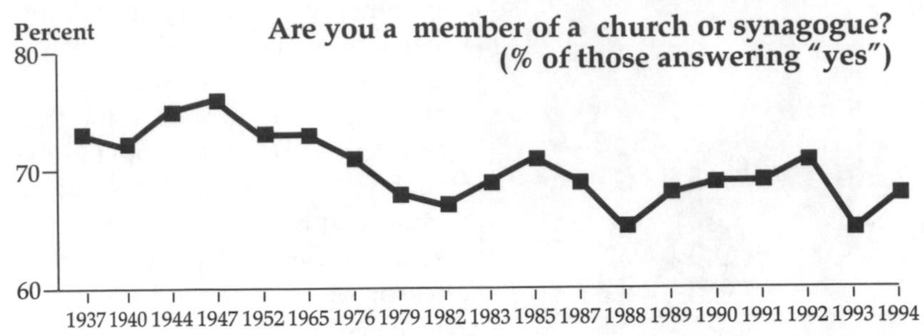

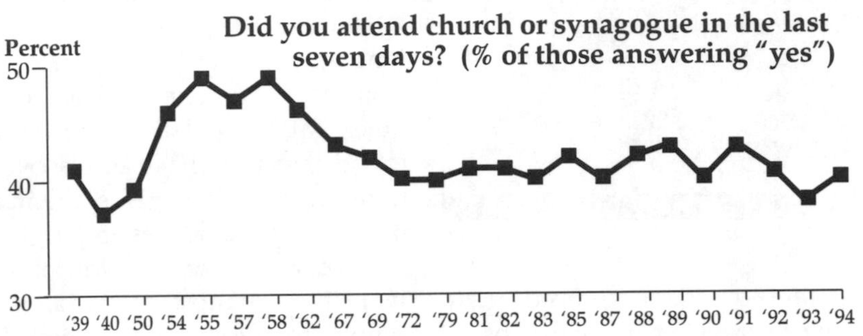

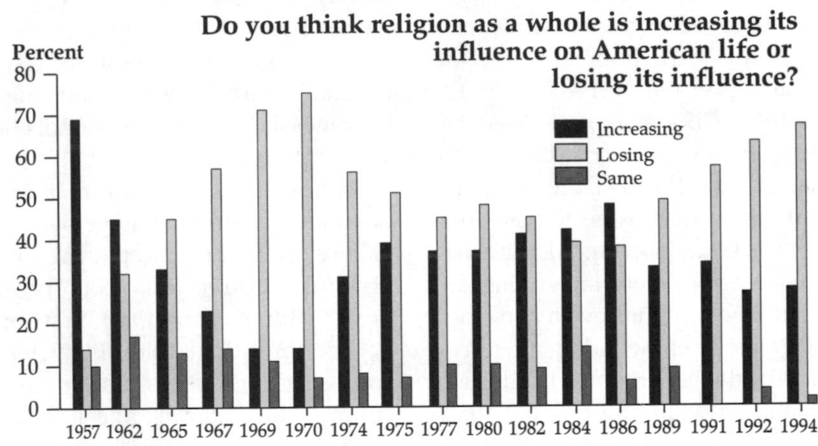

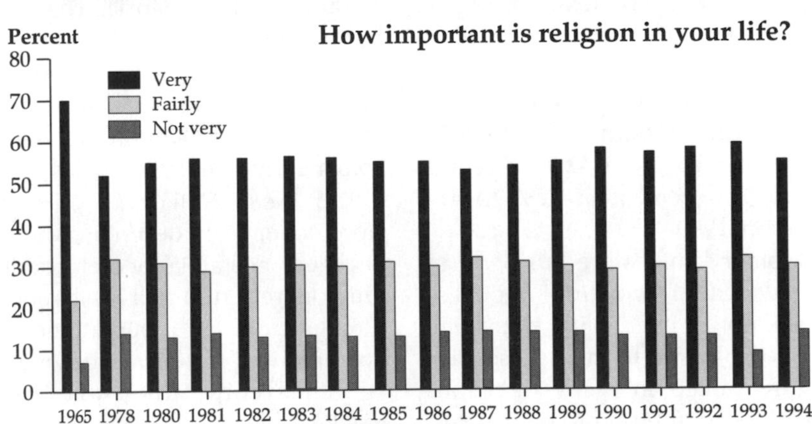

Note: Percentages do not add to 100% because those expressing no opinion are not included.

Source: The Gallup Organization

felt in individual faiths. Among Jews, says Sylvia Barack Fishman, a professor of contemporary American Jewish Life at Brandeis University, the revival can be seen in the "explosion in publishing of Jewish books, particularly by young authors."

"In the 1950s, Jewish literature portrayed the Jew as sort of an insider-outsider who would see things about American life that insiders couldn't see," she says. "Now they're writing about what it's like to be Jewish for Jews." The new pride in Jewish identity, she adds, also shows up in the movement for Jewish private schools, which are now in every major metropolitan area. "In the 1960s, public schools were valued by Jews as an Americanizing force, but now there's a feeling that when religious study is relegated to only two hours a day, there's less staying power."

Roman Catholics, too, are revisiting the religion of their birth, says the Rev. L. Michael Curtin, director of the Catholic Information Center in Washington, D.C., because of "the stable values and the optimism that faith gives people facing the future." Curtin has counseled many seekers in their 30s and 40s — women in particular — who've just experienced the death of their parents or grandparents. "After the funeral, they often sit with their alienated brothers and sisters going over their lives and find that the faith is deeply human and forgiving," he adds. "The things they were hurt by, the things for which they rejected the institutions, have ceased to have importance, and the emotional resentment has faded."

African-American churches are "among the [fastest]-growing elements of a national resurgence of searching for meaning and religious truth," says Bishop Charles E. Blake, pastor of the 12,000-member West Angeles Church of God in Christ in Los Angeles. He says the most rapidly growing groups are the young adults and middle-aged parishioners. "We've been through the phases — there was the militant period, the flower children, the period of disillusionment where people just chased the dollar, and now there's the deep conviction that if truth is to be found, it's in religion," he says.

Finally, the recent political activism of the religious right has helped fuel a campaign to recruit among evangelicals. [5] While liberal and moderate churches have struggled to maintain membership since 1950, conservative and Pentecostal denominations have seen their totals double and triple in the past four decades.

In response to the coming of the baby-boomers, church and temple leaders have been tailoring their growth strategies to demographics, just like advertisers and entertainment companies. Seminars on "boomers and church growth" are common for clergy in training. A Jewish temple in Caldwell, N.J., has special services for the children of baby-boomers called "Torah for Tots." Many churches are trying to lure-in busy families with Saturday night church services. A Baptist church in Pensacola, Fla., offers a 22-minute service with a crisp 10-minute sermon, says Richard Schramm, director of the American Baptist News Service.

Such mass-marketing, however, has irked academic skeptics as well as critics concerned about theological purity (*see below*). Baby-boomers "trying to find moral and spiritual structures and an anchoring point in their personal lives won't be fulfilled through many of the traditional churches and temples," says Edward Shafranske, a professor of psychology at Pepperdine University in Malibu, Calif. "What makes it difficult is that baby-boomers are looking for the spiritual and the transcendental rather than rules and codes. They're looking for a sophisticated church, one that responds in the context of dialogue, rather than an authoritarian, top-down bureaucratic structure."

Despite Americans' claims of interest in personal spirituality, the percentage of those who attend weekly worship services remains at only about 40 percent, according to a June 1994 Gallup Poll. The 10 largest denominations in the National Council of Churches' annual listing showed little or no growth in 1991-92, with modest 2 percent gains by the Baptists, Catholics and Mormons. [6] The Episcopal and Presbyterian churches each have cut their national staffs drastically in the past few years. [7] And the Gallup Poll's Princeton Religious Research Center reported in September that while 8 of 10 Americans say they adhere to a Judeo-Christian faith, many could not name any of the four Gospels or all of the Ten Commandments.

The secular culture that has been mainstream for decades continues to look askance at religious fervor. "To be devoutly religious, after all, is to believe in some aspect of the supernatural, whether the belief involves a certainty that God parted the Red Sea so that the Israelites could escape, a conviction that Jesus Christ is the Son of God or a sense that a powerful sentience beyond human ken is prepared, for whatever reason, to intervene in human affairs," Yale University law Professor Stephen Carter wrote in his influential 1993 book *The Culture of Disbelief*. "The message of contemporary culture seems to be that it is perfectly all right to *believe* that stuff . . . but you really ought to keep it to yourself." [8]

In the long-term, religious groups may find that the multitudes of boomers won't be enough to sustain congregations. California researcher George Barna, who has polled extensively on religion and lifestyle, says that the baby-boomers' much-touted return to religion began in 1987 and quickly leveled off in 1991. "The churches have more boomers than they did in the mid-1980s," he says,

Conservative Faiths on the Rise

Total membership in conservative religious groups increased from 1950 to 1990, while more liberal faiths declined.

	1950 (in millions)	1990 (in millions)	Percent of 1950 membership
Liberal Protestant (includes Episcopalians, Presbyterians and others)	7.6	6.9	91%
Moderate Protestant (includes Evangelical Lutherans, United Methodists and others)	15.9	15.7	99%
Roman Catholic	28.6	58.6	205%
Latter-day Saints	1.2	4.5	360%
Conservative Protestant (includes Baptists, Lutherans-Missouri Synod and others)	9.6	19.4	203%
Pentecostal/Holiness Protestant (includes Assemblies of God, Church of the Nazarene and others)	1.0	3.2	313%

Sources: David A. Roozen and C. Kirk Hadaway, Church and Denominational Growth, *1993;* Yearbook of American and Canadian Churches "but they're now showing up once every 4-6 weeks instead of 3-4 times a month, and there's less voluntarism and less from them in donations."

Barna and others have noted that churches are turning their attention to the 68 million Americans of the "baby-bust" cohort — the so-called Generation X — whose members are now in their 20s.

These successors to the boomers were recently described by *Christianity Today* magazine as the children of "social phenomena like AIDS, MTV, environmental catastrophe and the lingering economic threat of a multi-trillion-dollar federal deficit." They are "the children of divorce, with 50 percent coming from broken homes; and they are the children of two-job families, where parents often were not around." Relatively ungrounded in the basics their elders received in Sunday school, they are the first "post-Christian generation," the magazine said. [9]

The question of whether targeting the younger generations with modern marketing will revitalize religion in America raises doubts among clergy and scholars. As historians Barry Kosmin and Seymour Lachman put it, "How significant is religious doctrine to the American man or woman of religious affiliation when studies cite the reasons for joining a particular church to be the friendliness of the congregation, the church's closeness to the individual's home, the desire to be needed and wanted, the personality of the clergyman and, in last place, the worship service?" [10]

How the country responds to the new push to spread religion will hinge largely on the following question:

Should organized religion cater to the nation's new generations?

"Boomers, for the most part, do not attend church or synagogue out of obligation or family loyalty," writes Catholic University sociologist Dean R. Hoge." They feel no guilt if they abandon churchgoing, and they feel little need to go for the sake of appearances or respectability. If they go to church it is to get something. [11]

To meet the demand for that "something," today's churches conduct market research. They offer such family amenities as child care and singles groups. They use guitars and synthesizers to modernize their music. Some harness multimedia technology, replacing hymnals with lyrics flashed on a big screen. (*See "At Issue," p. 1049.*)

Many of the fastest-growing churches — notably the so-called "megachurches" with more than 2,000 congregants — now dispense with denominational labels. "A lot of Baptist churches are using 'community church' in the title because of the decline in brand-name loyalty," says Loren B. Mead, founder of the Alban Institute in Bethesda, Md., which studies how congregations grow.

Willow Creek Community Church

Sixteen thousand people attend services each week at Willow Creek Community Church, South Barrington, Ill.

"Baby-boomers and busters live in such a self-oriented, computerized, impersonal society, they're looking for a relationship with God rather than a religion," says Jeff Chitwood, associate minister for youth at the South Side Christian Church in Springfield, Ill. The modest-sized church, not affiliated with a national hierarchy, offers services with contemporary music, "but it is not a rock-and-roll band per se," he says. What is different about the music, he says, is the use of "praise chants, simple phrases or basic truths, often from the Book of Psalms, that focus on a personal approach directly to God, rather than the traditional hymn that uses four verses and a chorus to tell a story."

As for doctrine, the new generations reflect their upbringing in secular times. "In an age of competing ideologies, where there is a perception that a belief system is an ideology," says Roozen, "many of the highly educated baby-boomers take a relativistic approach to claims of truth. Experiential expression for many of them is primary, even among evangelical Christian groups with rigid doctrines. The theology has changed," he says, "from one that sees God as a judge with wrath and damnation, to one that says, 'Jesus is my friend.' "

Such free-wheeling spirituality is alarming to many in established churches and temples. The "consumer mentality" of ultramodern churches, Roozen says, is criticized for putting the focus of religious authority on subjective things. Such churches are attacked by "evangelical theologians who maintain a conservative, Calvinist dual emphasis on the Bible and reason," he says. "They are also hit from the left for not being reasoned or cognitive enough, for being too middle-class oriented and for forgetting about the poor."

Richard Cizik, a policy analyst with the National Association of Evangelicals, bemoans the fact that baby-boomers are deciding whether to return to church not on the basis of doctrine and theology but on whether their "needs are being met. A common joke around churches is that the most important way to attract new members is to have a nursery and ladies' restroom that's large enough for changing diapers," he says. "There's a lot of church-shopping, and many of these *needs* are merely *wants*. But evangelical churches are doctrinal. We care whether you believe in something, in values that are important. Many of these people aren't going back to church to serve but to be served."

Catholic baby-boomers, says Curtin, are likely to be fair-weather parishioners. "But they come because they treasure friendship more than any other generation, and they want their children to enjoy Easter and Christmas," he says. The domination by the boomers, he notes, has also changed the mix of charitable donations to churches. "It's not as heavily loaded toward the needy and the homeless, and is more oriented toward the environment and politics," he says. [12]

William Easum, a consultant on congregation growth and formerly pastor at Colonial Hills United Methodist Church in San Antonio, Texas, has written books attempting to guide churches through the modern temptations. "More and more churches allow the choir to sit in the congregation," he writes in *How to Reach Baby Boomers*. "This gives them the freedom to be part of the music ministry and sit with families. By the end of this decade many mainstream pastors may discontinue wearing robes because of [the boomers'] dislike for institutions and formality." But to be effective as clergy, he cautions, the goal of "preaching is not just to make people feel good but to direct them to examine how they relate to Christ. They are passionate about ministry and view it from a life-and-death perspective. Ministry is not just one way to live life; it is the only way to live." [13]

Debates about modernizing the church frequently refer to the "seeker movement," the spiritual questing of church-shy baby-boomers. The most prominent exemplar is Willow Creek Community Church in South Barrington, Ill., which draws some 16,000 parishioners weekly to services in a spacious, modern setting featuring jazz, theater-style seats and friendly parking attendants equipped with walkie-talkies. [14]

With parishioners whose median age is 38 — the median age of the baby-boom generation — Willow Creek attracts people who are "looking for an encounter with God to change their value system," says Assistant Pastor Lee Strobel. "Usually, they are unchurched. A lot are successful, have gone through a marriage or two, have large bank accounts. They have succeeded in life but know this is not it. Their kids need a framework to confront the unraveling of society morally, with all the poverty and troubles of the inner city. They know Clinton can't fix it, their parents can't fix it, government can't fix it, the schools can't fix it. So they're looking for a God."

Willow Creek is described by its

Changing Religious Attitudes, 1940-1991

The declining religious climate in the U.S., as measured by pollsters using eight key indicators, reflects the millions of baby-boomers coming of age in the 1960s who lost interest in religion.

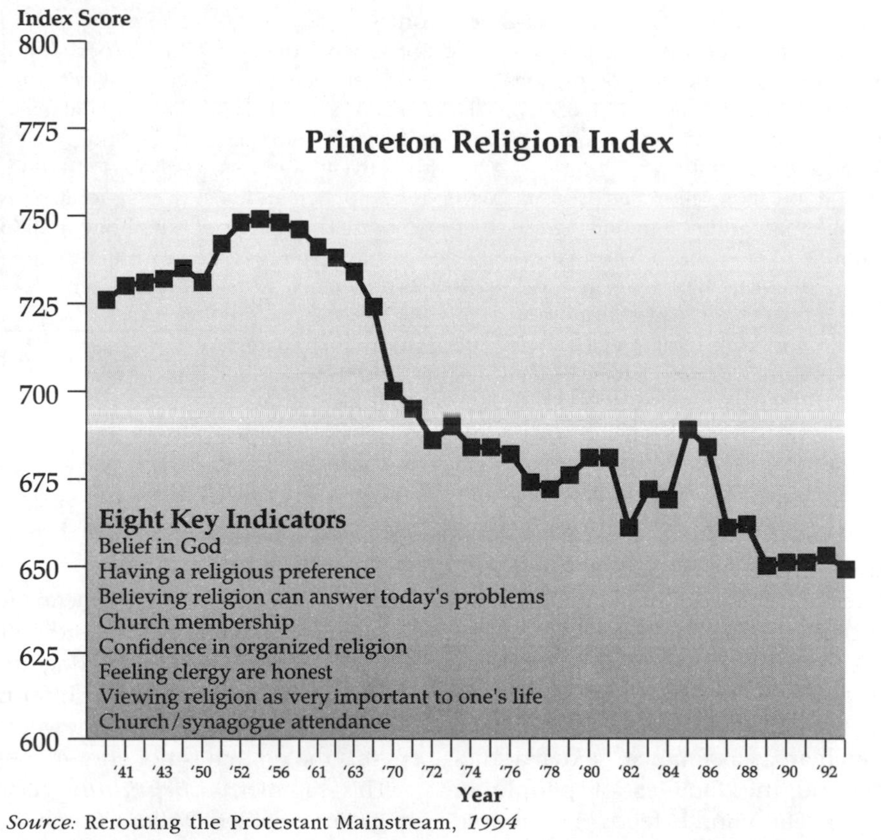

Source: Rerouting the Protestant Mainstream, *1994*

Counting Congregations Is No Easy Matter

Getting an accurate count of Americans' religious affiliations has long been tricky. That's because the decennial U.S. census omits any type of "What is your religion?" question, census officials believing that such queries are forbidden by the separation of church and state.

Consequently, many scholars have assumed there were no government figures for religious affiliation for most of U.S. history. Actually, the federal government from 1850-1936 did conduct and publish at regular intervals the Census of Religious Bodies. That voluntary survey, however, polled religious institutions rather than individuals, and so is ignored by many analysts.

The resulting gap in census data, complain religion historians Roger Finke and Rodney Starke, means that "for every church in the nation, we know details such as the value of the church buildings and land, the number of organizations sponsored by each and the seating capacity of the church. But we have no information on how many of these pew seats were ever filled." [1]

In 1946, the Census Bureau embarked upon a religion census, but it was quickly abandoned after resistance from Congress and from smaller religions. In 1957, the Census Bureau performed a voluntary survey in anticipation of possible inclusion of a religion query in the 1960 census. [2] Most of the data from that one-time effort was destroyed.

Most membership data since the late 1930s were derived from private national polling and from the denominations' internal head counts. Each of these methods brings complications. Poll-takers must distinguish between someone who identifies with a religion and one who actively practices one. Protestant churches, for example, tend to demand a formal entry and commitment from their members. The Roman Catholic Church has no formal criteria and is often willing to count everyone who lives in a local parish as a member. Jews, by contrast, have to be born to the faith or convert.

The samples used by the two most important pollsters, the Gallup Organization in Princeton, N.J., and the National Opinion Research Center in Chicago, "seldom include more than several hundred of the smaller religious denominations, and often considerably fewer, reflecting the fact that most religious groups constitute less than 2 percent of the total American population," note scholars Barry A. Kosmin and Seymour P. Lachman. "These surveys can never provide a profile of such groups as Jehovah's Witnesses or Hindus." [3]

The membership tallies often cited come from interdenominational groups such as the National Council of Churches and the Southern Baptist Convention. Here accuracy can suffer, too, because the written reports that congregations forward to central offices can contain clerical errors, notes David A. Roozen, professor of religion and society at Connecticut's Hartford Seminary Center for Social and Religious Research. "The numbers can also be overstated because some denominations don't prune their rolls," he says. "Inconsistencies creep in because some denominations include people of all ages while others include only adults." Generally, Roozen adds, tallies from congregations tend to be more reliable if the denomination's financial contributions to the central office are based on parish head counts.

The closest thing to a detailed religious census is compiled by the Glenmary Research Center in Atlanta, Ga., which since the late 1950s has offered a county-by-county breakdown of membership in the country's 30 top Christian denominations.

Two other surveys in recent years have added greatly to the religion database. In 1990, the National Jewish Population Survey, sponsored by the Council of Jewish Federations in New York City, produced an estimate of households in the country with at least one Jew and asked questions about Jewish practices and temple involvement.

Seeking an overall religious portrait of the country, scholars at the City University of New York in 1991 published the National Survey of Religious Identification. Based on a telephone poll of 113,000 Americans contacted over a 13-month period, it is seen as "the largest and most comprehensive poll ever on religious loyalties." [4]

[1] Roger Finke and Rodney Starke, *The Churching of America, 1776-1990: Winners and Losers in Our Religious Economy* (1992), p. 12.

[2] Barry A. Kosmin and Seymour P. Lachman, *One Nation Under God* (1993), p. 6.

[3] *Ibid.*, p. 4.

[4] *Ibid.*, p. 2.

pastor, Bill Hybels, as "a bona fide Protestant, evangelical, interdenominational church committed to exaltation, edification, evangelism and social action." The church sponsors 100 internal ministries and support groups in such areas as finance, sexual addiction and the families of people in prison. The church feeds 350 people a month and has given away 85 cars to single mothers.

Perhaps its most notable means for attracting new members, according to Strobel, is its policy of instructing first-timers not to contribute to the offering plate, a way of assuring the newcomers that the church is not after money.

This summer, *Christianity Today* magazine profiled Willow Creek and asked Hybels to respond to a series of published critiques of the seeker movement. [15] It cited author John MacArthur, who argued in his book *Ashamed of the Gospel* that "One cannot follow a market-driven strategy and remain faithful to scripture. Preachers who concern themselves with user-friendliness cannot fearlessly proclaim the whole counsel of God."

The magazine cited Os Guinness,

author of *Dining with the Devil,* who wrote: "Totally planned, professionally orchestrated, single-purposed environments may be as 'effective' for evangelism in megachurches as they are for selling in megamalls. But when everything is controlled . . . who controls the church and who controls the controllers?"

Hybels replied that Willow Creek does not engage in the more aggressive marketing practices, such as advertising, billboards or distributing pamphlets in neighborhoods. He did, however, defend the use of modern media. "The word *entertainment,* of course, is emotive by nature," he said. "And yes, we do use drama, contemporary Christian music and multimedia presentations. But they are never used for the sake of titillation. I think it's good to ask: Who was the master composer? Who created the arts? Whose idea was it to communicate the truth through a wide variety of artistic genres? I think it was God. Then why has the church narrowed its options and selected a talking head as its only form of communicating the most important message on the planet?"

Hybels' colleague Strobel elaborates: "Our statement of faith is mainstream," he says. "We don't water down, transform or soft-pedal. We use the 20th century multimedia of TV generation, but are careful to maintain the message and the integrity of the gospel."

Pollster Barna believes church efforts to cater to baby-boomers have failed. "In general, there is only a small minority of churchgoers who actually experience God, so the boomers were skeptical when most of them didn't," he says. More concretely, "the churches talked a lot about parenting, but did little hands-on training. There is a feeling of despair among pastors who don't know what to do. Some are trying cell-group ministries, of 8-10 people, but the number of adult participants has been cut in half in the last four years. That's because of a lack of strong leadership, good teaching, direction and training. Many try to do too much. You can use the modern style of video screens and computer-literate language, but the key is a personal relationship with God and individual spiritual training."

Dean Kelley, an adviser to the National Council of Churches and a longtime observer of church growth, says that the use of music with a beat and high-tech-communications are not new developments, and that the evangelical movement has been using them successfully for years. The difference is that "in the evangelical and fundamentalist churches, all these are ancillary to the very vigorous promulgation of meaning or doctrine or mutual expectations of what is Christian conduct," he says. "Child care and singles groups are not much help in giving religion meaning. In strong churches, those things are ancillary to a core of central meaning, not a facade that doesn't have much inside." ■

BACKGROUND

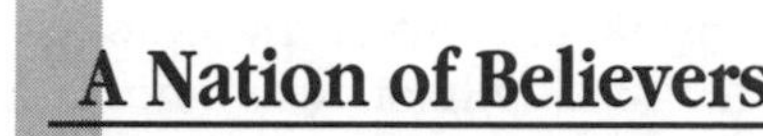

A Nation of Believers

At the time of the American Revolution, only 17 percent of Ameri-

Religious Groups in the U.S.

Catholics and Baptists are the two largest religious groups in the country. About 86 percent of Americans belong to Christian denominations, 8 percent list no religious affiliation and 3.3 percent are non-Christians, according to a poll of 113,000 Americans.

Religious Denomination	Estimated Adult Members (millions)	Estimated Percent of U.S. Adults
Roman Catholic	46.0	26.2%
Baptist	40.0	19.4
Protestant	17.1	9.7
Methodist	14.1	8.0
Lutheran	9.1	5.2
Christian	7.9	4.5
Presbyterian	5.0	2.8
Jewish	3.1	1.8
Pentecostal	3.1	1.8
Episcopalian	3.0	1.7
Mormon/Latter-day Saints	2.5	1.4
Churches of Christ	1.6	1.0
Jehovah's Witness	1.4	0.8
Seventh-Day Adventist	.67	
Assemblies of God	.66	
Holiness/Holy	.61	
Church of the Nazarene	.55	
Church of God	.53	
Muslim/Islamic	.53	
Unitarian Universalist	.50	
Orthodox (Eastern)	.50	
Congregationalist	.44	
Buddhist	.40	
Evangelical	.24	
Mennonite	.23	
Hindu	.23	
Christian Science	.21	
Church of the Brethren	.20	
"Born Again"	.20	
Non-denominational	.20	

Note: Percentages do not add up to 100% because very small religious groups are not listed, and some people polled refused to answer.

Sources: One Nation Under God, *1993; National Survey of Religious Identification, 1991* cans belonged to a church. By the Civil War that had risen to 37 percent. After a postwar dip, the number of adherents rose to 50 percent by 1906. By 1926, it hit 56 percent and in 1980 was up to 62 percent. [16] According to a June Gallup Poll, 68 percent belong to a church or temple.

Compared with other countries, the United States is a highly religious nation. An international Gallup Poll of youth ages 18-24 taken in the early 1980s put America at the top of industrial nations: 90 percent of the Americans polled said religion was important to them, compared with 80 percent of Brazilians, 68 percent of South Koreans, 38 percent of Japanese and 4 percent of Chinese. [17]

Still, having been founded as a haven for religious dissidents and having eschewed an official religion, the United States also has been the home of the secular, which has held its ground for more than three centuries. As scholars Kosmin and Lachman note, "the ratio of the number of U.S. residents in 1990 (250 million) to the number of churches (more than 255,000) is almost the same as in 1650." [18]

In the years after World War II, as the nation turned inward and families flocked to the tranquility of suburbia, American religiosity reached a historic high. Gallup surveys showed that 94 percent believed in God. A *Ladies' Home Journal* survey showed 90 percent engaging in prayer, with 86 percent regarding the Bible as the divinely inspired word of God. The laying down of suburban tracts brought with it a boom in church construction. In the late 1940s, churches and synagogues owned some $7 billion in property in the United States. They took in $700 million-$800 million annually and gave $200 million to charities and $150 million to parochial schools. [19]

"Everybody knows that church life is booming in the U.S., and there are plenty of statistics to prove it," effused *Time* magazine in 1955. "There is so much momentum in the United Lutheran Church these days," said the denomination's president, "that the leaders have to keep moving to avoid having their troops — the rank and file of pastors and congregations — run over them." [20]

Other church leaders, however, were skeptical that the boom would last. *Christianity Today* editorialized in 1957 that "it would be too much to say that the soul of the nation has undergone repentance and revival." [21]

The Baby-Boomers

The skepticism proved prophetic. The baby-boom generation, reared, some said, too permissively under the child-care advice of Dr. Benjamin Spock, was soon to come of age in the turbulent 1960s and give the religious establishment a jolt.

Pushed toward rebellion by the civil rights movement, the Vietnam War and the rise of the counterculture, baby-boomers began rejecting the religion handed down from their parents for a multiplicity of reasons. "The environment that used to set up a gravitational pull toward the church in the late 1950s and '60s eroded," says the Alban Institute's Mead. "Other options became available," and church was no longer "just part of the furniture."

States and localities, for example, began loosening the blue laws that had long forbade stores and public entertainment from doing business on the Sunday Sabbath. "Sunday evening church services were stopped dead by the 'Ed Sullivan Show' in the 1960s," Mead adds.

Two scholars who watched the transformation of American life have noted: "Our parents never worried about whether we would grow up Christian. The church was the only show in town. On Sundays, the town closed down. One could not even buy a gallon of gas. There was a traffic jam on Sunday mornings at 9:45, when all went to their respective Sunday schools. . . . When and how did it change? Although it may sound trivial, one of us is tempted to date the shift [to] a Sunday evening in 1963. Then, in Greenville, S.C., in defiance of the state's time-honored blue laws, the Fox theater opened on Sunday. . . . That evening has come to represent a watershed in the history of Christiandom, South Carolina-style. On that night, Greenville — the last pocket of resistance to secularity in the Western world — served notice that it would no longer be a prop for the church." [22]

"God is Dead"

By 1966, the *Time* magazine that a decade earlier had trumpeted the boom in religion announced on its cover that "God is Dead." Churches began to split along political lines, rent by such issues as Vietnam, civil rights, the sexual revolution and feminism.

Scholars began to analyze the impact on church attendance. "During the 1950s," writes Roof, "studies showed that college-educated men and women were more likely than the less educated to participate in organized religion. . . . Since the '60s, however, these patterns have changed. The polls show a gradual decline in religious attendance that is more pronounced among the college-educated than for any other category. . . . Now there are only slight differences in participation across educational lines." [23]

From 1965-75, mainline churches suffered a 10 percent drop in membership and a 30 percent decline in baptisms, according to Roozen and his colleagues. From 1958-68, "every major mainline denomination either was involved in a merger, or involved in serious discussions about church union. Such involvements appear to have generated stronger reactions, and more opposition and alienation, than the social-action controversies." [24]

The mass departures constituted a "seismic shift" in American religion, wrote Martin E. Marty, a professor at

Continued on p. 1044

Chronology

1950s *The postwar baby-boom and rise of the suburbs contribute to an increase in church and temple construction.*

1952
Gallup Poll shows 75 percent of Americans think religion is very important in their lives.

1955
Time and *Newsweek* run cover stories on the boom in church attendance.

1957
Census Bureau conducts preliminary survey of religious affiliations; results later destroyed.

1960s *Trend toward secularization accelerates; local jurisdictions abandon blue laws forbidding stores to open on Sundays; counterculture arises amid youthful alienation from older generation's authority.*

1960
John F. Kennedy overcomes the issue of his Catholicism in the presidential campaign.

1965
Gallup Poll shows 70 percent of Americans think religion is very important in their own lives; church membership begins decline.

April 8, 1966
Time magazine cover story declares "God is Dead."

1970s *Counterculture spawns new interest in Eastern religions and New Age movements. Evangelicals experience growth while other organized religions remain static or decline.*

1972
National Council of Churches publishes Dean Kelley's controversial book *Why Conservative Churches Are Growing*, which describes liberal, permissive churches as "weak" and says they are shrinking because they demand little commitment from members.

1975
Gallup Poll shows that adults under 30 are more than twice as likely as older generations to get interested in yoga, transcendental meditation and Eastern religions.

1976
Presidential candidate Jimmy Carter reveals he is a "born-again Christian," raising the visibility of traditional religion in modern life.

1978
Gallup Poll shows 52 percent of Americans think religion is very important in their lives.

1980s *Conservative shift in political climate fuels evangelical movement; baby-boomers, entering long-delayed parenthood, begin returning to religion and become targets of church recruitment.*

1984
Gallup Poll shows 56 percent of Americans think religion is very important in their lives.

February 1987
Washingtonian magazine cover story on baby-boomers returning to church declares that "God is Back."

1990s *The baby-boomers' return to religion tapers off; churches begin focusing on "baby-bust" generation, which has little grounding in religion.*

April 1991
Release of largest religious-affiliation survey in history, involving 113,000 Americans interviewed by researchers at City University of New York.

1992
World Methodist Church reports its North American membership remained at 15 million from 1962-92 but in Asia and Africa members swelled from 2 million to more than 5 million.

March 1994
President Clinton gives in-depth interview on his religious faith to the TV networks' first full-time religion reporter.

June 1994
Gallup Poll shows 55 percent of Americans think religion is very important in their lives, but only about 40 percent attend weekly worship services.

Americans Applaud Faith at the White House . . .

Seventy-eight percent of Americans believe "the president should be a moral and spiritual role model for the rest of the country," according to a *U.S. News & World Report* poll taken last March.

That was the month President Clinton, a Southern Baptist, gave a revealing interview to ABC News on the role of religion in his life, declaring, "I do not believe I could do my job as president, much less continue to grow as a person, in the absence of my faith in God." [1]

Six months later, Hillary Rodham Clinton took her turn, describing to *Newsweek* how much she relies on her Methodist faith and prompting the newsweekly to dub the Clintons "perhaps the most openly religious First Couple this century has seen." [2]

But does faith at the White House affect the religious practices of average Americans?

"Not directly," say observers of religion and politics. The presidency is "relatively irrelevant" to changes in the country's religiosity, says Loren Mead, founder of the Alban Institute in Bethesda, Md., which studies how congregations grow. "The president is like a rowboat — when the tide goes up, he's on top of it to articulate what's happening in society with religion, but when the tide goes down, he stops."

Charles W. Dunn, a Clemson University political scientist and editor of the book *American Political Theology,* says the American people take the president's religion in stride. "The president is not the general on the theological battlefield," he says. "He responds to public pressure, using the language of civil religion that attracts but doesn't alienate."

Dunn notes that presidential rhetoric often employs theological terms: sacred office, saving the presidency, faith and trust in leadership, bully pulpit. "The president's faith doesn't necessarily have any bearing on policy, and appearances are more important than reality, Dunn adds. "But appearances are absolutely critical because Americans do look at the president through a religious lens."

An example of how presidents respond to public devoutness came in 1952, Dunn says, when the Republican presidential nominee, Dwight D. Eisenhower, went from having no religious affiliation to Presbyterianism. At the same time, his opponent, Democrat Adlai E. Stevenson II, switched from the Lutheran to the Unitarian church. "They each picked a solid, mainstream, acceptable denomination," Dunn notes. The presidency has also had a moderating influence on men who previously were heavily religious, Dunn says, citing James A. Garfield and Warren G. Harding.

The Founding Fathers, many of whom adhered to deism (the belief that God created the universe and then left mankind alone), drafted the Constitution to prohibit religious tests for candidates for government office. But America's Judeo-Christian heritage remained influential. Thomas Jefferson proposed using an image of the Israelites during the Exodus on the nation's Great Seal, and presidents from George Washington on have been sworn-in using a Bible.

Abraham Lincoln was well-known for uttering biblical phrases, and his assassination, Dunn notes, led one noted political scientist to call him "the martyred Christ of democracy's passion play."

President William McKinley, facing a crisis in the Philippines in the late 1890s, acknowledged to colleagues that he got down on his knees and prayed over the issue before deciding that the U.S. must capture the Philippines

All the presidents except three — Thomas Jefferson, Abraham Lincoln and Andrew Johnson — have belonged to specific denominations.

Episcopalian
Washington
Madison
Monroe
W.H. Harrison
Tyler
Taylor
Pierce
Arthur
F.D. Roosevelt
Ford
Reagan
Bush

Presbyterian
Jackson
Polk
Buchanan
Cleveland
B. Harrison
Wilson
Eisenhower

Unitarian
J. Adams
J.Q. Adams
Fillmore
Taft

Baptist
Harding
Truman
Carter
Clinton

Methodist
Grant
Hayes
McKinley

Disciples of Christ
Garfield
L.B. Johnson

Dutch Reformed
Van Buren
T. Roosevelt

Society of Friends (Quaker)
Hoover
Nixon

Congregationalist
Coolidge

Roman Catholic
Kennedy

Continued from p. 1042

the University of Chicago Divinity School. In 1976, he wrote that "mainline churches suffer in times of cultural crisis and disintegration, when they receive blame for what goes wrong in society but are bypassed when people look for new ways to achieve social identity and location." [25]

The changes affected all areas of life. The proportion of Americans who considered premarital sex morally wrong dropped from 4 out of 5 in 1959 to less than 1 in 2 in 1973. [26] A Gallup Poll in 1975 would show that adults under 30 were more than twice as likely as older generations to get interested in yoga, transcendental meditation and Eastern religions.

Seeking to explain the religious sea change, Kelley of the National Council of Churches shook up organized religions with a widely noted 1972 book, *Why Conservative Churches Are Grow-*

. . . But Don't Get Religion From the President

and "civilize and Christianize" the Filipinos. [3]

Woodrow Wilson, the son of a clergyman, continually described the mission of the United States as the "liberation and salvation of the world." [4] Calvin Coolidge remarked that the very foundations of American society "rested so much on the teachings of the Bible that it would be difficult to support them if faith in these teachings should cease to be practically universal in our country." [5]

Franklin D. Roosevelt, Dunn notes, promoted his redistributionist economic reforms with such New Testament imagery as "the money-changers have fled from their high seats in the temple of civilization." Harry S Truman declared that "no problem on this Earth" was tough enough to withstand "the flame of a genuine revival of religious faith." [6]

Eisenhower told his countryman that "without God, there could be no American form of government, nor an American way of life." Lyndon B. Johnson used biblical parables to justify the 1965 Voting Rights Act and once spoke of "a covenant with this land [that] was meant one day to inspire the hopes of all mankind." [7]

John F. Kennedy, though as willing as any modern president to have his picture taken with the Rev. Billy Graham, had to tread carefully when it came to religion and guard against charges that his Catholicism would make him subservient to the pope. In an April 1960 campaign speech, he said that "the president is not elected to be protector of the faith — or guardian of the public morals. His attendance at church on Sunday should be his business alone, not a showcase for the nation." [8]

The modern president most associated with strong religious conviction is Jimmy Carter, who startled the public in 1976 with his off-the-cuff declaration that he was a "born-again Christian." It is a conviction that continues guiding Carter's actions in his political and diplomatic work as an ex-president.

Ronald Reagan, though declining to attend church because of what he said were security risks, encouraged the conservative evangelical movements that gathered steam in the 1970s and '80s and spoke of America in theological terms, as in his 1982 remark: "This anointed land was set apart in an uncommon way." [9]

When Bill and Hillary Clinton began displaying their devoutness, the religious and political communities — predictably — were divided in their reactions. Those who oppose Clinton's policies were the more skeptical. As ABC News observed, "Clinton's declaration that 'I try not to pray for personal advantage, but to think of others, [to] help me to do a better job,' poses a dilemma for evangelicals. He sounds like one of them, but they voted against him." [10]

The Rev. Jerry Falwell, a longtime leader of the religious right who blasts Clinton for his positions on abortion and gay rights, called him a "master manipulator." But James Dunn, executive director of the Baptist Joint Committee on Public Affairs in Washington, applauded the sincerity of the way Clinton applies his faith to social issues, noting how Clinton is knowledgeable about scripture and can sing hymns from memory. [11]

Methodist leaders had a similarly upbeat reaction to Hillary Clinton's religious revelations, which included the news that she believes that prayer is effective, and that she is not troubled, as some feminists are, by the traditional reference to God as "He."

Joe Hale, general secretary of the World Methodist Council in Lake Junaluska, N.C., says: "It is always a good thing when a government leader has a moral foundation and a practicing faith. It is a positive development for the Methodist religion, but Methodism is only a street address in a faith we share with a lot of other people. We're not using it to promote Methodism."

---

[1] *U.S. News & World Report,* April 4, 1994, p. 54.

[2] *Newsweek,* Oct. 31, 1994, p. 23.

[3] Charles W. Dunn (ed.), *American Political Theology: Historical Perspective and Theoretical Analysis* (1984), p. 159.

[4] Barry A. Kosmin and Seymour P. Lachman, *One Nation Under God* (1993), p. 22.

[5] Robert Wuthnow, *The Restructuring of American Religion* (1988), p. 42.

[6] *Ibid.,* p. 66.

[7] Kosmin and Lachman, *op. cit.,* p. 22.

[8] *CQ Almanac,* 1960, p. 810.

[9] Kosmin and Lachman, *op. cit.,* p. 23.

[10] Burt Solomon, "His Embrace of Religion Gives Clinton a Political Boost," *National Journal,* April 16, 1994, p. 912.

[11] *The Washington Post,* March 10, 1994.

ing. He categorized churches as strong (theologically conservative) and weak (theologically permissive). Strong churches offer a total, closed belief system that is deemed sufficient for all purposes and needs no revision, he said. They have a distinctive code of conduct, strict discipline over members in matters of belief and practice, demand high energy and commitment and maintain a missionary zeal. Weak churches, by contrast, embrace relativism, permissiveness, individualism, pluralism and a lack of enforcement. They demand little commitment from members and maintain a preference for dialogue with outsiders rather than attempting to convert them. [27]

With the exception of the conservative, evangelical movement, which gained members steadily during the 1970s, the departure from churches would continue into the '80s. Back in

Continued on p. 1047

A Fading Church Revived by Baby-Boomers

St. Mary's hit rock bottom in 1985. The stately stone church in Arlington that had once boasted Northern Virginia's largest Episcopal congregation was drawing only 50-75 parishioners, most of them elderly. Church revenues were outpaced by operating expenses, and a mere four children were enrolled in the Sunday school.

Today, St. Mary's has been resurrected. It packs in 350-400 devotees at weekly services, and its Sunday School bustles with the energy of 130 kids. The chief reason, says its rector, the Rev. Andrew T. P. Merrow, is that "the Holy Spirit is alive and active." A more visible factor is the return of the baby-boomers, the thirty- and fortysomethings who form the core of St. Mary's.

"People in the Washington area work too hard, play too hard, are overeducated and over-stressed," Merrow says. "Many of them are asking themselves, 'If this is all there is, what will I do with that?' "

What's more, the large portion of boomers who are parents "are finding that kids ask the darnedest questions," Merrow says. "'Why did the kitty die?' It sends parents into a tizzy. They want ways to talk about the big issues of life, death and war, and they want a sense that their kids know their Bible stories and who God is."

The Rev. Andrew T. P. Merrow, Rector, St. Mary's Episcopal Church

With modern children being exposed much earlier to the threats of early sex, drugs and violence, "the rules of parenting are totally different from how our parents raised us," Merrow adds. "Parents nowadays struggle with questions of authority. 'Is my kid my friend or what?' So they come here and meet other parents and find that they are not in this alone."

The tale of Merrow's arrival at St. Mary's is one of irony and spiritual significance. "I felt called to come here," says the 39-year-old, recounting how he'd often visited the church from his boyhood home in nearby Alexandria, where his father was also a clergyman. He grew up hearing the story of how during St. Mary's heyday back in the 1950s, its rector had called Merrow's father and asked him to come over to administer last rites to his deathly ill son. The elder Merrow proceeded to stun the grieving father by praying instead for the boy's recovery, declaring that the spirit had so moved him. The boy is alive and well to this day.

When a troubled St. Mary's began looking for a new rector in 1983, Merrow expressed his interest, despite having not reached the age of 30 and having served only as an assistant rector at Christ Church in Alexandria. "The bishop said, 'You're too young, I like you too much,' but I told him I had a sense this is where I'm supposed to be," he says.

The church's conservative trustees were initially cold, but Merrow impressed them when he said his first act as rector would be to put some prominent signs in the churchyard to shout out the schedule of services to the world. And he applied needed financial know-how, helping administer a new nonprofit foundation devoted to education and community outreach. The shaky church had established the foundation just before his arrival after selling off some land at a busy intersection.

Merrow's youth became one of his assets as he adopted the Episcopal Church's modern prayer book and began attracting young families. He concentrated on instilling "the good habit" of church attendance in people who are often more inclined to "spend Sundays reading *The New York Times* or playing tennis," he says. "It's a warm, friendly congregation that genuinely welcomes strangers." The newcomers come from all religious backgrounds, and many of them are ex-Catholics.

Tucked in the pews at St. Mary's are brochures giving details of the church's child-care program. And there's a pamphlet listing the church's program of community grants — to a hospice, a literary council, a disaster-relief fund, a homeless shelter.

Growth of a congregation, however, "is a byproduct of something else rather than a goal," Merrow says. "All I set about doing was preaching the Gospel, and the way you grow is when, say, a woman goes back to her neighborhood and taps into the spiritual hunger and tells people, 'Come to my church.' "

There is also a constant struggle to prevent the church from becoming a club, he says. That's why the vestry insisted on earmarking $50,000 a year for outreach to the community. "It's a spiritual component to keep ourselves honest and not ingrown," he says.

Merrow disagrees with the common portrait of boomers as being preoccupied with their personal needs. More noticeable, he says, is how lackadaisical many are about learning scripture. "They do all this research to buy a car or choose a doctor or school, yet they don't tackle religion with the same intellectual vigor," he says.

Whether or not St. Mary's sustains its growth spurt, Merrow has his work cut out for him. "Our generation is the bloom on a plant that our parents grounded in the church," he says. "It has to be grounded again, because the real issue facing the church is the next generation, which has no basic grounding in religion."

Continued from p. 1045
1955, the Gallup Poll had shown that only 1 in 25 Americans did not adhere to the faith of their childhood. By 1985, that had climbed to 1 in 3.[28]

Why the Baby-Boomers Left

The reasons why the boomers abandoned church pews ranged from the abstract to the mundane. Analysts cited psychologist Abraham Maslow's theories about the "hierarchy of needs" to explain how economic prosperity had altered young people's values. Now they were able to concentrate less on careers and the material benefits promised as rewards by religion and more on the environment, self-expression and independent ideas.[29]

To an extent, however, rebelliousness occurs in every generation. "The determined avoidance of organized religion during the late teens and early 20s," writes Barna, "is not so much a reasoned and impassioned resistance to God or other spiritual realities as a flexing of their independence from the older generations and their prevailing models of structure, authority and order."[30]

A survey of Presbyterian boomers who left the church pointed to personal convenience and lifestyle changes as the reasons. In response to a survey by a team of sociologists, 32 percent cited home and family commitments; 31 percent cited time constraints or "laziness"; and a final third cited a disagreement with the religious doctrine, a perception of hypocrisy among church members or a loss of faith.[31]

The eventual return of many baby-boomers in the 1980s was hypothesized as early as the '60s. According to Mead, counterculture politics would become conservative, and family responsibilities would put formerly rebellious boomers into roles as teachers and leaders. "Children make their parents grow up," said one Presbyterian baby-boomer. "They force them into taking stands where before you've just been saying, 'Well, this is OK, that is OK.' "[32] ■

CURRENT SITUATION

Enter the Young

The much-noted return of baby-boomers to religion is already showing signs of abating. The test of long-term commitment seems to come when the boomers' children finish high school and leave home.

"By the early 1990s, the first empty-nest boomers are evident in national survey data, and their worship attendance is significantly lower than that of boomers in active parenting roles," writes Roozen. "The inevitable and relatively massive transition of the boomers out of active parenting roles should exert considerable downward pressure on overall levels of religious participation for at least the next 20 years."[33]

Churches and temples have responded by turning their attention to the baby-busters of "Generation X." The attitudes of this generation were recently explored in *Sojourners,* a magazine for social-activist Christians. "After the anger and the tears, the repentance and the forgiving," wrote a 27-year-old seeking involvement with a church, "you will be surprised by how much we want and need the fathers and mothers we always expected to lose too soon." Said another twentysomething: "The leadership we desire is open and mentoring, not top-down, distant or self-justified. Instead of idolizing leadership or expecting superhuman perfection, honest companions and humble guides will do just fine."[34]

Barna's surveys show that baby-busters are even less churched than boomers. While having a close relationship with God is important to 70 percent of boomers, it's important to only 64 percent of busters, compared with 79 or 85 percent of older generations, he writes. Still, 91 percent of busters believe in God or a higher power. Some 52 percent say they are religious, but only 34 percent said they had attended services in the past week, compared with 49 percent of older groups who went to church.[35]

Tim Downs, a communications specialist for the Campus Crusade for Christ in Raleigh, N.C ., says his group is witnessing "an upswing in interest and willingness of students to talk about religion after a flat period of the past 10 years." Back in the early 1970s, he says, the group's approach to proseletyzing among college students was "materialistic and argumentative, with lots of debates over whether spiritual reality was a ridiculous concept. Nowadays, people are reading books about angels and are willing to discuss whether there are ultimate truths, and whether one religion has more to offer than another."

The problem, Downs adds, is that today's pluralism and ultra-tolerance concerning different religions clashes with his group's convictions that Christ "made some pretty exclusive statements. To talk about the uniqueness of Jesus is seen as bigotry." Still, the Generation Xers are "pragmatists with eclectic worldviews who are really happy living with contradictions and inconsistencies — they wear a navy blue suit with Nike shoes," he says. "Fewer of them have been to Sunday school, so unlike 20 years ago, we have to start from ground zero: 'This is the Bible, it's 66 books.' "

Disputes Over Lifestyles and Politics

Nearly all the churches and temples seeking to recruit new members will be buffeted by disputes over policies, politics and lifestyle issues. The Catholic Church in particular was in the spotlight in September for its active opposition to abortion education at a world conference on population growth in Cairo, Egypt. The Vatican's refusal to permit the ordination of women as Catholic priests also has drawn protests from feminists, politicians and even from nuns.

Homosexuality continues to be a divisive issue, particularly for fundamentalist denominations that point to a biblical passage calling it an "abomination." Conservative Dallas, Texas, meanwhile, is the home of the nation's largest predominantly gay and lesbian congregation. The 1,400 parishioners at Hope Metropolitan Community Church have been dealing almost weekly with the deaths of members and friends from AIDS. Rector Michael Piazza responds to the "abomination" charge by saying that overpopulation has rendered that verse out of date. [36]

Among evangelicals, one of the hottest movements is Youth for Christ, which is sponsoring the "True Love Waits" chastity campaign among teens and young adults. A rally in Los Angeles this summer drew 5,000, and a compact disc of songs has sold 70,000 copies. [37]

In what may be taken as a slap at the baby-boomers, a Baptist church in Santa Clarita, Calif., recently canceled the day-care services it had long provided in the community, citing the need to promote traditional family values. "By having a preschool at this church, we are signaling that we think it's OK for parents to leave their children for 10 to 12 hours a day," said Mike Long, chairman of the Board of Elders. "We didn't want to give that message." [38] ■

OUTLOOK

Sources of Growth

The many volumes that have analyzed recent religious trends in America have focused on the effects of the 1960s counterculture, the rising education levels of a secular population and the socioeconomic patterns in church affiliation. But none of these has been found to be a major determinant of today's decisions to join or not to join.

The key factors, say Hoge and his colleagues, are, first, personal religious beliefs, and second, "adult experience and family situation — marital history and current marital status, number of children, distance of residence from the home community and recent experiences with church." [39]

And these forces play out differently in different communities. In the Baptist and Methodist churches, for example, the major sources of new members are African-Americans, Hispanics, Asians and Native Americans. Hispanics are flocking to churches enough to become the subject of a special section in this year's *Yearbook of American and Canadian Churches.* "Not only are there more Spanish-language congregations in the U.S. than ever," writes Barna, "but we find a growing number of Protestant denominations aggressively seeking new ways to reach this burgeoning segment." [40]

The relative flatness of mainline church growth in the United States in some cases has been offset in other parts of the world. The World Methodist Church, for example, reports that while its North American membership remained at 15 million from 1962-92, it swelled from 1 million members each in Africa and Asia in 1962 to a total of more than 5 million in 1992.

Geography is important in matters of faith. The 1991 Gallup Youth Survey showed that 94 percent of teens in the Midwest believe in Heaven, but only 84 percent of those in the East do. Similarly, 55 percent of teens in the South read the Bible, compared with only 31 percent in the East and 45 in the West.

Another key factor is gender. While 66 percent of women told Gallup in 1991 that religion is important to them, only 48 percent of men said so. Only 6 percent of women said they had no faith, vs. 11 percent of men. [41]

Many women schooled by the feminist movement have objected to the "patriarchal" values of traditional churches, and more than a few baby-boomer women have been offended by a sermon that discourages mothers from working outside the home. But for the most part, says Roozen, such objections haven't "affected these women's relationship to their church because they can find a church that is relatively relaxed or permissive toward women, or they can gravitate to cells within their own church."

Similarly, the 1960s sexual revolution that set the younger generations apart from their parents has not discouraged female membership in strict-minded churches. "People I talk to say women were losers in the sexual revolution," says the Rev. Curtin, citing a women's magazine poll of baby-boomer women saying that if they had it to do over again, a half to two-thirds would have come to marriage as virgins.

Another prod to religious exploration, notes James Gormally, a clinical psychologist in Silver Spring, Md., comes from the increasingly popular 12-step recovery process offered by Alcoholics Anonymous and other support groups. "There's a spirituality in trying to connect with a power higher than yourself," he says. Also, "we tend to associate religion with sense of identity, and so this is an area one can turn to if one is having problems with identity."

Psychology Professor Shafranske says there is very good research showing that people who turn to religion can improve their behavior in such areas as substance abuse, sexual practices and social life. "What matters in the correlation with higher mental health isn't whether the person participates in religion but

Continued on p. 1051

At Issue:

Should churches market themselves to baby boomers and younger generations?

yes

LEE STROBEL
Assistant pastor, Willow Creek Community Church, South Barrington, Ill.

FROM *INSIDE THE MIND OF UNCHURCHED HARRY & MARY: HOW TO REACH FRIENDS AND FAMILY WHO AVOID GOD AND THE CHURCH*

Unfortunately, many Christians who say they want to bring the Gospel to the unchurched of their community don't actually know any irreligious people. To them, the unchurched are faceless entities with mysterious patterns of behavior. As a result, they end up inadvertently creating a church service or event more to their own tastes than to that of their target audience. . . .

A survey of 800 people in [one] U.S. urban area yielded [the following] responses for why people skipped church: Church people are cold and unfriendly. Sermons are boring and don't relate to real life. Going to church is a guilt trip. Churches don't care about you, all they want is your money. We're too busy; going to church is a waste of time. . . .

Actually these survey results should be encouraging to Christians. The reason is that with some prayer, planning and creativity, these complaints can be overcome without in any way compromising the Gospel.

In other words, these objections generally relate to the method that's used to communicate the Gospel, not to the message itself, and consequently we're free to use our God-given creativity to present Christ's message in new ways that our target audience will connect with. . . .

So instead of services that are boring, lifeless and predictable, they can be designed to reflect the excitement, adventure and, yes, even the sacrifice of Christianity. They can vary from week to week rather than being stuck in the same programming rut . . . .

Rather than being cold and unfriendly, churches can be warm and inclusive toward outsiders without smothering them. Instead of relying on guilt tactics, they can present a balanced picture of the faith that included God's grace, forgiveness and love, while still teaching about the reality of sin and the need for personal repentance.

Keep in mind there are at least 55 million unchurched adults in the country. Think how many might return to church if it were only more sensitive to their needs and relevant to their lives.

But how is this going to happen unless individual Christians make the decision to strategically team up with their church to turbo-charge their evangelistic efforts? They ought to be partners who are committed to assisting each other in the ongoing adventure of penetrating their community with the Gospel.

no

DOUGLAS D. WEBSTER
Pastor of adult ministry, Cherry Creek Presbyterian Church, San Diego, Calif.

FROM *SELLING JESUS: WHAT'S WRONG WITH MARKETING THE CHURCH*

It appears that we've become susceptible to the idolatrous moods of novelty, sentimentality and subjectivism. Churches now compete, not only among themselves but with popular culture, in a mood-producing quest for warmth and excitement. They are caught up in providing a diet of entertainment that does not satisfy the need for spiritual nourishment. . . .

Meeting people's physical and emotional needs are essential expressions of Christian obedience and love, but offering what I have heard pastors call "a dog-and-pony show" or "a song and dance" is not. . . .

Holy ambition discerns the difference between targeting a market niche and discovering Christ's mission for the church. It distinguishes between consumer-oriented felt needs and deep-seated spiritual needs. Holy zeal knows the difference between corporate excellence and the beauty of holiness. It warns against a pastor-centered church and favors a ministry-centered church. . . .

While market-driven churches are attracting thousands of individuals because of the personality of the "key man," felt-need satisfaction and special features, the household of faith is trying to work alongside Christ, following a pattern of conviction and obedience that has been in place since the apostles. . . .

The household of faith does not need a new campaign, a new program, a new cutting-edge strategy for marketing the church to baby-boomers. What it needs is a renewed commitment to the whole counsel of God, to Christian friendship and body life, to prayer and worship, to baptism and the Lord's Table, to meeting the needs of the poor. . . .

The issue for the church of the '90s is not that we become more innovative but that we become more prayerful. We need not assume new and unbiblical pressures.

John Maxwell, pastor of Skyline Wesleyan Church in San Diego, expresses a common fallacy: "When churches run out of new ideas or new programs, they stop growing." The result of this kind of thinking has been numerical growth at the expense of spiritual growth. The demand for novelty and excitement ends up distracting churches from becoming a household of faith. . . .

Instead of market sensitivity we need spiritual sensitivity. The church does not need 24-hour-a-day marketing agents competing for attention in the world as much as it needs men and women of God whose quiet lives, solid convictions and Christlike character authentically represent the Gospel.

News Media Paying More Attention to Religion

Americans can count on the media to report in detail on the fiery deaths of religious cultists, priests who sexually abuse children and television evangelists who misuse donated money. But the unspectacular story of ordinary religious faith — of the 80 million Americans who go to worship each week — seldom makes the evening news or Page One.

The reason, according to some observers, is a news profession dominated by secular people. "Members of the media are simply unchurched, which makes them uncomfortable covering religion," says Gene Kapp, vice president of public relations for the Christian Broadcasting Network in Virginia Beach, Va. "The media has long been uncertain how to handle stories about people of faith who don't put their faith on the shelf most of the week but integrate it into their lives."

"Journalists by their nature are anti-authoritarian, and we need to watch this tendency," Deborah Howell, Newhouse News Service Washington bureau chief, told the Religious Newswriters Association in May. [1]

The common result, critics say, is sensationalistic coverage of religion's negative aspects and neglect of an area that is central to many lives. A study of network evening news coverage compiled by the conservative Media Research Center in Alexandria, Va., found that of more than 18,000 stories broadcast in 1993, religion was the subject of only 211, and a fourth of those came during the pope's eight-day visit to the United States in August. [2]

There are signs, however, that the secular news industry is getting religion. ABC News, following years of lobbying by anchorman Peter Jennings, this year hired TV's first full-time religion news correspondent, a Dallas-based, born-again Christian named Peggy Wehmeyer.

Beefing up religious coverage has been the topic of numerous seminars and conferences among news professionals this year. Last spring, the Rev. Billy Graham addressed the American Society of Newspaper Editors with suggestions for bridging the cultural gap between the media and the religious community.

Time magazine senior political correspondent Laurence I. Barrett in 1993 urged fellow journalists to broaden themselves to avoid bias against the religious right. "It is easy to recognize that we need a broad, sensitivity check," he wrote. "Whatever we think of [the evangelical movement], we must get ourselves to church, if only as observers." [3]

Thomas J. Billitteri, news editor of the Religion News Service, says the top papers are giving more space to stories that "recognize religion is important to the lives of readers." Still, he says, only about 70 of the country's 1,700 daily newspapers have a full-time reporter or editor covering religion.

The notion of an anti-religious newsroom goes back at least to the 1960s. Edwin Diamond, a New York University-based media critic, says that when he worked at *Newsweek* in the '60s, the editors used the religion section as a dumping ground for mediocre writers and considered dropping the section as passé. "The editors were very secular-minded and uninspired by religion," he says. "God was dead — but, it turned out, only in the narrow Boston-New York-Washington corridor occupied by journalists." [4]

ABC-TV religion correspondent Peggy Wehmeyer

But a recent survey indicates that such attitudes are no longer widespread. A questionnaire sent to 1,700 journalists and clergy during the winter of 1992-93 by the First Amendment Center at Vanderbilt University showed that 72 percent of editors considered religion important in their lives. The report attributed the problems in coverage to ignorance rather than bias and recommended that religion reporters get more specialized education. [5]

Still, many argue against making religion a hot news topic. "Religion is a very personal matter in this country," says Cheryl Gould, vice president of NBC News. "Where some groups may feel something is important, others may not." [6]

Billitteri thinks the coverage is improving because the press is better at going beyond the religion-page stories of piety and Sunday activity to cover changes in religion as it "intersects with broad public issues. We live in a country where Islam now rivals Judaism as the second-largest religion," he notes. "We have to cover religion like we cover business or science, seeking to be fair, accurate and to seek diverse voices. We have to respect the intangible of faith, but still ask the hard questions when it comes to religion's effect on daily life."

---

[1] *Editor & Publisher*, May 21, 1994, p. 14.

[2] Thomas Johnson and Sandra L. Crawford, "Faith in a Box: Entertainment Television on Religion, 1993."

[3] *Columbia Journalism Review*, July-August 1993, p. 33.

[4] Stephen Bates, "Saturation of Church & Press?" *Mediacritic*, summer 1994, p. 48.

[5] John Dart and Jimmy Allen, "Bridging the Gap: Religion and the News Media," 1993.

[6] Quoted in Peter Ross Range, "God & the News: Why is This Woman the Only Religion Reporter on TV?" *TV Guide*, Aug. 6, 1994, p. 18.

Continued from p. 1048

whether his religion is intrinsically motivated," he says.

Softening Skepticism

In the everyday world of the 1990s, religion has hardly regained the exalted status it held in previous eras. Former U.S. Education Secretary William J. Bennett recently complained, "In America today, the only respectable form of bigotry is bigotry directed toward religious people." That's because religion "forces modern man to confront matters he would prefer to ignore." [42]

But many Americans who have long been skeptical, on intellectual grounds, for example, are warming. Widely noted was the convergence of science and religion implied in the work of physicist Stephen Hawking, who observed: "We shall know the mind of God when we arrive at a set of equations that unite contradictions of modern physics." [43]

In Silver Spring, a large group of lawyers, government officials and other professionals living the hectic modern life of career and families are also practicing orthodox Jews. They all live within walking distance of a temple so that at sundown on the Sabbath they can follow their religion by unplugging all appliances and walking, yarmulkes in place, to worship. [44]

Back in the 1950s, notes Fishman of Brandeis, many Jews focused on "social action and became idea-oriented, viewing ritual as primitive. Now they've reincorporated it, the '60s generation having proven that if ritual was to be discontinued as part of the structure, they would create their own rituals."

But efforts by churches to market themselves to the unchurched will likely continue to draw skeptics who deride the modern tendency toward piety on the run. "Where are the real religious prophets?" asks R. Laurence Moore in his 1994 book *Selling God*. "Can there be any in a country whose self-image rests on fast, friendly and guiltless consumption? It is not the taste of a Big Mac that sells it; it is the way it feeds the low-down common desire to be democratically unpretentious. Would-be religious prophets have to learn the ways of Disneyland in order to find their audience, but even that popular touch cannot give them the capacity to reach the many Americans who would feel perfectly comfortable at a prayer breakfast under McDonald's generous golden arches." [45]

Willow Creek Community Church

Willow Creek Community Church in South Barrington, Ill., feeds 350 people a month.

Barna says the larger issue is what happens to the general culture, which he says has been declining. "The church is the only positive institution that can have a long-term effect on restoring it. The [only] two possibilities are moral anarchy and widespread spiritual revival. We now have the perfect conditions for a revival: alienated people who are questioning and jumping from job to job. But it will only happen if churches are prepared, and they are not."

Hoge writes that religion will remain the primary place people turn to with questions of meaning in life, the main alternative being involvement in social causes and movements, which, he notes, attract a minority of Americans. "Religious needs are constant and eternal," he says. "The issue is what is the truest and best way to reach people. Jesus didn't say we have to have pipe organs."

What has been called into question, he adds, is the need for denominations. It's a debate that is "very threatening to people who love them and have given their lives to them. But denominations as we have known them are basically a 20th-century product. The issues that were so important in 1700 are less important now, so many denominations could merge."

The recent uptick in religiosity does hark back to less complicated times. After *U.S. News & World Report* published its cover story on religion last spring, a reader responded: "The headline 'In God We Trust' brought forth memories of the united America I miss and love. I recalled times filled with patriotism and flourishing religion based on seemingly forgotten ideals — integrity, pride, honor, decency, courage and respect. . . . To not have bought this issue seemed equivalent to not supporting an opportunity for a return to what we carelessly tossed by the wayside in the '60s." [46]

For More Information

Alban Institute, 4550 Montgomery Ave., Suite 433 North, Bethesda, Md. 20814-3341; (301) 718-4407. This non-denominational research, consulting and educational organization provides congregations with support and services.

American Jewish Committee, 165 East 56th St., New York, N.Y. 10022; (212) 751-4000. The committee is devoted to protecting civil and religious rights for all people. It compiles research on church-state issues, Israel and the Middle East and Jews in the U.S. and former Soviet Union.

Hartford Seminary Center for Social and Religious Research, 77 Sherman St., Hartford, Conn. 06105; (203) 232-4451. Founded in 1981, the center studies emerging issues in faith and religious practice.

National Council of Churches of Christ in the USA, 475 Riverside Dr., New York, N.Y. 10015; (212) 870-2227. Representing 32 Protestant, Anglican and Eastern Orthodox denominations, the council was formed in 1950 to promote "oneness in Jesus Christ" through research, publishing, education, refugee assistance and disaster relief.

As the country's largest and most talked about generation, the baby-boomers have clearly made their mark. At a Methodist church in the Midwest, a boomer told Roof, "Thirty years ago . . . ministers [said] rock and roll was the work of the devil and anybody that was dancing was going to hell. Last night this church had a fun night. The theme was the '50s. Our daughter got up there and danced with blue suede shoes. . . . I think that is part of the reason that some of us who may have dropped out have come back, because it's a different church today than it was 30 years ago." [47]

At the same time, however, religion has made its mark on the boomers. "You'd never see a bird out there by himself . . . just birds in a little flock," another baby-boomer told Roof. "I thought, that's the way life is supposed to be. You are supposed to be a part of something, and if you are really going to live life, religious[ly] or otherwise, you need to have relationships with people and with . . . something . . . you believe in." [48] ■

Notes

[1] David A. Roozen, "Empty Nest; Empty Pew: The Boomers Continue Through the Life-Cycle," unpublished paper, October 1993.

[2] Wade Clark Roof, *A Generation of Seekers: The Spiritual Journeys of the Baby Boom Generation* (1993), p. 8.

[3] Quoted in *TV Guide,* Aug. 6, 1994, p. 22.

[4] "Spiritual America," *U.S. News & World Report,* April 4, 1994, p. 48.

[5] For background, see "Religion and Politics," *The CQ Researcher,* Oct. 14, 1994, pp. 889-912, and "Muslims in America," *The CQ Researcher,* April 30, 1993, pp. 361-385.

[6] The Associated Press, March 19, 1994, citing the *Yearbook of American and Canadian Churches 1994.*

[7] *The New York Times,* Sept. 25, 1994.

[8] Stephen L. Carter, *The Culture of Disbelief: How American Law and Politics Trivialize Religious Devotion* (1993), p. 25.

[9] "Reaching the First Post-Christian Generation," *Christianity Today,* Sept. 12, 1994, p. 18.

[10] Barry A. Kosmin and Seymour P. Lachman, *One Nation Under God: Religion in Contemporary American Society* (1993), p. 14.

[11] Dean R. Hoge "What Do Baby Boomers Want From Their Churches?" *Congregations: The Alban Journal,* July-August 1994, p. 3. The magazine is published by the Alban Institute, Bethesda, Md.

[12] For background, see "Charitable Giving," *The CQ Researcher,* Nov. 12, 1993, pp. 1002-1025.

[13] William Easum, *How to Reach Baby Boomers* (1991), p. 120.

[14] *Chicago Tribune,* April 3, 1994.

[15] *Christianity Today,* July 18, 1994, p. 20.

[16] Roger Finke and Rodney Starke, *The Churching of America, 1976-1990* (1992), p. 15.

[17] Kosmin and Lachman, *op. cit.,* p. 8.

[18] *Ibid.,* p. 5.

[19] Robert Wuthnow, *The Restructuring of American Religion* (1988), pp. 17-20.

[20] Dean R. Hoge, Benton Johnson and Donald A. Luidens, *Vanishing Boundaries: The Religion of Mainline Protestant Baby Boomers* (1994), p. 2.

[21] *Ibid.,* p. 192.

[22] William Willimon and Stanley Hauerwas, quoted in Loren Mead, *The Once and Future Church* (1991) p. 23.

[23] Roof, *op. cit.,* p. 166.

[24] Wade Clark Roof, Jackson W. Carroll and David A. Roozen, *The Postwar Generation and Establishment Religion: Cross-Cultural Perspectives,* forthcoming book.

[25] Roof, Carroll and Roozen, *op. cit.,* p. 15.

[26] Wuthnow, *op. cit.,* p. 156.

[27] Summarized in Hoge, *op. cit.,* p. 18.

[28] Wuthnow, *op. cit.,* p. 88.

[29] Roof, Carroll and Roozen, *op. cit.,* p. xiii.

[30] George Barna, *The Invisible Generation* (1992), p. 151.

[31] Hoge et al., *op. cit.,* p. 47.

[32] *Ibid.,* p. 111.

[33] David A. Roozen, "Empty Nest, Empty Pew: The Boomers Continue Through the Life-Cycle," October 1993, unpublished paper.

[34] *Sojourners,* November 1994, pp. 9, 15.

[35] Barna, *op. cit.,* p. 30.

[36] *The New York Times,* Oct. 30, 1994.

[37] *The Nation,* Sept. 26, 1994, p. 306.

[38] *The Washington Post,* Oct. 23, 1994.

[39] Hoge, Johnson and Luidens, *op. cit.,* p. 172.

[40] *Yearbook of American and Canadian Churches 1994,* p. 9.

[41] Wuthnow, *op. cit.,* p. 225.

[42] "Revolt Against God," *Policy Review,* winter 1994, p. 19.

[43] Quoted by Bryan Appleyard, *The New York Times,* April 8, 1993.

[44] *Washingtonian,* April 1992, p. 58.

[45] R. Laurence Moore, *Selling God: American Religion in the Marketplace of Culture* (1994), p. 276.

[46] *U.S. News & World Report,* May 2, 1994, p. 8.

[47] Roof, *op. cit.,* p. 260.

[48] *Ibid.,* p. 153.

Bibliography

Selected Sources Used

Books

Barna, George, *The Invisible Generation: Baby Busters,* Barna Research Group, 1992.
A marketing analyst with a speciality in religion reports results of his surveys of Americans now in their 20s, contrasting their attitudes with those of older generations in areas of religion, values and career plans.

Easum, William, *How to Reach Baby Boomers,* Abingdon Press, 1991.
A church consultant who formerly was pastor of the Colonial Hills United Methodist Church in San Antonio, Texas, argues that unchurched baby-boomers can be recruited only if pastors and leaders help them move from a life-style of self-fulfillment to one of self-denial for the cause of Jesus Christ.

Finke, Roger, and Rodney Stark, *The Churching of America, 1976-1990: Winners and Losers in Our Religious Economy,* Rutgers University Press, 1992.
Two historians document the country's shift over two centuries from a place where most people took no part in organized religion to one where nearly two-thirds do.

Hoge, Dean R., Benton Johnson and Donald A. Luidens, *Vanishing Boundaries: The Religion of Mainline Protestant Baby Boomers,* Westminster/John Knox Press, 1994.
Three sociology professors analyze results of a survey of the religious habits of Presbyterian baby-boomers, quoting from in-depth interviews about why people leave or return to church.

Kosmin, Barry A., and Seymour P. Lachman, *One Nation Under God: Religion in Contemporary American Society,* Harmony Books, 1993.
Two professors at the City University of New York analyze results of "the most extensive survey of religious identification in 20th-century America."

Moore, R. Laurence, *Selling God: American Religion in the Marketplace of Culture,* Oxford University Press, 1994.
A fellow at the Woodrow Wilson International Center for Scholars analyzes the effects of the American economy and secular culture on religious practice and growth, warning that "readers offended by the suggestion that religion exerts an appeal analogous to that of a form of commercial entertainment" should avoid his book.

Roof, Wade Clark, *A Generation of Seekers: The Spiritual Journeys of the Baby Boom Generation,* Harper/San Francisco, 1993.
A professor of religion and society at the University of California-Santa Barbara uses interviews and statistical research to trace the trends in religious affiliation among Americans born from 1946-65.

Roozen, David A. and C. Kirk Hadaway, (eds.), *Church and Denominational Growth*, Abingdon Press, 1993.
A religion professor at Connecticut's Hartford Seminary and a former researcher at the Southern Baptist Convention edited these articles from 12 experts on church growth. They examine statistics and trends, analyze religious choices and argue that congregations, not denominations, are the key to growth.

Strobel, Lee, *Inside the Mind of Unchurched Harry & Mary: How to Reach Friends and Family Who Avoid God and the Church,* Zondervan Publishing House, 1993.
A former journalist who is now assistant pastor at the Willow Creek Community Church in South Barrington, Ill., offers advice for churches seeking to reach the baby-boomers with a Christian message.

Wuthnow, Robert, *The Restructuring of American Religion: Society and Faith Since World War II,* Princeton University Press, 1988.
A noted historian of religion traces the role religion has played in America over the past five decades, from the 1950s boom in church growth, through the decline of mainline churches in the '60s and '70s, to the resurgence — strongest among conservative, evangelical churches — in the '80s and '90s.

Articles

"Spiritual America," *U.S. News & World Report,* April 4, 1994, pp. 48-59.
This cover story explores the conflicting attitudes toward religion in the United States.

The Next Step

Additional information from UMI's Newspaper & Periodical Abstracts database

The Church and Abortion Rights

Bogert, Carroll, "Abortion and the fight for God," *Newsweek*, Oct. 17, 1994, p. 40.

While abortion foes claim that religious beliefs guide their actions, many abortion doctors have a religious zeal just as great. As they come under increasing attack, some of it violent, religious abortion doctors are seeking more support from the clergy.

"Dissent on abortion costs candidate her role in parish," *Boston Globe*, Oct. 9, 1994, p. 40.

Kathleen E. Caron, a state Senate candidate in Massachusetts, says she was told by a Catholic priest that she could no longer play a public role in the church because she has spoken out in favor of abortion rights.

General Interest

Bowman, Karlyn H., and Everett Carl Ladd, "Public opinion and demographic report: Faith in America," *American Enterprise*, September 1994, pp. 90-99.

A survey on religious faith in the U.S. is presented, focusing on religious practice, politics and religion, conservatism, demographics and other factors. A belief in God was affirmed by 95 percent of survey participants.

Shear, Michael D., "Bishop urges fair hearing for religious views," *The Washington Post*, Oct. 3, 1994, p. A8.

Roman Catholic Bishop Edward M. Egan urged the U.S.' leading jurists to help rid the country of "political correctness," which he said muzzles the voices of those who oppose abortion and support religious education.

Williams, Armstrong, "Virtue pays," *Forbes*, Oct. 10, 1994, p. 94.

A child with a religious orientation is much less likely to drop out of school, use drugs or commit crime. The evidence that suggests that civic virtue, along with strong personal morality, goes hand in hand with economic prosperity is discussed.

Politics and Religion

Carvajal, Doreen, and Gebe Martinez, "Clergy struggles to address volatile issues of Prop. 187," *Los Angeles Times*, Oct. 3, 1994, p. A1.

The top leaders of all of California's major religious denominations have attacked Proposition 187, the anti-illegal-immigrant measure on the November 1994 ballot. However, priests, ministers, rabbis and nuns are struggling to deliver the anti-187 message in a delicate manner that will persuade rather than alienate.

Gartner, Michael, "Religion and politics just don't mix," *USA Today*, Oct. 4, 1994, p. A2.

Gartner says that religion, which was supposed to have been buried as a political issue in 1960, is everywhere in politics in the '90s but that religion should still be kept out of government and vice versa.

Greenhouse, Linda, "A cross high above San Diego is dealt another setback," *The New York Times*, Oct. 12, 1994, p. A17.

The Supreme Court on Oct. 11, 1994, declined to review a ruling by the U.S. Court of Appeals for the 9th Circuit that a 43-ft. cross, a San Diego landmark, cannot remain on public land. Without comment, the justices turned down the city's appeal, which defended the cross as a historic property that had the secular purpose of honoring San Diego's war veterans.

Herman, Ken, "The candidates and the higher authority," *Houston Post*, Oct. 2, 1994, p. A1.

The religious views of Texas Gov. Ann Richards and Republican challenger George W. Bush, both of whom are Methodists, are discussed.

Jacobs, Sally, "Separation of politics, religion is often elusive," *Boston Globe*, Oct. 2, 1994, p. 1.

Although many U.S. citizens say that religion is not an issue when it comes to casting their votes, subjects like abortion, homosexuality and the role of women do raise the issue indirectly, since a candidate's religious beliefs may affect their views on controversial issues.

"Mitt Romney says Ted Kennedy needs a history lesson from JFK," *Detroit News*, Sept. 29, 1994, p. A2.

GOP Senate candidate Mitt Romney accused Sen. Edward T. Kennedy, D-Mass., of betraying John F. Kennedy's legacy by making an issue of Romney's religion. Romney is a former Mormon missionary and the son of three-time Michigan Gov. George Romney.

Niebuhr, Gustav, "Clinton talks about religion as his anchor," *The New York Times*, Oct. 4, 1994, p. A1.

Speaking to about 40 publishers, editors and reporters representing different Baptist denominations, President Clinton said on Oct. 3, 1994, that he read the Bible and other religious books for guidance and to cope with the isolation of the presidency. He defended his administration's stand on abortion rights, saying he had read Scripture that had been cited by religious conservatives opposed to abortion and found the passages ambiguous.

Strausberg, Chinta, "DNC chair: GOP has no trump card on morality," ***Chicago Defender,*** **Sept. 26, 1994, p. 9.**
Democratic National Committee Chair David Wilhelm has said the GOP does not have a trump card on morality and believes spirituality can curb crime.

Religion in the Schools

Curran, Charles E., "The elusive idea of a Catholic university," ***National Catholic Reporter,*** **Oct. 7, 1994, pp. 12-15.**
Institutional, historical and cultural changes have influenced the question of what it means to be a Catholic college or university. Issues concerning what constitutes a Catholic university and the advantages Catholic colleges and universities have over their secular counterparts are discussed.

Clough, Michael P., "Diminish students' resistance to biological evolution," ***American Biology Teacher,*** **October 1994, pp. 409-415.**
Few articles have provided instructional strategies for teachers in decreasing student and parent hostility toward evolution education. A brief overview of the arguments for teaching biological evolution and the arguments for not giving "scientific" creationism credibility is provided, and strategies for teaching the subject are discussed.

Merton, Andrew, "A moment of silence, please," ***Boston Globe,*** **Oct. 9, 1994, p. NH2.**
Merton comments that the current movement in New Hampshire to impose a five-minute period of silence at the beginning each public school day is not a bad thing.

O'Harrow, Robert Jr., and Debbi Wilgoren, "Conservatives press libraries: Fairfax loss looms, but limits gain hold," ***The Washington Post,*** **Oct. 10, 1994, p. A1.**
Christian activists and other conservatives have no intention of backing off efforts to limit access to books in public libraries. Despite the defeat of an effort to restrict children from library materials on topics such as suicide in Fairfax County, Va., other Washington, D.C., area movements have started.

Wells, Robert Marshall, "House gives its approval to school aid measure," ***Congressional Quarterly Weekly Report,*** **Oct. 1, 1994, pp. 2807-2808.**
On Sept. 30, 1994, the House adopted the conference report on the reauthorization of the 1965 Elementary and Secondary Education Act. The side issues of religion and sex may cause tumult in the Senate.

Religious Minorities

Golden, Daniel, "Diversity reshapes Mormon faith," ***Boston Globe,*** **Oct. 16, 1994, p. 1.**
The reshaping of the Mormon faith and the Church of Jesus Christ of Latter-day Saints is examined.

Horwitz, Donald P., and Richard S. Hirschhaut, "Card is not funny," ***Chicago Tribune,*** **Sept. 28, 1994, p. 24.**
In a letter to the editor, Horwitz and Hirschhaut of the Anti-Defamation League of B'nai B'rith say that the group shares the concerns expressed by members of the Muslim community over the so-called humor in greeting cards produced by Recycled Paper Products.

"Senate backs Indians' right to use peyote in religion," ***Congressional Quarterly Weekly Report,*** **Oct. 1, 1994, p. 2814.**
On Sept. 27, 1994, the Senate approved a bill that would protect the rights of Native Americans to ingest peyote during religious ceremonies. This bill and two others aimed at protecting the rights of Native Americans are discussed.

Sharif, Khadijah Fatinah, "Muslims making key political moves," ***American Muslim Journal,*** **Aug. 19, 1994, p. 1.**
All across America Muslims are successfully contesting political incumbents for leadership positions. Some specific situations are examined.

Women's Roles and Religion

Butturini, Paula, "Catholic women seek recognition of role in church," ***Boston Globe,*** **Sept. 29, 1994, p. 19.**
When Pope John Paul II convenes a worldwide synod of bishops to debate the role of nuns and priests for the new millennium, "women religious," who outnumber men 3-1, are hoping that the synod specifically acknowledges the role and importance of consecrated women in the church and gives them a larger voice.

Drozdiak, William, "Concern, criticism shroud ailing pope," ***The Washington Post,*** **Oct. 3, 1994, p. A11.**
Pope John Paul II's rejection of change in the role of women within the Catholic Church, along with his opposition to abortion and contraception, is causing some believers to question the direction of his papacy. The pope's failing health has also become an issue.

Farnham, Janice, and Mary Milligan, "Women religious and the World Synod of Bishops," ***America,*** **Oct. 15, 1994, pp. 22-23.**
An examination of the theological statements issued by the International Union of Superiors General for Women (ISUG) for consideration by the world Synod of Bishops is offered, and excerpts from the ISUG statement are presented. The statements reflect the hopes and struggles of women religious in the Roman Catholic Church of the 1990s.

Back Issues

Great Research on Current Issues Starts Right Here...Recent topics covered by The CQ Researcher are listed below. Before May 1991, reports were published under the name of Editorial Research Reports.®

MAY 1993
Head Start
High-Speed Rail
Children's Legal Rights
Muslims in America

JUNE 1993
Food Safety
Prostitution
Childhood Immunizations
National Service

JULY 1993
Electric Cars
Population Growth
Downward Mobility
Intelligence Testing

AUGUST 1993
Mental Illness
Bilingual Education
Foreign Policy Burden
School Funding

SEPTEMBER 1993
Suburban Crime
Public Housing
Supreme Court Preview
Immigration Reform

OCTOBER 1993
Airline Safety
Disaster Response
Science in the Courtroom
The Glass Ceiling

NOVEMBER 1993
Paying for Retirement
Charitable Giving
Privacy in the Workplace
Adoption

DECEMBER 1993
U.S. Vietnam-Relations
Learning Disabilities
Child Care
Space Program's Future

JANUARY 1994
Racial Tensions in Schools
South Africa's Future
Worker Retraining
Regulating Pesticides

FEBRUARY 1994
Prison Overcrowding
Water Quality
Religion in Schools
Juvenile Justice

MARCH 1994
Underground Economy
Education Standards
Gambling Boom
Private Management of Public Schools

APRIL 1994
Reproductive Ethics
U.S.-China Trade
Soccer in America
Talk Show Democracy

MAY 1994
Traffic Congestion
Women's Health Issues
Mutual Funds
Political Scandals

JUNE 1994
Education and Gender
Gun Control
Public Land Policy
Nuclear Arms Cleanup

JULY 1994
Dietary Supplements
Public Opinion and Foreign Policy
Crime Victims' Rights
Birth Control Choices

AUGUST 1994
Genetically Engineered Foods
Electing Minorities
Prozac Controversy
College Sports

SEPTEMBER 1994
Home Schooling
Welfare Experiments
Courts and the Media
Regulating Tobacco

OCTOBER 1994
Historic Preservation
Religion and Politics
Arts Funding
Economic Sanctions

NOVEMBER 1994
Sex on Campus
Blood Supply Safety
Testing Term Limits

Back issues are available for $4.00 (subscribers) or $7.00 (non-subscribers). Quantity discounts apply to orders over ten. To order, call Congressional Quarterly Customer Service at (202) 887-8621.

Binders are available for $16.00. To order call 1-800-638-1710. Please refer to stock number 648.

Future Topics

- ***Arms Sales***
- ***Farm Policy***
- ***Earthquake Research***

THE CQ Researcher

PUBLISHED BY CONGRESSIONAL QUARTERLY INC.

Farm Policy

Should federal farm programs be overhauled?

In 1995, Congress will draft legislation reauthorizing federal farm programs, as it does every five years. The basic design of these income and price support programs has changed very little since they were first conceived during the Great Depression of the 1930s, and a growing chorus of voices is calling for reform. Their common refrain is that the programs help those farmers who need it least, provide little or no help to the poorest farmers, make U.S. farm products uncompetitive in world markets and provide no lasting solution to the chronic problem of overproduction. While there is general agreement that current farm programs need some fixing, there is wide disagreement on what form the changes should take and how fast they should be made. Given such uncertainty, analysts expect a heated farm bill debate in 1995.

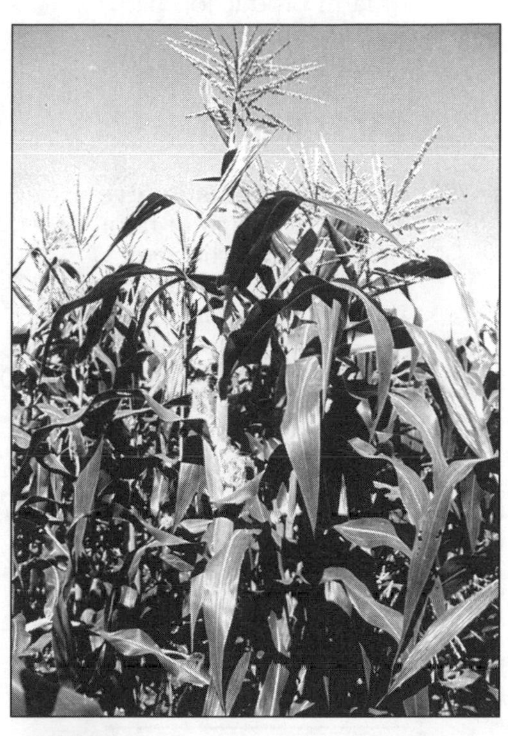

INSIDE THIS ISSUE

CQ Dec. 2, 1994 • Volume 4, No. 45 • Pages 1057-1080

Formerly Editorial Research Reports

COVER: U.S. DEPARTMENT OF AGRICULTURE

December 2, 1994
Volume 4, No. 45

EDITOR
Sandra Stencel

MANAGING EDITOR
Thomas J. Colin

ASSOCIATE EDITOR
Richard L. Worsnop

STAFF WRITERS
Charles S. Clark
Mary H. Cooper
Kenneth Jost

PRODUCTION EDITOR
Sarah E. Merritt

EDITORIAL ASSISTANT
Tonya Whitfield

GRAPHICS
P. Eloise Fuller

PUBLISHED BY
Congressional Quarterly Inc.

CHAIRMAN
Andrew Barnes

VICE CHAIRMAN
Andrew P. Corty

EDITOR AND PUBLISHER
Neil Skene

EXECUTIVE EDITOR
Robert W. Merry

ASSOCIATE PUBLISHER
John J. Coyle

MARKETING AND SALES DIRECTOR
Edward S. Hauck

The CQ Researcher (ISSN 1056-2036). Formerly Editorial Research Reports. Published weekly (48 times per year, not printed the first Friday of any month with five Fridays) by Congressional Quarterly Inc., 1414 22nd St., N.W., Washington, D.C. 20037. Rates are furnished upon request. Second-class postage paid at Washington, D.C. POSTMASTER: Send address changes to The CQ Researcher, 1414 22nd St., N.W., Washington, D.C. 20037.

Farm Policy

BY BARBARA MANTEL

THE ISSUES

Lee Schafer has been planting corn and soybeans on his 700-acre Brighton, Iowa, farm for 40 years, but this year is special. "It's one of our best years ever," he says. "We're in a fairly dry area, and we didn't anticipate a bumper [crop], but that's what we got."

Schafer averaged 180 bushels an acre on his 350 acres of corn, a record for him. And Schafer was not the only farmer who had a good year. The U.S. Department of Agriculture (USDA) has projected a record corn crop of 10 billion bushels in 1994.

But all this abundance has a downside. The record harvest, far outpacing demand, has pushed prices for corn to about $2 a bushel, 25 percent lower than prices six months ago. Still, Schafer says, "We're better off this year than we were last year. At least we have a crop to sell."

Massive flooding in the Midwest during the summer of 1993 turned Schafer's stretch of southeastern Iowa into "one of the Great Lakes" and cut his corn production in half. Last year, Schafer grossed about $233 an acre; this year he's looking at about $360 an acre, despite lower prices.

And that does not include the funds the federal government will kick in. When crop prices plummet, as they have this year, the government cushions the blow. Schafer expects to receive an additional 30 to 35 cents for each bushel of corn.

This income protection is part of what University of Minnesota professors Willard Cochrane and C. Ford Runge call the "social contract" between society and agriculture. "Politicians for most of the 20th century have praised farmers for their willingness to produce bountifully and promised them, in return, that their prices and incomes would be protected," they write in their 1992 book, *Reforming Farm Policy.*[1]

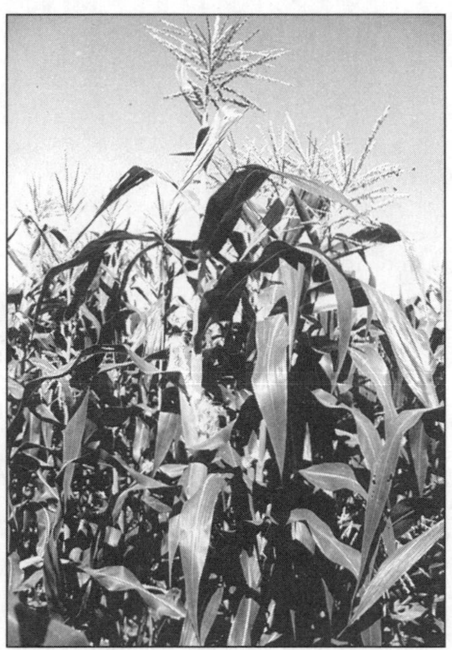

The government uses a complex, confusing and sometimes conflicting array of programs to support farm prices and incomes. The programs have been modified since they were first introduced during the Depression of the 1930s, but their core principle remains the same: a *quid pro quo* of government payments for idle acres.

The *quid* side of the equation works as follows: To help farmers get from harvest to sale, the USDA will loan a farmer money at a subsidized interest rate. After the harvest, the farmer can sell his crop in the marketplace and repay the government's loan with interest. If the market price for his crop has fallen too low, the farmer can forfeit his crop and keep the loan without penalty. In that case, the government essentially buys the farmer's crop. *(See box, p. 1060.)*

Whether the farmer repays the government loan or defaults, he is eligible to receive what are called deficiency payments. The government gives this money to farmers when the market price for their crop falls below some set government target. It's the 30 to 35 cents on the bushel that Schafer expects to get from the government.

These price and income support programs are voluntary, but if a farmer signs up for them, he must abide by the *quo* side of the agreement, known as the acreage reduction program. Before each growing season, the USDA must try to forecast world demand for a variety of crops, and then based on that forecast, it will require participating farmers to idle a certain number of acres to keep supply and demand in balance.

It's a tricky business. If the government idles too little land and "supplies exceed demand," write Cochrane and Runge, "prices will fall and deficiency payments will rise, leading to high commodity program spending. If it guesses too high, and supplies fall short of demand, prices will skyrocket. While farmers may be pleased, the general consuming public will not be."[2]

Critics of the current *quid pro quo* arrangement say it is out of date, unfair and inefficient. "The farm program philosophy has not changed significantly in decades, while farm management and ownership has," says Evan Stadlman, executive director of the Iowa Corn Growers Association. Large numbers of diversified family farms have given way to a much smaller number, and big, highly specialized farms now account for the bulk of farm production.

Defenders of the current system, including many farm-state politicians, say federal farm programs help keep the price of food relatively low. The American consumer "now spends about 10 cents out of every income dollar for the so-called market basket of food," Rep. Pat Roberts, R-Kan., told a gathering of farmers in Melvin, Ill., in June. "In Japan, Italy, France, Great Britain, the cost is double that. The point is, through the productivity of the American farmer and rancher — and yes, with the help of that

Federal Programs Supporting Farm Prices and Income

Non-Recourse Commodity Loans: Farmers put up their crops as collateral and obtain a loan from the U.S. Department of Agriculture's Commodity Credit Corporation to get them through the crop year. The loan is calculated using the "loan rate," a price per bushel, bale, pound or hundredweight — depending on the crop — set by the government. Farmers can either repay the loan with interest after selling their crop at the market price, or if the market price is below the loan rate, farmers can forfeit their crop to the government as full settlement of the loan.

Deficiency Payments: This is the primary method the government uses to support farm income for growers of wheat, feed grains, cotton and rice. It accounts for two-thirds of direct support to farmers. The program is voluntary, but in order for farmers to receive deficiency payments, they must agree to idle acres at the government's request and to comply with certain conservation provisions. Deficiency payments are triggered if the average market price for a crop falls below the crop's target price, which is set by the government. The actual payment rate equals the difference between the target price and the crop's market price or its loan rate, whichever is higher. For instance, the target price for corn is $2.75 per bushel; the market price is $2.09 per bushel (as of Nov. 25); and the loan rate is $1.89 per bushel. The payment rate would be 66 cents.

Multiple-Peril Crop Insurance: This program protects farmers from losses due to natural disasters. Congress reformed it in October 1994 to encourage greater farmer participation. Farmers who receive other farm program benefits, beginning in 1995, will be required to buy crop insurance. They will pay only a nominal processing fee for insurance covering catastrophic losses, and the government will subsidize private insurance providers to encourage farmers to buy supplemental insurance in the private sector.

Ad Hoc Disaster Assistance: Congress reformed this program in October as well. The revised program restricts the ability of Congress to pass disaster assistance legislation by requiring a pay-as-you-go approach. It also establishes a permanent disaster assistance fund for crops not eligible for crop insurance.

much maligned farm bill — the American consumer has 90 cents of every dollar to spend for health care, education, housing and all of the rest of the essentials to which we think we are entitled."

The terms of the social contract between agriculture and society will be the subject of intense debate next year, when Congress rewrites the legislation that authorizes farm programs, as it does every five years. Not only have critics of farm programs grown more vocal, but the 1994 elections swept a majority of Republicans into the House and Senate. Some prominent Republicans, including Rep. Dick Armey of Texas, in line to become House majority leader, have long proposed cutting farm programs.

But Republicans face a dilemma. They came to power promising a vote on a balanced-budget amendment, but they also received strong support from farm districts. "Dick Armey has worked in the past with Northeast liberals ... to cut some farm benefits," says William Browne, a political scientist at Central Michigan University. "But given the fact that Armey has to worry about keeping this new Republican majority in 1996, he's got to try not to alienate farm support. That's probably going to temper Armey's enthusiasm for farm program cuts. And Pat Roberts isn't going to stand still and watch farm programs be dismantled."

Roberts, the incoming chairman of the House Agriculture Committee, says he understands some spending cuts will be necessary. But, he adds, there's got to be a limit. "I think we're not only debating the details of the farm bill next year but also the entire rationale for even having a farm program. There's a sea change in Congress, with everyone rethinking government. Why not farm programs? And that's OK. It gives me a chance to educate members of Congress, including the new members."

Recent comments by Senate Republican leader Bob Dole of Kansas indicate that he, too, is likely to resist suggestions for drastic cutbacks in farm subsidies. Appearing on ABC-TV's "This Week With David Brinkley" Nov. 20, Dole said: "When people [have] asked me about farm programs, I [have] said, 'Sure, we'll cut farm programs if we cut everything else.' And I think that's the attitude we'll have."

As lawmakers prepare for next year's debate over the farm bill, here are some of the questions they are asking:

Should the government phase out its current menu of commodity programs and adopt just one program to guarantee farm revenue?

A number of individuals have suggested replacing current farm subsidy programs with a revenue guarantee designed to even out the fluctuations in farm income. [3] But many lawmakers say no plan will fly in Congress unless it has the backing of producers, and that's what makes the proposal of a group called the Iowa Farm Bill Study Team intriguing.

The participants in the study team are a who's who of Iowa agriculture: Agribusiness Association of Iowa, Iowa Corn Growers Association, Iowa Cattlemen's Association, Iowa Dairy Products Association, Iowa Farm Bureau Federation, Iowa Institute of

Cooperatives, Iowa Pork Producers Association, Iowa Poultry Association, Iowa Sheep Industry Association, Iowa Soybean Association and the National Farmers Organization. These groups formed the study team in June 1993 with the purpose of developing a proposal that Congress could consider during the 1995 farm bill debate.

Attesting to the plan's simplicity, its description takes up just a half-page in the study team's 22-page report, issued last February.[4] The group calls its approach revenue assurance, and it contains these key provisions:

- Three income-support programs — deficiency payments, disaster relief and crop insurance (*see box, p. 1060*) — would be eliminated.
- The government would no longer try to control supply by requiring farmers to idle acres.
- Each farmer would plant whatever crop he wanted and in whatever quantity he wanted as long as he complied with soil conservation plans. (*See story, p. 1074.*).
- The government would continue to make commodity loans to support prices.
- Each farmer's income would be guaranteed at 70 percent of his "normal crop revenue," which would be based on the farmer's income for the last five years.

The study team says its revenue assurance plan would "probably pay producers one year out of five instead of almost every year like the current program does. In the long run [it] will pay producers only when they need it and will save the government nearly $2 billion annually."

The study team's proposal addresses a number of longstanding concerns about current farm programs. One of the biggest complaints is that the largest farms receive the bulk of federal payments. In 1992, 15 percent of farms received roughly 90 percent of direct federal payments while more than 70 percent of the nation's farms received no government payments at all.[5]

The reason for this unequal distribution can be found in the way income supports are structured. Deficiency payments increase with acreage. The greater number of acres a farmer plants over the years, what's called his acreage base, the greater the deficiency payment.* And because deficiency payments reward size, critics say they actually accelerate the trend toward fewer, bigger farms by encouraging the owners of larger farms to buy up their smaller neighbors.

Under revenue assurance, payments would not be linked to farm size but rather to farm revenue. Farmers who have squeezed the most revenue out of their land in the past, no matter the number of acres, would receive the most payments in lean years. In this way, the study team says its plan promotes efficiency.

The study team also maintains that the current deficiency payments system works against the government's goal of controlling production and aligning supply and demand. After idling the number of acres required by the government, "producers are encouraged to produce the maximum number of acres [allowed] of these crops, no matter what the market dictates to them," the group states. "If the producers choose to plant less than this, they will reduce their payment."[6] Under revenue assurance, the team says, farmers would be encouraged to produce what the market dictates because federal payments would not be tied to the amount planted.

R. Michael Jenkins

"I think we're not only debating the details of the farm bill next year but also the entire rationale for even having a farm program."

— Rep. Pat Roberts, R-Kansas

The study team's report also criticizes the government's acreage reduction program, saying it puts U.S. farmers at a disadvantage in world markets. Last year half of all wheat, a fifth of all corn and a third of all soybeans produced in the U.S. were exported (*see p. 1070*). Those numbers could be higher, the study team said, if the acreage reduction program did not idle "productive farmland which makes the U.S. forfeit sales. . . . For every acre taken out of production in this country, an acre and a third comes into production somewhere in the world."[7]

Agricultural economist Richard Pottorff, of the private forecasting firm The WEFA Group, says the study team's plan has a number of potential benefits "that make it a program that needs a closer look." First of all, he says, "it saves the government money, at least based on the calculations of the study team, a test that any farm program proposal must pass."[8]

A report by five USDA economists said revenue assurance would stabilize farm income more effectively than

---

* The deficiency payment = (the target price) - (the loan rate or market price, whichever is higher) x (the farmer's base acreage) x (a government-calculated "average yield" per acre).

Reorganizing the Department of Agriculture

It's not just farm subsidies that will come under the budget ax in coming years. The bureaucracy that administers them is targeted for slimming as well. In October, Congress approved legislation that will put the Department of Agriculture (USDA), the government's fourth-largest agency, on the strictest diet since its creation 132 years ago.

President Abraham Lincoln established the department in 1862 "to acquire and to diffuse among the people of the United States useful information on subjects connected with agriculture in the most general and comprehensive sense of the word." The commissioner of Agriculture was authorized to conduct experiments, collect statistics and to collect, test and distribute new seeds and plants. [1]

During the next century, the department's mission expanded. In 1905, the USDA became the custodian of the country's national forests. After the Depression, the department became responsible for providing direct economic assistance to farmers. During the 1960s, the department began aiding consumers through such programs as food stamps and school lunches. Spending on these consumer programs swelled; by the early 1990s, spending on farm programs accounted for only about a quarter of the department's budget.

The 1990s also brought intense criticism of the department's organization and management, and not just from outsiders. Last August, Secretary of Agriculture Mike Espy told the Midwestern Governors Conference that the USDA had become "a bureaucratic Godzilla: a monster of overlapping services and endless paperwork."

The USDA has an annual budget of roughly $70 billion, with 115,000 employees working for 43 departments in more than 15,000 offices. A 1991 study by the General Accounting Office said the agency "administers its farm programs and services through one of the federal government's largest, most decentralized field structures. The structure reflects the era in which it was established — the 1930s when communication and transportation systems were greatly limited by geographic boundaries. Since then, the number of farmers has declined sharply, and telephones, computers and highways have increased farmers' access to information and assistance programs. . . . Yet, the basic USDA field structure has undergone few major adjustments." [2]

There have been many recommendations for major adjustments over the years. The Clinton administration announced its own restructuring plan on Sept. 7, 1993. Its basic elements were streamlining and realigning the headquarters' offices and functions, and closing or consolidating more than 1,200 field offices. USDA officials estimated that the plan would save $2.3 billion over 5 years, more than half of that coming from the anticipated elimination of 7,500 department jobs. After much debate, Congress passed the USDA reorganization legislation in early October 1994, and the president signed it into law Oct. 13. [3]

The centerpiece of the reorganization plan is the creation of a Consolidated Farm Service Agency within the USDA. It will oversee farm subsidy, farm lending and crop insurance programs — programs that had previously been administered by separate agencies, often in separate field offices. Now farmers will have one-stop shopping for services, something most farmers applaud.

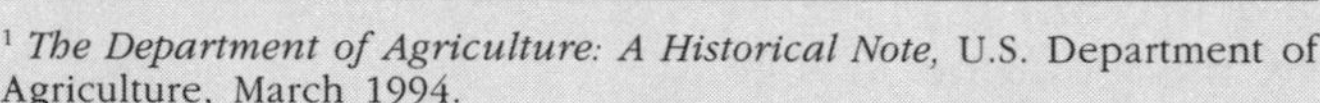

[1] *The Department of Agriculture: A Historical Note,* U.S. Department of Agriculture, March 1994.

[2] *Farm Agencies' Field Structure Needs Major Overhaul,* General Accounting Office, January 1991.

[3] See *CQ Weekly Report,* Oct. 8, 1994, pp. 2871-2872.

current programs. Under current law, deficiency payments kick in only when market prices fall below some predetermined target price. But there are years when farm income suffers not because of low prices, but because of poor harvests. In that situation, prices are actually driven higher because of tight supply, and farmers receive no deficiency payments. "The revenue guarantee approach might temper these extremes, giving farmers more stable incomes from year to year," the economists said. [9]

But analysts also see some potential problems with the study team's plan. Eliminating the acreage reduction program and putting the land that the program idles back in production could have serious implications, Pottorff says. "Just producing more doesn't mean we can sell more; and if we sell more it will probably be at significantly lower prices. At least until we drove a significant portion of the currently idled acreage back out of production, the revenue assurance program would probably mean excess supplies of many crops and *very* low prices." [10]

Others say that revenue guarantee programs are a mistake because they would prop up a farmer's income in bad times without any analysis of why his income had fallen. "They're like the doctor telling the patient to take two aspirins and go to bed," writes Robert Reinsel, an analyst with the USDA who favors keeping the current system of farm programs. "They leave the patient without any diagnosis of the problem, or a means to a cure." [11]

It's not known at this point how many farmers outside of the Iowa Farm Bill Study Team are interested in gutting farm programs and replacing them with some sort of revenue guarantee. National farm organizations are in somewhat of a bind because their Iowa affiliates support the revenue assurance approach while other affiliates do not. For instance, a proposal from the American Farm Bureau Federation's Illinois branch retains all basic commodity programs. As a result, the farm bureau has yet to take a position on revenue guarantees, although it has a task force studying the idea.

Mace Thornton, a spokesman for the farm bureau, says his group is "looking at a number of different proposals, and revenue assurance is just one of them. The bureau won't have a formal position until after its annual meeting of all of the affiliates, which concludes Jan. 12."

Is the growing industrialization of farm production bad for U.S. farmers and rural communities?

Over the past several decades, a decreasing number of farms has been producing an increasing share of the nation's total farm output. And many of them have become linked in tightly controlled networks to the suppliers who sell them feed and to the processors who buy their goods. Analysts call this the growing industrialization of U.S. agriculture.

This trend is most pronounced in the livestock sector, but it is slowly spreading to include grain producers as well. A vivid example of this industrialization is a company like ConAgra, based in Omaha, Neb.

ConAgra is the largest distributor of agricultural chemicals in North America, and one of the largest distributors of fertilizers. It is the largest turkey producer and second-largest broiler producer, and it makes its own poultry feed. It owns and operates hatcheries and contracts with farmers to raise the birds and then processes them in ConAgra facilities. It then sells them to consumers under the brand names Country Skillet and Swift Butterball or turns them into TV dinners and pot pies. [12]

In a transformation over the course of 40 years, raising poultry has gone from being a secondary enterprise on general purpose farms to being a highly specialized business. Now more than 90 percent of the country's poultry is produced by farmers under contract to food processors; the rest are produced by the processors themselves.

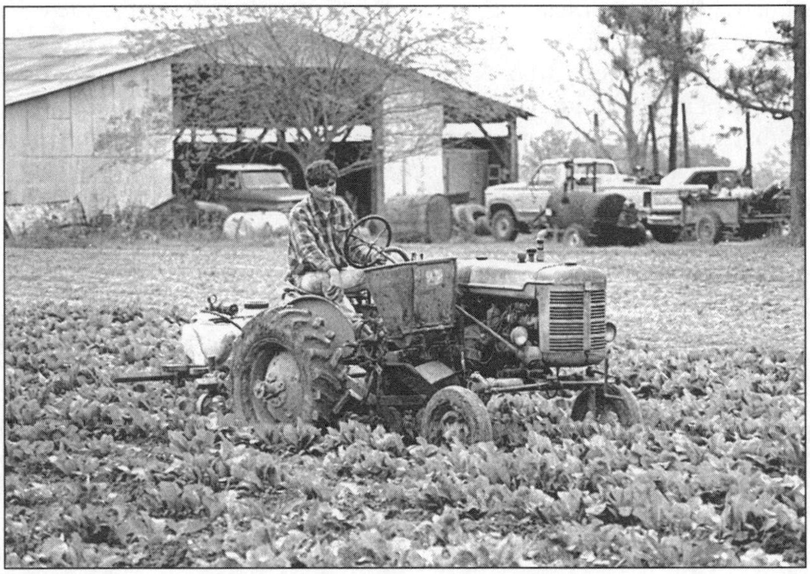

Clint W. Steib

Charles Glaser Jr. harvests his vegetables for local sale in Pointe Coupee Parrish, La.

This transformation recently has begun in the pork industry as well. In the Southeastern United States, more than half of the hogs are produced under contract. Farmers in the Midwest have been more reluctant to give up their independence, and less than 10 percent of the hogs there are produced under contract. But those numbers are expected to grow. [13]

Alan Barkema, a senior economist at the Federal Reserve Bank of Kansas City, says there are two key reasons for greater industrialization in the pork industry, the same reasons that earlier led to the consolidation of the poultry business. "First," he says, "consumers have become more discriminating, requiring the pork industry to design its product more carefully." And they can't do that without more control over what they buy from pork farmers. "Second, new technology is overhauling the pork industry," allowing it to respond to more demanding consumers. Sophisticated breeding techniques, climate-controlled living quarters, computers to track herd health and bio-engineered medicines to control disease are among the new tools available. [14]

But there is much disagreement about how the benefits of this industrialization are distributed among consumers, farmers, food processors and rural communities.

Most experts agree that consumers have benefited. According to a 1993 report by two USDA economists, "Increasing integration of farms and food processors can ensure greater control over food quality and safety for consumers. For example, potato processors often specify by contract the quality standards growers must meet, and tomato processors are increasingly specifying the use of chemical-reducing pest control methods." [15]

Lower prices are another benefit to consumers. According to data from The WEFA Group, the retail price of broilers dropped from $1.62 a pound in 1960 to $0.72 a pound in 1993, as industrialization improved the efficiency of poultry production and lowered its cost.

The impact on jobs, rural communities and farmers is more in dispute. A report by analysts at Virginia Polytechnic Institute studied the impact of contract swine production in the Southside region of the state. It concluded that the addition of a 72,000-sow complex would create more than 2,000 temporary construction jobs, roughly 1,000 permanent jobs and add millions of dollars in retail sales. [16]

But John Ikerd, a professor at the University of Missouri, says that while contracting may benefit one segment of the economy, it can harm several others. In Missouri, he estimated that a new $5 million investment in contract swine production would generate 40-50 new jobs but would displace approximately three times that number of independent hog farmers. [17]

For the farmers who do enter contracts, there are pros and cons. Under a typical poultry contract, a chicken farmer will supply the labor, the buildings, the equipment, utilities, the maintenance and make all tax and insurance payments and in exchange receive the chicks, the feed, technical assistance, medicines, management instructions and a guaranteed price from the processor. The farmer gives up much of his independence, but gains price stability. Yet some farmers are complaining, saying they feel like serfs on their own land.

"The biggest problem," says John Morrison, executive director of the National Contract Poultry Growers Association in Ruston, La., "is that the companies who process poultry have such tremendous economic power compared with the individual growers that they control the system."

Morrison's biggest complaint is that growers cannot negotiate their one-year contracts with processors; they either sign or they don't. And if they don't sign, they have nowhere to sell their birds. Morrison also complains that "growers can get poor chicks and poor feed from the processor, but can't send them back. You're obligated to take it, even though your income ultimately depends on the quality of the material you get."

Bill Roenigk, a senior vice president with the National Broiler Council in Washington, D.C., calls the Poultry Growers Association a "small group of dissident farmers," adding: "We know of no broiler company that does not have a wait-list with a significant number of farmers who have indicated a definite interest in growing broilers for that company. It would seem somewhat obvious that the contractual arrangement has excellent merit and rewards."

Independent pig farmers in the Midwest, who don't have the tradition of poultry contracting of the South, have great fears about letting the unknown into their states. Independent farmers in Iowa and Nebraska, for instance, have lobbied to keep laws on the books that make industrialization difficult. In Iowa, food processors are prohibited from owning their own feed lots, and they can't enter production contracts with pork farmers unless the processor is organized as a cooperative. But the barriers are gradually falling; this year lawmakers in Kansas changed their state regulations to allow growers to enter into contracts.

And contracting has begun to spread to grain farmers as well. Companies like Pioneer Hi-Bred International Inc. in Des Moines, Iowa, are signing contracts with grain producers who agree to use no pesticides. The grains are sold to food companies for pesticide-free consumer products. Biotechnology is also leading to increased contracting, with companies that have genetically engineered a new grain type contracting with producers in order to prevent unauthorized use and reproduction. [18] ■

BACKGROUND

Farm Programs Evolve

The core of government price and income support programs has changed comparatively little since their inception 60 years ago. The goals of the original lawmakers are the same as those of current members of Congress: to protect farm income and control surplus production.

The government's first attempt to support farm prices occurred during the farm depression of the 1920s, as farmers watched their exports shrink in both volume and value. Under a plan passed by Congress in 1924, the supply of crops in the domestic market would be limited to an amount that would drive up farm prices to desirable levels; the surplus crop would then be dumped on foreign markets for whatever it would bring. This mechanism lasted until 1926, and according to economists Cochrane and Runge, it "laid the groundwork for subsequent efforts to raise farm prices through government intervention." [19]

After the stock market crash in 1929, farm prices resumed their descent, falling more than 50 percent in three years. "For agriculture and rural America, it was the worst economic-social-political wrenching in history," write USDA historians Douglas Bowers, Wayne Rasmussen and Gladys Baker. "Farm foreclosures were the order of the day. Realized net income of farm operators in 1932 was less than one-third of what it had been in 1929." [20]

President Herbert Hoover and Congress responded with two policies that were doomed to failure. A Federal Farm Board was established in 1929 to buy up surplus crops, but the board did not have enough capital to prop up prices. Then, at the president's urging, Congress passed the Smoot-

Continued on p. 1066

Chronology

1930s *The first federal farm support programs are created during the Great Depression.*

1930
Congress passes the Smoot-Hawley Tariff Act, raising tariff duties to an all-time high. It results in worldwide protectionism and shut-off of U.S. farm exports.

May 12, 1933
Congress passes the Agricultural Adjustment Act, which attempts to control production by paying farmers to reduce acreage, gives the U.S. Department of Agriculture (USDA) authority to purchase and store commodities and sets inflexible price supports for crops.

1950s-1960s *Mass migration from farms to cities causes number of farms to sharply decline. Technological revolution improves farm efficiency, and remaining farms produce surplus crops of crisis proportions.*

1954
Congress introduces some flexibility into the price support mechanism, allowing the marketplace to play a larger role.

1961
Congress passes emergency legislation to control overproduction of crops, paying some farmers to take a percentage of their acreage out of production.

1965
Congress passes Food and Agriculture Act lowering price supports to world levels to promote American exports, and authorizes the USDA to make deficiency payments to support farm incomes but only to those farmers who agree to idle acreage.

1970s *Harvests fail around the world, boosting demand for U.S. crops. Surpluses disappear as exports boom. Farm numbers continue to shrink, and production becomes even more concentrated in the hands of a few.*

1973
Congress introduces the "target price" concept — a "what-it-ought-to-be" price — for measuring the size of income support, or deficiency payments, to farmers.

1980s *A worldwide recession and rising dollar reverse farm fortunes, leading to bankruptcies and foreclosures in first half of decade. Worldwide recovery and falling dollar increase U.S. exports and farm income in second half.*

1983
In response to the rising cost of federal farm programs and a growing surplus, the government begins the emergency payment-in-kind program. It keeps some farm benefits "off-budget" by paying farmers with USDA-owned stocks of crops rather than with cash.

1985
Congress passes a farm bill that continues basic farm programs of loans to support prices, deficiency payments to support incomes and acreage reduction to control production. Loan rates are ratcheted down to make U.S. crops competitive worldwide and acreage reductions are set high. The bill also creates several conservation programs, including the sodbuster and swampbuster programs.

1990s *Federal budget pressures and growing criticism of farm programs' effectiveness lead to calls for reform.*

1990
Federal deficit pressures and the enormous costs of the 1985 farm bill lead to "triple base" concept. It gives a farmer flexibility to plant any crop, except fruits or vegetables, on 15 percent of his acres; in exchange, he loses a proportionate amount of his deficiency payment. Conservation programs are extended and expanded.

1993
Congress eliminates subsidies for wool, mohair and honey.

January 1994
The Iowa Farm Bill Study Team introduces its revenue assurance plan to replace existing farm programs.

No-Till Farming Shows Skeptics . . .

Jim Consella is a trailblazer. Twenty years ago, when he first began using no-till techniques to grow corn and soybeans on his Lexington, Ill., farm, his neighbors were skeptical. People told him it would never work. Three years later, he converted his entire 640 acres to no-till and began converting his fellow farmers as well. Now roughly half of the farmers in his area use no-till techniques. "It's beginning to catch on," Consella says.

No-till farming means planting crops directly into the previous crop's stubble, with minimum soil disturbance. No plowing the earth under before planting; no vistas of fields with exposed black soil; and no large losses of topsoil to wind and water.

Nationwide, the amount of farmland planted using no-till methods has more than doubled since 1989; by last year, it accounted for 13 percent of total planted acres in the United States.

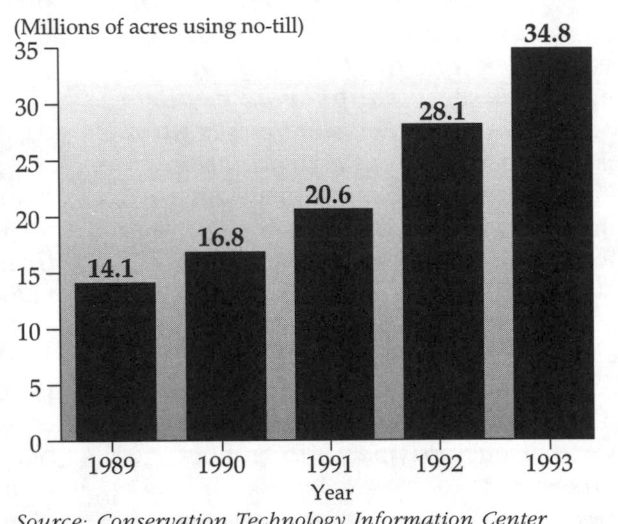

Source: Conservation Technology Information Center

The reduction in soil erosion is one of the main reasons for no-till's growing popularity. According to David Schertz, national agronomist with the Department of Agriculture's Soil Conservation Service, no-till farming can cut soil erosion by as much as 90 percent. It all depends on what kind of stubble is holding the topsoil in.

Planting into the stubble of high-residue crops like corn, wheat and sorghum controls erosion better than planting into the stubble of low-residue crops like soybeans and cotton. Because many farmers rotate crops, their erosion control rates will vary from year to year. For that reason, Schertz says, the total amount of topsoil saved because of the switch to no-till "is just too difficult to figure out because you have to make too many assumptions." Still, it's clear that no-till helps a great deal.

With reduced topsoil erosion comes a whole host of benefits: Zero-tillage improves the ability of soil to hold moisture by trapping snow and reducing water runoff; zero-till farmers, on average, have crop yields that are the same or better than farmers who use conventional techniques; zero-till farmers use their machinery less intensively, saving on repair and fuel costs; and zero-tillage reduces the time and labor needed to plant a crop. [1]

This benefit is particularly important to Jim Consella. "I farm part time. No-till allows me time for my other job," he says. "I get four weeks' vacation, and that gives me two weeks to plant and spray and two weeks to harvest. I couldn't do all that in that time if I were tilling."

There are drawbacks to no-till farming. Herbicides must replace plowing to kill weeds, and farmers must therefore become more knowledgeable about weed growth and herbicide application. Farmers also must learn new planting techniques and how to properly spread straw and chaff over their fields.

But studies of no-till farmers show that the advantages often outweigh the drawbacks and that no-till is at least as profitable, and often more profitable, than conventional farming.

The MAX (farming for maximum efficiency) program is one of the more thorough studies around. [2] It enrolls farmers who are willing to share information about their crop

Continued from p. 1064

Hawley Tariff Act of 1930, raising tariff duties to an all-time high.

"Today it is difficult to understand why Congress would take such an action," Cochrane and Runge write, "since it was well-known at the time that one of the principal causes of the agricultural depression of the 1920s was the loss of export markets following [World War I]." [21] The act set off a wave of protectionism around the world, and American farm exports plummeted.

A fresh approach was needed, and in 1933 Congress approved a farm policy that contained one basic feature — acreage control in exchange for government payments.

After World War II, two camps emerged with very different ideas about the future of farm policy, and the debate of that time still resonates today. One group wanted to reduce price supports and the government's role in agriculture while the second group wanted to maintain a high level of price supports. The second group won this debate, and high price supports continued through the 1950s.

In the postwar years, a technical revolution on American farms rapidly increased production. By the mid-1960s, the excess supply of crops had reached crisis levels. In 1965, Congress passed an agricultural act with some new twists. Price support levels were lowered to match world prices, helping to make American farm products competitive in world markets. The government would

. . . the Advantages of Giving Up the Plow

management techniques. MAX results in Iowa for 1993 show that those soybean farmers who used no-till had higher profits than farmers using all other planting methods. These no-till farmers had higher fertilizer costs and significantly higher pesticide costs, but they also had the lowest field operations costs and the highest yields.

Environmentalists are less comfortable with no-till than its practitioners. "Environmentalists are in an awkward situation with no-till," says Richard Wiles, director of agricultural pollution prevention for the Environmental Working Group, a nonprofit research organization in Washington, D.C. "It has some obvious benefits like soil conservation, but on the other hand, there hasn't been much research into whether you can do no-till with reduced herbicide use. It's generally assumed to be an either-or situation, with no-till meaning higher herbicide use. I'm not convinced that that's the case."

There are some heartening studies. One analysis using USDA data found that "during the first two or three years with a no-till system, operators often use more herbicides. However, once they become familiar with the no-till system and the weed seeds in the top few centimeters of the soil have been controlled, herbicide use declines to below that of the previous tillage system." [3]

What concerns environmentalists is what this herbicide use means for water quality. For surface water, the implications seem clear. According to a report by the Conservation Technology Information Center in West Lafayette, Ind., "controlled studies have shown that . . . runoff of common herbicides such as atrazine, alachlor and cyanazine has sometimes been reduced by 90 percent or more with no-till planting." [4] The reason is straightforward enough — less water runoff means less herbicide runoff from fields into surface water.

But what is good for surface water may not be so good for ground water, and there the studies are much less clear. While no-till farming reduces water running off a field, it increases the amount of water flowing into the ground. And the concern is that this in turn will increase the amount of pesticides and nitrates that find their way into the groundwater supply.

There are studies that show no-till farming reducing the amount of pesticide found in ground water; there also are studies that show no-till farming increasing the amount of pesticide in ground water. The results depend on how the pesticide was applied, the type of soil, how the pesticide reacts with the soil and the depth of the ground water. Researchers are currently working on developing control-released pesticides in granules as a way of cutting down on groundwater contamination.

But Dale Kemper, national program leader for soil management at the USDA's Agricultural Research Service, says "on balance, overall water quality is better with no-till. That's because any water that goes through the soil is usually filtered so that it has one-tenth of the contaminants than if it had come off as surface water."

Analysts expect to see no-till acreage continue to increase in 1994, helped in part by a provision of the 1985 farm bill called conservation compliance. It requires farmers with highly erodible acres to adopt and fully apply a government sponsored conservation plan by Jan. 1, 1995, or else risk losing all their USDA price-support payments and other farm program benefits. Switching to no-till is one way of meeting that deadline.

---

[1] *Zero-Tillage Production Manual,* Manitoba-North Dakota Zero Tillage Farmers' Association, 1991, p. 5.

[2] The Max program is sponsored by *Successful Farming* magazine, Conservation Technology Information Center and chemical maker Ciba Plant Protection, a division of Ciba-Geigy Corp.

[3] "Agricultural Resources: Inputs," U.S. Department of Agriculture, October 1993, p. 43.

[4] "Best Management Practices for Water Quality," Conservation Technology Information Center, undated, p. i. The center is a nonprofit, public-private partnership dedicated to encouraging profitable and environmentally sound agricultural management practices.

supplement farm incomes, when needed, but only farmers who agreed to participate in the government's production control program would receive these deficiency payments.

These strategies remained in effect, with only modest changes, throughout the 1970s. But there was one great drawback to them, according to Cochrane and Runge: "voluntary production control programs coupled with deficiency payments come with very high price tags for the federal government." [22]

1985 and 1990 Farm Bills

In the early 1980s, favorable weather and government miscalculations about how much acreage to idle combined to produce record-breaking crops. That plus a worldwide recession that cut sharply into U.S. exports pushed the farm sector into crisis and government payments and loans to levels never before seen.

In reaction, the government instituted the emergency payment-in-kind (PIK) program. PIK was designed to reduce the excess production of crops while keeping a portion of federal farm payments off-budget. PIK allowed the government to use stocks of crops already owned by the USDA to pay farmers to retire land. The farmers could then sell the crops and keep the revenue.

But farmers continued to suffer as the recession wore on and as real interest rates rose into the double digits, forcing many farmers who had taken on large amounts of debt during the boom of the 1970s over the edge.

Federal farm support programs were created during the Depression of the 1930s.

A second agricultural depression developed, setting the scene for the farm bill debate of 1985.

"No farm bill since the 1930s held out more promise for significant change in agricultural policy than the 1985 farm bill," writes USDA historian Bowers. "Conditions seemed ripe for a thoroughgoing reform of the 50-year-old system of price support and adjustment. . . . [B]y 1985, the USDA was administering an expensive program that hindered exports but had failed to reduce supply in line with lower demand." [23]

Just as in the years following World War II, a national debate ensued, with the administration of President Ronald Reagan proposing a more market-oriented policy and Democrats and many farm-state Republicans favoring the kind of strict supply controls that promised to push farm prices upward, not down. The debate provoked a year-long battle royale in Congress, with both sides keenly aware that the (then) Republican-controlled Senate was hanging in the balance.

The Food Security Act of 1985 was a compromise that continued all the basic farm programs, with neither mandatory supply controls nor significant free market reforms. And just as in the 1960s, price support levels were lowered to encourage exports while income protection was extended to make up the difference. But there was one important change. Environmental organizations, like the National Wildlife Federation, were taking a keen interest in farm legislation.

Environmentalists "saw an opportunity in the overproduction of the early 1980s . . . to require participants in price support programs to comply with conservation requirements," Bowers writes. And they succeeded. The conservation reserve program established by Congress in 1985 paid farmers to convert highly erodible acres to vegetative cover. The sodbuster and swampbuster programs used penalties to discourage farmers from converting highly erodible land and wetlands to crop use. (*See story, p. 1074.*)

The 1985 Food Security Act proved to be the most expensive farm bill of all time. With the federal budget deficit in the background, lawmakers writing the 1990 farm bill were looking for a way to cut spending. What they came up with was called the "triple base" concept. Acres would continue to be idled under an acreage reduction program but the remaining acres would be divided into two parts: a base that could be planted in program crops and on which farmers would continue to receive income support; and a "flexible" base, set at 15 percent of the total acres, that could be planted in any crop, except fruits or vegetables, and on which no payments would be made.

Deficit pressures continued after the 1990 bill was signed, and in 1993 Congress eliminated price subsidies for mohair, wool and honey. Pressure to reduce the federal budget deficit will again play an important role in next year's farm bill debate.

There are lessons to be learned from the history of farm programs, Cochrane and Runge write. Perhaps the most important is that technological changes in agriculture always seem to run ahead of political changes in farm programs, leading to "the repeated failure of domestic farm policy to control domestic production" and "a flow of benefits from those programs to fewer and fewer farmers on larger and larger farms." [24]

Changing Landscape

In the three decades following World War II, the farming landscape underwent a profound change. After the war, the industrial and service sectors of the economy began to expand, attracting people from farms and encouraging a large migration from rural areas to towns and cities. At the same time, technology was advancing and farmers were buying fertilizers and pesticides, larger machinery and better seeds, greatly increasing their productivity. As a result of these two trends, the number of farms sharply declined while those remaining grew larger.

Between 1945 and 1974, the number of farms fell from 5.9 million to 2.3

million, a decline of more than 100,000 farms a year. At the same time, the average size of farms nearly doubled to 440 acres. [25]

This was the most intense period of farm loss this century, belying the common impression that the trend toward fewer, larger farms is currently escalating. In fact, the rate of farm loss has slowed during the past two decades. Between 1974 and 1992, the last year that national census data for agriculture were available, the number of farms declined from 2.3 million to 1.9 million, while average farm size increased by just 51 acres, to 491 acres.

While the decline in the number of farms has slowed, the increase in the concentration of farm production and revenues in the hands of a few continues at a steady pace. A good way to measure this trend is to look at how many farms it takes to produce half of all farm sales. In 1940, 12 percent of the country's farms produced 50 percent of farm sales. By 1969, 8 percent of all farms were responsible for half of total farm sales. And by 1992, that figure had declined to just 3 percent.

The commercial farming sector is now basically made up of a few hundred thousand very large and very efficient farms. USDA economists R. Neal Peterson and Nora Brooks attribute this growing concentration to technological advances and the way they spread through the farm sector. "Larger, wealthier farmers are better positioned to adopt new methods and ideas and tools," they write. "The gap between large and small producers has increased in the process and, consequently, concentration has increased." [26]

And that has left the vast majority of farmers looking elsewhere for income. For most people, farming is now a part-time occupation. In 1991, more than two-thirds of farm households received more income from off the farm activities than from those on the farm. [27] Only about one-quarter of U.S. counties qualify as agribusiness counties — where farming and related industries employ a third or more of the labor force. For most rural areas, manufacturing and service jobs now are the main means of employment, and a great many farmers have come to rely on those jobs.

Another important change since World War II has been the growing specialization of farms. While there still remain farms that grow a variety of grains and raise livestock, the trend is away from that model. According to a USDA analysis, "Midwestern cash grain farms, suburban part-time cattle farms, Southern poultry producers and Western vegetable growers may have little in common. . . . [F]arms may be faring well in some industries and struggling in others — and each is affected differently by government farm policy." [28] New areas of agriculture are being developed as well, including aquaculture, herb farms and crops raised exclusively for industrial uses. Farmers no longer speak with a unified voice.

These changes in the farm sector of the past 50 years will continue, researchers say, but there is much disagreement about the pace. Some predict a massive wave of older farmers retiring in the next decade, selling their properties to larger neighbors and accelerating the trend toward consolidation. Others worry that the number of farms controlling production will shrink to such a point that together they will be able to set high food prices. Some USDA economists, in contrast, predict that future changes in agriculture will be ponderously slow.

"Farmers tend not to retire when others do," says David Harrington,

U.S. Agricultural Exports

Exports have been an important source of sales for U.S. farmers since the 1970s. Farm exports have risen in recent years, but they have not climbed back to the peak reached in 1981.

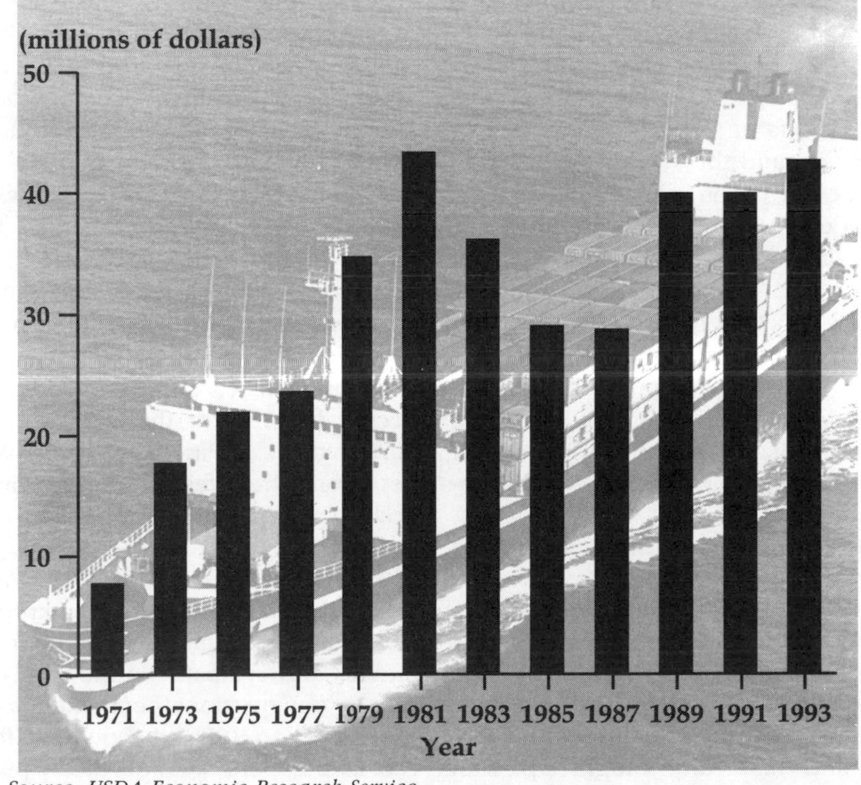

Source: USDA Economic Research Service

chief of the USDA's rural industry branch. "They tend to hold on to property longer," and "inheritance taxes at the state level favor holding farms right until death. So we expect change to continue to be gradual."

Impact of World Trade

The technological advances that have helped to put more production in the hands of fewer farmers have done so by increasing farm efficiency. But American farmers are not the only ones improving productivity. The United States now faces stiff competition from other countries that also have managed to lower their costs of production.

Exports have been an important source of sales to American farmers, especially beginning in the 1970s. Any disruption in exports, whether the result of increased competition from abroad or other factors, can cause great harm to the farm sector.

The 1970s

The early 1970s were a boom time for U.S. farm exports. Shortages of crops around the world, including in the Soviet Union, created an increasing demand for U.S farm products, helped along by the falling value of the dollar. U.S. grain exports nearly doubled between 1972 and 1973, and total agricultural exports increased by more than 25 percent. Stocks of surplus grain held by the government were virtually wiped out; stocks of government corn completely disappeared in 1973.

This was a profound change from a decade earlier, when farmers, in the midst of a technological revolution, were setting production records and surplus crops were reaching crisis levels. In 1973, "for the first time since the Korean War, it appeared that demand had fully caught up with supply and that demand would continue strong for at least several years," write USDA historians Bowers, Rasmussen and Baker.

It did continue, at least for a few years, and U.S. farmers enjoyed a new prosperity. The rise in world demand pushed up prices for wheat, feed grains, rice and cotton to new highs, and net farm income rose to record levels.

In 1974, government payments to farmers fell to the lowest level in nearly 20 years. Land values shot up, and a great many farmers went deep into debt to expand their operations. But there were "clouds on the horizon," the USDA historians write. "Greater dependence on export markets made commodities more vulnerable to sudden price swings due to economic and political events in other parts of the world." [29] In the 1980s, farm fortunes reversed with a vengeance.

The 1980s

On Jan. 4, 1980, President Jimmy Carter partially suspended agricultural exports to the Soviet Union in retaliation for that country's invasion of Afghanistan. The embargo unsettled foreign grain buyers and gave an advantage to America's competitors. Despite the turmoil, U.S. agricultural exports continued to rise in 1980.

But in 1982, U.S. farmers were not so lucky. Good weather helped to produce bumper crops for wheat, corn and other commodities at the same time that the world was sliding into recession. That recession, along with a strong dollar, "caused exports to decline in 1982 for the first time in eight years. . . . [P]rices fell and total net income from farming, in constant dollars, dropped to its lowest levels since 1933." [30]

This was the time of Farm Aid fundraising concerts, farm bankruptcies and heart-tugging testimony from farmers and sympathetic movie stars before congressional committees. [31] From 1983 to 1986, the outlook for U.S. farm exports was "decidedly pessimistic," said John Schnittker, an agricultural consultant in Santa Ynez, Calif., "as the dollar continued strong, as food crops refused to fail with any regularity in major importing or exporting countries, and as high price supports and inaction on export subsidies by U.S. officials left some U.S. commodities uncompetitive." [32]

In fact, U.S. farmers began to face intensifying competition from what had been one of their best importers — the European Community. High European tariffs were driving up European grain prices, encouraging European farmers to increase production and the European public to cut back consumption. The emerging surpluses had to go somewhere, and that was into the export market. Not only did U.S. sales to Europe suffer, but sales to the Soviet Union and the Middle East fell as the Europeans crowded out the Americans.

But the farm sector is like a roller coaster, and starting in 1986, new U.S. government export programs, a once again declining dollar, more competitive U.S. prices and increasing world demand all helped to contribute to a rebound in U.S. exports. Exports, have not, however, climbed back to the peak reached in 1981. (*See graph, p. 1069.*)

The 1990s and Beyond

With the recovery of U.S. exports has come a transformation in the type of goods sold. Demand for U.S. wheat, corn, soybeans and other bulk commodity products continues to suffer. Increased competition from Europe, Brazil and Argentina, the unstable economy in the former Soviet Union and the growing ability of China to feed itself and export its surplus have all taken their toll.

The bright spot is in exports of what analysts call high-value products — nuts, vegetables, fruits, meat, sugar and other goods that receive additional processing after leaving the farm. These now dominate U.S. farm exports.

From September 1993 to September 1994, high-value exports grew to $26 billion, making their share of total U.S.

agricultural exports 59 percent. [33] Increasing high-value sales also are expected to help push U.S. farm exports to record levels in Japan, Canada and Mexico, America's top three markets. Behind this shift are several factors: rising incomes in Asia and other newly industrialized countries that allow consumers there to buy these higher-priced goods; market promotion efforts; and trade liberalization agreements.

Many American farmers are hoping for additional benefits from trade liberalization. On Dec. 15, 1993, the United States and 116 other nations reached an historic agreement when they concluded the Uruguay Round of Multilateral Trade Negotiations under the auspices of the General Agreement on Tariffs and Trade — better known as GATT. * In essence, the agreement requires reductions in subsidized farm exports, cuts in import protection and the conversions of non-tariff barriers to tariffs or quotas, reductions in internal farm supports that skew world trade and an attempt to prevent the use of sanitary regulations as disguised trade barriers.

Congress was expected to vote on legislation implementing GATT the week of Nov. 28. Expectations about its impact on U.S. agricultural trade vary. (*See "At Issue," p. 1073.*) USDA economists are predicting that U.S. farm exports could increase to $4.7 billion in the year 2000 and to $8.7 billion in 2005. They also expect that export-related employment could climb by as a much as 112,000 in 2000 and by as much as 190,000 in 2005. All of this, they say, would raise farm prices, increase farm income and lower U.S. government spending on price and income support programs. [34]

But economists at The WEFA Group express a different view. "It is possible, and in fact probable, that the benefits of such an agreement have been grossly oversold," they wrote in a report to clients last winter. "This is especially true for the major grain and oilseed crops." [35]

Other analysts point out that there could be a political backlash to GATT because of public reaction to unemployment and other adjustment problems as these trade reforms are put in place. That could lead countries to look for ways to limit reform. Whatever the outcome, it will have a critical impact on American farmers, who, in Schnittker's view, have developed "a permanent dependence on exports." [36] ■

* There are currently 123 participating nations.

CURRENT SITUATION

1994: A Critical Year

No matter what grand plans different constituencies have for reinventing farm policy, hard economic realities usually rule the day, giving the crop year just before a farm bill debate added importance. And the realities of 1994 may make innovation a difficult sell in 1995.

"Great crops, lousy prices," is how Edward Lotterman, an agricultural economist with the Federal Reserve Bank of Minneapolis, sums up this year. The yield of almost every crop in the bank's district "is doing real well," Lotterman says. The problem is that this superabundance is overwhelming demand and prices are deteriorating.

In Iowa, the largest corn-producing state, Max Smith farms 2,000 acres in Knoxville and owns two small grain elevators that he rents out to about 250 other farmers. "This year for me is going to yield an excellent soybean crop and an above average corn crop," he says. But corn prices have dropped so low, down 25 percent since last spring, that farmers in his area are reluctant to sell and are trying to store their crops until prices bottom out.

The problem, Smith says, is "we're running out of room in our elevators and have begun to store grain on the ground." According to Smith, it's the poorest farmers who are getting hurt right now because they don't have money saved and so must sell at these low prices. "It's the old story; healthy farmers get ahead and poor farmers get further behind," says Smith.

Some farmers did lock-in the higher prices of the spring by hedging in the futures markets. But according to Lotterman of the Federal Reserve Bank, only about 5 to 10 percent of all farmers nationwide use the futures markets. "It's mostly the younger, larger farmers who do it," he says. So the vast majority are going to have to take what they can get. The same goes for the livestock sector, where beef and pork production are at record levels, and the excess supply is doing its work on prices.

At the same time that farmers are being paid less for the goods they produce, they are having to pay more in expenses: Interest rates are up, fertilizer prices are up and energy prices are rising. On top of that, government support payments are expected to drop by as much as $4 billion this year. (Deficiency payments were reduced in 1994 because of high market prices in the beginning of the year, the result of 1993's flood-induced short supply of crops.)

All this turmoil in the farm economy means one thing, says Pottorff of The WEFA Group. "It is virtually certain that farm income in 1994 and 1995 will be down from 1993 levels with the only real question being how much." [37] The WEFA Group, being in the forecasting business, is predicting a drop of 8 percent this year in what is called "net cash income."

But Pottorff is admonishing his clients to remember one thing: "While lower farm income levels over the next couple of years are probable, it is important to keep them in perspective. They are declining from the very high levels of 1992 and 1993."

And, he adds, "Projected net cash income levels in 1994 and 1995 of about $54.6 billion are still above the levels recorded in the late 1980s, a period of relatively favorable conditions for U.S. agriculture." In other words, the farm economy is softening, but it's still in relatively good shape. And compared with the crisis years of the early 1980s, the farm sector is doing great: Debt levels have been cut by a third, and profits have tripled.

Yet any weakening in farm incomes could influence the 1995 farm bill debate. According to The WEFA Group, "Congress may be less likely to adopt a new, untried approach to policy if there is an actual or perceived financial 'crisis' facing the farm sector. On the other hand, poor prices will trigger larger deficiency payments, highlighting the budget exposure that is embodied in current farm programs. One thing is certain, significant declines in farm income between now and next spring will bring agriculture issues back to the forefront and move them up several notches on the congressional and the administration's agenda." [38]

After the Flood

The flood was 40 days in reaching its greatest height, which was the 20th of April, and it was a beautiful thing to look upon the sea where there had been fields, for on each side of the river the water extended over twenty leagues of land, and all this area was navigated by canoes, and nothing was seen but the top of the tallest trees."

— Garciliaso de la Vega describing the DeSoto expedition on the banks of the Mississippi River, History of Hernando DeSoto, Lisbon, 1605. [39]

Some things never change, and flooding on the Mississippi River and its tributaries is one of them. One of the worst on record was "The Great Flood of 1993," as it's often referred to now.

Estimates of total damages range from $12 billion to $16 billion, with more than half in agriculture. Fields close to riverbanks were inundated with water, but many fields in upland areas did not escape harm: They were saturated by rain and so soggy that farmers could not plant. Livestock drowned, farm buildings were destroyed and equipment was ruined beyond repair. And as the water receded, some 60,000 acres were left smothered under two feet of sand.

Farmers in nine states suffered: Illinois, Iowa, Kansas, Minnesota, Missouri, Nebraska, North Dakota, South Dakota and Wisconsin, with Iowa and Missouri sustaining the greatest dollar amounts of damage.

Yet farm income in 1993 was the highest it had been in years. The crop may have been small, but prices were high as demand far exceeded supply, and farmers whose crops did not suffer from flood and rain benefited immensely. Even farmers whose crops were destroyed could at least sell the stockpiles they had accumulated during an abundant 1992, and sell them at high prices. Aid from the government also boosted income as the USDA paid out a total of $2.9 billion to farmers in the nine hard-hit states. (*See chart, p. 1075.*)

Disaster assistance accounted for more than half of that USDA flood relief, while crop insurance payments accounted for just a third. [40] And that is an example of what many analysts say has been a recurring problem in the face of natural calamities: not enough farmers have purchased crop insurance, assured in the knowledge that the federal government would bail them out with free disaster assistance after the fact. To try to address this problem, Congress in October passed a law reforming the crop insurance system. [41]

Under the old system, farmers could protect themselves from drought, flood, excess soil moisture, frost, hail, wind, insects and other natural perils by purchasing crop insurance from the USDA. Those who chose to buy the insurance were required to do so early in the crop year, however, and they could not insure the full value of the crop, only up to 75 percent of the expected yield.

The government did a number of things to encourage participation, including subsidizing up to 30 percent of the premiums. Yet many farmers did not buy the insurance, and not only because they knew emergency disaster assistance was available. In interviews, farmers said the 75 percent maximum coverage was too low and that flooding was relatively rare. [42]

Corn and soybean farmers had the lowest participation rates and wheat growers the highest. In Illinois, 44 percent of all farmers bought federal crop insurance last year; in Missouri it was just 24 percent; Wisconsin was the lowest at 11 percent; and North Dakota the highest at 93 percent. [43]

Federal crop insurance has been reformed before, in 1980. But most analysts consider that effort a failure because it did not succeed in eliminating federal disaster payments.

This year's law, signed by President Clinton on Oct. 13, aims to be different. Among other things, it requires that any farmer obtaining farm program benefits and loans must buy crop insurance, and it restricts the USDA's authority to offer disaster assistance. Premiums for catastrophic insurance are essentially eliminated and replaced with a nominal processing fee. And the government

Continued on p. 1075

At Issue:

Will the General Agreement on Tariffs and Trade (GATT) help U.S. agriculture?

yes

Dean Kleckner
President, American Farm Bureau Federation

WRITTEN FOR THE CQ RESEARCHER, NOVEMBER 1994

After seven years of negotiations, new trading rules are being considered by 123 nations. These rules will benefit U.S. agriculture, along with virtually every other sector of our economy and the economies of other countries.

The new GATT rules help U.S. agriculture. Agriculture is America's top growth industry. We export more farm products than we buy, earning a trade surplus. GATT will help us flex our competitive muscles.

New international trade language will lead to substantially improved access for U.S. farm exports. Our country is already relatively "open." GATT will require others to reduce their trade-distorting support payments, export subsidies and import protection. More exports mean more sales; more sales mean higher prices; higher prices mean higher profits; higher profits mean higher net income for farmers.

New trade regulations will substantially benefit the world economy. By eliminating import taxes, world income will increase as much as $5 trillion in the next 10 years. Higher world incomes mean more demand for our commodities. That increased demand could boost our foreign sales another $4.7 billion by 2000 and as much as $8.7 billion by 2005.

Increased farm exports mean more U.S. jobs — as many as 112,000 jobs in 2000, and as many as 190,000 in 2005.

Post-NAFTA [North American Free Trade Agreement] trade figures between Mexico and the U.S. are proof that liberalized trade works. Farmers want universal fair trade, but we'll take equitable bilateral and regional trade agreements when we can get them. Trade figures from the first six months after NAFTA's enactment prove us right.

Overall, U.S. exports to Mexico have risen by 17 percent, to $24.5 billion. This rise, coupled with our increased trade with Canada as a result of our U.S/Canada agreement, means as many as 100,000 new jobs have been created in the U.S. for Americans.

U.S. farm exports to Mexico are 11 percent higher than before the agreement and should end the year at $4.1 billion, a half billion dollars above last year, the pre-NAFTA year.

The new GATT agreement creates a World Trade Organization. Protectionists charge this new entity with all kinds of faults, including the suspension of U.S. self-determination, our sovereignty. Specific language in the agreement, in our Constitution and common sense refute the charges. No outside body is ever going to dictate rules to the U.S.

An example: Recently foreign car manufacturers complained to GATT, as is their right, about U.S. laws mandating fuel efficiency. The ruling was that the U.S. could do whatever we want, impose whatever penalties on our industries that we want — as long as we don't discriminate against foreign producers. So fuel standards, or labor requirements, or environmental constraints must apply to all — U.S. and foreign producers alike.

no

Larry Mitchell
Vice President for Government Relations, National Farmers Union

WRITTEN FOR THE CQ RESEARCHER, NOVEMBER 1994

The National Farmers Union disagrees with those who have identified agriculture as one of the big winners under GATT, and in doing so, we urge a closer look at the facts. The Food and Agriculture Research Institute, which does economic analysis for the House and Senate Agriculture committees, identifies the big winners in agriculture as corn producers, who will see about a 9-cent increase per bushel over the next eight years, and wheat producers, who could see an 8-cent-per-bushel increase in price at the farmgate over that same time period. A penny-a-bushel increase per year is in no way a big winner, and the accuracy of this projection is also questionable. The same team of economists predicted 18 months ago that this year's corn crop would be 8.2 billion bushels and sell for $2.09 per bushel. Tell that to Midwestern farmers trying to sell this year's 10-billion-bushel crop for $1.70 per bushel.

The projections for producers of cotton, rice and milk were not that good. In fact, according to a Texas A&M study of 22 dairy farms in 10 states, reductions in net worth by the year 2001 were projected for 87 percent of them.

What is the cost to agriculture for such a wonderful deal? To start with, there is the matter of $1.7 billion to be chopped from agriculture programs over the next five years to pay for the loss in tariff revenue due to GATT implementation. Additionally, U.S. agriculture will lose Section 22 of the Agricultural Adjustment Act of 1933, which authorizes the president to restrict imports by imposing quotas or fees if imports interfere with farm and food programs.

One other loss for U.S. agriculture is the demise of meat import laws. Just last month, as has been the case most years, it was announced that Australia and New Zealand would voluntarily restrict meat imports to the U.S. just short of the meat import law's level that automatically triggers restrictions. Will our friends from down under be as gracious when there is no longer a trigger level, or will inferior imports flood our domestic market, threaten our food supply and drive U.S. ranchers out of business?

GATT forces the U.S. to accept imports of agricultural products, even when there is a surplus. This is not free trade. Mandated imports of corn, wheat, dairy, peanut, rice and cotton will put farmers out of business and devastate our rural businesses, schools, churches and communities.

NFU recognizes that properly crafted trade agreements can be useful to lessen world trade tensions and increase development opportunities. However, poorly crafted trade agreements such as the Uruguay Round could heighten trade tensions and lower living standards of people living in countries involved, including the U.S.

Environmentalists' Role in the 1995 Farm Bill Debate

Environmentalists would like to use the 1995 farm bill as a vehicle to defend and strengthen soil and water conservation programs that were created in the 1985 and 1990 farm bills.

Some of the conservation programs use a stick to induce compliance: The conservation compliance provision requires farmers of highly erodible land to implement government approved soil erosion control plans by the beginning of next year or risk losing access to commodity program benefits. The sodbuster and swampbuster programs discourage the conversion of highly erodible land and wetlands to crop production also by threatening farmers with the loss of benefits.

Other measures use a carrot approach: The conservation reserve program pays farmers to voluntarily retire highly erodible land and plant it with vegetative cover under 10-to-15-year contracts; the water quality incentive program pays farmers to implement a water quality resource management plan; and the integrated farm management program encourages farmers to plant a portion of their fields in resource-conserving crops like legumes.

The effectiveness of these programs varies. Environmentalists complain that those programs that rely on penalties have not been properly enforced by the U.S. Department of Agriculture (USDA). "There's no method of checking on compliance" with the sodbuster and swampbuster programs, says Andrew Art, a policy analyst at the Environmental Working Group, a nonprofit environmental research organization based in Washington, D.C. "We need better tracking of violations."

The USDA's own inspector general, in a 1992 report, criticized his agency's Soil Conservation Service (SCS) for not properly enforcing the conservation compliance provision. [1]

Nevertheless, environmentalists say some conservation programs are working. Kenneth Cook, president of the Environmental Working Group, told a House subcommittee in August that "Soil erosion on highly erodible cropland has been reduced on tens of thousands of farms that had virtually no conservation practices in place on their highly erodible fields prior to the [1985 farm bill]. The benefits of these reductions on soil productivity, water quality and wildlife are still being documented. We believe those benefits have been substantial." [2]

The SCS estimates that when compliance plans are all fully in place, annual soil erosion on highly erodible land will be cut from 17.5 tons per acre to 6 tons an acre. Nationally that means a reduction of more than a billion tons a year. What Cook and other environmentalists want is stricter enforcement to bring those soil erosion numbers even lower.

The American Farm Bureau Federation argues that stricter enforcement is not what is needed. "People will do only the minimum required to comply with a mandate or regulation," the group says. The bureau would like to see more effort and money put into voluntary programs. "Voluntary, positive incentives win converts who will achieve greater environmental improvements than might otherwise be required," the bureau says. [3]

Possibly the most successful program in the USDA arsenal is the voluntary conservation reserve program. Under the program, grass or trees have been planted on more than 36 million acres, accomplishing the twin goals of reducing crop production and cutting soil erosion. Supporters say farmers like the program because it is voluntary and because the government payments farmers receive for retiring their fields are predictable and regular, unlike commodity program payments that fluctuate year to year depending on weather and market conditions.

Supporters of the conservation reserve program are concerned that it is scheduled to end, beginning next year. Both environmentalists and farmers worry about the impact on oversupply and conservation of returning millions of acres to crop production, and they are lobbying for an extension of the program. But in order for Congress to continue it, lawmakers will have to find a source of funds.

The problem is that there is no new money budgeted for extending conservation programs. And producers and environmental groups strongly disagree on where they might find some. Those who propose replacing commodity programs with some sort of revenue guarantee (*see p. 1060*) suggest using the resulting budget savings for what they call "green payments" to farmers. If that isn't possible, many environmentalists would like to simply divert money from traditional commodity programs to pay for conservation, an option that the American Farm Bureau Federation strenuously opposes.

The bureau has its own idea about a potential source of dollars: "If the timing is right, shifting funds from the Clean Water Act, the Endangered Species Act and/or the regulatory budgets of [the Environmental Protection Agency] and Department of Interior may be a possibility." [4] Or the bureau suggests that taxpayers could foot the bill, not by an increase in taxes but by giving farmers who comply with conservation programs a break on their local property taxes and federal income taxes.

The farm bureau is putting forward these ideas for extending conservation programs now because it is hoping to wield its influence before the formal debate begins. "This may be the best opportunity for farmers to take the lead in developing a farmer friendly conservation and environmental incentive program," the group says. [5]

[1] Office of the Inspector General, U.S. Department of Agriculture, *Audit Report No. 50600-3-KC,* August 1992.

[2] Testimony before the House Agriculture Subcommittee on Environment, Credit and Rural Development, Aug. 11, 1994.

[3] American Farm Bureau Policy Brief, "Conservation and Environmental Incentive Programs," undated.

[4] *Ibid.*

[5] *Ibid.*

Paying for 1993 Flood Damage

The Department of Agriculture paid a total of $2.9 billion to farmers in nine midwestern states hit hard by flooding in 1993. Disaster assistance accounted for more than half of the total, crop insurance for about a third.

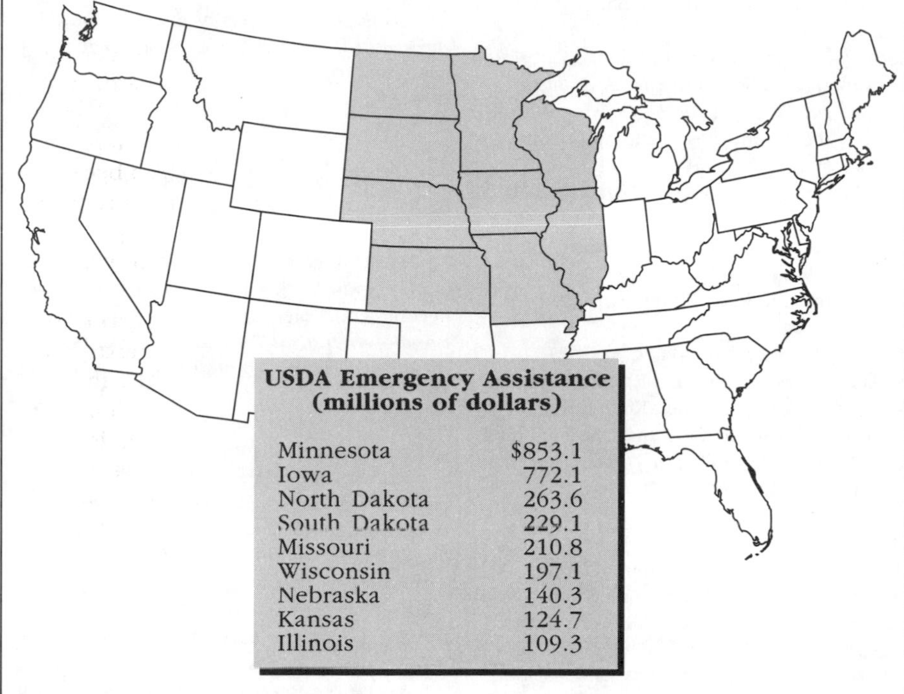

USDA Emergency Assistance (millions of dollars)

Minnesota	$853.1
Iowa	772.1
North Dakota	263.6
South Dakota	229.1
Missouri	210.8
Wisconsin	197.1
Nebraska	140.3
Kansas	124.7
Illinois	109.3

Continued from p. 1072

offers private insurance providers a subsidy to encourage farmers to buy supplemental insurance in the private marketplace. Of all the proposed reforms of federal farm programs, this was possibly the least controversial. ■

OUTLOOK

Chances of Reform

Congress will not begin its formal debate on the 1995 farm bill until next February and probably won't pass a bill until next summer or fall. But behind-the-scenes discussions already have begun, and conflicts within the new Republican majority are beginning to emerge.

Republicans find themselves in a predicament. They came to power pledging to balance the federal budget by cutting spending. Now this new majority must sort out where the cuts will fall.

"You're going to have some Republican ideologues who are going to want to cut farm programs to help balance the federal budget, but that's going to be difficult given the voting of the Farm Belt," which strongly backed Republican candidates, says Browne at Central Michigan University.

"This is going to be a real test for Republicans," Rep. Charles E. Schumer, D-N.Y., told *The Wall Street Journal*. "Are they really against all government subsidies, or just subsidies that affect Democratic constituencies, the poor and urban constituencies?" [44]

How these political currents will develop next year during the farm bill debate is difficult to predict, and what it may mean for radical reform of farm programs is hard to assess.

"Currently, adoption of [a radical] plan seems to be a long shot," Lotterman at the Federal Reserve Bank of Minneapolis wrote in a recent paper. [45] But Pottorff at The WEFA Group has a different view. "While in the past farm programs have changed fairly slowly, this does not ensure that there will be no radical changes this time around," he says. [46]

At a minimum, most analysts expect at least some cuts in farm subsidies. The question is how much. Among the obstacles facing those who want to hold the line on farm spending are the federal budget deficit, the decline in farm population, the suburbanization of Congress and continuing pressure from environmental groups.

• The federal budget deficit: The budget deficit played a key role in shaping farm policy in 1990, and three years later, urban members of Congress invoked the deficit when they voted to kill federal subsidies for wool, mohair and honey producers. Next year is expected to be no different. Farm advocates point out that federal spending on agriculture programs averages less than 1 percent of total government outlays while agriculture generates 16 percent of the country's gross domestic product.

• Suburbanization of Congress: As farm population has fallen and congressional districts have been redrawn, the influence of farmers has waned. Only 50 of the 435 members of the House come from districts that generate 10 percent or more of their income from agriculture. And those from outside rural areas may wish to redirect federal dollars to their constituencies.

"If Iowa farmers are smelling in the winds that it's going to be harder to sustain agricultural subsidies as they are now, they're right," Rep. Schumer said earlier this year. [47]

• Environmentalists' Clout: Beginning with the 1985 farm bill, Congress has used farm legislation to address its concern with the environment, creating voluntary conservation programs as well as programs that punish farmers if they don't comply.

Environmentalists like Kenneth Cook, president of the Environmental Working Group, a nonprofit environmental research organization in Washington, D.C., have helped to make these changes — a point noted by Rep. Roberts in his speech in Melvin, Ill., last June. "It has reached the point where in terms of policy, the real secretary of Agriculture may well be environmental activist Ken Cook," Roberts said.

Farmers themselves seem to be divided when it comes to keeping the current system of commodity payments. "There are as many growers who hate the programs as there are those who insist on them," political scientist Browne writes in his upcoming book, *Cultivating Congress: Constituents, Issues and Interests in Agricultural Policymaking*.

Browne says there have always been disagreements among farmers about farm programs, but he believes those divisions are wider today. It's increasingly difficult to find common ground among ranchers, wheat farmers, corn growers, pig farmers and growers of fruits and vegetables. "Today, farms are larger, more specialized, and farmers face different production problems even within the same state," Browne says.

These divisions among farmers also mean divisions among the politicians who represent them in Congress. All of this will come into play in next year's farm bill debate. ■

Barbara Mantel is a freelance writer in New York City.

Notes

[1] Willard Cochrane and C. Ford Runge, *Reforming Farm Policy: Toward a National Agenda* (1992), p. 5. Cochrane is professor emeritus and Runge is a professor in the Department of Agricultural and Applied Economics.

[2] *Ibid.*, p. 69.

[3] See David Harrington and Otto Doering, "Agricultural Policy Reform: A Proposal," *Choices*, First Quarter 1993. *Choices* is published by the American Agricultural Economics Association.

[4] *Findings of the 1995 Iowa Farm Bill Study Team*, Feb. 11, 1994, p. 10.

[5] *1992 Census of Agriculture*, Bureau of the Census, Volume AC92-A-51.

[6] Iowa Farm Bill Study Team, *op. cit.*, p. 4.

[7] *Ibid.*, p. 5.

[8] The WEFA Group, *Agri-View*, April 21, 1994. The WEFA Group is based in Bala Cynwyd, Pa.

[9] Joy Harwood, Dick Heifner, Keith Coble, Robert Dismukes and Sam Evans, "Streamlining Farm Policy: The Revenue Guarantee Approach," *The Agricultural Outlook*, U.S. Department of Agriculture, April 1994.

[10] The WEFA Group, *op. cit.*

[11] Letters, *Choices*, Second Quarter 1993, p. 43.

[12] William Heffernan, "Agricultural Profits: Who Gets Them Now, and Who Will in the Future?" undated paper. Heffernan is a professor of rural sociology at the University of Missouri.

[13] The WEFA Group, *Agri-View*, April 14, 1994.

[14] "The Changing U.S. Pork Industry," *Economic Review*, Second Quarter 1993, Federal Reserve Bank of Kansas City.

[15] H. Frederick Gale and David Harrington, writing in *The Agricultural Outlook*, U.S. Department of Agriculture, July 1993, p. 6.

[16] Suzanne Thornsbury, S. Murthy Kambhampaty and David Kenyon, "Economic Impact of a Swine Complex in Southside Virginia," Virginia Polytechnic Institute, 1993.

[17] John Ikerd, "The Economic Impacts of Increased Contract Swine Production in Missouri, Another Viewpoint," University of Missouri, undated.

[18] For background, see "Genetically Engineered Foods," *The CQ Researcher*, Aug. 5, 1994, pp. 673-696, and "Regulating Pesticides," *The CQ Researcher*, Jan. 28, 1994, pp. 73-96.

[19] Cochrane and Runge, *op. cit.*, p. 39.

[20] Douglas Bowers, Wayne Rasmussen and Gladys Baker, *History of Agricultural Price-Support and Adjustment Programs, 1933-84*, U.S. Department of Agriculture, December 1984, p. 1.

[21] Cochrane and Runge, *op. cit.*, p. 40.

[22] *Ibid.*, p. 49.

[23] Douglas Bowers, "Food Security Act of 1985," Draft, U.S. Department of Agriculture.

[24] Cochrane and Runge, *op. cit.*, p. 60.

[25] R. Neal Peterson and Nora Brooks, *The Changing Concentration of U.S. Agricultural Production During the 20th Century*, U.S. Department of Agriculture, July 1993.

[26] *Ibid.*

[27] "U.S. Farms — Diversity and Change," *The Agricultural Outlook*, U.S. Department of Agriculture, July 1993.

[28] *Ibid.*

[29] Bowers, Rasmussen and Baker, *op. cit.*

[30] *Ibid.*

[31] For background, see "Should Family Farms Be Saved?" *Editorial Research Reports*, May 6, 1988, pp. 233-243.

[32] John Schnittker, "An Assessment of International Export Market Development Efforts and Recommendations for the 1990s," in *International Agricultural Trade and Market Development Policy in the 1990s*, Chapter 14, p. 177-178.

[33] *Foreign Agricultural Trade of the U.S.*, U.S. Department of Agriculture Economic Research Service, November-December 1994.

[34] "Effects of the Uruguay Round Agreement on U.S. Agricultural Commodities," U.S. Department of Agriculture, March 1994.

[35] The WEFA Group, *Agri-View*, Feb. 24, 1994.

[36] Schnittker, *op. cit.*, p. 177.

[37] *U.S. Agriculture Executive Summary*, The WEFA Group, August 1994.

[38] *U.S. Agriculture Executive Summary*, The WEFA Group, July 1994.

[39] *Sharing the Challenge: Floodplain Management Into the 21st Century*, Report of the Interagency Floodplain Management Review Committee, June 1994.

[40] Emergency loans, grants and conservation payments accounted for the rest. For background, see "Disaster Response," *The CQ Researcher*, Oct. 15, 1993, pp. 889-912.

[41] See *CQ Weekly Report*, Oct. 8, 1994, pp. 2871-2872.

[42] *Sharing the Challenge, op. cit.*, p. 137.

[43] *Ibid.*, p. 29.

[44] Jackie Calmes, "Republicans Take Sides on Showing Commitment to Reduced Spending by Cutting Farm Subsidies," *The Wall Street Journal*, Nov. 15, 1994.

[45] Edward Lotterman, "The 1995 Farm Bill: Prospects for Change and Reform," Federal Reserve Bank of Minneapolis, September 1994.

[46] Richard Pottorff, "The Changing Focus of Agricultural Programs," The WEFA Group, 1994.

[47] Quoted in Peter T. Kilborn, "Iowa Farmers Rebel Against Subsidies, Seeking New Setup," *The New York Times*, July 25, 1994.

Bibliography

Selected Sources Used

Books

Browne, William P., *Cultivating Congress: Constituents, Issues and Interests in Agricultural Policymaking,* University Press of Kansas, 1995.
In his upcoming book, Browne, a political scientist at Central Michigan University, looks at how agricultural groups compete for congressional attention.

Cochrane, Willard W. and C. Ford Runge, *Reforming Farm Policy: Toward a National Agenda,* Iowa State University Press, 1992.
In this examination of federal farm programs, two University of Minnesota professors assert that current policy badly needs reforming because it is out of date and out of sync with the modern farm economy. They propose their own alternative.

Zigler, Allen and Burdette Loomis, *Interest Group Politics,* 4th edition, CQ Press, 1995.
This book is a compilation of recent research on interest group politics in the United States.

Articles

Barkema, Alan and Michael L. Cook, "The Changing U.S. Pork Industry: A Dilemma for Public Policy," *Economic Review,* Federal Reserve Bank of Kansas City, Second Quarter 1993.
This article documents the rapid changes in the nation's pork industry, as production shifts into the hands of fewer and larger farmers and thousands of small hog farmers disappear. The authors ask how government policy should balance the interests of traditional small farms against those of consumers who want high quality, lower cost products.

Hamilton, Neil D., "Agriculture without Farmers: How Industrialization is Restructuring Food Production," *Leopold Letter,* Iowa State University, spring 1991.
In this examination of the growing industrialization of agriculture, Drake University law Professor Hamilton argues that while food may be cheaper, there is little evidence that farmers benefit, that the environment improves or that rural communities prosper.

Harrington, David H. and Otto C. Doering III, "Agricultural Policy Reform: A Proposal," *Choices,* First Quarter 1993.
The authors propose a major restructuring of U.S. agricultural programs which they argue are too complex, distort trade and harm the environment. The two key features of their proposal are crop yield insurance and crop price stabilization. *Choices* is published by the American Agricultural Economics Association.

Sharples, Jerry, "World Events Shaping Future U.S. Agricultural Trade," *Choices,* Second Quarter 1994.
This article traces the world events that have influenced recent U.S. farm exports and makes predictions about trends in agricultural trade.

Reports and Studies

Bowers, Douglas E., Wayne D. Rasmussen and Gladys L. Baker, *History of Agricultural Price-Support and Adjustment Programs, 1933-81,* U.S. Department of Agriculture Economic Research Service, December 1984.
This report is a detailed history of federal farm programs from their inception onward. An updated report will be available by the end of 1994.

Cook, Kenneth A., *So Long, CRP,* Environmental Working Group, 1991.
This study presents data on the effectiveness of the Conservation Reserve Program (CRP) and the potential impact on agriculture and the environment of the program's expiration. Cook favors a continuation of a modified CRP.

Interagency Floodplain Management Review Committee, *Sharing the Challenge: Floodplain Management Into the 21st Century,* June 1994.
This report reviews the major causes and consequences of the 1993 Midwest flood and makes recommendations for better management of flood plains.

Iowa Farm Bill Study Team, *Findings of the 1995 Iowa Farm Bill Study Team,* February 1994.
The team, after studying current commodity programs and their perceived weaknesses, developed a proposal that would eliminate many current farm programs and replace them with a guarantee of farm revenue.

Lotterman, Edward, *The 1995 Farm Bill: Prospects for Change and Reform,* September 1994.
Agricultural economist Lotterman argues that Congress in 1995 will reauthorize current commodity programs with less funding and that there is little political support for extensive modifications of current policies

Midwestern Governors Conference, *Proposed Policy Objectives on the 1995 Farm Bill,* August 1994.
In this report from the 29th annual meeting of the conference, the governors argue for a go slow approach to proposals to overhaul current commodity programs.

Peterson, R. Neal and Nora L. Brooks, *The Changing Concentration of U.S. Agriculture Production During the 20th Century,* U.S. Department of Agriculture Economic Research Service, July 1993.
The authors document the growing concentration of farm production in the hands of fewer and larger farms.

The Next Step

Additional information from UMI's Newspaper & Periodical Abstracts database

Environmental Issues

Batie, Sandra S. and Craig A. Cox, "Soil and water quality: An agenda for agriculture — A summary," *Journal of Soil & Water Conservation,* September 1994, pp. 456-462.

A re-examination of the relationship between agriculture and the environment and attendant public policies resulted in some major contributions to the policy debate. These contributions to the farming systems agenda are discussed.

Betts, Kellyn, "Sustaining the Earth," *E: The Environmental Magazine,* September 1994, pp. 50-51.

Sustainable agriculture, which encompasses alternative farming practices aimed at minimizing or reducing environmental degradation, is discussed. Sustainable agriculture is a close relative of organic farming.

Epplin, Francis M, Ghazi A. Al-Sakkaf, and Thomas F. Peeper, "Impacts of alternative tillage methods for continuous wheat on grain yield and economics: Implications for conservation compliance," *Journal of Soil & Water Conservation,* July 1994, pp. 394-399.

By 1995, U.S. farmers who farm land classified as highly erodible and who wish to qualify for federal deficiency payments will be required to implement conservation compliance plans. Reasons behind this plan are examined.

Stauber, Karl N., "The futures of agriculture," *American Journal of Alternative Agriculture,* winter 1994, pp. 9-15.

The future of agriculture depends on what people believe and value and on their vision of the Common Good. Standards for the liberal, romantic and ecocentric visions of the Common Good are examined.

Zinn, Jeffrey and John Blodgett, "Agriculture meets the environment: Communicating perspectives," *Journal of Soil & Water Conservation,* March 1994, pp. 136-143.

The interjection of environmentalism into agricultural policy since 1989 is discussed. Although a greater understanding of each other has occurred, environmentalists and policy-makers have yet to develop sufficient empathy for each other's world view to fully establish a working partnership that will allow them to merge their strengths.

Farm Policies

"A Clinton farm bill," *The Washington Post,* Aug. 30, 1994, p. A20.

An editorial discusses the challenges of farm policy that will face the Clinton administration in 1995, noting that farm programs will be up for renewal, meaning fiscal pressure and demands from environmental and other groups to trim the subsidies.

Barkema, Alan and Mark Drabenstott, "A new agricultural policy for a new world market," *Economic Review* (Federal Reserve Bank of Kansas City), Second Quarter 1994, pp. 59-72.

A new farm bill will be enacted in 1995, and it will provide a propitious opportunity to re-evaluate the current bill in light of fundamental changes to the marketplace since the adoption of the 1990 bill. Recent developments in the world food market are examined. The U.S. will need to overhaul its agricultural policy if it is to excel in the future marketplace.

Benenson, Bob, "Custom puts farmers at odds with seed breeders and law," *Congressional Quarterly Weekly Report,* Aug. 6, 1994, p. 2245.

The House Agriculture Committee approved a bill on Aug. 3, 1994, to bring U.S. law into agreement with the 1991 international convention reinforcing patentlike protection of new plant varieties and preventing saved-seed sales between farmers. The bill, HR 2927, is discussed.

Day, Janet, "Groups gird for battle over farm bill," *Denver Post,* Feb. 19, 1994, p. D1.

Issues concerning the 1995 farm bill took center stage on Feb. 18, 1994, at the Governor's Agricultural Outlook Forum held at the Colorado Convention Center in Denver.

Kilborn, Peter T., "Iowa farmers rebel against subsidies, seeking new setup," *The New York Times,* July 25, 1994, p. A1.

Representatives of 11 leading farm organizations in Iowa have formed a coalition with the single purpose of pressuring Congress and the Clinton administration to scrap the system of farm subsidies in 1995, when a new five-year farm law is enacted.

Moseley, James R., "A shift in farm policy? The debate has begun," *Farm Journal* (Central Edition), Mid-March 1994, p. 22.

Most discussions of farm policy reform evolve around combining price support and disaster and crop insurance programs. Significant changes may be initiated by 1996.

Rose, Louis J., "Many farms harvest tax dollars," *St. Louis Post-Dispatch,* Sept. 4, 1994, p. B7.

Department of Agriculture officials are changing crop insurance rules so that farmers whose crops failed 70 percent of the time or more will be declared ineligible for the insurance or pay higher premiums.

Walker, Sam, "Fickle weather and low harvests may alter U.S. aid to corn farmers," *Christian Science Monitor,* May 17, 1994, p. 2.

A spate of freakish weather has prompted farmers across the corn belt to pay unusually close attention to the barometic pressure, and Congress, set to review U.S. farm policy in 1995, might be prompted to do away with the set-aside program in favor of a more market-oriented policy.

Zinn, Jeffrey, "Take your seats for the '95 farm bill," *Journal of Soil & Water Conservation,* September 1994, p. 418.

Many agricultural interests are likely to view the environmental elements of the farm bill as a defensive stand rather than as an offensive opportunity. The process of creating a farm bill and how conservation factors may affect it are discussed in an editorial.

Food Production and Consumption

Dahlberg, Kenneth A., "A transition from agriculture to regenerative food systems," *Futures,* March 1994, pp. 170-179.

Major transformations of industrial agriculture can be expected to occur as part of the larger transition to a post-fossil-fuel era. These transformations will occur not only because industrial agriculture is a major source of the unsustainability of industrial societies, but because it is itself unsustainable.

Hamilton, Neil, "Agriculture without farmers," *Successful Farming* (Iowa Edition), April 1994, pp. 28-29.

Industrialization is restructuring U.S. food production. Contract production is making farmers employees on their own land. Confronting this change in agriculture means reigniting the debate over agricultural industrialization.

Johnson, S. R., "How nutrition policy affects food and agricultural policy," *Journal of Nutrition,* September 1994, pp. 1871S-1877S.

The simple connection between nutrition policy and food and agricultural policy, which follows from the sovereignty of the consumer, is noted. If they are properly designed, food and agricultural policies can accelerate the process of adapting the production and distribution systems for agriculture and food to better meet the demands of the more informed consumer.

Karian, Steve, "Food for a change," *Dollars & Sense,* May 1994, pp. 30-31.

Understanding the central role of animal production in global agribusiness and developing a strategy to transform the Western food system are key challenges for progressives in the United States.

Myers, Lester H., "Food consumption data needs for food and agricultural policy," *Journal of Nutrition,* September 1994, pp. 1853S-1859S.

Food consumption data are essential for the management of government food and agriculture programs, but many food safety and nutritional well-being issues require specific food product consumption data for high risk groups. Data collection should be planned so that a balance is achieved between survey objectives and the practical constraints of obtaining accurate information.

GATT

Banks, Howard, "GATT will be good to farmers," *Forbes,* June 20, 1994, p. 35.

President Clinton can depend on farmers to support GATT because farmers will have the most to lose if GATT does not pass. The U.S. is the most efficient farming country. With GATT in place, it is likely that Asian countries will buy more U.S. food products.

Frydenlund, John, "More exports? Free farms' idle acres," *The New York Times,* Oct. 30, 1994, p. 3.

John Frydenlund contends that American farmers are unlikely to benefit from the GATT agreement because of "misguided domestic policies" insuring that their share of the global market will continue to shrink. Frydenlund criticizes the USDA's acreage-reduction programs and the conservation reserve program, which idle 15 percent of farmland each year, and the export enhancement program, which, he argues, actually depresses world prices.

Gunset, George, "Three gifts to farmers on horizon," *Chicago Tribune,* Jan. 10, 1994, p. 1.

Like the Magi, policy-makers presented farmers with three gifts at the end of 1993 that hold long-term promise for improved markets: NAFTA, GATT and ethanol. But no farmer is counting on a big boost from any of the three in 1994.

LaFranchi, Howard, "Tradition in turmoil: Dutch agriculture evolves," *Christian Science Monitor,* July 6, 1994, p. 7.

Dutch farmers are among the world's most efficient producers. But European Union and GATT agreements are imposing tough environmental rules, and all parties are engaging in debates over the country's agricultural future.

Lord Plumb of Coleshill, "The future of agriculture in the European Community," *SAIS Review,* winter 1994, pp. 53-60.

Challenges facing European agriculture include the reform of the Common Agricultural Policy, the new international trading rules of GATT and the impact of the opening of the Central European and Eastern European agriculture markets.

Back Issues

Great Research on Current Issues Starts Right Here...Recent topics covered by The CQ Researcher are listed below. Before May 1991, reports were published under the name of Editorial Research Reports.

MAY 1993
Cults in America
Preventing Teen Pregnancy
Software Piracy
National Parks

JUNE 1993
Food Safety
Prostitution
Childhood Immunizations
National Service

JULY 1993
Electric Cars
Population Growth
Downward Mobility
Intelligence Testing

AUGUST 1993
Mental Illness
Bilingual Education
Foreign Policy Burden
School Funding

SEPTEMBER 1993
Suburban Crime
Public Housing
Supreme Court Preview
Immigration Reform

Back issues are available for $4.00 (subscribers) or $7.00 (non-subscribers). Quantity discounts apply to orders over ten. To order, call Congressional Quarterly Customer Service at (202) 887-8621.

Binders are available for $16.00. To order call 1-800-638-1710. Please refer to stock number 648.

OCTOBER 1993
Airline Safety
Disaster Response
Science in the Courtroom
The Glass Ceiling

NOVEMBER 1993
Paying for Retirement
Charitable Giving
Privacy in the Workplace
Adoption

DECEMBER 1993
U.S. Vietnam-Relations
Learning Disabilities
Child Care
Space Program's Future

JANUARY 1994
Racial Tensions in Schools
South Africa's Future
Worker Retraining
Regulating Pesticides

FEBRUARY 1994
Prison Overcrowding
Water Quality
Religion in Schools
Juvenile Justice

MARCH 1994
Underground Economy
Education Standards
Gambling Boom
Private Management of Public Schools

APRIL 1994
Reproductive Ethics
U.S.-China Trade
Soccer in America
Talk Show Democracy

MAY 1994
Traffic Congestion
Women's Health Issues
Mutual Funds
Political Scandals

JUNE 1994
Education and Gender
Gun Control
Public Land Policy
Nuclear Arms Cleanup

JULY 1994
Dietary Supplements
Public Opinion and Foreign Policy
Crime Victims' Rights
Birth Control Choices

AUGUST 1994
Genetically Engineered Foods
Electing Minorities
Prozac Controversy
College Sports

SEPTEMBER 1994
Home Schooling
Welfare Experiments
Courts and the Media
Regulating Tobacco

OCTOBER 1994
Historic Preservation
Religion and Politics
Arts Funding
Economic Sanctions

NOVEMBER 1994
Sex on Campus
Blood Supply Safety
Testing Term Limits
Religion in America

Future Topics

- ***Earthquake Research***
- ***The Future of Television***
- ***Treating Addiction***

THE CQ Researcher
PUBLISHED BY CONGRESSIONAL QUARTERLY INC.

Arms Sales

Should the U.S. cut its weapons exports?

After the Cold War arms race ended between the United States and the Soviet Union, defense spending cuts rocked U.S. arms manufacturers. Many were forced to downsize or merge with competitors. To stay in business, weapons makers are focusing increasingly on exports. With defense firms from other nations cutting back on production, the United States has emerged as the undisputed leader in the vast international arms bazaar. The spread of regional conflicts around the globe has brought new buyers for fighter planes, tanks, missiles and other conventional arms, especially developing countries in the Near East and East Asia. The Clinton administration, meanwhile, is dismaying arms control advocates by promoting exports of weaponry as part of its campaign to enhance U.S. industrial competitiveness.

INSIDE THIS ISSUE

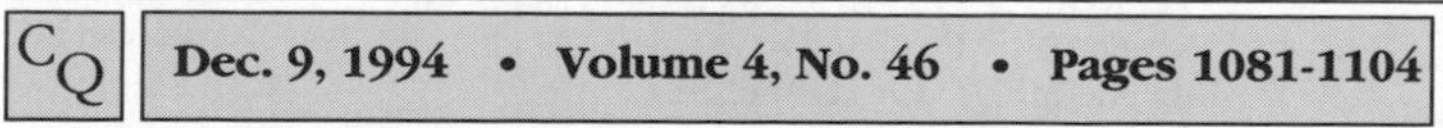

CQ Dec. 9, 1994 • Volume 4, No. 46 • Pages 1081-1104

Formerly Editorial Research Reports

THE ISSUES

BACKGROUND

CURRENT SITUATION

OUTLOOK

SIDEBARS AND GRAPHICS

FOR MORE INFORMATION

COVER: RECENT U.S. ARMS EXPORTS HAVE INCLUDED F-15 EAGLE FIGHTERS. (DEPARTMENT OF DEFENSE)

December 9, 1994
Volume 4, No. 46

The CQ Researcher (ISSN 1056-2036). Formerly Editorial Research Reports. Published weekly (48 times per year, not printed the first Friday of any month with five Fridays) by Congressional Quarterly Inc., 1414 22nd St., N.W., Washington, D.C. 20037. Rates are furnished upon request. Second-class postage paid at Washington, D.C. POSTMASTER: Send address changes to The CQ Researcher, 1414 22nd St., N.W., Washington, D.C. 20037.

Arms Sales

By Mary H. Cooper

The Issues

When the Berlin Wall came tumbling down and the Soviet Union disintegrated, a new era of peace and prosperity seemed on the horizon. There was hope that the billions of dollars fueling the Cold War arms race could be channeled into the civilian economy — the much-anticipated "peace dividend."

But five years later there is little talk of peace dividends or defense contractors converting to consumer products. The nuclear arms race between the two superpowers has ended, but regional conflicts from Bosnia to Rwanda to Sri Lanka have sparked races for conventional weapons — from missiles, jet fighters and tanks to rifles, grenades and land mines.

While defense spending by industrialized nations has been falling, total military spending in the developing world jumped 12 percent in 1990 and an additional 3 percent in 1991, hitting a new record high of $242 billion. A growing share of world arms sales goes to the Middle East, East Asia and South Asia. [1]

The makeup of the arms bazaar itself has changed as well. Once dominated by the U.S. and U.S.S.R. and a few lesser suppliers in Europe, it is now overwhelmingly dominated by one nation: the United States. To the dismay of arms control advocates, 70 percent of arms sold on the world market are made in the U.S.A., up from just 21 percent five years ago.

"I think it's a horrible trend," says Lawrence J. Korb, a senior fellow at the Brookings Institution and former assistant secretary of Defense in the Reagan administration.

During the Cold War, policy-makers' fears that U.S. arms exports might end up in Soviet hands led to restraints on arms transfers. Now the Soviet Union, and the restraints, are gone. "Without the normal brakes in the system," Korb says, "the only thing that's going to slow this thing down is that the arms buyers are going to run out of money. And to the extent that they buy military equipment, they're not going to buy other things" their citizens need.

But as industry spokesmen point out, the main reason for U.S. dominance of the arms market is the decline of its competitors. "U.S. exports of military equipment have been relatively constant for at least the last decade," says Joel L. Johnson, vice president for international affairs of the Aerospace Industries Association of America. "What happened is the world of transfers dropped from about $55 billion in 1985 down to around $22 billion in 1993," giving the United States a bigger percentage of the total.

Russia and the other successor states to the Soviet Union — once the world's leading arms supplier — are in deep economic crisis and have drastically curtailed weapons production and exports. Russia's share of exports dropped from a third of the market in 1989 to just 9 percent in 1993. [2]

Production also has been cut by the main producers in Eastern Europe, among them the Czech Republic (formerly part of Czechoslovakia), Poland and Hungary. Western European arms makers, led by France, the United Kingdom and Germany, cut production in response to defense budget cuts even before the Cold War's end. The value of arms exports by the three major Western European producers has fallen almost by half since 1989, to just $3.7 billion last year. [3]

U.S. arms exports, meanwhile, have remained fairly steady, averaging around $12 billion a year. Critics of arms sales say that at a time of shrinking markets the United States is setting a bad example to the rest of the world by hawking its lethal weapons overseas. Industry representatives respond that conventional arms are legitimate export products that serve the interests of both the United States and their customers, who are carefully screened through the federal licensing process. *

"Nine years out of 10 we're known as the merchants of death, and the next year we're the arsenal of democracy," Johnson says. "I'd feel more guilty selling sugar-coated breakfast cereal to kids than selling weapons to democratic nations. There are legitimate reasons for countries to defend themselves. I find it harder to come up with a good one for sugar-frosted cereal."

U.S. arms producers have stepped up their export efforts as a way to survive Pentagon budget cuts. Defense Department orders for new weapons have fallen by half since 1988, reach-

* U.S. arms exports go through one of two channels. The State Department's Office of Defense Trade Controls administers the Direct Commercial Sales program, which licenses manufacturers to deal directly with foreign governments or firms. Licenses are issued if there are no overriding foreign policy reasons not to approve the request. Most arms deals are made through the Foreign Military Sales program run by the Pentagon's Defense Security Assistance Agency, which purchases weapons from U.S. defense firms and transfers them overseas.

The Global Arms Market

Global arms sales have plummeted since the Cold War years. From a peak of about $46 billion in 1987, the value of weapons delivered dipped to about $22 billion in 1993, according to the Stockholm International Peace Research Institute. Cutbacks in defense spending have forced many arms makers to restructure their operations and to step up efforts to sell their goods overseas. Despite the changes, the industry remains highly concentrated, with five countries accounting for 86 percent of all arms deliveries.

Since the breakup of the Soviet Union, once the world's leading supplier, the United States has dominated the arms export market. In 1993, the U.S. supplied about 50 percent of the major conventional weapons sold globally. Bolstered by the sales of MiG-29 fighter jets to Hungary and Slovakia, Russia accounted for 21 percent of the export market and the European Union, led by Germany, France and the United Kingdom, supplied another 20 percent (*table at left*).

Arms importers also are concentrated among a relatively small group of nations, mostly in Asia and Europe. India, which is modernizing its armed services, led Asian importers in arms purchases, while Turkey, which also is modernizing its forces, led Europe in acquisitions (*table at right*). Turkey's purchases of new weapons are in addition to older weapons it is obtaining through "cascading" agreements with other NATO countries, by which it is acquiring older weapons deployed in Western Europe that are being phased out under terms of the 1990 Treaty on Conventional Armed Forces in Europe.

Since the 1991 gulf war, several Middle Eastern countries also have stepped up their arms purchases, especially Saudi Arabia, Kuwait and Israel. Completing deals made before the war, Egypt also continues to buy F-16 fighters and M-1A1 tanks.

Leading suppliers of major conventional weapons
(in billions of constant 1990 dollars)

Supplier	1993	1989-93
United States	$10.5	$56.6
U.S.S.R./Russia	4.5	35.4
West Germany/Germany	1.8	8.7
France	.9	7.8
United Kingdom	1.0	6.6
China	.4	5.7
Czechoslovakia/Czech Republic	.5	2.2
Netherlands	.3	1.9
Italy	.4	1.5
Israel	.2	1.1

Leading recipients of major conventional weapons
(in billions of constant 1990 dollars)

Recipient	1993	1989-93	Major suppliers (1987-91)*
India	$2.1	$10.5	U.S.S.R./Russia
Japan	1.0	8.3	U.S.
Saudi Arabia	1.3	8.0	U.K., U.S., China, France
Turkey	2.5	7.7	U.S., Germany (West)
Greece	.4	6.3	U.S., France
Afghanistan	0	6.3	U.S.S.R.
Germany (West)	.6	5.0	U.S.
Egypt	1.5	4.6	U.S.
Pakistan	.5	3.6	U.S., China
China	.8	3.4	U.S.S.R./Russia, Middle East

* From U.S. Arms Control and Disarmament Agency, *World Military Expenditures and Arms Transfers 1991-1992.*

Source: Stockholm International Peace Research Institute, *SIPRI Yearbook 1994.* SIPRI is an independent organization financed by the Swedish Parliament to monitor arms control issues.

ing a new low of $44 billion in 1994. Several weapons systems, including the General Dynamics Corp.'s M-1A2 tank and the McDonnell Douglas Corp.'s workhorse F-15 fighter aircraft, are being produced almost solely for export. "U.S. companies, as well as the Europeans, are out there beating the bushes more frantically and competing more nastily with each other," Johnson says.

Adds Richard Bitzinger, defense industry analyst at the Defense Budget Project, a Washington research group: "Today they are snapping up contracts that they would have turned up their noses at just five years ago." (*See table, p. 1086.*)

Both the Bush and Clinton administrations promised to help defense contractors convert their plants to produce civilian goods. But for the most part, military conversion has had only a limited impact. Many defense contractors, unable or reluctant to transform their production to civilian use, have followed the lead of the automakers and other heavy manufacturers by selling unproductive units, laying off workers or merging with competitors. In this environment, exports provide one of the few means to remain profitable.

The Cold War's demise has injected new energy into the decades-old debate over arms control. Once limited almost exclusively to weapons of mass destruction, the debate today focuses increasingly on conventional arms, especially their sale to Third World countries. (*See graph, p. 1088.*) Arms control advocates say exports cause untold misery in poor countries by diverting scarce resources away from investments in education, immunization and economic development. The U.N. Development Programme says that just 12 percent of the money developing countries now spend on military programs could provide primary health care and safe drinking water to all their citizens — and eliminate severe malnutrition. [4]

Arms control advocates condemn the United States' role as the leading provider of arms and call for policy changes that would greatly restrict sales. Bill Clinton supported that position during the 1992 presidential campaign against incumbent President George Bush, who had continued longstanding U.S. arms sale policies. While requiring licensing for most weapons exports, the Bush administration stepped up efforts to help American producers market their goods by promoting sales through foreign embassies and covering part of the costs of corporate participation in overseas trade shows.

Shortly after taking office, President Clinton initiated an overall review of that policy. Lawmakers also called for an end to export promotions, citing concerns over human-rights abuses by some buyers of U.S. weapons and the danger of sophisticated American arms falling into unfriendly hands. In 1993, Sen. Mark O. Hatfield, R-Ore., and Rep. Cynthia McKinney, D-Ga., introduced a bill to restrict arms exports based on these concerns. The Code of Conduct on Arms Transfer Act, which died in committee, would have barred arms exports to countries that are anti-democratic, violate human rights, attack other countries or refuse to report their arms deals to the United Nations.

Arms control advocates had hoped that new restrictions on U.S. arms exports would be announced as early as the summer of 1993. But the Clinton review has yet to be completed, and meanwhile the administration has helped promote weapons sales as part of its campaign to boost U.S. exports in general. "The irony is that we've probably never had as supportive an administration as this," Johnson says. "That doesn't mean they've been looser in terms of allowing a given sale. But when it comes to winning a specific sale, they've been as supportive as any administration in history."

Recent reports suggest that the Clinton administration will continue to help U.S. producers selling weapons abroad. In fact, while insisting that foreign policy interests will still guide decisions on arms sales, the administration reportedly will break with precedent by explicitly stating that domestic economic needs will be among the factors considered in arms sale questions.

Given the administration's likely shift away from tighter restrictions on arms sales, it is unclear whether the Republican sweep of both houses of Congress in last month's elections will have a great impact on arms transfer policy. The Republican Party's campaign promise to raise defense spend-

Among the most popular U.S. arms exports are (from left) AH-64A Apache attack helicopters, Stinger missiles and M-1A1 tanks. (Department of Defense photos)

Recent Major U.S. Arms Transfer Agreements

Saudi Arabia has been the biggest U.S. arms customer in the 1990s, reflecting its concern about security during and after the Persian Gulf War. Since 1990, it has spent about $22 billion on major arms purchases from U.S. firms. Taiwan and Kuwait were the next biggest spenders, at more than $5 billion each.

Purchasing country and year of agreement	Weapon	Contractor	Cost ($billions)
1994			
Western Europe (Belgium, Denmark, Netherlands, Norway)	F-16 fighter update	Lockheed	$1.3
Israel	F-15 fighters	McDonnell Douglas	N/A
Singapore	F-16 fighters	Lockheed	.9
1993			
Malaysia	F/A-18 fighters	McDonnell Douglas	1.6
France	E-2C surveillance planes	Grumman	.8
1992			
Saudi Arabia	F-15 fighters	McDonnell Douglas	9.0
Taiwan	F-16 fighters	General Dynamics	5.8
Finland	F/A-18 fighters	McDonnell Douglas	3.0
Kuwait	M-1A1 tanks	General Dynamics	3.0
Kuwait	Patriot missiles	Raytheon	2.5
Greece	F-16 fighters	General Dynamics	1.8
South Korea	AH-64 Apache helicopters	McDonnell Douglas	1.0
Israel	AH-64/UH-60 helicopters	McDonnell Douglas/Sikorsky	.9
Germany	D-500 surveillance planes	E-Systems	.8
Saudi Arabia	Hellfire missiles	Rockwell	.6
Saudi Arabia	F-15 training support aircraft	McDonnell Douglas	.5
Italy	AV-8B Harrier fighters	McDonnell Douglas	.4
Thailand	E-2C Hawkeye surveillance planes	Grumman	.4
1991			
Saudi Arabia	Patriot missiles	Raytheon	3.3
Turkey	F-16 fighters	General Dynamics	2.8
South Korea	F-16 fighters	General Dynamics	2.5
Switzerland	F/A-18 fighters	McDonnell Douglas	2.3
Egypt	F-16 fighters	Lockheed	1.6
United Arab Emirates	AH-64 helicopters	McDonnell Douglas	.7
Thailand	F-16 fighters	Lockheed	.5
Greece	AH-64 helicopters	McDonnell Douglas	.5
1990			
Saudi Arabia	Light armored vehicles/TOW missiles	GM Canada/Hughes	3.4
Saudi Arabia	M-1A2 tanks, M-2 Bradley infantry fighting vehicles/M-113 armored personnel carriers	General Dynamics/FMC	3.1
Saudi Arabia	F-15C/D fighters	McDonnell Douglas	2.0

Note: Transactions are reported in the year they were announced.

Source: Defense Budget Project

ing should mean a boost in procurement for defense contractors. At the same time, the promise to cut foreign aid, including military assistance, may dampen official support for exports.

"Congress has always been a little bit of a paper tiger when it comes to arms sales," says William Hartung, senior fellow at the World Policy Institute in New York City and author of a recent book on U.S. arms policy. "There were a few members who made a difference, but there were a lot of people who rhetorically were against arms sales but, when push came to shove, tended not to do anything that would actually limit sales. So in terms of policy changes, the election results may not be as big a loss [to arms control advocates] as they first appear."

As administration officials and lawmakers consider new restrictions on arms transfers, they must weigh the following issues:

Do arms exports enhance U.S. national security?

Throughout the Cold War, the primary security interest of the United

States was thwarting expansion by the Soviet Union and its Eastern European allies. That overriding priority governed arms transfer policy as well. Exports to developed countries, including the Western European NATO allies, were aimed at defending territory from Soviet attack. Concern over indirect Soviet involvement in Third World "proxy" conflicts often guided sales to developing countries as well. Israel, for example, the United States' chief recipient of military aid and weaponry, was armed to help protect U.S. interests in the region against hostile Arab countries — armed for the most part by the Soviet Union.

Spokesmen for the defense industry say the policy has been an unqualified success. "If you look at 60 years of the history of arms transfers starting with lend-lease to Britain and Russia, by and large we have gotten what we wanted," says Johnson. "We rolled back the Axis, the Soviet Union crumbled and most developing countries are moving toward democratic systems and market economies. That's a pretty good record."

But critics look at the same record to find evidence that arms sales have posed risks to U.S. security interests. According to Hartung, in at least three conflicts where the United States has intervened in recent years — Panama (1989), Iraq (1991) and Somalia (1992) — American soldiers have been endangered by the "boomerang effect" of previous U.S. arms sales to developing nations. "Iraq received machine tools, computer-testing equipment and other goods that were used to build howitzers and other arms for direct use in their war effort," Hartung says. "In both Somalia and Panama, the United States gave away a lot of weapons."

Industry spokesmen vehemently deny this allegation. "You'd be hard-pressed to show any example ever of a U.S. soldier facing a significant U.S. weapon system," Johnson says. "I'm not talking M-16s, which the Congress up until recently thought you ought to be able to buy at Woolworth's. I'm talking about tanks, missiles or airplanes. I can't think of any example in 60 years when that happened."

Department of Defense

Foreign orders for U.S. Patriot missiles increased after their use against Iraqi Scud missiles during the 1991 gulf war.

Hartung calls Johnson's position disingenuous. "The industry is asking us to show a picture of an Iraqi soldier holding a weapon with a sign that says 'Made in U.S.A.,' " Hartung says. "That's hard to document directly, but there no question that the United States contributed to these countries' military capability."

American weaponry can fall into the hands of potential enemies in various ways. When the Ayatollah Ruhollah Khomeini and his militant Islamic followers overthrew the shah of Iran, for example, they inherited one of the world's most sophisticated arsenals. As one of the United States' key allies in the Middle East, Shah Mohammed Reza Pahlavi had bought billions of dollars' worth of advanced American weaponry, including F-14 fighters.

But Johnson insists that such weapons pose little risk to U.S. security interests. "In the case of Iran, the F-14s mostly became inoperational," says Johnson, who estimates that Iran's ability to use its U.S.-supplied weapons may have lasted no more than three months. "None of them has ever fired a Phoenix missile at anybody because they simply couldn't support them without us. The more sophisticated the system, the more the customer needs us."

American arms also are stolen from overseas arsenals and transferred to hostile countries. According to the General Accounting Office, 40 shoulder-launched Stinger antiaircraft missiles sent to the Persian Gulf for use in the 1991 war against Iraq have vanished. "The Army does not know where these missiles are," the GAO reports.[5] In great demand for their accuracy and ease of handling, Stingers also disappeared by the hundreds after they were provided to anti-Soviet forces in Afghanistan during the 1980s.

The dangers posed by the covert sale or theft of U.S.-made arms has been heightened by what Michael T.

Arming the Third World

Russia was the leading arms supplier to Third World countries during the Cold War, but in 1990 the United States took over the lead.

Supplier	1986	1987	1988	1989	1990	1991	1992
United States	$3.3	$5.0	$8.7	$7.4	$13.5	$14.1	$14.8
Russia*	16.2	22.0	13.8	11.7	5.7	1.5	1.8
France	1.0	2.8	1.2	3.9	2.9	4.0	.2
United Kingdom	.8	.5	20.6	.8	.3	2.1	1.8
China	2.0	4.7	2.5	1.6	.5	.3	.3
Germany	.5	1.4	.2	.4	1.1	.7	.6
Italy	.6	.2	.2	.3	.1	.5	0

(in $ billions, not adjusted for inflation)

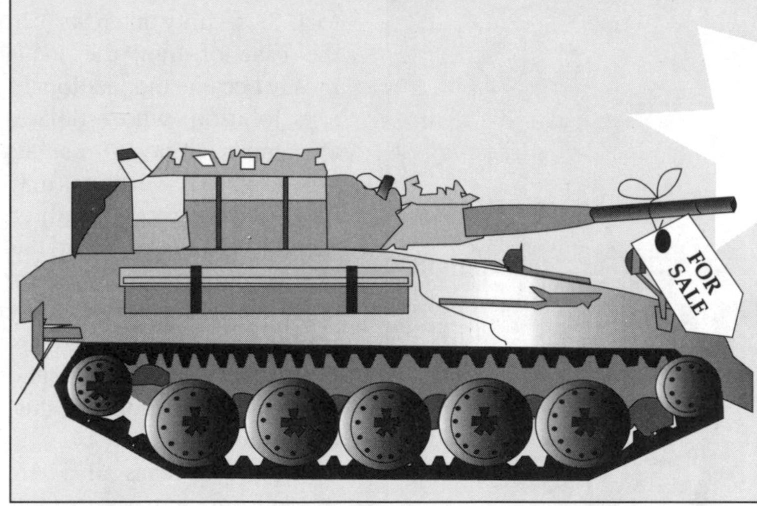

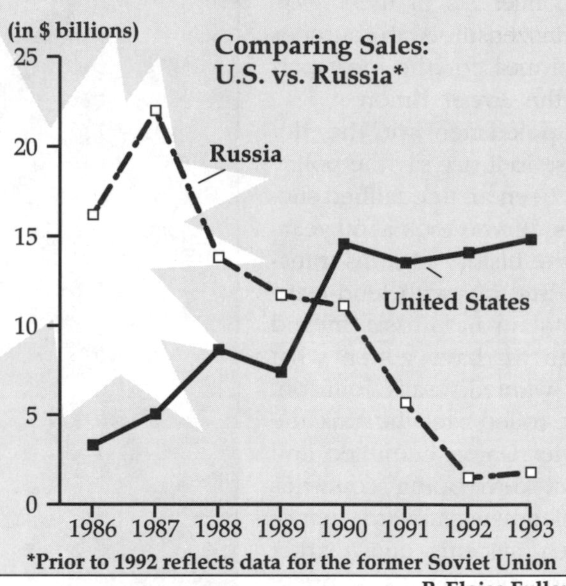

*Prior to 1992 reflects data for the former Soviet Union

P. Eloise Fuller

Source: Congressional Research Service

Klare calls the "deadly convergence" of trends in the post-Cold War era — the rise of Third World military powers such as Iraq and North Korea together with a growing stockpile of sophisticated weapons, including chemical and nuclear arms as well as conventional weapons.

"With the large supplies of conventional weapons now stockpiled in their military arsenals," he writes, "many of the Third World countries are capable of conducting combat operations over wide areas and at very high levels of violence — levels that one would expect from a major conflict in Europe. Battles fought on such a scale would pose a threat of catastrophic defeat to one side or the other, prompting the loser to resort to chemical or even nuclear weapons to avert disaster. . . . While still a remote possibility, this scenario represents the most plausible set of circumstances we can imagine today for the onset of a global nuclear war." [6]

Are U.S. arms sales to the Third World harmful to development?

While attention was focused on the superpowers during the Cold War, developing countries were increasing their military spending three times faster than the industrial countries. From 1960 to 1987, Third World military spending rose by 7.5 percent a year, rising from $24 billion to $145 billion. [7] After the Cold War began winding down, global arms sales fell by more than 10 percent a year, from $40 billion in 1985 to just $18 billion by 1992. But sales to developing countries during the same period only declined from 57 percent of the total to 51 percent.

Today, developing nations account for about two-thirds of global purchases of conventional weapons. Although the value of arms sales agreements and actual deliveries of weapons to these countries has declined in the post-Cold War period, Third World nations still took possession of $15 billion of military equipment in 1993 and ordered $20.4 billion more. [8]

Many of the leading purchasers of weapons, while technically defined as developing nations, are wealthy and provide their citizens with a broad array of social services. Saudi Arabia, for example, bought $10 billion worth of F-15s and other American weaponry in 1992 and is the United States' biggest arms customer. The world's leading oil producer, the Saudi kingdom provides its citizens free education and medical care and other services.

But even vast oil wealth has not insulated the Saudis from the perils of runaway defense spending. Coming at a time of declining oil prices, the kingdom's ambitious arms purchases have run the country into debt. Saudi Arabia, however, is better prepared than most arms importers to weather such financial setbacks.

While most of the world's arms purchases have come from wealthier developing countries in the Middle East and Northern Africa, a remarkable $95 billion a year in arms purchases have been made by some of the world's poorest countries. And money spent on weapons is often money denied to important social services.

India, for example, ordered 20 MiG-29 fighter aircraft from Russia in 1992 at a cost that could have provided basic education to all 15 million Indian girls without access to schooling. The same year, for the money it spent to buy 80 tanks from the United Kingdom, Nigeria could have immunized all 2 million of its unimmunized children and provided family-planning services to 17 million couples. For the cost of 28 U.S. missiles, South Korea could have immunized its 120,000 untreated children and provided safe water for 3.5 million people for three years. [9]

"Critics will say that the United States provides 75 percent of the sales to the Third World, and isn't that awful because it means that children aren't eating," Johnson says. "But if you look at who they're talking about, it's South Korea and Taiwan, which for the last three decades have had the two best economic growth records of any two countries ever in world history. It's Saudi Arabia and Kuwait, which up until now have provided free education and health care to their citizens."

By contrast, Johnson says, the United States sells far fewer weapons to poor countries, accounting for only 6 percent of the transfers to Africa, South Asia and Latin America. "The United States is essentially irrelevant to poor countries," he says. "They buy their stuff from other Third World countries and from Europe, Russia and China."

These comparisons, however, deal only with transfers of major weapons such as tanks and aircraft. Most arms sales to the Third World involve light weaponry such as grenades, rifles, land mines and munitions. (*See story, p. 1092.*) Because sales of most of these weapons are not monitored, estimates of the volume of small arms transfers vary broadly. But in developing countries that are ravaged by civil war, it is these weapons that usually cause most casualties. Machine guns and machetes, not F-16s or tanks, were the weapons of choice in Rwanda, where hundreds of thousands of minority Tutsis were slain earlier this year by rival Hutus, who controlled the government. [10]

Do arms exports help protect American jobs?

Pentagon procurement cutbacks have wreaked havoc in the defense industry. Since 1990, more than 600,000 employees of primary and secondary contractors have lost their jobs, reports the National Commission for Economic Conversion and Disarmament, a nonprofit group that supports military conversion.

Last year alone, some 164,000 workers were laid off. The most heavily affected contractors, accounting for 66 percent of last year's layoffs, were producers of aircraft and missile and space equipment. California, home to a disproportionate number of these contractors, suffered by far the largest number of layoffs, nearly 20,000 in 1993 alone. [11]

In response, defense contractors have stepped up export efforts. To do otherwise, they say, would condemn thousands more American workers to unemployment. Exports alone are keeping the production lines running for some U.S. weapon systems, including General Dynamics' M-1A2 tank factory in Lima, Ohio, and the McDonnell Douglas F-15 plant in St. Louis. Production of such complex weapons also generates jobs for scores of secondary contractors.

With procurement down, the U.S. defense budget is heavily weighted in favor of funding research and development for the next generation of weapons. "Development money is good for the [prime contractors] because it keeps their engineering teams going," Johnson says. "It doesn't help blue-collar workers or subcontractors, who make their living from things coming off the production lines. In that sense, exports are disproportionately important for the next three or four years." At that point, full production will start on weapons now being developed for the Defense Department.

While acknowledging the short-term economic benefits of arms exports, critics of this policy say that in the long run they do little or nothing to foster employment in the United States. Arms exports "postpone the day of reckoning for our economy adjusting to a lower level of defense spending," says Korb of the Brookings Institution. (*See "At Issue," p. 1097.*)

"I don't see arms sales as a savior by any stretch of the imagination of the defense industrial base," adds Bitzinger of the Defense Budget Project, "but do we let these industries wither up and die?" He cites the case of Lockheed's F-16 fighter, which is no longer on order by the Pentagon but is being made for export. Production of the next-generation fighter, the F-22, is years away. "We need to bridge the valley before picking up again with production of the F-22 at the turn of the century," he says. ■

BACKGROUND

The Nixon Doctrine

The United States' emergence as the world's leading arms merchant grew out of the high cost and poor results of America's participation in the Vietnam War. In the future, policy-makers decided, instead of intervening directly in foreign wars, the United States should help friendly nations by providing weapons and training — and then leaving them to do the fighting.

With a few little-noticed and apparently impromptu background comments to reporters during a 1969 stopover in Guam, President Richard M. Nixon enunciated what was to become the basis of future policy on arms sales. Except for situations involving the use or threatened use of nuclear weapons, he said Jan. 25, the United States would limit its role to providing economic and military aid to allied nations. "The objective of any American administration," the president said, "would be to avoid another war like Vietnam any place in the world." [12]

Later dubbed the "Nixon Doctrine," the new policy offered a means of containing Soviet influence in the Third World without risking American lives. It ushered in a huge increase in arms exports, from less than $2 billion a year at the time of Nixon's pronouncement to more than $16 billion a year by 1975.

Opponents of the new policy predicted that selling weapons abroad would only aggravate regional tensions and spark new conflicts. Nixon rejected the criticism, claiming that only Soviet allies used imported weapons for aggressive purposes while American allies only used U.S. arms for defense.

But the record proved Nixon wrong. In 1975, the same year it received $52 million in weaponry from the United States, Indonesia invaded neighboring East Timor. Protesters made clear during President Clinton's recent trip to Indonesia that the occupation continues even today.

As U.S. arms exports mushroomed, the United States ended up arming both sides in regional conflicts, such as India and Pakistan in their 1971 conflict, Israel and its Arab opponents and Greece and Turkey, which clashed over Turkey's occupation of northern Cyprus.

Closer to home, U.S. arms helped repressive regimes in Latin America cling to power. Chilean dictator Augusto Pinochet, whose military forces overthrew and assassinated leftist President Salvador Allende in 1973 with covert U.S. help, bought more than $80 million in American weapons the following year, helping him maintain his hold over the country for the next 18 years.

"The Nixon Doctrine gave the arms trade a bad name," Hartung writes, "and for good reason: It spawned an unprecedented spree of U.S.-supplied violence and repression by despots on three continents. But neither Nixon nor [national security adviser Henry A.] Kissinger showed any signs of caring about these harsh consequences of their arms sales policy, preoccupying themselves instead with its pivotal role in their new grand design for containing Soviet influence and keeping revolutionary and nationalist movements at bay." [13]

Nowhere did the Nixon Doctrine fare worse than in Iran. During the 1970s, Iran was the United States' leading customer for weapons and technical defense assistance. A staunch anti-communist, the shah served as the United States' main surrogate in the Middle East, a focus of intense Soviet interest. In a departure from the traditional practice of limiting overseas sales to obsolete military hardware, the Nixon administration provided the shah with some of the most sophisticated arms available, including the F-14, even before they were deployed to U.S. forces.

U.S. defense contractors responded by lobbying heavily for approval of more export proposals. "These economic factors," Hartung writes, "along with the obvious flaws in Nixon and Kissinger's original notion that the United States could reliably use arms sales to influence and control events halfway around the world, drove U.S. arms sales policy out of control." [14]

Curbing Arms Sales

Feeling its constitutional power over government appropriations threatened by the Nixon Doctrine and the subsequent explosion of arms exports, Congress belatedly moved to protect its "power of the purse." A 1974 amendment to the Foreign Assistance Act, sponsored by Sen. Gaylord Nelson, D-Wis., required Congress to be given 20-days' advance notice of major U.S. arms sales and empowered lawmakers to reject individual transactions. Also that year, Congress embargoed weapons sales to Turkey in retaliation for its occupation of northern Cyprus.

In 1975 Congress asserted greater control over covert arms transfers as well, passing an amendment introduced by Sen. Dick Clark, D-Iowa, that cut off covert shipments to the Angolan civil war. The Cold War proxy conflict pitted the Soviet-supported socialist government against U.S.-supported anti-communist rebels, including Jonas Savimbi's

Continued on p. 1092

Chronology

1960s *The Nixon Doctrine encourages U.S. arms exports.*

Jan. 25, 1969
President Richard M. Nixon, eager "to avoid another war like Vietnam any place in the world," announces a new policy emphasizing the use of economic and military aid to help friendly nations fight their own wars.

1970s *U.S. and Soviet arms flow to the Third World.*

1974
Congress requires the executive branch to notify lawmakers of major arms sales 20 days before they are finalized, thus giving Congress the option of rejecting proposed sales. Lawmakers block arms sales to Turkey after it occupies northern Cyprus.

1975
Indonesia invades neighboring East Timor, the same year Indonesia receives $52 million in weaponry from the United States. U.S. arms sales exceed $16 billion, up from $2 billion before the Nixon Doctrine took effect. Congress asserts greater control over transfers of covert arms, passing an amendment that cuts off shipments to Angola.

1976
Sen. Hubert H. Humphrey, D-Minn., tries to further curtail the executive branch's grip on arms sales with the 1976 Arms Export Control Act. Watered down to gain support from President Gerald R. Ford, the law extends the notification period required for arms sales to 30 days.

May 19, 1977
President Jimmy Carter issues Presidential Directive 13 seeking to reverse the Nixon Doctrine by requiring that arms transfers further U.S. security interests.

1978
Carter launches the Conventional Arms Transfer talks on limiting weapons transfers, but the initiative founders after several months due to policy disagreements within the Carter administration. Meanwhile, Carter completes the controversial sale of advanced weapons to Iran, the chief U.S. ally in the Persian Gulf. In December, the shah of Iran is overthrown, and anti-American revolutionaries take control of his U.S.-supplied arsenal.

1980s *Arms transfers peak at the Cold War's height.*

July 1981
Calling arms sales "an essential element of our global policy," President Ronald Reagan reverses Carter's stated policy of restraint, ushering in a period a rapid growth in arms sales. The next year, sales set a new record of more than $20 billion.

1982
An amendment sponsored by Rep. Edward P. Boland, D-Mass., prohibits aid to anti-communist "contra" rebels in Nicaragua. The stage is set for the Iran-contra scandal when members of the Reagan administration try to get around the law by raising money from buyers of American weapons and skimming the profits off covert sales of weapons to Iran to finance the contra rebellion.

1990s *World arms sales decline after the Cold War ends.*

1991
Weapons sales increase in the Persian Gulf region following Iraq's invasion of Kuwait and U.S. entry into the conflict. At the same time, President Bush announces his Middle East Arms Control Initiative and launches talks among the five permanent members of the United Nations Security Council to halt proliferation worldwide. Eighty-three countries agree to use the U.N. Register of Conventional Arms, a record of global arms transactions.

1992
Candidate Bill Clinton promises to reverse Bush's policy of promoting arms exports. A promised review of arms sale policy is delayed, however, as concern over massive defense industry layoffs prompts the administration to continue endorsing exports.

1993
The Code of Conduct on Arms Transfers Act is introduced. It would bar arms exports to countries that are anti-democratic, violate human rights or attack other countries. Hurt by defense procurement cuts, U.S. arms producers lay off 164,000 workers and turn increasingly to the export market to sell their products. Congress extends for three years a 1992 moratorium on the export of anti-personnel land mines.

The Human Toll From Small Arms

During the Cold War, concern about conventional arms focused on major weapons systems — the supersonic jet fighters, submarines, tanks and other major weapons capable of delivering bombs and artillery shells against the enemy.

But in many of today's conflicts, when poorly equipped troops often face one another, it is small arms that wreak the greatest havoc.

During the bloody civil war earlier this year in Rwanda, for example, rifles and grenades, as well as machetes, were used to slaughter hundreds of thousands of civilians. AK-47 machine guns from Romania, mortars and artillery guns from France, howitzers and land mines from Egypt and high-quality machine guns and rifles from South Africa fueled the genocide. According to Stephen D. Goose and Frank Smyth of the Human Rights Watch Arms Project, more than a dozen countries supplied small arms to both sides in the conflict.

"Small arms and light weapons have flooded nations like Rwanda, Sudan, Somalia and Bosnia-Herzegovina, not only fanning warfare but also undermining international efforts to embargo arms and to compel parties to respect human rights," they write. "Yet the international community has no viable mechanism to monitor the transfer of light and small weapons, and neither the United Nations nor the Clinton administration has demonstrated the leadership required to control that trade." [1]

While the market in major weapons has contracted since the end of the Cold War, analysts say the trade in small weapons is growing fast. They don't know how fast because efforts to monitor or control the flow of conventional weapons are limited to major weapons systems. No major arms producer, including the United States, controls small arms sales, nor are there international agreements that take this class of weaponry into account.

The most pernicious and indiscriminate of small arms is the anti-personnel land mine. Designed to maim as much as kill, land mines retain their lethal capability long after the fighting ends. After troops leave the battlefield, mines take their greatest toll among civilians — farmers who step on them while tilling their fields or children who mistake them for toys and pick them up.

The most common type is the blast mine, which is buried underground and activated when stepped on. "Detonation drives fragments of the mine, along with dirt, gravel, footwear and surrounding vegetation, up the victim's legs and body," writes United Nations Secretary General Boutros Boutros-Ghali in an appeal to curb land mine sales. "When not instantly deadly, blast mines almost always obliterate limbs or result in surgical amputation. Secondary injuries to the face and other parts of the body invariably occur." [2]

In Cambodia alone, scores of civilians are killed or maimed every day by mines left during the 12-year civil war that ended this year. Mozambique, Afghanistan, Somalia and Kuwait are among the countries where recent conflicts have left vast tracts of land studded with tens of thousands of undetonated mines. Retrieving these weapons is a laborious and highly risky task. The United Nations, which funds many land mine clearance programs around the world, estimates that it costs as much as $1,000 to retrieve each mine, which typically costs less than $25 to make. In Kuwait, where up to 7 million mines were laid during the 1991 gulf war, 84 mine-clearance workers have been killed or injured on the job, according to Boutros-Ghali.

Some arms producers have taken steps toward stemming the flow of these horrific weapons. In 1992, Congress approved a bill sponsored by Sen. Patrick J. Leahy, D-Vt., and Rep. Lane Evans, D-Ill., imposing a one-year moratorium on the export of anti-personnel land mines. Lawmakers in 1993 extended the ban for another three years. In 1992, the European Parliament demanded that all member states declare a five-year moratorium on mine exports.

But without multilateral support, such actions are doomed to failure. Between 500,000 and a million new land mines are deployed worldwide each year in conflicts throughout the world. In the face of such usage, Boutros-Ghali is calling for a new agreement to control the production and export of land mines. Meanwhile, he has asked U.N. members to create a trust fund to speed the removal of land mines.

[1] Stephen D. Goose and Frank Smyth, "Arming Genocide in Rwanda," *Foreign Affairs,* September/October 1994, p. 87.

[2] Boutros Boutros-Ghali, "The Land Mine Crisis," *Foreign Affairs,* September/October 1994, p. 9.

Continued from p. 1090

National Union for the Total Independence of Angola (UNITA).

The 1976 Arms Export Control Act sought to further curtail the executive branch's grip on arms sale policy. Introduced by Sen. Hubert H. Humphrey, D-Minn., the bill initially included a dollar limit on annual exports, but this and other tough provisions were eliminated in order to gain support from a skeptical President Gerald R. Ford.

In the end, the new law extended the notification period required for arms sales to 30 days and reaffirmed Congress' veto power over sales embodied in the Nelson amendment. To this day, however, Congress has never exercised its power to interrupt arms sales after notification.

Jimmy Carter's Initiative

President Jimmy Carter presented the first challenge to the Nixon Doctrine from the White House. "We cannot be both the world's leading champion of peace and the world's leading supplier of the weapons of war," he said during the 1976 presidential election campaign, promising to "increase the emphasis on peace and reduce the commerce in arms." [15]

Carter lost little time in making good on his promise. Within weeks of taking office in January 1977, his administration began drafting new guidelines for U.S. arms exports and contacted allies to begin negotiations on a multilateral arms control initiative.

On May 19, Carter outlined his new arms policy in Presidential Directive 13. Sharply reversing the Nixon Doctrine, Carter declared, "The virtually unrestrained spread of conventional weaponry threatens stability in every region of the world. . . . Because of the threat to world peace embodied in this spiralling arms traffic and because of the special responsibilities we bear as the largest arms seller, I believe that the United States must take steps to restrain its arms transfers." [16] P.D. 13 permitted future arms transfers only when they were shown to contribute to U.S. national security.

Carter's executive order also included several new controls over arms transfers, including:

- a dollar ceiling on the value of exports;
- a pledge not to provide more sophisticated arms to a region than those already present;
- a ban on production of advanced weapons solely for export;
- a ban on transfers of certain arms to Third World countries, and
- an end to the marketing of American weapons by U.S. embassy and military personnel overseas.

Multilateral negotiations, meanwhile, proceeded with the unexpected cooperation of the Soviet Union. Riding on the momentum created by other arms control initiatives, chiefly the 1972 Strategic Arms Limitation Treaty (SALT I), the Conventional Arms Transfer (CAT) talks started in early 1978. The talks focused on attempts to curb arms flows to certain regions.

Adamantly opposed to this approach, Carter's national security adviser, Zbigniew Brzezinski, insisted that U.S. negotiators quit the talks if their Soviet counterparts proposed limiting arms transfers to the Persian Gulf or East Asia. When the president failed to forcefully counter his adviser, other parties to the negotiations lost interest, and the talks foundered.

Carter's efforts to reverse the Nixon Doctrine also failed because of his own ambivalence toward arms sales. When asked to provide arms to protect U.S. security interests in the Middle East, including the shah's regime in Iran, Carter obliged. His decision in summer 1978 to sell Iran seven Airborne Warning and Control System (AWACS) planes and F-15s to Saudi Arabia, another key Persian Gulf ally, was seen as proof that P.D. 13 was open to negotiation.

In December 1978, only months after the AWACS deal was approved, the Nixon Doctrine's critics saw their worst nightmare come true. The shah was ousted by revolutionary forces led by the Ayatollah Khomeini, and billions of dollars in advanced U.S. military equipment fell into the hands of an anti-American government. Carter, who sank his own arms transfer policy through lack of commitment, lost his chance at re-election after Khomeini's forces took some 100 Americans hostage.

Arming the World

President Ronald Reagan's supply-side economic vision, combined with his call to "rearm America" against the perceived Soviet threat, was welcomed by the defense industry. Together with an unprecedented peacetime arms buildup at home, Reagan opened the door to arms sales, both overt and covert, in a strong reaffirmation of the Nixon Doctrine. Claiming the Soviet Union was arming revolution in El Salvador through Cuba and Nicaragua, the administration funneled arms and military assistance to shore up the Salvadoran military junta against a rebellion that began in 1979.

Reagan officially overturned Carter's stated policy of restraint with a July 1981 directive calling arms transfers "an essential element of our global policy" and repealing the controls on transfers delineated four years earlier

U.S. Army photo

TOW missiles were among the U.S. arms purchased by Saudi Arabia in 1991.

Top Arms Manufacturers, 1992

Nine of the world's 12 biggest arms manufacturers in 1992 were U.S. firms. Arms sales represented more than 50 percent of the business at five of the U.S. firms.

Manufacturer		Products	Arms Sales ($ billions)	% of Business	Total Employment
McDonnell Douglas	US	Aircraft, electronics, military vehicles	$9.3	53%	87,377
British Aerospace	UK	Aircraft, artillery, electronics, military vehicles, small arms/ ordnance	7.1	40	102,500
Lockheed	US	Aircraft	6.7	66	71,700
General Motors	US	Aircraft engines, electronics, military vehicles	5.4	4	750,000
Hughes Electronics (GM)	US	Aircraft, electronics	5.4	44	90,000
General Electric	US	Aircraft engines	5.3	9	268,000
Thomson S.A.	France	Electronics, military vehicles	5.0	37	100,768
Thomson -CSF (Thomson S.A.)	France	Electronics, military vehicles	5.0	77	42,350
Northrop	US	Aircraft	5.0	89	33,600
Raytheon	US	Electronics, military vehicles	4.8	53	63,900
Boeing	US	Aircraft, electronics, military vehicles	4.7	16	143,000
Martin Marietta	US	Military vehicles	4.4	74	56,000

Source: Stockholm International Peace Research Institute

in P.D. 13.[17] Rather than impede arms sales, the Reagan administration streamlined the process to facilitate them, ushering in a period of rapid growth in arms sales

The flood of arms sales was launched by the record-breaking $8.5 billion sale of five AWACS and other military equipment to Saudi Arabia in 1981 that gained congressional approval even over the opposition of the potent Israeli lobby. In 1982, more than $20 billion of U.S. weapons were sold overseas, exceeding the previous record set during the heyday of the Nixon Doctrine. U.S. defense contractors reaped immense benefit from the sales boost: For three years during the early 1980s, McDonnell Douglas made more than $1 billion in export revenue, while General Dynamics and General Electric tripled their foreign sales from 1981 to 1985.

Flouting past policy, the administration allowed some of the most sophisticated weapons to go to developing nations, including General Dynamics' F-16s, sold to South Korea, Pakistan and Venezuela. The sale to Pakistan also broke precedent by violating a provision of the Foreign Assistance Act prohibiting military aid to developing nations suspected of having nuclear weapons programs.

Human rights, a hallmark of the Carter administration's foreign policy, also fell by the wayside as a consideration in making arms deals. The first Reagan administration tripled weapons sales to Central and Latin America, including such repressive regimes as El Salvador, Guatemala and Argentina. Another fear of arms control advocates, that buyers of American weapons would be free to use them for their own aggressive purposes, also became evident during the Reagan years. Israel, a key recipient of American weaponry, used its military superiority to invade Lebanon in 1982, and Morocco's King Hassan employed U.S. M-60 tanks and aircraft to annex Western Sahara.

Reagan's escalation of the Cold War against the "evil empire" included active support of anti-communist forces, or "freedom fighters," opposing Soviet-backed governments throughout the developing world. The so-called "Reagan Doctrine," which involved arming insurgents in Angola, Afghanistan, Cambodia and Nicaragua, embroiled the administration in a far-reaching scandal over its violation of the law involving arms transfers.

After a 1982 amendment sponsored by Rep. Edward P. Boland, D-Mass., prohibited aid to contra forces in Nicaragua fighting the leftist Sandinista government, the administration raised money from Saudi Arabia and other recipients of U.S. arms. The second element of the Iran-contra scandal involved the deal arranged by Marine Lt. Col. Oliver L. North: arms with Iran in exchange for help in freeing American hostages held in Lebanon by pro-Iranian groups. Under the deal, Iran received more than 2,000 TOW anti-tank missiles, 80 Hawk antiaircraft missiles and spare parts for its F-14s. North skimmed the profits from the arms sales to help finance the contra insurgency. Three American hostages were released as a result of the illegal deal, but three more were seized.

Bush Follows Reagan Lead

Undeterred by the Iran-contra scandal, President Bush continued his predecessors' policy favoring overt and covert arms transfers. "When the economy was starting to go down, and Bush was cutting the defense budget, arms sales were one way to compensate," says Korb. "As a result, we begin to see the rapid growth in American arms sales in 1990-91 and continuing into 1992 and 1993."

One avenue for enhanced arms sales was the Bush administration's escalated War on Drugs, which focused heavily on interdiction of the cocaine trade at the source. Military assistance to Colombia, Bolivia, Peru and Ecuador — including attack helicopters, anti-tank weapons, grenade launchers and other arms — increased dramatically. In 1989 alone, Colombia was promised $65 million in military aid, more than it received in the preceding decade. Unfortunately, the military aid did little to curb drugs flowing into the United States. However, human rights groups documented a worsening of abuses by newly equipped military forces in the four nations.

Arms sales also were a crucial enticement in forging the alliance that repelled Iraq's August 1990 invasion of Kuwait. In exchange for their active participation in the 1991 gulf war, Saudi Arabia, Israel, Egypt, Turkey and other partners in Operation Desert Storm against Iraq received advanced U.S. weapons as well as promises of more to come.

"The trading of advanced U.S. weaponry for military cooperation in the gulf war," Hartung writes, "dramatically underscored the extent to which the initial Nixon/Kissinger concept of using arms sales in lieu of direct U.S. military intervention had come full circle to a policy of using arms sales to facilitate U.S. intervention." [18]

After the gulf war, Bush declared that one of his main goals was to curb the proliferation of weaponry to the highly unstable region. Bush's Middle East Arms Control Initiative, announced May 29, 1991, aimed at "halting the proliferation of conventional and unconventional weapons in the Middle East while supporting the legitimate need of every state in the region to defend itself." [19] At the same time, Bush launched an even more ambitious conventional arms control initiative, involving all five permanent members of the United Nations Security Council — the United States, the Soviet Union, France, the United Kingdom and China. The so-called P-5 talks, which opened in Paris July 8, focused on implementing "rules of restraint" governing conventional arms transfers.

But while it was calling for restraint at the negotiating table, the Bush administration continued allowing the sale of large quantities of arms. It announced agreements for $7 billion in sales to

Lockheed, the nation's third-largest arms maker, had $6.7 billion in aircraft sales in 1992. Due to defense cutbacks, Lockheed, McDonnell Douglas and Martin Marietta each have cut 50,000 jobs in the 1990s. Lockheed and Martin Marietta announced merger plans in August.

more than 10 countries in July alone. During the two years ending in August 1992, agreements were made to sell more than $23 billion in American weapons just to the Middle East.

The inconsistency in post-Cold War arms trade policy was due in large part to cutbacks in Pentagon orders for new weapons. The problem was not merely one of industry survival. Without export markets to absorb weapons, the industry said, entire weapons lines would have to be shut down, jeopardizing U.S. military readiness as well as throwing hundreds of thousands of workers into an already saturated labor market.

To oversee the new arms sale push, the administration created a new Office of Defense Trade Policy, one of whose functions was to speed the licensing process involving transfers of military equipment. Pentagon officials also assumed a more prominent role in promoting U.S. arms sales. By 1992, the last year of the Bush administration, arms sales approached $20 billion. ■

CURRENT SITUATION

Adjusting to Cuts

Cuts in defense spending, especially for procurement, have forced defense contractors to undergo wrenching changes. Spending for new weapons has fallen twice as fast as other parts of the defense budget. For fiscal 1995 it stands at $42 billion, down from $82 billion in fiscal 1991. Mirroring steps taken by the automobile and other manufacturing industries during the 1980s, weapons manufacturers have been forced to downsize their operations, sell or eliminate product lines and merge with competitors.

Since the beginning of the post-Cold War era in 1990, more than 600,000 defense-related jobs have disappeared, according to the National Commission for Economic Conversion and Disarmament. [20] Manufacturers of aircraft and missiles and space equipment were the hardest hit. McDonnell Douglas, Lockheed and Martin Marietta have each eliminated more than 50,000 jobs in the '90s.

Some of the leading defense contractors have tried to survive by selling off marginal product lines or merging with rivals. Lockheed, the third-largest arms maker, bought General Dynamics' F-16 fighter plant in Fort Worth, Texas. Martin Marietta, the second-largest defense contractor, took over General Electric Co.'s aerospace division and General Dynamics' space division. In August, the two behemoths announced they would merge. If the deal goes through, Lockheed Martin, with combined annual sales of $23 billion, would replace McDonnell Douglas as the country's — and the world's — leading weapons producer. The new defense giant reportedly is eyeing Northrup-Grumman, the product of a merger earlier this year, as another potential purchase. [21]

A few arms producers have stayed in business by converting part of their operations to civilian activities. Aerojet, for example, a California manufacturer of rocket motor cases, spacecraft pressure vessels and fuel tanks, now is developing storage tanks for natural-gas-fueled vehicles in collaboration with Pacific Gas & Electric. [22]

But for the most part, military conversion has not lived up to its initial promise as a key to survival for the defense industry. One of the main obstacles to conversion is the corporate culture that has been formed by years of dealing with the government, a reliable customer providing guaranteed orders over extended periods of time. "This kind of business doesn't make you Twinkletoes on your feet," says Johnson, who compares the current business environment to the beginning of the Ice Age. "We're a mastodon that has been carefully created by the government. When the temperature changes on us, we're going to freeze."

To survive at all, Johnson says, arms sales are not only essential but also good business strategy. "Even if we can make money with conversion, we're still going to export fighter aircraft," he says. "Businessmen don't wake up one morning and say, 'I think I'll get rid of that profitable line because I'm going to convert to another profitable line.' They can do both."

Calls for Restraint

It is just this kind of reasoning that prompts calls for curbs on arms exports. In the summer of 1993, more than 100 members of Congress sent a letter to the president asking him to press for an international agreement on curbs. That fall, Congress passed a three-year extension of a moratorium on U.S. exports of anti-personnel land mines, which kill and maim children and other civilians long after the soldiers have gone home.

Arms control advocates reject the industry's claim that the odds are pitted against them in selling weapons abroad. They say that blocking arms sale proposals under current law is difficult. Once a foreign government places an order, it is up to the president to authorize the transfer. Although Congress can stop the proposal, it needs a two-thirds majority to override the president's authorization.

The code of conduct proposed by Sen. Hatfield and Rep. McKinney in November 1993 would have strengthened the role of Congress in approving arms transfers. Under the proposed 1993

Continued on p. 1098

At Issue:

Do arms exports help the U.S. economy?

yes

Joel L. Johnson
Vice President, International Affairs, Aerospace Industries Association of America

FROM *TESTIMONY BEFORE THE HOUSE COMMITTEE ON FOREIGN AFFAIRS*, NOVEMBER 1993

Currently, roughly 20 percent of this country's production of conventional weapons is exported. . . . Over the remainder of the decade, exports of defense equipment will likely continue to climb as a percentage of production to 25 percent or more of conventional weapons production. This is both because domestic purchases will drop to somewhere around $50 billion-$60 billion, and because international purchases will hold constant at around $15 billion-$17 billion. In turn, the greater importance of exports to total production of defense products is likely to increase the attention paid to export markets by both industry and government.

There are several reasons for that outlook. Defense budgets in some regions of the world are increasing, not decreasing. . . . The U.S. military services, the Department of Defense (DOD), and civilian government agencies are beginning to recognize that exports can be important to hold down unit costs of DOD purchases, and even keep production lines open. . . .

Industry assumes our government will continue to pursue an active policy of encouraging sensible arms limitation agreements among supplier and user groups. But we also believe government should continue to allow U.S. defense equipment to be made available to friendly countries who have legitimate defense requirements. Furthermore, in such instances industry would argue that it is appropriate for our government to work with industry to see that such friendly countries purchase U.S. products rather than those of our competitors.

The U.S. government and our taxpayers benefit when countries buy our defense products. Exports of U.S. defense equipment to friendly countries can increase their ability to defend themselves and make joint activities easier through standardization of equipment. Such sales increase our influence on the purchasing country's actions, both because of the ties that are established between our defense establishment and theirs, and because their equipment will not be operable without continued U.S. support.

Economically, as already noted, foreign sales lower unit costs of equipment purchased by our own military. In some cases exports will be all that keep certain lines open — lines which provide the U.S. with a continued industrial base and trained manpower for use in an emergency, or as resources which can help launch new defense systems several years from now. And note that these industrial-base advantages are paid for by foreign taxpayers, rather than our own. Finally, it should be noted that, economically, defense exports have the same impact as all other exports — they create jobs and help our trade balance.

no

Dr. Caleb S. Rossiter
Director of the Project on Demilitarization and Democracy

FROM *TESTIMONY BEFORE THE HOUSE COMMITTEE ON FOREIGN AFFAIRS*, NOVEMBER 1993

I submit to this committee that in net terms, arms sales to developing countries actually cost the American economy jobs. How can that be?

The first reason is found in the dirty word of the arms exporting business: offsets. "Offsets" are agreements that American companies make with foreign arms purchasers that do indeed offset the payments the foreign economy makes for the arms purchase. Under offset agreements, the seller commits to using its connections to find markets for foreign goods and services in the United States. . . .

The second reason why arms exports cost jobs is that they drive up foreign aid spending. We spend about $5 billion a year in foreign aid to give away weapons, and that is money straight out of the taxpayer's pocket, so about a third of arms exports to developing countries create no jobs at all, since they are simply taking money from one taxpayer's pocket and putting it in another's, and giving away overseas what it bought. . . .

The third reason why arms exports cost jobs is found in the single biggest discretionary program in the U.S. budget, the Pentagon. Our force levels and defense spending are driven up and kept up by increased threats from foreign forces, and exporting sophisticated and even rudimentary weapons inevitably makes the world a more dangerous and therefore costly place. Let's take one specific example: $195 million worth of arms transfers to the Somali dictatorship in the 1980s. Yes, those sales maintained about 1,300 jobs, but they cost probably 10 times that many when the taxpayer had to come up with the $2 billion that the Pentagon has spent trying to clean up the disaster in Somalia that arose from arming that regime. . . .

The final, and probably most important reason, why arms exports cost American jobs is found in their impact on the international economy. Simply put, our economy is dependent on growth in developing countries, and that growth is being battered by wasteful military spending, by low levels of investment due to repression and political instability, and by the high cost of conflicts when they do break out. Again, let me be specific: Developing countries spend $200 billion a year on their armed forces, four times all foreign aid spending from all sources combined, and 20 times the level of U.S. foreign economic aid; according to econometric analyses by the Overseas Development Council, the recession in developing countries in the 1980s cost us 1.8 million U.S. export jobs [because] those countries couldn't afford to keep buying our exports at the same rate.

For More Information

Aerospace Industries Association of America, 1250 Eye St. N.W., Washington, D.C. 20005; (202) 371-8400. This membership group for U.S. aircraft manufacturers is also the leading representative of the U.S. defense industry. It favors policies that help American weapons producers export their products.

Defense Budget Project, 777 N. Capitol St. N.E., Suite 710, Washington, D.C. 20002; (202) 408-1517. This independent, nonprofit research organization studies national security policies and defense spending issues, including the role of arms exports in the defense industry's economic health.

Defense Security Assistance Agency, Defense Department, The Pentagon, Washington, D.C. 20301; (703) 695-5931. The agency develops arms transfer policy and administers the U.S. Foreign Military Sales program.

U.S. Arms Control and Disarmament Agency, 320 21st St. N.W., Washington, D.C. 20451; (202) 647-4800. The agency advises the president on arms control issues and provides information on current policy and agreements in force.

Continued from p. 1096

Code of Conduct on Arms Transfers Act, countries that are undemocratic, do not adequately protect human rights, are engaged in armed aggression or do not fully participate in the United Nations Register of Conventional Arms would not have been eligible for U.S. weapons without specific congressional approval. The legislation died in committee.

The U.N. Register is the main multilateral initiative in recent years to control the international arms trade. Created in 1991 by the General Assembly, the register attempts to make public all transfers of advanced weaponry. Because participation in the U.N. program is voluntary and makes no attempt to curb transfers, however, the register's impact on arms flows has been limited. Eighty-three countries have agreed to report their arms transactions in the register.

Arms control advocates say stronger international measures are needed. One frequently cited proposal is military conditionality. When deciding whether to make loans or grants, donor countries and multilateral organizations such as the International Monetary Fund and the World Bank would give preference to countries that abstain from buying or selling conventional weapons. But in the absence of a mandatory regime tracking arms transfers, donors have little evidence to go on when assessing a country's record. [23]

Clinton's Promise

During the 1992 presidential election campaign, candidate Bill Clinton pledged to seek limits on the sale of conventional weapons. The main focus of his campaign, however, was creating jobs and invigorating the domestic economy. At a time of declining fortunes in the defense industry, the conflict between creating jobs and limiting weapons production quickly became apparent. Challenged on the issue, Clinton endorsed a controversial plan by the Bush administration to sell 72 F-15 fighter planes to Saudi Arabia, in the name of protecting regional security — and thousands of jobs at McDonnell Douglas.

Despite these contradictions in policy goals, Clinton began his term with a pledge to review arms sale policy and announce the results as early as summer 1993. The Pentagon, meanwhile, refrained from actively promoting U.S. military hardware at the annual 1993 Paris air show, where arms makers from around the world show their goods and make deals.

Within a few months, however, the review on conventional arms sales was postponed. Lynn Davis, under secretary of State for international security affairs, said arms deals would be considered on a case-by-case basis, signalling no change in policy, pending the review, from previous administrations. Commerce Secretary Ronald H. Brown promptly included weapons among the U.S.-made products to be promoted in the administration's vigorous campaign to enhance U.S. exports.

Defense industry representatives say this help is only reasonable, given current restrictions on the sale of weapons to hostile countries. The first stage of a weapons sale involves gaining government approval, with congressional consent, that the sale is consistent with the security interests of the United States. It is only then that U.S. contractors can compete with foreign competitors for the deal. And it is during this second stage that the defense industry is clamoring for greater government support.

"If you say the sale is consistent with U.S. foreign policy interests, for heaven's sake, why would you want it to be a French sale?" Johnson asks. "Let Americans get the jobs rather than Frenchmen."

The defense industry is asking the government to help U.S. companies sell weapons overseas by creating a new lending facility similar to the Export-Import Bank of the United States to arrange loan guarantees. "Every other competitor we have has access to the same official credit institution that every other exporter does," Johnson says. "We want a finance facility that is comparable to Ex-Im Bank to provide loan guarantees" to help foreign buyers finance their arms purchases. ■

OUTLOOK

Tilt Toward Industry?

The Clinton administration has yet to issue the results of its long-awaited review of arms sale policy, but it appears increasingly likely that it will favor the defense industry over the arms control community. A draft policy statement reportedly under discussion within the administration would for the first time explicitly spell out domestic economic considerations to be weighed in the approval process for arms sales. [24]

"I think that what will come out of the Clinton review will be a relatively sensible, case-by-case approach, which they probably could have written in the first six weeks of the administration and saved themselves a lot of agony," Johnson says. "What I'm expecting is a steady-as-she-goes policy on the decision-making process with a slight nod toward the industrial base and a stronger recognition that once you've agreed that a sale makes sense, then by god the government is going to help make it an American sale."

Arms control advocates concur that the policy is likely to favor industry. "The administration seems to be whittling away at the arms control component of current policy and enlarging their view of it as a way to promote trade and support the defense industrial base," says Hartung. He is less sanguine than Johnson, however, about the prospects for the extension of loan guarantees and other marketing aids to arms exports. "Whether the administration heartily endorses the industry's request for loan guarantees may still be up in the air," he says. "President Clinton may have a hard time with that on the Hill, where guarantees may be perceived as caving in to special interests."

Some observers fear the emerging policy change poses grave security risks. "It may have some short-term benefits," says Korb, "but in the long term it will be disastrous for big issues, such as keeping sophisticated technology out of the hands of rogue nations. We will have no moral standing if we tell the Chinese or Russians not to export weapons when we control three-quarters of the world's arms market. It makes it very difficult for us to tell people that we're really sincere about a new arms control regime in the world." ■

Notes

[1] U.S. Arms Control and Disarmament Agency, *World Military Expenditures and Arms Transfers 1991-1992,* March 30, 1994. For background, see "U.S. Policy in Asia," *The CQ Researcher,* Nov. 27, 1992, pp. 1025-1048.

[2] Congressional Research Service, *Conventional Arms Transfers to the Third World, 1986-1993,* July 29, 1994, pp. 18-19.

[3] Stockholm International Peace Research Institute, *SIPRI Yearbook 1994* (1994), p. 484.

[4] United Nations Development Programme, *Human Development Report 1994,* March 16, 1994, p. 50. For background, see "Arms Control Negotiations," *Editorial Research Reports,* Feb. 22, 1985, pp. 145-168.

[5] Quoted in Stephen Barr, "GAO: Army's Missile Count Off Target," *The Washington Post,* Oct. 26, 1994.

[6] Michael T. Klare, "Deadly Convergence: The Perils of the Arms Trade," *World Policy Journal,* winter 1988-89, p. 143. Klare is director of the Five College Program in Peace and World Security Studies based at Hampshire College in Amherst, Mass. For background, see "Nuclear Proliferation," *The CQ Researcher,* June 5, 1992, pp. 481-504.

[7] United Nations Development Programme, *op. cit.,* March 16, 1994.

[8] Congressional Research Service, *op. cit.,* p. 5

[9] *Ibid.,* p. 54.

[10] See Stephen D. Goose and Frank Smyth, "Arming Genocide in Rwanda," *Foreign Affairs,* September/October 1994.

[11] Christine Evans-Klock and James Raffel, *National Defense Industry Layoffs, 1993: Analysis and Policy Recommendations,* National Commission for Economic Conversion and Disarmament, May 1993.

[12] Quoted in William D. Hartung, *And Weapons for All* (1994), p. 22. Unless otherwise noted, material in this section is based on Hartung's account. For background, see "Downsizing America's Armed Forces," *Editorial Research Reports,* June 8, 1990, pp. 317-332.

[13] *Ibid.,* p. 26.

[14] *Ibid.,* p. 29.

[15] *Ibid.,* pp. 63-64.

[16] *Ibid.,* p. 66.

[17] *Ibid.,* p. 93.

[18] *Ibid.,* p. 140.

[19] *Ibid.,* p. 147.

[20] Evans-Klock and Raffel, *op. cit.,* p. 2.

[21] See " 'This Is Going to Be the Biggest Kahuna Around,' " *Business Week,* Sept. 12, 1994, p. 32.

[22] *Ibid.,* p. 12.

[23] For a discussion of military conditionality, see Warwick J. McKibbin, "A New Military Equilibrium? Preventing Regional Conflicts in the Developing World," *The Brookings Review,* fall 1993.

[24] See R. Jeffrey Smith, "Administration Battles Over Arms Sales Policy," *The Washington Post,* Nov. 16, 1994.

Bibliography

Selected Sources Used

Books

Gansler, Jacques S., *Affording Defense,* MIT Press, 1989.

Written before the arms market changed following the Soviet Union's collapse, this account remains an illuminating analysis of the U.S. defense industry and its unique supply-and-demand structure.

Hartung, William D., *And Weapons for All,* HarperCollins, 1994.

Hartung, a fellow at the World Policy Institute in New York City, provides a critical review of arms sale policy, focusing on the United States. He favors a stricter regime to limit the transfer of advanced weapons.

Stockholm International Peace Research Institute, *SIPRI Yearbook 1994,* Oxford University Press, 1994.

SIPRI, an independent international institute studying arms control issues, provides one of the most authoritative analyses of international weapons flows. This year's chapter on conventional arms sales focuses on the near collapse of the Russian and Eastern European defense industries.

United National Development Programme, *Human Development Report 1994,* Oxford University Press, 1994.

Most conflicts in the 1990s are occurring in developing countries, which can ill afford the costs of buying weapons and waging war while their citizens lack basic social services, according to the U.N. agency.

Articles

Boutros Boutros-Ghali, "The Land Mine Crisis: A Humanitarian Disaster," *Foreign Affairs,* September/October 1994.

Anti-personnel land mines continue to kill and maim civilians long after hostilities cease in war-wracked countries from Cambodia to Kuwait. The United Nations secretary general calls for the creation of a new fund to retrieve these weapons and a moratorium on the export of new mines.

Stephen D. Goose and Frank Smyth, "Arming Genocide in Rwanda," *Foreign Affairs,* September/October 1994, pp. 86-96.

While arms transfer policy focuses on major weapons, small arms such as rifles and grenades wreak the greatest havoc in most conflicts, the authors write. With no viable controls on the transfer of small arms, more than a dozen countries supplied the genocide in Rwanda this year.

Michael T. Klare, "The Next Great Arms Race," *Foreign Affairs,* summer 1993, pp. 136-152.

Recent high-tech military sales to Taiwan, China and other countries of East and Southeast Asia suggest the beginnings of a regional arms race that could destabilize the entire region.

Eyal Press, "Prez Pampers Peddlers of Pain," *The Nation,* Oct. 3, 1994, pp. 340-344.

The Clinton administration has quietly shifted position from advocating restraint in arms sales to actively promoting them as a way to stem job losses in the U.S. defense industry and promote U.S. competitiveness through exports.

Nicholas ValÇry, "Military Aerospace," *The Economist,* Sept. 3, 1994.

This 18-page special survey examines the recent turmoil among major arms producers caused by defense cutbacks. Companies are turning to mergers and export promotion to survive in the post-Cold War era.

Reports and Studies

Nicole Ball, *Briefing Book on Conventional Arms Transfers,* Council for a Livable World Education Fund, August 1991.

An economic and military analysis of the arms trade, this brief report examines the supply and demand sides of the weapons market as well as financing arrangements and arms control initiatives aimed at curbing the weapons trade.

Richard F. Grimmett, *Conventional Arms Transfers to the Third World,* 1986-1993, Congressional Research Service, July 29, 1994.

Since the Cold War's end, the United States has emerged as the leading supplier of conventional weapons to developing countries, accounting for more than half the value of arms agreements since 1990.

U.S. Arms Control and Disarmament Agency, *World Military Expenditures and Arms Transfers 1991-1992,* March 1994.

In today's shrinking arms market, East Asia and the Persian Gulf region are principal sources of demand. Buyers are looking for sophisticated munitions and support equipment as well as major weapons, such as fighter aircraft and armored vehicles.

The Next Step

Additional information from UMI's Newspaper & Periodical Abstracts database

Areas of International Interest

"Arms sales: Boom," *The Economist,* Aug. 13, 1994, pp. 24-28.
At a time when worldwide arms transfers are falling fast, the U.S. has closed deals for the sale of $32 billion worth of arms abroad, an all-time high. Russia's share of arms deals dropped from 32 percent in 1989 to 9 percent in 1993.

"Main sellers of military equipment," *The Wall Street Journal,* Jan. 28, 1994, p. A6.
The US, China, Britain, France, Germany, Russia and other former Soviet states are among the leading sellers of military equipment on the world market. The main buyers are centered in the Middle East, South and Southeast Asia, the Far East, Europe, Africa and South America.

Meacher, Michael, "Bomb proof," *New Statesman & Society,* Oct. 14, 1994, pp. 18-19.
The Ferranti arms scandal reveals that the UK government colluded in illegal arms sales. Contracts with United Arab Emigrates, Pakistan and China are discussed.

Norton-Taylor, Richard, "Businessman denies lying to minister," *Guardian,* July 8, 1994, p. 4.
On July 7, 1994, British businessman Paul Henderson denied deceiving a government minister into believing machine-tool exports to Iraq would be used only for peaceful purposes. Henderson, who is at the center of the arms-to-Iraq affair, is the former managing director of Matrix Churchill.

Pallister, David, "Illicit arms sales to Indonesia," *Guardian,* Aug. 27, 1994, p. 8.
British defense contractors are being accused of selling arms to Indonesia against government guidelines that prohibit the sale of equipment that is likely to be used for internal repression. Several British companies that are filling Indonesian orders are briefly discussed.

"Peddling death to the poor," *The Economist,* June 4, 1994, p. 43.
A U.N. Development Program report notes that rich countries offer aid and promote peace in poor countries with one hand while shoveling in death with the other.

Smith, R. Jeffrey and Thomas W. Lippman, "Pakistan M-11 funding is reported," *The Washington Post,* Sept. 8, 1994, p. A32.
Pakistan has agreed to pay China an additional $15 million to help fund its purchase of M-11 ballistic missiles capable of targeting key Indian cities and eventually carrying nuclear weapons, according to a U.S. intelligence report.

Tyler, Patrick E., "Abuses of rights persist in China despite U.S. pleas," *The New York Times,* Aug. 29, 1994, p. A1.
In the three months since President Clinton renewed China's "most favored nation" trade status, human-rights conditions in China have continued to deteriorate, and relations with the U.S. remain mired in mistrust and contentiousness, Tyler writes. Before Commerce Secretary Ronald H. Brown arrived in Beijing the weekend of Aug. 27, 1994, the Chinese authorities ordered another clampdown on dissidents, placing many under effective house arrest. Although Brown's visit may pay dividends for American corporations, the political agenda remains soured by conflicts over trade, arms sales and human rights.

Bosnian Arms Embargo

"Bosnian embargo: Allowing arms sales now would throw gas on the fire," *Detroit News & Free Press,* June 12, 1994, p. F2.
An editorial comments that the bipartisan vote in the U.S. House urging an end to the Bosnian arms embargo was part rebuke to President Clinton, part a venting of frustration at a dirty war, and all wrong.

Morrison, David C., "How Bosnia is becoming a priority," *National Journal,* Aug. 20, 1994, pp. 1976-1977.
The Senate has approved an amendment to the fiscal 1995 defense appropriations bill directing President Clinton to lift the embargo on arms to Bosnia-Herzegovina by Nov. 15, 1994.

The Clinton Administration and Arms Policy

Feinstein, Lee, "Administration seeks to end ban on aid, arms transfers to Pakistan," *Arms Control Today,* January 1994, p. 29.
The Clinton administration has suggested the repeal of the 1985 "Pressler Amendment," which bars most U.S. foreign assistance and arms exports to Pakistan due to the status of Islamabad's nuclear weapons program.

Krauthammer, Charles, "Time for a little panic," *Time,* July 25, 1994, p. 74.
The question of why the Clinton administration is slashing defense spending in the face of possible nuclear weapons development in North Korea is addressed. It is argued that Clinton's arms controllers are the slaves of an obsolete treaty with the U.S.S.R.

Lancaster, John, "Administration helps arms makers promote goods at Singapore show," *The Washington Post,* Feb. 28, 1994, p. A6.
The Clinton administration spent an estimated $575,000 to help U.S. defense contractors promote their products at

Singapore's Asian Aerospace '94, a five-day international aircraft bazaar, a reversal of previous administration practice that has alarmed advocates of tighter controls on U.S. weapons exports.

"Look who's dominating the arms trade," ***The New York Times,*** **Aug. 20, 1994, p. A22.**
An editorial criticizes the Clinton administration for failing to formulate an arms sales policy and notes that the U.S.'s share of new arms deals in the Third World soared to 73 percent in 1993 from 56 percent in 1992.

Press, Eyal, "Arms sales and false economics: Prez pampers peddlers of pain," ***The Nation,*** **Oct. 3, 1994, pp. 340-344.**
The Clinton administration's policy on arms sales to foreign countries is discussed. Such exports reached $33.2 billion in President Clinton's first year, more than double what President Bush approved in 1992, and about three-quarters of those sales were to repressive or undemocratic governments.

"Still no policy on arms sales," ***The New York Times,*** **April 3, 1994, p. 10.**
An editorial criticizes the Clinton administration for failing to announce its policy on curbing arms sales.

Towell, Pat, "Senate retreats from mandate to arm Bosnian Muslims," ***Congressional Quarterly Weekly Report,*** **July 2, 1994, pp. 1812-1813.**
The Senate stopped one vote short of ordering President Clinton to ship arms to Bosnia-Herzegovina's Muslims on July 1, 1994. The vote came during debate on the $263.1 billion defense authorization bill.

Smith, R. Jeffrey, "Rights group assails U.S. arms sales policy," ***The Washington Post,*** **June 23, 1994, p. A22.**
Amnesty International USA criticized the Clinton administration for continuing to sell arms or provide military training to 19 nations that the group claims repeatedly have committed human rights abuses, including such U.S. allies as Saudi Arabia, Turkey, Egypt, Israel and Thailand.

Walker, Martin, "Clinton team at odds over plan to boost arms sales," ***Guardian,*** **Feb. 4, 1994, p. 11.**
A battle is brewing within the Clinton administration over federal subsidies for U.S. arms exports, which are designed to maintain American dominance of almost 60 percent of world arms sales, which resulted in contracts worth $31 billion in 1993. The conflict focuses on a new $1 billion export credit program.

"Washington wire: Arms sales," ***The Wall Street Journal,*** **July 15, 1994, p. A1.**
Arms sales have split the Clinton administration, according to *The Wall Street Journal.* The Pentagon and the Commerce Department have faced off against the State Department and the White House budget office in pressing to give the U.S. defense industry loan guarantees to finance exports.

Crisis in Rwanda

Morrison, David C., "Tilling the killing fields," ***National Journal,*** **May 14, 1994, p. 1161.**
Arms sales to countries such as Rwanda not only contribute to international instability but also are responsible for much of the civilian bloodshed. It is estimated that 200,000 people have been butchered in Rwanda since ethnic strife began in early April 1994.

"Rwanda's arms suppliers," ***The Washington Post,*** **June 15, 1994, p. A24.**
An editorial encourages the U.S. to demonstrate some restraint when it comes to arms sales to rogue states, noting that the imports of military weapons from France, Egypt and South Africa into Rwanda have helped push the estimated death toll toward a half-million and counting.

Schorr, Daniel, "Hard questions," ***New Leader,*** **July 4, 1994, pp. 3-4.**
The U.S. hesitated to term the massacres in Rwanda as genocide due to fear that the 1948 U.N. Genocide Convention might apply to the situation. The absurdity of this policy and the U.S.' failure to accurately interpret North Korea's suspension of arms shipments to Iran are discussed.

Smyth, Frank, "Cashing in on Rwanda's genocide," ***New Statesman & Society,*** **July 29, 1994, pp. 16-17.**
Automatic rifles are more plentiful than bicycles in Rwanda. France, Uganda, Egypt and South Africa are all profiting from arms sales there.

Iran-Contra Deal

McManus, Doyle, "Shultz's Iran-Contra criticisms surface," ***Los Angeles Times,*** **Jan. 20, 1994, p. A34.**
According to independent counsel Lawrence E. Walsh, former Secretary of State George P. Shultz considered George Bush a "superficial" politician who was "up to his ears" in the Iran-Contra scandal. Walsh's final report also said that Shultz himself knew more about the secret arms sale than he admitted.

"Report says Reagan was in cover-up," ***Chicago Tribune,*** **Jan. 18, 1994, p. 1.**
President Reagan authorized both the arms sales and military aid that became the focus of the Iran-Contra scandal and "knowingly participated or at least acquiesced" in a cover-up, independent counsel Lawrence E. Walsh concluded in his final report.

Russian Exports

Devroy, Ann, "U.S., Russia sign variety of pacts as talks focus on economics," ***The Washington Post,*** **Sept. 29, 1994, p. A25.**

President Clinton and Russian President Yeltsin ended two days of talks with a flurry of agreements aimed at speeding up the destruction of nuclear warheads, ending Russian arms sales to Iran and improving economic ties between the two nations.

Lauter, David, "Yeltsin pledges to end arms sales to Iran," *Los Angeles Times,* Sept. 29, 1994, p. A12.
Russian President Boris Yeltsin pledged on Sept. 28, 1994 to cut off future sales of weapons to Iran, but American officials quickly warned that the promise may contain huge loopholes that could render it meaningless. Russia will fulfill the terms of a contract with Iran, but will make no others.

Lockwood, Dunbar, "Russian defense budget continues downward spiral, says CIA, DIA," *Arms Control Today,* September 1994, p. 27.
Experts from the Defense Intelligence Agency and the CIA recently gave their annual testimony before the Joint Economic Committee. They gave estimates of Russian defense spending, weapons production and several other indices that show a continued downward spiral in Russia's military strength.

Sychov, Aleksandr, "Russia nearly doubles arms exports," *Current Digest of the Post-Soviet Press,* Oct. 19, 1994, p. 27.
Russia is once again becoming one of the world's leading arms exporters. Russia sold arms on foreign markets in 1993 that were worth an estimated $1.5 billion to $2 billion.

United States Arms Exportation Policy

Atkins, Arthur G., "U.S. again captures title of No. 1 arms exporter," *Arms Control Today,* September 1994, p. 31.
For the fourth straight year, the U.S. leads the world in conventional arms sales to developing countries. In 1993, U.S. weapons export agreements accounted for just under 73 percent of global aggregate sales to these countries.

Cole, Jeff, "Report assails defense-sector 'offset' deals," *The Wall Street Journal,* June 22, 1994, p. A5.
A draft of a GAO report concludes that the decline of the nation's defense industry is being hastened by side deals in foreign arms-sale contracts that place work with foreign companies and transfer technology to them.

Craddock, Ashley, "U.S. arms," *Mother Jones,* September 1994, pp. 41-48.
The U.S. has maintained high levels of production and dominated the global market by exporting the most sophisticated weapons worldwide. Military spending and the global weapons market are discussed.

Kemp, Geoffrey, "The continuing debate over U.S. arms sales: Strategic needs and the quest for arms limitations," *Annals of the American Academy of Political & Social Science,* September 1994, pp. 146-157.
Arms transfers between sovereign states have become a key and controversial ingredient of international relations. The continuing debate over U.S. arms sales, with regards to strategic needs and the quest for arms controls, is discussed.

Milhollin, Gary and Gerard White, "Proliferation in disguise," *The New York Times,* July 18, 1994, p. A15.
Gary Milhollin and Gerard White say that a bill sponsored by Rep. Sam Gejdenson, D-Conn., that would loosen some controls on the sale of strategic technology to other countries would make it easier for terrorist nations to build nuclear weapons, chemical weapons and the missiles to deliver them.

Noah, Timothy, "The world's most dangerous yard sale," *Washington Monthly,* Oct. 1994, pp. 24-28.
In efforts to increase the number of "public-private partnerships," the U.S. government sold hardware and blueprints for a nuclear bomb to an Idaho used-car salesman, Tom Johansen, who wants to sell them overseas. The details of how a private U.S. citizen could buy the guts of a nuclear bomb factory at a price comparable to what an ordinary middle-class American might pay for a house are discussed.

Saul, John Ralston, "A look at . . . Selling self-destruction — Arms addiction: How the West got hooked on exporting weapons," *The Washington Post,* Feb. 6, 1994, p. C3.
John Ralston Saul asserts that the most important capital good produced in the West today is armaments and discusses the historical foundation of the explosion in weapons production.

Schmitt, Eric, "U.S. arms merchants fatten share of sales to third world," *The New York Times,* Aug. 2, 1994, p. A6.
The Congressional Research Service reported on Aug. 1, 1994, that the U.S. increased its leading share of arms sales to the Third World in 1993, but overall sales to those countries continued a decline that started at the end of the cold war. Sales from the U.S. to third-world countries increased slightly to $14.8 billion in 1993 from $14.6 billion in 1992. But the share of America's sales in that period jumped to 73 percent from 56 percent of all weapons sales and sales agreements.

Tisdall, Simon, "Iraq 'used U.S. biotoxins in Gulf war'," *Guardian,* Feb. 11, 1994, p. 13.
The U.S. government licensed the export to Iraq of anthrax and other highly toxic biological agents that were subsequently used by Saddam Hussein against allied servicemen during the 1991 Persian Gulf War, according to a U.S. Senate investigation.

"U.S. emerges as top merchant in global arms trade," *National Catholic Reporter,* June 17, 1994, p. 28,
The fact that the U.S. is the top dealer in the world arms market is discussed in an editorial. By purchasing weapons from the U.S., poor nations are impoverishing their own people and creating new threats to world peace.

Back Issues

Great Research on Current Issues Starts Right Here...Recent topics covered by The CQ Researcher are listed below. Before May 1991, reports were published under the name of Editorial Research Reports.®

JUNE 1993
Food Safety
Prostitution
Childhood Immunizations
National Service

JULY 1993
Electric Cars
Population Growth
Downward Mobility
Intelligence Testing

AUGUST 1993
Mental Illness
Bilingual Education
Foreign Policy Burden
School Funding

SEPTEMBER 1993
Suburban Crime
Public Housing
Supreme Court Preview
Immigration Reform

OCTOBER 1993
Airline Safety
Disaster Response
Science in the Courtroom
The Glass Ceiling

Back issues are available for $4.00 (subscribers) or $7.00 (non-subscribers). Quantity discounts apply to orders over ten. To order, call Congressional Quarterly Customer Service at (202) 887-8621.

Binders are available for $16.00. To order call 1-800-638-1710. Please refer to stock number 648.

NOVEMBER 1993
Paying for Retirement
Charitable Giving
Privacy in the Workplace
Adoption

DECEMBER 1993
U.S. Vietnam-Relations
Learning Disabilities
Child Care
Space Program's Future

JANUARY 1994
Racial Tensions in Schools
South Africa's Future
Worker Retraining
Regulating Pesticides

FEBRUARY 1994
Prison Overcrowding
Water Quality
Religion in Schools
Juvenile Justice

MARCH 1994
Underground Economy
Education Standards
Gambling Boom
Private Management of Public Schools

APRIL 1994
Reproductive Ethics
U.S.-China Trade
Soccer in America
Talk Show Democracy

MAY 1994
Traffic Congestion
Women's Health Issues
Mutual Funds
Political Scandals

JUNE 1994
Education and Gender
Gun Control
Public Land Policy
Nuclear Arms Cleanup

JULY 1994
Dietary Supplements
Public Opinion and Foreign Policy
Crime Victims' Rights
Birth Control Choices

AUGUST 1994
Genetically Engineered Foods
Electing Minorities
Prozac Controversy
College Sports

SEPTEMBER 1994
Home Schooling
Welfare Experiments
Courts and the Media
Regulating Tobacco

OCTOBER 1994
Historic Preservation
Religion and Politics
Arts Funding
Economic Sanctions

NOVEMBER 1994
Sex on Campus
Blood Supply Safety
Testing Term Limits
Religion in America

DECEMBER 1994
Farm Policy

Future Topics

- ***Earthquake Research***
- ***The Video Revolution***
- ***Treating Addiction***

THE CQ Researcher

PUBLISHED BY CONGRESSIONAL QUARTERLY INC.

Earthquake Research

Will accurate quake prediction ever be possible?

Earthquakes continue to inspire awe and terror, as they have since ancient times. But now, because of the nation's prosperity, there are new concerns about the high rate of property damage in earthquake-prone areas. The quake that hit the Los Angeles area last January, for example, though moderate in scale, caused more than 60 deaths and $20 billion in destruction. The so-called Northridge quake sparked efforts to map Southern California's many geologic faults, where earthquakes commonly occur. But while understanding of earthquake dynamics is growing, geophysicists are less confident of their ability to predict major seismic events than they were 20 years ago. Meanwhile, seismologists caution that east of the Rockies, many parts of the central and eastern U.S. are at greater risk than residents think.

INSIDE THIS ISSUE

CQ Dec. 16, 1994 • Volume 4, No. 47 • Pages 1105-1128

Formerly Editorial Research Reports

EARTHQUAKE RESEARCH

THE ISSUES

BACKGROUND

CURRENT SITUATION

OUTLOOK

SIDEBARS AND GRAPHICS

FOR MORE INFORMATION

December 16, 1994
Volume 4, No. 47

The CQ Researcher (ISSN 1056-2036). Formerly Editorial Research Reports. Published weekly (48 times per year, not printed the first Friday of any month with five Fridays) by Congressional Quarterly Inc., 1414 22nd St., N.W., Washington, D.C. 20037. Rates are furnished upon request. Second-class postage paid at Washington, D.C. POSTMASTER: Send address changes to The CQ Researcher, 1414 22nd St., N.W., Washington, D.C. 20037.

COVER: APARTMENT BUILDING IN THE LOS ANGELES AREA DAMAGED BY THE JANUARY NORTHRIDGE EARTHQUAKE. PAGE 1107: AMERICAN RED CROSS WORKER ASSESSES DAMAGE FROM THE NORTHRIDGE QUAKE. (AMERICAN RED CROSS PHOTOS)

Earthquake Research

By Richard L. Worsnop

The Issues

It has been almost a year since an earthquake hit the Los Angeles area, causing some $20 billion in property damage. The so-called Northridge quake generated the most powerful ground motions ever recorded in a North American city — and was the costliest U.S. quake since San Francisco's legendary 1906 upheaval. But to judge by its Richter scale rating, it was a virtual pussycat.

The Northridge quake's relatively puny 6.7 rating prompted Southern Californians and scientists to wonder whether it was only a curtain-raiser for the long-dreaded "Big One." That's the 8-plus magnitude quake that many experts say will strike Southern California in the next 30 years or so. *

Like other major earthquakes of recent decades, Northridge spurred efforts to upgrade building codes and draft more comprehensive maps of the geologic faults where quakes mainly occur. Indeed, since the quake occurred on a previously unknown fault, it underscored how far scientists are from making accurate quake forecasts.

"To have a universal way of predicting all serious earthquakes everywhere will probably never be possible," says seismologist Bruce A. Bolt of the University of California-Berkeley.

But the scientists who are seeking better ways to predict where and when earthquakes will occur — and how powerful they will be — aren't giving up. And many, including Bolt, think progress is being made. The use of paleoseismology — the study of ancient earthquakes — is providing new clues to earthquake frequency. And scientists hope to be able to use super-fast computers to analyze initial shock waves as part of an earthquake early-warning system. Similarly, there is hope for a way to pick up early signs that tsunamis, the giant ocean waves caused by earthquakes, are bearing down on coastal areas.

Meanwhile, public-policy officials and engineering experts are working on ways to mitigate the effects of earthquakes through new building techniques and the passage of tougher building ordinances. A key player in that effort is the federal National Earthquake Hazards Reduction Program (NEHRP).

In any case, most Americans tend to regard earthquakes as a problem that affects only Californians and Alaskans on a regular basis. And the nation's earthquake history tends to justify this complacency. But many areas east of the Rockies are at higher risk of seismic damage than their residents think, and state and regional earthquake-preparedness groups are trying to raise public awareness of the threat.

It promises to be a hard sell, given the human impulse to assume disasters always happen to someone else, regardless of the posted odds. In the meantime, two questions often figure prominently in discussions of earthquake-linked research and policy-making:

Will scientists ever be able to predict major earthquakes?

Twenty years ago, many seismologists were confident that earthquake prediction was tantalizingly within their reach — that the place, time and magnitude of a major quake could be specified within fairly close limits. Such accuracy would enable emergency preparedness officials to save more lives and minimize property damage.

A report issued in 1975 by a National Academy of Sciences panel reflected the prevailing optimism. It noted that established methods of pinpointing areas at high risk of seismic damage were backward-looking, depending as they did on the past incidence of quakes and the mapping of fault structures. In contrast, newly developed earthquake prediction methods "rely primarily on premonitory signs, such as changing physical properties of rocks under stress and surface tilting, that occur in advance of a quake." The report added that "Prediction capability does not lessen the importance of other approaches to earthquake mitigation, but it adds one potentially telling weapon to the arsenal." [1]

At the time, China reigned as the world leader in earthquake prediction. Its reputation rested largely on a forecast made Feb. 4, 1975, that within 24 hours a strong earthquake would hit Haicheng, Manchuria. The warning had been based on a string of smaller tremors, which were diagnosed as foreshocks. That evening, a 7.3-magnitude quake struck the area. Though property damage was heavy, there were relatively few deaths in Haicheng, which had been evacuated.

However, there was no warning a year later when a 7.8-magnitude quake struck Tangshan, an industrial city of 1 million residents about 100 miles east of Beijing. Official reports estimated that 250,000 persons died in the July 27, 1976, disaster, including about 100 in Beijing.

* Northridge sits near the 650-mile-long San Andreas Fault, which extends south from Point Arena, 110 miles north of San Francisco, to the Gulf of California. (*See diagram, p. 1108.*)

The San Andreas Fault

The San Andreas Fault runs for about 650 miles through coastal California. During earthquakes, the western and eastern sides of the fault move in opposite directions. Diagram shows how shock waves emanate from the focus and epicenter of an earthquake.

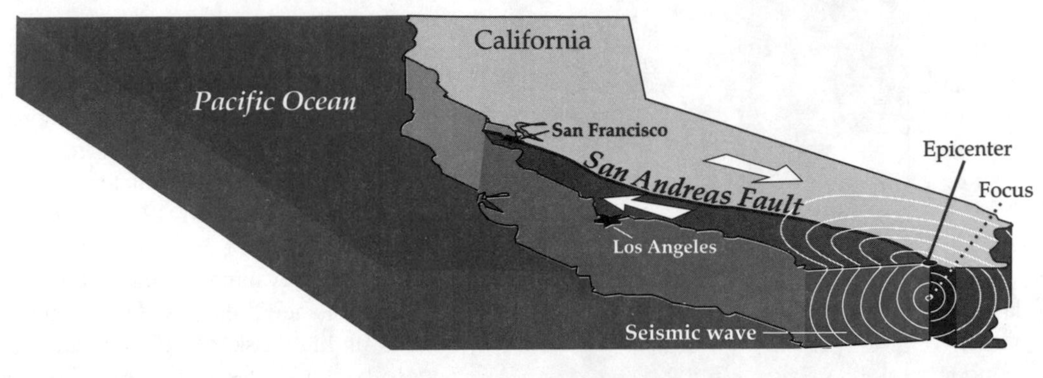

After the Tangshan quake, researchers focused on potential precursors, including foreshocks and changes in underground electrical signals, magnetic fields and the shape of the land. So far, though, none has emerged as a window to the future.

The successful Haicheng prediction, for example, suggested that closely spaced foreshocks could signal the imminent approach of a killer quake. But subsequent research has established that earthquakes follow no set script. "Some earthquakes have foreshocks, and others do not," said Max Wyss, a seismologist at the University of Alaska-Fairbanks. [2]

Similarly, unexplained bulges in the Earth's surface along fault zones are not necessarily earthquake warning flags. Rainfall, drying or natural slumping can cause such deformations. And changes in the electrical resistivity or magnetic fields of ground water beneath fault zones also have proved unreliable as quake precursors.

To many observers, the so-called Parkfield experiment underscored the limitations of earthquake prediction. In 1985, citing research by three prominent seismologists, the National Earthquake Prediction Evaluation Council said there was a 95 percent probability of a moderate earthquake (magnitude 5.5 to 6) near Parkfield, Calif., by the end of 1992. [3] This first prediction by the council, an arm of the U.S. Geological Survey (USGS), seemed well within reason: Parkfield, roughly midway between Los Angeles and San Francisco, had experienced earthquakes that big or bigger every 22 years, on average, for at least a century. [4]

In response, USGS installed a network of instruments to collect detailed data about seismic and geologic movement around Parkfield. Indeed, at the time Parkfield was said to be the world's most heavily monitored earthquake site. Arrays of digital seismographs recorded the size and location of all tremors in the area, including microearthquakes below magnitude 1. These readings were then relayed by satellite to computers at USGS offices in Menlo Park, Calif.

In mid-October 1992, just weeks before the prediction deadline, a 4.7-magnitude earthquake rattled Parkfield. USGS scientists, thinking that the tremor might be a precursor of the stronger shock they were waiting for, intensified their vigil. But 1992 passed without further seismic events worth noting.

"As a test of the theory by which we thought we could make the Parkfield prediction, the experiment was pretty clearly a failure," says USGS geophysicist Lucile M. Jones. But at the same time, "It was successful in that we now understand more about the earthquake process. An experiment is a failure only when it doesn't teach you anything."

The inexactness of the Parkfield forecast called into question a cherished tenet of earthquake prediction. The seismic-gap theory, as it is known, holds that stress accumulates in each section of a fault over time. It also assumes that the fault segment most likely to give way in an earthquake is the one that has been inactive the longest — the "gap" in a seismically active line.

Even before the Parkfield experiment ended, the seismic-gap hypothesis had come under intense scrutiny. Seismologists Yan Y. Kagan and David D. Jackson of the University of California-Los Angeles (UCLA) asserted in 1991 that an effort to apply the theory to fault zones in the Pacific Rim (*see map, p. 1114*) had failed to forecast 40 large earthquakes between 1979 and 1989. [5] Other experts raised the possibility that events long assumed to be part of a related series, like the Parkfield quakes, actually might have occurred along different fault lines.

Dismayed by the lack of progress in earthquake prediction, some geophysicists have thrown up their hands. "We fundamentally don't understand how earthquakes work," said Stanford University's Mark Zoback. "After all these years, we don't have a clue." Since traditional models of fault behavior have proved unreliable, "we don't have a basis on which to build a strategy" for making predictions, he added. [6]

Still, many believers in earthquake prediction have kept the faith. "Some of us never lost our optimism," says UCLA geophysicist Leon Knopoff. "The problems associated with earthquake prediction were difficult ones, and were not solvable just by throwing good insights and high tech at them." In his view, quake prediction "remains a tough nut to crack — but it's a crackable nut."

Knopoff helped to organize a National Academy of Sciences colloquium on earthquake prediction to be held next Feb. 10-11 at the University of California-Irvine. One of the conference's key topics will be what scientists call earthquake clustering. "If earthquakes don't cluster, then there's really no hope for that particular approach to prediction," says Knopoff. "There's no way to predict random events." Other areas to be covered include laboratory measurements, theory and modelling and paleoseismology, or the study of earthquakes that occurred in prehistoric times (*see p. 1116*).

Seismologist Bolt believes that "all science worthy of the name has a predictive side to it." He also feels seismologists should focus on "the doable part" of earthquake prediction, which he defines as determining "what the ground-shaking will be like" when a great earthquake strikes. "That's difficult enough to do," says Bolt, "but I think we're making great headway there."

In some limited ways, earthquake prediction is on the verge of becoming a reality. Because high-speed computers can analyze earthquake shock waves in less time than the waves last, "researchers may soon be able to anticipate the effects of an initial tremor, enabling railroads to stop or slow their trains and permit elevator systems to halt at the nearest floor," Corey S. Powell wrote in *Scientific American*.[7] Moreover, a Harvard University research team hopes to develop an automated warning system to predict the height and arrival time of the earthquake-generated sea waves called tsunamis many hours before they hit distant shores.

In the view of geophysicist Keiiti Aki of the Southern California Earthquake Center, progress being made in the United States suggests quake prediction has entered "a sort of revival" phase. "We shouldn't give it up," he says. "That's the message I'm hearing these days."

An earthquake that measured 6.9 on the Richter scale caused $30 million in property damage and injured 91 persons near El Centro, Calif., in 1979.

National Geophysical Data Center

In China and Japan, by comparison, seismic prediction studies never underwent a slump, says Aki, noting, "It's easier to do long-term science there." In the United States, however, the science review cycle is much shorter. "If you don't get any results for three years," Aki says, "you're in trouble — in getting additional funding, for example."

Does the U.S. earthquake hazard reduction program need restructuring?

Though most Americans doubtless don't know it, the federal government operates a National Earthquake Hazards Reduction Program (NEHRP). Established under legislation approved in 1977, NEHRP is administered jointly by the USGS, National Science Foundation (NST), National Institute for Standards and Technology (NIST) and the Federal Emergency Management Agency (FEMA). USGS and NSF conduct earth-science and engineering research on the causes and effects of earthquakes. NIST seeks to devise building-code provisions for enhancing earthquake resistance. FEMA, designated as the "lead agency," handles overall program coordination and helps state and local governments, private groups and individuals to implement hazard-reduction measures. *

Given the program's bureaucratic structure, it was perhaps inevitable that calls for a more streamlined chain of command would eventually be heard. (*See "At Issue," p. 1121.*) That's what the NEHRP advisory committee recommended last January in a report that is still being debated by federal and state earthquake policy-makers.[8]

NEHRP's "primary failure," declared the report, "has been a lack of strate-

* The "Contract With America" unveiled by House Republicans in September included a proposal to abolish the USGS and other federal agencies, including the Bureau of Mines. Under the plan, the USGS earthquake program would be absorbed by the National Science Foundation.

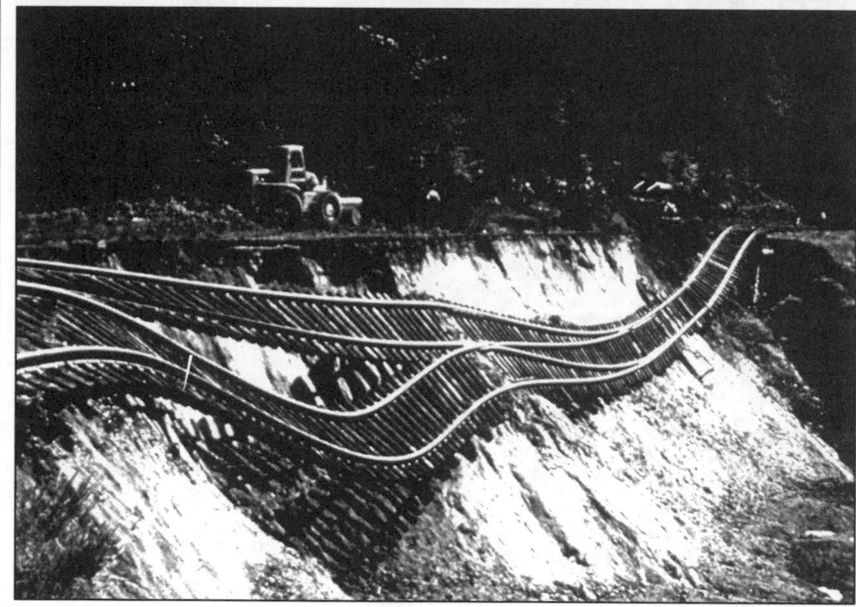

Snakelike fence and severe highway damage were caused by a magnitude 7.1 earthquake at Hebgen Lake, Mont., in 1959. Timber and highway damage was estimated at $11 million; 28 persons died.

Railroad tracks outside Olympia, Wash., were damaged when hillside fill slid away during a magnitude 6.5 quake in Seattle in 1965, killing seven and causing $12.5 million in damage.

National Geophysical Data Center (all)

gic planning that would guide program focus and balance, an inability to develop program priorities that reflect user needs and some lack of an ability to procure necessary knowledge, particularly in engineering and the social sciences."

To provide a firmer sense of direction, the report urged "the establishment of a single entity to manage and direct the program." This step, the report argued, would "permit initiation of prioritized projects of problem-focused research, particularly in the engineering and socioeconomic areas, as well as enhanc[e] NEHRP's already-existing capability for that in the earth-sciences area." [9]

Criticism of the advisory committee's recommendation came quickly. In a published response in April 1993, USGS agreed with some of the panel's proposals but challenged the main one. The "major drawback" to the "single-management entity," said USGS, "is that it would impose a new layer of bureaucracy on the management of NEHRP. . . . The rules and requirements of the new management entity would be added on top of the existing bureaucracy. The proposed new entity would control the financial resources of the [four existing NEHRP] agencies but not their personnel resources. Effective program management is very difficult when authority over financial and personnel resources [is] vested in different agencies." [10]

Klaus H. Jacob, senior research scientist at Columbia University's Lamont-Doherty Earth Observatory in Palisades, N.Y., also found fault with the advisory committee's plan. Testifying before a House subcommittee considering reauthorization of the hazard-reduction pro-

Measuring Earthquake Strength

If a powerful earthquake hit downtown Los Angeles during a weekday rush hour, the toll in lives and property losses would be staggering. But if a quake of identical strength were to strike the middle of Greenland, it probably would go unnoticed except by seismologists.

Earthquake damage, in other words, is not necessarily a reliable guide to earthquake strength — and vice versa. For this reason, scientists generally express earthquake severity in terms of both magnitude (size of ground waves) and intensity (observed effects). The two yardsticks, used in tandem, give a more rounded picture than either can do alone.

The measure of earthquake magnitude most familiar to Americans was devised in 1935 by Charles F. Richter of the California Institute of Technology. The Richter scale gauges the size of an earthquake at its source. Measurements are based on data captured by seismographs, instruments that convert the ground motion of an earthquake into a visible record or seismogram.

Richter scale magnitudes are expressed in whole numbers and decimals so that they are easy to grasp. Although the scale begins at zero, most of the quakes reported by the news media range from 3-8. However, these figures can be misleading because they are based on a logarithmic scale. This means that an increase of one whole number on the scale represents a tenfold increase in earthquake magnitude.

As an expression of raw earthquake power, however, each whole number on the Richter scale represents the release of about 32 times more energy than the preceding whole number. Thus, a 7.0 magnitude earthquake releases 32 times more energy than a 6.0 magnitude quake — and more than 1,000 times more energy than a 5.0 quake.

Though the Richter scale remains popular with the media, many U.S. and foreign seismologists prefer to use a scale that they say offers a more accurate profile of earthquake strength. When this yardstick is applied to notable past quakes, the new numbers sometimes are strikingly different from the original Richter figures.

Measuring earthquake intensity is a somewhat subjective exercise, since it relies largely on eyewitness observation. In 1902, Gieseppe Mercalli, an Italian seismologist, created the first scale for measuring earthquake intensity. It was revised in 1931 by two American seismologists, Harry O. Wood and Frank Neumann, to take into account tall buildings, motor vehicles, underground water mains and the like. Their Modified Mercalli scale (MMS) consists of 12 levels of increasing intensity, each designated by a Roman numeral, ranging from I (imperceptible shaking) to XII (catastrophic destruction).

After widely felt earthquakes, the U.S. Geological Survey mails questionnaires to postmasters in the affected area asking for information that helps determine intensity values.

gram, Jacob said the single-agency remedy "tries to cure failures in substance by changes in administrative form." Though the panel's proposal was "well-intended," he felt it could "jeopardize the now-effective elements in NEHRP, while providing no guarantee that less productive elements would perform any better under the new structure." In Jacob's opinion, the solution "lies not in administrative revisions at the top, but in rewarding competition, quality, professional performance and visionary planning at all levels, from bottom up as much as top down." [11]

The fate of the advisory committee's January 1993 proposal still is uncertain. Separate reviews of NEHRP's administrative structure are being conducted by the Office of Science and Technology Policy, a presidential advisory body, and the Office of Technology Assessment, which supplies Congress with information and analyses on the political, physical, economic and social effects of technological applications. According to a spokeswoman for the USGS Office of Earthquakes, Volcanoes and Engineering in Reston, Va., no further action on the matter is likely for several months. ■

BACKGROUND

Fatal Faults

Trembling of the Earth inspired special terror in ancient times. Many ancients thought earthquakes were the work of wrathful gods. Aristotle theorized that they were caused by winds that had become trapped in underground caverns and shook the ground in trying to escape. Thus arose the belief — still prevalent in many places — that earthquakes occur on windless days.

Some disasters cited in ancient chronicles may have been earthquake-related. In the Bible, for instance, Chapter 19 of "Genesis" relates that "brimstone and fire" rained from the skies when Sodom and Gomorrah were "overthrown" for their wickedness. Scholars now speculate that the two cities lay astride a seismically active rift running from present-day Turkey to the Red Sea. Thus, seismologist Leon Reiter believes that the biblical passage "probably depicts the occurrence of a massive earthquake, and perhaps an associated fire, some 4,000 years ago." [12]

Although geologists and seismologists are uncertain when earthquakes will occur, they do know where. Fault zones tend to be concentrated in areas with actively building mountains (often including volcanoes) or in deep oceanic

The "great San Francisco earthquake" of 1906 caused sidewalks to shift and destroyed City Hall. Poor construction was an important factor in its destruction. Four hundred fifty people died in the quake and resulting fires. (National Geophysical Data Center)

belts. The largest seismic zone in the world — the so-called "Ring of Fire" — surrounds the Pacific Basin and includes the fault systems of the west coasts of South and North America, the Aleutian Islands, the Japan-Kuriles belt, the Philippine Islands, New Zealand and many South Pacific islands. (*See map, p. 1114.*)

An estimated 80 percent of the world's earthquakes originate in the so-called circum-Pacific zone. A second earthquake belt, sometimes called the Alpide zone, begins in the Azores, passes through the Mediterranean Ocean and the Near East, skirts the northern border of India and slices through Sumatra and Indonesia to join the circum-Pacific zone in New Guinea.

The best-known suboceanic earthquake belt is associated with the mid-Atlantic ridge. Actually a submarine mountain chain, the ridge stretches along the full north-south length of the Atlantic, thrusting above the surface in Iceland, the Azores, Ascension Island and the Tristan da Cunha islands. Other suboceanic ridges — some associated with earthquakes, some not — lie in the Pacific, Indian and Arctic oceans.

The discovery in July 1967 of a Minoan city on the Aegean island of Thera led to speculation that the fabled island of Atlantis might actually have been the site of the Minoan civilization whose home was the island of Crete. The fall of this ancient culture coincided with a great volcanic eruption that occurred around 1400 B.C. Similarly fragmentary evidence indicates that 45,000 persons were killed in 856 A.D. and 180,000 killed in 893-4 A.D. by earthquakes in what is now Iran.

Indeed, Plato noted in *Timaeus,* one of his dialogues: "There occurred violent earthquakes and floods, and in a single day and night of misfortune all . . . warlike men in a body sank into the earth, and the island of Atlantis in like manner disappeared into the depths of the sea."

Curious Nobleman Advances Earthquake Science

The earthquake that devastated Lisbon, Portugal, on Nov. 1, 1755, was the first great quake to be observed in anything approaching a scientific manner, thanks to a nobleman's curiosity. According to author Charles Davison, "By order of the Marquez de Pombal, a list of questions [about the earthquake] was sent to every parish in the country," and if that list "had been drawn up at the present day, it could hardly have been more complete." [13]

The questionnaire asked respondents to estimate the duration of the shock, its effects on bodies of water and the times and intensities of aftershocks. It also sought information on parish population, the number of persons killed and houses destroyed and the extent of damage from earthquake-related fires.

These records indicate with reasonable accuracy that during the six or seven minutes of the Lisbon quake, at least 30,000 persons were killed and all large public buildings and 12,000 dwellings were demolished. Many people died while attending mass. A fire followed that burned for six days. It was estimated that the area shaken was four times as large as Europe.

The quake was remarkable for its effect on water. It generated tsunamis 60 feet high in Cadiz, Spain, and 12 feet high on the Caribbean island of Martinique. Water in lakes and ponds as far away as Sweden sloshed back and forth for hours — a phenomenon known as a seiche.

Afterwards, Voltaire wrote in *Candide,* three-quarters of Lisbon had been destroyed, and "the Portuguese pundits could not think of any better way of preventing total ruin than to treat the people to a splendid auto-da-fé, for the University of Coimbra had declared that the spectacle of a number of people being ceremoniously burned over a slow fire was an infallible way of preventing an earthquake."

Continued on p. 1114

Chronology

18th Century

***The first earthquake to be observed scientifically is memorialized in Voltaire's* Candide.**

Nov. 1, 1755
After Lisbon, Portugal, is rocked by an earthquake, a Portuguese nobleman sends a questionnaire to every parish in the country asking about the quake.

19th Century

Some of the most destructive U.S. earthquakes of the 1800s occur east of the Rocky Mountains.

1811-1812
The area surrounding New Madrid, Mo., is shaken by innumerable earthquakes, many of them major, for more than a year. In the process, the Mississippi's course is altered and a large, new lake is formed in northwestern Tennessee.

Aug. 31, 1886
An earthquake in Charleston, S.C., kills 60 people and is felt throughout South Carolina and North Carolina as well as parts of Georgia and Virginia.

1900s-1920s

Severe earthquakes hit the United States and Japan.

1902
Gieseppe Mercalli, an Italian seismologist, devises the first scale for measuring earthquake intensity.

April 18, 1906
Much of San Francisco is destroyed by an 8.3-magnitude earthquake and the resulting fires, but only about 450 deaths are recorded.

Sept. 1, 1923
An 8.3-magnitude quake destroys much of Tokyo and Yokohama and kills 140,000 persons.

1930s

Seismologists develop more precise ways to measure earthquake force and damage.

1931
American seismologists Harry O. Wood and Frank Neumann devise the Modified Mercalli scale of earthquake intensity to take into account such modern features as tall buildings and automobiles.

1935
Charles F. Richter, a seismologist at the California Institute of Technology, develops a scale for gauging the force generated by earthquakes.

1960s

The strongest recorded earthquake in U.S. history strikes far from population or industrial centers.

March 27, 1964
An 8.5-magnitude quake causes substantial damage over 50,000 square miles of Alaska but results in only 114 deaths.

1970s

State and federal governments become more involved in earthquake research and mitigation.

1972
California's Seismic Study Zone Act prohibits new construction anywhere in the state near or across active faults.

1974
The California Seismic Safety Commission is established.

July 28, 1976
An 8.2-magnitude quake strikes Tangshan, China, causing an estimated 250,000 deaths.

Oct. 7, 1977
President Jimmy Carter signs the Earthquake Hazards Reduction Act.

1980s-1990s

Two sizable earthquakes just five years apart cause Californians to think anew about the "Big One."

Oct. 17, 1989
The 7.1-magnitude Loma Prieta earthquake strikes the San Francisco Bay area, causing $6 billion in damages and at least 62 deaths.

Jan. 5, 1990
President George Bush issues an executive order requiring that all new buildings constructed or leased by federal agencies meet "appropriate seismic design and construction standards."

Jan. 17, 1994
A 6.7-magnitude quake centered in the Northridge area of Los Angeles kills at least 61 people and causes some $20 billion in damages.

Oct. 19, 1994
President Clinton signs a bill reauthorizing the Earthquake Hazards Reduction Act for two years.

The Earth's Movable Plates

The Earth's crust is made up of a number of segments, called tectonic plates, which are in constant motion. Most earthquakes occur along the boundaries of the plates as the plates collide. The boundaries of the major plates are formed by mid-oceanic ridges and trenches.

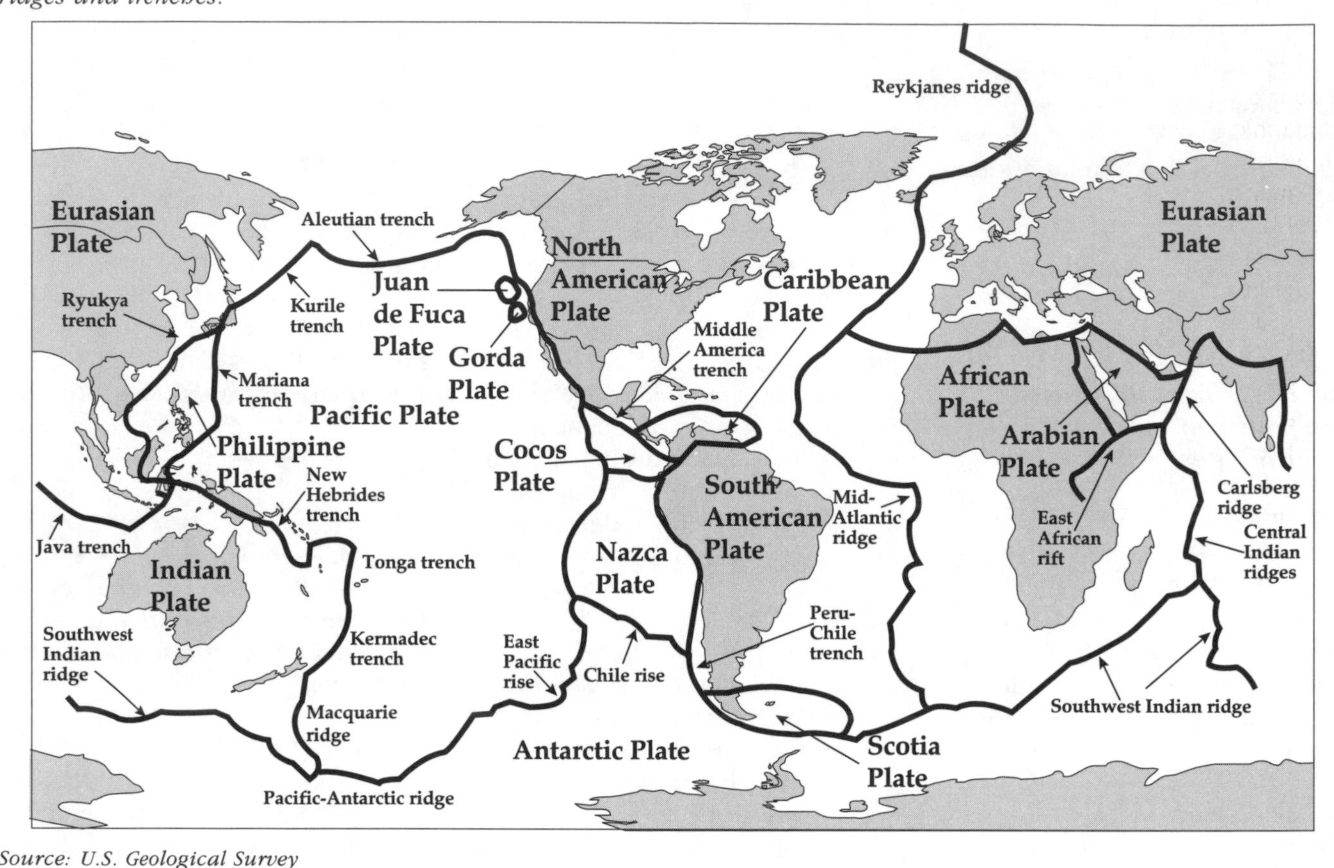

Source: U.S. Geological Survey

Continued from p. 1112

U.S. Disasters

Probably the most destructive earthquakes in U.S. history occurred in the vicinity of New Madrid, Mo., early in the last century. (*See story, p. 1118.*) Residents of that small Mississippi River community were awakened on the morning of Dec. 16, 1811, by the sounds of creaking walls and falling crockery. There followed a series of earthquakes that continued, several each day, for more than a year. Two of them, on Jan. 23, 1812, and Feb. 7, were just as severe as the first. The principal shocks were felt over an area of more than a million square miles, from New Orleans and all along the Atlantic seaboard. "The largest earthquake," wrote seismologist Bolt, "awakened President [James] Madison in the White House, rang church bells in Boston and tumbled chimneys in Cincinnati." [14]

Most of the earthquakes' lasting physical effects were confined to the lower Mississippi River and its bottom lands, which consisted of a thin layer of earth, clay, silt and gravel overlying a water-saturated bed of sand. Steady shaking caused much of this unconsolidated material to sink, forming swamps in some places and lakes in others. Numerous bluffs lining the river banks collapsed, and several islands in the Mississippi vanished.

John James Audubon, the famed ornithologist, experienced one of the New Madrid quakes while riding a horse in Kentucky. "The ground rose and fell in successive furrows like the ruffled waters of a lake," he wrote. "The Earth waved like a field of corn before the breeze." [15]

Almost 75 years after the New Madrid events, another area not regarded as seismically active experienced a major quake. On Aug. 31, 1886, a fault ruptured near Charleston, S.C., triggering a quake that seismologists say would have registered between 6.7 and 7 on the Richter scale. Sixty seconds of intense shaking resulted in 60 deaths and some $23 million in damages in an area extending 120 miles from the epicenter. Within 6 to 8 minutes, tremors were felt as far away as Chicago, New York City and St. Louis.

Havoc in San Francisco and Alaska

While the New Madrid and Charleston quakes may have been the most geographically extensive in American history, the "great San Francisco earthquake" of April 18, 1906, is probably the most renowned. * It provided the best example of visible faulting in recent times, and the fire it caused was one of the most destructive in U.S. history. Four hundred and fifty people perished.

The quake struck shortly after 5 a.m. There were two main shocks lasting 40 seconds and 25 seconds. Structural damage was severe on filled land but minimal on solid rock. The destruction stemmed chiefly from fires started by overturned stoves, collapsing chimneys and fractured gas pipes. Broken water mains left firefighters virtually helpless. In the end, bringing the fires under control required a stern measure — the use of dynamite to create firebreaks.

Because the earthquake area had been surveyed shortly before the disaster and again afterwards, scientists were able to calculate its range. They found that topographic upheaval extended along the San Andreas Fault for more than 250 miles. Until then, geologists thought fault movements were predominantly vertical, or up and down. (*See diagram, p. 1108.*) But the 1906 event, with its horizontal displacements of 15 to 20 feet and scattered vertical upthrusts of only 2 to 3 feet, prompted second thoughts. [16]

The 8.5-magnitude Alaska earthquake of March 27, 1964, was the strongest U.S. temblor yet recorded on seismographs. Tremors were felt in a 1-million-square-mile area; the damage zone covered an estimated 50,000 square miles. According to the Commerce Department's Environmental Science Services Administration, the quake caused the deaths of 131 persons and $750 million in property damage in Alaska and along the Pacific Coast. The agency also noted that seismic waves were recorded in Antarctica 22 1/2 hours after the quake and caused water to oscillate in Key West, Fla., nearly 4,000 miles away.

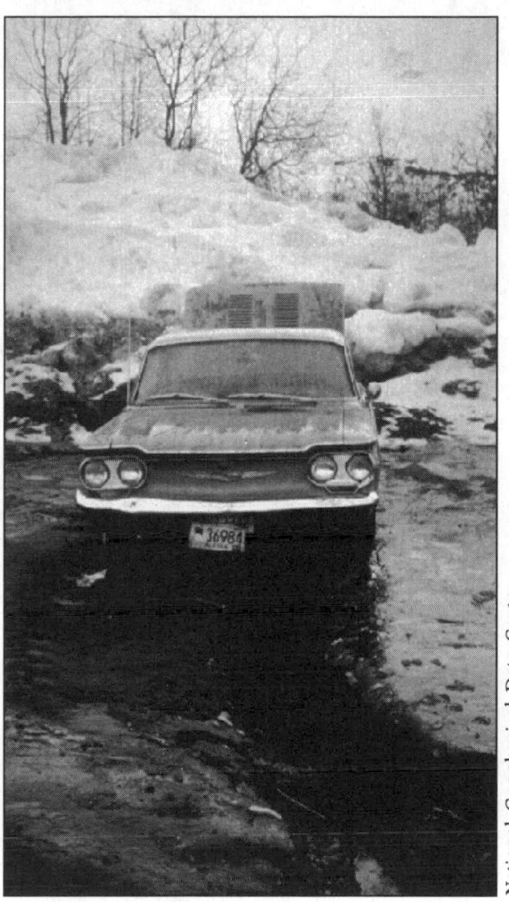

National Geophysical Data Center

Car straddles a crack in pavement caused by lateral spreading in the 8.5-magnitude Alaska quake in 1964, one of the largest of the century. It caused an estimated $750 million in damage over a 50,000-square-mile area and 131 deaths.

Geographic displacement was substantial: Mountains on Kodiak Island and the Kenai Peninsula subsided 7 feet or more. The ocean floor rose in an area measuring 480 miles by 127 miles. The biggest upheaval was 50 feet — the largest ever recorded — between Kodiak and Montague islands.

In the popular mind, earthquakes are ranked mainly by the number of deaths they cause. By this measure, the Alaska quake barely merits a footnote; the 1976 quake that claimed approximately 250,000 lives at Tangshan, China, was the most lethal of this century (*see p. 1107*).

Until last January's Northridge disaster, the 7.1-magnitude quake that shook the San Francisco Bay area Oct. 17, 1989, had been the most publicized U.S. seismic event of recent years. The quake struck shortly before the start of a World Series game at San Francisco's Candlestick Park, and millions of television viewers witnessed its immediate aftermath. The quake caused TV transmission to go dead momentarily, just as the game announcers were exchanging startled glances on camera. When power was restored, the announcers reported what had happened and shifted from the baseball game, which was quickly canceled, to disaster coverage.

The Loma Prieta * earthquake, as it was named, resulted in at least 62 deaths and 3,700 injuries and more than $6 billion in property damage. Communications cables and power lines broke and sections of elevated freeways collapsed; even the San Francisco Bay Bridge was damaged. As in 1906, devastation was especially severe in areas built on filled land, such as San Francisco's Marina district.

Only weeks before Loma Prieta, scientists had identified the Santa Cruz Mountains near Santa Clara as a likely earthquake site. After a 5.2-magnitude quake shook the area Aug. 8, the California Office of Emergency Services warned there was a "slightly increased likelihood" of further seismic activity in the same area that "could involve an earthquake as large as 6.2 magnitude."

* The earthquake that struck the San Francisco area Oct. 21, 1868, also was known as the "great San Francisco earthquake."

* Loma Prieta, meaning "dark mountain," is the highest peak in the Santa Cruz Mountains, where the earthquake was centered.

National Geophysical Data Center

Rows of lettuce were offset by ground shifts during the 1979 El Centro, Calif., quake. Growers suffered heavy damage to drainage canals, irrigation ditches and subsurface drain tiles.

Searching for Answers

Though geophysicists are still un able to predict exactly when and where major earthquakes will strike and how strong they'll be, they have greatly broadened their knowledge of earthquake mechanics over the past quarter-century. As recently as the 1960s, for example, scientists knew that seismic and volcanic events often occurred along the geologic faults that are common in "young" mountain ranges and deep ocean ridges. But they lacked a unifying hypothesis to explain why such areas are so seismically restless.

The discovery of plate tectonics in the 1970s supplied the answer. Earth's outer crust, scientists found, is not a seamless whole like an orange skin but rather a patchwork of plates. Floating on the Earth's semimolten mantle, the 60-mile-thick plates are constantly shifting — up to 4 inches a year. As they move, the plates grind against one another, producing the powerful forçes that create the tectonics, or deformations, of the Earth's surface that are associated with earthquakes.

An estimated 95 percent of all earthquakes occur at plate boundaries, either at the oceanic ridges where the plates are tearing apart or at the point where one plate bumps into another. The world's largest seismic zone — the "Ring of Fire" — is actually the lengthy boundary separating the Pacific plate from adjacent continental plates.

When an ocean plate collides offshore with a continental plate, the oceanic plate is driven beneath the continental plate, creating a seismically active undersea fault called a subduction zone. Many of the world's greatest earthquakes, including the 1964 quake in Alaska and the 1923 quake in Tokyo, occurred along subduction zones.

The 5 percent of earthquakes that occur far from plate boundaries are called mid-plate or intra-plate quakes and are still poorly understood. The New Madrid earthquakes of 1811-1812 are perhaps the most famous examples of such seismic events.

Geophysicists have found that some earthquakes are at least partially manmade. Lake Mead, in Arizona and Nevada, formed when the Hoover Dam was erected across the Colorado River, is a case in point, says Bolt. "Before the lake's creation [in 1935], there had been no historical record of earthquake activity in the area, but afterward small earthquakes became frequent," he noted. "Moreover, local seismographic stations, established after the filling of the reservoir, showed that the number of shocks correlated rather closely with changes in reservoir loading." [17]

Similarly, Denver residents were puzzled by a series of earthquakes that began rattling the area in spring 1962. Investigators found that the U.S. Army had just begun pumping chemical wastes from the nearby Rocky Mountain Arsenal into a 12,000-foot well. The earthquakes — Denver's first in 80 years — began a month later. In the following three years, the city experienced more than 700 additional minor tremors. Geologists finally concluded that the well was responsible, and its use was discontinued. Though the amount of waste stored was not great, the column of liquid was so high it exerted tremendous pressure on adjacent rocks.

Unlocking secrets of "fossil earthquakes"

A prime area of current earthquake research is paleoseismology, or the study of "fossil earthquakes" from prehistoric times. The discipline is especially useful to geophysicists in North America, which has a relatively short historical record. Bolt ranks paleoseismology among "the most important advances" in geophysics of the past 20 years, because it has helped "establish the rate of accumulation of strain along faults in many parts of the world."

Paleoseismology's basic technique calls for digging a trench across a fault and examining the exposed rock and sediment strata for evidence of past earthquakes. Such evidence can be direct (dramatic fault offsets) or indirect (signs of sand deposits or landslides typically linked to strong ground shaking). After identifying these traces, paleoseismologists determine their age through radiocarbon dating. The next step is ascertaining the time gap between successive earthquakes. This establishes the area's earthquake recurrence period. For example, if quakes happened in 1600, 1650, 1750 and 1825, the recurrence range is 50-100 years, and the average interval is 75 years.

The pioneering work in paleoseismology was done in the late 1970s by Kerry Sieh, a California Institute of Technology geologist. Working at Pallet Creek along the San Andreas Fault, Sieh found evidence of 12 earthquakes dating back to 260 A.D. He calculated that major quakes occurred in the vicinity every 50 to 300 years and that the average interval was about 150 years. The fault had not ruptured in that area since 1857, when one of the strongest earthquakes in U.S. history struck near Fort Tejon. [18]

Sieh's work led to a widely publicized 1980 FEMA prediction that Southern California was due for the "Big One" — a catastrophic earthquake of magnitude 8.3. [19] A more recent USGS report, which included more up-to-date paleoseismic research, said in July 1988 that there was a 60 percent chance of a large and damaging earthquake (magnitude 7.5 to 8) along the southern part of the San Andreas Fault over the next 30 years. [20]

Reducing Hazards

Even as seismologists continue probing for better ways to predict quakes, lawmakers and scientists are working for ways to minimize their effects. After the 1906 earthquake, for example, San Francisco installed an auxiliary water system, independent of the municipal supply, for use in future earthquake-fire emergencies. A more far-reaching preventive measure followed the 1933 earthquake at Long Beach, Calif., which heavily damaged 85 public schools. The disaster prompted passage of the Field Act, which required all California schools to be designed to resist earthquakes.

Other hazard-reduction measures followed still other quakes. After the 1971 Sylmar quake in Los Angeles, for example, California legislators passed the 1972 Seismic Study Zone Act, barring new construction anywhere in the state across faults or in designated zones near active faults. Two years later, the California Seismic Safety Commission was established to develop a statewide earthquake policy. And the 1989 Loma Prieta quake gave rise to legislation empowering the California Department of Transportation to retrofit bridges and overpasses to increase their resistance to seismic shock.

The federal government stepped up its seismic research role after President Jimmy Carter signed the Earthquake Hazards Reduction Act into law in 1977. The legislation, which nearly doubled federal spending on earthquake prediction and related matters, established a multiagency National Earthquake Hazards Reduction Program (NEHRP). Direction of NEHRP is divided among four agencies: FEMA, USGS, the National Institute of Standards and Technology and the National Science Foundation.

President George Bush reaffirmed the government's commitment to seismic hazard reduction by issuing an executive order in January 1990 requiring that all new buildings constructed or leased by federal agencies meet "appropriate seismic design and construction standards." In coming years, the order is expected to prod states and localities to upgrade their own seismic safety standards for new construction. ■

CURRENT SITUATION

Focus on Northridge

For the past year, the Jan. 17 Northridge earthquake has been a prime focus of U.S. seismological research. Reasons for the interest are

National Geophysical Data Center

The 6.7-magnitude Coalinga earthquake in central California in 1983 caused the roof to collapse on this house in the downtown area, where 59 of 139 buildings collapsed or were heavily damaged. Total damage was estimated at $31 million. Newer buildings of reinforced concrete blocks or prefabricated metal had little structural damage.

Eastern U.S. at Risk, Too

People living east of the Rockies may have less to fear from earthquakes than West Coasters, but they don't enjoy blanket immunity. As the headline on a U.S. Geological Survey fact sheet put it, "Earthquakes Aren't Just in California: Washington, D.C.-Baltimore Area and Much of East Have Felt Tremors."

No place in the country, in fact, has undergone more topographic upheaval from earthquakes than the region centered around New Madrid, Mo. — a Mississippi River community near the point where Arkansas, Missouri and Tennessee meet. In the winter of 1811-1812, the area was shaken by three of the strongest tremors in the nation's history, as well as numerous smaller ones (*see p. 1114*). A major quake also struck Charleston, S.C., in 1886.

What puzzles seismologists about earthquakes in the central and eastern United States is exactly why they happen at all. The Pacific Coast states clearly are affected by the colliding oceanic and North American crustal plates, but farther inland the North American plate does not come in contact with other plates. Some geophysicists suspect that seismic stresses are somehow transmitted throughout the North American plate, reactivating long-quiescent, deeply buried faults in the mid-continental area.

Indeed, Western faults — such as the dramatic, 650-mile-long San Andreas fault — often are clearly visible at ground level, but Eastern faults tend to lay buried, even after a quake. Recent research on the New Madrid region, geophysicist Bruce A. Bolt of the University of California-Berkeley wrote, indicated that "faults under the Mississippi [River] . . . are deeply buried under river mud and marine sediments deposited on the floor of an ancient sea." [1]

Despite the geological differences between the West Coast and areas to the east, geophysicists and seismologists from the different regions have much in common. "We use a lot of research and information from people who visit here from California," says James Wilkinson, a mitigation specialist for the Central United States Earthquake Consortium, in Memphis, Tenn. "Their data are definitely transferable." In fact, he adds, "Many areas in California are geologically similar to ours," citing soil composition in the San Francisco Bay region and the Central Mississippi Valley as an example.

Wilkinson notes also that the East Coast as a whole is more at risk of a destructive earthquake than many residents think. "New York is due for one," he says. "You don't hear much about it, but New York is definitely due." Wilkinson adds that researchers "are just now reporting that the Appalachian Mountains are very active, and they don't know why. The activity extends from Birmingham [Ala.] to northern Georgia and on up from there. I think it's going to prompt further research in coming years."

[1] Bruce A. Bolt, *Earthquakes and Geological Discovery,* (1993), p. 119.

not hard to find. For one thing, Northridge was the first quake since the Long Beach, Calif., temblor of 1933 to occur directly beneath a U.S. urban area. Moreover, as a group of scientists recently noted, "It produced the strongest ground motions ever instrumentally recorded in an urban setting in North America and the greatest financial losses from a natural disaster since [the San Francisco earthquake and fire of] 1906." [21]

The quake struck at 4:30 a.m. Casualties included 61 deaths, more than 7,000 injuries treated at hospitals and at least 20,000 people left without shelter. Economic losses, including severe damage to three major freeways, have been estimated at $20 billion. And yet the earthquake's magnitude was "only" 6.7 on the Richter scale — not nearly strong enough to qualify as the 8-plus "Big One" some seismologists have been predicting for the area.

According to USGS official Kaye M. Shedlock, "an extremely critical lesson" of Northridge is that "the 'Big One' on the San Andreas Fault may not be the most damaging earthquake facing Los Angeles." Northridge showed, he said, that "a moderate-to-large earthquake on any of the faults underlying the city will result in large amounts of damage and the loss of life." Because the precise location of many Los Angeles-area faults is not known, Shedlock urged that "a geologic hazards mapping effort" be undertaken to help strengthen building codes. [22]

Actually, the Northridge quake caused "extensive but not devastating" structural damage, scientists from USGS and the Southern California Earthquake Center (SCEC) found. "About 3,000 buildings were deemed unsafe by building inspectors," they reported, "which is only a small fraction of the buildings in the region of strong shaking, and many of those are repairable." On the other hand, they noted that two-to-four-story residences built over carports suffered severe damage. Such buildings are common in Los Angeles and Tokyo, which also is seismically unstable. [23]

California, like most other states, has both a state building code and local building codes. Seismic provisions of the California codes typically are updated after major earthquakes in the state reveal shortcomings. "There's a general belief among [Californians] that our construction code is such that all buildings are earthquake-proof," said Thomas Tobin, director of the state's Seismic Safety Commission. "Nothing could be further from the truth." [24]

Seismologists say that much of the Northridge property damage, in fact, was non-structural and could have been prevented or limited. Such simple steps as "securing computers, water pipes, ceiling tiles and bookcases could save billions of dollars in future earthquakes." [25]

USGS geophysicist Jones notes that it takes little effort to anchor home electronic equipment to a desk or table with Velcro strips, bolt bookcases to walls with L-brackets, or install latches on kitchen cupboards. In the Northridge quake, she says, "a million households had home electronics thrown to the floor. If the cost of that equipment was several thousand dollars per household, the damage total starts getting pretty substantial in a hurry."

Fault-Mapping Project

Jones has been involved in a fault-mapping project that USGS and SCEC scientists began this fall. The aim was not to improve geophysicists' ability to predict individual earthquakes in Southern California but to arrive at more accurate probabilities of ground-shaking in the area over the next 30 years.

To this end, a research vessel operated by the National Science Foundation began firing short, underwater air-gun bursts on Oct. 13 about 25 miles off the coast. A network of some 200 onshore seismographs analyzed the resulting shock waves to form a more detailed image of the rocks and faults lying six to 20 miles below the Earth's surface, where the most damaging earthquakes usually originate.

Phase II of the mapping project, launched in October, involved detonating some 60 charges as far as 140 feet below ground between Seal Beach (near Long Beach) and Barstow (a desert community about 100 miles inland). Some 400 seismographs were installed to monitor the explosions, which were not big enough to trigger an earthquake.

The next step is publishing a technical report on the project findings in the *Bulletin of the Seismological Society of America.* The report also is being recast into non-technical form for structural engineers, emergency-preparedness personnel and the general public. Jones says the publication goal is 5 million copies by April.

A key section of the 32-page brochure will explain what individuals can do to mitigate the effects of earthquakes. "The traditional approach stressed first aid and storing emergency supplies of food and water," says Jones. "The underlying idea was that you're going to have to suffer, and then we'll help you pick up the pieces." Jones hopes the new brochure will "get the message across that you don't have to sit and wait and take whatever comes along. There's actually a lot that can be done on an individual basis to save money and prevent injury in earthquakes." Preventive measures include:

• Bolting the house to its foundation. Many California houses constructed before 1940 aren't bolted to the foundation. It costs around $2,000 — "not an insignificant amount," says Jones, "but much less than the cost of repairing major earthquake damage."

• Strapping water heaters to the joists of interior walls. "Water heaters are very top-heavy and tend to fall over and pull the gas line out of the wall if an earthquake shakes them," Jones says. Fires commonly result.

Other Regions at Risk?

As the USGS-SCEC project moves closer to completion, evidence continues to accumulate that the Pacific Coast between Northern California and Canada's Vancouver Island faces an earthquake hazard comparable to that along the San Andreas Fault. Until the mid-1980s, most geologists believed there was little possibility of a major earthquake in the Pacific Northwest (also called Cascadia). Since there was no historical record of a great quake in the region where the offshore Juan de Fuca plate moves under the North American plate, they assumed that plate movement was proceeding without the buildup of stress that causes faults to rupture.

That view came under challenge in

National Geophysical Data Center

The most deadly structural failure during the 1989 Loma Prieta earthquake in California occurred when sections of Interstate 880 in Oakland felll into the lower roadway, killing 41 motorists. Damage to the region's roadways was put at $1.5 billion.

Tsunami Power

An 18-foot-high tsunami wave (above) spawned by a 1946 earthquake in Alaska's Aleutian Islands strikes the island of Hawaii, more than 2,000 miles from the quake's epicenter.

The powerful surge of a tsunami wave rammed a plank through a truck tire during the 8.5-magnitude Alaska earthquake of 1964. The wave that struck the tiny community of Whittier reached more than 90 feet above the low-tide mark, killing 13 people and causing $10 million in damage, including the destruction of two saw mills, a petroleum tank farm and the Alaska Railroad depot.

National Geophysical Data Center

the mid-1980s, when Thomas H. Heaton of USGS and other geophysicists argued that the Cascadia plate boundary differs little in terms of earthquake potential from other subduction zones despite its quiescence in recent decades. Also at that time, the first evidence of past seismic activity in the region came to light. Scientists reported finding ancient coastal marshes and forests that had been buried as sections of the Cascadia shoreline abruptly sank, presumably in an earthquake.

Subsequent research has lent further support to the theory that Cascadia may be subject to infrequent great earthquakes. For instance, damaging earthquakes in Northern California in 1992 and in Oregon in 1993 revealed "the potential for significant seismic activity in this region," U.S. and Canadian scientists reported in September. They noted that several geological studies suggest that the region may have been affected by large earthquakes approximately 300 years ago. [26]

Indeed, *Science* recently presented evidence from a number of research papers that an earthquake occurred less than 1,100 years ago not far from Seattle. One finding suggested that "Seattle and Vancouver may be at greater risk [from a moderate-size quake] than anticipated, for such a shallow, nearby earthquake would be much more devastating than even a great earthquake on the distant Cascadia subduction zone." [27]

However, the Pacific Northwest is not believed to be in imminent danger. After analyzing the record of prehistoric earthquakes compiled by other researchers, seismologists Kevin Coopersmith and Robert Youngs of Geomatrix Consultants, a San Francisco engineering firm, concluded in July that each site along the Pacific Northwest coast experiences a great earthquake once every 450 years, give or take 200 years. They were unable to say, however, whether the entire region would be hit by a single, powerful quake or several smaller ones. [28]

Regional Groups Challenge Complacency

Regional organizations have done much in recent years to bring earthquake research to the attention of a broader audience. One such group is the 14-state Western States Seismic Policy Council (WSSPC), which sponsors annual conferences on seismic hazard mitigation. Upgrading state building codes is an ongoing concern.

The Nashville-based Central United States Earthquake Consortium (CUSEC), which monitors seismic activity in the New Madrid seismic zone, shares WSSPC's goals. However, the midcontinental U.S. tends to be complacent about earthquakes, says James Wilkinson, a CUSEC mitigation specialist. "We'll have a tremor in the 3-

Continued on p. 1122

At Issue:

Should the National Earthquake Hazards Reduction Program (NEHRP) be restructured?

yes

FROM *REPORT OF THE ADVISORY COMMITTEE OF THE NATIONAL EARTHQUAKE HAZARDS REDUCTION PROGRAM*, JANUARY 1993

The committee believes that considerable earthquake risk mitigation has taken place across the country in recent years, in part because of information, assistance and stimulation provided by the National Earthquake Hazards Reduction Program (NEHRP) and the program agencies. Each day, in many areas of the country, seismic resistance is incorporated into designs for buildings and other facilities, and siting decisions are made to minimize the adverse impact of natural hazards. Techniques for evaluation of existing buildings have been developed and are in use, and guidelines for strengthening existing hazardous structures are in preparation. . . . Promulgation of Executive Order 12699, requiring seismic design in new federal construction, has been an especially important step.

There is a widespread belief, however, with which the committee agrees, that progress in earthquake risk reduction is not proceeding as rapidly as society has a right to expect or as Congress, in enacting the NEHRP legislation, contemplated. This situation is due, in part, to the difficulty, if not the impossibility, within the existing program structure to formulate prioritized goals and to focus available funds and other resources on implementation. It is also recognized that a major impediment to adoption of earthquake mitigation measures is the lack of incentives in the program for state and local jurisdictions and for individuals.

Therefore, the committee recommends that Congress consider changes to the management structure and program-delivery structure of NEHRP that address the major issues outlined above. The most crucial changes to be considered should be (1) to create a single managing NEHRP entity with the authority and responsibility to (a) develop and submit to [the Office of Management and Budget] and the Congress a single program budget, and (b) manage and direct the resources of NEHRP into efforts that are strategically based, priority ranked, and problem focused; and (2) to establish incentives for adoption and enforcement of earthquake risk-reduction measures by state and local governments and by private organizations and individuals. . . .

Revision of the management structure, through the establishment of a single entity to manage and direct the program, will permit initiation of prioritized projects of problem-focused research particularly in the engineering and socioeconomic areas as well as enhancing NEHRP's already existing capability for that in the earth sciences area. To support the decision-making process of the revised structure, a knowledge assessment effort should be started with the objective of defining the strengths and weaknesses of our current data in all areas of the earthquake problem. Such assessment should be a continuing activity within NEHRP because it is essential for priority setting and program formulation.

no

FROM *U.S. GEOLOGICAL SURVEY RESPONSE TO THE REPORT OF THE ADVISORY COMMITTEE OF THE NATIONAL EARTHQUAKE HAZARDS REDUCTION PROGRAM*, APRIL 1993.

The advisory committee recommends a new management structure for NEHRP, in which a single management entity (outside the NEHRP agencies) would have authority for planning, budgeting, directing and evaluating the program components housed in each of the NEHRP agencies. Clearly, there are shortcomings with the current management. But would the single management entity proposed for NEHRP be effective? We believe not.

A major drawback to the proposed management solution is that it would impose a new layer of bureaucracy on the management of NEHRP. The structure of the NEHRP agencies will remain, and their rules and requirements will not disappear. The rules and requirements of the new management entity would be added on top of the existing bureaucracy. The proposed new entity would control the financial resources of the agencies but not their personnel resources. Effective program management is very difficult when authority over financial and personnel resources are vested in different entities.

Also of substantial concern is the notion that the new management entity would be the primary advocate of NEHRP with the end-users of NEHRP products and with government agencies, university and other researchers and practitioners. In our extensive experience working in the seismic regions, we find that users of our information want and need to talk directly to those who developed the information. Our staff is in daily contact, for example, with state and local emergency response groups, such as the California Office of Emergency Services, state geological surveys and regional groups, such as the Central United States Earthquake Consortium. . . .

Finally, the model of a single management entity external to the four NEHRP agencies departs from standard government organization and from normal funding and management practices. Accordingly, the model is likely to meet resistance from the Congress and the Executive Branch, unless it is vastly superior to conventional management models. The proposed entity would be in conflict with the relevant Cabinet secretaries and agency heads and [the Office of Management and Budget] in making decisions affecting agency programs. We question that the single entity model is superior to a participatory model.

We advocate that the management of NEHRP reside within the four principal NEHRP agencies, as it is now, but that the current management structure be strengthened to 1) address the concerns of the Advisory Committee regarding policy direction, strategic planning and program integration, and 2) harness more effectively the talents and resources of the NEHRP agencies. We propose a participatory management model that would counteract deficiencies in the current management structure.

Japan Waits for the Really Big One

Californians aren't alone in worrying about the "Big One" — a monster 8-plus earthquake. Japanese citizens inhabit a land even more subject to seismic disturbance than the U.S. West Coast. Indeed, one of the most powerful quakes of the century leveled much of Tokyo and Yokohama on Sept. 1, 1923. Since then, the country has maintained a vigil for hints that another killer quake was poised to strike the same area.

Thus far, signals have been mixed. Seismologists generally agree a catastrophic temblor is unlikely to return to the region again in the foreseeable future. They do worry, however, that a nearby undersea fault is overdue for rupture. Their concern centers on the Suruga Trough, about 100 miles southwest of Tokyo, which has not had a major seismic disaster since 1854.

Geography has fated Japan to be forever earthquake-prone. The country lies at the eastern edge of the Eurasian tectonic plate, which rubs against both the Pacific and Philippine Sea plates at a point less than 100 miles south of Tokyo. Japan, moreover, is often battered by tsunamis, the great sea waves that are triggered by quakes occurring far beneath the Pacific or along coastal areas on the other side of the ocean.

National Geophysical Data Center

Soil compaction caused apartment buildings to topple during the 1964 7.4-magnitude quake in Niigata, Japan, which damaged or destroyed more than 12,000 sturctures and killed 26 persons.

Japan was reminded of its seismic vulnerability Oct. 5, when a powerful quake measuring 7.9 on the Richter scale struck not far off the east coast of Hokkaido, the northernmost large island in the Japanese chain. Despite the force of the tremor, there were few casualties and little property damage.

However, a quake of that magnitude in the Tokyo area doubtless would have global economic aftershocks. The Great Kwanto Earthquake of 1923 caused an estimated 140,000 deaths and more than $50 billion in property damage (in today's dollars). At that time, it should be remembered, Japan was a poor, largely agrarian country, and the Tokyo-Yokohama region contained only a fraction of the current population.

Today, the sprawling Tokyo region is Japan's center of government, population, industry, finance and culture. Perhaps no other world capital, with the possible exception of Buenos Aires, so dominates the rest of its country.

"In order to re-create a situation in the United States similar to that which exists in Japan, where a quarter of the population and an even greater fraction of resources is concentrated around the capital," wrote journalist Peter Hadfield, "it would be necessary to envisage Los Angeles, New York, Chicago, Washington, Houston, New Orleans, Philadelphia and Detroit, plus the next 42-largest cities of the United States — whose combined populations equal one-quarter the population of the United States — with all their attendant financial, political, mercantile and petroleum-refining resources, grouped together into one continuous urban conglomeration. That is the proportion of Japan's resources now grouped into the Tokyo metropolitan area. Put *that* on top of the San Andreas Fault and watch the sparks fly." [1]

In short, said Hadfield, a major quake in Tokyo could spark a worldwide financial crisis as Japan liquidated its overseas investments to obtain capital for rebuilding. In March 1989, he noted, the Tokai Bank estimated that reconstruction costs after such a disaster could amount to as much as $850 billion. More recent estimates place the figure at more than $1 trillion.

Japan's monster quake, should it occur, could well be remembered as the "Biggest One."

---

[1] Peter Hadfield, *Sixty Seconds That Will Change the World* (1991), p. 170.

Continued from p. 1120

3.5 [magnitude] range, and people will feel it, but they won't take it seriously," he says. "That just creates a challenge for us to convince them that there really is a threat."

Persuading New Englanders that earthquakes pose a hazard for them presumably would require an even harder sell, since the six-state area has been free of major tremors for almost 250 years. [29] Nonetheless, the New England Seismic Advisory Council was formed in 1991 to promote earthquake awareness and mitigation. As with WSSPC and CUSEC, strengthening building codes is a key objective.

President Clinton reaffirmed the federal government's commitment to earthquake research when he signed a bill Oct. 19 reauthorizing the Earthquake Hazards Reduction Act for two years. Among other provisions, the measure required the four agencies running the program to assess the nation's earthquake-monitoring facilities and report the findings to Congress within nine months.

Technologies developed under the hazard-reduction program "were demonstrated successfully" in the Northridge earthquake, said Sen. John D. Rockefeller IV, D-W.Va., shortly before the Senate approved the bill Sept. 30. "Still, $6 billion was paid out by private insurers in addition to the $9 billion in federal assistance," Rockefeller added. "Due to the high costs of earthquake damage, it is in all our interests to continue supporting national research and technology efforts to mitigate [earthquake] losses." ■

OUTLOOK

New Policies Needed?

Geophysicists, insurers and public-policy makers are alarmed by evidence indicating that the economic cost of earthquakes is on the rise. For instance, projections released in August by Stanford University experts said the most serious quake expected in the next 50 years in three cities — Los Angeles, San Francisco and Tokyo — would cause half the casualties but almost twice the damage estimated earlier.

The Stanford projections suggested, in turn, that the philosophy underlying modern building codes may need re-examination. At present, such codes are designed primarily to save lives, not to limit damage, maintain functions or provide for easy repair. Now, however, structural engineers are considering ways of amending the codes to take more account of damageability and functionality issues.

According to Katherine A. Frohmberg, information systems manager for the National Information Service for Earthquake Engineering in Richmond, Calif., "What's being talked about is performance-based design, where the code allows a potential owner to decide whether he wants his building constructed just to life-safety standards, the minimum criteria, or to resist a large earthquake with no structural damage. The latter option obviously would cost a good deal more."

It follows that a performance-based code "would be arranged in steps," Frohmberg adds. "The more safety and the less structural damage you want, the more stringent the building-code provisions will be." A committee of the Structural Engineers Association of California is currently drafting a framework for procedures to assure predictable seismic performance. If all goes well, the procedures will be made part of the state's Uniform Building Code.

Determining the cost of each seismic-performance option in advance of construction will be difficult, says Frohmberg, because "it'll depend on the building's size and type of construction and, above all, on which seismic zone it's in. A very complex cost-estimation formula would have to be set up."

A basic technique for enhancing the seismic performance of a building, bridge or elevated highway involves isolating it from its base or foundation, thus reducing the ground motion transmitted to the structure. One widely used seismic-isolation system relies on layered rubber and steel pads with lead cores. When installed under a structure's supporting columns, the pads act as shock absorbers, dissipating the energy imparted by earthquake shaking.

The system was used in the construction of a University of Southern California hospital in downtown Los Angeles, completed in 1991. According to Ronald L. Mayes, president of Dynamic Isolation Systems of Berkeley, Calif., "This hospital functioned continuously throughout the 1994 Northridge earthquake and suffered no damage — not even a vase or a bottle in the pharmacy toppled over." [30]

However, seismic isolation and other performance-based structural techniques are not widely used in the United States. "Civil engineers in this

National Geophysical Data Center

A landslide destroyed at least 75 houses in an Anchorage subdivision during the devastating 8.5 magnitude Alaska earthquake in 1964.

FOR MORE INFORMATION

Center for Earthquake Research and Information, University of Memphis, Memphis, TN 38152; (901) 678-2007. The center seeks to enhance understanding of the geologic structures and earthquake hazards of the region's seismic zones.

Office of Earthquakes, Volcanoes and Engineering, U.S. Geological Survey, 12201 Sunrise Valley Dr., Reston, VA 22092; (703) 648-6714. The office conducts geologic, geophysical and engineering studies, including assessments of hazards from earthquakes, volcanoes and landslides.

Seismological Society of America, El Cerrito Professional Building, Suite 201, El Cerrito, CA 94530; (510) 525-5474. The society promotes research on seismology and encourages the adoption of earthquake-resistant construction techniques.

Southern California Earthquake Center, University of Southern California, University Park, Los Angeles CA 90089-0740; (213) 740-5843. The center has been mapping hidden faults that pose potential earthquake threats to Southern California.

country are very conservative," complained Shih-Chi Liu, director of the National Science Foundation's five-year research project to explore such construction strategies. Liu also decried the "lengthy and frustrating process" of changing building codes to embrace innovative technologies. [31]

But the situation may be changing, thanks in part to lessons learned from the Northridge earthquake. "Thus far, building codes have been designed only for life safety," says Frohmberg. "But now I think the feeling is, 'Well, we've pretty much accomplished that goal.' Now we have to deal with the economic cost, which is turning out to be far more than we imagined." ■

Notes

[1] National Research Council Panel on the Public Policy Implications of Earthquake Prediction, *Earthquake Prediction and Public Policy* (1975), p. 24.

[2] Quoted by Robert F. Service, "Hope Fades for Earthquake Prediction," *Science,* June 17, 1994, p. 1657. For background, see "Disaster Response," *The CQ Researcher,* Oct. 15, 1993, pp. 889-912.

[3] The seismologists were Allan G. Lindh and William H. Bakun of USGS in Menlo Park, Calif., and Thomas V. McEvilly of the University of California-Berkeley.

[4] The last previous earthquake in that size range to strike Parkfield occurred in 1966. The evaluation council's prediction assumed a 22-year interval plus a five-year margin of error. For background, see "Slow Progress in Earthquake Prediction," *Editorial Research Reports,* July 15, 1988, pp. 354-370.

[5] Yan Y. Kagan and David D. Jackson, "Seismic Gap Hypothesis: 10 Years After," *Journal of Geophysical Research,* Dec. 10, 1991, pp. 21419-21431.

[6] Quoted by Richard A. Kerr, "Weak Faults: Breaking Out All Over," *Science,* March 6, 1992, p. 1210.

[7] Corey S. Powell, "Fast Moves," *Scientific American,* August 1993, p. 22.

[8] *Report of the Advisory Committee of the National Earthquake Hazards Reduction Program* (NEHRP), January 1993.

[9] *Ibid.,* pp. 5, 7.

[10] U.S. Geological Survey, *Response to the Report of the Advisory Committee of the National Earthquake Hazards Reduction Program,* April 1993, pp. 4-5.

[11] Testimony before House Science, Space and Technology Subcommittee on Science, June 15, 1993.

[12] Leon Reiter, *Earthquake Hazard Analysis: Issues and Insights* (1990), p. 30.

[13] Charles Davison, *Great Earthquakes* (1936), p. 3.

[14] Bruce A. Bolt, *Earthquakes and Geological Discovery* (1993), p. 11.

[15] Quoted by Robert M. Hamilton and Arch C. Johnston, eds., "Tecumseh's Prophecy: Preparing for the Next New Madrid Earthquake," 1990, p. 12 (U.S. Geological Survey Circular 1066).

[16] A fault whose movement is predominantly horizontal is called a strike-slip fault; a fault with predominantly vertical movement is called a dip-slip fault. Along many faults, movement is both horizontal and vertical.

[17] Bolt, *op. cit.,* p. 72.

[18] Because the region was sparsely settled, only two deaths were attributed to the Fort Tejon quake, whose magnitude is believed to have been about the same as the 1906 San Francisco quake.

[19] Federal Emergency Management Agency, *An Assessment of the Consequences and Preparations for a Catastrophic California Earthquake: Findings and Actions Taken* (1980), p. 3.

[20] U.S. Geological Survey, *Probabilities of Large Earthquakes Occurring in California on the San Andreas Fault* (Open File Report 88-398, July 1988), p. 51.

[21] U.S. Geological Survey and the Southern California Earthquake Center, "The Magnitude 6.7 Northridge, California, Earthquake of 17 January 1994," *Science,* Oct. 21, 1994, p. 389.

[22] Testimony before U.S. House Committee on Science, Space and Technology, March 2, 1994. Shedlock is chief of the USGS Earthquake and Landslide Hazards branch in Denver.

[23] U.S. Geological Survey and Southern California Earthquake Center, *op. cit.,* pp. 394-95.

[24] Quoted in *The Washington Post,* Feb. 8, 1994, p. A6.

[25] *Ibid.*

[26] A.M. Truhu, et al., "Crustal Architecture of the Cascadia Forearc," *Science,* Oct. 14, 1994, p. 237.

[27] John Adams, "Paleoseismology: A Search for Ancient Earthquakes in Puget Sound," *Science,* Dec. 4, 1992, p. 1593.

[28] Bernice Wuethrich, "It's Official: Quake Danger in Northwest Rivals California's," *Science,* Sept. 23, 1994, p. 1802.

[29] The largest known earthquake in New England occurred in 1755 off the coast of Cape Ann, Mass., northeast of Gloucester. Seismologists estimate its magnitude at 6.0.

[30] Testimony before House Committee on Science, Space and Technology, March 2, 1994.

[31] Quoted by Corey S. Powell, "Shaking Quakes," *Scientific American,* April 1994, p. 113.

Bibliography

Selected Sources Used

Books

Berke, Philip R., and Timothy Beatley, *Planning for Earthquakes: Risk, Politics and Policy,* The Johns Hopkins University Press, 1992.
Berke and Beatley look at earthquake hazard-reduction programs in California, Utah and South Carolina to illustrate how communities in different parts of the country try to limit the risk of seismic destruction.

Bolt, Bruce A., *Earthquakes and Geological Discovery,* Scientific American Library, 1993.
Bolt, a past president of the Seismological Society of America, explains why earthquakes occur, how they're measured and how their destructive effects can be minimized. He also examines some of history's most famous quakes and summarizes the lessons drawn from them.

Hadfield, Peter, *Sixty Seconds That Will Change the World: The Coming Tokyo Earthquake,* Charles E. Tuttle, 1991.
The centerpiece of Hadfield's book is one of the greatest natural disasters of the 20th century — the earthquake that devastated Tokyo and Yokohama in 1923. Because the area has experienced no seismic event of similar size since then, some geophysicists feel it is overdue for another "Big One." If that happens, writes Hadfield, the economic consequences could be severe for the entire industrialized world.

Olson, Richard Stuart, *The Politics of Earthquake Prediction,* Princeton University Press, 1989.
Olson shows how political considerations can influence earthquake prediction. He presents the case history of a prediction (which turned out to be wrong) by two U.S. government scientists that a series of major quakes would strike Lima, Peru, in the early 1980s.

Reiter, Leon, *Earthquake Hazard Analysis: Issues and Insights,* Columbia University Press, 1990.
Reiter, a seismologist formerly employed by the U.S. Nuclear Regulatory Commission, describes the various types of earthquake ground movement as well as basic concepts of seismic-hazard analysis.

Tazieff, Haroun, *Earthquake Prediction,* McGraw-Hill, 1992.
Tazieff, former director of research at the French National Scientific Research Center, examines the mechanics of earthquakes and then discusses earthquake prediction and hazard-reduction measures.

Articles

Adams, John, "Paleoseismology: A Search for Ancient Earthquakes in Puget Sound," Science, Dec. 4, 1992.
Adams explains how the relatively new scientific discipline of paleoseismology — the study of ancient earthquakes — can add to the limited knowledge about U.S. earthquakes.

Bolt, Bruce A., "Balance of Risks and Benefits in Preparation for Earthquakes," *Science,* Jan. 11, 1991.
Bolt examines the difficulties of predicting an earthquake and of applying the knowledge gained after one occurs.

Reports and Studies

Office of Earthquakes and Natural Hazards, Federal Emergency Management Agency, *Report of the Advisory Committee of the National Earthquake Hazards Reduction Program (NEHRP),* January 1993.
The advisory committee created a stir last year by suggesting that NEHRP, divided among four agencies, is hamstrung by a top-heavy chain of command.

Subcommittee on Science, U.S. House Committee on Science, Space and Technology, *The Reauthorization of the Earthquake Hazards Reduction Act* (published proceedings of hearing held June 15, 1993).
Witnesses offer their views on the effectiveness of the federal earthquake hazard reduction program during its first 16 years.

U.S. Geological Survey, *Goals, Opportunities and Priorities for the USGS Earthquake Hazards Reduction Program,* 1992.
The federal agency chiefly responsible for earthquake research sets forth the objectives it feels need attention.

U.S. Geological Survey, *Tecumseh's Prophecy: Preparing for the Next New Madrid Earthquake,* 1990.
This study reviews the long series of earthquakes that struck the New Madrid, Mo., area in 1811 and 1812. It also describes the unstable geological features that triggered the year-long string of temblors.

U.S. House Committee on Science, Space and Technology, *Lessons Learned From the Northridge Earthquake* (published proceedings of hearing held March 2, 1994).
Government officials, business executives and academic experts present their views on the earthquake that struck the San Fernando Valley last January.

The Next Step

Additional information from UMI's Newspaper & Periodical Abstracts database

Earthquake Research

Coghlan, Andy, "Quake buildings keep their bearings," ***New Scientist,*** **May 15, 1993, p. 21.**
Earthquake engineers in the U.S. claim that buildings can survive massive earthquakes if they are erected on top of specialized steel ball bearings. The bearings absorb the energy of the earthquake and stabilize the building.

Davidson, Keay, "Earthquake research gets short shrift from feds," ***San Francisco Chronicle,*** **Feb. 20, 1994, p. B4.**
In a series on earthquakes, as California's quake activity increases and experts express growing fear of a geo-catastrophe, funding for the U.S. Geological Survey's earthquake research efforts in 1994 is dwindling. Reasons for the cash shortages are examined.

Green, Harry W. II., "Solving the paradox of deep earthquakes," ***Scientific American,*** **September 1994, pp. 64-71.**
Deep earthquakes should not, in theory, be possible, and yet they occur. New research reveals the cause of deep earthquakes.

Powell, Corey S., "Fast moves," ***Scientific American,*** **August 1993, pp. 22-24.**
The speed at which seismologists can analyze the abrupt shifts of faults in earthquakes is surpassing the swiftness of the shock waves. The advancements in seismic analysis are discussed.

Reich, Kenneth, "Experts say small quakes may warn seconds before big one," ***Los Angeles Times,*** **Dec. 8, 1993, p. A3.**
On Dec. 7, 1993, presentations at the annual meeting of the American Geophysical Union said the discovery that temblors in the 4 and 5 magnitude range occurred in seconds before both the Loma Prieta and Landers, Calif., earthquakes gives scientists hopes of one day being able to forewarn of big quakes.

Ruff, Larry J., "Learning from the whispers," ***Nature,*** **Aug. 12, 1993, pp. 576-577.**
The idea of earthquake interaction is an essential part of quake research. Scientists are presenting convincing evidence that the large Landers earthquake in Southern California directly triggered quakes in 14 different sites.

Earthquakes in California

Beroza, G., G. Carver, L. Dengler, J. Eaton, et al, "The Cape Mendocino, California, Earthquakes of April 1992: Subduction at the Triple Junction," ***Science,*** **July 23, 1993, pp. 433-438.**
The April 25, 1992, Cape Mendocino thrust earthquake demonstrated that the North America-Gorda plate boundary is seismogenic. The earthquakes that shook Northern California in early 1992 are studied.

Bock, Yehuda, "Crustal deformation and earthquakes," ***Geotimes,*** **June 1994, pp. 16-18.**
The crustal deformation of Southern California is constantly being monitored by a growing number of Global Positioning System (GPS) monitoring stations. The area is being monitored in an effort to find a relationship between plate boundary deformation and the occurrence of earthquakes.

DelVecchio, Rick, "Faults found in quake relief," ***San Francisco Chronicle,*** **March 3, 1994, p. A29.**
Earthquake housing relief in California is shortchanging those who need it most, according to a University of California-Berkeley study. Government aid goes most swiftly to occupants of single-family homes and last to people who live in multiple-unit housing.

Dietsch, Deborah K., "Earthquake intervention," ***Architecture: The AIA Journal,*** **March 1994, p. 15.**
The damage caused by the January 1994, Los Angeles earthquake proves the need for advanced seismic devices and testing methods for buildings, notes an editorial. Money and lives could be saved by investing in seismic research.

Goodavage, Maria, "Earthquake Study Reassesses Risk of Big One," ***USA Today,*** **Dec. 8, 1992, p. A3.**
The chances of the "Big One" devastating Southern California may be much lower that previously predicted, according to new earthquake findings.

Graham, David, "A closer look at the San Andreas fault," ***Popular Science,*** **January 1994, p. 31.**
Scientists hope to dig tunnels into the San Andreas Fault from a six-mile-deep borehole. It is hoped that study of the rocks and conditions in the fault zone will provide clues to the prediction and processes of earthquakes.

Horgan, John, "The threat of buried thrust faults," ***Scientific American,*** **April 1994, p. 113.**
Geologists say that hidden thrust faults may pose a greater danger to California's cities than the San Andreas Fault.

Macilwain, Colin, "Earthquake centre was victim of cash curbs," ***Nature,*** **Jan. 27, 1994, p. 308.**
On Jan. 17, 1994, the day of the Los Angeles earthquake, the NSF informed the Southern California Earthquake Center in Los Angeles that its annual grant will be in-

creased by $1 million in 1994. The NSF hopes that the increase will take the heat off charges that the center is badly underfunded.

"New peril posed by inactive part of quake fault," *The New York Times,* March 27, 1994, p. 23.

Seismologists now say an inactive section of the San Andreas Fault west of Bakersfield, Calif., may pose more of a threat than once thought. Known as the Carrizo Plain segment, the section 100 miles northwest of Los Angeles had been given only a 10 percent chance of producing a strong earthquake, but Lisa Grant, a seismic geologist, has discovered that the area had been more seismically active than previously thought.

Rose, Frederick, "Science: Beneath Los Angeles, more earthquakes are lurking," *The Wall Street Journal,* March 22, 1994, p. B1.

Scientists studying the devastating January 1994, Los Angeles-area earthquake are increasingly concerned about their data on what happened and on the movement of the earth in the area. They fear that the likelihood of a truly large earthquake in the region is increasing.

Sanders, Christopher O., "Interaction of the San Jacinto and San Andreas fault zones, Southern California: Triggered earthquake migration and coupled recurrence intervals," *Science,* May 14, 1993, pp. 973-976.

Two lines of evidence suggest that large earthquakes that occur on either the San Jacinto fault zone or the San Andreas fault zone in Southern California may be triggered by large earthquakes that occur on the other. The research evidence is presented.

Schiffries, Craig M. and Thomas L. Henyey, "A possible earthquake deficit in Southern California," *Geotimes,* June 1994, p. 4.

Although there have been some powerful earthquakes in the Southern California area in the past few years, researchers say there is actually an earthquake deficit in the area. They have found that the geologic record and the results from satellite geodesy show that there have not been enough earthquakes in the area to account for the rates of movement.

"Waiting for the earth to move," *The Economist,* Nov. 20, 1993, p. 100.

Seismologists from around the world gathered at Parkfield, Calif., in November 1993 to study a predicted earthquake. Parkfield has averaged an earthquake every 22 years since records began in 1857. On Nov. 14, 1993, a 4.8 Richter scale reading was observed in Parkfield.

International

Kanamori, Hiroo and Masayuki Kikuchi, "The 1992 Nicaragua earthquake: A slow tsunami earthquake associated with subducted sediments," *Nature,* Feb. 25, 1993, pp. 714-716.

Seismograms of sufficiently high quality are presented from the 1992 Nicaragua tsunami earthquake. It was concluded that the Nicaragua earthquake was a slow thrust earthquake that occurred on the subduction interface between the Cocos and North American plates.

Pendick, Daniel, "Slow-motion slip may drive tsunami surprise," *Science News,* Feb. 27, 1993, p. 135.

Seismic measurements taken during the September 1992 Nicaraguan earthquake offer evidence that tsunami earthquakes stem from a slow-slip motion between oceanic plates. The research is discussed.

"Science Times: Major Tokyo quake would cost $1.2 trillion, study says," *The New York Times,* Sept. 20, 1994, p. C9.

The economic damage that would be caused by a major earthquake in Tokyo could reach $1.2 trillion, enough to send tremors through global economic markets and disrupt the economies of other countries, according to a professor of civil engineering at Stanford University, Haresh Shah. The results of the study, not yet published, indicated that the predicted economic damage of earthquakes in Tokyo, San Francisco Bay and Los Angeles would be twice as great as previously estimated while the number of deaths would be cut in half.

Predicting Earthquakes

"Can animals predict earthquakes?" *Current Science,* Jan. 14, 1994, p. 14.

Scientists are studying whether certain animals such as clams, alligators and catfish can predict earthquakes. Each species exhibits different behavior patterns just before an earthquake.

Goodavage, Maria, "We Told You So, Calif. Town Tells Quake Predictors," *USA Today,* Oct. 23, 1992, p. A11.

The strong earthquake that geologists predicted could hit Parkfield, Calif., between Oct. 19-22, 1992, did not happen, and residents are not the least bit surprised. Since 1985, the government has invested $19 million in quake research in the town, and the warning was the first ever issued.

Monastersky, Richard, "Electrical clues precede some tremors," *Science News,* Dec. 18, 1993, p. 407.

Research on electrical precursors of earthquakes is discussed. Unusual changes in the Earth's voltage were detected in the weeks before the four strong earthquakes that hit Japan between 1991 and 1993.

"Unpredictable earthquakes," *Science Teacher,* March 1994, pp. 10-12.

New seismology research shows that large earthquakes occur at irregular and unpredictable intervals on a segment of an earthquake fault rather than breaking the segment periodically like clockwork. The implications of the research for seismologists are discussed.

Back Issues

Great Research on Current Issues Starts Right Here...Recent topics covered by The CQ Researcher are listed below. Before May 1991, reports were published under the name of Editorial Research Reports.®

JUNE 1993
Food Safety
Prostitution
Childhood Immunizations
National Service

JULY 1993
Electric Cars
Population Growth
Downward Mobility
Intelligence Testing

AUGUST 1993
Mental Illness
Bilingual Education
Foreign Policy Burden
School Funding

SEPTEMBER 1993
Suburban Crime
Public Housing
Supreme Court Preview
Immigration Reform

OCTOBER 1993
Airline Safety
Disaster Response
Science in the Courtroom
The Glass Ceiling

NOVEMBER 1993
Paying for Retirement
Charitable Giving
Privacy in the Workplace
Adoption

DECEMBER 1993
U.S. Vietnam-Relations
Learning Disabilities
Child Care
Space Program's Future

JANUARY 1994
Racial Tensions in Schools
South Africa's Future
Worker Retraining
Regulating Pesticides

FEBRUARY 1994
Prison Overcrowding
Water Quality
Religion in Schools
Juvenile Justice

MARCH 1994
Underground Economy
Education Standards
Gambling Boom
Private Management of Public Schools

APRIL 1994
Reproductive Ethics
U.S.-China Trade
Soccer in America
Talk Show Democracy

MAY 1994
Traffic Congestion
Women's Health Issues
Mutual Funds
Political Scandals

JUNE 1994
Education and Gender
Gun Control
Public Land Policy
Nuclear Arms Cleanup

JULY 1994
Dietary Supplements
Public Opinion and Foreign Policy
Crime Victims' Rights
Birth Control Choices

AUGUST 1994
Genetically Engineered Foods
Electing Minorities
Prozac Controversy
College Sports

SEPTEMBER 1994
Home Schooling
Welfare Experiments
Courts and the Media
Regulating Tobacco

OCTOBER 1994
Historic Preservation
Religion and Politics
Arts Funding
Economic Sanctions

NOVEMBER 1994
Sex on Campus
Blood Supply Safety
Testing Term Limits
Religion in America

DECEMBER 1994
Farm Policy
Arms Sales

Back issues are available for $4.00 (subscribers) or $7.00 (non-subscribers). Quantity discounts apply to orders over ten. To order, call Congressional Quarterly Customer Service at (202) 887-8621.

Binders are available for $16.00. To order call 1-800-638-1710. Please refer to stock number 648.

Future Topics

- ***The Future of Television***
- ***Treating Addiction***
- ***Child Custody and Support***

THE
CQ Researcher

PUBLISHED BY CONGRESSIONAL QUARTERLY INC.

The Future of Television

Who will deliver the video revolution if there is one?

Something new is coming to television: video on demand, video games, interactive shopping and a dazzling array of entertainment and informational services that viewers control from their own homes. The nation's cable systems and local telephone companies are in a high-stakes race to deliver this video cornucopia within the next few years. The country's second largest cable operator, Time Warner Cable, launched its first commercial interactive television service this month in Orlando, Fla. Meanwhile, most of the big regional phone companies are waiting for approval to build new video networks to offer "video dial tone" service for homes and businesses. Some industry experts, however, question whether customers will buy the new services, while public interest groups fear the costs may be passed on to local telephone customers.

INSIDE

THIS ISSUE

CQ Dec. 23, 1994 • Volume 4, No. 48 • Pages 1129-1152

Formerly Editorial Research Reports

THE FUTURE OF TELEVISION

THE ISSUES

BACKGROUND

CURRENT SITUATION

OUTLOOK

SIDEBARS AND GRAPHICS

FOR FURTHER INFORMATION

COVER ART: BARBARA SASSA-DANIELS

December 23, 1994
Volume 4, No. 48

EDITOR
Sandra Stencel

MANAGING EDITOR
Thomas J. Colin

ASSOCIATE EDITOR
Richard L. Worsnop

STAFF WRITERS
Charles S. Clark
Mary H. Cooper
Kenneth Jost

PRODUCTION EDITOR
Sarah E. Merritt

EDITORIAL ASSISTANT
Tonya Whitfield

GRAPHICS
P. Eloise Fuller

PUBLISHED BY
Congressional Quarterly Inc.

CHAIRMAN
Andrew Barnes

VICE CHAIRMAN
Andrew P. Corty

EDITOR AND PUBLISHER
Neil Skene

EXECUTIVE EDITOR
Robert W. Merry

ASSOCIATE PUBLISHER
John J. Coyle

MARKETING AND SALES DIRECTOR
Edward S. Hauck

The CQ Researcher (ISSN 1056-2036). Formerly Editorial Research Reports. Published weekly (48 times per year, not printed the first Friday of any month with five Fridays) by Congressional Quarterly Inc., 1414 22nd St., N.W., Washington, D.C. 20037. Rates are furnished upon request. Second-class postage paid at Washington, D.C. POSTMASTER: Send address changes to The CQ Researcher, 1414 22nd St., N.W., Washington, D.C. 20037.

The Future of Television

BY KENNETH JOST

THE ISSUES

Imagine you're home on a Saturday night with nothing to do — nothing but watch television, that is. But this is not your father's television. It's television of the future.

Click a button and the screen fills with a menu of options: entertainment, children's programs, shopping, video games. Make a selection and the screen fills with more options. Recent movies, listed by subject or alphabetically by title; favorite episodes from classic TV series; nature documentaries; cartoons; or a televised shopping catalog from one of the nation's leading retailers.

Click another button and the screen presents your selection, then and there. No need to wait for an appointed time for the movie to start — or go to the video store. No need to wait until the home shopping channel shows the item you want to buy, or brave the weather and traffic outside your home.

Until recently, scenes like these would have seemed like the stuff of science fiction. But some TV viewers around the country have already seen the future of television in tests being conducted by telephone and cable companies. And if those companies have their way, millions more will have the chance to watch, and interact with, this new wave of television within a matter of years, not decades.

On Dec. 14, Time Warner Cable, the nation's second-largest cable operator, unveiled its vision of the future in Orlando, Fla.: the Full Service Network with video on demand, video games and home shopping. "With digital interactivity, consumers are in total control of the programming they bring into their homes," declared Time Warner Chairman Gerald Levin.

Bell Atlantic, one of the seven regional phone companies created a decade ago in the court-ordered

breakup of American Telephone & Telegraph Co. (AT&T), is hoping to get regulatory approval soon to offer a similar service to thousands of its customers in Northern Virginia.

"I'll bring the movie theater into the home. I'll bring the retail store into the home," says Robert Townsend, director of marketing for Bell Atlantic Video Services in Reston, Va. "Eventually, I'll bring the workplace into the home. I'll bring the school into the home."

The world of television has already changed dramatically in the past 20 years. The era when the three commercial networks — NBC, CBS and ABC — had television all to themselves ended with the rise of cable television beginning in the mid-1970s. Today, viewers are accustomed to "channel-surfing" on cable systems that carry dozens of channels, including over-the-air broadcast stations as well as channels devoted exclusively to news, sports, music, old movies, TV reruns and shopping.

"Cable's objective was to add choice, and there is no question we were remarkably successful in doing that," says Stephen Effros, president of the Cable Telecommunications Association, a trade association representing smaller cable systems.

Now local telephone companies are seeking approval to build new video networks to deliver even more programming into the homes of millions of viewers. Roy Neel, president of the U.S. Telephone Association (USTA), the trade association for local exchange carriers, says that allowing telephone companies to offer home video services will give consumers "exponentially greater choices, probably at reduced prices because of competition."

But the cable industry and some consumer groups warn that the "telcos" will use their control of local telephone service to subsidize the new video services, soaking phone customers for billions of dollars and setting up unfair competition with established cable systems.

"The cost of local telephone service will be artificially inflated to help defray the cost of investment in the network in order for them to pay for the cost of video services," says Bradley Stillman, legislative counsel for the Consumer Federation of America. The organization has joined with cable groups in urging Congress and the Federal Communications Commission (FCC) to impose additional regulatory safeguards before allowing the telephone companies into the home video business.

Rich D'Amato, senior director for public affairs for the National Cable Television Association (NCTA), the largest cable trade group, says cable companies are concerned about unfair competition. "If you're able to use a revenue stream not associated with the product you're providing, and we are unable to do so, you have a tremendous advantage in being able to price the service," he explains.

Telephone industry officials respond that cable forces are merely trying to thwart competition. "This is a red herring being raised by a special

Viewing the Future of Television Today

Karl Willard and his family helped demonstrate the future of television last week by playing a game of gin rummy with the chairman of the world's largest entertainment company. The Willards played from a network control center outside Orlando, Fla., while Gerald Levin, chairman and CEO of Time Warner, was seated in a hotel ballroom a mile away.

The Willards are among the first customers for Time Warner Cable's Full Service Network, which debuted last week in Orlando for a crowd of 500 reporters, industry executives and guests. Levin showed off this 21st-century marvel by playing cards with the Willards on screen. Levin also demonstrated the service's "video on demand" component by using a remote control device to call up the Time Warner film "Wyatt Earp."[1]

Visitors to Bell Atlantic Video Services' (BVS) new production center outside Washington, D.C., can see similar demonstrations of interactive television. BVS publicists use an ordinary telephone to dial up a menu on the TV screen. The menu displays four choices: Entertainment, Learning and Lifestyles, Children's Programming and Shopping.

Reuters

Brad Willard, 12, of Orlando, Fla., holds Time Warner Cable's new remote control device during a Dec. 14 demonstration of the company's new interactive television system.

Navigate through the menu, make a selection, punch in a security number and the choice appears — in this case, the blockbuster film "The Firm." Punch one button to fast-forward past the credits. Punch another to freeze the Tom Cruise chase scene, or another to rewind and see it again. If the phone cord is accidentally disconnected, plug it back in, and the movie resumes right where it stopped. When the film is over, there is no trip to the video store — and the bill comes in the mail at the end of the month.

Elsewhere in the BVS facility in Reston, Va., a visitor sees the gleaming "video server" that feeds the network: massively parallel supercomputers that hold 360 titles now and can be expanded later. The two-story building also houses a digital production center, where engineers sit in environmentally controlled production rooms and convert recent films, episodes from classic TV series and the like into bits of digital video for multichannel transmission.

Engineers say the digital versions are as good as the original, and an untrained eye detects no difference. But video purists disagree. "None of the demonstrations that I've seen lead me to believe that what we're going to get is exactly in line with the hopes that the industry built up," says Lancelot Braithwaite, technical editor of the magazine *Video Week*. "There will be some picture degradation."

So far, BVS engineers have produced about 700 titles — from full-length films to half-hour cartoons. In Orlando, the Full Service Network opened with a library of 36 films. Increasing the inventory is one critical task for all the video-on-demand networks. A typical video rental store has upwards of 2,000 titles, although recent releases account for the bulk of the business.

The immediate task, however, is to get TV viewers accustomed to the idea of video on demand, home shopping and interactive video games and to find out what they will pay for the new services. In Orlando, a movie on the Full Service Network costs $2.95; three simple video games can be ordered for $1 a day. At BVS, the menu shows $3.25 as the price for a movie, but publicists say pricing has yet to be decided. Blockbuster video stores in the Washington area charge $3 for most films and $2.50 for recent releases.

[1] *USA Today*, Dec. 15, 1994, p. 1B; *Orlando Sentinel*, Dec. 15, 1994, p. A1.

interest group that would rather not have us in their business," says Eric Rabe, executive director for public relations for Bell Atlantic Corp. "We stand a good chance of providing competition for customers, and, of course, it scares the cable companies to death."

The looming competition comes at a time when both the cable and telephone industries face difficult challenges.

Cable companies are coping with complex price regulations Congress ordered in 1992 after a wave of public complaints about rate increases and poor service under deregulation.[1] Cable viewership has plateaued, and advertising revenue was hurt by the recession, although it is now back on the upswing.

The 1992 cable law also required big cable companies to make programming available to a fledgling competitor: the direct broadcast satellite (DBS) industry. The law has helped the biggest DBS operator — DirecTV, a Los Angeles-based subsidiary of General Motors Hughes Electronics — to win 250,000 subscribers since it began offering a 150-channel service nationally in October.

Local telephone companies are also contending with new companies that want a piece of their business. These companies — called competitive access providers or CAPs — offer discounted service to business customers by bypassing the local telephone network — and taking revenues away from the main phone companies.

In addition, cable companies themselves are trying to move into the telephone business. Time Warner Cable won the right to offer basic telephone service in Rochester, N.Y., earlier this year. "We want to get into the local telephone loop," says NCTA's D'Amato. "We see that not only as a lucrative business, but as a way of providing additional services."

Gerald Levin, chairman and CEO of Time Warner Inc. demonstrates the company's new interactive television system in Orlando, Fla., Dec. 14. At left is Jim Chiddix, a senior vice president for Time Warner Cable.

This competition for basic telephone service has intensified the desire among the seven "Baby Bells" to eliminate restrictions imposed on them with the breakup of AT&T. The consent decree that ended the federal antitrust suit against AT&T barred the newly created regional companies from offering long-distance service, manufacturing phone equipment or providing information services.

The companies have urged the federal judge handling the case, the FCC and Congress to ease those restrictions and let them move into new lines of business. The FCC handed the companies an important victory in 1992 when it adopted rules allowing local telephone companies to construct new video networks and operate them as common carriers for other programmers.

The so-called "information superhighway" bills considered in Congress this year would have gone further by letting phone companies provide video programming themselves over the new networks. They also would have eliminated the restrictions on long distance and equipment manufacturing. But some of the Baby Bells worked to help kill the legislation because of a provision in one of the bills, backed by the cable industry, that would have barred phone companies from video programming until there was free competition for local phone service.

Even without legislation, however, telephone companies and cable companies alike are busy testing ways to provide new television services. Time Warner's Full Service Network in Orlando and Bell Atlantic's video-on-demand service in Northern Virginia are among the two dozen or so tests of interactive television being conducted around the country. (*See map, p. 1134.*)

Meanwhile, five of the Baby Bells and GTE, an independent phone company, are awaiting action by the FCC on applications to build "video dial tone" systems in their service areas. * According to the Center for Media Education, a public interest group in Washington, the plans would serve more than 8 million homes — about 9 percent of U.S. homes with telephones. (*See chart, p. 1142.*)

So far, the FCC has approved only one video dial tone application, giving Bell Atlantic permission to build a network in Dover Township, N.J., a well-to-do suburb midway between Philadelphia and New York. But the FCC cleared the way for action on the other applications in October when it rejected pleas by the cable industry and consumer groups to devise special rules to prevent the phone companies from cross-subsidization before acting on the video dial tone applications.

In Congress and within the Clinton administration, sentiment is strongly in favor of easing the restrictions on telephone companies. Vice President Al Gore linked the legislation to his vision of an information superhighway connecting homes, schools, libraries, hospitals and workplaces to a dazzling array of information and communication services.

Some advocacy groups, however, question whether the industries involved really will use their new freedoms to produce that kind of communications cornucopia. Instead, they fear that telephone and cable companies alike will merely provide more home shopping and recycled entertainment programming.

"Their agenda is to maximize revenues and to give little back in the

* Video dial tone is the phrase used to describe the technology that would allow telephone companies to offer video programs over their lines.

Testing Interactive Television

Almost every major telecommunications company is experimenting with interactive television, which allows nearly instantaneous two-way communication. Most of the experiments are technical tests to see if the technology works. Many are also marketing tests to see if consumers actually want the new services, which may include video on demand, home shopping and interactive games. The map below shows the major tests in operation or under development.

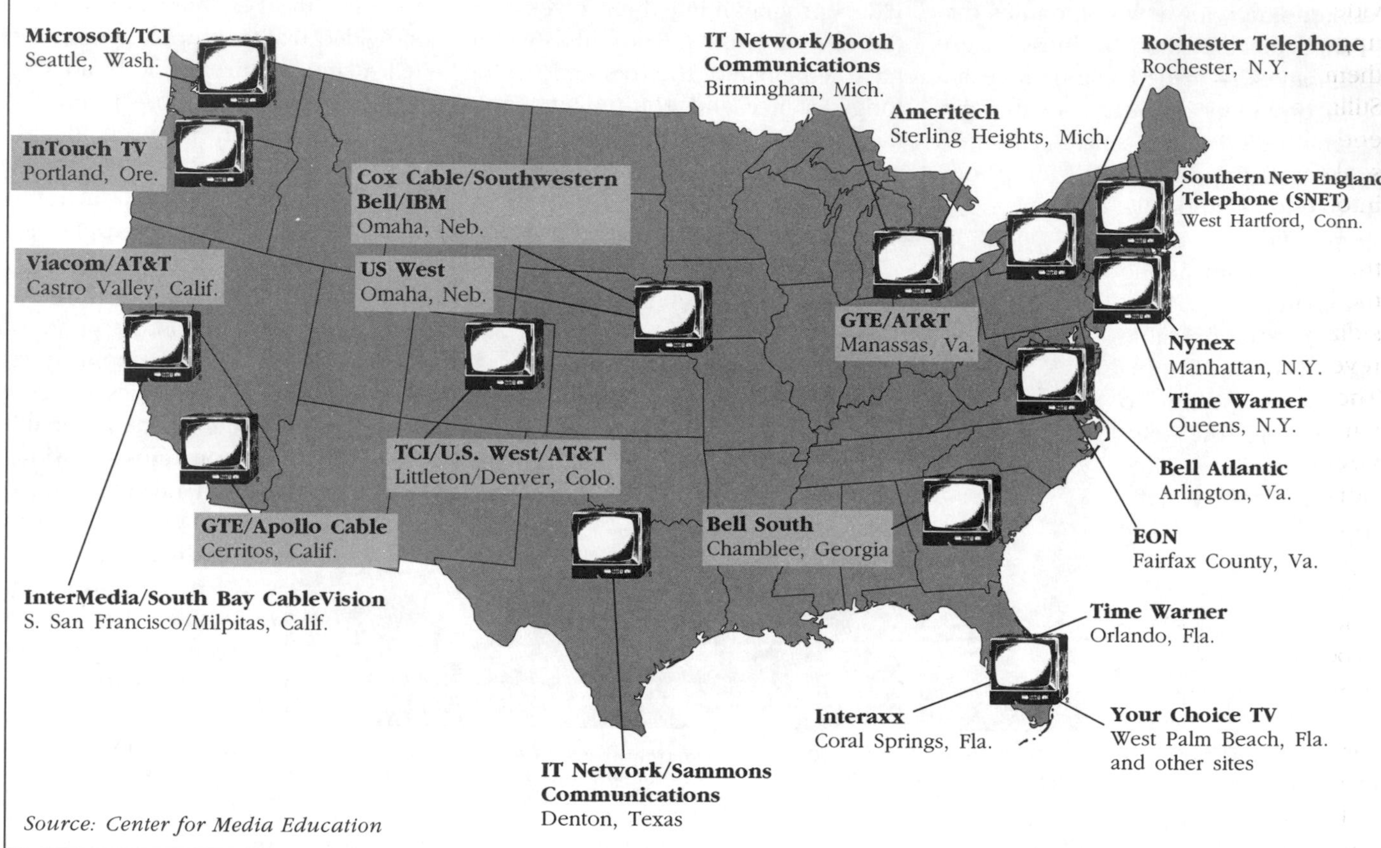

Source: Center for Media Education

terms of public interest," says Jeffrey Chester, executive director of the Center for Media Education.

The center joined with other public interest groups in supporting a provision opposed by the phone companies to require them to reserve up to 20 percent of the new video networks for public access. Even some industry observers who oppose that kind of regulation acknowledge that telephone companies may not bring about a television revolution overnight.

"We've been going through a cycle of hype and rediscovery of reality," says W. Russell Neuman, a professor of international communications at Tufts University and research fellow at the Media Lab at the Massachusetts Institute of Technology (MIT). "The new 500-channel universe will be mostly retransmission at different times of the day of the same kinds of programming that we saw in the four- or five-channel universe."

Industry officials, however, continue to promise a marvelous new television future if the economics and regulatory environment can be worked out. "The debut of the Full Service Network is a turning point for the communications industry," Time Warner's Levin said last week.

"The telecommunications industry is being revolutionized as we speak," says Bell Atlantic spokesman Rabe. "Who's going to be there first is a pointless game. We're all moving there fast."

As the rival industries move toward creating a new world of home video services, here are some of the major questions being debated:

Should Congress or the FCC tighten regulatory safeguards before telephone companies are allowed to provide home video services?

Telephone companies say they are ready to begin providing new video services as soon as they get a green light from the FCC or from Congress. But the cable industry, supported by consumer groups, wants to delay the new services until stronger safeguards are in place.

"You can't have a level playing field when one of the competitors has been a government-created monopoly for 60 years," says Effros of the Cable Telecommunications Association.

"We want to make sure that the video services pay for the network upgrades or the major portion of them," says the Consumer Federation's Stillman. Otherwise, he warns, "it will end up with the consumer being soaked so that the company can get into the video business."

The cable-consumer coalition asked the FCC for special rules to prevent the local phone companies from subsidizing the new video ventures with revenues from telephone customers. The cable industry asked Congress to bar telcos from providing video services until cable systems win permission from state regulators to compete in providing local telephone service.

"You need to let a competitor to such a dominant provider get up and running before you allow that dominant carrier to begin poaching into the new entrant's business," says NCTA's D'Amato.

The FCC rejected the plea for cross-subsidization rules but promised to examine the issue before acting on individual telco applications to build video dial tone systems. In Congress, last-minute lobbying by some of the Baby Bells over restrictions on their entry into video services helped derail communications legislation that had already been approved by the House and by a Senate committee.

Telephone industry officials argue that cable companies are merely trying to delay competition. "They are using every trick to keep us out of this business," says Bell Atlantic's Rabe.

He maintains that regulatory authorities have found no basis for worrying about cross-subsidization. The regulators are in a better position to judge whether there is a cross-subsidy than the special interest group, he says. As for requiring competition in local phone service before allowing telcos into video services, Rabe says state regulatory bodies are already moving in that direction.

Experts who have worked as consultants to the two industries differ about the risks of anti-competitive behavior by the telephone companies.

Bruce Owen, president of Economists Inc., a Washington consulting firm that has done work for the broadcasting and cable industries, has starkly warned that the telephone companies will crush their cable competitors. In a book on the economics of the video industry published in 1992, Owen said any competition between telcos and cable was "likely to be short-lived, ending in a monopoly by the telephone company, whether or not economically justified." [2]

Today, Owen still doubts that the FCC can prevent the telcos from cross-subsidizing the new video ventures. "The regulation of telephone companies engaged in cross-subsidization in the past has been a failure," says Owen, who worked on the antitrust case against AT&T as a Justice Department attorney in the late 1970s. "That was one of the reasons for the breakup of AT&T."

But Harry Shooshan, a partner in the consulting firm Strategic Policy Research Inc., which has prepared studies for the telephone industry, argues that telephone companies will be at a competitive disadvantage as they move into video services.

"The telcos have zero market share to begin with, and they will be competing with an entrenched monopolist, cable, and butting heads with a new industry, direct broadcast satellite," says Shooshan, who served as chief counsel to the House Communications Subcommittee in the 1970s. "If you place a lot of regulatory requirements on telco entry, then it seems to me you kill this thing in its infancy."

Should regulation of cable television be eased because of increased competition in video services?

As the cable industry braced for competition from local telephone companies, it also continued to complain about Congress' decision in 1992 to regulate subscriber rates and impose other restrictions on cable operations. Cable forces insisted the law had reduced the industry's ability to provide new channels or upgrade cable systems.

"It's certainly taken a bite out of revenues," says NCTA's D'Amato. "It's taken a bite of our ability to invest in new technologies, new services."

Nonetheless, cable operators have blunted the effects of rate regulation through a strategy called "retiering." Since the law provided for rate regulation only of "basic service," many cable systems shifted some channels from the lowest-priced package to a higher "tier" that was not subject to rate regulation. Thus, even though most customers saw basic rates fall as a result of the law, many others wound up paying as much as before — or even more — as cable systems revised their offerings.

In addition, the FCC last month gave cable systems freedom to raise rates when they add new channels. NCTA President Decker Anstrom said the FCC's move would provide cable systems "some much needed, although very limited, incentives for investments in programming." [3]

More broadly, however, Anstrom has said the cable industry wants to ease the rules for lifting rate regulation altogether. The 1992 law provides for deregulating a cable operator's rates if another multichannel provider — wireless cable, satellite broadcaster or telephone company — is available to 50 percent of households in the service area and attains a 15 percent market share.

In an interview in *Broadcasting & Cable* magazine, Anstrom said he believes the threshold is too high. "When a competitor enters a market, I suspect long before you lose 15 percent of your customers, you've begun to adapt in terms of offering

Set-Top Boxes: The Keys to the Future

First there were rabbit ears and rooftop antennas. Then came the cable converter box and the satellite dish. Now a new piece of TV-viewing equipment is coming: a set-top device that performs the functions of a cable converter and a personal computer.

"Right now, a cable TV set-top box is essentially a switching device," says Daniel Weitzner, general counsel of the Electronic Frontier Foundation in Washington. "In a more advanced environment, it's going to have to do more. It's going to contain the operating system of the interactive age."

The set-top box of the future will contain a computer to decompress the digital video signal that will be used for video on demand and interactive television. Viewers can also use the set-top box to navigate through entertainment libraries with hundreds of titles, browse through home shopping catalogs, play video games and send and receive messages from other subscribers.

Time Warner

The Home Communications Terminal built by Scientific-Atlanta and Silicon Graphics and the companion remote control device allow families to access Time Warner's Full Service Network.

This 21st-century electronic marvel is not in stores yet, though. "All the companies have made it seem as though the technology is already available and ready to be deployed," says Bruce Heiman, a Washington, D.C., attorney who represents Microsoft Corp., one of the many high-tech firms working on set-top box designs. "In many instances, perhaps most, this is not the case. The technology is at the lab or in the field."

Last week, two of Microsoft's rivals in this high-stakes technological race — Scientific-Atlanta and Silicon Graphics — did debut their digital set-top box when Time Warner Cable unveiled its interactive Full Service Network in Orlando, Fla. Families chosen by the companies to demonstrate the network described the box and companion remote control device as easy to use.

The companies need to do more than make the set-top box user-friendly, however. They also have to make the devices affordable. In Orlando, Time Warner customers are getting the equipment for free right now. The prototypes cost thousands of dollars to manufacture, but the companies hope to bring the price down to $300 or so with technological improvements and increased production.

Another issue is compatibility. Lawmakers, regulators and many industry observers say the set-top box needs to be designed to access any network — cable, telephone or direct broadcast satellite (DBS) — so that consumers do not need separate equipment for each. "If you think your VCRs are hard to program now, imagine having five of them," Andrew Lippman, associate director of the Media Lab at the Massachusetts Institute of Technology, told the House Telecommunications Subcommittee in February.

Industry observers also warn that a "closed system" would give too much power to the network operator. "If the network operator has total control over what the set-top box does and who gets to use it, then the network operator will really have bottleneck control over the whole interactive network," Weitzner says.

Lippman says the danger of a closed system has been reduced with the creation of an international council earlier this year that is trying to develop industrywide standards for video on demand. But Heiman, Microsoft's attorney, warns that setting standards now may hinder innovation. "The most important thing to do is to try to make sure the government doesn't prematurely choose a standard," Heiman says.

Meanwhile, Lippman cites another important development: the widespread deployment of digital set-top boxes for use with DBS systems. "That makes real all the stuff we in the lab are talking about," he says.

"By next Christmas, you'll see a lot of new things in your stores," Lippman adds. "Things will happen very fast because somebody's doing something, and they're succeeding."

better product, lower prices, better service," Anstrom said. [4]

Cable's consumer allies on telco issues part company on rate regulation questions. The Consumer Federation's Stillman says cable companies "have not been terribly hurt" by the cable law. "They're adding subscribers, and they're making money," he says. If cable companies' profits have declined since passage of the 1992 act, Stillman says, the reason is that "there was a determination that they were making excess profits as a monopoly at the expense of their customers."

The cable industry also wants to reconsider the provision of the 1992 law that guarantees direct broadcast satellite distributors access to cable programming. Congress imposed the requirement because of accusations that big cable companies that had interests in programming services and also operated local cable systems had refused to deal with their potential DBS competitors.

Supporters say the law has helped DBS establish itself as a cable competitor. "We have been encouraged by the beginnings of the competition from direct broadcast satellite, which is a direct consequence of the 1992 cable act," says Andrew Jay Schwartzman, director of the Media Access Project, a public interest telecommunications law firm.

But NCTA's Anstrom says DBS's new standing makes the program access requirement unnecessary — and unfair to cable operators that are not guaranteed access to exclusive DBS network programs.

"At a time when satellite services are delivering virtually every [cable] network . . . and when satellite firms have exclusive deals to deliver NFL [National Football League] game packages, isn't it time to reassess the laws on program access?" Anstrom asked in a speech to the Federal Communications Bar Association in October.

Satellite broadcasters, however, say it is too early to think about changing the law. "We have about 250,000 subscribers; the cable industry has about 60 million," says Jim Ramo, executive vice president of DirecTV. "There will come a time when we will be able to be considered an effective competitor in the media landscape. But until then, [the law] is a necessary linchpin to protect our business and to create competition."

Do consumers want — and will they pay for — expanded video services?

The companies that are ready to offer home viewers expanded video services such as video on demand and interactive television enthuse over the benefits customers will receive. Bell Atlantic Video says its video on demand service will offer viewers "the best of cable and the best of video rental stores." Time Warner Cable says its Full Service Network will "enrich customers' lives by providing them greater choice, control and convenience."

Company officials believe they can develop markets for these new services, but they acknowledge the difficulty in translating futuristic predictions into economically viable businesses. "Just when the money's going to flow, I can't tell you today," says Townsend of Bell Atlantic Video Services.

Townsend lists the problems that new video services have to surmount to be successful. Viewers must be convinced they are really getting a valuable new service. The price has to be competitive. And the service has to be easy to use — even for viewers who still do not know how to program their VCRs. "It's got to be intuitively clear to my 7-year-old kid and my 70-year-old mother," Townsend says.

For their part, cable industry officials say they expect stiff competition from the telephone companies. "There's no question that we think they're going to be formidable competitors," Anstrom told *Broadcasting & Cable*. "We would expect that as they build out their plant, they'll begin to take customers away from cable companies." [5]

But Anstrom said cable companies have some advantages. "We think we probably understand more about the television business," he said. And other industry observers note that telephone companies have traditionally been better at designing new products and services than bringing them to the market — as exemplified by AT&T's multimillion-dollar flop with the video telephone.

Moreover, some industry observers have questioned whether the public will find the new video services sufficiently attractive to pay for them on a long-term basis. Those doubts are reinforced by recent studies by groups outside the telephone industry.

The latest of the studies — a survey of about 1,200 cable subscribers conducted for Hewlett-Packard Co. — found that consumers were interested in video on demand and interactive television. But those surveyed said they were willing to pay, on average, about $29 per month for the services — around the current level of existing cable service. [6]

A survey by the Times Mirror Center for The People and The Press also cast doubt on potential consumer demand for new video services. The survey found that even though cable subscribers were somewhat more satisfied with television than people who received only over-the-air broadcasting, premium cable channels or pay-per-view services added very little in terms of consumer satisfaction. [7] "It's kind of like the Bruce Springsteen song — '57 channels (and nothing on)'," says Andrew Kohut, director of the media company-funded research center.

Telephone industry officials and many communications observers minimize these doubts. They say that consumers may be skeptical about a new service before it is on the market, but will buy it once it really is available. "It will probably be entertainment that drives the early deployment of the system, but once it's out there, there are going to be thousands of applications," says Bell Atlantic's Rabe.

Townsend is also confident that consumers will pay for the new services. But he acknowledges that there is no way to know in advance whether video innovators have found a viable economic strategy. "When will we know if we're right?" he asks. "After it happens. We never know where we're going until after we've been there." ■

BACKGROUND

Birth of Broadcasting

Commercial broadcasting began in the United States in the 1920s in a disorderly rush of entrepreneurship that broadcasters themselves asked the government to straighten out. [8] Pioneer broadcasters ranging from General Electric and Westinghouse to backyard tinkerers started up hundreds of radio stations. Secretary of Commerce Herbert Hoover tried to use the Radio Act of 1912 to prevent interference among stations, but courts ruled he had exceeded his authority under the law. Broadcasters asked Congress to step in.

The resulting Radio Act of 1927 created the Federal Radio Commission to issue station licenses, allocate frequency bands to various services, assign frequencies to specific stations and control station power. Seven years later, at the urging of President Franklin D. Roosevelt, Congress broadened the federal role by directing a renamed Federal Communications Commission to regulate broadcasting in the public interest. The commission was also given power over telephone and telegraph service.

Two networks had emerged to provide programs for this new medium. In 1926, the Radio Corporation of America, created by government charter seven years earlier to control U.S. patents for radio, gave birth to the first of the network giants: the National Broadcasting Co. With a distinctive three-chime identification, NBC began providing programs the next year through two networks: the "Red" and the "Blue" networks. A competitor was formed in 1927 — the Columbia Phonograph Broadcasting System, later renamed the Columbia Broadcasting System, CBS.

The early development of television also started in the 1920s. By the late 1930s, the new technology was being used for limited commercial purposes to broadcast baseball games, concerts and special events. But World War II interrupted the advance of commercial television.

With the end of the war, television was poised to grow as rapidly as radio had two decades earlier. But, again, the industry was moving faster than the government's regulatory machinery. The FCC received so many applications for TV licenses that it decided in 1948 to freeze the licensing process. Four years later, the commission adopted the channel allocation scheme that survives to this day: designating channels 2 through 13 for very high frequency (VHF) stations and creating room for an additional 70 channels in the ultra high frequency (UHF) portion of the broadcast spectrum.

Since receivers were not equipped to pick up stations in the UHF spectrum, the allocation scheme had the effect of limiting the growth of the new medium to the three or four stations that could be assigned to each viewing area without interfering with other stations. The principal beneficiaries were the three commercial broadcasting networks: NBC, CBS and ABC, which had been created in 1943 after a government antitrust suit forced NBC to divest itself of one of its two networks. Each of the three networks owned five VHF stations — the limit set by FCC rules — and they established affiliations with other stations in most metropolitan areas.

For the next two decades, the three networks essentially had television all to themselves. The FCC had reserved channels for educational use, but educational stations had little money for equipment or programming until Congress passed the Public Broadcasting Act in 1967. UHF stations also grew slowly until after Congress, in 1962, acted to spur their growth by mandating that TV receivers be equipped to receive VHF and UHF stations. And without a fourth network to provide original programming, the early UHF stations had little to offer viewers besides reruns and primitive local programming.

The FCC established a web of regulations over broadcasters, but the rules were weakly enforced. The commission had non-binding guidelines for programming and commercial limits that stations readily satisfied at license renewal time. Few stations were ever denied renewal or sanctioned for violating the more controversial rules.

Some public interest groups tried to put teeth into the regulations, but today even the architects of the earlier system pronounce it a failure. "It is a total failure. It is a charade," says telecommunications policy expert Henry Geller, who served as general counsel of the FCC from 1964 to 1970 and as head of the National Telecommunications and Information Administration under President Jimmy Carter.

Growth of Cable TV

From inauspicious beginnings, cable television has emerged in the past 20 years to become a major rival of over-the-air broadcasters. The credit for "inventing" cable TV goes to an appliance dealer in rural Pennsylvania who, in the late 1940s, built a large antenna on a mountaintop and then connected it to homes by a network of wires — all for the purpose of boosting his sales of TV receivers in an area with no local station at the time.[9]

Through the 1950s, this applied technology — called "community antenna television," or CATV — spread slowly, bringing TV to unserved communities and improving reception in others. Then in 1961, a cable operator in San Diego had the idea of bringing in TV stations from another city, Los Angeles. For the first time, cable had a service to offer in cities already served by three or more stations.

Beginning in the 1950s, troubled broadcasters asked the FCC to regulate the emerging industry. Initially, the FCC said no, but in 1965 the commission adopted its first cable rules limiting the importation of distant signals in order to protect local broadcasters from competition.

The Supreme Court upheld the rules in 1968, saying they were "reasonably ancillary" to the FCC's regulatory power

Continued on p. 1140

Chronology

1900-1950 ***Telephone moves from novelty to necessity under universal service philosophy of Bell system. Broadcasting is born with creation of national radio networks and establishment of first local television stations.***

1900
The Bell telephone company emerges after several reorganizations under the control of a national holding company: American Telephone and Telegraph Co. — now AT&T.

1927
Experimental television program is sent by wire between New York and Washington by Bell Telephone Laboratories.

1934
Congress creates the Federal Communications Commission (FCC) to regulate interstate communications, including broadcasting and telephone service.

April 30, 1941
FCC authorizes commercial TV operation to start the following July 1 on 10 commercial stations.

Sept. 30, 1948
FCC freezes new television licensing because of flood of applications.

—— • ——

1950-1970

Broadcasting matures, while cable television develops as a means to improve reception of local TV stations. Telephones and televisions become virtually universal.

April 14, 1952
FCC lifts freeze on television licenses, approving plan for 12 VHF channels and 70 UHF channels.

1961
San Diego cable operator is first to import television signals from another city — Los Angeles — for distribution to subscribers.

1965
FCC issues first rules regulating cable television, restricting importation of distant signals to promote development of UHF stations.

—— • ——

1970s ***Cable television grows, as new services are offered and FCC eases regulations. AT&T faces competition in long-distance service.***

Nov. 20, 1974
U.S. government files antitrust suit against AT&T, claiming company monopolizes long-distance service and phone equipment manufacturing.

Sept. 30, 1975
Home Box Office (HBO), a subsidiary of Time Inc., begins distribution of movies for cable systems by satellite.

—— • ——

1980s ***Cable television expands to reach most households. Broadcasters lose audiences to cable and face financial woes. Federal antitrust suit leads to breakup of AT&T.***

Jan. 8, 1982
AT&T agrees to settle federal antitrust suit by spinning off local exchange companies. The so-called Baby Bells come into being on Jan. 1, 1984, under court-ordered constraints against providing information services.

Oct. 11, 1984
Congress approves Cable Communications Policy Act, deregulating cable rates. Act codifies the FCC's rule prohibiting telephone companies from operating cable systems within their service areas.

—— • ——

1990s ***Telephone companies press for freedom to provide home video services. Broadcasters and cable operators brace for entry of new competitors.***

July 25, 1991
Federal judge modifies the 1982 consent decree governing the breakup of AT&T to allow regional Bell companies to offer information services.

July 16, 1992
FCC approves video dial tone rules, permitting local telephone companies to operate video delivery system on common carrier basis.

Oct. 5, 1992
Congress enacts cable reregulation bill. Telco-cable crossownership ban is retained.

Aug. 24, 1993
Federal court in Virginia clears way for Bell Atlantic's C&P Telephone Co. to provide television programming within its Alexandria, Va., service area.

Oct. 20, 1994
FCC reaffirms video dial tone rules, rejecting pleas by cable industry to slow telcos' entry into home video service.

Broadcasters Say They Can Be Part of a 'Multichannel' World

With all the attention focused on exotic television services being developed by cable systems and telephone companies, the nation's broadcasters feel more than a little neglected. Broadcasters say they can help bring the multichannel world into the home, too, but they want Congress first to change the law to give them more freedom in using parts of the broadcast spectrum.

A controversial provision included in telecommunications legislation considered in the House and the Senate last year would allow TV stations to provide additional services over their current frequencies or over a portion of the spectrum that has been reserved for high-definition television. [1]

The National Association of Broadcasters (NAB), which lobbied for the provision, said TV stations could use digital technology to give viewers expanded news coverage or targeted information such as local school closings. "Once digital transmission of broadcasting occurs, we could have minicable systems," says John Abel, the NAB's executive vice president of operations.

The broadcasters' provision drew little attention during the legislative process last year. But a public interest lobbyist, Andrew Jay Schwartzman of the Media Access Project, calls it a "greedy spectrum grab."

"They want to take a large chunk of spectrum that was kept fallow for high-definition television, and they want permission to utilize it for all manner of other services, many of them revenue-generating, non-broadcast services," Schwartzman says. "They don't want to pay what other people are paying for spectrum, and they do not want to compete with any other potential applicants for the spectrum by auction or otherwise."

Abel responds tartly: "I'm surprised that Mr. Schwartzman doesn't recognize that we can broadcast even more free to the public than we have in the past."

The debate over the spectrum flexibility issue comes when broadcast regulatory issues have all but disappeared. In the 1980s, the Federal Communications Commission (FCC) largely deregulated commercial broadcasting. It permitted postcard renewal of broadcast licenses, repealed rules limiting the sale of broadcast properties and eliminated the fairness doctrine, which required balance in coverage of public issues.

The broadcasting industry also rebounded after some difficult financial times in the mid-1980s as the networks lost audiences to cable. Nonetheless, broadcasters have been left out of the talk about video on demand and interactive television even though broadcasting is what most people watch most of the time today.

The three major broadcasting networks, which used to control about 98 percent of prime-time viewing, still have 63 percent of that audience. The most popular single cable channel — the Turner Broadcasting System (TBS) — has only a 3.8 percent share of overall TV viewing. [2]

Abel also notes that broadcasting is more widespread than cable. About 98 percent of U.S. households have television sets, but only 63 percent have cable. TV is also more universal than telephones, which are found in only 94 percent of homes.

Broadcasters have had a difficult relationship with cable. They tried to stifle it with regulation from the 1950s through the '70s, but lost that battle by the '80s. Then when Congress reregulated cable in 1992, broadcasters won enactment of two provisions that required cable operators either to carry all local TV stations for free or to pay for using their signal -- at the broadcaster's option.

The cable industry demonstrated its enhanced clout, however, by simply refusing to pay for retransmission of broadcast signals. The three networks all caved in, agreeing to use of their signals for no monetary compensation. Meanwhile, the cable industry challenged the "must-carry" provision in court. In June, the U.S. Supreme Court ordered a lower federal court to reconsider its decision upholding the law.

So far, broadcasters say they have no problem with telephone companies getting into the video business — in part because telephone companies plan to include broadcast stations in their services. "They knew that by saying that, they would get our support," Abel says.

But there could be a regulatory hurdle to the telephone companies' so-called "will carry" plan. The FCC has asked for comment on whether preferential access for broadcasters would violate the rules requiring telephone companies to operate as common carriers and serve programmers on a neutral basis.

However that issue is resolved, broadcasters are trying to emphasize that the future of television includes wireless as well as wire-line delivery systems. "This country is being brainwashed that the information highway is only wire-line," says Abel. "That's one model, and it's going to be there, but broadcasting is a better model."

[1] For background, see "A High-Tech, High Stakes HDTV Gamble," *Editorial Research Reports,* Feb. 17, 1989, pp. 89-103.

[2] A.C. Nielsen data for third quarter, 1994, cited in *The Wall Street Journal,* Nov. 29, 1994, p. B1.

Continued from p. 1138

over broadcasting. Four years later, the justices upheld FCC rules that imposed public interest rules on cable systems, including a requirement that some channels be reserved for public, educational or governmental uses.

Cable television grew slowly, partly because of the regulatory constraints and also because of economic factors: high capital costs and low demand. Then, in 1975, Home Box Office, a fledgling subsidiary of Time Inc., began distributing programming of its own via satellite. Other "premium cable" services followed, and cable suddenly became a more attractive service. By the early 1980s, most big cities were either wired or considering applications for franchises for the right to build cable systems.

By the late 1970s, the FCC had begun to loosen its regulation of cable. But the local franchising process proved to be more difficult for the still infant industry. Before granting franchises, local governments typically set the rates cable operators could charge subscribers, imposed some service and programming obligations and required the payment of an often hefty franchising fee. For relief, the cable industry turned to Congress, which responded in 1984 by ordering the deregulation of rates beginning in 1987. The Cable Communications Policy Act also limited franchising fees to 5 percent of revenues and gave cable operators procedural rights at franchise renewal time.

Predictably, cable rates jumped after 1987. The cable industry said it used the new moneys to improve service and expand programming. In fact, cable systems were offering more and more channels, including some original programming as well as a widening variety of movies, TV reruns, music, sports, news and public affairs and educational programming. Many customers, however, saw the bigger monthly cable bills as evidence that they being gouged by a deregulated monopoly.

After several years of lobbying, Congress decided in 1992 to reregulate cable rates by enacting, over President George Bush's veto, the Cable Television Consumer Protection and Competition Act. In addition to directing the FCC to regulate cable rates, the act contained the program-access provision to benefit satellite broadcasters and a "must-carry" provision requiring cable operators to carry local TV stations. Broadcasters worried that cable systems could use their "bottleneck" powers to black out TV stations that competed with cable for viewers and ad dollars.

The cable industry worked to avoid the act's strictures. The "retiering" strategy protected cable operators from sharp revenue losses. And in response to complaints that the regulations discouraged systems from adding new channels, the FCC last month agreed to let cable operators raise rates by up to $1.50 per month for six new channels.

Cable companies also sought to undo the "must-carry" provision with a federal court suit attacking it as a violation of their First Amendment rights. A three-judge federal court upheld the law in 1993, but the Supreme Court in June ordered the panel to re-examine the justifications Congress gave for passing the law. The high court's decision handed cable an important legal victory. The justices said that cable was not subject to the same kind of regulation as broadcasting since the rationale for regulating broadcasters — spectrum scarcity — did not apply to cable operators. [10]

'Telcos' Enter the Fray

While the cable industry fought with broadcasters in court, a more serious battle was looming in the marketplace with a new competitor: the telephone industry. Experts and officials across the political spectrum were hailing the telephone companies as the agents of wider competition and expanded choice in telecommunications. The cable industry, which had built itself up by taking away viewers from the giant TV networks, now faced competition from an industry with even more daunting financial resources, technological expertise and political clout.

The telephone companies clamoring to provide home video services in the 1990s had been born 10 years earlier in the biggest corporate restructuring in U.S. history: the court-ordered breakup of AT&T. [11]

Television was far from anyone's mind when the Justice Department first moved against AT&T in 1974. A small company called Microwave Communications Inc. — now MCI — was trying to break into the long-distance telephone business, but facing stiff resistance from AT&T. MCI mapped out a private antitrust lawsuit and, in 1973, also pressed its case on a lawyer in the department's antitrust division, Philip Verveer. After an investigation, Verveer recommended filing an antitrust suit seeking the dismantling of AT&T. In November 1974, the suit was approved by Attorney General William Saxbe, who had been appointed near the end of the Watergate scandal and carried over by President Gerald R. Ford.

In settling the suit eight years later, AT&T gave up its local operating companies valued at $80 billion — about two-thirds of the corporate giant's overall worth. AT&T kept the long-distance business and planned to get into other, unregulated lines of business, such as computers. For their part, the seven reorganized "regional Bell operating companies" continued largely as regulated monopoly local telephone carriers. The consent decree agreed to by the government and AT&T prohibited the Baby Bells from manufacturing telephone equipment, providing long-distance service or getting into information services.

The Baby Bells quickly began to chafe under the strictures. They pressed Congress and federal Judge Harold Greene, who was overseeing the implementation of the decree, for permission to get into some of the prohibited businesses. But Congress could not agree on legislation, and Greene generally resisted easing the consent decree.

In April 1990, however, the federal appeals court in Washington effectively forced Greene to reverse his refusal to let the Baby Bells into some lines of information services. Greene reluctantly gave way on the issue in July 1991, but stayed the ruling pending an appeal. In October, the appeals court dissolved

Video Dial Tone Applications

GTE and five regional telephone companies — Ameritech, Bell Atlantic, Nynex, Pacific Telesis and US West — have filed applications with the Federal Communications Commission to provide video programs over their phone lines on a permanent basis. If approved, these plans would serve more than 8 million homes — about 9 percent of the homes in the United States with telephones.

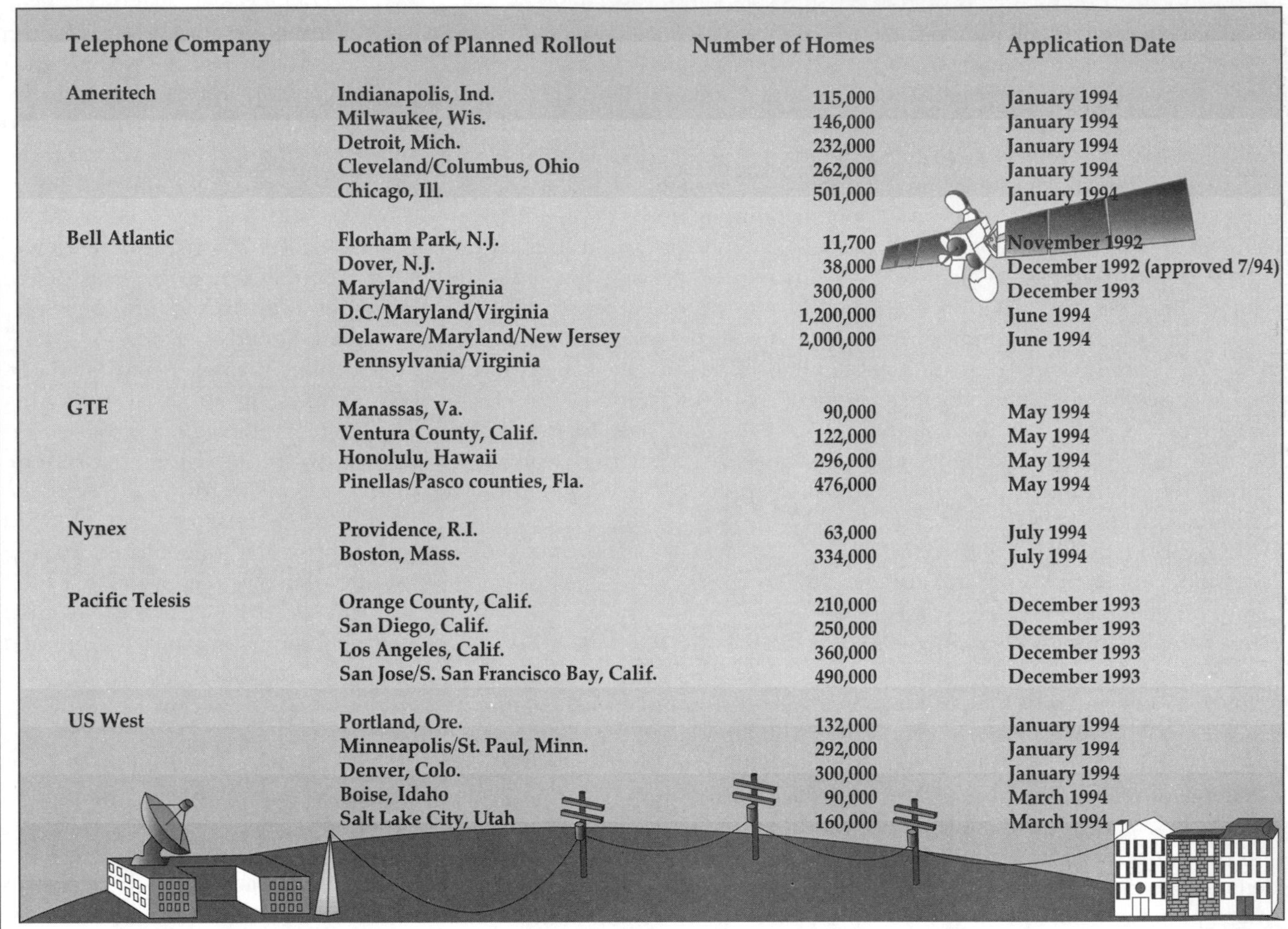

Telephone Company	Location of Planned Rollout	Number of Homes	Application Date
Ameritech	Indianapolis, Ind.	115,000	January 1994
	Milwaukee, Wis.	146,000	January 1994
	Detroit, Mich.	232,000	January 1994
	Cleveland/Columbus, Ohio	262,000	January 1994
	Chicago, Ill.	501,000	January 1994
Bell Atlantic	Florham Park, N.J.	11,700	November 1992
	Dover, N.J.	38,000	December 1992 (approved 7/94)
	Maryland/Virginia	300,000	December 1993
	D.C./Maryland/Virginia	1,200,000	June 1994
	Delaware/Maryland/New Jersey Pennsylvania/Virginia	2,000,000	June 1994
GTE	Manassas, Va.	90,000	May 1994
	Ventura County, Calif.	122,000	May 1994
	Honolulu, Hawaii	296,000	May 1994
	Pinellas/Pasco counties, Fla.	476,000	May 1994
Nynex	Providence, R.I.	63,000	July 1994
	Boston, Mass.	334,000	July 1994
Pacific Telesis	Orange County, Calif.	210,000	December 1993
	San Diego, Calif.	250,000	December 1993
	Los Angeles, Calif.	360,000	December 1993
	San Jose/S. San Francisco Bay, Calif.	490,000	December 1993
US West	Portland, Ore.	132,000	January 1994
	Minneapolis/St. Paul, Minn.	292,000	January 1994
	Denver, Colo.	300,000	January 1994
	Boise, Idaho	90,000	March 1994
	Salt Lake City, Utah	160,000	March 1994

Source: Center for Media Education

the stay — clearing the way for the Baby Bells to offer information services.

The ruling had no effect on one major curb on the Baby Bells: a statutory ban on a telephone company providing video services within its service area. The FCC had first banned telephone companies from owning cable systems in 1970 out of fear that telcos would refuse to let a competing cable system use telephone poles to hang its wires. Congress effectively codified the ban in its 1984 cable deregulation act, aiming to prevent discrimination against cable systems and also to promote diversity in media ownership.

By the late 1980s, communications policy-makers in Congress and in the Reagan and Bush administrations were beginning to advocate allowing telephone companies to provide cable services on a common carrier basis. In 1991, the FCC proposed rules to allow telcos to provide a so-called "video dial tone" and asked for comment on permitting phone companies to engage in their own video programming, too. The commission adopted the video dial tone rules in June 1992 and at the same time recommended to Congress that the cross-ownership ban be repealed.

When Congress failed to act by year's end, Bell Atlantic, one of the most aggressive of the Baby Bells in entering new lines of business, decided to contest the cross-ownership ban in court. After being turned down for an application to operate a cable system in Alexandria, Va., the Washington-area C&P Telephone Co. asked a federal judge to rule that the ban on cable service violated the First Amendment. None of the other Bell companies joined the suit. But in August 1993 Judge T. S. Ellis agreed.

In his ruling, Ellis said the absolute bar against telephone companies' providing video programming in their service areas went further than necessary to prevent discriminatory practices against cable systems or to encourage diversity in media ownership. The ruling paved the way for Bell Atlantic to set up full-fledged competitors for cable systems throughout the mid-Atlantic region. While the government said it would appeal the ruling, other Bell companies decided to file similar suits.

By late 1994, four other federal courts had issued similar rulings in suits filed by other Baby Bells: Ameritech, Bell South, Nynex and US West. And in November, the federal appeals court in Richmond, Va., upheld Ellis' original ruling in Bell Atlantic's case. The legal barriers to competition between telcos and cable had fallen. Now two industries were poised to compete in bringing the multichannel TV world into American living rooms.

Technology Moves On

Technological advances also played a major part in increasing the number of choices viewers were being given since the 1970s. The capacity on cable systems grew to 20 channels in the 1960s and to 100 or more channels in the '70s through improvements in the basic network technology of coaxial copper wire. The future world of 500 channels or more depends on two new technologies: fiber optics and digital television.

Fiber optics permits the transmission of enormous amounts of information by sending a laser beam over a hair-thin fiber made of the purest glass. Alexander Graham Bell had explored the use of light as a transmitting medium as early as 1880. But it was not until 1970 that the New York-based company Corning Glass successfully demonstrated the technology.

Fiber offers a number of advantages over copper wire. It uses a cheaper raw material (sand), is easier to maintain and is more secure. Most importantly, fiber offers vastly more bandwidth. John Malone, chief executive of TCI, the nation's largest cable company, told a cable trade show in late 1990 that the use of fiber would permit 200-channel systems by the year 2000. [12]

Malone claimed that cable would be first among its competitors to use fiber to the fullest. But telephone companies were not standing still. Some of the Baby Bells were rapidly installing optic fiber for local exchange service. And some policy-makers favored giving the local telephone companies greater incentives, through accelerated depreciation, to replace existing copper wire networks with optic fiber precisely to improve their competitive position against cable.

Digital television offers an even greater potential for increased signal capacity for cable or telephone video providers. Over-the-air broadcasters also can use digitization to send more signal over existing frequencies.

As John Heilemann of *The Economist* explained in a comprehensive report on the future of television earlier this year, television currently uses analogue signals — continuous electrical waves that directly simulate the characteristics of their source. A digital signal consists instead of bits of information, represented by ones or zeros. Digitization has already transformed the music business with compact discs. Now, advocates of digital television say, video can have the same distortion-free quality. [13]

More important, digital signals can be compressed to permit more information to be transmitted over whatever medium is chosen — copper wire, optic fiber or broadcast frequency. General Instrument Corp., the Chicago telecommunications equipment manufacturer that achieved the major breakthrough in digital compression in June 1990, says the technology allows 10 television programs to be carried simultaneously over a single channel. [14] In December 1992, General Instrument reached an agreement with cable giant TCI that envisioned deployment of digital television in 1 million American homes beginning this year.

Digital signals held out the additional prospect of opening up the era of interactive television. A TV viewer equipped with a computer can capture the digital signal and transform it — deleting objectionable scenes from a film or combining segments from different programs.

By 1992, the futuristic predictions were the talk of the telecommunications industries. But even as the "500-channel" world beckoned technologists and executives, many people in and around the industry were raising questions.

"There is no crying demand from consumers for additional services and interactive TV right now," Joseph Segal, founder of the QVC shopping network, told *The Wall Street Journal*. [15] Visionaries in both the cable and telephone industries were convinced otherwise. But they had many obstacles — technological, economic and political — to overcome before they could bring the new services to market. ■

CURRENT SITUATION

Competition Heats Up

Television futurists look to competition between telephone companies and cable systems to be the driving force behind the arrival of expanded services such as video on demand and interactive television. The regulatory barriers that stand in the way of that competition are being lowered, but they have not fallen completely.

The FCC took the most important step by adopting rules for telephone companies to construct video networks within their local service areas. When the FCC reaffirmed that decision in October, Bell Atlantic's vice president for external affairs, Edward Young, said the action "will result in millions of Americans having a choice between at least two video providers." [16]

In its decision, the FCC retained a variety of requirements that telephone companies had sought to eliminate or ease. The video network must be large enough to accommodate multiple programmers and capable of expansion later to serve additional programmers. A telephone company cannot lease all or substantially all the capacity to a single "anchor programmer." In addition, the telcos must file a tariff showing how they plan to recover the costs of constructing the network through video revenues.

Cable and consumer forces warned that the commission's refusal to issue more specific cost allocation may mean that phone customers end up bearing the cost of building an expensive network needed primarily for video services. In any event, the telephone companies will have to go through complex and inevitably contentious rate proceedings before getting permission to begin construction of the video dial tone systems.

So far, the FCC has granted only Bell Atlantic's application to build a video dial tone system in Dover Township, N.J. The company expects to begin deploying the system by next summer. Telephone industry officials hope approval of the 25 other pending applications will be forthcoming soon, but FCC officials have not laid out specific timetables. In October, the commission declined for now to adopt rules to streamline the process.

The local telephone industry wanted Congress to pass legislation this year that would have written into law the right to provide video services and to enter the lucrative long-distance market. After the House passed legislation along those lines in June, however, some telephone companies objected to a provision in the Senate version of the bill that called for delaying telcos' entry into video services until cable operators won the reciprocal right to provide local telephone service. A lobbying campaign led by three of the Baby Bells — Ameritech of Chicago, BellSouth of Atlanta and US West of Denver — helped kill the bill. [17]

Cable and telephone industry lobbyists traded recriminations over the failure of the legislation. Cable officials said the telcos were simply protecting their regulated monopoly, while telephone industry officials said the bill was imbalanced in favor of cable companies.

Cable interests kept up the pressure on the issue after the legislative stalemate. Time Warner Cable applied to the Ohio Public Utilities Commission in late October for permission to provide phone service to residential and business customers throughout the state. In the same week, three other big cable companies — TCI, Comcast Corp. and Cox Enterprises — announced plans to join with long-distance carrier Sprint to form a new company to compete with local telephone companies.

The moves toward competition for basic telephone service added to the image of a coming information revolution with dramatic changes for all telecommunications services: voice and data as well as video. But despite several years of breathless predictions, the many players in the brave new world of television were finding it more difficult than expected to bring new services on line.

Mergers and Deals

Both the telephone and cable industries have been going through significant restructurings to try to meet the variety of technological and entrepreneurial challenges of the new world of telecommunications.

A year ago, major cable and telephone companies were eyeing mergers to speed the construction of an interactive information superhighway. The mergers seemed to be ideal marriages. Cable companies had television knowhow and programming. Telephone companies had technical knowledge and steady cash flow. In the biggest of the planned deals, Bell Atlantic and TCI agreed in October 1993 on a consolidation valued at $16 billion. Two months later, Southwestern Bell and Cox Enterprises announced plans for a $5 billion merger.

Both deals collapsed this year, however. The companies said the FCC's cable regulations had reduced the value of the mergers. But industry observers also said it was difficult to marry two very different kinds of companies and — in the case of the Bell Atlantic-TCI combination — two hard-charging industry executives: Bell Atlantic Chairman Raymond Smith and TCI's John Malone. [18]

With cable marriages on the rocks, telephone companies decided to turn to Hollywood for partners in their television ventures. In August, three of the Baby Bells — Ameritech, BellSouth and Southwestern Bell (now SBC Communications) — formed a video programming venture with the Walt Disney Co. In late October, three other Bell companies — Bell Atlantic, Nynex and Pacific Telesis — struck a deal with the king of Hollywood dealmakers: Michael Ovitz, head of Creative Artists Agency (CAA). The plan calls for Ovitz to be the main adviser to a newly formed media company that will produce programming for the phone companies' new

Continued on p. 1146

At Issue:

Should Congress and the FCC make it easier for local telephone companies to begin providing video services?

yes

RAYMOND W. SMITH
Chairman, Bell Atlantic Corp.

FROM *A SPEECH TO THE PRACTICING LAW INSTITUTE*, DEC. 5, 1994.

Customers want more than "plain old telephone service" — or, for that matter, "plain old television service." They want information at their fingertips, video on demand, a telephone number that follows them wherever they go and an on-line connection to their bank, their children's school, their doctor, their favorite retailer, their video store and their office. They want choice, control and convenience — not just in communications, but in video entertainment as well. . . .

No industry in the country is better prepared to bring these benefits to the American consumer than the local exchange industry. In just the last year, billions of dollars have been pledged for the building of a broadband intelligent network that would bring the information age to millions of homes across the country. The . . . applications filed to date with the [Federal Communications Commission] represent more than $3.6 billion of investment covering 8.8 million homes across this country.

But so far only one application for commercial video dial tone service has been approved — for 38,000 homes in Dover Township, N.J.

The FCC took a huge step in the direction of consumer choice in October when the commission reaffirmed and clarified its rules for video dial tone and put to bed . . . the bogus issue of "cross-subsidies" for the video network. The VDT ruling sets the record straight: that a regulated telephone company . . . cannot raise prices on basic services to somehow "subsidize" the building of a video network. . . .

I believe the FCC now has the opportunity to follow up on this initiative by acting swiftly on the pending . . . applications for building the broadband highway. [Smith then criticized cable industry filings that he said had delayed FCC action and proposed that Congress eliminate altogether the requirement for phone companies to obtain FCC approval before construction of video networks.]

. . . Billions of dollars of investment capital are on the table. Scores of innovative new products and services are — or soon will be — in the pipeline. But unless we take action, these benefits will be available around the world long before they reach American consumers.

I said a year ago that Bell Atlantic would roll out the video dial tone platform and bring competition to the video marketplace by December 1994, and we will — in Rome, Italy. It's high time we got the green light to do the same thing here. Bell Atlantic will benefit — but so will competitors, consumers and the American economy.

no

DECKER ANSTROM
President, National Cable Television Association

FROM *TESTIMONY TO SENATE COMMERCE COMMITTEE*, MAY 4, 1994.

Local phone companies have clearly demonstrated their eagerness to become providers of video services. In fact, they have exerted tremendous efforts over the past five years to change current laws and regulations that prevent them from doing so.

The cable television industry and others have historically opposed the telephone companies' efforts out of concern that they would exercise their monopoly power to unfairly compete in the video market. But the cable industry does not contend that these cross-ownership restrictions should be maintained forever. Indeed, the cable industry acknowledges that the question is no longer *whether* the phone companies will someday be allowed to provide video services, but rather *when* and under what circumstances. . . .

The government must take steps to ensure that when phone companies do enter the video market, they will not be able to exercise monopoly power and impede the development of a truly competitive market. The current restrictions . . . were created in response to clearly identified abuses that occurred over several decades and continue to this day. Therefore, in loosening these restrictions, lawmakers must proceed carefully to ensure that the telcos' anti-competitive practices are not permitted to recur. . . .

Ensuring that competition develops in the local telephone loop is the single most important safeguard that lawmakers can enact because it will substantially reduce the telephone companies' ability to shift unregulated costs to monopoly services. . . .

Other safeguards can also help ensure that phone companies refrain from anti-competitive behavior. For example, phone companies should be required to deliver video services and develop any programming through separate subsidiaries. . . . Strict rules on cost allocations and the treatment of intangible assets should also be established to ensure that unregulated costs are not inappropriately apportioned to regulated services. . . .

Consumers will benefit from a diverse, competitive telecommunications environment that features multiple networks and multiple providers. Multiple networks will minimize the cost of the service to consumers by encouraging companies to provide competitive rates and to offer the specialization that consumers demand. . . .

Many cable companies are already laying the foundation for a national information superhighway. It is imperative that government policies ensure it can be used to its fullest potential.

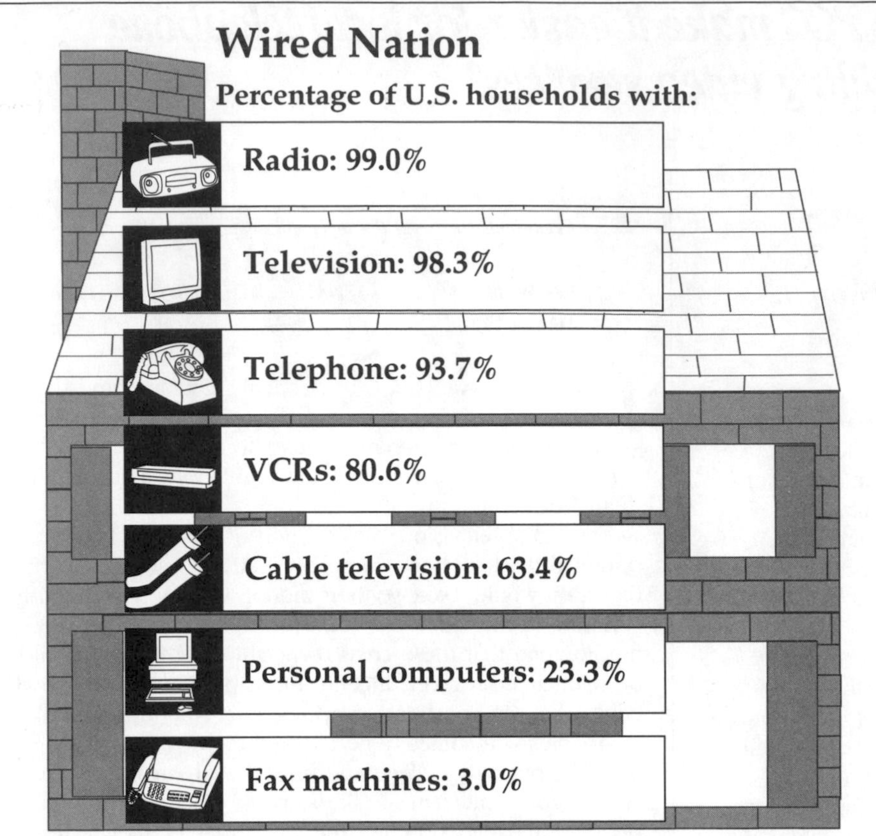

Wired Nation
Percentage of U.S. households with:
Radio: 99.0%
Television: 98.3%
Telephone: 93.7%
VCRs: 80.6%
Cable television: 63.4%
Personal computers: 23.3%
Fax machines: 3.0%

Sources: U.S. Energy Information Administration, Broadcasting & Cable Yearbook, *Census Bureau, Television Advertising Bureau, Radio Advertising Bureau and National Cable TV Association*

Continued from p. 1144

video networks; the three Bells also formed a second company to work on network technology issues.

Meanwhile, the cable industry is preparing to meet the looming competition from phone companies by consolidating. [19] Industry leader TCI announced plans in August to merge with midsized TeleCable Corporation in a $1 billion deal that would give TCI about 11 million subscribers — nearly one-fourth of the nation's cable households. Earlier in the summer, Cox Cable acquired Times Mirror Cable to move into third place of the so-called multisystem operators. And in September, second-ranking Time Warner Cable formed a joint venture with companies controlled by the billionaire Newhouse family to manage cable systems with about 4 million subscribers. Time Warner will continue to operate most of its systems separately.

The consolidations reflected a strategy called "clustering" — merging companies with systems in adjacent or overlapping markets. Industry observers say the strategy permits some economies through joint promotions and advertising sales. In addition, the geographically merged cable companies will be better positioned to compete with telephone companies on their turf: basic telephone service. "Phone companies don't serve one little neighborhood here and there," one unnamed federal official explained to a reporter. "They serve huge territories." [20]

Getting to Market

When the cable industry gathered for its annual Western Cable Show in Anaheim, Calif., this month, one leading cable executive warned against the dangers of unrealistic expectations for the new services being planned for television. "We now insist on everything appearing on schedule, perfectly realized," Barry Diller, chairman of the QVC shopping network, told the Cable Television and Administration Marketing conference. "And when it doesn't appear like that, as often happens, it's dismissed as a failure." [21]

By that standard, the variety of trial runs and market tests for video on demand and interactive television have been less than complete successes. Delays have been common, for a variety of technological, business and regulatory reasons. Time Warner Cable, for example, had planned to roll out its Full Service Network in Orlando this spring, but technical problems forced a delay. Now that the initial market test has begun, the company is setting no timetable for moving to broader offerings.

"We will be doing this for as long as we need to refine the interactive businesses, not just to refine the technology but to learn which interactive businesses customers want and what they're willing to pay," says Michael Luftman, vice president for corporate communications at Time Warner Cable's headquarters in Stamford, Conn.

Consumer demand for the new services remains questionable, however. Time Warner began its test in Orlando with only a handful of customers. [22] "Right now, it seems that people have a great deal of reluctance to pay a premium for movies on demand," says Neuman of Tufts University.

Cable and telephone company executives presented a more upbeat side during a panel discussion at the Western Cable Show. Marguerite Moreland, director of TCI Technology, said the company was encouraged by results of its video on demand test in suburban Denver. Subscribers made more buys than anticipated, she said, and reported little difficulty in ordering the programming. An executive with Southern New England Telephone Co. (SNET) said her company was pleased with its video on demand test in West Hartford, Conn.

Angela Hundley, director of programmer relations for SNET Multi-Media Services, said subscribers chose old movies and special interest programs as well as newly released films.[23]

Demand for home shopping — an equally important segment to make the service economically viable — is also uncertain. Lawrence Plumb, media relations director for Bell Atlantic Video, says the $60 million mail catalog business shows that people will shop from home. But retailers will have to find out what products can be sold from a TV screen. "This is a learning experience," Plumb says. "We expect some failures."

Despite the difficulties and uncertainties, telephone industry officials continue to look on video networks as a valuable business opportunity that will also benefit consumers. "This is a major business for us," says Bell Atlantic spokesman Rabe. "We see video dial tone as part of the construction of an information superhighway that will create the ability to make a broadband connection between any two users. It's the telephone network of the future." ■

OUTLOOK

Testing, Testing

The future of television may be coming, but the industries that will bring it to you are still adjusting their sets.

The market for video on demand or other interactive services remains unproven. Several of the planned market tests, such as Bell Atlantic's service in Northern Virginia and US West's plans for a combined video and telephone network in Omaha, Neb., are still awaiting regulatory approval. Other trials have been delayed for business reasons.[24]

Cable and telephone companies alike say they simply do not know how much money consumers are willing to spend on the new services. So far, tests indicate consumers will not pay much more than $3 for a video on demand movie — about the price in the video rental store. Even at that price, Plumb worries that customers who order several movies may have "sticker shock" when their monthly phone bill arrives.

The technology for the expanded video services also remains unproven. For the companies, one basic but critical problem is how to make sure that customers do not get a busy signal when they request a particular movie. For consumers, the expanded services will require new equipment: a "set-top" box with computer capability. But the product is not on the shelves yet. Rival companies are still working on the design and trying to figure out to how to get the cost down from thousands of dollars to a figure consumers can afford — perhaps $300 or so. (*See story, p. 1136.*)

In the meantime, cable companies are moving in a variety of ways to meet the anticipated competition from telephone companies. For one thing, cable programmers are offering more so-called niche channels. The Arts and Entertainment Networks (A&E) will launch a new History Channel on Jan. 1. Its rival Discovery Networks plans to counter with four new channels in April: a competing history channel called Time Traveler and channels on nature (Animal Planet), science (Quark!) and homes (Living).[25]

Satirists have conjured up an image of more and more niche channels aimed at ever more specialized audiences. But Effros of the Cable Telecommunications Association says the number of full-time channels may be nearing a limit. "I don't think you're going to get a massive number of new 24-hour-a-day channels," he says. "Instead, the technology has advanced to the point where people are going to be selecting programs instead of channels."

The cable industry also moved to shore up its battered image with consumers with an industrywide program announced last month that calls on local cable operators to offer a free month's service if they fail to meet scheduled service appointments. And the industry is bracing for more consolidations. Cable pioneer Ted Turner told the Western Cable Show this month that he expects there will not be more than four or five cable companies a year from now.[26]

For their part, the telephone companies trying to get into the video business are largely on hold — waiting for action by the FCC or Congress to dismantle regulatory barriers. In a speech to a lawyers' group this month, Bell Atlantic Chairman Smith called for repealing the Communications Act provision that requires telephone companies to get regulatory approval for building video networks. "I urge the Congress to do exactly that and let the building of the information superhighway commence," Smith told the Practicing Law Institute on Dec. 5.

When local telephone companies do finally get into the video business, they will face the crucial market test of attracting customers. While cable companies may worry about competing against entrenched phone companies, some experts close to the telephone industry wonder whether the local exchange carriers (LECs) will do well in the market.

"There's a big question mark about how big a share of the market the LECs can win," says consultant Shooshan. "Cable and direct broadcast satellites have a significant head start. The LECs are going to have to offer a tremendous added value to get customers."

Still, Shooshan sees benefits for consumers even if the telephone companies do not gain a significant share of the market. For example, he says Bell Atlantic's bid to offer video services in Alexandria, Va., spurred the existing cable system, owned by Jones Intercable Co., to upgrade service and add channels without raising rates.

FOR MORE INFORMATION

Center for Media Education, 1511 K St., N.W., Suite 518, Washington, D.C. 20005; (202) 628-2620. The center, founded in 1991, has worked on a variety of telecommunications issues, including children's television and public access.

National Association of Broadcasters, 1771 N St., N.W., Washington, D.C. 20036; (202) 429-5300. The NAB is the broadcasting industry's principal trade association, representing about 975 commercial television stations and 5,000 radio stations.

National Cable Television Association, 1724 Massachusetts Ave., N.W., Washington, D.C. 20036; (202) 775-3550. NCTA is the cable television industry's largest trade association, representing member companies that serve about 90 percent of the nation's cable TV subscribers.

United States Telephone Association, 1401 H St., N.W., suite 600, Washington, D.C. 20005-2136; (202) 326-7300. USTA represents more than 1,400 companies, including the seven regional Bell operating companies, or "Baby Bells," that provide local telephone service in the United States.

In Congress, lawmakers will try again to write legislation to encourage more competition in all types of telecommunications services. Sen. Larry Pressler, the South Dakota Republican slated to become chairman of the Senate Commerce Committee, told reporters after the election that new legislation would be less regulatory than the bill that the Baby Bells helped kill this fall. But reaching a consensus among the affected industries on a wide range of issues, including competition in long-distance and local phone service, will be difficult.[27]

Consumer and public interest groups are watching this process with apprehension. Schwartzman of the Media Access Project says he is troubled by Pressler's comments after the election and by the stand taken by Senate GOP leader Robert Dole of Kansas against the previous bill. He says he fears Senate Republicans may write legislation deregulating both cable and telephone industries before there is effective competition either in home video or local telephone service.

Chester of the Center for Media Education says he is concerned that legislation will not provide public access to the new video networks. "The marketplace alone will not meet the information needs of the public," he says. "That's why we founded public broadcasting. That's why we passed the Children's Television Act," which was aimed at increasing programs for children on television.

The prevailing view in government and industry circles today, however, looks to competition instead of regulation to bring expanded services to viewers. "The most important thing is to put the telephone companies and cable companies into meaningful competition," says Tufts Professor Neuman. He foresees the time when most viewers will choose to have as many as four or more video delivery systems: over-the-air broadcasting, satellite broadcasting, cable and telephone.

Cable and telephone companies are talking less grandly about a "two-wire world," but some industry observers question whether viewers will be willing to pay for even that much choice on their TV screens. And broadcasters are questioning the basic premise that viewers should have to depend on either cable or telephone to meet their television needs.

"We are the universal medium," says John Abel, executive vice president for operations at the National Association of Broadcasters. "The wire-line carriers are going to charge for subscription, and they're going to charge extra for [extra services]. We're free."

Whatever the ultimate outcome, the business rivalries show that the new wave of television will be more complex for the industries involved as well as for viewers. But it remains to be seen whether this brave new world of television will bring the cultural enrichment and political empowerment that its most hopeful advocates predict — or merely glue viewers to the screen for additional hours of mindless entertainment and commercial messages. For the answer to that question, viewers will have to stay tuned. ■

Notes

[1] For background, see "Does Cable TV Need More Regulation?" *Editorial Research Reports,* Dec. 7, 1990, pp. 697-711.

[2] Bruce M. Owen and Steven S. Wildman, *Video Economics* (1992), p. 256.

[3] Quoted in *The Wall Street Journal,* Nov. 11, 1994, p. A3.

[4] *Broadcasting & Cable,* Aug. 8, 1994, p. 19.

[5] *Ibid.*

[6] *The Wall Street Journal,* Nov. 29, 1994, p. B6.

[7] Times Mirror Center for The People and The Press, "The Role of Technology in American Life," May 1994. Also see "Pay-Per-View TV," *The CQ Researcher,* Oct. 4, 1991, pp. 729-752.

[8] See Eric Barnouw, *Tube of Plenty: The Evolution of American Television* (2nd rev. ed., 1990).

[9] See *Broadcasting and Cable Yearbook, 1994,* pp. xvii-xviii; *NTIA Telecomm 2000,* pp. 546-550.

[10] See Kenneth Jost, *The Supreme Court Yearbook, 1993-1994,* Congressional Quarterly, 1994, pp. 52-55.

[11] See Steve Coll, *The Deal of the Century: The Breakup of AT&T* (1986); "Breaking Up AT&T," *Editorial Research Reports,* Dec. 16, 1983, pp. 941-964.

[12] *Broadcasting,* Dec. 3, 1990, p. 39, cited in Henry Geller, "Fiber Optics: An Opportunity for a New Policy," Annenberg Washington Program, 1991, pp. 9-10.

[13] See John Heilemann, "Feeling for the Future: A Survey of Television," *The Economist,* Feb. 12, 1994, pp. 5-6.

[14] See General Instrument Corp., *1993 Annual Report,* pp. 9, 18.

[15] *The Wall Street Journal,* Nov. 29, 1993, p. A5.

[16] Quoted in *Broadcasting & Cable,* Oct. 24, 1994, p. 6.

[17] See *Congressional Quarterly Weekly Report,* Sept. 24, 1994, pp. 2669-2670.

[18] See *The Wall Street Journal,* April 7, 1994, p. B1. For extensive coverage of the failed Bell Atlantic-TCI merger, see *The Wall Street Journal,* Oct. 14, 1993; Feb. 25, 1994.

[19] See *Broadcasting & Cable,* Aug. 15, 1994, pp. 36-37.

[20] Quoted in *The Washington Post,* Sept. 13, 1994, p. D1.

[21] Quoted in *Broadcasting & Cable,* Dec. 5, 1994, p. 32.

[22] *USA Today,* Dec. 15, 1994, p. B1.

[23] *Broadcasting & Cable,* Dec. 5, 1994, pp. 32, 40.

[24] See *The New York Times,* Dec. 12, 1994, pp. D1, D7.

[25] *Broadcasting & Cable,* Nov. 21, 1994, p. 20.

[26] *Broadcasting & Cable,* Dec. 5, 1994, p. 7.

[27] *The Wall Street Journal,* Nov. 16, 1994, p. A3; *Congressional Quarterly Weekly Report,* Nov. 26, 1994, pp. 3406-3408.

Bibliography

Selected Sources Used

Books

Barnouw, Erik, *Tube of Plenty: The Evolution of American Television* (2d. rev. ed.), Oxford University Press, 1990.

Barnouw, professor emeritus of dramatic arts at Columbia University, traces the history of television from the earliest days of broadcasting through the rise of cable and development of fiber optics in the 1980s. The book includes a 12-page chronology and 19 pages of bibliographical notes. For a more detailed account through the 1960s, see Barnouw's three-volume work, *A History of Broadcasting* (Oxford University Press, 1966, 1968, 1970).

***Broadcasting & Cable Yearbook, 1994,* Broadcasting/ R.R. Bowker, 1994.**

This authoritative annual reference book includes a summary history, an overview of federal regulations, economic and financial statistics and an annotated bibliography of books, periodicals and videos on the broadcasting and cable industries.

Carter, T. Barton, Marc A. Franklin and Jay B. Wright, *The First Amendment and the Fifth Estate* (3rd ed.), Foundation Press, 1992.

This casebook comprehensively covers the history of and current developments in the regulation of broadcasting, cable and other telecommunications technologies. The latest annual supplement, for 1994, includes some of the recent rulings affecting entry of telephone companies into home video services.

Firestone, Charles (ed.), *Television for the 21st Century: The Next Wave,* The Aspen Institute, 1993.

The book includes papers or comments from 11 contributors to a 1992 conference exploring the technological, economic, legal and social issues for television in the 21st century.

Johnson, Leland, *Toward Competition in Cable Television,* MIT Press and American Enterprise Institute, 1994.

Johnson, a telecommunications consultant recently retired from the RAND Corporation, outlines steps to facilitate competition for cable television from telephone companies and direct broadcast satellites.

Articles

Andrews, Edmund L., "Time Warner's 'Time Machine,'" *The New York Times,* Dec. 12, 1994, p. D1; "A Launching Pad for the Video Revolution," *The New York Times,* Oct. 26, 1994, p. D1.

Andrews, who covers telecommunications for *The New York Times,* wrote informative stories about Bell Atlantic's plans for video on demand in Northern Virginia and Time Warner Cable's Full Service Network in Orlando, Fla. The most recent story includes a general survey of the status of video on demand and interactive television.

Heilemann, John, "Feeling for the Future: A Survey of Television," *The Economist,* Feb. 12, 1994, pp. 1-18.

This comprehensive survey and forecast by a correspondent for the British-based newsweekly concludes that unpredictability will be the hallmark of the new multimedia age that is dawning for television.

"Testing Television's Future," *InfoActive,* Center for Media Education, September/October 1994.

This public interest group's newsletter provides an overview of the status of video on demand and interactive television tests with a focus on issues of public access.

Reports and Studies

Geller, Henry, "Fiber Optics: An Opportunity for a New Policy," Annenberg Washington Program, 1991.

Geller, a leading communications expert and former official in the Federal Communications Commission and the National Telecommunications and Information Administration, advocates steps to permit and encourage telephone companies to provide home video services. The report also contains an insightful overview of the history of broadcasting and cable regulation. In a more recent paper, Geller calls for overhauling regulation of all three video providers: broadcasting, cable and telephone ("1995-2005: Regulatory Reform for Principal Electronic Media," Annenberg Washington Program, 1994).

"The Information Arena: Making Communications Policy for the Next Generation," *Congressional Quarterly Weekly Report,* May 14, 1994 [supplement].

The 74-page special report covers the range of issues considered by Congress in the unsuccessful effort to enact telecommunications legislation in 1994. The report includes a chronology of events from 1876 through 1994 and capsule descriptions of the various telecommunications industries, including broadcasting, cable and local and long-distance telephone companies.

U.S. Department of Commerce, National Telecommunications and Information Administration, *NTIA Telecomm 2000: Charting the Course for a New Century,* 1988.

This 672-page report contains background studies and deregulatory policy recommendations on broadcasting, cable and other telecommunications industries. The report was prepared under the direction of Alfred Sikes, then head of the NTIA and later chairman of the FCC.

The Next Step

Additional information from UMI's Newspaper & Periodical Abstracts database

Baby Bells and the TV Industry

Cauley, Leslie and Laura Landro, "Three Baby Bells may sign video deal with Michael Ovitz's Hollywood agency," *The Wall Street Journal,* Aug. 15, 1994, p. B8.

Bell Atlantic Corp., Nynex Corp. and Pacific Telesis Group are close to signing a pact with Hollywood power broker Michael Ovitz's Creative Artists Agency that aims to create a network to deliver video programming into the homes of phone customers.

Fitzgerald, Kate, David J. Wallace, "The first Baby Bell gets a green light," *Advertising Age,* July 18, 1994, p. 23.

Bell Atlantic Corp. has received FCC permission to build a "commercial video dial tone" network to compete directly with cable TV operators. Beginning in 1995, Bell Atlantic will offer video services to some 38,000 homes in the Toms River, N.J., area.

Greenwald, John, "Lights, Camera, Dial tone," *Time,* Sept. 5, 1994, pp. 56-57.

The Baby Bells are turning to Hollywood in their race with cable companies to wire U.S. homes for two-way TV. As Congress considers a sweeping deregulation bill that would give cable and phone companies broad latitude to invade each other's territories, it is clear that the Baby Bells do not intend to lose this battle.

Huber, Peter, "Telefeuds," *Forbes,* Feb. 14, 1994, p. 154.

The Baby Bells are invading each other's turf through alliances with out-of-region cable operators. A new monopoly emerging from these alliances is completely implausible.

"To compete with Baby Bells, ALC needs partners," *Detroit News,* Aug. 4, 1994, p. E3.

Long-distance company ALC Communications Corp. of Bingham Farms, Mich., is talking with phone and cable companies about teaming up to provide local phone service should regulators allow competition against the Baby Bells, the company's top executive said.

Zitner, Aaron, "Nynex, Baby Bells, superagent in interactive TV deal," *Boston Globe,* Nov. 1, 1994, p. 39.

Stepping further from their core telephone business and into television, Nynex Corp. and two other regional Bell companies confirmed that they had teamed up with Hollywood "superagent" Michael Ovitz to acquire, create and distribute TV programs and interactive services.

Cable Industry

Jessell, Harry A., "Telco, cable take infohighway sides," *Broadcasting & Cable,* Sept. 19, 1994, p. 62.

The cable TV industry is backing the so-called information superhighway legislation that is struggling through Congress, but telephone companies have generally opposed it. The two contrasting views of the legislation are discussed.

Keller, John J. and Mark Robichaux, "Sprint, 3 cable firms to form phone venture," *The Wall Street Journal,* Oct. 25, 1994, p. A3.

Sprint Corp. and cable giants Tele-Communications Inc., Cox Enterprises Inc. and Comcast Corp. have agreed to form a new telecommunications company to fight for customers of the Baby Bells and new wireless giant AT&T Corp. on all fronts. Wireless and wired phone services and newer multimedia video and information offerings will be delivered over phone and cable networks.

Samuels, Gary, "Partner or die," *Forbes,* Sept. 12, 1994, pp. 128-130.

Cable TV operators need to upgrade their systems to carry telephone calls or RBOCs will spend the necessary money to allow them to offer video programming in their own regions. The cable industry's problem is discussed.

"Sprint to announce alliance with three cable giants," *The New York Times,* Oct. 25, 1994, p. D4.

The Sprint Corp. will announce a venture with three cable TV companies that will offer local telephone services and set up a national wireless communication network. The venture with Tele-Communications Inc., the Comcast Corp. and Cox Enterprises Inc. will use radio frequencies that are being auctioned by the FCC in December.

Stern, Christopher, "Telcos close in on cable," *Broadcasting & Cable,* Oct. 24, 1994, p. 6.

The FCC has adopted new "video dial tone" (VDT) rules that have edged telephone companies closer to entering the cable TV business. Before telephone companies can compete for cable subscribers, individual VDT networks and rates must be approved.

"Telecoms alliances: The future, sort of," *The Economist,* Oct. 29, 1994, pp. 74-79.

Alliances between telephone companies and cable-TV firms are cropping up. On Oct. 20, 1994, Nynex, Bell Atlantic and US West linked their cellular operations with AirTouch Communications, a cellular group.

Zier, Julie A., "Economic forecast: Blue skies ahead," *Broadcasting & Cable,* Oct. 10, 1994, p. 27.

Panelists discuss the future of TV networks, cable and telcos.

The Future of Networks

Dorfman, Dan and David Lieberman, "Viacom may have its eye on CBS bid," *USA Today,* Nov. 21, 1994, p. B1.
CBS chief Laurence Tisch appears determined to make a deal for his TV network, but ITT has become the latest potential buyer to find the price too high. Now Viacom, the giant entertainment and publishing company, is taking a preliminary look at CBS.

Jensen, Elizabeth, Daniel Pearl, "Time-NBC pact would face slew of hurdles," *The Wall Street Journal,* Sept. 2, 1994, p. A3.
Regulatory rules, some of which date back to the pre-television era, could block an accord as Time Warner Inc. explores the possibility of buying part or all of General Electric Co.'s NBC Network.

Lieberman, David, "CBS sidesteps rival with Westinghouse deal," *USA Today,* July 15, 1994, p. B1.
CBS has struck a far-reaching deal with Westinghouse Broadcasting, a power in TV stations and daytime programming known as Group W. CBS was clearly pleased to announce the deal so soon after it was rocked by the collapse of its planned merger with home shopping channel QVC.

Wright, Bob, "What Fox can teach us," *The Wall Street Journal,* June 9, 1994, p. A14.
Bob Wright says Rupert Murdoch, through the acquisition of 12 former ABC, CBS and NBC affiliates, has set the TV world on its ear. Wright says TV networks and stations are still subject to outdated rules that were drawn up in the early days of radio and broadcasters must be free to compete in order to serve consumers' expectations in the present and the future on the information superhighway.

Interactive TV

Enrico, Dottie, "Viewers want a smart tube," *USA Today,* Nov. 21, 1994, p. B1.
Videos on demand and banking and check-writing services are what consumers most want from interactive TV, according to a survey from ad agency BBDO New York. The survey of 3,500 Compu-Serve subscribers is one of the most extensive on-line samplings of opinion about the desirability of services on the information superhighway.

Lippman, John, "Betting on a high-tech jackpot," *Los Angeles Times,* Nov. 18, 1994, p. A1.
Giant media corporations are maneuvering to reap a multibillion-dollar windfall by backing little-known entrepreneur David Lockton, who would pump off-track betting and the lottery into the nation's living rooms via interactive TV.

Maney, Kevin, "TCI taps video-game market for cable TV," *USA Today,* Oct. 21, 1994, p. B1.
Tele-Communications Inc. will invest $85 million in Acclaim Entertainment and get a 10 percent stake in the fee-for-play video games market. The companies will also create a venture to develop games for use on interactive TV networks.

Markoff, John, "Phone companies hit interactive-TV snags," *The New York Times,* Oct. 1, 1994, p. A43.
Efforts of telephone companies to profit from cable TV setbacks in the creation of interactive TV projects have become hampered by their own technological problems.

Legislative Initiatives

Andrews, Edmund L., "Bill to revamp communications dies in Congress," *The New York Times,* Sept. 24, 1994, p. A1.
Amid feuding between rival industry groups, sweeping legislation to overhaul U.S. telecommunications laws, intended to permit open competition between telephone and cable TV companies, collapsed in the Senate on Sept. 23, 1994.

Andrews, Edmund L., "The phone-law static," *The New York Times,* Sept. 26, 1994, p. D1.
The collapse of efforts in the Senate to overhaul communications law is likely to give telephone and cable-TV companies a temporary reprieve from the prospect of increased competition. But the day when people can choose between local phone companies and cable systems may be delayed for years in many places, and some companies are unlikely to invest as much in future technology until the regulatory climate is clearer.

McAvoy, Kim, "House bills would alter telcom landscape," *Broadcasting & Cable,* July 4, 1994, p. 34.
The House of Representatives has passed two major telecommunications bills: one that would permit the regional Bell operating companies to enter the long-distance telephone business and manufacture telecommunications equipment and one that would open local telephone markets to competition and permit telephone companies to enter the cable TV business. The two measures are discussed.

Mills, Mike, "Pressler wants phone, cable brakes off," *The Washington Post,* Nov. 16, 1994, p. C2.
Sen. Larry Pressler, R-S.D., the incoming chairman of the Senate Commerce, Science and Transportation Committee, urged the Clinton administration to work with him to pass a telecommunications bill that would impose far fewer regulations than one that died in Congress in 1994.

Shiver, Jube Jr., "Senate panel, phone firms tentatively reach accord," *Los Angeles Times,* Aug. 9, 1994, p. D1.
In a breakthrough that could salvage negotiations over telecommunications reform, the Baby Bell telephone companies and the Senate Commerce Committee on Aug. 8, 1994, reached a tentative agreement on a bill for competition among cable TV operators, local phone companies and long distance carriers.

Back Issues

Great Research on Current Issues Starts Right Here...Recent topics covered by The CQ Researcher are listed below. Before May 1991, reports were published under the name of Editorial Research Reports.

JUNE 1993
Food Safety
Prostitution
Childhood Immunizations
National Service

JULY 1993
Electric Cars
Population Growth
Downward Mobility
Intelligence Testing

AUGUST 1993
Mental Illness
Bilingual Education
Foreign Policy Burden
School Funding

SEPTEMBER 1993
Suburban Crime
Public Housing
Supreme Court Preview
Immigration Reform

OCTOBER 1993
Airline Safety
Disaster Response
Science in the Courtroom
The Glass Ceiling

Back issues are available for $4.00 (subscribers) or $7.00 (non-subscribers). Quantity discounts apply to orders over ten. To order, call Congressional Quarterly Customer Service at (202) 887-8621.

Binders are available for $16.00. To order call 1-800-638-1710. Please refer to stock number 648.

NOVEMBER 1993
Paying for Retirement
Charitable Giving
Privacy in the Workplace
Adoption

DECEMBER 1993
U.S. Vietnam-Relations
Learning Disabilities
Child Care
Space Program's Future

JANUARY 1994
Racial Tensions in Schools
South Africa's Future
Worker Retraining
Regulating Pesticides

FEBRUARY 1994
Prison Overcrowding
Water Quality
Religion in Schools
Juvenile Justice

MARCH 1994
Underground Economy
Education Standards
Gambling Boom
Private Management of Public Schools

APRIL 1994
Reproductive Ethics
U.S.-China Trade
Soccer in America
Talk Show Democracy

MAY 1994
Traffic Congestion
Women's Health Issues
Mutual Funds
Political Scandals

JUNE 1994
Education and Gender
Gun Control
Public Land Policy
Nuclear Arms Cleanup

JULY 1994
Dietary Supplements
Public Opinion and Foreign Policy
Crime Victims' Rights
Birth Control Choices

AUGUST 1994
Genetically Engineered Foods
Electing Minorities
Prozac Controversy
College Sports

SEPTEMBER 1994
Home Schooling
Welfare Experiments
Courts and the Media
Regulating Tobacco

OCTOBER 1994
Historic Preservation
Religion and Politics
Arts Funding
Economic Sanctions

NOVEMBER 1994
Sex on Campus
Blood Supply Safety
Testing Term Limits
Religion in America

DECEMBER 1994
Farm Policy
Arms Sales
Earthquake Research

Future Topics

- ***Treating Addiction***
- ***Child Custody and Support***
- ***Parental Involvement in Education***

The CQ Researcher

Subject-Title Index

January 1991-December 1994

NOTE: Weekly CQ Researcher reports are indexed by title under boldface subject headings. Titles are followed by the date of the report and the number of the first page. Page numbers followed by asterisks refer to sidebars or the "At Issue" pro/con feature. Issues dated before May 10, 1991, were published under the name of Editorial Research Reports.